The Unicode Standard

Version 2.0

The Unicode Consortium

Addison-Wesley Developers Press

Reading, Massachusetts · Menlo Park, California · New York
Don Mills, Ontario · Harlow, England · Amsterdam
Bonn · Sydney · Singapore · Tokyo · Madrid · San Juan
Paris · Seoul · Milan · Mexico City · Taipei

Many of the designations used by manufacturers and sellers to distinguish their products are claimed as trademarks. Where those designations appear in this book, and Addison-Wesley was aware of a trademark claim, the designations have been printed in initial capital letters.

The authors and publisher have taken care in preparation of this book, but make no expressed or implied warranty of any kind and assume no responsibility for errors or omissions. No liability is assumed for incidental or consequential damages in connection with or arising out of the use of the information or programs contained herein.

The *Unicode Character Database* is provided as-is by Unicode ®, Inc. No claims are made as to fitness for any particular purpose. No warranties of any kind are expressed or implied. The recipient agrees to determine applicability of information provided. If this file has been purchased on magnetic media, the sole remedy for any claim will be exchange of defective media within ninety days of receipt.

ISBN 0-201-48345-9

A-W Developers Press is a division of Addison-Wesley Publishing Company, Inc.

This book is set in Minion, designed by Rob Slimbach at Adobe Systems, Inc. It was set on an Apple Macintosh computer using FrameMaker 4. The character names list and index were created on a Xerox document creation system. ASMUS, Inc. provided custom software for chart layout. Taligent, Inc. provided custom software for names lists, chart layout, and Han cross-references. DecoType supplied glyphs for Arabic characters.

The Unicode ® Consortium is a registered trademark, and Unicode™ is a trademark of Unicode, Inc. The Unicode logo is a trademark of Unicode, Inc., and may be registered in some jurisdictions.

Adobe ® and PostScript ® are registered trademarks, and Minion™ is a trademark of Adobe Systems, Inc.

Apple ® and Macintosh ® are registered trademarks of Apple Computer, Inc.

CJK ® is a registered trademark and servicemark of the Research Libraries Group, Inc.

FrameMaker ® is a registered trademark of Frame Technology Corporation.

IBM ® is a registered trademark of International Business Machines Corporation.

Intel ® is a registered trademark of Intel Corporation.

ITC Zapf Dingbats ® is a registered trademark of the International Typeface Corporation.

Microsoft ® , Windows ®, and Win32 ® are registered trademarks, and Windows NT ™ is a trademark of Microsoft Corporation.

Motorola ® is a registered trademark of Motorola Corporation.

Xerox ® is a registered trademark of Xerox Corporation.

All other company and product names are trademarks or registered trademarks of the company or manufacturer respectively.

2 3 4 5 6 7 8 9 10 CRK 00999897
Second printing, February 1997

Addison-Wesley books are available for bulk purchases by corporations, institutions, and other organizations. For more information please contact the Corporate, Government, and Special Sales Department at (800) 238-9682.

Find A-W Developers Press on the World-Wide Web at: `http://www.aw.com/devpress/`

Acknowledgments

The production of *The Unicode Standard: Worldwide Character Encoding, Version 2.0* is due to the dedication of many individuals over considerable time. All of the authors and reviewers have contributed to the authorship, editing, and review of this standard. We would also like to acknowledge the major contributions of the following individuals, which were central to the design, authorship, and review of this book:

Glenn Adams, for overall integration of the original sources for Version 2.0 into a continuous text in FrameMaker, his refinements of Devanagari shaping behavior, his initial work on expanded versions of the glossary and *Chapter 3, Conformance*, and his editing of the Indic portions of *Chapter 6, Character Block Descriptions.*

Joan Aliprand, for her painstaking compilation and editing of the references, her contributions to Hebrew character descriptions, and her writing and editing of the front matter, back cover, and *Chapter 1, Introduction.*

Joe Becker, for his initial work and promotion of a 16-bit full encoding and his contributions to the creation and editing of this book.

Mark Davis, for his project management of the book editing, his development of algorithms for canonical equivalence, conjoining Hangul, Bidirectionality, and Arabic, Devanagari and Tamil shaping, his development of Line and Paragraph separators, sentinel value U+FFFF, his development and extension of the *Unicode Character Database*, his development of source material for *Chapter 5, Implementation Guidelines*, his editing of *Chapter 3, Conformance*, all the figures in this book, the software for printing the character name lists, and his meticulous editing of the final draft.

Asmus Freytag, for his extensive work on practical application of the Unicode Standard, his development of strategies for handling byte ordering, his development of Hangul code chart printing software, his coordination and development of enhancements to the bidirectionality algorithm, his contributions to a full set of symbols, his development of source material for *Chapter 5, Implementation Guidelines*, and his editing of *Chapter 2, General Structure* and *Chapter 5, Implementation Guidelines.*

John Jenkins, for his development of printing software for the character charts and Han cross-reference tables and for development and supervision of the Unicode font.

Rick McGowan, for his development of the algorithm for canonical equivalence, his early work in Tibetan, his extensive work in the development of Draft Proposals for additional scripts, his development and extension of the *Unicode Character Database*, and his editing of *Appendix A, Transformation Formats, Appendix B, Submitting New Characters*, and *Appendix C, Relationship to ISO/IEC 10646.*

Lisa Moore, for her work in organizing and refining *Chapter 4, Character Properties,* and the Hebrew cantillation marks.

Michel Suignard, for his extension of software for printing Hangul code charts.

Ken Whistler, for his extensive and crucial efforts in the development of the character database in Version 1.0 and its update for Version 2.0, his major contributions to the development of Indic, IPA, and symbols, his editing of the vast majority of *Chapter 6, Character Block Descriptions*, and his meticulous editing of the final draft.

In addition to the contributors noted above, principal reviewers were Tim Greenwood, Mike Ksar, and Lloyd Honomichl. Editorial assistance was provided by Steve Greenfield. Mark Davis and Ken Whistler collected and reconciled the overwhelming amount of review feedback and then edited the final copy of the text. Mark Davis is responsible for the book design.

The technical content of *The Unicode Standard* is the responsibility of the Unicode Technical Committee, composed of representatives from many different companies. At the time of publication, these representatives were Joan Aliprand (Research Libraries Group), Jürgen Bettels (Digital), Don Carroll (Hewlett-Packard), David O. Craig (NCR), Peter Edberg (Apple), John Gioia (IBM), Bill Hall (Novell), Lloyd Honomichl (Novell), Tatsuo Kobayashi (Justsystem), Mike Ksar (Hewlett-Packard), Michael Kung (Silicon Graphics), John McConnell (Apple), Mike McKenna (Sybase), Rick McGowan (NeXT), Gianni Mariani (Silicon Graphics), Lisa Moore (IBM), Ali Özer (NeXT), Gary Roberts (NCR), Murray Sargent (Microsoft), Karen Smith-Yoshimura (Research Libraries Group), Michel Suignard (Microsoft), V. S. Umamaheswaran (IBM), Ken Whistler (Sybase), and Arnold F. Winkler (Unisys). Other individuals who participated in the work of the Unicode Technical Committee include John Bale (Hewlett-Packard), Alan Barrett (Lotus), Ed Batutis (Lotus), Joe Becker (Xerox), Mark Davis (Taligent), James Do (Mentor Graphics), David Goldsmith (Taligent), Tim Greenwood, John H. Jenkins (Taligent), T. J. Kang (Hangul & Computer Company), Stephen P. Oksala (Unisys), and Andy Witkowski (Oracle).

Many of the individuals mentioned above were also responsible for Version 1.0 (published in 1991–92). Although they did not contribute directly to this version of the Unicode Standard, we also acknowledge the important contributions of the following people: Cora Chang, for her meticulous cross-checking of Han standards mappings; Lee Collins, for his painstaking work in the integration and extension of mappings from many different sources to produce the first Unicode Han unification, and his later contributions to Tibetan; David Goldsmith, for his development of UTF-7; Tim Greenwood, for his development of character databases and mappings; Lori Hoerth, for her development of character databases and mappings; Liao Huan-Mei, for her development of character databases and mappings; Mike Kernaghan, for his operational management of Unicode, Inc., which has enabled the production of the Unicode technical work; Michel Suignard, for first mapping large sections of the alphabetic Microsoft/IBM code pages, which provided the first handle on compatibility requirements for the Unicode Standard; Isai Scheinberg, for his pivotal work in guiding the Unicode Standard through the intricacies of the ISO standards development process, his development and coordination of enhancements to the Bidirectionality algorithm, and the inclusion of CJK and Arabic compatibility forms; Layne Cannon and Stuart Smith, for the Byte Order Mark.

Other significant contributors to the original version of *The Unicode Standard: Worldwide Character Encoding* were John Bennett, F. Avery Bishop, Joe Bosurgi, Andy Daniels, Burwell Davis, Bill English, Masami Hasegawa, Greg Hullander, Mike Kernaghan, Eric Mader, Dave Opstad, Jony Rosenne, Bill Tuthill, J G. Van Stee, and Glenn Wright.

Version 2.0 benefited from the advice and assistance of the following individuals: Tesring Choergual (Tibetan Languages Institute), S. G. Hong (Microsoft Korea), T. J. Kang (Hangul & Computer Company, Ltd.), Mao Yong Gang (Chinese Electronics Standardization Institute), Prof. Nyima Trashi (Tibetan University), and Prof. Norzhang Wujen (Institute of Social Sciences of Tibet). The contributions of Mati Allouche (IBM), Gadi Doran (Accent), Peter Lofting (Laserquill), and Prof. Robert Chilton (Asian Classics Input Project) are also acknowledged. Won-Seop Lee (Korea Industrial Advancement Administration) and Yang Kyoo Choo (University of California at Berkeley) provided assistance with references.

The support given to creation of *The Unicode Standard: Worldwide Character Encoding, Version 2.0* by member corporations has been crucial. Particular thanks for facilities, equipment, and resources are owed to Apple, ASMUS, Inc., Frame Technology, IBM, Microsoft, NeXT, The Research Libraries Group, Stonehand, Sybase, Taligent, and Xerox.

We would also like to thank the members of international standards bodies for their close cooperation in areas of mutual interest; in particular, the members of ISO JTC1/SC2/WG2 and the members of the Ideographic Rapporteur Group, especially the Convener of WG2, Mike Ksar, Editor Bruce Paterson, and the Rapporteur of the IRG, Zhang Zhoucai.

While we gratefully acknowledge the contribution of all persons named in this section, any errors or omissions in this work are the responsibility of the Unicode Consortium.

Unicode Consortium Members and Directors

Current Full Members

Apple Computer, Inc.
Digital Equipment Corporation
Hewlett-Packard Company
IBM Corporation
Justsystem Corporation
Microsoft Corporation
MGI Software Corporation
NCR
NeXT Software, Inc.
Novell, Inc.
The Research Libraries Group, Inc.
Silicon Graphics, Inc.
Spyglass, Inc.
Sybase, Inc.
Unisys Corporation

Current Associate Members

Accent Software International, Ltd.
Adobe Systems, Inc.
Alis Technologies, Inc.
ASMUS, Inc.
Bitstream, Inc.
Data Research Associates
Dynalab, Inc.
Eidetic Systems Corporation
Electronic Book Technologies, Inc.
Folio Corporation
FTP Software
Gamma Productions, Inc.
Getty Art History Information Program
Hangul & Computer Company, Ltd.
Innovative Interfaces, Inc.
InterBold
Knight-Ridder Information, Inc.
Language Analysis Systems, Inc.
Logos Research Systems, Inc.
Lotus Development Corporation
Monotype Typography, Inc.
Netscape Communications Corporation
OCLC, Inc.
Oracle Corporation
Progress Software Corporation
Reuters, Ltd.
Royal Library, Sweden
SHARE, Inc.
Software AG
Taligent, Inc.
University of Washington
VTLS, Inc.
Xerox Corporation

Current Liaison Members

Center of Computer & Information Development Research (China)
ECMA
TCVN/TC (The Vietnamese General Dept. for Standardization, Metrology, & Quality Control/ Technical Committee)
WG2-Korea

Current Members of the Board of Directors

Janet Buschert (Hewlett-Packard Company)
Tatsuo L. Kobayashi (Justsystem Corporation)
Ilene H. Lang (Digital Equipment Corporation)
Elizabeth G. Nichols (IBM Corporation)
Dr. Mike Potel (Taligent, Inc.)
Franz G. Rau (Microsoft Corporation)
Dr. David R. Richards (Research Libraries Group, Inc.)
Kazuya Watanabe (Novell, Inc.)

Former Members of the Board of Directors

Jerry Barbar (Aldus Corporation)
Robert M. Carr (Go Corporation)
John Gage (Sun Microsystems Computer Corporation)
Paul Hegarty (NeXT Software, Inc.)
Dr. Gary G. Hendrix (Symantec Corporation)
Dick Holleman (IBM Corporation)
Charles Irby (Metaphor, Inc.)
Jay E. Israel (Novell, Inc.)
Paul Maritz (Microsoft Corporation)
Stephen P. Oksala (Unisys Corporation)
Rick Spitz (Apple Computer, Inc.)
Lawrence Tesler (Apple Computer, Inc.)
Guy "Bud" Tribble (NeXT Software, Inc.)
Gayn B. Winters (Digital Equipment Corporation)

Contents

Figures

Tables

Preface

This book, *The Unicode Standard, Version 2.0,* is the authoritative source of information on the Unicode character encoding standard, an international character code for information processing that includes all major scripts of the world. As well as encoding characters used for written communication in a simple and consistent manner, the Unicode Standard defines character properties and algorithms for use in implementations.

The Unicode Consortium, incorporated in 1991 as *Unicode, Inc.*, has the charter to maintain the Unicode Standard and promote its use worldwide. Members of the Consortium include major corporations and institutions involved in international computing. Membership is open to any organization or individual interested in contributing to the design, implementation, and promotion of the Unicode Standard.

Version 2.0 consolidates and expands on material from earlier publications.

- *The Unicode Standard*, Version 1.0, Volume 1 (1991)
- *The Unicode Standard*, Version 1.0, Volume 2 (1992)
- *The Unicode Standard*, Version 1.1, Prepublication Edition (1993)

In addition, it documents decisions made by the Unicode Technical Committee since 1993. The major additions in Version 2.0 are

- comprehensive new information about how to implement the standard
- a substantially clarified specification of conformance
- the full encoding of modern Korean Hangul
- the full encoding of the Tibetan script
- the surrogate mechanism for future character extension

The Unicode Standard maintains consistency with the International Standard ISO/IEC 10646-1:1993 (including recent amendments), as specified in *Appendix C, Relationship to ISO/IEC 10646* in this book.

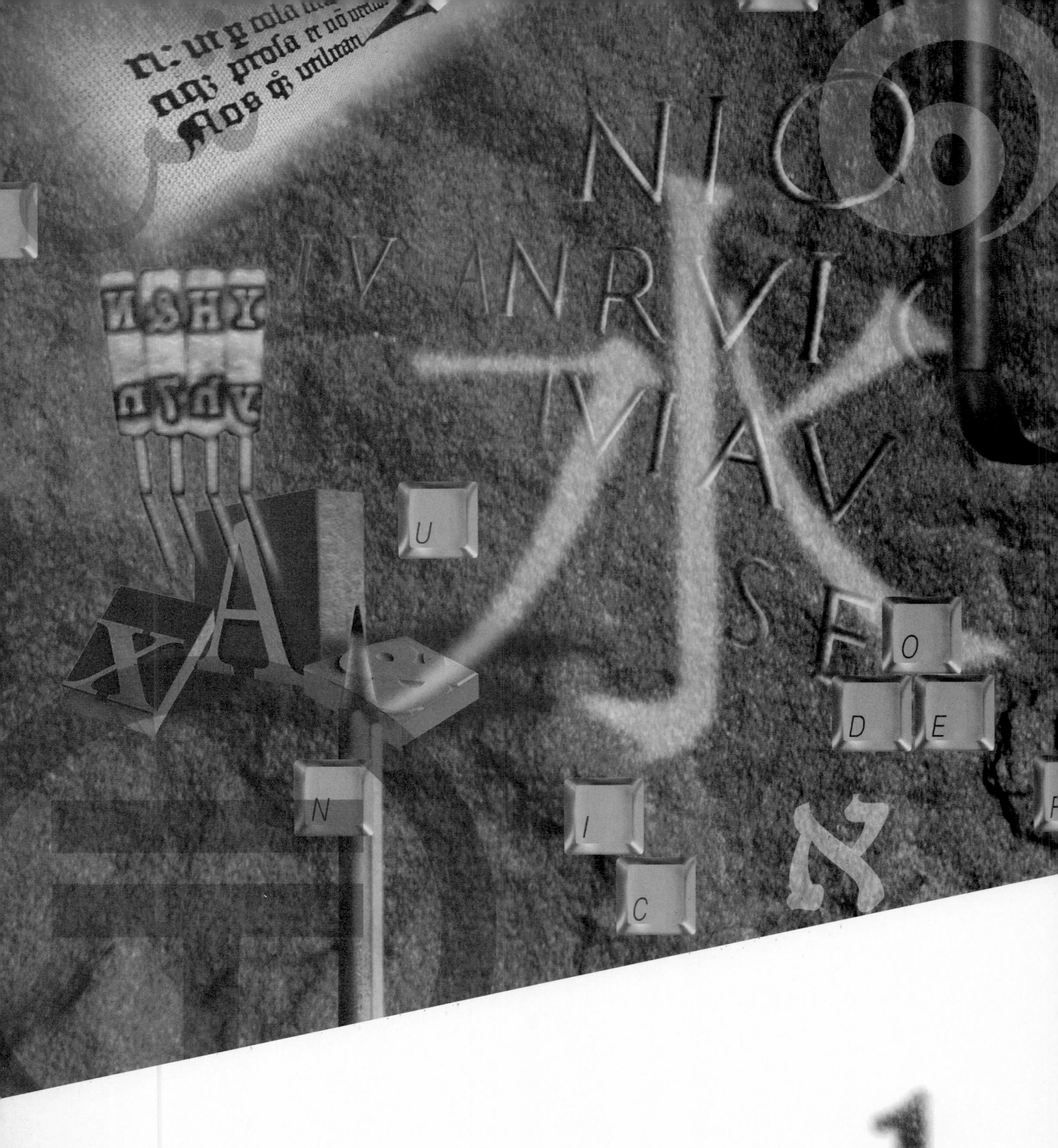

1

INTRODUCTION

Chapter 1

Introduction

The Unicode Standard is a fixed-width, uniform encoding scheme for written characters and text. The repertoire of this international character code for information processing includes characters for the major scripts of the world, as well as technical symbols in common use. The Unicode character encoding treats alphabetic characters, ideographic characters, and symbols identically, which means that they can be used in any mixture and with equal facility. The Unicode Standard is modeled on the ASCII character set, but uses a 16-bit encoding to support full multilingual text. No escape sequence or control code is required to specify any character in any language.

Figure 1-1. Wide ASCII

ASCII/8859-1 Text

A	0100 0001
S	0101 0011
C	0100 0011
I	0100 1001
I	0100 1001
/	0010 1111
8	0011 1000
8	0011 1000
5	0011 0101
9	0011 1001
-	0010 1101
1	0011 0001
	0010 0000
t	0111 0100
e	0110 0101
x	0111 1000
t	0111 0100

Unicode Text

A	0000 0000 0100 0001
S	0000 0000 0101 0011
C	0000 0000 0100 0011
I	0000 0000 0100 1001
I	0000 0000 0100 1001
	0000 0000 0010 0000
天	0101 1001 0010 1001
地	0101 0111 0011 0000
	0000 0000 0010 0000
س	0000 0110 0011 0011
ل	0000 0110 0100 0100
ا	0000 0110 0011 0111
م	0000 0110 0100 0101
	0000 0000 0010 0000
α	0000 0011 1011 0001
≰	0010 0010 0111 0000
γ	0000 0011 1011 0011

The Unicode Standard specifies a numerical value and a name for each of its characters; in this respect, it is similar to other character encoding standards from ASCII onwards (see Figure 1-1). The Unicode Standard is code-for-code identical with International Standard ISO/IEC 10646-1:1993, *Information Technology—Universal Multiple-Octet Coded Character Set (UCS)—Part 1: Architecture and Basic Multilingual Plane.*

As well as assigning character codes and names, the Unicode Standard provides other information not found in conventional character set standards, but crucial for using character encoding in implementations. The Unicode Standard defines properties for characters and includes application data such as case mapping tables and mappings to the repertoires of international, national, and industry character sets. The Unicode Consortium provides this additional information to ensure consistency in interchange of Unicode data.

1.1 Design Goals

The primary goal of the development effort for the Unicode Standard was to remedy two serious problems common to most multilingual computer programs: overloading of the font mechanism when encoding characters, and use of multiple, inconsistent character codes due to conflicting national and industry character standards. The ASCII 7-bit code space and its 8-bit extensions, although used in most computing systems, are limited to 128 and 256 code positions, respectively. These 7- and 8-bit code spaces are inadequate in the global computing environment.

When the Unicode project began in 1988, groups most affected by the lack of a consistent international character standard included the publishers of scientific and mathematical software, newspaper and book publishers, bibliographic information services, and academic researchers. More recently, the computer industry has adopted an increasingly global outlook, building international software that can be easily adapted to meet the needs of particular locations and cultures. The explosive growth of the Internet has added to the demand for a character set standard that can be used all over the world.

The designers of the Unicode Standard envisioned a uniform method of character identification which would be more efficient and flexible than previous encoding systems. The new system would be complete enough to satisfy the needs of technical and multilingual computing and would encode a broad range of characters for professional quality typesetting and desktop publishing worldwide.

The original design goals of the Unicode Standard were established as:

- ***Universal.*** The repertoire must be large enough to encompass all characters that were likely to be used in general text interchange, including those in major international, national, and industry character sets.
- ***Efficient.*** Plain text, composed of a sequence of fixed-width characters, provides an extremely useful model because it is simple to parse: software does not have to maintain state, look for special escape sequences, or search forward or backward through text to identify characters.
- ***Uniform.*** A fixed character code allows efficient sorting, searching, display, and editing of text.
- ***Unambiguous.*** Any given 16-bit value always represents the same character.

Figure 1-2 demonstrates some of these features, contrasting Unicode encoding to mixtures of single-byte character sets, with escape sequences to shift the meanings of bytes.

1.2 Coverage

The Unicode Standard, Version 2.0 contains 38,885 characters from the world's scripts. These characters are more than sufficient not only for modern communication, but also for

Figure 1-2. Universal, Efficient, and Unambiguous

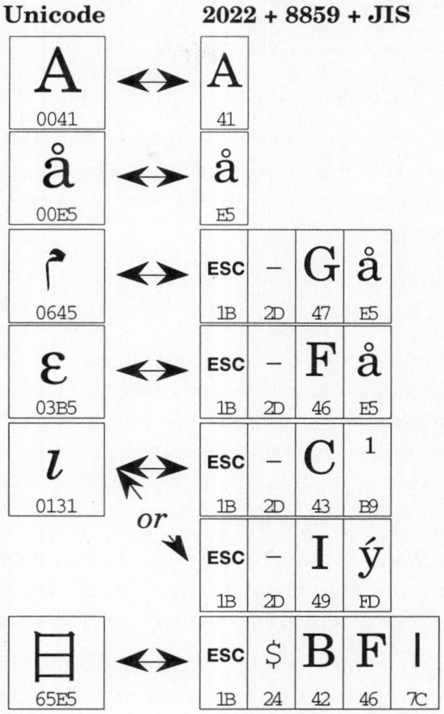

the classical forms of many languages. Languages that can be encoded include Russian, Arabic, Anglo-Saxon, Greek, Hebrew, Thai, and Sanskrit. The unified Han subset contains 20,902 ideographic characters defined by national and industry standards of China, Japan, Korea, and Taiwan. In addition, the Unicode Standard includes mathematical operators and technical symbols, geometric shapes, and dingbats. Overall character allocation and the code ranges are detailed in *Chapter 2, General Structure.*

Included in the Unicode Standard are characters from all major international standards approved and published before December 31, 1990, in particular, the ISO International Register of Character Sets, the ISO/IEC 6937 and ISO/IEC 8859 families of standards, as well as ISO/IEC 8879 (SGML). Other primary sources included bibliographic standards used in libraries (such as ISO/IEC 5426 and ANSI Z39.64), the most prominent national standards, and various industry standards in very common use (including code pages and character sets from Adobe, Apple, Fujitsu, Hewlett-Packard, IBM, Lotus, Microsoft, NEC, WordPerfect, and Xerox). The complete Hangul repertoire of Korean National Standard KS C 5601 was added in Version 2.0. For a complete list of ISO and national standards used as sources, see the bibliography.

The Unicode Standard does not encode idiosyncratic, personal, novel, rarely exchanged, or private-use characters, nor does it encode logos or graphics. Artificial entities, whose sole function is to serve transiently in the input of text, are excluded. Graphologies unrelated to text, such as musical and dance notations, are outside the scope of the Unicode Standard. Font variants are explicitly not encoded. The Unicode Standard includes a *Private Use Area,* which may be used to assign codes to characters not included in the repertoire of the Unicode Standard.

The Unicode Consortium (see *Section 1.4, The Unicode Consortium*) periodically develops proposals for new scripts. The Consortium welcomes the submission of new characters for possible inclusion in the Unicode Standard. (For instructions on how to submit characters to the Unicode Consortium, see *Appendix B, Submitting New Characters.*)

1.3 About This Book

This book defines Version 2.0 of the Unicode Standard. The general principles and architecture of the Unicode Standard, requirements for conformance, and guidelines for implementers precede the actual coding information. The accompanying CD-ROM carries tables of use to implementers.

Chapter 2 sets forth the fundamental principles underlying the Unicode Standard and covers specific topics such as text processes, overall character properties, and the use of nonspacing marks.

Chapter 3 constitutes the formal statement of conformance. It opens with the conformance clauses themselves, which are followed by sections that define more precisely terms used in the clauses. The remainder of this chapter presents the normative algorithms for three processes: the canonical ordering of combining marks, the encoding of Korean Hangul syllables by conjoining *jamo*, and the formatting of bidirectional text.

Chapter 4 describes character properties, both normative (required) and informative. Since code charts alone are not sufficient for implementation, the Unicode Standard also specifies character properties, some of which are required for conformance.

Chapter 5 discusses implementation issues, including compression, strategies for dealing with unknown and missing characters, and transcoding to other standards.

Chapter 6 contains character block descriptions, part of the coding information in the Unicode Standard. A character block generally contains characters from a single script (for example, *Tibetan*) or is a collection of a particular type of character (for example, *Mathematical Operators*). A character block description gives basic information about the script or collection and may discuss specific characters.

Chapter 7 presents the individual characters, arranged by character block. An overview of a particular character block is given by means of a code chart. With the exception of the blocks for East Asian ideographs and Korean hangul syllables, the individual characters of a block are identified in the accompanying names list.

Chapter 8 provides a radical/stroke index to East Asian ideographs.

Appendix A describes the various encoding forms that may be applied to Unicode character data to meet particular needs, for example, UTF-7 to facilitate the exchange of Unicode data in 7-bit environments.

Appendix B gives instructions on how to submit characters for consideration as additions to the Unicode Standard.

Appendix C gives the details of the merger of the Unicode Standard and ISO/IEC 10646, which occurred in 1991.

Appendix D lists the changes to the Unicode Standard since Version 1.0.

Appendix E describes the history of Han Unification in the Unicode Standard.

The appendices are followed by a glossary of terms, a bibliography, and two indices: an index to Unicode characters and an index to the text of Chapters 1 through 8.

The major table on the CD-ROM is the *Unicode Character Database*, which gives character codes, character names (with Version 1.0 name if different), character properties, and decompositions for decomposable or compatibility characters. The CD-ROM also includes property-based mapping tables (for example, tables for case) and transcoding tables for international, national, and industry character sets (including the Han cross-reference table). (For the complete contents of the CD-ROM, see its *READ ME* file.)

Notational Conventions

Throughout this book, certain typographic conventions are used. In running text, an individual Unicode value is expressed as *U+nnnn*, where *nnnn* is a four digit number in hexadecimal notation, using the digits 0–9 and the letters A–F (for 10 through 15 respectively). In tables, the *U+* may be omitted for brevity.

- U+0416 is the Unicode value for the character named CYRILLIC CAPITAL LETTER ZHE.

A range of Unicode values is expressed as U+xxxx →U+yyyy or U+xxxx — U+yyyy, where *xxxx* and *yyyy* are the first and last Unicode values in the range, and the arrow or long dash indicates a contiguous range.

- The range U+0900→U+097F contains 128 character values.

All Unicode characters have unique names, which are identical to those of the English language version of International Standard ISO/IEC 10646. Unicode character names contain only uppercase Latin letters A through Z, space, and hyphen-minus; this convention makes it easy to generate computer language identifiers automatically from the names. Unified East Asian ideographs are named CJK UNIFIED IDEOGRAPH-X, where X is replaced with the hexadecimal Unicode value; for example, CJK UNIFIED IDEOGRAPH-4E00. The names of Hangul syllables are generated algorithmically; for details, see Hangul Syllable Names in *Section 3.10, Combining Jamo Behavior.*

In running text, a formal Unicode name is shown in small capitals (for example, GREEK SMALL LETTER MU), and alternative names (aliases) appear in italics (for example, *umlaut*). Italics are also used to refer to a text element that is not explicitly encoded (for example, *pasekh alef*), or to set off a foreign word (for example, the Welsh word *ynghyd*).

The symbols used in the character names list are described at the beginning of *Chapter 7, Code Charts.*

In the text of this book, the word "Unicode" if used alone as a noun refers to the Unicode Standard or a Unicode character value.

1.4 The Unicode Consortium

The Unicode Consortium was incorporated in January 1991, under the name Unicode, Inc., to promote the Unicode Standard as an international encoding system for information interchange, to aid in its implementation, and to maintain quality control over future revisions. The Unicode Consortium is the central focus and contact point for conducting these activities.

To further these goals, the Unicode Consortium cooperates with the International Organization for Standardization (ISO). The Consortium holds a Class C liaison membership with ISO/IEC JTC1/SC2; it participates both in the work of JTC1/SC2/WG2 (the working group within ISO responsible for computer character sets) and in the work of the Ideographic Rapporteur Group of WG2. The Consortium is a member company of ANSI Subcommittee X3L2. In addition, member representatives in many countries also work with their national standards bodies.

A number of standards organizations are Liaison Members of the Unicode Consortium: ECMA (a European-based organization for standardizing information and communication systems), Association of Common Chinese Code of the Center for Computer & Information Development Research (China), and the Technical Committee on Information Technology of the Viet Nam General Department for Standardization, Metrology, and Quality Control (TCVN/TC), and the WG2 standards committee of Korea.

Membership in the Unicode Consortium is open to organizations and individuals anywhere in the world who support the Unicode Standard and who would like to assist in its extension and widespread implementation. Full and Associate Members represent a broad spectrum of corporations and organizations in the computer and information processing industry. The Consortium is supported through the volunteer efforts of employees of member companies and individual members, and financially through membership dues.

The Unicode Technical Committee

The Unicode Technical Committee (UTC) is the working group within the Consortium responsible for the creation, maintenance, and quality of the Unicode Standard. The UTC controls all technical input to the standard and makes associated content decisions. UTC members represent the companies that are Full and Associate Members of the Consortium. Observers are welcome to attend UTC meetings and may participate in the discussions, since the intent of the UTC is to act as an open forum for the free exchange of technical ideas.

1.5 The Unicode Standard and ISO/IEC 10646

During 1991, the Unicode Consortium and the International Organization for Standardization (ISO) recognized that a single, universal character code was highly desirable. Mutually acceptable changes were made to Version 1.0 of the Unicode Standard and to the first ISO/IEC Draft International Standard DIS 10646.1, and their repertoires were merged into a single character encoding in January 1992. After international ballot and editorial changes to accommodate comments, the final ISO standard was published in May 1993 as ISO/IEC 10646-1:1993, *Information Technology—Universal Multiple-Octet Coded Character Set (UCS)—Part 1: Architecture and Basic Multilingual Plane.*

In accord with the merger agreement, a revision of the Unicode Standard was published in 1993 as *Unicode Technical Report, No. 4*, with the title: *The Unicode Standard, Version 1.1, Prepublication Edition.* Version 1.1 of the Unicode Standard specified a repertoire and set of code assignments identical to those of the new ISO/IEC standard.

After the initial release of ISO/IEC 10646 and the Unicode Standard Version 1.1, both ISO JTC1/SC2/WG2 (the ISO working group responsible for ISO/IEC 10646) and the Unicode Technical Committee continued to develop the merged standard. These developments lead to Version 2.0 of the Unicode Standard, incorporating the first seven amendments made to or proposed for ISO/IEC 10646. (For details, see *Appendix C, Relationship to ISO/IEC 10646*, and *Appendix D, Cumulative Changes.)*

1.6 Resources

On-line Information Sources

The Unicode Consortium provides a number of on-line resources for obtaining information and data about the Unicode Standard. They are

- the World-Wide Web site at URL `http://www.unicode.org`
- the anonymous FTP site at URL `ftp://unicode.org`

Use account name `anonymous`, and specify your electronic mail address as the password

- the mailing list `unicode@unicode.org`

Note that this is a mailing list, not a listserv. To be added or removed, send a request to

- `unicode-request@unicode.org`

How to Contact the Unicode Consortium

Contact the Consortium for membership inquiries and to order publications (including additional copies of this book).

- Electronic mail address: `unicode-inc@unicode.org`
- Postal address:

  P.O. Box 700519
  San Jose, CA 95170-0519
  U.S.A.

- Telephone: +1 (408) 777-3721
- Fax: +1 (408) 777-3784
- Courier deliveries only: 10000 Torre Ave, Cupertino, CA 95014, U.S.A.

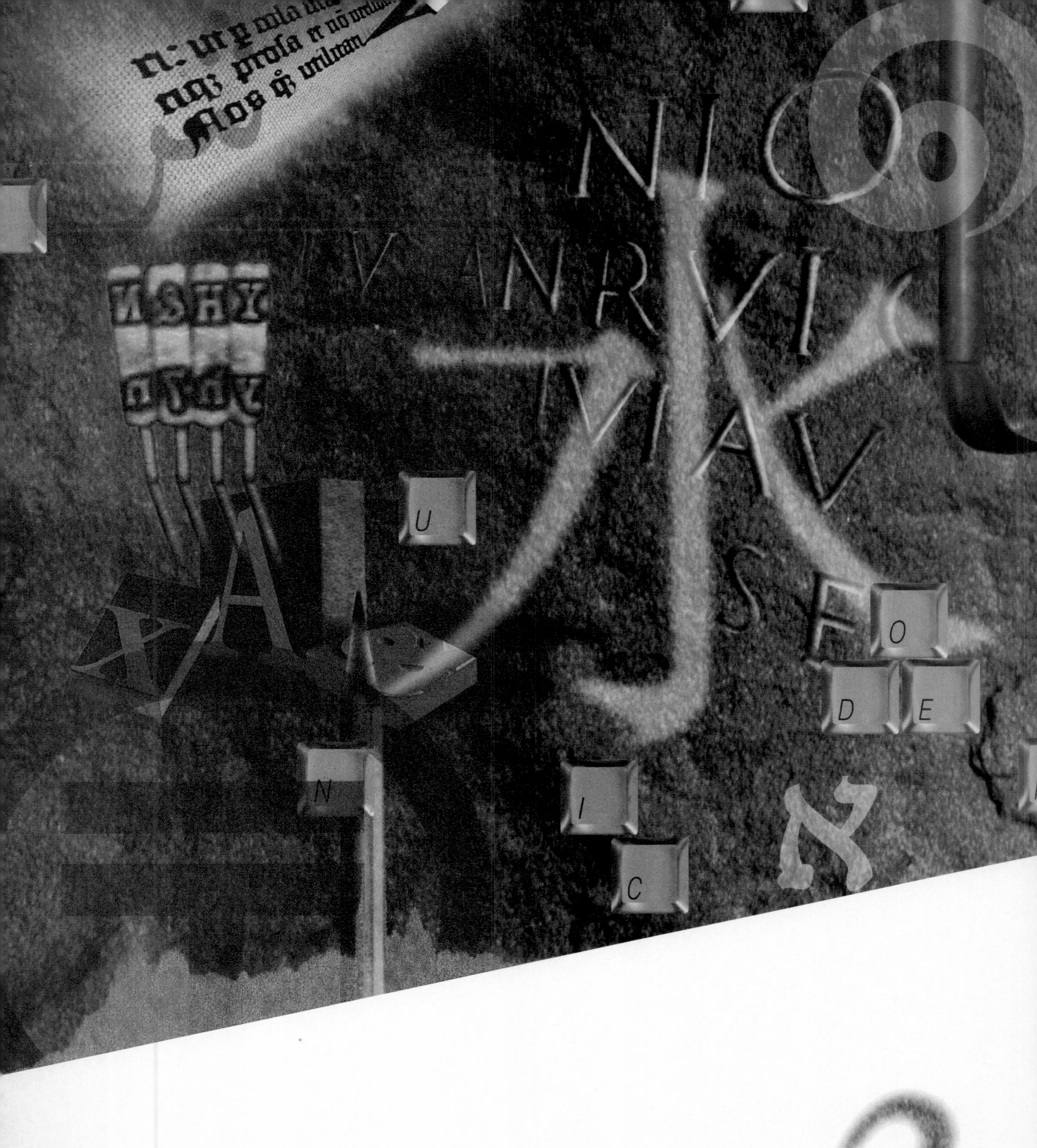

2 GENERAL STRUCTURE

Chapter 2

General Structure

This chapter discusses the fundamental principles governing the design of the Unicode Standard and presents an overview of its main features. It includes discussion of text processes, unification principles, allocation of codespace, character properties, and a description of non-spacing marks and how they are employed in Unicode character encoding. This chapter also discusses the general requirements for creating a text-processing system that conforms to the Unicode Standard. The formal requirements for conformance are in *Chapter 3, Conformance.* Character properties, both normative and informative, are in *Chapter 4, Character Properties.* A set of guidelines for implementers is in *Chapter 5, Implementation Guidelines.*

2.1 Architectural Context

A character code standard such as the Unicode Standard enables the implementation of useful processes operating on textual data. The interesting end products are not the character codes but the text processes, since these directly serve the needs of a system's users. Character codes are like nuts and bolts — minor, but essential and ubiquitous components used in many different ways in the construction of computer software systems. No single design of a character set can be optimal for all uses, so the architecture of the Unicode Standard strikes a balance among several competing requirements.

Basic Text Processes

Most computer systems provide low-level functionality for a small number of basic text processes from which more sophisticated text-processing capabilities are built. The following text processes are supported by most computer systems to some degree:

- Rendering characters visible (including ligatures, contextual forms, and so on)
- Breaking lines while rendering (including hyphenation)
- Modifying appearance, such as point size, kerning, underlining, slant, and weight (light, demi, bold, and so on)
- Determining units such as "word" and "sentence"
- Interacting with users in processes such as selecting and highlighting text
- Modifying keyboard input and editing stored text through insertion and deletion
- Comparing text in operations such as determining sort order of two strings, or filtering or matching strings
- Analyzing text content in operations such as spell-checking, hyphenation, and parsing morphology (that is, determining word roots, stems, and affixes)

- Treating text as bulk data for operations such as compressing and decompressing, truncating, transmitting, and receiving

Text Elements, Code Elements, and Text Processes

One of the more profound challenges in designing a world-wide character encoding stems from the fact that for each text process, written languages differ in what is considered a fundamental unit of text, or a *text element.*

For example, in German, the letter combination "ck" is a text element for the process of hyphenation (where it appears as "k-k"), but not for the process of sorting; in Spanish, the combination "ll" may be a text element for the traditional process of sorting (where it is sorted between "l" and "m"), but not for the process of rendering; and in English, the objects "A" and "a" are usually distinct text elements for the process of rendering, but generally not distinct for the process of spell-checking. The text elements in a given language depend upon the specific text process; a text element for spell checking may have different boundaries from a text element for sorting.

A character encoding standard provides the fundamental units of encoding, that is, the *code elements* or characters, which must exist in a unique relationship to the assigned numerical *code points.* These code elements are the smallest addressable units of stored text.

The design of the character encoding must provide precisely the set of code elements that allow programmers to design applications capable of implementing a variety of text processes in the desired languages. These code elements may not map directly to any particular set of text elements that are used by one of these processes.

Text Processes and Encoding

In the case of English text using an encoding such as ASCII, the relationships between the encoding and the basic text processes built on it are seemingly straightforward: characters are generally rendered visible one by one in distinct rectangles from left to right in linear order. Thus one character code inside the computer corresponds to one logical character in a process such as simple English rendering.

When designing an international and multilingual text encoding such as the Unicode Standard, the relationship between the encoding and implementation of basic text processes must be considered explicitly, for several reasons:

- Many assumptions about character rendering that hold true for English fail for other writing systems. Unlike English, characters in other writing systems are not necessarily rendered visible one by one in rectangles from left to right. In many cases, character positioning is quite complex and does not proceed in a linear fashion. (See the Arabic and Devanagari subsections in *Section 6.1, General Scripts Area* for detailed examples of this.)

- It is not always obvious that one set of text characters is an optimal encoding for a given language. For example, there exist two approaches for the encoding of accented characters commonly used in French or Swedish: ISO/IEC 8859 defines letters such as "ä" and "ö" as individual characters, whereas ISO/IEC 6937 and ISO/IEC 5426 represent them by composition instead. In the Swedish language both of these are considered distinct letters of the alphabet, following the letter "z". In French, the diaeresis on a vowel merely marks it as being pronounced in isolation. In practice both encodings can be used to implement either language.

- No encoding can support all basic text processes equally well. As a result, some

> trade-offs are necessary. For example, ASCII defines separate codes for uppercase and lowercase letters. This causes some text processes, such as rendering, to be carried out more easily, but other processes, such as comparison, to be more difficult. A different encoding design for English, such as case-shift control codes, would have had the opposite effect. In designing a new encoding for complex scripts, such trade-offs must be evaluated and decisions made explicitly, rather than unconsciously.

For these reasons, design of the Unicode Standard is not specific to the design of particular basic text-processing algorithms. Instead it provides an encoding that can be used with a wide variety of algorithms.

In particular, sorting and string comparison algorithms *cannot* assume that the assignment of Unicode character code numbers provides an alphabetical ordering for lexicographic string comparison. In general, culturally expected sorting orders require arbitrarily complex sorting algorithms. The expected sort sequence for the same characters differs across languages; thus, in general, no single acceptable lexicographic ordering exists. (See *Section 5.15, Sorting and Searching* for implementation guidelines.)

Text processes supporting many languages are often more complex than they are for English. The character encoding design of the Unicode Standard strives to minimize this additional complexity, enabling modern computer systems to interchange, render, and manipulate text in a user's own script and language—and possibly in other languages as well.

2.2 Unicode Design Principles

The design of the Unicode Standard reflects the following ten fundamental principles (see Table 2-1). Not all of these principles can be satisfied simultaneously. The design strikes a balance between maintaining consistency for the sake of simplicity and efficiency, and maintaining compatibility for interchange with existing standards.

Table 2-1. The Ten Unicode Design Principles

Principle	Statement
Sixteen-bit characters	Unicode character codes have a uniform width of 16 bits.
Full encoding	The full 16-bit codespace is available to encode characters.
Characters, not glyphs	The Unicode Standard encodes characters, not glyphs.
Semantics	Characters have well-defined semantics.
Plain text	The Unicode Standard encodes plain text.
Logical order	The default for memory representation is logical order.
Unification	The Unicode Standard unifies duplicate characters within scripts across languages.
Dynamic composition	The Unicode Standard allows for the dynamic composition of accented forms.
Equivalent sequence	For static precomposed forms, the Unicode Standard provides a mapping to the equivalent dynamically composed sequence of characters.
Convertibility	Accurate convertibility is guaranteed between the Unicode Standard and other widely accepted standards.

Sixteen-Bit Characters

Unicode character codes have a uniform width of 16 bits. Plain Unicode text consists of pure 16-bit Unicode character sequences. For compatibility with existing environments, two lossless transformations for converting 16-bit Unicode values into forms appropriate for 8- or 7-bit environments have been defined:

- UTF-8 (UCS Transformation Format-8) is the standard method for transforming Unicode values into a sequence of 8-bit codes. UTF-8 is not intended to replace the base 16-bit form of Unicode encoding but may be used where needed; for example, when transmitting data through 8-bit oriented protocols.
- UTF-7 (UCS Transformation Format-7) is the standard interchange format available for use in environments that strip the eighth bit, principally 7-bit Internet exchange. See Internet Working Group RFC-1642.

The UTF-8 and UTF-7 transformations are fully described in *Appendix A, Transformation Formats.*

Full Encoding

The full 16-bit codespace (over 65,000 code positions) is available to represent characters. (See *Section 2.3, Unicode Allocation,* on how these characters are allocated in this standard.) There are over 18,000 unassigned code positions that are available for future allocation. This number far exceeds anticipated character encoding requirements for modern and most archaic characters.

One million additional characters are accessible through the *surrogate extension mechanism*, where two 16-bit code values represent a single character. This number far exceeds anticipated character encoding requirements for all world characters and symbols.

This extension mechanism will allow implementations access to rare characters in the future. Two groups, each consisting of 1,024 code positions, are reserved for this purpose and are used in pairs to represent over 1 million additional characters. These code positions are called surrogates. In this version of the Unicode Standard, *none of the these additional surrogates has been assigned.*

The surrogate mechanism is designed to coexist well with the basic form of 16-bit encoding. (See *Section 3.7, Surrogates,* for the definition of this mechanism and *Section 5.5, Handling Surrogate Characters,* for implementation guidelines.)

Characters, Not Glyphs

The Unicode Standard draws a distinction between *characters,* which are the smallest components of written language that have semantic value, and *glyphs,* which represent the shapes that characters can have when they are rendered or displayed. There are various relationships between character and glyph: a single glyph may correspond to a single character, or to a number of characters, or multiple glyphs may result from a single character. The distinction between characters and glyphs is illustrated in Figure 2-1.

Unicodecharactersrepresentprimarily,butnotexclusively,theletters,punctuation,and other signs that comprise natural language text and technical notation. Characters are represented by code values that reside only in a memory representation, as strings in memory, or on disk. The Unicode Standard deals only with character codes.

In contrast to characters, glyphs appear on the screen or paper as particular representations of one or more characters. A repertoire of glyphs comprises a font. Glyph shape and methods of identifying and selecting glyphs are the responsibility of individual font vendors and of appropriate standards and are not part of the Unicode Standard.

Figure 2-1. Characters Versus Glyphs

Glyph	Unicode Character(s)
A A A A A 𝔄 A A	U+0041 LATIN CAPITAL LETTER A
a a a *a a* a a a	U+0061 LATIN SMALL LETTER A
ﬁ ﬁ	U+0066 LATIN SMALL LETTER F + U+0069 LATIN SMALL LETTER I
ه ـه ـهـ هـ	U+0647 ARABIC LETTER HEH

For certain scripts, such as Arabic and the various Indic scripts, the number of glyphs needed to display a given script may be significantly larger than the number of characters encoding the basic units of that script. The number of glyphs may also depend on the orthographic style supported by the font. For example, an Arabic font intended to support the *Nastaliq* style of Arabic script may possess many thousands of glyphs. However, the character encoding employs the same few dozen letters regardless of the font style used to depict the character data in context.

A font and its associated rendering process define an arbitrary mapping from Unicode values to glyphs. Some of the glyphs in a font may be independent forms for individual characters, while others may be rendering forms that do not directly correspond to any one character.

The process of mapping from characters in the memory representation to glyphs is one aspect of text rendering. The final appearance of rendered text may depend on context (neighboring characters in the memory representation), variations in typographic design of the fonts used, and formatting information (point size, superscript, subscript, and so on). The results on screen or paper can differ considerably from the prototypical shape of a letter or character (see Figure 2-2).

For all scripts there is an archetypical relation between character code sequences and resulting glyphic appearance. For the Latin script this is simple and well known; for several other scripts it is documented in this standard. However, in all cases, fine typography requires a more elaborated set of rules than given here. The Unicode Standard documents the default relation between character sequences and glyphic appearance solely for the purpose of ensuring that the same text content is always stored with the same, and therefore interchangeable, sequence of character codes.

Semantics

Characters have well-defined semantics. Character property tables are provided for use in parsing, sorting, and other algorithms requiring semantic knowledge about the code points. See *Section 5.13, Locating Text Element Boundaries, Section 5.14, Identifiers*, and *Section 5.15, Sorting and Searching* for suggested implementations. The properties identified by the Unicode Standard include numeric, spacing, combination, and directionality properties (see *Chapter 4, Character Properties*). Additional properties may be defined as needed from time to time. In general, neither the character name nor its location in the code table designates its properties (but see also *Section 4.1, Case*).

Plain Text

Plain text is a pure sequence of character codes; plain Unicode-encoded text is a sequence of Unicode character codes. In contrast, *fancy text*, also known as *rich text*, is any text rep-

Figure 2-2. Unicode Character Code to Rendered Glyph

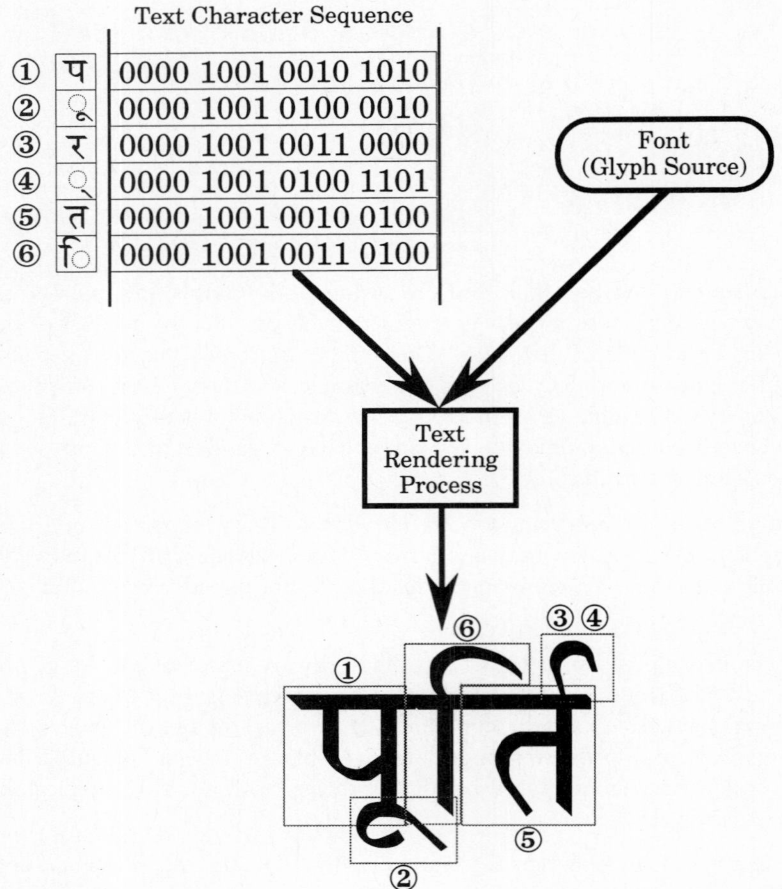

resentation consisting of plain text plus added information such as language identifier, font size, color, hypertext links, and so on. For example, the text of this book, a multifont text as formatted by a desktop publishing system, is fancy text.

There are many kinds of data structures that can be built into fancy text. To give but one example, in fancy text containing ideographs an application may store the phonetic readings of ideographs somewhere in the fancy text structure.

The simplicity of plain text gives it a natural role as a major structural element of fancy text. SGML, HTML, or TEX are examples of fancy text fully represented as plain text streams, interspersing plain text data with sequences of characters that represent the additional data structures. Many popular word processing packages rely on a buffer of plain text to represent the content and implement links to a parallel store of formatting data.

The relative functional roles of both plain and fancy text are well established:

- Plain text is public, standardized, and universally readable.
- Fancy text representation may be implementation-specific or proprietary.
- Plain text is the underlying content stream to which formatting can be applied.

While there are fancy text formats that have been standardized or made public, the majority of fancy text designs are vehicles for particular implementations and are not necessarily readable by other implementations. Since fancy text equals plain text plus added information, the extra information in fancy text can always be stripped away to reveal the "pure" text underneath. This operation is familiar, for example, in word processing systems that use both their own private fancy format and plain ASCII text file format as a universal, if limited, means of exchange. Thus, by default, plain text represents the *basic, interchangeable content of text.*

Since plain text represents character content, it has no inherent appearance. It requires a rendering process to make it visible. If the same plain text sequence is given to disparate rendering processes, there is no expectation that rendered text in each instance should have the same appearance. All that is required from disparate rendering processes is to make the text legible according to the intended reading. Therefore, the relationship between appearance and content of plain text may be stated as follows:

> *Plain text must contain enough information to permit the text to be rendered legibly, and nothing more.*

The Unicode Standard encodes plain text. The distinction between data encoded in the Unicode Standard and other forms of data in the same data stream is the function of a higher-level protocol and is not specified by the Unicode Standard itself. The 64 control code positions of ISO/IEC 2022 (commonly used with ISO/IEC 646 and ISO/IEC 8859) are retained for compatibility and may be used to implement such protocols. (See *Section 2.6, Controls and Control Sequences.*)

Logical Order

For all scripts Unicode text is stored in *logical order* in the memory representation, corresponding to the order in which text is typed on the keyboard. In some circumstances the order of characters is different from this logical order when the text is displayed or printed. Where needed to ensure legibility, the Unicode Standard defines the conversion of Unicode text from the memory representation to readable (displayed) text. The distinction between logical order and display order for reading is shown in Figure 2-3.

Figure 2-3. Bidirectional Ordering

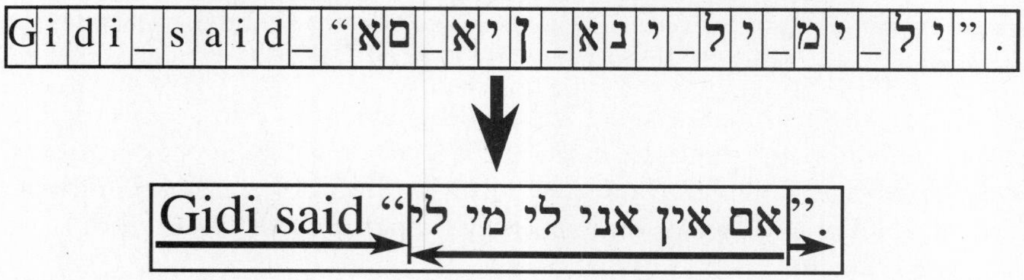

G i d i _ s a i d _ “ א ם _ א י ן _ א נ י _ ל י _ מ י _ ל י ” .

Gidi said “אם אין אני לי מי לי”.

When text in this example is ordered for display, the glyph that represents the first character of the English text is at the left. The logical start character of the Hebrew text, however, is represented by the Hebrew glyph closest to the right margin. The succeeding Hebrew glyphs are laid out to the left.

Logical order applies even when characters of different dominant direction are mixed: left-to-right (Greek, Cyrillic, Latin) with right-to-left (Arabic, Hebrew), or with vertical script. Properties of directionality inherent in characters generally determine the correct display order of text. This inherent directionality is occasionally insufficient to render plain text legibly. This situation can arise when scripts of different directionality are mixed. The Unicode Standard includes characters to specify changes in direction. *Chapter 3, Conformance* provides rules for the correct presentation of text containing left-to-right and right-to-left scripts.

For the most part, logical order corresponds to the *phonetic order*. The only current exceptions are the Thai and Lao scripts, which employ visual ordering; in these two scripts, users traditionally type in visual order rather than phonetic order.

Characters such as the *short i* in Devanagari are displayed before the characters that they logically follow in the memory representation. (See the Devanagari subsection in *Section 6.1, General Scripts Area* for further explanation.)

Combining marks (accent marks in the Greek, Cyrillic and Latin scripts, vowel marks in Arabic and Devanagari, and so on) do not appear linearly in the final rendered text. In a Unicode character code string, all such characters *follow* the base character that they modify (for example, Roman "ã" is stored as "a" followed by combining "˜" when not stored in a precomposed form). The combining marks are generally articulated in phonetic order after their base character.

Unification

The Unicode Standard avoids duplicate encoding of characters by unifying them within scripts across languages; characters that are equivalent in form are given a single code. Common letters, punctuation marks, symbols, and diacritics are given one code each, regardless of language, as are common Chinese/Japanese/Korean (CJK) ideographs. (See *Section 6.4, CJK Ideographs Area*).

Care has been taken not to make artificial distinctions among characters. Thus, for example, IPA characters are unified with the Latin alphabet. Users may become confused when they see an *Å* on the screen but their search dialog does not find it. The reason this occurs is that what they see on the screen is *not* an *Å* (*A-ring*)—it is an *Å* (*Ångström*). It is quite normal for many characters to have different usages, such as *comma* "," for either thousands-separator (English) or decimal-separator (French). The Unicode Standard avoids duplication of characters due to specific usage in different languages, duplicating characters *only* to support compatibility with base standards.

The Unicode Standard does not attempt to encode features such as language, font, size, positioning, glyphs, and so forth. For example, it does not preserve language as a part of character encoding: just as French *i grecque*, German *ypsilon*, and English *wye* are all represented by the same character code, "Y" U+0057, so too are Chinese *zi*, Japanese *ji*, and Korean *ja* all represented as the same character code, 字 U+5B57.

In determining whether or not to unify variant ideograph forms across standards, the Unicode Standard follows the principles described in *Section 6.4, CJK Ideographs Area*. Where these principles determine that two forms constitute a trivial (*wazukana*) difference, the Unicode Standard assigns a single code. Otherwise, separate codes are assigned.

Compatibility characters. Compatibility characters are those that would not have been encoded (except for compatibility) because they are in some sense variants of characters that have already been coded. The prime examples are the glyph variants in the Compatibility Area: half-width characters, Arabic contextual form glyphs, Arabic ligatures, and so on.

The Compatibility Area contains a large number of compatibility characters, but the Unicode Standard also contains many compatibility characters that are not in the Compatibility Area. Examples of these include Roman numerals, such as the IV "character." By the time a distinct area for such characters was created, it was impractical to move those characters to that area. Nevertheless, it is important to be able to identify which characters are compatibility characters so that Unicode-based systems can treat them in a uniform way.

Identifying a character A as a compatibility variant of another character B implies that generally A can be remapped to B without loss of information other than formatting. Such remapping cannot always take place because many of the compatibility characters are in place just to allow systems to maintain one-to-one mappings to existing code sets. In such cases, a remapping would lose information that is felt to be important in the original set. Compatibility mappings are called out in *Section 7.1, Character Names List.* Because replacing a character by its compatibly equivalent character or character sequence may change the information in the text, implementation has to proceed with due caution. A good use of these mappings may not be in transcoding, but in providing the correct equivalence for searching and sorting.

Dynamic Composition

The Unicode Standard allows for the dynamic composition of accented forms. Combining characters used to create composite forms are productive. Because the process of character composition is open-ended, new forms with modifying marks may be created from a combination of base characters followed by combining characters. For example, the diaeresis, "¨", may be combined with all vowels and a number of consonants in languages using the Latin script or any other script.

In the Unicode Standard, all combining characters are encoded following the base characters to which they apply. The sequence of Unicode characters U+0061 LATIN SMALL LETTER A "a" + U+0308 COMBINING DIAERESIS "¨" + U+0075 LATIN SMALL LETTER U "u" unambiguously encodes "äu" not "aü."

Equivalent Sequence

Some text elements can be encoded either as static precomposed forms or by dynamic composition. Common precomposed forms such as U+00DC LATIN CAPITAL LETTER U WITH DIAERESIS "Ü" are included for compatibility with current standards. For static precomposed forms the standard provides a mapping to the canonically equivalent dynamically composed sequence of characters.

In many cases different sequences of Unicode characters are considered equivalent. For example, a precomposed character may be represented as a composed character sequence (see Figure 2-4).

Figure 2-4. Equivalent Sequences

B + Ä → B + A + ¨

LJ + A → L + J + A

In such cases the Unicode Standard does not prescribe one particular sequence; each of the sequences in the examples are equivalent. Systems may choose to normalize Unicode text to one particular sequence, such as normalizing composed character sequences into precomposed characters or vice-versa. Therefore, any distinctions made by applications or users are not guaranteed to be interchangeable. (For implementation guidelines see *Section 5.9, Normalization*).

Convertibility

Character identity is preserved for interchange with a number of different base standards, which included national, international, and vendor standards. Where variant forms (or even the same form) are given separate codes within one base standard, they are also kept separate within the Unicode Standard. This guarantees that there will always be a mapping between the Unicode Standard and base standards.

Accurate convertibility is guaranteed between the Unicode Standard and other standards in wide usage as of May 1993. In general, a single code value in another standard will correspond to a single code value in the Unicode Standard. However, sometimes a single code value in another standard corresponds to a sequence of code values in the Unicode Standard, or vice versa. Conversion between Unicode text and text in other character codes must in general be done by explicit table-mapping processes. (See also *Section 5.7, Transcoding to Other Standards.*)

2.3 Unicode Allocation

All codes in the Unicode Standard are equally accessible electronically; the exact assignment of character codes is of minor consequence for information processing. But, for the convenience of people who will use them, the codes are grouped by linguistic and functional categories.

Allocation Areas

Figure 2-5 provides an overview of the Unicode code space allocation. The Unicode Standard code space is divided into several areas, which are themselves divided into character blocks.

- The *General Scripts Area*, consisting of alphabetic and syllabic scripts that have relatively small character sets, such as Latin, Cyrillic, Greek, Hebrew, Arabic, Devanagari, and Thai
- The *Symbols Area*, including a large variety of symbols and dingbats, for punctuation, mathematics, chemistry, technical, and other specialized usage
- The *CJK Phonetics and Symbols Area,* including punctuation, symbols, and phonetics for Chinese, Japanese, and Korean
- The *CJK Ideographs Area*, consisting of 20,902 unified CJK ideographs
- The *Hangul Syllables Area*, consisting of 11,172 precomposed Korean Hangul syllables
- The *Surrogates Area*, consisting of 1024 low-half surrogates and 1024 high-half surrogates that are used in the surrogate extension method to access over one million codes for future expansion
- The *Private Use Area*, containing 6,400 code positions used for defining user- or vendor-specific characters
- The *Compatibility and Specials Area*, containing characters from widely used corporate and national standards that have other representations in Unicode encoding, and several special-use characters

The allocation of characters into areas reflects the evolution of the Unicode Standard and is not intended to define the usage of characters in implementations. For example, there are many characters included in the standard solely for reasons of compatibility with other standards but not coded in the Compatibility Area; there are many general-purpose symbols and punctuation in the CJK Auxiliary Area, while the Hangul *conjoining jamo* are in the General Scripts Area.

Figure 2-5. Unicode Allocation

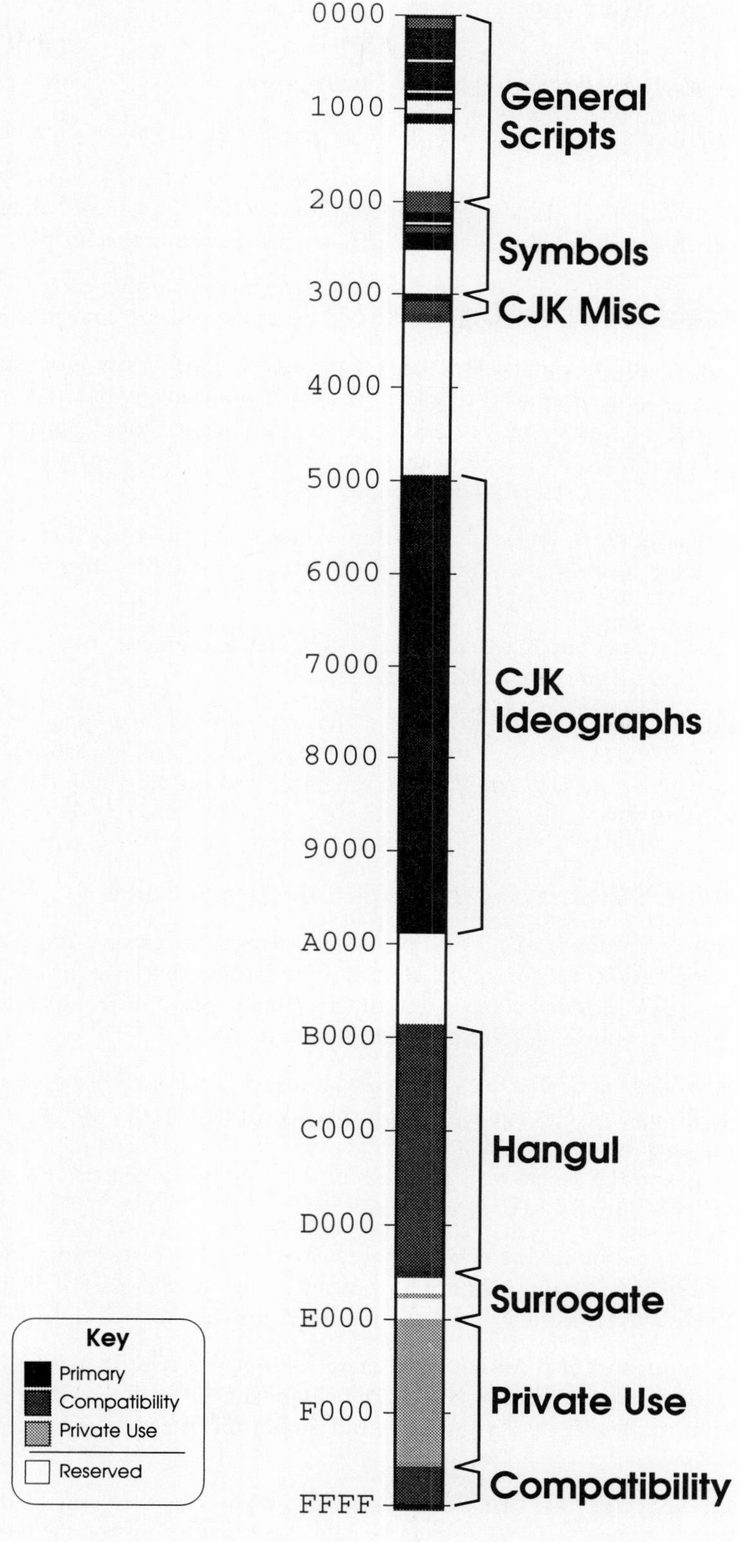

A Private Use Area gives the Unicode Standard the necessary flexibility and matches widespread practice in existing standards; successful interchange requires agreement between sender and receiver regarding interpretation of private use codes.

Code Space Assignment for Graphic Characters

The predominant characteristics of code space assignment in the Unicode Standard are as follows:

- Where there is a single accepted standard for a script, the Unicode Standard generally follows it for the relative order of characters within that script.
- The first 256 codes follow precisely the arrangement of ISO/IEC 8859-1 (Latin 1), of which 7-bit ASCII (ISO/IEC 646) comprises the first 128 code positions.
- Characters with common characteristics are located together contiguously. For example, the primary Arabic character block was modeled after ISO/IEC 8859-6. The Arabic script characters used in Persian, Urdu, and other languages, but not included in ISO/IEC 8859-6, are allocated after the primary Arabic character block. Right-to-left scripts are grouped together.
- Codes that represent letters, punctuation, symbols, and diacritics that are generally shared by multiple languages or scripts are grouped together in several locations.
- The Unicode Standard makes no pretense to correlate character code allocation with language-dependent collation or case.
- Unified CJK ideographs are arranged according to the Unified Repertoire and Ordering (URO) Version 2.0 published by the ISO JTC1/SC2/WG2 Ideographic Rapporteur Group. This ordering is roughly based on a radical and stroke count order.

Non-Graphic Characters, Reserved and Unassigned Codes

All code points except those mentioned below are reserved for graphic characters. Code points unassigned in this version of the Unicode Standard are available for assignment in later versions of the Unicode Standard to characters of any script. Existing characters will not be reassigned or removed except in extreme circumstances.[1]

- Sixty-five codes (U+0000→U+001F and U+007F→U+009F) are reserved specifically as control codes. Of the control codes, *null* (U+0000) can be used as a string terminator as in the C language, *tab* (U+0009) retains its customary meaning, and the others may be interpreted according to ISO/IEC 6429. (See *Section 2.6, Controls and Control Sequences.*)
- Two codes are not used to encode characters: U+FFFF is reserved for internal use (as a sentinel) and should not be transmitted or stored as part of plain text. U+FFFE is also reserved. Its presence may indicate byte-swapped Unicode data.
- A contiguous area of codes has been set aside for private use. Characters in this area will never be defined by the Unicode Standard. These codes can be freely used for characters of any purpose, but successful interchange requires an

1. Removal or movement of characters requires approval by a supermajority of Unicode Consortium members. The only cases where this has happened were in the process of merging with ISO/IEC 10646 and in accommodating the addition of the full repertoire of Korean characters.

agreement between sender and receiver on their interpretation.

- 2K codes have been allocated for use in the extension mechanism surrogates. There are no escape sequences to access other code spaces, as it is not necessary to maintain state or check for escape sequences.

2.4 Special Character and Non-Character Values

Byte Order Mark

The canonical encoding form of Unicode plain text as a sequence of 16-bit codes is sensitive to the byte ordering that is used when serializing text into a sequence of bytes, such as when writing to a file or transferring across a network. Some processors place the least significant byte in the initial position, while others place the most significant byte in the initial position. Ideally, all implementations of the Unicode Standard would follow only one set of byte order rules, but this would force one class of processors to swap the byte order on reading and writing plain text files, even when the file never leaves the system on which it was created.

To have an efficient way to indicate which byte order is used in a text, the Unicode Standard contains two code values, U+FEFF ZERO WIDTH NO-BREAK SPACE (*byte order mark*) and U+FFFE (not a character code), which are the byte-ordered mirror images of each other. The *byte order mark* is not a control character that selects the byte order of the text; rather its function is to notify recipients which byte ordering is used in a file.

Unicode Signature. The sequence FE_{16}, FF_{16} may serve as an implicit marker to identify a file as containing Unicode text. This sequence is exceedingly rare at the outset of text files using other character encodings, single- or multiple-byte.

For example, in systems that employ ISO Latin 1 (ISO/IEC 8859-1) or the Microsoft Windows ANSI Code Page 1252, this sequence constitutes the string *thorn* + *y umlaut* "þÿ"; in systems that employ the Apple Macintosh™ Roman character set or the Adobe Standard Encoding, this sequence represents *ogonek* + *hacek* "˛ˇ"; in systems that employ other common IBM PC Code Pages (e.g., CP 437, 850, etc.), this sequence represents *black square* + *no-break space* "■ ".

Strictly speaking, however, employment as a signature constitutes a particular use of a Unicode character, and there is nothing in this standard itself that requires or endorses this usage. Systems that employ the Unicode character encoding as their interchange code should consider prepending the U+FEFF *byte order mark* to each plain text file and removing initial *byte order marks* during processing. The *byte order mark* has legitimate use as zero width no-break space in the middle of text streams; it should not be filtered there. See the Specials subsection of *Section 6.8, Compatibility Area and Specials* for more information on the use of *byte order mark*.

Special Non-Character Values

U+FFFF and U+FFFE. These code values are *not* used to represent Unicode characters. U+FFFF is reserved for private program use as a sentinel or other signal. (Notice that U+FFFF is a 16-bit representation of –1 in two's-complement notation.) Programs receiving this code are not required to interpret it in any way. It is good practice, however, to recognize this code as a non-character value and to take appropriate action, such as indicating possible corruption of the text. U+FFFE is similar in all respects to U+FFFF, except that it is also the mirror image of U+FEFF ZERO WIDTH NO-BREAK SPACE (*byte order mark*). The presence of a U+FFFE constitutes a strong hint that the text in question is byte-reversed.

Separators

Line and Paragraph Separator. The Unicode Standard provides two unambiguous characters, U+2028 LINE SEPARATOR and U+2029 PARAGRAPH SEPARATOR, to separate lines and paragraphs. A new line is begun after each line separator. A new paragraph is begun after each paragraph separator. Since these are separator codes, it is not necessary either to start the first line or paragraph or to end the last line or paragraph with them. Doing so would indicate that there was an empty paragraph or line following. The paragraph separator can be inserted between paragraphs of text. Its use allows the creation of plain text files, which can be laid out on a different line width at the receiving end. The line separator can be used to indicate an unconditional end of line. These are considered the canonical form of denoting line and paragraph boundaries in Unicode plain text.

Interaction with CR/LF. The Unicode Standard does not prescribe specific semantics for U+000D CARRIAGE RETURN (CR) and U+000A LINE FEED (LF). These codes are provided to represent any CR or LF characters employed by a higher-level protocol or retained in text translated from other standards. It is left to each application to interpret these codes, to decide whether to require their use, and to determine whether CR/LF pairs or single codes are needed.

Layout and Format Control Characters

The Unicode Standard defines several characters, which are used to control joining behavior, bidirectional ordering control, and alternate formats for display. These characters are explicitly defined as not affecting line breaking behavior. Unlike space characters or other delimiters, they do not serve to indicate word, line, or other unit boundaries. Their specific use in layout and formatting is described in the General Punctuation section of *Chapter 6, Character Block Descriptions*.

The Replacement Character

U+FFFD REPLACEMENT CHARACTER is the general substitute character in the Unicode Standard. It can be substituted for any "unknown" character in another encoding that cannot be mapped in terms of known Unicode values (see *Section 5.4, Unknown and Missing Characters*).

2.5 Combining Characters

Combining Characters. Characters intended to be positioned relative to an associated base character are depicted in the character code charts above, below, or through a dotted circle. They are also annotated in the names list or in the character property lists as "combining," as "diacritic," or as "non-spacing" characters. When rendered, the glyphs that depict these characters are intended to be positioned relative to the glyph depicting the preceding base character in some combination and not to occupy a spacing position by themselves. This is the motivation for the terms "combining" and "non-spacing." The spacing or non-spacing properties of a combining character are really properties of the glyph used to depict a combining character, since, in certain scripts (for example, Tamil) a combining character may be depicted with either depending on the context.

Diacritics. Diacritics are the principal class of combining characters used with European alphabets. In the Unicode Standard, the term "diacritic" is defined very broadly to include accents as well as other non-spacing marks.

All diacritics can be applied to any base character and are available for use with any script. There is a separate block for symbol diacritics, generally intended to be used with symbol base characters. There are additional combining characters in the blocks for particular scripts with which they are primarily used. As with other characters, the allocation of a combining character to one block or another identifies only its primary usage; it is not intended to define or limit the range of characters to which it may be applied. *In the Unicode Standard, all sequences of character codes are permitted.*

Other Combining Characters. Some scripts, such as Hebrew, Arabic, and the scripts of India and Southeast Asia, also have combining characters indicated in the charts in relation to dotted circles to show their position relative to the base character. Many of these non-spacing marks encode vowel letters; as such they are not generally referred to as "diacritics."

Sequence of Base Characters and Diacritics

In the Unicode Standard, all combining characters are to be used in sequence following the base characters to which they apply. The sequence of Unicode characters U+0061 LATIN SMALL LETTER A "a" + U+0308 COMBINING DIAERESIS "¨" + U+0075 LATIN SMALL LETTER U "u" unambiguously encodes "äu" not "aü."

The ordering convention used by the Unicode Standard is consistent with the logical order of combining characters in Semitic and Indic scripts, the great majority of which (logically or phonetically) follow the base characters with respect to which they are positioned. To avoid the complication of defining and implementing combining characters on both sides of base characters, the Unicode Standard specifies that all combining characters must follow their base characters. This convention conforms to the way modern font technology handles the rendering of non-spacing graphical forms (glyphs) so that mapping from character memory representation order to font rendering order is simplified. It is different from the convention used in ISO/IEC 6937 and the bibliographic standard ISO/IEC 5426.

A sequence of base character plus one or more combining characters generally has the same properties as the base character, except for the case of enclosing diacritics that convey a symbol property. For example U+2460 CIRCLED DIGIT ONE has the same property as U+0031 DIGIT ONE followed by U+20DD COMBINING ENCLOSING CIRCLE.

Figure 2-6. Indic Vowel Signs

फ + ि◌ → फि

In the charts for Indian scripts, some vowels are depicted to the left of dotted circles (see Figure 2.6). This is a special case to be carefully distinguished from that of general combining diacritical mark characters. Such vowel signs are rendered to the left of a consonant letter or consonant cluster, even though their logical order in the Unicode encoding follows the consonant letter. The decision to code these in pronunciation order and not in visual order is also consistent with the ISCII standard.

Multiple Combining Characters

There are instances where more than one diacritical mark is applied to a single base character (see Figure 2-7). The Unicode Standard does not restrict the number of combining characters that may follow a base character. The following discussion summarizes the treatment of multiple combining characters. (For the formal algorithm, see *Chapter 3, Conformance.*)

Figure 2-7. Stacking Sequences

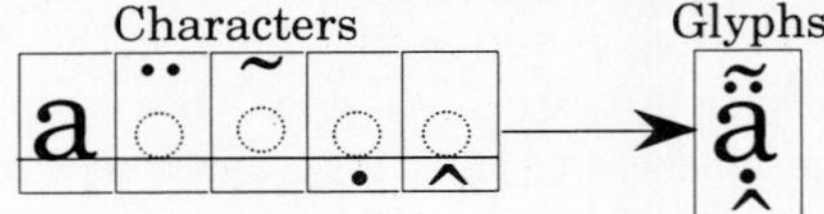

1. If the combining characters can interact typographically—for example, a U+0304 COMBINING MACRON and a U+0308 COMBINING DIAERESIS—then the order of graphic display is determined by the order of coded characters (see Figure 2-8). The diacritics or other combining characters are positioned from the base character's glyph outward. Combining characters placed above a base character will be stacked vertically, starting with the first encountered in the logical store and continuing for as many marks above as are required by the character codes following the base character. For combining characters placed below a base character, the situation is reversed, with the combining characters starting from the base character and stacking downward.

Figure 2-8. Interacting Combining Characters

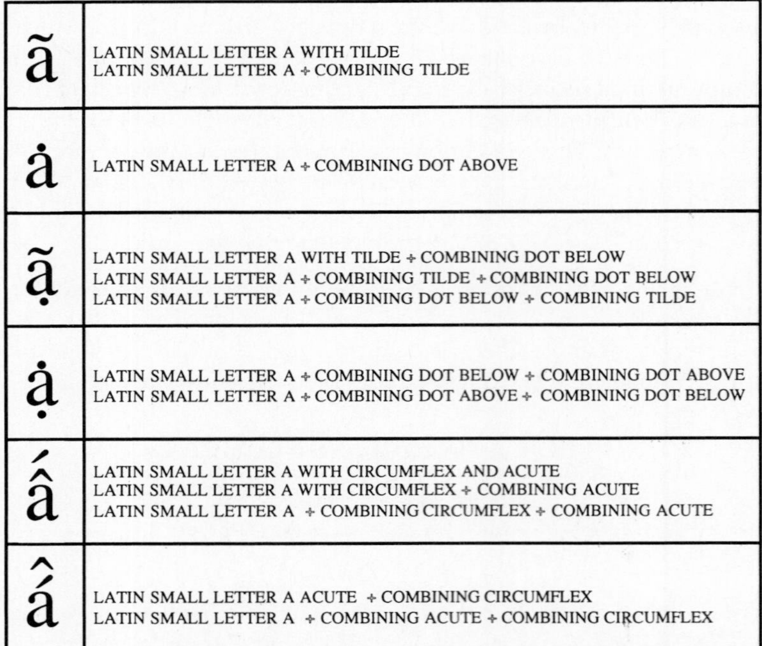

ã	LATIN SMALL LETTER A WITH TILDE LATIN SMALL LETTER A + COMBINING TILDE
ȧ	LATIN SMALL LETTER A + COMBINING DOT ABOVE
ạ̃	LATIN SMALL LETTER A WITH TILDE + COMBINING DOT BELOW LATIN SMALL LETTER A + COMBINING TILDE + COMBINING DOT BELOW LATIN SMALL LETTER A + COMBINING DOT BELOW + COMBINING TILDE
ạ̇	LATIN SMALL LETTER A + COMBINING DOT BELOW + COMBINING DOT ABOVE LATIN SMALL LETTER A + COMBINING DOT ABOVE + COMBINING DOT BELOW
ấ	LATIN SMALL LETTER A WITH CIRCUMFLEX AND ACUTE LATIN SMALL LETTER A WITH CIRCUMFLEX + COMBINING ACUTE LATIN SMALL LETTER A + COMBINING CIRCUMFLEX + COMBINING ACUTE
á̂	LATIN SMALL LETTER A ACUTE + COMBINING CIRCUMFLEX LATIN SMALL LETTER A + COMBINING ACUTE + COMBINING CIRCUMFLEX

An example of multiple combining characters above the base character is found in Thai, where a consonant letter can have above it one of the vowels U+0E34 through U+0E37 and, above that, one of four tone marks U+0E48 through U+0E4B. The order of character codes that produces this graphic display is base consonant character, vowel character, then tone mark character.

2. Some specific combining characters override the default stacking behavior by being positioned horizontally rather than stacking, or by ligaturing with an

adjacent non-spacing mark (see Figure 2-9). When positioned horizontally, the order of codes is reflected by positioning in the dominant order of the script with which they are used. For example, in a left-to-right script, horizontal accents would be coded left-to-right.

Figure 2-9. Overriding Behavior

ἄ	GREEK SMALL LETTER ALPHA + COMBINING COMMA ABOVE (psili) + COMBINING ACUTE ACCENT (oxia)
ά̓	GREEK SMALL LETTER ALPHA + COMBINING ACUTE ACCENT (oxia) + COMBINING COMMA ABOVE (psili)

Prominent characters that show such override behavior are associated with specific scripts or alphabets. For example, when used with the Greek script, the "breathing marks" U+0313 COMBINING COMMA ABOVE (*psili*) and U+0314 COMBINING REVERSED COMMA ABOVE (*dasia*) require that, when used together with a following acute or grave accent, they be rendered side-by-side above their base letter rather than the accent marks being stacked above the breathing marks. The order of codes here is *base character code + breathing mark code + accent mark code*. This is one example of the language-dependent nature of rendering combining diacritical marks.

Multiple Base Characters

When the glyphs representing two base characters merge to form a ligature, then the combining characters must be rendered correctly in relation to the ligated glyph (see Figure 2-10). Internally, the software has to distinguish between the non-spacing marks that apply to positions relative to the first part of the ligature glyph and those that apply to the second. (For a discussion of general methods of positioning non-spacing marks, see *Section 5.11, Stategies for Handling Non-Spacing Marks.*)

Figure 2-10. Multiple Base Characters

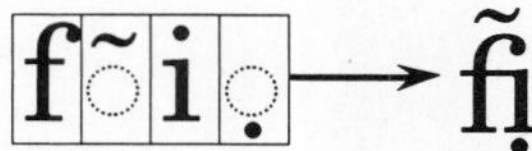

Multiple base characters do not commonly occur in most scripts. However, in some scripts, such as Arabic, this situation occurs quite often when vowel marks are used. This is because of the large number of ligatures in Arabic, where each element of a ligature is a consonant, which in turn can have a vowel mark attached to it. Ligatures can even occur with three or more characters merging; vowel marks may be attached to each part.

Spacing Clones of European Diacritical Marks

By convention, diacritical marks used by the Unicode Standard may be exhibited in (apparent) isolation by applying them to U+0020 SPACE or to U+00A0 NO BREAK SPACE. This might be done, for example, when talking about the diacritical mark itself as a mark, rather than using it in its normal way in text. The Unicode Standard separately encodes clones of many common European diacritical marks that are spacing characters, largely to provide compatibility with existing character set standards. These related characters are cross-referenced in the names list in *Chapter 7, Code Charts.*

2.6 Controls and Control Sequences

Control Characters

The Unicode Standard provides 65 code values for the representation of control characters. These ranges are U+0000→U+001F and U+007F→U+009F, which correspond to the 8-bit controls 00_{16} to $1F_{16}$ (C0 controls) and $7F_{16}$ to $9F_{16}$ (*delete* and C1 controls). For example, the 8-bit version of *horizontal tab* (HT) is at 09_{16}; the Unicode Standard encodes *tab* at U+0009. When converting control codes from existing 8-bit text, they are merely zero extended to the full 16 bits of Unicode characters.

Programs that conform to the Unicode Standard may treat these 16-bit control codes in exactly the same way as they treat their 7- and 8-bit equivalents in other protocols, such as ISO/IEC 2022 and ISO/IEC 6429. Such usage constitutes a higher-level protocol and is beyond the scope of the Unicode Standard. Similarly, the use of ISO/IEC 6429:1992 control sequences (extended to 16-bits) for controlling bidirectional formatting is a legitimate higher-level protocol layered on top of the plain text of the Unicode Standard. As with all higher-level protocols, sender and receiver must agree upon a common protocol beforehand.

Escape Characters. In converting text containing escape sequences to the Unicode character encoding, text must be converted to the equivalent Unicode characters. Converting escape sequences into Unicode characters on a character-by-character basis (for instance, ESC–A turns into U+001B ESCAPE, U+0041 LATIN CAPITAL LETTER A) allows the reverse conversion to be performed without forcing the conversion program to recognize the escape sequence as such.

Control Code Sequences Encoding Additional Information about Text. If a system does use sequences beginning with control codes to embed additional information about text (such as formatting attributes or structure), then such sequences form a higher-level protocol outside the scope of the Unicode Standard. Such higher-level protocols are not specified by the Unicode Standard; their existence cannot be assumed without a separate agreement between the parties interchanging such data.

Representing Control Sequences

Control sequences can be represented in the Unicode encoding but must then be represented in terms of 16-bit characters. For example, suppose that an application allows embedded font information to be transmitted by means of an 8-bit sequence. In the following, the notation **^A** refers to the C0 control code 01_{16}, **^B** refers to the C0 control code 02_{16}, and so on:

^ATimes**^B** = **01**,54,69,6D,65,73,**02**

Then the corresponding sequence of Unicode character codes would be

^ATimes**^B** = **0001**,0054,0069,006D,0065,0073,**0002**

That is, each Unicode character code is a 16-bit zero-extended code value of the corresponding 8-bit code value.

Where the embedded data is not interpreted as a sequence of characters by the protocol, it could be encoded as:

^ATimes**^B** = **0001**,5469,6D65,7300,**0002**

The data could never be encoded as

^ATimes^B = **01**54,696D,6573,**02**00

because in the Unicode character encoding this sequence represents four characters—LATIN CAPITAL LETTER R ACUTE (U+0154), two Han characters (U+696D and U+6573 respectively), and LATIN CAPITAL LETTER A WITH DOUBLE GRAVE (U+0200). None of these is a control character. If a control sequence contains embedded binary data, then the data bytes do not necessarily need to be zero-extended as the control sequence constitutes a higher protocol. However, doing so allows code conversion algorithms to succeed even in the absence of explicit knowledge of employed control sequences.

2.7 Conforming to the Unicode Standard

Chapter 3, Conformance, specifies the set of unambiguous criteria to which a Unicode-conformant implementation must adhere so that it can interoperate with other conformant implementations. The following section gives examples of conformance and non-conformance to complement the formal statement of conformance.

An implementation that conforms to the Unicode Standard has the following characteristics:

- It treats characters as 16-bit units.

  U+2020 (that is, 2020_{16}) is the single Unicode character DAGGER '†', *not* two ASCII spaces.

- It interprets characters according to the identities, properties, and rules defined for them in this standard.

  U+2423 is '␣' OPEN BOX, *not* 'い' *hiragana small i* (which is the meaning of the bytes 2423_{16} in JIS).

  U+00D4 'Ô' is equivalent to U+004F 'O' followed by U+0302 '^', but *not equivalent to* U+0302 followed by U+004F.

  U+05D0 'א' followed by U+05D1 'ב' looks like 'בא', *not* 'אב' when displayed.

- It does not use unassigned codes.

  U+2073 is unassigned and not usable for '³' (*superscript 3*) or any other character.

- It does not corrupt unknown characters.

  U+2029 is PARAGRAPH SEPARATOR and should not be dropped by applications that do not yet support it.

  U+03A1 "Ρ" GREEK CAPITAL LETTER RHO should not be changed to U+00A1 (first byte dropped), U+0050 (mapped to Latin letter *P*), U+A103 (bytes reversed), nor to anything but U+03A1.

However, it is acceptable for that implementation:

- To support only a subset of the Unicode characters

  An application may not provide mathematical symbols, or the Thai script.

- To transform data knowingly

  Uppercase conversion: 'a' transformed to 'A'

Romaji to kana: 'kyo' transformed to キョ

247D "(10)" decomposed to 0028 0031 0030 0029

- To build higher-level protocols on the character set

  Compression of characters

  Use of rich text file formats

- To define characters in the Private Use Area

  Examples of characters that might be encoded in the Private Use Area are supplementary ideographic characters (*gaiji*) or existing corporate logo characters.

Code conversion from other standards to the Unicode Standard will be considered conformant if the matching table produces accurate conversions in both directions.

Characters Not Used in a Subset

The Unicode Standard does not require that an application be capable of interpreting and rendering all of the Unicode characters in order to be conformant. Many systems will have fonts only for some scripts, but not for others; sorting and other text-processing rules may be implemented only for a limited set of languages. As a result, there is a subset of characters which an implementation is able to interpret.

The Unicode Standard provides no formalized method for identifying this subset. Furthermore, this subset is typically different for different aspects of an implementation. For example, an application may be able to read, write, and store any 16-bit character, be able to sort one subset according to the rules of one or more languages (and the rest arbitrarily), but only have access to fonts for a single script. The same implementation may be able to render additional scripts as soon as additional fonts are installed in its environment. Therefore, the subset of interpretable characters is typically not a static concept.

Conformance to the Unicode Standard *implies* that whenever text purports to be unmodified, uninterpretable characters must not be removed or altered. (See also *Section 3.1, Conformance Requirements.)*

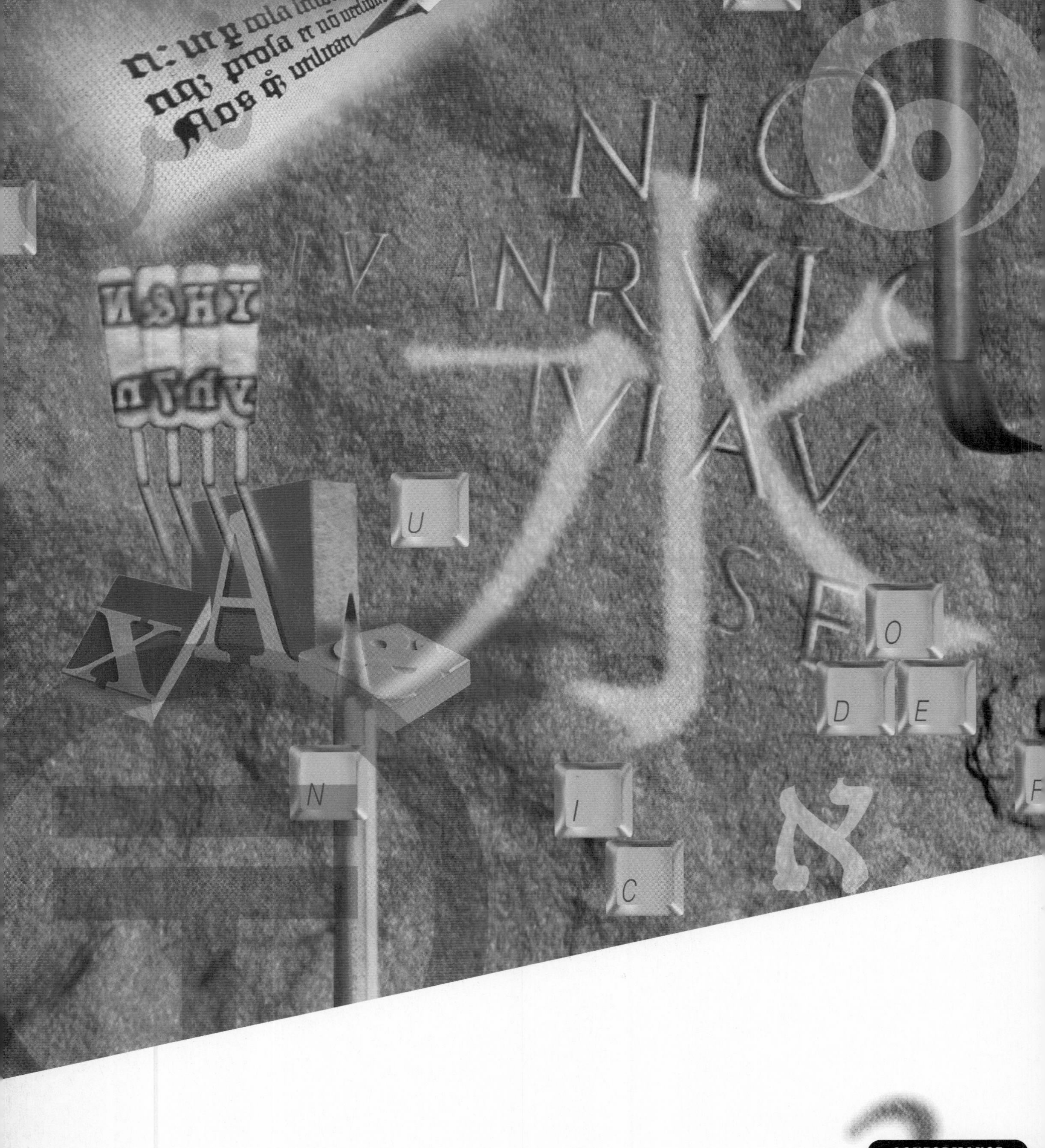

3 CONFORMANCE

Chapter 3

Conformance

This chapter defines conformance to the Unicode Standard in terms of the principles and encoding architecture it embodies. The first section consists of the conformance clauses, followed by sections that define more precisely the technical terms used in those clauses. The remaining sections contain the formal algorithms that are part of conformance and referred to by the conformance clause. These algorithms specify the required results rather than the specific implementation; all implementations that produce results identical to the results of the formal algorithms are conformant.

In this chapter, conformance subclauses are identified with a letter *C*. Definitions are identified with the letter *D*. Bulleted items are explanatory comments regarding definitions or subclauses.

3.1 Conformance Requirements

This section specifies the formal conformance requirements for processes implementing the Unicode Standard, Version 2.0. Note that this clause has been revised from the previous versions of the Unicode Standard (Versions 1.0 and 1.1). These revisions do not change the substance of the conformance requirements previously set forth but are formalized and extended to allow for the use of surrogates. Implementations that satisfied the conformance clause of the previous versions of the Unicode Standard (Versions 1.0 and 1.1) will satisfy this revised clause.

Byte Ordering

C1 *A process shall interpret Unicode code values as 16-bit quantities.*

- This means that Unicode values can be stored in native 16-bit machine words.
- For information on transformations of Unicode text, see *Appendix A, Transformation Formats*. For information on use of `wchar_t` or other programming language types to represent Unicode values, see *Section 5.1, ANSI/ISO C* `wchar_t`.

C2 *The Unicode Standard does not specify any order of bytes inside a Unicode value.*

- Machine architectures differ in the *ordering* of whether the most significant byte or the least significant byte comes first. These are known as "big-endian" and "little-endian" orders, respectively.

C3 *A process shall interpret a Unicode value that has been serialized into a sequence of bytes, by most significant byte first, in the absence of higher-level protocols.*

- The majority of all interchange occurs with processes running on the same or a similar configuration. This makes intra-domain interchange of Unicode text in the domain-specific byte order fully conformant and limits the role of the canonical byte order to interchange of Unicode text across domain, or where the nature of the originating domain is unknown. (For a discussion of the use of *byte order mark* to indicate byte orderings, see *Section 2.4, Special Character and Non-Character Values.)*

Invalid Code Values

C4 *A process shall not interpret an unpaired high- or low-surrogate as an abstract character.*

C5 *A process shall not interpret either U+FFFE or U+FFFF as an abstract character.*

C6 *A process shall not interpret any unassigned code value as an abstract character.*

- These clauses do not preclude the assignment of certain generic semantics (for example, rendering with a glyph indicating the character block) that allow graceful behavior in the presence of code values that are outside a supported subset, or code values that are unpaired surrogates.
- Private Use code values are assigned, but can be given any interpretation by conformant processes.

Interpretation

C7 *A process shall interpret a coded character representation according to the character semantics established by this standard, if that process does interpret that coded character representation.*

- The above restriction does not preclude internal transformations that are never visible external to the process.

C8 *A process shall not assume that it is required to interpret any particular coded character representation.*

- Any means for specifying a subset of characters that a process can interpret is outside the scope of this standard.
- The semantics of a code value in the Private Use Area is outside the scope of this standard.
- These clauses are not intended to preclude enumerations or specifications of the characters that a process or system is able to interpret, but they do separate supported subset enumerations from the question of conformance. In real life, any system may occasionally receive an unfamiliar character code that it is unable to interpret.

C9 *A process shall not assume that the interpretations of two canonical-equivalent character sequences are distinct.*

- Even processes that normally do not distinguish between canonical-equivalent character sequences can have reasonable exception behavior. Some examples of this behavior include graceful fallback processing by processes unable to support correct positioning of non-spacing marks; "Show Hidden Text" modes that reveal memory representation structure; and ignoring collating behavior of combining sequences that are not part of the repertoire of a specified language.

Modification

C10 *A process shall make no change in a valid coded character representation other than the possible replacement of character sequences by their canonical-equivalent sequences, if that process purports not to modify the interpretation of that coded character representation.*

- Replacement of a character sequence by a compatibility equivalent sequence does modify the interpretation of the text.
- Replacement or deletion of a character sequence that the process cannot or does not interpret does modify the interpretation of the text.
- Changing the bit or byte ordering when transforming between different machine architectures does not modify the interpretation of the text.

3.2 Semantics

This and the following sections more precisely define the terms that are used in the conformance clauses.

D1 *normative properties and behavior.* The following are normative character properties and normative behavior of the Unicode Standard:

- Simple Properties
- Character Combination
- Canonical Decompositio
- Compatibility Decomposition
- Surrogate Property
- Bidirectional behavior, as interpreted according to the Unicode bidirectional algorithm
- Combining Jamo Behavior, as interpreted according to *Section 3.10, Combining Jamo Behavior*

D2 *character semantics:* the semantics of a character are established by its character name, representative glyph, and normative properties and behavior.

- A character may have a broader range of use than the most literal interpretation of its name might indicate; coded representation, name, and representative glyph need to be taken in context when establishing the semantics of a character. For example, U+002E FULL STOP can represent a sentence period, an abbreviation period, a decimal number separator in English, a thousands number separator in German, and so on.
- Consistency with the representative glyph does not require that the images be identical or even graphically similar; rather, it means that both images are generally recognized to be representations of the same character. Representing the character U+0061 LATIN SMALL LETTER A by the glyph "X" would violate its character identity.
- Some normative behavior is default behavior; this behavior can be overridden by higher-level protocols. However, in the absence of such protocols, the behavior must be observed in order to follow the character semantics.

- The Character Combination properties and the Canonical Ordering Behavior are not overridable by higher-level protocols.

3.3 Characters and Coded Representations

D3 *abstract character:* a unit of information used for the organization, control, or representation of textual data.

- When representing data, the nature of that data is generally symbolic as opposed to some other kind of data (for example, numeric, aural, or visual). Examples of such symbolic data include letters, ideographs, digits, punctuation, technical symbols, and dingbats.
- An abstract character has no concrete form.
- The abstract characters defined by the Unicode Standard are known as Unicode abstract characters.

D4 *abstract character sequence:* an ordered sequence of abstract characters.

D5 *code value:* the minimal bit combination that can represent a unit of encoded text for processing or interchange.

- This term is variously referred to as a *code element*, a *code position*, a *code point*, and a *code set value* in the industry.
- The code values in the Unicode Standard are 16-bit combinations. These code values are also known as *Unicode values* for short.

D6 *coded character representation:* an ordered sequence of one or more code values which is associated with an abstract character in a given character repertoire.

- A Unicode abstract character is represented by a single Unicode code value; the only exception to this are surrogate pairs (which are provided for future extension, but are not currently used to represent any abstract characters).

D7 *coded character sequence:* an ordered sequence of coded character representations.

Unless specified otherwise for clarity, in the text of the Unicode Standard the term *character* alone generally designates a coded character representation. Similarly, the term *character sequence* alone generally designates a coded character sequence.

D8 *higher-level protocol:* any agreement on the interpretation of Unicode characters that extends beyond the scope of this standard. Such an agreement need not be formally announced in data; it may be implicit in the context.

3.4 Simple Properties

The Unicode Standard, Version 2.0 defines the normative simple character properties of *case, numeric value, directionality,* and *mirrored. Chapter 4, Character Properties,* contains explicit mappings of characters to character properties. These represent the default properties for conformant processes in the absence of explicit, overriding, higher-level protocols. Additional properties that are specific to particular characters (such as the definition and use of the Right-Left Override character or zero-width spaces) are discussed in the relevant sections of this standard.

- The *Unicode Character Database* contains additional properties, such as category and case mappings, that are informative rather than normative.

The interpretation of some properties (such as the case of a character) are independent of context, while the interpretation of others (such as directionality) are applicable to a character sequence as a whole, rather than to the individual characters that compose the sequence.

D9 *directionality property:* a property of every graphic character which determines its horizontal ordering as specified in *Section 3.11, Bidirectional Behavior.*

- Interpretation of directional properties according to the Unicode Bidirectional Algorithm is needed for layout of right-to-left scripts such as Arabic and Hebrew.

D10 *mirrored property:* the property of characters whose images are mirrored horizontally in text that is laid out from right to left (versus left to right).

- In other words, U+0028 LEFT PARENTHESIS is interpreted as an opening parenthesis; in a left-to-right context, this will appear as "(", while in a right-to-left context, this will be mirrored and appear as ")".
- This is the default behavior in Unicode text. (For more information, see the block description for the General Punctuation subsection in *Section 6.2, Symbols Area.*)

D11 *special character properties:* The behavior of most characters does not require special attention in this standard. However, certain characters exhibit special behavior, which is described in the character block descriptions. These characters are listed in *Section 3.8, Special Character Properties.*

D12 *Private Use:* Unicode values from U+E000 to U+F8FF and surrogate pairs (see *Section 3.7, Surrogates*) whose high surrogate is from U+DB80 to U+DBFF are available for private use.

3.5 Combination

D13 *base character:* a character that does not graphically combine with preceding characters.

- Most Unicode characters are base characters. This sense of graphic combination does not preclude the presentation of base characters from adopting different contextual forms or participating in ligatures.

D14 *combining character:* a character that graphically combines with a preceding base character. The combining character is said to *apply* to that base character.

- These are characters that are not used in isolation (unless they are being described), including such characters as accents, diacritics, Hebrew points, Arabic vowel signs, and Indic matras.
- Even though a combining character is intended to be presented in graphical combination with base character, circumstances may arise where either (1) no base character precedes the combining character, or (2) a process is unable to perform graphical combination. In both of these cases, a process may present a combining character without graphical combination; that is, it may present it as if it were a base character.
- The representative images of combining characters are depicted with a dotted circle in the code charts; when presented in graphical combination with a pre-

ceding base character, that base character is intended to appear in the position occupied by the dotted circle.

- Combining characters take on the properties of their base character (except for their combining property).

D15 *non-spacing mark:* a combining character whose positioning in presentation is dependent on its base character. It generally does not consume space along the visual baseline in and of itself.

- Such characters may be large enough to affect the placement of their base character relative to preceding and succeeding base characters. For example, a circumflex applied to an "i" may affect spacing ("î"), as might the character U+20DD COMBINING ENCLOSING CIRCLE.

D16 *spacing mark:* a combining character that is not a non-spacing mark.

- Examples include U+093F DEVANAGARI VOWEL SIGN I. In general, the behavior of spacing marks does not differ greatly from that of base characters.

D17 *combining character sequence:* a character sequence consisting of a base character followed by one or more combining characters.

- This is also referred to as a *composite character sequence.*

3.6 Decomposition

D18 *decomposable character:* a character that is equivalent to a sequence of one or more other characters, according to the decomposition mappings found in the names list of *Section 7.1, Character Names List Entries.* This may also be known as a *precomposed* character or *composite* character.

D19 *decomposition:* a sequence of one or more characters that is equivalent to a decomposable character. A full decomposition of a character sequence results from decomposing each of the characters in the sequence until no characters can be further decomposed.

Compatibility Decomposition

D20 *compatibility decomposition:* the decomposition of a character which results from recursively applying *both* the compatibility mappings *and* the canonical mappings found in the names list of *Section 7.1, Character Names List Entries* until no characters can be further decomposed, and then reordering non-spacing marks according to *Section 3.9, Canonical Ordering Behavior.*

- A compatibility decomposition may remove formatting information.

D21 *compatibility character:* a character that has a compatibility decomposition.

- Compatibility characters are included in the Unicode Standard only to represent distinctions in other base standards and would not otherwise have been encoded. However, replacing a compatibility character by its decomposition may lose round-trip convertibility with a base standard.

D22 *compatibility equivalent:* two character sequences are said to be compatibility equivalents if their full compatibility decompositions are identical.

Canonical Decomposition

D23 *canonical decomposition:* the decomposition of a character which results from recursively applying the canonical mappings found in the names list of *Section 7.1, Character Names List Entries* until no characters can be further decomposed, and then reordering non-spacing marks according to *Section 3.9, Canonical Ordering Behavior.*

- The canonical mappings are a subset of the compatibility mappings; however, a canonical decomposition does not remove formatting information.

D24 *canonical equivalent:* two character sequences are said to be canonical equivalents if their full canonical decompositions are identical.

- For example, the sequences <*o, combining-diaeresis*> and <*ö*> are canonical equivalents, which is a Unicode property. This should not be confused with language-specific collation or matching, which may add additional equivalencies. For example, in Swedish, *ö* is treated as a completely different letter from *o*, collated after *z*. In German, *ö* is weakly equivalent to *oe* and collated with *oe*. In English, *ö* is just an *o* with a diacritic that indicates that it is pronounced separately from the previous letter (as in *coöperate*) and is collated with *o*.

3.7 Surrogates

D25 *high-surrogate:* A Unicode code value in the range U+D800 through U+DBFF.

D26 *low-surrogate:* A Unicode code value in the range U+DC00 through U+DFFF.

D27 *surrogate pair:* a coded character representation for a single abstract character which consists of a sequence of two Unicode values, where the first value of the pair is a high-surrogate and the second is a low-surrogate.

- Unlike combining characters, which have independent semantics and properties, high- and low-surrogates have no interpretation when they do not appear as part of a surrogate pair, other than being a surrogate.
- Surrogate pairs are designed to allow represention of rare characters in future extensions of the Unicode Standard. There are no such currently assigned characters in this version of the standard. (For more information, see *Section 6.6, Surrogates Area.*)

D28 *Unicode scalar value:* a number N from 0 to $10FFFF_{16}$ defined by applying the following algorithm to a character sequence S (the numeric constants are in hexadecimal):

N = U	If S is a single, non-surrogate value <U>
N = (H – D800) * 400 + (L – DC00) + 10000	If S is a surrogate pair <H, L>

- Unicode scalar values are defined for use by standards such as SGML that require a scalar value associated with abstract characters.
- This algorithm is identical with the ISO/IEC 10646 algorithm used to transform UTF-16 into UCS-4 (for more information, see *Appendix C, Relationship to ISO/IEC 10646*).

3.8 Special Character Properties

The behavior of most characters does not require special attention in this standard. However, the following characters exhibit special behavior, which is described in *Chapter 6, Character Block Descriptions*, and in *Chapter 4, Character Properties*.

- Line boundary control

FEFF	ZERO WIDTH NO-BREAK SPACE
2011	NON-BREAKING HYPHEN
0020	SPACE
00A0	NO-BREAK SPACE
2000	EN QUAD
2002	EN SPACE
2003	EM SPACE
2004	THREE-PER-EM SPACE
2005	FOUR-PER-EM SPACE
2006	SIX-PER-EM SPACE
2007	FIGURE SPACE
2008	PUNCTUATION SPACE
2009	THIN SPACE
200A	HAIR SPACE
200B	ZERO WIDTH SPACE

- Hyphenation control

00AD	SOFT HYPHEN
2010	HYPHEN
2011	NON-BREAKING HYPHEN

- Text separators

2028	LINE SEPARATOR
2029	PARAGRAPH SEPARATOR
0009	HORIZONTAL TAB

- Fraction formatting

2044	FRACTION SLASH

- Special behavior with non-spacing marks

0131	LATIN SMALL LETTER DOTLESS I
0069	LATIN SMALL LETTER I
0020	SPACE
00A0	NO-BREAK SPACE

- Double non-spacing marks

0360	COMBINING DOUBLE TILDE
0361	COMBINING DOUBLE INVERTED BREVE

- Joining

200C	ZERO WIDTH NON-JOINER
200D	ZERO WIDTH JOINER

- Bidirectional ordering

200E	LEFT-TO-RIGHT MARK
200F	RIGHT-TO-LEFT MARK
202A	LEFT-TO-RIGHT EMBEDDING
202B	RIGHT-TO-LEFT EMBEDDING
202C	POP DIRECTIONAL FORMATTING
202D	LEFT-TO-RIGHT OVERRIDE
202E	RIGHT-TO-LEFT OVERRIDE

- Alternate formatting

  206A INHIBIT SYMMETRIC SWAPPING
  206B ACTIVATE SYMMETRIC SWAPPING
  206C INHIBIT ARABIC FORM SHAPING
  206D ACTIVATE ARABIC FORM SHAPING
  206E NATIONAL DIGIT SHAPES
  206F NOMINAL DIGIT SHAPES

- Indic dead-character formation

  094D DEVANAGARI SIGN VIRAMA
  09CD BENGALI SIGN VIRAMA
  0A4D GURMUKHI SIGN VIRAMA
  0ACD GUJARATI SIGN VIRAMA
  0B4D ORIYA SIGN VIRAMA
  0BCD TAMIL SIGN VIRAMA
  0C4D TELUGU SIGN VIRAMA
  0CCD KANNADA SIGN VIRAMA
  0D4D MALAYALAM SIGN VIRAMA
  0F84 TIBETAN SIGN HALANTA

- Code conversion fallback

  FFFD REPLACEMENT CHARACTER

- Byte order control

  FEFF ZERO WIDTH NO-BREAK SPACE

3.9 Canonical Ordering Behavior

The purpose of this section is to provide unambiguous interpretation of a combining character sequence. In the Unicode Standard, the order of characters in a combining character sequence is interpreted according to the following principles.

- In the Unicode Standard, all combining characters are encoded following the base characters to which they apply. The Unicode sequence U+0061 LATIN SMALL LETTER A "a" + U+0308 COMBINING DIAERESIS "¨" + U+0075 LATIN SMALL LETTER U "u" is unambiguously interpreted (and displayed) as "äu", not "aü."
- Enclosing non-spacing marks surround all previous characters up to and including the base character (see Figure 3-1). They thus successively surround previous enclosing non-spacing marks.

Figure 3-1. Enclosing Marks

a + ◌⃞ + ◌̈ + ◌⃝ ➡ ä⃞⃝

- Double diacritics always bind more loosely than other non-spacing marks. When rendering, the double diacritic will float above other diacritics, excluding enclosing diacritics (see Figure 3-2).

Figure 3-2. Positioning of Double Diacritics

o + ◌̂ + ◌͠ + o + ◌̈ ➡ ô͠ö

o + ◌͠ + ◌̂ + o + ◌̈ ➡ ô͠ö

- Combining marks with the same combining class are generally positioned graphically outwards from the base character they modify. Some specific non-spacing marks override the default stacking behavior by being positioned side-by-side rather than stacking, or by ligaturing with an adjacent non-spacing mark. When positioned side-by-side, the order of codes is is reflected by positioning in the dominant order of the script with which they are used.
- If combining characters have different combining classes—for example, when one non-spacing mark is above a base character form and another is below—then no distinction of graphic form nor semantic will result.

The following subsections formalize these principles in terms of a normative list of combining classes and an algorithmic statement of how to use those combining classes to unambiguously interpret a combining character sequence.

Combining Classes

The Unicode Standard treats sequences of non-spacing marks as equivalent if they do not typographically interact. The Canonical Ordering Algorithm defines a method for determining which sequences interact and a canonical ordering of these sequences for use in equivalence comparisons.

D29 *combining class:* a numeric value given to each combining Unicode character that determines which other combining characters it typographically interacts with.

- See *Section 4.2, Combining Classes,* for a list of the combining classes for Unicode characters.

Characters have the same class if they interact typographically, different classes if they do not.

➡ Enclosing characters and spacing combining characters have the class of base characters.

➡ The particular numeric value of the combining class does not have any special signficance; the intent of providing the numeric values is *only* to distinguish the combining classes as being different, for use in equivalence comparisons.

Collation processes may not require correct sorting outside of a given domain and may not choose to invoke the canonical ordering algorithm for excluded characters. For example, a Greek collation process may not need to sort Cyrillic letters properly; in that case, it does not have to maximally decompose and reorder Cyrillic letters and may just choose to sort them according to Unicode order.

Canonical Ordering

The canonical ordering of a decomposed character sequence results essentially by sorting each sequence of non-spacing marks according to their combining class. However, enclosing non-spacing marks are treated like base characters. Base characters never sort relative to one another, so the amount of work in the algorithm depends on the number of non-spacing marks in a row. With few occurrances of more than one non-spacing mark in a row, an implementation of this algorithm will be extremely fast. (The algorithm represents a logical description of the process. Optimized algorithms can be used in implementations as long as they are equivalent; that is, they produce the same result.)

More explicitly, the canonical ordering of a decomposed character sequence *D* results from the following algorithm.

R1 ***For each character x in D, let p(x) be the combining class of x.***

R2 ***Whenever any pair (A, B) of adjacent characters in D are such that $p(B) \neq 0$ & $p(A) > p(B)$, exchange them.***

R3 ***Repeat step R2 until no exchanges can be made among any of the characters in D.***

Examples of this ordering appear in Table 3-1.

Table 3-1. Sample Combining Classes

Combining class	Abbreviation	Code	Unicode Name
0	a	0061	LATIN SMALL LETTER A
220	underdot	0323	COMBINING DOT BELOW
230	diaeresis	0308	COMBINING DIAERESIS
230	breve	0306	COMBINING BREVE
0	a-underdot	1EA0	LATIN CAPITAL LETTER A WITH DOT BELOW
0	a-diaeresis	00C4	LATIN CAPITAL LETTER A WITH DIAERESIS
0	a-breve	0102	LATIN CAPITAL LETTER A WITH BREVE

a + underdot + diaeresis ⇨ *a + underdot + diaeresis*

a + diaeresis + underdot ⇨ *a + underdot + diaeresis*

Since *underdot* has a lower combining class than *diaeresis*, the algorithm will return the *a*, then the *underdot*, then the *diaeresis*. However, since *diaeresis* and *breve* have the same combining class (because they interact typographically), they do not rearrange.

a + breve + diaeresis ⇏ *a + diaeresis + breve*

a + diaeresis + breve ⇏ *a + breve + diaeresis*

Thus, we get the results shown in Table 3-2 when applying the algorithm.

Table 3-2. Canonical Ordering Results

Original	Decompose	Sort	Result
a-diaeresis + underdot	a + diaeresis + underdot	a + underdot + diaeresis	a + underdot + diaeresis
a + diaeresis + underdot		a + underdot + diaeresis	a + underdot + diaeresis
a + underdot + diaeresis			a + underdot + diaeresis
a-underdot + diaeresis	a + underdot + diaeresis		a + underdot + diaeresis
a-diaeresis + breve	a + diaeresis + breve		a + diaeresis + breve
a + diaeresis + breve			a + diaeresis + breve
a + breve + diaeresis			a + breve + diaeresis
a-breve + diaeresis	a + breve + diaeresis		a + breve + diaeresis

3.10 Combining Jamo Behavior

The Unicode Standard contains both a large set of precomposed modern Hangul syllables and a set of conjoining Hangul *jamo*, which can be used to encode archaic syllable blocks as well as modern syllable blocks. This section describes how to

- determine the syllable boundaries in a sequence of conjoining jamo characters
- compose jamo characters into Hangul syllables
- decompose Hangul syllables into a sequence of jamo characters
- algorithmically determine the names of the Hangul syllable characters

(For more information, see *Section 6.5, Hangul Syllables Area,* and the Hangul Jamo subsection in *Section 6.1, General Scripts Area.*)

The *jamo* characters can be classified into three sets of characters: *choseong* (leading consonants, or syllable-initial characters), *jungseong* (vowels, or syllable-peak characters), and *jongseong* (trailing consonants, or syllable-final characters). In the following discussion, these jamo are abbreviated by L (leading consonant), V (vowel) and T (trailing consonant); syllable breaks are shown by *middle dots* "·"; and non-jamo shown by X.

Syllable Boundaries

In rendering, a sequence of jamos are displayed as a series of syllable blocks. The following rules specify how to divide up an arbitrary sequence of *jamo* (including non-canonical sequences) into these syllable blocks. In these rules, a *choseong filler* (L_f) is treated as a *choseong* character, and a *jungseong filler* (V_f) is treated as a *jungseong*.

Within any sequence of characters, a syllable break occurs between the pairs of characters shown in Table 3-3. All other sequences of Hangul jamo are considered to be part of the same syllable.

Table 3-3. Hangul Syllable Break Rules

Condition	Example
Any conjoining *jamo* and any non-*jamo*	L·X, V·X, T·X, X·L, X·V, X·T
A *jongseong* (trailing) and *choseong* (leading)	T·L
A *jungseong* (vowel) and a *choseong* (leading)	V·L
A *jongseong* (trailing) and *jungseong* (vowel)	T·V

Canonical Syllables

A canonical syllable block is composed of a sequence of *choseong* followed by a sequence of *jungseong* and optionally a sequence of *jongseong* (e.g., $S = LV$ or LVT). A sequence of non-canonical syllable blocks can be transformed into a sequence of canonical syllable blocks by inserting *choseong* fillers and *jungseong* fillers.

Examples. In Table 3.4, row (1) shows syllable breaks in a canonical sequence, row (2) shows syllable breaks in a non-canonical sequence, and row (3) shows how the sequence in (2) could be transformed into canonical form by inserting fillers into each syllable.

Table 3-4. Syllable Break Examples

No.	Sequence		Sequence with syllable breaks marked
1	$LVTLVLVLV_fL_fVL_fV_fT$	→	$LVT \cdot LV \cdot LV \cdot LV_f \cdot L_fV \cdot L_fV_fT$
2	LLTVLTLTVVLL	→	LLT · V · LT · LT · VV · LL
3	LLTVLTLTVVLL	→	$LLV_fT \cdot L_fV \cdot LV_fT \cdot LV_fT \cdot L_fVV \cdot LLV_f$

Hangul Syllable Composition

The following algorithm describes how to take a sequence of characters C and compose Hangul syllables. First define the following constants (the first four are hexadecimal Unicode character values and the remainder are decimal).

```
SBase  = AC00
LBase  = 1100
VBase  = 1161
TBase  = 11A7
```

```
SCount = 11172
LCount = 19
VCount = 21
TCount = 28
NCount = VCount * TCount
```

1. Process C by composing the conjoining jamo wherever possible, according to the decomposition rules in *Chapter 7, Code Charts*. (Typical interchange of conjoining jamo will be in precomposed forms. In such cases, this step not be necessary. Raw keyboard data, on the other hand, may be in decomposed form.)

2. Let *i* represent the current position in the sequence C. Compute the following indices, which represent the ordinal number (zero-based) for each of the components of a syllable, and the index *j*, which represents the index of the last character in the syllable.

```
LIndex = C[i] - LBase
VIndex = C[i+1] - VBase
TIndex = C[i+2] - TBase
j      = i + 2
```

3. If either of the first two characters are not in bounds (neither 0 <= LIndex < LCount nor 0 <= VIndex < VCount), then increment *i* and continue.

4. If the third character is out of bounds (TIndex <= 0 or TIndex >= TCount), then it is not part of the syllable. Reset the following:

```
TIndex = 0
j      = i + 1
```

5. Now replace the characters C[i] through C[j] by the Hangul syllable S, and set *i* to be *j*+1.

```
S      = (LIndex * VCount + VIndex) * TCount + TIndex + SBase.
```

Example:

With the first three characters being

1111	ᄑ	HANGUL CHOSEONG PHIEUPH
1171	ᅱ	HANGUL JUNGSEONG WI
11B6	ᆶ	HANGUL JONGSEONG RIEUL-HIEUH

We compute the following indices:

```
LIndex = 17
VIndex = 16
TIndex = 15
```

And replace the three characters by

```
S      = [(17 * 21) + 16] * 28 + 15 + SBase
       = D4DB
       = 퓛
```

Hangul Syllable Decomposition

The following describes the reverse mapping—how to take Hangul syllable S and derive the decomposition character sequence C.

1. Compute the index of the syllable:

```
SIndex = S - SBase
```

2. If S is in the range (0 <= S < SCount) then compute the components as follows:

```
L       = LBase + TRUNC(SIndex / NCount)
V       = VBase + TRUNC(MOD(SIndex, NCount) / TCount)
T       = TBase + MOD(SIndex, TCount)
```

3. If T = TBase, then there is no trailing character, so replace S by the sequence <L, V>. Otherwise, there is a trailing character, so replace S by the sequence <L, V, T>.

Example:

```
L       = LBase + 17
V       = VBase + 16
T       = TBase + 15
D4DB → 1111, 1171, 11B6
```

Hangul Syllable Name

The character names for Hangul syllables are derived from the decomposition by starting with the words HANGUL SYLLABLE and adding the short name of each decomposition component in order, separated by spaces (see *Section 4.4, Jamo Short Names*). For example, for U+D4DB, derive the decomposition, as shown in the preceding example. This produces the following three-character sequence

U+1111 HANGUL CHOSEONG PHIEUPH
U+1171 HANGUL JUNGSEONG WI
U+11B6 HANGUL JONGSEONG RIEUL-HIEUH

The character name for U+D4DB is then generated as HANGUL SYLLABLE PWIRH

3.11 Bidirectional Behavior

The Unicode Standard prescribes a memory representation order known as logical order. When text is presented in horizontal lines, most scripts display characters from left to right. However, there are several scripts (such as Arabic or Hebrew) where the natural ordering of horizontal text is from right to left. If all of the text has the same horizontal direction, then the ordering of the display text is unambiguous. However, when bidirectional text (a mixture of left-to-right and right-to-left horizontal text) is present, some ambiguities can arise in determining the ordering of the displayed characters.

This section describes the algorithm used to determine the directionality for bidirectional Unicode text. The algorithm extends the implicit model currently employed by a number of existing implementations and adds explicit controls for special circumstances. In most cases, there is no need to include additional information with the text to obtain correct display ordering. However, when necessary, additional information can be included in the text by means of a small set of directional formatting codes.

In general, the Unicode Standard does not supply formatting codes; formatting is left up to higher-level protocols. However, in the case of bidirectional text, there are circumstances where an implicit bidirectional ordering is not sufficient to produce comprehensible text. To deal with these cases, a minimal set of directional formatting codes is defined to control the ordering of characters when rendered. This allows exact control of the display ordering for legible interchange and also ensures that plain text used for simple items like filenames or labels can always be correctly ordered for display.

The directional formatting codes are used *only* to influence the display ordering of text. In all other respects they are ignored—they have no effect on the comparison of text, nor on word breaks, parsing, or numeric analysis. The ordering of bidirectional text depends upon the directional properties of the text. *Section 4.3, Directionality* lists the ranges of characters that have each particular directional character type.

Directional Formatting Codes

Two types of explicit codes are used to modify the standard implicit Unicode bidirectional algorithm. In addition, there are implicit ordering codes, the *right-to-left* and *left-to-right* marks. All of these codes are limited to the current directional block; that is, their effects are terminated by a *block separator.* The directional types left-to-right and right-to-left are called *strong types*, and characters of those types are called strong directional characters. The directional types associated with numbers are called *weak types*, and characters of those types are called weak directional characters.

Explicit Directional Embedding. The following codes signal that a piece of text is to be treated as embedded. For example, an English quotation in the middle of an Arabic sentence could be marked as being embedded left-to-right text. If there were a Hebrew phrase in the middle of the English quotation, then that phrase could be marked as being embedded right-to-left. The following codes allow for nested embeddings.

LRE	Left-to-Right Embedding	Treat the following text as embedded left-to-right.
RLE	Right-to-Left Embedding	Treat the following text as embedded right-to-left.

The precise meaning of these codes will be made clear in the discussion of the algorithm. The effect of right-left line direction, for example, can be accomplished by simply embedding the text with RLE...PDF as seen next.

Explicit Directional Overrides. The following codes allow the bidirectional character types to be overridden when required for special cases, such as for part numbers. The following codes allow for nested directional overrides.

RLO	Right-to-Left Override	Force following characters to be treated as strong right-to-left characters.
LRO	Left-to-Right Override	Force following characters to be treated as strong left-to-right characters.

The precise meaning of these codes will be made clear in the discussion of the algorithm. The right-to-left override, for example, can be used to force a part number made of mixed English, digits and Hebrew letters to be written from right to left.

Terminating Explicit Directional Code. The following code terminates the effects of the last explicit code (either embedding or override) and restores the bidirectional state to what it was before that code was encountered.

PDF	Pop Directional Format	Restore the bidirectional state to what it was before the last LRE, RLE, RLO, LRO.

Implicit Directional Marks. These characters are very light-weight codes. They act exactly like right-to-left or left-to-right characters, except that they do not display (or have any other semantic effect). Their use is often more convenient than the explicit embeddings or overrides, since their scope is much more local (as will be made clear in the following).

RLM	Right-to-Left Mark	Right-to-left zero width character
LRM	Left-to-Right Mark	Left-to-right zero-width character

There is no special mention of the implicit directional marks in the following algorithm. That is because their effect on bidirectional ordering is exactly the same as a corresponding strong directional character; the only difference is that they do not appear in the display.

Basic Display Algorithm

This algorithm may be coded differently for speed, but logically speaking it proceeds in two main phases. The input is a stream of text, up to a block separator (such as a paragraph separator).

- Resolution of the embedding levels of the text. In this phase, the directional character types, plus the explicit controls, are used to produce resolved embedding levels.
- Reordering the text on a line-by-line basis, using the resolved embedding levels.

Embedding levels are numbers that indicate the embedding level of text. ("Embedding levels" in this text are determined both by override controls and by embedding controls.) Odd-numbered levels are right-to-left, and even-numbered levels are left-to-right. The minimum embedding level of text is zero, and the maximum depth is level 15. (The reason for having a limitation is to provide a precise stack limit for implementations to guarantee the same results. Fifteen levels is far more than sufficient for ordering; the display becomes rather muddied with more than a small number of embeddings!)

For example, in a particular piece of text, Level 0 is plain English text, Level 1 is plain Arabic text, possibly embedded within English level 0 text. Level 2 is English text, possibly embedded within Arabic level 1 text, and so on. Unless their direction is overridden, English text and numbers will always be an even level; Arabic text (excluding numbers) will always be an odd level. The exact meaning of the embedding level will become clear when the reordering algorithm is discussed, but the following provides an example of how the algorithm works.

Example. In the following examples, case is used to indicate different implicit character types for those unfamiliar with right-to-left letters. Uppercase letters stand for right-to-left characters (such as Arabic or Hebrew), while lowercase letters stand for left-to-right characters (such as English or Russian).

Memory:	`car is THE CAR in arabic`
Character types:	`LLL-LL-RRR-RRR-LL-LLLLLL`
Resolved levels:	`000000011111110000000000`

Notice that the neutral character (space) between THE and CAR gets the level of the surrounding characters. This is how the implicit directional marks have an effect; by inserting appropriate directional marks around neutral characters, the level of the neutral characters can be changed.

Combining characters always attach to preceding base character in the memory representation; this is logically *before* the bidirectional algorithm is applied. Hence, the glyph representing a combining character does not necessarily attach to the glyph, which is visually on its left in Arabic and Hebrew text. Depending on the line orientation and the placement direction of base letterform glyphs, it may, for example, attach to the glyph on the left, or on the right, or above.

Bidirectional Character Types

For the purpose of the bidirectional algorithm, characters have the types shown in Table 3-5. (For a specification of the bidirectional character types for a given Unicode value, see *Chapter 4, Character Properties.)*

Table 3-5. Bidirectional Character Types

Type	*Category*	*Description*	*Scope*
L	Strong	Left-to-Right	Most alphabetic, syllabic, Han ideographic characters, LRM.
R	Strong	Right-to-Left	Arabic and Hebrew alphabets, punctuation specific to those scripts, RLM
EN	Weak	European Number	European digits, Eastern Arabic-Indic digits, ...
ES	Weak	European Number Separator	Figure Space, Full Stop (Period), Solidus (Slash), ...
ET	Weak	European Number Terminator	Plus Sign, Minus Sign, Degree, Currency symbols, ...
AN	Weak	Arabic Number	Arabic-Indic digits, Arabic decimal & thousands separators, ...
CS	Weak	Common Number Separator	Colon, Comma,...
B	Separator	Block Separator	Paragraph Separator, Line Separator
S	Separator	Segment Separator	Tab
WS	Neutral	Whitespace	Space, No-Break Space, General Punctuation Spaces,...
ON	Neutral	Other Neutrals	All other characters

➡ The term *European digits* is used to refer to decimal forms common in Europe and elsewhere, and *Arabic-Indic digits* to refer to the native Arabic forms. (See the Arabic subsection in *Section 6.1, General Scripts Area,* for more details on naming digits.)

Table 3-6 lists additional abbreviations used in the examples.

Table 3-6. BIDI Example Abbreviations

Symbol	Description
AL	Arabic Letter
HL	Hebrew Letter
N	Neutral or Separator (B, S, WS, ON)
sot	Start of text
eot	End of text
e	The text ordering type (L or R) that matches the embedding level direction

Resolving Embedding Levels

Combining character types and explicit codes to produce a list of resolved levels lies at the heart of the bidirectional algorithm. This resolution process consists of seven steps: determining the base level; determining explicit embedding levels and directions; determining explicit overrides; determining embedding and override terminations; resolving weak types; resolving neutral types; and resolving implicit embedding levels.

The Base Level. First, determine the *base embedding level,* which determines the default horizontal orientation of the text in the current block.

B1. *In the text, find the first strong directional character, RLE, LRE, RLO, or LRO. (Because block separators delimit text in this algorithm, this will generally be the first strong character after a block separator or at the very beginning of the text.)*

B2. *If the first strong directional character in the text is right-to-left, RLE, or RLO, then set the base level to one; otherwise, set it to zero.*

The direction of the base embedding level is called the *base direction*. In some contexts this is also known as the *global direction* or the *block direction*.

Explicit Levels and Directions. All explicit embedding levels are determined from the embedding and override codes. The directional level indicates both how deeply the text is embedded and the basic directional flow of the text. Each even level is a left-to-right embedding, and each odd level is a right-to-left embedding. Only levels from 0 to 15 are valid.

E1. *Begin at the base embedding level. Set the directional override status to neutral.*

E2. *With each RLE, remember (push) the current embedding level and override status. Reset the current level to the least greater odd level (if it would be valid), and reset the override status to neutral.*

For example, level 0 → 1; levels 1, 2 → 3; levels 3, 4 → 5; ...13, 14 → 15; above 14, no change (don't change levels with LRE if the new level would be invalid).

E3. *With each LRE, remember (push) the current level and override status. Reset the current level to the least greater even level (if it would be valid), and reset the override status to neutral.*

For example, levels 0, 1 → 2; levels 2, 3 → 4; levels 4, 5 → 6; ...12, 13 → 14; above 13, no change (don't change levels with LRE if the new level would be invalid).

Explicit Overrides. A directional override changes all of the following characters within the current explicit embedding level to a given value and sets the embedding level as with the embedding codes.

O1. *With each RLO, remember (push) the current override status and embedding level. Reset the current override status to be right-to-left, and reset the current level to the least greater odd level (if it would be valid).*

O2. *With each LRO, remember (push) the current override status and embedding level. Reset the current override status to be left-to-right, and reset the current level to the least greater even level (if it would be valid.).*

O3. *Whenever the directional override status is not neutral, reset the current character type to the directional override status.*

Resetting levels works as described for embeddings in the previous section. For example, if the directional override status is neutral, then all intermediate characters retain their normal values: Arabic characters stay R, Latin characters stay L, neutrals stay N, and so on. If the directional override status is R, then all characters become R.

Terminating Embeddings and Overrides. There is a single code to terminate the scope of the current explicit code, whether an embedding or a directional override. All codes and pushed states are completely popped at block separators.

T4. *With each PDF, restore (pop) the last remembered (pushed) bidirectional state (embedding level and directional override). If there is no pushed state, ignore PDF.*

➥ Higher level protocols may choose to interpret PDFs that occur when there is no pushed state. For example, a presentation engine may receive blocks of processed Unicode text divided into lines. If the complexity of the text is limited by the higher-level protocol, then PDF can be interpreted significantly.

T5. *All explicit directional embeddings and overrides are completely terminated at block separators. Return to the state as of B1.*

All overrides and resolution of weak types and neutrals take effect within the bounds of an embedding; that is, nothing within an embedding or override will affect the character direction of codes outside of that embedding, and vice versa. The one exception is in resolving neutrals (see N4 in the subsection "Resolving Neutral Types" in this chapter).

Now that all of the directional override controls have had their effect, apply T6.

T6. *Remove implicit and explicit directional formatting codes.*

Resolving Weak Types. The text is now parsed for numbers. This pass will change the directional types European Number Separator, European Number Terminator, and Common Number Separator to be European Number text, Arabic Number text, or Other Neutral text. The text to be scanned may have already had its type altered by directional overrides. If so, then it will not parse as numeric.

P0. *Search backwards from each instance of a European number until the first strong character (or block boundary) is found. If a character is found before a block boundary, and if that character belongs to the Arabic block, then change the type of the European number to Arabic number:*

```
AL,EN      →   AL,AN
AL,N,EN    →   AL,N,AN
sot,EN     →   sot,EN
L,EN       →   L,EN
HL,EN      →   HL,EN
```

P1. *Separators change to numbers when surrounded by appropriate numbers:*

```
EN,ES,EN   →   EN,EN,EN
EN,CS,EN   →   EN,EN,EN
AN,CS,AN   →   AN,AN,AN
```

P2. *Terminators change to numbers when adjacent to an appropriate number:*

```
EN,ET      →   EN,EN
ET,EN      →   EN,EN
```

P3. *Otherwise, separators and terminators change to Other Neutral:*

```
AN,ET      →   AN,N
L,ES,EN    →   L,N,EN
EN,CS,AN   →   EN,N,AN
...
```

Resolving Neutral Types. The next phase resolves the direction of the neutrals. The results of this phase are that all neutrals become either R or L. Generally, neutral characters take on the direction of the surrounding text. In case of a conflict, they take on the embedding level. End-of-text and start-of-text are treated as if there were a character of the embedding level at that position.

N1. *A sequence of neutrals takes the direction of the surrounding strong text.*

```
R N R      →   R R R
L N L      →   L L L
```

N2. *Where there is a conflict in adjacent strong directions, a sequence of neutrals takes the global direction.*

```
L N R      →   L e R
R N L      →   R e L
```

Since end-of-text (eot) and start-of-text (sot) are treated as if they were characters of the embedding level at that position, the following examples are covered by this rule:

```
L N eot    →   L e eot
R N eot    →   R e eot
sot N L    →   sot e L
sot N R    →   sot e R
```

N3. *For the purpose of resolving neutrals,*
(a) European numbers are treated as though they were the type of the previous strong letter.
(b) If there is no previous strong letter, European number are treated as though they had the base direction.
(c) Arabic numbers are treated as though they were R but do not affect the treatment of European numbers as in (a) and (b).
The following are examples:

```
R N EN N R  →   R R EN R R
R N EN N L  →   R R EN e L
L N EN N R  →   L L EN e R
L N EN N L  →   L L EN L L
R N AN N R  →   R R AN R R
R N AN N L  →   R R AN e L
L N AN N R  →   L e AN R R
L N AN N L  →   L e AN e L
```

N4. *When processing adjacent neutrals, any embedded text will be treated as if it were a single strong character of the appropriate direction. The following examples illustrate the effects on neutrals.*

```
R N [LRO <text> PDF] N L → R e LRO <text> PDF L L
R N [RLE <text> PDF] N L → R R RLE <text> PDF e L
```

Examples. A list of numbers separated by neutrals and embedded in a directional run will come out in the run's order.

Storage:	`he said "THE VALUES ARE 123, 456, 789, OK".`
Display:	`he said "KO ,789 ,456 ,123 ERA SEULAV EHT".`

In this case, both the comma and the space between the numbers take on the direction of the surrounding text (uppercase = right-to-left), ignoring the numbers. The commas are not considered part of the number since they are not surrounded on both sides (see number parsing). However, if there is an adjacent left-to-right sequence, then European numbers will adopt that direction:

Storage:	`he said "IT IS A bmw 500, OK."`
Display:	`he said ".KO ,bmw 500 A SI TI"`

Resolving Implicit Levels. In the final phase, the embedding level of text may be increased, based upon the resolved character type. Right-to-left text will always have an odd level, and left-to-right and numeric text will always have an even level. In addition, numeric text will always have a higher level than the base level, except in one special case. This results in the following rules:

I1. *If the global direction is even (left-to-right), then the right-to-left text goes up one level. Numeric text (AN) goes up two levels. Numeric text (EN) goes up two levels unless preceeded by left-to-right text.*

I2. *If the global direction is odd (right-to-left), then the left-to-right text and numeric text (EN or AN) goes up one level.*

Table 3-7 summarizes the results of the implicit algorithm. The "(L)" indicates a preceding character type.

Table 3-7. Resolving Implicit Levels

Embedding Level (EL)	*Sequence Type*	*Result*
Even	L	EL
	R	EL+1
	AN	EL+2
	EN	EL+2
	(L) EN	EL
Odd	R	EL
	L	EL+1
	AN	EL+1
	EN	EL+1

Reordering Resolved Levels

The following algorithm describes the logical process of finding the correct display order. As before, this logical process is not necessarily the actual implementation, which may diverge for efficiency. As opposed to resolution phases, this algorithm acts on a per-line basis.

L1. *Reset the embedding level of segment separators and trailing white space (including block separators) to be the base embedding level.*

In combination with the following rule, this means that trailing white space will appear at the visual end of the line (in the base direction). Tabulation will always have a consistent direction within a directional block.

L2. *From the highest level found in the text to the lowest odd level on each line, reverse any sequence of characters that are at that level or higher.*

This reverses a progressively larger series of substrings. The following four examples illustrate this:

Memory: `car means CAR.`
Resolved levels: `00000000001110`
Reverse level 1: `car means RAC.`

Memory: `car MEANS CAR.`
Resolved levels: `22211111111111`
Reverse level 2: `rac MEANS CAR.`
Reverse levels 1,2: `.RAC SNAEM car`

Memory: `he said "car MEANS CAR."`
Resolved levels: `000000000222111111111100`
Reverse level 2: `he said "rac MEANS CAR."`
Reverse levels 1,2: `he said "RAC SNAEM car."`

Memory: `DID YOU SAY 'he said "car MEANS CAR"'?`
Resolved levels: `11111111111122222222224443333333333211`
Reverse level 4: `DID YOU SAY 'he said "rac MEANS CAR"'?`
Reverse levels 3,4: `DID YOU SAY 'he said "RAC SNAEM car"'?`

Reverse levels 2-4: `DID YOU SAY '"rac MEANS CAR" dias eh'?`

Reverse levels 1-4: `?'he said "RAC SNAEM car"' YAS UOY DID`

A character that possesses the mirrored property as specified by *Section 4.7, Mirrored,* should be depicted by a mirrored glyph if the resolved directionality of that character is odd. For example, U+0028 LEFT PARENTHESIS—which is interpreted in the Unicode Standard as an opening parenthesis—appears as "(" when its resolved level is even, and as the mirrored glyph ")" when its resolved level is odd.

Bidirectional Conformance

The bidirectional algorithm specifies part of the intrinsic semantics of right-to-left characters. In the absence of a higher-level protocol that specifically supercedes the interpretation of directionality, systems that interpret these characters must achieve results identical to the implicit bidirectional algorithm when rendering.

Explicit Formatting Codes. As with any Unicode characters, systems do not have to make use of any particular explicit directional formatting code (although it is not generally useful to include a terminating code without including the initiator). Generally, conforming systems will fall into three classes:

- No bidirectional formatting. This implies that the system does not visually interpret characters from right-to-left scripts.
- Implicit bidirectionality. The implicit bidirectional algorithm and the implicit directional marks RLM and LRM are supported.
- Full bidirectionality. Both the implicit bidirectional algorithm and both the implicit and explicit directional formatting codes are supported: RLM, LRM, LRE, RLE, LRO, RLO, PDF.

Higher-Level Protocols. The following are concrete examples of how systems may apply higher-level protocols to the ordering of bidirectional text.

- Override the basic level embedding (global direction). A higher-level protocol may provide for overriding the basic level embedding, such as on a field, paragraph, document, or system level.
- Override the number handling to provide for more (or less) sophisticated number parsing. For example, different types of numbers can be parsed differently; however, this may require fancy text information such as language.
- Supplement or override the directional overrides or embedding codes by providing information via stylesheets about the embedding level or character direction.
- Remap the number shapes to match those of another set. For example, remap the Arabic number shapes to have the same appearance as the European numbers.

When text using a higher-level protocol is to be converted to Unicode plain text, formatting codes can be inserted to ensure that the order matches that of the higher-level protocol, or (as in the last example) the appropriate characters can be substituted.

Vertical Text. In the case of vertical line orientation, these formatting codes and the rest of the bidirectional algorithm is inoperative if the glyphs are ordered uniformly from top to bottom. The bidirectional algorithm applies where characters can have different ordering directions. In the case of Hebrew text, vertical lines usually follow a vertical baseline in which each character is oriented as normal (with no rotation), with characters ordered from top to bottom whether they are Hebrew, numbers, or Latin. When setting text using the Arabic script in vertical lines, it is more common to employ a horizontal baseline that is rotated by 90° counterclockwise so that the characters are ordered from top to bottom. If embedded Latin text and numbers are rotated 90° clockwise (so that the characters are also ordered from top to bottom), then all characters in the line are also ordered from top to bottom. In all of these cases, all the characters have the same ordering direction, so the bidirectional algorithm does not apply.

The bidirectional algorithm *does* come into effect when some characters are ordered from bottom to top. For example, this happens with a mixture of Arabic and Latin glyphs when all the glyphs are rotated uniformally 90° clockwise. (The choice of whether text is to be presented horizontally or vertically, or whether text is to be rotated, is not specified by the Unicode Standard, and is left up to higher-level protocols.)

Usage

Because of the implicit character types and the heuristics for resolving neutral and numeric directional behavior, the implicit bidirectional ordering will generally produce the correct display without any further work. However, problematic cases may occur when a right-to-left paragraph begins with left-to-right characters, or there are nested segments of different-direction text, or there are weak characters on directional boundaries. In these cases, embeddings or directional marks may be required to get the right display. Part numbers may also require directional overrides.

The most common problematic case is that of neutrals on the boundary of an embedded language. This can be addressed by setting the level of the embedded text correctly. For example, with all the text at level 0 the following occurs:

Memory:	`he said "MEANS CAR!", and expired.`
Display:	`he said "RAC SNAEM!", and expired.`

If the exclamation mark is to be part of the Arabic quotation, then the user can select the text MEANS CAR! and explicitly mark it as embedded Arabic, which produces the following result:

Display:	`he said "!RAC SNAEM", and expired.`

Another method of doing this is to place a right directional mark (RLM) after the exclamation mark. Since the exclamation mark is now not on a directional boundary, this produces the correct result.

4 CHARACTER PROPERTIES

Chapter 4

Character Properties

This chapter describes the attributes of character properties defined by the Unicode Standard and gives mappings of characters to specific character properties. As specified in *Chapter 3, Conformance*, the Unicode Standard defines both normative and informative properties. The normative character properties of the Unicode Standard are given in the Table 4-1, and the informative character properties are given in Table 4-2. Also included in the tables is the location of each property's description and where the list of characters with that property can be found.

Table 4-1. Normative Character Properties

Property	Description	List
Case	Chapter 4	Chapter 7 [a]
Combining Classes	Chapter 3	Chapter 4
Combining Jamo	Chapter 3	Chapter 7
Decomposition (Canonical and Compatibility)	Chapter 3	Chapter 7
Directionality	Chapter 4	Chapter 4
Jamo Short Name	Chapter 3	Chapter 4
Numeric Value	Chapter 4	Chapter 4
Private Use	Chapter 3	None
Special Character Properties	Chapter 6	Chapter 3
Surrogate Property	Chapter 3	None
Mirrored	Chapter 3	Chapter 4
Unicode 2.0 Character Names	Chapter 7	Chapter 7

a. These properties are listed by individual character where they are not obvious. Full listings are provided in the *Unicode Character Database* on the CD-ROM.

Table 4-2. Informative Character Properties

Property	Description	List
Case Mapping	Chapter 4	CD-ROM
Dashes	Chapter 6	Chapter 6
Fullwidth and Halfwidth	Chapter 6	Chapter 7
Letters (Alphabetic and Ideographic)	Chapter 4	CD-ROM
Line Breaking	Chapter 6	Chapter 3
Mathematical Property	Chapter 4	Chapter 4
Spaces	Chapter 6	Chapter 6
Unicode 1.0 Names	Chapter 4	CD-ROM

Disclaimer

The content of all character property tables has been verified as far as possible by the Unicode Consortium. However, the Unicode Consortium does not guarantee that the tables printed in this volume or on the CD-ROM are correct in every detail, and it is not responsible for errors that may occur either in the character property tables or in software that implements these tables.

4.1 Case

Case is a normative property of characters in certain alphabets whereby characters are considered to be variants of a single letter. These variants, which may differ markedly in shape and size, are called the *uppercase* letter (also known as *capital* or *majuscule*) and the *lowercase* letter (also known as *small* or *minuscule*). The uppercase letter is generally larger than the lowercase letter.

Because of the inclusion of certain composite characters for compatibility, such as U+01F1 LATIN CAPITAL LETTER DZ, there is a third case, called *titlecase*, which is used where the first character of a word is to be capitalized. An example of such a character is U+01F2 LATIN CAPITAL LETTER D WITH SMALL LETTER Z. The three case forms are UPPERCASE, Titlecase, lowercase.

For those scripts that have case (Latin, Greek, Cyrillic, and Armenian), the case of a Unicode character can be obtained from the character's name. This is true for only these four scripts. Uppercase characters contain the word *capital* in their names. Lowercase characters contain the word *small*. The word *small* in the names of characters from scripts other than the four just listed has nothing to do with case. (Note that while the archaic Georgian script contained upper- and lowercase pairs, they are rarely used in modern Georgian. See the Georgian subsection in *Section 6.1, General Scripts Area*).

Case mappings. The lowercase letter default case mapping is between the small character and the capital character. The Unicode Standard case mapping tables, which are informative, are on the CD-ROM.

In a few instances, upper- and lowercase mappings may differ from language to language between writing systems that employ the same letters. Examples include Turkish ("ı", U+0131 LATIN SMALL LETTER DOTLESS I maps to "I", U+0049 LATIN CAPITAL LETTER I) and French ("é", U+00E9 LATIN SMALL LETTER E WITH ACUTE generally maps to "É", U+00C9 LATIN CAPITAL LETTER E WITH ACUTE, but in some circumstances may map to "E", U+0045 LATIN CAPITAL LETTER E). However, in general the vast majority of case mappings are uniform across languages.

It is important to note that casing operations do not always provide a round-trip mapping. Also, since many characters are really caseless (most of the IPA block, for example), uppercasing a string does not mean that it will no longer contain any lowercase letters.

Because there are many more lowercase forms than there are uppercase or titlecase, it is recommended that the lowercase form be used for normalization, such as when strings are case-folded for loose comparison or indexing.

➥ Case correspondences are not always one-to-one: the result of case folding may be a different character length than in the source string (for example, U+00DF LATIN SMALL LETTER SHARP S (ß) becomes "SS" in uppercase).

4.2 Combining Classes

Each combining character has a normative canonical *combining class*. This class is used with the Canonical Ordering Algorithm to determine which combining characters interact typographically and to determine the canonical ordering of sequences of combining characters. Class *zero* combining characters act like base letters for the purpose of determining canonical order. Combining characters with non-zero classes participate in re-ordering for the purpose of determining the canonical form of sequences of characters. (See *Section 3.9, Canonical Ordering Behavior*, for a description of the algorithm.)

The list of combining characters and their canonical combining class appears in Table 4-3. Most combining characters are non-spacing. The spacing, class zero combining characters are so noted.

Table 4-3. Combining Classes

Code	Class	Name
Spacing		
U+0903	0	DEVANAGARI SIGN VISARGA
U+093E	0	DEVANAGARI VOWEL SIGN AA
U+0940	0	DEVANAGARI VOWEL SIGN II
U+0949	0	DEVANAGARI VOWEL SIGN CANDRA O
U+094A	0	DEVANAGARI VOWEL SIGN SHORT O
U+094B	0	DEVANAGARI VOWEL SIGN O
U+094C	0	DEVANAGARI VOWEL SIGN AU
U+0982	0	BENGALI SIGN ANUSVARA
U+0983	0	BENGALI SIGN VISARGA
U+09BE	0	BENGALI VOWEL SIGN AA
U+09C0	0	BENGALI VOWEL SIGN II
U+09D7	0	BENGALI AU LENGTH MARK
U+0A3E	0	GURMUKHI VOWEL SIGN AA
U+0A40	0	GURMUKHI VOWEL SIGN II
U+0A83	0	GUJARATI SIGN VISARGA
U+0ABE	0	GUJARATI VOWEL SIGN AA
U+0AC0	0	GUJARATI VOWEL SIGN II
U+0AC9	0	GUJARATI VOWEL SIGN CANDRA O
U+0ACB	0	GUJARATI VOWEL SIGN O
U+0ACC	0	GUJARATI VOWEL SIGN AU
U+0B02	0	ORIYA SIGN ANUSVARA
U+0B03	0	ORIYA SIGN VISARGA
U+0B3E	0	ORIYA VOWEL SIGN AA
U+0B40	0	ORIYA VOWEL SIGN II
U+0B57	0	ORIYA AU LENGTH MARK
U+0B82	0	TAMIL SIGN ANUSVARA
U+0B83	0	TAMIL SIGN VISARGA
U+0BBE	0	TAMIL VOWEL SIGN AA
U+0BBF	0	TAMIL VOWEL SIGN I
U+0BC1	0	TAMIL VOWEL SIGN U
U+0BC2	0	TAMIL VOWEL SIGN UU
U+0BD7	0	TAMIL AU LENGTH MARK
U+0C01	0	TELUGU SIGN CANDRABINDU
U+0C02	0	TELUGU SIGN ANUSVARA
U+0C03	0	TELUGU SIGN VISARGA
U+0C41	0	TELUGU VOWEL SIGN U
U+0C42	0	TELUGU VOWEL SIGN UU
U+0C43	0	TELUGU VOWEL SIGN VOCALIC R
U+0C44	0	TELUGU VOWEL SIGN VOCALIC RR
U+0C82	0	KANNADA SIGN ANUSVARA
U+0C83	0	KANNADA SIGN VISARGA
U+0CBE	0	KANNADA VOWEL SIGN AA
U+0CC1	0	KANNADA VOWEL SIGN U
U+0CC2	0	KANNADA VOWEL SIGN UU
U+0CC3	0	KANNADA VOWEL SIGN VOCALIC R
U+0CC4	0	KANNADA VOWEL SIGN VOCALIC RR
U+0CD5	0	KANNADA LENGTH MARK
U+0CD6	0	KANNADA AI LENGTH MARK
U+0D02	0	MALAYALAM SIGN ANUSVARA
U+0D03	0	MALAYALAM SIGN VISARGA

Table 4-3. Combining Classes (Continued)

Code	Class	Name
U+0D3E	0	MALAYALAM VOWEL SIGN AA
U+0D3F	0	MALAYALAM VOWEL SIGN I
U+0D40	0	MALAYALAM VOWEL SIGN II
U+0D57	0	MALAYALAM AU LENGTH MARK
U+0F7F	0	TIBETAN SIGN RNAM BCAD
Split		
U+09CB	0	BENGALI VOWEL SIGN O
U+09CC	0	BENGALI VOWEL SIGN AU
U+0B48	0	ORIYA VOWEL SIGN AI
U+0B4B	0	ORIYA VOWEL SIGN O
U+0B4C	0	ORIYA VOWEL SIGN AU
U+0BCA	0	TAMIL VOWEL SIGN O
U+0BCB	0	TAMIL VOWEL SIGN OO
U+0BCC	0	TAMIL VOWEL SIGN AU
U+0CC0	0	KANNADA VOWEL SIGN II
U+0CC7	0	KANNADA VOWEL SIGN EE
U+0CC8	0	KANNADA VOWEL SIGN AI
U+0CCA	0	KANNADA VOWEL SIGN O
U+0CCB	0	KANNADA VOWEL SIGN OO
U+0D4A	0	MALAYALAM VOWEL SIGN O
U+0D4B	0	MALAYALAM VOWEL SIGN OO
U+0D4C	0	MALAYALAM VOWEL SIGN AU
Reordrant		
U+093F	0	DEVANAGARI VOWEL SIGN I
U+09BF	0	BENGALI VOWEL SIGN I
U+09C8	0	BENGALI VOWEL SIGN AI
U+09C7	0	BENGALI VOWEL SIGN E
U+0A3F	0	GURMUKHI VOWEL SIGN I
U+0ABF	0	GUJARATI VOWEL SIGN I
U+0B47	0	ORIYA VOWEL SIGN E
U+0BC6	0	TAMIL VOWEL SIGN E
U+0BC7	0	TAMIL VOWEL SIGN EE
U+0BC8	0	TAMIL VOWEL SIGN AI
U+0D46	0	MALAYALAM VOWEL SIGN E
U+0D47	0	MALAYALAM VOWEL SIGN EE
U+0D48	0	MALAYALAM VOWEL SIGN AI
Enclosing		
U+20DD	0	COMBINING ENCLOSING CIRCLE
U+20DE	0	COMBINING ENCLOSING SQUARE
U+20DF	0	COMBINING ENCLOSING DIAMOND
U+20E0	0	COMBINING ENCLOSING CIRCLE BACKSLASH
Surrounding		
U+06DD	0	ARABIC END OF AYAH
U+06DE	0	ARABIC START OF RUB EL HIZB
Overlays /Interior		
U+0334	1	COMBINING TILDE OVERLAY
U+0335	1	COMBINING SHORT STROKE OVERLAY
U+0336	1	COMBINING LONG STROKE OVERLAY
U+0337	1	COMBINING SHORT SOLIDUS OVERLAY
U+0338	1	COMBINING LONG SOLIDUS OVERLAY
U+20D2	1	COMBINING LONG VERTICAL LINE OVERLAY
U+20D3	1	COMBINING SHORT VERTICAL LINE OVERLAY
U+20D8	1	COMBINING RING OVERLAY
U+20D9	1	COMBINING CLOCKWISE RING OVERLAY
U+20DA	1	COMBINING ANTICLOCKWISE RING OVERLAY
U+20E1	1	COMBINING LEFT RIGHT ARROW ABOVE
Tibetan Subjoined Letters		
U+0F90	6	TIBETAN SUBJOINED LETTER KA
U+0F91	6	TIBETAN SUBJOINED LETTER KHA
U+0F92	6	TIBETAN SUBJOINED LETTER GA
U+0F93	6	TIBETAN SUBJOINED LETTER GHA

Table 4-3. Combining Classes (Continued)

Code	Class	Name
U+0F94	6	TIBETAN SUBJOINED LETTER NGA
U+0F95	6	TIBETAN SUBJOINED LETTER CA
U+0F97	6	TIBETAN SUBJOINED LETTER JA
U+0F99	6	TIBETAN SUBJOINED LETTER NYA
U+0F9A	6	TIBETAN SUBJOINED LETTER TTA
U+0F9B	6	TIBETAN SUBJOINED LETTER TTHA
U+0F9C	6	TIBETAN SUBJOINED LETTER DDA
U+0F9D	6	TIBETAN SUBJOINED LETTER DDHA
U+0F9E	6	TIBETAN SUBJOINED LETTER NNA
U+0F9F	6	TIBETAN SUBJOINED LETTER TA
U+0FA0	6	TIBETAN SUBJOINED LETTER THA
U+0FA1	6	TIBETAN SUBJOINED LETTER DA
U+0FA2	6	TIBETAN SUBJOINED LETTER DHA
U+0FA3	6	TIBETAN SUBJOINED LETTER NA
U+0FA4	6	TIBETAN SUBJOINED LETTER PA
U+0FA5	6	TIBETAN SUBJOINED LETTER PHA
U+0FA6	6	TIBETAN SUBJOINED LETTER BA
U+0FA7	6	TIBETAN SUBJOINED LETTER BHA
U+0FA8	6	TIBETAN SUBJOINED LETTER MA
U+0FA9	6	TIBETAN SUBJOINED LETTER TSA
U+0FAA	6	TIBETAN SUBJOINED LETTER TSHA
U+0FAB	6	TIBETAN SUBJOINED LETTER DZA
U+0FAC	6	TIBETAN SUBJOINED LETTER DZHA
U+0FAD	6	TIBETAN SUBJOINED LETTER WA
U+0FB1	6	TIBETAN SUBJOINED LETTER YA
U+0FB2	6	TIBETAN SUBJOINED LETTER RA
U+0FB3	6	TIBETAN SUBJOINED LETTER LA
U+0FB4	6	TIBETAN SUBJOINED LETTER SHA
U+0FB5	6	TIBETAN SUBJOINED LETTER SSA
U+0FB6	6	TIBETAN SUBJOINED LETTER SA
U+0FB7	6	TIBETAN SUBJOINED LETTER HA
U+0FB9	6	TIBETAN SUBJOINED LETTER KSSA
Nuktas		
U+093C	7	DEVANAGARI SIGN NUKTA
U+09BC	7	BENGALI SIGN NUKTA
U+0A3C	7	GURMUKHI SIGN NUKTA
U+0ABC	7	GUJARATI SIGN NUKTA
U+0B3C	7	ORIYA SIGN NUKTA
Kana Voiced Marks		
U+3099	8	COMBINING KATAKANA-HIRAGANA VOICED SOUND MARK
U+309A	8	COMBINING KATAKANA-HIRAGANA SEMI-VOICED SOUND MARK
Viramas		
U+094D	9	DEVANAGARI SIGN VIRAMA
U+09CD	9	BENGALI SIGN VIRAMA
U+0A4D	9	GURMUKHI SIGN VIRAMA
U+0ACD	9	GUJARATI SIGN VIRAMA
U+0B4D	9	ORIYA SIGN VIRAMA
U+0BCD	9	TAMIL SIGN VIRAMA
U+0C4D	9	TELUGU SIGN VIRAMA
U+0CCD	9	KANNADA SIGN VIRAMA
U+0D4D	9	MALAYALAM SIGN VIRAMA
U+0F84	9	TIBETAN MARK HALANTA
Fixed Position Classes		
U+05B0	10	HEBREW POINT SHEVA
U+05B1	11	HEBREW POINT HATAF SEGOL
U+05B2	12	HEBREW POINT HATAF PATAH
U+05B3	13	HEBREW POINT HATAF QAMATS
U+05B4	14	HEBREW POINT HIRIQ
U+05B5	15	HEBREW POINT TSERE
U+05B6	16	HEBREW POINT SEGOL
U+05B7	17	HEBREW POINT PATAH

Table 4-3. Combining Classes (Continued)

Code	Class	Name
U+05B8	18	HEBREW POINT QAMATS
U+05B9	19	HEBREW POINT HOLAM
U+05BB	20	HEBREW POINT QUBUTS
U+05BC	21	HEBREW POINT DAGESH OR MAPIQ
U+05BD	22	HEBREW POINT METEG
U+05BF	23	HEBREW POINT RAFE
U+05C1	24	HEBREW POINT SHIN DOT
U+05C2	25	HEBREW POINT SIN DOT
U+FB1E	26	HEBREW POINT JUDEO-SPANISH VARIKA
U+064B	27	ARABIC FATHATAN
U+064C	28	ARABIC DAMMATAN
U+064D	29	ARABIC KASRATAN
U+064E	30	ARABIC FATHA
U+064F	31	ARABIC DAMMA
U+0650	32	ARABIC KASRA
U+0651	33	ARABIC SHADDA
U+0652	34	ARABIC SUKUN
U+0670	35	ARABIC LETTER SUPERSCRIPT ALEF
U+0902	36	DEVANAGARI SIGN ANUSVARA
U+0901	37	DEVANAGARI SIGN CANDRABINDU
U+0941	38	DEVANAGARI VOWEL SIGN U
U+0942	39	DEVANAGARI VOWEL SIGN UU
U+0943	40	DEVANAGARI VOWEL SIGN VOCALIC R
U+0944	41	DEVANAGARI VOWEL SIGN VOCALIC RR
U+0945	42	DEVANAGARI VOWEL SIGN CANDRA E
U+0946	43	DEVANAGARI VOWEL SIGN SHORT E
U+0947	44	DEVANAGARI VOWEL SIGN E
U+0948	45	DEVANAGARI VOWEL SIGN AI
U+0951	46	DEVANAGARI STRESS SIGN UDATTA
U+0952	47	DEVANAGARI STRESS SIGN ANUDATTA
U+0962	48	DEVANAGARI VOWEL SIGN VOCALIC L
U+0963	49	DEVANAGARI VOWEL SIGN VOCALIC LL
U+0981	50	BENGALI SIGN CANDRABINDU
U+09C1	51	BENGALI VOWEL SIGN U
U+09C2	52	BENGALI VOWEL SIGN UU
U+09C3	53	BENGALI VOWEL SIGN VOCALIC R
U+09C4	54	BENGALI VOWEL SIGN VOCALIC RR
U+09E2	55	BENGALI VOWEL SIGN VOCALIC L
U+09E3	56	BENGALI VOWEL SIGN VOCALIC LL
U+0A02	57	GURMUKHI SIGN BINDI
U+0A41	58	GURMUKHI VOWEL SIGN U
U+0A42	59	GURMUKHI VOWEL SIGN UU
U+0A47	60	GURMUKHI VOWEL SIGN EE
U+0A48	61	GURMUKHI VOWEL SIGN AI
U+0A4B	62	GURMUKHI VOWEL SIGN OO
U+0A4C	63	GURMUKHI VOWEL SIGN AU
U+0A70	64	GURMUKHI TIPPI
U+0A71	65	GURMUKHI ADDAK
U+0A82	66	GUJARATI SIGN ANUSVARA
U+0A81	67	GUJARATI SIGN CANDRABINDU
U+0AC1	68	GUJARATI VOWEL SIGN U
U+0AC2	69	GUJARATI VOWEL SIGN UU
U+0AC3	70	GUJARATI VOWEL SIGN VOCALIC R
U+0AC4	71	GUJARATI VOWEL SIGN VOCALIC RR
U+0AC5	72	GUJARATI VOWEL SIGN CANDRA E
U+0AC7	73	GUJARATI VOWEL SIGN E
U+0AC8	74	GUJARATI VOWEL SIGN AI
U+0B01	75	ORIYA SIGN CANDRABINDU
U+0B3F	76	ORIYA VOWEL SIGN I
U+0B41	77	ORIYA VOWEL SIGN U
U+0B42	78	ORIYA VOWEL SIGN UU

Table 4-3. Combining Classes (Continued)

Code	Class	Name
U+0B43	79	ORIYA VOWEL SIGN VOCALIC R
U+0BC0	80	TAMIL VOWEL SIGN II
U+0C3E	81	TELUGU VOWEL SIGN AA
U+0C3F	82	TELUGU VOWEL SIGN I
U+0C40	83	TELUGU VOWEL SIGN II
U+0C46	84	TELUGU VOWEL SIGN E
U+0C47	85	TELUGU VOWEL SIGN EE
U+0C48	86	TELUGU VOWEL SIGN AI
U+0C4A	87	TELUGU VOWEL SIGN O
U+0C4B	88	TELUGU VOWEL SIGN OO
U+0C4C	89	TELUGU VOWEL SIGN AU
U+0C55	90	TELUGU LENGTH MARK
U+0C56	91	TELUGU AI LENGTH MARK
U+0CBF	92	KANNADA VOWEL SIGN I
U+0CC6	93	KANNADA VOWEL SIGN E
U+0CCC	94	KANNADA VOWEL SIGN AU
U+0D41	95	MALAYALAM VOWEL SIGN U
U+0D42	96	MALAYALAM VOWEL SIGN UU
U+0D43	97	MALAYALAM VOWEL SIGN VOCALIC R
U+0E31	98	THAI CHARACTER MAI HAN-AKAT
U+0E34	99	THAI CHARACTER SARA I
U+0E35	100	THAI CHARACTER SARA II
U+0E36	101	THAI CHARACTER SARA UE
U+0E37	102	THAI CHARACTER SARA UEE
U+0E38	103	THAI CHARACTER SARA U
U+0E39	104	THAI CHARACTER SARA UU
U+0E3A	105	THAI CHARACTER PHINTHU
U+0E47	106	THAI CHARACTER MAITAIKHU
U+0E48	107	THAI CHARACTER MAI EK
U+0E49	108	THAI CHARACTER MAI THO
U+0E4A	109	THAI CHARACTER MAI TRI
U+0E4B	110	THAI CHARACTER MAI CHATTAWA
U+0E4C	111	THAI CHARACTER THANTHAKHAT
U+0E4D	112	THAI CHARACTER NIKHAHIT
U+0EB1	113	LAO VOWEL SIGN MAI KAN
U+0EB4	114	LAO VOWEL SIGN I
U+0EB5	115	LAO VOWEL SIGN II
U+0EB6	116	LAO VOWEL SIGN Y
U+0EB7	117	LAO VOWEL SIGN YY
U+0EB8	118	LAO VOWEL SIGN U
U+0EB9	119	LAO VOWEL SIGN UU
U+0EBB	120	LAO VOWEL SIGN MAI KON
U+0EBC	121	LAO SEMIVOWEL SIGN LO
U+0EC8	122	LAO TONE MAI EK
U+0EC9	123	LAO TONE MAI THO
U+0ECA	124	LAO TONE MAI TI
U+0ECB	125	LAO TONE MAI CATAWA
U+0ECC	126	LAO CANCELLATION MARK
U+0ECD	127	LAO NIGGAHITA
U+0E4E	128	THAI CHARACTER YAMAKKAN
U+0F71	129	TIBETAN VOWEL SIGN AA
U+0F72	130	TIBETAN VOWEL SIGN I
U+0F73	131	TIBETAN VOWEL SIGN II
U+0F74	132	TIBETAN VOWEL SIGN U
U+0F75	133	TIBETAN VOWEL SIGN UU
U+0F76	134	TIBETAN VOWEL SIGN VOCALIC R
U+0F77	135	TIBETAN VOWEL SIGN VOCALIC RR
U+0F78	136	TIBETAN VOWEL SIGN VOCALIC L
U+0F79	137	TIBETAN VOWEL SIGN VOCALIC LL
U+0F7A	138	TIBETAN VOWEL SIGN E
U+0F7B	139	TIBETAN VOWEL SIGN EE

Table 4-3. Combining Classes (Continued)

Code	Class	Name
U+0F7C	140	TIBETAN VOWEL SIGN O
U+0F7D	141	TIBETAN VOWEL SIGN OO
U+0F7E	142	TIBETAN VOWEL SIGN RJES SU NGA RO
U+0F80	143	TIBETAN VOWEL SIGN REVERSED I
U+0F81	144	TIBETAN VOWEL SIGN REVERSED II
Below Attached		
U+0321	202	COMBINING PALATALIZED HOOK BELOW
U+0322	202	COMBINING RETROFLEX HOOK BELOW
U+0327	202	COMBINING CEDILLA
U+0328	202	COMBINING OGONEK
Above Right Attached		
U+031B	216	COMBINING HORN
U+0F39	216	TIBETAN MARK TSA -PHRU
Below Left		
U+302A	218	IDEOGRAPHIC LEVEL TONE MARK
Below		
U+0316	220	COMBINING GRAVE ACCENT BELOW
U+0317	220	COMBINING ACUTE ACCENT BELOW
U+0318	220	COMBINING LEFT TACK BELOW
U+0319	220	COMBINING RIGHT TACK BELOW
U+031C	220	COMBINING LEFT HALF RING BELOW
U+031D	220	COMBINING UP TACK BELOW
U+031E	220	COMBINING DOWN TACK BELOW
U+031F	220	COMBINING PLUS SIGN BELOW
U+0320	220	COMBINING MINUS SIGN BELOW
U+0323	220	COMBINING DOT BELOW
U+0324	220	COMBINING DIAERESIS BELOW
U+0325	220	COMBINING RING BELOW
U+0326	220	COMBINING COMMA BELOW
U+0329	220	COMBINING VERTICAL LINE BELOW
U+032A	220	COMBINING BRIDGE BELOW
U+032B	220	COMBINING INVERTED DOUBLE ARCH BELOW
U+032C	220	COMBINING CARON BELOW
U+032D	220	COMBINING CIRCUMFLEX ACCENT BELOW
U+032E	220	COMBINING BREVE BELOW
U+032F	220	COMBINING INVERTED BREVE BELOW
U+0330	220	COMBINING TILDE BELOW
U+0331	220	COMBINING MACRON BELOW
U+0332	220	COMBINING LOW LINE
U+0333	220	COMBINING DOUBLE LOW LINE
U+0339	220	COMBINING RIGHT HALF RING BELOW
U+033A	220	COMBINING INVERTED BRIDGE BELOW
U+033B	220	COMBINING SQUARE BELOW
U+033C	220	COMBINING SEAGULL BELOW
U+0345	220	COMBINING GREEK YPOGEGRAMMENI
U+0591	220	HEBREW ACCENT ETNAHTA
U+0596	220	HEBREW ACCENT TIPEHA
U+059B	220	HEBREW ACCENT TEVIR
U+05A3	220	HEBREW ACCENT MUNAH
U+05A4	220	HEBREW ACCENT MAHAPAKH
U+05A5	220	HEBREW ACCENT MERKHA
U+05A6	220	HEBREW ACCENT MERKHA KEFULA
U+05A7	220	HEBREW ACCENT DARGA
U+05AA	220	HEBREW ACCENT YERAH BEN YOMO
U+06E3	220	ARABIC SMALL LOW SEEN
U+06EA	220	ARABIC EMPTY CENTRE LOW STOP
U+06ED	220	ARABIC SMALL LOW MEEM
U+0F18	220	TIBETAN ASTROLOGICAL SIGN -KHYUD PA
U+0F19	220	TIBETAN ASTROLOGICAL SIGN SDONG TSHUGS
U+0F35	220	TIBETAN MARK NGAS BZUNG NYI ZLA
U+0F37	220	TIBETAN MARK NGAS BZUNG SGOR RTAGS

Table 4-3. Combining Classes (Continued)

Code	Class	Name
U+0F3E	220	TIBETAN SIGN YAR TSHES
U+0F3F	220	TIBETAN SIGN MAR TSHES
Below Right		
U+059A	222	HEBREW ACCENT YETIV
U+05AD	222	HEBREW ACCENT DEHI
U+302D	222	IDEOGRAPHIC ENTERING TONE MARK
Left		
U+302E	224	HANGUL SINGLE DOT TONE MARK
U+302F	224	HANGUL DOUBLE DOT TONE MARK
Above Left		
U+302B	228	IDEOGRAPHIC RISING TONE MARK
Above		
U+0300	230	COMBINING GRAVE ACCENT
U+0301	230	COMBINING ACUTE ACCENT
U+0302	230	COMBINING CIRCUMFLEX ACCENT
U+0303	230	COMBINING TILDE
U+0304	230	COMBINING MACRON
U+0305	230	COMBINING OVERLINE
U+0306	230	COMBINING BREVE
U+0307	230	COMBINING DOT ABOVE
U+0308	230	COMBINING DIAERESIS
U+0309	230	COMBINING HOOK ABOVE
U+030A	230	COMBINING RING ABOVE
U+030B	230	COMBINING DOUBLE ACUTE ACCENT
U+030C	230	COMBINING CARON
U+030D	230	COMBINING VERTICAL LINE ABOVE
U+030E	230	COMBINING DOUBLE VERTICAL LINE ABOVE
U+030F	230	COMBINING DOUBLE GRAVE ACCENT
U+0310	230	COMBINING CANDRABINDU
U+0311	230	COMBINING INVERTED BREVE
U+0312	230	COMBINING TURNED COMMA ABOVE
U+0313	230	COMBINING COMMA ABOVE
U+0314	230	COMBINING REVERSED COMMA ABOVE
U+033D	230	COMBINING X ABOVE
U+033E	230	COMBINING VERTICAL TILDE
U+033F	230	COMBINING DOUBLE OVERLINE
U+0340	230	COMBINING GRAVE TONE MARK
U+0341	230	COMBINING ACUTE TONE MARK
U+0342	230	COMBINING GREEK PERISPOMENI
U+0343	230	COMBINING GREEK KORONIS
U+0344	230	COMBINING GREEK DIALYTIKA TONOS
U+0483	230	COMBINING CYRILLIC TITLO
U+0484	230	COMBINING CYRILLIC PALATALIZATION
U+0485	230	COMBINING CYRILLIC DASIA PNEUMATA
U+0486	230	COMBINING CYRILLIC PSILI PNEUMATA
U+0592	230	HEBREW ACCENT SEGOL
U+0593	230	HEBREW ACCENT SHALSHELET
U+0594	230	HEBREW ACCENT ZAQEF QATAN
U+0595	230	HEBREW ACCENT ZAQEF GADOL
U+0597	230	HEBREW ACCENT REVIA
U+0598	230	HEBREW ACCENT ZARQA
U+0599	230	HEBREW ACCENT PASHTA
U+059C	230	HEBREW ACCENT GERESH
U+059D	230	HEBREW ACCENT GERESH MUQDAM
U+059E	230	HEBREW ACCENT GERSHAYIM
U+059F	230	HEBREW ACCENT QARNEY PARA
U+05A0	230	HEBREW ACCENT TELISHA GEDOLA
U+05A1	230	HEBREW ACCENT PAZER
U+05A8	230	HEBREW ACCENT QADMA
U+05A9	230	HEBREW ACCENT TELISHA QETANA
U+05AB	230	HEBREW ACCENT OLE

Table 4-3. Combining Classes (Continued)

Code	Class	Name
U+05AC	230	HEBREW ACCENT ILUY
U+05AE	230	HEBREW ACCENT ZINOR
U+05AF	230	HEBREW MARK MASORA CIRCLE
U+05C4	230	HEBREW MARK UPPER DOT
U+06D7	230	ARABIC SMALL HIGH LIGATURE QAF WITH LAM WITH ALEF MAKSURA
U+06D8	230	ARABIC SMALL HIGH MEEM INITIAL FORM
U+06D9	230	ARABIC SMALL HIGH LAM ALEF
U+06DA	230	ARABIC SMALL HIGH JEEM
U+06DB	230	ARABIC SMALL HIGH THREE DOTS
U+06DC	230	ARABIC SMALL HIGH SEEN
U+06DF	230	ARABIC SMALL HIGH ROUNDED ZERO
U+06E0	230	ARABIC SMALL HIGH UPRIGHT RECTANGULAR ZERO
U+06E1	230	ARABIC SMALL HIGH DOTLESS HEAD OF KHAH
U+06E2	230	ARABIC SMALL HIGH MEEM ISOLATED FORM
U+06E4	230	ARABIC SMALL HIGH MADDA
U+06E7	230	ARABIC SMALL HIGH YEH
U+06E8	230	ARABIC SMALL HIGH NOON
U+06EB	230	ARABIC EMPTY CENTRE HIGH STOP
U+06EC	230	ARABIC ROUNDED HIGH STOP WITH FILLED CENTRE
U+0953	230	DEVANAGARI GRAVE ACCENT
U+0954	230	DEVANAGARI ACUTE ACCENT
U+0B56	230	ORIYA AI LENGTH MARK
U+0F82	230	TIBETAN SIGN NYI ZLA NAA DA
U+0F83	230	TIBETAN SIGN SNA LDAN
U+0F86	230	TIBETAN MARK LCI RTAGS
U+0F87	230	TIBETAN MARK YANG RTAGS
U+0F88	230	TIBETAN MARK LCE TSA CAN
U+0F89	230	TIBETAN MARK MCHU CAN
U+0F8A	230	TIBETAN MARK GRU CAN RGYINGS
U+0F8B	230	TIBETAN MARK GRU MED RGYINGS
U+20D0	230	COMBINING LEFT HARPOON ABOVE
U+20D1	230	COMBINING RIGHT HARPOON ABOVE
U+20D4	230	COMBINING ANTICLOCKWISE ARROW ABOVE
U+20D5	230	COMBINING CLOCKWISE ARROW ABOVE
U+20D6	230	COMBINING LEFT ARROW ABOVE
U+20D7	230	COMBINING RIGHT ARROW ABOVE
U+20DB	230	COMBINING THREE DOTS ABOVE
U+20DC	230	COMBINING FOUR DOTS ABOVE
U+FE20	230	COMBINING LIGATURE LEFT HALF
U+FE21	230	COMBINING LIGATURE RIGHT HALF
U+FE22	230	COMBINING DOUBLE TILDE LEFT HALF
U+FE23	230	COMBINING DOUBLE TILDE RIGHT HALF
Above Right		
U+0315	232	COMBINING COMMA ABOVE RIGHT
U+031A	232	COMBINING LEFT ANGLE ABOVE
U+302C	232	IDEOGRAPHIC DEPARTING TONE MARK
Double Above		
U+0360	234	COMBINING DOUBLE TILDE
U+0361	234	COMBINING DOUBLE INVERTED BREVE

4.3 Directionality

Directional behavior is interpreted according to the Unicode Bidirectional Algorithm (see *Section 3.11, Bidirectional Behavior*). For this purpose, all characters of the Unicode Standard possess a normative *directional* type. The directional types left-to-right and right-to-left are called *strong types*, and characters of these types are called strong directional characters. Left-to-right types include most alphabetic and syllabic characters, as well as all Han ideographic characters. Right-to-left types include Arabic, Hebrew, and punctuation specific to those scripts. In addition, the Unicode Bidirectional Algorithm also uses *weak types* and *neutrals*.

As with other character properties, Compatibility Area characters have the same directional properties as the characters they map to. The directional type of all unassigned code values is not defined. This is also true of unassigned code values falling within the ranges used in the following table; for brevity, not all unassigned code values in the ranges are called out separately where there are gaps. As characters are assigned in future versions of the Unicode Standard, their properties will be documented.

It is recommended that unassigned code values be given the property of neutral for compatibility with future versions of this standard where these code points are assigned. That choice is most likely to produce acceptable rendering.

Table 4-4 gives the directional type of Unicode characters.

Table 4-4. Bidirectional Character Types

Type	Sym	Category	Description	Values
Strong	**L**	*Left-to-Right*	Miscellaneous	`U+0026, U+0040`
			Latin letters	`U+0041→U+005A, U+0061→U+007A, U+00C0→U+00D6, U+00D8→U+00F6, U+00F8→U+00FF`
			Extended Latin→Modifier Letters	`U+0100→U+02FF`
			Combining Diacriticals	`U+0300→U+036F`
			Greek→Armenian	`U+0370→U+058F`
			Devanagari→Thai Character Phinthu	`U+0900→U+0E3A`
			Thai Character Sara E→Hangul Jamo	`U+0E40→U+11FF`
			Latin Extended Additional→Greek Extended	`U+1E00→U+1FFF`
			Left-to-Right Mark	`U+200E`
			Symbol Diacritics	`U+20D0→U+20FF`
			Roman Numerals	`U+2160→U+2182`
			Hiragana→Han	`U+3040→U+9FFF`
	R	*Right-to-Left*	Arabic and Hebrew	`U+0590→U+065F, U+066D→U+06EF`
			Right-to-Left Mark	`U+200F`
Weak	**EN**	*European Number*	European Digits	`U+0030→U+0039`
			Eastern Arabic-Indic Digits	`U+06F0→U+06F9`
			Superscript and Subscript Digits	`U+00B2→U+00B3, U+00B9, U+2070, U+2074→U+2079, U+2080→U+2089`
	ES	*European Number Separator*	Full Stop (Period)	`U+002E`
			Solidus (Slash)	`U+002F`
			Figure Space	`U+2007`
	ET	*European Number Terminator*	Number Sign	`U+0023`

Table 4-4. Bidirectional Character Types (Continued)

Type	Sym	Category	Description	Values
			Currency symbols	U+0024, U+00A2→U+00A5, U+0E3F, U+20A0→U+20CF
			Percents	U+0025, U+066A
			Plus Sign	U+002B
			Hyphen-Minus	U+002D
			Degree	U+00B0
			Plus-Minus	U+00B1
			Prime (Minute)	U+2032
			Double Prime (Second)	U+2033
			Superscript Plus and Minus	U+207A, U+207B
			Subscript Plus and Minus	U+208A, U+208B
			Minus Sign	U+2212
			Minus-Plus	U+2213
	AN	*Arabic Number*	Arabic-Indic Digits	U+0660→U+0669
			Arabic Decimal and Thousands Separators	U+066B, U+066C
	CS	*Common Number Separator*	Comma	U+002C
			Colon	U+003A
Separators	**B**	*Block Separator*	Line Separator	U+2028
			Paragraph Separator	U+2029
	S	*Segment Separator*	Horizontal Tab	U+0009
Neutrals	**WS**	*Whitespace*	Space	U+0020
			No-Break Space	U+00A0
			General Punctuation Spaces	U+2000→U+2006, U+2008→U+200B, U+3000, U+FEFF
	ON	*Other Neutrals*	Punctuation, Symbols	All other characters

The definition of control code semantics is generally outside of the scope of the Unicode Standard (see *Section 2.6, Controls and Control Sequences*). Implementers should interpret the type of characters such as *carriage return, line feed, group separator,* and so on according to the closest semantics to the types given here, such as interpreting *carriage return* (when used as paragraph separator) as being a block separator. However, U+0009 HORIZONTAL TAB is interpreted as a segment separator, which indicates that in a line containing tabs, the tab-delimited segments go in the base level direction (see *Section 3.11, Bidirectional Behavior*).

Since horizontal Han ideographic characters are generally arranged from left to right when written in horizontally oriented lines, they have the left-to-right directional character type. (When they need to be written from right to left in horizontal lines, their direction can be overridden, as discussed in the *Section 3.11, Bidirectional Behavior.*)

4.4 Jamo Short Names

The *jamo short name* is the normative property of the Unicode conjoining Hangul *jamo* characters. These short names are used to determine the character names that are derived when decomposing Hangul syllables into their decomposition sequence.

Table 4-5. Jamo Short Names

Value	Short Name	Unicode Name
U+1100	G	HANGUL CHOSEONG KIYEOK
U+1101	GG	HANGUL CHOSEONG SSANGKIYEOK
U+1102	N	HANGUL CHOSEONG NIEUN
U+1103	D	HANGUL CHOSEONG TIKEUT
U+1104	DD	HANGUL CHOSEONG SSANGTIKEUT
U+1105	L	HANGUL CHOSEONG RIEUL
U+1106	M	HANGUL CHOSEONG MIEUM
U+1107	B	HANGUL CHOSEONG PIEUP
U+1108	BB	HANGUL CHOSEONG SSANGPIEUP
U+1109	S	HANGUL CHOSEONG SIOS
U+110A	SS	HANGUL CHOSEONG SSANGSIOS
U+110B		HANGUL CHOSEONG IEUNG
U+110C	J	HANGUL CHOSEONG CIEUC
U+110D	JJ	HANGUL CHOSEONG SSANGCIEUC
U+110E	C	HANGUL CHOSEONG CHIEUCH
U+110F	K	HANGUL CHOSEONG KHIEUKH
U+1110	T	HANGUL CHOSEONG THIEUTH
U+1111	P	HANGUL CHOSEONG PHIEUPH
U+1112	H	HANGUL CHOSEONG HIEUH
U+1161	A	HANGUL JUNGSEONG A
U+1162	AE	HANGUL JUNGSEONG AE
U+1163	YA	HANGUL JUNGSEONG YA
U+1164	YAE	HANGUL JUNGSEONG YAE
U+1165	EO	HANGUL JUNGSEONG EO
U+1166	E	HANGUL JUNGSEONG E
U+1167	YEO	HANGUL JUNGSEONG YEO
U+1168	YE	HANGUL JUNGSEONG YE
U+1169	O	HANGUL JUNGSEONG O
U+116A	WA	HANGUL JUNGSEONG WA
U+116B	WAE	HANGUL JUNGSEONG WAE
U+116C	OE	HANGUL JUNGSEONG OE
U+116D	YO	HANGUL JUNGSEONG YO
U+116E	U	HANGUL JUNGSEONG U
U+116F	WEO	HANGUL JUNGSEONG WEO
U+1170	WE	HANGUL JUNGSEONG WE
U+1171	WI	HANGUL JUNGSEONG WI
U+1172	YU	HANGUL JUNGSEONG YU
U+1173	EU	HANGUL JUNGSEONG EU
U+1174	YI	HANGUL JUNGSEONG YI
U+1175	I	HANGUL JUNGSEONG I
U+11A8	G	HANGUL JONGSEONG KIYEOK
U+11A9	GG	HANGUL JONGSEONG SSANGKIYEOK
U+11AA	GS	HANGUL JONGSEONG KIYEOK-SIOS
U+11AB	N	HANGUL JONGSEONG NIEUN
U+11AC	NJ	HANGUL JONGSEONG NIEUN-CIEUC
U+11AD	NH	HANGUL JONGSEONG NIEUN-HIEUH
U+11AE	D	HANGUL JONGSEONG TIKEUT
U+11AF	L	HANGUL JONGSEONG RIEUL
U+11B0	LG	HANGUL JONGSEONG RIEUL-KIYEOK

Table 4-5. Jamo Short Names (Continued)

Value	Short Name	Unicode Name
U+11B1	LM	HANGUL JONGSEONG RIEUL-MIEUM
U+11B2	LB	HANGUL JONGSEONG RIEUL-PIEUP
U+11B3	LS	HANGUL JONGSEONG RIEUL-SIOS
U+11B4	LT	HANGUL JONGSEONG RIEUL-THIEUTH
U+11B5	LP	HANGUL JONGSEONG RIEUL-PHIEUPH
U+11B6	LH	HANGUL JONGSEONG RIEUL-HIEUH
U+11B7	M	HANGUL JONGSEONG MIEUM
U+11B8	B	HANGUL JONGSEONG PIEUP
U+11B9	BS	HANGUL JONGSEONG PIEUP-SIOS
U+11BA	S	HANGUL JONGSEONG SIOS
U+11BB	SS	HANGUL JONGSEONG SSANGSIOS
U+11BC	NG	HANGUL JONGSEONG IEUNG
U+11BD	J	HANGUL JONGSEONG CIEUC
U+11BE	C	HANGUL JONGSEONG CHIEUCH
U+11BF	K	HANGUL JONGSEONG KHIEUKH
U+11C0	T	HANGUL JONGSEONG THIEUTH
U+11C1	P	HANGUL JONGSEONG PHIEUPH
U+11C2	H	HANGUL JONGSEONG HIEUH

4.5 Letters

Letter. This is an informative property of characters that are used to write words. This includes characters such as capital letters, small letters, ideographs, hangul, and spacing modifier letters. Combining marks generally assume the letter property of the preceding base character. For example, when searching for word boundaries, combining characters don't break from previous letters. The letter property mappings can be obtained from the CD-ROM accompanying the standard.

There are two informative character properties that specify subsets of all letters, alphabetic and ideographic.

Alphabetic. This is the property of the primary units of alphabets and syllabaries, both combining and non-combining. It also includes modifier letters and letterlike symbols that are compatibility equivalents to alphabetic letters. The following is a list of all characters in the Unicode Standard which have the alphabetic property (see *Section 5.14, Identifiers*).

```
0041..005A, 0061..007A, 00AA      , 00B5      , 00BA      , 00C0..00D6,
00D8..00F6, 00F8..01F5, 01FA..0217, 0250..02A8, 02B0..02B8, 02BB..02C1,
02E0..02E4, 037A      , 0386      , 0388..038A, 038C      , 038E..03A1,
03A3..03CE, 03D0..03D6, 03DA      , 03DC      , 03DE      , 03E0      ,
03E2..03F3, 0401..040C, 040E..044F, 0451..045C, 045E..0481, 0490..04C4,
04C7..04C8, 04CB..04CC, 04D0..04EB, 04EE..04F5, 04F8..04F9, 0531..0556,
0559..055A, 0561..0587, 05D0..05EA, 05F0..05F2, 0621..063A, 0641..0652,
0670..06B7, 06BA..06BE, 06C0..06CE, 06D0..06D3, 06D5..06DC, 06E1..06E8,
06ED      , 0901..0903, 0905..0939, 093D..094C, 0958..0963, 0981..0983,
0985..098C, 098F..0990, 0993..09A8, 09AA..09B0, 09B2      , 09B6..09B9,
09BE..09C4, 09C7..09C8, 09CB..09CC, 09D7      , 09DC..09DD, 09DF..09E3,
09F0..09F1, 0A02      , 0A05..0A0A, 0A0F..0A10, 0A13..0A28, 0A2A..0A30,
0A32..0A33, 0A35..0A36, 0A38..0A39, 0A3E..0A42, 0A47..0A48, 0A4B..0A4C,
0A8F..0A91, 0A93..0AA8, 0AAA..0AB0, 0AB2..0AB3, 0AB5..0AB9, 0ABD..0AC5,
0AC7..0AC9, 0ACB..0ACC, 0AE0      , 0B01..0B03, 0B05..0B0C, 0B0F..0B10,
0B13..0B28, 0B2A..0B30, 0B32..0B33, 0B36..0B39, 0B3D..0B43, 0B47..0B48,
0B4B..0B4C, 0B56..0B57, 0B5C..0B5D, 0B5F..0B61, 0B82..0B83, 0B85..0B8A,
0B8E..0B90, 0B92..0B95, 0B99..0B9A, 0B9C      , 0B9E..0B9F, 0BA3..0BA4,
```

```
0BA8..0BAA, 0BAE..0BB5, 0BB7..0BB9, 0BBE..0BC2, 0BC6..0BC8, 0BCA..0BCC,
0BD7      , 0C01..0C03, 0C05..0C0C, 0C0E..0C10, 0C12..0C28, 0C2A..0C33,
0C35..0C39, 0C3E..0C44, 0C46..0C48, 0C4A..0C4C, 0C55..0C56, 0C60..0C61,
0C82..0C83, 0C85..0C8C, 0C8E..0C90, 0C92..0CA8, 0CAA..0CB3, 0CB5..0CB9,
0CBE..0CC4, 0CC6..0CC8, 0CCA..0CCC, 0CD5..0CD6, 0CDE      , 0CE0..0CE1,
0D02..0D03, 0D05..0D0C, 0D0E..0D10, 0D12..0D28, 0D2A..0D39, 0D3E..0D43,
0D46..0D48, 0D4A..0D4C, 0D57      , 0D60..0D61, 0E01..0E2E, 0E30..0E3A,
0E40..0E45, 0E47      , 0E4D      , 0E81..0E82, 0E84      , 0E87..0E88,
0E8A      , 0E8D      , 0E94..0E97, 0E99..0E9F, 0EA1..0EA3, 0EA5      ,
0EA7      , 0EAA..0EAB, 0EAD..0EAE, 0EB0..0EB9, 0EBB..0EBD, 0EC0..0EC4,
0ECD      , 0EDC..0EDD, 0F40..0F47, 0F49..0F69, 0F71..0F81, 0F90..0F95,
0F97      , 0F99..0FAD, 0FB1..0FB7, 0FB9      , 10A0..10C5, 10D0..10F6,
1100..1159, 115F..11A2, 11A8..11F9, 1E00..1E9B, 1EA0..1EF9, 1F00..1F15,
1F18..1F1D, 1F20..1F45, 1F48..1F4D, 1F50..1F57, 1F59      , 1F5B      ,
1F5D      , 1F5F..1F7D, 1F80..1FB4, 1FB6..1FBC, 1FBE      , 1FC2..1FC4,
1FC6..1FCC, 1FD0..1FD3, 1FD6..1FDB, 1FE0..1FEC, 1FF2..1FF4, 1FF6..1FFC,
207F      , 2102      , 2107      , 210A..2113, 2115      , 2118..211D,
2124      , 2126      , 2128      , 212A..212D, 212F..2131, 2133..2138,
2160..2182, 3041..3094, 30A1..30FA, 3105..312C, 3131..318E, AC00..D7A3,
FB00..FB06, FB13..FB17, FB1F..FB28, FB2A..FB36, FB38..FB3C, FB3E      ,
FB40..FB41, FB43..FB44, FB46..FBB1, FBD3..FD3D, FD50..FD8F, FD92..FDC7,
FDF0..FDFB, FE70..FE72, FE74      , FE76..FEFC, FF21..FF3A, FF41..FF5A,
FF66..FF6F, FF71..FF9D, FFA0..FFBE, FFC2..FFC7, FFCA..FFCF, FFD2..FFD7,
FFDA..FFDC.
```

Ideographic. This is the property of the Unified Han Set and other Han characters. The following is a list of all characters in the Unicode Standard which have the ideographic property. See *Section 5.14, Identifiers.*

```
4E00..9FA5, F900..FA2D, 3007, 3021..3029
```

4.6 Numeric Value

Numeric value is a normative property of characters that represent *numbers.* This includes characters such as fractions, subscripts, superscripts, Roman numerals, currency numerators, encircled numbers, and script-specific digits. In many traditional numbering systems, letters are used with a numeric value. Examples include Greek and Hebrew letters, and Latin letters used in outlines (II.A.1.b). These are special cases and are not included here as numbers.

Decimal digits form a large subcategory of numbers consisting of those digits that can be used to form decimal-radix numbers. This includes script-specific digits. Decimal digits do not include characters such as Roman numerals (1 + 5 = 15 = fifteen, but I + V = IV = four), subscripts, or superscripts. Numbers other than decimal digits can be used in numerical expressions, but it is up to the user to determine the specialized uses.

The Unicode Standard assigns distinct codes to the forms of digits that are specific to a given script or language. Examples are the digits used with the Arabic script, Chinese numbers, or those of the Indic languages. For naming conventions, see the introduction to the Arabic subsection of *Section 6.1, General Scripts Area.*

Table 4-6 gives the numeric values of Unicode characters that can represent numbers. (Some CJK ideographs also have numeric values, but are not included in Table 4-6 in this version of the Unicode Standard.)

Table 4-6. Numeric Properties

Value	Decimal	Number	Name
U+0030	✔	0	DIGIT ZERO
U+0031	✔	1	DIGIT ONE
U+0032	✔	2	DIGIT TWO
U+0033	✔	3	DIGIT THREE

Table 4-6. Numeric Properties (Continued)

Value	Decimal	Number	Name
U+0034	✔	4	DIGIT FOUR
U+0035	✔	5	DIGIT FIVE
U+0036	✔	6	DIGIT SIX
U+0037	✔	7	DIGIT SEVEN
U+0038	✔	8	DIGIT EIGHT
U+0039	✔	9	DIGIT NINE
U+00B2		2	SUPERSCRIPT TWO
U+00B3		3	SUPERSCRIPT THREE
U+00B9		1	SUPERSCRIPT ONE
U+00BC		1/4	VULGAR FRACTION ONE QUARTER
U+00BD		1/2	VULGAR FRACTION ONE HALF
U+00BE		3/4	VULGAR FRACTION THREE QUARTERS
U+0660	✔	0	ARABIC-INDIC DIGIT ZERO
U+0661	✔	1	ARABIC-INDIC DIGIT ONE
U+0662	✔	2	ARABIC-INDIC DIGIT TWO
U+0663	✔	3	ARABIC-INDIC DIGIT THREE
U+0664	✔	4	ARABIC-INDIC DIGIT FOUR
U+0665	✔	5	ARABIC-INDIC DIGIT FIVE
U+0666	✔	6	ARABIC-INDIC DIGIT SIX
U+0667	✔	7	ARABIC-INDIC DIGIT SEVEN
U+0668	✔	8	ARABIC-INDIC DIGIT EIGHT
U+0669	✔	9	ARABIC-INDIC DIGIT NINE
U+06F0	✔	0	EXTENDED ARABIC-INDIC DIGIT ZERO
U+06F1	✔	1	EXTENDED ARABIC-INDIC DIGIT ONE
U+06F2	✔	2	EXTENDED ARABIC-INDIC DIGIT TWO
U+06F3	✔	3	EXTENDED ARABIC-INDIC DIGIT THREE
U+06F4	✔	4	EXTENDED ARABIC-INDIC DIGIT FOUR
U+06F5	✔	5	EXTENDED ARABIC-INDIC DIGIT FIVE
U+06F6	✔	6	EXTENDED ARABIC-INDIC DIGIT SIX
U+06F7	✔	7	EXTENDED ARABIC-INDIC DIGIT SEVEN
U+06F8	✔	8	EXTENDED ARABIC-INDIC DIGIT EIGHT
U+06F9	✔	9	EXTENDED ARABIC-INDIC DIGIT NINE
U+0966	✔	0	DEVANAGARI DIGIT ZERO
U+0967	✔	1	DEVANAGARI DIGIT ONE
U+0968	✔	2	DEVANAGARI DIGIT TWO
U+0969	✔	3	DEVANAGARI DIGIT THREE
U+096A	✔	4	DEVANAGARI DIGIT FOUR
U+096B	✔	5	DEVANAGARI DIGIT FIVE
U+096C	✔	6	DEVANAGARI DIGIT SIX
U+096D	✔	7	DEVANAGARI DIGIT SEVEN
U+096E	✔	8	DEVANAGARI DIGIT EIGHT
U+096F	✔	9	DEVANAGARI DIGIT NINE
U+09E6	✔	0	BENGALI DIGIT ZERO
U+09E7	✔	1	BENGALI DIGIT ONE
U+09E8	✔	2	BENGALI DIGIT TWO
U+09E9	✔	3	BENGALI DIGIT THREE
U+09EA	✔	4	BENGALI DIGIT FOUR
U+09EB	✔	5	BENGALI DIGIT FIVE
U+09EC	✔	6	BENGALI DIGIT SIX
U+09ED	✔	7	BENGALI DIGIT SEVEN
U+09EE	✔	8	BENGALI DIGIT EIGHT
U+09EF	✔	9	BENGALI DIGIT NINE
U+09F4		1	BENGALI CURRENCY NUMERATOR ONE
U+09F5		2	BENGALI CURRENCY NUMERATOR TWO
U+09F6		3	BENGALI CURRENCY NUMERATOR THREE
U+09F7		4	BENGALI CURRENCY NUMERATOR FOUR
U+09F8		-	BENGALI CURRENCY NUMERATOR ONE LESS THAN THE DENOMINATOR
U+09F9		16	BENGALI CURRENCY DENOMINATOR SIXTEEN
U+0A66	✔	0	GURMUKHI DIGIT ZERO
U+0A67	✔	1	GURMUKHI DIGIT ONE

Table 4-6. Numeric Properties (Continued)

Value	Decimal	Number	Name
U+0A68	✔	2	GURMUKHI DIGIT TWO
U+0A69	✔	3	GURMUKHI DIGIT THREE
U+0A6A	✔	4	GURMUKHI DIGIT FOUR
U+0A6B	✔	5	GURMUKHI DIGIT FIVE
U+0A6C	✔	6	GURMUKHI DIGIT SIX
U+0A6D	✔	7	GURMUKHI DIGIT SEVEN
U+0A6E	✔	8	GURMUKHI DIGIT EIGHT
U+0A6F	✔	9	GURMUKHI DIGIT NINE
U+0AE6	✔	0	GUJARATI DIGIT ZERO
U+0AE7	✔	1	GUJARATI DIGIT ONE
U+0AE8	✔	2	GUJARATI DIGIT TWO
U+0AE9	✔	3	GUJARATI DIGIT THREE
U+0AEA	✔	4	GUJARATI DIGIT FOUR
U+0AEB	✔	5	GUJARATI DIGIT FIVE
U+0AEC	✔	6	GUJARATI DIGIT SIX
U+0AED	✔	7	GUJARATI DIGIT SEVEN
U+0AEE	✔	8	GUJARATI DIGIT EIGHT
U+0AEF	✔	9	GUJARATI DIGIT NINE
U+0B66	✔	0	ORIYA DIGIT ZERO
U+0B67	✔	1	ORIYA DIGIT ONE
U+0B68	✔	2	ORIYA DIGIT TWO
U+0B69	✔	3	ORIYA DIGIT THREE
U+0B6A	✔	4	ORIYA DIGIT FOUR
U+0B6B	✔	5	ORIYA DIGIT FIVE
U+0B6C	✔	6	ORIYA DIGIT SIX
U+0B6D	✔	7	ORIYA DIGIT SEVEN
U+0B6E	✔	8	ORIYA DIGIT EIGHT
U+0B6F	✔	9	ORIYA DIGIT NINE
U+0BE7	✔	1	TAMIL DIGIT ONE
U+0BE8	✔	2	TAMIL DIGIT TWO
U+0BE9	✔	3	TAMIL DIGIT THREE
U+0BEA	✔	4	TAMIL DIGIT FOUR
U+0BEB	✔	5	TAMIL DIGIT FIVE
U+0BEC	✔	6	TAMIL DIGIT SIX
U+0BED	✔	7	TAMIL DIGIT SEVEN
U+0BEE	✔	8	TAMIL DIGIT EIGHT
U+0BEF	✔	9	TAMIL DIGIT NINE
U+0BF0		10	TAMIL NUMBER TEN
U+0BF1		100	TAMIL NUMBER ONE HUNDRED
U+0BF2		1000	TAMIL NUMBER ONE THOUSAND
U+0C66	✔	0	TELUGU DIGIT ZERO
U+0C67	✔	1	TELUGU DIGIT ONE
U+0C68	✔	2	TELUGU DIGIT TWO
U+0C69	✔	3	TELUGU DIGIT THREE
U+0C6A	✔	4	TELUGU DIGIT FOUR
U+0C6B	✔	5	TELUGU DIGIT FIVE
U+0C6C	✔	6	TELUGU DIGIT SIX
U+0C6D	✔	7	TELUGU DIGIT SEVEN
U+0C6E	✔	8	TELUGU DIGIT EIGHT
U+0C6F	✔	9	TELUGU DIGIT NINE
U+0CE6	✔	0	KANNADA DIGIT ZERO
U+0CE7	✔	1	KANNADA DIGIT ONE
U+0CE8	✔	2	KANNADA DIGIT TWO
U+0CE9	✔	3	KANNADA DIGIT THREE
U+0CEA	✔	4	KANNADA DIGIT FOUR
U+0CEB	✔	5	KANNADA DIGIT FIVE
U+0CEC	✔	6	KANNADA DIGIT SIX
U+0CED	✔	7	KANNADA DIGIT SEVEN
U+0CEE	✔	8	KANNADA DIGIT EIGHT
U+0CEF	✔	9	KANNADA DIGIT NINE
U+0D66	✔	0	MALAYALAM DIGIT ZERO

Table 4-6. Numeric Properties (Continued)

Value	Decimal	Number	Name
U+0D67	✔	1	MALAYALAM DIGIT ONE
U+0D68	✔	2	MALAYALAM DIGIT TWO
U+0D69	✔	3	MALAYALAM DIGIT THREE
U+0D6A	✔	4	MALAYALAM DIGIT FOUR
U+0D6B	✔	5	MALAYALAM DIGIT FIVE
U+0D6C	✔	6	MALAYALAM DIGIT SIX
U+0D6D	✔	7	MALAYALAM DIGIT SEVEN
U+0D6E	✔	8	MALAYALAM DIGIT EIGHT
U+0D6F	✔	9	MALAYALAM DIGIT NINE
U+0E50	✔	0	THAI DIGIT ZERO
U+0E51	✔	1	THAI DIGIT ONE
U+0E52	✔	2	THAI DIGIT TWO
U+0E53	✔	3	THAI DIGIT THREE
U+0E54	✔	4	THAI DIGIT FOUR
U+0E55	✔	5	THAI DIGIT FIVE
U+0E56	✔	6	THAI DIGIT SIX
U+0E57	✔	7	THAI DIGIT SEVEN
U+0E58	✔	8	THAI DIGIT EIGHT
U+0E59	✔	9	THAI DIGIT NINE
U+0ED0	✔	0	LAO DIGIT ZERO
U+0ED1	✔	1	LAO DIGIT ONE
U+0ED2	✔	2	LAO DIGIT TWO
U+0ED3	✔	3	LAO DIGIT THREE
U+0ED4	✔	4	LAO DIGIT FOUR
U+0ED5	✔	5	LAO DIGIT FIVE
U+0ED6	✔	6	LAO DIGIT SIX
U+0ED7	✔	7	LAO DIGIT SEVEN
U+0ED8	✔	8	LAO DIGIT EIGHT
U+0ED9	✔	9	LAO DIGIT NINE
U+0F20	✔	0	TIBETAN DIGIT ZERO
U+0F21	✔	1	TIBETAN DIGIT ONE
U+0F22	✔	2	TIBETAN DIGIT TWO
U+0F23	✔	3	TIBETAN DIGIT THREE
U+0F2D	✔	4	TIBETAN DIGIT FOUR
U+0F25	✔	5	TIBETAN DIGIT FIVE
U+0F26	✔	6	TIBETAN DIGIT SIX
U+0F27	✔	7	TIBETAN DIGIT SEVEN
U+0F28	✔	8	TIBETAN DIGIT EIGHT
U+0F29	✔	9	TIBETAN DIGIT NINE
U+0F2A		1/2	TIBETAN DIGIT HALF ONE
U+0F2B		3/2	TIBETAN DIGIT HALF TWO
U+0F2C		5/2	TIBETAN DIGIT HALF THREE
U+0F2D		7/2	TIBETAN DIGIT HALF FOUR
U+0F2E		9/2	TIBETAN DIGIT HALF FIVE
U+0F2F		11/2	TIBETAN DIGIT HALF SIX
U+0F30		13/2	TIBETAN DIGIT HALF SEVEN
U+0F31		15/2	TIBETAN DIGIT HALF EIGHT
U+0F32		17/2	TIBETAN DIGIT HALF NINE
U+0F33		-1/2	TIBETAN DIGIT HALF ZERO
U+2070		0	SUPERSCRIPT ZERO
U+2074		4	SUPERSCRIPT FOUR
U+2075		5	SUPERSCRIPT FIVE
U+2076		6	SUPERSCRIPT SIX
U+2077		7	SUPERSCRIPT SEVEN
U+2078		8	SUPERSCRIPT EIGHT
U+2079		9	SUPERSCRIPT NINE
U+2080		0	SUBSCRIPT ZERO
U+2081		1	SUBSCRIPT ONE
U+2082		2	SUBSCRIPT TWO
U+2083		3	SUBSCRIPT THREE
U+2084		4	SUBSCRIPT FOUR

Table 4-6. Numeric Properties (Continued)

Value	Decimal	Number	Name
U+2085		5	SUBSCRIPT FIVE
U+2086		6	SUBSCRIPT SIX
U+2087		7	SUBSCRIPT SEVEN
U+2088		8	SUBSCRIPT EIGHT
U+2089		9	SUBSCRIPT NINE
U+2153		1/3	VULGAR FRACTION ONE THIRD
U+2154		2/3	VULGAR FRACTION TWO THIRDS
U+2155		1/5	VULGAR FRACTION ONE FIFTH
U+2156		2/5	VULGAR FRACTION TWO FIFTHS
U+2157		3/5	VULGAR FRACTION THREE FIFTHS
U+2158		4/5	VULGAR FRACTION FOUR FIFTHS
U+2159		1/6	VULGAR FRACTION ONE SIXTH
U+215A		5/6	VULGAR FRACTION FIVE SIXTHS
U+215B		1/8	VULGAR FRACTION ONE EIGHTH
U+215C		3/8	VULGAR FRACTION THREE EIGHTHS
U+215D		5/8	VULGAR FRACTION FIVE EIGHTHS
U+215E		7/8	VULGAR FRACTION SEVEN EIGHTHS
U+215F		1	FRACTION NUMERATOR ONE
U+2160		1	ROMAN NUMERAL ONE
U+2161		2	ROMAN NUMERAL TWO
U+2162		3	ROMAN NUMERAL THREE
U+2163		4	ROMAN NUMERAL FOUR
U+2164		5	ROMAN NUMERAL FIVE
U+2165		6	ROMAN NUMERAL SIX
U+2166		7	ROMAN NUMERAL SEVEN
U+2167		8	ROMAN NUMERAL EIGHT
U+2168		9	ROMAN NUMERAL NINE
U+2169		10	ROMAN NUMERAL TEN
U+216A		11	ROMAN NUMERAL ELEVEN
U+216B		12	ROMAN NUMERAL TWELVE
U+216C		50	ROMAN NUMERAL FIFTY
U+216D		100	ROMAN NUMERAL ONE HUNDRED
U+216E		500	ROMAN NUMERAL FIVE HUNDRED
U+216F		1000	ROMAN NUMERAL ONE THOUSAND
U+2170		1	SMALL ROMAN NUMERAL ONE
U+2171		2	SMALL ROMAN NUMERAL TWO
U+2172		3	SMALL ROMAN NUMERAL THREE
U+2173		4	SMALL ROMAN NUMERAL FOUR
U+2174		5	SMALL ROMAN NUMERAL FIVE
U+2175		6	SMALL ROMAN NUMERAL SIX
U+2176		7	SMALL ROMAN NUMERAL SEVEN
U+2177		8	SMALL ROMAN NUMERAL EIGHT
U+2178		9	SMALL ROMAN NUMERAL NINE
U+2179		10	SMALL ROMAN NUMERAL TEN
U+217A		11	SMALL ROMAN NUMERAL ELEVEN
U+217B		12	SMALL ROMAN NUMERAL TWELVE
U+217C		50	SMALL ROMAN NUMERAL FIFTY
U+217D		100	SMALL ROMAN NUMERAL ONE HUNDRED
U+217E		500	SMALL ROMAN NUMERAL FIVE HUNDRED
U+217F		1000	SMALL ROMAN NUMERAL ONE THOUSAND
U+2180		1000	ROMAN NUMERAL ONE THOUSAND C D
U+2181		5000	ROMAN NUMERAL FIVE THOUSAND
U+2182		10000	ROMAN NUMERAL TEN THOUSAND
U+2460		1	CIRCLED DIGIT ONE
U+2461		2	CIRCLED DIGIT TWO
U+2462		3	CIRCLED DIGIT THREE
U+2463		4	CIRCLED DIGIT FOUR
U+2464		5	CIRCLED DIGIT FIVE
U+2465		6	CIRCLED DIGIT SIX
U+2466		7	CIRCLED DIGIT SEVEN
U+2467		8	CIRCLED DIGIT EIGHT

Table 4-6. Numeric Properties (Continued)

Value	Decimal	Number	Name
U+2468		9	CIRCLED DIGIT NINE
U+2469		10	CIRCLED NUMBER TEN
U+246A		11	CIRCLED NUMBER ELEVEN
U+246B		12	CIRCLED NUMBER TWELVE
U+246C		13	CIRCLED NUMBER THIRTEEN
U+246D		14	CIRCLED NUMBER FOURTEEN
U+246E		15	CIRCLED NUMBER FIFTEEN
U+246F		16	CIRCLED NUMBER SIXTEEN
U+2470		17	CIRCLED NUMBER SEVENTEEN
U+2471		18	CIRCLED NUMBER EIGHTEEN
U+2472		19	CIRCLED NUMBER NINETEEN
U+2473		20	CIRCLED NUMBER TWENTY
U+2474		1	PARENTHESIZED DIGIT ONE
U+2475		2	PARENTHESIZED DIGIT TWO
U+2476		3	PARENTHESIZED DIGIT THREE
U+2477		4	PARENTHESIZED DIGIT FOUR
U+2478		5	PARENTHESIZED DIGIT FIVE
U+2479		6	PARENTHESIZED DIGIT SIX
U+247A		7	PARENTHESIZED DIGIT SEVEN
U+247B		8	PARENTHESIZED DIGIT EIGHT
U+247C		9	PARENTHESIZED DIGIT NINE
U+247D		10	PARENTHESIZED NUMBER TEN
U+247E		11	PARENTHESIZED NUMBER ELEVEN
U+247F		12	PARENTHESIZED NUMBER TWELVE
U+2480		13	PARENTHESIZED NUMBER THIRTEEN
U+2481		14	PARENTHESIZED NUMBER FOURTEEN
U+2482		15	PARENTHESIZED NUMBER FIFTEEN
U+2483		16	PARENTHESIZED NUMBER SIXTEEN
U+2484		17	PARENTHESIZED NUMBER SEVENTEEN
U+2485		18	PARENTHESIZED NUMBER EIGHTEEN
U+2486		19	PARENTHESIZED NUMBER NINETEEN
U+2487		20	PARENTHESIZED NUMBER TWENTY
U+2488		1	DIGIT ONE FULL STOP
U+2489		2	DIGIT TWO FULL STOP
U+248A		3	DIGIT THREE FULL STOP
U+248B		4	DIGIT FOUR FULL STOP
U+248C		5	DIGIT FIVE FULL STOP
U+248D		6	DIGIT SIX FULL STOP
U+248E		7	DIGIT SEVEN FULL STOP
U+248F		8	DIGIT EIGHT FULL STOP
U+2490		9	DIGIT NINE FULL STOP
U+2491		10	NUMBER TEN FULL STOP
U+2492		11	NUMBER ELEVEN FULL STOP
U+2493		12	NUMBER TWELVE FULL STOP
U+2494		13	NUMBER THIRTEEN FULL STOP
U+2495		14	NUMBER FOURTEEN FULL STOP
U+2496		15	NUMBER FIFTEEN FULL STOP
U+2497		16	NUMBER SIXTEEN FULL STOP
U+2498		17	NUMBER SEVENTEEN FULL STOP
U+2499		18	NUMBER EIGHTEEN FULL STOP
U+249A		19	NUMBER NINETEEN FULL STOP
U+249B		20	NUMBER TWENTY FULL STOP
U+24EA		0	CIRCLED DIGIT ZERO
U+2776		1	DINGBAT NEGATIVE CIRCLED DIGIT ONE
U+2777		2	DINGBAT NEGATIVE CIRCLED DIGIT TWO
U+2778		3	DINGBAT NEGATIVE CIRCLED DIGIT THREE
U+2779		4	DINGBAT NEGATIVE CIRCLED DIGIT FOUR
U+277A		5	DINGBAT NEGATIVE CIRCLED DIGIT FIVE
U+277B		6	DINGBAT NEGATIVE CIRCLED DIGIT SIX
U+277C		7	DINGBAT NEGATIVE CIRCLED DIGIT SEVEN
U+277D		8	DINGBAT NEGATIVE CIRCLED DIGIT EIGHT

Table 4-6. Numeric Properties (Continued)

Value	Decimal	Number	Name
U+277E		9	DINGBAT NEGATIVE CIRCLED DIGIT NINE
U+277F		10	DINGBAT NEGATIVE CIRCLED NUMBER TEN
U+2780		1	DINGBAT CIRCLED SANS-SERIF DIGIT ONE
U+2781		2	DINGBAT CIRCLED SANS-SERIF DIGIT TWO
U+2782		3	DINGBAT CIRCLED SANS-SERIF DIGIT THREE
U+2783		4	DINGBAT CIRCLED SANS-SERIF DIGIT FOUR
U+2784		5	DINGBAT CIRCLED SANS-SERIF DIGIT FIVE
U+2785		6	DINGBAT CIRCLED SANS-SERIF DIGIT SIX
U+2786		7	DINGBAT CIRCLED SANS-SERIF DIGIT SEVEN
U+2787		8	DINGBAT CIRCLED SANS-SERIF DIGIT EIGHT
U+2788		9	DINGBAT CIRCLED SANS-SERIF DIGIT NINE
U+2789		10	DINGBAT CIRCLED SANS-SERIF NUMBER TEN
U+278A		1	DINGBAT NEGATIVE CIRCLED SANS-SERIF DIGIT ONE
U+278B		2	DINGBAT NEGATIVE CIRCLED SANS-SERIF DIGIT TWO
U+278C		3	DINGBAT NEGATIVE CIRCLED SANS-SERIF DIGIT THREE
U+278D		4	DINGBAT NEGATIVE CIRCLED SANS-SERIF DIGIT FOUR
U+278E		5	DINGBAT NEGATIVE CIRCLED SANS-SERIF DIGIT FIVE
U+278F		6	DINGBAT NEGATIVE CIRCLED SANS-SERIF DIGIT SIX
U+2790		7	DINGBAT NEGATIVE CIRCLED SANS-SERIF DIGIT SEVEN
U+2791		8	DINGBAT NEGATIVE CIRCLED SANS-SERIF DIGIT EIGHT
U+2792		9	DINGBAT NEGATIVE CIRCLED SANS-SERIF DIGIT NINE
U+2793		10	DINGBAT NEGATIVE CIRCLED SANS-SERIF NUMBER TEN
U+3007		0	IDEOGRAPHIC NUMBER ZERO
U+3021		1	HANGZHOU NUMERAL ONE
U+3022		2	HANGZHOU NUMERAL TWO
U+3023		3	HANGZHOU NUMERAL THREE
U+3024		4	HANGZHOU NUMERAL FOUR
U+3025		5	HANGZHOU NUMERAL FIVE
U+3026		6	HANGZHOU NUMERAL SIX
U+3027		7	HANGZHOU NUMERAL SEVEN
U+3028		8	HANGZHOU NUMERAL EIGHT
U+3029		9	HANGZHOU NUMERAL NINE
U+3280		1	CIRCLED IDEOGRAPH ONE
U+3281		2	CIRCLED IDEOGRAPH TWO
U+3282		3	CIRCLED IDEOGRAPH THREE
U+3283		4	CIRCLED IDEOGRAPH FOUR
U+3284		5	CIRCLED IDEOGRAPH FIVE
U+3285		6	CIRCLED IDEOGRAPH SIX
U+3286		7	CIRCLED IDEOGRAPH SEVEN
U+3287		8	CIRCLED IDEOGRAPH EIGHT
U+3288		9	CIRCLED IDEOGRAPH NINE
U+3289		10	CIRCLED IDEOGRAPH TEN
U+FF10	✔	0	FULLWIDTH DIGIT ZERO
U+FF11	✔	1	FULLWIDTH DIGIT ONE
U+FF12	✔	2	FULLWIDTH DIGIT TWO
U+FF13	✔	3	FULLWIDTH DIGIT THREE
U+FF14	✔	4	FULLWIDTH DIGIT FOUR
U+FF15	✔	5	FULLWIDTH DIGIT FIVE
U+FF16	✔	6	FULLWIDTH DIGIT SIX
U+FF17	✔	7	FULLWIDTH DIGIT SEVEN
U+FF18	✔	8	FULLWIDTH DIGIT EIGHT
U+FF19	✔	9	FULLWIDTH DIGIT NINE

4.7 Mirrored

Mirrored is the normative property of character pairs such as parentheses whose images are mirrored horizontally in text that is laid out from right to left. For example, U+0028 LEFT PARENTHESIS is interpreted as *opening parenthesis*; in a left-to-right context, this will appear as "(", while in a right-to-left context, this will appear as the mirrored glyph ")". The list of mirrored characters appears in Table 4-7.

Table 4-7. Mirrored Characters

Value	Name
U+0028	LEFT PARENTHESIS
U+0029	RIGHT PARENTHESIS
U+003C	LESS-THAN SIGN
U+003E	GREATER-THAN SIGN
U+005B	LEFT SQUARE BRACKET
U+005D	RIGHT SQUARE BRACKET
U+007B	LEFT CURLY BRACKET
U+007D	RIGHT CURLY BRACKET
U+2045	LEFT SQUARE BRACKET WITH QUILL
U+2046	RIGHT SQUARE BRACKET WITH QUILL
U+207D	SUPERSCRIPT LEFT PARENTHESIS
U+207E	SUPERSCRIPT RIGHT PARENTHESIS
U+208D	SUBSCRIPT LEFT PARENTHESIS
U+208E	SUBSCRIPT RIGHT PARENTHESIS
U+2201	COMPLEMENT
U+2202	PARTIAL DIFFERENTIAL
U+2203	THERE EXISTS
U+2204	THERE DOES NOT EXIST
U+2208	ELEMENT OF
U+2209	NOT AN ELEMENT OF
U+220A	SMALL ELEMENT OF
U+220B	CONTAINS AS MEMBER
U+220C	DOES NOT CONTAIN AS MEMBER
U+220D	SMALL CONTAINS AS MEMBER
U+2211	N-ARY SUMMATION
U+2215	DIVISION SLASH
U+2216	SET MINUS
U+221A	SQUARE ROOT
U+221B	CUBE ROOT
U+221C	FOURTH ROOT
U+221D	PROPORTIONAL TO
U+221F	RIGHT ANGLE
U+2220	ANGLE
U+2221	MEASURED ANGLE
U+2222	SPHERICAL ANGLE
U+2224	DOES NOT DIVIDE
U+2226	NOT PARALLEL TO
U+222B	INTEGRAL
U+222C	DOUBLE INTEGRAL
U+222D	TRIPLE INTEGRAL
U+222E	CONTOUR INTEGRAL
U+222F	SURFACE INTEGRAL
U+2230	VOLUME INTEGRAL
U+2231	CLOCKWISE INTEGRAL
U+2232	CLOCKWISE CONTOUR INTEGRAL
U+2233	ANTICLOCKWISE CONTOUR INTEGRAL
U+2239	EXCESS
U+223B	HOMOTHETIC
U+223C	TILDE OPERATOR
U+223D	REVERSED TILDE

Table 4-7. Mirrored Characters (Continued)

Value	Name
U+223E	INVERTED LAZY S
U+223F	SINE WAVE
U+2240	WREATH PRODUCT
U+2241	NOT TILDE
U+2242	MINUS TILDE
U+2243	ASYMPTOTICALLY EQUAL TO
U+2244	NOT ASYMPTOTICALLY EQUAL TO
U+2245	APPROXIMATELY EQUAL TO
U+2246	APPROXIMATELY BUT NOT ACTUALLY EQUAL TO
U+2247	NEITHER APPROXIMATELY NOR ACTUALLY EQUAL TO
U+2248	ALMOST EQUAL TO
U+2249	NOT ALMOST EQUAL TO
U+224A	ALMOST EQUAL OR EQUAL TO
U+224B	TRIPLE TILDE
U+224C	ALL EQUAL TO
U+2252	APPROXIMATELY EQUAL TO OR THE IMAGE OF
U+2253	IMAGE OF OR APPROXIMATELY EQUAL TO
U+2254	COLON EQUALS
U+2255	EQUALS COLON
U+225F	QUESTIONED EQUAL TO
U+2260	NOT EQUAL TO
U+2262	NOT IDENTICAL TO
U+2264	LESS-THAN OR EQUAL TO
U+2265	GREATER-THAN OR EQUAL TO
U+2266	LESS-THAN OVER EQUAL TO
U+2267	GREATER-THAN OVER EQUAL TO
U+2268	LESS-THAN BUT NOT EQUAL TO
U+2269	GREATER-THAN BUT NOT EQUAL TO
U+226A	MUCH LESS-THAN
U+226B	MUCH GREATER-THAN
U+226E	NOT LESS-THAN
U+226F	NOT GREATER-THAN
U+2270	NEITHER LESS-THAN NOR EQUAL TO
U+2271	NEITHER GREATER-THAN NOR EQUAL TO
U+2272	LESS-THAN OR EQUIVALENT TO
U+2273	GREATER-THAN OR EQUIVALENT TO
U+2274	NEITHER LESS-THAN NOR EQUIVALENT TO
U+2275	NEITHER GREATER-THAN NOR EQUIVALENT TO
U+2276	LESS-THAN OR GREATER-THAN
U+2277	GREATER-THAN OR LESS-THAN
U+2278	NEITHER LESS-THAN NOR GREATER-THAN
U+2279	NEITHER GREATER-THAN NOR LESS-THAN
U+227A	PRECEDES
U+227B	SUCCEEDS
U+227C	PRECEDES OR EQUAL TO
U+227D	SUCCEEDS OR EQUAL TO
U+227E	PRECEDES OR EQUIVALENT TO
U+227F	SUCCEEDS OR EQUIVALENT TO
U+2280	DOES NOT PRECEDE
U+2281	DOES NOT SUCCEED
U+2282	SUBSET OF
U+2283	SUPERSET OF
U+2284	NOT A SUBSET OF
U+2285	NOT A SUPERSET OF
U+2286	SUBSET OF OR EQUAL TO
U+2287	SUPERSET OF OR EQUAL TO
U+2288	NEITHER A SUBSET OF NOR EQUAL TO
U+2289	NEITHER A SUPERSET OF NOR EQUAL TO
U+228A	SUBSET OF WITH NOT EQUAL TO
U+228B	SUPERSET OF WITH NOT EQUAL TO
U+228C	MULTISET

Table 4-7. Mirrored Characters (Continued)

Value	Name
U+228F	SQUARE IMAGE OF
U+2290	SQUARE ORIGINAL OF
U+2291	SQUARE IMAGE OF OR EQUAL TO
U+2292	SQUARE ORIGINAL OF OR EQUAL TO
U+2298	CIRCLED DIVISION SLASH
U+22A2	RIGHT TACK
U+22A3	LEFT TACK
U+22A6	ASSERTION
U+22A7	MODELS
U+22A8	TRUE
U+22A9	FORCES
U+22AA	TRIPLE VERTICAL BAR RIGHT TURNSTILE
U+22AB	DOUBLE VERTICAL BAR DOUBLE RIGHT TURNSTILE
U+22AC	DOES NOT PROVE
U+22AD	NOT TRUE
U+22AE	DOES NOT FORCE
U+22AF	NEGATED DOUBLE VERTICAL BAR DOUBLE RIGHT TURNSTILE
U+22B0	PRECEDES UNDER RELATION
U+22B1	SUCCEEDS UNDER RELATION
U+22B2	NORMAL SUBGROUP OF
U+22B3	CONTAINS AS NORMAL SUBGROUP
U+22B4	NORMAL SUBGROUP OF OR EQUAL TO
U+22B5	CONTAINS AS NORMAL SUBGROUP OR EQUAL TO
U+22B6	ORIGINAL OF
U+22B7	IMAGE OF
U+22B8	MULTIMAP
U+22BE	RIGHT ANGLE WITH ARC
U+22BF	RIGHT TRIANGLE
U+22C9	LEFT NORMAL FACTOR SEMIDIRECT PRODUCT
U+22CA	RIGHT NORMAL FACTOR SEMIDIRECT PRODUCT
U+22CB	LEFT SEMIDIRECT PRODUCT
U+22CC	RIGHT SEMIDIRECT PRODUCT
U+22CD	REVERSED TILDE EQUALS
U+22D0	DOUBLE SUBSET
U+22D1	DOUBLE SUPERSET
U+22D6	LESS-THAN WITH DOT
U+22D7	GREATER-THAN WITH DOT
U+22D8	VERY MUCH LESS-THAN
U+22D9	VERY MUCH GREATER-THAN
U+22DA	LESS-THAN EQUAL TO OR GREATER-THAN
U+22DB	GREATER-THAN EQUAL TO OR LESS-THAN
U+22DC	EQUAL TO OR LESS-THAN
U+22DD	EQUAL TO OR GREATER-THAN
U+22DE	EQUAL TO OR PRECEDES
U+22DF	EQUAL TO OR SUCCEEDS
U+22E0	DOES NOT PRECEDE OR EQUAL
U+22E1	DOES NOT SUCCEED OR EQUAL
U+22E2	NOT SQUARE IMAGE OF OR EQUAL TO
U+22E3	NOT SQUARE ORIGINAL OF OR EQUAL TO
U+22E4	SQUARE IMAGE OF OR NOT EQUAL TO
U+22E5	SQUARE ORIGINAL OF OR NOT EQUAL TO
U+22E6	LESS-THAN BUT NOT EQUIVALENT TO
U+22E7	GREATER-THAN BUT NOT EQUIVALENT TO
U+22E8	PRECEDES BUT NOT EQUIVALENT TO
U+22E9	SUCCEEDS BUT NOT EQUIVALENT TO
U+22EA	NOT NORMAL SUBGROUP OF
U+22EB	DOES NOT CONTAIN AS NORMAL SUBGROUP
U+22EC	NOT NORMAL SUBGROUP OF OR EQUAL TO
U+22ED	DOES NOT CONTAIN AS NORMAL SUBGROUP OR EQUAL
U+22F0	UP RIGHT DIAGONAL ELLIPSIS
U+22F1	DOWN RIGHT DIAGONAL ELLIPSIS

Table 4-7. Mirrored Characters (Continued)

Value	Name
U+2308	LEFT CEILING
U+2309	RIGHT CEILING
U+230A	LEFT FLOOR
U+230B	RIGHT FLOOR
U+2320	TOP HALF INTEGRAL
U+2321	BOTTOM HALF INTEGRAL
U+2329	LEFT-POINTING ANGLE BRACKET
U+232A	RIGHT-POINTING ANGLE BRACKET
U+3008	LEFT ANGLE BRACKET
U+3009	RIGHT ANGLE BRACKET
U+300A	LEFT DOUBLE ANGLE BRACKET
U+300B	RIGHT DOUBLE ANGLE BRACKET
U+300C	LEFT CORNER BRACKET
U+300D	RIGHT CORNER BRACKET
U+300E	LEFT WHITE CORNER BRACKET
U+300F	RIGHT WHITE CORNER BRACKET
U+3010	LEFT BLACK LENTICULAR BRACKET
U+3011	RIGHT BLACK LENTICULAR BRACKET
U+3014	LEFT TORTOISE SHELL BRACKET
U+3015	RIGHT TORTOISE SHELL BRACKET
U+3016	LEFT WHITE LENTICULAR BRACKET
U+3017	RIGHT WHITE LENTICULAR BRACKET
U+3018	LEFT WHITE TORTOISE SHELL BRACKET
U+3019	RIGHT WHITE TORTOISE SHELL BRACKET
U+301A	LEFT WHITE SQUARE BRACKET
U+301B	RIGHT WHITE SQUARE BRACKET

4.8 Unicode 1.0 Names

The *Unicode 1.0 character name* is an informative property of the characters defined in the Unicode Standard Version 1.0. The names of Unicode characters were changed in the process of merging with ISO/IEC 10646. The 1.0 character names can be obtained from the CD-ROM accompanying the standard or from the ftp site. (See also *Appendix D, Cumulative Changes.*)

4.9 Mathematical Property

The mathematical property is an informative property of characters that are used as operators in mathematical formulas. The mathematical property may be useful in algorithms that deal with the display of mathematical text and formulas. However, a number of these characters have multiple usages and may also occur with non-mathematical semantics. For example, U+002D HYPHEN-MINUS may also be used as a hyphen—and not as a mathematical minus sign. Other characters, including some alphabetic, numeric, punctuation, spaces, arrows, and geometric shapes, are also used in mathematical expressions, but are even more dependent on the context for their identification. The following list of Unicode characters have the mathematical property.

```
0028..002B, 002D, 002F, 003C..003E, 005B..005E, 007B..007E, 00AC, 00B1,
00D7, 00F7, 20A6, 2032..2034, 2044, 20D2..20E1, 2190..2194, 21D2, 21D4,
2200..22F1, 2308..230B, 2320..2321, 2329..232A
```

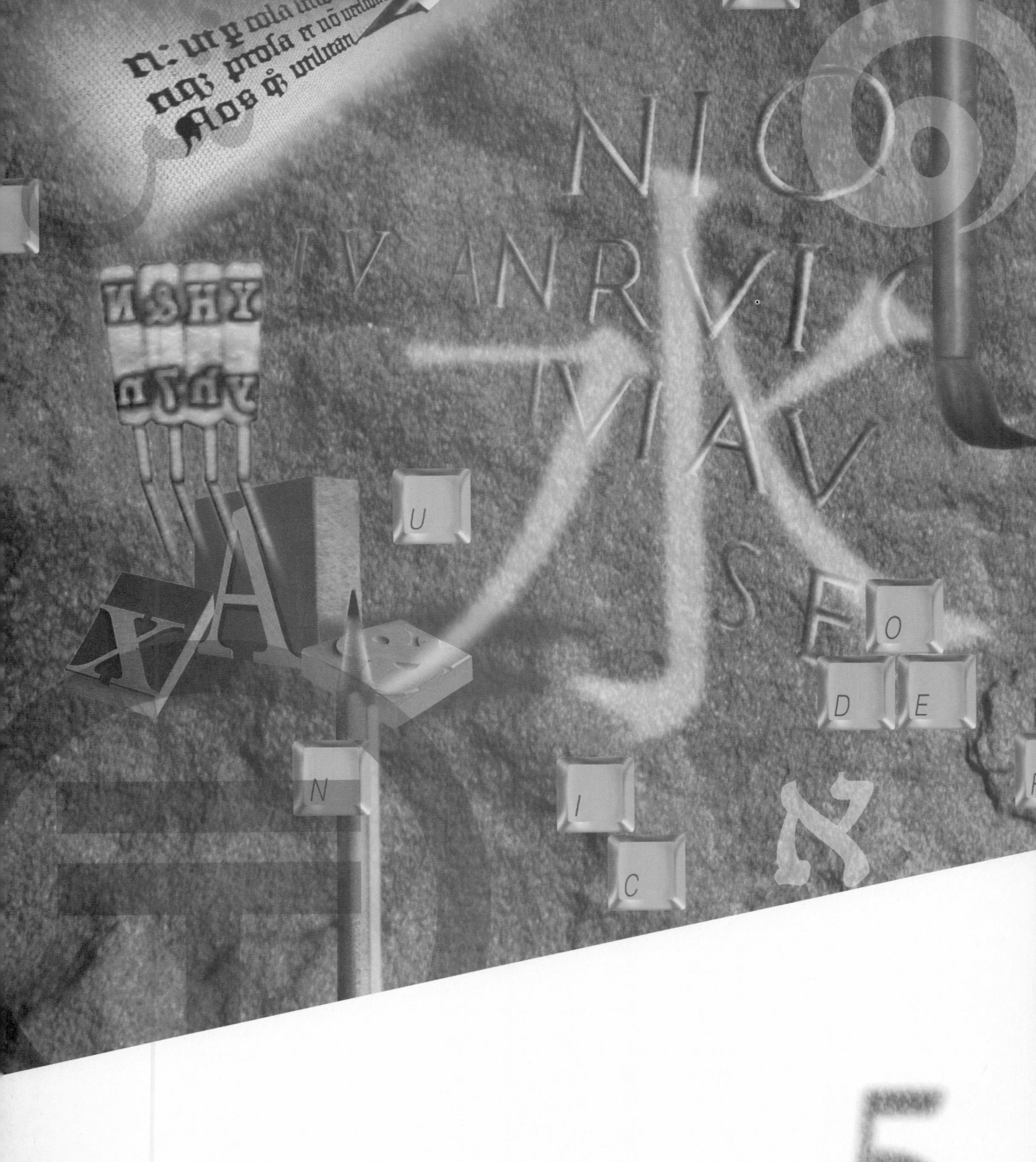

5 IMPLEMENTATION GUIDELINES

Chapter 5

Implementation Guidelines

It is possible to implement a substantial subset of the Unicode Standard as "wide-ASCII" with little change to existing programming practice. However, the Unicode Standard also provides for languages and writing systems that have more complex behavior than English. Whether implementing a new operating system from the ground up or enhancing existing programming environments or applications, dealing with this more complex behavior requires examining many aspects of programming practice and conventions in use today.

This chapter covers a series of short, self-contained topics that are useful to the implementer. The information and examples presented in this chapter will help implementers understand and apply the design and features of the Unicode Standard and will promote good practice in implementations conforming to the Unicode Standard. They are meant as guidelines and therefore are not binding on the implementer. The material is divided into three broad areas: basic programming, character semantics, and text handling.

5.1 ANSI/ISO C wchar_t

With the `wchar_t` wide character type, ANSI/ISO C provides for inclusion of fixed width, wide characters. ANSI/ISO C leaves the semantics of the wide character set to the specific implementation but requires that the characters from the portable C execution set correspond to their wide character equivalents by zero extension. The Unicode characters in the ASCII range U+0020 to U+007E satisfy these conditions. Thus, if an implementation uses ASCII to code the portable C execution set, the use of the Unicode character set for the `wchar_t` type, with a width of 16 bits, fulfills the requirement.

The width of `wchar_t` is compiler-specific and can be as little as 8 bits. Because of this, programs that need to be portable across any C or C++ compiler should not use `wchar_t` for storing Unicode text. The `wchar_t` type is intended for storing compiler-defined wide characters, which may be Unicode characters in some compilers. However, programmers can use a macro or typedef (for example, `UNICHAR`) which can be compiled as `unsigned short` or `wchar_t` depending on the target compiler and platform. This allows correct compilation on different platforms and compilers. Where a 16-bit implementation of `wchar_t` is guaranteed, such macros or typedefs may be predefined (for example, `TCHAR` on the Win32 API).

On systems where the native character type or `wchar_t` are implementated as 32-bit quantities, an implementation may transiently use 32-bit quantities to represent Unicode characters during processing. The internals of this representation are treated as a black box and are not Unicode conformant. In particular, any API or runtime library interfaces that accept strings of 32-bit characters are not Unicode conformant. If such an implementation interchanges 16-bit Unicode characters with the outside world, then this interchange can be conformant as long as the interface for this interchange complies with the requirements of *Chapter 3, Conformance.*

5.2 Compression and Transmission

Using the Unicode character encoding may increase the amount of storage or memory space dedicated to the text portion of files. Compressing Unicode-encoded files or strings can be an attractive option. Compression always constitutes a higher-level protocol and makes interchange dependent on knowledge of the compression method employed.

File-Based Compression. There are commercially available compression algorithms, such as LZW, that, given enough context, will compress files to something near their theoretical minimum. Assume for example that a particular text takes 1000 bytes to encode in ASCII and that the compressed size is 437 bytes. When the same text is encoded using Unicode characters (taking 2000 bytes) and is then compressed properly, the resulting size will still be 437 bytes. Since Unicode-encoded text is composed from a 16-bit token set, algorithms such as LZW, which are sensitive to the width of the individual tokens, may stand to gain from being reimplemented based on 16-bit tokens.

Compression can be effective in eliminating the size overhead of a Unicode encoding without the cost of added complexity when it is built into the underlying support layer (such as modem transmission protocols or file system).

String-Based Compression. Occasionally it is necessary to compress short strings of text in isolation, or in a manner that allows access and substitution of text without decompression. In these specialized cases, string-based compression schemes must be used. However, compression employed at a level where it is visible to the text-processing parts of the program reintroduces the kind of complexities found in multibyte or other stateful encodings, which the Unicode character encoding was designed to avoid.

The Unicode codespace is arranged such that characters within the same script are generally contiguous, except for shared punctuation. A simple compression algorithm might run-length encode the most significant byte. Because of shared punctuation, better results are achieved by using two windows of 128 characters: one permanent window spanning the characters U+0000 → U+007F (equivalent to ASCII), and one sliding window whose start value can be set by escape codes.

Transformation forms defined in *Appendix A, Transformation Formats,* have different storage characteristics. For example, as long as text contains only characters from the Basic Latin (ASCII) block, it occupies the same amount of space whether it is encoded with the UTF-8 transformation format or using ASCII codes. On the other hand, text consisting of ideographs encoded with UTF-8 will require more space than equivalent Unicode-encoded text.

7-bit or 8-bit Transmission

Some transmission protocols use ASCII control codes for flow control. Others, including some UNIX mailers, are notorious for their restrictions to 7-bit ASCII. In these cases, transmissions of Unicode-encoded text must be encapsulated. A number of encapsulation protocols exist today, such as `uuencode` and `BinHex`. These can be combined with compression in the same pass, thereby reducing the transmission overhead.

Alternatively, the UTF-7 and UTF-8 Transformation Formats described in *Appendix A, Transformation Formats,* may be used to transmit Unicode-encoded data through 7-bit or 8-bit transmission paths.

5.3 Language Information

The knowledge of the language of a given Unicode-encoded text is not explicitly specified by the character encoding itself; rather, a higher-level protocol is required to specify the language that a given text represents. Note that it may be possible to determine the language of a text based on its content heuristically, without any explicit language information. The accuracy of such a determination is based on the effectiveness of the heuristic. For example, text containing Hangul characters may reasonably be inferred to represent the Korean language since no other language employs the Hangul script. However, text containing Hebrew characters may or may not represent the Hebrew language since a number of unrelated languages use this script (for example, Hebrew (Ivrit), Yiddish, Judezmo (Ladino), and so on).

Language information is important to facilitate certain kinds of processing of character data. For example, correct searching, spell checking, and grammar checking of multilingual text certainly require language information to be marked for parts of the text. Even rendering may make use of language knowledge (see *Section 5.11, Strategies for Handling Non-Spacing Marks*).

The Unicode Standard does not encode language information. Therefore, if some aspect of character processing or display requires the discrimination of different uses of a single character according to language or writing system (that is, a particular linguistic and orthographic use of a particular character), a higher-level protocol is needed to specify the necessary language or orthographic bindings. An example of such a higher level protocol is the use of a language attribute as in SGML (Standard Generalized Markup Language) text encodings.

Languages in common use are covered by systems of language identifiers maintained by ISO as well as by vendors for use with their systems.

5.4 Unknown and Missing Characters

This section briefly discusses how users or implementers might deal with characters that are not supported, or which, though supported, are unavailable for legible rendering.

Unassigned and Private Use Character Codes

There are two classes of character code values which even a "complete" implementation of the Unicode Standard cannot necessarily interpret correctly:

- Character code values that are unassigned
- Character code values in the Private Use Area for which no private agreement exists

An implementation should not attempt to interpret such code values. Some options for rendering such unknown code values include printing the character code value as four hexadecimal digits, printing a black or white box, using appropriate glyphs such as for unassigned and for private use, or simply displaying nothing. In no case should an implementation *assume* anything else about the character's properties, nor should it blindly delete such characters. It should not unintentionally transform them into something else.[1]

Interpretable but Unrenderable Characters

An implementation may receive a character that is an assigned character in the Unicode character encoding, but be unable to render it because it does not have a font for it, or is otherwise incapable of rendering it appropriately.

In this case, an implementation might be able to provide further limited feedback to the user's queries such as being able to sort the data properly, show its script, or otherwise display it in a default manner. An implementation can distinguish between unrenderable (but assigned) characters, and unassigned code values by printing the former with distinctive glyphs that give some general indication of their type, such as [L], [Я], [Θ], [ŏ], [か], [த], [ش], [क], [ש], [가], [漢], and so on.

5.5 Handling Surrogate Characters

Surrogates were carefully designed to be a simple and efficient extension mechanism that works well with older implementations and does not fall prey to many of the problems of multibyte encodings. They provide a mechanism for encoding extremely rare characters without requiring the use of 32-bit characters. Since only infrequently used characters will be assigned to surrogate pairs, implementations do not need to handle these pairs initially; vendors may choose to support them as market conditions require. *(No surrogate pairs are currently assigned, except for private use.)*

High surrogates and low surrogates are assigned to disjoint ranges of code positions. Non-surrogate characters can never be assigned to these ranges. Since the high- and low-surrogate ranges are disjoint, determining character boundaries requires at most scanning one preceding or following Unicode code value, without regard to any other context. This enables efficient random access, which is not possible with encodings such as Shift-JIS.

In well-formed text, a low surrogate can be preceded only by a high surrogate (not by a low surrogate or non-surrogate) and a high surrogate can be followed only by a low surrogate (not by a high surrogate or non-surrogate).

Surrogates are also designed to work well with implementations that do not recognize them. For example, the valid sequence of Unicode characters [0048] [0069] [0020] [D800] [DC00] [0021] [0021] would be interpreted by a Unicode 1.0-conformant implementation as: "Hi <*unrecognized*><*unrecognized*>!!" This is only slightly worse than a Unicode 2.0 conformant implementation that did not support that surrogate pair, and so interpreted the sequence as: "Hi <*unrecognized*>!!"

So long as an implementation does not remove either surrogate or insert another character between them, the data integrity is maintained. Moreover, even if the data is corrupted, the data corruption is localized (unlike some multibyte encodings like Shift-JIS or EUC); corrupting a single Unicode value affects only a single character. Because the high and low sur-

1. There are also some character code values that were assigned in a previous version of the Unicode Standard but that have become unassigned because the characters have been moved (see *Appendix D, Cumulative Changes*). Such code values should be recognized and converted into the correct Unicode 2.0 character code values where possible. In some cases, a Unicode 2.0 application may still need to emit Unicode 1.1 character codes to communicate with some Unicode 1.1 applications.

rogates are disjoint and always occur in pairs, this prevents the errors from propagating through the rest of the text.

Implementations can have different levels of support for surrogates, based on two primary issues:

- Does the implementation interpret a surrogate pair as the assigned single character?
- Does the implementation guarantee the integrity of a surrogate pair?

The decisions on these issues give rise to three reasonable levels of support for surrogates as shown in Table 5-1.

Table 5-1. Surrogate Support Levels

Support Level	Interpretation	Integrity of pairs
None	No pairs	Does not guarantee
Weak	Non-null subset of pairs	Does not guarantee
Strong	Non-null subset of pairs	Guarantees

Example: The following sentence could be displayed in three different ways, assuming that both the weak and strong implementations have Phoenician fonts but no hieroglyphics: "The Greek letter α corresponds to *<hieroglyphic-high><hieroglyphic-low>* and to *<Phoenician-high><Phoenician-low>*." The ■ in Table 5-2 represents any visual representation of an uninterpretable single character by the implementation.

Table 5-2. Surrogate Level Examples

None	"The Greek letter α corresponds to ■ ■ and to ■ ■."
Weak	"The Greek letter α corresponds to ■ ■ and to *<Phoenician>*."
Strong	"The Greek letter α corresponds to ■ and to *<Phoenician>*."

Many implementations that handle advanced features of the Unicode Standard can easily be modified to support a weak surrogate implementation. For example:

- Text collation can be handled by treating those surrogate pairs as "grouped characters," much as "ij" in Dutch or "ll" in traditional Spanish.
- Text entry can be handled by having a keyboard generate two Unicode values with a single keypress, much as an Arabic keyboard can have a "*lam-alef*" key that generates a sequence of two characters, *lam* and *alef.*
- Character display and measurement can be handled by treating specific surrogate pairs as ligatures, in the same way as "f" and "i" are joined to form the single glyph "ﬁ".
- Truncation can be handled with the same mechanism as used to keep combining marks with base characters. (For more information, see *Section 5.13, Locating Text Element Boundaries.*)

Users are prevented from damaging the text if a text editor keeps *insertion points* (also known as *carets*) on character boundaries. As with text-element boundaries, the lowest-level string-handling routines (such as `wcschr`) do not necessarily need to be modified to prevent surrogates from being damaged. In practice it is sufficient that only certain higher-level processes (such as those just noted) be aware of surrogate pairs; the lowest-level routines can continue to function on sequences of 16-bit Unicode code values without having to treat surrogates specially.

5.6 Handling Numbers

There are many sets of characters that represent decimal digits in different scripts. Systems that interpret those characters numerically should provide the correct numerical values. For example, the sequence U+0968 DEVANAGARI DIGIT TWO, U+0966 DEVANAGARI DIGIT ZERO should be numerically interpreted as having the value twenty.

When converting binary numerical values to a visual form, digits can be chosen from different scripts. For example, the value *twenty* can either be represented by U+0032 DIGIT TWO, U+0030 DIGIT ZERO, or by U+0968 DEVANAGARI DIGIT TWO, U+0966 DEVANAGARI DIGIT ZERO, or by U+0662 ARABIC-INDIC DIGIT TWO, U+0660 ARABIC-INDIC DIGIT ZERO. It is recommended that systems allow users to choose the format of the resulting digits by replacing the appropriate occurrence of U+0030 DIGIT ZERO with U+0660 ARABIC-INDIC DIGIT ZERO, and so on. (See *Chapter 4, Character Properties,* for tables providing the information needed to implement formatting and scanning numerical values.)

Fullwidth variants of the ASCII digits are simply compatibility variants of regular digits and should be treated as regular Western digits.

The Roman numerals and East Asian ideographic numerals are decimal numeral writing systems, but they are not formally decimal radix digit systems. This is another way of saying that you cannot do a 1-1 transcoding to forms such as 123456.789. Both of them are appropriate only for positive integer writing.

It is also possible to write numbers in two ways with ideographic digits. For example, Figure 5-1 shows how the number 1,234 can be written.

Figure 5-1. Ideographic Numbers

一千二百三十四

or

一二三四

Supporting these digits for numerical parsing means that implementations have to be smart about distinguishing these two cases.

Digits often occur in situations where they need to be parsed, but are not part of numbers. One such example is alphanumeric identifiers (see *Section 5.14, Identifiers*).

It is only at a second level (for example, when implementing a full mathematical formula parser) that considerations such as superscripting become crucial for interpretation.

5.7 Transcoding to Other Standards

The Unicode Standard exists in a world of other text and character encoding standards, some private, some national, some international. One of the major strengths of the Unicode Standard is the number of other important standards that it incorporates. In many cases, decisions on whether to unify characters or not were influenced by distinctions made in established and widely used standards, in order to allow round-trip transcoding.

Conversion of characters between standards is not always a straightforward proposition. There are many characters that have mixed semantics in one standard and may correspond to more than one character in another. Sometimes standards give duplicate encodings for one and the same character; at other times the interpretation of a whole set of characters may depend on the application. Finally, there are subtle differences in what a standard may consider a character.

To assist and guide implementers, *The Unicode Standard, Version 2.0* provides a series of mapping tables on the accompanying CD-ROM. Each of these tables consist of one-to-one mappings from the Unicode Standard to another published character standard. They include occasional multiple mappings. Their primary function is to identify the characters in these standards in the context of the Unicode Standard. In many cases, data conversion between the Unicode Standard and other standards will be application-dependent or context-sensitive.

Disclaimer

The content of all mapping tables has been verified as far as possible by the Unicode Consortium. However, the Unicode Consortium does not guarantee that the tables are correct in every detail. The mapping tables are provided for informational purposes only. The Unicode Consortium is not responsible for errors that may occur either in the mapping tables printed in this volume or on the CD-ROM, or in software that implements those tables. All implementers should check the relevant international, national, and vendor standards in cases where ambiguity of interpretation may occur.

Issues

The Unicode Standard can be used as a pivot to transcode among *n* different standards. This reduces the number of mapping tables an implementation needs from $O(n^2)$ to $O(n)$. Generally mapping *tables*—as opposed to algorithmic transformation—are required to map between the Unicode Standard and another standard. Table lookup yields much better performance than even simple algorithmic conversions, as can be implemented between JIS and Shift-JIS.

Tables and Virtual Memory

Tables require space. Even small character sets often map to characters from several different blocks in the Unicode Standard, and so, in at least one direction, contain 64K entries.

Flat Tables. If diskspace is not at issue, virtual memory architectures have proven to yield acceptable working set sizes even for flat tables. This is because frequency of usage among characters differs widely and even small character sets contain many characters not used over large stretches of average text. Not only that, but data intended to be mapped into a given character set generally does not contain characters from all blocks of the Unicode Standard (usually only a few blocks at a time need be transcoded to a given character set). This leaves large sections of the 64K sized reverse mapping tables (containing the default character, or unmappable character entry) unused—and therefore paged to disk. Similar results obtain for other types of tables needed to implement the Unicode Standard.

Ranges. It may be tempting to "optimize" these tables for space by providing elaborate provisions for nested ranges or similar devices. Given the branch penalties on modern, highly pipelined processor architectures, this leads to unnecessary performance penalties. A better way is a two- or three-stage table (trie) as described next, which can be coded without any test or branch instructions.

Two-Stage Tables. Two-stage (high-byte) tables are a commonly employed mechanism to reduce table size (see Table 5-2). They use an array of 256 pointers and a default value. If a pointer is NULL, the returned value is the default. Otherwise the pointer references a block of 256 values.

Figure 5-2. Two-Stage Tables

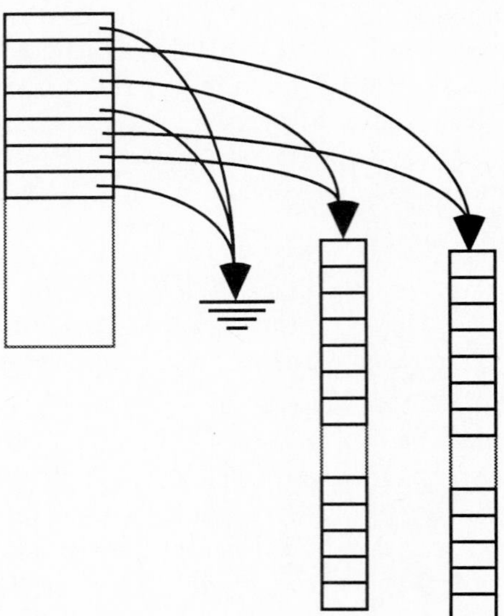

Optimized Two-Stage Table. Wherever any blocks are identical, the pointers just point to the same block. For transcoding tables, this occurs generally for a block containing only mappings to the "default" or "unmappable" character. Instead of using NULL pointers and a default value, one "shared" block of 256 default entries is created. This block is pointed to by all first-stage table entries, for which no character value can be mapped. By avoiding tests and branches, this provides access time that approaches the simple array access, but at a great savings in storage.

It is a simple matter, given an arbitrary 64K table, to write a small utility that can calculate the optimal number of stages and their width, but it is hard to improve on 8:8 two-stage tables because of their simplicity and ease of addressing 8 bits.

5.8 Handling Properties

The Unicode Standard provides detailed information on character properties (see *Chapter 4, Character Properties,* and the *Unicode Character Database* on the accompanying CD-ROM). These properties can be used by implementers to implement a variety of low level processes. Fully language aware and higher level processes will need additional information.

A two-stage table, as described in *Section 5.7, Transcoding to Other Standards*, can also be used to handle mapping to character properties or other information indexed by character code. For example, the data from the *Unicode Character Database* on the accompanying CD-ROM can be represented in memory very efficiently as a set of two-stage tables.

Individual properties are common to large sets of characters and therefore lend themselves to implementations using the shared blocks.

Many popular implementations are influenced by the POSIX model, which provides functions for separate properties, such as `isalpha`, `isdigit`, and so on. Implementers of

Unicode-based systems and internationalization libraries need to take care to extend these concepts to the full set of Unicode characters correctly.

In Unicode-encoded text, combining characters participate fully. In addition to providing callers with information as to which characters have the combining property, implementers and writers of language standards need to provide for the fact that combining characters assume the property of the preceding base character (see also *Section 5.14, Identifiers*). Other important properties, such as sort weights, may also depend on a character's context.

Because the Unicode Standard provides such a rich set of properties, implementers will find it useful to allow access to several properties at a time, possibly returning a string of bit-fields, one per character in the input string.

In the past, many existing standards, like the C language standard, have assumed very minimalist "portable character sets" and geared their functions to operations on this set. As this practice is about to change and Unicode encoding itself is increasingly becoming *the* portable character set, implementers are advised to distinguish between historical limitations and true requirements when implementing specifications for particular text processes.

5.9 Normalization

Converting to and from Canonical Form. The Unicode Standard contains explicit codes for the most frequently used accented characters. These characters can also be composed; in the case of accented letters, characters can be composed from a base character and non-spacing mark(s).

The Unicode Standard provides a table of normative spellings (maximal decompositions) of characters that can be composed of a base character plus one or more non-spacing marks. These tables can be used to unify spelling in a standard manner. Implementations that are 'liberal' in what they accept, but 'conservative' in what they issue, will have the least compatibility problems.

➥ The decomposition mappings are specific to a particular version of the Unicode Standard. Changes may occur as the result of character additions in the future. When new precomposed characters are added, mappings between those characters and correcsponding composed character sequences will also be added. The Unicode Standard, Version 2.0 includes the Tibetan script, which has a number of precomposed characters as well as combining marks; the decompositions for these new precomposed characters are included in the *Unicode Character Database* on the CD-ROM. Similarly, if a new combining mark is added to this standard, it may allow decompositions for precomposed characters that did not have decompositions before.

Figure 5-3. Normalization

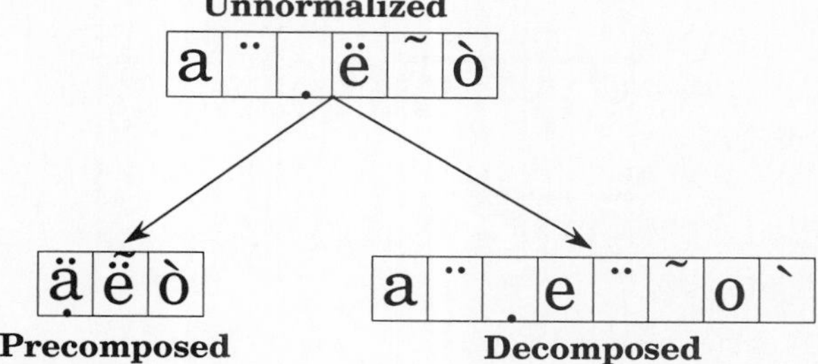

Normalization. Systems may normalize Unicode-encoded text to one particular sequence, such as normalizing composed character sequences into precomposed characters or vice versa (see Figure 5-3).

Compared to the *possible* combinations, only a relatively small number of precomposed base character plus non-spacing marks have independent Unicode character values; most existed in dominant standards.

Systems that cannot handle non-spacing marks can normalize to precomposed characters, which provides for most modern Latin-based languages. Such systems can use fall-back rendering techniques to at least visually indicate combinations that they cannot handle (see the "Fall-back Rendering" subsection of *Section 5.12, Rendering Non-Spacing Marks*).

In systems that *can* handle non-spacing marks, it may be useful to normalize so as to eliminate precomposed characters. This allows such systems to have a homogeneous representation of composed characters and always have a consistent treatment of such characters. However, in most cases, it does not require too much extra work to support both forms, which is the simpler route.

Such systems may also normalize to a particular ordering of non-spacing marks. As stated in *Section 3.9, Canonical Ordering Behavior*, non-spacing marks that do not interact typographically can occur in any order after the base character. The Unicode Standard does not impose a particular order on non-interacting non-spacing marks for a number of reasons. The principle reason becomes clear when we consider a sequence that is "out of order." In that case, the only reasonable interpretation is that it should have the same interpretation as the sequence in canonical order.

(For further information see *Chapter 3, Conformance; Chapter 4, Character Properties;* and *Section 2.5, Combining Characters.*)

5.10 Editing and Selection

Consistent Text Elements

A user interface for editing is most intuitive when the text elements are consistent (see Figure 5-4). In particular, the editing actions of deletion, selection, mouse-clicking, and cursor-key movement should act as though they have a consistent set of boundaries. For example, hitting a leftwards-arrow should result in the same cursor location as delete. *This synchronization gives a consistent, single model for editing characters.*

Figure 5-4. Consistent Character Boundaries

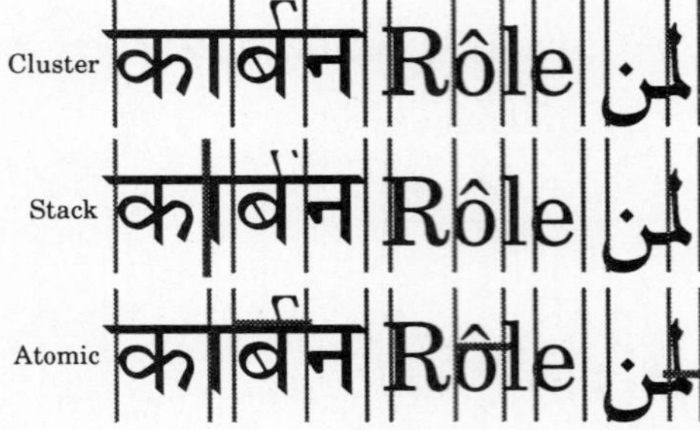

Three types of boundaries are generally useful in editing and selecting within words.

Cluster Boundaries. Cluster boundaries occur in scripts such as Devanagari. Selection or deletion using cluster boundaries means that an entire cluster (such as *ka* + *vowel sign a*) or a composed character (*o* + *circumflex*) is selected or deleted as a single unit.

Stacked Boundaries. Stacked boundaries are generally somewhat finer than cluster boundaries. Free standing elements (such as *vowel sign a*) can be independently selected and deleted, but any elements that "stack" (such as *o* + *circumflex*, or vertical ligatures such as Arabic *lam* + *meem*) can only be selected as a single unit. Stacked boundaries treat all composed character sequences as single entities, much like precomposed characters.

Atomic Character Boundaries. The use of atomic character boundaries is closest to selection of individual Unicode characters. However, most modern systems indicate selection with some sort of rectangular highlighting. This places restrictions on the consistency of editing because some sequences of characters do not linearly progress from the start of the line. When characters stack, there are two mechanisms used to visually indicate partial selection: linear and non-linear boundaries.

Linear Boundaries. Use of linear boundaries treats the entire width of the resultant glyph as belonging to the first character of the sequence, and the remaining characters in the backing-store representation as having no width and being visually afterwards.

This is the simplest mechanism and one that is currently in use on the Macintosh and some other systems. The advantage of this system is that it requires very little additional implementation work. The disadvantage is that it is never easy to select narrow characters, let alone a zero-width character. Mechanically, it requires the user to select just to the right of the non-spacing mark and drag to just to the left. It also does not allow the selection of individual non-spacing marks if there are more than one.

Non-Linear Boundaries. Use of linear boundaries divides any stacked element into parts. For example, picking a point halfway across a *lam* + *meem* ligature can represent the division between the characters. One can either allow highlighting with multiple rectangles or use another method such as coloring the individual characters.

Notice that with more work, a precomposed character can behave in deletion as if it were a composed character sequence with atomic character boundaries. This involves deriving the character's decomposition on the fly to get the components to be used in simulation. For example, deletion occurs by decomposing, removing the last character, then recomposing (if more than one character remains). However, this technique does not work in general editing and selection.

In most systems, the character is the smallest addressable item in text, so the selection and assignment of properties (such as font, color, letterspacing, and so on) is done on a per character basis. There is no good way to simulate this addressability with precomposed characters. Systematically modifying all text editing to address parts of characters would be quite inefficient.

Just as there is no single notion of text element, there is no single notion of editing character boundaries. At different times, users may want different degrees of granularity in the editing process. Two different methods suggest themselves. First, the user may set a global preference for the character boundaries. Second, the user may have alternate commands mechanisms, such as Shift-Delete, which are more (or less) fine than the default mode.

5.11 Strategies for Handling Non-Spacing Marks

By following these guidelines, a programmer should be able to implement systems and routines that provide for the effective and efficient use of non-spacing marks in a wide variety of applications and systems. The programmer also has the choice between minimal techniques that apply to the vast majority of existing systems or more sophisticated techniques that apply to more demanding situations, such as higher-end DTP (desktop publishing).

In this section, the terms *non-spacing mark* and *combining character* are be used interchangeably. The terms *diacritic, accent, stress mark, Hebrew point, Arabic vowel,* and others are sometimes used instead of the term *non-spacing mark.* (They refer to particular types of non-spacing marks.)

A relatively small number of implementation features are needed to support non-spacing marks. Different possible levels of implementation are also possible. A minimal system yields good results and is relatively simple to implement. Most of the features required by such a system are modifications of existing software.

Since non-spacing marks are required for a number of languages such as Arabic, Hebrew, and the languages of the Indian subcontinent, many vendors already have systems capable of dealing with these characters and can use their experience to produce general-purpose software for handling these characters in the Unicode Standard.

Rendering. A fixed set of composite character sequences can be rendered effectively by means of fairly simple substitution. Wherever a sequence of base character plus one or more non-spacing combining marks occurs, a glyph representing the combined form can be substituted. In simple, monospaced character rendering, a non-spacing combining mark has a zero advance width, and a composite character sequence will have the same width as the base character. When truncating strings, it is always easiest to truncate starting from the end and working backwards. A trailing non-spacing mark will then not be separated from the preceding base character.

A more sophisticated rendering system can take into account more subtle variations in widths and kerning with non-spacing marks or account for those cases where the composite character sequence has a different advance width than the base character, but such rendering systems are not necessary for the large majority of applications. Such systems can also supply more sophisticated truncation routines. (See also *Section 5.12, Rendering Non-Spacing Marks.*)

Other Processes. Correct multilingual comparison routines must already be able to compare a sequence of characters as one, or one character as if it were a sequence. Such routines can also handle composite character sequences when supplied the appropriate data. When searching strings, remember to check for additional non-spacing marks in the target string which may affect the interpretation of the last matching character.

Line-break algorithms generally use state machines for determining word breaks. Such algorithms can also be easily adapted to prevent separation of non-spacing marks from base characters. (See also the discussion in *Section 5.15, Sorting and Searching; Section 5.9, Normalization;* and *Section 5.13, Locating Text Element Boundaries.*)

Keyboard Input

A common implementation for the input of composed character sequences is the use of so-called *dead keys.* These match the mechanics used by typewriters to generate such sequences through overtyping the base character after the non-spacing mark. In computer implementations, keyboards enter a special state when a dead key is pressed for the accent and emit a precomposed character only when one of a limited number of "legal" base characters is entered. It is straightforward to adapt such a system to emit composed character sequences or precomposed characters as needed. While typists, especially in the Latin script, are trained on systems working in this way, many scripts in the Unicode Standard (including the Latin script) may be implemented according to the handwriting sequence, in which users type the base character first, followed by the accents or other non-spacing marks (see Figure 5-5).

Figure 5-5. Dead Keys Versus Handwriting Sequence

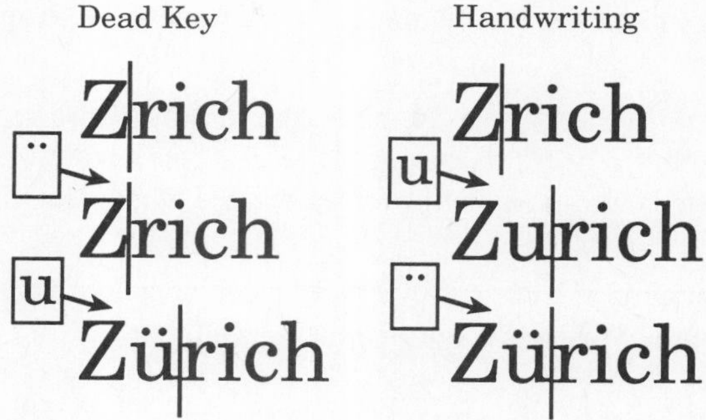

In the case of handwriting sequence, each keystroke produces a distinct, natural change on the screen; there are no hidden states. To add an accent to any existing character, the user positions the insertion point (*caret*) after the character and types the accent.

Truncation

There are two types of truncation: truncation by character count and truncation by displayed width. Truncation by character count can entail loss (be lossy) or be lossless.

Truncation by character count is used where, due to storage restrictions, a limited number of characters can be entered into a field, or where text is broken into buffers for transmission and other purposes. The latter case can be lossless if buffers are recombined seamlessly before processing or if lookahead is performing for possible combining character sequences straddling buffers.

When fitting data into a field of limited length, some information will be lost. Truncating at a text element boundary (for example, on the last composed character sequence boundary or even last word boundary) is often preferable to truncating after the last code element (see Figure 5-6). (See *Section 5.13, Locating Text Element Boundaries.*)

Figure 5-6. Truncating Composed Character Sequences

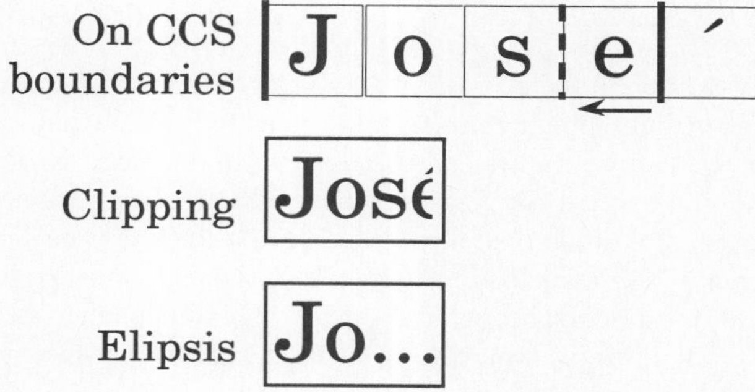

Truncation by displayed width is used for visual display in a narrow field. In this case, truncation is on the basis of the width of the resulting string rather than a character count. In simple systems it is easiest to truncate by width, starting from the end and working backwards by subtracting character widths as one goes. Since a trailing non-spacing mark does not contribute to the measurement of the string, the result will not separate non-spacing marks from their base characters.

If the textual environment is more sophisticated, the widths of characters may depend on their context, due to effects such as kerning, ligating, or contextual formation. For such systems, the width of a composed character, such as an *ï*, may be different than the width of a narrow base character alone. To handle these cases, a final check should be made on any truncation result derived from successive subtractions.

A different option is simply to clip the characters graphically. However, this may look ugly, and if the clipping occurs between characters, it may not give any visual feedback that characters are being omitted. A graphic or ellipsis can be used to give this visual feedback.

5.12 Rendering Non-Spacing Marks

This discussion assumes the use of proportional fonts, where the widths of individual characters can vary. Various techniques can be used with monospaced fonts, but in general, it is only possible to get a semblance of a correct rendering in these fonts, especially with international characters.

In this section, the terms *non-spacing mark* and *combining character* are be used interchangeably. The terms *diacritic, accent, stress mark, Hebrew point, Arabic vowel,* and others are sometimes used instead of the term *non-spacing mark*. (They refer to particular types of non-spacing marks.)

When rendering a sequence consisting of more than one non-spacing mark, the non-spacing marks should, by default, be stacked outwards from the base character. That is, if two non-spacing marks appear over a base character, then the first non-spacing mark should appear on top of the base character, and the second non-spacing mark on top of the first. If two non-spacing marks appear under a base character, then the first non-spacing mark should appear beneath the base character, and the second non-spacing mark below the first (see *Section 2.5, Combining Characters*). This default treatment of multiple, potentially interacting non-spacing marks is known as the inside-out rule (see Figure 5-7).

Figure 5-7. Inside-Out Rule

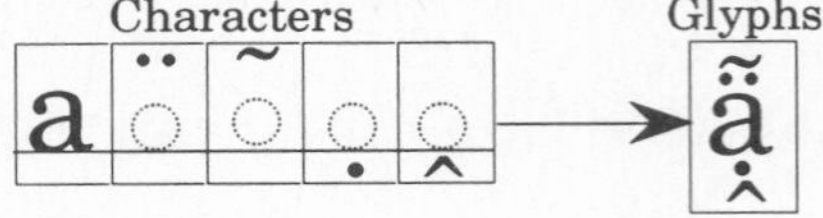

This default behavior may be altered based on typographic preferences or based on knowledge of the specific orthographic treatment to be given to multiple non-spacing marks in the context of a particular writing system. For example, in the modern Vietnamese writing system, an acute or grave accent (serving as a tone mark) may be positioned slightly to one side of a circumflex accent rather than directly above it. If the text to be displayed is known to employ a different typographic convention (either implicitly through knowledge of the language of the text or explicitly through rich-text style bindings), then an alternative positioning may be given to multiple non-spacing marks instead of that specified by the default inside-out rule just discussed.

Fall-back Rendering. There are several methods of dealing with an unknown composed character sequence which is outside of a fixed, renderable set (see Figure 5-8). One method (*Show Hidden*) indicates the inability to draw the sequence by drawing the base character

Figure 5-8. Fallback Rendering

first and then rendering the non-spacing mark as an individual unit—with the non-spacing mark position on a dotted circle. (This convention is used in the Code Charts.)

Another method (*Simple Overlap*) uses default fixed positioning for an overlapping zero-width non-spacing mark, generally placed far away from possible base characters. For example, the default positioning of a circumflex can be above the ascent, which will place it above capital letters. Even though this will not be particularly attractive for letters such as *g-circumflex*, the result should generally be recognizable in the case of single non-spacing marks.

There is a degenerate case, where a non-spacing mark occurs as the first character in the text, or where it is separated from its base character by a *line separator, paragraph separator,* or other formatting character that causes a positional separation. In those cases, it is recommended that the non-spacing mark be shown with the *Show Hidden* alternative.

Bidirectional Positioning. In bidirectional text, the non-spacing marks are reordered *with* their base characters; that is, they visually apply to the same base character after the algorithm is used (see Figure 5-9). There are a few ways to accomplish this.

Figure 5-9. Bidirectional Placement

Backing store

Screen Order

Glyph Metrics

Aligned Glyphs

The simplest method is similar to the *Simple Overlap* fallback method. In the bidirectional algorithm, combining marks take the level of their base character. In that case, Arabic and Hebrew non-spacing marks would come to the left of their base characters. The font is designed so that instead of overlapping to the left, the Arabic and Hebrew non-spacing marks overlap to the right. In Figure 5-9, the "glyph metrics" line shows the pen start and end for each glyph with such a design. After aligning the start and end points, the final result shows each non-spacing mark attached to the corresponding base letter. More sophisticated rendering could then apply the positioning methods outlined in the next section.

With some rendering software, it may be necessary to have the non-spacing mark glyphs consistently ordered to the right of the base character glyphs. In that case, a second pass can be done after producing the "screen order" to put the odd-level non-spacing marks on the right of their base characters. Since the levels of non-spacing marks will be the same as their base characters, this pass can swap the order of non-spacing marks glyphs and base character glyphs in right-left (odd) levels. (See *Section 3.11, Bidirectional Behavior.*)

Justification. Typically, full justification of text adds extra space at space characters in order to widen a line; however, if there are too few (or no) space characters, some systems add extra letterspace between characters (see Figure 5-10). This process needs to be modified if zero-width non-spacing marks are present in the text. Otherwise, the non-spacing marks will be separate from their base characters.

Figure 5-10. Justification

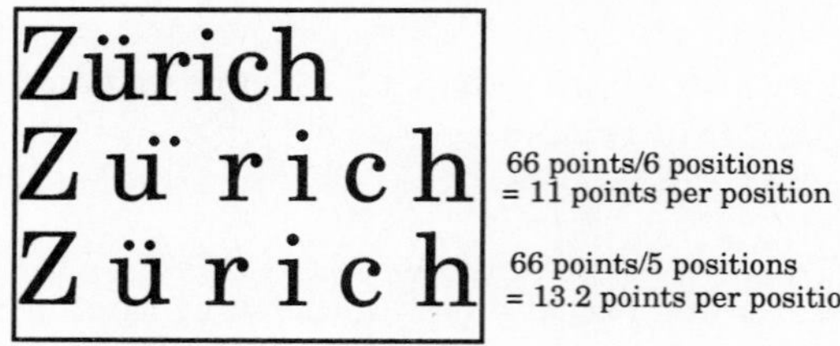

Since non-spacing marks always follow their base character, proper justification adds letterspace between characters only if the second character is a base character.

Positioning Methods

There are a number of different methods of positioning non-spacing marks so that they are in the correct location relative to the base character and previous non-spacing marks.

Positioning with Ligatures. A fixed set of composed character sequences can be rendered effectively by means of fairly simple substitution (see Figure 5-11). Wherever the glyphs representing a sequence of <base character, non-spacing mark> occurs, a glyph representing the combined form is substituted. Since the non-spacing mark has a zero advance width, the composed character sequence will automatically have the same width as the base character. (More sophisticated text rendering systems may take further measures to account for those cases where the composed character sequence kerns differently or has a slightly different advance width than the base character.)

Figure 5-11. Positioning with Ligatures

a + ◌̈ ➡ ä

A + ◌̈ ➡ Ä

(f + i ➡ ﬁ)

Positioning with ligatures is perhaps the simplest method of supporting non-spacing marks. Whenever there is a small, fixed set, such as the those corresponding to the precomposed characters of 8859-1 (Latin1), this method is straightforward to apply. Since the composed character sequence has the same width as the base character, rendering, measurement and editing of these characters is much easier than for the general case of ligatures.

If a composed character sequence does not ligate, then one of the two following methods can be applied. If they are not available, then a fallback method can be used.

Positioning with Contextual Forms. A more general method of dealing with positioning of non-spacing marks is to use contextual formation (see Figure 5-12). In this case, there are several different glyphs corresponding to different positions of the accents. Base glyphs generally fall in to a fairly small number of classes, based upon their general shape and width. According to the class of the base glyph, a particular glyph is chosen for a non-spacing mark.

Figure 5-12. Positioning with Contextual Forms

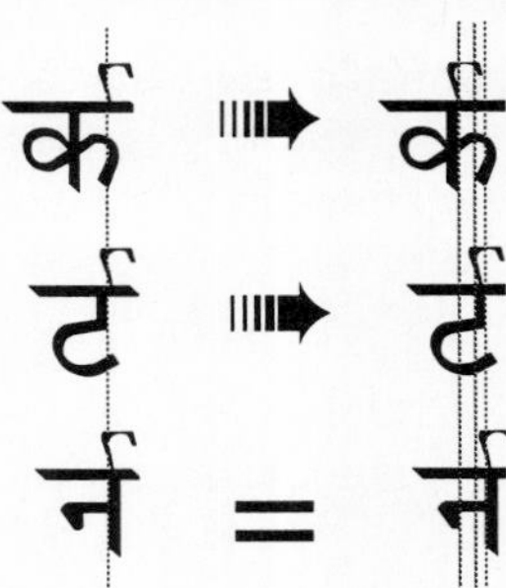

In general cases, a number of different heights of glyphs can be chosen to allow stacking of glyphs, at least for a few deep (when these bounds are exceeded, then the fallback methods can be used). This method can be combined with the ligature method so that in specific cases ligatures can be used to get fine variations in position and shape.

Positioning with Enhanced Kerning. A third technique for positioning diacritics is an extension of the normal process of kerning to be both horizontal and vertical (see Figure 5-13). Typically, kerning is a process of mapping from pairs of glyphs to a positioning offset. For example, in the word "To" the "o" should nest slightly under the "T". An extension of this maps to both a *vertical* and a *horizontal* offset, allowing glyphs to be arbitrarily positioned.

Figure 5-13. Positioning with Enhanced Kerning

For effective use in the general case, the kerning process must also be extended to handle more than simple kerning pairs, since multiple diacritics may occur after a base letter.

Positioning with enhanced kerning can be combined with the ligature method so that in specific cases ligatures can be used to get fine variations in position and shape.

5.13 Locating Text Element Boundaries

A string of Unicode-encoded text often needs to be broken up into text elements programmatically. Common examples of text elements include what users think of as characters, words, lines, and sentences. The precise determination of text elements may vary according to locale, even as to what constitutes a character. The goal of matching user perceptions cannot always be met because the text alone does not always contain enough information to unambiguously decide boundaries. For example, the *period* (U+002E FULL STOP) is used ambiguously, sometimes for end-of-sentence, sometimes for abbreviations, and sometimes for numbers. In most cases, however, programmatic text boundaries can match user perceptions quite closely, or at least not surprise the user.

Rather than concentrate on algorithmically searching for text elements themselves, it simplifies computation to look instead at detecting the *boundaries* between those text elements. The determination of those boundaries is often critical to the performance of general software, so it is important to be able to make such determination as quickly as possible.

The following example boundary determination mechanism provides a straightforward and efficient way to determine word boundaries. It builds upon the uniform character representation of the Unicode Standard, while handling the large number of characters and special features such as combining marks and surrogates in an effective manner. Since this boundary determination mechanism lends itself to a completely data-driven implementation, it can be customized to particular locales according to special language or user requirements without recoding.

However, for some languages this simple method is not sufficient. For example, Thai line-breaking requires the use of dictionary lookup, analogous to English hyphenation. An implementation therefore may need to provide means to override or subclass the standard, fast mechanism described in the "Boundary Specification" subsection in this section.

The large character set of the Unicode Standard and its representational power place requirements on both the specification of text element boundaries and the underlying implementation. The specification needs to allow for the designation of large sets of characters sharing the same characteristics (for example, uppercase letters), while the implementation must provide quick access and matches to those large sets.

The mechanism also must handle special features of the Unicode Standard, such as combining or non-spacing marks, conjoining *jamo*, and surrogate characters.

The following discussion looks at two aspects of text element boundaries: the specification and the underlying implementation. Specification means a way for programmers and localizers to programmatically specify where boundaries can occur.

Boundary Specification

A boundary specification defines different sets of characters, then lists the rules for boundaries in terms of those sets. The sets of characters are specified as a list, where each element of the list is

- a literal character
- a range of characters
- a property of a Unicode character, as defined in the Unicode Character Database
- a removal of the following elements from the list

These elements take the following form in practice:

List		Meaning
a		Literal character a.
¬Y		Remove Y from the list
U+NNNN		Unicode character value, where N is an uppercase hexadecimal digit (0–9, A–F)
a-b		The range of all valid characters from the Unicode value a through b.
[YY]		Unicode character property from Unicode Character Database:
Lu	=	Uppercase Letter
Ll	=	Lowercase Letter
Lt	=	Titlecase Letter
Lm	=	Modifier Letter (includes spacing versions of non-spacing marks)
Lo	=	Other Letter
Mn	=	Non-Spacing Mark
Mc	=	Combining Mark (other than non-spacing; may reorder or surround)
Nd	=	Decimal Number
No	=	Other Number
Pd	=	Dash Punctuation
Ps	=	Open Punctuation
Pe	=	Close Punctuation
Po	=	Other Punctuation
Sm	=	Math Symbol
Sc	=	Currency Symbol
So	=	Other Symbol
Zs	=	Space Separator
Zl	=	Line Separator
Zp	=	Paragraph Separator
Cc	=	Control or Format Character
Co	=	Other Character (for example, private use)
Cn	=	Non-Character (that is, not part of the Unicode Standard, Version 2.0)

A series of rules specifies a set of circumstances where a text element boundary can occur. The rules use fairly normal regular expression notation. The most interesting addition is a symbol that marks the position of a boundary, which can occur at any point in a rule.

Notation	Match
‡	position of boundary
¬X	characters not in X (or end-of-text or start-of-text)
X | Y	characters in either X or Y
X & Y	characters in both X and Y
X Y	a sequence of characters, the first in X, and second in Y
X*	zero or more characters in X
X+	one or more characters in X
{ X }	zero or one character in X
(X)	grouping, for application of above operations

There is always a boundary at the very start and at the very end of a string of text. As with typical regular expressions, the longest match possible is used. For example, in the following, the boundary is placed after as many Y's as possible:

$$X\,Y^{*} \quad ‡ \quad \neg X \tag{2}$$

(In the text the rules are numbered for reference.) Some additional constraints are reflected in the specification. These constraints make the implementation significantly simpler and more efficient and have not been found to be limitations for natural language use.

1. ***Limited context.*** Given boundaries at positions X and Y, then the position of any other boundaries between X and Y does not depend on characters outside of X and Y (so long as X and Y remain boundary positions).

   For example, with boundaries at "ab‡cde", changing "a" to "A" cannot introduce a new boundary, such as at "Ab‡cd‡e".

2. ***Single boundaries.*** Each rule has exactly one boundary position. Because of (1), this is more a limitation on the specification methods, since a rule with two boundaries could generally be expressed as two rules.

   For example, a rule "ab‡cd‡ef" could be broken into "ab‡cd" and "cd‡ef".

3. ***No conflicts.*** Two rules cannot have initial portions that match the same text, but with different boundary positions.

   For example: "x‡abc" and "a‡bc" cannot be part of the same boundary specification.

4. ***No overlapping sets.*** For efficiency, two character sets in a specification cannot intersect. A later character set definition will *override* a previous one, removing its characters from the previous set.

   For example: in the following, the second set specification removes "AEIOUaeiou" from the first.

   Let = [Lu][Ll][Lt][Lm][Lo]

   EngVowel = AEIOUaeiou

5. ***No more than 256 sets.*** This is purely an implementation detail to save on storage.

6. ***Ignore degenerates.*** Implementations need not make special provisions to get marginally better behavior for degenerate cases that never occur in practice, such as an *A* followed by an Indic combining mark.

Example Specifications

Different issues are present with different types of boundaries, as the following discussion and examples should make clear. In this section the rules are somewhat simplified, and not all edge cases are included. In particular, characters such as control characters and format characters do not cause breaks. This would complicate each of the examples (and is so left as an exercise for the reader). In addition, it is intended that the rules themselves are localizable; the examples provided here are not valid for all locales.

Rather than listing the contents of the character sets in these examples, the contents are explained instead. An *underscore* ("_") is used to indicate a space in examples.

If an implementation uses a state table, the performance does not depend on the complexity or number of rules. The only feature that does affect performance is the number of characters that may match *after* the boundary position in a rule that is matched.

Character Boundaries

As far as a user is concerned, the underlying representation of text is not important, but it is paramount that an editing interface present a uniform implementation of what the user thinks of as characters. Character representations should behave as a unit in terms of mouse selection, arrow key movement, backspacing, and so on. For example, if an accented character is represented by a combining character sequence, then using the right arrow key should skip from the start of the base character to the end of the last combining character. This is analogous to a system using conjoining *jamo* to represent Hangul syllables, where they are treated as single characters for editing. In those circumstances where end users need character counts (which is actually rather rare), the counts need to correspond to the users' perception of what constitutes a character.

The principal requirements for general character boundaries are the handling of combining marks, Hangul conjoining *jamo*, and surrogate characters.

Character Sets

¶	Paragraph Separator, Line Separator
Nsm	Non-spacing mark
L	Hangul leading jamo
V	Hangul vowel jamo
T	Hangul trailing jamo
Hs	High Surrogate
Ls	Low Surrogate

Rules

Always break after paragraph separators, even when they are followed by combining marks. Also, always break before paragraph separators (but that is caught by rule 2 anyway).

¶ ‡ (1

Break before base characters (non-combining characters). Notice that it is also necessary to exclude some other characters that might not break from preceding characters, depending on other context.

‡ ¬(*Nsm* | *Ls* | *L* | *V* | *T*) (2

Break around Hangul syllables. The first rule breaks before Hangul syllables, while the others break except within an allowable sequence. Notice that there are no breaks before combining marks, so that they can apply to Hangul syllables.

¬(*L* | *V* | *T*) ‡ *L* | *V* | *T* (3

L ‡ ¬(*L* | *V* | *T* | *Nsm*) (4

V ‡ ¬(*V* | *T* | *Nsm*) (5

T ‡ ¬(*T* | *Nsm*) (6

Break around isolated surrogates (degenerate cases). Note to keep combining marks from applying to an isolated surrogate.

¬*Hs* ‡ *Ls* (7

Hs ‡ ¬*Ls* (8

¬*Hs Ls* ‡ (9

Note: The only combining marks that are not non-spacing marks are certain Indic matras. These characters do not have the simple behavior of non-spacing marks; Indic clusters (such as defined in the Devanagari subsection in*Section 6.1, General Scripts Area*) have a more complex structure and may or may not be considered by users to be single characters. Where they are, the preceding rules would be amended to not break within sequences of the following form (where Con = consonant & Cm = combining mark):

Con (Virama Con)* Cm*

Word Boundaries. Word boundaries are used in a number of different contexts. The most familiar ones are for double-click mouse selection, "move to next word," and detection of whole words for search and replace.

For the search and replace option of "find whole word," the rules are fairly clear. The boundaries are between letters and non-letters. Trailing spaces cannot be counted as part of a word, since then searching for "abc" would fail on "abc_".

For word selection, the rules are somewhat less clear. Some programs include trailing spaces, while others include neighboring punctuation. Where words do not include trailing spaces, sometimes programs treat the individual spaces as separate words; other times they treat a whole string of spaces as a single word. (The latter fits better with usage in search and replace.)

➥ Word boundaries can also be used in so-called *intelligent cut and paste.* With this feature, if the user cuts a piece of text on word boundaries, adjacent spaces are collapsed to a single space. For example, cutting "quick" from "The_quick_fox" would leave "The_ _fox". Intelligent cut and paste collapses this to "The_fox".

This discussion outlines the case where boundaries occur between letters and non-letters, and there are no boundaries between non-letters. The discussion also includes Japanese words (for word selection). In Japanese, words are not delimited by spaces. Instead, a heuristic rule is used in which strings of either kanji (ideographs) or katakana characters (optionally followed by strings of hiragana characters) are considered words.

Character Sets

¶	Paragraph Separator, Line Separator
Let	Letter
Mid	hyphen, apostrophe (")
Nsm	non-spacing mark
Hira	Hiragana
Kata	Katakana
Han	Han ideograph (Kanji)

Rules

Always break after paragraph separators.

¶ ‡ *(1*

Break between letters and non-letters. Include trailing non-spacing marks as part of a letter.

¬ (Let | Nsm) ‡ ***Let*** *(2*

Let Nsm* ‡ ***¬Let*** *(3*

Handle Japanese specially for word selection. Treat clusters of kanji or katakana (with or without following hiragana) as single words. Break when preceded by other characters (such as punctuation). Include non-spacing marks.

¬ (Hira | Kata | Han | Nsm) ‡ ***Hira | Kata | Han*** *(4*

Hira Nsm* ‡ ***¬Hira*** *(5*

$$\textit{Kata Nsm*} \quad ‡ \quad \neg(\textit{Hira} \mid \textit{Kata}) \qquad (6$$

$$\textit{Han Nsm*} \quad ‡ \quad \neg(\textit{Hira} \mid \textit{Han}) \qquad (7$$

➥ One could also generally break between any letters of different scripts. In practice—except for languages that do not use spaces—this is a degenerate case.

Line Boundaries. Line boundaries determine acceptable locations for line-wrap to occur without hyphenation. (More sophisticated line wrap also makes use of hyphenation, but generally only in cases where the natural line-wrap yields inadequate results.) Note that this is very similar to word boundaries but *not* generally identical.

For the purposes of line-break, a composed character sequence should generally be treated as though it had the same properties as the base character. The non-spacing marks should not be separated from the base character.

Non-spacing marks may be exhibited in isolation; that is, over a space or non-breaking space. In that case, the the whole composed character sequence is treated as a unit. If the composed character sequence consists of a *no-break space* followed by non-spacing marks, then it does not generally allow linebreaks before or after the sequence. If the composed character sequence consists of any other space followed by non-spacing marks, then it generally does allow linebreaks before or after the sequence.

There is a degenerate case where a non-spacing mark occurs as the first character in the text or after a line or paragraph separator. In that case, the most consistent treatment for line-break is to treat the non-spacing mark as though it were applied to a space.

Character Sets

¶	Paragraph Separator, Line Separator
Sp	Space separator
Nb	Non-breaking space, non-breaking hyphen, zero-width non-breaking space
Nsm	Non-spacing mark
Ideo	Hiragana, Katakana, Bopomofo, Han
Open	Open Punctuation
Close	Close Punctuation, Period, Comma,...

Rules

Always break after paragraph separators.

$$\P \quad ‡ \qquad (1$$

Break between trailing spaces and other characters. Include non-spacing marks, since a non-spacing mark applied to a space is used to allow presentation of the non-spacing mark in isolation.

$$\textit{Sp Nsm*} \quad ‡ \quad \neg(\textit{Sp} \mid \textit{Nsm} \mid \textit{Nb}) \qquad (2$$

Handle ideographs specially. Break around ideographs except for opening and closing punctuation characters (also known as *taboo* characters) and non-spacing marks.

$$\textit{Ideo Nsm*} \quad ‡ \quad \neg\textit{Close} \qquad (3$$

$$\neg(\textit{Open Nsm*}) \quad ‡ \quad \textit{Ideo} \qquad (4$$

Sentence Boundaries. Sentence boundaries are often used for triple-click or some other method of selecting or iterating through blocks of text that are larger than single words.

Plain text provides inadequate information for determining good sentence boundaries. Periods, for example, can either signal the end of a sentence, indicate abbreviations, or be used for decimal points. Without analyzing the text semantically, it is impossible to be certain which of these usages is intended (and sometimes ambiguities still remain).

Character Sets

¶	Paragraph Separator, Line Separator
Sp	Space separator
Term	!?
Dot	Period
Cap	Uppercase, Titlecase & non-cased letters
Lower	Lowercase

Rules

Always break after paragraph separators.

¶ ‡ (1

Break after sentence terminators, but include non-spacing marks, closing punctuation, and trailing spaces, and (optionally) a paragraph separator.

Term Close* Sp* {¶} ‡ (2

Handle period specially, since it may be an abbreviation or numeric period—and not the end of a sentence. Don't break if it is followed by a lowercase letter instead of uppercase.

Dot Close* Sp+ ‡ ***Open* ¬Lower*** (3

Random Access. A further complication is introduced by random access (see Figure 5-14). When iterating through a string from beginning to end, the preceding approach works well. It guarantees a limited context, and allows a fresh start at each boundary to find the next boundary. By constructing a state table for the reverse direction from the same specification of the rules, reverse searches are possible. However, suppose that the user wants to iterate starting at a random point in the text. If the starting point does not provide enough context to allow the correct set of rules to be applied, then one could fail to find a valid boundary point. For example, suppose a user clicked after the first space in "?_ _A". On a forward iteration searching for a sentence boundary, one would fail to find the boundary before the "A", because the "?" hadn't been seen yet.

A second set of rules to determine a "safe" starting point provides a solution. Iterate backwards with this second set of rules until a safe starting point is located, then iterate forwards from there. Iterate forwards to find boundaries that were between the starting point and the safe point; discard these. The desired boundary is the first one which is not less than the starting point.

Figure 5-14. Random Access

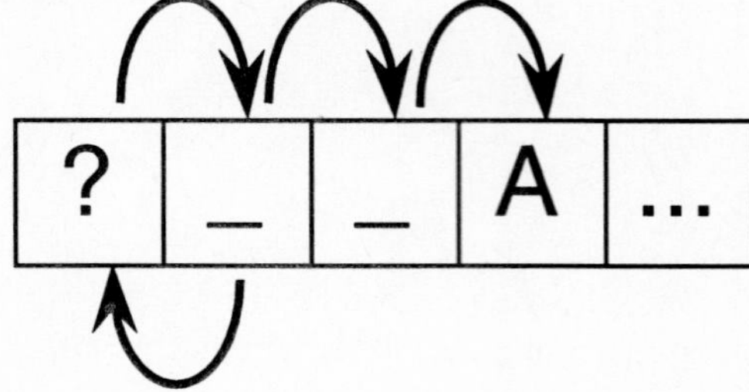

This process would represent a significant performance cost if it had to be performed on every search. However, this functionality could be wrapped up in an iterator object, which preserves the information as to whether it currently is at a valid boundary point. Only if it is reset to an arbitrary location in the text is this extra backup processing performed.

5.14 Identifiers

A common task facing an implementer of the Unicode Standard is the provision of a parsing and/or lexing engine for identifiers. In order to assist in the standard treatment of identifiers in Unicode character-based parsers, the following guidelines are provided for the definition of identifier syntax.

Note that the task of parsing for identifiers and the one of locating word boundaries are related tasks and it is straightforward to restate the sample syntax provided here in the form just discussed for locating text element boundaries. In this section, a more traditional BNF-style syntax is presented to facilitate incorporation into existing standards.

The formal syntax provided here is intended to capture the general intent that an identifier consists of a string of characters that starts with a letter or an ideograph, and then follows with any number of letters, ideographs, digits, or underscores. Each programming language standard has its own identifier syntax; different programming languages have different conventions for the use of certain characters from the ASCII range ($, @, #,_) in identifiers. To extend such a syntax to cover the full behavior of a Unicode implementation, implementers only need to combine these specific rules with the sample syntax provided here.

These rules are no more complex than current rules in the common programming languages, except that they include more characters of different types.

The innovations in the sample identifier syntax to cover the Unicode Standard correctly include the following:

1. Incorporation of proper handling of combining marks
2. Allowance for layout and format control characters, which should be ignored when parsing identifiers
3. Inclusion of extenders such as U+00B7 MIDDLE DOT
4. Inclusion of U+FF3F FULLWIDTH LOW LINE as equivalent to U+005F LOW LINE

Combining Marks. Combining marks must be accounted for in identifier syntax. A composed character sequence consisting of a base character followed by any number of combining marks must be valid for an identifier. This results from the conformance rules in *Chapter 3, Conformance,* regarding interpretation of canonical-equivalent character sequences.

The four enclosing combining marks (U+20DD → U+20E0) are given special treatment in the syntactic definition of <ident_combining_char> because the composite characters that result from their composition with letters (for example, U+24B6 CIRCLED CAPITAL LATIN LETTER A) are themselves not valid constituents of identifiers.

Layout and Format Control Characters. The Unicode characters that are used to control joining behavior, bidirectional ordering control, and alternate formats for display are explicitly defined as not affecting breaking behavior. Unlike space characters or other delimiters, they do not serve to indicate word, line, or other unit boundaries. Accordingly, they are explicitly assigned to an ignorable character class for the purposes of identifier definition. Some implementations may choose to filter out these ignorable characters; this has the advantage that two identifiers that appear to be identical will more likely *be* identical.

Extenders. U+00B7 MIDDLE DOT participates in the canonical decomposition of Unicode characters that are otherwise valid as elements of identifiers (for example, U+013F LATIN CAPITAL LETTER L WITH MIDDLE DOT). Treating middle dot as a letter extender that is valid in an identifier is consistent with the treatment of modifier letters as valid elements of identifiers and also parallels the treatment of letter plus diacritic combining marks.

Specific Character Additions. Specific identifier syntaxes can be treated as slight modifications of the generic syntax based on character properties. Thus, for example, SQL identifiers allow underscore as an identifier part (but not an identifier start); C identifiers allow underscore for either an identifier part or an identifier start. The syntax defined next shows inclusion of underscore for identifier part to illustrate that the <underscore> class should include U+FF3F FULLWIDTH LOW LINE, as well as the ASCII-derived underscore (U+005F LOW LINE) common to many character sets.

Terminology

<x>	indicates a named syntactic entity
{x}	indicates a set, defined either by specification of character properties, or by enumeration of coded character values
x–y	indicates set subtraction
+/–[x]	indicates presence or absence of the character property within the brackets
(x)	indicates grouping
x*	indicates occurrence of a sequence of zero or more instances of a syntactic entity

Terminal Classes

<alphabetic_char>	::=	{ +[alphabetic] }
<initial_alphabetic_char>	::=	{ +[alphabetic] –[combining] }
<combining_char>	::=	{ +[combining] }
<ideographic_char>	::=	{ +[ideographic] }
<decimal_digit_char>	::=	{ +[decimaldigit] }
<enclosing_char>	::=	{ 20DD, 20DE, 20DF, 20E0 }
<zw_layout_char>	::=	{ 200C, 200D, 200E, 200F }
<bidi_format_char>	::=	{ 202A, 202B, 202C, 202D, 202E }
<alt_format_char>	::=	{ 206A, 206B, 206C, 206D, 206E, 206F }
<zw_nonbreak_space>	::=	{ FEFF }
<underscore>	::=	{ 005F, FF3F }
<extender>	::=	{ 00B7, 02D0, 02D1, 0387, 0640, 0E46, 0EC6, 3005, 3031..3035, 309B..309D, 309E, 30FC..30FE, FF70, FF9E, FF9F}

Syntactic Rules

<ident_combining_char>	::=	<combining_char> – <enclosing_char>
<ident_ignorable_char>	::=	<zw_layout_char> | <bidi_format_char> | <alt_format_char> | <zw_nonbreak_space>
<identifier_start>	::=	<initial_alphabetic_char> | <ideographic_char>

<identifier_part>	::=	<alphabetic_char> | <ideographic_char> | <decimal_digit_char> | <ident_combining_char> | <underscore> | <extender> | <ident_ignorable_char>
<identifier>	::=	<identifier_start> (<identifier_part>)*

Character Properties

The exact list of characters with a given property is given in *Chapter 4, Character Properties.*

[decimaldigit] is a normative property of the Unicode Standard.

[combining] is a normative property of the Unicode Standard.

[ideographic] is an informative property of: the Unified Han set (U+4E00 ⟶ U+9FA5); the Compatibility Han characters (U+F900 ⟶ U+FA2D); U+3007 IDEOGRAPHIC NUMBER ZERO; and the Hangzhou-style numerals, (U+3021⟶ U+3029).

Other Unicode characters may involve ideographs, but these are either treated as neutral symbols (for example, circled ideograph symbols) or require special formatting that disqualifies them from participation in identifiers (for example, Kanbun symbols).

[alphabetic] is a informative property of the primary units of alphabets and/or syllabaries, whether combining or non-combining; composite characters that are canonically equivalent to a combining character sequence of an alphabetic base character plus one or more combining characters; letter digraphs; contextual variants of alphabetic characters; ligatures of alphabetic characters; contextual variants of ligatures; modifier letters; letterlike symbols that are compatibility equivalents of single alphabetic letters; and miscellaneous letter elements, notably U+00AA FEMININE ORDINAL INDICATOR and U+00BA MASCULINE ORDINAL INDICATOR.

5.15 Sorting and Searching

Sorting and searching overlap in that both implement degrees of *equivalence* of terms to be compared. In the case of searching, equivalence defines when terms match (for example, it determines when case distinctions are meaningful). In the case of sorting, equivalence affects their proximity in a sorted list. These determinations of equivalence always depend on the application and language, but for an implementation supporting the Unicode Standard, sorting and searching must also take into account the Unicode Character Equivalence and Canonical Ordering defined in *Chapter 3, Conformance.*

This section also discusses issues of adapting sublinear text searching algorithms, providing for fast text searching while still maintaining language-sensitivity, and using the same ordering algorithms that are used for collation.

Culturally Expected Sorting

Sort orders vary from culture to culture, and many specific applications require variations. Sort order can be by word or sentence, case sensitive or insensitive, ignoring accents or not; it can also be either phonetic or based on the appearance of the character (such as ordering by stroke and radical for East Asian ideographs). Phonetic sorting of Han characters requires use of either a look-up dictionary of words or special programs to maintain an associated phonetic spelling for the words in the text.

Languages vary not only regarding which types of sorts to use (and in which order they are to be applied), but also in what constitutes a fundamental element for sorting. Swedish treats U+00C4 LATIN CAPITAL LETTER A WITH DIAERESIS as an individual letter, sorting it after *z* in the alphabet; however, German sorts it either like *ae* or like other accented forms of *ä* following *a*. Spanish traditionally sorted the digraph *ll* as if it were a letter between *l* and *m*. Examples from other languages (and scripts) abound.

As a result, it is neither possible to arrange characters in an encoding in an order so that simple binary string comparison produces the desired collation order, nor is it possible to provide single-level sort-weight tables. (The latter implies that character encoding details have only an indirect impact on culturally expected sorting.)

To address the complexities of culturally expected sorting, a multilevel comparison algorithm is typically employed.[1] Each character in string is given several categories of *sort weights*. Categories can include alphabetic, case, and diacritic weights, among others.

In a first pass, these weights are accumulated into a *sort key* for the string. At the end of the first pass, the sort key contains a string of alphabetic weights, followed by a string of case weights, and so on. In a second pass, these substrings are compared by order of importance so that case and accent differences can either be fully ignored or applied only where needed to differentiate otherwise identical sort strings.

The first pass of this scheme looks very similar to the decomposition of Unicode characters into base character and accent. The fact that the Unicode Standard allows multiple spellings (composed and composite) of the same accented letter turns out not to matter at all. If anything, a completely decomposed text stream can simplify the first implementation of sorting.

To provide a powerful, table-based approach to natural-language collation using Unicode characters, implementers need to consider providing full functionality for these features of language-sensitive algorithmic sorting:

- four collation levels
- French or normal orientation
- grouped or expanding characters
- ordering of unmapped characters
- more than one level of ignorable characters.

Unicode Character Equivalence

Section 3.6, Decomposition, and *Section 3.9, Canonical Ordering Behavior,* define equivalent sequences and provide an exact algorithm for determining when two sequences are equivalent. Equivalent sequences of Unicode characters should be collated as exactly the same, no matter what the underlying storage is. Figure 5-15 gives two examples of this.

Compatibility characters—especially where they have the same appearance—should also be collated exactly the same (for example, U+00C5 *Å* LATIN CAPITAL LETTER A WITH RING ABOVE and U+212B *Å* ANGSTROM SIGN).

Similar Characters

Languages differ in what they consider similar characters, but users generally want characters that are similar (such as upper- and lowercase) to sort close to each other but not to be

1. A good example can be found in Denis Garneau, *Keys to Sort and Search for Culturally-Expected Results* (IBM document number GG24-3516, June 1, 1990), which addresses the problem for western European languages, Arabic and Hebrew.

Figure 5-15. Character Equivalence

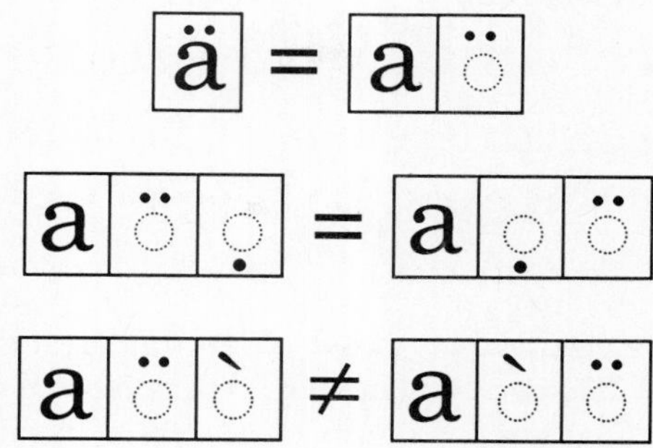

collated exactly the same way. Were upper- and lowercase to collate identically, words differing only in case would appear in random order (see Figure 5-16). The same is true for treating accented characters.

Typically, there is an ordering among these similar characters. In English dictionaries, for example, lowercase precedes uppercase (the reverse of what happens with a naïve ASCII comparison). However, this ordering only applies when the strings are the same in all other respects. If this were not so, *Aachen* would sort after *azure*. Characters with accents often sort close to the base character, but different accents on the same base character always sort in a given order.

Figure 5-16. Naïve Comparison

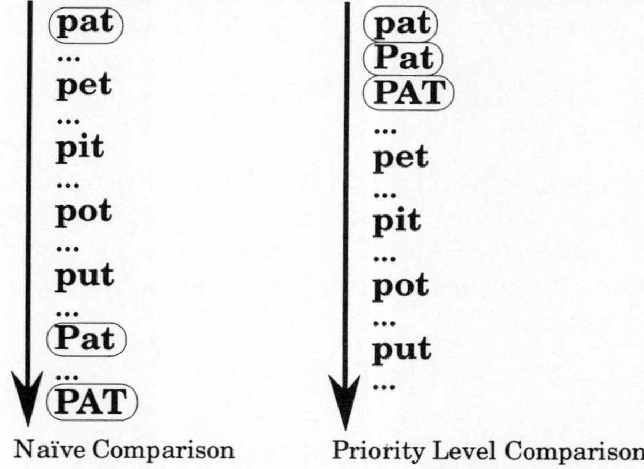

Levels of Comparison

The way to handle these problems is to use multiple levels of comparison and attach only a secondary or tertiary difference to the letters based on their case or accents (see Figure 5-17). Thus we get these rules:

R1 ***Count secondary differences—only if there are no primary differences.***

R2 ***Count tertiary differences—only if there are no primary or secondary differences.***

Figure 5-17. Levels of Comparison

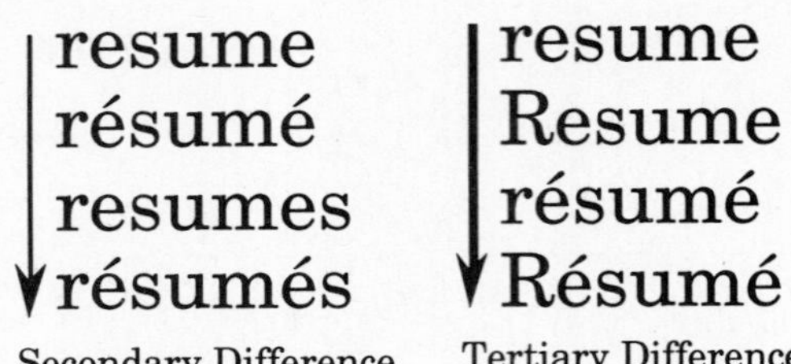

In English and similar languages, accents make only a secondary difference, and case differences make only a tertiary difference. Ignorable characters are counted as secondary or tertiary differences. In other languages and scripts, other features map to secondary or tertiary differences.

Figure 5-18. Orientation

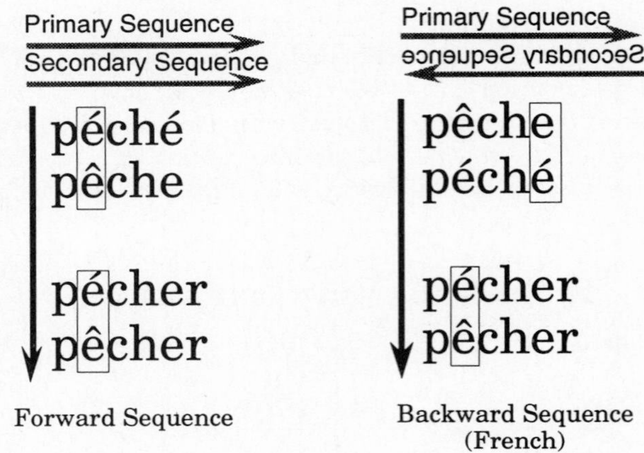

French presents an interesting special case. In French sorting, the differences in accents later in the string are more important than those earlier in the string. In Figure 5-18, the two pairs of words are identical in the first five base characters. In English the first accents are the most significant ones, but in French, the first accents from the end are as the boxes show.

Ignorable Characters

Another class of interesting cases are ignorable characters (see Figure 5-19), such as spaces, hyphens, and some other punctuation. In this case, the character itself is ignored unless there are no stronger differences in the string.

Figure 5-19. Ignorable Characters

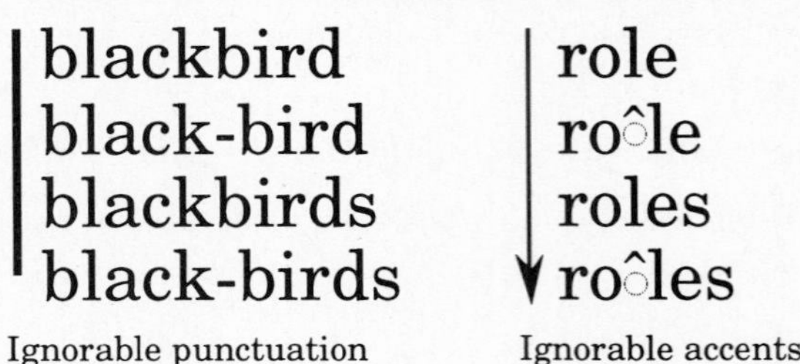

The general rule is

R3 Treat ignorable characters as a primary or secondary difference.

Multiple Mappings

With many language collations such as traditional Spanish or German, one character may compare as if it were two, or two characters can compare as if they were one character (see Figure 5-20). In traditional Spanish orthography, "Ch" sorts as a single letter, that is, after "Cz"; otherwise it would come before "Ci". In traditional German, "ö" sorts as if it were "oe", putting it after "od" and before "of".

Figure 5-20. Multiple Mappings

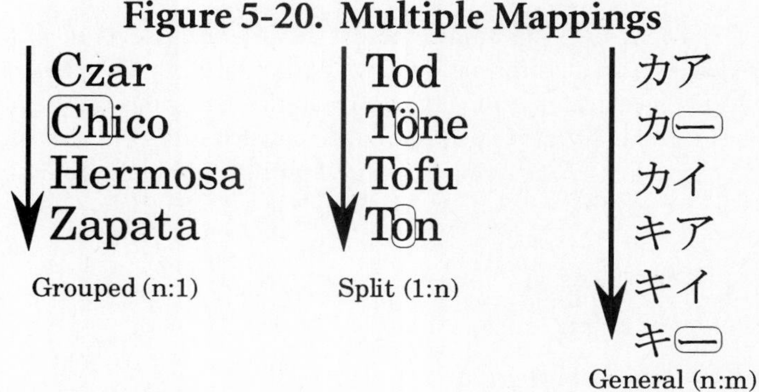

In Japanese, a ー *length mark* lengthens the vowel of the preceding character; depending on the vowel the result will sort in a different order. For example, after the character カ "ka" the ー *length mark* indicates a long "a" and comes after ア "a", while after the character キ "ki" the ー *length mark* indicates a long "i", and comes after イ "i".

Look at the second character in each word in the third column of the figure. There are three different characters in the second position: ア "a", ー *length mark,* and イ "i". The general rule is

R4 N characters may compare as if they were M

Collating Out-of-Scope Characters

Collation implements an ordering that matches the expectations of the user, based on rules of the user's language. Lists of terms encoded using the Unicode Standard may easily come from many different languages. These are all sorted according to the custom of the user's language.

For scripts and characters outside the use of a particular language, explicit rules may not exist. For example, Swedish and French have clear and different rules on sorting *ä* (either after *z* or as an accented character with a secondary difference from *a*), but neither defines a particular sorting order for the Han ideographs. Implementations supporting the Unicode Standard therefore typically provide a default ordering (like the culturally neutral ordering for ideographs used in this standard). Sorting for a Japanese user would still sort upper- and lowercase Latin letters in proximity. The *relative* ordering of scripts is typically configurable.

R5 Default to a common or culturally neutral ordering for out-of-scope characters

Unmapped Characters

Another option is to treat out-of-scope characters as irrelevant. Such characters can include box forms, dingbats, and perhaps also alphabets that are not of concern for the user base of an implementation. Characters irrelevant to a collation sequence are usually not assigned weights; this saves space in the collation sequence. However, to provide a definitive sorting order, a position needs to be specified in the collation sequence for any unassigned character. For efficiency, collate any unassigned characters in Unicode bit order.

R6 Collate irrelevant characters in Unicode bit order, in a specified position.

Parameterization

For effective use of collation, programmers need to have a certain level of control and need to be able to get back sufficient information. One of the outputs needs to be the place in the string where a difference occurs, so that common initial substrings can be found. Notice that this position may be different in the two different strings. Because of multiple mappings, the first 3 characters in one string might be equivalent to the first 4 in the other.

Input

- Specify language rule
- Relative order of scripts
- Allows specification of precision

Output

- First point in each string where different.
- Direction and precision of difference

Processing

- Can preprocess strings for fast comparison
- Or process just as much as needed for stand-alone

Optimizations

Multiple-level comparison requires a bit more work than binary comparison. While real life studies put the overhead at around 50 percent, it often pays to first transform terms to be sorted into equivalent *sortkeys,* which result in the same sorted list when subjected to a simple and fast binary comparison. (In the standard C library, the function `wcsxfrm` provides such a transformation.) These sortkeys might consist of a string of base weights followed by strings for weights used for secondary and tertiary differences, as just discussed. Unlike Unicode code values, sortkeys don't need to be 16-bit based. Thus, highly optimized functions, such as the `strcmp` function from the standard C library, can be used.

Sortkeys can also be stored, obviating recomputation when a list needs to be re-sorted. Another straightforward optimization is to *compare as you go.* For each string, sort weights are assembled into sort keys only until a difference is located. This reduces computation when a difference is found early in the string.

Searching

Searching is subject to many of the same issues as comparison, such as a choice of a weak, strong, or exact match. Additional features are often added, such as only matching words (that is, there is a word boundary on each side of the match). One technique is to code a fast search for a weak match. When a candidate is found, then additional tests can be made for additional criteria (such as matching diacriticals, word match, case match, and so on).

When searching strings, remember to check for trailing non-spacing marks in the target string that may affect the interpretation of the last matching character. That is, if you search for "San Jose", you may find a match in the string "Visiting San José, Costa Rica is a..." If you are searching for an exact (diacritic) match, then you want reject this match. If you are searching for a weak match, then you want to accept the match, but be sure to include any trailing non-spacing marks when you return the location and length of the target substring. The mechanisms discussed in *Section 5.13, Locating Text Element Boundaries,* can be used for this.

Once important of weak equivalence is case-insensitive searching. Many traditional implemenations map both the search string and the target text to uppercase. However, case mappings are language-dependent and *not* unambiguous (see *Section 4.1, Case,* and the Latin subsection in *Section 6.1, General Scripts Area*). The preferred method of implementing case insensitivity uses the same mechanisms and tables as discussed in the sorting discussions in the beginning of this section. In particular, it is advisable for many applications (for example, file systems) to treat a particular set of characters (i, I, ı *dotless-i,* İ *capital i with dot*) as a single equivalency class to guarantee reasonable results for Turkish.

A related issue can arise because of inaccurate mappings from external character sets. To deal with this, characters that are easily confused by users can be kept in a weak equivalency class (đ *d-bar,* ð *eth,* Đ *capital d-bar,* Đ *capital eth*). This tends to do a better job of meeting users' expectations when searching for named files or other objects.

Sublinear Searching

International searching is clearly possible using the information in the collation, just by using brute force. However, this represents an *O(m*n)* algorithm in the worst case and *O(m)* in common cases, where *n* is the number of characters in the pattern that is searched for, and *m* is the number of characters in the target to be searched.

There are a number of algorithms that allow for fast searching of simple text, using sublinear algorithms. These algorithms use only *O(m/n)* in common cases, by skipping over characters in the target. Several implementers have adapted one of these algorithms to search text pre-transformed according to a collation algorithm, which allows for fast searching with native-language matching (see Figure 5-21).

Figure 5-21. Sublinear Searching

```
The_quick_brown...
quicX
 ~~quick~~
  ~~quick~~
   ~~quick~~
     quic(k)
```

The main problems with adapting language aware collation algorithm for sublinear searching are caused by multiple mappings and ignorables. Additionally, sublinear algorithms precompute tables of information. Mechanisms like the two-stage tables introduced in Figure 5-2 are efficient tools in reducing memory requirements.

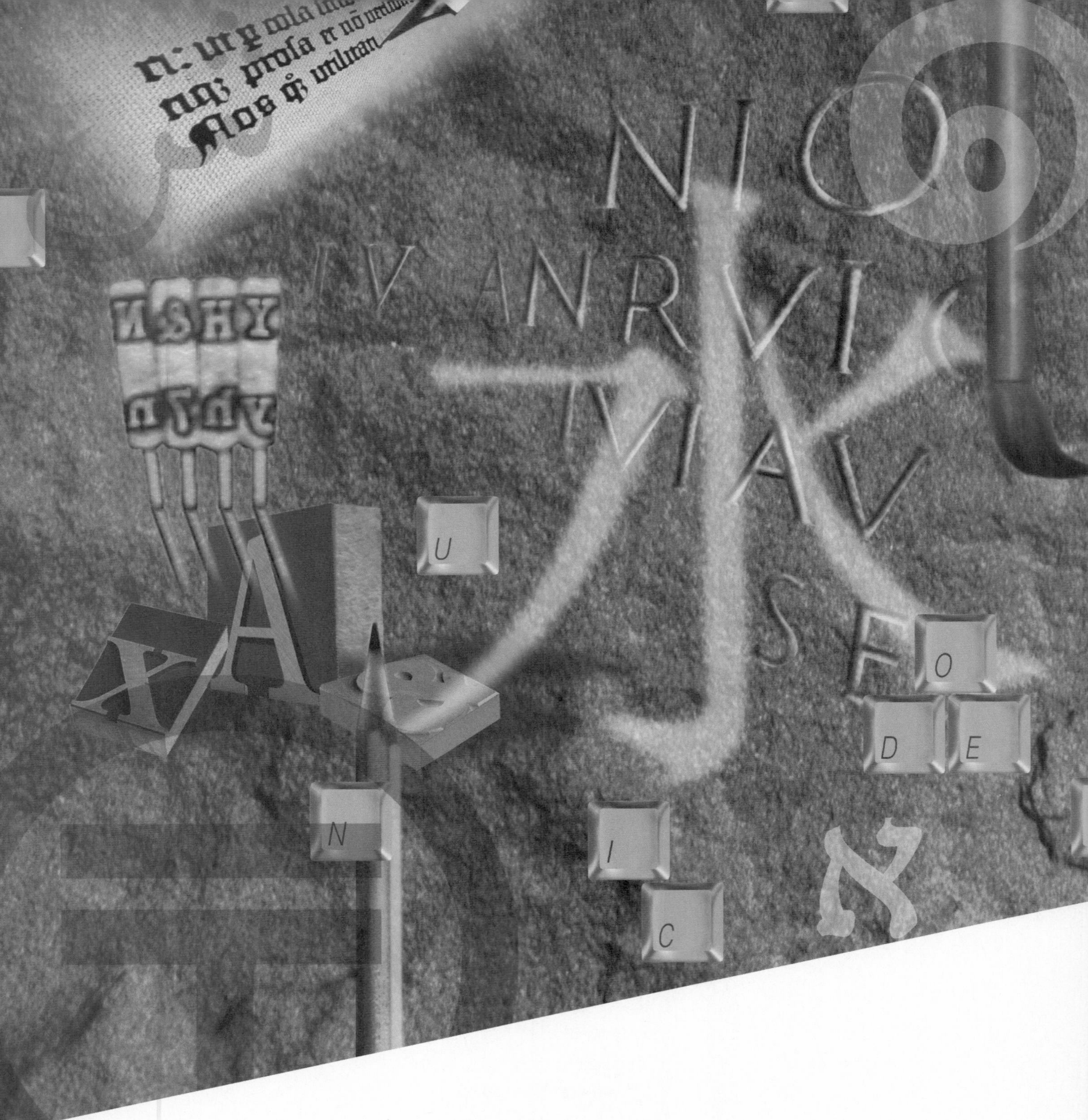

CHARACTER BLOCK

6

DESCRIPTIONS

Chapter 6

Character Block Descriptions

The character codes in the character charts constitute the core of the Unicode Standard. The characters cover modern communication and computer usage in the major scripts of the world. The coverage consists of over 2,700 alphabetic (or syllabic) letters, over 1,300 textual symbols, over 800 CJK phonetics and symbols, 11,172 Korean Hangul syllables, and over 21,000 Han (East Asian ideographic) characters.

Characters are organized into related groups called *blocks*. The following block descriptions are written so that they can be read alone, but by themselves they are not sufficient to implement the Unicode character encoding. It is also vital to understand the general architecture of the Unicode Standard (see *Chapter 2, General Structure,* and *Chapter 3, Conformance*).

The character blocks and the block descriptions are ordered by their code range location. Thus, the character blocks are ordered in the following sequence: the General Scripts Area, the Symbols Area, the CJK Phonetics and Symbols Area, the CJK Ideographs Area, the Hangul Syllables Area, the Surrogates Area, the Private Use Area, and the Compatibility Area and Specials. (See Figure 2-5 for an overview of scripts included in this version of the Unicode Standard.)

In the Unicode Standard, character blocks generally contain characters from a single script. In many cases a script is fully represented in its character block. There are, however, important exceptions, most notably in the area of punctuation characters. Punctuation characters occur in several widely separated places in the character blocks, including Basic Latin, Latin-1 Supplement, General Punctuation, and CJK Symbols and Punctuation, as well as occasional characters in character blocks for specific scripts. It is intended that punctuation characters, for example U+002C COMMA or U+2022 BULLET, be encoded only once, rather than being encoded again and again for particular scripts; such general purpose punctuation may be used for any script or mixture of scripts.

6.1 General Scripts Area

The General Scripts Area includes the encoding of all Latin and other non-ideographic script characters. This includes Greek, Cyrillic, Hebrew, Arabic, the numerous Indic scripts, Georgian, Armenian, Tibetan, Thai, and Lao (see Figure 6-1).

Figure 6-1. General Scripts

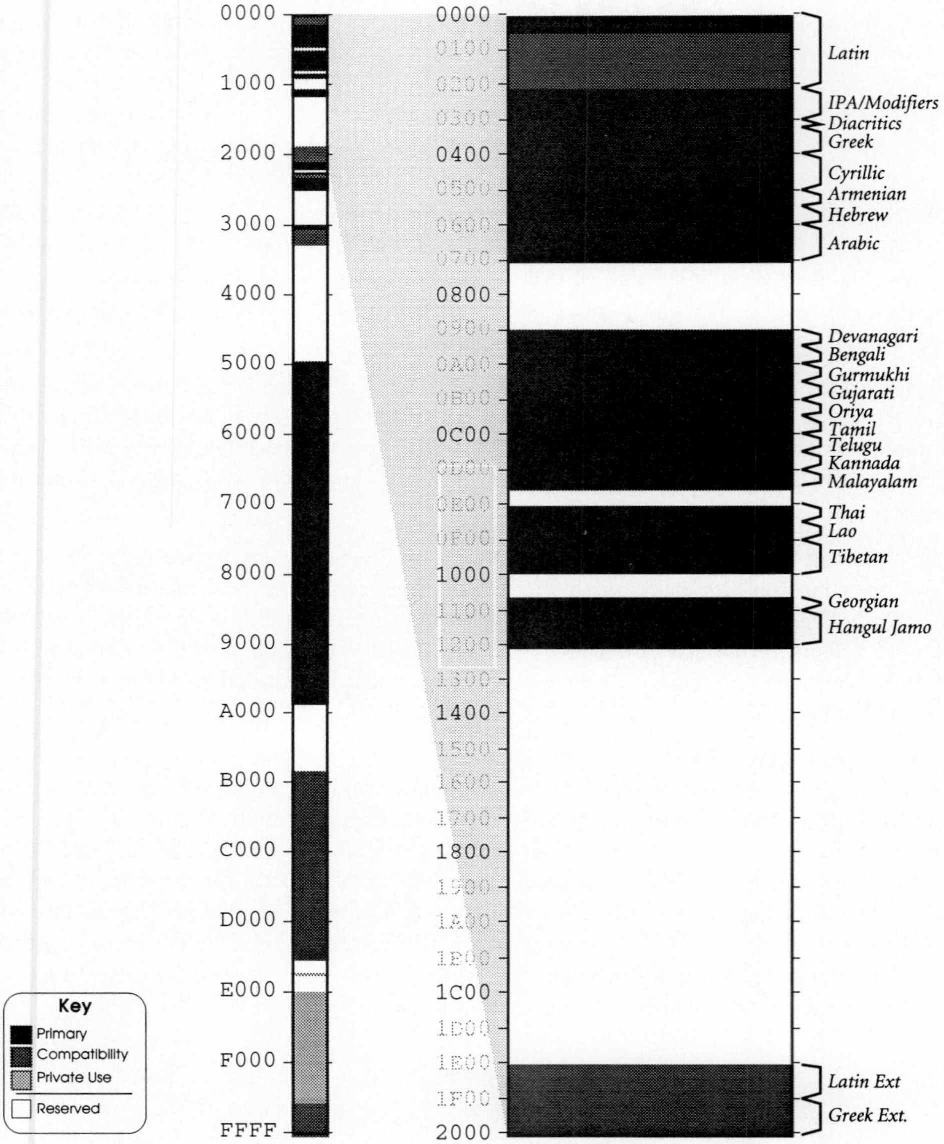

0000
1000
2000
3000
4000
5000
6000
7000
8000
9000
A000
B000
C000
D000
E000
F000
FFFF

0000
0400
0800
0C00
1000
1400
1800
1C00
2000

Latin
IPA/Modifiers
Diacritics
Greek
Cyrillic
Armenian
Hebrew
Arabic
Devanagari
Bengali
Gurmukhi
Gujarati
Oriya
Tamil
Telugu
Kannada
Malayalam
Thai
Lao
Tibetan
Georgian
Hangul Jamo
Latin Ext
Greek Ext.

Key
Primary
Compatibility
Private Use
Reserved

Basic Latin: U+0000—U+007F

Standards. The Unicode Standard adapts the ASCII (ISO 646) 7-bit standard by retaining the semantics and numeric code values, merely supplying enough leading zeros to convert them into 16-bit values. The content and arrangement of the ASCII standard is far from optimal in the context of a 16-bit space, but the Unicode Standard retains it without change because of its prevalence in existing usage. The ASCII (ANSI X3.4) standard is identical to ISO/IEC 646:1991-IRV.

ASCII C0 Control Codes and Delete. The Unicode Standard makes no specific use of these control codes, but it provides for the passage of the numeric code values intact, neither adding to nor subtracting from their semantics. The semantics of the C0 controls (U+0000→U+001F) and *delete* (U+007F) are generally determined by the application with which they are used. However, in the absence of specific application uses, they may be interpreted according to the semantics specified in ISO 6429. The only C0 control code that has specified semantics in the Unicode Standard is U+0009 HORIZONTAL TAB. (For more information on control codes, see *Section 2.4, Special Character and Non-Character Values.*)

There is a simple one-to-one mapping between 7-bit (and 8-bit) control codes and Unicode control codes: every 7-bit (or 8-bit) control code is simply zero-extended to a 16-bit code. For example, if LINE FEED (0A) is to be used for terminal control, then the text "WX<LF>YZ" would be transmitted in plain Unicode text as the following 16-bit values: "0057 0058 000A 0059 005A." Any interpretation of these control codes is outside the scope of the Unicode Standard; programmers should refer to a relevant standard (for example, ISO 6429) that specifies control code interpretations.

ASCII Graphic Characters. Some of the non-letter characters in this range suffer from overburdened usage as a result of the limited number of codes in a 7-bit space. Some coding consequences of this are discussed in the following subsections "Encoding Characters with Multiple Semantic Values" and "Loose versus Precise Semantics." The rather haphazard ASCII collection of punctuation and mathematical signs are isolated from the larger body of Unicode punctuation, signs, and symbols (which are encoded in ranges starting at U+2000) only because the relative locations within ASCII are so widely used in standards and software.

Encoding Characters with Multiple Semantic Values. Code values in the ASCII range are well established and used in widely varying implementations. The Unicode Standard therefore provides only minimal specifications on the typographic appearance of corresponding glyphs. For example, the value U+0024 ($) (derived from ASCII 24) has the semantic *dollar sign*, leaving open the question of whether the dollar sign is to be rendered with one vertical stroke or two. The Unicode value U+0024 refers to the *dollar sign semantic*, not to its precise appearance. Likewise, for other characters in this range that have alternative glyphs, the Unicode character is displayed with the basic or most common glyph; rendering software may present any other graphical form of that character.

Loose versus Precise Semantics. Some ASCII characters have multiple uses, either through ambiguity in the original standards or through accumulated reinterpretations of a limited codeset. For example, 27 hex is defined in ANSI X3.4 as *apostrophe (closing single quotation mark; acute accent)* and 2D hex as *hyphen minus*. In general, the Unicode Standard provides the same interpretation for the equivalent code values, without adding to or subtracting from their semantics. The Unicode Standard supplies *unambiguous* codes elsewhere for the most useful particular interpretations of these ASCII values; the corresponding unambiguous characters are cross-referenced in the character names list for this block. (For a complete list of space characters and dash characters in the Unicode Standard, see the General Punctuation subsection of *Section 6.2, Symbols Area.*)

Diacritics. ASCII contains four codes that are ambiguous regarding whether they denote combining characters or separate spacing characters. In the Unicode encoding, the corresponding code points (U+005E CIRCUMFLEX ACCENT ^; U+005F LOW LINE _; U+0060 GRAVE ACCENT `; U+007E TILDE ~) are restricted to use as spacing characters. The Unicode Standard provides unambiguous combining characters in other blocks which can be used to represent accented Latin letters by means of composed character sequences.

Semantics of Paired Punctuation. Paired punctuation marks such as parentheses (U+0028, U+0029), square brackets (U+005B, U+005D), and braces (U+007B, U+007D) are interpreted semantically rather than graphically in the context of bidirectional or vertical texts; that is, *these characters have consistent semantics but alternative glyphs depending upon the directional flow rendered by a given software program.* The software must ensure that the rendered glyph is the correct one. When interpreted semantically rather than graphically, characters containing the qualifier "LEFT" are taken to denote *opening*; characters containing the qualifer "RIGHT" are taken to denote *closing*. For example, U+0028 LEFT PARENTHESIS and U+0029 RIGHT PARENTHESIS are interpreted as opening and closing parenthesis, respectively, in the context of bidirectional or vertical texts. In a right-to-left directional flow, U+0028 is rendered as ")". In a left-to-right flow, the same character is rendered as "(".

Encoding Structure. The character block for Basic Latin characters is divided into the following ranges:

U+0000	→	U+001F	ASCII C0 control codes
U+0020	→	U+007E	ASCII graphic characters
U+007F			ASCII *delete* (also a control code)

Latin-1 Supplement: U+0080—U+00FF

Standards. ISO 8859-1, also known as Latin-1, extends ASCII by providing additional letters for major languages of Europe (listed in the next paragraph). Like ASCII, the Latin-1 set also includes a miscellaneous set of punctuation and mathematical signs. Punctuation, signs, and symbols not included in the Basic Latin and Latin-1 Supplement blocks are encoded in character blocks starting with the General Punctuation block.

Languages. The languages supported by the Latin-1 supplement include Danish, Dutch, Faroese, Finnish, Flemish, German, Icelandic, Irish, Italian, Norwegian, Portuguese, Spanish, and Swedish. Many other languages can be written with this set of letters, including Hawaiian, Indonesian, and Swahili.

C1 Control Codes. In extending the 7-bit encoding system of ASCII to an 8-bit system, ISO/IEC 4873 (on which the 8859 family of character standards are based) introduced 32 additional control codes in the range 80–9F hex. Like the C0 control codes, the Unicode Standard makes no specific use of these C1 control codes, but provides for the passage of their numeric code values intact, neither adding to nor subtracting from their semantics. The semantics of the C1 controls (U+0080→U+009F) are generally determined by the application with which they are used. However, in the absence of specific application uses, they may be interpreted according to the semantics specified in ISO 6429.

Diacritics. ISO 8859-1 contains four characters that are ambiguous regarding whether they denote combining characters or separate spacing characters. In the Unicode Standard, the corresponding codepoints (U+00A8 DIAERESIS, U+00AF MACRON, U+00B4 ACUTE ACCENT, and U+00B8 CEDILLA) are restricted to use as spacing characters. The Unicode Standard provides unambiguous combining characters in the character block for Combining Diacritical Marks which can be used to represent accented Latin letters by means of composed character sequences. U+00B0 DEGREE SIGN is also occasionally used ambiguously by implementations of ISO 8859-1 to denote a spacing form of a diacritic ring above a letter; in the Unicode Standard, that spacing diacritical mark is denoted unambiguously by U+02DA RING ABOVE.

U+00AD SOFT HYPHEN indicates a hyphenation point, where a line-break is preferred when a word is to be hyphenated. Depending on the script, the visible rendering of this character when a line break occurs may differ (for example, in some scripts it is rendered as a *hyphen* -, while in others it may be invisible). See also U+2027 HYPHENATION POINT. For a complete list of dash characters in the Unicode Standard, see the General Punctuation character block description.

U+00A0 NO-BREAK SPACE is included for compatibility with existing standards. The nominal width is the same as U+0020 SPACE, but the NO-BREAK SPACE indicates that, under normal circumstances, no line breaks are permitted between it and surrounding characters, unless the preceding or following character is a line or paragraph separator. U+00A0 NO-BREAK SPACE is equivalent to the following coded character sequence: U+FEFF ZERO WIDTH NO-BREAK SPACE + U+0020 SPACE + U+FEFF ZERO WIDTH NO-BREAK SPACE. For a complete list of space characters in the Unicode Standard, see the General Punctuation character block description.

Ordinals. U+00AA FEMININE ORDINAL INDICATOR and U+00BA MASCULINE ORDINAL INDICATOR can be depicted with an underscore, but many modern fonts show them as superscripted Latin letters with no underscore. In sorting and searching these characters should be treated as weakly equivalent to their Latin character equivalents.

Quotation Marks. The characters U+00AB LEFT-POINTING DOUBLE ANGLE QUOTATION MARK « and U+00BB RIGHT-POINTING DOUBLE ANGLE QUOTATION MARK », also known as *guillemets*, are interpreted semantically rather than graphically in the context of bidirectional or vertical texts. Like the parenthesis and bracket characters of the Basic Latin block, these characters are interpreted as opening and closing characters, respectively, when used in a bidirectional or vertical text. The rendering mechanism must select the appropriately shaped glyph form to depict the character according to its directional context.

Encoding Structure. The Latin-1 Supplement character block is divided into the following ranges:

U+0080	→	U+009F	C1 control codes
U+00A0	→	U+00FF	Latin-1 graphic characters

Latin Extended-A: U+0100—U+017F

The Latin Extended-A block contains a collection of letters which, when added to the letters contained in the Basic Latin and Latin-1 Supplement blocks, allow for the representation of most European languages that employ the Latin script. Many other languages can also be written with the characters in this block. Most of these characters are equivalent to precomposed combinations of base character forms and combining diacritical marks. These combinations may also be represented by means of composed character sequences. See *Section 2.5, Combining Characters.*

Standards. This block includes characters contained in International Standard ISO 8859 – Part 2. Latin alphabet No. 2, Part 3. Latin alphabet No. 3, Part 4. Latin alphabet No. 4, and Part 9. Latin alphabet No. 5. Many of the other graphic characters contained in these standards, such as punctuation, signs, symbols, and diacritical marks, are already encoded in the Latin-1 Supplement block. Other characters from these parts of ISO 8859 are encoded in other blocks, primarily in the Spacing Modifier Letters block (U+02B0→U+02FF) and in the character blocks starting at and following the General Punctuation block.

Languages. Most languages supported by this block also require the concurrent use of characters contained in the Basic Latin and Latin-1 Supplement blocks. When combined with these two blocks, the Latin Extended-A block supports Afrikaans, Breton, Basque, Catalan, Croatian, Czech, Esperanto, Estonian, French, Frisian, Greenlandic, Hungarian, Latin, Latvian, Lithuanian, Maltese, Polish, Provençal, Rhaeto-Romanic, Romanian, Romany, Sami, Slovak, Slovenian, Sorbian, Turkish, Welsh, and many others.

Alternative Graphics. Some characters have alternative representations, although they have a common semantic. When Czech is printed in books, letter/apostrophe forms are frequently used. In typewritten or handwritten documents, letter/hacek forms are preferred.

Exceptional Case Pairs. The characters U+0130 LATIN CAPITAL LETTER I WITH DOT ABOVE and U+0131 LATIN SMALL LETTER DOTLESS I (used primarily in Turkish) are assumed to take ASCII "i" and "I" as their case alternates, respectively. This mapping makes the corresponding reverse mapping language-specific; mapping in both directions requires special attention from the implementor (see *Section 5.15, Sorting and Searching*).

Diacritics on i. A dotted (normal) i followed by a top non-spacing mark loses the dot in rendering. Thus, in the word *naïve* the *ï* could be spelled with *i + diaeresis*. Just as Cyrillic A is not equivalent to Latin A, a *dotted-i* is not equivalent to a Turkish *dotless-i + overdot*, nor are other cases of accented *dotted-i* equivalent to accented *dotless-i* (for example, i + ¨ ≠ ı + ¨).

To express the forms sometimes used in the Baltic (where the dot is retained under a top accent), use *i + overdot + accent* (see Figure 6-2).

Figure 6-2. Diacritics on i

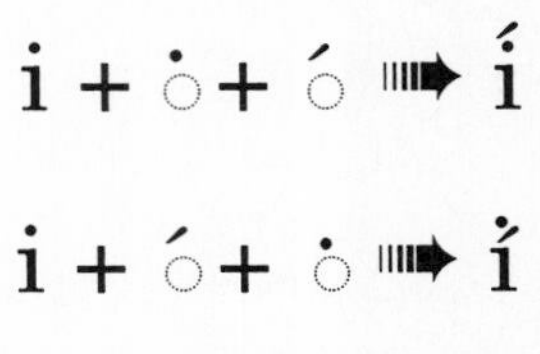

i + ◌̇ + ◌́ ➡ i̇́

i + ◌́ + ◌̇ ➡ í̇

Encoding Structure. The characters are grouped according to their base letter without regard for diacritics. Small letters immediately follow their capital letter counterparts.

U+0100 → U+017F Latin Extended-A characters

Latin Extended-B: U+0180—U+024F

The Latin Extended-B block contains letter forms used to extend Latin scripts to represent additional languages. It also contains phonetic symbols not included in the International Phonetic Alphabet (see the IPA Extensions block, U+0250→U+02AF).

Standards. This block covers, among other things, characters in ISO 6438 Documentation—African coded character set for bibliographic information interchange, *Pinyin* Latin transcription characters from the People's Republic of China national standard GB 2312 and from the Japanese national standard JIS X 0212, and Sami characters from ISO 8859 Part 10. *Latin alphabet No. 6.*

Arrangement. The characters are arranged in a nominal alphabetical order, followed by a small collection of Latinate forms. Upper- and lowercase pairs are placed together where possible, but in many instances the other case form is encoded at some distant location and so is cross-referenced. Variations on the same base letter are arranged in the following order: turned, inverted, hook attachment, stroke extension or modification, different style (script), small cap, modified basic form, ligature, and Greek-derived.

Croatian Digraphs Matching Serbian Cyrillic Letters. Serbo-Croatian is a single language with paired alphabets: a Latin script (Croatian) and a Cyrillic script (Serbian). A set of digraph codes is provided solely for compatibility purposes. There are two potential uppercase forms for each digraph, depending on whether only the initial letter is to be capitalized (title case), or both (all uppercase). The Unicode Standard offers both forms so that software can convert one form to the other without changing font sets. The appropriate cross-references are given for the lowercase letters. For more information about canonical equivalence, see *Chapter 3, Conformance.*

Pinyin Diacritic-Vowel Combinations. The Chinese standard GB 2312, as well as the Japanese standard JIS X 0212, includes a set of codes for *Pinyin,* used for Latin transcription of Mandarin Chinese. Most of the letters used in Pinyin romanization (even those with combining diacritical marks) are already covered in the preceding Latin blocks. The group of 16 characters provided here completes the Pinyin character set specified in GB 2312 and JIS X 0212.

Case Pairs. A number of characters in this block are uppercase forms of characters whose lowercase form is part of some other grouping. Many of these came from the International Phonetic Alphabet; they acquired novel uppercase forms when they were adopted into Latinscript-basedwritingsystems.Occasionally,however,*alternative*uppercaseforms arose in this process. In some instances, research has shown that alternative uppercase forms are merely variants of the same character. If so, such variants are assigned a single Unicode value, as is the case of U+01B7 LATIN CAPITAL LETTER EZH. But when research has shown that two uppercase forms are actually used in different ways, then they are given different codes; such is the case for U+018E LATIN CAPITAL LETTER REVERSED E and U+018F LATIN CAPITAL LETTER SCHWA. In this instance, the shared lowercase form is copied: U+01DD LATIN SMALL LETTER TURNED E is a copy of U+0259 LATIN SMALL LETTER SCHWA to enable unique case-pair mappings if desired.

For historical reasons, the names of some case pairs differ. For example, U+018E LATIN CAPITAL LETTER REVERSED E is the uppercase of U+01DD LATIN SMALL LETTER TURNED E—not of U+0258 LATIN SMALL LETTER REVERSED E. (For default case mappings of Unicode characters, see *Chapter 4, Character Properties.*)

Languages. Some indication of language or other usage is given for most characters within the names lists accompanying the character charts.

Encoding Structure. The character block for Latin Extended-B is divided into the following ranges:

U+0180	→	U+01C3	General Extended Latin
U+01C4	→	U+01CC	Croatian digraphs matching Serbian Cyrillic letters
U+01CD	→	U+01DC	Pinyin diacritic-vowel combinations
U+01DD	→	U+01F5	Additional Latin characters
U+01FA	→	U+01FF	Additional Latin characters from ISO 8859-10 (for Sami)
U+0200	→	U+0217	Croatian vowels with tone marks

IPA Extensions: U+0250—U+02AF

The IPA Extensions block contains primarily the unique symbols of the International Phonetic Alphabet (IPA), which is a standard system for indicating specific speech sounds. The IPA was first introduced in 1886 and has undergone occasional revisions of content and usage since that time. The Unicode Standard covers all single symbols and all diacritics in the last published IPA revision (1989), as well as a few symbols in former IPA usage which are no longer currently sanctioned. A few symbols have been added to this block that are part of the transcriptional practices of Sinologists, Americanists, and other linguists. Some of these practices have usages independent of the IPA and may use characters from other Latin blocks rather than IPA forms. Note also that a few non-standard or obsolete phonetic symbols are encoded in the Latin Extended-B block.

An essential feature of IPA is the use of combining diacritical marks. IPA diacritical mark characters are coded in the Combining Diacritical Marks block, U+0300→U+036F. In IPA, diacritical marks can be freely applied to base form letters to indicate fine degrees of phonetic differentiation required for precise recording of different languages. In the Unicode Standard, all diacritical marks are encoded in sequence *after the base characters to which they apply.* (For more details, see the block description for Combining Diacritical Marks, and *Section 2.5, Combining Characters.*)

Standards. The characters in this block are taken from the 1989 revision of the International Phonetic Alphabet, published by the International Phonetic Association. The International Phonetic Association standard considers IPA to be a separate alphabet, so it includes the entire Latin lowercase alphabet *a–z*, a number of extended Latin letters such as U+0153 LATIN SMALL LIGATURE OE œ, and a few Greek letters and other symbols as separate and distinct characters. In contrast, the Unicode Standard does not duplicate the Latin lowercase letters *a–z*, nor other Latin or Greek letters in encoding IPA. Note that unlike other character standards referenced by the Unicode Standard, IPA constitutes an extended alphabet and phonetic transcriptional standard, rather than a character encoding standard.

Unifications. The IPA symbols are unified as much as possible with other letters (though not with non-letter symbols like U+222B INTEGRAL ∫.) The IPA symbols have also been adopted into the Latin-based alphabets of many written languages (such as in Africa). It is futile to attempt to distinguish a transcription from an actual alphabet in such cases. Therefore, many IPA symbols are found outside the IPA Extensions block. IPA symbols that are not found in the IPA Extensions block are listed as cross-references at the beginning of the character names list for this block.

IPA Alternates. In a few cases IPA practice has, over time, produced alternate forms, such as U+0269 LATIN SMALL LETTER IOTA "ɩ" versus U+026A LATIN LETTER SMALL CAPITAL I "ɪ." The Unicode Standard provides separate encodings for the two alternate forms due to the fact that they are used in a meaningfully distinct fashion.

Case Pairs. IPA does not sanction case distinctions; in effect, its phonetic symbols are all lowercase. When IPA symbols are adopted into a particular alphabet as used by a given written language (as has occurred for example, in Africa) they acquire uppercase forms. Since these uppercase forms are not themselves IPA symbols, they are generally encoded in the Latin Extended-B block (or other Latin extension blocks) and are cross-referenced with the IPA names list.

Typographic Variants. IPA includes typographic variants of certain Latin and Greek letters that would ordinarily be considered variations of font style rather than of character identity, such as SMALL CAPITAL letter forms. Examples include a typographic variant of the Greek letter *phi* ɸ, as well as the borrowed letter Greek *iota* ɩ, which has a unique Latin uppercase form. These forms are encoded as separate characters in the Unicode Standard because they have distinct semantics in plain text.

Affricate Digraph Ligatures. IPA officially sanctions six digraph ligatures used in transcription of coronal affricates. These are encoded at U+02A3→U+02A8. The IPA digraph ligatures are explicitly defined in IPA and also have possible semantic values that make them not simply rendering forms. Thus, for example, while U+02A6 LATIN SMALL LETTER TS DIGRAPH is a transcription for the sounds that could also be transcribed in IPA as U+0074 U+0073, "ts," the choice of the digraph ligature may be the result of a deliberate distinction made by the transcriber regarding the systematic phonetic status of the affricate. It cannot be a choice left up to rendering software whether to ligate or not based on the font available. This ligature also differs in typographical design from the ts ligature found in some old-style fonts.

Encoding Structure. The IPA Extensions block is arranged in approximate alphabetical order according to the Latin letter that is graphically most similar to each symbol. This has nothing to do with a phonetic arrangement of the IPA letters. This block may be divided into the following ranges:

U+0250	→	U+0298	Pre-1989 IPA characters and other phonetic symbols
U+0299	→	U+02A2	Post-1989 IPA extensions and older IPA symbols
U+02A3	→	U+02A8	IPA digraph ligatures

Spacing Modifier Letters: U+02B0—U+02FF

Modifier letters are an assorted collection of small signs that are generally used to indicate modifications of a preceding letter. A few may modify the following letter, and some may serve as independent letters. These signs are distinguished from diacritical marks in that modifier letters are treated as free-standing, spacing characters. They are distinguished from similar or identical appearing punctuation or symbols by the fact that the members of this block are considered to be letter characters that do not break up a word. They have the "letter" character property (see *Chapter 4, Character Properties*). The majority of these signs are phonetic modifiers, including the characters required for coverage of the International Phonetic Alphabet (IPA).

Phonetic Usage. Modifier letters have relatively well-defined phonetic interpretations. Their usage is generally to indicate a specific articulatory modification of a sound represented by another letter, or to convey a particular level of stress or tone. In phonetic usage, the modifier letters are sometimes called "diacritics," which is correct in the logical sense that they are modifiers of the preceding letter. However, in the Unicode Standard, the term diacritical marks refers specifically to non-spacing marks, whereas the codes in this block specify *spacing characters*. For this reason, many of the modifier letters in this block correspond to separate diacritical mark codes, which are cross-referenced in *Section 7.1, Character Names List Entries*.

Encoding Principles. This block includes characters that may have different semantic values attributed to them in different contexts. It also includes multiple characters that may represent the same semantic values—there is no necessary one-to-one relationship. The intention of the Unicode encoding is not to resolve the variations in usage, but merely to supply implementers with a set of useful forms to choose from. The list of usages given for each modifier letter should not be considered exhaustive. For example, the glottal stop (Arabic *hamza*) in Latin transliteration has been variously represented by the characters U+02BC MODIFIER LETTER APOSTROPHE, U+02BE MODIFER LETTER RIGHT HALF RING, and U+02C0 MODIFER LETTER GLOTTAL STOP. Conversely, an apostrophe can have several uses; for a list, see the entry for U+02BC MODIFIER LETTER APOSTROPHE in the character names list. There are also instances where an IPA modifier letter is explicitly equated in semantic value to an IPA non-spacing diacritic form.

Latin Superscripts. Graphically, some of the phonetic modifier signs are raised or superscripted, some are lowered or subscripted, and some are vertically centered. Only those few forms that have specific usage in IPA or other major phonetic systems are encoded.

Spacing Clones of Diacritics. Some corporate standards explicitly specify spacing and non-spacing forms of combining diacritical marks, and the Unicode Standard provides matching codes for these interpretations when practical. A number of the spacing forms are covered in the Basic Latin and Latin-1 Supplement blocks. The six common European diacritics that do not have encodings there are added as spacing characters in the current block. These forms can have multiple semantics, such as U+02D9 DOT ABOVE, used as an indicator of the Mandarin Chinese fifth tone.

Rhotic Hook. U+02DE MODIFIER LETTER RHOTIC HOOK IS defined in IPA as a free-standing modifier letter. However, in common usage it is treated as a ligated hook on a baseform letter. Hence, U+0259 LATIN SMALL LETTER SCHWA + U+02DE MODIFIER LETTER RHOTIC HOOK may be treated as equivalent to U+025A LATIN SMALL LETTER SCHWA WITH HOOK.

Tone Letters. U+02E5→U+02E9 comprise a set of basic tone letters, defined in IPA and commonly used in detailed tone transcription of African and other languages. Each tone letter refers to one of five distinguishable tone levels. In order to represent contour tones, the tone letters are used in combinations. The rendering of contour tones follows a regular set of ligation rules that result in a graphic image of the contour (see Figure 6-3).

Figure 6-3. Tone Letters

˥ + ˩ = ˥˩

Encoding Structure. The character block for Modifier Letters is divided into the following ranges:

U+02B0	→	U+02B8,	Phonetic modifiers derived from Latin letters
U+02E0	→	U+02E4	
U+02B9	→	U+02D7,	Miscellaneous phonetic modifiers
U+02DE			
U+02D8	→	U+02DD	Spacing clones of non-spacing diacritic marks
U+02E5	→	U+02E9	IPA tone letters

Combining Diacritical Marks: U+0300—U+036F

The combining diacritical marks in this block are intended for general use with any script. Diacritical marks specific to some particular script are encoded with the alphabet for that script. Diacritical marks that are primarily used with symbols are defined in the Combining Diacritical Marks for Symbols character block (U+20D0→U+20FF).

Standards. The combining diacritical marks are derived from a variety of sources, including IPA, ISO 5426, and ISO 6937.

Sequence of Base Letters and Diacritics. In the Unicode character encoding, all non-spacing marks, including diacritics, are encoded *after* the base character. For example, the Unicode character sequence U+0061 "a" LATIN SMALL LETTER A, U+0308 "◌̈" COMBINING DIAERESIS, U+0075 "u" LATIN SMALL LETTER U unambiguously encodes "äu", *not* "aü".

The Unicode Standard convention is consistent with the logical order of other non-spacing marks in Semitic and Indic scripts, the great majority of which follow the base characters with respect to which they are positioned. This convention is also in line with the way modern font technology handles the rendering of non-spacing glyphic forms, so that mapping from character memory representation to rendered glyphs is simplified. (For more information on the use of diacritical marks, see *Chapter 2, General Structure,* and *Chapter 3, Conformance.*)

Diacritics Positioned Over Two Base Characters. IPA and a few languages such as Tagalog use diacritics that are applied to two base form characters. These marks apply to the previous base character—just like all other combining non-spacing marks—but hang over the following letter as well. The two characters U+0360 COMBINING DOUBLE TILDE and U+0361 COMBINING DOUBLE INVERTED BREVE are intended to be displayed as depicted in Figure 6-4.

Figure 6-4. Double Diacritics

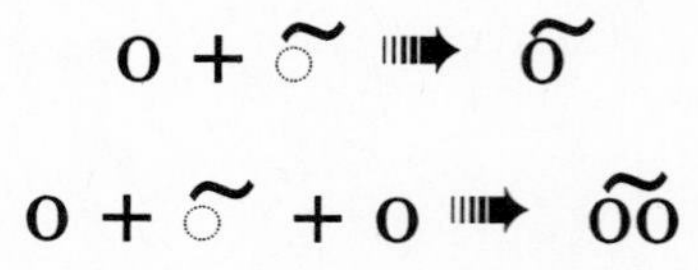

o + ◌͠ ➡ o͠

o + ◌͠ + o ➡ o͠o

These double diacritics always bind more loosely than other non-spacing marks and thus sort at the end in the canonical representation. When rendering, the double diacritic will float above other diacritics (excluding surrounding diacritics), as in Figure 6-5.

Figure 6-5. Ordering of Double Diacritics

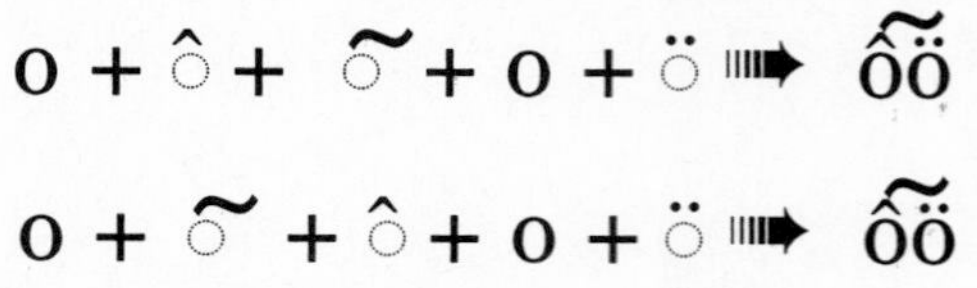

o + ◌̂ + ◌͠ + o + ◌̈ ➡ ô͠ö

o + ◌͠ + ◌̂ + o + ◌̈ ➡ ô͠ö

Marks as Spacing Characters. By convention, combining marks may be exhibited in (apparent) isolation by applying them to U+0020 SPACE or to U+00A0 NO-BREAK SPACE. This might be done, for example, when referring to the diacritical mark itself as a mark, rather than using it in its normal way in text. The use of U+0020 SPACE versus U+00A0 NO-BREAK SPACE affects line-breaking behavior.

In charts and illustrations in this standard, the combining nature of these marks is illustrated by applying them to U+25CC DOTTED CIRCLE, as shown in the examples throughout this standard.

The Unicode Standard separately encodes clones of many common European diacritical marks as spacing characters. These related characters are cross-referenced in the character names list.

Encoding Principles. Because non-spacing marks have such a wide variety of applications, the characters in this block may have multiple semantic values. For example, U+0308 = *diaeresis* = *umlaut* = *double derivative.* There are also cases of several different Unicode characters for equivalent semantic values; variants of CEDILLA include at least U+0312 COMBINING TURNED COMMA ABOVE, U+0326 COMBINING COMMA BELOW, and U+0327 COMBINING CEDILLA. (For more information about the difference between non-spacing marks and combining characters, see *Chapter 2, General Structure.*)

Encoding Structure. The character block for general combining diacritical marks is divided into the following ranges:

U+0300	→	U+0333,	Ordinary diacritics
U+0339	→	U+033F	
U+0334	→	U+0338	Overstruck diacritics
U+0340	→	U+0341	Vietnamese tone mark diacritics (usage strongly discouraged)
U+0342	→	U+0345	Greek diacritics
U+0360	→	U+0361	Double diacritics

Greek: U+0370—U+03FF

The Greek script is used for writing the Greek language and (in an extended variant) the Coptic language. The Greek script had a strong influence in the development of the Latin and Cyrillic scripts.

The Greek script is written in linear sequence from left to right with the occasional use of non-spacing marks. Greek letters come in upper- and lowercase pairs.

Standards. The Unicode encoding of Greek is based on ISO 8859-7, which is equivalent to the Greek national standard ELOT 928. The Unicode Standard encodes Greek characters in the same relative positions as in ISO 8859-7. A number of variant and archaic characters are taken from the bibliographic standard ISO 5428.

Polytonic Greek. Polytonic Greek, used for ancient Greek (classical and Byzantine), may be encoded using either composite character sequences or precomposed base plus diacritic combinations. For the latter, see the Greek Extended character block (U+1F00→U+1FFF).

Non-spacing Marks. Several non-spacing marks commonly used with the Greek script are found in the Combining Diacritical Marks range (see Table 6-1).

Table 6-1. Non-Spacing Marks Used with Greek

Code	Name	Alternate
U+0300	COMBINING GRAVE ACCENT	*varia*
U+0301	COMBINING ACUTE ACCENT	*oxia*
U+0302	COMBINING CIRCUMFLEX ACCENT	
U+0303	COMBINING TILDE	
U+0304	COMBINING MACRON	
U+0306	COMBINING BREVE	
U+0308	COMBINING DIAERESIS	*dialytika*
U+030D	COMBINING VERTICAL LINE ABOVE	*tonos*
U+0313	COMBINING COMMA ABOVE	*psili*
U+0314	COMBINING REVERSED COMMA ABOVE	*dasia*
U+0342	COMBINING GREEK PERISPOMENI	
U+0343	COMBINING GREEK KORONIS	
U+0344	COMBINING GREEK DIALYTIKA TONOS	
U+0345	COMBINING GREEK YPOGEGRAMMENI	

Since the marks in that range are encoded by shape, not by meaning, they are appropriate for use in Greek where applicable. Multiple non-spacing marks applied onto the same baseform character are to be spelled as the base form character followed by the non-spacing mark characters in sequence. The order of non-spacing marks is from the base form outward. (See the general rules for applying non-spacing marks in *Section 2.5, Combining Characters.*)

U+0342 COMBINING GREEK PERISPOMENI may appear as either a circumflex or a tilde: α̂ versus α̃. Because of this variation in form, the perispomeni was encoded distinctly from U+0303 COMBINING TILDE.

U+0313 COMBINING COMMA ABOVE and U+0343 COMBINING GREEK KORONIS both take the form of a raised comma over a baseform letter. U+0343 COMBINING GREEK KORONIS was included for compatibility reasons; U+0313 COMBINING COMMA ABOVE is the preferred form for general use.

The non-spacing mark *ypogegrammeni* (also known as *iota-subscript* in Engish) can be applied to the vowels *alpha*, *eta*, and *omega* to represent historic diphthongs. This mark appears as a small *iota* below the vowel. When applied to uppercase vowels, it can also be rendered as a small *iota* at the lower right-hand corner of the vowel.

Archaic representations of Greek words (which did not have lowercase or accents) use the Greek capital letter *iota* following the vowel for these diphthongs. Forms of the *iota* that follow the vowel are called *prosgegrammeni* (also known as *iota-adscript* in English). Such archaic representations require special case mapping.

Variant Letterforms. Variant forms of certain Greek letters are encoded as separate characters in ISO 8859-7 and ISO 5428; therefore, these forms are also included in the Unicode character set. These include U+03C2 GREEK SMALL LETTER FINAL SIGMA and U+03D0 GREEK BETA SYMBOL.

Greek Letters as Symbols. For compatibility purposes, a few Greek letters are separately encoded as symbols in other character blocks. Examples include U+00B5 MICRO SIGN µ in the Latin-1 Supplement character block and U+2126 OHM SIGN Ω in the Letterlike Symbols character block. Characters from the Greek block may be used for these symbols.

Punctuation-like Characters. The question of which punctuation-like characters are uniquely Greek and which ones can be unified with generic Western punctuation has no definitive answer. The Greek question mark U+037E GREEK QUESTION MARK *erotimatiko* ";" is encoded for compatible use by systems that treat it as a sentence-final punctuation distinct from the semicolon.

Historic Letters. Historic Greek letters have been retained from ISO 5428.

Coptic-Unique Letters. The Coptic script is regarded primarily as a stylistic variant of the Greek alphabet. The letters unique to Coptic are encoded in a separate range at the end of the Greek character block. Those characters may be used together with the basic Greek characters to represent the complete Coptic alphabet. Coptic text may be rendered using a font that contains the Coptic style of depicting the characters it shares with the Greek alphabet. Texts that mix Greek and Coptic languages together must employ appropriate font style associations.

Encoding Structure. The character block for the Greek script is divided into the following ranges:

U+0374	→	U+037E	Greek punctuation and *ypogegrammameni* not from ISO 8859-7, coded in relative positions where there are uncoded gaps in ISO 8859-7
U+0384	→	U+03CE	Greek letters, punctuation, and diacritical marks from ISO 8859-7 (except for those characters unified into other blocks)
U+03D0	→	U+03D6,	Variant Greek letterforms
U+03F0	→	U+03F3	
U+03DA	→	U+03E1	Archaic letters
U+03E2	→	U+03EF	Coptic-unique letters

Cyrillic: U+0400—U+04FF

The Cyrillic script is a member of the family of scripts strongly influenced by the Greek script. Cyrillic has traditionally been used for writing various Slavic languages, among which Russian is predominant. In the 19th and early 20th centuries, Cyrillic was extended to write the non-Slavic minority languages of the former Soviet Union. The Cyrillic script is written in linear sequence from left to right with the occasional use of non-spacing marks. Cyrillic letters come in upper- and lowercase pairs.

Standards. The Cyrillic block of the Unicode Standard is based on ISO 8859-5. The Unicode Standard encodes Cyrillic characters in the same relative positions as in 8859-5.

Unifications. Latin characters included in those alphabets that use both Latin and Cyrillic letters are not given duplicate Cyrillic encodings. Examples include *q* and *w* for Kurdish and U+0292 LATIN SMALL LETTER EZH for Abkhasian.

Historic Letters. The historic form of the Cyrillic alphabet is treated as a font style variation of modern Cyrillic because the historic forms are relatively close to the modern appearance and because some of them are still in modern use in languages other than Russian (for example, U+0406 CYRILLIC CAPITAL LETTER I "I" is used in modern Ukrainian and Byelorussian). Since the historic Cyrillic characters encoded in Unicode (U+0460 → U+0486) rarely occur in modern form, these letters are shown in the charts in an archaic font. A complete Old Cyrillic set would be obtained by rendering the whole Cyrillic section (that is, U+0400 → U+0486) in that same style.

Extended Cyrillic. These are the letters used in alphabets for minority languages of the former Soviet Union. The scripts of some of these languages have often been revised in the past; the Unicode Standard includes only the alphabets in current use, not the rejected old letterforms.

Glagolitic. The history of the creation of the Slavic scripts and their relationship has been lost. The Unicode Standard regards Glagolitic as a *separate* script from Cyrillic, not as a font change from Cyrillic. This is primarily because Glagolitic appears unrecognizably different from Cyrillic, and secondarily because Glagolitic has not grown to match the expansion of Cyrillic. The Glagolitic script is not currently supported by the Unicode Standard.

Encoding Structure. The character block for the Cyrillic script is divided into the following ranges:

U+0400	→	U+045F	Cyrillic characters from ISO 8859-5 (except for those characters unified into other blocks as specified above)
U+0460	→	U+0481	Historic Cyrillic letters
U+0482	→	U+0486	Historic miscellaneous signs and diacritics
U+0490	→	U+04CC	Extended Cyrillic letters
U+04D0	→	U+04F9	Cyrillic letter with diacritic combinations and other compatibility additions

Armenian: U+0530—U+058F

The Armenian script is used primarily for writing the Armenian language. The script is written from left to right and generally does not use diacritics (except for the modifier letters specified below). It does have upper- and lowercase pairs.

Modifier Letters. In modern Armenian typography, the small marks in the group called Armenian modifier letters are placed above and to the right of other letters so that they occupy a letter position of their own. Therefore, in the Unicode Standard they are treated as spacing letters rather than as non-spacing marks.

Encoding Structure. The character block for the Armenian script is divided into the following ranges:

U+0531	→	U+0556	Uppercase letters
U+0559	→	U+055F	Modifier letters
U+0561	→	U+0586	Lowercase letters
U+0589			Punctuation

Hebrew: U+0590—U+05FF

The Hebrew script is used for writing the Hebrew language as well as Yiddish, Judezmo (Ladino), and a number of other languages. Vowels and various other marks are written as *points,* which are applied to consonantal base letters; these marks are usually omitted in Hebrew, except for liturgical texts and other special applications. Five Hebrew letters assume a different graphic form when last in a word.

The Hebrew script is written from right to left. (For a general discussion of character ordering including right-to-left scripts, see *Section 3.11, Bidirectional Behavior.*)

Standards. ISO 8859-8—Part 8. *Latin/Hebrew Alphabet.* The Unicode Standard encodes the Hebrew alphabetic characters in the same relative positions as in ISO 8859-8; however, there are no points or Hebrew punctuation characters in ISO 8859-8.

Vowels and Other Marks of Pronunciation. These combining marks, generically called *points* in the context of Hebrew, indicate vowels or other modifications of consonantal letters. General rules for applying combining marks are given in *Section 2.5, Combining Characters.* Hebrew-specific behavior is described here.

Hebrew points can be separated into four classes: *Dagesh*, *Shin Dot* and *Sin Dot*, *vowels*, and *diacritics.* Each class has its own positioning rules.

Dagesh, U+05BC HEBREW POINT DAGESH, has the form of a dot that appears inside the letter that it affects. Dagesh is not a vowel, but a diacritic that affects the pronunciation of a consonant. The same base consonant can also have a vowel and/or other diacritics. *Dagesh* is the only element that goes inside a letter.

Shin dot, U+05C1 HEBREW POINT SHIN DOT, and *sin dot*, U+05C2 HEBREW POINT SIN DOT, have the form of dots that appear respectively on the upper right and upper left side of the base letter *shin*, U+05E9 HEBREW LETTER SHIN. These two dots are mutually exclusive and occur only after the base letter *shin*. The same base letter can also have a *dagesh*, a vowel, and other diacritics. *Shin* and *sin* are two Hebrew consonants that are differentiated only by the adjunction of a *shin dot* or a *sin dot* to the base character *shin*.

Points representing vowels all appear below the base character that they affect, except for *holam*, U+05B9 HEBREW POINT HOLAM, which appears above left. There is never more than one vowel for a base character, and a base charcter may have no vowel at all. The following points represent vowels: U+05B0 → U+05B9, U+05BB.

Three points are diacritics: U+05BD, U+05BF, U+FB1E. *Metag* goes below the base character it affects; *rafe* and *varika* go above.

Shin and Sin. Separate characters for the dotted letters *shin* and *sin* are not included in this block. When it is necessary to distinguish between the two forms, they should be encoded as U+05E9 HEBREW LETTER SHIN followed by the appropriate dot (U+05C1 or U+05C2). This is consistent with Israeli standard encoding. For compatibility purposes, presentation forms of shin are available in the compatibility zone at U+FB2A HEBREW LETTER SHIN WITH SHIN DOT and U+FB2B HEBREW LETTER SHIN WITH SIN DOT.

Cantillation Marks. Cantillation marks are used in publishing liturgical texts including the Bible. There are various historical schools of cantillation marking; the set of marks included in the Unicode Standard follow the pre-publication version of Israeli national standard IS 1311.2.

Positioning. Marks may combine with vowels and other points, and there are complex typographic rules for positioning these combinations.

The latitudinal placement (meaning above, below, or inside) of points and marks is very well defined and has no exceptions. The longitudinal placement (meaning left, right or center) of points is very well defined and has no exceptions. The longitude of marks is not well defined, and convention allows for the different placement of marks relative to their base character.

When points and marks are located below the same base letter, the point always comes first (on the right) and the mark after it (on the left), except for the marks *yetiv*, U+059A HEBREW ACCENT YETIV, and *dehi*, U+05AD HEBREW ACCENT DEHI, which come first (on the right) and are followed (on the left) by the point.

These rules are followed when points and marks are located above the same base letter:

- If the point is *holam*, all cantillation marks precede it (on the right), except *pashta*, U+0599 HEBREW ACCENT PASHTA.
- *Pashta* always follows (goes to the left of) points.
- *Holam* on a sin consonant (*shin* base + *sin dot*) follows (goes to the left of) the *sin dot*.
- *Shin dot* and *sin dot* are generally represented closer vertically to the base letter than other points and marks which go above.

Punctuation. Most punctuation marks used with the Hebrew script are not given independent codes (that is, they are unified with Latin punctuation), except for the few cases where the mark has a unique form in Hebrew, namely: U+05BE HEBREW PUNCTUATION MAQAF, U+05C0 HEBREW PUNCTUATION PASEQ, U+05C3 HEBREW PUNCTUATION SOF PASUQ, U+05F3 HEBREW PUNCTUATION GERESH, and U+05F4 HEBREW PUNCTUATION GERSHAYIM. See also U+FB1E HEBREW POINT JUDEO-SPANISH VARIKA. Note that for paired punctuation such as parentheses, the glyphs chosen to represent U+0028 LEFT PARENTHESIS and U+0029 RIGHT PARENTHESIS will depend upon the direction of the rendered text.

Final (Contextual Variant) Letterforms. Variant forms of five Hebrew letters are encoded as separate characters in all Hebrew standards; therefore this practice is followed in the Unicode Standard. These five variant forms are encoded in this block rather than the compatibility zone in order to retain structural consistency between this block and ISO 8859-8.

Other Presentation Forms. For compatibility purposes, a number of additional presentation forms of Hebrew letters and letter combinations are encoded in the compatibility zone in the range U+FB1F→U+FB4F. These presentation forms include wide and alternative variant forms of certain letters, precomposed combinations of letters or positional letter forms and points, and ligatures.

Yiddish Digraphs. These are considered to be independent characters in Yiddish. The Unicode Standard has included them as separate characters in order to distinguish certain letter combinations in Yiddish text; for example, to distinguish the digraph *double vav* from an occurrence of a consonontal *vav* followed by a vocalic *vav*. The use of digraphs is consistent with standard Yiddish orthography. Other letters of the Yiddish alphabet, such as *pasekh alef*, can be composed from other characters.

Encoding Structure. The character block for the Hebrew script is divided into the following ranges:

U+0591	→	U+05AF	Cantillation marks and accents
U+05B0	→	U+05C4,	Points and punctuation
U+05F3	→	U+05F4	
U+05D0	→	U+05EA	Hebrew letters
U+05F0	→	U+05F2	Yiddish digraphs

Arabic: U+0600—U+06FF

The Arabic script is used for writing the Arabic language and has been extended for representing a number of other languages, such as Persian, Urdu, Pashto, Sindhi, and Kurdish. Some languages, such as Indonesian/Malay, Turkish, and Ingush, formerly used the Arabic script and now employ the Latin or Cyrillic scripts.

The Arabic script is cursive, even in its printed form (see Figure 6-6). As a result, the same letter may be written in different forms depending on how it joins with its neighbors. Vowels and various other marks may be written as combining marks called *harakat*, which are applied to consonantal base letters. In normal writing, however, these *harakat* are omitted.

The Arabic script is written from right to left. (For a general discussion of character ordering including right-to-left scripts, see *Section 3.11, Bidirectional Behavior.*)

Figure 6-6. Reversal and Cursive Connection

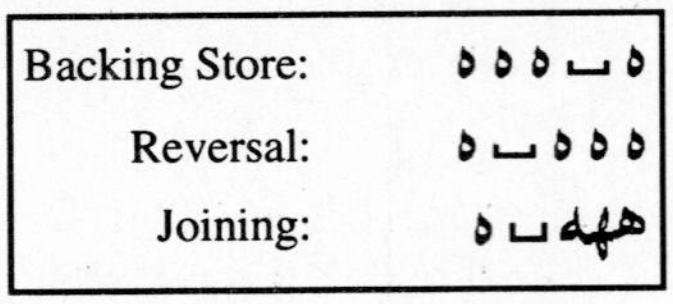

Backing Store:

Reversal:

Joining:

Standards. ISO 8859-6—Part 6. *Latin/Arabic Alphabet.* The Unicode Standard encodes the basic Arabic characters in the same relative positions as in ISO 8859-6. ISO 8859-6, in turn, is based on ECMA-114, which was based on ASMO 449.

Encoding Principles. The basic set of Arabic letters is well defined. Each letter receives only one Unicode character value in the basic Arabic block, no matter how many different contextual appearances it may exhibit in text. Each Arabic letter in the Unicode Standard may be said to represent the inherent semantic identity of the letter. A word is spelled as a sequence of these letters. The graphic form (glyph) shown in the Unicode character chart for an Arabic letter (usually the form of the letter when standing by itself) is not the identity of that character. (See also *Section 6.8, CompatibilityArea and Specials.*)

Punctuation. Most punctuation marks used with the Arabic script are not given independent codes (that is, they are unified with Latin punctuation), except for the few cases where the mark has a significantly different appearance in Arabic, namely: U+060C ARABIC COMMA, U+061B ARABIC SEMICOLON, U+061F ARABIC QUESTION MARK, and U+066A ARABIC PERCENT SIGN. Note that for paired punctuation such as parentheses, the glyphs chosen to represent U+0028 LEFT PARENTHESIS and U+0029 RIGHT PARENTHESIS will depend upon the direction of the rendered text.

The Non-Joiner and the Joiner. The Unicode Standard provides two user-selectable zero-width formatting codes: U+200C ZERO WIDTH NON-JOINER and U+200D ZERO WIDTH JOINER (see Figure 6-7, Figure 6-8, and Figure 6-9). The use of a non-joiner between two letters prevents them from forming a cursive connection with each other when rendered. Examples include the Persian plural suffix, some Persian proper names, and Ottoman Turkish vowels. For further discussion of joiners and non-joiners, see the General Punctuation block description.

Figure 6-7. Using Joiner

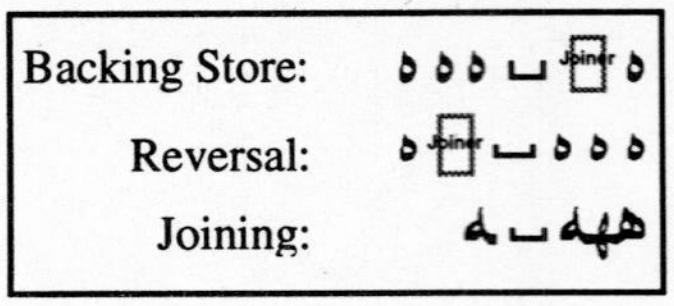

Backing Store:

Reversal:

Joining:

Figure 6-8. Using Non-Joiner

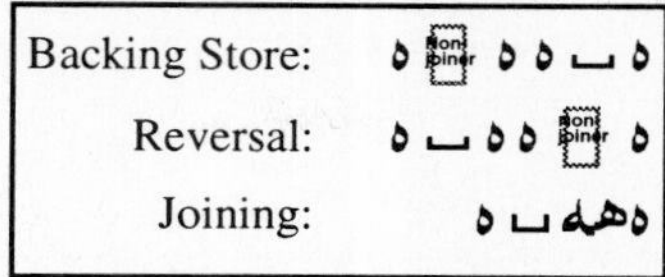

Figure 6-9. Combinations of Joiner and Non-Joiner

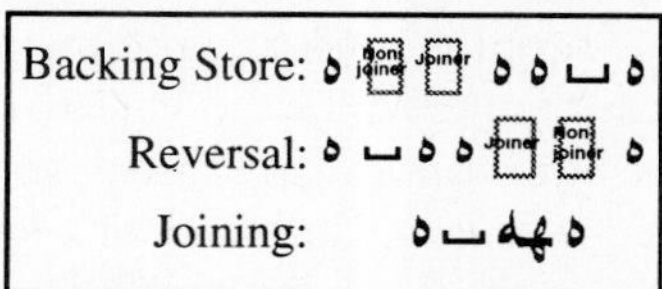

Harakat (Vowel) Non-Spacing Marks. *Harakat* are marks that indicate vowels or other modifications of consonant letters. The occurrence of a character in the *harakat* range and its depiction in relation to a dashed circle constitute an assertion that this character is intended to be applied via some process *to the character that precedes it* in the text stream, the base character. General rules for applying non-spacing marks are given in the Combining Diacritical Marks block description section. The few marks that are placed after (to the left of) the base character are treated as ordinary spacing characters in the Unicode Standard. The Unicode Standard does not specify a sequence order in case of multiple *harakat* applied to the same Arabic base character since there is no possible ambiguity of interpretation. (For more information about the canonical ordering of non-spacing marks, see *Chapter 2, General Structure,* and *Chapter 3, Conformance.*)

Arabic-Indic Digits. The names for the forms of decimal digits vary widely across different languages. The decimal numbering system originated in India (Devanagari ०१२३...) and was subsequently adopted in the Arabic world with a different appearance (Arabic ٠١٢٣...). The Europeans adopted decimal numbers from the Arabic world, although once again the forms of the digits changed greatly (European 0123...). The European forms were later adopted widely around the world and are used even in many Arabic-speaking countries in North Africa. In each case, the interpretation of decimal numbers remained the same. However, the forms of the digits changed to a degree that they are no longer recognizably the same characters. Because of the origin of these characters, the European decimal numbers are widely known as "Arabic numerials" or "Hindi-Arabic numerals," while the decimal numbers in use in the Arabic world are widely known there as "Hindi numbers."

The Unicode Standard includes both *Indic* digits (including forms used with different Indic scripts), *Arabic* digits (with forms used in most of the Arabic world), and *European* digits (now used internationally). Because of this, the traditional names could not be retained without confusion. In addition, there are two main variants of the Arabic digits—those used in Iran and Pakistan (here called *Eastern Arabic-Indic*) and those used in other parts of the Arabic world. The Persian and Urdu variant digits are given separate codes in the Unicode Standard to account for the differences in appearance and directional treatment when rendering them. (For a complete discussion of directional formatting in the Unicode Standard, see *Section 3.11, Bidirectional Behavior.*)

In summary, the Unicode Standard uses the names shown in Table 6-2. These names have been chosen to reduce the confusion involved in the use of the decimal number forms. They do not have any normative content; as with the choice of any other names, they are meant to be unique distinguishing labels and should not be viewed as favoring one culture over another.

Table 6-2. Digit Names

Name	Code Points	Forms
European	U+0030 → U+0039	0123456789
Arabic-Indic	U+0660 → U+0669	٠١٢٣٤٥٦٧٨٩
Eastern Arabic-Indic	U+06F0 → U+06F9	۰۱۲۳۴۵۶۷۸۹
Indic (Devanagari)	U+0966 → U+096F	०१२३४५६७८९

Extended Arabic Letters. Arabic script is used to write major languages, such as Persian and Urdu, but it has also been used to transcribe some relatively obscure languages, such as Baluchi and Lahnda, which have little tradition in printed typography. As a result, the set of characters encoded in this section unavoidably contains spurious forms. The Unicode Standard encodes multiple forms of the Extended Arabic letters and variant digits because the character forms and usages are not well documented for a number of languages. This approach was felt to be the most practical in the interest of minimizing the risk of omitting valid characters.

Languages. The languages using a given character are occasionally indicated, even though this information is incomplete. When such an annotation ends with an ellipsis (...), then the languages cited are merely the known principal ones among many.

Minimum Rendering Requirements. The cursive nature of the Arabic script imposes special requirements on display or rendering processes that are not typically found in Latin script-based systems. A display process must convert between the logical order in which Arabic characters are placed in backing store and the visual (or physical) order required by the display device. (See *Section 3.11, Bidirectional Behavior*, for a description of the conversion between logical and visual orders.)

At a minimum, a display process must also select an appropriate glyph to depict each Arabic letter according to its immediate *joining* context; furthermore, it must substitute certain ligature glyphs for sequences of Arabic characters. The remainder of this section specifies a minimum set of rules that provide legible Arabic joining and ligature substitution behavior.

Joining Classes. Each Arabic letter must be depicted by one of a number of possible contextual glyph forms. The appropriate form is determined on the basis of its *joining class* and the joining class of adjacent characters. Each Arabic character falls into one of the classes shown in Table 6-3 (see the end of this block description for a complete list).

Table 6-3. Arabic Joining Classes

Joining Class	Members
Right-joining:	ALEF, DAL, THAL, RA, ZAIN ,
Left-joining:	*none*
Dual-joining:	BAA, TAA, THAA, JEEM ...
Join-causing:	ZERO WIDTH JOINER, TATWEEL (*kashida*)
Non-joining:	ZERO WIDTH NON-JOINER and all spacing characters (other than the above), including HAMZAH, HIGH HAMZA, spaces, digits, punctuation, non-Arabic letters, and so on.
Transparent:	All combining marks and format marks, including FATHATAN, DAMMATAN, FATHAH, DAMMAH, KASRAH, SHADDAH, SUKUN, ALEF ABOVE, RIGHT-LEFT MARK, and so on.

In addition to the above classes, two superset classes will be employed as follows: a *right-join causing* character is either a dual-joining, right-joining or join-causing character; a *left-*

join causing character is either a dual-joining, left-joining or join-causing character. Here *right* and *left* refer to visual order.

Joining Rules. The following rules describe the joining behavior of Arabic letters in terms of their display (visual) order. In other words, the positions of letterforms in the included examples are presented as they would appear on the screen *after* the bidirectional algorithm has reordered the characters of a line of text.

➥ An implementation may choose to restate the following rules according to logical order so as to apply *before* the bidirectional algorithm's reordering phase. In this case, the words *right* and *left* as used in this section would become *preceding* and *following*.

In the following rules, if *X* refers to a character, then various glyph types representing that character are referred to as show in Table 6-4.

Table 6-4. Arabic Glyph Types

Glyph Types	Description
X_n	Nominal glyph form as it appears in the code charts.
X_r	Right-joining glyph form (both right-joining and dual-joining characters may employ this form).
X_l	Left-joining glyph form (both left-joining and dual-joining characters may employ this form).
X_m	Dual-joining (medial) glyph form which joins on both left and right (only dual-joining characters employ this form).

R1 ***Transparent characters do not affect the joining behavior of base (spacing) characters. For example:***

MEEM.N + SHADDAH.N + LAM.N ➡ MEEM.R + SHADDAH.N + LAM.L

م + ◌ّ + ل ➡ ـم + ◌ّ + لـ ➡ لمّ

R2 ***A right-joining character X that has a right join-causing character on the right will adopt the form*** X_r.
For example:

ALEF.N + TATWEEL.N ➡ ALEF.R + TATWEEL.N

ا + ـ ➡ ـا + ـ ➡ ـا

R3 ***A left-joining character X that has a join-causing character on the left will adopt the form*** X_l.

R4 ***A dual-joining character X that has a join-causing character on the right and a join-causing character on the left will adopt the form*** X_m. ***For example:***

TATWEEL.N + MEEM.N + TATWEEL.N ➡ TATWEEL.N + MEEM.M + TATWEEL.N

ـ + م + ـ ➡ ـ + ـمـ + ـ ➡ ـمـ

R5 ***A dual-joining character X that has a join-causing character on the right and no join-causing character on the left will adopt the form*** X_r. ***For example:***

MEEM.N + TATWEEL.N ➞ MEEM.R + TATWEEL.N

م + ـ ➞ مـ + ـ ➞ مـ

R6 ***A dual-joining character X that has a join-causing character on the left and no join-causing character on the right will adopt the form X_l. For example:***

TATWEEL.N + MEEM.N ➞ TATWEEL.N + MEEM.L

ـ + م ➞ ـ + ـم ➞ ـم

R7 ***If none of the above rules apply to a character X, then it will adopt the nominal form X_n.***

As just noted, the ZERO WIDTH NON-JOINER may be used to prevent joining, as in the Persian (Farsi) plural suffix or Ottoman Turkish vowels.

Ligature Classes. Certain types of ligatures are obligatory in Arabic script regardless of font design. Many other optional ligatures are possible, depending on font design. Since they are optional, those ligatures are not covered.

For the purpose of describing the obligatory Arabic ligatures, certain Unicode characters fall into the following classes (see the end of this block description for a complete list):

Alef-types: MADDAH-ON-ALEF, HAMZAH ON ALEF ...

Lam-types: LAM, LAM WITH SMALL V, LAM WITH DOT ABOVE ...

These two classes are designated below as *ALEF* and *LAM*, respectively.

Ligature Rules. The following rules describe the formation of ligatures. They are applied after the preceding joining rules. Like the joining rules just discussed, the following rules describe ligature behavior of Arabic letters in terms of their display (visual) order.

In the following rules, if *X* and *Y* refer to characters, then various glyph types representing combinations of these characters are referred to as as shown in Table 6-5.

Table 6-5. Ligature Notation

Symbol	Description
$(X.Y)_n$	Nominal ligature glyph form representing a combination of an X_r form and a Y_l form.
$(X.Y)_r$	Right-joining ligature glyph form representing a combination of an X_r form and a Y_m form.
$(X.Y)_l$	Left-joining ligature glyph form representing a combination of an X_m form and a Y_l form.
$(X.Y)_m$	Dual-joining (medial) ligature glyph form representing a combination of an X_m form and a Y_m form.

R1 ***Transparent characters do not affect the ligating behavior of base (non-transparent) characters. For example:***

ALEF.R + FATHAH.N + LAM.L ➞ LAM-ALEF.N + FATHAH.N

R2 ***Any sequence with $ALEF_r$ on the left and LAM_m on the right will form the ligature $(ALEF.LAM)_l$. For example:***

ـا + ـلـ ➞ ـلا (not ـلـا)

R3 ***Any sequence with*** *$ALEF_r$* ***on the left and*** *LAM_l* ***on the right will form the ligature*** *$(ALEF.LAM)_n$.* ***For example:***

ﺎ + ﻟ ➡ ﻻ (not ﺎﻟ)

➡ From the perspective of logical (or reading) order, the preceding *(ALEF.LAM)* ligature forms are referred to as LAM-ALEF forms. The difference is due to the use of visual order rather than logical order to state ligature rules.

Optional Features. There are many other ligatures and contextual forms that are optional—depending on the font and application—such as the following:

ﳎ, ﳍ, ﲜ, ﳉ, ﲏ

In addition, the context-sensitive placement of non-spacing vowels such as FATHA can greatly improve the appearance of Arabic text.

Arabic Character Joining Types. The Tables 6-6, 6-7, 6-8, and 6-9 provide a detailed list of the Arabic characters that are either right-joining or dual-joining. All other Arabic characters (aside from TATWEEL) are non-joining, including U+06D5 ARABIC LETTER AE. For brevity in the names, the words TWO, THREE, and FOUR are abbreviated using digits.

Most of the extended Arabic characters are merely variations on the basic Arabic shapes, with additional or different marks. For compatibility, many precomposed forms are included.

In some cases there are characters that occur only at the end of words in correct spelling; these are called *trailing characters*. Examples include TEH MARBUTA, ALEF MAQSURAH, and DAMMATAN. When trailing characters are joining (such as TEH MARBUTA), they are classed as right-joining (even when similarly-shaped characters are dual-joining). When trailing characters do not join or cause joining (such as DAMMATAN), they are classed as transparent, which treats all combining marks similarly.

NOTE. In the case of U+0647 HEH, the glyph HEH_l is also shown in the code chart box. This is often done to reduce the chance of misidentifying HEH as U+0665 ARABIC INDIC DIGIT FIVE, which has a very similar shape. The nominal form of HEH is the isolate form, which looks like U+06D5 ARABIC LETTER AE. In the case of U+06C1 HEH GOAL, the nominal form is not even listed; it also resembles ARABIC LETTER AE.

The characters in these tables are grouped by shape and not by standard Arabic alphabetical order.

Table 6-6. Dual-Joining Arabic Characters

Group	CHAR .N	CHAR .R	CHAR .M	CHAR .L	Other Characters with Similar Shaping Behavior
BAA	ب	ﺐ	ﺒ	ﺑ	TAA, THAA, TAA WITH SMALL TAH, TAA WITH 2 DOTS VERTICAL ABOVE, BAA WITH 2 DOTS VERTICAL BELOW, TAA WITH RING, TAA WITH 3 DOTS ABOVE DOWNWARD, TAA WITH 3 DOTS BELOW, TAA WITH 4 DOTS ABOVE, BAA WITH 4 DOTS BELOW
NOON	ن	ﻦ	ﻨ	ﻧ	DOTLESS NOON, DOTLESS NOON WITH SMALL TAH, NOON WITH RING, NOON WITH 3 DOTS ABOVE

Table 6-6. Dual-Joining Arabic Characters (Continued)

Group	CHAR .N	CHAR .R	CHAR .M	CHAR .L	Other Characters with Similar Shaping Behavior
YA	ي	ـي	ـيـ	يـ	HIGH HAMZAH YA, HAMZAH ON YA, DOTLESS YEH, YA WITH SMALL V, YA WITH 2 DOTS VERTICAL BELOW, YA WITH 3 DOTS BELOW
HAA	ج	ـج	ـحـ	حـ	JEEM, KHAA, HAMZAH ON HAA, HAA WITH 2 DOTS VERTICAL ABOVE, HAA WITH MIDDLE 2 DOTS, HAA WITH MIDDLE 2 DOTS VERTICAL, HAA WITH 3 DOTS ABOVE, HAA WITH MIDDLE 3 DOTS DOWNWARD, HAA WITH MIDDLE 4 DOTS
SEEN	س	ـس	ـشـ	سـ	
SAD	ص	ـص	ـصـ	صـ	DAD, SAD WITH 2 DOTS BELOW, SAD WITH 3 DOTS ABOVE
TAH	ط	ـط	ـطـ	طـ	DHAH, TAH WITH 3 DOTS ABOVE
AIN	ع	ـع	ـعـ	عـ	GHAIN, AIN WITH 3 DOTS ABOVE
FA	ڡ	ـڡ	ـفـ	فـ	DOTLESS FA, FAH WITH DOT MOVED BELOW, FA WITH DOT BELOW, FA WITH 3 DOTS ABOVE, FA WITH 3 DOTS BELOW, FA WITH 4 DOTS ABOVE
QAF	ق	ـق	ـقـ	قـ	QAF WITH DOT ABOVE, QAF WITH 3 DOTS ABOVE
MEEM	م	ـم	ـمـ	مـ	
KNOTTED HA	ہ	ـہ	ـهـ | ـہـ	ھـ	
HA	ہ	ـہ	ـهـ | ـہـ	هـ	
HA GOAL	ہ	ـہ	ـهـ | ـہـ	هـ	HA GOAL, HAMZAH ON HA GOAL
CAF	ك	ـك	ـکـ	کـ	CAF WITH DOT ABOVE, CAF WITH 3 DOTS ABOVE, CAF WITH 3 DOTS BELOW
SWASH CAF	ڪ	ـڪ	ـڪـ	ڪـ	
GAF	گ	ـگ	ـگـ	گـ	OPEN CAF, CAF WITH RING, GAF WITH RING, GAF WITH 2 DOTS ABOVE, GAF WITH 2 DOTS BELOW, GAF WITH 2 DOTS VERTICAL BELOW, GAF WITH 3 DOTS ABOVE
LAM	ل	ـل	ـلـ	لـ	LAM WITH SMALL V, LAM WITH DOT ABOVE, LAM WITH 3 DOTS ABOVE

Table 6-7. Right-Joining Arabic Characters

Group	CHAR.N	CHAR.R	Other Characters with Similar Shaping Behavior
ALEF	ا	ـا	ALEF, HAMZAH ON ALEF, MADDAH ON ALEF, HAMZAH UNDER ALEF, WAVY HAMZAH ON ALEF, HIGH HAMZAH ALEF
WAW	و	ـو	HAMZAH ON WAW, HAMZAH ON WAW, HIGH HAMZAH WAW, HIGH HAMZAH WAW WITH DAMMAH, WAW WITH RING, WAW WITH BAR, WAW WITH SMALL V, WAW WITH DAMMAH, WAW WITH ALEF ABOVE, WAW WITH INVERTED SMALL V, WAW WITH 2 DOTS ABOVE, WAW WITH 3 DOTS ABOVE
DAL	د	ـد	THAL, DAL WITH SMALL TAH, DALL WITH RING, DALL WITH DOT BELOW, DAL WITH DOT BELOW AND SMALL TAH, DAL WITH 2 DOTS, DAL WITH 2 DOTS BELOW, DALL WITH 3 DOTS ABOVE, DALL WITH 3 DOTS ABOVE DOWNWARD, DAL WITH 4 DOTS ABOVE,
RA	ر	ـر	ZAIN, RA WITH SMALL TAH, RA WITH SMALL V, RA WITH RING, RA WITH DOT BELOW, RA WITH SMALL V BELOW, RA WITH DOT BELOW AND DOT ABOVE, RA WITH 2 DOTS ABOVE, RA WITH 3 DOTS ABOVE, RA WITH 4 DOTS ABOVE
TAA MARBUTAH	ة	ـة	
TAA MARBUTAH GOAL	ۃ	ـۃ	HAMZAH ON HA
ALEF MAQSURAH	ى	ـى	YA WITH TAIL
YA BAREE	ے	ـے	HAMZAH ON YA BARREE

Table 6-8. Other Arabic Character Joining Classes

Class	Members
Link-causing	ZERO WIDTH JOINER, TATWEEL
Non-linking	ZERO WIDTH NON-JOINER, and all spacing characters (other than those mentioned above) are non-linking, including: HAMZAH, HIGH HAMZAH, HAMZAT WASL ON ALEF, spaces, digits, punctuation, non-Arabic letters, and so on).
Transparent	All combining marks and format marks are irrelevant, including: FATHATAN, DAMMATAN, FATHAH, DAMMAH, KASRAH, SHADDAH, SUKUN, ALEF ABOVE, RIGHT-LEFT MARK, and so on.

Table 6-9. Indexed Arabic Character Joining Classes

Unic.	Name	Link	Link Group
0622	MADDAH ON ALEF	R	ALEF
0623	HAMZAH ON ALEF	R	ALEF
0624	HAMZAH ON WAW	R	WAW
0625	HAMZAH UNDER ALEF	R	ALEF
0626	HAMZAH ON YA	D	YA
0627	ALEF	R	ALEF
0628	BAA	D	BAA
0629	TAA MARBUTAH	R	TAA MARBUTAH
062A	TAA	D	BAA
062B	THAA	D	BAA
062C	JEEM	D	HAA

Table 6-9. Indexed Arabic Character Joining Classes

Unic.	Name	Link	Link Group
062D	HAA	D	HAA
062E	KHAA	D	HAA
062F	DAL	R	DAL
0630	THAL	R	DAL
0631	RA	R	RA
0632	ZAIN	R	RA
0633	SEEN	D	SEEN
0634	SHEEN	D	SEEN
0635	SAD	D	SAD
0636	DAD	D	SAD
0637	TAH	D	TAH
0638	DHAH	D	TAH
0639	AIN	D	AIN
063A	GHAIN	D	AIN
0640	TATWEEL	C	<no shaping>
0641	FA	D	FA
0642	QAF	D	QAF
0643	CAF	D	CAF
0644	LAM	D	LAM
0645	MEEM	D	MEEM
0646	NOON	D	NOON
0647	HA	D	HA
0648	WAW	R	WAW
0649	ALEF MAQSURAH	R	ALEF MAQSURAH
064A	YA	D	YA
0671	HAMZAT WASL ON ALEF	U	<no shaping>
0672	WAVY HAMZAH ON ALEF	R	ALEF
0673	WAVY HAMZAH UNDER ALEF	R	ALEF
0674	HIGH HAMZAH	U	<no shaping>
0675	HIGH HAMZAH ALEF	R	ALEF
0676	HIGH HAMZAH WAW	R	WAW
0677	HIGH HAMZAH WAW WITH DAMMAH	R	WAW
0678	HIGH HAMZAH YA	D	YA
0679	TAA WITH SMALL TAH	D	BAA
067A	TAA WITH 2 DOTS VERTICAL ABOVE	D	BAA
067B	BAA WITH 2 DOTS VERTICAL BELOW	D	BAA
067C	TAA WITH RING	D	BAA
067D	TAA WITH 3 DOTS ABOVE DOWNWARD	D	BAA
067E	TAA WITH 3 DOTS BELOW	D	BAA
067F	TAA WITH 4 DOTS ABOVE	D	BAA
0680	BAA WITH 4 DOTS BELOW	D	BAA
0681	HAMZAH ON HAA	D	HAA
0682	HAA WITH 2 DOTS VERTICAL ABOVE	D	HAA
0683	HAA WITH MIDDLE 2 DOTS	D	HAA
0684	HAA WITH MIDDLE 2 DOTS VERTICAL	D	HAA
0685	HAA WITH 3 DOTS ABOVE	D	HAA
0686	HAA WITH MIDDLE 3 DOTS DOWNWARD	D	HAA
0687	HAA WITH MIDDLE 4 DOTS	D	HAA
0688	DAL WITH SMALL TAH	R	DAL
0689	DAL WITH RING	R	DAL
068A	DAL WITH DOT BELOW	R	DAL
068B	DAL WITH DOT BELOW AND SMALL TAH	R	DAL
068C	DAL WITH 2 DOTS ABOVE	R	DAL
068D	DAL WITH 2 DOTS BELOW	R	DAL
068E	DAL WITH 3 DOTS ABOVE	R	DAL
068F	DAL WITH 3 DOTS ABOVE DOWNWARD	R	DAL
0690	DAL WITH 4 DOTS ABOVE	R	DAL
0691	RA WITH SMALL TAH	R	RA
0692	RA WITH SMALL V	R	RA
0693	RA WITH RING	R	RA
0694	RA WITH DOT BELOW	R	RA

Table 6-9. Indexed Arabic Character Joining Classes

Unic.	Name	Link	Link Group
0695	RA WITH SMALL V BELOW	R	RA
0696	RA WITH DOT BELOW AND DOT ABOVE	R	RA
0697	RA WITH 2 DOTS ABOVE	R	RA
0698	RA WITH 3 DOTS ABOVE	R	RA
0699	RA WITH 4 DOTS ABOVE	R	RA
069A	SEEN WITH DOT BELOW AND DOT ABOVE	D	SEEN
069B	SEEN WITH 3 DOTS BELOW	D	SEEN
069C	SEEN WITH 3 DOTS BELOW AND 3 DOTS ABOVE	D	SEEN
069D	SAD WITH 2 DOTS BELOW	D	SAD
069E	SAD WITH 3 DOTS ABOVE	D	SAD
069F	TAH WITH 3 DOTS ABOVE	D	TAH
06A0	AIN WITH 3 DOTS ABOVE	D	AIN
06A1	DOTLESS FA	D	FA
06A2	FA WITH DOT MOVED BELOW	D	FA
06A3	FA WITH DOT BELOW	D	FA
06A4	FA WITH 3 DOTS ABOVE	D	FA
06A5	FA WITH 3 DOTS BELOW	D	FA
06A6	FA WITH 4 DOTS ABOVE	D	FA
06A7	QAF WITH DOT ABOVE	D	QAF
06A8	QAF WITH 3 DOTS ABOVE	D	QAF
06A9	OPEN CAF	D	GAF
06AA	SWASH CAF	D	SWASH CAF
06AB	CAF WITH RING	D	GAF
06AC	CAF WITH DOT ABOVE	D	CAF
06AD	CAF WITH 3 DOTS ABOVE	D	CAF
06AE	CAF WITH 3 DOTS BELOW	D	CAF
06AF	GAF	D	GAF
06B0	GAF WITH RING	D	GAF
06B1	GAF WITH 2 DOTS ABOVE	D	GAF
06B2	GAF WITH 2 DOTS BELOW	D	GAF
06B3	GAF WITH 2 DOTS VERTICAL BELOW	D	GAF
06B4	GAF WITH 3 DOTS ABOVE	D	GAF
06B5	LAM WITH SMALL V	D	LAM
06B6	LAM WITH DOT ABOVE	D	LAM
06B7	LAM WITH 3 DOTS ABOVE	D	LAM
06BA	DOTLESS NOON	D	NOON
06BB	DOTLESS NOON WITH SMALL TAH	D	NOON
06BC	NOON WITH RING	D	NOON
06BD	NOON WITH 3 DOTS ABOVE	D	NOON
06BE	KNOTTED HA	D	KNOTTED HA
06C0	HAMZAH ON HA	R	TAA MARBUTAH
06C1	HA GOAL	D	HA GOAL
06C2	HAMZAH ON HA GOAL	R	HAMZAH ON HA GOAL
06C3	TAA MARBUTAH GOAL	R	HAMZAH ON HA GOAL
06C4	WAW WITH RING	R	WAW
06C5	WAW WITH BAR	R	WAW
06C6	WAW WITH SMALL V	R	WAW
06C7	WAW WITH DAMMAH	R	WAW
06C8	WAW WITH ALEF ABOVE	R	WAW
06C9	WAW WITH INVERTED SMALL V	R	WAW
06CA	WAW WITH 2 DOTS ABOVE	R	WAW
06CB	WAW WITH 3 DOTS ABOVE	R	WAW
06CC	DOTLESS YA	D	YA
06CD	YA WITH TAIL	R	ALEF MAQSURAH
06CE	YA WITH SMALL V	D	YA
06D0	YA WITH 2 DOTS VERTICAL BELOW	D	YA
06D1	YA WITH 3 DOTS BELOW	D	YA
06D2	YA BARREE	R	YA BARREE
06D3	HAMZAH ON YA BARREE	R	YA BARREE
06D5	AE	U	<no shaping>

Encoding Structure. The Arabic block is divided into the following ranges:

U+060C	→	U+061F	Arabic-unique punctuation from 8859-6
U+0621	→	U+064A	Arabic letters and tatweel from 8859-6
U+064B	→	U+0652	Combining characters from 8859-6
U+0660	→	U+0669	Arabic-Indic digits
U+066A	→	U+066D	Arabic punctuation
U+0670			Additional combining character
U+0671	→	U+06D5	Extended Arabic characters
U+06D6	→	U+06ED	Extended Arabic characters (Koranic extensions)
U+06F0	→	U+06F9	Eastern Arabic-Indic digits

Devanagari: U+0900—U+097F

The Devanagari script is used for writing classical Sanskrit and its modern historical derivative, Hindi. Extensions to Devanagari are used to write other related languages of India (such as Marathi) and of Nepal (Nepali). In addition, the Devanagari script is used to write the following languages: Awadhi, Bagheli, Bhatneri, Bhili, Bihari, Braj Bhasha, Chhattisgarhi, Garhwali, Gondi (Betul, Chhindwara, and Mandla dialects), Harauti, Ho, Jaipuri, Kachchhi, Kanauji, Konkani, Kului, Kumaoni, Kurku, Kurukh, Marwari, Mundari, Newari, Palpa, and Santali.

All other Indian scripts, as well as the Sinhala script of Sri Lanka and the Southeast Asian scripts (Thai, Lao, Khmer, and Burmese), are historically connected with the Devanagari script as descendants of the ancient Brahmi script, and the entire family of scripts shares a large number of structural features.

The principles of the Indian scripts are covered in some detail in this introduction to the Devanagari script. The remaining introductions to the Indian scripts are abbreviated but highlight any differences from Devanagari where appropriate.

Standards. The Devanagari block of the Unicode Standard is based on ISCII-1988 (Indian Standard Code for Information Interchange). The ISCII standard of 1988 differs from and is an update of earlier ISCII standards issued in 1983 and in 1986.

The Unicode Standard encodes Devanagari characters in the same relative position as those coded in positions A0-$F4_{16}$ in the ISCII-1988 standard. The same character code layout is followed for eight other Indian scripts in the Unicode Standard: Bengali, Gurmukhi, Gujarati, Oriya, Tamil, Telugu, Kannada, and Malayalam. This parallel code layout emphasizes the structural similarities of the Brahmi scripts and follows the stated intention of the Indian coding standards to enable one-to-one mappings between analogous coding positions in different scripts in the family. Sinhala, Thai, Lao, Khmer, and Burmese depart to a greater extent from the Devanagari structural pattern, so the Unicode Standard does not attempt to provide any direct mappings for these scripts to the Devanagari order.

In November 1991, at the time the Unicode Standard, Version 1.0, was published, the Bureau of Indian Standards published a new version of ISCII in Indian Standard (IS) 13194:1991. This new version partially modified the layout and repertoire of the ISCII-1988 standard. Because of these events, the Unicode Standard does not precisely follow the layout of the current version of ISCII. Nevertheless, the Unicode Standard remains a superset of the ISCII-1991 repertoire except for a number of new Vedic extension characters defined in IS 13194:1991 *Annex G—Extended Character Set for Vedic.* Modern, non-Vedic texts encoded with ISCII-1991 may be automatically converted to Unicode code values and back to their original encoding without loss of information.

Encoding Principles. The writing systems that employ Devanagari and other Indian scripts constitute a cross between syllabic writing systems and phonemic writing systems (alphabets). The effective unit of these writing systems is the orthographic syllable, consisting of a consonant and vowel (*CV*) core and, optionally, one or more preceding consonants, with a canonical structure of ((*C*)*C*)*CV*. The orthographic syllable need not correspond exactly with a phonological syllable, especially when a consonant cluster is involved, but the writing system is built on phonological principles and tends to correspond quite closely to pronunciation.

The orthographic syllable is built up of alphabetic pieces, the actual letters of the Devanagari script. These consist of three distinct character types: consonant letters, independent vowels, and dependent vowel signs. In a text sequence, these characters are stored in logical (phonetic) order.

Rendering Devanagari Characters. Devanagari characters, like characters from many other scripts, can combine or change shape depending on their context. A character's appearance is affected by its ordering with respect to other characters, the font used to render the character, and the application or system environment. These variables can cause the appearance of Devanagari characters to be different from their nominal glyphs (used in the code charts).

Additionally, a few Devanagari characters cause a change in the order of the displayed characters. This reordering is not commonly seen in non-Indic scripts and occurs independently of any bidirectional character reordering that might be required.

Consonant Letters. The consonant letters each represent a single consonantal sound but also have the peculiarity of having an *inherent vowel*, generally the short vowel /a/ in Devanagari and the other Indian scripts. Thus, U+0915 DEVANAGARI LETTER KA represents not just /k/ but /ka/. In the presence of a dependent vowel, however, the inherent vowel associated with a consonant letter is overridden by the dependent vowel.

Consonant letters may also be rendered as *half-forms*, which are presentation forms used to depict the initial consonant in consonant clusters. These half-consonant forms do not have an inherent vowel. Their rendered forms in Devanagari often resemble the full consonant but are missing the vertical stem, which marks a syllabic core. (The stem glyph is graphically and historically related to the sign denoting the inherent /a/ vowel.)

Some Devanagari consonant letters are depicted with alternate presentation forms whose choice depends upon neighboring consonants. This is especially true of U+0930 DEVANAGARI LETTER RA, which has numerous different forms, both as the initial and as the final element of a consonant cluster. Only the nominal forms rather than the contextual alternates are depicted in the code chart. In certain cases, however, more than one nominal form is depicted for a single character, where a common stylistic alternate of a nominal form exists.

The traditional Sanskrit/Devanagari alphabetic encoding order for consonants follows articulatory phonetic principles, starting with velar consonants and moving forward to bilabial consonants, followed by liquids and then fricatives. ISCII and the Unicode Standard both observe this traditional order.

Independent Vowel Letters. The independent vowels in Devanagari are letters that stand on their own. The writing system treats independent vowels as orthographic CV syllables in which the consonant is null. The independent vowel letters are used to write syllables which start with a vowel.

Dependent Vowel Signs (Matras). The dependent vowels serve as the common manner of writing non-inherent vowels and are generally referred to as *vowel signs*, or as *matras* in Sanskrit. The dependent vowels do not stand alone; rather, they are visibly depicted in combination with a base letterform. A single consonant, or a consonant cluster, may have a dependent vowel applied to it to indicate the vowel quality of the syllable, when it is different from the inherent vowel. Explicit appearance of a dependent vowel in a syllable overrides the inherent vowel of a single consonant letter.

The greatest variation among different Indian scripts is found in the way that the dependent vowels are applied to base letterforms. Devanagari has a collection of non-spacing dependent vowel signs that may appear above or below a consonant letter, as well as spacing dependent vowel signs that may occur to the right or to the left of a consonant letter or consonant cluster. Other Indian scripts generally have one or more of these forms, but what is a non-spacing mark in one script may be a spacing mark in another. Also, some of the Indian scripts have single dependent vowels that are indicated by two or more glyph components—and those glyph components may *surround* a consonant letter both to the left and right or may occur both above and below it.

The Devanagari script has only one character denoting a left-side dependent vowel sign: U+093F DEVANAGARI VOWEL SIGN I. Other Indian scripts either have no such vowel signs (Telugu and Kannada) or as many as three of these signs (Bengali, Tamil, and Malayalam).

A one-to-one correspondence exists between the independent vowels and the dependent vowel signs. Independent vowels are sometimes represented by a sequence consisting of the independent form of the vowel /a/ followed by a dependent vowel sign. For example, Figure 6-10 illustrates this relationship (see the notation formally described in the "Rules for Rendering" later in this section).

Figure 6-10. Dependent versus Independent Vowels

/a/ + Dependent Vowel		Independent Vowel
$A_n + I_{lvs} \rightarrow I_{lvs} + A_n$	≈	I_n
अ + ि → िअ	≈	इ
$A_n + U_{vs} \rightarrow A_n + U_{vs}$	≈	U_n
अ + ु → अु	≈	उ

The combination of the independent form of the default vowel /a/ (in the Devanagari script, U+0905 DEVANAGARI LETTER A) with a dependent vowel sign may be viewed as an alternative spelling of the phonetic information normally represented by an isolated independent vowel form. However, these two representations should not be considered equivalent for the purposes of rendering. Higher-level text processes may choose to consider these alternative spellings equivalent in terms of information content; however, such an equivalence is not stipulated by this standard.

Virama. Devanagari and other Indian scripts employ a sign known as the *virama*, *halant*, or vowel omission sign. A *virama* sign (for example, U+094D DEVANAGARI SIGN VIRAMA) nominally serves to cancel (or kill) the inherent vowel of the consonant to which it is applied. The *virama* functions as a combining character, its shape varying from script to script. When a consonant has lost its inherent vowel by the application of *virama*, it is known as a *dead consonant*; in contrast, a *live consonant* is a consonant that retains its inherent vowel or is written with an explicit dependent vowel sign. In the Unicode Standard, a dead consonant is defined as a sequence consisting of a consonant letter followed by a *virama*. The default rendering for a dead consonant is to position the *virama* as a combining mark bound to the consonant letterform.

For example, if C_n denotes the nominal form of consonant C, and C_d denotes the dead consonant form, then a dead consonant is encoded as shown in Figure 6-11

Figure 6-11. Dead Consonants

$$TA_n + VIRAMA_n \rightarrow TA_d$$

त + ् → त्

Consonant Conjuncts. The Indian scripts are noted for a large number of consonant conjunct forms that serve as orthographic abbreviations (ligatures) of two or more adjacent letterforms. This abbreviation takes place only in the context of a *consonant cluster.* An orthographic consonant cluster is defined as a sequence of characters which represent one or more dead consonants (denoted C_d) followed by a normal, *live* consonant letter (denoted C_l) or an independent vowel letter.

Under normal circumstances, a consonant cluster is depicted with a conjunct glyph if such a glyph is available in the current font(s). In the absence of a conjunct glyph, the one or more dead consonants that form part of the cluster are depicted using half-form glyphs; or, in the absence of half-form glyphs, the dead consonants are depicted using the nominal consonant forms combined with visible *virama* signs (see Figure 6-12).

Figure 6-12. Conjunct Formations

(1) $GA_d + GHA_l \rightarrow GA_h + GHA_n$

ग् + घ → ग्घ

(2) $KA_d + KA_l \rightarrow K.KA_n$

क् + क → क्क

(3) $KA_d + SSHA_l \rightarrow K.SSHA_n$

क् + ष → क्ष

(4) $RA_d + RI_n \rightarrow RI_n + RA_{sup}$

र् + ऋ → र्ऋ

Anumber of types of conjunct formations appear in these examples: (1) a half-form of *GA* in its combination with the full form of *GHA*; (2) a vertical conjunct *K.KA*; (3) a fully ligated conjunct *K.SSHA,* in which the components are no longer distinct; and (4) a rare conjunct formed with an independent vowel letter, in this case the vowel letter *RI* (also known as *VOCALIC R*). Note that in example (4), the dead consonant RA_d is depicted with the non-spacing combining mark RA_{sup} (*repha*).

A well-designed Indian script font may contain hundreds of conjunct glyphs, but they are not encoded as Unicode characters because they are the result of ligation of distinct letters. Indian script rendering software must be able to map appropriate combinations of characters in context to the appropriate conjunct glyphs in fonts. (See "Rendering of Devanagari Script" later in this section.)

When an independent vowel appears as the terminal element of a consonant cluster, as in example (4) in Figure 6-12, the independent vowel should not be depicted as a dependent vowel sign, but as an independent vowel letterform.

Explicit Virama. Normally a *virama* character serves to create dead consonants which are, in turn, combined with subsequent consonants in order to form conjuncts. This behavior usually results in a *virama* sign not being depicted visually. Occasionally, however, this default behavior is not desired when a dead consonant should be excluded from conjunct formation, in which case the *virama* sign is visibly rendered. In order to accomplish this, the Unicode Standard adopts the convention of placing the character U+200C ZERO WIDTH NON-JOINER immediately after the encoded dead consonant that is to be excluded from conjunct formation. In this case, the *virama* sign is always depicted as appropriate for the consonant to which it is attached.

For example, in Figure 6-13, the use of ZERO WIDTH NON-JOINER prevents the default formation of the conjunct form क्ष ($K.SSHA_n$).

Explicit Half-Consonants. When a dead consonant participates in forming a conjunct, the dead consonant form is often absorbed into the conjunct form, such that it is no longer distinctly visible. In other contexts, however, the dead consonant may remain visible as a *half-consonant form.* In general, a half-consonant form is distinguished from the nominal

Figure 6-13. Preventing Conjunct Forms

$$KA_d + ZWNJ + SSHA_l \rightarrow KA_d + SSHA_n$$

क् + ZWNJ + ष → क्‌ष

consonant form by the loss of its inherent vowel stem, a vertical stem appearing to the right-side of the consonant form. In other cases, the vertical stem remains but some part of its right-side geometry is missing.

In certain cases, it is desirable to prevent a dead consonant from full conjunct formation yet still not appear with an explicit *virama*. In these cases, the half-form of the consonant is used. In order to explicitly encode a half consonant form, the Unicode Standard adopts the convention of placing the character U+200D ZERO WIDTH JOINER immediately after the encoded dead consonant. The ZERO WIDTH JOINER denotes a non-visible letter that presents linking or cursive joining behavior on either side (that is, to the previous or following letter). Therefore, in the present context, the ZERO WIDTH JOINER may be considered to present a context to which a preceding dead consonant may join in order to create the half-form of the consonant.

For example, if C_h denotes the half-form glyph of consonant C, then a half consonant form is encoded as shown in Figure 6-14.

Figure 6-14. Half-Consonants

$$KA_d + ZWJ + SSHA_l \rightarrow KA_h + SSHA_n$$

क् + ZWJ + ष → क्‍ष

➥ In the absence of the ZERO WIDTH JOINER, this sequence would normally produce the full conjunct form क्ष ($K.SSHA_n$).

This encoding of half consonant forms also applies in the absence of a base letterform; that is, this technique may also be used to encode independent half-forms, as shown in Figure 6-15.

Figure 6-15. Independent Half-Forms

$$GA_d \; + \; ZWJ \; \rightarrow \; GA_h$$

ग् + ZWJ → ग्‍

Consonant Forms. In summary, each consonant may be encoded such that it denotes a live consonant, a dead consonant that may be absorbed into a conjunct, or the half-form of a dead consonant (see Figure 6-16).

Rules for Rendering. The following provides more formal and complete rules for minimal rendering of Devanagari as part of a plain text sequence. It describes the mapping between Unicode characters and the glyphs in a Devanagari font. It also describes the combining and ordering of those glyphs.

Figure 6-16. Consonant Forms

क	→ क	KA_l
क + ◌्	→ क्	KA_d
क + ◌् + ZWJ	→ क्‍	KA_h

These rules provide minimal requirements for legibly rendering interchanged Devanagari text. As with any script, a more complex procedure can add rendering characteristics, depending on the font and application.

It is important to emphasize that in a font that is capable of rendering Devanagari, the set of glyphs is greater than the number of Devanagari Unicode characters.

Notation. In the next set of rules, the following notation applies:

C_n	Nominal glyph form of consonant *C* as it appears in the code charts.
C_l	A live consonant, depicted identically to C_n.
C_d	Glyph depicting the dead consonant form of consonant *C*.
C_h	Glyph depicting the half consonant form of consonant *C*.
L_n	Nominal glyph form of a conjunct ligature consisting of two or more component consonants. A conjunct ligature composed of two consonants *X* and *Y* is also denoted $X.Y_n$.
RA_{sup}	A non-spacing combining mark glyph form of the U+0930 DEVANAGARI LETTER RA positioned above or attached to the upper part of a base glyph form. This form is also known as *REPHA*.
RA_{sub}	A non-spacing combining mark glyph form of the U+0930 DEVANAGARI LETTER RA positioned below or attached to the lower part of a base glyph form.
V_{vs}	Glyph depicting the dependent vowel sign form of a vowel *V*.
$VIRAMA_n$	The nominal glyph form non-spacing combining mark depicting U+094D DEVANAGARI SIGN VIRAMA.

➥ A *virama* character is not always depicted; when it is depicted, it adopts this non-spacing mark form.

Dead Consonant Rule. The following rule logically precedes the application of any other rule in order to form a dead consonant. Once formed, a dead consonant may be subject to other rules described next .

R1 ***When a consonant C_n precedes a $VIRAMA_n$, it is considered to be a dead consonant C_d. A consonant C_n that does not precede $VIRAMA_n$ is considered to be a live consonant C_l.***

$$TA_n + VIRAMA_n \rightarrow TA_d$$

त + ् → त्

Consonant RA Rules. The character U+0930 DEVANAGARI LETTER RA takes one of a number of visual forms depending on its context in a consonant cluster. By default, this letter is depicted with its nominal glyph form (as shown in the code charts); however, in two contexts, it is depicted using a non-spacing glyph form that combines with a base letterform.

R2 ***If the dead consonant RA_d precedes either a consonant or an independent vowel, then it is replaced by the superscript non-spacing mark RA_{sup}, which is positioned so that it applies to the logically subsequent element in the memory representation.***

$$RA_d + KA_l \rightarrow KA_l + RA_{sup}$$ *Displayed Output*

र् + क → क + ◌र्‍ → र्क

$$RA^1_d + RA^2_d \rightarrow RA^2_d + RA^1_{sup}$$

र् + र् → र् + ◌र्‍ → र्र्

R3 ***If the superscript mark RA_{sup} is to be applied to a dead consonant and that dead consonant is combined with another consonant to form a conjunct ligature, then the mark is positioned so that it applies to the conjunct ligature form as a whole.***

$$RA_d + JA_d + NYA_l \rightarrow J.NYA_n + RA_{sup}$$ *Displayed Output*

र् + ज् + ञ → ज्ञ + ◌र्‍ → र्ज्ञ

R4 ***If the superscript mark RA_{sup} is to be applied to a dead consonant that is subsequently replaced by its half-consonant form, then the mark is positioned so that it applies to the form that serves as the base of the consonant cluster.***

$$RA_d + GA_d + GHA_l \rightarrow GA_h + GHA_l + RA_{sup}$$ *Displayed Output*

र् + ग् + घ → ग + घ + ◌र्‍ → र्ग्घ

R5 ***If the dead consonant RA_d precedes*** ZERO WIDTH JOINER, ***then the half consonant form RA_h, known as the eyelash-RA, is used instead of RA_{sup}. This form of RA is commonly used in writing certain languages such as Marathi.***

$$RA_d + ZWJ \rightarrow RA_h$$

र् + ZWJ → ऱ्‍

R6 ***Except for the dead consonant RA_d, when a dead consonant C_d precedes the live consonant RA_l, then C_d is replaced with its nominal form C_n, and RA is replaced***

by the subscript non-spacing mark RA_{sub}, which is positioned so that it applies to C_n.

$$\text{THA}_d + \text{RA}_l \rightarrow \text{THA}_n + \text{RA}_{sub} \quad \textit{Displayed Output}$$

ठ् + र → ठ + ◌्र → ठ्र

R7 ***For certain consonants, the mark RA_{sub} may graphically combine with the consonant to form a conjunct ligature form. These combinations, such as the one shown here, are further addressed by the Ligature Rules described shortly.***

$$\text{PHA}_d + \text{RA}_l \rightarrow \text{PHA}_n + \text{RA}_{sub} \quad \textit{Displayed Output}$$

फ् + र → फ + ◌्र → फ्र

R8 ***If a dead consonant (other than RA_d) precedes RA_d, then the substitution of RA for RA_{sub} is performed as described above; however, the VIRAMA that formed RA_d remains so as to form a dead consonant conjunct form.***

$$\text{TA}_d + \text{RA}_d \rightarrow \text{TA}_n + \text{RA}_{sub} + \text{VIRAMA}_n \rightarrow \text{T.RA}_d$$

त् + र् → त + ◌्र + ◌् → त्र्

A dead consonant conjunct form that contains an absorbed RA_d may subsequently combine to form a multipart conjunct form.

$$\text{T.RA}_d + \text{YA}_l \rightarrow \text{T.R.YA}_n$$

त्र् + य → त्र्य

Modifier Mark Rules. In addition to vowel signs, three other types of combining marks may be applied to a component of an orthographic syllable or to the syllable as a whole. These three types of marks are *nukta*, *bindus*, and *svaras*.

R9 ***The nukta sign, which modifies a consonant form, is placed immediately after the consonant in the memory representation and is attached to that consonant in rendering. If the consonant represents a dead consonant, then NUKTA should precede VIRAMA in the memory representation.***

$$\text{KA}_n + \text{NUKTA}_n + \text{VIRAMA}_n \rightarrow \text{QA}_d$$

क + ◌़ + ◌् → क़्

R10 ***The other modifying marks, bindus and svaras, apply to the orthographic syllable as a whole and should follow (in the memory representation) all other characters that constitute the syllable. In particular, the bindus should follow any vowel signs, and the svaras should come last. The relative placement of these marks is horizontal rather than vertical; the horizontal rendering order may vary according to typographic concerns.***

$$KA_n + AA_{vs} + CANDRABINDU_n$$

क + ◌ा + ◌ँ → काँ

Ligature Rules. Subsequent to the application of the rules just described, a set of rules governing ligature formation apply. The precise application of these rules depends on the availability of glyphs in the current font(s) being used to display the text.

R11 ***If a dead consonant immediately precedes another dead consonant or a live consonant, then the first dead consonant may join the subsequent element to form a two-part conjunct ligature form.***

$JA_d + NYA_l \rightarrow J.NYA_n$ $\quad$ $TTA_d + TTHA_l \rightarrow TT.TTHA_n$

ज् + ञ → ज्ञ $\quad$ ट् + ठ → ट्ठ

R12 ***A conjunct ligature form can itself behave as a dead consonant and enter into further, more complex ligatures.***

$$SA_d + TA_d + RA_n \rightarrow SA_d + T.R.A_n \rightarrow S.T.RA_n$$

स् + त् + र → स् + त्र → स्त्र

A conjunct ligature form can also produce a half-form.

$$K.SSHA_d + YA_l \rightarrow K.SSH_h + YA_n$$

क्ष् + य → क्ष्य

R13 ***If a nominal consonant or conjunct ligature form precedes RA_{sub} as a result of the application of rule R2, then the consonant or ligature form may join with RA_{sub} to form a multipart conjunct ligature (see rule R2 for more information).***

$KA_n + RA_{sub} \rightarrow K.RA_n$ $\quad$ $PHA_n + RA_{sub} \rightarrow PH.RA_n$

क + ◌्र → क्र $\quad$ फ + ◌्र → फ्र

R14 ***In some cases, other combining marks will also combine with a base consonant, either attaching at a non-standard location or changing shape. In minimal rendering there are only two cases, RA_l with U_{vs}*** or ***UU_{vs}.***

$RA_l + U_{vs} \rightarrow RU_n$ $\quad$ $RA_l + UU_{vs} \rightarrow RUU_n$

र + ◌ु → रु $\quad$ र + ◌ू → रू

Memory Representation and Rendering Order. The order for storage of plain text in Devanagari and all other Indian scripts generally follows phonetic order; that is, a CV syllable with a dependent vowel is always encoded as a consonant letter C followed by a vowel sign V in the memory representation. This order is employed by the ISCII standard and corresponds with both the phonetic and keying order of textual data (see Figure 6-17).

Figure 6-17. Rendering Order

Character Order	Glyph Order
KA_n + I_{lvs} →	I_{lvs} + KA_n
क + ि◌ →	कि

Since Devanagari and other Indian scripts have some dependent vowels that must be depicted to the left side of their consonant letter, the software that renders the Indian scripts must be able to reorder elements in mapping from the logical (character) store to the presentational (glyph) rendering. For example, if C_n denotes the nominal form of consonant C and V_{lvs} denotes a left-side dependent vowel sign form of vowel V, then a reordering of glyphs with respect to encoded characters occurs as just shown.

R15 ***When the dependent vowel*** I_{lvs} ***is used to override the inherent vowel of a syllable, it is always written to the extreme left of the orthographic syllable. If the orthographic syllable contains a consonant cluster, then this vowel is always depicted to the left of that cluster. For example:***

$$TA_d + RA_l + I_{lvs} \rightarrow T.RA_n + I_{lvs} \rightarrow I_{lvs} + T.RA_d$$

त् + र + ि◌ → त्र + ि◌ → त्रि

Sample Half Forms. Table 6-10 shows examples of half-consonant forms that are commonly used with the Devanagari script. These forms are glyphs, not characters. These forms may be encoded explicitly using ZERO WIDTH JOINER as shown; in normal conjunct formation, they may be used spontaneously to depict a dead consonant in combination with subsequent consonant forms.

Table 6-10. Sample Half-Forms

क	◌्	ZWJ	क्‍
ख	◌्	ZWJ	ख्‍
ग	◌्	ZWJ	ग्‍
घ	◌्	ZWJ	घ्‍
च	◌्	ZWJ	च्‍
ज	◌्	ZWJ	ज्‍
झ	◌्	ZWJ	झ्‍
ञ	◌्	ZWJ	ञ्‍
ण	◌्	ZWJ	ण्‍
त	◌्	ZWJ	त्‍
थ	◌्	ZWJ	थ्‍
ध	◌्	ZWJ	ध्‍

न	◌्	ZWJ	न्‍
प	◌्	ZWJ	प्‍
फ	◌्	ZWJ	फ्‍
ब	◌्	ZWJ	ब्‍
भ	◌्	ZWJ	भ्‍
म	◌्	ZWJ	म्‍
य	◌्	ZWJ	य्‍
ल	◌्	ZWJ	ल्‍
व	◌्	ZWJ	व्‍
श	◌्	ZWJ	श्‍
ष	◌्	ZWJ	ष्‍
स	◌्	ZWJ	स्‍

Sample Ligatures. Table 6-11 shows examples of conjunct ligature forms that are commonly used with the Devanagari script. These forms are glyphs, not characters. Not every writing system that employs this script uses all of these forms; in particular, many of these forms are used only in writing Sanskrit texts. Furthermore, individual fonts may provide fewer or more ligature forms than are depicted here.

Table 6-11. Sample Ligatures

क	◌्	क	क्क
क	◌्	त	क्त
क	◌्	र	क्र
क	◌्	ष	क्ष
ङ	◌्	क	ङ्क
ङ	◌्	ख	ङ्ख
ङ	◌्	ग	ङ्ग
ङ	◌्	घ	ङ्घ
ञ	◌्	ज	ञ्ज
ज	◌्	ञ	ज्ञ
द	◌्	घ	द्घ
द	◌्	द	द्द
द	◌्	ध	द्ध
द	◌्	ब	द्ब
द	◌्	भ	द्भ
द	◌्	म	द्म
द	◌्	य	द्य
द	◌्	व	द्व
ट	◌्	ट	ट्ट

ट	◌्	ठ	ट्ठ
ठ	◌्	ठ	ठ्ठ
ड	◌्	ग	ड्ग
ड	◌्	ड	ड्ड
ड	◌्	ढ	ड्ढ
त	◌्	त	त्त
त	◌्	र	त्र
न	◌्	न	न्न
फ	◌्	र	फ्र
श	◌्	र	श्र
ह	◌्	म	ह्म
ह	◌्	य	ह्य
ह	◌्	ल	ह्ल
ह	◌्	व	ह्व
ह		◌ृ	हृ
र		◌ु	रु
र		◌ू	रू
स	◌्	त्र	स्त्र

Sample Half Ligature Forms. In addition to half form glyphs of individual consonants, half forms are also used to depict conjunct ligature forms. A sample of such forms is shown in Table 6-12. These forms are glyphs, not characters. These forms may be encoded explicitly using ZERO WIDTH JOINER as shown; in normal conjunct formation, they may be used spontaneously to depict a conjunct ligature in combination with subsequent consonant forms.

Combining Marks. Devanagari and other Indian scripts have a number of combining marks that could be considered diacritic. One class of these, known as *bindus*, is represented by U+0901 DEVANAGARI SIGN CANDRABINDU and U+0902 DEVANAGARI SIGN ANUSVARA. These indicate nasalization or final nasal closure of a syllable. U+093C DEVANAGARI SIGN NUKTA is a true diacritic. It is used to extend the basic set of consonant letters by

Table 6-12. Sample Half-Ligature Forms

क	◌्	ष	◌्	ZWJ	क्ष्‍
ज	◌्	ञ	◌्	ZWJ	ज्ञ्‍
त	◌्	त	◌्	ZWJ	त्त्‍
त	◌्	र	◌्	ZWJ	त्र्‍
श	◌्	र	◌्	ZWJ	श्र्‍

modifying them (with a subscript dot in Devanagari) to create new letters. U+0951→U+0954 are a set of combining marks used in transcription of Sanskrit texts.

Digits. Each Indian script has a distinct set of digits appropriate to that script. These may or may not be used in ordinary text in that script. European digits have displaced the Indian script forms in modern usage in many of the scripts. Some Indian scripts—notably Tamil—lack a distinct digit for zero.

Punctuation and Symbols. U+0964 DEVANAGARI DANDA is similar to full stop. Corresponding forms occur in many other Indian scripts. U+0965 DEVANAGARI DOUBLE DANDA marks the end of a verse in traditional texts.

Many modern languages written in the Devanagari script intersperse punctuation derived from the Latin script. Thus U+002C COMMA and U+002E FULL STOP are freely used in writing Hindi, and the *danda* is usually restricted to more traditional texts.

Encoding Structure. The Unicode Standard organizes the nine principal Indian scripts in blocks of 128 encoding points each. The first six columns in each script are isomorphic with the ISCII-1988 encoding, except that the last eleven positions (U+0955→U+095F in Devanagari, for example), which are unassigned or undefined in ISCII-1988, are used in the Unicode encoding.

The seventh column in each of these scripts, along with the last eleven positions in the sixth column, represent additional character assignments in the Unicode Standard which are matched across all nine scripts. For example, positions U+xx66→U+xx6F or U+xxE6→U+xxEF code the Indic script digits for each script.

The eighth column for each script is reserved for script-specific additions that do not correspond from one Indian script to the next.

The character block for the Devanagari script is divided into the following specific ranges:

U+0901	→	U+0903	Various signs
U+0905	→	U+0914	Independent vowels
U+0915	→	U+0939	Consonants
U+093C	→	U+093D	Various signs
U+093E	→	U+094C	Dependent vowel signs
U+094D			Devanagari *virama*
U+0950	→	U+0954	Various signs
U+0958	→	U+095F	Additional consonants composed with Nukta
U+0960	→	U+0961	Additional independent vowels
U+0962	→	U+0963	Additional dependent vowel signs
U+0964	→	U+0965	Additional punctuation
U+0966	→	U+096F	Devanagari digits
U+0970			Devanagari-specific addition: abbreviation sign

Bengali: U+0980—U+09FF

The Bengali script is a North Indian script closely related to Devanagari. It is used to write the Bengali language primarily in West Bengal state (India) and in the nation of Bangladesh. It is also used to write Assamese in Assam (India) and a number of other minority languages (Daphla, Garo, Hallam, Khasi, Manipuri, Mizo, Naga, Munda, Rian, and Santali) in northeastern India.

Two-Part Vowel Signs. The Bengali script, along with a number of other Indian scripts, makes use of two-part vowel signs; these are vowels in which one half of the vowel is placed on each side of a consonant letter or cluster; for example: U+09CB BENGALI VOWEL SIGN O and U+09CC BENGALI VOWEL SIGN AU. The vowel signs are coded in each case in the position in the charts isomorphic with the corresponding vowel in Devanagari. Hence U+09CC BENGALI VOWEL SIGN AU is isomorphic with U+094C DEVANAGARI VOWEL SIGN AU. In order to provide compatibility with existing implementations of the scripts that use two-part vowel signs, the Unicode Standard explicitly encodes the right half part of these vowel signs; for example, U+09D7 BENGALI AU LENGTH MARK represents the right half part glyph component of U+09CC BENGALI VOWEL SIGN AU.

Special Characters. U+09F2 →U+09F9 are a series of Bengali additions for writing currency and fractions.

Rendering Behavior. For rendering of the Bengali script, see the rules for rendering in the Devanagari block description.

Encoding Structure. The character block for the Bengali script is divided into the following ranges:

U+0980	→	U+09EF	Follow the Devanagari prototype
U+09F0	→	U+09F9	Bengali-specific additions

Gurmukhi: U+0A00—U+0A7F

The Gurmukhi script is a North Indian script historically derived from an older script called Lahnda. It is quite closely related to Devanagari structurally. Gurmukhi is used to write the Punjabi language in the Punjab in India.

Rendering Behavior. For rendering of the Gurmukhi script, see the rules for rendering in the Devanagari block description.

Encoding Structure. The character block for the Gurmukhi script is divided into the following ranges:

U+0A00	→	U+0A6F	Follow the Devanagari prototype
U+0A70	→	U+0A75	Gurmukhi-specific additions: letters, diacritics

Gujarati: U+0A80—U+0AFF

The Gujarati script is a North Indian script closely related to Devanagari. It is most obviously distinguished from Devanagari by not having a horizontal bar for its letterforms, a characteristic of the older Kaithi script to which Gujarati is related. The Gujarati script is used to write the Gujarati language of the Gujarat state in India.

Rendering Behavior. For rendering of the Gujarati script, see the rules for rendering in the Devanagari block description.

Encoding Structure. The block for the Gujarati script is divided into the following ranges:

U+0A80 → U+0AEF Follow the Devanagari prototype

Oriya: U+0B00—U+0B7F

The Oriya script is a North Indian script structurally similar to Devanagari, but with semi-circular lines at the top of most letters instead of the straight horizontal bars of Devanagari. The actual shapes of the letters, particularly for vowel signs, show similarities to Tamil. The Oriya script is used to write the Oriya language, of Orissa state, India, as well as minority languages such as Khondi and Santali.

Special Characters. U+0B57 ORIYA AU LENGTH MARK is provided as an encoding for the right side of the surroundrant vowel U+0B4C ORIYA VOWEL SIGN AU.

Rendering Behavior. For rendering of the Oriya script, see the rules for rendering in the Devanagari block description.

Encoding Structure. The block for the Oriya script is divided into the following ranges:

U+0B00	→	U+0B6F	Follow the Devanagari prototype
U+0B70			Oriya-specific addition

Tamil: U+0B80—U+0BFF

The Tamil script is a South Indian script. South Indian scripts are structurally related to the North Indian scripts, but they are used to write Dravidian languages of southern India and of Sri Lanka, which are genetically unrelated to the North Indian languages such as Hindi, Bengali, and Gujarati. The shapes of letters in the South Indian scripts are generally quite distinct from the shapes of letters in Devanagari and its related scripts. This is partly a result of the fact that the South Indian scripts were originally carved with needles on palm leaves, a technology that apparently favored rounded letter shapes rather than square, block-like shapes.

The Tamil script is used to write the Tamil language of Tamil Nadu state in India as well as minority languages such as Badaga. Tamil is also used in Sri Lanka, Singapore, and parts of Malaysia. The Tamil script has fewer consonants than the other Indian scripts. It also lacks conjunct consonant forms. Instead of conjunct consonant forms, the *virama* (U+0BCD) is normally fully depicted in Tamil text.

Naming Conventions for Mid Vowels. The Unicode character encoding for Tamil uses a distinct set of naming conventions for mid vowels in the South Indian (Dravidian) scripts. These conventions are illustrated by U+0B8E TAMIL LETTER E and U+0B8F TAMIL LETTER EE, to be contrasted with the isomorphic positions in Devanagari: U+090E DEVANAGARI LETTER SHORT E and U+090F DEVANAGARI LETTER E. The Dravidian languages have a regular length distinction in the mid vowels which is not reflected in normal Devanagari. U+090E DEVANAGARI LETTER SHORT E is an addition to Devanagari to enable transcription of the Dravidian short vowel forms. The naming conventions are chosen to best reflect the actual nature of the vowels in question in the Dravidian scripts, as well as in Devanagari and the other North Indian scripts.

Special Characters. U+0BD7 TAMIL AU LENGTH MARK is provided as an encoding for the right side of the surroundrant (or two-part) vowel U+0BCC TAMIL VOWEL SIGN AU.

Rendering of Tamil Script. The South Indic scripts function in much the same way as Devanagari, with the additional feature of two-part vowels. As in the Devanagari example, the words "TAMIL LETTER" and "TAMIL VOWEL SIGN" will be omitted where this does not cause ambiguity.

It is important to emphasize that in a font that is capable of rendering Tamil, the set of glyphs is greater than the number of Tamil characters.

Table 6-13 is a summary of the Tamil letters.

Table 6-13. Tamil Letter Summary

க KA	ங NGA	ச CA	ஜ JA	ஞ NYA	ட TTA	ண NNA	த TA	ந NA	ன NNNA	ப PA	
ம MA	ய YA	ர RA	ற RRA	ல LA	ள LLA	ழ LLLA	வ VA	ஷ SSA	ஸ SA	ஹ HA	
அ A	ஆ AA	இ I	ஈ II	உ U	ஊ UU	எ E	ஏ EE	ஐ AI	ஒ O	ஓ OO	ஔ AU
A	ா AA	ி I	ீ II	ு U	ூ UU	ெ E	ே EE	ை AI	ொ O	ோ OO	ௌ AU
் VIRAMA	ௗ AU LENGTH										

Independent versus Dependent Vowels. As with Devanagari, the dependent vowel signs are not equivalent to a sequence of *virama* + independent vowel. For example:

ண + ி ≠ ண + ் + இ

As in the case of Devanagari, a consonant cluster is any sequence of one or more consonants separated by viramas, possibly terminated with a *virama*.

Two-Part Vowels. Certain Indic vowels consist of two discontiguous elements. As in other cases of discontiguous elements, there are two sequences of Unicode values that can be used to express equivalent spellings. This is similar to the case of letters such as "â", which can either be spelled with "a" followed by non-spacing "^", or spelled with a single Unicode character "â".

ொ (0BCA) ≈ ெ + ா (0BC6 + 0BBE)
ோ (0BCB) ≈ ே + ா (0BC7 + 0BBE)
ௌ (0BCC) ≈ ெ + ௗ (0BC7 + 0BD7)

Note that the ௗ in the third example is *not* U+0BB3 TAMIL LETTER LLA; it is rather U+0BD7 TAMIL AU LENGTH MARK.

If the precomposed forms are used in the memory representation instead of the separate characters, then a similar transformation occurs in the rendering process. The precomposed form on the left is transformed into the two separate forms equivalent to those on the right, which are then subject to vowel reordering, as below. Thus in rendering:

ொ → ெ + ா
ோ → ே + ா
ௌ → ெ + ௗ

Vowel Reordering. As shown in Table 6-14, the following vowels are always reordered in front of the previous consonant cluster, similar to the rendering behavior of the DEVANAGARI VOWEL SIGN I.

ெ (0BC6) ே (0BC7) ை (0BC8)

Table 6-14. Vowel Reordering

Memory Representation			Display
க	ெ	→	கெ
க	ே	→	கே
க	ை	→	கை

The same effect occurs with the results of vowel splitting (see Table 6-15).

Table 6-15. Vowel Splitting and Reordering

Memory Representation				Display
க	◌ொ		→	கொ
க	◌ெ	ா	→	கொ
க	◌ோ		→	கோ
க	◌ே	ா	→	கோ
க	◌ௌ		→	கௌ
க	◌ெ	ள	→	கௌ

In both cases, the ordering of the elements is *unambiguous*: the consonant (cluster) occurs *first* in the memory representation. The vowel ஔ also has two discontinuous parts and can also be composed using the AU LENGTH MARK.

Ligatures. The following examples illustrate the range of ligatures available in Tamil. These changes take place after vowel reordering and vowel splitting. Unlike Devanagari, there are very few conjunct consonants; most ligatures are located between a vowel and a neighboring consonant.

1. Conjunct consonants.

க + ◌் + ஷ → க்ஷ

As with Devanagari, vowel reordering occurs around conjunct consonants. For example:

க + ◌் + ஷ + ◌ெ + ா → க்ஷொ

2. The vowel ா optionally ligates with ண, ன, or ற on its left:

ண + ா → ணா

ன + ா → னா

ற + ா → றா

Since this process takes place after reordering and splitting, the following ligatures may also occur:

Separate Vowels	*Precomposed Vowels*
ண + ◌ெ + ா → ணொ	ண + ◌ொ → ணொ
ண + ◌ே + ா → ணோ	ண + ◌ோ → ணோ
ன + ◌ெ + ா → னொ	ன + ◌ொ → னொ
ன + ◌ே + ா → னோ	ன + ◌ோ → னோ
ற + ◌ெ + ா → றொ	ற + ◌ொ → றொ
ற + ◌ே + ா → றோ	ற + ◌ோ → றோ

3. The vowel signs ி and ீ form ligatures with ட on their left.

ட + ி → டி

ட + ீ → டீ

These vowels often change shape or position slightly in order to link up with the appropriate shape of the consonant on their left:

ல + ி → லி

ல + ீ → லீ

4. The vowel signs ு and ூ typically change form or ligate (see Table 6-16).

Table 6-16. Ligating Vowel Signs

x	*x* + ு	*x* + ூ
க	கு	கூ
ங	ஙு	ஙூ
ச	சு	சூ
ஞ	ஞு	ஞூ
ட	டு	டூ
ண	ணு	ணூ
த	து	தூ
ந	நு	நூ
ன	னு	னூ

x	*x* + ு	*x* + ூ
ப	பு	பூ
ம	மு	மூ
ய	யு	யூ
ர	ரு	ரூ
ற	று	றூ
ல	லு	லூ
ள	ளு	ளூ
ழ	ழு	ழூ
வ	வு	வூ

To the right of ஜ, ஷ, ஸ, ஹ, or க்ஷ, these forms have a spacing form (see Table 6-18).

Figure 6-18. Spacing Forms of Vowels

ஜ + ு → ஜு

ஜ + ூ → ஜூ

5. The vowel sign ◌ை changes to ◌ை to the left of ண, ன, ல, or ள.

◌ை	+	ண	→	ணை
◌ை	+	ன	→	னை
◌ை	+	ல	→	லை
◌ை	+	ள	→	ளை

Remember that this change takes place after the vowel reordering; in the first example, the vowel ◌ை follows ண in the memory representation. After vowel reordering, it is on the left of ண, and thus changes form. The complete process is

$$\text{ண} + \text{◌ை} \rightarrow \text{◌ை} + \text{ண} \rightarrow \text{ணை}$$

6. The consonant ர changes shape to ா.

This occurs when the ா form of ர U+0BB0 TAMIL LETTER RA would not be confused with the nominal form ா of U+0BBE TAMIL VOWEL SIGN AA (for example, when ர is combined with ◌், ◌ி, or ◌ீ).

ர + ◌் → ா + ◌்

ர + ◌ி → ா + ◌ி

ர + ◌ீ → ா + ◌ீ

Encoding Structure. The character block for the Tamil script is divided into the following ranges:

U+0B80	→	U+0BEF	Follows the Devanagari prototype
U+0BF0	→	U+0BF2	Tamil-specific additions

Telugu: U+0C00—U+0C7F

The Telugu script is a South Indian script used to write the Telugu language of Andhra Pradesh state in India, as well as minority languages such as Gondi (Adilabad and Koi dialects) and Lambadi.

Rendering Behavior. For rendering of the Telugu script, see the rules for rendering in the Tamil block description. Take note that, unlike Tamil, the Telugu script writes conjunct consonants with subscripted letters. There are also numerous consonant letters with contextual shape changes when used in conjuncts. Some vowel signs also change their shape in specified combinations.

Special Characters. U+0C55 TELUGU LENGTH MARK is provided as an encoding for the second element of the vowel U+0C47 TELUGU VOWEL SIGN EE. U+0C56 TELUGU AI LENGTH MARK is provided as an encoding for the second element of the surroundrant vowel U+0C48 TELUGU VOWEL SIGN AI. The length marks are both non-spacing characters.

Encoding Structure. The character block for the Telugu script is divided into the following ranges:

U+0C00 → U+0C6F Follow the Devanagari prototype

Kannada: U+0C80—U+0CFF

The Kannada script is a South Indian script used to write the Kannada (or Kanarese) language of Karnataka state, as well as minority languages such as Tulu.

The Kannada script is very closely related to the Telugu script both with regard to the shapes of the letters and in the way conjunct consonants behave.

Special Characters. U+0CD5 KANNADA LENGTH MARK is provided as an encoding for the right side of the two-part vowel U+0CC7 KANNADA VOWEL SIGN EE. U+0CD6 KANNADA AI LENGTH MARK is provided as an encoding for the right side of the two-part vowel U+0CC8 KANNADA VOWEL SIGN AI. The Kannada two-part vowels actually consist of a non-spacing element above the consonant letter and one or more spacing letters to the right of the consonant letter.

Encoding Structure. The character block for the Kannada script is divided into the following ranges:

U+0C80	→	U+0CEF	Follow the Devanagari prototype

Malayalam: U+0D00—U+0D7F

The Malayalam script is a South Indian script used to write the Malayalam language of Kerala state.

The shapes of Malayalam letters closely resemble those of Tamil. However, Malayalam has a very full and complex set of conjunct consonant forms.

Special Characters. U+0D57 MALAYALAM AU LENGTH MARK is provided as an encoding for the right side of the two-part vowel U+0D4C MALAYALAM VOWEL SIGN AU.

Encoding Structure. The character block for the Malayalam script is divided into the following ranges:

U+0D00 → U+0D6F Follow the Devanagari prototype

Thai: U+0E00—U+0E7F

The Thai script is used to write Thai and other Southeast Asian languages, such as Kuy, Lavna, and Pali. It is a member of the Indic family of scripts descended from Brahmi. Thai modifies the original Brahmi letter shapes and extends the number of letters to accommodate features unique to the Thai language, including tone marks derived from superscript digits.

Standards. Thai layout in the Unicode Standard is based on the Thai Industrial Standard 620-2529.

General Principles of the Thai Script. In common with the Indic scripts, each Thai letter is a consonant possessing an inherent vowel sound. Thai letters further feature inherent tones. The inherent vowel and tone can be varied by means of modifiers attached to the base consonant letter. These modifier letters consist of combining vowel signs, combining tone marks, and independent vowel letters. The combining signs and marks follow the modified consonant in the memory representation. However, the independent vowels are treated as other independent letters and precede or follow the consonant depending on their visual position. This encoding for Thai differs from the other Indic scripts since the latter always place vowels *after* the consonant that precedes them phonetically. The difference is necessitated by the encoding practice commonly employed with Thai character data as represented by the Thai Industrial Standards.

Thai Punctuation. Common Thai punctuation includes U+0E46 THAI CHARACTER MAIYAMOK to mark repetition of preceding letters and U+0E5A THAI CHARACTER ANGKHANKHU for ellipsis. U+0E5B THAI CHARACTER KHOMUT marks the beginning of religious texts. Thai also uses punctuation marks such as U+002E FULL STOP and U+002C COMMA, encoded in the ASCII and Latin1 blocks.

Thai Transcription of Pali and Sanskrit. The Thai script is frequently used to write Pali and Sanskrit. When so used, consonant clusters are represented by the explicit use of U+0E3A THAI CHARACTER PHINTHU (*virama*) to mark the removal of the inherent vowel. There is no conjoining behavior, unlike other Indic scripts. U+0E4D THAI CHARACTER NIKHAHIT is the Pali *nigghahita* and Sanskrit *anusvara*. U+0E30 THAI CHARACTER SARA A is the Sanskrit visarga. U+0E24 THAI CHARACTER RU and U+0E26 THAI CHARACTER LU are vocalic /r/ and /l/, with U+0E45 THAI CHARACTER LAKKHANGYAO used to indicate their lengthening.

Encoding Structure. The character block for the Thai script is divided into the following ranges:

U+0E01	→	U+0E2E	Consonant letters
U+0E2F			Punctuation
U+0E30	→	U+0E3A	Vowel signs
U+0E3F			Currency symbol (Baht)
U+0E40	→	U+0E44	Vowel signs
U+0E45	→	U+0E46	Punctuation
U+0E47			Vowel sign
U+0E48	→	U+0E4B	Tone marks (diacritics)
U+0E4C	→	U+0E4D	Vowel signs
U+0E4E	→	U+0E4F	Miscellaneous signs
U+0E50	→	U+0E59	Thai digits
U+0E5A	→	U+0E5B	Miscellaneous signs

Lao: U+0E80—U+0EFF

The Lao language and script are closely related to Thai. The Unicode Standard encodes the Lao script in the same relative order as Thai.

There are a few additional letters in Lao that have no match in Thai. These are

U+0EBB LAO VOWEL SIGH MAI KON

U+0EBC LAO SEMIVOWEL SIGN LO

U+0EBD LAO SEMIVOWEL SIGN NYO

The preceding two semivowel signs are the last remnants of the system of subscript medials, which in Burmese also includes original "rw." In Burmese and Khmer there is a full set of subscript consonant forms used for conjuncts. Thai no longer uses any of these; Lao has just the two.

There are also two ligatures in the Unicode character encoding for Lao: U+0EDC LAO HO NO and U+0EDD LAO HO MO. These correspond to sequences of [h] plus [n] or [h] plus [m] without ligating. Their function in Lao is to provide versions of the [n] and [m] consonants with a different inherent tonal implication.

Encoding Structure. The character block for the Lao script is divided into the following ranges:

U+0E80	→	U+0ED9	Follows the Thai prototype (see exceptions just noted)
U+0EDC	→	U+0EDD	Lao digraphs

Tibetan: U+0F00—U+0FBF

The Tibetan script is used for writing Tibetan and related languages, such as Ladakhi and Lahuli, spoken in the Himalayan region, including Tibet, Bhutan, India, and Nepal. The Tibetan script is a member of the Indic family of scripts descended from Brahmi. The original Brahmi letter shapes can still be clearly discerned in Tibetan, but Tibetan removes the Brahmi voiced aspirates and adds letters for Tibetan sounds not found in Brahmi.

General Principles of the Tibetan Script. As in all Indic scripts, each Tibetan letter is a consonant containing an inherent vowel sound. Tibetan letters each also contain an inherent tone related to the voicing or non-voicing of the original Brahmi letters; this is not marked in the script. As in other Indic scripts, the inherent vowels are modified by means of floating, non-spacing characters attached to the base letter. Removal of the inherent vowel is not always marked in native Tibetan words and must be determined from context.

Consonant clusters are rendered in Tibetan as conjuncts formed by stacking letters along a vertical axis. Because of the prevalence of this practice and to simplify other operations, the Tibetan script contains two encodings of each consonant, used in the following manner: conjuncts are represented in the text stream by placing one or more of the subjoined letter forms following one of the nominal forms; vowel signs come after the clusters thus formed.

Tibetan Punctuation. Common Tibetan punctuation includes U+0F0D *shey* to mark phrases. *Shey* is doubled (U+0F0E) to mark full stops. U+0F11 *rinchenpungshey* is a decorative variant. U+0F0B *intersyllabic tsek* is a syllable delimiter. There are no interword or interphrase spaces in Tibetan. Line breaks normally occur at word boundaries (which are always marked with U+0F0C *tsek*). When a multisyllable word must be broken at the end of a line, three *tseks* are used to indicate the continuation, in a manner similar to western hyphenation. U+0F08 *drulshey* is sometimes used at the beginning (and less frequently the end) of a text.

The character U+0F04 *goyik* is an honorific flourish, double and triple forms of which are used at the beginnings of texts. It normally joins with one or two more occurrences of the same character to form ligatures and is almost never used alone; it is often followed by *shey* in a decorative form.

The *Wheel of Dharma*, which occurs sometimes in Tibetan texts, is encoded in the Miscellaneous Symbols block at U+2638.

The two characters U+0F3C *left ang khang* and U+0F3D *right ang khang* are paired punctuation, typically used together forming a roof over one or more digits, in which case kerning or special ligatures may be required for proper rendering; they may also be used much as a single closing parenthesis is used in forming lists. The marks U+0F3E *yue chu* and U+0F3F *ye chu* are paired signs used to combine with digits; special glyphs or compositional metrics are required for their use.

Tibetan Half-Numbers. The *half-number* forms (U+0F2A → U+0F33) are peculiar to Tibetan, though other scripts (for example, Bengali) have similar fractional concepts. The value of each half-number is 0.5 less than the number within which they appear.

Tibetan Transcription of Sanskrit. Tibetan is also used to write Sanskrit. The Sanskrit retroflex letters are retained. The voiced aspirates are represented by conjuncts formed of consonants placed above the letter U+0F67 *ha*; the relevant aspirates for Sanskrit are encoded within this block at U+0F93 *subjoined gha*, U+0F9D *subjoined ddha*, U+0FA2 *subjoined dha*, U+0FA7 *subjoined bha*, and U+0FAC *subjoined dzha*. The conjunct *kshr* is at U+0FB9. U+0F7F *namchey* is the *visarga* (see the Devanagari block description), and U+0F7E *ngaro* is the *anusvara*.

To maintain consistency in transliterated texts and for ease in transmission and searching, it is recommended that implementations of Sanskrit in the Tibetan script use the precomposed forms of aspirated letters (and *kshr*) whenever possible, rather than implementing these as completely decomposed stacks. However, implementations must ensure that decomposed stacks and precomposed forms are treated interpreted equivalently (see *Section 3.6, Decomposition*).

When the Tibetan script is used to write Sanskrit, consonants are frequently stacked in ways that do not occur in native Tibetan words; this usually indicates deletion of one or more vowel sounds. The stacking behavior is usually indicated by a number of subjoined consonants following a nominal consonant without any break between them. In some rare cases, head or subjoined forms need to be displayed in a manner conflicting with normal, contextual rendering of the script. In those cases, the *virama* (U+0F84) may be inserted between consonants to signal the other, less common, behavior. The letters *wa* (U+0F5D), *ra* (U+0F62), and *ya* (U+0F61) typically change shape when subscripted via subjoining; the nominal changed forms are shown in the chart for Tibetan. (Unchanged forms are possible through the mechanism of *virama* insertion.)

U+0F09 *enumeration* is a list enumerator used at the start of administrative letters in Bhutan, as is U+0F0A *petition honorific.* U+0F3A TIBETAN MARK GUG RTAGS GYON and U+0F3B TIBETAN MARK GUG RTAGS GYAS are paired punctuation marks (brackets). The sign U+0F39 *trang se* is a non-spacing mark corresponding to the flagged ends on characters such as U+0F59 *tsa*; it is sometimes used to form new letters for sounds that do not occur in the traditional script, such as *fa* and *va*.

Encoding Structure. The character block for the Tibetan script is divided into the following ranges:

U+0F00	→	U+0F1F,	Tibetan syllables, punctuation, and symbols
U+0F34	→	U+0F3F	
U+0F20	→	U+0F29	Tibetan digits
U+0F2A	→	U+0F33	Tibetan half-numbers
U+0F40	→	U+0F69	Tibetan nominal letterforms
U+0F71	→	U+0F8B	Tibetan combining vowels and other combining marks
U+0F90	→	U+0FB9	Tibetan subjoined letterforms

Georgian: U+10A0—U+10FF

The Georgian script is used primarily for writing the Georgian language. Upper- and lowercase pairs exist primarily in archaic forms of the script.

Archaic Script Form. The modern Georgian script is a lowercase style called *mkhedruli* (soldier's). It originated as the secular derivative of a form called *khutsuri* (ecclesiastical) that had uppercase and lowercase pairs. Although no longer used in most modern texts, the *khutsuri* style is still used for liturgical purposes; the Unicode Standard encodes the uppercase form of *khutsuri* as well as the lowercase letters of modern Georgian.

Georgian Paragraph Separator. The Georgian paragraph separator has a distinct representation, so it has been separately encoded at U+10FB. It is intended to be used in conjunction with U+2029 PARAGRAPH SEPARATOR, rather than as a replacement for it. See the discussion of the *paragraph separator* in the General Punctuation block.

Other Punctuation. For the Georgian full stop, use U+0589 ARMENIAN FULL STOP.

Encoding Structure. The character block for the Georgian script is divided into the following ranges:

U+10A0	→	U+10C5	Historic (uppercase) letters
U+10D0	→	U+10F0	Modern letters
U+10F1	→	U+10F6	Archaic (lowercase) letters
U+10FB			Punctuation

Hangul Jamo: U+1100—U+11FF

Korean Hangul may be considered to be a syllabic script. As opposed to many other syllabic scripts, the syllables are formed from a set of alphabetic components in a regular fashion. These alphabetic components are called jamo.

The Unicode Standard contains both the complete set of precomposed modern Hangul syllable blocks, and the set of conjoining Hangul jamo in this block. This set of conjoining Hangul jamo can be used to encode all modern and ancient syllable blocks. For a description of conjoining jamo behavior and precomposed Hangul Syllables, see *Section 3.10, Combining Jamo Behavior,* and the Hangul Syllables character block description (U+AC00 → U+D7A3).

The Hangul jamo are divided into three classes: *choseong* (leading consonants, or syllable-initial characters), *jungseong* (vowels, or syllable-peak characters), and *jongseong* (trailing consonants, or syllable-final characters). In the following discussion, these can be abbreviated by *L* (leading consonant), *V* (vowel), and *T* (trailing consonant).

For use in composition, there are two invisible filler characters that act as placeholders for *choseong* or *jungseong*: U+115F HANGUL CHOSEONG FILLER and U+1160 HANGUL JUNGSEONG FILLER.

Collation. The unit of collation in Korean text is normally the Hangul syllable block. Because of the arrangement of the conjoining jamo, their sequences may be collated with a binary comparison. For example, in comparing (a) *LVTLV* against (b) *LVLV,* the first syllable block (*LVT*) should be compared against the second (*LV*). Supposing the first two characters are identical—since all trailing consonants have binary values greater than all leading consonants—the *T* would compare as greater than the second *L* in (b). This produces the correct ordering between the strings. The positions of the fillers in the code charts were also chosen with this in mind.

➥ As with any coded characters, collation cannot depend simply on a binary comparison. Odd sequences such as superfluous fillers will produce an incorrect sort, as will cases where a non-jamo character follows a sequence (such as comparing *LVT* against *LVx*, where *x* is a Unicode character above U+11FF, such as U+3000 IDEOGRAPHIC SPACE).

If mixtures of precomposed syllable blocks and jamo are collated, the easiest approach is to decompose the precomposed syllable blocks into conjoining jamo before comparing.

Encoding Structure. The character block for the Hangul Jamo is divided into the following ranges:

U+1100	→ U+1159	Choseong (leading consonants)
U+115F		CHOSEONG FILLER (leading filler)
U+1160		JUNGSEONG FILLER (vowel filler)
U+1161	→ U+11A2	Jungseong (vowels)
U+11A8	→ U+11F9	Jongseong (trailing consonants)

Latin Extended Additional: U+1E00—U+1EFF

The characters in this block constitute a number of precomposed combinations of Latin letters with one or more general diacritical marks. These characters were added to the Unicode Standard as a result of the process of merging the Unicode Standard with the developing ISO 10646 standard. Each of the characters contained in this block may be alternatively representated with a base letter followed by one or more general diacritical mark characters found in the Combining Diacritical Marks block. A canonical form for such alternative representations is specified in *Chapter 3, Conformance.*

Vietnamese Vowel Plus Tone Mark Combinations. A portion of this block (U+1EA0 → U+1EF9) comprises vowel letters of the modern Vietnamese alphabet (quốc ngữ) combined with a diacritic mark which denotes the phonemic tone that applies to the syllable. In the modern Vietnamese alphabet, there are 12 vowel letters and five tone marks

Figure 6-19. Vietnamese Letters and Tone Marks

a ă â e ê i o ô ơ u ư y

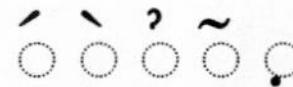

Some implementations of Vietnamese systems prefer storing the combination of vowel letter and tone mark as a singly encoded element; other implementations prefer storing the vowel letter and tone mark separately. The former implementations will use characters defined in this block along with combination forms defined in the Latin-1 Supplement and Latin Extended-A character blocks; the latter implementations will use the basic vowel letters in the Basic Latin, Latin-1 Supplement, and Latin Extended-A blocks along with characters from the Combining Diacritical Marks block. For these latter implementations, the characters U+0300 COMBINING GRAVE, U+0309 COMBINING HOOK ABOVE, U+0303 COMBINING TILDE, U+0301 COMBINING ACUTE, and U+0323 COMBINING DOT BELOW should be given preference in representing the Vietnamese tone marks.

Encoding Structure. The Latin Extended Additional character block is divided into the following ranges:

U+1E00	→	U+1E9B	Additional Latin letter with diacritic combinations
U+1EA0	→	U+1EF9	Vietnamese vowel plus tone mark combinations

Greek Extended: U+1F00—U+1FFF

The characters in this block constitute a number of precomposed combinations of Greek letters with one or more general diacritical marks; in addition, a number of spacing forms of Greek diacritical marks are provided here. These characters were added to the Unicode Standard as a result of the process of merging the Unicode Standard with the developing ISO 10646 standard. In particular, these characters facilitate the representation of Polytonic Greek texts in a compatible manner with existing implementations of Polytonic Greek.

Each of the characters contained in this block may be alternatively representated with a base letter from the Greek block followed by one or more general diacritical mark characters found in the Combining Diacritical Marks block. A canonical form for such alternative representations is specified in *Chapter 3, Conformance.*

Spacing Diacritics. Sixteen additional spacing diacritic marks are provided in this character block for use in the representation of Polytonic Greek texts. Each of these has an alternative representation for use with systems that support non-spacing marks. The Unicode Standard considers the non-spacing alternative forms to be the canonical Unicode representation of the information represented by the spacing forms. The non-spacing alternatives appear in Table 6-17.

Table 6-17. Greek Spacing and Non-Spacing Pairs

Spacing Form	Non-Spacing Form
1FBD GREEK KORONIS	0313 COMBINING COMMA ABOVE
037A GREEK YPOGEGRAMMENI	0345 COMBINING YPOGEGRAMMENI
1FBF GREEK PSILI	0313 COMBINING COMMA ABOVE
1FC0 GREEK PERISPOMENI	0342 COMBINING GREEK PERISPOMENI
1FC1 GREEK DIALYTIKA AND PERISPOMENI	0308 COMBINING DIAERESIS + 0342 COMBINING GREEK PERISPOMENI
1FCD GREEK PSILI AND VARIA	0313 COMBINING COMMA ABOVE + 0300 COMBINING GRAVE ACCENT
1FCE GREEK PSILI AND OXIA	0313 COMBINING COMMA ABOVE + 0301 COMBINING ACUTE ACCENT
1FCF GREEK PSILI AND PERISPOMENI	0313 COMBINING COMMA ABOVE + 0342 COMBINING GREEK PERISPOMENI
1FDD GREEK DASIA AND VARIA	0314 COMBINING REVERSED COMMA ABOVE + 0300 COMBINING GRAVE ACCENT
1FDE GREEK DASIA AND OXIA	0314 COMBINING REVERSED COMMA ABOVE + 0301 COMBINING ACUTE ACCENT
1FDF GREEK DASIA AND PERISPOMENI	0314 COMBINING REVERSED COMMA ABOVE + 0342 COMBINING GREEK PERISPOMENI
1FED GREEK DIALYTIKA AND VARIA	0308 COMBINING DIAERESIS + 0300 COMBINING GRAVE ACCENT
1FEE GREEK DIALYTIKA AND OXIA	0308 COMBINING DIAERESIS + 0301 COMBINING ACUTE ACCENT
1FEF GREEK VARIA	0300 COMBINING GRAVE ACCENT
1FFD GREEK OXIA	0301 COMBINING ACUTE ACCENT
1FFE GREEK DASIA	0314 COMBINING REVERSED COMMA ABOVE

Canonicalization of Spacing Forms. When canonicalizing the spacing forms, the spacing status of the implied usage must be taken into account. Unless information is present to the contrary, these spacing forms would be translated to U+0020 SPACE followed by the non-spacing form equivalents shown in Table 6-17.

In archaic forms of Greek, U+0345 COMBINING GREEK YPOGEGRAMMENI and the precomposed forms that contain it have special case mappings. (See the Greek character block description for more information.)

Encoding Structure. The Greek Extended character block is divided into the following ranges:

U+1F00	→	U+1FBC,	Additional Greek letter with diacritic combinations
U+1FC2	→	U+1FCC,	
U+1FD0	→	U+1FDB,	
U+1FE0	→	U+1FEC,	
U+1FF2	→	U+1FFC	
U+1FBD	→	U+1FC1,	Additional Greek spacing diacritics
U+1FCD	→	U+1FCF,	
U+1FDD	→	U+1FDF,	
U+1FED	→	U+1FEF,	
U+1FFD	→	U+1FFE	

6.2 Symbols Area

The Symbols Area of the Unicode Standard includes the encoding of symbolic characters, including punctuation, numbers, pictures for control codes, and dingbats (see Figure 6-20).

Figure 6-20. Symbols

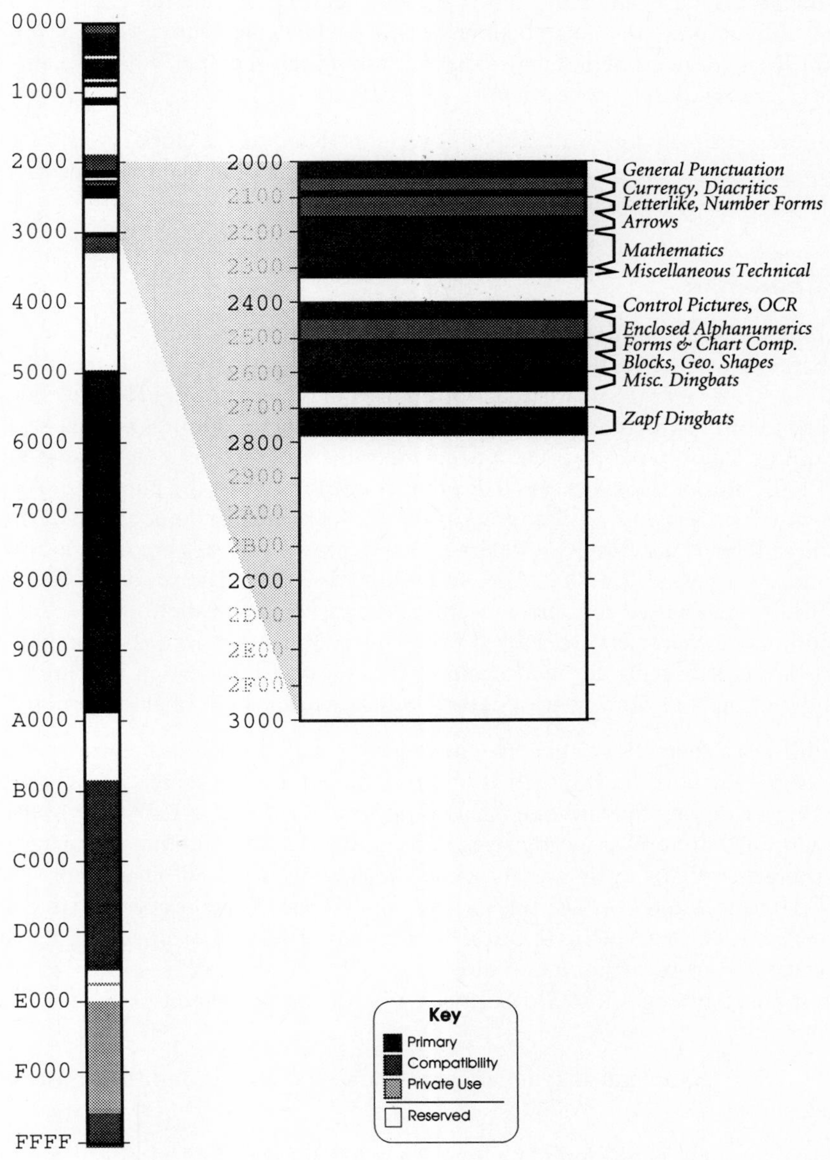

General Punctuation: U+2000—U+206F

General Punctuation combines punctuation characters and character-like elements used to achieve certain text layout effects. Some punctuation characters can be used with many different scripts. Many general punctuation characters can also be found in the Basic Latin (ASCII) and Latin-1 Supplement blocks.

In many cases, current standards include generic characters for punctuation instead of the more precisely specified characters used in printing. Examples include the single and double quotes, period, dash, and space. The Unicode Standard includes these generic characters, but also encodes the unambiguous characters independently: various forms of quotation mark, decimal period, em-dash, en-dash, minus, hyphen, em-space, en-space, hair-space, zero-width space, and so on.

Punctuation principally used with a specific script is found in the block corresponding to that script, such as U+061B ARABIC SEMICOLON "؛" or the punctuation used with ideographs in the CJK Symbols block.

Space Characters

Typographical Space Characters. Spaces generally have the semantics of being word-break characters. Other than that, the main difference is in the width of the characters. U+2000 → U+2006 are standard quad widths used in typography. U+2007 FIGURE SPACE is intended to be used as a thousands separator in cases where countries use space to separate groups of digits. Typically it has a fixed width the same size as a digit in a particular font. U+2007 FIGURE SPACE behaves like a numeric separator for the purposes of bidirectional layout. (See *Section 3.11, Bidirectional Behavior*, for a detailed discussion of the Unicode Bidirectional Algorithm.) U+2008 PUNCTUATION SPACE is a space defined to be the same width as a period. U+2009 THIN SPACE and U+200A HAIR SPACE are successively smaller-width spaces used for narrow word gaps and for justification of type. All of the fixed-width space characters are derived from conventional (hot lead) typography. Their functions are mostly replaced by algorithmic kerning and justification in computerized typography. Characters drawn with a dotted box are invisible in normal rendering.

Zero-width space characters can be used in languages that have no visible word spacing in order to represent word-breaks, such as in Thai or Japanese. There are several varieties of zero-width spaces; the standard one is the *word-break space* U+200B ZERO WIDTH SPACE, used to add soft word breaks in languages without word spaces. Additionally, there are two format characters that can be used in controlling cursive forms of characters, U+200D ZERO WIDTH JOINER and U+200C ZERO WIDTH NON-JOINER. These properties are mutually orthogonal: U+200B ZERO WIDTH SPACE does not affect joining or direction; the joiners neither cause a word-break nor have a direction; the directional spaces neither cause word-breaks nor affect joining. U+200B ZERO WIDTH SPACE may be significant for searching or sorting operations.

➥ It is important to note that not all space characters have word- or line-breaking properties.

Space characters may also be found in other character blocks in the Unicode Standard. The complete list of space characters, including the joiners and directional spaces, appears in Table 6-18.

Other Punctuation

Dashes and Hyphen. U+2010 HYPHEN represents the hyphen as found in words such as "left-to-right." It differs from U+002D HYPHEN-MINUS in that the latter has an ambiguous

Table 6-18. Unicode Space Characters

Code	Name
U+0020	SPACE
U+00A0	NO-BREAK SPACE
U+2000	EN QUAD
U+2001	EM QUAD
U+2002	EN SPACE
U+2003	EM SPACE
U+2004	THREE-PER-EM SPACE
U+2005	FOUR-PER-EM SPACE
U+2006	SIX-PER-EM SPACE
U+2007	FIGURE SPACE
U+2008	PUNCTUATION SPACE
U+2009	THIN SPACE
U+200A	HAIR SPACE
U+200B	ZERO WIDTH SPACE
U+200C	ZERO WIDTH NON-JOINER
U+200D	ZERO WIDTH JOINER
U+200E	LEFT-TO-RIGHT MARK
U+200F	RIGHT-TO-LEFT MARK
U+3000	IDEOGRAPHIC SPACE
U+FEFF	ZERO WIDTH NO-BREAK SPACE

semantic value. U+2011 NON-BREAKING HYPHEN is present for compatibility with existing standards. U+2011 NON-BREAKING HYPHEN has the same semantic as U+2010 HYPHEN, but should not be broken across lines.

U+2012 FIGURE DASH is present for compatibility with existing standards; it has the same (ambiguous) semantic as the U+002D HYPHEN-MINUS, but has the same width as digits (if they are monospaced). U+2013 EN DASH is used to indicate a range of values, such as 1973–1984. It should be distinguished from the U+2122 MINUS, which is an arithmetic operator; however, typographers have typically used U+2013 EN DASH in typesetting to represent the *minus sign.* For general compatibility in interpreting formulas, U+002D HYPHEN-MINUS, U+2012 FIGURE DASH, and U+2212 MINUS SIGN should each be taken as indicating a *minus sign*, as in "x = a - b."

U+2014 EM DASH is used to make a break—like this—in the flow of a sentence. It is commonly represented with a typewriter as a double-hyphen. In older mathematical typography, U+2014 EM DASH is also used to indicate a *binary minus sign.* U+2015 HORIZONTAL BAR is used to introduce quoted text in some typographic styles.

Dashes and hyphen characters may also be found in other character blocks in the Unicode Standard. The complete list of dash and hyphen characters appears in Table 6-19.

Table 6-19. Unicode Dash Characters

Code	Name
U+002D	HYPHEN-MINUS
U+00AD	SOFT HYPHEN
U+2010	HYPHEN
U+2011	NON-BREAKING HYPHEN
U+2012	FIGURE DASH
U+2013	EN DASH
U+2014	EM DASH
U+2015	HORIZONTAL BAR (= *quotation dash*)
U+207B	SUPERSCRIPT MINUS
U+208B	SUBSCRIPT MINUS
U+2212	MINUS SIGN
U+301C	WAVE DASH
U+3030	WAVY DASH

Quotation Marks. U+201A SINGLE LOW-9 QUOTATION MARK, U+201E DOUBLE LOW-9 QUOTATION MARK, U+2039 SINGLE LEFT-POINTING ANGLE QUOTATION MARK, and U+203A SINGLE RIGHT-POINTING ANGLE QUOTATION MARK have heterogeneous semantics. They may represent opening or closing quotation marks depending on usage.

Hyphenation Point. U+2027 HYPHENATION POINT is a raised dot used to indicate correct word breaking as in dic·tion·ar·ies. This is a punctuation mark, to be distinguished from U+00B7 MIDDLE DOT, which has multiple semantics.

Fraction Slash. U+2044 FRACTION SLASH is used between digits to form numeric fractions such as 2/3, 3/9, and so on. The standard form of a fraction built using the fraction slash is defined as follows: Any sequence of one or more decimal digits, followed by the fraction slash, followed by any sequence of one or more decimal digits. Such a fraction should be displayed as a unit, such as ¾ or as $\frac{3}{4}$. The precise choice of display can depend upon additional formatting information.

If the displaying software is incapable of mapping the fraction to a unit, then it can also be displayed as a simple linear sequence as a fall-back (for example, 3/4). If the fraction is to be separated from a previous number, then a space can be used, choosing the appropriate width (normal, thin, zero-width, and so on). For example, 1 + ZERO-WIDTH SPACE + 3 + FRACTION SLASH + 4 displays as 1¾.

Spacing Overscore. U+203E OVERLINE is the above-the-line counterpart to U+005F LOW LINE. It is a spacing character, not to be confused with U+0305 COMBINING OVERLINE. As with all over- or underscores, a sequence of these characters should connect in an unbroken line. The overscoring characters also must be distinguished from U+0304 COMBINING MACRON, which does not connect horizontally in this way.

Layout Controls

The Non-Joiner and Joiner. In some fonts for some scripts, consecutive characters in a text stream may be rendered via adjacent glyphs that cursively join to each other, so as to emulate connected handwriting. For example, cursive joining is implemented in nearly all fonts for the Arabic scripts, and in a few handwriting-like fonts for the Latin script.

Cursive rendering is implemented by joining glyphs in the font, plus a process that selects the particular joining glyph to represent each individual character occurrence, based on the joining nature of its neighboring characters. This glyph selection is implemented in some combination between the rendering engine and the font itself.

In cases where cursive joining is implemented, there are occasions when an author may wish to override the normal automatic selection of joining glyphs. Typically, this is done to achieve one of the following effects:

- Cause non-default joining appearance (for example, as is sometimes required in writing Persian using the Arabic script).
- Exhibit the joining-variant glyphs themselves in isolation.

The Unicode Standard provides a means to influence joining glyph selection, by means of the two characters U+200C *zero width non-joiner* and U+200D *zero width joiner*. Logically, these characters do not modify the contextual selection process itself, but rather they *change the context* of a particular character occurrence. By providing a non-joining neighbor character where otherwise the neighbor would be joining, or vice-versa, they deceive the rendering process into selecting a different joining glyph.

(1) Prevent joining appearance. For example,

ص U+0635 ARABIC LETTER SAD

ZWNJ U+200C ZERO WIDTH NON-JOINER

ل U+0644 ARABIC LETTER LAM

would be rendered as ص‌ل (that is, the normal cursive joining of the interior *sad* and *lam* is overridden). Without the ZERO WIDTH NON-JOINER it would be rendered as صل.

(2) Exhibit joining glyphs in isolation. For example,

ZWJ U+200D ZERO WIDTH JOINER

غ U+063A ARABIC LETTER GHAIN

ZWJ U+200D ZERO WIDTH JOINER

would be rendered as ‍غ‍. (That is, the medial glyph form of the *ghain* appears in isolation. Without the ZERO WIDTH JOINER before and after, it would be rendered as غ.)

➥ The preceding examples are adapted from the Iranian national coded character set standard, ISIRI 3342, which defines these characters as "pseudo space" and "pseudo connection," respectively.

The function of the ZERO WIDTH JOINER may also have a particular interpretation in specific scripts. For example, in Indic scripts it provides an invisible neighbor to which a dead consonant may join in order to induce a half-consonant form (see the Devanagari character block description). It also has specially defined usage in Tibetan (see the Tibetan character block description).

ZERO WIDTH NON-JOINER or ZERO WIDTH JOINER are format control characters. As with other such characters, they should be ignored by processes that analyze text content. For example, a spell-checker or find/replace operation should filter them out. (See *Section 2.4, Special Character and Non-Character Values,* for a general discussion of format control characters.)

The effect of these characters in display depends on the context in which they are found. Adding a ZERO WIDTH JOINER between characters that are already cursively connected will have no effect. Adding a ZERO WIDTH NON-JOINER between characters that are unconnected will also have no effect. For example, any number of ZERO-WIDTH NON-JOINER or ZERO-WIDTH JOINER characters sprinkled into an English text stream will have no effect on its appearance when rendered in a typical non-cursive Latin font.

Although ZERO WIDTH JOINER and ZERO-WIDTH NON-JOINER should not affect ligating behavior, in some systems they may break up ligatures by interrupting the character sequence required to form the ligature. As illustration, a cursive Latin font would produce the following results:

Memory Representation	**Rendering**	
f i s h	f- -i- -s- -h	
	ﬁ- -s- -h	optionally using a ligature
f ZWJ i s h	f- -i- -s- -h	
	ﬁ- -s- -h	optionally using a ligature
f ZWNJ i s h	f i- -s- -h	
f ZWJ ZWNJ i s h	f- i- -s- -h	
f ZWNJ ZWJ i s h	f -i- -s- -h	

Usage of optional ligatures such as *fi* is not currently controlled by any codes within the Unicode Standard but is determined by protocols or resources external to the text sequence.

Bidirectional Ordering Codes. These codes are used in the Bidirectional Algorithm, described in *Chapter 3, Conformance*. Systems that handle bidirectional scripts (Arabic and Hebrew) should be sensitive to these codes. The codes appear in Table 6-20.

Table 6-20. Bidirectional Ordering Codes

Code	Name	Abbrev.
U+200E	LEFT-TO-RIGHT MARK	(LRM)
U+200F	RIGHT-TO-LEFT MARK	(RLM)
U+202A	LEFT-TO-RIGHT EMBEDDING	(LRE)
U+202B	RIGHT-TO-LEFT EMBEDDING	(RLE)
U+202C	POP DIRECTIONAL FORMATTING	(PDF)
U+202D	LEFT-TO-RIGHT OVERRIDE	(RLO)
U+202E	RIGHT-TO-LEFT OVERRIDE	(LRO)

As with the other zero-width character codes, except for their effect on the layout of the text in which they are contained, the bidirectional ordering characters can be ignored by the processing software. For non-layout text processing, such as sorting, searching and so on, the zero-width layout characters may be ignored. However, when modifying text, care should be taken to maintain these characters correctly, since the matching pairs of zero-width formatting characters must be coordinated (see *Chapter 3, Conformance*).

U+200E LEFT-TO-RIGHT MARK and U+200F RIGHT-TO-LEFT MARK have the semantics of a an invisible character of zero width, except that while a normal space is directionally neutral, these characters have strong directionality. These characters are intended to be used to resolve cases of ambiguous directionality in the context of bidirectional texts. Unlike U+200B ZERO WIDTH SPACE, these characters carry no word break semantics. (See *Section 3.11, Bidirectional Behavior*, for more information.)

Line and Paragraph Separator. For historical reasons, carriage-return and line-feed are not used consistently across different systems. The Unicode Standard provides (and encourages use of) the *line* and *paragraph separator* characters to provide clear information about where line and paragraph boundaries occur. This is also required for use with the Bidirectional Algorithm (see *Chapter 3, Conformance*).

A paragraph separator indicates where a new paragraph should start. This could cause, for example, the line to be broken, the interparagraph line spacing to be applied, and indentation of the first line. A line separator indicates that a line-break should occur at this point; although the text continues on the next line, it does not start a new paragraph: no interparagraph line spacing nor paragraphic indentation is applied. Since these are separator codes, it is not necessary to start the first line or paragraph, nor end the last line or paragraph with them.

Alternate Format Characters

There are three pairs of alternate format characters encoded in this block:

- Symmetric swapping format characters used to control the glyphs which depict characters such as "(". (The default state is *activated*.)
- Character shaping selectors used to control the shaping behavior of the Arabic compatibility characters. (The default state is *inhibited*.)

- Numeric shape selectors codes used to override the normal shapes of the Western Digits. (The default state is *nominal.*)

The use of these character shaping selectors and digit shapes codes is *strongly* discouraged in the Unicode Standard. Instead, the appropriate character codes should be used with the default state. For example, if contextual forms for Arabic characters are desired, then the nominal characters should be used, and not the presentation forms with the shaping selectors. Similarly, if the Arabic digit forms are desired then the explicit characters should be used, such as U+0660 ARABIC-INDIC DIGIT ZERO.

Symmetric Swapping. The symmetric swapping format characters are used in conjunction with the class of left/right-handed pairs of characters (symmetric characters) such as parentheses. The characters thus affected are listed in *Section 4.7, Mirrored*. They indicate whether the interpretation of the term LEFT or RIGHT in the character names should be interpreted as meaning *opening* or *closing*, respectively. They do not nest. The default state of symmetric swapping may be set by a higher level protocol or standard, such as ISO 6429. In the absence of such a protocol, the default state is *activated.*

From the point of encountering U+206A INHIBIT SYMMETRIC SWAPPING format character up to a subsequent U+206B ACTIVATE SYMMETRIC SWAPPING (if any), the symmetric characters will be interpreted and rendered as left and right.

From the point of encountering U+206B ACTIVATE SYMMETRIC SWAPPING format character up to a subsequent U+206A INHIBIT SYMMETRIC SWAPPING (if any), the symmetric characters will be interpreted and rendered as opening and closing. This state (*activated*) is the default state in the absence of any symmetric swapping code or a higher level protocol.

Character Shaping Selectors. The character shaping selector format characters are used in conjunction with Arabic presentation forms. During the presentation process, certain letterforms may be joined together in cursive connection or ligatures. The shaping selector codes indicate that the character shape determination (glyph selection) process used to achieve this presentation effect is to be either activated or inhibited. The shaping selector codes do not nest.

From the point of encountering a U+206C INHIBIT ARABIC FORM SHAPING format character up to a subsequent U+206D ACTIVATE ARABIC FORM SHAPING (if any), the character shaping determination process should be inhibited. If the backing store contains Arabic presentation forms (for example, U+FE80 → U+FEFC), then these forms should be presented without shape modification. This state (*inhibited*) is the default state in the absence of any character shaping selector or a higher level protocol.

From the point of encountering a U+206D ACTIVATE ARABIC FORM SHAPING format character up to a subsequent U+206C INHIBIT ARABIC FORM SHAPING (if any), any Arabic presentation forms which appear in the backing store should be presented with shape modification by means of the character shaping (glyph selection) process.

The shaping selectors have no effect on nominal Arabic characters (U+0660 → U+06FF) which are always subject to character shaping (glyph selection) and which are unaffected by these formatting codes.

Numeric Shape Selectors. The numeric shape selector format characters allow the selection of the shapes in which the digits U+0030 → U+0039 are to be rendered. These format characters do not nest.

From the point of encountering a U+206E NATIONAL DIGIT SHAPES format character up to a subsequent U+206F NOMINAL DIGIT SHAPES (if any), the European digits (U+0030 → U+0039) should be depicted using the appropriate national digit shapes as specified by means of appropriate agreements. For example, they could be displayed with shapes such as the ARABIC-INDIC DIGITS (U+0660 → U+0669). The actual character shapes (glyphs) used to display national digit shapes is not specified by the Unicode Standard.

From the point of encountering a U+206F NOMINAL DIGIT SHAPES format character up to a subsequent U+206E NATIONAL DIGIT SHAPES (if any), the European digits (U+0030 → U+0039) should be depicted using glyphs that represent the nominal digit shapes shown in the code tables for these digits. This state (*nominal*) is the default state in the absence of any numeric shape selector or a higher level protocol.

Encoding Structure. The character block for General Punctuation is divided into the following ranges:

U+2000	→	U+200A	Typographical space characters
U+200B			Zero-width space
U+200C	→	U+200F	Zero-width layout characters
U+2010	→	U+2027	Printing punctuation characters
U+2028	→	U+2029	Line and paragraph separators
U+202A	→	U+202E	Bidirectional ordering codes
U+2030	→	U+2046	Printing punctuation characters
U+206A	→	U+206F	Alternate format characters (usage strongly discouraged)

Superscripts and Subscripts: U+2070—U+209F

Superscripts and subscripts have been included in the Unicode Standard only to provide compatibility with existing character sets. In general, the Unicode character encoding does not attempt to describe the positioning of a character above or below the baseline in typographical layout. The superscript digits one, two, and three are coded in the Latin-1 Supplement block in order to obtain code point compatibility with ISO 8859-1.

Standards. The characters in this block are from sets registered with ECMA under ISO 2374 for use with ISO 2022.

Encoding Structure. The character block for Superscripts and Subscripts is divided into the following ranges:

U+2070	→	U+2079	Superscript numbers (gapped where the superscript is encoded in the Latin-1 Supplement block)
U+207A	→	U+207F	Superscript mathematical operators, punctuation, and letter
U+2080	→	U+2089	Subscript numbers
U+208A	→	U+208E	Subscript mathematical operators and punctuation

Currency Symbols: U+20A0—U+20CF

This block contains currency symbols not encoded in other blocks. Where the Unicode Standard follows the layout of an existing standard, such as for the ASCII, Latin 1, and Thai blocks, the currency symbols are encoded in those blocks, rather than here.

Unification. The Unicode Standard does not duplicate encodings where more than one currency is expressed with the same symbol. Many currency symbols are overstruck letters. There are therefore many minor variants, such as the U+0024 DOLLAR SIGN $, with one or two vertical bars, or other graphical variation. The Unicode Standard considers these variants to be typographical and provides a single encoding.

Claims that glyph variants of a certain currency symbol are used consistently to indicate a particular currency could not be substantiated upon further research. (See ISO/IEC DIS 10367, Annex B (informative) for an example of multiple renderings for U+00A3 POUND SIGN.)

The following table lists common currency symbols encoded in other blocks.

Dollar, milreis, escudo	U+0024	DOLLAR SIGN
Cent	U+00A2	CENT SIGN
Pound	U+00A3	POUND SIGN
General currency	U+00A4	CURRENCY SIGN
Yen or yuan	U+00A5	YEN SIGN
Dutch florin	U+0192	LATIN SMALL LETTER F WITH HOOK
Baht	U+0E3F	THAI CURRENCY SYMBOL BAHT

Encoding Structure. The character block for currency symbols is divided into the following ranges:

U+20A0 → U+20AB Currency symbols

Combining Marks for Symbols: U+20D0—U+20FF

Diacritical marks for symbols are generally applied to mathematical or technical symbols. These can be used to extend the range of the symbol set. For example, U+20D3 COMBINING SHORT VERTICAL LINE OVERLAY can be used to express negation. Its presentation may change in those circumstances, changing length or slant. That is, U+2261 IDENTICAL TO, followed by U+20D3 is equivalent to U+2262 NOT IDENTICAL TO. In this case, there was a precomposed form for the negated symbol. However, this is not always true, and U+20D3 can be used with other symbols to form the negation. For example, U+2258 CORRESPONDS TO followed by U+20D3 can be used to express *does not correspond to*, without requiring that a precomposed form be part of the Unicode Standard.

Other non-spacing characters can also be used in mathematical expressions, of course. For example, a U+0304 COMBINING MACRON is commonly used in propositional logic to indicate logical negation.

Enclosing Diacritics. These non-spacing characters are supplied for compatibility with existing standards, allowing individual base characters to be enclosed in several ways. For example, U+2460 CIRCLED DIGIT ONE א can be expressed as U+0030 DIGIT ONE "1" + U+20DD COMBINING ENCLOSING CIRCLE ○. As with other combining characters, this one can also be applied productively; *circled letter alef* can be produced by the sequence: U+05D0 HEBREW LETTER ALEF א + U+20DD COMBINING ENCLOSING CIRCLE ○. The combining enclosing diacritics cannot be used to enclose a sequence of base characters in plain text. For example, there is no way to represent U+246A CIRCLED NUMBER ELEVEN with the ENCLOSING CIRCLE, since there is no single character NUMBER ELEVEN.

Encoding Structure. The character block for Combining Marks for Symbols is divided into the following ranges:

U+20D0 → U+20E1 Symbol Diacritics

Letterlike Symbols: U+2100—U+214F

Letterlike symbols are symbols derived in some way from ordinary letters of an alphabetic script. This block includes symbols based on Latin, Greek, and Hebrew letters. These symbols are encoded for compatibility. In general, the usage of distinct codes for letterlike symbols that are merely font variants or alternative representations of other characters is strongly discouraged. When using letters as symbols in equations and formulae, as well as in other contexts, use normal alphabetic forms in the appropriate styles. For example, to represent degrees Celsius "°C", use a sequence of U+00B0 DEGREE SIGN + U+0043 LATIN CAPITAL LETTER C, rather than U+2103 DEGREE CELSIUS. For searching, treat these two sequences as identical.

Where the letterlike symbols have alphabetic equivalents, they collate in alphabetic sequence; otherwise, they should be treated as neutral symbols. The letterlike symbols may have different directional properties than normal letters; for example, the four transfinite cardinal symbols (U+2135 → U+2138) are used in ordinary mathematical text and do not share the strong right-to-left directionality of the Hebrew letters they are derived from.

Styles. The letterlike symbols constitute one of the few instances in which the Unicode Standard encodes stylistic variants of letters as distinct characters. For example, there are instances of black letter, double-struck, and script styles for certain Latin letters used as mathematical symbols. The choice of these stylistic variants for encoding reflects their common use as distinct symbols. It is recognized that a particular style can be applied to any Latin letter with a resulting semantic distinction in mathematical or logical text; applications that require such systematic stylistic semantics should achieve them by using styles directly, rather than by seeking to extend the character-by-character encoding of such variants in the Unicode Standard.

The black-letter style is often referred to as *Fraktur* or *Gothic* in various sources. Technically, Fraktur and Gothic typefaces are distinct designs from black letter, but no encoding distinctions are implied in the various symbol sources. The Unicode Standard simply uses black letter forms as the archetypes.

A similar consideration applies to the double-struck style. This style is not literally double-struck, but is instead an open outline design that gives the visual appearance of being struck twice with a horizontal shift. For encoding purposes this style can be considered equivalent to letterlike symbols rendered in outlined or shadowed typefaces to carry conventional semantic distinctions.

Standards. The Unicode Standard encodes letterlike symbols from many different national standards and corporate collections.

Encoding Structure. The character block for Letterlike Symbols is divided into the following ranges:

U+2100 → U+2138 Letterlike symbols

Number Forms: U+2150—U+218F

Number Form characters are encoded solely for compatibility with existing standards. The same considerations with respect to compatibility apply as noted in the discussion of Letterlike Symbols.

Fractions. The vulgar fraction characters encoded in this block can be equivalently represented using U+2044 FRACTION SLASH.

Roman Numerals. The Roman numerals can be composed of sequences of the appropriate Latin letters. U+2180 ROMAN NUMERAL ONE THOUSAND C D and U+216F ROMAN NUMERAL ONE THOUSAND are actually variants of the same glyph but are distinguished because of existing standards; similarly, the upper- and lowercase variants of Roman numerals have been separately encoded. U+2181 ROMAN NUMERAL FIVE THOUSAND, and U+2182 ROMAN NUMERAL TEN THOUSAND are distinct characters used in Roman Numerals, since they represent characters used in Roman numerals that do not have decompositions in the Unicode Standard.

Encoding Structure. The character block for Number Forms is divided into the following ranges:

U+2153	→	U+215F	Vulgar fractions
U+2160	→	U+2182	Roman numerals and small Roman numerals

Arrows: U+2190—U+21FF

Arrows are used for a variety of purposes: to imply directional relation, logical derivation or implication, or to represent the cursor control keys.

The Unicode Standard attempts to provide fairly complete encodings for generic arrow shapes, especially where there are established usages with well-defined semantics; the Unicode Standard does not attempt to encode every possible stylistic variant of arrows separately, especially where their use is mainly decorative. For most arrow variants, the Unicode Standard provides encodings in the two horizontal directions, often in the four cardinal directions. For the single and double arrows the Unicode Standard provides encodings in eight directions.

Standards. The Unicode Standard encodes arrows from many different national standards and corporate collections.

Unifications. Arrows expressing mathematical relations have been encoded in the arrows block. An example is U+21D2 RIGHTWARDS DOUBLE ARROW ⇒ may be the equivalent of *implies.*

Long and short arrow forms encoded in glyph standards or typesetting systems such as TEX are not represented by separate Unicode values.

Encoding Principles. Because the arrows have such a wide variety of applications, there may be several semantic values for the same Unicode character value: for example, U+21B5 DOWNWARDS ARROW WITH CORNER LEFTWARDS ↵ may be the equivalent of *carriage return*; U+2191 UPWARDS ARROW ↑ may be the equivalent of *increases* or *exponent.*

Encoding Structure. The character block for arrows is divided into the following ranges:

U+2190 → U+21EA Arrows

Mathematical Operators: U+2200—U+22FF

The Mathematical Operators block includes character encodings for operators, relations, geometric symbols, and a few other symbols with special usages confined largely to mathematical contexts.

In addition to the characters in this block, mathematical operators are also found in the Basic Latin (ASCII) and Latin-1 Supplement blocks. A few of the symbols from the Miscellaneous Technical block, and characters from General Punctuation are also used in mathematical notation. Latin letters in special font styles and used as mathematical operators, such as U+2118 SCRIPT CAPITAL P ℘, as well as the Hebrew letter *alef* used as the operator first transfinite cardinal encoded by U+2135 ALEF SYMBOL ℵ, are encoded in the block for letterlike symbols.

Standards. Many national standards' mathematical operators are covered by the characters encoded in this block. These standards include such special collections as ANSI Y10.20, ISO DIS 6862.2, ISO 8879, and the collection of the American Mathematical Society, as well as the original repertoire of TEX.

Encoding Principles. Mathematical operators often have more than one meaning. Therefore the encoding of this block is intentionally rather shape-based, with numerous instances in which several semantic values can be attributed to the same Unicode value. For example, U+2218 RING OPERATOR ∘ may be the equivalent of *white small circle* or *composite function* or *apl jot*. The Unicode Standard does not attempt to distinguish all the possible semantic values which may be applied to mathematical operators or relation symbols.

On the other hand, mathematical operators, and especially relation symbols, may appear in various standards, handbooks, and fonts with a large number of purely graphical variants. Where variants were recognizable as such from the sources, they were not encoded separately.

Unifications. Mathematical operators such as *implies* ⇒ and *if and only if* ↔ have been unified with the corresponding arrows (U+21D2 RIGHTWARDS DOUBLE ARROW and U+2194 LEFT RIGHT ARROW, respectively) in the Arrows block.

The operator U+2208 ELEMENT OF is occasionally rendered with a taller shape than shown in the code charts. Mathematical handbooks and standards consulted treat these as variants of the same glyph. U+220A SMALL ELEMENT OF is separately encoded, because some existing standards distinguish it from U+2208.

The operators U+226B MUCH GREATER-THAN and U+226A MUCH LESS-THAN are sometimes rendered in a nested shape. Since no semantic distinction applies, the Unicode Standard provides a single encoding for each of these operators.

A large class of unifications applies to variants of relation symbols involving equality, similarity, and/or negation. Variants involving one- or two-barred *equal signs*, one- or two-*tilde similarity signs*, and vertical or slanted *negation slashes* and *negation slashes* of different lengths are not separately encoded. Thus, for example, U+2288 NEITHER A SUBSET OF NOR EQUAL TO, is the archetype for at least six different glyph variants noted in various collections.

There are two instances in which essentially stylistic variants are separately encoded: U+2265 GREATER-THAN OR EQUAL TO is distinguished from U+2267 GREATER-THAN OVER EQUAL TO; the same distinction applies to U+2264 LESS-THAN OR EQUAL TO and U+2266 LESS-THAN OVER EQUAL TO. This exception to the general rule regarding variation results from requirements for character mapping to some Asian standards which distinguish the two forms.

Greek-Derived Symbols. Several mathematical operators derived from Greek characters have been given separate encodings to match usage in existing standards. These operators may occasionally occur in context with Greek-letter variables. These operators include U+2206 INCREMENT Δ, U+220F N-ARY PRODUCT ∏, and U+2211 N-ARY SUMMATION ∑.

Other duplicated Greek characters are those for U+00B5 MICRO SIGN µ in the Latin-1 Supplement block, U+2126 OHM SIGN Ω in Letterlike symbols, and several characters among the APL functional symbols in the Miscellaneous Technical block. All other Greek characters with special mathematical semantics are found in the Greek block since duplicates were not required for compatibility.

Miscellaneous Symbols. U+2212 MINUS SIGN − is a mathematical operator, to be distinguished from the ASCII-derived U+002D HYPHEN-MINUS -, which may look the same as minus sign, or may be shorter in length. (For a complete list of dashes in the Unicode Standard, see the General Punctuation character block description.) U+22EE → U+22F1 are a set of ellipses used in matrix notation.

Math Property. A list of characters with the math property are listed in *Chapter 4, Character Properties.*

Encoding Structure. The character block for Mathematical Operators is divided into the following ranges:

U+2200 → U+22F1 Mathematical operators

Miscellaneous Technical: U+2300—U+23FF

This block encodes technical symbols including keytop labels such as U+232B ERASE TO THE LEFT. Excluded from consideration were symbols that are not normally used in one-dimensional text but are intended for two-dimensional diagrammatic use, such as symbols for electronic circuits. An unusually large expansion space is provided since it is anticipated that there are a large number of technical symbols that could be considered for addition to the Unicode Standard.

Crops and Quine Corners. Crops and quine corners are most properly used in two-dimensional layout but may be referred to in plain text. The usage of crops and quine corners is as indicated in this diagram:

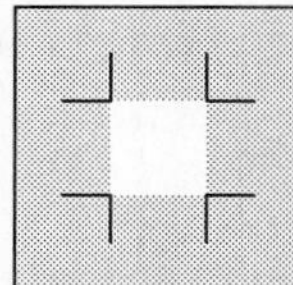

Use of crops

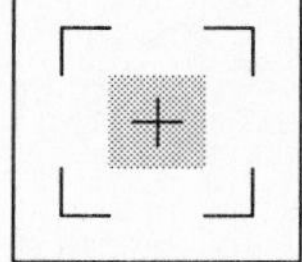

Use of quine corners

APL Functional Symbols. APL (A Programming Language) makes extensive use of functional symbols constructed by composition with other, more primitive functional symbols. It made extensive use of backspace and overstrike mechanisms in early computer implementations. While, in principle, functional composition is productive in APL, in practice, a relatively small set of composed functional symbols have become standard operators in APL. This relatively small set is encoded in entirety in this block. All other APL extensions can be encoded by composition of other Unicode characters. For example, the APL symbol *a underbar* can be represented by U+0061 LATIN SMALL LETTER A + U+0332 COMBINING LOW LINE.

Encoding Structure. The character block for Miscellaneous Technical symbols is divided into the following ranges:

U+2300	→	U+2307,	Miscellaneous symbols
U+2310	→	U+231B,	
U+2322	→	U+2323	
U+2308	→	U+230B	Ceilings and floors
U+230C	→	U+230F	Crops
U+231C	→	U+231F	Quine corners
U+2320	→	U+2321	Partial math symbols for compatibility
U+2324	→	U+2328,	Keyboard symbols
U+232B			
U+2329	→	U+232A	Bra and Ket
U+232C			Benzene ring
U+232D	→	U+2335	Technical drafting symbols
U+2336	→	U+237A	APL functional symbols

Control Pictures: U+2400—U+243F

The need to show the presence of the C0 control codes and the SPACE unequivocally when data is displayed has led to conventional representations for these non-graphic characters.

By definition, control codes themselves are manifested only by their action. However, it is sometimes necessary to show the position of a control code within a data stream. Conventional illustrations for the ASCII C0 control codes have been developed.

By definition, the SPACE is a blank graphic. Conventions have also been established for the visible representation of the space.

Standards. The CNS 11643 standard encodes characters for pictures of control codes. Standard representations for control characters have been defined, for example, in ANSI X3.32 and ISO 2047, but for the control code graphics U+2400 → U+241F only the semantic is encoded in the Unicode Standard. This allows a particular application to use the graphic representation it prefers.

Pictures for ASCII Space. Two specific glyphs are provided that may be used to represent the ASCII space character (U+2420 and U+2422).

Code Points for Pictures for Control Codes. The remaining code points in this block are not associated with specific glyphs, but rather are available to encode *any* desired pictorial representation of the given control code. The assumption is that the particular pictures used to represent control codes are often specific to different systems, and are not often the subject of text interchange between systems.

Encoding Structure. The character block for Control Pictures is divided into the following ranges:

U+2400 → U+241F U+0000→U+001F	Code points for pictures for control codes
U+2420, U+2422 → U+2423	Pictures for the ASCII space character
U+2421	Picture for *delete*
U+2424	Picture for *new line*

Optical Character Recognition: U+2440—U+245F

This block includes those symbolic characters of the OCR-A character set that do not correspond to ASCII characters, and magnetic ink character recognition (MICR) symbols used in check processing.

Standards. Both sets of symbols are specified in ISO 2033.

Encoding Structure. The character block for Optical Character Recognitions is divided into the following ranges:

U+2440	→ U+2445	OCR-A Symbols
U+2446	→ U+244A	MICR symbols

Enclosed Alphanumerics: U+2460—U+24FF

The enclosed numbers and Latin letters of this block come from several sources, chiefly East Asian standards, and are provided for compatibility with them.

Standards. Enclosed letters and numbers occur in the Korean National Standard, KS C 5601, and in the Chinese national standard, GB 2312, as well as in various East Asian industry standards.

The Zapf Dingbats character set in widespread industry use contains four sets of encircled numbers (including encircled zero). The black on white set that has numbers with serifs is encoded here (U+2460 → U+2468, and U+24EA). The other three sets are encoded in the range U+2776 → U+2793 in the Dingbats block.

Decompositions. The parenthesized letters or numbers may be decomposed to a sequence of opening parenthesis, letter or digit(s), closing parenthesis. The numbers with a period may be decomposed to digit(s), followed by a period. The encircled letters and single-digit numbers may be decomposed to letter or digit followed by U+20DD COMBINING ENCLOSING CIRCLE. Decompositions for the encircled numbers 10 through 20 are not supported in Unicode plain text. (For more information, see *Chapter 2, General Structure* and *Chapter 3, Conformance.*)

Encoding Structure. The character block for Enclosed Alphanumerics is divided into the following ranges:

U+2460	→	U+2473	Encircled numbers 1–20
U+2474	→	U+2487	Parenthesized numbers 1–20
U+2488	→	U+249B	Numbers with period 1–20
U+249C	→	U+24B5	Parenthesized small Latin a–z
U+24B6	→	U+24CF	Encircled capital Latin A–Z
U+24D0	→	U+24E9	Encircled small Latin a–z
U+24EA			Encircled number 0

Box Drawing: U+2500—U+257F

The characters in the Box Drawing block are encoded solely for compatibility with existing standards.

Standards. GB 2312, KS C 5601, and industry standards.

Encoding Structure. The character block for Box Drawing is divided into the following ranges:

U+2500	→	U+254F	Single-line box and line-drawing elements
U+2550	→	U+256C	Line-box drawing elements with double-line segments
U+256D	→	U+2570	Curved corner segments
U+2571	→	U+2573	Diagonal line segments and miscellaneous
U+2574	→	U+257F	Line end pieces and connectors

Block Elements: U+2580—U+259F

The Block Elements block represents a graphic compatibility zone in the Unicode Standard. A number of existing national and vendor standards, including IBM PC Code Page 437, contain a number of characters intended to enable a simple kind of display cell graphics by filling some fraction of each cell, or by filling each display cell by some degree of shading. The Unicode Standard does not encourage this kind of character-based graphics model but includes a minimal set of such characters for backward compatibility with the existing standards.

Half-block fill characters are included for each half of a display cell, plus a graduated series of vertical and horizontal fractional fills based on one-eighth parts. Also included is a series of shades based on one-quarter shadings. The fractional fills do not form a logically complete set but are intended only for backward compatibility.

Encoding Structure. The character block for Block Elements is divided into the following ranges:

U+2580	→	U+2590,	Display cell fractional fill characters
U+2594	→	U+2595	
U+2591	→	U+2593	Percent shade characters

Geometric Shapes: U+25A0—U+25FF

The Geometric Shapes are a collection of characters intended to encode prototypes for various commonly used geometrical shapes—mostly squares, triangles, and circles. The collection is somewhat arbitrary in scope; it is a compendium of shapes from various character and glyph standards. The typical distinctions more systematically encoded include black versus white, large versus small, basic shape (square versus triangle versus circle), orientation, and top versus bottom or left versus right part.

The hatched and cross-hatched squares at U+25A4 → U+25A9 derive from the Korean national standard (KS C 5601), in which they were probably intended as representations of fill patterns; however, since the semantics of those characters is insufficiently defined in that standard, the Unicode character encoding simply carries the glyphs themselves as geometric shapes to provide a mapping for that standard.

U+25CA LOZENGE ◊ is a typographical symbol seen in PostScript and in the Macintosh character set. It should be distinguished both from the generic U+25C7 WHITE DIAMOND and the U+2662 WHITE DIAMOND SUIT, as well as from another character sometimes called a lozenge, U+2311 SQUARE LOZENGE.

The squares and triangles at U+25E7 → U+25EE are derived from the Linotype font collection. U+25EF LARGE CIRCLE is included for compatibility with the JIS X 0208-1990 Japanese standard.

Standards. The Geometric Shapes are derived from a large range of national and vendor character standards.

Encoding Structure. The character block for Geometric Shapes is divided into the following ranges:

U+25A0 → U+25EF Geometric shapes based on various forms

Miscellaneous Symbols: U+2600—U+26FF

The Miscellaneous Symbols block consists of a very heterogenous collection of symbols that do not fit in any other Unicode character block and which tend to be rather pictographic in nature. The usage of these symbols is typically for text decorations, but they may also be treated as normal text characters in applications such as typesetting chess books, card game manuals, and horoscopes.

Characters in the Miscellaneous Symbols block may be rendered in more than one way, unlike characters in the Dingbats block, in which characters correspond to an explicit glyph. For example, both U+2641 EARTH and U+2645 URANUS have common alternative glyphs.

The order of the Miscellaneous Symbols is completely arbitrary, but an attempt has been made to keep like symbols together and to group subsets of them into meaningful orders. Some of these subsets include weather and astronomical symbols, pointing hands, religious and ideological symbols, the I Ching trigrams, planet and zodiacal symbols, chess pieces, card suits, and musical dingbats. (For other moon phases, see the circle-based shapes in the Geometric Shapes block.)

Corporate logos and collections of pictures of animals, vehicles, foods, and so on are not included since they tend either to be very specific in usage (logos, political party symbols) or nonconventional in appearance and semantic interpretation (pictures of cows or of cats; fizzing champagne bottles), and hence are inappropriate for encoding as characters. The Unicode Standard recommends that such items be incorporated in text via higher protocols that allow intermixing of graphic images with text, rather than by indefinite extension of the number of Miscellaneous Symbols encoded as characters. However, a large unassigned space has been set aside in this block with the expectation that other conventional sets of such symbols may be found appropriate for character encoding in the future.

No attempt is made to provide a complete character encoding for musical notation. The Unicode Standard considers musical notation to be a higher-order text format that requires two-dimensional layout control and complex structures.

Standards. The Miscellaneous Symbols are derived from a large range of national and vendor character standards.

Encoding Structure. The character block for Miscellaneous Symbols is divided into the following ranges:

U+2600	→	U+2603	Weather symbols
U+2604	→	U+262F,	Miscellaneous symbols
U+2638	→	U+263C,	
U+2645	→	U+2647,	
U+2668			
U+2630	→	U+2637	I-Ching symbols
U+263D	→	U+2644	Moon phases and planets
U+2648	→	U+2653	Signs of the zodiac
U+2654	→	U+265F	Chess pieces
U+2660	→	U+2667	Card suits
U+2669	→	U+266F	Musical symbols

Dingbats: U+2700—U+27BF

The Dingbats are a well-established set of symbols comprising the industry standard "Zapf Dingbat" font—currently available in most laser printers. Other series of Dingbats also exist but are not encoded in the Unicode Standard because they are not widely implemented in existing hardware and software as character-encoded fonts. Dingbats that are part of other standards have been encoded in the Geometrical Shapes, Enclosed Alphanumerics, and Miscellaneous Symbols blocks. The order of the remaining dingbats follows the PostScript encoding.

The Dingbats differ in their treatment in the Unicode Standard from all other characters. They are encoded as specific glyph shapes, rather than as glyphic archetypes for abstract characters that can be represented in different faces and styles. Thus, it would be incorrect to arbitrarily replace U+279D TRIANGLE-HEADED RIGHTWARDS ARROW ➝ with any other right arrow dingbat or with any of the generic arrows from the Arrows block (U+2190 → U+21FF). In other words, since the Zapf Dingbats refer to glyphs from a specific typeface, their semantic value *is* their shape.

Unifications. A number of the Dingbats represent shapes that overlap with regular Unicode symbol characters. Instead of coding both a Zapf Dingbat glyph shape and a separate character whose glyphic representation is normally indistinguishable from that shape, the Unicode Standard unifies the two. The characters in question include card suits, BLACK STAR, BLACK TELEPHONE, and BLACK RIGHT-POINTING INDEX (see "Miscellaneous Symbols"); BLACK CIRCLE and BLACK SQUARE (see "Geometric Shapes"); white encircled numbers 1 to 10 (see "Enclosed Alphanumerics"); and several generic arrows (see "Arrows"). These four entries appear elsewhere in this section.

The positions of these unified characters are left unassigned in the Dingbats block and are cross-referenced to the assigned positions in the other blocks. Applications may use alternative glyphs for representing those characters (as for any normal Unicode characters), including, of course, the exact shapes required for rendering them in the Zapf Dingbat font on an imaging device.

To illustrate this distinction, an application encoding an encircled digit one with U+2460 ① CIRCLED DIGIT ONE may render that encircled digit in any appropriate typeface—serif or sans serif, roman or italic, and with the circle rendered in different thicknesses. On the other hand, an application encoding an encircled digit one with the Dingbat U+2780 SANS SERIF CIRCLED DIGIT ONE ➀ requires an explicit sans serif glyph from the Zapf Dingbat font for rendering.

Encoding Structure. The character block for Dingbats is divided into the following ranges:

U+2701 → U+27BE ITC Zapf Dingbats, series 100 (with gaps for unifications)

6.3 CJK Phonetics and Symbols Area

The CJK Phonetics and Symbols Area of the Unicode Standard includes the encoding of phonetic characters, punctuation marks and symbols used in the CJK (Chinese, Japanese, Korean) writing systems (see Figure 6-21).

Figure 6-21. CJK Misc

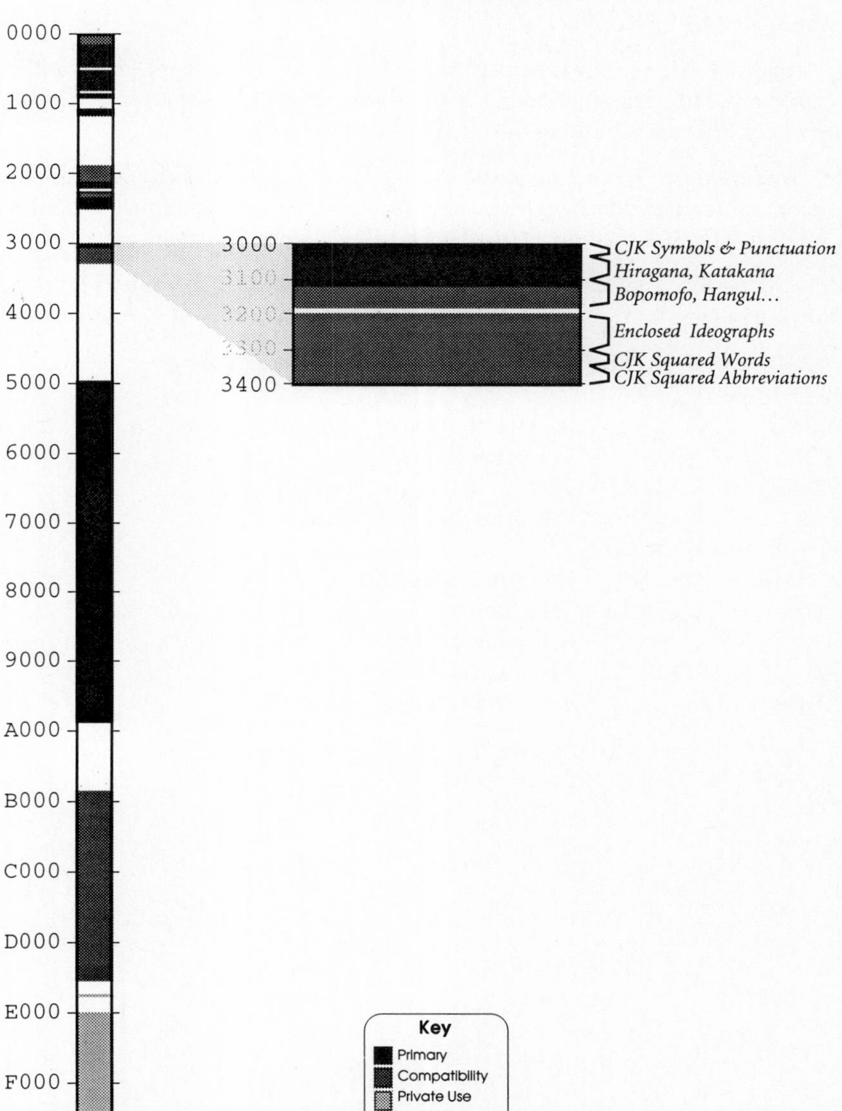

CJK Symbols and Punctuation: U+3000—U+303F

This block encodes punctuation marks and symbols used primarily by writing systems that employ Han ideographs. Most of these characters are found in East Asian standards.

U+3000 IDEOGRAPHIC SPACE is provided for compatibility. It is a fixed-width space appropriate for use with an ideographic font. U+301C WAVE DASH and U+3030 WAVY DASH are special forms of dashes found in East Asian character standards. (For a list of other space and dash characters in the Unicode Standard, see the General Punctuation character block description.)

U+3037 IDEOGRAPHIC TELEGRAPHIC LINE FEED SEPARATOR SYMBOL is a visible indicator of the line feed separator symbol used in the Chinese telegraphic code; it is comparable to the pictures of control codes found in the Control Pictures block.

U+303F IDEOGRAPHIC HALF-FILL SPACE is a visible indicator of a display cell filler used when ideographic characters have been split during display on systems using a double-byte character encoding. It is included in the Unicode Standard for compatibility.

Encoding Structure. The character block for CJK Punctuation and Symbols is divided into the following ranges:

U+3000	→	U+3003,	Ideographic space and punctuation
U+3005	→	U+3006	
U+3004			Japanese Industrial Standard symbol
U+3007			Ideographic zero
U+3008	→	U+3011	CJK quotation marks and brackets
U+3012	→	U+3020,	CJK symbols and brackets
U+3036	→	U+3037	
U+3021	→	U+3029	Hangzhou numerals
U+302A	→	U+302F	Tone marks
U+3030			CJK punctuation
U+3031	→	U+3035	Kana repeat marks
U+303F			Ideographic half-fill space

Hiragana: U+3040—U+309F

Hiragana is the cursive syllabary used to write Japanese words phonetically and also to write sentence particles and inflectional endings. Hiragana is commonly used as well to indicate the pronunciation of Japanese words. Hiragana syllables are phonetically equivalent to corresponding Katakana syllables.

Standards. The Hiragana block is based on the JIS X 0208-1990 standard, extended by the non-standard syllable U+3094 VU, which is included in some Japanese corporate standards.

Combining Marks. Hiragana and the related script Katakana use U+3099 COMBINING KATAKANA-HIRAGANA VOICED SOUND MARK and U+309A COMBINING KATAKANA-HIRAGANA SEMI-VOICED SOUND MARK to generate voiced and semi-voiced syllables from the base syllables, respectively. All common precomposed combinations of base syllable forms using these marks are already encoded as characters, and use of these precomposed forms is the predominant JIS usage. These combining marks must follow the base character to which they apply. As most implementations and JIS standard treat these as spacing characters, the Unicode Standard also contains two corresponding non-combining (spacing) marks at U+309B and U+309C.

Iteration Marks. The two characters U+309D HIRAGANA ITERATION MARK and U+309E HIRAGANA VOICED ITERATION MARK are punctuation-like characters that denote the iteration (repetition) of a previous syllable according to whether the repeated syllable has an unvoiced or voiced consonant, respectively.

Encoding Structure. The character block for the Hiragana script is divided into the following ranges:

U+3041	→	U+3093	Hiragana syllabary
U+3094			Extended Hiragana syllable form
U+3099	→	U+309A	Combining (non-spacing) diacritical marks
U+309B	→	U+309C	Non-Combining (spacing) diacritical marks
U+309D	→	U+309E	Iteration marks

Katakana: U+30A0—U+30FF

Katakana is the non-cursive syllabary used to write non-Japanese (usually Western) words phonetically in Japanese. Katakana is also used as well to write Japanese words with visual emphasis. Katakana syllables are phonetically equivalent to corresponding Hiragana syllables. Katakana contains two characters, U+30F5 KATAKANA LETTER SMALL KA and U+30F6 KATAKANA LETTER SMALL KE, which have no direct correspondent in Hiragana; these are used in special Japanese spelling conventions (for example, the spelling of placenames which include archaic Japanese connective particles).

Standards. The Katakana block is based on the JIS X 0208-1990 standard.

Punctuation-like Characters. U+30FB KATAKANA MIDDLE DOT is used to separate words when writing non-Japanese phrases. U+30FC KATAKANA-HIRAGANA PROLONGED SOUND MARK is used predominantly with Katakana and occasionally with Hiragana in order to denote a lengthened vowel of the previously written syllable. The two iteration marks, U+30FD KATAKANA ITERATION MARK and U+30FE KATAKANA VOICED ITERATION MARK serve the same function in Katakana writing that the two Hiragana iteration marks serve in Hiragana writing.

Encoding Structure. The character block for the Katakana script is divided into the following ranges:

U+30A1	→	U+30F6	Katakana syllabary
U+30F7	→	U+30FA	Extended Katakana syllable forms
U+30FB	→	U+30FC	Punctuation and vowel lengthening mark
U+30FD	→	U+30FE	Iteration marks

Bopomofo: U+3100—U+312F

Bopomofo are a set of characters used to annotate or teach the phonetics of Chinese, primarily the standard Mandarin language. They are used in dictionaries and teaching materials, not in the actual writing of Chinese text. The formal Chinese names for this alphabet are *Zhuyin-Zimu* ("phonetic alphabet") or *Zhuyin-Fuhao* ("phonetic symbols"), but the informal term Bopomofo (analogous to "ABCs") provides a more serviceable English name and is also used in China. The Bopomofo were developed as part of a populist literacy campaign following the 1911 revolution; thus they are acceptable to all branches of modern Chinese culture, although in the People's Republic of China their function has been largely taken over by the Pinyin romanization system.

Standards. The standard Mandarin set of Bopomofo are included in the People's Republic of China standard GB 2312 and in the Republic of China (Taiwan) standard CNS 11643.

Mandarin Tone Marks. Small modifier letters used to indicate the five Mandarin tones are part of the Bopomofo system, but in the Unicode Standard they have been unified into the Modifier Letter range, as follows:

first tone	U+02C9	MODIFIER LETTER MACRON
second tone	U+02CA	MODIFIER LETTER ACUTE ACCENT
third tone	U+02C7	CARON
fourth tone	U+02CB	MODIFIER LETTER GRAVE ACCENT
light tone	U+02D9	DOT ABOVE

Standard Mandarin Bopomofo. The order of Bopomofo letters is standard worldwide. The code offset of the first letter U+3105 BOPOMOFO LETTER B from a multiple of 16 is included to match the offset in the ISO-registered standard GB 2312. The character U+3127 BOPOMOFO LETTER I is usually written as a horizontal stroke when the Bopomofo text is set vertically; in the Unicode Standard this is considered to be a rendering variation; the variant is not assigned a separate character code.

Non-Mandarin Letters. These are very rarely used but are included for completeness. There are no standard Bopomofo letters for the phonetics of Cantonese or other dialects.

Encoding Structure. The character block for Bopomofo is divided into the following ranges:

U+3105	→	U+3129	Standard Mandarin Bopomofo
U+312A	→	U+312C	Dialect (non-Mandarin) letters

Hangul Compatibility Jamo: U+3130—U+318F

This block consists of spacing, non-conjoining Hangul consonant and vowel (jamo) elements. These characters are provided solely for compatibility with the KS C 5601 standard. Unlike the characters found in the Hangul Jamo block (U+1100 → U+11FF), the jamo characters in this block have no conjoining semantics.

The characters of this block are considered to be full-width forms in contrast with the Halfwidth Hangul Compatibility Jamo found at U+FFA0 → U+FFDF.

Standards. The Unicode Standard follows KS C 5601 for Hangul Jamo elements.

Encoding Structure. The character block for Hangul Elements is divided into the following ranges:

U+3131	→	U+3163	Modern Jamo elements
U+3164			Hangul fill character
U+3165	→	U+318E	Archaic Jamo elements

Kanbun: U+3190—U+319F

This block contains a set of Kanbun marks used in Japanese texts to indicate the Japanese reading order of classical Chinese texts. They are not encoded in any current character encoding standards but are widely used in literature. They are typically written in an annotation style to the left of each line of vertically-rendered Chinese text.

Encoding Structure. The character block for Kanbun is divided into the following ranges:

U+3190 → U+319F Kanbun marks

Enclosed CJK Letters and Months: U+3200—U+32FF

Standards. This block provides mapping for all the enclosed Hangul elements from Korean standard KS C 5601 as well as parenthesized ideographic characters from JIS X 0208-1990 standard, CNS 11643, and several corporate registries.

Encoding Structure. The character block for CJK parenthesized letters and ideographs is divided into the following ranges:

U+3200	→	U+320D	Parenthesized Hangul Jamo elements
U+320E	→	U+321C	Parenthesized Hangul syllables
U+3220	→	U+3229	Parenthesized number ideographs
U+322A	→	U+3243	Parenthesized ideographs
U+3260	→	U+326D	Circled Hangul Jamo elements
U+326E	→	U+327B	Circled Hangul syllables
U+327F			Korean standard symbol
U+3280	→	U+3289	Circled number ideographs
U+328A	→	U+32B0	Circled ideographs
U+32C0	→	U+32CB	Ideographic telegraph symbols for months
U+32D0	→	U+32FE	Circled Katakana

CJK Compatibility: U+3300—U+33FF

CJK squared Katakana words are Katakana-spelled words that fill a single display cell (em-square) when intermixed with CJK ideographs. Likewise, squared Latin abbreviation symbols are designed to fill a single character position when mixed with CJK ideographs.

These characters are provided solely for compatibility with existing character encoding standards.

Standards. CJK Compatibility characters are derived from the KS C 5601 and CNS 11643 national standards, and from various company registries.

Japanese Era Names. The Japanese era names refer to the following dates:

U+337B	SQUARE ERA NAME HEISEI	1989/1/7 to present day
U+337C	SQUARE ERA NAME SYOUWA	1926/12/24 to 1989/1/6
U+337D	SQUARE ERA NAME TAISYOU	1912/7/29 to 1926/12/23
U+337E	SQUARE ERA NAME MEIZI	1867 to 1912/7/28

Encoding Structure. The character block for CJK Compatibility characters is divided into the following ranges:

U+3300	→	U+3357	Squared symbolic Katakana words
U+3358	→	U+3370	Ideographic telegraph symbols for hours
U+3371	→	U+3376	Squared Latin abbreviation symbols
U+337B	→	U+337E	Japanese era names
U+337F			Squared Ideographic word ('corporation')
U+3380	→	U+33DD	Squared Latin abbreviation symbols
U+33E0	→	U+33FE	Ideographic telegraph symbols for days

6.4 CJK Ideographs Area

The CJK Ideographs Area of the Unicode Standard encodes the ideographic Han characters (see Figure 6-22).

Figure 6-22. CJK Ideographs

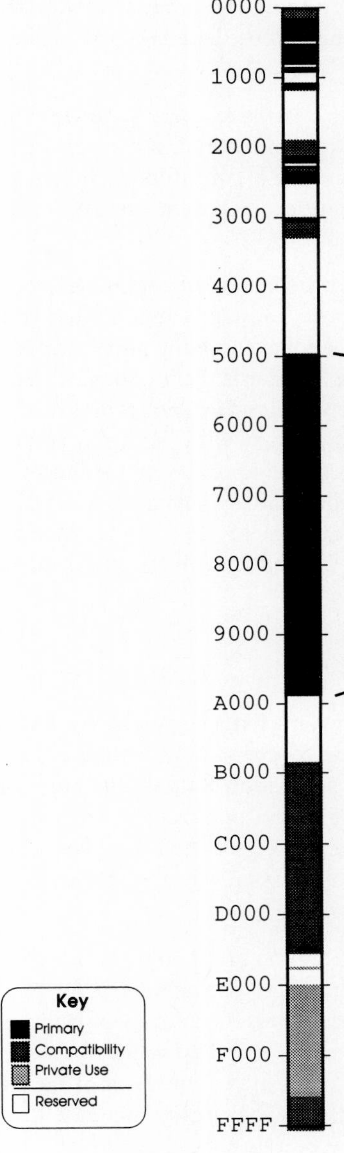

CJK Unified Ideographs: U+4E00—U+9FFF

This block contains a set of Unified Han ideographic characters used in the written Chinese, Japanese, and Korean languages.[1] The term *Han*, derived from *Han Dynasty*, refers generally to Chinese traditional culture. The Han ideographic characters comprise a coherent script, which was traditionally written vertically, with the vertical lines ordered from right-to-left. In modern usage, especially in technical works and in computer-rendered text, the Han script is written horizontally from left-to-right and is freely mixed with Latin or other scripts. When used in writing Japanese or Korean, the Han characters are interspersed with other scripts unique to those languages (Hiragana and Katakana for Japanese; Hangul syllables for Korean).

The Han ideographic characters constitute a very large set, numbering in the tens of thousands. They have a very long history of use in East Asia. Enormous compendia of Han ideographic characters exist because of a continuous, millenia-long scholarly tradition of collecting all Han character citations, including variant, mistaken, and nonce forms, into annotated character dictionaries.

Because of the very large size of the Han ideographic character repertoire, and because of the particular problems they pose for standardizing their encoding, this character block description is more extended than that for many other scripts. It is divided into the following subsections. First, there is a Standards section, describing the source standards for the repertoire encoded in the Unicode Standard. Following that is an extended discussion of the characteristics of the Han characters, with particular attention to the problem of unification of encoding for characters used for different languages. Then there is a formal statement of the principles behind the Unified Han character encoding adopted in the Unicode Standard and order of their arrangement. (For a detailed account of the background and history of development of the Unified Han character encoding, see also *Appendix E, Han Unification History.*)

CJK Standards

The Unicode Standard draws its Han character repertoire of 20,902 characters from a number of character standards. These source standards were categorized into two classes: those standards to which the Source Separation Rule should apply, and those to which this rule would not apply. This rule states that ideographs that are distinct in a source standard must not be unified. (For further discussion, see the Principles subsection later in this section.) The source standards to which this rule was applied are detailed in *Table 6-21 Primary Source Standards for Unified Han.*

This table gives a category label to each of the source standards for which the Source Separation Rules applies. The number of source characters for those standards is calculated as follows: The number of source characters consists of only those characters that are not already included from a prior source standard within its same category: G, T, J, or K. For example, only 2,352 characters of G_1 are counted out of the 6,866 characters in GB12345-90 since many characters from G_1 were already included through G_0. However, in some categories, such as the J category, every source character of each standard in that category is counted as a new inclusion since there is no overlap between the standards that comprise the category.

---

1. Although the term CJK—Chinese, Japanese, and Korean—is used throughout this text to describe the languages that currently use Han ideographic characters, it should be noted that earlier Vietnamese writing systems were based on Han ideographs. Consequently, the term CJKV would be more accurate in a historical sense. Han ideographs are still used for historical, religious, and pedagogical purposes in Vietnam.

Table 6-21. Primary Source Standards for Unified Han

Category	Standard	Number of Source Characters
G_0	GB2312-80	6,763
G_1	GB12345-90	2,352
G_3	GB7589-87	4,835
G_5	GB7590-87	2,842
G_7	General Use Characters for Modern Chinese	42
G_8	GB8565-88	290
T_1	CNS 11643-1986/1st plane	5,401
T_2	CNS 11643-1986/2nd plane	7,650
T_e	CNS 11643-1986/14th plane	4,198
J_0	JIS X 0208-1990	6,356
J_1	JIS X 0212-1990	5,801
K_0	KS C 5601-1987	4,620
K_1	KS C 5657-1991	2,856

Other contributing standards included by unification without the application of the Source Separation Rule are listed in Table 6-22 without a formal category label.

Table 6-22. Secondary Source Standards for Unified Han

Standard	Number of Source Characters
ANSI Z39.64-1989 (EACC)	13,053
Big-5 (Taiwan)	13,481
CCCII, level 1	4,808
GB 12052-89 (Korean)	94
JEF (Fujitsu)	3,149
PRC Telegraph Code	~8,000
Taiwan Telegraph Code (CCDC)	9,040
Xerox Chinese	9,776

In addition to the standards in the preceding two tables, the following standards were also included by unification without the application of the Source Separation Rule: Han Character Shapes Permitted for Personal Names (Japan) and IBM Selected Japanese and Korean ideographs.

General Characteristics of Han Ideographs

The authoritative Japanese dictionary *Kouzien*, defines Han characters to be

> characters that originated among the Chinese to write the Chinese language. They are now used in China, Japan, and Korea. They are logographic (each character represents a word, not just a sound) characters that developed from pictographic and ideographic principles. They are also used phonetically. In Japan they are generally called *kanzi* (Han, that is, Chinese, characters) including the "national characters"(*kokuzi*) such as *touge* (mountain pass), which have been created using the same principles. They are also called *mana* (true names, as opposed to *kana*, false or borrowed names).[1]

1. Lee Collins' translation from the Japanese, *Kouzien*, Izuru, Shinmura, ed. (Tokyo: Iwanami Syoten, 1983).

For many centuries, written Chinese was the accepted written standard throughout East Asia. The impact of the Chinese language and its written form on the modern East Asian languages is similar to the impact of Latin on the vocabulary and written forms of languages in the West. This is immediately visible in the mixture of Han characters and native phonetic scripts (*kana* in Japan, *hangul* in Korea) as now used in the orthographies of Japan and Korea (see Table 6-23).

Table 6-23. Common Han Characters

Han Character	*Chinese*[a]	*Japanese*	*Korean*	*English translation*
天	tian[1]	ten, ame	chen	heaven, sky
地	di[4]	ti, tuti	ci	earth, ground
人	ren[2]	zin, hito	in	man, person
山	shan[1]	san, yama	san	mountain
水	shui[3]	sui, mizu	swu	water
上	shang[4]	zyou, ue	sang	above
下	xia[4]	ka, sita	ha	below

a. The superscripted numbers in this table represent Chinese (Mandarin) tone marks.

The evolution of character shapes and semantic drift over the centuries has resulted in changes to the original forms and meanings. For example, the Chinese character 湯 *tang* (Japanese *tou* or *yu*, Korean *thang*), which originally meant "hot water," has come to mean "soup" in Chinese. "Hot water" remains the primary meaning in Japanese and Korean, while "soup" appears in more recent borrowings from Chinese, such as "soup noodles" (Japanese *tanmen*; Korean *thangmyen*.) Still, the identical appearance and similarities in meaning are dramatic and more than justify the concept of a unified Han script that transcends language.

The "nationality" of the Han characters became an issue only when each country began to create coded character sets (for example, China's GB 2312-80, Japan's JIS X 0208-1978, and Korea's KS C 5601-87) based on purely local needs. This problem appears to have arisen more from the priority placed on local requirements and lack of coordination with other countries, rather than out of conscious design. But the identity of the Han characters is fundamentally independent of language, as shown by dictionary definitions, vocabulary lists, and encoding standards.

Terminology. Several standard romanizations of the term used to refer to East Asian ideographic characters are commonly used. These include *hanzi* (Chinese), *kanzi* (Japanese), *kanji* (colloquial Japanese), *hanja* (Korean), and Chữ hán (Vietnamese). The standard English translations for these terms are interchangeable: Han character, Han ideographic character, East Asian ideographic character, or CJK ideographic character. For the purpose of clarity, the Unicode Standard uses some subset of the English terms when referring to these characters. The term *Kanzi* is used in reference to a specific Japanese government publication. The unrelated term *KangXi* (which is a Chinese reign name, rather than another romanization of "Han character") is used only when referring to the dictionary on which the Unified Repertoire and Ordering, Version 2.0 was based.

Distinguishing Han Character Usage Between Languages. There is some concern that unifying the Han characters may lead to confusion because they are sometimes used differently by the various East Asian languages. Computationally, Han character unification presents no more difficulty than employing a single Latin character set that is used to write languages as different as English and French. Programmers do not expect the characters 'c' 'h' 'a' and 't' alone to tell us whether *chat* is a French word for cat or an English word meaning "informal talk." Likewise, we depend on context to identify the American hood (of a car) with the British bonnet. Few computer users are confused by the fact that ASCII can also be used to represent such words as the Welsh word *ynghyd*, which are strange looking to English eyes. Although it would be convenient to identify words by language for programs such as spell-checkers, it is neither practical nor productive to encode a separate Latin character set for every language that uses it.

Similarly, the Han characters are often combined to "spell" words whose meaning may not be evident from the constituent characters. For example, the two characters "to cut" and "hand" mean "postal stamp" in Japanese, but the compound may appear to be nonsense to a speaker of Chinese or Korean (see Figure 6-23).

Figure 6-23. Han Spelling

切 + 手 = 1. Japanese "stamp".
2. Chinese "cut hand".

to cut hand

Even within one language, a computer requires context to distinguish the meanings of words represented by coded characters. The word *chuugoku* in Japanese, for example, may refer to China or to a district in central west Honshuu (see Figure 6-24).

Figure 6-24. Context for Characters

中 + 国 = 1. China
2. Chuugoku district of Honshuu

middle country

Coding these two characters as four so as to capture this distinction would probably cause more confusion and still not provide a general solution. The Unicode Standard leaves the issues of language tagging and word recognition up to a higher level of software and does not attempt to encode the language of the Han characters.

Sorting Han Ideographs. The Unicode Standard does not define a method by which ideographic characters are sorted; the requirements for sorting differ by locale and application. Possible collating sequences include phonetic, radical-stroke (*KangXi*, *Xinhua Zidian*, and so on), four-corner, and total stroke count. Raw character codes alone are seldom sufficient to achieve a useable ordering in any of these schemes; ancillary data is usually required. (See *Table 6-26 Han Ideograph Arrangement.*)

Character Glyphs. In form, Han characters are monospaced. Every character takes the same vertical and horizontal space, regardless of how simple or complex its particular form is. This follows from the long history of printing and typographical practice in China, which traditionally placed each character in a square cell. When written vertically, there are also a number of named cursive styles for Han characters, but the cursive forms of the characters tend to be quite idiosyncratic and are not implemented in general-purpose Han character fonts for computers.

There may be a wide variation in the glyphs used in different countries and for different applications. The most commonly used typefaces in one country may not be used in others.

The types of glyphs used to depict characters in the Han ideographic repertoire of the Unicode Standard have been constrained by available fonts. Users are advised to consult authoritative sources for the appropriate glyphs for individual markets and applications. It is assumed that most Unicode implementations will provide users with the ability to select the font (or mixture of fonts) that is most appropriate for a given application.

Principles

Three-Dimensional Conceptual Model. In order to develop the explicit rules for unification, a conceptual framework was developed to model the nature of Han ideographic characters. This model expresses written elements in terms of three primary attributes: semantic (meaning, function), abstract shape (general form), and actual shape (instantiated, typeface form). These attributes are graphically represented in three dimensions according to the X, Y, and Z axes (see Figure 6-25).

Figure 6-25. Three-Dimensional Conceptual Model

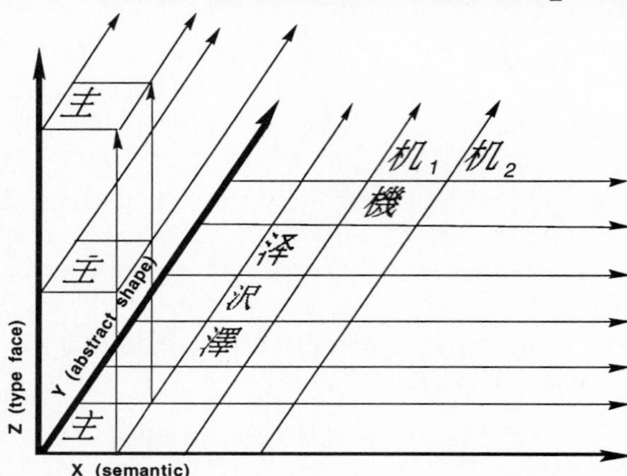

The semantic attribute (represented along the *X* axis) distinguishes characters by meaning and usage. Distinctions are made between entirely unrelated characters such as 澤 (marsh) and 機 (machine) as well as extensions or borrowings beyond the original semantic cluster such as 机$_1$ (a phonetic borrowing used as a simplified form of 機) and 机$_2$ (table, the original meaning).

The abstract shape attribute (the *Y* axis) distinguishes the variant forms of a single character with a single semantic attribute (that is, a character with a single position on the *X* axis).

The actual shape (typeface) attribute (the *Z* axis) is for differences of type design (the actual shape used in imaging) of each variant form.

Only characters that have the same abstract shape (that is, occupy a single point on the *X* and *Y* axes) are potential candidates for unification. *Z* axis typeface and semantic differences are generally ignored.

Unification Rules. The following rules were applied during the process of merging Han characters from the different source character sets:

R1 ***Source Separation Rule. If two ideographs are distinct in a primary source standard, then they are not unified.***

For example, the following ideographs would normally be subject to unification by rule R3; however, their unification is prevented since they are distinct in the primary source standard J_0 (JIS X 0208-1990) (see Figure 6-36).

Figure 6-26. Preserving Variants

剣 劍 剱 劔 劒 釼

"sword"

➥ This rule is sometimes called the *round-trip rule* since its goal is to facilitate a round-trip conversion of character data between a primary source standard and the Unicode Standard without loss of information.

R2 ***Non-Cognate Rule. In general, if two ideographs are unrelated in historical derivation (non-cognate characters), then they are not unified.***

For example, the following ideographs (in Figure 6-27) although visually quite similar, are nevertheless not unified since they are historically unrelated, and have distinct meanings.

Figure 6-27. Not Cognates, Not Unified

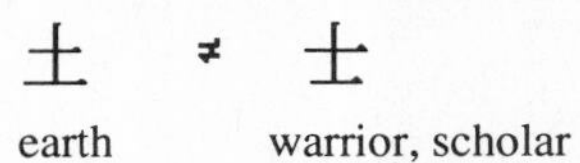

R3 ***By means of a two-level classification (described next), the abstract shape of each ideograph is determined. Any two ideographs that possess the same abstract shape are then unified provided their unification is not disallowed by either the source separation rule or the non-cognate rule.***

Two-Level Classification. Using the three-dimensional model, characters are analyzed in a two-level classification. The two-level classification distinguishes characters by abstract shape (*Y* axis) and actual shape of a particular typeface (*Z* axis). Variant forms are identified based on the difference of abstract shapes.

In order to determine differences in abstract shape and actual shape, the structure and features of each component of an ideograph is analyzed as follows.

Ideograph Component Structure. The component structure of each ideograph is examined. A component is a geometrical combination of primitive elements. Various ideographs can be configured with these components used in conjunction with other components. Some components can be combined to make a component more complicated in its structure. Therefore, an ideograph can be defined as a component tree with the entire ideograph as the root node and with the bottom nodes consisting of primitive elements (see Figures 6-28 and 6-29).

Figure 6-28. Component Structure

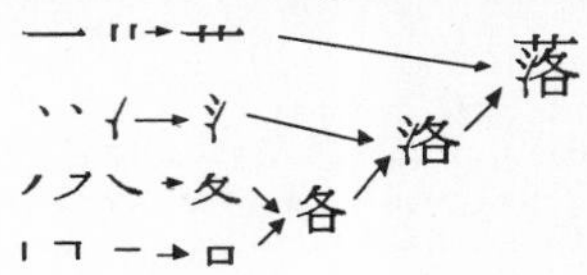

Figure 6-29. The Most Superior Node of a Component

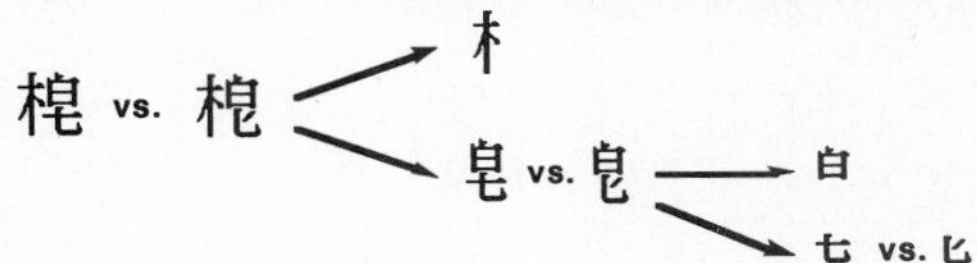

Ideograph Features. The following features of each ideograph to be compared are examined:

- Number of components
- Relative position of components in each complete ideograph
- Structure of a corresponding component
- Treatment in a source character set
- Radical contained in a component

Uniqueness. If one or more of these features are different between the ideographs compared, the ideographs are considered to have different abstract shapes and therefore are considered unique characters and are not unified.

Unification. If all these features are identical between the ideographs, the ideographs are considered to have the same abstract shape and are therefore unified.

The examples in Table 6-24 represent some typical differences in abstract character shape. The ideographs are therefore *not* unified.

Table 6-24. Ideographs Not Unified

Characters	Reason
崖 ≠ 厓	Different Number of Components
峰 ≠ 峯	Same Number of Components Placed in Different Relative Position
拡 ≠ 擴	Same Number and Same Relative Position of Components, Corresponding Components Structure Differently
区 ≠ 區	Characters Treated Differently in a Source Character Set
祕 ≠ 秘	Characters with Different Radical in a Component
爲 ≠ 為	Same Abstract Shape, Difference in Actual Shape

Differences in actual shape of ideographs that *have* been unified are illustrated in Table 6-25.

Table 6-25. Ideographs Unified

Characters	Reason
周 ≈ 周	Different Writing Sequence
雪 ≈ 雪	Differences in Overshoot at the Stroke Termination
酉 ≈ 酉	Differences in Contact of Strokes
鉅 ≈ 鉅	Differences in Protrusion at the Folded Corner of Strokes
亜 ≈ 亜	Differences in Bent Strokes
朱 ≈ 朱	Differences in Stroke Termination
父 ≈ 父	Differences in Accent at the Stroke Initiation
八 ≈ 八	Difference in Rooftop Modification
說 ≈ 説	Difference in Rotated Strokes/Dots[a]

a. These ideographs (having the same abstract shape) would have been unified except for the Source Separation Rule.

Han Ideograph Arrangment. The arrangement of the Unicode Han characters is based on the position of characters as they are listed in four major dictionaries. The *KangXi Zidian* was chosen as primary because it contains most of the source characters and because the dictionary itself and the principles of character ordering it employs are commonly used throughout East Asia.

The Han ideograph arrangement follows the index (page and position) of the dictionaries listed here with their priorities:

Table 6-26. Han Ideograph Arrangement

Priority	Dictionary	City	Publisher	Version
1	*KangXi Zidian*	Beijing	Zhonghua Bookstore, 1989	7th edition
2	*Dai Kanwa Ziten*	Tokyo	Taisyuukan Syoten, 1986	Revised edition
3	*Hanyu Da Zidian*	Chengdu	Sichuan Cishu Publishing, 1986	1st edition
4	*Dae Jaweon*	Seoul	Samseong Publishing Co. Ltd, 1988	1st edition

When a character is found in the *KangXi Zidian*, it follows the *KangXi Zidian* order. When it is not found in the *KangXi Zidian* and it is found in *Dai Kanwa Ziten*, it is given a position extrapolated from the *KangXi* position of the preceding character in *Dai Kanwa Ziten*. When it is not found in either *KanXi* or *Dai Kanwa*, then the *Hanyu Da Zidian* and *Dae Jaweon* dictionaries are consulted in a similar manner.

Ideographs with simplified *KangXi* radicals are placed in a group following the traditional *KangXi* radical from which the simplified radical is derived. For example, characters with the simplified radical 讠 corresponding to *KangXi* radical 言 follow the last non-simplified character having 言 as a radical. The arrangement for these simplified characters is that of the *Hanyu Da Zidian*.

The few characters which are not found in any of the four dictionaries are placed following characters with the same *KangXi* radical and stroke count.

Encoding Structure. The Unified CJK Ideographs block occupies range:

U+4E00 → U+9FA5 Unified CJK Ideograph Repertoire

➥ The form of the charts for the Unified CJK Ideographs block differs from that for other blocks; it is described in the introduction to *Chapter 7, Code Charts*. A full radical/stroke index is also provided in *Chapter 8, Han Radical-Stroke Index*, to help users locate characters in the main charts.

6.5 Hangul Syllables Area

The Hangul Syllables Area of the Unicode Standard encodes the Hangul syllable characters associated with the Korean writing system (see Figure 6-30).

Figure 6-30. Hangul Syllables

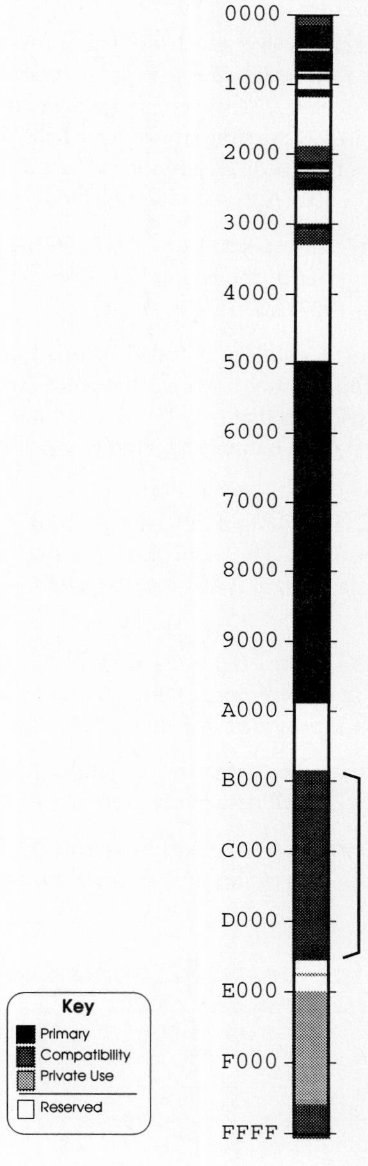

Hangul Syllables: U+AC00—U+D7A3

The Hangul script used in the Korean writing system consists of individual consonant and vowel letters (*jamo*) that are visually combined into square display cells to form entire syllable blocks. Hangul syllables may be encoded directly as precomposed combinations of individual jamo or as decomposed sequences of conjoining jamo. The latter encoding is supported by the Hangul Jamo block (U+1100 → U+11FF). The syllabic encoding method is described here.

Modern Hangul syllable blocks can be expressed with either two or three jamo, either in the form *consonant* + *vowel* or the form *consonant* + *vowel* + *consonant*. There are 19 possible leading (initial) consonants (*choseong*), 21 vowels (*jungeong*), and 27 trailing (final) consonants (*jongseong*). This results in 399 possible two-jamo syllable blocks and 10,773 possible three-jamo syllable blocks, for a total of 11,172 modern Hangul syllable blocks. This collection of 11,172 modern Hangul syllables encoded in this block is known as the *Johab* set.

Standards. The Hangul syllables are taken from KS C 5601-1992, representing the full Johab set. This represents a superset of the Hangul syllables encoded in earlier versions of Korean standards (KS C 5601 - 1987, KS C 5657 - 1991).

Equivalence. Each of the Hangul syllables encoded in this block may be encoded by an equivalent sequence of conjoining jamo; however, the converse is not true since there are thousands of archaic Hangul syllables that may be encoded only as a sequence of conjoining jamo. Implementations that use a conjoining jamo encoding are able to represent these archaic Hangul syllables.

Hangul Syllable Composition. The Hangul syllables can be derived from conjoining jamo by a regular process of composition. The algorithm that maps a sequence of conjoining jamo to the encoding point for a Hangul syllable in the Johab set is detailed in *Section 3.10, Combining Jamo Behavior.*

Hangul Syllable Decomposition. Conversely, any Hangul syllable from the Johab set can be decomposed into a sequence of conjoining jamo characters. The algorithm that details the formula for decomposition is provided in *Section 3.10, Combining Jamo Behavior.*

Hangul Syllable Name. The character name for Hangul syllables are derived algorithmically from the decomposition. (For full details, see *Section 3.10, Combining Jamo Behavior.*)

Hangul Syllable Representative Glyph. The representative glyph for a Hangul syllable can be formed from its decomposition based on the categorization of vowels shown in Table 6-25.

Table 6-27. Line-Based Placement of Jungseong

Vertical		Horizontal		Horizontal & Vertical	
1161	A	1169	O	116A	WA
1162	AE	116D	YO	116B	WAE
1163	YA	116E	U	116C	OE
1164	YAE	1172	YU	116F	WEO
1165	EO	1173	EU	1170	WE
1166	E			1171	WI
1167	YEO			1174	YI
1168	YE				
1175	I				

If the vowel of the syllable is based on a vertical line, place the leading consonant to its left. If the vowel is based on a horizontal line, place the preceding consonant above it. It the vowel is based on a combination of vertical and horizontal lines, place the preceding consonant above the horizontal line and to the left of the vertical line. In either case, place a following consonant, if any, below the middle of the resulting group.

In any particular font, the exact placement, shape and size of the components will vary according to the shapes of the other characters and the overall design of the font.

Encoding Structure. The character block for Hangul syllables is divided into the following ranges:

U+AC00 → U+D7A3 Hangul syllables in KSC 5601 order

6.6 Surrogates Area

The Surrogates Area of the Unicode Standard provides 2,048 character codes that are used in the surrogate extension method (see Figure 6-31).

Figure 6-31. Surrogates

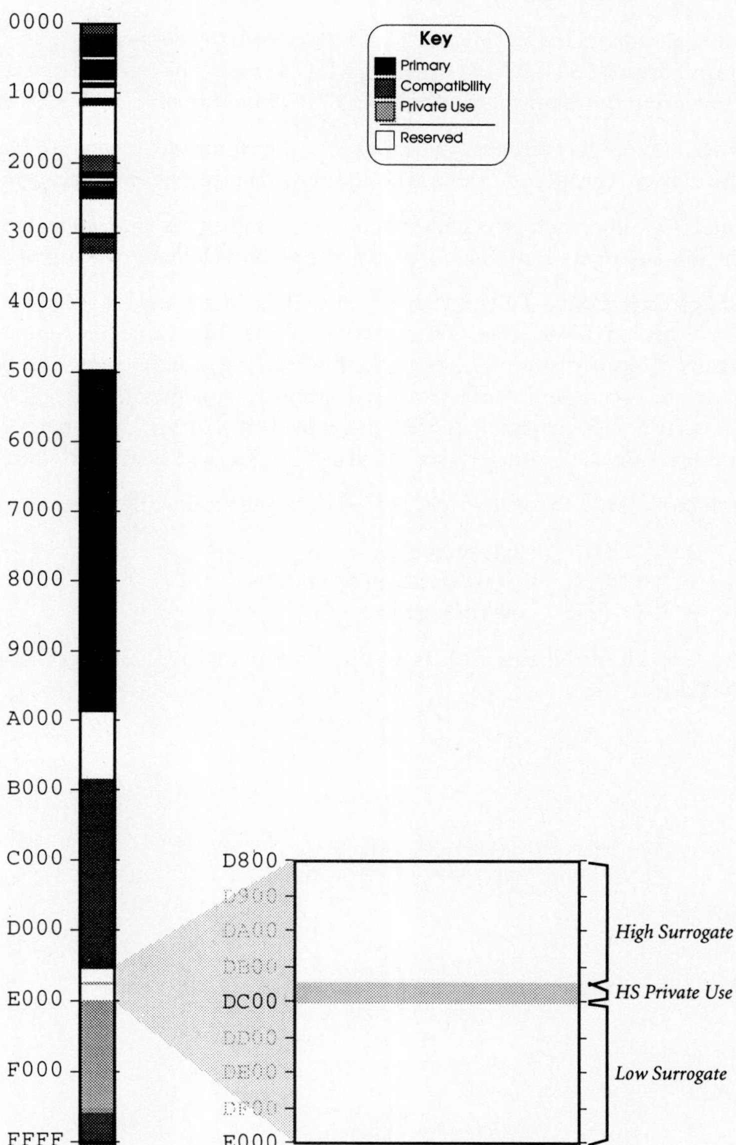

Surrogates Area: U+D800—U+DFFF

The Surrogates Area consists of 1,024 low-half surrogate code values and 1,024 high-half surrogate code values, which are interpreted in pairs to access over a million code points. Surrogate-pairs are designed to allow representation of rare characters in future extensions of the Unicode Standard. *There are no such characters currently assigned in this version of this standard.* (For the formal definition of a *surrogate-pair* and the role of surrogate-pairs in the Unicode Conformance Clause, see *Section 3.7, Surrogates.*)

The use of surrogate-pairs in the Unicode Standard is formally equivalent to the Universal Transformation Format-16 (UTF-16) defined in ISO 10646. (For a complete statement of the UTF-16 extension mechanism, see *Appendix C, Relationship to ISO/IEC 10646.*)

High Surrogate. The high surrogate code values are assigned to the range U+D800 → U+DBFF. The high surrogate code value is always the first element of a surrogate-pair.

Low Surrogate. The low surrogate code values are assigned to the range U+DC00 → U+DFFF. The low surrogate code value is always the second element of a surrogate-pair.

Private Use High Surrogates. The high surrogate code values from U+DB80 → U+DBFF are private use high surrogate code values (a total of 128 code values). Characters represented by means of a surrogate-pair, where the high surrogate code value is a private use high surrogate, are private use characters. This mechanism allows for a total of 131,072 (=128 × 1024) private use characters representable by means of surrogate-pairs. (For more information on private use characters, see the discussion of the Private Use Area.)

Encoding Structure. The Surrogate Area is divided into the following ranges:

U+D800	→	U+DB7F	High surrogates
U+DB80	→	U+DBFF	Private Use high surrogates
U+DC00	→	U+DFFF	Low surrogates

➥ There are no charts for this area, as no surrogate-pairs have assigned characters associated with them.

6.7 Private Use Area

The Private Use Area is reserved for use by software developers and end users who need a special set of characters for their application programs. The code points in this area are reserved for private use and do not have defined, interpretable semantics except by private agreement. (See Figure 6-32).

There are also private use characters defined by means of surrogate-pairs. (See the Surrogate Area description for a specification of how those private use characters are encoded.)

Figure 6-32. Private Use

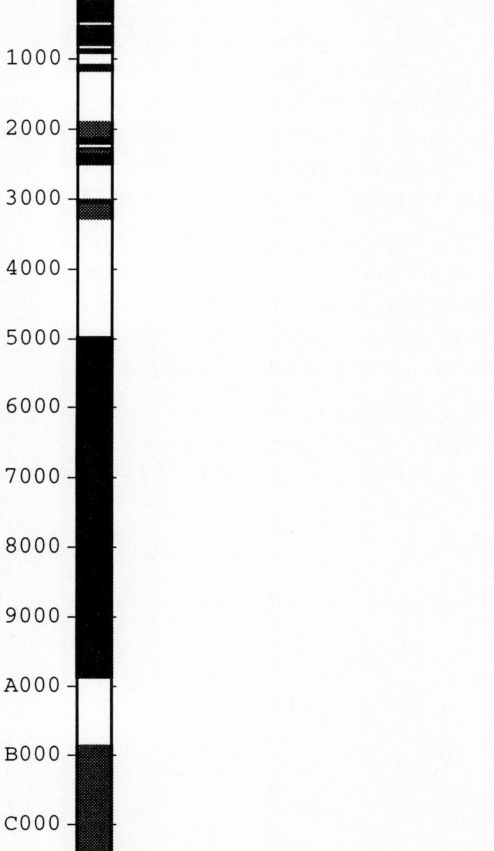

Private Use Area: U+E000—U+F8FF

Corporate Use Subarea. Systems vendors and/or software developers may need to reserve some private use characters for internal use by their software. The Corporate Use subarea is the preferred area for such reservations. Assignments of character semantics in this subarea could be completely internal, hidden from the end users, and used only for vendor-specific application support, or could be published as vendor-specific character assignments available to applications and end users. An example of the former case would be assignment of a character code to a system support operation such as <MOVE> or <COPY>; an example of the latter case would be assignment of a character code to a vendor-specific logo character such as Apple's *apple* character.

End User Subarea. The End User subarea is intended for private use character definition by end users, or for scratch allocations of character space by end user applications.

Allocation of Subareas. Vendors may choose to reserve private use codes in the Corporate Use subarea and make some defined portion of the End User subarea available for completely free end user definition. This convention is for the convenience of system vendors and software developers. No firm dividing line between the two subareas is defined, as different users may have different requirements. No provision is made in the Unicode Standard for avoiding a "stack-heap collision" between the two subareas in the Private Use Area.

Promotion of Private Use Characters. In future versions of the Unicode Standard, some characters that have been defined by one vendor or another in the Corporate Use subarea may be defined as regular Unicode characters if their usage is widespread enough that they become candidates for general use. These possibilities are to be distinguished from the treatment of characters defined in the Compatibility Area.

Encoding Structure. By convention, the Private Use Area is divided into a Corporate Use subarea, starting at U+F8FF and extending downward in values, and an End User subarea, starting at U+E000 and extending upward. The Private Use Area is divided into the following ranges:

U+E000 → U+F8FF Reserved for private use

➥ There are no charts for this area, as any character encoded in this area is privately defined.

6.8 Compatibility Area and Specials

The Compatibility Area is so named because it contains miscellaneous glyphs, contextual or orientational variants, vertical forms, and width variants that can legitimately be mapped to other characters in the Unicode Standard, but which require specific Unicode values for compatibility with pre-existing character standards. Canonical mappings between Compatibility Area characters and their regular counterparts can be found in the Character Names List.

Compatibility Area characters are provided solely for backwards compatibility to existing standards. The content of the Compatibility Area includes characters that are in use in existing implementations or standards, but whose semantics or usage is fundamentally at odds with the way in which the Unicode Standard generally handles characters. (See Figure 6-33).

Figure 6-33. Compatibility, Specials

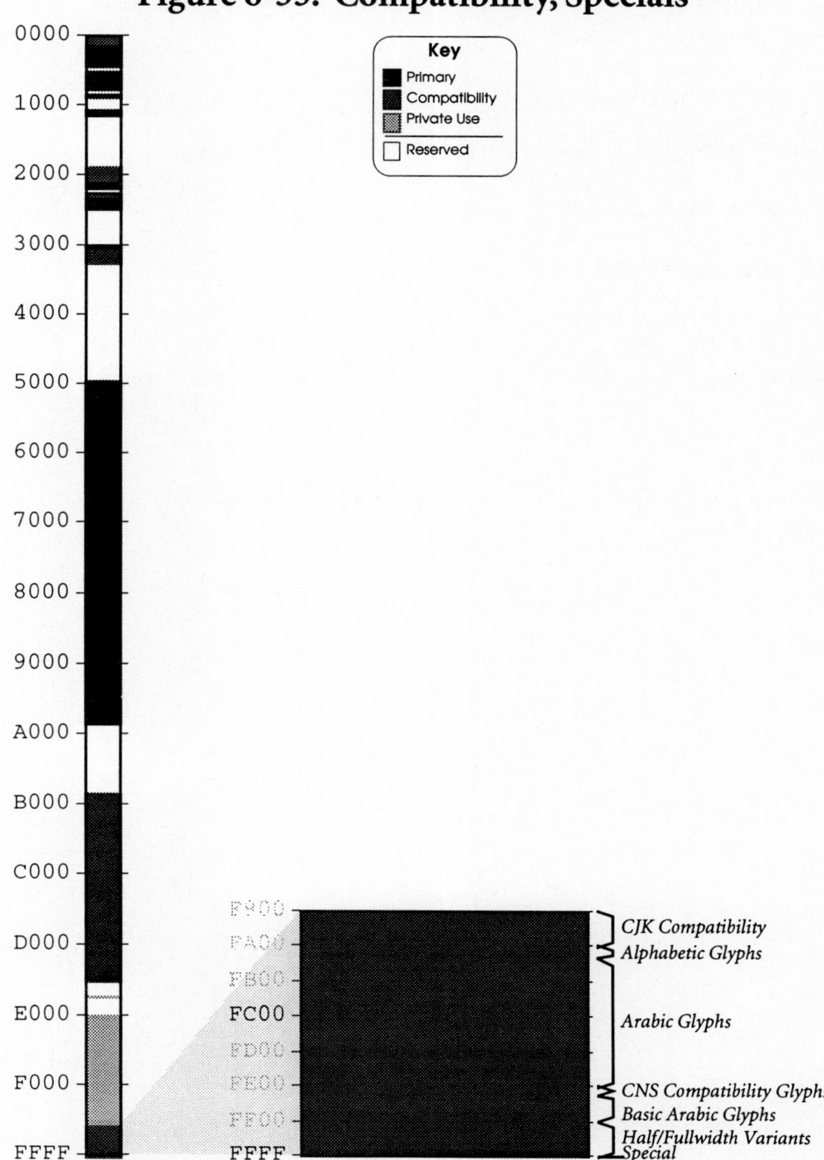

Note that not all compatibility characters are actually placed in this area; many characters outside of this area are also compatibility characters. These include superscript and subscript digits, precomposed combinations of Latin and Greek letterforms with one or more combining marks, certain letterlike symbols, non-conjoining Hangul Jamo, Hangul syllables, squared kana words and alphabetic units of measure, Han ideograph typeface (Z-axis) variants introduced by the source separation rule, and many others.

Conversely, the Compatibility Area *does* contain a small number of characters that are not compatibility characters. These include, for example, the Specials Block, U+FEFF ZERO WIDTH NO-BREAK SPACE, U+FB1E HEBREW POINT JUDEO-SPANISH VARIKA, and the ornate parentheses in the Arabic Presentation Forms-A Block.

The Specials block of the Compatibility Area contains code values that are interpreted neither as control nor graphic characters and which are provided to facilitate current software practices.

CJK Compatibility Ideographs: U+F900—U+FAFF

The Korean national standard KS C 5601-1987, which served as one of the primary source sets for the Unified CJK Ideograph Repertoire and Ordering 2.0, contains 268 duplicate encodings of identical ideograph forms in order to denote alternative pronunciations. That is, in certain cases, that standard encoded a single character multiple times in order to denote different linguistic uses. This is like encoding the letter 'a' five times to denote the different pronunciations it has in the words *hat, able, art, father, adrift.* Due to the source separation rule, these Korean characters could not be unified as required. Since they are in all ways identical in shape to their nominal counterparts, they are encoded separately from the primary CJK Unified Ideographs block.

In addition, another 34 ideographs that were duplicated in various regional and industry standards were encoded in this block in order to achieve round-trip conversion compatibility.

Encoding Structure. The CJK Compatibility Ideographs block is divided into the following ranges:

U+F900	→	U+FA0B	Pronunciation variants from KS C 5601-1987
U+FA0C	→	U+FA0D	Duplicates from Taiwan BIG5 Character Set
U+FA0E	→	U+FA2D	Duplicates from industry standards.

Alphabetic Presentation Forms: U+FB00—U+FB4F

This block is composed of a number of presentation forms commonly encoded with Latin, Armenian, and Hebrew texts. Each character in this block has a preferred encoding consisting of its components (in the case of ligatures and Hebrew pointed letters) or of its nominal counterpart (in the case of the wide Hebrew variants, U+FB1E HEBREW POINT JUDEO-SPANISH VARIKA, U+FB20 HEBREW LETTER ALTERNATIVE AYIN, and U+FB29 HEBREW LETTER ALTERNATIVE PLUS SIGN).

Encoding Structure. The Alphabetic Presentation Forms block is divided into the following ranges:

U+FB00	→	U+FB06	Latin ligatures
U+FB13	→	U+FB17	Armenian ligatures
U+FB1E			Variant of 05BF HEBREW POINT RAFE
U+FB1F			Hebrew ligature (Yiddish)
U+FB20			Variant of 05E2 HEBREW LETTER AYIN
U+FB21	→	U+FB28	Wide Hebrew letter variants
U+FB29			Hebrew variant of 002B PLUS SIGN
U+FB2A	→	U+FB36,	Hebrew pointed letters
U+FB38	→	U+FB3C,	
U+FB3E,			
U+FB40	→	U+FB41,	
U+FB43	→	U+FB44,	
U+FB46	→	U+FB4E	
U+FB4F			Hebrew ligature

Arabic Presentation Forms-A: U+FB50—U+FDFF

This block contains a list of presentation forms (glyphs) encoded as characters for compatibility. At the time of publication, there are no known implementations of all of these presentation forms. As with all other compatibility encodings, these characters have a preferred encoding that makes use of non-compatibility characters.

The presentation forms in this block consist of contextual (positional) variants of Extended Arabic letters, contextual variants of Arabic letter ligatures, spacing forms of Arabic diacritic combinations, contextual variants of certain Arabic letter/diacritic combinations, and Arabic phrase ligatures. (See also Arabic Presentation Forms-B U+FE70 → U+FEFE.)

The alternate (ornate) forms of parentheses for use with the Arabic script are not compatibility characters.

Encoding Structure. The Arabic Presentation Forms A block is divided into the following ranges:

U+FB50	→	U+FBB1,	Contextual variants of Extended Arabic letters
U+FBD3	→	U+FBE9	
U+FBFC	→	U+FBFF	Contextual variants of Extended Arabic letters (Farsi)
U+FBEA	→	U+FBFB,	Contextual variants of Extended Arabic ligatures
U+FC00	→	U+FC5D,	
U+FC64	→	U+FD3B	
U+FC5E	→	U+FC63	Spacing forms of Arabic diacritic combinations
U+FD3C	→	U+FD3D	Contextual variants of Arabic letter/diacritic combinations
U+FD3E			Ornate form of *left parenthesis*
U+FD3F			Ornate form of *right parenthesis*
U+FD50	→	U+FD8F,	Contextual variants of Arabic ligatures
U+FD92	→	U+FDC7	
U+FDF0	→	U+FDF1	Arabic phrase ligatures (Koranic stops)
U+FDF2	→	U+FDFB	Arabic phrase ligatures

Combining Half Marks: U+FE20—U+FE2F

This block consists of a number of presentation form (glyph) encodings which may be used to visually encode certain combining marks that apply to multiple base letterforms. These characters are intended to facilitate the support of such combining marks in simple implementations.

Unlike the other compatibility characters, these characters do not correspond to a single nominal character or a sequence of nominal characters; rather, a discontiguous sequence of these combining half marks corresponds to a single combining mark, as depicted in Figure 6-34.

Figure 6-34. Combining Half-Marks

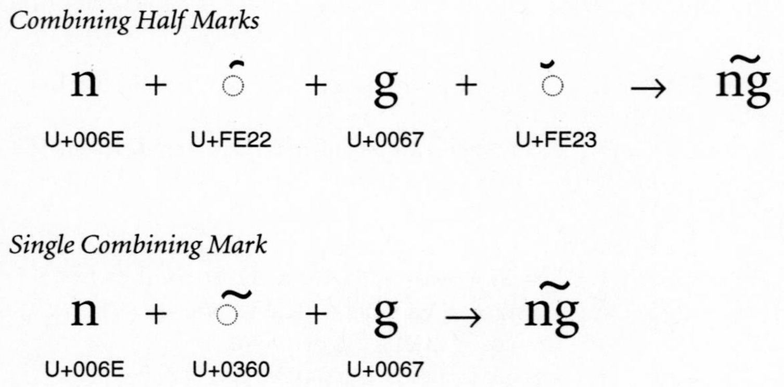

Combining Half Marks

n + ◌︢ + g + ◌︣ → n͠g

U+006E U+FE22 U+0067 U+FE23

Single Combining Mark

n + ◌͠ + g → n͠g

U+006E U+0360 U+0067

Encoding Structure. The Combining Half Marks block is divided into the following ranges:

U+FE20	→	U+FE21	Two halves of U+0361 COMBINING DOUBLE INVERTED BREVE
U+FE22	→	U+FE23	Two halves of U+0360 COMBINING DOUBLE TILDE

CJK Compatibility Forms: U+FE30—U+FE4F

A number of presentation forms are encoded in this block which are found in the Republic of China (Taiwan) national standard CNS 11643. These forms are often explicitly encoded when Chinese text is being set in vertical rather than horizontal lines. The preferred Unicode encoding is to encode the nominal characters that correspond to these vertical variants. Then, at display time, the appropriate glyph is selected according to the line orientation.

Encoding Structure. The CJK Compatibility Forms block is divided into the following ranges:

U+FE30 → U+FE4F Vertical punctuation variants from CNS 11643

Small Form Variants: U+FE50—U+FE6F

The Republic of China (Taiwan) national standard CNS 11643 also encodes a number of small variants of ASCII punctuation. The preferred Unicode encoding is to use the corresponding punctuation characters found in the ASCII block and use rich-text mechanisms (for example, font or font style bindings) to select the appropriate size and/or position of the displayed glyphs.

The characters of this block, while construed as fullwidth characters, are nevertheless depicted using small forms that are set in a fullwidth display cell. (See the discussion in the character block description for Halfwidth and Fullwidth Forms.)

Unifications. Two small form variants from CNS 11643/plane 1 were unified with other characters outside the ASCII block: 2131_{16} was unified with U+00B7 MIDDLE DOT, and 2261_{16} was unified with U+2215 DIVISION SLASH.

Encoding Structure. The Small Form Variants block is divided into the following ranges:

U+FE50 → U+FE6B Small punctuation variants from CNS 11643

Arabic Presentation Forms-B: U+FE70—U+FEFF

This block contains additional Arabic presentation forms comprised of spacing or *tatweel* forms of Arabic diacritics, contextual variants of primary Arabic letters, and the obligatory LAM-ALEF ligature. They are included here for compatibility with pre-existing standards and implementations that use these forms as characters. They can be replaced by letters from the Arabic block (U+0600 → U+06FF). Implementations can handle contextual glyph shaping by rendering rules when accessing glyphs from fonts, rather than by encoding contextual shapes as characters.

Spacing and Tatweel Forms of Arabic Diacritics. For compatibility with certain implementations, a set of spacing forms of the Arabic diacritics are provided here. The *tatweel* forms are combinations of the joining connector *tatweel* and a diacritic.

Zero Width No-Break Space. This character (U+FEFF), which is not an Arabic presentation form, is described in the Specials block (U+FFF0 → U+FFFF).

Encoding Structure. The Arabic Presentation Forms B block is divided into the following ranges:

U+FE70	→	U+FE72	Spacing/Tatweel forms of Arabic diacritics
U+FE74			Spacing forms of Arabic diacritic
U+FE76	→	U+FE7F	Spacing/Tatweel forms of Arabic diacritics
U+FE80	→	U+FEF4	Contextual variants of Arabic letters
U+FEF5	→	U+FEFC	Contextual variants of Arabic LAM-ALEF ligature
U+FEFF			*See Specials block description.*

Halfwidth and Fullwidth Forms: U+FF00—U+FFEF

In the context of East Asian coding systems, a double-byte character set (DBCS) such as JIS X 0208-1990 or KS C 5601-1987 is generally used together with a single-byte character set (SBCS), such as ASCII or a variant of ASCII. Text that is encoded with both a DBCS and SBCS is typically displayed such that the glyphs representing DBCS characters occupy two display cells where a display cell is defined in terms of the glyphs used to display the SBCS (ASCII) characters. In these systems, the two-display-cell width is known as the *fullwidth* or *zenkaku* form, while the one-display-cell width is known as the *halfwidth* or *hankaku* form.

Because of this mixture of display widths, certain characters often appear twice, once in fullwidth form in the DBCS repertoire and once in halfwidth form in the SBCS repertoire. In order to achieve round-trip conversion compatibility with such mixed encoding systems, it is necessary to encode both fullwidth and halfwidth forms of certain characters. This block consists of the additional forms needed to support conversion for existing texts which employ both forms.

In the context of conversion to and from such mixed width encodings, all characters in the General Scripts area should be construed as halfwidth (*hankaku*) characters. All characters in the CJK Phonetics and Symbols area and the Unified CJK Ideograph area, along with the characters in the CJK Compatibility Ideographs, CJK Compatibility Forms, and Small Form Variants blocks, should be construed as fullwidth (*zenkaku*) characters. Other Compatibility Area characters outside of the current block should be construed as halfwidth characters. The characters of the Symbols Area are neutral regarding their width semantics.

The characters in this block consist of fullwidth forms of the ASCII block (except SPACE), certain characters of the Latin-1 Supplement, and some currency symbols. In addition, this block contains halfwidth forms of the Katakana and Hangul Compatibility Jamo characters. Finally, a number of characters from the Symbols Area are replicated here (U+FFE8 → U+FFEE) with explicit halfwidth semantics.

As with other compatibility characters, the preferred Unicode encoding is to use the nominal counterparts of these characters and use rich text font or style bindings to select the appropriate glyph size and width.

Unifications. The fullwidth form of U+0020 SPACE is unified with U+3000 IDEOGRAPHIC SPACE.

Encoding Structure. The Halfwidth and Fullwidth Forms block is divided into the following ranges:

U+FF01	→	U+FF5E	Fullwidth ASCII
U+FF61	→	U+FF64	Halfwidth CJK punctuation
U+FF65	→	U+FF9F	Halfwidth Katakana
U+FFA0			Halfwidth Hangul Jamo filler
U+FFA1	→	U+FFDC	Halfwidth Hangul Jamo
U+FFE0	→	U+FFE6	Fullwidth punctuation and currency signs
U+FFE8	→	U+FFEE	Halfwidth forms, arrows, and shapes

Specials: U+FEFF, U+FFF0—U+FFFF

The fourteen Unicode values from U+FFF0 → U+FFFD are reserved for special character definitions. The only special character currently defined is U+FFFD REPLACEMENT CHARACTER, which is the general substitute character in the Unicode Standard. That character can be substituted for any "unknown" character in another encoding which cannot be mapped in terms of known Unicode values (see *Section 5.4, Unknown and Missing Characters*). In addition to these fourteen positions, two code values are specified here for use not as characters but as special signaling devices (described below).

U+FFFE. The 16-bit unsigned hexadecimal value U+FFFE is *not* a Unicode character value. Its occurrence in a stream of Unicode data strongly suggests that the Unicode characters should be byte-swapped before interpretation. U+FFFE should be interpreted only as an incorrectly byte-swapped version of U+FEFF ZERO WIDTH NO-BREAK SPACE, also known as the byte order mark.

Byte Order Mark. The code value U+FEFF *byte order mark* may be used at the beginning of a stream of coded characters to indicate that the characters following are Unicode characters.

The byte order mark is defined to be a signal of correct byte-order polarity. An application may use this signal character to explicitly enable the "big-endian" or "little-endian" byte order to be determined in Unicode text which may exist in either byte order (for example, in networks that mix Intel and Motorola or RISC CPU architectures for data storage). U+FEFF is the correct or legal order; finding a value U+FFFE is a signal that text of the incorrect byte order for an interpreting process has been encountered.

Encoding Form Signature. A character stream starting off with bytes FE and FF is unlikely to be ASCII text. Data streams (or files) that begin with U+FEFF *byte order mark* are likely to contain Unicode values. It is recommended that applications sending or receiving untyped data streams of coded characters use this signature.

The code value FEFF is assigned a signature role in Informative Annex F to ISO 10646. As specified in that annex, the code value FEFF may be used at the beginning of a stream of coded characters to indicate that the characters following are encode in the UCS-2 or UCS-4 representation, as follows:

Unicode encoding (UCS-2) signature:	FEFF
UCS-4 signature:	0000 FEFF

Since UCS-2 in ISO 10646 terminology is equivalent to the Unicode encoding, this convention for discerning between UCS-2 and UCS-4 forms of ISO 10646 is recommended to the attention of implementers of the Unicode Standard.

Zero Width No-Break Space. In addition to the meaning of *byte order mark*, the code value U+FEFF possesses the semantics of ZERO WIDTH NO-BREAK SPACE.

As ZERO WIDTH NO-BREAK SPACE, U+FEFF behaves like U+00A0 NO-BREAK SPACE in that it indicates the absence of word boundaries; however, the former has no width. For example, this character can be inserted after the fourth character in the text "base+delta" to indicate that there should be no line break between the "e" and the "+."

The characters U+2011 NON-BREAKING HYPHEN and U+00A0 NO-BREAK SPACE may also be expressed by using their counterparts U+2010 HYPHEN and U+0020 SPACE bracketed by ZERO WIDTH NO-BREAK SPACES. The ZERO WIDTH NO-BREAK SPACE can also be used in this manner to prevent line-breaking with other characters that do not have non-breaking variants, such as U+2009 THIN SPACE or U+2015 HORIZONTAL BAR.

This character has the opposite function from the U+200B ZERO WIDTH SPACE. The latter indicates a word boundary, except that it has no width. It can be used to indicate word boundaries in scripts such as Thai which do not use visible spaces to separate words.

The ZERO WIDTH NO-BREAK SPACE is not to be confused with U+200C ZERO WIDTH NON-JOINER. U+200C ZERO WIDTH NON-JOINER and U+200D ZERO WIDTH JOINER have no effect on word boundaries, while ZERO WIDTH NO-BREAK SPACE and ZERO WIDTH SPACE have no effect on joining or linking behavior. In other words, the ZERO WIDTH NO-BREAK SPACE and the ZERO WIDTH SPACE should be ignored when determining cursive joining behavior; the ZERO WIDTH NON-JOINER and ZERO WIDTH JOINER should be ignored when determining word boundaries. (For more discussion see the General Punctuation character block description.)

U+FFFF. The 16-bit unsigned hexadecimal value U+FFFF is *not* a Unicode character value; it may be used by an application as a error code or other non-character value. The specific interpretation of U+FFFF is not defined by the Unicode Standard, so it can be viewed as a kind of private-use non-character.

Encoding Structure. The Specials block is divided into the following ranges:

U+FEFF	ZERO WIDTH NON-BREAK SPACE (and byte order mark)
U+FFFD	Replacement character
U+FFFE	Not a character; byte swap required signal value
U+FFFF	Not a character

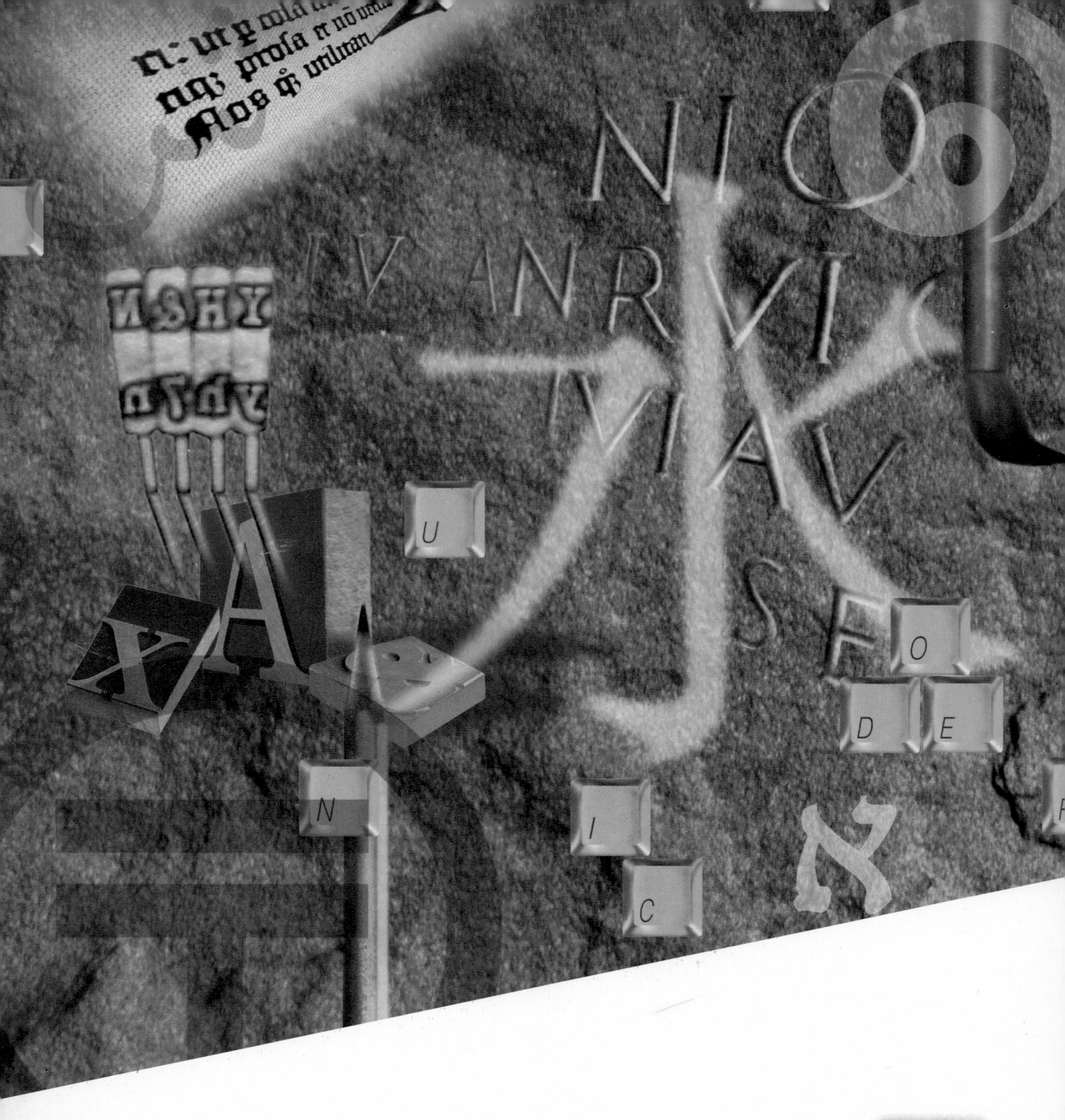

7

CODE CHARTS

Chapter 7

Code Charts

The code charts that follow present the individual characters of the Unicode Standard. The character repertoire is laid out in successive character blocks, described in *Chapter 6, Character Block Descriptions.* A character block always begins on the left-hand page with the character chart giving an overview of the character block as a whole.

A character names list follows the character chart (except for CJK ideographs and Hangul syllables, as discussed in this chapter). The character names list itemizes every character in the block and provides supplementary information in many cases.

An index to distinctive character names is at the back of this book; a full set of character names (including earlier Version 1.0 names) are in the *Unicode Character Database* on the CD-ROM.

7.1 Character Names List

The following illustration identifies the components of typical entries in the character names list.

code	*image*	*entry*	
00AF	¯	MACRON	*(Unicode name)*
		= SPACING MACRON	*(Version 1.0 name)*
		= overline	*(alternative name)*
		= APL overbar	
		• this is a spacing character	*(informative note)*
		→ 02C3 ˉ modifier letter macron	*(cross reference)*
		→ 0304 ◌̄ combining macron	
		→ 0305 ◌̅ combining overline	
		≈ 0020 SP + 0304 ◌̄	*(compatibility decomposition)*
00E5	å	LATIN SMALL LETTER A WITH RING ABOVE	
		= LATIN SMALL LETTER A RING	
		• Danish, Norwegian, Swedish	
		≡ 0061 a + 030A ◌̊	*(canonical decomposition)*

Images in the Code Charts and Character Lists

In all cases, a representative glyph is printed to represent a character. The image shown in a grid cell of a panel should not be considered to be the prescriptive form of a character; it is merely intended as a typical representation of the character encoded by the value. For example, U+0061 LATIN SMALL LETTER A can be represented by a or *a*.

Combining characters are shown with a dotted circle. A character that is shown as a name or abbreviation surrounded by a dashed box has no visible manifestation on its own.

Cross References

Cross referenced characters (preceded by →) have various characteristics: explicit inequality, the other member of a case pair, or some other linguistic relationship.

- ***Explicit inequality.*** The two characters are not identical, although the glyphs that depict them are identical or very close.

003A : COLON
→ 0589 : armenian full stop
→ 2236 : ratio

- ***Other linguistic relationship.*** These relationships include transliterations (such as between Serbian and Croatian), typographically unrelated characters used to represent the same sound, and so on.

01C9 lj LATIN SMALL LETTER LJ
→ 0459 љ cyrillic small letter lje
≈ 006C l + 006A j

Case Form Mappings

When a case mapping corresponds *solely* to a difference based on SMALL versus CAPITAL in the names of the characters, the case mapping is not given in the names list but is given only in the *Unicode Character Database* on the CD-ROM.

0041 A LATIN CAPITAL LETTER A

01F2 Dz LATIN CAPITAL LETTER D WITH SMALL LETTER Z
≈ 0044 D + 007A z

When the case mapping cannot be predicted from the name, the information is given in a note.

00DF ß LATIN SMALL LETTER SHARP S
= ess-zed
• German
• uppercase is "SS"
→ 03B2 β greek small letter beta

Decompositions

The decomposition sequence (one or more letters) given for a character is either its canonical decomposition or its compatibility decomposition. The canonical mapping is marked with an *identical to* symbol ≡.

00E5 å LATIN SMALL LETTER A WITH RING ABOVE
= LATIN SMALL LETTER A RING
• Danish, Norwegian, Swedish
≡ 0061 a + 030A ◌̊

212B Å ANGSTROM SIGN
→ 00C5 Å latin capital letter a with ring above
≡ 00C5 Å

Compatibility decompositions are marked with an *almost equal to* symbol ≈. Formatting information may be indicated inside angle brackets.

01F2 Dz LATIN CAPITAL LETTER D WITH SMALL LETTER Z
≈ 0044 D + 007A z

FF21 Ａ FULLWIDTH LATIN CAPITAL LETTER A
≈ <wide> + 0041 A

Decompositions are not necessarily full decompositions. For example, the decomposition for U+212B ANGSTROM SIGN can be further decomposed using the canonical decomposition for U+00C5 LATIN SMALL LETTER A WITH RING ABOVE. (For more information on decomposition, see *Section 3.6, Decomposition.*)

Information About Languages

An informative note may include a list of the language(s) using that character where this information is considered useful. For case pairs, the annotation is given only for the lowercase form, to avoid needless repetition. An ellipsis "..." indicates that the listed languages cited are merely the principal ones among many.

Reserved Characters

Character codes that are marked "<reserved>" are unassigned and reserved for future encoding. Reserved codes are indicated by a ▧ glyph.

FFFC ▧ <reserved>

Reserved codes may also have cross references to assigned characters located elsewhere.

0373 ▧ <reserved>
→ 00A3 £ pound sign

Character codes that are marked "<not a character>" are permanently unassigned; they will never be assigned a character. Reserved codes are indicated by a ■ glyph.

FFFF ■ <not a character>
• the value FFFF ■ is guaranteed not to be a Unicode character at all

7.2 CJK Unified Ideographs

A character names list is not provided for the *CJK Unified Ideographs* character block since the name of a unified ideograph simply consists of its Unicode value preceded by CJK UNIFIED IDEOGRAPH-. The character charts also take a different form, which show how the Unicode Han ideographic character set maps to several of the source standards (see Table 7-1). This table is also included on the CD-ROM.

Each Unicode character is shown with its Unicode value and a representative glyph. There are six additional fields for each of the primary source character sets. Characters with the compatibility range (U+F900 → U+FAFF) are also found within the main CJK range.

Table 7-1. Han Character Chart Entries

Key	Prefix	Subset	Code Format
G	0	GB 2312-80	Row/column
	1	GB 12345-80	
	3	GB 7589-87	
	5	GB 7590-87	
	7	General Purpose Han Characters for Modern Chinese	
	8	GB 8565-89	
J	0	JIS X 0208-1990	Row/column
	1	JIS X 0212-1990	
K	0	KS C 5601-1987	Row/column
	1	KS C 5657-1991	
B		Big Five	Hexadecimal
C	1	CNS 11643-1986 (1st plane)	Hexadecimal
	2	CNS 11643-1986 (2nd plane)	
	E	CNS 11643-1986 (14th plane)	
A		ANSI Z39.64-1989	Hexadecimal

Their placement is indicated by the small number beneath their Unicode code value in the charts.

➥ GB 2312-80 and GB 12345-80 are overlapping standards; most of the characters in the former are also found in the latter. Characters showing a mapping in the charts to GB 2312-80 may also be mapped into GB 12345-80. (For fuller information on how GB 12345-80 maps to Unicode, see the tables available on the CD-ROM.)

A radical/stroke index to CJK ideographs is in *Chapter 8, Han Radical Stroke Index.*

7.3 Hangul Syllables

A character names list is not provided for characters in the *Hangul Syllables Area* (U+AC00 → U+D7A3) since the name of a Hangul syllable can be determined by algorithm (as described in *Section 3.10, Combining Jamo Behavior*).

	000	001	002	003	004	005	006	007
0	NUL 0000	DLE 0010	SP 0020	0 0030	@ 0040	P 0050	` 0060	p 0070
1	STX 0001	DC1 0011	! 0021	1 0031	A 0041	Q 0051	a 0061	q 0071
2	SOT 0002	DC2 0012	" 0022	2 0032	B 0042	R 0052	b 0062	r 0072
3	ETX 0003	DC3 0013	# 0023	3 0033	C 0043	S 0053	c 0063	s 0073
4	EOT 0004	DC4 0014	$ 0024	4 0034	D 0044	T 0054	d 0064	t 0074
5	ENQ 0005	NAK 0015	% 0025	5 0035	E 0045	U 0055	e 0065	u 0075
6	ACK 0006	SYN 0016	& 0026	6 0036	F 0046	V 0056	f 0066	v 0076
7	BEL 0007	ETB 0017	' 0027	7 0037	G 0047	W 0057	g 0067	w 0077
8	BS 0008	CAN 0018	(0028	8 0038	H 0048	X 0058	h 0068	x 0078
9	HT 0009	EM 0019	) 0029	9 0039	I 0049	Y 0059	i 0069	y 0079
A	LF 000A	SUB 001A	* 002A	: 003A	J 004A	Z 005A	j 006A	z 007A
B	VT 000B	ESC 001B	+ 002B	; 003B	K 004B	[005B	k 006B	{ 007B
C	FF 000C	FS 001C	, 002C	< 003C	L 004C	\ 005C	l 006C	| 007C
D	CR 000D	GS 001D	- 002D	= 003D	M 004D	] 005D	m 006D	} 007D
E	SO 000E	RS 001E	. 002E	> 003E	N 004E	^ 005E	n 006E	~ 007E
F	SI 000F	US 001F	/ 002F	? 003F	O 004F	_ 005F	o 006F	DEL 007F

C0 controls

0000 NUL NULL
0001 STX START OF HEADING
0002 SOT START OF TEXT
0003 ETX END OF TEXT
0004 EOT END OF TRANSMISSION
0005 ENQ ENQUIRY
0006 ACK ACKNOWLEDGE
0007 BEL BELL
0008 BS BACKSPACE
0009 HT HORIZONTAL TABULATION
000A LF LINE FEED
000B VT VERTICAL TABULATION
000C FF FORM FEED
000D CR CARRIAGE RETURN
000E SO SHIFT OUT
000F SI SHIFT IN
0010 DLE DATA LINK ESCAPE
0011 DC1 DEVICE CONTROL ONE
0012 DC2 DEVICE CONTROL TWO
0013 DC3 DEVICE CONTROL THREE
0014 DC4 DEVICE CONTROL FOUR
0015 NAK NEGATIVE ACKNOWLEDGE
0016 SYN SYNCHRONOUS IDLE
0017 ETB END OF TRANSMISSION BLOCK
0018 CAN CANCEL
0019 EM END OF MEDIUM
001A SUB SUBSTITUTE
→ FFFD � replacement character
001B ESC ESCAPE
001C FS FILE SEPARATOR
001D GS GROUP SEPARATOR
001E RS RECORD SEPARATOR
001F US UNIT SEPARATOR

ASCII

0020 SP SPACE
• sometimes considered a control code
• other space characters: 2000 NQSP → 200A HSP
→ 00A0 NBSP no-break space
→ 200B ZWSP zero width space
→ 3000 IDSP ideographic space
→ FEFF ZWNBSP zero width no-break space

0021 ! EXCLAMATION MARK
= factorial
→ 00A1 ¡ inverted exclamation mark
→ 01C3 ǃ latin letter retroflex click
→ 203C ‼ double exclamation mark
→ 2762 ❢ heavy exclamation mark ornament

0022 " QUOTATION MARK
= APL quote
• neutral (vertical), used as opening or closing quotation mark
• preferred characters for paired quotation marks are 201C “ & 201D ”
→ 02BA ʺ modifier letter double prime
→ 030B ◌̋ combining double acute accent
→ 030E ◌̎ combining double vertical line above
→ 201C “ left double quotation mark
→ 201D ” right double quotation mark
→ 2033 ″ double prime

0023 # NUMBER SIGN
= pound sign

0024 $ DOLLAR SIGN
= milreis
= escudo
• glyph may have one or two vertical bars
• this code is unambiguously dollar sign, not "currency sign" or any other currency symbol
→ 00A4 ¤ currency sign

0025 % PERCENT SIGN
→ 066A ٪ arabic percent sign
→ 2030 ‰ per mille sign
→ 2031 ‱ per ten thousand sign

0026 & AMPERSAND

0027 ' APOSTROPHE
= APOSTROPHE-QUOTE
• neutral (vertical) glyph having mixed usage
• preferred character for apostrophe is 02BC ʼ
• preferred character for opening single quotation mark is 2018 ‘
• preferred character for closing single quotation mark is 2019 ’
→ 02B9 ʹ modifier letter prime
→ 02BC ʼ modifier letter apostrophe
→ 02C8 ˈ modifier letter vertical line
→ 0301 ◌́ combining acute accent
→ 2018 ‘ left single quotation mark
→ 2019 ’ right single quotation mark
→ 2032 ′ prime

0028 (LEFT PARENTHESIS
= OPENING PARENTHESIS

0029) RIGHT PARENTHESIS
= CLOSING PARENTHESIS
• see discussion on semantics of paired bracketing characters

002A * ASTERISK
→ 2217 ∗ asterisk operator
→ 2731 ✱ heavy asterisk

002B + PLUS SIGN

002C , COMMA
→ 060C ، arabic comma
→ 3001 、 ideographic comma

002D - HYPHEN-MINUS
= hyphen or minus sign
= hyphus
• used for either hyphen or minus sign
• other hyphen and dash characters: 2010 ‐ → 2015 ―
→ 2010 ‐ hyphen
→ 2011 ‑ non-breaking hyphen
→ 2212 − minus sign

002E . FULL STOP
= PERIOD
→ 06D4 ۔ arabic full stop
→ 3002 。 ideographic full stop

002F / SOLIDUS
= SLASH
= virgule
= shilling (British)
→ 01C0 ǀ latin letter dental click
→ 2044 ⁄ fraction slash
→ 2215 ∕ division slash

0030 0 DIGIT ZERO

0031 1 DIGIT ONE

0032 2 DIGIT TWO

0033 3 DIGIT THREE

0034 4 DIGIT FOUR

0035 5 DIGIT FIVE

0036 6 DIGIT SIX

0037 7 DIGIT SEVEN

0038 8 DIGIT EIGHT

0039 9 DIGIT NINE

003A : COLON
→ 0589 ։ armenian full stop
→ 2236 ∶ ratio

003B ; SEMICOLON
→ 037E ; greek question mark
→ 061B ؛ arabic semicolon

003C < LESS-THAN SIGN
→ 2039 ‹ single left-pointing angle quotation mark
→ 2329 〈 left-pointing angle bracket
→ 3008 〈 left angle bracket

003D = EQUALS SIGN
• other related characters: 2241 ≁ → 2263 ≣
→ 2260 ≠ not equal to
→ 2261 ≡ identical to

003E > GREATER-THAN SIGN
→ 203A › single right-pointing angle quotation mark
→ 232A 〉 right-pointing angle bracket
→ 3009 〉 right angle bracket

003F ? QUESTION MARK
→ 00BF ¿ inverted question mark
→ 037E ; greek question mark
→ 061F ؟ arabic question mark
→ 203D ‽ interrobang

0040 @ COMMERCIAL AT

0041 A LATIN CAPITAL LETTER A

0042 B LATIN CAPITAL LETTER B
→ 212C ℬ script capital b

0043 C LATIN CAPITAL LETTER C
→ 2102 ℂ double-struck capital c
→ 212D ℭ black-letter capital c

0044 D LATIN CAPITAL LETTER D

0045 E LATIN CAPITAL LETTER E
→ 2107 ℇ euler constant
→ 2130 ℰ script capital e

0046 F LATIN CAPITAL LETTER F
→ 2131 ℱ script capital f
→ 2132 Ⅎ turned capital f

0047 G LATIN CAPITAL LETTER G

0048 H LATIN CAPITAL LETTER H
→ 210B ℋ script capital h
→ 210C ℌ black-letter capital h
→ 210D ℍ double-struck capital h

0049 I LATIN CAPITAL LETTER I
• note alternative case mappings in Turkish
→ 0130 İ latin capital letter i with dot above
→ 0131 ı latin small letter dotless i
→ 2110 ℐ script capital i
→ 2111 ℑ black-letter capital i

004A J LATIN CAPITAL LETTER J

004B K LATIN CAPITAL LETTER K
→ 212A K kelvin sign

004C L LATIN CAPITAL LETTER L
→ 2112 ℒ script capital l

004D M LATIN CAPITAL LETTER M
→ 2133 ℳ script capital m

004E N LATIN CAPITAL LETTER N
→ 2115 ℕ double-struck capital n

004F O LATIN CAPITAL LETTER O

0050 P LATIN CAPITAL LETTER P
→ 2118 ℘ script capital p
→ 2119 ℙ double-struck capital p

0051 Q LATIN CAPITAL LETTER Q
→ 211A ℚ double-struck capital q

0052 R LATIN CAPITAL LETTER R
→ 211B ℛ script capital r
→ 211C ℜ black-letter capital r
→ 211D ℝ double-struck capital r

0053 S LATIN CAPITAL LETTER S

0054 T LATIN CAPITAL LETTER T

0055 U LATIN CAPITAL LETTER U

0056 V LATIN CAPITAL LETTER V
0057 W LATIN CAPITAL LETTER W
0058 X LATIN CAPITAL LETTER X
0059 Y LATIN CAPITAL LETTER Y
005A Z LATIN CAPITAL LETTER Z
→ 2124 ℤ double-struck capital z
→ 2128 ℨ black-letter capital z
005B [LEFT SQUARE BRACKET
= OPENING SQUARE BRACKET
• other bracket characters: 3008 〈 → 301B 〛
005C \ REVERSE SOLIDUS
= BACKSLASH
→ 2216 ∖ set minus
005D] RIGHT SQUARE BRACKET
= CLOSING SQUARE BRACKET
005E ^ CIRCUMFLEX ACCENT
= SPACING CIRCUMFLEX
• this is a spacing character
→ 02C4 ˄ modifier letter up arrowhead
→ 02C6 ˆ modifier letter circumflex accent
→ 0302 ̂ combining circumflex accent
→ 2303 ⌃ up arrowhead
≈ 0020 SP + 0302 ̂
005F _ LOW LINE
= SPACING UNDERSCORE
• this is a spacing character
→ 02CD ˍ modifier letter low macron
→ 0331 ̱ combining macron below
→ 0332 ̲ combining low line
→ 2017 ‗ double low line
≈ 0020 SP + 0332 ̲
0060 ` GRAVE ACCENT
= SPACING GRAVE
• this is a spacing character
→ 02CB ˋ modifier letter grave accent
→ 0300 ̀ combining grave accent
→ 2035 ‵ reversed prime
≈ 0020 SP + 0300 ̀
0061 a LATIN SMALL LETTER A
0062 b LATIN SMALL LETTER B
0063 c LATIN SMALL LETTER C
0064 d LATIN SMALL LETTER D
0065 e LATIN SMALL LETTER E
→ 212E ℮ estimated symbol
→ 212F ℯ script small e
0066 f LATIN SMALL LETTER F
0067 g LATIN SMALL LETTER G
→ 0261 ɡ latin small letter script g
→ 210A ℊ script small g
0068 h LATIN SMALL LETTER H
→ 04BB һ cyrillic small letter shha
→ 210E ℎ planck constant
0069 i LATIN SMALL LETTER I
• note alternative case mappings in Turkish
→ 0130 İ latin capital letter i with dot above
→ 0131 ı latin small letter dotless i
006A j LATIN SMALL LETTER J
006B k LATIN SMALL LETTER K
006C l LATIN SMALL LETTER L
→ 2113 ℓ script small l
006D m LATIN SMALL LETTER M
006E n LATIN SMALL LETTER N
006F o LATIN SMALL LETTER O
→ 2134 ℴ script small o
0070 p LATIN SMALL LETTER P
0071 q LATIN SMALL LETTER Q
0072 r LATIN SMALL LETTER R
0073 s LATIN SMALL LETTER S
0074 t LATIN SMALL LETTER T
0075 u LATIN SMALL LETTER U
0076 v LATIN SMALL LETTER V
0077 w LATIN SMALL LETTER W
0078 x LATIN SMALL LETTER X
0079 y LATIN SMALL LETTER Y
007A z LATIN SMALL LETTER Z
→ 01B6 ƶ latin small letter z with stroke
007B { LEFT CURLY BRACKET
= OPENING CURLY BRACKET
= opening brace
007C | VERTICAL LINE
= VERTICAL BAR
→ 01C0 ǀ latin letter dental click
→ 2223 ∣ divides
→ 2758 ❘ light vertical bar
007D } RIGHT CURLY BRACKET
= CLOSING CURLY BRACKET
= closing brace
007E ~ TILDE
• this is a spacing character
→ 02DC ˜ small tilde
→ 0303 ̃ combining tilde
→ 223C ∼ tilde operator
007F DEL DELETE
• control code

	008	009	00A	00B	00C	00D	00E	00F
0	CTRL 0080	CTRL 0090	NB SP 00A0	° 00B0	À 00C0	Đ 00D0	à 00E0	ð 00F0
1	CTRL 0081	CTRL 0091	¡ 00A1	± 00B1	Á 00C1	Ñ 00D1	á 00E1	ñ 00F1
2	CTRL 0082	CTRL 0092	¢ 00A2	^{2} 00B2	Â 00C2	Ò 00D2	â 00E2	ò 00F2
3	CTRL 0083	CTRL 0093	£ 00A3	^{3} 00B3	Ã 00C3	Ó 00D3	ã 00E3	ó 00F3
4	CTRL 0084	CTRL 0094	¤ 00A4	´ 00B4	Ä 00C4	Ô 00D4	ä 00E4	ô 00F4
5	CTRL 0085	CTRL 0095	¥ 00A5	µ 00B5	Å 00C5	Õ 00D5	å 00E5	õ 00F5
6	CTRL 0086	CTRL 0096	¦ 00A6	¶ 00B6	Æ 00C6	Ö 00D6	æ 00E6	ö 00F6
7	CTRL 0087	CTRL 0097	§ 00A7	· 00B7	Ç 00C7	× 00D7	ç 00E7	÷ 00F7
8	CTRL 0088	CTRL 0098	¨ 00A8	¸ 00B8	È 00C8	Ø 00D8	è 00E8	ø 00F8
9	CTRL 0089	CTRL 0099	© 00A9	^{1} 00B9	É 00C9	Ù 00D9	é 00E9	ù 00F9
A	CTRL 008A	CTRL 009A	ª 00AA	º 00BA	Ê 00CA	Ú 00DA	ê 00EA	ú 00FA
B	CTRL 008B	CTRL 009B	« 00AB	» 00BB	Ë 00CB	Û 00DB	ë 00EB	û 00FB
C	CTRL 008C	CTRL 009C	¬ 00AC	¼ 00BC	Ì 00CC	Ü 00DC	ì 00EC	ü 00FC
D	CTRL 008D	CTRL 009D	- 00AD	½ 00BD	Í 00CD	Ý 00DD	í 00ED	ý 00FD
E	CTRL 008E	CTRL 009E	® 00AE	¾ 00BE	Î 00CE	Þ 00DE	î 00EE	þ 00FE
F	CTRL 008F	CTRL 009F	¯ 00AF	¿ 00BF	Ï 00CF	ß 00DF	ï 00EF	ÿ 00FF

ISO 8859-1 (aka Latin1)

00A0 [NB SP] NO-BREAK SPACE
= NON-BREAKING SPACE
→ 0020 [SP] space
→ FEFF [ZWN BSP] zero width no-break space
≈ <noBreak> + 0020 [SP]

00A1 ¡ INVERTED EXCLAMATION MARK
• Spanish
→ 0021 ! exclamation mark

00A2 ¢ CENT SIGN

00A3 £ POUND SIGN
= pound sterling
→ 20A4 ₤ lira sign

00A4 ¤ CURRENCY SIGN
• other currency symbol characters: 20A0 ₠ → 20CF
→ 0024 $ dollar sign

00A5 ¥ YEN SIGN
= yuan sign
• glyph may have one or two crossbars

00A6 ¦ BROKEN BAR
= BROKEN VERTICAL BAR

00A7 § SECTION SIGN
• paragraph sign in some European usage

00A8 ¨ DIAERESIS
= SPACING DIAERESIS
• this is a spacing character
→ 0308 ̈ combining diaeresis
≈ 0020 [SP] + 0308 ̈

00A9 © COPYRIGHT SIGN
→ 2117 ℗ sound recording copyright

00AA ª FEMININE ORDINAL INDICATOR
• Spanish
≈ <super> + 0061 a

00AB « LEFT-POINTING DOUBLE ANGLE QUOTATION MARK
= LEFT POINTING GUILLEMET
• usually opening, sometimes closing
→ 226A ≪ much less-than
→ 300A 《 left double angle bracket

00AC ¬ NOT SIGN
→ 2310 ⌐ reversed not sign

00AD - SOFT HYPHEN
= discretionary hyphen

00AE ® REGISTERED SIGN
= REGISTERED TRADE MARK SIGN

00AF ¯ MACRON
= SPACING MACRON
= overline
= APL overbar
• this is a spacing character
→ 02C9 ˉ modifier letter macron
→ 0304 ̄ combining macron
→ 0305 ̅ combining overline
≈ 0020 [SP] + 0304 ̄

00B0 ° DEGREE SIGN
• this is a spacing character
→ 02DA ˚ ring above
→ 030A ̊ combining ring above
→ 2218 ∘ ring operator

00B1 ± PLUS-MINUS SIGN
= PLUS-OR-MINUS SIGN
→ 2213 ∓ minus-or-plus sign

00B2 ² SUPERSCRIPT TWO
= SUPERSCRIPT DIGIT TWO
= squared
→ 00B9 ¹ superscript one
≈ <super> + 0032 2

00B3 ³ SUPERSCRIPT THREE
= SUPERSCRIPT DIGIT THREE
= cubed
→ 00B9 ¹ superscript one
≈ <super> + 0033 3

00B4 ´ ACUTE ACCENT
= SPACING ACUTE
• this is a spacing character
→ 02B9 ʹ modifier letter prime
→ 02CA ˊ modifier letter acute accent
→ 0301 ́ combining acute accent
→ 2032 ′ prime
≈ 0020 [SP] + 0301 ́

00B5 µ MICRO SIGN
→ 03BC μ greek small letter mu
≈ 03BC μ

00B6 ¶ PILCROW SIGN
= PARAGRAPH SIGN
• section sign in some European usage
→ 2761 ❡ curved stem paragraph sign ornament

00B7 · MIDDLE DOT
= Georgian comma
= Greek middle dot
→ 2022 • bullet
→ 2024 ․ one dot leader
→ 2219 ∙ bullet operator
→ 22C5 ⋅ dot operator
→ 30FB ・ katakana middle dot

00B8 ¸ CEDILLA
= SPACING CEDILLA
• this is a spacing character
• other spacing accent characters: 02D8 ˘ → 02DB ˛
→ 0327 ̧ combining cedilla
≈ 0020 SP + 0327 ̧

00B9 ¹ SUPERSCRIPT ONE
= SUPERSCRIPT DIGIT ONE
• other superscript digit characters: 2070 ⁰ → 2079 ⁹
→ 00B2 ² superscript two
→ 00B3 ³ superscript three
≈ <super> + 0031 1

00BA º MASCULINE ORDINAL INDICATOR
• Spanish
≈ <super> + 006F o

00BB » RIGHT-POINTING DOUBLE ANGLE QUOTATION MARK
= RIGHT POINTING GUILLEMET
• usually closing, sometimes opening
→ 226B ≫ much greater-than
→ 300B 》 right double angle bracket

00BC ¼ VULGAR FRACTION ONE QUARTER
= FRACTION ONE QUARTER
• bar may be horizontal or slanted
≈ <fraction> + 0031 1 + 2044 ⁄ + 0034 4

00BD ½ VULGAR FRACTION ONE HALF
= FRACTION ONE HALF
• bar may be horizontal or slanted
≈ <fraction> + 0031 1 + 2044 ⁄ + 0032 2

00BE ¾ VULGAR FRACTION THREE QUARTERS
= FRACTION THREE QUARTERS
• bar may be horizontal or slanted
• other fraction characters: 2153 ⅓ → 215E ⅞
≈ <fraction> + 0033 3 + 2044 ⁄ + 0034 4

00BF ¿ INVERTED QUESTION MARK
= turned question mark
• Spanish
→ 003F ? question mark

00C0 À LATIN CAPITAL LETTER A WITH GRAVE
= LATIN CAPITAL LETTER A GRAVE
• (many of the following have similar name transformations)
≡ 0041 A + 0300 ̀

00C1 Á LATIN CAPITAL LETTER A WITH ACUTE
≡ 0041 A + 0301 ́

00C2 Â LATIN CAPITAL LETTER A WITH CIRCUMFLEX
≡ 0041 A + 0302 ̂

00C3 Ã LATIN CAPITAL LETTER A WITH TILDE
≡ 0041 A + 0303 ̃

00C4 Ä LATIN CAPITAL LETTER A WITH DIAERESIS
≡ 0041 A + 0308 ̈

00C5 Å LATIN CAPITAL LETTER A WITH RING ABOVE
= LATIN CAPITAL LETTER A RING
→ 212B Å angstrom sign
≡ 0041 A + 030A ̊

00C6 Æ LATIN CAPITAL LETTER AE
= LATIN CAPITAL LIGATURE AE

00C7 Ç LATIN CAPITAL LETTER C WITH CEDILLA
≡ 0043 C + 0327 ̧

00C8 È LATIN CAPITAL LETTER E WITH GRAVE
≡ 0045 E + 0300 ̀

00C9 É LATIN CAPITAL LETTER E WITH ACUTE
≡ 0045 E + 0301 ́

00CA Ê LATIN CAPITAL LETTER E WITH CIRCUMFLEX
≡ 0045 E + 0302 ̂

00CB Ë LATIN CAPITAL LETTER E WITH DIAERESIS
≡ 0045 E + 0308 ̈

00CC Ì LATIN CAPITAL LETTER I WITH GRAVE
≡ 0049 I + 0300 ̀

00CD Í LATIN CAPITAL LETTER I WITH ACUTE
≡ 0049 I + 0301 ́

00CE Î LATIN CAPITAL LETTER I WITH CIRCUMFLEX
≡ 0049 I + 0302 ̂

00CF Ï LATIN CAPITAL LETTER I WITH DIAERESIS
≡ 0049 I + 0308 ̈

00D0 Đ LATIN CAPITAL LETTER ETH
→ 00F0 ð latin small letter eth
→ 0110 Đ latin capital letter d with stroke
→ 0189 Đ latin capital letter african d

00D1 Ñ LATIN CAPITAL LETTER N WITH TILDE
≡ 004E N + 0303 ̃

00D2 Ò LATIN CAPITAL LETTER O WITH GRAVE
≡ 004F O + 0300 ̀

00D3 Ó LATIN CAPITAL LETTER O WITH ACUTE
≡ 004F O + 0301 ◌́
00D4 Ô LATIN CAPITAL LETTER O WITH CIRCUMFLEX
≡ 004F O + 0302 ◌̂
00D5 Õ LATIN CAPITAL LETTER O WITH TILDE
≡ 004F O + 0303 ◌̃
00D6 Ö LATIN CAPITAL LETTER O WITH DIAERESIS
≡ 004F O + 0308 ◌̈
00D7 × MULTIPLICATION SIGN
00D8 Ø LATIN CAPITAL LETTER O WITH STROKE
= LATIN CAPITAL LETTER O SLASH
→ 2205 ∅ empty set
00D9 Ù LATIN CAPITAL LETTER U WITH GRAVE
≡ 0055 U + 0300 ◌̀
00DA Ú LATIN CAPITAL LETTER U WITH ACUTE
≡ 0055 U + 0301 ◌́
00DB Û LATIN CAPITAL LETTER U WITH CIRCUMFLEX
≡ 0055 U + 0302 ◌̂
00DC Ü LATIN CAPITAL LETTER U WITH DIAERESIS
≡ 0055 U + 0308 ◌̈
00DD Ý LATIN CAPITAL LETTER Y WITH ACUTE
≡ 0059 Y + 0301 ◌́
00DE Þ LATIN CAPITAL LETTER THORN
00DF ß LATIN SMALL LETTER SHARP S
= ess-zed
• German
• uppercase is "SS"
→ 03B2 β greek small letter beta
00E0 à LATIN SMALL LETTER A WITH GRAVE
= LATIN SMALL LETTER A GRAVE
• (many of the following have similar name transformations)
≡ 0061 a + 0300 ◌̀
00E1 á LATIN SMALL LETTER A WITH ACUTE
≡ 0061 a + 0301 ◌́
00E2 â LATIN SMALL LETTER A WITH CIRCUMFLEX
≡ 0061 a + 0302 ◌̂
00E3 ã LATIN SMALL LETTER A WITH TILDE
• Portuguese
≡ 0061 a + 0303 ◌̃
00E4 ä LATIN SMALL LETTER A WITH DIAERESIS
≡ 0061 a + 0308 ◌̈
00E5 å LATIN SMALL LETTER A WITH RING ABOVE
= LATIN SMALL LETTER A RING
• Danish, Norwegian, Swedish
≡ 0061 a + 030A ◌̊
00E6 æ LATIN SMALL LETTER AE
= LATIN SMALL LIGATURE AE
• IPA
→ 0153 œ latin small ligature oe
00E7 ç LATIN SMALL LETTER C WITH CEDILLA
≡ 0063 c + 0327 ◌̧
00E8 è LATIN SMALL LETTER E WITH GRAVE
≡ 0065 e + 0300 ◌̀
00E9 é LATIN SMALL LETTER E WITH ACUTE
≡ 0065 e + 0301 ◌́
00EA ê LATIN SMALL LETTER E WITH CIRCUMFLEX
≡ 0065 e + 0302 ◌̂
00EB ë LATIN SMALL LETTER E WITH DIAERESIS
≡ 0065 e + 0308 ◌̈
00EC ì LATIN SMALL LETTER I WITH GRAVE
• Italian, Malagash
≡ 0069 i + 0300 ◌̀
00ED í LATIN SMALL LETTER I WITH ACUTE
≡ 0069 i + 0301 ◌́
00EE î LATIN SMALL LETTER I WITH CIRCUMFLEX
≡ 0069 i + 0302 ◌̂
00EF ï LATIN SMALL LETTER I WITH DIAERESIS
≡ 0069 i + 0308 ◌̈
00F0 ð LATIN SMALL LETTER ETH
• Icelandic, Faroese, old English, IPA
→ 00D0 Đ latin capital letter eth
00F1 ñ LATIN SMALL LETTER N WITH TILDE
≡ 006E n + 0303 ◌̃
00F2 ò LATIN SMALL LETTER O WITH GRAVE
≡ 006F o + 0300 ◌̀
00F3 ó LATIN SMALL LETTER O WITH ACUTE
≡ 006F o + 0301 ◌́
00F4 ô LATIN SMALL LETTER O WITH CIRCUMFLEX
≡ 006F o + 0302 ◌̂

00F5 õ LATIN SMALL LETTER O WITH TILDE
• Portuguese, Estonian
≡ 006F o + 0303 ̃

00F6 ö LATIN SMALL LETTER O WITH DIAERESIS
≡ 006F o + 0308 ̈

00F7 ÷ DIVISION SIGN

00F8 ø LATIN SMALL LETTER O WITH STROKE
= LATIN SMALL LETTER O SLASH
• Danish, Norwegian, Faroese, IPA

00F9 ù LATIN SMALL LETTER U WITH GRAVE
• French, Italian
≡ 0075 u + 0300 ̀

00FA ú LATIN SMALL LETTER U WITH ACUTE
≡ 0075 u + 0301 ́

00FB û LATIN SMALL LETTER U WITH CIRCUMFLEX
≡ 0075 u + 0302 ̂

00FC ü LATIN SMALL LETTER U WITH DIAERESIS
≡ 0075 u + 0308 ̈

00FD ý LATIN SMALL LETTER Y WITH ACUTE
• Czech, Slovak, Icelandic, Faroese, Malagash
≡ 0079 y + 0301 ́

00FE þ LATIN SMALL LETTER THORN
• Icelandic, old English, IPA
• Runic letter borrowed into Latin script

00FF ÿ LATIN SMALL LETTER Y WITH DIAERESIS
• French
→ 0178 Ÿ latin capital letter y with diaeresis
≡ 0079 y + 0308 ̈

	010	011	012	013	014	015	016	017
0	Ā 0100	Đ 0110	Ġ 0120	İ 0130	ŀ 0140	Ő 0150	Š 0160	Ű 0170
1	ā 0101	đ 0111	ġ 0121	ı 0131	Ł 0141	ő 0151	š 0161	ű 0171
2	Ă 0102	Ē 0112	Ģ 0122	Ĳ 0132	ł 0142	Œ 0152	Ţ 0162	Ų 0172
3	ă 0103	ē 0113	ģ 0123	ĳ 0133	Ń 0143	œ 0153	ţ 0163	ų 0173
4	Ą 0104	Ĕ 0114	Ĥ 0124	Ĵ 0134	ń 0144	Ŕ 0154	Ť 0164	Ŵ 0174
5	ą 0105	ĕ 0115	ĥ 0125	ĵ 0135	Ņ 0145	ŕ 0155	ť 0165	ŵ 0175
6	Ć 0106	Ė 0116	Ħ 0126	Ķ 0136	ņ 0146	Ŗ 0156	Ŧ 0166	Ŷ 0176
7	ć 0107	ė 0117	ħ 0127	ķ 0137	Ň 0147	ŗ 0157	ŧ 0167	ŷ 0177
8	Ĉ 0108	Ę 0118	Ĩ 0128	ĸ 0138	ň 0148	Ř 0158	Ũ 0168	Ÿ 0178
9	ĉ 0109	ę 0119	ĩ 0129	Ĺ 0139	ŉ 0149	ř 0159	ũ 0169	Ź 0179
A	Ċ 010A	Ě 011A	Ī 012A	ĺ 013A	Ŋ 014A	Ś 015A	Ū 016A	ź 017A
B	ċ 010B	ě 011B	ī 012B	Ļ 013B	ŋ 014B	ś 015B	ū 016B	Ż 017B
C	Č 010C	Ĝ 011C	Ĭ 012C	ļ 013C	Ō 014C	Ŝ 015C	Ŭ 016C	ż 017C
D	č 010D	ĝ 011D	ĭ 012D	Ľ 013D	ō 014D	ŝ 015D	ŭ 016D	Ž 017D
E	Ď 010E	Ğ 011E	Į 012E	ľ 013E	Ŏ 014E	Ş 015E	Ů 016E	ž 017E
F	ď 010F	ğ 011F	į 012F	Ŀ 013F	ŏ 014F	ş 015F	ů 016F	ſ 017F

European Latin

0100 Ā LATIN CAPITAL LETTER A WITH MACRON
≡ 0041 A + 0304 ◌̄

0101 ā LATIN SMALL LETTER A WITH MACRON
• Latvian, ...
≡ 0061 a + 0304 ◌̄

0102 Ă LATIN CAPITAL LETTER A WITH BREVE
≡ 0041 A + 0306 ◌̆

0103 ă LATIN SMALL LETTER A WITH BREVE
• Romanian, Vietnamese, ...
≡ 0061 a + 0306 ◌̆

0104 Ą LATIN CAPITAL LETTER A WITH OGONEK
≡ 0041 A + 0328 ◌̨

0105 ą LATIN SMALL LETTER A WITH OGONEK
• Polish, Lithuanian, ...
≡ 0061 a + 0328 ◌̨

0106 Ć LATIN CAPITAL LETTER C WITH ACUTE
≡ 0043 C + 0301 ◌́

0107 ć LATIN SMALL LETTER C WITH ACUTE
• Polish, Croatian, ...
→ 045B ћ cyrillic small letter tshe
≡ 0063 c + 0301 ◌́

0108 Ĉ LATIN CAPITAL LETTER C WITH CIRCUMFLEX
≡ 0043 C + 0302 ◌̂

0109 ĉ LATIN SMALL LETTER C WITH CIRCUMFLEX
• Esperanto
≡ 0063 c + 0302 ◌̂

010A Ċ LATIN CAPITAL LETTER C WITH DOT ABOVE
≡ 0043 C + 0307 ◌̇

010B ċ LATIN SMALL LETTER C WITH DOT ABOVE
• Maltese
≡ 0063 c + 0307 ◌̇

010C Č LATIN CAPITAL LETTER C WITH CARON
≡ 0043 C + 030C ◌̌

010D č LATIN SMALL LETTER C WITH CARON
• (many)
≡ 0063 c + 030C ◌̌

010E Ď LATIN CAPITAL LETTER D WITH CARON
• the form using caron/hacek is preferred in all contexts
≡ 0044 D + 030C ◌̌

010F ď LATIN SMALL LETTER D WITH CARON
• Czech, Slovak
• the form using apostrophe is preferred in typesetting
≡ 0064 d + 030C ◌̌

0110 Đ LATIN CAPITAL LETTER D WITH STROKE
→ 00D0 Ð latin capital letter eth
→ 0111 đ latin small letter d with stroke
→ 0189 Ɖ latin capital letter african d

0111 đ LATIN SMALL LETTER D WITH STROKE
• Croatian, Vietnamese, Lappish
→ 0110 Đ latin capital letter d with stroke
→ 0452 ђ cyrillic small letter dje

0112 Ē LATIN CAPITAL LETTER E WITH MACRON
≡ 0045 E + 0304 ◌̄

0113 ē LATIN SMALL LETTER E WITH MACRON
• Latvian, ...
≡ 0065 e + 0304 ◌̄

0114 Ĕ LATIN CAPITAL LETTER E WITH BREVE
≡ 0045 E + 0306 ◌̆

0115 ĕ LATIN SMALL LETTER E WITH BREVE
• Malay, ...
≡ 0065 e + 0306 ◌̆

0116 Ė LATIN CAPITAL LETTER E WITH DOT ABOVE
≡ 0045 E + 0307 ◌̇

0117 ė LATIN SMALL LETTER E WITH DOT ABOVE
• Lithuanian
≡ 0065 e + 0307 ◌̇

0118 Ę LATIN CAPITAL LETTER E WITH OGONEK
≡ 0045 E + 0328 ◌̨

0119 ę LATIN SMALL LETTER E WITH OGONEK
• Polish, Lithuanian, ...
≡ 0065 e + 0328 ◌̨

011A Ě LATIN CAPITAL LETTER E WITH CARON
≡ 0045 E + 030C ◌̌

011B ě LATIN SMALL LETTER E WITH CARON
• Czech, ...
≡ 0065 e + 030C ̌

011C Ĝ LATIN CAPITAL LETTER G WITH CIRCUMFLEX
≡ 0047 G + 0302 ̂

011D ĝ LATIN SMALL LETTER G WITH CIRCUMFLEX
• Esperanto
≡ 0067 g + 0302 ̂

011E Ğ LATIN CAPITAL LETTER G WITH BREVE
≡ 0047 G + 0306 ̆

011F ğ LATIN SMALL LETTER G WITH BREVE
• Turkish
→ 01E7 ǧ latin small letter g with caron
≡ 0067 g + 0306 ̆

0120 Ġ LATIN CAPITAL LETTER G WITH DOT ABOVE
≡ 0047 G + 0307 ̇

0121 ġ LATIN SMALL LETTER G WITH DOT ABOVE
• Maltese, ...
≡ 0067 g + 0307 ̇

0122 Ģ LATIN CAPITAL LETTER G WITH CEDILLA
≡ 0047 G + 0327 ̧

0123 ģ LATIN SMALL LETTER G WITH CEDILLA
• Latvian, Lappish
• there are three glyph variants
≡ 0067 g + 0327 ̧

0124 Ĥ LATIN CAPITAL LETTER H WITH CIRCUMFLEX
≡ 0048 H + 0302 ̂

0125 ĥ LATIN SMALL LETTER H WITH CIRCUMFLEX
• Esperanto
≡ 0068 h + 0302 ̂

0126 Ħ LATIN CAPITAL LETTER H WITH STROKE

0127 ħ LATIN SMALL LETTER H WITH STROKE
• Maltese, IPA, ...
→ 045B ћ cyrillic small letter tshe
→ 210F ℏ planck constant over two pi

0128 Ĩ LATIN CAPITAL LETTER I WITH TILDE
≡ 0049 I + 0303 ̃

0129 ĩ LATIN SMALL LETTER I WITH TILDE
• Greenlandic
≡ 0069 i + 0303 ̃

012A Ī LATIN CAPITAL LETTER I WITH MACRON
≡ 0049 I + 0304 ̄

012B ī LATIN SMALL LETTER I WITH MACRON
• Latvian, ...
≡ 0069 i + 0304 ̄

012C Ĭ LATIN CAPITAL LETTER I WITH BREVE
≡ 0049 I + 0306 ̆

012D ĭ LATIN SMALL LETTER I WITH BREVE
• Latin, ...
≡ 0069 i + 0306 ̆

012E Į LATIN CAPITAL LETTER I WITH OGONEK
≡ 0049 I + 0328 ̨

012F į LATIN SMALL LETTER I WITH OGONEK
• Lithuanian, ...
≡ 0069 i + 0328 ̨

0130 İ LATIN CAPITAL LETTER I WITH DOT ABOVE
= LATIN CAPITAL LETTER I DOT
• Turkish
• note case mapping
→ 0049 I latin capital letter i
→ 0069 i latin small letter i
≡ 0049 I + 0307 ̇

0131 ı LATIN SMALL LETTER DOTLESS I
• Turkish
• note case mapping
→ 0049 I latin capital letter i
→ 0069 i latin small letter i

0132 Ĳ LATIN CAPITAL LIGATURE IJ
≈ 0049 I + 004A J

0133 ĳ LATIN SMALL LIGATURE IJ
• Dutch
≈ 0069 i + 006A j

0134 Ĵ LATIN CAPITAL LETTER J WITH CIRCUMFLEX
≡ 004A J + 0302 ̂

0135 ĵ LATIN SMALL LETTER J WITH CIRCUMFLEX
• Esperanto
≡ 006A j + 0302 ̂

0136 Ķ LATIN CAPITAL LETTER K WITH CEDILLA
≡ 004B K + 0327 ̧

0137 ķ LATIN SMALL LETTER K WITH CEDILLA
• Latvian, ...
≡ 006B k + 0327 ̧

0138 ĸ LATIN SMALL LETTER KRA
• old Greenlandic

0139 Ĺ LATIN CAPITAL LETTER L WITH ACUTE
≡ 004C L + 0301 ◌́

013A ĺ LATIN SMALL LETTER L WITH ACUTE
• Slovak
≡ 006C l + 0301 ◌́

013B Ļ LATIN CAPITAL LETTER L WITH CEDILLA
≡ 004C L + 0327 ◌̧

013C ļ LATIN SMALL LETTER L WITH CEDILLA
• Latvian
≡ 006C l + 0327 ◌̧

013D Ľ LATIN CAPITAL LETTER L WITH CARON
≡ 004C L + 030C ◌̌

013E ľ LATIN SMALL LETTER L WITH CARON
• Slovak
• the form using apostrophe is preferred in typesetting
≡ 006C l + 030C ◌̌

013F Ŀ LATIN CAPITAL LETTER L WITH MIDDLE DOT
≈ 004C L + 00B7 ·

0140 ŀ LATIN SMALL LETTER L WITH MIDDLE DOT
• Catalan
≈ 006C l + 00B7 ·

0141 Ł LATIN CAPITAL LETTER L WITH STROKE

0142 ł LATIN SMALL LETTER L WITH STROKE
• Polish, ...
→ 019A ƚ latin small letter l with bar

0143 Ń LATIN CAPITAL LETTER N WITH ACUTE
≡ 004E N + 0301 ◌́

0144 ń LATIN SMALL LETTER N WITH ACUTE
• Polish, ...
≡ 006E n + 0301 ◌́

0145 Ņ LATIN CAPITAL LETTER N WITH CEDILLA
≡ 004E N + 0327 ◌̧

0146 ņ LATIN SMALL LETTER N WITH CEDILLA
• Latvian
≡ 006E n + 0327 ◌̧

0147 Ň LATIN CAPITAL LETTER N WITH CARON
≡ 004E N + 030C ◌̌

0148 ň LATIN SMALL LETTER N WITH CARON
• Czech, Slovak
≡ 006E n + 030C ◌̌

0149 ŉ LATIN SMALL LETTER N PRECEDED BY APOSTROPHE
= LATIN SMALL LETTER APOSTROPHE N
• Afrikaans
• this is not actually a single letter
≈ 02BC ʼ + 006E n

014A Ŋ LATIN CAPITAL LETTER ENG

014B ŋ LATIN SMALL LETTER ENG
• Sami, IPA, ...

014C Ō LATIN CAPITAL LETTER O WITH MACRON
≡ 004F O + 0304 ◌̄

014D ō LATIN SMALL LETTER O WITH MACRON
• Latvian, ...
≡ 006F o + 0304 ◌̄

014E Ŏ LATIN CAPITAL LETTER O WITH BREVE
≡ 004F O + 0306 ◌̆

014F ŏ LATIN SMALL LETTER O WITH BREVE
• Latin
≡ 006F o + 0306 ◌̆

0150 Ő LATIN CAPITAL LETTER O WITH DOUBLE ACUTE
≡ 004F O + 030B ◌̋

0151 ő LATIN SMALL LETTER O WITH DOUBLE ACUTE
• Hungarian
≡ 006F o + 030B ◌̋

0152 Œ LATIN CAPITAL LIGATURE OE

0153 œ LATIN SMALL LIGATURE OE
= LATIN ... LETTER O E
• French, IPA, ...
→ 00E6 æ latin small letter ae
→ 0276 ɶ latin letter small capital oe

0154 Ŕ LATIN CAPITAL LETTER R WITH ACUTE
≡ 0052 R + 0301 ◌́

0155 ŕ LATIN SMALL LETTER R WITH ACUTE
• Slovak, ...
≡ 0072 r + 0301 ◌́

0156 Ŗ LATIN CAPITAL LETTER R WITH CEDILLA
≡ 0052 R + 0327 ◌̧

0157 ŗ LATIN SMALL LETTER R WITH CEDILLA
• Latvian
≡ 0072 r + 0327 ◌̧

0158 Ř LATIN CAPITAL LETTER R WITH CARON
≡ 0052 R + 030C ̌

0159 ř LATIN SMALL LETTER R WITH CARON
• Czech, ...
≡ 0072 r + 030C ̌

015A Ś LATIN CAPITAL LETTER S WITH ACUTE
≡ 0053 S + 0301 ́

015B ś LATIN SMALL LETTER S WITH ACUTE
• Polish, ...
≡ 0073 s + 0301 ́

015C Ŝ LATIN CAPITAL LETTER S WITH CIRCUMFLEX
≡ 0053 S + 0302 ̂

015D ŝ LATIN SMALL LETTER S WITH CIRCUMFLEX
• Esperanto
≡ 0073 s + 0302 ̂

015E Ş LATIN CAPITAL LETTER S WITH CEDILLA
≡ 0053 S + 0327 ̧

015F ş LATIN SMALL LETTER S WITH CEDILLA
• Turkish, Romanian, ...
• the form using under-comma is taken to be a glyph variant
≡ 0073 s + 0327 ̧

0160 Š LATIN CAPITAL LETTER S WITH CARON
≡ 0053 S + 030C ̌

0161 š LATIN SMALL LETTER S WITH CARON
• (many)
≡ 0073 s + 030C ̌

0162 Ţ LATIN CAPITAL LETTER T WITH CEDILLA
≡ 0054 T + 0327 ̧

0163 ţ LATIN SMALL LETTER T WITH CEDILLA
• Romanian, ...
• the form using under-comma is taken to be a glyph variant
≡ 0074 t + 0327 ̧

0164 Ť LATIN CAPITAL LETTER T WITH CARON
• the form using caron/hacek is preferred in all contexts
≡ 0054 T + 030C ̌

0165 ť LATIN SMALL LETTER T WITH CARON
• Czech, Slovak
• the form using apostrophe is preferred in typesetting
≡ 0074 t + 030C ̌

0166 Ŧ LATIN CAPITAL LETTER T WITH STROKE

0167 ŧ LATIN SMALL LETTER T WITH STROKE
• Lappish

0168 Ũ LATIN CAPITAL LETTER U WITH TILDE
≡ 0055 U + 0303 ̃

0169 ũ LATIN SMALL LETTER U WITH TILDE
• Greenlandic
≡ 0075 u + 0303 ̃

016A Ū LATIN CAPITAL LETTER U WITH MACRON
≡ 0055 U + 0304 ̄

016B ū LATIN SMALL LETTER U WITH MACRON
• Latvian, Lithuanian, ...
≡ 0075 u + 0304 ̄

016C Ŭ LATIN CAPITAL LETTER U WITH BREVE
≡ 0055 U + 0306 ̆

016D ŭ LATIN SMALL LETTER U WITH BREVE
• Latin, Esperanto, ...
≡ 0075 u + 0306 ̆

016E Ů LATIN CAPITAL LETTER U WITH RING ABOVE
≡ 0055 U + 030A ̊

016F ů LATIN SMALL LETTER U WITH RING ABOVE
• Czech, ...
≡ 0075 u + 030A ̊

0170 Ű LATIN CAPITAL LETTER U WITH DOUBLE ACUTE
≡ 0055 U + 030B ̋

0171 ű LATIN SMALL LETTER U WITH DOUBLE ACUTE
• Hungarian
≡ 0075 u + 030B ̋

0172 Ų LATIN CAPITAL LETTER U WITH OGONEK
≡ 0055 U + 0328 ̨

0173 ų LATIN SMALL LETTER U WITH OGONEK
• Lithuanian
≡ 0075 u + 0328 ̨

0174 Ŵ LATIN CAPITAL LETTER W WITH CIRCUMFLEX
≡ 0057 W + 0302 ̂

0175 ŵ LATIN SMALL LETTER W WITH CIRCUMFLEX
- Welsh
≡ 0077 w + 0302 ̂

0176 Ŷ LATIN CAPITAL LETTER Y WITH CIRCUMFLEX
≡ 0059 Y + 0302 ̂

0177 ŷ LATIN SMALL LETTER Y WITH CIRCUMFLEX
- Welsh
≡ 0079 y + 0302 ̂

0178 Ÿ LATIN CAPITAL LETTER Y WITH DIAERESIS
- French
→ 00FF ÿ latin small letter y with diaeresis
≡ 0059 Y + 0308 ̈

0179 Ź LATIN CAPITAL LETTER Z WITH ACUTE
≡ 005A Z + 0301 ́

017A ź LATIN SMALL LETTER Z WITH ACUTE
- Polish, ...
≡ 007A z + 0301 ́

017B Ż LATIN CAPITAL LETTER Z WITH DOT ABOVE
≡ 005A Z + 0307 ̇

017C ż LATIN SMALL LETTER Z WITH DOT ABOVE
- Polish, ...
≡ 007A z + 0307 ̇

017D Ž LATIN CAPITAL LETTER Z WITH CARON
≡ 005A Z + 030C ̌

017E ž LATIN SMALL LETTER Z WITH CARON
- (many)
≡ 007A z + 030C ̌

017F ſ LATIN SMALL LETTER LONG S
≈ 0073 s

	018	019	01A	01B	01C	01D	01E	01F
0	ƀ 0180	Ɛ 0190	Ơ 01A0	ư 01B0	ǀ 01C0	ǐ 01D0	Ǡ 01E0	ǰ 01F0
1	Ɓ 0181	Ƒ 0191	ơ 01A1	Ʊ 01B1	ǁ 01C1	Ǒ 01D1	ǡ 01E1	Ǳ 01F1
2	Ƃ 0182	ƒ 0192	Ƣ 01A2	Ʋ 01B2	ǂ 01C2	ǒ 01D2	Ǣ 01E2	ǲ 01F2
3	ƃ 0183	Ɠ 0193	ƣ 01A3	Ƴ 01B3	ǃ 01C3	Ǔ 01D3	ǣ 01E3	ǳ 01F3
4	Ƅ 0184	Ɣ 0194	Ƥ 01A4	ƴ 01B4	Ǆ 01C4	ǔ 01D4	Ǥ 01E4	Ǵ 01F4
5	ƅ 0185	ƕ 0195	ƥ 01A5	Ƶ 01B5	ǅ 01C5	Ǖ 01D5	ǥ 01E5	ǵ 01F5
6	Ɔ 0186	Ɩ 0196	Ʀ 01A6	ƶ 01B6	ǆ 01C6	ǖ 01D6	Ǧ 01E6	
7	Ƈ 0187	Ɨ 0197	Ƨ 01A7	Ʒ 01B7	Ǉ 01C7	Ǘ 01D7	ǧ 01E7	
8	ƈ 0188	Ƙ 0198	ƨ 01A8	Ƹ 01B8	ǈ 01C8	ǘ 01D8	Ǩ 01E8	
9	Ɖ 0189	ƙ 0199	Ʃ 01A9	ƹ 01B9	ǉ 01C9	Ǚ 01D9	ǩ 01E9	
A	Ɗ 018A	ƚ 019A	ƪ 01AA	ƺ 01BA	Ǌ 01CA	ǚ 01DA	Ǫ 01EA	Ǻ 01FA
B	Ƌ 018B	ƛ 019B	ƫ 01AB	ƻ 01BB	ǋ 01CB	Ǜ 01DB	ǫ 01EB	ǻ 01FB
C	ƌ 018C	Ɯ 019C	Ƭ 01AC	Ƽ 01BC	ǌ 01CC	ǜ 01DC	Ǭ 01EC	Ǽ 01FC
D	ƍ 018D	Ɲ 019D	ƭ 01AD	ƽ 01BD	Ǎ 01CD	ǝ 01DD	ǭ 01ED	ǽ 01FD
E	Ǝ 018E	ƞ 019E	Ʈ 01AE	ƾ 01BE	ǎ 01CE	Ǟ 01DE	Ǯ 01EE	Ǿ 01FE
F	Ə 018F	Ɵ 019F	Ư 01AF	ƿ 01BF	Ǐ 01CF	ǟ 01DF	ǯ 01EF	ǿ 01FF

	020	021	022	023	024
0	Ȁ 0200	Ȑ 0210			
1	ȁ 0201	ȑ 0211			
2	Ȃ 0202	Ȓ 0212			
3	ȃ 0203	ȓ 0213			
4	Ȅ 0204	Ȕ 0214			
5	ȅ 0205	ȕ 0215			
6	Ȇ 0206	Ȗ 0216			
7	ȇ 0207	ȗ 0217			
8	Ȉ 0208				
9	ȉ 0209				
A	Ȋ 020A				
B	ȋ 020B				
C	Ȍ 020C				
D	ȍ 020D				
E	Ȏ 020E				
F	ȏ 020F				

Latin extended-B

0180 ƀ LATIN SMALL LETTER B WITH STROKE
• Americanist usage for phonetic beta
→ 03B2 β greek small letter beta
→ 2422 ␢ blank symbol

0181 Ɓ LATIN CAPITAL LETTER B WITH HOOK
→ 0253 ɓ latin small letter b with hook

0182 Ƃ LATIN CAPITAL LETTER B WITH TOPBAR

0183 ƃ LATIN SMALL LETTER B WITH TOPBAR
• Ex-Soviet minority language scripts
→ 0411 Б cyrillic capital letter be

0184 Ƅ LATIN CAPITAL LETTER TONE SIX

0185 ƅ LATIN SMALL LETTER TONE SIX
• Zhuang
• Zhuang tone three is Cyrillic ze
• Zhuang tone four is Cyrillic che
→ 01A8 ƨ latin small letter tone two
→ 01BD ƽ latin small letter tone five
→ 0437 з cyrillic small letter ze
→ 0447 ч cyrillic small letter che
→ 044C ь cyrillic small letter soft sign

0186 Ɔ LATIN CAPITAL LETTER OPEN O
• typographically a turned C
→ 0254 ɔ latin small letter open o

0187 Ƈ LATIN CAPITAL LETTER C WITH HOOK

0188 ƈ LATIN SMALL LETTER C WITH HOOK
• African

0189 Ɖ LATIN CAPITAL LETTER AFRICAN D
→ 00D0 Ð latin capital letter eth
→ 0110 Đ latin capital letter d with stroke
→ 0256 ɖ latin small letter d with tail

018A Ɗ LATIN CAPITAL LETTER D WITH HOOK
• African
→ 0257 ɗ latin small letter d with hook

018B Ƌ LATIN CAPITAL LETTER D WITH TOPBAR

018C ƌ LATIN SMALL LETTER D WITH TOPBAR
• Ex-Soviet minority language scripts

018D ƍ LATIN SMALL LETTER TURNED DELTA
• archaic phonetic for labialized dental fricative
• recommended spellings 007A z + 02B7 ʷ or 007A z + 032B ̫

018E Ǝ LATIN CAPITAL LETTER REVERSED E
= LATIN CAPITAL LETTER TURNED E
• Nigerian
• alternate uppercase usage to the following
→ 01DD ǝ latin small letter turned e

018F Ə LATIN CAPITAL LETTER SCHWA
• Azerbaijani, ...
→ 0259 ə latin small letter schwa

0190 Ɛ LATIN CAPITAL LETTER OPEN E
• African
→ 025B ɛ latin small letter open e
→ 2107 ℇ euler constant

0191 Ƒ LATIN CAPITAL LETTER F WITH HOOK
• African

0192 ƒ LATIN SMALL LETTER F WITH HOOK
= LATIN SMALL LETTER SCRIPT F
= Florin currency symbol (Dutch)
= function symbol

0193 Ɠ LATIN CAPITAL LETTER G WITH HOOK
• African
→ 0260 ɠ latin small letter g with hook

0194 Ɣ LATIN CAPITAL LETTER GAMMA
• African
→ 0263 ɣ latin small letter gamma

0195 ƕ LATIN SMALL LETTER HV
• Gothic

0196 Ɩ LATIN CAPITAL LETTER IOTA
• African
→ 0269 ɩ latin small letter iota

0197 Ɨ LATIN CAPITAL LETTER I WITH STROKE
= i bar
• African
• ISO 6438 gives lowercase as 026A ɪ, not 0268 ɨ
→ 026A ɪ latin letter small capital i

0198 Ƙ LATIN CAPITAL LETTER K WITH HOOK

0199 ƙ LATIN SMALL LETTER K WITH HOOK
• African

019A ƚ LATIN SMALL LETTER L WITH BAR
• Americanist phonetic usage
→ 0142 ł latin small letter l with stroke

019B ƛ LATIN SMALL LETTER LAMBDA WITH STROKE
= lambda bar
• Americanist phonetic usage

019C ɯ LATIN CAPITAL LETTER TURNED M
• Zhuang
→ 026F ɯ latin small letter turned m

019D Ɲ LATIN CAPITAL LETTER N WITH LEFT HOOK
• African
→ 0272 ɲ latin small letter n with left hook

019E ƞ LATIN SMALL LETTER N WITH LONG RIGHT LEG
• archaic phonetic for Japanese syllabic "n"
• recommended spelling 006E n + 0329 ̩

019F Ɵ LATIN CAPITAL LETTER O WITH MIDDLE TILDE
= LATIN CAPITAL LETTER BARRED O
= o bar
• note case mapping
• African, Ex-Soviet minority language scripts
→ 0275 ɵ latin small letter barred o

01A0 Ơ LATIN CAPITAL LETTER O WITH HORN
≡ 004F O + 031B ̛

01A1 ơ LATIN SMALL LETTER O WITH HORN
• Vietnamese
≡ 006F o + 031B ̛

01A2 Ƣ LATIN CAPITAL LETTER OI

01A3 ƣ LATIN SMALL LETTER OI
• old Azerbaijani

01A4 Ƥ LATIN CAPITAL LETTER P WITH HOOK

01A5 ƥ LATIN SMALL LETTER P WITH HOOK
• African

01A6 Ʀ LATIN LETTER YR
• old Norse
• from German Standard DIN 31624

01A7 Ƨ LATIN CAPITAL LETTER TONE TWO

01A8 ƨ LATIN SMALL LETTER TONE TWO
• Zhuang
• typographically a reversed S
→ 0185 ƅ latin small letter tone six

01A9 Ʃ LATIN CAPITAL LETTER ESH
• African
→ 0283 ʃ latin small letter esh
→ 03A3 Σ greek capital letter sigma

01AA ƪ LATIN LETTER REVERSED ESH LOOP
• archaic phonetic for labialized palato-alveolar or palatal fricative
• Twi
• recommended spellings 0283 ʃ + 02B7 ʷ, 00E7 ç + 02B7 ʷ, 0068 h + 0265 ɥ, etc.

01AB ƫ LATIN SMALL LETTER T WITH PALATAL HOOK
• archaic phonetic for palatalized alveolar or dental stop
• recommended spelling 0074 t + 02B2 ʲ

01AC Ƭ LATIN CAPITAL LETTER T WITH HOOK

01AD ƭ LATIN SMALL LETTER T WITH HOOK
• African

01AE Ʈ LATIN CAPITAL LETTER T WITH RETROFLEX HOOK
• African
→ 0288 ʈ latin small letter t with retroflex hook

01AF Ư LATIN CAPITAL LETTER U WITH HORN
≡ 0055 U + 031B ̛

01B0 ư LATIN SMALL LETTER U WITH HORN
• Vietnamese
≡ 0075 u + 031B ̛

01B1 Ʊ LATIN CAPITAL LETTER UPSILON
• African
• typographically based on turned capital Greek omega
→ 028A ʊ latin small letter upsilon
→ 2127 ℧ inverted ohm sign

01B2 Ʋ LATIN CAPITAL LETTER V WITH HOOK
= LATIN CAPITAL LETTER SCRIPT V
• African
→ 028B ʋ latin small letter v with hook

01B3 Ƴ LATIN CAPITAL LETTER Y WITH HOOK

01B4 ƴ LATIN SMALL LETTER Y WITH HOOK
• African

01B5 Ƶ LATIN CAPITAL LETTER Z WITH STROKE

01B6 ƶ LATIN SMALL LETTER Z WITH STROKE
= z bar
• variant of Latin "z"
→ 007A z latin small letter z

01B7 Ʒ LATIN CAPITAL LETTER EZH
= LATIN CAPITAL LETTER YOGH
• African
→ 0292 ʒ latin small letter ezh

01B8 Ƹ LATIN CAPITAL LETTER EZH REVERSED

01B9 ƹ LATIN SMALL LETTER EZH REVERSED
• archaic phonetic for voiced pharyngeal fricative
• sometimes typographically rendered with a turned digit 3
• recommended spelling 0295 ʕ
→ 0295 ʕ latin letter pharyngeal voiced fricative
→ 0639 ع arabic letter ain

01BA ƺ LATIN SMALL LETTER EZH WITH TAIL
• archaic phonetic for labialized voiced palato-alveolar or palatal fricative
• Twi
• recommended spellings 0292 ʒ + 02B7 ʷ or 006A j + 02B7 ʷ

01BB ƻ LATIN LETTER TWO WITH STROKE
• archaic phonetic for [dz] affricate
• recommended spellings 0292 ʒ or 0064 d + 007A z

01BC Ƽ LATIN CAPITAL LETTER TONE FIVE

01BD ƽ LATIN SMALL LETTER TONE FIVE
• Zhuang
→ 0185 ƅ latin small letter tone six

01BE ƾ LATIN LETTER INVERTED GLOTTAL STOP WITH STROKE
• archaic phonetic for [ts] affricate
• recommended spelling 0074 t + 0073 s

01BF ƿ LATIN LETTER WYNN
• Runic letter borrowed into Latin script
• replaced by "w" in modern transcriptions of Old English

01C0 ǀ LATIN LETTER DENTAL CLICK
= LATIN LETTER PIPE
• Khoisan tradition
• "c" in Zulu orthography
→ 002F / solidus
→ 007C | vertical line
→ 0287 ʇ latin small letter turned t
→ 2223 ∣ divides

01C1 ǁ LATIN LETTER LATERAL CLICK
= LATIN LETTER DOUBLE PIPE
• Khoisan tradition
• "x" in Zulu orthography
→ 0296 ʖ latin letter inverted glottal stop
→ 2225 ∥ parallel to

01C2 ǂ LATIN LETTER ALVEOLAR CLICK
= LATIN LETTER PIPE DOUBLE BAR
• Khoisan tradition
• no IPA equivalent
→ 2260 ≠ not equal to

01C3 ǃ LATIN LETTER RETROFLEX CLICK
= LATIN LETTER EXCLAMATION MARK
• Khoisan tradition
• "q" in Zulu orthography
→ 0021 ! exclamation mark
→ 0297 ʗ latin letter stretched c

Croatian digraphs matching Serbian Cyrillic letters

01C4 Ǆ LATIN CAPITAL LETTER DZ WITH CARON
≈ 0044 D + 017D Ž

01C5 ǅ LATIN CAPITAL LETTER D WITH SMALL LETTER Z WITH CARON
≈ 0044 D + 017E ž

01C6 ǆ LATIN SMALL LETTER DZ WITH CARON
→ 045F џ cyrillic small letter dzhe
≈ 0064 d + 017E ž

01C7 Ǉ LATIN CAPITAL LETTER LJ
≈ 004C L + 004A J

01C8 ǈ LATIN CAPITAL LETTER L WITH SMALL LETTER J
≈ 004C L + 006A j

01C9 ǉ LATIN SMALL LETTER LJ
→ 0459 љ cyrillic small letter lje
≈ 006C l + 006A j

01CA Ǌ LATIN CAPITAL LETTER NJ
≈ 004E N + 004A J

01CB ǋ LATIN CAPITAL LETTER N WITH SMALL LETTER J
≈ 004E N + 006A j

01CC ǌ LATIN SMALL LETTER NJ
→ 045A њ cyrillic small letter nje
≈ 006E n + 006A j

Pinyin diacritic-vowel combinations

01CD Ǎ LATIN CAPITAL LETTER A WITH CARON
≡ 0041 A + 030C ̌

01CE ǎ LATIN SMALL LETTER A WITH CARON
• Pinyin third tone
≡ 0061 a + 030C ̌

01CF Ǐ LATIN CAPITAL LETTER I WITH CARON
≡ 0049 I + 030C ̌

01D0 ǐ LATIN SMALL LETTER I WITH CARON
• Pinyin third tone
≡ 0069 i + 030C ̌

01D1 Ǒ LATIN CAPITAL LETTER O WITH CARON
≡ 004F O + 030C ̌

01D2 ǒ LATIN SMALL LETTER O WITH CARON
• Pinyin third tone
≡ 006F o + 030C ̌

01D3 Ǔ LATIN CAPITAL LETTER U WITH CARON
≡ 0055 U + 030C ̌

01D4 ǔ LATIN SMALL LETTER U WITH CARON
• Pinyin third tone
≡ 0075 u + 030C ̌

01D5 Ǖ LATIN CAPITAL LETTER U WITH DIAERESIS AND MACRON
≡ 00DC Ü + 0304 ̄

01D6 ǖ LATIN SMALL LETTER U WITH DIAERESIS AND MACRON
• Pinyin first tone
≡ 00FC ü + 0304 ̄

01D7 Ǘ LATIN CAPITAL LETTER U WITH DIAERESIS AND ACUTE
≡ 00DC Ü + 0301 ́

01D8 ǘ LATIN SMALL LETTER U WITH DIAERESIS AND ACUTE
• Pinyin second tone
≡ 00FC ü + 0301 ́

01D9 Ǚ LATIN CAPITAL LETTER U WITH DIAERESIS AND CARON
≡ 00DC Ü + 030C ̌

01DA ǚ LATIN SMALL LETTER U WITH DIAERESIS AND CARON
• Pinyin third tone
≡ 00FC ü + 030C ̌

01DB Ǜ LATIN CAPITAL LETTER U WITH DIAERESIS AND GRAVE
≡ 00DC Ü + 0300 ̀

01DC ǜ LATIN SMALL LETTER U WITH DIAERESIS AND GRAVE
• Pinyin fourth tone
≡ 00FC ü + 0300 ̀

Additions

01DD ǝ LATIN SMALL LETTER TURNED E
• Nigerian
• all other usages of schwa are 0259 ə
• note case mapping
→ 018E Ǝ latin capital letter reversed e
→ 0259 ə latin small letter schwa

01DE Ǟ LATIN CAPITAL LETTER A WITH DIAERESIS AND MACRON
≡ 00C4 Ä + 0304 ̄

01DF ǟ LATIN SMALL LETTER A WITH DIAERESIS AND MACRON
• Lappish
≡ 00E4 ä + 0304 ̄

01E0 Ǡ LATIN CAPITAL LETTER A WITH DOT ABOVE AND MACRON
≡ 0041 A + 0307 ̇ + 0304 ̄

01E1 ǡ LATIN SMALL LETTER A WITH DOT ABOVE AND MACRON
• Lappish
≡ 0061 a + 0307 ̇ + 0304 ̄

01E2 Ǣ LATIN CAPITAL LETTER AE WITH MACRON
≡ 00C6 Æ + 0304 ̄

01E3 ǣ LATIN SMALL LETTER AE WITH MACRON
• Lappish, Old English
≡ 00E6 æ + 0304 ̄

01E4 Ǥ LATIN CAPITAL LETTER G WITH STROKE

01E5 ǥ LATIN SMALL LETTER G WITH STROKE
• Lappish

01E6 Ǧ LATIN CAPITAL LETTER G WITH CARON
≡ 0047 G + 030C ̌

01E7 ǧ LATIN SMALL LETTER G WITH CARON
• Lappish; sometimes used in writing Turkish
→ 011F ğ latin small letter g with breve
≡ 0067 g + 030C ̌

01E8 Ǩ LATIN CAPITAL LETTER K WITH CARON
≡ 004B K + 030C ̌

01E9 ǩ LATIN SMALL LETTER K WITH CARON
• Lappish
≡ 006B k + 030C ̌

01EA Ǫ LATIN CAPITAL LETTER O WITH OGONEK
≡ 004F O + 0328 ̨

01EB ǫ LATIN SMALL LETTER O WITH OGONEK
• Lappish, Iroquoian
≡ 006F o + 0328 ̨

01EC Ǭ LATIN CAPITAL LETTER O WITH OGONEK AND MACRON
≡ 01EA Ǫ + 0304 ̄

01ED ǭ LATIN SMALL LETTER O WITH OGONEK AND MACRON
• Lappish
≡ 01EB ǫ + 0304 ̄

01EE Ǯ LATIN CAPITAL LETTER EZH WITH CARON
≡ 01B7 Ʒ + 030C ̌

01EF ǯ LATIN SMALL LETTER EZH WITH CARON
• Lappish
≡ 0292 ʒ + 030C ̌

01F0 ǰ LATIN SMALL LETTER J WITH CARON
• IPA
≡ 006A j + 030C ̌

01F1 Ǳ LATIN CAPITAL LETTER DZ
≈ 0044 D + 005A Z

01F2 ǲ LATIN CAPITAL LETTER D WITH SMALL LETTER Z
≈ 0044 D + 007A z

01F3 ǳ LATIN SMALL LETTER DZ
≈ 0064 d + 007A z

01F4 Ǵ LATIN CAPITAL LETTER G WITH ACUTE
≡ 0047 G + 0301 ́

01F5 ǵ LATIN SMALL LETTER G WITH ACUTE
≡ 0067 g + 0301 ́

01FA Ǻ LATIN CAPITAL LETTER A WITH RING ABOVE AND ACUTE
≡ 00C5 Å + 0301 ́

01FB ǻ LATIN SMALL LETTER A WITH RING ABOVE AND ACUTE
≡ 00E5 å + 0301 ́

01FC Ǽ LATIN CAPITAL LETTER AE WITH ACUTE
≡ 00C6 Æ + 0301 ́

01FD ǽ LATIN SMALL LETTER AE WITH ACUTE
≡ 00E6 æ + 0301 ́

01FE Ǿ LATIN CAPITAL LETTER O WITH STROKE AND ACUTE
≡ 00D8 Ø + 0301 ́

01FF ǿ LATIN SMALL LETTER O WITH STROKE AND ACUTE
≡ 00F8 ø + 0301 ́

0200 Ȁ LATIN CAPITAL LETTER A WITH DOUBLE GRAVE
≡ 0041 A + 030F ̏

0201 ȁ LATIN SMALL LETTER A WITH DOUBLE GRAVE
≡ 0061 a + 030F ̏

0202 Ȃ LATIN CAPITAL LETTER A WITH INVERTED BREVE
≡ 0041 A + 0311 ̑

0203 ȃ LATIN SMALL LETTER A WITH INVERTED BREVE
≡ 0061 a + 0311 ̑

0204 Ȅ LATIN CAPITAL LETTER E WITH DOUBLE GRAVE
≡ 0045 E + 030F ̏

0205 ȅ LATIN SMALL LETTER E WITH DOUBLE GRAVE
≡ 0065 e + 030F ̏

0206 Ȇ LATIN CAPITAL LETTER E WITH INVERTED BREVE
≡ 0045 E + 0311 ̑

0207 ȇ LATIN SMALL LETTER E WITH INVERTED BREVE
≡ 0065 e + 0311 ̑

0208 Ȉ LATIN CAPITAL LETTER I WITH DOUBLE GRAVE
≡ 0049 I + 030F ̏

0209 ȉ LATIN SMALL LETTER I WITH DOUBLE GRAVE
≡ 0069 i + 030F ̏

020A Ȋ LATIN CAPITAL LETTER I WITH INVERTED BREVE
≡ 0049 I + 0311 ̑

020B ȋ LATIN SMALL LETTER I WITH INVERTED BREVE
≡ 0069 i + 0311 ̑

020C Ȍ LATIN CAPITAL LETTER O WITH DOUBLE GRAVE
≡ 004F O + 030F ̏

020D ȍ LATIN SMALL LETTER O WITH DOUBLE GRAVE
≡ 006F o + 030F ̏

020E Ȏ LATIN CAPITAL LETTER O WITH INVERTED BREVE
≡ 004F O + 0311 ̑

020F ȏ LATIN SMALL LETTER O WITH INVERTED BREVE
≡ 006F o + 0311 ̑

0210 Ȑ LATIN CAPITAL LETTER R WITH DOUBLE GRAVE
≡ 0052 R + 030F ̏

0211 ȑ LATIN SMALL LETTER R WITH DOUBLE GRAVE
≡ 0072 r + 030F ̏

0212 Ȓ LATIN CAPITAL LETTER R WITH INVERTED BREVE
≡ 0052 R + 0311 ̑

0213 ȓ LATIN SMALL LETTER R WITH INVERTED BREVE
≡ 0072 r + 0311 ̑

0214 Ȕ LATIN CAPITAL LETTER U WITH DOUBLE GRAVE
≡ 0055 U + 030F ̏

0215 ȕ LATIN SMALL LETTER U WITH DOUBLE GRAVE
≡ 0075 u + 030F ̏

0216 Ȗ LATIN CAPITAL LETTER U WITH INVERTED BREVE
≡ 0055 U + 0311 ◌̑

0217 ȗ LATIN SMALL LETTER U WITH INVERTED BREVE
≡ 0075 u + 0311 ◌̑

	025	026	027	028	029	02A
0	ɐ 0250	ɠ 0260	ɰ 0270	ʀ 0280	ʐ 0290	ʠ 02A0
1	ɑ 0251	ɡ 0261	ɱ 0271	ʁ 0281	ʑ 0291	ʡ 02A1
2	ɒ 0252	ɢ 0262	ɲ 0272	ʂ 0282	ʒ 0292	ʢ 02A2
3	ɓ 0253	ɣ 0263	ɳ 0273	ʃ 0283	ʓ 0293	ʣ 02A3
4	ɔ 0254	ɤ 0264	ɴ 0274	ʄ 0284	ʔ 0294	ʤ 02A4
5	ɕ 0255	ɥ 0265	ɵ 0275	ʅ 0285	ʕ 0295	ʥ 02A5
6	ɖ 0256	ɦ 0266	ɶ 0276	ʆ 0286	ʖ 0296	ʦ 02A6
7	ɗ 0257	ɧ 0267	ɷ 0277	ʇ 0287	ʗ 0297	ʧ 02A7
8	ɘ 0258	ɨ 0268	ɸ 0278	ʈ 0288	ʘ 0298	ʨ 02A8
9	ə 0259	ɩ 0269	ɹ 0279	ʉ 0289	ʙ 0299	
A	ɚ 025A	ɪ 026A	ɺ 027A	ʊ 028A	ʚ 029A	
B	ɛ 025B	ɫ 026B	ɻ 027B	ʋ 028B	ʛ 029B	
C	ɜ 025C	ɬ 026C	ɼ 027C	ʌ 028C	ʜ 029C	
D	ɝ 025D	ɭ 026D	ɽ 027D	ʍ 028D	ʝ 029D	
E	ɞ 025E	ɮ 026E	ɾ 027E	ʎ 028E	ʞ 029E	
F	ɟ 025F	ɯ 026F	ɿ 027F	ʏ 028F	ʟ 029F	

IPA extensions

→ 00E6 æ latin small letter ae
→ 00E7 ç latin small letter c with cedilla
→ 00F0 ð latin small letter eth
→ 00F8 ø latin small letter o with stroke
→ 0127 ħ latin small letter h with stroke
→ 014B ŋ latin small letter eng
→ 0153 œ latin small ligature oe
→ 03B2 β greek small letter beta
→ 03B8 θ greek small letter theta
→ 03BB λ greek small letter lamda
→ 03C7 χ greek small letter chi

0250 ɐ LATIN SMALL LETTER TURNED A
• low central unrounded vowel

0251 ɑ LATIN SMALL LETTER ALPHA
= LATIN SMALL LETTER SCRIPT A
• low back unrounded vowel
→ 03B1 α greek small letter alpha

0252 ɒ LATIN SMALL LETTER TURNED ALPHA
• low back rounded vowel

0253 ɓ LATIN SMALL LETTER B WITH HOOK
• implosive bilabial stop
→ 0181 Ɓ latin capital letter b with hook

0254 ɔ LATIN SMALL LETTER OPEN O
• typographically a turned c
• lower-mid back rounded vowel
→ 0186 Ɔ latin capital letter open o

0255 ɕ LATIN SMALL LETTER C WITH CURL
• voiceless alveolo-palatal laminal fricative
• used in transcription of Mandarin Chinese
• sound spelled with 015B ś in Polish

0256 ɖ LATIN SMALL LETTER D WITH TAIL
= LATIN SMALL LETTER D RETROFLEX HOOK
• voiced retroflex stop
→ 0189 Đ latin capital letter african d

0257 ɗ LATIN SMALL LETTER D WITH HOOK
• implosive dental or alveolar stop
→ 018A Ɗ latin capital letter d with hook

0258 ɘ LATIN SMALL LETTER REVERSED E
• upper-mid central unrounded vowel

0259 ə LATIN SMALL LETTER SCHWA
• mid-central unrounded vowel
• variant uppercase form 018E Ǝ is associated with clone 01DD ǝ
→ 018F Ə latin capital letter schwa
→ 01DD ǝ latin small letter turned e

025A ɚ LATIN SMALL LETTER SCHWA WITH HOOK
• rhotacized schwa

025B ɛ LATIN SMALL LETTER OPEN E
= LATIN SMALL LETTER EPSILON
• lower-mid front unrounded vowel
→ 0190 Ɛ latin capital letter open e
→ 03B5 ε greek small letter epsilon

025C ɜ LATIN SMALL LETTER REVERSED OPEN E
• lower-mid central unrounded vowel

025D ɝ LATIN SMALL LETTER REVERSED OPEN E WITH HOOK
• rhotacized lower-mid central vowel

025E ɞ LATIN SMALL LETTER CLOSED REVERSED OPEN E
• lower-mid central rounded vowel

025F ɟ LATIN SMALL LETTER DOTLESS J WITH STROKE
• voiced palatal stop
• typographically a turned f
• "gy" in Hungarian orthography

0260 ɠ LATIN SMALL LETTER G WITH HOOK
• implosive velar stop
→ 0193 Ɠ latin capital letter g with hook

0261 ɡ LATIN SMALL LETTER SCRIPT G
• voiced velar stop
→ 0067 g latin small letter g

0262 ɢ LATIN LETTER SMALL CAPITAL G
• voiced uvular stop

0263 ɣ LATIN SMALL LETTER GAMMA
• voiced velar fricative
→ 0194 Ɣ latin capital letter gamma
→ 03B3 γ greek small letter gamma

0264 ɤ LATIN SMALL LETTER RAMS HORN
= LATIN SMALL LETTER BABY GAMMA
• upper-mid back unrounded vowel

0265 ɥ LATIN SMALL LETTER TURNED H
• voiced rounded palatal approximant

0266 ɦ LATIN SMALL LETTER H WITH HOOK
• breathy-voiced glottal fricative
→ 02B1 ʱ modifier letter small h with hook

0267 ɧ LATIN SMALL LETTER HENG WITH HOOK
• voiceless coarticulated velar and palato-alveolar fricative
• "tj" or "kj" in some Swedish dialects

0268 ɨ LATIN SMALL LETTER I WITH STROKE
= i bar
• high central unrounded vowel
• ISO 6438 gives lowercase of 0197 Ɨ as 026A ɪ, not 0268 ɨ

0269 ɩ LATIN SMALL LETTER IOTA
• semi-high front unrounded vowel
• obsoleted by IPA in 1989
• preferred use is 026A ɪ LATIN LETTER SMALL CAPITAL I
→ 0196 Ɩ latin capital letter iota
→ 03B9 ι greek small letter iota

026A ɪ LATIN LETTER SMALL CAPITAL I
• semi-high front unrounded vowel
• preferred IPA alternate
→ 0197 Ɨ latin capital letter i with stroke

026B ɫ LATIN SMALL LETTER L WITH MIDDLE TILDE
• velarized voiced alveolar lateral approximant

026C ɬ LATIN SMALL LETTER L WITH BELT
• voiceless alveolar lateral fricative

026D ɭ LATIN SMALL LETTER L WITH RETROFLEX HOOK
• voiced retroflex lateral

026E ɮ LATIN SMALL LETTER LEZH
• voiced lateral fricative
• "dhl" in Zulu orthography

026F ɯ LATIN SMALL LETTER TURNED M
• high back unrounded vowel
→ 019C Ɯ latin capital letter turned m

0270 ɰ LATIN SMALL LETTER TURNED M WITH LONG LEG
• voiced velar approximant

0271 ɱ LATIN SMALL LETTER M WITH HOOK
• voiced labiodental nasal

0272 ɲ LATIN SMALL LETTER N WITH LEFT HOOK
• voiced palatal nasal
→ 019D Ɲ latin capital letter n with left hook

0273 ɳ LATIN SMALL LETTER N WITH RETROFLEX HOOK
• voiced retroflex nasal

0274 ɴ LATIN LETTER SMALL CAPITAL N
• voiced uvular nasal

0275 ɵ LATIN SMALL LETTER BARRED O
= o bar
• rounded mid-central vowel, i.e. rounded schwa
• note case mapping
→ 019F Ɵ latin capital letter o with middle tilde
→ 03B8 θ greek small letter theta
→ 0473 ѳ cyrillic small letter fita

0276 ɶ LATIN LETTER SMALL CAPITAL OE
• low front rounded vowel
→ 0153 œ latin small ligature oe

0277 ɷ LATIN SMALL LETTER CLOSED OMEGA
• semi-high back rounded vowel
• obsoleted by IPA in 1989
• preferred use is 028A ʊ LATIN LETTER SMALL UPSILON

0278 ɸ LATIN SMALL LETTER PHI
• voiceless bilabial fricative
→ 03C6 ϕ greek small letter phi

0279 ɹ LATIN SMALL LETTER TURNED R
• voiced alveolar approximant
→ 02B4 ʴ modifier letter small turned r

027A ɺ LATIN SMALL LETTER TURNED R WITH LONG LEG
• voiced lateral flap

027B ɻ LATIN SMALL LETTER TURNED R WITH HOOK
• voiced retroflex approximant
→ 02B5 ʵ modifier letter small turned r with hook

027C ɼ LATIN SMALL LETTER R WITH LONG LEG
• voiced strident apico-alveolar trill
• sound spelled with 0159 ř in Czech

027D ɽ LATIN SMALL LETTER R WITH TAIL
= LATIN SMALL LETTER R HOOK
• voiced retroflex flap

027E ɾ LATIN SMALL LETTER R WITH FISHHOOK
• voiced alveolar flap or tap

027F ɿ LATIN SMALL LETTER REVERSED R WITH FISHHOOK
• apical dental vowel
• used in Sinological tradition
• IPA spelling - 007A z + 0329 ̩

0280 ʀ LATIN LETTER SMALL CAPITAL R
• voiced uvular trill

0281 ʁ LATIN LETTER SMALL CAPITAL INVERTED R
• voiced uvular fricative or approximant
→ 02B6 ʶ modifier letter small capital inverted r

0282 ʂ LATIN SMALL LETTER S WITH HOOK
• voiceless retroflex fricative

0283 ʃ LATIN SMALL LETTER ESH
• voiceless postalveolar fricative
→ 01A9 Σ latin capital letter esh
→ 222B ∫ integral

0284 ʄ LATIN SMALL LETTER DOTLESS J WITH STROKE AND HOOK
• implosive palatal stop
• typographically based on 025F ɟ, not on 0283 ʃ

0285 ʅ LATIN SMALL LETTER SQUAT REVERSED ESH
• apical retroflex vowel
• used in Sinological tradition
• IPA spelling - 0290 ʐ + 0329 ̩

0286 ʆ LATIN SMALL LETTER ESH WITH CURL
• palatalized voiceless postalveolar fricative
• suggested spelling - 0283 ʃ + 02B2 ʲ

0287 ʇ LATIN SMALL LETTER TURNED T
• dental click (sound of "tsk tsk")
→ 01C0 ǀ latin letter dental click

0288 ʈ LATIN SMALL LETTER T WITH RETROFLEX HOOK
• voiceless retroflex stop
→ 01AE Ʈ latin capital letter t with retroflex hook

0289 ʉ LATIN SMALL LETTER U BAR
• high central rounded vowel

028A ʊ LATIN SMALL LETTER UPSILON
• semi-high back rounded vowel
• preferred IPA alternate
→ 01B1 Ʊ latin capital letter upsilon
→ 03C5 υ greek small letter upsilon

028B ʋ LATIN SMALL LETTER V WITH HOOK
= LATIN SMALL LETTER SCRIPT V
• voiced labiodental approximant
→ 01B2 Ʋ latin capital letter v with hook
→ 03C5 υ greek small letter upsilon

028C ʌ LATIN SMALL LETTER TURNED V
= caret
= wedge
• lower-mid back unrounded vowel

028D ʍ LATIN SMALL LETTER TURNED W
• voiceless rounded labiovelar approximant

028E ʎ LATIN SMALL LETTER TURNED Y
• voiced lateral approximant

028F ʏ LATIN LETTER SMALL CAPITAL Y
• semi-high front rounded vowel

0290 ʐ LATIN SMALL LETTER Z WITH RETROFLEX HOOK
• voiced retroflex fricative

0291 ʑ LATIN SMALL LETTER Z WITH CURL
• voiced alveolo-palatal laminal fricative
• sound spelled with 017A ź in Polish

0292 ʒ LATIN SMALL LETTER EZH
= LATIN SMALL LETTER YOGH
= dram
• old Irish, old English
• voiced postalveolar fricative
→ 01B7 Ʒ latin capital letter ezh
→ 2125 ℥ ounce sign

0293 ʓ LATIN SMALL LETTER EZH WITH CURL
• palatalized voiced postalveolar fricative

0294 ʔ LATIN LETTER GLOTTAL STOP
→ 02C0 ˀ modifier letter glottal stop

0295 ʕ LATIN LETTER PHARYNGEAL VOICED FRICATIVE
= LATIN LETTER REVERSED GLOTTAL STOP
• voiced pharyngeal fricative
• ain
→ 01B9 ƹ latin small letter ezh reversed
→ 02C1 ˁ modifier letter reversed glottal stop

0296 ʖ LATIN LETTER INVERTED GLOTTAL STOP
• lateral click
→ 01C1 ǁ latin letter lateral click

0297 ʗ LATIN LETTER STRETCHED C
• palatal (or alveolar) click
→ 01C3 ǃ latin letter retroflex click
→ 2201 ∁ complement

0298 ʘ LATIN LETTER BILABIAL CLICK
= LATIN LETTER BULLSEYE
→ 2299 ⊙ circled dot operator

0299 ʙ LATIN LETTER SMALL CAPITAL B
• bilabial trill

029A ʚ LATIN SMALL LETTER CLOSED OPEN E
• lower-mid front rounded vowel
• non-IPA alternate for the preferred 0153 œ

029B ʛ LATIN LETTER SMALL CAPITAL G WITH HOOK
• voiced uvular implosive

029C ʜ LATIN LETTER SMALL CAPITAL H
• voiceless epiglotto-pharyngeal fricative

029D ʝ LATIN SMALL LETTER J WITH CROSSED-TAIL
• voiced palatal fricative

029E ʞ LATIN SMALL LETTER TURNED K
• proposed for velar click
• withdrawn by IPA in 1970

029F ʟ LATIN LETTER SMALL CAPITAL L
• velar lateral approximant

02A0 ʠ LATIN SMALL LETTER Q WITH HOOK
• voiceless uvular implosive

02A1 ʡ LATIN LETTER GLOTTAL STOP WITH STROKE
• voiced epiglottal-pharyngeal stop

02A2 ʢ LATIN LETTER REVERSED GLOTTAL STOP WITH STROKE
• voiced epiglottal-pharyngeal fricative

02A3 ʣ LATIN SMALL LETTER DZ DIGRAPH
• voiced dental affricate

02A4 ʤ LATIN SMALL LETTER DEZH DIGRAPH
• voiced postalveolar affricate

02A5 ʥ LATIN SMALL LETTER DZ DIGRAPH WITH CURL
• voiced alveolo-palatal affricate

02A6 ʦ LATIN SMALL LETTER TS DIGRAPH
• voiceless dental affricate

02A7 ʧ LATIN SMALL LETTER TESH DIGRAPH
• voiceless postalveolar affricate

02A8 ʨ LATIN SMALL LETTER TC DIGRAPH WITH CURL
• voiceless alveolo-palatal affricate

	02B	02C	02D	02E	02F
0	ʰ 02B0	ˀ 02C0	ː 02D0	ˠ 02E0	
1	ʱ 02B1	ˁ 02C1	ˑ 02D1	ˡ 02E1	
2	ʲ 02B2	˂ 02C2	˒ 02D2	ˢ 02E2	
3	ʳ 02B3	˃ 02C3	˓ 02D3	ˣ 02E3	
4	ʴ 02B4	˄ 02C4	˔ 02D4	ˤ 02E4	
5	ʵ 02B5	˅ 02C5	˕ 02D5	˥ 02E5	
6	ʶ 02B6	ˆ 02C6	˖ 02D6	˦ 02E6	
7	ʷ 02B7	ˇ 02C7	˗ 02D7	˧ 02E7	
8	ʸ 02B8	ˈ 02C8	˘ 02D8	˨ 02E8	
9	ʹ 02B9	ˉ 02C9	˙ 02D9	˩ 02E9	
A	ʺ 02BA	ˊ 02CA	˚ 02DA		
B	ʻ 02BB	ˋ 02CB	˛ 02DB		
C	ʼ 02BC	ˌ 02CC	˜ 02DC		
D	ʽ 02BD	ˍ 02CD	˝ 02DD		
E	ʾ 02BE	ˎ 02CE	˞ 02DE		
F	ʿ 02BF	ˏ 02CF			

Phonetic modifiers derived from Latin letters

02B0 ʰ MODIFIER LETTER SMALL H
• aspiration
≈ <super> + 0068 h

02B1 ʱ MODIFIER LETTER SMALL H WITH HOOK
• breathy voiced, murmured
→ 0266 ɦ latin small letter h with hook
→ 0324 ̤ combining diaeresis below
≈ <super> + 0266 ɦ

02B2 ʲ MODIFIER LETTER SMALL J
• palatalization
→ 0321 ̡ combining palatalized hook below
≈ <super> + 006A j

02B3 ʳ MODIFIER LETTER SMALL R
≈ <super> + 0072 r

02B4 ʴ MODIFIER LETTER SMALL TURNED R
→ 0279 ɹ latin small letter turned r
≈ <super> + 0279 ɹ

02B5 ʵ MODIFIER LETTER SMALL TURNED R WITH HOOK
→ 027B ɻ latin small letter turned r with hook
≈ <super> + 027B ɻ

02B6 ʶ MODIFIER LETTER SMALL CAPITAL INVERTED R
• preceding four used for r-coloring or r-offglides
→ 0281 ʁ latin letter small capital inverted r
≈ <super> + 0281 ʁ

02B7 ʷ MODIFIER LETTER SMALL W
• labialization
→ 032B ̫ combining inverted double arch below
≈ <super> + 0077 w

02B8 ʸ MODIFIER LETTER SMALL Y
• palatalization
• common Americanist substitution for 02B2 ʲ
≈ <super> + 0079 y

Miscellaneous phonetic modifiers

02B9 ʹ MODIFIER LETTER PRIME
• primary stress, emphasis
• transliteration of mjagkij znak (Cyrillic soft sign: palatalization)
→ 0027 ' apostrophe
→ 00B4 ´ acute accent
→ 02CA ˊ modifier letter acute accent
→ 0301 ́ combining acute accent
→ 0374 ʹ greek numeral sign
→ 2032 ′ prime

02BA ʺ MODIFIER LETTER DOUBLE PRIME
• exaggerated stress, contrastive stress
• transliteration of tverdyj znak (Cyrillic hard sign: no palatalization)
→ 0022 " quotation mark
→ 030B ̋ combining double acute accent
→ 2033 ″ double prime

02BB ʻ MODIFIER LETTER TURNED COMMA
• typographical alternate for 02BD ʽ or 02BF ʿ
→ 0312 ̒ combining turned comma above
→ 2018 ‘ left single quotation mark

02BC ʼ MODIFIER LETTER APOSTROPHE
= apostrophe
• glottal stop, glottalization, ejective; elision
• spacing clone of Greek smooth breathing mark
• this is the preferred character for apostrophe
→ 0027 ' apostrophe
→ 0313 ̓ combining comma above
→ 0315 ̕ combining comma above right
→ 055A ՚ armenian apostrophe
→ 2019 ’ right single quotation mark

02BD ʽ MODIFIER LETTER REVERSED COMMA
• weak aspiration
• spacing clone of Greek rough breathing mark
→ 0314 ̔ combining reversed comma above
→ 0559 ՙ armenian modifier letter left half ring
→ 201B ‛ single high-reversed-9 quotation mark

02BE ʾ MODIFIER LETTER RIGHT HALF RING
• transliteration of Arabic hamzah (glottal stop)
→ 055A ՚ armenian apostrophe
→ 0621 ء arabic letter hamza

02BF ʿ MODIFIER LETTER LEFT HALF RING
• transliteration of Arabic ain (voiced pharyngeal fricative)
→ 0559 ՙ armenian modifier letter left half ring
→ 0639 ع arabic letter ain

02C0 ˀ MODIFIER LETTER GLOTTAL STOP
• ejective or glottalized
• typographical alternate for 02BC ʼ or 02BE ʾ
→ 0294 ʔ latin letter glottal stop
→ 0309 ◌̉ combining hook above

02C1 ˁ MODIFIER LETTER REVERSED GLOTTAL STOP
• typographical alternate for 02BF ʿ
→ 0295 ʕ latin letter pharyngeal voiced fricative

02C2 ˂ MODIFIER LETTER LEFT ARROWHEAD
• fronted articulation

02C3 ˃ MODIFIER LETTER RIGHT ARROWHEAD
• backed articulation

02C4 ˄ MODIFIER LETTER UP ARROWHEAD
• raised articulation
→ 005E ^ circumflex accent
→ 2303 ⌃ up arrowhead

02C5 ˅ MODIFIER LETTER DOWN ARROWHEAD
• lowered articulation

02C6 ˆ MODIFIER LETTER CIRCUMFLEX ACCENT
• rising-falling tone, falling tone, secondary stress, etc.
→ 005E ^ circumflex accent
→ 0302 ◌̂ combining circumflex accent

02C7 ˇ CARON
= MODIFIER LETTER HACEK
• falling-rising tone
• Mandarin Chinese third tone
→ 030C ◌̌ combining caron

02C8 ˈ MODIFIER LETTER VERTICAL LINE
• primary stress, downstep
• precedes letter or syllable modified
→ 0027 ' apostrophe
→ 030D ◌̍ combining vertical line above

02C9 ˉ MODIFIER LETTER MACRON
• high level tone
• precedes or follows letter or syllable modified
• Mandarin Chinese first tone
→ 00AF ¯ macron
→ 0304 ◌̄ combining macron

02CA ˊ MODIFIER LETTER ACUTE ACCENT
• high-rising tone (IPA), high tone, primary stress
• Mandarin Chinese second tone
→ 00B4 ´ acute accent
→ 02B9 ʹ modifier letter prime
→ 0301 ◌́ combining acute accent
→ 0374 ʹ greek numeral sign
→ 055B ՛ armenian emphasis mark

02CB ˋ MODIFIER LETTER GRAVE ACCENT
• high-falling tone (IPA), low tone, secondary or tertiary stress
• Mandarin Chinese fourth tone
→ 0060 ` grave accent
→ 0300 ◌̀ combining grave accent
→ 055D ՝ armenian comma

02CC ˌ MODIFIER LETTER LOW VERTICAL LINE
• secondary stress
• precedes letter or syllable modified
→ 0329 ◌̩ combining vertical line below

02CD ˍ MODIFIER LETTER LOW MACRON
• low level tone
→ 005F _ low line
→ 0331 ◌̱ combining macron below

02CE ˎ MODIFIER LETTER LOW GRAVE ACCENT
• low-falling tone

02CF ˏ MODIFIER LETTER LOW ACUTE ACCENT
• low-rising tone
→ 0375 ͵ greek lower numeral sign

02D0 ː MODIFIER LETTER TRIANGULAR COLON
• length mark

02D1 ˑ MODIFIER LETTER HALF TRIANGULAR COLON
• half-length mark

02D2 ˒ MODIFIER LETTER CENTRED RIGHT HALF RING
• more rounded articulation

02D3 ˓ MODIFIER LETTER CENTRED LEFT HALF RING
• less rounded articulation

02D4 ˔ MODIFIER LETTER UP TACK
• vowel raising or closing
→ 031D ◌̝ combining up tack below
→ 0323 ◌̣ combining dot below

02D5 ˕ MODIFIER LETTER DOWN TACK
• vowel lowering or opening
→ 031C ̜ combining left half ring below
→ 031E ̞ combining down tack below

02D6 ˖ MODIFIER LETTER PLUS SIGN
• advanced or fronted articulation
→ 031F ̟ combining plus sign below

02D7 ˗ MODIFIER LETTER MINUS SIGN
• retracted or backed articulation
• glyph may have small end-serifs
→ 0320 ̠ combining minus sign below

Spacing clones of diacritics

02D8 ˘ BREVE
→ 0306 ̆ combining breve
≈ 0020 SP + 0306 ̆

02D9 ˙ DOT ABOVE
• Mandarin Chinese fifth tone (light or neutral)
→ 0307 ̇ combining dot above
≈ 0020 SP + 0307 ̇

02DA ˚ RING ABOVE
→ 00B0 ° degree sign
→ 030A ̊ combining ring above
≈ 0020 SP + 030A ̊

02DB ˛ OGONEK
→ 0328 ̨ combining ogonek
≈ 0020 SP + 0328 ̨

02DC ˜ SMALL TILDE
→ 007E ~ tilde
→ 0303 ̃ combining tilde
→ 223C ∼ tilde operator
≈ 0020 SP + 0303 ̃

02DD ˝ DOUBLE ACUTE ACCENT
→ 030B ̋ combining double acute accent
≈ 0020 SP + 030B ̋

Additions based on 1989 IPA

02DE ˞ MODIFIER LETTER RHOTIC HOOK
• rhotacization in vowel
• often ligated: 025A ɚ = 0259 ə + 02DE ˞; 025D ɝ = 025C ɜ + 02DE ˞

02DF ▨ <reserved>

02E0 ˠ MODIFIER LETTER SMALL GAMMA
• these modifier letters are occasionally used in transcription of affricates
≈ <super> + 0263 ɣ

02E1 ˡ MODIFIER LETTER SMALL L
≈ <super> + 006C l

02E2 ˢ MODIFIER LETTER SMALL S
≈ <super> + 0073 s

02E3 ˣ MODIFIER LETTER SMALL X
≈ <super> + 0078 x

02E4 ˤ MODIFIER LETTER SMALL REVERSED GLOTTAL STOP
≈ <super> + 0295 ʕ

Tone letters

02E5 ˥ MODIFIER LETTER EXTRA-HIGH TONE BAR

02E6 ˦ MODIFIER LETTER HIGH TONE BAR

02E7 ˧ MODIFIER LETTER MID TONE BAR

02E8 ˨ MODIFIER LETTER LOW TONE BAR

02E9 ˩ MODIFIER LETTER EXTRA-LOW TONE BAR

	030	031	032	033	034	035	036
0	0300	0310	0320	0330	0340		0360
1	0301	0311	0321	0331	0341		0361
2	0302	0312	0322	0332	0342		
3	0303	0313	0323	0333	0343		
4	0304	0314	0324	0334	0344		
5	0305	0315	0325	0335	0345		
6	0306	0316	0326	0336			
7	0307	0317	0327	0337			
8	0308	0318	0328	0338			
9	0309	0319	0329	0339			
A	030A	031A	032A	033A			
B	030B	031B	032B	033B			
C	030C	031C	032C	033C			
D	030D	031D	032D	033D			
E	030E	031E	032E	033E			
F	030F	031F	032F	033F			

Ordinary diacritics

0300 ̀ COMBINING GRAVE ACCENT
= Greek varia
→ 0060 ` grave accent
→ 02CB ˋ modifier letter grave accent

0301 ́ COMBINING ACUTE ACCENT
= stress mark
= Greek oxia
→ 0027 ' apostrophe
→ 00B4 ´ acute accent
→ 02B9 ʹ modifier letter prime
→ 02CA ˊ modifier letter acute accent

0302 ̂ COMBINING CIRCUMFLEX ACCENT
= hat
→ 005E ^ circumflex accent
→ 02C6 ˆ modifier letter circumflex accent

0303 ̃ COMBINING TILDE
• IPA: nasalization
• Vietnamese tone mark
→ 007E ~ tilde
→ 02DC ˜ small tilde

0304 ̄ COMBINING MACRON
= long
• distinguish from the following
→ 00AF ¯ macron
→ 02C9 ˉ modifier letter macron

0305 ̅ COMBINING OVERLINE
= overscore
• connects on left and right
→ 00AF ¯ macron

0306 ̆ COMBINING BREVE
= short
= Greek vrachy
→ 02D8 ˘ breve

0307 ̇ COMBINING DOT ABOVE
= derivative
• IPA (unofficial): palatalization
→ 02D9 ˙ dot above

0308 ̈ COMBINING DIAERESIS
= double dot above
= umlaut
= double derivative
= Greek dialytika
→ 00A8 ¨ diaeresis

0309 ̉ COMBINING HOOK ABOVE
• kerns left or right of circumflex over vowels
• Vietnamese tone mark
→ 02C0 ˀ modifier letter glottal stop

030A ̊ COMBINING RING ABOVE
→ 00B0 ° degree sign
→ 02DA ˚ ring above

030B ̋ COMBINING DOUBLE ACUTE ACCENT
• Hungarian, Chuvash
→ 0022 " quotation mark
→ 02BA ʺ modifier letter double prime
→ 02DD ˝ double acute accent

030C ̌ COMBINING CARON
= NON-SPACING HACEK
= V above
→ 02C7 ˇ caron

030D ̍ COMBINING VERTICAL LINE ABOVE
• Marshallese
= Greek tonos
→ 02C8 ˈ modifier letter vertical line
→ 0384 ΄ greek tonos

030E ̎ COMBINING DOUBLE VERTICAL LINE ABOVE
• Marshallese
→ 0022 " quotation mark

030F ̏ COMBINING DOUBLE GRAVE ACCENT
• Serbocroatian

0310 ̐ COMBINING CANDRABINDU
→ 0901 ँ devanagari sign candrabindu
≡ 0306 ̆ + 0307 ̇

0311 ̑ COMBINING INVERTED BREVE

0312 ̒ COMBINING TURNED COMMA ABOVE
= cedilla above
• Latvian
→ 02BB ʻ modifier letter turned comma

0313 ̓ COMBINING COMMA ABOVE
= Greek psili
= smooth breathing
→ 02BC ʼ modifier letter apostrophe
→ 0486 ҆ combining cyrillic psili pneumata
→ 055A ՚ armenian apostrophe

0314 ̔ COMBINING REVERSED COMMA ABOVE
= Greek dasia
= rough breathing
→ 02BD ʽ modifier letter reversed comma
→ 0485 ҅ combining cyrillic dasia pneumata
→ 0559 ՙ armenian modifier letter left half ring

0315 ̕ COMBINING COMMA ABOVE RIGHT
→ 02BC ʼ modifier letter apostrophe

0316 ̖ COMBINING GRAVE ACCENT BELOW

0317 ◌̗ COMBINING ACUTE ACCENT BELOW

0318 ◌̘ COMBINING LEFT TACK BELOW

0319 ◌̙ COMBINING RIGHT TACK BELOW

031A ◌̚ COMBINING LEFT ANGLE ABOVE
• IPA: unreleased stop

031B ◌̛ COMBINING HORN
• Vietnamese

031C ◌̜ COMBINING LEFT HALF RING BELOW
• IPA: open variety of vowel
→ 02D5 ˕ modifier letter down tack

031D ◌̝ COMBINING UP TACK BELOW
• IPA: vowel raising or closing
→ 02D4 ˔ modifier letter up tack

031E ◌̞ COMBINING DOWN TACK BELOW
• IPA: vowel lowering or opening
→ 02D5 ˕ modifier letter down tack

031F ◌̟ COMBINING PLUS SIGN BELOW
• IPA: advanced or fronted articulation
→ 02D6 ˖ modifier letter plus sign

0320 ◌̠ COMBINING MINUS SIGN BELOW
• IPA: retracted or backed articulation
• glyph may have small end-serifs
→ 02D7 ˗ modifier letter minus sign

0321 ◌̡ COMBINING PALATALIZED HOOK BELOW
• IPA: palatalization
→ 02B2 ʲ modifier letter small j

0322 ◌̢ COMBINING RETROFLEX HOOK BELOW
• IPA: retroflexion

0323 ◌̣ COMBINING DOT BELOW
• IPA: closer variety of vowel
• Americanist: retraction or retroflexion
• Semiticist: velarization or pharyngealization
• Vietnamese tone mark
→ 02D4 ˔ modifier letter up tack

0324 ◌̤ COMBINING DIAERESIS BELOW
• IPA: breathy-voice or murmur
→ 02B1 ʱ modifier letter small h with hook

0325 ◌̥ COMBINING RING BELOW
• IPA: voiceless
• Madurese

0326 ◌̦ COMBINING COMMA BELOW
• variant of the following

0327 ◌̧ COMBINING CEDILLA
→ 00B8 ¸ cedilla

0328 ◌̨ COMBINING OGONEK
• Americanist: nasalization
→ 02DB ˛ ogonek

0329 ◌̩ COMBINING VERTICAL LINE BELOW
• IPA: syllabic
• Yoruba
→ 02CC ˌ modifier letter low vertical line

032A ◌̪ COMBINING BRIDGE BELOW
• IPA: dental

032B ◌̫ COMBINING INVERTED DOUBLE ARCH BELOW
• IPA: labialization
→ 02B7 ʷ modifier letter small w

032C ◌̬ COMBINING CARON BELOW
• IPA: voiced
• Hittite

032D ◌̭ COMBINING CIRCUMFLEX ACCENT BELOW
• Americanist: fronted articulation

032E ◌̮ COMBINING BREVE BELOW

032F ◌̯ COMBINING INVERTED BREVE BELOW
• Americanist: fronted articulation (variant of 032D ◌̭)
• Indo-European: semivowel

0330 ◌̰ COMBINING TILDE BELOW
• IPA: creaky voice

0331 ◌̱ COMBINING MACRON BELOW
→ 005F _ low line
→ 02CD ˍ modifier letter low macron

0332 ◌̲ COMBINING LOW LINE
= underline
= underscore
• connects on left and right
→ 005F _ low line

0333 ◌̳ COMBINING DOUBLE LOW LINE
= double underline
= double underscore
• connects on left and right
→ 2017 ‗ double low line

Overstruck diacritics

0334 ◌̴ COMBINING TILDE OVERLAY
• IPA: velarization or pharyngealization

0335 ◌̵ COMBINING SHORT STROKE OVERLAY

0336 ◌̶ COMBINING LONG STROKE OVERLAY

0337 ◌̷ COMBINING SHORT SOLIDUS OVERLAY
= short slash overlay

0338 ◌̸ COMBINING LONG SOLIDUS OVERLAY
= long slash overlay

Additions

0339 ◌̹ COMBINING RIGHT HALF RING BELOW

033A ◌̺ COMBINING INVERTED BRIDGE BELOW

033B ◌̻ COMBINING SQUARE BELOW

033C ◌̼ COMBINING SEAGULL BELOW

033D ◌̽ COMBINING X ABOVE

033E ◌̾ COMBINING VERTICAL TILDE
• Cyrillic palatalization
→ 0484 ◌҄ combining cyrillic palatalization

033F ◌̿ COMBINING DOUBLE OVERLINE

Vietnamese tone marks

0340 ◌̀ COMBINING GRAVE TONE MARK
• kerns left of circumflex over vowels
≡ 0300 ◌̀

0341 ◌́ COMBINING ACUTE TONE MARK
• kerns right of circumflex over vowels
≡ 0301 ◌́

Additions for Greek

0342 ◌͂ COMBINING GREEK PERISPOMENI

0343 ◌̓ COMBINING GREEK KORONIS
≡ 0313 ◌̓

0344 ◌̈́ COMBINING GREEK DIALYTIKA TONOS
≡ 0308 ◌̈ + 030D ◌̍

0345 ◌ͅ COMBINING GREEK YPOGEGRAMMENI
= GREEK NON-SPACING IOTA BELOW
= iota subscript
→ 037A ͺ greek ypogegrammeni

0346 <reserved>
0347 <reserved>
0348 <reserved>
0349 <reserved>
034A <reserved>
034B <reserved>
034C <reserved>
034D <reserved>
034E <reserved>
034F <reserved>
0350 <reserved>
0351 <reserved>
0352 <reserved>
0353 <reserved>
0354 <reserved>
0355 <reserved>
0356 <reserved>
0357 <reserved>
0358 <reserved>
0359 <reserved>
035A <reserved>
035B <reserved>
035C <reserved>
035D <reserved>
035E <reserved>
035F <reserved>

Double diacritics

0360 ◌͠ COMBINING DOUBLE TILDE

0361 ◌͡ COMBINING DOUBLE INVERTED BREVE

	037	038	039	03A	03B	03C	03D	03E	03F
0			ΐ 0390	Π 03A0	ΰ 03B0	π 03C0	ϐ 03D0	Ϡ 03E0	ϰ 03F0
1			Α 0391	Ρ 03A1	α 03B1	ρ 03C1	ϑ 03D1		ϱ 03F1
2			Β 0392		β 03B2	ς 03C2	ϒ 03D2	Ϣ 03E2	ϲ 03F2
3			Γ 0393	Σ 03A3	γ 03B3	σ 03C3	ϓ 03D3	ϣ 03E3	ϳ 03F3
4	ʹ 0374	΄ 0384	Δ 0394	Τ 03A4	δ 03B4	τ 03C4	ϔ 03D4	Ϥ 03E4	
5	͵ 0375	΅ 0385	Ε 0395	Υ 03A5	ε 03B5	υ 03C5	ϕ 03D5	ϥ 03E5	
6		Ά 0386	Ζ 0396	Φ 03A6	ζ 03B6	φ 03C6	ϖ 03D6	Ϧ 03E6	
7		· 0387	Η 0397	Χ 03A7	η 03B7	χ 03C7		ϧ 03E7	
8		Έ 0388	Θ 0398	Ψ 03A8	θ 03B8	ψ 03C8		Ϩ 03E8	
9		Ή 0389	Ι 0399	Ω 03A9	ι 03B9	ω 03C9		ϩ 03E9	
A	ͺ 037A	Ί 038A	Κ 039A	Ϊ 03AA	κ 03BA	ϊ 03CA	Ϛ 03DA	Ϫ 03EA	
B			Λ 039B	Ϋ 03AB	λ 03BB	ϋ 03CB		ϫ 03EB	
C		Ό 038C	Μ 039C	ά 03AC	μ 03BC	ό 03CC	Ϝ 03DC	Ϭ 03EC	
D			Ν 039D	έ 03AD	ν 03BD	ύ 03CD		ϭ 03ED	
E	; 037E	Ύ 038E	Ξ 039E	ή 03AE	ξ 03BE	ώ 03CE	Ϟ 03DE	Ϯ 03EE	
F		Ώ 038F	Ο 039F	ί 03AF	ο 03BF			ϯ 03EF	

Based on ISO 8859-7

0370 <reserved>
→ 0345 ͅ combining greek ypogegrammeni

0371 <reserved>
→ 0314 ̔ combining reversed comma above

0372 <reserved>
→ 0313 ̓ combining comma above

0373 <reserved>
→ 00A3 £ pound sign

0374 ʹ GREEK NUMERAL SIGN
= GREEK UPPER NUMERAL SIGN
= dexia keraia
• for numeric use of letters
→ 02B9 ʹ modifier letter prime
→ 02CA ˊ modifier letter acute accent
≡ 02B9 ʹ

0375 ͵ GREEK LOWER NUMERAL SIGN
= aristeri keraia
• for numeric use of letters
→ 02CF ˏ modifier letter low acute accent

0376 <reserved>
→ 00A6 ¦ broken bar

0377 <reserved>
→ 00B6 ¶ pilcrow sign

0378 <reserved>
→ 0308 ̈ combining diaeresis

0379 <reserved>
→ 00A9 © copyright sign

037A ͺ GREEK YPOGEGRAMMENI
→ 0345 ͅ combining greek ypogegrammeni
≈ 0020 SP + 0345 ͅ

037B <reserved>
→ 00AB « left-pointing double angle quotation mark

037C <reserved>
→ 00AC ¬ not sign

037D <reserved>
→ 00AD - soft hyphen

037E ; GREEK QUESTION MARK
= erotimatiko
• sentence-final punctuation
→ 003B ; semicolon
→ 003F ? question mark
≡ 003B ;

037F <reserved>
→ 2015 ― horizontal bar

0380 <reserved>
→ 00B0 ° degree sign

0381 <reserved>
→ 00B1 ± plus-minus sign

0382 <reserved>
→ 00B2 ² superscript two

0383 <reserved>
→ 00B3 ³ superscript three

0384 ΄ GREEK TONOS
→ 030D ̍ combining vertical line above
≈ 0020 SP + 030D ̍

0385 ΅ GREEK DIALYTIKA TONOS
≡ 00A8 ¨ + 030D ̍

0386 Ά GREEK CAPITAL LETTER ALPHA WITH TONOS
≡ 0391 Α + 030D ̍

0387 · GREEK ANO TELEIA
→ 00B7 · middle dot
≡ 00B7 ·

0388 Έ GREEK CAPITAL LETTER EPSILON WITH TONOS
≡ 0395 Ε + 030D ̍

0389 Ή GREEK CAPITAL LETTER ETA WITH TONOS
≡ 0397 Η + 030D ̍

038A Ί GREEK CAPITAL LETTER IOTA WITH TONOS
≡ 0399 Ι + 030D ̍

038B <reserved>
→ 00BB » right-pointing double angle quotation mark

038C Ό GREEK CAPITAL LETTER OMICRON WITH TONOS
≡ 039F Ο + 030D ̍

038D <reserved>
→ 00BD ½ vulgar fraction one half

038E Ύ GREEK CAPITAL LETTER UPSILON WITH TONOS
≡ 03A5 Υ + 030D ̍

038F Ώ GREEK CAPITAL LETTER OMEGA WITH TONOS
≡ 03A9 Ω + 030D ̍

0390 ΐ GREEK SMALL LETTER IOTA WITH DIALYTIKA AND TONOS
≡ 03B9 ι + 0344 ̈́

0391 Α GREEK CAPITAL LETTER ALPHA

0392 Β GREEK CAPITAL LETTER BETA

0393 Γ GREEK CAPITAL LETTER GAMMA
= gamma function

0394 Δ GREEK CAPITAL LETTER DELTA
→ 2206 ∆ increment

0395 Ε GREEK CAPITAL LETTER EPSILON

0396 Ζ GREEK CAPITAL LETTER ZETA

0397 Η GREEK CAPITAL LETTER ETA

0398 Θ GREEK CAPITAL LETTER THETA

0399 Ι GREEK CAPITAL LETTER IOTA
= iota adscript

039A Κ GREEK CAPITAL LETTER KAPPA

039B Λ GREEK CAPITAL LETTER LAMDA
039C Μ GREEK CAPITAL LETTER MU
039D Ν GREEK CAPITAL LETTER NU
039E Ξ GREEK CAPITAL LETTER XI
039F Ο GREEK CAPITAL LETTER OMICRON
03A0 Π GREEK CAPITAL LETTER PI
→ 220F ∏ n-ary product
03A1 Ρ GREEK CAPITAL LETTER RHO
03A2 ▧ <reserved>
03A3 Σ GREEK CAPITAL LETTER SIGMA
→ 01A9 Ʃ latin capital letter esh
→ 2211 ∑ n-ary summation
03A4 Τ GREEK CAPITAL LETTER TAU
03A5 Υ GREEK CAPITAL LETTER UPSILON
03A6 Φ GREEK CAPITAL LETTER PHI
03A7 Χ GREEK CAPITAL LETTER CHI
03A8 Ψ GREEK CAPITAL LETTER PSI
03A9 Ω GREEK CAPITAL LETTER OMEGA
→ 2126 Ω ohm sign
→ 2127 ℧ inverted ohm sign
03AA Ϊ GREEK CAPITAL LETTER IOTA WITH DIALYTIKA
≡ 0399 Ι + 0308 ̈
03AB Ϋ GREEK CAPITAL LETTER UPSILON WITH DIALYTIKA
≡ 03A5 Υ + 0308 ̈
03AC ά GREEK SMALL LETTER ALPHA WITH TONOS
≡ 03B1 α + 030D ̍
03AD έ GREEK SMALL LETTER EPSILON WITH TONOS
≡ 03B5 ε + 030D ̍
03AE ή GREEK SMALL LETTER ETA WITH TONOS
≡ 03B7 η + 030D ̍
03AF ί GREEK SMALL LETTER IOTA WITH TONOS
≡ 03B9 ι + 030D ̍
03B0 ΰ GREEK SMALL LETTER UPSILON WITH DIALYTIKA AND TONOS
≡ 03C5 υ + 0344 ̈́
03B1 α GREEK SMALL LETTER ALPHA
→ 0251 ɑ latin small letter alpha
→ 221D ∝ proportional to
03B2 β GREEK SMALL LETTER BETA
→ 00DF ß latin small letter sharp s
→ 0180 ƀ latin small letter b with stroke
03B3 γ GREEK SMALL LETTER GAMMA
→ 0263 ɣ latin small letter gamma
03B4 δ GREEK SMALL LETTER DELTA
03B5 ε GREEK SMALL LETTER EPSILON
→ 025B ɛ latin small letter open e
03B6 ζ GREEK SMALL LETTER ZETA
03B7 η GREEK SMALL LETTER ETA
03B8 θ GREEK SMALL LETTER THETA
→ 0275 ɵ latin small letter barred o
→ 0473 ѳ cyrillic small letter fita
03B9 ι GREEK SMALL LETTER IOTA
→ 0269 ɩ latin small letter iota
→ 2129 ℩ turned greek small letter iota
03BA κ GREEK SMALL LETTER KAPPA
03BB λ GREEK SMALL LETTER LAMDA
03BC μ GREEK SMALL LETTER MU
→ 00B5 µ micro sign
03BD ν GREEK SMALL LETTER NU
03BE ξ GREEK SMALL LETTER XI
03BF ο GREEK SMALL LETTER OMICRON
03C0 π GREEK SMALL LETTER PI
• math constant 3.141592...
03C1 ρ GREEK SMALL LETTER RHO
03C2 ς GREEK SMALL LETTER FINAL SIGMA
03C3 σ GREEK SMALL LETTER SIGMA
03C4 τ GREEK SMALL LETTER TAU
03C5 υ GREEK SMALL LETTER UPSILON
→ 028A ʊ latin small letter upsilon
→ 028B ʋ latin small letter v with hook
03C6 φ GREEK SMALL LETTER PHI
→ 0278 ɸ latin small letter phi
03C7 χ GREEK SMALL LETTER CHI
03C8 ψ GREEK SMALL LETTER PSI
03C9 ω GREEK SMALL LETTER OMEGA
03CA ϊ GREEK SMALL LETTER IOTA WITH DIALYTIKA
≡ 03B9 ι + 0308 ̈
03CB ϋ GREEK SMALL LETTER UPSILON WITH DIALYTIKA
≡ 03C5 υ + 0308 ̈
03CC ό GREEK SMALL LETTER OMICRON WITH TONOS
≡ 03BF ο + 030D ̍
03CD ύ GREEK SMALL LETTER UPSILON WITH TONOS
≡ 03C5 υ + 030D ̍
03CE ώ GREEK SMALL LETTER OMEGA WITH TONOS
≡ 03C9 ω + 030D ̍
03CF ▧ <reserved>

Variant letterforms

03D0 ϐ GREEK BETA SYMBOL
03D1 ϑ GREEK THETA SYMBOL
• used as technical symbol
03D2 ϒ GREEK UPSILON WITH HOOK SYMBOL

03D3 ϓ GREEK UPSILON WITH ACUTE AND HOOK SYMBOL
≡ 03D2 ϒ + 030D ̍
03D4 ϔ GREEK UPSILON WITH DIAERESIS AND HOOK SYMBOL
≡ 03D2 ϒ + 0308 ̈
03D5 ϕ GREEK PHI SYMBOL
• used as technical symbol
03D6 ϖ GREEK PI SYMBOL
• used as technical symbol
• a variant of pi, looking like omega
03D7 <reserved>
→ 037E ; greek question mark
03D8 <reserved>
→ 0374 ʹ greek numeral sign
03D9 <reserved>
→ 0375 ͵ greek lower numeral sign

Archaic letters

03DA Ϛ GREEK LETTER STIGMA
03DB <reserved>
03DC Ϝ GREEK LETTER DIGAMMA
03DD <reserved>
03DE Ϟ GREEK LETTER KOPPA
03DF <reserved>
03E0 Ϡ GREEK LETTER SAMPI
03E1 <reserved>

Coptic-unique letters

03E2 Ϣ COPTIC CAPITAL LETTER SHEI
03E3 ϣ COPTIC SMALL LETTER SHEI
03E4 Ϥ COPTIC CAPITAL LETTER FEI
03E5 ϥ COPTIC SMALL LETTER FEI
03E6 Ϧ COPTIC CAPITAL LETTER KHEI
03E7 ϧ COPTIC SMALL LETTER KHEI
03E8 Ϩ COPTIC CAPITAL LETTER HORI
03E9 ϩ COPTIC SMALL LETTER HORI
03EA Ϫ COPTIC CAPITAL LETTER GANGIA
03EB ϫ COPTIC SMALL LETTER GANGIA
03EC Ϭ COPTIC CAPITAL LETTER SHIMA
03ED ϭ COPTIC SMALL LETTER SHIMA
03EE Ϯ COPTIC CAPITAL LETTER DEI
03EF ϯ COPTIC SMALL LETTER DEI

Additions

03F0 ϰ GREEK KAPPA SYMBOL
• used as technical symbol
03F1 ϱ GREEK RHO SYMBOL
• used as technical symbol
03F2 ϲ GREEK LUNATE SIGMA SYMBOL
03F3 ϳ GREEK LETTER YOT
03F4 <reserved>
→ 0385 ΅ greek dialytika tonos
03F5 <reserved>
→ 037A ͺ greek ypogegrammeni

	040	041	042	043	044	045	046	047
0		А 0410	Р 0420	а 0430	р 0440		Ѡ 0460	Ѱ 0470
1	Ё 0401	Б 0411	С 0421	б 0431	с 0441	ё 0451	ѡ 0461	ѱ 0471
2	Ђ 0402	В 0412	Т 0422	в 0432	т 0442	ђ 0452	Ѣ 0462	Ѳ 0472
3	Ѓ 0403	Г 0413	У 0423	г 0433	у 0443	ѓ 0453	ѣ 0463	ѳ 0473
4	Є 0404	Д 0414	Ф 0424	д 0434	ф 0444	є 0454	Ѥ 0464	Ѵ 0474
5	Ѕ 0405	Е 0415	Х 0425	е 0435	х 0445	ѕ 0455	ѥ 0465	ѵ 0475
6	І 0406	Ж 0416	Ц 0426	ж 0436	ц 0446	і 0456	Ѧ 0466	Ѷ 0476
7	Ї 0407	З 0417	Ч 0427	з 0437	ч 0447	ї 0457	ѧ 0467	ѷ 0477
8	Ј 0408	И 0418	Ш 0428	и 0438	ш 0448	ј 0458	Ѩ 0468	Ѹ 0478
9	Љ 0409	Й 0419	Щ 0429	й 0439	щ 0449	љ 0459	ѩ 0469	ѹ 0479
A	Њ 040A	К 041A	Ъ 042A	к 043A	ъ 044A	њ 045A	Ѫ 046A	Ѻ 047A
B	Ћ 040B	Л 041B	Ы 042B	л 043B	ы 044B	ћ 045B	ѫ 046B	ѻ 047B
C	Ќ 040C	М 041C	Ь 042C	м 043C	ь 044C	ќ 045C	Ѭ 046C	Ѽ 047C
D		Н 041D	Э 042D	н 043D	э 044D		ѭ 046D	ѽ 047D
E	Ў 040E	О 041E	Ю 042E	о 043E	ю 044E	ў 045E	Ѯ 046E	Ѿ 047E
F	Џ 040F	П 041F	Я 042F	п 043F	я 044F	џ 045F	ѯ 046F	ѿ 047F

	048	049	04A	04B	04C	04D	04E	04F
0	Ҁ 0480	Ґ 0490	Ҡ 04A0	Ұ 04B0	Ӏ 04C0	Ӑ 04D0	Ӡ 04E0	Ӱ 04F0
1	ҁ 0481	ґ 0491	ҡ 04A1	ұ 04B1	Ӂ 04C1	ӑ 04D1	ӡ 04E1	ӱ 04F1
2	҂ 0482	Ғ 0492	Ң 04A2	Ҳ 04B2	ӂ 04C2	Ӓ 04D2	Ӣ 04E2	Ӳ 04F2
3	◌҃ 0483	ғ 0493	ң 04A3	ҳ 04B3	Ӄ 04C3	ӓ 04D3	ӣ 04E3	ӳ 04F3
4	◌҄ 0484	Ҕ 0494	Ҥ 04A4	Ҵ 04B4	ӄ 04C4	Ӕ 04D4	Ӥ 04E4	Ӵ 04F4
5	◌҅ 0485	ҕ 0495	ҥ 04A5	ҵ 04B5		ӕ 04D5	ӥ 04E5	ӵ 04F5
6	◌҆ 0486	Җ 0496	Ҧ 04A6	Ҷ 04B6		Ӗ 04D6	Ӧ 04E6	
7		җ 0497	ҧ 04A7	ҷ 04B7	Ӈ 04C7	ӗ 04D7	ӧ 04E7	
8		Ҙ 0498	Ҩ 04A8	Ҹ 04B8	ӈ 04C8	Ә 04D8	Ө 04E8	Ӹ 04F8
9		ҙ 0499	ҩ 04A9	ҹ 04B9		ә 04D9	ө 04E9	ӹ 04F9
A		Қ 049A	Ҫ 04AA	Һ 04BA		Ӛ 04DA	Ӫ 04EA	
B		қ 049B	ҫ 04AB	һ 04BB	Ӌ 04CB	ӛ 04DB	ӫ 04EB	
C		Ҝ 049C	Ҭ 04AC	Ҽ 04BC	ӌ 04CC	Ӝ 04DC		
D		ҝ 049D	ҭ 04AD	ҽ 04BD		ӝ 04DD		
E		Ҟ 049E	Ү 04AE	Ҿ 04BE		Ӟ 04DE	Ӯ 04EE	
F		ҟ 049F	ү 04AF	ҿ 04BF		ӟ 04DF	ӯ 04EF	

Based on ISO 8859-5

0400 <reserved>
  → 00A0 no-break space
0401 Ё CYRILLIC CAPITAL LETTER IO
  ≡ 0415 Е + 0308 ◌̈
0402 Ђ CYRILLIC CAPITAL LETTER DJE
0403 Ѓ CYRILLIC CAPITAL LETTER GJE
  ≡ 0413 Г + 0301 ◌́
0404 Є CYRILLIC CAPITAL LETTER UKRAINIAN IE
0405 Ѕ CYRILLIC CAPITAL LETTER DZE
0406 І CYRILLIC CAPITAL LETTER BYELORUSSIAN-UKRAINIAN I
  → 04C0 Ӏ cyrillic letter palochka
0407 Ї CYRILLIC CAPITAL LETTER YI
  ≡ 0406 І + 0308 ◌̈
0408 Ј CYRILLIC CAPITAL LETTER JE
0409 Љ CYRILLIC CAPITAL LETTER LJE
040A Њ CYRILLIC CAPITAL LETTER NJE
040B Ћ CYRILLIC CAPITAL LETTER TSHE
040C Ќ CYRILLIC CAPITAL LETTER KJE
  ≡ 041A К + 0301 ◌́
040D <reserved>
  → 00AD - soft hyphen
040E Ў CYRILLIC CAPITAL LETTER SHORT U
  ≡ 0423 У + 0306 ◌̆
040F Џ CYRILLIC CAPITAL LETTER DZHE

Basic Russian alphabet

0410 А CYRILLIC CAPITAL LETTER A
0411 Б CYRILLIC CAPITAL LETTER BE
  → 0183 ƃ latin small letter b with topbar
0412 В CYRILLIC CAPITAL LETTER VE
0413 Г CYRILLIC CAPITAL LETTER GHE
0414 Д CYRILLIC CAPITAL LETTER DE
0415 Е CYRILLIC CAPITAL LETTER IE
0416 Ж CYRILLIC CAPITAL LETTER ZHE
0417 З CYRILLIC CAPITAL LETTER ZE
0418 И CYRILLIC CAPITAL LETTER I
0419 Й CYRILLIC CAPITAL LETTER SHORT I
  ≡ 0418 И + 0306 ◌̆
041A К CYRILLIC CAPITAL LETTER KA
041B Л CYRILLIC CAPITAL LETTER EL
041C М CYRILLIC CAPITAL LETTER EM
041D Н CYRILLIC CAPITAL LETTER EN
041E О CYRILLIC CAPITAL LETTER O
041F П CYRILLIC CAPITAL LETTER PE
0420 Р CYRILLIC CAPITAL LETTER ER
0421 С CYRILLIC CAPITAL LETTER ES
0422 Т CYRILLIC CAPITAL LETTER TE
0423 У CYRILLIC CAPITAL LETTER U
  → 0478 Ѹ cyrillic capital letter uk
  → 04AF ү cyrillic small letter straight u
0424 Ф CYRILLIC CAPITAL LETTER EF
0425 Х CYRILLIC CAPITAL LETTER HA
0426 Ц CYRILLIC CAPITAL LETTER TSE
0427 Ч CYRILLIC CAPITAL LETTER CHE
0428 Ш CYRILLIC CAPITAL LETTER SHA
0429 Щ CYRILLIC CAPITAL LETTER SHCHA
042A Ъ CYRILLIC CAPITAL LETTER HARD SIGN
042B Ы CYRILLIC CAPITAL LETTER YERU
042C Ь CYRILLIC CAPITAL LETTER SOFT SIGN
042D Э CYRILLIC CAPITAL LETTER E
042E Ю CYRILLIC CAPITAL LETTER YU
042F Я CYRILLIC CAPITAL LETTER YA
0430 а CYRILLIC SMALL LETTER A
0431 б CYRILLIC SMALL LETTER BE
0432 в CYRILLIC SMALL LETTER VE
0433 г CYRILLIC SMALL LETTER GHE
0434 д CYRILLIC SMALL LETTER DE
0435 е CYRILLIC SMALL LETTER IE
0436 ж CYRILLIC SMALL LETTER ZHE
0437 з CYRILLIC SMALL LETTER ZE
  → 0185 ƅ latin small letter tone six
0438 и CYRILLIC SMALL LETTER I
0439 й CYRILLIC SMALL LETTER SHORT I
  ≡ 0438 и + 0306 ◌̆
043A к CYRILLIC SMALL LETTER KA
043B л CYRILLIC SMALL LETTER EL
043C м CYRILLIC SMALL LETTER EM
043D н CYRILLIC SMALL LETTER EN
043E о CYRILLIC SMALL LETTER O
043F п CYRILLIC SMALL LETTER PE
0440 р CYRILLIC SMALL LETTER ER
0441 с CYRILLIC SMALL LETTER ES
0442 т CYRILLIC SMALL LETTER TE
0443 у CYRILLIC SMALL LETTER U
0444 ф CYRILLIC SMALL LETTER EF
0445 х CYRILLIC SMALL LETTER HA
0446 ц CYRILLIC SMALL LETTER TSE
0447 ч CYRILLIC SMALL LETTER CHE
  → 0185 ƅ latin small letter tone six
0448 ш CYRILLIC SMALL LETTER SHA
0449 щ CYRILLIC SMALL LETTER SHCHA
044A ъ CYRILLIC SMALL LETTER HARD SIGN
044B ы CYRILLIC SMALL LETTER YERU

044C ь CYRILLIC SMALL LETTER SOFT SIGN
→ 0185 ƅ latin small letter tone six
044D э CYRILLIC SMALL LETTER E
044E ю CYRILLIC SMALL LETTER YU
044F я CYRILLIC SMALL LETTER YA

Based on ISO 8859-5

0450 ▧ <reserved>
→ 2116 № numero sign
0451 ё CYRILLIC SMALL LETTER IO
• Russian, ...
≡ 0435 е + 0308 ̈
0452 ђ CYRILLIC SMALL LETTER DJE
• Serbian
→ 0111 đ latin small letter d with stroke
0453 ѓ CYRILLIC SMALL LETTER GJE
• Macedonian
≡ 0433 г + 0301 ́
0454 є CYRILLIC SMALL LETTER UKRAINIAN IE
= Old Cyrillic yest
• Ukrainian, ...
0455 ѕ CYRILLIC SMALL LETTER DZE
= Old Cyrillic zelo
• Macedonian
0456 і CYRILLIC SMALL LETTER BYELORUSSIAN-UKRAINIAN I
= Old Cyrillic i
• Ukrainian, Byelorussian, ...
0457 ї CYRILLIC SMALL LETTER YI
• Ukrainian
≡ 0456 і + 0308 ̈
0458 ј CYRILLIC SMALL LETTER JE
• Serbian, Azerbaijan, Altaic
0459 љ CYRILLIC SMALL LETTER LJE
• Serbian, Macedonian
→ 01C9 lj latin small letter lj
045A њ CYRILLIC SMALL LETTER NJE
• Serbian, Macedonian
→ 01CC nj latin small letter nj
045B ћ CYRILLIC SMALL LETTER TSHE
= Old Cyrillic derv
• Serbian
→ 0107 ć latin small letter c with acute
→ 0127 ħ latin small letter h with stroke
→ 040B Ћ cyrillic capital letter tshe
→ 210F ℏ planck constant over two pi
045C ќ CYRILLIC SMALL LETTER KJE
• Macedonian
≡ 043A к + 0301 ́
045D ▧ <reserved>
→ 00A7 § section sign
045E ў CYRILLIC SMALL LETTER SHORT U
• Byelorussian, Uzbek, ...
≡ 0443 у + 0306 ̆
045F џ CYRILLIC SMALL LETTER DZHE
• Serbian, Macedonian, Abkhasian
→ 01C6 dž latin small letter dz with caron

Historic letters

0460 Ѡ CYRILLIC CAPITAL LETTER OMEGA
0461 ѡ CYRILLIC SMALL LETTER OMEGA
0462 Ѣ CYRILLIC CAPITAL LETTER YAT
0463 ѣ CYRILLIC SMALL LETTER YAT
0464 Ѥ CYRILLIC CAPITAL LETTER IOTIFIED E
0465 ѥ CYRILLIC SMALL LETTER IOTIFIED E
0466 Ѧ CYRILLIC CAPITAL LETTER LITTLE YUS
0467 ѧ CYRILLIC SMALL LETTER LITTLE YUS
0468 Ѩ CYRILLIC CAPITAL LETTER IOTIFIED LITTLE YUS
0469 ѩ CYRILLIC SMALL LETTER IOTIFIED LITTLE YUS
046A Ѫ CYRILLIC CAPITAL LETTER BIG YUS
046B ѫ CYRILLIC SMALL LETTER BIG YUS
046C Ѭ CYRILLIC CAPITAL LETTER IOTIFIED BIG YUS
046D ѭ CYRILLIC SMALL LETTER IOTIFIED BIG YUS
046E Ѯ CYRILLIC CAPITAL LETTER KSI
046F ѯ CYRILLIC SMALL LETTER KSI
0470 Ѱ CYRILLIC CAPITAL LETTER PSI
0471 ѱ CYRILLIC SMALL LETTER PSI
0472 Ѳ CYRILLIC CAPITAL LETTER FITA
0473 ѳ CYRILLIC SMALL LETTER FITA
→ 0275 ɵ latin small letter barred o
→ 03B8 θ greek small letter theta
0474 Ѵ CYRILLIC CAPITAL LETTER IZHITSA
0475 ѵ CYRILLIC SMALL LETTER IZHITSA
0476 Ѷ CYRILLIC CAPITAL LETTER IZHITSA WITH DOUBLE GRAVE ACCENT
≡ 0474 Ѵ + 030F ̏
0477 ѷ CYRILLIC SMALL LETTER IZHITSA WITH DOUBLE GRAVE ACCENT
≡ 0475 ѵ + 030F ̏
0478 Ѹ CYRILLIC CAPITAL LETTER UK
• basic Old Cyrillic uk is unified with CYRILLIC LETTER U
→ 0423 У cyrillic capital letter u
0479 ѹ CYRILLIC SMALL LETTER UK

047A Ѻ CYRILLIC CAPITAL LETTER ROUND OMEGA
047B ѻ CYRILLIC SMALL LETTER ROUND OMEGA
047C Ѽ CYRILLIC CAPITAL LETTER OMEGA WITH TITLO
047D ѽ CYRILLIC SMALL LETTER OMEGA WITH TITLO
047E Ѿ CYRILLIC CAPITAL LETTER OT
047F ѿ CYRILLIC SMALL LETTER OT
0480 Ҁ CYRILLIC CAPITAL LETTER KOPPA
0481 ҁ CYRILLIC SMALL LETTER KOPPA

Historic miscellaneous

0482 ҂ CYRILLIC THOUSANDS SIGN
0483 ҃ COMBINING CYRILLIC TITLO
0484 ҄ COMBINING CYRILLIC PALATALIZATION
→ 033E ̾ combining vertical tilde
0485 ҅ COMBINING CYRILLIC DASIA PNEUMATA
→ 0314 ̔ combining reversed comma above
0486 ҆ COMBINING CYRILLIC PSILI PNEUMATA
→ 0313 ̓ combining comma above
0487 <reserved>
0488 <reserved>
0489 <reserved>
048A <reserved>
048B <reserved>
048C <reserved>
048D <reserved>
048E <reserved>
048F <reserved>

Extended Cyrillic

0490 Ґ CYRILLIC CAPITAL LETTER GHE WITH UPTURN
0491 ґ CYRILLIC SMALL LETTER GHE WITH UPTURN
• Old Ukrainian
0492 Ғ CYRILLIC CAPITAL LETTER GHE WITH STROKE
0493 ғ CYRILLIC SMALL LETTER GHE WITH STROKE
• Azerbaijani, Bashkir, ...
• full bar form preferred
0494 Ҕ CYRILLIC CAPITAL LETTER GHE WITH MIDDLE HOOK
0495 ҕ CYRILLIC SMALL LETTER GHE WITH MIDDLE HOOK
• Abkhasian, Yakut
0496 Җ CYRILLIC CAPITAL LETTER ZHE WITH DESCENDER
0497 җ CYRILLIC SMALL LETTER ZHE WITH DESCENDER
• Tatar, ...
0498 Ҙ CYRILLIC CAPITAL LETTER ZE WITH DESCENDER
0499 ҙ CYRILLIC SMALL LETTER ZE WITH DESCENDER
• Bashkir
• cedilla form preferred
049A Қ CYRILLIC CAPITAL LETTER KA WITH DESCENDER
049B қ CYRILLIC SMALL LETTER KA WITH DESCENDER
• Abkhasian, Tajik, ...
049C Ҝ CYRILLIC CAPITAL LETTER KA WITH VERTICAL STROKE
049D ҝ CYRILLIC SMALL LETTER KA WITH VERTICAL STROKE
• Azerbaijan
049E Ҟ CYRILLIC CAPITAL LETTER KA WITH STROKE
049F ҟ CYRILLIC SMALL LETTER KA WITH STROKE
• Abkhasian
04A0 Ҡ CYRILLIC CAPITAL LETTER BASHKIR KA
04A1 ҡ CYRILLIC SMALL LETTER BASHKIR KA
• Bashkir
04A2 Ң CYRILLIC CAPITAL LETTER EN WITH DESCENDER
04A3 ң CYRILLIC SMALL LETTER EN WITH DESCENDER
• Bashkir, ...
04A4 Ҥ CYRILLIC CAPITAL LIGATURE EN GHE
04A5 ҥ CYRILLIC SMALL LIGATURE EN GHE
• Altaic, Mari, Yakut
04A6 Ҧ CYRILLIC CAPITAL LETTER PE WITH MIDDLE HOOK
04A7 ҧ CYRILLIC SMALL LETTER PE WITH MIDDLE HOOK
• Abkhasian
04A8 Ҩ CYRILLIC CAPITAL LETTER ABKHASIAN HA
04A9 ҩ CYRILLIC SMALL LETTER ABKHASIAN HA
• Abkhasian

04AA Ҫ CYRILLIC CAPITAL LETTER ES WITH DESCENDER
04AB ҫ CYRILLIC SMALL LETTER ES WITH DESCENDER
• Bashkir, Chuvash
• cedilla form preferred
04AC Ҭ CYRILLIC CAPITAL LETTER TE WITH DESCENDER
04AD ҭ CYRILLIC SMALL LETTER TE WITH DESCENDER
• Abkhasian
04AE Ү CYRILLIC CAPITAL LETTER STRAIGHT U
04AF ү CYRILLIC SMALL LETTER STRAIGHT U
• stem is straight, unlike LETTER U
• Azerbaijan, Bashkir, ...
→ 0423 У cyrillic capital letter u
04B0 Ұ CYRILLIC CAPITAL LETTER STRAIGHT U WITH STROKE
04B1 ұ CYRILLIC SMALL LETTER STRAIGHT U WITH STROKE
• Kazakh
04B2 Ҳ CYRILLIC CAPITAL LETTER HA WITH DESCENDER
04B3 ҳ CYRILLIC SMALL LETTER HA WITH DESCENDER
• Abkhasian, Tajik, ...
04B4 Ҵ CYRILLIC CAPITAL LIGATURE TE TSE
04B5 ҵ CYRILLIC SMALL LIGATURE TE TSE
• Abkhasian
04B6 Ҷ CYRILLIC CAPITAL LETTER CHE WITH DESCENDER
04B7 ҷ CYRILLIC SMALL LETTER CHE WITH DESCENDER
• Abkhasian, Tajik
04B8 Ҹ CYRILLIC CAPITAL LETTER CHE WITH VERTICAL STROKE
04B9 ҹ CYRILLIC SMALL LETTER CHE WITH VERTICAL STROKE
• Azerbaijan
04BA Һ CYRILLIC CAPITAL LETTER SHHA
04BB һ CYRILLIC SMALL LETTER SHHA
• basically just a Latin "h", but uppercase form 04BA Һ is closer to an inverted che (0427 Ч)
• Azerbaijan, Bashkir, ...
→ 0068 h latin small letter h
04BC Ҽ CYRILLIC CAPITAL LETTER ABKHASIAN CHE
04BD ҽ CYRILLIC SMALL LETTER ABKHASIAN CHE
• Abkhasian
• represents a "che"
04BE Ҿ CYRILLIC CAPITAL LETTER ABKHASIAN CHE WITH DESCENDER
04BF ҿ CYRILLIC SMALL LETTER ABKHASIAN CHE WITH DESCENDER
• Abkhasian
04C0 Ӏ CYRILLIC LETTER PALOCHKA
• aspiration sign in many Caucasian languages
• has no "lowercase form", i.e. is case-invariant
→ 0406 І cyrillic capital letter byelorussian-ukrainian i
04C1 Ӂ CYRILLIC CAPITAL LETTER ZHE WITH BREVE
≡ 0416 Ж + 0306 ̆
04C2 ӂ CYRILLIC SMALL LETTER ZHE WITH BREVE
• Moldavian
≡ 0436 ж + 0306 ̆
04C3 Ӄ CYRILLIC CAPITAL LETTER KA WITH HOOK
04C4 ӄ CYRILLIC SMALL LETTER KA WITH HOOK
• Khanty, Chukchi
04C5 <reserved>
→ 049A Қ cyrillic capital letter ka with descender
04C6 <reserved>
→ 049B қ cyrillic small letter ka with descender
04C7 Ӈ CYRILLIC CAPITAL LETTER EN WITH HOOK
04C8 ӈ CYRILLIC SMALL LETTER EN WITH HOOK
• Khanty, Chukchi
04C9 <reserved>
→ 04B2 Ҳ cyrillic capital letter ha with descender
04CA <reserved>
→ 04B3 ҳ cyrillic small letter ha with descender
04CB Ӌ CYRILLIC CAPITAL LETTER KHAKASSIAN CHE
04CC ӌ CYRILLIC SMALL LETTER KHAKASSIAN CHE
• Khakassian
04CD <reserved>
04CE <reserved>
04CF <reserved>
04D0 Ӑ CYRILLIC CAPITAL LETTER A WITH BREVE
≡ 0410 А + 0306 ̆

04D1 ӑ CYRILLIC SMALL LETTER A WITH BREVE
≡ 0430 а + 0306 ̆

04D2 Ӓ CYRILLIC CAPITAL LETTER A WITH DIAERESIS
≡ 0410 А + 0308 ̈

04D3 ӓ CYRILLIC SMALL LETTER A WITH DIAERESIS
≡ 0430 а + 0308 ̈

04D4 Ӕ CYRILLIC CAPITAL LIGATURE A IE
≡ 00C6 Æ

04D5 ӕ CYRILLIC SMALL LIGATURE A IE
≡ 00E6 æ

04D6 Ӗ CYRILLIC CAPITAL LETTER IE WITH BREVE
≡ 0415 Е + 0306 ̆

04D7 ӗ CYRILLIC SMALL LETTER IE WITH BREVE
≡ 0435 е + 0306 ̆

04D8 Ә CYRILLIC CAPITAL LETTER SCHWA
≡ 018F Ə

04D9 ә CYRILLIC SMALL LETTER SCHWA
≡ 0259 ə

04DA Ӛ CYRILLIC CAPITAL LETTER SCHWA WITH DIAERESIS
≡ 018F Ə + 0308 ̈

04DB ӛ CYRILLIC SMALL LETTER SCHWA WITH DIAERESIS
≡ 0259 ə + 0308 ̈

04DC Ӝ CYRILLIC CAPITAL LETTER ZHE WITH DIAERESIS
≡ 0416 Ж + 0308 ̈

04DD ӝ CYRILLIC SMALL LETTER ZHE WITH DIAERESIS
≡ 0436 ж + 0308 ̈

04DE Ӟ CYRILLIC CAPITAL LETTER ZE WITH DIAERESIS
≡ 0417 З + 0308 ̈

04DF ӟ CYRILLIC SMALL LETTER ZE WITH DIAERESIS
≡ 0437 з + 0308 ̈

04E0 Ӡ CYRILLIC CAPITAL LETTER ABKHASIAN DZE
≡ 01B7 Ʒ

04E1 ӡ CYRILLIC SMALL LETTER ABKHASIAN DZE
≡ 0292 ʒ

04E2 Ӣ CYRILLIC CAPITAL LETTER I WITH MACRON
≡ 0418 И + 0304 ̄

04E3 ӣ CYRILLIC SMALL LETTER I WITH MACRON
≡ 0438 и + 0304 ̄

04E4 Ӥ CYRILLIC CAPITAL LETTER I WITH DIAERESIS
≡ 0418 И + 0308 ̈

04E5 ӥ CYRILLIC SMALL LETTER I WITH DIAERESIS
≡ 0438 и + 0308 ̈

04E6 Ӧ CYRILLIC CAPITAL LETTER O WITH DIAERESIS
≡ 041E О + 0308 ̈

04E7 ӧ CYRILLIC SMALL LETTER O WITH DIAERESIS
≡ 043E о + 0308 ̈

04E8 Ө CYRILLIC CAPITAL LETTER BARRED O
≡ 019F Ɵ

04E9 ө CYRILLIC SMALL LETTER BARRED O
≡ 0275 ɵ

04EA Ӫ CYRILLIC CAPITAL LETTER BARRED O WITH DIAERESIS
≡ 019F Ɵ + 0308 ̈

04EB ӫ CYRILLIC SMALL LETTER BARRED O WITH DIAERESIS
≡ 0275 ɵ + 0308 ̈

04EC <reserved>

04ED <reserved>

04EE Ӯ CYRILLIC CAPITAL LETTER U WITH MACRON
≡ 0423 У + 0304 ̄

04EF ӯ CYRILLIC SMALL LETTER U WITH MACRON
≡ 0443 у + 0304 ̄

04F0 Ӱ CYRILLIC CAPITAL LETTER U WITH DIAERESIS
≡ 0423 У + 0308 ̈

04F1 ӱ CYRILLIC SMALL LETTER U WITH DIAERESIS
≡ 0443 у + 0308 ̈

04F2 Ӳ CYRILLIC CAPITAL LETTER U WITH DOUBLE ACUTE
≡ 0423 У + 030B ̋

04F3 ӳ CYRILLIC SMALL LETTER U WITH DOUBLE ACUTE
≡ 0443 у + 030B ̋

04F4 Ӵ CYRILLIC CAPITAL LETTER CHE WITH DIAERESIS
≡ 0427 Ч + 0308 ̈

04F5 ӵ CYRILLIC SMALL LETTER CHE WITH DIAERESIS
≡ 0447 ч + 0308 ̈

04F6 <reserved>

04F7 <reserved>

04F8 Ӹ CYRILLIC CAPITAL LETTER YERU WITH DIAERESIS
≡ 042B Ы + 0308 ̈

04F9 ӹ CYRILLIC SMALL LETTER YERU WITH DIAERESIS
≡ 044B ы + 0308 ̈

	053	054	055	056	057	058
0		Հ 0540	Ր 0550		հ 0570	ր 0580
1	Ա 0531	Ձ 0541	Ց 0551	ա 0561	ձ 0571	ց 0581
2	Բ 0532	Ղ 0542	Ւ 0552	բ 0562	ղ 0572	ւ 0582
3	Գ 0533	Ճ 0543	Փ 0553	գ 0563	ճ 0573	փ 0583
4	Դ 0534	Մ 0544	Ք 0554	դ 0564	մ 0574	ք 0584
5	Ե 0535	Յ 0545	Օ 0555	ե 0565	յ 0575	օ 0585
6	Զ 0536	Ն 0546	Ֆ 0556	զ 0566	ն 0576	ֆ 0586
7	Է 0537	Շ 0547		է 0567	շ 0577	և 0587
8	Ը 0538	Ո 0548		ը 0568	ո 0578	
9	Թ 0539	Չ 0549	ՙ 0559	թ 0569	չ 0579	։ 0589
A	Ժ 053A	Պ 054A	՚ 055A	ժ 056A	պ 057A	
B	Ի 053B	Ջ 054B	՛ 055B	ի 056B	ջ 057B	
C	Լ 053C	Ռ 054C	՜ 055C	լ 056C	ռ 057C	
D	Խ 053D	Ս 054D	՝ 055D	խ 056D	ս 057D	
E	Ծ 053E	Վ 054E	՞ 055E	ծ 056E	վ 057E	
F	Կ 053F	Տ 054F	՟ 055F	կ 056F	տ 057F	

Uppercase letters

0530 ▧ <reserved>

0531 Ա ARMENIAN CAPITAL LETTER AYB

0532 Բ ARMENIAN CAPITAL LETTER BEN

0533 Գ ARMENIAN CAPITAL LETTER GIM

0534 Դ ARMENIAN CAPITAL LETTER DA

0535 Ե ARMENIAN CAPITAL LETTER ECH

0536 Զ ARMENIAN CAPITAL LETTER ZA

0537 Է ARMENIAN CAPITAL LETTER EH

0538 Ը ARMENIAN CAPITAL LETTER ET

0539 Թ ARMENIAN CAPITAL LETTER TO

053A Ժ ARMENIAN CAPITAL LETTER ZHE

053B Ի ARMENIAN CAPITAL LETTER INI

053C Լ ARMENIAN CAPITAL LETTER LIWN

053D Խ ARMENIAN CAPITAL LETTER XEH

053E Ծ ARMENIAN CAPITAL LETTER CA

053F Կ ARMENIAN CAPITAL LETTER KEN

0540 Հ ARMENIAN CAPITAL LETTER HO

0541 Ձ ARMENIAN CAPITAL LETTER JA

0542 Ղ ARMENIAN CAPITAL LETTER GHAD

0543 Ճ ARMENIAN CAPITAL LETTER CHEH

0544 Մ ARMENIAN CAPITAL LETTER MEN

0545 Յ ARMENIAN CAPITAL LETTER YI

0546 Ն ARMENIAN CAPITAL LETTER NOW

0547 Շ ARMENIAN CAPITAL LETTER SHA

0548 Ո ARMENIAN CAPITAL LETTER VO

0549 Չ ARMENIAN CAPITAL LETTER CHA

054A Պ ARMENIAN CAPITAL LETTER PEH

054B Ջ ARMENIAN CAPITAL LETTER JHEH

054C Ռ ARMENIAN CAPITAL LETTER RA

054D Ս ARMENIAN CAPITAL LETTER SEH

054E Վ ARMENIAN CAPITAL LETTER VEW

054F Տ ARMENIAN CAPITAL LETTER TIWN

0550 Ր ARMENIAN CAPITAL LETTER REH

0551 Ց ARMENIAN CAPITAL LETTER CO

0552 Ւ ARMENIAN CAPITAL LETTER YIWN

0553 Փ ARMENIAN CAPITAL LETTER PIWR

0554 Ք ARMENIAN CAPITAL LETTER KEH

0555 Օ ARMENIAN CAPITAL LETTER OH

0556 Ֆ ARMENIAN CAPITAL LETTER FEH

0557 ▧ <reserved>

0558 ▧ <reserved>

Modifier letters

0559 ՙ ARMENIAN MODIFIER LETTER LEFT HALF RING
→ 02BD ʽ modifier letter reversed comma
→ 02BF ʿ modifier letter left half ring
→ 0314 ◌̔ combining reversed comma above

055A ՚ ARMENIAN APOSTROPHE
= ARMENIAN MODIFIER LETTER RIGHT HALF RING
→ 02BC ʼ modifier letter apostrophe
→ 02BE ʾ modifier letter right half ring
→ 0313 ◌̓ combining comma above

055B ՛ ARMENIAN EMPHASIS MARK
= shesht
→ 02CA ˊ modifier letter acute accent

055C ՜ ARMENIAN EXCLAMATION MARK
= batsaganchakan nshan

055D ՝ ARMENIAN COMMA
= boot
→ 02CB ˋ modifier letter grave accent

055E ՞ ARMENIAN QUESTION MARK
= hartsakan nshan

055F ՟ ARMENIAN ABBREVIATION MARK
= patiw

Lowercase letters

0560 ▧ <reserved>

0561 ա ARMENIAN SMALL LETTER AYB

0562 բ ARMENIAN SMALL LETTER BEN

0563 գ ARMENIAN SMALL LETTER GIM

0564 դ ARMENIAN SMALL LETTER DA

0565 ե ARMENIAN SMALL LETTER ECH

0566 զ ARMENIAN SMALL LETTER ZA

0567 է ARMENIAN SMALL LETTER EH

0568 ը ARMENIAN SMALL LETTER ET

0569 թ ARMENIAN SMALL LETTER TO

056A ժ ARMENIAN SMALL LETTER ZHE

056B ի ARMENIAN SMALL LETTER INI

056C լ ARMENIAN SMALL LETTER LIWN

056D խ ARMENIAN SMALL LETTER XEH

056E ծ ARMENIAN SMALL LETTER CA

056F կ ARMENIAN SMALL LETTER KEN

0570 հ ARMENIAN SMALL LETTER HO

0571 ձ ARMENIAN SMALL LETTER JA

0572 ղ ARMENIAN SMALL LETTER GHAD

0573 ճ ARMENIAN SMALL LETTER CHEH

0574 մ ARMENIAN SMALL LETTER MEN

0575 յ ARMENIAN SMALL LETTER YI

0576 ն ARMENIAN SMALL LETTER NOW

0577 շ ARMENIAN SMALL LETTER SHA
0578 ո ARMENIAN SMALL LETTER VO
0579 չ ARMENIAN SMALL LETTER CHA
057A պ ARMENIAN SMALL LETTER PEH
057B ջ ARMENIAN SMALL LETTER JHEH
057C ռ ARMENIAN SMALL LETTER RA
057D ս ARMENIAN SMALL LETTER SEH
057E վ ARMENIAN SMALL LETTER VEW
057F տ ARMENIAN SMALL LETTER TIWN
0580 ր ARMENIAN SMALL LETTER REH
0581 ց ARMENIAN SMALL LETTER CO
0582 ւ ARMENIAN SMALL LETTER YIWN
0583 փ ARMENIAN SMALL LETTER PIWR
0584 ք ARMENIAN SMALL LETTER KEH
0585 օ ARMENIAN SMALL LETTER OH
0586 ֆ ARMENIAN SMALL LETTER FEH
0587 և ARMENIAN SMALL LIGATURE ECH YIWN
≈ 0565 ե + 0582 ւ
0588 <reserved>

Punctuation

0589 ։ ARMENIAN FULL STOP
= vertsaket
• may also be used for Georgian
→ 003A : colon

	059	05A	05B	05C	05D	05E	05F
0		05A0	05B0	׀ 05C0	א 05D0	נ 05E0	װ 05F0
1	0591	05A1	05B1	05C1	ב 05D1	ס 05E1	ױ 05F1
2	0592		05B2	05C2	ג 05D2	ע 05E2	ײ 05F2
3	0593	05A3	05B3	׃ 05C3	ד 05D3	ף 05E3	׳ 05F3
4	0594	05A4	05B4	05C4	ה 05D4	פ 05E4	״ 05F4
5	0595	05A5	05B5		ו 05D5	ץ 05E5	
6	0596	05A6	05B6		ז 05D6	צ 05E6	
7	0597	05A7	05B7		ח 05D7	ק 05E7	
8	0598	05A8	05B8		ט 05D8	ר 05E8	
9	0599	05A9	05B9		י 05D9	ש 05E9	
A	059A	05AA			ך 05DA	ת 05EA	
B	059B	05AB	05BB		כ 05DB		
C	059C	05AC	05BC		ל 05DC		
D	059D	05AD	05BD		ם 05DD		
E	059E	05AE	־ 05BE		מ 05DE		
F	059F	05AF	05BF		ן 05DF		

Cantillation marks

0590 <reserved>
0591 ◌֑ HEBREW ACCENT ETNAHTA
0592 ◌֒ HEBREW ACCENT SEGOL
0593 ◌֓ HEBREW ACCENT SHALSHELET
0594 ◌֔ HEBREW ACCENT ZAQEF QATAN
0595 ◌֕ HEBREW ACCENT ZAQEF GADOL
0596 ◌֖ HEBREW ACCENT TIPEHA
0597 ◌֗ HEBREW ACCENT REVIA
0598 ◌֘ HEBREW ACCENT ZARQA
0599 ◌֙ HEBREW ACCENT PASHTA
059A ◌֚ HEBREW ACCENT YETIV
059B ◌֛ HEBREW ACCENT TEVIR
059C ◌֜ HEBREW ACCENT GERESH
059D ◌֝ HEBREW ACCENT GERESH MUQDAM
059E ◌֞ HEBREW ACCENT GERSHAYIM
059F ◌֟ HEBREW ACCENT QARNEY PARA
05A0 ◌֠ HEBREW ACCENT TELISHA GEDOLA
05A1 ◌֡ HEBREW ACCENT PAZER
05A2 <reserved>
05A3 ◌֣ HEBREW ACCENT MUNAH
05A4 ◌֤ HEBREW ACCENT MAHAPAKH
05A5 ◌֥ HEBREW ACCENT MERKHA
05A6 ◌֦ HEBREW ACCENT MERKHA KEFULA
05A7 ◌֧ HEBREW ACCENT DARGA
05A8 ◌֨ HEBREW ACCENT QADMA
05A9 ◌֩ HEBREW ACCENT TELISHA QETANA
05AA ◌֪ HEBREW ACCENT YERAH BEN YOMO
05AB ◌֫ HEBREW ACCENT OLE
05AC ◌֬ HEBREW ACCENT ILUY
05AD ◌֭ HEBREW ACCENT DEHI
05AE ◌֮ HEBREW ACCENT ZINOR
05AF ◌֯ HEBREW MARK MASORA CIRCLE

Points and punctuation

05B0 ◌ְ HEBREW POINT SHEVA
05B1 ◌ֱ HEBREW POINT HATAF SEGOL
05B2 ◌ֲ HEBREW POINT HATAF PATAH
05B3 ◌ֳ HEBREW POINT HATAF QAMATS
05B4 ◌ִ HEBREW POINT HIRIQ
05B5 ◌ֵ HEBREW POINT TSERE
05B6 ◌ֶ HEBREW POINT SEGOL
05B7 ◌ַ HEBREW POINT PATAH
• furtive Patah is not a distinct character
05B8 ◌ָ HEBREW POINT QAMATS
05B9 ◌ֹ HEBREW POINT HOLAM
05BA <reserved>
05BB ◌ֻ HEBREW POINT QUBUTS
05BC ◌ּ HEBREW POINT DAGESH OR MAPIQ
= shuruq
• falls within the base letter
05BD ◌ֽ HEBREW POINT METEG
= siluq
05BE ־ HEBREW PUNCTUATION MAQAF
05BF ◌ֿ HEBREW POINT RAFE
05C0 ׀ HEBREW PUNCTUATION PASEQ
= legarmeh
• may be treated as spacing punctuation, not as a point
05C1 ◌ׁ HEBREW POINT SHIN DOT
05C2 ◌ׂ HEBREW POINT SIN DOT
05C3 ׃ HEBREW PUNCTUATION SOF PASUQ
05C4 ◌ׄ HEBREW MARK UPPER DOT
05C5 <reserved>
05C6 <reserved>
05C7 <reserved>
05C8 <reserved>
05C9 <reserved>
05CA <reserved>
05CB <reserved>
05CC <reserved>
05CD <reserved>
05CE <reserved>
05CF <reserved>

Based on ISO 8859-8

05D0 א HEBREW LETTER ALEF
= aleph
→ 2135 ℵ alef symbol
05D1 ב HEBREW LETTER BET
→ 2136 ℶ bet symbol
05D2 ג HEBREW LETTER GIMEL
→ 2137 ℷ gimel symbol
05D3 ד HEBREW LETTER DALET
→ 2138 ℸ dalet symbol
05D4 ה HEBREW LETTER HE
05D5 ו HEBREW LETTER VAV
05D6 ז HEBREW LETTER ZAYIN
05D7 ח HEBREW LETTER HET
05D8 ט HEBREW LETTER TET
05D9 י HEBREW LETTER YOD
05DA ך HEBREW LETTER FINAL KAF
05DB כ HEBREW LETTER KAF
05DC ל HEBREW LETTER LAMED

05DD ם HEBREW LETTER FINAL MEM
05DE מ HEBREW LETTER MEM
05DF ן HEBREW LETTER FINAL NUN
05E0 נ HEBREW LETTER NUN
05E1 ס HEBREW LETTER SAMEKH
05E2 ע HEBREW LETTER AYIN
05E3 ף HEBREW LETTER FINAL PE
05E4 פ HEBREW LETTER PE
05E5 ץ HEBREW LETTER FINAL TSADI
05E6 צ HEBREW LETTER TSADI
= zade
05E7 ק HEBREW LETTER QOF
05E8 ר HEBREW LETTER RESH
05E9 ש HEBREW LETTER SHIN
05EA ת HEBREW LETTER TAV
05EB <reserved>
05EC <reserved>
05ED <reserved>
05EE <reserved>
05EF <reserved>

Yiddish digraphs

05F0 װ HEBREW LIGATURE YIDDISH DOUBLE VAV
= tsvey vovn
05F1 ױ HEBREW LIGATURE YIDDISH VAV YOD
05F2 ײ HEBREW LIGATURE YIDDISH DOUBLE YOD
= tsvey yudn

Additional punctuation

05F3 ׳ HEBREW PUNCTUATION GERESH
05F4 ״ HEBREW PUNCTUATION GERSHAYIM
05F5 <reserved>
→ FB1E ◌ﬞ hebrew point judeo-spanish varika

	060	061	062	063	064	065	066	067
0				ذ 0630	ـ 0640	◌ِ 0650	٠ 0660	◌ٰ 0670
1			ء 0621	ر 0631	ف 0641	◌ّ 0651	١ 0661	ٱ 0671
2			آ 0622	ز 0632	ق 0642	◌ْ 0652	٢ 0662	ٲ 0672
3			أ 0623	س 0633	ك 0643		٣ 0663	ٳ 0673
4			ؤ 0624	ش 0634	ل 0644		٤ 0664	ٴ 0674
5			إ 0625	ص 0635	م 0645		٥ 0665	ٵ 0675
6			ئ 0626	ض 0636	ن 0646		٦ 0666	ٶ 0676
7			ا 0627	ط 0637	ه 0647		٧ 0667	ٷ 0677
8			ب 0628	ظ 0638	و 0648		٨ 0668	ٸ 0678
9			ة 0629	ع 0639	ى 0649		٩ 0669	ٹ 0679
A			ت 062A	غ 063A	ي 064A		٪ 066A	ٺ 067A
B		؛ 061B	ث 062B		◌ً 064B		٫ 066B	ٻ 067B
C	، 060C		ج 062C		◌ٌ 064C		٬ 066C	ټ 067C
D			ح 062D		◌ٍ 064D		٭ 066D	ٽ 067D
E			خ 062E		◌َ 064E			پ 067E
F		؟ 061F	د 062F		◌ُ 064F			ٿ 067F

	068	069	06A	06B	06C	06D	06E	06F
0	ڀ 0680	ڐ 0690	ڠ 06A0	ڰ 06B0	ۀ 06C0	ې 06D0	◌۠ 06E0	۰ 06F0
1	ځ 0681	ڑ 0691	ڡ 06A1	ڱ 06B1	ہ 06C1	ۑ 06D1	◌ۡ 06E1	۱ 06F1
2	ڂ 0682	ڒ 0692	ڢ 06A2	ڲ 06B2	ۂ 06C2	ے 06D2	◌ۢ 06E2	۲ 06F2
3	ڃ 0683	ړ 0693	ڣ 06A3	ڳ 06B3	ۃ 06C3	ۓ 06D3	◌ۣ 06E3	۳ 06F3
4	ڄ 0684	ڔ 0694	ڤ 06A4	ڴ 06B4	ۄ 06C4	۔ 06D4	◌ۤ 06E4	۴ 06F4
5	څ 0685	ڕ 0695	ڥ 06A5	ڵ 06B5	ۅ 06C5	ە 06D5	ۥ 06E5	۵ 06F5
6	چ 0686	ږ 0696	ڦ 06A6	ڶ 06B6	ۆ 06C6	◌ۖ 06D6	ۦ 06E6	۶ 06F6
7	ڇ 0687	ڗ 0697	ڧ 06A7	ڷ 06B7	ۇ 06C7	◌ۗ 06D7	◌ۧ 06E7	۷ 06F7
8	ڈ 0688	ژ 0698	ڨ 06A8		ۈ 06C8	◌ۘ 06D8	◌ۨ 06E8	۸ 06F8
9	ډ 0689	ڙ 0699	ک 06A9		ۉ 06C9	◌ۙ 06D9	۩ 06E9	۹ 06F9
A	ڊ 068A	ښ 069A	ڪ 06AA	ں 06BA	ۊ 06CA	◌ۚ 06DA	◌۪ 06EA	
B	ڋ 068B	ڛ 069B	ګ 06AB	ڻ 06BB	ۋ 06CB	◌ۛ 06DB	◌۫ 06EB	
C	ڌ 068C	ڜ 069C	ڬ 06AC	ڼ 06BC	ی 06CC	◌ۜ 06DC	◌۬ 06EC	
D	ڍ 068D	ڝ 069D	ڭ 06AD	ڽ 06BD	ۍ 06CD	۝ 06DD	◌ۭ 06ED	
E	ڎ 068E	ڞ 069E	ڮ 06AE	ھ 06BE	ێ 06CE	۞ 06DE		
F	ڏ 068F	ڟ 069F	گ 06AF			◌۟ 06DF		

Based on ISO 8859-6

0600 ▧ <reserved>
→ 00A0 NBSP no-break space
0601 ▧ <reserved>
0602 ▧ <reserved>
0603 ▧ <reserved>
0604 ▧ <reserved>
→ 00A4 ¤ currency sign
0605 ▧ <reserved>
0606 ▧ <reserved>
0607 ▧ <reserved>
0608 ▧ <reserved>
0609 ▧ <reserved>
060A ▧ <reserved>
060B ▧ <reserved>
060C ، ARABIC COMMA
→ 002C , comma
060D ▧ <reserved>
→ 00AD - soft hyphen
060E ▧ <reserved>
060F ▧ <reserved>
0610 ▧ <reserved>
0611 ▧ <reserved>
0612 ▧ <reserved>
0613 ▧ <reserved>
0614 ▧ <reserved>
0615 ▧ <reserved>
0616 ▧ <reserved>
0617 ▧ <reserved>
0618 ▧ <reserved>
0619 ▧ <reserved>
061A ▧ <reserved>
061B ؛ ARABIC SEMICOLON
→ 003B ; semicolon
061C ▧ <reserved>
061D ▧ <reserved>
061E ▧ <reserved>
061F ؟ ARABIC QUESTION MARK
→ 003F ? question mark
0620 ▧ <reserved>
0621 ء ARABIC LETTER HAMZA
→ 02BE ʾ modifier letter right half ring
0622 آ ARABIC LETTER ALEF WITH MADDA ABOVE
0623 أ ARABIC LETTER ALEF WITH HAMZA ABOVE
0624 ؤ ARABIC LETTER WAW WITH HAMZA ABOVE
0625 إ ARABIC LETTER ALEF WITH HAMZA BELOW
0626 ئ ARABIC LETTER YEH WITH HAMZA ABOVE
0627 ا ARABIC LETTER ALEF
0628 ب ARABIC LETTER BEH
0629 ة ARABIC LETTER TEH MARBUTA
062A ت ARABIC LETTER TEH
062B ث ARABIC LETTER THEH
062C ج ARABIC LETTER JEEM
062D ح ARABIC LETTER HAH
062E خ ARABIC LETTER KHAH
062F د ARABIC LETTER DAL
0630 ذ ARABIC LETTER THAL
0631 ر ARABIC LETTER REH
0632 ز ARABIC LETTER ZAIN
0633 س ARABIC LETTER SEEN
0634 ش ARABIC LETTER SHEEN
0635 ص ARABIC LETTER SAD
0636 ض ARABIC LETTER DAD
0637 ط ARABIC LETTER TAH
0638 ظ ARABIC LETTER ZAH
0639 ع ARABIC LETTER AIN
→ 01B9 ƹ latin small letter ezh reversed
→ 02BF ʿ modifier letter left half ring
063A غ ARABIC LETTER GHAIN
063B ▧ <reserved>
063C ▧ <reserved>
063D ▧ <reserved>
063E ▧ <reserved>
063F ▧ <reserved>
0640 ـ ARABIC TATWEEL
= kashida
• inserted to stretch characters
0641 ف ARABIC LETTER FEH
0642 ق ARABIC LETTER QAF
0643 ك ARABIC LETTER KAF
0644 ل ARABIC LETTER LAM
0645 م ARABIC LETTER MEEM
0646 ن ARABIC LETTER NOON
0647 ه ARABIC LETTER HEH
0648 و ARABIC LETTER WAW
0649 ى ARABIC LETTER ALEF MAKSURA
064A ي ARABIC LETTER YEH

Points from ISO 8859-6

064B ◌ً ARABIC FATHATAN
064C ◌ٌ ARABIC DAMMATAN
064D ◌ٍ ARABIC KASRATAN
064E ◌َ ARABIC FATHA
064F ◌ُ ARABIC DAMMA
0650 ◌ِ ARABIC KASRA

0651 ◌ّ ARABIC SHADDA

0652 ◌ْ ARABIC SUKUN

0653 <reserved>

0654 <reserved>

0655 <reserved>

0656 <reserved>

0657 <reserved>

0658 <reserved>

0659 <reserved>

065A <reserved>

065B <reserved>

065C <reserved>

065D <reserved>

065E <reserved>

065F <reserved>

Arabic-Indic digits

0660 ٠ ARABIC-INDIC DIGIT ZERO

0661 ١ ARABIC-INDIC DIGIT ONE

0662 ٢ ARABIC-INDIC DIGIT TWO

0663 ٣ ARABIC-INDIC DIGIT THREE

0664 ٤ ARABIC-INDIC DIGIT FOUR

0665 ٥ ARABIC-INDIC DIGIT FIVE

0666 ٦ ARABIC-INDIC DIGIT SIX

0667 ٧ ARABIC-INDIC DIGIT SEVEN

0668 ٨ ARABIC-INDIC DIGIT EIGHT

0669 ٩ ARABIC-INDIC DIGIT NINE

066A ٪ ARABIC PERCENT SIGN
→ 0025 % percent sign

066B ٫ ARABIC DECIMAL SEPARATOR

066C ٬ ARABIC THOUSANDS SEPARATOR

066D ٭ ARABIC FIVE POINTED STAR

066E <reserved>

066F <reserved>

Point

0670 ◌ٰ ARABIC LETTER SUPERSCRIPT ALEF

Extended Arabic letters

0671 ٱ ARABIC LETTER ALEF WASLA
• Arabic

0672 ٲ ARABIC LETTER ALEF WITH WAVY HAMZA ABOVE
• Baluchi, Kashmiri

0673 ٳ ARABIC LETTER ALEF WITH WAVY HAMZA BELOW
• Baluchi, Kashmiri

0674 ٴ ARABIC LETTER HIGH HAMZA
• Kazakh
• forms digraphs

0675 ٵ ARABIC LETTER HIGH HAMZA ALEF
• Kazakh

0676 ٶ ARABIC LETTER HIGH HAMZA WAW
• Kazakh

0677 ٷ ARABIC LETTER U WITH HAMZA ABOVE
• Kazakh

0678 ٸ ARABIC LETTER HIGH HAMZA YEH
• Kazakh

0679 ٹ ARABIC LETTER TTEH
• Urdu

067A ٺ ARABIC LETTER TTEHEH
• Sindhi

067B ٻ ARABIC LETTER BEEH
• Sindhi

067C ټ ARABIC LETTER TEH WITH RING
• Pashto

067D ٽ ARABIC LETTER TEH WITH THREE DOTS ABOVE DOWNWARDS
• Sindhi

067E پ ARABIC LETTER PEH
• Persian, Urdu, ...

067F ٿ ARABIC LETTER TEHEH
• Sindhi

0680 ڀ ARABIC LETTER BEHEH
• Sindhi

0681 ځ ARABIC LETTER HAH WITH HAMZA ABOVE
• Pashto

0682 ڂ ARABIC LETTER HAH WITH TWO DOTS VERTICAL ABOVE
• Pashto

0683 ڃ ARABIC LETTER NYEH
• Sindhi

0684 ڄ ARABIC LETTER DYEH
• Sindhi

0685 څ ARABIC LETTER HAH WITH THREE DOTS ABOVE
• Pashto

0686 چ ARABIC LETTER TCHEH
• Persian, Urdu, ...

0687 ڇ ARABIC LETTER TCHEHEH
• Sindhi

0688 ڈ ARABIC LETTER DDAL
• Urdu

0689 ډ ARABIC LETTER DAL WITH RING
• Pashto

068A ڊ ARABIC LETTER DAL WITH DOT BELOW
• Sindhi

068B ڋ ARABIC LETTER DAL WITH DOT BELOW AND SMALL TAH
• Lahnda

068C ڌ ARABIC LETTER DAHAL
• Sindhi

068D ڍ ARABIC LETTER DDAHAL
• Sindhi

068E ڎ ARABIC LETTER DUL
• Sindhi

068F ڏ ARABIC LETTER DAL WITH THREE DOTS ABOVE DOWNWARDS
• Sindhi

0690 ڐ ARABIC LETTER DAL WITH FOUR DOTS ABOVE
• Urdu

0691 ڑ ARABIC LETTER RREH
• Urdu

0692 ڒ ARABIC LETTER REH WITH SMALL V
• Kurdish

0693 ړ ARABIC LETTER REH WITH RING
• Pashto

0694 ڔ ARABIC LETTER REH WITH DOT BELOW
• Kurdish

0695 ڕ ARABIC LETTER REH WITH SMALL V BELOW
• Kurdish

0696 ږ ARABIC LETTER REH WITH DOT BELOW AND DOT ABOVE
• Pashto

0697 ڗ ARABIC LETTER REH WITH TWO DOTS ABOVE
• Dargwa

0698 ژ ARABIC LETTER JEH
• Persian, Urdu, ...

0699 ڙ ARABIC LETTER REH WITH FOUR DOTS ABOVE
• Sindhi

069A ښ ARABIC LETTER SEEN WITH DOT BELOW AND DOT ABOVE
• Pashto

069B ڛ ARABIC LETTER SEEN WITH THREE DOTS BELOW
• Uighur

069C ڜ ARABIC LETTER SEEN WITH THREE DOTS BELOW AND THREE DOTS ABOVE
• Moroccan Arabic

069D ڝ ARABIC LETTER SAD WITH TWO DOTS BELOW
• Turkic

069E ڞ ARABIC LETTER SAD WITH THREE DOTS ABOVE
• Berber

069F ڟ ARABIC LETTER TAH WITH THREE DOTS ABOVE
• old Hausa

06A0 ڠ ARABIC LETTER AIN WITH THREE DOTS ABOVE
• old Malay

06A1 ڡ ARABIC LETTER DOTLESS FEH
• Adighe

06A2 ڢ ARABIC LETTER FEH WITH DOT MOVED BELOW
• Maghrib Arabic

06A3 ڣ ARABIC LETTER FEH WITH DOT BELOW
• Ingush

06A4 ڤ ARABIC LETTER VEH
• Arabic for foreign words

06A5 ڥ ARABIC LETTER FEH WITH THREE DOTS BELOW
• Arabic for foreign words

06A6 ڦ ARABIC LETTER PEHEH
• Sindhi

06A7 ڧ ARABIC LETTER QAF WITH DOT ABOVE
• Maghrib Arabic

06A8 ڨ ARABIC LETTER QAF WITH THREE DOTS ABOVE
• Tunisian Arabic

06A9 ک ARABIC LETTER KEHEH
• Persian, Urdu, ...

06AA ڪ ARABIC LETTER SWASH KAF
• (various)

06AB ګ ARABIC LETTER KAF WITH RING
• Pashto

06AC ڬ ARABIC LETTER KAF WITH DOT ABOVE
• old Malay

06AD ڭ ARABIC LETTER NG
• Uighur, Kazakh, old Malay, ...

06AE ڮ ARABIC LETTER KAF WITH THREE DOTS BELOW
• Berber

06AF گ ARABIC LETTER GAF
• Persian, Urdu, ...

06B0 ڰ ARABIC LETTER GAF WITH RING
• Lahnda

06B1 ڱ ARABIC LETTER NGOEH
• Sindhi

06B2 ڲ ARABIC LETTER GAF WITH TWO DOTS BELOW
• Sindhi

06B3 ڳ ARABIC LETTER GUEH
• Sindhi

06B4 ڴ ARABIC LETTER GAF WITH THREE DOTS ABOVE
• Sindhi

06B5 ARABIC LETTER LAM WITH SMALL V
• Kurdish

06B6 ARABIC LETTER LAM WITH DOT ABOVE
• Kurdish

06B7 ARABIC LETTER LAM WITH THREE DOTS ABOVE
• Kurdish

06B8 <reserved>

06B9 <reserved>

06BA ARABIC LETTER NOON GHUNNA
• Urdu

06BB ARABIC LETTER RNOON
• Sindhi

06BC ARABIC LETTER NOON WITH RING
• Pashto

06BD ARABIC LETTER NOON WITH THREE DOTS ABOVE
• old Malay

06BE ARABIC LETTER HEH DOACHASHMEE
• Urdu
• forms aspirate digraphs

06BF <reserved>

06C0 ARABIC LETTER HEH WITH YEH ABOVE
• Persian

06C1 ARABIC LETTER HEH GOAL
• Urdu

06C2 ARABIC LETTER HEH GOAL WITH HAMZA ABOVE
• Urdu

06C3 ARABIC LETTER TEH MARBUTA GOAL
• Urdu

06C4 ARABIC LETTER WAW WITH RING
• Kashmiri

06C5 ARABIC LETTER KIRGHIZ OE
• Kirghiz

06C6 ARABIC LETTER OE
• Uighur, Kurdish, Kazah

06C7 ARABIC LETTER U
• Kirghiz

06C8 ARABIC LETTER YU
• Uighur

06C9 ARABIC LETTER KIRGHIZ YU
• Kazakh, Kirghiz

06CA ARABIC LETTER WAW WITH TWO DOTS ABOVE
• Kurdish

06CB ARABIC LETTER VE
• Uighur, Kazakh

06CC ARABIC LETTER FARSI YEH
• Arabic, Persian, Urdu, ...

06CD ARABIC LETTER YEH WITH TAIL
• Pashto, Sindhi

06CE ARABIC LETTER YEH WITH SMALL V
• Kurdish

06CF <reserved>

06D0 ARABIC LETTER E
• Pashto, Uighur

06D1 ARABIC LETTER YEH WITH THREE DOTS BELOW
• old Malay

06D2 ARABIC LETTER YEH BARREE
• Urdu

06D3 ARABIC LETTER YEH BARREE WITH HAMZA ABOVE
• Urdu

06D4 ARABIC FULL STOP
• Urdu

06D5 ARABIC LETTER AE
• Uighur, Kazakh, Kirghiz

06D6 ARABIC SMALL HIGH LIGATURE SAD WITH LAM WITH ALEF MAKSURA

06D7 ARABIC SMALL HIGH LIGATURE QAF WITH LAM WITH ALEF MAKSURA

06D8 ARABIC SMALL HIGH MEEM INITIAL FORM

06D9 ARABIC SMALL HIGH LAM ALEF

06DA ARABIC SMALL HIGH JEEM

06DB ARABIC SMALL HIGH THREE DOTS

06DC ARABIC SMALL HIGH SEEN

06DD ARABIC END OF AYAH

06DE ARABIC START OF RUB EL HIZB

06DF ARABIC SMALL HIGH ROUNDED ZERO

06E0 ARABIC SMALL HIGH UPRIGHT RECTANGULAR ZERO

06E1 ARABIC SMALL HIGH DOTLESS HEAD OF KHAH

06E2 ARABIC SMALL HIGH MEEM ISOLATED FORM

06E3 ARABIC SMALL LOW SEEN

06E4 ARABIC SMALL HIGH MADDA

06E5 ARABIC SMALL WAW

06E6 ARABIC SMALL YEH

06E7 ARABIC SMALL HIGH YEH

06E8 ARABIC SMALL HIGH NOON

06E9 ARABIC PLACE OF SAJDAH

06EA ARABIC EMPTY CENTRE LOW STOP

06EB ◌۫ ARABIC EMPTY CENTRE HIGH STOP

06EC ◌۬ ARABIC ROUNDED HIGH STOP WITH FILLED CENTRE

06ED ◌ۭ ARABIC SMALL LOW MEEM

06EE <reserved>

06EF <reserved>

Eastern Arabic-Indic digits (Persian and Urdu)

06F0 ۰ EXTENDED ARABIC-INDIC DIGIT ZERO

06F1 ۱ EXTENDED ARABIC-INDIC DIGIT ONE

06F2 ۲ EXTENDED ARABIC-INDIC DIGIT TWO

06F3 ۳ EXTENDED ARABIC-INDIC DIGIT THREE

06F4 ۴ EXTENDED ARABIC-INDIC DIGIT FOUR
- different glyphs in Persian and Urdu

06F5 ۵ EXTENDED ARABIC-INDIC DIGIT FIVE
- Persian and Urdu share glyph different from Arabic

06F6 ۶ EXTENDED ARABIC-INDIC DIGIT SIX
- Persian glyph different from Arabic

06F7 ۷ EXTENDED ARABIC-INDIC DIGIT SEVEN
- Urdu glyph different from Arabic

06F8 ۸ EXTENDED ARABIC-INDIC DIGIT EIGHT

06F9 ۹ EXTENDED ARABIC-INDIC DIGIT NINE

	090	091	092	093	094	095	096	097
0		ऐ 0910	ठ 0920	र 0930	◌ी 0940	ॐ 0950	ॠ 0960	॰ 0970
1	◌ँ 0901	ऑ 0911	ड 0921	ऱ 0931	◌ु 0941	◌॑ 0951	ॡ 0961	
2	◌ं 0902	ऒ 0912	ढ 0922	ल 0932	◌ू 0942	◌॒ 0952	◌ॢ 0962	
3	◌ः 0903	ओ 0913	ण 0923	ळ 0933	◌ृ 0943	◌॓ 0953	◌ॣ 0963	
4		औ 0914	त 0924	ऴ 0934	◌ॄ 0944	◌॔ 0954	। 0964	
5	अ 0905	क 0915	थ 0925	व 0935	◌ॅ 0945		॥ 0965	
6	आ 0906	ख 0916	द 0926	श 0936	◌ॆ 0946		० 0966	
7	इ 0907	ग 0917	ध 0927	ष 0937	◌े 0947		१ 0967	
8	ई 0908	घ 0918	न 0928	स 0938	◌ै 0948	क़ 0958	२ 0968	
9	उ 0909	ङ 0919	ऩ 0929	ह 0939	◌ॉ 0949	ख़ 0959	३ 0969	
A	ऊ 090A	च 091A	प 092A		◌ॊ 094A	ग़ 095A	४ 096A	
B	ऋ 090B	छ 091B	फ 092B		◌ो 094B	ज़ 095B	५ 096B	
C	ऌ 090C	ज 091C	ब 092C	◌़ 093C	◌ौ 094C	ड़ 095C	६ 096C	
D	ऍ 090D	झ 091D	भ 092D	ऽ 093D	◌् 094D	ढ़ 095D	७ 096D	
E	ऎ 090E	ञ 091E	म 092E	◌ा 093E		फ़ 095E	८ 096E	
F	ए 090F	ट 091F	य 092F	◌ि 093F		य़ 095F	९ 096F	

Based on ISCII 1988

Various signs

0900 ▧ <reserved>
0901 ँ DEVANAGARI SIGN CANDRABINDU
= anunasika
→ 0310 ̐ combining candrabindu
0902 ं DEVANAGARI SIGN ANUSVARA
= bindu
0903 ः DEVANAGARI SIGN VISARGA
0904 ▧ <reserved>

Independent vowels

0905 अ DEVANAGARI LETTER A
0906 आ DEVANAGARI LETTER AA
0907 इ DEVANAGARI LETTER I
0908 ई DEVANAGARI LETTER II
0909 उ DEVANAGARI LETTER U
090A ऊ DEVANAGARI LETTER UU
090B ऋ DEVANAGARI LETTER VOCALIC R
090C ऌ DEVANAGARI LETTER VOCALIC L
090D ऍ DEVANAGARI LETTER CANDRA E
090E ऎ DEVANAGARI LETTER SHORT E
• for transcribing Dravidian short e
090F ए DEVANAGARI LETTER E
0910 ऐ DEVANAGARI LETTER AI
0911 ऑ DEVANAGARI LETTER CANDRA O
0912 ऒ DEVANAGARI LETTER SHORT O
• for transcribing Dravidian short o
0913 ओ DEVANAGARI LETTER O
0914 औ DEVANAGARI LETTER AU

Consonants

0915 क DEVANAGARI LETTER KA
0916 ख DEVANAGARI LETTER KHA
0917 ग DEVANAGARI LETTER GA
0918 घ DEVANAGARI LETTER GHA
0919 ङ DEVANAGARI LETTER NGA
091A च DEVANAGARI LETTER CA
091B छ DEVANAGARI LETTER CHA
091C ज DEVANAGARI LETTER JA
091D झ DEVANAGARI LETTER JHA
091E ञ DEVANAGARI LETTER NYA
091F ट DEVANAGARI LETTER TTA
0920 ठ DEVANAGARI LETTER TTHA
0921 ड DEVANAGARI LETTER DDA
0922 ढ DEVANAGARI LETTER DDHA
0923 ण DEVANAGARI LETTER NNA
0924 त DEVANAGARI LETTER TA
0925 थ DEVANAGARI LETTER THA
0926 द DEVANAGARI LETTER DA
0927 ध DEVANAGARI LETTER DHA
0928 न DEVANAGARI LETTER NA
0929 ऩ DEVANAGARI LETTER NNNA
• for transcribing Tamil alveolar n
≡ 0928 न + 093C ़
092A प DEVANAGARI LETTER PA
092B फ DEVANAGARI LETTER PHA
092C ब DEVANAGARI LETTER BA
092D भ DEVANAGARI LETTER BHA
092E म DEVANAGARI LETTER MA
092F य DEVANAGARI LETTER YA
0930 र DEVANAGARI LETTER RA
0931 ऱ DEVANAGARI LETTER RRA
• for transcribing Tamil alveolar r
≡ 0930 र + 093C ़
0932 ल DEVANAGARI LETTER LA
0933 ळ DEVANAGARI LETTER LLA
0934 ऴ DEVANAGARI LETTER LLLA
• for transcribing Tamil l
≡ 0933 ळ + 093C ़
0935 व DEVANAGARI LETTER VA
0936 श DEVANAGARI LETTER SHA
0937 ष DEVANAGARI LETTER SSA
0938 स DEVANAGARI LETTER SA
0939 ह DEVANAGARI LETTER HA

Various signs

093A ▧ <reserved>
093B ▧ <reserved>
093C ़ DEVANAGARI SIGN NUKTA
• for extending the alphabet to new letters
093D ऽ DEVANAGARI SIGN AVAGRAHA

Dependent vowel signs

093E ा DEVANAGARI VOWEL SIGN AA
093F ि DEVANAGARI VOWEL SIGN I
• stands to the left of the consonant
0940 ी DEVANAGARI VOWEL SIGN II
0941 ु DEVANAGARI VOWEL SIGN U
0942 ू DEVANAGARI VOWEL SIGN UU
0943 ृ DEVANAGARI VOWEL SIGN VOCALIC R
0944 ॄ DEVANAGARI VOWEL SIGN VOCALIC RR
0945 ॅ DEVANAGARI VOWEL SIGN CANDRA E
= candra

0946 ◌ॆ DEVANAGARI VOWEL SIGN SHORT E
• for transcribing Dravidian vowels

0947 ◌े DEVANAGARI VOWEL SIGN E

0948 ◌ै DEVANAGARI VOWEL SIGN AI

0949 ◌ॉ DEVANAGARI VOWEL SIGN CANDRA O

094A ◌ॊ DEVANAGARI VOWEL SIGN SHORT O
• for transcribing Dravidian vowels

094B ◌ो DEVANAGARI VOWEL SIGN O

094C ◌ौ DEVANAGARI VOWEL SIGN AU

Various signs

094D ◌् DEVANAGARI SIGN VIRAMA
= halant
• suppresses inherent vowel

094E <reserved>

094F <reserved>

0950 ॐ DEVANAGARI OM

0951 ◌॑ DEVANAGARI STRESS SIGN UDATTA

0952 ◌॒ DEVANAGARI STRESS SIGN ANUDATTA

0953 ◌॓ DEVANAGARI GRAVE ACCENT

0954 ◌॔ DEVANAGARI ACUTE ACCENT

0955 <reserved>

0956 <reserved>

0957 <reserved>

Additional consonants

0958 क़ DEVANAGARI LETTER QA
≡ 0915 क + 093C ◌़

0959 ख़ DEVANAGARI LETTER KHHA
≡ 0916 ख + 093C ◌़

095A ग़ DEVANAGARI LETTER GHHA
≡ 0917 ग + 093C ◌़

095B ज़ DEVANAGARI LETTER ZA
≡ 091C ज + 093C ◌़

095C ड़ DEVANAGARI LETTER DDDHA
≡ 0921 ड + 093C ◌़

095D ढ़ DEVANAGARI LETTER RHA
≡ 0922 ढ + 093C ◌़

095E फ़ DEVANAGARI LETTER FA
≡ 092B फ + 093C ◌़

095F य़ DEVANAGARI LETTER YYA
≡ 092F य + 093C ◌़

Generic additions

0960 ॠ DEVANAGARI LETTER VOCALIC RR

0961 ॡ DEVANAGARI LETTER VOCALIC LL

0962 ◌ॢ DEVANAGARI VOWEL SIGN VOCALIC L

0963 ◌ॣ DEVANAGARI VOWEL SIGN VOCALIC LL

0964 । DEVANAGARI DANDA
= phrase separator

0965 ॥ DEVANAGARI DOUBLE DANDA

0966 ० DEVANAGARI DIGIT ZERO

0967 १ DEVANAGARI DIGIT ONE

0968 २ DEVANAGARI DIGIT TWO

0969 ३ DEVANAGARI DIGIT THREE

096A ४ DEVANAGARI DIGIT FOUR

096B ५ DEVANAGARI DIGIT FIVE

096C ६ DEVANAGARI DIGIT SIX

096D ७ DEVANAGARI DIGIT SEVEN

096E ८ DEVANAGARI DIGIT EIGHT

096F ९ DEVANAGARI DIGIT NINE

Devanagari-specific additions

0970 ॰ DEVANAGARI ABBREVIATION SIGN

	098	099	09A	09B	09C	09D	09E	09F
0		ঐ 0990	ঠ 09A0	র 09B0	◌ী 09C0		ৠ 09E0	ৰ 09F0
1	◌ঁ 0981		ড 09A1		◌ু 09C1		ৡ 09E1	ৱ 09F1
2	◌ং 0982		ঢ 09A2	ল 09B2	◌ূ 09C2		◌ৢ 09E2	৲ 09F2
3	◌ঃ 0983	ও 0993	ণ 09A3		◌ৃ 09C3		◌ৣ 09E3	৳ 09F3
4		ঔ 0994	ত 09A4		◌ৄ 09C4			৴ 09F4
5	অ 0985	ক 0995	থ 09A5					৵ 09F5
6	আ 0986	খ 0996	দ 09A6	শ 09B6			০ 09E6	৶ 09F6
7	ই 0987	গ 0997	ধ 09A7	ষ 09B7	◌ে 09C7	◌ৗ 09D7	১ 09E7	৷ 09F7
8	ঈ 0988	ঘ 0998	ন 09A8	স 09B8	◌ৈ 09C8		২ 09E8	৸ 09F8
9	উ 0989	ঙ 0999		হ 09B9			৩ 09E9	৹ 09F9
A	ঊ 098A	চ 099A	প 09AA				৪ 09EA	৺ 09FA
B	ঋ 098B	ছ 099B	ফ 09AB		◌ো 09CB		৫ 09EB	
C	ঌ 098C	জ 099C	ব 09AC	◌় 09BC	◌ৌ 09CC	ড় 09DC	৬ 09EC	
D		ঝ 099D	ভ 09AD		◌্ 09CD	ঢ় 09DD	৭ 09ED	
E		ঞ 099E	ম 09AE	◌া 09BE			৮ 09EE	
F	এ 098F	ট 099F	য 09AF	◌ি 09BF		য় 09DF	৯ 09EF	

Based on ISCII 1988

Various signs

0980 <reserved>
0981 ◌ঁ BENGALI SIGN CANDRABINDU
0982 ◌ং BENGALI SIGN ANUSVARA
0983 ◌ঃ BENGALI SIGN VISARGA
0984 <reserved>

Independent vowels

0985 অ BENGALI LETTER A
0986 আ BENGALI LETTER AA
0987 ই BENGALI LETTER I
0988 ঈ BENGALI LETTER II
0989 উ BENGALI LETTER U
098A ঊ BENGALI LETTER UU
098B ঋ BENGALI LETTER VOCALIC R
098C ঌ BENGALI LETTER VOCALIC L
098D <reserved>
098E <reserved>
098F এ BENGALI LETTER E
0990 ঐ BENGALI LETTER AI
0991 <reserved>
0992 <reserved>
0993 ও BENGALI LETTER O
0994 ঔ BENGALI LETTER AU

Consonants

0995 ক BENGALI LETTER KA
0996 খ BENGALI LETTER KHA
0997 গ BENGALI LETTER GA
0998 ঘ BENGALI LETTER GHA
0999 ঙ BENGALI LETTER NGA
099A চ BENGALI LETTER CA
099B ছ BENGALI LETTER CHA
099C জ BENGALI LETTER JA
099D ঝ BENGALI LETTER JHA
099E ঞ BENGALI LETTER NYA
099F ট BENGALI LETTER TTA
09A0 ঠ BENGALI LETTER TTHA
09A1 ড BENGALI LETTER DDA
09A2 ঢ BENGALI LETTER DDHA
09A3 ণ BENGALI LETTER NNA
09A4 ত BENGALI LETTER TA
09A5 থ BENGALI LETTER THA
09A6 দ BENGALI LETTER DA
09A7 ধ BENGALI LETTER DHA
09A8 ন BENGALI LETTER NA
09A9 <reserved>
09AA প BENGALI LETTER PA
09AB ফ BENGALI LETTER PHA
09AC ব BENGALI LETTER BA
= Bengali va, wa
09AD ভ BENGALI LETTER BHA
09AE ম BENGALI LETTER MA
09AF য BENGALI LETTER YA
09B0 র BENGALI LETTER RA
≡ 09AC ব + 09BC ◌়
09B1 <reserved>
09B2 ল BENGALI LETTER LA
09B3 <reserved>
09B4 <reserved>
09B5 <reserved>
09B6 শ BENGALI LETTER SHA
09B7 ষ BENGALI LETTER SSA
09B8 স BENGALI LETTER SA
09B9 হ BENGALI LETTER HA

Various signs

09BA <reserved>
09BB <reserved>
09BC ◌় BENGALI SIGN NUKTA
• for extending the alphabet to new letters
09BD <reserved>

Dependent vowel signs

09BE ◌া BENGALI VOWEL SIGN AA
09BF ি◌ BENGALI VOWEL SIGN I
• stands to the left of the consonant
09C0 ◌ী BENGALI VOWEL SIGN II
09C1 ◌ু BENGALI VOWEL SIGN U
09C2 ◌ূ BENGALI VOWEL SIGN UU
09C3 ◌ৃ BENGALI VOWEL SIGN VOCALIC R
09C4 ◌ৄ BENGALI VOWEL SIGN VOCALIC RR
09C5 <reserved>
09C6 <reserved>
09C7 ে◌ BENGALI VOWEL SIGN E
• stands to the left of the consonant
09C8 ৈ◌ BENGALI VOWEL SIGN AI
• stands to the left of the consonant
09C9 <reserved>
09CA <reserved>
09CB ◌ো BENGALI VOWEL SIGN O
• pieces on both sides of the consonant
≡ 09C7 ে◌ + 09BE ◌া
09CC ◌ৌ BENGALI VOWEL SIGN AU
• pieces on both sides of the consonant
≡ 09C7 ে◌ + 09D7 ◌ৗ

Various signs

09CD ্ BENGALI SIGN VIRAMA
= halant
09CE <reserved>
09CF <reserved>
09D0 <reserved>
09D1 <reserved>
09D2 <reserved>
09D3 <reserved>
09D4 <reserved>
09D5 <reserved>
09D6 <reserved>
09D7 ৗ BENGALI AU LENGTH MARK

Additional consonants

09D8 <reserved>
09D9 <reserved>
09DA <reserved>
09DB <reserved>
09DC ড় BENGALI LETTER RRA
≡ 09A1 ড + 09BC ়
09DD ঢ় BENGALI LETTER RHA
≡ 09A2 ঢ + 09BC ়
09DE <reserved>
09DF য় BENGALI LETTER YYA
≡ 09AF য + 09BC ়

Generic additions

09E0 ৠ BENGALI LETTER VOCALIC RR
09E1 ৡ BENGALI LETTER VOCALIC LL
09E2 ৢ BENGALI VOWEL SIGN VOCALIC L
09E3 ৣ BENGALI VOWEL SIGN VOCALIC LL
09E4 <reserved>
09E5 <reserved>
09E6 ০ BENGALI DIGIT ZERO
09E7 ১ BENGALI DIGIT ONE
09E8 ২ BENGALI DIGIT TWO
09E9 ৩ BENGALI DIGIT THREE
09EA ৪ BENGALI DIGIT FOUR
09EB ৫ BENGALI DIGIT FIVE
09EC ৬ BENGALI DIGIT SIX
09ED ৭ BENGALI DIGIT SEVEN
09EE ৮ BENGALI DIGIT EIGHT
09EF ৯ BENGALI DIGIT NINE

Bengali-specific additions

09F0 ৰ BENGALI LETTER RA WITH MIDDLE DIAGONAL
• Assamese
09F1 ৱ BENGALI LETTER RA WITH LOWER DIAGONAL
= BENGALI LETTER VA WITH LOWER DIAGONAL
• Assamese
09F2 ৲ BENGALI RUPEE MARK
09F3 ৳ BENGALI RUPEE SIGN
09F4 ৴ BENGALI CURRENCY NUMERATOR ONE
09F5 ৵ BENGALI CURRENCY NUMERATOR TWO
09F6 ৶ BENGALI CURRENCY NUMERATOR THREE
09F7 ৷ BENGALI CURRENCY NUMERATOR FOUR
09F8 ৸ BENGALI CURRENCY NUMERATOR ONE LESS THAN THE DENOMINATOR
09F9 ৹ BENGALI CURRENCY DENOMINATOR SIXTEEN
09FA ৺ BENGALI ISSHAR

	0A0	0A1	0A2	0A3	0A4	0A5	0A6	0A7
0		ਐ 0A10	ਠ 0A20	ਰ 0A30	◌ੀ 0A40			◌ੰ 0A70
1			ਡ 0A21		◌ੁ 0A41			◌ੱ 0A71
2	◌ਂ 0A02		ਢ 0A22	ਲ 0A32	◌ੂ 0A42			ੲ 0A72
3		ਓ 0A13	ਣ 0A23	ਲ਼ 0A33				ੳ 0A73
4		ਔ 0A14	ਤ 0A24					ੴ 0A74
5	ਅ 0A05	ਕ 0A15	ਥ 0A25	ਵ 0A35				
6	ਆ 0A06	ਖ 0A16	ਦ 0A26	ਸ਼ 0A36			੦ 0A66	
7	ਇ 0A07	ਗ 0A17	ਧ 0A27		◌ੇ 0A47		੧ 0A67	
8	ਈ 0A08	ਘ 0A18	ਨ 0A28	ਸ 0A38	◌ੈ 0A48		੨ 0A68	
9	ਉ 0A09	ਙ 0A19		ਹ 0A39		ਖ਼ 0A59	੩ 0A69	
A	ਊ 0A0A	ਚ 0A1A	ਪ 0A2A			ਗ਼ 0A5A	੪ 0A6A	
B		ਛ 0A1B	ਫ 0A2B		◌ੋ 0A4B	ਜ਼ 0A5B	੫ 0A6B	
C		ਜ 0A1C	ਬ 0A2C	◌਼ 0A3C	◌ੌ 0A4C	ੜ 0A5C	੬ 0A6C	
D		ਝ 0A1D	ਭ 0A2D		◌੍ 0A4D		੭ 0A6D	
E		ਞ 0A1E	ਮ 0A2E	◌ਾ 0A3E		ਫ਼ 0A5E	੮ 0A6E	
F	ਏ 0A0F	ਟ 0A1F	ਯ 0A2F	ਿ◌ 0A3F			੯ 0A6F	

Based on ISCII 1988

Various signs

0A00		<reserved>
0A01		<reserved>
0A02	◌ਂ	GURMUKHI SIGN BINDI
0A03		<reserved>
0A04		<reserved>

Independent vowels

0A05	ਅ	GURMUKHI LETTER A
0A06	ਆ	GURMUKHI LETTER AA
0A07	ਇ	GURMUKHI LETTER I
0A08	ਈ	GURMUKHI LETTER II
0A09	ਉ	GURMUKHI LETTER U
0A0A	ਊ	GURMUKHI LETTER UU
0A0B		<reserved>
0A0C		<reserved>
0A0D		<reserved>
0A0E		<reserved>
0A0F	ਏ	GURMUKHI LETTER EE
0A10	ਐ	GURMUKHI LETTER AI
0A11		<reserved>
0A12		<reserved>
0A13	ਓ	GURMUKHI LETTER OO
0A14	ਔ	GURMUKHI LETTER AU

Consonants

0A15	ਕ	GURMUKHI LETTER KA
0A16	ਖ	GURMUKHI LETTER KHA
0A17	ਗ	GURMUKHI LETTER GA
0A18	ਘ	GURMUKHI LETTER GHA
0A19	ਙ	GURMUKHI LETTER NGA
0A1A	ਚ	GURMUKHI LETTER CA
0A1B	ਛ	GURMUKHI LETTER CHA
0A1C	ਜ	GURMUKHI LETTER JA
0A1D	ਝ	GURMUKHI LETTER JHA
0A1E	ਞ	GURMUKHI LETTER NYA
0A1F	ਟ	GURMUKHI LETTER TTA
0A20	ਠ	GURMUKHI LETTER TTHA
0A21	ਡ	GURMUKHI LETTER DDA
0A22	ਢ	GURMUKHI LETTER DDHA
0A23	ਣ	GURMUKHI LETTER NNA
0A24	ਤ	GURMUKHI LETTER TA
0A25	ਥ	GURMUKHI LETTER THA
0A26	ਦ	GURMUKHI LETTER DA
0A27	ਧ	GURMUKHI LETTER DHA
0A28	ਨ	GURMUKHI LETTER NA
0A29		<reserved>
0A2A	ਪ	GURMUKHI LETTER PA
0A2B	ਫ	GURMUKHI LETTER PHA
0A2C	ਬ	GURMUKHI LETTER BA
0A2D	ਭ	GURMUKHI LETTER BHA
0A2E	ਮ	GURMUKHI LETTER MA
0A2F	ਯ	GURMUKHI LETTER YA
0A30	ਰ	GURMUKHI LETTER RA
0A31		<reserved>
0A32	ਲ	GURMUKHI LETTER LA
0A33	ਲ਼	GURMUKHI LETTER LLA
0A34		<reserved>
0A35	ਵ	GURMUKHI LETTER VA
0A36	ਸ਼	GURMUKHI LETTER SHA
0A37		<reserved>
0A38	ਸ	GURMUKHI LETTER SA
0A39	ਹ	GURMUKHI LETTER HA

Various signs

0A3A		<reserved>
0A3B		<reserved>
0A3C	◌਼	GURMUKHI SIGN NUKTA • for extending the alphabet to new letters
0A3D		<reserved>

Dependent vowel signs

0A3E	◌ਾ	GURMUKHI VOWEL SIGN AA
0A3F	ਿ◌	GURMUKHI VOWEL SIGN I • stands to the left of the consonant
0A40	◌ੀ	GURMUKHI VOWEL SIGN II
0A41	◌ੁ	GURMUKHI VOWEL SIGN U
0A42	◌ੂ	GURMUKHI VOWEL SIGN UU
0A43		<reserved>
0A44		<reserved>
0A45		<reserved>
0A46		<reserved>
0A47	◌ੇ	GURMUKHI VOWEL SIGN EE
0A48	◌ੈ	GURMUKHI VOWEL SIGN AI
0A49		<reserved>
0A4A		<reserved>
0A4B	◌ੋ	GURMUKHI VOWEL SIGN OO
0A4C	◌ੌ	GURMUKHI VOWEL SIGN AU
0A4D	◌੍	GURMUKHI SIGN VIRAMA
0A4E		<reserved>
0A4F		<reserved>
0A50		<reserved>
0A51		<reserved>
0A52		<reserved>

0A53 <reserved>
0A54 <reserved>
0A55 <reserved>
0A56 <reserved>
0A57 <reserved>

Additional consonants

0A58 <reserved>
0A59 ਖ਼ GURMUKHI LETTER KHHA
≡ 0A16 ਖ + 0A3C ਼
0A5A ਗ਼ GURMUKHI LETTER GHHA
≡ 0A17 ਗ + 0A3C ਼
0A5B ਜ਼ GURMUKHI LETTER ZA
≡ 0A1C ਜ + 0A3C ਼
0A5C ੜ GURMUKHI LETTER RRA
≡ 0A21 ਡ + 0A3C ਼
0A5D <reserved>
0A5E ਫ਼ GURMUKHI LETTER FA
≡ 0A2B ਫ + 0A3C ਼
0A5F <reserved>

Generic additions

0A60 <reserved>
0A61 <reserved>
0A62 <reserved>
0A63 <reserved>
0A64 <reserved>
0A65 <reserved>
0A66 ੦ GURMUKHI DIGIT ZERO
0A67 ੧ GURMUKHI DIGIT ONE
0A68 ੨ GURMUKHI DIGIT TWO
0A69 ੩ GURMUKHI DIGIT THREE
0A6A ੪ GURMUKHI DIGIT FOUR
0A6B ੫ GURMUKHI DIGIT FIVE
0A6C ੬ GURMUKHI DIGIT SIX
0A6D ੭ GURMUKHI DIGIT SEVEN
0A6E ੮ GURMUKHI DIGIT EIGHT
0A6F ੯ GURMUKHI DIGIT NINE

Gurmukhi-specific additions

0A70 ੰ GURMUKHI TIPPI
• nasalization
0A71 ੱ GURMUKHI ADDAK
• doubles following consonant
0A72 ੲ GURMUKHI IRI
• base for vowels
0A73 ੳ GURMUKHI URA
• base for vowels
0A74 ੴ GURMUKHI EK ONKAR
• God is One

	0A8	0A9	0AA	0AB	0AC	0AD	0AE	0AF
0		ઐ 0A90	ઠ 0AA0	ર 0AB0	◌ી 0AC0	ૐ 0AD0	ૠ 0AE0	
1	◌ઁ 0A81	ઑ 0A91	ડ 0AA1		◌ુ 0AC1			
2	◌ં 0A82		ઢ 0AA2	લ 0AB2	◌ૂ 0AC2			
3	◌ઃ 0A83	ઓ 0A93	ણ 0AA3	ળ 0AB3	◌ૃ 0AC3			
4		ઔ 0A94	ત 0AA4		◌ૄ 0AC4			
5	અ 0A85	ક 0A95	થ 0AA5	વ 0AB5	◌ૅ 0AC5			
6	આ 0A86	ખ 0A96	દ 0AA6	શ 0AB6			૦ 0AE6	
7	ઇ 0A87	ગ 0A97	ધ 0AA7	ષ 0AB7	◌ે 0AC7		૧ 0AE7	
8	ઈ 0A88	ઘ 0A98	ન 0AA8	સ 0AB8	◌ૈ 0AC8		૨ 0AE8	
9	ઉ 0A89	ઙ 0A99		હ 0AB9	◌ૉ 0AC9		૩ 0AE9	
A	ઊ 0A8A	ચ 0A9A	પ 0AAA				૪ 0AEA	
B	ઋ 0A8B	છ 0A9B	ફ 0AAB		◌ો 0ACB		૫ 0AEB	
C		જ 0A9C	બ 0AAC	◌઼ 0ABC	◌ૌ 0ACC		૬ 0AEC	
D	ઍ 0A8D	ઝ 0A9D	ભ 0AAD	ઽ 0ABD	◌્ 0ACD		૭ 0AED	
E		ઞ 0A9E	મ 0AAE	◌ા 0ABE			૮ 0AEE	
F	એ 0A8F	ટ 0A9F	ય 0AAF	િ◌ 0ABF			૯ 0AEF	

Based on ISCII 1988

Various signs

0A80 <reserved>
0A81 ◌ઁ GUJARATI SIGN CANDRABINDU
0A82 ◌ં GUJARATI SIGN ANUSVARA
0A83 ◌ઃ GUJARATI SIGN VISARGA
0A84 <reserved>

Independent vowels

0A85 અ GUJARATI LETTER A
0A86 આ GUJARATI LETTER AA
0A87 ઇ GUJARATI LETTER I
0A88 ઈ GUJARATI LETTER II
0A89 ઉ GUJARATI LETTER U
0A8A ઊ GUJARATI LETTER UU
0A8B ઋ GUJARATI LETTER VOCALIC R
0A8C <reserved>
0A8D ઍ GUJARATI VOWEL CANDRA E
0A8E <reserved>
0A8F એ GUJARATI LETTER E
0A90 ઐ GUJARATI LETTER AI
0A91 ઑ GUJARATI VOWEL CANDRA O
0A92 <reserved>
0A93 ઓ GUJARATI LETTER O
0A94 ઔ GUJARATI LETTER AU

Consonants

0A95 ક GUJARATI LETTER KA
0A96 ખ GUJARATI LETTER KHA
0A97 ગ GUJARATI LETTER GA
0A98 ઘ GUJARATI LETTER GHA
0A99 ઙ GUJARATI LETTER NGA
0A9A ચ GUJARATI LETTER CA
0A9B છ GUJARATI LETTER CHA
0A9C જ GUJARATI LETTER JA
0A9D ઝ GUJARATI LETTER JHA
0A9E ઞ GUJARATI LETTER NYA
0A9F ટ GUJARATI LETTER TTA
0AA0 ઠ GUJARATI LETTER TTHA
0AA1 ડ GUJARATI LETTER DDA
0AA2 ઢ GUJARATI LETTER DDHA
0AA3 ણ GUJARATI LETTER NNA
0AA4 ત GUJARATI LETTER TA
0AA5 થ GUJARATI LETTER THA
0AA6 દ GUJARATI LETTER DA
0AA7 ધ GUJARATI LETTER DHA
0AA8 ન GUJARATI LETTER NA
0AA9 <reserved>
0AAA પ GUJARATI LETTER PA
0AAB ફ GUJARATI LETTER PHA
0AAC બ GUJARATI LETTER BA
0AAD ભ GUJARATI LETTER BHA
0AAE મ GUJARATI LETTER MA
0AAF ય GUJARATI LETTER YA
0AB0 ર GUJARATI LETTER RA
0AB1 <reserved>
0AB2 લ GUJARATI LETTER LA
0AB3 ળ GUJARATI LETTER LLA
0AB4 <reserved>
0AB5 વ GUJARATI LETTER VA
0AB6 શ GUJARATI LETTER SHA
0AB7 ષ GUJARATI LETTER SSA
0AB8 સ GUJARATI LETTER SA
0AB9 હ GUJARATI LETTER HA

Various signs

0ABA <reserved>
0ABB <reserved>
0ABC ◌઼ GUJARATI SIGN NUKTA
• for extending the alphabet to new letters
0ABD ઽ GUJARATI SIGN AVAGRAHA

Dependent vowel signs

0ABE ◌ા GUJARATI VOWEL SIGN AA
0ABF ◌િ GUJARATI VOWEL SIGN I
• stands to the left of the consonant
0AC0 ◌ી GUJARATI VOWEL SIGN II
0AC1 ◌ુ GUJARATI VOWEL SIGN U
0AC2 ◌ૂ GUJARATI VOWEL SIGN UU
0AC3 ◌ૃ GUJARATI VOWEL SIGN VOCALIC R
0AC4 ◌ૄ GUJARATI VOWEL SIGN VOCALIC RR
0AC5 ◌ૅ GUJARATI VOWEL SIGN CANDRA E
0AC6 <reserved>
0AC7 ◌ે GUJARATI VOWEL SIGN E
0AC8 ◌ૈ GUJARATI VOWEL SIGN AI
0AC9 ◌ૉ GUJARATI VOWEL SIGN CANDRA O
0ACA <reserved>
0ACB ◌ો GUJARATI VOWEL SIGN O
0ACC ◌ૌ GUJARATI VOWEL SIGN AU

Various signs

0ACD ◌્ GUJARATI SIGN VIRAMA
0ACE <reserved>

0ACF ▧ <reserved>
0AD0 ૐ GUJARATI OM
0AD1 ▧ <reserved>
0AD2 ▧ <reserved>
0AD3 ▧ <reserved>
0AD4 ▧ <reserved>
0AD5 ▧ <reserved>
0AD6 ▧ <reserved>
0AD7 ▧ <reserved>
0AD8 ▧ <reserved>
0AD9 ▧ <reserved>
0ADA ▧ <reserved>
0ADB ▧ <reserved>
0ADC ▧ <reserved>
0ADD ▧ <reserved>
0ADE ▧ <reserved>
0ADF ▧ <reserved>

Generic additions

0AE0 ૠ GUJARATI LETTER VOCALIC RR
0AE1 ▧ <reserved>
0AE2 ▧ <reserved>
0AE3 ▧ <reserved>
0AE4 ▧ <reserved>
0AE5 ▧ <reserved>
0AE6 ૦ GUJARATI DIGIT ZERO
0AE7 ૧ GUJARATI DIGIT ONE
0AE8 ૨ GUJARATI DIGIT TWO
0AE9 ૩ GUJARATI DIGIT THREE
0AEA ૪ GUJARATI DIGIT FOUR
0AEB ૫ GUJARATI DIGIT FIVE
0AEC ૬ GUJARATI DIGIT SIX
0AED ૭ GUJARATI DIGIT SEVEN
0AEE ૮ GUJARATI DIGIT EIGHT
0AEF ૯ GUJARATI DIGIT NINE

	0B0	0B1	0B2	0B3	0B4	0B5	0B6	0B7
0		ଐ 0B10	ଠ 0B20	ର 0B30	◌ୀ 0B40		ୠ 0B60	୰ 0B70
1	◌ଁ 0B01		ଡ 0B21		◌ୁ 0B41		ୡ 0B61	
2	◌ଂ 0B02		ଢ 0B22	ଲ 0B32	◌ୂ 0B42			
3	◌ଃ 0B03	ଓ 0B13	ଣ 0B23	ଳ 0B33	◌ୃ 0B43			
4		ଔ 0B14	ତ 0B24					
5	ଅ 0B05	କ 0B15	ଥ 0B25					
6	ଆ 0B06	ଖ 0B16	ଦ 0B26	ଶ 0B36		◌ୖ 0B56	୦ 0B66	
7	ଇ 0B07	ଗ 0B17	ଧ 0B27	ଷ 0B37	◌େ 0B47	◌ୗ 0B57	୧ 0B67	
8	ଈ 0B08	ଘ 0B18	ନ 0B28	ସ 0B38	◌ୈ 0B48		୨ 0B68	
9	ଉ 0B09	ଙ 0B19		ହ 0B39			୩ 0B69	
A	ଊ 0B0A	ଚ 0B1A	ପ 0B2A				୪ 0B6A	
B	ଋ 0B0B	ଛ 0B1B	ଫ 0B2B		◌ୋ 0B4B		୫ 0B6B	
C	ଌ 0B0C	ଜ 0B1C	ବ 0B2C	◌଼ 0B3C	◌ୌ 0B4C	ଡ଼ 0B5C	୬ 0B6C	
D		ଝ 0B1D	ଭ 0B2D	ଽ 0B3D	◌୍ 0B4D	ଢ଼ 0B5D	୭ 0B6D	
E		ଞ 0B1E	ମ 0B2E	◌ା 0B3E			୮ 0B6E	
F	ଏ 0B0F	ଟ 0B1F	ଯ 0B2F	◌ି 0B3F		ୟ 0B5F	୯ 0B6F	

Based on ISCII 1988

Various signs

0B00 <reserved>

0B01 ◌ଁ ORIYA SIGN CANDRABINDU

0B02 ◌ଂ ORIYA SIGN ANUSVARA

0B03 ◌ଃ ORIYA SIGN VISARGA

0B04 <reserved>

Independent vowels

0B05 ଅ ORIYA LETTER A

0B06 ଆ ORIYA LETTER AA

0B07 ଇ ORIYA LETTER I

0B08 ଈ ORIYA LETTER II

0B09 ଉ ORIYA LETTER U

0B0A ଊ ORIYA LETTER UU

0B0B ଋ ORIYA LETTER VOCALIC R

0B0C ଌ ORIYA LETTER VOCALIC L

0B0D <reserved>

0B0E <reserved>

0B0F ଏ ORIYA LETTER E

0B10 ଐ ORIYA LETTER AI

0B11 <reserved>

0B12 <reserved>

0B13 ଓ ORIYA LETTER O

0B14 ଔ ORIYA LETTER AU

Consonants

0B15 କ ORIYA LETTER KA

0B16 ଖ ORIYA LETTER KHA

0B17 ଗ ORIYA LETTER GA

0B18 ଘ ORIYA LETTER GHA

0B19 ଙ ORIYA LETTER NGA

0B1A ଚ ORIYA LETTER CA

0B1B ଛ ORIYA LETTER CHA

0B1C ଜ ORIYA LETTER JA

0B1D ଝ ORIYA LETTER JHA

0B1E ଞ ORIYA LETTER NYA

0B1F ଟ ORIYA LETTER TTA

0B20 ଠ ORIYA LETTER TTHA

0B21 ଡ ORIYA LETTER DDA

0B22 ଢ ORIYA LETTER DDHA

0B23 ଣ ORIYA LETTER NNA

0B24 ତ ORIYA LETTER TA

0B25 ଥ ORIYA LETTER THA

0B26 ଦ ORIYA LETTER DA

0B27 ଧ ORIYA LETTER DHA

0B28 ନ ORIYA LETTER NA

0B29 <reserved>

0B2A ପ ORIYA LETTER PA

0B2B ଫ ORIYA LETTER PHA

0B2C ବ ORIYA LETTER BA
= Oriya va, wa

0B2D ଭ ORIYA LETTER BHA

0B2E ମ ORIYA LETTER MA

0B2F ଯ ORIYA LETTER YA

0B30 ର ORIYA LETTER RA

0B31 <reserved>

0B32 ଲ ORIYA LETTER LA

0B33 ଳ ORIYA LETTER LLA

0B34 <reserved>

0B35 <reserved>
→ 0B2C ବ oriya letter ba

0B36 ଶ ORIYA LETTER SHA

0B37 ଷ ORIYA LETTER SSA

0B38 ସ ORIYA LETTER SA

0B39 ହ ORIYA LETTER HA

Various signs

0B3A <reserved>

0B3B <reserved>

0B3C ◌଼ ORIYA SIGN NUKTA
• for extending the alphabet to new letters

0B3D ଽ ORIYA SIGN AVAGRAHA

Dependent vowel signs

0B3E ◌ା ORIYA VOWEL SIGN AA

0B3F ◌ି ORIYA VOWEL SIGN I

0B40 ◌ୀ ORIYA VOWEL SIGN II

0B41 ◌ୁ ORIYA VOWEL SIGN U

0B42 ◌ୂ ORIYA VOWEL SIGN UU

0B43 ◌ୃ ORIYA VOWEL SIGN VOCALIC R

0B44 <reserved>

0B45 <reserved>

0B46 <reserved>

0B47 ◌େ ORIYA VOWEL SIGN E
• stands to the left of the consonant

0B48 ◌ୈ ORIYA VOWEL SIGN AI
• pieces left of and above the consonant
≡ 0B47 ◌େ + 0B56 ◌ୖ

0B49 <reserved>

0B4A <reserved>

0B4B ◌ୋ ORIYA VOWEL SIGN O
• pieces on both sides of the consonant
≡ 0B47 ◌େ + 0B3E ◌ା

0B4C ◌ୌ ORIYA VOWEL SIGN AU
• pieces on both sides of the consonant
≡ 0B47 ◌େ + 0B57 ◌ୗ

Various signs

0B4D ୍ ORIYA SIGN VIRAMA
0B4E <reserved>
0B4F <reserved>
0B50 <reserved>
0B51 <reserved>
0B52 <reserved>
0B53 <reserved>
0B54 <reserved>
0B55 <reserved>
0B56 ୖ ORIYA AI LENGTH MARK
0B57 ୗ ORIYA AU LENGTH MARK

Additional consonants

0B58 <reserved>
0B59 <reserved>
0B5A <reserved>
0B5B <reserved>
0B5C ଡ଼ ORIYA LETTER RRA
≡ 0B21 ଡ + 0B3C ଼
0B5D ଢ଼ ORIYA LETTER RHA
≡ 0B22 ଢ + 0B3C ଼
0B5E <reserved>
0B5F ୟ ORIYA LETTER YYA
≡ 0B2F ଯ + 0B3C ଼

Generic additions

0B60 ୠ ORIYA LETTER VOCALIC RR
0B61 ୡ ORIYA LETTER VOCALIC LL
0B62 <reserved>
0B63 <reserved>
0B64 <reserved>
0B65 <reserved>
0B66 ୦ ORIYA DIGIT ZERO
0B67 ୧ ORIYA DIGIT ONE
0B68 ୨ ORIYA DIGIT TWO
0B69 ୩ ORIYA DIGIT THREE
0B6A ୪ ORIYA DIGIT FOUR
0B6B ୫ ORIYA DIGIT FIVE
0B6C ୬ ORIYA DIGIT SIX
0B6D ୭ ORIYA DIGIT SEVEN
0B6E ୮ ORIYA DIGIT EIGHT
0B6F ୯ ORIYA DIGIT NINE

Oriya-specific addition

0B70 ୰ ORIYA ISSHAR

	0B8	0B9	0BA	0BB	0BC	0BD	0BE	0BF
0		ஐ 0B90		ர 0BB0	◌ீ 0BC0			௰ 0BF0
1				ற 0BB1	◌ு 0BC1			௱ 0BF1
2	◌ஂ 0B82	ஒ 0B92		ல 0BB2	◌ூ 0BC2			௲ 0BF2
3	◌ஃ 0B83	ஓ 0B93	ண 0BA3	ள 0BB3				
4		ஔ 0B94	த 0BA4	ழ 0BB4				
5	அ 0B85	க 0B95		வ 0BB5				
6	ஆ 0B86				◌ெ 0BC6			
7	இ 0B87			ஷ 0BB7	◌ே 0BC7	◌ௗ 0BD7	௧ 0BE7	
8	ஈ 0B88		ந 0BA8	ஸ 0BB8	◌ை 0BC8		௨ 0BE8	
9	உ 0B89	ங 0B99	ன 0BA9	ஹ 0BB9			௩ 0BE9	
A	ஊ 0B8A	ச 0B9A	ப 0BAA		◌ொ 0BCA		௪ 0BEA	
B					◌ோ 0BCB		௫ 0BEB	
C		ஜ 0B9C			◌ௌ 0BCC		௬ 0BEC	
D					◌் 0BCD		௭ 0BED	
E	எ 0B8E	ஞ 0B9E	ம 0BAE	◌ா 0BBE			௮ 0BEE	
F	ஏ 0B8F	ட 0B9F	ய 0BAF	◌ி 0BBF			௯ 0BEF	

Based on ISCII 1988

Various signs

0B80 <reserved>
0B81 <reserved>
0B82 ◌ஂ TAMIL SIGN ANUSVARA
0B83 ◌ஃ TAMIL SIGN VISARGA
0B84 <reserved>

Independent vowels

0B85 அ TAMIL LETTER A
0B86 ஆ TAMIL LETTER AA
0B87 இ TAMIL LETTER I
0B88 ஈ TAMIL LETTER II
0B89 உ TAMIL LETTER U
0B8A ஊ TAMIL LETTER UU
0B8B <reserved>
0B8C <reserved>
0B8D <reserved>
0B8E எ TAMIL LETTER E
0B8F ஏ TAMIL LETTER EE
0B90 ஐ TAMIL LETTER AI
0B91 <reserved>
0B92 ஒ TAMIL LETTER O
0B93 ஓ TAMIL LETTER OO
0B94 ஔ TAMIL LETTER AU
≡ 0B92 ஒ + 0BD7 ◌ௗ

Consonants

0B95 க TAMIL LETTER KA
0B96 <reserved>
0B97 <reserved>
0B98 <reserved>
0B99 ங TAMIL LETTER NGA
0B9A ச TAMIL LETTER CA
0B9B <reserved>
0B9C ஜ TAMIL LETTER JA
0B9D <reserved>
0B9E ஞ TAMIL LETTER NYA
0B9F ட TAMIL LETTER TTA
0BA0 <reserved>
0BA1 <reserved>
0BA2 <reserved>
0BA3 ண TAMIL LETTER NNA
0BA4 த TAMIL LETTER TA
0BA5 <reserved>
0BA6 <reserved>
0BA7 <reserved>
0BA8 ந TAMIL LETTER NA
0BA9 ன TAMIL LETTER NNNA
0BAA ப TAMIL LETTER PA
0BAB <reserved>
0BAC <reserved>
0BAD <reserved>
0BAE ம TAMIL LETTER MA
0BAF ய TAMIL LETTER YA
0BB0 ர TAMIL LETTER RA
0BB1 ற TAMIL LETTER RRA
0BB2 ல TAMIL LETTER LA
0BB3 ள TAMIL LETTER LLA
0BB4 ழ TAMIL LETTER LLLA
0BB5 வ TAMIL LETTER VA
0BB6 <reserved>
0BB7 ஷ TAMIL LETTER SSA
0BB8 ஸ TAMIL LETTER SA
0BB9 ஹ TAMIL LETTER HA
0BBA <reserved>
0BBB <reserved>
0BBC <reserved>
0BBD <reserved>

Dependent vowel signs

0BBE ◌ா TAMIL VOWEL SIGN AA
0BBF ◌ி TAMIL VOWEL SIGN I
0BC0 ◌ீ TAMIL VOWEL SIGN II
0BC1 ◌ு TAMIL VOWEL SIGN U
0BC2 ◌ூ TAMIL VOWEL SIGN UU
0BC3 <reserved>
0BC4 <reserved>
0BC5 <reserved>
0BC6 ◌ெ TAMIL VOWEL SIGN E
• stands to the left of the consonant
0BC7 ◌ே TAMIL VOWEL SIGN EE
• stands to the left of the consonant
0BC8 ◌ை TAMIL VOWEL SIGN AI
• stands to the left of the consonant
0BC9 <reserved>
0BCA ◌ொ TAMIL VOWEL SIGN O
• pieces on both sides of the consonant
≡ 0BC6 ◌ெ + 0BBE ◌ா
0BCB ◌ோ TAMIL VOWEL SIGN OO
• pieces on both sides of the consonant
≡ 0BC7 ◌ே + 0BBE ◌ா
0BCC ◌ௌ TAMIL VOWEL SIGN AU
• pieces on both sides of the consonant
≡ 0BC6 ◌ெ + 0BD7 ◌ௗ

Various signs

0BCD ◌் TAMIL SIGN VIRAMA

0BCE		<reserved>
0BCF		<reserved>
0BD0		<reserved>
0BD1		<reserved>
0BD2		<reserved>
0BD3		<reserved>
0BD4		<reserved>
0BD5		<reserved>
0BD6		<reserved>
0BD7	ௗ	TAMIL AU LENGTH MARK
0BD8		<reserved>
0BD9		<reserved>
0BDA		<reserved>
0BDB		<reserved>
0BDC		<reserved>
0BDD		<reserved>
0BDE		<reserved>
0BDF		<reserved>

Generic additions

0BE0		<reserved>
0BE1		<reserved>
0BE2		<reserved>
0BE3		<reserved>
0BE4		<reserved>
0BE5		<reserved>
0BE6		<reserved> → 0030 0 digit zero
0BE7	௧	TAMIL DIGIT ONE
0BE8	௨	TAMIL DIGIT TWO
0BE9	௩	TAMIL DIGIT THREE
0BEA	௪	TAMIL DIGIT FOUR
0BEB	௫	TAMIL DIGIT FIVE
0BEC	௬	TAMIL DIGIT SIX
0BED	௭	TAMIL DIGIT SEVEN
0BEE	௮	TAMIL DIGIT EIGHT
0BEF	௯	TAMIL DIGIT NINE

Tamil-specific additions

0BF0	௰	TAMIL NUMBER TEN
0BF1	௱	TAMIL NUMBER ONE HUNDRED
0BF2	௲	TAMIL NUMBER ONE THOUSAND

Based on ISCII 1988

Various signs

0C00 <reserved>
0C01 ◌ఁ TELUGU SIGN CANDRABINDU
0C02 ◌ం TELUGU SIGN ANUSVARA
0C03 ◌ః TELUGU SIGN VISARGA
0C04 <reserved>

Independent vowels

0C05 అ TELUGU LETTER A
0C06 ఆ TELUGU LETTER AA
0C07 ఇ TELUGU LETTER I
0C08 ఈ TELUGU LETTER II
0C09 ఉ TELUGU LETTER U
0C0A ఊ TELUGU LETTER UU
0C0B ఋ TELUGU LETTER VOCALIC R
0C0C ఌ TELUGU LETTER VOCALIC L
0C0D <reserved>
0C0E ఎ TELUGU LETTER E
0C0F ఏ TELUGU LETTER EE
0C10 ఐ TELUGU LETTER AI
0C11 <reserved>
0C12 ఒ TELUGU LETTER O
0C13 ఓ TELUGU LETTER OO
0C14 ఔ TELUGU LETTER AU

Consonants

0C15 క TELUGU LETTER KA
0C16 ఖ TELUGU LETTER KHA
0C17 గ TELUGU LETTER GA
0C18 ఘ TELUGU LETTER GHA
0C19 ఙ TELUGU LETTER NGA
0C1A చ TELUGU LETTER CA
0C1B ఛ TELUGU LETTER CHA
0C1C జ TELUGU LETTER JA
0C1D ఝ TELUGU LETTER JHA
0C1E ఞ TELUGU LETTER NYA
0C1F ట TELUGU LETTER TTA
0C20 ఠ TELUGU LETTER TTHA
0C21 డ TELUGU LETTER DDA
0C22 ఢ TELUGU LETTER DDHA
0C23 ణ TELUGU LETTER NNA
0C24 త TELUGU LETTER TA
0C25 థ TELUGU LETTER THA
0C26 ద TELUGU LETTER DA
0C27 ధ TELUGU LETTER DHA
0C28 న TELUGU LETTER NA
0C29 <reserved>
0C2A ప TELUGU LETTER PA
0C2B ఫ TELUGU LETTER PHA
0C2C బ TELUGU LETTER BA
0C2D భ TELUGU LETTER BHA
0C2E మ TELUGU LETTER MA
0C2F య TELUGU LETTER YA
0C30 ర TELUGU LETTER RA
0C31 ఱ TELUGU LETTER RRA
0C32 ల TELUGU LETTER LA
0C33 ళ TELUGU LETTER LLA
0C34 <reserved>
0C35 వ TELUGU LETTER VA
0C36 శ TELUGU LETTER SHA
0C37 ష TELUGU LETTER SSA
0C38 స TELUGU LETTER SA
0C39 హ TELUGU LETTER HA
0C3A <reserved>
0C3B <reserved>
0C3C <reserved>
0C3D <reserved>

Dependent vowel signs

0C3E ◌ా TELUGU VOWEL SIGN AA
0C3F ◌ి TELUGU VOWEL SIGN I
0C40 ◌ీ TELUGU VOWEL SIGN II
0C41 ◌ు TELUGU VOWEL SIGN U
0C42 ◌ూ TELUGU VOWEL SIGN UU
0C43 ◌ృ TELUGU VOWEL SIGN VOCALIC R
0C44 ◌ౄ TELUGU VOWEL SIGN VOCALIC RR
0C45 <reserved>
0C46 ◌ె TELUGU VOWEL SIGN E
0C47 ◌ే TELUGU VOWEL SIGN EE
0C48 ◌ై TELUGU VOWEL SIGN AI
≡ 0C46 ◌ె + 0C56 ◌ౖ
0C49 <reserved>
0C4A ◌ొ TELUGU VOWEL SIGN O
0C4B ◌ో TELUGU VOWEL SIGN OO
0C4C ◌ౌ TELUGU VOWEL SIGN AU

Various signs

0C4D ◌్ TELUGU SIGN VIRAMA
0C4E <reserved>
0C4F <reserved>
0C50 <reserved>
0C51 <reserved>
0C52 <reserved>

0C53 <reserved>
0C54 <reserved>
0C55 ౕ TELUGU LENGTH MARK
0C56 ౖ TELUGU AI LENGTH MARK
0C57 <reserved>
0C58 <reserved>
0C59 <reserved>
0C5A <reserved>
0C5B <reserved>
0C5C <reserved>
0C5D <reserved>
0C5E <reserved>
0C5F <reserved>

Generic additions

0C60 ౠ TELUGU LETTER VOCALIC RR
0C61 ౡ TELUGU LETTER VOCALIC LL
0C62 <reserved>
0C63 <reserved>
0C64 <reserved>
0C65 <reserved>
0C66 ౦ TELUGU DIGIT ZERO
0C67 ౧ TELUGU DIGIT ONE
0C68 ౨ TELUGU DIGIT TWO
0C69 ౩ TELUGU DIGIT THREE
0C6A ౪ TELUGU DIGIT FOUR
0C6B ౫ TELUGU DIGIT FIVE
0C6C ౬ TELUGU DIGIT SIX
0C6D ౭ TELUGU DIGIT SEVEN
0C6E ౮ TELUGU DIGIT EIGHT
0C6F ౯ TELUGU DIGIT NINE

0C8 0C9 0CA 0CB 0CC 0CD 0CE 0CF
0 1 2 3 4 5 6 7 8 9 A B C D E F
0C82 0C83 0C85 0C86 0C87 0C88 0C89 0C8A 0C8B 0C8C 0C8E 0C8F
0C90 0C92 0C93 0C94 0C95 0C96 0C97 0C98 0C99 0C9A 0C9B 0C9C 0C9D 0C9E 0C9F
0CA0 0CA1 0CA2 0CA3 0CA4 0CA5 0CA6 0CA7 0CA8 0CAA 0CAB 0CAC 0CAD 0CAE 0CAF
0CB0 0CB1 0CB2 0CB3 0CB5 0CB6 0CB7 0CB8 0CB9 0CBE 0CBF
0CC0 0CC1 0CC2 0CC3 0CC4 0CC6 0CC7 0CC8 0CCA 0CCB 0CCC 0CCD
0CD5 0CD6 0CDE
0CE0 0CE1 0CE6 0CE7 0CE8 0CE9 0CEA 0CEB 0CEC 0CED 0CEE 0CEF

Based on ISCII 1988

Various signs

0C80		<reserved>
0C81		<reserved>
0C82	◌ಂ	KANNADA SIGN ANUSVARA
0C83	◌ಃ	KANNADA SIGN VISARGA
0C84		<reserved>

Independent vowels

0C85	ಅ	KANNADA LETTER A
0C86	ಆ	KANNADA LETTER AA
0C87	ಇ	KANNADA LETTER I
0C88	ಈ	KANNADA LETTER II
0C89	ಉ	KANNADA LETTER U
0C8A	ಊ	KANNADA LETTER UU
0C8B	ಋ	KANNADA LETTER VOCALIC R
0C8C	ಌ	KANNADA LETTER VOCALIC L
0C8D		<reserved>
0C8E	ಎ	KANNADA LETTER E
0C8F	ಏ	KANNADA LETTER EE
0C90	ಐ	KANNADA LETTER AI
0C91		<reserved>
0C92	ಒ	KANNADA LETTER O
0C93	ಓ	KANNADA LETTER OO
0C94	ಔ	KANNADA LETTER AU

Consonants

0C95	ಕ	KANNADA LETTER KA
0C96	ಖ	KANNADA LETTER KHA
0C97	ಗ	KANNADA LETTER GA
0C98	ಘ	KANNADA LETTER GHA
0C99	ಙ	KANNADA LETTER NGA
0C9A	ಚ	KANNADA LETTER CA
0C9B	ಛ	KANNADA LETTER CHA
0C9C	ಜ	KANNADA LETTER JA
0C9D	ಝ	KANNADA LETTER JHA
0C9E	ಞ	KANNADA LETTER NYA
0C9F	ಟ	KANNADA LETTER TTA
0CA0	ಠ	KANNADA LETTER TTHA
0CA1	ಡ	KANNADA LETTER DDA
0CA2	ಢ	KANNADA LETTER DDHA
0CA3	ಣ	KANNADA LETTER NNA
0CA4	ತ	KANNADA LETTER TA
0CA5	ಥ	KANNADA LETTER THA
0CA6	ದ	KANNADA LETTER DA
0CA7	ಧ	KANNADA LETTER DHA
0CA8	ನ	KANNADA LETTER NA
0CA9		<reserved>
0CAA	ಪ	KANNADA LETTER PA
0CAB	ಫ	KANNADA LETTER PHA
0CAC	ಬ	KANNADA LETTER BA
0CAD	ಭ	KANNADA LETTER BHA
0CAE	ಮ	KANNADA LETTER MA
0CAF	ಯ	KANNADA LETTER YA
0CB0	ರ	KANNADA LETTER RA
0CB1	ಱ	KANNADA LETTER RRA
0CB2	ಲ	KANNADA LETTER LA
0CB3	ಳ	KANNADA LETTER LLA
0CB4		<reserved>
0CB5	ವ	KANNADA LETTER VA
0CB6	ಶ	KANNADA LETTER SHA
0CB7	ಷ	KANNADA LETTER SSA
0CB8	ಸ	KANNADA LETTER SA
0CB9	ಹ	KANNADA LETTER HA
0CBA		<reserved>
0CBB		<reserved>
0CBC		<reserved>
0CBD		<reserved>

Dependent vowel signs

0CBE	◌ಾ	KANNADA VOWEL SIGN AA
0CBF	◌ಿ	KANNADA VOWEL SIGN I
0CC0	◌ೀ	KANNADA VOWEL SIGN II ≡ 0CBF ◌ಿ + 0CD5 ◌ೕ
0CC1	◌ು	KANNADA VOWEL SIGN U
0CC2	◌ೂ	KANNADA VOWEL SIGN UU
0CC3	◌ೃ	KANNADA VOWEL SIGN VOCALIC R
0CC4	◌ೄ	KANNADA VOWEL SIGN VOCALIC RR
0CC5		<reserved>
0CC6	◌ೆ	KANNADA VOWEL SIGN E
0CC7	◌ೇ	KANNADA VOWEL SIGN EE ≡ 0CC6 ◌ೆ + 0CD5 ◌ೕ
0CC8	◌ೈ	KANNADA VOWEL SIGN AI ≡ 0CC6 ◌ೆ + 0CD6 ◌ೖ
0CC9		<reserved>
0CCA	◌ೊ	KANNADA VOWEL SIGN O ≡ 0CC6 ◌ೆ + 0CC2 ◌ೂ
0CCB	◌ೋ	KANNADA VOWEL SIGN OO ≡ 0CC6 ◌ೆ + 0CC2 ◌ೂ + 0CD5 ◌ೕ
0CCC	◌ೌ	KANNADA VOWEL SIGN AU

Various signs

0CCD	◌್	KANNADA SIGN VIRAMA
0CCE		<reserved>
0CCF		<reserved>

0CD0 <reserved>
0CD1 <reserved>
0CD2 <reserved>
0CD3 <reserved>
0CD4 <reserved>
0CD5 ◌ೕ KANNADA LENGTH MARK
0CD6 ◌ೖ KANNADA AI LENGTH MARK
0CD7 <reserved>

Additional consonants

0CD8 <reserved>
0CD9 <reserved>
0CDA <reserved>
0CDB <reserved>
0CDC <reserved>
0CDD <reserved>
0CDE ೞ KANNADA LETTER FA
0CDF <reserved>

Generic additions

0CE0 ೠ KANNADA LETTER VOCALIC RR
0CE1 ೡ KANNADA LETTER VOCALIC LL
0CE2 <reserved>
0CE3 <reserved>
0CE4 <reserved>
0CE5 <reserved>
0CE6 ೦ KANNADA DIGIT ZERO
0CE7 ೧ KANNADA DIGIT ONE
0CE8 ೨ KANNADA DIGIT TWO
0CE9 ೩ KANNADA DIGIT THREE
0CEA ೪ KANNADA DIGIT FOUR
0CEB ೫ KANNADA DIGIT FIVE
0CEC ೬ KANNADA DIGIT SIX
0CED ೭ KANNADA DIGIT SEVEN
0CEE ೮ KANNADA DIGIT EIGHT
0CEF ೯ KANNADA DIGIT NINE

	0D0	0D1	0D2	0D3	0D4	0D5	0D6	0D7
0		ഐ 0D10	ഠ 0D20	ര 0D30	◌ീ 0D40		ൠ 0D60	
1			ഡ 0D21	റ 0D31	◌ു 0D41		ൡ 0D61	
2	◌ം 0D02	ഒ 0D12	ഢ 0D22	ല 0D32	◌ൂ 0D42			
3	◌ഃ 0D03	ഓ 0D13	ണ 0D23	ള 0D33	◌ൃ 0D43			
4		ഔ 0D14	ത 0D24	ഴ 0D34				
5	അ 0D05	ക 0D15	ഥ 0D25	വ 0D35				
6	ആ 0D06	ഖ 0D16	ദ 0D26	ശ 0D36	◌െ 0D46		൦ 0D66	
7	ഇ 0D07	ഗ 0D17	ധ 0D27	ഷ 0D37	◌േ 0D47	◌ൗ 0D57	൧ 0D67	
8	ഈ 0D08	ഘ 0D18	ന 0D28	സ 0D38	◌ൈ 0D48		൨ 0D68	
9	ഉ 0D09	ങ 0D19		ഹ 0D39			൩ 0D69	
A	ഊ 0D0A	ച 0D1A	പ 0D2A		◌ൊ 0D4A		൪ 0D6A	
B	ഋ 0D0B	ഛ 0D1B	ഫ 0D2B		◌ോ 0D4B		൫ 0D6B	
C	ഌ 0D0C	ജ 0D1C	ബ 0D2C		◌ൌ 0D4C		൬ 0D6C	
D		ഝ 0D1D	ഭ 0D2D		◌് 0D4D		൭ 0D6D	
E	എ 0D0E	ഞ 0D1E	മ 0D2E	◌ാ 0D3E			൮ 0D6E	
F	ഏ 0D0F	ട 0D1F	യ 0D2F	◌ി 0D3F			൯ 0D6F	

Based on ISCII 1988

Various signs

0D00 <reserved>
0D01 <reserved>
0D02 ◌ം MALAYALAM SIGN ANUSVARA
0D03 ◌ഃ MALAYALAM SIGN VISARGA
0D04 <reserved>

Independent vowels

0D05 അ MALAYALAM LETTER A
0D06 ആ MALAYALAM LETTER AA
0D07 ഇ MALAYALAM LETTER I
0D08 ഈ MALAYALAM LETTER II
0D09 ഉ MALAYALAM LETTER U
0D0A ഊ MALAYALAM LETTER UU
0D0B ഋ MALAYALAM LETTER VOCALIC R
0D0C ഌ MALAYALAM LETTER VOCALIC L
0D0D <reserved>
0D0E എ MALAYALAM LETTER E
0D0F ഏ MALAYALAM LETTER EE
0D10 ഐ MALAYALAM LETTER AI
0D11 <reserved>
0D12 ഒ MALAYALAM LETTER O
0D13 ഓ MALAYALAM LETTER OO
0D14 ഔ MALAYALAM LETTER AU

Consonants

0D15 ക MALAYALAM LETTER KA
0D16 ഖ MALAYALAM LETTER KHA
0D17 ഗ MALAYALAM LETTER GA
0D18 ഘ MALAYALAM LETTER GHA
0D19 ങ MALAYALAM LETTER NGA
0D1A ച MALAYALAM LETTER CA
0D1B ഛ MALAYALAM LETTER CHA
0D1C ജ MALAYALAM LETTER JA
0D1D ഝ MALAYALAM LETTER JHA
0D1E ഞ MALAYALAM LETTER NYA
0D1F ട MALAYALAM LETTER TTA
0D20 ഠ MALAYALAM LETTER TTHA
0D21 ഡ MALAYALAM LETTER DDA
0D22 ഢ MALAYALAM LETTER DDHA
0D23 ണ MALAYALAM LETTER NNA
0D24 ത MALAYALAM LETTER TA
0D25 ഥ MALAYALAM LETTER THA
0D26 ദ MALAYALAM LETTER DA
0D27 ധ MALAYALAM LETTER DHA
0D28 ന MALAYALAM LETTER NA
0D29 <reserved>
0D2A പ MALAYALAM LETTER PA
0D2B ഫ MALAYALAM LETTER PHA
0D2C ബ MALAYALAM LETTER BA
0D2D ഭ MALAYALAM LETTER BHA
0D2E മ MALAYALAM LETTER MA
0D2F യ MALAYALAM LETTER YA
0D30 ര MALAYALAM LETTER RA
0D31 റ MALAYALAM LETTER RRA
0D32 ല MALAYALAM LETTER LA
0D33 ള MALAYALAM LETTER LLA
0D34 ഴ MALAYALAM LETTER LLLA
0D35 വ MALAYALAM LETTER VA
0D36 ശ MALAYALAM LETTER SHA
0D37 ഷ MALAYALAM LETTER SSA
0D38 സ MALAYALAM LETTER SA
0D39 ഹ MALAYALAM LETTER HA
0D3A <reserved>
0D3B <reserved>
0D3C <reserved>
0D3D <reserved>

Dependent vowel signs

0D3E ◌ാ MALAYALAM VOWEL SIGN AA
0D3F ◌ി MALAYALAM VOWEL SIGN I
0D40 ◌ീ MALAYALAM VOWEL SIGN II
0D41 ◌ു MALAYALAM VOWEL SIGN U
0D42 ◌ൂ MALAYALAM VOWEL SIGN UU
0D43 ◌ൃ MALAYALAM VOWEL SIGN VOCALIC R
0D44 <reserved>
0D45 <reserved>
0D46 ◌െ MALAYALAM VOWEL SIGN E
• stands to the left of the consonant
0D47 ◌േ MALAYALAM VOWEL SIGN EE
• stands to the left of the consonant
0D48 ◌ൈ MALAYALAM VOWEL SIGN AI
• stands to the left of the consonant
0D49 <reserved>
0D4A ◌ൊ MALAYALAM VOWEL SIGN O
• pieces on both sides of the consonant
≡ 0D46 ◌െ + 0D3E ◌ാ
0D4B ◌ോ MALAYALAM VOWEL SIGN OO
• pieces on both sides of the consonant
≡ 0D47 ◌േ + 0D3E ◌ാ
0D4C ◌ൌ MALAYALAM VOWEL SIGN AU
• pieces on both sides of the consonant
≡ 0D46 ◌െ + 0D57 ◌ൗ

Various signs

0D4D ് MALAYALAM SIGN VIRAMA
= vowel half-u
0D4E <reserved>
0D4F <reserved>
0D50 <reserved>
0D51 <reserved>
0D52 <reserved>
0D53 <reserved>
0D54 <reserved>
0D55 <reserved>
0D56 <reserved>
0D57 ൗ MALAYALAM AU LENGTH MARK
0D58 <reserved>
0D59 <reserved>
0D5A <reserved>
0D5B <reserved>
0D5C <reserved>
0D5D <reserved>
0D5E <reserved>
0D5F <reserved>

Generic additions

0D60 ൠ MALAYALAM LETTER VOCALIC RR
0D61 ൡ MALAYALAM LETTER VOCALIC LL
0D62 <reserved>
0D63 <reserved>
0D64 <reserved>
0D65 <reserved>
0D66 ൦ MALAYALAM DIGIT ZERO
0D67 ൧ MALAYALAM DIGIT ONE
0D68 ൨ MALAYALAM DIGIT TWO
0D69 ൩ MALAYALAM DIGIT THREE
0D6A ൪ MALAYALAM DIGIT FOUR
0D6B ൫ MALAYALAM DIGIT FIVE
0D6C ൬ MALAYALAM DIGIT SIX
0D6D ൭ MALAYALAM DIGIT SEVEN
0D6E ൮ MALAYALAM DIGIT EIGHT
0D6F ൯ MALAYALAM DIGIT NINE

	0E0	0E1	0E2	0E3	0E4	0E5	0E6	0E7
0		ฐ 0E10	ภ 0E20	ะ 0E30	เ 0E40	๐ 0E50		
1	ก 0E01	ฑ 0E11	ม 0E21	◌ั 0E31	แ 0E41	๑ 0E51		
2	ข 0E02	ฒ 0E12	ย 0E22	า 0E32	โ 0E42	๒ 0E52		
3	ฃ 0E03	ณ 0E13	ร 0E23	ำ 0E33	ใ 0E43	๓ 0E53		
4	ค 0E04	ด 0E14	ฤ 0E24	◌ิ 0E34	ไ 0E44	๔ 0E54		
5	ฅ 0E05	ต 0E15	ล 0E25	◌ี 0E35	ๅ 0E45	๕ 0E55		
6	ฆ 0E06	ถ 0E16	ฦ 0E26	◌ึ 0E36	ๆ 0E46	๖ 0E56		
7	ง 0E07	ท 0E17	ว 0E27	◌ื 0E37	◌็ 0E47	๗ 0E57		
8	จ 0E08	ธ 0E18	ศ 0E28	◌ุ 0E38	◌่ 0E48	๘ 0E58		
9	ฉ 0E09	น 0E19	ษ 0E29	◌ู 0E39	◌้ 0E49	๙ 0E59		
A	ช 0E0A	บ 0E1A	ส 0E2A	◌ฺ 0E3A	◌๊ 0E4A	๚ 0E5A		
B	ซ 0E0B	ป 0E1B	ห 0E2B		◌๋ 0E4B	๛ 0E5B		
C	ฌ 0E0C	ผ 0E1C	ฬ 0E2C		◌์ 0E4C			
D	ญ 0E0D	ฝ 0E1D	อ 0E2D		◌ํ 0E4D			
E	ฎ 0E0E	พ 0E1E	ฮ 0E2E		◌๎ 0E4E			
F	ฏ 0E0F	ฟ 0E1F	ฯ 0E2F	฿ 0E3F	๏ 0E4F			

Based on TIS 620-2529

Consonants

0E00 ▧ <reserved>
0E01 ก THAI CHARACTER KO KAI
0E02 ข THAI CHARACTER KHO KHAI
0E03 ฃ THAI CHARACTER KHO KHUAT
0E04 ค THAI CHARACTER KHO KHWAI
0E05 ฅ THAI CHARACTER KHO KHON
0E06 ฆ THAI CHARACTER KHO RAKHANG
0E07 ง THAI CHARACTER NGO NGU
0E08 จ THAI CHARACTER CHO CHAN
0E09 ฉ THAI CHARACTER CHO CHING
0E0A ช THAI CHARACTER CHO CHANG
0E0B ซ THAI CHARACTER SO SO
0E0C ฌ THAI CHARACTER CHO CHOE
0E0D ญ THAI CHARACTER YO YING
0E0E ฎ THAI CHARACTER DO CHADA
0E0F ฏ THAI CHARACTER TO PATAK
0E10 ฐ THAI CHARACTER THO THAN
0E11 ฑ THAI CHARACTER THO NANGMONTHO
0E12 ฒ THAI CHARACTER THO PHUTHAO
0E13 ณ THAI CHARACTER NO NEN
0E14 ด THAI CHARACTER DO DEK
0E15 ต THAI CHARACTER TO TAO
0E16 ถ THAI CHARACTER THO THUNG
0E17 ท THAI CHARACTER THO THAHAN
0E18 ธ THAI CHARACTER THO THONG
0E19 น THAI CHARACTER NO NU
0E1A บ THAI CHARACTER BO BAIMAI
0E1B ป THAI CHARACTER PO PLA
0E1C ผ THAI CHARACTER PHO PHUNG
0E1D ฝ THAI CHARACTER FO FA
0E1E พ THAI CHARACTER PHO PHAN
0E1F ฟ THAI CHARACTER FO FAN
0E20 ภ THAI CHARACTER PHO SAMPHAO
0E21 ม THAI CHARACTER MO MA
0E22 ย THAI CHARACTER YO YAK
0E23 ร THAI CHARACTER RO RUA
0E24 ฤ THAI CHARACTER RU
• independent vowel letter used to write Pali
0E25 ล THAI CHARACTER LO LING
0E26 ฦ THAI CHARACTER LU
• independent vowel letter used to write Pali
0E27 ว THAI CHARACTER WO WAEN
0E28 ศ THAI CHARACTER SO SALA
0E29 ษ THAI CHARACTER SO RUSI
0E2A ส THAI CHARACTER SO SUA
0E2B ห THAI CHARACTER HO HIP
0E2C ฬ THAI CHARACTER LO CHULA
0E2D อ THAI CHARACTER O ANG
0E2E ฮ THAI CHARACTER HO NOKHUK

Sign

0E2F ฯ THAI CHARACTER PAIYANNOI
• ellipsis, abbreviation

Vowels

0E30 ะ THAI CHARACTER SARA A
0E31 ◌ั THAI CHARACTER MAI HAN-AKAT
0E32 า THAI CHARACTER SARA AA
0E33 ำ THAI CHARACTER SARA AM
≡ 0E4D ◌ํ + 0E32 า
0E34 ◌ิ THAI CHARACTER SARA I
0E35 ◌ี THAI CHARACTER SARA II
0E36 ◌ึ THAI CHARACTER SARA UE
0E37 ◌ื THAI CHARACTER SARA UEE
0E38 ◌ุ THAI CHARACTER SARA U
0E39 ◌ู THAI CHARACTER SARA UU
0E3A ◌ฺ THAI CHARACTER PHINTHU
• Pali virama
0E3B ▧ <reserved>
0E3C ▧ <reserved>
0E3D ▧ <reserved>
0E3E ▧ <reserved>

Currency symbol

0E3F ฿ THAI CURRENCY SYMBOL BAHT

Vowels

0E40 เ THAI CHARACTER SARA E
0E41 แ THAI CHARACTER SARA AE
0E42 โ THAI CHARACTER SARA O
0E43 ใ THAI CHARACTER SARA AI MAIMUAN
0E44 ไ THAI CHARACTER SARA AI MAIMALAI

Signs

0E45 ๅ THAI CHARACTER LAKKHANGYAO
0E46 ๆ THAI CHARACTER MAIYAMOK
• repetition

Vowel

0E47 ◌็ THAI CHARACTER MAITAIKHU

Tone marks

0E48 ่ THAI CHARACTER MAI EK
0E49 ้ THAI CHARACTER MAI THO
0E4A ๊ THAI CHARACTER MAI TRI
0E4B ๋ THAI CHARACTER MAI CHATTAWA

Signs

0E4C ์ THAI CHARACTER THANTHAKHAT
• cancellation mark
0E4D ํ THAI CHARACTER NIKHAHIT
• final nasal
0E4E ๎ THAI CHARACTER YAMAKKAN
0E4F ๏ THAI CHARACTER FONGMAN

Digits

0E50 ๐ THAI DIGIT ZERO
0E51 ๑ THAI DIGIT ONE
0E52 ๒ THAI DIGIT TWO
0E53 ๓ THAI DIGIT THREE
0E54 ๔ THAI DIGIT FOUR
0E55 ๕ THAI DIGIT FIVE
0E56 ๖ THAI DIGIT SIX
0E57 ๗ THAI DIGIT SEVEN
0E58 ๘ THAI DIGIT EIGHT
0E59 ๙ THAI DIGIT NINE

Signs

0E5A ๚ THAI CHARACTER ANGKHANKHU
0E5B ๛ THAI CHARACTER KHOMUT

	0E8	0E9	0EA	0EB	0EC	0ED	0EE	0EF
0				ະ 0EB0	ເ 0EC0	໐ 0ED0		
1	ກ 0E81		ມ 0EA1	◌ັ 0EB1	ແ 0EC1	໑ 0ED1		
2	ຂ 0E82		ຢ 0EA2	າ 0EB2	ໂ 0EC2	໒ 0ED2		
3			ຣ 0EA3	ຳ 0EB3	ໃ 0EC3	໓ 0ED3		
4	ຄ 0E84	ດ 0E94		◌ິ 0EB4	ໄ 0EC4	໔ 0ED4		
5		ຕ 0E95	ລ 0EA5	◌ີ 0EB5		໕ 0ED5		
6		ຖ 0E96		◌ຶ 0EB6	ໆ 0EC6	໖ 0ED6		
7	ງ 0E87	ທ 0E97	ວ 0EA7	◌ື 0EB7		໗ 0ED7		
8	ຈ 0E88			◌ຸ 0EB8	◌່ 0EC8	໘ 0ED8		
9		ນ 0E99		◌ູ 0EB9	◌້ 0EC9	໙ 0ED9		
A	ຊ 0E8A	ບ 0E9A	ສ 0EAA		◌໊ 0ECA			
B		ປ 0E9B	ຫ 0EAB	◌ົ 0EBB	◌໋ 0ECB			
C		ຜ 0E9C		◌ຼ 0EBC	◌໌ 0ECC	ໜ 0EDC		
D	ຍ 0E8D	ຝ 0E9D	ອ 0EAD	ຽ 0EBD	◌ໍ 0ECD	ໝ 0EDD		
E		ພ 0E9E	ຮ 0EAE					
F		ຟ 0E9F	ຯ 0EAF					

Based on TIS 620-2529

Consonants

0E80 <reserved>
0E81 ກ LAO LETTER KO
0E82 ຂ LAO LETTER KHO SUNG
0E83 <reserved>
0E84 ຄ LAO LETTER KHO TAM
0E85 <reserved>
0E86 <reserved>
0E87 ງ LAO LETTER NGO
0E88 ຈ LAO LETTER CO
0E89 <reserved>
0E8A ຊ LAO LETTER SO TAM
0E8B <reserved>
0E8C <reserved>
0E8D ຍ LAO LETTER NYO
0E8E <reserved>
0E8F <reserved>
0E90 <reserved>
0E91 <reserved>
0E92 <reserved>
0E93 <reserved>
0E94 ດ LAO LETTER DO
0E95 ຕ LAO LETTER TO
0E96 ຖ LAO LETTER THO SUNG
0E97 ທ LAO LETTER THO TAM
0E98 <reserved>
0E99 ນ LAO LETTER NO
0E9A ບ LAO LETTER BO
0E9B ປ LAO LETTER PO
0E9C ຜ LAO LETTER PHO SUNG
0E9D ຝ LAO LETTER FO TAM
0E9E ພ LAO LETTER PHO TAM
0E9F ຟ LAO LETTER FO SUNG
0EA0 <reserved>
0EA1 ມ LAO LETTER MO
0EA2 ຢ LAO LETTER YO
0EA3 ຣ LAO LETTER LO LING
0EA4 <reserved>
0EA5 ລ LAO LETTER LO LOOT
0EA6 <reserved>
0EA7 ວ LAO LETTER WO
0EA8 <reserved>
0EA9 <reserved>
0EAA ສ LAO LETTER SO SUNG
0EAB ຫ LAO LETTER HO SUNG
0EAC <reserved>
0EAD ອ LAO LETTER O
0EAE ຮ LAO LETTER HO TAM

Sign

0EAF ຯ LAO ELLIPSIS

Vowels

0EB0 ະ LAO VOWEL SIGN A
0EB1 ◌ັ LAO VOWEL SIGN MAI KAN
• vowel shortener
0EB2 າ LAO VOWEL SIGN AA
0EB3 ຳ LAO VOWEL SIGN AM
≡ 0ECD ◌ໍ + 0EB2 າ
0EB4 ◌ິ LAO VOWEL SIGN I
0EB5 ◌ີ LAO VOWEL SIGN II
0EB6 ◌ຶ LAO VOWEL SIGN Y
0EB7 ◌ື LAO VOWEL SIGN YY
0EB8 ◌ຸ LAO VOWEL SIGN U
0EB9 ◌ູ LAO VOWEL SIGN UU
0EBA <reserved>

Vowel

0EBB ◌ົ LAO VOWEL SIGN MAI KON

Signs

0EBC ◌ຼ LAO SEMIVOWEL SIGN LO
0EBD ຽ LAO SEMIVOWEL SIGN NYO
0EBE <reserved>
0EBF <reserved>

Vowels

0EC0 ເ LAO VOWEL SIGN E
0EC1 ແ LAO VOWEL SIGN EI
0EC2 ໂ LAO VOWEL SIGN O
0EC3 ໃ LAO VOWEL SIGN AY
0EC4 ໄ LAO VOWEL SIGN AI
0EC5 <reserved>

Sign

0EC6 ໆ LAO KO LA
• repetition
0EC7 <reserved>

Tone marks

0EC8 ◌່ LAO TONE MAI EK
0EC9 ◌້ LAO TONE MAI THO
0ECA ◌໊ LAO TONE MAI TI
0ECB ◌໋ LAO TONE MAI CATAWA

Signs

0ECC ໌ LAO CANCELLATION MARK
0ECD ໍ LAO NIGGAHITA
• final nasal
0ECE <reserved>
0ECF <reserved>

Digits

0ED0 ໐ LAO DIGIT ZERO
0ED1 ໑ LAO DIGIT ONE
0ED2 ໒ LAO DIGIT TWO
0ED3 ໓ LAO DIGIT THREE
0ED4 ໔ LAO DIGIT FOUR
0ED5 ໕ LAO DIGIT FIVE
0ED6 ໖ LAO DIGIT SIX
0ED7 ໗ LAO DIGIT SEVEN
0ED8 ໘ LAO DIGIT EIGHT
0ED9 ໙ LAO DIGIT NINE
0EDA <reserved>
0EDB <reserved>

Digraphs

0EDC ໜ LAO HO NO
≈ 0EAB ຫ + 0E99 ນ
0EDD ໝ LAO HO MO
≈ 0EAB ຫ + 0EA1 ມ

	0F0	0F1	0F2	0F3	0F4	0F5	0F6	0F7
0	ༀ 0F00	༐ 0F10	༠ 0F20	༰ 0F30	ཀ 0F40	ཐ 0F50	འ 0F60	
1	༁ 0F01	༑ 0F11	༡ 0F21	༱ 0F31	ཁ 0F41	ད 0F51	ཡ 0F61	◌ཱ 0F71
2	༂ 0F02	༒ 0F12	༢ 0F22	༲ 0F32	ག 0F42	དྷ 0F52	ར 0F62	◌ི 0F72
3	༃ 0F03	༓ 0F13	༣ 0F23	༳ 0F33	གྷ 0F43	ན 0F53	ལ 0F63	◌ཱི 0F73
4	༄ 0F04	༔ 0F14	༤ 0F24	༴ 0F34	ང 0F44	པ 0F54	ཤ 0F64	◌ུ 0F74
5	༅ 0F05	༕ 0F15	༥ 0F25	◌༵ 0F35	ཅ 0F45	ཕ 0F55	ཥ 0F65	◌ཱུ 0F75
6	༆ 0F06	༖ 0F16	༦ 0F26	༶ 0F36	ཆ 0F46	བ 0F56	ས 0F66	◌ྲྀ 0F76
7	༇ 0F07	༗ 0F17	༧ 0F27	◌༷ 0F37	ཇ 0F47	བྷ 0F57	ཧ 0F67	◌ཷ 0F77
8	༈ 0F08	◌༘ 0F18	༨ 0F28	༸ 0F38		མ 0F58	ཨ 0F68	◌ླྀ 0F78
9	༉ 0F09	◌༙ 0F19	༩ 0F29	◌༹ 0F39	ཉ 0F49	ཙ 0F59	ཀྵ 0F69	◌ཹ 0F79
A	༊ 0F0A	༚ 0F1A	༪ 0F2A	༺ 0F3A	ཊ 0F4A	ཚ 0F5A		◌ེ 0F7A
B	་ 0F0B	༛ 0F1B	༫ 0F2B	༻ 0F3B	ཋ 0F4B	ཛ 0F5B		◌ཻ 0F7B
C	༌ 0F0C	༜ 0F1C	༬ 0F2C	༼ 0F3C	ཌ 0F4C	ཛྷ 0F5C		◌ོ 0F7C
D	། 0F0D	༝ 0F1D	༭ 0F2D	༽ 0F3D	ཌྷ 0F4D	ཝ 0F5D		◌ཽ 0F7D
E	༎ 0F0E	༞ 0F1E	༮ 0F2E	◌༾ 0F3E	ཎ 0F4E	ཞ 0F5E		◌ཾ 0F7E
F	༏ 0F0F	༟ 0F1F	༯ 0F2F	◌༿ 0F3F	ཏ 0F4F	ཟ 0F5F		◌ཿ 0F7F

	0F8	0F9	0FA	0FB
0	◌ྀ 0F80	◌ྐ 0F90	◌ྠ 0FA0	
1	◌ཱྀ 0F81	◌ྑ 0F91	◌ྡ 0FA1	◌ྱ 0FB1
2	◌ྂ 0F82	◌ྒ 0F92	◌ྡྷ 0FA2	◌ྲ 0FB2
3	◌ྃ 0F83	◌ྒྷ 0F93	◌ྣ 0FA3	◌ླ 0FB3
4	◌྄ 0F84	◌ྔ 0F94	◌ྤ 0FA4	◌ྴ 0FB4
5	྅ 0F85	◌ྕ 0F95	◌ྥ 0FA5	◌ྵ 0FB5
6	◌྆ 0F86		◌ྦ 0FA6	◌ྶ 0FB6
7	◌྇ 0F87	◌ྗ 0F97	◌ྦྷ 0FA7	◌ྷ 0FB7
8	◌ྈ 0F88		◌ྨ 0FA8	
9	◌ྉ 0F89	◌ྙ 0F99	◌ྩ 0FA9	◌ྐྵ 0FB9
A	◌ྊ 0F8A	◌ྚ 0F9A	◌ྪ 0FAA	
B	◌ྋ 0F8B	◌ྛ 0F9B	◌ྫ 0FAB	
C		◌ྜ 0F9C	◌ྫྷ 0FAC	
D		◌ྜྷ 0F9D	◌ྭ 0FAD	
E		◌ྞ 0F9E		
F		◌ྟ 0F9F		

Syllables

0F00 ༀ TIBETAN SYLLABLE OM
0F01 ༁ TIBETAN MARK GTER YIG MGO TRUNCATED A
= ter yik go a thung
0F02 ༂ TIBETAN MARK GTER YIG MGO -UM RNAM BCAD MA
= ter yik go wum nam chey ma
0F03 ༃ TIBETAN MARK GTER YIG MGO -UM GTER TSHEG MA
= ter yik go wum ter tsek ma

Marks and signs

0F04 ༄ TIBETAN MARK INITIAL YIG MGO MDUN MA
= yik go dun ma
0F05 ༅ TIBETAN MARK CLOSING YIG MGO SGAB MA
= yik go kab ma
0F06 ༆ TIBETAN MARK CARET YIG MGO PHUR SHAD MA
= yik go pur shey ma
0F07 ༇ TIBETAN MARK YIG MGO TSHEG SHAD MA
= yik go tsek shey ma
0F08 ༈ TIBETAN MARK SBRUL SHAD
= drul shey
0F09 ༉ TIBETAN MARK BSKUR YIG MGO
= kur yik go
0F0A ༊ TIBETAN MARK BKA- SHOG YIG MGO
= ka sho yik go
0F0B ་ TIBETAN MARK INTERSYLLABIC TSHEG
= tsek
0F0C ༌ TIBETAN MARK DELIMITER TSHEG BSTAR
= tsek tar
0F0D ། TIBETAN MARK SHAD
= shey
0F0E ༎ TIBETAN MARK NYIS SHAD
= nyi shey
0F0F ༏ TIBETAN MARK TSHEG SHAD
= tsek shey
0F10 ༐ TIBETAN MARK NYIS TSHEG SHAD
= nyi tsek shey
0F11 ༑ TIBETAN MARK RIN CHEN SPUNGS SHAD
= rinchen pung shey
0F12 ༒ TIBETAN MARK RGYA GRAM SHAD
= gya tram shey
0F13 ༓ TIBETAN MARK CARET -DZUD RTAGS ME LONG CAN
= dzu ta me long chen
0F14 ༔ TIBETAN MARK GTER TSHEG
= ter tsek
0F15 ༕ TIBETAN LOGOTYPE SIGN CHAD RTAGS
= che ta
0F16 ༖ TIBETAN LOGOTYPE SIGN LHAG RTAGS
= hlak ta
0F17 ༗ TIBETAN ASTROLOGICAL SIGN SGRA GCAN -CHAR RTAGS
= trachen char ta
0F18 ༘ TIBETAN ASTROLOGICAL SIGN -KHYUD PA
= kyu pa
0F19 ༙ TIBETAN ASTROLOGICAL SIGN SDONG TSHUGS
= dong tsu
0F1A ༚ TIBETAN SIGN RDEL DKAR GCIG
= deka chig
0F1B ༛ TIBETAN SIGN RDEL DKAR GNYIS
= deka nyi
0F1C ༜ TIBETAN SIGN RDEL DKAR GSUM
= deka sum
0F1D ༝ TIBETAN SIGN RDEL NAG GCIG
= dena chig
0F1E ༞ TIBETAN SIGN RDEL NAG GNYIS
= dena nyi
0F1F ༟ TIBETAN SIGN RDEL DKAR RDEL NAG
= deka dena

Digits

0F20 ༠ TIBETAN DIGIT ZERO
0F21 ༡ TIBETAN DIGIT ONE
0F22 ༢ TIBETAN DIGIT TWO
0F23 ༣ TIBETAN DIGIT THREE
0F24 ༤ TIBETAN DIGIT FOUR
0F25 ༥ TIBETAN DIGIT FIVE
0F26 ༦ TIBETAN DIGIT SIX
0F27 ༧ TIBETAN DIGIT SEVEN
0F28 ༨ TIBETAN DIGIT EIGHT
0F29 ༩ TIBETAN DIGIT NINE
0F2A ༪ TIBETAN DIGIT HALF ONE
0F2B ༫ TIBETAN DIGIT HALF TWO
0F2C ༬ TIBETAN DIGIT HALF THREE
0F2D ༭ TIBETAN DIGIT HALF FOUR
0F2E ༮ TIBETAN DIGIT HALF FIVE
0F2F ༯ TIBETAN DIGIT HALF SIX
0F30 ༰ TIBETAN DIGIT HALF SEVEN
0F31 ༱ TIBETAN DIGIT HALF EIGHT
0F32 ༲ TIBETAN DIGIT HALF NINE
0F33 ༳ TIBETAN DIGIT HALF ZERO

Marks and signs

0F34 ༴ TIBETAN MARK BSDUS RTAGS
= du ta

0F35 ༵ TIBETAN MARK NGAS BZUNG NYI ZLA
= nge zung nyi da

0F36 ༶ TIBETAN MARK CARET -DZUD RTAGS BZHI MIG CAN
= dzu ta shi mig chen

0F37 ༷ TIBETAN MARK NGAS BZUNG SGOR RTAGS
= nge zung gor ta

0F38 ༸ TIBETAN MARK CHE MGO
= che go

0F39 ༹ TIBETAN MARK TSA -PHRU
= tsa tru

0F3A ༺ TIBETAN MARK GUG RTAGS GYON
= gug ta yun

0F3B ༻ TIBETAN MARK GUG RTAGS GYAS
= gug ta ye

0F3C ༼ TIBETAN MARK ANG KHANG GYON
= ang kang yun

0F3D ༽ TIBETAN MARK ANG KHANG GYAS
= ang kang ye

0F3E ༾ TIBETAN SIGN YAR TSHES
= yar tse

0F3F ༿ TIBETAN SIGN MAR TSHES
= mar tse

Consonants

0F40 ཀ TIBETAN LETTER KA

0F41 ཁ TIBETAN LETTER KHA

0F42 ག TIBETAN LETTER GA

0F43 གྷ TIBETAN LETTER GHA
≡ 0F42 ག + 0FB7 ྷ

0F44 ང TIBETAN LETTER NGA

0F45 ཅ TIBETAN LETTER CA

0F46 ཆ TIBETAN LETTER CHA

0F47 ཇ TIBETAN LETTER JA

0F48 <reserved>

0F49 ཉ TIBETAN LETTER NYA

0F4A ཊ TIBETAN LETTER TTA

0F4B ཋ TIBETAN LETTER TTHA

0F4C ཌ TIBETAN LETTER DDA

0F4D ཌྷ TIBETAN LETTER DDHA
≡ 0F4C ཌ + 0FB7 ྷ

0F4E ཎ TIBETAN LETTER NNA

0F4F ཏ TIBETAN LETTER TA

0F50 ཐ TIBETAN LETTER THA

0F51 ད TIBETAN LETTER DA

0F52 དྷ TIBETAN LETTER DHA
≡ 0F51 ད + 0FB7 ྷ

0F53 ན TIBETAN LETTER NA

0F54 པ TIBETAN LETTER PA

0F55 ཕ TIBETAN LETTER PHA

0F56 བ TIBETAN LETTER BA

0F57 བྷ TIBETAN LETTER BHA
≡ 0F56 བ + 0FB7 ྷ

0F58 མ TIBETAN LETTER MA

0F59 ཙ TIBETAN LETTER TSA

0F5A ཚ TIBETAN LETTER TSHA

0F5B ཛ TIBETAN LETTER DZA

0F5C ཛྷ TIBETAN LETTER DZHA
≡ 0F5B ཛ + 0FB7 ྷ

0F5D ཝ TIBETAN LETTER WA

0F5E ཞ TIBETAN LETTER ZHA

0F5F ཟ TIBETAN LETTER ZA

0F60 འ TIBETAN LETTER -A

0F61 ཡ TIBETAN LETTER YA

0F62 ར TIBETAN LETTER RA

0F63 ལ TIBETAN LETTER LA

0F64 ཤ TIBETAN LETTER SHA

0F65 ཥ TIBETAN LETTER SSA

0F66 ས TIBETAN LETTER SA

0F67 ཧ TIBETAN LETTER HA

0F68 ཨ TIBETAN LETTER A

0F69 ཀྵ TIBETAN LETTER KSSA
≡ 0F40 ཀ + 0FB5 ྵ

0F6A <reserved>

0F6B <reserved>

0F6C <reserved>

0F6D <reserved>

0F6E <reserved>

0F6F <reserved>

Dependent vowel signs

0F70 <reserved>

0F71 ཱ TIBETAN VOWEL SIGN AA

0F72 ི TIBETAN VOWEL SIGN I

0F73 ཱི TIBETAN VOWEL SIGN II
≡ 0F71 ཱ + 0F72 ི

0F74 ུ TIBETAN VOWEL SIGN U

0F75 ཱུ TIBETAN VOWEL SIGN UU
≡ 0F74 ུ + 0F71 ཱ

0F76 ྲྀ TIBETAN VOWEL SIGN VOCALIC R
≡ 0FB2 ྲ + 0F80 ྀ

0F77 ཷ TIBETAN VOWEL SIGN VOCALIC RR
≡ 0F76 ྲྀ + 0F71 ཱ

0F78 ླྀ TIBETAN VOWEL SIGN VOCALIC L
≡ 0FB3 ླ + 0F80 ྀ

0F79 ◌ཹ TIBETAN VOWEL SIGN VOCALIC LL
≡ 0F78 ◌ླྀ + 0F71 ◌ཱ

0F7A ◌ེ TIBETAN VOWEL SIGN E

0F7B ◌ཻ TIBETAN VOWEL SIGN EE

0F7C ◌ོ TIBETAN VOWEL SIGN O

0F7D ◌ཽ TIBETAN VOWEL SIGN OO

Various

0F7E ◌ཾ TIBETAN SIGN RJES SU NGA RO
= je su nga ro
= anusvara

0F7F ◌ཿ TIBETAN SIGN RNAM BCAD
= nam chey
= visarga

0F80 ◌ྀ TIBETAN VOWEL SIGN REVERSED I

0F81 ◌ཱྀ TIBETAN VOWEL SIGN REVERSED II
≡ 0F80 ◌ྀ + 0F71 ◌ཱ

Marks and signs

0F82 ◌ྂ TIBETAN SIGN NYI ZLA NAA DA
= nyi da na da

0F83 ◌ྃ TIBETAN SIGN SNA LDAN
= nan de

0F84 ◌྄ TIBETAN MARK HALANTA

0F85 ྅ TIBETAN MARK PALUTA

0F86 ◌྆ TIBETAN SIGN LCI RTAGS
= ji ta

0F87 ◌྇ TIBETAN SIGN YANG RTAGS
= yang ta

0F88 ྈ TIBETAN SIGN LCE TSA CAN
= che tsa chen

0F89 ྉ TIBETAN SIGN MCHU CAN
= chu chen

0F8A ྊ TIBETAN SIGN GRU CAN RGYINGS
= tru chen ging

0F8B ྋ TIBETAN SIGN GRU MED RGYINGS
= tru me ging

0F8C <reserved>

0F8D <reserved>

0F8E <reserved>

0F8F <reserved>

Subjoined consonants

0F90 ◌ྐ TIBETAN SUBJOINED LETTER KA

0F91 ◌ྑ TIBETAN SUBJOINED LETTER KHA

0F92 ◌ྒ TIBETAN SUBJOINED LETTER GA

0F93 ◌ྒྷ TIBETAN SUBJOINED LETTER GHA
≡ 0F92 ◌ྒ + 0FB7 ◌ྷ

0F94 ◌ྔ TIBETAN SUBJOINED LETTER NGA

0F95 ◌ྕ TIBETAN SUBJOINED LETTER CA

0F96 <reserved>

0F97 ◌ྗ TIBETAN SUBJOINED LETTER JA

0F98 <reserved>

0F99 ◌ྙ TIBETAN SUBJOINED LETTER NYA

0F9A ◌ྚ TIBETAN SUBJOINED LETTER TTA

0F9B ◌ྛ TIBETAN SUBJOINED LETTER TTHA

0F9C ◌ྜ TIBETAN SUBJOINED LETTER DDA

0F9D ◌ྜྷ TIBETAN SUBJOINED LETTER DDHA
≡ 0F9C ◌ྜ + 0FB7 ◌ྷ

0F9E ◌ྞ TIBETAN SUBJOINED LETTER NNA

0F9F ◌ྟ TIBETAN SUBJOINED LETTER TA

0FA0 ◌ྠ TIBETAN SUBJOINED LETTER THA

0FA1 ◌ྡ TIBETAN SUBJOINED LETTER DA

0FA2 ◌ྡྷ TIBETAN SUBJOINED LETTER DHA
≡ 0FA1 ◌ྡ + 0FB7 ◌ྷ

0FA3 ◌ྣ TIBETAN SUBJOINED LETTER NA

0FA4 ◌ྤ TIBETAN SUBJOINED LETTER PA

0FA5 ◌ྥ TIBETAN SUBJOINED LETTER PHA

0FA6 ◌ྦ TIBETAN SUBJOINED LETTER BA

0FA7 ◌ྦྷ TIBETAN SUBJOINED LETTER BHA
≡ 0FA6 ◌ྦ + 0FB7 ◌ྷ

0FA8 ◌ྨ TIBETAN SUBJOINED LETTER MA

0FA9 ◌ྩ TIBETAN SUBJOINED LETTER TSA

0FAA ◌ྪ TIBETAN SUBJOINED LETTER TSHA

0FAB ◌ྫ TIBETAN SUBJOINED LETTER DZA

0FAC ◌ྫྷ TIBETAN SUBJOINED LETTER DZHA
≡ 0FAB ◌ྫ + 0FB7 ◌ྷ

0FAD ◌ྭ TIBETAN SUBJOINED LETTER WA

0FAE <reserved>

0FAF <reserved>

0FB0 <reserved>

0FB1 ◌ྱ TIBETAN SUBJOINED LETTER YA

0FB2 ◌ྲ TIBETAN SUBJOINED LETTER RA

0FB3 ◌ླ TIBETAN SUBJOINED LETTER LA

0FB4 ◌ྴ TIBETAN SUBJOINED LETTER SHA

0FB5 ◌ྵ TIBETAN SUBJOINED LETTER SSA

0FB6 ◌ྶ TIBETAN SUBJOINED LETTER SA

0FB7 ◌ྷ TIBETAN SUBJOINED LETTER HA

0FB8 <reserved>

0FB9 ◌ྐྵ TIBETAN SUBJOINED LETTER KSSA
≡ 0F90 ◌ྐ + 0FB5 ◌ྵ

	10A	10B	10C	10D	10E	10F
0	Ⴀ 10A0	Ⴐ 10B0	Ⴠ 10C0	ა 10D0	რ 10E0	ჰ 10F0
1	Ⴁ 10A1	Ⴑ 10B1	Ⴡ 10C1	ბ 10D1	ს 10E1	ჱ 10F1
2	Ⴂ 10A2	Ⴒ 10B2	Ⴢ 10C2	გ 10D2	ტ 10E2	ჲ 10F2
3	Ⴃ 10A3	Ⴓ 10B3	Ⴣ 10C3	დ 10D3	უ 10E3	ჳ 10F3
4	Ⴄ 10A4	Ⴔ 10B4	Ⴤ 10C4	ე 10D4	ფ 10E4	ჴ 10F4
5	Ⴅ 10A5	Ⴕ 10B5	Ⴥ 10C5	ვ 10D5	ქ 10E5	ჵ 10F5
6	Ⴆ 10A6	Ⴖ 10B6		ზ 10D6	ღ 10E6	ჶ 10F6
7	Ⴇ 10A7	Ⴗ 10B7		თ 10D7	ყ 10E7	
8	Ⴈ 10A8	Ⴘ 10B8		ი 10D8	შ 10E8	
9	Ⴉ 10A9	Ⴙ 10B9		კ 10D9	ჩ 10E9	
A	Ⴊ 10AA	Ⴚ 10BA		ლ 10DA	ც 10EA	
B	Ⴋ 10AB	Ⴛ 10BB		მ 10DB	ძ 10EB	჻ 10FB
C	Ⴌ 10AC	Ⴜ 10BC		ნ 10DC	წ 10EC	
D	Ⴍ 10AD	Ⴝ 10BD		ო 10DD	ჭ 10ED	
E	Ⴎ 10AE	Ⴞ 10BE		პ 10DE	ხ 10EE	
F	Ⴏ 10AF	Ⴟ 10BF		ჟ 10DF	ჯ 10EF	

Archaic uppercase alphabet (Khutsuri)

10A0	Ⴀ	GEORGIAN CAPITAL LETTER AN
10A1	Ⴁ	GEORGIAN CAPITAL LETTER BAN
10A2	Ⴂ	GEORGIAN CAPITAL LETTER GAN
10A3	Ⴃ	GEORGIAN CAPITAL LETTER DON
10A4	Ⴄ	GEORGIAN CAPITAL LETTER EN
10A5	Ⴅ	GEORGIAN CAPITAL LETTER VIN
10A6	Ⴆ	GEORGIAN CAPITAL LETTER ZEN
10A7	Ⴇ	GEORGIAN CAPITAL LETTER TAN
10A8	Ⴈ	GEORGIAN CAPITAL LETTER IN
10A9	Ⴉ	GEORGIAN CAPITAL LETTER KAN
10AA	Ⴊ	GEORGIAN CAPITAL LETTER LAS
10AB	Ⴋ	GEORGIAN CAPITAL LETTER MAN
10AC	Ⴌ	GEORGIAN CAPITAL LETTER NAR
10AD	Ⴍ	GEORGIAN CAPITAL LETTER ON
10AE	Ⴎ	GEORGIAN CAPITAL LETTER PAR
10AF	Ⴏ	GEORGIAN CAPITAL LETTER ZHAR
10B0	Ⴐ	GEORGIAN CAPITAL LETTER RAE
10B1	Ⴑ	GEORGIAN CAPITAL LETTER SAN
10B2	Ⴒ	GEORGIAN CAPITAL LETTER TAR
10B3	Ⴓ	GEORGIAN CAPITAL LETTER UN
10B4	Ⴔ	GEORGIAN CAPITAL LETTER PHAR
10B5	Ⴕ	GEORGIAN CAPITAL LETTER KHAR
10B6	Ⴖ	GEORGIAN CAPITAL LETTER GHAN
10B7	Ⴗ	GEORGIAN CAPITAL LETTER QAR
10B8	Ⴘ	GEORGIAN CAPITAL LETTER SHIN
10B9	Ⴙ	GEORGIAN CAPITAL LETTER CHIN
10BA	Ⴚ	GEORGIAN CAPITAL LETTER CAN
10BB	Ⴛ	GEORGIAN CAPITAL LETTER JIL
10BC	Ⴜ	GEORGIAN CAPITAL LETTER CIL
10BD	Ⴝ	GEORGIAN CAPITAL LETTER CHAR
10BE	Ⴞ	GEORGIAN CAPITAL LETTER XAN
10BF	Ⴟ	GEORGIAN CAPITAL LETTER JHAN
10C0	Ⴠ	GEORGIAN CAPITAL LETTER HAE
10C1	Ⴡ	GEORGIAN CAPITAL LETTER HE
10C2	Ⴢ	GEORGIAN CAPITAL LETTER HIE
10C3	Ⴣ	GEORGIAN CAPITAL LETTER WE
10C4	Ⴤ	GEORGIAN CAPITAL LETTER HAR
10C5	Ⴥ	GEORGIAN CAPITAL LETTER HOE
10C6		<reserved>
10C7		<reserved>
10C8		<reserved>
10C9		<reserved>
10CA		<reserved>
10CB		<reserved>
10CC		<reserved>
10CD		<reserved>
10CE		<reserved>
10CF		<reserved>

Modern alphabet (Mkhedruli)

= Archaic lowercase alphabet

10D0	ა	GEORGIAN LETTER AN
10D1	ბ	GEORGIAN LETTER BAN
10D2	გ	GEORGIAN LETTER GAN
10D3	დ	GEORGIAN LETTER DON
10D4	ე	GEORGIAN LETTER EN
10D5	ვ	GEORGIAN LETTER VIN
10D6	ზ	GEORGIAN LETTER ZEN
10D7	თ	GEORGIAN LETTER TAN
10D8	ი	GEORGIAN LETTER IN
10D9	კ	GEORGIAN LETTER KAN
10DA	ლ	GEORGIAN LETTER LAS
10DB	მ	GEORGIAN LETTER MAN
10DC	ნ	GEORGIAN LETTER NAR
10DD	ო	GEORGIAN LETTER ON
10DE	პ	GEORGIAN LETTER PAR
10DF	ჟ	GEORGIAN LETTER ZHAR
10E0	რ	GEORGIAN LETTER RAE
10E1	ს	GEORGIAN LETTER SAN
10E2	ტ	GEORGIAN LETTER TAR
10E3	უ	GEORGIAN LETTER UN
10E4	ფ	GEORGIAN LETTER PHAR
10E5	ქ	GEORGIAN LETTER KHAR
10E6	ღ	GEORGIAN LETTER GHAN
10E7	ყ	GEORGIAN LETTER QAR
10E8	შ	GEORGIAN LETTER SHIN
10E9	ჩ	GEORGIAN LETTER CHIN
10EA	ც	GEORGIAN LETTER CAN
10EB	ძ	GEORGIAN LETTER JIL
10EC	წ	GEORGIAN LETTER CIL
10ED	ჭ	GEORGIAN LETTER CHAR
10EE	ხ	GEORGIAN LETTER XAN
10EF	ჯ	GEORGIAN LETTER JHAN
10F0	ჰ	GEORGIAN LETTER HAE

Archaic letters

10F1	ჱ	GEORGIAN LETTER HE
10F2	ჲ	GEORGIAN LETTER HIE
10F3	ჳ	GEORGIAN LETTER WE
10F4	ჴ	GEORGIAN LETTER HAR
10F5	ჵ	GEORGIAN LETTER HOE
10F6	ჶ	GEORGIAN LETTER FI
10F7		<reserved>
10F8		<reserved>
10F9		<reserved>

10FA ▧ <reserved>

Punctuation

10FB ჻ GEORGIAN PARAGRAPH SEPARATOR

	110	111	112	113	114	115	116	117
0	ᄀ 1100	ᄐ 1110	ᄠ 1120	ᄰ 1130	ᅀ 1140	ᅐ 1150	HJF 1160	ᅰ 1170
1	ᄁ 1101	ᄑ 1111	ᄡ 1121	ᄱ 1131	ᅁ 1141	ᅑ 1151	ᅡ 1161	ᅱ 1171
2	ᄂ 1102	ᄒ 1112	ᄢ 1122	ᄲ 1132	ᅂ 1142	ᅒ 1152	ᅢ 1162	ᅲ 1172
3	ᄃ 1103	ᄓ 1113	ᄣ 1123	ᄳ 1133	ᅃ 1143	ᅓ 1153	ᅣ 1163	ᅳ 1173
4	ᄄ 1104	ᄔ 1114	ᄤ 1124	ᄴ 1134	ᅄ 1144	ᅔ 1154	ᅤ 1164	ᅴ 1174
5	ᄅ 1105	ᄕ 1115	ᄥ 1125	ᄵ 1135	ᅅ 1145	ᅕ 1155	ᅥ 1165	ᅵ 1175
6	ᄆ 1106	ᄖ 1116	ᄦ 1126	ᄶ 1136	ᅆ 1146	ᅖ 1156	ᅦ 1166	ᅶ 1176
7	ᄇ 1107	ᄗ 1117	ᄧ 1127	ᄷ 1137	ᅇ 1147	ᅗ 1157	ᅧ 1167	ᅷ 1177
8	ᄈ 1108	ᄘ 1118	ᄨ 1128	ᄸ 1138	ᅈ 1148	ᅘ 1158	ᅨ 1168	ᅸ 1178
9	ᄉ 1109	ᄙ 1119	ᄩ 1129	ᄹ 1139	ᅉ 1149	ᅙ 1159	ᅩ 1169	ᅹ 1179
A	ᄊ 110A	ᄚ 111A	ᄪ 112A	ᄺ 113A	ᅊ 114A		ᅪ 116A	ᅺ 117A
B	ᄋ 110B	ᄛ 111B	ᄫ 112B	ᄻ 113B	ᅋ 114B		ᅫ 116B	ᅻ 117B
C	ᄌ 110C	ᄜ 111C	ᄬ 112C	ᄼ 113C	ᅌ 114C		ᅬ 116C	ᅼ 117C
D	ᄍ 110D	ᄝ 111D	ᄭ 112D	ᄽ 113D	ᅍ 114D		ᅭ 116D	ᅽ 117D
E	ᄎ 110E	ᄞ 111E	ᄮ 112E	ᄾ 113E	ᅎ 114E		ᅮ 116E	ᅾ 117E
F	ᄏ 110F	ᄟ 111F	ᄯ 112F	ᄿ 113F	ᅏ 114F	HCF 115F	ᅯ 116F	ᅿ 117F

	118	119	11A	11B	11C	11D	11E	11F
0	ᆀ 1180	ᆐ 1190	ᆠ 11A0	ᆰ 11B0	ᇀ 11C0	ᇐ 11D0	ᇠ 11E0	ᇰ 11F0
1	ᆁ 1181	ᆑ 1191	ᆡ 11A1	ᆱ 11B1	ᇁ 11C1	ᇑ 11D1	ᇡ 11E1	ᇱ 11F1
2	ᆂ 1182	ᆒ 1192	ᆢ 11A2	ᆲ 11B2	ᇂ 11C2	ᇒ 11D2	ᇢ 11E2	ᇲ 11F2
3	ᆃ 1183	ᆓ 1193		ᆳ 11B3	ᇃ 11C3	ᇓ 11D3	ᇣ 11E3	ᇳ 11F3
4	ᆄ 1184	ᆔ 1194		ᆴ 11B4	ᇄ 11C4	ᇔ 11D4	ᇤ 11E4	ᇴ 11F4
5	ᆅ 1185	ᆕ 1195		ᆵ 11B5	ᇅ 11C5	ᇕ 11D5	ᇥ 11E5	ᇵ 11F5
6	ᆆ 1186	ᆖ 1196		ᆶ 11B6	ᇆ 11C6	ᇖ 11D6	ᇦ 11E6	ᇶ 11F6
7	ᆇ 1187	ᆗ 1197		ᆷ 11B7	ᇇ 11C7	ᇗ 11D7	ᇧ 11E7 •	ᇷ 11F7
8	ᆈ 1188	ᆘ 1198	ᆨ 11A8	ᆸ 11B8	ᇈ 11C8	ᇘ 11D8	ᇨ 11E8	ᇸ 11F8
9	ᆉ 1189	ᆙ 1199	ᆩ 11A9	ᆹ 11B9	ᇉ 11C9	ᇙ 11D9	ᇩ 11E9	ᇹ 11F9
A	ᆊ 118A	ᆚ 119A	ᆪ 11AA	ᆺ 11BA	ᇊ 11CA	ᇚ 11DA	ᇪ 11EA	
B	ᆋ 118B	ᆛ 119B	ᆫ 11AB	ᆻ 11BB	ᇋ 11CB	ᇛ 11DB	ᇫ 11EB	
C	ᆌ 118C	ᆜ 119C	ᆬ 11AC	ᆼ 11BC	ᇌ 11CC	ᇜ 11DC	ᇬ 11EC	
D	ᆍ 118D	ᆝ 119D	ᆭ 11AD	ᆽ 11BD	ᇍ 11CD	ᇝ 11DD	ᇭ 11ED	
E	ᆎ 118E	ᆞ 119E	ᆮ 11AE	ᆾ 11BE	ᇎ 11CE	ᇞ 11DE	ᇮ 11EE	
F	ᆏ 118F	ᆟ 119F	ᆯ 11AF	ᆿ 11BF	ᇏ 11CF	ᇟ 11DF	ᇯ 11EF	

Korean combining alphabet

Initial consonants

1100 ᄀ HANGUL CHOSEONG KIYEOK
1101 ᄁ HANGUL CHOSEONG SSANGKIYEOK
≈ 1100 ᄀ + 1100 ᄀ
1102 ᄂ HANGUL CHOSEONG NIEUN
1103 ᄃ HANGUL CHOSEONG TIKEUT
1104 ᄄ HANGUL CHOSEONG SSANGTIKEUT
≈ 1103 ᄃ + 1103 ᄃ
1105 ᄅ HANGUL CHOSEONG RIEUL
1106 ᄆ HANGUL CHOSEONG MIEUM
1107 ᄇ HANGUL CHOSEONG PIEUP
1108 ᄈ HANGUL CHOSEONG SSANGPIEUP
≈ 1107 ᄇ + 1107 ᄇ
1109 ᄉ HANGUL CHOSEONG SIOS
110A ᄊ HANGUL CHOSEONG SSANGSIOS
≈ 1109 ᄉ + 1109 ᄉ
110B ᄋ HANGUL CHOSEONG IEUNG
110C ᄌ HANGUL CHOSEONG CIEUC
110D ᄍ HANGUL CHOSEONG SSANGCIEUC
≈ 110C ᄌ + 110C ᄌ
110E ᄎ HANGUL CHOSEONG CHIEUCH
110F ᄏ HANGUL CHOSEONG KHIEUKH
1110 ᄐ HANGUL CHOSEONG THIEUTH
1111 ᄑ HANGUL CHOSEONG PHIEUPH
1112 ᄒ HANGUL CHOSEONG HIEUH
1113 ᄓ HANGUL CHOSEONG NIEUN-KIYEOK
≈ 1102 ᄂ + 1100 ᄀ
1114 ᄔ HANGUL CHOSEONG SSANGNIEUN
≈ 1102 ᄂ + 1102 ᄂ
1115 ᄕ HANGUL CHOSEONG NIEUN-TIKEUT
≈ 1102 ᄂ + 1103 ᄃ
1116 ᄖ HANGUL CHOSEONG NIEUN-PIEUP
≈ 1102 ᄂ + 1107 ᄇ
1117 ᄗ HANGUL CHOSEONG TIKEUT-KIYEOK
≈ 1103 ᄃ + 1100 ᄀ
1118 ᄘ HANGUL CHOSEONG RIEUL-NIEUN
≈ 1105 ᄅ + 1102 ᄂ
1119 ᄙ HANGUL CHOSEONG SSANGRIEUL
≈ 1105 ᄅ + 1105 ᄅ
111A ᄚ HANGUL CHOSEONG RIEUL-HIEUH
≈ 1105 ᄅ + 1112 ᄒ
111B ᄛ HANGUL CHOSEONG KAPYEOUNRIEUL
≈ 1105 ᄅ + 110B ᄋ
111C ᄜ HANGUL CHOSEONG MIEUM-PIEUP
≈ 1106 ᄆ + 1107 ᄇ
111D ᄝ HANGUL CHOSEONG KAPYEOUNMIEUM
≈ 1106 ᄆ + 110B ᄋ
111E ᄞ HANGUL CHOSEONG PIEUP-KIYEOK
≈ 1107 ᄇ + 1100 ᄀ
111F ᄟ HANGUL CHOSEONG PIEUP-NIEUN
≈ 1107 ᄇ + 1102 ᄂ
1120 ᄠ HANGUL CHOSEONG PIEUP-TIKEUT
≈ 1107 ᄇ + 1103 ᄃ
1121 ᄡ HANGUL CHOSEONG PIEUP-SIOS
≈ 1107 ᄇ + 1109 ᄉ
1122 ᄢ HANGUL CHOSEONG PIEUP-SIOS-KIYEOK
≈ 1107 ᄇ + 1109 ᄉ + 1100 ᄀ
1123 ᄣ HANGUL CHOSEONG PIEUP-SIOS-TIKEUT
≈ 1107 ᄇ + 1109 ᄉ + 1103 ᄃ
1124 ᄤ HANGUL CHOSEONG PIEUP-SIOS-PIEUP
≈ 1107 ᄇ + 1109 ᄉ + 1107 ᄇ
1125 ᄥ HANGUL CHOSEONG PIEUP-SSANGSIOS
≈ 1107 ᄇ + 1109 ᄉ + 1109 ᄉ
1126 ᄦ HANGUL CHOSEONG PIEUP-SIOS-CIEUC
≈ 1107 ᄇ + 1109 ᄉ + 110C ᄌ
1127 ᄧ HANGUL CHOSEONG PIEUP-CIEUC
≈ 1107 ᄇ + 110C ᄌ
1128 ᄨ HANGUL CHOSEONG PIEUP-CHIEUCH
≈ 1107 ᄇ + 110E ᄎ
1129 ᄩ HANGUL CHOSEONG PIEUP-THIEUTH
≈ 1107 ᄇ + 1110 ᄐ
112A ᄪ HANGUL CHOSEONG PIEUP-PHIEUPH
≈ 1107 ᄇ + 1111 ᄑ
112B ᄫ HANGUL CHOSEONG KAPYEOUNPIEUP
≈ 1107 ᄇ + 110B ᄋ
112C ᄬ HANGUL CHOSEONG KAPYEOUNSSANGPIEUP
≈ 1107 ᄇ + 1107 ᄇ + 110B ᄋ
112D ᄭ HANGUL CHOSEONG SIOS-KIYEOK
≈ 1109 ᄉ + 1100 ᄀ
112E ᄮ HANGUL CHOSEONG SIOS-NIEUN
≈ 1109 ᄉ + 1102 ᄂ
112F ᄯ HANGUL CHOSEONG SIOS-TIKEUT
≈ 1109 ᄉ + 1103 ᄃ

1130 ᄰ HANGUL CHOSEONG SIOS-RIEUL
≈ 1109 ᄉ + 1105 ᄅ
1131 ᄱ HANGUL CHOSEONG SIOS-MIEUM
≈ 1109 ᄉ + 1106 ᄆ
1132 ᄲ HANGUL CHOSEONG SIOS-PIEUP
≈ 1109 ᄉ + 1107 ᄇ
1133 ᄳ HANGUL CHOSEONG SIOS-PIEUP-KIYEOK
≈ 1109 ᄉ + 1107 ᄇ + 1100 ᄀ
1134 ᄴ HANGUL CHOSEONG SIOS-SSANGSIOS
≈ 1109 ᄉ + 1109 ᄉ + 1109 ᄉ
1135 ᄵ HANGUL CHOSEONG SIOS-IEUNG
≈ 1109 ᄉ + 110B ᄋ
1136 ᄶ HANGUL CHOSEONG SIOS-CIEUC
≈ 1109 ᄉ + 110C ᄌ
1137 ᄷ HANGUL CHOSEONG SIOS-CHIEUCH
≈ 1109 ᄉ + 110E ᄎ
1138 ᄸ HANGUL CHOSEONG SIOS-KHIEUKH
≈ 1109 ᄉ + 110F ᄏ
1139 ᄹ HANGUL CHOSEONG SIOS-THIEUTH
≈ 1109 ᄉ + 1110 ᄐ
113A ᄺ HANGUL CHOSEONG SIOS-PHIEUPH
≈ 1109 ᄉ + 1111 ᄑ
113B ᄻ HANGUL CHOSEONG SIOS-HIEUH
≈ 1109 ᄉ + 1112 ᄒ
113C ᄼ HANGUL CHOSEONG CHITUEUMSIOS
113D ᄽ HANGUL CHOSEONG CHITUEUMSSANGSIOS
≈ 113C ᄼ + 113C ᄼ
113E ᄾ HANGUL CHOSEONG CEONGCHIEUMSIOS
113F ᄿ HANGUL CHOSEONG CEONGCHIEUMSSANGSIOS
≈ 113E ᄾ + 113E ᄾ
1140 ᅀ HANGUL CHOSEONG PANSIOS
1141 ᅁ HANGUL CHOSEONG IEUNG-KIYEOK
≈ 110B ᄋ + 1100 ᄀ
1142 ᅂ HANGUL CHOSEONG IEUNG-TIKEUT
≈ 110B ᄋ + 1103 ᄃ
1143 ᅃ HANGUL CHOSEONG IEUNG-MIEUM
≈ 110B ᄋ + 1106 ᄆ
1144 ᅄ HANGUL CHOSEONG IEUNG-PIEUP
≈ 110B ᄋ + 1107 ᄇ
1145 ᅅ HANGUL CHOSEONG IEUNG-SIOS
≈ 110B ᄋ + 1109 ᄉ
1146 ᅆ HANGUL CHOSEONG IEUNG-PANSIOS
≈ 110B ᄋ + 1140 ᅀ
1147 ᅇ HANGUL CHOSEONG SSANGIEUNG
≈ 110B ᄋ + 110B ᄋ
1148 ᅈ HANGUL CHOSEONG IEUNG-CIEUC
≈ 110B ᄋ + 110C ᄌ
1149 ᅉ HANGUL CHOSEONG IEUNG-CHIEUCH
≈ 110B ᄋ + 110E ᄎ
114A ᅊ HANGUL CHOSEONG IEUNG-THIEUTH
≈ 110B ᄋ + 1110 ᄐ
114B ᅋ HANGUL CHOSEONG IEUNG-PHIEUPH
≈ 110B ᄋ + 1111 ᄑ
114C ᅌ HANGUL CHOSEONG YESIEUNG
114D ᅍ HANGUL CHOSEONG CIEUC-IEUNG
≈ 110C ᄌ + 110B ᄋ
114E ᅎ HANGUL CHOSEONG CHITUEUMCIEUC
114F ᅏ HANGUL CHOSEONG CHITUEUMSSANGCIEUC
≈ 114E ᅎ + 114E ᅎ
1150 ᅐ HANGUL CHOSEONG CEONGCHIEUMCIEUC
1151 ᅑ HANGUL CHOSEONG CEONGCHIEUMSSANGCIEUC
≈ 1150 ᅐ + 1150 ᅐ
1152 ᅒ HANGUL CHOSEONG CHIEUCH-KHIEUKH
≈ 110E ᄎ + 110F ᄏ
1153 ᅓ HANGUL CHOSEONG CHIEUCH-HIEUH
≈ 110E ᄎ + 1112 ᄒ
1154 ᅔ HANGUL CHOSEONG CHITUEUMCHIEUCH
1155 ᅕ HANGUL CHOSEONG CEONGCHIEUMCHIEUCH
1156 ᅖ HANGUL CHOSEONG PHIEUPH-PIEUP
≈ 1111 ᄑ + 1107 ᄇ
1157 ᅗ HANGUL CHOSEONG KAPYEOUNPHIEUPH
≈ 1111 ᄑ + 110B ᄋ
1158 ᅘ HANGUL CHOSEONG SSANGHIEUH
≈ 1112 ᄒ + 1112 ᄒ
1159 ᅙ HANGUL CHOSEONG YEORINHIEUH
115A <reserved>
115B <reserved>
115C <reserved>

115D <reserved>

115E <reserved>

115F HANGUL CHOSEONG FILLER

Medial vowels

1160 HANGUL JUNGSEONG FILLER

1161 ᅡ HANGUL JUNGSEONG A

1162 ᅢ HANGUL JUNGSEONG AE
≈ 1161 ᅡ + 1175 ᅵ

1163 ᅣ HANGUL JUNGSEONG YA

1164 ᅤ HANGUL JUNGSEONG YAE
≈ 1163 ᅣ + 1175 ᅵ

1165 ᅥ HANGUL JUNGSEONG EO

1166 ᅦ HANGUL JUNGSEONG E
≈ 1165 ᅥ + 1175 ᅵ

1167 ᅧ HANGUL JUNGSEONG YEO

1168 ᅨ HANGUL JUNGSEONG YE
≈ 1167 ᅧ + 1175 ᅵ

1169 ᅩ HANGUL JUNGSEONG O

116A ᅪ HANGUL JUNGSEONG WA
≈ 1169 ᅩ + 1161 ᅡ

116B ᅫ HANGUL JUNGSEONG WAE
≈ 1169 ᅩ + 1161 ᅡ + 1175 ᅵ

116C ᅬ HANGUL JUNGSEONG OE
≈ 1169 ᅩ + 1175 ᅵ

116D ᅭ HANGUL JUNGSEONG YO

116E ᅮ HANGUL JUNGSEONG U

116F ᅯ HANGUL JUNGSEONG WEO
≈ 116E ᅮ + 1165 ᅥ

1170 ᅰ HANGUL JUNGSEONG WE
≈ 116E ᅮ + 1165 ᅥ + 1175 ᅵ

1171 ᅱ HANGUL JUNGSEONG WI
≈ 116E ᅮ + 1175 ᅵ

1172 ᅲ HANGUL JUNGSEONG YU

1173 ᅳ HANGUL JUNGSEONG EU

1174 ᅴ HANGUL JUNGSEONG YI
≈ 1173 ᅳ + 1175 ᅵ

1175 ᅵ HANGUL JUNGSEONG I

1176 ᅶ HANGUL JUNGSEONG A-O
≈ 1161 ᅡ + 1169 ᅩ

1177 ᅷ HANGUL JUNGSEONG A-U
≈ 1161 ᅡ + 116E ᅮ

1178 ᅸ HANGUL JUNGSEONG YA-O
≈ 1163 ᅣ + 1169 ᅩ

1179 ᅹ HANGUL JUNGSEONG YA-YO
≈ 1163 ᅣ + 116D ᅭ

117A ᅺ HANGUL JUNGSEONG EO-O
≈ 1165 ᅥ + 1169 ᅩ

117B ᅻ HANGUL JUNGSEONG EO-U
≈ 1165 ᅥ + 116E ᅮ

117C ᅼ HANGUL JUNGSEONG EO-EU
≈ 1165 ᅥ + 1173 ᅳ

117D ᅽ HANGUL JUNGSEONG YEO-O
≈ 1167 ᅧ + 1169 ᅩ

117E ᅾ HANGUL JUNGSEONG YEO-U
≈ 1167 ᅧ + 116E ᅮ

117F ᅿ HANGUL JUNGSEONG O-EO
≈ 1169 ᅩ + 1165 ᅥ

1180 ᆀ HANGUL JUNGSEONG O-E
≈ 1169 ᅩ + 1166 ᅦ

1181 ᆁ HANGUL JUNGSEONG O-YE
≈ 1169 ᅩ + 1168 ᅨ

1182 ᆂ HANGUL JUNGSEONG O-O
≈ 1169 ᅩ + 1169 ᅩ

1183 ᆃ HANGUL JUNGSEONG O-U
≈ 1169 ᅩ + 116E ᅮ

1184 ᆄ HANGUL JUNGSEONG YO-YA
≈ 116D ᅭ + 1163 ᅣ

1185 ᆅ HANGUL JUNGSEONG YO-YAE
≈ 116D ᅭ + 1164 ᅤ

1186 ᆆ HANGUL JUNGSEONG YO-YEO
≈ 116D ᅭ + 1167 ᅧ

1187 ᆇ HANGUL JUNGSEONG YO-O
≈ 116D ᅭ + 1169 ᅩ

1188 ᆈ HANGUL JUNGSEONG YO-I
≈ 116D ᅭ + 1175 ᅵ

1189 ᆉ HANGUL JUNGSEONG U-A
≈ 116E ᅮ + 1161 ᅡ

118A ᆊ HANGUL JUNGSEONG U-AE
≈ 116E ᅮ + 1162 ᅢ

118B ᆋ HANGUL JUNGSEONG U-EO-EU
≈ 116E ᅮ + 1165 ᅥ + 1173 ᅳ

118C ᆌ HANGUL JUNGSEONG U-YE
≈ 116E ᅮ + 1168 ᅨ

118D ᆍ HANGUL JUNGSEONG U-U
≈ 116E ᅮ + 116E ᅮ

118E ᆎ HANGUL JUNGSEONG YU-A
≈ 1172 ᅲ + 1161 ᅡ

118F ᆏ HANGUL JUNGSEONG YU-EO
≈ 1172 ᅲ + 1165 ᅥ

1190 ᆐ HANGUL JUNGSEONG YU-E
≈ 1172 ᅲ + 1166 ᅦ

1191 ᆑ HANGUL JUNGSEONG YU-YEO
≈ 1172 ᅲ + 1167 ᅧ

1192 ᆒ HANGUL JUNGSEONG YU-YE
≈ 1172 ᅲ + 1168 ᅨ

1193 ᆓ HANGUL JUNGSEONG YU-U
≈ 1172 ᅲ + 116E ᅮ

1194 ᆔ HANGUL JUNGSEONG YU-I
≈ 1172 ᅲ + 1175 ᅵ

1195 ᆕ HANGUL JUNGSEONG EU-U
≈ 1173 ᅳ + 116E ᅮ

1196 ᆖ HANGUL JUNGSEONG EU-EU
≈ 1173 ᅳ + 1173 ᅳ

1197 ᆗ HANGUL JUNGSEONG YI-U
≈ 1174 ᅴ + 116E ᅮ

1198 ᆘ HANGUL JUNGSEONG I-A
≈ 1175 ᅵ + 1161 ᅡ

1199 ᆙ HANGUL JUNGSEONG I-YA
≈ 1175 ᅵ + 1163 ᅣ

119A ᆚ HANGUL JUNGSEONG I-O
≈ 1175 ᅵ + 1169 ᅩ

119B ᆛ HANGUL JUNGSEONG I-U
≈ 1175 ᅵ + 116E ᅮ

119C ᆜ HANGUL JUNGSEONG I-EU
≈ 1175 ᅵ + 1173 ᅳ

119D ᆝ HANGUL JUNGSEONG I-ARAEA
≈ 1175 ᅵ + 119E ᆞ

119E ᆞ HANGUL JUNGSEONG ARAEA

119F ᆟ HANGUL JUNGSEONG ARAEA-EO
≈ 119E ᆞ + 1165 ᅥ

11A0 ᆠ HANGUL JUNGSEONG ARAEA-U
≈ 119E ᆞ + 116E ᅮ

11A1 ᆡ HANGUL JUNGSEONG ARAEA-I
≈ 119E ᆞ + 1175 ᅵ

11A2 ᆢ HANGUL JUNGSEONG SSANGARAEA
≈ 119E ᆞ + 119E ᆞ

11A3 <reserved>

11A4 <reserved>

11A5 <reserved>

11A6 <reserved>

11A7 <reserved>

Final consonants

11A8 ᆨ HANGUL JONGSEONG KIYEOK

11A9 ᆩ HANGUL JONGSEONG SSANGKIYEOK
≈ 11A8 ᆨ + 11A8 ᆨ

11AA ᆪ HANGUL JONGSEONG KIYEOK-SIOS
≈ 11A8 ᆨ + 11BA ᆺ

11AB ᆫ HANGUL JONGSEONG NIEUN

11AC ᆬ HANGUL JONGSEONG NIEUN-CIEUC
≈ 11AB ᆫ + 11BD ᆽ

11AD ᆭ HANGUL JONGSEONG NIEUN-HIEUH
≈ 11AB ᆫ + 11C2 ᇂ

11AE ᆮ HANGUL JONGSEONG TIKEUT

11AF ᆯ HANGUL JONGSEONG RIEUL

11B0 ᆰ HANGUL JONGSEONG RIEUL-KIYEOK
≈ 11AF ᆯ + 11A8 ᆨ

11B1 ᆱ HANGUL JONGSEONG RIEUL-MIEUM
≈ 11AF ᆯ + 11B7 ᆷ

11B2 ᆲ HANGUL JONGSEONG RIEUL-PIEUP
≈ 11AF ᆯ + 11B8 ᆸ

11B3 ᆳ HANGUL JONGSEONG RIEUL-SIOS
≈ 11AF ᆯ + 11BA ᆺ

11B4 ᆴ HANGUL JONGSEONG RIEUL-THIEUTH
≈ 11AF ᆯ + 11C0 ᇀ

11B5 ᆵ HANGUL JONGSEONG RIEUL-PHIEUPH
≈ 11AF ᆯ + 11C1 ᇁ

11B6 ᆶ HANGUL JONGSEONG RIEUL-HIEUH
≈ 11AF ᆯ + 11C2 ᇂ

11B7 ᆷ HANGUL JONGSEONG MIEUM

11B8 ᆸ HANGUL JONGSEONG PIEUP

11B9 ᆹ HANGUL JONGSEONG PIEUP-SIOS
≈ 11B8 ᆸ + 11BA ᆺ

11BA ᆺ HANGUL JONGSEONG SIOS

11BB ᆻ HANGUL JONGSEONG SSANGSIOS
≈ 11BA ᆺ + 11BA ᆺ

11BC ᆼ HANGUL JONGSEONG IEUNG

11BD ᆽ HANGUL JONGSEONG CIEUC

11BE ᆾ HANGUL JONGSEONG CHIEUCH

11BF ᆿ HANGUL JONGSEONG KHIEUKH

11C0 ᇀ HANGUL JONGSEONG THIEUTH

11C1 ᇁ HANGUL JONGSEONG PHIEUPH

11C2 ᇂ HANGUL JONGSEONG HIEUH

11C3 ᇃ HANGUL JONGSEONG KIYEOK-RIEUL
≈ 11A8 ᆨ + 11AF ᆯ

11C4 ᇄ HANGUL JONGSEONG KIYEOK-SIOS-KIYEOK
≈ 11A8 ᆨ + 11BA ᆺ + 11A8 ᆨ

11C5 ᇅ HANGUL JONGSEONG NIEUN-KIYEOK
≈ 11AB ᆫ + 11A8 ᆨ

11C6 ᇆ HANGUL JONGSEONG NIEUN-TIKEUT
≈ 11AB ᆫ + 11AE ᆮ

11C7 ᇇ HANGUL JONGSEONG NIEUN-SIOS
≈ 11AB ᆫ + 11BA ᆺ

11C8 ᇈ HANGUL JONGSEONG NIEUN-PANSIOS
≈ 11AB ᆫ + 11EB ᇫ

11C9 ᇉ HANGUL JONGSEONG NIEUN-THIEUTH
≈ 11AB ᆫ + 11C0 ᇀ

11CA ᇊ HANGUL JONGSEONG TIKEUT-KIYEOK
≈ 11AE ᆮ + 11A8 ᆨ

11CB ᇋ HANGUL JONGSEONG TIKEUT-RIEUL
≈ 11AE ᆮ + 11AF ᆯ

11CC ᇌ HANGUL JONGSEONG RIEUL-KIYEOK-SIOS
≈ 11AF ᆯ + 11A8 ᆨ + 11BA ᆺ

11CD ᇍ HANGUL JONGSEONG RIEUL-NIEUN
≈ 11AF ᆯ + 11AB ᆫ

11CE ᇎ HANGUL JONGSEONG RIEUL-TIKEUT
≈ 11AF ᆯ + 11AE ᆮ

11CF ᇏ HANGUL JONGSEONG RIEUL-TIKEUT-HIEUH
≈ 11AF ᆯ + 11AE ᆮ + 11C2 ᇂ

11D0 ᇐ HANGUL JONGSEONG SSANGRIEUL
≈ 11AF ᆯ + 11AF ᆯ

11D1 ᇑ HANGUL JONGSEONG RIEUL-MIEUM-KIYEOK
≈ 11AF ᆯ + 11B7 ᆷ + 11A8 ᆨ

11D2 ᇒ HANGUL JONGSEONG RIEUL-MIEUM-SIOS
≈ 11AF ᆯ + 11B7 ᆷ + 11BA ᆺ

11D3 ᇓ HANGUL JONGSEONG RIEUL-PIEUP-SIOS
≈ 11AF ᆯ + 11B8 ᆸ + 11BA ᆺ

11D4 ᇔ HANGUL JONGSEONG RIEUL-PIEUP-HIEUH
≈ 11AF ᆯ + 11B8 ᆸ + 11C2 ᇂ

11D5 ᇕ HANGUL JONGSEONG RIEUL-KAPYEOUNPIEUP
≈ 11AF ᆯ + 11B8 ᆸ + 11BC ᆼ

11D6 ᇖ HANGUL JONGSEONG RIEUL-SSANGSIOS
≈ 11AF ᆯ + 11BA ᆺ + 11BA ᆺ

11D7 ᇗ HANGUL JONGSEONG RIEUL-PANSIOS
≈ 11AF ᆯ + 11EB ᇫ

11D8 ᇘ HANGUL JONGSEONG RIEUL-KHIEUKH
≈ 11AF ᆯ + 11BF ᆿ

11D9 ᇙ HANGUL JONGSEONG RIEUL-YEORINHIEUH
≈ 11AF ᆯ + 11F9 ᇹ

11DA ᇚ HANGUL JONGSEONG MIEUM-KIYEOK
≈ 11B7 ᆷ + 11A8 ᆨ

11DB ᇛ HANGUL JONGSEONG MIEUM-RIEUL
≈ 11B7 ᆷ + 11AF ᆯ

11DC ᇜ HANGUL JONGSEONG MIEUM-PIEUP
≈ 11B7 ᆷ + 11B8 ᆸ

11DD ᇝ HANGUL JONGSEONG MIEUM-SIOS
≈ 11B7 ᆷ + 11BA ᆺ

11DE ᇞ HANGUL JONGSEONG MIEUM-SSANGSIOS
≈ 11B7 ᆷ + 11BA ᆺ + 11BA ᆺ

11DF ᇟ HANGUL JONGSEONG MIEUM-PANSIOS
≈ 11B7 ᆷ + 11EB ᇫ

11E0 ᇠ HANGUL JONGSEONG MIEUM-CHIEUCH
≈ 11B7 ᆷ + 11BE ᆾ

11E1 ᇡ HANGUL JONGSEONG MIEUM-HIEUH
≈ 11B7 ᆷ + 11C2 ᇂ

11E2 ᇢ HANGUL JONGSEONG KAPYEOUNMIEUM
≈ 11B7 ᆷ + 11BC ᆼ

11E3 ᇣ HANGUL JONGSEONG PIEUP-RIEUL
≈ 11B8 ᆸ + 11AF ᆯ

11E4 ᇤ HANGUL JONGSEONG PIEUP-PHIEUPH
≈ 11B8 ᆸ + 11C1 ᇁ

11E5 ᇥ HANGUL JONGSEONG PIEUP-HIEUH
≈ 11B8 ᆸ + 11C2 ᇂ

11E6 ᇦ HANGUL JONGSEONG KAPYEOUNPIEUP
≈ 11B8 ᆸ + 11BC ᆼ

11E7 ᇧ HANGUL JONGSEONG SIOS-KIYEOK
≈ 11BA ᆺ + 11A8 ᆨ

11E8 ᇨ HANGUL JONGSEONG SIOS-TIKEUT
≈ 11BA ᆺ + 11AE ᆮ

11E9 ᇩ HANGUL JONGSEONG SIOS-RIEUL
≈ 11BA ᆺ + 11AF ᆯ

11EA ᇪ HANGUL JONGSEONG SIOS-PIEUP
≈ 11BA ᆺ + 11B8 ᆸ

11EB ᇫ HANGUL JONGSEONG PANSIOS

11EC ᇬ HANGUL JONGSEONG IEUNG-KIYEOK
≈ 11BC ᆼ + 11A8 ᆨ

11ED ᇭ HANGUL JONGSEONG IEUNG-SSANGKIYEOK
≈ 11BC ᆼ + 11A8 ᆨ + 11A8 ᆨ

11EE ᇮ HANGUL JONGSEONG SSANGIEUNG
≈ 11BC ᆼ + 11BC ᆼ

11EF ᇯ HANGUL JONGSEONG IEUNG-KHIEUKH
≈ 11BC ᆼ + 11BF ᆿ

11F0 ᇰ HANGUL JONGSEONG YESIEUNG

11F1 ᇱ HANGUL JONGSEONG YESIEUNG-SIOS
≈ 11F0 ᇰ + 11BA ᆺ

11F2 ᇲ HANGUL JONGSEONG YESIEUNG-PANSIOS
≈ 11F0 ᇰ + 11EB ᇫ

11F3 ᇳ HANGUL JONGSEONG PHIEUPH-PIEUP
≈ 11C1 ᇁ + 11B8 ᆸ

11F4 ᇴ HANGUL JONGSEONG KAPYEOUNPHIEUPH
≈ 11C1 ᇁ + 11BC ᆼ

11F5 ᇵ HANGUL JONGSEONG HIEUH-NIEUN
≈ 11C2 ᇂ + 11AB ᆫ

11F6 ᇶ HANGUL JONGSEONG HIEUH-RIEUL
≈ 11C2 ᇂ + 11AF ᆯ

11F7 ᇷ HANGUL JONGSEONG HIEUH-MIEUM
≈ 11C2 ᇂ + 11B7 ᆷ

11F8 ᇸ HANGUL JONGSEONG HIEUH-PIEUP
≈ 11C2 ᇂ + 11B8 ᆸ

11F9 ᇹ HANGUL JONGSEONG YEORINHIEUH

	1E0	1E1	1E2	1E3	1E4	1E5	1E6	1E7
0	Ḁ 1E00	Ḑ 1E10	Ḡ 1E20	Ḱ 1E30	Ṁ 1E40	Ṑ 1E50	Ṡ 1E60	Ṱ 1E70
1	ḁ 1E01	ḑ 1E11	ḡ 1E21	ḱ 1E31	ṁ 1E41	ṑ 1E51	ṡ 1E61	ṱ 1E71
2	Ḃ 1E02	Ḓ 1E12	Ḣ 1E22	Ḳ 1E32	Ṃ 1E42	Ṓ 1E52	Ṣ 1E62	Ṳ 1E72
3	ḃ 1E03	ḓ 1E13	ḣ 1E23	ḳ 1E33	ṃ 1E43	ṓ 1E53	ṣ 1E63	ṳ 1E73
4	Ḅ 1E04	Ḕ 1E14	Ḥ 1E24	Ḵ 1E34	Ṅ 1E44	Ṕ 1E54	Ṥ 1E64	Ṵ 1E74
5	ḅ 1E05	ḕ 1E15	ḥ 1E25	ḵ 1E35	ṅ 1E45	ṕ 1E55	ṥ 1E65	ṵ 1E75
6	Ḇ 1E06	Ḗ 1E16	Ḧ 1E26	Ḷ 1E36	Ṇ 1E46	Ṗ 1E56	Ṧ 1E66	Ṷ 1E76
7	ḇ 1E07	ḗ 1E17	ḧ 1E27	ḷ 1E37	ṇ 1E47	ṗ 1E57	ṧ 1E67	ṷ 1E77
8	Ḉ 1E08	Ḙ 1E18	Ḩ 1E28	Ḹ 1E38	Ṉ 1E48	Ṙ 1E58	Ṩ 1E68	Ṹ 1E78
9	ḉ 1E09	ḙ 1E19	ḩ 1E29	ḹ 1E39	ṉ 1E49	ṙ 1E59	ṩ 1E69	ṹ 1E79
A	Ḋ 1E0A	Ḛ 1E1A	Ḫ 1E2A	Ḻ 1E3A	Ṋ 1E4A	Ṛ 1E5A	Ṫ 1E6A	Ṻ 1E7A
B	ḋ 1E0B	ḛ 1E1B	ḫ 1E2B	ḻ 1E3B	ṋ 1E4B	ṛ 1E5B	ṫ 1E6B	ṻ 1E7B
C	Ḍ 1E0C	Ḝ 1E1C	Ḭ 1E2C	Ḽ 1E3C	Ṍ 1E4C	Ṝ 1E5C	Ṭ 1E6C	Ṽ 1E7C
D	ḍ 1E0D	ḝ 1E1D	ḭ 1E2D	ḽ 1E3D	ṍ 1E4D	ṝ 1E5D	ṭ 1E6D	ṽ 1E7D
E	Ḏ 1E0E	Ḟ 1E1E	Ḯ 1E2E	Ḿ 1E3E	Ṏ 1E4E	Ṟ 1E5E	Ṯ 1E6E	Ṿ 1E7E
F	ḏ 1E0F	ḟ 1E1F	ḯ 1E2F	ḿ 1E3F	ṏ 1E4F	ṟ 1E5F	ṯ 1E6F	ṿ 1E7F

	1E8	1E9	1EA	1EB	1EC	1ED	1EE	1EF
0	Ẁ 1E80	Ẑ 1E90	Ạ 1EA0	Ằ 1EB0	Ề 1EC0	Ố 1ED0	Ỡ 1EE0	Ự 1EF0
1	ẁ 1E81	ẑ 1E91	ạ 1EA1	ằ 1EB1	ề 1EC1	ố 1ED1	ỡ 1EE1	ự 1EF1
2	Ẃ 1E82	Ẓ 1E92	Ả 1EA2	Ẳ 1EB2	Ể 1EC2	Ồ 1ED2	Ợ 1EE2	Ỳ 1EF2
3	ẃ 1E83	ẓ 1E93	ả 1EA3	ẳ 1EB3	ể 1EC3	ồ 1ED3	ợ 1EE3	ỳ 1EF3
4	Ẅ 1E84	Ẕ 1E94	Ấ 1EA4	Ẵ 1EB4	Ễ 1EC4	Ổ 1ED4	Ụ 1EE4	Ỵ 1EF4
5	ẅ 1E85	ẕ 1E95	ấ 1EA5	ẵ 1EB5	ễ 1EC5	ổ 1ED5	ụ 1EE5	ỵ 1EF5
6	Ẇ 1E86	ẖ 1E96	Ầ 1EA6	Ặ 1EB6	Ệ 1EC6	Ỗ 1ED6	Ủ 1EE6	Ỷ 1EF6
7	ẇ 1E87	ẗ 1E97	ầ 1EA7	ặ 1EB7	ệ 1EC7	ỗ 1ED7	ủ 1EE7	ỷ 1EF7
8	Ẉ 1E88	ẘ 1E98	Ẩ 1EA8	Ẹ 1EB8	Ỉ 1EC8	Ộ 1ED8	Ứ 1EE8	Ỹ 1EF8
9	ẉ 1E89	ẙ 1E99	ẩ 1EA9	ẹ 1EB9	ỉ 1EC9	ộ 1ED9	ứ 1EE9	ỹ 1EF9
A	Ẋ 1E8A	ẚ 1E9A	Ẫ 1EAA	Ẻ 1EBA	Ị 1ECA	Ớ 1EDA	Ừ 1EEA	
B	ẋ 1E8B	ẛ 1E9B	ẫ 1EAB	ẻ 1EBB	ị 1ECB	ớ 1EDB	ừ 1EEB	
C	Ẍ 1E8C		Ậ 1EAC	Ẽ 1EBC	Ọ 1ECC	Ờ 1EDC	Ử 1EEC	
D	ẍ 1E8D		ậ 1EAD	ẽ 1EBD	ọ 1ECD	ờ 1EDD	ử 1EED	
E	Ẏ 1E8E		Ắ 1EAE	Ế 1EBE	Ỏ 1ECE	Ở 1EDE	Ữ 1EEE	
F	ẏ 1E8F		ắ 1EAF	ế 1EBF	ỏ 1ECF	ở 1EDF	ữ 1EEF	

Latin extended additional

1E00 Ḁ LATIN CAPITAL LETTER A WITH RING BELOW
≡ 0041 A + 0325 ̥

1E01 ḁ LATIN SMALL LETTER A WITH RING BELOW
≡ 0061 a + 0325 ̥

1E02 Ḃ LATIN CAPITAL LETTER B WITH DOT ABOVE
≡ 0042 B + 0307 ̇

1E03 ḃ LATIN SMALL LETTER B WITH DOT ABOVE
≡ 0062 b + 0307 ̇

1E04 Ḅ LATIN CAPITAL LETTER B WITH DOT BELOW
≡ 0042 B + 0323 ̣

1E05 ḅ LATIN SMALL LETTER B WITH DOT BELOW
≡ 0062 b + 0323 ̣

1E06 Ḇ LATIN CAPITAL LETTER B WITH LINE BELOW
≡ 0042 B + 0331 ̱

1E07 ḇ LATIN SMALL LETTER B WITH LINE BELOW
≡ 0062 b + 0331 ̱

1E08 Ḉ LATIN CAPITAL LETTER C WITH CEDILLA AND ACUTE
≡ 00C7 Ç + 0301 ́

1E09 ḉ LATIN SMALL LETTER C WITH CEDILLA AND ACUTE
≡ 00E7 ç + 0301 ́

1E0A Ḋ LATIN CAPITAL LETTER D WITH DOT ABOVE
≡ 0044 D + 0307 ̇

1E0B ḋ LATIN SMALL LETTER D WITH DOT ABOVE
≡ 0064 d + 0307 ̇

1E0C Ḍ LATIN CAPITAL LETTER D WITH DOT BELOW
≡ 0044 D + 0323 ̣

1E0D ḍ LATIN SMALL LETTER D WITH DOT BELOW
≡ 0064 d + 0323 ̣

1E0E Ḏ LATIN CAPITAL LETTER D WITH LINE BELOW
≡ 0044 D + 0331 ̱

1E0F ḏ LATIN SMALL LETTER D WITH LINE BELOW
≡ 0064 d + 0331 ̱

1E10 Ḑ LATIN CAPITAL LETTER D WITH CEDILLA
≡ 0044 D + 0327 ̧

1E11 ḑ LATIN SMALL LETTER D WITH CEDILLA
≡ 0064 d + 0327 ̧

1E12 Ḓ LATIN CAPITAL LETTER D WITH CIRCUMFLEX BELOW
≡ 0044 D + 032D ̭

1E13 ḓ LATIN SMALL LETTER D WITH CIRCUMFLEX BELOW
≡ 0064 d + 032D ̭

1E14 Ḕ LATIN CAPITAL LETTER E WITH MACRON AND GRAVE
≡ 0112 Ē + 0300 ̀

1E15 ḕ LATIN SMALL LETTER E WITH MACRON AND GRAVE
≡ 0113 ē + 0300 ̀

1E16 Ḗ LATIN CAPITAL LETTER E WITH MACRON AND ACUTE
≡ 0112 Ē + 0301 ́

1E17 ḗ LATIN SMALL LETTER E WITH MACRON AND ACUTE
≡ 0113 ē + 0301 ́

1E18 Ḙ LATIN CAPITAL LETTER E WITH CIRCUMFLEX BELOW
≡ 0045 E + 032D ̭

1E19 ḙ LATIN SMALL LETTER E WITH CIRCUMFLEX BELOW
≡ 0065 e + 032D ̭

1E1A Ḛ LATIN CAPITAL LETTER E WITH TILDE BELOW
≡ 0045 E + 0330 ̰

1E1B ḛ LATIN SMALL LETTER E WITH TILDE BELOW
≡ 0065 e + 0330 ̰

1E1C Ḝ LATIN CAPITAL LETTER E WITH CEDILLA AND BREVE
≡ 0114 Ĕ + 0327 ̧

1E1D ḝ LATIN SMALL LETTER E WITH CEDILLA AND BREVE
≡ 0115 ĕ + 0327 ̧

1E1E Ḟ LATIN CAPITAL LETTER F WITH DOT ABOVE
≡ 0046 F + 0307 ̇

1E1F ḟ LATIN SMALL LETTER F WITH DOT ABOVE
≡ 0066 f + 0307 ̇

1E20 Ḡ LATIN CAPITAL LETTER G WITH MACRON
≡ 0047 G + 0304 ̄

1E21 ḡ LATIN SMALL LETTER G WITH MACRON
≡ 0067 g + 0304 ̄

1E22 Ḣ LATIN CAPITAL LETTER H WITH DOT ABOVE
≡ 0048 H + 0307 ̇

1E23 ḣ LATIN SMALL LETTER H WITH DOT ABOVE
≡ 0068 h + 0307 ̇

1E24 Ḥ LATIN CAPITAL LETTER H WITH DOT BELOW
≡ 0048 H + 0323 ◌̣

1E25 ḥ LATIN SMALL LETTER H WITH DOT BELOW
≡ 0068 h + 0323 ◌̣

1E26 Ḧ LATIN CAPITAL LETTER H WITH DIAERESIS
≡ 0048 H + 0308 ◌̈

1E27 ḧ LATIN SMALL LETTER H WITH DIAERESIS
≡ 0068 h + 0308 ◌̈

1E28 Ḩ LATIN CAPITAL LETTER H WITH CEDILLA
≡ 0048 H + 0327 ◌̧

1E29 ḩ LATIN SMALL LETTER H WITH CEDILLA
≡ 0068 h + 0327 ◌̧

1E2A Ḫ LATIN CAPITAL LETTER H WITH BREVE BELOW
≡ 0048 H + 032E ◌̮

1E2B ḫ LATIN SMALL LETTER H WITH BREVE BELOW
≡ 0068 h + 032E ◌̮

1E2C Ḭ LATIN CAPITAL LETTER I WITH TILDE BELOW
≡ 0049 I + 0330 ◌̰

1E2D ḭ LATIN SMALL LETTER I WITH TILDE BELOW
≡ 0069 i + 0330 ◌̰

1E2E Ḯ LATIN CAPITAL LETTER I WITH DIAERESIS AND ACUTE
≡ 00CF Ï + 0301 ◌́

1E2F ḯ LATIN SMALL LETTER I WITH DIAERESIS AND ACUTE
≡ 00EF ï + 0301 ◌́

1E30 Ḱ LATIN CAPITAL LETTER K WITH ACUTE
≡ 004B K + 0301 ◌́

1E31 ḱ LATIN SMALL LETTER K WITH ACUTE
≡ 006B k + 0301 ◌́

1E32 Ḳ LATIN CAPITAL LETTER K WITH DOT BELOW
≡ 004B K + 0323 ◌̣

1E33 ḳ LATIN SMALL LETTER K WITH DOT BELOW
≡ 006B k + 0323 ◌̣

1E34 Ḵ LATIN CAPITAL LETTER K WITH LINE BELOW
≡ 004B K + 0331 ◌̱

1E35 ḵ LATIN SMALL LETTER K WITH LINE BELOW
≡ 006B k + 0331 ◌̱

1E36 Ḷ LATIN CAPITAL LETTER L WITH DOT BELOW
≡ 004C L + 0323 ◌̣

1E37 ḷ LATIN SMALL LETTER L WITH DOT BELOW
≡ 006C l + 0323 ◌̣

1E38 Ḹ LATIN CAPITAL LETTER L WITH DOT BELOW AND MACRON
≡ 1E36 Ḷ + 0304 ◌̄

1E39 ḹ LATIN SMALL LETTER L WITH DOT BELOW AND MACRON
≡ 1E37 ḷ + 0304 ◌̄

1E3A Ḻ LATIN CAPITAL LETTER L WITH LINE BELOW
≡ 004C L + 0331 ◌̱

1E3B ḻ LATIN SMALL LETTER L WITH LINE BELOW
≡ 006C l + 0331 ◌̱

1E3C Ḽ LATIN CAPITAL LETTER L WITH CIRCUMFLEX BELOW
≡ 004C L + 032D ◌̭

1E3D ḽ LATIN SMALL LETTER L WITH CIRCUMFLEX BELOW
≡ 006C l + 032D ◌̭

1E3E Ḿ LATIN CAPITAL LETTER M WITH ACUTE
≡ 004D M + 0301 ◌́

1E3F ḿ LATIN SMALL LETTER M WITH ACUTE
≡ 006D m + 0301 ◌́

1E40 Ṁ LATIN CAPITAL LETTER M WITH DOT ABOVE
≡ 004D M + 0307 ◌̇

1E41 ṁ LATIN SMALL LETTER M WITH DOT ABOVE
≡ 006D m + 0307 ◌̇

1E42 Ṃ LATIN CAPITAL LETTER M WITH DOT BELOW
≡ 004D M + 0323 ◌̣

1E43 ṃ LATIN SMALL LETTER M WITH DOT BELOW
≡ 006D m + 0323 ◌̣

1E44 Ṅ LATIN CAPITAL LETTER N WITH DOT ABOVE
≡ 004E N + 0307 ◌̇

1E45 ṅ LATIN SMALL LETTER N WITH DOT ABOVE
≡ 006E n + 0307 ◌̇

1E46 Ṇ LATIN CAPITAL LETTER N WITH DOT BELOW
≡ 004E N + 0323 ◌̣

1E47 ṇ LATIN SMALL LETTER N WITH DOT BELOW
≡ 006E n + 0323 ◌̣

1E48 Ṉ LATIN CAPITAL LETTER N WITH LINE BELOW
≡ 004E N + 0331 ◌̱

1E49 ṉ LATIN SMALL LETTER N WITH LINE BELOW
≡ 006E n + 0331 ◌̱

1E4A Ṋ LATIN CAPITAL LETTER N WITH CIRCUMFLEX BELOW
≡ 004E N + 032D ◌̭

1E4B ṋ LATIN SMALL LETTER N WITH CIRCUMFLEX BELOW
≡ 006E n + 032D ◌̭

1E4C Ṍ LATIN CAPITAL LETTER O WITH TILDE AND ACUTE
≡ 00D5 Õ + 0301 ◌́

1E4D ṍ LATIN SMALL LETTER O WITH TILDE AND ACUTE
≡ 00F5 õ + 0301 ◌́

1E4E Ṏ LATIN CAPITAL LETTER O WITH TILDE AND DIAERESIS
≡ 00D5 Õ + 0308 ◌̈

1E4F ṏ LATIN SMALL LETTER O WITH TILDE AND DIAERESIS
≡ 00F5 õ + 0308 ◌̈

1E50 Ṑ LATIN CAPITAL LETTER O WITH MACRON AND GRAVE
≡ 014C Ō + 0300 ◌̀

1E51 ṑ LATIN SMALL LETTER O WITH MACRON AND GRAVE
≡ 014D ō + 0300 ◌̀

1E52 Ṓ LATIN CAPITAL LETTER O WITH MACRON AND ACUTE
≡ 014C Ō + 0301 ◌́

1E53 ṓ LATIN SMALL LETTER O WITH MACRON AND ACUTE
≡ 014D ō + 0301 ◌́

1E54 Ṕ LATIN CAPITAL LETTER P WITH ACUTE
≡ 0050 P + 0301 ◌́

1E55 ṕ LATIN SMALL LETTER P WITH ACUTE
≡ 0070 p + 0301 ◌́

1E56 Ṗ LATIN CAPITAL LETTER P WITH DOT ABOVE
≡ 0050 P + 0307 ◌̇

1E57 ṗ LATIN SMALL LETTER P WITH DOT ABOVE
≡ 0070 p + 0307 ◌̇

1E58 Ṙ LATIN CAPITAL LETTER R WITH DOT ABOVE
≡ 0052 R + 0307 ◌̇

1E59 ṙ LATIN SMALL LETTER R WITH DOT ABOVE
≡ 0072 r + 0307 ◌̇

1E5A Ṛ LATIN CAPITAL LETTER R WITH DOT BELOW
≡ 0052 R + 0323 ◌̣

1E5B ṛ LATIN SMALL LETTER R WITH DOT BELOW
≡ 0072 r + 0323 ◌̣

1E5C Ṝ LATIN CAPITAL LETTER R WITH DOT BELOW AND MACRON
≡ 1E5A Ṛ + 0304 ◌̄

1E5D ṝ LATIN SMALL LETTER R WITH DOT BELOW AND MACRON
≡ 1E5B ṛ + 0304 ◌̄

1E5E Ṟ LATIN CAPITAL LETTER R WITH LINE BELOW
≡ 0052 R + 0331 ◌̱

1E5F ṟ LATIN SMALL LETTER R WITH LINE BELOW
≡ 0072 r + 0331 ◌̱

1E60 Ṡ LATIN CAPITAL LETTER S WITH DOT ABOVE
≡ 0053 S + 0307 ◌̇

1E61 ṡ LATIN SMALL LETTER S WITH DOT ABOVE
≡ 0073 s + 0307 ◌̇

1E62 Ṣ LATIN CAPITAL LETTER S WITH DOT BELOW
≡ 0053 S + 0323 ◌̣

1E63 ṣ LATIN SMALL LETTER S WITH DOT BELOW
≡ 0073 s + 0323 ◌̣

1E64 Ṥ LATIN CAPITAL LETTER S WITH ACUTE AND DOT ABOVE
≡ 015A Ś + 0307 ◌̇

1E65 ṥ LATIN SMALL LETTER S WITH ACUTE AND DOT ABOVE
≡ 015B ś + 0307 ◌̇

1E66 Ṧ LATIN CAPITAL LETTER S WITH CARON AND DOT ABOVE
≡ 0160 Š + 0307 ◌̇

1E67 ṧ LATIN SMALL LETTER S WITH CARON AND DOT ABOVE
≡ 0161 š + 0307 ◌̇

1E68 Ṩ LATIN CAPITAL LETTER S WITH DOT BELOW AND DOT ABOVE
≡ 1E62 Ṣ + 0307 ◌̇

1E69 ṩ LATIN SMALL LETTER S WITH DOT BELOW AND DOT ABOVE
≡ 1E63 ṣ + 0307 ◌̇

1E6A Ṫ LATIN CAPITAL LETTER T WITH DOT ABOVE
≡ 0054 T + 0307 ◌̇

1E6B ṫ LATIN SMALL LETTER T WITH DOT ABOVE
≡ 0074 t + 0307 ◌̇

1E6C Ṭ LATIN CAPITAL LETTER T WITH DOT BELOW
≡ 0054 T + 0323 ◌̣

1E6D ṭ LATIN SMALL LETTER T WITH DOT BELOW
≡ 0074 t + 0323 ◌̣

1E6E Ṯ LATIN CAPITAL LETTER T WITH LINE BELOW
≡ 0054 T + 0331 ◌̱

1E6F ṯ LATIN SMALL LETTER T WITH LINE BELOW
≡ 0074 t + 0331 ◌̱

1E70 Ṱ LATIN CAPITAL LETTER T WITH CIRCUMFLEX BELOW
≡ 0054 T + 032D ◌̭

1E71 ṱ LATIN SMALL LETTER T WITH CIRCUMFLEX BELOW
≡ 0074 t + 032D ◌̭

1E72 Ṳ LATIN CAPITAL LETTER U WITH DIAERESIS BELOW
≡ 0055 U + 0324 ◌̤

1E73 ṳ LATIN SMALL LETTER U WITH DIAERESIS BELOW
≡ 0075 u + 0324 ◌̤

1E74 Ṵ LATIN CAPITAL LETTER U WITH TILDE BELOW
≡ 0055 U + 0330 ◌̰

1E75 ṵ LATIN SMALL LETTER U WITH TILDE BELOW
≡ 0075 u + 0330 ◌̰

1E76 Ṷ LATIN CAPITAL LETTER U WITH CIRCUMFLEX BELOW
≡ 0055 U + 032D ◌̭

1E77 ṷ LATIN SMALL LETTER U WITH CIRCUMFLEX BELOW
≡ 0075 u + 032D ◌̭

1E78 Ṹ LATIN CAPITAL LETTER U WITH TILDE AND ACUTE
≡ 0168 Ũ + 0301 ◌́

1E79 ṹ LATIN SMALL LETTER U WITH TILDE AND ACUTE
≡ 0169 ũ + 0301 ◌́

1E7A Ṻ LATIN CAPITAL LETTER U WITH MACRON AND DIAERESIS
≡ 016A Ū + 0308 ◌̈

1E7B ṻ LATIN SMALL LETTER U WITH MACRON AND DIAERESIS
≡ 016B ū + 0308 ◌̈

1E7C Ṽ LATIN CAPITAL LETTER V WITH TILDE
≡ 0056 V + 0303 ◌̃

1E7D ṽ LATIN SMALL LETTER V WITH TILDE
≡ 0076 v + 0303 ◌̃

1E7E Ṿ LATIN CAPITAL LETTER V WITH DOT BELOW
≡ 0056 V + 0323 ◌̣

1E7F ṿ LATIN SMALL LETTER V WITH DOT BELOW
≡ 0076 v + 0323 ◌̣

1E80 Ẁ LATIN CAPITAL LETTER W WITH GRAVE
≡ 0057 W + 0300 ◌̀

1E81 ẁ LATIN SMALL LETTER W WITH GRAVE
≡ 0077 w + 0300 ◌̀

1E82 Ẃ LATIN CAPITAL LETTER W WITH ACUTE
≡ 0057 W + 0301 ◌́

1E83 ẃ LATIN SMALL LETTER W WITH ACUTE
≡ 0077 w + 0301 ◌́

1E84 Ẅ LATIN CAPITAL LETTER W WITH DIAERESIS
≡ 0057 W + 0308 ◌̈

1E85 ẅ LATIN SMALL LETTER W WITH DIAERESIS
≡ 0077 w + 0308 ◌̈

1E86 Ẇ LATIN CAPITAL LETTER W WITH DOT ABOVE
≡ 0057 W + 0307 ◌̇

1E87 ẇ LATIN SMALL LETTER W WITH DOT ABOVE
≡ 0077 w + 0307 ◌̇

1E88 Ẉ LATIN CAPITAL LETTER W WITH DOT BELOW
≡ 0057 W + 0323 ◌̣

1E89 ẉ LATIN SMALL LETTER W WITH DOT BELOW
≡ 0077 w + 0323 ◌̣

1E8A Ẋ LATIN CAPITAL LETTER X WITH DOT ABOVE
≡ 0058 X + 0307 ◌̇

1E8B ẋ LATIN SMALL LETTER X WITH DOT ABOVE
≡ 0078 x + 0307 ◌̇

1E8C Ẍ LATIN CAPITAL LETTER X WITH DIAERESIS
≡ 0058 X + 0308 ◌̈

1E8D ẍ LATIN SMALL LETTER X WITH DIAERESIS
≡ 0078 x + 0308 ◌̈

1E8E Ẏ LATIN CAPITAL LETTER Y WITH DOT ABOVE
≡ 0059 Y + 0307 ◌̇

1E8F ẏ LATIN SMALL LETTER Y WITH DOT ABOVE
≡ 0079 y + 0307 ◌̇

1E90 Ẑ LATIN CAPITAL LETTER Z WITH CIRCUMFLEX
≡ 005A Z + 0302 ̂

1E91 ẑ LATIN SMALL LETTER Z WITH CIRCUMFLEX
≡ 007A z + 0302 ̂

1E92 Ẓ LATIN CAPITAL LETTER Z WITH DOT BELOW
≡ 005A Z + 0323 ̣

1E93 ẓ LATIN SMALL LETTER Z WITH DOT BELOW
≡ 007A z + 0323 ̣

1E94 Ẕ LATIN CAPITAL LETTER Z WITH LINE BELOW
≡ 005A Z + 0331 ̱

1E95 ẕ LATIN SMALL LETTER Z WITH LINE BELOW
≡ 007A z + 0331 ̱

1E96 ẖ LATIN SMALL LETTER H WITH LINE BELOW
≡ 0068 h + 0331 ̱

1E97 ẗ LATIN SMALL LETTER T WITH DIAERESIS
≡ 0074 t + 0308 ̈

1E98 ẘ LATIN SMALL LETTER W WITH RING ABOVE
≡ 0077 w + 030A ̊

1E99 ẙ LATIN SMALL LETTER Y WITH RING ABOVE
≡ 0079 y + 030A ̊

1E9A ẚ LATIN SMALL LETTER A WITH RIGHT HALF RING

1E9B ẛ LATIN SMALL LETTER LONG S WITH DOT ABOVE
≡ 017F ſ + 0307 ̇

1E9C <reserved>

1E9D <reserved>

1E9E <reserved>

1E9F <reserved>

1EA0 Ạ LATIN CAPITAL LETTER A WITH DOT BELOW
≡ 0041 A + 0323 ̣

1EA1 ạ LATIN SMALL LETTER A WITH DOT BELOW
≡ 0061 a + 0323 ̣

1EA2 Ả LATIN CAPITAL LETTER A WITH HOOK ABOVE
≡ 0041 A + 0309 ̉

1EA3 ả LATIN SMALL LETTER A WITH HOOK ABOVE
≡ 0061 a + 0309 ̉

1EA4 Ấ LATIN CAPITAL LETTER A WITH CIRCUMFLEX AND ACUTE
≡ 00C2 Â + 0301 ́

1EA5 ấ LATIN SMALL LETTER A WITH CIRCUMFLEX AND ACUTE
≡ 00E2 â + 0301 ́

1EA6 Ầ LATIN CAPITAL LETTER A WITH CIRCUMFLEX AND GRAVE
≡ 00C2 Â + 0300 ̀

1EA7 ầ LATIN SMALL LETTER A WITH CIRCUMFLEX AND GRAVE
≡ 00E2 â + 0300 ̀

1EA8 Ẩ LATIN CAPITAL LETTER A WITH CIRCUMFLEX AND HOOK ABOVE
≡ 00C2 Â + 0309 ̉

1EA9 ẩ LATIN SMALL LETTER A WITH CIRCUMFLEX AND HOOK ABOVE
≡ 00E2 â + 0309 ̉

1EAA Ẫ LATIN CAPITAL LETTER A WITH CIRCUMFLEX AND TILDE
≡ 00C2 Â + 0303 ̃

1EAB ẫ LATIN SMALL LETTER A WITH CIRCUMFLEX AND TILDE
≡ 00E2 â + 0303 ̃

1EAC Ậ LATIN CAPITAL LETTER A WITH CIRCUMFLEX AND DOT BELOW
≡ 00C2 Â + 0323 ̣

1EAD ậ LATIN SMALL LETTER A WITH CIRCUMFLEX AND DOT BELOW
≡ 00E2 â + 0323 ̣

1EAE Ắ LATIN CAPITAL LETTER A WITH BREVE AND ACUTE
≡ 0102 Ă + 0301 ́

1EAF ắ LATIN SMALL LETTER A WITH BREVE AND ACUTE
≡ 0103 ă + 0301 ́

1EB0 Ằ LATIN CAPITAL LETTER A WITH BREVE AND GRAVE
≡ 0102 Ă + 0300 ̀

1EB1 ằ LATIN SMALL LETTER A WITH BREVE AND GRAVE
≡ 0103 ă + 0300 ̀

1EB2 Ẳ LATIN CAPITAL LETTER A WITH BREVE AND HOOK ABOVE
≡ 0102 Ă + 0309 ̉

1EB3 ẳ LATIN SMALL LETTER A WITH BREVE AND HOOK ABOVE
≡ 0103 ă + 0309 ̉

1EB4 Ẵ LATIN CAPITAL LETTER A WITH BREVE AND TILDE
≡ 0102 Ă + 0303 ̃

1EB5 ẵ LATIN SMALL LETTER A WITH BREVE AND TILDE
≡ 0103 ă + 0303 ̃

1EB6 Ặ LATIN CAPITAL LETTER A WITH BREVE AND DOT BELOW
≡ 0102 Ă + 0323 ̣

1EB7 ặ LATIN SMALL LETTER A WITH BREVE AND DOT BELOW
≡ 0103 ă + 0323 ◌̣

1EB8 Ẹ LATIN CAPITAL LETTER E WITH DOT BELOW
≡ 0045 E + 0323 ◌̣

1EB9 ẹ LATIN SMALL LETTER E WITH DOT BELOW
≡ 0065 e + 0323 ◌̣

1EBA Ẻ LATIN CAPITAL LETTER E WITH HOOK ABOVE
≡ 0045 E + 0309 ◌̉

1EBB ẻ LATIN SMALL LETTER E WITH HOOK ABOVE
≡ 0065 e + 0309 ◌̉

1EBC Ẽ LATIN CAPITAL LETTER E WITH TILDE
≡ 0045 E + 0303 ◌̃

1EBD ẽ LATIN SMALL LETTER E WITH TILDE
≡ 0065 e + 0303 ◌̃

1EBE Ế LATIN CAPITAL LETTER E WITH CIRCUMFLEX AND ACUTE
≡ 00CA Ê + 0301 ◌́

1EBF ế LATIN SMALL LETTER E WITH CIRCUMFLEX AND ACUTE
≡ 00EA ê + 0301 ◌́

1EC0 Ề LATIN CAPITAL LETTER E WITH CIRCUMFLEX AND GRAVE
≡ 00CA Ê + 0300 ◌̀

1EC1 ề LATIN SMALL LETTER E WITH CIRCUMFLEX AND GRAVE
≡ 00EA ê + 0300 ◌̀

1EC2 Ể LATIN CAPITAL LETTER E WITH CIRCUMFLEX AND HOOK ABOVE
≡ 00CA Ê + 0309 ◌̉

1EC3 ể LATIN SMALL LETTER E WITH CIRCUMFLEX AND HOOK ABOVE
≡ 00EA ê + 0309 ◌̉

1EC4 Ễ LATIN CAPITAL LETTER E WITH CIRCUMFLEX AND TILDE
≡ 00CA Ê + 0303 ◌̃

1EC5 ễ LATIN SMALL LETTER E WITH CIRCUMFLEX AND TILDE
≡ 00EA ê + 0303 ◌̃

1EC6 Ệ LATIN CAPITAL LETTER E WITH CIRCUMFLEX AND DOT BELOW
≡ 00CA Ê + 0323 ◌̣

1EC7 ệ LATIN SMALL LETTER E WITH CIRCUMFLEX AND DOT BELOW
≡ 00EA ê + 0323 ◌̣

1EC8 Ỉ LATIN CAPITAL LETTER I WITH HOOK ABOVE
≡ 0049 I + 0309 ◌̉

1EC9 ỉ LATIN SMALL LETTER I WITH HOOK ABOVE
≡ 0069 i + 0309 ◌̉

1ECA Ị LATIN CAPITAL LETTER I WITH DOT BELOW
≡ 0049 I + 0323 ◌̣

1ECB ị LATIN SMALL LETTER I WITH DOT BELOW
≡ 0069 i + 0323 ◌̣

1ECC Ọ LATIN CAPITAL LETTER O WITH DOT BELOW
≡ 004F O + 0323 ◌̣

1ECD ọ LATIN SMALL LETTER O WITH DOT BELOW
≡ 006F o + 0323 ◌̣

1ECE Ỏ LATIN CAPITAL LETTER O WITH HOOK ABOVE
≡ 004F O + 0309 ◌̉

1ECF ỏ LATIN SMALL LETTER O WITH HOOK ABOVE
≡ 006F o + 0309 ◌̉

1ED0 Ố LATIN CAPITAL LETTER O WITH CIRCUMFLEX AND ACUTE
≡ 00D4 Ô + 0301 ◌́

1ED1 ố LATIN SMALL LETTER O WITH CIRCUMFLEX AND ACUTE
≡ 00F4 ô + 0301 ◌́

1ED2 Ồ LATIN CAPITAL LETTER O WITH CIRCUMFLEX AND GRAVE
≡ 00D4 Ô + 0300 ◌̀

1ED3 ồ LATIN SMALL LETTER O WITH CIRCUMFLEX AND GRAVE
≡ 00F4 ô + 0300 ◌̀

1ED4 Ổ LATIN CAPITAL LETTER O WITH CIRCUMFLEX AND HOOK ABOVE
≡ 00D4 Ô + 0309 ◌̉

1ED5 ổ LATIN SMALL LETTER O WITH CIRCUMFLEX AND HOOK ABOVE
≡ 00F4 ô + 0309 ◌̉

1ED6 Ỗ LATIN CAPITAL LETTER O WITH CIRCUMFLEX AND TILDE
≡ 00D4 Ô + 0303 ◌̃

1ED7 ỗ LATIN SMALL LETTER O WITH CIRCUMFLEX AND TILDE
≡ 00F4 ô + 0303 ◌̃

1ED8 Ộ LATIN CAPITAL LETTER O WITH CIRCUMFLEX AND DOT BELOW
≡ 00D4 Ô + 0323 ◌̣

1ED9 ộ LATIN SMALL LETTER O WITH CIRCUMFLEX AND DOT BELOW
≡ 00F4 ô + 0323 ◌̣

1EDA Ớ LATIN CAPITAL LETTER O WITH HORN AND ACUTE
≡ 01A0 Ơ + 0301 ◌́

1EDB ớ LATIN SMALL LETTER O WITH HORN AND ACUTE
≡ 01A1 ơ + 0301 ́

1EDC Ờ LATIN CAPITAL LETTER O WITH HORN AND GRAVE
≡ 01A0 Ơ + 0300 ̀

1EDD ờ LATIN SMALL LETTER O WITH HORN AND GRAVE
≡ 01A1 ơ + 0300 ̀

1EDE Ở LATIN CAPITAL LETTER O WITH HORN AND HOOK ABOVE
≡ 01A0 Ơ + 0309 ̉

1EDF ở LATIN SMALL LETTER O WITH HORN AND HOOK ABOVE
≡ 01A1 ơ + 0309 ̉

1EE0 Ỡ LATIN CAPITAL LETTER O WITH HORN AND TILDE
≡ 01A0 Ơ + 0303 ̃

1EE1 ỡ LATIN SMALL LETTER O WITH HORN AND TILDE
≡ 01A1 ơ + 0303 ̃

1EE2 Ợ LATIN CAPITAL LETTER O WITH HORN AND DOT BELOW
≡ 01A0 Ơ + 0323 ̣

1EE3 ợ LATIN SMALL LETTER O WITH HORN AND DOT BELOW
≡ 01A1 ơ + 0323 ̣

1EE4 Ụ LATIN CAPITAL LETTER U WITH DOT BELOW
≡ 0055 U + 0323 ̣

1EE5 ụ LATIN SMALL LETTER U WITH DOT BELOW
≡ 0075 u + 0323 ̣

1EE6 Ủ LATIN CAPITAL LETTER U WITH HOOK ABOVE
≡ 0055 U + 0309 ̉

1EE7 ủ LATIN SMALL LETTER U WITH HOOK ABOVE
≡ 0075 u + 0309 ̉

1EE8 Ứ LATIN CAPITAL LETTER U WITH HORN AND ACUTE
≡ 01AF Ư + 0301 ́

1EE9 ứ LATIN SMALL LETTER U WITH HORN AND ACUTE
≡ 01B0 ư + 0301 ́

1EEA Ừ LATIN CAPITAL LETTER U WITH HORN AND GRAVE
≡ 01AF Ư + 0300 ̀

1EEB ừ LATIN SMALL LETTER U WITH HORN AND GRAVE
≡ 01B0 ư + 0300 ̀

1EEC Ử LATIN CAPITAL LETTER U WITH HORN AND HOOK ABOVE
≡ 01AF Ư + 0309 ̉

1EED ử LATIN SMALL LETTER U WITH HORN AND HOOK ABOVE
≡ 01B0 ư + 0309 ̉

1EEE Ữ LATIN CAPITAL LETTER U WITH HORN AND TILDE
≡ 01AF Ư + 0303 ̃

1EEF ữ LATIN SMALL LETTER U WITH HORN AND TILDE
≡ 01B0 ư + 0303 ̃

1EF0 Ự LATIN CAPITAL LETTER U WITH HORN AND DOT BELOW
≡ 01AF Ư + 0323 ̣

1EF1 ự LATIN SMALL LETTER U WITH HORN AND DOT BELOW
≡ 01B0 ư + 0323 ̣

1EF2 Ỳ LATIN CAPITAL LETTER Y WITH GRAVE
≡ 0059 Y + 0300 ̀

1EF3 ỳ LATIN SMALL LETTER Y WITH GRAVE
≡ 0079 y + 0300 ̀

1EF4 Ỵ LATIN CAPITAL LETTER Y WITH DOT BELOW
≡ 0059 Y + 0323 ̣

1EF5 ỵ LATIN SMALL LETTER Y WITH DOT BELOW
≡ 0079 y + 0323 ̣

1EF6 Ỷ LATIN CAPITAL LETTER Y WITH HOOK ABOVE
≡ 0059 Y + 0309 ̉

1EF7 ỷ LATIN SMALL LETTER Y WITH HOOK ABOVE
≡ 0079 y + 0309 ̉

1EF8 Ỹ LATIN CAPITAL LETTER Y WITH TILDE
≡ 0059 Y + 0303 ̃

1EF9 ỹ LATIN SMALL LETTER Y WITH TILDE
≡ 0079 y + 0303 ̃

	1F0	1F1	1F2	1F3	1F4	1F5	1F6	1F7
0	ἀ 1F00	ἐ 1F10	ἠ 1F20	ἰ 1F30	ὀ 1F40	ὐ 1F50	ὠ 1F60	ὰ 1F70
1	ἁ 1F01	ἑ 1F11	ἡ 1F21	ἱ 1F31	ὁ 1F41	ὑ 1F51	ὡ 1F61	ά 1F71
2	ἂ 1F02	ἒ 1F12	ἢ 1F22	ἲ 1F32	ὂ 1F42	ὒ 1F52	ὢ 1F62	ὲ 1F72
3	ἃ 1F03	ἓ 1F13	ἣ 1F23	ἳ 1F33	ὃ 1F43	ὓ 1F53	ὣ 1F63	έ 1F73
4	ἄ 1F04	ἔ 1F14	ἤ 1F24	ἴ 1F34	ὄ 1F44	ὔ 1F54	ὤ 1F64	ὴ 1F74
5	ἅ 1F05	ἕ 1F15	ἥ 1F25	ἵ 1F35	ὅ 1F45	ὕ 1F55	ὥ 1F65	ή 1F75
6	ἆ 1F06		ἦ 1F26	ἶ 1F36		ὖ 1F56	ὦ 1F66	ὶ 1F76
7	ἇ 1F07		ἧ 1F27	ἷ 1F37		ὗ 1F57	ὧ 1F67	ί 1F77
8	Ἀ 1F08	Ἐ 1F18	Ἠ 1F28	Ἰ 1F38	Ὀ 1F48		Ὠ 1F68	ὸ 1F78
9	Ἁ 1F09	Ἑ 1F19	Ἡ 1F29	Ἱ 1F39	Ὁ 1F49	Ὑ 1F59	Ὡ 1F69	ό 1F79
A	Ἂ 1F0A	Ἒ 1F1A	Ἢ 1F2A	Ἲ 1F3A	Ὂ 1F4A		Ὢ 1F6A	ὺ 1F7A
B	Ἃ 1F0B	Ἓ 1F1B	Ἣ 1F2B	Ἳ 1F3B	Ὃ 1F4B	Ὓ 1F5B	Ὣ 1F6B	ύ 1F7B
C	Ἄ 1F0C	Ἔ 1F1C	Ἤ 1F2C	Ἴ 1F3C	Ὄ 1F4C		Ὤ 1F6C	ὼ 1F7C
D	Ἅ 1F0D	Ἕ 1F1D	Ἥ 1F2D	Ἵ 1F3D	Ὅ 1F4D	Ὕ 1F5D	Ὥ 1F6D	ώ 1F7D
E	Ἆ 1F0E		Ἦ 1F2E	Ἶ 1F3E			Ὦ 1F6E	
F	Ἇ 1F0F		Ἧ 1F2F	Ἷ 1F3F		Ὗ 1F5F	Ὧ 1F6F	

	1F8	1F9	1FA	1FB	1FC	1FD	1FE	1FF
0	ᾀ 1F80	ᾐ 1F90	ᾠ 1FA0	ᾰ 1FB0	῀ 1FC0	ῐ 1FD0	ῠ 1FE0	
1	ᾁ 1F81	ᾑ 1F91	ᾡ 1FA1	ᾱ 1FB1	῁ 1FC1	ῑ 1FD1	ῡ 1FE1	
2	ᾂ 1F82	ᾒ 1F92	ᾢ 1FA2	ᾲ 1FB2	ῂ 1FC2	ῒ 1FD2	ῢ 1FE2	ῲ 1FF2
3	ᾃ 1F83	ᾓ 1F93	ᾣ 1FA3	ᾳ 1FB3	ῃ 1FC3	ΐ 1FD3	ΰ 1FE3	ῳ 1FF3
4	ᾄ 1F84	ᾔ 1F94	ᾤ 1FA4	ᾴ 1FB4	ῄ 1FC4		ῤ 1FE4	ῴ 1FF4
5	ᾅ 1F85	ᾕ 1F95	ᾥ 1FA5				ῥ 1FE5	
6	ᾆ 1F86	ᾖ 1F96	ᾦ 1FA6	ᾶ 1FB6	ῆ 1FC6	ῖ 1FD6	ῦ 1FE6	ῶ 1FF6
7	ᾇ 1F87	ᾗ 1F97	ᾧ 1FA7	ᾷ 1FB7	ῇ 1FC7	ῗ 1FD7	ῧ 1FE7	ῷ 1FF7
8	ᾈ 1F88	ᾘ 1F98	ᾨ 1FA8	Ᾰ 1FB8	Ὲ 1FC8	Ῐ 1FD8	Ῠ 1FE8	Ὸ 1FF8
9	ᾉ 1F89	ᾙ 1F99	ᾩ 1FA9	Ᾱ 1FB9	Έ 1FC9	Ῑ 1FD9	Ῡ 1FE9	Ό 1FF9
A	ᾊ 1F8A	ᾚ 1F9A	ᾪ 1FAA	Ὰ 1FBA	Ὴ 1FCA	Ὶ 1FDA	Ὺ 1FEA	Ὼ 1FFA
B	ᾋ 1F8B	ᾛ 1F9B	ᾫ 1FAB	Ά 1FBB	Ή 1FCB	Ί 1FDB	Ύ 1FEB	Ώ 1FFB
C	ᾌ 1F8C	ᾜ 1F9C	ᾬ 1FAC	ᾼ 1FBC	ῌ 1FCC		Ῥ 1FEC	ῼ 1FFC
D	ᾍ 1F8D	ᾝ 1F9D	ᾭ 1FAD	᾽ 1FBD	῍ 1FCD	῝ 1FDD	῭ 1FED	´ 1FFD
E	ᾎ 1F8E	ᾞ 1F9E	ᾮ 1FAE	ι 1FBE	῎ 1FCE	῞ 1FDE	΅ 1FEE	῾ 1FFE
F	ᾏ 1F8F	ᾟ 1F9F	ᾯ 1FAF	᾿ 1FBF	῏ 1FCF	῟ 1FDF	` 1FEF	

Greek extended

1F00 ἀ GREEK SMALL LETTER ALPHA WITH PSILI
≡ 03B1 α + 0313 ◌̓

1F01 ἁ GREEK SMALL LETTER ALPHA WITH DASIA
≡ 03B1 α + 0314 ◌̔

1F02 ἂ GREEK SMALL LETTER ALPHA WITH PSILI AND VARIA
≡ 1F00 ἀ + 0300 ◌̀

1F03 ἃ GREEK SMALL LETTER ALPHA WITH DASIA AND VARIA
≡ 1F01 ἁ + 0300 ◌̀

1F04 ἄ GREEK SMALL LETTER ALPHA WITH PSILI AND OXIA
≡ 1F00 ἀ + 0301 ◌́

1F05 ἅ GREEK SMALL LETTER ALPHA WITH DASIA AND OXIA
≡ 1F01 ἁ + 0301 ◌́

1F06 ἆ GREEK SMALL LETTER ALPHA WITH PSILI AND PERISPOMENI
≡ 1F00 ἀ + 0342 ◌͂

1F07 ἇ GREEK SMALL LETTER ALPHA WITH DASIA AND PERISPOMENI
≡ 1F01 ἁ + 0342 ◌͂

1F08 Ἀ GREEK CAPITAL LETTER ALPHA WITH PSILI
≡ 0391 Α + 0313 ◌̓

1F09 Ἁ GREEK CAPITAL LETTER ALPHA WITH DASIA
≡ 0391 Α + 0314 ◌̔

1F0A Ἂ GREEK CAPITAL LETTER ALPHA WITH PSILI AND VARIA
≡ 1F08 Ἀ + 0300 ◌̀

1F0B Ἃ GREEK CAPITAL LETTER ALPHA WITH DASIA AND VARIA
≡ 1F09 Ἁ + 0300 ◌̀

1F0C Ἄ GREEK CAPITAL LETTER ALPHA WITH PSILI AND OXIA
≡ 1F08 Ἀ + 0301 ◌́

1F0D Ἅ GREEK CAPITAL LETTER ALPHA WITH DASIA AND OXIA
≡ 1F09 Ἁ + 0301 ◌́

1F0E Ἆ GREEK CAPITAL LETTER ALPHA WITH PSILI AND PERISPOMENI
≡ 1F08 Ἀ + 0342 ◌͂

1F0F Ἇ GREEK CAPITAL LETTER ALPHA WITH DASIA AND PERISPOMENI
≡ 1F09 Ἁ + 0342 ◌͂

1F10 ἐ GREEK SMALL LETTER EPSILON WITH PSILI
≡ 03B5 ε + 0313 ◌̓

1F11 ἑ GREEK SMALL LETTER EPSILON WITH DASIA
≡ 03B5 ε + 0314 ◌̔

1F12 ἒ GREEK SMALL LETTER EPSILON WITH PSILI AND VARIA
≡ 1F10 ἐ + 0300 ◌̀

1F13 ἓ GREEK SMALL LETTER EPSILON WITH DASIA AND VARIA
≡ 1F11 ἑ + 0300 ◌̀

1F14 ἔ GREEK SMALL LETTER EPSILON WITH PSILI AND OXIA
≡ 1F10 ἐ + 0301 ◌́

1F15 ἕ GREEK SMALL LETTER EPSILON WITH DASIA AND OXIA
≡ 1F11 ἑ + 0301 ◌́

1F16 <reserved>

1F17 <reserved>

1F18 Ἐ GREEK CAPITAL LETTER EPSILON WITH PSILI
≡ 0395 Ε + 0313 ◌̓

1F19 Ἑ GREEK CAPITAL LETTER EPSILON WITH DASIA
≡ 0395 Ε + 0314 ◌̔

1F1A Ἒ GREEK CAPITAL LETTER EPSILON WITH PSILI AND VARIA
≡ 1F18 Ἐ + 0300 ◌̀

1F1B Ἓ GREEK CAPITAL LETTER EPSILON WITH DASIA AND VARIA
≡ 1F19 Ἑ + 0300 ◌̀

1F1C Ἔ GREEK CAPITAL LETTER EPSILON WITH PSILI AND OXIA
≡ 1F18 Ἐ + 0301 ◌́

1F1D Ἕ GREEK CAPITAL LETTER EPSILON WITH DASIA AND OXIA
≡ 1F19 Ἑ + 0301 ◌́

1F1E <reserved>

1F1F <reserved>

1F20 ἠ GREEK SMALL LETTER ETA WITH PSILI
≡ 03B7 η + 0313 ◌̓

1F21 ἡ GREEK SMALL LETTER ETA WITH DASIA
≡ 03B7 η + 0314 ◌̔

1F22 ἢ GREEK SMALL LETTER ETA WITH PSILI AND VARIA
≡ 1F20 ἠ + 0300 ◌̀

1F23 ἣ GREEK SMALL LETTER ETA WITH DASIA AND VARIA
≡ 1F21 ἡ + 0300 ◌̀

1F24 ἤ GREEK SMALL LETTER ETA WITH PSILI AND OXIA
≡ 1F20 ἠ + 0301 ◌́

1F25 ἥ GREEK SMALL LETTER ETA WITH DASIA AND OXIA
≡ 1F21 ἡ + 0301 ◌́

1F26 ἦ GREEK SMALL LETTER ETA WITH PSILI AND PERISPOMENI
≡ 1F20 ἠ + 0342 ◌͂

1F27 ἧ GREEK SMALL LETTER ETA WITH DASIA AND PERISPOMENI
≡ 1F21 ἡ + 0342 ͂

1F28 Ἠ GREEK CAPITAL LETTER ETA WITH PSILI
≡ 0397 Η + 0313 ̓

1F29 Ἡ GREEK CAPITAL LETTER ETA WITH DASIA
≡ 0397 Η + 0314 ̔

1F2A Ἢ GREEK CAPITAL LETTER ETA WITH PSILI AND VARIA
≡ 1F28 Ἠ + 0300 ̀

1F2B Ἣ GREEK CAPITAL LETTER ETA WITH DASIA AND VARIA
≡ 1F29 Ἡ + 0300 ̀

1F2C Ἤ GREEK CAPITAL LETTER ETA WITH PSILI AND OXIA
≡ 1F28 Ἠ + 0301 ́

1F2D Ἥ GREEK CAPITAL LETTER ETA WITH DASIA AND OXIA
≡ 1F29 Ἡ + 0301 ́

1F2E Ἦ GREEK CAPITAL LETTER ETA WITH PSILI AND PERISPOMENI
≡ 1F28 Ἠ + 0342 ͂

1F2F Ἧ GREEK CAPITAL LETTER ETA WITH DASIA AND PERISPOMENI
≡ 1F29 Ἡ + 0342 ͂

1F30 ἰ GREEK SMALL LETTER IOTA WITH PSILI
≡ 03B9 ι + 0313 ̓

1F31 ἱ GREEK SMALL LETTER IOTA WITH DASIA
≡ 03B9 ι + 0314 ̔

1F32 ἲ GREEK SMALL LETTER IOTA WITH PSILI AND VARIA
≡ 1F30 ἰ + 0300 ̀

1F33 ἳ GREEK SMALL LETTER IOTA WITH DASIA AND VARIA
≡ 1F31 ἱ + 0300 ̀

1F34 ἴ GREEK SMALL LETTER IOTA WITH PSILI AND OXIA
≡ 1F30 ἰ + 0301 ́

1F35 ἵ GREEK SMALL LETTER IOTA WITH DASIA AND OXIA
≡ 1F31 ἱ + 0301 ́

1F36 ἶ GREEK SMALL LETTER IOTA WITH PSILI AND PERISPOMENI
≡ 1F30 ἰ + 0342 ͂

1F37 ἷ GREEK SMALL LETTER IOTA WITH DASIA AND PERISPOMENI
≡ 1F31 ἱ + 0342 ͂

1F38 Ἰ GREEK CAPITAL LETTER IOTA WITH PSILI
≡ 0399 Ι + 0313 ̓

1F39 Ἱ GREEK CAPITAL LETTER IOTA WITH DASIA
≡ 0399 Ι + 0314 ̔

1F3A Ἲ GREEK CAPITAL LETTER IOTA WITH PSILI AND VARIA
≡ 1F38 Ἰ + 0300 ̀

1F3B Ἳ GREEK CAPITAL LETTER IOTA WITH DASIA AND VARIA
≡ 1F39 Ἱ + 0300 ̀

1F3C Ἴ GREEK CAPITAL LETTER IOTA WITH PSILI AND OXIA
≡ 1F38 Ἰ + 0301 ́

1F3D Ἵ GREEK CAPITAL LETTER IOTA WITH DASIA AND OXIA
≡ 1F39 Ἱ + 0301 ́

1F3E Ἶ GREEK CAPITAL LETTER IOTA WITH PSILI AND PERISPOMENI
≡ 1F38 Ἰ + 0342 ͂

1F3F Ἷ GREEK CAPITAL LETTER IOTA WITH DASIA AND PERISPOMENI
≡ 1F39 Ἱ + 0342 ͂

1F40 ὀ GREEK SMALL LETTER OMICRON WITH PSILI
≡ 03BF ο + 0313 ̓

1F41 ὁ GREEK SMALL LETTER OMICRON WITH DASIA
≡ 03BF ο + 0314 ̔

1F42 ὂ GREEK SMALL LETTER OMICRON WITH PSILI AND VARIA
≡ 1F40 ὀ + 0300 ̀

1F43 ὃ GREEK SMALL LETTER OMICRON WITH DASIA AND VARIA
≡ 1F41 ὁ + 0300 ̀

1F44 ὄ GREEK SMALL LETTER OMICRON WITH PSILI AND OXIA
≡ 1F40 ὀ + 0301 ́

1F45 ὅ GREEK SMALL LETTER OMICRON WITH DASIA AND OXIA
≡ 1F41 ὁ + 0301 ́

1F46 <reserved>

1F47 <reserved>

1F48 Ὀ GREEK CAPITAL LETTER OMICRON WITH PSILI
≡ 039F Ο + 0313 ̓

1F49 Ὁ GREEK CAPITAL LETTER OMICRON WITH DASIA
≡ 039F Ο + 0314 ̔

1F4A Ὂ GREEK CAPITAL LETTER OMICRON WITH PSILI AND VARIA
≡ 1F48 Ὀ + 0300 ̀

1F4B Ὃ GREEK CAPITAL LETTER OMICRON WITH DASIA AND VARIA
≡ 1F49 Ὁ + 0300 ̀

1F4C Ὄ GREEK CAPITAL LETTER OMICRON WITH PSILI AND OXIA
≡ 1F48 Ὀ + 0301 ◌́

1F4D Ὅ GREEK CAPITAL LETTER OMICRON WITH DASIA AND OXIA
≡ 1F49 Ὁ + 0301 ◌́

1F4E <reserved>

1F4F <reserved>

1F50 ὐ GREEK SMALL LETTER UPSILON WITH PSILI
≡ 03C5 υ + 0313 ◌̓

1F51 ὑ GREEK SMALL LETTER UPSILON WITH DASIA
≡ 03C5 υ + 0314 ◌̔

1F52 ὒ GREEK SMALL LETTER UPSILON WITH PSILI AND VARIA
≡ 1F50 ὐ + 0300 ◌̀

1F53 ὓ GREEK SMALL LETTER UPSILON WITH DASIA AND VARIA
≡ 1F51 ὑ + 0300 ◌̀

1F54 ὔ GREEK SMALL LETTER UPSILON WITH PSILI AND OXIA
≡ 1F50 ὐ + 0301 ◌́

1F55 ὕ GREEK SMALL LETTER UPSILON WITH DASIA AND OXIA
≡ 1F51 ὑ + 0301 ◌́

1F56 ὖ GREEK SMALL LETTER UPSILON WITH PSILI AND PERISPOMENI
≡ 1F50 ὐ + 0342 ◌͂

1F57 ὗ GREEK SMALL LETTER UPSILON WITH DASIA AND PERISPOMENI
≡ 1F51 ὑ + 0342 ◌͂

1F58 <reserved>

1F59 Ὑ GREEK CAPITAL LETTER UPSILON WITH DASIA
≡ 03A5 Υ + 0314 ◌̔

1F5A <reserved>

1F5B Ὓ GREEK CAPITAL LETTER UPSILON WITH DASIA AND VARIA
≡ 1F59 Ὑ + 0300 ◌̀

1F5C <reserved>

1F5D Ὕ GREEK CAPITAL LETTER UPSILON WITH DASIA AND OXIA
≡ 1F59 Ὑ + 0301 ◌́

1F5E <reserved>

1F5F Ὗ GREEK CAPITAL LETTER UPSILON WITH DASIA AND PERISPOMENI
≡ 1F59 Ὑ + 0342 ◌͂

1F60 ὠ GREEK SMALL LETTER OMEGA WITH PSILI
≡ 03C9 ω + 0313 ◌̓

1F61 ὡ GREEK SMALL LETTER OMEGA WITH DASIA
≡ 03C9 ω + 0314 ◌̔

1F62 ὢ GREEK SMALL LETTER OMEGA WITH PSILI AND VARIA
≡ 1F60 ὠ + 0300 ◌̀

1F63 ὣ GREEK SMALL LETTER OMEGA WITH DASIA AND VARIA
≡ 1F61 ὡ + 0300 ◌̀

1F64 ὤ GREEK SMALL LETTER OMEGA WITH PSILI AND OXIA
≡ 1F60 ὠ + 0301 ◌́

1F65 ὥ GREEK SMALL LETTER OMEGA WITH DASIA AND OXIA
≡ 1F61 ὡ + 0301 ◌́

1F66 ὦ GREEK SMALL LETTER OMEGA WITH PSILI AND PERISPOMENI
≡ 1F60 ὠ + 0342 ◌͂

1F67 ὧ GREEK SMALL LETTER OMEGA WITH DASIA AND PERISPOMENI
≡ 1F61 ὡ + 0342 ◌͂

1F68 Ὠ GREEK CAPITAL LETTER OMEGA WITH PSILI
≡ 03A9 Ω + 0313 ◌̓

1F69 Ὡ GREEK CAPITAL LETTER OMEGA WITH DASIA
≡ 03A9 Ω + 0314 ◌̔

1F6A Ὢ GREEK CAPITAL LETTER OMEGA WITH PSILI AND VARIA
≡ 1F68 Ὠ + 0300 ◌̀

1F6B Ὣ GREEK CAPITAL LETTER OMEGA WITH DASIA AND VARIA
≡ 1F69 Ὡ + 0300 ◌̀

1F6C Ὤ GREEK CAPITAL LETTER OMEGA WITH PSILI AND OXIA
≡ 1F68 Ὠ + 0301 ◌́

1F6D Ὥ GREEK CAPITAL LETTER OMEGA WITH DASIA AND OXIA
≡ 1F69 Ὡ + 0301 ◌́

1F6E Ὦ GREEK CAPITAL LETTER OMEGA WITH PSILI AND PERISPOMENI
≡ 1F68 Ὠ + 0342 ◌͂

1F6F Ὧ GREEK CAPITAL LETTER OMEGA WITH DASIA AND PERISPOMENI
≡ 1F69 Ὡ + 0342 ◌͂

1F70 ὰ GREEK SMALL LETTER ALPHA WITH VARIA
≡ 03B1 α + 0300 ◌̀

1F71 ά GREEK SMALL LETTER ALPHA WITH OXIA
≡ 03B1 α + 0301 ◌́

1F72 ὲ GREEK SMALL LETTER EPSILON WITH VARIA
≡ 03B5 ε + 0300 ◌̀

1F73 έ GREEK SMALL LETTER EPSILON WITH OXIA
≡ 03B5 ε + 0301 ◌́

1F74 ὴ GREEK SMALL LETTER ETA WITH VARIA
≡ 03B7 η + 0300 ◌̀

1F75 ή GREEK SMALL LETTER ETA WITH OXIA
≡ 03B7 η + 0301 ◌́

1F76 ὶ GREEK SMALL LETTER IOTA WITH VARIA
≡ 03B9 ι + 0300 ◌̀

1F77 ί GREEK SMALL LETTER IOTA WITH OXIA
≡ 03B9 ι + 0301 ◌́

1F78 ὸ GREEK SMALL LETTER OMICRON WITH VARIA
≡ 03BF ο + 0300 ◌̀

1F79 ό GREEK SMALL LETTER OMICRON WITH OXIA
≡ 03BF ο + 0301 ◌́

1F7A ὺ GREEK SMALL LETTER UPSILON WITH VARIA
≡ 03C5 υ + 0300 ◌̀

1F7B ύ GREEK SMALL LETTER UPSILON WITH OXIA
≡ 03C5 υ + 0301 ◌́

1F7C ὼ GREEK SMALL LETTER OMEGA WITH VARIA
≡ 03C9 ω + 0300 ◌̀

1F7D ώ GREEK SMALL LETTER OMEGA WITH OXIA
≡ 03C9 ω + 0301 ◌́

1F7E <reserved>

1F7F <reserved>

1F80 ᾀ GREEK SMALL LETTER ALPHA WITH PSILI AND YPOGEGRAMMENI
≡ 1F00 ἀ + 0345 ◌ͅ

1F81 ᾁ GREEK SMALL LETTER ALPHA WITH DASIA AND YPOGEGRAMMENI
≡ 1F01 ἁ + 0345 ◌ͅ

1F82 ᾂ GREEK SMALL LETTER ALPHA WITH PSILI AND VARIA AND YPOGEGRAMMENI
≡ 1F02 ἂ + 0345 ◌ͅ

1F83 ᾃ GREEK SMALL LETTER ALPHA WITH DASIA AND VARIA AND YPOGEGRAMMENI
≡ 1F03 ἃ + 0345 ◌ͅ

1F84 ᾄ GREEK SMALL LETTER ALPHA WITH PSILI AND OXIA AND YPOGEGRAMMENI
≡ 1F04 ἄ + 0345 ◌ͅ

1F85 ᾅ GREEK SMALL LETTER ALPHA WITH DASIA AND OXIA AND YPOGEGRAMMENI
≡ 1F05 ἅ + 0345 ◌ͅ

1F86 ᾆ GREEK SMALL LETTER ALPHA WITH PSILI AND PERISPOMENI AND YPOGEGRAMMENI
≡ 1F06 ἆ + 0345 ◌ͅ

1F87 ᾇ GREEK SMALL LETTER ALPHA WITH DASIA AND PERISPOMENI AND YPOGEGRAMMENI
≡ 1F07 ἇ + 0345 ◌ͅ

1F88 ᾈ GREEK CAPITAL LETTER ALPHA WITH PSILI AND PROSGEGRAMMENI
≡ 1F08 Ἀ + 0345 ◌ͅ

1F89 ᾉ GREEK CAPITAL LETTER ALPHA WITH DASIA AND PROSGEGRAMMENI
≡ 1F09 Ἁ + 0345 ◌ͅ

1F8A ᾊ GREEK CAPITAL LETTER ALPHA WITH PSILI AND VARIA AND PROSGEGRAMMENI
≡ 1F0A Ἂ + 0345 ◌ͅ

1F8B ᾋ GREEK CAPITAL LETTER ALPHA WITH DASIA AND VARIA AND PROSGEGRAMMENI
≡ 1F0B Ἃ + 0345 ◌ͅ

1F8C ᾌ GREEK CAPITAL LETTER ALPHA WITH PSILI AND OXIA AND PROSGEGRAMMENI
≡ 1F0C Ἄ + 0345 ◌ͅ

1F8D ᾍ GREEK CAPITAL LETTER ALPHA WITH DASIA AND OXIA AND PROSGEGRAMMENI
≡ 1F0D Ἅ + 0345 ◌ͅ

1F8E ᾎ GREEK CAPITAL LETTER ALPHA WITH PSILI AND PERISPOMENI AND PROSGEGRAMMENI
≡ 1F0E Ἆ + 0345 ◌ͅ

1F8F ᾏ GREEK CAPITAL LETTER ALPHA WITH DASIA AND PERISPOMENI AND PROSGEGRAMMENI
≡ 1F0F Ἇ + 0345 ◌ͅ

1F90 ᾐ GREEK SMALL LETTER ETA WITH PSILI AND YPOGEGRAMMENI
≡ 1F20 ἠ + 0345 ◌ͅ

1F91 ᾑ GREEK SMALL LETTER ETA WITH DASIA AND YPOGEGRAMMENI
≡ 1F21 ἡ + 0345 ◌ͅ

1F92 ᾒ GREEK SMALL LETTER ETA WITH PSILI AND VARIA AND YPOGEGRAMMENI
≡ 1F22 ἢ + 0345 ◌ͅ

1F93 ᾓ GREEK SMALL LETTER ETA WITH DASIA AND VARIA AND YPOGEGRAMMENI
≡ 1F23 ἣ + 0345 ◌ͅ

1F94 ᾔ GREEK SMALL LETTER ETA WITH PSILI AND OXIA AND YPOGEGRAMMENI
≡ 1F24 ἤ + 0345 ͅ

1F95 ᾕ GREEK SMALL LETTER ETA WITH DASIA AND OXIA AND YPOGEGRAMMENI
≡ 1F25 ἥ + 0345 ͅ

1F96 ᾖ GREEK SMALL LETTER ETA WITH PSILI AND PERISPOMENI AND YPOGEGRAMMENI
≡ 1F26 ἦ + 0345 ͅ

1F97 ᾗ GREEK SMALL LETTER ETA WITH DASIA AND PERISPOMENI AND YPOGEGRAMMENI
≡ 1F27 ἧ + 0345 ͅ

1F98 ᾘ GREEK CAPITAL LETTER ETA WITH PSILI AND PROSGEGRAMMENI
≡ 1F28 Ἠ + 0345 ͅ

1F99 ᾙ GREEK CAPITAL LETTER ETA WITH DASIA AND PROSGEGRAMMENI
≡ 1F29 Ἡ + 0345 ͅ

1F9A ᾚ GREEK CAPITAL LETTER ETA WITH PSILI AND VARIA AND PROSGEGRAMMENI
≡ 1F2A Ἢ + 0345 ͅ

1F9B ᾛ GREEK CAPITAL LETTER ETA WITH DASIA AND VARIA AND PROSGEGRAMMENI
≡ 1F2B Ἣ + 0345 ͅ

1F9C ᾜ GREEK CAPITAL LETTER ETA WITH PSILI AND OXIA AND PROSGEGRAMMENI
≡ 1F2C Ἤ + 0345 ͅ

1F9D ᾝ GREEK CAPITAL LETTER ETA WITH DASIA AND OXIA AND PROSGEGRAMMENI
≡ 1F2D Ἥ + 0345 ͅ

1F9E ᾞ GREEK CAPITAL LETTER ETA WITH PSILI AND PERISPOMENI AND PROSGEGRAMMENI
≡ 1F2E Ἦ + 0345 ͅ

1F9F ᾟ GREEK CAPITAL LETTER ETA WITH DASIA AND PERISPOMENI AND PROSGEGRAMMENI
≡ 1F2F Ἧ + 0345 ͅ

1FA0 ᾠ GREEK SMALL LETTER OMEGA WITH PSILI AND YPOGEGRAMMENI
≡ 1F60 ὠ + 0345 ͅ

1FA1 ᾡ GREEK SMALL LETTER OMEGA WITH DASIA AND YPOGEGRAMMENI
≡ 1F61 ὡ + 0345 ͅ

1FA2 ᾢ GREEK SMALL LETTER OMEGA WITH PSILI AND VARIA AND YPOGEGRAMMENI
≡ 1F62 ὢ + 0345 ͅ

1FA3 ᾣ GREEK SMALL LETTER OMEGA WITH DASIA AND VARIA AND YPOGEGRAMMENI
≡ 1F63 ὣ + 0345 ͅ

1FA4 ᾤ GREEK SMALL LETTER OMEGA WITH PSILI AND OXIA AND YPOGEGRAMMENI
≡ 1F64 ὤ + 0345 ͅ

1FA5 ᾥ GREEK SMALL LETTER OMEGA WITH DASIA AND OXIA AND YPOGEGRAMMENI
≡ 1F65 ὥ + 0345 ͅ

1FA6 ᾦ GREEK SMALL LETTER OMEGA WITH PSILI AND PERISPOMENI AND YPOGEGRAMMENI
≡ 1F66 ὦ + 0345 ͅ

1FA7 ᾧ GREEK SMALL LETTER OMEGA WITH DASIA AND PERISPOMENI AND YPOGEGRAMMENI
≡ 1F67 ὧ + 0345 ͅ

1FA8 ᾨ GREEK CAPITAL LETTER OMEGA WITH PSILI AND PROSGEGRAMMENI
≡ 1F68 Ὠ + 0345 ͅ

1FA9 ᾩ GREEK CAPITAL LETTER OMEGA WITH DASIA AND PROSGEGRAMMENI
≡ 1F69 Ὡ + 0345 ͅ

1FAA ᾪ GREEK CAPITAL LETTER OMEGA WITH PSILI AND VARIA AND PROSGEGRAMMENI
≡ 1F6A Ὢ + 0345 ͅ

1FAB ᾫ GREEK CAPITAL LETTER OMEGA WITH DASIA AND VARIA AND PROSGEGRAMMENI
≡ 1F6B Ὣ + 0345 ͅ

1FAC ᾬ GREEK CAPITAL LETTER OMEGA WITH PSILI AND OXIA AND PROSGEGRAMMENI
≡ 1F6C Ὤ + 0345 ͅ

1FAD ᾭ GREEK CAPITAL LETTER OMEGA WITH DASIA AND OXIA AND PROSGEGRAMMENI
≡ 1F6D Ὥ + 0345 ͅ

1FAE ᾮ GREEK CAPITAL LETTER OMEGA WITH PSILI AND PERISPOMENI AND PROSGEGRAMMENI
≡ 1F6E Ὦ + 0345 ͅ

1FAF ᾯ GREEK CAPITAL LETTER OMEGA WITH DASIA AND PERISPOMENI AND PROSGEGRAMMENI
≡ 1F6F Ὧ + 0345 ͅ

1FB0 ᾰ GREEK SMALL LETTER ALPHA WITH VRACHY
≡ 03B1 α + 0306 ◌̆

1FB1 ᾱ GREEK SMALL LETTER ALPHA WITH MACRON
≡ 03B1 α + 0304 ◌̄

1FB2 ᾲ GREEK SMALL LETTER ALPHA WITH VARIA AND YPOGEGRAMMENI
≡ 1F70 ὰ + 0345 ◌ͅ

1FB3 ᾳ GREEK SMALL LETTER ALPHA WITH YPOGEGRAMMENI
≡ 03B1 α + 0345 ◌ͅ

1FB4 ᾴ GREEK SMALL LETTER ALPHA WITH OXIA AND YPOGEGRAMMENI
≡ 1F71 ά + 0345 ◌ͅ

1FB5 <reserved>

1FB6 ᾶ GREEK SMALL LETTER ALPHA WITH PERISPOMENI
≡ 03B1 α + 0342 ◌͂

1FB7 ᾷ GREEK SMALL LETTER ALPHA WITH PERISPOMENI AND YPOGEGRAMMENI
≡ 1FB6 ᾶ + 0345 ◌ͅ

1FB8 Ᾰ GREEK CAPITAL LETTER ALPHA WITH VRACHY
≡ 0391 Α + 0306 ◌̆

1FB9 Ᾱ GREEK CAPITAL LETTER ALPHA WITH MACRON
≡ 0391 Α + 0304 ◌̄

1FBA Ὰ GREEK CAPITAL LETTER ALPHA WITH VARIA
≡ 0391 Α + 0300 ◌̀

1FBB Ά GREEK CAPITAL LETTER ALPHA WITH OXIA
≡ 0391 Α + 0301 ◌́

1FBC ᾼ GREEK CAPITAL LETTER ALPHA WITH PROSGEGRAMMENI
≡ 0391 Α + 0345 ◌ͅ

1FBD ᾽ GREEK KORONIS
≈ 0020 [SP] + 0313 ◌̓

1FBE ι GREEK PROSGEGRAMMENI
≡ 0399 Ι

1FBF ᾿ GREEK PSILI
≈ 0020 [SP] + 0313 ◌̓

1FC0 ῀ GREEK PERISPOMENI
≈ 0020 [SP] + 0342 ◌͂

1FC1 ῁ GREEK DIALYTIKA AND PERISPOMENI
≡ 00A8 ¨ + 0342 ◌͂

1FC2 ῂ GREEK SMALL LETTER ETA WITH VARIA AND YPOGEGRAMMENI
≡ 1F74 ὴ + 0345 ◌ͅ

1FC3 ῃ GREEK SMALL LETTER ETA WITH YPOGEGRAMMENI
≡ 03B7 η + 0345 ◌ͅ

1FC4 ῄ GREEK SMALL LETTER ETA WITH OXIA AND YPOGEGRAMMENI
≡ 1F75 ή + 0345 ◌ͅ

1FC5 <reserved>

1FC6 ῆ GREEK SMALL LETTER ETA WITH PERISPOMENI
≡ 03B7 η + 0342 ◌͂

1FC7 ῇ GREEK SMALL LETTER ETA WITH PERISPOMENI AND YPOGEGRAMMENI
≡ 1FC6 ῆ + 0345 ◌ͅ

1FC8 Ὲ GREEK CAPITAL LETTER EPSILON WITH VARIA
≡ 0395 Ε + 0300 ◌̀

1FC9 Έ GREEK CAPITAL LETTER EPSILON WITH OXIA
≡ 0395 Ε + 0301 ◌́

1FCA Ὴ GREEK CAPITAL LETTER ETA WITH VARIA
≡ 0397 Η + 0300 ◌̀

1FCB Ή GREEK CAPITAL LETTER ETA WITH OXIA
≡ 0397 Η + 0301 ◌́

1FCC ῌ GREEK CAPITAL LETTER ETA WITH PROSGEGRAMMENI
≡ 0397 Η + 0345 ◌ͅ

1FCD ῍ GREEK PSILI AND VARIA
≡ 1FBF ᾿ + 0300 ◌̀

1FCE ῎ GREEK PSILI AND OXIA
≡ 1FBF ᾿ + 0301 ◌́

1FCF ῏ GREEK PSILI AND PERISPOMENI
≡ 1FBF ᾿ + 0342 ◌͂

1FD0 ῐ GREEK SMALL LETTER IOTA WITH VRACHY
≡ 03B9 ι + 0306 ◌̆

1FD1 ῑ GREEK SMALL LETTER IOTA WITH MACRON
≡ 03B9 ι + 0304 ◌̄

1FD2 ῒ GREEK SMALL LETTER IOTA WITH DIALYTIKA AND VARIA
≡ 03CA ϊ + 0300 ◌̀

1FD3 ΐ GREEK SMALL LETTER IOTA WITH DIALYTIKA AND OXIA
≡ 03CA ϊ + 0301 ◌́

1FD4 <reserved>

1FD5 <reserved>

1FD6 ῖ GREEK SMALL LETTER IOTA WITH PERISPOMENI
≡ 03B9 ι + 0342 ◌͂

1FD7 ῗ GREEK SMALL LETTER IOTA WITH DIALYTIKA AND PERISPOMENI
≡ 03CA ϊ + 0342 ◌͂

1FD8 Ῐ GREEK CAPITAL LETTER IOTA WITH VRACHY
≡ 0399 Ι + 0306 ◌̆

1FD9 Ῑ GREEK CAPITAL LETTER IOTA WITH MACRON
≡ 0399 Ι + 0304 ◌̄

1FDA Ὶ GREEK CAPITAL LETTER IOTA WITH VARIA
≡ 0399 Ι + 0300 ◌̀

1FDB Ί GREEK CAPITAL LETTER IOTA WITH OXIA
≡ 0399 Ι + 0301 ◌́

1FDC <reserved>

1FDD ῝ GREEK DASIA AND VARIA
≡ 1FFE ῾ + 0300 ◌̀

1FDE ῞ GREEK DASIA AND OXIA
≡ 1FFE ῾ + 0301 ◌́

1FDF ῟ GREEK DASIA AND PERISPOMENI
≡ 1FFE ῾ + 0342 ◌͂

1FE0 ῠ GREEK SMALL LETTER UPSILON WITH VRACHY
≡ 03C5 υ + 0306 ◌̆

1FE1 ῡ GREEK SMALL LETTER UPSILON WITH MACRON
≡ 03C5 υ + 0304 ◌̄

1FE2 ῢ GREEK SMALL LETTER UPSILON WITH DIALYTIKA AND VARIA
≡ 03CB ϋ + 0300 ◌̀

1FE3 ΰ GREEK SMALL LETTER UPSILON WITH DIALYTIKA AND OXIA
≡ 03CB ϋ + 0301 ◌́

1FE4 ῤ GREEK SMALL LETTER RHO WITH PSILI
≡ 03C1 ρ + 0313 ◌̓

1FE5 ῥ GREEK SMALL LETTER RHO WITH DASIA
≡ 03C1 ρ + 0314 ◌̔

1FE6 ῦ GREEK SMALL LETTER UPSILON WITH PERISPOMENI
≡ 03C5 υ + 0342 ◌͂

1FE7 ῧ GREEK SMALL LETTER UPSILON WITH DIALYTIKA AND PERISPOMENI
≡ 03CB ϋ + 0342 ◌͂

1FE8 Ῠ GREEK CAPITAL LETTER UPSILON WITH VRACHY
≡ 03A5 Υ + 0306 ◌̆

1FE9 Ῡ GREEK CAPITAL LETTER UPSILON WITH MACRON
≡ 03A5 Υ + 0304 ◌̄

1FEA Ὺ GREEK CAPITAL LETTER UPSILON WITH VARIA
≡ 03A5 Υ + 0300 ◌̀

1FEB Ύ GREEK CAPITAL LETTER UPSILON WITH OXIA
≡ 03A5 Υ + 0301 ◌́

1FEC Ῥ GREEK CAPITAL LETTER RHO WITH DASIA
≡ 03A1 Ρ + 0314 ◌̔

1FED ῭ GREEK DIALYTIKA AND VARIA
≡ 00A8 ¨ + 0300 ◌̀

1FEE ΅ GREEK DIALYTIKA AND OXIA
≡ 00A8 ¨ + 0301 ◌́

1FEF ` GREEK VARIA
≡ 0060 `

1FF0 <reserved>

1FF1 <reserved>

1FF2 ῲ GREEK SMALL LETTER OMEGA WITH VARIA AND YPOGEGRAMMENI
≡ 1F7C ὼ + 0345 ◌ͅ

1FF3 ῳ GREEK SMALL LETTER OMEGA WITH YPOGEGRAMMENI
≡ 03C9 ω + 0345 ◌ͅ

1FF4 ῴ GREEK SMALL LETTER OMEGA WITH OXIA AND YPOGEGRAMMENI
≡ 1F79 ό + 0345 ◌ͅ

1FF5 <reserved>

1FF6 ῶ GREEK SMALL LETTER OMEGA WITH PERISPOMENI
≡ 03C9 ω + 0342 ◌͂

1FF7 ῷ GREEK SMALL LETTER OMEGA WITH PERISPOMENI AND YPOGEGRAMMENI
≡ 1FF6 ῶ + 0345 ◌ͅ

1FF8 Ὸ GREEK CAPITAL LETTER OMICRON WITH VARIA
≡ 039F Ο + 0300 ◌̀

1FF9 Ό GREEK CAPITAL LETTER OMICRON WITH OXIA
≡ 039F Ο + 0301 ◌́

1FFA Ὼ GREEK CAPITAL LETTER OMEGA WITH VARIA
≡ 03A9 Ω + 0300 ◌̀

1FFB Ώ GREEK CAPITAL LETTER OMEGA WITH OXIA
≡ 03A9 Ω + 0301 ◌́

1FFC ῼ GREEK CAPITAL LETTER OMEGA WITH PROSGEGRAMMENI
≡ 03A9 Ω + 0345 ◌ͅ

1FFD ´ GREEK OXIA
≡ 00B4 ´

1FFE ῾ GREEK DASIA
≈ 0020 SP + 0314 ◌̔

	200	201	202	203	204	205	206
0	NQ SP 2000	‐ 2010	† 2020	‰ 2030	⁀ 2040		
1	MQ SP 2001	‑ 2011	‡ 2021	‱ 2031	⁁ 2041		
2	EN SP 2002	‒ 2012	• 2022	′ 2032	⁂ 2042		
3	EM SP 2003	– 2013	‣ 2023	″ 2033	⁃ 2043		
4	3/M SP 2004	— 2014	․ 2024	‴ 2034	⁄ 2044		
5	4/M SP 2005	― 2015	‥ 2025	‵ 2035	⁅ 2045		
6	6/M SP 2006	‖ 2016	… 2026	‶ 2036	⁆ 2046		
7	F SP 2007	‗ 2017	‧ 2027	‷ 2037			
8	P SP 2008	‘ 2018	L SEP 2028	‸ 2038			
9	TH SP 2009	’ 2019	P SEP 2029	‹ 2039			
A	H SP 200A	‚ 201A	LRE 202A	› 203A			I SS 206A
B	ZW SP 200B	‛ 201B	RLE 202B	※ 203B			A SS 206B
C	ZW NJ 200C	“ 201C	PDF 202C	‼ 203C			I AFS 206C
D	ZW J 200D	” 201D	LRO 202D	‽ 203D			A AFS 206D
E	LRM 200E	„ 201E	RLO 202E	‾ 203E			NA DS 206E
F	RLM 200F	‟ 201F		‿ 203F			NO DS 206F

General punctuation

2000 [NQSP] EN QUAD
≡ 2002 [ENSP]

2001 [MQSP] EM QUAD
≡ 2003 [EMSP]

2002 [ENSP] EN SPACE
≈ 0020 [SP]

2003 [EMSP] EM SPACE
≈ 0020 [SP]

2004 [3/MSP] THREE-PER-EM SPACE
≈ 0020 [SP]

2005 [4/MSP] FOUR-PER-EM SPACE
≈ 0020 [SP]

2006 [6/MSP] SIX-PER-EM SPACE
≈ 0020 [SP]

2007 [FSP] FIGURE SPACE
≈ <noBreak> + 0020 [SP]

2008 [PSP] PUNCTUATION SPACE
≈ 0020 [SP]

2009 [THSP] THIN SPACE
≈ 0020 [SP]

200A [HSP] HAIR SPACE
≈ 0020 [SP]

200B [ZWSP] ZERO WIDTH SPACE

200C [ZWNJ] ZERO WIDTH NON-JOINER
= ZWNJ ("zwinj")

200D [ZWJ] ZERO WIDTH JOINER
= ZWJ ("zawj")

200E [LRM] LEFT-TO-RIGHT MARK
= LRM

200F [RLM] RIGHT-TO-LEFT MARK
= RLM

2010 ‐ HYPHEN
→ 002D - hyphen-minus

2011 ‑ NON-BREAKING HYPHEN
→ 002D - hyphen-minus
≈ <noBreak> + 2010 ‐

2012 ‒ FIGURE DASH

2013 – EN DASH

2014 — EM DASH
→ 30FC ー katakana-hiragana prolonged sound mark

2015 ― HORIZONTAL BAR
= QUOTATION DASH
• long dash introducing quoted text

2016 ‖ DOUBLE VERTICAL LINE
• used in pairs to indicate norm of a matrix
→ 2225 ∥ parallel to

2017 ‗ DOUBLE LOW LINE
= SPACING DOUBLE UNDERSCORE
• this is a spacing character
→ 005F _ low line
→ 0333 ̳ combining double low line
≈ 0020 [SP] + 0333 ̳

2018 ‘ LEFT SINGLE QUOTATION MARK
= SINGLE TURNED COMMA QUOTATION MARK
• this is the preferred character for opening single quotation mark
→ 0027 ' apostrophe
→ 02BB ʻ modifier letter turned comma
→ 275B ❛ heavy single turned comma quotation mark ornament

2019 ’ RIGHT SINGLE QUOTATION MARK
= SINGLE COMMA QUOTATION MARK
• this is the preferred character for closing single quotation mark
→ 0027 ' apostrophe
→ 02BC ʼ modifier letter apostrophe
→ 275C ❜ heavy single comma quotation mark ornament

201A ‚ SINGLE LOW-9 QUOTATION MARK
= LOW SINGLE COMMA QUOTATION MARK
• usually opening, sometimes closing, in European usage

201B ‛ SINGLE HIGH-REVERSED-9 QUOTATION MARK
= SINGLE REVERSED COMMA QUOTATION MARK
• glyph variant of 2018 ‘
→ 02BD ʽ modifier letter reversed comma

201C “ LEFT DOUBLE QUOTATION MARK
= DOUBLE TURNED COMMA QUOTATION MARK
• this is the preferred character for opening quotation mark
→ 0022 " quotation mark
→ 275D ❝ heavy double turned comma quotation mark ornament
→ 301D 〝 reversed double prime quotation mark

201D ” RIGHT DOUBLE QUOTATION MARK
= DOUBLE COMMA QUOTATION MARK
• this is the preferred character for closing quotation mark
→ 0022 " quotation mark
→ 2033 ″ double prime
→ 275E ❞ heavy double comma quotation mark ornament
→ 301E 〞 double prime quotation mark

201E „ DOUBLE LOW-9 QUOTATION MARK
= LOW DOUBLE COMMA QUOTATION MARK
• usually opening, sometimes closing, in European usage
→ 301F 〟 low double prime quotation mark

201F ‟ DOUBLE HIGH-REVERSED-9 QUOTATION MARK
= DOUBLE REVERSED COMMA QUOTATION MARK
• glyph variant of 201C “

2020 † DAGGER

2021 ‡ DOUBLE DAGGER

2022 • BULLET
= black small circle
→ 00B7 · middle dot
→ 2024 . one dot leader
→ 2219 ∙ bullet operator
→ 25D8 ◘ inverse bullet
→ 25E6 ◦ white bullet

2023 ‣ TRIANGULAR BULLET
→ 220E ∎ end of proof
→ 25B8 ▸ black right-pointing small triangle

2024 . ONE DOT LEADER
→ 00B7 · middle dot
→ 2022 • bullet
→ 2219 ∙ bullet operator
≈ 002E .

2025 ‥ TWO DOT LEADER
≈ 002E . + 002E .

2026 … HORIZONTAL ELLIPSIS
= three dot leader
→ 22EE ⋮ vertical ellipsis
≈ 002E . + 002E . + 002E .

2027 ‧ HYPHENATION POINT

2028 LINE SEPARATOR
• may be used to represent this semantic unambiguously

2029 PARAGRAPH SEPARATOR
• may be used to represent this semantic unambiguously

202A LEFT-TO-RIGHT EMBEDDING
= LRE

202B RIGHT-TO-LEFT EMBEDDING
= RLE

202C POP DIRECTIONAL FORMATTING
= PDF

202D LEFT-TO-RIGHT OVERRIDE
= LRO

202E RIGHT-TO-LEFT OVERRIDE
= RLO

202F <reserved>

2030 ‰ PER MILLE SIGN
→ 0025 % percent sign

2031 ‱ PER TEN THOUSAND SIGN
→ 0025 % percent sign

2032 ′ PRIME
= minutes
= feet
→ 0027 ' apostrophe
→ 00B4 ´ acute accent
→ 02B9 ʹ modifier letter prime

2033 ″ DOUBLE PRIME
= seconds
= inches
→ 0022 " quotation mark
→ 02BA ʺ modifier letter double prime
→ 201D ” right double quotation mark
→ 3003 〃 ditto mark
→ 301E 〞 double prime quotation mark
≈ 2032 ′ + 2032 ′

2034 ‴ TRIPLE PRIME
≈ 2032 ′ + 2032 ′ + 2032 ′

2035 ‵ REVERSED PRIME
→ 0060 ` grave accent

2036 ‶ REVERSED DOUBLE PRIME
→ 301D 〝 reversed double prime quotation mark
≈ 2035 ‵ + 2035 ‵

2037 ‷ REVERSED TRIPLE PRIME
≈ 2035 ‵ + 2035 ‵ + 2035 ‵

2038 ‸ CARET

2039 ‹ SINGLE LEFT-POINTING ANGLE QUOTATION MARK
= LEFT POINTING SINGLE GUILLEMET
• usually opening, sometimes closing
→ 003C < less-than sign
→ 2329 〈 left-pointing angle bracket
→ 3008 〈 left angle bracket

203A › SINGLE RIGHT-POINTING ANGLE QUOTATION MARK
= RIGHT POINTING SINGLE GUILLEMET
• usually closing, sometimes opening
→ 003E > greater-than sign
→ 232A 〉 right-pointing angle bracket
→ 3009 〉 right angle bracket

203B ※ REFERENCE MARK
= Japanese kome
= Urdu paragraph separator

203C ‼ DOUBLE EXCLAMATION MARK
→ 0021 ! exclamation mark
≈ 0021 ! + 0021 !

203D ‽ INTERROBANG
→ 003F ? question mark

203E ‾ OVERLINE
= SPACING OVERSCORE
≈ 0020 SP + 0305 ̅

203F ‿ UNDERTIE
= Greek enotikon

2040 ⁀ CHARACTER TIE

2041 ⁁ CARET INSERTION POINT
• proofreader's mark: insert here
→ 22CC ⋌ right semidirect product

2042 ⁂ ASTERISM

2043 ⁃ HYPHEN BULLET

2044 ⁄ FRACTION SLASH
• for composing arbitrary fractions
→ 002F / solidus
→ 2215 ∕ division slash

2045 ⁅ LEFT SQUARE BRACKET WITH QUILL

2046 ⁆ RIGHT SQUARE BRACKET WITH QUILL

2047 <reserved>
2048 <reserved>
2049 <reserved>
204A <reserved>
204B <reserved>
204C <reserved>
204D <reserved>
204E <reserved>
204F <reserved>
2050 <reserved>
2051 <reserved>
2052 <reserved>
2053 <reserved>
2054 <reserved>
2055 <reserved>
2056 <reserved>
2057 <reserved>
2058 <reserved>
2059 <reserved>
205A <reserved>
205B <reserved>
205C <reserved>
205D <reserved>
205E <reserved>
205F <reserved>
2060 <reserved>
2061 <reserved>
2062 <reserved>
2063 <reserved>
2064 <reserved>
2065 <reserved>
2066 <reserved>
2067 <reserved>
2068 <reserved>
2069 <reserved>

206A INHIBIT SYMMETRIC SWAPPING
206B ACTIVATE SYMMETRIC SWAPPING
206C INHIBIT ARABIC FORM SHAPING
206D ACTIVATE ARABIC FORM SHAPING
206E NATIONAL DIGIT SHAPES
206F NOMINAL DIGIT SHAPES

	207	208	209
0	^{0} 2070	$_{0}$ 2080	
1		$_{1}$ 2081	
2		$_{2}$ 2082	
3		$_{3}$ 2083	
4	^{4} 2074	$_{4}$ 2084	
5	^{5} 2075	$_{5}$ 2085	
6	^{6} 2076	$_{6}$ 2086	
7	^{7} 2077	$_{7}$ 2087	
8	^{8} 2078	$_{8}$ 2088	
9	^{9} 2079	$_{9}$ 2089	
A	$^{+}$ 207A	$_{+}$ 208A	
B	$^{-}$ 207B	$_{-}$ 208B	
C	$^{=}$ 207C	$_{=}$ 208C	
D	$^{(}$ 207D	$_{(}$ 208D	
E	$^{)}$ 207E	$_{)}$ 208E	
F	^{n} 207F		

Superscripts and subscripts

2070 ^{0} SUPERSCRIPT ZERO
≈ <super> + 0030 0

2071 <reserved>
→ 00B9 ^{1} superscript one

2072 <reserved>
→ 00B2 ^{2} superscript two

2073 <reserved>
→ 00B3 ^{3} superscript three

2074 ^{4} SUPERSCRIPT FOUR
≈ <super> + 0034 4

2075 ^{5} SUPERSCRIPT FIVE
≈ <super> + 0035 5

2076 ^{6} SUPERSCRIPT SIX
≈ <super> + 0036 6

2077 ^{7} SUPERSCRIPT SEVEN
≈ <super> + 0037 7

2078 ^{8} SUPERSCRIPT EIGHT
≈ <super> + 0038 8

2079 ^{9} SUPERSCRIPT NINE
≈ <super> + 0039 9

207A $^{+}$ SUPERSCRIPT PLUS SIGN
≈ <super> + 002B +

207B $^{-}$ SUPERSCRIPT MINUS
≈ <super> + 2212 −

207C $^{=}$ SUPERSCRIPT EQUALS SIGN
≈ <super> + 003D =

207D $^{(}$ SUPERSCRIPT LEFT PARENTHESIS
≈ <super> + 0028 (

207E $^{)}$ SUPERSCRIPT RIGHT PARENTHESIS
≈ <super> + 0029)

207F ^{n} SUPERSCRIPT LATIN SMALL LETTER N
≈ <super> + 006E n

2080 $_{0}$ SUBSCRIPT ZERO
≈ <sub> + 0030 0

2081 $_{1}$ SUBSCRIPT ONE
≈ <sub> + 0031 1

2082 $_{2}$ SUBSCRIPT TWO
≈ <sub> + 0032 2

2083 $_{3}$ SUBSCRIPT THREE
≈ <sub> + 0033 3

2084 $_{4}$ SUBSCRIPT FOUR
≈ <sub> + 0034 4

2085 $_{5}$ SUBSCRIPT FIVE
≈ <sub> + 0035 5

2086 $_{6}$ SUBSCRIPT SIX
≈ <sub> + 0036 6

2087 $_{7}$ SUBSCRIPT SEVEN
≈ <sub> + 0037 7

2088 $_{8}$ SUBSCRIPT EIGHT
≈ <sub> + 0038 8

2089 $_{9}$ SUBSCRIPT NINE
≈ <sub> + 0039 9

208A $_{+}$ SUBSCRIPT PLUS SIGN
≈ <sub> + 002B +

208B $_{-}$ SUBSCRIPT MINUS
≈ <sub> + 2212 −

208C $_{=}$ SUBSCRIPT EQUALS SIGN
≈ <sub> + 003D =

208D $_{(}$ SUBSCRIPT LEFT PARENTHESIS
≈ <sub> + 0028 (

208E $_{)}$ SUBSCRIPT RIGHT PARENTHESIS
≈ <sub> + 0029)

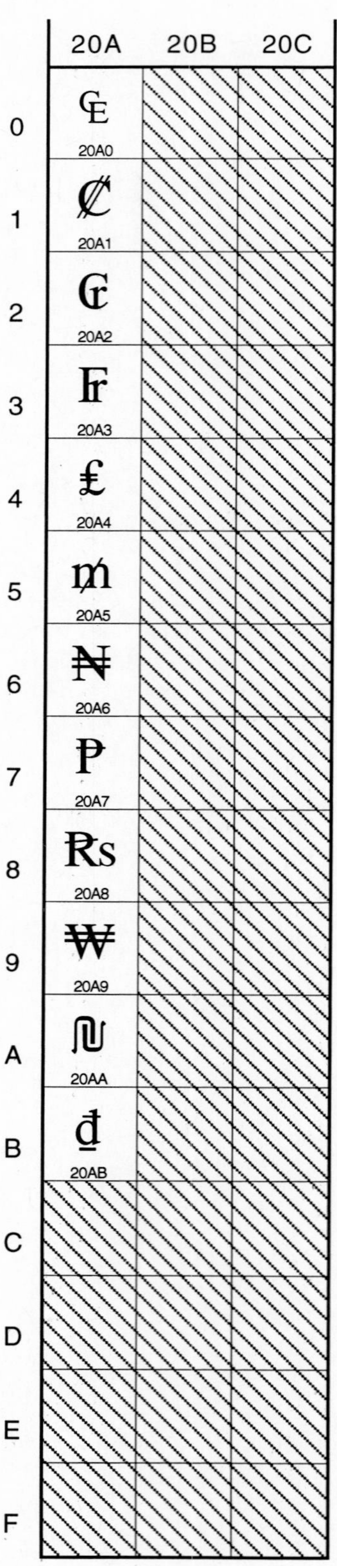
20A
20B
20C
0
20A0
1
20A1
2
20A2
3
20A3
4
20A4
5
20A5
6
20A6
7
20A7
8
20A8
9
20A9
A
20AA
B
20AB
C
D
E
F

Currency symbols

→ 0024 $ dollar sign
→ 00A2 ¢ cent sign
→ 00A3 £ pound sign
→ 00A4 ¤ currency sign
→ 00A5 ¥ yen sign
→ 09F2 ৲ bengali rupee mark
→ 09F3 ৳ bengali rupee sign
→ 0E3F ฿ thai currency symbol baht

20A0 ₠ EURO-CURRENCY SIGN

20A1 ₡ COLON SIGN
• Costa Rica, El Salvador

20A2 ₢ CRUZEIRO SIGN
• Brazil

20A3 ₣ FRENCH FRANC SIGN
• France

20A4 ₤ LIRA SIGN
• Italy, Turkey
→ 00A3 £ pound sign

20A5 ₥ MILL SIGN
• USA (1/10 cent)

20A6 ₦ NAIRA SIGN
• Nigeria

20A7 ₧ PESETA SIGN
• Spain

20A8 ₨ RUPEE SIGN
• India
≈ 0052 R + 0073 s

20A9 ₩ WON SIGN
• Korea

20AA ₪ NEW SHEQEL SIGN
• Israel

20AB ₫ DONG SIGN
• Vietnam

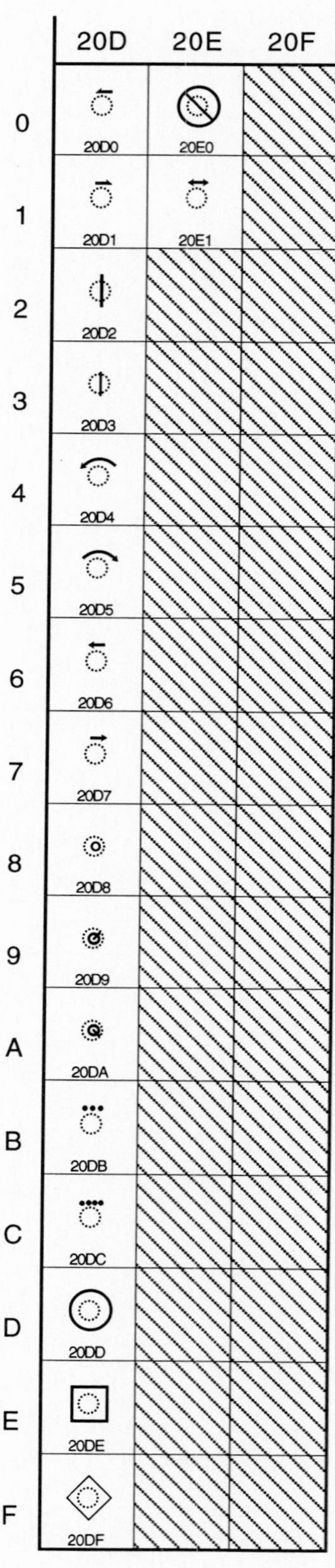

20D
20E
20F
0
1
2
3
4
5
6
7
8
9
A
B
C
D
E
F
20D0
20D1
20D2
20D3
20D4
20D5
20D6
20D7
20D8
20D9
20DA
20DB
20DC
20DD
20DE
20DF
20E0
20E1

Combining diacritical marks for symbols

20D0 ◌⃐ COMBINING LEFT HARPOON ABOVE
20D1 ◌⃑ COMBINING RIGHT HARPOON ABOVE
• vector
20D2 ◌⃒ COMBINING LONG VERTICAL LINE OVERLAY
20D3 ◌⃓ COMBINING SHORT VERTICAL LINE OVERLAY
• negation
20D4 ◌⃔ COMBINING ANTICLOCKWISE ARROW ABOVE
20D5 ◌⃕ COMBINING CLOCKWISE ARROW ABOVE
• rotation
20D6 ◌⃖ COMBINING LEFT ARROW ABOVE
20D7 ◌⃗ COMBINING RIGHT ARROW ABOVE
• vector
20D8 ◌⃘ COMBINING RING OVERLAY
20D9 ◌⃙ COMBINING CLOCKWISE RING OVERLAY
20DA ◌⃚ COMBINING ANTICLOCKWISE RING OVERLAY
20DB ◌⃛ COMBINING THREE DOTS ABOVE
= third derivative
20DC ◌⃜ COMBINING FOUR DOTS ABOVE
= fourth derivative

Enclosing diacritics

20DD ◌⃝ COMBINING ENCLOSING CIRCLE
= JIS composition circle
→ 25CB ○ white circle
→ 25EF ◯ large circle
→ 3007 〇 ideographic number zero
20DE ◌⃞ COMBINING ENCLOSING SQUARE
20DF ◌⃟ COMBINING ENCLOSING DIAMOND
20E0 ◌⃠ COMBINING ENCLOSING CIRCLE BACKSLASH
• prohibition

Additional diacritics

20E1 ◌⃡ COMBINING LEFT RIGHT ARROW ABOVE
• tensor

	210	211	212	213	214
0	℀ 2100	ℐ 2110	℠ 2120	ℰ 2130	
1	℁ 2101	ℑ 2111	℡ 2121	ℱ 2131	
2	ℂ 2102	ℒ 2112	™ 2122	Ⅎ 2132	
3	℃ 2103	ℓ 2113	℣ 2123	ℳ 2133	
4	℄ 2104	℔ 2114	ℤ 2124	ℴ 2134	
5	℅ 2105	ℕ 2115	℥ 2125	ℵ 2135	
6	℆ 2106	№ 2116	Ω 2126	ℶ 2136	
7	ℇ 2107	℗ 2117	℧ 2127	ℷ 2137	
8	℈ 2108	℘ 2118	ℨ 2128	ℸ 2138	
9	℉ 2109	ℙ 2119	℩ 2129		
A	ℊ 210A	ℚ 211A	K 212A		
B	ℋ 210B	ℛ 211B	Å 212B		
C	ℌ 210C	ℜ 211C	ℬ 212C		
D	ℍ 210D	ℝ 211D	ℭ 212D		
E	ℎ 210E	℞ 211E	℮ 212E		
F	ℏ 210F	℟ 211F	ℯ 212F		

Letterlike symbols

2100 ℀ ACCOUNT OF

2101 ℁ ADDRESSED TO THE SUBJECT

2102 ℂ DOUBLE-STRUCK CAPITAL C
= the set of complex numbers
→ 0043 C latin capital letter c
≈ <font> + 0043 C

2103 ℃ DEGREE CELSIUS
= degrees Centigrade
≈ 00B0 ° + 0043 C

2104 ℄ CENTRE LINE SYMBOL
= clone

2105 ℅ CARE OF

2106 ℆ CADA UNA

2107 ℇ EULER CONSTANT
→ 0045 E latin capital letter e
→ 0190 Ɛ latin capital letter open e
≈ 0190 Ɛ

2108 ℈ SCRUPLE

2109 ℉ DEGREE FAHRENHEIT
≈ 00B0 ° + 0046 F

210A ℊ SCRIPT SMALL G
= real number symbol
→ 0067 g latin small letter g
≈ <font> + 0067 g

210B ℋ SCRIPT CAPITAL H
= Hamiltonian function
→ 0048 H latin capital letter h
≈ <font> + 0048 H

210C ℌ BLACK-LETTER CAPITAL H
→ 0048 H latin capital letter h
≈ <font> + 0048 H

210D ℍ DOUBLE-STRUCK CAPITAL H
→ 0048 H latin capital letter h
≈ <font> + 0048 H

210E ℎ PLANCK CONSTANT
→ 0068 h latin small letter h
≈ <font> + 0068 h

210F ℏ PLANCK CONSTANT OVER TWO PI
→ 0127 ħ latin small letter h with stroke
→ 045B ћ cyrillic small letter tshe
≈ <font> + 0127 ħ

2110 ℐ SCRIPT CAPITAL I
→ 0049 I latin capital letter i
≈ <font> + 0049 I

2111 ℑ BLACK-LETTER CAPITAL I
= imaginary part
→ 0049 I latin capital letter i
≈ <font> + 0049 I

2112 ℒ SCRIPT CAPITAL L
= Laplace symbol
→ 004C L latin capital letter l
≈ <font> + 004C L

2113 ℓ SCRIPT SMALL L
= liter
→ 006C l latin small letter l
≈ <font> + 006C l

2114 ℔ L B BAR SYMBOL
= pounds

2115 ℕ DOUBLE-STRUCK CAPITAL N
= natural number
→ 004E N latin capital letter n
≈ <font> + 004E N

2116 № NUMERO SIGN
≈ 004E N + 006F o

2117 ℗ SOUND RECORDING COPYRIGHT
= published
→ 00A9 © copyright sign

2118 ℘ SCRIPT CAPITAL P
= per
= power set
= Weierstrass elliptic function
→ 0050 P latin capital letter p
≈ <font> + 0050 P

2119 ℙ DOUBLE-STRUCK CAPITAL P
→ 0050 P latin capital letter p
≈ <font> + 0050 P

211A ℚ DOUBLE-STRUCK CAPITAL Q
= the set of rational numbers
→ 0051 Q latin capital letter q
≈ <font> + 0051 Q

211B ℛ SCRIPT CAPITAL R
= Riemann Integral
→ 0052 R latin capital letter r
≈ <font> + 0052 R

211C ℜ BLACK-LETTER CAPITAL R
= REAL PART SYMBOL
→ 0052 R latin capital letter r
≈ <font> + 0052 R

211D ℝ DOUBLE-STRUCK CAPITAL R
= the set of real numbers
→ 0052 R latin capital letter r
≈ <font> + 0052 R

211E ℞ PRESCRIPTION TAKE
= recipe
= cross ratio

211F ℟ RESPONSE

2120 ℠ SERVICE MARK
≈ <super> + 0053 S + 004D M

2121 ℡ TELEPHONE SIGN
≈ <super> + 0054 T + 0045 E + 004C L

2122 ™ TRADE MARK SIGN
≈ <super> + 0054 T + 004D M

2123 ℣ VERSICLE

2124 ℤ DOUBLE-STRUCK CAPITAL Z
= the set of integers
→ 005A Z latin capital letter z
≈ <font> + 005A Z

2125 ℥ OUNCE SIGN
→ 0292 ʒ latin small letter ezh

2126 Ω OHM SIGN
= resistance
→ 03A9 Ω greek capital letter omega
≡ 03A9 Ω

2127 ℧ INVERTED OHM SIGN
= conductance
• typographically a turned greek capital letter omega
→ 01B1 Ʊ latin capital letter upsilon
→ 03A9 Ω greek capital letter omega

2128 ℨ BLACK-LETTER CAPITAL Z
→ 005A Z latin capital letter z
≈ <font> + 005A Z

2129 ℩ TURNED GREEK SMALL LETTER IOTA
• unique element fulfilling a description (logic)
→ 03B9 ι greek small letter iota

212A K KELVIN SIGN
= degrees Kelvin
→ 004B K latin capital letter k
≡ 004B K

212B Å ANGSTROM SIGN
→ 00C5 Å latin capital letter a with ring above
≡ 00C5 Å

212C ℬ SCRIPT CAPITAL B
= Bernoulli function
→ 0042 B latin capital letter b
≈ <font> + 0042 B

212D ℭ BLACK-LETTER CAPITAL C
→ 0043 C latin capital letter c
≈ <font> + 0043 C

212E ℮ ESTIMATED SYMBOL
• used in European packaging
→ 0065 e latin small letter e

212F ℯ SCRIPT SMALL E
= error
→ 0065 e latin small letter e
≈ <font> + 0065 e

2130 ℰ SCRIPT CAPITAL E
= EMF (Electro-Magnetic Force)
→ 0045 E latin capital letter e
≈ <font> + 0045 E

2131 ℱ SCRIPT CAPITAL F
= Fourier transform
→ 0046 F latin capital letter f
≈ <font> + 0046 F

2132 Ⅎ TURNED CAPITAL F
→ 0046 F latin capital letter f

2133 ℳ SCRIPT CAPITAL M
= M-matrix (physics)
→ 004D M latin capital letter m
≈ <font> + 004D M

2134 ℴ SCRIPT SMALL O
= order; of inferior order to
→ 006F o latin small letter o
≈ <font> + 006F o

2135 ℵ ALEF SYMBOL
= first transfinite cardinal (countable)
→ 05D0 א hebrew letter alef
≈ 05D0 א

2136 ℶ BET SYMBOL
= second transfinite cardinal (the continuum)
→ 05D1 ב hebrew letter bet
≈ 05D1 ב

2137 ℷ GIMEL SYMBOL
= third transfinite cardinal (functions of a real variable)
→ 05D2 ג hebrew letter gimel
≈ 05D2 ג

2138 ℸ DALET SYMBOL
= fourth transfinite cardinal
→ 05D3 ד hebrew letter dalet
≈ 05D3 ד

	215	216	217	218
0		Ⅰ 2160	ⅰ 2170	ↀ 2180
1		Ⅱ 2161	ⅱ 2171	ↁ 2181
2		Ⅲ 2162	ⅲ 2172	ↂ 2182
3	⅓ 2153	Ⅳ 2163	ⅳ 2173	
4	⅔ 2154	Ⅴ 2164	ⅴ 2174	
5	⅕ 2155	Ⅵ 2165	ⅵ 2175	
6	⅖ 2156	Ⅶ 2166	ⅶ 2176	
7	⅗ 2157	Ⅷ 2167	ⅷ 2177	
8	⅘ 2158	Ⅸ 2168	ⅸ 2178	
9	⅙ 2159	Ⅹ 2169	ⅹ 2179	
A	⅚ 215A	Ⅺ 216A	ⅺ 217A	
B	⅛ 215B	Ⅻ 216B	ⅻ 217B	
C	⅜ 215C	Ⅼ 216C	ⅼ 217C	
D	⅝ 215D	Ⅽ 216D	ⅽ 217D	
E	⅞ 215E	Ⅾ 216E	ⅾ 217E	
F	⅟ 215F	Ⅿ 216F	ⅿ 217F	

Number forms

2150 <reserved>
→ 00BC ¼ vulgar fraction one quarter

2151 <reserved>
→ 00BD ½ vulgar fraction one half

2152 <reserved>
→ 00BE ¾ vulgar fraction three quarters

2153 ⅓ VULGAR FRACTION ONE THIRD
≈ <fraction> + 0031 1 + 2044 ⁄ + 0033 3

2154 ⅔ VULGAR FRACTION TWO THIRDS
≈ <fraction> + 0032 2 + 2044 ⁄ + 0033 3

2155 ⅕ VULGAR FRACTION ONE FIFTH
≈ <fraction> + 0031 1 + 2044 ⁄ + 0035 5

2156 ⅖ VULGAR FRACTION TWO FIFTHS
≈ <fraction> + 0032 2 + 2044 ⁄ + 0035 5

2157 ⅗ VULGAR FRACTION THREE FIFTHS
≈ <fraction> + 0033 3 + 2044 ⁄ + 0035 5

2158 ⅘ VULGAR FRACTION FOUR FIFTHS
≈ <fraction> + 0034 4 + 2044 ⁄ + 0035 5

2159 ⅙ VULGAR FRACTION ONE SIXTH
≈ <fraction> + 0031 1 + 2044 ⁄ + 0036 6

215A ⅚ VULGAR FRACTION FIVE SIXTHS
≈ <fraction> + 0035 5 + 2044 ⁄ + 0036 6

215B ⅛ VULGAR FRACTION ONE EIGHTH
≈ <fraction> + 0031 1 + 2044 ⁄ + 0038 8

215C ⅜ VULGAR FRACTION THREE EIGHTHS
≈ <fraction> + 0033 3 + 2044 ⁄ + 0038 8

215D ⅝ VULGAR FRACTION FIVE EIGHTHS
≈ <fraction> + 0035 5 + 2044 ⁄ + 0038 8

215E ⅞ VULGAR FRACTION SEVEN EIGHTHS
≈ <fraction> + 0037 7 + 2044 ⁄ + 0038 8

215F ⅟ FRACTION NUMERATOR ONE
≈ <fraction> + 0031 1 + 2044 ⁄

2160 Ⅰ ROMAN NUMERAL ONE
≈ 0049 I

2161 Ⅱ ROMAN NUMERAL TWO
≈ 0049 I + 0049 I

2162 Ⅲ ROMAN NUMERAL THREE
≈ 0049 I + 0049 I + 0049 I

2163 Ⅳ ROMAN NUMERAL FOUR
≈ 0049 I + 0056 V

2164 Ⅴ ROMAN NUMERAL FIVE
≈ 0056 V

2165 Ⅵ ROMAN NUMERAL SIX
≈ 0056 V + 0049 I

2166 Ⅶ ROMAN NUMERAL SEVEN
≈ 0056 V + 0049 I + 0049 I

2167 Ⅷ ROMAN NUMERAL EIGHT
≈ 0056 V + 0049 I + 0049 I + 0049 I

2168 Ⅸ ROMAN NUMERAL NINE
≈ 0049 I + 0058 X

2169 Ⅹ ROMAN NUMERAL TEN
≈ 0058 X

216A Ⅺ ROMAN NUMERAL ELEVEN
≈ 0058 X + 0049 I

216B Ⅻ ROMAN NUMERAL TWELVE
≈ 0058 X + 0049 I + 0049 I

216C Ⅼ ROMAN NUMERAL FIFTY
≈ 004C L

216D Ⅽ ROMAN NUMERAL ONE HUNDRED
≈ 0043 C

216E Ⅾ ROMAN NUMERAL FIVE HUNDRED
≈ 0044 D

216F Ⅿ ROMAN NUMERAL ONE THOUSAND
≈ 004D M

2170 ⅰ SMALL ROMAN NUMERAL ONE
≈ 0069 i

2171 ⅱ SMALL ROMAN NUMERAL TWO
≈ 0069 i + 0069 i

2172 ⅲ SMALL ROMAN NUMERAL THREE
≈ 0069 i + 0069 i + 0069 i

2173 ⅳ SMALL ROMAN NUMERAL FOUR
≈ 0069 i + 0076 v

2174 ⅴ SMALL ROMAN NUMERAL FIVE
≈ 0076 v

2175 ⅵ SMALL ROMAN NUMERAL SIX
≈ 0076 v + 0069 i

2176 ⅶ SMALL ROMAN NUMERAL SEVEN
≈ 0076 v + 0069 i + 0069 i

2177 ⅷ SMALL ROMAN NUMERAL EIGHT
≈ 0076 v + 0069 i + 0069 i + 0069 i

2178 ⅸ SMALL ROMAN NUMERAL NINE
≈ 0069 i + 0078 x

2179 ⅹ SMALL ROMAN NUMERAL TEN
≈ 0078 x

217A ⅺ SMALL ROMAN NUMERAL ELEVEN
≈ 0078 x + 0069 i

217B ⅻ SMALL ROMAN NUMERAL TWELVE
≈ 0078 x + 0069 i + 0069 i

217C ⅼ SMALL ROMAN NUMERAL FIFTY
≈ 006C l

217D c SMALL ROMAN NUMERAL ONE HUNDRED
≈ 0063 c

217E d SMALL ROMAN NUMERAL FIVE HUNDRED
≈ 0064 d

217F m SMALL ROMAN NUMERAL ONE THOUSAND
≈ 006D m

2180 ↀ ROMAN NUMERAL ONE THOUSAND C D

2181 ↁ ROMAN NUMERAL FIVE THOUSAND

2182 ↂ ROMAN NUMERAL TEN THOUSAND

	219	21A	21B	21C	21D	21E	21F
0	← 2190	↠ 21A0	↰ 21B0	⇀ 21C0	⇐ 21D0	⇠ 21E0	
1	↑ 2191	↡ 21A1	↱ 21B1	⇁ 21C1	⇑ 21D1	⇡ 21E1	
2	→ 2192	↢ 21A2	↲ 21B2	⇂ 21C2	⇒ 21D2	⇢ 21E2	
3	↓ 2193	↣ 21A3	↳ 21B3	⇃ 21C3	⇓ 21D3	⇣ 21E3	
4	↔ 2194	↤ 21A4	↴ 21B4	⇄ 21C4	⇔ 21D4	⇤ 21E4	
5	↕ 2195	↥ 21A5	↵ 21B5	⇅ 21C5	⇕ 21D5	⇥ 21E5	
6	↖ 2196	↦ 21A6	↶ 21B6	⇆ 21C6	⇖ 21D6	⇦ 21E6	
7	↗ 2197	↧ 21A7	↷ 21B7	⇇ 21C7	⇗ 21D7	⇧ 21E7	
8	↘ 2198	↨ 21A8	↸ 21B8	⇈ 21C8	⇘ 21D8	⇨ 21E8	
9	↙ 2199	↩ 21A9	↹ 21B9	⇉ 21C9	⇙ 21D9	⇩ 21E9	
A	↚ 219A	↪ 21AA	↺ 21BA	⇊ 21CA	⇚ 21DA	⇪ 21EA	
B	↛ 219B	↫ 21AB	↻ 21BB	⇋ 21CB	⇛ 21DB		
C	↜ 219C	↬ 21AC	↼ 21BC	⇌ 21CC	⇜ 21DC		
D	↝ 219D	↭ 21AD	↽ 21BD	⇍ 21CD	⇝ 21DD		
E	↞ 219E	↮ 21AE	↾ 21BE	⇎ 21CE	⇞ 21DE		
F	↟ 219F	↯ 21AF	↿ 21BF	⇏ 21CF	⇟ 21DF		

Arrows

2190 ← LEFTWARDS ARROW
2191 ↑ UPWARDS ARROW
2192 → RIGHTWARDS ARROW
2193 ↓ DOWNWARDS ARROW
2194 ↔ LEFT RIGHT ARROW
2195 ↕ UP DOWN ARROW
2196 ↖ NORTH WEST ARROW
2197 ↗ NORTH EAST ARROW
2198 ↘ SOUTH EAST ARROW
2199 ↙ SOUTH WEST ARROW
219A ↚ LEFTWARDS ARROW WITH STROKE
219B ↛ RIGHTWARDS ARROW WITH STROKE
219C ↜ LEFTWARDS WAVE ARROW
219D ↝ RIGHTWARDS WAVE ARROW
219E ↞ LEFTWARDS TWO HEADED ARROW
219F ↟ UPWARDS TWO HEADED ARROW
21A0 ↠ RIGHTWARDS TWO HEADED ARROW
21A1 ↡ DOWNWARDS TWO HEADED ARROW
= form FEED
21A2 ↢ LEFTWARDS ARROW WITH TAIL
21A3 ↣ RIGHTWARDS ARROW WITH TAIL
21A4 ↤ LEFTWARDS ARROW FROM BAR
21A5 ↥ UPWARDS ARROW FROM BAR
21A6 ↦ RIGHTWARDS ARROW FROM BAR
21A7 ↧ DOWNWARDS ARROW FROM BAR
= depth symbol
21A8 ↨ UP DOWN ARROW WITH BASE
21A9 ↩ LEFTWARDS ARROW WITH HOOK
21AA ↪ RIGHTWARDS ARROW WITH HOOK
21AB ↫ LEFTWARDS ARROW WITH LOOP
21AC ↬ RIGHTWARDS ARROW WITH LOOP
21AD ↭ LEFT RIGHT WAVE ARROW
21AE ↮ LEFT RIGHT ARROW WITH STROKE
21AF ↯ DOWNWARDS ZIGZAG ARROW
= electrolysis
21B0 ↰ UPWARDS ARROW WITH TIP LEFTWARDS
21B1 ↱ UPWARDS ARROW WITH TIP RIGHTWARDS
21B2 ↲ DOWNWARDS ARROW WITH TIP LEFTWARDS
21B3 ↳ DOWNWARDS ARROW WITH TIP RIGHTWARDS
21B4 ↴ RIGHTWARDS ARROW WITH CORNER DOWNWARDS
= line FEED
21B5 ↵ DOWNWARDS ARROW WITH CORNER LEFTWARDS
= carriage return
= new line
21B6 ↶ ANTICLOCKWISE TOP SEMICIRCLE ARROW
21B7 ↷ CLOCKWISE TOP SEMICIRCLE ARROW
21B8 ↸ NORTH WEST ARROW TO LONG BAR
= home
21B9 ↹ LEFTWARDS ARROW TO BAR OVER RIGHTWARDS ARROW TO BAR
= tab with shift tab
21BA ↺ ANTICLOCKWISE OPEN CIRCLE ARROW
21BB ↻ CLOCKWISE OPEN CIRCLE ARROW
21BC ↼ LEFTWARDS HARPOON WITH BARB UPWARDS
21BD ↽ LEFTWARDS HARPOON WITH BARB DOWNWARDS
21BE ↾ UPWARDS HARPOON WITH BARB RIGHTWARDS
21BF ↿ UPWARDS HARPOON WITH BARB LEFTWARDS
21C0 ⇀ RIGHTWARDS HARPOON WITH BARB UPWARDS
21C1 ⇁ RIGHTWARDS HARPOON WITH BARB DOWNWARDS
21C2 ⇂ DOWNWARDS HARPOON WITH BARB RIGHTWARDS
21C3 ⇃ DOWNWARDS HARPOON WITH BARB LEFTWARDS
21C4 ⇄ RIGHTWARDS ARROW OVER LEFTWARDS ARROW
21C5 ⇅ UPWARDS ARROW LEFTWARDS OF DOWNWARDS ARROW
21C6 ⇆ LEFTWARDS ARROW OVER RIGHTWARDS ARROW
21C7 ⇇ LEFTWARDS PAIRED ARROWS
21C8 ⇈ UPWARDS PAIRED ARROWS
21C9 ⇉ RIGHTWARDS PAIRED ARROWS
21CA ⇊ DOWNWARDS PAIRED ARROWS
21CB ⇋ LEFTWARDS HARPOON OVER RIGHTWARDS HARPOON
21CC ⇌ RIGHTWARDS HARPOON OVER LEFTWARDS HARPOON
21CD ⇍ LEFTWARDS DOUBLE ARROW WITH STROKE
21CE ⇎ LEFT RIGHT DOUBLE ARROW WITH STROKE
21CF ⇏ RIGHTWARDS DOUBLE ARROW WITH STROKE

21D0 ⇐ LEFTWARDS DOUBLE ARROW
21D1 ⇑ UPWARDS DOUBLE ARROW
21D2 ⇒ RIGHTWARDS DOUBLE ARROW
21D3 ⇓ DOWNWARDS DOUBLE ARROW
21D4 ⇔ LEFT RIGHT DOUBLE ARROW
21D5 ⇕ UP DOWN DOUBLE ARROW
21D6 ⇖ NORTH WEST DOUBLE ARROW
21D7 ⇗ NORTH EAST DOUBLE ARROW
21D8 ⇘ SOUTH EAST DOUBLE ARROW
21D9 ⇙ SOUTH WEST DOUBLE ARROW
21DA ⇚ LEFTWARDS TRIPLE ARROW
21DB ⇛ RIGHTWARDS TRIPLE ARROW
21DC ⇜ LEFTWARDS SQUIGGLE ARROW
21DD ⇝ RIGHTWARDS SQUIGGLE ARROW
21DE ⇞ UPWARDS ARROW WITH DOUBLE STROKE
= page up
21DF ⇟ DOWNWARDS ARROW WITH DOUBLE STROKE
= page down
21E0 ⇠ LEFTWARDS DASHED ARROW
21E1 ⇡ UPWARDS DASHED ARROW
21E2 ⇢ RIGHTWARDS DASHED ARROW
21E3 ⇣ DOWNWARDS DASHED ARROW
21E4 ⇤ LEFTWARDS ARROW TO BAR
= leftward tab
21E5 ⇥ RIGHTWARDS ARROW TO BAR
= rightward tab
21E6 ⇦ LEFTWARDS WHITE ARROW
21E7 ⇧ UPWARDS WHITE ARROW
= shift
21E8 ⇨ RIGHTWARDS WHITE ARROW
21E9 ⇩ DOWNWARDS WHITE ARROW
21EA ⇪ UPWARDS WHITE ARROW FROM BAR
= caps lock

	220	221	222	223	224	225	226	227
0	∀ 2200	∐ 2210	∠ 2220	∰ 2230	≀ 2240	≐ 2250	≠ 2260	≰ 2270
1	∁ 2201	∑ 2211	∡ 2221	∱ 2231	≁ 2241	≑ 2251	≡ 2261	≱ 2271
2	∂ 2202	− 2212	∢ 2222	∲ 2232	≂ 2242	≒ 2252	≢ 2262	≲ 2272
3	∃ 2203	∓ 2213	∣ 2223	∳ 2233	≃ 2243	≓ 2253	≣ 2263	≳ 2273
4	∄ 2204	∔ 2214	∤ 2224	∴ 2234	≄ 2244	≔ 2254	≤ 2264	≴ 2274
5	∅ 2205	∕ 2215	∥ 2225	∵ 2235	≅ 2245	≕ 2255	≥ 2265	≵ 2275
6	∆ 2206	∖ 2216	∦ 2226	∶ 2236	≆ 2246	≖ 2256	≦ 2266	≶ 2276
7	∇ 2207	∗ 2217	∧ 2227	∷ 2237	≇ 2247	≗ 2257	≧ 2267	≷ 2277
8	∈ 2208	∘ 2218	∨ 2228	∸ 2238	≈ 2248	≘ 2258	≨ 2268	≸ 2278
9	∉ 2209	∙ 2219	∩ 2229	∹ 2239	≉ 2249	≙ 2259	≩ 2269	≹ 2279
A	∊ 220A	√ 221A	∪ 222A	∺ 223A	≊ 224A	≚ 225A	≪ 226A	≺ 227A
B	∋ 220B	∛ 221B	∫ 222B	∻ 223B	≋ 224B	≛ 225B	≫ 226B	≻ 227B
C	∌ 220C	∜ 221C	∬ 222C	∼ 223C	≌ 224C	≜ 225C	≬ 226C	≼ 227C
D	∍ 220D	∝ 221D	∭ 222D	∽ 223D	≍ 224D	≝ 225D	≭ 226D	≽ 227D
E	∎ 220E	∞ 221E	∮ 222E	∾ 223E	≎ 224E	≞ 225E	≮ 226E	≾ 227E
F	∏ 220F	∟ 221F	∯ 222F	∿ 223F	≏ 224F	≟ 225F	≯ 226F	≿ 227F

	228	229	22A	22B	22C	22D	22E	22F
0	⊀ 2280	⊐ 2290	⊠ 22A0	⊰ 22B0	⋀ 22C0	⋐ 22D0	⋠ 22E0	⋰ 22F0
1	⊁ 2281	⊑ 2291	⊡ 22A1	⊱ 22B1	⋁ 22C1	⋑ 22D1	⋡ 22E1	⋱ 22F1
2	⊂ 2282	⊒ 2292	⊢ 22A2	⊲ 22B2	⋂ 22C2	⋒ 22D2	⋢ 22E2	
3	⊃ 2283	⊓ 2293	⊣ 22A3	⊳ 22B3	⋃ 22C3	⋓ 22D3	⋣ 22E3	
4	⊄ 2284	⊔ 2294	⊤ 22A4	⊴ 22B4	⋄ 22C4	⋔ 22D4	⋤ 22E4	
5	⊅ 2285	⊕ 2295	⊥ 22A5	⊵ 22B5	⋅ 22C5	⋕ 22D5	⋥ 22E5	
6	⊆ 2286	⊖ 2296	⊦ 22A6	⊶ 22B6	⋆ 22C6	⋖ 22D6	⋦ 22E6	
7	⊇ 2287	⊗ 2297	⊧ 22A7	⊷ 22B7	⋇ 22C7	⋗ 22D7	⋧ 22E7	
8	⊈ 2288	⊘ 2298	⊨ 22A8	⊸ 22B8	⋈ 22C8	⋘ 22D8	⋨ 22E8	
9	⊉ 2289	⊙ 2299	⊩ 22A9	⊹ 22B9	⋉ 22C9	⋙ 22D9	⋩ 22E9	
A	⊊ 228A	⊚ 229A	⊪ 22AA	⊺ 22BA	⋊ 22CA	⋚ 22DA	⋪ 22EA	
B	⊋ 228B	⊛ 229B	⊫ 22AB	⊻ 22BB	⋋ 22CB	⋛ 22DB	⋫ 22EB	
C	⊌ 228C	⊜ 229C	⊬ 22AC	⊼ 22BC	⋌ 22CC	⋜ 22DC	⋬ 22EC	
D	⊍ 228D	⊝ 229D	⊭ 22AD	⊽ 22BD	⋍ 22CD	⋝ 22DD	⋭ 22ED	
E	⊎ 228E	⊞ 229E	⊮ 22AE	⊾ 22BE	⋎ 22CE	⋞ 22DE	⋮ 22EE	
F	⊏ 228F	⊟ 229F	⊯ 22AF	⊿ 22BF	⋏ 22CF	⋟ 22DF	⋯ 22EF	

Mathematical operators

2200 ∀ FOR ALL

2201 ∁ COMPLEMENT
→ 0297 ʗ latin letter stretched c

2202 ∂ PARTIAL DIFFERENTIAL

2203 ∃ THERE EXISTS

2204 ∄ THERE DOES NOT EXIST
≡ 2203 ∃ + 0338 ̸

2205 ∅ EMPTY SET
= null set
= diameter symbol
→ 00D8 Ø latin capital letter o with stroke

2206 ∆ INCREMENT
= Laplace operator
= forward difference
→ 0394 Δ greek capital letter delta
→ 25B3 △ white up-pointing triangle

2207 ∇ NABLA
= Laplace operator (written with superscript 2)
= backward difference
= del
→ 25BD ▽ white down-pointing triangle

2208 ∈ ELEMENT OF

2209 ∉ NOT AN ELEMENT OF
≡ 2208 ∈ + 0338 ̸

220A ∊ SMALL ELEMENT OF

220B ∋ CONTAINS AS MEMBER
= such that

220C ∌ DOES NOT CONTAIN AS MEMBER
≡ 220B ∋ + 0338 ̸

220D ∍ SMALL CONTAINS AS MEMBER

220E ∎ END OF PROOF
= qed
→ 2023 ‣ triangular bullet

220F ∏ N-ARY PRODUCT
= product sign
→ 03A0 Π greek capital letter pi

2210 ∐ N-ARY COPRODUCT
= coproduct sign

2211 ∑ N-ARY SUMMATION
= summation sign
→ 03A3 Σ greek capital letter sigma

2212 − MINUS SIGN
→ 002D - hyphen-minus

2213 ∓ MINUS-OR-PLUS SIGN
→ 00B1 ± plus-minus sign

2214 ∔ DOT PLUS

2215 ∕ DIVISION SLASH
• generic division operator
→ 002F / solidus
→ 2044 ⁄ fraction slash

2216 ∖ SET MINUS
→ 005C \ reverse solidus

2217 ∗ ASTERISK OPERATOR
→ 002A * asterisk

2218 ∘ RING OPERATOR
= composite function
= APL jot
→ 00B0 ° degree sign
→ 25E6 ◦ white bullet

2219 ∙ BULLET OPERATOR
→ 00B7 · middle dot
→ 2022 • bullet
→ 2024 ․ one dot leader

221A √ SQUARE ROOT
= radical sign
→ 2713 ✓ check mark

221B ∛ CUBE ROOT

221C ∜ FOURTH ROOT

221D ∝ PROPORTIONAL TO
→ 03B1 α greek small letter alpha

221E ∞ INFINITY

221F ∟ RIGHT ANGLE

2220 ∠ ANGLE

2221 ∡ MEASURED ANGLE

2222 ∢ SPHERICAL ANGLE
= angle arc

2223 ∣ DIVIDES
= such that
= APL stile
→ 007C | vertical line
→ 01C0 ǀ latin letter dental click

2224 ∤ DOES NOT DIVIDE
≡ 2223 ∣ + 0338 ̸

2225 ∥ PARALLEL TO
→ 01C1 ǁ latin letter lateral click
→ 2016 ‖ double vertical line

2226 ∦ NOT PARALLEL TO
≡ 2225 ∥ + 0338 ̸

2227 ∧ LOGICAL AND
= wedge

2228 ∨ LOGICAL OR
= vee

2229 ∩ INTERSECTION
= cap

222A ∪ UNION
= cup

222B ∫ INTEGRAL
→ 0283 ʃ latin small letter esh

222C ∬ DOUBLE INTEGRAL
≈ 222B ∫ + 222B ∫

222D ∭ TRIPLE INTEGRAL
≈ 222B ∫ + 222B ∫ + 222B ∫

222E ∮ CONTOUR INTEGRAL

222F ∯ SURFACE INTEGRAL
≈ 222E ∮ + 222E ∮
2230 ∰ VOLUME INTEGRAL
≈ 222E ∮ + 222E ∮ + 222E ∮
2231 ∱ CLOCKWISE INTEGRAL
2232 ∲ CLOCKWISE CONTOUR INTEGRAL
2233 ∳ ANTICLOCKWISE CONTOUR INTEGRAL
2234 ∴ THEREFORE
2235 ∵ BECAUSE
2236 ∶ RATIO
→ 003A : colon
2237 ∷ PROPORTION
2238 ∸ DOT MINUS
= symmetric difference
2239 ∹ EXCESS
223A ∺ GEOMETRIC PROPORTION
223B ∻ HOMOTHETIC
223C ∼ TILDE OPERATOR
= varies with (proportional to)
= difference between
= similar to
= APL tilde
= cycle
= not
→ 007E ~ tilde
→ 02DC ˜ small tilde
223D ∽ REVERSED TILDE
= lazy S
• reversed tilde and lazy S are glyph variants
223E ∾ INVERTED LAZY S
= most positive
223F ∿ SINE WAVE
= alternating current
2240 ≀ WREATH PRODUCT
2241 ≁ NOT TILDE
≡ 007E ~ + 0338 ̸
2242 ≂ MINUS TILDE
2243 ≃ ASYMPTOTICALLY EQUAL TO
2244 ≄ NOT ASYMPTOTICALLY EQUAL TO
≡ 2243 ≃ + 0338 ̸
2245 ≅ APPROXIMATELY EQUAL TO
2246 ≆ APPROXIMATELY BUT NOT ACTUALLY EQUAL TO
2247 ≇ NEITHER APPROXIMATELY NOR ACTUALLY EQUAL TO
≡ 2245 ≅ + 0338 ̸
2248 ≈ ALMOST EQUAL TO
= asymptotic to
2249 ≉ NOT ALMOST EQUAL TO
≡ 2248 ≈ + 0338 ̸
224A ≊ ALMOST EQUAL OR EQUAL TO
224B ≋ TRIPLE TILDE
224C ≌ ALL EQUAL TO
• reversed tilde and lazy S are glyph variants
224D ≍ EQUIVALENT TO
224E ≎ GEOMETRICALLY EQUIVALENT TO
224F ≏ DIFFERENCE BETWEEN
2250 ≐ APPROACHES THE LIMIT
2251 ≑ GEOMETRICALLY EQUAL TO
2252 ≒ APPROXIMATELY EQUAL TO OR THE IMAGE OF
= nearly equals
2253 ≓ IMAGE OF OR APPROXIMATELY EQUAL TO
2254 ≔ COLON EQUALS
2255 ≕ EQUALS COLON
2256 ≖ RING IN EQUAL TO
2257 ≗ RING EQUAL TO
= approximately equal to
2258 ≘ CORRESPONDS TO
2259 ≙ ESTIMATES
= corresponds to
225A ≚ EQUIANGULAR TO
225B ≛ STAR EQUALS
225C ≜ DELTA EQUAL TO
= equiangular
= equal to by definition
225D ≝ EQUAL TO BY DEFINITION
225E ≞ MEASURED BY
225F ≟ QUESTIONED EQUAL TO
2260 ≠ NOT EQUAL TO
→ 003D = equals sign
→ 01C2 ǂ latin letter alveolar click
≡ 003D = + 0338 ̸
2261 ≡ IDENTICAL TO
2262 ≢ NOT IDENTICAL TO
≡ 2261 ≡ + 0338 ̸
2263 ≣ STRICTLY EQUIVALENT TO
2264 ≤ LESS-THAN OR EQUAL TO
2265 ≥ GREATER-THAN OR EQUAL TO
2266 ≦ LESS-THAN OVER EQUAL TO
2267 ≧ GREATER-THAN OVER EQUAL TO
2268 ≨ LESS-THAN BUT NOT EQUAL TO
2269 ≩ GREATER-THAN BUT NOT EQUAL TO
226A ≪ MUCH LESS-THAN
→ 00AB « left-pointing double angle quotation mark
226B ≫ MUCH GREATER-THAN
→ 00BB » right-pointing double angle quotation mark

226C ≬ BETWEEN
= plaintiff
= quantic

226D ≭ NOT EQUIVALENT TO
≡ 224D ≍ + 0338 ̸

226E ≮ NOT LESS-THAN
≡ 003C < + 0338 ̸

226F ≯ NOT GREATER-THAN
≡ 003E > + 0338 ̸

2270 ≰ NEITHER LESS-THAN NOR EQUAL TO
≡ 2264 ≤ + 0338 ̸

2271 ≱ NEITHER GREATER-THAN NOR EQUAL TO
≡ 2265 ≥ + 0338 ̸

2272 ≲ LESS-THAN OR EQUIVALENT TO

2273 ≳ GREATER-THAN OR EQUIVALENT TO

2274 ≴ NEITHER LESS-THAN NOR EQUIVALENT TO
≡ 2272 ≲ + 0338 ̸

2275 ≵ NEITHER GREATER-THAN NOR EQUIVALENT TO
≡ 2273 ≳ + 0338 ̸

2276 ≶ LESS-THAN OR GREATER-THAN

2277 ≷ GREATER-THAN OR LESS-THAN

2278 ≸ NEITHER LESS-THAN NOR GREATER-THAN
≡ 2276 ≶ + 0338 ̸

2279 ≹ NEITHER GREATER-THAN NOR LESS-THAN
≡ 2277 ≷ + 0338 ̸

227A ≺ PRECEDES
= lower rank than
→ 22B0 ⊰ precedes under relation

227B ≻ SUCCEEDS
= higher rank than
→ 22B1 ⊱ succeeds under relation

227C ≼ PRECEDES OR EQUAL TO

227D ≽ SUCCEEDS OR EQUAL TO

227E ≾ PRECEDES OR EQUIVALENT TO

227F ≿ SUCCEEDS OR EQUIVALENT TO

2280 ⊀ DOES NOT PRECEDE
≡ 227A ≺ + 0338 ̸

2281 ⊁ DOES NOT SUCCEED
≡ 227B ≻ + 0338 ̸

2282 ⊂ SUBSET OF

2283 ⊃ SUPERSET OF

2284 ⊄ NOT A SUBSET OF
≡ 2282 ⊂ + 0338 ̸

2285 ⊅ NOT A SUPERSET OF
≡ 2283 ⊃ + 0338 ̸

2286 ⊆ SUBSET OF OR EQUAL TO

2287 ⊇ SUPERSET OF OR EQUAL TO

2288 ⊈ NEITHER A SUBSET OF NOR EQUAL TO
≡ 2286 ⊆ + 0338 ̸

2289 ⊉ NEITHER A SUPERSET OF NOR EQUAL TO
≡ 2287 ⊇ + 0338 ̸

228A ⊊ SUBSET OF WITH NOT EQUAL TO

228B ⊋ SUPERSET OF WITH NOT EQUAL TO

228C ⊌ MULTISET

228D ⊍ MULTISET MULTIPLICATION

228E ⊎ MULTISET UNION

228F ⊏ SQUARE IMAGE OF

2290 ⊐ SQUARE ORIGINAL OF

2291 ⊑ SQUARE IMAGE OF OR EQUAL TO

2292 ⊒ SQUARE ORIGINAL OF OR EQUAL TO

2293 ⊓ SQUARE CAP

2294 ⊔ SQUARE CUP

2295 ⊕ CIRCLED PLUS
= direct sum
= vector pointing into page
→ 2641 ♁ earth

2296 ⊖ CIRCLED MINUS
= symmetric difference

2297 ⊗ CIRCLED TIMES
= tensor product
= vector pointing into page

2298 ⊘ CIRCLED DIVISION SLASH

2299 ⊙ CIRCLED DOT OPERATOR
= direct product
= vector pointing out of page
→ 0298 ʘ latin letter BILABIAL CLICK
→ 2609 ☉ sun

229A ⊚ CIRCLED RING OPERATOR
→ 25CE ◎ bullseye

229B ⊛ CIRCLED ASTERISK OPERATOR

229C ⊜ CIRCLED EQUALS

229D ⊝ CIRCLED DASH

229E ⊞ SQUARED PLUS

229F ⊟ SQUARED MINUS

22A0 ⊠ SQUARED TIMES
→ 2612 ☒ ballot box with x

22A1 ⊡ SQUARED DOT OPERATOR

22A2 ⊢ RIGHT TACK
= turnstile
= proves, implies, yields
= reducible

22A3 ⊣ LEFT TACK
= reverse turnstile
= non-theorem, does not yield

22A4 ⊤ DOWN TACK

22A5 ⊥ UP TACK
 = orthogonal to
 = perpendicular
 • APL and other uses

22A6 ⊦ ASSERTION
 = reduces to

22A7 ⊧ MODELS

22A8 ⊨ TRUE
 = statement is true, valid
 = is a tautology
 = satisfies
 = results in

22A9 ⊩ FORCES

22AA ⊪ TRIPLE VERTICAL BAR RIGHT TURNSTILE

22AB ⊫ DOUBLE VERTICAL BAR DOUBLE RIGHT TURNSTILE

22AC ⊬ DOES NOT PROVE
 ≡ 22A2 ⊢ + 0338 ̸

22AD ⊭ NOT TRUE
 ≡ 22A8 ⊨ + 0338 ̸

22AE ⊮ DOES NOT FORCE
 ≡ 22A9 ⊩ + 0338 ̸

22AF ⊯ NEGATED DOUBLE VERTICAL BAR DOUBLE RIGHT TURNSTILE
 ≡ 22AB ⊫ + 0338 ̸

22B0 ⊰ PRECEDES UNDER RELATION
 → 227A ≺ precedes

22B1 ⊱ SUCCEEDS UNDER RELATION
 → 227B ≻ succeeds

22B2 ⊲ NORMAL SUBGROUP OF

22B3 ⊳ CONTAINS AS NORMAL SUBGROUP

22B4 ⊴ NORMAL SUBGROUP OF OR EQUAL TO

22B5 ⊵ CONTAINS AS NORMAL SUBGROUP OR EQUAL TO

22B6 ⊶ ORIGINAL OF

22B7 ⊷ IMAGE OF

22B8 ⊸ MULTIMAP

22B9 ⊹ HERMITIAN CONJUGATE MATRIX

22BA ⊺ INTERCALATE

22BB ⊻ XOR

22BC ⊼ NAND

22BD ⊽ NOR

22BE ⊾ RIGHT ANGLE WITH ARC

22BF ⊿ RIGHT TRIANGLE

22C0 ⋀ N-ARY LOGICAL AND

22C1 ⋁ N-ARY LOGICAL OR

22C2 ⋂ N-ARY INTERSECTION

22C3 ⋃ N-ARY UNION

22C4 ⋄ DIAMOND OPERATOR
 → 25C7 ◇ white diamond

22C5 ⋅ DOT OPERATOR
 → 00B7 · middle dot

22C6 ⋆ STAR OPERATOR
 • APL
 → 2605 ★ black star

22C7 ⋇ DIVISION TIMES

22C8 ⋈ BOWTIE
 → 2445 ⑅ ocr bow tie

22C9 ⋉ LEFT NORMAL FACTOR SEMIDIRECT PRODUCT

22CA ⋊ RIGHT NORMAL FACTOR SEMIDIRECT PRODUCT

22CB ⋋ LEFT SEMIDIRECT PRODUCT

22CC ⋌ RIGHT SEMIDIRECT PRODUCT
 → 2041 ⁁ caret insertion point

22CD ⋍ REVERSED TILDE EQUALS

22CE ⋎ CURLY LOGICAL OR

22CF ⋏ CURLY LOGICAL AND

22D0 ⋐ DOUBLE SUBSET

22D1 ⋑ DOUBLE SUPERSET

22D2 ⋒ DOUBLE INTERSECTION

22D3 ⋓ DOUBLE UNION

22D4 ⋔ PITCHFORK
 = proper intersection

22D5 ⋕ EQUAL AND PARALLEL TO
 → 2317 ⌗ viewdata square

22D6 ⋖ LESS-THAN WITH DOT

22D7 ⋗ GREATER-THAN WITH DOT

22D8 ⋘ VERY MUCH LESS-THAN

22D9 ⋙ VERY MUCH GREATER-THAN

22DA ⋚ LESS-THAN EQUAL TO OR GREATER-THAN

22DB ⋛ GREATER-THAN EQUAL TO OR LESS-THAN

22DC ⋜ EQUAL TO OR LESS-THAN

22DD ⋝ EQUAL TO OR GREATER-THAN

22DE ⋞ EQUAL TO OR PRECEDES

22DF ⋟ EQUAL TO OR SUCCEEDS

22E0 ⋠ DOES NOT PRECEDE OR EQUAL
 ≡ 227C ≼ + 0338 ̸

22E1 ⋡ DOES NOT SUCCEED OR EQUAL
 ≡ 227D ≽ + 0338 ̸

22E2 ⋢ NOT SQUARE IMAGE OF OR EQUAL TO
 ≡ 2291 ⊑ + 0338 ̸

22E3 ⋣ NOT SQUARE ORIGINAL OF OR EQUAL TO
 ≡ 2292 ⊒ + 0338 ̸

22E4 ⋤ SQUARE IMAGE OF OR NOT EQUAL TO

22E5 ⋥ SQUARE ORIGINAL OF OR NOT EQUAL TO

22E6 ⋦ LESS-THAN BUT NOT EQUIVALENT TO

22E7 ⋧ GREATER-THAN BUT NOT EQUIVALENT TO

22E8 ⋨ PRECEDES BUT NOT EQUIVALENT TO

22E9 ⋩ SUCCEEDS BUT NOT EQUIVALENT TO

22EA ⋪ NOT NORMAL SUBGROUP OF
≡ 22B2 ⊲ + 0338 ̸

22EB ⋫ DOES NOT CONTAIN AS NORMAL SUBGROUP
≡ 22B3 ⊳ + 0338 ̸

22EC ⋬ NOT NORMAL SUBGROUP OF OR EQUAL TO
≡ 22B4 ⊴ + 0338 ̸

22ED ⋭ DOES NOT CONTAIN AS NORMAL SUBGROUP OR EQUAL
≡ 22B5 ⊵ + 0338 ̸

22EE ⋮ VERTICAL ELLIPSIS
• these four ellipses are used for matrix row/column ellision
→ 2026 … horizontal ellipsis

22EF ⋯ MIDLINE HORIZONTAL ELLIPSIS

22F0 ⋰ UP RIGHT DIAGONAL ELLIPSIS

22F1 ⋱ DOWN RIGHT DIAGONAL ELLIPSIS

	230	231	232	233	234	235	236	237
0	⌀ 2300	⌐ 2310	⌠ 2320	⌰ 2330	⍀ 2340	⍐ 2350	⍠ 2360	⍰ 2370
1		⌑ 2311	⌡ 2321	⌱ 2331	⍁ 2341	⍑ 2351	⍡ 2361	⍱ 2371
2	⌂ 2302	⌒ 2312	⌢ 2322	⌲ 2332	⍂ 2342	⍒ 2352	⍢ 2362	⍲ 2372
3	⌃ 2303	⌓ 2313	⌣ 2323	⌳ 2333	⍃ 2343	⍓ 2353	⍣ 2363	⍳ 2373
4	⌄ 2304	⌔ 2314	⌤ 2324	⌴ 2334	⍄ 2344	⍔ 2354	⍤ 2364	⍴ 2374
5	⌅ 2305	⌕ 2315	⌥ 2325	⌵ 2335	⍅ 2345	⍕ 2355	⍥ 2365	⍵ 2375
6	⌆ 2306	⌖ 2316	⌦ 2326	⌶ 2336	⍆ 2346	⍖ 2356	⍦ 2366	⍶ 2376
7	⌇ 2307	⌗ 2317	⌧ 2327	⌷ 2337	⍇ 2347	⍗ 2357	⍧ 2367	⍷ 2377
8	⌈ 2308	⌘ 2318	⌨ 2328	⌸ 2338	⍈ 2348	⍘ 2358	⍨ 2368	⍸ 2378
9	⌉ 2309	⌙ 2319	〈 2329	⌹ 2339	⍉ 2349	⍙ 2359	⍩ 2369	⍹ 2379
A	⌊ 230A	⌚ 231A	〉 232A	⌺ 233A	⍊ 234A	⍚ 235A	⍪ 236A	⍺ 237A
B	⌋ 230B	⌛ 231B	⌫ 232B	⌻ 233B	⍋ 234B	⍛ 235B	⍫ 236B	
C	⌌ 230C	⌜ 231C	⌬ 232C	⌼ 233C	⍌ 234C	⍜ 235C	⍬ 236C	
D	⌍ 230D	⌝ 231D	⌭ 232D	⌽ 233D	⍍ 234D	⍝ 235D	⍭ 236D	
E	⌎ 230E	⌞ 231E	⌮ 232E	⌾ 233E	⍎ 234E	⍞ 235E	⍮ 236E	
F	⌏ 230F	⌟ 231F	⌯ 232F	⌿ 233F	⍏ 234F	⍟ 235F	⍯ 236F	

Miscellaneous technical

2300 ⌀ DIAMETER SIGN
2301 ⌁ <reserved>
2302 ⌂ HOUSE
2303 ⌃ UP ARROWHEAD
→ 005E ^ circumflex accent
→ 02C4 ˄ modifier letter up arrowhead
2304 ⌄ DOWN ARROWHEAD
2305 ⌅ PROJECTIVE
2306 ⌆ PERSPECTIVE
2307 ⌇ WAVY LINE
→ 3030 〰 wavy dash
2308 ⌈ LEFT CEILING
= APL upstile
2309 ⌉ RIGHT CEILING
230A ⌊ LEFT FLOOR
= APL downstile
230B ⌋ RIGHT FLOOR
230C ⌌ BOTTOM RIGHT CROP
• set of four "crop" corners, arranged facing outward
230D ⌍ BOTTOM LEFT CROP
230E ⌎ TOP RIGHT CROP
230F ⌏ TOP LEFT CROP
2310 ⌐ REVERSED NOT SIGN
= beginning of line
→ 00AC ¬ not sign
2311 ⌑ SQUARE LOZENGE
2312 ⌒ ARC
2313 ⌓ SEGMENT
2314 ⌔ SECTOR
2315 ⌕ TELEPHONE RECORDER
2316 ⌖ POSITION INDICATOR
2317 ⌗ VIEWDATA SQUARE
→ 22D5 ⋕ equal and parallel to
2318 ⌘ PLACE OF INTEREST SIGN
= COMMAND KEY
2319 ⌙ TURNED NOT SIGN
= line marker
231A ⌚ WATCH
231B ⌛ HOURGLASS
231C ⌜ TOP LEFT CORNER
• set of four "quine" corners, for quincuncial arrangement
231D ⌝ TOP RIGHT CORNER
231E ⌞ BOTTOM LEFT CORNER
231F ⌟ BOTTOM RIGHT CORNER
2320 ⌠ TOP HALF INTEGRAL
2321 ⌡ BOTTOM HALF INTEGRAL
2322 ⌢ FROWN
2323 ⌣ SMILE
2324 ⌤ UP ARROWHEAD BETWEEN TWO HORIZONTAL BARS
= ENTER KEY
2325 ⌥ OPTION KEY
2326 ⌦ ERASE TO THE RIGHT
= DELETE TO THE RIGHT KEY
2327 ⌧ X IN A RECTANGLE BOX
= CLEAR KEY
2328 ⌨ KEYBOARD
2329 〈 LEFT-POINTING ANGLE BRACKET
= BRA
→ 003C < less-than sign
→ 2039 ‹ single left-pointing angle quotation mark
→ 3008 〈 left angle bracket
≡ 3008 〈
232A 〉 RIGHT-POINTING ANGLE BRACKET
= KET
→ 003E > greater-than sign
→ 203A › single right-pointing angle quotation mark
→ 3009 〉 right angle bracket
≡ 3009 〉
232B ⌫ ERASE TO THE LEFT
= DELETE TO THE LEFT KEY
232C ⌬ BENZENE RING
232D ⌭ CYLINDRICITY
232E ⌮ ALL AROUND-PROFILE
232F ⌯ SYMMETRY
2330 ⌰ TOTAL RUNOUT
2331 ⌱ DIMENSION ORIGIN
2332 ⌲ CONICAL TAPER
2333 ⌳ SLOPE
2334 ⌴ COUNTERBORE
2335 ⌵ COUNTERSINK

APL

2336 ⌶ APL FUNCTIONAL SYMBOL I-BEAM
2337 ⌷ APL FUNCTIONAL SYMBOL SQUISH QUAD
2338 ⌸ APL FUNCTIONAL SYMBOL QUAD EQUAL
2339 ⌹ APL FUNCTIONAL SYMBOL QUAD DIVIDE
233A ⌺ APL FUNCTIONAL SYMBOL QUAD DIAMOND
233B ⌻ APL FUNCTIONAL SYMBOL QUAD JOT
233C ⌼ APL FUNCTIONAL SYMBOL QUAD CIRCLE
233D ⌽ APL FUNCTIONAL SYMBOL CIRCLE STILE

233E ⌾ APL FUNCTIONAL SYMBOL CIRCLE JOT
233F ⌿ APL FUNCTIONAL SYMBOL SLASH BAR
2340 ⍀ APL FUNCTIONAL SYMBOL BACKSLASH BAR
2341 ⍁ APL FUNCTIONAL SYMBOL QUAD SLASH
2342 ⍂ APL FUNCTIONAL SYMBOL QUAD BACKSLASH
2343 ⍃ APL FUNCTIONAL SYMBOL QUAD LESS-THAN
2344 ⍄ APL FUNCTIONAL SYMBOL QUAD GREATER-THAN
2345 ⍅ APL FUNCTIONAL SYMBOL LEFTWARDS VANE
2346 ⍆ APL FUNCTIONAL SYMBOL RIGHTWARDS VANE
2347 ⍇ APL FUNCTIONAL SYMBOL QUAD LEFTWARDS ARROW
2348 ⍈ APL FUNCTIONAL SYMBOL QUAD RIGHTWARDS ARROW
2349 ⍉ APL FUNCTIONAL SYMBOL CIRCLE BACKSLASH
234A ⍊ APL FUNCTIONAL SYMBOL DOWN TACK UNDERBAR
234B ⍋ APL FUNCTIONAL SYMBOL DELTA STILE
234C ⍌ APL FUNCTIONAL SYMBOL QUAD DOWN CARET
234D ⍍ APL FUNCTIONAL SYMBOL QUAD DELTA
234E ⍎ APL FUNCTIONAL SYMBOL DOWN TACK JOT
234F ⍏ APL FUNCTIONAL SYMBOL UPWARDS VANE
2350 ⍐ APL FUNCTIONAL SYMBOL QUAD UPWARDS ARROW
2351 ⍑ APL FUNCTIONAL SYMBOL UP TACK OVERBAR
2352 ⍒ APL FUNCTIONAL SYMBOL DEL STILE
2353 ⍓ APL FUNCTIONAL SYMBOL QUAD UP CARET
2354 ⍔ APL FUNCTIONAL SYMBOL QUAD DEL
2355 ⍕ APL FUNCTIONAL SYMBOL UP TACK JOT
2356 ⍖ APL FUNCTIONAL SYMBOL DOWNWARDS VANE
2357 ⍗ APL FUNCTIONAL SYMBOL QUAD DOWNWARDS ARROW
2358 ⍘ APL FUNCTIONAL SYMBOL QUOTE UNDERBAR
2359 ⍙ APL FUNCTIONAL SYMBOL DELTA UNDERBAR
235A ⍚ APL FUNCTIONAL SYMBOL DIAMOND UNDERBAR
235B ⍛ APL FUNCTIONAL SYMBOL JOT UNDERBAR
235C ⍜ APL FUNCTIONAL SYMBOL CIRCLE UNDERBAR
235D ⍝ APL FUNCTIONAL SYMBOL UP SHOE JOT
235E ⍞ APL FUNCTIONAL SYMBOL QUOTE QUAD
235F ⍟ APL FUNCTIONAL SYMBOL CIRCLE STAR
2360 ⍠ APL FUNCTIONAL SYMBOL QUAD COLON
2361 ⍡ APL FUNCTIONAL SYMBOL UP TACK DIAERESIS
2362 ⍢ APL FUNCTIONAL SYMBOL DEL DIAERESIS
2363 ⍣ APL FUNCTIONAL SYMBOL STAR DIAERESIS
2364 ⍤ APL FUNCTIONAL SYMBOL JOT DIAERESIS
2365 ⍥ APL FUNCTIONAL SYMBOL CIRCLE DIAERESIS
2366 ⍦ APL FUNCTIONAL SYMBOL DOWN SHOE STILE
2367 ⍧ APL FUNCTIONAL SYMBOL LEFT SHOE STILE
2368 ⍨ APL FUNCTIONAL SYMBOL TILDE DIAERESIS
2369 ⍩ APL FUNCTIONAL SYMBOL GREATER-THAN DIAERESIS
236A ⍪ APL FUNCTIONAL SYMBOL COMMA BAR
236B ⍫ APL FUNCTIONAL SYMBOL DEL TILDE
236C ⍬ APL FUNCTIONAL SYMBOL ZILDE
236D ⍭ APL FUNCTIONAL SYMBOL STILE TILDE
236E ⍮ APL FUNCTIONAL SYMBOL SEMICOLON UNDERBAR
236F ⍯ APL FUNCTIONAL SYMBOL QUAD NOT EQUAL
2370 ⍰ APL FUNCTIONAL SYMBOL QUAD QUESTION
2371 ⍱ APL FUNCTIONAL SYMBOL DOWN CARET TILDE
2372 ⍲ APL FUNCTIONAL SYMBOL UP CARET TILDE
2373 ⍳ APL FUNCTIONAL SYMBOL IOTA
2374 ⍴ APL FUNCTIONAL SYMBOL RHO

2375 ⍵ APL FUNCTIONAL SYMBOL OMEGA
2376 ⍶ APL FUNCTIONAL SYMBOL ALPHA UNDERBAR
2377 ⍷ APL FUNCTIONAL SYMBOL EPSILON UNDERBAR
2378 ⍸ APL FUNCTIONAL SYMBOL IOTA UNDERBAR
2379 ⍹ APL FUNCTIONAL SYMBOL OMEGA UNDERBAR
237A ⍺ APL FUNCTIONAL SYMBOL ALPHA

	240	241	242	243
0	NUL 2400	DLE 2410	SP 2420	
1	SOH 2401	DC1 2411	DEL 2421	
2	STX 2402	DC2 2412	ƀ 2422	
3	ETX 2403	DC3 2413	␣ 2423	
4	EOT 2404	DC4 2414	N_L 2424	
5	ENQ 2405	NAK 2415		
6	ACK 2406	SYN 2416		
7	BEL 2407	ETB 2417		
8	BS 2408	CAN 2418		
9	HT 2409	EM 2419		
A	LF 240A	SUB 241A		
B	VT 240B	ESC 241B		
C	FF 240C	FS 241C		
D	CR 240D	GS 241D		
E	SO 240E	RS 241E		
F	SI 240F	US 241F		

Graphic pictures for control codes

2400 ␀ SYMBOL FOR NULL

2401 ␁ SYMBOL FOR START OF HEADING

2402 ␂ SYMBOL FOR START OF TEXT

2403 ␃ SYMBOL FOR END OF TEXT

2404 ␄ SYMBOL FOR END OF TRANSMISSION

2405 ␅ SYMBOL FOR ENQUIRY

2406 ␆ SYMBOL FOR ACKNOWLEDGE

2407 ␇ SYMBOL FOR BELL

2408 ␈ SYMBOL FOR BACKSPACE

2409 ␉ SYMBOL FOR HORIZONTAL TABULATION

240A ␊ SYMBOL FOR LINE FEED

240B ␋ SYMBOL FOR VERTICAL TABULATION

240C ␌ SYMBOL FOR FORM FEED

240D ␍ SYMBOL FOR CARRIAGE RETURN

240E ␎ SYMBOL FOR SHIFT OUT

240F ␏ SYMBOL FOR SHIFT IN

2410 ␐ SYMBOL FOR DATA LINK ESCAPE

2411 ␑ SYMBOL FOR DEVICE CONTROL ONE

2412 ␒ SYMBOL FOR DEVICE CONTROL TWO

2413 ␓ SYMBOL FOR DEVICE CONTROL THREE

2414 ␔ SYMBOL FOR DEVICE CONTROL FOUR

2415 ␕ SYMBOL FOR NEGATIVE ACKNOWLEDGE

2416 ␖ SYMBOL FOR SYNCHRONOUS IDLE

2417 ␗ SYMBOL FOR END OF TRANSMISSION BLOCK

2418 ␘ SYMBOL FOR CANCEL

2419 ␙ SYMBOL FOR END OF MEDIUM

241A ␚ SYMBOL FOR SUBSTITUTE

241B ␛ SYMBOL FOR ESCAPE

241C ␜ SYMBOL FOR FILE SEPARATOR

241D ␝ SYMBOL FOR GROUP SEPARATOR

241E ␞ SYMBOL FOR RECORD SEPARATOR

241F ␟ SYMBOL FOR UNIT SEPARATOR

2420 ␠ SYMBOL FOR SPACE

2421 ␡ SYMBOL FOR DELETE

2422 ␢ BLANK SYMBOL
• graphic for space
→ 0180 ƀ latin small letter b with stroke

2423 ␣ OPEN BOX
• graphic for space

2424 ␤ SYMBOL FOR NEWLINE

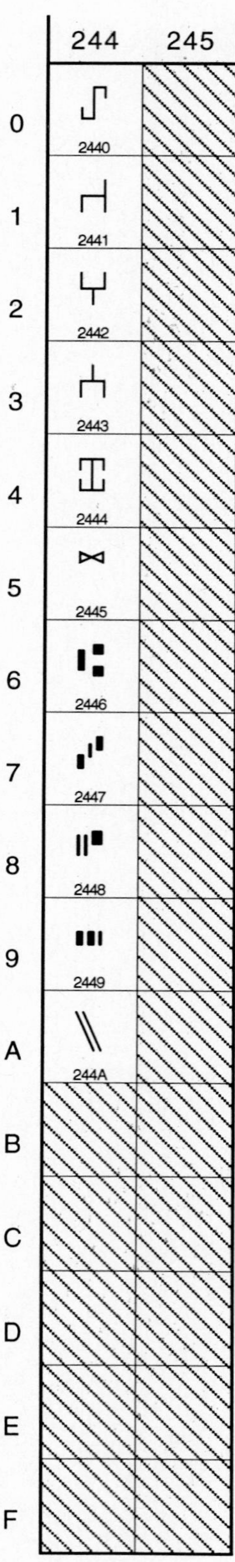

OCR

2440 ⑀ OCR HOOK
2441 ⑁ OCR CHAIR
2442 ⑂ OCR FORK
2443 ⑃ OCR INVERTED FORK
2444 ⑄ OCR BELT BUCKLE
2445 ⑅ OCR BOW TIE
→ 22C8 ⋈ bowtie
2446 ⑆ OCR BRANCH BANK IDENTIFICATION
= transit
2447 ⑇ OCR AMOUNT OF CHECK
2448 ⑈ OCR DASH
= on us
2449 ⑉ OCR CUSTOMER ACCOUNT NUMBER
= dash
244A ⑊ OCR DOUBLE BACKSLASH

	246	247	248	249	24A	24B	24C	24D	24E	24F
0	① 2460	⑰ 2470	⒀ 2480	⒐ 2490	⒠ 24A0	⒰ 24B0	Ⓚ 24C0	ⓐ 24D0	ⓠ 24E0	
1	② 2461	⑱ 2471	⒁ 2481	⒑ 2491	⒡ 24A1	⒱ 24B1	Ⓛ 24C1	ⓑ 24D1	ⓡ 24E1	
2	③ 2462	⑲ 2472	⒂ 2482	⒒ 2492	⒢ 24A2	⒲ 24B2	Ⓜ 24C2	ⓒ 24D2	ⓢ 24E2	
3	④ 2463	⑳ 2473	⒃ 2483	⒓ 2493	⒣ 24A3	⒳ 24B3	Ⓝ 24C3	ⓓ 24D3	ⓣ 24E3	
4	⑤ 2464	⑴ 2474	⒄ 2484	⒔ 2494	⒤ 24A4	⒴ 24B4	Ⓞ 24C4	ⓔ 24D4	ⓤ 24E4	
5	⑥ 2465	⑵ 2475	⒅ 2485	⒕ 2495	⒥ 24A5	⒵ 24B5	Ⓟ 24C5	ⓕ 24D5	ⓥ 24E5	
6	⑦ 2466	⑶ 2476	⒆ 2486	⒖ 2496	⒦ 24A6	Ⓐ 24B6	Ⓠ 24C6	ⓖ 24D6	ⓦ 24E6	
7	⑧ 2467	⑷ 2477	⒇ 2487	⒗ 2497	⒧ 24A7	Ⓑ 24B7	Ⓡ 24C7	ⓗ 24D7	ⓧ 24E7	
8	⑨ 2468	⑸ 2478	⒈ 2488	⒘ 2498	⒨ 24A8	Ⓒ 24B8	Ⓢ 24C8	ⓘ 24D8	ⓨ 24E8	
9	⑩ 2469	⑹ 2479	⒉ 2489	⒙ 2499	⒩ 24A9	Ⓓ 24B9	Ⓣ 24C9	ⓙ 24D9	ⓩ 24E9	
A	⑪ 246A	⑺ 247A	⒊ 248A	⒚ 249A	⒪ 24AA	Ⓔ 24BA	Ⓤ 24CA	ⓚ 24DA	⓪ 24EA	
B	⑫ 246B	⑻ 247B	⒋ 248B	⒛ 249B	⒫ 24AB	Ⓕ 24BB	Ⓥ 24CB	ⓛ 24DB		
C	⑬ 246C	⑼ 247C	⒌ 248C	⒜ 249C	⒬ 24AC	Ⓖ 24BC	Ⓦ 24CC	ⓜ 24DC		
D	⑭ 246D	⑽ 247D	⒍ 248D	⒝ 249D	⒭ 24AD	Ⓗ 24BD	Ⓧ 24CD	ⓝ 24DD		
E	⑮ 246E	⑾ 247E	⒎ 248E	⒞ 249E	⒮ 24AE	Ⓘ 24BE	Ⓨ 24CE	ⓞ 24DE		
F	⑯ 246F	⑿ 247F	⒏ 248F	⒟ 249F	⒯ 24AF	Ⓙ 24BF	Ⓩ 24CF	ⓟ 24DF		

Circled numbers

2460 ① CIRCLED DIGIT ONE
≈ <circle> + 0031 1

2461 ② CIRCLED DIGIT TWO
≈ <circle> + 0032 2

2462 ③ CIRCLED DIGIT THREE
≈ <circle> + 0033 3

2463 ④ CIRCLED DIGIT FOUR
≈ <circle> + 0034 4

2464 ⑤ CIRCLED DIGIT FIVE
≈ <circle> + 0035 5

2465 ⑥ CIRCLED DIGIT SIX
≈ <circle> + 0036 6

2466 ⑦ CIRCLED DIGIT SEVEN
≈ <circle> + 0037 7

2467 ⑧ CIRCLED DIGIT EIGHT
≈ <circle> + 0038 8

2468 ⑨ CIRCLED DIGIT NINE
≈ <circle> + 0039 9

2469 ⑩ CIRCLED NUMBER TEN
≈ <circle> + 0031 1

246A ⑪ CIRCLED NUMBER ELEVEN
≈ <circle> + 0031 1 + 0030 0

246B ⑫ CIRCLED NUMBER TWELVE
≈ <circle> + 0031 1 + 0032 2

246C ⑬ CIRCLED NUMBER THIRTEEN
≈ <circle> + 0031 1 + 0033 3

246D ⑭ CIRCLED NUMBER FOURTEEN
≈ <circle> + 0031 1 + 0034 4

246E ⑮ CIRCLED NUMBER FIFTEEN
≈ <circle> + 0031 1 + 0035 5

246F ⑯ CIRCLED NUMBER SIXTEEN
≈ <circle> + 0031 1 + 0036 6

2470 ⑰ CIRCLED NUMBER SEVENTEEN
≈ <circle> + 0031 1 + 0037 7

2471 ⑱ CIRCLED NUMBER EIGHTEEN
≈ <circle> + 0031 1 + 0038 8

2472 ⑲ CIRCLED NUMBER NINETEEN
≈ <circle> + 0031 1 + 0039 9

2473 ⑳ CIRCLED NUMBER TWENTY
≈ <circle> + 0032 2 + 0030 0

Parenthesized numbers

2474 ⑴ PARENTHESIZED DIGIT ONE
≡ 0028 (+ 0031 1 + 0029)

2475 ⑵ PARENTHESIZED DIGIT TWO
≡ 0028 (+ 0032 2 + 0029)

2476 ⑶ PARENTHESIZED DIGIT THREE
≡ 0028 (+ 0033 3 + 0029)

2477 ⑷ PARENTHESIZED DIGIT FOUR
≡ 0028 (+ 0034 4 + 0029)

2478 ⑸ PARENTHESIZED DIGIT FIVE
≡ 0028 (+ 0035 5 + 0029)

2479 ⑹ PARENTHESIZED DIGIT SIX
≡ 0028 (+ 0036 6 + 0029)

247A ⑺ PARENTHESIZED DIGIT SEVEN
≡ 0028 (+ 0037 7 + 0029)

247B ⑻ PARENTHESIZED DIGIT EIGHT
≡ 0028 (+ 0038 8 + 0029)

247C ⑼ PARENTHESIZED DIGIT NINE
≡ 0028 (+ 0039 9 + 0029)

247D ⑽ PARENTHESIZED NUMBER TEN
≡ 0028 (+ 0031 1 + 0030 0 + 0029)

247E ⑾ PARENTHESIZED NUMBER ELEVEN
≡ 0028 (+ 0031 1 + 0031 1 + 0029)

247F ⑿ PARENTHESIZED NUMBER TWELVE
≡ 0028 (+ 0031 1 + 0032 2 + 0029)

2480 ⒀ PARENTHESIZED NUMBER THIRTEEN
≡ 0028 (+ 0031 1 + 0033 3 + 0029)

2481 ⒁ PARENTHESIZED NUMBER FOURTEEN
≡ 0028 (+ 0031 1 + 0034 4 + 0029)

2482 ⒂ PARENTHESIZED NUMBER FIFTEEN
≡ 0028 (+ 0031 1 + 0035 5 + 0029)

2483 ⒃ PARENTHESIZED NUMBER SIXTEEN
≡ 0028 (+ 0031 1 + 0036 6 + 0029)

2484 ⒄ PARENTHESIZED NUMBER SEVENTEEN
≡ 0028 (+ 0031 1 + 0037 7 + 0029)

2485 ⒅ PARENTHESIZED NUMBER EIGHTEEN
≡ 0028 (+ 0031 1 + 0038 8 + 0029)

2486 ⒆ PARENTHESIZED NUMBER NINETEEN
≡ 0028 (+ 0031 1 + 0039 9 + 0029)

2487 ⒇ PARENTHESIZED NUMBER TWENTY
≡ 0028 (+ 0032 2 + 0030 0 + 0029)

Numbers period

2488 ⒈ DIGIT ONE FULL STOP
≡ 0031 1 + 002E .

2489 ⒉ DIGIT TWO FULL STOP
≡ 0032 2 + 002E .

248A ⒊ DIGIT THREE FULL STOP
≡ 0033 3 + 002E .

248B ⒋ DIGIT FOUR FULL STOP
≡ 0034 4 + 002E .

248C ⒌ DIGIT FIVE FULL STOP
≡ 0035 5 + 002E .

248D ⒍ DIGIT SIX FULL STOP
≡ 0036 6 + 002E .

248E ⒎ DIGIT SEVEN FULL STOP
≡ 0037 7 + 002E .

248F ⒏ DIGIT EIGHT FULL STOP
≡ 0038 8 + 002E .

2490 9. DIGIT NINE FULL STOP
≡ 0039 9 + 002E .

2491 10. NUMBER TEN FULL STOP
≡ 0031 1 + 0030 0 + 002E .

2492 11. NUMBER ELEVEN FULL STOP
≡ 0031 1 + 0031 1 + 002E .

2493 12. NUMBER TWELVE FULL STOP
≡ 0031 1 + 0032 2 + 002E .

2494 13. NUMBER THIRTEEN FULL STOP
≡ 0031 1 + 0033 3 + 002E .

2495 14. NUMBER FOURTEEN FULL STOP
≡ 0031 1 + 0034 4 + 002E .

2496 15. NUMBER FIFTEEN FULL STOP
≡ 0031 1 + 0035 5 + 002E .

2497 16. NUMBER SIXTEEN FULL STOP
≡ 0031 1 + 0036 6 + 002E .

2498 17. NUMBER SEVENTEEN FULL STOP
≡ 0031 1 + 0037 7 + 002E .

2499 18. NUMBER EIGHTEEN FULL STOP
≡ 0031 1 + 0038 8 + 002E .

249A 19. NUMBER NINETEEN FULL STOP
≡ 0031 1 + 0039 9 + 002E .

249B 20. NUMBER TWENTY FULL STOP
≡ 0032 2 + 0030 0 + 002E .

Parenthesized Latin letters

249C (a) PARENTHESIZED LATIN SMALL LETTER A
≡ 0028 (+ 0061 a + 0029)

249D (b) PARENTHESIZED LATIN SMALL LETTER B
≡ 0028 (+ 0062 b + 0029)

249E (c) PARENTHESIZED LATIN SMALL LETTER C
≡ 0028 (+ 0063 c + 0029)

249F (d) PARENTHESIZED LATIN SMALL LETTER D
≡ 0028 (+ 0064 d + 0029)

24A0 (e) PARENTHESIZED LATIN SMALL LETTER E
≡ 0028 (+ 0065 e + 0029)

24A1 (f) PARENTHESIZED LATIN SMALL LETTER F
≡ 0028 (+ 0066 f + 0029)

24A2 (g) PARENTHESIZED LATIN SMALL LETTER G
≡ 0028 (+ 0067 g + 0029)

24A3 (h) PARENTHESIZED LATIN SMALL LETTER H
≡ 0028 (+ 0068 h + 0029)

24A4 (i) PARENTHESIZED LATIN SMALL LETTER I
≡ 0028 (+ 0069 i + 0029)

24A5 (j) PARENTHESIZED LATIN SMALL LETTER J
≡ 0028 (+ 006A j + 0029)

24A6 (k) PARENTHESIZED LATIN SMALL LETTER K
≡ 0028 (+ 006B k + 0029)

24A7 (l) PARENTHESIZED LATIN SMALL LETTER L
≡ 0028 (+ 006C l + 0029)

24A8 (m) PARENTHESIZED LATIN SMALL LETTER M
≡ 0028 (+ 006D m + 0029)

24A9 (n) PARENTHESIZED LATIN SMALL LETTER N
≡ 0028 (+ 006E n + 0029)

24AA (o) PARENTHESIZED LATIN SMALL LETTER O
≡ 0028 (+ 006F o + 0029)

24AB (p) PARENTHESIZED LATIN SMALL LETTER P
≡ 0028 (+ 0070 p + 0029)

24AC (q) PARENTHESIZED LATIN SMALL LETTER Q
≡ 0028 (+ 0071 q + 0029)

24AD (r) PARENTHESIZED LATIN SMALL LETTER R
≡ 0028 (+ 0072 r + 0029)

24AE (s) PARENTHESIZED LATIN SMALL LETTER S
≡ 0028 (+ 0073 s + 0029)

24AF (t) PARENTHESIZED LATIN SMALL LETTER T
≡ 0028 (+ 0074 t + 0029)

24B0 (u) PARENTHESIZED LATIN SMALL LETTER U
≡ 0028 (+ 0075 u + 0029)

24B1 (v) PARENTHESIZED LATIN SMALL LETTER V
≡ 0028 (+ 0076 v + 0029)

24B2 (w) PARENTHESIZED LATIN SMALL LETTER W
≡ 0028 (+ 0077 w + 0029)

24B3 (x) PARENTHESIZED LATIN SMALL LETTER X
≡ 0028 (+ 0078 x + 0029)

24B4 (y) PARENTHESIZED LATIN SMALL LETTER Y
≡ 0028 (+ 0079 y + 0029)

24B5 (z) PARENTHESIZED LATIN SMALL LETTER Z
≡ 0028 (+ 007A z + 0029)

Circled Latin letters

24B6 Ⓐ CIRCLED LATIN CAPITAL LETTER A
≈ <circle> + 0041 A

24B7 Ⓑ CIRCLED LATIN CAPITAL LETTER B
≈ <circle> + 0042 B
24B8 Ⓒ CIRCLED LATIN CAPITAL LETTER C
≈ <circle> + 0043 C
24B9 Ⓓ CIRCLED LATIN CAPITAL LETTER D
≈ <circle> + 0044 D
24BA Ⓔ CIRCLED LATIN CAPITAL LETTER E
≈ <circle> + 0045 E
24BB Ⓕ CIRCLED LATIN CAPITAL LETTER F
≈ <circle> + 0046 F
24BC Ⓖ CIRCLED LATIN CAPITAL LETTER G
≈ <circle> + 0047 G
24BD Ⓗ CIRCLED LATIN CAPITAL LETTER H
≈ <circle> + 0048 H
24BE Ⓘ CIRCLED LATIN CAPITAL LETTER I
≈ <circle> + 0049 I
24BF Ⓙ CIRCLED LATIN CAPITAL LETTER J
≈ <circle> + 004A J
24C0 Ⓚ CIRCLED LATIN CAPITAL LETTER K
≈ <circle> + 004B K
24C1 Ⓛ CIRCLED LATIN CAPITAL LETTER L
≈ <circle> + 004C L
24C2 Ⓜ CIRCLED LATIN CAPITAL LETTER M
≈ <circle> + 004D M
24C3 Ⓝ CIRCLED LATIN CAPITAL LETTER N
≈ <circle> + 004E N
24C4 Ⓞ CIRCLED LATIN CAPITAL LETTER O
≈ <circle> + 004F O
24C5 Ⓟ CIRCLED LATIN CAPITAL LETTER P
≈ <circle> + 0050 P
24C6 Ⓠ CIRCLED LATIN CAPITAL LETTER Q
≈ <circle> + 0051 Q
24C7 Ⓡ CIRCLED LATIN CAPITAL LETTER R
≈ <circle> + 0052 R
24C8 Ⓢ CIRCLED LATIN CAPITAL LETTER S
≈ <circle> + 0053 S
24C9 Ⓣ CIRCLED LATIN CAPITAL LETTER T
≈ <circle> + 0054 T
24CA Ⓤ CIRCLED LATIN CAPITAL LETTER U
≈ <circle> + 0055 U
24CB Ⓥ CIRCLED LATIN CAPITAL LETTER V
≈ <circle> + 0056 V
24CC Ⓦ CIRCLED LATIN CAPITAL LETTER W
≈ <circle> + 0057 W
24CD Ⓧ CIRCLED LATIN CAPITAL LETTER X
≈ <circle> + 0058 X
24CE Ⓨ CIRCLED LATIN CAPITAL LETTER Y
≈ <circle> + 0059 Y
24CF Ⓩ CIRCLED LATIN CAPITAL LETTER Z
≈ <circle> + 005A Z
24D0 ⓐ CIRCLED LATIN SMALL LETTER A
≈ <circle> + 0061 a
24D1 ⓑ CIRCLED LATIN SMALL LETTER B
≈ <circle> + 0062 b
24D2 ⓒ CIRCLED LATIN SMALL LETTER C
≈ <circle> + 0063 c
24D3 ⓓ CIRCLED LATIN SMALL LETTER D
≈ <circle> + 0064 d
24D4 ⓔ CIRCLED LATIN SMALL LETTER E
≈ <circle> + 0065 e
24D5 ⓕ CIRCLED LATIN SMALL LETTER F
≈ <circle> + 0066 f
24D6 ⓖ CIRCLED LATIN SMALL LETTER G
≈ <circle> + 0067 g
24D7 ⓗ CIRCLED LATIN SMALL LETTER H
≈ <circle> + 0068 h
24D8 ⓘ CIRCLED LATIN SMALL LETTER I
≈ <circle> + 0069 i
24D9 ⓙ CIRCLED LATIN SMALL LETTER J
≈ <circle> + 006A j
24DA ⓚ CIRCLED LATIN SMALL LETTER K
≈ <circle> + 006B k
24DB ⓛ CIRCLED LATIN SMALL LETTER L
≈ <circle> + 006C l
24DC ⓜ CIRCLED LATIN SMALL LETTER M
≈ <circle> + 006D m
24DD ⓝ CIRCLED LATIN SMALL LETTER N
≈ <circle> + 006E n
24DE ⓞ CIRCLED LATIN SMALL LETTER O
≈ <circle> + 006F o
24DF ⓟ CIRCLED LATIN SMALL LETTER P
≈ <circle> + 0070 p
24E0 ⓠ CIRCLED LATIN SMALL LETTER Q
≈ <circle> + 0071 q
24E1 ⓡ CIRCLED LATIN SMALL LETTER R
≈ <circle> + 0072 r
24E2 ⓢ CIRCLED LATIN SMALL LETTER S
≈ <circle> + 0073 s
24E3 ⓣ CIRCLED LATIN SMALL LETTER T
≈ <circle> + 0074 t
24E4 ⓤ CIRCLED LATIN SMALL LETTER U
≈ <circle> + 0075 u
24E5 ⓥ CIRCLED LATIN SMALL LETTER V
≈ <circle> + 0076 v
24E6 ⓦ CIRCLED LATIN SMALL LETTER W
≈ <circle> + 0077 w
24E7 ⓧ CIRCLED LATIN SMALL LETTER X
≈ <circle> + 0078 x
24E8 ⓨ CIRCLED LATIN SMALL LETTER Y
≈ <circle> + 0079 y
24E9 ⓩ CIRCLED LATIN SMALL LETTER Z
≈ <circle> + 007A z

Additional circled numbers

24EA ⓪ CIRCLED DIGIT ZERO
≈ <circle> + 0030 0

	250	251	252	253	254	255	256	257
0	─ 2500	┐ 2510	┠ 2520	┰ 2530	╀ 2540	═ 2550	╠ 2560	╰ 2570
1	━ 2501	┑ 2511	┡ 2521	┱ 2531	╁ 2541	║ 2551	╡ 2561	╱ 2571
2	│ 2502	┒ 2512	┢ 2522	┲ 2532	╂ 2542	╒ 2552	╢ 2562	╲ 2572
3	┃ 2503	┓ 2513	┣ 2523	┳ 2533	╃ 2543	╓ 2553	╣ 2563	╳ 2573
4	┄ 2504	└ 2514	┤ 2524	┴ 2534	╄ 2544	╔ 2554	╤ 2564	╴ 2574
5	┅ 2505	┕ 2515	┥ 2525	┵ 2535	╅ 2545	╕ 2555	╥ 2565	╵ 2575
6	┆ 2506	┖ 2516	┦ 2526	┶ 2536	╆ 2546	╖ 2556	╦ 2566	╶ 2576
7	┇ 2507	┗ 2517	┧ 2527	┷ 2537	╇ 2547	╗ 2557	╧ 2567	╷ 2577
8	┈ 2508	┘ 2518	┨ 2528	┸ 2538	╈ 2548	╘ 2558	╨ 2568	╸ 2578
9	┉ 2509	┙ 2519	┩ 2529	┹ 2539	╉ 2549	╙ 2559	╩ 2569	╹ 2579
A	┊ 250A	┚ 251A	┪ 252A	┺ 253A	╊ 254A	╚ 255A	╪ 256A	╺ 257A
B	┋ 250B	┛ 251B	┫ 252B	┻ 253B	╋ 254B	╛ 255B	╫ 256B	╻ 257B
C	┌ 250C	├ 251C	┬ 252C	┼ 253C	╌ 254C	╜ 255C	╬ 256C	╼ 257C
D	┍ 250D	┝ 251D	┭ 252D	┽ 253D	╍ 254D	╝ 255D	╭ 256D	╽ 257D
E	┎ 250E	┞ 251E	┮ 252E	┾ 253E	╎ 254E	╞ 255E	╮ 256E	╾ 257E
F	┏ 250F	┟ 251F	┯ 252F	┿ 253F	╏ 254F	╟ 255F	╯ 256F	╿ 257F

Form and chart components

2500 ─ BOX DRAWINGS LIGHT HORIZONTAL
= Videotex Mosaic DG 15

2501 ━ BOX DRAWINGS HEAVY HORIZONTAL

2502 │ BOX DRAWINGS LIGHT VERTICAL
= Videotex Mosaic DG 14

2503 ┃ BOX DRAWINGS HEAVY VERTICAL

2504 ┄ BOX DRAWINGS LIGHT TRIPLE DASH HORIZONTAL

2505 ┅ BOX DRAWINGS HEAVY TRIPLE DASH HORIZONTAL

2506 ┆ BOX DRAWINGS LIGHT TRIPLE DASH VERTICAL

2507 ┇ BOX DRAWINGS HEAVY TRIPLE DASH VERTICAL

2508 ┈ BOX DRAWINGS LIGHT QUADRUPLE DASH HORIZONTAL

2509 ┉ BOX DRAWINGS HEAVY QUADRUPLE DASH HORIZONTAL

250A ┊ BOX DRAWINGS LIGHT QUADRUPLE DASH VERTICAL

250B ┋ BOX DRAWINGS HEAVY QUADRUPLE DASH VERTICAL

250C ┌ BOX DRAWINGS LIGHT DOWN AND RIGHT
= Videotex Mosaic DG 16

250D ┍ BOX DRAWINGS DOWN LIGHT AND RIGHT HEAVY

250E ┎ BOX DRAWINGS DOWN HEAVY AND RIGHT LIGHT

250F ┏ BOX DRAWINGS HEAVY DOWN AND RIGHT

2510 ┐ BOX DRAWINGS LIGHT DOWN AND LEFT
= Videotex Mosaic DG 17

2511 ┑ BOX DRAWINGS DOWN LIGHT AND LEFT HEAVY

2512 ┒ BOX DRAWINGS DOWN HEAVY AND LEFT LIGHT

2513 ┓ BOX DRAWINGS HEAVY DOWN AND LEFT

2514 └ BOX DRAWINGS LIGHT UP AND RIGHT
= Videotex Mosaic DG 18

2515 ┕ BOX DRAWINGS UP LIGHT AND RIGHT HEAVY

2516 ┖ BOX DRAWINGS UP HEAVY AND RIGHT LIGHT

2517 ┗ BOX DRAWINGS HEAVY UP AND RIGHT

2518 ┘ BOX DRAWINGS LIGHT UP AND LEFT
= Videotex Mosaic DG 19

2519 ┙ BOX DRAWINGS UP LIGHT AND LEFT HEAVY

251A ┚ BOX DRAWINGS UP HEAVY AND LEFT LIGHT

251B ┛ BOX DRAWINGS HEAVY UP AND LEFT

251C ├ BOX DRAWINGS LIGHT VERTICAL AND RIGHT
= Videotex Mosaic DG 20

251D ┝ BOX DRAWINGS VERTICAL LIGHT AND RIGHT HEAVY
= Videotex Mosaic DG 03

251E ┞ BOX DRAWINGS UP HEAVY AND RIGHT DOWN LIGHT

251F ┟ BOX DRAWINGS DOWN HEAVY AND RIGHT UP LIGHT

2520 ┠ BOX DRAWINGS VERTICAL HEAVY AND RIGHT LIGHT

2521 ┡ BOX DRAWINGS DOWN LIGHT AND RIGHT UP HEAVY

2522 ┢ BOX DRAWINGS UP LIGHT AND RIGHT DOWN HEAVY

2523 ┣ BOX DRAWINGS HEAVY VERTICAL AND RIGHT

2524 ┤ BOX DRAWINGS LIGHT VERTICAL AND LEFT
= Videotex Mosaic DG 21

2525 ┥ BOX DRAWINGS VERTICAL LIGHT AND LEFT HEAVY
= Videotex Mosaic DG 04

2526 ┦ BOX DRAWINGS UP HEAVY AND LEFT DOWN LIGHT

2527 ┧ BOX DRAWINGS DOWN HEAVY AND LEFT UP LIGHT

2528 ┨ BOX DRAWINGS VERTICAL HEAVY AND LEFT LIGHT

2529 ┩ BOX DRAWINGS DOWN LIGHT AND LEFT UP HEAVY

252A ┪ BOX DRAWINGS UP LIGHT AND LEFT DOWN HEAVY

252B ┫ BOX DRAWINGS HEAVY VERTICAL AND LEFT

252C ┬ BOX DRAWINGS LIGHT DOWN AND HORIZONTAL
= Videotex Mosaic DG 22

252D ┭ BOX DRAWINGS LEFT HEAVY AND RIGHT DOWN LIGHT

252E ┮ BOX DRAWINGS RIGHT HEAVY AND LEFT DOWN LIGHT

252F ┯ BOX DRAWINGS DOWN LIGHT AND HORIZONTAL HEAVY
= Videotex Mosaic DG 02

2530 ┰ BOX DRAWINGS DOWN HEAVY AND HORIZONTAL LIGHT

2531 ┱ BOX DRAWINGS RIGHT LIGHT AND LEFT DOWN HEAVY

2532 ┲ BOX DRAWINGS LEFT LIGHT AND RIGHT DOWN HEAVY

2533 ┳ BOX DRAWINGS HEAVY DOWN AND HORIZONTAL

2534 ┴ BOX DRAWINGS LIGHT UP AND HORIZONTAL
= Videotex Mosaic DG 23

2535 ┵ BOX DRAWINGS LEFT HEAVY AND RIGHT UP LIGHT

2536 ┶ BOX DRAWINGS RIGHT HEAVY AND LEFT UP LIGHT

2537 ┷ BOX DRAWINGS UP LIGHT AND HORIZONTAL HEAVY
= Videotex Mosaic DG 01

2538 ┸ BOX DRAWINGS UP HEAVY AND HORIZONTAL LIGHT

2539 ┹ BOX DRAWINGS RIGHT LIGHT AND LEFT UP HEAVY

253A ┺ BOX DRAWINGS LEFT LIGHT AND RIGHT UP HEAVY

253B ┻ BOX DRAWINGS HEAVY UP AND HORIZONTAL

253C ┼ BOX DRAWINGS LIGHT VERTICAL AND HORIZONTAL
= Videotex Mosaic DG 24

253D ┽ BOX DRAWINGS LEFT HEAVY AND RIGHT VERTICAL LIGHT

253E ┾ BOX DRAWINGS RIGHT HEAVY AND LEFT VERTICAL LIGHT

253F ┿ BOX DRAWINGS VERTICAL LIGHT AND HORIZONTAL HEAVY
= Videotex Mosaic DG 13

2540 ╀ BOX DRAWINGS UP HEAVY AND DOWN HORIZONTAL LIGHT

2541 ╁ BOX DRAWINGS DOWN HEAVY AND UP HORIZONTAL LIGHT

2542 ╂ BOX DRAWINGS VERTICAL HEAVY AND HORIZONTAL LIGHT

2543 ╃ BOX DRAWINGS LEFT UP HEAVY AND RIGHT DOWN LIGHT

2544 ╄ BOX DRAWINGS RIGHT UP HEAVY AND LEFT DOWN LIGHT

2545 ╅ BOX DRAWINGS LEFT DOWN HEAVY AND RIGHT UP LIGHT

2546 ╆ BOX DRAWINGS RIGHT DOWN HEAVY AND LEFT UP LIGHT

2547 ╇ BOX DRAWINGS DOWN LIGHT AND UP HORIZONTAL HEAVY

2548 ╈ BOX DRAWINGS UP LIGHT AND DOWN HORIZONTAL HEAVY

2549 ╉ BOX DRAWINGS RIGHT LIGHT AND LEFT VERTICAL HEAVY

254A ╊ BOX DRAWINGS LEFT LIGHT AND RIGHT VERTICAL HEAVY

254B ╋ BOX DRAWINGS HEAVY VERTICAL AND HORIZONTAL

254C ╌ BOX DRAWINGS LIGHT DOUBLE DASH HORIZONTAL

254D ╍ BOX DRAWINGS HEAVY DOUBLE DASH HORIZONTAL

254E ╎ BOX DRAWINGS LIGHT DOUBLE DASH VERTICAL

254F ╏ BOX DRAWINGS HEAVY DOUBLE DASH VERTICAL

2550 ═ BOX DRAWINGS DOUBLE HORIZONTAL

2551 ║ BOX DRAWINGS DOUBLE VERTICAL

2552 ╒ BOX DRAWINGS DOWN SINGLE AND RIGHT DOUBLE

2553 ╓ BOX DRAWINGS DOWN DOUBLE AND RIGHT SINGLE

2554 ╔ BOX DRAWINGS DOUBLE DOWN AND RIGHT

2555 ╕ BOX DRAWINGS DOWN SINGLE AND LEFT DOUBLE

2556 ╖ BOX DRAWINGS DOWN DOUBLE AND LEFT SINGLE

2557 ╗ BOX DRAWINGS DOUBLE DOWN AND LEFT

2558 ╘ BOX DRAWINGS UP SINGLE AND RIGHT DOUBLE

2559 ╙ BOX DRAWINGS UP DOUBLE AND RIGHT SINGLE

255A ╚ BOX DRAWINGS DOUBLE UP AND RIGHT

255B ╛ BOX DRAWINGS UP SINGLE AND LEFT DOUBLE

255C ╜ BOX DRAWINGS UP DOUBLE AND LEFT SINGLE

255D ╝ BOX DRAWINGS DOUBLE UP AND LEFT

255E ╞ BOX DRAWINGS VERTICAL SINGLE AND RIGHT DOUBLE

255F ╟ BOX DRAWINGS VERTICAL DOUBLE AND RIGHT SINGLE

2560 ╠ BOX DRAWINGS DOUBLE VERTICAL AND RIGHT

2561 ╡ BOX DRAWINGS VERTICAL SINGLE AND LEFT DOUBLE

2562 ╢ BOX DRAWINGS VERTICAL DOUBLE AND LEFT SINGLE
2563 ╣ BOX DRAWINGS DOUBLE VERTICAL AND LEFT
2564 ╤ BOX DRAWINGS DOWN SINGLE AND HORIZONTAL DOUBLE
2565 ╥ BOX DRAWINGS DOWN DOUBLE AND HORIZONTAL SINGLE
2566 ╦ BOX DRAWINGS DOUBLE DOWN AND HORIZONTAL
2567 ╧ BOX DRAWINGS UP SINGLE AND HORIZONTAL DOUBLE
2568 ╨ BOX DRAWINGS UP DOUBLE AND HORIZONTAL SINGLE
2569 ╩ BOX DRAWINGS DOUBLE UP AND HORIZONTAL
256A ╪ BOX DRAWINGS VERTICAL SINGLE AND HORIZONTAL DOUBLE
256B ╫ BOX DRAWINGS VERTICAL DOUBLE AND HORIZONTAL SINGLE
256C ╬ BOX DRAWINGS DOUBLE VERTICAL AND HORIZONTAL
256D ╭ BOX DRAWINGS LIGHT ARC DOWN AND RIGHT
256E ╮ BOX DRAWINGS LIGHT ARC DOWN AND LEFT
256F ╯ BOX DRAWINGS LIGHT ARC UP AND LEFT
2570 ╰ BOX DRAWINGS LIGHT ARC UP AND RIGHT
2571 ╱ BOX DRAWINGS LIGHT DIAGONAL UPPER RIGHT TO LOWER LEFT
2572 ╲ BOX DRAWINGS LIGHT DIAGONAL UPPER LEFT TO LOWER RIGHT
2573 ╳ BOX DRAWINGS LIGHT DIAGONAL CROSS
2574 ╴ BOX DRAWINGS LIGHT LEFT
2575 ╵ BOX DRAWINGS LIGHT UP
2576 ╶ BOX DRAWINGS LIGHT RIGHT
2577 ╷ BOX DRAWINGS LIGHT DOWN
2578 ╸ BOX DRAWINGS HEAVY LEFT
2579 ╹ BOX DRAWINGS HEAVY UP
257A ╺ BOX DRAWINGS HEAVY RIGHT
257B ╻ BOX DRAWINGS HEAVY DOWN
257C ╼ BOX DRAWINGS LIGHT LEFT AND HEAVY RIGHT
257D ╽ BOX DRAWINGS LIGHT UP AND HEAVY DOWN
257E ╾ BOX DRAWINGS HEAVY LEFT AND LIGHT RIGHT
257F ╿ BOX DRAWINGS HEAVY UP AND LIGHT DOWN

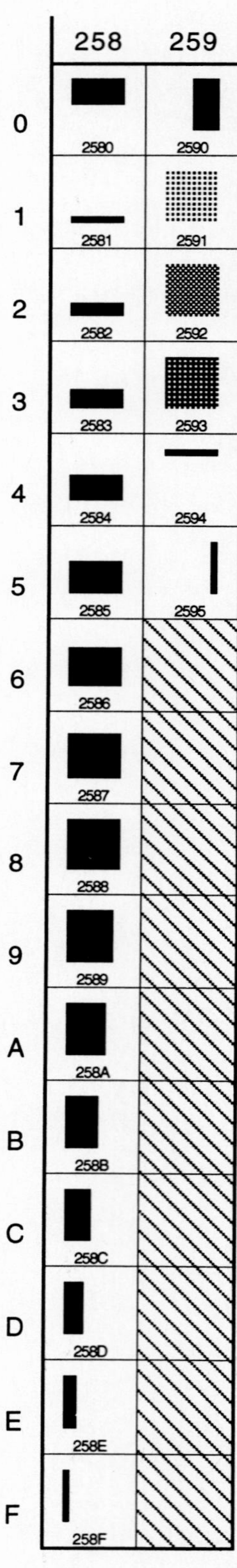
258
259
0
2580
2590
1
2581
2591
2
2582
2592
3
2583
2593
4
2584
2594
5
2585
2595
6
2586
7
2587
8
2588
9
2589
A
258A
B
258B
C
258C
D
258D
E
258E
F
258F

Block elements

2580 ▀ UPPER HALF BLOCK
2581 ▁ LOWER ONE EIGHTH BLOCK
2582 ▂ LOWER ONE QUARTER BLOCK
2583 ▃ LOWER THREE EIGHTHS BLOCK
2584 ▄ LOWER HALF BLOCK
2585 ▅ LOWER FIVE EIGHTHS BLOCK
2586 ▆ LOWER THREE QUARTERS BLOCK
2587 ▇ LOWER SEVEN EIGHTHS BLOCK
2588 █ FULL BLOCK
= solid
2589 ▉ LEFT SEVEN EIGHTHS BLOCK
258A ▊ LEFT THREE QUARTERS BLOCK
258B ▋ LEFT FIVE EIGHTHS BLOCK
258C ▌ LEFT HALF BLOCK
258D ▍ LEFT THREE EIGHTHS BLOCK
258E ▎ LEFT ONE QUARTER BLOCK
258F ▏ LEFT ONE EIGHTH BLOCK
2590 ▐ RIGHT HALF BLOCK
2591 ░ LIGHT SHADE
• 25
2592 ▒ MEDIUM SHADE
• 50
2593 ▓ DARK SHADE
• 75
2594 ▔ UPPER ONE EIGHTH BLOCK
2595 ▕ RIGHT ONE EIGHTH BLOCK

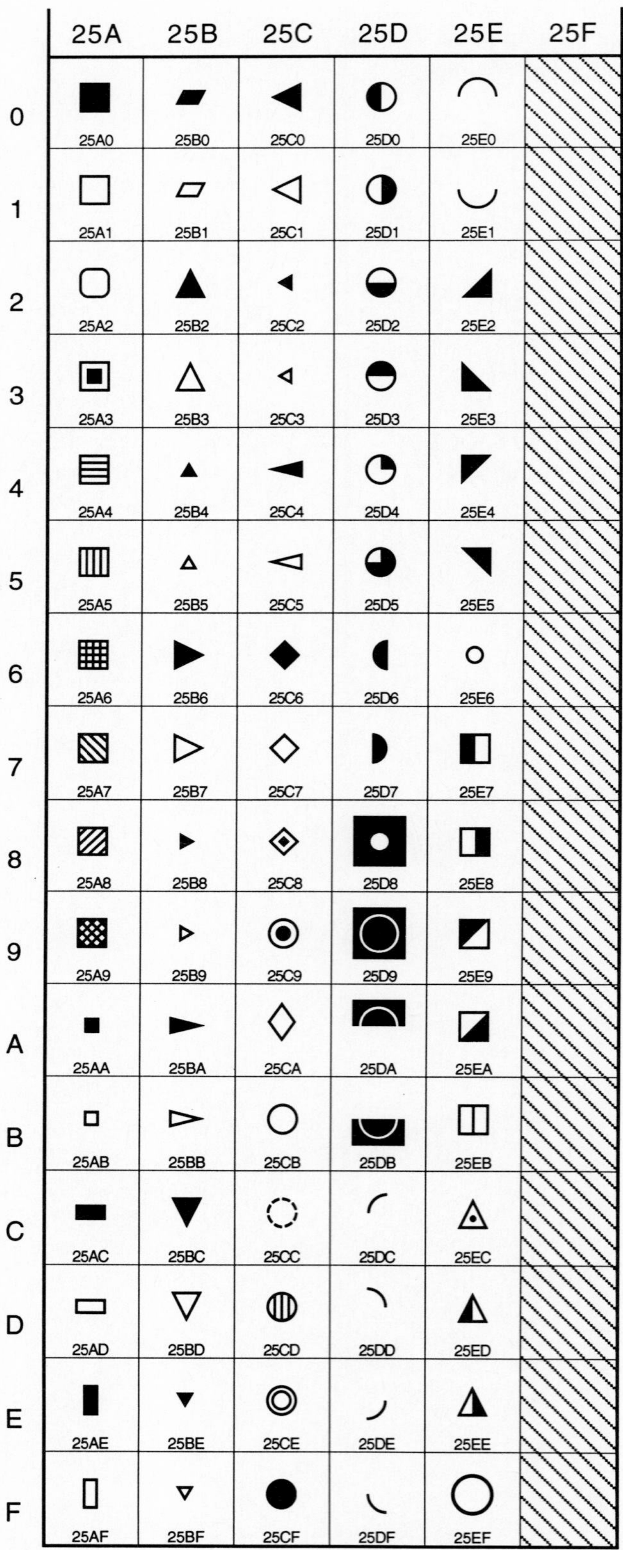

Geometric shapes

25A0 ■ BLACK SQUARE
25A1 □ WHITE SQUARE
= quadrature
→ 2610 ☐ ballot box
25A2 ▢ WHITE SQUARE WITH ROUNDED CORNERS
25A3 ▣ WHITE SQUARE CONTAINING BLACK SMALL SQUARE
25A4 ▤ SQUARE WITH HORIZONTAL FILL
25A5 ▥ SQUARE WITH VERTICAL FILL
25A6 ▦ SQUARE WITH ORTHOGONAL CROSSHATCH FILL
25A7 ▧ SQUARE WITH UPPER LEFT TO LOWER RIGHT FILL
25A8 ▨ SQUARE WITH UPPER RIGHT TO LOWER LEFT FILL
25A9 ▩ SQUARE WITH DIAGONAL CROSSHATCH FILL
25AA ▪ BLACK SMALL SQUARE
25AB ▫ WHITE SMALL SQUARE
25AC ▬ BLACK RECTANGLE
25AD ▭ WHITE RECTANGLE
25AE ▮ BLACK VERTICAL RECTANGLE
= histogram marker
25AF ▯ WHITE VERTICAL RECTANGLE
25B0 ▰ BLACK PARALLELOGRAM
25B1 ▱ WHITE PARALLELOGRAM
25B2 ▲ BLACK UP-POINTING TRIANGLE
25B3 △ WHITE UP-POINTING TRIANGLE
= trine
→ 2206 ∆ increment
25B4 ▴ BLACK UP-POINTING SMALL TRIANGLE
25B5 ▵ WHITE UP-POINTING SMALL TRIANGLE
25B6 ▶ BLACK RIGHT-POINTING TRIANGLE
25B7 ▷ WHITE RIGHT-POINTING TRIANGLE
25B8 ▸ BLACK RIGHT-POINTING SMALL TRIANGLE
→ 2023 ‣ triangular bullet
25B9 ▹ WHITE RIGHT-POINTING SMALL TRIANGLE
25BA ► BLACK RIGHT-POINTING POINTER
25BB ▻ WHITE RIGHT-POINTING POINTER
= forward arrow indicator
25BC ▼ BLACK DOWN-POINTING TRIANGLE
25BD ▽ WHITE DOWN-POINTING TRIANGLE
→ 2207 ∇ nabla
25BE ▾ BLACK DOWN-POINTING SMALL TRIANGLE
25BF ▿ WHITE DOWN-POINTING SMALL TRIANGLE
25C0 ◀ BLACK LEFT-POINTING TRIANGLE
25C1 ◁ WHITE LEFT-POINTING TRIANGLE
25C2 ◂ BLACK LEFT-POINTING SMALL TRIANGLE
25C3 ◃ WHITE LEFT-POINTING SMALL TRIANGLE
25C4 ◄ BLACK LEFT-POINTING POINTER
25C5 ◅ WHITE LEFT-POINTING POINTER
= backward arrow indicator
25C6 ◆ BLACK DIAMOND
→ 2666 ♦ black diamond suit
25C7 ◇ WHITE DIAMOND
→ 22C4 ⋄ diamond operator
→ 2662 ♢ white diamond suit
25C8 ◈ WHITE DIAMOND CONTAINING BLACK SMALL DIAMOND
25C9 ◉ FISHEYE
= tainome (Japanese, a kind of bullet)
25CA ◊ LOZENGE
→ 2662 ♢ white diamond suit
25CB ○ WHITE CIRCLE
→ 20DD ⃝ combining enclosing circle
→ 25EF ◯ large circle
→ 3007 〇 ideographic number zero
25CC ◌ DOTTED CIRCLE
25CD ◍ CIRCLE WITH VERTICAL FILL
25CE ◎ BULLSEYE
→ 229A ⊚ circled ring operator
25CF ● BLACK CIRCLE
25D0 ◐ CIRCLE WITH LEFT HALF BLACK
25D1 ◑ CIRCLE WITH RIGHT HALF BLACK
25D2 ◒ CIRCLE WITH LOWER HALF BLACK
25D3 ◓ CIRCLE WITH UPPER HALF BLACK
25D4 ◔ CIRCLE WITH UPPER RIGHT QUADRANT BLACK
25D5 ◕ CIRCLE WITH ALL BUT UPPER LEFT QUADRANT BLACK
25D6 ◖ LEFT HALF BLACK CIRCLE
25D7 ◗ RIGHT HALF BLACK CIRCLE
25D8 ◘ INVERSE BULLET
→ 2022 • bullet
→ 25E6 ◦ white bullet
25D9 ◙ INVERSE WHITE CIRCLE
25DA ◚ UPPER HALF INVERSE WHITE CIRCLE

25DB ◛ LOWER HALF INVERSE WHITE CIRCLE
25DC ◜ UPPER LEFT QUADRANT CIRCULAR ARC
25DD ◝ UPPER RIGHT QUADRANT CIRCULAR ARC
25DE ◞ LOWER RIGHT QUADRANT CIRCULAR ARC
25DF ◟ LOWER LEFT QUADRANT CIRCULAR ARC
25E0 ◠ UPPER HALF CIRCLE
25E1 ◡ LOWER HALF CIRCLE
25E2 ◢ BLACK LOWER RIGHT TRIANGLE
25E3 ◣ BLACK LOWER LEFT TRIANGLE
25E4 ◤ BLACK UPPER LEFT TRIANGLE
25E5 ◥ BLACK UPPER RIGHT TRIANGLE
25E6 ◦ WHITE BULLET
→ 2022 • bullet
→ 2218 ∘ ring operator
→ 25D8 ◘ inverse bullet
25E7 ◧ SQUARE WITH LEFT HALF BLACK
25E8 ◨ SQUARE WITH RIGHT HALF BLACK
25E9 ◩ SQUARE WITH UPPER LEFT DIAGONAL HALF BLACK
25EA ◪ SQUARE WITH LOWER RIGHT DIAGONAL HALF BLACK
25EB ◫ WHITE SQUARE WITH VERTICAL BISECTING LINE
25EC ◬ WHITE UP-POINTING TRIANGLE WITH DOT
25ED ◭ UP-POINTING TRIANGLE WITH LEFT HALF BLACK
25EE ◮ UP-POINTING TRIANGLE WITH RIGHT HALF BLACK
25EF ◯ LARGE CIRCLE
→ 20DD ⃝ combining enclosing circle
→ 25CB ○ white circle
→ 3007 〇 ideographic number zero

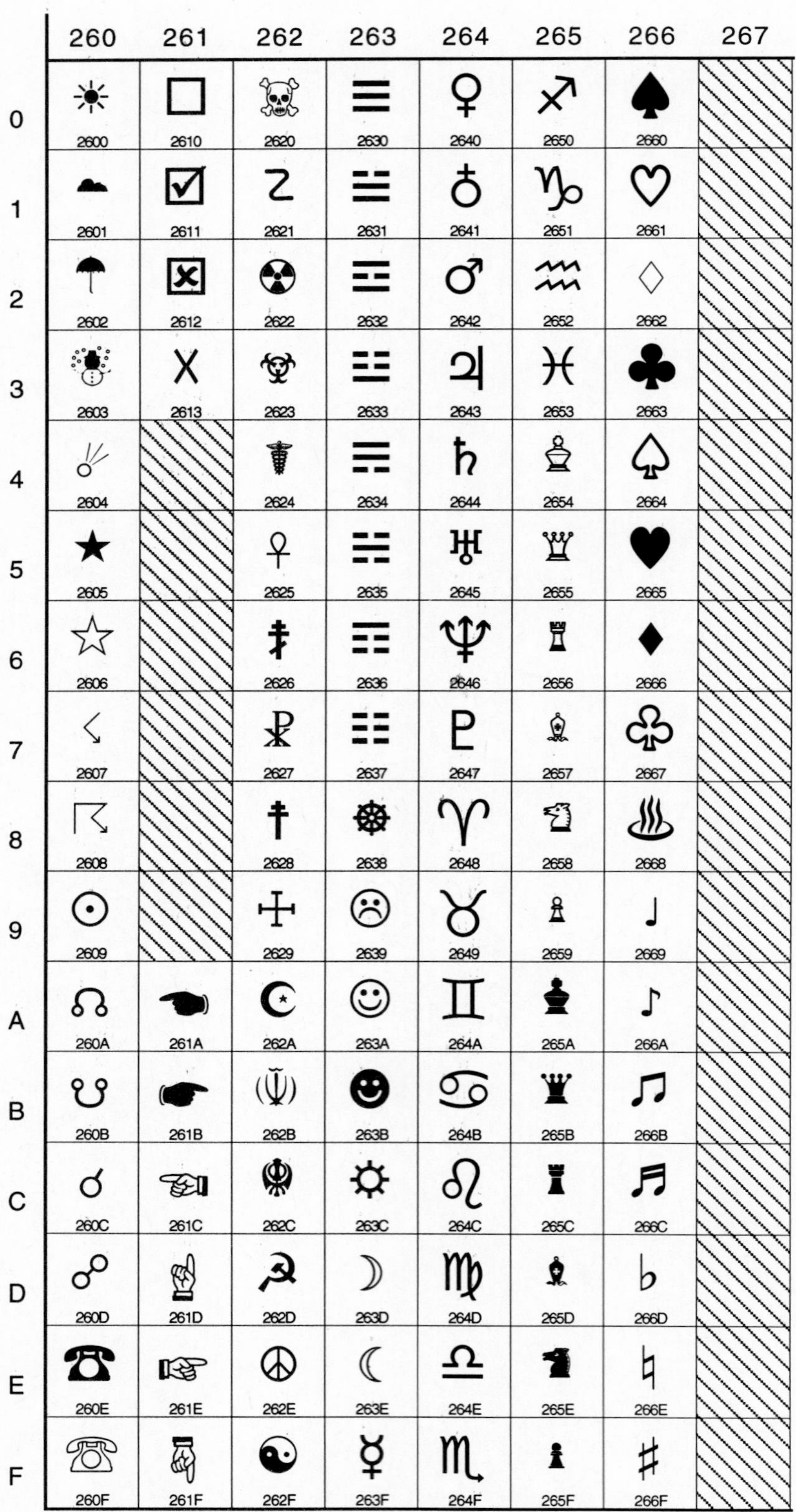

Miscellaneous symbols

2600 ☀ BLACK SUN WITH RAYS
= clear weather
→ 2609 ☉ sun

2601 ☁ CLOUD
= cloudy weather

2602 ☂ UMBRELLA
= rainy weather

2603 ☃ SNOWMAN
= snowy weather

2604 ☄ COMET

2605 ★ BLACK STAR
→ 22C6 ⋆ star operator

2606 ☆ WHITE STAR
→ 2729 ✩ stress outlined white star

2607 ☇ LIGHTNING

2608 ☈ THUNDERSTORM

2609 ☉ SUN
→ 2299 ⊙ circled dot operator
→ 2600 ☀ black sun with rays
→ 263C ☼ white sun with rays

260A ☊ ASCENDING NODE

260B ☋ DESCENDING NODE

260C ☌ CONJUNCTION

260D ☍ OPPOSITION

260E ☎ BLACK TELEPHONE

260F ☏ WHITE TELEPHONE

2610 ☐ BALLOT BOX
→ 25A1 □ white square

2611 ☑ BALLOT BOX WITH CHECK

2612 ☒ BALLOT BOX WITH X
→ 22A0 ⊠ squared times

2613 ☓ SALTIRE
= St. Andrew's Cross
→ 2717 ✗ ballot x

2614 <reserved>

2615 <reserved>

2616 <reserved>

2617 <reserved>

2618 <reserved>

2619 <reserved>

261A ☚ BLACK LEFT POINTING INDEX

261B ☛ BLACK RIGHT POINTING INDEX

261C ☜ WHITE LEFT POINTING INDEX

261D ☝ WHITE UP POINTING INDEX

261E ☞ WHITE RIGHT POINTING INDEX

261F ☟ WHITE DOWN POINTING INDEX

2620 ☠ SKULL AND CROSSBONES
= poison

2621 ☡ CAUTION SIGN

2622 ☢ RADIOACTIVE SIGN

2623 ☣ BIOHAZARD SIGN

2624 ☤ CADUCEUS

2625 ☥ ANKH

2626 ☦ ORTHODOX CROSS

2627 ☧ CHI RHO

2628 ☨ CROSS OF LORRAINE

2629 ☩ CROSS OF JERUSALEM

262A ☪ STAR AND CRESCENT

262B ☫ FARSI SYMBOL
= SYMBOL OF IRAN

262C ☬ ADI SHAKTI

262D ☭ HAMMER AND SICKLE

262E ☮ PEACE SYMBOL

262F ☯ YIN YANG

2630 ☰ TRIGRAM FOR HEAVEN
= qian2

2631 ☱ TRIGRAM FOR LAKE
= dui4

2632 ☲ TRIGRAM FOR FIRE
= li2

2633 ☳ TRIGRAM FOR THUNDER
= zhen4

2634 ☴ TRIGRAM FOR WIND
= xun4

2635 ☵ TRIGRAM FOR WATER
= kan3

2636 ☶ TRIGRAM FOR MOUNTAIN
= gen4

2637 ☷ TRIGRAM FOR EARTH
= kun1

2638 ☸ WHEEL OF DHARMA

2639 ☹ WHITE FROWNING FACE

263A ☺ WHITE SMILING FACE
= have a nice day!

263B ☻ BLACK SMILING FACE

263C ☼ WHITE SUN WITH RAYS
= compass
→ 2609 ☉ sun

263D ☽ FIRST QUARTER MOON

263E ☾ LAST QUARTER MOON

263F ☿ MERCURY

2640 ♀ FEMALE SIGN
= Venus

2641 ♁ EARTH
→ 2295 ⊕ circled plus

2642 ♂ MALE SIGN
= Mars

2643 ♃ JUPITER

2644 ♄ SATURN

2645 ♅ URANUS

2646 ♆ NEPTUNE

2647 ♇ PLUTO

2648 ♈ ARIES
2649 ♉ TAURUS
264A ♊ GEMINI
264B ♋ CANCER
264C ♌ LEO
264D ♍ VIRGO
= minim (alternate glyph)
264E ♎ LIBRA
264F ♏ SCORPIUS
= minim, drop
2650 ♐ SAGITTARIUS
2651 ♑ CAPRICORN
2652 ♒ AQUARIUS
2653 ♓ PISCES
2654 ♔ WHITE CHESS KING
2655 ♕ WHITE CHESS QUEEN
2656 ♖ WHITE CHESS ROOK
2657 ♗ WHITE CHESS BISHOP
2658 ♘ WHITE CHESS KNIGHT
2659 ♙ WHITE CHESS PAWN
265A ♚ BLACK CHESS KING
265B ♛ BLACK CHESS QUEEN
265C ♜ BLACK CHESS ROOK
265D ♝ BLACK CHESS BISHOP
265E ♞ BLACK CHESS KNIGHT
265F ♟ BLACK CHESS PAWN
2660 ♠ BLACK SPADE SUIT
2661 ♡ WHITE HEART SUIT
2662 ♢ WHITE DIAMOND SUIT
→ 25C7 ◇ white diamond
→ 25CA ◊ lozenge
2663 ♣ BLACK CLUB SUIT
= shamrock
2664 ♤ WHITE SPADE SUIT
2665 ♥ BLACK HEART SUIT
= valentine
→ 2764 ❤ heavy black heart
2666 ♦ BLACK DIAMOND SUIT
→ 25C6 ◆ black diamond
2667 ♧ WHITE CLUB SUIT
2668 ♨ HOT SPRINGS
2669 ♩ QUARTER NOTE
266A ♪ EIGHTH NOTE
266B ♫ BEAMED EIGHTH NOTES
266C ♬ BEAMED SIXTEENTH NOTES
266D ♭ MUSIC FLAT SIGN
266E ♮ MUSIC NATURAL SIGN
266F ♯ MUSIC SHARP SIGN

	270	271	272	273	274	275	276	277
0		2710	2720	2730	2740	2750		
1	2701	2711	2721	2731	2741	2751	2761	
2	2702	2712	2722	2732	2742	2752	2762	
3	2703	2713	2723	2733	2743		2763	
4	2704	2714	2724	2734	2744		2764	
5		2715	2725	2735	2745		2765	
6	2706	2716	2726	2736	2746	2756	2766	2776
7	2707	2717	2727	2737	2747		2767	2777
8	2708	2718		2738	2748	2758		2778
9	2709	2719	2729	2739	2749	2759		2779
A		271A	272A	273A	274A	275A		277A
B		271B	272B	273B	274B	275B		277B
C	270C	271C	272C	273C		275C		277C
D	270D	271D	272D	273D	274D	275D		277D
E	270E	271E	272E	273E		275E		277E
F	270F	271F	272F	273F	274F			277F

	278	279	27A	27B
0	➀ 2780	➐ 2790	➠ 27A0	
1	➁ 2781	➑ 2791	➡ 27A1	➱ 27B1
2	➂ 2782	➒ 2792	➢ 27A2	➲ 27B2
3	➃ 2783	➓ 2793	➣ 27A3	➳ 27B3
4	➄ 2784	➔ 2794	➤ 27A4	➴ 27B4
5	➅ 2785		➥ 27A5	➵ 27B5
6	➆ 2786		➦ 27A6	➶ 27B6
7	➇ 2787		➧ 27A7	➷ 27B7
8	➈ 2788	➘ 2798	➨ 27A8	➸ 27B8
9	➉ 2789	➙ 2799	➩ 27A9	➹ 27B9
A	➊ 278A	➚ 279A	➪ 27AA	➺ 27BA
B	➋ 278B	➛ 279B	➫ 27AB	➻ 27BB
C	➌ 278C	➜ 279C	➬ 27AC	➼ 27BC
D	➍ 278D	➝ 279D	➭ 27AD	➽ 27BD
E	➎ 278E	➞ 279E	➮ 27AE	➾ 27BE
F	➏ 278F	➟ 279F	➯ 27AF	

Zapf dingbats

Code	Glyph	Name
2700		<reserved>
2701	✁	UPPER BLADE SCISSORS
2702	✂	BLACK SCISSORS
2703	✃	LOWER BLADE SCISSORS
2704	✄	WHITE SCISSORS
2705		<reserved> → 260E ☎ black telephone
2706	✆	TELEPHONE LOCATION SIGN
2707	✇	TAPE DRIVE
2708	✈	AIRPLANE
2709	✉	ENVELOPE
270A		<reserved> → 261B ☛ black right pointing index
270B		<reserved> → 261E ☞ white right pointing index
270C	✌	VICTORY HAND
270D	✍	WRITING HAND
270E	✎	LOWER RIGHT PENCIL
270F	✏	PENCIL
2710	✐	UPPER RIGHT PENCIL
2711	✑	WHITE NIB
2712	✒	BLACK NIB
2713	✓	CHECK MARK → 221A √ square root
2714	✔	HEAVY CHECK MARK
2715	✕	MULTIPLICATION X
2716	✖	HEAVY MULTIPLICATION X
2717	✗	BALLOT X → 2613 ☓ saltire
2718	✘	HEAVY BALLOT X
2719	✙	OUTLINED GREEK CROSS
271A	✚	HEAVY GREEK CROSS
271B	✛	OPEN CENTRE CROSS
271C	✜	HEAVY OPEN CENTRE CROSS
271D	✝	LATIN CROSS
271E	✞	SHADOWED WHITE LATIN CROSS
271F	✟	OUTLINED LATIN CROSS
2720	✠	MALTESE CROSS
2721	✡	STAR OF DAVID
2722	✢	FOUR TEARDROP-SPOKED ASTERISK
2723	✣	FOUR BALLOON-SPOKED ASTERISK
2724	✤	HEAVY FOUR BALLOON-SPOKED ASTERISK
2725	✥	FOUR CLUB-SPOKED ASTERISK
2726	✦	BLACK FOUR POINTED STAR
2727	✧	WHITE FOUR POINTED STAR
2728		<reserved> → 2605 ★ black star
2729	✩	STRESS OUTLINED WHITE STAR → 2606 ☆ white star
272A	✪	CIRCLED WHITE STAR
272B	✫	OPEN CENTRE BLACK STAR
272C	✬	BLACK CENTRE WHITE STAR
272D	✭	OUTLINED BLACK STAR
272E	✮	HEAVY OUTLINED BLACK STAR
272F	✯	PINWHEEL STAR
2730	✰	SHADOWED WHITE STAR
2731	✱	HEAVY ASTERISK → 002A * asterisk
2732	✲	OPEN CENTRE ASTERISK
2733	✳	EIGHT SPOKED ASTERISK
2734	✴	EIGHT POINTED BLACK STAR
2735	✵	EIGHT POINTED PINWHEEL STAR
2736	✶	SIX POINTED BLACK STAR = sextile
2737	✷	EIGHT POINTED RECTILINEAR BLACK STAR
2738	✸	HEAVY EIGHT POINTED RECTILINEAR BLACK STAR
2739	✹	TWELVE POINTED BLACK STAR
273A	✺	SIXTEEN POINTED ASTERISK = starburst
273B	✻	TEARDROP-SPOKED ASTERISK
273C	✼	OPEN CENTRE TEARDROP-SPOKED ASTERISK
273D	✽	HEAVY TEARDROP-SPOKED ASTERISK
273E	✾	SIX PETALLED BLACK AND WHITE FLORETTE
273F	✿	BLACK FLORETTE
2740	❀	WHITE FLORETTE
2741	❁	EIGHT PETALLED OUTLINED BLACK FLORETTE
2742	❂	CIRCLED OPEN CENTRE EIGHT POINTED STAR
2743	❃	HEAVY TEARDROP-SPOKED PINWHEEL ASTERISK
2744	❄	SNOWFLAKE
2745	❅	TIGHT TRIFOLIATE SNOWFLAKE
2746	❆	HEAVY CHEVRON SNOWFLAKE
2747	❇	SPARKLE
2748	❈	HEAVY SPARKLE
2749	❉	BALLOON-SPOKED ASTERISK = jack
274A	❊	EIGHT TEARDROP-SPOKED PROPELLER ASTERISK
274B	❋	HEAVY EIGHT TEARDROP-SPOKED PROPELLER ASTERISK = turbofan

274C <reserved>
→ 25CF ● black circle

274D ❍ SHADOWED WHITE CIRCLE

274E <reserved>
→ 25A0 ■ black square

274F ❏ LOWER RIGHT DROP-SHADOWED WHITE SQUARE

2750 ❐ UPPER RIGHT DROP-SHADOWED WHITE SQUARE

2751 ❑ LOWER RIGHT SHADOWED WHITE SQUARE

2752 ❒ UPPER RIGHT SHADOWED WHITE SQUARE

2753 <reserved>
→ 25B2 ▲ black up-pointing triangle

2754 <reserved>
→ 25BC ▼ black down-pointing triangle

2755 <reserved>
→ 25C6 ◆ black diamond

2756 ❖ BLACK DIAMOND MINUS WHITE X

2757 <reserved>
→ 25D7 ◗ right half black circle

2758 ❘ LIGHT VERTICAL BAR
→ 007C | vertical line

2759 ❙ MEDIUM VERTICAL BAR

275A ❚ HEAVY VERTICAL BAR

275B ❛ HEAVY SINGLE TURNED COMMA QUOTATION MARK ORNAMENT
→ 2018 ‘ left single quotation mark

275C ❜ HEAVY SINGLE COMMA QUOTATION MARK ORNAMENT
→ 2019 ’ right single quotation mark

275D ❝ HEAVY DOUBLE TURNED COMMA QUOTATION MARK ORNAMENT
→ 201C “ left double quotation mark

275E ❞ HEAVY DOUBLE COMMA QUOTATION MARK ORNAMENT
→ 201D ” right double quotation mark

275F <reserved>

2760 <reserved>

2761 ❡ CURVED STEM PARAGRAPH SIGN ORNAMENT
→ 00B6 ¶ pilcrow sign

2762 ❢ HEAVY EXCLAMATION MARK ORNAMENT
→ 0021 ! exclamation mark

2763 ❣ HEAVY HEART EXCLAMATION MARK ORNAMENT

2764 ❤ HEAVY BLACK HEART
→ 2665 ♥ black heart suit

2765 ❥ ROTATED HEAVY BLACK HEART BULLET

2766 ❦ FLORAL HEART

2767 ❧ ROTATED FLORAL HEART BULLET

2768 <reserved>
→ 2663 ♣ black club suit

2769 <reserved>
→ 2666 ♦ black diamond suit

276A <reserved>
→ 2665 ♥ black heart suit

276B <reserved>
→ 2660 ♠ black spade suit

276C <reserved>
→ 2460 ① circled digit one

276D <reserved>
→ 2461 ② circled digit two

276E <reserved>
→ 2462 ③ circled digit three

276F <reserved>
→ 2463 ④ circled digit four

2770 <reserved>
→ 2464 ⑤ circled digit five

2771 <reserved>
→ 2465 ⑥ circled digit six

2772 <reserved>
→ 2466 ⑦ circled digit seven

2773 <reserved>
→ 2467 ⑧ circled digit eight

2774 <reserved>
→ 2468 ⑨ circled digit nine

2775 <reserved>
→ 2469 ⑩ circled number ten

2776 ❶ DINGBAT NEGATIVE CIRCLED DIGIT ONE

2777 ❷ DINGBAT NEGATIVE CIRCLED DIGIT TWO

2778 ❸ DINGBAT NEGATIVE CIRCLED DIGIT THREE

2779 ❹ DINGBAT NEGATIVE CIRCLED DIGIT FOUR

277A ❺ DINGBAT NEGATIVE CIRCLED DIGIT FIVE

277B ❻ DINGBAT NEGATIVE CIRCLED DIGIT SIX

277C ❼ DINGBAT NEGATIVE CIRCLED DIGIT SEVEN

277D ❽ DINGBAT NEGATIVE CIRCLED DIGIT EIGHT

277E ❾ DINGBAT NEGATIVE CIRCLED DIGIT NINE

277F ❿ DINGBAT NEGATIVE CIRCLED NUMBER TEN

2780 ➀ DINGBAT CIRCLED SANS-SERIF DIGIT ONE

2781 ➁ DINGBAT CIRCLED SANS-SERIF DIGIT TWO

2782 ③ DINGBAT CIRCLED SANS-SERIF DIGIT THREE
2783 ④ DINGBAT CIRCLED SANS-SERIF DIGIT FOUR
2784 ⑤ DINGBAT CIRCLED SANS-SERIF DIGIT FIVE
2785 ⑥ DINGBAT CIRCLED SANS-SERIF DIGIT SIX
2786 ⑦ DINGBAT CIRCLED SANS-SERIF DIGIT SEVEN
2787 ⑧ DINGBAT CIRCLED SANS-SERIF DIGIT EIGHT
2788 ⑨ DINGBAT CIRCLED SANS-SERIF DIGIT NINE
2789 ⑩ DINGBAT CIRCLED SANS-SERIF NUMBER TEN
278A ➊ DINGBAT NEGATIVE CIRCLED SANS-SERIF DIGIT ONE
278B ➋ DINGBAT NEGATIVE CIRCLED SANS-SERIF DIGIT TWO
278C ➌ DINGBAT NEGATIVE CIRCLED SANS-SERIF DIGIT THREE
278D ➍ DINGBAT NEGATIVE CIRCLED SANS-SERIF DIGIT FOUR
278E ➎ DINGBAT NEGATIVE CIRCLED SANS-SERIF DIGIT FIVE
278F ➏ DINGBAT NEGATIVE CIRCLED SANS-SERIF DIGIT SIX
2790 ➐ DINGBAT NEGATIVE CIRCLED SANS-SERIF DIGIT SEVEN
2791 ➑ DINGBAT NEGATIVE CIRCLED SANS-SERIF DIGIT EIGHT
2792 ➒ DINGBAT NEGATIVE CIRCLED SANS-SERIF DIGIT NINE
2793 ➓ DINGBAT NEGATIVE CIRCLED SANS-SERIF NUMBER TEN
2794 ➔ HEAVY WIDE-HEADED RIGHTWARDS ARROW
2795 <reserved>
→ 2192 → rightwards arrow
2796 <reserved>
→ 2194 ↔ left right arrow
2797 <reserved>
→ 2195 ↕ up down arrow
2798 ➘ HEAVY SOUTH EAST ARROW
2799 ➙ HEAVY RIGHTWARDS ARROW
279A ➚ HEAVY NORTH EAST ARROW
279B ➛ DRAFTING POINT RIGHTWARDS ARROW
279C ➜ HEAVY ROUND-TIPPED RIGHTWARDS ARROW
279D ➝ TRIANGLE-HEADED RIGHTWARDS ARROW
279E ➞ HEAVY TRIANGLE-HEADED RIGHTWARDS ARROW
279F ➟ DASHED TRIANGLE-HEADED RIGHTWARDS ARROW
27A0 ➠ HEAVY DASHED TRIANGLE-HEADED RIGHTWARDS ARROW
27A1 ➡ BLACK RIGHTWARDS ARROW
27A2 ➢ THREE-D TOP-LIGHTED RIGHTWARDS ARROWHEAD
27A3 ➣ THREE-D BOTTOM-LIGHTED RIGHTWARDS ARROWHEAD
27A4 ➤ BLACK RIGHTWARDS ARROWHEAD
27A5 ➥ HEAVY BLACK CURVED DOWNWARDS AND RIGHTWARDS ARROW
27A6 ➦ HEAVY BLACK CURVED UPWARDS AND RIGHTWARDS ARROW
27A7 ➧ SQUAT BLACK RIGHTWARDS ARROW
27A8 ➨ HEAVY CONCAVE-POINTED BLACK RIGHTWARDS ARROW
27A9 ➩ RIGHT-SHADED WHITE RIGHTWARDS ARROW
27AA ➪ LEFT-SHADED WHITE RIGHTWARDS ARROW
27AB ➫ BACK-TILTED SHADOWED WHITE RIGHTWARDS ARROW
27AC ➬ FRONT-TILTED SHADOWED WHITE RIGHTWARDS ARROW
27AD ➭ HEAVY LOWER RIGHT-SHADOWED WHITE RIGHTWARDS ARROW
27AE ➮ HEAVY UPPER RIGHT-SHADOWED WHITE RIGHTWARDS ARROW
27AF ➯ NOTCHED LOWER RIGHT-SHADOWED WHITE RIGHTWARDS ARROW
27B0 <reserved>
27B1 ➱ NOTCHED UPPER RIGHT-SHADOWED WHITE RIGHTWARDS ARROW
27B2 ➲ CIRCLED HEAVY WHITE RIGHTWARDS ARROW
27B3 ➳ WHITE-FEATHERED RIGHTWARDS ARROW
27B4 ➴ BLACK-FEATHERED SOUTH EAST ARROW
27B5 ➵ BLACK-FEATHERED RIGHTWARDS ARROW
27B6 ➶ BLACK-FEATHERED NORTH EAST ARROW
27B7 ➷ HEAVY BLACK-FEATHERED SOUTH EAST ARROW

27B8 ➸ HEAVY BLACK-FEATHERED RIGHTWARDS ARROW
27B9 ➹ HEAVY BLACK-FEATHERED NORTH EAST ARROW
27BA ➺ TEARDROP-BARBED RIGHTWARDS ARROW
27BB ➻ HEAVY TEARDROP-SHANKED RIGHTWARDS ARROW
27BC ➼ WEDGE-TAILED RIGHTWARDS ARROW
27BD ➽ HEAVY WEDGE-TAILED RIGHTWARDS ARROW
27BE ➾ OPEN-OUTLINED RIGHTWARDS ARROW

	300	301	302	303
0	ID SP 3000	【 3010	〠 3020	〰 3030
1	、 3001	】 3011	〡 3021	〱 3031
2	。 3002	〒 3012	〢 3022	〲 3032
3	〃 3003	〓 3013	〣 3023	〳 3033
4	〄 3004	〔 3014	〤 3024	〴 3034
5	々 3005	〕 3015	〥 3025	〵 3035
6	〆 3006	〖 3016	〦 3026	〶 3036
7	〇 3007	〗 3017	〧 3027	〷 3037
8	〈 3008	〘 3018	〨 3028	
9	〉 3009	〙 3019	〩 3029	
A	《 300A	〚 301A	◌〪 302A	
B	》 300B	〛 301B	◌〫 302B	
C	「 300C	〜 301C	◌〬 302C	
D	」 300D	〝 301D	◌〭 302D	
E	『 300E	〞 301E	◌〮 302E	
F	』 300F	〟 301F	◌〯 302F	〿 303F

CJK symbols and punctuation

3000 ⟦ID SP⟧ IDEOGRAPHIC SPACE
→ 0020 ⟦SP⟧ space
≈ <wide> + 0020 ⟦SP⟧

3001 、 IDEOGRAPHIC COMMA
→ 002C , comma

3002 。 IDEOGRAPHIC FULL STOP
→ 002E . full stop

3003 〃 DITTO MARK
→ 2033 ″ double prime

3004 〄 JAPANESE INDUSTRIAL STANDARD SYMBOL

3005 々 IDEOGRAPHIC ITERATION MARK

3006 〆 IDEOGRAPHIC CLOSING MARK

3007 〇 IDEOGRAPHIC NUMBER ZERO
→ 20DD ⃝ combining enclosing circle
→ 25CB ○ white circle
→ 25EF ◯ large circle

3008 〈 LEFT ANGLE BRACKET
→ 003C < less-than sign
→ 2039 ‹ single left-pointing angle quotation mark
→ 2329 〈 left-pointing angle bracket

3009 〉 RIGHT ANGLE BRACKET
→ 003E > greater-than sign
→ 203A › single right-pointing angle quotation mark
→ 232A 〉 right-pointing angle bracket

300A 《 LEFT DOUBLE ANGLE BRACKET
→ 00AB « left-pointing double angle quotation mark

300B 》 RIGHT DOUBLE ANGLE BRACKET
→ 00BB » right-pointing double angle quotation mark

300C 「 LEFT CORNER BRACKET

300D 」 RIGHT CORNER BRACKET
• used as quotation marks

300E 『 LEFT WHITE CORNER BRACKET

300F 』 RIGHT WHITE CORNER BRACKET
• used as quotation marks

3010 【 LEFT BLACK LENTICULAR BRACKET

3011 】 RIGHT BLACK LENTICULAR BRACKET

3012 〒 POSTAL MARK

3013 〓 GETA MARK
• substitute for ideograph not in font

3014 〔 LEFT TORTOISE SHELL BRACKET

3015 〕 RIGHT TORTOISE SHELL BRACKET

3016 〖 LEFT WHITE LENTICULAR BRACKET

3017 〗 RIGHT WHITE LENTICULAR BRACKET

3018 〘 LEFT WHITE TORTOISE SHELL BRACKET

3019 〙 RIGHT WHITE TORTOISE SHELL BRACKET

301A 〚 LEFT WHITE SQUARE BRACKET

301B 〛 RIGHT WHITE SQUARE BRACKET

301C 〜 WAVE DASH
• JIS punctuation
→ 3030 〰 wavy dash

301D 〝 REVERSED DOUBLE PRIME QUOTATION MARK
→ 201C “ left double quotation mark
→ 2036 ‶ reversed double prime

301E 〞 DOUBLE PRIME QUOTATION MARK
→ 201D ” right double quotation mark
→ 2033 ″ double prime

301F 〟 LOW DOUBLE PRIME QUOTATION MARK
→ 201E „ double low-9 quotation mark

3020 〠 POSTAL MARK FACE

Hangzhou-style numerals

3021 〡 HANGZHOU NUMERAL ONE

3022 〢 HANGZHOU NUMERAL TWO

3023 〣 HANGZHOU NUMERAL THREE

3024 〤 HANGZHOU NUMERAL FOUR

3025 〥 HANGZHOU NUMERAL FIVE

3026 〦 HANGZHOU NUMERAL SIX

3027 〧 HANGZHOU NUMERAL SEVEN

3028 〨 HANGZHOU NUMERAL EIGHT

3029 〩 HANGZHOU NUMERAL NINE

Diacritics

302A 〪 IDEOGRAPHIC LEVEL TONE MARK

302B 〫 IDEOGRAPHIC RISING TONE MARK

302C 〬 IDEOGRAPHIC DEPARTING TONE MARK

302D 〭 IDEOGRAPHIC ENTERING TONE MARK

302E 〮 HANGUL SINGLE DOT TONE MARK

302F 〯 HANGUL DOUBLE DOT TONE MARK

Other CJK symbols

3030 〰 WAVY DASH
→ 2307 ⌇ wavy line
→ 301C 〜 wave dash

3031 〱 VERTICAL KANA REPEAT MARK

3032 〲 VERTICAL KANA REPEAT WITH VOICED SOUND MARK
• the preceding two semantic characters are preferred to the following three glyphic forms

3033 〳 VERTICAL KANA REPEAT MARK UPPER HALF

3034 〴 VERTICAL KANA REPEAT WITH VOICED SOUND MARK UPPER HALF
• the preceding two are glyphs used in conjunction with the following glyph

3035 〵 VERTICAL KANA REPEAT MARK LOWER HALF

3036 〶 CIRCLED POSTAL MARK
≈ 3012 〒

3037 〷 IDEOGRAPHIC TELEGRAPH LINE FEED SEPARATOR SYMBOL

3038 <reserved>

3039 <reserved>

303A <reserved>

303B <reserved>

303C <reserved>

303D <reserved>

303E <reserved>

303F 〿 IDEOGRAPHIC HALF FILL SPACE

	304	305	306	307	308	309
0		ぐ 3050	だ 3060	ば 3070	む 3080	ゐ 3090
1	ぁ 3041	け 3051	ち 3061	ぱ 3071	め 3081	ゑ 3091
2	あ 3042	げ 3052	ぢ 3062	ひ 3072	も 3082	を 3092
3	ぃ 3043	こ 3053	っ 3063	び 3073	ゃ 3083	ん 3093
4	い 3044	ご 3054	つ 3064	ぴ 3074	や 3084	ゔ 3094
5	ぅ 3045	さ 3055	づ 3065	ふ 3075	ゅ 3085	
6	う 3046	ざ 3056	て 3066	ぶ 3076	ゆ 3086	
7	ぇ 3047	し 3057	で 3067	ぷ 3077	ょ 3087	
8	え 3048	じ 3058	と 3068	へ 3078	よ 3088	
9	ぉ 3049	す 3059	ど 3069	べ 3079	ら 3089	◌゙ 3099
A	お 304A	ず 305A	な 306A	ぺ 307A	り 308A	◌゚ 309A
B	か 304B	せ 305B	に 306B	ほ 307B	る 308B	゛ 309B
C	が 304C	ぜ 305C	ぬ 306C	ぼ 307C	れ 308C	゜ 309C
D	き 304D	そ 305D	ね 306D	ぽ 307D	ろ 308D	ゝ 309D
E	ぎ 304E	ぞ 305E	の 306E	ま 307E	ゎ 308E	ゞ 309E
F	く 304F	た 305F	は 306F	み 307F	わ 308F	

Based on JIS X 0208 Ì

3040 ⊘ <reserved>

3041 ぁ HIRAGANA LETTER SMALL A

3042 あ HIRAGANA LETTER A

3043 ぃ HIRAGANA LETTER SMALL I

3044 い HIRAGANA LETTER I

3045 ぅ HIRAGANA LETTER SMALL U

3046 う HIRAGANA LETTER U

3047 ぇ HIRAGANA LETTER SMALL E

3048 え HIRAGANA LETTER E

3049 ぉ HIRAGANA LETTER SMALL O

304A お HIRAGANA LETTER O

304B か HIRAGANA LETTER KA

304C が HIRAGANA LETTER GA
≡ 304B か + 3099 ♂

304D き HIRAGANA LETTER KI

304E ぎ HIRAGANA LETTER GI
≡ 304D き + 3099 ♂

304F く HIRAGANA LETTER KU

3050 ぐ HIRAGANA LETTER GU
≡ 304F く + 3099 ♂

3051 け HIRAGANA LETTER KE

3052 げ HIRAGANA LETTER GE
≡ 3051 け + 3099 ♂

3053 こ HIRAGANA LETTER KO

3054 ご HIRAGANA LETTER GO
≡ 3053 こ + 3099 ♂

3055 さ HIRAGANA LETTER SA

3056 ざ HIRAGANA LETTER ZA
≡ 3055 さ + 3099 ♂

3057 し HIRAGANA LETTER SI
= SHI

3058 じ HIRAGANA LETTER ZI
= JI (not unique)
≡ 3057 し + 3099 ♂

3059 す HIRAGANA LETTER SU

305A ず HIRAGANA LETTER ZU
≡ 3059 す + 3099 ♂

305B せ HIRAGANA LETTER SE

305C ぜ HIRAGANA LETTER ZE
≡ 305B せ + 3099 ♂

305D そ HIRAGANA LETTER SO

305E ぞ HIRAGANA LETTER ZO
≡ 305D そ + 3099 ♂

305F た HIRAGANA LETTER TA

3060 だ HIRAGANA LETTER DA
≡ 305F た + 3099 ♂

3061 ち HIRAGANA LETTER TI
= CHI

3062 ぢ HIRAGANA LETTER DI
= JI (not unique)
≡ 3061 ち + 3099 ♂

3063 っ HIRAGANA LETTER SMALL TU
= SMALL TSU

3064 つ HIRAGANA LETTER TU
= TSU

3065 づ HIRAGANA LETTER DU
= ZU (not unique)
≡ 3064 つ + 3099 ♂

3066 て HIRAGANA LETTER TE

3067 で HIRAGANA LETTER DE
≡ 3066 て + 3099 ♂

3068 と HIRAGANA LETTER TO

3069 ど HIRAGANA LETTER DO
≡ 3068 と + 3099 ♂

306A な HIRAGANA LETTER NA

306B に HIRAGANA LETTER NI

306C ぬ HIRAGANA LETTER NU

306D ね HIRAGANA LETTER NE

306E の HIRAGANA LETTER NO

306F は HIRAGANA LETTER HA

3070 ば HIRAGANA LETTER BA
≡ 306F は + 3099 ♂

3071 ぱ HIRAGANA LETTER PA
≡ 306F は + 309A ♂

3072 ひ HIRAGANA LETTER HI

3073 び HIRAGANA LETTER BI
≡ 3072 ひ + 3099 ♂

3074 ぴ HIRAGANA LETTER PI
≡ 3072 ひ + 309A ♂

3075 ふ HIRAGANA LETTER HU
= FU

3076 ぶ HIRAGANA LETTER BU
≡ 3075 ふ + 3099 ♂

3077 ぷ HIRAGANA LETTER PU
≡ 3075 ふ + 309A ♂

3078 へ HIRAGANA LETTER HE

3079 べ HIRAGANA LETTER BE
≡ 3078 へ + 3099 ♂

307A ぺ HIRAGANA LETTER PE
≡ 3078 へ + 309A ♂

307B ほ HIRAGANA LETTER HO

307C ぼ HIRAGANA LETTER BO
≡ 307B ほ + 3099 ♂

307D ぽ HIRAGANA LETTER PO
≡ 307B ほ + 309A ♂

307E ま HIRAGANA LETTER MA

307F み HIRAGANA LETTER MI

3080 む HIRAGANA LETTER MU

3081 め HIRAGANA LETTER ME

3082 も HIRAGANA LETTER MO

3083 ゃ HIRAGANA LETTER SMALL YA
3084 や HIRAGANA LETTER YA
3085 ゅ HIRAGANA LETTER SMALL YU
3086 ゆ HIRAGANA LETTER YU
3087 ょ HIRAGANA LETTER SMALL YO
3088 よ HIRAGANA LETTER YO
3089 ら HIRAGANA LETTER RA
308A り HIRAGANA LETTER RI
308B る HIRAGANA LETTER RU
308C れ HIRAGANA LETTER RE
308D ろ HIRAGANA LETTER RO
308E ゎ HIRAGANA LETTER SMALL WA
308F わ HIRAGANA LETTER WA
3090 ゐ HIRAGANA LETTER WI
3091 ゑ HIRAGANA LETTER WE
3092 を HIRAGANA LETTER WO
3093 ん HIRAGANA LETTER N
3094 ゔ HIRAGANA LETTER VU
≡ 3046 う + 3099 ◌゙
3095 <reserved>
3096 <reserved>
3097 <reserved>
3098 <reserved>
3099 ◌゙ COMBINING KATAKANA-HIRAGANA VOICED SOUND MARK
309A ◌゚ COMBINING KATAKANA-HIRAGANA SEMI-VOICED SOUND MARK
309B ゛ KATAKANA-HIRAGANA VOICED SOUND MARK
≈ 0020 SP + 3099 ◌゙
309C ゜ KATAKANA-HIRAGANA SEMI-VOICED SOUND MARK
≈ 0020 SP + 309A ◌゚
309D ゝ HIRAGANA ITERATION MARK
309E ゞ HIRAGANA VOICED ITERATION MARK
≡ 309D ゝ + 3099 ◌゙

	30A	30B	30C	30D	30E	30F
0		グ 30B0	ダ 30C0	バ 30D0	ム 30E0	ヰ 30F0
1	ァ 30A1	ケ 30B1	チ 30C1	パ 30D1	メ 30E1	ヱ 30F1
2	ア 30A2	ゲ 30B2	ヂ 30C2	ヒ 30D2	モ 30E2	ヲ 30F2
3	ィ 30A3	コ 30B3	ッ 30C3	ビ 30D3	ャ 30E3	ン 30F3
4	イ 30A4	ゴ 30B4	ツ 30C4	ピ 30D4	ヤ 30E4	ヴ 30F4
5	ゥ 30A5	サ 30B5	ヅ 30C5	フ 30D5	ュ 30E5	ヵ 30F5
6	ウ 30A6	ザ 30B6	テ 30C6	ブ 30D6	ユ 30E6	ヶ 30F6
7	ェ 30A7	シ 30B7	デ 30C7	プ 30D7	ョ 30E7	ヷ 30F7
8	エ 30A8	ジ 30B8	ト 30C8	ヘ 30D8	ヨ 30E8	ヸ 30F8
9	ォ 30A9	ス 30B9	ド 30C9	ベ 30D9	ラ 30E9	ヹ 30F9
A	オ 30AA	ズ 30BA	ナ 30CA	ペ 30DA	リ 30EA	ヺ 30FA
B	カ 30AB	セ 30BB	ニ 30CB	ホ 30DB	ル 30EB	・ 30FB
C	ガ 30AC	ゼ 30BC	ヌ 30CC	ボ 30DC	レ 30EC	ー 30FC
D	キ 30AD	ソ 30BD	ネ 30CD	ポ 30DD	ロ 30ED	ヽ 30FD
E	ギ 30AE	ゾ 30BE	ノ 30CE	マ 30DE	ヮ 30EE	ヾ 30FE
F	ク 30AF	タ 30BF	ハ 30CF	ミ 30DF	ワ 30EF	

Based on JIS X 0208

30A0 ▧ <reserved>
30A1 ァ KATAKANA LETTER SMALL A
30A2 ア KATAKANA LETTER A
30A3 ィ KATAKANA LETTER SMALL I
30A4 イ KATAKANA LETTER I
30A5 ゥ KATAKANA LETTER SMALL U
30A6 ウ KATAKANA LETTER U
30A7 ェ KATAKANA LETTER SMALL E
30A8 エ KATAKANA LETTER E
30A9 ォ KATAKANA LETTER SMALL O
30AA オ KATAKANA LETTER O
30AB カ KATAKANA LETTER KA
30AC ガ KATAKANA LETTER GA
≡ 30AB カ + 3099 ♂
30AD キ KATAKANA LETTER KI
30AE ギ KATAKANA LETTER GI
≡ 30AD キ + 3099 ♂
30AF ク KATAKANA LETTER KU
30B0 グ KATAKANA LETTER GU
≡ 30AF ク + 3099 ♂
30B1 ケ KATAKANA LETTER KE
30B2 ゲ KATAKANA LETTER GE
≡ 30B1 ケ + 3099 ♂
30B3 コ KATAKANA LETTER KO
30B4 ゴ KATAKANA LETTER GO
≡ 30B3 コ + 3099 ♂
30B5 サ KATAKANA LETTER SA
30B6 ザ KATAKANA LETTER ZA
≡ 30B5 サ + 3099 ♂
30B7 シ KATAKANA LETTER SI
= SHI
30B8 ジ KATAKANA LETTER ZI
= JI (not unique)
≡ 30B7 シ + 3099 ♂
30B9 ス KATAKANA LETTER SU
30BA ズ KATAKANA LETTER ZU
≡ 30B9 ス + 3099 ♂
30BB セ KATAKANA LETTER SE
30BC ゼ KATAKANA LETTER ZE
≡ 30BB セ + 3099 ♂
30BD ソ KATAKANA LETTER SO
30BE ゾ KATAKANA LETTER ZO
≡ 30BD ソ + 3099 ♂
30BF タ KATAKANA LETTER TA
30C0 ダ KATAKANA LETTER DA
≡ 30BF タ + 3099 ♂
30C1 チ KATAKANA LETTER TI
= CHI
30C2 ヂ KATAKANA LETTER DI
= JI (not unique)
≡ 30C1 チ + 3099 ♂
30C3 ッ KATAKANA LETTER SMALL TU
= SMALL TSU
30C4 ツ KATAKANA LETTER TU
= TSU
30C5 ヅ KATAKANA LETTER DU
= ZU (not unique)
≡ 30C4 ツ + 3099 ♂
30C6 テ KATAKANA LETTER TE
30C7 デ KATAKANA LETTER DE
≡ 30C6 テ + 3099 ♂
30C8 ト KATAKANA LETTER TO
30C9 ド KATAKANA LETTER DO
≡ 30C8 ト + 3099 ♂
30CA ナ KATAKANA LETTER NA
30CB ニ KATAKANA LETTER NI
30CC ヌ KATAKANA LETTER NU
30CD ネ KATAKANA LETTER NE
30CE ノ KATAKANA LETTER NO
30CF ハ KATAKANA LETTER HA
30D0 バ KATAKANA LETTER BA
≡ 30CF ハ + 3099 ♂
30D1 パ KATAKANA LETTER PA
≡ 30CF ハ + 309A ♂
30D2 ヒ KATAKANA LETTER HI
30D3 ビ KATAKANA LETTER BI
≡ 30D2 ヒ + 3099 ♂
30D4 ピ KATAKANA LETTER PI
≡ 30D2 ヒ + 309A ♂
30D5 フ KATAKANA LETTER HU
= FU
30D6 ブ KATAKANA LETTER BU
≡ 30D5 フ + 3099 ♂
30D7 プ KATAKANA LETTER PU
≡ 30D5 フ + 309A ♂
30D8 ヘ KATAKANA LETTER HE
30D9 ベ KATAKANA LETTER BE
≡ 30D8 ヘ + 3099 ♂
30DA ペ KATAKANA LETTER PE
≡ 30D8 ヘ + 309A ♂
30DB ホ KATAKANA LETTER HO
30DC ボ KATAKANA LETTER BO
≡ 30DB ホ + 3099 ♂
30DD ポ KATAKANA LETTER PO
≡ 30DB ホ + 309A ♂
30DE マ KATAKANA LETTER MA
30DF ミ KATAKANA LETTER MI
30E0 ム KATAKANA LETTER MU
30E1 メ KATAKANA LETTER ME
30E2 モ KATAKANA LETTER MO
30E3 ャ KATAKANA LETTER SMALL YA
30E4 ヤ KATAKANA LETTER YA
30E5 ュ KATAKANA LETTER SMALL YU

30E6 ユ KATAKANA LETTER YU
30E7 ョ KATAKANA LETTER SMALL YO
30E8 ヨ KATAKANA LETTER YO
30E9 ラ KATAKANA LETTER RA
30EA リ KATAKANA LETTER RI
30EB ル KATAKANA LETTER RU
30EC レ KATAKANA LETTER RE
30ED ロ KATAKANA LETTER RO
30EE ヮ KATAKANA LETTER SMALL WA
30EF ワ KATAKANA LETTER WA
30F0 ヰ KATAKANA LETTER WI
30F1 ヱ KATAKANA LETTER WE
30F2 ヲ KATAKANA LETTER WO
30F3 ン KATAKANA LETTER N
30F4 ヴ KATAKANA LETTER VU
≡ 30A6 ウ + 3099 ゙
30F5 ヵ KATAKANA LETTER SMALL KA
30F6 ヶ KATAKANA LETTER SMALL KE
30F7 ヷ KATAKANA LETTER VA
≡ 30EF ワ + 3099 ゙
30F8 ヸ KATAKANA LETTER VI
≡ 30F0 ヰ + 3099 ゙
30F9 ヹ KATAKANA LETTER VE
≡ 30F1 ヱ + 3099 ゙
30FA ヺ KATAKANA LETTER VO
≡ 30F2 ヲ + 3099 ゙
30FB ・ KATAKANA MIDDLE DOT
→ 00B7 · middle dot
30FC ー KATAKANA-HIRAGANA PROLONGED SOUND MARK
→ 2014 — em dash
30FD ヽ KATAKANA ITERATION MARK
30FE ヾ KATAKANA VOICED ITERATION MARK
≡ 30FD ヽ + 3099 ゙

	310	311	312
0		ㄐ 3110	ㄠ 3120
1		ㄑ 3111	ㄡ 3121
2		ㄒ 3112	ㄢ 3122
3		ㄓ 3113	ㄣ 3123
4		ㄔ 3114	ㄤ 3124
5	ㄅ 3105	ㄕ 3115	ㄥ 3125
6	ㄆ 3106	ㄖ 3116	ㄦ 3126
7	ㄇ 3107	ㄗ 3117	ㄧ 3127
8	ㄈ 3108	ㄘ 3118	ㄨ 3128
9	ㄉ 3109	ㄙ 3119	ㄩ 3129
A	ㄊ 310A	ㄚ 311A	ㄪ 312A
B	ㄋ 310B	ㄛ 311B	ㄫ 312B
C	ㄌ 310C	ㄜ 311C	ㄬ 312C
D	ㄍ 310D	ㄝ 311D	
E	ㄎ 310E	ㄞ 311E	
F	ㄏ 310F	ㄟ 311F	

Based on GB 2312

→ 02C7 ˇ caron
→ 02C9 ˉ modifier letter macron
→ 02CA ˊ modifier letter acute accent
→ 02CB ˋ modifier letter grave accent
→ 02D9 ˙ dot above

3100 <reserved>
3101 <reserved>
3102 <reserved>
3103 <reserved>
3104 <reserved>
3105 ㄅ BOPOMOFO LETTER B
3106 ㄆ BOPOMOFO LETTER P
3107 ㄇ BOPOMOFO LETTER M
3108 ㄈ BOPOMOFO LETTER F
3109 ㄉ BOPOMOFO LETTER D
310A ㄊ BOPOMOFO LETTER T
310B ㄋ BOPOMOFO LETTER N
310C ㄌ BOPOMOFO LETTER L
310D ㄍ BOPOMOFO LETTER G
310E ㄎ BOPOMOFO LETTER K
310F ㄏ BOPOMOFO LETTER H
3110 ㄐ BOPOMOFO LETTER J
3111 ㄑ BOPOMOFO LETTER Q
3112 ㄒ BOPOMOFO LETTER X
3113 ㄓ BOPOMOFO LETTER ZH
3114 ㄔ BOPOMOFO LETTER CH
3115 ㄕ BOPOMOFO LETTER SH
3116 ㄖ BOPOMOFO LETTER R
3117 ㄗ BOPOMOFO LETTER Z
3118 ㄘ BOPOMOFO LETTER C
3119 ㄙ BOPOMOFO LETTER S
311A ㄚ BOPOMOFO LETTER A
311B ㄛ BOPOMOFO LETTER O
311C ㄜ BOPOMOFO LETTER E
311D ㄝ BOPOMOFO LETTER EH
311E ㄞ BOPOMOFO LETTER AI
311F ㄟ BOPOMOFO LETTER EI
3120 ㄠ BOPOMOFO LETTER AU
3121 ㄡ BOPOMOFO LETTER OU
3122 ㄢ BOPOMOFO LETTER AN
3123 ㄣ BOPOMOFO LETTER EN
3124 ㄤ BOPOMOFO LETTER ANG
3125 ㄥ BOPOMOFO LETTER ENG
3126 ㄦ BOPOMOFO LETTER ER
3127 ㄧ BOPOMOFO LETTER I
3128 ㄨ BOPOMOFO LETTER U
3129 ㄩ BOPOMOFO LETTER IU

Dialect (non-Mandarin) letters

312A ㄪ BOPOMOFO LETTER V
312B ㄫ BOPOMOFO LETTER NG
312C ㄬ BOPOMOFO LETTER GN

	313	314	315	316	317	318
0		ㅀ 3140	ㅐ 3150	ㅠ 3160	ㅰ 3170	ㆀ 3180
1	ㄱ 3131	ㅁ 3141	ㅑ 3151	ㅡ 3161	ㅱ 3171	ㆁ 3181
2	ㄲ 3132	ㅂ 3142	ㅒ 3152	ㅢ 3162	ㅲ 3172	ㆂ 3182
3	ㄳ 3133	ㅃ 3143	ㅓ 3153	ㅣ 3163	ㅳ 3173	ㆃ 3183
4	ㄴ 3134	ㅄ 3144	ㅔ 3154	HF 3164	ㅴ 3174	ㆄ 3184
5	ㄵ 3135	ㅅ 3145	ㅕ 3155	ㅥ 3165	ㅵ 3175	ㆅ 3185
6	ㄶ 3136	ㅆ 3146	ㅖ 3156	ㅦ 3166	ㅶ 3176	ㆆ 3186
7	ㄷ 3137	ㅇ 3147	ㅗ 3157	ㅧ 3167	ㅷ 3177	ㆇ 3187
8	ㄸ 3138	ㅈ 3148	ㅘ 3158	ㅨ 3168	ㅸ 3178	ㆈ 3188
9	ㄹ 3139	ㅉ 3149	ㅙ 3159	ㅩ 3169	ㅹ 3179	ㆉ 3189
A	ㄺ 313A	ㅊ 314A	ㅚ 315A	ㅪ 316A	ㅺ 317A	ㆊ 318A
B	ㄻ 313B	ㅋ 314B	ㅛ 315B	ㅫ 316B	ㅻ 317B	ㆋ 318B
C	ㄼ 313C	ㅌ 314C	ㅜ 315C	ㅬ 316C	ㅼ 317C	ㆌ 318C
D	ㄽ 313D	ㅍ 314D	ㅝ 315D	ㅭ 316D	ㅽ 317D	ㆍ 318D
E	ㄾ 313E	ㅎ 314E	ㅞ 315E	ㅮ 316E	ㅾ 317E	ㆎ 318E
F	ㄿ 313F	ㅏ 314F	ㅟ 315F	ㅯ 316F	ㅿ 317F	

Based on KS C 5601

Modern letters

3130 ▧ <reserved>
3131 ㄱ HANGUL LETTER KIYEOK
≈ 1100 ᄀ
3132 ㄲ HANGUL LETTER SSANGKIYEOK
≈ 1101 ᄁ
3133 ㄳ HANGUL LETTER KIYEOK-SIOS
≈ 11AA ᆪ
3134 ㄴ HANGUL LETTER NIEUN
≈ 1102 ᄂ
3135 ㄵ HANGUL LETTER NIEUN-CIEUC
≈ 11AC ᆬ
3136 ㄶ HANGUL LETTER NIEUN-HIEUH
≈ 11AD ᆭ
3137 ㄷ HANGUL LETTER TIKEUT
≈ 1103 ᄃ
3138 ㄸ HANGUL LETTER SSANGTIKEUT
≈ 1104 ᄄ
3139 ㄹ HANGUL LETTER RIEUL
≈ 1105 ᄅ
313A ㄺ HANGUL LETTER RIEUL-KIYEOK
≈ 11B0 ᆰ
313B ㄻ HANGUL LETTER RIEUL-MIEUM
≈ 11B1 ᆱ
313C ㄼ HANGUL LETTER RIEUL-PIEUP
≈ 11B2 ᆲ
313D ㄽ HANGUL LETTER RIEUL-SIOS
≈ 11B3 ᆳ
313E ㄾ HANGUL LETTER RIEUL-THIEUTH
≈ 11B4 ᆴ
313F ㄿ HANGUL LETTER RIEUL-PHIEUPH
≈ 11B5 ᆵ
3140 ㅀ HANGUL LETTER RIEUL-HIEUH
≈ 111A ᄚ
3141 ㅁ HANGUL LETTER MIEUM
≈ 1106 ᄆ
3142 ㅂ HANGUL LETTER PIEUP
≈ 1107 ᄇ
3143 ㅃ HANGUL LETTER SSANGPIEUP
≈ 1108 ᄈ
3144 ㅄ HANGUL LETTER PIEUP-SIOS
≈ 1121 ᄡ
3145 ㅅ HANGUL LETTER SIOS
≈ 1109 ᄉ
3146 ㅆ HANGUL LETTER SSANGSIOS
≈ 110A ᄊ
3147 ㅇ HANGUL LETTER IEUNG
≈ 110B ᄋ
3148 ㅈ HANGUL LETTER CIEUC
≈ 110C ᄌ
3149 ㅉ HANGUL LETTER SSANGCIEUC
≈ 110D ᄍ
314A ㅊ HANGUL LETTER CHIEUCH
≈ 110E ᄎ
314B ㅋ HANGUL LETTER KHIEUKH
≈ 110F ᄏ
314C ㅌ HANGUL LETTER THIEUTH
≈ 1110 ᄐ
314D ㅍ HANGUL LETTER PHIEUPH
≈ 1111 ᄑ
314E ㅎ HANGUL LETTER HIEUH
≈ 1112 ᄒ
314F ㅏ HANGUL LETTER A
≈ 1161 ᅡ
3150 ㅐ HANGUL LETTER AE
≈ 1162 ᅢ
3151 ㅑ HANGUL LETTER YA
≈ 1163 ᅣ
3152 ㅒ HANGUL LETTER YAE
≈ 1164 ᅤ
3153 ㅓ HANGUL LETTER EO
≈ 1165 ᅥ
3154 ㅔ HANGUL LETTER E
≈ 1166 ᅦ
3155 ㅕ HANGUL LETTER YEO
≈ 1167 ᅧ
3156 ㅖ HANGUL LETTER YE
≈ 1168 ᅨ
3157 ㅗ HANGUL LETTER O
≈ 1169 ᅩ
3158 ㅘ HANGUL LETTER WA
≈ 116A ᅪ
3159 ㅙ HANGUL LETTER WAE
≈ 116B ᅫ
315A ㅚ HANGUL LETTER OE
≈ 116C ᅬ
315B ㅛ HANGUL LETTER YO
≈ 116D ᅭ
315C ㅜ HANGUL LETTER U
≈ 116E ᅮ
315D ㅝ HANGUL LETTER WEO
≈ 116F ᅯ
315E ㅞ HANGUL LETTER WE
≈ 1170 ᅰ
315F ㅟ HANGUL LETTER WI
≈ 1171 ᅱ
3160 ㅠ HANGUL LETTER YU
≈ 1172 ᅲ
3161 ㅡ HANGUL LETTER EU
≈ 1173 ᅳ
3162 ㅢ HANGUL LETTER YI
≈ 1174 ᅴ
3163 ㅣ HANGUL LETTER I
≈ 1175 ᅵ

Special character

3164 HANGUL FILLER
= HANGUL CAE OM
≈ 1160

Archaic letters

3165 ㅥ HANGUL LETTER SSANGNIEUN
≈ 1114 ᄔ

3166 ㅦ HANGUL LETTER NIEUN-TIKEUT
≈ 1115 ᄕ

3167 ㅧ HANGUL LETTER NIEUN-SIOS
≈ 11C7 ᇇ

3168 ㅨ HANGUL LETTER NIEUN-PANSIOS
≈ 11C8 ᇈ

3169 ㅩ HANGUL LETTER RIEUL-KIYEOK-SIOS
≈ 11CC ᇌ

316A ㅪ HANGUL LETTER RIEUL-TIKEUT
≈ 11CE ᇎ

316B ㅫ HANGUL LETTER RIEUL-PIEUP-SIOS
≈ 11D3 ᇓ

316C ㅬ HANGUL LETTER RIEUL-PANSIOS
≈ 11D7 ᇗ

316D ㅭ HANGUL LETTER RIEUL-YEORINHIEUH
≈ 11D9 ᇙ

316E ㅮ HANGUL LETTER MIEUM-PIEUP
≈ 111C ᄜ

316F ㅯ HANGUL LETTER MIEUM-SIOS
≈ 11DD ᇝ

3170 ㅰ HANGUL LETTER MIEUM-PANSIOS
≈ 11DF ᇟ

3171 ㅱ HANGUL LETTER KAPYEOUNMIEUM
≈ 111D ᄝ

3172 ㅲ HANGUL LETTER PIEUP-KIYEOK
≈ 111E ᄞ

3173 ㅳ HANGUL LETTER PIEUP-TIKEUT
≈ 1120 ᄠ

3174 ㅴ HANGUL LETTER PIEUP-SIOS-KIYEOK
≈ 1122 ᄢ

3175 ㅵ HANGUL LETTER PIEUP-SIOS-TIKEUT
≈ 1123 ᄣ

3176 ㅶ HANGUL LETTER PIEUP-CIEUC
≈ 1127 ᄧ

3177 ㅷ HANGUL LETTER PIEUP-THIEUTH
≈ 1129 ᄩ

3178 ㅸ HANGUL LETTER KAPYEOUNPIEUP
≈ 112B ᄫ

3179 ㅹ HANGUL LETTER KAPYEOUNSSANGPIEUP
≈ 112C ᄬ

317A ㅺ HANGUL LETTER SIOS-KIYEOK
≈ 112D ᄭ

317B ㅻ HANGUL LETTER SIOS-NIEUN
≈ 112E ᄮ

317C ㅼ HANGUL LETTER SIOS-TIKEUT
≈ 112F ᄯ

317D ㅽ HANGUL LETTER SIOS-PIEUP
≈ 1132 ᄲ

317E ㅾ HANGUL LETTER SIOS-CIEUC
≈ 1136 ᄶ

317F ㅿ HANGUL LETTER PANSIOS
≈ 1140 ᅀ

3180 ㆀ HANGUL LETTER SSANGIEUNG
≈ 1147 ᅇ

3181 ㆁ HANGUL LETTER YESIEUNG
• archaic velar nasal
≈ 114C ᅌ

3182 ㆂ HANGUL LETTER YESIEUNG-SIOS
≈ 11F1 ᇱ

3183 ㆃ HANGUL LETTER YESIEUNG-PANSIOS
≈ 11F2 ᇲ

3184 ㆄ HANGUL LETTER KAPYEOUNPHIEUPH
≈ 1157 ᅗ

3185 ㆅ HANGUL LETTER SSANGHIEUH
≈ 1158 ᅘ

3186 ㆆ HANGUL LETTER YEORINHIEUH
• archaic glottal stop
≈ 1159 ᅙ

3187 ㆇ HANGUL LETTER YO-YA
≈ 1184 ᆄ

3188 ㆈ HANGUL LETTER YO-YAE
≈ 1185 ᆅ

3189 ㆉ HANGUL LETTER YO-I
≈ 1188 ᆈ

318A ㆊ HANGUL LETTER YU-YEO
≈ 1191 ᆑ

318B ㆋ HANGUL LETTER YU-YE
≈ 1192 ᆒ

318C ㆌ HANGUL LETTER YU-I
≈ 1194 ᆔ

318D ㆍ HANGUL LETTER ARAEA
≈ 119E ᆞ

318E ㆎ HANGUL LETTER ARAEAE
≈ 11A1 ᆡ

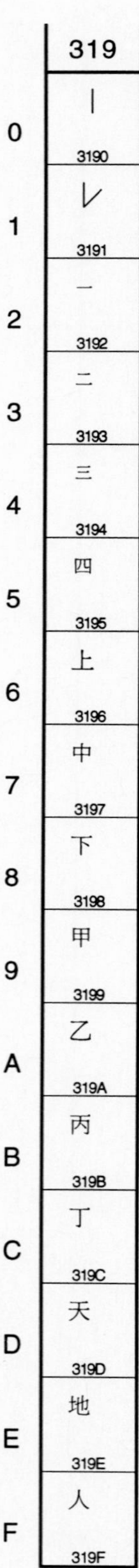
319
0
丨
3190
1
㆑
3191
2
一
3192
3
二
3193
4
三
3194
5
四
3195
6
上
3196
7
中
3197
8
下
3198
9
甲
3199
A
乙
319A
B
丙
319B
C
丁
319C
D
天
319D
E
地
319E
F
人
319F

Kanbun

3190 ㆐ IDEOGRAPHIC ANNOTATION LINKING MARK

3191 ㆑ IDEOGRAPHIC ANNOTATION REVERSE MARK

3192 ㆒ IDEOGRAPHIC ANNOTATION ONE MARK
≈ <super> + 4E00

3193 ㆓ IDEOGRAPHIC ANNOTATION TWO MARK
≈ <super> + 4E8C

3194 ㆔ IDEOGRAPHIC ANNOTATION THREE MARK
≈ <super> + 4E09

3195 ㆕ IDEOGRAPHIC ANNOTATION FOUR MARK
≈ <super> + 56DB

3196 ㆖ IDEOGRAPHIC ANNOTATION TOP MARK
≈ <super> + 4E0A

3197 ㆗ IDEOGRAPHIC ANNOTATION MIDDLE MARK
≈ <super> + 4E2D

3198 ㆘ IDEOGRAPHIC ANNOTATION BOTTOM MARK
≈ <super> + 4E0B

3199 ㆙ IDEOGRAPHIC ANNOTATION FIRST MARK
≈ <super> + 7532

319A ㆚ IDEOGRAPHIC ANNOTATION SECOND MARK
≈ <super> + 4E59

319B ㆛ IDEOGRAPHIC ANNOTATION THIRD MARK
≈ <super> + 4E19

319C ㆜ IDEOGRAPHIC ANNOTATION FOURTH MARK
≈ <super> + 4E01

319D ㆝ IDEOGRAPHIC ANNOTATION HEAVEN MARK
≈ <super> + 5929

319E ㆞ IDEOGRAPHIC ANNOTATION EARTH MARK
≈ <super> + 5730

319F ㆟ IDEOGRAPHIC ANNOTATION MAN MARK
≈ <super> + 4EBA

	320	321	322	323	324	325	326	327
0	㈀ 3200	㈐ 3210	㈠ 3220	㈰ 3230	㉀ 3240		㉠ 3260	㉰ 3270
1	㈁ 3201	㈑ 3211	㈡ 3221	㈱ 3231	㉁ 3241		㉡ 3261	㉱ 3271
2	㈂ 3202	㈒ 3212	㈢ 3222	㈲ 3232	㉂ 3242		㉢ 3262	㉲ 3272
3	㈃ 3203	㈓ 3213	㈣ 3223	㈳ 3233	㉃ 3243		㉣ 3263	㉳ 3273
4	㈄ 3204	㈔ 3214	㈤ 3224	㈴ 3234			㉤ 3264	㉴ 3274
5	㈅ 3205	㈕ 3215	㈥ 3225	㈵ 3235			㉥ 3265	㉵ 3275
6	㈆ 3206	㈖ 3216	㈦ 3226	㈶ 3236			㉦ 3266	㉶ 3276
7	㈇ 3207	㈗ 3217	㈧ 3227	㈷ 3237			㉧ 3267	㉷ 3277
8	㈈ 3208	㈘ 3218	㈨ 3228	㈸ 3238			㉨ 3268	㉸ 3278
9	㈉ 3209	㈙ 3219	㈩ 3229	㈹ 3239			㉩ 3269	㉹ 3279
A	㈊ 320A	㈚ 321A	㈪ 322A	㈺ 323A			㉪ 326A	㉺ 327A
B	㈋ 320B	㈛ 321B	㈫ 322B	㈻ 323B			㉫ 326B	㉻ 327B
C	㈌ 320C	㈜ 321C	㈬ 322C	㈼ 323C			㉬ 326C	
D	㈍ 320D		㈭ 322D	㈽ 323D			㉭ 326D	
E	㈎ 320E		㈮ 322E	㈾ 323E			㉮ 326E	
F	㈏ 320F		㈯ 322F	㈿ 323F			㉯ 326F	㉿ 327F

	328	329	32A	32B	32C	32D	32E	32F
0	㊀ 3280	㊐ 3290	㊠ 32A0	㊰ 32B0	㋀ 32C0	㋐ 32D0	㋠ 32E0	㋰ 32F0
1	㊁ 3281	㊑ 3291	㊡ 32A1		㋁ 32C1	㋑ 32D1	㋡ 32E1	㋱ 32F1
2	㊂ 3282	㊒ 3292	㊢ 32A2		㋂ 32C2	㋒ 32D2	㋢ 32E2	㋲ 32F2
3	㊃ 3283	㊓ 3293	㊣ 32A3		㋃ 32C3	㋓ 32D3	㋣ 32E3	㋳ 32F3
4	㊄ 3284	㊔ 3294	㊤ 32A4		㋄ 32C4	㋔ 32D4	㋤ 32E4	㋴ 32F4
5	㊅ 3285	㊕ 3295	㊥ 32A5		㋅ 32C5	㋕ 32D5	㋥ 32E5	㋵ 32F5
6	㊆ 3286	㊖ 3296	㊦ 32A6		㋆ 32C6	㋖ 32D6	㋦ 32E6	㋶ 32F6
7	㊇ 3287	㊗ 3297	㊧ 32A7		㋇ 32C7	㋗ 32D7	㋧ 32E7	㋷ 32F7
8	㊈ 3288	㊘ 3298	㊨ 32A8		㋈ 32C8	㋘ 32D8	㋨ 32E8	㋸ 32F8
9	㊉ 3289	㊙ 3299	㊩ 32A9		㋉ 32C9	㋙ 32D9	㋩ 32E9	㋹ 32F9
A	㊊ 328A	㊚ 329A	㊪ 32AA		㋊ 32CA	㋚ 32DA	㋪ 32EA	㋺ 32FA
B	㊋ 328B	㊛ 329B	㊫ 32AB		㋋ 32CB	㋛ 32DB	㋫ 32EB	㋻ 32FB
C	㊌ 328C	㊜ 329C	㊬ 32AC			㋜ 32DC	㋬ 32EC	㋼ 32FC
D	㊍ 328D	㊝ 329D	㊭ 32AD			㋝ 32DD	㋭ 32ED	㋽ 32FD
E	㊎ 328E	㊞ 329E	㊮ 32AE			㋞ 32DE	㋮ 32EE	㋾ 32FE
F	㊏ 328F	㊟ 329F	㊯ 32AF			㋟ 32DF	㋯ 32EF	

Parenthesized Hangul elements

3200 ㈀ PARENTHESIZED HANGUL KIYEOK
≈ 0028 (+ 1100 ᄀ + 0029)

3201 ㈁ PARENTHESIZED HANGUL NIEUN
≈ 0028 (+ 1102 ᄂ + 0029)

3202 ㈂ PARENTHESIZED HANGUL TIKEUT
≈ 0028 (+ 1103 ᄃ + 0029)

3203 ㈃ PARENTHESIZED HANGUL RIEUL
≈ 0028 (+ 1105 ᄅ + 0029)

3204 ㈄ PARENTHESIZED HANGUL MIEUM
≈ 0028 (+ 1106 ᄆ + 0029)

3205 ㈅ PARENTHESIZED HANGUL PIEUP
≈ 0028 (+ 1107 ᄇ + 0029)

3206 ㈆ PARENTHESIZED HANGUL SIOS
≈ 0028 (+ 1109 ᄉ + 0029)

3207 ㈇ PARENTHESIZED HANGUL IEUNG
≈ 0028 (+ 110B ᄋ + 0029)

3208 ㈈ PARENTHESIZED HANGUL CIEUC
≈ 0028 (+ 110C ᄌ + 0029)

3209 ㈉ PARENTHESIZED HANGUL CHIEUCH
≈ 0028 (+ 110E ᄎ + 0029)

320A ㈊ PARENTHESIZED HANGUL KHIEUKH
≈ 0028 (+ 110F ᄏ + 0029)

320B ㈋ PARENTHESIZED HANGUL THIEUTH
≈ 0028 (+ 1110 ᄐ + 0029)

320C ㈌ PARENTHESIZED HANGUL PHIEUPH
≈ 0028 (+ 1111 ᄑ + 0029)

320D ㈍ PARENTHESIZED HANGUL HIEUH
≈ 0028 (+ 1112 ᄒ + 0029)

Parenthesized Hangul syllables

320E ㈎ PARENTHESIZED HANGUL KIYEOK A
≈ 0028 (+ 1100 ᄀ + 1161 ᅡ + 0029)

320F ㈏ PARENTHESIZED HANGUL NIEUN A
≈ 0028 (+ 1102 ᄂ + 1161 ᅡ + 0029)

3210 ㈐ PARENTHESIZED HANGUL TIKEUT A
≈ 0028 (+ 1103 ᄃ + 1161 ᅡ + 0029)

3211 ㈑ PARENTHESIZED HANGUL RIEUL A
≈ 0028 (+ 1105 ᄅ + 1161 ᅡ + 0029)

3212 ㈒ PARENTHESIZED HANGUL MIEUM A
≈ 0028 (+ 1106 ᄆ + 1161 ᅡ + 0029)

3213 ㈓ PARENTHESIZED HANGUL PIEUP A
≈ 0028 (+ 1107 ᄇ + 1161 ᅡ + 0029)

3214 ㈔ PARENTHESIZED HANGUL SIOS A
≈ 0028 (+ 1109 ᄉ + 1161 ᅡ + 0029)

3215 ㈕ PARENTHESIZED HANGUL IEUNG A
≈ 0028 (+ 110B ᄋ + 1161 ᅡ + 0029)

3216 ㈖ PARENTHESIZED HANGUL CIEUC A
≈ 0028 (+ 110C ᄌ + 1161 ᅡ + 0029)

3217 ㈗ PARENTHESIZED HANGUL CHIEUCH A
≈ 0028 (+ 110E ᄎ + 1161 ᅡ + 0029)

3218 ㈘ PARENTHESIZED HANGUL KHIEUKH A
≈ 0028 (+ 110F ᄏ + 1161 ᅡ + 0029)

3219 ㈙ PARENTHESIZED HANGUL THIEUTH A
≈ 0028 (+ 1110 ᄐ + 1161 ᅡ + 0029)

321A ㈚ PARENTHESIZED HANGUL PHIEUPH A
≈ 0028 (+ 1111 ᄑ + 1161 ᅡ + 0029)

321B ㈛ PARENTHESIZED HANGUL HIEUH A
≈ 0028 (+ 1112 ᄒ + 1161 ᅡ + 0029)

321C ㈜ PARENTHESIZED HANGUL CIEUC U
≈ 0028 (+ 110C ᄌ + 116E ᅮ + 0029)

321D <reserved>

321E <reserved>

321F <reserved>

Parenthesized ideographs

3220 ㈠ PARENTHESIZED IDEOGRAPH ONE
≈ 0028 (+ 4E00 + 0029)

3221 ㈡ PARENTHESIZED IDEOGRAPH TWO
≈ 0028 (+ 4E8C + 0029)

3222 ㈢ PARENTHESIZED IDEOGRAPH THREE
≈ 0028 (+ 4E09 + 0029)

3223 ㈣ PARENTHESIZED IDEOGRAPH FOUR
≈ 0028 (+ 56DB + 0029)

3224 ㈤ PARENTHESIZED IDEOGRAPH FIVE
≈ 0028 (+ 4E94 + 0029)

3225 ㈥ PARENTHESIZED IDEOGRAPH SIX
≈ 0028 (+ 516D + 0029)

3226 ㈦ PARENTHESIZED IDEOGRAPH SEVEN
≈ 0028 (+ 4E03 + 0029)

3227 ㈧ PARENTHESIZED IDEOGRAPH EIGHT
≈ 0028 (+ 516B + 0029)

3228 ㈨ PARENTHESIZED IDEOGRAPH NINE
≈ 0028 (+ 4E5D + 0029)

3229 ㈩ PARENTHESIZED IDEOGRAPH TEN
≈ 0028 (+ 5341 + 0029)

322A ㈪ PARENTHESIZED IDEOGRAPH MOON
• Monday
≈ 0028 (+ 6708 + 0029)

322B ㈫ PARENTHESIZED IDEOGRAPH FIRE
• Tuesday
≈ 0028 (+ 706B + 0029)

322C ㈬ PARENTHESIZED IDEOGRAPH WATER
• Wednesday
≈ 0028 (+ 6C34 + 0029)

322D ㈭ PARENTHESIZED IDEOGRAPH WOOD
• Thursday
≈ 0028 (+ 6728 + 0029)

322E ㈮ PARENTHESIZED IDEOGRAPH METAL
• Friday
≈ 0028 (+ 91D1 + 0029)

322F ㈯ PARENTHESIZED IDEOGRAPH EARTH
• Saturday
≈ 0028 (+ 571F + 0029)

3230 ㈰ PARENTHESIZED IDEOGRAPH SUN
• Sunday
≈ 0028 (+ 65E5 + 0029)

3231 ㈱ PARENTHESIZED IDEOGRAPH STOCK
• incorporated
≈ 0028 (+ 682A + 0029)

3232 ㈲ PARENTHESIZED IDEOGRAPH HAVE
• limited
≈ 0028 (+ 6709 + 0029)

3233 ㈳ PARENTHESIZED IDEOGRAPH SOCIETY
• company
≈ 0028 (+ 793E + 0029)

3234 ㈴ PARENTHESIZED IDEOGRAPH NAME
≈ 0028 (+ 540D + 0029)

3235 ㈵ PARENTHESIZED IDEOGRAPH SPECIAL
≈ 0028 (+ 7279 + 0029)

3236 ㈶ PARENTHESIZED IDEOGRAPH FINANCIAL
≈ 0028 (+ 8CA1 + 0029)

3237 ㈷ PARENTHESIZED IDEOGRAPH CONGRATULATION
≈ 0028 (+ 795D + 0029)

3238 ㈸ PARENTHESIZED IDEOGRAPH LABOR
≈ 0028 (+ 52B4 + 0029)

3239 ㈹ PARENTHESIZED IDEOGRAPH REPRESENT
≈ 0028 (+ 4EE3 + 0029)

323A ㈺ PARENTHESIZED IDEOGRAPH CALL
≈ 0028 (+ 547C + 0029)

323B ㈻ PARENTHESIZED IDEOGRAPH STUDY
≈ 0028 (+ 5B66 + 0029)

323C ㈼ PARENTHESIZED IDEOGRAPH SUPERVISE
≈ 0028 (+ 76E3 + 0029)

323D ㈽ PARENTHESIZED IDEOGRAPH ENTERPRISE
≈ 0028 (+ 4F01 + 0029)

323E ㈾ PARENTHESIZED IDEOGRAPH RESOURCE
≈ 0028 (+ 8CC7 + 0029)

323F ㈿ PARENTHESIZED IDEOGRAPH ALLIANCE
≈ 0028 (+ 5354 + 0029)

3240 ㉀ PARENTHESIZED IDEOGRAPH FESTIVAL
≈ 0028 (+ 796D + 0029)

3241 ㉁ PARENTHESIZED IDEOGRAPH REST
≈ 0028 (+ 4F11 + 0029)

3242 ㉂ PARENTHESIZED IDEOGRAPH SELF
• from
≈ 0028 (+ 81EA + 0029)

3243 ㉃ PARENTHESIZED IDEOGRAPH REACH
• to
≈ 0028 (+ 81F3 + 0029)

3244 <reserved>
3245 <reserved>
3246 <reserved>
3247 <reserved>
3248 <reserved>
3249 <reserved>
324A <reserved>
324B <reserved>
324C <reserved>
324D <reserved>
324E <reserved>
324F <reserved>
3250 <reserved>
3251 <reserved>
3252 <reserved>
3253 <reserved>
3254 <reserved>
3255 <reserved>
3256 <reserved>
3257 <reserved>
3258 <reserved>
3259 <reserved>
325A <reserved>
325B <reserved>
325C <reserved>

325D <reserved>
325E <reserved>
325F <reserved>

Circled Hangul elements

3260 ㉠ CIRCLED HANGUL KIYEOK
≈ <circle> + 1100 ㄱ
3261 ㉡ CIRCLED HANGUL NIEUN
≈ <circle> + 1102 ㄴ
3262 ㉢ CIRCLED HANGUL TIKEUT
≈ <circle> + 1103 ㄷ
3263 ㉣ CIRCLED HANGUL RIEUL
≈ <circle> + 1105 ㄹ
3264 ㉤ CIRCLED HANGUL MIEUM
≈ <circle> + 1106 ㅁ
3265 ㉥ CIRCLED HANGUL PIEUP
≈ <circle> + 1107 ㅂ
3266 ㉦ CIRCLED HANGUL SIOS
≈ <circle> + 1109 ㅅ
3267 ㉧ CIRCLED HANGUL IEUNG
≈ <circle> + 110B ㅇ
3268 ㉨ CIRCLED HANGUL CIEUC
≈ <circle> + 110C ㅈ
3269 ㉩ CIRCLED HANGUL CHIEUCH
≈ <circle> + 110E ㅊ
326A ㉪ CIRCLED HANGUL KHIEUKH
≈ <circle> + 110F ㅋ
326B ㉫ CIRCLED HANGUL THIEUTH
≈ <circle> + 1110 ㅌ
326C ㉬ CIRCLED HANGUL PHIEUPH
≈ <circle> + 1111 ㅍ
326D ㉭ CIRCLED HANGUL HIEUH
≈ <circle> + 1112 ㅎ

Circled Hangul syllables

326E ㉮ CIRCLED HANGUL KIYEOK A
≈ <circle> + 1100 ㄱ + 1161 ㅏ
326F ㉯ CIRCLED HANGUL NIEUN A
≈ <circle> + 1102 ㄴ + 1161 ㅏ
3270 ㉰ CIRCLED HANGUL TIKEUT A
≈ <circle> + 1103 ㄷ + 1161 ㅏ
3271 ㉱ CIRCLED HANGUL RIEUL A
≈ <circle> + 1105 ㄹ + 1161 ㅏ
3272 ㉲ CIRCLED HANGUL MIEUM A
≈ <circle> + 1106 ㅁ + 1161 ㅏ
3273 ㉳ CIRCLED HANGUL PIEUP A
≈ <circle> + 1107 ㅂ + 1161 ㅏ
3274 ㉴ CIRCLED HANGUL SIOS A
≈ <circle> + 1109 ㅅ + 1161 ㅏ
3275 ㉵ CIRCLED HANGUL IEUNG A
≈ <circle> + 110B ㅇ + 1161 ㅏ
3276 ㉶ CIRCLED HANGUL CIEUC A
≈ <circle> + 110C ㅈ + 1161 ㅏ
3277 ㉷ CIRCLED HANGUL CHIEUCH A
≈ <circle> + 110E ㅊ + 1161 ㅏ
3278 ㉸ CIRCLED HANGUL KHIEUKH A
≈ <circle> + 110F ㅋ + 1161 ㅏ
3279 ㉹ CIRCLED HANGUL THIEUTH A
≈ <circle> + 1110 ㅌ + 1161 ㅏ
327A ㉺ CIRCLED HANGUL PHIEUPH A
≈ <circle> + 1111 ㅍ + 1161 ㅏ
327B ㉻ CIRCLED HANGUL HIEUH A
≈ <circle> + 1112 ㅎ + 1161 ㅏ
327C <reserved>
327D <reserved>
327E <reserved>

Symbol

327F ㉿ KOREAN STANDARD SYMBOL

Circled ideographs

3280 ㊀ CIRCLED IDEOGRAPH ONE
= maru-iti, symbol of unification
≈ <circle> + 4E00
3281 ㊁ CIRCLED IDEOGRAPH TWO
≈ <circle> + 4E8C
3282 ㊂ CIRCLED IDEOGRAPH THREE
≈ <circle> + 4E09
3283 ㊃ CIRCLED IDEOGRAPH FOUR
≈ <circle> + 56DB
3284 ㊄ CIRCLED IDEOGRAPH FIVE
≈ <circle> + 4E94
3285 ㊅ CIRCLED IDEOGRAPH SIX
≈ <circle> + 516D
3286 ㊆ CIRCLED IDEOGRAPH SEVEN
≈ <circle> + 4E03
3287 ㊇ CIRCLED IDEOGRAPH EIGHT
≈ <circle> + 516B
3288 ㊈ CIRCLED IDEOGRAPH NINE
≈ <circle> + 4E5D
3289 ㊉ CIRCLED IDEOGRAPH TEN
≈ <circle> + 5341
328A ㊊ CIRCLED IDEOGRAPH MOON
• Monday
≈ <circle> + 6708
328B ㊋ CIRCLED IDEOGRAPH FIRE
• Tuesday
≈ <circle> + 706B
328C ㊌ CIRCLED IDEOGRAPH WATER
• Wednesday
≈ <circle> + 6C34
328D ㊍ CIRCLED IDEOGRAPH WOOD
• Thursday
≈ <circle> + 6728

328E ㊎ CIRCLED IDEOGRAPH METAL
• Friday
≈ <circle> + 91D1

328F ㊏ CIRCLED IDEOGRAPH EARTH
• Saturday
≈ <circle> + 571F

3290 ㊐ CIRCLED IDEOGRAPH SUN
• Sunday
≈ <circle> + 65E5

3291 ㊑ CIRCLED IDEOGRAPH STOCK
• incorporated
≈ <circle> + 682A

3292 ㊒ CIRCLED IDEOGRAPH HAVE
• limited
≈ <circle> + 6709

3293 ㊓ CIRCLED IDEOGRAPH SOCIETY
• company
≈ <circle> + 793E

3294 ㊔ CIRCLED IDEOGRAPH NAME
≈ <circle> + 540D

3295 ㊕ CIRCLED IDEOGRAPH SPECIAL
≈ <circle> + 7279

3296 ㊖ CIRCLED IDEOGRAPH FINANCIAL
≈ <circle> + 8CA1

3297 ㊗ CIRCLED IDEOGRAPH CONGRATULATION
≈ <circle> + 795D

3298 ㊘ CIRCLED IDEOGRAPH LABOR
≈ <circle> + 52B4

3299 ㊙ CIRCLED IDEOGRAPH SECRET
≈ <circle> + 79D8

329A ㊚ CIRCLED IDEOGRAPH MALE
≈ <circle> + 7537

329B ㊛ CIRCLED IDEOGRAPH FEMALE
≈ <circle> + 5973

329C ㊜ CIRCLED IDEOGRAPH SUITABLE
≈ <circle> + 9069

329D ㊝ CIRCLED IDEOGRAPH EXCELLENT
≈ <circle> + 512A

329E ㊞ CIRCLED IDEOGRAPH PRINT
• name seal
≈ <circle> + 5370

329F ㊟ CIRCLED IDEOGRAPH ATTENTION
≈ <circle> + 6CE8

32A0 ㊠ CIRCLED IDEOGRAPH ITEM
≈ <circle> + 9805

32A1 ㊡ CIRCLED IDEOGRAPH REST
• holiday
≈ <circle> + 4F11

32A2 ㊢ CIRCLED IDEOGRAPH COPY
≈ <circle> + 5199

32A3 ㊣ CIRCLED IDEOGRAPH CORRECT
≈ <circle> + 6B63

32A4 ㊤ CIRCLED IDEOGRAPH HIGH
≈ <circle> + 4E0A

32A5 ㊥ CIRCLED IDEOGRAPH CENTRE
≈ <circle> + 4E2D

32A6 ㊦ CIRCLED IDEOGRAPH LOW
≈ <circle> + 4E0B

32A7 ㊧ CIRCLED IDEOGRAPH LEFT
≈ <circle> + 5DE6

32A8 ㊨ CIRCLED IDEOGRAPH RIGHT
≈ <circle> + 53F3

32A9 ㊩ CIRCLED IDEOGRAPH MEDICINE
≈ <circle> + 533B

32AA ㊪ CIRCLED IDEOGRAPH RELIGION
≈ <circle> + 5B97

32AB ㊫ CIRCLED IDEOGRAPH STUDY
≈ <circle> + 5B66

32AC ㊬ CIRCLED IDEOGRAPH SUPERVISE
≈ <circle> + 76E3

32AD ㊭ CIRCLED IDEOGRAPH ENTERPRISE
≈ <circle> + 4F01

32AE ㊮ CIRCLED IDEOGRAPH RESOURCE
≈ <circle> + 8CC7

32AF ㊯ CIRCLED IDEOGRAPH ALLIANCE
≈ <circle> + 5354

32B0 ㊰ CIRCLED IDEOGRAPH NIGHT
≈ <circle> + 591C

32B1 <reserved>

32B2 <reserved>

32B3 <reserved>

32B4 <reserved>

32B5 <reserved>

32B6 <reserved>

32B7 <reserved>

32B8 <reserved>

32B9 <reserved>

32BA <reserved>

32BB <reserved>

32BC <reserved>

32BD <reserved>

32BE <reserved>

32BF <reserved>

32C0 ㋀ IDEOGRAPHIC TELEGRAPH SYMBOL FOR JANUARY
≈ 0031 1 + 6708

32C1 ㋁ IDEOGRAPHIC TELEGRAPH SYMBOL FOR FEBRUARY
≈ 0032 2 + 6708

32C2 ㋂ IDEOGRAPHIC TELEGRAPH SYMBOL FOR MARCH
≈ 0033 3 + 6708

32C3 ㋃ IDEOGRAPHIC TELEGRAPH SYMBOL FOR APRIL
≈ 0034 4 + 6708

32C4 ㋄ IDEOGRAPHIC TELEGRAPH SYMBOL FOR MAY
≈ 0035 5 + 6708

32C5 ㋅ IDEOGRAPHIC TELEGRAPH SYMBOL FOR JUNE
≈ 0036 6 + 6708

32C6 ㋆ IDEOGRAPHIC TELEGRAPH SYMBOL FOR JULY
≈ 0037 7 + 6708

32C7 ㋇ IDEOGRAPHIC TELEGRAPH SYMBOL FOR AUGUST
≈ 0038 8 + 6708

32C8 ㋈ IDEOGRAPHIC TELEGRAPH SYMBOL FOR SEPTEMBER
≈ 0039 9 + 6708

32C9 ㋉ IDEOGRAPHIC TELEGRAPH SYMBOL FOR OCTOBER
≈ 0031 1 + 0030 0 + 6708

32CA ㋊ IDEOGRAPHIC TELEGRAPH SYMBOL FOR NOVEMBER
≈ 0031 1 + 0031 1 + 6708

32CB ㋋ IDEOGRAPHIC TELEGRAPH SYMBOL FOR DECEMBER
≈ 0031 1 + 0032 2 + 6708

32CC <reserved>

32CD <reserved>

32CE <reserved>

32CF <reserved>

Circled Katakana

32D0 ㋐ CIRCLED KATAKANA A
≈ <circle> + 30A2 ア

32D1 ㋑ CIRCLED KATAKANA I
≈ <circle> + 30A4 イ

32D2 ㋒ CIRCLED KATAKANA U
≈ <circle> + 30A6 ウ

32D3 ㋓ CIRCLED KATAKANA E
≈ <circle> + 30A8 エ

32D4 ㋔ CIRCLED KATAKANA O
≈ <circle> + 30AA オ

32D5 ㋕ CIRCLED KATAKANA KA
≈ <circle> + 30AB カ

32D6 ㋖ CIRCLED KATAKANA KI
≈ <circle> + 30AD キ

32D7 ㋗ CIRCLED KATAKANA KU
≈ <circle> + 30AF ク

32D8 ㋘ CIRCLED KATAKANA KE
≈ <circle> + 30B1 ケ

32D9 ㋙ CIRCLED KATAKANA KO
≈ <circle> + 30B3 コ

32DA ㋚ CIRCLED KATAKANA SA
≈ <circle> + 30B5 サ

32DB ㋛ CIRCLED KATAKANA SI
≈ <circle> + 30B7 シ

32DC ㋜ CIRCLED KATAKANA SU
≈ <circle> + 30B9 ス

32DD ㋝ CIRCLED KATAKANA SE
≈ <circle> + 30BB セ

32DE ㋞ CIRCLED KATAKANA SO
≈ <circle> + 30BD ソ

32DF ㋟ CIRCLED KATAKANA TA
≈ <circle> + 30BF タ

32E0 ㋠ CIRCLED KATAKANA TI
≈ <circle> + 30C1 チ

32E1 ㋡ CIRCLED KATAKANA TU
≈ <circle> + 30C4 ツ

32E2 ㋢ CIRCLED KATAKANA TE
≈ <circle> + 30C6 テ

32E3 ㋣ CIRCLED KATAKANA TO
≈ <circle> + 30C8 ト

32E4 ㋤ CIRCLED KATAKANA NA
≈ <circle> + 30CA ナ

32E5 ㋥ CIRCLED KATAKANA NI
≈ <circle> + 30CB ニ

32E6 ㋦ CIRCLED KATAKANA NU
≈ <circle> + 30CC ヌ

32E7 ㋧ CIRCLED KATAKANA NE
≈ <circle> + 30CD ネ

32E8 ㋨ CIRCLED KATAKANA NO
≈ <circle> + 30CE ノ

32E9 ㋩ CIRCLED KATAKANA HA
≈ <circle> + 30CF ハ

32EA ㋪ CIRCLED KATAKANA HI
≈ <circle> + 30D2 ヒ

32EB ㋫ CIRCLED KATAKANA HU
≈ <circle> + 30D5 フ

32EC ㋬ CIRCLED KATAKANA HE
≈ <circle> + 30D8 ヘ

32ED ㋭ CIRCLED KATAKANA HO
≈ <circle> + 30DB ホ

32EE ㋮ CIRCLED KATAKANA MA
≈ <circle> + 30DE マ

32EF ㋯ CIRCLED KATAKANA MI
≈ <circle> + 30DF ミ

32F0 ㋰ CIRCLED KATAKANA MU
≈ <circle> + 30E0 ム

32F1 ㋱ CIRCLED KATAKANA ME
≈ <circle> + 30E1 メ

32F2 ㋲ CIRCLED KATAKANA MO
≈ <circle> + 30E2 モ

32F3 ㋳ CIRCLED KATAKANA YA
≈ <circle> + 30E4 ヤ

32F4 ㋴ CIRCLED KATAKANA YU
≈ <circle> + 30E6 ユ

32F5 ㋵ CIRCLED KATAKANA YO
≈ <circle> + 30E8 ヨ

32F6 ㋶ CIRCLED KATAKANA RA
≈ <circle> + 30E9 ラ

32F7 ㋷ CIRCLED KATAKANA RI
≈ <circle> + 30EA リ

32F8 ㋸ CIRCLED KATAKANA RU
≈ <circle> + 30EB ル

32F9 ㋹ CIRCLED KATAKANA RE
≈ <circle> + 30EC レ

32FA ㋺ CIRCLED KATAKANA RO
≈ <circle> + 30ED ロ

32FB ㋻ CIRCLED KATAKANA WA
≈ <circle> + 30EF ワ

32FC ㋼ CIRCLED KATAKANA WI
≈ <circle> + 30F0 ヰ

32FD ㋽ CIRCLED KATAKANA WE
≈ <circle> + 30F1 ヱ

32FE ㋾ CIRCLED KATAKANA WO
≈ <circle> + 30F2 ヲ

	330	331	332	333	334	335	336	337
0	アパート 3300	ギガ 3310	サンチーム 3320	ピコ 3330	ポンド 3340	ユアン 3350	8点 3360	24点 3370
1	アルファ 3301	ギニー 3311	シリング 3321	ビル 3331	ホール 3341	リットル 3351	9点 3361	hPa 3371
2	アンペア 3302	キュリー 3312	センチ 3322	ファラッド 3332	ホーン 3342	リラ 3352	10点 3362	da 3372
3	アール 3303	ギルダー 3313	セント 3323	フィート 3333	マイクロ 3343	ルピー 3353	11点 3363	AU 3373
4	イニング 3304	キロ 3314	ダース 3324	ブッシェル 3334	マイル 3344	ルーブル 3354	12点 3364	bar 3374
5	インチ 3305	キログラム 3315	デシ 3325	フラン 3335	マッハ 3345	レム 3355	13点 3365	oV 3375
6	ウォン 3306	キロメートル 3316	ドル 3326	ヘクタール 3336	マルク 3346	レントゲン 3356	14点 3366	pc 3376
7	エスクード 3307	キロワット 3317	トン 3327	ペソ 3337	マンション 3347	ワット 3357	15点 3367	
8	エーカー 3308	グラム 3318	ナノ 3328	ペニヒ 3338	ミクロン 3348	0点 3358	16点 3368	
9	オンス 3309	グラムトン 3319	ノット 3329	ヘルツ 3339	ミリ 3349	1点 3359	17点 3369	
A	オーム 330A	クルゼイロ 331A	ハイツ 332A	ペンス 333A	ミリバール 334A	2点 335A	18点 336A	
B	カイリ 330B	クローネ 331B	パーセント 332B	ページ 333B	メガ 334B	3点 335B	19点 336B	平成 337B
C	カラット 330C	ケース 331C	パーツ 332C	ベータ 333C	メガトン 334C	4点 335C	20点 336C	昭和 337C
D	カロリー 330D	コルナ 331D	バーレル 332D	ポイント 333D	メートル 334D	5点 335D	21点 336D	大正 337D
E	ガロン 330E	コーポ 331E	ピアストル 332E	ボルト 333E	ヤード 334E	6点 335E	22点 336E	明治 337E
F	ガンマ 330F	サイクル 331F	ピクル 332F	ホン 333F	ヤール 334F	7点 335F	23点 336F	株式会社 337F

	338	339	33A	33B	33C	33D	33E	33F
0	pA 3380	Hz 3390	cm^2 33A0	ps 33B0	kΩ 33C0	lm 33D0	1日 33E0	17日 33F0
1	nA 3381	kHz 3391	m^2 33A1	ns 33B1	MΩ 33C1	ln 33D1	2日 33E1	18日 33F1
2	μA 3382	MHz 3392	km^2 33A2	μs 33B2	a.m. 33C2	log 33D2	3日 33E2	19日 33F2
3	mA 3383	GHz 3393	mm^3 33A3	ms 33B3	Bq 33C3	lx 33D3	4日 33E3	20日 33F3
4	kA 3384	THz 3394	cm^3 33A4	pV 33B4	cc 33C4	mb 33D4	5日 33E4	21日 33F4
5	KB 3385	μℓ 3395	m^3 33A5	nV 33B5	cd 33C5	mil 33D5	6日 33E5	22日 33F5
6	MB 3386	Mℓ 3396	km^3 33A6	μV 33B6	C/kg 33C6	mol 33D6	7日 33E6	23日 33F6
7	GB 3387	dℓ 3397	m/s 33A7	mV 33B7	Co. 33C7	pH 33D7	8日 33E7	24日 33F7
8	cal 3388	kℓ 3398	m/s^2 33A8	kV 33B8	dB 33C8	p.m. 33D8	9日 33E8	25日 33F8
9	kcal 3389	fm 3399	Pa 33A9	MV 33B9	Gy 33C9	PPM 33D9	10日 33E9	26日 33F9
A	pF 338A	nm 339A	kPa 33AA	pW 33BA	ha 33CA	PR 33DA	11日 33EA	27日 33FA
B	nF 338B	μm 339B	MPa 33AB	nW 33BB	HP 33CB	sr 33DB	12日 33EB	28日 33FB
C	μF 338C	mm 339C	GPA 33AC	μW 33BC	in 33CC	Sv 33DC	13日 33EC	29日 33FC
D	μg 338D	cm 339D	rad 33AD	mW 33BD	KK 33CD	Wb 33DD	14日 33ED	30日 33FD
E	mg 338E	km 339E	rad/s 33AE	kW 33BE	KM 33CE		15日 33EE	31日 33FE
F	kg 338F	mm^2 339F	rad/s^2 33AF	MW 33BF	kt 33CF		16日 33EF	

Squared Katakana words

3300 ㌀ SQUARE APAATO
• apartment
≈ <square> + 30A2 ア + 30D1 パ + 30FC ー + 30C8 ト

3301 ㌁ SQUARE ARUHUA
• alpha
≈ <square> + 30A2 ア + 30EB ル + 30D5 フ + 30A1 ァ

3302 ㌂ SQUARE ANPEA
• ampere
≈ <square> + 30A2 ア + 30F3 ン + 30DA ペ + 30A2 ア

3303 ㌃ SQUARE AARU
• are (unit of area)
≈ <square> + 30A2 ア + 30FC ー + 30EB ル

3304 ㌄ SQUARE ININGU
• inning
≈ <square> + 30A4 イ + 30CB ニ + 30F3 ン + 30B0 グ

3305 ㌅ SQUARE INTI
• inch
≈ <square> + 30A4 イ + 30F3 ン + 30C1 チ

3306 ㌆ SQUARE UON
• won (Korean currency)
≈ <square> + 30A6 ウ + 30A9 ォ + 30F3 ン

3307 ㌇ SQUARE ESUKUUDO
• escudo (Portuguese currency)
≈ <square> + 30A8 エ + 30B9 ス + 30AF ク + 30FC ー + 30C9 ド

3308 ㌈ SQUARE EEKAA
• acre
≈ <square> + 30A8 エ + 30FC ー + 30AB カ + 30FC ー

3309 ㌉ SQUARE ONSU
• ounce
≈ <square> + 30AA オ + 30F3 ン + 30B9 ス

330A ㌊ SQUARE OOMU
• ohm
≈ <square> + 30AA オ + 30FC ー + 30E0 ム

330B ㌋ SQUARE KAIRI
• kai-ri: nautical mile
≈ <square> + 30AB カ + 30A4 イ + 30EA リ

330C ㌌ SQUARE KARATTO
• carat
≈ <square> + 30AB カ + 30E9 ラ + 30C3 ッ + 30C8 ト

330D ㌍ SQUARE KARORII
• calorie
≈ <square> + 30AB カ + 30ED ロ + 30EA リ + 30FC ー

330E ㌎ SQUARE GARON
• gallon
≈ <square> + 30AC ガ + 30ED ロ + 30F3 ン

330F ㌏ SQUARE GANMA
• gamma
≈ <square> + 30AC ガ + 30F3 ン + 30DE マ

3310 ㌐ SQUARE GIGA
• giga-
≈ <square> + 30AE ギ + 30AC ガ

3311 ㌑ SQUARE GINII
• guinea
≈ <square> + 30AE ギ + 30CB ニ + 30FC ー

3312 ㌒ SQUARE KYURII
• curie
≈ <square> + 30AD キ + 30E5 ュ + 30EA リ + 30FC ー

3313 ㌓ SQUARE GIRUDAA
• guilder
≈ <square> + 30AE ギ + 30EB ル + 30C0 ダ + 30FC ー

3314 ㌔ SQUARE KIRO
• kilo-
≈ <square> + 30AD キ + 30ED ロ

3315 ㌕ SQUARE KIROGURAMU
• kilogram
≈ <square> + 30AD キ + 30ED ロ + 30B0 グ + 30E9 ラ + 30E0 ム

3316 ㌖ SQUARE KIROMEETORU
• kilometer
≈ <square> + 30AD キ + 30ED ロ + 30E1 メ + 30FC ー + 30C8 ト + 30EB ル

3317 ㌗ SQUARE KIROWATTO
• kilowatt
≈ <square> + 30AD キ + 30ED ロ + 30EF ワ + 30C3 ッ + 30C8 ト

3318 ㌘ SQUARE GURAMU
• gram
≈ <square> + 30B0 グ + 30E9 ラ + 30E0 ム

3319 ㌙ SQUARE GURAMUTON
• gram ton
≈ <square> + 30B0 グ + 30E9 ラ + 30E0 ム + 30C8 ト + 30F3 ン

331A ㌚ SQUARE KURUZEIRO
• cruzeiro (Brazilian currency)
≈ <square> + 30AF ク + 30EB ル + 30BC ゼ + 30A4 イ + 30ED ロ

331B ㌛ SQUARE KUROONE
• krone
≈ <square> + 30AF ク + 30ED ロ + 30FC ー + 30CD ネ

331C ㌜ SQUARE KEESU
• case
≈ <square> + 30B1 ケ + 30FC ー + 30B9 ス

331D ㌝ SQUARE KORUNA
• koruna (Czech currency)
≈ <square> + 30B3 コ + 30EB ル + 30CA ナ

331E ㌞ SQUARE KOOPO
• co-op
≈ <square> + 30B3 コ + 30FC ー + 30DD ポ

331F ㌟ SQUARE SAIKURU
• cycle
≈ <square> + 30B5 サ + 30A4 イ + 30AF ク + 30EB ル

3320 ㌠ SQUARE SANTIIMU
• centime
≈ <square> + 30B5 サ + 30F3 ン + 30C1 チ + 30FC ー + 30E0 ム

3321 ㌡ SQUARE SIRINGU
• shilling
≈ <square> + 30B7 シ + 30EA リ + 30F3 ン + 30B0 グ

3322 ㌢ SQUARE SENTI
• centi-
≈ <square> + 30BB セ + 30F3 ン + 30C1 チ

3323 ㌣ SQUARE SENTO
• cent
≈ <square> + 30BB セ + 30F3 ン + 30C8 ト

3324 ㌤ SQUARE DAASU
• dozen
≈ <square> + 30C0 ダ + 30FC ー + 30B9 ス

3325 ㌥ SQUARE DESI
• deci-
≈ <square> + 30C7 デ + 30B7 シ

3326 ㌦ SQUARE DORU
• dollar
≈ <square> + 30C9 ド + 30EB ル

3327 ㌧ SQUARE TON
• ton
≈ <square> + 30C8 ト + 30F3 ン

3328 ㌨ SQUARE NANO
• nano-
≈ <square> + 30CA ナ + 30CE ノ

3329 ㌩ SQUARE NOTTO
• knot, nautical mile
≈ <square> + 30CE ノ + 30C3 ッ + 30C8 ト

332A ㌪ SQUARE HAITU
• heights
≈ <square> + 30CF ハ + 30A4 イ + 30C4 ツ

332B ㌫ SQUARE PAASENTO
• percent
≈ <square> + 30D1 パ + 30FC ー + 30BB セ + 30F3 ン + 30C8 ト

332C ㌬ SQUARE PAATU
• parts
≈ <square> + 30D1 パ + 30FC ー + 30C4 ツ

332D ㌭ SQUARE BAARERU
• barrel
≈ <square> + 30D0 バ + 30FC ー + 30EC レ + 30EB ル

332E ㌮ SQUARE PIASUTORU
• piaster
≈ <square> + 30D4 ピ + 30A2 ア + 30B9 ス + 30C8 ト + 30EB ル

332F ㌯ SQUARE PIKURU
• picul (unit of weight)
≈ <square> + 30D4 ピ + 30AF ク + 30EB ル

3330 ㌰ SQUARE PIKO
• pico-
≈ <square> + 30D4 ピ + 30B3 コ

3331 ㌱ SQUARE BIRU
• building
≈ <square> + 30D3 ビ + 30EB ル

3332 ㌲ SQUARE HUARADDO
• farad
≈ <square> + 30D5 フ + 30A1 ァ + 30E9 ラ + 30C3 ッ + 30C9 ド

3333 ㌳ SQUARE HUIITO
• feet
≈ <square> + 30D5 フ + 30A3 ィ + 30FC ー + 30C8 ト

3334 ㌴ SQUARE BUSSYERU
• bushel
≈ <square> + 30D6 ブ + 30C3 ッ + 30B7 シ + 30A7 ェ + 30EB ル

3335 ㌵ SQUARE HURAN
• franc
≈ <square> + 30D5 フ + 30E9 ラ + 30F3 ン

3336 ㌶ SQUARE HEKUTAARU
• hectare
≈ <square> + 30D8 ヘ + 30AF ク + 30BF タ + 30FC ー + 30EB ル

3337 ㌷ SQUARE PESO
• peso
≈ <square> + 30DA ペ + 30BD ソ

3338 ㌸ SQUARE PENIHI
• pfennig
≈ <square> + 30DA ペ + 30CB ニ + 30D2 ヒ

3339 ㌹ SQUARE HERUTU
• hertz
≈ <square> + 30D8 ヘ + 30EB ル + 30C4 ツ

333A ㌺ SQUARE PENSU
• pence
≈ <square> + 30DA ペ + 30F3 ン + 30B9 ス

333B ㌻ SQUARE PEEZI
• page
≈ <square> + 30DA ペ + 30FC ー + 30B8 ジ

333C ㌼ SQUARE BEETA
• beta
≈ <square> + 30D9 ベ + 30FC ー + 30BF タ

333D ㌽ SQUARE POINTO
• point
≈ <square> + 30DD ポ + 30A4 イ + 30F3 ン + 30C8 ト

333E ㌾ SQUARE BORUTO
• volt, bolt
≈ <square> + 30DC ボ + 30EB ル + 30C8 ト

333F ㌿ SQUARE HON
• hon: volume
≈ <square> + 30DB ホ + 30F3 ン

3340 ㍀ SQUARE PONDO
• pound
≈ <square> + 30DD ポ + 30F3 ン + 30C9 ド

3341 ㍁ SQUARE HOORU
• hall
≈ <square> + 30DB ホ + 30FC ー + 30EB ル

3342 ㍂ SQUARE HOON
• horn
≈ <square> + 30DB ホ + 30FC ー + 30F3 ン

3343 ㍃ SQUARE MAIKURO
• micro-
≈ <square> + 30DE マ + 30A4 イ + 30AF ク + 30ED ロ

3344 ㍄ SQUARE MAIRU
• mile
≈ <square> + 30DE マ + 30A4 イ + 30EB ル

3345 ㍅ SQUARE MAHHA
• mach
≈ <square> + 30DE マ + 30C3 ッ + 30CF ハ

3346 ㍆ SQUARE MARUKU
• mark
≈ <square> + 30DE マ + 30EB ル + 30AF ク

3347 ㍇ SQUARE MANSYON
• mansion
≈ <square> + 30DE マ + 30F3 ン + 30B7 シ + 30E7 ョ + 30F3 ン

3348 ㍈ SQUARE MIKURON
• micron
≈ <square> + 30DF ミ + 30AF ク + 30ED ロ + 30F3 ン

3349 ㍉ SQUARE MIRI
• milli-
≈ <square> + 30DF ミ + 30EA リ

334A ㍊ SQUARE MIRIBAARU
• millibar
≈ <square> + 30DF ミ + 30EA リ + 30D0 バ + 30FC ー + 30EB ル

334B ㍋ SQUARE MEGA
• mega-
≈ <square> + 30E1 メ + 30AC ガ

334C ㍌ SQUARE MEGATON
• megaton
≈ <square> + 30E1 メ + 30AC ガ + 30C8 ト + 30F3 ン

334D ㍍ SQUARE MEETORU
• meter
≈ <square> + 30E1 メ + 30FC ー + 30C8 ト + 30EB ル

334E ㍎ SQUARE YAADO
• yard
≈ <square> + 30E4 ヤ + 30FC ー + 30C9 ド

334F ㍏ SQUARE YAARU
• yard
≈ <square> + 30E4 ヤ + 30FC ー + 30EB ル

3350 ㍐ SQUARE YUAN
• yuan (Chinese currency)
≈ <square> + 30E6 ユ + 30A2 ア + 30F3 ン

3351 ㍑ SQUARE RITTORU
• liter
≈ <square> + 30EA リ + 30C3 ッ + 30C8 ト + 30EB ル

3352 ㍒ SQUARE RIRA
• lira
≈ <square> + 30EA リ + 30E9 ラ

3353 ㍓ SQUARE RUPII
• rupee
≈ <square> + 30EB ル + 30D4 ピ + 30FC ー

3354 ㍔ SQUARE RUUBURU
• ruble
≈ <square> + 30EB ル + 30FC ー + 30D6 ブ + 30EB ル

3355 ㍕ SQUARE REMU
• rem (unit of radiation)
≈ <square> + 30EC レ + 30E0 ム

3356 ㍖ SQUARE RENTOGEN
• roentgen
≈ <square> + 30EC レ + 30F3 ン + 30C8 ト + 30B2 ゲ + 30F3 ン

3357 ㍗ SQUARE WATTO
• watt
≈ <square> + 30EF ワ + 30C3 ッ + 30C8 ト

3358 ㍘ IDEOGRAPHIC TELEGRAPH SYMBOL FOR HOUR ZERO
≈ <square> + 0030 0 + 70B9

3359 ㍙ IDEOGRAPHIC TELEGRAPH SYMBOL FOR HOUR ONE
≈ 0031 1 + 70B9

335A ㍚ IDEOGRAPHIC TELEGRAPH SYMBOL FOR HOUR TWO
≈ 0032 2 + 70B9

335B ㍛ IDEOGRAPHIC TELEGRAPH SYMBOL FOR HOUR THREE
≈ 0033 3 + 70B9

335C ㍜ IDEOGRAPHIC TELEGRAPH SYMBOL FOR HOUR FOUR
≈ 0034 4 + 70B9

335D ㍝ IDEOGRAPHIC TELEGRAPH SYMBOL FOR HOUR FIVE
≈ 0035 5 + 70B9

335E ㍞ IDEOGRAPHIC TELEGRAPH SYMBOL FOR HOUR SIX
≈ 0036 6 + 70B9

335F ㍟ IDEOGRAPHIC TELEGRAPH SYMBOL FOR HOUR SEVEN
≈ 0037 7 + 70B9

3360 ㍠ IDEOGRAPHIC TELEGRAPH SYMBOL FOR HOUR EIGHT
≈ 0038 8 + 70B9

3361 ㍡ IDEOGRAPHIC TELEGRAPH SYMBOL FOR HOUR NINE
≈ 0039 9 + 70B9

3362 ㍢ IDEOGRAPHIC TELEGRAPH SYMBOL FOR HOUR TEN
≈ 0031 1 + 0030 0 + 70B9

3363 ㍣ IDEOGRAPHIC TELEGRAPH SYMBOL FOR HOUR ELEVEN
≈ 0031 1 + 0031 1 + 70B9

3364 ㍤ IDEOGRAPHIC TELEGRAPH SYMBOL FOR HOUR TWELVE
≈ 0031 1 + 0032 2 + 70B9

3365 ㍥ IDEOGRAPHIC TELEGRAPH SYMBOL FOR HOUR THIRTEEN
≈ 0031 1 + 0033 3 + 70B9

3366 ㍦ IDEOGRAPHIC TELEGRAPH SYMBOL FOR HOUR FOURTEEN
≈ 0031 1 + 0034 4 + 70B9

3367 ㍧ IDEOGRAPHIC TELEGRAPH SYMBOL FOR HOUR FIFTEEN
≈ 0031 1 + 0035 5 + 70B9

3368 ㍨ IDEOGRAPHIC TELEGRAPH SYMBOL FOR HOUR SIXTEEN
≈ 0031 1 + 0036 6 + 70B9

3369 ㍩ IDEOGRAPHIC TELEGRAPH SYMBOL FOR HOUR SEVENTEEN
≈ 0031 1 + 0037 7 + 70B9

336A ㍪ IDEOGRAPHIC TELEGRAPH SYMBOL FOR HOUR EIGHTEEN
≈ 0031 1 + 0038 8 + 70B9

336B ㍫ IDEOGRAPHIC TELEGRAPH SYMBOL FOR HOUR NINETEEN
≈ 0031 1 + 0039 9 + 70B9

336C ㍬ IDEOGRAPHIC TELEGRAPH SYMBOL FOR HOUR TWENTY
≈ 0032 2 + 0030 0 + 70B9

336D ㍭ IDEOGRAPHIC TELEGRAPH SYMBOL FOR HOUR TWENTY-ONE
≈ 0032 2 + 0031 1 + 70B9

336E ㍮ IDEOGRAPHIC TELEGRAPH SYMBOL FOR HOUR TWENTY-TWO
≈ 0032 2 + 0032 2 + 70B9

336F ㍯ IDEOGRAPHIC TELEGRAPH SYMBOL FOR HOUR TWENTY-THREE
≈ 0032 2 + 0033 3 + 70B9

3370 ㍰ IDEOGRAPHIC TELEGRAPH SYMBOL FOR HOUR TWENTY-FOUR
≈ 0032 2 + 0034 4 + 70B9

3371 hPa SQUARE HPA
≈ <square> + 0068 h + 0050 P + 0061 a

3372 da SQUARE DA
≈ <square> + 0064 d + 0061 a

3373 AU SQUARE AU
≈ <square> + 0041 A + 0055 U

3374 bar SQUARE BAR
≈ <square> + 0062 b + 0061 a + 0072 r

3375 oV SQUARE OV
≈ <square> + 006F o + 0056 V

3376 pc SQUARE PC
≈ <square> + 0070 p + 0063 c

3377 <reserved>

3378 <reserved>

3379 <reserved>

337A ▧ <reserved>

Japanese era names

337B 平成 SQUARE ERA NAME HEISEI
≈ <square> + 5E73 + 6210

337C 昭和 SQUARE ERA NAME SYOUWA
≈ <square> + 662D + 548C

337D 大正 SQUARE ERA NAME TAISYOU
≈ <square> + 5927 + 6B63

337E 明治 SQUARE ERA NAME MEIZI
≈ <square> + 660E + 6CBB

Japanese corporation

337F 株式会社 SQUARE CORPORATION
= kabusiki-gaisya
• incorporated
≈ <square> + 682A + 5F0F + 4F1A + 793E

Squared Latin abbreviations

3380 pA SQUARE PA AMPS
≈ <square> + 0070 p + 0041 A

3381 nA SQUARE NA
≈ <square> + 006E n + 0041 A

3382 μA SQUARE MU A
≈ <square> + 03BC μ + 0041 A

3383 mA SQUARE MA
≈ <square> + 006D m + 0041 A

3384 kA SQUARE KA
≈ <square> + 006B k + 0041 A

3385 KB SQUARE KB
≈ <square> + 004B K + 0042 B

3386 MB SQUARE MB
≈ <square> + 004D M + 0042 B

3387 GB SQUARE GB
≈ <square> + 0047 G + 0042 B

3388 cal SQUARE CAL
≈ <square> + 0063 c + 0061 a + 006C l

3389 kcal SQUARE KCAL
≈ <square> + 006B k + 0063 c + 0061 a + 006C l

338A pF SQUARE PF
≈ <square> + 0070 p + 0046 F

338B nF SQUARE NF
≈ <square> + 006E n + 0046 F

338C μF SQUARE MU F
≈ <square> + 03BC μ + 0046 F

338D μg SQUARE MU G
≈ <square> + 03BC μ + 0067 g

338E mg SQUARE MG
≈ <square> + 006D m + 0067 g

338F kg SQUARE KG
≈ <square> + 006B k + 0067 g

3390 Hz SQUARE HZ
≈ <square> + 0048 H + 007A z

3391 kHz SQUARE KHZ
≈ <square> + 006B k + 0048 H + 007A z

3392 MHz SQUARE MHZ
≈ <square> + 004D M + 0048 H + 007A z

3393 GHz SQUARE GHZ
≈ <square> + 0047 G + 0048 H + 007A z

3394 THz SQUARE THZ
≈ <square> + 0054 T + 0048 H + 007A z

3395 μℓ SQUARE MU L
≈ <square> + 03BC μ + 2113 ℓ

3396 Mℓ SQUARE ML
≈ <square> + 006D m + 2113 ℓ

3397 dℓ SQUARE DL
≈ <square> + 0064 d + 2113 ℓ

3398 kℓ SQUARE KL
≈ <square> + 006B k + 2113 ℓ

3399 fm SQUARE FM
≈ <square> + 0066 f + 006D m

339A nm SQUARE NM
≈ <square> + 006E n + 006D m

339B μm SQUARE MU M
≈ <square> + 03BC μ + 006D m

339C mm SQUARE MM
≈ <square> + 006D m + 006D m

339D cm SQUARE CM
≈ <square> + 0063 c + 006D m

339E km SQUARE KM
≈ <square> + 006B k + 006D m

339F mm^2 SQUARE MM SQUARED
≈ <square> + 006D m + 006D m + 00B2 ^{2}

33A0 cm^2 SQUARE CM SQUARED
≈ <square> + 0063 c + 006D m + 00B2 ^{2}

33A1 m^2 SQUARE M SQUARED
≈ <square> + 006D m + 00B2 ^{2}

33A2 km^2 SQUARE KM SQUARED
≈ <square> + 006B k + 006D m + 00B2 ^{2}

33A3 mm^3 SQUARE MM CUBED
≈ <square> + 006D m + 006D m + 00B3 ^{3}

33A4 cm^3 SQUARE CM CUBED
≈ <square> + 0063 c + 006D m + 00B3 ^{3}

33A5 m^3 SQUARE M CUBED
≈ <square> + 006D m + 00B3 ^{3}

33A6 km^3 SQUARE KM CUBED
≈ <square> + 006B k + 006D m + 00B3 ^{3}

33A7 m/s SQUARE M OVER S
≈ <square> + 006D m + 2215 / + 0073 s

33A8 m/s^2 SQUARE M OVER S SQUARED
≈ <square> + 006D m + 2215 / + 0073 s + 00B2 ^{2}

33A9 Pa SQUARE PA
≈ <square> + 0050 P + 0061 a

33AA kPa SQUARE KPA
≈ <square> + 006B k + 0050 P + 0061 a

33AB MPa SQUARE MPA
≈ <square> + 004D M + 0050 P + 0061 a

33AC GPA SQUARE GPA
≈ <square> + 0047 G + 0050 P + 0061 a

33AD rad SQUARE RAD
≈ <square> + 0072 r + 0061 a + 0064 d

33AE rad/s SQUARE RAD OVER S
≈ <square> + 0072 r + 0061 a + 0064 d + 2215 / + 0073 s

33AF rad/s^2 SQUARE RAD OVER S SQUARED
≈ <square> + 0072 r + 0061 a + 0064 d + 2215 / + 0073 s + 00B2 ^{2}

33B0 ps SQUARE PS
≈ <square> + 0070 p + 0073 s

33B1 ns SQUARE NS
≈ <square> + 006E n + 0073 s

33B2 μs SQUARE MU S
≈ <square> + 03BC μ + 0073 s

33B3 ms SQUARE MS
≈ <square> + 006D m + 0073 s

33B4 pV SQUARE PV
≈ <square> + 0070 p + 0056 V

33B5 nV SQUARE NV
≈ <square> + 006E n + 0056 V

33B6 μV SQUARE MU V
≈ <square> + 03BC μ + 0056 V

33B7 mV SQUARE MV
≈ <square> + 006D m + 0056 V

33B8 kV SQUARE KV
≈ <square> + 006B k + 0056 V

33B9 MV SQUARE MV MEGA
≈ <square> + 004D M + 0056 V

33BA pW SQUARE PW
≈ <square> + 0070 p + 0057 W

33BB nW SQUARE NW
≈ <square> + 006E n + 0057 W

33BC μW SQUARE MU W
≈ <square> + 03BC μ + 0057 W

33BD mW SQUARE MW
≈ <square> + 006D m + 0057 W

33BE kW SQUARE KW
≈ <square> + 006B k + 0057 W

33BF MW SQUARE MW MEGA
≈ <square> + 004D M + 0057 W

33C0 kΩ SQUARE K OHM
≈ <square> + 006B k + 03A9 Ω

33C1 MΩ SQUARE M OHM
≈ <square> + 004D M + 03A9 Ω

33C2 a.m. SQUARE AM
≈ <square> + 0061 a + 002E . + 006D m + 002E .

33C3 Bq SQUARE BQ
≈ <square> + 0042 B + 0071 q

33C4 cc SQUARE CC
≈ <square> + 0063 c + 0063 c

33C5 cd SQUARE CD
≈ <square> + 0063 c + 0064 d

33C6 C/kg SQUARE C OVER KG
≈ <square> + 0043 C + 2215 / + 006B k + 0067 g

33C7 Co. SQUARE CO
≈ <square> + 0043 C + 006F o + 002E .

33C8 dB SQUARE DB
≈ <square> + 0064 d + 0042 B

33C9 Gy SQUARE GY
≈ <square> + 0047 G + 0079 y

33CA ha SQUARE HA
≈ <square> + 0068 h + 0061 a

33CB HP SQUARE HP
≈ <square> + 0048 H + 0050 P

33CC in SQUARE IN
≈ <square> + 0069 i + 006E n

33CD KK SQUARE KK
≈ <square> + 004B K + 004B K

33CE KM SQUARE KM CAPITAL
≈ <square> + 004B K + 004D M

33CF kt SQUARE KT
≈ <square> + 006B k + 0074 t

33D0 lm SQUARE LM
≈ <square> + 006C l + 006D m

33D1 ln SQUARE LN
≈ <square> + 006C l + 006E n

33D2 log SQUARE LOG
≈ <square> + 006C l + 006F o + 0067 g

33D3 lx SQUARE LX
≈ <square> + 006C l + 0078 x

33D4 mb SQUARE MB SMALL
≈ <square> + 006D m + 0062 b

33D5 mil SQUARE MIL
≈ <square> + 006D m + 0069 i + 006C l

33D6 mol SQUARE MOL
≈ <square> + 006D m + 006F o + 006C l

33D7 pH SQUARE PH
≈ <square> + 0050 P + 0048 H

33D8 p.m. SQUARE PM
≈ <square> + 0070 p + 002E . + 006D m + 002E .

33D9 PPM SQUARE PPM
≈ <square> + 0050 P + 0050 P + 004D M

33DA PR SQUARE PR
≈ <square> + 0050 P + 0052 R

33DB sr SQUARE SR
≈ <square> + 0073 s + 0072 r

33DC Sv SQUARE SV
≈ <square> + 0053 S + 0076 v

33DD Wb SQUARE WB
≈ <square> + 0057 W + 0062 b

33DE <reserved>

33DF <reserved>

33E0 1日 IDEOGRAPHIC TELEGRAPH SYMBOL FOR DAY ONE
≈ 0031 1 + 65E5

33E1 2日 IDEOGRAPHIC TELEGRAPH SYMBOL FOR DAY TWO
≈ 0032 2 + 65E5

33E2 3日 IDEOGRAPHIC TELEGRAPH SYMBOL FOR DAY THREE
≈ 0033 3 + 65E5

33E3 4日 IDEOGRAPHIC TELEGRAPH SYMBOL FOR DAY FOUR
≈ 0034 4 + 65E5

33E4 5日 IDEOGRAPHIC TELEGRAPH SYMBOL FOR DAY FIVE
≈ 0035 5 + 65E5

33E5 6日 IDEOGRAPHIC TELEGRAPH SYMBOL FOR DAY SIX
≈ 0036 6 + 65E5

33E6 7日 IDEOGRAPHIC TELEGRAPH SYMBOL FOR DAY SEVEN
≈ 0037 7 + 65E5

33E7 8日 IDEOGRAPHIC TELEGRAPH SYMBOL FOR DAY EIGHT
≈ 0038 8 + 65E5

33E8 9日 IDEOGRAPHIC TELEGRAPH SYMBOL FOR DAY NINE
≈ 0039 9 + 65E5

33E9 10日 IDEOGRAPHIC TELEGRAPH SYMBOL FOR DAY TEN
≈ 0031 1 + 0030 0 + 65E5

33EA 11日 IDEOGRAPHIC TELEGRAPH SYMBOL FOR DAY ELEVEN
≈ 0031 1 + 0031 1 + 65E5

33EB 12日 IDEOGRAPHIC TELEGRAPH SYMBOL FOR DAY TWELVE
≈ 0031 1 + 0032 2 + 65E5

33EC 13日 IDEOGRAPHIC TELEGRAPH SYMBOL FOR DAY THIRTEEN
≈ 0031 1 + 0033 3 + 65E5

33ED 14日 IDEOGRAPHIC TELEGRAPH SYMBOL FOR DAY FOURTEEN
≈ 0031 1 + 0034 4 + 65E5

33EE 15日 IDEOGRAPHIC TELEGRAPH SYMBOL FOR DAY FIFTEEN
≈ 0031 1 + 0035 5 + 65E5

33EF 16日 IDEOGRAPHIC TELEGRAPH SYMBOL FOR DAY SIXTEEN
≈ 0031 1 + 0036 6 + 65E5

33F0 17日 IDEOGRAPHIC TELEGRAPH SYMBOL FOR DAY SEVENTEEN
≈ 0031 1 + 0037 7 + 65E5

33F1 18日 IDEOGRAPHIC TELEGRAPH SYMBOL FOR DAY EIGHTEEN
≈ 0031 1 + 0038 8 + 65E5

33F2 19日 IDEOGRAPHIC TELEGRAPH SYMBOL FOR DAY NINETEEN
≈ 0031 1 + 0039 9 + 65E5

33F3 20日 IDEOGRAPHIC TELEGRAPH SYMBOL FOR DAY TWENTY
≈ 0032 2 + 0030 0 + 65E5

33F4 21日 IDEOGRAPHIC TELEGRAPH SYMBOL FOR DAY TWENTY-ONE
≈ 0032 2 + 0031 1 + 65E5

33F5 22日 IDEOGRAPHIC TELEGRAPH SYMBOL FOR DAY TWENTY-TWO
≈ 0032 2 + 0032 2 + 65E5

33F6 23日 IDEOGRAPHIC TELEGRAPH SYMBOL FOR DAY TWENTY-THREE
≈ 0032 2 + 0033 3 + 65E5

33F7 24日 IDEOGRAPHIC TELEGRAPH SYMBOL FOR DAY TWENTY-FOUR
≈ 0032 2 + 0034 4 + 65E5

33F8 25日 IDEOGRAPHIC TELEGRAPH SYMBOL FOR DAY TWENTY-FIVE
≈ 0032 2 + 0035 5 + 65E5

33F9 26日 IDEOGRAPHIC TELEGRAPH SYMBOL FOR DAY TWENTY-SIX
≈ 0032 2 + 0036 6 + 65E5

33FA 27日 IDEOGRAPHIC TELEGRAPH SYMBOL FOR DAY TWENTY-SEVEN
≈ 0032 2 + 0037 7 + 65E5

33FB ㏻ IDEOGRAPHIC TELEGRAPH
SYMBOL FOR DAY TWENTY-EIGHT
≈ 0032 2 + 0038 8 + 65E5

33FC ㏼ IDEOGRAPHIC TELEGRAPH
SYMBOL FOR DAY TWENTY-NINE
≈ 0032 2 + 0039 9 + 65E5

33FD ㏽ IDEOGRAPHIC TELEGRAPH
SYMBOL FOR DAY THIRTY
≈ 0033 3 + 0030 0 + 65E5

33FE ㏾ IDEOGRAPHIC TELEGRAPH
SYMBOL FOR DAY THIRTY-ONE
≈ 0033 3 + 0031 1 + 65E5

Code	Char	G	J	K	B	C	A
4E00	一	0-5027	0-1676	0-7673	A440	1-4421	213021
4E01	丁	0-2201	0-3590	0-7943	A442	1-4423	213022
4E02	丂	5-1601	1-1601				
4E03	七	0-3863	0-2823	0-8650	A443	1-4424	213023
4E04	丄		1-1602			E-2126	
4E05	丅		1-1603			E-2125	
4E06	丆						
4E07	万	0-4582	0-4392	0-5618	C945	2-2126	274F22
4E08	丈	0-5341	0-3070	0-7759	A456	1-4437	213027
4E09	三	0-4093	0-2716	0-6318	A454	1-4435	213024
4E0A	上	0-4147	0-3069	0-6330	A457	1-4438	213026
4E0B	下	0-4734	0-1828	0-8927	A455	1-4436	213025
4E0C	丌	0-5602	1-1604		C946	2-2127	2D332A
4E0D	不	0-1827	0-4152	0-6084	A4A3	1-4462	21302A
4E0E	与	0-5175	0-4531		C94F	2-212F	275432
4E0F	丏	3-1601			C94D	2-212D	216424
4E10	丐	0-5604	0-4802		A4A2	1-4461	213029
4E11	丑	0-1983	0-1715	0-8568	A4A1	1-4460	275D30
4E12	丒		1-1605				
4E13	专	0-5508					273B3F
4E14	且	0-3950	0-1978	0-8306	A542	1-4562	21302B
4E15	丕	0-5607	0-4803	0-6164	A541	1-4561	21302E
4E16	世	0-4232	0-3204	0-6506	A540	1-4560	21302D
4E17	丗		0-5034				2D302D
4E18	丘	0-3980	0-2154	0-4688	A543	1-4563	21302F
4E19	丙	0-1791	0-4226	0-6016	A4FE	1-455F	21302C
4E1A	业	0-5021					27452D
4E1B	丛	0-2052					27352B
4E1C	东	0-2211					274426
4E1D	丝	0-4331					27513B
4E1E	丞	0-5609	0-3071	0-6710	A5E0	1-4722	213031
4E1F	丟		1-1606	1-7742	A5E1	1-4723	213030
4E20	丠	5-1603				E-2262	
4E21	両		0-4630			E-2261	333323
4E22	丢	0-2210				E-2263	
4E23	丣		1-1607				
4E24	两	0-3329	1-1608			E-243F	273323
4E25	严	0-4947					27375A
4E26	並	8-1286	0-4234	1-6582	A8C3	1-4B64	213032
4E27	丧	0-4105					273663
4E28	丨	0-5613	1-1609			E-2121	216429
4E29	丩	5-1628					
4E2A	个	0-2486	0-4804			E-212C	273224
4E2B	丫	0-4930	1-1610	1-7002	A458	1-4439	283E22
4E2C	丬	0-6760					4C5541
4E2D	中	0-5448	0-3570	0-8173	A4A4	1-4463	213034
4E2E	丮		1-1611		C950	2-2130	
4E2F	丯		1-1612				
4E30	丰	0-2365	1-1613	1-6612	A4A5	1-4464	275958
4E31	丱	3-1617	0-4805	1-5762	C963	2-2143	21642E
4E32	串	0-2014	0-2290	0-4590	A6EA	1-486B	213035
4E33	丳	3-1608			CBB1	2-2531	
4E34	临	0-3357					275425
4E35	丵		1-1614				
4E36	丶	0-5628	0-4806			E-2122	216431
4E37	丷						
4E38	丸	0-4572	0-2061	0-9215	A459	1-443A	213037
4E39	丹	0-2104	0-3516	0-5101	A4A6	1-4465	213038
4E3A	为	0-4610					274951
4E3B	主	0-5487	0-2871	0-8111	A544	1-4564	213039
4E3C	丼		0-4807		C964	2-2144	2D3053
4E3D	丽	0-3286				E-2740	276256
4E3E	举	0-3057					275434
4E3F	丿	0-5615	0-4808			E-2123	216433
4E40	乀		1-1615				
4E41	乁		1-1616				
4E42	乂	3-1610	0-4809	0-7149	C940	2-2121	216434
4E43	乃	0-3643	0-3921	0-5012	A444	1-4425	21303A
4E44	乄		1-1617				
4E45	久	0-3035	0-2155	0-4689	A45B	1-443C	21303B
4E46	乆					E-2130	
4E47	乇	0-5617	1-1618		C947	2-2128	275644
4E48	么	0-3520			A45C	1-443D	276260
4E49	义	0-5069				E-212E	275242
4E4A	乊						
4E4B	之	0-5414	0-3923	0-8193	A4A7	1-4466	21303D
4E4C	乌	0-4658					27495D
4E4D	乍	0-5307	0-3867	0-6231	A545	1-4565	213041
4E4E	乎	0-2685	0-2435	0-9126	A547	1-4567	213040
4E4F	乏	0-2306	0-4319	0-8925	A546	1-4566	21303F
4E50	乐	0-3254					27454E
4E51	乑		1-1619				
4E52	乒	0-3825			A5E2	1-4724	213042
4E53	乓	0-3750			A5E3	1-4725	213043
4E54	乔	0-3939				E-2345	27366F
4E55	乕		0-7341				395643
4E56	乖	0-2552	0-4810	0-4650	A8C4	1-4B65	213044
4E57	乗		0-3072			E-2B22	2D3045
4E58	乘	0-1943	0-4811	0-6711	ADBC	1-537D	213045
4E59	乙	0-5050	0-1821	0-7564	A441	1-4422	213046
4E5A	乚		1-1620				
4E5B	乛						
4E5C	乜	0-5631	1-1621		C941	2-2122	21643C
4E5D	九	0-3037	0-2269	0-4690	A445	1-4426	213047
4E5E	乞	0-3882	0-2480	0-4387	A45E	1-443F	213049
4E5F	也	0-5018	0-4473	0-6905	A45D	1-443E	213048
4E60	习	0-4716					27524D
4E61	乡	0-4771					275C70
4E62	乢		0-5406			E-2146	695626
4E63	乣	3-3083	1-1622			E-2145	
4E64	乤						
4E65	乥						
4E66	书	0-4273					274355
4E67	乧			1-6174			
4E68	乨	5-1631	1-1623			E-2264	
4E69	乩	0-5632	1-1624		A5E4	1-4726	2D4F41
4E6A	乪						
4E6B	乫			0-4265			
4E6C	乬			1-5608			
4E6D	乭			0-5244			
4E6E	乮						
4E6F	乯						
4E70	买	0-3482					27597A
4E71	乱	0-3450	0-4580			E-2440	27304D
4E72	乲						
4E73	乳	0-4073	0-3893	0-7465	A8C5	1-4B66	21304B
4E74	乴		1-1625				
4E75	乵		1-1626				
4E76	乶			0-6067			
4E77	乷			0-6313			
4E78	乸						
4E79	乹		1-1627			E-2B23	33304C
4E7A	乺						
4E7B	乻						
4E7C	乼			1-7779			
4E7D	乽						
4E7E	乾	0-3912	0-2005	0-4375	B0AE	1-5871	21304C
4E7F	乿	5-1632	1-1628		D44B	2-334E	

4E8

	Char	G	J	K	B	C	A
0	亀		0-2121			E-396C	2D632D
1	乾					E-396E	39304C
2	亂	1-3450	0-4812	0-5315	B6C3	1-632A	21304D
3	亃	5-1634			DCB1	2-4156	
4	亄	5-1633			DCB2	2-4157	
5	亅	8-1591	0-4813			E-2124	216446
6	了	0-3343	0-4627	0-5485	A446	1-4427	274D73
7	亇					E-212D	
8	予	0-5172	0-4529	0-6988	A4A9	1-4468	27595E
9	争	0-5389	0-3372			E-2265	2D4A3B
A	亊		0-4815				4B3050
B	事	0-4234	0-2786	0-6232	A8C6	1-4B67	213050
C	二	0-2294	0-3883	0-7603	A447	1-4428	213051
D	亍	0-5601	1-1629		C948	2-2129	275747
E	于	0-5158	0-4818	0-7345	A45F	1-4440	213052
F	亏	0-3187		1-7314		E-2131	27564C

4E9

	Char	G	J	K	B	C	A
0	亐			0-7407			
1	云	0-5238	0-1730	0-7386	A4AA	1-4469	275F54
2	互	0-2705	0-2463	0-9127	A4AC	1-446B	213055
3	亓	0-5633			C951	2-2131	33332A
4	五	0-4669	0-2462	0-7173	A4AD	1-446C	213054
5	井	0-3014	0-1670	0-7944	A4AB	1-446A	213053
6	亖		1-1630				
7	亗		1-1631			E-216C	3F4629
8	亘	0-5608	0-4743	0-4870		E-2266	513057
9	亙		0-4742	1-5966	A5E5	1-4727	213057
A	亚	0-4939					273058
B	些	0-4809	0-2619	0-6233	A8C7	1-4B68	213059
C	亜		0-1601			E-2442	2D3058
D	亝		1-1632			E-2742	
E	亞	1-4939	0-4819	0-6812	A8C8	1-4B69	213058
F	亟	0-5629	0-4820	1-5941	AB45	1-4F67	21305A

4EA

	Char	G	J	K	B	C	A
0	亠	0-5779	0-4821				216450
1	亡	0-4586	0-4320	0-5644	A460	1-4441	21305B
2	亢	0-3126	0-4822	0-8981	A4AE	1-446D	216451
3	亣					E-2147	
4	交	0-2927	0-2482	0-4663	A5E6	1-4728	21305E
5	亥	0-2605	0-1671	0-9004	A5E8	1-472A	21305D
6	亦	0-5064	0-4382	0-7018	A5E7	1-4729	21305C
7	产	0-1890					274B7A
8	亨	0-2664	0-2192	0-9091	A6EB	1-486C	21305F
9	亩	0-3622					274C2D
A	亪						
B	享	0-4777	0-2193	0-9029	A8C9	1-4B6A	213060
C	京	0-3009	0-2194	0-4440	A8CA	1-4B6B	213061
D	亭	0-4504	0-3666	0-7945	AB46	1-4F68	213062
E	亮	0-3333	0-4628	0-5353	AB47	1-4F69	213063
F	亯		1-1633			E-2B26	333060

4EB

	Char	G	J	K	B	C	A
0	亰		0-4823			E-2B25	2D3061
1	亱					E-2B27	
2	亲	0-3955				E-2B24	27582C
3	亳	0-5781	0-4824	1-6517	ADBD	1-537E	216452
4	亴			1-7315			
5	亵	0-5784					275777
6	亶	3-1855	0-4825	0-5102	DCB3	2-4158	216455
7	亷					E-4033	
8	亸	8-1202					
9	亹	3-1858	1-1634	1-6485	F6D6	2-6D44	216458
A	人	0-4043	0-3145	0-7649	A448	1-4429	213064
B	亻	0-5673					
C	亼					E-2132	21645A
D	亽						
E	亾					E-2133	
F	亿	0-5058					27325A

4EC

	Char	G	J	K	B	C	A
0	什	0-4218	0-2926	0-6807	A4B0	1-446F	4B4B77
1	仁	0-4042	0-3146	0-7650	A4AF	1-446E	213066
2	仂	0-5676	0-4830		C952	2-2132	4B682E
3	仃	0-5674	1-1635		A4B1	1-4470	213068
4	仄	0-5638	0-4828	0-8617	A4B7	1-4476	213069
5	仅	0-2986				E-2149	273249
6	仆	0-3845	0-4829	1-6618	A4B2	1-4471	273255
7	仇	0-1980	0-2156	0-4691	A4B3	1-4472	21306C
8	仈	3-1660			C954	2-2134	216461
9	仉	0-5675			C953	2-2133	21645E
A	今	0-2981	0-2603	0-4849	A4B5	1-4474	213065
B	介	0-2973	0-1880	0-4331	A4B6	1-4475	21306D
C	仌	5-1728				E-214C	
D	仍	0-4052	0-4827	0-7704	A4B4	1-4473	21306B
E	从	0-2051	0-4826			E-214B	273D6C
F	仏		0-4209			E-214A	2D3132

4ED

	Char	G	J	K	B	C	A
0	仐		1-1636				
1	仑	0-3456					27314F
2	仒						
3	仓	0-1854					27316C
4	仔	0-5548	0-2738	0-7708	A54A	1-456A	213074
5	仕	0-4243	0-2737	0-6234	A54B	1-456B	213070
6	他	0-4391	0-3430	0-8666	A54C	1-456C	213071
7	仗	0-5344	0-4831	0-7760	A54D	1-456D	213075
8	付	0-2422	0-4153	0-6085	A549	1-4569	21306F
9	仙	0-4741	0-3271	0-6425	A550	1-4570	213076
A	仚	3-1657	1-1637		C96A	2-214A	
B	仛	5-1741	1-1638				
C	仜	5-1739			C966	2-2146	
D	仝	0-5758	0-0124	0-5246	C969	2-2149	2D3543
E	仞	0-5680	0-4832	1-7460	A551	1-4571	213072
F	仟	0-3910	0-4834	0-8421	A561	1-4623	2D3458

4EE

	Char	G	J	K	B	C	A
0	仠	5-1738	1-1639			E-216D	
1	仡	0-5678	1-1640	1-8511	C968	2-2148	21646B
2	仢	5-1742	1-1641				
3	代	0-2090	0-3469	0-5159	A54E	1-456E	213073
4	令	0-3378	0-4665	0-5421	A54F	1-456F	21306E
5	以	0-5052	0-1642	0-7604	A548	1-4568	213077
6	仦					E-2172	
7	仧					E-2170	
8	仨	0-5677	1-1642		C965	2-2145	216463
9	仩				C967	2-2147	
A	仪	0-5039					273259
B	仫	0-5679					70586F
C	们	0-3539					273173
D	仭		0-4833				4B3072
E	仮	5-1756	0-1830	1-5501		E-226F	4B3231
F	仯	5-1753	1-1643			E-2268	

4EF

	Char	G	J	K	B	C	A
0	仰	0-4986	0-2236	0-6870	A5F5	1-4737	213128
1	仱	3-1666	1-1644		C9B0	2-216F	
2	仲	0-5457	0-3571	0-8174	A5F2	1-4734	213124
3	仳	0-5682	1-1645	1-6675	A5F6	1-4738	213126
4	仴	5-1757			C9BA	2-2179	
5	仵	0-5685	1-1646	1-7203	C9AE	2-216D	216527
6	件	0-2894	0-2379	0-4376	A5F3	1-4735	213127
7	价	0-2859	0-4835	0-4332	C9B2	2-2171	27325D
8	仸	5-1755				E-226B	
9	仹	5-1746				E-2267	
A	仺					E-2276	
B	任	0-4046	0-3904	0-7682	A5F4	1-4736	21307C
C	仼					E-226E	
D	份	0-2361	1-1647		A5F7	1-4739	333D54
E	仾		1-1648				
F	仿	0-2334	1-1649	1-6536	A5E9	1-472B	213078

4F0

	Char	G	J	K	B	C	A
0	伀	3-1667	1-1650	1-7728	C9B1	2-2170	21652A
1	企	0-3883	0-2075	0-4874	A5F8	1-473A	213125
2	伂	5-1749	1-1651		C9B5	2-2174	
3	伃	3-1672	1-1652			E-226D	216475
4	伄	3-1671			C9B9	2-2178	
5	伅	5-1752			C9B6	2-2175	
6	伆	3-1668				E-226C	
7	伇	5-1759				E-2274	216528
8	伈	3-1670	1-1653		C9B3	2-2172	216472
9	伉	0-5688	0-4836	0-8982	A5EA	1-472C	213079
A	伊	0-5033	0-1643	0-7605	A5EC	1-472E	21307D
B	伋	3-1661	1-1654	0-4863	A5F9	1-473B	21652C
C	伌		1-1655				
D	伍	0-4673	0-2464	0-7174	A5EE	1-4730	393054
E	伎	0-2831	0-2076	0-4875	C9AB	2-216A	216473
F	伏	0-2392	0-4190	0-6049	A5F1	1-4733	213123

4F1

	Char	G	J	K	B	C	A
0	伐	0-2305	0-4018	0-5973	A5EF	1-4731	213122
1	休	0-4861	0-2157	0-9344	A5F0	1-4732	213121
2	伒		1-1656		C9BB	2-217A	
3	伓	5-1750			C9B8	2-2177	
4	伔				C9AF	2-216E	
5	伕	5-1747	1-1657		A5ED	1-472F	21307E
6	伖		1-1658			E-2270	
7	众	0-5458	1-1659			E-2277	274D56
8	优	0-5137			C9AC	2-216B	273266
9	伙	0-2779	1-1660		A5EB	1-472D	273923
A	会	0-2765	0-1881			E-2275	27435A
B	伛	0-5681					27677C
C	伜		0-4871			E-2273	276649
D	伝	5-1748	0-3733		C9B4	2-2173	393246
E	伞	0-4101					273244
F	伟	0-4616					273233

4F2

	Char	G	J	K	B	C	A
0	传	0-2011					273246
1	伡	8-1404					
2	伢	0-5683			C9B7	2-2176	21647C
3	伣	8-9013					
4	伤	0-4143					27324C
5	伥	0-5686					273226
6	伦	0-3455					27322D
7	伧	0-5687					273243
8	伨	5-1758				E-2272	
9	伩	5-1760					
A	伪	0-4617					273256
B	伫	0-5689					4B312D
C	伬				C9AD	2-216C	
D	伭	3-1681			CA66	2-2328	
E	伮		1-1661				
F	伯	0-1814	0-3976	0-5955	A742	1-4924	213141

4F3

	Char	G	J	K	B	C	A
0	估	0-2532	0-4838	1-5674	A6F4	1-4875	213134
1	伱		1-1662			E-2450	
2	伲	0-5703				E-2448	2D3140
3	伳	5-1766	1-1664		CA67	2-2329	
4	伴	0-1673	0-4028	0-5865	A6F1	1-4872	21312C
5	伵	5-1774	1-1665			E-244F	
6	伶	0-3370	0-4666	0-5422	A744	1-4926	213144
7	伷	5-1772	1-1666			E-2446	
8	伸	0-4176	0-3113	0-6763	A6F9	1-487A	21313A
9	伹	5-1771	1-1667			E-2445	
A	伺	0-4337	0-2739	0-6235	A6F8	1-4879	21312F
B	伻	5-1768	1-1668		CA5B	2-227B	216532
C	似	0-4338	0-2787	0-6236	A6FC	1-487D	21313D
D	伽	0-5704	0-1832	0-4201	A6F7	1-4878	213137
E	伾	3-1676	1-1669		CA60	2-2322	21653F
F	伿	5-1773			CA68	2-232A	

4F4

	Char	G	J	K	B	C	A
0	佀		1-1670			E-244E	
1	佁	3-1688			CA64	2-2326	
2	佂	5-1764	1-1671	1-7650		E-2449	
3	佃	0-2172	0-3649	0-7876	A6FA	1-487B	21313B
4	佄	5-1765				E-244B	
5	佅	3-1673				E-2443	
6	但	0-2111	0-3502	0-5103	A6FD	1-487E	213139
7	佇	1-5689	0-4842	0-7823	A6EE	1-486F	21312D
8	佈		1-1672	0-8847	A747	1-4929	213138
9	佉	3-1675	1-1673	1-5835	CA5D	2-227D	21653A
A	佊	3-1686				E-2444	
B	佋	5-1776	1-1674	1-6868		E-244C	
C	佌	3-1693	1-1675		CBBD	2-253D	21656C
D	位	0-4627	0-1644	0-7440	A6EC	1-486D	21312B
E	低	0-2145	0-3667	0-7824	A743	1-4925	213142
F	住	0-5501	0-2927	0-8112	A6ED	1-486E	21312A

4F5

	Char	G	J	K	B	C	A
0	佐	0-5584	0-2620	0-8105	A6F5	1-4876	213135
1	佑	0-5151	0-4504	0-7346	A6F6	1-4877	213136
2	佒	3-1678	1-1676		CA62	2-2324	
3	体	0-4469	0-3446	1-6645	CA5E	2-227E	27615A
4	佔		1-1677	1-7633	A6FB	1-487C	21313C
5	何	0-2646	0-1831	0-8928	A6F3	1-4874	213133
6	佖	3-1685	1-1678	1-8257	CA5A	2-227A	
7	佗	0-5702	0-4841	1-8112	A6EF	1-4870	21312E
8	佘	0-5760	1-1679		CA65	2-2327	216536
9	余	0-5164	0-4530	0-6989	A745	1-4927	276076
A	佚	0-5693	0-4837	0-7674	A748	1-492A	21654E
B	佛	0-2380	0-4839	0-6154	A6F2	1-4873	213132
C	作	0-5587	0-2678	0-7734	A740	1-4922	21313F
D	佝	0-5694	0-4840	1-5836	A746	1-4928	213143
E	佞	0-5690	0-5304	1-6031	A6F0	1-4871	213130
F	佟	0-5701	1-1680	1-8169	CA63	2-2325	21654F

4F6

	Char	G	J	K	B	C	A
0	你	0-3667	1-1663		A741	1-4923	213140
1	佡	3-1679			CA69	2-232B	
2	佢	3-1662			CA5C	2-227C	216537
3	佣	0-5122	1-1681		A6FE	1-4921	21313E
4	佤	0-5684			CA5F	2-2321	216539
5	佥	0-5761					276775
6	佦					E-6448	216540
7	佧	0-5691			CA61	2-2323	216544
8	佨					E-6449	21654D
9	佩	0-3769	0-4848	0-8805	A8D8	1-4B79	213154
A	佪	5-1788	1-1682	1-8443	CBBF	2-253F	
B	佫	3-1713			CBCB	2-254B	
C	佬	0-3248	1-1683		A8D0	1-4B71	21314D
D	佭	5-1789				E-2747	
E	佮	3-1709	1-1684		CBCC	2-254C	
F	佯	0-4980	0-4851	0-6926	A8CB	1-4B6C	213146

4F7

	Char	G	J	K	B	C	A
0	佰	0-1659	0-4849	0-5956	A8D5	1-4B76	2D4C7E
1	佱		1-1685				
2	佲	5-1790				E-274F	
3	佳	0-2849	0-1834	0-4202	A8CE	1-4B6F	213149
4	佴	0-5706			CBB9	2-2539	216561
5	併		0-4227		A8D6	1-4B77	213147
6	佶	0-5705	0-4843	0-4945	CBB8	2-2538	216562
7	佷	5-1792	1-1686		CBBC	2-253C	
8	佸	3-1705	1-1687	1-5777	CBC3	2-2543	216573
9	佹	3-1710	1-1688	1-5908	CBC1	2-2541	216570
A	佺	3-1708	1-1689	0-7877	A8DE	1-4C21	21657B
B	佻	0-5712	0-4847	1-7686	A8D9	1-4B7A	213152
C	佼	0-5714	0-2483	1-5816	CBB3	2-2533	216557
D	佽	3-1715	1-1690	1-7832	CBB5	2-2535	21655C
E	佾	0-5711	1-1691	0-7675	A8DB	1-4B7C	213156
F	使	0-4225	0-2740	0-6237	A8CF	1-4B70	21314A

4F8

	Char	G	J	K	B	C	A
0	侀	5-1781			CBB6	2-2536	216560
1	侁	3-1703	1-1692	0-6764	CBC2	2-2542	216572
2	侂	3-1714	1-1693		CBC9	2-2549	216556
3	侃	0-5709	0-2006	0-4241	A8D4	1-4B75	213151
4	侄	0-5422	1-1694	0-8273	CBBB	2-253B	2D396E
5	侅	3-1716	1-1701		CBB4	2-2534	
6	來	1-3220	0-4852	0-5346	A8D3	1-4B74	21314C
7	侇	3-1691			CBB7	2-2537	
8	侈	0-1962	0-4844	0-8622	A8D7	1-4B78	213153
9	侉	0-5708	1-1702	1-5744	CBBA	2-253A	4B5861
A	侊	3-1694	1-1703	0-4634		E-2744	
B	例	0-3293	0-4667	0-5439	A8D2	1-4B73	21314E
C	侌		1-1704			E-2751	
D	侍	0-4244	0-2788	0-6720	A8CD	1-4B6E	213148
E	侎		1-1705			E-2748	
F	侏	0-5710	0-4845	0-8113	A8DC	1-4B7D	213155

4F9

	Char	G	J	K	B	C	A
0	侐	3-1706	1-1706		CBC4	2-2544	216577
1	侑	0-5707	0-4850	0-7466	A8DD	1-4B7E	216566
2	侒	5-1791	1-1707		CBC8	2-2548	21655B
3	侓		1-1708			E-2743	
4	侔	0-5716	1-1709	1-6441	CBC6	2-2546	21656E
5	侕				CBCA	2-254A	216567
6	侖	1-3456	0-4853	0-5534	A8DA	1-4B7B	21314F
7	侗	0-2217	1-1710	1-6149	CBBE	2-253E	21656D
8	侘	3-1717	0-4846	0-8307	CBB2	2-2532	21655A
9	侙	3-1689	1-1711				
A	侚	3-1711	1-1712	1-6937	CBC0	2-2540	216571
B	供	0-2509	0-2201	0-4574	A8D1	1-4B72	21314B
C	侜	3-1707		1-7743	CBC5	2-2545	216576
D	依	0-5032	0-1645	0-7578	A8CC	1-4B6D	213145
E	侞	3-1719	1-1713		CBC7	2-2547	
F	侟	5-1783	1-1714			E-274C	

4FA

	Char	G	J	K	B	C	A
0	侠	0-4732	0-2202			E-2749	27315D
1	価		0-1833			E-274B	33325D
2	侢	5-1782				E-274A	216564
3	侣	0-3434				E-274D	2D315F
4	侤						
5	侥	0-2936					273251
6	侦	0-5376					273238
7	侧	0-1864					273235
8	侨	0-3940					273258
9	侩	0-3175					273260
A	侪	0-5713					276871
B	侫		0-5305				4B3130
C	侬	0-5715					27325E
D	侭		0-4389				2D3263
E	侮	0-4674	0-4178	0-5718	AB56	1-4F78	213166
F	侯	0-2678	0-2484	0-9305	AB4A	1-4F6C	21315A

4FB

	Char	G	J	K	B	C	A
0	侰	5-1809				E-2B2D	
1	侱	3-1731				E-2B2E	
2	侲	3-1727	1-1715	1-7811	CDE0	2-2922	
3	侳	3-1734			CDE8	2-292A	
4	侴	3-1893				E-2B36	
5	侵	0-3954	0-3115	0-8653	AB49	1-4F6B	213159
6	侶		0-4623	0-5366	AB51	1-4F73	21315F
7	侷		1-1716		AB5D	1-5021	216626
8	侸	3-1726				E-2B2C	
9	侹	3-1704	1-1717		CDEE	2-2930	216643
A	侺	5-1801			CDEC	2-292E	
B	侻	3-1737	1-1718	1-8139	CDE7	2-2929	
C	侼	3-1724	1-1719				
D	侽		1-1720			E-6263	
E	侾		1-1721			E-2B2B	
F	便	0-1767	0-4256	0-8821	AB4B	1-4F6D	21315B

4FC

	Char	G	J	K	B	C	A
0	俀	5-1805	1-1722		CDED	2-292F	
1	俁		1-1723	1-7316	CDE3	2-2925	216637
2	係	1-8882	0-2324	0-4485	AB59	1-4F7B	213169
3	促	0-2057	0-3405	0-8521	AB50	1-4F72	213162
4	俄	0-2277	0-1868	0-6813	AB58	1-4F7A	213168
5	俅	0-5720	1-1724	1-5837	CDDE	2-287E	216627
6	俆	5-1804	1-1725			E-2B32	21663E
7	俇	3-1735			CDEA	2-292C	
8	俈	5-1802	1-1726			E-2B2F	
9	俉	3-1725	1-1727	0-7175	CDE1	2-2923	216629
A	俊	0-3101	0-2951	0-8153	AB54	1-4F76	213165
B	俋	3-1732	1-1728		CDE2	2-2924	
C	俌	5-1793	1-1729	1-6590		E-2B33	
D	俍	3-1740	1-1730		CDDD	2-287D	21657C
E	俎	0-5762	0-4857	0-8027	AB5B	1-4F7D	21316A
F	俏	0-3946	1-1731	1-6869	AB4E	1-4F70	21315E

4FD

	Char	G	J	K	B	C	A
0	俐	0-3294	0-4862	1-6356	AB57	1-4F79	213167
1	俑	0-5724	0-4860	0-7321	AB4D	1-4F6F	213158
2	俒	5-1808	1-1732			E-2B28	
3	俓	3-1687		0-4441	CDDF	2-2921	
4	俔	3-1663	0-4855	0-9053	CDE4	2-2926	216635
5	俕	3-1739				E-2B29	
6	俖	5-1794			CDEB	2-292D	
7	俗	0-4355	0-3415	0-6552	AB55	1-4F77	21316B
8	俘	0-2393	0-4858	1-6619	AB52	1-4F74	213163
9	俙	3-1733			CDE6	2-2928	
A	俚	0-5721	0-4861	0-5554	AB5A	1-4F7C	213160
B	俛		0-4859	1-6433	CDE9	2-292B	21663B
C	俜	0-5723	1-1733		CDE5	2-2927	216633
D	保	0-1703	0-4261	0-6033	AB4F	1-4F71	213161
E	俞	0-5165			AB5C	1-4F7E	21315C
F	俟	0-5725	0-4856	0-6238	AB53	1-4F75	213164

4FE

	Char	G	J	K	B	C	A
0	俠	1-4732	1-1734	0-9079	AB4C	1-4F6E	21315D
1	信	0-4837	0-3114	0-6765	AB48	1-4F6A	213157
2	俢		1-1735				
3	俣	0-5722	0-4383	1-7204		E-2B35	4B6637
4	俤	3-1738	0-4863				216622
5	俥	5-1751	0-4864			E-2B34	21662A
6	俦	0-5717					273265
7	俧					E-644A	21662C
8	俨	0-5718					27326B
9	俩	0-3309					273179
A	俪	0-5719					27326A
B	俫	8-9018					
C	俬				CDEF	2-2931	
D	俭	0-2883					273261
E	修	0-4862	0-2904	0-6583	ADD7	1-543A	213227
F	俯	0-2409	0-4877	0-6086	ADC1	1-5424	21316F

4FF

	Char	G	J	K	B	C	A
0	俰	5-1822	1-1736	1-8412		E-2F48	
1	俱	0-3067		0-4692	ADD1	1-5434	213222
2	俲		1-1737			E-2F4D	394243
3	俳	0-5729	0-3948	0-5936	ADD6	1-5439	213228
4	俴	3-1674		1-7916	D0D0	2-2D71	216659
5	俵	3-1741	0-4122	0-8881	D0CF	2-2D70	216652
6	俶	3-1749	0-4872	1-6930	D0D4	2-2D75	216661
7	俷	5-1826			D0D5	2-2D76	
8	俸	0-5726	0-4280	0-6068	ADC4	1-5427	213174
9	俹	3-1690				E-2F44	
A	俺	0-1619	0-1822	0-6979	ADCD	1-5430	21317E
B	俻					E-2F58	333240
C	俼		1-1738			E-2F4C	
D	俽	5-1823	1-1739			E-2F56	
E	俾	0-5734	0-4876	1-6676	ADDA	1-543D	21322B
F	俿	5-1815	1-1740			E-2F46	

	500	502	504	506
0	倀 G 1-5686 J 1-1741 K 1-7869 B ADCE C 1-5431 A 213226	倠 G 3-1750 J K B D0D8 C 2-2D79 A	偀 G 5-1812 J 1-1763 K B D463 C 2-3366 A	偠 G 5-1834 J 1-1777 K 1-7280 B D450 C 2-3353 A
1	倁 G J 1-1742 K B C A	倡 G 0-1911 J 0-4873 K 0-8359 B ADD2 C 1-5435 A 213223	偁 G 5-1841 J 1-1764 K B D457 C 2-335A A 216741	偡 G 3-1762 J K B D44E C 2-3351 A
2	倂 G J K 0-6017 B C E-2F4B A 2D3147	倢 G 3-1748 J 1-1756 K 1-7952 B D0CC C 2-2D6D A 21664E	偂 G J 1-1765 K B C E-343C A	偢 G 3-1774 J 1-1778 K 1-7972 B D45A C 2-335D A
3	倃 G J K B C E-2F49 A 21322A	倣 G J 0-4279 K 0-5907 B ADC0 C 1-5423 A 3F3078	偃 G 0-5740 J 0-4880 K 0-6971 B B0B3 C 1-5876 A 213234	偣 G 5-1843 J 1-1779 K B D460 C 2-3363 A
4	倄 G 3-1751 J 1-1743 K B C E-2F47 A	値 G J 0-3545 K 0-8623 B C E-2F4E A 21317C	偄 G 3-1765 J K 1-6017 B C E-343F A	偤 G 5-1845 J K B D461 C 2-3364 A
5	倅 G 3-1755 J 0-4870 K 1-6948 B D0C9 C 2-2D6A A 216649	倥 G 0-5737 J 0-4869 K 1-5732 B ADC3 C 1-5426 A 213172	偅 G 5-1837 J 1-1766 K B D45C C 2-335F A	健 G 0-2901 J 0-2382 K 0-4377 B B0B7 C 1-587A A 213230
6	倆 G 1-3309 J 0-4879 K 0-5354 B ADC7 C 1-542A A 213179	倦 G 0-3075 J 0-2381 K 0-4770 B ADC2 C 1-5425 A 213170	偆 G 3-1761 J 1-1767 K B D462 C 2-3365 A	偦 G 5-1848 J 1-1780 K B C E-3440 A
7	倇 G 3-1759 J 1-1744 K B D0CA C 2-2D6B A 21664C	倧 G 3-1758 J 1-1757 K 0-8082 B D0D9 C 2-2D7A A	假 G 0-2857 J 0-4881 K 0-4203 B B0B2 C 1-5875 A 213231	偧 G 5-1835 J 1-1781 K B C A
8	倈 G 3-1728 J K B C E-2F4F A 2D314C	倨 G 0-5738 J 0-4866 K 0-4358 B ADD0 C 1-5433 A 213175	偈 G 0-5742 J 0-4885 K 0-4407 B D455 C 2-3358 A 216739	偨 G 3-1787 J K B D85B C 2-3A3F A
9	倉 G 1-1854 J 0-3350 K 0-8358 B ADDC C 1-543F A 21316C	倩 G 0-5727 J 0-4874 K 1-7917 B ADC5 C 1-5428 A 213178	偉 G 1-4616 J 0-1646 K 0-7441 B B0B6 C 1-5879 A 213233	偩 G 3-1712 J K B D45E C 2-3361 A
A	倊 G J 1-1745 K B C A	倪 G 0-3663 J 0-4868 K 0-7150 B ADD9 C 1-543C A 21322C	偊 G 3-1775 J 1-1768 K 1-7317 B D459 C 2-335C A	偪 G J 1-1782 K 1-8269 B D44D C 2-3350 A 21672A
B	個 G 1-2486 J 0-2436 K 0-4333 B ADD3 C 1-5436 A 213224	倫 G 1-3455 J 0-4649 K 0-5535 B ADDB C 1-543E A 21322D	偋 G 5-1847 J K B D452 C 2-3355 A	偫 G 3-1776 J K B D45F C 2-3362 A 21674D
C	倌 G 0-5736 J 1-1746 K B ADBE C 1-5421 A 213171	倬 G 0-5730 J 0-4875 K 0-8680 B D0D3 C 2-2D74 A 216666	偌 G 0-5728 J 1-1769 K B B0B4 C 1-5877 A 213239	偬 G 0-5744 J 0-4888 K B C E-344B A 21674A
D	倍 G 0-1722 J 0-3960 K 0-5935 B ADBF C 1-5422 A 21316E	倭 G 0-5733 J 0-4733 K 0-7262 B ADD8 C 1-543B A 213229	偍 G 3-1767 J K B D456 C 2-3359 A	偭 G 3-1764 J 1-1783 K B B0C1 C 1-5926 A 216731
E	倎 G 5-1818 J 1-1747 K B D0DD C 2-2D7E A	倮 G 0-5732 J 1-1758 K 1-6183 B C E-2F51 A 21665E	偎 G 0-5743 J 1-1770 K 1-7271 B B0B9 C 1-587C A 213237	偮 G 3-1768 J K B D464 C 2-3367 A
F	倏 G 0-5731 J 0-6439 K 1-6931 B B0BF C 1-5924 A 21323B	倯 G 5-1813 J K B D0DB C 2-2D7C A	偏 G 0-3811 J 0-4248 K 0-8822 B B0BE C 1-5923 A 21322F	偯 G 3-1777 J K B B0C0 C 1-5925 A 216722

	501	503	505	507
0	倐 G J 1-1748 K B C E-2F53 A 216669	倰 G 3-1742 J 1-1759 K 1-6354 B D0CD C 2-2D6E A	偐 G 5-1844 J 0-4884 K B C E-3444 A 216723	偰 G 5-1831 J 1-1784 K 1-6840 B D44C C 2-334F A 216725
1	們 G 1-3539 J 0-4878 K 0-5790 B ADCC C 1-542F A 213173	倱 G 5-1816 J K B D0DC C 2-2D7D A	偑 G 3-1669 J 1-1771 K B D467 C 2-336A A	偱 G J 1-1785 K B C E-3443 A
2	倒 G 0-2125 J 0-3761 K 0-5178 B ADCB C 1-542E A 21317B	倲 G 3-1677 J 1-1760 K B C E-2F43 A	偒 G 5-1745 J 1-1772 K B C E-3441 A	偲 G 3-1770 J 0-2837 K 1-6957 B D454 C 2-3357 A 21673C
3	倓 G 3-1757 J 1-1749 K B D0CB C 2-2D6C A 21664D	倳 G 3-1744 J 1-1761 K B D0D1 C 2-2D72 A	偓 G 3-1782 J 1-1773 K 1-7013 B D451 C 2-3354 A 216729	偳 G 3-1772 J K B D465 C 2-3368 A
4	倔 G 0-3083 J 0-4867 K 1-5891 B ADCF C 1-5432 A 213176	倴 G 3-1747 J K B C A	偔 G 3-1771 J K B C E-3442 A	側 G 1-1864 J 0-3406 K 0-8616 B B0BC C 1-5921 A 213235
5	倕 G 5-1821 J K B D45B C 2-335E A 216746	倵 G 5-1810 J 1-1762 K B D0DA C 2-2D7B A	偕 G 0-5741 J 0-4883 K 0-9005 B B0BA C 1-587D A 21323A	偵 G 1-5376 J 0-3669 K 0-7947 B B0BB C 1-587E A 213238
6	倖 G J 0-2486 K 0-9024 B ADC6 C 1-5429 A 213177	倶 G J 0-2270 K B C E-2F50 A	偖 G J 0-4887 K 1-7833 B C E-2F57 A 21672C	偶 G 0-3728 J 0-2286 K 0-7347 B B0B8 C 1-587B A 213236
7	倗 G 3-1753 J 1-1750 K B D0D6 C 2-2D77 A	倷 G 3-1746 J K B D0D2 C 2-2D73 A 21665B	偗 G J 1-1774 K B D466 C 2-3369 A	偷 G 0-4521 J K B B0BD C 1-5922 A 21323C
8	倘 G 0-4440 J 1-1751 K 1-6094 B ADD5 C 1-5438 A 213221	倸 G J K B C E-2F54 A	偘 G J K 1-5522 B C E-3447 A 21673B	偸 G J 0-4889 K 0-8762 B C E-344C A
9	候 G 0-2682 J 0-2485 K 0-9306 B ADD4 C 1-5437 A 213225	倹 G J 0-2380 K B C E-2F55 A 2D3261	偙 G 3-1779 J 1-1775 K B C E-343D A	偹 G J K B C E-344A A
A	倚 G 0-5048 J 0-4865 K 0-7579 B ADCA C 1-542D A 21317D	债 G 0-5314 J K B C A 273247	做 G 0-5586 J 0-4886 K 0-8114 B B0B5 C 1-5878 A 213232	偺 G J K B B0AF C 1-5872 A 216748
B	倛 G 5-1811 J 1-1752 K B D0CE C 2-2D6F A	倻 G 3-1743 J 1-1786 K 0-6906 B C A	偛 G 3-1773 J K B D458 C 2-335B A	偻 G 0-5745 J K B C E-3445 A 276822
C	倜 G 0-5735 J 1-1753 K 0-8406 B D0D7 C 2-2D78 A 216662	值 G 0-5421 J K B ADC8 C 1-542B A 4B317C	停 G 0-4503 J 0-3668 K 0-7946 B B0B1 C 1-5874 A 21322E	偼 G J K B C E-3446 A
D	倝 G 5-8327 J 1-1754 K B C E-2F45 A	倽 G 5-1825 J K B C A 216679	偝 G 5-1836 J K B D453 C 2-3356 A 216738	偽 G J 0-2122 K B B0B0 C 1-5873 A 213256
E	倞 G 3-1754 J 1-1755 K 0-4442 B D0C8 C 2-2D69 A 216646	倾 G 0-3967 J K B C A 27324A	偞 G 3-1763 J K B D44F C 2-3352 A	偾 G 0-5739 J K B C A 276842
F	借 G 0-2972 J 0-2858 K 0-8308 B ADC9 C 1-542C A 27562E	倿 G J K B C E-644B A 216648	偟 G 5-1839 J 1-1776 K B D45D C 2-3360 A 21674B	偿 G 0-1905 J K B C A 273267

508

	Char	G	J	K	B	C	A
0	傀	0-3194	0-4890	0-4651	B3C8	1-5E2E	213242
1	傁	5-1838	1-1787			E-3975	
2	傂	5-1856			D85E	2-3A42	
3	傃	3-1783	1-1788		D857	2-3A3B	
4	傄	3-1786	1-1789				
5	傅	0-2421	0-4892	0-6087	B3C5	1-5E2B	21323F
6	傆	5-1854	1-1790				
7	傇	5-1832			D85F	2-3A43	
8	傈	0-3292				E-3971	21675C
9	傉	3-1785				E-3972	
A	傊		1-1791				
B	傋	3-1784		1-5555	D855	2-3A39	
C	傌				D858	2-3A3C	21675A
D	傍	0-1688	0-4321	0-5908	B3C4	1-5E2A	21323D
E	傎	5-1853	1-1792		D859	2-3A3D	216762
F	傏	5-1862	1-1793			E-396F	

50A

	Char	G	J	K	B	C	A
0	傠	3-1684	1-1809				
1	傡		1-1810				
2	傢	1-8833	1-1811	1-5502	B3C3	1-5E29	21323E
3	傣	0-2086			D856	2-3A3A	216757
4	傤	8-1407					
5	傥	0-5746					276948
6	傦					E-644D	216767
7	傧	0-5747					273262
8	储	0-2002					273269
9	傩	0-5748					276944
A	傪	3-1760	1-1812			E-4039	
B	傫	3-1808				E-403C	
C	催	0-2063	0-2637	0-8542	B6CA	1-6331	21324B
D	傭	1-5122	0-4535	0-7322	B6C4	1-632B	213245
E	傮	3-1804		1-7687	DCB7	2-415C	
F	傯		1-1813		B6CD	1-6334	21324D

50C

	Char	G	J	K	B	C	A
0	僀	5-1833	1-1818				
1	僁	3-1810			DCBE	2-4163	
2	僂	1-5745	0-4904	1-6332	DCBC	2-4161	216822
3	僃		1-1819			E-403D	
4	僄	3-1805	1-1820	1-8236	DCB8	2-415D	
5	僅	1-2986	0-2247	0-4833	B6C8	1-632F	213249
6	僆	3-1729			DCB6	2-415B	
7	僇	3-1815	1-1821		B6CE	1-6335	216771
8	僈	3-1806			DCBB	2-4160	
9	僉	1-5761	0-4901	0-8450	DCC2	2-4167	216775
A	僊		0-4902	0-6426	DCB9	2-415E	21677B
B	僋	3-1752			DCC1	2-4166	
C	僌	5-1814	1-1822			E-4036	
D	働	8-1290	0-3815			E-403E	21682E
E	僎	3-1826	1-1823		B9B6	1-677C	21683B
F	像	0-4781	0-3392	0-6332	B9B3	1-6779	213257

50E

	Char	G	J	K	B	C	A
0	僠				E0FE	2-4926	
1	僡	5-1873				E-4570	
2	僢	5-1879	1-1831	1-7918		E-4575	
3	僣		0-4909		E0FD	2-4925	2D3253
4	僤	3-1756	1-1832		E0F8	2-487E	
5	僥	1-2936	0-4907	0-7273	B9AE	1-6774	213251
6	僦	0-5754	1-1833	1-8027	E0F0	2-4876	216835
7	僧	0-4114	0-3346	0-6712	B9AC	1-6772	21324E
8	僨	1-5739	1-1834		E0F3	2-4879	216842
9	僩	3-1736	1-1835	1-8284	B9B7	1-677D	
A	僪	3-1828			E0F6	2-487C	
B	僫	5-1852				E-4571	
C	僬	0-5753		1-7973	E0FA	2-4922	216855
D	僭	0-5752	0-4908	0-8348	B9B0	1-6776	213253
E	僮	0-5755	0-4910	1-6150	B9AD	1-6773	21324F
F	僯	3-1822	1-1836		E0FC	2-4924	216834

509

	Char	G	J	K	B	C	A
0	傐		1-1794				
1	傑	8-1289	0-2370	0-4388	B3C7	1-5E2D	213241
2	傒	5-1858	1-1801	1-8369	D85D	2-3A41	21676A
3	傓	5-1863	1-1802				
4	傔	3-1794	1-1803	1-5633	D853	2-3A37	21674E
5	傕	3-1802			D852	2-3A36	216764
6	傖	1-5687	1-1804	1-7870	B3C9	1-5E2F	213243
7	傗	3-1793				E-3970	
8	傘	1-4101	0-2717	0-6301	B3CA	1-5E30	213244
9	備	1-1724	0-4087	0-6165	B3C6	1-5E2C	213240
A	傚		0-4891	1-8456	B3CB	1-5E31	216753
B	傛	3-1801	1-1805	1-7304	D851	2-3A35	216752
C	傜	5-1857	1-1806		D85C	2-3A40	21676C
D	傝	3-1791		1-8143	D85A	2-3A3E	
E	傞	3-1781	1-1807	1-6741	D854	2-3A38	216750
F	傟	5-1859	1-1808				

50B

	Char	G	J	K	B	C	A
0	傰	3-1809	1-1814		DCBD	2-4162	
1	傱	3-1665			DCC0	2-4165	
2	傲	0-1633	0-4894	0-7176	B6C6	1-632D	213248
3	傳	1-2011	0-4903	0-7878	B6C7	1-632E	213246
4	傴	1-5681	0-4893	1-5838	DCBA	2-415F	21677C
5	債	1-5314	0-2636	0-8380	B6C5	1-632C	213247
6	傶	5-1867			DCC3	2-4168	
7	傷	1-4143	0-2993	0-6331	B6CB	1-6332	21324C
8	傸	5-1869			DCC4	2-4169	
9	傹	3-1812	1-1815			E-403A	
A	傺	0-5749	1-1816		DCBF	2-4164	21682C
B	傻	0-4121			B6CC	1-6333	21325F
C	傼					E-4037	
D	傽	3-1811	1-1817	1-7530	DCB4	2-4159	
E	傾	1-3967	0-2325	0-4443	B6C9	1-6330	21324A
F	傿	3-1803		1-7111	DCB5	2-415A	

50D

	Char	G	J	K	B	C	A
0	僐	5-1881	1-1824			E-456B	
1	僑	1-3940	0-2203	0-4664	B9B4	1-677A	213258
2	僒	3-1824				E-634C	
3	僓	3-1769	1-1825		E0F9	2-4921	
4	僔	3-1823	1-1826		E0F1	2-4877	216832
5	僕	1-3845	0-4345	0-6050	B9B2	1-6778	213255
6	僖	0-5750	0-4905	0-9374	B9AF	1-6775	213252
7	僗	3-1723			E0F2	2-4878	
8	僘		1-1827			E-456E	
9	僙	5-1865				E-456C	216846
A	僚	0-3337	0-4629	0-5486	B9B1	1-6777	213254
B	僛	3-1818		1-5968	E0F5	2-487B	
C	僜	3-1827	1-1828			E-456D	
D	僝	3-1825	1-1829		E0F7	2-487D	21683C
E	僞	1-4617	0-4906	0-7442		E-4576	
F	僟		1-1830			E-634D	

50F

	Char	G	J	K	B	C	A
0	僰	3-1658			E0FB	2-4923	216844
1	僱		1-1837		B9B5	1-677B	213250
2	僲		1-1849				
3	僳	0-4359			E0F4	2-487A	216841
4	僴					E-4574	21683A
5	僵	0-2909	0-4912	1-5556	BBF8	1-6C23	21325C
6	僶	5-1819	1-1838		E4EC	2-4F54	
7	僷					E-4B29	
8	僸	3-1830			E4E9	2-4F51	
9	價	1-2859	0-4911	0-4204	BBF9	1-6C24	21325D
A	僺		1-1839				
B	僻	0-3807	0-4240	0-5988	BBF7	1-6C22	21325B
C	僼	5-1886				E-4B2B	216861
D	僽	3-1832			E4F0	2-4F58	21686A
E	僾	3-1792	1-1840	1-7052	E4ED	2-4F55	216868
F	僿	3-1833		0-6239	E4E6	2-4F4E	

510

	Char	G	J	K	B	C	A
0	儀	1-5039	0-2123	0-7580	BBF6	1-6C21	213259
1	儁		0-4914	0-8154		E-4B2D	21686D
2	儂	1-5715	0-4915	1-6041	BBFA	1-6C25	21325E
3	儃	5-1888	1-1841	1-7919	E4E7	2-4F4F	
4	億	1-5058	0-1815	0-6966	BBF5	1-6B7E	21325A
5	儅	3-1701			BBFD	1-6C28	21685F
6	儆	0-5751	1-1842	0-4444	E4EA	2-4F52	216865
7	儇	0-5756	1-1843	1-8343	E4EB	2-4F53	216866
8	儈	1-3175	1-1844		BBFB	1-6C26	213260
9	儉	1-2883	0-4913	0-4391	BBFC	1-6C27	213261
A	儊				E4F1	2-4F59	
B	儋	0-5757	1-1845	1-6082	E4EE	2-4F56	216869
C	儌		1-1846		E4EF	2-4F57	2D3251
D	儍	5-1887	1-1847			E-4B2C	
E	儎	5-1850	1-1848			E-4B27	21685B
F	儏					E-644E	216867

511

	Char	G	J	K	B	C	A
0	儐	1-5747	1-1850	1-6724	BEAA	1-7033	213262
1	儑	3-1834			E8F8	2-5643	
2	儒	0-4069	0-2884	0-7467	BEA7	1-7030	213264
3	儓	5-1890		1-6117	E8F5	2-5640	216872
4	儔	1-5717	0-4918	1-7744	BEA9	1-7032	213265
5	儕	1-5713	0-4917	1-7669	BEAB	1-7034	216871
6	儖		0-4916			E-5031	695130
7	儗		1-1851	1-7436	E8F6	2-5641	2D4228
8	儘	1-8837	0-4854	1-7812	BEA8	1-7031	213263
9	儙		1-1852				
A	儚	3-1829	0-4919	1-6427	E8F7	2-5642	216878
B	儛	5-1893	1-1853	1-6472		E-5035	
C	儜	3-1683	1-1854	1-6032	E8F4	2-563F	
D	儝		1-1855			E-5030	
E	儞		1-1856			E-5034	2D3944
F	償	1-1905	0-2994	0-6333	C076	1-7341	213267

512

	Char	G	J	K	B	C	A
0	儠	3-1839			ECBD	2-5C49	
1	儡	0-3260	0-4920	0-5477	C077	1-7342	213268
2	儢	3-1788		1-6227	ECBB	2-5C47	
3	儣	5-1743	1-1857				
4	儤	3-1837		1-8224	ECBC	2-5C48	216929
5	儥	3-1745		1-7408	ECBA	2-5C46	
6	儦	3-1838			ECB9	2-5C45	21687E
7	儧	5-1872	1-1858	1-7843		E-5441	
8	儨		1-1859			E-5440	
9	儩	3-1820			ECBE	2-5C4A	21692B
A	優	1-5137	0-4505	0-7348	C075	1-7340	213266
B	儫	5-1894		1-8377		E-5033	
C	儬		1-1860				
D	儭	3-1778	1-1861		EFB8	2-6144	
E	儮				EFB9	2-6145	
F	儯		1-1862			E-5752	

513

	Char	G	J	K	B	C	A
0	儰	3-1722			E4E8	2-4F50	
1	儱	5-1767	1-1863	1-6301	EFB7	2-6143	216930
2	儲	1-2002	0-4457	0-7825	C078	1-7343	213269
3	儳	3-1842	1-1864	1-7853	C35F	1-782B	216940
4	儴	5-1906	1-1865		F1EB	2-6537	
5	儵		1-1866	1-6932	F1EC	2-6538	21693E
6	儶	3-1843				E-5C32	
7	儷	1-5719	0-4922	0-5367	C4D7	1-7A62	21326A
8	儸	5-1820	1-1867		C4D8	1-7A63	
9	儹	5-1904	1-1868	1-7844	F5C1	2-6B4F	216947
A	儺	1-5748	0-4921	0-4951	F5C0	2-6B4E	216944
B	儻	1-5746	0-4924	1-6101	C56C	1-7B58	216948
C	儼	1-5718	0-4923	0-6980	C56B	1-7B57	21326B
D	儽				F7D0	2-6E7D	
E	儾	3-1844				E-606F	
F	儿	0-2289	0-4925		A449	1-442A	27327A

514

	Char	G	J	K	B	C	A
0	兀	0-5603	0-4926	0-7220	A461	1-4442	21326C
1	允	0-5242	0-1684	0-7535	A4B9	1-4478	21326E
2	兂		1-1869				
3	元	0-5210	0-2421	0-7410	A4B8	1-4477	21326D
4	兄	0-4854	0-2327	0-9092	A553	1-4573	213270
5	充	0-1968	0-2928	0-8586	A552	1-4572	21326F
6	兆	0-5355	0-3591	0-8028	A5FC	1-473E	213271
7	兇		0-2204	0-9352	A5FB	1-473D	213273
8	先	0-4740	0-3272	0-6427	A5FD	1-473F	213274
9	光	0-2566	0-2487	0-4635	A5FA	1-473C	213272
A	兊		1-1870			E-2278	
B	克	0-3143	0-2578	0-4826	A74A	1-492C	27336B
C	兌		0-4928	0-8726	A749	1-492B	213275
D	免	0-3566	0-4440	0-5683	A74B	1-492D	213277
E	兎		0-3738	0-8745		E-2454	2D3279
F	兏		1-1871				

515

	Char	G	J	K	B	C	A
0	児		0-2789			E-2453	33327A
1	兑	0-2250				E-2451	
2	兒	1-2289	0-4927	0-6814	A8E0	1-4C23	21327A
3	兓	5-3490	1-1872				
4	兔	0-4535	0-4929		A8DF	1-4C22	213279
5	兕	0-5778	1-1873	1-6958	A8E1	1-4C24	213278
6	兖	0-5780				E-2752	27327B
7	兗		1-1874	1-7134	AB5E	1-5022	21327B
8	兘		1-1875				
9	兙				A259	1-2279	216951
A	党	0-2119	0-3762	1-6102	D0DE	2-2E21	27626F
B	兛				A25A	1-227A	216952
C	兜	0-2221	0-1985	0-5263	B0C2	1-5927	21327C
D	兝				A25C	1-227C	216955
E	兞				A25B	1-227B	216956
F	兟	3-4140	1-1876		D860	2-3A44	216958

516

	Char	G	J	K	B	C	A
0	兠					E-3976	216A73
1	兡				A25D	1-227D	216959
2	兢	0-3004	0-4930	0-4871	B9B8	1-677E	21327D
3	兣				A25E	1-227E	21695C
4	兤		1-1877			E-5E25	
5	入	0-4075	0-3894	0-7693	A44A	1-442B	21327E
6	兦		1-1878			E-2134	2D305B
7	內			0-5014	A4BA	1-4479	213321
8	全	0-4011	0-3320	0-7879	A5FE	1-4740	213322
9	兩	1-3329	0-4932	0-5355	A8E2	1-4C25	213323
A	兪		0-4933	0-7468		E-2B37	
B	八	0-1643	0-4012	0-8802	A44B	1-442C	213324
C	公	0-2511	0-2488	0-4575	A4BD	1-447C	213327
D	六	0-3389	0-4727	0-5531	A4BB	1-447A	213325
E	兮	0-5766	0-4934	0-9117	A4BC	1-447B	213326
F	兯						

517

	Char	G	J	K	B	C	A
0	兰	0-3228					27563E
1	共	0-2518	0-2206	0-4576	A640	1-4741	213328
2	兲					E-227A	
3	关	0-2556					275E69
4	兴	0-4843					275433
5	兵	0-1788	0-4228	0-6018	A74C	1-492E	213329
6	其	0-3868	0-3422	0-4876	A8E4	1-4C27	21332A
7	具	0-3063	0-2281	0-4693	A8E3	1-4C26	21332B
8	典	0-2168	0-3721	0-7880	A8E5	1-4C28	21332C
9	兹	0-5540				E-2E7B	215521
A	兺						
B	养	0-4988					276071
C	兼	0-2870	0-2383	0-4434	ADDD	1-5440	21332D
D	兽	0-4262					274B2B
E	兾		1-1879			E-403F	
F	兿					E-6453	3F5631

518

	Char	G	J	K	B	C	A
0	冀	0-2829	0-4935	0-4877	BEAC	1-7035	21332E
1	冁	0-5770					277360
2	冂	0-5671	0-4936			E-2127	216967
3	冃		1-1880				
4	冄		1-1881			E-214D	216969
5	内	0-3658	0-3866			E-2148	4B3321
6	円		0-1763	0-6987		E-214E	4B3772
7	冇	3-1654			C94E	2-212E	216425
8	冈	0-2452					273B6E
9	冉	0-4029	0-4939	1-7150	A554	1-4574	21332F
A	冊		0-2693	0-8392	A555	1-4575	213330
B	冋		1-1882			E-2178	
C	册	0-1865	0-4938			E-2179	333330
D	再	0-5257	0-2638	0-7802	A641	1-4742	213331
E	冎	5-1719	1-1883				
F	冏	3-1655	0-4940	1-5642	CA6A	2-232C	21696E

51A

	Char	G	J	K	B	C	A
0	冠	0-2558	0-2007	0-4614	AB61	1-5025	213337
1	冡	5-1984	1-1886			E-2F5B	21697B
2	冢	0-5803	0-4947		ADE0	1-5443	2D3852
3	冣		1-1887	1-8069		E-2F59	21697C
4	冤	0-5209	0-4945	1-7341	ADDE	1-5441	2D7E6A
5	冥	0-5804	0-4429	0-5702	ADDF	1-5442	213339
6	冦		0-4946			E-2F5A	4B3B22
7	冧						
8	冨	5-1985	0-4158			E-344D	2D3B27
9	冩		0-4948				4B3B37
A	冪		0-4949	0-5681	BEAD	1-7036	216A22
B	冫	0-5791	0-4950				216A23
C	冬	0-2212	0-3763	0-5247	A556	1-4576	276276
D	冭		1-1888				
E	冮	3-1859					
F	冯	0-2375					27612D

51C

	Char	G	J	K	B	C	A
0	净	0-3027					39476F
1	凁	3-1861				E-2B3B	
2	凂		1-1894			E-2B3D	
3	凃	5-1975				E-2B3E	51384D
4	凄	0-3864	0-3208	0-8402	D0E2	2-2E25	2D475F
5	凅	3-1864	0-4957	1-5675	D0E3	2-2E26	4B476C
6	准	0-5528	0-2958	0-8155	ADE3	1-5446	27484B
7	凇	0-5801				E-2F5E	216A46
8	凈	1-3027	1-1901		D0E4	2-2E27	3F476F
9	凉	0-3325	0-4958	0-5356		E-2F5F	2D475B
A	凊	3-1863		1-7957	D0E1	2-2E24	216A43
B	凋	0-2182	0-3592	0-8029	ADE4	1-5447	4B5F49
C	凌	0-3372	0-4631	0-5548	ADE2	1-5445	213341
D	凍	1-2219	0-3764	0-5248	ADE1	1-5444	213340
E	凎	3-1865			D0E5	2-2E28	
F	减	0-2885	1-1902			E-344F	2D4829

51E

	Char	G	J	K	B	C	A
0	几	0-2824	0-4960	1-5909	A44C	1-442D	273C6B
1	凡	0-2318	0-4362	0-5977	A45A	1-443B	213036
2	凢		1-1909			E-212F	
3	凣					E-2135	216A68
4	凤	0-2379				E-2151	276233
5	凥	5-3041	1-1910			E-217B	
6	処		0-2972				4B5647
7	凧		0-3492				222664
8	凨	5-1940				E-2322	
9	凩		0-4962	1-6456			69515E
A	凪		0-3868				694664
B	凫	0-5776					4D5973
C	凬	5-1942				E-245B	
D	凭	0-3830	0-4963	1-6738		E-2759	273F3F
E	凮		1-1911				
F	凯	0-3113					273348

519

	Char	G	J	K	B	C	A
0	冐		0-7078			E-2755	2D3332
1	冑		0-4941		AB60	1-5024	213333
2	冒	0-3516	0-4333	0-5719	AB5F	1-5023	213332
3	冓	3-1605	0-4942	1-5839	D0E0	2-2E23	216971
4	冔	3-4027			D0DF	2-2E22	216970
5	冕	0-3565	0-4943	0-5684	B0C3	1-5928	213334
6	冖	0-5802	0-4944			E-2128	216975
7	冗	0-4063	0-3073	0-7323	A4BE	1-447D	213336
8	冘	3-1869	1-1884	1-7371	C955	2-2135	
9	写	0-4820	0-2844			E-217A	273B37
A	冚						
B	军	0-3092					275B34
C	农	0-3709					275B64
D	冝		1-1885			E-2457	
E	冞	3-1870			CBCD	2-254D	
F	冟	3-1871				E-2B39	

51B

	Char	G	J	K	B	C	A
0	冰	0-1789	0-4954	1-6737	A642	1-4743	21333C
1	冱	0-5792	0-4952	1-8378	C9BC	2-217B	216A26
2	冲	0-1969	0-4953	1-8061		E-227E	27574A
3	决	0-3086	0-4951			E-227D	2D466D
4	冴		0-2667			E-227C	516A26
5	况	0-3186	0-4955			E-2459	2D4730
6	冶	0-5017	0-4474	0-6907	A74D	1-492F	21333D
7	冷	0-3268	0-4668	0-5350	A74E	1-4930	21333E
8	冸	5-1966	1-1889			E-245A	
9	冹	5-1964			CA6B	2-232D	
A	冺		1-1890				
B	冻	0-2219					273340
C	冼	0-5794	1-1891		CBCE	2-254E	216A35
D	冽	0-5793	0-4956	0-5409	A8E6	1-4C29	4B4741
E	冾	5-1972	1-1892		CBCF	2-254F	
F	冿	5-1974	1-1893				

51D

	Char	G	J	K	B	C	A
0	凐	5-1979			D468	2-336B	216A4F
1	凑	0-2053	1-1903			E-344E	216A4E
2	凒	5-1971	1-1904	1-7437		E-397D	
3	凓		1-1905			E-397A	216A54
4	凔	3-1860		1-7871	D861	2-3A45	
5	凕	3-1866	1-1906				
6	凖		0-5037			E-397E	4B484B
7	凗	5-1981			DCC5	2-416A	
8	凘	3-1867	1-1907		E140	2-4927	
9	凙					E-4B2F	216A63
A	凚	3-1868				E-4B2E	
B	凛	0-3361	0-4959	1-6351		E-4B30	333344
C	凜		0-8405	0-5547	BBFE	1-6C29	213344
D	凝	0-3693	0-2237	0-7574	BEAE	1-7037	213345
E	凞		1-1908	0-9375	E8F9	2-5644	
F	凟	5-1976				E-5442	216A66

51F

	Char	G	J	K	B	C	A
0	凰	0-2743	0-4964	0-9237	B0C4	1-5929	213347
1	凱	1-3113	0-1914	0-4334	B3CD	1-5E33	213348
2	凲		1-1912				
3	凳	0-2142	1-1913	1-6175	B9B9	1-6821	213349
4	凴		1-1914	1-6739		E-457A	333F3F
5	凵	0-5941	0-4965		C942	2-2123	216A78
6	凶	0-4855	0-2207	0-9353	A4BF	1-447E	273273
7	凷	5-1987	1-1915				216A79
8	凸	0-4525	0-3844	0-8440	A559	1-4579	21334D
9	凹	0-1628	0-1790	0-7274	A557	1-4577	21334C
A	出	0-1986	0-2948	0-8583	A558	1-4578	21334B
B	击	0-2787					274176
C	凼	0-5942					2D3C6A
D	函	0-2615	0-4001	0-8962	A8E7	1-4C2A	21334E
E	凾		0-4966			E-275A	33334E
F	凿	0-5268					275E4B

520

	Char	G	J	K	B	C	A
0	刀	0-2122	0-3765	0-5179	A44D	1-442E	21334F
1	刁	0-2183	1-1916	1-7688	A44E	1-442F	213350
2	刂	0-5654	1-1917				2D334F
3	刃	0-4048	0-3147	0-7651	A462	1-4443	213351
4	刄		0-4967			E-2136	4B3351
5	刅		1-1918			E-2152	
6	分	0-2354	0-4212	0-6134	A4C0	1-4521	213353
7	切	0-3948	0-3258	0-7923	A4C1	1-4522	213352
8	刈	0-5655	0-2002	0-7152	A4C2	1-4523	213354
9	刉	3-1881			C9BE	2-214C	
A	刊	0-3115	0-2009	0-4242	A55A	1-457A	213355
B	刋		0-4968			E-217D	4B3355
C	刌	3-2142			C96B	2-214B	
D	刍	0-5927					27545C
E	刎	0-5656	0-4970	0-5791	A646	1-4747	213359
F	刏	3-4394				E-2325	

522

	Char	G	J	K	B	C	A
0	删	0-4130				E-2461	
1	刡	5-2026			CA6E	2-2330	
2	刢	5-2023	1-1924				
3	刣					E-245C	
4	判	0-3748	0-4029	0-8787	A750	1-4932	21335A
5	別		0-4244	0-6012	A74F	1-4931	21335B
6	刦			1-5613		E-245E	2D3428
7	刧		0-4971	1-5614		E-245D	393428
8	刨	0-3757	1-1925		A753	1-4935	21335D
9	利	0-3291	0-4588	0-5555	A751	1-4933	21335E
A	刪		0-4972	0-6302	A752	1-4934	21335C
B	别	0-1780				E-2460	4B335B
C	刬	8-9028					
D	刭	0-5657					276B3E
E	刮	0-2546	0-4973	0-4630	A8ED	1-4C30	27605E
F	刯					E-275B	

524

	Char	G	J	K	B	C	A
0	剀	0-5660					273376
1	剁	0-2271			A8EF	1-4C32	213366
2	剂	0-2833					273423
3	剃	0-4474	0-3670	0-8479	AB63	1-5027	213368
4	剄	1-5657	0-4977	1-5643	CDF0	2-2932	216B3E
5	剅	3-7832	1-1930			E-2B3F	
6	剆				CBD3	2-2553	
7	則	1-5282	0-3407	0-8646	AB68	1-502C	21336D
8	剈	3-1892				E-2B40	
9	剉		1-1931	1-7738	CDF1	2-2933	216B43
A	削	0-4787	0-2679	0-6291	AB64	1-5028	21336C
B	剋	1-8840	0-4978	0-4827	AB67	1-502B	21336B
C	剌	0-5661	0-4979	0-5323	AB66	1-502A	21336A
D	前	0-3916	0-3316	0-7881	AB65	1-5029	213369
E	剎				AB62	1-5026	
F	剏		0-4976			E-2B43	336B33

526

	Char	G	J	K	B	C	A
0	剠	3-1901	1-1938			E-2F60	216B47
1	剡	0-5663	1-1939	0-6470	D0E6	2-2E29	2E3172
2	剢	5-2040			D0EC	2-2E2F	
3	剣		0-2385			E-2F66	4B3421
4	剤		0-2662			E-2F61	333423
5	剥	0-1694	0-3977			E-2F63	2D3372
6	剦		1-1940				
7	剧	0-3071				E-2F64	27337E
8	剨	5-2046				E-3450	216B5E
9	剩	0-4203	0-4984	0-7705	B3D1	1-5E37	213377
A	剪	0-2884	0-4982	0-7882	B0C5	1-592A	213373
B	剫	3-1907			D469	2-336C	
C	剬	3-1905			D46B	2-336E	
D	剭	3-1909			D46A	2-336D	
E	剮	1-2548	1-1941		D46C	2-336F	216B5B
F	副	0-2417	0-4191	0-6089	B0C6	1-592B	213374

521

	Char	G	J	K	B	C	A
0	刐	5-2018			C9BF	2-217D	
1	刑	0-4844	0-2326	0-9093	A644	1-4745	213356
2	划	0-2714	1-1919		A645	1-4746	27337C
3	刓	3-1882	1-1920	1-7259	C9BD	2-217C	216B24
4	刔		0-4969			E-2324	2D4029
5	刕	5-2002	1-1921			E-2326	
6	刖	0-7530	1-1922	1-7355	A647	1-4748	216B26
7	列	0-3348	0-4683	0-5410	A643	1-4744	213357
8	刘	0-3385	1-1923			E-2327	273422
9	则	0-5282					27336D
A	刚	0-2453					273370
B	创	0-2020					273378
C	刜	3-1886			CA6C	2-232E	216B2A
D	初	0-1985	0-2973	0-8488	AAEC	1-4F4F	21574E
E	刞	5-2022			CA6D	2-232F	
F	刟					E-245F	396E2F

523

	Char	G	J	K	B	C	A
0	到	0-2129	0-3794	0-5180	A8EC	1-4C2F	213362
1	刱	5-2003	1-1926	1-7872	CBD4	2-2554	216B33
2	刲	3-1887	1-1927	1-5922	CBD1	2-2551	216B37
3	刳	0-5658	0-4974	1-5676	CBD2	2-2552	216B39
4	刴					E-275E	
5	刵	3-6437	1-1928		CBD0	2-2550	216B36
6	制	0-5438	0-3209	0-8004	A8EE	1-4C31	27576C
7	刷	0-4302	0-2694	0-6576	A8EA	1-4C2D	213361
8	券	0-4015	0-2384	0-4771	A8E9	1-4C2C	21335F
9	刹	0-4118	0-4975	0-8343		E-275F	213367
A	刺	0-2044	0-2741	0-7709	A8EB	1-4C2E	213363
B	刻	0-3144	0-2579	0-4230	A8E8	1-4C2B	213360
C	刼		1-1929			E-275D	333428
D	刽	0-2584					276B7A
E	刾					E-644F	4B576C
F	刿	0-5659					276B79

525

	Char	G	J	K	B	C	A
0	剐	0-2548					276B5B
1	剑	0-2903					273421
2	剒	5-2037			D0E8	2-2E2B	216B4C
3	剓	5-2005				E-2F68	
4	剔	0-4462	0-4981	0-8408	ADE7	1-544A	213371
5	剕	3-8453	1-1932	1-6677	D0EB	2-2E2E	216B53
6	剖	0-3842	0-4322	0-6088	ADE5	1-5448	21336F
7	剗	3-1885	1-1933	1-7519		E-2F65	335E2F
8	剘	5-2036	1-1934				
9	剙					E-2F62	
A	剚	3-1894	1-1935	1-6742	D0E7	2-2E2A	216B4B
B	剛	1-2453	0-2568	0-4307	ADE8	1-544B	213370
C	剜	0-5664	1-1936		ADE6	1-5449	21336E
D	剝			0-5846	ADE9	1-544C	213372
E	剞	0-5662	0-4980	1-5969	D0E9	2-2E2C	216B4D
F	剟	3-1903	1-1937	1-7934	D0EA	2-2E2D	216B50

527

	Char	G	J	K	B	C	A
0	剰		0-3074			E-3A23	333377
1	剱		0-4991				453421
2	割	0-2478	0-1968	0-8960	B3CE	1-5E34	213375
3	剳		0-4985			E-3A21	2D6B5F
4	剴	1-5660	0-4983	1-5572	B3CF	1-5E35	213376
5	創	1-2020	0-3347	0-8360	B3D0	1-5E36	213378
6	剶	3-1910				E-3451	
7	剷		1-1942	1-6764	B6D0	1-6337	395E2F
8	剸	3-1883	1-1943		DCC7	2-416C	216B6B
9	剹		1-1944			E-4041	
A	剺	3-3936		1-6357	DCC6	2-416B	
B	剻	5-2064			DCC8	2-416D	
C	剼	5-2045			DCC9	2-416E	
D	剽	0-5666	0-4987	0-8882	B6D1	1-6338	21337A
E	剾	3-1884				E-4040	
F	剿	0-2943	0-4986	0-8489	B6CF	1-6336	21337B

528

		G	J	K	B	C	A
0	劀	5-2073	1-1945		E141	2-4928	
1	劁	0-5668			E142	2-4929	216B75
2	劂	0-5667	1-1946	1-5910	B9BB	1-6823	216B74
3	劃	1-2714	0-1936	0-9281	B9BA	1-6822	21337C
4	劄				E35A	2-4C61	
5	劅		1-1947				
6	劆					E-4B31	
7	劇	1-3071	0-2364	0-4828	BC40	1-6C2A	21337E
8	劈	0-3792	0-4992	0-5989	BC41	1-6C2B	21337D
9	劉	1-3385	0-4613	0-5517	BC42	1-6C2C	213422
A	劊	1-2584	1-1948		BC44	1-6C2E	216B7A
B	劋	3-1918			E4F2	2-4F5A	
C	劌	1-5659	1-1949		E4F3	2-4F5B	216B79
D	劍	1-2903	0-4988	0-4392	BC43	1-6C2D	213421
E	劎					E-4B32	
F	劏						

529

		G	J	K	B	C	A
0	劐	0-5669				E-5036	216B7C
1	劑	1-2833	0-4993	0-8005	BEAF	1-7038	213423
2	劒		0-4990	0-4393			2D3421
3	劓	0-5670	1-1950	1-7438	BEB0	1-7039	216C21
4	劔		0-4989			E-5037	
5	劕	5-2043	1-1951				
6	劖	3-1923	1-1952		F1ED	2-6539	216C27
7	劗	5-2078	1-1953	1-7845	F5C3	2-6B51	
8	劘	3-1925	1-1954	1-6384	F5C2	2-6B50	216C29
9	劙	3-1926			F7D1	2-6E7E	216C2C
A	劚	5-2071	1-1955			E-602C	216C2B
B	力	0-3306	0-4647	0-5384	A44F	1-4430	213424
C	劜	5-2079	1-1956			E-2137	
D	劝	0-4016				E-2154	27343D
E	办	0-1676				E-2153	275B5F
F	功	0-2506	0-2489	0-4577	A55C	1-457C	213425

52A

		G	J	K	B	C	A
0	加	0-2851	0-1835	0-4205	A55B	1-457B	213426
1	务	0-4681					273433
2	劢	0-5929					2D343C
3	劣	0-3351	0-4684	0-5411	A648	1-4749	213427
4	劤	3-4419	1-1957	0-4834			
5	劥		1-1958				
6	劦	3-1928	1-1959		C9C0	2-217E	216C2E
7	劧		1-1960				
8	动	0-2215				E-2328	273434
9	助	0-5490	0-2985	0-8030	A755	1-4937	213429
A	努	0-3712	0-3756	0-5029	A756	1-4938	21342B
B	劫	0-2957	0-2569	0-4404	A754	1-4936	213428
C	劬	0-5930	0-5002	1-5840	A757	1-4939	21342A
D	劭	0-5931	0-5003	1-7974	CA6F	2-2331	216C31
E	劮	3-1929			CA70	2-2332	216C33
F	劯		1-1961				

52B

		G	J	K	B	C	A
0	劰		1-1962				
1	励	0-3288	0-4669				27343C
2	劲	0-3002					27342F
3	劳	0-3245				E-2463	273435
4	労		0-4711			E-2462	4B3435
5	劵		0-5005			E-2761	2D335F
6	劶		1-1963				
7	劷		1-1964				
8	劸		1-1965				
9	効	8-1291	0-2490			E-2760	334243
A	劺	3-1934	1-1966				
B	劻	3-1931	1-1967		A8F1	1-4C34	216C37
C	劼	3-1932	0-5004		CBD5	2-2555	216C38
D	劽		1-1968			E-625A	
E	劾	0-5932	0-1915	0-9022	A8F0	1-4C33	21342C
F	势	0-4238				E-2762	273438

52C

		G	J	K	B	C	A
0	勀	5-2083	1-1969		CDF2	2-2934	
1	勁	1-3002	0-5006	0-4445	AB6C	1-5030	21342F
2	勂				CDF3	2-2935	
3	勃	0-1810	0-4354	0-5890	AB6B	1-502F	21342E
4	勄		1-1970			E-2B48	
5	勅		0-3628	0-8647		E-2B46	2E363F
6	勆		1-1971				
7	勇	0-5134	0-4506	0-7324	AB69	1-502D	21342D
8	勈		1-1972				
9	勉	0-3567	0-4257	0-5685	AB6A	1-502E	213430
A	勊	5-2084				E-2B47	216C3C
B	勋	0-4911					273436
C	勌		1-1973	1-5902		E-2F6F	
D	勍	3-1936	0-5007	0-4446	D0ED	2-2E30	216C3D
E	勎	5-2086				E-2F6C	
F	勏		1-1974			E-2F6A	

52D

		G	J	K	B	C	A
0	勐	0-5934				E-2F6D	216C40
1	勑		1-1975			E-2F6E	216C41
2	勒	0-3253	0-8053	0-5545	B0C7	1-592C	213432
3	勓	5-2090			D46E	2-3371	
4	勔	5-8763	1-1976			E-3452	216C46
5	動	1-2215	0-3816	0-5249	B0CA	1-592F	213434
6	勖	0-5935	1-1977	0-7377	D46D	2-3370	216C48
7	勗	5-4228	0-5008		B1E5	1-5B2B	214357
8	勘	0-3117	0-2010	0-4275	B0C9	1-592E	213431
9	務	1-4681	0-4419	0-5766	B0C8	1-592D	213433
A	勚	8-9035					
B	勛	1-4911	1-1978	0-9318	B3D4	1-5E3A	213436
C	勜	5-2094	1-1979				
D	勝	1-4204	0-3001	0-6713	B3D3	1-5E39	213437
E	勞	1-3245	0-5009	0-5444	B3D2	1-5E38	213435
F	募	0-3628	0-4271	0-5720	B6D2	1-6339	21343A

52E

		G	J	K	B	C	A
0	勠		0-5013	1-6344		E-4045	453F6D
1	勡	5-2101	1-1980	1-8237		E-4044	216C4E
2	勢	1-4238	0-3210	0-6507	B6D5	1-633C	213438
3	勣		0-5010	0-7851	B6D6	1-633D	216C4C
4	勤	0-3958	0-2248	0-4835	B6D4	1-633B	213439
5	勥	5-2104	1-1981				
6	勦		0-5011	1-7975	B6D3	1-633A	33337B
7	勧		0-2011			E-4046	2D343D
8	勨	3-1942	1-1982				
9	勩	3-1937	1-1983		E143	2-492A	216C53
A	勪		1-1984			E-4621	
B	勫	5-2103			E144	2-492B	
C	勬	3-1944	1-1985				
D	勭	3-1943				E-457E	
E	勮	3-1945				E-4B33	
F	勯	5-2106			E4F5	2-4F5D	

52F

		G	J	K	B	C	A
0	勰	0-5936	1-1986		BC45	1-6C2F	216C58
1	勱	1-5929	1-1987		E4F4	2-4F5C	216C5A
2	勲		0-2314			E-4D2C	4B3436
3	勳	8-1351	0-5014	0-9319	BEB1	1-703A	2D3436
4	勴	3-1939	1-1988		ECBF	2-5C4B	
5	勵	1-3288	0-5015	0-5368	C079	1-7344	21343C
6	勶	5-2107	1-1989				
7	勷	3-1947	1-1990		F1EE	2-653A	216C5E
8	勸	1-4016	0-5016	0-4772	C455	1-7961	21343D
9	勹	0-5772	0-5017				216C61
A	勺	0-4155	0-2859	0-7735	A463	1-4444	216C62
B	勻			0-4818	A4C3	1-4524	21343E
C	勼	5-1912			C956	2-2136	216C64
D	勽	5-1911				E-2155	
E	勾	0-2520	0-2491	0-4694	A4C4	1-4525	2D3539
F	勿	0-4680	0-4462	0-5808	A4C5	1-4526	213440

Code	Char	G	J	K	B	C	A
5300	匀	0-5240	1-1991			E-2156	
5301	匁		0-4472	1-6478			694C68
5302	匂		0-3887	1-6024			694677
5303	匃		1-1992	1-5573		E-2223	216C6A
5304	匄					E-2222	
5305	包	0-1692	0-4281	0-8848	A55D	1-457D	213441
5306	匆	0-2050	0-5018		A55E	1-457E	213442
5307	匇					E-2224	216C69
5308	匈	0-4857	0-5019	0-9354	A649	1-474A	213443
5309	匉	5-1913			CA71	2-2333	
530A	匊	5-1917	1-1993	1-5884	CBD6	2-2556	216C6E
530B	匋	5-1915	1-1994		CBD7	2-2557	216C6F
530C	匌	3-1845	1-2001	1-8305			
530D	匍	0-5773	0-5021	0-8849	AB6D	1-5031	213444
530E	匎				D0EE	2-2E31	
530F	匏	0-6243	0-5023	0-8850	B0CC	1-5931	213446
5310	匐	0-5775	0-5022	0-6051	B0CB	1-5930	213445
5311	匑	5-1924	1-2002		D863	2-3A47	216C77
5312	匒	3-1846			D862	2-3A46	
5313	匓		1-2003				
5314	匔	3-1849				E-5038	
5315	匕	0-5616	0-5024	0-6166	A450	1-4431	213447
5316	化	0-2715	0-1829	0-9189	A4C6	1-4527	213448
5317	北	0-1717	0-4344	0-6133	A55F	1-4621	213449
5318	匘	5-1930	1-2004				
5319	匙	0-1955	0-2692	0-6721	B0CD	1-5932	21344A
531A	匚	0-5646	0-5025		C943	2-2124	216D23
531B	匛		1-2005				
531C	匜	3-1639	1-2006		C96C	2-214D	216D24
531D	匝	0-5249	0-3357		A560	1-4622	21344C
531E	匞		1-2007			E-2226	
531F	匟		1-2008		C9C2	2-2222	216D25
5320	匠	0-2919	0-3002	0-7761	A64B	1-474C	21344E
5321	匡	0-3179	0-2209	0-4636	A64A	1-474B	21344D
5322	匢				C9C1	2-2221	
5323	匣	0-4727	0-5026	0-4301	A758	1-493A	21344F
5324	匤					E-6450	
5325	匥	3-1641	1-2009			E-2465	
5326	匦	0-5648					276D2E
5327	匧	5-1701	1-2010	1-8357		E-2B49	
5328	匨		1-2011				
5329	匩		1-2012				
532A	匪	0-2343	0-4059	0-6167	ADEA	1-544D	213450
532B	匫	3-1644	1-2013				
532C	匬	3-1646	1-2014				
532D	匭	1-5648	1-2015		D46F	2-3372	216D2E
532E	匮	0-5649					273452
532F	匯	1-2767	0-5027	0-9261	B6D7	1-633E	213451
5330	匰	3-1645	1-2016		E145	2-492C	216D33
5331	匱	1-5649	0-5028	1-5911	B9BC	1-6824	213452
5332	匲		1-2017			E-4623	
5333	匳		0-5029			E-4B34	4B393F
5334	匴	3-1649			E8FA	2-5645	
5335	匵	5-1704	1-2018			E-5444	216D36
5336	匶			1-5841		E-5C34	
5337	匷				F3FD	2-686A	
5338	匸	8-0890	0-5030			E-2129	216D3A
5339	匹	0-3805	0-4104	0-8915	A4C7	1-4528	213453
533A	区	0-3988	0-2272			E-2157	273455
533B	医	0-5029	0-1669			E-2466	275D31
533C	匼	3-1642	1-2019		CBD8	2-2558	
533D	匽	3-1643	1-2020	1-7112	CDF4	2-2936	216D3E
533E	匾	0-5650	1-2021	1-8203	B0D0	1-5935	213454
533F	匿	0-3668	0-3831	0-5091	B0CE	1-5933	213456
5340	區	1-3988	0-5031	0-4701	B0CF	1-5934	213455
5341	十	0-4214	0-2929	0-6808	A451	1-4432	213457
5342	卂	5-1626	1-2022				
5343	千	0-3907	0-3273	0-8422	A464	1-4445	213458
5344	卄	5-1602		0-7694	A2CD	1-243F	
5345	卅	0-5606	0-5033	1-6779	A4CA	1-452B	213459
5346	卆		0-5032			E-2159	27345F
5347	升	0-4193	0-3003	0-6714	A4C9	1-452A	21345B
5348	午	0-4671	0-2465	0-7177	A4C8	1-4529	21345A
5349	卉	0-2760	0-5035	0-9333	A563	1-4625	21345D
534A	半	0-1675	0-4030	0-5866	A562	1-4624	21345C
534B	卋		1-2024			E-232A	39302D
534C	卌	3-1602	1-2023		C96D	2-214E	216D41
534D	卍	5-1623	0-5036	0-5619	C9C3	2-2223	216D42
534E	华	0-2710					27553C
534F	协	0-4813				E-232B	273460
5350	卐	5-1630				E-232D	
5351	卑	0-1716	0-4060	0-6168	A8F5	1-4C38	213462
5352	卒	0-5568	0-3420	0-8079	A8F2	1-4C35	21345F
5353	卓	0-5531	0-3478	0-8681	A8F4	1-4C37	213461
5354	協	1-4813	0-2208	0-9080	A8F3	1-4C36	213460
5355	单	0-2105				E-2763	273668
5356	卖	0-3484					275A2F
5357	南	0-3647	0-3878	0-4985	AB6E	1-5032	213463
5358	単		0-3517			E-2B4A	4B3668
5359	卙	5-1641	1-2025				
535A	博	0-1809	0-3978	0-5847	B3D5	1-5E3B	213464
535B	卛		1-2026				
535C	卜	0-1823	0-4346	0-6052	A452	1-4433	275573
535D	卝	5-1712				E-215A	216D4B
535E	卞	0-1769	0-5038	0-6006	A4CB	1-452C	213466
535F	卟	0-6318				E-2227	216E58
5360	占	0-5328	0-3274	0-7931	A565	1-4627	27313C
5361	卡	0-3108	1-2027	1-7525	A564	1-4626	213467
5362	卢	0-3412					274D3F
5363	卣	0-5653	1-2028		CA72	2-2334	216D4C
5364	卤	0-3417					295D3C
5365	卥		1-2029			E-6451	216D4E
5366	卦	0-5652	0-2321	0-4647	A8F6	1-4C39	213469
5367	卧	0-4652				E-2A5C	2D5424
5368	卨	3-1653		0-6457			
5369	卩	0-5864	0-5039			E-212A	275C6B
536A	卪						
536B	卫	0-4632					275749
536C	卬	3-1874	1-2030	1-7047	C957	2-2137	216D53
536D	卭	5-2142	1-2031			E-2228	
536E	卮	0-5620	0-5040	1-8074	A567	1-4629	21346B
536F	卯	0-3514	0-1712	0-5754	A566	1-4628	21346A
5370	印	0-5101	0-1685	0-7652	A64C	1-474D	21346C
5371	危	0-4603	0-2077	0-7443	A64D	1-474E	21346D
5372	卲	3-1875	1-2032	1-6870	CA73	2-2335	216D57
5373	即	0-2820	0-3408	1-7781	A759	1-493B	21346E
5374	却	0-4020	0-2149	0-4231		E-2467	2D3473
5375	卵	0-3449	0-4581	0-5316	A75A	1-493C	21346F
5376	卶	5-1989				E-2765	
5377	卷	0-3077	0-5043	0-4773	A8F7	1-4C3A	27407B
5378	卸	0-4822	0-1823	1-6743	A8F8	1-4C3B	213471
5379	卹		1-2033	1-8502	A8F9	1-4C3C	3F3E47
537A	卺	0-5865		1-5945		E-2766	216D58
537B	卻		0-5042	1-5516	AB6F	1-5033	213473
537C	卼	5-2357			CDF5	2-2937	
537D	卽			0-8177		E-2B4B	2D346E
537E	卾		1-2034	1-7014			
537F	卿	0-3968	0-2210	0-4447	ADEB	1-544E	213474

538

	Char	G	J	K	B	C	A
0	厀					E-4047	216D5D
1	厁						
2	厂	0-1907	0-5044		C944	2-2125	273D2C
3	厃	5-2009	1-2035				
4	厄	0-2282	0-4481	0-6888	A4CC	1-452D	213475
5	厅	0-4492					273D2F
6	历	0-3290				E-215B	274349
7	厇	5-1647	1-2036				
8	厈		1-2037				
9	厉	0-3287				E-2229	27347B
A	厊	5-1648			C9C4	2-2224	
B	压	0-4925				E-232F	273869
C	厌	0-4965					27347A
D	厍	0-5639					276D6D
E	厎	3-1621	1-2038		CA74	2-2336	216D64
F	厏	5-1653			CA75	2-2337	

53A

	Char	G	J	K	B	C	A
0	厠	1-1862	0-5046	0-8618		E-3454	2D3C7E
1	厡		1-2043				
2	厢	0-4765					2D3C7D
3	厣	0-5641					276E2A
4	厤		1-2044		D864	2-3A48	216D7A
5	厥	0-5642	0-5048	0-4780	B3D6	1-5E3C	213479
6	厦	0-4735	0-5047	0-8929		E-3A28	4B3D24
7	厧	5-1671			D865	2-3A49	
8	厨	0-1988	0-3163			E-3A27	333D28
9	厩	0-3039	0-1725			E-404A	3A284C
A	厪	5-1673	1-2045	1-5946		E-4049	
B	厫	5-1670	1-2046			E-4048	216D7B
C	厬	3-1632			E146	2-492D	
D	厭	1-4965	0-1762	0-7084	B9BD	1-6825	21347A
E	厮	0-5643	0-5049	1-6959		E-4625	2D3D29
F	厯		1-2047				222D56

53C

	Char	G	J	K	B	C	A
0	叀		1-2055				
1	叁	0-4094				E-2769	33347D
2	参	0-1846	0-2718			E-276A	27347D
3	參	1-1846	0-5052	0-8349	B0D1	1-5936	21347D
4	叄					E-3455	
5	叅		1-2056	1-7854		E-3A29	
6	叆	8-9037					
7	叇	8-9038					
8	又	0-5154	0-4384	0-7349	A453	1-4434	21347E
9	叉	0-1870	0-2621	0-8309	A465	1-4446	213521
A	及	0-2816	0-2158	0-4864	A4CE	1-452F	213523
B	友	0-5149	0-4507	0-7350	A4CD	1-452E	213522
C	双	0-4311	0-3348			E-215E	275F4E
D	反	0-2320	0-4031	0-5867	A4CF	1-4530	213524
E	収		0-2893			E-2160	33423D
F	叏		1-2057				

53E

	Char	G	J	K	B	C	A
0	叠	0-2194	1-2064			E-404B	2D4C3C
1	叡		0-1735	0-7153	E8FB	2-5646	2D4D65
2	叢	1-2052	0-3349	0-8531	C24F	1-763B	21352B
3	口	0-3158	0-2493	0-4702	A466	1-4447	21352C
4	古	0-2537	0-2437	0-4515	A56A	1-462C	21352E
5	句	0-3068	0-2271	0-4703	A579	1-463B	213539
6	另	0-3377	1-2065	1-6259	A574	1-4636	213535
7	叧		1-2066				
8	叨	0-6322	0-5059	1-6123	A56F	1-4631	213534
9	叩	0-6321	0-3501	0-4516	A56E	1-4630	213531
A	只	0-5427	0-3494	0-8194	A575	1-4637	21353C
B	叫	0-2948	0-2211	0-4803	A573	1-4635	213537
C	召	0-5357	0-3004	0-6515	A56C	1-462E	213536
D	叭	0-1640	0-5060	0-8803	A57A	1-463C	21353B
E	叮	0-2203	0-5058	1-7651	A56D	1-462F	21352F
F	可	0-3141	0-1836	0-4206	A569	1-462B	213530

539

	Char	G	J	K	B	C	A
0	厐	8-1401					
1	厑						
2	厒				CBD9	2-2559	
3	厓	5-1655	1-2039	0-6877		E-2767	216D66
4	厔	3-1622	1-2040		CBDA	2-255A	216D67
5	厕	0-1862					273C7E
6	厖	3-1624	0-5045	1-6537	CDF7	2-2939	2D3D2D
7	厗	3-1626			CDF6	2-2938	
8	厘	0-3269	0-4650	0-5556	CDF9	2-293B	275D3D
9	厙	1-5639	1-2041		CDF8	2-293A	216D6D
A	厚	0-2681	0-2492	0-9307	AB70	1-5034	213476
B	厛					E-6452	2D3D2F
C	厜	3-1630			D470	2-3373	
D	厝	0-5640	1-2042	1-7689	ADED	1-5450	213477
E	厞	5-1661			D0EF	2-2E32	
F	原	0-5213	0-2422	0-7411	ADEC	1-544F	213478

53B

	Char	G	J	K	B	C	A
0	厰		0-5050			E-4626	4B3D2C
1	厱	3-1625				E-4B35	
2	厲	1-3287	1-2048	1-6228	BC46	1-6C30	21347B
3	厳		0-2423			E-5445	4B375A
4	厴	1-5641	1-2049		F1EF	2-653B	
5	厵	5-1685	1-2050				216E2C
6	厶	0-5944	0-5051			E-212B	274F25
7	厷	5-2109	1-2051			E-215C	
8	厸		1-2052				
9	厹	3-1948		1-5842	C958	2-2138	216E2E
A	厺		1-2053			E-222A	
B	去	0-4005	0-2178	0-4359	A568	1-462A	21347C
C	厼						
D	厽	5-2111	1-2054				
E	厾	3-1616				E-2331	
F	县	0-4756					455164

53D

	Char	G	J	K	B	C	A
0	叐					E-222B	216E3E
1	发	0-2302					274C7B
2	叒	5-2122	1-2058			E-2333	
3	叓		1-2059				
4	叔	0-4269	0-2939	0-6650	A8FB	1-4C3E	213526
5	叕	5-2125	1-2060			E-276B	
6	取	0-4001	0-2872	0-8602	A8FA	1-4C3D	213525
7	受	0-4260	0-2885	0-6584	A8FC	1-4C3F	213527
8	变	0-1768					27594B
9	叙	0-4880	0-2986			E-2B50	2D4249
A	叚		1-2061			E-2B4F	216E48
B	叛	0-3749	0-4032	0-5868	AB71	1-5035	213528
C	叜	5-2126				E-2B4E	333529
D	叝		1-2062			E-2B4D	
E	叞	5-2127	1-2063				
F	叟	0-5937	0-5055	1-6909	ADEE	1-5451	213529

53F

	Char	G	J	K	B	C	A
0	台	0-4408	0-3470	0-8727	A578	1-463A	213538
1	叱	0-6319	0-2824	0-8274	A577	1-4639	21353A
2	史	0-4223	0-2743	0-6240	A576	1-4638	21353D
3	右	0-5150	0-1706	0-7351	A56B	1-462D	213532
4	叴	5-2369		1-5843		E-2231	
5	叵	0-5647	1-2067	1-8171	A572	1-4634	21344B
6	叶	0-5022	0-1980	1-8358		E-222D	27554F
7	号	0-2637	0-2570			E-222E	27564A
8	司	0-4330	0-2742	0-6241	A571	1-4633	21352D
9	叹	0-4430				E-222F	27372C
A	叺		0-5061				69525D
B	叻	0-6323			A57B	1-463D	216E57
C	叼	0-2180			A570	1-4632	213533
D	叽	0-6320					273740
E	叾						
F	叿	5-2371				E-2335	

540

	Char	G	J	K	B	C	A
0	吀					E-2337	
1	吁	0-5185	0-5062	1-7318	A653	1-4754	275055
2	吂	3-2149	1-2068				
3	吃	0-1952	0-2141	0-9362	A659	1-475A	213547
4	各	0-2487	0-1938	0-4232	A655	1-4756	213546
5	吅	5-2376				E-2339	33365A
6	吆	0-6326			A65B	1-475C	216E68
7	吇	5-2380			C9C5	2-2225	
8	合	0-2647	0-2571	0-8974	A658	1-4759	275E5D
9	吉	0-2810	0-2140	0-4946	A64E	1-474F	213540
A	吊	0-2185	0-3663	0-7852	A651	1-4752	213544
B	吋	8-0883	0-1705	1-8013	A654	1-4755	21353F
C	同	0-4512	0-3817	0-5250	A650	1-4751	213543
D	名	0-3591	0-4430	0-5703	A657	1-4758	213545
E	后	0-2683	0-2501	0-9308	A65A	1-475B	273D65
F	吏	0-3284	0-4589	0-5557	A64F	1-4750	213542

542

	Char	G	J	K	B	C	A
0	吠	0-2345	0-4342	0-8837	A770	1-4952	21355A
1	吡	0-6333	1-2071			E-2479	216E76
2	吢	5-5074				E-247E	216F26
3	吣	0-6336				E-2475	216F27
4	吤	5-2392			CAA5	2-2345	
5	吥	3-2152			CA7D	2-233F	
6	否	0-2381	0-4061	0-6090	A75F	1-4941	213559
7	吧	0-1641	1-2072		A761	1-4943	213553
8	吨	0-2254	1-2073		CAA4	2-2344	273744
9	吩	0-2352	0-5070	0-6135	A768	1-494A	213567
A	吪	3-2159	1-2074		CA78	2-233A	216F24
B	含	0-2612	0-2062	0-8963	A774	1-4956	213565
C	听	0-4493	0-5065	1-7414	A776	1-4958	27527B
D	吭	0-3152	0-5066		A75C	1-493E	21354D
E	吮	0-4317	0-5068	1-7584	A76D	1-494F	21355E
F	启	0-3884	1-2075			E-2524	27424F

544

	Char	G	J	K	B	C	A
0	呀	0-4929	0-5064	1-8270	A772	1-4954	213554
1	呁	3-2162			CAA3	2-2343	
2	呂		0-4704	0-5369	A766	1-4948	213564
3	呃	0-6332	1-2079		A763	1-4945	213558
4	呄		1-2080			E-2473	
5	呅	3-2164			CA7A	2-233C	216E6D
6	呆	0-2084	0-4282	1-6415	A762	1-4944	213556
7	呇		1-2081		CAA6	2-2346	
8	呈	0-1942	0-3672	0-7948	A765	1-4947	213560
9	呉		0-2466			E-247C	33355C
A	告	0-2470	0-2580	0-4517	A769	1-494B	21355F
B	呋	0-6327				E-2478	4D386F
C	呌					E-2474	216E6C
D	呍		1-2082			E-246D	
E	呎	8-0884	0-5072	1-7907	A760	1-4942	213551
F	呏		1-2083		CAA2	2-2342	216F21

546

	Char	G	J	K	B	C	A
0	呠	5-2407			CBEB	2-256B	
1	呡	5-2419			CBEA	2-256A	
2	呢	0-3656	1-2085	1-6059	A94F	1-4C51	213569
3	呣	3-2188			CBED	2-256D	216F4A
4	呤	0-6342	1-2086	1-6260	CBEF	2-256F	216F53
5	呥	3-2179			CBE4	2-2564	
6	呦	0-6347	1-2087	1-7372	CBE7	2-2567	216F52
7	呧	5-2413	1-2088		CBEE	2-256E	
8	周	0-5460	0-2894	0-8118	A950	1-4C52	213574
9	呩	5-2404	1-2089			E-2774	
A	呪		0-2886	0-8117		E-2778	2D3571
B	呫	3-2173	1-2090	1-7953	CBE1	2-2561	216F43
C	呬	3-2180			CBE5	2-2565	
D	呭	5-2406	1-2091			E-2775	216F3A
E	呮		1-2092				
F	呯	5-2410			CBE9	2-2569	

541

	Char	G	J	K	B	C	A
0	吐	0-4534	0-3739	0-8746	A652	1-4753	213541
1	向	0-4782	0-2494	0-9030	A656	1-4757	273755
2	吒	0-6324			A65C	1-475D	213548
3	吓	0-4737	1-2069			E-233A	273751
4	吔	3-2150					216E61
5	吕	0-3432				E-233B	333564
6	吖	0-6325				E-2334	705F39
7	吗	0-3480					27367A
8	吘	5-2387			CA7E	2-2340	
9	吙	5-2401			CA7B	2-233D	
A	吚		1-2070			E-2476	216E6F
B	君	0-3093	0-2315	0-4754	A767	1-4949	213550
C	吜	5-2403			CA7C	2-233E	
D	吝	0-3363	0-5071	0-5580	A75B	1-493D	21354E
E	吞	0-4544			A75D	1-493F	21354F
F	吟	0-5087	0-2267	0-7565	A775	1-4957	213566

543

	Char	G	J	K	B	C	A
0	吰	3-2153			CA76	2-2338	216E78
1	吱	0-5408	1-2076		A773	1-4955	213555
2	吲	0-6337				E-2477	216E70
3	吳			0-7179	A764	1-4946	21355C
4	吴	0-4666	1-2077			E-247B	2D355C
5	吵	0-1919	1-2078		A76E	1-4950	21355D
6	吶		0-5069	1-6054	A76F	1-4951	21355B
7	吷	3-2167			CA77	2-2339	
8	吸	0-4692	0-2159	0-9369	A76C	1-494E	213562
9	吹	0-2021	0-3165	0-8603	A76A	1-494C	213563
A	吺	3-2163				E-2470	
B	吻	0-4639	0-4213	0-5792	A76B	1-494D	213561
C	吼	0-2680	0-5067	0-9309	A771	1-4953	213557
D	吽	3-2157	0-5063	1-8464	CAA1	2-2341	216E7D
E	吾	0-4665	0-2467	0-7178	A75E	1-4940	213552
F	吿					E-2521	

545

	Char	G	J	K	B	C	A
0	呐	0-3637				E-247D	
1	呑		0-3861	0-8702		E-2522	
2	呒	0-6328					277267
3	呓	0-6329					273762
4	呔	0-6330			CA79	2-233B	216E79
5	呕	0-3727					27372E
6	呖	0-6331					27734C
7	呗	0-6334					277030
8	员	0-5217					27363E
9	呙	0-6335					276F69
A	呚					E-2523	
B	呛	0-3926					273722
C	呜	0-4656					273721
D	呝	5-2417		1-7072			
E	呞	3-2185	1-2084				
F	呟		0-5076			E-276E	216F2E

547

	Char	G	J	K	B	C	A
0	呰	3-2204	0-5079	1-7479	CE49	2-294A	216F68
1	呱	0-6341	0-5077	0-4518	A94B	1-4C4D	21357B
2	呲	0-6358			CE4D	2-294E	216F67
3	味	0-4622	0-4403	0-5811	A8FD	1-4C40	213568
4	呴	3-2182	1-2093		CBE6	2-2566	216F4B
5	呵	0-2639	0-5074	0-4207	A8FE	1-4C41	21356A
6	呶	0-6346	0-5083	1-6035	A94C	1-4C4E	21357A
7	呷	0-6340	0-5078		A945	1-4C47	21356E
8	呸	0-3762			A941	1-4C43	21356C
9	呹	3-2181				E-2771	
A	呺	3-2177			CBE2	2-2562	
B	呻	0-4175	0-5081	0-6766	A944	1-4C46	21356F
C	呼	0-2684	0-2438	0-9128	A949	1-4C4B	213573
D	命	0-3592	0-4431	0-5704	A952	1-4C54	213579
E	呾	3-2176			CBE3	2-2563	
F	呿	3-2168	1-2094	1-5582	CBDC	2-255C	216F37

548

	Char	G	J	K	B	C	A
0	咀	0-3055	0-5082	0-7826	A943	1-4C45	27373D
1	咁	3-2169	1-2101		CBDD	2-255D	
2	咂	0-6338			CBDF	2-255F	216F39
3	咃		1-2102				
4	咄	0-6345	0-5084	1-6147	A946	1-4C48	213572
5	咅	5-6190	1-2103			E-276C	
6	咆	0-3756	0-5086	0-8851	A948	1-4C4A	213575
7	咇	5-2418		1-8258	CBDB	2-255B	
8	咈	3-2186	1-2104		CBE0	2-2560	216F35
9	咉	3-2178	1-2105			E-2770	
A	咊					E-2779	
B	咋	0-5306	0-2680	1-6744	A951	1-4C53	213576
C	和	0-2645	0-4734	0-9190	A94D	1-4C4F	213577
D	咍	3-2187	1-2106	1-8317	CBE8	2-2568	216F49
E	咎	0-3044	0-5075	0-4704	A953	1-4C55	21357D
F	咏	0-5129	0-5073	1-7166		E-2773	2D584D

54A

	Char	G	J	K	B	C	A
0	咠	3-2191		1-7826	CE48	2-2949	
1	咡	3-2190	1-2112		CDFB	2-293D	216F58
2	咢	3-2205	0-5088	1-7015	CE4B	2-294C	216F66
3	咣	0-6359				E-2B57	705F5B
4	咤	0-6369	0-5103	0-8667		E-2B59	216F55
5	咥	3-2202	0-5090	1-8521	CDFD	2-293F	216F60
6	咦	0-6355	1-2113		AB78	1-503C	213626
7	咧	0-6354	1-2114		ABA8	1-504A	216F63
8	咨	0-5541	0-5094	0-7710	AB74	1-5038	213622
9	咩	0-6367	1-2115		ABA7	1-5049	21357E
A	咪	0-6368	1-2116		AB7D	1-5041	213621
B	咫	0-6975	0-5101	0-8201	ABA4	1-5046	213627
C	咬	0-5007	0-5091	0-4665	AB72	1-5036	213623
D	咭	0-6350	1-2117		CDFC	2-293E	216F5A
E	咮	3-2208	1-2118		CE43	2-2944	216F6D
F	咯	0-3109	0-5130	1-5517	ABA3	1-5045	213632

54C

	Char	G	J	K	B	C	A
0	哀	0-1607	0-1605	0-6878	AB73	1-5037	213624
1	品	0-3823	0-4142	0-8901	AB7E	1-5042	21362D
2	哂	0-6351	0-5102	1-6977	AB7B	1-503F	21362B
3	哃	3-2207		1-6151	CE40	2-2941	
4	哄	0-2669	0-5092	0-9179	ABA1	1-5043	21362A
5	哅	3-2212			CE46	2-2947	
6	哆	0-2263	1-2125	1-8075	CE47	2-2948	216F74
7	哇	0-4559	0-5087	1-7250	AB7A	1-503E	213628
8	哈	0-2594	0-5093	0-8975	ABA2	1-5044	213633
9	哉	0-5253	0-2640	0-7803	AB76	1-503A	213629
A	哊	3-2194	1-2126			E-2B55	
B	哋					E-6454	
C	哌	0-6363				E-2B63	4B357B
D	响	0-4776	1-2127			E-2B61	276036
E	哎	0-1605	1-2128		AB75	1-5039	21362F
F	哏	0-6371			CDFE	2-2940	216F5C

54E

	Char	G	J	K	B	C	A
0	哠	5-2448	1-2129		D144	2-2E46	
1	員	1-5217	0-1687	0-7412	ADFB	1-545E	21363E
2	哢	3-2215	0-5115		D0F1	2-2E34	216F7C
3	哣						
4	哤	3-2220			D0F6	2-2E39	21702A
5	哥	0-2471	0-5107	0-4208	ADF4	1-5457	21363A
6	哦	0-3722	0-5108	1-7003	AE40	1-5462	213643
7	哧	0-6374			D0F4	2-2E37	217025
8	哨	0-4158	0-3005	0-8490	ADEF	1-5452	21363D
9	哩	0-3308	0-4373	1-6358	ADF9	1-545C	21363F
A	哪	0-3636	1-2130		ADFE	1-5461	213637
B	哫	3-2223			D0FB	2-2E3E	
C	哬	5-2450	1-2131				
D	哭	0-3162	0-5113	0-4554	ADFA	1-545D	213640
E	哮	0-4788	0-5112	0-9286	ADFD	1-5460	21363B
F	哯	3-2156	1-2132			E-2F77	217032

549

	Char	G	J	K	B	C	A
0	咐	0-2432	0-5085	0-6091	A94A	1-4C4C	213578
1	咑	3-2172	1-2107		CBDE	2-255E	216F3B
2	咒	0-5468	0-5080		A947	1-4C49	213571
3	咓					E-276F	
4	咔	0-6339				E-2777	216F42
5	咕	0-2530	1-2108		A942	1-4C44	21356B
6	咖	0-3107	1-2109	1-5503	A940	1-4C42	21356D
7	咗						
8	咘	3-2171			CBEC	2-256C	
9	咙	0-3392					273756
A	咚	0-6343			A94E	1-4C50	21357C
B	咛	0-6344					27374E
C	咜		1-2110				216F2F
D	咝	0-6348					705F50
E	咞					E-2B5C	
F	咟	5-2424	1-2111			E-2B5D	

54B

	Char	G	J	K	B	C	A
0	咰	5-2433			CE4F	2-2950	
1	咱	0-5259	1-2119		ABA5	1-5047	213630
2	咲		0-2673			E-2B5B	334F71
3	咳	0-3140	0-1917	0-9006	AB79	1-503D	213625
4	咴	0-6352				E-2B54	705F54
5	咵	5-2425				E-2B5E	216F64
6	咶	3-2209			CE45	2-2946	
7	咷	5-2432	1-2120		CE42	2-2943	216F6A
8	咸	0-4744	0-5089	0-8964	AB77	1-503B	276250
9	咹	3-2213	1-2121			E-2B51	
A	咺	3-2192	1-2122		CDFA	2-293C	216F5B
B	咻	0-6361	1-2123	1-8491	ABA6	1-5048	213631
C	咼	1-6335	0-5105	1-5794	CE4A	2-294B	216F69
D	咽	0-4942	0-1686	0-7654	AB7C	1-5040	2D3758
E	咾	5-2422	0-5104		CE4C	2-294D	216F5E
F	咿	0-6362	1-2124	1-7446	ABA9	1-504B	216F71

54D

	Char	G	J	K	B	C	A
0	哐	0-6349				E-2B53	705F51
1	哑	0-4938					273649
2	哒	0-6353					277272
3	哓	0-6356					277255
4	哔	0-6357					277239
5	哕	0-6360					27727A
6	哖				CE44	2-2945	216F6C
7	哗	0-2709					335941
8	哘		0-5106				695326
9	哙	0-6364					27727E
A	哚	0-6365				E-2B58	705F61
B	哛						
C	哜	0-6366					277328
D	哝	0-6370					273747
E	哞	0-6372			CE4E	2-294F	216F6B
F	哟	0-5120					273671

54F

	Char	G	J	K	B	C	A
0	哰	3-2236				E-3021	
1	哱	3-2219		1-6531	D0FE	2-2E41	
2	哲	0-5360	0-3715	0-8441	ADF5	1-5458	21363C
3	哳	0-6378			D0F5	2-2E38	217027
4	哴	3-2237				E-2F74	
5	哵	3-2225				E-2F78	
6	哶	5-2446	1-2133			E-3022	217038
7	哷	3-2229			D142	2-2E44	217039
8	哸	3-2230			D143	2-2E45	
9	哹	3-2231				E-2F79	
A	哺	0-1824	0-5114	0-8852	ADF7	1-545A	213639
B	哻	5-2447			D141	2-2E43	
C	哼	0-2663	1-2134		ADF3	1-5456	213635
D	哽	0-6376	0-5111	1-5644	AE43	1-5465	217024
E	哾	5-2455	1-2135				
F	哿	0-5933	1-2136	1-5504	D0F8	2-2E3B	21702D

Code	Char	G	J	K	B	C	A
5500	唀		1-2137			E-2F7B	
5501	唁	0-4968	1-2138		ADF1	1-5454	213634
5502	唂	3-2228				E-2F7A	
5503	唃	3-2232			D146	2-2E48	
5504	唄	1-6334	0-1720	0-8806	D0F9	2-2E3C	217030
5505	唅	5-2452	1-2139		D0FD	2-2E40	
5506	唆	0-4384	0-2622	0-6242	ADF6	1-5459	213641
5507	唇	0-2029	0-3116	0-8238	AE42	1-5464	216F7D
5508	唈	3-2224	1-2140		D0FA	2-2E3D	217034
5509	唉	0-1606	1-2141	1-7053	ADFC	1-545F	213642
550A	唊	3-2201			D140	2-2E42	21702B
550B	唋	5-2451			D147	2-2E49	
550C	唌	3-2211	1-2142		D4A1	2-3424	
550D	唍		1-2143			E-2F73	
550E	唎	3-2226	1-2144	0-5558	D145	2-2E47	21703E
550F	唏	0-6381	0-5109	1-8522	AE44	1-5466	217046
5510	唐	0-4438	0-3766	0-5148	ADF0	1-5453	213636
5511	唑	0-6382			D0FC	2-2E3F	217047
5512	唒				D0F3	2-2E36	
5513	唓	3-2154				E-2F76	
5514	唔	0-6377	0-5110	1-7205	ADF8	1-545B	213638
5515	唕		1-2145				
5516	唖		0-1602				
5517	唗	3-2217			D0F2	2-2E35	217023
5518	唘					E-2F7E	21702E
5519	唙	5-2453				E-3025	
551A	唚	3-2238			D0F7	2-2E3A	216F7B
551B	唛	0-6373					277234
551C	唜			0-5637			
551D	唝	8-9065					
551E	唞						
551F	唟						
5520	唠	0-6375					273732
5521	唡	8-0885					
5522	唢	0-6379					277169
5523	唣	0-6380					217044
5524	唤	0-2729					27366D
5525	唥						
5526	唦	3-2235			D0F0	2-2E33	
5527	唧	0-6383			AE41	1-5463	21365E
5528	唨					E-6721	
5529	唩	3-2253				E-345F	
552A	唪	0-6384	1-2146		D477	2-337A	21705D
552B	唫		1-2147	1-5955		E-3468	
552C	唬	0-2703			B0E4	1-5949	213651
552D	唭	5-2457			D4A7	2-342A	217059
552E	售	0-4259	0-5120	1-6910	B0E2	1-5947	213657
552F	唯	0-4608	0-4503	0-7470	B0DF	1-5944	213656
5530	唰	0-6407			D47C	2-3421	217068
5531	唱	0-1910	0-3007	0-8361	B0DB	1-5940	21364F
5532	唲	3-2254	1-2148		D4A2	2-3425	
5533	唳	0-6406	0-5126	1-6229	B0E6	1-594B	213645
5534	唴	3-2234			D476	2-3379	
5535	唵	3-2246	1-2149	0-6858	D47B	2-337E	21706B
5536	唶	3-2242	1-2150		D47A	2-337D	217061
5537	唷	0-6401			ADF2	1-5455	
5538	唸		0-5125		B0E1	1-5946	213659
5539	唹	5-2475	0-5116		D4A5	2-3428	217057
553A	唺	3-2250				E-3466	
553B	唻	3-2221	1-2151		D4A8	2-342B	
553C	唼	0-6394	1-2152	1-6780	D473	2-3376	217053
553D	唽	5-2460	1-2153				
553E	唾	0-4557	0-3435	0-8668	B3E8	1-5E4E	213653
553F	唿	0-6392				E-3467	217079
5540	啀	3-2245	0-5117	1-7054	D4A9	2-342C	21706A
5541	啁	0-6390	1-2154		B0E7	1-594C	21707B
5542	啂	5-2471		1-6052			
5543	啃	0-3148			B0D9	1-593E	213650
5544	啄	0-5536	0-3479	0-8682	B0D6	1-593B	21364D
5545	啅	3-2247	0-5122		D47E	2-3423	217070
5546	商	0-4144	0-3006	0-6334	B0D3	1-5938	213646
5547	啇	5-1950	1-2155				
5548	啈	3-2240			D4A6	2-3429	217058
5549	啉	0-6388	1-2156			E-345B	217064
554A	啊	0-1601	1-2157		B0DA	1-593F	21364C
554B	啋	5-2470			D4AA	2-342D	
554C	啌	3-2261	0-5119			E-3458	21704E
554D	啍	3-2257	1-2158		D474	2-3377	217050
554E	啎				D4A4	2-3427	
554F	問	1-4642	0-4468	0-5793	B0DD	1-5942	213648
5550	啐	0-6393	1-2159		D475	2-3378	217055
5551	啑		1-2160		D478	2-337B	21705A
5552	啒	5-2478			D47D	2-3422	
5553	啓	1-3884	0-2328	0-4486		E-3462	21424F
5554	啔	5-2477				E-3461	39424F
5555	啕	0-6391			B0DE	1-5943	213655
5556	啖	0-6402	0-5123	0-5126	B0DC	1-5941	213644
5557	啗	8-1293	0-5124	1-6083	B0E8	1-594D	2D3644
5558	啘	3-2262	1-2161			E-3457	
5559	啙	3-3889				E-3A36	21714B
555A	啚	5-2473	1-2162			E-3464	217051
555B	啛	5-2463	1-2163				
555C	啜	0-6408	0-5121	1-7935	B0E3	1-5948	21364E
555D	啝	5-2468	0-5127			E-345E	69533B
555E	啞	1-4938	1-2164	0-6815	B0D7	1-593C	213649
555F	啟				B1D2	1-5A76	2D424F
5560	啠		1-2165				
5561	啡	0-2340	1-2166		B0D8	1-593D	213652
5562	啢				D479	2-337C	217060
5563	啣		0-5118	0-8965	B0E5	1-594A	213654
5564	啤	0-3801	1-2167		B0E0	1-5945	213658
5565	啥	0-4122			D4A3	2-3426	21707D
5566	啦	0-3218	1-2168		B0D5	1-593A	21364A
5567	啧	0-6385					273727
5568	啨	3-2239				E-3459	
5569	啩						
556A	啪	0-3730			B0D4	1-5939	21364B
556B	啫					E-6457	
556C	啬	0-5636					273678
556D	啭	0-6389					27375C
556E	啮	0-3686					277345
556F	啯	8-9067					
5570	啰	8-1592					
5571	啱					E-6456	
5572	啲					E-6722	
5573	啳					E-6455	21704D
5574	啴	8-1224					
5575	啵	0-6403			D471	2-3374	21704B
5576	啶	0-6404			D472	2-3375	21704F
5577	啷	0-6405			D86A	2-3A4E	217125
5578	啸	0-4805					273733
5579	啹						
557A	啺	5-2379				E-3A3C	
557B	啻	0-6420	0-5133	1-6960	B3D7	1-5E3D	21365C
557C	啼	0-4468	0-5138	0-8006	B3DA	1-5E40	21365D
557D	啽	3-2279		1-7036	D875	2-3A59	
557E	啾	0-6417	0-5134	1-8028	B3EE	1-5E54	21366E
557F	啿		1-2169		D878	2-3A5C	

558

	Char	G	J	K	B	C	A
0	喀	0-3106	0-5129	0-4351	B3D8	1-5E3E	21365B
1	喁	0-6415	1-2170	1-7241	D871	2-3A55	217144
2	喂	0-4625	1-2171		B3DE	1-5E44	213669
3	喃	0-6411	0-5139	1-6021	B3E4	1-5E4A	213666
4	善	0-4138	0-3317	0-6428	B5BD	1-6143	21523F
5	喅	5-2487				E-3A31	
6	喆	8-1362	1-2172	0-8442		E-3A38	21712F
7	喇	0-3214	0-5141	0-5290	B3E2	1-5E48	213660
8	喈	0-6414	1-2173		D86E	2-3A52	217134
9	喉	0-2677	0-2502	0-9310	B3EF	1-5E55	213670
A	喊	0-2616	0-5131	0-8966	B3DB	1-5E41	213665
B	喋	0-6409	0-3593	1-7954	B3E3	1-5E49	213662
C	喌	5-2491			D876	2-3A5A	
D	喍				DCD7	2-417C	
E	喎		1-2174		D87B	2-3A5F	217145
F	喏	0-6386	1-2175		D86F	2-3A53	217149

559

	Char	G	J	K	B	C	A
0	喐						
1	喑	0-6419	1-2176	1-7428	D866	2-3A4A	217123
2	喒		1-2177		D873	2-3A57	217151
3	喓	3-2266	1-2178	1-7281	D86D	2-3A51	21712D
4	喔	0-6424	1-2179	1-7016	B3E1	1-5E47	21365F
5	喕	5-2484			D879	2-3A5D	
6	喖	5-2482				E-3A2E	
7	喗	3-2214	1-2180			E-3A2A	
8	喘	0-2013	0-5135	0-8423	B3DD	1-5E43	21366C
9	喙	0-6425	0-5128	0-9334	B3F1	1-5E57	217152
A	喚	1-2729	0-2013	0-9216	B3EA	1-5E50	21366D
B	喛	3-2280				E-3A33	
C	喜	0-4718	0-2078	0-9376	B3DF	1-5E45	213661
D	喝	0-2640	0-1969	0-4266	B3DC	1-5E42	21366B
E	喞		0-5136	1-7782		E-3A40	39365E
F	喟	0-6416	0-5132	1-7357	B3E7	1-5E4D	21366A

55A

	Char	G	J	K	B	C	A
0	喠	3-2276				E-3A34	
1	喡	3-2151			D87A	2-3A5E	
2	喢	5-2493			D86C	2-3A50	
3	喣	3-4866	1-2181	1-8465	D872	2-3A56	
4	喤	3-2277	1-2182	1-8436	D874	2-3A58	217150
5	喥	5-2503			D868	2-3A4C	
6	喦	5-2490			D877	2-3A5B	
7	喧	0-4890	0-2386	0-9329	B3D9	1-5E3F	21365A
8	喨	3-2282	0-5142	1-6221	D867	2-3A4B	217126
9	喩		0-5140	0-7471		E-3A42	
A	喪	1-4105	0-3351	0-6335	B3E0	1-5E46	213663
B	喫		0-2142	0-4950	B3F0	1-5E56	2D3547
C	喬	1-3939	0-2212	0-4666	B3EC	1-5E52	21366F
D	喭	3-2284	1-2183		D869	2-3A4D	217127
E	單	1-2105	0-5137	0-5104	B3E6	1-5E4C	213668
F	喯	5-2462				E-3A3B	

55B

	Char	G	J	K	B	C	A
0	喰		0-2284	1-6974			396074
1	喱	0-6412			B3ED	1-5E53	213667
2	喲	1-5120	1-2184		B3E9	1-5E4F	213671
3	喳	0-5291			B3E5	1-5E4B	213664
4	喴	3-2267				E-3A2F	217136
5	喵	0-6387			D870	2-3A54	217147
6	営		0-1736				4B4A2E
7	喷	0-3771					273745
8	喸						
9	喹	0-6413					70602D
A	喺					E-6723	
B	喻	0-5187			B3EB	1-5E51	213672
C	喼						
D	喽	0-6422					273731
E	喾	0-6423					27735A
F	喿	3-3429	1-2185		DCD5	2-417A	

55C

	Char	G	J	K	B	C	A
0	嗀	3-4714			DCD1	2-4176	
1	嗁		1-2186			E-4051	217178
2	嗂	5-2519			DCE0	2-4227	
3	嗃	3-2293	1-2187		DCCA	2-416F	21715E
4	嗄	0-6436	0-5146		DCD3	2-4178	217165
5	嗅	0-4865	0-5144	0-9311	B6E5	1-634C	21367E
6	嗆	1-3926	1-2188		B6E6	1-634D	213722
7	嗇	1-5636	0-5207	0-6364	B6DE	1-6345	213678
8	嗈	5-2525			DCDC	2-4223	
9	嗉	0-6428	1-2189	1-6871	B6E8	1-634F	21715F
A	嗊	3-2218			DCCF	2-4174	217161
B	嗋	3-2301	1-2190		DCCE	2-4173	
C	嗌	0-6441	1-2191		DCCC	2-4171	217158
D	嗍	0-6442			DCDE	2-4225	21715B
E	嗎	1-3480	1-2192		B6DC	1-6343	21367A
F	嗏	3-2265			DCD8	2-417D	21716F

55D

	Char	G	J	K	B	C	A
0	嗐	5-2523			DCCD	2-4172	217159
1	嗑	0-6430	1-2193	1-8306	B6DF	1-6346	213675
2	嗒	0-6410	1-2194		DCD6	2-417B	217170
3	嗓	0-4104	1-2201		B6DA	1-6341	213679
4	嗔	0-6433	0-5149	0-8239	DCD2	2-4177	217164
5	嗕	3-2290			DCD9	2-417E	
6	嗖	0-6418			DCDB	2-4222	217177
7	嗗	3-2273	1-2202			E-404E	
8	嗘		1-2203				
9	嗙	3-2294			DCDF	2-4226	21715D
A	嗚	1-4656	0-5143	0-7180	B6E3	1-634A	213721
B	嗛	5-2522	1-2204	1-5634	DCCB	2-4170	21715A
C	嗜	0-4240	0-5147	0-4878	B6DD	1-6344	213676
D	嗝	0-6435			DCD0	2-4175	217162
E	嗞	3-2285	1-2205			E-3A2B	21715C
F	嗟	0-6421	0-5145	0-8310	B6D8	1-633F	213674

55E

	Char	G	J	K	B	C	A
0	嗠			1-6192			
1	嗡	0-4643			B6E4	1-634B	213723
2	嗢	3-2270	1-2206	1-7239	DCDA	2-4221	2D7143
3	嗣	0-4335	0-2744	0-6243	B6E0	1-6347	21367B
4	嗤	0-6445	0-5148	0-8624	B6E1	1-6348	21367D
5	嗥	0-6438			B6E7	1-634E	217175
6	嗦	0-6434			B6DB	1-6342	213677
7	嗧				A25F	1-2321	216C50
8	嗨	0-6443			B6D9	1-6340	213673
9	嗩	1-6379	1-2207		DCD4	2-4179	217169
A	嗪	0-6426				E-404C	70603A
B	嗫	0-6431					27375D
C	嗬	0-6432					4B356A
D	嗭						
E	嗮					E-6725	
F	嗯	0-6437			B6E2	1-6349	21367C

55F

	Char	G	J	K	B	C	A
0	嗰					E-6724	
1	嗱						
2	嗲	0-6439			DCDD	2-4224	217179
3	嗳	0-6440					27374B
4	嗴					E-6458	217156
5	嗵	0-6444					70604C
6	嗶	1-6357	1-2208		B9CD	1-6835	217239
7	嗷	0-6427	0-5151	1-7206	B9C8	1-6830	213728
8	嗸	5-2514				E-462E	217227
9	嗹	5-2445	0-5156		E155	2-493C	21722B
A	嗺	3-2308			E151	2-4938	
B	嗻	3-2313				E-4628	217224
C	嗼	5-2515			E14B	2-4932	
D	嗽	0-4352	0-5154	0-6585	B9C2	1-682A	21372B
E	嗾	0-6453	0-5153	0-8119	B9BE	1-6826	213726
F	嗿	3-2255	1-2209	1-8140	E154	2-493B	217244

560

	Char	G	J	K	B	C	A
0	嘀	0-6454			B9BF	1-6827	213724
1	嘁	0-6450			E14E	2-4935	217236
2	嘂	3-2307			E150	2-4937	21723C
3	嘃					E-4629	
4	嘄	5-2472		1-5817	E153	2-493A	
5	嘅		1-2210			E-4636	21712A
6	嘆	1-4430	0-3518	0-8703	B9C4	1-682C	21372C
7	嘇	3-2264				E-462C	
8	嘈	0-6448	1-2211	1-7690	B9CB	1-6833	213729
9	嘉	0-2846	0-1837	0-4209	B9C5	1-682D	21372D
A	嘊	5-2529	1-2212				
B	嘋	5-2526				E-462A	
C	嘌	0-6449		1-8238	E149	2-4930	217231
D	嘍	1-6422	1-2213	1-6333	B9C6	1-682E	213731
E	嘎	0-2434	1-2214	1-7028	B9C7	1-682F	21372F
F	嘏	0-5637	1-2215		E14C	2-4933	217228

562

	Char	G	J	K	B	C	A
0	嘠					E-645A	21725D
1	嘡	3-2306					
2	嘢					E-6459	
3	嘣	0-6452					706054
4	嘤	0-6451					27375B
5	嘥						
6	嘦	3-2311				E-4650	
7	嘧	0-6455			E147	2-492E	21717E
8	嘨					E-4630	
9	嘩	1-2709	0-1862	1-8413	BC4D	1-6C37	2D5941
A	嘪	5-2438			E547	2-4F6E	217260
B	嘫	5-2545				E-4B41	21726B
C	嘬	0-6460	1-2220	1-8019	E544	2-4F6B	217264
D	嘭	0-6456				E-4B38	706058
E	嘮	1-6375			BC47	1-6C31	213732
F	嘯	1-4805	0-5166	0-6516	BC53	1-6C3D	213733

564

	Char	G	J	K	B	C	A
0	噀	3-2326	1-2230		E541	2-4F68	217252
1	噁	1-8816	1-2231	1-7207	E4FA	2-4F62	217258
2	噂	3-2325	0-1729	1-7764	E4F7	2-4F5F	217247
3	噃	5-2544	1-2232				
4	噄	5-2536	1-2233			E-4B3E	
5	噅	3-2165			D86B	2-3A4F	
6	噆	3-2318	1-2234		E4FD	2-4F65	
7	噇	3-2323				E-4B37	
8	噈	3-2321			E4F6	2-4F5E	
9	噉		1-2235	1-6084	E4FC	2-4F64	217257
A	噊	3-2327			E4FB	2-4F63	
B	噋	3-2322	1-2236	1-8159		E-4B3B	21724B
C	噌	0-6465	0-3325		E4F8	2-4F60	217248
D	噍	0-6461	1-2237	1-7976		E-4B43	217269
E	噎	0-5013	0-5157	1-7149	BC4F	1-6C39	213734
F	噏	5-2543	1-2238	1-8517		E-4B45	21726C

566

	Char	G	J	K	B	C	A
0	噠	1-6353	1-2241		E8FD	2-5648	217272
1	噡	5-2558	1-2242			E-5040	
2	噢	0-6462	1-2243		BEBE	1-7047	21374C
3	噣	3-2333	1-2244		E942	2-564C	
4	噤	0-6468	0-5165	1-5956	BEB6	1-703F	213742
5	噥	1-6370		1-6042	BEBA	1-7043	213747
6	噦	1-6360	1-2245		E941	2-564B	21727A
7	噧	3-2147				E-503B	
8	器	0-3887	0-2079	0-4879	BEB9	1-7042	213749
9	噩	0-5612	1-2246	1-7017	BEB5	1-703E	213743
A	噪	0-5275	0-5168	1-7691	BEB8	1-7041	213748
B	噫	0-6470	0-5164	0-9377	BEB3	1-703C	213741
C	噬	0-4241	0-5167	1-6807	BEBD	1-7046	21374D
D	噭	3-2334	1-2247	1-5819	E943	2-564D	21727C
E	噮				E8FE	2-5649	
F	噯	1-6440	1-2248	1-7055	BEBC	1-7045	21374B

561

	Char	G	J	K	B	C	A
0	嘐	3-2315	1-2216	1-5818	B9CC	1-6834	217235
1	嘑		1-2217			E-4634	393573
2	嘒	3-2302	1-2218	1-8370	E14A	2-4931	217225
3	嘓	3-2249			E14F	2-4936	217238
4	嘔	1-3727	0-5150	0-4705	B9C3	1-682B	21372E
5	嘕	3-2303			E148	2-492F	
6	嘖	1-6385	0-5152	1-7890	B9C9	1-6831	213727
7	嘗	1-1902	0-3008	0-6336	B9C1	1-6829	213730
8	嘘	0-4874	0-1719			E-4633	
9	嘙		1-2219				
A	嘚	3-2309					
B	嘛	0-3479	0-5155		B9C0	1-6828	213725
C	嘜	1-6373			E14D	2-4934	217234
D	嘝				E152	2-4939	217242
E	嘞	0-6447				E-4631	21722E
F	嘟	0-6429			B9CA	1-6832	21372A

563

	Char	G	J	K	B	C	A
0	嘰	1-6320	1-2221		BC54	1-6C3E	213740
1	嘱	0-5486	0-3092			E-4B3D	273764
2	嘲	0-1916	0-5162	0-8031	BC4A	1-6C34	213736
3	嘳	5-2488	1-2222		E542	2-4F69	
4	嘴	0-5576	0-5160	0-8604	BC4C	1-6C36	21373D
5	嘵	1-6356	1-2223		E4F9	2-4F61	217255
6	嘶	0-4327	0-5161	0-6722	BC52	1-6C3C	213735
7	嘷		1-2224	1-8379		E-4B44	21373E
8	嘸	1-6328	0-5163	1-6473	E546	2-4F6D	217267
9	嘹	0-6458	1-2225	1-6319	BC49	1-6C33	213738
A	嘺	3-2210			E548	2-4F6F	
B	嘻	0-4691	1-2226	1-8523	BC48	1-6C32	213737
C	嘼	5-2541	1-2227				
D	嘽	3-2260	1-2228		E543	2-4F6A	217261
E	嘾	3-2317			E545	2-4F6C	
F	嘿	0-2657	1-2229	1-6477	BC4B	1-6C35	21373C

565

	Char	G	J	K	B	C	A
0	噐	5-2540	0-5158			E-4B40	2D3749
1	噑					E-4635	
2	噒					E-4B3C	
3	噓			0-9038	BC4E	1-6C38	21373B
4	噔	0-6466	1-2239			E-4B39	21725E
5	噕						
6	噖	5-2537				E-4B3F	
7	噗	0-6459			BC50	1-6C3A	213739
8	噘	0-6457			E4FE	2-4F66	21725C
9	噙	0-6463			BEE2	1-703B	21373F
A	噚				E540	2-4F67	
B	噛		0-1990				
C	噜	0-6464					273754
D	噝	1-6348					
E	噞	3-2227	1-2240		E945	2-564F	
F	噟	5-2938				E-503F	21726F

567

	Char	G	J	K	B	C	A
0	噰	5-2559			E8FC	2-5647	21726E
1	噱	0-6469	1-2249		BEBB	1-7044	21374A
2	噲	1-6364	1-2250	1-8110	E944	2-564E	21727E
3	噳	3-2331			E940	2-564A	21727B
4	噴	1-3771	0-4214	0-6136	BC51	1-6C3B	213745
5	噵		1-2251				
6	噶	0-2433		1-5533	BEBF	1-7048	217278
7	噷	3-2335			E946	2-5650	
8	噸	1-2254	0-3853	1-8160	BEB7	1-7040	213744
9	噹	1-8811			BEB4	1-703D	213746
A	噺		0-4024	1-6978			694838
B	噻	0-6471				E-503D	706067
C	噼	0-6472					217270
D	噽	5-2303				E-5448	
E	噾	5-2570			BCC6	2-5C52	
F	噿	5-2572			BCC8	2-5C54	

568

	Char	G	J	K	B	C	A
0	嚀	1-6344	0-5170	1-6033	C07B	1-7346	21374E
1	嚁	5-2571			E0C9	2-5C55	
2	嚂	3-2292			E0C7	2-5C53	
3	嚃	3-2332			E0C5	2-5C51	
4	嚄	3-2329	1-2252	1-8452	E0C4	2-5C50	217335
5	嚅	0-6473	1-2253		C07D	1-7348	213750
6	嚆	0-6467	0-5169	0-9287	E0C3	2-5C4F	217334
7	嚇	1-4737	0-1937	1-8271	C07E	1-7349	213751
8	嚈	3-2193	1-2254				
9	嚉					E-5449	
A	嚊	5-2567	0-5171			E-5447	217337
B	嚋	5-2440	1-2255				
C	嚌	1-6366	1-2256		E0C1	2-5C4D	217328
D	嚍	5-2437			E0C2	2-5C4E	
E	嚎	0-2631			C07A	1-7345	21374F
F	嚏	0-4471	0-5174	1-7961	C0A1	1-734A	

569

	Char	G	J	K	B	C	A
0	嚐				C07C	1-7347	213752
1	嚑					E-645D	217336
2	嚒					E-645B	
3	嚓	0-6474			E0C0	2-5C4C	217325
4	嚔	5-2575	0-5173			E-575B	213753
5	嚕	1-6464	1-2257		C250	1-763C	213754
6	嚖	5-2574				E-575A	
7	嚗	3-2341			EFBC	2-6148	
8	嚘	3-2339			EFBA	2-6146	
9	嚙	1-3686	1-2258	1-5820	EFBF	2-614B	217345
A	嚚	3-2342	1-2259	1-7415	EFBD	2-6149	217342
B	嚛	3-2184				E-5758	
C	嚜	3-2343			EFBB	2-6147	217341
D	嚝	5-2377	1-2260		EFBE	2-614A	
E	嚞	5-2304	1-2261			E-5759	21733E
F	嚟		1-2262			E-5757	

56A

	Char	G	J	K	B	C	A
0	嚠		0-5172			E-575C	4B4937
1	嚡						
2	嚢		0-3925				
3	嚣	0-4789					27375E
4	嚤						
5	嚥		0-5175	0-7031	C360	1-782C	213758
6	嚦	1-6331	1-2263		F1F2	2-653E	21734C
7	嚧	3-2174	1-2264		F1F3	2-653F	
8	嚨	1-3392	1-2265		C456	1-782D	213756
9	嚩	3-2336	1-2266				
A	嚪	5-2533			F1F4	2-6540	
B	嚫	3-2283	1-2267		F1F0	2-653C	
C	嚬	5-2554	1-2268	0-6213	F1F5	2-6541	21734E
D	嚭	3-2103	1-2269		F1F1	2-653D	21734B
E	嚮	1-8885	0-5176	0-9031	C251	1-763D	213755
F	嚯	0-6475				E-5A2D	4D3359

56B

	Char	G	J	K	B	C	A
0	嚰					E-645E	213757
1	嚱		1-2270				
2	嚲	3-1857			F3FE	2-686B	217353
3	嚳	1-6423	1-2271	1-5709	F441	2-686D	21735A
4	嚴	1-4947	0-5178	0-6981	C459	1-7964	21375A
5	嚵	3-2347			F440	2-686C	
6	嚶	1-6451	0-5177	1-7076	C458	1-7963	21375B
7	嚷	0-4034	1-2272		C457	1-7962	213759
8	嚸					E-6726	
9	嚹					E-6727	
A	嚺					E-645C	217332
B	嚻					E-5E26	
C	嚼	0-2932	0-5180	0-7736	C45A	1-7965	21375F
D	嚽	5-2563			F5C5	2-6B53	
E	嚾	3-2346	1-2273		F5C6	2-6B54	
F	嚿						

56C

	Char	G	J	K	B	C	A
0	囀	1-6389	0-5183	1-7585	C4DA	1-7A65	21375C
1	囁	1-6431	0-5181	1-6855	C4D9	1-7A64	21375D
2	囂	1-4789	0-5179	1-8457	C4DB	1-7A66	21375E
3	囃		0-5182	1-7526	F5C4	2-6B52	21735B
4	囄					E-6728	
5	囅	1-5770	1-2274		F6D8	2-6D46	217360
6	囆	5-2485			F6D7	2-6D45	
7	囇					E-5F40	
8	囈	1-6329	0-5184	1-7178	C56D	1-7B59	213762
9	囉	1-8851	1-2275	1-6184	C56F	1-7B5B	213761
A	囊	0-3650	1-2276	0-5005	C56E	1-7B5A	213760
B	囋	3-2345	1-2277		F6D9	2-6D47	
C	囌	1-8874	1-2280		C5C8	1-7C34	39563C
D	囍		1-2281	0-9378	F8A6	2-7034	217367
E	囎		0-5185				695375
F	囏	5-7488	1-2278				217362

56D

	Char	G	J	K	B	C	A
0	囐	5-2552	1-2279				
1	囑	1-5486	0-5186	0-8522	C5F1	1-7C5D	213764
2	囒					E-6071	
3	囓		0-5187		F8A5	2-7033	2D7345
4	囔	0-6476			F8EE	2-707C	21736A
5	囕						
6	囖						
7	囗	0-6477	0-5188		C949	2-212A	21736B
8	囘		0-4937			E-2177	4B3768
9	囙		1-2282				
A	囚	0-3984	0-2892	0-6586	A57D	1-463F	213766
B	四	0-4336	0-2745	0-6244	A57C	1-463E	213765
C	囜		1-2283				
D	囝	0-6478	1-2284		A65F	1-4760	21736D
E	回	0-2756	0-1883	0-9262	A65E	1-475F	213768
F	囟	0-5622	1-2285	1-6979	C9C7	2-2227	217370

56E

	Char	G	J	K	B	C	A
0	因	0-5082	0-1688	0-7655	A65D	1-475E	213767
1	囡	0-6479	1-2286		C9C6	2-2226	21736F
2	团	0-4537					273773
3	団		0-3536			E-233E	4B3773
4	囤	0-2258	1-2287		A779	1-495B	213769
5	囥	3-2351	1-2288		CAA9	2-2349	
6	囦	5-2587	1-2289	1-7135		E-252C	
7	囧	5-2586	1-2290		CAA8	2-2348	217377
8	囨		1-2291				
9	囩	3-2349				E-2526	
A	囪				A777	1-4959	21376B
B	囫	0-6481	1-2293	1-8406	A77A	1-495C	217375
C	囬					E-252B	2D3768
D	园	0-5216	1-2294			E-252A	273771
E	囮	3-2350	0-5189	1-7251	CAA7	2-2347	217376
F	囯					E-2529	27376F

56F

	Char	G	J	K	B	C	A
0	困	0-3207	0-2604	0-4561	A778	1-495A	274D57
1	囱	0-2049	1-2292			E-2548	
2	囲		0-1647			E-2527	393770
3	図		0-3162			E-2528	4B3774
4	围	0-4607					273770
5	囵	0-6480					27742E
6	囶		1-2301			E-2822	
7	囷	3-2352	1-2302	1-5939	CBF0	2-2570	21737E
8	囸	5-2588				E-277D	
9	囹	0-6482	0-5190	0-5423	CBF1	2-2571	217421
A	固	0-2544	0-2439	0-4519	A954	1-4C56	21376C
B	囻					E-277C	217379
C	囼	5-2589				E-2821	
D	国	0-2590	0-2581			E-277B	4B376F
E	图	0-4528					273774
F	囿	0-6483	0-5192	1-7373	ABAA	1-504C	217424

570

	Char	G	J	K	B	C	A
0	圀	5-2590	0-5191			E-2B65	2D376F
1	圁	3-2355	1-2303	1-7416	D148	2-2E4A	
2	圂	3-2354	1-2304	1-8401	D149	2-2E4B	217429
3	圃	0-3852	0-4264	0-8853	AE45	1-5467	21376D
4	圄	0-6484	0-5193	0-6956	AE46	1-5468	217428
5	圅					E-3027	217427
6	圆	0-5218					273772
7	圇	1-6480	1-2305		D4AC	2-342F	21742E
8	圈	0-4006	0-5201	0-4774	B0E9	1-594E	21376E
9	圉	0-6486	0-5194	1-7106	B0EB	1-5950	21742D
A	圊	0-6485	1-2306	1-7958	D4AB	2-342E	21742C
B	國	1-2590	0-5202	0-4748	B0EA	1-594F	21376F
C	圌	3-2356	1-2307		D87C	2-3A60	217430
D	圍	1-4607	0-5203	0-7444	B3F2	1-5E58	213770
E	圎					E-3A44	
F	圏		0-2387			E-3A43	

571

	Char	G	J	K	B	C	A
0	圐	3-2357					
1	圑		1-2308				
2	園	1-5216	0-1764	0-7414	B6E9	1-6350	213771
3	圓	1-5218	0-5204	0-7413	B6EA	1-6351	213772
4	圔	3-2358			DCE1	2-4228	217432
5	圕		1-2309			E-4052	217431
6	圖	1-4528	0-5206	0-5181	B9CF	1-6837	213774
7	圗					E-4637	
8	團	1-4537	0-5205	0-5105	B9CE	1-6836	213773
9	圙	3-2360					
A	圚	5-2592	1-2310		E549	2-4F70	217435
B	圛	3-2353	1-2311		E948	2-5652	217436
C	圜	0-6487	0-5208	1-7342	E947	2-5651	217437
D	圝		1-2312			E-5F41	217439
E	圞	3-2359			F96B	2-715A	21743A
F	土	0-4533	0-3758	0-8747	A467	1-4448	213775

572

	Char	G	J	K	B	C	A
0	圠	5-2152	1-2313		C959	2-2139	
1	圡	5-2151				E-2161	
2	圢	5-2153	1-2314		C96E	2-214F	
3	圣	0-4205	1-2315		C96F	2-2150	27526F
4	圤	5-2154	1-2316			E-2234	217441
5	圥		1-2317	1-6288			
6	圦		0-5209				695429
7	圧		0-1621			E-6249	4B3869
8	在	0-5258	0-2663	0-7804	A662	1-4763	21377A
9	圩	0-5955	1-2318		A666	1-4767	217443
A	圪	0-5957	1-2319		C9C9	2-2229	21744C
B	圫	5-2158					
C	圬	0-5956	1-2320	1-7208	A664	1-4765	343A5B
D	圭	0-2571	0-2329	0-4804	A663	1-4764	213777
E	圮	0-5960	1-2321	1-6678	C9C8	2-2228	217442
F	圯	0-5961	1-2322		A665	1-4766	213778

573

	Char	G	J	K	B	C	A
0	地	0-2156	0-3547	0-8202	A661	1-4762	213779
1	圱	5-2157				E-2341	
2	圲	3-1965				E-2342	
3	圳	0-5958	1-2323		A660	1-4761	21377B
4	圴	3-1966	1-2324		C9CA	2-222A	
5	圵					E-233F	
6	圶	5-2314				E-2340	
7	圷		0-5210				69542A
8	圸		0-5211				217448
9	圹	0-5959					27386B
A	场	0-1901					27384A
B	圻	0-5963	0-5213	0-4880	A7A6	1-4966	2D3830
C	圼	5-4144				E-2531	
D	圽	5-2166	1-2325			E-253E	
E	圾	0-2788	1-2326	1-5960	A7A3	1-4963	213824
F	圿	5-2164	1-2327			E-2530	21746A

574

	Char	G	J	K	B	C	A
0	址	0-5423	0-5214	0-8203	A77D	1-495F	213821
1	坁	5-2165			CAAA	2-234A	
2	坂	0-5964	0-2668	0-8788		E-2540	395E71
3	坃	5-2160				E-2536	
4	坄	3-1978				E-252F	
5	坅	3-1976	1-2328		CAAB	2-234B	217465
6	坆	5-2163	1-2329			E-253C	
7	均	0-3089	0-2249	0-4819	A7A1	1-4961	213822
8	坈	3-1979				E-252D	
9	坉	3-1970			CAAD	2-234D	217463
A	坊	0-2327	0-4323	0-5909	A77B	1-495D	21377D
B	坋	3-1977			CAAE	2-234E	217468
C	坌	0-5948	1-2330	1-6646	CAAC	2-234C	217469
D	坍	0-4414	1-2331	0-5127	A77E	1-4960	213823
E	坎	0-3118	0-5212	0-4276	A7A2	1-4962	213825
F	坏	0-2721	0-5215	1-6549	A7A5	1-4965	27386E

575

	Char	G	J	K	B	C	A
0	坐	0-5588	0-2633	0-8106	A7A4	1-4964	273C77
1	坑	0-3151	0-2503	0-4353	A77C	1-495E	21377C
2	坒	5-4033	1-2332		CAAF	2-234F	
3	坓					E-2532	
4	坔	5-5266				E-2541	
5	坕					E-2542	
6	坖					E-2533	
7	块	0-3173				E-2538	273856
8	坘					E-2537	
9	坙					E-645F	
A	坚	0-2865					2D383F
B	坛	0-4419					273864
C	坜	0-5962					27386F
D	坝	0-1651					273871
E	坞	0-4675					273855
F	坟	0-2356				E-2535	273860

576

	Char	G	J	K	B	C	A
0	坠	0-5525					273861
1	坡	0-3834	0-5219	0-8771	A959	1-4C5B	21382B
2	坢	3-1987	1-2333		CBFE	2-257E	
3	坣	5-2175				E-2825	
4	坤	0-3204	0-2605	0-4562	A95B	1-4C5D	21382C
5	坥	3-1982	1-2334			E-2823	
6	坦	0-4425	0-3519	0-8704	A95A	1-4C5C	21382D
7	坧	5-2172	1-2335	1-7908		E-2826	21747A
8	坨	0-5971	1-2336	1-7447	CC40	2-2621	217470
9	坩	0-5965	0-5216	1-5539	A958	1-4C5A	213829
A	坪	0-3826	0-3658	0-8832	A957	1-4C59	213828
B	坫	0-5967	1-2337		CBF5	2-2575	2D3C70
C	坬	3-1985					
D	坭	0-5972	1-2338		CBF4	2-2574	217477
E	坮	5-2185	1-2339	0-5161		E-2828	21752A
F	坯	0-3787	1-2340	1-6550	CBF2	2-2572	33386E

577

	Char	G	J	K	B	C	A
0	坰	3-1984	1-2341	0-4448	CBF7	2-2577	217526
1	坱	3-1983	1-2342	1-7048	CBF6	2-2576	217528
2	坲	3-1990			CBF3	2-2573	
3	坳	0-5974	1-2343	1-7282	CBFC	2-257C	217535
4	坴	5-2171	1-2344		CBFD	2-257D	217479
5	坵		1-2345	0-4706	CBFA	2-257A	217531
6	坶	0-5973			CBF8	2-2578	21752D
7	坷	0-3132	1-2346	1-5505	A956	1-4C58	21382A
8	坸	5-2180		1-5844		E-2829	
9	坹	5-2182	1-2347				
A	坺	3-1981	1-2348				
B	坻	0-5970	1-2349	1-7789	CBFB	2-257B	217532
C	坼	0-5969	1-2350	0-8683	A95C	1-4C5E	21382F
D	坽	5-2178			CC41	2-2622	
E	坾	5-2168	1-2351				
F	坿	8-1361	0-5220			E-282A	217530

578

	Char	G	J	K	B	C	A
0	垀	3-1986			CBF9	2-2579	
1	垁	5-2177	1-2352			E-2824	
2	垂	0-2025	0-3166	0-6587	ABAB	1-504D	21382E
3	垃	0-3212	1-2353		A955	1-4C57	213827
4	垄	0-3402					27386D
5	垅	0-5966					27785A
6	垆	0-5968					27785E
7	垇	5-2176					
8	垈		0-5218	0-5160			217533
9	垉		0-5221				21752E
A	垊					E-6460	217475
B	型	0-4845	0-2331	0-9094	ABAC	1-504E	213831
C	垌	0-5977	1-2354	1-6152	CE54	2-2955	217549
D	垍	3-2002				E-2B69	
E	垎	5-2202				E-2B68	
F	垏	5-2205			CE5A	2-295B	

579

	Char	G	J	K	B	C	A
0	垐	3-2007				E-2B6C	217539
1	垑	3-2005				E-2B67	
2	垒	0-3261				E-2B6A	27386C
3	垓	0-5982	0-5222	0-9007	ABB2	1-5054	21753A
4	垔	5-6367	1-2355		CE58	2-2959	217545
5	垕	5-2194	1-2364	1-8466	CE5E	2-295F	21755B
6	垖	5-2193				E-2B71	
7	垗	3-2003	1-2356		CE55	2-2956	21754B
8	垘	3-1994			CE59	2-295A	
9	垙	5-2191	1-2357		CE5B	2-295C	217548
A	垚	5-2187	1-2358		CE5D	2-295E	217543
B	垛	0-2266			CE57	2-2958	217552
C	垜		1-2359			E-2B70	
D	垝	3-2004	1-2360		CE56	2-2957	21754E
E	垞	3-2009	1-2361	1-8113	CE51	2-2952	21753F
F	垟	3-2008	1-2362		CE52	2-2953	217538

57A

	Char	G	J	K	B	C	A
0	垠	0-5983	0-5223	0-7557	ABAD	1-504F	213830
1	垡	0-5950	1-2363			E-2B6B	217557
2	垢	0-2524	0-2504	0-4707	ABAF	1-5051	213834
3	垣	0-5211	0-1932	0-7415	ABAE	1-5050	213832
4	垤	0-5976	0-5225	1-7820	CE53	2-2954	217547
5	垥	5-2201			CE5C	2-295D	
6	垦	0-3149				E-2B6D	273867
7	垧	0-5980	1-2365			E-2B72	217554
8	垨		1-2366			E-2B6E	
9	垩	0-5949	1-2367				27383E
A	垪		0-5226				69543A
B	垫	0-2170					27385A
C	垬		1-2368			E-2B66	
D	垭	0-5975					277638
E	垮	0-3169			ABB1	1-5053	213833
F	垯	7-0101					

57B

	Char	G	J	K	B	C	A
0	垰		0-5227				69543B
1	垱	8-9041					
2	垲	0-5978					277748
3	垳		0-5224				695438
4	垴	0-5981					705B71
5	垵	5-2203			CE50	2-2951	217540
6	垶	5-2216			D153	2-2E55	
7	垷	3-1973				E-302A	
8	垸	0-5989	1-2369	1-7260	D152	2-2E54	21755F
9	垹	5-2186			D157	2-2E59	
A	垺	3-2015			D14E	2-2E50	
B	垻					E-3030	4B3871
C	垼	3-2014			D151	2-2E53	
D	垽	3-2018	1-2370	1-7417	D150	2-2E52	
E	垾	3-2012				E-302F	21756C
F	垿	3-2017			D154	2-2E56	

57C

	Char	G	J	K	B	C	A
0	埀		0-5217			E-3038	4B382E
1	埁	5-2213			D158	2-2E5A	
2	埂	0-2501			AE47	1-5469	213836
3	埃	0-1603	0-5228	0-6879	AE4A	1-546C	213839
4	埄	5-2215				E-3034	217622
5	埅	5-2206				E-3035	
6	埆	3-2016	0-5229	1-5518	D14F	2-2E51	21757E
7	埇	5-2219	1-2371	0-7325	D155	2-2E57	217560
8	埈		1-2372	0-8156		E-3033	
9	埉	5-2189		1-8359		E-3028	
A	埊	5-2722				E-3037	
B	埋	0-3481	0-4368	0-5656	AE49	1-546B	213838
C	埌	3-2020	1-2373		D14A	2-2E4C	
D	埍	3-2013				E-302B	
E	城	0-1939	0-3075	0-6482	ABB0	1-5052	213837
F	埏	0-5979	1-2374	1-7136	D4BA	2-343D	21765A

57D

	Char	G	J	K	B	C	A
0	埐	3-2021			D156	2-2E58	
1	埑	5-2209		1-7936		E-3036	
2	埒	0-5988	0-5231	1-6207	D14D	2-2E4F	217577
3	埓		0-5232				4B7577
4	埔	0-3850	0-5230		AE48	1-546A	213835
5	埕	0-5984	1-2375		D14C	2-2E4E	217573
6	埖		0-5234				695442
7	埗	5-2210					
8	埘	0-5985					277742
9	埙	0-5987					277745
A	埚	0-5986					27767A
B	埛					E-3032	217571
C	埜		0-3924	1-7080	D4B1	2-3434	335D3B
D	埝	0-5994	1-2376			E-346E	21765B
E	埞	5-2229	1-2377			E-3471	
F	域	0-5182	0-1672	0-7020	B0EC	1-5951	21383D

57E

	Char	G	J	K	B	C	A
0	埠	0-1826	0-4154	0-6092	B0F0	1-5955	213843
1	埡	1-5975	1-2394		D4C1	2-3444	
2	埢	3-2035			D4AF	2-3432	
3	埣	5-2227	0-5235		D4BD	2-3440	217629
4	埤	0-5993	1-2378	1-6679	B0F1	1-5956	213842
5	埥	5-2220			D4BF	2-3442	
6	埦	5-2230	1-2379			E-3472	21762D
7	埧	3-2027	1-2380		D4C5	2-3448	
8	埨	3-1975				E-3474	
9	埩	3-2006	1-2381		D4C9	2-344C	
A	埪	3-2038				E-3469	
B	埫	5-2226					
C	埬	5-2174			D4C0	2-3443	217635
D	埭	0-6004	1-2382	1-8150	D4B4	2-3437	217631
E	埮	3-2037			D4BC	2-343F	
F	埯	0-5991				E-346B	217643

57F

	Char	G	J	K	B	C	A
0	埰	3-2032	1-2383	0-8381	D4CA	2-344D	217652
1	埱	5-2224			D4C8	2-344B	
2	埲	3-2023			D4BE	2-3441	
3	埳			1-5540	D4B9	2-343C	217658
4	埴	0-5990	0-3093	0-6748	D4B2	2-3435	21763D
5	埵	3-2030	1-2384		D8A6	2-3A68	217726
6	埶	3-2025	1-2385		D4B0	2-3433	21762C
7	執	1-5420	0-2825	0-8291	B0F5	1-595A	21383B
8	埸	0-5992	1-2386		D4B7	2-343A	21764E
9	培	0-3764	0-3961	0-5938	B0F6	1-595B	21383A
A	基	0-2789	0-2080	0-4881	B0F2	1-5957	21383C
B	埻	3-2033		1-7765	D4AD	2-3430	21762A
C	埼	3-2026	0-2675	0-4882	D4C3	2-3446	2D3C21
D	埽	0-6003	1-2387	1-6872	D4B5	2-3438	21764D
E	埾	5-2221	1-2388			E-346F	
F	埿	5-2228	1-2389			E-3475	

580

	Char	G	J	K	B	C	A
0	堀	0-6005	0-4357	0-4760	D4B3	2-3436	217633
1	堁	3-2028			D4C6	2-3449	217648
2	堂	0-4435	0-3818	0-5149	B0F3	1-5958	213840
3	堃	8-1573	1-2390	1-5714		E-3476	21762B
4	堄	3-2031	1-2391		D4CC	2-344F	217659
5	堅	1-2865	0-2388	0-4417	B0ED	1-5952	21383F
6	堆	0-2249	0-3447	0-8756	B0EF	1-5954	213841
7	堇	0-6132			D4BB	2-343E	217636
8	堈	3-1971	1-2392	0-4308	D4B6	2-3439	
9	堉	3-2034	1-2393	0-7528	AE4B	1-546D	21756A
A	堊	1-5949	0-5233	0-6830	B0EE	1-5953	21383E
B	堋	0-6001	0-5236	1-6672	D4B8	2-343B	217656
C	堌	3-2029	1-2401		D4C7	2-344A	217650
D	堍	0-6002	1-2402		D4CB	2-344E	217640
E	堎	3-2024			D4C2	2-3445	217639
F	堏					E-6461	21763B

581

	Char	G	J	K	B	C	A
0	堐				D4C4	2-3447	21763E
1	堑	0-3921					27385B
2	堒					E-6462	217649
3	堓					E-6463	217651
4	堔				D4AE	2-3431	
5	堕	0-2273	0-3436				273862
6	堖	1-5981					
7	堗	5-2247		1-6148			
8	堘					E-3A4A	217723
9	堙	0-6007	0-5237	1-7461	D8A1	2-3A63	217669
A	堚	3-2010				E-3A45	
B	堛	5-2233	1-2403		D8AA	2-3A6C	217667
C	堜				D8A9	2-3A6B	
D	堝	1-5986	0-5238	1-5745	B3FA	1-5E60	21767A
E	堞	0-6006	1-2404	0-8460	D8A2	2-3A64	21766C
F	堟	5-2249	1-2405			E-3A47	

582

	Char	G	J	K	B	C	A
0	堠	0-6009	1-2406	1-8467	B3FB	1-5E61	21772B
1	堡	0-1704	0-5240	0-6034	B3F9	1-5E5F	21384B
2	堢	5-2243				E-3A50	
3	堣	5-2237		1-7319	D8A4	2-3A66	
4	堤	0-2144	0-3673	0-8007	B3F6	1-5E5C	213849
5	堥	3-2056			D8A8	2-3A6A	
6	堦		1-2407	1-5662		E-3A4C	2D5F2C
7	堧	5-2235	1-2408	0-7032	D8A3	2-3A65	217671
8	堨	3-2045			D8A5	2-3A67	217676
9	堩				D87D	2-3A61	
A	堪	0-3116	0-2014	0-4277	B3F4	1-5E5A	213847
B	堫	3-2050				E-6336	
C	堬	5-2244				2-3A74	
D	堭	3-2048	1-2409		D8B2	2-3A73	217729
E	堮	5-2239			D8AE	2-3A70	217678
F	堯	1-5002	0-8401	0-7275	B3F3	1-5E59	213845

583

	Char	G	J	K	B	C	A
0	堰	0-4963	0-1765	0-6972	B3F7	1-5E5D	213848
1	報	1-1708	0-4283	0-6035	B3F8	1-5E5E	213844
2	堲	3-2022	1-2410		D14B	2-2E4D	
3	堳	3-2055			D8AB	2-3A6D	21766A
4	場	1-1901	0-3076	0-7762	B3F5	1-5E5B	21384A
5	堵	0-2234	0-3740	0-5182	B0F4	1-5959	213846
6	堶	5-2234			D8AD	2-3A6F	
7	堷				D87E	2-3A62	
8	堸	5-2167			D8B0	2-3A72	
9	堹	5-2241	1-2411		D8AF	2-3A71	
A	堺	5-2238	0-2670	0-4487		E-3A4E	2D4C2C
B	堻				D8B3	2-3A75	
C	堼	3-2041				E-3A49	
D	堽	3-2059	0-5246		DCEF	2-4236	217749
E	堾	3-2040				E-3A4B	
F	堿		1-2412		D8AC	2-3A6E	21766D

584

	Char	G	J	K	B	C	A
0	塀		0-4229	1-6583			21775F
1	塁		0-4661				4B386C
2	塂	8-1572					
3	塃	3-2043					
4	塄	0-6008					21767D
5	塅	3-2047				E-6337	
6	塆	8-9053					
7	塇					E-6464	21765F
8	塈	3-2054			D8A7	2-3A69	217721
9	塉	3-2065	1-2413	1-7909	DCE7	2-422E	
A	塊	1-3173	0-1884	0-4652	B6F4	1-635B	213856
B	塋	1-6067	0-5242	0-7111	B6F7	1-635E	217737
C	塌	0-4390	1-2414	1-8144	B6F2	1-6359	213851
D	塍	0-7583	1-2415	1-6955	DCE6	2-422D	21774D
E	塎	3-2068			DCEA	2-4231	217730
F	塏	1-5978	1-2416	0-4335	DCE5	2-422C	217748

585

	Char	G	J	K	B	C	A
0	塐	5-2250	1-2417	1-6873		E-4057	
1	塑	0-4360	0-3326	0-6517	B6BC	1-6353	21384F
2	塒	1-5985	0-5245	1-6961	B6F6	1-635D	217742
3	塓	3-2070			DCE2	2-4229	217747
4	塔	0-4394	0-3767	0-8718	B6F0	1-6357	213854
5	塕	3-2061	1-2418		DCE9	2-4230	
6	塖	5-2254				E-405B	21774E
7	塗	1-4531	0-3741	0-5183	B6EE	1-6355	21384D
8	塘	0-4433	0-3768	0-5150	B6ED	1-6354	21384E
9	塙	3-2063	0-4025	1-5677	DCBC	2-4233	217735
A	塚	8-1418	0-3645	0-8532	B6EF	1-6356	213852
B	塛				DCEE	2-4235	
C	塜	5-2258				E-4056	
D	塝	5-2256			DCEB	2-4232	217733
E	塞	0-4091	0-2641	0-6361	B6EB	1-6352	21384C
F	塟		1-2419			E-405E	2D5550

586

	Char	G	J	K	B	C	A
0	塠	3-2049				E-405C	
1	塡		1-2420	0-7883		E-4058	
2	塢	1-4675	0-5241	0-7181	B6F5	1-635C	213855
3	塣				DCF0	2-4237	
4	塤	1-5987	1-2421	0-9320	DCE4	2-422B	217745
5	塥	0-6010			DCED	2-4234	21773D
6	塦					E-405D	
7	塧	5-2257	1-2422			E-6343	
8	塨	3-2057	1-2423		DCE3	2-422A	
9	塩		0-1786	1-7151		E-405A	2D6251
A	塪					E-4059	
B	填	0-4478	0-3722		B6F1	1-6358	213850
C	塬	0-6011				E-4054	217740
D	塭				B6F3	1-635A	213853
E	塮	3-2060					
F	塯				DCE8	2-422F	

587

	Char	G	J	K	B	C	A
0	塰		0-5243				69544B
1	塱	5-2259			DCF1	2-4238	
2	塲		0-5239			E-4643	2D384A
3	塳	3-2062				E-463E	
4	塴	3-2075			E15D	2-4944	
5	塵	1-1930	0-3148	0-8240	B9D0	1-6838	213859
6	塶				E163	2-494A	
7	塷	5-2211				E-4642	
8	塸	3-1969	1-2424			E-463C	
9	塹	1-3921	0-5247	0-8350	B9D6	1-683D	21385B
A	塺	3-9201			E15F	2-4946	
B	塻	5-2252			E166	2-494D	
C	塼		1-2425	0-7884	E157	2-493E	217761
D	塽	5-2267		1-6786	B9D7	1-683F	21776B
E	塾	0-5951	0-2946	0-6651	B9D1	1-6839	213858
F	塿	3-2052	1-2426		E15C	2-4943	21776F

Code	Char	G	J	K	B	C	A
5880	墀	0-6015	1-2427	1-7790	BC55	1-6C3F	21385F
5881	墁	0-6012	1-2428	1-6392	E15B	2-4942	217770
5882	墂	5-2265			E164	2-494B	
5883	境	0-3019	0-2213	0-4449	B9D2	1-683A	213857
5884	墄	3-2074				E-463D	
5885	墅	0-4291	0-5248	0-6374	B9D6	1-683E	21385C
5886	墆	3-2042			E15A	2-4941	
5887	墇	3-2078	1-2429		E160	2-4947	
5888	墈	3-2071	1-2430		E165	2-494C	217763
5889	墉	0-6013	1-2431	0-7326	E156	2-493D	21775C
588A	墊	1-2170	1-2432	1-7634	B9D4	1-683C	21385A
588B	墋	5-2231			E15E	2-4945	
588C	墌	3-2077	1-2433			E-463A	
588D	墍		1-2434	1-5970		E-4645	
588E	墎	3-2064			E162	2-4949	21775A
588F	墏	5-2245	1-2435		E168	2-494F	
5890	墐	3-2072	1-2436	1-5947	E158	2-493F	217765
5891	墑	5-2273			E161	2-4948	
5892	墒	0-4142				E-4638	217758
5893	墓	0-3625	0-4272	0-5755	B9D3	1-683B	21385D
5894	墔	5-2271	1-2437		E167	2-494E	
5895	墕	5-2262				E-4641	
5896	墖		1-2438			E-4644	2D3854
5897	増		0-3393			E-4640	4B385E
5898	墘	3-2073			E159	2-4940	217768
5899	墙	0-3929					274A46
589A	墚	0-6014					217755
589B	墛					E-6465	217760
589C	墜	1-5525	0-3638	0-8545	BC59	1-6C43	213861
589D	墝	5-2190	1-2439	1-7283	E54B	2-4F72	346622
589E	增	0-5286		0-8182	BC57	1-6C41	21385E
589F	墟	0-4870	0-5250	0-9039	BC56	1-6C40	213863
58A0	墠	3-2036	1-2440		E54D	2-4F74	21782E
58A1	墡	3-2087	1-2441	1-6824	E552	2-4F79	21777E
58A2	墢	5-2183	1-2442			E-4B46	
58A3	墣	3-2081		1-6603	E54E	2-4F75	217830
58A4	墤					E-4B50	
58A5	墥	3-2086			E551	2-4F78	
58A6	墦	3-2085	1-2443		BC5C	1-6C46	217832
58A7	墧					E-4B51	
58A8	墨	0-3611	0-4347	0-5788	BEA5	1-702E	216267
58A9	墩	0-2253	1-2444	0-5234	BC5B	1-6C45	21777B
58AA	墪					E-4B4B	
58AB	墫	5-2302	0-5251	1-7766	E54A	2-4F71	2D4550
58AC	墬	5-2277			E550	2-4F77	
58AD	墭	5-2268				E-463F	21782B
58AE	墮	1-2273	0-5256	0-8669	BC5A	1-6C44	213862
58AF	墯	5-2281			E54F	2-4F76	
58B0	墰	5-2278		1-6085		E-4B4D	
58B1	墱	5-2282	1-2445	1-6176	E54C	2-4F73	217824
58B2	墲	3-1967	1-2446			E-4B49	
58B3	墳	1-2356	0-4215	0-6137	BC58	1-6C42	213860
58B4	墴	5-2263				E-4B4F	
58B5	墵					E-4B4C	
58B6	墶	3-1992					
58B7	墷	3-2001				E-4B47	
58B8	墸		0-5255				695457
58B9	墹		0-5249				695451
58BA	墺	3-2084	0-5252	0-7182	E94D	2-5657	21784C
58BB	墻	1-3929	0-5254	0-7763		E-504A	2D4A46
58BC	墼	0-5952	1-2448		E94F	2-5659	217841
58BD	墽	3-2089			E94A	2-5654	
58BE	墾	1-3149	0-2606	0-4243	BEC1	1-704A	213867
58BF	墿	5-2184			E94C	2-5656	217849
58C0	壀					E-504B	
58C1	壁	0-1758	0-4241	0-5990	BEC0	1-7049	213866
58C2	壂	3-2090	1-2449		E94E	2-5658	
58C3	壃			1-5557		E-5048	
58C4	壄		1-2447			E-504C	
58C5	壅	0-5953	0-5257	0-7221	BEC3	1-704C	213865
58C6	壆	3-1988			E950	2-565A	21784B
58C7	壇	1-4419	0-3537	0-5106	BEC2	1-704B	213864
58C8	壈		1-2450		E949	2-5653	21783A
58C9	壉				E94B	2-5655	
58CA	壊		0-1885			E-5049	2D386E
58CB	壋	3-1993					
58CC	壌		0-3077				4B3870
58CD	壍	5-2275	1-2451			E-544B	
58CE	壎		1-2452	0-9321	C0A5	1-734E	217856
58CF	壏	3-2058			ECCC	2-5C58	
58D0	壐	5-2181	1-2453			E-544C	
58D1	壑	0-5954	0-5259	0-8941	C0A4	1-734D	21386A
58D2	壒	5-2284	1-2454		ECCD	2-5C59	217854
58D3	壓	1-4925	0-5258	0-6866	C0A3	1-734C	213869
58D4	壔	3-2011	1-2455	1-6124	ECCB	2-5C57	
58D5	壕	0-2630	0-2572	0-9129	C0A2	1-734B	213868
58D6	壖	3-2091	1-2456		ECCA	2-5C56	217850
58D7	壗		0-5260				69545C
58D8	壘	1-3261	0-5262	0-5504	C253	1-763F	21386C
58D9	壙	1-5959	0-5261	0-4637	C252	1-763E	21386B
58DA	壚	1-5968	1-2457	1-6274	F1F6	2-6542	21785E
58DB	壛	5-2274			F1F8	2-6544	
58DC	壜		0-5264	1-6086		E-5A2F	347431
58DD	壝	3-2083	1-2458	1-7374	F1F7	2-6543	
58DE	壞	1-2721	0-5253	0-4653	C361	1-782E	21386E
58DF	壟	1-3402	0-5266	0-5470	C362	1-782F	21386D
58E0	壠	1-5966				E-5A2E	21785A
58E1	壡		1-2459				
58E2	壢	1-5962	1-2460		C363	1-7830	21386F
58E3	壣				F442	2-686E	
58E4	壤	0-4032	0-5265	0-6929	C45B	1-7966	213870
58E5	壥		0-5263				69545F
58E6	壦					E-5E28	
58E7	壧	5-2207			F7D3	2-6F22	
58E8	壨				F7D2	2-6F21	
58E9	壩	1-1651	1-2461		C5F2	1-7C5E	213871
58EA	壪	3-2051					
58EB	士	0-4231	0-2746	0-6245	A468	1-4449	213872
58EC	壬	0-4041	0-3149	0-7683	A4D0	1-4531	213873
58ED	壭						
58EE	壮	0-5519	0-3352			E-2343	273874
58EF	壯	1-5519	0-5267	0-7764	A7A7	1-4967	213874
58F0	声	0-4189	0-3228			E-2545	275274
58F1	壱		0-1677			E-2543	4B3021
58F2	売		0-3968			E-2544	395A2F
58F3	壳	0-3139	1-2462			E-282D	27463C
58F4	壴	3-2101			CE5F	2-2960	
58F5	壵					E-2B77	
58F6	壶	0-2688					273876
58F7	壷		0-3659			E-3477	2D3876
58F8	壸	8-9058					
58F9	壹	0-5028	0-5269	0-7676	B3FC	1-5E62	333021
58FA	壺	1-2688	0-5268	0-9130	B3FD	1-5E63	213876
58FB	壻		0-5270	0-6375		E-3A52	2D3A2F
58FC	壼	3-2102	0-5271		DCF2	2-4239	21786C
58FD	壽	1-4257	0-5272	0-6588	B9D8	1-6840	213877
58FE	壾	5-2294			E169	2-4950	
58FF	壿				E553	2-4F7A	

Code	Char	G	J	K	B	C	A
5900	夀					E-6466	2D3877
5901	夁					E-504D	
5902	夂	0-6626	0-5273			E-2139	217870
5903	夃	5-2121			C95A	2-213A	
5904	处	0-2006				E-2235	275647
5905	夅	5-2875	1-2463			E-2344	
5906	夆	3-2620	1-2464	1-6613	CAB0	2-2350	217873
5907	备	0-1724					273240
5908	夈			1-7549		E-2B7A	
5909	変		0-4249			E-2B79	4B594B
590A	夊	8-0891	0-5274			E-213A	4B7874
590B	夋	3-1949	1-2465			E-2546	
590C	夌	3-2621	1-2466		CC42	2-2623	
590D	复	0-2420			CE60	2-2961	273D6F
590E	夎	3-2623			D159	2-2E5B	
590F	夏	0-4736	0-1838	0-8930	AE4C	1-546E	213878
5910	夐	3-1879	0-5275	1-8364		E-4646	21787A
5911	夑					E-6560	22545C
5912	夒	3-2624	1-2467		F1F9	2-6545	
5913	夓		1-2468				
5914	夔	0-5771	1-2469	0-4883	C4DC	1-7A67	213879
5915	夕	0-4706	0-4528	0-6410	A469	1-444A	21387A
5916	外	0-4566	0-1916	0-7266	A57E	1-4640	21387B
5917	夗	3-2616			C970	2-2151	
5918	夘		0-5041			E-2236	2D346A
5919	夙	0-5777	0-2940	0-6652	A667	1-4768	21387C
591A	多	0-2264	0-3431	0-5093	A668	1-4769	21387D
591B	夛		0-5276				4B387D
591C	夜	0-5025	0-4475	0-6908	A95D	1-4C5F	21387E
591D	夝	5-2865	1-2471				
591E	夞						
591F	够	0-2527				E-3479	2D3921
5920	夠				B0F7	1-595C	213921
5921	夡	5-2868	1-2472				
5922	夢	1-3546	0-4420	0-5751	B9DA	1-6842	213924
5923	夣		1-2473			E-405F	
5924	夤	0-6625	1-2474	1-7462	B9DB	1-6843	213922
5925	夥	0-6623	0-5278	1-5746	B9D9	1-6841	213923
5926	夦					E-4B53	
5927	大	0-2083	0-3471	0-5162	A46A	1-444B	213925
5928	夨	5-2311	1-2475				
5929	天	0-4476	0-3723	0-8424	A4D1	1-4532	213928
592A	太	0-4411	0-3432	0-8728	A4D3	1-4534	213926
592B	夫	0-2382	0-4155	0-6093	A4D2	1-4533	213927
592C	夬	3-1615	0-5279	1-8111	C95B	2-213B	217928
592D	夭	0-5618	0-5280	0-7276	A4D4	1-4535	213929
592E	央	0-4975	0-1791	0-6871	A5A1	1-4641	21392A
592F	夯	0-2627	1-2476	1-8312	C971	2-2152	21792B
5930	夰	5-2313	1-2477			E-2238	
5931	失	0-4207	0-2826	0-6787	A5A2	1-4642	21392B
5932	夲	5-2312	0-5281			E-2237	334369
5933	夳		1-2478				
5934	头	0-4523				E-2239	276046
5935	夵	5-2315	1-2479				
5936	夶		1-2480			E-2347	
5937	夷	0-5036	0-1648	0-7608	A669	1-476A	21392C
5938	夸	0-3168	0-5282	1-5747	A66A	1-476B	275861
5939	夹	0-2848					27392E
593A	夺	0-2265					273940
593B	夻						
593C	夼	0-6237			C9CB	2-222B	217930
593D	夽	3-2107				E-2549	
593E	夾	1-2848	0-5283	0-9081	A7A8	1-4968	21392E
593F	夿	3-2111	1-2481				
5940	奀	3-2108			CAB1	2-2351	217933
5941	奁	0-6238					27393F
5942	奂	0-5928					4B3938
5943	奃	3-2113	1-2482				
5944	奄	0-4957	0-1766	0-6982	A961	1-4C63	213933
5945	奅	3-2114			CC43	2-2624	
5946	奆	3-2109	1-2483				
5947	奇	0-3870	0-2081	0-4884	A95F	1-4C61	213932
5948	奈	0-3646	0-3864	0-5015	A960	1-4C62	213931
5949	奉	0-2378	0-4284	0-6069	A95E	1-4C60	213930
594A	奊	3-1991			D15A	2-2E5C	
594B	奋	0-2360				E-282E	273941
594C	奌					E-282F	
594D	奍					E-6467	217938
594E	奎	0-3192	0-5287	0-4805	ABB6	1-5058	213936
594F	奏	0-5564	0-3353	0-8120	ABB5	1-5057	213937
5950	奐	1-5928	0-5286	0-9217	ABB7	1-5059	213938
5951	契	0-3885	0-2332	0-4488	ABB4	1-5056	213935
5952	奒	5-2327	1-2484			E-2B7C	
5953	奓	3-2119	1-2485	1-7834	CE61	2-2962	217943
5954	奔	0-1728	0-4359	0-6138	A962	1-4C64	21392F
5955	奕	0-6240	0-5285	0-9049	ABB3	1-5055	213934
5956	奖	0-2917					277954
5957	套	0-4455	0-3769	0-8763	AE4D	1-546F	213939
5958	奘	0-6242	0-5289	1-7531	AE4E	1-5470	21393A
5959	奙		1-2486				
595A	奚	0-6241	0-5288	0-9008	AE4F	1-5471	21393B
595B	奛		1-2487			E-347B	
595C	奜	3-8454			D4CD	2-3450	21794B
595D	奝	3-2123	1-2488			E-347C	
595E	奞	3-2121	1-2489			E-347D	
595F	奟	3-2122	1-2490				
5960	奠	0-2176	0-5291	0-7885	B3FE	1-5E64	21393C
5961	奡	3-1606	1-2491		D8B4	2-3A76	21794F
5962	奢	0-4161	0-5290	0-6246	B0F8	1-595D	21393D
5963	奣	3-3979	1-2492			E-3A53	
5964	奤	3-2124				E-3A54	
5965	奥	0-1634	0-1792				4B393E
5966	奦	3-2127				E-4060	
5967	奧		0-5292	0-7183	B6F8	1-635F	21393E
5968	奨		0-3009			E-4061	4B7954
5969	奩	1-6238	0-5294	1-6254	B9DD	1-6845	21393F
596A	奪	1-2265	0-3505	0-8712	B9DC	1-6844	213940
596B	奫	3-2129	1-2493	0-7536	E16A	2-4951	
596C	奬	1-2917	0-5293	0-7765		E-4648	217954
596D	奭	3-2128	1-2494	0-6411	BC5D	1-6C47	217955
596E	奮	1-2360	0-4219	0-6139	BEC4	1-704D	213941
596F	奯	3-2117	1-2501				
5970	奰	3-2130			EFC0	2-614C	
5971	奱				F6DA	2-6D48	
5972	奲	5-2340	1-2502		F7D4	2-6F23	
5973	女	0-3714	0-2987	0-5019	A46B	1-444C	213942
5974	奴	0-3711	0-3759	0-5031	A5A3	1-4643	213943
5975	奵	3-2790	1-2503			E-223B	
5976	奶	0-3644	1-2504	1-6025	A5A4	1-4644	213944
5977	奷				C9D1	2-2231	
5978	奸	0-2873	0-5301	0-4244	A66C	1-476D	213947
5979	她	0-4393	1-2505		A66F	1-4770	213949
597A	奺	3-2793				E-234B	
597B	奻	5-3134	1-2506		C9CF	2-222F	
597C	奼	3-2792	1-2507		C9CD	2-222D	217965
597D	好	0-2635	0-2505	0-9131	A66E	1-476F	213948
597E	奾	5-3131			C9D0	2-2230	
597F	奿				C9D2	2-2232	

598

	Char	G	J	K	B	C	A
0	妀				C9CC	2-222C	
1	妁	0-6989	0-5302		A671	1-4772	21394B
2	如	0-4071	0-3901	0-6993	A670	1-4771	21394A
3	妃	0-6990	0-4062	0-6169	A66D	1-476E	213946
4	妄	0-4593	0-4449	0-5645	A66B	1-476C	213945
5	妅	5-3129			C9CE	2-222E	
6	妆	0-5517				E-234D	273953
7	妇	0-2430					273A27
8	妈	0-3472					273A36
9	妉	5-3144				E-2555	
A	妊	0-4049	0-3905	0-7684	A7B3	1-4973	213956
B	妋	5-3136	1-2508				
C	妌	3-2802	1-2509			E-254C	
D	妍	0-6991	0-5311		A7B0	1-4970	217A44
E	妎	3-2810	1-2510		CAB6	2-2356	
F	妏	5-3143			CAB9	2-2359	

59A

	Char	G	J	K	B	C	A
0	妠	3-2809			CAB4	2-2354	217971
1	妡	5-3140			CABB	2-235B	
2	妢	3-2811			CAB7	2-2357	
3	妣	0-6994	0-5306	1-6680	A7AD	1-496D	213950
4	妤	0-7005	1-2515		A7B1	1-4971	21394F
5	妥	0-4555	0-3437	0-8670	A7B4	1-4974	213955
6	妦	5-3135			CAB2	2-2352	
7	妧	3-2803	1-2516	1-7261	CABA	2-235A	217969
8	妨	0-2333	0-4324	0-5910	A7AB	1-496B	21394C
9	妩	0-6992					273A45
A	妪	0-6993					273A3B
B	妫	0-7003					277C36
C	妬		0-3742	0-8764		E-2841	2D394D
D	妭	3-2821	1-2517			E-2833	
E	妮	0-3661	1-2518		A967	1-4C69	21395A
F	妯	0-7008	1-2519	1-8055	A96F	1-4C71	213960

59C

	Char	G	J	K	B	C	A
0	姀	5-3154			CC51	2-2632	
1	姁	3-2827	1-2525		CC4A	2-262B	217A3E
2	姂	3-2813				E-2837	
3	姃	3-2818	1-2526	0-7949	CC4D	2-262E	
4	姄		1-2527			E-2835	
5	姅	3-2832			A972	1-4C74	217A24
6	姆	0-3623	0-5308	0-5721	A969	1-4C6B	21395D
7	姇	5-3155			CC54	2-2635	
8	姈	3-2826	1-2528	1-6261	CC52	2-2633	
9	姉		0-2748	0-7711		E-283F	333963
A	姊	0-7002	1-2529		A96E	1-4C70	213963
B	始	0-4228	0-2747	0-6723	A96C	1-4C6E	213965
C	姌	3-2825			CC49	2-262A	
D	姍		1-2530	1-6765	A96B	1-4C6D	21395F
E	姎	3-2824			CC47	2-2628	
F	姏	3-2819			CC46	2-2627	217A28

59E

	Char	G	J	K	B	C	A
0	姠	5-3172			CE73	2-2974	
1	姡	3-2849			CE62	2-2963	
2	姢					E-2C2C	
3	姣	0-7015	1-2535	1-5821	ABBB	1-505D	213967
4	姤	3-2852	1-2536	1-5845	CE6C	2-296D	217A61
5	姥	0-3249	0-1724	1-6442	ABBE	1-5060	21396D
6	姦		0-2015	0-4245	ABC1	1-5063	213971
7	姧	5-2141	1-2537			E-2C2E	
8	姨	0-5044	0-5309	0-7609	ABBC	1-505E	21396C
9	姩	3-2846			CE70	2-2971	
A	姪		0-4437	0-8275	ABBF	1-5061	21396E
B	姫	5-3163	0-4117			E-2C23	213978
C	姬	0-2807		0-9379	AE56	1-5478	
D	姭				CE76	2-2977	
E	姮	3-2839	1-2538	0-8983	CE64	2-2965	217A4F
F	姯	5-3169	1-2539			E-2C24	

599

	Char	G	J	K	B	C	A
0	妐	3-2812			CAB8	2-2358	217A21
1	妑	3-2816		1-8172			
2	妒	0-2242	1-2511	1-8166	A7AA	1-496A	21394D
3	妓	0-2843	0-2124	0-4885	A7B2	1-4972	213951
4	妔	3-2814				E-254B	
5	妕		1-2512				
6	妖	0-4993	0-4537	0-7277	A7AF	1-496F	213957
7	妗	0-7001	1-2513	0-4850	CAB5	2-2355	21797C
8	妘	3-2805			CAB3	2-2353	21796B
9	妙	0-3578	0-4415	0-5756	A7AE	1-496E	213954
A	妚	5-3137				E-2556	21796F
B	妛		0-5412			E-2553	69562C
C	妜	3-2815				E-254E	
D	妝	1-5517	0-5303	1-7532	A7A9	1-4969	213953
E	妞	0-7004			A7AC	1-496C	213952
F	妟	5-4146	1-2514			E-2551	

59B

	Char	G	J	K	B	C	A
0	妰	5-3153	1-2520			E-2838	
1	妱				CC4F	2-2630	
2	妲	0-7007	0-5307	1-6077	CC48	2-2629	217A35
3	妳	8-1370	1-2521		A970	1-4C72	393944
4	妴	3-2828			CC53	2-2634	
5	妵	3-2830			CC44	2-2625	217A25
6	妶	3-2831			CC4B	2-262C	
7	妷		1-2522			E-2845	217A3A
8	妸	5-3148				E-2840	217A2C
9	妹	0-3535	0-4369	0-5657	A966	1-4C68	21395C
A	妺	3-2817	1-2523		CC45	2-2626	217A2A
B	妻	0-3862	0-2642	0-8403	A964	1-4C66	213959
C	妼	3-2834	1-2524		CC4C	2-262D	
D	妽				CC50	2-2631	
E	妾	0-7010	0-3010	0-8461	A963	1-4C65	213958
F	妿	5-3157				E-283D	

59D

	Char	G	J	K	B	C	A
0	姐	0-2967	0-1625	0-7827	A96A	1-4C6C	21395E
1	姑	0-2535	0-2440	0-4520	A968	1-4C6A	21395B
2	姒	0-7006	1-2531	1-6745	A971	1-4C73	213961
3	姓	0-4853	0-3211	0-6483	A96D	1-4C6F	213962
4	委	0-4615	0-1649	0-7445	A965	1-4C67	213966
5	姕	3-2843				E-2C26	
6	姖	3-2807			CC4E	2-262F	
7	姗	0-7009				E-2846	
8	姘	0-7016			ABB9	1-505B	21396A
9	姙		0-5312	0-7685		E-2C2D	2D3956
A	姚	0-5006	0-5313	0-7278	ABC0	1-5062	213972
B	姛	3-2845			CE6F	2-2970	
C	姜	0-2910	0-5310	0-4309	ABB8	1-505A	275624
D	姝	0-7013	1-2532	0-8115	CE67	2-2968	217A5E
E	姞	3-2838	1-2533	1-6010	CE63	2-2964	217A52
F	姟	5-3179	1-2534			E-2C21	

59F

	Char	G	J	K	B	C	A
0	姰	3-2856				E-2C25	
1	姱	3-2841	1-2540		CE66	2-2967	217A50
2	姲	5-3182	1-2541		CE6D	2-296E	
3	姳	5-3176			CE71	2-2972	
4	姴	5-3165	1-2542		CE75	2-2976	
5	姵	5-3175			CE72	2-2973	
6	姶	3-2854	0-1608		CE6B	2-296C	217A5D
7	姷	5-3164	1-2543		CE6E	2-296F	
8	姸			0-7033		E-2C2B	2D7A44
9	姹	0-7017				E-2C29	217A43
A	姺	3-2847		1-6980	CE68	2-2969	217A5F
B	姻	0-5086	0-1689	0-7656	ABC3	1-5065	213970
C	姼	3-2857			CE6A	2-296B	
D	姽	3-2855			CE69	2-296A	217A56
E	姾				CE74	2-2975	
F	姿	0-5543	0-2749	0-7712	ABBA	1-505C	213969

5A0

	Char	G	J	K	B	C	A
0	娀	3-2837	1-2544		CE65	2-2966	217A51
1	威	0-4594	0-1650	0-7446	ABC2	1-5064	21396F
2	娂	5-3162				E-2C2A	
3	娃	0-4562	0-1603	0-7263	ABBD	1-505F	21396B
4	娄	0-3406	1-2545			E-2C28	273A28
5	娅	0-7011					277B3C
6	娆	0-7012					277D2B
7	娇	0-2931					273A44
8	娈	0-7014					277D74
9	娉	0-7019	0-5318	1-6740	AE5C	1-547E	217A78
A	娊	5-3139			D162	2-2E64	
B	娋	5-3188				E-3040	
C	娌	0-7018	1-2546		AE5B	1-547D	21397C
D	娍	3-2842	1-2547			E-2C27	
E	娎	3-2868	1-2548				
F	娏				D160	2-2E62	

5A1

	Char	G	J	K	B	C	A
0	娐	3-2872				E-6270	
1	娑	0-7022	0-5316	0-6247	AE50	1-5472	213973
2	娒	5-3191	1-2549			E-304F	217A7E
3	娓	0-7024	1-2550	1-6486	AE55	1-5477	213977
4	娔	3-2860				E-304A	
5	娕	3-2862			D15F	2-2E61	
6	娖	3-2869			D15C	2-2E5E	217A75
7	娗	3-2848			D161	2-2E63	
8	娘	0-3679	0-4428	0-5006	AE51	1-5473	213974
9	娙	3-2835		1-8365	D15B	2-2E5D	
A	娚		0-5319			E-304E	4B3666
B	娛			0-7184	AE54	1-5476	21397B
C	娜	0-3640	0-5317	0-4954	AE52	1-5474	213976
D	娝	3-2866				E-303E	
E	娞	5-3192	1-2551		D163	2-2E65	
F	娟	0-3074	0-5315	0-7034	AE53	1-5475	21397A

5A2

	Char	G	J	K	B	C	A
0	娠	0-4179	0-3117	0-6767	AE57	1-5479	213979
1	娡	5-3185				E-303B	
2	娢					E-3045	
3	娣	0-7023	1-2552	1-7670	AE58	1-547A	213975
4	娤		1-2553			E-3048	
5	娥	0-2280	0-5314	0-6816	AE5A	1-547C	21397E
6	娦					E-3052	
7	娧	3-2874	1-2554	1-8151			
8	娨	5-3189	1-2555				
9	娩	0-3568	0-4258	0-5620	AE59	1-547B	21397D
A	娪	3-2863	1-2556			E-303C	217A6E
B	娫	3-2850				E-3522	
C	娬	5-3193				E-3538	217B41
D	娭	3-2876	1-2557	1-7056	D15D	2-2E5F	
E	娮				D15E	2-2E60	
F	娯		0-2468			E-304D	4B397B

5A3

	Char	G	J	K	B	C	A
0	娰		1-2558				
1	娱	0-5173				E-304B	2D397B
2	娲	0-7020					277C24
3	娳				D164	2-2E66	
4	娴	0-7021					273A41
5	娵	3-2881	0-5323	1-8029	D4D4	2-3457	217B3D
6	娶	0-4002	0-5324	0-8605	B0F9	1-595E	213A24
7	娷	3-2894			D8C2	2-3B26	
8	娸	3-2880			D4D3	2-3456	217B3A
9	娹	5-3211			D4E6	2-3469	
A	娺	3-2911				E-3528	
B	娻	3-2822				E-3524	
C	娼	0-7029	0-3011	0-8362	B140	1-5964	213A29
D	娽	3-2909				E-3531	
E	娾	3-2887			D4E4	2-3467	
F	娿			1-7004		E-3533	2D3A26

5A4

	Char	G	J	K	B	C	A
0	婀	0-7025	0-5320	1-7005	B0FE	1-5963	213A26
1	婁	1-3406	0-4712	0-5505	B0FA	1-595F	213A28
2	婂	5-3208			D4ED	2-3470	
3	婃				D4DD	2-3460	
4	婄	3-2906	1-2559		D4E0	2-3463	
5	婅		1-2560			E-352E	
6	婆	0-3837	0-3944	0-8772	B143	1-5967	213A21
7	婇		1-2561		D4EA	2-346D	
8	婈	5-3201	1-2562		D4E2	2-3465	
9	婉	0-4581	0-5322	0-7238	B0FB	1-5960	213A22
A	婊	0-7027			B144	1-5968	213A25
B	婋	5-3204				E-352A	
C	婌	5-3202	1-2563	1-6933	D4E7	2-346A	
D	婍	3-2888			D4E5	2-3468	
E	婎	3-2903				E-352F	
F	婏	3-2905				E-353B	

5A5

	Char	G	J	K	B	C	A
0	婐		1-2564	1-7252	D4D6	2-3459	217B48
1	婑	3-2901			D4EB	2-346E	
2	婒				D4DF	2-3462	
3	婓	3-8456			D4DA	2-345D	
4	婔					E-353A	
5	婕	0-7028	1-2565		D4D0	2-3453	217B3E
6	婖				D4EC	2-346F	
7	婗	3-2902			D4DC	2-345F	
8	婘	3-2907			D4CF	2-3452	
9	婙	5-3177				E-3539	
A	婚	0-2773	0-2607	0-9170	B142	1-5966	213A2B
B	婛				D4E1	2-3464	
C	婜	3-2808			D4EE	2-3471	
D	婝				D4DE	2-3461	
E	婞	3-2879	1-2566		D4D2	2-3455	217B3B
F	婟	3-2892			D4D7	2-345A	

5A6

	Char	G	J	K	B	C	A
0	婠	3-2908			D4CE	2-3451	217B2C
1	婡	3-2867				E-3527	
2	婢	0-7030	0-5325	0-6170	B141	1-5965	213A2A
3	婣		1-2567	1-7463		E-353C	2D3970
4	婤	3-2904			D4DB	2-345E	217B52
5	婥	5-3203	1-2568		D4D8	2-345B	217B49
6	婦	1-2430	0-4156	0-6094	B0FC	1-5961	213A27
7	婧	0-7026	1-2569	1-7652	D4D1	2-3454	217B31
8	婨	5-3141				E-3530	
9	婩	3-2893			D4E9	2-346C	
A	婪	0-3223	0-5326	1-6209	B0FD	1-5962	213A23
B	婫	3-2891				E-352B	
C	婬		0-5321		D4D9	2-345C	334770
D	婭	1-7011	1-2570		D4D5	2-3458	217B3C
E	婮					E-3529	
F	婯					E-3534	

5A7

	Char	G	J	K	B	C	A
0	婰	5-3206			D4E8	2-346B	
1	婱					E-3532	
2	婲			1-8414			
3	婳	8-9125				E-3537	
4	婴	0-5104					273A4A
5	婵	0-7031				E-3535	273A43
6	婶	0-4184					273A4B
7	婷	0-7035	1-2571	1-7653	B440	1-5E65	213A2C
8	婸	3-2801			D8BB	2-3A7D	
9	婹	5-3217				E-3A75	
A	婺	0-7036	1-2572		D8B8	2-3A7A	217B6A
B	婻	3-2914	1-2573		D8C9	2-3B2D	
C	婼	3-2882			D8BD	2-3B21	217C28
D	婽	5-3232			D8CA	2-3B2E	
E	婾		1-2574			E-3A7C	
F	婿	0-4886	0-4427	1-6808	B442	1-5E67	213A2F

5A8

	Char	G	J	K	B	C	A
0	媀	3-2919				E-3A63	
1	媁	3-2804				E-3A61	
2	媂	3-2927				E-3A58	
3	媃	3-2934			D8C6	2-3B2A	
4	媄	5-3228		1-6487	D8C3	2-3B27	
5	媅	3-2913				E-3A5B	
6	媆	5-3218				E-3A77	
7	媇					E-3A72	
8	媈					E-3A59	
9	媉	3-2933				E-3A60	
A	媊	3-2930			D8C4	2-3B28	217B65
B	媋	5-3212	1-2575		D8C7	2-3B2B	
C	媌	3-2883			D8CB	2-3B2F	217C22
D	媍			1-6620		E-3A7B	
E	媎	5-3194			D4E3	2-3466	
F	媏	5-3221			D8CD	2-3B31	

5AA

	Char	G	J	K	B	C	A
0	媠	3-2915	1-2583			E-3A73	217B75
1	媡					E-3A5A	
2	媢	3-2918	1-2584	1-6443	D8B9	2-3A7B	217C26
3	媣	3-2932				E-3A57	
4	媤			0-6724		E-3A7A	
5	媥	5-3231			D8BE	2-3B22	
6	媦	3-2920			D8BC	2-3A7E	217C21
7	媧	1-7020	1-2585	1-7270	B445	1-5E6A	217C24
8	媨	3-2931				E-3A56	
9	媩	5-3216			D8C8	2-3B2C	
A	媪	0-7033		1-7209		E-3A79	217C52
B	媫					E-3A78	
C	媬		1-2586		D8BF	2-3B23	217C31
D	媭	8-9127					
E	媮	8-1371			D8C1	2-3B25	217C34
F	媯				D8B5	2-3A77	217C36

5AC

	Char	G	J	K	B	C	A
0	嫀	5-3235			DD41	2-4247	
1	嫁	0-2862	0-1839	0-4210	B6F9	1-6360	213A33
2	嫂	0-4109	0-5331	0-6589	B741	1-6367	213A38
3	嫃	5-3241				E-4067	
4	嫄	5-3244	1-2601	0-7417	DCF4	2-423B	217C41
5	嫅	3-2928				E-4066	
6	嫆	5-3252	1-2602		DCFE	2-4245	
7	嫇	3-2940			DCF3	2-423A	
8	嫈	3-2820	1-2603	1-7077	DCFC	2-4243	217C39
9	嫉	0-2821	0-2827	0-8276	B6FA	1-6361	213A34
A	嫊	5-3237			DD42	2-4248	
B	嫋		0-5330	1-6046	DCF5	2-423C	2D3A47
C	嫌	0-4751	0-2389	0-9078	B6FB	1-6362	213A32
D	嫍				DD45	2-424B	
E	嫎	3-2938				E-4064	
F	嫏	5-3209	1-2604			E-3A6B	217B69

5AE

	Char	G	J	K	B	C	A
0	嫠	0-7043	1-2607	1-6359	E175	2-495C	217C6E
1	嫡	0-2153	0-3568	0-7853	B9DE	1-6846	213A3A
2	嫢	3-2878		1-5923	E174	2-495B	
3	嫣	0-7044	0-5333	1-7113	B9E4	1-684C	213A3D
4	嫤	3-2941				E-464C	
5	嫥	3-2806	1-2608	1-7586	E16D	2-4954	217C6D
6	嫦	0-7047	0-5335	0-8984	B9DF	1-6847	213A40
7	嫧	3-2877				E-464A	
8	嫨	3-2942			E17B	2-4962	
9	嫩	0-3659	0-5336	0-5076	B9E0	1-6848	213A3E
A	嫪	3-2951	1-2609		E16F	2-4956	217C72
B	嫫	0-7038		1-6444	E172	2-4959	217C7C
C	嫬	5-3260			E177	2-495E	
D	嫭	3-2946		1-8380	E171	2-4958	
E	嫮	5-3257	1-2610	1-8381	E16C	2-4953	
F	嫯	5-3236		1-7210		E-464F	

5A9

	Char	G	J	K	B	C	A
0	媐	3-2936	1-2576		DD47	2-424D	217C4A
1	媑	5-3223				E-3A66	
2	媒	0-3529	0-3962	0-5658	B443	1-5E68	213A2E
3	媓	3-2924	1-2577	1-8437	D8CE	2-3B32	217C30
4	媔	3-2916			D8B6	2-3A78	
5	媕	3-2926		1-7037	D8C0	2-3B24	217C35
6	媖	3-2884	1-2578			E-3A62	217C29
7	媗	5-3230			D8C5	2-3B29	
8	媘					E-3A5C	
9	媙		1-2579			E-3A5E	
A	媚	0-3536	0-5327	0-5812	B441	1-5E66	213A2D
B	媛	0-7034	0-4118	0-7416	B444	1-5E69	213A31
C	媜	3-2844	1-2580		D8CC	2-3B30	217C27
D	媝	5-3222			D8CF	2-3B33	
E	媞	3-2917	1-2581		D8BA	2-3A7C	217C25
F	媟	5-3215	1-2582	1-6841	D8B7	2-3A79	217B71

5AB

	Char	G	J	K	B	C	A
0	媰	3-2829			DCFA	2-4241	
1	媱	5-3247	1-2587		DCF8	2-423F	217C5B
2	媲	0-7039	1-2588		B742	1-6368	213A37
3	媳	0-4717	1-2589	1-6975	B740	1-6366	213A39
4	媴	5-3239			DD43	2-4249	
5	媵	0-7584	1-2590	1-7478	DCF9	2-4240	217C3E
6	媶	5-3214			DD44	2-424A	
7	媷	5-3242			DD40	2-4246	217C45
8	媸	0-7042	1-2591		DCF7	2-423E	217C4F
9	媹	5-3249			DD46	2-424C	
A	媺	5-3245	1-2592	1-6488	DCF6	2-423D	217C50
B	媻	5-3246	1-2593	1-6523	DCFD	2-4244	
C	媼		0-5328	1-7228	B6FE	1-6365	213A30
D	媽	1-3472	0-5332	1-6385	B6FD	1-6364	213A36
E	媾	0-7037	0-5329	1-5846	B6FC	1-6363	213A35
F	媿		1-2594	1-5804	DCFB	2-4242	2D3F2A

5AD

	Char	G	J	K	B	C	A
0	嫐		0-5344			E-406A	453666
1	嫑					E-6468	217C49
2	嫒	0-7040					277D48
3	嫓					E-6469	217C59
4	嫔	0-7041					273A48
5	嫕	3-2944			E16E	2-4955	
6	嫖	0-7046	0-5337	1-8239	B9E2	1-684A	213A3C
7	嫗	1-6993	0-5334	1-5847	B9E1	1-6849	213A3B
8	嫘	0-7048			B9E3	1-684B	213A3F
9	嫙	3-2950		1-6825	E17A	2-4961	
A	嫚	3-2947	1-2605	1-6393	E170	2-4957	217C7B
B	嫛	3-2943		1-7179	E176	2-495D	
C	嫜	0-7049	1-2606		E16B	2-4952	217C60
D	嫝				E179	2-4960	
E	嫞	3-2949			E178	2-495F	
F	嫟	5-3238			E17C	2-4963	

5AF

	Char	G	J	K	B	C	A
0	嫰					E-4653	
1	嫱	0-7045					277D40
2	嫲						
3	嫳	5-3258			E173	2-495A	
4	嫴	5-3265			E555	2-4F7C	
5	嫵	1-6992	1-2611		BC61	1-6C4B	213A45
6	嫶	3-2956	1-2612	1-7977	E558	2-5021	
7	嫷	5-3262			E557	2-4F7E	
8	嫸	3-2960			E55A	2-5023	
9	嫹				E55C	2-5025	
A	嫺		0-5338	1-8285		E-4B5C	2D3A41
B	嫻	1-7021	0-5339	1-8286	BC5F	1-6C49	213A41
C	嫼	3-2955				E-4B58	
D	嫽	3-2954	1-2613	1-6320	E556	2-4F7D	217D2A
E	嫾					E-4B54	
F	嫿	3-2885			E554	2-4F7B	217D26

Code	Char	G	J	K	B	C	A
5B00	嬀	1-7003	1-2614	1-5924		E-4B5E	
5B01	嬁		1-2615		E55D	2-5026	
5B02	嬂	5-3151			E55B	2-5024	
5B03	嬃	3-2925			E559	2-5022	217D38
5B04	嬄					E-4B56	
5B05	嬅	3-2851		0-9191	E55F	2-5028	
5B06	嬆	3-2957				E-4B5A	
5B07	嬇	3-2921			E55E	2-5027	
5B08	嬈	1-7012	1-2616	1-7284	BC63	1-6C4D	217D2B
5B09	嬉	0-7050	0-2082	0-9380	BC5E	1-6C48	213A42
5B0A	嬊					E-4B5B	
5B0B	嬋	1-7031	0-5341	0-6429	BC60	1-6C4A	213A43
5B0C	嬌	1-2931	0-5340	0-4667	BC62	1-6C4C	213A44
5B0D	嬍					E-4B5D	217D2E
5B0E	嬎	3-2958				E-4B5F	
5B0F	嬏	5-3267			E560	2-5029	
5B10	嬐	3-2870			E957	2-5661	
5B11	嬑					E-5050	
5B12	嬒	3-2853				E-5053	
5B13	嬓				E956	2-5660	
5B14	嬔				E955	2-565F	
5B15	嬕	5-3158				E-5051	
5B16	嬖	0-7052	0-5342	0-8838	E958	2-5662	217D3E
5B17	嬗	0-7051	1-2617		E951	2-565B	217D3D
5B18	嬘					E-504F	
5B19	嬙	1-7045	1-2619	1-7533	E952	2-565C	217D40
5B1A	嬚	3-2964			E95A	2-5664	
5B1B	嬛	3-2963	1-2620	1-8344	E953	2-565D	217D47
5B1C	嬜	3-2965				E-5054	
5B1D	嬝		1-2621		BBC5	1-704E	213A47
5B1E	嬞	5-3264			E95C	2-5666	
5B1F	嬟	3-2794				E-504E	
5B20	嬠	5-3270			E95B	2-5665	
5B21	嬡	1-7040	1-2622		E954	2-565E	217D48
5B22	嬢		0-3078			E-5056	4B3974
5B23	嬣	3-2833			BCD1	2-5C5D	
5B24	嬤	5-3278			C0A8	1-7351	213A49
5B25	嬥	3-2967	1-2623	1-7692	BCCF	2-5C5B	
5B26	嬦	5-3184			BCD4	2-5C60	
5B27	嬧	5-3183			BCD3	2-5C5F	
5B28	嬨	5-3273		1-7480	E959	2-5663	
5B29	嬩	3-2791				E-5450	
5B2A	嬪	1-7041	0-5345	0-6214	C0A7	1-7350	213A48
5B2B	嬫					E-544E	
5B2C	嬬	3-2966	0-3660		BCD2	2-5C5E	217D52
5B2D	嬭		1-2624	1-6026	BCCE	2-5C5A	333944
5B2E	嬮	3-1623			BCD6	2-5C62	
5B2F	嬯	5-3276			BCD5	2-5C61	
5B30	嬰	1-5104	0-1737	1-7168	C0A6	1-734F	213A4A
5B31	嬱	5-3261				E-5452	
5B32	嬲	0-7053	0-5343	1-6047	BCD0	2-5C5C	217D59
5B33	嬳	3-2962				E-544F	
5B34	嬴	0-5788	1-2618	1-7167	BBC6	1-704F	213A46
5B35	嬵					E-5451	
5B36	嬶		0-5346				69554E
5B37	嬷	0-7054				E-5453	4B3A49
5B38	嬸	1-4184	1-2625		C254	1-7640	213A4B
5B39	嬹	3-2970				E-5A31	
5B3A	嬺	5-3275				E-5761	
5B3B	嬻	3-2886				E-575E	
5B3C	嬼	3-2858			EFC1	2-614D	
5B3D	嬽				F1FA	2-6546	
5B3E	嬾		0-5347	1-6194	F1FB	2-6547	333F55
5B3F	嬿	3-2968		1-7137	F1FC	2-6548	217D63
5B40	孀	0-7055	0-5350	0-6337	C45C	1-7967	213A4C
5B41	孁		1-2626				
5B42	孂	3-2972				E-5C36	
5B43	孃	8-9457	0-5348	0-6930	C45D	1-7968	2D3974
5B44	孄	5-3268				E-5C39	
5B45	孅	3-2973	0-5349	1-6848	F443	2-686F	217D6E
5B46	孆	5-3259				E-5C3A	
5B47	孇	5-3146			F5C8	2-6B56	
5B48	孈	3-2975			F5C7	2-6B55	
5B49	孉	5-3282				E-5E29	
5B4A	孊	3-2976				E-5F42	
5B4B	孋	3-2865	1-2627		F6DB	2-6D49	217D76
5B4C	孌	1-7014	1-2628	1-6244	F6DC	2-6D4A	217D74
5B4D	孍	3-2859			F7D5	2-6F24	
5B4E	孎	3-2961			F8A7	2-7035	
5B4F	孏					E-6073	
5B50	子	0-5551	0-2750	0-7713	A46C	1-444D	213A4D
5B51	孑	0-7061	0-5351	0-9074	A46D	1-444E	213A4E
5B52	孒		1-2629				
5B53	孓	0-7062			A46E	1-444F	213A4F
5B54	孔	0-3155	0-2506	0-4578	A4D5	1-4536	213A50
5B55	孕	0-5248	0-5352	0-7706	A5A5	1-4645	213A51
5B56	孖	3-2978	1-2630	1-7481	C9D3	2-2233	217D7C
5B57	字	0-5554	0-2790	0-7714	A672	1-4773	213A52
5B58	存	0-2070	0-3424	0-8077	A673	1-4774	213A53
5B59	孙	0-4379					273A5B
5B5A	孚	0-7058	0-5353	0-6101	A7B7	1-4977	273A5F
5B5B	孛	0-5635	0-5354	1-8188	A7B8	1-4978	217E21
5B5C	孜	0-5546	0-2758	0-7715	A7B6	1-4976	213A55
5B5D	孝	0-4802	0-2507	0-9288	A7B5	1-4975	213A54
5B5E	孞		1-2631				
5B5F	孟	0-3547	0-4450	0-5675	A973	1-4C75	213A57
5B60	孠					E-2848	
5B61	孡	5-3302		1-8152			
5B62	孢	0-7063			CC55	2-2636	217E23
5B63	季	0-2830	0-2108	0-4489	A975	1-4C77	213A58
5B64	孤	0-2534	0-2441	0-4521	A974	1-4C76	213A59
5B65	孥	0-7059	0-5355	1-6036	CC56	2-2637	217E24
5B66	学	0-4907	0-1956			E-625C	273A60
5B67	孧					E-646A	217E25
5B68	孨	5-3306	1-2632				
5B69	孩	0-2602	0-5356	0-9009	ABC4	1-5066	213A5A
5B6A	孪	0-3447				E-2C2F	273A63
5B6B	孫	1-4379	0-3425	0-6561	AE5D	1-5521	213A5B
5B6C	孬	0-5611			D165	2-2E67	217E28
5B6D	孭						
5B6E	孮	5-3308	1-2633		D4F0	2-3473	217E2A
5B6F	孯		1-2634				
5B70	孰	0-4275	0-5357	0-6653	B145	1-5969	213A5C
5B71	孱	0-6978	0-5403	0-7747	B447	1-5E6C	213A5E
5B72	孲				D4EF	2-3472	
5B73	孳	0-7060	0-5358		B446	1-5E6B	213A5D
5B74	孴	3-4005				E-4071	
5B75	孵	0-2385	0-5359	0-6102	B9E5	1-684D	213A5F
5B76	孶			1-7482		E-4072	
5B77	孷	5-4136			E17D	2-4964	
5B78	學	1-4907	0-5360	0-8942	BBC7	1-7050	213A60
5B79	孹					E-5057	
5B7A	孺	0-4070	0-5362	0-7472	C0A9	1-7352	213A61
5B7B	孻	5-3305			BCD7	2-5C63	217E30
5B7C	孼		1-2635	0-6977		E-5A34	217E31
5B7D	孽	0-3685	1-2636		C45E	1-7969	213A62
5B7E	孾		1-2637			E-5C3B	
5B7F	孿	1-3447	1-2638	1-6766	C570	1-7B5C	213A63

Code	Char	G	J	K	B	C	A
5B80	宀	0-6918	0-5363			E-213B	217E32
5B81	宁	0-3694	1-2639	1-7559	C972	2-2153	273B32
5B82	宂			1-7305		E-223D	453336
5B83	它	0-4392	0-5364		A5A6	1-4646	274A53
5B84	宄	0-6919	1-2640		C973	2-2154	217E34
5B85	宅	0-5312	0-3480	0-5175	A676	1-4777	213A68
5B86	宆		1-2641			E-2350	
5B87	宇	0-5178	0-1707	0-7352	A674	1-4775	213A65
5B88	守	0-4256	0-2873	0-6590	A675	1-4776	213A66
5B89	安	0-1618	0-1634	0-6844	A677	1-4778	213A67
5B8A	宊	5-2982	1-2642	1-5506			
5B8B	宋	0-4346	0-3355	0-6568	A7BA	1-497A	213A6A
5B8C	完	0-4574	0-2016	0-7239	A7B9	1-4979	213A69
5B8D	宍	5-2986	0-2821			E-255A	2D5323
5B8E	宎	5-2984	1-2643		CABC	2-235C	
5B8F	宏	0-2674	0-2508	0-4659	A7BB	1-497B	213A6B
5B90	宐		1-2644				
5B91	宑		1-2645				
5B92	宒				CABD	2-235D	
5B93	宓	0-6921	1-2646	0-6053	CC57	2-2638	217E43
5B94	宔	3-2725	1-2647			E-284C	
5B95	宕	0-6920	0-3770	0-8721	CC58	2-2639	217E40
5B96	宖	5-2987	1-2648	0-9283		E-284A	
5B97	宗	0-5558	0-2901	0-8083	A976	1-4C78	213A6C
5B98	官	0-2557	0-2017	0-4615	A978	1-4C7A	213A6F
5B99	宙	0-5470	0-3572	0-8121	A97A	1-4C7C	213A70
5B9A	定	0-2208	0-3674	0-7950	A977	1-4C79	213A6D
5B9B	宛	0-4580	0-1624	0-7240	A97B	1-4C7D	213A71
5B9C	宜	0-5043	0-2125	0-7581	A979	1-4C7B	213A6E
5B9D	宝	0-1706	0-4285			E-284E	273B39
5B9E	实	0-4221				E-284B	273B31
5B9F	実		0-2834			E-284D	4B3B31
5BA0	宠	0-1972					273B38
5BA1	审	0-4183					273B36
5BA2	客	0-3145	0-2150	0-4352	ABC8	1-506A	213A76
5BA3	宣	0-4891	0-3275	0-6430	ABC5	1-5067	213A73
5BA4	室	0-4250	0-2828	0-6788	ABC7	1-5069	213A75
5BA5	宥	0-6922	0-4508	0-7473	ABC9	1-506B	213A72
5BA6	宦	0-2734	0-5365	0-9218	ABC6	1-5068	213A74
5BA7	宧	3-2729			D166	2-2E68	217E52
5BA8	宨		1-2649		CE77	2-2978	
5BA9	宩		1-2650				
5BAA	宪	0-4760					273F3E
5BAB	宫	0-2512				E-2C32	
5BAC	宬	3-2727	1-2651	0-6484	D168	2-2E6A	217E49
5BAD	宭	3-2731	1-2652		D167	2-2E69	
5BAE	宮		0-2160	0-4764	AE63	1-5527	213A7C
5BAF	宯		1-2653				
5BB0	宰	0-5255	0-2643	0-7805	AE5F	1-5523	213A77
5BB1	宱	5-3004	1-2654				
5BB2	宲		1-2655				
5BB3	害	0-2606	0-1918	0-9010	AE60	1-5524	213A7E
5BB4	宴	0-4971	0-1767	0-7035	AE62	1-5526	213A7B
5BB5	宵	0-4792	0-3012	0-6518	AE64	1-5528	213A7A
5BB6	家	0-2850	0-1840	0-4211	AE61	1-5525	27323E
5BB7	宷		1-2656			E-3057	217E55
5BB8	宸	0-6923	0-5366	0-6768	AE66	1-552A	213A78
5BB9	容	0-4061	0-4538	0-7327	AE65	1-5529	213A7D
5BBA	宺		1-2657				
5BBB	宻					E-3056	
5BBC	宼		1-2658			E-3055	
5BBD	宽	0-3177					273B35
5BBE	宾	0-1786					275A29
5BBF	宿	0-4362	0-2941	0-6654	B14A	1-596E	213B26
5BC0	寀		1-2659	0-8382	D4F2	2-3475	
5BC1	寁	3-2732	1-2660		D4F1	2-3474	217E59
5BC2	寂	0-2837	0-2868	0-7854	B149	1-596D	213B25
5BC3	寃		0-5367	0-7418		E-3541	217E6A
5BC4	寄	0-2836	0-2083	0-4886	B148	1-596C	213B24
5BC5	寅	0-5090	0-3850	0-7657	B147	1-596B	213B23
5BC6	密	0-3560	0-4409	0-5843	B14B	1-596F	213B21
5BC7	寇	0-3160	0-5368	0-4708	B146	1-596A	213B22
5BC8	寈					E-353F	
5BC9	寉	5-3010	0-5369				217E60
5BCA	寊	5-2989			D8D5	2-3B39	
5BCB	寋	5-1991			D8D2	2-3B36	
5BCC	富	0-2427	0-4157	0-6103	B449	1-5E6E	213B27
5BCD	寍	5-3016	1-2661		D8D1	2-3B35	
5BCE	寎	3-2735			D8D6	2-3B3A	
5BCF	寏	5-3007	1-2662				
5BD0	寐	0-3534	0-5371	0-5659	B44B	1-5E70	213B29
5BD1	寑				D8D4	2-3B38	
5BD2	寒	0-2614	0-2008	0-8946	B448	1-5E6D	213B28
5BD3	寓	0-5202	0-2287	0-7353	B44A	1-5E6F	213B2A
5BD4	寔		0-5370	0-6749	D8D3	2-3B37	217E68
5BD5	寕					E-3A7E	
5BD6	寖	5-3021	1-2663	1-8103	DD48	2-424E	217E6E
5BD7	寗		1-2664	0-5028		E-4074	217E75
5BD8	寘		1-2665	1-8076	DD49	2-424F	395230
5BD9	寙	5-3020	1-2666		DD4A	2-4250	
5BDA	寚		1-2667			E-4075	
5BDB	寛		0-2018			E-4076	
5BDC	寜					E-4073	
5BDD	寝	0-3962	0-3118			E-6345	273B2E
5BDE	寞	0-3615	0-5375	0-5612	B9E6	1-684E	213B30
5BDF	察	0-1876	0-2701	0-8344	B9EE	1-6856	213B33
5BE0	寠	5-3015	1-2668		E17E	2-4965	217E79
5BE1	寡	0-2549	0-1841	0-4591	B9E8	1-6850	213B2B
5BE2	寢	1-3962	0-5374	0-8654	B9EC	1-6854	213B2E
5BE3	寣	3-2740			E1A1	2-4966	
5BE4	寤	0-6927	0-5372	0-7185	B9ED	1-6855	213B2F
5BE5	寥	0-3340	0-5376	0-7279	B9E9	1-6851	213B2C
5BE6	實	1-4221	0-5373	0-6789	B9EA	1-6852	213B31
5BE7	寧	1-3694	0-3911	0-5027	B9E7	1-684F	213B32
5BE8	寨	0-5315	0-6045	0-8383	B9EB	1-6853	213B2D
5BE9	審	1-4183	0-3119	0-6791	BC66	1-6C50	213B36
5BEA	寪	3-2724			D8D0	2-3B34	217E7E
5BEB	寫	1-4820	0-5377	0-6248	BC67	1-6C51	213B37
5BEC	寬	1-3177		0-4616	BC65	1-6C4F	213B35
5BED	寭			1-8371			
5BEE	寮	0-6928	0-4632	0-5487	BC64	1-6C4E	213B34
5BEF	寯		1-2669	0-8157	E95D	2-5667	222225
5BF0	寰	0-6930	0-5378	1-8423	BBC8	1-7051	222224
5BF1	寱	5-3027	1-2670		BCD8	2-5C64	
5BF2	寲	5-3026			BCD9	2-5C65	
5BF3	寳		0-5380			E-5A35	393B39
5BF4	寴	3-2734	1-2671				
5BF5	寵	1-1972	0-3594	0-8533	C364	1-7831	213B38
5BF6	寶	1-1706	0-5379	0-6036	C45F	1-796A	213B39
5BF7	寷	3-2723				E-5E2A	
5BF8	寸	0-2071	0-3203	0-8527	A46F	1-4450	213B3A
5BF9	对	0-2252				E-223E	273B43
5BFA	寺	0-4334	0-2791	0-6249	A678	1-4779	213B3B
5BFB	寻	0-4916					273B42
5BFC	导	0-2128					273B44
5BFD	寽	5-4671	1-2672			E-255E	
5BFE	対		0-3448			E-255C	4B3B43
5BFF	寿	0-4257	0-2887			E-255D	273877

Code	Char	G	J	K	B	C	A
5C00	尀	5-2359				E-2850	222233
5C01	封	0-2366	0-4185	0-6070	ABCA	1-506C	213B3C
5C02	専		0-3276				2D3B3F
5C03	尃	3-2143			D169	2-2E6B	
5C04	射	0-4168	0-2845	0-6250	AE67	1-552B	213B3D
5C05	尅	8-1365	0-5381	1-5942		E-3058	2D336B
5C06	将	0-2911	0-3013			E-3059	273B40
5C07	將	1-2911	0-5382	0-7766	B14E	1-5972	213B40
5C08	專	1-5508	0-5383	0-7886	B14D	1-5971	213B3F
5C09	尉	0-4630	0-1651	0-7447	B14C	1-5970	213B3E
5C0A	尊	0-5580	0-3426	0-8078	B44C	1-5E71	213B41
5C0B	尋	1-4916	0-3150	0-6792	B44D	1-5E72	213B42
5C0C	尌	5-2362	1-2673	1-7745	D8D7	2-3B3B	
5C0D	對	1-2252	0-5384	0-5163	B9EF	1-6857	213B43
5C0E	導	1-2128	0-3819	0-5184	BEC9	1-7052	213B44
5C0F	小	0-4801	0-3014	0-6519	A470	1-4451	213B45
5C10	尐				C95C	2-213C	
5C11	少	0-4157	0-3015	0-6520	A4D6	1-4537	213B46
5C12	尒				C974	2-2155	2D4A45
5C13	尓		0-5385			E-624A	4B4A45
5C14	尔	0-2291		1-7448		E-223F	274A45
5C15	尕	0-7056			C9D4	2-2234	22223C
5C16	尖	0-2866	0-3277	0-8451	A679	1-477A	213B47
5C17	尗	5-3283	1-2674				
5C18	尘	0-1930				E-2352	273859
5C19	尙			0-6338		E-2851	
5C1A	尚	0-4148	0-3016		A97C	1-4C7E	213B48
5C1B	尛	5-3286				E-2C34	
5C1C	尜	0-7057					4B372F
5C1D	尝	0-1902					273730
5C1E	尞	5-3289	1-2675			E-3B24	
5C1F	尟		1-2676	1-6826	DD4B	2-4251	3F6179
5C20	尠		0-5386	1-6827		E-4078	396179
5C21	尡					E-6525	223930
5C22	尢	0-6244	0-5387		A471	1-4452	222246
5C23	尣		1-2677				
5C24	尤	0-5140	0-4464	0-7354	A4D7	1-4538	213B49
5C25	尥	0-6245			C9D5	2-2235	222248
5C26	尦		1-2678				
5C27	尧	0-5002					273845
5C28	尨	3-5686	0-5388	0-5911	CABE	2-235E	2D632B
5C29	尩		1-2679				
5C2A	尪	3-2131			CABF	2-235F	22224B
5C2B	尫		1-2680	1-7267		E-255F	
5C2C	尬	0-6246	1-2681		A7BC	1-497C	213B4A
5C2D	尭		0-2238				
5C2E	尮		1-2682				
5C2F	尯	3-2134				E-2C35	222252
5C30	尰	5-2351	1-2683		D8D8	2-3B3C	
5C31	就	0-3045	0-2902	0-8606	B44E	1-5E73	213B4B
5C32	尲	5-2353	1-2684				22225B
5C33	尳	5-2350			DD4C	2-4252	
5C34	尴	0-6247					273B4C
5C35	尵	5-2349	1-2685				
5C36	尶		1-2686			E-5454	
5C37	尷	1-6247			C0AA	1-7353	213B4C
5C38	尸	0-4212	0-5389	0-6725	A472	1-4453	213B4D
5C39	尹	0-5092	0-5390	0-7537	A4A8	1-4467	21303E
5C3A	尺	0-1963	0-2860	0-8409	A4D8	1-4539	213B4E
5C3B	尻	0-6974	0-3112	0-4522	C975	2-2156	222263
5C3C	尼	0-3665	0-3884	0-5089	A5A7	1-4647	213B4F
5C3D	尽	0-3001	0-3152			E-2354	273263
5C3E	尾	0-4618	0-4088	0-5813	A7C0	1-4A22	213B53
5C3F	尿	0-3682	0-3902	0-5067	A7BF	1-4A21	213B52
5C40	局	0-3054	0-2241	0-4749	A7BD	1-497D	213B50
5C41	屁	0-3808	0-5391	1-6681	A7BE	1-497E	213B51
5C42	层	0-1867					273B61
5C43	屃	7-0103					
5C44	屄	3-2750			CC59	2-263A	222265
5C45	居	0-3051	0-2179	0-4360	A97E	1-4D22	213B55
5C46	屆		0-5392	0-4490	A9A1	1-4D23	213B54
5C47	屇	5-3047		1-7587	CC5A	2-263B	
5C48	屈	0-3992	0-2294	0-4761	A97D	1-4D21	213B56
5C49	屉	0-4475				E-2854	222267
5C4A	届	0-2976	0-3847			E-2855	2D3B54
5C4B	屋	0-4661	0-1816	0-7209	ABCE	1-5070	213B58
5C4C	屌	3-2751			CE78	2-2979	
5C4D	屍		0-2751	0-6727	ABCD	1-506F	213B59
5C4E	屎	0-4226	0-5393	0-6726	ABCB	1-506D	213B57
5C4F	屏	0-3833	0-5402		ABCC	1-506E	213B5D
5C50	屐	0-6976	0-5401	1-5943	AE6A	1-552E	213B5C
5C51	屑	0-4828	0-2293	0-6458	AE68	1-552C	213B5B
5C52	屒	3-2754				E-305A	
5C53	屓	3-2745	0-5394			E-305B	4C2330
5C54	屔	5-3056			D16B	2-2E6D	
5C55	展	0-5325	0-3724	0-7887	AE69	1-552D	213B5A
5C56	屖	3-2756			D16A	2-2E6C	
5C57	屗					E-646B	222235
5C58	屘				AE5E	1-5522	217E27
5C59	屙	0-6977	1-2687		D4F3	2-3476	222279
5C5A	屚	5-3059	1-2688				
5C5B	屛			0-6019		E-3543	27415A
5C5C	屜	5-3061	1-2689		B150	1-5974	213B5F
5C5D	屝	3-2758			B151	1-5975	22227B
5C5E	属	0-4284	0-3416			E-3B26	273B63
5C5F	屟	5-3062				E-3B25	22227C
5C60	屠	0-4532	0-3743	0-5185	B14F	1-5973	213B5E
5C61	屡	0-3437	0-2840			E-3544	273B60
5C62	屢	1-3437	1-2690	0-5506	B9F0	1-6858	213B60
5C63	屣	0-6979	1-2691		E1A2	2-4967	222323
5C64	層	1-1867	0-3356	0-8621	BC68	1-6C52	213B61
5C65	履	0-3436	0-4590	0-5559	BC69	1-6C53	213B62
5C66	屦	0-6980					28232B
5C67	屧	5-3073	1-2692		E561	2-502A	222329
5C68	屨	1-6980	1-2693	1-5848	C0AB	1-7354	22232B
5C69	屩	3-2760	1-2694		EFC2	2-614E	4B5A7E
5C6A	屪	5-3076			EFC3	2-614F	
5C6B	屫	5-3069				E-5A38	
5C6C	屬	1-4284	0-5404	0-6553	C4DD	1-7A68	213B63
5C6D	屭	5-3072	1-2701		F8A8	2-7036	222330
5C6E	屮	0-6988	0-5405		C94B	2-212B	222331
5C6F	屯	0-4545	0-3854	0-5274	A4D9	1-453A	213B64
5C70	屰	5-1725	1-2702				
5C71	山	0-4129	0-2719	0-6303	A473	1-4454	213B65
5C72	屲	5-2651					
5C73	屳	5-1734		1-6828	C977	2-2158	222339
5C74	屴	3-2431	1-2703		C976	2-2157	222337
5C75	屵	5-2652	1-2704				
5C76	屶		0-5407				4C233F
5C77	屷					E-646C	22233B
5C78	屸	3-2432				E-2355	
5C79	屹	0-5057	0-5408	0-9363	A67A	1-477B	213B66
5C7A	屺	0-6508	1-2705	1-5971	C9D7	2-2237	22233C
5C7B	屻	5-2660	1-2706		C9D8	2-2238	
5C7C	屼	3-2433	1-2707		C9D6	2-2236	222340
5C7D	屽	5-2656	1-2708				
5C7E	屾	5-2657			C9D9	2-2239	
5C7F	屿	0-5176					273C2D

5C8

	Char	G	J	K	B	C	A
0	岀					E-235A	
1	岁	0-4374					274629
2	岂	0-3881					275954
3	岃						
4	岄					E-2561	
5	岅					E-2566	
6	岆				CAC7	2-2367	
7	岇		1-2709				
8	岈	0-6512	1-2710	1-8272	CAC2	2-2362	222349
9	岉				CAC4	2-2364	
A	岊	3-2444	1-2711	1-7630	CAC6	2-2366	
B	岋	5-2658			CAC3	2-2363	
C	岌	0-6507	0-5409	1-5961	A7C4	1-4A26	213B68
D	岍	0-6509			CAC0	2-2360	22234B
E	岎	3-2442				E-2562	
F	岏	3-2435	1-2712	1-7262	CAC1	2-2361	222346

5C9

	Char	G	J	K	B	C	A
0	岐	0-6510	0-2084	0-4887	A7C1	1-4A23	213B67
1	岑	0-6515	0-5410	0-7752	A7C2	1-4A24	213B69
2	岒	5-2663	1-2713	1-5635	CAC5	2-2365	
3	岓	5-2662			CAC8	2-2368	
4	岔	0-1877	0-5411	1-7835	A7C3	1-4A25	213B6A
5	岕	3-2439			CAC9	2-2369	
6	岖	0-6511					273C2B
7	岗	0-2458					393B6E
8	岘	0-6513					282441
9	岙	0-6514					22234D
A	岚	0-6516					273C28
B	岛	0-2126					273B79
C	岜	0-6517				E-2563	706131
D	岝	5-2668	1-2714	1-7511	CC68	2-2649	
E	岞	3-2456				E-285D	
F	岟	3-2455	1-2715		CC62	2-2643	

5CA

	Char	G	J	K	B	C	A
0	岠	5-2661	1-2716		CC5D	2-263E	222357
1	岡	1-2452	0-1812	0-4310	A9A3	1-4D25	213B6E
2	岢	0-6519	1-2717		CC65	2-2646	22235C
3	岣	0-6524	1-2718	1-5849	CC63	2-2644	22236B
4	岤	5-2674			CC5C	2-263D	
5	岥	5-2679		1-8173	CC69	2-264A	
6	岦	5-2673	1-2719	1-6383	CC6C	2-264D	222355
7	岧	3-2461		1-7978	CC67	2-2648	222361
8	岨	3-2453	0-3327	1-7560	CC60	2-2641	222366
9	岩	0-4950	0-2068	0-6859	A9A5	1-4D27	273C33
A	岪	3-2460	1-2720	1-6664	CC66	2-2647	
B	岫	0-6522	0-5413	0-6591	A9A6	1-4D28	213B6F
C	岬	0-6521	0-4408	0-4302	CC61	2-2642	222367
D	岭	0-3375		1-6262	CC64	2-2645	22236F
E	岮	5-2675			CC5B	2-263C	
F	岯	3-2447			CC5F	2-2640	

5CB

	Char	G	J	K	B	C	A
0	岰	3-2464			CC6B	2-264C	
1	岱	0-6523	0-3450	0-5164	A9A7	1-4D29	213B71
2	岲		1-2721				
3	岳	0-5232	0-1957	0-6831	A9A8	1-4D2A	273C2E
4	岴	5-2669	1-2722			E-285E	
5	岵	0-6518	1-2723	0-9132	CC5E	2-263F	222360
6	岶	5-2670	0-5415		CC6A	2-264B	22236C
7	岷	0-6526	0-5417	0-5830	A9A2	1-4D24	213B6B
8	岸	0-1622	0-2063	0-6845	A9A4	1-4D26	213B6C
9	岹	5-2678				E-285C	
A	岺	5-2671	1-2724	0-5425		E-285F	
B	岻	3-2457	0-5414			E-2857	69562E
C	岼		0-5416				695630
D	岽	0-6520					342453
E	岾		0-5419	0-7932			695633
F	岿	0-3189					282647

5CC

	Char	G	J	K	B	C	A
0	峀			0-6592			
1	峁	0-6525				E-2858	22236D
2	峂	3-2458					
3	峃	8-9082					
4	峄	0-6527					282626
5	峅		0-5418				695632
6	峆	5-2693			CEAB	2-2A2C	
7	峇	5-2694	0-5420		CEA4	2-2A25	222430
8	峈				CEAA	2-2A2B	
9	峉	3-2475	1-2725		CEA3	2-2A24	
A	峊	5-2692			CEA5	2-2A26	
B	峋	0-6530	1-2726		CE7D	2-297E	22242B
C	峌	3-2470			CE7B	2-297C	
D	峍					E-2C3F	
E	峎	3-2479			CEAC	2-2A2D	
F	峏	5-2684			CEA9	2-2A2A	

5CD

	Char	G	J	K	B	C	A
0	峐	3-2478			CE79	2-297A	
1	峑					E-2C3B	
2	峒	0-6528	1-2727	1-6153	ABD0	1-5072	222428
3	峓	3-2468			CEA7	2-2A28	222378
4	峔	5-2682			CEA8	2-2A29	
5	峕					E-646D	222370
6	峖	5-2704			CEA6	2-2A27	
7	峗	3-2474	1-2729		CE7C	2-297D	
8	峘	3-2466			CE7A	2-297B	
9	峙	0-5437	0-5421	0-8625	ABCF	1-5071	213B72
A	峚	5-2685			CEA2	2-2A23	
B	峛	3-2467			CE7E	2-2A21	
C	峜	5-2701				E-2C3C	222431
D	峝		1-2728			E-2C42	222429
E	峞	5-2703			CEA1	2-2A22	
F	峟	5-2683			CEAD	2-2A2E	

5CE

	Char	G	J	K	B	C	A
0	峠		0-3829	0-6339			222426
1	峡	0-4731	0-2214			E-2C3E	273B74
2	峢					E-2C41	
3	峣	8-9084					
4	峤	0-6529					282577
5	峥	0-6531				E-2C43	4B3C23
6	峦	0-3445				E-2C3D	273C31
7	峧	3-2476					
8	峨	0-2275	0-1869	0-6817	AE6F	1-5533	213B77
9	峩		0-5422	1-7006		E-3063	2D3B77
A	峪	0-5188	0-5427		AE6E	1-5532	213B7A
B	峫	3-2471				E-305F	22243C
C	峬	5-2708			D16C	2-2E6E	
D	峭	0-3945	0-5425	1-7979	AE6B	1-552F	213B75
E	峮	3-2502	1-2730		D16E	2-2E70	
F	峯		0-4287	0-6071		E-3064	2D3B78

5CF

	Char	G	J	K	B	C	A
0	峰	0-2369	0-4286	0-6072	AE70	1-5534	213B78
1	峱	3-3622	1-2731	1-6037	D16F	2-2E71	222446
2	峲	5-2715	1-2732				
3	峳	3-2486				E-3061	
4	峴	1-6513	1-2733	0-9054	AE73	1-5537	222441
5	峵	5-2721				E-3062	
6	島	1-2126	0-3771	0-5186	AE71	1-5535	213B79
7	峷	5-2718			D170	2-2E72	
8	峸				CEAE	2-2A2F	
9	峹	5-2716			D172	2-2E74	
A	峺	5-2709	0-5424			E-305E	4B4E39
B	峻	0-3094	0-2952	0-8158	AE6D	1-5531	213B76
C	峼	3-2485				E-6271	
D	峽	1-4731	0-5423	0-9082	AE6C	1-5530	213B74
E	峾	3-2493				E-6272	
F	峿	3-2482			D16D	2-2E6F	22243B

5D0

	Char	G	J	K	B	C	A
0	崀	3-2501			D171	2-2E73	222434
1	崁	3-2481	1-2734		AE72	1-5536	213B73
2	崂	0-6532					282569
3	崃	0-6533					282458
4	崄	8-9087					
5	崅	8-1580					
6	崆	0-6539	1-2735	1-5733	B153	1-5977	213B7C
7	崇	0-1971	0-3182	0-6693	B152	1-5976	213B7B
8	崈					E-354B	2D3B7B
9	崉					E-3548	
A	崊					E-3547	
B	崋		0-5428		D4F5	2-3478	39553C
C	崌	3-2516			D4F9	2-347C	222452
D	崍	1-6533	1-2736	0-5347	D4FB	2-347E	222458
E	崎	0-3873	0-2674	0-4888	B154	1-5978	213C21
F	崏				D4FE	2-3523	

5D2

	Char	G	J	K	B	C	A
0	崠	3-2449			D4F8	2-347B	222453
1	崡	5-2737				E-3546	222454
2	崢	1-6531	0-5436	1-7555	B157	1-597B	213C23
3	崣	3-2510	1-2739		D542	2-3526	
4	崤	0-6537	1-2740	1-8458	B15C	1-5A22	222469
5	崥	3-2511			D4FD	2-3522	
6	崦	0-6535	1-2741	1-7119	D4FC	2-3521	22245A
7	崧	0-6534	1-2742	0-6694	B15D	1-5A23	222457
8	崨	3-2506			D4FA	2-347D	
9	崩	0-1732	0-4288	0-6158	B159	1-597D	213C24
A	崪	3-2513				E-354E	
B	崫	3-2517	1-2738				
C	崬	1-6520				E-354A	
D	崭	0-5324					273C2A
E	崮	0-6536			D544	2-3528	22245D
F	崯	5-2730				E-3554	

5D4

	Char	G	J	K	B	C	A
0	嵀	5-2740			D8F0	2-3B54	
1	嵁	3-2519		1-5541	D8DC	2-3B40	
2	嵂	3-2530	1-2748	1-6346	D8E9	2-3B4D	222531
3	嵃	3-2533	1-2749		D8DA	2-3B3E	
4	嵄					E-3B27	
5	嵅				D8F1	2-3B55	
6	嵆	5-2745	1-2750			E-3B37	
7	嵇	0-7990			B452	1-5E77	22252D
8	嵈		1-2751			E-3B2A	
9	嵉	5-2751			D8EB	2-3B4F	
A	嵊	0-6551	1-2755		DD4F	2-4255	222544
B	嵋	0-6550	0-5443	0-5814	D8DD	2-3B41	222474
C	嵌	0-3922	0-5440	0-4278	B44F	1-5E74	213C27
D	嵍					E-3B2E	
E	嵎	3-2524	0-5442	1-7320	D8E1	2-3B45	222528
F	嵏	3-2531				E-3B34	

5D6

	Char	G	J	K	B	C	A
0	嵠	5-2761	1-2757			E-4121	
1	嵡	5-2762	1-2758				
2	嵢	5-2664	1-2759		DD56	2-425C	22254A
3	嵣	3-2544			DD4E	2-4254	
4	嵤	5-2665	1-2760			E-407C	
5	嵥	5-2763			DD50	2-4256	
6	嵦	5-2689				E-407A	
7	嵧	5-2764			DD55	2-425B	
8	嵨	3-2443			DD54	2-425A	
9	嵩	0-6552	0-3183	0-6701	B743	1-6369	213C29
A	嵪	5-2765	1-2761				
B	嵫	0-6549			D8DB	2-3B3F	22253A
C	嵬	0-6545	0-5444	0-7267	DD52	2-4258	222549
D	嵭		1-2762			E-4079	
E	嵮	5-2755				E-407D	
F	嵯	0-6547	0-2623	0-8311	B744	1-636A	222539

5D1

	Char	G	J	K	B	C	A
0	崐			1-5715		E-3551	2D3C22
1	崑	8-1367	0-5434	0-4563	B158	1-597C	213C22
2	崒	5-2732	1-2737		D541	2-3525	22244A
3	崓	3-2508				E-3552	
4	崔	0-2062	0-5435	0-8543	B15A	1-597E	213C25
5	崕	5-2725	0-5429	1-7057		E-354F	4B3B7E
6	崖	0-4934	0-1919	0-6880	B156	1-597A	213B7E
7	崗	1-2458	0-5430	0-4311	B15E	1-5A24	2D3B6E
8	崘		0-5439			E-3555	2D3C26
9	崙	8-1368	0-5438	0-5536	B15B	1-5A21	213C26
A	崚	3-2504	0-5437		D4F7	2-347A	222450
B	崛	0-6540	0-5433	1-5892	B155	1-5979	213B7D
C	崜	3-2509				E-3B2B	
D	崝	3-2503			D4F6	2-3479	
E	崞	0-6538			D4F4	2-3477	222449
F	崟	3-2512	0-5432	1-7429	D543	2-3527	2E257B

5D3

	Char	G	J	K	B	C	A
0	崰				D540	2-3524	
1	崱	3-2472	1-2743		D8E7	2-3B4B	
2	崲	5-2746			D8EE	2-3B52	22252F
3	崳	5-2749			D8E3	2-3B47	
4	崴	0-6543	1-2744	1-7272	B451	1-5E76	222477
5	崵	5-2659			D8DF	2-3B43	
6	崶	3-2518			D8EF	2-3B53	222471
7	崷	3-2537			D8D9	2-3B3D	
8	崸				D8EC	2-3B50	
9	崹	3-2534	1-2745		D8EA	2-3B4E	
A	崺	3-2535			D8E4	2-3B48	
B	崻	5-2748				E-3B36	
C	崼	3-2523			D8ED	2-3B51	
D	崽	0-6544	1-2746	1-7550	D8E6	2-3B4A	222527
E	崾	0-6542				E-3B28	222472
F	崿	3-2527	1-2747		D8DE	2-3B42	222525

5D5

	Char	G	J	K	B	C	A
0	嵐	1-6516	0-4582	0-5325	B450	1-5E75	213C28
1	嵑	3-2525	1-2753		D8E0	2-3B44	
2	嵒		0-5441		D8E5	2-3B49	222526
3	嵓	5-2744		1-7038		E-3B33	
4	嵔	5-2742		1-7273			
5	嵕	5-2750	1-2752		D8E2	2-3B46	
6	嵖	3-2522					
7	嵗					E-3B31	222476
8	嵘	0-6541					282632
9	嵙		1-2754		D8E8	2-3B4C	22252C
A	嵚	8-9092					
B	嵛	0-6546				E-3B2D	4C2532
C	嵜		0-5431				4B3C21
D	嵝	0-6548					28255A
E	嵞				DD53	2-4259	
F	嵟	5-2757	1-2756				

5D7

	Char	G	J	K	B	C	A
0	嵰	3-2545	1-2763				
1	嵱	3-2546		1-7306	DD4D	2-4253	
2	嵲	3-2542			DD51	2-4257	
3	嵳		0-5445				4C2539
4	嵴	0-6553					222534
5	嵵					E-646E	22253F
6	嵶		0-5446				69564E
7	嵷	3-2440			E1A9	2-496E	
8	嵸	3-2441				E-465C	
9	嵹	3-2568	1-2764		E1B0	2-4975	222550
A	嵺	3-2556	1-2765		E1A7	2-496C	
B	嵻					E-4654	
C	嵼	3-2477			E1AE	2-4973	
D	嵽	3-2520			E1A5	2-496A	
E	嵾		1-2766		E1AD	2-4972	222560
F	嵿	3-2507	1-2767		E1B1	2-4976	

5D8

	Char	G	J	K	B	C	A
0	嶀				E1A4	2-4969	
1	嶁	1-6548	1-2768	1-6334	E1A8	2-496D	22255A
2	嶂	0-6554	0-5449	1-7534	E1A3	2-4968	22254D
3	嶃		1-2769			E-4656	
4	嶄	1-5324	0-5448	1-7855	B9F1	1-6859	213C2A
5	嶅	8-9093					
6	嶆	3-2549			E1A6	2-496B	
7	嶇	1-6511	0-5447	0-4709	B9F2	1-685A	213C2B
8	嶈	3-2532	1-2770		E1AC	2-4971	
9	嶉	3-2552			E1AB	2-4970	
A	嶊	3-2551	1-2771		E1AA	2-496F	
B	嶋	5-2672	0-3772	0-5187		E-4659	2D3B79
C	嶌		0-5426			E-465A	4B3B79
D	嶍	3-2555			E1AF	2-4974	
E	嶎					E-646F	222551
F	嶏	5-2775				E-4B65	

5D9

	Char	G	J	K	B	C	A
0	嶐		0-5455			E-4B66	695657
1	嶑					E-4B63	
2	嶒	3-2567	1-2772	1-7786	E565	2-502E	222566
3	嶓	3-2564	1-2773		E567	2-5030	222575
4	嶔	3-2528	1-2774	1-5957	BC6B	1-6C55	22257B
5	嶕	3-2562	1-2775	1-7980	E568	2-5031	
6	嶖	5-2781				E-4B6B	
7	嶗	1-6532			E563	2-502C	222569
8	嶘	5-2739				E-4B67	
9	嶙	0-6555	1-2776	1-6370	E562	2-502B	222568
A	嶚	5-2776			E56C	2-5035	
B	嶛	3-2559	1-2777			E-4B69	
C	嶜	3-2560			E56A	2-5033	
D	嶝	0-6556	0-5451	0-5281	BC6A	1-6C54	213C2C
E	嶞	3-2554			E56D	2-5036	
F	嶟	3-2566	1-2778		E564	2-502D	

5DA

	Char	G	J	K	B	C	A
0	嶠	1-6529	1-2779	0-4668	E569	2-5032	222577
1	嶡	3-2558			E56B	2-5034	222573
2	嶢	3-2469	0-5450	0-7282	E566	2-502F	22256A
3	嶣	5-2779				E-4B6A	
4	嶤	5-2687				E-4B68	
5	嶥					E-6470	
6	嶦	3-2575				E-5058	
7	嶧	1-6527	1-2780	1-7130	E961	2-566B	222626
8	嶨	3-2459			E966	2-5670	
9	嶩	5-2706			E960	2-566A	
A	嶪	3-2452		0-6985	E965	2-566F	
B	嶫		1-2781	1-7125		E-505B	
C	嶬	3-2434	0-5452		E95E	2-5668	22257E
D	嶭	3-2574			E968	2-5672	
E	嶮	3-2487	0-5453	1-8336	E964	2-566E	22262F
F	嶯				E969	2-5673	

5DB

	Char	G	J	K	B	C	A
0	嶰	3-2576	1-2782	1-8318	E963	2-566D	22262A
1	嶱	3-2557			E95F	2-5669	
2	嶲		1-7084		E967	2-5671	
3	嶳	5-2785				E-505A	
4	嶴	5-2780	1-2783		E96A	2-5674	22262E
5	嶵				E962	2-566C	
6	嶶					E-6471	222630
7	嶷	0-6558	0-5456	1-7439	BCDA	2-5C66	222636
8	嶸	1-6541	1-2784	0-7114	C0AF	1-7358	222632
9	嶹	5-2707	1-2785			E-5457	
A	嶺	1-3375	0-4670	0-5426	C0AD	1-7356	213C2F
B	嶻	3-2578				E-5459	
C	嶼	1-5176	0-5457	0-6376	C0AC	1-7355	213C2D
D	嶽		0-5454	0-6832	C0AE	1-7357	213C2E
E	嶾	3-2579				E-5455	
F	嶿					E-6472	222634

5DC

	Char	G	J	K	B	C	A
0	巀				EFC4	2-6150	
1	巁	3-2446				E-5762	
2	巂	5-3123			F172	2-643E	
3	巃	3-2448	1-2786		F1FD	2-6549	22263E
4	巄	5-2667				E-5A39	
5	巅	0-6559					273C32
6	巆	3-2548			F444	2-6870	
7	巇	3-2584	1-2787		F445	2-6871	222644
8	巈					E-5C3D	
9	巉	3-2585	0-5458	1-7856	C460	1-796B	222646
A	巊	3-2553				E-5C3C	
B	巋	1-3189	1-2788	1-5925	F5C9	2-6B57	222647
C	巌		0-2064			E-5C3E	4B3C33
D	巍	0-4601	0-5459	0-7268	C4DE	1-7A69	213C30
E	巎	5-2802	1-2790				
F	巏	3-2583			F5CA	2-6B58	

5DD

	Char	G	J	K	B	C	A
0	巐	5-2801	1-2789			E-5E2D	
1	巑	3-2582		1-7846	F6DE	2-6D4C	
2	巒	1-3445	0-5461	0-5621	C572	1-7B5E	213C31
3	巓		0-5460	1-7588		E-5F43	4B3C32
4	巔	1-6559			C571	1-7B5D	213C32
5	巕				F6DD	2-6D4B	
6	巖	8-1369	0-5462	0-6860	C5C9	1-7C35	213C33
7	巗					E-6030	
8	巘	3-2571	1-2791		F7D6	2-6F25	22264E
9	巙		1-2792				
A	巚			1-8333			
B	巛	0-7161	0-5463			E-213C	222650
C	巜	5-1629					222652
D	川	0-2008	0-3278	0-8425	A474	1-4455	213C34
E	州	0-5461	0-2903	0-8122	A67B	1-477C	213C35
F	巟	5-1944			C9DA	2-223A	

5DE

	Char	G	J	K	B	C	A
0	巠		1-2793		CACA	2-236A	
1	巡	0-4918	0-2968	0-6662	A8B5	1-4B56	215B69
2	巢	0-1918		0-6521	B15F	1-5A25	213C36
3	巣		0-3367			E-3557	2D3C36
4	巤	5-3369	1-2794			E-4B6C	222656
5	工	0-2504	0-2509	0-4579	A475	1-4456	213C37
6	左	0-5583	0-2624	0-8107	A5AA	1-464A	213C3A
7	巧	0-3941	0-2510	0-4669	A5A9	1-4649	213C39
8	巨	0-3062	0-2180	0-4361	A5A8	1-4648	213C38
9	巩	0-2514	1-2801				276023
A	巪						
B	巫	0-4655	0-5464	0-5767	A7C5	1-4A27	213C3B
C	巬						
D	巭						
E	差	0-1878	0-2625	0-8312	AE74	1-5538	213C3C
F	巯	0-5947					282659

5DF

	Char	G	J	K	B	C	A
0	巰	1-5947			DD57	2-425D	
1	己	0-2826	0-2442	0-4889	A476	1-4457	213C3D
2	已	0-5049	0-5465	0-7611	A477	1-4458	213C3E
3	巳	0-4340	0-4406	0-6251	A478	1-4459	213C3F
4	巴	0-1645	0-3935	0-8773	A4DA	1-453B	213C40
5	巵		0-5466	1-8077		E-2567	4B346B
6	巶	5-3080				E-2860	
7	巷	0-4779	0-2511	0-8985	ABD1	1-5073	213C41
8	巸	3-2765	1-2802				
9	巹	5-3081	1-2803	1-5948	CEAF	2-2A30	
A	巺					E-2C45	
B	巻		0-2012			E-2C44	
C	巼						
D	巽	0-5767	0-3507	0-6562	B453	1-5E78	213C42
E	巾	0-2977	0-2250	0-4378	A479	1-445A	213C43
F	巿	5-2594			C95D	2-213D	

5E0

	Char	G	J	K	B	C	A
0	帀		1-2804			E-2163	222662
1	币	0-1750					273C5E
2	市	0-4248	0-2752	0-6728	A5AB	1-464B	213C44
3	布	0-1828	0-4159	0-8854	A5AC	1-464C	273138
4	帄	5-2601			C978	2-2159	
5	帅	0-4307					273C4F
6	帆	0-2311	0-4033	0-5978	A67C	1-477D	213C46
7	帇	5-7123	1-2805				
8	师	0-4206				E-235C	273C51
9	帉	5-2606		1-6647		E-2568	
A	帊	3-2369			CACB	2-236B	
B	帋	8-1366	0-5467			E-256B	2D5124
C	希	0-4703	0-2085	0-9381	A7C6	1-4A28	274F36
D	帍	5-5067	1-2806				
E	帎	5-2608			CACC	2-236C	
F	帏	0-6488					282736

5E1

	Char	G	J	K	B	C	A
0	帐	0-5342					273C52
1	帑	0-6491	0-5470	0-8722	A9AE	1-4D30	213C4D
2	帒	5-2611	1-2807			E-2862	222677
3	帓	3-2370				E-2861	
4	帔	0-6490	1-2808		CC6E	2-264F	222672
5	帕	0-3733	1-2809	1-6407	A9AC	1-4D2E	213C4B
6	帖	0-4491	0-3601	0-8462	A9AB	1-4D2D	213C4A
7	帗	3-2372			CC6D	2-264E	222673
8	帘	0-3317	1-2810		A9A9	1-4D2B	275048
9	帙	0-6489	0-5469	0-8277	CC6F	2-2650	222676
A	帚	0-5467	0-5468	1-8030	A9AA	1-4D2C	213C49
B	帛	0-1815	0-5471	0-5957	A9AD	1-4D2F	213C4C
C	帜	0-5436					273C60
D	帝	0-2159	0-3675	0-8008	ABD2	1-5074	213C4E
E	帞	3-2375				E-2C46	
F	帟	3-2380	1-2811		ABD4	1-5076	222678

5E2

	Char	G	J	K	B	C	A
0	帠		1-2812		CEB3	2-2A34	
1	帡	3-2381			CEB0	2-2A31	22267B
2	帢	3-2378			CEB1	2-2A32	222722
3	帣	3-2382			CEB2	2-2A33	22267A
4	帤	3-2383			CEB4	2-2A35	
5	帥	1-4307	0-3167	0-6593	ABD3	1-5075	213C4F
6	带	0-2088					273C53
7	帧	0-5401					273C58
8	帨	3-2387	1-2814	1-6864	D174	2-2E76	222724
9	帩	3-2386			D173	2-2E75	
A	帪	3-2385				E-3066	
B	師	1-4206	0-2753	0-6252	AE76	1-553A	213C51
C	帬					E-3069	2D5760
D	席	0-4715	0-3242	0-6412	AE75	1-5539	27555D
E	帮	0-1679	1-2813			E-3068	273C61
F	帯		0-3451			E-306A	4B3C53

5E3

	Char	G	J	K	B	C	A
0	帰		0-2102			E-3067	3F462B
1	帱	0-6492					28275F
2	帲		1-2815			E-355B	
3	帳	1-5342	0-3602	0-7767	B162	1-5A28	213C52
4	帴	3-2371			D546	2-352A	
5	帵	3-2393	1-2816			E-3559	
6	帶	1-2088	0-5472	0-5165	B161	1-5A27	213C53
7	帷	0-6501	0-5473	1-7375	B163	1-5A29	213C55
8	常	0-1903	0-3079	0-6340	B160	1-5A26	213C54
9	帹	3-2391				E-3558	
A	帺	3-2389				E-355A	
B	帻	0-6493					282747
C	帼	0-6494					273C5C
D	帽	0-3517	0-4325	0-5722	B455	1-5E7A	213C57
E	帾	3-2388	1-2817		D545	2-3529	
F	帿			0-9312			

5E4

	Char	G	J	K	B	C	A
0	幀	1-5401	0-5476	0-7951	B456	1-5E7B	213C58
1	幁				D8F3	2-3B57	
2	幂	0-3561				E-3979	222739
3	幃	1-6488	0-5475	1-7358	B457	1-5E7C	222736
4	幄	0-6502	0-5474	0-6833	D8F2	2-3B56	222735
5	幅	0-2389	0-4193	0-8875	B454	1-5E79	213C56
6	幆	3-2404				E-3B3A	
7	幇		0-5483	0-5912		E-3B3B	2D3C61
8	幈	5-2632				E-3B3D	222748
9	幉		1-2820				
A	幊				DD5A	2-4260	
B	幋	5-2635	1-2818		DD5C	2-4262	
C	幌	0-2747	0-4358	0-9238	B745	1-636B	213C59
D	幍	5-2636			DD5B	2-4261	
E	幎	3-2417	0-5477	1-6431	DD59	2-425F	22273F
F	幏	3-2416			DD58	2-425E	

5E5

	Char	G	J	K	B	C	A
0	幐	3-4554	1-2819				
1	幑		1-2821				
2	幒	3-2420				E-465D	
3	幓	3-2401			E1B4	2-4979	
4	幔	0-6503	0-5479	1-6394	B9F7	1-685F	213C5B
5	幕	0-3627	0-4375	0-5613	B9F5	1-685D	213C5D
6	幖	3-2419	1-2822				
7	幗	1-6494	0-5478		B9F6	1-685E	213C5C
8	幘	1-6493	1-2823	1-7891	E1B2	2-4977	222747
9	幙				E1B3	2-4978	
A	幚					E-4B6D	
B	幛	0-6504	1-2824		B9F3	1-685B	213C5A
C	幜	5-2643	1-2825		E571	2-503A	
D	幝	3-2392			E56F	2-5038	
E	幞	0-6505	1-2826	1-6604		E-4B70	222757
F	幟	1-5436	0-5480	0-8626	BC6D	1-6C57	213C60

5E6

	Char	G	J	K	B	C	A
0	幠	3-2367			E570	2-5039	
1	幡	0-6506	0-4008	0-5963	BC6E	1-6C58	222758
2	幢	0-2017	0-5481	0-5151	BC6C	1-6C56	213C5F
3	幣	1-1750	0-4230	0-8839	B9F4	1-685C	213C5E
4	幤		0-5482				4B3C5E
5	幥					E-6473	
6	幦	3-2425			E96D	2-5677	
7	幧	5-2646			E96B	2-5675	
8	幨	3-2424	1-2827	1-7944	E96C	2-5676	22275D
9	幩	3-2402			E56E	2-5037	
A	幪	3-2423	1-2828	1-6458	ECDC	2-5C68	222760
B	幫	1-1679	1-2829	1-6538	C0B0	1-7359	213C61
C	幬	1-6492	1-2830	1-7746	ECDB	2-5C67	22275F
D	幭	3-2426	1-2831		EFC5	2-6151	222764
E	幮		1-2832		EFC6	2-6152	222763
F	幯	5-2610			E96E	2-5678	

5E7

	Char	G	J	K	B	C	A
0	幰	3-2427	1-2833	1-8334	F1FE	2-654A	222765
1	幱	5-2644		1-6201		E-6677	
2	干	0-2441	0-2019	0-4246	A47A	1-445B	27304C
3	平	0-3829	0-4231	0-8833	A5AD	1-464D	213C63
4	年	0-3674	0-3915	0-5020	A67E	1-4821	213C65
5	幵		0-5484		C9DB	2-223B	22276D
6	并	0-1802	0-5485		A67D	1-477E	273032
7	幷			0-6020		E-2863	
8	幸	0-4850	0-2512	0-9025	A9AF	1-4D31	2D3177
9	幹	1-2441	0-2020	0-4247	B746	1-636C	3F304C
A	幺	0-7159	0-5486	1-7285		E-213D	456260
B	幻	0-2735	0-2424	0-9219	A4DB	1-453C	213C68
C	幼	0-5155	0-4536	0-7474	A5AE	1-464E	213C69
D	幽	0-5136	0-4509	0-7475	ABD5	1-5077	213C6A
E	幾	1-2824	0-2086	0-4890	B458	1-5E7D	213C6B
F	广	0-2567	0-5488	1-7120		E-213E	273D2A

5E8

	Char	G	J	K	B	C	A
0	庀	0-6647	1-2834		C979	2-215A	222777
1	庁	5-2885	0-3603			E-2247	333D2F
2	庂	5-2887			C97A	2-215B	
3	広		0-2513			E-2248	333D2A
4	庄	0-5515	0-3017	0-7768	C9DC	2-223C	27552D
5	庅					E-6678	2D6260
6	庆	0-3976					273F2E
7	庇	0-1751	0-4063	0-6171	A7C8	1-4A2A	213C6D
8	庈	3-2632			CAD0	2-2370	
9	庉	5-2892			CACE	2-236E	
A	床	0-2018	0-3018	0-6341	A7C9	1-4A2B	213C6E
B	庋	0-6649	1-2835	1-5972	CACD	2-236D	22277E
C	庌	3-2630			CACF	2-236F	
D	庍	5-2894			CAD1	2-2371	
E	庎	5-2901	1-2836				
F	序	0-4882	0-2988	0-6377	A7C7	1-4A29	213C6C

5E9

	Char	G	J	K	B	C	A
0	庐	0-3414				E-256E	273D2E
1	庑	0-6648					282868
2	庒					E-256D	
3	库	0-3166					273C76
4	应	0-5106					273F4A
5	底	0-2155	0-3676	0-7828	A9B3	1-4D35	213C73
6	庖	0-6650	0-4289	1-8225	A9B4	1-4D36	213C71
7	店	0-2174	0-3725	0-7933	A9B1	1-4D33	213C70
8	庘	3-2634				E-2865	
9	庙	0-3577				E-2867	273D2B
A	庚	0-2493	0-2514	0-4450	A9B0	1-4D32	213C6F
B	庛	3-2641			CEB8	2-2A39	
C	府	0-2414	0-4160	0-6104	A9B2	1-4D34	213C72
D	庝	3-2638				E-2868	
E	庞	0-3751					273D2D
F	废	0-2347					273D27

5EA

	Char	G	J	K	B	C	A
0	庠	0-6652	0-5489	0-6342	ABD6	1-5078	213C74
1	庡	3-2646				E-2C48	
2	庢	5-2906	1-2837		CEB7	2-2A38	
3	庣	3-2645			CEB9	2-2A3A	
4	庤	3-2639	1-2838		CEB6	2-2A37	22282F
5	庥	0-6651	1-2839		CEBA	2-2A3B	222835
6	度	0-2240	0-3757	0-5188	ABD7	1-5079	213C75
7	座	0-5589	0-2634	0-8108	AE79	1-553D	213C77
8	庨	3-2649	1-2840		D175	2-2E77	
9	庩	3-2654				E-306C	
A	庪	3-2653	1-2841		D177	2-2E79	
B	庫	1-3166	0-2443	0-4523	AE77	1-553B	213C76
C	庬	5-2917	1-2842		D178	2-2E7A	
D	庭	0-4505	0-3677	0-7952	AE78	1-553C	213C78
E	庮	3-2651			D176	2-2E78	
F	庯	3-2650				E-306B	222836

5EB

	Char	G	J	K	B	C	A
0	庰	3-2647			CEB5	2-2A36	
1	庱	3-2657	1-2843		D547	2-352B	
2	庲	3-2652			D54A	2-352E	
3	庳	0-6656	1-2844	1-6682	D54B	2-352F	22284B
4	庴	3-2658			D548	2-352C	
5	庵	0-6654	0-1635	0-6861	B167	1-5A2D	213C7C
6	庶	0-4292	0-2978	0-6378	B166	1-5A2C	213C7B
7	康	0-3121	0-2515	0-4312	B164	1-5A2A	213C79
8	庸	0-5125	0-4539	0-7328	B165	1-5A2B	213C7A
9	庹	0-6653			D549	2-352D	222842
A	庺	5-2923				E-3561	
B	庻					E-3560	
C	庼	8-9110					
D	庽		1-2845	1-7321		E-3B3F	2D3B2A
E	庾	0-6655	1-2846	0-7476	B168	1-5A2E	213D21
F	庿	5-2919	1-2847			E-3B40	2D3D2B

5EC

	Char	G	J	K	B	C	A
0	廀					E-3B3E	
1	廁		0-5490	1-8072	B45A	1-5F21	213C7E
2	廂		0-5491	0-6343	B45B	1-5F22	213C7D
3	廃		0-3949				4B3D27
4	廄	5-2927			B45C	1-5F23	22284C
5	廅	3-2672			DD5D	2-4263	
6	廆	3-2670	1-2848		DD5F	2-4265	
7	廇	3-2674			DD61	2-4267	
8	廈	8-1359	0-5492	0-8931	B748	1-636E	213D24
9	廉	0-3314	0-4687	0-5415	B747	1-636D	213D23
A	廊	0-3240	0-4713	0-5338	B459	1-5E7E	213D22
B	廋	3-2669	1-2850	1-6911	DD60	2-4266	222855
C	廌	3-2675	1-2849		DD5E	2-4264	222851
D	廍					E-6474	222857
E	廎	3-2661	1-2851		E1B8	2-497D	222861
F	廏		0-5494			E-4661	

5ED

	Char	G	J	K	B	C	A
0	廐		0-5493	0-4710		E-4660	2E284C
1	廑	0-6659	1-2852	1-5949	E1B6	2-497B	22285B
2	廒	0-6658	1-2853		E1BC	2-4A23	22285A
3	廓	0-3210	0-1939	0-4609	B9F8	1-6860	213D25
4	廔	5-2926	1-2854		E1BD	2-4A24	22285F
5	廕		1-2855	1-7430	E1BA	2-4A21	22285C
6	廖	0-3346	0-5501	0-5488	B9F9	1-6861	213D26
7	廗	3-2666			E1B7	2-497C	
8	廘	3-2678			E1B5	2-497A	
9	廙	3-2677			E1BB	2-4A22	222860
A	廚		0-5504	0-8123	BC70	1-6C5A	213D28
B	廛	0-6660	0-5505	0-7888	E573	2-503C	4C2867
C	廜	3-2679	1-2856		E1B9	2-497E	
D	廝		0-5503	1-6962	BC72	1-6C5C	213D29
E	廞	3-2667	1-2857	1-8516	E574	2-503D	
F	廟	1-3577	0-4132	0-5757	BC71	1-6C5B	213D2B

5EE

	Char	G	J	K	B	C	A
0	廠	1-1907	0-3019	0-8363	BC74	1-6C5E	213D2C
1	廡	1-6648	0-5507	1-6474	E575	2-503E	222868
2	廢	1-2347	0-5506	0-8840	BC6F	1-6C59	213D27
3	廣	1-2567	0-5502	0-4638	BC73	1-6C5D	213D2A
4	廤						
5	廥	3-2644	1-2858	1-5805	E973	2-567D	
6	廦	3-2682			E971	2-567B	
7	廧	5-2932		1-7535	E970	2-567A	22286D
8	廨	0-6661	0-5508	1-8319	E972	2-567C	222871
9	廩		0-5509	1-6352	E96F	2-5679	334F37
A	廪	0-6662				E-505C	
B	廫		1-2859				
C	廬	1-3414	0-5510	0-5370	C366	1-7833	213D2E
D	廭					E-6475	22287C
E	廮	5-2933			F446	2-6872	
F	廯	5-2940			F447	2-6873	

5EF

	Char	G	J	K	B	C	A
0	廰		0-5513			E-5C3F	4B3D2F
1	廱	5-2943	0-5511	1-7242	F5CB	2-6B59	222921
2	廲	5-2915			F6DF	2-6D4D	
3	廳	1-4492	0-5512	0-8470	C655	1-7D22	213D2F
4	廴	0-5940	0-5514			E-213F	222923
5	廵					E-2361	2D5B69
6	延	0-4951	0-1768	0-7037	A9B5	1-4D37	213D32
7	廷	0-4502	0-3678	0-7953	A7CA	1-4A2C	213D30
8	廸		0-5515			E-2869	335B70
9	廹					E-286B	
A	建	0-2908	0-2390	0-4379	ABD8	1-507A	213D33
B	廻		0-1886	0-9263		E-2C4C	453768
C	廼		0-3922			E-2C4B	39303A
D	廽					E-306E	
E	廾	0-6235	0-5516		A47B	1-445C	2D3D34
F	廿	0-5605	0-3891	1-7477	A4DC	1-453D	213D34

5F0

	Char	G	J	K	B	C	A
0	开	0-3110					275E53
1	弁	0-5945	0-4259	0-6007	A5AF	1-464F	4B5B5E
2	异	0-5076	1-2860		C9DD	2-223D	274C34
3	弃	0-3890	0-5517	1-5973		E-256F	27446D
4	弄	0-3710	0-4714	0-5471	A7CB	1-4A2D	213D36
5	弅				CAD2	2-2372	
6	弆	3-2104	1-2861			E-286D	
7	弇	3-2106	1-2862	1-5542	CEBB	2-2A3C	222935
8	弈	0-6236	1-2863	1-8339	ABD9	1-507B	213D37
9	弉		0-5518				4B393A
A	弊	0-1755	0-4232	0-8841	B9FA	1-6862	213D38
B	弋	0-6314	0-5521	1-7457	A47C	1-445D	22293A
C	弌	5-2363	0-4801			E-2164	2D3021
D	弍	5-2364	0-4817			E-2249	2D3051
E	弎	5-2365	1-2864			E-2362	
F	式	0-4229	0-2816	0-6750	A6A1	1-4822	213D39

5F1

	Char	G	J	K	B	C	A
0	弐		0-3885				4B3051
1	弑	0-6317	0-5522	0-6729		E-3B42	
2	弒				B749	1-636F	213D3A
3	弓	0-2513	0-2161	0-4765	A47D	1-445E	213D3B
4	弔		0-3604	0-8032	A4DD	1-453E	213D3D
5	引	0-5093	0-1690	0-7658	A4DE	1-453F	213D3C
6	弖		0-5523				695737
7	弗	0-2405	0-4206	0-6155	A5B1	1-4651	213D3F
8	弘	0-2675	0-2516	0-9180	A5B0	1-4650	213D3E
9	弙	3-2767	1-2865				
A	弚	5-1723			C9DE	2-223E	
B	弛	0-1958	0-3548	0-7612	A6A2	1-4823	213D40
C	弜	3-2769	1-2866				
D	弝	5-3087	1-2867		CAD3	2-2373	
E	弞	3-2771				E-2571	
F	弟	0-2160	0-3679	0-8009	A7CC	1-4A2E	213D41

5F2

	Char	G	J	K	B	C	A
0	张	0-5337					273D47
1	弡	5-3086	1-2868			E-286E	
2	弢	3-2775	1-2869	1-6125	CC71	2-2652	22294B
3	弣	3-2772	1-2870		CC72	2-2653	22294C
4	弤	3-2773	1-2871		CC73	2-2654	22294D
5	弥	0-3554	0-4479	1-6489		E-2870	273D4C
6	弦	0-4750	0-2425	0-9055	A9B6	1-4D38	213D42
7	弧	0-2701	0-2444	0-9133	A9B7	1-4D39	213D43
8	弨	3-2776	1-2872		CC70	2-2651	22294A
9	弩	0-6983	0-5524	0-5032	A9B8	1-4D3A	213D44
A	弪	0-6982					282951
B	弫		1-2873				
C	弬		1-2874				
D	弭	0-6984	0-5525	1-6490	ABDA	1-507C	213D45
E	弮	3-2779	1-2875		CEBC	2-2A3D	
F	弯	0-4568	0-5531			E-2C4D	273D4D

5F3

	Char	G	J	K	B	C	A
0	弰	3-2780	1-2876		D17A	2-2E7C	222952
1	弱	0-4085	0-2869	0-6916	AE7A	1-553E	213D46
2	弲	3-2781				E-306F	
3	弳	1-6982			D179	2-2E7B	222951
4	弴	5-3094	1-2877	1-6144		E-3562	
5	張	1-5337	0-3605	0-7769	B169	1-5A2F	213D47
6	弶	3-2784	1-2878		D54C	2-3530	
7	強		0-2215		B16A	1-5A30	333D48
8	弸	3-2783	0-5526		D54D	2-3531	222958
9	弹	0-2115				E-3563	273D4B
A	强	0-3931		0-4313		E-3B47	213D48
B	弻	5-3104	1-2879			E-3B45	
C	弼	0-6986	0-4111	0-8916	B45D	1-5F24	213D49
D	弽	5-3102	1-2880				
E	弾		0-3538			E-3B44	4B3D4B
F	弿	5-3108	1-2881				

5F4

	Char	G	J	K	B	C	A
0	彀	0-7616	1-2882	1-5850	DD62	2-4268	22295C
1	彁		0-5527				69573B
2	彂					E-4122	
3	彃	3-2778			E1BF	2-4A26	
4	彄	3-2770	1-2883		E1BE	2-4A25	22295F
5	彅		1-2884				
6	彆	1-8804		1-6580	B9FB	1-6863	213D4A
7	彇	5-3101	1-2885				
8	彈	1-2115	0-5528	0-8705	BC75	1-6C5F	213D4B
9	彉	5-3109			E576	2-503F	
A	彊		0-2216	0-4314	BECA	1-7053	2D3D48
B	彋	5-3114			E974	2-567E	
C	彌	1-3554	0-5529	0-5815	C0B1	1-735A	213D4C
D	彍	3-2768	1-2886			E-5763	222962
E	彎	1-4568	0-5530	0-5622	C573	1-7B5F	213D4D
F	彏	3-2789			F7D8	2-6F27	

5F5

	Char	G	J	K	B	C	A
0	彐	0-6970	1-2887			E-2140	222968
1	彑		0-5532			E-2141	2E2968
2	归	0-2573				E-224A	27462B
3	当	0-2117	0-3786			E-2351	273746
4	彔		1-2888	1-6289	CC74	2-2655	222969
5	录	0-3428				E-2871	275D74
6	彖	0-6972	0-5533	0-5107	CEBD	2-2A3E	22296A
7	彗	0-6971	0-5534	0-9118	B16B	1-5A31	213D4E
8	彘	0-6973	1-2889	1-7962	D8F4	2-3B58	22296C
9	彙	1-8829	0-5535	0-9336	B74A	1-6370	213D4F
A	彚					E-4123	
B	彛		1-2890	0-7613		E-505E	
C	彜	5-3039	0-5520				2D3D50
D	彝	0-5045	0-5519	1-7449	C255	E-5764	213D50
E	彞					1-7641	
F	彟	8-1429					

5F6

	Char	G	J	K	B	C	A
0	彠	5-3038	1-2891			E-6164	222970
1	彡	0-6574	0-5536			E-2142	222971
2	形	0-4846	0-2333	0-9101	A7CE	1-4A30	213D51
3	彣	5-4886	1-2892			E-2572	222972
4	彤	0-4514	1-2893	1-6154	A7CD	1-4A2F	213D52
5	彥				ABDB	1-507D	213D53
6	彦	0-4969	0-4107	0-6973		E-2C50	453D53
7	彧	3-3816	1-2894	0-7378	D17B	2-2E7D	222974
8	彨	8-1428					
9	彩	0-1842	0-2644	0-8384	B16D	1-5A33	213D55
A	彪	0-1775	0-4123	0-8883	B343	1-5D29	215646
B	彫		0-3606	0-8033	B16E	1-5A34	395F49
C	彬	0-1782	0-4143	0-6215	B16C	1-5A32	213D54
D	彭	0-3777	0-5537	0-8816	B45E	1-5F25	213D57
E	彮	5-2862				E-4124	
F	彯	5-2863	1-2901		E1C0	2-4A27	

5F7

	Char	G	J	K	B	C	A
0	彰	0-5335	0-3020	0-8364	B9FC	1-6864	213D58
1	影	0-5116	0-1738	0-7115	BC76	1-6C60	213D59
2	彲	5-2858	1-2902			E-5F45	222978
3	彳	0-6560	0-5538		C94C	2-212C	222979
4	彴	3-2588	1-2903		C9DF	2-223F	22297C
5	彵		1-2904				
6	彶	5-2806			CAD5	2-2375	
7	彷	0-6561	0-5539	0-5913	A7CF	1-4A31	333078
8	彸	3-2589	1-2905		CAD4	2-2374	
9	役	0-5059	0-4482	0-7021	A7D0	1-4A32	213D5B
A	彺		1-2906				
B	彻	0-1925					273D74
C	彼	0-1743	0-4064	0-8908	A9BC	1-4D3E	213D5F
D	彽	5-2814	1-2907		CC77	2-2658	
E	彾	5-2812	1-2908		CC76	2-2657	
F	彿		0-5542	0-6156	A9BB	1-4D3D	213D5E

5F8

	Char	G	J	K	B	C	A
0	往	0-4589	0-1793	0-7257	A9B9	1-4D3B	213D5C
1	征	0-5387	0-3212	0-7954	A9BA	1-4D3C	273D76
2	徂	0-6562	0-5541	1-7693	CC75	2-2656	222A23
3	徃		0-5540			E-2876	4B3D5C
4	径	0-3022	0-2334			E-2875	273D67
5	待	0-2093	0-3452	0-5166	ABDD	1-5121	213D60
6	徆	5-2815			CEBE	2-2A3F	
7	徇	0-6563	0-5546	0-6663	ABE0	1-5124	213D64
8	很	0-2660	0-5544	1-8505	ABDC	1-507E	213D61
9	徉	0-6564	1-2909	1-7089	ABE2	1-5126	222A27
A	徊	0-2718	0-5543	0-9264	ABDE	1-5122	213D63
B	律	0-3441	0-4607	0-5540	ABDF	1-5123	213D62
C	後	0-6565	0-2469	0-9313	ABE1	1-5125	213D65
D	徍		1-2910			E-6264	
E	徎	3-2593				E-3070	
F	徏		1-2911			E-3072	2F4A4A

5FA

	Char	G	J	K	B	C	A
0	徠	1-6566	0-5550	0-5348	B174	1-5A3A	33314C
1	御	0-5189	0-2470	0-6957	B173	1-5A39	2D4E79
2	徢		1-2915				
3	徣			1-7836			
4	徤		1-2918				
5	徥	3-2604			D8F6	2-3B5A	
6	徦	5-2835			D8F5	2-3B59	
7	徧		1-2916	1-8204		E-3B4B	2D5C3F
8	徨	0-6569	0-5551	0-9239	B461	1-5F28	2D5C40
9	復	1-2420	0-4192	0-6054	B45F	1-5F26	213D6F
A	循	0-4913	0-2959	0-6664	B460	1-5F27	213D71
B	徫	5-2807	1-2917		D8F7	2-3B5B	
C	徬	5-2838	1-2919	1-6539	B74B	1-6371	213D72
D	徭	0-6570	0-5552	1-7286	DD64	2-426A	2E7328
E	微	0-4602	0-4089	0-5816	B74C	1-6372	213D73
F	徯	3-2605	1-2920	1-8372	DD63	2-4269	222A46

5FC

	Char	G	J	K	B	C	A
0	忀	5-2854			F448	2-6874	
1	忁				F449	2-6875	
2	忂	5-2855				E-5E2F	
3	心	0-4836	0-3120	0-6793	A4DF	1-4540	213D78
4	忄	0-6664	1-2924				
5	必	0-1756	0-4112	0-8917	A5E2	1-4652	213D79
6	忆	0-5068					273F48
7	忇	3-4914	1-2925			E-224D	
8	忈	5-5072	1-2926			E-6251	333066
9	忉	0-6665	1-2927	1-6126	C97B	2-215C	222A57
A	忊	3-4913				E-224C	
B	忋	5-5138	1-2928				
C	忌	0-2841	0-2087	0-4891	A7D2	1-4A34	213D7C
D	忍	0-4044	0-3906	0-7659	A7D4	1-4A36	213E21
E	忎					E-2578	222A67
F	忏	0-6667			C9E2	2-2242	273F58

5FE

	Char	G	J	K	B	C	A
0	忠	0-5450	0-3573	0-8587	A9BE	1-4D40	213E23
1	忡	0-6671	1-2935	1-8062	CADD	2-237D	222A78
2	忢		1-2936				
3	忣	5-5137			CADF	2-2421	
4	忤	0-6672	0-5556	1-7211	CADE	2-237E	222A7B
5	忥	3-4403			CC79	2-265A	
6	忦	3-4930				E-2576	
7	忧	0-5139				E-2574	273F33
8	忨	5-5139	1-2937	1-7263	CADA	2-237A	
9	忩		1-2938			E-287E	
A	忪	0-6676	1-2939		A7D8	1-4A3A	222E24
B	快	0-3176	0-1887	0-8665	A7D6	1-4A38	213E22
C	忬	5-5151	1-2940			E-257C	
D	忭	0-6677	1-2941	1-6571	CAD9	2-2379	222A68
E	忮	0-6669	1-2942	1-5974	CADB	2-237B	222A72
F	忯	3-4933	1-2943		CAE1	2-2423	

5F9

	Char	G	J	K	B	C	A
0	徐	0-4876	0-2989	0-6379	AE7D	1-5541	213D68
1	徑	1-3022	0-5545	0-4451	AE7C	1-5540	213D67
2	徒	0-4529	0-3744	0-5189	AE7B	1-553F	213D66
3	従		0-2930			E-3071	2D3D6C
4	徔					E-6476	222A2B
5	徕	0-6566					4B314C
6	徖		1-2912		D54F	2-3533	
7	得	0-2135	0-3832	0-5280	B16F	1-5A35	213D6A
8	徘	0-3739	0-5549	0-5939	B172	1-5A38	213D69
9	徙	0-6567	0-5548	0-6253	B170	1-5A36	213D6B
A	徚					E-6477	222A3D
B	徛	3-2602			D54E	2-3532	
C	徜	0-6568	1-2913	1-6787	B175	1-5A3B	222A39
D	徝	5-2828	1-2914				
E	從	1-2051	0-5547	0-8084	B171	1-5A37	213D6C
F	徟				D550	2-3534	

5FB

	Char	G	J	K	B	C	A
0	徰		1-2921				
1	徱		1-2922				
2	徲	3-2609			E577	2-5040	
3	徳		0-3833			E-4663	333D75
4	徴		0-3607			E-4664	2D3D76
5	徵	0-6571		0-8303	BC78	1-6C62	213D76
6	徶	3-2607			E1C1	2-4A28	
7	德	0-2134		0-5176	BC77	1-6C61	213D75
8	徸	5-2844	1-2923			E-4B72	
9	徹	1-1925	0-3716	0-8443	B9FD	1-6865	213D74
A	徺					E-6478	333251
B	徻				ECDE	2-5722	
C	徼	0-6572	0-5553	1-7287	E975	2-5721	222A50
D	徽	0-2753	0-2111	0-9337	C0B2	1-735B	213D77
E	徾				ECDD	2-5C69	
F	徿	5-2809			F240	2-654B	

5FD

	Char	G	J	K	B	C	A
0	忐	0-7694	1-2929	1-8141	CAD8	2-2378	222A63
1	忑	0-7693	1-2930		CAD7	2-2377	222A5F
2	忒	0-6315	1-2931	1-8170	CAD6	2-2376	222A61
3	忓	3-4915	1-2932			E-2366	
4	忔	3-4918	1-2933		C9E1	2-2241	
5	忕	3-4916			C9E0	2-2240	
6	忖	0-6666	0-5554	0-8528	A6A4	1-4825	213D7D
7	志	0-5430	0-2754	0-8204	A7D3	1-4A35	27586D
8	忘	0-4592	0-4326	0-5646	A7D1	1-4A33	213D7B
9	忙	0-3506	0-4327	0-5647	A6A3	1-4824	213D7A
A	忚	3-4921				E-2367	
B	忛					E-2369	
C	応		0-1794			E-2577	4B3F4A
D	忝	0-6735	0-5559	1-7945	A9BD	1-4D3F	213E26
E	忞	3-4730	1-2934	1-6505	CC78	2-2659	343875
F	忟			1-6506		E-257B	

5FF

	Char	G	J	K	B	C	A
0	忰		0-5613			E-2622	273E57
1	忱	0-1932	0-5558	1-8104	A7D5	1-4A37	213E24
2	忲	5-5141	1-2944			E-2621	
3	忳	3-4927	1-2945		CADC	2-237C	
4	忴	3-4932			CAE5	2-2427	
5	念	0-3678	0-3916	0-5023	A9C0	1-4D42	213E27
6	忶	5-5140	1-2946			E-257D	
7	忷	5-5146			CAE2	2-2424	
8	忸	0-6678	0-5557	1-6056	A7D7	1-4A39	222A73
9	忹	3-4923				E-2623	
A	忺	3-4934	1-2947		CAE0	2-2422	
B	忻	0-4835	0-5555	1-8506	CAE3	2-2425	2D4574
C	忼	5-5148	1-2948	1-5558		E-257A	
D	忽	0-2686	0-2590	0-9176	A9BF	1-4D41	213E25
E	忾	0-6673				E-2575	273F29
F	忿	0-2362	0-5561	0-6140	A9C1	1-4D43	213E28

600

	Char	G	J	K	B	C	A
0	怀	0-2719			CAE4	2-2426	273F54
1	态	0-4412					273F28
2	怂	0-4343					273F3B
3	怃	0-6668					282E52
4	怄	0-6670					282D74
5	怅	0-6674					273E5E
6	怆	0-6675					273F2B
7	怇	5-5143	1-2949			E-2878	
8	怈	5-5153				E-2922	222B31
9	怉	3-4944			CCAF	2-266E	
A	怊	0-6687	1-2950	1-7981	CCA2	2-2661	222B36
B	怋	3-4946			CC7E	2-265F	
C	怌	5-5156			CCAE	2-266D	222B37
D	怍	0-6684	1-2951	1-7512	CCA9	2-2668	222B45
E	怎	0-5285	0-5567		ABE7	1-512B	213E35
F	怏	0-6683	0-5573	0-6872	A9C2	1-4D44	213E2F

601

	Char	G	J	K	B	C	A
0	怐	3-4941	0-5565		CCAA	2-2669	222B46
1	怑	5-5165			CCAD	2-266C	
2	怒	0-3713	0-3760	0-5033	ABE3	1-5127	213E37
3	怓	3-4948	1-2952		CCAC	2-266B	222B50
4	怔	0-5390	1-2953	1-7654	A9C3	1-4D45	213E29
5	怕	0-3734	0-5570	1-8174	A9C8	1-4D4A	213E36
6	怖	0-1832	0-4161	0-8855	A9C6	1-4D48	213E2D
7	怗	3-4937	1-2954	1-7955	CCA3	2-2662	222B3C
8	怘	5-5077	1-2955			E-6266	
9	怙	0-6679	0-5564	1-8382	CC7C	2-265D	222B30
A	怚	3-4938	1-2956		CCA5	2-2664	
B	怛	0-6682	0-5569	1-6078	A9CD	1-4D4F	222B38
C	怜	0-3315	0-4671	0-5427	CCB0	2-266F	273F4B
D	思	0-4328	0-2755	0-6254	ABE4	1-5128	213E2E
E	怞	3-4939			CCA6	2-2665	
F	怟	5-5163	1-2957				

602

	Char	G	J	K	B	C	A
0	怠	0-2101	0-3453	0-8729	ABE5	1-5129	213E31
1	怡	0-6689	0-5562	0-7614	A9C9	1-4D4B	213E30
2	怢	3-4940			CCA8	2-2667	
3	怣	5-5079				E-2C5A	
4	怤	3-4882	1-2958		CBCD	2-2A4E	
5	急	0-2817	0-2162	0-4865	ABE6	1-512A	213E33
6	怦	0-6681	0-5572	1-8214	CC7B	2-265C	222B2A
7	性	0-4852	0-3213	0-6485	A9CA	1-4D4C	213E34
8	怨	0-5225	0-1769	0-7419	ABE8	1-512C	213E32
9	怩	0-6685	0-5566	1-6060	A9CB	1-4D4D	222B2C
A	怪	0-2554	0-1888	0-4654	A9C7	1-4D49	213E2B
B	怫	0-6686	0-5571		A9CC	1-4D4E	222B2D
C	怬	5-5160			CCA7	2-2666	
D	怭	3-4945	1-2959		CC7A	2-265B	
E	怮	3-4950			CCAB	2-266A	
F	怯	0-3951	0-2217	0-4405	A9C4	1-4D46	213E2C

603

	Char	G	J	K	B	C	A
0	怰	5-5164				E-2877	
1	怱		0-5568			E-2C5B	336C6B
2	怲	3-4935			CC7D	2-265E	
3	怳		1-2960	1-8438	CCA4	2-2663	222B3D
4	怴	3-4936			CCA1	2-2660	
5	怵	0-6680	1-2961		A9C5	1-4D47	213E2A
6	怶	3-4949				E-287A	
7	怷				CEBF	2-2A40	
8	怸	5-5078					
9	怹	3-4883			CBC0	2-2A41	222B4B
A	怺		0-5574				69576A
B	总	0-5560					27516D
C	怼	0-7701					282E7E
D	怽					E-2921	
E	怾						
F	怿	0-6688					282E5C

604

	Char	G	J	K	B	C	A
0	恀	3-4966	1-2962		CBCA	2-2A4B	
1	恁	0-7705	0-5576	0-7686	D1A1	2-2F23	222B71
2	恂	0-6694	0-5586	0-6665	CBCB	2-2A4C	222B74
3	恃	0-4249	0-5584	0-6730	ABEE	1-5132	213E3B
4	恄				CBCE	2-2A4F	
5	恅	3-4953			CBC4	2-2A45	
6	恆		0-5581	1-8313	ABED	1-5131	213E40
7	恇	3-4951	1-2963	1-5783	CBC6	2-2A47	222B5A
8	恈	3-4974	1-2964	1-6445		E-6267	
9	恉	5-5178	1-2965		CBC7	2-2A48	222B5E
A	恊	5-5183	0-5580	1-8360		E-2C60	393460
B	恋	0-3321	0-4688			E-3079	273F5C
C	恌	3-4965	1-2966		CBC9	2-2A4A	222B6F
D	恍	0-2748	0-5582	0-9240	ABE9	1-512D	213E41
E	恎	3-4960				E-2C56	
F	恏					E-3073	

605

	Char	G	J	K	B	C	A
0	恐	0-3154	0-2218	0-4580	AEA3	1-5545	213E3D
1	恑	5-5177	1-2967			E-2C57	
2	恒	0-2667	0-2517	0-8986		E-2C5D	2D3E40
3	恓	3-4956			CBC5	2-2A46	222B5F
4	恔	3-4969	1-2968		CBC1	2-2A42	222B53
5	恕	0-4301	0-2990	0-6380	AEA4	1-5546	213E49
6	恖		1-2969			E-307E	
7	恗	3-4957	1-2970				
8	恘				CBCF	2-2A50	
9	恙	0-7706	0-5589	0-6931	AE7E	1-5542	213E38
A	恚	0-7703	0-5575	1-7127	D17D	2-2F21	2E2B5B
B	恛	3-4962			CBC8	2-2A49	
C	恜	3-4952				E-2C54	
D	恝	0-7702	1-2971	0-4631	D17C	2-2E7E	222B57
E	恞	5-5172			CBC3	2-2A44	
F	恟	5-5179	0-5579	1-8503	CBCC	2-2A4D	222B76

606

	Char	G	J	K	B	C	A
0	恠		0-5563	1-5806		E-2C5F	2D3E2B
1	恡		1-2972			E-2C61	222B7A
2	恢	0-2754	0-1890	0-9265	ABEC	1-5130	213E3F
3	恣	0-7707	0-5583	0-7716	AEA1	1-5543	213E39
4	恤	0-4884	0-5585	0-9349	ABF2	1-5136	213E47
5	恥		0-3549	0-8627	AEA2	1-5544	213E3C
6	恦				CED0	2-2A51	
7	恧	0-7704	1-2973		D17E	2-2F22	222B68
8	恨	0-2662	0-2608	0-8947	ABEB	1-512F	213E3A
9	恩	0-2287	0-1824	0-7558	AEA6	1-5548	213E43
A	恪	0-6701	0-5577	0-4233	ABF1	1-5135	213E46
B	恫	0-2218	0-5588	1-8162	ABF0	1-5134	213E42
C	恬	0-4481	0-5587	0-5024	ABEF	1-5133	213E44
D	恭	0-2507	0-2219	0-4581	AEA5	1-5547	213E3E
E	恮	3-4963			CED1	2-2A52	
F	息	0-4702	0-3409	0-6751	AEA7	1-5549	213E45

607

	Char	G	J	K	B	C	A
0	恰	0-3901	0-1970	0-9370	ABEA	1-512E	213E48
1	恱		1-2974				
2	恲	3-4972			CBC2	2-2A43	
3	恳	0-3150				E-307A	273F4E
4	恴					E-3078	
5	恵		0-2335			E-307B	2D3E60
6	恶	0-2281					277258
7	恷		0-5578				222B72
8	恸	0-6690					273F3A
9	恹	0-6691					282E79
A	恺	0-6693					282D5E
B	恻	0-6692					273E70
C	恼	0-3653				E-2C5C	273E7E
D	恽	0-6702					282D34
E	恾	3-4954	1-2975			E-3076	
F	恿	0-5133	1-2976		B176	1-5A3C	213E4C

608

	Char	G	J	K	B	C	A
0	悀	3-5002			D1A4	2-2F26	
1	悁	3-4985	0-5590	1-7138	D1A6	2-2F28	222C2D
2	悂	3-4983	1-2977				
3	悃	0-6707	0-5593	1-5716	D1A8	2-2F2A	222C30
4	悄	0-3936	0-5601	1-7982	AEA8	1-554A	213E50
5	悅			0-7077	AEAE	1-5550	
6	悆	5-5093	1-2978		D553	2-3537	
7	悇	3-4988			D1AC	2-2F2E	
8	悈	3-4976	1-2979		D1A3	2-2F25	
9	悉	0-4704	0-2829	0-6790	B178	1-5A3E	213E53
A	悊	5-5091	1-2980		D551	2-3535	222C24
B	悋	5-5187	0-5607	1-6371		E-3122	33354E
C	悌	0-6709	0-3680	0-8010	AEAD	1-554F	213E4A
D	悍	0-2623	0-5591	0-8948	AEAB	1-554D	213E51
E	悎	3-4987	1-2981		D1AE	2-2F30	
F	悏	3-4959		1-8361			

609

	Char	G	J	K	B	C	A
0	悐	5-5094			D552	2-3536	
1	悑		1-2982				
2	悒	0-6708	0-5605	1-7433	D1A5	2-2F27	222C2B
3	悓		1-2983			E-3125	
4	悔	0-2758	0-1889	0-9266	AEAC	1-554E	213E54
5	悕	3-4989	1-2984	1-8524	D1A9	2-2F2B	222C3A
6	悖	0-6703	0-5603	0-8807	AEAF	1-5551	213E4F
7	悗	3-4992	0-5604	1-6479	D1AB	2-2F2D	222C32
8	悘	3-4886	1-2985			E-3568	
9	悙	3-4993				E-3074	
A	悚	0-6704	0-5594	0-6569	AEAA	1-554C	213E4E
B	悛	0-6710	0-5602	0-7889	D1AA	2-2F2C	2E2B74
C	悜	3-4984			D1AD	2-2F2F	
D	悝	0-6706	1-2986		D1A7	2-2F29	222C2C
E	悞		1-2987			E-3127	222C2F
F	悟	0-4682	0-2471	0-7186	AEA9	1-554B	213E4D

60A

	Char	G	J	K	B	C	A
0	悠	0-5138	0-4510	0-7477	B179	1-5A3F	213E55
1	悡					E-3571	
2	悢	3-5001	1-2988	1-6222	D1A2	2-2F24	
3	患	0-2728	0-2021	0-9220	B177	1-5A3D	213E52
4	悤		1-2989	0-8534		E-3572	396C6B
5	悥		1-2990				
6	悦	0-5235	0-1757			E-3123	213E4B
7	悧	5-5186	0-5606	0-5560		E-3128	222C34
8	您	0-3690	1-2991		B17A	1-5A40	213E56
9	悩		0-3926			E-3121	4B3E7E
A	悪		0-1613			E-356F	393E61
B	悫	0-7708					282D79
C	悬	0-4892					273F56
D	悭	0-6705					282D77
E	悮	8-1358				E-3126	
F	悯	0-3585					273F41

60B

	Char	G	J	K	B	C	A
0	悰	3-5024	1-2992	0-8085	D555	2-3539	222C42
1	悱	0-6713	1-2993	1-6683	D55E	2-3542	222C60
2	悲	0-1715	0-4065	0-6172	B464	1-5F2B	213E66
3	悳		0-5560	0-5177		E-3B54	222C54
4	悴	0-6718	0-5612	0-8592	B17C	1-5A42	213E57
5	悵	1-6674	0-5616	1-7873	B1A3	1-5A47	213E5E
6	悶	1-3538	0-4469	0-5831	B465	1-5F2C	213E5C
7	悷	3-5026	1-2994		D560	2-3544	
8	悸	0-2834	0-5609	0-4491	B1AA	1-5A4E	213E68
9	悹	3-4892			D8F9	2-3B5D	
A	悺	5-5201			D556	2-353A	
B	悻	0-6712	1-3001	1-8330	B1A2	1-5A46	213E5F
C	悼	0-2131	0-3773	0-5190	B1A5	1-5A49	213E65
D	悽		0-5614	0-8404	B17E	1-5A44	33475F
E	悾	3-5025	1-3002	1-5734	D554	2-3538	222C46
F	悿	3-5004			D562	2-3546	

60C

	Char	G	J	K	B	C	A
0	惀	3-4931			D565	2-3549	
1	惁	3-4890			D949	2-3B6C	
2	惂		1-3003				
3	惃	3-5012			D563	2-3547	
4	惄	3-4891	1-3004	1-6029	D8FD	2-3B61	222C5D
5	情	0-3973	0-3080	0-7955	B1A1	1-5A45	213E5B
6	惆	0-6716	0-5615	1-8031	B1A8	1-5A4C	213E67
7	惇	3-5021	0-3855	0-5235	B1AC	1-5A50	222C3E
8	惈	3-5011	1-3005		D55D	2-3541	
9	惉	5-5108	1-3006	1-7946	D8F8	2-3B5C	
A	惊	0-3010	1-3007		D561	2-3545	27614B
B	惋	0-4579	1-3008	1-7264	B17B	1-5A41	213E59
C	惌	5-5109			D8FA	2-3B5E	
D	惍				D564	2-3548	
E	惎	3-4889	1-3009		D8FC	2-3B60	222C4E
F	惏		1-3010	1-6210	D559	2-353D	222C51

60D

	Char	G	J	K	B	C	A
0	惐	3-5006				E-356A	
1	惑	0-2783	0-4739	0-9167	B462	1-5F29	213E5D
2	惒	5-5105				E-3B56	
3	惓	3-5022	0-5611	1-5903	D557	2-353B	222C47
4	惔	3-5023	1-3011		D558	2-353C	222C48
5	惕	0-4472	1-3012	1-7910	B1A7	1-5A4B	213E64
6	惖	5-5102				E-3B55	
7	惗	3-5019				E-356E	
8	惘	0-6715	0-5617	1-6409	B1A6	1-5A4A	213E63
9	惙	3-5029	1-3013	1-7937	D55B	2-353F	222C53
A	惚	0-6717	0-2591	0-9177	B1AB	1-5A4F	213E69
B	惛	3-5020	1-3014	1-8402	D55F	2-3543	222C69
C	惜	0-4707	0-3243	0-6413	B1A4	1-5A48	213E62
D	惝	0-6714	1-3015	1-7874	D55C	2-3540	222C56
E	惞		1-3016			E-3579	
F	惟	0-4609	0-1652	0-7478	B1A9	1-5A4D	213E6A

60E

	Char	G	J	K	B	C	A
0	惠	0-2761	0-5610	0-9119	B466	1-5F2D	213E60
1	惡	1-2281	0-5608	0-6834	B463	1-5F2A	213E61
2	惢	3-4893	1-3017	1-6906	D8FB	2-3B5F	222C66
3	惣		0-3358			E-3B58	222C62
4	惤				D55A	2-353E	
5	惥		1-3018			E-3B59	222C67
6	惦	0-2175			B17D	1-5A43	213E58
7	惧	0-3069	0-5592			E-3576	273F5B
8	惨	0-1850	0-2720				273F38
9	惩	0-1945				E-3B5A	222C6E
A	惪					E-3B4D	2D3D75
B	惫	0-1725					273F47
C	惬	0-6711					273E6C
D	惭	0-1849					273F31
E	惮	0-2112				E-3574	273F44
F	惯	0-2563					273F39

60F

	Char	G	J	K	B	C	A
0	惰	0-2272	0-3438	0-8671	B46B	1-5F32	213E6F
1	惱	1-3653	0-5629	0-5061	B46F	1-5F36	213E7E
2	惲	1-6702	1-3019	1-7335	D940	2-3B63	222D34
3	想	0-4775	0-3359	0-6344	B751	1-6377	213E6D
4	惴	0-6723	0-5624	1-8064	B46D	1-5F34	213E76
5	惵	5-5205	1-3020		D944	2-3B67	
6	惶	0-2744	0-5621	0-9241	B471	1-5F38	213E7B
7	惷		0-5622	1-7767	DD65	2-426B	2D573B
8	惸	5-5215	1-3021	1-5645	D946	2-3B69	222D3B
9	惹	0-4039	0-2870	0-6909	B753	1-6379	213E74
A	惺	0-4842	0-5625	0-6486	B469	1-5F30	213E71
B	惻	1-6692	0-5628	0-8619	B46C	1-5F33	213E70
C	惼	3-5046	1-3022	1-8205	D947	2-3B6A	222D41
D	惽	5-5220	1-3023			E-3B5E	222C7C
E	惾	3-5041			D948	2-3B6B	
F	惿	3-5035			D94E	2-3B71	

Code	Char	G	J	K	B	C	A
6100	愀	0-6724	0-5623	1-7983	B473	1-5F3A	213E79
6101	愁	0-1978	0-2905	0-6594	B754	1-637A	213E7A
6102	愂		1-3024				
6103	愃	3-5045	0-5626	1-6829	D94A	2-3B6D	222C73
6104	愄	5-5211			D94F	2-3B72	
6105	愅	5-5204			D943	2-3B66	
6106	愆	0-7709	0-5620	0-4380	B75E	1-6426	222D43
6107	愇	3-4924	1-3025			E-3B4F	
6108	愈	0-5190	0-4492	0-7479	B755	1-637B	213E7D
6109	愉	0-5168	0-4491	0-7480	B472	1-5F39	213E7C
610A	愊	3-5034	1-3026		D941	2-3B64	222D2A
610B	愋	3-5040			D950	2-3B73	
610C	愌	3-4991	1-3027			E-3B51	
610D	愍	0-7710	0-5630	0-5832	B75D	1-6425	222C7D
610E	愎	0-6725	0-5631	0-8820	B470	1-5F37	213E78
610F	意	0-5066	0-1653	0-7582	B74E	1-6374	213E6B
6110	愐	5-5208	1-3028		D94D	2-3B70	222D2C
6111	愑	5-5222	1-3029			E-3B5D	
6112	愒	3-5036	1-3030		B474	1-5F3B	222D32
6113	愓	3-4922	1-3031		D945	2-3B68	
6114	愔	3-5042	1-3032	1-7431	D8FE	2-3B62	222C70
6115	愕	0-6721	0-5619	0-6835	B46A	1-5F31	213E73
6116	愖	3-5032	1-3033		D942	2-3B65	
6117	愗	3-4901	1-3034				
6118	愘	5-5218			D94B	2-3B6E	
6119	愙	5-5115	1-3035			E-412B	222C75
611A	愚	0-5162	0-2282	0-7355	B74D	1-6373	213E72
611B	愛	1-1614	0-1606	0-6881	B752	1-6378	213E77
611C	愜	1-6711	1-3036	1-8362	B467	1-5F2E	213E6C
611D	愝	5-5207			D94C	2-3B6F	
611E	愞	5-5209	1-3037			E-3B61	
611F	感	0-2448	0-2022	0-4279	B750	1-6376	213E6E
6120	愠	0-6719				E-3B62	2D3F27
6121	愡		0-5627			E-3B63	222D3F
6122	愢	3-5038	1-3038			E-3B50	
6123	愣	0-6722			B468	1-5F2F	213E75
6124	愤	0-2363					273F42
6125	愥					E-6479	222D37
6126	愦	0-6720					282E4C
6127	愧	0-3202	0-5635	0-4655	B75C	1-6424	213F2A
6128	愨	5-5118	0-5634		E1C3	2-4A2A	2E2D79
6129	愩	3-4977			DD70	2-4276	222D50
612A	愪	3-4986	1-3039			E-4129	
612B	愫	0-6726	1-3040		DD68	2-426E	222D4E
612C	愬		0-5639	1-6874	E1C2	2-4A29	2D6856
612D	愭	3-5050		1-5975			
612E	愮	3-5055			DD6C	2-4272	
612F	愯				DD6E	2-4274	
6130	愰	3-5052	1-3041	0-9242		E-4127	222D58
6131	愱		1-3042			E-412C	
6132	愲	3-5039			DD6B	2-4271	
6133	愳					E-466F	333F5B
6134	愴	1-6675	0-5640	0-8365	B75B	1-6423	213F2B
6135	愵	5-5236	1-3043				
6136	愶	5-5237	1-3044		DD6A	2-4270	
6137	愷	1-6693	1-3045	0-4336	B75F	1-6427	222D5E
6138	愸	5-5113				E-466E	
6139	愹		1-3046				
613A	愺	3-5033				E-4128	
613B	愻	5-5088			E1D2	2-4A39	
613C	愼		0-5638	0-6769		E-466C	213F24
613D	愽		0-5641			E-412E	2D3464
613E	愾	1-6673	0-5633	0-4337	B75A	1-6422	213F29
613F	愿	0-5224	0-5637	0-7420	BA40	1-6867	276055
6140	慀	3-5057			DD71	2-4277	
6141	慁	3-4902	1-3047		E1C4	2-4A2B	222D5B
6142	慂		0-5642	0-7329		E-466D	393E4C
6143	慃	3-5058				E-412A	
6144	慄		0-5643	0-5541	B758	1-637E	334449
6145	慅	3-5048	1-3048		DD69	2-426F	
6146	慆	3-5056	1-3049	1-6127	DD6D	2-4273	222D61
6147	慇		0-5632	0-7559	B9FE	1-6866	213F2C
6148	慈	0-2040	0-2792	0-7717	B74F	1-6375	213F21
6149	慉	5-5234	1-3050		DD66	2-426C	222D48
614A	慊	0-6727	0-5636	0-4435	DD67	2-426D	222D4A
614B	態	1-4412	0-3454	0-8730	BA41	1-6868	213F28
614C	慌	0-2737	0-2518	0-9243	B757	1-637D	213F26
614D	慍		0-5618	1-7229	B759	1-6421	213F27
614E	慎	0-4187	0-3121		B756	1-637C	3F3F24
614F	慏				DD6F	2-4275	
6150	慐					E-647A	222D51
6151	慑	0-4169					273F59
6152	慒	3-5060		1-7729	E1C8	2-4A2F	
6153	慓	5-5239	0-5656	0-8884	E1C9	2-4A30	222D7B
6154	慔	5-5227			E1CE	2-4A35	
6155	慕	0-3629	0-4273	0-5723	BC7D	1-6C67	213F37
6156	慖	3-5013			E1D5	2-4A3C	
6157	慗	3-4905				E-4B73	
6158	慘	1-1850	0-5646	0-8351	BA47	1-686E	213F38
6159	慙		0-5647	0-8352		E-4B7E	2D3F31
615A	慚	1-1849	0-5648	1-7857	BA46	1-686D	213F31
615B	慛	5-5243			E1D0	2-4A37	
615C	慜	5-5123				E-4B74	222E2F
615D	慝	0-7711	0-5655	0-8768	BC7C	1-6C66	213F32
615E	慞	5-5246	1-3051		E1C5	2-4A2C	222D66
615F	慟	1-6690	0-5654	0-8749	BA45	1-686C	213F3A
6160	慠	5-5224	1-3052	1-7212		E-4671	
6161	慡	5-5240			E1D4	2-4A3B	
6162	慢	0-3493	0-4393	0-5623	BA43	1-686A	213F35
6163	慣	1-2563	0-2023	0-4617	BA44	1-686B	213F39
6164	慤	1-7708		0-4234		E-4B7C	222D79
6165	慥	3-5053	0-5652		E1D1	2-4A38	222E2D
6166	慦	3-4907			E5AA	2-5051	
6167	慧	0-2759	0-2337	0-9120	BC7A	1-6C64	213F2F
6168	慨	0-3114	0-1920	0-4338	B46E	1-5F35	213F22
6169	慩	5-5184				E-4672	
616A	慪	1-6670			E1D3	2-4A3A	222D74
616B	慫	1-4343	0-5649	0-8086	BCA3	1-6C6B	213F3B
616C	慬	3-5059	1-3053		E1CB	2-4A32	
616D	慭	7-0142					
616E	慮	1-3439	0-4624	0-5371	BC7B	1-6C65	213F36
616F	慯	5-5161	0-5651			E-466A	222E2C
6170	慰	0-4631	0-1654	0-7448	BCA2	1-6C6A	213F30
6171	慱	3-4925	0-5653	1-6068	E1C6	2-4A2D	222D70
6172	慲	5-5226	1-3054		E1CA	2-4A31	
6173	慳	1-6705	0-5644	1-5523	E1C7	2-4A2E	222D77
6174	慴		0-5650	1-6952	E1CD	2-4A34	222D68
6175	慵	0-6728	0-5657	1-7307	BA48	1-686F	222D67
6176	慶	1-3976	0-2336	0-4452	BC79	1-6C63	213F2E
6177	慷	0-3122	0-5645	0-4315	BA42	1-6869	213F2D
6178	慸	5-5112	1-3055			E-4C21	
6179	慹	5-5084			E57A	2-5043	
617A	慺	3-5043		1-6335	E1CF	2-4A36	
617B	慻		1-3056			E-4668	
617C	慼		1-3057		BCA1	1-6C69	213F34
617D	慽			0-8410		E-4673	
617E	慾		0-4561	0-7315	BCA4	1-6C6C	213F3C
617F	憀		1-3058				

Code	Char	G	J	K	B	C	A
6180	憀	3-5068	1-3059		E1CC	2-4A33	
6181	憁	3-5063	1-3060	0-8535		E-466B	
6182	憂	1-5139	0-4511	0-7356	BC7E	1-6C68	213F33
6183	憃	3-4904	1-3061	1-7308	E579	2-5042	222D6B
6184	憄		1-3062				
6185	憅					E-4C23	2D3F3A
6186	憆	5-5242				E-4674	
6187	憇		0-5660			E-4C24	273F45
6188	憈	5-5241				E-4B77	
6189	憉				E57E	2-5047	
618A	憊	1-1725	0-5664	0-6173	BECE	1-7057	213F47
618B	憋	0-1779	1-3063		E578	2-5041	222E23
618C	憌	5-5114			E9A3	2-572E	
618D	憍	5-5175	1-3064	1-5822	E5A9	2-5050	222E55
618E	憎	0-5287	0-3394	0-8183	BCA8	1-6C70	213F40
618F	憏	5-5245				E-4B7A	
6190	憐	1-3315	0-4689	0-5391	BCA6	1-6C6E	213F4B
6191	憑	1-3830	0-5665	0-6227	BECC	1-7055	213F3F
6192	憒	1-6720	1-3065	1-5912	E5A6	2-504D	222E4C
6193	憓	3-5069	1-3066		E5A2	2-5049	
6194	憔	0-6730	0-5662	0-8491	BCAC	1-6C74	213F46
6195	憕	3-5079				E-4B76	
6196	憖	3-4906	0-5659	1-7418	E978	2-5725	222E45
6197	憗		1-3067			E-5068	222E46
6198	憘		1-3068	0-9383		E-4C28	
6199	憙	3-4908	0-5658	0-9382		E-5067	2D3661
619A	憚	1-2112	0-5663	0-8706	BCAA	1-6C72	213F44
619B	憛	3-5070			E5A1	2-5048	
619C	憜	5-5248	1-3069			E-4C29	222E42
619D	憝	0-7713	1-3070		E976	2-5723	222E32
619E	憞	3-5077				E-4C25	
619F	憟	5-5251	1-3071		E5A5	2-504C	
61A0	憠		1-3072				
61A1	憡	5-5254			E5A8	2-504F	
61A2	憢	5-5173			E57D	2-5046	222E3D
61A3	憣	3-5074				E-4B79	
61A4	憤	1-2363	0-4216	0-6141	BCAB	1-6C73	213F42
61A5	憥	5-5089	1-3073				
61A6	憦	3-4980				E-4B75	222E33
61A7	憧	0-6731	0-3820	0-5251	BCA5	1-6C6D	213F3D
61A8	憨	0-2609	1-3074	1-5543	E977	2-5724	222E40
61A9	憩	0-7712	0-2338	0-4408	BECD	1-7056	213F45
61AA	憪	3-4994	1-3075		E5A7	2-504E	
61AB	憫	1-3585	0-5666	0-5833	BCA7	1-6C6F	213F41
61AC	憬	0-6729	0-5661	0-4453	BCA9	1-6C71	213F43
61AD	憭	3-5071	1-3076		E5A4	2-504B	222E47
61AE	憮	1-6668	0-5667	0-5768	BCAD	1-6C75	222E52
61AF	憯	3-5072		1-7858	E5A3	2-504A	222E43
61B0	憰	3-5080			E57C	2-5045	
61B1	憱	3-5076			E57B	2-5044	
61B2	憲	1-4760	0-2391	0-9042	BECB	1-7054	213F3E
61B3	憳				E5AB	2-5052	
61B4	憴	5-5191			E97A	2-5727	
61B5	憵	5-5128			ECE0	2-5C6B	
61B6	憶	1-5068	0-1817	0-6967	BED0	1-7059	213F48
61B7	憷	0-6732				E-5061	706340
61B8	憸	3-4990	1-3077	1-6849	E9A2	2-572D	222E6A
61B9	憹	3-4973	1-3078			E-5063	
61BA	憺	3-5087	0-5675	0-5128	E97E	2-572B	222E68
61BB	憻	3-5088		1-8134		E-506A	
61BC	憼	5-5125	1-3079	1-5646	ECE1	2-5C6C	
61BD	憽					E-5064	
61BE	憾	0-2622	0-2024	0-4280	BED1	1-705A	213F4C
61BF	憿	3-5086			E9A1	2-572C	
61C0	懀	3-4964	1-3080			E-5066	
61C1	懁	3-5085	1-3081		E97C	2-5729	
61C2	懂	0-2214	1-3082		C0B4	1-735D	213F4D
61C3	懃		0-5673	0-4836	ECDF	2-5C6A	393439
61C4	懄					E-506C	
61C5	懅	3-5083			E979	2-5726	
61C6	懆	3-5084	0-5674	1-7694	E97B	2-5728	222E5D
61C7	懇	1-3150	0-2609	0-4248	C0B5	1-735E	213F4E
61C8	懈	0-4824	0-5672	0-9011	BED3	1-705C	213F4F
61C9	應	1-5106	0-5670	0-7575	C0B3	1-735C	213F4A
61CA	懊	0-1635	0-5669	0-7188	BED2	1-705B	213F50
61CB	懋	0-7714	0-5676	0-5769	C0B7	1-7360	222E5A
61CC	懌	1-6688	0-5668	1-7131	E97D	2-572A	222E5C
61CD	懍		0-5678		BECF	1-7058	213F49
61CE	懎		1-3083			E-5062	
61CF	懏		1-3084			E-5065	
61D0	懐		0-1891			E-506B	2D3F54
61D1	懑	0-7715					4B3F51
61D2	懒	0-3233					273F55
61D3	懓					E-6679	
61D4	懔	0-6733					
61D5	懕	3-1629	1-3085	1-7152			
61D6	懖	5-5122			EFCF	2-615B	
61D7	懗			1-8273			
61D8	懘	3-4910			EFC7	2-6153	
61D9	懙	3-4917				E-5461	
61DA	懚					E-545F	
61DB	懛	5-5256				E-545C	
61DC	懜		1-3086			E-545E	222E7D
61DD	懝		1-3087			E-545D	
61DE	懞	1-8854	1-3088	1-6459	ECE7	2-5C72	3F5564
61DF	懟	1-7701	1-3089	1-6118	EFC8	2-6154	222E7E
61E0	懠	3-4968			ECE3	2-5C6E	222E71
61E1	懡	3-5091	1-3090				
61E2	懢	5-5229	1-3091			E-545B	
61E3	懣	1-7715	0-5680	1-6480	C256	1-7642	213F51
61E4	懤	3-4975			ECE5	2-5C70	
61E5	懥	3-5090	1-3094		ECE4	2-5C6F	222E77
61E6	懦	0-3719	0-5679	0-4955	C0B6	1-735F	213F52
61E7	懧		1-3092		ECE2	2-5C6D	
61E8	懨	1-6691			ECE6	2-5C71	
61E9	懩		1-3093		EFD0	2-615C	
61EA	懪	5-5257			EFCC	2-6158	
61EB	懫	3-5016			EFCE	2-615A	
61EC	懬		1-3101				
61ED	懭	3-4920	1-3102		EFC9	2-6155	
61EE	懮	3-5092			EFCA	2-6156	
61EF	懯	5-5131	1-3103				
61F0	懰	3-4967			EFCD	2-6159	
61F1	懱	3-5089			EFCB	2-6157	
61F2	懲	1-1945	0-3608	0-8304	C367	1-7834	213F53
61F3	懳					E-5765	222F29
61F4	懴		0-5683				333F58
61F5	懵	0-6734			C36A	1-7837	213F57
61F6	懶	1-3233	0-5681	0-5291	C369	1-7836	213F55
61F7	懷	1-2719	0-5671	0-9267	C368	1-7835	213F54
61F8	懸	1-4892	0-2392	0-9056	C461	1-796C	213F56
61F9	懹	3-5101			F44A	2-6876	
61FA	懺	1-6667	0-5682	0-8353	C462	1-796D	213F58
61FB	懻	5-5258			F241	2-654C	
61FC	懼	1-3069	0-5686	0-4711	C4DF	1-7A6A	213F5B
61FD	懽		0-5685	1-8424	F5CC	2-6B5A	2D4621
61FE	懾	1-4169	0-5687	1-6856	C4E0	1-7A6B	213F59
61FF	懿	0-6018	0-5684	0-7583	C574	1-7B60	213F5A

620

	Char	G	J	K	B	C	A
0	戀	1-3321	0-5688	0-5392	C5CA	1-7C36	213F5C
1	戁	3-4903	1-3104		F7D9	2-6F28	222F3D
2	戂	3-5102				E-5F46	
3	戃	5-5230	1-3105		F7DA	2-6F29	
4	戄	3-5103	1-3106		F7DB	2-6F2A	222F41
5	戅	5-5135				E-613E	
6	戆	0-7716					282F43
7	戇	1-7716	1-3107	0-5152	F9BA	2-722A	222F43
8	戈	0-2474	0-5689	0-4592	A4E0	1-4541	213F5D
9	戉	5-4002	0-5690		C97C	2-215D	222F44
A	戊	0-4676	0-4274	0-5770	A5B3	1-4653	213F5E
B	戋	0-7407					282F47
C	戌	0-4871	0-5692	0-6689	A6A6	1-4827	213F61
D	戍	0-4289	0-5691	0-6601	A6A7	1-4828	213F60
E	戎	0-4054	0-2931	0-7552	A6A5	1-4826	213F5F
F	戏	0-4723				E-236B	273F6F

621

	Char	G	J	K	B	C	A
0	成	0-1941	0-3214	0-6487	A6A8	1-4829	213F62
1	我	0-4650	0-1870	0-6818	A7DA	1-4A3C	213F64
2	戒	0-2968	0-1892	0-4492	A7D9	1-4A3B	213F63
3	戓		1-3108			E-2625	
4	戔	1-7407	0-5693	1-7520	CCB1	2-2670	222F47
5	戕	0-6762	1-3109	1-7536	A9CF	1-4D51	213F66
6	或	0-2782	0-1631	0-9168	A9CE	1-4D50	213F65
7	戗	0-7408					282F66
8	战	0-5329				E-2C63	273F6E
9	戙	5-4009			D1AF	2-2F31	
A	戚	0-3861	0-3244	0-8411	B1AD	1-5A51	213F68
B	戛	0-7409	0-5694		B1AE	1-5A52	213F67
C	戜	5-4012	1-3110				
D	戝		0-7635				4B5A23
E	戞		0-5701	1-7029		E-3B64	2D3F67
F	戟	0-7410	0-2365	0-4829	B475	1-5F3C	213F69

622

	Char	G	J	K	B	C	A
0	戠	5-8888	1-3111		DD72	2-4278	
1	戡	0-7412	0-5702	0-4281	B760	1-6428	213F6A
2	戢	0-7411	1-3112	1-7827	B761	1-6429	213F6B
3	戣	3-3821	1-3113		DD74	2-427A	222F56
4	戤	0-7414			DD76	2-427C	222F5D
5	戥	0-7413			DD75	2-427B	222F5B
6	戦		0-3279				2D3F6E
7	戧	1-7408	1-3114	1-7875	E1D7	2-4A3E	
8	戨	5-4023				E-4676	
9	戩	1-7415	1-3115	1-7589	E1D6	2-4A3D	222F61
A	截	0-2956	0-5703	0-7924	BA49	1-6870	213F6C
B	戫	5-4790	1-3116		E1D8	2-4A3F	
C	戬	0-7415				E-4675	4C2F61
D	戭	3-3823			E5AC	2-5053	222F67
E	戮	0-3430	0-5704	0-5532	BCAE	1-6C76	213F6D
F	戯		0-2126			E-4C2C	2D3F6F

623

	Char	G	J	K	B	C	A
0	戰	1-5329	0-5705	0-7890	BED4	1-705D	213F6E
1	戱			0-9384		E-506D	
2	戲	1-4723	0-5706	1-8525	C0B8	1-7361	213F6F
3	戳	0-2033	0-5707	1-7840	C257	1-7643	213F71
4	戴	0-2087	0-3455	0-5167	C0B9	1-7362	213F70
5	戵	5-4031		1-5851		E-5F48	
6	戶			0-9134	A4E1	1-4542	213F72
7	户	0-2707				E-2165	
8	戸		0-2445			E-2166	
9	戹		1-3117	1-7073		E-224E	222F6E
A	戺	3-4875			CAE6	2-2428	222F6F
B	戻		0-4465			E-2628	4B3F74
C	戼					E-2629	
D	戽	0-7670	1-3118		CCB2	2-2671	222F70
E	戾	0-7669		0-5372	A9D1	1-4D53	213F74
F	房	0-2331	0-4328	0-5914	A9D0	1-4D52	213F73

624

	Char	G	J	K	B	C	A
0	所	0-4389	0-2974	0-6522	A9D2	1-4D54	213F75
1	扁	0-1766	0-5708	0-8823	ABF3	1-5137	213F76
2	扂	3-4878	1-3119		CED2	2-2A53	
3	扃	0-7671	1-3120	1-5647	CED3	2-2A54	222F75
4	扄		1-3121				
5	扅	3-4879				E-3129	222F78
6	扆	3-4880	1-3122		D1B0	2-2F32	222F77
7	扇	0-4140	0-3280	0-6431	AEB0	1-5552	274975
8	扈	0-7672	0-7829	0-9135	B1AF	1-5A53	213F78
9	扉	0-7673	0-4066	0-6174	B476	1-5F3D	213F79
A	扊	3-4881		1-7153	D951	2-3B74	222F79
B	手	0-4254	0-2874	0-6602	A4E2	1-4543	213F7A
C	扌	0-6248	1-3123				
D	才	0-1837	0-2645	0-7806	A47E	1-445F	28736D
E	扎	0-5290	0-5709	1-7851	A4E3	1-4544	275129
F	扏	3-4151				E-2250	

625

	Char	G	J	K	B	C	A
0	扐	3-4152	1-3124		C97D	2-215E	222F7A
1	扑	0-3843	1-3125	1-6605	A5B7	1-4657	27416E
2	扒	0-1639	1-3126	1-6551	A5B6	1-4656	214021
3	打	0-2082	0-3439	0-8672	A5B4	1-4654	213F7D
4	扔	0-4051	1-3127		A5B5	1-4655	213F7E
5	払	5-4352	0-4207				2D403F
6	扖		1-3128				
7	扗			1-7551		E-236F	
8	托	0-4548	0-3481	0-8685	A6AB	1-482C	214024
9	扙	5-4353			C9E9	2-2249	
A	扚	3-4159	1-3129		C9EB	2-224B	22302B
B	扛	0-3124	0-5712	1-5559	A6AA	1-482B	214022
C	扜		1-3130		C9E3	2-2243	
D	扝	3-4154				E-236C	
E	扞		0-5710		C9E4	2-2244	222F7C
F	扟	3-4160				E-236D	

626

	Char	G	J	K	B	C	A
0	扠	3-4162	0-5713		C9EA	2-224A	223028
1	扡	3-4161			C9E6	2-2246	
2	扢	3-4157			C9E8	2-2248	22302C
3	扣	0-3159	0-5711	1-5852	A6A9	1-482A	214023
4	扤	3-4155	1-3131		C9E5	2-2245	
5	扥				C9EC	2-224C	
6	扦	0-3904			C9E7	2-2247	22302D
7	执	0-5420				E-236E	27383B
8	扨		0-5714	1-7464			223026
9	扩	0-3209					27422A
A	扪	0-6249					27407E
B	扫	0-4108					27407D
C	扬	0-4979					27413F
D	扭	0-3704	1-3132		A7E1	1-4A43	21402E
E	扮	0-1671	0-4217	0-6142	A7EA	1-4A4C	214036
F	扯	0-1922	1-3133		A7E8	1-4A4A	214031

627

	Char	G	J	K	B	C	A
0	扰	0-4037			CAF0	2-2432	27422E
1	扱	3-4158	0-1623	0-4866	CAED	2-242F	2D4147
2	扲	3-4174			CAF5	2-2437	
3	扳	0-1666	1-3134	1-6524	A7E6	1-4A48	214037
4	扴	5-4364			CAF6	2-2438	
5	扵	5-4365				E-2639	4B3052
6	扶	0-2386	0-4162	0-6106	A7DF	1-4A41	214028
7	扷				CAF3	2-2435	
8	扸	5-4363				E-262E	
9	批	0-3790	0-4067	0-6175	A7E5	1-4A47	21402B
A	扺	3-4177	1-3135	1-7791	CAEF	2-2431	4B4053
B	扻	5-4366			CAEE	2-2430	
C	扼	0-2283	0-5715	0-6889	A7E3	1-4A45	21402F
D	扽	3-4167	1-3136		CAF4	2-2436	
E	找	0-5350	0-5718	1-7701	A7E4	1-4A46	214030
F	承	0-1948	0-3021	0-6715	A9D3	1-4D55	21402A

628

	Char	G	J	K	B	C	A
0	技	0-2828	0-2127	0-4892	A7DE	1-4A40	21402C
1	抁	3-4182			CAF1	2-2433	
2	抂		0-5716			E-262A	223043
3	抃	3-4178	0-5723	1-6572	CAE7	2-2429	2D404C
4	抄	0-1913	0-3022	0-8492	A7DB	1-4A3D	214032
5	抅	5-4368				E-2637	223046
6	抆	3-4179		1-6481	A7EE	1-4A50	223031
7	抇	3-4168			CAEC	2-242E	
8	抈	3-4176			CAF2	2-2434	
9	抉	0-3081	0-5717	0-4428	A7E0	1-4A42	214029
A	把	0-1649	0-3936	0-8774	A7E2	1-4A44	21402D
B	抋	3-4181				E-262F	
C	抌	3-4180			CAE8	2-242A	
D	抍	3-4171	1-3137			E-2636	
E	抎	3-4164	1-3138		CAE9	2-242B	223032
F	抏	3-4163	1-3139		CAEA	2-242C	

62A

	Char	G	J	K	B	C	A
0	抠	0-3157					28337B
1	抡	0-3453					274136
2	抢	0-3932					274155
3	抣					E-647B	223041
4	护	0-2704					275948
5	报	0-1708				E-2632	273844
6	抦	5-4373	1-3141			E-2931	223056
7	抧	5-4377				E-292A	
8	抨	0-3774	1-3142	1-8215	A9E1	1-4D63	21403C
9	抩	5-4378			CCBE	2-267D	
A	抪	3-4186			CCB7	2-2676	
B	披	0-3791	0-4068	0-8909	A9DC	1-4D5E	214044
C	抬	0-4407	0-5813	1-8153	A9EF	1-4D71	21404D
D	抭	3-4203			CCB3	2-2672	
E	抮	3-4193			CCBA	2-2679	
F	抯	5-4376			CCBC	2-267B	

62C

	Char	G	J	K	B	C	A
0	拀					E-2934	
1	拁					E-2932	
2	拂	0-2387	0-5736	0-6157	A9D8	1-4D5A	21403F
3	拃	3-4192					22306A
4	拄	0-5484	1-3149	1-7747	A9D6	1-4D58	21403A
5	担	0-2103	0-3520	1-6069		E-2933	274222
6	拆	0-1880	0-5730	1-8125	A9EE	1-4D70	214056
7	拇	0-3620	0-5737	0-5771	A9E6	1-4D68	21404E
8	拈	0-3673	0-5732	0-5025	A9E0	1-4D62	21404A
9	拉	0-3213	0-5739	0-5335	A9D4	1-4D56	214039
A	拊	0-6252	0-5735	1-6622	CCB9	2-2678	2D4171
B	拋				A9DF	1-4D61	214045
C	拌	0-1672	0-5734	0-5869	A9D5	1-4D57	21403B
D	拍	0-3736	0-3979	0-5848	A9E7	1-4D69	214052
E	拎	0-3364	1-3150		A9F0	1-4D72	214054
F	拏		0-5728	0-4957	CED4	2-2A55	2D4067

62E

	Char	G	J	K	B	C	A
0	拠		0-2182			E-2936	39417C
1	拡		0-1940			E-292F	33422A
2	拢	0-3403					274231
3	拣	0-2880					27413C
4	拤	3-4188				E-2929	223061
5	拥	0-5121					274174
6	拦	0-3225					274233
7	拧	0-3701					274226
8	拨	0-1806					274166
9	择	0-5281					27417E
A	拪	5-4388	1-3154			E-2C6D	
B	拫	3-4221			CEDA	2-2A5B	
C	括	0-3208	0-1971	0-4632	AC41	1-5144	214065
D	拭	0-4235	0-3101	0-6752	ABF8	1-513C	21405C
E	拮	0-6255	0-5741	0-4947	ABFA	1-513E	21405E
F	拯	0-5392	0-5746	0-8185	AC40	1-5143	21405F

629

	Char	G	J	K	B	C	A
0	抐	3-4169	1-3140				
1	抑	0-5054	0-4562	0-6968	A7ED	1-4A4F	214034
2	抒	0-4267	0-5719	0-6381	A7E7	1-4A49	214027
3	抓	0-5505	0-5720		A7EC	1-4A4E	214038
4	抔	3-4166	0-5724	1-6621	CAEB	2-242D	2D404F
5	投	0-4522	0-3774	0-8765	A7EB	1-4A4D	214033
6	抖	0-2222	0-5721	1-6165	A7DD	1-4A3F	214025
7	抗	0-3125	0-2519	0-8987	A7DC	1-4A3E	214026
8	折	0-5359	0-3262	0-7925	A7E9	1-4A4B	214035
9	抙	5-4361				E-2635	
A	抚	0-2407					274171
B	抛	0-3755	0-5738	0-8856		E-2633	334045
C	抜		0-4020			E-2634	4B4046
D	抝					E-2638	22304B
E	択		0-3482			E-2631	33417E
F	抟	0-6250					28336F

62B

	Char	G	J	K	B	C	A
0	抰	3-4190			CCBF	2-267E	
1	抱	0-1707	0-4290	0-8857	A9EA	1-4D6C	21404F
2	抲	3-4185				E-2926	
3	抳	5-4383	1-3143		CCBB	2-267A	
4	抴	5-4372			CCB4	2-2673	
5	抵	0-2154	0-3681	0-7829	A9E8	1-4D6A	214053
6	抶	3-4191	1-3144		CCB8	2-2677	223069
7	抷		1-3145			E-2928	
8	抸	3-4175			CCC0	2-2721	
9	抹	0-3608	0-4385	0-5638	A9D9	1-4D5B	214040
A	抺		1-3146			E-2925	
B	抻	0-6251	0-5727		CCBD	2-267C	2D313A
C	押	0-4926	0-1801	0-6867	A9E3	1-4D65	214048
D	抽	0-1973	0-3574	0-8546	A9E2	1-4D64	214047
E	抾	3-4183	1-3147		CCB6	2-2675	
F	抿	0-3582	1-3148		A9D7	1-4D59	21403E

62D

	Char	G	J	K	B	C	A
0	拐	0-2553	0-1893	0-4656	A9E4	1-4D66	214049
1	拑	5-4371	0-5726	1-5636	CCB5	2-2674	223057
2	拒	0-3060	0-2181	0-4362	A9DA	1-4D5C	214041
3	拓	0-4556	0-3483	0-8412	A9DD	1-4D5F	214042
4	拔	0-1646	0-5722	0-5891	A9DE	1-4D60	214046
5	拕	5-4381	1-3151	1-8114		E-292E	334050
6	拖	0-4547	1-3152	0-8673	A9EC	1-4D6E	214050
7	拗	0-6254	0-5725	0-7283	A9ED	1-4D6F	214055
8	拘	0-3048	0-2520	0-4712	A9EB	1-4D6D	214051
9	拙	0-5530	0-3259	0-8080	A9E5	1-4D67	21404B
A	拚	0-6253	1-3153		A9E9	1-4D6B	21404C
B	招	0-5348	0-3023	0-8493	A9DB	1-4D5D	214043
C	拜	0-1661	0-5733	0-5940	ABF4	1-5138	21403D
D	拝		0-3950			E-2930	4B403D
E	拞					E-2937	
F	拟	0-3666				E-2935	274228

62F

	Char	G	J	K	B	C	A
0	拰	3-4214			CEE6	2-2A67	
1	拱	0-2516	0-5742	0-4582	ABFD	1-5141	214062
2	拲	5-4334	1-3155		D1B1	2-2F33	
3	拳	0-4013	0-2393	0-4775	AEB1	1-5553	21405A
4	拴	0-4309	1-3156		AC43	1-5146	214066
5	拵	3-4209	0-5747	1-7727	CED7	2-2A58	223125
6	拶	0-6257	0-2702	1-7852	CEDF	2-2A60	223137
7	拷	0-3129	0-2573	0-4524	ABFE	1-5142	214060
8	拸	3-4217			CEDE	2-2A5F	
9	拹	3-4222			CEDB	2-2A5C	
A	拺	3-4207			CEE3	2-2A64	
B	拻				CEE5	2-2A66	
C	拼	0-3820	1-3157		ABF7	1-513B	214059
D	拽	0-5507	1-3158	1-7180	ABFB	1-513F	214063
E	拾	0-4216	0-2906	0-6706	AC42	1-5145	2D3457
F	拿	0-3635	0-5729	0-4958	AEB3	1-5555	214067

630

	Char	G	J	K	B	C	A
0	挀				CEE0	2-2A61	
1	持	0-1954	0-2793	0-8205	ABF9	1-513D	21405D
2	挂	0-2550	0-5744	1-5801	AC45	1-5148	274123
3	挃	3-4210	1-3159		CED9	2-2A5A	
4	挄	5-4393	1-3160			E-2C6F	
5	挅					E-2C70	
6	挆	5-4404					
7	指	0-5424	0-2756	0-8206	ABFC	1-5140	214061
8	挈	0-7492	0-5745		AEB2	1-5554	21405B
9	按	0-1620	0-1636	0-6846	ABF6	1-513A	214057
A	挊		1-3161				
B	挋	3-4206	1-3162		CED6	2-2A57	
C	挌	5-4407	0-5740	1-5615	CEDD	2-2A5E	223131
D	挍	5-4409	1-3163		CED5	2-2A56	223072
E	挎	0-3170			CED8	2-2A59	2E337B
F	挏	3-4212			CEDC	2-2A5D	

631

	Char	G	J	K	B	C	A
0	挐		1-3164	1-6012	D1B2	2-2F34	
1	挑	0-4484	0-3609	0-5191	AC44	1-5147	214064
2	挒	5-4390		1-6251			
3	挓	5-4411	1-3165		CEE1	2-2A62	
4	挔				CEE2	2-2A63	
5	挕	5-4387			CEE4	2-2A65	
6	挖	0-4558	1-3166		ABF5	1-5139	214058
7	挗					E-2C6C	
8	挘		1-3167				
9	挙		0-2183			E-3132	4B5434
A	挚	0-5431					27415B
B	挛	0-3446				E-3133	274237
C	挜	8-9244					
D	挝	0-4646					4C3474
E	挞	0-4402					274177
F	挟	0-4814	0-2220			E-2C6B	27406C

632

	Char	G	J	K	B	C	A
0	挠	0-3651					274168
1	挡	0-2118				E-2C6E	27417A
2	挢	0-6256					283462
3	挣	0-5385					4B412A
4	挤	0-2823					274225
5	挥	0-2751					274142
6	挦	8-9245					
7	挧		0-5743				69594B
8	挨	0-1604	0-1607	1-7058	AEC1	1-5563	214074
9	挩		1-3168		D1BE	2-2F40	
A	挪	0-3718	1-3169	1-6013	AEBF	1-5561	21406A
B	挫	0-2076	0-2635	0-8109	AEC0	1-5562	214073
C	挬	5-4416			D1B4	2-2F36	
D	挭	5-4417	1-3170		D1C4	2-2F46	
E	挮	3-4237				E-312C	
F	振	0-5381	0-3122	0-8241	AEB6	1-5558	21406D

633

	Char	G	J	K	B	C	A
0	挰	3-4229				E-312F	
1	挱					E-3135	22313A
2	挲	0-7493			D566	2-354A	2E313A
3	挳				D1C6	2-2F48	
4	挴	3-4231			D1C0	2-2F42	
5	挵		1-3171			E-3138	223145
6	挶	3-4239	1-3172		D1B7	2-2F39	223149
7	挷	5-4385				E-3137	
8	挸	5-4360			D1C9	2-2F4B	
9	挹	0-6258	1-3173	1-7434	D1BA	2-2F3C	223154
A	挺	0-4506	0-3682	0-7956	AEBC	1-555E	214075
B	挻	3-4213		0-7041	D57D	2-3561	
C	挼	8-1579	1-3174		D1BD	2-2F3F	22315A
D	挽	0-4576	0-4052	0-5624	AEBE	1-5560	21412E
E	挾	1-4814	0-5749	0-9083	AEB5	1-5557	21406C
F	挿		0-3362			E-313C	4B4147

634

	Char	G	J	K	B	C	A
0	捀	3-4234			D1CB	2-2F4D	
1	捁	3-4230	1-3175		D1BF	2-2F41	
2	捂	0-4670	1-3176	1-7213	AEB8	1-555A	214069
3	捃	0-6260	1-3177	1-5888	D1B8	2-2F3A	223144
4	捄		1-3178	1-5853	D1B5	2-2F37	22314A
5	捅	0-4517			D1B6	2-2F38	223142
6	捆	0-3206	1-3179	1-5717	AEB9	1-555B	27513D
7	捇	5-4414			D1C5	2-2F47	
8	捈	3-4232			D1CC	2-2F4E	
9	捉	0-5529	0-3410	0-8321	AEBB	1-555D	214071
A	捊	5-4428	1-3180		D1BC	2-2F3E	
B	捋	0-6259	1-3181		D1BB	2-2F3D	22315C
C	捌	0-1638	0-2711	0-8804	AEC3	1-5565	2D3324
D	捍	0-2620	0-5750	1-8287	AEC2	1-5564	2E2F7C
E	捎	0-4151	1-3182	1-6875	AEB4	1-5556	21406E
F	捏	0-3683	0-5752	0-4983	AEBA	1-555C	21406F

635

	Char	G	J	K	B	C	A
0	捐	0-3072	0-5748	0-7040	AEBD	1-555F	214070
1	捑				D1C8	2-2F4A	
2	捒	5-4418	1-3183			E-312E	
3	捓	5-4391	1-3184			E-3139	223147
4	捔	3-4233	1-3185		D1C2	2-2F44	22315F
5	捕	0-1822	0-4265	0-8858	AEB7	1-5559	21406B
6	捖	5-4431			D1B3	2-2F35	
7	捗	3-4227	0-3629	1-7911	D1CA	2-2F4C	223158
8	捘	3-4240	1-3186		D1C1	2-2F43	22315B
9	捙				D1C3	2-2F45	
A	捚	5-4425			D1C7	2-2F49	
B	捛		1-3187			E-3130	
C	捜		0-3360			E-313B	2D4154
D	捝	3-4236				E-3136	
E	捞	0-3244					274165
F	损	0-4380					27414F

636

	Char	G	J	K	B	C	A
0	捠					E-647C	223132
1	捡	0-2881					274224
2	换	0-2727					454146
3	捣	0-2123					274153
4	捤					E-647D	223148
5	捥	5-4457	1-3188		D567	2-354B	
6	捦	5-4449	1-3189			E-3631	
7	捧	0-3785	0-4291	0-6073	B1B7	1-5A5B	214121
8	捨	1-4165	0-2846	0-6255	B1CB	1-5A6F	214135
9	捩	0-6270	0-5764	1-6252	B1CA	1-5A6E	214077
A	捪	5-4451				E-3627	
B	捫	1-6249	0-5763	1-6482	B1BF	1-5A63	21407E
C	捬	5-4453	1-3190			E-3629	22316C
D	捭	0-6267	1-3191		D579	2-355D	223241
E	据	0-3061	0-3188	0-4363	D575	2-3559	27417C
F	捯	3-4247			D572	2-3556	

637

	Char	G	J	K	B	C	A
0	捰				D5A6	2-3568	
1	捱	0-6263	1-3192	1-7059	B1BA	1-5A5E	214125
2	捲	1-8839	0-2394	0-4776	B1B2	1-5A56	21407B
3	捳	3-4251				E-3626	
4	捴		1-3193			E-3632	33516D
5	捵	5-4447	1-3194		D577	2-355B	22322F
6	捶	0-2023	0-5757	1-8032	B4A8	1-5F4D	214131
7	捷	0-2961	0-3025	0-8463	B1B6	1-5A5A	21407C
8	捸		1-3201		D5A1	2-3563	
9	捹					E-3622	
A	捺	0-6264	0-3872	0-4984	B1CC	1-5A70	223226
B	捻	0-3677	0-3917	0-5026	B1C9	1-5A6D	214134
C	捼		1-3202		D57B	2-355F	22323A
D	捽	3-4256	1-3203		D56A	2-354E	223168
E	捾	3-4259				E-357C	
F	捿	5-4443	1-3204	0-6382		E-362B	223173

638

	Char	G	J	K	B	C	A
0	掀	0-4738	0-5755	1-8507	B1C8	1-5A6C	214137
1	掁	3-4172			D5A3	2-3565	223179
2	掂	0-2164	1-3205		D569	2-354D	22316B
3	掃	1-4108	0-3361	0-6523	B1BD	1-5A61	21407D
4	掄	1-3453	1-3206	1-6345	B1C1	1-5A65	214136
5	掅	3-4241			D5A2	2-3564	
6	掆					E-3623	22322A
7	掇	0-2262	1-3207	1-7938	D573	2-3557	223225
8	授	0-4258	0-2888	0-6603	B1C2	1-5A66	21412C
9	掉	0-2184	0-5760	0-5192	B1BC	1-5A60	214128
A	掊	0-6269	1-3208	1-6623	D568	2-354C	3F404F
B	掋	5-4454				E-357D	
C	掌	0-5338	0-3024	0-7770	B478	1-5F3F	214127
D	掍	3-4250			D5A5	2-3567	
E	掎	0-6265	0-5754	1-5976	D571	2-3555	223227
F	掏	0-4445	0-5759	1-6128	B1C7	1-5A6B	214132

639

	Char	G	J	K	B	C	A
0	掐	0-3894	1-3209		D574	2-3558	22323B
1	掑				D5A4	2-3566	
2	排	0-3737	0-3951	0-5941	B1C6	1-5A6A	21412F
3	掓	5-4444				E-3624	
4	掔	3-4141	1-3210		D952	2-3B75	
5	掕	3-4242	1-3211				
6	掖	0-5020	0-5753	0-6890	B1B3	1-5A57	214079
7	掗	3-4205			D56F	2-3553	22317B
8	掘	0-3082	0-2301	0-4762	B1B8	1-5A5C	214122
9	掙	1-5385	1-3212		B1C3	1-5A67	21412A
A	掚	5-4420	1-3213				
B	掛		0-1961	0-4648	B1BE	1-5A62	214123
C	掜	3-4252		1-7181	D578	2-355C	
D	掝	3-4245			D56E	2-3552	
E	掞	3-4257	1-3214		D56C	2-3550	223172
F	掟	3-4258	0-5761	1-7655	D57E	2-3562	22316E

63A

	Char	G	J	K	B	C	A
0	掠	0-3451	0-4611	0-5351	B1B0	1-5A54	214078
1	採		0-2646	0-8385	B1C4	1-5A68	21412B
2	探	0-4429	0-3521	0-8714	B1B4	1-5A58	214129
3	掣	0-1924	0-5758		B477	1-5F3E	214130
4	掤	3-4253	1-3215		D57C	2-3560	
5	接	0-2951	0-3260	0-7940	B1B5	1-5A59	214076
6	掦	5-4446	1-3216				
7	控	0-3156	0-2521	0-4583	B1B1	1-5A55	21407A
8	推	0-4538	0-3168	0-8547	B1C0	1-5A64	214133
9	掩	0-4958	0-1770	0-6983	B1BB	1-5A5F	214126
A	措	0-2075	0-3328	0-8034	B1B9	1-5A5D	214124
B	掫	3-4243	0-5756		D570	2-3554	22317D
C	掬	0-6268	0-2137	1-5885	B1C5	1-5A69	21412D
D	掭	0-6261	1-3217		D56D	2-3551	22323D
E	掮	0-6271	1-3218		D57A	2-355E	223239
F	掯	3-4248	1-3219		D576	2-355A	223230

63B

	Char	G	J	K	B	C	A
0	掰	0-7494			D954	2-3B77	223238
1	掱	3-4145			D953	2-3B76	223237
2	掲		0-2339			E-362D	2D4141
3	掳	0-3416					27417D
4	掴	0-6266	0-3647				274160
5	掵		0-5762				69595E
6	掶					E-647E	22316A
7	掷	0-5432					27422B
8	掸	0-2107					283457
9	掹						
A	掺	0-1884				E-362E	28342C
B	掻		0-3363				
C	掼	0-6272					28342E
D	掽		1-3220		D56B	2-354F	22324F
E	掾	0-6282	0-5765	1-7139	D964	2-3C29	223270
F	掿	5-4438				E-3B71	

63C

	Char	G	J	K	B	C	A
0	揀	1-2880	0-5767	0-4249	B47A	1-5F41	21413C
1	揁	5-4392	1-3221			E-3B70	
2	揂	5-4481			D96A	2-3C2F	
3	揃	3-4282	0-3423	1-7590	D959	2-3B7C	223250
4	揄	0-6277	0-5773	0-7481	D967	2-3C2C	223279
5	揅	5-4343	1-3222		DD77	2-427D	223266
6	揆	0-6281	0-5768	0-4806	B47D	1-5F44	214138
7	揇	5-4460			D96B	2-3C30	
8	揈	5-4474	1-3223		D96E	2-3C33	
9	揉	0-4064	0-5770	1-7376	B47C	1-5F43	214139
A	揊	5-4461			D95C	2-3C21	
B	揋	5-4465			D96D	2-3C32	
C	揌	5-4466			D96C	2-3C31	
D	揍	0-5565			B47E	1-5F45	21413A
E	揎	0-6279	1-3224		D955	2-3B78	2D4066
F	描	0-3572	0-4133	0-5758	B479	1-5F40	214143

63D

	Char	G	J	K	B	C	A
0	提	0-4465	0-3683	0-8011	B4A3	1-5F48	21413E
1	揑		1-3225			E-3B73	223276
2	插	0-1869	0-5771		B4A1	1-5F46	214147
3	揓	5-4478	1-3226		D969	2-3C2E	223247
4	揔	5-4473	1-3227				
5	揕	3-4264	1-3228		D95F	2-3C24	22325C
6	揖	0-5030	0-4512	0-7571	B4A5	1-5F4A	214140
7	揗				D970	2-3C35	22327B
8	揘	3-4277			D968	2-3C2D	
9	揙	3-4285			D971	2-3C36	
A	揚	1-4979	0-4540	0-6932	B4AD	1-5F52	21413F
B	換	1-2727	0-2025	0-9221	B4AB	1-5F50	214146
C	揜	3-4279	1-3229		D966	2-3C2B	22327A
D	揝	5-4475			D965	2-3C2A	223273
E	揞	0-6278				E-3B67	223243
F	揟	3-4288		1-6809	D963	2-3C28	

63E

	Char	G	J	K	B	C	A
0	揠	0-6275	1-3230	1-7030	D95D	2-3C22	22325B
1	握	0-4653	0-1614	0-6836	B4A4	1-5F49	21413B
2	揢	3-4284				E-3B66	
3	揣	0-2007	0-5769	1-8065	B4A2	1-5F47	214144
4	揤	3-4238			D1B9	2-2F3B	
5	揥	3-4281	1-3231		D956	2-3B79	223244
6	揦	3-4268				E-3B68	223258
7	揧	5-4342			DDB7	2-433D	
8	揨	5-4477			D957	2-3B7A	
9	揩	0-3111	0-5766	1-5574	B47B	1-5F42	21413D
A	揪	0-3030	1-3232		B4AA	1-5F4F	214148
B	揫			1-8033	DD79	2-4321	223272
C	揬	5-4484	1-3233				
D	揭	0-2950		0-4409	B4A6	1-5F4B	214141
E	揮	1-2751	0-2088	0-9338	B4A7	1-5F4C	214142
F	揯				D958	2-3B7B	

63F

	Char	G	J	K	B	C	A
0	揰	5-4467			D96F	2-3C34	
1	揱	3-4146			DD78	2-427E	
2	揲	0-6273	1-3234	1-6842	D960	2-3C25	22325E
3	揳	3-4263	1-3235		D95B	2-3B7E	
4	援	0-5214	0-1771	0-7421	B4A9	1-5F4E	214145
5	揵	3-4260	1-3236	1-5602	D961	2-3C26	223252
6	揶	0-6262	0-5772	0-6910	D95E	2-3C23	22325D
7	揷			0-6326		E-3B72	
8	揸	0-6274	1-3237			E-3B6D	22325F
9	揹		1-3238		B4AE	1-5F53	22326A
A	揺		0-4541			E-6339	
B	揻	3-4270					
C	揼						
D	揽	0-3231					27423B
E	揾	3-4273				E-3B6F	
F	揿	0-6276					283466

Code	Char	G	J	K	B	C	A
6400	搀	0-1883					274234
6401	搁	0-2473					274229
6402	搂	0-3407					27415F
6403	搃					E-6521	3F516D
6404	搄	3-4283					
6405	搅	0-2933					27423A
6406	搆		0-5776	1-5854	B770	1-6438	2D4539
6407	搇					E-4149	223359
6408	搈	3-4304				E-4132	
6409	搉		1-3239	1-5519	DD7C	2-4324	22334C
640A	搊	3-4194	1-3240		DDB1	2-4337	223351
640B	搋	0-6285			DDB6	2-433C	2E3028
640C	搌	0-6288			DDAA	2-4330	223331
640D	損	1-4380	0-3427	0-6563	B76C	1-6434	21414F
640E	搎	3-4223			DDBB	2-4341	223338
640F	搏	0-1811	0-5783	0-5849	B769	1-6431	21414D
6410	搐	0-2004	1-3241		DD7A	2-4322	223322
6411	搑	3-4265				E-413A	
6412	搒	3-4302	1-3242	1-6540	DD7B	2-4323	22327E
6413	搓	0-2074	0-5777		B762	1-642A	21414C
6414	搔	0-4106	1-3243	0-6524	B76B	1-6433	21414E
6415	搕	5-4493			DDA4	2-432A	223336
6416	搖		0-5774	0-7284	B76E	1-6436	214152
6417	搗	1-2123	0-5781	0-5193	B76F	1-6437	214153
6418	搘	5-4492	1-3244		DDA5	2-432B	223337
6419	搙	3-4290				E-4138	
641A	搚	5-4520			DDB2	2-4338	
641B	搛	0-6286			DDB8	2-433E	223329
641C	搜	0-4349	0-5751	0-6604	B76A	1-6432	214154
641D	搝	5-4507				E-413E	
641E	搞	0-2467	1-3245		B764	1-642C	214149
641F	搟	5-4421			DDA3	2-4329	
6420	搠	0-6287	1-3246		DD7D	2-4325	22332B
6421	搡	0-6290			DDBA	2-4340	22333D
6422	搢	3-4289	1-3247	0-8242	DDA8	2-432E	22333B
6423	搣	3-4291			DDA9	2-432F	
6424	搤		1-3248	1-7074	DD7E	2-4326	22332C
6425	搥		1-3249	1-8034	DDB4	2-433A	334131
6426	搦	0-6289	0-5778		DDAB	2-4331	22332F
6427	搧	5-4518			DDB5	2-433B	4B4975
6428	搨		0-5782	1-8145	DDAD	2-4333	2D4150
6429	搩		1-3250			E-413D	
642A	搪	0-4434	1-3251	1-6103	B765	1-642D	21414A
642B	搫	3-4148		1-6525	E1D9	2-4A40	
642C	搬	0-1665	0-4034	0-5870	B768	1-6430	214156
642D	搭	0-2078	0-3775	0-8719	B766	1-642E	214150
642E	搮				DDB9	2-433F	
642F	搯	5-4509	1-3252	1-6129	DDB0	2-4336	2D4132
6430	搰	3-4275	1-3253	1-5728	DDAC	2-4332	223344
6431	搱	3-4306				E-4136	
6432	搲	3-4303				E-4133	
6433	搳	5-4517			DDA1	2-4327	
6434	搴	0-6926	0-5775		BA53	1-687A	223324
6435	搵		1-3254		DDAF	2-4335	223348
6436	搶	1-3932	0-5779	1-7876	B76D	1-6435	214155
6437	搷	5-4501			DDA7	2-432D	
6438	搸	5-4488				E-4134	
6439	搹	5-4503			DDA6	2-432C	
643A	携	0-4815	0-2340	0-9345		E-4148	4B4236
643B	搻	5-4344				E-4725	22335B
643C	搼	5-4516				E-4142	
643D	搽	0-1875	1-3255		B767	1-642F	214151
643E	搾		0-2681	0-8322	B763	1-642B	21414B
643F	搿	0-7501	1-3256		E1EE	2-4A55	22335D
6440	摀				DDB3	2-4339	223353
6441	摁	0-6284			DDAE	2-4334	223345
6442	摂		0-3261				4B4235
6443	摃				DDA2	2-4328	394022
6444	摄	0-4167					274235
6445	摅	0-6283					283546
6446	摆	0-1658				E-4144	274230
6447	摇	0-5001				E-4145	2D4152
6448	摈	0-1787					28352A
6449	摉					E-6676	
644A	摊	0-4415					274238
644B	摋	3-4215	1-3257		E1E9	2-4A50	
644C	摌	3-4218				E-4678	
644D	摍	5-4537			E1DA	2-4A41	
644E	摎	3-4324	0-5787		E1E5	2-4A4C	223423
644F	摏	5-4523	1-3258			E-4728	22336A
6450	摐	3-4173			E1EC	2-4A53	
6451	摑	1-6266	1-3259		BA51	1-6878	214160
6452	摒	0-6280	1-3260		B4AC	1-5F51	21415A
6453	摓	5-4511	1-3261		E1EA	2-4A51	
6454	摔	0-4304	1-3262		BA4C	1-6873	214159
6455	摕	3-4266				E-467E	
6456	摖	3-4320				E-4724	
6457	摗	3-4310				E-467A	
6458	摘	0-5310	0-3706	0-7855	BA4B	1-6872	214157
6459	摙	3-4226			E1F1	2-4A58	
645A	摚	3-4317	1-3263				
645B	摛		1-3264		E1DB	2-4A42	223368
645C	摜	1-6272	1-3265		E1E8	2-4A4F	22342E
645D	摝	3-4321	1-3266		E1DC	2-4A43	
645E	摞	0-6291			E1E7	2-4A4E	223428
645F	摟	1-3407	1-3267		BA4F	1-6876	21415F
6460	摠	5-4531	1-3268	0-8536	E1EB	2-4A52	
6461	摡	3-4286	1-3269		D962	2-3C27	
6462	摢	3-4316				E-4721	
6463	摣	3-4315	1-3270				
6464	摤	5-4527				E-472A	223424
6465	摥				E1F2	2-4A59	
6466	摦	3-4314			E1E3	2-4A4A	
6467	摧	0-2061	0-5784	1-8020	BA52	1-6879	214161
6468	摨	5-4555			E5BA	2-5061	
6469	摩	0-3606	0-4364	0-5604	BCAF	1-6C77	214158
646A	摪	5-4476				E-4723	
646B	摫	5-4435			E1F0	2-4A57	22336C
646C	摬	3-4322			E1EF	2-4A56	
646D	摭	0-6293	1-3271	1-7912	BA54	1-687B	394042
646E	摮	3-4147			E5AD	2-5054	
646F	摯	1-5431	0-5785	0-8207	BCB0	1-6C78	21415B
6470	摰	3-4149			E5AE	2-5055	
6471	摱	3-4318				E-4722	
6472	摲	3-4246			E1DF	2-4A46	
6473	摳	1-3157	1-3272	1-5855	E1E0	2-4A47	22337B
6474	摴	5-4528	1-3273		E1DD	2-4A44	223376
6475	摵	3-4313			E1E2	2-4A49	
6476	摶	1-6250	0-5786		E1DE	2-4A45	22336F
6477	摷	5-4540			E1F3	2-4A5A	
6478	摸	0-3594	0-4446	0-5724	BA4E	1-6875	21415C
6479	摹	0-3601		0-5725	BCB1	1-6C79	21415D
647A	摺	0-6301	0-3202	0-7941	BA50	1-6877	21415E
647B	摻	1-1884	1-3274	1-6850	BA55	1-687C	22342C
647C	摼	3-4228				E-467B	
647D	摽	3-4312	1-3275	1-8240	E1E1	2-4A48	223378
647E	摾	5-4557				E-4729	
647F	摿				E1ED	2-4A54	

648

	Char	G	J	K	B	C	A
0	撀					E-4C2D	
1	撁					E-4726	
2	撂	0-3344			E1E6	2-4A4D	223427
3	撃		0-2366			E-4C35	2D4176
4	撄	0-6292					28355B
5	撅	0-3079	1-3276	1-5913	E5B1	2-5058	2D4122
6	撆	5-4345				E-4C38	
7	撇	0-3818	1-3277		BA4A	1-6871	214164
8	撈	1-3244	0-5793	0-5446	BCB4	1-6C7C	214165
9	撉	5-4346			E9AA	2-5735	
A	撊	3-4235			E5B6	2-505D	
B	撋	5-4430			E5B5	2-505C	
C	撌	3-4274			E5B7	2-505E	
D	撍	3-4329				E-4C30	
E	撎	3-4326				E-4C2F	
F	撏	3-4220	1-3278		E5B4	2-505B	223442

64A

	Char	G	J	K	B	C	A
0	撠	3-4328			E5B0	2-5057	
1	撡	5-4559	1-3286			E-4C3E	
2	撢	5-4546			BCC2	1-6D2C	22344E
3	撣	1-2107	1-3287		E5B8	2-505F	
4	撤	0-1923	0-3717	0-8444	BA4D	1-6874	214163
5	撥	1-1806	0-5791	0-5892	BCB7	1-6D21	214166
6	撦		1-3288		E1E4	2-4A4B	2D4031
7	撧					E-4C3F	223465
8	撨	3-4331	1-3289			E-4C34	
9	撩	0-3335	0-5792	1-6321	BCBA	1-6D24	21416B
A	撪					E-4C3D	
B	撫	1-2407	0-4179	0-5772	BCBE	1-6D28	214171
C	撬	0-3943	1-3290		BCC0	1-6D2A	214172
D	播	0-1805	0-3937	0-8775	BCBD	1-6D27	21416F
E	撮	0-2073	0-2703	0-8541	BCBC	1-6D26	21416D
F	撯	5-4535				E-4C3A	

64C

	Char	G	J	K	B	C	A
0	擀	0-6306				E-5070	3A2F7C
1	擁	1-5121	0-4542	0-7222	BED6	1-705F	214174
2	擂	0-3262	0-5807		BEDD	1-7066	214178
3	擃	5-4412			E9AB	2-5736	
4	擄	1-3416	1-3301	0-5447	BEDB	1-7064	21417D
5	擅	0-4135	0-5803	0-8426	BED5	1-705E	214173
6	擆	3-4308				E-4C32	
7	擇	1-5281	0-5804	0-8741	BEDC	1-7065	21417E
8	擈					E-5077	
9	擉	5-4568	1-3302	1-7841	E9A8	2-5733	
A	擊	1-2787	1-3303	0-4410	C0BB	1-7364	214176
B	擋	1-2118	1-3304		BED7	1-7060	21417A
C	擌		1-3305				
D	操	0-1857	0-3364	0-8035	BEDE	1-7067	21417B
E	擎	0-3970	1-3306	0-4454	C0BA	1-7363	214221
F	擏	5-4544			E9A7	2-5732	

64E

	Char	G	J	K	B	C	A
0	擠	1-2823	0-5811	1-7671	C0BD	1-7366	214225
1	擡	5-4572	0-5812	0-5168		E-5467	22352D
2	擢	0-6310	0-3707	0-8687	C0C2	1-736B	223533
3	擣		0-5814	1-6130	ECEA	2-5C75	2D4153
4	擤	0-6309	1-3311		ECEC	2-5C77	223538
5	擥	5-4333	1-3312	0-5326		E-576B	22352E
6	擦	0-1833	0-2704	0-8345	C0BF	1-7368	214227
7	擧		0-5809	0-4365		E-576D	2D5434
8	擨	5-4575			ECED	2-5C78	
9	擩	3-4348	1-3313		ECE9	2-5C74	
A	擪	3-1628	1-3314			E-576C	
B	擫	5-4389			ECEB	2-5C76	223531
C	擬	1-3666	0-2128	0-7584	C0C0	1-7369	214228
D	擭	3-4340	1-3315	1-8415	C0C3	1-736C	223536
E	擮					E-5469	
F	擯	1-1787	0-5815	1-6725	ECE8	2-5C73	22352A

649

	Char	G	J	K	B	C	A
0	撐		1-3279	1-8157	BCB5	1-6C7D	223454
1	撑	0-1937	1-3280	0-8743		E-4C3B	21416C
2	撒	0-4086	0-2721	0-6314	BCBB	1-6D25	21416A
3	撓	1-3651	0-5790	0-7285	BCB8	1-6D22	214168
4	撔	5-4548				E-4C31	
5	撕	0-4326	0-5789	1-6810	BCB9	1-6D23	214169
6	撖	0-6294			E5AF	2-5056	22344D
7	撗	5-4525			E5B2	2-5059	
8	撘		1-3281		E5BC	2-5063	223461
9	撙	0-6304	1-3282	1-7768	BCC1	1-6D2B	22343F
A	撚		0-3918	0-5021	BCBF	1-6D29	214170
B	撛	3-4337	1-3283			E-4C2E	
C	撜	3-4339			E5B3	2-505A	
D	撝	5-4370	1-3284	1-8489	D95A	2-3B7D	22343C
E	撞	0-5518	0-3821	0-5153	BCB2	1-6C7A	214162
F	撟	1-6256	1-3285	1-5823	E5B9	2-5060	223462

64B

	Char	G	J	K	B	C	A
0	撰	0-5511	0-3281	0-8328	BCB6	1-6C7E	214167
1	撱				E5BB	2-5062	
2	撲	1-3843	0-4348	0-5850	BCB3	1-6C7B	21416E
3	撳	1-6276	1-3291		BCC3	1-6D2D	223466
4	撴	3-4336				E-4C39	
5	撵	0-3676					27422C
6	撶					E-6522	22345B
7	撷	0-6302					283542
8	撸	0-6303					4C354A
9	撹		0-1941			E-4C37	4B423A
A	撺	0-6305					283561
B	撻	1-4402	0-5805	0-5121	BED8	1-7061	214177
C	撼	0-2619	0-5794	1-5544	BED9	1-7062	214179
D	撽	3-4342	1-3292		E9A9	2-5734	
E	撾	1-4646	1-3293	1-5748	BEE2	1-706B	223474
F	撿	1-2881	1-3294	1-5611	BEDF	1-7068	214224

64D

	Char	G	J	K	B	C	A
0	擐	0-6307	1-3307	1-8425	E9A6	2-5731	223475
1	擑	3-4330	1-3308			E-5076	
2	擒	0-3960	0-5802	0-4851	BEE0	1-7069	214223
3	擓					E-506F	22346C
4	擔	1-2103	0-5731	0-5129	BEE1	1-706A	214222
5	擕		1-3309	1-8492		E-5079	
6	擖	3-4327			E9A5	2-5730	
7	擗	0-6308	1-3310	1-6565	E9A4	2-572F	22346A
8	擘	0-7502	0-5806	0-5991	C0BC	1-7365	214175
9	擙				E9AE	2-5739	
A	據	1-3061	0-5801	0-4364	BEDA	1-7063	21417C
B	擛				E9AC	2-5737	
C	擜					E-5075	
D	擝						
E	擞	0-4351					27422F
F	擟					E-5464	

64F

	Char	G	J	K	B	C	A
0	擰	1-3701	1-3316		C0BE	1-7367	214226
1	擱	1-2473	0-5808	1-5520	C0C1	1-736A	214229
2	擲	1-5432	0-5819	0-8413	C259	1-7645	21422B
3	擳	3-4184			E9AD	2-5738	
4	擴	1-3209	0-5818	0-9210	C258	1-7644	21422A
5	擵		1-3317				
6	擶		0-5817			E-576A	695A31
7	擷	1-6302	1-3318		C25E	1-764A	223542
8	擸	3-4354			EFD4	2-6160	
9	擹					E-5770	
A	擺	1-1658	0-5820	0-8776	C25C	1-7648	214230
B	擻	1-4351	1-3319		C25D	1-7649	21422F
C	擼	1-6303			EFD7	2-6163	
D	擽	3-4201	0-5822		EFD3	2-615F	22354B
E	擾	1-4037	0-3081	0-7286	C25A	1-7646	21422E
F	擿	3-4349	1-3320		EFD1	2-615D	

650

	Char	G	J	K	B	C	A
0	攀	0-3742	0-5821	0-5871	C36B	1-7838	21422D
1	攁	5-4578	1-3321		EFD5	2-6161	
2	攂	5-4583		1-6308			
3	攃	3-4347			EFD6	2-6162	
4	攄	1-6283	1-3322	0-8744	EFD2	2-615E	223546
5	攅	5-4543	0-5825			E-576E	
6	攆	1-3676			C25B	1-7647	21422C
7	攇	3-4357		1-8335	F242	2-654D	
8	攈	5-4587	1-3323			E-5A3B	22354F
9	攉	0-6311	1-3324		F245	2-6550	223553
A	攊		1-3325	1-6238		E-5A3C	
B	攋	3-4341				E-5A3A	
C	攌	3-4356			F246	2-6551	
D	攍	5-4588			F244	2-654F	
E	攎	3-4189			F247	2-6552	
F	攏	1-3403	1-3326	1-6302	C36C	1-7839	214231

651

	Char	G	J	K	B	C	A
0	攐	5-4590			F243	2-654E	
1	攑	5-4482				E-5E31	
2	攒	0-5260					28356D
3	攓	5-4601	1-3327		F44E	2-687A	
4	攔	1-3225	1-3328	1-6202	C464	1-796F	214233
5	攕	5-4592			F44D	2-6879	
6	攖	1-6292	1-3329		F44C	2-6878	22355B
7	攗	3-4359			F44B	2-6877	
8	攘	0-4033	0-5823	0-6933	C463	1-796E	214232
9	攙	1-1883	1-3330	1-7859	C465	1-7970	214234
A	攚					E-6523	223559
B	攛	1-6305	1-3331		F5CD	2-6B5B	223561
C	攜		0-5824		C4E2	1-7A6D	214236
D	攝	1-4167	0-5780	0-6478	C4E1	1-7A6C	214235
E	攞	5-4448	1-3332			E-5F4A	
F	攟	5-4605	1-3333			E-5F4B	2E3144

652

	Char	G	J	K	B	C	A
0	攠	3-4361			F6E1	2-6D4F	
1	攡	3-4301			F6E0	2-6D4E	
2	攢	1-5260	1-3334	1-7847	F6E3	2-6D51	22356D
3	攣	1-3446	0-5827	0-5393	C5CB	1-7C37	214237
4	攤	1-4415	0-5826	1-8135	C575	1-7B61	214238
5	攥	0-6312			F7DD	2-6F2C	223572
6	攦	3-4225	1-3335		F6E2	2-6D50	
7	攧	3-4355				E-5F49	223569
8	攨					E-6032	2E3328
9	攩		1-3336		F7DC	2-6F2B	22356F
A	攪	1-2933	0-5788	0-4670	C5CD	1-7C39	21423A
B	攫	0-3080	0-5828	0-9211	C5CC	1-7C38	214239
C	攬	1-3231	0-5816	0-5327	C5F3	1-7C5F	21423B
D	攭	5-4606			F8A9	2-7037	
E	攮	0-6313	1-3337		F8EF	2-707D	223577
F	支	0-5407	0-2757	0-8208	A4E4	1-4545	21423C

653

	Char	G	J	K	B	C	A
0	攰						
1	攱	5-6191	1-3338			E-2C72	
2	攲	3-3572		1-5977	D972	2-3C37	
3	攳	5-3834			E9AF	2-573A	
4	攴	0-7423	0-5829			E-2167	2D416E
5	攵	0-7522	0-5830			E-2168	217874
6	收	0-4253	0-5832	0-6605	A6AC	1-482D	21423D
7	攷		0-5831	0-4525	CAF7	2-224D	2D525D
8	攸	0-5692	0-5833	0-7482	A7F1	1-4A53	22362C
9	改	0-2436	0-1894	0-4339	A7EF	1-4A51	21423E
A	攺	5-3078	1-3339				
B	攻	0-2505	0-2522	0-4584	A7F0	1-4A52	21423F
C	攼	5-2139	1-3340				
D	攽	5-4121	1-3341	1-6526	CCC1	2-2722	
E	放	0-2337	0-4292	0-5915	A9F1	1-4D73	214240
F	政	0-5394	0-3215	0-7957	AC46	1-5149	214241

654

	Char	G	J	K	B	C	A
0	敀	5-5951				E-2C74	
1	敁	5-4079			CEE7	2-2A68	22357C
2	敂					E-2C76	223634
3	敃	5-4122	1-3342		CEE8	2-2A69	
4	敄	5-6292				E-2C73	
5	故	0-2542	0-2446	0-4526	AC47	1-514A	214242
6	敆	3-3905			D1CE	2-2F50	
7	敇		1-3343				
8	效	0-4807	0-5835	0-9289	AEC4	1-5566	214243
9	敉	0-8445	1-3344	1-6491	AEC5	1-5567	223636
A	敊	3-3903			D1CD	2-2F4F	
B	敋					E-313D	
C	敌	0-2148					274252
D	敍		0-5838	0-6383		E-3637	
E	敎			0-4671		E-3636	334244
F	敏	0-3584	0-4150	0-5834	B1D3	1-5A77	21424A

655

	Char	G	J	K	B	C	A
0	敐	5-7824	1-3345				
1	救	0-3040	0-2163	0-4713	B1CF	1-5A73	214246
2	敒		1-3346				
3	敓				D5A7	2-3569	
4	敔	3-3932	1-3347	1-7107	B1D6	1-5A7A	22363E
5	敕	0-7523	0-5837	1-8092	B1D5	1-5A79	22363F
6	敖	0-1629	0-5836	0-7189	B1CE	1-5A72	214245
7	敗	1-1660	0-3952	0-8808	B1D1	1-5A75	214247
8	敘		0-5839		B1D4	1-5A78	214249
9	教	0-2944	0-2221		B1D0	1-5A74	214244
A	敚	5-4129				E-3634	
B	敛	0-3318					274256
C	敜	3-3934			D976	2-3C3B	
D	敝	0-1754	0-5841	1-8220	B1CD	1-5A71	214248
E	敞	0-1908	0-5840	0-8366	B4AF	1-5F54	21424E
F	敟	5-4132	1-3348			E-3B74	

656

	Char	G	J	K	B	C	A
0	敠	5-4101	1-3349			E-3B75	
1	敡	5-4092				E-3B76	223647
2	敢	0-2450	0-2026	0-4282	B4B1	1-5F56	21424C
3	散	0-4102	0-2722	0-6304	B4B2	1-5F57	21424D
4	敤	5-4091			D975	2-3C3A	
5	敥				D978	2-3C3D	
6	敦	0-2256	0-3856	0-5236	B4B0	1-5F55	21424B
7	敧	3-3907	1-3350		D973	2-3C38	223645
8	敨				D977	2-3C3C	
9	敩	8-9223					
A	敪				D974	2-3C39	
B	敫	0-7524	1-3351			E-414B	226055
C	敬	0-3020	0-2341	0-4455	B771	1-6439	214250
D	敭			0-6934		E-414E	22364F
E	敮	3-3918				E-6346	
F	敯	5-4110			DDBC	2-4342	

657

	Char	G	J	K	B	C	A
0	数	0-4293	0-3184			E-414D	274254
1	敱	3-3904				E-4730	
2	敲	0-3935	0-5842	0-4527	BA56	1-687D	214251
3	敳				E1F4	2-4A5B	
4	整	0-5391	0-3216	0-7958	BEE3	1-706C	214255
5	敵	1-2148	0-3708	0-7856	BCC4	1-6D2E	214252
6	敶	5-4131			E5BD	2-5064	
7	敷	0-2383	0-4163	0-6107	BCC5	1-6D2F	214253
8	數	1-4293	0-5843	0-6606	BCC6	1-6D30	214254
9	敹	3-3938			E5BF	2-5066	
A	敺		1-3352		E5BE	2-5065	223654
B	敻				E5C0	2-5067	
C	敼				E9B1	2-573C	
D	敽		1-3353				
E	敾			0-6432			
F	敿	3-3931			E9B0	2-573B	2E3654

658

	Char	G	J	K	B	C	A
0	斀	3-3924			ECEF	2-5C7A	
1	斁	3-3929	1-3354	1-6166	ECEE	2-5C79	
2	斂	1-3318	0-5844	0-5416	C0C4	1-736D	214256
3	斃	1-1748	0-5845	0-8842	C0C5	1-736E	214257
4	斄	3-3940			F248	2-6553	
5	斅	5-4094	1-3355	0-9290		E-5C41	223664
6	斆	3-3935					
7	文	0-4636	0-4224	0-5794	A4E5	1-4546	214258
8	斈	5-4887	0-5361			E-2558	2D3A60
9	斉		0-3238			E-2939	33627D
A	斊		1-3356				
B	斋	0-5311				E-3140	2D627E
C	斌	0-1783	0-4144	0-6216	D979	2-3C3E	22366E
D	斍					E-3638	335830
E	斎		0-2656			E-3639	27627E
F	斏	8-1373					

659

	Char	G	J	K	B	C	A
0	斐	0-7619	0-4069	0-6176	B4B4	1-5F59	21425A
1	斑	0-1663	0-4035	0-5872	B4B3	1-5F58	214259
2	斒	5-4890	1-3357		DDBD	2-4343	223670
3	斓	0-7621					283671
4	斔	5-4891			EFD8	2-6164	
5	斕	1-7621	1-3358		C4E3	1-7A6E	223671
6	斖				F7DE	2-6F2D	
7	斗	0-2223	0-3745	0-5264	A4E6	1-4547	276167
8	斘		1-3359				
9	料	0-3347	0-4633	0-5489	ABC6	1-5568	21425C
A	斚					E-3142	
B	斛	0-8590	0-5847	0-4555	B1D8	1-5A7C	223675
C	斜	0-4817	0-2848	0-6256	B1D7	1-5A7B	21425D
D	斝	3-4869	1-3360	1-5507	D97A	2-3C3F	223677
E	斞	5-5062			D97B	2-3C40	
F	斟	0-5369	0-5848	0-8288	B772	1-643A	21425E

65A

	Char	G	J	K	B	C	A
0	斠	3-4871	1-3361		E1F5	2-4A5C	22367A
1	斡	0-4651	0-1622	0-6854	BA57	1-687E	21425F
2	斢	3-9185			E9B2	2-573D	
3	斣	3-4873	1-3362				
4	斤	0-2979	0-2252	0-4837	A4E7	1-4548	214260
5	斥	0-1966	0-3245	0-8414	A5B8	1-4658	214261
6	斦	5-4661	1-3363			E-293B	223723
7	斧	0-2411	0-4164	0-6108	A9F2	1-4D74	214262
8	斨	3-2625			CCC2	2-2723	223722
9	斩	0-5322					274263
A	斪	5-4663			CEE9	2-2A6A	
B	斫	0-7729	0-5849	0-7737	AC48	1-514B	214E2D
C	斬	1-5322	0-2734	0-8354	B1D9	1-5A7D	214263
D	断	0-2247	0-3539			E-363A	274266
E	斮		1-3364		D97C	2-3C41	223727
F	斯	0-4325	0-2759	0-6257	B4B5	1-5F5A	214264

65B

	Char	G	J	K	B	C	A
0	新	0-4834	0-3123	0-6770	B773	1-643B	214265
1	斱			1-7513			
2	斲		1-3365	1-7842	E5C1	2-5068	
3	斳	5-4668	1-3366		E5C2	2-5069	
4	斴		1-3367				
5	斵					E-546B	2E3729
6	斶	3-4422			ECF0	2-5C7B	22372A
7	斷	1-2247	0-5850	0-5108	C25F	1-764B	214266
8	斸	3-4421			F8F0	2-707E	22372C
9	方	0-2329	0-4293	0-5916	A4E8	1-4549	214267
A	斺	3-4732				E-293C	
B	斻	5-4901			CCC3	2-2724	
C	於	0-7622	0-1787	0-6958	A9F3	1-4D75	393052
D	施	0-4209	0-2760	0-6731	AC49	1-514C	214269
E	斾					E-2C77	
F	斿	5-4902	1-3368	1-7377	CEEA	2-2A6B	22372F

65C

	Char	G	J	K	B	C	A
0	旀						
1	旁	0-3752	0-5853	0-5917	ABC7	1-5569	21426A
2	旂	8-1394	1-3369	1-5978	D1D2	2-2F54	223734
3	旃	0-7625	0-5851	1-7591	D1D0	2-2F52	223732
4	旄	0-7624	0-5854	1-6446	D1D1	2-2F53	223733
5	旅	0-3435	0-4625	0-5373	ABC8	1-556A	21426B
6	旆	0-7623	0-5852	1-8189	D1CF	2-2F51	223731
7	旇	3-4736				E-363C	
8	旈		1-3370				
9	旉	5-4904	1-3371			E-363F	
A	旊	3-4735		1-6541		E-363D	
B	旋	0-4893	0-3291	0-6433	B1DB	1-5B21	21426D
C	旌	0-7626	0-5855	0-7959	B1DC	1-5B22	21426E
D	旍	5-4908			D5A8	2-356A	
E	旎	0-7627	1-3372		B1DD	1-5B23	21426C
F	族	0-5569	0-3418	0-8073	B1DA	1-5A7E	21426F

65D

	Char	G	J	K	B	C	A
0	旐	3-4738	1-3373		D97D	2-3C42	22373B
1	旑					E-3B79	
2	旒	0-7628	0-5856	0-5518	D97E	2-3C43	22373C
3	旓	3-4739			DDBE	2-4344	
4	旔		1-3374				
5	旕						
6	旖	0-7629	1-3375		BA59	1-6922	214271
7	旗	0-3876	0-2090	0-4893	BA58	1-6921	214270
8	旘		1-3376				
9	旙		0-5858				4C3744
A	旚	5-4911			ECF1	2-5C7C	
B	旛	3-4741	0-5857		EFD9	2-6165	223744
C	旜	5-4914				E-5A3F	223745
D	旝	3-4737			F24A	2-6555	223747
E	旞	3-4742			F249	2-6554	
F	旟	3-4733	1-3377		F44F	2-687B	223748

65E

	Char	G	J	K	B	C	A
0	无	0-4662	0-5859	0-5773		E-2169	274966
1	旡	5-3488	0-5860		C95E	2-213E	22374A
2	既	0-2840	0-2091		AC4A	1-514D	214272
3	旣			0-4894		E-3641	2D4272
4	旤					E-4150	22374E
5	日	0-4053	0-3892	0-7677	A4E9	1-454A	214273
6	旦	0-2109	0-3522	0-5109	A5B9	1-4659	27565A
7	旧	0-3041	0-2176			E-2251	275435
8	旨	0-5428	0-2761	0-8209	A6AE	1-482F	214278
9	早	0-5271	0-3365	0-8036	A6AD	1-482E	214275
A	旪	5-4222				E-2373	
B	旫					E-2372	
C	旬	0-4914	0-2960	0-6666	A6AF	1-4830	214276
D	旭	0-4881	0-1616	0-7379	A6B0	1-4831	214277
E	旮	0-7424			C9EE	2-224F	2D4277
F	旯	0-7425			C9ED	2-224E	334277

65F

	Char	G	J	K	B	C	A
0	旰	0-7426	1-3378		CAF8	2-2439	223755
1	旱	0-2621	0-5861	0-8949	A7F2	1-4A54	214279
2	旲	3-3942	1-3379	1-6119	CAFB	2-243C	
3	旳	5-4145			CAFA	2-243B	
4	旴	3-3941	1-3380	0-7357	CAF9	2-243A	223754
5	旵	3-3943	1-3381		CAFC	2-243D	
6	时	0-4217				E-263D	27432D
7	旷	0-3185					27434D
8	旸	8-9225					
9	旹		1-3382			E-625E	
A	旺	0-4590	0-1802	0-7258	A9F4	1-4D76	21427A
B	旻	3-3953	0-5865	0-5835	CCC9	2-272A	22375B
C	旼	3-3952		0-5836	CCC5	2-2726	22375C
D	旽	5-4151		0-5237	CCCE	2-272F	
E	旾		1-3383			E-2943	
F	旿	3-3947	1-3384	0-7190		E-293E	

660

	Char	G	J	K	B	C	A
0	昀	0-7432	1-3385	1-7409	A9FB	1-4D7D	21427E
1	昁					E-2942	
2	昂	0-1626	0-2523		A9F9	1-4D7B	214323
3	昃	0-7430	0-5864	1-8073	CCCA	2-272B	223764
4	昄	3-3949	1-3386		CCC6	2-2727	22376D
5	昅				CCCD	2-272E	
6	昆	0-3205	0-2611	0-4564	A9F8	1-4D7A	21427B
7	昇	8-1380	0-3026	0-6716	AA40	1-4E23	2D345B
8	昈	3-3955	1-3387		CCC8	2-2729	
9	昉	3-3954	1-3388	0-5918	CCC4	2-2725	22375A
A	昊	0-7427	0-5863	0-9136	A9FE	1-4E22	22375E
B	昋	3-3945			CCCB	2-272C	
C	昌	0-1893	0-3027	0-8367	A9F7	1-4D79	21427D
D	昍	5-4152	1-3389		CCCC	2-272D	
E	明	0-3587	0-4432	0-5705	A9FA	1-4D7C	214321
F	昏	0-2772	0-2610	0-9171	A9FC	1-4D7E	214324

661

	Char	G	J	K	B	C	A
0	昐	5-4154		0-6143	CCD0	2-2731	
1	昑	5-4153	1-3390	0-4852	CCCF	2-2730	22376A
2	昒	3-3950	1-3391		CCC7	2-2728	
3	易	0-5055	0-1655	0-7022	A9F6	1-4D78	214322
4	昔	0-4684	0-3246	0-6414	A9F5	1-4D77	21427C
5	昕	0-7431	1-3392	0-9358	A9FD	1-4E21	22376B
6	昖	5-4155	1-3393				
7	昗	5-4156				E-2940	
8	昘					E-2941	
9	昙	0-7428					283955
A	昚					E-2C7E	2D3F24
B	昛			1-5583		E-2C7A	
C	昜	5-4161	0-5870		CEEF	2-2A70	2D5F2E
D	昝	0-7435	1-3394		CEF5	2-2A76	2E3A26
E	昞	5-4159	1-3401	0-6021		E-2D23	22377C
F	星	0-4839	0-3217	0-6488	AC50	1-5153	21432A

662

	Char	G	J	K	B	C	A
0	映	0-5119	0-1739	0-7117	AC4D	1-5150	214329
1	昡	3-3963	1-3402	1-8345	CEEC	2-2A6D	223772
2	昢	3-3965	1-3403		CEF1	2-2A72	
3	昣		1-3404			E-2C7C	
4	昤	5-4163	1-3405	1-6263	AC53	1-5156	22382C
5	春	0-2026	0-2953	0-8580	AC4B	1-514E	214325
6	昦	5-4160	1-3406		CEF0	2-2A71	
7	昧	0-3533	0-4370	0-5660	AC4E	1-5151	214326
8	昨	0-5582	0-2682	0-7738	AC51	1-5154	21432B
9	昩	3-3956	1-3407			E-2C79	
A	昪	3-3966	1-3408				
B	昫	3-3962	1-3409	1-5856	CEF3	2-2A74	223828
C	昬		1-3410			E-2C7D	223775
D	昭	0-5349	0-3028	0-6525	AC4C	1-514F	214328
E	昮	5-4158	1-3411		CEF8	2-2A79	
F	是	0-4239	0-3207	0-6732	AC4F	1-5152	214327

663

	Char	G	J	K	B	C	A
0	昰		1-3412	0-8932		E-2D21	2D4327
1	昱	0-7437	1-3413	0-7380	AC52	1-5155	22376E
2	昲	3-3964			CEED	2-2A6E	
3	昳	3-3960	1-3414		CEF2	2-2A73	223827
4	昴	0-7436	0-5869	0-5759	CEF6	2-2A77	22382B
5	昵	0-7439	0-5867	1-6065	CEEE	2-2A6F	223777
6	昶	0-7438	0-5868	0-8368	CEEB	2-2A6C	2D4343
7	昷	5-4226	1-3416	1-7230		E-2D24	
8	昸					E-2D25	
9	昹	5-4164	1-3415		CEF7	2-2A78	
A	昺	3-3957		0-6022	CEF4	2-2A75	22377D
B	昻			0-6873		E-2D22	
C	昼	0-5471	0-3575			E-2C37	274332
D	昽	8-9228					
E	显	0-4752					276058
F	昿		0-5906				4B434D

664

	Char	G	J	K	B	C	A
0	晀		1-3417			E-3146	
1	晁	0-7443	0-5874	0-8037	AED0	1-5572	2F5E7D
2	時	1-4217	0-2794	0-6733	AEC9	1-556B	21432D
3	晃	0-2746	0-2524	0-9244	AECC	1-556E	214330
4	晄	5-4167	0-5872	0-9245		E-314C	394330
5	晅	3-3968	1-3418		AECF	1-5571	223831
6	晆		1-3419			E-3144	
7	晇	3-3969			D1D5	2-2F57	
8	晈	5-4170		1-5824		E-3149	
9	晉	1-2990	0-5873	0-8243	AECA	1-556C	21432F
A	晊	5-4166	1-3420		D1D3	2-2F55	
B	晋	0-2990	0-3124	0-8244		E-3148	33432F
C	晌	0-4146	1-3421	1-6788	AECE	1-5570	214331
D	晍					E-314D	
E	晎		1-3423	1-8407		E-3145	
F	晏	0-7444	0-5871	0-6847	AECB	1-556D	21432C

665

	Char	G	J	K	B	C	A
0	晐	3-3971				E-3143	
1	晑		1-3422		D1D6	2-2F58	
2	晒	0-4125	0-2715		AECD	1-556F	21432E
3	晓	0-4794					274348
4	晔	0-7442					28395C
5	晕	0-5246					274341
6	晖	0-7445					274340
7	晗	0-7447	1-3424			E-3642	22384D
8	晘	5-4173	1-3425				
9	晙	3-3978	1-3426	0-8159	D5AC	2-356E	223849
A	晚	0-4577			B1DF	1-5B25	214336
B	晛	3-3946	1-3427	0-9057	D5AB	2-356D	223848
C	晜	5-4176	1-3428		D5AD	2-356F	22383E
D	晝	1-5471	0-5876	0-8124	B1DE	1-5B24	214332
E	晞	3-3976	0-5875	0-9385	B1E3	1-5B29	22384C
F	晟	0-7441	0-5880	0-6489	D1D4	2-2F56	223832

666

	Char	G	J	K	B	C	A
0	晠		1-3429			E-314B	
1	晡	0-7446	1-3430	1-8226	D5AA	2-356C	22383F
2	晢	3-3975	0-5881	1-7631	D5AE	2-3570	2D433B
3	晣	5-4172				E-3644	
4	晤	0-4678	0-5877	0-7191	B1E0	1-5B26	214333
5	晥	5-4177		0-9223	D5A9	2-356B	22383D
6	晦	0-2762	0-1902	0-9268	B1E2	1-5B28	214335
7	晧	5-4174	0-5878	0-9137		E-3645	22384A
8	晨	0-1931	0-5879	0-6771	B1E1	1-5B27	214334
9	晩		0-4053	0-5625		E-3C26	
A	晪		1-3432		D9A7	2-3C4A	
B	晫	3-3981	1-3433	0-8688		E-3B7D	
C	晬	3-3985	1-3434	1-6912	D9A2	2-3C45	223851
D	晭	5-4181				E-3C25	223866
E	普	0-3853	0-4165	0-6037	B4B6	1-5F5B	214338
F	景	0-3016	0-2342	0-4456	B4BA	1-5F5F	214337

667

	Char	G	J	K	B	C	A
0	晰	0-4690	0-5882	1-6817	B4B7	1-5F5C	21433B
1	晱	5-4183			D9A5	2-3C48	
2	晲	3-3983			D9A8	2-3C4B	
3	晳	8-1382	1-3436	0-6415		E-3C23	223860
4	晴	0-3971	0-3218	0-8471	B4B8	1-5F5D	214339
5	晵	3-3987	1-3437				
6	晶	0-3007	0-3029	0-7960	B4B9	1-5F5E	21433C
7	晷	0-7448	1-3439	0-4792	B4BE	1-5F63	223868
8	晸	3-3989	1-3440	0-7961	DDC7	2-434D	22385A
9	晹	3-3982	1-3441		D9A6	2-3C49	
A	智	0-5439	0-3550	0-8210	B4BC	1-5F61	21433D
B	晻		1-3442	1-7039	D9A3	2-3C46	2D433E
C	晼	3-3986	1-3444		D9A1	2-3C44	
D	晽	3-3980				E-3B7C	
E	晾	0-3332	1-3435		B4BD	1-5F62	223850
F	晿		1-3438			E-3B7E	

668

	Char	G	J	K	B	C	A
0	暀	5-4180	1-3443		D9A4	2-3C47	
1	暁		0-2239			E-3C24	2D4348
2	暂	0-5261					274344
3	暃		0-5883				695A73
4	暄	0-7449	0-5887	0-9330	B779	1-6441	223870
5	暅	3-4003					
6	暆	3-4001			DDBF	2-4345	
7	暇	0-4730	0-1843	0-4212	B776	1-643E	21433F
8	暈	1-5246	0-5884	0-9327	B777	1-643F	214341
9	暉	1-7445	0-5886	0-9339	B775	1-643D	214340
A	暊	5-4165			DDC4	2-434A	22387A
B	暋	3-4004	1-3445	1-6507	DDC3	2-4349	223875
C	暌	0-7450	1-3446	1-5926	DDC0	2-4346	223871
D	暍	3-3992	1-3447		B77B	1-6443	22387D
E	暎	8-1381	0-5885	0-7118		E-415B	2D4329
F	暏	5-4178				E-4156	

669

	Char	G	J	K	B	C	A
0	暐	5-4148	1-3448	0-7449	DDC2	2-4348	223876
1	暑	0-4278	0-2975	0-6384	B4BB	1-5F60	21433A
2	暒	5-4187	1-3449			E-4159	
3	暓	5-4189				E-4151	223872
4	暔	3-3990			DDC6	2-434C	223879
5	暕	3-3991			DDC1	2-4347	
6	暖	0-3715	0-3540	0-4976	B778	1-6440	214342
7	暗	0-1621	0-1637	0-6862	B774	1-643C	21433E
8	暘	3-3944	0-5888	0-6935	B77A	1-6442	22387C
9	暙	5-4186	1-3450		DDC5	2-434B	
A	暚	3-4007	1-3451			E-4734	
B	暛	3-4002	1-3452				
C	暜		1-3453			E-4735	
D	暝	0-7452	0-5889	0-5706	BA5C	1-6925	223932
E	暞			1-5825			
F	暟	3-3970	1-3454		E1F8	2-4A5F	

66A

	Char	G	J	K	B	C	A
0	暠		1-3455	0-4528	E1F7	2-4A5E	22392A
1	暡	5-4203			E1F6	2-4A5D	
2	暢	1-1909	0-3610	0-8369	BA5A	1-6923	214343
3	暣	3-3948		1-5979			
4	暤	5-4202	1-3456			E-4739	
5	暥	5-4201				E-4733	
6	暦		0-4681			E-4737	2D4349
7	暧	0-7451					27434B
8	暨	0-8463			BA5B	1-6924	214347
9	暩				E5C5	2-506C	
A	暪	5-4191			E5C8	2-506F	223941
B	暫	1-5261	0-2735	0-7753	BCC8	1-6D32	214344
C	暬	3-4009		1-6843		E-4C44	223943
D	暭		1-3457			E-4C46	
E	暮	0-3626	0-4275	0-5726	BCC7	1-6D31	214346
F	暯	5-4192			E5C9	2-5070	

66B

	Char	G	J	K	B	C	A
0	暰				E5C4	2-506B	
1	暱		1-3458	1-6066	BCCA	1-6D34	223947
2	暲	5-4207	1-3459	0-7771	E5C6	2-506D	22393A
3	暳	5-4206		0-9121		E-4C41	
4	暴	0-1709	0-4329	0-8876	BCC9	1-6D33	214345
5	暵	3-4010	1-3460	1-8288	E5C3	2-506A	223940
6	暶	3-4012				E-4C40	
7	暷	5-4149			E5C7	2-506E	
8	暸	5-4211	0-5902	1-6322	BEE9	1-7072	4B4D73
9	暹	0-6963	0-5891	0-6471	BEE6	1-706F	21434A
A	暺	5-4182			E9BB	2-5746	
B	暻	5-4212	1-3461	0-4457	E9BA	2-5745	22395A
C	暼		0-5894			E-4C43	695A7E
D	暽	5-4214			E9B9	2-5744	
E	暾	0-7453	0-5893	0-5238	E9B4	2-573F	22394F
F	暿	5-4208	1-3462	1-8526		E-507D	

66C

	Char	G	J	K	B	C	A
0	曀	3-4014	1-3463	1-7128	E9B5	2-5740	223954
1	曁		0-5890	1-5980		E-5123	4B4347
2	曂		1-3464				
3	曃	3-4013	1-3465			E-507A	
4	曄	1-7442	0-5901	0-7105	BEE7	1-7070	22395C
5	曅	5-4168		1-7162		E-507E	
6	曆	1-8847		0-5385	BEE4	1-706D	214349
7	曇	1-7428	0-3862	0-5130	BEE8	1-7071	223955
8	曈	3-4017	1-3466		E9B3	2-573E	22394E
9	曉	1-4794	0-5892	0-9291	BEE5	1-706E	214348
A	曊	5-4188			E9B6	2-5741	
B	曋	5-4210			E9B7	2-5742	
C	曌	3-4016	1-3467		E9BC	2-5747	
D	曍					E-5122	2E3936
E	曎		1-3468			E-5471	
F	曏		1-3469		E9B8	2-5743	223960

66D

	Char	G	J	K	B	C	A
0	曐					E-546F	
1	曑					E-5470	
2	曒	3-4020			BCF2	2-5C7D	
3	曓			1-8227			
4	曔	3-4015	1-3470			E-546C	
5	曕					E-546D	
6	曖	1-7451	0-5903	0-6882	C0C7	1-7370	21434B
7	曗					E-5472	
8	曘	3-4021			EFDC	2-6168	
9	曙	0-4279	0-2976	0-6385	C0C6	1-736F	21434C
A	曚	5-4217	0-5904	1-6460	EFDA	2-6166	223971
B	曛	0-7454	1-3471	1-8475	EFDB	2-6167	223972
C	曜	0-7455	0-4543	0-7288	C260	1-764C	39525B
D	曝	0-3856	0-3988	0-8877	C36E	1-783B	21434E
E	曞				F24B	2-6556	
F	曟		1-3472			E-5A43	

66E

	Char	G	J	K	B	C	A
0	曠	1-3185	0-5905	0-4639	C36D	1-783A	21434D
1	曡					E-5A42	223976
2	曢					E-6526	223973
3	曣	3-4023		1-7140	F451	2-687D	
4	曤				F452	2-687E	
5	曥	3-3959				E-5C42	
6	曦	0-7456	0-5907	0-9386	C466	1-7971	21434F
7	曧					E-5C43	
8	曨	3-3958	1-3473	1-6303	F450	2-687C	223978
9	曩	0-7457	0-5908	1-6023	C4E4	1-7A6F	22397C
A	曪			1-6185			
B	曫		1-3474		F7DF	2-6F2E	
C	曬	1-4125	1-3475	1-6907	C5CE	1-7C3A	2D432E
D	曭	3-4006			F8AA	2-7038	
E	曮	3-3973	1-3476	1-7121	F8AB	2-7039	
F	曯			1-8007		E-613F	

66F

	Char	G	J	K	B	C	A
0	曰	0-5227	0-5909	0-7256	A4EA	1-454B	214350
1	曱						
2	曲	0-3990	0-2242	0-4556	A6B1	1-4832	214351
3	曳	0-5023	0-1740	0-7154	A6B2	1-4833	214352
4	更	0-2492	0-2525	0-4458	A7F3	1-4A55	214353
5	曵		0-5910			E-2641	4B4352
6	曶	3-4024			CCD1	2-2732	
7	曷	0-7434	0-5911	0-4267	AC54	1-5157	214354
8	書	1-4273	0-2981	0-6386	AED1	1-5573	214355
9	曹	0-1860	0-3366	0-8039	B1E4	1-5B2A	214356
A	曺		1-3477	0-8038			
B	曻		1-3431				
C	曼	0-3492	0-5056	0-5626	B0D2	1-5937	21352A
D	曽		0-3330				4B4358
E	曾	0-5288	0-3329	0-8184	B4BF	1-5F64	214358
F	替	0-4470	0-3456	0-8480	B4C0	1-5F65	214359

670

	Char	G	J	K	B	C	A
0	最	0-5578	0-2639	0-8544	B3CC	1-5E32	213335
1	朁	3-4025			D9A9	2-3C4C	
2	朂					E-6527	334357
3	會	1-2765	0-4882	0-9269	B77C	1-6444	21435A
4	朄	3-1609			E1FA	2-4A61	
5	朅	3-2079	1-3478	1-5609	E1F9	2-4A60	223A28
6	朆	5-1727				E-5124	216C7B
7	朇		1-3479				
8	月	0-5234	0-2378	0-7437	A4EB	1-454C	21435B
9	有	0-5148	0-4513	0-7483	A6B3	1-4834	21435C
A	朊	0-7535			CCD2	2-2733	22775C
B	朋	0-3783	0-4294	0-6159	AA42	1-4E25	21435E
C	朌	5-4689		1-6527		E-2945	
D	服	0-2394	0-4194	0-6055	AA41	1-4E24	21435D
E	朎		1-3480			E-2D27	
F	朏	3-4471	0-5912		CEF9	2-2A7A	223A30

671

	Char	G	J	K	B	C	A
0	朐	0-7552			CEFA	2-2A7B	223A31
1	朑					E-6632	227775
2	朒	3-4481			D1D7	2-2F59	223A33
3	朓	3-4486	1-3481		D1D8	2-2F5A	223A34
4	朔	0-4323	0-2683	0-6293	AED2	1-5574	214361
5	朕	0-7562	0-3631	0-8289	AED3	1-5575	214360
6	朖		0-5913			E-3648	2D435F
7	朗	0-3242	0-4715	0-5339	AED4	1-5576	21435F
8	朘	3-4514			D5AF	2-3571	223A39
9	朙	5-4719	1-3482			E-3647	223A38
A	朚	5-4175				E-3646	
B	望	0-4591	0-4330	0-5648	B1E6	1-5B2C	214362
C	朜		1-3483				
D	朝	0-1915	0-3611	0-8040	B4C2	1-5F67	214363
E	朞		0-5914	0-4901		E-3C29	2D4364
F	期	0-3858	0-2092	0-4902	B4C1	1-5F66	214364

672

	Char	G	J	K	B	C	A
0	朠		1-3484		DDC8	2-434E	22792E
1	朡	3-4550			DF7A	2-4641	
2	朢		1-3485		E1FB	2-4A62	2D4362
3	朣	5-4777		1-6155	E9BD	2-5748	223A47
4	朤					E-5126	
5	朥					E-6633	22797E
6	朦	0-7592	0-5915	0-5752	C261	1-764D	395564
7	朧	1-7542	0-5916	0-5472	C467	1-7972	214366
8	木	0-3630	0-4458	0-5742	A4EC	1-454D	214367
9	朩						
A	未	0-4620	0-4404	0-5817	A5BC	1-465C	21436B
B	末	0-3609	0-4386	0-5639	A5BD	1-465D	21436A
C	本	0-1730	0-4360	0-6066	A5BB	1-465B	214369
D	札	0-5293	0-2705	0-8346	A5BE	1-465E	276B5F
E	朮		0-5918	0-8584	A5BA	1-465A	275746
F	术	0-4285				E-2252	455746

673

	Char	G	J	K	B	C	A
0	朰						
1	朱	0-5476	0-2875	0-8125	A6B6	1-4837	21436F
2	朲	3-3237				E-2377	
3	朳	3-3238	1-3486	1-8186	C9F6	2-2257	
4	朴	0-3851	0-4349	0-5851	A6B5	1-4836	274558
5	朵	0-2268			A6B7	1-4838	2D4370
6	朶		0-5920	0-8674		E-2378	214370
7	朷	3-3240	0-5923			E-2375	695B37
8	朸	3-3241	0-5922		C9F1	2-2252	2E2F7A
9	朹	3-3239			C9F0	2-2251	
A	机	0-2790	0-2089	0-4785	C9F3	2-2254	27455D
B	朻	5-3526			C9F2	2-2253	
C	朼	5-3525			C9F5	2-2256	
D	朽	0-4864	0-2164	0-9314	A6B4	1-4835	21436D
E	朾	3-3236	1-3487		C9EF	2-2250	223A4C
F	朿	3-1603	0-5919		C9F4	2-2255	223A4E

674

	Char	G	J	K	B	C	A
0	杀	0-4117					27463B
1	杁		0-5921				4C3A55
2	杂	0-5251					275F4B
3	权	0-4008					274570
4	杄	3-3246				E-2648	
5	杅	3-3242	1-3488	1-7322	CAFD	2-243E	223A5B
6	杆	0-2443	0-5924	0-4250	A7FD	1-4A5F	2D4461
7	杇	3-3243	1-3489		CAFE	2-243F	223A5C
8	杈	0-7230	1-3490		CB43	2-2443	223A68
9	杉	0-4128	0-3189	0-6320	A7FC	1-4A5E	214379
A	杊					E-2649	223A71
B	杋				CB47	2-2447	
C	杌	0-7227	1-3491		CB42	2-2442	223A66
D	杍	5-3530			CB45	2-2445	
E	李	0-3278	0-4591	0-5561	A7F5	1-4A57	214373
F	杏	0-4851	0-1641	0-9026	A7F6	1-4A58	214378

675

	Char	G	J	K	B	C	A
0	材	0-1836	0-2664	0-7807	A7F7	1-4A59	214375
1	村	0-2069	0-3428	0-8529	A7F8	1-4A5A	214372
2	杒	3-3252				E-2645	
3	杓	0-7228	0-2861	0-8885	A840	1-4A61	223A6E
4	杔	3-3247	1-3492			E-2644	
5	杕	3-3244	1-3493		CB41	2-2441	223A61
6	杖	0-5340	0-3083	0-7772	A7FA	1-4A5C	214376
7	杗	3-3250			A841	1-4A62	223A58
8	杘	3-2744				E-2647	
9	杙	3-3245	0-5927		CB40	2-2440	223A67
A	杚	5-3528			CB46	2-2446	
B	杛					E-2642	
C	杜	0-2237	0-3746	0-5265	A7F9	1-4A5B	214374
D	杝	3-3251	1-3494		CB44	2-2444	223A60
E	杞	0-7229	0-5925	0-4903	A7FB	1-4A5D	214371
F	束	0-4288	0-3411	0-6554	A7F4	1-4A56	214377

676

	Char	G	J	K	B	C	A
0	杠	0-2460	0-5926	1-5560	A7FE	1-4A60	2D453A
1	条	0-4485	0-3082			E-264A	274463
2	杢		0-4461				694C5D
3	杣		0-5928				223A6B
4	杤		0-5929				4C3B60
5	来	0-3220	0-4572			E-6257	27314C
6	杦		1-3501				
7	杧	3-3249					
8	杨	0-4978					27452A
9	杩	0-7231					283F5C
A	杪	0-7234	0-5934	1-7984	AA57	1-4E3A	223B32
B	杫	3-3261				E-2947	
C	杬	3-3255	1-3502	1-7343	CCD4	2-2735	
D	杭	0-2628	0-2526	0-8988	AA43	1-4E26	21437B
E	杮	3-3258	1-3503				
F	杯	0-1713	0-3953	0-5942	AA4D	1-4E30	214425

677

	Char	G	J	K	B	C	A
0	杰	0-2960	0-5931	0-4389	AA4E	1-4E31	273241
1	東	1-2211	0-3776	0-5252	AA46	1-4E29	214426
2	杲	0-7429	0-5862	1-5678	AA58	1-4E3B	223B30
3	杳	0-7235	0-5866	0-5760	AA48	1-4E2B	214427
4	杴	5-3542	1-3504		CCDC	2-273D	
5	杵	0-7238	0-2147	0-7830	AA53	1-4E36	214429
6	杶	3-3259	1-3505		CCD7	2-2738	223B23
7	杷	0-7243	0-3939	0-8777	AA49	1-4E2C	214422
8	杸	5-3543			CCE6	2-2747	
9	杹	3-3263			CCE7	2-2748	
A	杺	5-3544			CCDF	2-2740	
B	杻	3-3271	1-3506	0-5078	CCD8	2-2739	223B21
C	杼	0-7244	0-5933	1-7561	AA56	1-4E39	223A78
D	杽	5-3535			CCE4	2-2745	
E	松	0-4341	0-3030	0-6570	AA51	1-4E34	21442D
F	板	0-1669	0-4036	0-8789	AA4F	1-4E32	275E65

678

	Char	G	J	K	B	C	A
0	枀	5-3541				E-2952	2D442D
1	极	0-2811	1-3507		CCE5	2-2746	274526
2	枂	3-3266				E-2949	
3	枃	3-3267			CCE3	2-2744	
4	构	0-2525	1-3508		CCDB	2-273C	274539
5	枅	3-3253	0-5939		CCD3	2-2734	223A7C
6	枆	5-3536			CCDA	2-273B	
7	枇	0-7233	0-4090	0-6177	AA4A	1-4E2D	214421
8	枈	3-3824				E-625F	
9	枉	0-4587	0-5930	0-7259	AA50	1-4E33	21437E
A	枊	3-3269				E-294A	
B	枋	0-7242	0-5936	0-5919	AA44	1-4E27	21437C
C	枌	3-3265	0-5935	1-6648	CCDE	2-273F	223B49
D	枍	5-3539			CCDD	2-273E	223B48
E	枎	3-3254	1-3509		CCD5	2-2736	
F	枏		1-3510	0-4987		E-294F	223B2E

67A

	Char	G	J	K	B	C	A
0	枠		0-4740				223B3B
1	枡		0-5938				223B3F
2	枢	0-4264	0-3185			E-294E	274549
3	枣	0-5270				E-294C	27447A
4	枤					E-6528	223B28
5	枥	0-7232					284340
6	枦		0-5937				4C4345
7	枧	0-7237					283D30
8	枨	0-7239					283D6E
9	枩		0-5932				4B442D
A	枪	0-3925					274540
B	枫	0-2367					27452F
C	枬					E-6529	223B39
D	枭	0-7241					274468
E	枮	5-3552			CF5B	2-2B3D	223B79
F	枯	0-3161	0-2447	0-4529	AC5C	1-515F	214433

67C

	Char	G	J	K	B	C	A
0	柀	3-3302	1-3525		CF44	2-2B26	
1	柁	0-7262	0-3440	1-8115	CEFB	2-2A7C	335445
2	柂	3-3283	1-3526		CF51	2-2B33	223C23
3	柃	0-7258	1-3527		CF61	2-2B43	223C2B
4	柄	0-1790	0-4233	0-6023	AC60	1-5163	214432
5	柅	3-3293	1-3528	1-6061	CF46	2-2B28	223B58
6	柆	5-3559	0-5954		CF58	2-2B3A	2D4039
7	柇	3-3282				E-2D2D	
8	柈	3-3291	1-3529		CEFD	2-2A7E	223B51
9	柉		1-3530		CF5F	2-2B41	
A	柊	3-3286	0-4102	1-7730	CF60	2-2B42	223C26
B	柋				CF63	2-2B45	
C	柌	5-3560			CF5A	2-2B3C	223B54
D	柍	3-3278			CF4B	2-2B2D	
E	柎	3-3284	0-5953		CF53	2-2B35	223C28
F	柏	0-1656	0-3980	0-5958	AC66	1-5169	214440

67E

	Char	G	J	K	B	C	A
0	柠	0-3691					274563
1	柡		1-3535				
2	柢	0-7260	0-5950	1-7562	AC6B	1-516E	223C29
3	柣	3-3281			CF50	2-2B32	223C24
4	柤	5-3555	0-5947		CF48	2-2B2A	223B6F
5	查	0-1873			AC64	1-5167	21443A
6	柦	5-3554	1-3536		CF5C	2-2B3E	
7	柧	5-3558	0-5955		CF54	2-2B36	223C2F
8	柨	3-3276				E-2D2A	
9	柩	0-7249	0-5945	0-4715	AC5E	1-5161	214437
A	柪	3-3305			CF62	2-2B44	
B	柫				CF47	2-2B29	
C	柬	0-2877	0-5943	0-4251	AC5A	1-515D	214439
D	柭	3-3277			CF59	2-2B3B	
E	柮	3-3294	0-5951		CF4F	2-2B31	223B7C
F	柯	0-3134	0-5941	0-4215	AC5F	1-5162	214436

679

	Char	G	J	K	B	C	A
0	析	0-4686	0-3247	0-6416	AA52	1-4E35	21442B
1	枑	3-3260	1-3511		CCE1	2-2742	223B25
2	枒				CCD6	2-2737	223B22
3	枓	3-3270	1-3512	0-5266	AA55	1-4E38	223A75
4	枔	5-3540			CCE8	2-2749	
5	枕	0-5377	0-4377	0-8655	AA45	1-4E28	21437D
6	枖	5-3537	1-3513			E-2948	
7	林	0-3354	0-4651	0-5589	AA4C	1-4E2F	214424
8	枘	0-7236	1-3514	1-7182	CCD9	2-273A	223B31
9	枙	5-3533	1-3515	1-7253	CCE2	2-2743	223B26
A	枚	0-3522	0-4371	0-5661	AA54	1-4E37	21442A
B	枛		1-3516				
C	果	0-2591	0-1844	0-4593	AA47	1-4E2A	214428
D	枝	0-5406	0-2762	0-8211	AA4B	1-4E2E	214423
E	枞	0-7240					27454F
F	枟	3-3256			CCE0	2-2741	223A7A

67B

	Char	G	J	K	B	C	A
0	枰	0-7250	1-3517	0-8834	AC69	1-516C	223B5F
1	枱	5-3563	1-3518			E-2D36	3A3B7D
2	枲	3-1951	1-3519	1-6963	CF56	2-2B38	223B7E
3	枳	0-7255	0-5944	0-8212	CF4C	2-2B2E	223B77
4	枴		0-5942		AC62	1-5165	2D4049
5	枵	0-7253	1-3520		CF4A	2-2B2C	223B72
6	架	0-2860	0-1845	0-4213	AC5B	1-515E	214438
7	枷	0-2847	0-5940	0-4214	CF45	2-2B27	223B64
8	枸	0-7259	0-5946	0-4714	AC65	1-5168	21443F
9	枹	3-3289	0-5952		CF52	2-2B34	223C21
A	枺	3-3272			CEFE	2-2B21	
B	枻	3-3274	1-3521		CF41	2-2B23	223B5C
C	枼	5-3550	1-3522			E-2D2E	
D	枽		1-3523				
E	枾			0-6734			
F	枿	3-3273				E-2D30	

67D

	Char	G	J	K	B	C	A
0	某	0-3619	0-4331	0-5727	AC59	1-515C	214434
1	柑	0-2444	0-2027	0-4283	AC61	1-5164	214435
2	柒	0-3866	1-3531	0-8651	AC6D	1-5170	33485E
3	染	0-4030	0-3287	0-7088	AC56	1-5159	21442E
4	柔	0-4065	0-2932	0-7485	AC58	1-515B	214431
5	柕					E-2D31	
6	柖	3-3301				E-2D2B	
7	柗		1-3532	1-6903		E-2D3A	
8	柘	0-7247	0-3651	1-7483	CF43	2-2B25	223B63
9	柙	0-7252	1-3533	1-8307	AC6A	1-516D	223B70
A	柚	0-7254	0-4514	0-7486	AC63	1-5166	21443C
B	柛	5-3556			CF5D	2-2B3F	223B71
C	柜	0-2581	1-3534		CF40	2-2B22	274565
D	柝	0-7256	0-5949	0-8689	AC6C	1-516F	223C2D
E	柞	0-5585	0-5948	1-7514	AC67	1-516A	21443E
F	柟			1-6022	CF49	2-2B2B	223B74

67F

	Char	G	J	K	B	C	A
0	柰	0-7245	1-3537	0-5016	CF55	2-2B37	2D3931
1	柱	0-5489	0-3576	0-8126	AC57	1-515A	21442F
2	柲	3-3292	1-3538		CEFC	2-2A7D	223C2A
3	柳	0-3388	0-4488	0-5519	AC68	1-516B	214441
4	柴	0-1881	0-2838	0-6735	AEE3	1-5627	214450
5	柵		0-2684	0-8393	AC5D	1-5160	21443D
6	柶	3-3280	1-3539	0-6258	CF4E	2-2B30	223B7A
7	柷	3-3279	1-3540		CF4D	2-2B2F	223B75
8	柸	3-3275			CF42	2-2B24	223B61
9	柹		1-3524	1-6964		E-2951	223B44
A	柺				CF5E	2-2B40	21443B
B	査		0-2626	0-6259		E-2D34	
C	柼				CF57	2-2B39	223B4C
D	柽	0-7263					28405E
E	柾		0-4379	0-7962		E-2D32	2D4437
F	柿	0-4233	0-1933		AC55	1-5158	214430

680

	Char	G	J	K	B	C	A
0	栀	0-7257				E-2D39	274469
1	栁					E-2D37	
2	栂		0-3646				223B6D
3	栃		0-3842	1-8444			223B60
4	栄		0-1741				4B4537
5	栅	0-5304				E-2D38	
6	栆					E-652B	223B78
7	标	0-1774					274547
8	栈	0-5327					274476
9	栉	0-7246					27456C
A	栊	0-7248					284339
B	栋	0-2216					274471
C	栌	0-7251					284345
D	栍						
E	栎	0-7261					284333
F	栏	0-3224					27456E

681

	Char	G	J	K	B	C	A
0	栐					E-652A	223B4E
1	树	0-4287					274555
2	栒	3-3326		0-6667	D1EC	2-2F6E	223C59
3	栓	0-4308	0-3282	0-7891	AEEA	1-562E	214456
4	栔	5-3564	1-3542		D1ED	2-2F6F	223C36
5	栕	5-3568				E-315D	
6	栖	0-3860	0-3220	0-6387	D1E1	2-2F63	27446E
7	栗	0-3285	0-2310	0-5542	AEDF	1-5623	214449
8	栘	3-3328			AEEB	1-562F	
9	栙	3-3327	1-3543			E-3157	
A	栚	3-3333			D1DA	2-2F5C	
B	栛	3-3336				E-3153	
C	栜	3-3308			D1E3	2-2F65	
D	栝	0-7273	1-3544	1-5778	D1EB	2-2F6D	2D4562
E	栞		0-5957	1-5524		E-315B	223C38
F	栟	3-3332	1-3545		D1D9	2-2F5B	223D65

682

	Char	G	J	K	B	C	A
0	栠	5-3576			D1F4	2-2F76	
1	校	0-4803	0-2527	0-4672	AED5	1-5577	214443
2	栢		0-1992	0-5959		E-315E	2D4440
3	栣					E-3164	
4	栤					E-3150	
5	栥				D1F3	2-2F75	
6	栦				D1EE	2-2F70	
7	栧	5-3573	1-3547			E-315F	
8	栨	5-3581	1-3546		D1EF	2-2F71	
9	栩	0-7282	0-5959		AEDD	1-5621	21444C
A	株	0-5474	0-1984	0-8127	AEE8	1-562C	214453
B	栫	3-3311	0-5965		D1E5	2-2F67	223C47
C	栬	3-3329	1-3548			E-3156	
D	栭	3-3310	1-3549		D1E6	2-2F68	223C48
E	栮	5-3567		1-7450	D1F0	2-2F72	
F	栯	3-3309	1-3550	0-7381	D1E7	2-2F69	

683

	Char	G	J	K	B	C	A
0	栰		1-3551			E-3163	
1	栱	3-3307	1-3552	1-5735	D1E2	2-2F64	223C40
2	栲	0-7264	0-5962	1-5679	D1DC	2-2F5E	223C41
3	栳	0-7265	1-3553		D1DD	2-2F5F	223C3B
4	栴	5-3575	0-3283	1-7592	D1EA	2-2F6C	223C58
5	栵	3-3313			D1E4	2-2F66	223C42
6	栶					E-3154	
7	样	0-4989				E-314F	274544
8	核	0-2643	0-1943	0-9023	AED6	1-5578	214444
9	根	0-2489	0-2612	0-4838	AEDA	1-557C	21444E
A	栺	3-3325			D1F2	2-2F74	
B	栻	3-3306	1-3554	1-6976	D1DE	2-2F60	223C43
C	格	0-2481	0-1942	0-4411	AEE6	1-562A	214455
D	栽	0-5252	0-2647	0-7808	AEE2	1-5626	21444A
E	栾	0-7279				E-315A	223C31
F	栿	3-3319	1-3555				

684

	Char	G	J	K	B	C	A
0	桀	0-7278	0-5960	0-4390	AEE5	1-5629	214452
1	桁	0-7276	0-2369	0-8989	AEEC	1-5630	2D5440
2	桂	0-2580	0-2343	0-4493	AEDB	1-557D	214447
3	桃	0-4450	0-3777	0-5194	AEE7	1-562B	214451
4	桄	0-7270	1-3556	1-5784	D1E9	2-2F6B	223C4F
5	桅	0-4606	1-3557		AEE9	1-562D	214454
6	框	0-3182	0-5958	1-5785	AED8	1-557A	214446
7	桇					E-3159	
8	案	0-1624	0-1638	0-6848	AED7	1-5579	214442
9	桉	0-7281		1-7024	D1DB	2-2F5D	223C30
A	桊	0-7280	1-3558				2E3D62
B	桋	3-3315			D1DF	2-2F61	223C37
C	桌	0-5532	1-3559		AEE0	1-5624	2D447D
D	桍	3-3312	0-5961		D1F1	2-2F73	223C4A
E	桎	0-7268	0-5963	0-8278	D1E8	2-2F6A	223C44
F	桏				D1E0	2-2F62	

685

	Char	G	J	K	B	C	A
0	桐	0-4509	0-2245	0-5253	AEE4	1-5628	21444D
1	桑	0-4103	0-2312	0-6345	AEE1	1-5625	21444B
2	桒		1-3541			E-2D2F	2D444B
3	桓	0-2724	0-2028	0-9224	AED9	1-557B	214445
4	桔	0-2959	0-2143	0-4948	AEDC	1-557E	214448
5	桕	0-7274	1-3560			E-3162	3A4034
6	桖	3-3321				E-3158	
7	桗		1-3561				
8	桘		1-3562			E-3161	
9	桙		0-5966			E-3160	4C3A5B
A	桚					E-652D	223C65
B	桛		1-3563				
C	桜		0-2689				4B456F
D	桝		0-4381				223C55
E	桞					E-652C	223C56
F	桟		0-2723				4B4476

686

	Char	G	J	K	B	C	A
0	桠	0-7266					4C3B22
1	桡	0-7267					284140
2	桢	0-7269					27452B
3	档	0-2121	0-5967				27455F
4	桤	0-7271					284027
5	桥	0-3937					27455B
6	桦	0-7275					274557
7	桧	0-7277	0-4116				274562
8	桨	0-2916					27454C
9	桩	0-5514					274546
A	桪	8-9176					
B	桫	0-7288	1-3564		D5C4	2-3628	223C68
C	桬	5-3612				E-3655	223C69
D	桭	3-3347		0-8245	D5B4	2-3576	223D25
E	桮		1-3565		D5B5	2-3577	2D4425
F	桯	3-3351	1-3566	1-7656	D5B9	2-357B	223D34

687

	Char	G	J	K	B	C	A
0	桰	5-3606	1-3567			E-3660	
1	桱	3-3304	1-3568		D5C8	2-362C	
2	桲	3-3343	1-3569		D5C5	2-3629	223D21
3	桳					E-364E	
4	桴	0-7285	0-5979	1-6624	D5BE	2-3622	223D3B
5	桵	3-3365	1-3570		D5BD	2-3621	223D3C
6	桶	0-4516	0-1819	0-8750	B1ED	1-5B33	21445A
7	桷	0-7286	0-5968	1-5521	D5C1	2-3625	223D3F
8	桸	3-3362			D5D0	2-3634	
9	桹	5-3613	1-3571		D5B0	2-3572	223C6B
A	桺		1-3572			E-365B	
B	桻	5-3608	1-3573		D5D1	2-3635	223D43
C	桼	5-3605	1-3574		D5C3	2-3627	
D	桽				D5D5	2-3639	
E	桾	5-3614	0-5985	1-5889	D5C9	2-362D	223C72
F	桿		0-5969	0-4252	B1EC	1-5B32	214461

	688	68A	68C	68E
0	梀 G 3-3344 J K B D5C7 C 2-362B A	梠 G 3-3317 J 0-5981 K 1-6230 B D5CD C 2-3631 A 223D33	检 G 0-2876 J K B C A 274561	棠 G 0-4436 J 0-6011 K 0-5154 B B4C5 C 1-5F6A A 214477
1	梁 G 0-3326 J 0-4634 K 0-5357 B B1E7 C 1-5B2D A 214457	梡 G 3-3368 J 1-3583 K 0-7241 B B1FB C 1-5B41 A	棁 G 3-3367 J K B C E-3656 A	棡 G 3-3262 J 0-5992 K B D9BB C 2-3C5E A 223E33
2	梂 G 3-3350 J 1-3575 K B B1FC C 1-5B42 A 223C76	梢 G 0-4150 J 0-3031 K 0-8494 B B1E9 C 1-5B2F A 214460	棂 G 0-7289 J K B C A 284350	棢 G J K B C E-3C3D A
3	梃 G 0-7272 J 0-5976 K 1-7657 B B1F2 C 1-5B38 A 21446A	梣 G 3-3359 J 1-3584 K 1-6989 B D5BA C 2-357C A 223D39	棃 G J K B C E-3C45 A 223E40	棣 G 0-7306 J 0-6008 K 1-7963 B B4D0 C 1-5F75 A 214470
4	梄 G 5-3589 J 1-3576 K B C E-3657 A	梤 G 5-3616 J K B D5CF C 2-3633 A	棄 G 1-3890 J 0-2094 K 0-4905 B B1F3 C 1-5B39 A 21446D	棤 G J K B D9B6 C 2-3C59 A
5	梅 G 0-3523 J 0-3963 K 0-5662 B B1F6 C 1-5B3C A 214466	梥 G 5-3011 J 1-3585 K B C E-3654 A 22697E	棅 G 5-3630 J 1-3591 K 0-6024 B C E-3C41 A	棥 G J 1-3608 K B C E-3C32 A
6	梆 G 0-1680 J 1-3577 K 1-6542 B B1F5 C 1-5B3B A 214465	梦 G 0-3546 J 0-5277 K B C E-3478 A 273924	棆 G 3-3264 J 0-6018 K B D9C3 C 2-3C66 A 223E49	棦 G 5-3580 J K B D9D1 C 2-3C74 A
7	梇 G 3-3338 J K B D5B1 C 2-3573 A	梧 G 0-4664 J 0-2472 K 0-7192 B B1EF C 1-5B35 A 21445C	棇 G J K B D9D9 C 2-3C7C A 223E4B	棧 G 1-5327 J 0-6002 K 0-7748 B B4CC C 1-5F71 A 214476
8	梈 G 3-3366 J 1-3578 K B C A	梨 G 0-3270 J 0-4592 K 0-5562 B B1F9 C 1-5B3F A 214467	棈 G 5-3618 J 1-3592 K B D9CE C 2-3C71 A	棨 G 3-3412 J 1-3609 K 0-4501 B D9C9 C 2-3C6C A 223E3E
9	梉 G J K B D5CE C 2-3632 A	梩 G 3-3353 J 1-3586 K B D5BC C 2-357E A 223D2E	棉 G 0-3562 J 0-4441 K 0-5686 B B4D6 C 1-5F7B A 214522	棩 G 5-3665 J K B D9D6 C 2-3C79 A
A	梊 G 5-3592 J K B D5D4 C 2-3638 A	梪 G 3-3345 J 1-3587 K B D5C6 C 2-362A A	棊 G J 0-5987 K 1-5981 B C E-3C38 A 2D4472	棪 G 3-3408 J 1-3610 K B D9B0 C 2-3C53 A 223D64
B	梋 G 3-3356 J K B D5CC C 2-3630 A 223D32	梫 G 3-3369 J K B D5B7 C 2-3579 A	棋 G 0-3869 J 0-2093 K 0-4904 B B4D1 C 1-5F76 A 214472	棫 G 3-3379 J 1-3611 K B D9B5 C 2-3C58 A 223D6F
C	梌 G 3-3361 J K B D5D3 C 2-3637 A	梬 G 3-3354 J K B D5BB C 2-357D A	棌 G 5-3632 J 1-3593 K 1-7888 B D9BD C 2-3C60 A	棬 G 3-3405 J 1-3612 K 1-5904 B D9AF C 2-3C52 A 223D62
D	梍 G 5-3602 J 0-5984 K B C A	梭 G 0-4383 J 0-5972 K 0-6260 B B1F4 C 1-5B3A A 214464	棍 G 0-2587 J 0-5994 K 0-4566 B B4D2 C 1-5F77 A 214479	棭 G J 1-3613 K B C E-3C2A A
E	梎 G 3-3360 J K B C E-3651 A 223D44	梮 G 3-3372 J 1-3588 K B D5B6 C 2-3578 A	棎 G 5-3640 J K B D9CD C 2-3C70 A	森 G 0-4113 J 0-3125 K 0-6321 B B4CB C 1-5F70 A 214473
F	梏 G 0-7284 J 0-5971 K 0-4557 B D5C0 C 2-3624 A 223D40	梯 G 0-4461 J 0-3684 K 0-8012 B B1E8 C 1-5B2E A 214459	棏 G J 1-3594 K B C E-3C3E A	棯 G 3-3389 J 0-6012 K B D9C2 C 2-3C65 A 223E47

	689	68B	68D	68F
0	梐 G 3-3349 J K B D5B2 C 2-3574 A 223C7A	械 G 0-4821 J 0-1903 K 0-4494 B B1F1 C 1-5B37 A 21445B	棐 G 3-8458 J 1-3601 K 1-6684 B D9C6 C 2-3C69 A 223E38	棰 G 0-7302 J 1-3614 K B DDDE C 2-4364 A 223E3F
1	梑 G 5-3607 J K B D5D2 C 2-3636 A	梱 G 3-3355 J 0-2613 K 0-4565 B B1EE C 1-5B34 A 214462	棑 G 3-3382 J 1-3602 K B D9D3 C 2-3C76 A 223E37	棱 G 0-3266 J 1-3615 K B D9B1 C 2-3C54 A 223D73
2	梒 G 5-3604 J K B D5C2 C 2-3626 A	梲 G J 1-3589 K B D5BF C 2-3623 A 223C6E	棒 G 0-1684 J 0-4332 K 0-6074 B B4CE C 1-5F73 A 21446F	棲 G 1-3860 J 0-3219 K 0-6388 B B4CF C 1-5F74 A 21446E
3	梓 G 0-7287 J 0-1620 K 0-7809 B B1EA C 1-5B30 A 214458	梳 G 0-4265 J 0-5964 K 0-6526 B AEDE C 1-5622 A 21445F	棓 G 3-3402 J 1-3603 K B D9AB C 2-3C4E A 223D58	棳 G 3-3415 J K B D9BA C 2-3C5D A 223D7B
4	梔 G J 0-5973 K 0-8628 B B1F7 C 1-5B3D A 214469	梴 G 3-3320 J K B D9C0 C 2-3C63 A 223D4B	棔 G 3-3391 J 0-6001 K B D9D5 C 2-3C78 A 223E46	棴 G 5-3634 J K B D9D2 C 2-3C75 A
5	梕 G 5-3617 J K B C E-365A A	梵 G 0-7283 J 0-5980 K 0-5979 B B1EB C 1-5B31 A 21445E	棕 G 0-5556 J 0-6003 K 0-8087 B B4C4 C 1-5F69 A 21446B	棵 G 0-3135 J 1-3616 K B B4CA C 1-5F6F A 214478
6	梖 G 5-3534 J 1-3579 K B D5CB C 2-362F A	梶 G 3-3371 J 0-1965 K 0-5818 B C E-364C A 223C74	棖 G 1-7239 J 1-3604 K 1-7658 B D9B3 C 2-3C56 A 223D6E	棶 G 3-3348 J 1-3617 K B D9B7 C 2-3C5A A
7	梗 G 0-2503 J 0-2528 K 0-4459 B B1F0 C 1-5B36 A 21445D	梷 G J K B C E-3652 A	棗 G 1-5270 J 0-6007 K 0-8042 B B4C7 C 1-5F6C A 21447A	棷 G 3-3375 J K B D9B4 C 2-3C57 A
8	梘 G 1-7237 J 1-3580 K B C E-364D A 223D30	梸 G 5-3594 J K B C E-365E A	棘 G 0-2812 J 0-5989 K 0-4830 B B4C6 C 1-5F6B A 21447B	棸 G 5-3620 J K B D9C5 C 2-3C68 A
9	梙 G 5-3593 J K B C E-365C A	梹 G 5-3601 J 0-5978 K B C E-365F A 2D4564	棙 G 3-3411 J 1-3605 K B C A	棹 G 0-7294 J 0-6010 K 0-5201 B B4CD C 1-5F72 A 21447D
A	梚 G J 1-3581 K B C E-3650 A	梺 G J 0-5982 K B C A 4B6258	棚 G 0-3779 J 0-3510 K 0-6160 B B4D7 C 1-5F7C A 21447E	棺 G 0-2555 J 0-2029 K 0-4618 B B4C3 C 1-5F68 A 21446C
B	梛 G 5-3583 J 0-5975 K 1-6014 B D5CA C 2-362E A 223C71	梻 G J 1-3590 K B C A	棛 G 5-3638 J K B C E-3653 A	棻 G 3-3342 J 1-3618 K 1-6649 B B4D9 C 1-5F7E A 223E2D
C	梜 G 3-3314 J 1-3582 K B D5B3 C 2-3575 A 223D22	梼 G 8-9177 J 0-3778 K B C A 284257	棜 G 3-3404 J 1-3606 K B D9AD C 2-3C50 A	棼 G 0-7291 J 1-3619 K 1-6650 B D9C8 C 2-3C6B A 223D79
D	條 G 1-4485 J 0-5974 K 0-8041 B B1F8 C 1-5B3E A 214463	梽 G 3-3339 J K B C A	棝 G 5-3627 J 1-3607 K B D9CF C 2-3C72 A	棽 G 3-3378 J 1-3620 K B D9C7 C 2-3C6A A 223D78
E	梞 G 3-3373 J K B C E-364B A	梾 G 7-0104 J K B C A	棞 G 5-3628 J K B D9D0 C 2-3C73 A 223E2A	棾 G J K B C E-3C31 A
F	梟 G 1-7241 J 0-5970 K 0-9292 B B1FA C 1-5B40 A 214468	梿 G 8-1379 J K B C A	棟 G 1-2216 J 0-3779 K 0-5254 B B4C9 C 1-5F6E A 214471	棿 G J K B C E-3C42 A

Code	Char	G	J	K	B	C	A
6900	椀		0-4748	0-7242		E-3C39	346126
6901	椁	0-7304	0-5986	1-5757		E-3C3B	2D4543
6902	椂	5-3641				E-3C34	
6903	椃	5-3624				E-3C2F	
6904	椄	3-3403	0-6006	1-7644	D9AC	2-3C4F	223D59
6905	椅	0-5046	0-1656	0-7585	B4C8	1-5F6D	214475
6906	椆	3-3390	1-3621		D9D4	2-3C77	
6907	椇	3-3383			D9BC	2-3C5F	223E21
6908	椈	3-3392	0-5988		D9BE	2-3C61	223E39
6909	椉		1-3622			E-3C37	223D5C
690A	椊	3-3394	1-3623		D9CB	2-3C6E	223D5B
690B	椋	0-7303	0-4426	1-6223	D9CA	2-3C6D	223D56
690C	椌	3-3410	0-5993		D9AA	2-3C4D	223D53
690D	植	0-5418	0-3102	0-6753	B4D3	1-5F78	214474
690E	椎	0-5521	0-3639	0-8548	B4D5	1-5F7A	214521
690F	椏	1-7266	0-5983		D9E2	2-3C55	2E3B22
6910	椐	0-7307	1-3624		D9B9	2-3C5C	223D6A
6911	椑	3-3387	1-3625	1-6685	D9C1	2-3C64	223E44
6912	椒	0-2923	0-6005	0-8501	B4D4	1-5F79	21447C
6913	椓	3-3381	1-3626		D9B8	2-3C5B	223D7C
6914	椔	3-3416			D9C4	2-3C67	
6915	椕	5-3633			D9D7	2-3C7A	
6916	椖		1-3627				
6917	椗		1-3628		D9CC	2-3C6F	223D51
6918	椘					E-3C3C	334527
6919	椙		0-3190	1-7877			223E24
691A	椚		0-6015				223E23
691B	椛		0-1981				223E2B
691C	検		0-2401			E-3C44	4B4561
691D	椝	8-1377					
691E	椞					E-3C33	
691F	椟	0-7292					27456B
6920	椠	0-7293					284056
6921	椡		0-6017				695C31
6922	椢		0-5990				4C3F7A
6923	椣		0-6016				695C30
6924	椤	0-7301					284366
6925	椥		0-6009		D9D8	2-3C7B	695C29
6926	椦		0-5991				695B7B
6927	椧			0-5707			
6928	椨		0-6013				695C2D
6929	椩					E-652F	223D5D
692A	椪	3-3406	0-6014		D9AE	2-3C51	223D63
692B	椫	8-9188					
692C	椬					E-652E	223D50
692D	椭	0-4554					274553
692E	椮					E-3C40	
692F	椯	3-3430			DDF2	2-4378	
6930	椰	0-5012	0-6031	0-6911	B7A6	1-644C	214524
6931	椱	3-3434	1-3629			E-4165	
6932	椲	5-3532			DDF0	2-4376	223E66
6933	椳	3-3428	1-3630		DDDB	2-4361	223E7E
6934	椴	0-7318	0-3846	1-6070	DDE0	2-4366	223F3A
6935	椵	3-3446	1-3631		DDD9	2-435F	
6936	椶		0-6004	1-7731		E-4177	2D446B
6937	椷				DDBC	2-4372	223E73
6938	椸	3-3443	1-3632		DDCB	2-4351	223E55
6939	椹	0-7309	0-6027	1-8105	DDD2	2-4358	223E6E
693A	椺						
693B	椻	5-3651	1-3633		DDEA	2-4370	
693C	椼	5-3668			DDF4	2-437A	
693D	椽	0-2010	0-6029	0-7043	DDDC	2-4362	223F32
693E	椾					E-4168	2D502B
693F	椿	0-2027	0-3656	0-8581	DDCF	2-4355	223E60
6940	楀	3-3436			DDE2	2-4368	
6941	楁	5-3680			DDE7	2-436D	
6942	楂	0-7311	1-3634	1-6746	DDD3	2-4359	2D443A
6943	楃	5-3681				E-416B	
6944	楄	3-3445			DDE4	2-436A	223F3D
6945	楅	3-3421	1-3635		DDD0	2-4356	223E64
6946	楆	5-3654				E-415D	
6947	楇	3-3357				E-4175	
6948	楈	5-3683			DDD7	2-435D	223E6B
6949	楉	3-3377	1-3636		DDD8	2-435E	
694A	楊	1-4978	0-4544	0-6937	B7A8	1-644E	21452A
694B	楋	5-3652			DDEB	2-4371	
694C	楌	5-3677			DDE9	2-436F	
694D	楍					E-4173	
694E	楎	3-3334	1-3637		DDCC	2-4352	223E7B
694F	楏	5-3656		1-5927	DDEE	2-4374	
6950	楐	5-3661				E-4174	
6951	楑	5-3684			DDEF	2-4375	
6952	楒	5-3662			DDF1	2-4377	223F21
6953	楓	1-2367	0-4186	0-8903	B7AC	1-6452	21452F
6954	楔	0-4808	0-6024	0-6459	B7A4	1-644A	214523
6955	楕	3-3422	0-3442	0-8675		E-416F	4B4553
6956	楖	3-3370			D5B8	2-357A	
6957	楗	0-7305	1-3638	0-4381	DDD4	2-435A	223E5F
6958	楘	3-3448			DDE6	2-436C	223E5D
6959	楙	3-3447	0-6030	0-5774	DDD5	2-435B	2D6468
695A	楚	0-1994	0-3331	0-8502	B7A1	1-6447	214527
695B	楛	3-3376	1-3639		B7B1	1-6457	223F25
695C	楜		0-6021		DDED	2-4373	4B533B
695D	楝	0-7312	0-6034	1-6245	B7AF	1-6455	223E65
695E	楞	0-3267	0-6033	0-5549	B7AB	1-6451	21452C
695F	楟	3-3440			DDCA	2-4350	
6960	楠	0-7310	0-3879	0-4988	B7A3	1-6449	214528
6961	楡		0-6032	0-7488		E-4179	
6962	楢	3-3444	0-3874	0-7489	DDCD	2-4353	223E58
6963	楣	0-7325	1-3640	0-5819	B7B0	1-6456	223E6A
6964	楤	5-3671	1-3641			E-4178	
6965	楥		1-3642	1-7344	DDDD	2-4363	
6966	楦	0-7324	1-3643		DDC9	2-434F	283F30
6967	楧	5-3621				E-4176	
6968	楨	1-7269	1-3644	0-7963	B7A9	1-644F	21452B
6969	楩	3-3435	1-3645		DDE1	2-4367	223F3B
696A	楪	3-3419	0-6036	1-7645	DDD1	2-4357	223E70
696B	楫	0-7314	0-6023	0-8179	B7AA	1-6450	214529
696C	楬	3-3427	1-3646	1-5534	DDDA	2-4360	223E7A
696D	業	1-5021	0-2240	0-6986	B77E	1-6446	21452D
696E	楮	0-7290	0-6026	0-7831	B4D8	1-5F7D	223E69
696F	楯	3-3438	0-2961	0-6668	DDE3	2-4369	223F3E
6970	楰	3-3386	1-3647		D9BF	2-3C62	
6971	楱	0-7308	1-3648		DDCE	2-4354	223E61
6972	楲	3-3423	1-3649				
6973	楳		0-3964	1-6416		E-416D	2D4466
6974	楴	3-3442	0-6028		DDE8	2-436E	223E53
6975	極	1-2811	0-2243	0-4831	B7A5	1-644B	214526
6976	楶	5-3676			DDE5	2-436B	
6977	楷	0-3112	0-6020	0-9012	B7A2	1-6448	214525
6978	楸	0-7317	0-6022	0-8549	DDDF	2-4365	223F35
6979	楹	0-7326	0-6019	0-7119	B7AD	1-6453	21452E
697A	楺	5-3685	1-3650		DDD6	2-435C	
697B	楻	5-3667	1-3651		DDF3	2-4379	223F37
697C	楼	0-3405	0-4716			E-416A	27454A
697D	楽		0-1958			E-417B	2D454E
697E	楾		0-6025				695C39
697F	楿		1-3652				

Code	Char	G	J	K	B	C	A
6980	榀	0-7315	1-3653				223E7D
6981	榁		0-6035				695C43
6982	概	0-2437	0-1921		B7A7	1-644D	214545
6983	榃	3-5876			DEC6	2-452C	
6984	榄	0-7313					274571
6985	榅	3-3426				E-4172	
6986	榆	0-5160			B7AE	1-6454	214530
6987	榇	0-7320					284337
6988	榈	0-7321					27456A
6989	榉	0-7323					284359
698A	榊		0-2671				223F44
698B	榋						
698C	榌						
698D	榍	0-7339	1-3654		E24A	2-4A70	223F59
698E	榎	5-3703	0-1761	1-5508	E248	2-4A6E	223F6A
698F	榏	3-3477				E-473A	
6990	榐	3-3482			E25E	2-4B26	
6991	榑	5-3701	0-6052	1-6625	E246	2-4A6C	223F5A
6992	榒		1-3655			E-473D	
6993	榓	5-3721			E258	2-4A7E	
6994	榔	0-3238	0-4717	1-6212	B77D	1-6445	214534
6995	榕	0-7337	0-6055	0-7330	BA5F	1-6928	214532
6996	榖	3-4717	1-3656		E242	2-4A68	22454D
6997	榗	3-3459			E25D	2-4B25	
6998	榘	0-7316	1-3657	1-5857		E-4751	2D4E24
6999	榙	5-3648			E247	2-4A6D	
699A	榚	5-3715			E255	2-4A7B	
699B	榛	0-7327	0-3126	0-8246	BA64	1-692D	214538
699C	榜	0-1681	0-6054	0-5920	BA5D	1-6926	214533
699D	榝	3-3324				E-474E	
699E	榞	5-3704			E25B	2-4B23	223F65
699F	榟			1-7552		E-4746	
69A0	榠	3-3481	0-6053		E240	2-4A66	223F45
69A1	榡	5-3689	1-3658		E25A	2-4B22	
69A2	榢	5-3718				E-4747	
69A3	榣	3-3472			BA6F	1-6938	22402D
69A4	榤	5-3710		1-5610	E251	2-4A77	22402E
69A5	榥	3-3465	1-3659	0-9246	E261	2-4B29	223F75
69A6	榦		1-3660	1-5525	BA6D	1-6936	45304C
69A7	榧	0-7328	0-6050	0-6178	E249	2-4A6F	223F61
69A8	榨	0-5305	1-3661		BA5E	1-6927	214531
69A9	榩	5-3706			E24B	2-4A71	
69AA	榪	1-7231			E259	2-4B21	223F5C
69AB	榫	0-7330	1-3662		BA67	1-6930	21453C
69AC	榬	3-3451			E244	2-4A6A	
69AD	榭	0-7331	1-3663	1-6747	BA6B	1-6934	21453E
69AE	榮	1-4057	0-6038	0-7120	BA61	1-692A	214537
69AF	榯	3-3352	1-3664		E24D	2-4A73	
69B0	榰	3-3452		1-7792	E243	2-4A69	
69B1	榱	0-7333	0-6067	1-8021	E1FC	2-4A63	223F46
69B2	榲		0-6037			E-473E	2E3F2D
69B3	榳	5-3674			E257	2-4A7D	
69B4	榴	0-3381	0-6056	0-5520	BA68	1-6931	214541
69B5	榵	5-3644			E260	2-4B28	
69B6	榶	3-3476			E1FD	2-4A64	
69B7	榷	0-4022	1-3665	1-5826	BA65	1-692E	214536
69B8	榸	3-3450	1-3666				
69B9	榹	3-3470			E253	2-4A79	
69BA	榺		1-3667			E-6352	
69BB	榻	0-7329	0-6048	0-8720	BA66	1-692F	21453B
69BC	榼	3-3454	1-3668	1-8308	E245	2-4A6B	223F60
69BD	榽	3-3474			E250	2-4A76	
69BE	榾	3-3432	0-6043	1-5729	E24C	2-4A72	223F77
69BF	榿	1-7271	0-6040		E24E	2-4A74	224027
69C0	槀			1-5680		E-4743	
69C1	槁	0-7334	0-6041	0-4530	BA60	1-6929	214535
69C2	槂	5-3585			E25F	2-4B27	
69C3	槃	3-3471	0-6049	0-5873	BA6E	1-6937	224038
69C4	槄	3-3473			E24F	2-4A75	
69C5	槅	3-3462	1-3669			E-473B	2D4444
69C6	槆	3-3420			E262	2-4B2A	
69C7	槇		0-8402	1-7593			4C3F68
69C8	槈	5-3702	1-3670			E-473C	
69C9	槉	5-3712			E1FE	2-4A65	
69CA	槊	0-7335	0-6046	1-6760	E254	2-4A7A	223F51
69CB	構	1-2525	0-2529	0-4716	BA63	1-692C	214539
69CC	槌	0-7319	0-3640	0-8757	BA6C	1-6935	21453D
69CD	槍	1-3925	0-3368	0-8370	BA6A	1-6933	214540
69CE	槎	0-7322	0-6044	1-7837	E241	2-4A67	223F50
69CF	槏	3-3478			E256	2-4A7C	
69D0	槐	0-2717	0-6039	0-4657	BA69	1-6932	21453F
69D1	槑		1-3671			E-4745	223F78
69D2	槒					E-4748	
69D3	槓		0-6042	1-5736	BA62	1-692B	21453A
69D4	槔	0-7332			E252	2-4A78	224034
69D5	槕					E-474D	223F7E
69D6	槖	5-2301	1-3672			E-4744	223F6D
69D7	槗		1-3673				
69D8	様		0-4545			E-4C54	4B4544
69D9	槙	3-3460	0-4374		E25C	2-4B24	223F68
69DA	槚	8-9206					
69DB	槛	0-2887					274566
69DC	槜	3-3468					
69DD	槝		0-6047				695C4F
69DE	槞		0-6057				4C4339
69DF	槟	0-7336					274564
69E0	槠	0-7338					28433A
69E1	槡					E-474C	
69E2	槢	3-3512	1-3674		E5D5	2-507C	
69E3	槣	5-3744				E-4742	2E3645
69E4	槤	5-3591			E5D1	2-5078	
69E5	槥	3-3485	1-3675	1-8373	E5CD	2-5074	22404C
69E6	槦	3-3506		1-7309	E5E1	2-512A	224046
69E7	槧	1-7293	0-6065	1-7860	E5DE	2-5127	224056
69E8	槨		0-6058	0-4610	BCCD	1-6D37	214543
69E9	槩			1-5575		E-4C64	22404D
69EA	槪			0-4340		E-4C60	4B4545
69EB	槫	3-3257	0-6071		E5E5	2-512E	224057
69EC	槬	3-3492			E5D4	2-507B	
69ED	槭	0-7342	0-6069	1-6802	BCD8	1-6D42	224064
69EE	槮	3-3414	1-3676		E5DB	2-5124	22407C
69EF	槯	3-3502	1-3677			E-4C4F	
69F0	槰	5-3709				E-4C51	224123
69F1	槱	3-3491	1-3678		E5D0	2-5077	22405B
69F2	槲	0-7346	0-6064	1-5710	E5DA	2-5123	224124
69F3	槳	1-2916	1-3679		BCD5	1-6D3F	21454C
69F4	槴	5-3746			E5EE	2-5137	
69F5	槵	3-3501	1-3680				
69F6	槶	5-3626			E5EB	2-5134	223F7A
69F7	槷	3-3487			E5DD	2-5126	
69F8	槸	5-3724			E5CE	2-5075	
69F9	槹		0-6063	1-5681		E-4C5F	22416C
69FA	槺	5-3741				E-4C57	
69FB	槻	3-3374	0-3648	0-4807	E5E2	2-512B	395829
69FC	槼				E5E4	2-512D	224050
69FD	槽	0-1859	0-3369	0-8043	BCD1	1-6D3B	214548
69FE	槾	5-3732	1-3681		E5D8	2-5121	
69FF	槿	0-7340	0-6061	0-4839	E5D3	2-507A	22405F

6A0

		G	J	K	B	C	A
0	樀	3-3507	1-3682	1-7577	E5CA	2-5071	224041
1	樁	1-5514	1-3683		BCCE	1-6D38	214546
2	樂	1-3254	0-6059	0-6837	BCD6	1-6D40	21454E
3	樃		1-3684				
4	樄	5-3615			E5E7	2-5130	
5	樅	1-7240	0-6066	1-7732	BCD7	1-6D41	21454F
6	樆	3-3475			E5CB	2-5072	
7	樇	5-3707			E5ED	2-5136	
8	樈	5-3743			E5E0	2-5129	
9	樉	3-3493			E5E6	2-512F	
A	樊	0-2314	0-6072	0-5964	BCD4	1-6D3E	21454D
B	樋	3-3484	0-4085	1-8163		E-4C4D	22404B
C	樌	5-3642	0-6078			E-4C50	224075
D	樍	5-3619			E5E3	2-512C	
E	樎	3-3510				E-4C47	
F	樏	3-3494	1-3685		E5EA	2-5133	224076

6A2

		G	J	K	B	C	A
0	樠	3-3456	1-3690		E5D2	2-5079	224060
1	模	0-3603	0-4447	0-5728	BCD2	1-6D3C	21454B
2	樢	3-3287	0-6088			E-4C52	2F252D
3	樣	1-4989	0-6075	0-6938	BCCB	1-6D35	214544
4	樤	5-3609	1-3691			E-4C62	
5	樥	5-3693			E5E9	2-5132	
6	樦	5-3736			E5EC	2-5135	
7	樧				E5D9	2-5122	
8	樨	0-7356	1-3692		E9CA	2-5755	22413F
9	権		0-2402			E-4C5E	4B4570
A	横	0-2665	0-1803			E-4C59	4B4556
B	樫		0-1963	1-5621			22405E
C	樬	3-3503				E-4C61	
D	樭					E-6530	224068
E	樮		0-6051				695C53
F	樯	0-7341					28422B

6A4

		G	J	K	B	C	A
0	橀	5-3770			E5DF	2-5128	
1	橁	5-3765			E9CE	2-5759	
2	橂					E-5128	
3	橃	5-3562		1-6560		E-512B	224139
4	橄	0-7347	0-6077	0-4284	BEF1	1-707A	214554
5	橅	5-3531	1-3706			E-5140	
6	橆		1-3707		E9DD	2-5768	
7	橇	0-3933	0-6082	1-8070	BEF5	1-707E	214559
8	橈	1-7267	0-6086	0-7290	BEF8	1-7123	224140
9	橉	3-3529	1-3708		E9C0	2-574B	
A	橊		1-3709	1-6339		E-513B	
B	橋	1-3937	0-2222	0-4673	BEF4	1-707D	21455B
C	橌	5-3611				E-5131	
D	橍	5-3610			E9DB	2-5766	
E	橎	5-3766	1-3710		E9DC	2-5767	
F	橏	3-3527			E9D2	2-575D	

6A6

		G	J	K	B	C	A
0	橠	5-3768			E9D6	2-5761	
1	橡	0-4780	0-3843	0-6346	BEF3	1-707C	21455A
2	橢	1-4554	0-6083	1-8116	BEF2	1-707B	214553
3	橣	5-3772				E-5127	224129
4	橤		1-3717		E9D0	2-575B	22416D
5	橥	0-7345					4C433F
6	橦	3-3525	0-6085	1-6156	E9BF	2-574A	2D3C5F
7	橧	3-3531	1-3718		E9C1	2-574C	224137
8	橨	3-3418			E9C3	2-574E	
9	橩	5-3752			E9D5	2-5760	
A	橪	3-3523	1-3719		E9CF	2-575A	
B	橫			0-9284	BEEE	1-7077	214556
C	橬	3-3520				E-512E	
D	橭	5-3753			E9C6	2-5751	
E	橮	5-3672				E-5132	
F	橯	5-3587			E9D4	2-575F	

6A1

		G	J	K	B	C	A
0	樐					E-4C5B	45456D
1	樑	8-1378	1-3686	0-5358	BCD9	1-6D43	22403E
2	樒	5-3745	0-6073	1-6515		E-4C56	22403D
3	樓	1-3405	0-6076	0-5507	BCD3	1-6D3D	21454A
4	樔	5-3749	0-6070	1-6876	E5DC	2-5125	224128
5	樕	3-3490	1-3687		E5CF	2-5076	
6	樖	5-3738			E5EF	2-5138	
7	樗	0-7343	0-3584	0-7832	E5CC	2-5073	224054
8	樘	0-7344			E5E8	2-5131	22406E
9	標	1-1774	0-4124	0-8886	BCD0	1-6D3A	214547
A	樚	5-3742	1-3688			E-4C4A	
B	樛	3-3513	0-6060	1-5928	E5D6	2-507D	224067
C	樜	3-3504				E-4C49	
D	樝	5-3731	1-3689		E5D7	2-507E	224072
E	樞	1-4264	0-6068	0-8550	BCCF	1-6D39	214549
F	樟	0-5333	0-3032	0-7773	BCCC	1-6D36	214542

6A3

		G	J	K	B	C	A
0	樰		1-3693				
1	樱	0-5103					27456F
2	樲	3-3417	1-3694		E9C2	2-574D	22413B
3	樳	3-3335				E-512C	22413A
4	樴		1-3701		E9BE	2-5749	
5	樵	0-7352	0-3033	0-8503	BEF6	1-7121	21455C
6	樶	5-3759	0-6080			E-513C	224153
7	樷		1-3702			E-5138	
8	樸	1-3851	0-6087	0-5852	BEEB	1-7074	214558
9	樹	1-4287	0-2889	0-6607	BEF0	1-7079	214555
A	樺	1-7275	0-1982	0-9192	BEEC	1-7075	214557
B	樻	5-3660	1-3703	1-5914	E9CC	2-5757	
C	樼	5-3774			E9D7	2-5762	
D	樽	0-7355	0-3514	0-8160	BEEA	1-7073	214550
E	樾	0-7348	1-3704		E9C4	2-574F	224145
F	樿	3-3407	1-3705		E9CD	2-5758	224158

6A5

		G	J	K	B	C	A
0	橐	0-7350	1-3711	1-8126	E9D1	2-575C	224141
1	橑	3-3519	1-3712		E9C9	2-5754	22414F
2	橒		1-3713	0-7388		E-5129	224142
3	橓	5-3767		0-6669		E-513E	
4	橔	3-3524			E9D3	2-575E	
5	橕	5-3758	1-3714		E9DA	2-5765	
6	橖	5-3757	1-3715		E9D9	2-5764	224151
7	橗	3-3488				E-512F	
8	橘	0-7357	0-2144	0-4825	BEEF	1-7078	214551
9	橙	0-1940	0-6084	0-5282	BEED	1-7076	214552
A	橚	3-3413		1-6934	E9CB	2-5756	22413C
B	橛	0-7351	1-3716		E9C8	2-5753	224147
C	橜					E-5144	22414B
D	橝	3-3518			E9C5	2-5750	
E	橞	5-3755			E9D8	2-5763	22414A
F	機	1-2790	0-2101	0-4906	BEF7	1-7122	21455D

6A7

		G	J	K	B	C	A
0	橰					E-5141	
1	橱	0-1987	1-3720			E-513A	4B4569
2	橲		0-6079				224143
3	橳		1-3721				
4	橴						
5	橵			1-6767			
6	橶				E9C7	2-5752	
7	橷					E-6531	224146
8	橸		0-6081				695C71
9	橹	0-7354					27456D
A	橺					E-6532	224156
B	橻						
C	橼	0-7358					284335
D	橽	5-3570				E-5475	22417E
E	橾	3-3541	1-3722		C0CF	1-7378	224236
F	橿	3-3537	0-1964	1-5561	ED45	2-5D31	224222

6A8

	Char	G	J	K	B	C	A
0	檀	0-4420	0-3541	0-5110	C0C8	1-7371	21455E
1	檁		1-3723		ECF5	2-5D22	2E4174
2	檂	5-3582				E-547B	
3	檃		1-3724		ED41	2-5D2D	
4	檄	0-4713	0-6092	0-4412	C0CA	1-7373	214560
5	檅	5-3574			ED48	2-5D34	
6	檆	5-3791	1-3725			E-5521	
7	檇		1-3726		ECFC	2-5D29	22424A
8	檈	3-3542				E-547C	
9	檉	1-7263	1-3727	0-7964	ECF7	2-5D24	224223
A	檊	3-3536				E-5476	
B	檋	3-3457	1-3728				
C	檌	5-3785			ED49	2-5D35	
D	檍	3-3545	0-6090	0-6969	ECF3	2-5C7E	224173
E	檎	0-7353	0-2473	0-4853	ECFE	2-5D2B	22424B
F	檏					E-5527	

6AA

	Char	G	J	K	B	C	A
0	檠	0-7349	0-6091	1-5648	C0D2	1-737B	224242
1	檡	3-3303			ECFA	2-5D27	
2	檢	1-2876	0-6093	0-4394	C0CB	1-7374	214561
3	檣	1-7341	0-6094	0-7774	C0CE	1-7377	22422B
4	檤	5-3771			ED43	2-5D2F	
5	檥	5-3529	1-3734		ECF6	2-5D23	224177
6	檦	5-3782			ED46	2-5D32	
7	檧	3-3517				E-5478	
8	檨	3-3528			ED42	2-5D2E	224175
9	檩	0-7361					
A	檪		0-6112			E-5529	4C4333
B	檫	0-7363	1-3735			E-5774	224251
C	檬	0-3542	0-6108		C263	1-764F	214568
D	檭	5-3733			EFE7	2-6173	
E	檮	3-3337	0-5977	1-6131	C268	1-7654	224257
F	檯	1-8877	1-3736		C269	1-7655	223B7D

6AC

	Char	G	J	K	B	C	A
0	櫀	5-3793				E-577D	
1	櫁	5-3806	0-6074			E-577A	2E403D
2	櫂		0-6105	0-5202	C267	1-7653	39447D
3	櫃	1-2581	0-6104	0-4786	C264	1-7650	214565
4	櫄	5-3801				E-5822	
5	櫅	3-3331			EFDD	2-6169	
6	櫆	3-3543	1-3743		EFE1	2-616D	
7	櫇	5-3748			EFE5	2-6171	
8	櫈		1-3745			E-577B	224255
9	櫉		1-3744				2D4569
A	櫊					E-6533	224264
B	櫋	3-3556			F251	2-655C	
C	櫌	5-3809	1-3746		F24E	2-6559	224325
D	櫍	3-3388			F257	2-6562	224334
E	櫎	3-3248				E-5A44	
F	櫏				F256	2-6561	

6AE

	Char	G	J	K	B	C	A
0	櫠	3-3401			F24D	2-6558	
1	櫡	3-3550			EFE0	2-616C	
2	櫢	5-3790				E-5A48	
3	櫣	3-3458				E-5A46	
4	櫤		1-3753				
5	櫥				C36F	1-783C	214569
6	櫦					E-6534	224279
7	櫧	1-7338	1-3754		F24C	2-6557	22433A
8	櫨	1-7251	0-4007		F456	2-6924	224345
9	櫩	3-3509				E-5C49	
A	櫪	1-7232	0-6114	1-6240	F455	2-6923	224340
B	櫫				F255	2-6560	22433F
C	櫬	1-7320	1-3755	1-8093	C468	1-7973	224337
D	櫭	3-3552				E-5775	22427E
E	櫮	5-3813			F459	2-6927	
F	櫯				F45A	2-6928	

6A9

	Char	G	J	K	B	C	A
0	檐	0-7360	0-6089	1-7947	C0D1	1-737A	224247
1	檑	0-7359	1-3729		ED44	2-5D30	224224
2	檒	5-4848			ED4A	2-5D36	22422A
3	檓	5-3787			ECFD	2-5D2A	
4	檔	1-2121		1-6104	C0C9	1-7372	21455F
5	檕				ED40	2-5D2C	
6	檖	3-3530			ECF4	2-5D21	224179
7	檗	0-7362	0-6101	0-5992	C0D0	1-7379	2D563F
8	檘					E-5523	4B563F
9	檙	5-3760				E-547A	224234
A	檚	5-3779			ED47	2-5D33	
B	檛	3-3316	1-3730		ECF9	2-5D26	224237
C	檜	1-7277	0-5956	0-9270	C0CC	1-7375	214562
D	檝		1-3731	1-7784		E-5524	224235
E	檞	3-3544	1-3732		ECFB	2-5D28	224249
F	檟	3-3463	1-3733	1-5509	ECF8	2-5D25	224226

6AB

	Char	G	J	K	B	C	A
0	檰	3-3514	1-3737			E-5777	
1	檱		1-3738			E-5821	
2	檲					E-5776	
3	檳	1-7336	0-6107	0-6217	C262	1-764E	214564
4	檴	3-3535	1-3739		EFE6	2-6172	224268
5	檵	3-3553				E-5778	
6	檶	5-3590		1-7155	EFE3	2-616F	
7	檷	3-3290			EFE4	2-6170	
8	檸	1-3691	0-6106		C266	1-7652	214563
9	檹	5-3805			EFDE	2-616A	
A	檺				EFE2	2-616E	
B	檻	1-2887	0-6103	0-8967	C265	1-7651	214566
C	檼	5-3803		1-7419		E-577E	
D	檽	3-3549	1-3740		EFDF	2-616B	
E	檾	5-7348	1-3741			E-5779	
F	檿	3-1627	1-3742	1-7154		E-5823	22425D

6AD

	Char	G	J	K	B	C	A
0	櫐		1-3747		F254	2-655F	
1	櫑	5-3810	0-6110		F24F	2-655A	224328
2	櫒					E-5A4F	
3	櫓	1-7354	0-4706	0-5448	C372	1-783F	21456D
4	櫔	5-3551	1-3748			E-5A45	
5	櫕	5-3750	1-3749			E-5A4E	
6	櫖		1-3750				
7	櫗	3-3546				E-5A47	
8	櫘	5-3807				E-5A4D	
9	櫙	3-3341			F250	2-655B	
A	櫚	1-7321	0-6113	0-5374	C371	1-783E	21456A
B	櫛	1-7246	0-2291	0-8178	C0CD	1-7376	21456C
C	櫜	3-3554	1-3751	1-5682	F253	2-655E	
D	櫝	1-7292	1-3752	1-6142	C370	1-783D	21456B
E	櫞	1-7358	0-6109	1-7141	F258	2-6563	224335
F	櫟	1-7261	0-6111	1-6239	F252	2-655D	224333

6AF

	Char	G	J	K	B	C	A
0	櫰	3-3560	1-3756		F454	2-6922	
1	櫱		1-3757		F458	2-6926	224344
2	櫲	5-3812	1-3758				
3	櫳	1-7248			F453	2-6921	224339
4	櫴	5-3781				E-5C47	
5	櫵					E-6535	224348
6	櫶	5-3818		0-9043			
7	櫷						
8	櫸	1-7323			F5D1	2-6B5F	224359
9	櫹	3-3489			F457	2-6925	
A	櫺	5-3819	0-6118		C4E7	1-7A72	224350
B	櫻	1-5103	0-6115	0-6901	C4E5	1-7A70	21456F
C	櫼	3-3561	1-3759	1-7948	F5CF	2-6B5D	
D	櫽	3-3511	1-3760			E-5E35	22434E
E	櫾	5-3820				E-5E34	
F	櫿					E-5E33	

Code	Char	G	J	K	B	C	A
6B00	欀	3-3563			F5D2	2-6B60	
6B01	欁	5-3720				E-5E37	224352
6B02	欂	3-3559	1-3761	1-6518	F5CE	2-6B5C	
6B03	欃	3-3562	1-3762	1-7861	F5D0	2-6B5E	224358
6B04	欄	1-3224	0-4583	0-5317	C4E6	1-7A71	21456E
6B05	欅		0-6116				4C4359
6B06	欆	5-3548	1-3763			E-5F4F	
6B07	欇	3-3455	1-3764			E-5F4E	
6B08	欈	5-3822			F6E5	2-6D53	
6B09	欉		1-3765		F6E6	2-6D54	224360
6B0A	權	1-4008	0-6062	0-4777	C576	1-7B62	214570
6B0B	欋	3-3564			F6E4	2-6D52	
6B0C	欌			0-7775			
6B0D	欍					E-6536	22435F
6B0E	欎					E-6537	224361
6B0F	欏	1-7301	1-3766		F7E2	2-6F31	
6B10	欐	3-3346	1-3767		C5CF	1-7C3B	
6B11	欑	5-3816	1-3768	1-7848	F7E0	2-6F2F	224367
6B12	欒	1-7279	0-6119	0-5318	F7E1	2-6F30	394944
6B13	欓	3-3464			F8AC	2-703A	
6B14	欔	3-3566				E-6074	
6B15	欕						
6B16	欖	1-7313	0-6120	0-5328	C656	1-7D23	214571
6B17	欗		1-3769		F8F3	2-7123	22436E
6B18	欘	3-3533			F8F1	2-7121	
6B19	欙				F8F2	2-7122	22436D
6B1A	欚	3-3567			F8F4	2-7124	
6B1B	欛	5-3824	1-3770			E-6140	
6B1C	欜	3-3568				E-6165	
6B1D	欝		0-1721			E-6141	2D616A
6B1E	欞	1-7289	1-3771	1-6264	F9BB	2-722B	224372
6B1F	欟		0-6122				695D36
6B20	欠	0-3923	0-2371	0-9366	A4ED	1-454E	4B5227
6B21	次	0-2046	0-2801	0-8313	A6B8	1-4839	214573
6B22	欢	0-2722				E-2379	274621
6B23	欣	0-4832	0-2253	0-9359	AA59	1-4E3C	214574
6B24	欤	0-7603	1-3772				27457E
6B25	欥	5-4225			CCE9	2-274A	
6B26	欦	3-4618				E-2953	
6B27	欧	0-3723	0-1804			E-2954	27457C
6B28	欨	5-4807	1-3773		CF64	2-2B46	
6B29	欩	3-4624				E-6269	
6B2A	欪	3-4623				E-2D3C	
6B2B	欫		1-3774			E-3166	
6B2C	欬		1-3775	1-8320	D1F5	2-2F77	22437E
6B2D	欭	3-4632			D1F7	2-2F79	
6B2E	欮	5-4811				E-3165	
6B2F	欯	3-4627	1-3776		D1F6	2-2F78	
6B30	欰	5-6870				E-3167	
6B31	欱	3-4634			D1F8	2-2F7A	
6B32	欲	0-5191	0-4563	0-7316	B1FD	1-5B43	273F3C
6B33	欳				D5D7	2-363B	
6B34	欴				D1F9	2-2F7B	
6B35	欵		1-3777			E-3662	22442A
6B36	欶	3-4636	1-3778		D5D6	2-363A	
6B37	欷	0-7604	0-6124	1-8527	D5D8	2-363C	22442C
6B38	欸	3-4638	0-6123	1-7060	D5D9	2-363D	2D3642
6B39	欹	0-7605	0-6126	1-7440	D9DA	2-3C7D	224432
6B3A	欺	0-3859	0-2129	0-4907	B4DB	1-6022	214577
6B3B	欻	3-4644	1-3779	1-8481	D9DB	2-3C7E	22442D
6B3C	欼	5-4815			D9DD	2-3D22	
6B3D	欽	1-3953	0-2254	0-9367	B4DC	1-6023	214578
6B3E	款	0-3178	0-2030	0-4619	B4DA	1-6021	214576
6B3F	欿	3-4642	1-3780	1-5545	D9DC	2-3D21	224435
6B40	歀	5-4817				E-417D	22443A
6B41	歁	3-4646			DDFA	2-4422	224438
6B42	歂	5-4819			DDF8	2-437E	22443B
6B43	歃	0-7606	0-6129	1-6781	DDF7	2-437D	22443C
6B44	歄	3-4637				E-417C	
6B45	歅	5-4818			DDF6	2-437C	
6B46	歆	0-7607	1-3781	0-9368	DDF5	2-437B	224437
6B47	歇	0-4810	0-6128	0-9046	B7B2	1-6458	214579
6B48	歈	3-4650			DDF9	2-4421	22443E
6B49	歉	0-3924	0-6130	1-5637	BA70	1-6939	21457A
6B4A	歊	3-9180	1-3782		E263	2-4B2B	22443F
6B4B	歋	5-4821			E265	2-4B2D	
6B4C	歌	0-2472	0-1846	0-4216	BA71	1-693A	21457B
6B4D	歍	3-4619	1-3783		E264	2-4B2C	
6B4E	歎		0-3523	0-8707	BCDB	1-6D45	224446
6B4F	歏	3-4654				E-4C66	
6B50	歐	1-3723	0-6131	0-4717	BCDA	1-6D44	21457C
6B51	歑	5-4825			E5F0	2-5139	
6B52	歒		1-3784			E-4C65	
6B53	歓		0-2031			E-4C67	4B4621
6B54	歔	5-4824	0-6133	1-8332	E9DF	2-576A	22444C
6B55	歕	5-4816			E9DE	2-5769	22444E
6B56	歖	5-4828	1-3785		E9E0	2-576B	
6B57	歗	5-4814				E-5146	22444A
6B58	歘	5-4829	1-3786			E-5145	
6B59	歙	0-7608	0-6132	1-8518	BEF9	1-7124	21457D
6B5A	歚			1-6830			
6B5B	歛		0-6134	1-5546	ED4B	2-5D37	334256
6B5C	歜	3-4656			C0D3	1-737C	224451
6B5D	歝	5-4808	1-3787			E-552B	
6B5E	歞	3-4657			EFE8	2-6174	224453
6B5F	歟	1-7603	0-6135	0-7002	C26A	1-7656	21457E
6B60	歠	3-4659	1-3788	1-7939	F259	2-6564	224454
6B61	歡	1-2722	0-6136	0-9222	C577	1-7B63	214621
6B62	止	0-5425	0-2763	0-8213	A4EE	1-454F	2D353C
6B63	正	0-5393	0-3221	0-7965	A5BF	1-465F	214623
6B64	此	0-2043	0-2601	0-8314	A6B9	1-483A	214624
6B65	步	0-1829		0-6038	A842	1-4A63	214625
6B66	武	0-4668	0-4180	0-5775	AA5A	1-4E3D	214627
6B67	歧	0-3871	1-3789	1-5982	AA5B	1-4E3E	4B3B67
6B68	歨	5-4064				E-2955	
6B69	歩		0-4266			E-2956	
6B6A	歪	0-4565	0-4736	0-7264	AC6E	1-5171	214628
6B6B	歫	5-4063	1-3790			E-2D3D	22445B
6B6C	歬	5-4067				E-3168	22445D
6B6D	歭	5-4066			D1FA	2-2F7C	
6B6E	歮	5-4069	1-3791			E-3C49	22445F
6B6F	歯		0-2785			E-3C47	336321
6B70	歰	5-4075	1-3792				
6B71	歱	5-4074				E-417E	224461
6B72	歲	1-4374		0-6508	B7B3	1-6459	214629
6B73	歳		0-2648			E-4221	
6B74	歴		0-4682			E-4753	4B462A
6B75	歵	3-3888	1-3793				
6B76	歶				E6D1	2-5259	
6B77	歷	1-3290		0-5386	BEFA	1-7125	21462A
6B78	歸	1-2573	0-6137	0-4793	C26B	1-7657	21462B
6B79	歹	0-2085	0-6138		A4EF	1-4550	21462C
6B7A	歺					E-2253	2D462C
6B7B	死	0-4332	0-2764	0-6261	A6BA	1-483B	21462D
6B7C	歼	0-2863					274638
6B7D	歽		1-3794				
6B7E	歾	5-3927	1-3801		CCEB	2-274C	22446B
6B7F	歿		0-6139	0-5749	AA5C	1-4E3F	21462E

6B8

	Char	G	J	K	B	C	A
0	殀		0-6140	1-7288	CCEA	2-274B	2D3929
1	殁	0-7366				E-2958	4B462E
2	殂	0-7367	1-3802	1-7702	CF65	2-2B47	224471
3	殃	0-4974	0-6142	0-6874	AC6F	1-5172	21462F
4	殄	0-7369	0-6141	0-8247	CF66	2-2B48	224473
5	殅	5-3931	1-3803				
6	殆	0-2089	0-4356	0-8731	AC70	1-5173	214630
7	殇	0-7368					274635
8	殈	3-3686			D1FC	2-2F7E	
9	殉	0-4919	0-2962	0-6670	AEEE	1-5632	214632
A	殊	0-4266	0-2876	0-6608	AEED	1-5631	214631
B	残	0-1848	0-2736			E-316A	274633
C	殌				D5DE	2-3642	
D	殍	0-7372	0-6143	1-8241	D5DC	2-3640	224479
E	殎				D5DD	2-3641	
F	殏				D5DB	2-363F	

6BA

	Char	G	J	K	B	C	A
0	殠	5-3954	1-3807		E268	2-4B30	
1	殡	0-7375				E-4754	274637
2	殢	3-3709	1-3808	1-7964	E5F3	2-513C	224536
3	殣	3-3715	1-3809		E5F2	2-513B	224535
4	殤	1-7368	0-6147	1-6789	BCDC	1-6D46	214635
5	殥	3-3716			E5F1	2-513A	
6	殦				E5F4	2-513D	
7	殧	3-3718			E9E1	2-576C	
8	殨	5-3946	1-3810				
9	殩		1-3811				
A	殪	0-7376	0-6148		E9E2	2-576D	224538
B	殫	1-7373	0-6149	1-8136	E9E3	2-576E	224539
C	殬		1-3812				
D	殭		1-3813	1-5562	ED4C	2-5D38	22453B
E	殮	1-7371	1-3814	0-5417	C0D4	1-737D	214636
F	殯	1-7375	0-6150	0-6218	C26C	1-7658	214637

6BC

	Char	G	J	K	B	C	A
0	毀		0-5244		B7B4	1-645A	21463D
1	毁	0-2757		0-9335		E-4226	
2	毂	0-7617					275B52
3	毃	5-8972	1-3820		E269	2-4B31	
4	毄		1-3821	1-5616	E26A	2-4B32	
5	毅	0-5067	0-2103	0-7586	BCDD	1-6D47	21463F
6	毆	1-3725	0-6156	0-4718	BCDE	1-6D48	214640
7	毇	3-4727			E9E5	2-5770	
8	毈	5-4880			E9E4	2-576F	224554
9	毉	5-4884	1-3822		EFE9	2-6175	
A	毊	5-4882			F7E3	2-6F32	
B	毋	0-4667	0-6157	0-5776	A4F0	1-4551	214641
C	毌	3-5104	1-3823		C960	2-2140	
D	母	0-3624	0-4276	0-5729	A5C0	1-4660	214642
E	毎		0-4372			E-237A	
F	每	0-3531		0-5663	A843	1-4A64	214643

6BE

	Char	G	J	K	B	C	A
0	毠				CF6A	2-2B4C	
1	毡	0-5317	1-3826			E-2D42	28464C
2	毢	5-4612			D242	2-3025	
3	毣	3-7569	1-3827		D241	2-3024	
4	毤				D1FE	2-3022	
5	毥	3-4366				E-316E	
6	毦	3-6440	1-3828		D1FD	2-3021	
7	毧		1-3829		D243	2-3026	22456F
8	毨	3-4365			D240	2-3023	224571
9	毩					E-316C	
A	毪	0-7504				E-316D	224570
B	毫	0-2633	0-6161	0-9138	B240	1-5B45	214649
C	毬		0-6160	0-4719	B241	1-5B46	2D4B45
D	毭	3-7835				E-3666	
E	毮		1-3830				
F	毯	0-4426	0-6163	1-6087	B4E0	1-6027	21464A

6B9

	Char	G	J	K	B	C	A
0	殐	3-3689				E-3664	
1	殑	3-3688		1-5967	D5DA	2-363E	
2	殒	0-7370					4B5F35
3	殓	0-7371					274636
4	殔	3-3706			D9DE	2-3D23	
5	殕	3-3704	0-6145		D9E1	2-3D26	22447B
6	殖	0-5419	0-3103	0-6754	B4DE	1-6025	214634
7	殗	3-3702	1-3804		D9DF	2-3D24	
8	殘	1-1848	0-6144	0-7749	B4DD	1-6024	214633
9	殙	3-3703			D9E0	2-3D25	224525
A	殚	0-7373					284539
B	殛	0-7374	1-3805		DDFB	2-4423	224529
C	殜	3-3708				E-4222	
D	殝	3-3713				E-6354	
E	殞	1-7370	0-6146	0-7389	E266	2-4B2E	3F5F35
F	殟	3-3710	1-3806		E267	2-4B2F	

6BB

	Char	G	J	K	B	C	A
0	殰	3-3694	1-3815		F25A	2-6565	22453D
1	殱		0-6152				4B4638
2	殲	1-2863	0-6151	0-6472	C4E8	1-7A73	214638
3	殳	0-7615	0-6153	1-6913	C95F	2-213F	22453F
4	殴	0-3725	0-1805			E-2959	274640
5	段	0-2246	0-3542	0-5111	AC71	1-5174	214639
6	殶	3-4709			CF67	2-2B49	
7	殷	0-5083	0-6154	0-7560	AEEF	1-5633	21463A
8	殸	5-4869	1-3816				
9	殹	3-4711	1-3817				
A	殺	1-4117	0-2706	0-6315	B1FE	1-5B44	21463B
B	殻	1-3139	0-1944			E-3665	33463C
C	殼	5-4872	0-6155	0-4235	B4DF	1-6026	21463C
D	殽		1-3818	1-8459	D9E2	2-3D27	224547
E	殾		1-3819			E-3C4B	
F	殿	0-2178	0-3734	0-7892	B7B5	1-645B	21463E

6BD

	Char	G	J	K	B	C	A
0	毐	3-2094			CB48	2-2448	
1	毑	3-5105				E-295A	
2	毒	0-2230	0-3839	0-5224	AC72	1-5175	214644
3	毓	0-5625	0-6158	0-7530	B7B6	1-645C	2D532C
4	比	0-1740	0-4070	0-6179	A4F1	1-4552	214646
5	毕	0-1747					274C33
6	毖	0-1749	1-3824	0-6180	CF68	2-2B4A	22455B
7	毗	0-3794		0-6181	AC73	1-5176	214647
8	毘		0-4091	0-6182	CF69	2-2B4B	2D4647
9	毙	0-1748					274257
A	毚	3-1880	1-3825	1-7862	C0D5	1-737E	224560
B	毛	0-3511	0-4451	0-5730	A4F2	1-4553	214648
C	毜					E-6538	224562
D	毝					E-6539	224563
E	毞	5-4034			CCBC	2-274D	
F	毟		0-6159				224565

6BF

	Char	G	J	K	B	C	A
0	毰	3-4374			D9E3	2-3D28	
1	毱	5-4619	1-3831				
2	毲	3-4375			D9E4	2-3D29	
3	毳	0-7505	0-6162	1-8071	D9E5	2-3D2A	22462C
4	毴	5-4617				E-3C4D	
5	毵	0-7507					284642
6	毶					E-653A	22462A
7	毷	5-4623	1-3832		DE41	2-4427	
8	毸	3-4379			DE42	2-4428	224633
9	毹	0-7508	1-3833		DE40	2-4426	224638
A	毺	5-4624				E-4228	224637
B	毻	5-4622			DDFD	2-4424	
C	毼	3-4378			DDFE	2-4425	
D	毽	0-7506			B7B7	1-645D	21464B
E	毾	3-4384			E26B	2-4B33	
F	毿	1-7507	1-3834	1-6775	E5F7	2-5140	224642

6C0

	Char	G	J	K	B	C	A
0	氀	3-4381			E5F6	2-513F	
1	氁				E5F5	2-513E	
2	氂		1-3835		E5F8	2-5141	2D4A60
3	氃	3-4389			E9E7	2-5772	
4	氄	3-4391	1-3836		E9E6	2-5771	224648
5	氅	0-7509	1-3837	1-7878	BEFB	1-7126	22464A
6	氆	0-7511			E9E8	2-5773	224644
7	氇	0-7510					284651
8	氈	1-5317	0-6165	0-7893	C0D6	1-7421	22464C
9	氉	5-4635	1-3838		ED4D	2-5D39	
A	氊					E-552D	
B	氋	3-4392			EFEA	2-6176	
C	氌	1-7510			F25B	2-6566	224651
D	氍	0-7512	1-3839		F6E7	2-6D55	224652
E	氎		1-3840				
F	氏	0-4247	0-2765	0-6811	A4F3	1-4554	21464C

6C1

	Char	G	J	K	B	C	A
0	氐	0-5621	1-3841	1-7563	A5C2	1-4662	21464E
1	民	0-3581	0-4417	0-5837	A5C1	1-4661	21464D
2	氒	5-4792	1-3842				
3	氓	0-3505	0-6166	0-5676	AA5D	1-4E40	21464F
4	气	0-3888	0-6167		C961	2-2141	274655
5	氕	0-7513			C97E	2-215F	224659
6	氖	0-3642			A6BB	1-483C	214650
7	気		0-2104				4B4655
8	氘	0-7514			C9F7	2-2258	22465A
9	氙	0-7515	1-3843		CB49	2-2449	22465B
A	氚	0-7516			CB4A	2-244A	22465C
B	氛	0-2353	0-6168	1-6651	AA5E	1-4E41	214651
C	氜	5-4640				E-295D	
D	氝	5-4641			CCED	2-274E	22465E
E	氞					E-653B	
F	氟	0-2390	1-3844		AC74	1-5177	214652

6C2

	Char	G	J	K	B	C	A
0	氠				CF6B	2-2B4D	224660
1	氡	0-7517			CF6C	2-2B4E	224662
2	氢	0-3966					274658
3	氣	1-3888	0-6170	0-4908	AEF0	1-5634	214655
4	氤	0-7519	0-6169	1-7465	AEF4	1-5638	214657
5	氥	8-1383			D244	2-3027	
6	氦	0-2604	1-3845		AEF3	1-5637	214654
7	氧	0-4985	1-3846		AEF1	1-5635	214653
8	氨	0-1617	1-3847		AEF2	1-5636	214656
9	氩	0-7518					284668
A	氪	0-7520			D5DF	2-3643	224664
B	氫	1-3966			B242	1-5B47	214658
C	氬	1-7518	1-3848		B4E3	1-602A	224668
D	氭	5-4642				E-3C4E	224666
E	氮	0-2110	1-3849		B4E1	1-6028	214659
F	氯	0-3440			B4E2	1-6029	21465B

6C3

	Char	G	J	K	B	C	A
0	氰	0-3972			D9E6	2-3D2B	224667
1	氱	5-4638				E-4229	
2	氲	0-7521				E-422A	
3	氳		1-3850	1-7231	BA72	1-693B	21465A
4	水	0-4314	0-3169	0-6609	A4F4	1-4555	21465C
5	氵	0-6763	1-3851				
6	氶	5-1624	1-3852		C9A1	2-2160	
7	氷		0-4125	0-6228		E-2257	33333C
8	永	0-5132	0-1742	0-7121	A5C3	1-4663	21465D
9	氹	5-5264				E-2254	21643F
A	氺		1-3853				
B	氻	5-5278	1-3854		C9A4	2-2163	224670
C	氼	5-5265				E-2421	
D	氽	0-5759					513B52
E	氾	8-1574	0-4037	0-5980	A5C6	1-4666	394735
F	氿	3-5115	1-3855	1-5915	C9A3	2-2162	224674

6C4

	Char	G	J	K	B	C	A
0	汀	0-4501	0-3685	0-7966	A5C5	1-4665	214660
1	汁	0-5413	0-2933	0-8180	A5C4	1-4664	21465E
2	求	0-3983	0-2165	0-4720	A844	1-4A65	214661
3	汃	3-5114		1-8187	C9A2	2-2161	
4	汄					E-2258	
5	汅					E-2259	
6	汆	0-5764			C9F8	2-2259	224678
7	汇	0-2767					273451
8	汈	3-5116					
9	汉	0-2626					274857
A	汊	0-6766	1-3856		C9FC	2-225D	22467C
B	汋	3-5122	1-3857	1-7515	C9FE	2-225F	22472B
C	汌	3-5119			CA40	2-2260	
D	汍	3-5121	1-3858		A6C5	1-4846	224727
E	汎		0-4038	0-5981	A6C6	1-4847	2D4735
F	汏	3-5117	1-3859	1-6120	C9FB	2-225C	

6C5

	Char	G	J	K	B	C	A
0	汐	0-4711	0-2814	0-6417	A6C1	1-4842	214668
1	汑					E-237D	
2	汒	5-5280	1-3860	1-6410	C9F9	2-225A	22467A
3	汓	5-5281				E-2425	
4	汔	0-6764	1-3861	1-8512	C9FD	2-225E	22472C
5	汕	0-4139	0-6172	0-6305	A6C2	1-4843	214667
6	汖					E-2655	
7	汗	0-2625	0-2032	0-8950	A6BD	1-483E	214663
8	汘	3-5118				E-237C	
9	汙		1-3862	1-7214	A6BE	1-483F	214665
A	汚		0-1788	0-7193		E-2423	
B	汛	0-4920	1-3863	1-6981	A6C4	1-4845	224726
C	汜	0-6765	1-3864	1-6748	C9FA	2-225B	224724
D	汝	0-4074	0-3882	0-7003	A6BC	1-483D	214669
E	汞	0-2515	0-6171	0-9181	A845	1-4A66	214662
F	江	0-2913	0-2530	0-4316	A6BF	1-4840	214664

6C6

	Char	G	J	K	B	C	A
0	池	0-1956	0-3551	0-8214	A6C0	1-4841	214666
1	污	0-4659			A6C3	1-4844	334665
2	汢		0-6173				22467B
3	汣					E-653C	22472D
4	汤	0-4432					27482D
5	汥	3-5132			CB5B	2-245B	224742
6	汦	3-5149			CB59	2-2459	
7	汧	3-5125	1-3922		CB4C	2-244C	224739
8	汨	0-6772	0-6181	0-4571	A851	1-4A72	214673
9	汩	0-6773			CB53	2-2453	22474A
A	汪	0-4584	0-6174	0-7260	A84C	1-4A6D	21466E
B	汫	3-5126	1-3865		CB4D	2-244D	
C	汬	5-5267				E-2964	224738
D	汭	3-5141	1-3866	0-7155	CB55	2-2455	22474C
E	汮	5-5291				E-2650	224752
F	汯	3-5136	1-3867		CB52	2-2452	224747

6C7

	Char	G	J	K	B	C	A
0	汰	0-4413	0-3433	0-8732	A84F	1-4A70	214672
1	汱	3-5134			CB51	2-2451	
2	汲	0-2819	0-2166	0-4867	A856	1-4A77	214671
3	汳	3-5145	0-6182		CB5A	2-245A	2E4731
4	汴	0-6774	1-3868	1-8185	A858	1-4A79	224731
5	汵	3-5148				E-2653	
6	汶	0-6775	1-3869	0-5801	A85A	1-4A7B	224733
7	汷	3-5120				E-237E	
8	汸	3-5154	1-3870		CB4B	2-244B	224730
9	汹	0-4858	1-3871			E-2657	2D4746
A	決		0-2372	0-4429	A84D	1-4A6E	21466D
B	汻	3-5143	1-3872		CB5C	2-245C	
C	汼	3-5144				E-2651	
D	汽	0-3891	0-2105	0-4909	A854	1-4A75	214679
E	汾	0-2358	0-6180	0-6144	A857	1-4A78	214678
F	汿	5-5301				E-264C	

6C8

	Char	G	J	K	B	C	A
0	沀	3-5107			CD45	2-2765	
1	沁	0-3963	0-6178	0-6794	A847	1-4A68	21466B
2	沂	0-5042	0-6175	0-4910	A85E	1-4B21	22475A
3	沃	0-4654	0-4564	0-7210	A855	1-4A76	21467B
4	沄	3-5129		1-7336	CB4E	2-244E	22473B
5	沅	0-6768	1-3873	0-7422	A84A	1-4A6B	274841
6	沆	0-6776	1-3874	0-8990	A859	1-4A7A	224732
7	沇	5-5294	1-3875	0-7044	CB56	2-2456	224751
8	沈	0-4182	0-3632	0-8656	A848	1-4A69	274931
9	沉	0-1933	1-3876	1-8106	A849	1-4A6A	214676
A	沊	5-5268			CD43	2-2763	
B	沋	3-5135			CB4F	2-244F	
C	沌	0-6771	0-3857	0-5239	A850	1-4A71	21466F
D	沍	3-5138	0-6176	1-8383	A85B	1-4A7C	4B6A26
E	沎	5-5289			CB5D	2-245D	
F	沏	0-3867			CB50	2-2450	224740

6CA

	Char	G	J	K	B	C	A
0	沠					E-265C	22475C
1	没	0-3527	0-4355			E-2659	33467A
2	沢		0-3484			E-2656	4B4921
3	沣	0-6767					284F5D
4	沤	0-3729					284C41
5	沥	0-3304					27493B
6	沦	0-3457					274777
7	沧	0-1855					274848
8	沨	8-9280					
9	沩	0-6777					284D58
A	沪	0-2706				E-265B	27484F
B	沫	0-3613	0-4387	0-5640	AA6A	1-4E4D	214725
C	沬	3-5156		1-6417	AA7A	1-4E5D	224767
D	沭	0-6780			CCF5	2-2756	22476E
E	沮	0-3058	0-6192	0-7833	AA71	1-4E54	21472D
F	沯	5-5270				E-2D4E	224770

6CC

	Char	G	J	K	B	C	A
0	泀	5-5316			CD47	2-2767	224764
1	況		0-2223	0-9247	AA70	1-4E53	214730
2	泂	3-5168	1-3886	0-9102	CCF9	2-275A	22477D
3	泃	3-5174			CCFB	2-275C	
4	泄	0-4825	0-6185	0-6460	AA6E	1-4E51	214729
5	泅	0-3986	0-6190	1-6914	AA73	1-4E56	214732
6	泆	3-5169	1-3887	1-7471	CCFC	2-275D	224826
7	泇	3-5179			CD4A	2-276A	
8	泈	5-5314				E-296D	
9	泉	0-4010	0-3284	0-8427	AC75	1-5178	21473A
A	泊	0-1820	0-3981	0-5853	AA79	1-4E5C	214738
B	泋	3-5158				E-6261	
C	泌	0-3558	0-4071	0-8918	AA63	1-4E46	214739
D	泍	3-5160	1-3888		CD49	2-2769	
E	泎	5-5310				E-296C	224828
F	泏	3-5178	1-3889		CD4D	2-276D	

6CE

	Char	G	J	K	B	C	A
0	泠	0-6786	1-3903	1-6265	AA7E	1-4E61	22482F
1	泡	0-3761	0-4302	0-8860	AA77	1-4E5A	214736
2	波	0-1808	0-3940	0-8778	AA69	1-4E4C	21472B
3	泣	0-3892	0-2167	0-7572	AA5F	1-4E42	214721
4	泤	5-5293				E-2969	
5	泥	0-3664	0-3705	0-5090	AA64	1-4E47	214726
6	泦	3-5177				E-6260	
7	泧	3-5165	1-3904		CCF6	2-2757	
8	注	0-5502	0-3577	0-8128	AA60	1-4E43	27584C
9	泩	5-5309	1-3905		CD4E	2-276E	224829
A	泪	0-3265	0-6205			E-2967	274759
B	泫	0-6789	1-3906	0-9058	CCF0	2-2751	224762
C	泬	3-5176	1-3907		CCEF	2-2750	
D	泭	3-5170			CCFD	2-275E	
E	泮	0-6790	1-3908	0-5874	CCF1	2-2752	224763
F	泯	0-6793	0-6203	0-5838	AA7B	1-4E5E	224766

6C9

	Char	G	J	K	B	C	A
0	沐	0-6769	0-6184	0-5743	A84E	1-4A6F	214670
1	沑	3-5155				E-264D	
2	沒		0-6183	0-5750	A853	1-4A74	21467A
3	沓	0-7719	0-2303	0-5143	CCEE	2-274F	22474D
4	沔	0-6770	1-3877	0-5687	A85C	1-4A7D	22473E
5	沕	3-5151	1-3878	0-5809	CB57	2-2457	224756
6	沖	8-1352	0-1813	0-8588	A852	1-4A73	214674
7	沗		1-3879			E-2963	
8	沘	3-5137	1-3880	1-6686	A85D	1-4A7E	
9	沙	0-4119	0-2627	0-6262	A846	1-4A67	214677
A	沚	3-5139	0-6177	0-8215	CB54	2-2454	22474B
B	沛	0-3770	0-6179	0-8809	A84B	1-4A6C	21466A
C	沜	5-5288	1-3881		CB58	2-2458	
D	沝	5-5269			CD44	2-2764	224749
E	沞	3-5131				E-264E	
F	沟	0-2521	1-3882			E-2652	27483D

6CB

	Char	G	J	K	B	C	A
0	沰	3-5162	1-3883	1-8127	CD4B	2-276B	
1	沱	0-6791	0-6193	1-8117	AA62	1-4E45	21467C
2	沲	0-6785	1-3884			E-296B	2D467C
3	河	0-2651	0-1847	0-8933	AA65	1-4E48	214728
4	沴	3-5172	1-3885		CD42	2-2762	224833
5	沵	8-9282					
6	沶	3-5157			CCF3	2-2754	
7	沷	3-5163			CCF7	2-2758	
8	沸	0-2348	0-4208	0-6183	AA6D	1-4E50	214723
9	油	0-5145	0-4493	0-7490	AA6F	1-4E52	21472E
A	沺	3-5167	0-6201		CCFA	2-275B	22477A
B	治	0-5446	0-2803	0-8629	AA76	1-4E59	214734
C	沼	0-5351	0-3034	0-6527	AA68	1-4E4B	21472C
D	沽	0-2533	0-6188	0-4531	AA66	1-4E49	214727
E	沾	0-5320	0-6194	0-8452	AA67	1-4E4A	214731
F	沿	0-4956	0-1772	0-7045	AA75	1-4E58	214737

6CD

	Char	G	J	K	B	C	A
0	泐	0-6778	1-3890	1-6350	CCF8	2-2759	2E4670
1	泑	3-5181	1-3891	1-7378	CD4F	2-276F	224830
2	泒	3-5171	1-3892		CD40	2-2760	224832
3	泓	0-6792	0-6187	0-9182	AA6C	1-4E4F	214724
4	泔	0-6779	1-3893	1-5547	CCF4	2-2755	2E6F35
5	法	0-2308	0-4301	0-5986	AA6B	1-4E4E	21472A
6	泖	0-6787	1-3894		AA7D	1-4E60	335461
7	泗	0-6784	0-6189	0-6263	AA72	1-4E55	214733
8	泘	5-5313				E-296A	224824
9	泙	3-5164	0-6204	1-8216	CCF2	2-2753	2E492F
A	泚	3-5194	1-3901	1-7484	CF75	2-2B57	22485C
B	泛	0-2326	0-6202	0-5982	AA78	1-4E5B	214735
C	泜	3-5173	1-3902	1-7793	AA7C	1-4E5F	
D	泝		0-6191	1-6877	CD41	2-2761	33483B
E	泞	0-3702			CD46	2-2766	274927
F	泟	5-5302				E-2965	

6CF

	Char	G	J	K	B	C	A
0	泰	0-4409	0-3457	0-8733	AEF5	1-5639	214722
1	泱	0-6783	0-6186	1-7049	AA74	1-4E57	21472F
2	泲	3-5150	1-3909		CCFE	2-275F	22482D
3	泳	0-5130	0-1743	0-7122	AA61	1-4E44	21467E
4	泴	5-5272	1-3910			E-2D4F	
5	泵	0-1735			ACA6	1-5229	224772
6	泶	0-7720					284E3E
7	泷	0-6781					284F26
8	泸	0-6782					284F39
9	泹				CD4C	2-276C	
A	泺	0-6788					454738
B	泻	0-4826					274932
C	泼	0-3835					27486C
D	泽	0-5283					274921
E	泾	0-6794					27474E
F	泿	3-5216				E-2D46	

Code	Char	G	J	K	B	C	A
6D00	洀	5-5335			CF7C	2-2B5E	22486C
6D01	洁	0-2964			CFA1	2-2B61	27486F
6D02	洂	5-5339				E-2D50	
6D03	洃	5-5323			CFA4	2-2B64	
6D04	洄	0-6807	1-3911	1-8445	CF77	2-2B59	22485B
6D05	洅	5-5320				E-2D48	
6D06	洆					E-2D4A	
6D07	洇	0-6806	1-3912	1-7466	CFA7	2-2B67	22485A
6D08	洈	5-5338			CFAA	2-2B6A	
6D09	洉	5-5333			CFAC	2-2B6C	
6D0A	洊	3-5188	1-3913	1-7920	CF74	2-2B56	224850
6D0B	洋	0-4983	0-4546	0-6939	AC76	1-5179	21473C
6D0C	洌	0-6803	0-6216	0-5412	AC7B	1-517E	214741
6D0D	洍	5-5349			D249	2-302C	
6D0E	洎	0-6809	1-3914		ACAD	1-5230	224867
6D0F	洏	3-5187	1-3915		CFA5	2-2B65	22484F
6D10	洐	5-5334			CFAD	2-2B6D	
6D11	洑	3-5205	1-3916	0-6039	CF7B	2-2B5D	22486B
6D12	洒	0-4087	0-6215	1-6865	CF73	2-2B55	274941
6D13	洓	3-5186	1-3917			E-2D49	
6D14	洔	3-5184				E-2D47	
6D15	洕	3-5206				E-2D4D	
6D16	洖				D264	2-3047	
6D17	洗	0-4720	0-3286	0-6509	AC7E	1-5223	214743
6D18	洘	3-5185			CFA2	2-2B62	
6D19	洙	0-6808	0-6212	0-6610	CF78	2-2B5A	224864
6D1A	洚	0-6814	1-3918		CF7A	2-2B5C	334740
6D1B	洛	0-3469	0-4576	0-5306	ACA5	1-5228	214745
6D1C	洜					E-317A	
6D1D	洝	3-5215			CF7D	2-2B5F	224837
6D1E	洞	0-2220	0-3822	0-5255	AC7D	1-5222	214742
6D1F	洟	3-5191	0-6206	1-7451	CF70	2-2B52	33474A
6D20	洠	5-5341			CFA8	2-2B68	
6D21	洡	3-5183				E-2D4B	
6D22	洢	5-5332			CFAB	2-2B6B	
6D23	洣	3-5214				E-2D45	
6D24	洤	5-5336				E-2D57	22486D
6D25	津	0-2982	0-3637	0-8248	AC7A	1-517D	21473E
6D26	洦	5-5322	1-3919			E-2D53	22484D
6D27	洧	0-6802	1-3920	0-7491	ACA8	1-522B	22484E
6D28	洨	3-5209	1-3921		CF6D	2-2B4F	22483B
6D29	洩	8-1575	0-1744	0-6461	ACAA	1-522D	2D4729
6D2A	洪	0-2673	0-2531	0-9183	AC78	1-517B	214740
6D2B	洫	0-6810	0-6209	1-8340	ACAE	1-5231	22486A
6D2C	洬	3-5207		1-6891	CFA9	2-2B69	
6D2D	洭	3-5182			CF6F	2-2B51	
6D2E	洮	0-6812	1-3923	1-6132	ACAB	1-522E	224860
6D2F	洯	5-5273	1-3924		D25E	2-3041	
6D30	洰	5-5284			CD48	2-2768	
6D31	洱	0-2293	1-3925		AC7C	1-5221	21473F
6D32	洲	0-5462	0-2907	0-8129	AC77	1-517A	21473D
6D33	洳	0-6818	0-6214		CF76	2-2B58	22486F
6D34	洴	3-5213			CF6E	2-2B50	22492F
6D35	洵	0-6813	0-6213	0-6671	ACAC	1-522F	224861
6D36	洶		0-6208	0-9355	ACA4	1-5227	214746
6D37	洷	3-5193			CFA3	2-2B63	
6D38	洸	3-5202	0-6211	0-4640	ACA9	1-522C	2E4D3D
6D39	洹	0-6801	1-3926	0-7423	ACA7	1-522A	224844
6D3A	洺	3-5208		1-6440	CF79	2-2B5B	224862
6D3B	活	0-2778	0-1972	0-9232	ACA1	1-5224	214744
6D3C	洼	0-4561	1-3927	1-7254	CF71	2-2B53	274F5C
6D3D	洽	0-3902	0-6210	0-9371	ACA2	1-5225	214747
6D3E	派	0-3741	0-3941	0-8779	ACA3	1-5226	214748
6D3F	洿	3-5189	1-3928		CF72	2-2B54	224851
6D40	浀	5-5327			CFA6	2-2B66	
6D41	流	0-3387	0-4614	0-5521	AC79	1-517C	21473B
6D42	浂	5-5340			CF7E	2-2B60	
6D43	浃	0-6804					284934
6D44	浄	8-1353	0-3084			E-2D55	33476F
6D45	浅	0-3919	0-3285			E-2D51	274768
6D46	浆	0-2912					274863
6D47	浇	0-2929					274871
6D48	浈	0-6805					284E28
6D49	浉	8-9283					
6D4A	浊	0-5539					274922
6D4B	测	0-1866					274830
6D4C	浌						
6D4D	浍	0-6811					284E42
6D4E	济	0-2835					274926
6D4F	浏	0-6815					274937
6D50	浐	8-9288					
6D51	浑	0-2775					274833
6D52	浒	0-6816					284C2E
6D53	浓	0-3708					27487C
6D54	浔	0-6817					284D2B
6D55	浕	8-9290					
6D56	浖	5-5360				E-3177	
6D57	浗		1-3929			E-3173	
6D58	浘	3-5242			D24C	2-302F	
6D59	浙	0-5367	0-6222	0-7926	AEFD	1-5641	21474D
6D5A	浚	0-3103	0-6220	0-8161	AF43	1-5646	214755
6D5B	浛	3-5234				E-3179	
6D5C	浜	0-6826	0-4145	0-6219		E-3226	394928
6D5D	浝	5-5353				E-3176	
6D5E	浞	0-6823	1-3930		D255	2-3038	22493E
6D5F	浟	3-5231	1-3931		D25B	2-303E	
6D60	浠	0-6827			D257	2-303A	224946
6D61	浡	3-5221	1-3932	1-6532	D24A	2-302D	224928
6D62	浢	3-5223			D24D	2-3030	
6D63	浣	0-6829	0-6217	0-7243	D246	2-3029	224873
6D64	浤	3-5238	0-6219	1-5812	D247	2-302A	2E4747
6D65	浥	3-5228	1-3933	1-7435	AF4A	1-564D	22493C
6D66	浦	0-3854	0-1726	0-8861	AEFA	1-563E	21474C
6D67	浧	3-5226	1-3934	1-7169	D256	2-3039	224940
6D68	浨				D25F	2-3042	
6D69	浩	0-2638	0-2532	0-9139	AF45	1-5648	214756
6D6A	浪	0-3243	0-4718	0-5340	AEF6	1-563A	214749
6D6B	浫	3-5240				E-316F	
6D6C	浬	8-0886	0-1929	0-5563	AF40	1-5643	214750
6D6D	浭	3-5222			D24E	2-3031	224925
6D6E	浮	0-2401	0-4166	0-6109	AF42	1-5645	214753
6D6F	浯	0-6820	1-3935		D24F	2-3032	224926
6D70	浰	3-5230	1-3936		D259	2-303C	22494C
6D71	浱	5-5351				E-3222	
6D72	浲	5-5363				E-3225	
6D73	浳					E-3172	
6D74	浴	0-5201	0-4565	0-7317	AF44	1-5647	214754
6D75	浵	3-5235			D268	2-304B	
6D76	浶	3-5239			D248	2-302B	
6D77	海	0-2603	0-1904	0-9013	AEFC	1-5640	214757
6D78	浸	0-2994	0-3127	0-8657	AEFB	1-563F	21474B
6D79	浹	1-6804	0-6221	0-9084	AF48	1-564B	224934
6D7A	浺	3-5237			D245	2-3028	
6D7B	浻	5-5358			D266	2-3049	
6D7C	浼	0-6828	1-3937		D25A	2-303D	22494B
6D7D	浽	3-5233			D267	2-304A	
6D7E	浾	5-5345			D261	2-3044	
6D7F	浿	3-5140		0-8810	D253	2-3036	224939

6D8

	Char	G	J	K	B	C	A
0	涀	3-5142			D262	2-3045	
1	涁	5-5350				E-3221	22492C
2	涂	0-4531	1-3938	1-6133	D25C	2-303F	27384D
3	涃	5-5357			D265	2-3048	
4	涄	5-5356			D263	2-3046	
5	涅	0-3689	0-6226	0-7078	AF49	1-564C	22493B
6	涆	5-5354			D254	2-3037	
7	涇	1-6794	1-3939	0-4460	AEF9	1-563D	21474E
8	消	0-4791	0-3035	0-6528	AEF8	1-563C	21474F
9	涉	0-4170		0-6479	AF41	1-5644	214752
A	涊	3-5243			AF47	1-564A	22492E
B	涋				D260	2-3043	
C	涌	0-5131	0-4516	0-7331	AF46	1-5649	27477D
D	涍	3-5219		0-9293	D251	2-3034	
E	涎	0-4749	0-6223	0-7046	B243	1-5B48	214775
F	涏	3-5204				E-3178	

6DA

	Char	G	J	K	B	C	A
0	涠	0-6822					284D49
1	涡	0-4648					274831
2	涢	8-9292					
3	涣	0-2733					4B4835
4	涤	0-2151					224A3D
5	涥					E-653D	224877
6	润	0-4083					27486D
7	涧	0-2907					27486E
8	涨	0-5339					274855
9	涩	0-4112					27492E
A	涪	0-2402	1-3946	1-6626	B265	1-5B6A	22495C
B	涫	0-6842		1-5763	D5E1	2-3645	224959
C	涬	3-5248	1-3947		D5E5	2-3649	22496A
D	涭	5-5387				E-366F	
E	涮	0-6844			B252	1-5B57	214760
F	涯	0-4936	0-1922	0-6883	B250	1-5B55	214766

6DC

	Char	G	J	K	B	C	A
0	淀	0-2177	0-4568	0-7967	D5E0	2-3644	27487B
1	淁	3-5276				E-366A	
2	淂	3-5259			D5FC	2-3660	
3	淃	3-5278		0-4778		E-366B	
4	淄	0-5545	1-3953	0-8630	B264	1-5B69	214778
5	淅	0-6832	0-6240	0-6418	B258	1-5B5D	214764
6	淆	0-4793	0-6234	0-9294	B263	1-5B68	214776
7	淇	0-6831	0-6231	0-4911	B24E	1-5B53	214762
8	淈	3-5283	1-3954	1-5893	D5EC	2-3650	
9	淉	3-5260			D5FE	2-3662	
A	淊	3-5273	1-3955		D5F6	2-365A	
B	淋	0-3360	0-4652	0-5590	B24F	1-5B54	214763
C	淌	0-4442	0-6237		B249	1-5B4E	21476A
D	淍	3-5271			D645	2-3668	
E	淎	5-5371	1-3956			E-366C	
F	淏	3-5258	1-3957	0-9140	D5FD	2-3661	

6DE

	Char	G	J	K	B	C	A
0	淠	0-6836	1-3962	1-6688	D5ED	2-3651	2E4E5D
1	淡	0-2113	0-3524	0-5131	B248	1-5B4D	21475E
2	淢	3-5252	1-3963	1-7132	D5E7	2-364B	22496C
3	淣	5-5382			D646	2-3669	
4	淤	0-5157	0-6243	1-7108	B24A	1-5B4F	21475C
5	淥		1-3964	1-6290	D5F1	2-3655	2E4C35
6	淦	0-6838	0-6232	1-5548	B268	1-5B6D	224A4A
7	淧					E-3674	
8	淨		0-6238	0-7968	B262	1-5B67	21476F
9	淩	3-5247	1-3965		D5E6	2-364A	22496E
A	淪	1-3457	0-6245	0-5537	B25F	1-5B64	214777
B	淫	0-5089	0-1692	0-7566	B25D	1-5B62	214770
C	淬	0-2067	0-6235	1-6949	B266	1-5B6B	224960
D	淭				D5F8	2-365C	
E	淮	0-2720	0-6246	0-9271	B261	1-5B66	214773
F	淯	5-5390	1-3966		D252	2-3035	224935

6D9

	Char	G	J	K	B	C	A
0	涐				D269	2-304C	
1	涑	0-6819	1-3940	0-6555	D250	2-3033	224929
2	涒	3-5241	1-3941		D24B	2-302E	22487D
3	涓	0-6824	0-6218	0-7047	AEFE	1-5642	214751
4	涔	0-6825	1-3942	1-7522	AF4B	1-564E	224943
5	涕	0-4473	0-6224	0-8481	AEF7	1-563B	21474A
6	涖		1-3943	1-6360		E-3227	22494F
7	涗		1-3944		D258	2-303B	
8	涘	3-5244	1-3945		D25D	2-3040	224948
9	涙		0-4662			E-317D	4B4759
A	涚	3-5236				E-317B	
B	涛	0-4446	0-3783			E-317C	27492D
C	涜		0-3834				
D	涝	0-3252					284D27
E	涞	0-6821					284971
F	涟	0-3316					274859

6DB

	Char	G	J	K	B	C	A
0	涰					E-367A	
1	涱	5-5287				E-3721	
2	液	0-5026	0-1753	0-6891	B247	1-5B4C	21475D
3	涳	5-5392			D5E3	2-3647	
4	涴	3-5281	1-3948	1-7265	D5E2	2-3646	22495A
5	涵	0-2613	0-6230	0-8968	B25B	1-5B60	214767
6	涶	3-5264				E-3C50	
7	涷	3-5166	1-3949	1-6157	D5E8	2-364C	22496B
8	涸	0-2652	0-6233	1-8468	B255	1-5B5A	21476C
9	涹	3-5265	1-3950			E-3672	
A	涺	5-5401			D5FA	2-365E	
B	涻	5-5385			D647	2-366A	
C	涼		0-4635	1-6224	B244	1-5B49	21475B
D	涽	3-5272	1-3951		D5F7	2-365B	
E	涾	3-5284			D5F0	2-3654	
F	涿	0-6835	1-3952	1-8128	B267	1-5B6C	22497B

6DD

	Char	G	J	K	B	C	A
0	淐	3-5262			D640	2-3663	
1	淑	0-4271	0-2942	0-6655	B251	1-5B56	21476D
2	淒		0-6239	1-7902	B259	1-5B5E	21475F
3	淓	5-5348			D642	2-3665	224A2D
4	淔	3-5250			D5EA	2-364E	
5	淕	3-5246	0-6244		D5FB	2-365F	22496D
6	淖	0-3655	1-3958	1-6048	D5EF	2-3653	2D514A
7	淗	5-5388			D644	2-3667	
8	淘	0-4452	0-3781	0-5203	B25E	1-5B63	214771
9	淙	0-6840	0-6242	0-8088	B246	1-5B4B	214758
A	淚			0-5508	B25C	1-5B61	214759
B	淛		1-3959		D5F4	2-3658	224A39
C	淜	3-5270			D5F2	2-3656	224A36
D	淝	0-6839	1-3960	1-6687	D5F3	2-3657	224A35
E	淞	0-6833	0-6236	0-6571	B253	1-5B58	214765
F	淟	3-5263	1-3961		D5EE	2-3652	224A2A

6DF

	Char	G	J	K	B	C	A
0	淰	3-5269	1-3967		D5F9	2-365D	224A46
1	深	0-4178	0-3128	0-6802	B260	1-5B65	21476E
2	淲	3-5257			D641	2-3664	
3	淳	0-2030	0-2963	0-6672	B245	1-5B4A	21475A
4	淴	3-5275	1-3968		D5F5	2-3659	
5	淵	1-5208	0-4205	0-7048	B257	1-5B5C	214774
6	淶	1-6821	1-3969	1-6218	D5E9	2-364D	224971
7	混	0-2776	0-2614	0-9172	B256	1-5B5B	21476B
8	淸			0-8472		E-367C	4B4761
9	淹	0-4945	0-6227	0-6984	B254	1-5B59	214769
A	淺	1-3919	0-6241	0-8428	B24C	1-5B51	214768
B	添	0-4477	0-3726	0-8453	B24B	1-5B50	214772
C	淼	0-7721	1-3970	1-6468	D9E7	2-3D2C	224A32
D	淽	5-5347			D643	2-3666	
E	淾	5-8516				E-3C5D	
F	淿					E-3728	

6E0

	Char	G	J	K	B	C	A
0	渀	3-5255	1-3971		D5EB	2-364F	
1	渁					E-3726	
2	渂	5-5378				E-3723	
3	渃	3-5249			D9FC	2-3D41	
4	渄		1-3972			E-3670	
5	清	0-3969	0-3222		B24D	1-5B52	214761
6	渆					E-3677	
7	渇		0-1973			E-3724	2D482F
8	済		0-2649			E-3676	3F4926
9	渉		0-3036			E-3725	
A	渊	0-5208	0-6229			E-3679	274774
B	渋		0-2934				4B492E
C	渌	0-6843				E-367D	4C4C35
D	渍	0-5553					274854
E	渎	0-6834					274933
F	渏					E-653E	224979

6E1

	Char	G	J	K	B	C	A
0	渐	0-2905					27485A
1	渑	0-6837					284E30
2	渒	5-5383				E-3729	224A44
3	渓		0-2344				4B484A
4	渔	0-5170					274865
5	渕		0-6228				454774
6	渖	0-6841					4B4931
7	渗	0-4188		0-6322		E-3727	274864
8	渘	3-5338				E-3C54	
9	渙	1-2733	0-6250	0-9225	B541	1-6047	214835
A	渚	0-6830	0-2977	0-7834	B25A	1-5B5F	214822
B	減	8-1354	0-2426	0-4285	B4EE	1-6035	214829
C	渜	3-5293			D9F6	2-3D3B	
D	渝	0-5169	0-6265	1-8167	B4FC	1-6043	214836
E	渞		1-3973			E-3C52	
F	渟	3-5320	0-6259	0-7969	D9EA	2-3D2F	224A4C

6E2

	Char	G	J	K	B	C	A
0	渠	0-3994	0-2184	0-4366	B4EB	1-6032	21477E
1	渡	0-2241	0-3747	0-5204	B4E7	1-602E	21477A
2	渢	3-5152	1-3974		DA49	2-3D4D	224B42
3	渣	0-5292	0-6254	0-6264	B4ED	1-6034	214827
4	渤	0-1819	0-6263	0-5893	B4F1	1-6038	214828
5	渥	0-6855	0-1615	0-6838	B4EC	1-6033	21482A
6	渦	1-4648	0-1718	0-7230	B4F5	1-603C	214831
7	渧	3-5325	1-3975		DA4D	2-3D51	224A50
8	渨	3-5309		1-7274	DA44	2-3D48	224B22
9	温	0-4634	0-1825			E-3C6B	2D4845
A	渪	5-5417				E-3C6D	224B40
B	渫	0-6845	0-6256	0-6462	D9F1	2-3D36	334729
C	測	1-1866	0-3412	0-8620	B4FA	1-6041	214830
D	渭	0-4628	0-6247	0-7450	B4F4	1-603B	21482E
E	渮	5-5373	0-6249		D9FD	2-3D42	224B2E
F	港	0-2459	0-2533	0-8991	B4E4	1-602B	214824

6E3

	Char	G	J	K	B	C	A
0	渰	3-5315			DA4A	2-3D4E	224B33
1	渱	3-5310			DA43	2-3D47	224B26
2	渲	0-6854	1-3976	0-6434	B4E8	1-602F	21477C
3	渳	3-5335			D9F7	2-3D3C	
4	渴	0-3142		0-4268	B4F7	1-603E	21482F
5	渵				DA55	2-3D59	
6	渶	5-5374	1-3977	0-7123	DA56	2-3D5A	224B30
7	渷			1-7142			
8	游	0-5146	0-6266	0-7493	B4E5	1-602C	21477B
9	渹	3-5317	1-3978		DA48	2-3D4C	224B36
A	渺	0-3576	0-6261	0-5761	B4F9	1-6040	21482C
B	渻	5-5414	1-3979		D9FB	2-3D40	
C	渼	3-5329	1-3980	0-5820	D9ED	2-3D32	224A58
D	渽	3-5287		0-7810	D9EE	2-3D33	
E	渾	1-2775	0-6253	0-9173	B4FD	1-6044	214833
F	渿	5-5409			D9F2	2-3D37	

6E4

	Char	G	J	K	B	C	A
0	湀	5-5427			D9F9	2-3D3E	
1	湁	3-5294			D9F3	2-3D38	
2	湂					E-3C5A	
3	湃	0-3740	0-6260	0-5943	B4FB	1-6042	214834
4	湄	0-6856	1-3981	0-5821	B544	1-604A	224A6B
5	湅	3-5292	1-3982	1-6246	D9EF	2-3D34	
6	湆	3-5324			D9E8	2-3D2D	
7	湇	5-5421			D9E9	2-3D2E	
8	湈		1-3983			E-3C56	
9	湉	3-5332	1-3984		D9EB	2-3D30	224A55
A	湊		0-4411	0-8130	B4EA	1-6031	21482B
B	湋	3-5128	1-3985		D9F8	2-3D3D	224A62
C	湌	5-5419				E-3C6E	224B41
D	湍	0-4536	0-6258	0-5112	B4F8	1-603F	214832
E	湎	0-6847	0-6262	1-6434	B542	1-6048	224A77
F	湏		1-3986			E-3C58	224A74

6E5

	Char	G	J	K	B	C	A
0	湐	5-5410				E-3C69	
1	湑	3-5337	1-3987	1-6811	D9FA	2-3D3F	224A6A
2	湒	3-5305	1-3988		DA53	2-3D57	
3	湓	0-6852	1-3989	1-6652	DA4B	2-3D4F	224B34
4	湔	0-6853	1-3990	1-7594	B4E6	1-602D	214779
5	湕	5-5394			DA51	2-3D55	
6	湖	0-2694	0-2448	0-9141	B4F2	1-6039	214823
7	湗	5-5403	1-3991			E-3C66	
8	湘	0-4770	0-3037	0-6347	B4F0	1-6037	214826
9	湙	3-5322				E-3C64	
A	湚				DA57	2-3D5B	
B	湛	0-5331	0-3525	0-5132	B4EF	1-6036	214821
C	湜	3-5304	1-3992	0-6755	DA41	2-3D45	224B24
D	湝	3-5301	1-3993		D9F4	2-3D39	224B31
E	湞	1-6805	1-3994	0-7970	D9FE	2-3D43	224B28
F	湟	0-6850	0-6252	0-9248	B547	1-604D	334730

6E6

	Char	G	J	K	B	C	A
0	湠	3-5311			DA45	2-3D49	
1	湡	3-5307			DA42	2-3D46	
2	湢	3-5291	1-4001		D9F0	2-3D35	224A66
3	湣	5-5425	1-4002	1-6508	B543	1-6049	224A6D
4	湤	3-5327			DA4F	2-3D53	
5	湥	5-5424			DA4C	2-3D50	
6	湦	3-5308			DA54	2-3D58	
7	湧	8-1355	0-4515	0-7332	B4E9	1-6030	21477D
8	湨	3-5303	1-4003		DA40	2-3D44	
9	湩	3-5313			B546	1-604C	224B38
A	湪	3-5339				E-3C5B	
B	湫	0-6848	0-6255	0-8551	DA47	2-3D4B	224B39
C	湬	5-5276				E-423A	
D	湭	3-5331				E-3C60	
E	湮	0-6846	0-6248	0-7660	B4F3	1-603A	214825
F	湯	1-4432	0-3782	0-8723	B4F6	1-603D	21482D

6E7

	Char	G	J	K	B	C	A
0	湰	3-5318				E-3C5C	
1	湱	3-5285			DA46	2-3D4A	224B37
2	湲	3-5316	0-6251	0-7424	B545	1-604B	224B32
3	湳	3-5290	1-4004	0-4989	D9F5	2-3D3A	224A71
4	湴	3-5279			D5E4	2-3648	
5	湵					E-3C51	
6	湶	5-5416	0-6257			E-3C6C	224B3E
7	湷				DA50	2-3D54	
8	湸	5-5420			DA4E	2-3D52	
9	湹	5-5411			DA52	2-3D56	
A	湺			0-6040			
B	湻		1-4005			E-3C62	
C	湼					E-6542	2E493B
D	湽		1-4006				
E	湾	0-4569	0-4749			E-3C63	274943
F	湿	0-4210	0-2830				274844

6E8

	Char	G	J	K	B	C	A
0	満		0-4394			E-3C68	4B4858
1	溁	8-1461					
2	溂		0-6267				695E63
3	溃	0-3203					274878
4	溄					E-6540	224B2C
5	溅	0-2906					274934
6	溆	0-6851				E-633D	2E4C7B
7	溇	8-9307					
8	溈				D9EC	2-3D31	224D58
9	溉	0-2440			B540	1-6046	214866
A	溊					E-653F	224A60
B	溋					E-6541	224B3B
C	溌		0-4014				
D	溍	3-5343	1-4007		DE61	2-4447	
E	溎	3-5344			DE60	2-4446	224B5E
F	溏	0-6871	0-6279	1-6105	DE46	2-442C	224B4A

6EA

	Char	G	J	K	B	C	A
0	溠	3-5328	1-4010		DE4B	2-4431	224B4F
1	溡	5-5355			DE63	2-4449	
2	溢	0-5071	0-1678	0-7678	B7B8	1-645E	21483C
3	溣	5-5330			DE6A	2-4450	
4	溤	5-5282			DE62	2-4448	224B75
5	溥	0-6863	0-6280	0-6110	B7C1	1-6467	21483F
6	溦	3-5350			DE57	2-443D	2E4A6B
7	溧	0-6864	1-4011	1-6347	B7CC	1-6472	224B5A
8	溨	5-5431				E-422E	224B57
9	溩	3-5153				E-4236	
A	溪	0-4710	0-6268	0-4502	B7CB	1-6471	21484A
B	溫			0-7214	B7C5	1-646B	214845
C	溬					E-4240	
D	溭	3-5349	1-4012				
E	溮	3-5201	1-4013		DE69	2-444F	
F	溯	0-4361	0-6274	0-6529	B7B9	1-645F	21483B

6EC

	Char	G	J	K	B	C	A
0	滀	3-5361	1-4018		DE47	2-442D	
1	滁	0-1992	1-4019		DE51	2-4437	224B63
2	滂	0-6872	0-6281	0-5921	B7BC	1-6462	214839
3	滃	3-5355	1-4020	1-7243	DE5B	2-4441	224C21
4	滄	1-1855	0-6275	0-8371	B7C9	1-646F	214848
5	滅	1-3580	0-4439	0-5694	B7C0	1-6466	214842
6	滆	3-5346			DE4E	2-4434	
7	滇	0-2165	1-4021		B7BF	1-6465	214843
8	滈	3-5358	1-4022	1-8384	DE45	2-442B	224B48
9	滉	3-5348	0-6270	0-9249	DE53	2-4439	224B6A
A	滊		1-4023		DE67	2-444D	224B7C
B	滋	0-5544	0-2802	0-7718	B4FE	1-6045	214847
C	滌	1-2151	0-6294	0-8415	BAB0	1-6957	214867
D	滍	3-5368	1-4024		DE56	2-443C	
E	滎	1-6094	1-4025	0-9103	E26C	2-4B34	224B43
F	滏	0-6870	1-4026		DE58	2-443E	224B79

6EE

	Char	G	J	K	B	C	A
0	滠	0-6860					284F61
1	满	0-3490					274858
2	滢	0-6862					284E66
3	滣	5-5435				E-4245	
4	滤	0-3443					274936
5	滥	0-3236					27492B
6	滦	0-3448				E-423F	274944
7	滧	8-1576					
8	滨	0-1785				E-423B	274928
9	滩	0-4418				E-4246	274942
A	滪	8-9313					
B	滫	3-5353	1-4027		E2AA	2-4B50	224C77
C	滬	1-2706	0-6286	1-8385	BAAD	1-6954	21484F
D	滭	3-5192	1-4028	1-8259	E27D	2-4B45	
E	滮	3-5376	1-4029		E2A4	2-4B4A	224C61
F	滯	1-5445	0-6292	0-8482	BAA2	1-6949	21485F

6E9

	Char	G	J	K	B	C	A
0	源	0-5220	0-2427	0-7425	B7BD	1-6463	214841
1	溑	3-5225				E-4230	
2	溒	3-5342			DE5F	2-4445	224B59
3	溓	3-5363	1-4008		DE49	2-442F	224B4D
4	溔	3-5362			DE4A	2-4430	
5	溕			1-6461			
6	準	1-5528	0-2964	0-8162	B7C7	1-646D	21484B
7	溗	3-5352			DE68	2-444E	
8	溘	0-6859	0-6269	1-8309	B7C2	1-6468	214840
9	溙	5-5429	1-4009		DE5E	2-4444	
A	溚	3-5288				E-4233	
B	溛	5-5450			DE43	2-4429	224B45
C	溜	0-3379	0-4615	0-5522	B7C8	1-646E	21484C
D	溝	1-2521	0-2534	0-4721	B7BE	1-6464	21483D
E	溞	5-5428			DE52	2-4438	
F	溟	0-6873	0-6282	0-5708	DE48	2-442E	224B46

6EB

	Char	G	J	K	B	C	A
0	溰	5-5328			DE55	2-443B	
1	溱	0-6858	1-4014	0-8249	DE4C	2-4432	224B51
2	溲	0-6849	0-6276	1-6915	DE59	2-443F	224C26
3	溳	3-5227	1-4015		DE65	2-444B	224B6C
4	溴	0-6869			B7CD	1-6473	224C24
5	溵	5-5445		1-7420		E-4239	224C29
6	溶	0-4060	0-4547	0-7333	B7BB	1-6461	214838
7	溷	0-6867	0-6271	1-8403	DE54	2-443A	224B6D
8	溸	5-5430				E-422D	
9	溹	5-5434			DE4D	2-4433	
A	溺	0-3671	0-3714	0-5092	B7C4	1-646A	2D3B52
B	溻	0-6866	1-4016			E-4231	224B69
C	溼				B7C3	1-6469	214844
D	溽	0-6865	0-6273	1-7302	DE50	2-4436	224B61
E	溾	3-5314			DE5A	2-4440	
F	溿	5-5437	1-4017		DE64	2-444A	

6ED

	Char	G	J	K	B	C	A
0	滐	5-5446			DE66	2-444C	
1	滑	0-2712	0-1974	0-9233	B7C6	1-646C	214846
2	滒	3-5345			DE4F	2-4435	
3	滓	0-5550	0-6272	0-7811	B7BA	1-6460	214837
4	滔	0-4447	0-6277	0-5205	B7CA	1-6470	214849
5	滕	0-7588	0-6278	1-6177	BCF0	1-6D5A	224B7D
6	滖				DE44	2-442A	
7	滗	0-6868					284D59
8	滘	3-5367			DE5D	2-4443	224B49
9	滙			1-8446		E-4244	224B60
A	滚	0-2586				E-423E	2D4850
B	滛					E-4247	
C	滜	5-5442			DE5C	2-4442	
D	滝		0-3476			E-423D	4C4F26
E	滞	0-5445	0-3458				27485F
F	滟	0-6857					285029

6EF

	Char	G	J	K	B	C	A
0	滰	3-5389				E-4756	
1	滱	3-5393			E26E	2-4B36	
2	滲	1-4188	0-6290		BAAF	1-6956	214864
3	滳	3-5390				E-4757	
4	滴	0-2146	0-3709	0-7857	BA77	1-6940	21484E
5	滵	3-5402		1-6516	E26D	2-4B35	
6	滶	3-5340			E2B0	2-4B56	224C42
7	滷	1-3417	0-6303	1-6275	BAB1	1-6958	2F5D3C
8	滸	1-6816	0-6287	0-9142	E271	2-4B39	224C2E
9	滹	0-6879	1-4030		E2A3	2-4B49	224C60
A	滺	5-5464	.			E-4765	224C76
B	滻	3-5210	1-4031		E273	2-4B3B	
C	滼	3-5373			E2B3	2-4B59	
D	滽	3-5387	1-4032		E2AF	2-4B55	224C34
E	滾		0-6288	0-4567	BA75	1-693E	214850
F	滿	1-3490	0-6264	0-5627	BAA1	1-6948	214858

6F0

	Char	G	J	K	B	C	A
0	漀	3-5111			E653	2-515B	224C44
1	漁	1-5170	0-2189	0-6959	BAAE	1-6955	214865
2	漂	0-3815	0-4126	0-8887	BA7D	1-6946	21485D
3	漃	3-5394			E26F	2-4B37	
4	漄		1-4033	1-7061		E-4763	
5	漅	5-5469			E2AE	2-4B54	
6	漆	0-3865	0-2831	0-8652	BAA3	1-694A	21485E
7	漇	3-5384			E2AB	2-4B51	
8	漈	3-5386	1-4034		E2B8	2-4B5E	224C78
9	漉	0-6885	0-2587	1-6291	E275	2-4B3D	224C35
A	漊	3-5330	1-4035		E27E	2-4B46	224C5A
B	漋	5-5468				E-4C78	224D44
C	漌	5-5458	1-4036	1-5950		E-475B	
D	漍	3-5261	1-4037		E2B6	2-4B5C	
E	漎	3-5146			E2AC	2-4B52	224C79
F	漏	0-3409	0-4719	0-5509	BA7C	1-6945	214856

6F2

	Char	G	J	K	B	C	A
0	漠	0-3614	0-3989	0-5614	BA7A	1-6943	214862
1	漡	5-5312			E2B9	2-4B5F	
2	漢	1-2626	0-2033	0-8951	BA7E	1-6947	214857
3	漣	1-3316	0-4690	0-5394	BAA7	1-694E	214859
4	漤	0-6877					224C4B
5	漥	3-5401			E270	2-4B38	
6	漦	3-3937	1-4042		E5FA	2-5143	224C3F
7	漧				E279	2-4B41	
8	漨	3-5357				E-475E	
9	漩	0-6886	1-4043		BA78	1-6941	214851
A	漪	0-6884	1-4044	1-7441	BAAC	1-6953	214868
B	漫	0-3494	0-4401	0-5628	BAA9	1-6950	214860
C	漬	1-5553	0-3650	0-8216	BA7B	1-6944	214854
D	漭	0-6861	1-4051	1-6411	E2A5	2-4B4B	224C65
E	漮	3-5388			E274	2-4B3C	
F	漯	0-6880	1-4045		BAAA	1-6951	214861

6F4

	Char	G	J	K	B	C	A
0	潀				E2A6	2-4B4C	
1	潁	1-8203	0-6283	0-7124	E5F9	2-5142	224C62
2	潂					E-4762	
3	潃				E2AD	2-4B53	
4	潄					E-4761	2D485C
5	潅		0-2035				4B4940
6	潆	0-6875					4C4F24
7	潇	0-6876					27493D
8	潈					E-6544	
9	潉					E-6545	224C6B
A	潊					E-4766	
B	潋	0-6882					284E41
C	潌					E-6543	
D	潍	0-4611					284E62
E	潎	3-5377			E276	2-4B3E	
F	潏	3-5431	1-4052	1-7411	E644	2-514C	

6F6

	Char	G	J	K	B	C	A
0	潠	5-5492			BCF2	1-6D5C	224D30
1	潡	5-5485	1-4061	1-6145	E654	2-515C	
2	潢	0-6874	1-4062	0-9250	E643	2-514B	224D3D
3	潣	5-5366			E65E	2-5166	224C3D
4	潤	1-4083	0-2965	0-7540	BCED	1-6D57	21486D
5	潥	3-5412				E-4C6B	
6	潦	0-3342	0-6319	1-6323	BCE3	1-6D4D	214877
7	潧	5-5490			E657	2-515F	
8	潨	3-5420	1-4063				
9	潩	3-5378			E65B	2-5163	
A	潪	3-5417			E660	2-5168	
B	潫	3-5424			E655	2-515D	
C	潬	3-5280	1-4064		E649	2-5151	224D4B
D	潭	0-4422	0-6312	0-5133	BCE6	1-6D50	214873
E	潮	0-1917	0-3612	0-8045	BCE9	1-6D53	214875
F	潯	1-6817	0-6309	1-6990	BCF1	1-6D5B	224D2B

6F1

	Char	G	J	K	B	C	A
0	漐	3-5109				E-4C6A	
1	漑		0-6284	0-4341		E-4764	4B4866
2	漒	3-5430			E27C	2-4B44	224C3E
3	漓	0-3276	0-6302	1-6361	BA76	1-693F	284F6B
4	演	0-4961	0-1773	0-7049	BA74	1-693D	214852
5	漕	0-6878	0-3370	0-8044	BAA8	1-694F	21485B
6	漖	5-5456	1-4038				
7	漗					E-475F	
8	漘	3-5374	1-4039		E27A	2-4B42	224C51
9	漙	3-5130		1-6071	E277	2-4B3F	224C43
A	漚	1-3729	1-4040	1-5858	E278	2-4B40	224C41
B	漛		1-4041			E-475A	
C	漜	3-5372			E2B2	2-4B58	
D	漝	3-5405				E-475C	
E	漞	5-5386			E2B7	2-4B5D	
F	漟	5-5461			E2B5	2-4B5B	224C57

6F3

	Char	G	J	K	B	C	A
0	漰	3-5381	1-4046	1-6673	E2A7	2-4B4D	224C6D
1	漱	0-4294	0-6291	0-6611	BAA4	1-694B	21485C
2	漲	1-5339	0-6293	0-8372	BAA6	1-694D	214855
3	漳	0-5336	1-4047	1-7537	BA73	1-693C	21484D
4	漴	3-5382				E-475D	224C67
5	漵				E2A9	2-4B4F	224C7B
6	漶	0-6881	1-4048		E2A1	2-4B47	224C5E
7	漷	3-5359			E272	2-4B3A	224C30
8	漸	1-2905	0-3318	0-7934	BAA5	1-694C	21485A
9	漹	3-5370			E2B1	2-4B57	
A	漺	3-5375			E2B4	2-4B5A	
B	漻	3-5406	1-4049		E27B	2-4B43	224C3C
C	漼	3-5380	1-4050	1-8022	E2A8	2-4B4E	
D	漽	5-5491				E-4C74	
E	漾	0-4990	0-6301	1-7090	BA79	1-6942	214853
F	漿	1-2912	0-6289	0-7776	BCDF	1-6D49	214863

6F5

	Char	G	J	K	B	C	A
0	潐	3-5419			E64E	2-5156	
1	潑	1-3835	1-4053	0-5894	BCE2	1-6D4C	21486C
2	潒	5-5465	1-4054		E64D	2-5155	
3	潓	3-5411	1-4055		E659	2-5161	
4	潔	1-2964	0-2373	0-4430	BCE4	1-6D4E	21486F
5	潕	3-5127			E64B	2-5153	224D5A
6	潖	3-5407					
7	潗	5-5482	1-4056	0-8292	E64F	2-5157	224D62
8	潘	0-3743	0-6315	0-5875	BCEF	1-6D59	214879
9	潙	1-6777	1-4057	1-5929		E-4C7D	
A	潚	3-5282	1-4058	0-6656	E646	2-514E	224D2F
B	潛	1-3917	0-6310	0-7754	BCE7	1-6D51	214874
C	潜	0-3917	0-3288	1-7523		E-4C73	2D4874
D	潝	3-5423	1-4059	1-8519	E652	2-515A	224D68
E	潞	0-3426	1-4060	0-5449	E9F0	2-577B	224E2E
F	潟	3-5418	0-1967	0-6419	BCF3	1-6D5D	224D63

6F7

	Char	G	J	K	B	C	A
0	潰	1-3203	0-3657	0-4787	BCEC	1-6D56	214878
1	潱					E-4C75	
2	潲	0-6891			E64C	2-5154	224D5F
3	潳	3-5403			E2A2	2-4B48	
4	潴	0-6883	0-6344	1-7564		E-4C7E	2E4E72
5	潵	3-5409				E-4C6C	
6	潶				E648	2-5150	
7	潷	1-6868			E65F	2-5167	
8	潸	0-6890	0-6306	1-6768	BCE8	1-6D52	214876
9	潹	5-5473				E-4C79	
A	潺	0-6893	0-6305	0-7750	BCEB	1-6D55	214870
B	潻				E661	2-5169	
C	潼	0-6892	0-6314	0-5256	BCE0	1-6D4A	214869
D	潽	3-5425	1-4065	0-6041	E656	2-515E	
E	潾	3-5426	1-4066	0-5581	E5FB	2-5144	224D23
F	潿	1-6822			E65C	2-5164	

Code	Char	G	J	K	B	C	A
6F80	澀	1-4112	0-6308		C0DF	1-742A	21492E
6F81	澁		0-6307	0-6327		E-4C7A	33492E
6F82	澂	8-1356	0-6313	1-7828	E64A	2-5152	2D486B
6F83	澃		1-4067				
6F84	澄	0-1946	0-3201	0-8305	BCE1	1-6D4B	21486B
6F85	澅	3-5253			E645	2-514D	
6F86	澆	1-2929	0-6304	1-7289	BCE5	1-6D4F	214871
6F87	澇	1-3252	1-4068		E5FC	2-5145	224D27
6F88	澈	0-1926	1-4069	0-8445	BAAB	1-6952	21486A
6F89	澉	0-6887		1-5549	E641	2-5149	224D3A
6F8A	澊	3-5427				E-6363	
6F8B	澋	5-5476	1-4070	1-8453	E65A	2-5162	224D4D
6F8C	澌	0-6889	1-4071	1-6965	E642	2-514A	224D3C
6F8D	澍	0-6888	1-4072	0-8131	E640	2-5148	224D37
6F8E	澎	0-3776	0-6316	0-8817	BCEA	1-6D54	214872
6F8F	澏	5-5478				E-4C7B	
6F90	澐		1-4073	0-7390	E658	2-5160	224D35
6F91	澑		0-6317			E-4C77	4B484C
6F92	澒	5-5404	1-4074	1-8408	E5FE	2-5147	224D39
6F93	澓	3-5421	1-4075		E651	2-5159	
6F94	澔	5-5483	1-4076	0-9143	E650	2-5158	2D4756
6F95	澕	5-5331			E65D	2-5165	224C64
6F96	澖		1-4077		E647	2-514F	
6F97	澗	1-2907	0-2034	0-4253	BCEE	1-6D58	21486E
6F98	澘	5-5474		1-6769			
6F99	澙					E-6547	4C4D63
6F9A	澚		1-4078				
6F9B	澛	8-1464					
6F9C	澜	0-3229					27493F
6F9D	澝					E-6546	224D24
6F9E	澞	5-5507			E9F3	2-577E	
6F9F	澟		1-4079	1-6353		E-5156	224D74
6FA0	澠	1-6837	1-4080		BF49	1-7133	224E30
6FA1	澡	0-5272	0-6322	1-7703	BEFE	1-7129	21487E
6FA2	澢	5-5326			EA40	2-582C	
6FA3	澣		0-6321	0-8952	E9EB	2-5776	2E4873
6FA4	澤	1-5283	0-6323	0-8742	BF41	1-712B	214921
6FA5	澥	3-5442	1-4081		E9F7	2-5824	224E40
6FA6	澦	3-5369	1-4082		BF48	1-7132	224D79
6FA7	澧	0-6902	1-4083	0-5440	BF43	1-712D	21487D
6FA8	澨	3-5440	1-4084	1-6812	E9F5	2-5822	224E3C
6FA9	澩	1-7720			ED4F	2-5D3B	
6FAA	澪	3-5434	0-6326		E9FB	2-5828	224E21
6FAB	澫	5-5279			EA42	2-582E	
6FAC	澬	3-5360			E9FA	2-5827	
6FAD	澭	5-5511			E9E9	2-5774	
6FAE	澮	1-6811	1-4085	0-9272	E9F8	2-5825	224E42
6FAF	澯	5-5506	1-4086	0-8329	EA44	2-5830	224E37
6FB0	澰	3-5232	1-4087		EA46	2-5832	224E41
6FB1	澱	1-2177	0-3735	0-7894	BEFD	1-7128	21487B
6FB2	澲	5-5305			EA45	2-5831	
6FB3	澳	0-1636	0-6320	0-7194	BF44	1-712E	214925
6FB4	澴	3-5438			BF4A	1-7134	224E35
6FB5	澵		1-4088			E-5154	
6FB6	澶	0-6904	1-4089	1-7601	BF47	1-7131	224D73
6FB7	澷					E-5158	
6FB8	澸				E9FE	2-582B	
6FB9	澹	0-6903	0-6324	0-5134	BF46	1-7130	33475E
6FBA	澺	3-5444			E9F9	2-5826	
6FBB	澻	3-5428				E-514D	
6FBC	澼	3-5446	1-4090		E9ED	2-5778	224D7D
6FBD	澽	3-5435			E9F2	2-577D	
6FBE	澾	3-5190		0-5122		E-5150	
6FBF	澿	5-5503			E9FD	2-582A	224E25
6FC0	激	0-2804	0-2367	0-4413	BF45	1-712F	214924
6FC1	濁	1-5539	0-3489	0-8690	BF42	1-712C	214922
6FC2	濂	0-6905	0-6318	0-5418	BEFC	1-7127	21487A
6FC3	濃	1-3708	0-3927	0-5056	BF40	1-712A	21487C
6FC4	濄	5-5325			E9F1	2-577C	
6FC5	濅	5-5514	1-4091				
6FC6	濆	3-5286	0-6325	1-6653	E5FD	2-5146	224D7C
6FC7	濇		1-4092	1-6803	E9EC	2-5777	224E26
6FC8	濈	3-5415	1-4093		E9EF	2-577A	224E2F
6FC9	濉	0-6901		1-6916	EA41	2-582D	224E2D
6FCA	濊	3-5203	1-4094	0-7156	E9F4	2-5821	224E32
6FCB	濋	5-5504			E9EA	2-5775	
6FCC	濌	3-5112			ED4E	2-5D3A	
6FCD	濍	5-5472			EA43	2-582F	
6FCE	濎	3-5414			E9EE	2-5779	
6FCF	濏	5-5494			E9FC	2-5829	
6FD0	濐					E-4C71	
6FD1	濑	0-6894					27493A
6FD2	濒	0-1784					27493C
6FD3	濓					E-5155	
6FD4	濔	3-5175	0-6330		ED51	2-5D3D	224E50
6FD5	濕	1-4210	0-6328	0-6705	C0E3	1-742E	2D4844
6FD6	濖	3-5437				E-5530	
6FD7	濗					E-552F	
6FD8	濘	1-3702	0-6331	1-6034	C0D7	1-7422	214927
6FD9	濙	3-5289				E-5535	224E43
6FDA	濚	5-5408	1-4101	0-7125		E-5536	224E44
6FDB	濛	1-8853	0-6334	1-6462	C0DB	1-7426	
6FDC	濜	3-5217			ED53	2-5D3F	
6FDD	濝				ED59	2-5D45	
6FDE	濞	0-6908	1-4102	1-6689	ED57	2-5D43	224E5D
6FDF	濟	1-2835	0-6327	0-8013	C0D9	1-7424	214926
6FE0	濠	0-6909	0-2574	0-9144	C0DA	1-7425	214929
6FE1	濡	0-6906	0-3908	0-7501	C0E1	1-742C	21492C
6FE2	濢	3-5455			ED5A	2-5D46	
6FE3	濣	5-5518			ED52	2-5D3E	
6FE4	濤	1-4446	0-6225	0-5206	C0DC	1-7427	21492D
6FE5	濥	3-5452				E-5531	
6FE6	濦	5-5524			ED56	2-5D42	
6FE7	濧	3-5180			ED55	2-5D41	
6FE8	濨	5-5513	1-4103		ED5B	2-5D47	
6FE9	濩	3-5433	1-4104	0-9145	C0E2	1-742D	224E56
6FEA	濪					E-5537	
6FEB	濫	1-3236	0-4584	0-5329	C0DD	1-7428	21492B
6FEC	濬	8-1357	0-6329	0-8163	C0E0	1-742B	334755
6FED	濭	3-5432			ED54	2-5D40	
6FEE	濮	0-6907	0-6333	1-6606	C0E4	1-742F	224E5E
6FEF	濯	0-6910	0-3485	0-8691	C0DE	1-7429	21492A
6FF0	濰	1-4611	1-4105		C0E5	1-7430	224E62
6FF1	濱	1-1785	0-6332	0-6220	C0D8	1-7423	214928
6FF2	濲				ED58	2-5D44	
6FF3	濳	5-5529	0-6311	1-7524		E-5A55	4B4874
6FF4	濴			1-7170	ED50	2-5D3C	
6FF5	濵		1-4106			E-5159	
6FF6	濶		0-7973			E-5539	2D5E61
6FF7	濷				EFF7	2-6225	
6FF8	濸					E-6548	224E57
6FF9	濹		1-4107				
6FFA	濺	1-2906	0-6337	1-7921	C271	1-765D	214934
6FFB	濻				EFF4	2-6222	
6FFC	濼	1-6788	1-4108		EFF6	2-6224	2D4738
6FFD	濽		1-4109			E-5828	
6FFE	濾	1-3443	0-6341	0-5375	C26F	1-765B	214936
6FFF	濿	5-5303			EFF2	2-617E	

700							
0	瀀	G 3-5457	J 1-4110	K	B EFF3	C 2-6221	A
1	瀁	G 3-5453	J 0-6339	K 0-6940	B EFEE	C 2-617A	A 2D4853
2	瀂	G 5-5484	J	K	B	C E-582A	A
3	瀃	G 5-5479	J	K	B	C E-5827	A
4	瀄	G 3-5159	J	K	B E9F6	C 2-5823	A
5	瀅	G 1-6862	J 1-4111	K 0-9104	B EFEF	C 2-617B	A 224E66
6	瀆	G 1-6834	J 1-4112	K 0-5225	B C270	C 1-765C	A 214933
7	瀇	G 3-5123	J 1-4113	K 1-7268	B EFEB	C 2-6177	A
8	瀈	G 5-5493	J	K	B	C E-5826	A
9	瀉	G 1-4826	J 0-6335	K 0-6265	B C26D	C 1-7659	A 214932
A	瀊	G	J	K	B EFF8	C 2-6226	A
B	瀋	G 1-6841	J 0-6336	K 0-6803	B C26E	C 1-765A	A 214931
C	瀌	G 3-5463	J	K	B EFEC	C 2-6178	A 224E67
D	瀍	G 3-5462	J 1-4114	K	B EFED	C 2-6179	A 224E6A
E	瀎	G 3-5448	J	K	B EFF1	C 2-617D	A
F	瀏	G 1-6815	J 0-6340	K 0-5523	B C273	C 1-765F	A 214937

701							
0	瀐	G 5-5526	J	K	B	C E-5829	A
1	瀑	G 0-3857	J 0-6338	K 0-8878	B C272	C 1-765E	A 214935
2	瀒	G	J	K 1-6804	B	C	A
3	瀓	G	J	K 1-7829	B	C E-582B	A
4	瀔	G 3-5456	J	K	B EFF0	C 2-617C	A
5	瀕	G 1-1784	J 0-4146	K 0-6221	B C378	C 1-7845	A 21493C
6	瀖	G 3-5466	J	K	B F25F	C 2-656A	A
7	瀗	G 3-5470	J 1-4115	K	B F265	C 2-6570	A
8	瀘	G 1-6782	J 0-6346	K 0-5450	B C379	C 1-7846	A 224F39
9	瀙	G 3-5323	J	K	B F25C	C 2-6567	A
A	瀚	G 0-6911	J 0-6343	K 0-8953	B C376	C 1-7843	A 214939
B	瀛	G 0-6913	J 0-6342	K 0-7126	B C373	C 1-7840	A 214938
C	瀜	G 3-5465	J	K 0-7553	B F267	C 2-6572	A
D	瀝	G 1-3304	J 0-6345	K 0-5387	B C377	C 1-7844	A 21493B
E	瀞	G 5-5515	J 0-3852	K 0-7971	B	C E-5A52	A 224F2B
F	瀟	G 1-6876	J 0-6347	K 0-6530	B C374	C 1-7841	A 21493D

702							
0	瀠	G 1-6875	J 1-4116	K	B F25E	C 2-6569	A 224F24
1	瀡	G 3-5454	J	K	B F261	C 2-656C	A 224F35
2	瀢	G 3-5416	J	K	B F262	C 2-656D	A
3	瀣	G 0-6912	J 1-4117	K 0-9014	B F263	C 2-656E	A 224F3A
4	瀤	G 3-5469	J	K	B F266	C 2-6571	A
5	瀥	G 5-5531	J	K	B	C E-5A54	A
6	瀦	G	J 0-3585	K 1-7565	B EFF5	C 2-6223	A 224E72
7	瀧	G 1-6781	J 0-3477	K 0-5473	B F25D	C 2-6568	A 224F26
8	瀨	G 1-6894	J	K 0-5478	B C375	C 1-7842	A 21493A
9	瀩	G	J	K	B F264	C 2-656F	A
A	瀪	G	J	K	B F268	C 2-6934	A
B	瀫	G 3-5464	J	K	B F260	C 2-656B	A
C	瀬	G	J 0-3205	K	B	C E-5A53	A 2D493A
D	瀭	G	J	K	B	C E-654A	A 224F31
E	瀮	G	J	K	B	C E-6549	A 224F2F
F	瀯	G 3-5371	J 1-4118	K 0-7127	B F45D	C 2-692B	A

703							
0	瀰	G 1-8856	J 0-6348	K 1-6492	B C46A	C 1-7975	A 333D4C
1	瀱	G 3-5471	J	K	B F460	C 2-692E	A
2	瀲	G 1-6882	J 0-6350	K 1-6255	B C46B	C 1-7976	A 2E4E41
3	瀳	G 5-5406	J	K	B F468	C 2-6937	A
4	瀴	G 3-5383	J 1-4119	K	B F45F	C 2-692D	A 224F51
5	瀵	G 0-6915	J	K	B F45C	C 2-692A	A 224F44
6	瀶	G	J	K	B	C E-5C51	A
7	瀷	G 3-5477	J 1-4120	K 0-7643	B F45E	C 2-692C	A
8	瀸	G 3-5472	J	K 1-7949	B F462	C 2-6930	A
9	瀹	G 0-6914	J 1-4121	K	B F465	C 2-6933	A 224F53
A	瀺	G 3-5474	J	K	B F464	C 2-6932	A 224F54
B	瀻	G 5-5532	J	K	B F467	C 2-6936	A
C	瀼	G 3-5475	J 1-4122	K 1-7091	B F45B	C 2-6929	A 224F41
D	瀽	G 3-5476	J	K	B	C E-5C4F	A
E	瀾	G 1-3229	J 0-6349	K 0-5319	B C469	C 1-7974	A 21493F
F	瀿	G 5-5536	J	K	B F463	C 2-6931	A

704							
0	灀	G 5-5534	J	K	B F466	C 2-6935	A
1	灁	G	J	K	B F469	C 2-6938	A
2	灂	G 3-5473	J	K	B F461	C 2-692F	A
3	灃	G 1-6767	J 1-4123	K	B F5D3	C 2-6B61	A 224F5D
4	灄	G 1-6860	J 1-4124	K 1-6857	B F5D4	C 2-6B62	A 224F61
5	灅	G 3-5480	J	K	B F5D8	C 2-6B66	A
6	灆	G 5-5502	J	K	B F5D9	C 2-6B67	A
7	灇	G	J	K	B	C E-5E3C	A 224F67
8	灈	G 3-5479	J 1-4125	K	B F5D6	C 2-6B64	A
9	灉	G 3-5483	J 1-4126	K	B F5D7	C 2-6B65	A 224F69
A	灊	G 3-5478	J 1-4127	K	B F5D5	C 2-6B63	A
B	灋	G	J 1-4128	K	B	C E-5E3A	A
C	灌	G 0-2564	J 0-6285	K 0-4620	B C4E9	C 1-7A74	A 214940
D	灍	G 5-5512	J	K	B	C E-5E3B	A
E	灎	G	J 1-4133	K 1-7156	B	C	A
F	灏	G 0-6916	J	K	B	C	A 284F7D

705							
0	灐	G	J	K 0-9105	B	C	A
1	灑	G 1-4087	J 0-6351	K 0-6578	B C578	C 1-7B64	A 214941
2	灒	G 3-5468	J	K	B F6EB	C 2-6D59	A 224F71
3	灓	G 3-5110	J	K 1-6203	B	C E-6036	A
4	灔	G	J 1-4129	K	B	C E-5F52	A
5	灕	G 1-3276	J 1-4130	K	B F6E8	C 2-6D56	A 224F6B
6	灖	G 3-5484	J	K	B F6E9	C 2-6D57	A
7	灗	G	J	K	B F6EA	C 2-6D58	A
8	灘	G 1-4418	J 0-3871	K 0-8708	B C579	C 1-7B65	A 214942
9	灙	G 3-5347	J	K	B	C E-6037	A 224F78
A	灚	G 5-5423	J	K	B F7E5	C 2-6F34	A
B	灛	G 3-5392	J	K	B F7E4	C 2-6F33	A
C	灜	G	J	K	B	C E-654B	A 224F73
D	灝	G 1-6916	J 1-4131	K 0-9146	B F8AF	C 2-703D	A 224F7D
E	灞	G 0-6917	J 1-4132	K 1-8175	B C5F4	C 1-7C60	A 224F7B
F	灟	G 3-5429	J	K	B F8AD	C 2-703B	A

706							
0	灠	G 5-5413	J	K	B F8B0	C 2-703E	A
1	灡	G	J	K	B F8AE	C 2-703C	A 224F7C
2	灢	G	J	K	B F8F5	C 2-7125	A
3	灣	G 1-4569	J 0-6352	K 0-5629	B C657	C 1-7D24	A 214943
4	灤	G 1-3448	J 1-4134	K	B C665	C 1-7D32	A 214944
5	灥	G 5-5972	J 1-4135	K	B F9A3	C 2-7171	A 225027
6	灦	G	J	K	B F96C	C 2-715B	A 225025
7	灧	G 1-6857	J	K	B	C E-6179	A 225029
8	灨	G	J	K	B F9A2	C 2-7170	A 225028
9	灩	G	J	K 1-7157	B F9D0	C 2-723E	A
A	灪	G 3-5486	J	K	B F9D1	C 2-723F	A
B	火	G 0-2780	J 0-1848	K 0-9193	B A4F5	C 1-4556	A 214945
C	灬	G 0-7665	J 1-4136	K	B	C	A
D	灭	G 0-3580	J	K	B	C	A 274842
E	灮	G	J 1-4137	K	B	C E-2428	A 2D3272
F	灯	G 0-2138	J 0-3784	K 1-7659	B	C E-2426	A 274A24

707							
0	灰	G 0-2750	J 0-1905	K 0-9273	B A6C7	C 1-4848	A 214946
1	灱	G 5-4915	J	K	B CA41	C 2-2261	A
2	灲	G	J	K	B	C E-2427	A
3	灳	G	J	K	B	C E-242B	A
4	灴	G 5-4917	J	K	B CB5E	C 2-245E	A 225039
5	灵	G 0-3373	J 1-4138	K	B	C E-2662	A 275F6F
6	灶	G 0-5278	J 1-4139	K	B A85F	C 1-4B22	A 214947
7	灷	G 3-4744	J	K	B	C E-265F	A
8	灸	G 0-3036	J 0-2168	K 0-4722	B A862	C 1-4B25	A 214949
9	灹	G 3-4746	J	K	B	C E-265E	A
A	灺	G 5-4918	J	K	B CB5F	C 2-245F	A 22503B
B	灻	G	J	K	B	C E-2663	A
C	灼	G 0-5538	J 0-2862	K 0-7739	B A860	C 1-4B23	A 214948
D	災	G	J 0-2650	K 0-7812	B A861	C 1-4B24	A 21494A
E	灾	G 0-5254	J 1-4140	K 1-7553	B	C E-2660	A 27494A
F	灿	G 0-1851	J	K	B	C	A 274A31

708

	Char	G	J	K	B	C	A
0	炀	0-7630					27496F
1	炁	5-3491	1-4141	1-5983		E-2977	22504A
2	炂	3-4757			CD58	2-2778	
3	炃	5-4925			CD5A	2-277A	
4	炄	5-4930			CD55	2-2775	225049
5	炅	0-7433	1-4142	0-4461	CD52	2-2772	2D526B
6	炆	3-4759	1-4143	1-6483	CD54	2-2774	225042
7	炇	5-4923				E-2974	
8	炈	3-4758				E-2970	225056
9	炉	0-3415	0-4707			E-2975	274A37
A	炊	0-2022	0-3170	0-8607	AAA4	1-4E65	21494F
B	炋					E-296F	
C	炌	3-4755				E-2979	225059
D	炍					E-2976	
E	炎	0-4955	0-1774	0-7090	AAA2	1-4E63	21494C
F	炏	5-4928				E-2972	

709

	Char	G	J	K	B	C	A
0	炐	3-4748				E-2971	
1	炑	5-4921			CD56	2-2776	
2	炒	0-1920	0-6354	0-8504	AAA3	1-4E64	21494D
3	炓	5-4929			CD53	2-2773	225040
4	炔	0-4018	1-4144		CD50	2-2770	39526B
5	炕	0-3127	1-4145	1-8314	AAA1	1-4E62	21494B
6	炖	0-7632	1-4146		CD57	2-2777	225048
7	炗	5-4920	1-4147				
8	炘	3-4754	1-4148	0-9360	CD51	2-2771	225057
9	炙	0-5443	0-6353	0-7719	AAA5	1-4E66	21494E
A	炚	5-4157		0-4641	CD59	2-2779	
B	炛	5-4924	1-4149				
C	炜	0-7631					285252
D	炝	0-7633					28533C
E	炞	8-1374					
F	炟	3-4764			CFAF	2-2B6F	

70A

	Char	G	J	K	B	C	A
0	炠	3-4765				E-2D5E	
1	炡	5-4933		0-7972	CFB3	2-2B73	225062
2	炢	3-4760				E-2D5C	
3	炣	3-4761				E-2D5A	225063
4	炤		1-4150	0-6531	ACB7	1-523A	2D4971
5	炥	3-4770				E-2D58	
6	炦	3-4763				E-626A	
7	炧	3-4767				E-2D65	22506F
8	炨	5-4939				E-2D62	
9	炩	5-4937			CFB6	2-2B76	225073
A	炪	3-4771				E-2D5F	
B	炫	0-7637	1-4151	0-9059	ACAF	1-5232	214950
C	炬	0-3070	0-6357	0-4367	ACB2	1-5235	214952
D	炭	0-4431	0-3526	0-8709	ACB4	1-5237	214955
E	炮	0-3758	0-6360	1-8228	ACB6	1-5239	214956
F	炯	0-3028	0-6355	0-9106	ACB3	1-5236	214954

70B

	Char	G	J	K	B	C	A
0	炰	3-4864	1-4152	1-8229	CFB2	2-2B72	2D4956
1	炱	0-7638	1-4153		CFB1	2-2B71	2E506D
2	炲	5-4940				E-2D64	
3	炳	0-1794	0-6359	0-6025	ACB1	1-5234	214953
4	炴	3-4766	1-4154		CFB4	2-2B74	
5	炵	3-4769			CFB5	2-2B75	225071
6	炶	5-4936				E-2D63	
7	炷	0-7636	1-4155	0-8132	CFAE	2-2B6E	22505C
8	炸	0-5308	0-6358	0-7740	ACB5	1-5238	214957
9	点	0-2167	0-3732	0-7935		E-2D68	27626A
A	為		0-1657		ACB0	1-5233	214951
B	炻	0-7634				E-2D5D	706C42
C	炼	0-3322					27496A
D	炽	0-1967					274A21
E	炾				CFB0	2-2B70	
F	炿					E-654D	225072

70C

	Char	G	J	K	B	C	A
0	烀	0-7635					706C43
1	烁	0-4324					274A36
2	烂	0-3235					274A38
3	烃	0-4494					285150
4	烄	3-4781				E-3228	
5	烅	5-4954			D277	2-305A	
6	烆	5-4955			D278	2-305B	22513D
7	烇	3-4778			D279	2-305C	22513B
8	烈	0-3350	0-4685	0-5413	AF50	1-5653	21495B
9	烉					E-6279	
A	烊	0-7640	1-4156	1-7092	AF4C	1-564F	214958
B	烋	5-5055	0-6362	0-9346	D26E	2-3051	225138
C	烌	5-4953				E-322A	
D	烍	5-4951			D276	2-3059	
E	烎				D27B	2-305E	
F	烏	1-4658	0-1708	0-7201	AF51	1-5654	21495D

70D

	Char	G	J	K	B	C	A
0	烐	5-4956				E-322B	22513A
1	烑	5-4957	1-4157		D26C	2-304F	22512E
2	烒	5-4942			D272	2-3055	
3	烓	5-4943	1-4158	1-5663	D26B	2-304E	22507D
4	烔	5-4949	1-4159		D275	2-3058	22512B
5	烕	3-3818	1-4160			E-3231	
6	烖		1-4161			E-322F	33494A
7	烗	5-4958			D271	2-3054	
8	烘	0-2670	1-4162	0-9184	AF4D	1-5650	21495A
9	烙	0-3251	0-6364	0-5307	AF4F	1-5652	21495C
A	烚	3-4779			D27A	2-305D	22513C
B	烛	0-5482				E-3229	274A30
C	烜	3-4773	1-4163	1-8482	D26A	2-304D	22507C
D	烝	3-4865	0-6363	0-8186	D26D	2-3050	225122
E	烞	5-4945			D273	2-3056	
F	烟	0-4944	0-6361	0-7051		E-322D	2D496B

70E

	Char	G	J	K	B	C	A
0	烠	3-4774			D274	2-3057	225128
1	烡				D27C	2-305F	225123
2	烢	5-4959			D270	2-3053	
3	烣	5-4948				E-322C	225126
4	烤	0-3130	1-4164		AF4E	1-5651	214959
5	烥					E-654F	22507B
6	烦	0-2319					27496D
7	烧	0-4153					274A26
8	烨	0-7639					285424
9	烩	0-2766					274A33
A	烪					E-654E	225078
B	烫	0-4444					27497E
C	烬	0-2993					28544F
D	热	0-4040					27497D
E	烮					E-3230	
F	烯	0-4709			E26D	1-5B72	225167

70F

	Char	G	J	K	B	C	A
0	烰	5-4969			D64E	2-3671	
1	烱	8-1456	0-6356	0-4462		E-3730	2D4954
2	烲	3-4786				E-3732	
3	烳	3-4784			D650	2-3673	225148
4	烴	1-4494			D64C	2-366F	225150
5	烵	5-4944				E-372F	
6	烶	5-4952			D658	2-367B	225160
7	烷	0-4573			D64A	2-366D	225142
8	烸	5-4966			D657	2-367A	
9	烹	0-3775	0-4303	0-8818	E269	1-5B6E	21495E
A	烺	3-4793	1-4165		D648	2-366B	22513F
B	烻	3-4777			DA5B	2-3D5F	
C	烼	3-4785			D652	2-3675	
D	烽	0-2373	0-6366	0-6075	E26C	1-5B71	214961
E	烾					E-3735	217627
F	烿	5-4970			D653	2-3676	

710

	Char	G	J	K	B	C	A
0	焀	5-4968			D656	2-3679	225168
1	焁	3-4790				E-372E	
2	焂	5-4967			D65A	2-367D	
3	焃	5-4962	1-4166			E-372C	22514C
4	焄	5-5058	1-4167	0-9322	D64F	2-3672	225144
5	焅	5-4965	1-4168				
6	焆	3-4788	1-4169		D654	2-3677	
7	焇	3-4787	1-4170			E-372D	
8	焈					E-3731	
9	焉	0-4941	0-6365	0-6974	B26A	1-5B6F	21495F
A	焊	0-2624			B26B	1-5B70	214960
B	焋		1-4171		D659	2-367C	
C	焌	3-4802	1-4172	0-8164	D64D	2-3670	22515C
D	焍	3-4792			D649	2-366C	
E	焎	5-5057			D65B	2-367E	
F	焏		1-4173			E-3733	

712

	Char	G	J	K	B	C	A
0	焠	5-4981	1-4175	1-6950	DA58	2-3D5C	22516E
1	無	1-4662	0-4421	0-5777	B54C	1-6052	214966
2	焢				DA60	2-3D64	
3	焣				DA5E	2-3D62	
4	焤					E-3C7D	
5	焥	3-4814			DA5F	2-3D63	
6	焦	0-2925	0-3039	0-8505	B54A	1-6050	214968
7	焧	5-4978				E-3C7C	
8	焨				DA63	2-3D67	
9	焩	5-4979					22523B
A	焪	3-4813				E-3C6F	
B	焫	5-4963	1-4176			E-3C7A	
C	焬					E-3C72	
D	焭	5-1936	1-4177	1-5650		E-3D21	225175
E	焮	5-4977		1-8508	DA5C	2-3D60	225243
F	焯	0-7644	1-4178	1-7516	DA5A	2-3D5E	225235

714

	Char	G	J	K	B	C	A
0	煀						
1	煁	3-4816	1-4182		DE70	2-4456	225256
2	煂				DE77	2-445D	
3	煃	3-4818			DE79	2-445F	22525C
4	煄	5-4991			DEA1	2-4465	225270
5	煅	0-7649	1-4183			E-4257	2D5E24
6	煆	3-4826	1-4184	1-8274	B7DA	1-6522	225251
7	煇		1-4185	0-9340	DE6B	2-4451	225262
8	煈	5-4927				E-424C	
9	煉	1-3322	0-4691	0-5401	B7D2	1-6478	21496A
A	煊	0-7651	1-4186	0-9331		E-424E	2E3870
B	煋	3-4821	1-4187		DE7A	2-4460	225260
C	煌	0-2745	0-6374	0-9251	B7D7	1-647D	214974
D	煍				DEA2	2-4466	
E	煎	0-2869	0-3289	0-7901	B7CE	1-6474	214969
F	煏	3-4817				E-4251	225254

716

	Char	G	J	K	B	C	A
0	煠	5-4984	1-4194		DE6F	2-4455	225257
1	煡				DE76	2-445C	
2	煢	1-6068	0-6373	1-5649	DE72	2-4458	345175
3	煣	3-4827			DE6E	2-4454	
4	煤	0-3526	0-3965	0-5664	B7D1	1-6477	21496C
5	煥	1-2732	0-6369	0-9226	B7D8	1-647E	214973
6	煦	0-7667	0-6372	0-9315	B7D6	1-647C	214970
7	照	0-5353	0-3040	0-8046	B7D3	1-6479	214971
8	煨	0-7648	1-4201	1-7275	B7DB	1-6523	225265
9	煩	1-2319	0-4049	0-5965	B7D0	1-6476	21496D
A	煪	3-4824			DE75	2-445B	
B	煫	5-5001				E-424F	
C	煬	1-7630	0-6376	0-6941	B7D5	1-647B	21496F
D	煭					E-4259	
E	煮	0-5483	0-2849	0-7720	B54E	1-6054	214963
F	煯					E-4249	

711

	Char	G	J	K	B	C	A
0	焐	0-7641			D651	2-3674	22514A
1	焑					E-6550	225155
2	焒					E-6551	225156
3	焓	0-7642			D655	2-3678	225166
4	焔		0-1775				
5	焕	0-2732					4B4973
6	焖	0-7643					274A25
7	焗	3-4794			D64B	2-366E	
8	焘	0-7666					345452
9	焙	0-1726	0-6368	0-5944	B548	1-604E	214962
A	焚	0-2357	0-4218	0-6145	B549	1-604F	214964
B	焛				DA65	2-3D69	
C	焜	3-4807	0-6367	1-8404	B54F	1-6055	22522E
D	焝	3-4810				E-3C74	
E	焞	3-4811	1-4174	0-5240	DA59	2-3D5D	22516C
F	焟	3-4803			DA62	2-3D66	

713

	Char	G	J	K	B	C	A
0	焰	0-4970	1-4179	0-7091	B54B	1-6051	214967
1	焱	0-7645	1-4180	1-8341	DA5D	2-3D61	225174
2	焲	5-4980			DA61	2-3D65	
3	焳					E-3C7B	334968
4	焴	5-4982				E-3C79	22516D
5	焵	3-4750				E-3C71	225228
6	然	0-4027	0-3319	0-7052	B54D	1-6053	214965
7	焷	3-4809				E-3C73	
8	焸	3-4808	1-4181			E-3C77	
9	焹					E-6553	225227
A	焺	5-4976			DA64	2-3D68	
B	焻	5-4975				E-6554	22522C
C	焼		0-3038				2D4A26
D	焽					E-6555	225232
E	焾						
F	焿					E-6552	22516F

715

	Char	G	J	K	B	C	A
0	煐	3-4804	1-4188	0-7128	DE7D	2-4463	225269
1	煑					E-4258	
2	煒	1-7631	1-4189	1-7359	DE6D	2-4453	225252
3	煓	3-4822			DE7E	2-4464	22526B
4	煔	3-4825			DE6C	2-4452	
5	煕		0-6370				
6	煖		0-6375	0-4978	B7DC	1-6524	334342
7	煗		1-4190	1-6018		E-4252	
8	煘	5-4987			DE78	2-445E	
9	煙		0-1776	0-7053	B7CF	1-6475	21496B
A	煚	3-4806	1-4191		DEA3	2-4467	22525D
B	煛	3-4831				E-483C	2E525D
C	煜	0-7647	1-4192	0-7382	B7D4	1-647A	21496E
D	煝	5-5002			DE71	2-4457	225255
E	煞	0-4123	1-4193	0-6316	B7D9	1-6521	214972
F	煟	5-4989			DE7C	2-4462	225267

717

	Char	G	J	K	B	C	A
0	煰				DE7B	2-4461	
1	煱					E-6559	225266
2	煲	0-7650			DE73	2-4459	225276
3	煳	0-7646					22525A
4	煴	3-4820				E-4253	
5	煵					E-6557	225259
6	煶					E-6558	22525E
7	煷					E-6556	225248
8	煸	0-7652			DE74	2-445A	225278
9	煹		1-4202				
A	煺	0-7653					4C523A
B	煻	3-4836			E2C1	2-4B67	22527C
C	煼	5-4938				E-476F	225336
D	煽	0-4131	0-3290	0-6435	BAB4	1-695B	214975
E	煾					E-476E	
F	煿	5-5005				E-476C	

	718	71A	71C	71E
0	熀 G 3-4832 J 1-4203 K 1-7163 B E2BD C 2-4B63 A 22532B	熠 G 0-7658 J 1-4210 K 1-6953 B E666 C 2-516E A 225352	燀 G 3-4812 J 1-4218 K B EA4C C 2-5838 A 225422	燠 G 0-7659 J 0-6390 K 1-7334 B C0EE C 1-7439 A 225447
1	熁 G 3-4838 J K B E2C3 C 2-4B69 A	熡 G J K B E66E C 2-5176 A	燁 G 1-7639 J 1-4219 K 0-7107 B EA4D C 2-5839 A 225424	燡 G 3-4772 J K B ED5C C 2-5D48 A 22543F
2	熂 G 3-4752 J K B E2BF C 2-4B65 A	熢 G J 1-4211 K 0-6076 B C E-4D2A A	燂 G 3-4849 J K B EA48 C 2-5834 A 225375	燢 G J K B ED62 C 2-5D4E A
3	熃 G 5-5013 J K B C E-4770 A	熣 G 5-5019 J K B C E-4D24 A	燃 G 0-4028 J 0-3919 K 0-7055 B BF55 C 1-713F A 214A2A	燣 G J K B C E-553C A
4	熄 G 0-4708 J 0-6379 K 0-6756 B BAB6 C 1-695D A 214979	熤 G 3-4847 J K 1-7458 B E66D C 2-5175 A 225351	燄 G J 1-4220 K B BF56 C 1-7140 A 214A2B	燤 G 3-4745 J K B ED60 C 2-5D4C A
5	熅 G J 1-4204 K 1-7232 B E2BE C 2-4B64 A 225332	熥 G 3-4839 J K B E66B C 2-5173 A 225342	燅 G 5-5028 J K B EA47 C 2-5833 A 225377	燥 G 0-5279 J 0-3371 K 0-8047 B C0EA C 1-7435 A 214A2F
6	熆 G 5-5003 J K B E2C2 C 2-4B68 A	熦 G 5-5018 J K B C E-4D29 A	燆 G 3-4776 J K B EA56 C 2-5842 A	燦 G 1-1851 J 0-2724 K 0-8330 B C0E9 C 1-7434 A 214A31
7	熇 G 3-4834 J 1-4205 K 1-8460 B E2BA C 2-4B60 A 22527B	熧 G 3-4756 J K B E671 C 2-5179 A	燇 G 5-5033 J K B EA51 C 2-583D A 225369	燧 G 0-7661 J 0-6392 K 0-6612 B C0E6 C 1-7431 A 214A2D
8	熈 G J 0-6371 K B C E-4772 A 4B4977	熨 G 0-7657 J 0-6381 K 1-7360 B BCF7 C 1-6D61 A 21497B	燈 G 1-2138 J 0-3785 K 0-5283 B BF4F C 1-7139 A 214A24	燨 G J K B ED5E C 2-5D4A A 225436
9	熉 G 3-4789 J K 0-7391 B E2BC C 2-4B62 A 22532C	熩 G 5-5025 J K B E668 C 2-5170 A 22533F	燉 G 3-4853 J 0-6387 K 0-5241 B BF4C C 1-7136 A 214A22	燩 G 3-4857 J K B C E-553E A
A	熊 G 0-4860 J 0-2307 K 0-7408 B BAB5 C 1-695C A 214978	熪 G 5-5020 J K B E66F C 2-5177 A	燊 G 3-3532 J K B EA50 C 2-583C A 22536D	燪 G 5-5029 J K B C E-5543 A
B	熋 G 5-5012 J K B C E-476A A	熫 G J K B C E-4D28 A	燋 G 3-4851 J 1-4221 K 1-7985 B EA4E C 2-583A A 225429	燫 G 3-4858 J K B C E-5540 A 225432
C	熌 G J 1-4206 K B C E-476D A	熬 G 0-1630 J 0-6382 K 0-7202 B BCF5 C 1-6D5F A 21497C	燌 G 5-4983 J 1-4222 K B C E-5163 A	燬 G J 0-6391 K 1-8485 B C0EC C 1-7437 A 214A32
D	熍 G J K B C E-476B A	熭 G 3-4840 J K B C E-4D25 A	燍 G 3-4848 J K B C E-6374 A	燭 G 1-5482 J 0-3104 K 0-8523 B C0EB C 1-7436 A 214A30
E	熎 G J K B C E-4768 A	熮 G 3-4846 J K B C E-4D22 A	燎 G 0-3339 J 0-6389 K 0-5490 B BF52 C 1-713C A 214A29	燮 G 0-5938 J 0-5057 K 0-6480 B C0E8 C 1-7433 A 214A2C
F	熏 G 0-4912 J 0-6377 K 0-9323 B E2C0 C 2-4B66 A 2D4A34	熯 G 3-4841 J 1-4212 K 1-6831 B E663 C 2-516B A 22534E	燏 G 3-4855 J K B EA52 C 2-583E A 22536F	燯 G 3-4856 J K B C E-5541 A

	719	71B	71D	71F
0	熐 G J K B E2BB C 2-4B61 A	熰 G 3-4749 J 1-4213 K B E665 C 2-516D A	燐 G J 0-4653 K 0-5582 B BF4D C 1-7137 A 214A23	燰 G J K B ED61 C 2-5D4D A
1	熑 G 3-4837 J K B C E-4767 A	熱 G 1-4040 J 0-3914 K 0-7080 B BCF6 C 1-6D60 A 21497D	燑 G 5-5032 J K B C E-515E A 225367	燱 G 5-5040 J K B ED5D C 2-5D49 A
2	熒 G 1-5111 J 1-4207 K 0-9107 B BAB7 C 1-695E A 225323	熲 G 3-6485 J 1-4214 K 1-5651 B E662 C 2-516A A 225347	燒 G 1-4153 J 0-6386 K 0-6532 B BF4E C 1-7138 A 214A26	燲 G J K B ED5F C 2-5D4B A
3	熓 G J K B C E-655B A	熳 G 0-7655 J 1-4215 K B E672 C 2-517A A 225357	燓 G 5-5030 J 1-4223 K B C E-5166 A	燳 G J K B C E-5542 A 22543D
4	熔 G 0-4059 J 0-4548 K 0-7334 B BAB2 C 1-6959 A 2D5E26	熴 G J K B C E-655C A 225359	燔 G 0-7660 J 0-6388 K 0-5966 B EA4F C 2-583B A 225426	燴 G 1-2766 J K B C0ED C 1-7438 A 214A33
5	熕 G J 0-6380 K B C A 695F70	熵 G 0-7656 J K B E669 C 2-5171 A 22533E	燕 G 0-4964 J 0-1777 K 0-7056 B BF50 C 1-713A A 214A28	燵 G J 0-6393 K B C A 22543A
6	熖 G J K B C E-655A A 225333	熶 G 5-5031 J K B C E-5162 A	燖 G 3-4782 J 1-4224 K 1-6991 B EA4B C 2-5837 A 225370	燶 G J K B C A
7	熗 G 1-7633 J K B E2C4 C 2-4B6A A 22533C	熷 G 5-5034 J K B C E-515A A 22536A	燗 G J 0-6383 K B C A 4B4A38	燷 G 5-5038 J K B C A
8	熘 G 0-7654 J K B C A 225339	熸 G 3-4850 J K B EA4A C 2-5836 A 22537C	燘 G 5-4971 J K B EA54 C 2-5840 A	燸 G 3-4859 J 1-4228 K B C277 C 1-7663 A
9	熙 G 0-4685 J 0-8406 K 0-9387 B BAB3 C 1-695A A 214977	熹 G 0-7668 J 0-6384 K 0-9388 B BF51 C 1-713B A 214A27	燙 G 1-4444 J 1-4225 K 1-8146 B BF53 C 1-713D A 21497E	燹 G 0-7662 J 0-6401 K 1-8528 B EFFB C 2-6229 A 225456
A	熚 G 3-4775 J 1-4208 K B E667 C 2-516F A 225355	熺 G 5-5027 J 1-4216 K 0-9389 B C E-5160 A 225372	燚 G 3-4854 J 1-4226 K B EA57 C 2-5843 A	燺 G 5-5044 J K B C E-582D A
B	熛 G 3-4843 J 1-4209 K 1-8242 B E664 C 2-516C A 22534A	熻 G 3-4852 J K B C E-515C A	燛 G J K B EA58 C 2-5844 A	燻 G J 0-6378 K 0-9324 B C274 C 1-7660 A 214A34
C	熜 G 3-4845 J K B E670 C 2-5178 A	熼 G 3-4844 J K B EA55 C 2-5841 A	燜 G 1-7643 J 1-4227 K B BF54 C 1-713E A 214A25	燼 G 1-2993 J 0-6394 K 0-6772 B C275 C 1-7661 A 22544F
D	熝 G 5-5023 J K B E66A C 2-5172 A	熽 G 3-4815 J K B EA53 C 2-583F A	燝 G J K B C E-655D A 225421	燽 G 5-4961 J K B EFFD C 2-622B A
E	熞 G 5-4964 J K B E66C C 2-5174 A 225346	熾 G 1-1967 J 0-6385 K 0-8631 B BF4B C 1-7135 A 214A21	燞 G J K B C E-655E A 22542A	燾 G 1-7666 J 1-4229 K 0-5207 B C276 C 1-7662 A 2E5452
F	熟 G 0-4276 J 0-2947 K 0-6657 B BCF4 C 1-6D5E A 21497A	熿 G 5-5015 J 1-4217 K B EA49 C 2-5835 A 22537A	營 G 1-5110 J 0-5159 K 0-7129 B C0E7 C 1-7432 A 214A2E	燿 G 8-1376 J 0-6402 K 0-7292 B EFFA C 2-6228 A 33525B

Code	Char	G	J	K	B	C	A
7200	爀	5-5041	1-4230	0-9050		E-582E	
7201	爁	3-4829			EFF9	2-6227	
7202	爂				F26C	2-6576	
7203	爃	5-4985			EFFC	2-622A	
7204	爄	3-4762				E-5A56	
7205	爅	5-5048			F26D	2-6577	
7206	爆	0-1712	0-3990	0-8879	C37A	1-7847	214A35
7207	爇	3-7534	1-4231	1-6844	F26B	2-6575	225461
7208	爈	3-4828	1-4232			E-5A57	
7209	爉	3-4860	1-4233				
720A	爊	5-5050			F26A	2-6574	22545E
720B	爋			1-8476		E-5C59	225471
720C	爌	3-4747		1-5786	F269	2-6573	22544B
720D	爍	1-4324	0-6403	1-6761	C37B	1-7848	214A36
720E	爎					E-655F	22545B
720F	爏	5-4922				E-5C56	
7210	爐	1-3415	0-6404	0-5451	C46C	1-7977	214A37
7211	爑	5-5047				E-5C58	
7212	爒					E-5C55	
7213	爓	5-5024	1-4234		F46A	2-6939	225469
7214	爔	3-4861		1-8529	F46B	2-693A	
7215	爕					E-5A58	225466
7216	爖	5-4935				E-5C53	
7217	爗		1-4235	1-7164		E-5C57	225460
7218	爘					E-6561	22546E
7219	爙	5-5053			F5DC	2-6B6A	
721A	爚	5-5052	1-4236	1-7081	F5DB	2-6B69	225479
721B	爛	1-3235	0-6405	0-5320	C4EA	1-7A75	214A38
721C	爜					E-5F53	
721D	爝	0-7663	1-4237		F5DA	2-6B68	225521
721E	爞				F6EC	2-6D5A	
721F	爟	3-4862	1-4238	1-5764	F6ED	2-6D5B	22547D
7220	爠					E-5F54	
7221	爡	3-4819				E-6039	
7222	爢				F7E6	2-6F35	
7223	爣	3-4830			F8B1	2-703F	
7224	爤		1-4239			E-6143	
7225	爥	5-5036		1-8008		E-6142	225529
7226	爦				F8F6	2-7126	22552A
7227	爧				F9BC	2-722C	
7228	爨	0-7664	0-6406	1-7849	C679	1-7D46	214A39
7229	爩				F9C6	2-7240	
722A	爪	0-5506	0-3662	0-8048	A4F6	1-4557	214A3A
722B	爫		1-4240				
722C	爬	0-3732	0-6408	0-8780	AAA6	1-4E67	214A3C
722D	爭	1-5389	0-6407	0-7819	AAA7	1-4E68	214A3B
722E	爮	3-4423				E-2D69	
722F	爯	5-4674	1-4241				
7230	爰	0-7528	0-6409	0-7426	ACB8	1-523B	214A3D
7231	爱	0-1614					273E77
7232	爲	1-4610	0-6410	0-7451		E-3D22	
7233	爳						
7234	爴		1-4242				
7235	爵	0-3084	0-2863	0-7741	C0EF	1-743A	214A3E
7236	父	0-2424	0-4167	0-6111	A4F7	1-4558	214A3F
7237	爷	0-5015					274A42
7238	爸	0-1654	1-4243	1-8176	AAA8	1-4E69	214A40
7239	爹	0-2189	1-4244	1-6067	AF52	1-5655	214A41
723A	爺	1-5015	0-4476	0-6912	B7DD	1-6525	214A42
723B	爻	0-5619	0-6411	0-9301	A4F8	1-4559	214A43
723C	爼		0-6412			E-2D6B	4B316A
723D	爽	0-4312	0-3354	0-6348	B26E	1-5B73	214A44
723E	爾	1-2291	0-2804	0-7619	BAB8	1-695F	214A45
723F	爿	0-6761	0-6413		C962	2-2142	225541
7240	牀		0-6414	0-6349		E-297C	2D3C6E
7241	牁	3-2626	1-4245		CFB7	2-2B77	225543
7242	牂	3-2628	1-4246	1-7538	D27D	2-3060	225544
7243	牃		1-4247				
7244	牄	5-2880			E2C5	2-4B6B	
7245	牅		1-4248				
7246	牆		0-6415	0-7777	C0F0	1-743B	214A46
7247	片	0-3812	0-4250	0-8824	A4F9	1-455A	214A47
7248	版	0-1670	0-4039	0-8790	AAA9	1-4E6A	214A48
7249	牉	3-4412			CFB8	2-2B78	
724A	牊	5-4653			CFB9	2-2B79	
724B	牋		0-6416	1-7602	DA66	2-3D6A	33502B
724C	牌	0-3738	0-3955	0-8811	B550	1-6056	214A49
724D	牍	0-7525					274A4C
724E	牎		1-4249			E-425D	
724F	牏	3-4415	1-4250		DEA4	2-4468	225551
7250	牐		1-4251			E-425C	22554F
7251	牑	3-4416				E-425B	
7252	牒	0-7526	0-3613	0-8464	B7DE	1-6526	214A4A
7253	牓		1-4252	1-6543	E2C6	2-4B6C	225552
7254	牔			1-6519			
7255	牕		1-4253			E-4D2E	225553
7256	牖	0-7527	1-4254	1-7379	BCF8	1-6D62	214A4B
7257	牗					E-4D2D	
7258	牘	1-7525	0-6417	0-5226	C37C	1-7849	214A4C
7259	牙	0-4932	0-1871	0-6819	A4FA	1-455B	214A4D
725A	牚	3-3827	1-4255	1-8158	DA67	2-3D6B	225556
725B	牛	0-3703	0-2177	0-7358	A4FB	1-455C	214A4E
725C	牜		1-4256				
725D	牝	0-7482	0-4438	0-6222	A6C9	1-484A	214A50
725E	牞	5-4291	1-4257		CA42	2-2262	
725F	牟	0-3618	0-4422	0-5731	A6C8	1-4849	214A4F
7260	牠		1-4258		A865	1-4B28	214A53
7261	牡	0-3621	0-1820	0-5732	A864	1-4B27	214A52
7262	牢	0-3246	0-4720	0-5479	A863	1-4B26	214A51
7263	牣	3-4087	1-4259		CB60	2-2460	225559
7264	牤	3-4086				E-2664	
7265	牥	3-4093				E-2A21	
7266	牦	0-7483				E-2A22	3F4A60
7267	牧	0-3633	0-4350	0-5744	AAAA	1-4E6B	214A54
7268	牨	5-4302	1-4260			E-2A23	
7269	物	0-4679	0-4210	0-5810	AAAB	1-4E6C	214A55
726A	牪	5-4294			CD5B	2-277B	
726B	牫		1-4261				
726C	牬				CFBA	2-2B7A	
726D	牭	3-4102				E-2D6D	
726E	牮	0-7480	1-4262		CFBD	2-2B7D	225563
726F	牯	0-7484	1-4263	1-5683	ACBA	1-523D	214A56
7270	牰				CFBB	2-2B7B	
7271	牱		1-4264				
7272	牲	0-4192	0-3223	0-6369	ACB9	1-523C	214A57
7273	牳	3-4104			CFBC	2-2B7C	225561
7274	牴		0-6418	1-7566	ACBB	1-523E	214A58
7275	牵	0-3903					274A5A
7276	牶	5-4311			D2A2	2-3063	225566
7277	牷	3-4107	1-4265		D2A1	2-3062	225568
7278	牸	3-4109	1-4266	1-7485	D27E	2-3061	
7279	特	0-4456	0-3835	0-8769	AF53	1-5656	214A59
727A	牺	0-4694				E-3236	274A62
727B	牻	5-4313	1-4267		D65D	2-3722	
727C	牼	3-4103	1-4268		D65E	2-3723	22556D
727D	牽	1-3903	0-2403	0-4418	B26F	1-5B74	214A5A
727E	牾	0-7485	0-6419		D65C	2-3721	22556B
727F	牿	0-7486	1-4269		D65F	2-3724	225571

Code	Char	G	J	K	B	C	A
7280	犀	0-4712	0-2652	0-6389	B552	1-6058	214A5C
7281	犁	0-3271	0-6421	0-5564	B270	1-5B75	214A5B
7282	犂		0-6420			E-3D24	2D4A5B
7283	犃	3-4116				E-3D23	
7284	犄	0-7487	1-4270		B551	1-6057	214A5D
7285	犅	3-4090			DA6B	2-3D6F	
7286	犆	3-4114			DA6A	2-3D6E	
7287	犇	8-1583	0-6422	1-6654		E-3D25	2D392F
7288	犈	5-4320			DA68	2-3D6C	
7289	犉	3-4115	1-4271		DA69	2-3D6D	225574
728A	犊	0-2231					274A61
728B	犋	0-7488			DA6C	2-3D70	22557C
728C	犌	5-4323			DEA6	2-446A	
728D	犍	0-7489	1-4272	1-5603	DEA5	2-4469	225622
728E	犎	3-4119	1-4273		DEA9	2-446D	
728F	犏	0-7490					225628
7290	犐	3-4120			DEA8	2-446C	
7291	犑	5-4321			DEA7	2-446B	
7292	犒	0-7491	0-6423	1-8386	BAB9	1-6960	214A5F
7293	犓	5-4305	1-4274		E2C9	2-4B6F	
7294	犔	3-4091				E-4775	
7295	犕	3-4122			E2C8	2-4B6E	
7296	犖	1-6093	0-6424	1-6193	BABA	1-6961	214A5E
7297	犗	3-4127			E2C7	2-4B6D	
7298	犘	5-8982			E673	2-517B	
7299	犙	3-4117				E-4D2F	
729A	犚	5-4327			E674	2-517C	
729B	犛		1-4275		BCF9	1-6D63	214A60
729C	犜						
729D	犝	5-4329			EA59	2-5845	
729E	犞				EA5A	2-5846	
729F	犟	0-7481					4C5638
72A0	犠		0-2130				4B4A62
72A1	犡	3-4101			F272	2-657C	
72A2	犢	1-2231	0-6425	0-5227	C37D	1-784A	214A61
72A3	犣	3-4136			F271	2-657B	
72A4	犤	3-4126			F270	2-657A	
72A5	犥	3-4135			F26E	2-6578	
72A6	犦	3-4134			F26F	2-6579	
72A7	犧	1-4694	0-6426	0-9390	C4EB	1-7A76	214A62
72A8	犨	3-4137	1-4276		F46C	2-693B	225648
72A9	犩	3-4138			F6EE	2-6D5C	
72AA	犪	3-4139			F8F7	2-7127	
72AB	犫	5-4331				E-617B	22564C
72AC	犬	0-4014	0-2404	0-4419	A4FC	1-455D	214A63
72AD	犭	0-6575	1-4277				
72AE	犮		1-4278		C9A5	2-2164	
72AF	犯	0-2324	0-4040	0-5983	A5C7	1-4667	214A64
72B0	犰	0-6576			C9A6	2-2165	22564E
72B1	犱		1-4279			E-242C	
72B2	犲	5-3846	0-6428			E-242D	2D5960
72B3	犳	3-3576		1-7517			
72B4	犴	0-6577	1-4280	1-7025	CA43	2-2263	22564F
72B5	犵	5-3848		1-8532	CA44	2-2264	225652
72B6	状	0-5520	0-3085			E-266B	274A68
72B7	犷	0-6578					274B2A
72B8	犸	0-6579					28575E
72B9	犹	0-5144	0-6427			E-2669	274A79
72BA	犺	3-3584			CB66	2-2466	
72BB	犻	3-3577				E-2666	
72BC	犼	5-3854				E-2667	225656
72BD	犽	3-3579			CB62	2-2462	
72BE	犾		1-4281			E-266A	
72BF	犿	3-3583			CB61	2-2461	
72C0	狀	1-5520		0-6350	AAAC	1-4E6D	214A68
72C1	狁	0-6581	1-4282		CB65	2-2465	22565B
72C2	狂	0-3181	0-2224	0-4642	A867	1-4B2A	214A66
72C3	狃	0-6580	0-6429		CB63	2-2463	225658
72C4	狄	0-2150	0-6431	0-7858	A866	1-4B29	214A65
72C5	狅	3-3580			CB67	2-2467	
72C6	狆		0-6430		CB64	2-2464	225651
72C7	狇		1-4283			E-2668	
72C8	狈	0-1723					274A72
72C9	狉	3-3589	1-4284	1-6690	CD5F	2-2821	225667
72CA	狊	3-5713			CFBE	2-2B7E	
72CB	狋	3-3587			CD5D	2-277D	
72CC	狌	3-3593	1-4285		CD64	2-2826	22566C
72CD	狍	0-6583				E-2A26	22566F
72CE	狎	0-6582	0-6432	0-6868	AAAD	1-4E6E	214A69
72CF	狏	5-3858				E-2A2A	
72D0	狐	0-2692	0-2449	0-9147	AAB0	1-4E71	214A6B
72D1	狑	5-3859			CD65	2-2827	
72D2	狒	0-6584	0-6433	1-6691	CD61	2-2823	225664
72D3	狓	3-3605				E-2A27	
72D4	狔	5-3863			CD62	2-2824	
72D5	狕	5-3865	1-4286				
72D6	狖	3-3603	1-4287		CD5C	2-277C	225660
72D7	狗	0-2523	0-2273	0-4723	AAAF	1-4E70	214A6A
72D8	狘	3-3590	1-4288		CD5E	2-277E	
72D9	狙	0-3049	0-3332	0-7835	AAAE	1-4E6F	214A67
72DA	狚	3-3591			CD63	2-2825	
72DB	狛	3-3594	0-2593			E-2A28	22566E
72DC	狜				CD60	2-2822	
72DD	狝	8-9213					
72DE	狞	0-3692					274B28
72DF	狟	5-3866	1-4289		CFC2	2-2C24	
72E0	狠	0-2661	0-6435		ACBD	1-5240	214A6E
72E1	狡	0-2938	0-6436	0-4674	ACBE	1-5241	214A6C
72E2	狢	5-3872	0-6434	1-8278		E-2D75	4B5964
72E3	狣	5-3871			CFC5	2-2C27	
72E4	狤	3-3606			CFBF	2-2C21	
72E5	狥		1-4290	1-6938		E-2D74	225679
72E6	狦				CFC4	2-2C26	
72E7	狧	3-3613				E-2D70	
72E8	狨	0-6585		1-7413	CFC0	2-2C22	225673
72E9	狩	0-6587	0-2877	0-6613	ACBC	1-523F	214A6D
72EA	狪	3-3611			CFC3	2-2C25	
72EB	狫	3-3607			CFC1	2-2C23	225676
72EC	独	0-2232	0-3840			E-2D73	274B27
72ED	狭	0-4733	0-2225			E-2D71	274A70
72EE	狮	0-4208					274B23
72EF	狯	0-6586					274B22
72F0	狰	0-5388					4B4A78
72F1	狱	0-5192					274A7E
72F2	狲	0-6588					28575F
72F3	狳	0-6592	1-4291		D2A8	2-3069	22572E
72F4	狴	0-6589	1-4292	1-8221	D2A5	2-3066	225724
72F5	狵	5-3878				E-3238	
72F6	狶	5-3882			D2A7	2-3068	
72F7	狷	0-6590	0-6438	1-5622	AF58	1-565B	214A73
72F8	狸	0-3274	0-3512	0-5565	AF57	1-565A	2D5965
72F9	狹	1-4733	0-6437	0-9085	AF55	1-5658	214A70
72FA	狺	0-6594	1-4293	1-7421	D2A4	2-3065	22567E
72FB	狻	0-6601	1-4294	1-6770	D2A9	2-306A	22572C
72FC	狼	0-3239	0-4721	0-5341	AF54	1-5657	214A6F
72FD	狽	1-1723	0-3966	0-8812	AF56	1-5659	214A72
72FE	狾	5-3879	1-4301		D2A6	2-3067	225725
72FF	狿	3-3615			D667	2-372C	

730

	Char	G	J	K	B	C	A
0	猀				D2A3	2-3064	
1	猁	0-6591			D2AA	2-306B	22572D
2	猂		1-4302			E-3239	225729
3	猃	0-6593					28582B
4	猄	3-3633	1-4303				
5	猅		1-4304				
6	猆	3-8459				E-3D26	
7	猇	3-3625	1-4305		D662	2-3727	22573B
8	猈	3-3630			D666	2-372B	
9	猉			1-5984			
A	猊	0-6605	0-6441	0-7157	D665	2-372A	2F5D5C
B	猋	3-3574	1-4306		DA6E	2-3D72	225735
C	猌				DA79	2-3D7D	
D	猍	3-3620	1-4307				
E	猎	0-3352				E-373B	274B2C
F	猏				D668	2-372D	

731

	Char	G	J	K	B	C	A
0	猐					E-373A	
1	猑	3-3626			D663	2-3728	
2	猒	5-3840	1-4308		DA6D	2-3D71	
3	猓	0-6603	1-4309	1-5749	E274	1-5B79	214A76
4	猔	3-3635					
5	猕	0-6608					285836
6	猖	0-1894	0-6443	0-8373	E273	1-5B78	214A77
7	猗	0-6602	0-6440	1-7442	D661	2-3726	225736
8	猘	3-3627	1-4310	1-7672	D664	2-3729	22573E
9	猙	1-5388	1-4311	1-7556	E275	1-5B7A	214A78
A	猚	3-3629				E-3739	
B	猛	0-3545	0-4452	0-5677	E272	1-5B77	214A75
C	猜	0-1834	0-6442	0-6736	E271	1-5B76	214A74
D	猝	0-6607	0-6444	0-8081	D660	2-3725	225731
E	猞	0-6606	1-4312		D669	2-372E	225742
F	猟		0-4636				4B4B2C

732

	Char	G	J	K	B	C	A
0	猠						
1	猡	0-6604					274B2F
2	猢	0-6609	1-4313	1-8387	DA70	2-3D74	22574A
3	猣	5-3901			DA77	2-3D7B	
4	猤	3-3645	1-4314			E-3D27	
5	猥	0-6611	0-6448	0-7269	E554	1-605A	214A7C
6	猦				DA76	2-3D7A	
7	猧	3-3621	1-4315	1-7255	DA73	2-3D77	22574E
8	猨		1-4316	1-7345		E-3D2E	225755
9	猩	0-4841	0-6447	0-6490	E556	1-605C	214A7B
A	猪	0-5477	0-3586	0-7836		E-3D29	
B	猫	0-3508	0-3913	0-5762		E-3D2B	22574F
C	猬	0-6612	1-4317			E-3D2A	22574D
D	猭	3-3646			DA75	2-3D79	
E	献	0-4755	0-2405			E-4261	274B2E
F	猯	5-3894	0-6446			E-3D2D	225752

733

	Char	G	J	K	B	C	A
0	猰	3-3638			DA6F	2-3D73	
1	猱	0-6614	1-4318	1-6038	DA71	2-3D75	225746
2	猲	3-3641	1-4319		DA74	2-3D78	22574C
3	猳	5-3904			DA72	2-3D76	
4	猴	0-2679	0-6445	1-8469	E555	1-605B	214A7D
5	猵	3-3644	1-4320		DA78	2-3D7C	
6	猶	1-5144	0-4517	0-7502	E553	1-6059	214A79
7	猷	0-7364	0-4518	0-7503	B7DF	1-6527	214A7A
8	猸	0-6613				E-3D28	225749
9	猹	0-6610					70622A
A	猺	3-3652	1-4321		DEAD	2-4471	225762
B	猻	1-6588	1-4322		DEAC	2-4470	22575F
C	猼	3-3650			DEAA	2-446E	
D	猽	5-3911	1-4323				
E	猾	0-2711	0-6449	0-9234	B7E2	1-652A	214B22
F	猿	0-5219	0-1778	0-7427	B7E1	1-6529	214B21

734

	Char	G	J	K	B	C	A
0	獀	3-3642			DEAE	2-4472	225765
1	獁	1-6579				E-425F	
2	獂	3-3651			DEAB	2-446F	
3	獃		1-4324	1-7062	E2CA	2-4B70	2D3556
4	獄	1-5192	0-2586	0-7211	BABB	1-6962	214A7E
5	獅	1-4208	0-2766	0-6266	B7E0	1-6528	214B23
6	獆	5-3907				E-4262	
7	獇					E-6562	22575A
8	獈					E-6563	22575B
9	獉	5-3905			DEB0	2-4474	22575C
A	獊	3-3581			DEAF	2-4473	
B	獋					E-4D30	225821
C	獌	3-3658			E2CD	2-4B73	
D	獍	0-6616	1-4325		E2CB	2-4B71	225768
E	獎		0-6450		BCFA	1-6D64	517954
F	獏	3-3649	0-6451			E-4779	4B5963

735

	Char	G	J	K	B	C	A
0	獐	0-6615	1-4326	0-7779	BABC	1-6963	214B24
1	獑	3-3623			E2CC	2-4B72	
2	獒	0-7365	1-4327	0-7203	E676	2-517E	22576B
3	獓	3-3648				E-4778	
4	獔					E-477A	
5	獕	3-3659				E-4777	
6	獖	3-3639	1-4328				
7	獗	0-6617	0-6453	0-4781	BCFB	1-6D65	214B26
8	獘		1-4329	1-8222	E675	2-517D	22577B
9	獙				E67E	2-5228	
A	獚	3-3656			E67D	2-5227	
B	獛				E67B	2-5225	
C	獜	3-3668		1-6372			
D	獝	3-3669	1-4330		E67A	2-5224	225774
E	獞	5-3914	1-4331		E677	2-5221	225772
F	獟	5-3868	1-4332		E678	2-5222	

736

	Char	G	J	K	B	C	A
0	獠	0-6618	1-4333	1-6324	E679	2-5223	225779
1	獡	3-3665			E67C	2-5226	
2	獢	3-3614			E6A1	2-5229	22577E
3	獣		0-2935				4B4B2B
4	獤						
5	獥	3-3671			EA5F	2-584B	
6	獦	3-3664	1-4334		EA5C	2-5848	
7	獧		1-4335		EA5D	2-5849	225825
8	獨	1-2232	0-6455	0-5228	BF57	1-7141	214B27
9	獩	5-3869	1-4336	1-7183	EA5B	2-5847	
A	獪	1-6586	0-6454	0-9274	EA61	2-584D	2D4B22
B	獫	1-6593	1-4337	1-8337	EA60	2-584C	22582B
C	獬	0-6619	1-4338	1-8321	EA5E	2-584A	225829
D	獭	0-4401					274B2D
E	獮	3-3602	1-4339		ED64	2-5D50	
F	獯	0-6620	1-4340	1-8477	ED65	2-5D51	22582F

737

	Char	G	J	K	B	C	A
0	獰	1-3692	0-6456	0-7130	C0F1	1-743C	214B28
1	獱	3-3654	1-4341			E-5549	
2	獲	1-2781	0-1945	0-9282	C0F2	1-743D	214B29
3	獳	3-3672			ED63	2-5D4F	
4	獴	3-3670					
5	獵	1-3352	0-6458	0-5420	C279	1-7665	214B2C
6	獶	3-3674			EFFE	2-622C	
7	獷	1-6578	1-4342	1-5787	C278	1-7664	214B2A
8	獸	1-4262	0-6457	0-6614	C37E	1-784B	214B2B
9	獹	5-3857	1-4343				
A	獺	1-4401	0-6460	0-5123	C3A1	1-784C	214B2D
B	獻	1-4755	0-6459	0-9044	C46D	1-7978	214B2E
C	獼	1-6608	1-4344	1-6493	F46E	2-693D	225836
D	獽	3-3681			F46D	2-693C	
E	獾	0-6621			F5DD	2-6B6B	225838
F	獿	5-3920			F6EF	2-6D5D	

738

	Char	G	J	K	B	C	A
0	玀	1-6604	1-4345		C57A	1-7B66	214B2F
1	玁	3-3618	1-4346	1-8338	F7E8	2-6F37	22583B
2	玂	5-3918			F7E7	2-6F36	
3	玃	3-3683	1-4347		F7E9	2-6F38	
4	玄	0-4894	0-2428	0-9060	A5C8	1-4668	214B30
5	玅		1-4348		CFC6	2-2C28	2D3954
6	玆	3-1852	1-4349	0-7721	AF59	1-565C	
7	率	0-3442	0-4608	0-6567	B276	1-5B7B	214B31
8	玈	5-1951		1-6276	D66A	2-372F	22583F
9	玉	0-5181	0-2244	0-7212	A5C9	1-4669	214B32
A	玊	3-3085			C9A7	2-2166	
B	王	0-4585	0-1806	0-7261	A4FD	1-455E	214B33
C	玌	5-3375				E-225A	
D	玍	3-3084				E-216B	216437
E	玎	0-7164	1-4350	0-7973	CA45	2-2265	225842
F	玏	3-3086				E-242F	

739

	Char	G	J	K	B	C	A
0	玐	5-3377	1-4351				
1	玑	0-7165					274B64
2	玒	3-3089			CB6C	2-246C	225847
3	玓	5-3381	1-4352		CB6A	2-246A	22584C
4	玔	5-3380		0-8429	CB6B	2-246B	22584D
5	玕	3-3087	1-4353	1-5526	CB68	2-2468	225846
6	玖	0-3033	0-2274	0-4724	A868	1-4B2B	214B34
7	玗	3-3088	1-4354	0-7359	CB69	2-2469	225848
8	玘	3-3091	1-4355	0-4912		E-266E	
9	玙	8-9140					
A	玚	8-1242					
B	玛	0-3474					274B5E
C	玜	5-3390	1-4356			E-2A33	
D	玝	5-3388			CD6D	2-282F	
E	玞	5-3383	1-4357	1-6627		E-2A2D	225851
F	玟	0-7168	1-4358	0-5839	AAB3	1-4E74	214B35

73A

	Char	G	J	K	B	C	A
0	玠	3-3103	1-4359	1-5576	CD6B	2-282D	225863
1	玡	3-3102			CD67	2-2829	
2	玢	0-7167	1-4360		CD6A	2-282C	225862
3	玣	5-3394				E-2A2C	
4	玤	3-3093			CD66	2-2828	
5	玥	3-3106	1-4361		AAB5	1-4E76	22585D
6	玦	3-3107	1-4362	1-5630	CD69	2-282B	225852
7	玧	5-3401		0-7541		E-2A2B	
8	玨	5-3382			AAB2	1-4E73	214B36
9	玩	0-4570	0-2065	0-7244	AAB1	1-4E72	214B37
A	玪	5-3389	1-4363			E-2A32	
B	玫	0-3521	1-4364	1-6418	AAB4	1-4E75	214B38
C	玬	5-3391			CD6C	2-282E	
D	玭	5-3386	1-4365	0-6223	CD68	2-282A	
E	玮	0-7166					285A47
F	环	0-2723				E-2A2F	274B67

73B

	Char	G	J	K	B	C	A
0	现	0-4754					274B47
1	玱	8-9142					
2	玲	0-3365	0-4672	0-5428	ACC2	1-5245	214B3E
3	玳	0-7173	0-6462	0-5169	ACC5	1-5248	2E5A40
4	玴	5-3403			CFCE	2-2C30	
5	玵	5-3402	1-4366		CFCD	2-2C2F	
6	玶	3-3108			CFCC	2-2C2E	225867
7	玷	0-7172	1-4367	1-7635	ACBF	1-5242	214B3B
8	玸	3-3113			CFD5	2-2C37	
9	玹	3-3114	1-4368	0-9061	CFCB	2-2C2D	
A	玺	0-7184					274B69
B	玻	0-1803	0-6464	1-8177	ACC1	1-5244	214B39
C	玼	3-3121	1-4369		D2AF	2-3070	225935
D	玽	3-3111	1-4370			E-2D78	
E	玾	5-3404			CFD2	2-2C34	
F	玿	5-3408	1-4371		CFD0	2-2C32	22586F

73C

	Char	G	J	K	B	C	A
0	珀	0-7174	0-6465	0-5854	ACC4	1-5247	214B3C
1	珁					E-2D7B	
2	珂	0-7170	0-1849	0-4217	CFC8	2-2C2A	22586A
3	珃	5-3405			CFD3	2-2C35	
4	珄					E-2D77	
5	珅	3-3110	1-4372		CFCA	2-2C2C	
6	珆	3-3117	1-4373	1-7452	CFD4	2-2C36	
7	珇	3-3109			CFD1	2-2C33	
8	珈	0-7176	0-6461	1-5510	CFC9	2-2C2B	225870
9	珉	0-7175	1-4374	0-5840		E-2D7A	2D4B35
A	珊	0-4126	0-2725	0-6306	ACC0	1-5243	214B3A
B	珋	5-3406	1-4375		CFD6	2-2C38	
C	珌	3-3115	1-4376	0-8919	CFC7	2-2C29	22587D
D	珍	0-5368	0-3633	0-8250	ACC3	1-5246	214B3F
E	珎		0-6463			E-2D7E	2D4B3F
F	珏	0-7169	1-4377	0-4236		E-2D79	225868

73D

	Char	G	J	K	B	C	A
0	珐	0-2309				E-2D7C	22586B
1	珑	0-7171					274B6B
2	珒	3-3134	1-4378	1-7813	D2B4	2-3075	
3	珓	3-3132	1-4379		D2AB	2-306C	225921
4	珔	5-3410			D2B6	2-3077	22592F
5	珕	3-3137				E-323E	
6	珖	3-3122	1-4380	0-4643	D2AE	2-306F	225932
7	珗				D2B9	2-307A	
8	珘	5-3415			D2BA	2-307B	
9	珙	0-7178	1-4381	0-4585	D2AC	2-306D	22592A
A	珚	5-3413			D2B8	2-3079	
B	珛	3-3119			D2B5	2-3076	225930
C	珜	5-3418			D2B3	2-3074	
D	珝	3-3138	1-4382	0-9316	D2B7	2-3078	
E	珞	0-7183	0-6468	0-5308	AF5F	1-5662	22593A
F	珟	3-3128				E-3240	

73E

	Char	G	J	K	B	C	A
0	珠	0-5473	0-2878	0-8133	AF5D	1-5660	214B42
1	珡		1-4383			E-3247	
2	珢	3-3136		1-7422		E-323C	
3	珣	3-3129	1-4384	0-6673	D2B1	2-3072	225938
4	珤	5-3414		0-6042		E-3246	
5	珥	0-7177	0-6466	0-7620	D2AD	2-306E	225928
6	珦	3-3125	1-4385	0-9032		E-3241	22593C
7	珧	0-7182	1-4386		D2B0	2-3071	225936
8	珨	3-3127			D2BB	2-307C	
9	珩	0-7181	1-4387	0-9108	D2B2	2-3073	22593F
A	珪	5-3409	0-2330	0-4808	AF5E	1-5661	225927
B	珫	3-3133		1-8063	CFCF	2-2C31	
C	珬	3-3118				E-323D	
D	班	0-1664	0-4041	0-5876	AF5A	1-565D	214B40
E	珮	5-3417	0-6467	1-8190	AF5C	1-565F	214B41
F	珯					E-6564	22592B

73F

	Char	G	J	K	B	C	A
0	珰	8-9146					
1	珱		0-6494				4C5C3A
2	珲	0-7185					274B57
3	珳					E-373D	
4	珴	5-3426	1-4388		D678	2-373D	
5	珵	3-3142	1-4389	1-7660	D66D	2-3732	225954
6	珶	3-3148			D66B	2-3730	225945
7	珷	5-3433	1-4390	0-5778		E-3D38	225970
8	珸	3-3141	0-6473		D66C	2-3731	22594A
9	珹	3-3120	1-4391	0-6491		E-323F	
A	珺	3-3149	1-4392		D673	2-3738	225947
B	珻		1-4393			E-3740	
C	珼	5-3387			D674	2-3739	
D	珽	3-3124	1-4394	0-7974	D670	2-3735	22595A
E	現	1-4754	0-2429	0-9062	B27B	1-5C22	214B47
F	珿	3-3143	1-4401		D675	2-373A	

740

	Char	G	J	K	B	C	A
0	玲	3-3147	1-4402		D672	2-3737	
1	琁	5-3427	1-4403	0-6436	D66F	2-3734	
2	琂	5-3431				E-373C	
3	球	0-3982	0-2169	0-4725	B279	1-5B7E	214B45
4	琄	5-3425	1-4404	1-8346	D66E	2-3733	
5	琅	0-3237	0-6470	0-5342	B277	1-5B7C	214B43
6	理	0-3277	0-4593	0-5566	B27A	1-5C21	214B48
7	琇	3-3144	1-4405	0-6615	D671	2-3736	22595C
8	琈	3-3146			D679	2-373E	
9	琉	0-3380	0-4616	0-5524	AF5B	1-565E	214B44
A	琊	0-7180	1-4406		B278	1-5B7D	214B46
B	琋	5-3428			D677	2-373C	
C	琌				D676	2-373B	
D	琍				B27C	1-5C23	214B49
E	琎	8-9150					
F	琏	0-7186					285B21

741

	Char	G	J	K	B	C	A
0	琐	0-4386					274B5F
1	琑		1-4407				
2	琒					E-6565	22595E
3	琓			0-7245			
4	琔	5-3443				E-3D36	225969
5	琕	5-3439				E-3D3A	225A30
6	琖				DA7E	2-3E24	225978
7	琗	5-3441				E-3D2F	
8	琘	5-3440				E-3D3B	
9	琙	3-3151				E-3D32	
A	琚	0-7202	1-4408		DAA1	2-3E25	225971
B	琛	0-7201	1-4409	0-8658	B560	1-6066	225A2A
C	琜	5-3422				E-3D39	
D	琝	5-3437			DAA7	2-3E2B	
E	琞					E-426D	
F	琟	3-3157				E-3D35	

742

	Char	G	J	K	B	C	A
0	琠	5-3438		0-7902	DAA9	2-3E2D	225A28
1	琡	3-3154		0-6658	DAA2	2-3E26	
2	琢	0-5533	0-3486	0-8692	B55A	1-6060	214B50
3	琣	5-3442			DAA6	2-3E2A	
4	琤	3-3130	1-4410	1-7557	DAA5	2-3E29	225A2B
5	琥	0-7190	0-6472	0-9148	B55B	1-6061	214B51
6	琦	0-7189	1-4411	0-4913	B561	1-6067	22597A
7	琧	5-3482				E-4264	
8	琨	0-7191	1-4412	0-4568	B562	1-6068	225A21
9	琩	5-3436	1-4413		DAA8	2-3E2C	225A23
A	琪	0-7187	1-4414	0-4914	B558	1-605E	214B4E
B	琫	3-3150	1-4415	0-6077	DA7D	2-3E23	22596E
C	琬	0-7194	1-4416	0-7246	DA7B	2-3E21	22596A
D	琭	3-3160	1-4417		DAA3	2-3E27	225A2D
E	琮	0-7193	1-4418	0-8089	DA7A	2-3D7E	225966
F	琯	3-3158	1-4419	0-4621	B55F	1-6065	225967

743

	Char	G	J	K	B	C	A
0	琰	0-7192	1-4420	0-7092	DA7C	2-3E22	22596C
1	琱		1-4421	1-7704	DAA4	2-3E28	3F5F49
2	琲	3-3153	0-6474	1-6552	DAAA	2-3E2E	225A2C
3	琳	0-3353	0-4654	0-5591	B559	1-605F	214B4F
4	琴	0-3957	0-2255	0-4854	B55E	1-6064	214B4D
5	琵	0-3793	0-4092	0-6185	B55C	1-6062	214B4B
6	琶	0-3735	0-3942	0-8781	B55D	1-6063	214B4C
7	琷	5-3432					
8	琸			0-8693		E-3D33	
9	琹		1-4422			E-3D3C	223D66
A	琺		0-6475	0-5987	B557	1-605D	214B4A
B	琻					E-6566	225A32
C	琼	0-3977				E-3D37	225963
D	琽					E-4268	
E	琾	5-3450				E-4275	
F	琿	1-7185	0-6477	0-9174	B7E9	1-6531	214B57

744

	Char	G	J	K	B	C	A
0	瑀	3-3166	1-4423	0-7360	DEB7	2-447B	225A5D
1	瑁	0-7203	0-6480	0-5733	B7E8	1-6530	214B56
2	瑂	3-3169			DEBB	2-4521	225A45
3	瑃	3-3161	1-4424	0-8582		E-426F	
4	瑄	3-3168	1-4425	0-6437	DEB1	2-4475	225A36
5	瑅	5-3447		1-7673		E-4274	
6	瑆	3-3164	1-4426	1-6862	DEBC	2-4522	
7	瑇		1-4427			E-426E	225A40
8	瑈	3-3171				E-4266	
9	瑉	5-3455				E-4271	
A	瑊	3-3163			DEB2	2-4476	225A4A
B	瑋	1-7166	1-4428	0-7452	DEB3	2-4477	225A47
C	瑌	5-3445				E-4273	
D	瑍	5-3429	1-4429		DEBD	2-4523	
E	瑎	5-3446		1-8322	DEBA	2-447E	
F	瑏	5-3453			DEB8	2-447C	

745

	Char	G	J	K	B	C	A
0	瑐				DEB9	2-447D	
1	瑑	3-3172	1-4430		DEB5	2-4479	225A56
2	瑒	3-3092	1-4431		DEB4	2-4478	225A4F
3	瑓					E-4267	
4	瑔	5-3452			DEBE	2-4524	225A5B
5	瑕	0-7206	0-6476	0-8934	B7E5	1-652D	214B53
6	瑖	5-3451				E-426B	
7	瑗	0-7205	1-4432	0-7428	DEB6	2-447A	225A55
8	瑘	5-3434				E-4270	225A43
9	瑙	0-7207	0-6479	0-5037	B7EA	1-6532	214B5B
A	瑚	0-2687	0-2474	0-9149	B7E4	1-652C	214B55
B	瑛	0-7188	0-1745	0-7132	B7EB	1-6533	214B58
C	瑜	0-7204	0-6481	0-7505	B7EC	1-6534	214B5A
D	瑝	3-3165	1-4433	1-8439		E-426A	225A5A
E	瑞	0-4080	0-3180	0-6390	B7E7	1-652F	214B59
F	瑟	0-4110	0-6478	0-6702	B7E6	1-652E	214B54

746

	Char	G	J	K	B	C	A
0	瑠		0-4660	0-5525		E-4825	225A78
1	瑡					E-477E	
2	瑢	3-3182	1-4434	0-7335	E2CE	2-4B74	225A61
3	瑣	1-4386	0-6484	1-6908	BABE	1-6965	214B5F
4	瑤		0-8404	0-7293	BABD	1-6964	214B60
5	瑥	5-3448		0-7215		E-477C	
6	瑦	5-3392	1-4435			E-477D	
7	瑧	5-3456	1-4436		E2D3	2-4B79	
8	瑨	3-3175	1-4437	0-8251		E-4822	225A6B
9	瑩	1-5108	0-6482	0-9109	BCFC	1-6D66	214B5D
A	瑪	1-3474	0-6485	0-5605	BABF	1-6966	214B5E
B	瑫	3-3180	1-4438			E-4821	
C	瑬	3-3210				E-477B	
D	瑭	0-7209	1-4439	1-6106	BAC1	1-6968	225A60
E	瑮	3-3178	1-4440		E2D4	2-4B7A	225A69
F	瑯		0-6471	0-5343	B7E3	1-652B	2D4B43

747

	Char	G	J	K	B	C	A
0	瑰	0-2569	0-6483	1-5807	BAC0	1-6967	214B61
1	瑱	3-3177	1-4441	1-7603	E2D0	2-4B76	225A6A
2	瑲	3-3105	1-4442	1-7879	E2D2	2-4B78	225A79
3	瑳	3-3167	0-2628	1-7838	E2CF	2-4B75	225A62
4	瑴	5-4876				E-4827	225A68
5	瑵	3-3170			E2D1	2-4B77	
6	瑶	0-4994	0-6486			E-4823	
7	瑷	0-7208					274B68
8	瑸	8-9159					
9	瑹	5-3458			E6AB	2-5233	
A	瑺	3-3185				E-4D31	225B30
B	瑻	5-3444				E-4D3B	
C	瑼	5-3384			E6AA	2-5232	225B22
D	瑽	3-3104		1-7733	E6A7	2-522F	225B3E
E	瑾	0-7210	0-6487	0-4840	BD40	1-6D69	225B28
F	瑿	3-3211			EA62	2-584E	

748

	Char	G	J	K	B	C	A
0	璀	0-7213	1-4443	1-8023	BD41	1-6D6A	225B38
1	璁	0-7214	1-4444		E6A6	2-522E	225B3C
2	璂	3-3183		0-4915		E-4D39	225B27
3	璃	0-3307	0-4594	0-5567	BCFE	1-6D68	214B5C
4	璄	5-3464				E-4D36	225A7A
5	璅	5-3465	1-4445		E6A8	2-5230	225B3F
6	璆	3-3186	1-4446	1-5859	E6A5	2-522D	225B2D
7	璇	0-7215	1-4447	0-6438	E6A2	2-522A	225A7B
8	璈	3-3173			E6A9	2-5231	225A7E
9	璉	1-7186	1-4448	0-5402	E6A3	2-522B	225B21
A	璊	3-3174		1-6484	E6A4	2-522C	225B2A
B	璋	0-7216	0-6488	0-7780	BCFD	1-6D67	214B62
C	璌					E-4D35	
D	璍					E-6568	225B56
E	璎	0-7212					285C3A
F	璏	3-3194	1-4449				

749

	Char	G	J	K	B	C	A
0	璐	0-7220	1-4450		ED69	2-5D55	225B6A
1	璑	3-3094	1-4451				
2	璒	5-3469	1-4452		EA66	2-5852	
3	璓	5-3457				E-4D3A	
4	璔				EA65	2-5851	
5	璕	3-3135			EA67	2-5853	
6	璖					E-516A	
7	璗	3-3208			ED66	2-5D52	225B40
8	璘	3-3192	1-4453	0-5583	BF5A	1-7144	225B43
9	璙	3-3188	1-4454			E-6375	
A	璚	5-3470	1-4455		EA63	2-584F	225B45
B	璛	3-3159				E-5167	
C	璜	0-7211	1-4456	0-9252	BF58	1-7142	214B63
D	璝	5-3449		1-5808		E-516C	225B55
E	璞	0-7217	0-6489	0-5855	BF5C	1-7146	225B57
F	璟	3-3189	1-4457	0-4463	BF5B	1-7145	225B54

74A

	Char	G	J	K	B	C	A
0	璠	3-3190	1-4458		EA64	2-5850	225B59
1	璡	3-3140	1-4459	0-8252	EA68	2-5854	225B5D
2	璢		0-6469			E-516B	2E5A78
3	璣	1-7165	1-4460	0-4916	BF59	1-7143	214B64
4	璤					E-6567	225B4D
5	璥	3-3187		0-4464	ED6D	2-5D59	225B6C
6	璦	1-7208	1-4461		C0F5	1-7440	214B68
7	璧	0-7221	0-6490	0-5993	C27A	1-7666	214B65
8	璨	0-7218	1-4462	0-8331	C0F6	1-7441	225B6E
9	璩	0-7219	1-4463		C0F3	1-743E	214B66
A	璪	3-3203	1-4464	0-8049	ED6A	2-5D56	225B69
B	璫	3-3123	1-4465	1-6107	ED68	2-5D54	225B67
C	璬	3-3204				E-554F	
D	璭				ED6B	2-5D57	
E	璮		1-4466			E-554B	
F	璯	3-3126	1-4467		ED6E	2-5D5A	

74B

	Char	G	J	K	B	C	A
0	環	1-2723	0-2036	0-9227	C0F4	1-743F	214B67
1	璱	5-3471	1-4468		ED6C	2-5D58	225B61
2	璲	3-3193	1-4469	0-6616	ED67	2-5D53	225B60
3	璳					E-554D	
4	璴					E-6569	225B66
5	璵	3-3090	1-4470	0-7005	F042	2-622F	225C28
6	璶	5-3420			F045	2-6232	
7	璷	3-3206			F275	2-6621	
8	璸	3-3181			F040	2-622D	225B76
9	璹	3-3139	1-4471	0-6659		E-582F	
A	璺	0-7223			F46F	2-693E	225C29
B	璻	5-3475	1-4472		F046	2-6233	
C	璼	5-3459				E-5830	
D	璽	1-7184	0-2805	0-6362	C3A2	1-784D	214B69
E	璾	3-3131			F044	2-6231	
F	璿		1-4473	0-6439	C27B	1-7667	225C25

74C

	Char	G	J	K	B	C	A
0	瓀	3-3205			F041	2-622E	225B7A
1	瓁	3-3201			F043	2-6230	
2	瓂				F047	2-6234	
3	瓃	5-3476			F276	2-6622	
4	瓄	3-3152				E-5A5A	
5	瓅	5-3407			F274	2-657E	225C31
6	瓆			0-8279			
7	瓇					E-5A5C	
8	瓈		1-4474			E-5A5D	225C30
9	瓉	5-3466	1-4475			E-5A5B	
A	瓊	1-3977	0-6491	0-4465	C3A3	1-784E	214B6A
B	瓋				F273	2-657D	
C	瓌		1-4476			E-5C5E	225C32
D	瓍					E-5C5C	
E	瓎					E-5C5F	
F	瓏	1-7171	0-6492	0-5474	C46E	1-7979	214B6B

74D

	Char	G	J	K	B	C	A
0	瓐		1-4477			E-5C5D	
1	瓑	5-3385				E-5C60	
2	瓒	0-7222					285C40
3	瓓	3-3191	1-4478			E-5E3D	
4	瓔	1-7212	0-6493	0-7134	C4ED	1-7A78	225C3A
5	瓕	3-3209			F6F1	2-6D5F	
6	瓖	5-3479			C4EC	1-7A77	225C38
7	瓗	5-3480			F6F3	2-6D61	
8	瓘	3-3207	1-4479	0-4622	F6F0	2-6D5E	225C3D
9	瓙				F6F2	2-6D60	
A	瓚	1-7222	1-4480	0-8332	C5D0	1-7C3C	225C40
B	瓛	3-3202	1-4481	1-8426	F8E2	2-7040	225C41
C	瓜	0-2547	0-1727	0-4594	A5CA	1-466A	214B6C
D	瓝	3-6071			CD6E	2-2830	
E	瓞	0-8012	1-4482		D2BC	2-307D	225C47
F	瓟	5-5975	1-4483		D2BD	2-307E	

74E

	Char	G	J	K	B	C	A
0	瓠	0-8013	0-6501	0-9150	B27D	1-5C24	214B6D
1	瓡	5-5977			DEBF	2-4525	
2	瓢	0-3816	0-4127	0-8888	BF5D	1-7147	214B6E
3	瓣	0-1674	0-6502	0-8791	C3A4	1-784F	214B6F
4	瓤	0-4031	1-4484		C57B	1-7B67	225C50
5	瓥				F8B3	2-7041	
6	瓦	0-4563	0-2004	0-7231	A5CB	1-466B	214B70
7	瓧		0-6503				225C52
8	瓨	5-2143	1-4485		CD6F	2-2831	
9	瓩	8-0887	0-6504	1-7922	A260	1-2322	225C54
A	瓪	3-3830	1-4486				
B	瓫	5-4040	1-4487			E-2E22	
C	瓬	5-4894			CFD7	2-2C39	
D	瓭	3-3832				E-2E21	
E	瓮	0-4645	0-6505	0-7223	CFD8	2-2C3A	225C5C
F	瓯	0-7417	1-4488			E-2E24	274B74

74F

	Char	G	J	K	B	C	A
0	瓰		0-6507				225C5A
1	瓱		0-6508				225C58
2	瓲		0-6506	1-8161			696126
3	瓳	3-3833				E-3248	
4	瓴	0-7418	1-4489		D2BE	2-3121	225C61
5	瓵	5-4046			D2BF	2-3122	
6	瓶	0-3831	0-4151		B27E	1-5C25	214B71
7	瓷	0-2041	0-6510	0-7722	B2A1	1-5C26	214B72
8	瓸		0-6509				225C63
9	瓹	3-3848				E-3D3D	
A	瓺	3-4404	1-4490				
B	瓻	3-3849	1-4491		DAAB	2-3E2F	225C66
C	瓼		1-4492				
D	瓽	3-3854			DEC2	2-4528	
E	瓾	3-3857			DEC1	2-4527	
F	瓿	0-7419	1-4493		DEC0	2-4526	225C67

750

	Char	G	J	K	B	C	A
0	甀	3-3856			E2D5	2-4B7B	
1	甁			0-6026		E-4277	
2	甂	3-3869			E2D6	2-4B7C	
3	甃	3-3866	0-6512	1-8035	E2D7	2-4B7D	225C77
4	甄	0-5371	0-6511	0-4420	BAC2	1-6969	214B73
5	甅		0-6513				225C71
6	甆	5-4053	1-4494			E-4828	2D4B72
7	甇	5-4042			E6AD	2-5235	225C7D
8	甈	3-3870			E6AC	2-5234	
9	甉	3-3872				E-4D3D	
A	甊	3-3868				E-516D	
B	甋	3-3875			EA69	2-5855	
C	甌	1-7417	0-6514	1-5860	BF5E	1-7148	214B74
D	甍	0-6189	0-6516	1-6428	BF5F	1-7149	225D28
E	甎		0-6515	1-7604		E-516E	225D25
F	甏	0-7420			ED72	2-5D5E	225D2D

752

	Char	G	J	K	B	C	A
0	甠		1-4504				
1	甡	3-5940	1-4505		D2C0	2-3123	225D42
2	產				B2A3	1-5C28	214B7A
3	産	1-1890	0-2726	0-6307		E-3745	454B7A
4	甤	5-7833	1-4506			E-3D3E	225D44
5	甥	0-4191	0-1789	0-6371	B563	1-6069	214B7C
6	甦	8-1285	0-6520	0-6533	B564	1-606A	214B7B
7	甧		1-4507				
8	用	0-5135	0-4549	0-7336	A5CE	1-466E	214B7D
9	甩	0-4306	1-4508		A5CF	1-466F	214B7E
A	甪	3-1612	1-4509		CA46	2-2266	2D5833
B	甫	0-2406	0-4267	0-6043	A86A	1-4B2D	214C22
C	甬	0-8014	0-6521	0-7337	A869	1-4B2C	214C21
D	甭	0-1734			ACC7	1-524A	214C23
E	甮	3-1613			CFD9	2-2C3B	
F	甯	0-6924	1-4510		DAAC	2-3E30	225D49

754

	Char	G	J	K	B	C	A
0	畀	0-7815	1-4516		CD71	2-2833	225D51
1	畁	5-1614				E-2A38	
2	畂					E-2A35	
3	畃		1-4517				
4	畄		0-6523			E-2A36	274C31
5	畅	0-1909					274343
6	畆		0-6528			E-2E27	394C2D
7	畇	3-5867	1-4518	0-4820	CFDA	2-2C3C	225D58
8	畈	0-7818	1-4519		CFDB	2-2C3D	225D5A
9	畉	5-5807	0-6526			E-2E25	69613A
A	畊		0-6525	1-5652		E-2E28	225D55
B	畋	0-7817	0-5834	1-7605	ACCB	1-524E	225D59
C	界	0-2971	0-1906	0-4503	ACC9	1-524C	214C2C
D	畍		0-6524			E-2E2A	334C2C
E	畎	0-7816	1-4520	1-5623	ACCA	1-524D	225D57
F	畏	0-4623	0-1658	0-7270	ACC8	1-524B	214C2B

756

	Char	G	J	K	B	C	A
0	畠		0-4011	1-7606			69482B
1	畡	5-5817	1-4526			E-3746	
2	畢	1-1747	0-4113	0-8920	B2A6	1-5C2B	214C33
3	畣	5-5815			D67B	2-3740	225D67
4	畤	3-5872	0-6531	1-8078	D67A	2-373F	225D62
5	略	0-3452	0-4612	0-5352	B2A4	1-5C29	214C35
6	畦	0-3872	0-2345	0-9347	B2A5	1-5C2A	214C32
7	畧		0-6532	1-6220		E-3749	2D4C35
8	畨					E-3747	
9	畩		0-6530				69613E
A	番	0-2312	0-4054	0-5967	B566	1-606C	214C37
B	畫	1-2713	0-6533	1-8416	B565	1-606B	214C36
C	畬	3-5874			DAAE	2-3E32	225D6B
D	畭		0-6534			E-3D43	345D6B
E	畮					E-3D42	2D4C2D
F	畯	3-5875	1-4527	0-8165	DAAD	2-3E31	225D69

751

	Char	G	J	K	B	C	A
0	甐	3-3879			ED6F	2-5D5B	
1	甑	0-7421	0-2589	0-8187	ED70	2-5D5C	225D2C
2	甒	3-3214	1-4501		ED71	2-5D5D	225D32
3	甓	0-7422	0-6518	1-6566	F049	2-6236	225D33
4	甔	3-3882			F048	2-6235	
5	甕		0-6517	0-7224	C27C	1-7668	214B75
6	甖		1-4502		F277	2-6623	2E742E
7	甗	3-3884	1-4503		F5DE	2-6B6C	225D39
8	甘	0-2442	0-2037	0-4286	A5CC	1-466C	214B76
9	甙	0-6316					705F30
A	甚	0-4185	0-3151	0-6804	ACC6	1-5249	214B77
B	甛	5-5578		0-8454		E-3744	
C	甜	0-4480	0-3728		B2A2	1-5C27	214B78
D	甝	3-6545			DEC3	2-4529	
E	甞		0-6519	1-6790		E-4278	2D3730
F	生	0-4190	0-3224	0-6370	A5CD	1-466D	214B79

753

	Char	G	J	K	B	C	A
0	田	0-4479	0-3736	0-7903	A5D0	1-4670	214C24
1	由	0-5141	0-4519	0-7506	A5D1	1-4671	214C26
2	甲	0-2855	0-2535	0-4303	A5D2	1-4672	214C25
3	申	0-4174	0-3129	0-6773	A5D3	1-4673	214C27
4	甴						
5	电	0-2171					275F55
6	甶	5-5792	1-4511				
7	男	0-3648	0-3543	0-4991	A86B	1-4B2E	214C28
8	甸	0-2173	0-5020	0-7904	A86C	1-4B2F	214C29
9	甹	3-1607	1-4512		CB6E	2-246E	
A	町	0-7814	0-3614	0-7975	CB6D	2-246D	225D4D
B	画	0-2713	0-1872			E-2A37	274C36
C	甼		0-6522				696136
D	甽	5-5803	1-4513		AAB6	1-4E77	214C2A
E	甾	0-7162	1-4514		CD72	2-2834	225D52
F	甿	3-5864	1-4515	1-6429	CD70	2-2832	225D4F

755

	Char	G	J	K	B	C	A
0	畐	3-5865	1-4521			E-2E26	
1	畑	8-1375	0-4010	0-7905			225068
2	畒		1-4522				
3	畓			0-5144			22477B
4	畔	0-3747	0-4042	0-5877	AF60	1-5663	214C2F
5	畕	5-5810				E-324E	
6	畖	3-5870				E-324D	
7	畗	5-1946	1-4523			E-3250	
8	畘	3-5869				E-324F	
9	留	0-3384	0-4617	0-5526	AF64	1-5667	214C31
A	畚	0-5946	0-6529	1-6655	AF63	1-5666	214C30
B	畛	0-7819	0-6527	0-8253	D2C1	2-3124	225D60
C	畜	0-4883	0-3560	0-8569	AF62	1-5665	214C2E
D	畝	1-3622	0-3206	0-5779	AF61	1-5664	214C2D
E	畞		1-4524			E-3251	
F	畟	5-5812	1-4525		D2C2	2-3125	225D5F

757

	Char	G	J	K	B	C	A
0	異		0-1659	0-7622	B2A7	1-5C2C	214C34
1	畱		1-4528			E-3D44	225D75
2	畲	0-7820					285D6B
3	畳		0-3086				4B4C3C
4	畴	0-1975	0-6539				274C3B
5	畵			0-9194			4B4C36
6	當	1-2117	0-6536	0-5155	B7ED	1-6535	214C39
7	畷	3-5879	0-3877		DEC5	2-452B	225D71
8	畸	0-2791	0-6535	0-4917	B7EE	1-6536	214C38
9	畹	0-7821	1-4529		DEC4	2-452A	225D6D
A	畺	5-1611	1-4530	0-4317		E-427B	225D6E
B	畻		1-4531				
C	畼	5-5805	1-4532				
D	畽	5-5822	1-4533		E2D8	2-4B7E	225D79
E	畾	3-5883	1-4534		E6AE	2-5236	
F	畿	0-7160	0-2106	0-4918	BD42	1-6D6B	225D7E

758

	Char	G	J	K	B	C	A
0	疀	5-3371			EA6A	2-5856	
1	疁	3-5884	1-4535			E-5170	
2	疂		0-6542				3F4C3C
3	疃	0-7822				E-5552	225E25
4	疄	3-5885			ED73	2-5D5F	
5	疅		1-4536				
6	疆	0-2914	0-6537	0-4318	C3A6	1-7851	214C3A
7	疇	1-1975	0-6538	0-8134	C3A5	1-7850	214C3B
8	疈	3-5889		1-6567			
9	疉		0-6541			E-5C62	454C3C
A	疊	1-2194	0-6540	0-8465	C57C	1-7B68	214C3C
B	疋	0-8166	0-4105	0-8921	A5D4	1-4674	2D3453
C	疌	5-1606			CD73	2-2835	
D	疍	3-6382					
E	疎		0-3334	0-6535		E-3D45	2D4C3E
F	疏	0-4272	0-3333	0-6534	E2A8	1-5C2D	214C3E

75A

	Char	G	J	K	B	C	A
0	疠	0-8061					274C71
1	疡	0-4981					274C60
2	疢	3-6248	1-4543		ACCF	1-5252	225E37
3	疣	0-8064	0-6547	1-7323	ACD0	1-5253	225E3B
4	疤	0-1644	1-4544		ACCD	1-5250	214C43
5	疥	0-2974	0-6546	0-4342	ACCE	1-5251	214C45
6	疦	3-6250				E-2E2B	
7	疧	3-6246			CFDC	2-2C3E	
8	疨	3-6242				E-2E2F	
9	疩			1-8066			
A	疪	5-6072			CFDD	2-2C3F	
B	疫	0-5063	0-1754	0-7025	ACCC	1-524F	214C44
C	疬	0-8063					286032
D	疭	7-0114					
E	疮	0-2015					274C6A
F	疯	0-2372					274C63

75C

	Char	G	J	K	B	C	A
0	痀	5-6089	1-4548	1-5862	D2C7	2-312A	
1	痁	3-6254	1-4549		D2C4	2-3127	225E4E
2	痂	0-8072	0-6548	0-4218	AF6D	1-5670	225E4A
3	痃	0-8071	0-6550	1-8347		E-3252	225E44
4	痄	0-8068	1-4550		D2C6	2-3129	225E51
5	病	0-1801	0-4134	0-6027	AF66	1-5669	214C47
6	痆	3-6262	1-4551				
7	症	0-5402	0-3041	0-8188	AF67	1-566A	214C46
8	痈	0-5124					28603A
9	痉	0-3023					274C56
A	痊	0-4012	0-6557	1-7607	B2AC	1-5C31	214C51
B	痋	5-6103			D6A1	2-3744	
C	痌	5-6104	1-4552		D6A2	2-3745	225E5E
D	痍	0-8074	0-6556	0-7623	B2AD	1-5C32	225E58
E	痎	3-6274	1-4553	1-8323	D67C	2-3741	
F	痏	3-6266	1-4554		D67E	2-3743	225E5C

75E

	Char	G	J	K	B	C	A
0	痠	5-6124	1-4558		B56D	1-6073	225E72
1	痡	3-6279	1-4559		DAB1	2-3E35	225E66
2	痢	0-3301	0-4601	0-5569	B567	1-606D	214C57
3	痣	0-8075	0-6560	1-7794	B569	1-606F	214C53
4	痤	0-8078	1-4560	1-7739	DAB5	2-3E39	225E71
5	痥	3-6288				E-3D47	
6	痦	0-8077			DAB2	2-3E36	225E67
7	痧	0-8080	1-4561	1-6749	DAAF	2-3E33	225E63
8	痨	0-8076					274C6D
9	痩		0-3373				
A	痪	0-2730					274C62
B	痫	0-8079					4C5F69
C	痬	3-6302	1-4562				
D	痭	3-6307			DED2	2-4538	
E	痮	5-6075	1-4563			E-427C	
F	痯	3-6309	1-4564		DEC7	2-452D	

759

	Char	G	J	K	B	C	A
0	疐	5-1646	1-4537		E2D9	2-4C21	225E2C
1	疑	0-5041	0-2131	0-7587	BAC3	1-696A	214C3F
2	疒	0-8058	1-4538			E-225B	225E2D
3	疓	5-6064	1-4539			E-2673	
4	疔	0-8059	0-6543	1-7661	CB6F	2-246F	225E2E
5	疕	3-6239	1-4540		CB70	2-2470	225E31
6	疖	0-8060					4C6022
7	疗	0-3338					274C6E
8	疘				CD74	2-2836	225E35
9	疙	0-2477	1-4541	1-8513	AAB8	1-4E79	214C41
A	疚	0-3046	0-6544	1-5861	AAB9	1-4E7A	214C42
B	疛	3-6240				E-2A3A	
C	疜		1-4542				
D	疝	0-8062	0-6545	0-6308	AAB7	1-4E78	214C40
E	疞					E-2A3B	
F	疟	0-3717					274C61

75B

	Char	G	J	K	B	C	A
0	疰	0-8070			D2C3	2-3126	225E43
1	疱	0-8069	0-6555	0-8862		E-3257	225E50
2	疲	0-3803	0-4072	0-8910	AF68	1-566B	214C49
3	疳	0-8065	0-6549	0-4287	AF69	1-566C	214C48
4	疴	0-8066	1-4545	1-7007		E-3255	225E47
5	疵	0-2035	0-6551	0-7723	B2AB	1-5C30	214C50
6	疶	5-6082			D2C9	2-312C	
7	疷	5-6088					
8	疸	0-8067	0-6553	0-5124	AF6E	1-5671	2E5F6F
9	疹	0-5378	0-3130	0-8254	AF6C	1-566F	214C4D
A	疺	3-6245	1-4546		D2CA	2-312D	225E3E
B	疻	3-6256			D2C5	2-3128	
C	疼	0-4459	0-6554	0-5257	AF6B	1-566E	214C4C
D	疽	0-3050	0-6552	0-7837	AF6A	1-566D	214C4A
E	疾	0-2818	0-2832	0-8280	AF65	1-5668	214C4B
F	疿		1-4547		D2C8	2-312B	225E46

75D

	Char	G	J	K	B	C	A
0	痐				D6A4	2-3747	225E5F
1	痑	3-6273			D6A3	2-3746	
2	痒	0-4987	0-6558	0-6942	D67D	2-3742	274C73
3	痓	3-6269		1-8079		E-374A	
4	痔	0-5444	0-2806	0-8632	B2A9	1-5C2E	214C4F
5	痕	0-2659	0-2615	0-9361	B2AA	1-5C2F	214C4E
6	痖	0-8073					285E7A
7	痗	3-6285	1-4555		DAB6	2-3E3A	225E73
8	痘	0-2227	0-3787	0-5267	B56B	1-6071	214C54
9	痙	1-3023	0-6559	0-4466	B56A	1-6070	214C56
A	痚	5-6111			DAB0	2-3E34	
B	痛	0-4520	0-3643	0-8752	B568	1-606E	214C52
C	痜		1-4556				
D	痝	3-6281			DAB3	2-3E37	
E	痞	0-3806	0-6561	1-6692	B56C	1-6072	214C55
F	痟	3-6282	1-4557		DAB4	2-3E38	

75F

	Char	G	J	K	B	C	A
0	痰	0-4421	0-6566	0-5135	B7F0	1-6538	214C5A
1	痱	0-8082	1-4565		B7F3	1-653B	214C5C
2	痲		0-6568	0-5606	B7F2	1-653A	214C5B
3	痳	8-1588	0-6569	1-6382	B7F7	1-653F	4B4C5B
4	痴	0-1953	0-3552	0-8633	B7F6	1-653E	214C5D
5	痵	5-6130			DED3	2-4539	
6	痶	3-6303			DED1	2-4537	
7	痷	3-6293			DECA	2-4530	
8	痸	3-6306			DECE	2-4534	
9	痹	0-1752	1-4566	1-6693	DECD	2-4533	225F21
A	痺		0-6567	0-6186	B7F4	1-653C	214C5F
B	痻	5-6136			DED0	2-4536	
C	痼	0-8083	0-6564	0-4532	DECC	2-4532	225F22
D	痽	5-6132			DED4	2-453A	
E	痾		0-6562		DECB	2-4531	345E47
F	痿	0-8084	0-6563	1-7361	B7F5	1-653D	214C5E

Code	Char	G	J	K	B	C	A
7600	瘀	0-8086	1-4567	0-6960	B7EF	1-6537	214C59
7601	瘁	0-2065	0-6565	1-8067	B7F1	1-6539	214C58
7602	瘂	1-8073	1-4568			E-427D	225E7A
7603	瘃	0-8081	1-4569		DEC9	2-452F	225E7E
7604	瘄	3-6291	1-4570				
7605	瘅	0-8087					285F6F
7606	瘆	7-0115					
7607	瘇	3-6320	1-4571	1-7734		E-482B	
7608	瘈	3-6312	1-4572	1-5664	E2DB	2-4C23	225F2C
7609	瘉		0-6572	1-7380	BAC7	1-696E	393E7D
760A	瘊	0-8090	1-4573		E2DF	2-4C27	225F3C
760B	瘋	1-2372	0-6570	1-8250	BAC6	1-696D	214C63
760C	瘌	0-8088	1-4574		E2DC	2-4C24	225F2E
760D	瘍	1-4981	0-6571	0-6943	BAC5	1-696C	214C60
760E	瘎	3-6314				E-4829	
760F	瘏	3-6290	1-4575		DEC8	2-452E	225F2F
7610	瘐	0-8085		1-7381	DECF	2-4535	225F3B
7611	瘑	3-6284			E2DE	2-4C26	
7612	瘒		1-4576				
7613	瘓	1-2730	1-4577		BAC8	1-696F	214C62
7614	瘔	5-6126			E2E0	2-4C28	
7615	瘕	0-8093	1-4578	1-8275	E2DD	2-4C25	225F2D
7616	瘖		1-4579		E2DA	2-4C22	225F29
7617	瘗	0-8089					285F48
7618	瘘	0-8092					285F5E
7619	瘙	0-8094	1-4580	0-6536	E6B1	2-5239	225F47
761A	瘚	5-6161			E6B5	2-523D	225F3F
761B	瘛	0-8101	1-4581		E6B7	2-523F	225F40
761C	瘜	5-6158	1-4582		E6B3	2-523B	
761D	瘝	3-6326	1-4583		E6B2	2-523A	225F4C
761E	瘞	1-8089	1-4584		E6B0	2-5238	225F48
761F	瘟	0-4633	0-6573	0-7216	BD45	1-6D6E	214C67
7620	瘠	0-8104	0-6575	0-8416	BD43	1-6D6C	214C65
7621	瘡	1-2015	0-6576	0-8374	BD48	1-6D71	214C6A
7622	瘢	0-8103	0-6577	0-5878	BD49	1-6D72	225F50
7623	瘣	3-6321	1-4585		E6B4	2-523C	
7624	瘤	0-3386	0-6578	0-5527	BD46	1-6D6F	214C68
7625	瘥	0-8091	1-4586		E6AF	2-5237	225F3E
7626	瘦	0-4261	1-4587	0-6617	BD47	1-6D70	214C69
7627	瘧	1-3717	0-6574	1-8279	BAC4	1-696B	214C61
7628	瘨	3-6324			E6B6	2-523E	
7629	瘩	0-2081	1-4588		BD44	1-6D6D	214C66
762A	瘪	0-1781					28602B
762B	瘫	0-4417					274C78
762C	瘬	5-6123				E-5171	
762D	瘭	0-8106	1-4589		EA6C	2-5858	225F54
762E	瘮	3-6311					
762F	瘯	5-6170		1-7726	EA6B	2-5857	225F51
7630	瘰	0-8107	0-6580	1-6186	EA73	2-585F	225F5F
7631	瘱	5-6155			EA6D	2-5859	
7632	瘲	3-6244	1-4590		EA72	2-585E	
7633	瘳	0-8112	1-4591	1-8036	EA6F	2-585B	225F5C
7634	瘴	0-5346	0-6579	1-7539	BF60	1-714A	214C6B
7635	瘵	0-8109	1-4592		EA71	2-585D	225F62
7636	瘶	5-6166				E-5173	
7637	瘷	5-6165				E-5172	
7638	瘸	0-4019	1-4593		BF61	1-714B	214C6C
7639	瘹	3-6305	1-4594				
763A	瘺	5-6173	1-4601		BF62	1-714C	
763B	瘻	1-8092	0-6581	0-5510		E-5174	225F5E
763C	瘼	0-8102	1-4602		EA70	2-585C	225F60
763D	瘽	5-6164			EA6E	2-585A	
763E	瘾	0-8111					274C76
763F	瘿	0-8108					286037
7640	癀	0-8105	1-4604				4C5F58
7641	癁		1-4605				
7642	療	1-3338	0-4637	0-5491	C0F8	1-7443	214C6E
7643	癃	0-8110	1-4606	1-6348	ED74	2-5D60	225F6A
7644	癄		1-4607			E-5555	
7645	癅		1-4608			E-5553	
7646	癆	1-8076	0-6584	1-6277	C0F7	1-7442	214C6D
7647	癇	1-8079	0-6582		ED77	2-5D63	225F69
7648	癈		0-6583	1-8223	ED75	2-5D61	225F67
7649	癉	1-8087	1-4609	1-6072	ED76	2-5D62	225F6F
764A	癊	3-6275	1-4603				
764B	癋		1-4610				
764C	癌	0-1609	0-2066	0-6863	C0F9	1-7444	214C6F
764D	癍	0-8113					225F6E
764E	癎	5-6121		0-4254		E-5554	225F68
764F	癏	5-6178				E-5834	
7650	癐	3-6272			F04D	2-623A	
7651	癑	5-6110				E-5833	
7652	癒	8-1384	0-4494	0-7508	C2A1	1-766B	333E7D
7653	癓	5-6180			F04E	2-623B	
7654	癔	0-8115					225F75
7655	癕	5-6183	1-4611	1-7244			
7656	癖	0-8117	0-4242	0-5994	C27D	1-7669	214C70
7657	癗	5-6177			F04F	2-623C	225F7B
7658	癘	1-8061	0-6586	1-6231	C27E	1-766A	214C71
7659	癙	3-6336	1-4612		F04C	2-6239	226024
765A	癚	5-6181			F050	2-623D	
765B	癛					E-5832	
765C	癜	0-8116	0-6585	1-7608	F04A	2-6237	225F7A
765D	癝	3-6337					
765E	癞	0-8114					274C75
765F	癟	1-1781	1-4613		C3A7	1-7852	22602B
7660	癠	5-6108			F278	2-6624	
7661	癡		0-6587	0-8634	C3A8	1-7853	2D4C5D
7662	癢	1-4987	0-6588	1-7093	C46F	1-797A	214C73
7663	癣	0-4902					274C77
7664	癤	1-8060	1-4614	0-7927	F04B	2-6238	226022
7665	癥	1-5402	1-4615	1-7830	C470	1-797B	214C74
7666	癦						
7667	癧	1-8063	0-6592	1-6241		E-5E3F	226032
7668	癨		0-6589	1-5758		E-5E3E	4B5F62
7669	癩	1-8114	0-6590	0-5293	C4EE	1-7A79	214C75
766A	癪		0-6591		F5DF	2-6B6D	226035
766B	癫	0-8118					274C79
766C	癬	1-4902	0-6593	0-6440	C57E	1-7B6A	214C77
766D	癭	1-8108	1-4616	1-7171	F6F4	2-6D62	226037
766E	癮	1-8111	1-4617	1-7423	C57D	1-7B69	214C76
766F	癯	0-8119	1-4618	1-5863		E-603B	226038
7670	癰	1-5124	0-6594	0-7225	F7EA	2-6F39	22603A
7671	癱	1-4417	1-4619	1-8137	C5F5	1-7C61	214C78
7672	癲	1-8118	0-6601	0-7906	C5F6	1-7C62	214C79
7673	癳					E-656A	
7674	癴		1-4620				
7675	癵				F9CC	2-723A	
7676	癶	5-6286	0-6602			E-225C	226040
7677	癷					E-656B	226041
7678	癸	0-2579	0-6603	0-4504	ACD1	1-5254	214C7A
7679	癹	3-6405			CFDE	2-2C40	
767A	発		0-4015				334C7B
767B	登	0-2139	0-3748	0-5284	B56E	1-6074	214C7C
767C	發	1-2302	0-6604	0-5901	B56F	1-6075	214C7B
767D	白	0-1655	0-3982	0-5960	A5D5	1-4675	214C7D
767E	百	0-1657	0-4120	0-5961	A6CA	1-484B	214C7E
767F	癿	3-6051			CA47	2-2267	

Code	Char	G	J	K	B	C	A
7680	皀	3-6052	0-6605	1-5962		E-2674	226048
7681	皁		1-4621	1-7705	CB71	2-2471	2D4D21
7682	皂	0-5277			A86D	1-4B30	214D21
7683	皃	5-5947	0-6606	1-6447		E-2676	275966
7684	的	0-2136	0-3710	0-7860	AABA	1-4E7B	214D22
7685	皅	3-6054	1-4622				
7686	皆	0-2952	0-1907	0-4343	ACD2	1-5255	214D24
7687	皇	0-2742	0-2536	0-9253	ACD3	1-5256	214D23
7688	皈	0-8007	0-6607		ACD4	1-5257	45462B
7689	皉	5-5957			D6A6	2-3749	
768A	皊	5-5954			D2CB	2-312E	
768B	皋	0-2462	0-6608	1-5684	AF6F	1-5672	22604A
768C	皌		1-4623				
768D	皍		1-4624				
768E	皎	0-8008	0-6609	0-4675	B2AE	1-5C33	214D26
768F	皏	3-6055			D6A5	2-3748	
7690	皐		0-2709	0-4533		E-374D	2E604A
7691	皑	0-1608					274D29
7692	皒	5-5963			DAB8	2-3E3C	
7693	皓	0-8009	0-6611	0-9151	B571	1-6077	214D28
7694	皔	3-6057				E-3D4C	
7695	皕	3-6056	1-4625		DAB7	2-3E3B	226052
7696	皖	0-4578	0-6610	1-8427	B570	1-6076	214D27
7697	皗	3-6060				E-427E	
7698	皘	3-6058				E-4321	
7699	皙	0-8010	0-6612		DED5	2-453B	226059
769A	皚	1-1608	0-6613	1-7063	BD4A	1-6D73	214D29
769B	皛	3-6063	1-4626	1-8461	E6BB	2-5243	
769C	皜		1-4627	1-8388	E6B8	2-5240	22605D
769D	皝	3-6061	1-4628		E6B9	2-5241	22605F
769E	皞	3-6062		1-8389	E6BA	2-5242	
769F	皟	3-6059	1-4629				
76A0	皠	3-6067	1-4630				
76A1	皡					E-5176	2E6060
76A2	皢	5-5956	1-4631				
76A3	皣	5-5959	1-4632			E-5556	
76A4	皤	0-8011	1-4633	1-8178	ED78	2-5D64	226065
76A5	皥		1-4634			E-5557	226066
76A6	皦	3-6068	1-4635		F051	2-623E	226067
76A7	皧	3-6064	1-4636				
76A8	皨		1-4637				
76A9	皩					E-5A5E	
76AA	皪	5-5955	1-4638		F471	2-6940	22606A
76AB	皫	3-6069			F470	2-693F	
76AC	皬	5-5970		1-8280			
76AD	皭	3-6070	1-4639		F6F5	2-6D63	22606D
76AE	皮	0-3804	0-4073	0-8911	A5D6	1-4676	214D2A
76AF	皯	3-6385			CD75	2-2837	
76B0	皰		0-6614		AF70	1-5673	214D2B
76B1	皱	0-5469					274D2D
76B2	皲	0-8168					466074
76B3	皳					E-3D4D	
76B4	皴	0-8169	0-6615	1-7769	B572	1-6078	214D2C
76B5	皵	3-6393			DED6	2-453C	
76B6	皶			1-6750			
76B7	皷		0-8373			E-4830	2D6275
76B8	皸	1-8168	0-6616	1-5890	E2E1	2-4C29	226074
76B9	皹		0-6617			E-482E	4C6074
76BA	皺	1-5469	0-6618	0-8552	BD4B	1-6D74	214D2D
76BB	皻	5-6282			EA74	2-5860	
76BC	皼					E-656C	336275
76BD	皽	3-6404	1-4640		F052	2-623F	226077
76BE	皾	5-6278			F472	2-6941	
76BF	皿	0-3583	0-2714	0-5709	A5D7	1-4677	214D2E
76C0	盀	3-1651				E-2677	
76C1	盁		1-4641			E-2678	
76C2	盂	0-5159	0-6619	0-7361	AABB	1-4E7C	214D2F
76C3	盃		0-3954	0-5945	ACD7	1-525A	334425
76C4	盄	5-5860			CFDF	2-2C41	
76C5	盅	0-5449	1-4642		ACD8	1-525B	334674
76C6	盆	0-3772	0-4363	0-6146	ACD6	1-5259	214D32
76C7	盇					E-2E32	2D4D34
76C8	盈	0-5115	0-1746	0-7135	ACD5	1-5258	214D31
76C9	盉	3-5964	1-4643		D2CC	2-312F	
76CA	益	0-5070	0-1755	0-7644	AF71	1-5674	214D33
76CB	盋		1-4644			E-325A	226123
76CC	盌		1-4645	1-7266		E-325B	226126
76CD	盍	0-7833	0-6620	1-8310	AF72	1-5675	214D34
76CE	盎	0-1627	1-4646	1-7050	AF73	1-5676	214D35
76CF	盏	0-5321					274D3A
76D0	盐	0-4946					276251
76D1	监	0-2864					274D3D
76D2	盒	0-2648	0-6622	0-8976	B2B0	1-5C35	214D37
76D3	盓	3-5929			D6A7	2-374A	
76D4	盔	0-3188	1-4647	1-8447	B2AF	1-5C34	214D36
76D5	盕	3-5930				E-3750	
76D6	盖	0-2439	0-6621	0-4344		E-3752	2D5561
76D7	盗	0-2133	0-3780			E-3751	2D4D38
76D8	盘	0-3744					274D3E
76D9	盙		1-4648	1-6591		E-3D4F	
76DA	盚	3-5931			DAB9	2-3E3D	
76DB	盛	0-4202	0-3225	0-6492	B2B1	1-5C36	214D39
76DC	盜		0-6125	0-5208	B573	1-6079	214D38
76DD	盝	3-5932			DED7	2-453D	
76DE	盞	1-5321	0-6623	0-7751	B7F8	1-6540	214D3A
76DF	盟	0-3543	0-4433	0-5679	B7F9	1-6541	214D3B
76E0	盠	5-5869	1-4649				
76E1	盡	1-3001	0-6624	0-8255	BAC9	1-6970	214D3C
76E2	盢					E-4831	
76E3	監	1-2864	0-2038	0-4288	BACA	1-6971	214D3D
76E4	盤	1-3744	0-4055	0-5879	BD4C	1-6D75	214D3E
76E5	盥	0-7834	0-6625	1-5765	BF64	1-714E	214D40
76E6	盦	3-5936	1-4650		EA75	2-5861	22613B
76E7	盧	1-3412	0-6626	0-5452	BF63	1-714D	214D3F
76E8	盨	3-5933	1-4651				
76E9	盩	3-5937			ED79	2-5D65	22613C
76EA	盪	8-1386	0-6627	1-8147	C0FA	1-7445	214D41
76EB	盫	5-5873				E-5835	
76EC	盬	3-5938	1-4652	1-5685	F053	2-6240	226140
76ED	盭	5-5874			F473	2-6942	226144
76EE	目	0-3631	0-4460	0-5745	A5D8	1-4678	214D42
76EF	盯	0-2202			A86E	1-4B31	214D43
76F0	盰	5-5684	1-4653		CD78	2-283A	
76F1	盱	0-7776	1-4654	1-7324	CD77	2-2839	226148
76F2	盲	0-3504	0-4453	0-5678	AABC	1-4E7D	214D44
76F3	盳	5-5687			CD76	2-2838	
76F4	直	0-5417	0-3630	0-8233	AABD	1-4E7E	214D45
76F5	盵	3-5702			CD79	2-283B	
76F6	盶	3-5710	1-4655				
76F7	盷	3-5724			CFE5	2-2C47	226153
76F8	相	0-4764	0-3374	0-6351	ACDB	1-525E	214D48
76F9	盹	0-7779	1-4656	1-6939	ACDA	1-525D	214D47
76FA	盺	3-5718			CFE7	2-2C49	
76FB	盻	3-5720	0-6629	1-8374	CFE6	2-2C48	226159
76FC	盼	0-3746	1-4657	0-5880	ACDF	1-5262	214D4B
76FD	盽					E-2E35	
76FE	盾	0-2260	0-2966	0-6674	ACDE	1-5261	214D4C
76FF	盿					E-2E33	

770

	Char	G	J	K	B	C	A
0	明	5-5692	1-4658				
1	省	0-4201	0-3042	0-6493	ACD9	1-525C	214D49
2	眂	5-5693					
3	眃	3-5712			CFE1	2-2C43	
4	眄	0-7777	0-6632	0-5688	CFE2	2-2C44	22614B
5	眅	3-5719			CFE3	2-2C45	
6	眆	5-5694	1-4659			E-626C	
7	眇	0-7780	0-6631	1-6469	ACE0	1-5263	226150
8	眈	0-7781	0-6630	0-8715	CFE0	2-2C42	22614F
9	眉	0-3528	0-4093	0-5822	ACDC	1-525F	214D46
A	眊	3-5717	1-4660	1-6448	CFE4	2-2C46	226154
B	看	0-3120	0-2039	0-4255	ACDD	1-5260	214D4A
C	県		0-2409	1-8348			4B5164
D	眍	0-7778					286272
E	眎		1-4661			E-3264	226160
F	眏	3-5737				E-325F	

771

	Char	G	J	K	B	C	A
0	眐	3-5729			D2CF	2-3132	
1	眑	3-5748			D2D3	2-3136	
2	眒	3-5736	1-4662		D2D1	2-3134	
3	眓	3-5734			D2D0	2-3133	
4	眔	3-5893	1-4663				
5	眕	3-5739	1-4664		D2D4	2-3137	
6	眖	3-5738				E-325E	
7	眗	3-5740	1-4665				
8	眘					E-3268	333F24
9	眙	0-7784	1-4666		D2D5	2-3138	2D4D71
A	眚	0-7782	1-4667	1-6805	D2D6	2-3139	22616D
B	眛	3-5727	0-6638	1-6419	D2CE	2-3131	226162
C	眜	3-5728	1-4668				
D	眝	5-5701			D2CD	2-3130	
E	眞		0-6635	0-8256		E-3759	214D4F
F	真	0-5370	0-3131		AF75	1-5678	2D4D4F

772

	Char	G	J	K	B	C	A
0	眠	0-3563	0-4418	0-5689	AF76	1-5679	214D4E
1	眡					E-3267	22616F
2	眢	0-7783	1-4669		D2D7	2-313A	22616C
3	眣	5-5708			D2D2	2-3135	
4	眤		0-6634			E-3265	226163
5	眥		0-6636	1-7486	D6B0	2-3753	226222
6	眦	0-7786	0-6637	1-7487		E-3755	286222
7	眧	5-5713			D2D8	2-313B	
8	眨	0-5303	1-4670	1-7527	AF77	1-567A	214D50
9	眩	0-4903	0-6633	0-9063	AF74	1-5677	214D4D
A	眪	3-5732				E-325C	
B	眫					E-3263	22615E
C	眬	8-9344					
D	眭	0-7785	1-4671		D6AA	2-374D	2E624F
E	眮	3-5753	1-4672				
F	眯	0-3548	1-4673		D6A9	2-374C	226176

773

	Char	G	J	K	B	C	A
0	眰	3-5752				E-3753	
1	眱	3-5751			D6AB	2-374E	226177
2	眲	3-5749			D6AC	2-374F	
3	眳	3-5760			D6AE	2-3751	
4	眴	3-5759	1-4674	1-6940	D6AD	2-3750	226226
5	眵	0-7787	1-4675		D6B2	2-3755	226225
6	眶	0-3184	1-4676		B2B5	1-5C3A	214D53
7	眷	0-3076	0-6639	0-4779	B2B2	1-5C37	214D51
8	眸	0-7788	0-6640	0-5734	B2B6	1-5C3B	214D54
9	眹	3-5765	1-4677		D6A8	2-374B	226175
A	眺	0-4487	0-3615	0-8050	B2B7	1-5C3C	214D55
B	眻	5-5722		1-7094	D6B1	2-3754	
C	眼	0-4959	0-2067	0-6849	B2B4	1-5C39	214D52
D	眽	3-5757	1-4678		D6AF	2-3752	
E	眾		1-4679	1-7780	B2B3	1-5C38	214D56
F	眿					E-3262	

774

	Char	G	J	K	B	C	A
0	着	0-5537	0-3569	0-8323		E-3757	226174
1	睁	0-5386					2D4D5F
2	睂		1-4680			E-3D56	
3	睃	0-7792				E-3D53	226235
4	睄	3-5772			DABC	2-3E40	
5	睅	3-5773	1-4681		DABE	2-3E42	226231
6	睆	3-5788	1-4682	1-8428	DABA	2-3E3E	
7	睇	0-7791	0-6641	1-7674	DABB	2-3E3F	22622D
8	睈	3-5774				E-3D51	
9	睉	3-5782				E-3D52	
A	睊	3-5776	1-4683		DABF	2-3E43	226233
B	睋	3-5778			DAC1	2-3E45	
C	睌	3-5784			DAC2	2-3E46	
D	睍	3-5716	1-4684	0-9064	DABD	2-3E41	226232
E	睎	3-5781	1-4685		DAC0	2-3E44	226237
F	睏	1-8842	1-4686		B574	1-607A	214D57

775

	Char	G	J	K	B	C	A
0	睐	0-7789					274D5D
1	睑	0-7790					28632C
2	睒	3-5804	1-4687	1-6851	DEDB	2-4541	22623E
3	睓	5-5736				E-4327	
4	睔	3-5722			DEE0	2-4546	
5	睕	3-5805			DED8	2-453E	
6	睖	3-5790	1-4688		DEDC	2-4542	226244
7	睗	3-5794	1-4689				
8	睘	5-5845				E-4328	226242
9	睙				DEE1	2-4547	
A	睚	0-7793	0-6642	1-7064	DEDD	2-4543	226245
B	睛	0-3006	0-6645	0-7976	B7FA	1-6542	214D59
C	睜	1-5386	1-4690		B843	1-654A	214D5F
D	睝					E-4325	
E	睞	1-7789	1-4691		B7FD	1-6545	214D5D
F	睟	3-5803	1-4692	1-6917	DED9	2-453F	22623A

776

	Char	G	J	K	B	C	A
0	睠		1-4693	1-5905	DEDA	2-4540	22623D
1	睡	0-4315	0-3171	0-6618	BACE	1-6975	214D67
2	睢	0-7801	1-4694	1-6918	B846	1-654D	22624F
3	督	0-2229	0-3836	0-5229	B7FE	1-6546	214D5E
4	睤	5-5735	1-4701			E-4326	
5	睥	0-7802	0-6646	1-6694	B844	1-654B	214D62
6	睦	0-3632	0-4351	0-5746	B7FC	1-6544	214D5B
7	睧	5-5739	1-4702		DEDF	2-4545	
8	睨	0-7794	0-6643	1-7184	B845	1-654C	214D61
9	睩	3-5809			DEDE	2-4544	
A	睪		1-4703		B841	1-6548	214D5A
B	睫	0-2962	0-6644	0-8466	B7FB	1-6543	214D58
C	睬	0-1839	1-4704		B842	1-6549	214D60
D	睭	3-5801			DEE2	2-4548	
E	睮	3-5824			E2E6	2-4C2E	
F	睯	3-5830			E2E8	2-4C30	226256

777

	Char	G	J	K	B	C	A
0	睰		1-4705				
1	睱	3-5828				E-4839	214D64
2	睲	3-5819	1-4706				
3	睳	5-5747	1-4707				
4	睴	3-5766	1-4708			E-4833	
5	睵	3-5814				E-4836	
6	睶	3-5812				E-4835	
7	睷	3-5808		1-5604		E-4834	
8	睸					E-4838	
9	睹	0-2235	0-6649	0-5209	B840	1-6547	214D5C
A	睺	3-5823	1-4709			E-483B	226260
B	睻	5-5752				E-483D	
C	睼	5-5748			E2E3	2-4C2B	
D	睽	0-7805	1-4710	1-5930	BACC	1-6973	214D63
E	睾	0-5626	0-6648	0-4534	E2E9	2-4C31	22625D
F	睿	0-7803	0-6647	0-7158	BACD	1-6974	214D65

778

	Char	G	J	K	B	C	A
0	瞀	0-7806	1-4711		E2E7	2-4C2F	226252
1	瞁	3-5817			E2E2	2-4C2A	
2	瞂	5-1688			E2E5	2-4C2D	
3	瞃				E2EA	2-4C32	
4	瞄	0-3573	1-4712		BACB	1-6972	214D66
5	瞅	0-1982			E2E4	2-4C2C	22625F
6	瞆	8-9345					
7	瞇				BD4E	1-6D77	214D68
8	瞈	5-5765			E6BF	2-5247	
9	瞉	3-4723			E6BE	2-5246	
A	瞊	5-5767				E-4D44	
B	瞋	8-1385	0-6651	0-8257	BD51	1-6D7A	226266
C	瞌	0-7807	1-4713		BD4F	1-6D78	214D6A
D	瞍	0-7804	1-4714	1-6919	E6BC	2-5244	22626A
E	瞎	0-4725	0-6650	1-8293	BD4D	1-6D76	214D69
F	瞏	5-5849			E6BD	2-5245	

77A

	Char	G	J	K	B	C	A
0	瞠	0-7810	0-6653	1-6108	BF65	1-714F	214D6E
1	瞡	5-5733			EA78	2-5864	
2	瞢	0-6211	1-4720	1-6463	EA7B	2-5867	226275
3	瞣				EA7C	2-5868	
4	瞤	3-5785				E-5559	
5	瞥	0-3819	0-4245	0-6013	BF68	1-7152	214D6F
6	瞦	3-5840				E-5558	
7	瞧	0-3938	1-4721		C140	1-744A	214D75
8	瞨				EDA3	2-5D6D	
9	瞩	0-5485				E-555B	274D7C
A	瞪	0-2141	1-4722	1-7831	C0FC	1-7447	214D71
B	瞫	3-5841			ED7B	2-5D67	
C	瞬	0-4318	0-2954	0-6675	C0FE	1-7449	214D74
D	瞭	1-8849	0-4638	0-5492	C141	1-744B	214D73
E	瞮		1-4723				
F	瞯	3-5786	1-4724			E-555C	

77C

	Char	G	J	K	B	C	A
0	矀	5-5784				E-583A	
1	矁					E-5839	2E625F
2	矂	3-5848			F054	2-6241	
3	矃		1-4728				
4	矄	3-5853			F27B	2-6627	
5	矅	3-5855				E-5A60	
6	矆	3-5847				E-5A5F	
7	矇	1-8855	0-6662	1-6464	C3A9	1-7854	4B5564
8	矈	5-5786					
9	矉	5-5768	1-4729	1-6726	F279	2-6625	
A	矊	3-5839			F27A	2-6626	
B	矋						
C	矌	3-5705			F474	2-6943	
D	矍	0-5939	0-6663	1-8419	F477	2-6946	226335
E	矎	3-5854			F475	2-6944	
F	矏				F476	2-6945	

77E

	Char	G	J	K	B	C	A
0	矠	3-6409	1-4736		DEE3	2-4549	
1	矡	3-6414		1-8420			
2	矢	0-4224	0-4480	0-6737	A5DA	1-467A	214E21
3	矣	0-5051	0-6667	0-7588	A86F	1-4B32	214E22
4	矤	5-3088	1-4737				
5	知	0-5410	0-3546	0-8217	AABE	1-4F21	214E23
6	矦	5-2011	1-4738			E-2E36	226352
7	矧	0-7982	0-3974	1-6982	CFE8	2-2C4A	22634F
8	矨				CFE9	2-2C4B	
9	矩	0-3056	0-2275	0-4727	AF78	1-567B	214E24
A	矪		1-4739				
B	矫	0-2935					274E27
C	矬	0-7983	1-4740		DAC4	2-3E48	226355
D	短	0-2244	0-3527	0-5113	B575	1-607B	214E25
E	矮	0-1611	0-6668	0-7265	B847	1-654E	214E26
F	矯	1-2935	0-2226	0-4676	C142	1-744C	214E27

779

	Char	G	J	K	B	C	A
0	瞐	3-5834				E-4D46	
1	瞑	0-7808	0-6652	0-5710	BD50	1-6D79	214D6B
2	瞒	0-3487					2D4D6D
3	瞓						
4	瞔		1-4715				
5	瞕	5-5776	1-4716		EA7D	2-5869	
6	瞖		1-4717	1-7185		E-517B	226273
7	瞗	3-5741			EAA1	2-586B	
8	瞘	1-7778				E-5179	226272
9	瞙	5-5756		1-6390	EA7E	2-586A	226276
A	瞚	5-5778	1-4718		EA76	2-5862	
B	瞛	3-5721			EA7A	2-5866	
C	瞜	3-5827			EA79	2-5865	
D	瞝				EA77	2-5863	
E	瞞	1-3487	0-6654	0-5630	BF66	1-7150	214D6D
F	瞟	0-7809	1-4719		BF67	1-7151	214D6C

77B

	Char	G	J	K	B	C	A
0	瞰	0-7811	0-6655	0-4289	C0FD	1-7448	214D72
1	瞱	3-5756	1-4725		EDA2	2-5D6C	
2	瞲	5-5781			ED7C	2-5D68	
3	瞳	0-4511	0-3823	0-5258	C0FB	1-7446	214D70
4	瞴	3-5711			EDA1	2-5D6B	
5	瞵	0-7812	1-4726		ED7A	2-5D66	22627A
6	瞶	3-5821	0-6656		ED7E	2-5D6A	226323
7	瞷	3-5787			ED7D	2-5D69	22627D
8	瞸					E-5836	
9	瞹	5-5764	0-6657	1-7065		E-5838	22632B
A	瞺	5-5719			F055	2-6242	
B	瞻	0-5316	0-6661	0-8455	C2A4	1-766E	214D78
C	瞼	1-7790	0-6659	0-4401	C2A5	1-766F	22632C
D	瞽	0-7813	0-6660	1-5686	C2A2	1-766C	214D76
E	瞾		1-4727			E-583B	226329
F	瞿	0-8636	0-6658	0-4726	C2A3	1-766D	214D77

77D

	Char	G	J	K	B	C	A
0	矐	3-5858			F5E0	2-6B6E	
1	矑	3-5735	1-4730			E-5E42	22633A
2	矒		1-4731				
3	矓	3-5733			C4EF	1-7A7A	214D7A
4	矔	3-5860			F7EB	2-6F3A	
5	矕	3-5762	1-4732		F8B4	2-7042	
6	矖	3-5770				E-6432	
7	矗	0-2003	0-6664	0-8524	C5F7	1-7C63	214D7B
8	矘	3-5833			F8F8	2-7128	
9	矙		1-4733	1-5550	F8F9	2-7129	
A	矚	1-5485	0-6665	1-8009	C666	1-7D33	214D7C
B	矛	0-3512	0-4423	0-5735	A5D9	1-4679	214D7D
C	矜	0-8170	0-6666	0-4872	ACE1	1-5264	214D7E
D	矝	5-6304				E-3269	
E	矞	3-6408	1-4734	1-7412	DAC3	2-3E47	226345
F	矟	5-6307	1-4735			E-3D57	226346

77F

	Char	G	J	K	B	C	A
0	矰	3-5947	1-4741	1-7787	EDA4	2-5D6E	226359
1	矱	3-5948	1-4742		F27C	2-6628	22635A
2	矲	5-5884			F478	2-6947	
3	石	0-4215	0-3248	0-6420	A5DB	1-467B	214E28
4	矴		1-4743			E-267B	22635C
5	矵					E-267C	
6	矶	0-7722					274E58
7	矷	5-5584			CDA1	2-2841	
8	矸	0-7723	1-4744		CD7A	2-283C	226367
9	矹	5-5581			CD7C	2-283E	
A	矺	3-5540		1-8129	CD7E	2-2840	
B	矻	3-5541	1-4745	1-5730	CD7D	2-283F	226368
C	矼	3-5539	0-6669	1-5563	CD7B	2-283D	226360
D	矽	0-4689		1-6818	AABF	1-4F22	214E29
E	矾	0-2315					274E5C
F	矿	0-3183					274E5B

780

	Char	G	J	K	B	C	A
0	砀	0-7724					286540
1	码	0-3475					274E4C
2	砂	0-4116	0-2629	0-6267	ACE2	1-5265	214E2A
3	砃	3-5555			CFF2	2-2C54	
4	砄	3-5557				E-2E39	
5	砅	5-5593	1-4746		CFED	2-2C4F	
6	砆	5-5585	1-4747		CFEA	2-2C4C	226371
7	砇	5-5590				E-2E3B	
8	砈					E-2E3E	
9	砉	0-7725	1-4748		CFF1	2-2C53	226370
A	砊	3-5556				E-2E37	
B	砋	3-5547				E-2E3A	
C	砌	0-3886	0-6670	1-7965	ACE4	1-5267	214E2C
D	砍	0-3119	1-4749		ACE5	1-5268	214E2B
E	砎	3-5550	1-4750		CFF0	2-2C52	
F	砏	3-5554		1-6656	CFEF	2-2C51	

782

	Char	G	J	K	B	C	A
0	砠	3-5564	0-6673		AFA3	1-5726	226435
1	砡	5-5594	1-4753		D2E1	2-3144	
2	砢	3-5562	1-4754	1-6187	D2DB	2-313E	22642D
3	砣	0-7740	1-4755		D2D9	2-313C	226427
4	砤	5-5605				E-326C	
5	砥	0-7738	0-3754	0-8218	AFA1	1-5724	214E35
6	砦	0-7746	0-2654	0-8386	D6B9	2-375C	226450
7	砧	0-5372	0-2146	0-8659	AF7A	1-567D	214E33
8	砨				D2DE	2-3141	
9	砩	0-7741			D2E2	2-3145	22642A
A	砪	5-5606			D2E4	2-3147	
B	砫	3-5570			D2E0	2-3143	226428
C	砬	0-7739		0-5594	D2DA	2-313D	226426
D	砭	0-7730	1-4756	1-8212	AFA2	1-5725	214E34
E	砮	3-5572	1-4757		D2DF	2-3142	226433
F	砯	3-5576			D2DD	2-3140	

784

	Char	G	J	K	B	C	A
0	础	0-2001					274E59
1	硁	8-9335					
2	硂	5-5609				E-3762	
3	硃	1-8907	1-4761	1-7748	B2B9	1-5C3E	214E38
4	硄	3-5582	1-4762				
5	硅	0-2572	0-6675	0-4809	D6BA	2-375D	22644B
6	硆	5-5610				E-3763	
7	硇	0-7748	1-4763			E-375D	226452
8	硈	3-5578	1-4764		D6B3	2-3756	226448
9	硉	3-5587			D6B5	2-3758	
A	硊	3-5586			D6B7	2-375A	
B	硋	5-5613				E-375F	
C	硌	0-7749	1-4765		D6B8	2-375B	226456
D	硍	3-5588			D6B6	2-3759	226444
E	硎	0-7742	1-4766		B2BA	1-5C3F	334E37
F	硏			0-7058		E-3761	4B4E37

786

	Char	G	J	K	B	C	A
0	硠	3-5604	1-4770	1-6213	DAC5	2-3E49	
1	硡	3-5603	1-4771				
2	硢	5-5624			DAD1	2-3E55	
3	硣		1-4772			E-3D59	
4	硤	1-7744	1-4773		DAC6	2-3E4A	226460
5	硥	3-5592			DAC7	2-3E4B	
6	硦	3-5589				E-3D5D	
7	硧	5-5628		1-7310			
8	硨	1-7726	1-4774	1-7839	DACF	2-3E53	22645A
9	硩	3-5593			DACE	2-3E52	
A	硪	0-7750	1-4775		DACB	2-3E4F	226466
B	硫	0-3382	0-4618	0-5528	B2B8	1-5C3D	214E36
C	硬	0-5118	0-2537	0-4467	B577	1-607D	214E39
D	硭	0-7743			DAC9	2-3E4D	22645B
E	确	0-4023	1-4776	1-8281	DACC	2-3E50	274E49
F	硯	1-4966	0-2407	0-7059	B578	1-607E	214E3B

781

	Char	G	J	K	B	C	A
0	砐	3-5542			CFEE	2-2C50	
1	砑	0-7728	1-4751	1-7008	CFEB	2-2C4D	226374
2	砒	0-3788	0-6671	0-6187	CFEC	2-2C4E	226378
3	砓				CFF3	2-2C55	
4	研	0-4948	0-2406		ACE3	1-5266	214E37
5	砕		0-2653			E-2E3D	274E3E
6	砖	0-5509					274E53
7	砗	0-7726					28645A
8	砘	0-7727					706D3B
9	砙					E-656D	226373
A	砚	0-4966					274E3B
B	砛					E-656E	226424
C	砜	0-7731					706D3F
D	砝	0-7732	1-4752		AF7C	1-5721	214E2F
E	砞					E-667C	
F	砟	0-7736			AFA4	1-5727	22643B

783

	Char	G	J	K	B	C	A
0	砰	0-3773	1-4758	1-8193	AF79	1-567C	214E2E
1	砱	3-5567			D2E5	2-3148	22643D
2	砲		0-4304	0-8863	AFA5	1-5728	3F4956
3	砳	3-5563			D2E3	2-3146	226432
4	破	0-3838	0-3943	0-8782	AF7D	1-5722	214E30
5	砵	3-5561	1-4759		D2DC	2-313F	226431
6	砶					E-326D	
7	砷	0-4173	1-4760		AF7E	1-5723	214E32
8	砸	0-5250			AF7B	1-567E	214E31
9	砹	0-7733					4C6376
A	砺	0-7734	0-3755				274E5D
B	砻	0-7735					286655
C	砼	0-7737					706D45
D	砽					E-656F	226438
E	砾	0-3289					274E5E
F	砿		0-2560				4B4E5B

785

	Char	G	J	K	B	C	A
0	硐	0-7747			D6BB	2-375E	22644E
1	硑	5-5614				E-3760	
2	硒	0-4688	1-4767		D6B4	2-3757	22644C
3	硓					E-6570	226449
4	硔					E-6571	22644A
5	硕	0-4322					274E45
6	硖	0-7744					286460
7	硗	0-7745					286622
8	硘					E-6572	22644F
9	硙	8-1468					
A	硚	8-9336					
B	硛						
C	硜	3-5575	1-4768	1-5579	DAC8	2-3E4C	226461
D	硝	0-4785	0-3043	0-8506	B576	1-607C	214E3A
E	硞	3-5601	1-4769		DAD0	2-3E54	
F	硟	3-5585				E-3D5C	

787

	Char	G	J	K	B	C	A
0	硰				DACD	2-3E51	
1	硱	5-5620			DACA	2-3E4E	
2	硲		0-4003				694823
3	硳						
4	硴		0-6677				69626D
5	硵	8-9337					
6	硶	5-5623				E-3D5A	226464
7	硷	0-2879					276252
8	硸	3-5617				E-4331	
9	硹	5-5630			DEEE	2-4554	
A	硺		1-4777			E-432D	
B	硻	5-5588			DEF2	2-4558	
C	硼	0-3780	0-6679	0-6161	B84E	1-6555	214E42
D	硽	3-5612				E-432E	
E	硾	3-5619	1-4778		E2F0	2-4C38	
F	硿	3-5627			B851	1-6558	22646C

788

	Char	G	J	K	B	C	A
0	碀	5-5612			DEF0	2-4556	
1	碁		0-2475	0-4919		E-4337	3F4472
2	碂	3-5626				E-4329	
3	碃	3-5605			DEED	2-4553	
4	碄				DEE8	2-454E	
5	碅	3-5618			DEEA	2-4550	
6	碆	3-5625	0-6678		DEEB	2-4551	226469
7	碇	0-7754	0-3686	0-7977	DEE4	2-454A	22646D
8	碈	5-5633				E-4335	
9	碉	0-2179			B84D	1-6554	214E40
A	碊	3-5559	1-4779			E-432B	
B	碋					E-4330	
C	碌	0-3421	0-6681	0-5462	B84C	1-6553	214E43
D	碍	0-1613	0-1923	0-6884		E-4334	274E5A
E	碎	0-4373	0-6676	0-6579	B848	1-654F	214E3E
F	碏	3-5607	1-4780	1-7518	DEE7	2-454D	226476

78A

	Char	G	J	K	B	C	A
0	碠	5-5642			E2F4	2-4C3C	
1	碡	0-7756	1-4783		DEEC	2-4552	226531
2	碢	5-5622			E2F6	2-4C3E	
3	碣	0-7757	0-6682	0-4269	BAD4	1-697B	226541
4	碤	3-5609	1-4787	1-7172	E2F7	2-4C3F	22653B
5	碥	0-7760			E2F3	2-4C3B	2D3F76
6	碦	3-5642				E-483E	
7	碧	0-1744	0-4243	0-6001	BAD1	1-6978	214E44
8	碨	3-5635	1-4788	1-7276	E2EF	2-4C37	226544
9	碩	1-4322	0-3257	0-6421	BAD3	1-697A	214E45
A	碪		0-6684		E2EC	2-4C34	2D4E33
B	碫	3-5637			E2F1	2-4C39	226548
C	碬	3-5643	1-4789		E2F5	2-4C3D	
D	碭	1-7724	1-4790	1-8148	E2EE	2-4C36	226540
E	碮	3-5634				E-483F	
F	碯	5-5645	0-6685			E-4845	2D4E5B

78C

	Char	G	J	K	B	C	A
0	磀					E-4D4A	
1	磁	0-2037	0-2807	0-7724	BACF	1-6976	214E4A
2	磂	5-5650				E-4D4D	
3	磃	3-5649			E6C8	2-5250	
4	磄	3-5652			E6C9	2-5251	
5	磅	0-1685	0-6692	0-5922	BD53	1-6D7C	214E4B
6	磆	5-5639	0-6687			E-4D48	4B4846
7	磇	5-5647	1-4804			E-4D4C	
8	磈	3-5638	1-4805	1-7277	E6C7	2-524F	22655E
9	磉	0-7763	1-4806		E6CA	2-5252	226556
A	磊	0-3258	0-6693	0-5480	BD55	1-6D7E	214E4F
B	磋	0-2072	0-6688	0-8315	BD52	1-6D7B	214E48
C	磌	3-5646	1-4807		E6C3	2-524B	226555
D	磍	3-5654			E6C0	2-5248	
E	磎	5-5649	1-4808	0-4505	E6C5	2-524D	
F	磏	3-5653		1-6256	E6C2	2-524A	

78E

	Char	G	J	K	B	C	A
0	磠	3-5594	1-4816	1-6049	EAAD	2-5877	226573
1	磡	3-5658	1-4817		EAA9	2-5873	22656F
2	磢	3-5660			EAAA	2-5874	
3	磣	1-7755			EAA7	2-5871	226577
4	磤	3-5650	1-4813				
5	磥	3-5661			EAA4	2-586E	
6	磦		1-4818				
7	磧	1-7751	0-6701	1-7578	BF6C	1-7156	22656A
8	磨	0-3605	0-4365	0-5608	BF69	1-7153	214E51
9	磩	3-5659			EAA3	2-586D	
A	磪	5-5656	1-4819	1-8024	EAA5	2-586F	
B	磫	3-5551				E-5222	
C	磬	0-7764	0-6694	0-4468	BF6B	1-7155	214E52
D	磭				EAAB	2-5875	
E	磮					E-6575	226576
F	磯	1-7722	0-1675	0-4920	C146	1-7450	214E58

789

	Char	G	J	K	B	C	A
0	碐	3-5606				E-432A	
1	碑	0-1714	0-4074	0-6188	B84F	1-6556	214E41
2	碒	5-5632				E-4336	22652C
3	碓	0-7752	0-1716	1-6121	B850	1-6557	226529
4	碔	5-5629	1-4781		DEE6	2-454C	226470
5	碕	3-5611	0-2676		DEE9	2-454F	333C21
6	碖	3-5553			DEF1	2-4557	22652D
7	碗	0-4575	0-4750	0-7247	B84A	1-6551	214E3D
8	碘	0-2166	1-4782		B84B	1-6552	214E3F
9	碙	3-5548			DEEF	2-4555	22647E
A	碚	0-7753	0-6680		DEE5	2-454B	22646B
B	碛	0-7751					28656A
C	碜	0-7755					286577
D	碝	3-5631	1-4784				
E	碞	5-5638	1-4785		E2F2	2-4C3A	226543
F	碟	0-2190	1-4786	1-6845	BAD0	1-6977	214E46

78B

	Char	G	J	K	B	C	A
0	碰	0-3786	1-4791		B849	1-6550	214E3C
1	碱	0-2878	1-4792			E-4844	2D6252
2	碲	0-7758	1-4793		E2EB	2-4C33	22652F
3	碳	0-4428	1-4794		BAD2	1-6979	214E47
4	碴	0-1874			E2ED	2-4C35	22653E
5	碵		0-6683				696273
6	碶	3-5629					226532
7	碷					E-6573	226539
8	碸	1-7731				E-4840	
9	碹	0-7759					4C6565
A	確	1-4023	0-1946	0-9212	BD54	1-6D7D	214E49
B	碻	3-5651	1-4801	0-9213	E6C1	2-5249	22654E
C	碼	1-3475	0-6691	0-5607	BD58	1-6E23	214E4C
D	碽	3-5590	1-4802				
E	碾	0-3675	0-6690	1-6030	BD56	1-6E21	214E4E
F	碿	3-5657	1-4803				

78D

	Char	G	J	K	B	C	A
0	磐	0-3745	0-4056	0-5881	BD59	1-6E24	214E50
1	磑	5-5608	0-6686	1-7066	E6C4	2-524C	226558
2	磒	5-5621	1-4809			E-4D4B	
3	磓	3-5639	1-4810			E-4D49	
4	磔	0-7761	0-6689	1-7892	E6C6	2-524E	226560
5	磕	0-3136	1-4811	1-5577	BD57	1-6E22	214E4D
6	磖		1-4812			E-5221	
7	磗						
8	磘					E-6574	22655A
9	磙	0-7762					4C6564
A	磚	1-5509	0-6702	1-7609	BF6A	1-7154	214E53
B	磛	3-5614	1-4814		EAA8	2-5872	22656E
C	磜	5-5657				E-5224	
D	磝	3-5644			EAA2	2-586C	
E	磞	3-5662			EAA6	2-5870	
F	磟		1-4815		EAAC	2-5876	226568

78F

	Char	G	J	K	B	C	A
0	磰	5-5664				E-5560	
1	磱					E-5562	
2	磲	0-7765	1-4820		EDAA	2-5D75	226579
3	磳	3-5672	1-4821		EDA5	2-5D6F	
4	磴	0-7767	0-6704	1-6178	C145	1-744F	214E55
5	磵	5-5625		0-4256			
6	磶	3-5668	1-4823				
7	磷	0-3355	1-4824	1-6373	C143	1-744D	214E54
8	磸					E-5561	
9	磹	3-5665			EDAC	2-5D77	226621
A	磺	0-2739	1-4825	1-5788	C144	1-744E	214E56
B	磻	3-5670	1-4826	0-5882	EDA8	2-5D72	226629
C	磼	3-5669		1-7528	EDA9	2-5D73	
D	磽	1-7745	0-6703	1-5827	EDA6	2-5D70	226622
E	磾	3-5624			EDAD	2-5D78	226627
F	磿	3-1635	1-4827		F056	2-5D74	

790

	Char	G	J	K	B	C	A
0	礀		1-4822				
1	礁	0-2924	0-3044	0-8507	C147	1-7451	214E57
2	礂				EDA7	2-5D71	
3	礃	5-5663					
4	礄	3-5584			EDAE	2-5D79	22662B
5	礅	0-7766			EDAB	2-5D76	22657E
6	礆		1-4828			E-5843	
7	礇		0-6705			E-583E	696325
8	礈	5-5665				E-5840	
9	礉	3-5675			F05A	2-6246	
A	礊					E-583F	
B	礋	3-5574				E-583C	
C	礌	3-5674	1-4829	1-6309	F057	2-6243	226632
D	礍					E-5842	
E	礎	1-2001	0-3335	0-8508	C2A6	1-7670	214E59
F	礏	5-5603		1-5963			

791

	Char	G	J	K	B	C	A
0	礐	3-5571	1-4830		F05B	2-6247	
1	礑		0-6707	1-6109	F05D	2-6249	226635
2	礒	3-5543	0-6706	1-7443	F05C	2-6248	22662E
3	礓	0-7768			F058	2-6244	226634
4	礔	5-5669			F059	2-6245	
5	礕					E-5844	
6	礖			0-7006			
7	礗	3-5655			F2A3	2-662D	
8	礘	3-5677				E-5A61	
9	礙	1-1613	0-6708	1-7067	C3AA	1-7855	214E5A
A	礚		1-4831			E-5A62	
B	礛	3-5648			F27E	2-662A	
C	礜		1-4832		F2A2	2-662C	
D	礝	5-5670			F27D	2-6629	
E	礞	0-7770	1-4833		F2A4	2-662E	226643
F	礟		1-4834				

792

	Char	G	J	K	B	C	A
0	礠		1-4835			E-5A63	
1	礡				F2A1	2-662B	
2	礢					E-6576	226646
3	礣	3-5676			F47A	2-6949	
4	礤	0-7769			F47D	2-694C	22664C
5	礥	3-5615	1-4836		F479	2-6948	
6	礦	1-3183	0-6672		C471	1-797C	214E5B
7	礧	3-5679	1-4837	1-6310	F47B	2-694A	22664D
8	礨	3-5680			F47C	2-694B	
9	礩	3-5622	1-4838		F47E	2-694D	226650
A	礪	1-7734	0-6674	0-5376	C472	1-797D	214E5D
B	礫	1-3289	0-6710	0-5388	C474	1-7A21	214E5E
C	礬	1-2315	0-6709	0-5883	C473	1-797E	214E5C
D	礭	5-5672	1-4839	1-8421	F5E1	2-6B6F	
E	礮					E-5E45	394956
F	礯	5-5652			F5E3	2-6B71	

793

	Char	G	J	K	B	C	A
0	礰	3-5546				E-5E43	
1	礱	1-7735	1-4840	1-6304	F5E2	2-6B70	226655
2	礲	5-5602				E-5E44	
3	礳	3-5683					
4	礴	0-7771	1-4841				22665D
5	礵	5-5674	1-4842		F6F6	2-6D64	
6	礶	5-5673					226660
7	礷	5-5666				E-603C	
8	礸				F8B5	2-7043	
9	礹	5-5616			F8FA	2-712A	
A	示	0-4230	0-2808	0-6738	A5DC	1-467C	214E5F
B	礻	0-7674	1-4843				
C	礼	0-3281	0-4673			E-2433	274E7C
D	礽	5-5544	1-4844		CB72	2-2472	226665
E	社	0-4171	0-2850	0-6268	AAC0	1-4F23	214E61
F	礿	3-5490	1-4845		CDA3	2-2843	226668

794

	Char	G	J	K	B	C	A
0	祀	0-7675	0-6711	0-6269	AAC1	1-4F24	214E60
1	祁	0-3878	0-2323	0-4921	AAC2	1-4F25	214E62
2	祂				CDA2	2-2842	226667
3	祃	8-9323					
4	祄	5-5546	1-4846		CFF8	2-2C5A	
5	祅		1-4847	1-7290	CFF7	2-2C59	214E63
6	祆	0-7676	1-4848	1-7923	ACE6	1-5269	226675
7	祇	8-9324	0-2132	0-4922	ACE9	1-526C	214E66
8	祈	0-3877	0-2107	0-4923	ACE8	1-526B	214E65
9	祉	0-7677	0-2767	0-8219	ACE7	1-526A	214E64
A	祊	3-5504	1-4849	1-8194	CFF4	2-2C56	22666A
B	祋	3-5503	1-4850		CFF6	2-2C58	
C	祌	3-5502			CFF5	2-2C57	
D	祍					E-6577	22666B
E	祎	8-1466					
F	祏	3-5505	1-4851		D2E8	2-314B	22667B

795

	Char	G	J	K	B	C	A
0	祐	3-5506	0-4520	0-7362	AFA7	1-572A	214E69
1	祑	5-5549	1-4852		D2EC	2-314F	226721
2	祒				D2EB	2-314E	
3	祓	0-7680	0-6717	1-6665	D2EA	2-314D	22667D
4	祔	3-5507	1-4853	1-6628	D2E6	2-3149	226723
5	祕		0-6716	1-6701	AFA6	1-5729	214E67
6	祖	0-5570	0-3336	0-8051	AFAA	1-572D	214E6A
7	祗	0-7683	0-6713	0-8220	AFAD	1-5730	214E6F
8	祘	5-5540	1-4854			E-326F	226677
9	祙	5-5547				E-3270	
A	祚	0-7681	0-6715	0-8052	AFAE	1-5731	214E6E
B	祛	0-7678	1-4855	0-4368	D2E7	2-314A	226679
C	祜	0-7679	1-4856	0-9152	D2E9	2-314C	22667A
D	祝	0-5503	0-2943	0-8570	AFAC	1-572F	214E6C
E	神	0-4181	0-3132	0-6774	AFAB	1-572E	214E6B
F	祟	0-4378	0-6714	1-6920	AFA9	1-572C	214E6D

796

	Char	G	J	K	B	C	A
0	祠	0-7684	0-6712	0-6270	AFA8	1-572B	214E68
1	祡	5-5541			D6C2	2-3765	
2	祢	0-7682	0-3910	1-6062		E-3272	293032
3	祣	5-5555			D6C0	2-3763	
4	祤				D6BC	2-375F	
5	祥	0-4773	0-3045	0-6352	B2BB	1-5C40	214E70
6	祦					E-3D5E	
7	祧	0-7686	1-4857	1-7706	D6BD	2-3760	22672A
8	票	0-3817	0-4128	0-8889	B2BC	1-5C41	214E71
9	祩	5-5554	1-4858		D6BE	2-3761	
A	祪	5-5556			D6BF	2-3762	
B	祫	3-5510	1-4859		D6C1	2-3764	22672D
C	祬	5-5552				E-3766	
D	祭	0-2832	0-2655	0-8014	B2BD	1-5C42	214E72
E	祮					E-3765	
F	祯	0-7685					274E78

797

	Char	G	J	K	B	C	A
0	祰	5-5559			DAD5	2-3E59	
1	祱	5-5560				E-3D5F	
2	祲	3-5513	1-4860		DAD4	2-3E58	226730
3	祳				DAD3	2-3E57	
4	祴	3-5511			DAD2	2-3E56	
5	祵					E-3D64	
6	祶					E-3D62	
7	祷	0-2127	0-3788				274E7D
8	祸	0-2786					274E77
9	祹	3-5518	1-4861		DEF6	2-455C	
A	祺	0-7687	0-6718	0-4924	B852	1-6559	214E73
B	祻		1-4862				
C	祼	3-5517	1-4863	1-5766	DEF3	2-4559	22673E
D	祽	5-5564			DEF5	2-455B	
E	祾	3-5514	1-4864			E-4338	
F	祿		0-6719	0-5463	B853	1-655A	214E75

798

	Char	G	J	K	B	C	A
0	禀	0-5787	0-6741	1-8249		E-433D	2D4F37
1	禁	0-2991	0-2256	0-4855	B854	1-655B	214E74
2	禂	5-5562			DEF4	2-455A	
3	禃	3-5515				E-4339	
4	禄	0-3427	0-4729			E-3D63	454E75
5	禅	0-7688	0-3321				274E7B
6	禆					E-6578	
7	禇					E-4848	
8	禈	5-5557			E341	2-4C48	
9	禉					E-4847	
A	禊	0-7689	0-6720	1-5665	E2F9	2-4C41	22674B
B	禋	3-5520	1-4865	1-7467	E2FA	2-4C42	22674F
C	禌		1-4866				
D	禍	1-2786	0-1850	0-9201	BAD7	1-697E	214E77
E	禎	1-7685	0-3687	0-7978	BAD5	1-697C	214E78
F	福	0-2403	0-4201	0-6056	BAD6	1-697D	214E76

799

	Char	G	J	K	B	C	A
0	禐	5-5568			E343	2-4C4A	
1	禑	3-5521	1-4867	0-7363			
2	禒				E342	2-4C49	
3	禓	3-5491	1-4868		E2FE	2-4C46	226755
4	禔	5-5566	1-4869	1-7675	E2FD	2-4C45	226754
5	禕	3-5494	1-4870		E2FC	2-4C44	22674E
6	禖	3-5519	1-4871		E2FB	2-4C43	226750
7	禗	3-5522			E340	2-4C47	
8	禘	3-5523	1-4872		E2F8	2-4C40	22674A
9	禙					E-6579	22674D
A	禚	0-7690			E6CB	2-5253	22675C
B	禛	3-5524	1-4873		E6D0	2-5258	226760
C	禜	3-5487	1-4874		E6CE	2-5256	
D	禝	5-5572	0-6721	1-7810		E-4D50	226764
E	禞					E-4D51	
F	禟	3-5527				E-4D4F	

79A

	Char	G	J	K	B	C	A
0	禠	3-5525			E6CD	2-5255	
1	禡	3-5492	1-4875		E6CC	2-5254	22675F
2	禢	5-5571			E6CF	2-5257	
3	禣					E-657A	226761
4	禤	3-5530			EAAE	2-5878	
5	禥	5-5574				E-5226	334E73
6	禦	1-8890	0-2190	0-6961	BF6D	1-7157	214E79
7	禧	0-7691	0-6722	0-9391	C148	1-7452	214E7A
8	禨	3-5489	1-4876	1-5985	EDB0	2-5D7B	226771
9	禩		1-4877			E-5227	22676E
A	禪	1-7688	0-6724	0-6441	C149	1-7453	214E7B
B	禫	3-5531	1-4878	1-6088	EDAF	2-5D7A	226770
C	禬	3-5509			F05F	2-624B	
D	禭	3-5532			F05E	2-624A	
E	禮	1-3281	0-6725	0-5441	C2A7	1-7671	214E7C
F	禯		1-4879			E-5845	

79B

	Char	G	J	K	B	C	A
0	禰	1-7682	0-3909	1-6063	F2A5	2-662F	226775
1	禱	1-2127	1-4880	0-5210	C3AB	1-7856	214E7D
2	禲	5-5548			F4A1	2-694E	
3	禳	0-7692	0-6726	0-6944	C5A1	1-7B6B	22677A
4	禴	5-5576	1-4881	1-7082	F6F7	2-6D65	22677B
5	禵	3-5534				E-603D	
6	禶	3-5535			F8B7	2-7045	
7	禷				F8B6	2-7044	
8	禸	5-1718	1-4882		C9A8	2-2167	226822
9	禹	0-5177	0-6727	0-7364	ACEA	1-526D	214E7E
A	禺	0-5614	0-6728	1-7245	ACEB	1-526E	226823
B	离	0-3275	1-4883	1-6362	D6C3	2-3766	275F4F
C	禼					E-657B	226825
D	禽	0-3961	0-2257	0-4856	B856	1-655D	214F21
E	禾	0-2644	0-1851	0-9202	A5DD	1-467D	214F23
F	禿		0-3837	0-5230	A872	1-4B35	214F26

79C

	Char	G	J	K	B	C	A
0	秀	0-4867	0-2908	0-6619	A871	1-4B34	214F24
1	私	0-4329	0-2768	0-6271	A870	1-4B33	214F25
2	秂		1-4884				
3	秃	0-4526				E-2A3E	
4	秄	5-5892	1-4885			E-2A3D	
5	秅	3-5949			CDA4	2-2844	
6	秆	0-2449		1-5527		E-2A3F	226828
7	秇		1-4886			E-2A42	
8	秈		1-4887		AAC4	1-4F27	22682A
9	秉	0-1792	0-6729	0-6028	AAC3	1-4F26	214F27
A	秊		1-4888	0-5022		E-2A44	2D3C65
B	秋	0-3979	0-2909	0-8553	ACEE	1-5271	214F29
C	秌					E-654C	225070
D	种	0-5454			CFFA	2-2C5C	274F3D
E	秎	3-5959			CFFD	2-2C5F	
F	秏	5-5893	1-4889		CFFB	2-2C5D	2D5267

79D

	Char	G	J	K	B	C	A
0	秐					E-2E42	2D5265
1	科	0-3138	0-1842	0-4601	ACEC	1-526F	214F28
2	秒	0-3575	0-4135	0-8509	ACED	1-5270	214F2A
3	秓	3-5955				E-2E40	
4	秔		1-4890			E-2E41	22682D
5	秕	0-7985	0-6730	0-6189	CFF9	2-2C5B	22682E
6	秖		1-4891		CFFC	2-2C5E	226832
7	秗					E-2E43	
8	秘	0-3556	0-4075	0-6190	AFB5	1-5738	4B4E67
9	秙	3-5960				E-3274	
A	秚		1-4892			E-3273	
B	秛	3-5971				E-3279	
C	秜	3-5969			D2F3	2-3156	
D	秝	5-5905	1-4893		D2F5	2-3158	226844
E	秞	3-5963	1-4894		D2F4	2-3157	
F	租	0-5566	0-3337	0-8053	AFB2	1-5735	214F2E

79E

	Char	G	J	K	B	C	A
0	秠	3-5961	1-4901		D2EF	2-3152	
1	秡		0-6733			E-3276	226842
2	秢	3-5966	1-4902	1-6266		E-327B	
3	秣	0-7987	0-6734	1-6408	AFB0	1-5733	214F2D
4	秤	0-1951	0-3973	0-8663	AFAF	1-5732	214F2B
5	秥		1-4903			E-3277	
6	秦	0-3956	0-3133	0-8258	AFB3	1-5736	214F2C
7	秧	0-4977	0-6731	0-6875	AFB1	1-5734	214F2F
8	秨	3-5965				E-3278	
9	秩	0-5440	0-3565	0-8281	AFB4	1-5737	214F30
A	秪	3-5967	1-4904	1-7801	D2F2	2-3155	
B	秫	0-7988	1-4905	1-8060	D2ED	2-3150	22683E
C	秬	3-5956	0-6732	1-5584	D2EE	2-3151	22683D
D	秭	0-7986	1-4906		D2F1	2-3154	226845
E	秮				D2F0	2-3153	
F	积	0-2793					274F44

79F

	Char	G	J	K	B	C	A
0	称	0-1938	0-3046			E-327C	274F3C
1	秱	3-5980	1-4907			E-3769	
2	秲	3-5973				E-3767	
3	秳	3-5982				E-376B	
4	秴	5-5910					
5	秵	3-5981				E-376A	
6	秶				D6C6	2-3769	
7	秷	3-5979			D6C7	2-376A	
8	秸	0-2953	1-4908	1-5535	D6C5	2-3768	226848
9	秹					E-376C	
A	秺	3-5987			D6C4	2-3767	
B	移	0-5038	0-1660	0-7625	B2BE	1-5C43	214F31
C	秼		1-4909				
D	秽	0-2764					274F4A
E	秾	8-9356					
F	秿	3-5990				E-3D65	

7A0

	Char	G	J	K	B	C	A
0	稀	0-4701	0-2109	0-9392	B57D	1-6125	214F36
1	稁			1-5687			
2	稂	0-7992	1-4910	1-6214	DAD6	2-3E5A	22684F
3	稃	0-7991	1-4911		DAD8	2-3E5C	22685C
4	稄	5-5920			DADA	2-3E5E	
5	稅			0-6510	B57C	1-6124	214F32
6	稆	0-7989					4C695C
7	稇	5-5916	1-4912			E-3D66	
8	稈		0-6735	0-4257	B57A	1-6122	214F34
9	稉		1-4913			E-3D69	226854
A	稊	3-6001	1-4914	1-7676	DAD7	2-3E5B	226850
B	程	0-1944	0-3688	0-7979	B57B	1-6123	214F35
C	稌	3-5992	1-4915	1-6134	DAD9	2-3E5D	226861
D	稍	0-4152	0-6736	0-8510	B579	1-6121	214F33
E	税	0-4316	0-3239			E-3D68	
F	稏	3-5975				E-4341	

7A1

	Char	G	J	K	B	C	A
0	稐	5-5901			DF41	2-4566	
1	稑	3-6002	1-4916		DEF7	2-455D	22686B
2	稒	3-6007			DEFA	2-4560	
3	稓	3-6003			DEFE	2-4564	
4	稔	0-7994	0-4413	0-7689	B85A	1-6561	214F3B
5	稕	5-5924	1-4917		DEFC	2-4562	
6	稖	5-5926					
7	稗	0-1662	0-4103	0-8813	DEFB	2-4561	226876
8	稘	5-5921	0-6737		DEF8	2-455E	22686C
9	稙	3-6004	0-6738	0-8234	DEF9	2-455F	22686F
A	稚	0-5441	0-3553	0-8635	B858	1-655F	214F3A
B	稛	3-6008	1-4918		DF40	2-4565	
C	稜		0-4639	0-5550	B857	1-655E	2E3D73
D	稝	3-6010				E-4344	
E	稞	0-7993	1-4919	1-5750	B85C	1-6563	226871
F	稟		0-6740	0-8902	B85B	1-6562	214F37

7A2

	Char	G	J	K	B	C	A
0	稠	0-1977	0-6739	0-8054	B859	1-6560	214F39
1	稡	5-5925	1-4920				
2	稢	3-6005			DEFD	2-4563	
3	稣	0-8653					274F46
4	稤						
5	稥					E-6524	223924
6	稦	3-5954			E349	2-4C50	
7	稧	3-6014	1-4921	1-6846			
8	稨	5-5933			E348	2-4C4F	
9	稩	3-6018				E-484B	
A	稪					E-484D	
B	稫	3-6016	1-4922		E344	2-4C4B	
C	稬					E-4850	226922
D	稭		1-4923			E-484F	22687E
E	種	1-5454	0-2879	0-8090	BAD8	1-6A21	214F3D
F	稯	3-6020	1-4924		E347	2-4C4E	

7A3

	Char	G	J	K	B	C	A
0	稰	3-6023	1-4925		E346	2-4C4D	
1	稱	1-1938	0-6742	0-8664	BAD9	1-6A22	214F3C
2	稲		0-1680			E-4852	4B4F43
3	稳	0-4640					274F4C
4	稴	3-6033	1-4926				
5	稵	5-5932	1-4927				
6	稶			0-7383			
7	稷	0-8002	0-6745	0-8235	BD5E	1-6E29	214F42
8	稸	5-5936	1-4928			E-4D55	
9	稹	0-8001	1-4929	1-7814	E6D2	2-525A	4C725D
A	稺		1-4930			E-4D56	
B	稻	0-2130	0-6743	0-5211	BD5F	1-6E2A	214F43
C	稼	0-2858	0-1852	0-4219	BD5B	1-6E26	214F3F
D	稽	0-2792	0-2346	0-4506	BD5D	1-6E28	214F41
E	稾		0-6744			E-4D5A	2D4F3E
F	稿	0-2469	0-2538	0-4535	BD5A	1-6E25	214F3E

7A4

	Char	G	J	K	B	C	A
0	穀	1-8822	0-2582	0-4558	BD5C	1-6E27	214F40
1	穁	3-6015				E-4D53	
2	穂		0-4270			E-4D57	2D4F48
3	穃		0-6746				69634E
4	穄	3-6036	1-4931		EAAF	2-5879	22693F
5	穅		1-4932	1-5564		E-522A	335065
6	穆	0-3634	0-4352	0-5747	BF70	1-715A	214F47
7	穇	3-6012	1-4933		EAB1	2-587B	22693E
8	穈	3-9202	1-4934		EAB0	2-587A	226939
9	穉		0-6748	0-8636		E-5564	334F3A
A	穊	3-6022			E345	2-4C4C	
B	穋	5-5940			BF72	1-715C	22693D
C	穌	1-8653	1-4935		BF71	1-715B	214F46
D	積	1-2793	0-3249	0-7861	BF6E	1-7158	214F44
E	穎	1-5117	0-1747	0-7136	BF6F	1-7159	214F45
F	穏		0-1826			E-522C	4B4F4C

7A5

	Char	G	J	K	B	C	A
0	穐		0-1612				4B4F29
1	穑	0-8003					274F49
2	穒						
3	穓					E-5229	
4	穔	5-5938			EDB5	2-5E22	
5	穕		1-4936				
6	穖	5-5885	1-4937		EDB3	2-5D7E	
7	穗	0-4375	0-6747	0-6620	C14A	1-7454	214F48
8	穘	3-5978			EDB4	2-5E21	
9	穙	3-6038	1-4938				
A	穚	5-5909			EDB6	2-5E23	
B	穛	3-6040			EDB2	2-5D7D	
C	穜	3-6041	1-4939		EDB1	2-5D7C	226940
D	穝		1-4940				
E	穞	8-1473					
F	穟	3-6043	1-4941		F060	2-624C	22694D

7A6

	Char	G	J	K	B	C	A
0	穠	3-5989	1-4942	1-6043	C2AA	1-7674	22694F
1	穡	1-8003	0-6749	0-6366	C2A8	1-7672	214F49
2	穢	1-2764	0-6750	0-7159	C2A9	1-7673	214F4A
3	穣		0-3087				4C695F
4	穤					E-5A66	
5	穥	5-5886	1-4943				
6	穦					E-5A65	
7	穧	3-5986	1-4944		F2A6	2-6630	
8	穨				F2A7	2-6631	
9	穩	1-4640	0-6751	0-7217	C3AD	1-7858	214F4C
A	穪		1-4945			E-5A67	
B	穫	1-8830	0-1947	0-9214	C3AC	1-7857	214F4B
C	穬	3-5950			F4A3	2-6950	
D	穭	5-5943	1-4946		F4A4	2-6951	
E	穮	3-6045			F4A2	2-694F	226957
F	穯					E-5C64	

7A7

	Char	G	J	K	B	C	A
0	穰	0-8006	0-6753	0-6945	F6F8	2-6D66	22695F
1	穱	3-6049			F6F9	2-6D67	
2	穲					E-6076	
3	穳	3-6047				E-6077	
4	穴	0-4908	0-2374	0-9075	A5DE	1-467E	214F4D
5	穵	5-6216	1-4947	1-7031	CA48	2-2268	226966
6	究	0-3031	0-2170	0-4728	A873	1-4B36	214F4E
7	穷	0-3978					274F5F
8	穸	0-8122	1-4948		CDA5	2-2845	226969
9	穹	0-8123	0-6754	0-4766	AAC6	1-4F29	214F4F
A	空	0-3153	0-2285	0-4586	AAC5	1-4F28	214F50
B	穻	5-6218			CDA6	2-2846	
C	穼	3-6353				E-2E44	
D	穽		0-6755	0-7980		E-2E47	395E6F
E	穾	5-6224	1-4949	1-7291	D040	2-2C61	
F	穿	0-2009	0-3292	0-8430	ACEF	1-5272	214F51

7A8

	Char	G	J	K	B	C	A
0	窀	0-8124	1-4950	1-6172	CFFE	2-2C60	22696B
1	突	0-4527	0-3845	0-5245	ACF0	1-5273	214F52
2	窂	5-6223	1-4951	1-6278		E-2E49	
3	窃	0-3952	0-3264	1-7632		E-2E48	274F64
4	窄	0-5313	0-2685	0-8324	AFB6	1-5739	214F53
5	窅	3-6356	1-4952	1-7292	D2F8	2-315B	226970
6	窆	0-8125	1-4953	1-8213	D2F6	2-3159	226975
7	窇	5-6233			D2FC	2-315F	
8	窈	0-8126	0-6756	0-7301	AFB7	1-573A	214F54
9	窉	5-6227			D2F7	2-315A	
A	窊	5-6232	1-4954	1-7256	D2FB	2-315E	226978
B	窋	5-6235	1-4955		D2F9	2-315C	
C	窌	3-6357			D2FA	2-315D	
D	窍	0-3947					274F61
E	窎	8-9381					
F	窏	3-6361			D6C8	2-376B	

7AA

	Char	G	J	K	B	C	A
0	窠	0-8129	1-4960	1-5751	B85E	1-6565	214F5B
1	窡	3-6368				E-4346	
2	窢	3-6364			DF43	2-4568	
3	窣	3-6367	1-4961	1-6901	DF42	2-4567	226A28
4	窤					E-4347	
5	窥	0-3190					274F60
6	窦	0-8128					274F63
7	窧					E-657C	226A2C
8	窨	0-8131			E34A	2-4C51	226A2E
9	窩	1-4649	0-6761	0-7232	BADB	1-6A24	214F5D
A	窪	1-4561	0-2306	0-7233	BADA	1-6A23	214F5C
B	窫	3-6369			E34B	2-4C52	
C	窬	0-8130	1-4962	1-7382	E34C	2-4C53	226A31
D	窭	0-8132					286A3C
E	窮	1-3978	0-2171	0-4767	BD61	1-6E2C	214F5F
F	窯		0-4550	0-7302	BD60	1-6E2B	214F5E

7AC

	Char	G	J	K	B	C	A
0	竀	3-6370			EDB8	2-5E25	
1	竁	3-6378			EDB9	2-5E26	
2	竂	5-6257				E-5568	
3	竃		0-1986				2D4947
4	竄	1-2060	0-6766	0-8333	C2AB	1-7675	214F62
5	竅	1-3947	0-6765	0-4811	C2AC	1-7676	214F61
6	竆		1-4968				
7	竇	1-8128	0-6769	0-5268	C475	1-7A22	214F63
8	竈	1-5278	0-6762	1-7707		E-5E49	4B4947
9	竉	5-6228	1-4969			E-5E48	
A	竊	1-3952	0-6770	0-7928	C5D1	1-7C3D	214F64
B	立	0-3302	0-4609	0-5601	A5DF	1-4721	214F65
C	竌		1-4970			E-267E	
D	竍		0-6771			E-2721	226A49
E	竎		1-4971				
F	竏		0-6772			E-2A47	226A4B

7AE

	Char	G	J	K	B	C	A
0	章	0-5334	0-3047	0-7781	B3B9	1-5D7D	216032
1	竡		0-6778			E-3773	226A5A
2	竢		0-6779	1-6751		E-3D71	2D3164
3	竣	0-3102	0-2955	0-8166	B5A4	1-612A	214F68
4	竤	5-6207			DADD	2-3E61	
5	童	0-4515	0-3824	0-5259	B5A3	1-6129	214F67
6	竦	0-8121	0-6780	1-6904	DADC	2-3E60	226A5E
7	竧	5-6206				E-3D70	
8	竨		1-4974				
9	竩		1-4975			E-4349	
A	竪	1-4290	0-3508	0-6621		E-434A	2D5957
B	竫	5-6202	1-4976		DF45	2-456A	226A66
C	竬		1-4977			E-4854	
D	竭	0-2963	0-6781	0-4270	BADC	1-6A25	214F69
E	竮	5-6214			E34D	2-4C54	
F	端	0-2243	0-3528	0-5114	BADD	1-6A26	214F6A

7A9

	Char	G	J	K	B	C	A
0	窐	5-6237	1-4956		D6CA	2-376D	
1	窑	0-5004	1-4957			E-3772	334F5E
2	窒	0-5447	0-3566	0-8282	B2BF	1-5C44	214F55
3	窓		0-3375	0-8375		E-3771	334F59
4	窔	5-6242	1-4958		D6C9	2-376C	22697A
5	窕	0-8127	0-6758	0-8055	B2C0	1-5C45	214F56
6	窖	0-2949	0-6760	1-5828	B5A2	1-6128	214F58
7	窗	0-2016	0-6757	1-7880	B5A1	1-6127	214F59
8	窘	0-3029	0-6759	0-4755	B57E	1-6126	214F57
9	窙	3-6362			DADB	2-3E5F	
A	窚	5-6238				E-3770	
B	窛			1-5864			
C	窜	0-2060					274F62
D	窝	0-4649					274F5D
E	窞	3-6366	1-4959		DF44	2-4569	226A2B
F	窟	0-3163	0-2302	0-4763	B85D	1-6564	214F5A

7AB

	Char	G	J	K	B	C	A
0	窰		0-6763			E-4D5B	2D4F5E
1	窱	5-6247			EAB5	2-5921	
2	窲	3-6373			E6D3	2-525B	
3	窳	0-8133	1-4963	1-7383	E6D5	2-525D	226A36
4	窴	3-6371			E6D4	2-525C	
5	窵	3-6358	1-4964		EAB4	2-587E	226A3E
6	窶	1-8132	0-6764	1-5865	EAB2	2-587C	226A3C
7	窷				EAB6	2-5922	
8	窸	3-6374			EAB3	2-587D	226A3D
9	窹		1-4965	1-7215			
A	窺	1-3190	0-1714	0-4810	BF73	1-715D	214F60
B	窻		1-4966	1-7881		E-522F	226A3F
C	窼		1-4967				
D	窽					E-522E	226A3A
E	窾	3-6377		1-5767	EDB7	2-5E24	
F	窿	0-3394	0-6767	1-6349	C14B	1-7455	226A43

7AD

	Char	G	J	K	B	C	A
0	竐					E-2E4E	
1	竑	3-6341	1-4972		D041	2-2C62	226A4F
2	竒		0-5284			E-2E4F	2D3932
3	竓		0-6774			E-2E4D	226A51
4	竔					E-2E4B	226A52
5	竕		0-6773			E-2E4C	226A54
6	竖	0-4290					275957
7	竗			0-5763			
8	竘	3-6344			D2FD	2-3160	
9	站	0-5330	0-6775	0-8355	AFB8	1-573B	214F66
A	竚		0-6776			E-3323	226A55
B	竛	3-6343	1-4973			E-3326	
C	竜	5-6193	0-4621			E-3327	33632B
D	竝		0-6777	0-6029		E-3324	2D3032
E	竞	0-3026					274F6B
F	竟	0-3025	0-8079	0-4469	B3BA	1-5D7E	216033

7AF

	Char	G	J	K	B	C	A
0	竰		0-6782			E-4855	226A6B
1	竱	3-6340	1-4978			E-5230	
2	竲	5-6215				E-5569	
3	竳	3-6351				E-556A	
4	竴		1-4979				
5	竵					E-5849	226A76
6	競	1-3026	0-2205	0-4470	C476	1-7A23	214F6B
7	竷				F4A5	2-6952	
8	竸		0-4931	1-5653		E-5F55	2D4F6B
9	竹	0-5481	0-3561	0-8151	A6CB	1-484C	214F6C
A	竺	0-8335	0-2819	0-8571	AAC7	1-4F2A	214F6D
B	竻	3-6738	1-4980		CDA7	2-2847	
C	竼					E-2E51	
D	竽	0-8336	1-4981	1-7325	ACF2	1-5275	214F6F
E	竾	5-6681	1-4982			E-2E50	226A7C
F	竿	0-2445	0-2040	0-4258	ACF1	1-5274	214F6E

Code	Char	G	J	K	B	C	A
7B00	笀				D042	2-2C63	
7B01	笁				D043	2-2C64	
7B02	笂		0-6783				696373
7B03	笃	0-8338					275039
7B04	笄	0-8339	0-6802		D340	2-3162	226B54
7B05	笅	5-6689			D342	2-3164	
7B06	笆	0-1642	0-6786	1-8179	AFB9	1-573C	214F70
7B07	笇	5-6691	1-4983				
7B08	笈	0-8337	0-2172	1-5964	D344	2-3166	226B2E
7B09	笉	3-6748			D347	2-3169	
7B0A	笊	0-8341	0-6785	1-7708	D345	2-3167	226B33
7B0B	笋	0-4381	0-6804			E-332B	275021
7B0C	笌	5-6687		1-7009			
7B0D	笍	3-6744				E-332A	
7B0E	笎	3-6739			D346	2-3168	
7B0F	笏	0-8343	0-6784	0-9178	D343	2-3165	226B2D
7B10	笐	3-6749			D2FE	2-3161	
7B11	笑	0-4806	0-3048	0-6537	AFBA	1-573D	214F71
7B12	笒	3-6745		1-5958	D348	2-316A	
7B13	笓	5-6685			D341	2-3163	
7B14	笔	0-1742	1-4984			E-332C	274F79
7B15	笕	0-8340					286B7C
7B16	笖	3-6751				E-3778	
7B17	笗	5-6706				E-3779	
7B18	笘	3-6755	0-6788	1-7636	D6D3	2-3776	226B44
7B19	笙	0-8347	0-6789	0-6373	B2C6	1-5C4B	214F77
7B1A	笚	3-6758			D6DC	2-3821	
7B1B	笛	0-2149	0-3711	0-7862	B2C3	1-5C48	214F75
7B1C	笜					E-3777	
7B1D	笝	5-6701			D6D5	2-3778	
7B1E	笞	0-8355	0-6790	0-8734	B2C7	1-5C4C	214F76
7B1F	笟	5-6702	1-4985			E-377B	226B4D
7B20	笠	0-8350	0-1962	0-5602	B2C1	1-5C46	214F72
7B21	笡	3-6757				E-3776	
7B22	笢	3-6763			D6D0	2-3773	
7B23	笣	5-6708	1-4986		D6DD	2-3822	
7B24	笤	0-8352			D6D1	2-3774	226B3F
7B25	笥	0-8351	0-3158	1-6752	D6CE	2-3771	226B36
7B26	符	0-2391	0-4168	0-6112	B2C5	1-5C4A	214F78
7B27	笧	5-6705	1-4987	1-7893			
7B28	笨	0-1731	0-6792	1-6657	B2C2	1-5C47	214F74
7B29	笩		1-4988			E-632D	
7B2A	笪	0-8346	1-4989		D6D4	2-3777	226B42
7B2B	笫	0-8342	1-4990		D6D7	2-377A	226B4A
7B2C	第	0-2158	0-3472	0-8015	B2C4	1-5C49	214F73
7B2D	笭	3-6760	1-4991	0-5429	D6D8	2-377B	
7B2E	笮	0-8348	1-4992		B2C8	1-5C4D	2E6C27
7B2F	笯	3-6765	1-4993	1-6039	D6D9	2-377C	
7B30	笰	3-6764	1-4994		D6CF	2-3772	
7B31	笱	0-8349	1-5001		D6D6	2-3779	226B47
7B32	笲	3-6766			D6DA	2-377D	
7B33	笳	0-8353	0-6787	1-5511	D6D2	2-3775	226B40
7B34	笴	5-6694	1-5002		D6CD	2-3770	
7B35	笵	5-6709	0-6791	1-6562	D6CB	2-376E	226B35
7B36	笶		0-6793			E-377A	4B4E21
7B37	笷					E-657D	226B4B
7B38	笸	0-8345			D6DB	2-377E	226B39
7B39	笹		0-2691	0-6511			226B27
7B3A	笺	0-2867					27502B
7B3B	笻	5-6692			DADF	2-376F	226B3B
7B3C	笼	0-3393					275050
7B3D	笽		1-5003				
7B3E	笾	0-8354					286B68
7B3F	笿	3-6782	1-5004				
7B40	筀	5-6711	1-5005		DAE4	2-3E68	
7B41	筁		1-5006			E-3D7B	
7B42	筂					E-3D78	
7B43	筃	3-6772				E-3D75	
7B44	筄	3-6780			DAE0	2-3E64	
7B45	筅	0-8358	0-6806	1-6832	DAE6	2-3E6A	226B61
7B46	筆	1-1742	0-4114	0-8922	B5A7	1-612D	214F79
7B47	筇	0-8344	1-5007		D6CC	2-3E63	226B55
7B48	筈	3-6776	0-4006	1-5779	DAE1	2-3E65	226B60
7B49	等	0-2140	0-3789	0-5285	B5A5	1-612B	214F7A
7B4A	筊	3-6784			DADE	2-3E62	226B52
7B4B	筋	0-2978	0-2258	0-4841	B5AC	1-6132	214F7E
7B4C	筌	0-8360	0-6805	0-7907	DAE2	2-3E66	226B62
7B4D	筍		0-6803	0-6676	B5AB	1-6131	215021
7B4E	筎	3-6787	1-5008		DAE3	2-3E67	226B63
7B4F	筏	0-2304	0-4021	0-5974	B5AD	1-6133	215022
7B50	筐	0-3180	0-6794	0-4644	B5A8	1-612E	214F7B
7B51	筑	0-5494	0-3562	0-8572	B5AE	1-6134	27503A
7B52	筒	0-4518	0-3791	0-8753	B5A9	1-612F	214F7D
7B53	筓			1-5666		E-3D79	
7B54	答	0-2080	0-3790	0-5145	B5AA	1-6130	215023
7B55	筕	3-6779	1-5009			E-3D72	
7B56	策	0-1863	0-2686	0-8394	B5A6	1-612C	214F7C
7B57	筗	5-6719				E-3D76	
7B58	筘	0-8356			DAE5	2-3E69	226B59
7B59	筙					E-657E	2E6C3E
7B5A	筚	0-8357					286D54
7B5B	筛	0-4124					27503C
7B5C	筜	8-1273					
7B5D	筝	0-8361	0-6824				2D502D
7B5E	筞					E-434F	2D4F7C
7B5F	筟	3-6807		1-6629			
7B60	筠	0-8362	1-5010	0-4821	B861	1-6568	215024
7B61	筡	5-6731			DF50	2-4575	
7B62	筢	0-8365				E-434C	226B74
7B63	筣	3-6805			DF53	2-4578	
7B64	筤	3-6811	1-5011		DF47	2-456C	226B6C
7B65	筥	3-6771	0-6808	1-5585	DF4C	2-4571	226B7E
7B66	筦		1-5012	1-5768	DF46	2-456B	226B68
7B67	筧	1-8340	0-6810	1-5624	B863	1-656A	226B7C
7B68	筨	5-6733				E-4355	
7B69	筩		1-5013	1-8164	DF4A	2-456F	226B6E
7B6A	筪		1-5014				
7B6B	筫	3-6743				E-434D	
7B6C	筬	3-6768	0-6813	0-6494		E-3D77	226B5B
7B6D	筭	3-6790	1-5015		DF48	2-456D	226B70
7B6E	筮	0-8363	0-6814	0-6391	B862	1-6569	226B75
7B6F	筯		1-5016			E-4354	226B7B
7B70	筰	3-6806	0-6811		DF4F	2-4574	226C27
7B71	筱	0-8367	0-6812	1-6878	DF4E	2-4573	226C26
7B72	筲	0-8366	1-5017		DF4B	2-4570	226B79
7B73	筳	3-6775	1-5018	1-7662	DF4D	2-4572	226C29
7B74	筴		0-6809		DF49	2-456E	226B76
7B75	筵	0-8359	0-6807	0-7061	BAE1	1-6A2A	215026
7B76	筶				DF52	2-4577	
7B77	筷	0-3174	1-5019		B85F	1-6566	215025
7B78	筸	3-6802			DF51	2-4576	226B7A
7B79	筹	0-1979				E-4351	27504D
7B7A	筺		0-6801				4B4F7B
7B7B	筻	0-8364					707360
7B7C	筼	7-0116					
7B7D	筽			0-7204			
7B7E	签	0-3909					27504B
7B7F	筿	8-9407					

7B8

	Char	G	J	K	B	C	A
0	简	0-2882					275041
1	箁	3-6822				E-4856	
2	箂	3-6794			E35D	2-4C64	
3	箃	3-6814				E-4858	
4	箄	3-6819	1-5020		BAE8	1-6A31	
5	箅	0-8375			E358	2-4C5F	226C41
6	箆		0-4247			E-4860	226C46
7	箇	8-1390	0-1853	0-4345	BAE7	1-6A30	2D3224
8	箈	3-6828			E34E	2-4C55	
9	箉		1-5021				
A	箊	3-6825			E350	2-4C57	
B	箋	1-2867	0-6821	0-7908	BAE0	1-6A29	21502B
C	箌				E355	2-4C5C	
D	箍	0-2531	0-6818	1-5688	E354	2-4C5B	226C3A
E	箎	5-6745	1-5022	1-8390	E357	2-4C5E	226C43
F	箏	1-8361	0-6823	0-7820	BAE5	1-6A2E	21502D

7B9

	Char	G	J	K	B	C	A
0	箐	0-8368	1-5023		E352	2-4C59	226C35
1	箑	3-6817	1-5024		E351	2-4C58	226C34
2	箒		0-6822	1-8038		E-485A	226C33
3	箓	8-9408				E-485E	
4	箔	0-1813	0-3983	0-5856	BAE4	1-6A2D	215028
5	箕	0-2794	0-4407	0-4925	BADF	1-6A28	215029
6	箖	3-6815	1-5025		E353	2-4C5A	
7	算	0-4367	0-2727	0-6309	BAE2	1-6A2B	21502C
8	箘	3-6818	0-6816		E359	2-4C60	226C44
9	箙	5-6754	0-6825	1-6607	E35B	2-4C62	226C48
A	箚	5-6751	0-6820	0-8316			
B	箛	3-6832	1-5026		E356	2-4C5D	
C	箜	0-8377	0-6819	1-5737	E34F	2-4C56	226C2D
D	箝	0-8373	0-6815	0-4436	BAE3	1-6A2C	21502A
E	箞		1-5027			E-4857	
F	箟	5-6746	0-6817			E-485D	4C6C46

7BA

	Char	G	J	K	B	C	A
0	箠		1-5028	1-8039	BD69	1-6E34	2E3E3F
1	管	0-2560	0-2041	0-4623	BADE	1-6A27	215027
2	箢	0-8378					70736E
3	箣	3-6816				E-485C	226C38
4	箤				E35C	2-4C63	
5	箥		1-5029				
6	箦	0-8369					286D47
7	箧	0-8370					286C58
8	箨	0-8374					286E56
9	箩	0-3465					275054
A	箪	0-8376	0-3529				275045
B	箫	0-8379					275042
C	箬	0-8372	1-5030		E6D9	2-5261	275038
D	箭	0-2893	0-3293	0-7909	BD62	1-6E2D	21502F
E	箮					E-4D5C	
F	箯	3-6850	1-5031		E6DB	2-5263	

7BB

	Char	G	J	K	B	C	A
0	箰	5-6765	1-5032				
1	箱	0-4768	0-4002	0-6353	BD63	1-6E2E	215031
2	箲	5-6769	1-5033			E-4D65	226C52
3	箳	5-6773				E-4D5D	
4	箴	0-8380	0-6830	0-7755	BD65	1-6E30	215032
5	箵	3-6841	1-5034		E6DE	2-5266	
6	箶	3-6837	1-5035				
7	箷	5-6767			E6D6	2-525E	
8	箸	0-8371	0-4004	0-7838	BAE6	1-6A2F	226C59
9	箹	3-6788			E6DC	2-5264	
A	箺		1-5036				
B	箻		1-5037				
C	箼		1-5038				
D	箽	3-6849	1-5039				
E	箾	3-6842		1-6879	E6D8	2-5260	226C60
F	箿	3-6845				E-4D60	

7BC

	Char	G	J	K	B	C	A
0	節	1-2958	0-3265	0-7929	B860	1-6567	215033
1	篁	0-8382	0-6827	0-9254	BD68	1-6E33	215035
2	篂		1-5040			E-6367	
3	篃	3-6861				E-6366	
4	範	1-2322	0-4047	0-5984	BD64	1-6E2F	215030
5	篅	3-6847	1-5041				
6	篆	0-5513	0-6831	0-7910	BD66	1-6E31	215034
7	篇	0-3810	0-4251	0-8825	BD67	1-6E32	21502E
8	篈	3-6835	1-5042				
9	築	1-5494	0-3559	0-8573	BF76	1-7160	21503A
A	篊	3-6858	1-5043	1-8409	E6DD	2-5265	
B	篋	1-8370	0-6826	1-8363	E6D7	2-525F	226C58
C	篌	0-8383	0-6828	1-8470	BD6A	1-6E35	226C6F
D	篍	3-6848				E-4D63	
E	篎	3-6844			E6DA	2-5262	
F	篏	5-6758	0-6829				226C5A

7BD

	Char	G	J	K	B	C	A
0	篐					E-6621	226C5C
1	篑	0-8381					275046
2	篒			0-6757			
3	篓	0-3408					27503E
4	篔	3-6804	1-5044	1-7337	EAC0	2-592C	226D2F
5	篕	5-6775			EABB	2-5927	
6	篖	3-6877	1-5045				
7	篗	3-6874	1-5046				
8	篘	3-6761			EAC5	2-5931	226D35
9	篙	0-2461	1-5047	1-5689	BF74	1-715E	215037
A	篚	0-8385	1-5048		EABD	2-5929	343E38
B	篛		1-5049	1-7083	BF78	1-7162	215038
C	篜	3-6883			EAC3	2-592F	
D	篝	0-8384	0-6832	1-5866	EABA	2-5926	226D22
E	篞	5-6789			EAB7	2-5923	
F	篟	3-6873			EAC6	2-5932	226D32

7BE

	Char	G	J	K	B	C	A
0	篠	3-6810	0-2836	0-6538	C151	1-745B	2E6C26
1	篡	0-2059			BF79	1-7163	21503B
2	篢	3-6791			EAC2	2-592E	
3	篣	3-6880			EAB8	2-5924	
4	篤	1-8338	0-3838	0-5231	BF77	1-7161	215039
5	篥	0-8386	0-6837		EABC	2-5928	226D24
6	篦	0-8387	0-6836	1-6702	BF7B	1-7165	2E6C46
7	篧	5-6791			EAB9	2-5925	
8	篨	3-6863	1-5050		EABE	2-592A	226D29
9	篩	1-4124	0-6833	0-6272	BF7A	1-7164	21503C
A	篪	0-8388	1-5051	1-7802	EAC1	2-592D	226D37
B	篫	5-6774			EAC4	2-5930	
C	篬	5-6690				E-5233	
D	篭		0-4722			E-5234	395050
E	篮	0-3226					27504C
F	篯	8-9409					

7BF

	Char	G	J	K	B	C	A
0	篰	3-6878			EDCB	2-5E38	226D3E
1	篱	0-3273			EDCC	2-5E39	275053
2	篲	5-6794	1-5052		EDBC	2-5E29	2D3D4E
3	篳	1-8357	0-6842	1-8260	EDC3	2-5E30	226D54
4	篴	5-6780	1-5053		EDC1	2-5E2E	226D4F
5	篵		1-5054				
6	篶		0-6846			E-556D	69644E
7	篷	0-3781	0-6843	1-6614	C14F	1-7459	215040
8	篸	5-6757	1-5055		EDC8	2-5E35	
9	篹		1-5056		EABF	2-592B	226D2E
A	篺	5-6802	1-5057			E-556B	
B	篻	3-6888			EDBF	2-5E2C	
C	篼	0-8391	1-5058			E-556E	226D5C
D	篽				EDC9	2-5E36	
E	篾	0-8390	1-5059	1-6438	C14E	1-7458	21503F
F	篿	3-6741			EDBE	2-5E2B	

7C0

	Char	G	J	K	B	C	A
0	簀	1-8369	0-6839	1-7894	EDBD	2-5E2A	226D47
1	簁	3-6893	1-5060		EDC7	2-5E34	
2	簂	5-6747	1-5061		EDC4	2-5E31	
3	簃	3-6892	1-5062		EDC6	2-5E33	226D5B
4	簄		1-5063				
5	簅	5-6722			EDBA	2-5E27	
6	簆		1-5064		EDCA	2-5E37	226D3B
7	簇	0-2056	0-6840	0-8074	C14C	1-7456	21503D
8	簈					E-5570	
9	簉	3-6872	1-5065	1-8040	EDC5	2-5E32	226D5A
A	簊	3-6884			EDCE	2-5E3B	
B	簋	0-8394	1-5066	1-5916	EDC2	2-5E2F	226D46
C	簌	0-8389	1-5067		C150	1-745A	226D4B
D	簍	1-3408	0-6845		C14D	1-7457	21503E
E	簎	3-6889	1-5068		EDC0	2-5E2D	
F	簏	0-8392	1-5069	1-6292	EDBB	2-5E28	226D41

7C2

	Char	G	J	K	B	C	A
0	簠	3-6906	1-5072	1-6592	F064	2-6250	226D63
1	簡	1-2882	0-2042	0-4259	C2B2	1-767C	215041
2	簢	5-6737			F06A	2-6256	
3	簣	1-8381	0-6847		C2B1	1-767B	215046
4	簤	5-6724				E-5851	
5	簥	3-6778	1-5073		F06B	2-6257	
6	簦	0-8403	1-5074		F068	2-6254	226D61
7	簧	0-2741	0-6848	0-9255	C2AE	1-7678	215044
8	簨	5-6825	1-5075		F069	2-6255	226D62
9	簩	3-6792			F062	2-624E	
A	簪	0-8402	0-6849	0-7756	C2AF	1-7679	215043
B	簫	1-8379	0-6852	0-6539	C2AD	1-7677	215042
C	簬	5-6832	1-5076		F2AB	2-6635	
D	簭				F066	2-6252	
E	簮					E-584C	
F	簯					E-6622	226D68

7C4

	Char	G	J	K	B	C	A
0	籀	0-8406	0-6858		C3B3	1-785E	226E2A
1	籁	0-8405					275051
2	籂					E-6624	226E3B
3	籃	1-3226	0-6855	0-5330	C478	1-7A25	21504C
4	籄	5-6801				E-5C66	
5	籅	5-6680			F4AA	2-6957	
6	籆	5-6827	1-5083				
7	籇	5-6840			F4A9	2-6956	
8	籈	3-6916			F4A7	2-6954	
9	籉				F4A6	2-6953	
A	籊	3-6922	1-5084		F4A8	2-6955	
B	籋	3-6762				E-5C65	
C	籌	1-1979	0-6854	0-8135	C477	1-7A24	21504D
D	籍	0-2814	0-3250	0-7863	C479	1-7A26	21504E
E	籎					E-6625	226E46
F	籏		0-6857				

7C6

	Char	G	J	K	B	C	A
0	籠	1-3393	0-6838	0-5475	C5A2	1-7B6C	215050
1	籡		1-5101				
2	籢					E-603E	
3	籣	3-6911	1-5102		C5D3	1-7C3F	226E5E
4	籤	1-8866	0-6862	0-8457	C5D2	1-7C3E	215052
5	籥	3-6930	0-6864	1-7084	C5D4	1-7C40	226E62
6	籦	3-6920			F7ED	2-6F3C	
7	籧	3-6926	1-5103	1-5586	F7EC	2-6F3B	226E5C
8	籨					E-6626	226E61
9	籩	1-8354	1-5104	1-6573	F8FB	2-712B	
A	籪	1-8393			F8B8	2-7046	
B	籫	3-6927			F8FC	2-712C	
C	籬	1-3273	0-6865	0-5570	C658	1-7D25	215053
D	籭	5-6729	1-5105			E-6144	
E	籮	1-3465	1-5106		C659	1-7D26	215054
F	籯	3-6932			F96D	2-715C	226E6F

7C1

	Char	G	J	K	B	C	A
0	簐	5-6743			EDCD	2-5E3A	
1	簑		0-6834		BF75	1-715F	215036
2	簒		0-5053	0-8334		E-5571	4B503B
3	簓		0-6841				696449
4	簔		0-6835				4B5036
5	簕	3-6886					
6	簖	0-8393					286E69
7	簗		0-6844				69644C
8	簘					E-556F	
9	簙	5-6813	1-5070		F063	2-624F	
A	簚	5-6816				E-5850	
B	簛	3-6903	1-5071			E-584E	
C	簜	3-6786			F061	2-624D	226D5F
D	簝	3-6907			F067	2-6253	
E	簞	1-8376		0-5115	C2B0	1-767A	215045
F	簟	0-8401	0-6850	1-7637	F065	2-6251	226D66

7C3

	Char	G	J	K	B	C	A
0	簰	5-6818			F06C	2-6258	226D75
1	簱		1-5077				4C6E42
2	簲					E-6623	
3	簳	3-6915	1-5078		F2A8	2-6632	
4	簴	5-6831	1-5079			E-5A6F	226E35
5	簵	3-6869				E-5A6E	226E27
6	簶	3-6913	1-5080				
7	簷		0-6851	1-7950	C3B2	1-785D	21504A
8	簸	0-8404	0-4086	1-8180	C3B0	1-785B	215049
9	簹	3-6769	1-5081		F2AA	2-6634	226E30
A	簺	3-6919	1-5082				
B	簻	5-6717			F2AC	2-6636	226E34
C	簼	5-6828			F2A9	2-6633	
D	簽	1-3909	0-6853	0-8456	C3B1	1-785C	21504B
E	簾	1-3317	0-4692	0-5419	C3AE	1-7859	215048
F	簿	0-1830	0-4277	0-6113	C3AF	1-785A	215047

7C5

	Char	G	J	K	B	C	A
0	籐	8-1391	0-6859	1-6179	C4F0	1-7A7B	21504F
1	籑		1-5086			E-5E4C	
2	籒		1-5087	1-7749			
3	籓	3-6924	1-5088		F5E5	2-6B73	
4	籔	3-6918	0-6856	1-6921	F5E4	2-6B72	4B5632
5	籕		1-5085				
6	籖		0-6863			E-5E4B	4B5052
7	籗	5-6848			F6FA	2-6D68	
8	籘		0-6860			E-5F58	2D504F
9	籙	3-6830	1-5089		F6FC	2-6D6A	226E59
A	籚	3-6756	1-5090		F6FE	2-6D6C	226E57
B	籛	3-6871	1-5091	1-7610	F6FD	2-6D6B	226E58
C	籜	1-8374	1-5092	1-8130	F6FB	2-6D69	226E56
D	籝	5-6850	1-5093			E-5F57	226E54
E	籞	3-6929	1-5094			E-603F	226E5B
F	籟	1-8405	0-6861	1-6311	C5A3	1-7B6D	215051

7C7

	Char	G	J	K	B	C	A
0	籰	5-6856	1-5107				
1	籱					E-623A	
2	籲	1-8891	1-5108	1-7384	C67E	1-7D4B	215055
3	米	0-3555	0-4238	0-5823	A6CC	1-484D	215056
4	籴	0-5765				E-2A49	287035
5	籵		0-6866		CDA8	2-2848	226E75
6	籶					E-2A48	
7	籷	3-7176				E-2E52	
8	籸	5-7053			D045	2-2C66	226E7A
9	籹	3-7177	1-5109		D046	2-2C67	
A	籺	5-7052			D044	2-2C65	
B	类	0-3264				E-2E54	276053
C	籼	0-8444	1-5110			E-2E53	34682A
D	籽	0-5549	1-5111		ACF3	1-5276	226E7D
E	籾		0-4466	1-7468			226E79
F	籿				D047	2-2C68	

7C8

	Char	G	J	K	B	C	A
0	粀				D048	2-2C69	
1	粁		0-2246	1-7924	D049	2-2C6A	226F21
2	粂		0-2309				693729
3	粃		0-6867	0-6191		E-3331	226F2A
4	粄	5-7056			D349	2-316B	
5	粅	5-7057			D34F	2-3171	
6	粆	3-7180	1-5112			E-332E	
7	粇		1-5113			E-3330	
8	粈	3-7182			D34D	2-316F	
9	粉	0-2359	0-4220	0-6147	AFBB	1-573E	215057
A	粊				D34B	2-316D	
B	粋		0-3172			E-3332	275060
C	粌				D34C	2-316E	
D	粍		0-4416	1-6449	D34E	2-3170	226F2C
E	粎					E-332D	226F28
F	粏		1-5114				

7C9

	Char	G	J	K	B	C	A
0	粐		0-6868				696464
1	粑	0-8446			D34A	2-316C	226F29
2	粒	0-3303	0-4619	0-5603	B2C9	1-5C4E	215058
3	粓	5-7059				E-377D	
4	粔	3-7179	1-5115		D6DE	2-3823	
5	粕	0-3841	0-3984	0-5857	B2CB	1-5C50	226F40
6	粖	5-7058			D6E0	2-3825	
7	粗	0-2054	0-3338	0-8056	B2CA	1-5C4F	215059
8	粘	0-5319	0-3920	0-7936	D6DF	2-3824	226F3B
9	粙	5-7060				E-377E	226F3A
A	粚	5-7062				E-3821	
B	粛		0-2945			E-383E	2D5321
C	粜	0-8448				E-3822	226F3E
D	粝	0-8447					287030
E	粞	0-8449	1-5116		DAE8	2-3E6C	226F45
F	粟	0-4358	0-1632	0-6556	B5AF	1-6135	21505A

7CA

	Char	G	J	K	B	C	A
0	粠	5-7069	1-5117			E-3E21	
1	粡	3-7187	0-6873		DAEA	2-3E6E	226F49
2	粢	0-8450	0-6871	1-7488	DAE7	2-3E6B	226F43
3	粣	3-7184			D6E1	2-3826	
4	粤	0-5233	0-6869	1-7356		E-3E23	
5	粥	0-5464	0-2001	0-8152	B5B0	1-6136	21505B
6	粦	8-1590	1-5118	1-6374		E-3E22	226F4C
7	粧		0-3049	0-7782		E-3D7E	226F42
8	粨		0-6874	1-6554	DAE9	2-3E6D	226F48
9	粩					E-6627	226F46
A	粪	0-2364					275068
B	粫		0-6872				4B506C
C	粬	5-7070					226F4A
D	粭		0-6870				696466
E	粮	0-3324	0-6878	0-5359		E-4358	27506B
F	粯	5-7055			DF56	2-457B	

7CB

	Char	G	J	K	B	C	A
0	粰		1-5119			E-435C	
1	粱	0-3327	0-6877	0-5360	B864	1-656B	21505D
2	粲	0-8451	0-6876	0-8336	DF54	2-4579	226F54
3	粳	0-3012	0-6875	0-4355	B865	1-656C	21505E
4	粴				DF55	2-457A	
5	粵				B866	1-656D	21505C
6	粶		1-5120				
7	粷	5-7078	1-5121			E-4862	
8	粸					E-4861	
9	粹	0-2066	0-6879	0-6622	BAE9	1-6A32	215060
A	粺		1-5122		E361	2-4C68	226F5E
B	粻	3-7181	1-5123		E35E	2-4C65	226F58
C	粼	0-8452	1-5124	1-6375	E360	2-4C67	226F5F
D	粽	0-8453	0-6880	1-7735	BAEA	1-6A33	21505F
E	精	0-3011	0-3226	0-7981	BAEB	1-6A34	215061
F	粿	5-7076	1-5125		E35F	2-4C66	226F59

7CC

	Char	G	J	K	B	C	A
0	糀		0-6881				696471
1	糁	0-8454					287022
2	糂	5-7080	0-6883			E-4D6F	226F64
3	糃	3-7178				E-4D71	
4	糄	3-7192	1-5126			E-4D6D	
5	糅	0-8459	0-6882	1-7385	E6DF	2-5267	226F69
6	糆	5-7085		1-6435		E-4D70	
7	糇	0-8455	1-5127			E-4D73	2F5158
8	糈	0-8458	1-5128		E6E0	2-5268	226F68
9	糉		1-5129			E-4D72	226F6F
A	糊	0-2693	0-2450	0-9153	BD6B	1-6E36	215062
B	糋	5-7090			E6E2	2-526A	
C	糌	0-8456			E6E1	2-5269	226F6D
D	糍	0-8457	1-5130			E-4D6E	4C6F43
E	糎		0-3324		A261	1-2323	226F66
F	糏	5-7102	1-5131				

7CD

	Char	G	J	K	B	C	A
0	糐				EACA	2-5936	
1	糑	3-7202			EACB	2-5937	
2	糒	3-7201	0-6885		EAC7	2-5933	226F71
3	糓	5-4878	1-5132			E-5237	
4	糔	3-7193	1-5133		EAC8	2-5934	
5	糕	0-2466	1-5134	1-5690	BF7C	1-7166	215064
6	糖	0-4439	0-3792	0-5156	BF7D	1-7167	215063
7	糗	0-8460	1-5135	1-5867	EAC9	2-5935	226F75
8	糘		0-6884				696474
9	糙	0-1858	1-5136	1-7709	C157	1-7461	21506A
A	糚		1-5137	1-7540		E-5575	
B	糛	5-7103				E-5574	
C	糜	0-3551	0-6886	1-6494	C153	1-745D	215066
D	糝	1-8454	1-5138	1-6776	C158	1-7462	227022
E	糞	1-2364	0-4221	0-6148	C154	1-745E	215068
F	糟	0-5267	0-3376	0-8057	C156	1-7460	215067

7CE

	Char	G	J	K	B	C	A
0	糠	0-3123	0-2539	0-4319	C152	1-745C	215065
1	糡	5-7107				E-5239	226F77
2	糢	5-7092	0-6887	1-6450	C155	1-745F	215069
3	糣	3-7206				E-5855	
4	糤	5-7109					
5	糥	5-7110		1-6015			
6	糦	5-7108	1-5139			E-5854	
7	糧	1-3324	0-4640	0-5361	C2B3	1-767D	21506B
8	糨	0-8461			EDCF	2-5E3C	226F7B
9	糩		1-5140				
A	糪	3-7210			F2AE	2-6638	
B	糫	3-7207	1-5141				
C	糬				F2AD	2-6637	
D	糭					E-6628	227028
E	糮				F4AB	2-6958	
F	糯	0-3720	0-6889	1-6016	C47A	1-7A27	21506C

7CF

	Char	G	J	K	B	C	A
0	糰	1-8880			C47B	1-7A28	22702E
1	糱	5-7117			F741	2-6D6E	
2	糲	1-8447	0-6890	1-6232	F5E6	2-6B74	227030
3	糳	5-7120				E-6169	
4	糴	1-5765	0-6891	1-7579	F740	2-6D6D	227035
5	糵	3-7211	1-5142			E-6040	
6	糶	1-8448	0-6892	1-7710	F8FD	2-712D	227039
7	糷				F9A4	2-7172	
8	糸	0-8473	0-2769	1-6432	A6CD	1-484E	4B513B
9	糹	1-7089					
A	糺	5-7545	0-6893	1-5931		E-2722	2D506F
B	系	0-4721	0-2347	0-4507	A874	1-4B37	21506E
C	糼	5-7547				E-2A4B	
D	糽	5-7546			CDA9	2-2849	
E	糾	1-3032	0-2174	0-4812	AAC8	1-4F2B	21506F
F	糿					E-2A4A	

7D0

	Char	G	J	K	B	C	A
0	紀	1-2845	0-2110	0-4926	ACF6	1-5279	215070
1	紁	5-7550			D04C	2-2C6D	
2	紂	1-7091	0-6901	0-8136	ACF4	1-5277	215071
3	紃	3-7618	1-5143	1-6941	D04A	2-2C6B	227044
4	約	1-5228	0-4483	0-6919	ACF9	1-527C	215074
5	紅	1-2676	0-2540	0-9185	ACF5	1-5278	215072
6	紆	1-7090	0-6894	0-7365	ACFA	1-527D	227042
7	紇	1-7092	1-5144	0-9364	ACF8	1-527B	215075
8	紈	1-7093	1-5145	0-9228	D04B	2-2C6C	227045
9	紉	1-4050	1-5146		ACF7	1-527A	215073
A	紊	0-4641	0-6904	0-5802	AFBF	1-5742	215078
B	紋	1-4638	0-4470	0-5803	AFBE	1-5741	215077
C	紌	5-7555			D35A	2-317C	
D	納	1-3641	0-3928	0-5001	AFC7	1-574A	215122
E	紎	5-7553			D353	2-3175	
F	紏	5-7560	1-5147		D359	2-317B	227049

7D1

	Char	G	J	K	B	C	A
0	紐	1-3706	0-4119	0-5079	AFC3	1-5746	21507E
1	紑	3-7621	1-5148		D352	2-3174	
2	紒	3-7626	1-5149		D358	2-317A	
3	紓	1-7103	1-5150	1-6813	D356	2-3178	22704A
4	純	1-2031	0-2967	0-6677	AFC2	1-5745	21507D
5	紕	1-7102	0-6903	1-6703	AFC4	1-5747	21507C
6	紖	3-7631	1-5151		D355	2-3177	
7	紗	1-4120	0-2851	0-6273	AFBD	1-5740	215121
8	紘	3-7622	0-2541	0-4660	D354	2-3176	227050
9	紙	1-5429	0-2770	0-8221	AFC8	1-574B	215124
A	級	1-2822	0-2173	0-4868	AFC5	1-5748	215123
B	紛	1-2355	0-4222	0-6149	AFC9	1-574C	215125
C	紜	1-7101	0-6902	1-7338	AFC6	1-5749	21507A
D	紝	3-7625	1-5152		D351	2-3173	227052
E	紞	3-7630	1-5153		D350	2-3172	227051
F	紟	3-7627			D357	2-3179	

7D2

	Char	G	J	K	B	C	A
0	素	0-4356	0-3339	0-6540	AFC0	1-5743	215079
1	紡	1-2336	0-4334	0-5923	AFBC	1-573F	215076
2	索	0-4387	0-2687	0-6367	AFC1	1-5744	21507B
3	紣		1-5154				
4	紤					E-3337	
5	紥					E-333B	2D5129
6	紦		1-5155				
7	紧	0-2984					275144
8	紨	3-7640			D6F0	2-3835	
9	紩	3-7637			D6E9	2-382E	22706C
A	紪		1-5156				
B	紫	0-5547	0-2771	0-7725	B5B5	1-613B	215135
C	紬	3-7636	0-3661	0-8137	D6E8	2-382D	2D514D
D	紭	5-7574	1-5157			E-3829	
E	紮		0-6907	0-8347	B2CF	1-5C54	215129
F	累	0-3259	0-4663	0-5511	B2D6	1-5C5B	21512E

7D3

	Char	G	J	K	B	C	A
0	細	1-4724	0-2657	0-6512	B2D3	1-5C58	21512C
1	紱	1-7106	1-5158	1-6666	B2D9	1-5C5E	227065
2	紲	1-7105	0-6908	1-6847	B2D8	1-5C5D	227062
3	紳	1-4180	0-3134	0-6775	B2D4	1-5C59	21512D
4	紴	3-7648				E-3826	
5	紵	3-7629	0-6910	0-7839	D6E2	2-3827	227059
6	紶	5-7564			D6E5	2-382A	
7	紷	3-7642				E-3827	
8	紸	3-7645			D6E4	2-3829	
9	紹	1-4160	0-3050	0-6541	B2D0	1-5C55	21512A
A	紺	1-7104	0-2616	0-4290	D6E6	2-382B	227061
B	紻	5-7567			D6EF	2-3834	
C	紼	1-7108	1-5159		B2D1	1-5C56	215128
D	紽	3-7647	1-5160		D6E3	2-3828	22705A
E	紾	3-7641	1-5161		D6EC	2-3831	227071
F	紿	1-7110	0-6909		D6ED	2-3832	22706A

7D4

	Char	G	J	K	B	C	A
0	絀	1-7109	1-5162		B2D2	1-5C57	21512F
1	絁	3-7639	1-5163		D6EA	2-382F	22706F
2	終	1-5453	0-2910	0-8091	B2D7	1-5C5C	215130
3	絃		0-2430	0-9065	B2CD	1-5C52	333D42
4	組	1-5573	0-3340	0-8058	B2D5	1-5C5A	21512B
5	絅	5-7569	0-6905	0-4471	D6E7	2-382C	227068
6	絆	1-1677	0-6911	0-5884	B2CC	1-5C51	215126
7	絇	3-7643	1-5164		D6EB	2-3830	
8	絈		1-5165			E-382E	
9	絉			1-6946		E-3824	
A	絊				D6EE	2-3833	
B	絋		0-6906				4C735D
C	経		0-2348			E-382B	33513C
D	絍	5-7587	1-5166	1-7473		E-3E34	
E	絎	1-7112	0-6914		DAFB	2-3F21	227134
F	絏		0-6918		DAF2	2-3E76	2E7062

7D5

	Char	G	J	K	B	C	A
0	結	1-2965	0-2375	0-4431	B5B2	1-6138	215134
1	絑	3-7658	1-5167		DAF9	2-3E7D	
2	絒				DAF6	2-3E7A	
3	絓	3-7649	1-5168		DAEE	2-3E72	22707C
4	絔	5-7579			DAF7	2-3E7B	
5	絕				B5B4	1-613A	215137
6	絖	5-7583	0-6913	1-5789	DAEF	2-3E73	2E735D
7	絗		1-5169			E-3E29	
8	絘	3-7666			DAEB	2-3E6F	
9	絙	3-7650	1-5170	1-8429		E-3E26	
A	絚		1-5171			E-3E2E	22707E
B	絛		0-6922	1-7712	B86C	1-6573	22715A
C	絜		1-5172	1-8355	DAF4	2-3E78	22707A
D	絝	1-7111	1-5173			E-3E2F	2D5773
E	絞	1-2942	0-2542	0-4677	B5B1	1-6137	215132
F	絟	3-7663			DAFA	2-3E7E	

7D6

	Char	G	J	K	B	C	A
0	絠	3-7651				E-3E28	
1	絡	1-3471	0-4577	0-5309	B5B8	1-613E	215138
2	絢	1-4904	0-1628	0-9066	B5BA	1-6140	215136
3	絣	3-7668	0-6919	1-6584	DAED	2-3E71	2E717C
4	絤	5-7578				E-3E2C	
5	絥	5-7586	1-5174				
6	給	1-2488	0-2175	0-4869	B5B9	1-613F	215139
7	絧	3-7656	1-5175		DAF0	2-3E74	227129
8	絨	1-4062	0-6916	0-7554	B5B3	1-6139	215133
9	絩	3-7664		1-7711	DAF8	2-3E7C	
A	絪	5-7584	1-5176	0-7663	DAF1	2-3E75	22712B
B	絫	5-7538			DAF5	2-3E79	22712C
C	絬	3-7660				E-3E2A	
D	絭	3-7605			DAF3	2-3E77	
E	絮	0-4885	0-6917	0-6392	B5B6	1-613C	21513A
F	絯	3-7667			DAEC	2-3E70	

7D7

	Char	G	J	K	B	C	A
0	絰	3-7655	1-5177	1-7821	B5BB	1-6141	227122
1	統	1-4519	0-3793	0-8754	B2CE	1-5C53	215131
2	絲	1-4331	0-6915	0-6274	B5B7	1-613D	21513B
3	絳	1-7113	0-6912	0-4320	B5BC	1-6142	227130
4	絴					E-3E24	
5	絵		0-1908			E-3E35	395179
6	絶	1-3088	0-3268	0-7930		E-3E33	
7	絷	0-8474					287275
8	絸	5-7557	1-5178			E-4367	
9	絹	1-3078	0-2408	0-4421	B868	1-656F	21513E
A	絺	3-7676	1-5179	1-8080	DF5D	2-4624	227158
B	絻	3-7680	1-5180		DF5F	2-4626	227154
C	絼	3-7679			DF61	2-4628	
D	絽	3-7657	0-6924		DF65	2-462C	22714F
E	絾	5-7581				E-3E2B	
F	絿	3-7673	1-5181	0-4729	DF5B	2-4622	227142

7D8

	Char	G	J	K	B	C	A
0	綀	5-7605			DF59	2-457E	
1	綁	1-1683	1-5182		B86A	1-6571	215140
2	綂		1-5183				
3	綃	1-7115	1-5184	1-7986	DF60	2-4627	22714D
4	綄	3-7682			DF64	2-462B	
5	綅	3-7683	1-5185		DF5C	2-4623	22713B
6	綆	1-7114	1-5186	1-5654	DF58	2-457D	227144
7	綇					E-4366	
8	綈	1-7116	1-5187		DF57	2-457C	227139
9	綉	1-4869	0-6921			E-4369	335172
A	綊	3-7653				E-4360	
B	綋	5-7611	1-5188			E-4362	227137
C	綌	3-7678	1-5189		DF62	2-4629	22715B
D	綍	5-7604	1-5190		DF5A	2-4621	227148
E	綎	3-7659		0-7982	DF5E	2-4625	22713D
F	綏	1-4371	0-6923	0-6623	B86B	1-6572	21513F

7DA

	Char	G	J	K	B	C	A
0	綠			0-5464	BAF1	1-6A3A	21514C
1	綡	5-7626			E378	2-4D21	
2	綢	1-1981	0-6934	0-8138	BAF7	1-6A40	21514D
3	綣	1-7125	0-6928	1-5906	E365	2-4C6C	227161
4	綤	5-7540				E-4874	
5	綥	5-7620		1-5986			
6	綦	0-8475	1-5202	1-5987	E375	2-4C7C	22716F
7	綧	5-7627	1-5203	1-7770	E362	2-4C69	
8	綨	5-7614				E-486D	
9	綩	3-7707		1-7346	E377	2-4C7E	
A	綪	3-7685	1-5204		E366	2-4C6D	227169
B	綫	1-4763	0-6932	1-6833		E-486E	33515C
C	綬	1-7123	0-2890	0-6624	BAFE	1-6A47	227178
D	維	1-4612	0-1661	0-7511	BAFB	1-6A44	21514E
E	綮	0-8476	0-6927	1-5667	E376	2-4C7D	227162
F	綯	3-7703	0-6935		E370	2-4C77	395773

7DC

	Char	G	J	K	B	C	A
0	緀	5-7618			E368	2-4C6F	
1	緁	5-7617			E367	2-4C6E	
2	緂	3-7706	1-5209		E364	2-4C6B	
3	緃	5-7622	1-5210				
4	緄	1-7121	1-5211	1-5718	E36C	2-4C73	227174
5	緅	3-7687	1-5212		E369	2-4C70	22716E
6	緆	3-7692	1-5213		E36D	2-4C74	
7	緇	1-7127	0-6930	0-8637	BAFD	1-6A46	215151
8	緈	3-7686				E-4868	
9	緉	3-7670			E379	2-4D22	22716B
A	緊	1-2984	0-2259	0-4944	BAF2	1-6A3B	215144
B	緋	1-7119	0-4076	0-6192	E36E	2-4C75	227167
C	緌	3-7693	1-5214	1-7386	E36F	2-4C76	
D	緍	5-7624	1-5215	1-6509		E-4871	
E	緎	3-7690	1-5216		E36B	2-4C72	22716A
F	総		0-3377			E-4873	4B516D

7DE

	Char	G	J	K	B	C	A
0	締	1-2162	0-3689	0-8483	BD6C	1-6E37	215152
1	緡	1-7137	0-6946	0-5841	E6E8	2-5270	227229
2	緢	3-7688	1-5220			E-4D78	
3	緣	1-5221		0-7062	BD74	1-6E3F	21515A
4	緤	5-7632	0-6942			E-4E24	22722B
5	緥		1-5221			E-4E2F	227249
6	緦	1-7133	1-5222	1-6966	E6EB	2-5273	22723E
7	緧	5-7646			E6E6	2-526E	
8	編	1-1764	0-4252	0-8826	BD73	1-6E3E	21515B
9	緩	1-2726	0-2043	0-7248	BD77	1-6E42	215159
A	緪		1-5223		E6E5	2-526D	22723A
B	緫		1-5224			E-4E2E	
C	緬	1-3569	0-4443	0-5691	BD71	1-6E3C	215157
D	緭	3-7717	1-5225			E-4D77	
E	緮	5-7641			E6EF	2-5277	
F	緯	1-4619	0-1662	0-7453	BD6E	1-6E39	215153

7D9

	Char	G	J	K	B	C	A
0	綐	3-7681				E-435E	
1	綑		1-5191		B869	1-6570	21513D
2	綒	5-7608			DF66	2-462D	
3	經	1-3013	0-6920	0-4472	B867	1-656E	21513C
4	綔				DF63	2-462A	
5	綕	5-7602				E-4364	
6	綖	3-7662	1-5192		E372	2-4C79	227159
7	綗		1-5193			E-4368	
8	綘	5-7609		1-6615		E-436A	
9	継		0-2349			E-4363	2D517D
A	続		0-3419				4B5221
B	綛		0-6925				22714B
C	綜	1-5559	0-3378	0-8092	BAEE	1-6A37	215141
D	綝	3-7689	1-5194		E36A	2-4C71	
E	綞	1-7122	1-5201		BD78	1-6E43	21515D
F	綟	3-7708	0-6938		E374	2-4C7B	227222

7DB

	Char	G	J	K	B	C	A
0	綰	1-7126	0-6939	1-5769	BAED	1-6A36	215143
1	綱	1-2457	0-2543	0-4321	BAF5	1-6A3E	215149
2	網	1-4588	0-4454	0-5649	BAF4	1-6A3D	215148
3	綳	1-1733	1-5205			E-4870	2D516A
4	綴	1-5526	0-3654	0-8446	BAF3	1-6A3C	215146
5	綵		0-6929	0-8387	BAF9	1-6A42	21514B
6	綶		1-5206			E-4869	
7	綷	3-7704	1-5207		E363	2-4C6A	
8	綸	1-3458	0-6937	0-5538	BAFA	1-6A43	215150
9	綹	1-7124	1-5208		E371	2-4C78	22717D
A	綺	1-7118	0-6926	0-4927	BAF6	1-6A3F	215147
B	綻	1-5332	0-3530	0-8710	BAEC	1-6A35	215142
C	綼	3-7701			E373	2-4C7A	
D	綽	1-2034	0-6931	0-7742	BAEF	1-6A38	21514A
E	綾	1-7117	0-1629	0-5551	BAF0	1-6A39	215145
F	綿	1-3564	0-4442	0-5690	BAF8	1-6A41	21514F

7DD

	Char	G	J	K	B	C	A
0	緐					E-6629	33516B
1	緑	1-3444	0-4648			E-486B	33514C
2	緒	1-4887	0-2979		BAFC	1-6A45	
3	緓					E-662B	
4	緔	1-7120					
5	緕		0-6978				69656E
6	緖			0-6393		E-4E22	215155
7	緗	1-7129	1-5217	1-6791	E6E7	2-526F	227231
8	緘	1-2874	0-6940	0-8969	BD70	1-6E3B	215156
9	緙	1-7128	1-5218		BD79	1-6E44	22722A
A	線		0-3294	0-6442	BD75	1-6E40	21515C
B	緛	3-7712			E6E4	2-526C	
C	緜		0-6936	1-6436		E-4D7C	227246
D	緝	1-2809	0-6941	0-8293	BD72	1-6E3D	215158
E	緞	1-2248	0-6943	0-5116	BD76	1-6E41	21515E
F	緟	5-7640			E6F0	2-5278	

7DF

	Char	G	J	K	B	C	A
0	緰	3-7719			E6EE	2-5276	
1	緱	1-7135	1-5226		E6ED	2-5275	227247
2	緲	1-7131	0-6945		BD7A	1-6E45	22723C
3	緳				E572	2-503B	
4	練	1-3323	0-4693	0-5403	BD6D	1-6E38	215154
5	緵	3-7720	1-5227			E-4E2B	22724B
6	緶	1-7134	1-5228	1-8206	E6EC	2-5274	227248
7	緷	3-7669			E6E3	2-526B	
8	緸	5-7634				E-4D75	
9	緹	1-7130	1-5229	1-7677	BD7B	1-6E46	227236
A	緺	3-7675	1-5230		E6EA	2-5272	
B	緻	1-8904	0-6944	0-8638	BD6F	1-6E3A	215163
C	緼	3-7714				E-4E28	4C7265
D	緽	5-7582				E-4E29	
E	緾	5-7635				E-4E25	
F	緿	5-7652				E-4E2C	

7E0

	Char	G	J	K	B	C	A
0	縀	5-7650	1-5219			E-4E27	
1	縁		0-1779			E-4D7E	4B515A
2	縂					E-4D7D	
3	縃				E6E9	2-5271	
4	縄		0-3876				4B5176
5	縅		0-6947				69654F
6	縆	5-7649					
7	縇					E-662A	
8	縈	1-6151	1-5231	1-7173	BFA2	1-716A	215161
9	縉	1-7138	0-6954	0-8259	BFA7	1-716F	22725E
A	縊	1-7143	0-6948	0-6892	BF7E	1-7168	215160
B	縋	1-7136	0-6955	1-8041	EAD8	2-5944	227253
C	縌	5-7648			EACF	2-593B	
D	縍	5-7659			EADB	2-5947	
E	縎	3-7718			EAD3	2-593F	
F	縏	3-7610			EAD9	2-5945	22726A

7E1

	Char	G	J	K	B	C	A
0	縐	1-7107	1-5232	1-8042	BFA8	1-7170	227269
1	縑	1-7144	1-5233	1-5638	BFA1	1-7169	21515F
2	縒	5-7645	0-6951		EACC	2-5938	227255
3	縓	3-7723			EAD2	2-593E	
4	縔	5-7662			EADC	2-5948	
5	縕		1-5234	0-7218	EAD5	2-5941	227265
6	縖	5-7661			EADA	2-5946	
7	縗	5-7658	1-5235	1-8025	EACE	2-593A	227250
8	縘			1-5668			
9	縙	3-7711				E-523B	
A	縚				EAD6	2-5942	34715A
B	縛	1-2431	0-3991	0-5858	BFA3	1-716B	215162
C	縜	3-7674	1-5236		EAD4	2-5940	
D	縝	1-7139	1-5237	0-8260	BFA6	1-716E	22725D
E	縞	1-7141	0-2842	0-9154	BFA5	1-716D	227251
F	縟	1-7140	0-6953	0-7318	EAD0	2-593C	22725F

7E2

	Char	G	J	K	B	C	A
0	縠	3-4726	1-5238	1-5711	EAD1	2-593D	22725B
1	縡	3-7726	0-6950	0-7813	EACD	2-5939	227252
2	縢	3-4588	0-6956	1-6180	EAD7	2-5943	227256
3	縣	1-4756	0-6949	0-9067	BFA4	1-716C	215164
4	縤	5-7653			EADE	2-594A	
5	縥				EADD	2-5949	
6	縦		0-2936			E-5240	4B516E
7	縧	1-4448	1-5239			E-523F	2E715A
8	縨		1-5240				
9	縩	3-7730			EDDA	2-5E47	
A	縪	3-7654			EDD6	2-5E43	
B	縫	1-2376	0-4305	0-6078	C15F	1-7469	21516C
C	縬	5-7665	1-5241			E-5579	
D	縭	1-7142	1-5242		EDD0	2-5E3D	227272
E	縮	1-4385	0-2944	0-8574	C159	1-7463	215165
F	縯	3-7734	1-5243	0-7064	C169	1-7473	227273

7E3

	Char	G	J	K	B	C	A
0	縰	3-7729			EDDC	2-5E49	
1	縱	1-5561	0-6952	0-8093	C161	1-746B	21516E
2	縲	1-7148	0-6964	1-6340	C15D	1-7467	215169
3	縳	3-7620	1-5244	1-5625	EDD3	2-5E40	
4	縴	1-8867			C164	1-746E	227271
5	縵	1-7147	0-6960	1-6401	C167	1-7471	227321
6	縶	1-8474	1-5245		EDDE	2-5E4B	227275
7	縷	1-3438	0-6963	0-5512	C15C	1-7466	215168
8	縸	3-7722			EDD5	2-5E42	
9	縹	1-7146	0-6961	1-8243	C165	1-746F	227279
A	縺	3-7672	0-6965		EDE0	2-5E4D	227277
B	縻	0-8767	0-6959	1-6501	EDDD	2-5E4A	22726D
C	縼	3-7731			EDD1	2-5E3E	
D	總	1-5560	0-6933	0-8537	C160	1-746A	21516D
E	績	1-2808	0-3251	0-7864	C15A	1-7464	215166
F	縿	3-7709	1-5246		C168	1-7472	227326

7E4

	Char	G	J	K	B	C	A
0	繀	3-7728			EDD8	2-5E45	
1	繁	0-2317	0-4043	0-5969	C163	1-746D	21516B
2	繂	3-7732			EDD2	2-5E3F	
3	繃		0-6962	0-6162	C15E	1-7468	21516A
4	繄	3-7611	1-5247	1-7186	EDDF	2-5E4C	22727D
5	繅	1-7150	1-5248	1-6880	C162	1-746C	21516F
6	繆	1-7149	0-6957	0-5780	C15B	1-7465	215167
7	繇	0-8477	1-5249	0-7303	EDD9	2-5E46	227328
8	繈			1-5565	C166	1-7470	2F2F5D
9	繉				EDD7	2-5E44	
A	繊		0-3301				4B5223
B	繋		0-2350				
C	繌				EDDB	2-5E48	
D	繍		0-2911			E-557A	
E	繎	5-7673	1-5250				
F	繏	3-7741				E-5859	

7E5

	Char	G	J	K	B	C	A
0	繐	3-7737	1-5251	1-6866	F06E	2-625A	227333
1	繑	3-7661			F074	2-6260	22732F
2	繒	1-7153	1-5252	0-8189	C2B9	1-7725	22732D
3	繓	5-7669			F077	2-6263	
4	織	1-5415	0-3105	0-8236	C2B4	1-767E	215171
5	繕	1-4141	0-3322	0-6443	C2B5	1-7721	215170
6	繖		0-6968	1-6771	F06F	2-625B	227337
7	繗	5-7675		1-6376	F076	2-6262	
8	繘	3-7742	1-5253		F071	2-625D	
9	繙		0-6970	1-6555	C2BA	1-7726	335259
A	繚	1-7152	0-6971	1-6325	C2B7	1-7723	215174
B	繛					E-585B	
C	繜	3-7738			F06D	2-6259	
D	繝		0-6967			E-5858	4D2F73
E	繞	1-4038	0-6969	0-7304	C2B6	1-7722	215173
F	繟	3-7705	1-5254		F073	2-625F	

7E6

	Char	G	J	K	B	C	A
0	繠	3-7614			F075	2-6261	
1	繡		1-5255	0-6625	C2B8	1-7724	215172
2	繢	1-7132	1-5256	1-5917	F072	2-625E	2D5179
3	繣	3-7691			F070	2-625C	
4	繤	3-7524				E-662C	
5	繥		1-5257				
6	繦	5-7676	0-6958			E-585A	
7	繧		0-6966				227334
8	繨	5-7580			F2B8	2-6642	227348
9	繩	1-4194	0-6974	0-6717	C3B7	1-7862	215176
A	繪	1-2770	0-6973	0-9275	C3B8	1-7863	215179
B	繫	1-8883	1-5258	0-4508	C3B4	1-785F	215175
C	繬	3-7727				E-5A72	
D	繭	1-2875	0-4390	0-4422	C3B5	1-7860	215177
E	繮	1-7154	1-5259			E-5A74	227349
F	繯	1-7157	1-5260	1-8349	F2B4	2-663E	227351

7E7

	Char	G	J	K	B	C	A
0	繰	1-7156	0-2311	0-8059	F2B2	2-663C	22734E
1	繱	3-7736				E-5A75	
2	繲	3-7743			F2B6	2-6640	
3	繳	1-2941	1-5261		C3BA	1-7864	227352
4	繴	3-7616			F2B7	2-6641	
5	繵	3-7744			F2B0	2-663A	
6	繶	3-7745		1-7110	F2AF	2-6639	
7	繷	5-7593			F2B3	2-663D	
8	繸	3-7739	1-5262		F2B1	2-663B	
9	繹	1-5079	0-6972	0-7026	C3B6	1-7861	215178
A	繺				F2B5	2-663F	
B	繻	3-7747	0-6976		F4AC	2-6959	227358
C	繼	1-2844	0-6975	0-4509	C47E	1-7A2B	21517D
D	繽	1-7145	0-6979	1-6727	C47D	1-7A2A	21517B
E	繾	1-7155	1-5263	1-5626	F4AD	2-695A	227359
F	繿		0-6981			E-5C6C	4B577E

Code	Char	G	J	K	B	C	A
7E80	纀	3-7749			F4AF	2-695C	
7E81	纁	3-7748	1-5264	1-8478	F4AE	2-695B	22735B
7E82	纂	0-5575	0-2728	0-8335	C4A1	1-7A2C	21517C
7E83	纃		0-6977				69656D
7E84	纄					E-5E53	
7E85	纅	3-7644				E-5E50	
7E86	纆	3-7751	1-5265		F5EB	2-6B79	227364
7E87	纇	3-6528	1-5266	1-6312	F5E8	2-6B76	22735E
7E88	纈	1-7151	0-6982	1-8533	F5E9	2-6B77	227360
7E89	纉		0-6983			E-5E51	2E7374
7E8A	纊	1-7094	1-5267	1-5790	F5E7	2-6B75	22735D
7E8B	纋	3-7750			F5EA	2-6B78	
7E8C	續	1-4888	0-6984	0-6557	C4F2	1-7A7D	215221
7E8D	纍	1-8845	1-5268	1-6341	F5EC	2-6B7A	33512E
7E8E	纎		0-6990			E-5E52	335223
7E8F	纏	1-1888	0-3727	0-7911	C4F1	1-7A7C	21517E
7E90	纐		0-6986				696576
7E91	纑	3-7634	1-5269		F742	2-6D6F	22736A
7E92	纒		0-6985			E-5F5A	4B517E
7E93	纓	1-5107	0-6987	0-7137	C5D5	1-7C41	215222
7E94	纔	1-8806	0-6988	1-7554	C5D7	1-7C43	22736D
7E95	纕	3-7754	1-5270		F7EE	2-6F3D	22736B
7E96	纖	1-4743	0-6989	0-6473	C5D6	1-7C42	215223
7E97	纗	3-7755			F8B9	2-7047	
7E98	纘	1-7158	1-5271	0-8337	F940	2-712F	227374
7E99	纙	5-7621			F942	2-7131	227373
7E9A	纚	3-7671	1-5272		F8FE	2-712E	227371
7E9B	纛	0-8478	0-6991	0-5232	F941	2-7130	227370
7E9C	纜	1-3234	0-6992	0-5331	C66C	1-7D39	215224
7E9D	纝		1-5273				
7E9E	纞		1-5274			E-6235	
7E9F	纟	0-7089					51513B
7EA0	纠	0-3032					27506F
7EA1	纡	0-7090					287042
7EA2	红	0-2676					275072
7EA3	纣	0-7091					275071
7EA4	纤	0-4743					275223
7EA5	纥	0-7092					275075
7EA6	约	0-5228					275074
7EA7	级	0-2822					275123
7EA8	纨	0-7093					287045
7EA9	纩	0-7094					28735D
7EAA	纪	0-2845					275070
7EAB	纫	0-4050					275073
7EAC	纬	0-4619					275153
7EAD	纭	0-7101					27507A
7EAE	纮	8-9452					
7EAF	纯	0-2031					27507D
7EB0	纰	0-7102					27507C
7EB1	纱	0-4120					275121
7EB2	纲	0-2457					275149
7EB3	纳	0-3641					275122
7EB4	纴	8-9453					
7EB5	纵	0-5561					27516E
7EB6	纶	0-3458					275150
7EB7	纷	0-2355					275125
7EB8	纸	0-5429					275124
7EB9	纹	0-4638					275077
7EBA	纺	0-2336					275076
7EBB	纻	8-1234					
7EBC	纼	8-9454					
7EBD	纽	0-3706					27507E
7EBE	纾	0-7103					28704A
7EBF	线	0-4763					27515C
7EC0	绀	0-7104					287061
7EC1	绁	0-7105					287062
7EC2	绂	0-7106					287065
7EC3	练	0-3323					275154
7EC4	组	0-5573					27512B
7EC5	绅	0-4180					27512D
7EC6	细	0-4724					27512C
7EC7	织	0-5415					275171
7EC8	终	0-5453					275130
7EC9	绉	0-7107					287269
7ECA	绊	0-1677					275126
7ECB	绋	0-7108					275128
7ECC	绌	0-7109					27512F
7ECD	绍	0-4160					27512A
7ECE	绎	0-5079					275178
7ECF	经	0-3013					27513C
7ED0	绐	0-7110					28706A
7ED1	绑	0-1683					275140
7ED2	绒	0-4062					275133
7ED3	结	0-2965					275134
7ED4	绔	0-7111					4B5773
7ED5	绕	0-4038					275173
7ED6	绖	8-9455					
7ED7	绗	0-7112					287134
7ED8	绘	0-2770					275179
7ED9	给	0-2488					275139
7EDA	绚	0-4904					275136
7EDB	绛	0-7113					287130
7EDC	络	0-3471					275138
7EDD	绝	0-3088					275137
7EDE	绞	0-2942					275132
7EDF	统	0-4519					275131
7EE0	绠	0-7114					287144
7EE1	绡	0-7115					28714D
7EE2	绢	0-3078					27513E
7EE3	绣	0-4869					275172
7EE4	绤	8-1235					
7EE5	绥	0-4371					27513F
7EE6	绦	0-4448					4C715A
7EE7	继	0-2844					27517D
7EE8	绨	0-7116					287139
7EE9	绩	0-2808					275166
7EEA	绪	0-4887					275155
7EEB	绫	0-7117					275145
7EEC	绬	8-1582					
7EED	续	0-4888					275221
7EEE	绮	0-7118					335147
7EEF	绯	0-7119					287167
7EF0	绰	0-2034					27514A
7EF1	绱	0-7120					4D4D61
7EF2	绲	0-7121					287174
7EF3	绳	0-4194					275176
7EF4	维	0-4612					27514E
7EF5	绵	0-3564					27514F
7EF6	绶	0-7123					287178
7EF7	绷	0-1733					4B516A
7EF8	绸	0-1981					27514D
7EF9	绹	8-1236					
7EFA	绺	0-7124					28717D
7EFB	绻	0-7125					287161
7EFC	综	0-5559					275141
7EFD	绽	0-5332					275142
7EFE	绾	0-7126					275143
7EFF	绿	0-3444					27514C

Code	Char	G	J	K	B	C	A
7F00	缀	0-5526					275146
7F01	缁	0-7127					275151
7F02	缂	0-7128					28722A
7F03	缃	0-7129					287231
7F04	缄	0-2874					275156
7F05	缅	0-3569					275157
7F06	缆	0-3234					275224
7F07	缇	0-7130					287236
7F08	缈	0-7131					28723C
7F09	缉	0-2809					275158
7F0A	缊	8-9456					
7F0B	缋	0-7132					4B5179
7F0C	缌	0-7133					28723E
7F0D	缍	0-7122					27515D
7F0E	缎	0-2248					27515E
7F0F	缏	0-7134					287248
7F10	缐	8-1581					
7F11	缑	0-7135					287247
7F12	缒	0-7136					287253
7F13	缓	0-2726					275159
7F14	缔	0-2162					275152
7F15	缕	0-3438					275168
7F16	编	0-1764					27515B
7F17	缗	0-7137					287229
7F18	缘	0-5221					27515A
7F19	缙	0-7138					28725E
7F1A	缚	0-2431					275162
7F1B	缛	0-7140					28725F
7F1C	缜	0-7139					28725D
7F1D	缝	0-2376					27516C
7F1E	缞	8-1487					
7F1F	缟	0-7141					287251
7F20	缠	0-1888					27517E
7F21	缡	0-7142					287272
7F22	缢	0-7143					275160
7F23	缣	0-7144					27515F
7F24	缤	0-7145					27517B
7F25	缥	0-7146					287279
7F26	缦	0-7147					287321
7F27	缧	0-7148					275169
7F28	缨	0-5107					275222
7F29	缩	0-4385					275165
7F2A	缪	0-7149					275167
7F2B	缫	0-7150					27516F
7F2C	缬	0-7151					287360
7F2D	缭	0-7152					275174
7F2E	缮	0-4141					275170
7F2F	缯	0-7153					28732D
7F30	缰	0-7154					287349
7F31	缱	0-7155					287359
7F32	缲	0-7156					28734E
7F33	缳	0-7157					287351
7F34	缴	0-2941					287352
7F35	缵	0-7158					287374
7F36	缶	0-8330	0-2044	0-6114	A6CE	1-484F	4B522B
7F37	缷			1-6753			
7F38	缸	0-2455	0-6993	0-8992	ACFB	1-527E	215226
7F39	缹	5-6661			D26F	2-3052	
7F3A	缺	0-4017	0-6994	0-4432	AFCA	1-574D	215227
7F3B	缻	5-6659	1-5276			E-3831	
7F3C	缼		1-5275				
7F3D	缽		1-5277		B2DA	1-5C5F	215228
7F3E	缾		1-5278	1-6585	DAFC	2-3F22	2D4B71
7F3F	缿	3-6729	1-5279	1-8315	DAFD	2-3F23	
7F40	罀					E-662D	
7F41	罁	5-6660				E-4877	
7F42	罂	0-8331					28742E
7F43	罃	3-6726	1-5280	1-7078	EADF	2-594B	227425
7F44	罄	0-8332	1-5281	1-5656	C16A	1-7474	215229
7F45	罅	0-8333	0-7001	1-8276	EDE1	2-5E4E	227428
7F46	罆	5-6669				E-557D	227427
7F47	罇		1-5282	1-7771		E-585C	334550
7F48	罈				C2BB	1-7727	2E7431
7F49	罉						
7F4A	罊				F2BA	2-6644	
7F4B	罋			1-7246	F2B9	2-6643	22742B
7F4C	罌	1-8331	0-7002	0-6902	C4A2	1-7A2D	22742E
7F4D	罍	3-6733	0-7003	1-6313	F5ED	2-6B7B	22742F
7F4E	罎	1-8878	0-7004	1-6089		E-5F5B	227431
7F4F	罏	3-6727	1-5283		F743	2-6D70	227432
7F50	罐	0-2562	0-7005	0-4624	C5F8	1-7C64	21522B
7F51	网	0-4588	0-7006		CA49	2-2269	275148
7F52	罒		1-5284				
7F53	罓		1-5285				
7F54	罔	0-5672	0-7008	0-5650	AAC9	1-4F2C	21522D
7F55	罕	0-2617	0-7007	0-8954	A875	1-4B38	21522C
7F56	罖						
7F57	罗	0-3462					275237
7F58	罘	0-7823	0-7009	1-6630	D04D	2-2C6E	2E7451
7F59	罙					E-2A4E	
7F5A	罚	0-2303					275233
7F5B	罛	3-5901	1-5286		D360	2-3224	227445
7F5C	罜	3-5903	1-5287		D35B	2-317D	
7F5D	罝	3-5894	1-5288	1-7567	D35F	2-3223	227443
7F5E	罞	5-5838			D35D	2-3221	
7F5F	罟	0-7825	0-7010	1-5691	AFCB	1-574E	21522E
7F60	罠	5-5837	0-7011	1-6510	D35E	2-3222	22743E
7F61	罡	0-7824	1-5289	1-5566	D35C	2-317E	22743F
7F62	罢	0-1653				E-333C	275235
7F63	罣		1-5290	1-5802	D6F1	2-3836	227447
7F64	罤		1-5291				
7F65	罥	3-5905	1-5292		DAFE	2-3F24	227450
7F66	罦	3-5907	1-5293	1-6631	DB40	2-3F25	227451
7F67	罧	3-5909	0-7014		DF69	2-4630	227455
7F68	罨	0-7827	0-7012	1-7122	DF6A	2-4631	227457
7F69	罩	0-5354	0-7013		B86E	1-6575	215231
7F6A	罪	0-5579	0-2665	0-8110	B86F	1-6576	215232
7F6B	罫	3-5908	0-2351	0-4649	DF68	2-462F	227454
7F6C	罬				DF6B	2-4632	
7F6D	罭	3-5910	1-5294		DF67	2-462E	227453
7F6E	置	0-5435	0-3554	0-8639	B86D	1-6574	215230
7F6F	罯	3-5913				E-4878	
7F70	罰	1-2303	0-4019	0-5975	BB40	1-6A48	215233
7F71	罱	0-7829	1-5301			E-4879	22745E
7F72	署	0-4280	0-2980	0-6394	B870	1-6577	21522F
7F73	罳	3-5912			E37A	2-4D23	227460
7F74	罴	0-7828					287472
7F75	罵		0-3945	0-5665	BD7C	1-6E47	215234
7F76	罶	3-5914			E6F1	2-5279	227463
7F77	罷	1-1653	0-4077	0-8783	BD7D	1-6E48	215235
7F78	罸		0-7015	1-6561		E-4E30	2D5233
7F79	罹	0-7830	0-5677	0-5571	BFA9	1-7171	215236
7F7A	罺	3-5920			EAE2	2-594E	
7F7B	罻	3-5918			EAE0	2-594C	
7F7C	罼	5-5839		1-8261	EAE1	2-594D	
7F7D	罽	3-5921	1-5302	1-5669	EDE4	2-5E51	22746C
7F7E	罾	0-7832	1-5303	1-7788	EDE3	2-5E50	22746B
7F7F	罿	3-5922	1-5304		EDE2	2-5E4F	22746A

7F8

	Char	G	J	K	B	C	A
0	羀		1-5305				
1	羁	0-7831					275238
2	羂	3-5916	0-7016	1-5627			2E7450
3	羃	5-5854	0-7018		F2BB	2-6645	4B6A22
4	羄	3-5919				E-6422	
5	羅	1-3462	0-4569	0-5294	C3B9	1-7865	215237
6	羆	1-7828	0-7017	1-6704	F2BC	2-6646	227472
7	羇	3-5924	0-7020	1-5988	F744	2-6D71	4B5238
8	羈	1-7831	0-7019	0-4928	C5F9	1-7C65	215238
9	羉				F8BA	2-7048	
A	羊	0-4982	0-4551	0-6947	A6CF	1-4850	215239
B	羋	5-1713	1-5306		AACB	1-4F2E	216330
C	羌	0-3928	0-7021	0-4322	AACA	1-4F2D	21523A
D	羍	5-2328	1-5307		D04F	2-2C70	
E	美	0-3532	0-4094	0-5824	ACFC	1-5321	21523B
F	羏	5-7025	1-5308			E-2E5D	

7F9

	Char	G	J	K	B	C	A
0	羐		1-5309				
1	羑	3-7172	1-5310		D04E	2-2C6F	22747A
2	羒	3-7151			D362	2-3226	
3	羓	3-7154				E-333D	
4	羔	0-2465	0-7022	0-4536	AFCC	1-574F	21523C
5	羕	3-7173			D6F2	2-3837	227524
6	羖	3-7152	1-5311	1-5692	D361	2-3225	22747E
7	羗		1-5312	1-5567		E-333F	227523
8	羘			1-7541			
9	羙					E-333E	
A	羚	0-3371	0-7025	0-5430	B2DC	1-5C61	21523E
B	羛	3-7174			D6F5	2-383A	
C	羜	3-7153	1-5313		D6F3	2-3838	
D	羝	0-8438	0-7024	1-7568	D6F4	2-3839	2D4A58
E	羞	0-4863	0-7023	0-6626	B2DB	1-5C60	21523D
F	羟	0-8439					287531

7FA

	Char	G	J	K	B	C	A
0	羠	3-7157			DB42	2-3F27	
1	羡	0-4759	1-5314		DB43	2-3F28	2D5240
2	羢		1-5315		DB41	2-3F26	22752C
3	羣		0-7026			E-436E	2D5241
4	群	0-4026	0-2318	0-4756	B873	1-657A	215241
5	羥	1-8439			DF6D	2-4634	
6	羦	3-7163	1-5316		DF6C	2-4633	
7	羧	0-8440			DF6E	2-4635	227533
8	羨		0-3302	0-6444	B872	1-6579	215240
9	義	1-5069	0-2133	0-7589	B871	1-6578	215242
A	羪		1-5317				
B	羫	5-7045		1-5568			
C	羬	3-7165			E6F2	2-527A	
D	羭	3-7166	1-5318		E6F4	2-527C	22753C
E	羮		0-7030			E-4E31	4B5247
F	羯	0-8441	0-7027	1-5536	BD7E	1-6E49	215243

7FB

	Char	G	J	K	B	C	A
0	羰	0-8442			E6F3	2-527B	22753B
1	羱	3-7168			EAE3	2-594F	22753F
2	羲	0-8443	0-7028	0-9393	BFAA	1-7172	215244
3	羳	5-7049			F079	2-6265	
4	羴		1-5319			E-585D	227540
5	羵	5-7046			F078	2-6264	227542
6	羶		0-7031	1-7611	C3BB	1-7866	215245
7	羷	5-7038			F2BD	2-6647	
8	羸	0-5790	0-7032	0-5572	C3BD	1-7868	215246
9	羹	0-2494	0-7029	0-4356	C3BC	1-7867	215247
A	羺	5-7050			F4B0	2-695D	
B	羻				F5EE	2-6B7C	
C	羼	0-6981	1-5320		C4F3	1-7A7E	22754A
D	羽	0-5180	0-1709	0-7366	A6D0	1-4851	215248
E	羾	3-7567			D050	2-2C71	22754C
F	羿	0-8464	1-5321		ACFD	1-5322	215249

7FC

	Char	G	J	K	B	C	A
0	翀	5-7505	1-5322		D365	2-3229	
1	翁	0-4644	0-1807	0-7226	AFCE	1-5751	21524B
2	翂	3-7570			D364	2-3228	
3	翃	3-7568	1-5323		D363	2-3227	227551
4	翄	5-7503				E-3342	2D524A
5	翅	0-1965	0-7034	0-6739	AFCD	1-5750	21524A
6	翆		0-7035			E-3343	275251
7	翇	5-7511			D6FB	2-3840	
8	翈	3-7575	1-5324				
9	翉	3-7573			D6FD	2-3842	
A	翊	0-8120	0-7036	0-7645	D6F6	2-383B	227557
B	翋	3-7581			D6F7	2-383C	
C	翌	0-5078	0-4566	0-7646	B2DD	1-5C62	21524C
D	翍	5-7512			D6F8	2-383D	
E	翎	0-8465	1-5325	0-5431	B2DE	1-5C63	21524E
F	翏	3-7578	1-5326		D6FC	2-3841	

7FD

	Char	G	J	K	B	C	A
0	翐	3-7577			D6F9	2-383E	
1	翑	3-7579			D6FA	2-383F	
2	習	1-4716	0-2912	0-6707	B2DF	1-5C64	21524D
3	翓	5-7513				E-3E37	
4	翔	0-4772	0-7038	0-6354	B5BE	1-6144	21524F
5	翕	0-8466	0-7037	0-9372	B5BF	1-6145	215250
6	翖			1-8520		E-3E38	
7	翗	5-7516			DB44	2-3F29	
8	翘	0-3944					275258
9	翙	8-1274					
A	翚	8-9451					
B	翛	3-1790	1-5327	1-6881	DF6F	2-4636	227567
C	翜	3-7583			DF70	2-4637	
D	翝					E-4372	
E	翞				E37E	2-4D27	
F	翟	0-2152	1-5328	0-7865	BB43	1-6A4B	215253

7FE

	Char	G	J	K	B	C	A
0	翠	0-2068	0-3173	0-8608	BB41	1-6A49	215251
1	翡	0-8468	0-7039	0-6193	BB42	1-6A4A	215252
2	翢	5-7519			E37B	2-4D24	
3	翣	3-7590	1-5329	1-6782	E37C	2-4D25	227568
4	翤			1-6967			
5	翥	0-8467	1-5330		E37D	2-4D26	22756F
6	翦	0-8469	0-7040	1-7612	E6F9	2-5323	22756C
7	翧	5-7524				E-4E32	
8	翨	3-7593	1-5331		E6FA	2-5324	
9	翩	0-8470	0-7041	0-8827	BDA1	1-6E4A	215254
A	翪	5-7523			E6F7	2-5321	
B	翫		0-2069	0-7249	E6F6	2-527E	227573
C	翬	3-7586	1-5332	1-8490	E6F8	2-5322	227572
D	翭	3-7594			E6F5	2-527D	
E	翮	0-8471	1-5333	1-8328	BFAD	1-7175	22757A
F	翯	3-7602	1-5334		EAE4	2-5950	227577

7FF

	Char	G	J	K	B	C	A
0	翰	0-2618	0-2045	0-8955	BFAB	1-7173	215255
1	翱	0-1631			BFAC	1-7174	21525A
2	翲	5-7527	1-5335		EDE6	2-5E53	
3	翳	0-8472	0-7042	1-7187	C16B	1-7475	215256
4	翴	5-7517			EDE5	2-5E52	
5	翵				EFA8	2-6134	
6	翶					E-557E	
7	翷	5-7529			F07A	2-6266	
8	翸	5-7521			F07B	2-6267	
9	翹	1-3944	0-7043	0-4678	C2BC	1-7728	215258
A	翺		1-5336	1-5693		E-5861	4B525A
B	翻	0-2313	0-4361	1-6556	C2BD	1-7729	215259
C	翼	0-5077	0-4567	0-7647	C16C	1-7476	215257
D	翽	3-7584	1-5337		F2BE	2-6648	227629
E	翾	3-7603	1-5338	1-8350	F2BF	2-6649	22762A
F	翿	3-7587	1-5339		F4B1	2-695E	22762C

800

	Char	G	J	K	B	C	A
0	耀	0-5011	0-4552	0-7305	C4A3	1-7A2E	21525B
1	老	0-3247	0-4723	0-5453	A6D1	1-4852	21525C
2	耂					E-667B	4B525C
3	考	0-3128	0-2545	0-4537	A6D2	1-4853	21525D
4	耄	0-7503	0-7046	1-6451	ACFE	1-5753	22762E
5	者	0-5363	0-2852	0-7726	AACC	1-4F2F	21525F
6	耆	0-7440	0-7045	0-4929	AFCF	1-5752	21525E
7	耇	3-6434	1-5340		D051	2-2C72	
8	耈	5-6336	1-5341			E-3836	227631
9	耉			0-4730			
A	耊	5-6340	1-5342			E-3344	
B	耋	0-8183	0-7047		B5C0	1-6146	227633
C	而	0-2288	0-2809	0-7627	A6D3	1-4854	215260
D	耍	0-4303	1-5343		AD41	1-5324	215262
E	耎	5-6374	1-5344		D052	2-2C73	227634
F	耏	3-6466	1-5345		D053	2-2C74	227636

801

	Char	G	J	K	B	C	A
0	耐	0-3645	0-3449	0-5017	AD40	1-5323	215261
1	耑		1-5346	1-6073	AD42	1-5325	227635
2	耒	0-8171	0-7048	1-6314	A6D4	1-4855	215263
3	耓		1-5347				
4	耔	0-8172	1-5348	1-7489	D054	2-2C75	227637
5	耕	0-2491	0-2544	0-4473	AFD1	1-5755	215264
6	耖	0-8173	1-5349	1-7987	D366	2-322A	227639
7	耗	0-2636	0-4455	0-5736	AFD3	1-5757	215267
8	耘	0-5237	0-7049	0-7392	AFD0	1-5754	215265
9	耙	0-1650	0-7050	1-8181	AFD2	1-5756	215266
A	耚	3-6419				E-3837	
B	耛	3-6420			D741	2-3845	
C	耜	0-8174	0-7051		B2E0	1-5C65	215268
D	耝	3-6417	1-5350			E-3839	22763E
E	耞	5-6319	1-5351	1-5512	D740	2-3844	22763D
F	耟		1-5352		D6FE	2-3843	22763B

802

	Char	G	J	K	B	C	A
0	耠	0-8175	1-5353				2E684E
1	耡		0-7052	1-6814	DF71	2-4638	2D5D68
2	耢	0-8176					344138
3	耣	3-6416				E-4922	
4	耤	5-6324	1-5354		E3A1	2-4D28	2D562E
5	耥	0-8177					22764B
6	耦	0-8178	1-5355	1-7326	BDA2	1-6E4B	22764C
7	耧	0-8179					287655
8	耨	0-8181	0-7053	1-6053	BFAE	1-7176	22764F
9	耩	0-8180			EAE6	2-5952	22764E
A	耪	0-3753			EAE5	2-5951	22764D
B	耫	3-6422				E-5621	
C	耬	1-8179	1-5356	1-6336	EDE7	2-5E54	
D	耭			0-4930			
E	耮	1-8176	1-5357			E-5862	
F	耯	5-6333				E-5C6F	

803

	Char	G	J	K	B	C	A
0	耰	3-6431	1-5358	1-7327	F5EF	2-6B7D	22765B
1	耱	0-8182					22765D
2	耲	3-6432					
3	耳	0-2290	0-2810	0-7628	A6D5	1-4856	215269
4	耴	3-6435	1-5359		CB73	2-2473	
5	耵	0-8184	1-5360		CDAA	2-284A	227660
6	耶	0-5014	0-4477	0-6913	AD43	1-5326	21526A
7	耷	0-6239	1-5361		D055	2-2C76	2E765F
8	耸	0-4342					275275
9	耹	5-6343	1-5362		D368	2-322C	227669
A	耺	3-6438	1-5363				
B	耻	0-1960	0-7055			E-3349	2D3E3C
C	耼		1-5364			E-3348	
D	耽	0-2102	0-3531	0-8716	AFD4	1-5758	21526C
E	耾	3-6439	1-5365		D367	2-322B	
F	耿	0-2502	0-7054	0-4474	AFD5	1-5759	21526B

804

	Char	G	J	K	B	C	A
0	聀		1-5366			E-3347	
1	聁					E-662F	22766B
2	聂	0-3684					275279
3	聃	0-8185		0-5136	D743	2-3847	227670
4	聄	5-6347	1-5367			E-383D	
5	聅	3-6441				E-383C	
6	聆	0-8186	0-7057	0-5432	B2E2	1-5C67	21526E
7	聇				D742	2-3846	
8	聈				D744	2-3848	
9	聉	3-6442				E-383B	
A	聊	0-3336	0-7056	0-5493	B2E1	1-5C66	21526D
B	聋	0-3391					27527A
C	职	0-5416					275278
D	聍	0-8187					28773F
E	聎	3-6448				E-3E3C	
F	聏	3-6445			DB46	2-3F2B	

805

	Char	G	J	K	B	C	A
0	聐	3-6443			DB47	2-3F2C	
1	聑	3-6444			DB45	2-3F2A	
2	聒	0-8188	0-7058	1-5780	B5C1	1-6147	22767B
3	聓					E-6729	
4	联	0-3310					275277
5	聕	3-6449		1-8391			
6	聖	1-4205	0-3227	0-6501	B874	1-657B	21526F
7	聗	3-6446				E-4373	
8	聘	0-3824	0-7059	0-6229	B875	1-657C	215270
9	聙	3-6450				E-6356	
A	聚	0-3059	0-7060	0-8609	BB45	1-6A4D	215272
B	聛	5-6351				E-4923	
C	聜				E3A3	2-4D2A	
D	聝	5-6349			E3A2	2-4D29	
E	聞	1-4637	0-4225	0-5804	BB44	1-6A4C	215271
F	聟		0-7061			E-4926	4B3A2F

806

	Char	G	J	K	B	C	A
0	聠		1-5368			E-3E3B	
1	聡		0-3379			E-4925	335276
2	聢		0-7062				22767E
3	聣					E-6630	227728
4	聤	3-6455	1-5369		E6FB	2-5325	
5	聥	3-6454				E-4E34	
6	聦		1-5370			E-4E36	
7	聧	5-6357			E6FC	2-5326	
8	聨		0-7063			E-4E37	4B5277
9	聩	0-8189					287739
A	聪	0-2047				E-4E35	275276
B	聫					E-4E38	
C	聬	5-6358			EAE7	2-5953	227732
D	聭	5-6356	1-5371				
E	聮					E-5243	
F	聯	1-3310	0-4694	0-5404	C170	1-747A	215277

807

	Char	G	J	K	B	C	A
0	聰	1-2047	0-7066	0-8538	C16F	1-7479	215276
1	聱	0-8190	1-5372	1-7216	C16D	1-7477	215273
2	聲	1-4189	0-7065	0-6502	C16E	1-7478	215274
3	聳	1-4342	0-7064	0-7338	C171	1-747B	215275
4	聴		0-3616			E-5622	2D527B
5	聵	1-8189	1-5373	1-7278	F07C	2-6268	227739
6	聶	1-3684	0-7067	1-6858	C2BF	1-772B	215279
7	職	1-5416	0-3106	0-8237	C2BE	1-772A	215278
8	聸	5-6364			F2C0	2-664A	
9	聹	1-8187	0-7068		F4B2	2-695F	22773F
A	聺					E-5C70	
B	聻	3-6459				E-5C71	22773E
C	聼					E-5C72	
D	聽	1-4493	0-7069	0-8473	C5A5	1-7B6F	21527B
E	聾	1-3391	0-4724	0-5476	C5A4	1-7B6E	21527A
F	聿	0-7718	0-7070	0-7551	A6D6	1-4857	21527C

808

	Char	G	J	K	B	C	A
0	肀	0-7717					4B527C
1	肁	5-5070	1-5374				
2	肂	3-3687			D1FB	2-2F7D	
3	肃	0-4364					275321
4	肄	0-5062	0-7071	0-7629	B877	1-657E	21527E
5	肅	1-4364	0-7073	0-6660	B5C2	1-6148	215321
6	肆	0-4333	0-7072	0-6275	B876	1-657D	2D3765
7	肇	0-5356	0-4005	0-8060	BB46	1-6A4E	215322
8	肈	5-7122	1-5375				
9	肉	0-4066	0-3889	0-7531	A6D7	1-4858	215323
A	肊	5-4680			C9A9	2-2168	227747
B	肋	0-3263	0-4730	0-5546	A6D8	1-4859	215324
C	肌	0-2801	0-4009	0-4931	A6D9	1-485A	215325
D	肍	3-4428				E-2435	
E	肎		1-5376			E-2436	227749
F	肏	3-1659			CDAB	2-284B	

80A

	Char	G	J	K	B	C	A
0	肠	0-1906					27535E
1	股	0-2541	0-2452	0-4538	AAD1	1-4F34	215334
2	肢	0-5411	0-2772	0-8222	AACF	1-4F32	215330
3	肣	3-4446			CDAD	2-284D	
4	肤	0-2384				E-2A56	27536E
5	肥	0-2342	0-4078	0-6194	AACE	1-4F31	21532F
6	肦		1-5379	1-6658		E-2A5B	22776A
7	肧		1-5380			E-2A58	227760
8	肨	3-4436				E-2A4F	
9	肩	0-2871	0-2410	0-4423	AAD3	1-4F36	215335
A	肪	0-2330	0-4335	0-5924	AAD5	1-4F38	21532D
B	肫	0-7538	1-5381	1-6942	AAD2	1-4F35	215331
C	肬	5-4683	0-7079			E-2A59	345E3B
D	肭	0-7539	0-7077	1-6055	CDB0	2-2850	2E3A33
E	肮	0-1625			CDAC	2-284C	276153
F	肯	0-3147	0-2546	0-4873	AAD6	1-4F39	215333

80C

	Char	G	J	K	B	C	A
0	胀	0-5345					275359
1	胁	0-4818					275344
2	胂	0-7547			D05B	2-2C7C	22777D
3	胃	0-4624	0-1663	0-7454	AD47	1-532A	21533C
4	胄	0-7548	0-7084	0-8116	AD48	1-532B	21533E
5	胅	3-4461			D05D	2-2C7E	
6	胆	0-2108	0-3532	1-6074		E-2E66	275379
7	胇	3-4470			D057	2-2C78	
8	胈	3-4455	1-5384		D05A	2-2C7B	
9	胉	5-4702			D063	2-2D26	
A	胊			1-5868	D061	2-2D24	
B	胋	3-4457				E-2E60	
C	背	0-1719	0-3956	0-5946	AD49	1-532C	215338
D	胍	0-7550	1-5385		D067	2-2D2A	22782F
E	胎	0-4405	0-3459	0-8735	AD4C	1-532F	21533F
F	胏	3-4447	1-5386		D064	2-2D27	22782D

80E

	Char	G	J	K	B	C	A
0	胠	3-4454	1-5392	1-5587	D058	2-2C79	227773
1	胡	0-2690	0-2453	0-9155	AD4A	1-532D	21533B
2	胢	5-4694				E-2E64	
3	胣	3-4462			D05E	2-2D21	
4	胤	0-5623	0-1693	0-7542	AD4E	1-5331	215341
5	胥	0-8167	0-7081	0-6401	AD45	1-5328	215339
6	胦	3-4459			D066	2-2D29	
7	胧	0-7542					274366
8	胨	0-7543					28786E
9	胩	0-7544					706B4C
A	胪	0-7545					275421
B	胫	0-7554					287855
C	胬	0-7032					706640
D	胭	0-7557	1-5393		AFDA	1-575E	215347
E	胮	5-4713	1-5394			E-334C	
F	胯	0-3172	0-7088	1-5694	AFE3	1-5767	227841

809

	Char	G	J	K	B	C	A
0	肐				CB76	2-2476	27534A
1	肑	3-4432				E-2724	
2	肒	3-4431			CB77	2-2477	
3	肓	0-7533	0-7075	1-8440	A877	1-4B3A	215326
4	肔	5-4681				E-2726	
5	肕	3-4434			CB74	2-2474	
6	肖	0-4804	0-3051	0-8511	A876	1-4B39	21532B
7	肗	3-4433				E-2725	
8	肘	0-5466	0-4110	1-7750	A879	1-4B3C	215328
9	肙	3-2155			CB75	2-2475	
A	肚	0-2239	0-7076	1-6167	A87B	1-4B3E	21532A
B	肛	0-2456	0-7074	0-8993	A87A	1-4B3D	215329
C	肜	0-7532	1-5377		CB78	2-2478	222973
D	肝	0-2446	0-2046	0-4260	A878	1-4B3B	215327
E	肞		1-5378				
F	肟	0-7531				E-2723	22774E

80B

	Char	G	J	K	B	C	A
0	肰	5-4682				E-2A52	227761
1	肱	0-7537	0-2547	0-4661	AAD0	1-4F33	215332
2	育	0-5193	0-1673	0-7532	A87C	1-4B3F	21532C
3	肳	3-4448				E-2A54	
4	肴	0-7540	0-2672	0-9302	AAD4	1-4F37	215336
5	肵	3-4443		1-5989	CDAF	2-284F	227769
6	肶	5-4684				E-2A57	
7	肷	0-7541					4C794E
8	肸	3-4444	1-5382		CDAE	2-284E	227768
9	肹	5-4687	1-5383				
A	肺	0-2346	0-3957	0-8843	AACD	1-4F30	21532E
B	肻					E-6631	335333
C	肼	0-7534					706B42
D	肽	0-7536					706B44
E	肾	0-4186					275358
F	肿	0-5455					275362

80D

	Char	G	J	K	B	C	A
0	胐				D05C	2-2C7D	
1	胑	3-4458			D059	2-2C7A	
2	胒	3-4469	1-5387			E-2E61	
3	胓	3-4456				E-2E5E	
4	胔	3-6722	1-5388		DB49	2-3F2E	227842
5	胕	3-4463	1-5389	1-6632	D062	2-2D25	
6	胖	0-3754	0-7086	1-6528	AD44	1-5327	215337
7	胗	0-7551	1-5390		D065	2-2D28	227830
8	胘	3-4467	1-5391		D056	2-2C77	
9	胙	0-7549	0-7082	1-7713	D05F	2-2D22	227827
A	胚	0-3763	0-7085	0-5947	AD46	1-5329	21533A
B	胛	0-7546	0-7080	0-4304	AD4B	1-532E	21533D
C	胜	0-4204			D060	2-2D23	273437
D	胝	0-7553	0-7083		AD4F	1-5332	22782A
E	胞	0-1691	0-4306	0-8864	AD4D	1-5330	215340
F	胟	5-4706				E-2E65	22777B

80F

	Char	G	J	K	B	C	A
0	胰	0-5040	1-5401		AFD8	1-575C	215342
1	胱	0-7555	0-7089	0-4645	AFD6	1-575A	215345
2	胲	0-7560	1-5402		D36A	2-322E	227833
3	胳	0-2476	1-5403		AFDE	1-5762	21534A
4	胴	0-7556	0-3825	0-5260	AFDB	1-575F	215346
5	胵	3-4478			D36C	2-3230	
6	胶	0-2926	1-5404			E-334A	27536C
7	胷			1-8504		E-3352	2D534B
8	胸	0-4856	0-2227	0-9356	AFDD	1-5761	21534B
9	胹	3-4475	1-5405		D36B	2-322F	227840
A	胺	0-1623	1-5406		D369	2-322D	227834
B	胻	3-4485			D36E	2-3232	
C	胼	0-7561	0-7106		AFE2	1-5766	3A787D
D	能	0-3660	0-3929	0-5086	AFE0	1-5764	215348
E	胾	3-3819	1-5407	1-7490	DB48	2-3F2D	227838
F	胿	3-4473				E-334B	

810

	Char	G	J	K	B	C	A
0	脀	3-4613			D36F	2-3233	
1	脁				D36D	2-3231	
2	脂	0-5412	0-2773	0-8223	AFD7	1-575B	215343
3	脃		1-5408			E-334E	22783C
4	脄	5-4709				E-334D	
5	脅	1-4818	0-2228	0-9086	AFD9	1-575D	215344
6	脆	0-2064	0-3240	0-8610	AFDC	1-5760	215349
7	脇		0-4738	0-9087		E-334F	2D5344
8	脈		0-4414	0-5670	AFDF	1-5763	21534D
9	脉	0-3486	0-7087	1-6424		E-2E63	27534D
A	脊	0-2825	0-3252	0-8417	AFE1	1-5765	21534C
B	脋		1-5409				
C	脌						
D	脍	0-7558					27537B
E	脎	0-7559					706B5B
F	脏	0-5264					275422

811

	Char	G	J	K	B	C	A
0	脐	0-3874					27537C
1	脑	0-3652					275365
2	脒	0-7563					706B5F
3	脓	0-3707					275378
4	脔	0-5785				E-3E44	287A56
5	脕	5-4722			D74E	2-3852	
6	脖	0-1817	1-5410	1-6533	B2E4	1-5C69	215350
7	脗		1-5411			E-3849	227866
8	脘	0-7568	1-5412	0-7250	D745	2-3849	22784B
9	脙	5-4717			D747	2-384B	
A	脚	0-2937	0-2151	0-4237		E-3847	2D5361
B	脛	1-7554	0-7090	0-4475	D748	2-384C	227855
C	脜		1-5413				
D	脝	5-4723			D750	2-3854	227849
E	脞	0-7566	1-5414		D74C	2-3850	227861
F	脟	3-4510			D74A	2-384E	

812

	Char	G	J	K	B	C	A
0	脠	3-4483	1-5415				
1	脡	3-4482			D74D	2-3851	227864
2	脢	3-4508			D751	2-3855	
3	脣		0-7092	0-6678	B2E5	1-5C6A	2D6F7D
4	脤	3-4493	1-5416	1-6983	B2E9	1-5C6E	227854
5	脥	3-4476			D746	2-384A	
6	脦	3-4501					
7	脧		1-5417	1-8026	D74F	2-3853	
8	脨	3-4490				E-632E	
9	脩	8-1288	0-7091	0-6627	B2E7	1-5C6C	215352
A	脪	3-4509				E-3841	227860
B	脫			0-8713	B2E6	1-5C6B	21534E
C	脬	0-7567	1-5418		D74B	2-384F	2D5340
D	脭	3-4506			D749	2-384D	
E	脮	3-4511				E-3842	
F	脯	0-2412	0-7093	0-8865	B2E3	1-5C68	21534F

813

	Char	G	J	K	B	C	A
0	脰	3-4491	1-5419	1-6168	B2E8	1-5C6D	227850
1	脱	0-4549	0-3506			E-3845	
2	脲	0-7569					4B3B52
3	脳		0-3930				4B5365
4	脴	5-4716				E-3848	
5	脵		1-5420				
6	脶	0-7565					287941
7	脷						
8	脸	0-3319					27537A
9	脹	1-5345	0-3617	0-8376	B5C8	1-614E	215359
A	脺	3-4527	1-5421	1-6922	DB51	2-3F36	227869
B	脻	3-4516				E-3E3E	
C	脼	3-4492	1-5422				
D	脽	3-4522			DB4F	2-3F34	
E	脾	0-3802	0-7103	0-6201	B5CA	1-6150	21535B
F	脿	5-4729					

814

	Char	G	J	K	B	C	A
0	腀	5-4688				E-3E43	
1	腁			1-6575		E-3E45	22787D
2	腂	3-4518				E-3E41	
3	腃	3-4529			DB4A	2-3F2F	
4	腄	3-4521			DFA1	2-4646	
5	腅	3-4530	1-5423			E-3E3D	
6	腆	0-4483	0-7102	1-7613	B5C9	1-614F	21535A
7	腇	5-4734	1-5424		DB4E	2-3F33	
8	腈	0-7570				E-3E40	22786D
9	腉	5-4735				E-3E42	
A	腊	0-3216	1-5425	1-6819	DB4B	2-3F30	27537E
B	腋	0-5024	0-7094	0-6893	B5C5	1-614B	215355
C	腌	0-7571	1-5426		B5CB	1-6151	227877
D	腍	3-4525			DB50	2-3F35	227925
E	腎	1-4186	0-3153	0-6776	B5C7	1-614D	215358
F	腏	3-4535			DB4D	2-3F32	

815

	Char	G	J	K	B	C	A
0	腐	0-2415	0-4169	0-6115	BB47	1-6A4F	215357
1	腑	0-2413	0-7105	0-6116	B5C6	1-614C	215356
2	腒	3-4533	1-5427	1-5588	DB4C	2-3F31	
3	腓	0-7572	0-7104	1-6705	B5CC	1-6152	22787C
4	腔	0-3927	0-2548	0-4323	B5C4	1-614A	215354
5	腕	0-4583	0-4751	0-7251	B5C3	1-6149	215353
6	腖	1-7543					
7	腗		1-5428				
8	腘	8-9253					
9	腙	0-7574					706B6A
A	腚	0-7575					22786A
B	腛	3-4558			DF77	2-463E	
C	腜	3-4538			DF75	2-463C	
D	腝	3-4541				E-437B	
E	腞	5-4754			DF7B	2-4642	
F	腟	5-4752	0-7121			E-437E	4C796B

816

	Char	G	J	K	B	C	A
0	腠	0-7577	1-5429	1-7751	DF73	2-463A	227932
1	腡	1-7565	1-5430		DFA2	2-4647	227941
2	腢	5-4747			DF78	2-463F	
3	腣	3-4552				E-4375	
4	腤	3-4551		1-7040	DF72	2-4639	
5	腥	0-4840	0-7109	0-6503	B87B	1-6624	21535F
6	腦	1-3652	0-7110	0-5064	B8A3	1-662A	215365
7	腧	0-7582	1-5431		DF7D	2-4644	227948
8	腨		1-5432				
9	腩	0-7578	1-5433		DF76	2-463D	22793B
A	腪	3-4489				E-4376	
B	腫	1-5455	0-2880	0-8094	B87E	1-6627	215362
C	腬	3-4559				E-4377	
D	腭	0-7581	1-5434	1-7018		E-4423	4D6047
E	腮	0-4089	0-7108		B87C	1-6625	215360
F	腯	3-4549	1-5435		DF7E	2-4645	22794B

817

	Char	G	J	K	B	C	A
0	腰	0-4992	0-2588	0-7306	B879	1-6622	21535D
1	腱	0-7576	0-7107	0-4382	B878	1-6621	21535C
2	腲	3-4546			DF79	2-4640	
3	腳				B87D	1-6626	215361
4	腴	0-7573	0-7111	1-7387	B5CD	1-6153	227947
5	腵	3-4557				E-437C	
6	腶	5-4749		1-6075	DF7C	2-4643	227946
7	腷	3-4540	1-5436	1-8256	DF74	2-463B	
8	腸	1-1906	0-3618	0-7783	B87A	1-6623	21535E
9	腹	0-2425	0-4202	0-6057	B8A1	1-6628	215363
A	腺	0-4757	0-3303	0-6445	B8A2	1-6629	215364
B	腻	0-3669					275371
C	腼	0-7579					22793C
D	腽	0-7580				E-4422	4C7959
E	腾	0-4458					276144
F	腿	0-4540	0-3460	0-8758	BB4C	1-6A54	215368

	818	81A	81C	81E
0	膀 G 0-1682 J 0-7115 K 0-5925 B BB48 C 1-6A50 A 215366	膠 G 1-2926 J 0-7117 K 0-4679 B BDA6 C 1-6E4F A 21536C	臀 G 0-4546 J 0-7129 K 0-5275 B C176 C 1-7522 A 215376	臠 G 1-5785 J 0-7140 K 1-6247 B F943 C 2-7132 A 227A56
1	膁 G 3-4565 J 1-5437 K B C E-4927 A	膡 G 3-4575 J K B C E-4E3A A	臁 G 0-7601 J K B C A 227A38	臡 G 5-6657 J 1-5464 K B F944 C 2-7133 A
2	膂 G 0-7586 J 0-7116 K 1-6233 B BB4D C 1-6A55 A 22794D	膢 G 3-4555 J 1-5448 K B E742 C 2-532B A	臂 G 0-1759 J 0-7130 K 0-6202 B C175 C 1-7521 A 215377	臢 G 3-4607 J K B C5D8 C 1-7C44 A 227A57
3	膃 G J 0-7112 K 1-7240 B E3A6 C 2-4D2D A 227959	膣 G 0-7589 J 0-7120 K 0-8283 B E6FD C 2-5327 A 22796B	臃 G 0-5123 J 1-5454 K B C173 C 1-747D A 215375	臣 G 0-1928 J 0-3135 K 0-6777 B A6DA C 1-485B A 215423
4	膄 G 5-4750 J 1-5439 K 1-6923 B C E-492A A	膤 G J 0-7119 K B C A 696733	臄 G 3-4592 J K B EDE9 C 2-5E56 A 227A3B	臤 G 5-6366 J 1-5465 K B C A
5	膅 G J 1-5440 K B C A	膥 G J K B C A	臅 G 3-4593 J 1-5455 K B EDEC C 2-5E59 A	臥 G J 0-1873 K 0-7234 B AAD7 C 1-4F3A A 215424
6	膆 G 5-4755 J 1-5441 K 1-6882 B E3A5 C 2-4D2C A 227952	膦 G 0-7602 J K B EAE9 C 2-5955 A 22797D	臆 G 0-5060 J 0-1818 K 0-6970 B C172 C 1-747C A 215373	臦 G J K B DB52 C 2-3F37 A
7	膇 G 3-4548 J K B E3A7 C 2-4D2E A	膧 G J K B EAF3 C 2-595F A	臇 G J K B EDED C 2-5E5A A	臧 G 0-7416 J 0-7141 K 0-7785 B BB4E C 1-6A56 A 227A5B
8	膈 G 0-7585 J 0-7113 K 0-4414 B BB4A C 1-6A52 A 21536A	膨 G 0-3782 J 0-4336 K 0-8819 B BFB1 C 1-7179 A 215372	臈 G J 0-7137 K B C E-5624 A 2D537E	臨 G 1-3357 J 0-4655 K 0-5592 B C17B C 1-7527 A 215425
9	膉 G 3-4564 J K B E3A4 C 2-4D2B A	膩 G 1-3669 J 0-7123 K 1-6064 B BFB0 C 1-7178 A 215371	臉 G 1-3319 J 0-7132 K B C179 C 1-7525 A 21537A	臩 G J K B EDEF C 2-5E5C A
A	膊 G 0-1818 J 0-7114 K 0-5859 B BB4B C 1-6A53 A 215369	膪 G 0-7590 J K B C E-5249 A 22797C	臊 G 0-7593 J 1-5456 K 1-7714 B EDEB C 2-5E58 A 227A3A	自 G 0-5552 J 0-2811 K 0-7727 B A6DB C 1-485C A 215426
B	膋 G 3-4611 J 1-5442 K 1-6326 B E3AA C 2-4D31 A 227951	膫 G 3-4580 J K B EAED C 2-5959 A	臋 G J 1-5453 K B C A	臫 G J 1-5466 K B C A
C	膌 G 5-4763 J K B E3A9 C 2-4D30 A	膬 G 5-4776 J K B EAEF C 2-595B A	臌 G 0-7591 J K B EDEA C 2-5E57 A 227A39	臬 G 0-8411 J 1-5467 K 1-7118 B AFE5 C 1-5769 A 215427
D	膍 G 5-4760 J K B E3A8 C 2-4D2F A	膭 G 3-4547 J K B C E-5247 A	臍 G 1-3874 J 0-7133 K 0-8016 B C2C0 C 1-772C A 21537C	臭 G 0-1984 J 0-2913 K 0-8611 B AFE4 C 1-5768 A 215428
E	膎 G 3-4563 J 1-5443 K B C A	膮 G 3-4477 J 1-5449 K B EAEA C 2-5956 A	臎 G 3-4605 J 1-5457 K B C E-5865 A 227A41	臮 G J K B DB53 C 2-3F38 A
F	膏 G 0-2464 J 0-2549 K 0-4539 B BB49 C 1-6A51 A 215367	膯 G 3-4590 J K B C E-5244 A	臏 G 1-7587 J 1-5458 K 1-6728 B C2C1 C 1-772D A 21537D	臯 G J K B C E-3E47 A

	819	81B	81D	81F
0	膐 G J 1-5438 K B C A	膰 G 3-4585 J 0-7124 K 1-6557 B EAEE C 2-595A A 227A2E	臐 G 3-4602 J K B F0A1 C 2-626B A 227A43	臰 G 5-6863 J 1-5468 K B C A
1	膑 G 0-7587 J K B C A 27537D	膱 G J K B EAE8 C 2-5954 A	臑 G 3-4601 J 0-7134 K 1-6040 B F07D C 2-6269 A 227A40	臱 G 3-6942 J 1-5469 K B C A
2	膒 G 3-4439 J K B C E-4E3B A	膲 G 3-4583 J 1-5450 K B EAF1 C 2-595D A	臒 G 3-4591 J K B F07E C 2-626A A	臲 G 5-6867 J 1-5470 K B EAF4 C 2-5960 A 227A65
3	膓 G J 0-7122 K B C E-4E3D A 2D535E	膳 G 0-4137 J 0-3323 K 0-6446 B BFAF C 1-7177 A 215370	臓 G J 0-3401 K B C A 4B5422	至 G 0-5433 J 0-2774 K 0-8224 B A6DC C 1-485D A 215429
4	膔 G 5-4769 J K B C E-4E39 A	膴 G 3-4437 J 1-5451 K 1-6475 B EAF0 C 2-595C A 227A2F	臔 G 3-4517 J K B C E-5A77 A	致 G 0-5434 J 0-3555 K 0-8640 B AD50 C 1-5333 A 275163
5	膕 G 3-4519 J 0-7118 K B E741 C 2-532A A 227975	膵 G 3-4568 J 0-7125 K 0-8593 B EAEC C 2-5958 A 227A2C	臕 G J 1-5459 K B F2C2 C 2-664C A 3A7970	臵 G J 1-5471 K B C A
6	膖 G J 1-5444 K B C E-4E3C A	膶 G J K B C A	臖 G 3-4615 J K B C E-5A78 A	臶 G 5-6444 J 1-5472 K 1-7925 B C E-3E48 A 227A68
7	膗 G 3-4571 J K B E744 C 2-532D A 227977	膷 G 3-4435 J K B EAF2 C 2-595E A 227A33	臗 G 5-4764 J 1-5460 K B F2C1 C 2-664B A	臷 G 5-4014 J K B DB54 C 2-3F39 A
8	膘 G 0-1776 J 1-5445 K B BDA8 C 1-6E51 A 227970	膸 G 5-4774 J 0-7127 K 1-6924 B C E-5623 A 4B6159	臘 G 1-3216 J 0-7136 K 0-5336 B C3BE C 1-7869 A 21537E	臸 G 3-6533 J 1-5473 K B DB55 C 2-3F3A A
9	膙 G 3-4589 J K B E743 C 2-532C A	膹 G 3-4537 J K 1-6659 B EAEB C 2-5957 A	臙 G J 0-7135 K 1-7143 B F4B4 C 2-6961 A 335347	臹 G J 1-5474 K B DB56 C 2-3F3B A
A	膚 G 1-2384 J 0-4170 K 0-6117 B BDA7 C 1-6E50 A 21536E	膺 G 0-6663 J 0-7131 K 0-7576 B C174 C 1-747E A 215374	臚 G 1-7545 J 0-7138 K 1-6234 B C4A4 C 1-7A2F A 215421	臺 G 1-4408 J 0-7142 K 0-5170 B BB4F C 1-6A57 A 21542B
B	膛 G 0-4437 J 1-5446 K B BDA3 C 1-6E4C A 21536D	膻 G 0-7594 J 1-5452 K B EDE8 C 2-5E55 A 227A37	臛 G 3-4606 J 1-5461 K B F4B3 C 2-6960 A 227A4B	臻 G 0-5373 J 0-7143 K 0-8261 B BFB2 C 1-717A A 21542C
C	膜 G 0-3604 J 0-4376 K 0-5615 B BDA4 C 1-6E4D A 21536F	膼 G 3-4479 J K B EDEE C 2-5E5B A	臜 G 7-0107 J K B C A	臼 G 0-3042 J 0-1717 K 0-4731 B A6DD C 1-485E A 21542D
D	膝 G 0-4705 J 0-4108 K 0-6703 B BDA5 C 1-6E4E A 21536B	膽 G 1-2108 J 0-7128 K 0-5137 B C178 C 1-7524 A 215379	臝 G J 1-5462 K 1-6188 B F5F0 C 2-6B7E A 227A4F	臽 G 5-2010 J 1-5475 K B C A
E	膞 G 3-4438 J 1-5447 K 1-7614 B E740 C 2-5329 A	膾 G 1-7558 J 0-7126 K 0-9276 B C17A C 1-7526 A 21537B	臞 G 5-4784 J 1-5463 K B F745 C 2-6D72 A 227A53	臾 G 0-8407 J 0-7144 K 0-7512 B AAD8 C 1-4F3B A 21542E
F	膟 G 3-4574 J K B E6FE C 2-5328 A 22796A	膿 G 1-3707 J 0-3931 K 0-5059 B C177 C 1-7523 A 215378	臟 G 1-5264 J 0-7139 K 0-7784 B C5A6 C 1-7B70 A 215422	臿 G 3-6934 J 1-5476 K B D068 C 2-2D2B A

820

	Char	G	J	K	B	C	A
0	舀	0-5008	1-5477		AFE6	1-576A	21542F
1	舁	0-8408	0-7145	1-7129	D370	2-3234	227A70
2	舂	0-8409	0-7146	1-7311	B2EA	1-5C6F	215430
3	舃	5-6860	1-5478	1-6820		E-3E49	227A74
4	舄	0-8410			DB57	2-3F3C	227A75
5	舅	0-3043	0-7147	0-4732	B8A4	1-662B	215431
6	舆	0-5163					275B53
7	與	1-5175	0-7148	0-7008	BB50	1-6A58	215432
8	興	1-4843	0-2229	0-9373	BFB3	1-717B	215433
9	舉	1-3057	0-5810		C17C	1-7528	215434
A	舊	1-3041	0-7149	0-4733	C2C2	1-772E	215435
B	舋	3-1614			F4B5	2-664D	227A77
C	舌	0-4164	0-3269	0-6463	A6DE	1-485F	215436
D	舍	0-4165	0-7150	0-6276	AAD9	1-4F3C	215437
E	舎		0-2843			E-2A5D	4B5437
F	舏		1-5479				

822

	Char	G	J	K	B	C	A
0	舠	3-6948			CDB1	2-2851	227B29
1	舡	0-8413	1-5485	0-4324	D069	2-2D2C	335446
2	舢	0-8414	1-5486		AD51	1-5334	21543F
3	舣	0-8415					4C4177
4	舤					E-2E68	
5	舥	3-6955			D372	2-3236	
6	舦						
7	舧	5-6884				E-3357	
8	舨	0-8418	1-5487		AFEA	1-576E	215443
9	舩		0-7153			E-3358	2D5446
A	航	0-2629	0-2550	0-8994	AFE8	1-576C	215440
B	舫	0-8419	0-7154	0-5926	AFE9	1-576D	215441
C	般	0-1667	0-4044	0-5885	AFEB	1-576F	215442
D	舭	0-8416				E-3355	227B2E
E	舮		0-7168				51456D
F	舯	0-8417			D371	2-3235	227B2F

824

	Char	G	J	K	B	C	A
0	艀	5-6902	0-7157	0-6118	DFA6	2-464B	227B47
1	艁	5-6894				E-4426	227B48
2	艂				DFA7	2-464C	
3	艃		1-5491				
4	艄	0-8425	1-5492		DFA5	2-464A	227B45
5	艅	5-6901	1-5493	0-7009	DFA8	2-464D	227B4A
6	艆	3-6968	1-5494				
7	艇	0-4507	0-3690	0-7983	B8A5	1-662C	215448
8	艈					E-6634	227B42
9	艉	0-8426			DFA4	2-4649	227B43
A	艊					E-492D	2D5447
B	艋	0-8427	1-5501		BB53	1-6A5B	227B4B
C	艌	5-6905				E-492E	
D	艍						
E	艎	5-6909	1-5502		E74A	2-5333	227B53
F	艏	0-8428	1-5503		E746	2-532F	227B50

826

	Char	G	J	K	B	C	A
0	艠		1-5507				
1	艡	5-6890			F2C4	2-664F	
2	艢		0-7164			E-5A7A	227B67
3	艣		1-5508		F2C5	2-6650	3F456D
4	艤	1-8415	0-7163	0-7590	F2C3	2-664E	344177
5	艥	5-6914				E-5A7B	
6	艦	1-2902	0-2047	0-8970	C4A5	1-7A30	21544B
7	艧		1-5509				
8	艨	0-8431	0-7165	1-6465	F4B6	2-6962	227B6B
9	艩	3-6964			F4B7	2-6963	
A	艪		0-7166	1-6279		E-5E55	33456D
B	艫	1-8421	0-7167	1-6280	F746	2-6D73	39456D
C	艬	3-6987			F7EF	2-6F3E	
D	艭	3-6956	1-5510		F8BB	2-7049	227B6F
E	艮	0-8462	0-2617	0-4261	A6E1	1-4862	21544C
F	良	0-3328	0-4641	0-5362	A87D	1-4B40	21544D

821

	Char	G	J	K	B	C	A
0	舐	0-8334	0-7151	1-7803	AFE7	1-576B	215438
1	舑	3-6734			D752	2-3856	
2	舒	0-4270	0-4816	0-6402	B5CE	1-6154	215439
3	舓	5-6675	1-5480			E-492B	
4	舔	0-4482	1-5481		BB51	1-6A59	21543A
5	舕	3-6736			E3AB	2-4D32	
6	舖	8-1586	0-7152	1-8230	E745	2-532E	2D5D65
7	舗		0-4262				4B5D65
8	舘	8-1585	0-2060			E-524A	2D6079
9	舙	5-6678	1-5482			E-5868	
A	舚	5-6679	1-5483			E-5A79	
B	舛	0-6622	0-3304	0-8431	A6DF	1-4860	21543B
C	舜	0-4320	0-2956	0-6679	B5CF	1-6155	21543C
D	舝	5-1625	1-5484		DFA3	2-4648	227B27
E	舞	0-4672	0-4181	0-5781	BB52	1-6A5A	21543D
F	舟	0-5459	0-2914	0-8139	A6E0	1-4861	21543E

823

	Char	G	J	K	B	C	A
0	舰	0-2902					27544B
1	舱	0-1853					27544A
2	舲	3-6958	1-5488		D757	2-385B	227B3A
3	舳	0-8422	0-7156	1-8056	D754	2-3858	227B35
4	舴	0-8423	1-5489		D756	2-385A	227B36
5	舵	0-2270	0-3441	0-8676	B2EB	1-5C70	215445
6	舶	0-1816	0-3985	0-5860	B2ED	1-5C72	215447
7	舷	0-4747	0-2431	0-9068	B2EC	1-5C71	215444
8	舸	0-8420	0-7155	1-5513	D753	2-3857	227B32
9	船	0-2012	0-3305	0-6447	B2EE	1-5C73	215446
A	舺	3-6957	1-5490		D755	2-3859	227B34
B	舻	0-8421					4B456D
C	舼	3-6961			DB58	2-3F3D	
D	舽	3-6963		1-6544	DB59	2-3F3E	
E	舾	0-8424					707438
F	舿				DB5A	2-3F3F	

825

	Char	G	J	K	B	C	A
0	艐	3-6973			E749	2-5332	
1	艑	3-6977	1-5504	1-8207	E74B	2-5334	
2	艒	3-6972			E748	2-5331	
3	艓	3-6971			E747	2-5330	
4	艔						
5	艕	3-6979			EAF5	2-5961	
6	艖	3-6975	1-5505		EAF6	2-5962	227B56
7	艗	5-6911			EAF7	2-5963	227B57
8	艘	0-4350	0-7159	1-6883	BFB4	1-717C	215449
9	艙	1-1853	0-7158	0-8377	BFB5	1-717D	21544A
A	艚	0-8429	0-7161	1-7715	EDF1	2-5E5E	227B5E
B	艛	3-6976			EDF0	2-5E5D	
C	艜	5-6907	1-5506		EDF2	2-5E5F	
D	艝		0-7160				69675C
E	艞	5-6915			F0A3	2-626D	
F	艟	0-8430	0-7162	1-6158	F0A2	2-626C	227B62

827

	Char	G	J	K	B	C	A
0	艰	0-2872					27544E
1	艱	1-2872	0-7169	0-4262	C17D	1-7529	21544E
2	色	0-4111	0-3107	0-6368	A6E2	1-4863	21544F
3	艳	0-4962					4B5959
4	艴	0-6985	1-5511	1-6667	D758	2-385C	2D342E
5	艵	3-6990			DB5B	2-3F40	
6	艶		0-1780	0-7093		E-5A7C	3F5959
7	艷	1-4962	0-7170		C641	1-7C6C	2D5959
8	艸	5-7124	0-7171	0-8512	CA4A	2-226A	227B77
9	艹	0-6019					
A	艺	0-5053					275631
B	艻		1-5512			E-2438	
C	艼	5-7125			CA4B	2-226B	
D	艽	0-6020	1-5513		CA4D	2-226D	276030
E	艾	0-1612	0-7172	0-6885	A6E3	1-4864	215450
F	艿	0-6021	1-5514		CA4E	2-226E	227B7D

	828	82A	82C	82E
0	芀 G 3-7215 J 1-5515 K B CA4C C 2-226C A	芠 G 3-7235 J 1-5529 K B CDB2 C 2-2852 A	苀 G 3-7236 J K B CDB3 C 2-2853 A	苠 G 0-6069 J 1-5550 K 1-6511 B D0A2 C 2-2D43 A 227C5A
1	芁 G 5-7128 J 1-5516 K B C A	芡 G 0-6045 J 1-5530 K 1-5612 B CDC0 C 2-2860 A 227C50	苁 G 0-6042 J K B C A 292535	苡 G 0-6051 J 0-7179 K 0-7630 B D077 C 2-2D3A A 227C73
2	节 G 0-2958 J K B C A 275033	芢 G 3-7231 J K 1-7469 B CDC6 C 2-2866 A	苂 G J K B CDC2 C 2-2862 A	苢 G 5-7161 J 1-5551 K B C E-2E78 A 227C6A
3	芃 G 3-7221 J 1-5517 K B CBA2 C 2-2522 A 227C2D	芣 G 3-7225 J 1-5531 K 1-6633 B AAE6 C 1-4F49 A 227C42	苃 G J K B CDC4 C 2-2864 A	苣 G 0-6036 J 0-7180 K 1-5589 B AD55 C 1-5338 A 215463
4	芄 G 0-6025 J 1-5518 K B CBA3 C 2-2523 A 227C28	芤 G 0-6050 J 1-5532 K B CDC3 C 2-2863 A 227C3C	苄 G 0-6048 J K B C E-2A5E A 705C50	苤 G 0-6054 J 1-5552 K B D0A1 C 2-2D42 A 227C64
5	芅 G 3-7219 J K B CB7B C 2-247B A	芥 G 0-2970 J 0-1909 K 0-4346 B AAE3 C 1-4F46 A 21545A	苅 G 5-7150 J 0-2003 K 1-7188 B C A 4B3354	若 G 0-4084 J 0-2867 K 0-6920 B AD59 C 1-533C A 215467
6	芆 G 3-7223 J K B C E-2728 A	芦 G 0-3411 J 0-1618 K 0-9156 B C E-2A6B A 27563A	苆 G J 1-5546 K B C A	苦 G 0-3164 J 0-2276 K 0-4540 B AD57 C 1-533A A 215465
7	芇 G 5-7134 J 1-5519 K B C A	芧 G 3-7242 J 1-5533 K 1-6815 B CDB9 C 2-2859 A 227C34	苇 G 0-4613 J K B C A 27554D	苧 G 1-6049 J 0-3587 K 0-7840 B AD52 C 1-5335 A 215460
8	芈 G 0-5634 J K B C A	芨 G 0-6024 J 1-5534 K 1-5965 B CDBF C 2-285F A 227C4C	苈 G 0-6034 J K B C A 292765	苨 G 3-7259 J 1-5553 K B D06F C 2-2D32 A
9	芉 G 3-7216 J 1-5520 K B C A	芩 G 0-6043 J 1-5535 K 0-4857 B CDC1 C 2-2861 A 227C46	苉 G 3-7227 J K B C E-2A68 A	苩 G 3-7252 J K B C E-2E72 A
A	芊 G 0-6023 J 1-5521 K 1-7926 B CBA1 C 2-2521 A 227C2E	芪 G 0-6046 J 1-5536 K 1-5990 B C E-2A66 A 227C53	苊 G 0-6035 J K B C A 705C43	苪 G 3-7244 J 1-5554 K B D07E C 2-2D41 A 227C5F
B	芋 G 0-5183 J 0-1682 K 0-7367 B A8A1 C 1-4B42 A 215452	芫 G 0-6030 J 0-7175 K 1-7347 B CDB4 C 2-2854 A 227C38	苋 G 0-6040 J K B C A 27552A	苫 G 0-4127 J 0-3849 K 1-7638 B D073 C 2-2D36 A 227C71
C	芌 G J K B C E-2729 A	芬 G 0-2350 J 0-7178 K 0-6150 B AAE2 C 1-4F45 A 215459	苌 G 0-6041 J K B C A 287E61	苬 G 5-7162 J K B D076 C 2-2D39 A
D	芍 G 0-4154 J 0-7173 K 0-7743 B A8A2 C 1-4B43 A 215453	芭 G 0-1637 J 0-3946 K 0-8784 B AADD C 1-4F40 A 215458	苍 G 0-1852 J K B C A 275567	苭 G 5-7172 J 1-5555 K B D0A5 C 2-2D46 A
E	芎 G 0-6026 J 1-5522 K 0-4768 B CB7C C 2-247C A 227C24	芮 G 0-6039 J 1-5537 K 0-7160 B CDBA C 2-285A A 227C45	苎 G 0-6049 J K B C A 275564	苮 G J K B C E-2E74 A
F	芏 G 0-6022 J K B CB7A C 2-247A A 227C27	芯 G 0-4830 J 0-3136 K 0-6805 B AAE4 C 1-4F47 A 227C31	苏 G 0-4353 J K B C A 27563C	苯 G 0-1729 J 1-5556 K B AD66 C 1-5349 A 227C62

	829	82B	82D	82F
0	芐 G 3-7217 J K B CB79 C 2-2479 A	芰 G 0-6033 J 1-5538 K 1-5991 B AAE7 C 1-4F4A A 227C3A	苐 G J 1-5547 K B C E-2E76 A 227C5B	苰 G 3-7261 J K B D07D C 2-2D40 A
1	芑 G 0-6027 J 1-5523 K B CB7D C 2-247D A 227C25	花 G 0-2708 J 0-1854 K 0-9203 B AAE1 C 1-4F44 A 21545D	苑 G 0-5223 J 0-1781 K 0-7429 B AD62 C 1-5345 A 21546F	英 G 0-5102 J 0-1749 K 0-7140 B AD5E C 1-5341 A 21546B
2	芒 G 0-3502 J 0-7174 K 0-5651 B A87E C 1-4B41 A 215451	芲 G J 1-5539 K B C E-2A6C A	苒 G 0-6059 J 0-7182 K 0-7094 B AD5C C 1-533F A 227C6D	苲 G 3-7251 J K B D078 C 2-2D3B A
3	芓 G 5-7139 J K B CB7E C 2-247E A	芳 G 0-2328 J 0-4307 K 0-5927 B AADA C 1-4F3D A 215454	苓 G 0-6063 J 0-4674 K 1-6267 B AD64 C 1-5347 A 21546D	苳 G 5-7167 J 0-7184 K 1-6159 B D0A4 C 2-2D45 A 227C7C
4	芔 G 5-3127 J 1-5524 K 1-8486 B D06A C 2-2D2D A	芴 G 0-6044 J 1-5540 K B CDBE C 2-285E A 227C4E	苔 G 0-4406 J 0-3461 K 0-8736 B AD61 C 1-5344 A 21546E	苴 G 0-6058 J 0-7183 K 1-7569 B D075 C 2-2D38 A 227C69
5	芕 G J K B C E-272B A	芵 G 5-7155 J K B CDB8 C 2-2858 A	苕 G 0-6070 J 1-5548 K 0-8513 B D071 C 2-2D34 A 227C65	苵 G 3-7250 J K B D079 C 2-2D3C A
6	芖 G J 1-5525 K B C A	芶 G 3-7234 J K B CDC5 C 2-2865 A	苖 G 3-7247 J K B D074 C 2-2D37 A	苶 G 3-7253 J 1-5557 K B D07C C 2-2D3F A 227C75
7	芗 G 0-6028 J K B C A 292577	芷 G 0-6038 J 1-5541 K 0-8226 B AAE9 C 1-4F4C A 227C44	苗 G 0-3571 J 0-4136 K 0-5764 B AD5D C 1-5340 A 21546A	苷 G 0-6053 J 1-5558 K B C E-2E69 A 227C60
8	芘 G 0-6037 J 1-5526 K 1-6706 B CDB6 C 2-2856 A 275568	芸 G 0-6031 J 0-2361 K 0-7393 B AAE5 C 1-4F48 A 4B5631	苘 G 0-6060 J K B C E-2E6A A 227C72	苸 G 5-7166 J K B C E-2E6E A
9	芙 G 0-6029 J 0-4171 K 0-6119 B AADC C 1-4F3F A 215456	芹 G 0-3959 J 0-2260 K 0-4842 B AAE0 C 1-4F43 A 21545E	苙 G 3-7255 J 0-7194 K B D06B C 2-2D2E A 227C55	苹 G 0-3827 J 0-7189 K 1-8217 B D06D C 2-2D30 A 27563B
A	芚 G 3-7228 J 1-5527 K 0-5276 B CDB5 C 2-2855 A 227C3F	芺 G 3-7230 J 1-5542 K B CDBD C 2-285D A	苚 G J 1-5549 K B C A	苺 G 5-7171 J 0-7185 K 1-6420 B D0A3 C 2-2D44 A 2D552E
B	芛 G 3-7239 J 1-5528 K B CDB7 C 2-2857 A	芻 G 1-5927 J 0-7177 K 0-8554 B AFBC C 1-5770 A 21545C	苛 G 0-3133 J 0-1855 K 0-4220 B AD56 C 1-5339 A 215464	苻 G 0-6062 J 0-7188 K 1-6634 B D07B C 2-2D3E A 227D22
C	芜 G 0-4663 J K B C E-2A60 A 27557C	芼 G 3-7229 J 1-5543 K 0-5737 B CDBB C 2-285B A 227C49	苜 G 0-6057 J 0-7192 K 1-6457 B AD60 C 1-5343 A 215469	苼 G 3-7249 J K B C E-2E6F A
D	芝 G 0-5405 J 0-2839 K 0-8225 B AADB C 1-4F3E A 215455	芽 G 0-4931 J 0-1874 K 0-6820 B AADE C 1-4F41 A 215457	苝 G 3-7245 J K B C E-2E6B A	苽 G 5-7165 J 1-5559 K 0-4541 B C E-2E7A A 227D24
E	芞 G 5-7145 J K B CDBC C 2-285C A	芾 G 0-6032 J 1-5544 K 1-6707 B AAE8 C 1-4F4B A 355E76	苞 G 0-1690 J 0-7190 K 0-8866 B AD63 C 1-5346 A 215470	苾 G 3-7258 J 1-5560 K 0-8923 B D06C C 2-2D2F A 227C57
F	芟 G 0-6047 J 0-7176 K 0-6323 B AADF C 1-4F42 A 21545B	芿 G 5-7148 J 1-5545 K 0-7707 B C A	苟 G 0-2522 J 0-7181 K 0-4734 B AD65 C 1-5348 A 215471	苿 G J K 1-6502 B C A

Code	Char	G	J	K	B	C	A
8300	茀	3-7260	1-5561	1-6668	D070	2-2D33	227C5C
8301	茁	0-5534	1-5562	0-8172	AD5F	1-5342	21546C
8302	茂	0-3515	0-4448	0-5782	AD5A	1-533D	215468
8303	范	0-2322	0-7187	0-5985	AD53	1-5336	275030
8304	茄	0-3949	0-1856	0-4221	AD58	1-533B	215466
8305	茅	0-3509	0-1993	0-5738	AD54	1-5337	215461
8306	茆	0-6066	0-7191		AD67	1-534A	2D5461
8307	茇	0-6056	1-5563		D06E	2-2D31	227C67
8308	茈	0-6075	1-5564	1-7491	D3A5	2-3247	2D4450
8309	茉	0-6052	0-7193	0-5641	AD5B	1-533E	215462
830A	茊		1-5565				
830B	茋		1-5566			E-2E79	
830C	茌	0-6061			D07A	2-2D3D	227D21
830D	茍				CE41	2-2942	
830E	茎	0-3005	0-2352			E-2E77	275529
830F	茏	0-6055					292752
8310	茐					E-6635	227C7B
8311	茑	0-6064					29252D
8312	茒					E-6637	227D54
8313	茓	3-7257					
8314	茔	0-6067					227C6E
8315	茕	0-6068					4C5175
8316	茖	3-7283	0-7203		D3A8	2-324A	227D56
8317	茗	0-6088	0-7212	0-5711	AFFA	1-577E	21547E
8318	茘		0-7213			E-3362	2D5476
8319	茙	3-7263			D376	2-323A	
831A	茚	0-6065					227D58
831B	茛	0-6102	1-5568	1-5528	D3A3	2-3245	227D35
831C	茜	0-6071	0-1611	1-7927	D37D	2-3241	2E7C2E
831D	茝	3-7293	1-5569	1-7889		E-384D	227D76
831E	茞	5-7178	1-5570		D3B2	2-3254	
831F	茟	5-7203	1-5571			E-3359	
8320	茠	3-7279			D3AA	2-324C	
8321	茡	3-7287	1-5572			E-335F	
8322	茢	3-7269	1-5573		D37E	2-3242	227D3F
8323	茣		0-7220	1-7217		E-385B	4C7D6A
8324	茤	3-7284			D3A9	2-324B	
8325	茥	5-7176			D378	2-323C	
8326	茦	3-7266			D37C	2-3240	
8327	茧	0-2875			D3B5	2-3257	275177
8328	茨	0-2036	0-1681	0-7728	AFFD	1-5823	227D29
8329	茩	5-7192			D3AD	2-324F	
832A	茪	5-7185		1-5791	D3A4	2-3246	
832B	茫	0-3503	0-7211	0-5652	AFED	1-5771	215472
832C	茬	0-1871	1-5574		D3B3	2-3255	227D40
832D	茭	0-6090	1-5575		D374	2-3238	27447C
832E	茮	3-7274	1-5576				
832F	茯	0-6082	0-7210	0-6058	D3AC	2-324E	227D52
8330	茰		1-5577				
8331	茱	0-6079	0-7205	0-6628	AFFC	1-5822	21547C
8332	茲		0-7204	1-7492	AFF7	1-577B	4B5521
8333	茳	0-6092	1-5578	1-5569	D373	2-3237	227D26
8334	茴	0-6078	0-7202	0-9277	AFF5	1-5779	21547A
8335	茵	0-5080	0-7201	0-7664	AFF4	1-5778	215479
8336	茶	0-1872	0-3567	0-5094	AFF9	1-577D	21547B
8337	茷	5-7189	1-5579		D3AB	2-324D	
8338	茸	0-4055	0-3491	0-7339	AFF1	1-5775	215475
8339	茹	0-4067	0-7207	0-7010	AFF8	1-577C	215523
833A	茺	0-6091	1-5580		D072	2-2D35	227C63
833B	茻				DB5C	2-3F41	
833C	茼	0-6077	1-5581	1-6160	D3A6	2-3248	227D48
833D	茽		1-5582				
833E	茾					E-2A5F	
833F	茿	5-7177			D37A	2-323E	
8340	荀	0-6087	0-7206	0-6680	AFFB	1-5821	21547D
8341	荁	3-7265			D37B	2-323F	
8342	荂	5-7182	1-5583		D3A1	2-3243	
8343	荃	0-6085	1-5584	1-7615	AFFE	1-5824	227D4D
8344	荄	3-7285	1-5585		D375	2-3239	227D2B
8345	荅	3-7280	0-7209		D3AF	2-3251	275023
8346	荆	0-3003				E-3E57	
8347	荇	0-6084	1-5586	0-9027	D3AE	2-3250	227D5F
8348	荈	3-7282			D3B6	2-3258	227D53
8349	草	0-1861	0-3380	0-8514	AFF3	1-5777	215478
834A	荊		0-2353	0-9110	AFF0	1-5774	215474
834B	荋	3-7267			D3B4	2-3256	
834C	荌	5-7202			D3B0	2-3252	
834D	荍		1-5587		D3A7	2-3249	227D4A
834E	荎	3-7271	1-5588		D3A2	2-3244	
834F	荏	0-6083	0-1733	0-7691	AFF6	1-577A	215522
8350	荐	0-2886	0-7208	1-7928	AFF2	1-5776	215477
8351	荑	0-6072	1-5589	0-7631	D377	2-323B	227D2E
8352	荒	0-2736	0-2551	0-9256	AFEE	1-5772	215473
8353	荓	3-7286	1-5630		D3B1	2-3253	
8354	荔	0-3283	1-5567		AFEF	1-5773	215476
8355	荕		1-5590				
8356	荖	3-7264	1-5591		D379	2-323D	227D3B
8357	荗		1-5592			E-335A	
8358	荘		0-3381			E-3363	2D552D
8359	荙	7-0102					
835A	荚	0-2852					275528
835B	荛	0-6073					29254B
835C	荜	0-6074					29247D
835D	荝	8-9429					
835E	荞	0-6081					292571
835F	荟	0-6086					292657
8360	荠	0-6089					292661
8361	荡	0-2120					275576
8362	荢					E-6636	
8363	荣	0-4057				E-2D33	274537
8364	荤	0-2771					275553
8365	荥	0-6094					284B43
8366	荦	0-6093					274A5E
8367	荧	0-5111					285323
8368	荨	0-6101					292546
8369	荩	0-6103					292668
836A	荪	0-6105					275563
836B	荫	0-5081					27556E
836C	荬	0-6104					292567
836D	荭	0-6106					29233C
836E	荮	0-6107					29233D
836F	药	0-5009					275635
8370	荰		1-5593				
8371	荱	3-7325				E-384E	
8372	荲	3-7308				E-3851	
8373	荳		0-7226	0-5269	D75E	2-3862	227D6D
8374	荴	3-7304			D760	2-3864	
8375	荵	3-7326	0-7227		D765	2-3869	227D7E
8376	荶				D779	2-387D	
8377	荷	0-2641	0-1857	0-8935	B2FC	1-5D23	215531
8378	荸	0-6109	1-5594		B2F2	1-5C77	215527
8379	荹	3-7305				E-3854	
837A	荺	3-7291			D75D	2-3861	
837B	荻	0-6122	0-1814	0-7866	B2FD	1-5D24	215533
837C	荼	0-6117	0-7224		B2FE	1-5D25	215532
837D	荽	0-6120	1-5601		D768	2-386C	2D5547
837E	荾	3-7328			D76F	2-3873	
837F	荿	5-7184	1-5602		D775	2-3879	227E21

838

	Char	G	J	K	B	C	A
0	莀	5-7212	1-5603			E-3850	
1	莁	5-7209			D762	2-3866	
2	莂	3-7311	1-5604				
3	莃	5-7226			D769	2-386D	
4	莄	5-7210	1-5605			E-384F	
5	莅	0-6116	0-7214	1-6363		E-385D	2D555B
6	莆	0-3846	1-5606		B340	1-5D26	2D555A
7	莇	5-7220	0-7222		D777	2-387B	227E25
8	莈				D772	2-3876	
9	莉	0-3282	0-7229	0-5573	B2FA	1-5D21	215530
A	莊	1-5515	0-7223	0-7786	B2F8	1-5C7D	21552D
B	莋	3-7313			D76E	2-3872	
C	莌	3-7322			D76A	2-386E	
D	莍	5-7217	1-5607		D75C	2-3860	
E	莎	0-4115	0-7221	0-6277	B2EF	1-5C74	215524
F	莏	5-7213			D761	2-3865	227D7A

83A

	Char	G	J	K	B	C	A
0	莠	0-6112	0-7228	1-7388	B2FB	1-5D22	21552F
1	莡	3-7309				E-3852	
2	莢	1-2852	0-7218	0-9088	B2F3	1-5C78	215528
3	莣	3-7320			D75A	2-385E	
4	莤	3-7303			D75F	2-3863	
5	莥	3-7317			D770	2-3874	
6	莦	3-7307	1-5616		D776	2-387A	227E23
7	莧	1-6040	1-5617		B341	1-5D27	21552A
8	莨	0-6125	0-7230	1-6215	D75B	2-385F	227D62
9	莩	0-6119	1-5618	0-6120	D767	2-386B	227E2B
A	莪	0-6113	0-7216	0-6821	D76D	2-3871	227E33
B	莫	0-3610	0-3992	0-5616	B2F6	1-5C7B	21552B
C	莬	5-7227	1-5619				
D	莭		1-5644			E-3858	227D67
E	莮				D778	2-387C	
F	莯				D771	2-3875	

83C

	Char	G	J	K	B	C	A
0	菀	0-6150	1-5622		DB60	2-3F45	2D546F
1	菁	0-6128	0-7239	0-8474	B5D7	1-615D	21553A
2	菂	3-7351		1-7580	DB7D	2-3F62	
3	菃				DBA7	2-3F6B	
4	菄	5-7158			DBAA	2-3F6E	
5	菅	0-6149	0-3191	0-4625	B5D5	1-615B	215539
6	菆	3-7333			DB68	2-3F4D	227E60
7	菇	0-2529	1-5623		DBA3	2-3F66	347D24
8	菈	3-7339			DB69	2-3F4E	
9	菉		1-5624	0-5465	DB77	2-3F5C	232229
A	菊	0-3053	0-2138	0-4750	B5E2	1-6168	215545
B	菋	3-7346			DB73	2-3F58	
C	菌	0-3090	0-2261	0-4822	B5DF	1-6165	215543
D	菍	5-7249				E-3E5E	
E	菎	5-7243	0-7234		DB74	2-3F59	227E79
F	菏	0-2642	1-5625		DB5D	2-3F42	227E41

83E

	Char	G	J	K	B	C	A
0	菠	0-1804	0-7242	1-8182	B5D4	1-615A	215535
1	菡	0-6153		1-8301	DB72	2-3F57	227E5A
2	菢	3-7338			DBAD	2-3F71	227E6B
3	菣				DB6B	2-3F50	
4	菤	5-7254			DB64	2-3F49	
5	菥	0-6130			DB6F	2-3F54	227E72
6	菦					E-3E5F	
7	菧	3-7356			DB63	2-3F48	
8	菨	5-7253	1-5631		DB61	2-3F46	
9	菩	0-3848	0-4278	0-6044	B5D0	1-6156	215536
A	菪	0-6148	1-5632		DBA5	2-3F68	227E52
B	菫		0-7233	0-4843	DB6A	2-3F4F	227E63
C	菬	5-7258			DBA8	2-3F6C	
D	菭	3-7359				E-3E4B	
E	菮				DBA9	2-3F6D	
F	華	1-2710	0-1858	0-9204	B5D8	1-615E	21553C

839

	Char	G	J	K	B	C	A
0	莐	5-7231			D759	2-385D	
1	莑	5-7228				E-3855	
2	莒	0-6076	1-5608	1-5590	B2F7	1-5C7C	21552C
3	莓	0-6114	0-7186	1-6421	B2F9	1-5C7E	21552E
4	莔	3-7312	1-5609		D766	2-386A	
5	莕	3-7294	1-5610		D763	2-3867	227D7C
6	莖	1-3005	0-7219	0-4476	B2F4	1-5C79	215529
7	莗				D773	2-3877	
8	莘	0-6123	1-5611	0-6778	B2F1	1-5C76	215525
9	莙	3-7324	1-5612		D764	2-3868	227E22
A	莚	5-7190	0-7215	1-7144	D77A	2-3F6A	232236
B	莛	0-6080	1-5613	1-7663	D76C	2-3870	227E2F
C	莜	0-6115	1-5614			E-385E	227E37
D	莝	3-7314	1-5615	1-7740	D76B	2-386F	
E	莞	0-6124	0-2048	0-7252	B2F0	1-5C75	215526
F	莟	3-7315	0-7217	1-8294		E-3857	227E38

83B

	Char	G	J	K	B	C	A
0	莰	0-6108			D774	2-3878	227D72
1	莱	0-3219	0-4573				275541
2	莲	0-3311					27556C
3	莳	0-6110					292375
4	莴	0-6111					275555
5	莵		0-7225				4D222A
6	莶	0-6118					292658
7	获	0-2781				E-385F	274B29
8	莸	0-6121					292574
9	莹	0-5108					227E26
A	莺	0-6126					276247
B	莻						
C	莼	0-6127					29243A
D	莽	0-3507	0-7247	0-5653	B2F5	1-5C7A	21553F
E	莾		1-5620	1-6412			
F	莿	5-7237	1-5621	1-7493	DB6C	2-3F51	227E6A

83D

	Char	G	J	K	B	C	A
0	菐		1-5626				
1	菑	8-1484	1-5627	1-8081	DBA4	2-3F67	232243
2	菒	3-7347				E-3E4F	
3	菓		0-1859	0-4602		E-3E59	227E7B
4	菔	0-6142	1-5628	1-6608	B5E8	1-616E	2D5573
5	菕	3-7232			DBA1	2-3F64	
6	菖	0-6137	0-3052	0-8378	DB75	2-3F5A	227E7D
7	菗	5-7238			DBAC	2-3F70	
8	菘	0-6131	0-7237	1-6947	DB70	2-3F55	227E71
9	菙	5-7246			DFC8	2-466D	
A	菚	5-7156				E-3E4D	
B	菛	5-7136			DBAF	2-3F73	
C	菜	0-1843	0-2658	0-8388	B5E6	1-616C	215544
D	菝	0-6135	1-5629		DB6E	2-3F53	395568
E	菞	3-7350			DB7A	2-3F5F	
F	菟	0-6143	0-3749	1-6135	B5E9	1-616F	23222A

83F

	Char	G	J	K	B	C	A
0	菰	0-6152	0-2454	0-4542	B5DD	1-6163	2E7D24
1	菱	0-3366	0-4109	0-5552	B5D9	1-615F	21553E
2	菲	0-2338	0-7243	0-6203	B5E1	1-6167	215546
3	菳	3-7353			DB7E	2-3F63	23223C
4	菴		0-7231	0-6864	B5DA	1-6160	2D3C7C
5	菵	3-7348			DB76	2-3F5B	
6	菶	3-7331	1-5633	1-6616	DB66	2-3F4B	227E57
7	菷	5-7263	0-7240				2D3C49
8	菸	0-6146	1-5634		B5D2	1-6158	4B496B
9	菹	0-6147	1-5635	0-7841	DB5E	2-3F43	227E43
A	菺	3-7361			DBA2	2-3F65	
B	菻	3-7334	0-7250		DBAB	2-3F6F	2D625F
C	菼	3-7358	1-5636		DB65	2-3F4A	227E56
D	菽	0-6136	0-7235	0-6661	B5E0	1-6166	232223
E	菾	3-7332			DBB0	2-3F74	
F	菿	3-7342			DB71	2-3F56	

Code	Char	G	J	K	B	C	A
8400	萀	3-7344				E-3E52	
8401	萁	0-6129	1-5637		DB6D	2-3F52	227E6D
8402	萂	5-7248				E-3E5C	
8403	萃	0-6145	0-7236	0-8594	B5D1	1-6157	215538
8404	萄	0-4449	0-3826	0-5212	B5E5	1-616B	215548
8405	萅	5-7241				E-3E5A	
8406	萆	0-6141	1-5638	1-6708	DB7C	2-3F61	335568
8407	萇	1-6041	0-7241	1-7542	B5E7	1-616D	227E61
8408	萈	3-7248				E-3E50	
8409	萉	5-7251			DB78	2-3F5D	
840A	萊	1-3219	1-5639	0-5349	B5DC	1-6162	215541
840B	萋	0-6134	0-7238	1-7903	B5D6	1-615C	21553B
840C	萌	0-3540	0-4308	0-5680	B5DE	1-6164	215542
840D	萍	0-3828	0-7244	0-8835	B5D3	1-6159	215534
840E	萎	0-4614	0-1664	0-7455	B5E4	1-616A	215547
840F	萏	0-6144	1-5640		DB79	2-3F5E	23222E
8410	萐	3-7337			DB67	2-3F4C	227E59
8411	萑	0-6140	1-5641		DB7B	2-3F60	232230
8412	萒	3-7357			DB62	2-3F47	
8413	萓	5-7260	0-7232		DBA6	2-3F69	227E53
8414	萔	5-7240				E-3E58	
8415	萕		1-5642				
8416	萖					E-3E5D	
8417	萗					E-3E56	
8418	萘	0-6133				E-3E4E	227E74
8419	萙		1-5643				
841A	萚	8-9436					
841B	萛				DBAE	2-3F72	
841C	萜	0-6138					705D46
841D	萝	0-3460					275642
841E	萞					E-6639	232225
841F	萟					E-3E5B	23222C
8420	萠		0-7246				4B5542
8421	萡					E-6638	227E45
8422	萢		0-7245				69684D
8423	萣				DB5F	2-3F44	227E51
8424	萤	0-5109					275724
8425	营	0-5110					274A2E
8426	萦	0-6151					275161
8427	萧	0-4784					275622
8428	萨	0-4088					27562A
8429	萩	3-7381	0-3975	0-8555	DFC7	2-466C	23232E
842A	萪	3-7382	0-7252			E-442D	23232D
842B	萫	5-7289			DFDD	2-4724	
842C	萬	1-4582	0-7263	0-5631	B855	1-655C	214F22
842D	萭	3-7385			DFCC	2-4671	
842E	萮	3-7388				E-4431	
842F	萯	3-7281	1-5645		DFCA	2-466F	
8430	萰	3-7373			DFB5	2-465A	
8431	萱	0-6170	0-1994	0-9332	B8A9	1-6630	21554B
8432	萲				DFC5	2-466A	232324
8433	萳	5-7270			DFD9	2-467E	
8434	萴	3-7277			DFC1	2-4666	
8435	萵	1-6111	0-7266	1-7257	B8B1	1-6638	215555
8436	萶	5-7268			DFD8	2-467D	
8437	萷	3-7377			DFBF	2-4664	
8438	萸	0-6139	0-7248	0-7513	B5E3	1-6169	215559
8439	萹	3-7407	1-5646	1-8208	DFCF	2-4674	23224C
843A	萺	5-7281			DFC0	2-4665	
843B	萻	5-7309			DFD6	2-467B	
843C	萼	0-6164	0-7253	1-7019	B8B0	1-6637	215554
843D	落	0-3468	0-4578	0-5310	B8A8	1-662F	215549
843E	萾	5-7317				E-443A	23226E
843F	萿	3-7405			DFAA	2-464F	
8440	葀	3-7376			DFB2	2-4657	
8441	葁					E-4435	
8442	葂	3-7392			DFCB	2-4670	
8443	葃	3-7379			DFC3	2-4668	
8444	葄	3-7391			DFDC	2-4723	
8445	葅	5-7303	1-5647		DFC6	2-466B	
8446	葆	0-6165	0-7262	1-6593	B8B6	1-663D	23233A
8447	葇	3-7414	1-5648		DFD7	2-467C	
8448	葈	3-7413	1-5649			E-442C	
8449	葉	1-5022	0-4553	0-7108	B8AD	1-6634	21554F
844A	葊	5-7302	1-5650	1-7041		E-443E	23233F
844B	葋	5-7304			DFC9	2-466E	
844C	葌	5-7316			DFD1	2-4676	
844D	葍	3-7371	1-5651		DFB6	2-465B	
844E	葎	3-7386	0-4610		DFD0	2-4675	232345
844F	葏	5-7314	1-5652			E-4427	
8450	葐	3-7390			DFE1	2-4728	
8451	葑	0-6155	1-5653	1-8251	DFB1	2-4656	23225C
8452	葒	1-6106	1-5654		DFD2	2-4677	23233C
8453	葓	3-7404				E-4433	232248
8454	葔				DFDF	2-4726	
8455	葕	5-7294				E-443F	
8456	葖	3-7406	1-5655		DFAB	2-4650	
8457	著	0-5488	0-3588	0-7842	B5DB	1-6161	21554E
8458	葘		1-5656			E-4440	
8459	葙	0-6157	1-5657		DFB9	2-465E	232266
845A	葚	0-6156	1-5658	1-6992	DFB8	2-465D	232262
845B	葛	0-2480	0-1975	0-4271	B8AF	1-6636	215552
845C	葜	0-6154	1-5659			E-4432	232329
845D	葝	3-7327			DFBC	2-4661	
845E	葞	3-7409			DFBE	2-4663	
845F	葟	3-7384			DFCD	2-4672	232335
8460	葠	8-1364	1-5660		DFDE	2-4725	232336
8461	葡	0-3847	0-4182	0-8867	B8B2	1-6639	215556
8462	葢	5-7276	0-7268			E-4438	335561
8463	董	0-2213	0-3801	0-5261	B8B3	1-663A	215557
8464	葤	1-6107	1-5661			E-4430	
8465	葥	3-7403	1-5662		DFB0	2-4655	
8466	葦	1-4613	0-1617	0-7456	B8AB	1-6632	21554D
8467	葧	3-7370	1-5663		DFB4	2-4659	
8468	葨	5-7282			DFDA	2-4721	
8469	葩	0-6166	0-7261	1-8183	B8B4	1-663B	215558
846A	葪	3-7393	1-5664	1-5670			
846B	葫	0-2689	0-7257	0-9157	B8AC	1-6633	215551
846C	葬	0-5265	0-3382	0-7787	B8AE	1-6635	215550
846D	葭	0-6171	0-7251	1-5514	B8B5	1-663C	232271
846E	葮		0-7259		DFE0	2-4727	232337
846F	葯	1-8887	0-7264	0-6921	DFD3	2-4678	2D5635
8470	葰	5-7293	1-5665		DFCE	2-4673	
8471	葱	0-2048	0-3912	1-8014		E-443C	232332
8472	葲					E-442F	
8473	葳	0-6158	1-5666	1-7362	DFBB	2-4660	232269
8474	葴	3-7374	1-5667		DFBA	2-465F	
8475	葵	0-3191	0-1610	0-4813	B8AA	1-6631	21554C
8476	葶	0-6167	1-5668		DFAC	2-4651	23224D
8477	葷	1-2771	0-7256	1-8479	B8A7	1-662E	215553
8478	葸	0-6163	1-5669		DFC4	2-4669	23227C
8479	葹	3-7394	0-7265		DFAD	2-4652	23224E
847A	葺	0-6161	0-4188	0-8181	DFC2	2-4667	232278
847B	葻	3-7233				E-442E	
847C	葼	3-7389	1-5670				
847D	葽	3-7372	1-5671		DFB7	2-465C	23225F
847E	葾				DFDB	2-4722	
847F	葿	3-7410				E-442A	

848

	Char	G	J	K	B	C	A
0	蒀	3-7378				E-4439	
1	蒁		1-5672				
2	蒂	0-2157	0-7260	1-7966	B8A6	1-662D	21554A
3	蒃					E-443B	
4	蒄		0-7255			E-4428	23227B
5	蒅		1-5673				
6	蒆				DFB3	2-4658	
7	蒇	0-6159					29255A
8	蒈	0-6160					705D5C
9	蒉	0-6162					292564
A	蒊						
B	蒋	0-2915	0-3053				275571
C	蒌	0-6168					292524
D	蒍				DFAF	2-4654	23256C
E	蒎	0-6169			DFD5	2-467A	23224A
F	蒏				DFAE	2-4653	

84A

	Char	G	J	K	B	C	A
0	蒠	3-7427			E3CD	2-4D54	
1	蒡	0-6182	0-7280	0-5928	E3AE	2-4D35	232350
2	蒢	3-7411			E3C1	2-4D48	
3	蒣	5-7335				E-493C	
4	蒤	5-7345			E3AD	2-4D34	
5	蒥	3-7433				E-4939	
6	蒦	3-7426	1-5678				
7	蒧	5-7328			E3BF	2-4D46	
8	蒨	3-7424	1-5679	1-7929	E3C8	2-4D4F	232432
9	蒩	5-7332	1-5680		E3C6	2-4D4D	
A	蒪	3-7418	1-5681		E3BA	2-4D41	
B	蒫	5-7311			E3B5	2-4D3C	
C	蒬	5-7350			E3B3	2-4D3A	
D	蒭	5-7168	0-7258	1-8043		E-4942	232429
E	蒮	5-7349			E3B4	2-4D3B	
F	蒯	0-5665	1-5682	1-5809	E3C7	2-4D4E	232427

84C

	Char	G	J	K	B	C	A
0	蓀	1-6105	1-5688	0-6564	BB5E	1-6A66	215563
1	蓁	0-6172	0-7277	1-7815	E3B8	2-4D3F	23235E
2	蓂	3-7444	1-5689	0-5712	E3B2	2-4D39	23237C
3	蓃					E-4936	
4	蓄	0-4878	0-3563	0-8575	BB57	1-6A5F	21555E
5	蓅	5-7346			DFD4	2-4679	
6	蓆	8-1578	0-7278	0-6422	BB56	1-6A5E	21555D
7	蓇	3-7380	1-5690		E3C3	2-4D4A	232379
8	蓈	5-7262	1-5691			E-4436	
9	蓉	0-4056	0-4554	0-7340	BB54	1-6A5C	21555F
A	蓊	0-6178	0-7267	1-7247	BB63	1-6A6B	232441
B	蓋	1-2439	0-1924	0-4347	BB5C	1-6A64	215561
C	蓌	3-7429	1-5692		E3C4	2-4D4B	
D	蓍	0-6173	0-7273	0-6741	E3B9	2-4D40	232368
E	蓎	5-7340			E3B1	2-4D38	
F	蓏	3-7428	1-5693		E3CC	2-4D53	23243F

84E

	Char	G	J	K	B	C	A
0	蓠	0-6181					292840
1	蓡					E-663C	3F347D
2	蓢					E-663A	
3	蓣	0-6187					292633
4	蓤					E-493D	
5	蓥	0-6186					294629
6	蓦	0-6175					276148
7	蓧	3-7318	1-5702		E773	2-535C	23252F
8	蓨	3-7425			E774	2-535D	
9	蓩	3-7447			E767	2-5350	
A	蓪	5-7352	1-5703		E766	2-534F	23245F
B	蓫	3-7420			E762	2-534B	23247C
C	蓬	0-3778	0-4309	0-6079	BDB4	1-6E5D	215574
D	蓭			1-7042		E-4E4F	
E	蓮	1-3311	0-4701	0-5405	BDAC	1-6E55	21556C
F	蓯	1-6042	1-5704	1-8015	E776	2-535F	232535

849

	Char	G	J	K	B	C	A
0	蒐		0-2915	0-6629	BB60	1-6A68	215566
1	蒑	5-7336			E3D3	2-4D5A	
2	蒒	3-7275	1-5674			E-4935	
3	蒓	1-6127	1-5675			E-4944	23243A
4	蒔	1-6110	0-2812	0-6740	E3C2	2-4D49	232375
5	蒕		1-5676			E-4933	232421
6	蒖	3-7417				E-4938	
7	蒗	0-6185			E3AC	2-4D33	232349
8	蒘				E3CA	2-4D51	
9	蒙	0-3541	0-4456	0-5753	BB58	1-6A60	215564
A	蒚	5-7326			E3BB	2-4D42	
B	蒛				E3C5	2-4D4C	
C	蒜	0-4366	0-4139	0-6310	BB5B	1-6A63	215560
D	蒝	3-7419			E3BE	2-4D45	232371
E	蒞	8-1363	1-5677		BB59	1-6A61	21555B
F	蒟	3-7438	0-7271	1-5869	E3AF	2-4D36	232353

84B

	Char	G	J	K	B	C	A
0	蒰	5-7337			E3D2	2-4D59	
1	蒱	5-7329	1-5683		E3BC	2-4D43	232370
2	蒲	0-3849	0-1987	0-8868	BB5A	1-6A62	21555A
3	蒳	3-7329				E-493B	
4	蒴	0-6184	1-5684	1-6762	E3B7	2-4D3E	23235C
5	蒵	3-7432				E-493A	
6	蒶	3-7330			E3CB	2-4D52	
7	蒷	5-7221				E-4941	
8	蒸	0-5384	0-3088	0-8190	BB5D	1-6A65	215562
9	蒹	0-6183	0-7269	1-5639	E3B6	2-4D3D	232358
A	蒺	0-6180	1-5685	1-7822	E3B0	2-4D37	232356
B	蒻	3-7445	0-7274	0-6922	E3C0	2-4D47	23235F
C	蒼	1-1852	0-3383	0-8379	BB61	1-6A69	215567
D	蒽	0-6176	1-5686			E-4932	23237A
E	蒾	3-7402	1-5687				
F	蒿	0-6179	0-7270	0-9158	BB55	1-6A5D	21555C

84D

	Char	G	J	K	B	C	A
0	蓐	0-6174	0-7276	1-7303	E3BD	2-4D44	232372
1	蓑	0-4382	0-4412	0-6278	BB62	1-6A6A	2D5036
2	蓒	5-7216			E3D0	2-4D57	
3	蓓	0-6177	1-5694	1-6553	BB5F	1-6A67	215565
4	蓔	5-7342			E3CF	2-4D56	
5	蓕	5-7323				E-493F	
6	蓖	0-1745	0-7279	1-6709	E3C9	2-4D50	232433
7	蓗				E3CE	2-4D55	
8	蓘	3-7435				E-493E	
9	蓙		0-7272				696868
A	蓚	5-7291	0-7275	0-6630		E-4943	232435
B	蓛	5-7327			E3D1	2-4D58	
C	蓜		1-5701				
D	蓝	0-3222					275629
E	蓞					E-663B	
F	蓟	0-2827					292651

84F

	Char	G	J	K	B	C	A
0	蓰	0-6191	1-5705		E775	2-535E	232534
1	蓱	5-7313	1-5706	1-8218	DFA9	2-464E	
2	蓲	3-7226	1-5707		E75F	2-5348	
3	蓳	5-7358			E763	2-534C	
4	蓴		0-7283	0-6681	E75D	2-5346	232466
5	蓵	3-7455				E-4E44	
6	蓶	3-7459			E770	2-5359	
7	蓷	3-7456	1-5708		E761	2-534A	232477
8	蓸	3-7452				E-4E42	
9	蓹	5-7391			E777	2-5360	
A	蓺	5-7354	1-5710		E75A	2-5343	
B	蓻	3-7270	1-5711		E758	2-5341	
C	蓼	0-6204	0-7290	0-5494	E764	2-534D	23247A
D	蓽	1-6074	1-5712	1-8262	E76E	2-5357	23247D
E	蓾	3-7306			E769	2-5352	
F	蓿	0-6203	0-7282		BDB6	1-6E5F	215569

850

	Char	G	J	K	B	C	A
0	蔀	3-7437	0-2835	1-6635	E74F	2-5338	23244D
1	蔁	3-7467				E-4E40	
2	蔂	3-7458	1-5713		E76D	2-5356	
3	蔃	3-7502	1-5714			E-4E4C	
4	蔄					E-4E46	
5	蔅					E-4E54	
6	蔆		0-7249	1-6355	BDB7	1-6E60	232446
7	蔇	3-7408	1-5715		DFBD	2-4662	2F252E
8	蔈	3-7453			E75B	2-5344	
9	蔉				E752	2-533B	
A	蔊	3-7470			E755	2-533E	
B	蔋	5-7373			E77B	2-5364	232447
C	蔌	0-6188	1-5716		E75C	2-5345	23246A
D	蔍	5-7369			E753	2-533C	
E	蔎	3-7288	1-5717		E751	2-533A	
F	蔏	3-7468			E74E	2-5337	

852

	Char	G	J	K	B	C	A
0	蔠	5-7266			E779	2-5362	
1	蔡	0-1844	0-7281	0-8389	BDB2	1-6E5B	215572
2	蔢	5-7375	1-5721				
3	蔣	1-2915	1-5722	0-7788	BDB1	1-6E5A	215571
4	蔤	3-7471	1-5723		E74C	2-5335	
5	蔥		1-5724	0-8539	BDB5	1-6E5E	215575
6	蔦	1-6064	0-3653	1-7716	E772	2-535B	23252D
7	蔧	3-7448	1-5725		E756	2-533F	
8	蔨	3-7461			E76A	2-5353	
9	蔩	5-7376			E750	2-5339	
A	蔪	3-7341	1-5726	1-7639	E75E	2-5347	
B	蔫	0-3672	1-5727		E759	2-5342	51496B
C	蔬	0-4263	0-7286	0-6542	BDAD	1-6E56	21556D
D	蔭	1-5081	0-1694	0-7567	BDAE	1-6E57	21556E
E	蔮				E76C	2-5355	
F	蔯	5-7234	1-5728	0-8262	E77D	2-5366	232472

854

	Char	G	J	K	B	C	A
0	蕀	3-7476	0-7291		EB40	2-596B	23254F
1	蕁	1-6101	0-7301	0-5138	EB43	2-596E	232546
2	蕂	3-7488				E-5252	23256D
3	蕃	0-6212	0-4057	0-5970	BFBB	1-7225	21557B
4	蕄	5-7229			EB45	2-5970	
5	蕅	5-7405			EAF9	2-5965	
6	蕆	1-6159	1-5733	1-7930	EB41	2-596C	23255A
7	蕇	5-7255			EB47	2-5972	
8	蕈	0-6206	0-7294		BFB8	1-7222	215579
9	蕉	0-2922	0-3054	0-8515	BFBC	1-7226	21557D
A	蕊	0-4079	0-2841	1-7189	BFB6	1-717E	215577
B	蕋		0-7303	1-7190		E-5259	395577
C	蕌					E-5250	
D	蕍	3-7493			EAFB	2-5967	
E	蕎	1-6081	0-2230	0-4680	EB4C	2-5977	232571
F	蕏	3-7465	1-5734				

856

	Char	G	J	K	B	C	A
0	蕠	5-7411	1-5745		EB51	2-597C	
1	蕡	3-7369	1-5746	1-6660	EAFD	2-5969	23254E
2	蕢	1-6162	1-5747		EB44	2-596F	232564
3	蕣	3-7487	0-7292	0-6682	EB48	2-5973	23256B
4	蕤	0-6208	1-5748	1-7390	EB42	2-596D	23255C
5	蕥	5-7382			EB56	2-5A23	
6	蕦	5-7301			EB53	2-597E	
7	蕧	3-7486			EB50	2-597B	
8	蕨	0-6207	0-4747	0-4782	BFB9	1-7223	21557A
9	蕩	1-2120	0-3802	0-8725	BFBA	1-7224	215576
A	蕪	1-4663	0-4183	0-5783	BFBE	1-7228	21557C
B	蕫	3-7490	1-5749	1-6161	EAFA	2-5966	
C	蕬	5-7173			EB57	2-5A24	
D	蕭	1-4784	0-7311	0-6543	BFBD	1-7227	215622
E	蕮	3-7484			EB4D	2-5978	
F	蕯	3-7473	1-5750			E-524F	

851

	Char	G	J	K	B	C	A
0	蔐	5-7370	1-5718				
1	蔑	0-3579	0-4246	0-5701	BDB0	1-6E59	292D51
2	蔒	5-7377			E765	2-534E	
3	蔓	0-3491	0-4402	0-5632	BDAF	1-6E58	21556F
4	蔔	1-8805	0-7289	0-6059	BDB3	1-6E5C	215573
5	蔕		0-7288	1-7967	E760	2-5349	232475
6	蔖	5-7361			E768	2-5351	
7	蔗	0-5365	0-7284	0-7729	BDA9	1-6E52	21556A
8	蔘	3-7365	0-7285	0-6324	E778	2-5361	23252A
9	蔙	5-7371			E77C	2-5365	
A	蔚	0-4621	0-1722	0-7405	BDAB	1-6E54	21556B
B	蔛	3-7466				E-4E4B	
C	蔜	5-7319	1-5719		E757	2-5340	
D	蔝	5-7362			E76B	2-5354	
E	蔞	1-6168	1-5720	0-5513	E76F	2-5358	232524
F	蔟	0-6193	0-7287	1-7752	E754	2-533D	232459

853

	Char	G	J	K	B	C	A
0	蔰				E77A	2-5363	
1	蔱				E771	2-535A	
2	蔲		1-5709				
3	蔳	5-7372	1-5729			E-4E4D	
4	蔴	8-1577	1-5730			E-4E4E	33625F
5	蔵	5-7360	0-3402			E-4E52	4E562B
6	蔶		1-5731				
7	蔷	0-3930					275626
8	蔸	0-6190					4C4146
9	蔹	0-6192					29282A
A	蔺	0-6194					275639
B	蔻	0-6202			E74D	2-5336	23245C
C	蔼	0-1610					275637
D	蔽	0-1746	0-4235	0-8844	BDAA	1-6E53	215568
E	蔾				EB49	2-5974	
F	蔿	3-7237	1-5732	0-7457		E-525A	

855

	Char	G	J	K	B	C	A
0	蕐		1-5735				
1	蕑	3-7321	1-5736		EB46	2-5971	23255F
2	蕒	1-6104	1-5737				
3	蕓	1-6031	1-5738	0-7394	EAFC	2-5968	23254D
4	蕔	3-7474			EB55	2-5A22	
5	蕕	1-6121	0-7304	1-7389	EB4F	2-597A	232574
6	蕖	0-6201	1-5739	1-5591	EAF8	2-5964	232536
7	蕗	3-7513	0-4189		EE46	2-5E72	232645
8	蕘	1-6073	0-7293	1-7293	EAFE	2-596A	23254B
9	蕙	0-6205	1-5740	0-9122	BFB7	1-7221	215578
A	蕚		0-7254			E-5258	2D5554
B	蕛	5-7387			EB4A	2-5975	
C	蕜	5-7383	1-5741			E-5254	
D	蕝	3-7416	1-5742		EB54	2-5A21	232576
E	蕞	0-6209	1-5743	1-7968	BFBF	1-7229	23255D
F	蕟		1-5744			E-5256	

857

	Char	G	J	K	B	C	A
0	蕰	3-7492				E-5255	
1	蕱				EB4B	2-5976	
2	蕲	0-6213					292768
3	蕳					E-663D	23255E
4	蕴	0-5244					27563D
5	蕵	5-7393			EB4E	2-5979	
6	蕶				EE53	2-5F21	
7	蕷	1-6187	0-7317		EE40	2-5E6C	232633
8	蕸	3-7501			EE45	2-5E71	232634
9	蕹	0-6219	1-5751		EE52	2-5E7E	23262D
A	蕺	0-6210	1-5752	1-7785	EE44	2-5E70	232642
B	蕻	0-6214	1-5753		EDFB	2-5E68	232636
C	蕼	5-7415			EE41	2-5E6D	
D	蕽		1-5754				
E	蕾	0-3257	0-7318	1-6315	C1A2	1-752C	215625
F	蕿		1-5755			E-562B	232632

858

	Char	G	J	K	B	C	A
0	薀		0-7305	1-7233	EDF4	2-5E61	232625
1	薁	3-7485	1-5756		EE4D	2-5E79	
2	薂	3-7516			EE4F	2-5E7B	
3	薃	3-7522			EDF3	2-5E60	
4	薄	0-1701	0-3986	0-5861	C1A1	1-752B	21557E
5	薅	0-6222	1-5757		EE51	2-5E7D	232656
6	薆	3-7431	1-5758	1-7068	EE49	2-5E75	23264E
7	薇	0-6217	0-7315	0-5825	C1A8	1-7532	215628
8	薈	1-6086	0-7307		EE50	2-5E7C	232657
9	薉	5-7187	1-5759	1-7191	EE42	2-5E6E	
A	薊	1-2827	0-7309	1-5671	C1AA	1-7534	232651
B	薋	3-7436	1-5760		EDF9	2-5E66	
C	薌	1-6028	1-5761	1-8331	EE52	2-597D	232577
D	薍	3-7517			EE4A	2-5E76	
E	薎	5-7421			EE47	2-5E73	
F	薏	0-6218	1-5762	0-7591	EDF5	2-5E62	232628

85A

	Char	G	J	K	B	C	A
0	薠	3-7439	1-5767		EDF8	2-5E65	
1	薡	3-7483			EE43	2-5E6F	
2	薢	3-7519	1-5768		EE4E	2-5E7A	232652
3	薣				EDFA	2-5E67	
4	薤	0-6215	0-7306	1-8324	EDFC	2-5E69	23263D
5	薥	5-7420	1-5769	1-8010			
6	薦	1-2886	0-3306	0-8432	C2CB	1-7535	395477
7	薧	5-7428	1-5770		EDF6	2-5E63	
8	薨	0-6216	0-7310	0-9328	C1A9	1-7533	232649
9	薩	1-4088	0-2707	0-6317	C2C4	1-7730	21562A
A	薪	0-4829	0-3137	0-6779	C17E	1-752A	215621
B	薫		0-2316			E-562C	
C	薬		0-4484			E-5630	335635
D	薭		1-5784				
E	薮	0-6220	0-4489				275632
F	薯	0-4277	0-2982	0-6403	C1A6	1-7530	21562C

85C

	Char	G	J	K	B	C	A
0	藀				F0A6	2-6270	
1	藁	0-6227	0-4746	0-4543		E-586F	23265D
2	藂	5-7433	1-5779		F0A8	2-6272	23266A
3	藃	3-7530			F0A7	2-6271	
4	藄				F0AD	2-6277	232670
5	藅	5-7286			F0B2	2-627C	
6	藆	5-7450			F0A5	2-626F	
7	藇	3-7218	1-5780		F0AC	2-6276	
8	藈				F0B1	2-627B	
9	藉	0-2969	0-7320	0-7730	C2C7	1-7733	21562E
A	藊	5-7444	1-5781				
B	藋	3-7533	1-5782		F0AF	2-6279	
C	藌	5-7451				E-586B	
D	藍	1-3222	0-4585	0-5332	C2C5	1-7731	215629
E	藎	1-6103	1-5783	0-6780	F0B0	2-627A	232668
F	藏	0-1856	0-7322	0-7790	C2C3	1-772F	21562B

85E

	Char	G	J	K	B	C	A
0	藠	3-7539	1-5788				
1	藡				F2CA	2-6655	
2	藢	5-7457			F2DA	2-6665	
3	藣	3-7422			F2D3	2-665E	
4	藤	0-4457	0-3803	0-5286	C3C3	1-786E	215633
5	藥	1-5009	0-7327	0-6923	C3C4	1-786F	215635
6	藦	3-7541	1-5789		F2D7	2-6662	23272C
7	藧					E-5B22	
8	藨	3-7542	1-5790		F2CB	2-6656	
9	藩	0-2310	0-4045	0-5971	C3BF	1-786A	215630
A	藪	1-6220	0-7314	0-6631	C3C1	1-786C	215632
B	藫	3-7544			F2C6	2-6651	
C	藬	5-7378			F2CE	2-6659	
D	藭	3-7323	1-5791		F2C8	2-6653	232731
E	藮	5-7463				E-5C7B	
F	藯	5-7458			F2D8	2-6663	

859

	Char	G	J	K	B	C	A
0	薐	3-7514	0-7319		EE55	2-5F23	232654
1	薑	1-8836	0-7308	0-4325	C1A4	1-752E	215624
2	薒					E-5628	
3	薓	5-7431	1-5763			E-5629	
4	薔	1-3930	0-7312	0-7789	C1A5	1-752F	215626
5	薕	3-7521			EDF7	2-5E64	
6	薖	3-7272			EE48	2-5E74	
7	薗		0-1782	1-7348		E-562D	232644
8	薘	3-7268	1-5764		EE54	2-5F22	232635
9	薙		0-3869	1-8082	EE4B	2-5E77	232650
A	薚				EDFD	2-5E6A	
B	薛	0-4906	0-7313	0-6464	C1A7	1-7531	215623
C	薜	0-6221	0-7316		C1A3	1-752D	215627
D	薝	3-7518	1-5765	1-6090	EE4C	2-5E78	
E	薞				EDFE	2-5E6B	
F	薟	1-6118	1-5766		EE56	2-5F24	

85B

	Char	G	J	K	B	C	A
0	薰	0-6225		0-9325	C2C8	1-7734	21562F
1	薱	3-7262			F0B3	2-627D	
2	薲	3-7441				E-586C	
3	薳	3-7507			F0A9	2-6273	23266E
4	薴	3-7256	1-5771		F0A4	2-626E	
5	薵	3-7290			F0AA	2-6274	
6	薶	5-7446	1-5772		F0B4	2-627E	23267E
7	薷	0-6224	1-5773		F0B8	2-6324	23266B
8	薸	3-7531	1-5774		F0B7	2-6323	23265A
9	薹	0-6223	0-7323		C2CA	1-7736	23266C
A	薺	1-6089	0-7321	0-8017	C2C9	1-7735	232661
B	薻					E-586E	
C	薼		1-5775				
D	薽	3-7511	1-5776		F0AB	2-6275	23266F
E	薾	3-7254	1-5777		F0B9	2-6325	232675
F	薿	3-7528	1-5778		F0AE	2-6278	232672

85D

	Char	G	J	K	B	C	A
0	藐	0-3574	0-7324	1-6470	C2C6	1-7732	21562D
1	藑	3-7527			F2D5	2-6660	
2	藒	5-7443			F0B5	2-6321	
3	藓	0-6226					275640
4	藔					E-663E	23272E
5	藕	0-3726	0-7325	0-7368	C3C2	1-786D	215634
6	藖	3-7345				E-5A7E	
7	藗	5-7435			F2CD	2-6658	
8	藘	3-7421	1-5785		F2D1	2-665C	232745
9	藙	3-7543			F2C9	2-6654	
A	藚	3-7335	1-5786		F2CC	2-6657	232739
B	藛	5-7169				E-5A7D	
C	藜	0-6228	0-7328	0-5377	F2D4	2-665F	23274C
D	藝	1-5053	0-7326	0-7161	C3C0	1-786B	215631
E	藞	3-7536			F2D9	2-6664	
F	藟	3-7537	1-5787		F2D2	2-665D	232743

85F

	Char	G	J	K	B	C	A
0	藰	5-7201			F2D6	2-6661	
1	藱	5-7447			F2C7	2-6652	
2	藲				F2CF	2-665A	
3	藳	3-7540	1-5792				
4	藴	1-5244				E-5B25	
5	藵					E-663F	23274E
6	藶	1-6034	1-5793		F4BE	2-696A	
7	藷		0-2983	0-7843	C3C5	1-7870	232728
8	藸				F2D0	2-665B	
9	藹	1-1610	0-7329	1-7069	C4A7	1-7A32	215637
A	藺	1-6194	0-7334	0-5584	C4A9	1-7A34	215639
B	藻	0-5269	0-3384	0-8061	C4A6	1-7A31	215636
C	藼		1-5794			E-5C76	232757
D	藽	5-7308		1-8094	F4C3	2-696F	
E	藾	3-7510	0-7333		F4BB	2-6967	23275E
F	藿	0-6229	1-5801	0-4611	F4B9	2-6965	23275B

Code	Char	G	J	K	B	C	A
8600	蘀	3-7340	1-5802	1-8131	F4BD	2-6969	232760
8601	蘁	5-7462			F4BA	2-6966	
8602	蘂		0-7302	0-7162		E-5C78	335577
8603	蘃					E-5C7C	
8604	蘄	1-6213	1-5803	1-5992	F4BF	2-696B	232768
8605	蘅	0-6231	1-5804		F4C1	2-696D	232771
8606	蘆	1-3411	0-7335	0-5454	C4AA	1-7A35	21563A
8607	蘇	1-4353	0-3341	0-6544	C4AC	1-7A37	21563C
8608	蘈	5-7423				E-5D22	
8609	蘉	3-7549			F4C0	2-696C	
860A	蘊		0-7330	0-7219	C4AD	1-7A38	21563D
860B	蘋	1-3827	0-7332	1-6729	C4AB	1-7A36	21563B
860C	蘌	3-7556			F4C2	2-696E	
860D	蘍		1-5805			E-5C7E	
860E	蘎		1-5806				
860F	蘏					E-5D23	
8610	蘐		1-5807			E-5C77	232754
8611	蘑	0-3602	1-5808		C4A8	1-7A33	215638
8612	蘒		1-5809				
8613	蘓		0-7331			E-5D21	2D563C
8614	蘔	5-7427					
8615	蘕					E-5E5B	
8616	蘖	0-6233	0-6117	0-6978		E-5E5A	51563F
8617	蘗	5-7476	0-6102	0-6002	C4F4	1-7B21	21563F
8618	蘘	3-7558	1-5810	1-7101	F5F1	2-6C21	
8619	蘙	3-7553	1-5811		F5F7	2-6C27	
861A	蘚	1-6226	0-7337	0-6448	C4F6	1-7B23	215640
861B	蘛	5-7467	1-5812		F4BC	2-6968	
861C	蘜	5-7468			F5F6	2-6C26	
861D	蘝					E-5E5C	
861E	蘞	1-6192	1-5813		F5FD	2-6C2D	
861F	蘟				F5F4	2-6C24	
8620	蘠				F5FB	2-6C2B	
8621	蘡	3-7460	1-5814		F5FA	2-6C2A	
8622	蘢	1-6055	0-7336	1-6305	F4B8	2-6964	232752
8623	蘣	3-7547			F5F5	2-6C25	
8624	蘤				F0B6	2-6322	232724
8625	蘥	3-7557			F5FE	2-6C2E	
8626	蘦	3-7554			F5F3	2-6C23	
8627	蘧	0-6230	1-5815	1-5592	F5F8	2-6C28	232822
8628	蘨	5-7473				E-5E58	
8629	蘩	0-6232	1-5816	1-6558	F5FC	2-6C2C	232826
862A	蘪	3-7560			F5F2	2-6C22	
862B	蘫	5-7429				E-5E56	232775
862C	蘬	3-7246			F74A	2-6D77	
862D	蘭	1-3228	0-4586	0-5321	C4F5	1-7B22	21563E
862E	蘮	3-7555			F5F9	2-6C29	
862F	蘯		0-6628	1-8149		E-5E57	4B4D41
8630	蘰		0-7338				696946
8631	蘱				F7F4	2-6F43	
8632	蘲				F74B	2-6D78	
8633	蘳	3-7552			F749	2-6D76	
8634	蘴				F747	2-6D74	
8635	蘵	5-7355			F748	2-6D75	
8636	蘶	5-7471	1-5817		F74C	2-6D79	232838
8637	蘷					E-6640	232832
8638	蘸	0-5326	1-5818		C5D9	1-7C45	215641
8639	蘹				F7F2	2-6F41	
863A	蘺	1-6181	1-5819		F7F0	2-6F3F	232840
863B	蘻				F7F5	2-6F44	
863C	蘼	0-6234	1-5820	1-6503	F7F3	2-6F42	23283E
863D	蘽	5-7484	1-5821			E-6043	
863E	蘾				F7F6	2-6F45	
863F	蘿	1-3460	0-7339	0-5301	C5DA	1-7C46	215642
8640	虀		1-5822		F7F1	2-6F40	23283F
8641	虁		1-2470	1-5993		E-602F	21787C
8642	虂		1-5823			E-6146	
8643	虃	5-7490			F8BC	2-704A	
8644	虄						
8645	虅					E-6641	23284C
8646	虆		1-5824		F945	2-7134	
8647	虇	5-7491			F946	2-7135	
8648	虈				F947	2-7136	
8649	虉	3-7535				E-6147	
864A	虊					E-617C	
864B	虋	3-7566			F9C7	2-7235	
864C	虌				F9BD	2-722D	
864D	虍	0-8214	0-7340		CA4F	2-226F	232859
864E	虎	0-2702	0-2455	0-9159	AAEA	1-4F4D	215643
864F	虏	0-3418					275648
8650	虐	0-3716	0-2152	0-8943	AD68	1-534B	215644
8651	虑	0-3439					273F36
8652	虒	3-1638	1-5825		D3B8	2-325A	216D74
8653	虓	3-6541	1-5826	1-8462	D3B7	2-3259	23285A
8654	虔	0-8215	0-7342	0-4383	B040	1-5825	215645
8655	處	1-2006	0-4961	0-8405	B342	1-5D28	215647
8656	虖	5-6452	1-5827		D77C	2-3921	333573
8657	虗		1-5828			E-3863	
8658	虘	5-6449	1-5829			E-3860	
8659	虙	5-6453	1-5830		D77B	2-387E	23285E
865A	虚	0-4873	0-2185			E-3861	
865B	虛			0-9040	B5EA	1-6170	215649
865C	虜	1-3418	0-4626	0-5455	B8B8	1-663F	215648
865D	虝		1-5831			E-3E61	
865E	虞	0-5161	0-2283	0-7369	B8B7	1-663E	21564B
865F	號	1-2637	0-7343	0-9160	B8B9	1-6640	21564A
8660	虠		1-5832				
8661	虡	3-6536	1-5833		E3D4	2-4D5B	232866
8662	虢	0-7529	1-5834		E77E	2-5367	232869
8663	虣	3-6546	1-5835		EB58	2-5A25	23286A
8664	虤	3-6547	1-5836		EB5A	2-5A27	
8665	虥	5-6461			EB59	2-5A26	
8666	虦	3-6543					
8667	虧	1-3187	0-7344	0-9348	C1AB	1-7536	21564C
8668	虨	3-2615			EB57	2-5F25	
8669	虩	3-6549	1-5837		F0BA	2-6326	232871
866A	虪	3-6550			F9A5	2-7173	
866B	虫	0-1970	0-3578	1-8487	A6E4	1-4865	275733
866C	虬	0-8216	1-5838	1-5932		E-272D	232878
866D	虭	5-6468			CDC9	2-2869	
866E	虮	0-8217			CDCA	2-286A	292C4C
866F	虯		1-5839	1-5933	CDC8	2-2868	23287C
8670	虰	3-6551			CDC7	2-2867	
8671	虱	0-4213	0-7345	1-6951	AAEB	1-4F4E	33567C
8672	虲					E-6642	23287B
8673	虳	5-6470			D0A9	2-2D4A	232926
8674	虴	5-6469			D0A7	2-2D48	
8675	虵		1-5840			E-2F23	
8676	虶	3-6553	1-5841			E-2E7C	
8677	虷	3-6552	1-5842		D0A6	2-2D47	
8678	虸	3-6554		1-7494		E-2E7E	
8679	虹	0-2671	0-3890	0-9186	AD69	1-534C	21564F
867A	虺	0-8219	1-5843	1-8488	AD6B	1-534E	232925
867B	虻	0-8221	0-1626	1-6430	AD6A	1-534D	23287E
867C	虼	0-8220			D0A8	2-2D49	232927
867D	虽	0-4368				E-2F24	275F4A
867E	虾	0-4726					27567A
867F	虿	0-8218					292C5D

Code	Char	G	J	K	B	C	A
8680	蚀	0-4220					275676
8681	蚁	0-5047					275735
8682	蚂	0-3476					275725
8683	蚃	8-9391					
8684	蚄	3-6569				E-3369	
8685	蚅	5-6475			D3C4	2-3266	
8686	蚆	5-6489			D3C1	2-3263	
8687	蚇	5-6487			D3BF	2-3261	
8688	蚈	3-6557	1-5877				
8689	蚉	5-4889				E-336C	
868A	蚊	0-4635	0-1867	0-5805	B041	1-5826	215652
868B	蚋	0-8224	0-7350	1-7192	D3C2	2-3264	23293D
868C	蚌	0-1686	0-7351	0-5929	B046	1-582B	215655
868D	蚍	0-8223	1-5844	1-6710	D3BC	2-325E	23293C
868E	蚎	5-6478			D3CB	2-326D	
868F	蚏	3-6567				E-336F	
8690	蚐				D3CD	2-326F	
8691	蚑	3-6559	1-5845		D3BD	2-325F	232936
8692	蚒	5-6484				E-336E	
8693	蚓	0-8230	0-7346	0-7666	B043	1-5828	215653
8694	蚔	5-6483			D3CE	2-3270	
8695	蚕	0-1847	0-2729	1-7931	D3C9	2-326B	275741
8696	蚖	3-6558	1-5846		D3BB	2-325D	23292E
8697	蚗	3-6570			D3C0	2-3262	
8698	蚘		1-5847		D3CA	2-326C	232939
8699	蚙	3-6566			D3C6	2-3268	
869A	蚚	3-6563	1-5848		D3C3	2-3265	
869B	蚛	3-6562				E-336B	
869C	蚜	0-4933	1-5849		B048	1-582D	232937
869D	蚝	0-8226			D3CC	2-326E	232942
869E	蚞				D3BE	2-3260	
869F	蚟	3-6556				E-336A	
86A0	蚠					E-3370	232946
86A1	蚡	5-6482	1-5850		D3C7	2-3269	2F5F45
86A2	蚢	3-6568			D3B9	2-325B	
86A3	蚣	0-8228	0-7347	0-4587	B047	1-582C	215656
86A4	蚤	0-5273	0-3934	0-8062	B044	1-5829	215654
86A5	蚥	5-6481			D3C5	2-3267	
86A6	蚦		1-5851			E-336D	232940
86A7	蚧	0-8227	1-5852		D3C8	2-326A	232948
86A8	蚨	0-8222	1-5853	1-6636	D3BA	2-325C	23292F
86A9	蚩	0-8231	0-7348	0-8641	B045	1-582A	215650
86AA	蚪	0-8229	0-7349	1-6169	B042	1-5827	215651
86AB	蚫		0-7359				69695B
86AC	蚬	0-8225					292A34
86AD	蚭		1-5854				
86AE	蚮	3-6582				E-3866	
86AF	蚯	0-8239	0-7353	1-5870	B34C	1-5D32	21565F
86B0	蚰	0-8236	0-7356	1-7391	D7A5	2-3928	232959
86B1	蚱	0-8238	1-5855	1-7901	B34B	1-5D31	21565E
86B2	蚲	3-6575				E-3864	
86B3	蚳	3-6584	1-5856		D7A8	2-392B	232960
86B4	蚴	0-8242	1-5857	1-7392	D7AB	2-392E	232963
86B5	蚵	0-8234	1-5858		B348	1-5D2E	215659
86B6	蚶	0-8232	0-7352		B346	1-5D2C	21565B
86B7	蚷	3-6560	1-5859		D77E	2-3923	
86B8	蚸	3-6583	1-5860		D7A9	2-392C	
86B9	蚹	3-6581	1-5861		D7A7	2-392A	
86BA	蚺	0-8237			D7A4	2-3927	232958
86BB	蚻	3-6573			D7AC	2-392F	
86BC	蚼	3-6585			D7AD	2-3930	
86BD	蚽	5-6493			D7AF	2-3932	
86BE	蚾	3-6591			D7B0	2-3933	
86BF	蚿	3-6586	1-5862		D77D	2-3922	23294B
86C0	蛀	0-5491	1-5863	1-7753	B345	1-5D2B	215657
86C1	蛁	3-6590	1-5864		D7A2	2-3925	
86C2	蛂	5-6494			D7A1	2-3924	
86C3	蛃	5-6492	1-5865		D7AE	2-3931	
86C4	蛄	0-8233	0-7354		B347	1-5D2D	21565C
86C5	蛅	3-6577	1-5866	1-7640	D7A3	2-3926	
86C6	蛆	0-3989	0-7355	1-7570	B349	1-5D2F	21565D
86C7	蛇	0-4163	0-2856	0-6279	B344	1-5D2A	215658
86C8	蛈	5-6503			D7A6	2-3929	
86C9	蛉	0-8240	0-7357	1-6268	B34D	1-5D33	232962
86CA	蛊	0-2538					27573F
86CB	蛋	0-2116	0-3533	0-5117	B34A	1-5D30	21565A
86CC	蛌	5-6505			D7AA	2-392D	
86CD	蛍		0-2354				4B5724
86CE	蛎	0-8235	0-1934				27573C
86CF	蛏	0-8241					292C55
86D0	蛐	0-8248			B5F1	1-6177	232977
86D1	蛑	0-8254	1-5867		DEBF	2-4025	23297A
86D2	蛒	3-6610	1-5868				
86D3	蛓	5-4015			DEB4	2-3F78	
86D4	蛔	0-2755	0-7360	0-9278	B5EE	1-6174	215663
86D5	蛕		1-5869			E-3E62	232974
86D6	蛖	3-6623			DFE7	2-472E	
86D7	蛗		1-5870		DEBD	2-4023	
86D8	蛘	0-8253			DEB1	2-3F75	232967
86D9	蛙	0-4560	0-1931	0-7235	B5EC	1-6172	215661
86DA	蛚	3-6604	1-5871		DEB6	2-3F7A	
86DB	蛛	0-5475	0-7365	0-8140	B5EF	1-6175	215664
86DC	蛜	5-6521	1-5872		DEBA	2-3F7E	
86DD	蛝	3-6616			DEB8	2-3F7C	
86DE	蛞	0-8250	0-7361	1-8435	B5F2	1-6178	23297E
86DF	蛟	0-8252	0-7364	0-4681	B5EB	1-6171	215660
86E0	蛠		1-5873				
86E1	蛡	3-6617				E-3E63	
86E2	蛢	3-6612			DEB2	2-3F76	
86E3	蛣	3-6602	1-5874	1-6011	DEB5	2-3F79	23296E
86E4	蛤	0-2482	0-4026	0-8977	B5F0	1-6176	215665
86E5	蛥	3-6611	1-5875				
86E6	蛦	3-6605			DEB3	2-3F77	
86E7	蛧	5-6518	1-5876				
86E8	蛨	3-6603			DEBE	2-4024	
86E9	蛩	0-8243	0-7362	1-5738	DEBC	2-4022	23296F
86EA	蛪	3-6594			DEB7	2-3F7B	
86EB	蛫	3-6608			DEB9	2-3F7D	
86EC	蛬	5-6511	0-7363	1-5739	DEBB	2-4021	232971
86ED	蛭	0-8246	0-4140	0-8284	B5ED	1-6173	215662
86EE	蛮	0-3489	0-4058			E-3E68	275742
86EF	蛯		0-7366				696962
86F0	蛰	0-5361					292B6E
86F1	蛱	0-8244					292A2F
86F2	蛲	0-8245					275732
86F3	蛳	0-8247					292B55
86F4	蛴	0-8251					292C61
86F5	蛵	3-6593			DFE8	2-472F	
86F6	蛶				DFEE	2-4735	
86F7	蛷	5-6536			DFE4	2-472B	
86F8	蛸	0-8257	0-3493	1-6884	DFEA	2-4731	232A33
86F9	蛹	0-5128	0-7376	1-7312	B8BA	1-6641	215667
86FA	蛺	1-8244	1-5878		DFE6	2-472D	232A2F
86FB	蛻		0-7372	1-6867	B8C0	1-6647	215666
86FC	蛼	5-6476	1-5879			E-4444	
86FD	蛽		1-5880			E-4445	
86FE	蛾	0-2274	0-1875	0-6822	B8BF	1-6646	21566C
86FF	蛿	5-6540				E-4449	

870

Code	Char	G	J	K	B	C	A
0	蜀	0-4281	0-7370	0-8525	B8BE	1-6645	21566B
1	蜁				DFED	2-4734	
2	蜂	0-2368	0-4310	0-6080	B8C1	1-6648	21566E
3	蜃	0-8255	0-7371	0-6781	B8C2	1-6649	215669
4	蜄	5-6532	1-5881		DFE3	2-472A	
5	蜅	3-6622	1-5882		DFF0	2-4737	
6	蜆	1-8225	0-7368	1-8351	B8C3	1-664A	232A34
7	蜇	0-8256	1-5883		B8BD	1-6644	215668
8	蜈	0-8258	0-7369	0-7205	B8BC	1-6643	21566A
9	蜉	0-8261	0-7374	1-6637	DFEC	2-4733	232A38
A	蜊	0-8259	0-7377	1-6364	B8C4	1-664B	232A3A
B	蜋		1-5884	1-6216	DFE2	2-4729	232A25
C	蜌	3-6624			DFE5	2-472C	
D	蜍	0-8260	0-7375		DFEF	2-4736	232A3E
E	蜎	3-6625	1-5885		DFEB	2-4732	232A36
F	蜏	3-6626	1-5886				

872

Code	Char	G	J	K	B	C	A
0	蜠	3-6631			E3E4	2-4D6B	
1	蜡	0-3215	1-5893	1-6754	E3DC	2-4D63	27573E
2	蜢	0-8276			BB67	1-6A6F	215672
3	蜣	0-8262	1-5894		E3D6	2-4D5D	232A43
4	蜤	5-6551			E3F1	2-4D78	
5	蜥	0-8265	0-7382	1-6821	BB68	1-6A70	215673
6	蜦	3-6565			E3EE	2-4D75	
7	蜧	5-6564			E3EF	2-4D76	
8	蜨		1-5901	1-7646	E3D7	2-4D5E	232A45
9	蜩	0-8272	0-7383	1-7717	BB6D	1-6A75	232A59
A	蜪	3-6636			E3E6	2-4D6D	
B	蜫	5-6556				E-494A	
C	蜬	5-6570			E3E0	2-4D67	
D	蜭				E3E7	2-4D6E	
E	蜮	0-8266	1-5902		E3DA	2-4D61	232A4B
F	蜯	5-6547	1-5903				

874

Code	Char	G	J	K	B	C	A
0	蝀	3-6576	1-5911	1-6162	E3D9	2-4D60	232A49
1	蝁				E3E1	2-4D68	
2	蝂	5-6560			E3ED	2-4D74	
3	蝃	5-6568	1-5912		E3DF	2-4D66	232A53
4	蝄	5-6557					232A55
5	蝅		1-5913			E-494E	
6	蝆				E3E3	2-4D6A	
7	蝇	0-5112				E-494B	275736
8	蝈	0-8269					2D572D
9	蝉	0-1885	0-3270				275734
A	蝊					E-6643	232A42
B	蝋		0-4725				
C	蝌	0-8282	0-7388	1-5752	BDC1	1-6E6A	21567D
D	蝍	3-6628	1-5914		DFE9	2-4730	232B33
E	蝎	0-4811	0-7389	0-4273	E7B2	2-5379	232B27
F	蝏	3-6657			E7BB	2-5424	232A6B

876

Code	Char	G	J	K	B	C	A
0	蝠	0-8280	0-7385	1-6609	BDBB	1-6E64	215677
1	蝡		1-5917		E7AB	2-5372	232B21
2	蝢	5-6512			E7BE	2-5427	
3	蝣	0-8286	0-7402		E7A2	2-5369	232A6D
4	蝤	0-8288	1-5918	1-7393	E7A3	2-536A	232A71
5	蝥	0-8290	1-5919	1-6452	E7BA	2-5423	232A73
6	蝦	1-4726	0-1860	0-8936	BDBC	1-6E65	21567A
7	蝧				E7BF	2-5428	
8	蝨		0-7392	0-6704	BDBE	1-6E67	21567C
9	蝩	3-6650			E7C0	2-5429	
A	蝪	5-6472	0-7403		E7B0	2-5377	232B24
B	蝫				E3D8	2-4D5F	
C	蝬				E7B6	2-537D	
D	蝭	3-6648			E7AF	2-5376	
E	蝮	0-8283	0-7393	1-6610	E7B8	2-5421	232B30
F	蝯		1-5920		E7B5	2-537C	232B2D

871

Code	Char	G	J	K	B	C	A
0	蜐	5-6527	1-5887				
1	蜑	5-6519	0-7373	1-6076	E3F4	2-4D7B	232A65
2	蜒	0-4949	0-7367		E3E9	2-4D70	232A66
3	蜓	0-8249	1-5888		B8BB	1-6642	21566D
4	蜔		1-5889				
5	蜕	0-4541				E-4446	
6	蜖					E-4448	
7	蜗	0-4647					2D567B
8	蜘	0-5409	0-3556	0-8227	BB6A	1-6A72	215675
9	蜙	5-6552	1-5890		E3DD	2-4D64	
A	蜚	0-8267	0-7384	0-6204	E3F2	2-4D79	232A5F
B	蜛				E3DE	2-4D65	
C	蜜	0-3559	0-4410	0-5844	BB65	1-6A6D	21566F
D	蜝	3-6629		1-5994		E-494F	
E	蜞	0-8264	1-5891		E3DB	2-4D62	232A4E
F	蜟	3-6639	1-5892				

873

Code	Char	G	J	K	B	C	A
0	蜰	3-6635			E3F3	2-4D7A	
1	蜱	0-8271	1-5904		E3EB	2-4D72	232A64
2	蜲	5-6558	1-5905		E3E5	2-4D6C	
3	蜳	5-6562			E3D5	2-4D5C	
4	蜴	0-8270	0-7378	1-7913	BB69	1-6A71	215674
5	蜵	3-6651		1-7145	E3EC	2-4D73	
6	蜶					E-4945	
7	蜷	0-8273	0-7380	1-5907	BB6C	1-6A74	232A44
8	蜸	5-6477			E3F0	2-4D77	
9	蜹	3-6620	1-5906			E-494C	232A5A
A	蜺		1-5907	1-7193	E3EA	2-4D71	2D5F63
B	蜻	0-8263	0-7381	1-7959	BB66	1-6A6E	215671
C	蜼	3-6633	1-5908		E3E8	2-4D6F	
D	蜽	5-6530	1-5909			E-4949	232A4C
E	蜾	0-8268	1-5910		E3E2	2-4D69	232A57
F	蜿	0-8274	0-7379	1-7349	BB64	1-6A6C	215670

875

Code	Char	G	J	K	B	C	A
0	蝐	5-6574			E7B1	2-5378	
1	蝑	3-6660			E7AD	2-5374	
2	蝒	3-6647			E7AA	2-5371	
3	蝓	0-8285	0-7401		BDC2	1-6E6B	232B35
4	蝔				E7A8	2-536F	
5	蝕	1-4220	0-3110	0-6758	BB6B	1-6A73	215676
6	蝖	3-6659			E7A1	2-5368	
7	蝗	0-2740	0-7391	0-9257	BDC0	1-6E69	21567E
8	蝘	3-6645	1-5915		E7A7	2-536E	232A79
9	蝙	0-8289	0-7394	1-8209	BDBF	1-6E68	215721
A	蝚	3-6661			E7AC	2-5373	
B	蝛	5-6572			E7A9	2-5370	
C	蝜	5-6524			E7B9	2-5422	
D	蝝	3-6662	1-5916		E7B4	2-537B	232B2E
E	蝞				E7AE	2-5375	
F	蝟		0-7386	0-7458	E7B3	2-537A	232B28

877

Code	Char	G	J	K	B	C	A
0	蝰	0-8281					4D2925
1	蝱		1-5921			E-4E5D	232A6C
2	蝲	3-6646	1-5922				
3	蝳	5-6571			E7A6	2-536D	
4	蝴	0-2691	0-7390	0-9161	BDB9	1-6E62	215679
5	蝵	5-6580			E7BD	2-5426	
6	蝶	0-2191	0-3619	0-7942	BDBA	1-6E63	215678
7	蝷				E7A4	2-536B	
8	蝸	1-4647	0-7387	0-7236	BDBD	1-6E66	21567B
9	蝹	5-6576			EB64	2-5A32	
A	蝺	5-6582			E7B7	2-537E	
B	蝻	0-8279	1-5923		E7BC	2-5425	232A7B
C	蝼	0-8287					27572C
D	蝽	0-8277				E-4E59	232A74
E	蝾	0-8278					292C64
F	蝿		0-3972				4B5736

878

	Char	G	J	K	B	C	A
0	螀	8-1388					
1	螁				EB61	2-5A2F	
2	螂	0-8275	0-7407	0-5344	EDB8	1-6E61	215723
3	螃	0-8306	1-5924	1-6545	BFC0	1-722A	215722
4	螄	1-8247	1-5925		EB6B	2-5A39	232B55
5	螅	0-8303	1-5926		EB67	2-5A35	232B53
6	螆	5-6585	1-5927				
7	螇	3-6669	1-5928		EB65	2-5A33	
8	螈	0-8302	1-5929		EB60	2-5A2E	232B48
9	螉	3-6670	1-5930		EB6F	2-5A3D	232B5D
A	螊	3-6673				E-525B	
B	螋	0-8284	1-5931			E-525D	232B54
C	螌	3-6668	1-5932	1-6529			
D	融	0-4058	0-4527	0-7555	BFC4	1-722E	215726
E	螎					E-525F	
F	螏	5-6605			EB5C	2-5A2A	

87A

	Char	G	J	K	B	C	A
0	螠	3-6672	1-5940				
1	螡					E-525E	395652
2	螢	1-5109	0-7405	0-9111	BFC3	1-722D	215724
3	螣	3-4587	1-5941	1-6181	EB66	2-5A34	232B3A
4	螤				F0CB	2-5A28	
5	螥					E-6645	
6	螦						
7	螧		1-5942				
8	螨	0-8293					70727D
9	螩					E-6644	232B58
A	螪	5-6606			EE59	2-5F27	
B	螫	0-8307	0-7414		C1B1	1-753C	21572A
C	螬	0-8309	1-5943		EE5D	2-5F2B	232B72
D	螭	0-8304	1-5944	1-6365	EE5A	2-5F28	232B60
E	螮	3-6644	1-5945		EE61	2-5F2F	232B78
F	螯	0-8292	0-7408		EE67	2-5F35	232B6F

87C

	Char	G	J	K	B	C	A
0	蟀	0-8316	0-7411	1-6902	C1AC	1-7537	215729
1	蟁		1-5950			E-5639	335652
2	蟂	3-6638			EE64	2-5F32	
3	蟃	3-6681			EE63	2-5F31	
4	蟄	1-5361	0-7415	0-8662	EE68	2-5F36	232B6E
5	蟅	3-6682			EE5B	2-5F29	
6	蟆	0-8301	0-7418		C1B0	1-753B	215730
7	蟇		0-7417	1-6387		E-563B	2D5730
8	蟈	1-8269	1-5951		C1B4	1-753F	21572D
9	蟉	3-6689	1-5952		EE62	2-5F30	
A	蟊	0-8317	1-5953	1-6453	EE69	2-5F37	2F2A73
B	蟋	0-8312	0-7409	1-6987	C1B5	1-7540	215731
C	蟌	5-6613			EE65	2-5F33	
D	蟍					E-5636	
E	蟎	1-8293	1-5954			E-5634	
F	蟏	8-9394					

87E

	Char	G	J	K	B	C	A
0	蟠	0-8320	0-7422	0-5886	C2CF	1-773A	232C47
1	蟡	5-6485			E7A5	2-536C	
2	蟢	3-6691	1-5961		F0BD	2-6329	232C37
3	蟣	1-8217	1-5962	1-6001	F0CA	2-6336	232C4C
4	蟤	3-6706	1-5963		F0C4	2-6330	
5	蟥	0-8308			F0C1	2-632D	4D2C3C
6	蟦	3-6643			F0BC	2-6328	
7	蟧	3-6621			F0BB	2-6327	
8	蟨	5-1681			F0D0	2-633B	
9	蟩	3-6694				E-5873	
A	蟪	0-8319	1-5964		F0C0	2-632C	232C34
B	蟫	3-6693	1-5965		F0BF	2-632B	232C39
C	蟬	1-1885		0-6449	C2CD	1-7738	215734
D	蟭	5-6626	1-5966		F0C8	2-6334	
E	蟮	0-8321				E-5874	232C2C
F	蟯	1-8245	0-7420	0-7308	C2CC	1-7737	215732

879

	Char	G	J	K	B	C	A
0	螐		1-5933		EB68	2-5A36	
1	螑				EB69	2-5A37	
2	螒	3-8427			EB5F	2-5A2D	
3	螓	0-8291	1-5934		EB5E	2-5A2C	232B3D
4	螔	3-6667			EB6C	2-5A3A	
5	螕	5-6603	1-5935				
6	螖	3-6649			EB62	2-5A30	
7	螗	0-8305	1-5936		EB5D	2-5A2B	2D572B
8	螘	5-6517	1-5937	1-7444	EB63	2-5A31	232B4C
9	螙	5-3762	1-5938			E-5262	232B45
A	螚	3-6676			EB6E	2-5A3C	
B	螛	3-6674			EB5B	2-5A29	
C	螜	3-6663			EB6D	2-5A3B	
D	螝	3-6652			EB6A	2-5A38	
E	螞	1-3476	1-5939	1-6386	BFC2	1-722C	215725
F	螟	0-3588	0-7406	0-5713	BFC1	1-722B	215727

87B

	Char	G	J	K	B	C	A
0	螰	3-6684			EE5C	2-5F2A	
1	螱	3-6688	1-5946			E-563A	
2	螲	3-6687			EE70	2-5F3E	
3	螳	0-8311	0-7416	0-5157	C1AE	1-7539	21572B
4	螴	5-6546		1-7816	EE6A	2-5F38	
5	螵	0-8310	1-5947		EE5F	2-5F2D	2F2A64
6	螶	5-6592			EE6B	2-5F39	
7	螷				EE66	2-5F34	
8	螸				EE6D	2-5F3B	
9	螹	5-6553			EE5E	2-5F2C	
A	螺	0-3461	0-4570	0-5302	C1B3	1-753E	21572F
B	螻	1-8287	0-7419	1-6337	C1B2	1-753D	21572C
C	螼	5-6610			EE60	2-5F2E	
D	螽	0-8314	0-7410	1-7736	EE6E	2-5F3C	232C24
E	螾	3-6686	1-5948		EE58	2-5F26	232B66
F	螿	3-6656	1-5949		EE6C	2-5F3A	232B7E

87D

	Char	G	J	K	B	C	A
0	蟐		0-7412				696A2C
1	蟑	0-8315			C1AD	1-7538	215728
2	蟒	0-8294	0-7429	1-6413	C1AF	1-753A	21572E
3	蟓	0-8313			F0C7	2-6333	232C48
4	蟔	3-6703			F0C5	2-6331	
5	蟕	5-6632	1-5955			E-5B28	
6	蟖	5-6622	1-5956			E-5876	232C3A
7	蟗	5-6624			F0CC	2-6337	
8	蟘	5-6581			F0C9	2-6335	
9	蟙	3-6580	1-5957		F0CD	2-6338	
A	蟚	5-6621	1-5958	1-8201		E-5878	
B	蟛	0-8318		1-8202	F0BE	2-632A	232C36
C	蟜	3-6607	1-5959		F0C6	2-6332	232C49
D	蟝	5-6616			F0D1	2-633C	
E	蟞	3-6680			EE6F	2-5F3D	
F	蟟	3-6701	1-5960		F0C2	2-632E	

87F

	Char	G	J	K	B	C	A
0	蟰	5-6565				E-5875	232C31
1	蟱		1-5967				
2	蟲	1-1970	0-7421	0-8589	C2CE	1-7739	215733
3	蟳	3-6615	1-5968		F0C3	2-632F	232C30
4	蟴	3-6692			F0CF	2-633A	
5	蟵					E-6646	232C3F
6	蟶	1-8241	0-7426		F2DE	2-6669	232C55
7	蟷	3-6606	0-7427	1-6110	F2DF	2-666A	232C57
8	蟸		1-5969			E-5B2C	
9	蟹	0-4823	0-1910	0-9015	C3C9	1-7874	215738
A	蟺	3-6709	1-5970		F2DC	2-6667	
B	蟻	1-5047	0-2134	0-7592	C3C6	1-7871	215735
C	蟼	5-6623			F2E4	2-666F	
D	蟽					E-5B27	
E	蟾	0-8324	0-7425	0-6474	C3CA	1-7875	232C5F
F	蟿		1-5971		F2E6	2-6671	

Code	Char	G	J	K	B	C	A
8800	蠀	3-6671			F2DB	2-6666	
8801	蠁	3-6555	1-5972		F0CE	2-6339	232C4D
8802	蠂				F2E8	2-6673	
8803	蠃	0-5789	1-5973		F2DD	2-6668	232C4F
8804	蠄						
8805	蠅	1-5112	0-7404	0-6718	C3C7	1-7872	215736
8806	蠆	1-8218	1-5974		F2E3	2-666E	232C5D
8807	蠇					E-5B29	
8808	蠈				F2E5	2-6670	
8809	蠉	3-6707	1-5975		F2E0	2-666B	
880A	蠊	0-8325	1-5976		F2E7	2-6672	232C50
880B	蠋	3-6708	1-5977		F2E2	2-666D	232C5C
880C	蠌	3-6592			F2E1	2-666C	
880D	蠍		0-7424	1-5537	C3C8	1-7873	215737
880E	蠎		0-7428			E-5877	33572E
880F	蠏		0-7423			E-5B2B	335738
8810	蠐	1-8251	1-5978		F4C5	2-6971	232C61
8811	蠑	1-8278	0-7430	1-7174	F4C6	2-6972	232C64
8812	蠒		1-5980			E-5D25	
8813	蠓	0-8323	1-5981		F4C8	2-6974	232C6A
8814	蠔		1-5982		C4AE	1-7A39	215739
8815	蠕	0-4068	0-7432	1-7146	C4AF	1-7A3A	21573A
8816	蠖	0-8322	0-7431		F4C9	2-6975	232C6B
8817	蠗	3-6715			F4C7	2-6973	
8818	蠘	3-6712	1-5983			E-5D24	232C66
8819	蠙	3-6675	1-5979		F4C4	2-6970	232C63
881A	蠚	3-6713	1-5984			E-5E5D	
881B	蠛	0-8326	1-5985		F642	2-6C31	232C7A
881C	蠜	5-6641	1-5986		F645	2-6C34	232C73
881D	蠝	5-6643			F641	2-6C30	
881E	蠞		1-5987				
881F	蠟	1-3215	1-5988	0-5337	C4FA	1-7B27	21573E
8820	蠠				F643	2-6C32	
8821	蠡	0-8327	0-7434	1-6235	C4F9	1-7B26	21573D
8822	蠢	0-2032	0-7433	0-8167	C4F8	1-7B25	21573B
8823	蠣	1-8235	0-7358	0-5378	C4F7	1-7B24	21573C
8824	蠤				F644	2-6C33	
8825	蠥				F751	2-6D7E	
8826	蠦	3-6578			F74F	2-6D7C	
8827	蠧	5-2306	0-7438			E-5F5F	4B5740
8828	蠨	3-6678	1-5989		F74E	2-6D7B	232D23
8829	蠩	5-6607			F640	2-6C2F	
882A	蠪	3-5693			F750	2-6D7D	
882B	蠫				F646	2-6C35	
882C	蠬				F74D	2-6D7A	
882D	蠭	5-6645	1-5990			E-6045	232D32
882E	蠮	3-6718	1-5991		F7F9	2-6F48	232D2E
882F	蠯				F7D7	2-6F26	
8830	蠰	3-6719	1-5992		F7F7	2-6F46	
8831	蠱	1-2538	0-7435	0-4544	C5DB	1-7C47	21573F
8832	蠲	0-7835	1-5993	1-5628	F7F8	2-6F47	232D2A
8833	蠳	5-6612			F7FA	2-6F49	
8834	蠴					E-6647	232C72
8835	蠵	3-6721	1-5994		F8BF	2-704D	
8836	蠶	1-1847	0-7436	0-7757	C5FA	1-7C66	215741
8837	蠷	3-6720			F8BE	2-704C	
8838	蠸	3-6717			F8BD	2-704B	
8839	蠹	0-8328	0-7437	1-6170	C5FB	1-7C67	215740
883A	蠺		1-6001				
883B	蠻	1-3489	0-7439	0-5633	C65A	1-7D27	215742
883C	蠼	0-8329	1-6002		F96E	2-715D	232D3C
883D	蠽				F9A7	2-7175	
883E	蠾	3-6705			F9A6	2-7174	
883F	蠿				F9A8	2-7176	
8840	血	0-4910	0-2376	0-9076	A6E5	1-4866	215743
8841	衁	3-6943	1-6003		D0AA	2-2D4B	232D41
8842	衂		0-7441			E-2F26	232D42
8843	衃	5-6869	1-6004		D3CF	2-3271	
8844	衄	0-8412	0-7440	1-6058	D3D0	2-3272	232D44
8845	衅	0-4838	1-6005			E-386A	275D35
8846	衆	1-5458	0-2916	0-8175		E-3E6A	4B4D56
8847	衇					E-3E69	232D4B
8848	衈	3-6944	1-6006		DBC0	2-4026	
8849	衉	3-6945	1-6007				
884A	衊	1-8858	1-6008	1-6439	F647	2-6C36	232D51
884B	衋	3-7213	1-6009		F8C0	2-704E	
884C	行	0-4848	0-2552	0-9028	A6E6	1-4867	215744
884D	衍	0-4960	0-6207	0-7066	AD6C	1-534F	215745
884E	衎	3-2590	1-6010	1-5529	D0AB	2-2D4C	232D53
884F	衏	3-2592				E-3371	
8850	衐					E-6648	232D57
8851	衑		1-6011				
8852	衒	3-2603	0-7442	0-9069	D7B1	2-3934	232D56
8853	術	1-4285	0-2949	0-6690	B34E	1-5D34	215746
8854	衔	0-4746					275D61
8855	衕		1-6012		DBC2	2-4028	232D5A
8856	衖		1-6013		DBC1	2-4027	232D59
8857	街	0-2954	0-1925	0-4222	B5F3	1-6179	215747
8858	衘		1-6014			E-444D	
8859	衙	0-4935	0-7443	0-6823	B8C5	1-664C	215748
885A	衚		1-6015		E7C1	2-542A	232D5F
885B	衛	1-4632	0-1750	0-7459	BDC3	1-6E6C	215749
885C	衜	5-2846	1-6016			E-4E5F	232D5E
885D	衝	1-1969	0-3055	0-8590	BDC4	1-6E6D	21574A
885E	衞		0-7444	1-7363		E-5263	2D6749
885F	衟	5-2848	1-6017			E-5264	
8860	衠	3-2610	1-6018				
8861	衡	0-2666	0-2553	0-9112	BFC5	1-722F	21574B
8862	衢	0-6573	0-7445	0-4735	C5FC	1-7C68	21574C
8863	衣	0-5034	0-1665	0-7593	A6E7	1-4868	21574D
8864	衤	0-8134	1-6019				
8865	补	0-1825					275762
8866	衦	5-6930				E-2F27	
8867	衧	5-6931			D0AC	2-2D4D	
8868	表	0-1777	0-4129	0-8890	AAED	1-4F50	21574F
8869	衩	0-8135	1-6020		D0AE	2-2D4F	232D69
886A	衪	5-6936			D0AD	2-2D4E	
886B	衫	0-4132	0-7446	0-6325	AD6D	1-5350	215750
886C	衬	0-1936					275822
886D	衭	3-7010			D3D1	2-3273	232D6D
886E	衮	0-5782		1-5719		E-3374	2D575B
886F	衯	3-7019			D3D8	2-327A	
8870	衰	0-4305	0-3174	0-6581	B049	1-582E	215753
8871	衱	3-7009	1-6021		D3D6	2-3278	
8872	衲	0-8136	0-7453	0-5004	D3D4	2-3276	232D75
8873	衳	3-7020				E-3377	
8874	衴	3-7023			D3DB	2-327D	
8875	衵	3-7015	0-7450		D3D2	2-3274	232D71
8876	衶	3-7016			D3D3	2-3275	
8877	衷	0-5452	0-3579	0-8591	B04A	1-582F	215754
8878	衸	3-7017				E-3372	
8879	衹	1-5427	1-6022		B04E	1-5833	232D7C
887A	衺					E-3373	232D6E
887B	衻		1-6023			E-3375	
887C	衼	3-7013			D3DC	2-327E	
887D	衽	0-8137	0-7451	1-7474	B04D	1-5832	232D79
887E	衾	0-8432	0-7448	0-4858	D3DA	2-327C	232D7E
887F	衿	0-8138	0-2262	0-4859	D3D7	2-3279	232D7D

Code	Char	G	J	K	B	C	A
8880	袀	3-7021	1-6024		D3D5	2-3277	
8881	袁	0-5212	0-7447	0-7430	B04B	1-5830	215752
8882	袂	0-8139	0-7454	0-5717	B04C	1-5831	215751
8883	袃				D3D9	2-327B	
8884	袄	0-1632				E-3376	27577D
8885	袅	0-8433					513A47
8886	袆	8-9416					
8887	袇					E-6649	
8888	袈	0-8434	0-2322	0-4223	B350	1-5D36	215755
8889	袉	3-7044			D7B2	2-3935	
888A	袊	3-7039				E-3872	
888B	袋	0-2092	0-3462	0-5171	B355	1-5D3B	21575A
888C	袌	5-1949			D7C2	2-3945	232E3B
888D	袍	0-3759	0-7460	0-8869	B354	1-5D3A	215759
888E	袎	5-6947			D7C4	2-3947	
888F	袏	3-7029				E-386E	
8890	袐	5-6946				E-3874	232E3A
8891	袑	3-7047			D7B8	2-393B	
8892	袒	0-4427	0-7456	0-5118	B352	1-5D38	215757
8893	袓	3-7033			D7C3	2-3946	
8894	袔	3-7028				E-386C	
8895	袕	3-7043			D7B3	2-3936	
8896	袖	0-4868	0-3421	0-6632	B353	1-5D39	215758
8897	袗	3-7038	0-7455	0-8263	D7BF	2-3942	232E45
8898	袘	3-7036	1-6025		D7BB	2-393E	
8899	袙	5-6943	0-7458		D7BD	2-3940	232E40
889A	袚	5-6942	1-6026		D7B7	2-393A	232E34
889B	袛	3-7040	1-6027	1-7571	D7BE	2-3941	
889C	袜	0-4564	1-6028			E-386B	275821
889D	袝	3-7037		1-6638			
889E	袞		0-7449	0-4569	B34F	1-5D35	21575B
889F	袟		1-6029		D7BA	2-393D	
88A0	袠		1-6030			E-3873	232E3D
88A1	袡	3-7035			D7B9	2-393C	
88A2	袢	0-8140	0-7459	1-6559	D7B5	2-3938	232E28
88A3	袣	3-7026				E-386D	
88A4	袤	0-5783	0-7461		D7C0	2-3943	232E2A
88A5	袥	3-7030				E-386F	
88A6	袦	3-7046				E-3871	
88A7	袧	3-7041			D7BC	2-393F	
88A8	袨	3-7042	1-6031		D7B4	2-3937	
88A9	袩	3-7032				E-3870	
88AA	袪	3-7025	1-6032	1-5593	D7B6	2-3939	232E2F
88AB	被	0-1727	0-4079	0-8912	B351	1-5D37	215756
88AC	袬				D7C1	2-3944	
88AD	袭	0-4714					275823
88AE	袮		0-7457				4D3032
88AF	袯	8-1261					
88B0	袰		0-7462				696A5E
88B1	袱	0-2404	0-7464		B5F6	1-617C	21575E
88B2	袲	3-1853			DBCD	2-4033	232E51
88B3	袳	3-7061					
88B4	袴		0-2451	0-4545		E-3E70	335773
88B5	袵		0-7452			E-3E72	2F2D79
88B6	袶				DBC9	2-402F	
88B7	袷	0-8142	0-1633		DBCB	2-4031	232E57
88B8	袸	3-7054			DBC6	2-402C	
88B9	袹	3-7052			DBC5	2-402B	
88BA	袺	3-7051	1-6033		DBC3	2-4029	232E4A
88BB	袻	3-7053				E-3E6D	
88BC	袼	0-8143			DBCA	2-4030	232E54
88BD	袽	3-7066	1-6034		DBCC	2-4032	232E59
88BE	袾	3-7058	1-6035		DBC8	2-402E	
88BF	袿	3-7050	0-7463			E-3E6F	232E49
88C0	裀	3-7057	1-6036	1-7470	DBC7	2-402D	232E4F
88C1	裁	0-1835	0-2659	0-7814	B5F4	1-617A	21575C
88C2	裂	0-3349	0-4686	0-5414	B5F5	1-617B	21575D
88C3	裃		0-7465				696A61
88C4	裄		0-7466				232E5A
88C5	装	0-5516	0-3385	1-7543			275765
88C6	裆	0-8141					27577C
88C7	裇						
88C8	裈	8-9419					
88C9	裉	0-8144			DBCF	2-4035	232E48
88CA	裊	1-8433	1-6037	1-6050	B8CD	1-6654	4B3A47
88CB	裋	3-7068	1-6038		DFF2	2-4739	232E5E
88CC	裌		1-6039		DFF8	2-473F	232E60
88CD	裍	5-6953	1-6040	1-5720	DFF3	2-473A	
88CE	裎	0-8146	1-6041		DFF4	2-473B	232E64
88CF	裏	1-3279	0-4602	0-5574		E-444E	215763
88D0	裐				DFF9	2-4740	
88D1	裑	5-6954	1-6042				
88D2	裒	0-5786	1-6043	1-6639	B8CF	1-6656	232E68
88D3	裓	3-7067	1-6044				
88D4	裔	0-5065	0-7467	0-7164	B8C7	1-664E	215764
88D5	裕	0-5203	0-4521	0-7514	B8CE	1-6655	215766
88D6	裖	3-7071			DFF1	2-4738	
88D7	裗	5-6958			DBC4	2-402A	
88D8	裘	0-8435	0-7468	1-5871	B8CA	1-6651	215761
88D9	裙	0-4025	0-7469	0-4757	B8C8	1-664F	215760
88DA	裚	5-6928			DFF7	2-473E	
88DB	裛	3-1854	1-6045		DFF6	2-473D	232E62
88DC	補	1-1825	0-4268	0-6045	B8C9	1-6650	215762
88DD	裝	1-5516	0-7470	0-7791	B8CB	1-6652	215765
88DE	裞	3-7075	1-6046		DFF5	2-473C	
88DF	裟	0-8436	0-2632	0-6280	B8C6	1-664D	21575F
88E0	裠					E-444F	335760
88E1	裡		0-4603	0-5575	B8CC	1-6653	2D5763
88E2	裢	0-8145					292F60
88E3	裣	0-8147					29302D
88E4	裤	0-3167					275773
88E5	裥	0-8148					292F72
88E6	裦					E-4E60	
88E7	裧	5-6975	1-6047		E3F6	2-4D7D	
88E8	裨	0-8152	0-7475	0-6205	BB74	1-6A7C	21576D
88E9	裩	5-6968				E-4959	
88EA	裪	5-6974				E-4952	
88EB	裫	3-7107			E442	2-4E2A	
88EC	裬	5-6960			E441	2-4E29	
88ED	裭					E-4957	
88EE	裮	5-6969			E3FB	2-4E24	
88EF	裯	3-7080	1-6048	1-7754	BB76	1-6A7E	232F23
88F0	裰	0-8154	1-6049		E440	2-4E28	232E7A
88F1	裱	0-8149	1-6050	1-8244	E3F7	2-4D7E	232E71
88F2	裲	3-7069	0-7476		E3F8	2-4E21	232E75
88F3	裳	0-4149	0-3056	0-6355	BB6E	1-6A76	215768
88F4	裴	0-3765	0-7474	0-5948	BB70	1-6A78	21576B
88F5	裵		1-6051	0-5949		E-4954	
88F6	裶	5-6966			E3FD	2-4E26	
88F7	裷	3-7084	1-6052		E3F5	2-4D7C	
88F8	裸	0-3467	0-4571	0-5303	BB72	1-6A7A	215769
88F9	裹	0-2592	0-7471	1-5753	BB71	1-6A79	21576A
88FA	裺	3-7078			E3F9	2-4E22	
88FB	裻	3-7005			E3FE	2-4E27	
88FC	裼	0-8151	0-7473		E3FC	2-4E25	232F21
88FD	製	1-8905	0-3229	0-8018	BB73	1-6A7B	21576C
88FE	裾	0-8153	0-3194	1-5594	E3FA	2-4E23	232E72
88FF	裿	3-7077				E-4951	

Code	Char	G	J	K	B	C	A
8900	褀	5-6961				E-4956	232E78
8901	褁		1-6053		DBCE	2-4034	
8902	褂	0-2551	0-7472		BB6F	1-6A77	215767
8903	褃	5-6967				E-4958	232F24
8904	褄		0-7477	1-7904			696A6D
8905	褅	5-6988			E7C2	2-542B	
8906	褆	3-7102	1-6054		E7C9	2-5432	232F35
8907	複	1-8820	0-4203	0-6060	BDC6	1-6E6F	393D6F
8908	褈	3-7106					
8909	褉	5-6977			E7CD	2-5436	232F2D
890A	褊	0-8159	0-7479	1-8210	BDCA	1-6E73	232F3D
890B	褋	3-7091			E7C5	2-542E	
890C	褌	3-7064	0-7478	1-5721	E7C3	2-542C	232F36
890D	褍	3-7104	1-6055				
890E	褎	3-1856	1-6056		E7CC	2-5435	2D5758
890F	褏	5-1957	1-6057			E-4E61	
8910	褐	0-2654	0-1976	0-4272	BDC5	1-6E6E	21576F
8911	褑	3-7110			E7CB	2-5434	
8912	褒	0-1693	0-4311	0-8870	BDC7	1-6E70	215772
8913	褓	0-8157	0-7480	0-6046	BDC8	1-6E71	215771
8914	褔	3-7092			E7C4	2-542D	
8915	褕	3-7109	1-6058	1-7394	BDC9	1-6E72	232F43
8916	褖	3-7113	1-6059		E7CA	2-5433	
8917	褗	5-6980			E7C6	2-542F	
8918	褘	3-7011	1-6060	0-7460	E7C7	2-5430	232F2F
8919	褙	0-8156	1-6061	0-5950	E7C8	2-5431	232F37
891A	褚	0-8150	1-6062	1-7572	BB75	1-6A7D	21576E
891B	褛	0-8158				E-4E62	275779
891C	褜		1-6063				
891D	褝		0-7492				4D2F7A
891E	褞	5-6983	0-7482		EB70	2-5A3E	232F54
891F	褟	3-7117			EB7C	2-5A4A	232F51
8920	褠	3-7114	1-6064				
8921	褡	0-8155			BFCA	1-7234	232F4E
8922	褢	5-1958			EB77	2-5A45	232F57
8923	褣	5-7005			EB79	2-5A47	
8924	褤	5-6990				E-5265	
8925	褥	0-4076	0-7483	0-7319	BFC8	1-7232	215775
8926	褦	3-7120	1-6065		EB71	2-5A3F	232F56
8927	褧	3-7006	1-6066	1-5657	EB75	2-5A43	232F4F
8928	褨	3-7111	1-6067				
8929	褩				EB78	2-5A46	
892A	褪	0-4542	0-7484	0-8759	BFC6	1-7230	215774
892B	褫	0-8161	0-7485	1-8083	BFC9	1-7233	215776
892C	褬				EB7B	2-5A49	
892D	褭				EB73	2-5A41	
892E	褮	3-7004			EB74	2-5A42	
892F	褯	3-7119			EB7A	2-5A48	232F45
8930	褰	0-6929	1-6068	1-5605	EB72	2-5A40	232F47
8931	褱	5-1961	1-6069		EB76	2-5A44	232F53
8932	褲	1-3167	1-6070		BFC7	1-7231	215773
8933	褳	1-8145			EE72	2-5F40	232F60
8934	褴	0-8160					275771
8935	褵	5-7002	1-6071		EE71	2-5F3F	232F5A
8936	褶	0-8162	0-7489	0-6708	C1B7	1-7542	215778
8937	褷	3-7126			EE77	2-5F45	
8938	褸	1-8158	0-7490	0-5514	C1B9	1-7544	215779
8939	褹	5-7007	1-6072			E-5640	
893A	褺	5-6926	1-6073	1-7956			
893B	褻	1-5784	0-7488	0-6465	C1B6	1-7541	215777
893C	褼	3-7130			EE73	2-5F41	
893D	褽	3-7007			C1BA	1-7545	
893E	褾	3-7122	1-6074		EE74	2-5F42	
893F	褿	3-7121				E-563F	
8940	襀	3-7076	1-6075			E-563D	
8941	襁	0-8163	0-7486	0-4326	EE75	2-5F43	232F5D
8942	襂	3-7089	1-6076		EE78	2-5F46	
8943	襃		0-7481			E-5642	335772
8944	襄	0-4769	0-7487	0-6949	C1B8	1-7543	21577A
8945	襅		1-6077				
8946	襆	3-7133	1-6078		F0D6	2-6341	232F7B
8947	襇	1-8148					232F72
8948	襈	3-7139				E-5879	
8949	襉		1-6079		F0D9	2-6344	
894A	襊	3-7134				E-587A	
894B	襋	3-7131			F0D3	2-633E	
894C	襌	3-7085	0-7491		F0D5	2-6340	232F7A
894D	襍		0-8023	1-7529		E-587C	233021
894E	襎	3-7135				E-587B	
894F	襏	3-7048	1-6080		F0D4	2-633F	232F6F
8950	襐	3-7127			F0D7	2-6342	
8951	襑	5-6952			F0D8	2-6343	
8952	襒	3-7124	1-6081		EE76	2-5F44	
8953	襓	5-6948			F0D2	2-633D	
8954	襔					E-664A	232F66
8955	襕	8-1262					
8956	襖	1-1632	0-1808	1-7218	C3CD	1-7878	21577D
8957	襗	3-7049	1-6082		F2BC	2-6677	
8958	襘	3-7060		1-5810	F2EF	2-667A	
8959	襙				F2F1	2-667C	
895A	襚	3-7137	1-6083		F2EA	2-6675	233024
895B	襛	3-7065	1-6084		F2EB	2-6676	233029
895C	襜	3-7142	1-6085	1-7951	F2EE	2-6679	23302C
895D	襝	1-8147			F2F0	2-667B	23302D
895E	襞	0-8437	0-7494	1-6568	C3CE	1-7879	233025
895F	襟	0-2983	0-2263	0-4860	C3CC	1-7877	21577B
8960	襠	1-8141	0-7493	1-6111	C3CB	1-7876	21577C
8961	襡	3-7141	1-6086		F2ED	2-6678	
8962	襢		1-6087		F2E9	2-6674	233023
8963	襣	3-7143	1-6088		F4CA	2-6976	
8964	襤	1-8160	0-7502	0-5333	C4B0	1-7A3B	21577E
8965	襥					E-5D29	
8966	襦	0-8164	0-7501		F4CB	2-6977	233031
8967	襧					E-5D28	
8968	襨						
8969	襩	5-6964			F649	2-6C38	
896A	襪	1-4564	0-7504	0-5642	C4FB	1-7B28	215821
896B	襫	3-7144	1-6089		F64B	2-6C3A	23303A
896C	襬	1-8801			C4FC	1-7B29	23303C
896D	襭	3-7129	0-7503	1-8534	F648	2-6C37	233037
896E	襮	3-7145	1-6090		F64A	2-6C39	23303B
896F	襯	1-1936	0-7505	1-8101	C5A8	1-7B72	215822
8970	襰	5-7019	1-6091				
8971	襱	3-7031			F752	2-6E21	
8972	襲	1-4714	0-2917	0-6709	C5A7	1-7B71	215823
8973	襳	3-7147	1-6092		F7FD	2-6F4C	
8974	襴	3-7136	0-7506	1-6204	F7FC	2-6F4B	233042
8975	襵	5-6992	1-6093				
8976	襶	3-7146			F7FB	2-6F4A	233041
8977	襷		0-7507				696B27
8978	襸	5-7023				E-6149	
8979	襹	3-7070			F948	2-7137	
897A	襺		1-6094		F949	2-7138	
897B	襻	0-8165	1-6101		F94B	2-713A	233049
897C	襼	3-7012	1-6102		F94A	2-7139	23304A
897D	襽		1-6103			E-617D	
897E	襾	8-0892	0-7508		CA50	2-2270	4B5824
897F	西	0-4687	0-3230	0-6404	A6E8	1-4869	215824

898

	Char	G	J	K	B	C	A
0	覀	8-1589					
1	要	0-5010	0-4555	0-7309	AD6E	1-5351	215825
2	覂	3-6463			D7C5	2-3948	
3	覃	0-8191	0-7509	0-5139	B5F7	1-617D	215826
4	覄					E-664B	233053
5	覅	3-6464			DFFA	2-4741	233055
6	覆	0-2418	0-4204	0-6061	C2D0	1-773B	3F3D6F
7	覇		0-3938	0-8814		E-5B2F	395F68
8	覈		0-7510	1-8329	F2F2	2-667D	394444
9	覉	5-6372	1-6104	1-6002		E-6046	335238
A	覊		0-7511			E-614A	2D5238
B	見	1-2891	0-2411	0-4424	A8A3	1-4B44	215828
C	覌					E-2F29	
D	覍		1-6105				
E	覎	5-4258					
F	規	1-2570	0-2112	0-4814	B357	1-5D3D	215829

899

	Char	G	J	K	B	C	A
0	覐		1-6106				
1	覑	3-4410				E-3876	233062
2	覒	3-4362				E-3875	
3	覓	1-3557	0-7512	0-5682	B356	1-5D3C	21582A
4	覔		1-6107			E-3877	
5	覕	5-4264	1-6108		DBD0	2-4036	
6	視	1-4251	0-2775	0-6742	B5F8	1-617E	21582B
7	覗	5-4265	0-3933	1-6755	DBD2	2-4038	233064
8	覘	1-7472	0-7513	1-7641	DBD1	2-4037	233066
9	覙	3-4063					
A	覚		0-1948			E-3E74	4B5830
B	覛	5-4266	1-6109		DFFB	2-4742	
C	覜		1-6110		B8D0	1-6657	23306B
D	覝	5-4268			E443	2-4E2B	
E	覞	3-4061			E446	2-4E2E	
F	覟	5-4269	1-6111		E445	2-4E2D	

89A

	Char	G	J	K	B	C	A
0	覠	3-4071	1-6112				
1	覡	1-7474	0-7514	0-4415	E444	2-4E2C	23306F
2	覢	5-4274			E7CE	2-5437	
3	覣	3-4074			E7D0	2-5439	
4	覤	5-6460			E7CF	2-5438	
5	覥	5-4272	1-6113			E-4E65	233076
6	覦	1-7476	0-7516		BFCC	1-7236	21582D
7	覧		0-4587			E-5266	2D5831
8	覨			1-7020			
9	覩		0-7515	0-5213		E-4E64	233079
A	親	1-3955	0-3138	0-8649	BFCB	1-7235	21582C
B	覫	3-4079				E-5646	
C	覬	1-7473	0-7517	1-6003	C1BB	1-7546	21582E
D	覭	3-4080			EE79	2-5F47	
E	覮				EE7B	2-5F49	
F	覯	1-7477	0-7518	1-5872	EE7A	2-5F48	23307D

89B

	Char	G	J	K	B	C	A
0	覰	5-4282	1-6114			E-587E	
1	覱	3-4073				E-587D	
2	覲	1-7478	0-7519	0-4844	C2D1	1-773C	21582F
3	観		0-2049			E-5921	4B5832
4	覴	5-4287	1-6115				
5	覵		1-6116			E-5B31	23312A
6	覶	5-4285	1-6117		F2F4	2-6721	23312C
7	覷	1-7479	1-6118	1-7905	F2F3	2-667E	23312B
8	覸	3-4070					
9	覹	5-4289			F4CC	2-6978	
A	覺	1-3085	0-7520	0-4238	C4B1	1-7A3C	215830
B	覻	5-4288				E-5D2A	2F312B
C	覼		1-6119			E-5E61	23312F
D	覽	1-3232	0-7521	0-5334	C4FD	1-7B2A	215831
E	覾	5-4275			F754	2-6E23	
F	覿	1-7475	0-7522	1-7581	F753	2-6E22	233132

89C

	Char	G	J	K	B	C	A
0	觀	1-2559	0-7523	0-4626	C65B	1-7D28	215832
1	见	0-2891					275828
2	观	0-2559					275832
3	觃	8-1447					
4	规	0-2570					275829
5	觅	0-3557					27582A
6	视	0-4251					27582B
7	觇	0-7472					293066
8	览	0-3232					275831
9	觉	0-3085					275830
A	觊	0-7473					27582E
B	觋	0-7474					29306F
C	觌	0-7475					293132
D	觍	8-1448					
E	觎	0-7476					27582D
F	觏	0-7477					29307D

89D

	Char	G	J	K	B	C	A
0	觐	0-7478					27582F
1	觑	0-7479					29312B
2	角	0-2939	0-1949	0-4239	A8A4	1-4B45	215833
3	觓	5-8092			D0AF	2-2D50	
4	觔	8-1292	1-6120	1-5951	AD6F	1-5352	334260
5	觕		1-6121		D7C8	2-394B	23313B
6	觖	0-8591	1-6122	1-5631	D7C6	2-3949	23313A
7	觗		1-6123				
8	觘	3-8222	1-6124				
9	觙	5-8094			D7C7	2-394A	
A	觚	0-8593	0-7524	1-5701	DBD4	2-403A	23313F
B	觛	5-8105			DBD5	2-403B	
C	觜	0-8594	0-7525	1-7501	E043	2-4749	233145
D	觝	3-8224	0-7526	1-7573	DBD3	2-4039	334A58
E	觞	0-8592					275835
F	觟	3-8229			DFFC	2-4743	

89E

	Char	G	J	K	B	C	A
0	觠	5-8110			E041	2-4747	
1	觡	3-8232			E040	2-4746	233147
2	觢	3-8228			E042	2-4748	
3	解	0-2966	0-1882	0-9016	B8D1	1-6658	215834
4	觤	5-8109			DFFE	2-4745	
5	觥	0-8601	1-6125	1-5813	DFFD	2-4744	233143
6	触	0-2005	0-3108		E044	2-474A	2D5836
7	觧		0-7527			E-4454	335834
8	觨				E449	2-4E31	
9	觩	3-8234	1-6126		E447	2-4E2F	23314C
A	觪	3-8235				E-495C	
B	觫	0-8602	1-6127		E448	2-4E30	23314D
C	觬	3-8238			E7D3	2-543C	
D	觭	3-8236	1-6128		E7D1	2-543A	233153
E	觮	5-8120				E-4E66	
F	觯	0-8603					293160

89F

	Char	G	J	K	B	C	A
0	觰	5-8115			E7D2	2-543B	
1	觱	3-8242	1-6129	1-8263	EB7D	2-5A4B	233158
2	觲	5-8127			EE7C	2-5F4A	
3	觳	0-7618	1-6130	1-5712	EE7D	2-5F4B	23315C
4	觴	1-8592	0-7528	0-6356	C2D2	1-773D	215835
5	觵	5-8128				E-5B32	23315E
6	觶	1-8603	1-6131		F2F5	2-6722	233160
7	觷	3-8226			F4CD	2-6979	233164
8	觸	1-2005	0-7529	0-8526	C4B2	1-7A3D	215836
9	觹		1-6132				
A	觺	3-8248			F64C	2-6C3B	
B	觻	3-8225			F755	2-6E24	
C	觼	5-8133			C5A9	1-7B73	
D	觽		1-6133				
E	觾	5-8135			F7FE	2-6F4D	
F	觿	3-8250	1-6134		F94C	2-713B	23316B

8A0

	Char	G	J	K	B	C	A
0	言	0-4952	0-2432	0-6975	A8A5	1-4B46	215837
1	訁	1-5805					
2	訂	1-2209	0-3691	0-7984	AD71	1-5354	215839
3	訃	1-2428	0-7530	0-6121	AD72	1-5355	21583A
4	訄	3-8251	1-6135		D0B0	2-2D51	23316E
5	訅	5-8149	1-6136			E-2F2A	
6	訆	5-8151				E-2F2C	23316C
7	訇	0-5774	1-6137	1-5814	D0B1	2-2D52	23316D
8	計	1-2838	0-2355	0-4510	AD70	1-5353	215838
9	訉	5-8154		1-6563			
A	訊	1-4922	0-3154	0-6782	B054	1-5839	215840
B	訋	3-8259				E-337B	
C	訌	1-5807	0-7533	0-9187	B052	1-5837	21583E
D	訍	3-8263				E-337A	233173
E	討	1-4454	0-3804	0-8748	B051	1-5836	21583D
F	訏	3-8257	1-6138		B058	1-583D	233170

8A1

	Char	G	J	K	B	C	A
0	訐	1-5806	0-7532	1-7032	B050	1-5835	21583B
1	訑	3-8260	1-6139	1-7453	B059	1-583E	233171
2	訒	3-8262	1-6140		D3DD	2-3321	233172
3	訓	1-4921	0-2317	0-9326	B056	1-583B	215843
4	訔	3-2491	1-6141	1-7424			
5	訕	1-5808	1-6142	1-6772	B053	1-5838	21583F
6	訖	1-3893	0-7531	0-9365	B057	1-583C	215841
7	託		0-3487	0-8694	B055	1-583A	215842
8	記	1-2839	0-2113	0-4932	B04F	1-5834	21583C
9	訙					E-337C	
A	訚	8-9114					
B	訛	1-2279	0-7534	0-7237	B35F	1-5D45	21584A
C	訜	5-8168				E-387E	
D	訝	1-4940	0-7535	0-6824	B359	1-5D3F	215846
E	訞	3-8270	1-6143		D7CC	2-394F	
F	訟	1-4347	0-3057	0-6572	B35E	1-5D44	21584B

8A2

	Char	G	J	K	B	C	A
0	訠	5-8173	1-6144			E-3923	
1	訡					E-3929	
2	訢	3-8271	1-6145	1-8509	B360	1-5D46	233225
3	訣	1-3087	0-2377	0-4433	B35A	1-5D40	215845
4	訤		1-6146				
5	訥	1-5811	0-7536	0-5077	B35B	1-5D41	215847
6	訦	5-8171	1-6147			E-3879	
7	訧	5-8160			D7CA	2-394D	23317A
8	訨	3-8267				E-387B	
9	訩	3-8274				E-3925	23317D
A	訪	1-2335	0-4312	0-5930	B358	1-5D3E	215844
B	訫	5-8172	1-6148			E-3922	
C	訬	3-8268	1-6149		D7CB	2-394E	
D	設	1-4172	0-3263	0-6466	B35D	1-5D43	215849
E	訮	3-8264				E-6330	
F	訯		1-6150				

8A3

	Char	G	J	K	B	C	A
0	訰	5-8161			D7C9	2-394C	
1	許	1-4877	0-2186	0-9041	B35C	1-5D42	215848
2	訲	3-8269				E-387A	
3	訳		0-4485				4B5946
4	訴	1-4363	0-3342	0-6545	B644	1-622B	215856
5	訵	5-8182	1-6151			E-3E7C	
6	訶	1-5813	0-7537	0-4224	B646	1-622D	2D356A
7	訷	5-8178	1-6152				
8	訸	3-8285				E-3E7D	
9	訹	3-8280			DBD8	2-403E	
A	診	1-5379	0-3139	0-8264	B645	1-622C	215857
B	註		0-3580	0-8141	B5F9	1-6221	21584C
C	証		0-3058	1-7664	B5FD	1-6225	39593F
D	訽	5-8188	1-6153			E-3F24	233240
E	訾	0-8604	1-6154	1-7502	B8E4	1-666B	233258
F	訿	3-8306			E049	2-474F	

8A4

	Char	G	J	K	B	C	A
0	詀	3-8281	1-6155		DBDA	2-4040	
1	詁	1-5812	0-7538	1-5702	B5FE	1-6226	215851
2	詂	5-8185				E-3E7E	
3	詃	5-8190	1-6156			E-3E75	
4	詄	3-8284			DBDD	2-4043	
5	詅	3-8286	1-6157		DBDE	2-4044	233242
6	詆	1-5814	0-7541	1-7574	B643	1-622A	215855
7	詇	3-8282	1-6158				
8	詈	0-7826	0-7542		DBE0	2-4046	233239
9	詉	5-8193	1-6159			E-3F21	
A	詊	3-8289			DBE2	2-4048	233228
B	詋	5-8180		1-7755		E-3F23	
C	詌	5-8174			DBE3	2-4049	
D	詍	3-8279	1-6160		DBD7	2-403D	
E	詎	1-5810	1-6161		DBD6	2-403C	23322A
F	詏	5-8202			DBE4	2-404A	

8A5

	Char	G	J	K	B	C	A
0	詐	1-5309	0-2630	0-6281	B642	1-6229	215854
1	詑	3-8291	0-3434	1-7454	DBE1	2-4047	233227
2	詒	1-5817	0-7540		DBDF	2-4045	23323C
3	詓	3-8278	1-6162				
4	詔	1-5815	0-3059	0-8063	B640	1-6227	215852
5	評	1-3832	0-4130	0-8836	B5FB	1-6223	21584E
6	詖	3-8301	1-6163	1-8252	B647	1-622E	233230
7	詗	3-8283	1-6164	1-8366	DBDB	2-4041	233237
8	詘	1-5816	1-6165	1-5894	DBDC	2-4042	23323B
9	詙				DBD9	2-403F	
A	詚	5-8176				E-3E78	
B	詛	1-5571	0-7539	0-7844	B641	1-6228	215853
C	詜	3-8294	1-6166				
D	詝	3-8276	1-6167			E-3F22	
E	詞	1-2042	0-2776	0-6282	B5FC	1-6224	21584F
F	詟	8-9341					

8A6

	Char	G	J	K	B	C	A
0	詠		0-1751	0-7141	B5FA	1-6222	21584D
1	詡	1-5828	1-6168	1-8471	E048	2-474E	233256
2	詢	1-4915	0-7546	0-6683	B8DF	1-6666	215865
3	詣	1-5072	0-2356	0-7165	B8DA	1-6661	21585E
4	詤					E-4460	
5	詥	3-8314	1-6169			E-4459	
6	試	1-4252	0-2778	0-6743	B8D5	1-665C	21585B
7	詧		1-6170			E-4463	2D3B33
8	詨	3-8319			B8E5	1-666C	
9	詩	1-4211	0-2777	0-6744	B8D6	1-665D	21585C
A	詪	3-8321				E-4455	
B	詫	1-1879	0-4745	1-8118	B8D2	1-6659	215858
C	詬	1-5824	0-7545	1-5873	B8E1	1-6668	215868
D	詭	1-2578	0-7544	0-4788	B8DE	1-6665	215863
E	詮	1-5825	0-3307	0-7912	B8E0	1-6667	215867
F	詯	3-8312				E-4458	

8A7

	Char	G	J	K	B	C	A
0	詰	1-5821	0-2145	0-9394	B8D7	1-665E	21585D
1	話	1-2716	0-4735	0-9205	B8DC	1-6663	215866
2	該	1-2435	0-1926	0-9017	B8D3	1-665A	215859
3	詳	1-4774	0-3060	0-6357	B8D4	1-665B	21585A
4	詴	5-8207			E050	2-4756	
5	詵	1-5823	1-6171	0-6450	E04D	2-4753	23325E
6	詶		1-6172		E045	2-474B	335D23
7	詷	3-8307	1-6173		E04A	2-4750	
8	詸	5-8221				E-445B	
9	詹	0-5318	1-6174	0-8458	B8E2	1-6669	215864
A	詺	5-8218	1-6175		E051	2-4757	
B	詻	3-8316	1-6176		B8E3	1-666A	2D3632
C	詼	1-5822	0-7543	1-8448	B8D9	1-6660	21585F
D	詽					E-445C	
E	詾	5-8217	1-6177			E-4461	2F317D
F	詿	1-5820	1-6178	1-5803	E047	2-474D	23324F

8A8

	Char	G	J	K	B	C	A
0	誀	5-8203	1-6179			E-4456	
1	誁	3-8320			E04F	2-4755	
2	誂	3-8315	0-7548	1-7718	E04B	2-4751	233259
3	誃	3-8317	1-6180		E04E	2-4754	
4	誄	1-5819	0-7549	1-6316	E04C	2-4752	23325D
5	誅	1-5479	0-7547	0-8142	B8DD	1-6664	215862
6	誆	1-5818	1-6181	1-5792	E046	2-474C	233250
7	誇	1-3168	0-2456	0-4603	B8D8	1-665F	215861
8	誈					E-445D	
9	誉	0-5194	0-4532				275949
A	誊	0-4460					275937
B	誋	3-8339	1-6182		E44C	2-4E34	
C	誌		0-2779	0-8228	BB78	1-6B22	21586D
D	認	1-4047	0-3907	0-7667	BB7B	1-6B25	215870
E	誎	3-8326				E-495F	
F	誏	5-8231	1-6183		E44E	2-4E36	233269

8A9

	Char	G	J	K	B	C	A
0	誐	3-8335	1-6184			E-4964	
1	誑	1-5831	0-7552	1-5793	BBA5	1-6B2D	215875
2	誒	1-5832	1-6185		E44D	2-4E35	333642
3	誓	0-4236	0-3232	0-6405	BB7D	1-6B27	21586E
4	誔	3-8308				E-4963	
5	誕	1-2114	0-3534	0-8711	BDCF	1-6E78	215923
6	誖		1-6186		E44F	2-4E37	23326F
7	誗	3-8333	1-6187				
8	誘	1-5153	0-4522	0-7515	BBA4	1-6B2C	215874
9	誙	3-8302	1-6188		E44B	2-4E33	
A	誚	1-5829	0-7555	1-7988	BBA6	1-6B2E	233271
B	誛	3-8338				E-495E	
C	誜	3-8341				E-4962	
D	誝					E-496B	
E	語	1-5179	0-2476	0-6962	BB79	1-6B23	21586C
F	誟		1-6189			E-4968	

8AA

	Char	G	J	K	B	C	A
0	誠	1-1947	0-3231	0-6504	B8DB	1-6662	215860
1	誡	1-2975	0-7551	0-4511	BB7C	1-6B26	21586B
2	誢			1-8352		E-4960	
3	誣	1-4660	0-7556	0-5784	BB7A	1-6B24	21586F
4	誤	1-4683	0-2477	0-7206	BB7E	1-6B28	215871
5	誥	1-5830	0-7553	0-4546	BBA2	1-6B2A	215873
6	誦	1-4348	0-7554	0-6573	BB77	1-6B21	21586A
7	誧	3-8325	1-6190	1-8231	BBA7	1-6B2F	
8	誨	1-2769	0-7550	0-9279	BBA3	1-6B2B	215872
9	誩		1-6191			E-4965	
A	說			0-6467	BBA1	1-6B29	215869
B	誫				E44A	2-4E32	
C	説	1-4321	0-3266			E-4966	
D	読		0-3841				4B594A
E	誮		1-6192				
F	誯	5-8239	1-6193			E-4E74	233331

8AB

	Char	G	J	K	B	C	A
0	誰	1-4313	0-3515	0-6633	BDD6	1-6F21	215922
1	誱	5-8237				E-4E67	
2	課	1-3146	0-1861	0-4604	BDD2	1-6E7B	21587C
3	誳	3-8355	1-6194			E-4E72	
4	誴	5-8245				E-4E70	
5	誵					E-4E6E	
6	誶	1-5839	1-6201		BDD9	1-6F24	23327E
7	誷	3-8348	1-6202			E-4E6C	
8	誸	3-8356			E7D6	2-543F	
9	誹	1-2344	0-4080	0-6206	BDDA	1-6F25	233338
A	誺	3-8328			E7E2	2-544B	
B	誻	5-8248	1-6203		E7DB	2-5444	
C	誼	1-5074	0-2135	0-7594	BDCB	1-6E74	215876
D	誽	3-8350			E7E3	2-544C	
E	誾	3-2703	1-6204	0-7561	E7DD	2-5446	233321
F	調	1-2187	0-3620	0-8064	BDD5	1-6E7E	21587D

8AC

	Char	G	J	K	B	C	A
0	諀	3-8352			E7DE	2-5447	
1	諁	3-8358				E-4E73	
2	諂	1-5838	0-7559	0-8459	BDD4	1-6E7D	215921
3	諃	3-8344	1-6205		E7E1	2-544A	
4	諄	1-5527	0-7557	0-6684	BDCE	1-6E77	215877
5	諅	5-8138			E7DF	2-5448	
6	諆	3-8342	1-6206		E7D5	2-543E	233327
7	談	1-4424	0-3544	0-5140	BDCD	1-6E76	215879
8	諈	3-8349	1-6207		EBAA	2-5A56	
9	諉	1-5835	1-6208	1-7364	BDD3	1-6E7C	21587E
A	諊	5-8243	1-6209			E-4E75	
B	請	1-3975	0-3233	0-8475	BDD0	1-6E79	21587A
C	諌		0-2050			E-4E69	2D5927
D	諍	1-5826	0-7558	0-7821	BDD8	1-6F23	233336
E	諎	3-8343				E-4E6A	
F	諏	1-5833	0-3159	0-8556	E7D4	2-543D	233325

8AD

	Char	G	J	K	B	C	A
0	諐					E-4E76	23333F
1	諑	1-5834	1-6210		E7D8	2-5441	23332C
2	諒	1-3334	0-4642	0-5363	BDCC	1-6E75	215878
3	諓	3-8277	1-6211		E7D7	2-5440	23332D
4	諔	3-8346	1-6212		E7D9	2-5442	233333
5	諕	3-8347	1-6213		E7DA	2-5443	
6	論	1-3459	0-4732	0-5469	BDD7	1-6F22	215924
7	諗	1-5837	1-6214		E7DC	2-5445	233340
8	諘	5-8234			E7E0	2-5449	
9	諙				E7E4	2-544D	
A	諚		0-7560				696B5C
B	諛	1-5836	0-7571	0-7516	BDDB	1-6F26	23333B
C	諜	1-2193	0-3621	0-8467	BFD2	1-723C	21592A
D	諝	3-8371	1-6215		EBA5	2-5A51	23334C
E	諞	1-5850	0-7570	1-8211	EBAB	2-5A57	233362
F	諟	5-8254	1-6216	1-6968	EBA8	2-5A54	233353

8AE

	Char	G	J	K	B	C	A
0	諠		0-7567	1-8483	EB7E	2-5A4C	39365A
1	諡		0-7575	0-6745	EBAC	2-5A58	233363
2	諢	1-5827	0-7568		EBA1	2-5A4D	233345
3	諣	3-8332				E-526A	
4	諤	1-5844	0-7564	1-7021	EBA7	2-5A53	233357
5	諥	5-8255				E-526B	
6	諦	1-5848	0-3692	0-8484	BFCD	1-7237	215925
7	諧	1-4819	0-7563	0-9018	BFD3	1-723D	215929
8	諨				EBAD	2-5A59	
9	諩					E-4E6F	2D593D
A	諪			0-7985		E-5267	
B	諫	1-5841	0-7561	0-4263	BFCF	1-7239	215927
C	諬		1-6217			E-526E	
D	諭	1-5845	0-4501	0-7517	BFD9	1-7243	215930
E	諮	1-5849	0-2780	0-7731	BFD4	1-723E	2D3622
F	諯	3-8365			EBAF	2-5A5B	

8AF

	Char	G	J	K	B	C	A
0	諰	3-8364	1-6218	1-6969	EBA9	2-5A55	
1	諱	1-2768	0-7565	0-9341	BFD0	1-723A	215928
2	諲	3-8360			EBA2	2-5A4E	
3	諳	1-5847	0-7562	1-7043	BFDA	1-7244	233344
4	諴	3-8361	1-6219	1-8302	EBA3	2-5A4F	23334F
5	諵	5-8252	1-6220		EBA4	2-5A50	233350
6	諶	1-5840	1-6221	0-6806	BFDB	1-7245	23334E
7	諷	1-2377	0-7569	0-8904	BFD8	1-7242	21592F
8	諸	1-5478	0-2984	0-8019	BDD1	1-6E7A	21587B
9	諹	3-8261				E-5269	
A	諺	1-4972	0-2433	0-6976	BFCE	1-7238	215926
B	諻	3-8368			EBB0	2-5A5C	
C	諼	1-5846	1-6222	1-8484	BFDC	1-7246	23335D
D	諽	3-8359				E-5268	
E	諾	1-3721	0-3490	0-4971	BFD5	1-723F	21592E
F	諿	3-8362	1-6223		EBAE	2-5A5A	

8B0

	Char	G	J	K	B	C	A
0	謀	1-3617	0-4337	0-5739	BFD1	1-723B	21592B
1	謁	1-5843	0-1758	0-6855	BFD6	1-7240	21592C
2	謂	1-4629	0-1666	0-7461	BFD7	1-7241	21592D
3	謃					E-664C	233356
4	謄	1-4460	0-3805	0-5287	C1C3	1-754E	215937
5	謅	1-5463	1-6224		EEA4	2-5F50	23337A
6	謆	3-8383	1-6225		EEAD	2-5F59	233379
7	謇	0-6932	0-7573	1-5606	EEAA	2-5F56	233364
8	謈	3-4019			EEAC	2-5F58	
9	謉	3-8369				E-5649	
A	謊	1-2749	1-6231		C1C0	1-754B	215935
B	謋	3-8380	1-6226		EEA5	2-5F51	233378
C	謌		0-7572	1-5515		E-564A	23336B
D	謍	3-8252			EEAB	2-5F57	
E	謎	1-3553	0-3870	0-5826	C1BC	1-7547	215933
F	謏	3-8367			EEA7	2-5F53	23337C

8B1

	Char	G	J	K	B	C	A
0	謐	1-5855	0-7577	0-5845	C1C4	1-754F	23337D
1	謑	3-8379	1-6227	1-8375	EEA3	2-5F4F	
2	謒				EEA8	2-5F54	
3	謓	5-8264			EEAF	2-5F5B	
4	謔	1-5842	0-7566	0-8944	EBA6	2-5A52	233359
5	謕	5-8267			EEA9	2-5F55	
6	謖	1-5853	0-7576	0-6558	EEA2	2-5F4E	233373
7	謗	1-1689	0-7578	0-5931	C1BD	1-7548	215931
8	謘	5-8271			EEA1	2-5F4D	
9	謙	1-3911	0-2412	0-4437	C1BE	1-7549	215932
A	謚	1-5854	0-7574	0-7648	EEB0	2-5F5C	2F3363
B	講	1-2918	0-2554	0-4327	C1BF	1-754A	215934
C	謜	3-8376	1-6228	1-7350	EEAE	2-5F5A	23336F
D	謝	1-4827	0-2853	0-6283	C1C2	1-754D	215938
E	謞	3-8381	1-6229		EE7E	2-5F4C	
F	謟	3-8378	1-6230			E-5648	233376

8B2

	Char	G	J	K	B	C	A
0	謠		0-7579	0-7310	C1C1	1-754C	215936
1	謡	1-5005	0-4556				4B5936
2	謢				EEA6	2-5F52	
3	謣	3-8387		1-7328	F0DC	2-6347	
4	謤	3-8385			F0EA	2-6355	
5	謥	5-8276			F0E5	2-6350	
6	謦	0-8605	0-7582	1-5658	F0E7	2-6352	23342D
7	謧	3-8382			F0DB	2-6346	
8	謨	1-5851	0-7585	0-5740	C2D3	1-773E	21593B
9	謩					E-592A	23343A
A	謪	5-8279			F0DA	2-6345	
B	謫	1-5856	0-7583	0-7867	C2D6	1-7741	233422
C	謬	1-3593	0-4121	0-5529	C2D5	1-7740	21593A
D	謭	1-5857	1-6232			E-5926	35347B
E	謮	5-8233			F0E9	2-6354	
F	謯	3-8388			F0E1	2-634C	

8B3

	Char	G	J	K	B	C	A
0	謰	3-8329	1-6233		F0DE	2-6349	
1	謱	3-8370			F0E4	2-634F	
2	謲	3-8357				E-5924	
3	謳	1-5809	0-7580	0-4736	F0DD	2-6348	233430
4	謴					E-5928	
5	謵	3-8392			F0DF	2-634A	
6	謶	5-8278			F0E8	2-6353	
7	謷	3-8254	1-6234	1-7219	F0E6	2-6351	23342A
8	謸	3-8373				E-5923	
9	謹	1-2987	0-2264	0-4845	C2D4	1-773F	215939
A	謺	3-8253			F0ED	2-6358	
B	謻	3-8389			F0EB	2-6356	
C	謼		1-6235		F0E2	2-634D	3F3573
D	謽	5-8144			F0EC	2-6357	
E	謾	1-3501	0-7584	1-6402	F0E3	2-634E	233438
F	謿	5-8288				E-5B34	23344F

8B4

	Char	G	J	K	B	C	A
0	譀	3-8390			F2F9	2-6726	
1	譁		0-7586	0-9206	C3CF	1-787A	215941
2	譂		1-6236		F341	2-672D	
3	譃	5-8273	1-6237	1-8472		E-5B35	
4	譄	5-8304	1-6238				
5	譅	3-8416	1-6239		F64F	2-6C3E	233473
6	譆		1-6240		C3D6	1-7923	23344A
7	譇	3-8386			F0E0	2-634B	
8	譈	5-8301	1-6241		F2F7	2-6724	233442
9	證	1-5404	0-7590	0-8191	C3D2	1-787D	21593F
A	譊	3-8305			F2F8	2-6725	233449
B	譋				F2FD	2-672A	
C	譌		0-7587	1-7258		E-5B36	233349
D	譍	5-2941	1-6246			E-5D33	23345F
E	譎	1-5860	0-7589	0-9350	C3D4	1-7921	21593E
F	譏	1-2805	0-7588	0-4933	C3D5	1-7922	215942

8B5

	Char	G	J	K	B	C	A
0	譐				F2F6	2-6723	
1	譑	3-8309			F340	2-672C	
2	譒	5-8294	1-6242		F342	2-672E	
3	譓	5-8291	1-6243		F2FA	2-6727	233448
4	譔		1-6244	1-6834	F2FC	2-6729	233444
5	譕	3-8266			F2FE	2-672B	
6	譖	1-5858	0-7591	1-7863	F2FB	2-6728	23344D
7	譗	3-8394			F343	2-672F	
8	識	1-4222	0-2817	0-6759	C3D1	1-787C	21593C
9	譙	1-5859	1-6245	1-7989	C3D7	1-7924	233459
A	譚	1-4423	0-7593	0-5141	C3D3	1-787E	215940
B	譛		0-7592				35344D
C	譜	1-3855	0-4172	0-6047	C3D0	1-787B	21593D
D	譝	5-8240			F4D0	2-697C	
E	譞	3-8405	1-6247				
F	譟		0-7601	1-7719	C4B7	1-7A42	2D3748

8B6

	Char	G	J	K	B	C	A
0	譠	3-8408			F4CE	2-697A	
1	譡	5-8210				E-5D30	
2	譢	3-8402				E-5D2C	
3	譣	3-8337	1-6248		F4D2	2-697E	
4	譤	3-8407				E-5D32	
5	譥	3-8256			F4D3	2-6A21	
6	警	0-3015	0-2357	0-4477	C4B5	1-7A40	215945
7	譧	3-8409			F4D4	2-6A22	
8	譨	5-8222			F4D1	2-697D	
9	譩	3-8410				E-5D2B	
A	譪	5-8287			F4CF	2-697B	
B	譫	1-5862	0-7594	1-6852	C4B8	1-7A43	233468
C	譬	0-3809	0-7602	0-6207	C4B4	1-7A3F	215944
D	譭		1-6249		F4D5	2-6A23	23346B
E	譮	3-8313				E-5D2E	
F	譯	1-5075	0-7603	0-7027	C4B6	1-7A41	215946

8B7

	Char	G	J	K	B	C	A
0	議	1-5073	0-2136	0-7601	C4B3	1-7A3E	215943
1	譱		0-7033	1-6835		E-5C6D	33523F
2	譲		0-3089				2D594C
3	譳	3-8411				E-642D	
4	譴	1-3920	0-7604	0-4425	C4FE	1-7B2B	215947
5	譵	5-8201				E-5E62	
6	譶	5-8148	1-6250				
7	護	1-2704	0-2478	0-9162	C540	1-7B2C	215948
8	譸	3-8322	1-6251		F64E	2-6C3D	233470
9	譹	5-8308	1-6252		F64D	2-6C3C	
A	譺	3-8415			F650	2-6C3F	
B	譻	5-8139			F651	2-6C40	
C	譼		1-6253			E-5E63	
D	譽	1-5194	0-7605	0-7166	C541	1-7B2D	215949
E	譾		1-6254		F756	2-6E25	23347B
F	譿	5-8309		1-8376	F75B	2-6E2A	

8B8

	Char	G	J	K	B	C	A
0	讀	1-2233	0-7606	0-5233	C5AA	1-7B74	21594A
1	讁		1-6255			E-5F61	233479
2	讂	3-8414			F758	2-6E27	
3	讃		0-2730			E-5F62	2D594F
4	讄	5-8311	1-6256		F757	2-6E26	
5	讅	3-8354	1-6257		F75A	2-6E29	233478
6	讆				F759	2-6E28	
7	讇	5-8281				E-6048	233526
8	讈				F843	2-6F51	
9	讉	3-8393		1-7401			
A	變	1-1768	0-5846	0-6008	C5DC	1-7C48	21594B
B	讋	3-5694	1-6258		F842	2-6F50	233523
C	讌	3-8419	0-7607	1-7147	F840	2-6F4E	2D4A28
D	讍		1-6259			E-6047	
E	讎	1-8637	0-7608	1-6925	F841	2-6F4F	2D306C
F	讏		1-6260				

8BA

	Char	G	J	K	B	C	A
0	讠	0-5805					455837
1	计	0-2838					275838
2	订	0-2209					275839
3	讣	0-2428					27583A
4	认	0-4047					275870
5	讥	0-2805					275942
6	讦	0-5806					27583B
7	讧	0-5807					27583E
8	讨	0-4454					27583D
9	让	0-4035					27594C
A	讪	0-5808					27583F
B	讫	0-3893					275841
C	讬	8-1287					
D	训	0-4921					275843
E	议	0-5073					275943
F	讯	0-4922					275840

8BC

	Char	G	J	K	B	C	A
0	诀	0-3087					275845
1	证	0-5404					27593F
2	诂	0-5812					275851
3	诃	0-5813					51356A
4	评	0-3832					27584E
5	诅	0-5571					275853
6	识	0-4222					27593C
7	诇	8-9484					
8	诈	0-5309					275854
9	诉	0-4363					275856
A	诊	0-5379					275857
B	诋	0-5814					275855
C	诌	0-5463					29337A
D	词	0-2042					27584F
E	诎	0-5816					29323B
F	诏	0-5815					275852

8BE

	Char	G	J	K	B	C	A
0	诠	0-5825					275867
1	诡	0-2578					275863
2	询	0-4915					275865
3	诣	0-5072					27585E
4	诤	0-5826					293336
5	该	0-2435					275859
6	详	0-4774					27585A
7	诧	0-1879					275858
8	诨	0-5827					293345
9	诩	0-5828					293256
A	诪	8-9485					
B	诫	0-2975					27586B
C	诬	0-4660					27586F
D	语	0-5179					27586C
E	诮	0-5829					293271
F	误	0-4683					275871

8B9

	Char	G	J	K	B	C	A
0	讐		0-2918	0-6634		E-6049	33306C
1	讑	3-8420				E-607B	
2	讒	1-1887	0-7609	0-8356	C5FE	1-7C6A	21594E
3	讓	1-4035	0-7610	0-6951	C5FD	1-7C69	21594C
4	讔	3-8391	1-6261		F8C1	2-704F	23352E
5	讕	1-3230	1-6262		F8C2	2-7050	23352D
6	讖	1-5863	0-7611	0-8357	C640	1-7C6B	21594D
7	讗	3-8421				E-614B	
8	讘	3-8374			F94D	2-713C	
9	讙		0-7612		F94E	2-713D	334621
A	讚		0-7613	0-8338	C667	1-7D34	21594F
B	讛	5-8158				E-616B	
C	讜	1-5852	1-6263	1-6112	C66D	1-7D3A	233537
D	讝	3-8323				E-617E	
E	讞	1-5861	1-6264	1-7114	F9A9	2-7177	473539
F	讟		1-6265		F9C8	2-7236	23353A

8BB

	Char	G	J	K	B	C	A
0	记	0-2839					27583C
1	讱	8-9482					
2	讲	0-2918					275934
3	讳	0-2768					275928
4	讴	0-5809					293430
5	讵	0-5810					29322A
6	讶	0-4940					275846
7	讷	0-5811					275847
8	许	0-4877					275848
9	讹	0-2279					27584A
A	论	0-3459					275924
B	讻	8-9483					
C	讼	0-4347					27584B
D	讽	0-2377					27592F
E	设	0-4172					275849
F	访	0-2335					275844

8BD

	Char	G	J	K	B	C	A
0	诐	7-0119					
1	译	0-5075					275946
2	诒	0-5817					29323C
3	诓	0-5818					293250
4	诔	0-5819					29325D
5	试	0-4252					27585B
6	诖	0-5820					29324F
7	诗	0-4211					27585C
8	诘	0-5821					27585D
9	诙	0-5822					27585F
A	诚	0-1947					275860
B	诛	0-5479					275862
C	诜	0-5823					29325E
D	话	0-2716					275866
E	诞	0-2114					275923
F	诟	0-5824					275868

8BF

	Char	G	J	K	B	C	A
0	诰	0-5830					275873
1	诱	0-5153					275874
2	诲	0-2769					275872
3	诳	0-5831					275875
4	说	0-4321					275869
5	诵	0-4348					27586A
6	诶	0-5832					4B3642
7	请	0-3975					27587A
8	诸	0-5478					27587B
9	诹	0-5833					293325
A	诺	0-3721					27592E
B	读	0-2233					27594A
C	诼	0-5834					29332C
D	诽	0-2344					293338
E	课	0-3146					27587C
F	诿	0-5835					27587E

Code	Char	G	J	K	B	C	A
8C00	谀	0-5836					29333B
8C01	谁	0-4313					275922
8C02	谂	0-5837					293340
8C03	调	0-2187					27587D
8C04	谄	0-5838					275921
8C05	谅	0-3334					275878
8C06	谆	0-5527					275877
8C07	谇	0-5839					29327E
8C08	谈	0-4424					275879
8C09	谉	8-9486					
8C0A	谊	0-5074					275876
8C0B	谋	0-3617					27592B
8C0C	谌	0-5840					29334E
8C0D	谍	0-2193					27592A
8C0E	谎	0-2749					275935
8C0F	谏	0-5841					275927
8C10	谐	0-4819					275929
8C11	谑	0-5842					293359
8C12	谒	0-5843					27592C
8C13	谓	0-4629					27592D
8C14	谔	0-5844					293357
8C15	谕	0-5845					275930
8C16	谖	0-5846					29335D
8C17	谗	0-1887					27594E
8C18	谘	0-5849					4B3622
8C19	谙	0-5847					293344
8C1A	谚	0-4972					275926
8C1B	谛	0-5848					275925
8C1C	谜	0-3553					275933
8C1D	谝	0-5850					293362
8C1E	谞	8-9487					
8C1F	谟	0-5851					27593B
8C20	谠	0-5852					293537
8C21	谡	0-5853					293373
8C22	谢	0-4827					275938
8C23	谣	0-5005					275936
8C24	谤	0-1689					275931
8C25	谥	0-5854					4D3363
8C26	谦	0-3911					275932
8C27	谧	0-5855					29337D
8C28	谨	0-2987					275939
8C29	谩	0-3501					293438
8C2A	谪	0-5856					473422
8C2B	谫	0-5857					47347B
8C2C	谬	0-3593					27593A
8C2D	谭	0-4423					275940
8C2E	谮	0-5858					29344D
8C2F	谯	0-5859					293459
8C30	谰	0-3230					29352D
8C31	谱	0-3855					27593D
8C32	谲	0-5860					27593E
8C33	谳	0-5861					293539
8C34	谴	0-3920					275947
8C35	谵	0-5862					293468
8C36	谶	0-5863					27594D
8C37	谷	0-2540	0-3511	0-4559	A8A6	1-4B47	274F40
8C38	谸	5-8049	1-6266				
8C39	谹	3-8193	1-6267		D7CD	2-3950	
8C3A	谺	5-8052	0-7614			E-392A	23353D
8C3B	谻	5-8057			D7CE	2-3951	
8C3C	谼	3-8201			E052	2-4758	
8C3D	谽	5-8060	1-6268		E450	2-4E38	
8C3E	谾	5-8063	1-6269		E7E5	2-544E	
8C3F	谿		0-7616	0-4512	C1C6	1-7551	215952
8C40	豀	5-8065				E-564D	233544
8C41	豁	0-2777	0-7615	0-9235	C1C5	1-7550	215951
8C42	豂	5-8066			F0EE	2-6359	233545
8C43	豃	3-8205			F344	2-6730	
8C44	豄	5-8061				E-5F64	
8C45	豅	3-8194	1-6270		F844	2-6F52	
8C46	豆	0-2225	0-3806	0-5271	A8A7	1-4B48	215953
8C47	豇	0-8488	1-6271	1-5570	D3DE	2-3322	23354B
8C48	豈	1-3881	0-7617	0-4934	B05A	1-583F	215954
8C49	豉	0-8489	1-6272	1-6970	B361	1-5D47	215955
8C4A	豊	3-7838	0-4313	0-8905	E054	2-475A	335958
8C4B	豋	5-7786	1-6273		E053	2-4759	23354D
8C4C	豌	0-4567	0-7618	0-7253	BDDC	1-6F27	215956
8C4D	豍	5-7788			E7E6	2-544F	
8C4E	豎		0-7619	1-6926	BDDD	1-6F28	215957
8C4F	豏	3-7846	1-6274		EEB1	2-5F5D	233550
8C50	豐	1-2365	0-7620		C2D7	1-7742	215958
8C51	豑	5-7789	1-6275			E-5D34	
8C52	豒					E-664D	
8C53	豓		1-6276			E-6221	
8C54	豔		1-6277		C676	1-7D43	215959
8C55	豕	0-8525	0-7621	0-6746	A8A8	1-4B49	233552
8C56	豖	3-7911		1-8057	CDCB	2-286B	
8C57	豗	3-2135	1-6278		D3DF	2-3323	233554
8C58	豘	5-7829	1-6279			E-392D	
8C59	豙	5-7830	1-6282				
8C5A	豚	0-7564	0-3858	0-5242	B362	1-5D48	21595A
8C5B	豛	3-7916	1-6280			E-392C	
8C5C	豜	3-7913			D7CF	2-3952	233555
8C5D	豝	3-7917	1-6281		D7D0	2-3953	233556
8C5E	豞	3-7920				E-3F2A	
8C5F	豟	3-7921			DBE5	2-404B	
8C60	豠	3-7918				E-3F29	
8C61	象	0-4783	0-3061	0-6358	B648	1-622F	273257
8C62	豢	0-2731	0-7622	1-8430	B8E6	1-666D	21595C
8C63	豣		1-6283			E-4464	
8C64	豤	5-7837	1-6284		E056	2-475C	
8C65	豥	5-7836			E055	2-475B	
8C66	豦	3-6535	1-6285		E057	2-475D	
8C67	豧	3-7923				E-496D	
8C68	豨	3-7924	1-6286	1-8530	E451	2-4E39	233563
8C69	豩	5-7839	1-6287		E452	2-4E3A	
8C6A	豪	0-2632	0-2575	0-9163	BBA8	1-6B30	21595D
8C6B	豫	0-5205	0-4814	0-7167	BFDD	1-7247	21595E
8C6C	豬		0-7623	1-7575	BDDE	1-6F29	21595F
8C6D	豭	3-7930	1-6288		BFDE	1-7248	233565
8C6E	豮	8-9461					
8C6F	豯	3-7933			EEB5	2-5F61	
8C70	豰	3-4728			EEB2	2-5F5E	
8C71	豱	5-7842			EEB4	2-5F60	
8C72	豲	3-7932			EEB3	2-5F5F	
8C73	豳	0-6557	1-6289	1-6730	C1C7	1-7552	23356D
8C74	豴	5-7847				E-592B	23356F
8C75	豵	3-7914	1-6290		F0EF	2-635A	233571
8C76	豶	3-7928	1-6291		F346	2-6732	233574
8C77	豷	3-7934			F345	2-6731	233573
8C78	豸	0-8584	0-7624	1-8084	CBA4	2-2524	23357B
8C79	豹	0-1710	0-4131	0-8891	B05C	1-5841	215961
8C7A	豺	0-1882	0-7625	0-6747	B05B	1-5840	215960
8C7B	豻	3-8207	1-6292		D3E0	2-3324	23357D
8C7C	豼		0-7633			E-392E	2F3639
8C7D	豽	3-8209			D7D1	2-3954	
8C7E	豾	5-8069	1-6293			E-3F2C	
8C7F	豿	3-8211				E-3F2B	

8C8

	Char	G	J	K	B	C	A
0	貀	5-8073			DBE7	2-404D	
1	貁	5-8072			DBE6	2-404C	
2	貂	0-8585	0-7626	0-8516	B649	1-6230	215962
3	貃	5-8070		1-6425		E-3F2D	
4	貄				E059	2-475F	
5	貅	0-8587	0-7628		E05A	2-4760	23362D
6	貆	3-8213	1-6294		E058	2-475E	23362A
7	貇	5-8079	1-6301			E-634A	
8	貈	5-8078				E-4465	23362E
9	貉	0-2649	0-7627		B8E8	1-666F	215964
A	貊	0-8586	0-7629	0-5671	B8E7	1-666E	215963
B	貋		1-6302				
C	貌	0-3518	0-4338	0-5741	BBAA	1-6B32	215966
D	貍		0-7630	1-6366	BBA9	1-6B31	215965
E	貎		0-7631			E-4E7A	355D5C
F	貏	3-8214			E7E7	2-5450	

8C9

	Char	G	J	K	B	C	A
0	貐	5-8084	1-6303		EBB3	2-5A5F	
1	貑	3-8216			EBB1	2-5A5D	
2	貒	3-8215	1-6304		EBB2	2-5A5E	
3	貓		1-6305	1-6471	BFDF	1-7249	215967
4	貔	0-8589	0-7632	1-6711	EEB7	2-5F63	233639
5	貕	3-8217			EEB6	2-5F62	
6	貖					E-564F	
7	貗				F0F2	2-635D	
8	貘	0-8588	0-7634	1-6426	F0F1	2-635C	2D5963
9	貙	3-8208	1-6306		F0F0	2-635B	
A	貚				F347	2-6733	
B	貛		1-6307			E-614D	233641
C	貜	5-8088	1-6308		F9AA	2-7178	
D	貝	1-1720	0-1913	0-8815	A8A9	1-4B4A	215968
E	貞	1-5374	0-3671	0-7986	AD73	1-5356	215969
F	貟	5-2110				E-2F2E	233643

8CA

	Char	G	J	K	B	C	A
0	負	1-2426	0-4173	0-6122	AD74	1-5357	21596A
1	財	1-1838	0-2666	0-7815	B05D	1-5842	21596C
2	貢	1-2517	0-2555	0-4588	B05E	1-5843	21596B
3	貣	3-2144			D3E2	2-3326	
4	貤	3-4032	1-6309		D3E1	2-3325	233644
5	貥				D7D2	2-3955	
6	貦	5-4233				E-3930	
7	貧	1-3822	0-4147	0-6224	B368	1-5D4E	215971
8	貨	1-2785	0-1863	0-9207	B366	1-5D4C	21596F
9	販	1-2323	0-4046	0-8792	B363	1-5D49	215972
A	貪	1-4416	0-7637	0-8717	B367	1-5D4D	215970
B	貫	1-2565	0-2051	0-4627	B365	1-5D4B	21596E
C	責	1-5280	0-3253	0-8401	B364	1-5D4A	21596D
D	貭		0-7636			E-3932	2D5A34
E	貮		0-7641			E-3931	513051
F	貯	1-5492	0-3589	0-7845	B64A	1-6231	215973

8CB

	Char	G	J	K	B	C	A
0	貰	1-7459	0-4467	0-6514	DBEA	2-4050	23364E
1	貱	3-4040				E-3F2F	
2	貲	1-7463	0-7639	1-7503	B8ED	1-6674	215A26
3	貳	1-2301	0-7640	0-7635	B64C	1-6233	333051
4	貴	1-2583	0-2114	0-4794	B651	1-6238	215978
5	貵				DBEC	2-4052	233652
6	貶	1-1765	0-7642	0-8831	B653	1-623A	21597B
7	買	1-3482	0-3967	0-5666	B652	1-6239	21597A
8	貸	1-2091	0-3463	0-5172	B655	1-623C	21597D
9	貹	3-4036	1-6310		DBEB	2-4051	233653
A	貺	1-7460	1-6311	1-8441	DBE8	2-404E	233651
B	費	1-2349	0-4081	0-6208	B64F	1-6236	215975
C	貼	1-4489	0-3729	0-8468	B64B	1-6232	215979
D	貽	1-7461	0-7638	0-7634	B64D	1-6234	21597C
E	貾	5-4237			DBE9	2-404F	
F	貿	1-3519	0-4339	0-5785	B654	1-623B	21597E

8CC

	Char	G	J	K	B	C	A
0	賀	1-2656	0-1876	0-8937	B650	1-6237	215977
1	賁	1-7458	0-7644	0-6151	B64E	1-6235	215976
2	賂	1-3424	0-4708	0-5481	B8EF	1-6676	215A28
3	賃	1-3362	0-3634	0-7692	B8EE	1-6675	215A27
4	賄	1-2763	0-4737	0-9280	B8EC	1-6673	215A25
5	賅	1-7464	1-6312		B8F0	1-6677	215A21
6	賆		1-6313	1-6576			
7	資	1-5542	0-2781	0-7732	B8EA	1-6671	215A22
8	賈	1-2854	0-7643	0-4225	B8EB	1-6672	215A24
9	賉		1-6314			E-4469	393E47
A	賊	1-5284	0-3417	0-7868	B8E9	1-6670	215A23
B	賋		1-6315				
C	賌	5-4241			E05B	2-4761	
D	賍		0-7660			E-4467	233657
E	賎		0-3308				4B5A31
F	賏		1-6316		E454	2-4E3C	

8CD

	Char	G	J	K	B	C	A
0	賐					E-4970	
1	賑	1-7466	0-3888	0-8265	BBAC	1-6B34	215A2A
2	賒	1-4162			BBAD	1-6B35	215A2B
3	賓	1-1786	0-4148	0-6225	BBAB	1-6B33	215A29
4	賔					E-4972	
5	賕	1-7468	1-6318		E453	2-4E3B	23365F
6	賖		1-6317			E-4971	
7	賗				E455	2-4E3D	
8	賘					E-664E	23365E
9	賙	5-4247	1-6319	1-7756	E7EA	2-5453	233674
A	賚	1-7467	0-7647	0-5482	E7EC	2-5455	233670
B	賛		0-2731			E-4E7E	2D5A3D
C	賜	1-2045	0-2782	0-6284	BDE7	1-6F32	215A33
D	賝	5-4248	1-6320		E7ED	2-5456	233672
E	賞	1-4145	0-3062	0-6359	BDE0	1-6F2B	215A32
F	賟				E7E9	2-5452	

8CE

	Char	G	J	K	B	C	A
0	賠	1-3766	0-3969	0-5951	BDDF	1-6F2A	215A2C
1	賡	1-6657	1-6321	1-5580	BDE9	1-6F34	23366A
2	賢	1-4745	0-2413	0-9071	BDE5	1-6F30	215A30
3	賣	1-3484	0-7646	0-5667	BDE6	1-6F31	215A2F
4	賤	1-2890	0-7645	0-8433	BDE2	1-6F2D	215A31
5	賥	3-4045			E7E8	2-5451	
6	賦	1-2419	0-4174	0-6123	BDE1	1-6F2C	215A2D
7	賧	1-7470			E7EE	2-5457	
8	賨	3-4046	1-6322		E7EB	2-5454	233667
9	賩					E-4E7D	233668
A	質	1-5442	0-2833	0-8285	BDE8	1-6F33	215A34
B	賫	1-7469				E-4F22	23366F
C	賬	1-5343	1-6323	1-7544	BDE3	1-6F2E	333C52
D	賭	1-2236	0-3750	0-5214	BDE4	1-6F2F	215A35
E	賮	5-4251			EBB5	2-5A61	233676
F	賯		1-6324			E-5275	

8CF

	Char	G	J	K	B	C	A
0	賰		1-6325		EBB7	2-5A63	
1	賱				EBB6	2-5A62	23367B
2	賲	3-4052	1-6326			E-5273	
3	賳				EBB8	2-5A64	
4	賴	1-3221		0-5483	BFE0	1-724A	215A36
5	賵	3-4051	1-6327		EBB4	2-5A60	23367C
6	賶					E-5651	
7	賷		1-6328			E-5652	233721
8	賸		1-6329		C1CB	1-7556	2D3377
9	賹	3-4055			EEB8	2-5F64	
A	賺	1-5512	0-7649		C1C8	1-7553	215A38
B	賻	1-7471	0-7650	0-6124	C1CC	1-7557	23367E
C	購	1-2526	0-2556	0-4737	C1CA	1-7555	215A3A
D	賽	1-4092	0-7648	0-6363	C1C9	1-7554	215A37
E	賾	1-5651	1-6330		F0F3	2-635E	233726
F	賿		1-6331				

8D0

	Char	G	J	K	B	C	A
0	贀	3-4056			F0F6	2-6361	
1	贁		1-6332				
2	贂				F0F5	2-6360	
3	贃		1-6333			E-592E	
4	贄	1-7462	0-7651	0-8230	F0F4	2-635F	233725
5	贅	1-5524	0-7652	0-8601	C2D8	1-7743	215A39
6	贆				F348	2-6734	
7	贇	3-4058	0-7654	0-7543	F349	2-6735	23372B
8	贈	1-5289	0-3403	0-8192	C3D8	1-7925	215A3B
9	贉	3-4057	1-6334		F34A	2-6736	23372D
A	贊	1-5262	0-7653	0-8339	C3D9	1-7926	215A3D
B	贋	1-5645	0-2070	1-7026		E-5B38	215A3C
C	贌					E-664F	233732
D	贍	1-4136	0-7656	0-6475	C4BA	1-7A45	215A3F
E	贎	3-4031				E-6428	
F	贏	1-5114	0-7655	1-7175	C4B9	1-7A44	215A3E

8D1

	Char	G	J	K	B	C	A
0	贐	1-7465	0-7657	1-6984	F652	2-6C41	23373A
1	贑					E-5E65	233739
2	贒		1-6335			E-5E66	23373B
3	贓		0-7659	0-7792	C542	1-7B2E	215A40
4	贔	3-4044	0-7661	1-6712	F653	2-6C42	23373D
5	贕	3-1619			F75C	2-6E2B	
6	贖	1-4274	0-7662	0-6559	C5AB	1-7B75	215A41
7	贗		1-6336		C5AC	1-7B76	
8	贘					E-6650	23373E
9	贙	3-4060			F845	2-6F53	
A	贚	3-4035				E-604A	
B	贛	1-2451	1-6337	1-5740	C642	1-7C6D	215A42
C	贜	1-5263				E-614E	
D	贝	0-1720					275968
E	贞	0-5374					275969
F	负	0-2426					27596A

8D2

	Char	G	J	K	B	C	A
0	贠	8-1412					
1	贡	0-2517					27596B
2	财	0-1838					27596C
3	责	0-5280					27596D
4	贤	0-4745					275A30
5	败	0-1660					274247
6	账	0-5343					393C52
7	货	0-2785					27596F
8	质	0-5442					275A34
9	贩	0-2323					275972
A	贪	0-4416					275970
B	贫	0-3822					275971
C	贬	0-1765					27597B
D	购	0-2526					275A3A
E	贮	0-5492					4B5973
F	贯	0-2565					27596E

8D3

	Char	G	J	K	B	C	A
0	贰	0-2301					453051
1	贱	0-2890					275A31
2	贲	0-7458					275976
3	贳	0-7459					29364E
4	贴	0-4489					275979
5	贵	0-2583					275978
6	贶	0-7460					293651
7	贷	0-2091					27597D
8	贸	0-3519					27597E
9	费	0-2349					275975
A	贺	0-2656					275977
B	贻	0-7461					27597C
C	贼	0-5284					275A23
D	贽	0-7462					293725
E	贾	0-2854					275A24
F	贿	0-2763					275A25

8D4

	Char	G	J	K	B	C	A
0	赀	0-7463					275A26
1	赁	0-3362					275A27
2	赂	0-3424					275A28
3	赃	0-5263					275A40
4	资	0-5542					275A22
5	赅	0-7464					275A21
6	赆	0-7465					29373A
7	赇	0-7468					29365F
8	赈	0-7466					275A2A
9	赉	0-7467					293670
A	赊	0-4162					275A2B
B	赋	0-2419					275A2D
C	赌	0-2236					275A35
D	赍	0-7469					47366F
E	赎	0-4274					275A41
F	赏	0-4145					275A32

8D5

	Char	G	J	K	B	C	A
0	赐	0-2045					275A33
1	赑	8-9234					
2	赒	8-1446					
3	赓	0-6657					29366A
4	赔	0-3766					275A2C
5	赕	0-7470					29366B
6	赖	0-3221					275A36
7	赗	8-9235					
8	赘	0-5524					275A39
9	赙	0-7471					29367E
A	赚	0-5512					275A38
B	赛	0-4092					275A37
C	赜	0-5651					293726
D	赝	0-5645					275A3C
E	赞	0-5262					275A3D
F	赟	8-1253					

8D6

	Char	G	J	K	B	C	A
0	赠	0-5289					275A3B
1	赡	0-4136					275A3F
2	赢	0-5114					275A3E
3	赣	0-2451					275A42
4	赤	0-1964	0-3254	0-7869	A8AA	1-4B4B	215A43
5	赥	5-7777	1-6338			E-3933	
6	赦	0-4166	0-2847	0-6285	B36A	1-5D50	215A45
7	赧	0-8486	0-7663	1-6019	B369	1-5D4F	215A44
8	赨	3-7827			E05C	2-4762	
9	赩	3-7828	1-6339		E05D	2-4763	
A	赪	8-9458					
B	赫	0-2653	0-1950	0-9051	BBAE	1-6B36	215A46
C	赬	3-7826	1-6340		EBB9	2-5A65	233748
D	赭	0-8487	0-7664	1-7504	BDEA	1-6F35	215A47
E	赮	5-7781	1-6341		EBBA	2-5A66	
F	赯	3-7830			EEB9	2-5F65	

8D7

	Char	G	J	K	B	C	A
0	走	0-5563	0-3386	0-8143	A8AB	1-4B4C	215A48
1	赱		0-7665			E-243A	2D5A48
2	赲	3-7778			D0E2	2-2D53	
3	赳	0-8481	0-7666	0-4815	AD76	1-5359	215A4A
4	赴	0-2416	0-4175	0-6125	AD75	1-5358	215A49
5	赵	0-5352					275A4F
6	赶	0-2447		1-5530	D3E3	2-3327	275A50
7	起	0-3880	0-2115	0-4935	B05F	1-5844	215A4B
8	赸	3-7780			D3E4	2-3328	233752
9	赹	5-7723			D7D5	2-3958	
A	赺	3-7786				E-3939	23375C
B	赻				D7D4	2-3957	
C	赼					E-3937	
D	赽	5-7725			D7D3	2-3956	
E	赾	3-7785				E-3935	
F	赿		1-6342			E-3938	

8D8

	Char	G	J	K	B	C	A
0	趀	5-7721			DBEE	2-4054	
1	趁	0-1935	0-7667	1-7817	B658	1-623F	215A4E
2	趂		1-6343			E-3F39	2D5A4E
3	趃	5-7728				E-3F34	
4	趄	0-8482	1-6344		DBED	2-4053	233761
5	超	0-1912	0-3622	0-8517	B657	1-623E	215A4C
6	趆	3-7788				E-3F37	
7	趇					E-3F30	
8	趈	5-7727	1-6345			E-3F33	
9	趉	3-7790			DBEF	2-4055	
A	越	0-5229	0-1759	0-7438	B656	1-623D	215A4D
B	趋	0-3987				E-3F38	275A53
C	趌				E05F	2-4765	
D	趍	5-7738	1-6346		E062	2-4768	233775
E	趎	3-7793		1-7757	E060	2-4766	
F	趏	5-7736			E061	2-4767	

8DA

	Char	G	J	K	B	C	A
0	趠	5-7749	1-6352	1-7990	E7EF	2-5458	
1	趡	3-7806			E7F1	2-545A	23382F
2	趢	3-7810				E-4F25	
3	趣	0-4004	0-2881	0-8612	BDEC	1-6F37	215A51
4	趤					E-4F23	
5	趥	5-7759			EBBB	2-5A67	
6	趦	5-7758	1-6353			E-5277	233833
7	趧	5-7754			EBBC	2-5A68	
8	趨	1-3987	0-3186	0-8557	C1CD	1-7558	215A53
9	趩	3-7816				E-5931	
A	趪	3-7815			F34C	2-6738	
B	趫	3-7794	1-6354	1-5829	F34E	2-673A	233852
C	趬	3-7792	1-6355		F34B	2-6737	
D	趭	3-7818			F34D	2-6739	
E	趮	5-7769			F4D6	2-6A24	
F	趯	3-7823	1-6356		F654	2-6C43	233859

8DC

	Char	G	J	K	B	C	A
0	跀	3-7955	1-6362			E-393D	
1	跁	3-7961			D7DA	2-395D	233872
2	跂	3-7949	0-7669	1-6004	D7D7	2-395A	233871
3	跃	0-5230					275B29
4	跄	0-8536					293A2E
5	跅	3-7968	1-6363		DBFB	2-4061	23392B
6	跆	0-8544	1-6364	0-8737	B660	1-6247	215A5C
7	跇	3-7963	1-6365		DBF3	2-4059	
8	跈	3-7969	1-6366		DBF9	2-405F	
9	跉	3-7970				E-3F3F	
A	跊		1-6367			E-3F3A	
B	跋	0-1647	0-7677	0-5902	B65B	1-6242	215A5A
C	跌	0-2188	0-7675	0-8286	B65E	1-6245	215A5E
D	跍				DBF2	2-4058	
E	跎	0-8541	1-6368	1-8119	B659	1-6240	215A57
F	跏	0-8542	0-7672	0-4226	DBF6	2-405C	233921

8DE

	Char	G	J	K	B	C	A
0	跠	5-7883			E068	2-476E	
1	跡		0-3255	0-7870	B8F1	1-6678	215A5F
2	跢	3-7986			E06F	2-4775	
3	跣	0-8548	0-7681	0-6451	E06E	2-4774	23393B
4	跤	0-8551	1-6374		B8F8	1-6721	23392F
5	跥		1-6375				2D5A63
6	跦	3-7981			B8F9	1-6722	23393A
7	跧	3-7983	1-6376		E070	2-4776	23393D
8	跨	0-3171	0-2457	0-4605	B8F3	1-667A	215A61
9	跩	3-7979			E06D	2-4773	233938
A	跪	0-2582	0-7678	1-5918	B8F7	1-667E	215A64
B	跫	0-8528	0-7679	1-5741	E072	2-4778	233935
C	跬	0-8545	1-6377	1-5934	E069	2-476F	233934
D	跭	3-7985				E-446B	
E	跮	3-7977			E06B	2-4771	
F	路	0-3423	0-4709	0-5456	B8F4	1-667B	215A65

8D9

	Char	G	J	K	B	C	A
0	趐	5-7741	1-6347	1-8356	E065	2-476B	
1	趑	0-8484	1-6348		E05E	2-4764	2F3833
2	趒				E066	2-476C	
3	趓	3-7801			E063	2-4769	
4	趔	0-8483			E064	2-476A	233771
5	趕	1-2447	1-6349		BBB0	1-6B38	215A50
6	趖	3-7804			E456	2-4E3E	233822
7	趗	3-7803				E-4975	
8	趘					E-4973	
9	趙	1-5352	0-7668	0-8065	BBAF	1-6B37	215A4F
A	趚					E-4974	
B	趛				E7F2	2-545B	
C	趜	3-7809			E7F0	2-5459	
D	趝	3-7807				E-4F26	
E	趞	5-7747	1-6350				
F	趟	0-4443	1-6351		BDEB	1-6F36	215A52

8DB

	Char	G	J	K	B	C	A
0	趰					E-6651	23385A
1	趱	0-8485					293866
2	趲	1-8485	1-6357	1-7850	F96F	2-715E	233866
3	足	0-5567	0-3413	0-8075	A8AC	1-4B4D	215A54
4	趴	0-3731			AD77	1-535A	215A55
5	趵	0-8532	1-6358		D3E5	2-3329	3B3922
6	趶				D3E7	2-332B	
7	趷		1-6359		D3E6	2-332A	
8	趸	0-8527					275B26
9	趹	3-7960	1-6360		D7D8	2-395B	233870
A	趺	0-8535	0-7671	0-6126	B36C	1-5D52	23386F
B	趻	3-7953	1-6361			E-393E	
C	趼	0-8534	1-6379		D7D6	2-3959	23386E
D	趽	3-7959				E-393A	
E	趾	0-5426	0-7670	0-8231	B36B	1-5D51	215A56
F	趿	0-8533			D7D9	2-395C	233873

8DD

	Char	G	J	K	B	C	A
0	跐	3-7978			E06C	2-4772	233927
1	跑	0-3760	1-6369		B65D	1-6244	215A5D
2	跒	3-7965				E-3F3B	
3	跓	5-7877			DBF1	2-4057	
4	跔	3-7972	1-6370			E-3F3E	
5	跕	3-7966	1-6371	1-7647	DBF7	2-405D	
6	跖	0-8537	0-7674	1-7914	DBF4	2-405A	233922
7	跗	0-8538	1-6372	1-6640	DBFA	2-4060	2F386F
8	跘	5-7878			DBF0	2-4056	
9	跙	3-7967	1-6373		DBF8	2-405E	
A	跚	0-8539	0-7673		B65C	1-6243	215A5B
B	跛	0-8543	0-7676	0-8785	B65F	1-6246	215A59
C	跜				DBF5	2-405B	
D	距	0-3064	0-2187	0-4369	B65A	1-6241	215A58
E	跞	0-8540					293A5F
F	跟	0-2490	0-7680	1-5952	B8F2	1-6679	215A60

8DF

	Char	G	J	K	B	C	A
0	跰	5-7884	1-6378		E067	2-476D	
1	跱	5-7880	1-6380	1-8085	E06A	2-4770	
2	跲	3-7984	1-6381		E071	2-4777	23393E
3	跳	0-4488	0-3623	0-5215	B8F5	1-667C	215A62
4	跴		1-6382		E073	2-4779	233936
5	践	0-2889	0-3309				275A68
6	跶	7-0118					
7	跷	0-8546					275A7E
8	跸	0-8547					293A40
9	跹	0-8549					293A5E
A	跺	0-2269			B8F6	1-667D	215A63
B	跻	0-8550					293A57
C	跼		0-7682	1-5886	BBB1	1-6B39	215A66
D	跽	0-8553	1-6383		E45B	2-4E43	233941
E	跾				E461	2-4E49	
F	跿	3-7987	0-7685		E459	2-4E41	233944

8E0

	Char	G	J	K	B	C	A
0	踀				E462	2-4E4A	
1	踁		1-6384			E-497B	233949
2	踂	3-7988			E458	2-4E40	
3	踃	3-7992			E45D	2-4E45	
4	踄	3-7991	1-6385		E463	2-4E4B	23394E
5	踅	0-8529	1-6386		E460	2-4E48	233946
6	踆	3-8004	1-6387	1-7772	E45F	2-4E47	233950
7	踇				E45E	2-4E46	
8	踈		0-7683	1-6885		E-497A	334C3E
9	踉	0-8552	0-7684	1-6225	E457	2-4E3F	23393F
A	踊	0-5127	0-4557	0-7341	E45C	2-4E44	275A71
B	踋		1-6388			E-4979	
C	踌	0-1976					275B28
D	踍				E45A	2-4E42	
E	踎						
F	踏	0-4404	0-3807	0-5146	BDF1	1-6F3C	215A6B

8E2

	Char	G	J	K	B	C	A
0	踠	3-8017	1-6392		E7F3	2-545C	
1	踡	5-7905	1-6393		BDF4	1-6F3F	233958
2	踢	0-4463	1-6394		BDF0	1-6F3B	215A69
3	踣	0-8559	1-6401		E7F4	2-545D	233954
4	踤	3-8014			E7F6	2-545F	
5	踥	3-8015			E7F5	2-545E	
6	踦	3-8008	1-6402		E7FD	2-5466	233966
7	踧	3-8010	1-6403		E7FE	2-5467	233967
8	踨					E-4F2C	335A7B
9	踩	0-1840			BDF2	1-6F3D	215A6C
A	踪	0-5557	0-7709	0-8101		E-4F2B	233952
B	踫				BDED	1-6F38	215A67
C	踬	0-8557					293A60
D	踭						
E	踮	0-8558			E7F7	2-5460	233957
F	踯	0-8560					275B2A

8E4

	Char	G	J	K	B	C	A
0	蹀	0-8562	1-6411	1-7648	EBC0	2-5A6C	233977
1	蹁	0-8568	1-6412		EBC5	2-5A71	23396F
2	蹂	0-8569	0-7690	0-7519	BFE4	1-724E	215A70
3	蹃	3-8007				E-527C	
4	蹄	0-4467	0-3693	0-8020	BFE1	1-724B	215A6E
5	蹅	3-8026			EBC1	2-5A6D	
6	蹆	5-7914				E-5654	233A26
7	蹇	0-6931	0-7701	0-4384	EEBF	2-5F6B	233A24
8	蹈	0-2124	0-7705	0-5216	C1D0	1-755B	215A76
9	蹉	0-8567	0-7702	0-8318	C1CE	1-7559	215A74
A	蹊	0-8572	0-7694	0-9123	C1D1	1-755C	215A77
B	蹋	0-4403	1-6413		C1CF	1-755A	215A75
C	蹌	1-8536	0-7703	1-7882	EEBE	2-5F6A	233A2E
D	蹍	3-8040	1-6414		EEBB	2-5F67	
E	蹎	5-7916	1-6415		EEBA	2-5F66	
F	蹏		1-6416	1-7679		E-5655	233A32

8E6

	Char	G	J	K	B	C	A
0	蹠		0-7708	0-8418	F0F9	2-6364	233A36
1	蹡	5-7913	1-6422		F142	2-636C	233A41
2	蹢	3-8043	1-6423		F0F8	2-6363	233A35
3	蹣	1-8571	0-7710	1-6403	C2DA	1-7745	215A78
4	蹤		0-7707	1-7737	C2DC	1-7747	215A7B
5	蹥	5-7886			F0FD	2-6368	
6	蹦	0-1736			C2DB	1-7746	215A7A
7	蹧				F0FE	2-6369	233A3B
8	蹨	3-8047				E-5B3A	
9	蹩	0-8531	1-6424		F144	2-636E	233A4B
A	蹪	3-8031			F352	2-673E	
B	蹫	5-7935				E-5B39	
C	蹬	0-2137	1-6425		C3DE	1-792B	215A7D
D	蹭	0-1868	1-6426		F34F	2-673B	233A48
E	蹮	5-7929					2F3A5E
F	蹯	0-8576	1-6427		F353	2-673F	334C37

8E1

	Char	G	J	K	B	C	A
0	踐	1-2889	0-7688	0-8434	BDEE	1-6F39	215A68
1	踑	5-7889	1-6389		E7FB	2-5464	
2	踒	3-8013			E841	2-5469	
3	踓	5-7901			E843	2-546B	
4	踔	0-8554	1-6390	1-8132	E840	2-5468	233968
5	踕	3-8009			E7F8	2-5461	
6	踖	3-8006	1-6391		E7FA	2-5463	233964
7	踗				E845	2-546D	
8	踘	5-7903			E842	2-546A	233969
9	踙				E7FC	2-5465	
A	踚	3-7952			E846	2-546E	
B	踛	5-7888			E7F9	2-5462	
C	踜	3-8005			E844	2-546C	
D	踝	0-8555	0-7686	1-5754	BDEF	1-6F3A	215A6A
E	踞	0-3065	0-7687	0-4370	BDF5	1-6F40	23395C
F	踟	0-8556	0-7689	1-7804	BDF3	1-6F3E	215A6D

8E3

	Char	G	J	K	B	C	A
0	踰		0-7692	0-7518	EBC6	2-5A72	233A21
1	踱	0-8566	1-6404		BFE2	1-724C	215A6F
2	踲	5-7912				E-527E	
3	踳	3-8022	1-6405		EBBD	2-5A69	
4	踴	1-5127	0-7693	1-7313	BFE3	1-724D	215A71
5	踵	0-8564	0-7691	0-8102	BFE6	1-7250	215A73
6	踶	3-8030	1-6406	1-7678	EBC2	2-5A6E	233979
7	踷		1-6407				
8	踸	3-8023	1-6408		EBBF	2-5A6B	
9	踹	0-8563	1-6409		BFE5	1-724F	215A72
A	踺	0-8561					70755D
B	踻	3-7993				E-527B	
C	踼	3-7946			EBC3	2-5A6F	
D	踽	0-8565	1-6410	1-7329	EBC4	2-5A70	23397E
E	踾	3-8027			EBBE	2-5A6A	
F	踿	5-7911			EBC7	2-5A73	

8E5

	Char	G	J	K	B	C	A
0	蹐	3-8038	0-7704		EEBD	2-5F69	233A30
1	蹑	0-8570					275B2B
2	蹒	0-8571					275A78
3	蹓	3-8037			EEBC	2-5F68	
4	蹔		1-6417		F145	2-636F	233A3A
5	蹕	1-8547	0-7711	1-8264	C2DE	1-7749	233A40
6	蹖				F0FB	2-6366	
7	蹗	5-7923			F0FA	2-6365	
8	蹘	3-8045				E-5932	
9	蹙	0-8530	0-7706	0-8576	C2D9	1-7744	215A79
A	蹚				F141	2-636B	233A3E
B	蹛	3-8025	1-6418		F140	2-636A	
C	蹜	3-8044	1-6419	1-8058	F0F7	2-6362	233A34
D	蹝	3-8042	1-6420		F143	2-636D	233A43
E	蹞	5-7891	1-6421		F0FC	2-6367	233A3F
F	蹟		0-3256	0-7871	C2DD	1-7748	2D5A5F

8E7

	Char	G	J	K	B	C	A
0	蹰	0-8573	1-6428			E-5B3B	293A46
1	蹱	5-7932	1-6429				
2	蹲	0-2255	0-7713	1-7773	C3DB	1-7928	215A7C
3	蹳	3-7975			F351	2-673D	
4	蹴	0-8577	0-2919	0-8577	C3E0	1-792D	233A45
5	蹵					E-5B3C	233A44
6	蹶	0-8574	0-7712	0-4783	C3DD	1-792A	215B21
7	蹷	5-1682				E-5B3D	
8	蹸	5-7933			F350	2-673C	
9	蹹	5-7931	1-6430				
A	蹺	1-8546	1-6431		C3DF	1-792C	215A7E
B	蹻		1-6432	1-5830	F354	2-6740	2D5A7E
C	蹼	0-8575	0-7714		C3DA	1-7927	215B22
D	蹽	3-8046					
E	蹾	3-8048					
F	蹿	0-2058					293A6B

Code	Char	G	J	K	B	C	A
8E80	躀						
8E81	躁	0-5274	0-7715	0-8066	C4BC	1-7A47	215B24
8E82	躂	3-7976	1-6433		C4BE	1-7A49	215B23
8E83	躃	3-8053	1-6434			E-5D37	233A52
8E84	躄	3-7943	0-7718		F4D9	2-6A27	233A53
8E85	躅	0-8578	0-7717	1-8011	C4BD	1-7A48	215B27
8E86	躆	3-8050			F4D7	2-6A25	
8E87	躇	0-1989	0-7716	0-7846	C3DC	1-7929	215B25
8E88	躈	3-8051			F4D8	2-6A26	
8E89	躉	1-8527	1-6435	1-6146	C4BB	1-7A46	215B26
8E8A	躊	1-1976	0-7720	0-8144	C543	1-7B2F	215B28
8E8B	躋	1-8550	0-7719	1-7680	C545	1-7B31	233A57
8E8C	躌				F656	2-6C45	
8E8D	躍	1-5230	0-4486	0-6924	C544	1-7B30	215B29
8E8E	躎				F655	2-6C44	
8E8F	躏	0-8579					275B2C
8E90	躐	0-8581	1-6436	1-6257	F761	2-6E30	233A62
8E91	躑	1-8560	0-7722	1-7915	C5AD	1-7B77	215B2A
8E92	躒	1-8540	1-6437		F760	2-6E2F	233A5F
8E93	躓	1-8557	0-7721	1-7805	C5AE	1-7B78	233A60
8E94	躔	0-8580	0-7723	1-7616	F75E	2-6E2D	233A5D
8E95	躕		1-6438		F75D	2-6E2C	233A46
8E96	躖				F762	2-6E31	
8E97	躗				F763	2-6E32	
8E98	躘	5-7875			F846	2-6F54	233A63
8E99	躙	5-7925	0-7724	1-6377		E-604B	233A72
8E9A	躚	1-8549	1-6439		F75F	2-6E2E	233A5E
8E9B	躛		1-6440				
8E9C	躜	0-8582					293A70
8E9D	躝		1-6441		F8C6	2-7054	
8E9E	躞	0-8583	1-6442		F8C3	2-7051	233A64
8E9F	躟	5-7943			F8C4	2-7052	
8EA0	躠	3-7944			F8C5	2-7053	
8EA1	躡	1-8570	0-7726	1-6859	C65C	1-7D29	215B2B
8EA2	躢	5-7937	1-6443			E-6150	
8EA3	躣	3-8057			F951	2-7140	
8EA4	躤	5-7944			F950	2-713F	
8EA5	躥	1-2058			F94F	2-713E	233A6B
8EA6	躦	1-8582			F970	2-715F	
8EA7	躧	5-7885	1-6444			E-616C	233A6F
8EA8	躨				F9BE	2-722E	
8EA9	躩	3-8058	1-6445	1-5759	F9AB	2-7179	233A71
8EAA	躪	1-8579	0-7725	0-5585	C66E	1-7D3B	215B2C
8EAB	身	0-4177	0-3140	0-6783	A8AD	1-4B4E	215B2D
8EAC	躬	0-2510	0-7727	0-4769	B060	1-5845	215B2E
8EAD	躭	8-1392	1-6446			E-393F	2D526C
8EAE	躮		1-6447				
8EAF	躯	0-3991	0-2277			E-3940	275B31
8EB0	躰	5-7985	0-7728			E-3F40	33615A
8EB1	躱		0-7730	1-8120		E-4473	2D5E2F
8EB2	躲	0-2267			B8FA	1-6723	215B2F
8EB3	躳		1-6448	1-5901		E-497D	233A78
8EB4	躴	3-8144				E-497C	
8EB5	躵		1-6449				
8EB6	躶					E-4F30	233A7D
8EB7	躷	5-7987				E-4F32	
8EB8	躸	3-8145				E-4F2F	
8EB9	躹					E-4F31	
8EBA	躺	0-4441	1-6450		BDF6	1-6F41	215B30
8EBB	躻		1-6451				
8EBC	躼					E-6652	233A7A
8EBD	躽	3-8147			EBC8	2-5A74	
8EBE	躾		0-7731				696D3F
8EBF	躿	3-8150				E-5935	
8EC0	軀	1-3991	1-6452	0-4738	C2DF	1-774A	215B31
8EC1	軁	3-8149	1-6453			E-5936	
8EC2	軂				F355	2-6741	
8EC3	軃	3-8146	1-6454			E-5B3F	
8EC4	軄		1-6455				
8EC5	軅		0-7732				696D40
8EC6	軆		0-7729	1-7969		E-5D38	2D615A
8EC7	軇		1-6456				
8EC8	軈		0-7733				696D41
8EC9	軉				F9AC	2-717A	233B2E
8ECA	車	1-1921	0-2854	0-8319	A8AE	1-4B4F	215B32
8ECB	軋	1-5294	0-7734	0-6856	AAEE	1-4F51	215B33
8ECC	軌	1-2576	0-2116	0-4789	AD79	1-535C	215B35
8ECD	軍	1-3092	0-2319	0-4758	AD78	1-535B	215B34
8ECE	軎	0-7406					233B31
8ECF	軏	3-3724	1-6457		B063	1-5848	233B2F
8ED0	軐	3-3726					
8ED1	軑	3-3723	1-6458		D3E8	2-332C	
8ED2	軒	1-4889	0-2414	0-9045	B061	1-5846	215B36
8ED3	軓				D3E9	2-332D	
8ED4	軔	1-7377	1-6459		B062	1-5847	215B37
8ED5	軕					E-6653	233B33
8ED6	軖	3-3728				E-3941	
8ED7	軗				D7DF	2-3962	
8ED8	軘	3-3730			D7DB	2-395E	
8ED9	軙					E-3947	
8EDA	軚						
8EDB	軛	1-7378	0-7735		B36D	1-5D53	215B39
8EDC	軜	3-3731	1-6460		D7DE	2-3961	
8EDD	軝	3-3733			D7DD	2-3960	
8EDE	軞	5-3963			D7DC	2-395F	
8EDF	軟	1-4077	0-3880	0-7067	B36E	1-5D54	215B38
8EE0	軠				D7E0	2-3963	
8EE1	軡				D7E1	2-3964	
8EE2	転		0-3730				4B5B55
8EE3	軣		0-7736				4B5B58
8EE4	軤	1-7385				E-3F45	
8EE5	軥	3-3743			DC43	2-4068	
8EE6	軦				DC41	2-4066	
8EE7	軧	3-3742			DC45	2-406A	
8EE8	軨	3-3741	1-6461	1-6269	DC46	2-406B	233B4B
8EE9	軩				DC4C	2-4071	
8EEA	軪	3-3747				E-3F47	
8EEB	軫	1-7384	0-7739	0-8266	DC48	2-406D	233B4F
8EEC	軬	3-1950			DC4A	2-406F	
8EED	軭	5-3970	1-6468				
8EEE	軮	5-3968	1-6462		DC42	2-4067	
8EEF	軯	3-3738			DBFC	2-4062	
8EF0	軰		1-6463				
8EF1	軱	3-3740	1-6464		DC49	2-406E	
8EF2	軲	1-7379				E-3F44	
8EF3	軳	3-3744				E-3F46	
8EF4	軴				DC4B	2-4070	
8EF5	軵	3-3739			DC44	2-4069	
8EF6	軶	5-3969			DC47	2-406C	
8EF7	軷	3-3737	1-6465		DBFD	2-4063	
8EF8	軸	1-5465	0-2820	0-8578	B662	1-6249	215B3B
8EF9	軹	1-7382	1-6466	1-7806	DC40	2-4065	233B42
8EFA	軺	1-7387	1-6467	1-7991	DBFE	2-4064	233B3F
8EFB	軻	1-7380	0-7738	0-4227	B661	1-6248	215B3A
8EFC	軼	1-7383	0-7737	1-7472	B663	1-624A	215B3C
8EFD	軽		0-2358			E-3F49	2D5B43
8EFE	軾	1-7388	0-7740	0-6760	B8FD	1-6726	215B3E
8EFF	軿	3-3755			E075	2-477B	

Code	Char	G	J	K	B	C	A
8F00	輀	3-3751	1-6469		E077	2-477D	233B56
8F01	輁	3-3749			E076	2-477C	
8F02	輂	3-3750	1-6470		E07B	2-4823	
8F03	較	1-2947	0-1951	0-4682	B8FB	1-6724	215B3D
8F04	輄					E-4476	
8F05	輅	1-7391	0-7742	0-5457	E078	2-477E	233B59
8F06	輆	3-3754			E074	2-477A	
8F07	輇	1-7390	1-6471	1-7617	E079	2-4821	233B5B
8F08	輈	3-3752	1-6472	1-7758	E07A	2-4822	233B5A
8F09	載	1-5256	0-2660	0-7816	B8FC	1-6725	215B3F
8F0A	輊	1-7389	0-7741		B8FE	1-6727	215B40
8F0B	輋	5-2710			E07C	2-4824	
8F0C	輌		0-7750				4B5B46
8F0D	輍				E467	2-4E4F	
8F0E	輎				E466	2-4E4E	
8F0F	輏		1-6473				
8F10	輐	5-3975	1-6474		E464	2-4E4C	
8F11	輑	3-3760			E465	2-4E4D	
8F12	輒	1-7392	0-7744	0-8469	BBB3	1-6B3B	215B42
8F13	輓		0-7746	0-5634	BBB5	1-6B3D	215B44
8F14	輔	1-2408	0-4269	0-6048	BBB2	1-6B3A	215B41
8F15	輕	1-3965	0-7743	0-4478	BBB4	1-6B3C	215B43
8F16	輖	3-3772	1-6475		E84D	2-5475	
8F17	輗	3-3769	1-6476		E84E	2-5476	233B75
8F18	輘	3-3764	1-6477		E849	2-5471	
8F19	輙		0-7745			E-4F36	2D5B42
8F1A	輚	3-3736			E84A	2-5472	
8F1B	輛	1-3330	0-7749	0-5364	BDF8	1-6F43	215B46
8F1C	輜	1-7402	0-7747	0-8642	BDFD	1-6F48	215B4B
8F1D	輝	1-2752	0-2117	0-9342	BDF7	1-6F42	215B48
8F1E	輞	1-7394	1-6478	0-5654	BDFE	1-6F49	233B6B
8F1F	輟	1-7401	0-7748	0-8447	BDF9	1-6F44	215B47
8F20	輠	3-3768	1-6479		E84B	2-5473	233B6E
8F21	輡	5-3976	1-6480				
8F22	輢	3-3765				E-4F33	
8F23	輣	3-3771	1-6481		E84C	2-5474	
8F24	輤	3-3761			E848	2-5470	
8F25	輥	1-2585	1-6482		BE40	1-6F4A	233B6D
8F26	輦	1-7393	0-7751	0-5406	BDFB	1-6F46	215B45
8F27	輧		1-6483	0-6030		E-4F35	233B51
8F28	輨	3-3775	1-6484	1-5770			
8F29	輩	1-1718	0-3958	0-5952	BDFA	1-6F45	215B49
8F2A	輪	1-3454	0-4656	0-5539	BDFC	1-6F47	215B4A
8F2B	輫	3-3766				E-4F34	
8F2C	輬	3-3773	1-6485		E847	2-546F	233B64
8F2D	輭		1-6486			E-5324	233B7D
8F2E	輮	3-3785	1-6487		EBCA	2-5A76	233B79
8F2F	輯	1-2813	0-2920	0-8294	BFE8	1-7252	215B4D
8F30	輰	3-3727		1-7102		E-5322	
8F31	輱					E-5321	
8F32	輲	3-3779			EBCC	2-5A78	
8F33	輳	1-7403	0-7752	0-8145	BFEA	1-7254	233B7A
8F34	輴	3-3781	1-6488		EBCF	2-5A7B	233C27
8F35	輵	5-3979	1-6489		EBCB	2-5A77	
8F36	輶	3-3783	1-6490		EBC9	2-5A75	233B78
8F37	輷	5-3980	1-6491		EBCE	2-5A7A	
8F38	輸	1-4268	0-4502	0-6635	BFE9	1-7253	215B4E
8F39	輹	3-3780	0-7754	0-6062	EBCD	2-5A79	233C26
8F3A	輺		1-6492				
8F3B	輻	1-2388	0-7753	0-6063	BFE7	1-7251	215B4C
8F3C	輼	3-3778				E-5325	2F3C2D
8F3D	輽					E-5659	
8F3E	輾	1-5323	0-7757	0-7913	C1D3	1-755E	215B50
8F3F	輿	1-5163	0-4533	0-7011	C1D6	1-7561	215B53
8F40	轀		1-6493	1-7234	EBC1	2-5F6D	233C2D
8F41	轁		1-6494			E-565A	
8F42	轂	1-7617	0-7756	1-5713	C1D4	1-755F	215B52
8F43	轃	3-3786	1-6501		EBC0	2-5F6C	
8F44	轄	1-4729	0-1977	0-8961	C1D2	1-755D	215B4F
8F45	轅	1-5215	0-7755	0-7431	C1D5	1-7560	215B51
8F46	轆	1-7404	0-7760	1-6293	F146	2-6370	233C30
8F47	轇	3-3801	1-6502		F147	2-6371	233C33
8F48	轈	5-3986			F148	2-6372	
8F49	轉	1-5510	0-7759	0-7914	C2E0	1-774B	215B55
8F4A	轊	5-3985				E-5937	233C31
8F4B	轋	5-3973			F149	2-6373	
8F4C	轌		0-7758				696D5A
8F4D	轍	1-5362	0-3718	0-8448	C2E1	1-774C	215B54
8F4E	轎	1-2946	0-7761	0-4683	C3E2	1-792F	215B57
8F4F	轏	3-3808	1-6503		F358	2-6744	
8F50	轐	5-3988			F359	2-6745	
8F51	轑	3-3804	1-6504		F357	2-6743	
8F52	轒	3-3777	1-6505	1-6661	F356	2-6742	233C3D
8F53	轓	3-3805	1-6506		F35A	2-6746	
8F54	轔	1-7405	1-6507	1-6378	C3E1	1-792E	215B56
8F55	轕	3-3803	1-6508		F4DD	2-6A2B	233C4B
8F56	轖	3-3792			F4DB	2-6A29	233C48
8F57	轗	5-3990	0-7762	1-5551	F4DC	2-6A2A	233C49
8F58	轘	3-3811	1-6509	1-8431	F4DE	2-6A2C	233C4C
8F59	轙	3-3725			F4DA	2-6A28	
8F5A	轚				F4DF	2-6A2D	
8F5B	轛	3-3746			F658	2-6C47	
8F5C	轜	5-3993	0-7763			E-5E67	233C4D
8F5D	轝		1-6510	0-7012	F659	2-6C48	233C53
8F5E	轞	5-3982	1-6511	1-8303	F657	2-6C46	233C4E
8F5F	轟	1-2668	0-2576	0-4662	C546	1-7B32	215B58
8F60	轠	3-3813			F764	2-6E33	
8F61	轡	1-6446	0-2305	1-6713	C5AF	1-7B79	215B59
8F62	轢	1-7386	0-7764	0-5389	F765	2-6E34	233C57
8F63	轣	3-3729	0-7765	1-6242	F848	2-6F56	233C59
8F64	轤	1-7381	0-7766	1-6281	F847	2-6F55	233C5A
8F65	轥	3-3812	1-6512			E-6222	
8F66	车	0-1921					275B32
8F67	轧	0-5294					275B33
8F68	轨	0-2576					275B35
8F69	轩	0-4889					275B36
8F6A	轪	7-0105					
8F6B	轫	0-7377					275B37
8F6C	转	0-5510					275B55
8F6D	轭	0-7378					275B39
8F6E	轮	0-3454					275B4A
8F6F	软	0-4077					275B38
8F70	轰	0-2668					275B58
8F71	轱	0-7379					293B3E
8F72	轲	0-7380					275B3A
8F73	轳	0-7381					293C5A
8F74	轴	0-5465					275B3B
8F75	轵	0-7382					293B42
8F76	轶	0-7383					275B3C
8F77	轷	0-7385					293B47
8F78	轸	0-7384					293B4F
8F79	轹	0-7386					293C57
8F7A	轺	0-7387					293B3F
8F7B	轻	0-3965					275B43
8F7C	轼	0-7388					275B3E
8F7D	载	0-5256					275B3F
8F7E	轾	0-7389					275B40
8F7F	轿	0-2946					275B57

8F8

	Char	G	J	K	B	C	A
0	辀	8-1251					
1	辁	0-7390					293B5B
2	辂	0-7391					293B59
3	较	0-2947					275B3D
4	辄	0-7392					275B42
5	辅	0-2408					275B41
6	辆	0-3330					275B46
7	辇	0-7393					275B45
8	辈	0-1718					275B49
9	辉	0-2752					275B48
A	辊	0-2585					293B6D
B	辋	0-7394					293B6B
C	辌	7-0106					
D	辍	0-7401					275B47
E	辎	0-7402					275B4B
F	辏	0-7403					293B7A

8FA

	Char	G	J	K	B	C	A
0	辠		1-6514			E-4478	2D5232
1	辡		1-6515			E-4A21	
2	辢			1-6208		E-4A22	2D5B5D
3	辣	0-3217	0-7769	0-5324	BBB6	1-6B3E	215B5D
4	辤		1-6516			E-4F37	233C65
5	辥	5-8317	1-6517			E-5327	233C66
6	辦	1-1676	1-6518	0-8793	BFEC	1-7256	215B5F
7	辧		0-5001			E-5326	2D5B5E
8	辨	0-1770	0-4994	0-6009	BFEB	1-7255	215B5E
9	辩	0-1771					275B61
A	辪					E-6654	
B	辫	0-1772					27517A
C	辬	5-8320				E-5938	
D	辭	1-2039	0-7770	0-6286	C3E3	1-7930	215B60
E	辮	1-1772	0-6980	1-6574	C47C	1-7A29	21517A
F	辯	1-1771	0-7771	0-6010	C547	1-7B33	215B61

8FC

	Char	G	J	K	B	C	A
0	迀	5-7992	1-6523	1-5531			
1	迁	0-3908	1-6524			E-2733	275C51
2	迂	0-5156	0-1710	0-7370	A8B1	1-4B52	275C3C
3	迃			1-7220			
4	迄	0-3889	0-4388	1-8514	A8B4	1-4B55	215B68
5	迅	0-4924	0-3155	0-6786	A8B3	1-4B54	215B67
6	迆	5-8002	1-6525		A8B2	1-4B53	215B66
7	过	0-2593				E-2731	275C3E
8	迈	0-3485					275C56
9	迉				CBA5	2-2525	
A	迊		1-6526			E-2A72	233C7A
B	迋	3-8155	1-6527		CDCD	2-286D	233C77
C	迌					E-2A70	
D	迍	3-8156	1-6528	1-6173	CDCF	2-286F	233C7D
E	迎	0-5113	0-2362	0-7142	AAEF	1-4F52	215B6A
F	迏					E-2A74	

8FE

	Char	G	J	K	B	C	A
0	迠		1-6533		D0B6	2-2D57	
1	迡	5-8012			D0B4	2-2D55	
2	迢	0-4486	0-7775	1-7992	AD7C	1-535F	215B6F
3	迣	3-8158	1-6534		D0B3	2-2D54	
4	迤	0-6938	1-6535	1-7455	ADA3	1-5364	233D2F
5	迥	0-6936	0-7774	1-8367	AD7E	1-5361	215B71
6	迦	0-6940	0-1864	0-4228	AD7B	1-535E	215B6E
7	迧					E-2F31	
8	迨	0-6942	1-6536	1-8154	ADA4	1-5365	2D5C2F
9	迩	0-6939	0-3886			E-2F32	2D5C5A
A	迪	0-2147	0-7776	0-7872	AD7D	1-5360	215B70
B	迫	0-3840	0-3987	0-5862	ADA2	1-5363	215B73
C	迬			1-7269			
D	迭	0-2192	0-3719	0-8287	ADA1	1-5362	274C3C
E	迮	0-6937	1-6537		D0B5	2-2D56	233D30
F	迯	5-8010	0-7777			E-2F33	2D5B7A

8F9

	Char	G	J	K	B	C	A
0	辐	0-2388					275B4C
1	辑	0-2813					275B4D
2	辒	8-1252					
3	输	0-4268					275B4E
4	辔	0-6446					275B59
5	辕	0-5215					275B51
6	辖	0-4729					275B4F
7	辗	0-5323					275B50
8	辘	0-7404					293C30
9	辙	0-5362					275B54
A	辚	0-7405					275B56
B	辛	0-4833	0-3141	0-6784	A8AF	1-4B50	215B5A
C	辜	0-2528	0-7767	0-4548	B664	1-624B	215B5B
D	辝		1-6513			E-3F4B	
E	辞	0-2039	0-2813			E-4477	275B60
F	辟	0-1757	0-7768	1-8253	B940	1-6728	215B5C

8FB

	Char	G	J	K	B	C	A
0	辰	0-1929	0-3504	0-8267	A8B0	1-4B51	215B62
1	辱	0-4072	0-3111	0-7320	B064	1-5849	215B63
2	農	1-3709	0-3932	0-5060	B941	1-6729	215B64
3	辳					E-4F39	
4	辴	5-7828			F35B	2-6747	
5	辵	3-8152	1-6519			E-272F	233C6C
6	辶	0-6933	1-6520				4D3C6C
7	辷		0-7772				233C6D
8	辸	5-7991	1-6521				
9	边	0-1763				E-243B	275C5B
A	辺		0-4253				4B5C5B
B	辻		0-3652	1-7001			233C6E
C	込		0-2594				233C70
D	辽	0-3341					275C52
E	达	0-2079	1-6522			E-2730	275C39
F	辿	3-8153	0-3509	1-7932	CBA6	2-2526	233C74

8FD

	Char	G	J	K	B	C	A
0	运	0-5243	1-6529				275C34
1	近	0-2992	0-2265	0-4846	AAF1	1-4F54	215B6B
2	迒	3-8157	1-6530		CDCC	2-286C	233C75
3	迓	0-6934	1-6531	1-7010	CDCE	2-286E	233C7B
4	返	0-2321	0-4254	0-5887	AAF0	1-4F53	215B6C
5	迕	0-6935	1-6532	1-7221	CDD1	2-2871	233D22
6	迖				CDD0	2-2870	
7	迗				CDD2	2-2872	
8	还	0-2725				E-2A73	275C57
9	这	0-5366				E-2A71	275B7D
A	迚		0-7773				233D21
B	进	0-2988					275C33
C	远	0-5222					275C44
D	违	0-4605					275C3A
E	连	0-3312					275B7E
F	迟	0-1957					275C50

8FF

	Char	G	J	K	B	C	A
0	述	0-4286	0-2950	0-6691	AD7A	1-535D	215B6D
1	迱	5-8011	1-6538			E-2F30	
2	迲			0-4406			
3	迳	0-6941					513D67
4	迴	1-8828	0-7779	1-8449	B06A	1-584F	333768
5	迵	3-8162	1-6539		D3EB	2-332F	
6	迶		1-6540		D3F1	2-3335	
7	迷	0-3552	0-4434	0-5827	B067	1-584C	215B76
8	迸	0-1737	0-7794	1-6586	B06E	1-5853	293D4E
9	迹	0-2803	0-7781	0-7873		E-3425	233D35
A	迺	8-1360	0-7782	1-6027	B069	1-584E	33303A
B	迻		1-6541		D3EE	2-3332	233D3C
C	迼	3-8160			D3F0	2-3334	
D	追	0-5523	0-3641	0-8558	B06C	1-5851	215B7B
E	迾	3-8161	1-6542		D3EA	2-332E	
F	迿	3-8164			D3ED	2-3331	

Code	Char	G	J	K	B	C	A
9000	退	0-4543	0-3464	0-8760	B068	1-584D	215B77
9001	送	0-4345	0-3387	0-6574	B065	1-584A	215B74
9002	适	0-4242	1-6543	0-4633	D3EC	2-3330	275C49
9003	逃	0-4451	0-3808	0-5217	B06B	1-5850	215B7A
9004	逄	0-6944	1-6544		D3EF	2-3333	233D3F
9005	逅	0-6943	0-7780	0-9317	B06D	1-5852	215B7C
9006	逆	0-3670	0-2153	0-7029	B066	1-584B	215B75
9007	逇						
9008	逈		1-6545	0-9113		E-3427	233D40
9009	选	0-4901				E-3426	275C4F
900A	逊	0-4923					275C45
900B	逋	0-6945	0-7789	0-8871	D7E3	2-3966	233D45
900C	逌	3-8169	1-6546	1-7402	D7E6	2-3969	233D48
900D	逍	0-6948	0-7786	0-6546	B370	1-5D56	215C26
900E	逎	3-8168	0-7805			E-394B	2F3D5D
900F	透	0-4524	0-3809	0-8766	B37A	1-5D60	215C2A
9010	逐	0-5480	0-3564	0-8579	B376	1-5D5C	215C24
9011	逑	0-6947	0-7783	0-4739	D7E4	2-3967	233D44
9012	递	0-2161				E-394A	275C48
9013	逓		0-3694			E-394E	2D5C48
9014	途	0-4530	0-3751	0-5218	B37E	1-5D64	215C2E
9015	逕	1-6941	0-7784	0-4479	B377	1-5D5D	2D3D67
9016	逖	0-6949	0-7788	1-7582	B37C	1-5D62	215C2C
9017	逗	0-2226	0-3164	0-5272	B372	1-5D58	215C22
9018	逘		1-6547				
9019	這	1-5366	0-3971	0-7847	B36F	1-5D55	215B7D
901A	通	0-4508	0-3644	0-8755	B371	1-5D57	215C28
901B	逛	0-2568	1-6548		B37D	1-5D63	215C2D
901C	逜	5-8017			D7E5	2-3968	
901D	逝	0-4237	0-3234	0-6406	B375	1-5D5B	215C23
901E	逞	0-1949	0-7787	0-5433	B378	1-5D5E	215C27
901F	速	0-4357	0-3414	0-6560	B374	1-5D5A	215C21
9020	造	0-5276	0-3404	0-8067	B379	1-5D5F	215C29
9021	逡	0-6950	0-7785	0-8168	D7E7	2-396A	233D49
9022	逢	0-2374	0-1609	0-6081	B37B	1-5D61	215C2B
9023	連	1-3312	0-4702	0-5407	B373	1-5D59	215B7E
9024	逤				D7E2	2-3965	
9025	逥					E-394C	
9026	逦	0-6946					275C5C
9027	逧		0-7790				696D7A
9028	逨	5-8018	1-6549			E-3F4F	
9029	逩		1-6550			E-3F50	33392F
902A	逪	5-8021	1-6552			E-3F4D	
902B	逫	3-8174				E-3F4C	
902C	逬		1-6553			E-3F51	
902D	逭	0-6953	1-6554		DC4D	2-4072	233D4A
902E	逮	0-2094	0-3465	0-8485	B665	1-624C	215C2F
902F	逯	0-6954	1-6551		DC4F	2-4074	233D58
9030	逰					E-3F55	
9031	週		0-2921	0-8146	B667	1-624E	215C31
9032	進	1-2988	0-3142	0-8268	B669	1-6250	215C33
9033	逳	3-8172	1-6555				
9034	逴	3-8171	1-6556	1-8133	DC4E	2-4073	233D57
9035	逵	0-6951	0-7792	0-4816	B666	1-624D	215C30
9036	逶	0-6952	0-7791	1-7365	B66A	1-6251	233D59
9037	逷	5-8025	1-6557			E-3F56	233D56
9038	逸	0-5061	0-1679	0-7679	B668	1-624F	215C32
9039	逹		0-7793				4B5C39
903A	逺					E-3F54	
903B	逻	0-3463				E-3F57	275C5D
903C	逼	0-1738	0-4115	0-8926	B947	1-672F	215C3B
903D	逽	3-8170			E0A3	2-4829	
903E	逾	0-5166	0-7807	0-7521	B94F	1-6737	215C42
903F	逿	3-8154	1-6558		E07E	2-4826	
9040	遀					E-447D	
9041	遁	0-2261	0-3859	0-5277	B950	1-6738	215C41
9042	遂	0-4376	0-3175	0-6636	B945	1-672D	215C37
9043	遃	3-8178	1-6559			E-4479	
9044	遄	0-6955	1-6560		E0A1	2-4827	233D6A
9045	遅		0-3557			E-447C	4B5C50
9046	遆	3-8179				E-447A	233D5B
9047	遇	0-5186	0-2288	0-7371	B94A	1-6732	215C3C
9048	遈					E-447B	
9049	遉		0-7806	1-7665	E0A2	2-4828	233D67
904A	遊		0-4523	0-7520	B943	1-672B	33477B
904B	運	1-5243	0-1731	0-7401	B942	1-672A	215C34
904C	遌	3-8177	1-6561			E-447E	
904D	遍	0-1773	0-4255	0-8828	B94D	1-6735	215C3F
904E	過	1-2593	0-1865	0-4606	B94C	1-6734	215C3E
904F	遏	0-2284	0-7801	1-7033	B94B	1-6733	215C3D
9050	遐	0-6958	0-7802	0-8938	B949	1-6731	215C38
9051	遑	0-6956	0-7803	0-9258	B94E	1-6736	215C40
9052	遒	0-6957	0-7804	1-7759	E07D	2-4825	233D5D
9053	道	0-2132	0-3827	0-5219	B944	1-672C	215C36
9054	達	1-2079	0-3503	0-5125	B946	1-672E	215C39
9055	違	1-4605	0-1667	0-7462	B948	1-6730	215C3A
9056	遖		0-7808				696E28
9057	遗	0-5037					275C53
9058	遘	0-6960	0-7809	1-5874	BBB8	1-6B40	215C43
9059	遙		0-8403	0-7311	BBBB	1-6B43	215C47
905A	遚					E-4A24	
905B	遛	0-6962	1-6562	1-6342	BBBF	1-6B47	233D78
905C	遜	1-4923	0-3429	0-6565	BBB9	1-6B41	215C45
905D	遝	3-8182	1-6563	0-5147	BBBE	1-6B46	233D75
905E	遞	1-2161	0-7810	0-8486	BBBC	1-6B44	215C48
905F	遟	5-8031				E-4A27	
9060	遠	1-5222	0-1783	0-7432	BBB7	1-6B3F	215C44
9061	遡		0-3344	0-6547		E-4A26	39483B
9062	遢	0-6961	1-6564		BBBD	1-6B45	233D74
9063	遣	0-3918	0-2415	0-4426	BBBA	1-6B42	215C46
9064	遤						
9065	遥	0-5003	0-4558				4B5C47
9066	遦	5-8028	1-6565				
9067	遧	5-8036	1-6566		E852	2-547A	
9068	遨	0-6959	0-7811	1-7222	BE43	1-6F4D	215C4B
9069	適	1-4242	0-3712	0-7874	BE41	1-6F4B	215C49
906A	遪	3-8173				E-4F3C	
906B	遫	3-8183			E853	2-547B	233D7B
906C	遬	3-8184	1-6567	1-6892			
906D	遭	0-5266	0-3388	0-8068	BE44	1-6F4E	215C4C
906E	遮	0-5358	0-2855	0-8320	BE42	1-6F4C	215C4A
906F	遯		0-7812	0-5278	E851	2-5479	233E25
9070	遰	3-8176	1-6568		E850	2-5478	233E21
9071	遱	3-8180				E-4F3B	
9072	遲	1-1957	0-7815	0-8232	BFF0	1-725A	215C50
9073	遳	3-8181			E84F	2-5477	
9074	遴	0-6964	1-6569		BFEE	1-7258	215C4E
9075	遵	0-5581	0-2969	0-8169	BFED	1-7257	215C4D
9076	遶		0-7813	1-7294	EBD0	2-5A7C	233E28
9077	遷	1-3908	0-3311	0-8435	BE45	1-6F4F	215C51
9078	選	1-4901	0-3310	0-6452	BFEF	1-7259	215C4F
9079	遹	3-8188	1-6570		EBD1	2-5A7D	233E26
907A	遺	1-5037	0-1668	0-7522	BFF2	1-725C	215C53
907B	遻	5-8039			EBD2	2-5A7E	233E2A
907C	遼	1-3341	0-4643	0-5501	BFF1	1-725B	215C52
907D	遽	0-6965	0-7817	0-4372	C1D8	1-7563	215C55
907E	遾	3-8189			EBC3	2-5F6F	
907F	避	0-1760	0-4082	0-8913	C1D7	1-7562	215C54

908

	Char	G	J	K	B	C	A
0	邀	0-4991	0-7819	0-7313	C1DC	1-7567	215C59
1	邁	1-3485	0-7818	0-5668	C1DA	1-7565	215C56
2	邂	0-6966	0-7816	0-9019	C1DB	1-7566	215C58
3	邃	0-6968	0-6768	0-6637	C2E3	1-774E	233E34
4	還	1-2725	0-2052	0-9229	C1D9	1-7564	215C57
5	邅	3-8190	1-6571	1-7618	EEC2	2-5F6E	233E2C
6	邆	3-8187			EED3	2-5B21	
7	邇	1-6939	0-7778	0-7636	C2E2	1-774D	215C5A
8	邈	0-6967	1-6572	0-5617	C2E4	1-774F	233E37
9	邉		0-7821			E-593A	2D5C5B
A	邊	1-1763	0-7820	0-6011	C3E4	1-7931	215C5B
B	邋	0-6969	1-6573		C3E5	1-7932	233E3A
C	邌	5-8042	1-6574	1-6236			
D	邍				F4E0	2-6A2E	
E	邎		1-6575				
F	邏	1-3463	0-7822	0-5304	C5DE	1-7C4A	215C5D

909

	Char	G	J	K	B	C	A
0	邐	1-6946	1-6576	1-6367	C5DD	1-7C49	215C5C
1	邑	0-5056	0-4524	0-7573	A8B6	1-4B57	215C5E
2	邒	3-8060				E-225E	
3	邓	0-2143				E-225D	275C75
4	邔				CA55	2-2275	
5	邕	0-7163	1-6577	0-7227	B06F	1-5854	215C5F
6	邖	3-2430				E-243C	
7	邗	0-5885	1-6578		CA52	2-2272	233E40
8	邘	3-8061	1-6579		CA53	2-2273	
9	邙	0-5888	1-6580	0-5655	CA51	2-2271	233E3F
A	邚					E-243D	
B	邛	0-5886	1-6581		CA54	2-2274	233E43
C	邜					E-6655	233E44
D	邝	0-5887					294031
E	邞				CBAA	2-252A	
F	邟	3-8066			CBA7	2-2527	

90A

	Char	G	J	K	B	C	A
0	邠	3-8065	1-6582	1-6731	CBAC	2-252C	233E54
1	邡	0-5890	1-6583		CBA8	2-2528	233E48
2	邢	0-4847	1-6584	0-9114	A8B7	1-4B58	215C61
3	那	0-3639	0-3865	0-4965	A8BA	1-4B5B	215C60
4	邤	3-4418				E-2735	
5	邥	3-8068	1-6585		CBA9	2-2529	
6	邦	0-1678	0-4314	0-5932	A8B9	1-4B5A	215C63
7	邧	3-8062			CBAB	2-252B	
8	邨	8-1570	0-7823	0-8530		E-2739	233E51
9	邩	3-4743				E-2734	
A	邪	0-4816	0-2857	0-6287	A8B8	1-4B59	215C62
B	邫					E-3951	
C	邬	0-5889					293F5C
D	邭					E-2A77	233E5F
E	邮	0-5142					275C6D
F	邯	0-2610	0-7824	0-4291	CDD5	2-2875	233E58

90B

	Char	G	J	K	B	C	A
0	邰	0-5902	1-6586	0-8738	CDD7	2-2877	233E5D
1	邱	0-3981	0-7825	0-4740	AAF4	1-4F57	215C65
2	邲	3-8069	1-6587		CDD3	2-2873	233E61
3	邳	0-5892	1-6588	1-6714	CDD6	2-2876	233E59
4	邴	0-5891	1-6589		CDD4	2-2874	2F4A2E
5	邵	0-4159	0-7826	0-6548	AAF2	1-4F55	215C64
6	邶	0-5893	1-6590		AAF5	1-4F58	233E5B
7	邷	3-3829				E-2A75	
8	邸	0-5901	0-3701	0-7848	AAF3	1-4F56	215C66
9	邹	0-5562				E-2A78	275C71
A	邺	0-5894					29402B
B	邻	0-3358					275C74
C	邼					E-2F35	
D	邽	3-8071	1-6591	1-5935	D0B8	2-2D59	233E6A
E	邾	0-5905	1-6593		D0BC	2-2D5D	233E72
F	邿	3-8072			D0B9	2-2D5A	

90C

	Char	G	J	K	B	C	A
0	郀	3-8075				E-2F38	
1	郁	0-5184	0-1674	0-7384	ADA7	1-5368	27616A
2	郂	3-8082				E-2F34	
3	郃	3-8080	1-6594	1-8311	ADA8	1-5369	233E79
4	郄	0-5907	1-6601	1-5944		E-2F3E	335F34
5	郅	0-5904	1-6602	1-7823	D0BB	2-2D5C	34782A
6	郆	3-8073				E-2F37	
7	郇	0-5908	1-6603		D0BD	2-2D5E	233E75
8	郈	3-8079	1-6604		D0BF	2-2D60	233E78
9	郉					E-2F3C	233E68
A	郊	0-2928	0-2557	0-4684	ADA5	1-5366	215C68
B	郋	3-6940			D0BE	2-2D5F	
C	郌		1-6592				
D	郍	3-6947				E-2F3B	
E	郎	0-3241	0-4726		ADA6	1-5367	215C67
F	郏	0-5903					293F23

90D

	Char	G	J	K	B	C	A
0	郐	0-5906					29402C
1	郑	0-5403					275C73
2	郒		1-6613				
3	郓	0-5909					293F4C
4	郔	3-8078			D7EE	2-3971	
5	郕	3-8076	1-6605		D0BA	2-2D5B	233E6F
6	郖	3-7833			D3F2	2-3336	
7	郗	0-5913	1-6606		D3FB	2-333F	233F2C
8	郘	3-8077	1-6607		D3F9	2-333D	233F27
9	郙	3-8087	1-6608		D3F4	2-3338	
A	郚	3-8089			D3F5	2-3339	
B	郛	0-5914	0-7830		D3FA	2-333E	233F28
C	郜	0-5912	1-6609	1-5703	D3FC	2-3340	233F2A
D	郝	0-2634	1-6610	1-8282	B071	1-5856	233F22
E	郞			0-5345		E-3429	
F	郟	1-5903	1-6611		D3F7	2-333B	233F23

90E

	Char	G	J	K	B	C	A
0	郠	3-8088			D3F3	2-3337	
1	郡	0-3104	0-2320	0-4759	B070	1-5855	215C6A
2	郢	0-5911	0-7827	1-7176	B072	1-5857	233F26
3	郣	3-8086			D3F6	2-333A	
4	郤	3-8192	0-7828		D3FD	2-3341	233F2D
5	郥		1-6612		D3F8	2-333C	
6	郦	0-5910					294040
7	郧	0-5239					293F5A
8	部	0-1831	0-4184	0-6127	B3A1	1-5D65	215C6B
9	郩	5-7964			D7F1	2-3974	
A	郪	3-8103		1-7906	D7E9	2-396C	233F2F
B	郫	0-5915	1-6615	1-6715	D7EF	2-3972	233F3E
C	郬				D7F0	2-3973	
D	郭	0-2589	0-1952	0-4612	B3A2	1-5D66	215C6C
E	郮					E-394F	
F	郯	0-5916	1-6616	1-6091	D7E8	2-396B	233F2E

90F

	Char	G	J	K	B	C	A
0	郰	3-8094	1-6617		D7EA	2-396D	233F32
1	郱	3-8083			D0B7	2-2D58	
2	郲	3-8090			D7EC	2-396F	233F34
3	郳	3-8105			D7ED	2-3970	233F3F
4	郴	0-1927	1-6618	1-8107	D7EB	2-396E	233F33
5	郵	1-5142	0-4525	0-7372	B66C	1-6253	215C6D
6	郶		1-6614			E-636C	
7	郷		0-2231			E-3952	
8	郸	0-2106					294021
9	郹	3-8108			DC56	2-407B	
A	郺				EED4	2-5B22	
B	郻				DC57	2-407C	
C	郼				DC54	2-4079	233F46
D	都	0-2228	0-3752	0-5220	B3A3	1-5D67	215C6E
E	郾	0-5917	1-6619		B66E	1-6255	233F47
F	郿	3-8114	1-6620		DC53	2-4078	233F4A

910

	Char	G	J	K	B	C	A
0	鄀	3-8101	1-6621		DC59	2-407E	233F4E
1	鄁				DC58	2-407D	
2	鄂	0-2285	0-7831	0-6839	B66B	1-6252	215C6F
3	鄃	3-8112			DC5C	2-4123	
4	鄄	0-5918	1-6622		DC52	2-4077	233F49
5	鄅	3-8110	1-6623		DC5B	2-4122	
6	鄆	1-5909	1-6624		DC50	2-4075	233F4C
7	鄇	3-8111			DC5A	2-4121	233F50
8	鄈	3-8115	1-6625		DC55	2-407A	
9	鄉	1-4771			B66D	1-6254	215C70
A	鄊					E-3F59	
B	鄋	3-8109			E0AA	2-4830	233F60
C	鄌	3-8120				E-4523	
D	鄍	3-8122	1-6626		E0A5	2-482B	
E	鄎	5-7969			E0AB	2-4831	
F	鄏	3-8118			E0A6	2-482C	233F57

911

	Char	G	J	K	B	C	A
0	鄐	3-8121	1-6627		E0A4	2-482A	
1	鄑	3-8117			E0A7	2-482D	233F58
2	鄒	1-5562	0-7832	0-8559	B951	1-6739	215C71
3	鄓					E-4524	
4	鄔	1-5889	1-6628		E0A9	2-482F	233F5C
5	鄕			0-9033		E-4525	
6	鄖	1-5239	1-6629		E0A8	2-482E	233F5A
7	鄗	3-9178	1-6630		B952	1-673A	
8	鄘	3-8126	1-6631		BBC1	1-6B49	233F63
9	鄙	0-1741	0-7833	0-6209	BBC0	1-6B48	215C72
A	鄚	3-8116	1-6632		E46E	2-4E56	233F72
B	鄛	3-8129			E471	2-4E59	
C	鄜	3-9211	1-6633		E469	2-4E51	233F64
D	鄝	3-8128			E46D	2-4E55	
E	鄞	0-5920	1-6634	1-7425	BBC2	1-6B4A	233F6A
F	鄟	3-8063			E46C	2-4E54	

912

	Char	G	J	K	B	C	A
0	鄠	3-8123	1-6635		E46A	2-4E52	233F66
1	鄡	3-8107			E470	2-4E58	
2	鄢	0-5919	1-6637	1-7115	E46B	2-4E53	233F67
3	鄣	0-5921	1-6638	1-7545	E468	2-4E50	
4	鄤	3-8124			E46F	2-4E57	233F71
5	鄥		1-6636			E-4A2A	233F74
6	鄦	3-3213			E859	2-5523	234024
7	鄧	1-2143	1-6639	0-5288	BE48	1-6F52	215C75
8	鄨	3-8059			F14A	2-6374	
9	鄩	3-8085	1-6640		E856	2-547E	
A	鄪	5-7967			E857	2-5521	
B	鄫	3-8133			E855	2-547D	233F79
C	鄬	3-8067			DC51	2-4076	
D	鄭	1-5403	0-3702	0-7987	BE47	1-6F51	215C73
E	鄮	3-8113	1-6641		E85A	2-5524	
F	鄯	0-5923	1-6642		E854	2-547C	233F77

913

	Char	G	J	K	B	C	A
0	鄰	1-3358	0-7835	1-6379	BE46	1-6F50	215C74
1	鄱	0-5922	1-6643	1-8184	BE49	1-6F53	215C76
2	鄲	1-2106	0-7834	0-5119	E858	2-5522	234021
3	鄳	3-8502			EBD5	2-5B23	
4	鄴	1-5894	1-6644	1-7126	BFF3	1-725D	23402B
5	鄵	3-8135			EBD6	2-5B24	
6	鄶	1-5906	1-6645		EBD7	2-5B25	23402C
7	鄷		1-6646			E-532B	
8	鄸	3-8134			EEC4	2-5F70	
9	鄹	0-5924	1-6647		C1DD	1-7568	215C77
A	鄺	1-5887	1-6648		F14B	2-6375	234031
B	鄻	3-8130			F14C	2-6376	234032
C	鄼		1-6649			E-593C	
D	鄽	5-7979	1-6650	1-7619		E-593B	
E	鄾	3-8137			F14D	2-6377	
F	鄿	5-7971			F35D	2-6749	

914

	Char	G	J	K	B	C	A
0	酀	5-7980			F35C	2-6748	
1	酁				F4E2	2-6A30	
2	酂	8-9477					
3	酃	0-5925	1-6651		F4E1	2-6A2F	23403B
4	酄	5-7982			F65B	2-6C4A	
5	酅	3-8139			F65C	2-6C4B	23403F
6	酆	0-5926			F65A	2-6C49	23403E
7	酇	3-8138	1-6652		F766	2-6E35	234041
8	酈	1-5910	1-6653	1-6243	C5B0	1-7B7A	234040
9	酉	0-5147	0-3851	0-7523	A8BB	1-4B5C	215C78
A	酊	0-8490	0-7836	0-7988	ADAA	1-536B	215C7A
B	酋	0-3985	0-2922	0-8560	ADA9	1-536A	215C79
C	酌	0-5535	0-2864	0-7744	B075	1-585A	215C7D
D	配	0-3768	0-3959	0-5953	B074	1-5859	215C7C
E	酎	0-8492	0-3581	0-8147	D440	2-3343	234043
F	酏	0-8493	1-6654		D441	2-3344	2F4053

915

	Char	G	J	K	B	C	A
0	酐	0-8491			D3FE	2-3342	234042
1	酑					E-342A	
2	酒	0-3038	0-2882	0-8148	B073	1-5858	215C7B
3	酓	3-7851	1-6655		D7F5	2-3978	
4	酔		0-3176			E-3955	275D2A
5	酕	3-7850			D7F6	2-3979	
6	酖		0-7837	1-8142	D7F2	2-3975	23404D
7	酗	0-4879	1-6656	1-8473	B3A4	1-5D68	215C7E
8	酘	3-7853	0-7838		D7F3	2-3976	234050
9	酙		1-6657			E-3954	234048
A	酚	0-2351	1-6658		D7F4	2-3977	234052
B	酛		1-6659				
C	酜					E-6657	234049
D	酝	0-5245					275D2F
E	酞	0-4410					704C2A
F	酟	3-7856			DC5F	2-4126	

916

	Char	G	J	K	B	C	A
0	酠				DC61	2-4128	
1	酡	0-8502	1-6660		DC5D	2-4124	234053
2	酢	0-8501	0-3161	0-8518	DC60	2-4127	4B5D2B
3	酣	0-2608	0-7839	1-5552	B66F	1-6256	215D21
4	酤	0-8494	1-6661	1-5704	DC5E	2-4125	234056
5	酥	0-4354	0-7840	1-6886	B670	1-6257	215D22
6	酦	7-0117					
7	酧		1-6662			E-4528	2D5D23
8	酨	3-3820			DD73	2-4279	
9	酩	0-8504	0-7841	0-5714	B955	1-673D	215D24
A	酪	0-3250	0-4579	0-5312	B954	1-673C	215D25
B	酫					E-4527	
C	酬	0-1974	0-2923	0-6638	B953	1-673B	215D23
D	酭	5-7804	1-6663				
E	酮	0-4510			E0AC	2-4832	234062
F	酯	0-8505			E0AD	2-4833	234061

917

	Char	G	J	K	B	C	A
0	酰	0-8503					707523
1	酱	0-2920					275D32
2	酲	0-8508	0-7843	1-7666	E473	2-4E5B	234068
3	酳	3-7868	0-7842		E475	2-4E5D	23406C
4	酴	0-8509	1-6664	1-6136	BBC6	1-6B4E	23406B
5	酵	0-2945	0-2558	0-9303	BBC3	1-6B4B	215D26
6	酶	0-3524		1-6422		E-4A2C	23406A
7	酷	0-3165	0-2583	0-9169	BBC5	1-6B4D	215D28
8	酸	0-4365	0-2732	0-6311	BBC4	1-6B4C	215D27
9	酹	0-8510	1-6665	1-6317	E474	2-4E5C	234069
A	酺	3-7865	1-6666		E472	2-4E5A	234066
B	酻		1-6667			E-4A2B	
C	酼					E-4A2D	
D	酽	0-8506					29415D
E	酾	0-8507					29415C
F	酿	0-3680					275D34

918

	Char	G	J	K	B	C	A
0	醀	3-7873			E861	2-552B	
1	醁	3-7876	1-6668		E85E	2-5528	234073
2	醂	3-7871	0-7846		E85F	2-5529	23406F
3	醃		1-6669	1-7123	BE4D	1-6F57	215D2C
4	醄	3-7874			E860	2-552A	
5	醅	0-8512	1-6670		E85B	2-5525	23406D
6	醆		1-6671		E85C	2-5526	234071
7	醇	0-2028	0-2970	0-6685	BE4A	1-6F54	215D29
8	醈	5-7810				E-4F3F	
9	醉	0-5577	0-7845	0-8613	BE4B	1-6F55	215D2A
A	醊	3-7878	1-6672		E85D	2-5527	234070
B	醋	0-2055	0-7844	0-8519	BE4C	1-6F56	215D2B
C	醌	0-8511				E-4F40	234072
D	醍	0-8514	0-3473	0-8021	EBDB	2-5B29	234124
E	醎	5-7813	1-6673			E-532D	23407E
F	醏				EBDC	2-5B2A	

91A

	Char	G	J	K	B	C	A
0	醠	5-7820			EBCC	2-5F78	
1	醡	5-7821	1-6680		EBCA	2-5F76	
2	醢	0-8516	0-7847	1-8325	EBC6	2-5F72	234130
3	醣	0-8517			C1DE	1-7569	215D2E
4	醤		0-3063				
5	醥				F14F	2-6379	
6	醦	3-7877	1-6681				
7	醧	5-7791			F150	2-637A	
8	醨	3-7886	1-6682		F14E	2-6378	234137
9	醩	5-7822				E-593D	
A	醪	0-8518	0-7850	1-6327	F152	2-637C	23413D
B	醫	1-5029	0-7848	0-7602	C2E5	1-7750	215D31
C	醬	1-2920	1-6683	0-7793	C2E6	1-7751	215D32
D	醭	0-8519	1-6684		F35F	2-674B	234147
E	醮	0-8520	1-6685	0-8520	C3E7	1-7934	234148
F	醯	0-8521	0-7849	0-9124	F151	2-637B	234141

91C

	Char	G	J	K	B	C	A
0	釀	1-3680	0-7854	0-6952	C643	1-7C6E	215D34
1	釁	1-4838	0-7855	1-8510	C65D	1-7D2A	215D35
2	釂	3-7905	1-6701		F8C9	2-7057	23415A
3	釃	1-8507	1-6702	1-6971	F971	2-7160	23415C
4	釄					E-616D	23415B
5	釅	1-8506	1-6703	1-7158	C66F	1-7D3C	
6	釆		0-4048		A8BC	1-4B5D	4B5D36
7	采	0-1841	0-2651	0-8390	AAF6	1-4F59	215D36
8	釈		0-2865				4B5D38
9	釉	0-5152	0-7856	0-7524	B956	1-673E	215D37
A	释	0-4245					275D38
B	釋	1-4245	0-7857	0-6423	C4C0	1-7A4B	215D38
C	里	0-3279	0-4604	0-5576	A8BD	1-4B5E	275763
D	重	0-5456	0-2937	0-8176	ADAB	1-536C	215D3A
E	野	0-5016	0-4478	0-6915	B3A5	1-5D69	215D3B
F	量	0-3331	0-4644	0-5365	B671	1-6258	215D3C

91E

	Char	G	J	K	B	C	A
0	釠					E-3431	
1	釡		0-7861				4B5D42
2	釢				D443	2-3346	234168
3	釣	1-2186	0-3664	0-8069	B3A8	1-5D6C	215D45
4	釤	1-7844	1-6710	1-6777	D7FC	2-3A21	234222
5	釥	3-8562	1-6711			E-3958	
6	釦		0-4353	1-5875	B3A7	1-5D6B	215D44
7	釧	1-7843	0-2292	0-8436	B3A9	1-5D6D	215D46
8	釨				D842	2-3A26	234171
9	釩	1-2316	1-6712		B3AB	1-5D6F	234179
A	釪	3-8554	1-6713	0-7373	D7FE	2-3A23	
B	釫				D840	2-3A24	
C	釬		1-6714		D7F7	2-397A	23416B
D	釭	3-8555	1-6715	1-5742	B3AA	1-5D6E	234169
E	釮		1-6716		D843	2-3A27	234173
F	釯		1-6717				

919

	Char	G	J	K	B	C	A
0	醐	0-8513	0-2479	1-8392	EBD9	2-5B27	23407D
1	醑	0-8515	1-6674		EBDA	2-5B28	23407B
2	醒	0-4849	0-3235	0-6505	BFF4	1-725E	215D2D
3	醓	3-7885	1-6675		EBD8	2-5B26	234125
4	醔		1-6676				
5	醕		1-6677			E-532C	
6	醖	1-5245				E-532F	2D5D2F
7	醗		0-4016				
8	醘		1-6678				
9	醙				EBC8	2-5F74	
A	醚	0-3549			EBC5	2-5F71	23412C
B	醛	0-4009			EBC7	2-5F73	234134
C	醜	1-1983	0-2925	0-8561	C1E0	1-756B	215D30
D	醝	3-7884			EBCB	2-5F77	23412B
E	醞		1-6679	1-7235	C1DF	1-756A	215D2F
F	醟	3-7854			EBC9	2-5F75	

91B

	Char	G	J	K	B	C	A
0	醰	3-7890	1-6686		F35E	2-674A	
1	醱	3-7858	1-6687	0-5903	C3E6	1-7933	234142
2	醲	3-7864	1-6688	1-6044	F4E5	2-6A33	23414C
3	醳	3-7859	1-6689		F4E6	2-6A34	
4	醴	0-8523	0-7852	0-5442	C4BF	1-7A4A	23414B
5	醵	0-8522	0-7851	0-4357	F4E4	2-6A32	23414D
6	醶	5-7808	1-6690				
7	醷	3-7901			F4E3	2-6A31	
8	醸		0-3090				4B5D34
9	醹	3-7902			F65D	2-6C4C	
A	醺	0-8524	0-7853		C548	1-7B34	215D33
B	醻		1-6691			E-5E68	395D23
C	醼		1-6692		F849	2-6F57	334A28
D	醽	3-7904	1-6693		F8C8	2-7056	234157
E	醾	3-7906			F8C7	2-7055	354156
F	醿		1-6694			E-607E	234156

91D

	Char	G	J	K	B	C	A
0	釐		0-7858	0-5577	C2E7	1-7752	215D3D
1	金	0-2980	0-2266	0-4949	AAF7	1-4F5A	215D3E
2	釒	1-7836					
3	釓	1-7837	1-6704		D0C1	2-2D62	234162
4	釔	1-7838	1-6705		D0C0	2-2D61	234161
5	釕	1-7841			D442	2-3345	234163
6	釖	5-8523	0-7859			E-3430	513421
7	釗	1-7840	1-6706	0-6582	B078	1-585D	215D41
8	釘	1-2204	0-3703	0-7989	B076	1-585B	215D40
9	釙	1-7839	1-6707		B07A	1-585F	234164
A	釚	5-8522	1-6708		D444	2-3347	
B	釛		0-7862			E-342D	4D4176
C	釜	0-2410	0-1988	0-6128	B079	1-585E	215D42
D	針	1-5375	0-3143	0-8660	B077	1-585C	215D3F
E	釞	5-8521	1-6709			E-342F	
F	釟		0-7860			E-342E	696E5C

91F

	Char	G	J	K	B	C	A
0	釰	3-8561	1-6718			E-3957	
1	釱	3-8556	1-6719		D7F9	2-397C	234177
2	釲	5-8524				E-3956	23416F
3	釳	3-8558			D7FA	2-397D	
4	釴	3-8557			D7F8	2-397B	234174
5	釵	1-7846	0-7864	0-8391	B3A6	1-5D6A	215D43
6	釶	5-8525	0-7865			E-3959	234172
7	釷	1-7842	1-6720		D841	2-3A25	23416A
8	釸				D7FB	2-397E	23417A
9	釹	1-7847	1-6721		D7FD	2-3A22	234221
A	釺	1-3905					
B	釻		1-6722				
C	釼		0-7863				333421
D	釽	5-8532	1-6723		DC6D	2-4134	
E	釾	5-8529				E-3F5D	234233
F	釿	5-8531	0-7867	1-5953	DC6C	2-4133	234248

920

	Char	G	J	K	B	C	A
0	鈀	1-7857	1-6724		DC6A	2-4131	234231
1	鈁	1-7853	1-6725		DC62	2-4129	234225
2	鈂	3-8572			DC71	2-4138	
3	鈃	3-8563			DC65	2-412C	23422F
4	鈄	1-7855	1-6726		DC6F	2-4136	234223
5	鈅		1-6727		DC76	2-413D	
6	鈆		1-6728		DC6E	2-4135	23424E
7	鈇	3-8564	1-6729	1-6641	B679	1-6260	23422E
8	鈈	1-7848				E-3F66	234236
9	鈉	1-3638	1-6730		B675	1-625C	215D4A
A	鈊	3-8573	1-6731		DC63	2-412A	234227
B	鈋	3-8568				E-3F60	
C	鈌	3-8574	1-6732		DC69	2-4130	
D	鈍	1-2259	0-3863	0-5279	B677	1-625E	215D48
E	鈎	1-2519	0-1935			E-3F68	2D5D56
F	鈏	3-8575			DC68	2-412F	

922

	Char	G	J	K	B	C	A
0	鈠	3-8571				E-3F5E	
1	鈡					E-6659	335E21
2	鈢					E-3F63	
3	鈣	1-2438	1-6740		B674	1-625B	215D47
4	鈤		1-6741		DC73	2-413A	23423B
5	鈥	1-7856	1-6742		DC64	2-412B	234228
6	鈦	1-7849	1-6743		DC67	2-412E	234237
7	鈧	1-7854			DC70	2-4137	
8	鈨		1-6744				23422C
9	鈩		0-7947				4D4862
A	鈪						
B	鈫					E-6658	234226
C	鈬		0-7869				4B5E3F
D	鈭				E4BA	2-4F22	
E	鈮	1-7874	1-6745		E0B7	2-483D	23425C
F	鈯	3-8587	1-6746			E-452E	

924

	Char	G	J	K	B	C	A
0	鉀	1-2856	1-6756	0-4305	B95B	1-6743	215D53
1	鉁			1-7818		E-4539	23432E
2	鉂	3-8579	1-6757				
3	鉃		1-6758				
4	鉄		0-3720			E-4538	335E3D
5	鉅	1-7850	0-7874	0-4373	B964	1-674C	2D3C38
6	鉆		1-6759		E0B9	2-483F	
7	鉇		1-6760				
8	鉈	1-7872	0-7877		E0AE	2-4834	234255
9	鉉	1-7871	0-7875	0-9072	B962	1-674A	234252
A	鉊		1-6761		E0B8	2-483E	
B	鉋		0-7880	1-8232	B95E	1-6746	215D54
C	鉌	5-8535			E0CA	2-4850	234326
D	鉍	1-7873	1-6762		B963	1-674B	234254
E	鉎	3-8581	1-6763	1-6806	E0C8	2-484E	234323
F	鉏		1-6764	1-6816	E0BC	2-4842	234271

926

	Char	G	J	K	B	C	A
0	鉠	5-8534	1-6770		E0BD	2-4843	234277
1	鉡	3-8584	1-6771		E0C1	2-4847	
2	鉢	1-1807	0-4013	0-5904		E-4533	2D5228
3	鉣				E0C5	2-484B	
4	鉤		0-7876	0-4741	B95F	1-6747	215D56
5	鉥	3-8576	1-6772	0-6692	E0B4	2-483A	
6	鉦	1-7859	0-3064	0-7990	E0B2	2-4838	234261
7	鉧	3-8591	1-6773		E0BE	2-4844	
8	鉨		1-6774				
9	鉩	5-8537	1-6775				
A	鉪					E-4532	
B	鉫					E-4535	23426C
C	鉬	1-7866			E0BB	2-4841	234270
D	鉭	1-7867			E0BA	2-4840	23426F
E	鉮	3-8578	1-6776			E-4536	
F	鉯		1-6777		E0BF	2-4845	

921

	Char	G	J	K	B	C	A
0	鈐	1-7852	1-6733	0-4402	B678	1-625F	215D4D
1	鈑	1-7851	0-7871	0-8794	B67A	1-6261	23424B
2	鈒	3-8559	1-6734	0-6328	DC6B	2-4132	234243
3	鈓		1-6735			E-3F69	
4	鈔	1-1914	0-7868	1-7993	B672	1-6259	215D4B
5	鈕	1-3705	0-7870		B673	1-625A	215D49
6	鈖		1-6736		DC77	2-413E	23424A
7	鈗			0-7545	DC75	2-413C	
8	鈘		1-6737			E-3F62	234232
9	鈙	5-8530			DC74	2-413B	
A	鈚	5-8528			DC66	2-412D	
B	鈛					E-3F65	
C	鈜		1-6738	1-8454	DC72	2-4139	234238
D	鈝		1-6739				
E	鈞	1-3091	0-7866	0-4823	B676	1-625D	215D4C
F	鈟			1-7720			

923

	Char	G	J	K	B	C	A
0	鈰	1-7870	1-6747		E0B0	2-4836	234251
1	鈱	5-8539			E0C3	2-4849	
2	鈲				E0CC	2-4852	
3	鈳	1-7861	1-6748		E0B3	2-4839	23425F
4	鈴	1-3369	0-4675	0-5434	B961	1-6749	215D58
5	鈵		1-6749	1-6587		E-452B	234268
6	鈶	3-8590	1-6750		E0C0	2-4846	23427E
7	鈷	1-7860	0-2458	1-5705	B957	1-673F	215D4F
8	鈸	1-7864	1-6751	1-6534	B959	1-6741	215D60
9	鈹	1-7875	1-6752		B965	1-674D	23426D
A	鈺	1-7858	1-6753	0-7213	E0B1	2-4837	234258
B	鈻	3-8580				E-4537	
C	鈼	3-8582	1-6754			E-452F	
D	鈽	1-7863			B95A	1-6742	215D51
E	鈾	1-5143	1-6755		B95C	1-6744	215D52
F	鈿	1-7868	0-7879	0-7915	B966	1-674E	234274

925

	Char	G	J	K	B	C	A
0	鉐		0-7881	1-6822	E0C6	2-484C	23426B
1	鉑	1-1812	1-6765		B960	1-6748	215D57
2	鉒	3-8583		1-7760	E0AF	2-4835	
3	鉓				E0C9	2-484F	
4	鉔				E0C4	2-484A	
5	鉕	1-7862				E-452A	
6	鉖				E0CB	2-4851	234327
7	鉗	1-3915	0-7873	0-4438	B958	1-6740	33502A
8	鉘		1-6766				
9	鉙		1-6767			E-452D	
A	鉚	1-3513	0-7886		B967	1-674F	23432B
B	鉛	1-3906	0-1784	0-7071	B95D	1-6745	215D55
C	鉜	5-8536	1-6768			E-4531	
D	鉝		1-6769			E-4529	
E	鉞	1-7865	0-7872	0-7439	E0B5	2-483B	234264
F	鉟					E-4534	

927

	Char	G	J	K	B	C	A
0	鉰		1-6778		E0C2	2-4848	
1	鉱		0-2559				514E5B
2	鉲				E0C7	2-484D	
3	鉳					E-665A	
4	鉴	0-2888					395E42
5	鉵	3-8607	1-6779				
6	鉶	3-8592	1-6780		E478	2-4E60	23433E
7	鉷	3-8594	1-6781	1-8410			234347
8	鉸	1-2934	1-6782	1-5831	BBC7	1-6B4F	215D59
9	鉹	3-8617	1-6783		E4A4	2-4E6A	
A	鉺	1-7879			E47A	2-4E62	234343
B	鉻	1-2485	1-6784		BBCC	1-6B55	215D5F
C	鉼	3-8618	1-6785	1-6589	BBD0	1-6B59	234337
D	鉽		1-6786		E4AD	2-4E73	
E	鉾	3-8619	0-4340	1-6454	E4B5	2-4E7B	234354
F	鉿	1-7894	1-6787		E4A6	2-4E6C	234362

Code	Char	G	J	K	B	C	A
9280	銀	1-5088	0-2268	0-7562	BBC8	1-6B51	215D5A
9281	銁					E-4A34	
9282	銂				E4AA	2-4E70	234333
9283	銃	1-7905	0-2938	0-8540	E0B6	2-483C	23432F
9284	銄					E-4A35	
9285	銅	1-4513	0-3828	0-5262	BBC9	1-6B52	215D5C
9286	銆				E4B1	2-4E77	
9287	銇	5-8541			E4B6	2-4E7C	
9288	銈	5-8542	1-6788		E4AE	2-4E74	234342
9289	銉		1-6789			E-4A2F	
928A	銊	3-8603	1-6790		E4B0	2-4E76	
928B	銋	3-8612		1-7475	E4B9	2-4F21	
928C	銌				E4B2	2-4E78	
928D	銍	3-8606	1-6791		E47E	2-4E66	23433F
928E	銎	0-8638	1-6792		E4A9	2-4E6F	234345
928F	銏					E-4530	
9290	銐	3-8546				E-4A38	
9291	銑	1-4719	0-3313	0-6453	BBD1	1-6B5A	23435B
9292	銒		1-6793			E-4A33	
9293	銓	1-7893	0-7884	0-7916	BBCD	1-6B56	215D60
9294	銔	3-8604			E47C	2-4E64	
9295	銕	5-8545	0-7878	1-7940	E4AB	2-4E71	395E3D
9296	銖	1-7889	0-7883	0-6639	BBCB	1-6B54	215D5E
9297	銗	3-8613	1-6794		E4A5	2-4E6B	
9298	銘	1-3590	0-4435	0-5715	BBCA	1-6B53	215D5D
9299	銙	3-8605	1-6801	1-5755	E4B3	2-4E79	
929A	銚	1-7902	0-3624	1-7721	E4A2	2-4E68	234355
929B	銛	3-8609	0-7885	1-6853	E479	2-4E61	23435D
929C	銜	1-4746	0-7882	0-8971	BBCE	1-6B57	215D61
929D	銝				E4B8	2-4E7E	
929E	銞					E-4A39	
929F	銟		1-6802				
92A0	銠	1-7878	1-6803		E47B	2-4E63	234346
92A1	銡	3-8593			E4AF	2-4E75	
92A2	銢				E4AC	2-4E72	23424F
92A3	銣	1-7908			E4A7	2-4E6D	234364
92A4	銤	5-8548	1-6804		E477	2-4E5F	234338
92A5	銥	1-5031	1-6805		E476	2-4E5E	234331
92A6	銦	1-7887			E4A1	2-4E67	234350
92A7	銧		1-6806		E4B4	2-4E7A	
92A8	銨	1-7907	1-6807		BBCF	1-6B58	234335
92A9	銩	1-7891			E4B7	2-4E7D	
92AA	銪	1-7880			E47D	2-4E65	234349
92AB	銫	1-7904	1-6808		E4A3	2-4E69	234358
92AC	銬	1-7877			BE52	1-6B50	215D5B
92AD	銭		0-3312			E-4A32	4B5D70
92AE	銮	0-8639				E-4A37	275E48
92AF	銯		1-6809				
92B0	銰					E-672A	
92B1	銱	1-7886				E-4A31	
92B2	銲		1-6810		BE5A	1-6F63	23442A
92B3	銳			0-7169	BE55	1-6F5E	215D64
92B4	銴	3-8549			E8A4	2-554D	
92B5	銵	5-8557			E8A1	2-5549	
92B6	銶	3-8623	1-6811	0-4742	E867	2-5531	234376
92B7	銷	1-4790	0-7889	0-6549	BE50	1-6F5A	215D66
92B8	銸	5-8552	1-6812			E-4F42	
92B9	銹	1-4866	0-7888	0-6640		E-4F50	2D5E3B
92BA	銺		1-6813				
92BB	銻	1-4464	1-6814		BE4F	1-6F59	215D63
92BC	銼	1-7917	1-6815		BE56	1-6F5F	215D69
92BD	銽		1-6816				
92BE	銾	5-8551				E-4F43	234379
92BF	銿		1-6817			E-4F41	
92C0	鋀	3-8621	1-6818		E865	2-552F	234377
92C1	鋁	1-3433	1-6819		BE54	1-6F5D	215D67
92C2	鋂	3-8626	1-6820		E871	2-553B	23443C
92C3	鋃	1-7922	1-6821		E863	2-552D	23436A
92C4	鋄				E864	2-552E	
92C5	鋅	1-4831	1-6822		BE4E	1-6F58	215D62
92C6	鋆	3-8548	1-6823	1-7410	E8A3	2-554C	234421
92C7	鋇	1-1721	1-6824		BE58	1-6F61	23442D
92C8	鋈	0-8640	1-6825		E874	2-553E	234366
92C9	鋉				E879	2-5543	
92CA	鋊	3-8628			E873	2-553D	23443A
92CB	鋋	3-8611	1-6826		EBEE	2-5B3C	
92CC	鋌	1-7890	1-6827	0-7991	E86F	2-5539	23443E
92CD	鋍	3-8620	1-6828		E877	2-5541	
92CE	鋎		1-6829		E875	2-553F	
92CF	鋏	1-7882	0-7887	0-9089	E868	2-5532	234427
92D0	鋐	3-8630	1-6830		E862	2-552C	23436F
92D1	鋑			1-7620	E87D	2-5547	234439
92D2	鋒	1-2370	0-4315	0-6082	BE57	1-6F60	215D6A
92D3	鋓		1-6831		E87E	2-5548	
92D4	鋔					E-4F48	
92D5	鋕	5-8550	1-6832		E878	2-5542	23437E
92D6	鋖	5-8558				E-4F49	
92D7	鋗	3-8625	1-6833	1-8353	E86D	2-5537	
92D8	鋘	5-8556	1-6834		E86B	2-5535	234431
92D9	鋙	5-8554	1-6835		E866	2-5530	23437A
92DA	鋚	5-8517				E-4F4B	
92DB	鋛					E-4F4E	23442F
92DC	鋜	3-8624	1-6836			E-4F44	234430
92DD	鋝	1-7918	1-6837		E86E	2-5538	234435
92DE	鋞	3-8589			E87B	2-5545	
92DF	鋟	1-7923	1-6838	1-8108	E86A	2-5534	234372
92E0	鋠	3-8622	1-6839		E87A	2-5544	
92E1	鋡	3-8629	1-6840		E8A2	2-554A	
92E2	鋢					E-4F51	
92E3	鋣	1-7884	1-6841				
92E4	鋤	1-1990	0-2991	0-6407	BE53	1-6F5C	215D68
92E5	鋥	1-7913	1-6842	1-7667		E-4F45	
92E6	鋦	1-7924			E876	2-5540	234375
92E7	鋧	3-8566	1-6843		E87C	2-5546	23442C
92E8	鋨	1-7916	1-6844		E872	2-553C	234441
92E9	鋩	3-8601	0-7890		E86C	2-5536	234433
92EA	鋪	1-3844	0-4263	0-8872	BE51	1-6F5B	215D65
92EB	鋫					E-4F52	234443
92EC	鋬	3-8550	1-6845				
92ED	鋭	1-4081	0-1752			E-4F4C	
92EE	鋮	1-7881	1-6846		E4A8	2-4E6E	234340
92EF	鋯	1-7915			E870	2-553A	234440
92F0	鋰	1-7914	1-6847		BE59	1-6F62	23442E
92F1	鋱	1-7911			E869	2-5533	234371
92F2	鋲		0-4138	1-6588			234448
92F3	鋳		0-3582			E-4F4D	2D5E43
92F4	鋴					E-665B	234425
92F5	鋵					E-665C	234445
92F6	鋶	1-7919				E-4A30	
92F7	鋷				EBF4	2-5B41	
92F8	鋸	1-3066	0-2188	0-4374	BFF7	1-7261	215D6D
92F9	鋹	3-8567	1-6848	1-7883	EBF3	2-5B40	23445D
92FA	鋺	3-8651	0-7892	1-7351	EBF0	2-5B3E	234454
92FB	鋻	3-8545	1-6849		EC44	2-5B50	
92FC	鋼	1-2454	0-2561	0-4328	BFFB	1-7265	215D71
92FD	鋽	3-8638		1-7722		E-5335	
92FE	鋾	5-8567			EC41	2-5B4D	234528
92FF	鋿	5-8564	1-6850		EBF8	2-5B45	

Code	Char	G	J	K	B	C	A
9300	錀	3-8570	1-6851		EC43	2-5B4F	
9301	錁	1-7930			EBE9	2-5B37	234472
9302	錂	5-8561	1-6852		EBF6	2-5B43	234462
9303	錃					E-533D	23444C
9304	錄			0-5466	BFFD	1-7267	215D74
9305	錅					E-533E	
9306	錆	1-7926	0-2712	1-7884	EBE1	2-5B2F	23445B
9307	錇	1-7934				E-5338	23444D
9308	錈	1-7935	1-6853		EBDF	2-5B2D	
9309	錉	5-8566			EC42	2-5B4E	
930A	錊	3-8648				E-5332	
930B	錋				EC40	2-5B4C	
930C	錌				EBFE	2-5B4B	
930D	錍	3-8643	1-6854		EBED	2-5B3B	
930E	錎	3-8646			EBEC	2-5B3A	
930F	錏	3-8602	0-7891	1-7011	EBE2	2-5B30	23445F
9310	錐	1-5522	0-3177	0-8562	C040	1-7269	215D75
9311	錑	3-8652	1-6855				
9312	錒	1-7925			EBE8	2-5B36	234466
9313	錓				EBF2	2-5B3F	
9314	錔	3-8656	1-6856		EBFD	2-5B4A	234522
9315	錕	1-7931	1-6857	1-5722	C043	1-726C	234474
9316	錖	5-8518			EC45	2-5B51	
9317	錗	3-8642				E-5336	
9318	錘	1-2024	0-3178	0-8563	C1E8	1-7573	215E22
9319	錙	1-7937	0-7901	1-8086	C045	1-726E	234532
931A	錚	1-7903	0-7903	0-7822	BFFE	1-7268	215D73
931B	錛	1-7928			EBE6	2-5B34	
931C	錜	3-8645	1-6858			E-5337	
931D	錝		1-6859		EBEF	2-5B3D	234453
931E	錞	3-8647	1-6860	0-6686	EBDE	2-5B2C	23444E
931F	錟	1-7936	1-6861	0-5142	EBE0	2-5B2E	234458
9320	錠	1-2207	0-3091	0-7992	BFF5	1-725F	215D6B
9321	錡	3-8632	1-6862	0-4936	C042	1-726B	23446C
9322	錢	1-3914	0-7902	0-7917	BFFA	1-7264	215D70
9323	錣	3-8654	0-7904	1-7941	EBE7	2-5B35	23446A
9324	錤	5-8562	1-6863	0-4937	EBF7	2-5B44	234464
9325	錥	3-8649	1-6864		EBF1	2-554B	
9326	錦	1-2985	0-2251	0-4862	C041	1-726A	215D76
9327	錧	3-8650	1-6865	1-5771	EBDD	2-5B2B	
9328	錨	1-3510	0-4137	0-5765	C1E3	1-756E	215D7D
9329	錩	3-8640	1-6866		EBF9	2-5B46	234476
932A	錪	3-8641	1-6867	1-7621	EBFC	2-5B49	234479
932B	錫	1-4693	0-2866	0-6424	BFFC	1-7266	215D72
932C	錬		0-4703	1-6163		E-533B	4B496A
932D	錭	5-8565			EBEB	2-5B39	
932E	錮	1-7932	0-7894	0-4549	C044	1-726D	234478
932F	錯	1-2077	0-2688	0-8325	BFF9	1-7263	215D6F
9330	錰					E-533C	
9331	錱					E-5339	23445A
9332	録	1-3428	0-4731			E-533A	
9333	錳	1-3544	1-6868		BFF8	1-7262	215D6E
9334	錴		1-6869		EBF5	2-5B42	
9335	錵		0-7906		EBFB	2-5B48	23447E
9336	錶	1-8803	1-6870		BFF6	1-7260	215D6C
9337	錷		1-6871				
9338	錸	1-7910			EBE4	2-5B32	234469
9339	錹				EBFA	2-5B47	
933A	錺		0-7905				23447C
933B	錻		0-7907				696F27
933C	錼				EBE5	2-5B33	
933D	錽	3-8634					
933E	錾	0-8641					294666
933F	錿					E-665D	23447B
9340	鍀	1-7929					234471
9341	鍁	1-4739					234531
9342	鍂					E-665E	23452F
9343	鍃	1-7933					
9344	鍄		0-7893				23444F
9345	鍅					E-5331	
9346	鍆	1-7845			EBEA	2-5B38	
9347	鍇	1-7939	1-6872		EED2	2-5F7E	23454D
9348	鍈	3-8631	1-6873	0-7144		E-5665	23456A
9349	鍉	5-8573	1-6874	1-6972	EED7	2-6025	23455D
934A	鍊			0-5408	C1E5	1-7570	33496A
934B	鍋	1-2588	0-3873	0-4607	C1E7	1-7572	215D7C
934C	鍌	3-8552			EEDD	2-602B	234535
934D	鍍	1-2238	0-3753	0-5221	C1E1	1-756C	215D77
934E	鍎				EEEC	2-6039	
934F	鍏	5-8526			EEE3	2-6031	23454C
9350	鍐		1-6875		EED8	2-6026	
9351	鍑	3-8664	1-6876		EED9	2-6027	23456E
9352	鍒		1-6877		EEE2	2-6030	
9353	鍓					E-5666	
9354	鍔	1-7941	0-3655	0-6840	C1EE	1-7579	234567
9355	鍕		1-6878		EEE1	2-602F	234566
9356	鍖	3-8658	0-7912		EED1	2-5F7D	234553
9357	鍗	3-8670	1-6879	1-7681	EEE0	2-602E	
9358	鍘	1-5301	1-6880		EED4	2-6022	23455E
9359	鍙				EEED	2-603A	
935A	鍚	3-8560	1-6881		C1ED	1-7578	23455F
935B	鍛	1-2245	0-3535	0-5120	C1EB	1-7576	215E24
935C	鍜		0-7908	1-8277	EED5	2-6023	234548
935D	鍝	3-8662		1-7330		E-565D	
935E	鍞		1-6882		EEE8	2-6036	
935F	鍟					E-5667	234562
9360	鍠	3-8665	0-7909		EEDA	2-6028	234573
9361	鍡				EEE7	2-6035	
9362	鍢					E-5664	
9363	鍣				EEE9	2-6037	
9364	鍤	1-7942	1-6883	1-6783	EED0	2-5F7C	23456F
9365	鍥	1-7938	1-6884		C1E6	1-7571	215D7A
9366	鍦	3-8671				E-565B	
9367	鍧	3-8669	1-6885		EEEA	2-6038	
9368	鍨					E-5668	
9369	鍩	1-7927	1-6886			E-565E	
936A	鍪	0-8642	1-6887		EEDE	2-602C	234547
936B	鍫			1-7994		E-566B	234571
936C	鍬	1-3934	0-2313	1-8001	C1EA	1-7575	215E23
936D	鍭	3-8667	1-6888		EEDB	2-6029	234572
936E	鍮	3-8668	0-7911	0-7525		E-5661	234577
936F	鍯		1-6889				
9370	鍰	1-7944	1-6890	1-8432	C1EC	1-7577	215D7E
9371	鍱	3-8659	1-6891		EEE4	2-6032	234554
9372	鍲	5-8577				E-5662	
9373	鍳		1-6892			E-5663	
9374	鍴	3-8663	1-6893			E-565F	23456B
9375	鍵	1-2892	0-2416	0-4385	C1E4	1-756F	215D79
9376	鍶	1-7940	1-6894		EED6	2-6024	234564
9377	鍷				EEE5	2-6033	23455C
9378	鍸					E-565C	
9379	鍹	5-8575			EEDF	2-602D	234541
937A	鍺	1-5364	1-6901		EBE3	2-5B31	234551
937B	鍻				EEE6	2-6034	
937C	鍼		0-7910	0-8661	EED3	2-6021	234556
937D	鍽		1-6902			E-5660	
937E	鍾	1-7981	0-3065	0-8103	C1E9	1-7574	215E21
937F	鍿		1-6903			E-566A	

Code	Char	G	B	J	C	K	A
9380	鎀		EEEB	1-6904	2-642F		
9381	鎁	5-8563		1-6905			
9382	鎂	1-3530	C1E2	1-6906	1-756D		215D78
9383	鎃		EECE		2-5F7A		
9384	鎄	1-7945					
9385	鎅						
9386	鎆				E-665F		234544
9387	鎇	1-7949					
9388	鎈	3-8672	F160	1-6907	2-642C		234623
9389	鎉	5-8586	F159		2-6425		23463C
938A	鎊	1-1687	C2E9	1-6908	1-7754	1-6546	215E25
938B	鎋	5-8592		1-6909	E-5943		23457E
938C	鎌		F154	0-1989	2-637E	0-4439	234622
938D	鎍	5-8583	F163	1-6910	2-6430		
938E	鎎		F15B		2-6427		
938F	鎏	0-8644	EEDC	1-6911	2-602A		234579
9390	鎐	3-8681			E-5940		
9391	鎑	3-8674	F165		2-6432		
9392	鎒	5-8584	F155	1-6912	2-6421		
9393	鎓	3-8682			E-5942		
9394	鎔		C2E8	0-7916	1-7753	0-7342	215E26
9395	鎕	5-8591	F15F	1-6913	2-642B		23457B
9396	鎖	1-4388	C2EA	0-2631	1-7755	0-6580	215E28
9397	鎗		C2F2	0-3389	1-775D	1-7558	23464F
9398	鎘	1-7951	C2F0	1-6914	1-775B		23462D
9399	鎙		F161		2-642D		
939A	鎚		C2F1	0-3642	1-775C	0-8564	234648
939B	鎛	3-8675	F157	1-6915	2-6423	1-6520	23462B
939C	鎜				E-5949		
939D	鎝	3-8660	F158		2-6424		
939E	鎞	3-8680	F15D	1-6916	2-6429		23464D
939F	鎟		F162		2-642E	1-6792	
93A0	鎠				E-593E		
93A1	鎡	3-8673	EECD	1-6917	2-5F79	1-7505	234627
93A2	鎢	1-4657	C2EB		1-7756		215E29
93A3	鎣	1-6186	F16A	1-6918	2-6437	0-9115	234629
93A4	鎤	5-8585	F167	1-6919	2-6434	1-8442	23463D
93A5	鎥		F16B		2-6761		
93A6	鎦	1-7954	F15E	1-6920	2-642A		234647
93A7	鎧	1-7888	F15A	0-1927	2-6426	0-4349	234642
93A8	鎨	5-8588	F168	1-6921	2-6435		
93A9	鎩	1-7901	F36A	1-6927	2-6756		23472F
93AA	鎪	1-7943	F15C		2-6428		23464A
93AB	鎫			1-6922			
93AC	鎬	1-2468	C2EE	0-7914	1-7759	0-9164	23457A
93AD	鎭			0-7915	E-5944	0-8269	4B5E27
93AE	鎮	1-5382	C2ED	0-3635	1-7758		215E27
93AF	鎯	5-8568	EECF		2-5F7B		
93B0	鎰	1-7955	C2EF	0-7913	1-775A	0-7680	234628
93B1	鎱		F164		2-6431		
93B2	鎲		F166		2-6433		
93B3	鎳	1-3688	C2EC		1-7757		215E2A
93B4	鎴		F169	1-6923	2-6436		
93B5	鎵	1-7956	F153	1-6924	2-637D		234621
93B6	鎶			1-6925			
93B7	鎷		F156		2-6422		23462A
93B8	鎸	1-7952			E-5946		
93B9	鎹			0-7917			234625
93BA	鎺			1-6926			
93BB	鎻				E-5945		234651
93BC	鎼				E-6661		234640
93BD	鎽				E-6662		234644
93BE	鎾				E-6660		234560
93BF	鎿	1-7953					
93C0	鏀	5-8555	F373		2-675F		
93C1	鏁	5-8606		1-6928	E-5B50		2D5E28
93C2	鏂	3-8565	F363		2-674F		
93C3	鏃	1-7963	C3EB	0-7923	1-7938	0-8076	215E2E
93C4	鏄	5-8527	F371	1-6929	2-675D		234664
93C5	鏅	3-8679		1-6930	E-5B44		
93C6	鏆	3-8655		1-6931	E-5B45		
93C7	鏇	1-7964	F361	1-6932	2-674D	1-6836	23465A
93C8	鏈	1-3320	C3EC	0-7926	1-7939	1-6248	215E31
93C9	鏉	5-8594		1-6933			
93CA	鏊	0-8643	F36C	1-6934	2-6758	1-7223	234663
93CB	鏋			1-6935	E-5B43	1-6404	
93CC	鏌	1-7950	F368	1-6936	2-6754	1-6391	23467C
93CD	鏍	1-7961	C3F1	1-6937	1-793E		215E36
93CE	鏎		F372		2-675E		
93CF	鏏	3-8685	F362		2-674E		
93D0	鏐	3-8693	F365	0-7925	2-6751		234673
93D1	鏑	1-7965	C3E9	0-3713	1-7936	0-7875	215E2C
93D2	鏒	3-8653	F374		2-6760		
93D3	鏓	3-8691		1-6938	E-5B48		23472C
93D4	鏔		F36D		2-6759		23465D
93D5	鏕	5-8603	F370		2-675C		
93D6	鏖	0-8773	C3EF	0-7918	1-793C	1-7224	215E2D
93D7	鏗	1-7912	C3F4	0-7919	1-7941	1-5581	215E30
93D8	鏘	1-7947	C3F2	0-7922	1-793F	1-7546	215E37
93D9	鏙	3-8689	F369	1-6939	2-6755		
93DA	鏚	5-8601	F364		2-6750		234672
93DB	鏛	5-8602			E-5B4D		234675
93DC	鏜	1-7959	C3ED	1-6940	1-793A	1-6113	215E33
93DD	鏝	1-7960	C3EE	0-7924	1-793B	1-6405	215E35
93DE	鏞	1-7962	F360	1-6941	2-674C	0-7343	234656
93DF	鏟	1-1889	C3EA	1-6942	1-7937	1-6773	215E2F
93E0	鏠	5-8590			E-5B4F		
93E1	鏡	1-3021	C3E8	0-2232	1-7935	0-4480	215E2B
93E2	鏢	1-7958	C3F0	1-6943	1-793D	1-8245	215E32
93E3	鏣		F36F		2-675B		
93E4	鏤	1-7946	C3F3	0-7927	1-7940	0-5515	215E34
93E5	鏥			0-7921	E-5B4A		23465F
93E6	鏦	3-8569	F36B	1-6944	2-6757	1-8016	234730
93E7	鏧		F375	1-6945	2-6762		234667
93E8	鏨	1-8641	C3F5	0-7920	1-7942	1-7864	234666
93E9	鏩	3-8635			E-5B41		
93EA	鏪				E-5B42		
93EB	鏫				E-5B4E		
93EC	鏬		F367		2-6753		
93ED	鏭				E-5B47		
93EE	鏮		F36E		2-675A		234657
93EF	鏯				E-6665		234674
93F0	鏰	3-8690					
93F1	鏱				E-6663		234653
93F2	鏲				E-6664		23465B
93F3	鏳				E-5D41		
93F4	鏴				E-5E6A		234827
93F5	鏵	1-7892	F4F3		2-6A41		234767
93F6	鏶		F542		2-6A50	0-8301	
93F7	鏷	1-7968	F4F5	1-6947	2-6A43		234769
93F8	鏸	3-8703	F4FC	1-6948	2-6A4A		
93F9	鏹	1-7974	F366	1-6946	2-6752		234662
93FA	鏺	3-8588	F4FA	1-6949	2-6A48		234749
93FB	鏻	3-8708	F4E9	1-6950	2-6A37	1-6380	23473D
93FC	鏼		F540		2-6A4E		
93FD	鏽		C4C3	1-6951	1-7A4E		215E3B
93FE	鏾	3-8702	F4ED		2-6A3B		
93FF	鏿		F4FE		2-6A4D		

Code	Char	G	J	K	B	C	A
9400	鐀	5-8574			F4F4	2-6A42	
9401	鐁		1-6952				
9402	鐂		1-6953			E-5D43	
9403	鐃	1-7883	0-7931	1-6051	C4C2	1-7A4D	215E39
9404	鐄	3-8687	1-6954	0-9285		E-5D3C	234759
9405	鐅	5-8519				E-5D3F	
9406	鐆	5-8515			F544	2-6A52	23475D
9407	鐇	3-8707	0-7932		F4F6	2-6A44	23476A
9408	鐈	3-8610	1-6955			E-5D3E	
9409	鐉		1-6956		F4FB	2-6A49	234755
940A	鐊				F4FD	2-6A4C	
940B	鐋	1-7906			F4E7	2-6A35	234732
940C	鐌	3-8692			F541	2-6A4F	
940D	鐍	3-8711	1-6957		F4F2	2-6A40	23474E
940E	鐎	3-8705	1-6958		F4F7	2-6A45	23476F
940F	鐏	3-8709	1-6959	1-7774	F4EB	2-6A39	23473B
9410	鐐	1-3345	0-7933	1-6328	F4EF	2-6A3D	234760
9411	鐑				F543	2-6A51	234771
9412	鐒	1-7909			F4F9	2-6A47	
9413	鐓	1-7970	0-7930	1-6122	F4E8	2-6A36	234734
9414	鐔	1-7966	0-7929	1-6993	F4EC	2-6A3A	234758
9415	鐕	3-8704	1-6960		F4EE	2-6A3C	
9416	鐖	3-8553	1-6961		F4F8	2-6A46	
9417	鐗		1-6962			E-5D3D	
9418	鐘	1-5451	0-3066	0-8104	C4C1	1-7A4C	2D5E21
9419	鐙	1-7975	0-3810	1-6182	F4F1	2-6A3F	23474D
941A	鐚		0-7928			E-5D44	2F445F
941B	鐛					E-5D45	
941C	鐜	5-8520				E-5D47	
941D	鐝	1-7967					
941E	鐞					E-5D42	
941F	鐟		1-6963			E-5D3A	
9420	鐠	1-7972			F4EA	2-6A38	23473C
9421	鐡		0-7937				4B5E3D
9422	鐢					E-6666	23475C
9423	鐣					E-6667	234762
9424	鐤					E-6668	23482D
9425	鐥	5-8611		0-6454			
9426	鐦	1-7920					234750
9427	鐧	1-7921				E-5D46	234751
9428	鐨	1-7948			F4F0	2-6A3E	
9429	鐩	5-8612			F661	2-6C50	234779
942A	鐪	3-8639		1-6282	F666	2-6C54	
942B	鐫		0-7935	0-7918	C54F	1-7B3B	234835
942C	鐬	3-8608			F668	2-6C56	
942D	鐭	5-8610				E-5E6D	234836
942E	鐮	1-3313	1-6964		C549	1-7B35	215E3A
942F	鐯	3-8686	1-6965				
9430	鐰	3-8714			F664	2-6C52	
9431	鐱	3-8627	1-6966		F66A	2-6C58	234838
9432	鐲	1-7977	1-6967		C54E	1-7B3A	215E40
9433	鐳	1-3256	1-6968		C54A	1-7B36	215E3C
9434	鐴	3-8717	1-6969				
9435	鐵	1-4490	0-7936	0-8449	C54B	1-7B37	215E3D
9436	鐶	3-8715	0-7934	1-8433	F660	2-6C4F	234828
9437	鐷				F667	2-6C55	234830
9438	鐸	1-7876	0-3488	0-8701	C54D	1-7B39	215E3F
9439	鐹	5-8546			F665	2-6C53	
943A	鐺	1-7885	0-7938	1-6114	C54C	1-7B38	215E3E
943B	鐻	3-8713	1-6970		F65F	2-6C4E	23482B
943C	鐼	3-8657			F663	2-6A4B	
943D	鐽		1-6972		F662	2-6C51	23477C
943E	鐾	0-8645					4D477B
943F	鐿	1-7978	1-6971		F65E	2-6C4D	234774
9440	鑀				F669	2-6C57	234832
9441	鑁		0-7939				234837
9442	鑂			1-8480		E-5F69	
9443	鑃		1-6973			E-5F6E	
9444	鑄	1-5493	0-7941	0-8149	C5B1	1-7B7B	215E43
9445	鑅	5-8571	1-6974		F76D	2-6E3C	234840
9446	鑆				F770	2-6E3F	
9447	鑇	5-8547			F76C	2-6E3B	
9448	鑈	5-8538	1-6975		F76E	2-6E3D	
9449	鑉				F76F	2-6E3E	
944A	鑊	1-7976	1-6976	1-8422	F769	2-6E38	23484A
944B	鑋	3-8551			F76A	2-6E39	
944C	鑌	1-7957	1-6977	1-6732	F767	2-6E36	23483E
944D	鑍					E-5F6A	
944E	鑎					E-5F6C	
944F	鑏	3-8585			F76B	2-6E3A	
9450	鑐	3-8719			F768	2-6E37	234842
9451	鑑		0-2053	0-4292	C5B2	1-7B7C	215E42
9452	鑒	1-2888	0-7940	0-4293	C5B3	1-7B7D	335E42
9453	鑓		0-4490				694C7A
9454	鑔	1-7979				E-5F6B	
9455	鑕	3-8644	1-6978	1-7824	F84B	2-6F59	23485D
9456	鑖	3-8718				E-6052	
9457	鑗				F84D	2-6F5B	
9458	鑘	3-8720				E-6431	
9459	鑙		1-6979				
945A	鑚		0-7952			E-6055	2D5E4A
945B	鑛		0-7942	0-4646		E-6054	2D4E5B
945C	鑜		1-6980			E-6056	
945D	鑝	5-8613			F84C	2-6F5A	
945E	鑞	3-8722	0-7945	1-6211	F84E	2-6F5C	23485E
945F	鑟		1-6981			E-604F	
9460	鑠	1-7869	0-7943	1-6763	C5E0	1-7C4C	215E45
9461	鑡	3-8637	1-6982			E-6053	
9462	鑢	3-8677	0-7944	1-6237	F84A	2-6F58	234858
9463	鑣	1-7980	1-6983	1-8246	C5DF	1-7C4B	215E44
9464	鑤				C5E1	1-7C4D	234857
9465	鑥	1-7969				E-6057	23485C
9466	鑦					E-666A	234853
9467	鑧					E-6669	23483D
9468	鑨	3-8577	1-6984		F8CB	2-7059	
9469	鑩				F8CC	2-705A	
946A	鑪		0-7946	1-6283	C644	1-7C6F	234862
946B	鑫	0-8646	1-6985		F8CA	2-7058	234868
946C	鑬					E-6122	
946D	鑭	1-7971	1-6986		F953	2-7142	234869
946E	鑮	5-8618	1-6987		F952	2-7141	
946F	鑯	5-8619	1-6988		F954	2-7143	23486C
9470	鑰	1-5231	0-7948	1-7085	C65F	1-7D2C	215E47
9471	鑱	3-8723	1-6989	1-7865	F955	2-7144	23486D
9472	鑲	1-4766	1-6990	1-7103	C65E	1-7D2B	215E46
9473	鑳				F956	2-7145	
9474	鑴	3-8724			F972	2-7161	
9475	鑵		0-7949	1-5772	F975	2-7164	2D522B
9476	鑶				F974	2-7163	
9477	鑷	1-3687	0-7950	1-6860	C668	1-7D35	234871
9478	鑸				F973	2-7162	
9479	鑹	1-7973					
947A	鑺	5-8620				E-616F	
947B	鑻					E-6223	
947C	鑼	1-3464	0-7953	1-6189	C672	1-7D3F	215E49
947D	鑽	1-5574	0-7951	0-8340	C670	1-7D3D	215E4A
947E	鑾	1-8639	0-7954	1-6205	C671	1-7D3E	215E48
947F	鑿	1-5268	0-7956	0-8326	C677	1-7D44	215E4B

948

	Char	G	J	K	B	C	A
0	钀	3-8712			F9C0	2-7230	
1	钁	5-8621	0-7955		F9C1	2-7231	23487C
2	钂	3-8678			F9BF	2-722F	23487B
3	钃	3-8710	1-6992		F9C9	2-7237	
4	钄		1-6991			E-6236	
5	钅	0-7836					455D3E
6	钆	0-7837					294162
7	钇	0-7838					294161
8	针	0-5375					275D3F
9	钉	0-2204					275D40
A	钊	0-7840					275D41
B	钋	0-7839					294164
C	钌	0-7841					294163
D	钍	0-7842					29416A
E	钎	0-3905					29416B
F	钏	0-7843					275D46

94A

	Char	G	J	K	B	C	A
0	钠	0-3638					275D4A
1	钡	0-1721					29442D
2	钢	0-2454					275D71
3	钣	0-7851					29424B
4	钤	0-7852					275D4D
5	钥	0-5231					275E47
6	钦	0-3953					274578
7	钧	0-3091					275D4C
8	钨	0-4657					275E29
9	钩	0-2519					275D56
A	钪	0-7854					294224
B	钫	0-7853					294225
C	钬	0-7856					294228
D	钭	0-7855					294223
E	钮	0-3705					275D49
F	钯	0-7857					294231

94C

	Char	G	J	K	B	C	A
0	铀	0-5143					275D52
1	铁	0-4490					275E3D
2	铂	0-1812					275D57
3	铃	0-3369					275D58
4	铄	0-7869					275E45
5	铅	0-3906					275D55
6	铆	0-3513					29432B
7	铇	8-1294					
8	铈	0-7870					294251
9	铉	0-7871					294252
A	铊	0-7872					294255
B	铋	0-7873					294254
C	铌	0-7874					29425C
D	铍	0-7875					29426D
E	铎	0-7876					275E3F
F	铏	8-1303					

94E

	Char	G	J	K	B	C	A
0	铠	0-7888					294642
1	铡	0-5301					29455E
2	铢	0-7889					275D5E
3	铣	0-4719					29435B
4	铤	0-7890					29443E
5	铥	0-7891					294359
6	铦	8-1306					
7	铧	0-7892					294767
8	铨	0-7893					275D60
9	铩	0-7901					29472F
A	铪	0-7894					294362
B	铫	0-7902					294355
C	铬	0-2485					275D5F
D	铭	0-3590					275D5D
E	铮	0-7903					275D73
F	铯	0-7904					294358

949

	Char	G	J	K	B	C	A
0	钐	0-7844					294222
1	钑	8-9494					
2	钒	0-2316					294179
3	钓	0-2186					275D45
4	钔	0-7845					294475
5	钕	0-7847					294221
6	钖	8-1301					
7	钗	0-7846					275D43
8	钘	8-1302					
9	钙	0-2438					275D47
A	钚	0-7848					474236
B	钛	0-7849					294237
C	钜	0-7850					4B3C38
D	钝	0-2259					275D48
E	钞	0-1914					275D4B
F	钟	0-5451					275E21

94B

	Char	G	J	K	B	C	A
0	钰	0-7858					294258
1	钱	0-3914					275D70
2	钲	0-7859					294261
3	钳	0-3915					27502A
4	钴	0-7860					275D4F
5	钵	0-1807					335228
6	钶	0-7861					29425F
7	钷	0-7862					294260
8	钸	0-7863					275D51
9	钹	0-7864					275D50
A	钺	0-7865					294264
B	钻	0-5574					275E4A
C	钼	0-7866					474270
D	钽	0-7867					29426F
E	钾	0-2856					275D53
F	钿	0-7868					294274

94D

	Char	G	J	K	B	C	A
0	铐	0-7877					275D5B
1	铑	0-7878					294346
2	铒	0-7879					294343
3	铓	8-1304					
4	铔	8-1305					
5	铕	0-7880					294349
6	铖	0-7881					294340
7	铗	0-7882					294427
8	铘	0-7884					29437D
9	铙	0-7883					275E39
A	铚	8-1264					
B	铛	0-7885					275E3E
C	铜	0-4513					275D5C
D	铝	0-3433					275D67
E	铞	0-7886					29434F
F	铟	0-7887					294350

94F

	Char	G	J	K	B	C	A
0	铰	0-2934					275D59
1	铱	0-5031					294331
2	铲	0-1889					275E2F
3	铳	0-7905					29432F
4	铴	0-7906					294732
5	铵	0-7907					294335
6	银	0-5088					275D5A
7	铷	0-7908					294364
8	铸	0-5493					275E43
9	铹	0-7909					29473E
A	铺	0-3844					275D65
B	铻	8-1492					
C	铼	0-7910					294469
D	铽	0-7911					294371
E	链	0-3320					275E31
F	铿	0-7912					275E30

950

	Char	G	J	K	B	C	A
0	销	0-4790					275D66
1	锁	0-4388					275E28
2	锂	0-7914					29442E
3	锃	0-7913					29442B
4	锄	0-1990					275D68
5	锅	0-2588					275D7C
6	锆	0-7915					294440
7	锇	0-7916					294441
8	锈	0-4866					275E3B
9	锉	0-7917					275D69
A	锊	0-7918					294435
B	锋	0-2370					275D6A
C	锌	0-4831					275D62
D	锍	0-7919					29436C
E	锎	0-7920					294750
F	锏	0-7921					294751

952

	Char	G	J	K	B	C	A
0	锠	8-1309					
1	锡	0-4693					275D72
2	锢	0-7932					294478
3	锣	0-3464					275E49
4	锤	0-2024					275E22
5	锥	0-5522					275D75
6	锦	0-2985					275D76
7	锧	8-1310					
8	锨	0-4739					294531
9	锩	0-7935					294457
A	锪	0-7933					4D472C
B	锫	0-7934					29444D
C	锬	0-7936					294458
D	锭	0-2207					275D6B
E	键	0-2892					275D79
F	锯	0-3066					275D6D

954

	Char	G	J	K	B	C	A
0	镀	0-2238					275D77
1	镁	0-3530					275D78
2	镂	0-7946					275E34
3	镃	8-1312					
4	镄	0-7948					4D4754
5	镅	0-7949					29454E
6	镆	0-7950					29467C
7	镇	0-5382					275E27
8	镈	7-0120					
9	镉	0-7951					29462D
A	镊	0-3687					294871
B	镋	7-0121					
C	镌	0-7952					4D4835
D	镍	0-3688					275E2A
E	镎	0-7953					4D446B
F	镏	0-7954					294647

956

	Char	G	J	K	B	C	A
0	镠	8-1266					
1	镡	0-7966					294758
2	镢	0-7967					29475E
3	镣	0-3345					294760
4	镤	0-7968					294769
5	镥	0-7969					29485C
6	镦	0-7970					294734
7	镧	0-7971					294869
8	镨	0-7972					29473C
9	镩	0-7973					29486F
A	镪	0-7974					294662
B	镫	0-7975					29474D
C	镬	0-7976					29484A
D	镭	0-3256					275E3C
E	镮	8-1313					
F	镯	0-7977					275E40

951

	Char	G	J	K	B	C	A
0	锐	0-4081					275D64
1	锑	0-4464					275D63
2	锒	0-7922					29436A
3	锓	0-7923					294372
4	锔	0-7924					294375
5	锕	0-7925					294466
6	锖	0-7926					29445B
7	锗	0-5364					294551
8	锘	0-7927					294568
9	错	0-2077					275D6F
A	锚	0-3510					275D7D
B	锛	0-7928					29446D
C	锜	8-1308					
D	锝	0-7929					294471
E	锞	0-7930					294472
F	锟	0-7931					294474

953

	Char	G	J	K	B	C	A
0	锰	0-3544					275D6E
1	锱	0-7937					294532
2	锲	0-7938					275D7A
3	锳	8-1307					
4	锴	0-7939					29454D
5	锵	0-7947					275E37
6	锶	0-7940					294564
7	锷	0-7941					294567
8	锸	0-7942					29456F
9	锹	0-3934					275E23
A	锺	0-7981					455E21
B	锻	0-2245					275E24
C	锼	0-7943					29464A
D	锽	8-1311					
E	锾	0-7944					275D7E
F	锿	0-7945					4D4832

955

	Char	G	J	K	B	C	A
0	镐	0-2468					29457A
1	镑	0-1687					275E25
2	镒	0-7955					294628
3	镓	0-7956					294621
4	镔	0-7957					29483E
5	镕	7-0143					
6	镖	0-7958					275E32
7	镗	0-7959					275E33
8	镘	0-7960					275E35
9	镙	0-7961					275E36
A	镚	8-1265					
B	镛	0-7962					294656
C	镜	0-3021					275E2B
D	镝	0-7965					275E2C
E	镞	0-7963					275E2E
F	镟	0-7964					29465A

957

	Char	G	J	K	B	C	A
0	镰	0-3313					275E3A
1	镱	0-7978					294774
2	镲	0-7979					29483F
3	镳	0-7980					275E44
4	镴	8-1314					
5	镵	8-1393					
6	镶	0-4766					275E46
7	長	1-1904	0-3625	0-7794	AAF8	1-4F5B	215E4C
8	镸	5-4643	1-6993				
9	镹		1-6994			E-6323	
A	镺	3-4405			D844	2-3A28	
B	镻				DC78	2-413F	
C	镼	5-4649			E8A5	2-554E	
D	镽	3-4409			F376	2-6763	
E	镾	5-4644	1-7001				
F	长	0-1904					275E4C

Code	Char	G	J	K	B	C	A
9580	門	1-3537	0-4471	0-5806	AAF9	1-4F5C	215E4D
9581	閁					E-2F40	
9582	閂	1-6737	0-7957		ADAC	1-536D	215E4E
9583	閃	1-4133	0-3314	0-6476	B07B	1-5860	215E4F
9584	閄		1-7002				
9585	閅					E-3432	23492E
9586	閆	1-6738			D845	2-3A29	3F5E60
9587	閇		0-7958			E-395C	2D5E50
9588	閈	3-2683	1-7003	1-8289	D846	2-3A2A	234930
9589	閉	1-1753	0-4236	0-8845	B3AC	1-5D70	215E50
958A	閊		0-7959	1-6774			696F5B
958B	開	1-3110	0-1911	0-4350	B67D	1-6264	215E53
958C	閌	1-6742	1-7004		DC7A	2-4141	234931
958D	閍	5-2947	1-7005		DC79	2-4140	
958E	閎	1-6740	1-7006	1-5815	B6A3	1-6268	234936
958F	閏	1-4082	0-1728	0-7546	B67C	1-6263	215E52
9590	閐				DC7B	2-4142	
9591	閑	1-4748	0-2055	0-8956	B67E	1-6265	215E54
9592	閒			0-8957	B6A2	1-6267	215E56
9593	間	1-2868	0-2054	0-4264	B6A1	1-6266	215E55
9594	閔	1-6741	0-7960	0-5842	B67B	1-6262	215E51
9595	閕	3-2686				E-3F6C	
9596	閖		0-7961				696F5D
9597	閗					E-666B	234934
9598	閘	1-5302	0-7962	0-4306	B968	1-6750	215E57
9599	閙		0-7963			E-453C	4B6168
959A	閚					E-453A	
959B	閛	3-2690			E0D0	2-4856	
959C	閜	3-2689			E0CE	2-4854	
959D	閝		1-7007				
959E	閞		1-7008		E0CF	2-4855	
959F	閟	3-2693	1-7009	1-6716	E0CD	2-4853	234938
95A0	閠		0-7964				23493A
95A1	閡	1-2650	1-7010		BBD2	1-6B5B	215E58
95A2	関		0-2056			E-4A3D	4B5E69
95A3	閣	1-2483	0-1953	0-4240	BBD5	1-6B5E	215E5B
95A4	閤	1-8825	0-2562	0-8978	BBD7	1-6B60	215E5D
95A5	閥	1-2307	0-4022	0-5976	BBD6	1-6B5F	215E5C
95A6	閦	3-2702	1-7011				
95A7	閧		0-7966			E-4A3E	2D362A
95A8	閨	1-2575	0-7965	0-4817	BBD3	1-6B5C	215E59
95A9	閩	1-3586	1-7012	1-6512	BBD4	1-6B5D	215E5A
95AA	閪						
95AB	閫	1-6745	1-7013	1-5723	E8A7	2-5550	234944
95AC	閬	1-6747	1-7014	1-6217	E8A6	2-554F	234942
95AD	閭	1-6744	0-7967	0-5379	BE5B	1-6F64	215E5F
95AE	閮	5-2958			E8A8	2-5551	
95AF	閯					E-4F53	
95B0	閰				E8A9	2-5552	
95B1	閱			0-7083	BE5C	1-6F65	215E5E
95B2	閲	1-5236	0-1760			E-4F55	
95B3	閳					E-4F56	
95B4	閴		1-7015				
95B5	閵	5-2969			EC4D	2-5B59	
95B6	閶	1-6749	1-7016	1-7885	EC4B	2-5B57	23494F
95B7	閷	3-3363			EEF3	2-6040	
95B8	閸					E-5342	
95B9	閹	1-4943	0-7970	1-7124	EC49	2-5B55	23494D
95BA	閺	5-2967	1-7017		EC4A	2-5B56	23494E
95BB	閻	1-4954	0-7969	0-7102	C046	1-726F	215E60
95BC	閼	1-6753	0-7968	0-6857	EC46	2-5B52	234948
95BD	閽	1-6752	1-7018	1-8405	EC4E	2-5B5A	234952
95BE	閾	1-6748	0-7971	1-7133	EC48	2-5B54	234949
95BF	閿	1-6751	1-7019		EC4C	2-5B58	234950
95C0	闀	3-2709			EEEF	2-603C	
95C1	闁					E-5344	
95C2	闂					E-5340	
95C3	闃	1-6754	0-7974	1-5617	EEF1	2-603E	234965
95C4	闄	3-2711				E-566D	
95C5	闅				EEF2	2-603F	
95C6	闆	1-8802	1-7020		C1F3	1-757E	215E65
95C7	闇		0-1639	0-6865	EEEE	2-603B	33433E
95C8	闈	1-6739	1-7021	1-7366	C1F2	1-757D	215E64
95C9	闉	3-2710	1-7022		EEF0	2-603D	234959
95CA	闊	1-3211	0-7972	0-9236	C1EF	1-757A	215E61
95CB	闋	1-6755	1-7023	1-5632	C1F0	1-757B	215E62
95CC	闌	1-3227	0-7976	1-6206	C1F1	1-757C	215E63
95CD	闍	3-2704	0-7975	1-6137	EC47	2-5B53	23494A
95CE	闎					E-666C	23495D
95CF	闏						
95D0	闐	1-6757	1-7024		C2F5	1-7760	215E68
95D1	闑	3-2716	1-7025		F16E	2-643A	234964
95D2	闒	3-2715	1-7026		F16C	2-6438	234962
95D3	闓	3-2701	1-7027	1-5578	F16D	2-6439	234963
95D4	闔	1-6756	0-7978	0-8979	C2F3	1-775E	4B5E5D
95D5	闕	1-6758	0-7977	0-4784	C2F6	1-7761	234960
95D6	闖	1-2019	0-7979	0-8770	C2F4	1-775F	215E67
95D7	闗					E-594B	
95D8	闘		0-3814			E-594A	4B6167
95D9	闙		1-7028				
95DA	闚		1-7029	1-5936	F377	2-6764	234966
95DB	闛	3-2717			F378	2-6765	
95DC	關	1-2556	0-7980	0-4628	C3F6	1-7943	215E69
95DD	闝	5-2968	1-7030			E-5B53	
95DE	闞	1-6759	1-7031	1-8304	F545	2-6A53	234969
95DF	闟	3-2719	1-7032		F547	2-6A55	
95E0	闠	3-2713	1-7033	1-5919	F546	2-6A54	23496A
95E1	闡	1-1891	0-7981	0-8437	C4C4	1-7A4F	215E6A
95E2	闢	1-8859	0-7983	0-6003	C550	1-7B3C	215E6B
95E3	闣	3-2694			F66D	2-6C5B	
95E4	闤	3-2720	1-7034		F66C	2-6C5A	234972
95E5	闥	1-6743	0-7982	1-6079	F66B	2-6C59	23496F
95E6	闦		1-7035				
95E7	闧					E-666D	234976
95E8	门	0-3537					275E4D
95E9	闩	0-6737					275E4E
95EA	闪	0-4133					275E4F
95EB	闫	0-6738					
95EC	闬	8-9112					
95ED	闭	0-1753					275E50
95EE	问	0-4642					273648
95EF	闯	0-2019					275E67
95F0	闰	0-4082					275E52
95F1	闱	0-6739					275E64
95F2	闲	0-4748					275E54
95F3	闳	0-6740					294936
95F4	间	0-2868					275E55
95F5	闵	0-6741					275E51
95F6	闶	0-6742					474931
95F7	闷	0-3538					273E5C
95F8	闸	0-5302					275E57
95F9	闹	0-3654					276168
95FA	闺	0-2575					275E59
95FB	闻	0-4637					275271
95FC	闼	0-6743					29496F
95FD	闽	0-3586					275E5A
95FE	闾	0-6744					275E5F
95FF	闿	8-9113					

960

	Char	G	J	K	B	C	A
0	阀	0-2307					275E5C
1	阁	0-2483					275E5B
2	阂	0-2650					275E58
3	阃	0-6745					294944
4	阄	0-6746					295574
5	阅	0-5236					275E5E
6	阆	0-6747					294942
7	阇	8-9115					
8	阈	0-6748					294949
9	阉	0-4943					29494D
A	阊	0-6749					29494F
B	阋	0-6750					29556C
C	阌	0-6751					294950
D	阍	0-6752					294952
E	阎	0-4954					275E60
F	阏	0-6753					294948

961

	Char	G	J	K	B	C	A
0	阐	0-1891					275E6A
1	阑	0-3227					275E63
2	阒	0-6754					29495A
3	阓	8-9116					
4	阔	0-3211					275E61
5	阕	0-6755					275E62
6	阖	0-6756					515E5D
7	阗	0-6757					275E68
8	阘	8-1216					
9	阙	0-6758					294960
A	阚	0-6759					294969
B	阛	8-9117					
C	阜	0-2423	0-4176	0-6129	AAFA	1-4F5D	215E6C
D	阝	0-5866	1-7036			E-2143	4B5E6C
E	阞	3-8510	1-7037		C9AA	2-2169	23497A
F	队	0-2251					275F2B

962

	Char	G	J	K	B	C	A
0	阠				CA58	2-2278	
1	阡	0-5868	0-7984	0-8438	A6E9	1-486A	215E6D
2	阢	0-5867	1-7038		CA56	2-2276	23497C
3	阣	5-8468			CA59	2-2279	
4	阤	3-8511	1-7039	1-8087	CA57	2-2277	23497B
5	阥		1-7040				
6	阦		1-7041			E-273B	
7	阧	5-8474				E-273A	234A21
8	阨		0-7985	1-7075	CBAE	2-252E	333475
9	阩					E-273F	
A	阪	0-5870	0-2669	0-8801	A8C1	1-4B62	215E71
B	阫	3-8512				E-273C	
C	阬		1-7042		A8C2	1-4B63	2D377C
D	阭	3-8514			CBB0	2-2530	
E	阮	0-4078	0-7986	0-7254	A8BF	1-4B60	215E70
F	阯		0-7987	1-7807	CBAF	2-252F	2D3821

963

	Char	G	J	K	B	C	A
0	阰	3-8513			CBAD	2-252D	
1	阱	0-5869	1-7043		A8C0	1-4B61	215E6F
2	防	0-2332	0-4341	0-5933	A8BE	1-4B5F	215E6E
3	阳	0-4984	1-7044			E-273D	275F2E
4	阴	0-5085				E-273E	275F2A
5	阵	0-5383					275E7B
6	阶	0-2955					275F2C
7	阷	3-8515	1-7045			E-2A79	
8	阸	5-8479	1-7046				
9	阹	3-8516	1-7047		CDD8	2-2878	
A	阺	3-8517	1-7048		CDDB	2-287B	
B	阻	0-5572	0-3343	0-8070	AAFD	1-4F60	215E74
C	阼	0-5872	1-7049		CDDA	2-287A	234A32
D	阽	0-5871	1-7050		CDD9	2-2879	234A30
E	阾	5-8477				E-2A7C	
F	阿	0-1602	0-1604	0-6825	AAFC	1-4F5F	215E73

964

	Char	G	J	K	B	C	A
0	陀	0-4551	0-3443	0-8677	AAFB	1-4F5E	215E72
1	陁	5-8476	1-7051			E-2A7B	
2	陂	0-5873	0-7988	0-8914	AB40	1-4F62	234A2F
3	陃				CDDC	2-287C	
4	附	0-2429	0-4177	0-6130	AAFE	1-4F61	215E75
5	际	0-2842					275F37
6	陆	0-3429					275F24
7	陇	0-3404					275F3C
8	陈	0-1934					275F23
9	陉	0-5874					294A46
A	陊	5-8483			D0C6	2-2D67	
B	陋	0-3410	0-7991	0-5516	ADAE	1-536F	215E78
C	陌	0-3616	0-7989	0-5672	ADAF	1-5370	215E77
D	降	0-2921	0-2563	0-4329	ADB0	1-5371	215E79
E	陎				D0C7	2-2D68	
F	陏	3-8520	0-7990		D0C3	2-2D64	

965

	Char	G	J	K	B	C	A
0	限	0-4762	0-2434	0-8958	ADAD	1-536E	215E76
1	陑	3-8521			D0C4	2-2D65	234A3C
2	陒	5-8482	1-7052				
3	陓	3-8522			D0C5	2-2D66	
4	陔	0-5875	1-7053		D0C2	2-2D63	2D753A
5	陕	0-4134					294A44
6	陖	5-8485	1-7054			E-3436	234A4B
7	陗		1-7055				
8	陘	1-5874	1-7056	1-8368	B0A4	1-5867	234A46
9	陙	3-8527				E-3434	
A	陚	3-8532				E-395E	
B	陛	0-1761	0-4237	0-8846	B0A1	1-5864	215E7C
C	陜		0-7993	0-8980	D445	2-3348	234A44
D	陝	1-4134	0-8001	0-6477	B0A2	1-5865	215E7E
E	陞	8-1571	0-7994	0-6719	B0A5	1-5868	39345B
F	陟	0-5876	0-8002	0-8419	D446	2-3349	234A4A

966

	Char	G	J	K	B	C	A
0	陠	5-8484				E-3433	234A42
1	陡	0-2224	1-7057	1-6171	B07E	1-5863	215E7D
2	院	0-5226	0-1701	0-7434	B07C	1-5861	215E7A
3	陣	1-5383	0-3156	0-8270	B07D	1-5862	215E7B
4	除	0-1993	0-2992	0-8022	B0A3	1-5866	215F21
5	陥		0-2057				2D5F28
6	陦		0-8003				697023
7	陧	0-5877					4D4A6C
8	陨	0-5241					2D5F35
9	险	0-4753					275F3A
A	陪	0-3767	0-3970	0-5954	B3AD	1-5D71	215F22
B	陫	5-8488			D849	2-3A2D	
C	陬	0-5878	0-8005	1-8044	B3B5	1-5D79	234A51
D	陭	3-8533			D848	2-3A2C	
E	陮	5-8489	1-7058			E-3961	
F	陯				D84B	2-3A2F	

967

	Char	G	J	K	B	C	A
0	陰	1-5085	0-1702	0-7568	B3B1	1-5D75	215F2A
1	陱	5-8492			D84A	2-3A2E	
2	陲	0-5879	0-8004	1-6927	B6AB	1-6270	215F26
3	陳	1-1934	0-3636	0-8271	B3AF	1-5D73	215F23
4	陴	0-5880	1-7059	1-6717	B3B2	1-5D76	215F29
5	陵	0-3374	0-4645	0-5553	B3AE	1-5D72	215F25
6	陶	0-4453	0-3811	0-5222	B3B3	1-5D77	215F27
7	陷	0-4761	0-7992	0-8972	B3B4	1-5D78	215F28
8	陸	1-3429	0-4606	0-5533	B3B0	1-5D74	215F24
9	陹					E-3965	
A	険		0-2417				4B5F3A
B	陻		1-7060			E-3F71	234A5D
C	陼	5-8486	1-7061	1-7576	D847	2-3A2B	
D	陽	1-4984	0-4559	0-6953	B6A7	1-626C	215F2E
E	陾	3-8535	1-7062		DC7D	2-4144	234A62
F	陿		1-7063			E-3F72	234A5E

968

	Char	G	J	K	B	C	A
0	陲				DCA3	2-4148	
1	陻	5-8501	1-7064			E-3F73	
2	陼		1-7065			E-3F75	234A6D
3	隃	3-8537	1-7066		DCA2	2-4147	234A6E
4	隄		1-7067	1-7682	B6AC	1-6271	234A63
5	隅	0-5171	0-2289	0-7374	B6A8	1-626D	215F2F
6	隆	0-3401	0-4620	0-5544	B6A9	1-626E	215F30
7	隇	3-8534			DC7C	2-4143	
8	隈	0-5881	0-2308		DC7E	2-4145	234A65
9	隉	1-5877	1-7068		DCA1	2-4146	234A6C
A	隊	1-2251	0-3466	0-5173	B6A4	1-6269	215F2B
B	隋	0-4369	0-7101	0-6641	B6A6	1-626B	215F2D
C	隌	5-8502				E-3F70	
D	隍	0-5882	0-8006	0-9259	B6AA	1-626F	215F31
E	階	1-2955	0-1912	0-4513	B6A5	1-626A	215F2C
F	随	0-4370	0-3179			E-4540	275F39

969

	Char	G	J	K	B	C	A
0	隐	0-5094					275F3B
1	隑	3-8524	1-7069	1-6005	E0D3	2-4859	
2	隒	3-8539			E0D1	2-4857	
3	隓	5-8504			E0D2	2-4858	
4	隔	0-2484	0-1954	0-4416	B96A	1-6752	215F33
5	隕	1-5241	0-8008	0-7402	B96B	1-6753	215F35
6	隖		1-7070			E-4542	234A79
7	隗	0-5883	0-8009	1-7279	E0D4	2-485A	234A7A
8	隘	0-1615	0-8007	0-6886	B969	1-6751	215F32
9	隙	0-4722	0-2368	0-4832	BBD8	1-6B61	215F34
A	隚		1-7071				
B	際	1-2842	0-2661	0-8023	BBDA	1-6B63	215F37
C	障	0-5347	0-3067	0-7801	BBD9	1-6B62	215F36
D	隝	5-8478	1-7072			E-4A45	
E	隞	3-8538			E4BB	2-4F23	
F	隟	5-8511	1-7073			E-4A46	

96A

	Char	G	J	K	B	C	A
0	隠		0-1703			E-4A44	2D5F3B
1	隡				E4BC	2-4F24	
2	隢				E8AB	2-5554	
3	隣		0-4657	0-5586		E-4F5A	2D5C74
4	隤	3-8536	1-7074	1-8165	E8AA	2-5553	234B2F
5	隥	5-8512	1-7075			E-4F5B	
6	隦		1-7076				
7	隧	0-4377	0-8011	0-6642	C047	1-7270	215F38
8	隨	1-4370	0-7814	0-6643	C048	1-7271	215F39
9	隩	3-8541	1-7077	1-7225	EC4F	2-5B5B	234B35
A	險	1-4753	0-8010	0-9047	C049	1-7272	215F3A
B	隫	5-8494				E-5348	
C	隬				EEF6	2-6043	
D	隭					E-5670	
E	隮	3-8525	1-7078		EEF4	2-6041	234B37
F	隯		1-7079			E-566F	

96B

	Char	G	J	K	B	C	A
0	隰	0-5884	0-8014	1-6954	EEF5	2-6042	234B3B
1	隱	1-5094	0-8012	0-7563	C1F4	1-7621	215F3B
2	隲		0-8013			E-5671	234B3C
3	隳	0-6736	1-7080	1-8493	F16F	2-643B	234B3E
4	隴	1-3404	0-8015	1-6306	C3F7	1-7944	215F3C
5	隵					E-5D49	
6	隶	0-3305	0-8016	1-7456		E-2A7D	275F3D
7	隷		0-4676	0-5443		E-5349	335F3D
8	隸	1-3305	0-8017	1-6272	C1F5	1-7622	215F3D
9	隹	0-8631	0-8018	1-8045	AB41	1-4F63	234B48
A	隺	3-1872	1-7081			E-6325	
B	隻	1-8902	0-3241	0-8420	B0A6	1-5869	215F3E
C	隼	0-8632	0-4027	1-7775	D447	2-334A	234B49
D	隽	0-8633				E-3439	2D5F46
E	难	0-3649					275F50
F	隿				D84C	2-3A30	

96C

	Char	G	J	K	B	C	A
0	雀	0-4024	0-3193	0-7745	B3B6	1-5D7A	215F3F
1	雁	0-4967	0-2071	0-6850	B6AD	1-6272	215F43
2	雂	5-8449			DCA4	2-4149	
3	雃	5-8447			DCA6	2-414B	
4	雄	0-4859	0-4526	0-7409	B6AF	1-6274	215F42
5	雅	0-4937	0-1877	0-6826	B6AE	1-6273	215F44
6	集	0-2815	0-2924	0-8302	B6B0	1-6275	215F41
7	雇	0-2545	0-2459	0-4550	B6B1	1-6276	215F40
8	雈				DCA5	2-414A	
9	雉	0-7984	0-8021	0-8643	B96E	1-6756	215F47
A	雊	3-8506	1-7082		B96F	1-6757	234B53
B	雋		0-8020	0-8170	B96D	1-6755	215F46
C	雌	0-2038	0-2783	0-7733	BBDB	1-6B64	215F48
D	雍	0-5126	0-8022	0-7228	B96C	1-6754	215F45
E	雎	0-8634	0-8019	0-7849	E0D5	2-485B	234B52
F	雏	0-1991					275F4D

96D

	Char	G	J	K	B	C	A
0	雐	3-6537				E-4A47	
1	雑		0-2708			E-4A49	2D5F4B
2	雒	0-8635	1-7083		BBDC	1-6B65	234B57
3	雓				E8AC	2-5555	
4	雔	5-8455			EC50	2-5B5C	
5	雕	0-2181	0-8026	0-8071	C04A	1-7273	215F49
6	雖	1-4368	0-7413	0-6644	C1F6	1-7623	215F4A
7	雗	5-8331			F170	2-643C	
8	雘	3-7529	1-7085		F174	2-6440	234B66
9	雙	1-4311	0-5054	0-6810	C2F9	1-7764	215F4E
A	雚	5-7440	1-7086	1-5773	F171	2-643D	
B	雛	1-1991	0-3187	0-8565	C2FA	1-7765	215F4D
C	雜	1-5251	0-8024	0-7758	C2F8	1-7763	215F4B
D	雝		1-7087	1-7248	F175	2-6441	234B67
E	雞		1-7088	1-5672	C2FB	1-7766	215F4C
F	雟	3-2580	1-7089		F173	2-643F	234B64

96E

	Char	G	J	K	B	C	A
0	雠	0-8637					4B306C
1	雡	5-8461			F379	2-6766	
2	離	1-3275	0-4605	0-5578	C2F7	1-7762	215F4F
3	難	1-3649	0-3881	0-4981	C3F8	1-7945	215F50
4	雤					E-5E70	
5	雥	5-8463			F8CD	2-705B	
6	雦					E-6125	
7	雧	5-3825				E-622F	
8	雨	0-5174	0-1711	0-7375	AB42	1-4F64	215F51
9	雩	0-8607	1-7090	0-7376	B3B8	1-5D7C	234B71
A	雪	0-4909	0-3267	0-6468	B3B7	1-5D7B	215F52
B	雫		0-2822				693C36
C	雬					E-3F7E	
D	雭	5-8332				E-3F7C	
E	雮					E-3F7B	
F	雯	0-8609	1-7091	0-5807	B6B2	1-6277	215F53

96F

	Char	G	J	K	B	C	A
0	雰		0-4223	0-6152	DCA8	2-414D	234B76
1	雱	3-8428	1-7092		DCA7	2-414C	234B74
2	雲	1-5238	0-1732	0-7403	B6B3	1-6278	215F54
3	雳	0-8608					275F6E
4	雴					E-4546	234B77
5	雵				E0D9	2-485F	234B7A
6	零	0-3367	0-4677	0-5435	B973	1-675B	215F58
7	雷	0-3255	0-4575	0-5484	B970	1-6758	215F56
8	雸				E0D8	2-485E	
9	雹	0-1702	0-8027	0-5863	B972	1-675A	215F57
A	雺	5-8336	1-7093	1-6466	E0D6	2-485C	234B78
B	電	1-2171	0-3737	0-7919	B971	1-6759	215F55
C	雼					E-4547	
D	雽				E0D7	2-485D	
E	雾	0-4677					275F67
F	雿	5-8342			E4BD	2-4F25	234C22

970

	Char	G	J	K	B	C	A
0	需	0-4872	0-2891	0-6645	BBDD	1-6B66	215F59
1	霁	0-8611					275F6B
2	霂	3-8435	1-7094		E8AF	2-5558	234C27
3	霃	5-8346	1-7101				
4	霄	0-4786	0-8028	1-6887	BE5D	1-6F66	215F5B
5	霅	3-8434	1-7102	1-6784	E8AD	2-5556	234C2A
6	霆	0-8610	0-8029	0-7993	BE5E	1-6F67	215F5D
7	震	0-5380	0-3144	0-8272	BE5F	1-6F68	215F5A
8	霈	0-8612	0-8030	1-8191	E8AE	2-5557	234C29
9	霉	0-3525	1-7103	1-6423	BE60	1-6F69	215F5C
A	霊		0-4678			E-4F60	4B5F6F
B	霋	5-8349			EC51	2-5B5D	
C	霌			1-7761		E-5350	
D	霍	0-2784	0-8025	1-5760	C04E	1-7277	215F62
E	霎	0-8614	0-8032	1-6785	C04B	1-7274	215F5F
F	霏	0-8613	0-8034	1-6718	C050	1-7279	215F61

971

	Char	G	J	K	B	C	A
0	霐	5-8354			EC53	2-5B5F	
1	霑		0-8033	0-7937	C04C	1-7275	215F5E
2	霒	5-2112			EC52	2-5B5E	
3	霓	0-3662	0-8031	0-7171	C04F	1-7278	215F63
4	霔	5-8353		1-7762		E-534D	
5	霕					E-534C	
6	霖	0-3356	0-8035	0-5593	C04D	1-7276	215F60
7	霗					E-5351	
8	霘				EEF9	2-6046	
9	霙	3-8436	0-8036	0-7146	EEFB	2-6048	234C3E
A	霚		1-7104			E-5674	
B	霛	5-8362	1-7105			E-5675	234C38
C	霜	0-4310	0-3390	0-6360	C1F7	1-7624	215F64
D	霝	5-8357	1-7106		EEFA	2-6047	234C3D
E	霞	0-4728	0-1866	0-8939	C1F8	1-7625	215F65
F	霟				EEF8	2-6045	

972

	Char	G	J	K	B	C	A
0	霠	5-8360			EEF7	2-6044	
1	霡	3-8443	1-7107				
2	霢	5-8364	1-7108		F177	2-6443	234C49
3	霣	3-8433	1-7109	1-7339	F176	2-6442	234C47
4	霤	3-8445	0-8037		C2FC	1-7767	234C4A
5	霥				F178	2-6444	
6	霦	3-8446		1-6733	F37E	2-676B	234C50
7	霧	1-4677	0-4424	0-5786	C3FA	1-7947	215F67
8	霨	5-8370	1-7110		F37D	2-676A	234C4E
9	霩	5-8365			F37A	2-6767	
A	霪	0-8615	0-8038	1-7432	C3F9	1-7946	215F66
B	霫	3-8447			F37B	2-6768	
C	霬				F37C	2-6769	
D	霭	0-8616					275F6D
E	霮	3-8449			F548	2-6A56	
F	霯				F549	2-6A57	

973

	Char	G	J	K	B	C	A
0	霰	0-8617	0-8039	0-6312	C4C5	1-7A50	234C58
1	霱	5-8378	1-7111			E-5D4F	234C52
2	露	0-3422	0-4710	0-5458	C553	1-7B3F	215F6A
3	霳	5-8371	1-7112			E-5D4C	
4	霴					E-5D4E	
5	霵	3-8448			F66E	2-6C5C	
6	霶	5-8380				E-5E72	234C5C
7	霷					E-5E71	
8	霸	0-1652	0-5917	1-8192	C551	1-7B3D	215F68
9	霹	0-3789	0-8040	0-6004	C552	1-7B3E	215F69
A	霺				F66F	2-6C5D	
B	霻					E-666E	
C	霼	3-4401				E-5F71	
D	霽	1-8611	0-8041	0-8024	C5B4	1-7B7E	215F6B
E	霾	0-8618	0-8042		C5B5	1-7C21	215F6C
F	霿	3-8450			F771	2-6E40	

974

	Char	G	J	K	B	C	A
0	靀	5-8379				E-5F72	
1	靁	5-8383	1-7113			E-6059	234C6A
2	靂	1-8608	0-8046	0-5390	C645	1-7C70	215F6E
3	靃	3-8452	1-7114		F8CF	2-705D	
4	靄	1-8616	0-8043	0-6887	C647	1-7C72	215F6D
5	靅	3-1953				E-6126	
6	靆	3-1955	0-8044	1-7970	F8CE	2-705C	234C6C
7	靇	5-8335			F8D0	2-705E	234C6B
8	靈	1-3373	0-8045	0-5436	C646	1-7C71	215F6F
9	靉	3-1954	0-8047	1-7070	F957	2-7146	234C6E
A	靊		1-7115				
B	靋				F9AD	2-717B	
C	靌			1-6594			
D	靍					E-666F	
E	靎		1-7116				
F	靏		1-7117				

975

	Char	G	J	K	B	C	A
0	靐					E-6245	
1	靑			0-8476		E-2A7E	4B5F70
2	青	0-3964	0-3236		AB43	1-4F65	215F70
3	靓	0-8606					294C76
4	靔	8-1490					
5	靕		1-7118			E-4549	
6	靖	0-3024	0-4487	0-7994	B974	1-675C	215F71
7	靗	5-8325	1-7119				
8	靘	3-8424	1-7120		E4BE	2-4F26	234C75
9	静	0-3018	0-3237			E-4A4C	335F73
A	靚	1-8606	1-7121	1-7668	E8B0	2-5559	234C76
B	靛	0-2169	1-7122	1-7622	C051	1-727A	215F72
C	靜	1-3018	0-8048	0-8001	C052	1-727B	215F73
D	靝	5-8324		1-7933		E-594F	234C78
E	非	0-2339	0-4083	0-6210	AB44	1-4F66	215F74
F	靟	3-8461				E-4021	234C7B

976

	Char	G	J	K	B	C	A
0	靠	0-3131	0-8049	1-5706	BE61	1-6F6A	215F75
1	靡	0-3550	0-8351	0-5828	C3FB	1-7948	215F76
2	面	0-3570	0-4444	0-5692	ADB1	1-5372	27625E
3	靣		1-7123			E-2B21	
4	靤	5-8765	0-8050			E-4A4E	234C7D
5	靥	0-5644					275F79
6	靦	3-8963	0-8051	1-7623	C053	1-727C	215F78
7	靧	3-8969	1-7124			E-5E73	234D25
8	靨	1-5644	0-8052	1-7165	C5E2	1-7C4E	215F79
9	革	0-2479	0-1955	0-9052	ADB2	1-5373	215F7A
A	靪	5-8702	1-7125		D84D	2-3A31	
B	靫	3-8903	0-8054				234D2C
C	靬	3-8891			DCA9	2-414E	
D	靭		0-3157	0-7669		E-4024	4B602D
E	靮	3-8902	1-7126		DCAB	2-4150	234D30
F	靯	3-8893				E-4022	

977

	Char	G	J	K	B	C	A
0	靰	3-8894			DCAA	2-414F	
1	靱		0-8055				2D602D
2	靲	3-8906			E0DD	2-4863	
3	靳	0-2989	1-7127	1-5954	E0DA	2-4860	234D35
4	靴	0-4905	0-2304	0-9208	B975	1-675D	215F7C
5	靵			1-6057			
6	靶	0-1648	1-7128		B976	1-675E	215F7B
7	靷	3-8909	1-7129	0-7670	E0DB	2-4861	234D31
8	靸	3-8901	1-7130		E0DC	2-4862	234D32
9	靹		0-8056			E-454B	697058
A	靺	3-8910	0-8060	0-5643	E4C0	2-4F28	234D38
B	靻	3-8912	1-7131		E4C5	2-4F2D	
C	靼	0-8716	0-8058	1-6080	BBDE	1-6B67	215F7D
D	靽	3-8914	1-7132		E4BF	2-4F27	
E	靾	5-8709			E4C1	2-4F29	
F	靿	3-8918	1-7133		E4C8	2-4F30	234D43

Code	Char	G	J	K	B	C	A
9780	鞀	5-8717	1-7134	1-6138	E4C3	2-4F2B	234D3A
9781	鞁	3-8917	0-8059	1-8254	E4C7	2-4F2F	234D3C
9782	鞂				E4C4	2-4F2C	
9783	鞃	3-8916			E4C2	2-4F2A	234D37
9784	鞄	3-8913	0-1983	1-8233	E4C6	2-4F2E	234D40
9785	鞅	0-8717	0-8057	1-7051	BBDF	1-6B68	215F7E
9786	鞆		0-8061				69705D
9787	鞇	3-8921				E-4F62	
9788	鞈	3-8923			E8B3	2-555C	
9789	鞉	5-8723	1-7135			E-4F63	234D49
978A	鞊	5-8718			E8B1	2-555A	
978B	鞋	0-4812	0-8062	0-9125	BE63	1-6F6C	216022
978C	鞌					E-4F64	2D6021
978D	鞍	0-1616	0-1640	0-6851	BE62	1-6F6B	216021
978E	鞎				E8B2	2-555B	
978F	鞏	1-2514	0-8063	0-4589	BE64	1-6F6D	216023
9790	鞐		0-8064				697060
9791	鞑	0-8718					276029
9792	鞒	0-8719					4B4559
9793	鞓	3-8925				E-5353	
9794	鞔	0-8720			EC56	2-5B62	234D54
9795	鞕	5-8729	1-7136				
9796	鞖		1-7137				
9797	鞗	5-1885	1-7138		EC55	2-5B61	216879
9798	鞘	0-3942	0-3068	1-8002	C054	1-727D	216024
9799	鞙	3-8926	1-7139		EC54	2-5B60	
979A	鞚	3-8934	1-7140		EEFC	2-6049	234D5C
979B	鞛	5-8737				E-567A	234D59
979C	鞜	3-8938	0-8065		EEFE	2-604B	234D62
979D	鞝	5-8735			EF41	2-604D	
979E	鞞	3-8931	1-7141		EF40	2-604C	
979F	鞟	3-8932	1-7142			E-567B	234D5A
97A0	鞠	0-3047	0-2139	0-4751	C1F9	1-7626	216025
97A1	鞡	3-8930			EEFD	2-604A	
97A2	鞢	3-8939	1-7143		F1A1	2-644B	
97A3	鞣	0-8723	0-8068	1-7403	C2FD	1-7768	216026
97A4	鞤				F17D	2-6449	
97A5	鞥	3-8945			F1A2	2-644C	234D78
97A6	鞦	1-8868	0-8067	1-8046	C2FE	1-7769	216027
97A7	鞧	3-8948					
97A8	鞨	3-8942	0-8066	0-4274	F17B	2-6447	234D71
97A9	鞩					E-5950	
97AA	鞪	5-8746			F17E	2-644A	
97AB	鞫	0-8722	0-7581	0-4752	F17C	2-6448	234D74
97AC	鞬	3-8936	1-7144	1-5607	F179	2-6445	234D6A
97AD	鞭	0-1762	0-4260	0-8829	C340	1-776A	216028
97AE	鞮	3-8941	1-7145		F17A	2-6446	234D70
97AF	鞯	0-8721					294E43
97B0	鞰						
97B1	鞱	5-8753	1-7146	1-6139		E-5B5F	
97B2	鞲	0-8724	1-7147			E-5B5D	234D7A
97B3	鞳	3-8940	0-8069		F3A1	2-676C	234E24
97B4	鞴	0-8725	0-8070	1-6719		E-5B5E	234D7C
97B5	鞵		1-7148			E-5B60	234E26
97B6	鞶	5-8752	1-7149		F3A3	2-676E	
97B7	鞷				F3A2	2-676D	
97B8	鞸	5-8719	1-7150	1-8265		E-5D50	234E2D
97B9	鞹	3-8953	1-7151	1-5761	F54A	2-6A58	234E29
97BA	鞺		1-7152			E-5D51	
97BB	鞻	3-8947			F54B	2-6A59	
97BC	鞼	3-8943	1-7153				
97BD	鞽	1-8719				E-5E75	
97BE	鞾		1-7154			E-5E74	234E35
97BF	鞿	3-8890	1-7155		F670	2-6C5E	
97C0	韀	5-8761				E-5F73	234E38
97C1	韁		1-7156	1-5571	C5B7	1-7C23	21602A
97C2	韂	3-8957					
97C3	韃	1-8718	0-8071	1-6081	C5B6	1-7C22	216029
97C4	韄	3-8956	1-7157		F84F	2-6F5D	
97C5	韅	3-8958	1-7158		F850	2-6F5E	234E3B
97C6	韆	1-8865	0-8072	0-8439	C648	1-7C73	21602B
97C7	韇	3-8929	1-7159		F8D1	2-705F	
97C8	韈		0-8073			E-6128	335821
97C9	韉	1-8721	1-7160		C669	1-7D36	234E43
97CA	韊		1-7161			E-623B	
97CB	韋	1-4604	0-8074	0-7463	ADB3	1-5374	21602C
97CC	韌	1-4045	1-7162		B6B4	1-6279	21602D
97CD	韍	3-3218	1-7163	1-6669	E4CA	2-4F32	234E4C
97CE	韎	3-3217	1-7164		E4C9	2-4F31	234E4B
97CF	韏	3-3225			E8B5	2-555E	
97D0	韐	3-3224	1-7165	1-5554	E8B4	2-555D	234E4E
97D1	韑		1-7166				
97D2	韒	5-3510				E-5355	
97D3	韓	1-2611	0-2058	0-8959	C1FA	1-7627	21602E
97D4	韔	3-3216	1-7167		EF43	2-604F	234E51
97D5	韕				EF42	2-604E	
97D6	韖	5-3517			F1A5	2-644F	
97D7	韗	3-3226	1-7168		F1A3	2-644D	
97D8	韘	3-3228	1-7169		F1A6	2-6450	234E53
97D9	韙	1-7224	1-7170	1-7367	F1A4	2-644E	234E54
97DA	韚					E-5951	
97DB	韛	3-3231	1-7174				
97DC	韜	1-7226	0-8075	0-5223	C3FC	1-7949	21602F
97DD	韝	3-3230	1-7171	1-5876	F3A4	2-676F	234E59
97DE	韞	1-7225	1-7172	1-7236	F3A5	2-6770	234E5C
97DF	韟	5-3519			F3A6	2-6771	
97E0	韠	3-3223	1-7173	1-8266			234E5E
97E1	韡	5-3506	1-7175	1-7368	F671	2-6C5F	234E60
97E2	韢	3-3233				E-5E76	
97E3	韣	3-3235			F772	2-6E41	
97E4	韤		1-7176			E-6129	395821
97E5	韥				F8D2	2-7060	
97E6	韦	0-4604					27602C
97E7	韧	0-4045					27602D
97E8	韨	8-9166					
97E9	韩	0-2611					27602E
97EA	韪	0-7224					294E54
97EB	韫	0-7225					294E5C
97EC	韬	0-7226					27602F
97ED	韭	0-3034	0-8076	1-5877	ADB4	1-5375	216030
97EE	韮		0-3903	1-5878		E-454F	2D6030
97EF	韯	5-4026	1-7177			E-4F65	222F69
97F0	韰	3-8973			EC57	2-5B63	
97F1	韱	5-4029	1-7178	1-6854	EF44	2-6050	
97F2	韲		0-8078	1-7683		E-5B61	4D5F7B
97F3	音	0-5084	0-1827	0-7569	ADB5	1-5376	216031
97F4	韴		1-7179				
97F5	韵	0-5247	0-8081	1-7340		E-4550	234E6C
97F6	韶	0-4156	0-8080	0-6550	BBE0	1-6B69	216034
97F7	韷		1-7180				
97F8	韸	5-8892	1-7181		EC58	2-5B64	
97F9	韹	5-8901			C341	1-776B	
97FA	韺	5-8893	1-7182	1-7177	F1A7	2-6451	234E73
97FB	韻		0-1704	0-7404	C3FD	1-794A	216035
97FC	韼					E-5D53	
97FD	韽	3-9118			F54C	2-6A5A	
97FE	韾				F54D	2-6A5B	
97FF	響	1-4776	0-2233	0-9034	C554	1-7B40	216036

980

	Char	G	J	K	B	C	A
0	頀	5-8903		0-9165	F851	2-6F5F	2E4E56
1	頁	1-5019	0-4239	0-9077	ADB6	1-5377	216037
2	頂	1-2205	0-3626	0-8002	B3BB	1-5E21	216038
3	頃	1-3974	0-2602	0-4481	B3BC	1-5E22	216039
4	頄	5-6375			D84E	2-3A32	
5	項	1-4778	0-2564	0-9003	B6B5	1-627A	21603A
6	順	1-4319	0-2971	0-6687	B6B6	1-627B	21603B
7	頇	1-8192	1-7183		DCAC	2-4151	234E79
8	須	1-4875	0-3160	0-6646	B6B7	1-627C	21603C
9	頉	3-3887					
A	頊	1-7179	1-7184	0-7385	B97A	1-6762	21603E
B	頋					E-4552	2D6056
C	頌	1-4344	0-8083	0-6575	B97C	1-6764	216042
D	頍	3-3571	1-7186	1-5937	E0DF	2-4865	234E7E
E	頎	1-8193	1-7187	1-6006	E0E0	2-4866	234F23
F	頏	1-8194	0-8082	1-8316	E0DE	2-4864	234E7B

982

	Char	G	J	K	B	C	A
0	頠	3-6484	1-7192		E8BB	2-5564	234F37
1	頡	1-8201	0-8086	1-8535	BE65	1-6F6E	216045
2	頢	3-6735				E-4F67	
3	頣		1-7193	1-6985		E-636E	
4	頤	1-5035	0-8085		C05B	1-7326	21604C
5	頥		1-7208				
6	頦	1-8204	1-7194	1-8326	E8B8	2-5561	234F2C
7	頧	5-6391			E8BD	2-5566	
8	頨	5-7514			E8BA	2-5563	
9	頩	3-6486			E8B9	2-5562	
A	頪	3-7186				E-4F66	
B	頫		1-7201	1-6642	BE66	1-6F6F	234F34
C	頬		0-4343				
D	頭	1-4523	0-3812	0-5273	C059	1-7324	216046
E	頮	5-6407	1-7202	1-8450		E-535C	234F40
F	頯	3-6491	1-7203		EC5A	2-5B66	234F44

984

	Char	G	J	K	B	C	A
0	顀	3-8508				E-5726	
1	顁	5-6422			EF45	2-6051	
2	顂	5-6402		1-6318		E-637B	
3	顃				EF4A	2-6056	
4	顄	5-6423	1-7210		EF46	2-6052	234F4E
5	顅	3-6501			EF49	2-6055	
6	顆	1-3137	0-8089	0-4608	C1FB	1-7628	21604D
7	顇		1-7211	1-8068		E-5728	234F4B
8	顈	5-6421		1-5655	EDD4	2-5E41	
9	顉	5-8543			EF48	2-6054	
A	顊	5-8464	1-7212		EF47	2-6053	
B	顋		0-8091	1-6973		E-5959	234F62
C	題	1-4466	0-3474	0-8025	C344	1-776E	216050
D	額	1-2278	0-1959	0-6894	C342	1-776C	21604F
E	顎	1-8206	0-1960	0-6841	C345	1-776F	216051
F	顏		0-8090		C343	1-776D	21604E

986

	Char	G	J	K	B	C	A
0	顠	3-6521			F54E	2-6A5C	
1	顡	3-6523				E-642A	
2	顢	1-8209	1-7220		F54F	2-6A5D	234F77
3	顣	5-6432	1-7221		F550	2-6A5E	
4	顤	3-6479			F672	2-6C60	
5	顥	1-8211	1-7222	0-9166	C556	1-7B42	235021
6	顦		1-7223	1-8003		E-5E78	235022
7	顧	1-2543	0-2460	0-4551	C555	1-7B41	216056
8	顨	5-2310				E-5E77	234F7E
9	顩	3-6490			F774	2-6E43	
A	顪	3-6480	1-7224		F773	2-6E42	
B	顫	1-1892	0-8092	0-7921	C5B8	1-7C24	216057
C	顬	1-8212	1-7225			E-605D	235029
D	顭					E-605E	
E	顮	3-6520				E-605C	
F	顯	1-4752	0-8093	0-9073	C5E3	1-7C4F	216058

981

	Char	G	J	K	B	C	A
0	預	1-5204	0-4534	0-7172	B977	1-675F	21603D
1	頑	1-4571	0-2072	0-7255	B978	1-6760	21603F
2	頒	1-1668	0-4050	0-5888	B97B	1-6763	216041
3	頓	1-2257	0-3860	0-5243	B979	1-6761	216040
4	頔	3-6473	1-7188			E-4A54	
5	頕	3-6472				E-4A55	
6	頖	5-6388	1-7189	1-6530	E4CB	2-4F33	234F26
7	頗	1-3836	0-3192	0-8786	BBE1	1-6B6A	216043
8	領	1-3376	0-4646	0-5437	BBE2	1-6B6B	216044
9	頙	5-6385	1-7185			E-4A52	
A	頚		0-2359			E-4A56	4B6048
B	頛	5-6321			E8BC	2-5565	
C	頜	1-8202	1-7190		BE67	1-6F70	
D	頝	5-6393			E8B7	2-5560	
E	頞	3-6487	1-7191	1-7034	E8B6	2-555F	234F2D
F	頟					E-4F69	234F38

983

	Char	G	J	K	B	C	A
0	頰	1-2853	1-7204	0-9090	C055	1-727E	216047
1	頱					E-5359	
2	頲	3-6482	1-7205		EC5B	2-5B67	234F45
3	頳	5-7780	1-7206			E-535A	234F3D
4	頴		0-1748			E-5228	2D4F45
5	頵	3-6493	1-7207		EC59	2-5B65	
6	頶					E-5358	
7	頷	1-8205	0-8087	1-7044	C058	1-7323	21604B
8	頸	1-3017	0-8084	0-4482	C056	1-7321	216048
9	頹			0-8761	C05A	1-7325	21604A
A	頺					E-535D	
B	頻	1-3821	0-4149	0-6226	C057	1-7322	216049
C	頼		0-4574			E-535B	395A36
D	頽	1-4539	0-8088			E-535F	
E	頾		1-7209				234F66
F	頿	5-6425		1-7506		E-595B	

985

	Char	G	J	K	B	C	A
0	顐	5-6401			F1A8	2-6452	
1	顑	3-6505	1-7213		F1A9	2-6453	
2	顒	3-6506	1-7214	1-7249	F1AA	2-6454	234F60
3	顓	1-8207	1-7215	1-7624	C346	1-7770	216052
4	顔	1-4953	0-2073	0-6852		E-5956	45604E
5	顕		0-2418			E-5958	336058
6	顖	5-6428	1-7216			E-5B65	234F72
7	顗	3-6481	1-7217		F3AA	2-6775	234F6F
8	願	1-5224	0-2074	0-7435	C440	1-794C	216055
9	顙	1-8210	1-7218	1-6793	F3A8	2-6773	234F6B
A	顚		1-7219	0-7920			336054
B	顛	1-2163	0-3731		C441	1-794D	216054
C	顜	3-6513			F3A7	2-6772	234F6A
D	顝	3-8985			F3A9	2-6774	
E	類	1-3264	0-4664	0-5530	C3FE	1-794B	216053
F	顟	3-6524			F551	2-6A5F	

987

	Char	G	J	K	B	C	A
0	顰	1-8213	0-8094	1-6734	C649	1-7C74	21605A
1	顱	1-3413	0-8101	1-6284	C660	1-7D2D	216059
2	顲	3-6532			F958	2-7147	
3	顳	1-8208	0-8103	1-6861	F9AE	2-717C	235030
4	顴	1-4007	0-8102	1-5774	F9AF	2-717D	235031
5	页	0-5019					276037
6	顶	0-2205					276038
7	顷	0-3974					276039
8	顸	0-8192					294E79
9	项	0-4778					27603A
A	顺	0-4319					27603B
B	须	0-4875					27603C
C	顼	0-7179					27603E
D	顽	0-4571					27603F
E	顾	0-2543					276056
F	顿	0-2257					276040

988

	Char	G	J	K	B	C	A
0	颀	0-8193					294F23
1	颁	0-1668					276041
2	颂	0-4344					276042
3	颃	0-8194					294E7B
4	预	0-5204					27603D
5	颅	0-3413					276059
6	领	0-3376					276044
7	颇	0-3836					276043
8	颈	0-3017					276048
9	颉	0-8201					276045
A	颊	0-2853					276047
B	颋	8-9387					
C	颌	0-8202					4D4F39
D	颍	0-8203					284C62
E	颎	8-9388					
F	颏	0-8204					294F2C

98A

	Char	G	J	K	B	C	A
0	颠	0-2163					276054
1	颡	0-8210					294F6B
2	颢	0-8211					295021
3	颣	8-9390					
4	颤	0-1892					276057
5	颥	0-8212					295029
6	颦	0-8213					27605A
7	颧	0-4007					295031
8	風	1-2371	0-4187	0-8906	ADB7	1-5378	21605B
9	颩	3-4662			DCAD	2-4152	
A	颪		0-8104				697124
B	颫		1-7226				
C	颬	3-4665			E0E1	2-4867	
D	颭	3-4670	1-7227	1-7642	E4CC	2-4F34	235039
E	颮	1-7609	1-7228		E4CD	2-4F35	
F	颯	1-7610	0-8105	0-6329	BBE3	1-6B6C	21605C

98C

	Char	G	J	K	B	C	A
0	飀	3-4703			F675	2-6C63	23504E
1	飁	3-4706			F552	2-6A60	
2	飂	3-4707	1-7236	1-6329	F553	2-6A61	
3	飃		0-8109			E-5D56	336062
4	飄	1-3814	0-8108	0-8893	C4C6	1-7A51	216062
5	飅		1-7237				
6	飆	1-7613	0-8110		F674	2-6C62	235053
7	飇			0-8892		E-5E7B	
8	飈	1-7614	1-7238			E-5E79	355053
9	飉	5-4862		1-6330	F673	2-6C61	
A	飊					E-5E7A	
B	飋	5-4863		1-6988	F775	2-6E44	
C	飌	5-4866	1-7239		F9B0	2-717E	
D	飍	3-4690				E-6225	
E	风	0-2371					27605B
F	飏	8-9255					

98E

	Char	G	J	K	B	C	A
0	飠	1-6627					
1	飡	5-1980	1-7240	0-6566		E-3967	23505F
2	飢	1-8831	0-2118	0-4938	B0A7	1-586A	216065
3	飣	3-9041	1-7241		D448	2-334B	235060
4	飤					E-6670	235061
5	飥	3-9042	1-7242		D84F	2-3A33	235063
6	飦	5-8842	1-7243	1-7625		E-3968	
7	飧	0-6624	1-7244	1-6893	B6B8	1-627D	216066
8	飨	0-8747					295222
9	飩	1-6629	0-8111		B6BB	1-6322	216067
A	飪	1-6631	1-7245	1-7476	B6B9	1-627E	216069
B	飫	1-6632	0-8112	1-7109	DCAE	2-4153	23506C
C	飬					E-455B	
D	飭	1-6633	0-5012	0-8648	B6BD	1-6324	216068
E	飮		0-6127	0-7570			21606A
F	飯	1-2325	0-4051	0-5889	B6BA	1-6321	21606B

989

	Char	G	J	K	B	C	A
0	颐	0-5035					27604C
1	频	0-3821					276049
2	颒	8-1477					
3	颓	0-4539					27604A
4	颔	0-8205					27604B
5	颕	8-1387					
6	颖	0-5117					454F45
7	颗	0-3137					27604D
8	题	0-4466					276050
9	颙	8-9389					
A	颚	0-8206					276051
B	颛	0-8207					276052
C	颜	0-4953					27604E
D	额	0-2278					27604F
E	颞	0-8208					295030
F	颟	0-8209					294F77

98B

	Char	G	J	K	B	C	A
0	颰	5-4839	1-7229				
1	颱	1-8876	0-8106	0-8739	BBE4	1-6B6D	21605D
2	颲	3-4676		1-6253	E8BE	2-5567	
3	颳	1-8823			BE68	1-6F71	21605E
4	颴		1-7230				235040
5	颵	3-4683				E-5361	
6	颶	1-7611	0-8107	1-5879	C1FC	1-7629	21605F
7	颷	5-4851	1-7231			E-572A	
8	颸	3-4693	1-7232		F1AB	2-6455	235048
9	颹	3-4664				E-595C	
A	颺	3-4663	1-7233	1-7104	C347	1-7771	216060
B	颻	5-4858	1-7234		F3AD	2-6778	23504D
C	颼	1-7612		1-6928	C442	1-794E	216061
D	颽	5-4844			F3AC	2-6777	
E	颾	3-4702			F3AE	2-6779	
F	颿		1-7235	1-6564	F3AB	2-6776	23504A

98D

	Char	G	J	K	B	C	A
0	飐	8-1259					
1	飑	0-7609					4D503A
2	飒	0-7610					27605C
3	飓	0-7611					27605F
4	飔	8-9256					
5	飕	0-7612					276061
6	飖	8-1454					
7	飗	8-9257					
8	飘	0-3814					276062
9	飙	0-7613					295053
A	飚	0-7614					4D5053
B	飛	1-2341	0-4084	0-6211	ADB8	1-5379	216063
C	飜		0-7044	0-5972		E-5E7C	2D5259
D	飝					E-6226	
E	飞	0-2341					276063
F	食	0-4219	0-3109	0-6761	ADB9	1-537A	216064

98F

	Char	G	J	K	B	C	A
0	飰					E-402B	45606B
1	飱			1-6894		E-455C	
2	飲	1-5091	0-1691		B6BC	1-6323	
3	飳	3-9053	1-7246			E-4554	
4	飴	1-6634	0-1627	0-7639	B97E	1-6766	21606D
5	飵	3-9051				E-4559	
6	飶	3-9056	1-7247		E0E2	2-4868	
7	飷	3-9049				E-4557	
8	飸					E-4A5D	
9	飹				E0E3	2-4869	
A	飺	5-8839			E8C0	2-5569	
B	飻	5-8849		1-7942			
C	飼	1-4339	0-2784	0-6288	B97D	1-6765	21606C
D	飽	1-1705	0-4316	0-8873	B9A1	1-6767	21606E
E	飾	1-4246	0-3094	0-6762	B9A2	1-6768	21606F
F	飿	3-9057				E-4558	

990

	Char	G	J	K	B	C	A
0	餀	5-8848			E4CF	2-4F37	
1	餁					E-4A5E	
2	餂	3-9060	1-7248		E4CE	2-4F36	235128
3	餃	1-2940	0-8113	0-4685	BBE5	1-6B6E	216070
4	餄	3-9061					
5	餅	1-1793	0-4463		BBE6	1-6B6F	216078
6	餆					E-4A5B	
7	餇		1-7249		E4D0	2-4F38	235124
8	餈		1-7250		E8BF	2-5568	2E6F43
9	餉	1-6635	0-8114	0-9035	BBE8	1-6B71	216073
A	養	1-4988	0-4560	0-6955	BE69	1-6F72	216071
B	餋	5-8840					
C	餌	1-2292	0-1734	0-7640	BBE7	1-6B70	216072
D	餍	0-8748					276126
E	餎	3-9062				E-667A	
F	餏	3-9064					

991

	Char	G	J	K	B	C	A
0	餐	0-1845	0-2733	0-8341	C05C	1-7327	216074
1	餑	1-6636	1-7251		E8C1	2-556A	235132
2	餒	1-3657	0-8115	1-6045	BE6B	1-6F74	216075
3	餓	1-2286	0-1878	0-6827	BE6A	1-6F73	216077
4	餔	3-9067	0-8116	1-8234	E8C2	2-556B	235130
5	餕	3-9074	1-7252	1-7776	E8C5	2-556E	235138
6	餖	3-9069	1-7253		E8C3	2-556C	23512F
7	餗	3-9068	1-7254		E8C4	2-556D	235131
8	餘	1-5164	0-8117	0-7014	BE6C	1-6F75	216076
9	餙					E-4F6B	
A	餚		1-7255	1-8463	C061	1-732C	235147
B	餛	1-6638	1-7256		C05F	1-732A	21607B
C	餜	3-9078	1-7257			E-5365	235140
D	餝	5-8858	0-8119			E-5366	4B606F
E	餞	1-2904	0-8120	0-7922	C05E	1-7329	21607A
F	餟	5-8868	1-7258		EC5D	2-5B69	23513B

992

	Char	G	J	K	B	C	A
0	餠		0-8122	0-6031		E-5364	2D6078
1	餡	1-4758	0-8118		C060	1-732B	21607C
2	餢		1-7259			E-5362	
3	餣	3-9077				E-5363	
4	餤	3-9083	0-8121		EC5C	2-5B68	23513A
5	餥	3-8462			EF4B	2-6057	
6	餦	3-9045	1-7260	1-7547			
7	餧		1-7261	1-7369	EC5E	2-5B6A	235145
8	館	1-2561	0-2059	0-4629	C05D	1-7328	216079
9	餩	3-9081			EC5F	2-5B6B	235143
A	餪	3-9086		1-6020	EF4E	2-605A	235151
B	餫	3-9066	1-7262		EF4C	2-6058	235156
C	餬		0-8123	1-8393	EF4D	2-6059	235150
D	餭	3-9089			EF52	2-605E	
E	餮	0-8749	0-8124	1-7943	C34B	1-7775	23514F
F	餯	3-9091			EF51	2-605D	

993

	Char	G	J	K	B	C	A
0	餰	5-8871		1-7626	EF54	2-6060	
1	餱		1-7263	1-8474	EF53	2-605F	235158
2	餲	3-9087	1-7264		EF50	2-605C	235155
3	餳	1-6628	1-7265	1-6115	EF4F	2-605B	235153
4	餴	3-9076	1-7266				
5	餵		1-7267		C1FD	1-762A	21607D
6	餶	3-9088				E-5962	
7	餷	1-6639					
8	餸					E-5961	
9	餹		1-7268	1-6116		E-5966	395063
A	餺	3-9093	1-7269		F1AE	2-6458	235160
B	餻		1-7270			E-5965	23515C
C	餼	1-6630	1-7271	1-8531	F1AD	2-6457	235166
D	餽		0-8125	1-5920	C34A	1-7774	216122
E	餾	1-3383	0-8126		C348	1-7772	21607E
F	餿	1-6640			C349	1-7773	216121

994

	Char	G	J	K	B	C	A
0	饀	5-8876	1-7272			E-5963	235164
1	饁	3-9092	1-7273		F1AC	2-6456	235161
2	饂		0-8127	1-7237		E-6671	235154
3	饃	1-6641			F3B1	2-677C	235170
4	饄					E-5B69	
5	饅	1-3488	0-8129	0-5635	C443	1-794F	216123
6	饆	3-9058	1-7274				
7	饇	3-9044	1-7275		F3B0	2-677B	23516C
8	饈	1-6642	1-7276	1-6929	F3AF	2-677A	23516A
9	饉	1-6643	0-8128	0-4847	C444	1-7950	23516D
A	饊	1-6644					
B	饋	1-3201	0-8131	0-4790	F558	2-6A66	4B6122
C	饌	1-6645	0-8134	0-8342	F557	2-6A65	235172
D	饍		1-7277	0-6455		E-5D58	235171
E	饎	3-9103	1-7278		F555	2-6A63	235173
F	饏					E-5E7E	

995

	Char	G	J	K	B	C	A
0	饐	3-9104	0-8130	1-7445	F554	2-6A62	235174
1	饑	1-2802	0-8132	0-4939	C4C8	1-7A53	216125
2	饒	1-4036	0-8133	0-7314	C4C7	1-7A52	216124
3	饓				F559	2-6A67	
4	饔	0-8751	1-7279	0-7229	F776	2-6E45	23517B
5	饕	0-8750	0-8135	1-6140	C5B9	1-7C25	23517E
6	饖	5-8853			F677	2-6C65	
7	饗	1-8747	0-2234	0-9036	C557	1-7B43	235222
8	饘	3-9109	1-7280		F676	2-6C64	23517A
9	饙	5-8869	1-7281		F556	2-6A64	
A	饚					E-5F78	
B	饛	3-9107	1-7282		F777	2-6E46	
C	饜	1-8748	1-7283	1-7159	C5E4	1-7C50	216126
D	饝					E-612A	235229
E	饞	1-1886	1-7284	1-7866	C661	1-7D2E	216127
F	饟		1-7285		F959	2-7148	23522B

996

	Char	G	J	K	B	C	A
0	饠	3-9080	1-7286				
1	饡	3-9111			F9B1	2-7221	
2	饢	1-6646					
3	饣	0-6627					456064
4	饤	8-1335					
5	饥	0-2802					276065
6	饦	8-1336					
7	饧	0-6628					295153
8	饨	0-6629					276067
9	饩	0-6630					295166
A	饪	0-6631					276069
B	饫	0-6632					29506C
C	饬	0-6633					276068
D	饭	0-2325					27606B
E	饮	0-5091					27606A
F	饯	0-2904					27607A

997

	Char	G	J	K	B	C	A
0	饰	0-4246					27606F
1	饱	0-1705					27606E
2	饲	0-4339					27606C
3	饳	7-0140					
4	饴	0-6634					27606D
5	饵	0-2292					276072
6	饶	0-4036					276124
7	饷	0-6635					276073
8	饸	8-1337					
9	饹	8-1338					
A	饺	0-2940					276070
B	饻	8-1339					
C	饼	0-1793					276078
D	饽	0-6636					295132
E	饾	8-1340					
F	饿	0-2286					276077

998		G	J	K	B	C	A
0	馀	0-6637					456076
1	馁	0-3657					276075
2	馂	8-1341					
3	馃	8-1342					
4	馄	0-6638					27607B
5	馅	0-4758					27607C
6	馆	0-2561					276079
7	馇	0-6639					706247
8	馈	0-3201					516122
9	馉	7-0141					
A	馊	0-6640					276121
B	馋	0-1886					276127
C	馌	8-1230					
D	馍	0-6641					295170
E	馎	8-1343					
F	馏	0-3383					27607E

999		G	J	K	B	C	A
0	馐	0-6642					29516A
1	馑	0-6643					29516D
2	馒	0-3488					276123
3	馓	0-6644					295175
4	馔	0-6645					295172
5	馕	0-6646					70624E
6	首	0-4255	0-2883	0-6647	ADBA	1-537B	216128
7	馗	0-5624	0-8136	1-5938	D850	2-3A34	23522F
8	馘	0-5769	0-8137	1-5811	EF55	2-6061	235230
9	香	0-4767	0-2565	0-9037	ADBB	1-537C	216129
A	馚	5-8814				E-455F	
B	馛	3-9009	1-7287				
C	馜	3-9011			E4D2	2-4F3A	
D	馝	3-9010	1-7288	0-8924	E4D1	2-4F39	
E	馞	3-9012			EC60	2-5B6C	
F	馟		1-7289				

99A		G	J	K	B	C	A
0	馠	3-9014				E-5368	
1	馡	5-8816			EF57	2-6063	23523C
2	馢					E-5730	
3	馣	5-8815		1-7045	EF56	2-6062	23523B
4	馤	3-9016				E-5967	
5	馥	0-8005	0-8138	0-6064	C34C	1-7776	21612A
6	馦	3-9017	1-7290		F3B2	2-677D	23523E
7	馧	3-9015			F3B3	2-677E	
8	馨	0-6016	0-1930	0-9116	C4C9	1-7A54	21612B
9	馩	5-8817				E-5F21	235241
A	馪	3-9018				E-6060	235242
B	馫				F9B2	2-7222	
C	馬	1-3477	0-3947	0-5609	B0A8	1-586B	21612C
D	馭	1-5206	0-8139	0-6963	B6BF	1-6326	21612E
E	馮	1-2375	0-8140	0-8907	B6BE	1-6325	21612D
F	馯	3-2981			E0E4	2-486A	

99B		G	J	K	B	C	A
0	馰	5-3310	1-7291	1-7583	E0E6	2-486C	
1	馱	1-4552	1-7292	0-8678	B9A4	1-676A	216130
2	馲	3-2983	1-7293		E0E5	2-486B	
3	馳	1-1959	0-3558	0-8644	B9A3	1-6769	21612F
4	馴	1-4917	0-3875	0-6688	B9A5	1-676B	216131
5	馵	3-2982	1-7294		E0E7	2-486D	235249
6	馶	3-2985				E-4A63	
7	馷					E-4A62	
8	馸	3-2989				E-4A66	
9	馹	3-2987	1-7301	0-7681	E4D4	2-4F3C	235253
A	馺	3-2984	1-7302		E4D6	2-4F3E	
B	馻				E4D5	2-4F3D	
C	馼		0-8141			E-4A61	23524E
D	馽	5-3312	1-7303		E4D8	2-4F40	235254
E	馾	3-2992				E-4A60	
F	馿		1-7304			E-4A6C	23524D

99C		G	J	K	B	C	A
0	駀					E-4A64	
1	駁	1-1821	0-3993	0-5864	BBE9	1-6B72	216132
2	駂	3-2990			E4D7	2-4F3F	
3	駃	3-2993	1-7305		E4D3	2-4F3B	23524F
4	駄		0-3444	1-8155		E-4A6A	4B6130
5	駅		0-1756				3F614C
6	駆		0-2278				4B6147
7	駇				E4D9	2-4F41	
8	駈		0-2279	1-5880		E-4F73	2D6147
9	駉	3-3007	1-7306	1-5659	E8CC	2-5575	235265
A	駊	3-3013				E-4F6D	
B	駋				E8CF	2-5578	
C	駌				E8D1	2-557A	
D	駍	3-3003			E8C7	2-5570	
E	駎				E8CB	2-5574	
F	駏	3-2986		1-5601	E8C8	2-5571	

99D		G	J	K	B	C	A
0	駐	1-5504	0-3583	0-8150	BE6E	1-6F77	216133
1	駑	1-7069	0-8146	0-5044	BE71	1-6F7A	21613A
2	駒	1-3052	0-2280	0-4743	BE73	1-6F7C	216138
3	駓	3-2994	1-7307		E8C9	2-5572	235261
4	駔	1-7064	1-7308		E8CA	2-5573	235263
5	駕	1-2861	0-1879	0-4229	BE72	1-6F7B	216135
6	駖	3-3009			E8CD	2-5576	
7	駗	3-3008			E8D0	2-5579	
8	駘	1-7070	0-8145	1-8156	E8CE	2-5577	235269
9	駙	1-7066	1-7309	0-6131	BE74	1-6F7D	216139
A	駚	3-3006	1-7310			E-4F6E	
B	駛	1-4227	0-8143	1-6756	BE70	1-6F79	216137
C	駜	3-3012	1-7311	1-8267	E8C6	2-556F	
D	駝	1-4553	0-8144	0-8679	BE6D	1-6F76	216134
E	駞		1-7312	1-8121		E-4F72	2D6134
F	駟	1-7065	0-8142	0-6289	BE6F	1-6F78	216136

99E		G	J	K	B	C	A
0	駠					E-4F74	
1	駡	1-3478				E-5370	335234
2	駢	1-7073	0-8156	1-6577	C063	1-732E	21613F
3	駣	3-3020			EC66	2-5B72	23527B
4	駤	3-3017			EC64	2-5B70	
5	駥	5-3314			EC63	2-5B6F	
6	駦					E-5371	
7	駧	5-3319	1-7313		EC69	2-5B75	
8	駨	3-3021		1-6943		E-536B	
9	駩				EC68	2-5B74	
A	駪	5-3323	1-7314	1-6986	EC67	2-5B73	23527C
B	駫		1-7315			E-536C	
C	駬	5-3316	1-7316		EC62	2-5B6E	235274
D	駭	1-2607	0-8147	0-9020	C062	1-732D	21613B
E	駮		0-8148	1-6521	EC61	2-5B6D	2D6132
F	駯					E-536A	

99F		G	J	K	B	C	A
0	駰	3-3018	1-7317		EC65	2-5B71	23527A
1	駱	1-3470	0-8149	0-5313	C064	1-732F	21613C
2	駲		0-8150				697152
3	駳					E-5734	
4	駴	3-3025	1-7318		EF5A	2-6066	23532A
5	駵	5-3326	1-7319			E-5737	
6	駶				EF5E	2-606A	
7	駷	3-3026			EF5B	2-6067	
8	駸	3-3038	0-8152	1-8109	EF5D	2-6069	235329
9	駹	3-3027	1-7320		EF5C	2-6068	
A	駺	3-3037			EF59	2-6065	
B	駻	3-3029	0-8151	1-8290	EF5F	2-606B	235330
C	駼	3-3033			EF62	2-606E	
D	駽	3-3030	1-7321	1-8354	EF60	2-606C	235331
E	駾	3-3036	1-7322		EF61	2-606D	
F	駿	1-3105	0-2957	0-8171	C240	1-762C	21613E

9A0

	Char	G	J	K	B	C	A
0	騀	3-3032				E-5733	
1	騁	1-1950	0-8153	0-6230	C1FE	1-762B	21613D
2	騂	3-3035	1-7323	1-6863	EF58	2-6064	235324
3	騃		1-7324	1-7071	EF63	2-606F	333556
4	騄	5-3333	1-7325	1-6294	F1B3	2-645D	235344
5	騅	1-7077	0-8155	1-8047	F1B6	2-6460	235347
6	騆				F1B8	2-6462	
7	騇	3-3044			F1B7	2-6461	
8	騈			0-6032		E-596A	4B613F
9	騉	3-3042			F1B1	2-645B	23533F
A	騊	3-3046			F1B5	2-645F	
B	騋	3-3028	1-7326	1-6219	F1B0	2-645A	23533E
C	騌		1-7327			E-596B	2D6162
D	騍	1-7076		1-5756	F1B2	2-645C	
E	騎	1-3879	0-2119	0-4940	C34D	1-7777	216140
F	騏	1-7075	0-8154	0-4941	F1AF	2-6459	23533D

9A1

	Char	G	J	K	B	C	A
0	騐		1-7328			E-596D	235348
1	騑	3-3041	1-7329	1-6720	F1B4	2-645E	235345
2	騒		0-3391				4B6145
3	験		0-2419				4B614D
4	騔				F3C0	2-682D	
5	騕	5-3336			F3B5	2-6822	
6	騖	1-7080	1-7330	1-6476	C445	1-7951	216142
7	騗	3-3061				E-5B6F	
8	騘			1-8017		E-5B6D	
9	騙	1-3813	0-8157	0-8830	C446	1-7952	216141
A	騚				F3B4	2-6821	
B	騛			1-6721	F3B9	2-6826	
C	騜	3-3058			F3BF	2-682C	
D	騝	5-3332			F3B7	2-6824	
E	騞	3-3050	1-7331		F3BE	2-682B	
F	騟	3-3060				E-5B6C	

9A2

	Char	G	J	K	B	C	A
0	騠	3-3054	1-7332		F3BB	2-6828	23534F
1	騡					E-5B6E	
2	騢	3-3062	1-7333		F3BA	2-6827	23534D
3	騣		1-7334		F3BD	2-682A	336162
4	騤	3-3063	1-7335		F3B8	2-6825	23534C
5	騥				F3B6	2-6823	
6	騦	5-3338				E-5B6B	
7	騧	3-3031	1-7336		F3BC	2-6829	235352
8	騨		0-3445				
9	騩	3-3059			F560	2-6A6E	
A	騪	3-3057			F55E	2-6A6C	
B	騫	1-6925	0-8158	0-4386	C4CA	1-7A55	216143
C	騬	3-3068			F55D	2-6A6B	
D	騭	1-7079	1-7337	1-7783	F563	2-6A71	235360
E	騮	1-7082	1-7338		F561	2-6A6F	23536A
F	騯	5-3343				E-5D5A	235359

9A3

	Char	G	J	K	B	C	A
0	騰	1-4458	0-3813	0-5289	C4CB	1-7A56	216144
1	騱	3-3069			F55C	2-6A6A	
2	騲	3-3052			F55A	2-6A68	235364
3	騳	5-3311	1-7339				
4	騴				F55B	2-6A69	
5	騵	3-3066	1-7340	1-7352	C4CD	1-7A58	235361
6	騶	1-7067	1-7341	0-8566	F55F	2-6A6D	235369
7	騷	1-4107	0-8159	0-6551	C4CC	1-7A57	216145
8	騸	1-7083	1-7342	1-6837	F562	2-6A70	23535A
9	騹	5-3346			F678	2-6C66	
A	騺	3-3016			F67E	2-6C6C	
B	騻	5-3347				E-5F24	235374
C	騼					E-5F22	
D	騽	3-3073			F679	2-6C67	
E	騾	1-3466	0-8164	1-6190	C55B	1-7B47	216149
F	騿				F6A1	2-6C6D	

9A4

	Char	G	J	K	B	C	A
0	驀	1-6175	0-8162	0-5673	C55A	1-7B46	216148
1	驁	1-7081	1-7344	1-7226	F67D	2-6C6B	235370
2	驂	1-7078	0-8161	1-7867	F67C	2-6C6A	235379
3	驃	1-7084	0-8163	0-8894	C559	1-7B45	216146
4	驄	1-7085	1-7345	1-8018	F67B	2-6C69	23537A
5	驅	1-3993	0-8160	0-4744	C558	1-7B44	216147
6	驆				F67A	2-6C68	
7	驇		1-7343				
8	驈	3-3078			F77D	2-6E4C	23537D
9	驉	3-3072			F7A1	2-6E4E	
A	驊	1-7072	1-7346	1-8417	F77E	2-6E4D	235427
B	驋	3-3014	1-7347				
C	驌	3-3048	1-7348	1-6935	F77B	2-6E4A	23537E
D	驍	1-7071	0-8166	0-9304	C5BB	1-7C27	235422
E	驎	3-3076	1-7349	1-6381	F778	2-6E47	
F	驏	1-7086		1-7521	F77C	2-6E4B	

9A5

	Char	G	J	K	B	C	A
0	驐	3-3075			F7A3	2-6E50	
1	驑		1-7350			E-5F79	
2	驒	3-3047		1-8138	F7A2	2-6E4F	235424
3	驓				F779	2-6E48	
4	驔	3-3074	1-7351		F77A	2-6E49	
5	驕	1-2930	0-8165	0-4686	C5BA	1-7C26	21614A
6	驖	3-3079	1-7352		F852	2-6F60	23542C
7	驗	1-4973	0-8168	0-9048	C5E7	1-7C53	21614D
8	驘			1-6191		E-6062	23542A
9	驙	3-3081			F853	2-6F61	
A	驚	1-3010	0-2235	0-4483	C5E5	1-7C51	21614B
B	驛	1-7068	0-8167	0-7030	C5E6	1-7C52	21614C
C	驜	3-3005				E-6061	
D	驝	5-3350	1-7353				
E	驞				F8D3	2-7061	
F	驟	1-5472	0-8169	0-8614	C64A	1-7C75	21614E

9A6

	Char	G	J	K	B	C	A
0	驠				F976	2-7165	
1	驡	3-5688				E-6172	
2	驢	1-3431	0-8170	0-5380	C66A	1-7D37	21614F
3	驣					E-6173	
4	驤	1-7088	0-8172	1-7105	F9B3	2-7223	235433
5	驥	1-7087	0-8171	0-4942	C66B	1-7D38	216150
6	驦	3-3082			F9B4	2-7224	235434
7	驧	5-3354			F9B5	2-7225	
8	驨	5-3356			F9C3	2-7233	
9	驩		0-8173	0-9230	F9C2	2-7232	3F4621
A	驪	1-7074	0-8175	0-5381	C67A	1-7D47	216151
B	驫	3-3023	0-8174		F9CD	2-723B	23543A
C	马	0-3477					27612C
D	驭	0-5206					27612E
E	驮	0-4552					276130
F	驯	0-4917					276131

9A7

	Char	G	J	K	B	C	A
0	驰	0-1959					27612F
1	驱	0-3993					276147
2	驲	8-9132					
3	驳	0-1821					276132
4	驴	0-3431					27614F
5	驵	0-7064					295263
6	驶	0-4227					276137
7	驷	0-7065					276136
8	驸	0-7066					276139
9	驹	0-3052					276138
A	驺	0-7067					295369
B	驻	0-5504					276133
C	驼	0-4553					276134
D	驽	0-7069					27613A
E	驾	0-2861					276135
F	驿	0-7068					27614C

9A8

		G	J	K	B	C	A
0	骀	0-7070					295269
1	骁	0-7071					295422
2	骂	0-3478					275234
3	骃	8-9133					
4	骄	0-2930					27614A
5	骅	0-7072					295427
6	骆	0-3470					27613C
7	骇	0-2607					27613B
8	骈	0-7073					27613F
9	骉	8-9134					
A	骊	0-7074					276151
B	骋	0-1950					27613D
C	验	0-4973					27614D
D	骍	8-9135					
E	骎	8-9136					
F	骏	0-3105					27613E

9AA

		G	J	K	B	C	A
0	骠	0-7084					276146
1	骡	0-3466					276149
2	骢	0-7085					29537A
3	骣	0-7086					295421
4	骤	0-5472					27614E
5	骥	0-7087					276150
6	骦	8-9138					
7	骧	0-7088					295433
8	骨	0-2539	0-2592	0-4573	B0A9	1-586C	216152
9	骩					E-402F	
A	骪		1-7354	1-7370			
B	骫	3-8977			E0E9	2-486F	235441
C	骬	3-8976	1-7355				
D	骭	3-8975	0-8176		E0E8	2-486E	23543F
E	骮	5-8776	1-7356				
F	骯	1-1625	1-7357		BBEA	1-6B73	216153

9AC

		G	J	K	B	C	A
0	髀	0-8734	0-8179	1-6722	F1B9	2-6463	235459
1	髁	0-8733	1-7366		C34E	1-7778	235457
2	髂	0-8736			F3C1	2-682E	23545A
3	髃	5-8794	1-7367				
4	髄		0-3181			E-5D61	2D6159
5	髅	0-8735					276158
6	髆	5-8804	1-7368	1-6522	F566	2-6A74	
7	髇				F564	2-6A72	
8	髈		1-7369			E-5D60	23545D
9	髉	3-9005				E-5D5E	
A	髊	5-8803			F565	2-6A73	
B	髋	0-8737					29546D
C	髌	0-8738					4B537D
D	髍				F6A2	2-6C6E	
E	髎	3-9006	1-7370			E-5F25	
F	髏	1-8735	0-8180	1-6338	C55C	1-7B48	216158

9AE

		G	J	K	B	C	A
0	髠	5-8907	1-7378			E-4032	235476
1	髡	0-8753		1-5724	B9A6	1-676C	2F5476
2	髢	3-9120	0-8186			E-4561	235477
3	髣		0-8187	1-6547	E4DB	2-4F43	393078
4	髤	3-9121	1-7379			E-4A6F	
5	髥		1-7380	0-7103		E-4A73	
6	髦	0-8754	0-8188	1-6455	BBEC	1-6B75	394A60
7	髧	3-9124	1-7381		E4DC	2-4F44	235521
8	髨					E-4A71	
9	髩	5-8909	1-7382			E-4A70	
A	髪		0-4017			E-4A72	4B615F
B	髫	0-8756	0-8190	1-8004	E8D4	2-557D	235527
C	髬	3-9127	1-7383		E8D3	2-557C	
D	髭	0-8758	0-4106	1-7507	C068	1-7333	216161
E	髮	1-8817	0-8191	0-5905	BE76	1-7021	21615F
F	髯	0-8755	0-8189		BE77	1-7022	23552A

9A9

		G	J	K	B	C	A
0	骐	0-7075					29533D
1	骑	0-3879					276140
2	骒	0-7076					295340
3	骓	0-7077					295347
4	骔	8-1372					
5	骕	8-9137					
6	骖	0-7078					295379
7	骗	0-3813					276141
8	骘	0-7079					295360
9	骙	8-1237					
A	骚	0-4107					276145
B	骛	0-7080					276142
C	骜	0-7081					295370
D	骝	0-7082					29536A
E	骞	0-6925					276143
F	骟	0-7083					29535A

9AB

		G	J	K	B	C	A
0	骰	0-8727	0-8177	1-8168	BBEB	1-6B74	216154
1	骱	0-8726			E4DA	2-4F42	235443
2	骲	3-8981	1-7358				
3	骳	3-8983			E8D2	2-557B	235445
4	骴	3-8988	1-7359		EC6C	2-5B78	
5	骵		1-7360			E-4F77	
6	骶	0-8730	1-7361			E-4F76	235449
7	骷	0-8728			BE75	1-6F7E	216155
8	骸	0-2601	0-1928	0-9021	C065	1-7330	216156
9	骹	3-8991	1-7362	1-5832	EC6A	2-5B76	
A	骺	0-8731					235450
B	骻	3-8986	1-7363		EC6D	2-5B79	23544C
C	骼	0-8732	0-8178	1-5618	C066	1-7331	216157
D	骽					E-573A	235454
E	骾		1-7364		EF64	2-6070	2F575F
F	骿	3-8992	1-7365	1-6578	EC6B	2-5B77	

9AD

		G	J	K	B	C	A
0	髐	3-8987	1-7371		F7A4	2-6E51	235466
1	髑	0-8739	0-8181	1-8012	C5EA	1-7C56	23546A
2	髒	1-8894	1-7372		C5BC	1-7C28	21615B
3	髓	0-4372	0-8182	0-6648	C5E8	1-7C54	216159
4	體	1-4469	0-8183	0-8487	C5E9	1-7C55	21615A
5	髕	1-8738	1-7373		F8D4	2-7062	33537D
6	髖	1-8737	1-7374	1-5775	C662	1-7D2F	23546D
7	髗		1-7375	1-6285		E-6174	2D6421
8	高	0-2463	0-2566	0-4552	B0AA	1-586D	21615C
9	髙					E-6334	
A	髚					E-4A6E	
B	髛		1-7376				
C	髜		1-7377		F1BA	2-6464	235472
D	髝	3-9182				E-5F7B	
E	髞	3-9183	0-8184			E-6063	697174
F	髟	0-8752	0-8185	1-8247	D449	2-334C	235474

9AF

		G	J	K	B	C	A
0	髰			1-7971			
1	髱		0-8193		E8D7	2-5622	69717D
2	髲	3-9130	1-7384	1-8255	E8D6	2-5621	235528
3	髳	3-9131	1-7385		E8D5	2-557E	
4	髴		0-8192	1-6670		E-4F79	2D3D5E
5	髵	3-9134	1-7386			E-5375	
6	髶	3-9133			EC6E	2-5B7A	
7	髷		0-8194		EC71	2-5B7D	69717E
8	髸					E-5374	
9	髹	0-8759	1-7387	1-8494	EC70	2-5B7C	235532
A	髺	3-9135	1-7388	1-5781	EC6F	2-5B7B	
B	髻	0-8757	0-8201	1-5673	C067	1-7332	216160
C	髼	5-8931			EF68	2-6074	
D	髽	3-9139	1-7389	1-7741	EF66	2-6072	235535
E	髾	3-9138			EF65	2-6071	
F	髿	3-9142	1-7390				

Code	Char	G	J	K	B	C	A
9B00	鬀		1-7391			E-573B	23553B
9B01	鬁	5-8929	1-7392		EF67	2-6073	235536
9B02	鬂		1-7393	1-6735		E-573C	235538
9B03	鬃	0-5555	1-7394		C34F	1-7779	216162
9B04	鬄	3-9143	1-7401		F1BC	2-6466	23553E
9B05	鬅	5-8934	1-7402	1-6674	F1BD	2-6467	235541
9B06	鬆	1-4341	0-8202	1-6905	C350	1-777A	216163
9B07	鬇	3-9136				E-596F	
9B08	鬈	0-8760	1-7403		F1BB	2-6465	23553C
9B09	鬉		1-7404			E-5B71	
9B0A	鬊	3-9151		1-6944	F3C3	2-6830	
9B0B	鬋	3-9155	1-7405	1-7627	F3C2	2-682F	235543
9B0C	鬌	3-9152	1-7406		F3C5	2-6832	
9B0D	鬍	1-8826	1-7407	1-8394	C447	1-7953	216164
9B0E	鬎	5-8937	1-7408		F3C4	2-6831	235547
9B0F	鬏	0-8761					70775D
9B10	鬐	3-9158	1-7409	1-6007	F567	2-6A75	23554F
9B11	鬑	3-9164			F569	2-6A77	23554E
9B12	鬒	3-9160	1-7410	1-7819	F568	2-6A76	2F5E66
9B13	鬓	0-8762					276166
9B14	鬔					E-5F27	
9B15	鬕	3-9159			F6A3	2-6C6F	
9B16	鬖	3-9150	1-7411	1-6778	F6A6	2-6C72	
9B17	鬗	5-8943			F6A4	2-6C70	
9B18	鬘	3-9165	0-8203	1-6406	F6A5	2-6C71	235554
9B19	鬙	3-9166	1-7412	1-6956	F7A5	2-6E52	
9B1A	鬚	1-8886	0-8204	0-6649	C5BD	1-7C29	216165
9B1B	鬛		1-7413				
9B1C	鬜	3-9141	1-7414				
9B1D	鬝					E-6672	235556
9B1E	鬞	5-8922			F854	2-6F62	
9B1F	鬟	0-8763	0-8205	1-8434	F855	2-6F63	23555E
9B20	鬠	5-8918	1-7415		F856	2-6F64	
9B21	鬡	3-9129				E-612C	
9B22	鬢	1-8762	0-8206	1-6736	C64B	1-7C76	216166
9B23	鬣	0-8764	0-8207	1-6258	C663	1-7D30	235566
9B24	鬤	3-9170			F9B6	2-7226	
9B25	鬥	1-2223	0-8208		B0AB	1-586E	216167
9B26	鬦		1-7416			E-4A75	
9B27	鬧	1-3654	0-8209	0-5502	BE78	1-7023	216168
9B28	鬨		0-8210	1-8411	C069	1-7334	33362A
9B29	鬩	1-6750	0-8211	1-8342	F1BE	2-6468	23556C
9B2A	鬪		0-8212	0-8767		E-5D62	396167
9B2B	鬫		1-7417		F7A6	2-6E53	
9B2C	鬬					E-612E	
9B2D	鬭		1-7418			E-6433	235573
9B2E	鬮	1-6746	0-8213	1-5881	F9C4	2-7166	4D5574
9B2F	鬯	0-5943	0-8214	1-7886	D44A	2-334D	235576
9B30	鬰					E-6228	
9B31	鬱	1-5184	0-6121	0-7406	C67B	1-7D48	21616A
9B32	鬲	0-5610	0-8215	1-5619	B0AC	1-586F	21616B
9B33	鬳	3-6539	1-7419		BC72	2-5B7E	
9B34	鬴	5-8957	1-7420			E-573E	23557D
9B35	鬵	3-9175	1-7421		F1BF	2-6469	235622
9B36	鬶	8-1254					
9B37	鬷	3-9176	1-7422		F3C6	2-6833	235623
9B38	鬸					E-5D63	
9B39	鬹	3-9174	1-7423				
9B3A	鬺	3-9172	1-7424	1-6794	F6A7	2-6C73	
9B3B	鬻	0-6987	0-6888		F7A7	2-6E54	39505B
9B3C	鬼	0-2577	0-2120	0-4801	B0AD	1-5870	21616C
9B3D	鬽	5-8820	1-7425			E-4562	
9B3E	鬾	3-9020			E4DD	2-4F45	
9B3F	鬿	3-9021			E4DE	2-4F46	
9B40	魀	5-8822				E-4A78	
9B41	魁	0-3193	0-1901	0-4658	BBED	1-6B76	21616D
9B42	魂	0-2774	0-2618	0-9175	BBEE	1-6B77	21616E
9B43	魃	0-8741	0-8217	0-5906	E8D9	2-5624	235636
9B44	魄	0-3839	0-8216	0-5962	BE7A	1-7025	216170
9B45	魅	0-8740	0-4405	0-5669	BE79	1-7024	21616F
9B46	魆	3-9023			E8D8	2-5623	
9B47	魇	0-8742					276173
9B48	魈	0-8744	1-7426	1-6888	EF69	2-6075	23563A
9B49	魉	0-8743				E-573F	29563C
9B4A	魊	3-9030			F1C0	2-646A	
9B4B	魋	3-9032	1-7427	1-8048	F1C2	2-646C	235641
9B4C	魌	3-9029	1-7428		F1C1	2-646B	
9B4D	魍	0-8745	0-8219	1-6414	C353	1-777D	23563E
9B4E	魎	1-8743	0-8220	1-6226	C352	1-777C	23563C
9B4F	魏	0-4626	0-8218	0-7464	C351	1-777B	216171
9B50	魐	5-8833				E-5D64	
9B51	魑	0-8746	0-8221	1-6368	C55E	1-7B4A	235647
9B52	魒				F6A8	2-6C74	
9B53	魓					E-5F28	
9B54	魔	0-3607	0-4366	0-5610	C55D	1-7B49	216172
9B55	魕	3-9019	1-7429		F7A9	2-6E56	
9B56	魖	3-9034	1-7430		F7A8	2-6E55	
9B57	魗	5-8829	1-7431			E-612F	
9B58	魘	1-8742	0-8222	1-7160	C64C	1-7C77	216173
9B59	魙	5-8835			F8D5	2-7063	
9B5A	魚	1-5167	0-2191	0-6964	B3BD	1-5E23	216174
9B5B	魛	3-8727	1-7432		E0EA	2-4870	
9B5C	魜	5-8622					
9B5D	魝	3-8726				E-4563	
9B5E	魞		1-7433				
9B5F	魟	3-8728			E4E1	2-4F49	
9B60	魠	3-8730			E4DF	2-4F47	
9B61	魡	5-8627	1-7434		E4E0	2-4F48	
9B62	魢	3-8732					
9B63	魣	3-8749	1-7435			E-4F7E	
9B64	魤	5-8637			E8E2	2-562D	
9B65	魥	5-8628	1-7436				
9B66	魦	5-8634	1-7437	1-6757	E8DD	2-5628	
9B67	魧	3-8746			E8DA	2-5625	
9B68	魨	3-8737	1-7438		E8E1	2-562C	235663
9B69	魩					E-4F7C	
9B6A	魪	3-8742	1-7439				
9B6B	魫	3-8747	1-7440			E-4F7B	
9B6C	魬	3-8741	1-7441		E8E3	2-562E	
9B6D	魭	5-8630	1-7442				
9B6E	魮	3-8738	1-7443				
9B6F	魯	1-3419	0-4705	0-5459	BE7C	1-7027	216176
9B70	魰				E8E0	2-562B	
9B71	魱	3-8739			E8DC	2-5627	
9B72	魲					E-4F7D	
9B73	魳	5-8631	1-7444				
9B74	魴	1-8648	0-8223	1-6548	E8DB	2-5626	23565D
9B75	魵	3-8745	1-7445		E8DF	2-562A	
9B76	魶	5-8635			E8DE	2-5629	
9B77	魷	1-8647	1-7446		BE7B	1-7026	216175
9B78	魸		1-7447				
9B79	魹		1-7448				
9B7A	魺	3-8754			BC7D	2-5C2B	
9B7B	魻	3-8756			BC78	2-5C26	
9B7C	魼	3-8752			BC76	2-5C24	
9B7D	魽	5-8642			BCA1	2-5C2D	23567B
9B7E	魾	3-8755			BC77	2-5C25	
9B7F	魿	3-8762	1-7449				

Code	Char	G	J	K	B	C	A
9B80	鮀	3-8766	1-7450	1-8122	EC73	2-5C21	235672
9B81	鮁	1-8649					
9B82	鮂	3-8759			EC79	2-5C27	
9B83	鮃	1-8650	0-8225	1-8219		E-5378	235721
9B84	鮄	3-8768	1-7451			E-537A	
9B85	鮅	3-8767	1-7452		EC74	2-5C22	
9B86	鮆	3-8779	1-7453		EF72	2-607E	235749
9B87	鮇	3-8750	1-7454		EC75	2-5C23	
9B88	鮈	3-8764			ECA2	2-5C2E	
9B89	鮉		1-7455			E-5423	
9B8A	鮊	3-8761	1-7456				
9B8B	鮋	3-8757	1-7457			E-537C	
9B8C	鮌	5-8648				E-5421	235673
9B8D	鮍	3-8769	1-7458				
9B8E	鮎	1-8651	0-1630	0-7938		E-5425	235729
9B8F	鮏	5-8647	1-7459			E-537D	
9B90	鮐	1-8656	1-7460		EC7C	2-5C2A	23572B
9B91	鮑	1-1711	0-8226	0-8874	C06A	1-7335	216177
9B92	鮒	1-8654	0-4211	1-6643	EC7B	2-5C29	235731
9B93	鮓	3-8760	0-8224	1-7508	EC7A	2-5C28	23572E
9B94	鮔		1-7461			E-5379	
9B95	鮕				EC7E	2-5C2C	23567A
9B96	鮖		0-8227				69723B
9B97	鮗		0-8228	1-6164			23572F
9B98	鮘					E-6673	235732
9B99	鮙					E-5744	235743
9B9A	鮚	1-8658	1-7462		EF6A	2-6076	23573D
9B9B	鮛	3-8778			EF6D	2-6079	
9B9C	鮜	3-8788					
9B9D	鮝	1-8663	1-7463			E-5745	235739
9B9E	鮞	1-8660	1-7464		EF6C	2-6078	235742
9B9F	鮟	3-8803	0-8229	0-6853		E-5740	235736
9BA0	鮠	3-8791	0-8230		EF74	2-6122	23574E
9BA1	鮡	3-8790			EF6F	2-607B	
9BA2	鮢				EF73	2-6121	
9BA3	鮣	3-8763				E-5742	
9BA4	鮤	3-8775			EF71	2-607D	
9BA5	鮥	3-8793			EF70	2-607C	
9BA6	鮦	3-8781	1-7465		EF6E	2-607A	
9BA7	鮧	3-8777	1-7466	1-7684			
9BA8	鮨	3-8792	0-8231	1-7808	EF6B	2-6077	23573F
9BA9	鮩	3-8801	1-7467				
9BAA	鮪	1-8659	0-4378	1-7404	C243	1-762F	21617A
9BAB	鮫	1-8662	0-2713	0-4687	C242	1-762E	216178
9BAC	鮬	3-8774	1-7468				
9BAD	鮭	1-8657	0-2690	1-8327	C244	1-7630	23573C
9BAE	鮮	1-4742	0-3315	0-6456	C241	1-762D	216179
9BAF	鮯				EF75	2-6123	
9BB0	鮰	3-8783	1-7469				
9BB1	鮱		1-7470				
9BB2	鮲		1-7471				
9BB3	鮳	3-8772					
9BB4	鮴		0-8232				697240
9BB5	鮵				F1C8	2-6472	
9BB6	鮶	3-8814			F1CB	2-6475	
9BB7	鮷	5-8664	1-7472				
9BB8	鮸	3-8813	1-7473		F1C9	2-6473	
9BB9	鮹	3-8808	0-8235	1-6889	F1CD	2-6477	235766
9BBA	鮺	5-7044					
9BBB	鮻		1-7474			E-5974	23576B
9BBC	鮼		1-7475				
9BBD	鮽				F1CE	2-6478	
9BBE	鮾		1-7476				
9BBF	鮿	3-8804	1-7477		F1C6	2-6470	23575E
9BC0	鯀	1-8671	0-8233		C358	1-7824	23576E
9BC1	鯁	1-8665	1-7478	1-5660	F1C7	2-6471	23575F
9BC2	鯂					E-5973	
9BC3	鯃				F1C5	2-646F	
9BC4	鯄	5-8658			F1CC	2-6476	
9BC5	鯅	3-8787				E-5B74	
9BC6	鯆	3-8806	0-8236	1-8235	F1C4	2-646E	23575D
9BC7	鯇	1-8673	1-7479		F1C3	2-646D	235756
9BC8	鯈	3-1819	1-7480		C357	1-7823	235772
9BC9	鯉	1-3280	0-2481	0-5579	C355	1-7821	21617C
9BCA	鯊	1-8672	0-8234	1-6758	C354	1-777E	21617B
9BCB	鯋					E-5976	
9BCC	鯌					E-5975	
9BCD	鯍					E-5743	
9BCE	鯎		1-7481				
9BCF	鯏		0-8237				697245
9BD0	鯐		1-7482				
9BD1	鯑		0-8238				697246
9BD2	鯒	3-8815	0-8239			E-5971	235759
9BD3	鯓				F1CA	2-6474	23576C
9BD4	鯔	1-8686	0-8243	1-8088	F3CF	2-683C	235834
9BD5	鯕	3-8819			F3D5	2-6842	235823
9BD6	鯖	1-8675	0-2710	0-8477	C44A	1-7956	23577A
9BD7	鯗	5-8663	1-7483		F3D0	2-683D	235777
9BD8	鯘	5-8671	1-7484				
9BD9	鯙				F3D3	2-6840	
9BDA	鯚	3-8825			F3D7	2-6844	
9BDB	鯛	1-8684	0-3468	1-7723	C44B	1-7957	23582D
9BDC	鯜				F3D2	2-683F	
9BDD	鯝	1-8681	1-7485				
9BDE	鯞	3-8830			F3CA	2-6837	
9BDF	鯟		1-7486			E-5B75	
9BE0	鯠				F3C9	2-6836	
9BE1	鯡	1-8678	0-8244		F3D6	2-6843	23582C
9BE2	鯢	1-8682	0-8241	1-7194	F3CD	2-683A	23582F
9BE3	鯣	5-8668	0-8240			E-5B77	4D5858
9BE4	鯤	1-8679	0-8242	0-4570	F3CB	2-6838	235827
9BE5	鯥	3-8818	1-7487		F3D4	2-6841	
9BE6	鯦	5-8675			F3CC	2-6839	
9BE7	鯧	1-8680	1-7488		C449	1-7955	21617E
9BE8	鯨	1-3008	0-2363	0-4484	C448	1-7954	21617D
9BE9	鯩	3-8743				E-5B79	
9BEA	鯪	1-8676	1-7489		F3C7	2-6834	
9BEB	鯫	1-8677	1-7490		F3C8	2-6835	23577C
9BEC	鯬	5-8670			F3D1	2-683E	
9BED	鯭						
9BEE	鯮	3-8828				E-5B7A	
9BEF	鯯		1-7491				
9BF0	鯰	1-8683	0-8248		F3CE	2-683B	235831
9BF1	鯱		0-8247				23582B
9BF2	鯲		0-8246				69724E
9BF3	鯳		1-7492				
9BF4	鯴	1-8685					
9BF5	鯵		0-1619				4D594E
9BF6	鯶	5-8656				E-5D6F	
9BF7	鯷	3-8841	1-7493	1-7685	F56C	2-6A7A	
9BF8	鯸	3-8849	1-7494		F56F	2-6A7D	
9BF9	鯹		1-7501			E-5D71	
9BFA	鯺	5-8665	1-7502				
9BFB	鯻	3-8837				E-5D67	
9BFC	鯼	5-8680				E-5D69	
9BFD	鯽	1-8674	1-7503		C356	1-7822	216223
9BFE	鯾	3-8846				E-5D6A	
9BFF	鯿	1-8693	1-7504			E-5D74	23583E

9C0

	Char	G	J	K	B	C	A
0	鰀		1-7505			E-5D75	
1	鰁	3-8848					
2	鰂	3-8784	1-7506			E-5D6E	235852
3	鰃	3-8844					
4	鰄		0-8258			E-5D68	23584D
5	鰅	3-8842			F56D	2-6A7B	
6	鰆	3-8835	0-8254		F573	2-6B23	235843
7	鰇				F571	2-6B21	
8	鰈	1-8688	0-8255	1-7649	F56B	2-6A79	23584B
9	鰉	1-8692	0-8251		F576	2-6B26	23585C
A	鰊	3-8839	0-8257	1-6249		E-5D66	235849
B	鰋	3-8836	1-7507		F56A	2-6A78	
C	鰌		0-8253	1-8049		E-5D76	2D6222
D	鰍	1-8690	0-1966	0-8567	C4CF	1-7A5A	216222
E	鰎	5-8677			F572	2-6B22	
F	鰏	3-8838	1-7508				

9C1

	Char	G	J	K	B	C	A
0	鰐	1-8689	0-4744	0-6842		E-5D73	235854
1	鰑		1-7509				
2	鰒	1-8691	0-8256	0-6065	F56E	2-6A7C	235859
3	鰓	1-4090	0-8252	1-6801	C4CE	1-7A59	216221
4	鰔	5-8678	0-8250		F575	2-6B25	23584C
5	鰕	3-8855	0-8249	0-8940		E-5D72	235844
6	鰖		1-7510				
7	鰗				F574	2-6B24	
8	鰘		1-7511				
9	鰙		1-7512				
A	鰚		1-7513				
B	鰛	3-8843	0-8260			E-5D70	2F5870
C	鰜	3-8865	1-7514		F6AB	2-6C77	235866
D	鰝	3-8862			F6AA	2-6C76	
E	鰞		1-7515				
F	鰟	3-8863				E-5F2C	

9C2

	Char	G	J	K	B	C	A
0	鰠	1-8694					
1	鰡	3-8861	0-8263		F6B1	2-6C7D	235878
2	鰢		1-7516				
3	鰣	1-8669	1-7517		F6AD	2-6C79	23586E
4	鰤	3-8780	0-8262	1-6759	F6B0	2-6C7C	235879
5	鰥	1-8704	0-8261	0-9231	C560	1-7B4C	216225
6	鰦	3-8853	1-7518				
7	鰧	3-4604	1-7519			E-642F	
8	鰨	1-8703	1-7520		F6AE	2-6C7A	235871
9	鰩	1-8705	1-7521		F6AF	2-6C7B	
A	鰪	3-8857	1-7522				
B	鰫	5-8685			F6A9	2-6C75	
C	鰬	3-8859			F6AC	2-6C78	
D	鰭	1-8702	0-4141	1-6008	C55F	1-7B4B	216224
E	鰮		0-8259	1-7238		E-5F2A	235870
F	鰯	3-8866	0-1683	1-7086			235869

9C3

	Char	G	J	K	B	C	A
0	鰰		0-8264				697260
1	鰱	1-8667	1-7523	1-6250	C5BF	1-7C2B	216226
2	鰲	1-8701	0-8266	0-7207	F7B4	2-6E61	235925
3	鰳	1-8706			F7AF	2-6E5C	23592A
4	鰴	3-2612			F7B3	2-6E60	
5	鰵	1-8710	1-7524	1-6513		E-6025	235932
6	鰶	3-8868	1-7525		F7B6	2-6E63	
7	鰷	1-8670	1-7526		F7B2	2-6E5F	235934
8	鰸	3-8736				E-5F7E	
9	鰹	1-8668	0-1979	1-5629	F7AE	2-6E5B	235929
A	鰺	3-8833	0-8245	1-6890		E-6023	47594E
B	鰻	1-8709	0-1723	0-5636	C5C1	1-7C2D	216228
C	鰼	3-8872			F7B1	2-6E5E	
D	鰽	5-8687	1-7527		F7B5	2-6E62	
E	鰾	1-8707	0-8268	1-8248	C5C0	1-7C2C	216227
F	鰿	3-8816			F7AC	2-6E59	

9C4

	Char	G	J	K	B	C	A
0	鱀	3-8854			F570	2-6A7E	
1	鱁	3-8858	1-7528		F7B0	2-6E5D	
2	鱂	3-8850					
3	鱃	3-8864	1-7529				
4	鱄	3-8734	1-7530		F7AD	2-6E5A	235926
5	鱅	1-8711	1-7531			E-6022	
6	鱆	5-8689	0-8267		F7AA	2-6E57	23587E
7	鱇	3-8869	0-8265	0-4330			235930
8	鱈	1-8708	0-3513		F7AB	2-6E58	235928
9	鱉	1-1778	1-7532	0-6014	C5BE	1-7C2A	21622C
A	鱊	3-8879	1-7533		F85A	2-6F68	
B	鱋				F85C	2-6F6A	
C	鱌				F85F	2-6F6D	
D	鱍	3-8770			F85B	2-6F69	
E	鱎	3-8786	1-7534		F860	2-6F6E	
F	鱏	3-8878	1-7535	1-6994		E-6065	

9C5

	Char	G	J	K	B	C	A
0	鱐	3-8829	1-7536		F859	2-6F67	
1	鱑	5-8686				E-6066	235945
2	鱒	1-8714	0-4380	1-7777	F857	2-6F65	235938
3	鱓		1-7537	1-6838		E-6068	2D6229
4	鱔	1-8713	1-7538		C5EB	1-7C57	216229
5	鱕				F85D	2-6F6B	
6	鱖	1-8712	1-7539		C5ED	1-7C59	21622B
7	鱗	1-3359	0-4658	0-5587	C5EC	1-7C58	21622A
8	鱘	1-8664	1-7540		F858	2-6F66	23593B
9	鱙				F85E	2-6F6C	
A	鱚	3-8876	0-8269				697265
B	鱛		1-7541				
C	鱜		1-7548				
D	鱝	1-8687	1-7542			E-6132	
E	鱞	5-8694	1-7543		F8DA	2-7068	
F	鱟	1-8655	1-7544		C64D	1-7C78	235955

9C6

	Char	G	J	K	B	C	A
0	鱠	3-8789	0-8270	1-8451	F8DB	2-7069	235956
1	鱡	5-8683				E-6133	
2	鱢	5-8693			F8D9	2-7067	
3	鱣	3-8883	1-7545	1-7628	F8D6	2-7064	235949
4	鱤	3-8882					
5	鱥	3-8782				E-6134	
6	鱦	5-8669			F8D8	2-7066	
7	鱧	1-8715	0-8271	1-6273	F8D7	2-7065	23594F
8	鱨	3-8840	1-7550		F95A	2-7149	23595B
9	鱩		1-7546				
A	鱪		1-7547				
B	鱫		1-7549				
C	鱬	3-8885				E-6159	
D	鱭	1-8661			F95C	2-714B	235958
E	鱮	3-8729	1-7551		F95B	2-714A	23595E
F	鱯	3-8880				E-615B	23595C

9C7

	Char	G	J	K	B	C	A
0	鱰		1-7552				
1	鱱				F979	2-7169	
2	鱲	3-8889	1-7553				
3	鱳	3-8765			F978	2-7168	
4	鱴	3-8884			F977	2-7167	
5	鱵	3-8888	1-7554		F97A	2-716A	
6	鱶		0-8272			E-6175	355739
7	鱷		1-7555		C673	1-7D40	21622D
8	鱸	1-8652	0-8273	1-6286	C674	1-7D41	21622E
9	鱹				F9CA	2-7238	
A	鱺	1-8666			F9CE	2-723C	23596B
B	鱻		1-7556	1-6839		E-6241	336179
C	鱼	0-5167					276174
D	鱽	7-0122					
E	鱾	7-0123					
F	鱿	0-8647					276175

9C8

	Char	G	J	K	B	C	A
0	鲀	8-1315					
1	鲁	0-3419					276176
2	鲂	0-8648					29565D
3	鲃	7-0124					
4	鲄	8-1316					
5	鲅	0-8649					29593A
6	鲆	0-8650					295721
7	鲇	0-8651					295729
8	鲈	0-8652					27622E
9	鲉	7-0125					
A	鲊	8-1317					
B	鲋	0-8654					295731
C	鲌	7-0126					
D	鲍	0-1711					276177
E	鲎	0-8655					295955
F	鲏	7-0127					

9CA

	Char	G	J	K	B	C	A
0	鲠	0-8665					29575F
1	鲡	0-8666					29596B
2	鲢	0-8667					276226
3	鲣	0-8668					295929
4	鲤	0-3280					27617C
5	鲥	0-8669					29586E
6	鲦	0-8670					4D5934
7	鲧	0-8671					29576E
8	鲨	0-8672					27617B
9	鲩	0-8673					295756
A	鲪	7-0128					
B	鲫	0-8674					276223
C	鲬	7-0129					
D	鲭	0-8675					29577A
E	鲮	0-8676					295822
F	鲯	7-0130					

9CC

	Char	G	J	K	B	C	A
0	鳀	8-1324					
1	鳁	8-1325					
2	鳂	7-0134					
3	鳃	0-4090					276221
4	鳄	0-8689					295854
5	鳅	0-8690					276222
6	鳆	0-8691					295859
7	鳇	0-8692					29585C
8	鳈	7-0135					
9	鳉	7-0133					
A	鳊	0-8693					29583E
B	鳋	0-8694					29586A
C	鳌	0-8701					295925
D	鳍	0-8702					276224
E	鳎	0-8703					295871
F	鳏	0-8704					276225

9CE

	Char	G	J	K	B	C	A
0	鳠	8-1328					
1	鳡	7-0138					
2	鳢	0-8715					29594F
3	鳣	8-1329					
4	鳤	7-0139					
5	鳥	1-3681	0-3627	0-8072	B3BE	1-5E24	21622F
6	鳦	3-6084	1-7557	1-7427	DCAF	2-4154	
7	鳧	5-5983	0-8274	0-6132	E0ED	2-4873	235973
8	鳨	3-6085				E-4564	
9	鳩	1-8015	0-4023	0-4745	B9A7	1-676D	216230
A	鳪	3-1652			E0EB	2-4871	
B	鳫		0-8279			E-4566	2D5F43
C	鳬	1-5776	0-8275			E-2F42	2F5973
D	鳭	3-1876			E0EC	2-4872	
E	鳮					E-4568	
F	鳯					E-4567	

9C9

	Char	G	J	K	B	C	A
0	鲐	0-8656					29572B
1	鲑	0-8657					29573C
2	鲒	0-8658					29573D
3	鲓	8-1318					
4	鲔	0-8659					27617A
5	鲕	0-8660					295742
6	鲖	8-1319					
7	鲗	8-1320					
8	鲘	8-1321					
9	鲙	8-1322					
A	鲚	0-8661					295958
B	鲛	0-8662					276178
C	鲜	0-4742					276179
D	鲝	8-1481					
E	鲞	0-8663					295739
F	鲟	0-8664					29593B

9CB

	Char	G	J	K	B	C	A
0	鲰	0-8677					29577C
1	鲱	0-8678					29582C
2	鲲	0-8679					295827
3	鲳	0-8680					27617E
4	鲴	0-8681					295828
5	鲵	0-8682					29582F
6	鲶	0-8683					295831
7	鲷	0-8684					29582D
8	鲸	0-3008					27617D
9	鲹	7-0131					
A	鲺	0-8685					295825
B	鲻	0-8686					295834
C	鲼	0-8687					295940
D	鲽	0-8688					29584B
E	鲾	7-0132					
F	鲿	8-1323					

9CD

	Char	G	J	K	B	C	A
0	鳐	0-8705					4D5875
1	鳑	7-0136					
2	鳒	8-1326					
3	鳓	0-8706					29592A
4	鳔	0-8707					276227
5	鳕	0-8708					295928
6	鳖	0-1778					27622C
7	鳗	0-8709					276228
8	鳘	0-8710					295932
9	鳙	0-8711					295921
A	鳚	7-0137					
B	鳛	8-1327					
C	鳜	0-8712					27622B
D	鳝	0-8713					276229
E	鳞	0-3359					27622A
F	鳟	0-8714					295938

9CF

	Char	G	J	K	B	C	A
0	鳰		0-8276				235974
1	鳱	5-2140			E4E2	2-4F4A	
2	鳲	3-2749	1-7558		E4E3	2-4F4B	235977
3	鳳	1-2379	0-4317	0-6083	BBF1	1-6B7A	216233
4	鳴	1-3589	0-4436	0-5716	BBEF	1-6B78	216232
5	鳵				E4E4	2-4F4C	
6	鳶	1-8016	0-3848	0-7073	BBF0	1-6B79	216231
7	鳷	3-3570	1-7559		E8E8	2-5633	235A23
8	鳸	5-5069				E-5027	235A2C
9	鳹	3-6101	1-7560		E8EB	2-5636	
A	鳺	3-6089			E8E5	2-5630	
B	鳻	3-6102			E8EC	2-5637	
C	鳼	3-4731			E8E4	2-562F	
D	鳽	3-6088			E8E6	2-5631	
E	鳾	3-6090				E-502A	
F	鳿	3-3112			E8E7	2-5632	

Code	Char	G	J	K	B	C	A
9D00	鴀	3-6091			E8EA	2-5635	
9D01	鴁	3-6092				E-5024	
9D02	鴂	3-6108	1-7562			E-502B	235A21
9D03	鴃	5-6001	0-8280	1-5620	BEA1	1-702A	235A22
9D04	鴄	5-5992			E8EF	2-563A	235A24
9D05	鴅	3-6107			E8EE	2-5639	
9D06	鴆	1-8018	0-8281	1-7825	BE7D	1-7028	216234
9D07	鴇	1-8017	0-3830	1-6601	E8E9	2-5634	235A28
9D08	鴈		0-8278	1-7027	E8ED	2-5638	335F43
9D09	鴉	1-4927	0-8277	0-6828	BE7E	1-7029	216235
9D0A	鴊	3-6109				E-542D	
9D0B	鴋	3-4734	1-7561				
9D0C	鴌			1-6617		E-5025	
9D0D	鴍	5-4888				E-5022	
9D0E	鴎		0-1810				
9D0F	鴏					E-542A	
9D10	鴐	5-6008			ECAC	2-5C38	
9D11	鴑		1-7563				
9D12	鴒	3-6118	0-8289	1-6270	C06F	1-733A	21623B
9D13	鴓	3-6124				E-542C	
9D14	鴔	3-6104			ECA7	2-5C33	
9D15	鴕	1-4550	0-8288	1-8123	C06B	1-7336	216236
9D16	鴖	3-6125				E-5436	
9D17	鴗	3-6345	1-7564		ECA4	2-5C30	
9D18	鴘	3-6127	1-7565	1-6579	ECAA	2-5C36	
9D19	鴙	5-5879		1-8089	ECAD	2-5C39	
9D1A	鴚	3-6111				E-5433	
9D1B	鴛	1-5207	0-1785	0-7436	C070	1-733B	21623A
9D1C	鴜		1-7566				
9D1D	鴝	1-8022	1-7567		ECA9	2-5C35	235A44
9D1E	鴞	3-6115	1-7568		ECA6	2-5C32	235A3F
9D1F	鴟	1-8023	0-8286	1-8090	ECAE	2-5C3A	235A48
9D20	鴠	3-6114			ECA5	2-5C31	
9D21	鴡	5-6003				E-5437	
9D22	鴢	3-6128			ECAB	2-5C37	
9D23	鴣	1-8019	0-8285	1-5707	C06C	1-7337	216237
9D24	鴤	5-6005				E-5429	
9D25	鴥	3-6123			ECA3	2-5C2F	235A30
9D26	鴦	1-4976	0-8283	0-6876	C06D	1-7338	216239
9D27	鴧					E-5435	
9D28	鴨	1-4928	0-1991	0-6869	C06E	1-7339	216238
9D29	鴩				ECA8	2-5C34	
9D2A	鴪		0-8282			E-5432	235A2F
9D2B	鴫		0-2818				693C32
9D2C	鴬		0-1809				4B6247
9D2D	鴭				EFA9	2-6135	
9D2E	鴮				EF7A	2-6128	
9D2F	鴯	1-8025	1-7569		EF7B	2-6129	
9D30	鴰	1-8027	1-7570	1-5782	EF7E	2-612C	235A65
9D31	鴱	3-6110			EF7C	2-612A	
9D32	鴲	3-6137	1-7571				
9D33	鴳	5-6020	1-7572		EF76	2-6124	
9D34	鴴	3-6136	1-7573				
9D35	鴵					E-574D	
9D36	鴶			1-7035	EF79	2-6127	235A53
9D37	鴷	3-6131			EFA5	2-6131	
9D38	鴸				EF7D	2-612B	
9D39	鴹	5-7036				E-5748	
9D3A	鴺	5-6013	1-7574				
9D3B	鴻	1-2672	0-2567	0-9188	C245	1-7631	21623C
9D3C	鴼	5-6017	1-7575				
9D3D	鴽	3-6140	1-7577		EFA7	2-6133	235A6B
9D3E	鴾		0-8292		EFA4	2-6130	235A63
9D3F	鴿	1-2475	0-8291		C246	1-7632	21623D
9D40	鵀	3-6135			EFA6	2-6132	235A69
9D41	鵁	3-6139	0-8290	1-5833	EF77	2-6125	235A4F
9D42	鵂	1-8028	1-7578	1-8501	EFA2	2-612E	235A68
9D43	鵃	3-6959	1-7579		EFA3	2-612F	
9D44	鵄	5-6442	0-8287	1-8091		E-574A	2F5A48
9D45	鵅	3-6138	1-7576		EFA1	2-612D	
9D46	鵆		0-8293				4D5A6C
9D47	鵇		1-7580				
9D48	鵈		0-8294				69727E
9D49	鵉					E-6675	4B624F
9D4A	鵊	3-6132	1-7581		F1D2	2-647C	
9D4B	鵋				F1D4	2-647E	
9D4C	鵌	3-6152			F1D7	2-6523	
9D4D	鵍	3-6158				E-5979	
9D4E	鵎	3-6155				E-597B	
9D4F	鵏	3-6144			F1D1	2-647B	
9D50	鵐	3-6142	0-8305			E-597D	4D5C6B
9D51	鵑	1-3073	0-8304	0-4427	C359	1-7825	21623F
9D52	鵒	1-8033			F1D9	2-6525	235B2A
9D53	鵓	1-8030	1-7582	1-6535	F1D0	2-647A	235A75
9D54	鵔	3-6159	1-7583	1-7778	F1DA	2-6526	
9D55	鵕	5-6026				E-597E	
9D56	鵖	3-6151			F1D6	2-6522	
9D57	鵗	3-6154			F1D8	2-6524	
9D58	鵘				F1DC	2-6528	
9D59	鵙	5-4238	0-8306		F1D5	2-6521	235A7B
9D5A	鵚				F1DD	2-6529	235B26
9D5B	鵛	3-6126			F1D3	2-647D	
9D5C	鵜	1-8035	0-1713		F1CF	2-6479	235A70
9D5D	鵝	1-2276	0-8301	0-6829	C35A	1-7826	216241
9D5E	鵞		0-8302	1-7012		E-5A22	2D6241
9D5F	鵟	3-6157	1-7584		F1DB	2-6527	
9D60	鵠	1-8032	0-2584	0-4560	C35B	1-7827	216240
9D61	鵡	1-8036	0-4425	0-5787	C44D	1-7959	21623E
9D62	鵢		1-7586				
9D63	鵣		1-7585			E-597A	
9D64	鵤		0-8303				697323
9D65	鵥		1-7587				
9D66	鵦					E-5B7D	
9D67	鵧				EF78	2-6126	
9D68	鵨				F3F1	2-685E	
9D69	鵩	3-6169	1-7588	1-6611	F3E8	2-6855	235B47
9D6A	鵪	1-8038	1-7589		C44F	1-795B	216244
9D6B	鵫	3-6164	1-7590		F3E4	2-6851	
9D6C	鵬	1-3784	0-4318	0-6163	C450	1-795C	216245
9D6D	鵭					E-5C27	
9D6E	鵮	3-6171				E-5C22	
9D6F	鵯	1-8039	0-8311	1-8268	F3ED	2-685A	235B52
9D70	鵰		1-7591	1-7724	F3E7	2-6854	335F49
9D71	鵱				F3DD	2-684A	
9D72	鵲	1-4021	0-8307	0-7746	C44E	1-795A	216243
9D73	鵳	3-6176			F3EA	2-6857	
9D74	鵴				F3E5	2-6852	
9D75	鵵	3-6170			F3E6	2-6853	
9D76	鵶		1-7592			E-5C25	2D6235
9D77	鵷	3-6175	1-7593	1-7353	F3D8	2-6845	235B2C
9D78	鵸	3-6161			F3DF	2-684C	235B3F
9D79	鵹	5-6030			F3EE	2-685B	
9D7A	鵺		0-8312			E-5B7E	235B2F
9D7B	鵻	3-6168	1-7594	1-8050	F3EB	2-6858	235B4D
9D7C	鵼	3-6174	1-7601				
9D7D	鵽	3-6180			F3E3	2-6850	
9D7E	鵾	3-6165	1-7602	1-5725		E-5C26	235B42
9D7F	鵿				F3EF	2-685C	

9D8

	Char	G	J	K	B	C	A
0	鶀	5-6028			F3DE	2-684B	
1	鶁				F3D9	2-6846	
2	鶂	5-6031			F3EC	2-6859	
3	鶃	3-6167	1-7603			E-5C24	235B4F
4	鶄	3-8423	1-7604	1-7960	F3DB	2-6848	
5	鶅	3-6181			F3E9	2-6856	
6	鶆	3-6145	1-7605		F3E0	2-684D	
7	鶇	1-8020	0-8309		F3F0	2-685D	235B35
8	鶈	3-6162			F3DC	2-6849	
9	鶉	1-8040	0-8308	1-6945	C44C	1-7958	216242
A	鶊	3-6172	1-7606		F3DA	2-6847	235B2E
B	鶋	3-6178			F3E1	2-684E	
C	鶌	3-6179			F3E2	2-684F	
D	鶍		1-7607				
E	鶎		1-7608				
F	鶏		0-2360				4B5F4C

9DA

	Char	G	J	K	B	C	A
0	鶠	3-6182			F5A1	2-6B2F	
1	鶡	3-6187	1-7615	1-5538	F5A6	2-6B34	235B6A
2	鶢				F5A8	2-6B36	
3	鶣	5-6037			F5AB	2-6B39	
4	鶤	5-6021	0-8314	1-5726	F579	2-6B29	235B66
5	鶥	1-8044				E-5D7A	
6	鶦				F5AF	2-6B3D	
7	鶧				F5B0	2-6B3E	
8	鶨				F5A9	2-6B37	
9	鶩	1-8045	0-8315	0-5748	F5AD	2-6B3B	235B59
A	鶪	3-6186	1-7616		F5A4	2-6B32	235B67
B	鶫		0-8310				4D5B35
C	鶬	3-6105	1-7617	1-7887	F6C1	2-6D2F	235C34
D	鶭				F6C4	2-6D32	
E	鶮	5-8973	1-7618			E-5F35	
F	鶯	1-6126	0-8284	0-6903	C561	1-7B4D	216247

9DC

	Char	G	J	K	B	C	A
0	鷀	1-8043					235B79
1	鷁	3-6213	0-8318	1-7459	F6B5	2-6D23	235B7A
2	鷂	1-8046	0-8324	1-7301	C563	1-7B4F	216248
3	鷃	3-6205	1-7624		F6BB	2-6D29	235C27
4	鷄	1-2806	0-8317	0-4514		E-5F36	2D5F4C
5	鷅	5-6038			F6BA	2-6D28	
6	鷆		0-8322				4D5B7E
7	鷇	3-4724	1-7625	1-5882	F6B6	2-6D24	235C22
8	鷈				F6C2	2-6D30	
9	鷉	3-6209	1-7626				
A	鷊	3-9173	1-7627		F6B7	2-6D25	
B	鷋	3-6204			F7BB	2-6E68	
C	鷌				F6C5	2-6D33	
D	鷍				F6C7	2-6D35	
E	鷎	3-6208			F6BE	2-6D2C	
F	鷏		0-8323		F6B8	2-6D26	235B7E

9DE

	Char	G	J	K	B	C	A
0	鷠		1-7635				
1	鷡				F869	2-6F77	
2	鷢	3-1636			F86E	2-6F7C	
3	鷣				F864	2-6F72	
4	鷤	5-6032			F867	2-6F75	
5	鷥	1-8024	1-7636		C5EE	1-7C5A	21624B
6	鷦	1-8052	0-8328	1-8005	F86B	2-6F79	235C6C
7	鷧		1-7637				
8	鷨				F872	2-7022	
9	鷩	3-6217	1-7638	1-6581	F7C0	2-6E6D	235C4F
A	鷪			1-7079			
B	鷫	3-6177	1-7639	1-6936	F865	2-6F73	235C5F
C	鷬				F86F	2-6F7D	
D	鷭	3-6223	0-8329		F873	2-7023	235C6A
E	鷮	3-6134	1-7640		F86A	2-6F78	235C6D
F	鷯	1-8051	0-8330		F863	2-6F71	235C65

9D9

	Char	G	J	K	B	C	A
0	鶐				F57D	2-6B2D	
1	鶑					E-5C23	
2	鶒	3-6183	1-7609		F57B	2-6B2B	235B5E
3	鶓	1-8037	1-7610				
4	鶔				F5A2	2-6B30	
5	鶕		1-7611			E-5D79	
6	鶖	3-6189	1-7612	1-8051	F5AE	2-6B3C	235B70
7	鶗	5-6034	1-7613		F5A5	2-6B33	
8	鶘	1-8041	1-7614		F57C	2-6B2C	235B60
9	鶙	3-6194			F578	2-6B28	
A	鶚	1-8042	0-8313	1-7022	F5A7	2-6B35	235B6B
B	鶛	3-6185			F57E	2-6B2E	
C	鶜				F5A3	2-6B31	
D	鶝	3-6184			F57A	2-6B2A	
E	鶞				F5AA	2-6B38	
F	鶟				F577	2-6B27	

9DB

	Char	G	J	K	B	C	A
0	鶰	3-6149				E-5F31	
1	鶱	3-6214	1-7619		F6C3	2-6D31	235B74
2	鶲	3-6210	0-8316		F6C8	2-6D36	235C36
3	鶳				F6C6	2-6D34	
4	鶴	1-2655	0-3665	0-8945	C562	1-7B4E	216246
5	鶵	5-6006	1-7620	1-8052	F6BD	2-6D2B	
6	鶶				F6B3	2-6D21	235B76
7	鶷				F6B2	2-6C7E	
8	鶸	5-6042	0-8320	1-7087	C564	1-7B50	235B7B
9	鶹	3-6211	1-7621	1-6343	F6BF	2-6D2D	235C32
A	鶺	3-6212	0-8321		F6C0	2-6D2E	235B7C
B	鶻	1-8729	0-8319	1-5731	F6BC	2-6D2A	235C28
C	鶼	1-8047	1-7622		F6B4	2-6D22	235B77
D	鶽	3-6207				E-5F32	
E	鶾	5-8330			F6B9	2-6D27	
F	鶿		1-7623	1-7509	F5AC	2-6B3A	

9DD

	Char	G	J	K	B	C	A
0	鷐	5-6048			F7BC	2-6E69	
1	鷑				F7BE	2-6E6B	
2	鷒				F7B8	2-6E65	
3	鷓	1-8049	0-8326	1-7510	C5C2	1-7C2E	216249
4	鷔	3-6203	1-7628				
5	鷕	3-6218	1-7629		F7C5	2-6E72	
6	鷖	3-6216	1-7630	1-7201	F7C3	2-6E70	235C45
7	鷗	1-3724	1-7631	0-4746	C5C3	1-7C2F	21624A
8	鷘	5-6044			F7C2	2-6E6F	
9	鷙	1-8026	0-8325	1-7809	F7C1	2-6E6E	235C3E
A	鷚	1-8050	1-7632		F7BA	2-6E67	
B	鷛	5-6050			F7B7	2-6E64	
C	鷜	3-6201			F7BD	2-6E6A	
D	鷝				F7C6	2-6E73	
E	鷞	5-6046	1-7633		F7B9	2-6E66	235C46
F	鷟	3-6219	1-7634		F7BF	2-6E6C	235C3A

9DF

	Char	G	J	K	B	C	A
0	鷰		1-7641	1-7148	F86D	2-6F7B	3F4A28
1	鷱			1-5708			
2	鷲	1-8053	0-4741	0-8615	F86C	2-6F7A	235C57
3	鷳	1-8034	1-7642	1-8291	F871	2-7021	235C5C
4	鷴		1-7643		F870	2-6F7E	
5	鷵				F7C4	2-6E71	
6	鷶				F868	2-6F76	
7	鷷				F862	2-6F70	
8	鷸	1-8054	0-8327	0-9351	F866	2-6F74	235C5B
9	鷹	1-5105	0-3475	0-7577	C64E	1-7C79	21624C
A	鷺	1-8056	0-2677	0-5460	C64F	1-7C7A	21624D
B	鷻	5-6056			F861	2-6F6F	
C	鷼					E-606C	
D	鷽	3-6121	0-8331	1-8283	F8E6	2-7074	235C7E
E	鷾	5-6059	1-7644		F8DD	2-706B	
F	鷿			1-6569	F8E5	2-7073	

Code	Char	G	J	K	B	C	A
9E00	鸀	3-6231			F8E2	2-7070	
9E01	鸁	3-6233			F8E3	2-7071	
9E02	鸂	3-6234	1-7646		F8DC	2-706A	225021
9E03	鸃	3-6087			F8DF	2-706D	
9E04	鸄				F8E7	2-7075	
9E05	鸅	5-6010			F8E1	2-706F	
9E06	鸆	3-6228			F8E0	2-706E	
9E07	鸇	3-6232	1-7647	1-7629	F8DE	2-706C	235C71
9E08	鸈					E-6135	
9E09	鸉	3-6143			F8E4	2-7072	
9E0A	鸊	3-6235	1-7645				
9E0B	鸋	3-6122			F95D	2-714C	
9E0C	鸌	1-8055					
9E0D	鸍				F95E	2-714D	
9E0E	鸎		1-7648			E-615D	235D27
9E0F	鸏	3-6226		1-6467	F960	2-714F	
9E10	鸐	5-6060	1-7649		F95F	2-714E	
9E11	鸑	3-6193	1-7650		F962	2-7151	235D2B
9E12	鸒		1-7651		F961	2-7150	
9E13	鸓	3-6237			F97C	2-716C	
9E14	鸔				F97B	2-716B	
9E15	鸕	1-8021	1-7652	1-6287	F9B7	2-7227	235D36
9E16	鸖		1-7653			E-6229	
9E17	鸗	3-5691			F9B8	2-7228	
9E18	鸘	3-6238				E-6230	235D37
9E19	鸙		1-7654		F9C5	2-7234	
9E1A	鸚	1-8048	0-8332	0-6904	C678	1-7D45	21624E
9E1B	鸛	1-8057	0-8333	1-5776	C67C	1-7D49	235D3A
9E1C	鸜	5-6061	1-7655	1-5883		E-6238	235D39
9E1D	鸝	1-8031	1-7656		F9CF	2-723D	235D3B
9E1E	鸞	1-8029	0-8334	0-5322	C67D	1-7D4A	21624F
9E1F	鸟	0-3681					27622F
9E20	鸠	0-8015					276230
9E21	鸡	0-2806					275F4C
9E22	鸢	0-8016					276231
9E23	鸣	0-3589					276232
9E24	鸤	8-1267					
9E25	鸥	0-3724					27624A
9E26	鸦	0-4927					276235
9E27	鸧	8-9360					
9E28	鸨	0-8017					295A28
9E29	鸩	0-8018					276234
9E2A	鸪	0-8019					276237
9E2B	鸫	0-8020					295B35
9E2C	鸬	0-8021					295D36
9E2D	鸭	0-4928					276238
9E2E	鸮	8-9361					
9E2F	鸯	0-4976					276239
9E30	鸰	8-9362					
9E31	鸱	0-8023					295A48
9E32	鸲	0-8022					295A44
9E33	鸳	0-5207					27623A
9E34	鸴	8-9363					
9E35	鸵	0-4550					276236
9E36	鸶	0-8024					27624B
9E37	鸷	0-8026					295C3E
9E38	鸸	0-8025					295A59
9E39	鸹	0-8027					295A65
9E3A	鸺	0-8028					295A68
9E3B	鸻	7-0108					
9E3C	鸼	7-0109					
9E3D	鸽	0-2475					27623D
9E3E	鸾	0-8029					27624F
9E3F	鸿	0-2672					27623C
9E40	鹀	8-1268					
9E41	鹁	0-8030					295A75
9E42	鹂	0-8031					295D3B
9E43	鹃	0-3073					27623F
9E44	鹄	0-8032					276240
9E45	鹅	0-2276					276241
9E46	鹆	0-8033					295B2A
9E47	鹇	0-8034					295C49
9E48	鹈	0-8035					295A70
9E49	鹉	0-8036					27623E
9E4A	鹊	0-4021					276243
9E4B	鹋	0-8037					295B6C
9E4C	鹌	0-8038					276244
9E4D	鹍	8-9364					
9E4E	鹎	0-8039					295B52
9E4F	鹏	0-3784					276245
9E50	鹐	8-1269					
9E51	鹑	0-8040					276242
9E52	鹒	8-9365					
9E53	鹓	8-9366					
9E54	鹔	8-9367					
9E55	鹕	0-8041					295B60
9E56	鹖	8-9368					
9E57	鹗	0-8042					295B6B
9E58	鹘	0-8729					295C28
9E59	鹙	8-9369					
9E5A	鹚	0-8043					295B79
9E5B	鹛	0-8044					295B5C
9E5C	鹜	0-8045					295B59
9E5D	鹝	8-1270					
9E5E	鹞	0-8046					276248
9E5F	鹟	7-0111					
9E60	鹠	8-1271					
9E61	鹡	8-9370					
9E62	鹢	8-9371					
9E63	鹣	0-8047					295B77
9E64	鹤	0-2655					276246
9E65	鹥	8-9372					
9E66	鹦	0-8048					27624E
9E67	鹧	0-8049					276249
9E68	鹨	0-8050					295C47
9E69	鹩	0-8051					295C65
9E6A	鹪	0-8052					295C6C
9E6B	鹫	0-8053					295C57
9E6C	鹬	0-8054					295C5B
9E6D	鹭	0-8056					27624D
9E6E	鹮	7-0113					
9E6F	鹯	8-9373					
9E70	鹰	0-5105					27624C
9E71	鹱	0-8055					295D29
9E72	鹲	7-0112					
9E73	鹳	0-8057					295D3A
9E74	鹴	8-9374					
9E75	鹵	1-8850	0-8335	0-5461	B3BF	1-5E25	235D3C
9E76	鹶	3-7937					
9E77	鹷			1-6271			
9E78	鹸		0-2420				
9E79	鹹	1-8884	0-8336	0-8973	C4D0	1-7A5B	216250
9E7A	鹺	1-8526	1-7657		F6C9	2-6D37	235D42
9E7B	鹻		1-7658	1-5553		E-5F37	235D43
9E7C	鹼	1-2879	1-7659		C650	1-7C7B	216252
9E7D	鹽	1-4946	0-8337	0-7104	C651	1-7C7C	216251
9E7E	鹾	0-8526					295D42
9E7F	鹿	0-3425	0-2815	0-5467	B3C0	1-5E26	216253

Code	Char	G	J	K	B	C	A
9E80	麀	3-9210	1-7660	1-7331	E0EE	2-4874	235D47
9E81	麁	5-2013	0-8338			E-4569	4D5D49
9E82	麂	0-8768	1-7661	1-5921	B9A8	1-676E	216254
9E83	麃	3-9214	1-7662		E8F0	2-563B	235D48
9E84	麄	5-8992	1-7663	1-8053		E-502C	235D49
9E85	麅	3-9217	1-7664			E-5439	
9E86	麆	3-9215			ECB0	2-5C3C	
9E87	麇	0-8769	1-7665		ECB1	2-5C3D	235D4F
9E88	麈	0-8770	0-8339		ECAF	2-5C3B	235D4B
9E89	麉				EFAB	2-6137	
9E8A	麊	5-7106			EFAA	2-6136	
9E8B	麋	0-8771	0-8340	1-6504	C247	1-7633	216255
9E8C	麌	3-9219	0-8341	1-7332	F1DF	2-652B	235D58
9E8D	麍				EFAC	2-6138	
9E8E	麎		1-7666		F1DE	2-652A	
9E8F	麏		1-7667	1-5940			
9E90	麐					E-5A24	235D55
9E91	麑	3-9221	0-8344	1-7202	F3F3	2-6860	235D5C
9E92	麒	0-8772	0-8342	0-4943	C451	1-795D	216257
9E93	麓	0-3420	0-4728	0-5468	C453	1-795F	216258
9E94	麔	3-9222			F3F2	2-685F	
9E95	麕	5-9002	0-8343			E-5C29	235D5A
9E96	麖	3-9223	1-7668				
9E97	麗	1-3286	0-4679	0-5382	C452	1-795E	216256
9E98	麘		1-7669			E-5E21	
9E99	麙	3-9224			F5B1	2-6B3F	
9E9A	麚				F5B3	2-6B41	
9E9B	麛	3-9225	1-7670		F5B2	2-6B40	235D5D
9E9C	麜	3-9226			F6CA	2-6D38	
9E9D	麝	0-8774	0-8345	0-6290	C565	1-7B51	216259
9E9E	麞		1-7671	1-7548		E-5F3A	235D66
9E9F	麟	0-8775	0-4659	0-5588	C5EF	1-7C5B	21625A
9EA0	麠				F8E8	2-7076	
9EA1	麡				F963	2-7152	
9EA2	麢					E-6231	
9EA3	麣					E-623F	
9EA4	麤		1-7672	1-8054	F9D2	2-7241	2F5D49
9EA5	麥	1-3483	0-8346	0-5674	B3C1	1-5E27	21625B
9EA6	麦	0-3483	0-3994			E-2547	27625B
9EA7	麧	5-7692			E4E5	2-4F4D	
9EA8	麨	5-7701	1-7673				
9EA9	麩	1-8479	0-8347	1-6644	BEA2	1-702B	21625C
9EAA	麪		0-8349	1-6437		E-502F	33625E
9EAB	麫					E-502E	
9EAC	麬		1-7674			E-543A	
9EAD	麭		0-8350		ECB3	2-5C3F	235D77
9EAE	麮	3-7764	1-7675		ECB2	2-5C3E	
9EAF	麯	1-8869	1-7676	1-5887		E-5750	235D79
9EB0	麰	3-7768	1-7677		EFAD	2-6139	235D7A
9EB1	麱	5-7706				E-5A26	
9EB2	麲					E-5A25	
9EB3	麳	3-7769	1-7678				
9EB4	麴	0-8480	1-7679	0-4753	C454	1-7960	21625D
9EB5	麵	1-8857	1-7680	0-5693	C4D1	1-7A5C	21625E
9EB6	麶				F7C7	2-6E74	
9EB7	麷	3-7759			F9CB	2-7239	
9EB8	麸	0-8479	0-8348				27625C
9EB9	麹		0-2577				
9EBA	麺		0-4445				
9EBB	麻	0-3473	0-4367	0-5611	B3C2	1-5E28	21625F
9EBC	麼		0-5487		BBF2	1-6B7B	216260
9EBD	麽	0-8765		1-6388		E-4B22	4B6260
9EBE	麾	0-8766	0-6164	0-9343	BEA3	1-702C	216261
9EBF	麿		0-4391	1-6389			694B7B
9EC0	黀	3-9205			F3F4	2-6861	
9EC1	黁	3-9207				E-5E22	235E30
9EC2	黂	3-9206			F874	2-7024	
9EC3	黃			0-9260	B6C0	1-6327	216262
9EC4	黄	0-2738	0-1811			E-396A	2D6262
9EC5	黅	3-9184		1-5959		E-543C	
9EC6	黆		1-7681			E-543B	235E35
9EC7	黇	3-9186					
9EC8	黈		1-7682		EFAE	2-613A	235E37
9EC9	黉	0-5768					2F5E42
9ECA	黊	3-9187				E-5A28	
9ECB	黋	3-9190	1-7683				
9ECC	黌	1-5768	0-8352	1-8455	C664	1-7D31	235E42
9ECD	黍	0-4282	0-2148	0-6408	B6C1	1-6328	216263
9ECE	黎	0-3272	0-8353	0-5383	BEA4	1-702D	216264
9ECF	黏	0-8004	0-8354	1-7643	C248	1-7634	216265
9ED0	黐	3-9258	0-8355	1-6369	F875	2-7025	235E4A
9ED1	黑	0-2658		0-9357	B6C2	1-6329	216266
9ED2	黒		0-2585			E-396B	4B6266
9ED3	黓	3-9230			E8F1	2-563C	235E4C
9ED4	黔	0-3913	0-8356	0-4403	C072	1-733D	216269
9ED5	黕	3-9235	1-7684		ECB4	2-5C40	
9ED6	黖	3-9234		1-6009	ECB5	2-5C41	
9ED7	黗	3-9233				E-543D	
9ED8	默	0-3612	0-6452	0-5789	C071	1-733C	216268
9ED9	黙		0-4459				4B6268
9EDA	黚	3-9236		1-5640	EFAF	2-613B	235E53
9EDB	黛	0-8776	0-3467	0-5174	C24C	1-7638	21626C
9EDC	黜	0-8777	0-8357	0-8585	C24A	1-7636	21626B
9EDD	黝	0-8778	0-8359	1-7405	C24B	1-7637	21626D
9EDE	點	1-2167	0-8358	0-7939	C249	1-7635	21626A
9EDF	黟	0-8780	1-7685		F1E0	2-652C	235E55
9EE0	黠	0-8779	0-8360	1-8536	C35C	1-7828	21626E
9EE1	黡	8-9006					
9EE2	黢	0-8781					
9EE3	黣	3-9239				E-5C2A	235E57
9EE4	黤	5-9025	1-7686		F5B5	2-6B43	
9EE5	黥	0-8784	0-8361	1-5661	F5B4	2-6B42	235E59
9EE6	黦	3-9241			F5B7	2-6B45	
9EE7	黧	0-8783	1-7687		F5B6	2-6B44	235E5C
9EE8	黨	1-2119	0-8362	0-5158	C4D2	1-7A5D	21626F
9EE9	黩	0-8782					276272
9EEA	黪	0-8785					295E6A
9EEB	黫	5-9031			F6CB	2-6D39	
9EEC	黬	3-9244	1-7688				
9EED	黭	3-9245	1-7689		F6CD	2-6D3B	
9EEE	黮	3-9243	1-7690	1-6092	F6CC	2-6D3A	235E60
9EEF	黯	0-8786	0-8363	1-7046	C566	1-7B52	216270
9EF0	黰	5-9036	1-7691		F7C8	2-6E75	235E66
9EF1	黱	5-4786	1-7692			E-6029	
9EF2	黲	1-8785	1-7693	1-7868	F876	2-7026	
9EF3	黳	3-9246			F877	2-7027	
9EF4	黴	1-8852	0-8364	0-5829	C5F0	1-7C5C	216271
9EF5	黵	3-9249	1-7694	1-6093	F964	2-7153	
9EF6	黶	3-1637	0-8365	1-7161	F97D	2-716D	235E6F
9EF7	黷	1-8782	0-8366	1-6143	C675	1-7D42	216272
9EF8	黸	5-9018	1-7701				
9EF9	黹	0-7773	0-8367		DCB0	2-4155	235E74
9EFA	黺			1-6662	ECB6	2-5C42	
9EFB	黻	0-7774	0-8368	1-6671	EFB0	2-613C	235E76
9EFC	黼	0-7775	0-8369	1-6602	F3F5	2-6862	235E77
9EFD	黽	1-8628	0-8370	1-6514	E0EF	2-4875	235E7A
9EFE	黾	0-8628				E-2772	295E7A
9EFF	黿	1-8629	1-7702	1-7354	EFB1	2-613D	235E7C

9F0

	Char	G	J	K	B	C	A
0	黿	5-8438		1-8059	F1E2	2-652E	
1	鼁	5-8439			F1E1	2-652D	
2	鼂	5-8440	1-7703	1-7725		E-5A29	235E7D
3	鼃		1-7704			E-5C2D	
4	鼄	5-8443		1-7763		E-5C2E	2D5664
5	鼅	5-8444				E-5F3C	2D5675
6	鼆	3-8505			F878	2-7028	
7	鼇		0-8371	0-7208	C652	1-7C7D	216273
8	鼈		0-8372	0-6015		E-615F	2D622C
9	鼉	1-8630	1-7705	1-8124	F965	2-7154	
A	鼊			1-6570	F97E	2-716E	
B	鼋	0-8629					295E7C
C	鼌	8-1491					
D	鼍	0-8630					295F2B
E	鼎	0-2206	0-3704	0-8003	B9A9	1-676F	216274
F	鼏	3-1873	1-7706		E8F2	2-563D	235F2F

9F1

	Char	G	J	K	B	C	A
0	鼐	0-5630	1-7707	1-6028	E8F3	2-563E	235F31
1	鼑		1-7708				
2	鼒	3-9227	1-7709		ECB7	2-5C43	235F32
3	鼓	0-2536	0-2461	0-4553	B9AA	1-6770	216275
4	鼔	5-4103	1-7710			E-456A	
5	鼕	1-8814	0-8374		C35D	1-7829	216276
6	鼖	5-9054	1-7711		F1E3	2-652F	235F33
7	鼗	0-5627	1-7712	1-6141		E-5C30	235F34
8	鼘				F6CF	2-6D3D	
9	鼙	0-6017	1-7713	1-6723	C567	1-7B53	216277
A	鼚	3-9259	1-7714		F6D0	2-6D3E	235F37
B	鼛	3-9263	1-7715		F6CE	2-6D3C	
C	鼜	3-9265			F879	2-7029	
D	鼝	3-9266				E-6160	
E	鼞				F8E9	2-7077	
F	鼟	3-9267	1-7716				

9F2

	Char	G	J	K	B	C	A
0	鼠	0-4283	0-3345	0-6409	B9AB	1-6771	216278
1	鼡		0-8375				4B6278
2	鼢	0-8787	1-7717	1-6663	EFB4	2-6140	235F45
3	鼣				EFB3	2-613F	
4	鼤	3-9270			EFB2	2-613E	
5	鼥	3-9272			F1E4	2-6530	
6	鼦	5-9063	1-7718			E-5A2B	235F49
7	鼧	3-9277				E-5A2A	
8	鼨	3-9276			F1E8	2-6534	
9	鼩	3-9275			F1E7	2-6533	
A	鼪	3-9274	1-7719		F1E6	2-6532	
B	鼫	3-9271	1-7720	1-6823	F1E5	2-6531	235F48
C	鼬	0-8788	0-8376	1-7406	C35E	1-782A	216279
D	鼭				F3F6	2-6863	
E	鼮	3-9278			F5B9	2-6B47	
F	鼯	0-8789	1-7721	1-7227	C4D3	1-7A5E	235F53

9F3

	Char	G	J	K	B	C	A
0	鼰				F5B8	2-6B46	
1	鼱	3-9281	1-7722		F6D1	2-6D3F	
2	鼲	3-9280	1-7723		F7CB	2-6E78	
3	鼳	3-9283			F7CA	2-6E77	
4	鼴		1-7724	1-7116	C5C4	1-7C30	21627A
5	鼵	3-9284			F7C9	2-6E76	
6	鼶	3-9286			F87C	2-702C	
7	鼷	0-8791	1-7725		F87B	2-702B	235F5F
8	鼸	3-9288		1-5641	F87A	2-702A	
9	鼹	0-8790	1-7726	1-7117		E-606D	235F5E
A	鼺		1-7727				
B	鼻	0-1739	0-4101	0-6212	BBF3	1-6B7C	21627B
C	鼼	5-9069	1-7728				
D	鼽	0-8792	1-7729		ECB8	2-5C44	235F64
E	鼾	0-8793	0-8377	1-8292	C24D	1-7639	21627C
F	鼿	5-9070	1-7730				

9F4

	Char	G	J	K	B	C	A
0	齀				F3F7	2-6864	
1	齁	3-9290	1-7731		F3F8	2-6865	235F69
2	齂				F7CC	2-6E79	
3	齃	5-9076	1-7732		F87D	2-702D	
4	齄	0-8794	1-7733				4D5F70
5	齅	5-9077	1-7734			E-613B	235F6D
6	齆	3-9291	1-7735		F8EA	2-7078	235F6F
7	齇	5-9078	1-7736		F966	2-7155	
8	齈				F9B9	2-7229	235F71
9	齉	3-9292			F9D4	2-7243	235F73
A	齊	1-3875	0-8378	0-8026	BBF4	1-6B7D	21627D
B	齋	1-5311	0-6723	0-7817	C24E	1-763A	21627E
C	齌	3-7003			F1E9	2-6535	
D	齍	5-6920			F3F9	2-6866	
E	齎		0-7658	0-7818	F6D2	2-6D40	235F79
F	齏	1-7620	0-8077		F87E	2-702E	235F7B

9F5

	Char	G	J	K	B	C	A
0	齐	0-3875				E-2370	27627D
1	齑	0-7620					295F7B
2	齒	1-1961	0-8379	0-8645	BEA6	1-702F	216321
3	齓	5-8393	1-7737			E-543E	
4	齔	1-8619	0-8380	1-8102	EFB5	2-6141	235F7C
5	齕	3-8464	1-7738	1-8515	F1EA	2-6536	235F7E
6	齖	3-8466	1-7739		F3FA	2-6867	
7	齗	3-8467	1-7740	1-7426	F3FB	2-6868	236023
8	齘	3-8468	1-7741		F3FC	2-6869	
9	齙	1-8621			F5BE	2-6B4C	
A	齚	3-8473	1-7742			E-5E24	
B	齛	5-8405			F5BA	2-6B48	
C	齜	1-8623			C568	1-7B54	216326
D	齝	3-8476	1-7743		F5BD	2-6B4B	
E	齞	3-8472	1-7744		F5BC	2-6B4A	
F	齟	1-8620	0-8382	0-7850	C4D4	1-7A5F	216322

9F6

	Char	G	J	K	B	C	A
0	齠	1-8622	0-8383	1-8006	F5BB	2-6B49	236028
1	齡	1-3368	0-8384	0-5438	C4D6	1-7A61	216324
2	齢		0-4680				4B6324
3	齣	1-8810	0-8381		C4D5	1-7A60	216323
4	齤	3-8481			F6D4	2-6D42	
5	齥				F6D3	2-6D41	
6	齦	1-8624	0-8385	1-5532	C569	1-7B55	216325
7	齧		0-8386	0-6469	C56A	1-7B56	337345
8	齨	5-8415	1-7745				
9	齩		1-7746	1-5834		E-5F3E	333623
A	齪	1-8626	0-8388	0-8327	C5C6	1-7C32	216328
B	齫	5-8417		1-5727	F7CD	2-6E7A	
C	齬	1-8625	0-8387	0-6965	C5C5	1-7C31	216327
D	齭	5-8423	1-7747				
E	齮	3-8486	1-7748		F8A3	2-7031	23603F
F	齯	3-8487	1-7749		F8A4	2-7032	236040

9F7

	Char	G	J	K	B	C	A
0	齰	5-8420	1-7750		F8A2	2-7030	
1	齱	3-8485	1-7751		F8A1	2-702F	
2	齲	1-4003	0-8390	1-7333	C654	1-7D21	21632A
3	齳	3-8482	1-7752				
4	齴	3-8491			F8EB	2-7079	
5	齵	3-8489	1-7753		F8EC	2-707A	
6	齶		0-8391	1-7023	F8ED	2-707B	236047
7	齷	1-8627	0-8389	0-6843	C653	1-7C7E	216329
8	齸	5-8432			F967	2-7156	
9	齹				F96A	2-7159	
A	齺	3-8474	1-7754		F969	2-7158	
B	齻	3-8492			F968	2-7157	
C	齼	3-8501				E-6233	
D	齽	3-8494	1-7755				
E	齾	3-8493			F9D3	2-7242	
F	齿	0-1961					276321

	9F8	9FA	9FC	9FE
0	龀 G 0-8619 J K B C A 295F7C	龠 G 0-5763 J 0-8394 K 1-7088 B EFB6 C 2-6142 A 23606B	G J K B C A	G J K B C A
1	龁 G 8-9491 J K B C A	龡 G 5-9079 J 1-7764 K B C E-5F3F A	G J K B C A	G J K B C A
2	龂 G 8-9492 J K B C A	龢 G J 1-7765 K 1-8418 B F7CF C 2-6E7C A 393577	G J K B C A	G J K B C A
3	龃 G 0-8620 J K B C A 276322	龣 G 5-9083 J 1-7766 K B C E-6161 A	G J K B C A	G J K B C A
4	龄 G 0-3368 J K B C A 276324	龤 G J K B F9A1 C 2-716F A 236072	G J K B C A	G J K B C A
5	龅 G 0-8621 J K B C A 29602B	龥 G 5-9080 J 1-7767 K 1-7407 B C E-6177 A 236071	G J K B C A	G J K B C A
6	龆 G 0-8622 J K B C A 296028	G J K B C A	G J K B C A	G J K B C A
7	龇 G 0-8623 J K B C A 276326	G J K B C A	G J K B C A	G J K B C A
8	龈 G 0-8624 J K B C A 276325	G J K B C A	G J K B C A	G J K B C A
9	龉 G 0-8625 J K B C A 276327	G J K B C A	G J K B C A	G J K B C A
A	龊 G 0-8626 J K B C A 276328	G J K B C A	G J K B C A	G J K B C A
B	龋 G 0-4003 J K B C A 27632A	G J K B C A	G J K B C A	G J K B C A
C	龌 G 0-8627 J K B C A 276329	G J K B C A	G J K B C A	G J K B C A
D	龍 G 1-3390 J 0-4622 K 0-5503 B C073 C 1-733E A 21632B	G J K B C A	G J K B C A	G J K B C A
E	龎 G 5-1652 J K 1-6307 B C E-5755 A 23605B	G J K B C A	G J K B C A	G J K B C A
F	龏 G 3-5687 J 1-7756 K B C A	G J K B C A	G J K B C A	G J K B C A

	9F9	9FB	9FD	9FF
0	龐 G 1-3751 J 1-7757 K 0-5934 B C365 C 1-7832 A 213D2D	G J K B C A	G J K B C A	G J K B C A
1	龑 G 3-5689 J 1-7758 K B F5BF C 2-6B4D A	G J K B C A	G J K B C A	G J K B C A
2	龒 G J 1-7759 K 1-6331 B F6D5 C 2-6D43 A	G J K B C A	G J K B C A	G J K B C A
3	龓 G 3-5692 J K B C E-602B A 236061	G J K B C A	G J K B C A	G J K B C A
4	龔 G 1-2508 J 1-7760 K 1-5743 B C5C7 C 1-7C33 A 21632C	G J K B C A	G J K B C A	G J K B C A
5	龕 G 1-7772 J 0-8392 K 0-4294 B F7CE C 2-6E7B A 236062	G J K B C A	G J K B C A	G J K B C A
6	龖 G 3-5690 J 1-7761 K B C A	G J K B C A	G J K B C A	G J K B C A
7	龗 G 5-5680 J 1-7762 K B C E-6242 A	G J K B C A	G J K B C A	G J K B C A
8	龘 G J K B F9D5 C 2-7244 A	G J K B C A	G J K B C A	G J K B C A
9	龙 G 0-3390 J K B C A 27632B	G J K B C A	G J K B C A	G J K B C A
A	龚 G 0-2508 J K B C A 27632C	G J K B C A	G J K B C A	G J K B C A
B	龛 G 0-7772 J K B C A 296062	G J K B C A	G J K B C A	G J K B C A
C	龜 G 1-2574 J 0-8393 K 0-4747 B C074 C 1-733F A 21632D	G J K B C A	G J K B C A	G J K B C A
D	龝 G 5-5919 J 0-6752 K 1-8037 B C E-5E47 A 2D4F29	G J K B C A	G J K B C A	G J K B C A
E	龞 G 5-8091 J 1-7763 K B C A	G J K B C A	G J K B C A	G J K B C A
F	龟 G 0-2574 J K B C A 27632D	G J K B C A	G J K B C A	G J K B C A

	AC0	AC1	AC2	AC3	AC4	AC5	AC6	AC7	AC8	AC9	ACA	ACB	ACC	ACD
0	가 AC00	감 AC10	갠 AC20	갰 AC30	걀 AC40	걐 AC50	걠 AC60	거 AC70	검 AC80	겐 AC90	겠 ACA0	결 ACB0	곀 ACC0	곐 ACD0
1	각 AC01	갑 AC11	갡 AC21	갱 AC31	걁 AC41	걑 AC51	걡 AC61	걱 AC71	겁 AC81	겑 AC91	겡 ACA1	겱 ACB1	곁 ACC1	곑 ACD1
2	갂 AC02	값 AC12	갢 AC22	갲 AC32	걂 AC42	걒 AC52	걢 AC62	걲 AC72	겂 AC82	겒 AC92	겢 ACA2	겲 ACB2	곂 ACC2	곒 ACD2
3	갃 AC03	갓 AC13	갣 AC23	갳 AC33	걃 AC43	걓 AC53	걣 AC63	걳 AC73	것 AC83	겓 AC93	겣 ACA3	겳 ACB3	곃 ACC3	곓 ACD3
4	간 AC04	갔 AC14	갤 AC24	갴 AC34	걄 AC44	걔 AC54	걤 AC64	건 AC74	겄 AC84	겔 AC94	겤 ACA4	겴 ACB4	계 ACC4	곔 ACD4
5	갅 AC05	강 AC15	갥 AC25	갵 AC35	걅 AC45	걕 AC55	걥 AC65	걵 AC75	겅 AC85	겕 AC95	겥 ACA5	겵 ACB5	곅 ACC5	곕 ACD5
6	갆 AC06	갖 AC16	갦 AC26	갶 AC36	걆 AC46	걖 AC56	걦 AC66	걶 AC76	겆 AC86	겖 AC96	겦 ACA6	겶 ACB6	곆 ACC6	곖 ACD6
7	갇 AC07	갗 AC17	갧 AC27	갷 AC37	걇 AC47	걗 AC57	걧 AC67	걷 AC77	겇 AC87	겗 AC97	겧 ACA7	겷 ACB7	곇 ACC7	곗 ACD7
8	갈 AC08	갘 AC18	갨 AC28	갸 AC38	걈 AC48	걘 AC58	걨 AC68	걸 AC78	겈 AC88	겘 AC98	겨 ACA8	겸 ACB8	곈 ACC8	곘 ACD8
9	갉 AC09	같 AC19	갩 AC29	갹 AC39	걉 AC49	걙 AC59	걩 AC69	걹 AC79	겉 AC89	겙 AC99	격 ACA9	겹 ACB9	곉 ACC9	곙 ACD9
A	갊 AC0A	갚 AC1A	갪 AC2A	갺 AC3A	걊 AC4A	걚 AC5A	걪 AC6A	걺 AC7A	겊 AC8A	겚 AC9A	겪 ACAA	겺 ACBA	곊 ACCA	곚 ACDA
B	갋 AC0B	갛 AC1B	갫 AC2B	갻 AC3B	걋 AC4B	걛 AC5B	걫 AC6B	걻 AC7B	겋 AC8B	겛 AC9B	겫 ACAB	겻 ACBB	곋 ACCB	곛 ACDB
C	갌 AC0C	개 AC1C	갬 AC2C	갼 AC3C	걌 AC4C	걜 AC5C	걬 AC6C	걼 AC7C	게 AC8C	겜 AC9C	견 ACAC	겼 ACBC	곌 ACCC	곜 ACDC
D	갍 AC0D	객 AC1D	갭 AC2D	갽 AC3D	걍 AC4D	걝 AC5D	걭 AC6D	걽 AC7D	겍 AC8D	겝 AC9D	겭 ACAD	경 ACBD	곍 ACCD	곝 ACDD
E	갎 AC0E	갞 AC1E	갮 AC2E	갾 AC3E	걎 AC4E	걞 AC5E	걮 AC6E	걾 AC7E	겎 AC8E	겞 AC9E	겮 ACAE	겾 ACBE	곎 ACCE	곞 ACDE
F	갏 AC0F	갟 AC1F	갯 AC2F	갿 AC3F	걏 AC4F	걟 AC5F	걯 AC6F	걿 AC7F	겏 AC8F	겟 AC9F	겯 ACAF	겿 ACBF	곏 ACCF	곟 ACDF

	ACE	ACF	AD0	AD1	AD2	AD3	AD4	AD5	AD6	AD7	AD8	AD9	ADA	ADB
0	고 ACE0	곰 ACF0	관 AD00	괐 AD10	괠 AD20	괰 AD30	굀 AD40	교 AD50	굠 AD60	군 AD70	궀 AD80	궐 AD90	궠 ADA0	궰 ADB0
1	곡 ACE1	곱 ACF1	괁 AD01	광 AD11	괡 AD21	괱 AD31	굁 AD41	굑 AD51	굡 AD61	굱 AD71	궁 AD81	궑 AD91	궡 ADA1	궱 ADB1
2	곢 ACE2	곲 ACF2	괂 AD02	괒 AD12	괢 AD22	괲 AD32	굂 AD42	굒 AD52	굢 AD62	굲 AD72	궂 AD82	궒 AD92	궢 ADA2	궲 ADB2
3	곣 ACE3	곳 ACF3	괃 AD03	괓 AD13	괣 AD23	괳 AD33	굃 AD43	굓 AD53	굣 AD63	굳 AD73	궃 AD83	궓 AD93	궣 ADA3	궳 ADB3
4	곤 ACE4	곴 ACF4	괄 AD04	괔 AD14	괤 AD24	괴 AD34	굄 AD44	굔 AD54	굤 AD64	굴 AD74	궄 AD84	궔 AD94	궤 ADA4	궴 ADB4
5	곥 ACE5	공 ACF5	괅 AD05	괕 AD15	괥 AD25	괵 AD35	굅 AD45	굕 AD55	굥 AD65	굵 AD75	궅 AD85	궕 AD95	궥 ADA5	궵 ADB5
6	곦 ACE6	곶 ACF6	괆 AD06	괖 AD16	괦 AD26	괶 AD36	굆 AD46	굖 AD56	굦 AD66	굶 AD76	궆 AD86	궖 AD96	궦 ADA6	궶 ADB6
7	곧 ACE7	곷 ACF7	괇 AD07	괗 AD17	괧 AD27	괷 AD37	굇 AD47	굗 AD57	굧 AD67	굷 AD77	궇 AD87	궗 AD97	궧 ADA7	궷 ADB7
8	골 ACE8	곸 ACF8	괈 AD08	괘 AD18	괨 AD28	괸 AD38	굈 AD48	굘 AD58	굨 AD68	굸 AD78	궈 AD88	궘 AD98	궨 ADA8	궸 ADB8
9	곩 ACE9	곹 ACF9	괉 AD09	괙 AD19	괩 AD29	괹 AD39	굉 AD49	굙 AD59	굩 AD69	굹 AD79	궉 AD89	궙 AD99	궩 ADA9	궹 ADB9
A	곪 ACEA	곺 ACFA	괊 AD0A	괚 AD1A	괪 AD2A	괺 AD3A	굊 AD4A	굚 AD5A	굪 AD6A	굺 AD7A	궊 AD8A	궚 AD9A	궪 ADAA	궺 ADBA
B	곫 ACEB	곻 ACFB	괋 AD0B	괛 AD1B	괫 AD2B	괻 AD3B	굋 AD4B	굛 AD5B	굫 AD6B	굻 AD7B	궋 AD8B	궛 AD9B	궫 ADAB	궻 ADBB
C	곬 ACEC	과 ACFC	괌 AD0C	괜 AD1C	괬 AD2C	괼 AD3C	굌 AD4C	굜 AD5C	구 AD6C	굼 AD7C	권 AD8C	궜 AD9C	궬 ADAC	궼 ADBC
D	곭 ACED	곽 ACFD	괍 AD0D	괝 AD1D	괭 AD2D	괽 AD3D	굍 AD4D	굝 AD5D	국 AD6D	굽 AD7D	궍 AD8D	궝 AD9D	궭 ADAD	궽 ADBD
E	곮 ACEE	곾 ACFE	괎 AD0E	괞 AD1E	괮 AD2E	괾 AD3E	굎 AD4E	굞 AD5E	굮 AD6E	굾 AD7E	궎 AD8E	궞 AD9E	궮 ADAE	궾 ADBE
F	곯 ACEF	곿 ACFF	괏 AD0F	괟 AD1F	괯 AD2F	괿 AD3F	굏 AD4F	굟 AD5F	굯 AD6F	굿 AD7F	궏 AD8F	궟 AD9F	궯 ADAF	궿 ADBF

	ADC	ADD	ADE	ADF	AE0	AE1	AE2	AE3	AE4	AE5	AE6	AE7	AE8	AE9
0	귀 ADC0	귐 ADD0	균 ADE0	귰 ADF0	글 AE00	긐 AE10	긠 AE20	기 AE30	김 AE40	깐 AE50	깠 AE60	깰 AE70	꺀 AE80	꺐 AE90
1	귁 ADC1	귑 ADD1	귡 ADE1	귱 ADF1	긁 AE01	긑 AE11	긡 AE21	긱 AE31	깁 AE41	깑 AE51	깡 AE61	깱 AE71	꺁 AE81	꺑 AE91
2	귂 ADC2	귒 ADD2	귢 ADE2	귲 ADF2	긂 AE02	긒 AE12	긢 AE22	긲 AE32	깂 AE42	깒 AE52	깢 AE62	깲 AE72	꺂 AE82	꺒 AE92
3	귃 ADC3	귓 ADD3	귣 ADE3	귳 ADF3	긃 AE03	긓 AE13	긣 AE23	긳 AE33	깃 AE43	깓 AE53	깣 AE63	깳 AE73	꺃 AE83	꺓 AE93
4	귄 ADC4	귔 ADD4	귤 ADE4	귴 ADF4	긄 AE04	긔 AE14	긤 AE24	긴 AE34	깄 AE44	깔 AE54	깤 AE64	깴 AE74	꺄 AE84	꺔 AE94
5	귅 ADC5	귕 ADD5	귥 ADE5	귵 ADF5	긅 AE05	긕 AE15	긥 AE25	긵 AE35	깅 AE45	깕 AE55	깥 AE65	깵 AE75	꺅 AE85	꺕 AE95
6	귆 ADC6	귖 ADD6	귦 ADE6	귶 ADF6	긆 AE06	긖 AE16	긦 AE26	긶 AE36	깆 AE46	깖 AE56	깦 AE66	깶 AE76	꺆 AE86	꺖 AE96
7	귇 ADC7	귗 ADD7	귧 ADE7	귷 ADF7	긇 AE07	긗 AE17	긧 AE27	긷 AE37	깇 AE47	깗 AE57	깧 AE67	깷 AE77	꺇 AE87	꺗 AE97
8	귈 ADC8	귘 ADD8	귨 ADE8	그 ADF8	금 AE08	긘 AE18	긨 AE28	길 AE38	깈 AE48	깘 AE58	깨 AE68	깸 AE78	꺈 AE88	꺘 AE98
9	귉 ADC9	귙 ADD9	귩 ADE9	극 ADF9	급 AE09	긙 AE19	긩 AE29	긹 AE39	깉 AE49	깙 AE59	깩 AE69	깹 AE79	꺉 AE89	꺙 AE99
A	귊 ADCA	귚 ADDA	귪 ADEA	귺 ADFA	긊 AE0A	긚 AE1A	긪 AE2A	긺 AE3A	깊 AE4A	깚 AE5A	깪 AE6A	깺 AE7A	꺊 AE8A	꺚 AE9A
B	귋 ADCB	귛 ADDB	귫 ADEB	귻 ADFB	긋 AE0B	긛 AE1B	긫 AE2B	긻 AE3B	깋 AE4B	깛 AE5B	깫 AE6B	깻 AE7B	꺋 AE8B	꺛 AE9B
C	귌 ADCC	규 ADDC	귬 ADEC	근 ADFC	긌 AE0C	긜 AE1C	긬 AE2C	긼 AE3C	까 AE4C	깜 AE5C	깬 AE6C	깼 AE7C	꺌 AE8C	꺜 AE9C
D	귍 ADCD	귝 ADDD	귭 ADED	귽 ADFD	긍 AE0D	긝 AE1D	긭 AE2D	긽 AE3D	깍 AE4D	깝 AE5D	깭 AE6D	깽 AE7D	꺍 AE8D	꺝 AE9D
E	귎 ADCE	귞 ADDE	귮 ADEE	귾 ADFE	긎 AE0E	긞 AE1E	긮 AE2E	긾 AE3E	깎 AE4E	깞 AE5E	깮 AE6E	깾 AE7E	꺎 AE8E	꺞 AE9E
F	귏 ADCF	귟 ADDF	귯 ADEF	귿 ADFF	긏 AE0F	긟 AE1F	긯 AE2F	긿 AE3F	깏 AE4F	깟 AE5F	깯 AE6F	깿 AE7F	꺏 AE8F	꺟 AE9F

	AEA	AEB	AEC	AED	AEE	AEF	AF0	AF1	AF2	AF3	AF4	AF5	AF6	AF7
0	꺠 AEA0	꺰 AEB0	껀 AEC0	껐 AED0	껠 AEE0	껰 AEF0	꼀 AF00	꼐 AF10	꼠 AF20	꼰 AF30	꽀 AF40	꽐 AF50	꽠 AF60	꽰 AF70
1	꺡 AEA1	꺱 AEB1	껁 AEC1	껑 AED1	껡 AEE1	껱 AEF1	꼁 AF01	꼑 AF11	꼡 AF21	꼱 AF31	꽁 AF41	꽑 AF51	꽡 AF61	꽱 AF71
2	꺢 AEA2	꺲 AEB2	껂 AEC2	껒 AED2	껢 AEE2	껲 AEF2	꼂 AF02	꼒 AF12	꼢 AF22	꼲 AF32	꽂 AF42	꽒 AF52	꽢 AF62	꽲 AF72
3	꺣 AEA3	꺳 AEB3	껃 AEC3	껓 AED3	껣 AEE3	껳 AEF3	꼃 AF03	꼓 AF13	꼣 AF23	꼳 AF33	꽃 AF43	꽓 AF53	꽣 AF63	꽳 AF73
4	꺤 AEA4	꺴 AEB4	껄 AEC4	껔 AED4	껤 AEE4	껴 AEF4	꼄 AF04	꼔 AF14	꼤 AF24	꼴 AF34	꽄 AF44	꽔 AF54	꽤 AF64	꽴 AF74
5	꺥 AEA5	꺵 AEB5	껅 AEC5	껕 AED5	껥 AEE5	껵 AEF5	꼅 AF05	꼕 AF15	꼥 AF25	꼵 AF35	꽅 AF45	꽕 AF55	꽥 AF65	꽵 AF75
6	꺦 AEA6	꺶 AEB6	껆 AEC6	껖 AED6	껦 AEE6	껶 AEF6	꼆 AF06	꼖 AF16	꼦 AF26	꼶 AF36	꽆 AF46	꽖 AF56	꽦 AF66	꽶 AF76
7	꺧 AEA7	꺷 AEB7	껇 AEC7	껗 AED7	껧 AEE7	껷 AEF7	꼇 AF07	꼗 AF17	꼧 AF27	꼷 AF37	꽇 AF47	꽗 AF57	꽧 AF67	꽷 AF77
8	꺨 AEA8	꺸 AEB8	껈 AEC8	께 AED8	껨 AEE8	껸 AEF8	꼈 AF08	꼘 AF18	꼨 AF28	꼸 AF38	꽈 AF48	꽘 AF58	꽨 AF68	꽸 AF78
9	꺩 AEA9	꺹 AEB9	껉 AEC9	껙 AED9	껩 AEE9	껹 AEF9	꼉 AF09	꼙 AF19	꼩 AF29	꼹 AF39	꽉 AF49	꽙 AF59	꽩 AF69	꽹 AF79
A	꺪 AEAA	꺺 AEBA	껊 AECA	껚 AEDA	껪 AEEA	껺 AEFA	꼊 AF0A	꼚 AF1A	꼪 AF2A	꼺 AF3A	꽊 AF4A	꽚 AF5A	꽪 AF6A	꽺 AF7A
B	꺫 AEAB	꺻 AEBB	껋 AECB	껛 AEDB	껫 AEEB	껻 AEFB	꼋 AF0B	꼛 AF1B	꼫 AF2B	꼻 AF3B	꽋 AF4B	꽛 AF5B	꽫 AF6B	꽻 AF7B
C	꺬 AEAC	꺼 AEBC	껌 AECC	껜 AEDC	껬 AEEC	껼 AEFC	꼌 AF0C	꼜 AF1C	꼬 AF2C	꼼 AF3C	꽌 AF4C	꽜 AF5C	꽬 AF6C	꽼 AF7C
D	꺭 AEAD	꺽 AEBD	껍 AECD	껝 AEDD	껭 AEED	껽 AEFD	꼍 AF0D	꼝 AF1D	꼭 AF2D	꼽 AF3D	꽍 AF4D	꽝 AF5D	꽭 AF6D	꽽 AF7D
E	꺮 AEAE	꺾 AEBE	껎 AECE	껞 AEDE	껮 AEEE	껾 AEFE	꼎 AF0E	꼞 AF1E	꼮 AF2E	꼾 AF3E	꽎 AF4E	꽞 AF5E	꽮 AF6E	꽾 AF7E
F	꺯 AEAF	꺿 AEBF	껏 AECF	껟 AEDF	껯 AEEF	껿 AEFF	꼏 AF0F	꼟 AF1F	꼯 AF2F	꼿 AF3F	꽏 AF4F	꽟 AF5F	꽯 AF6F	꽿 AF7F

	AF8	AF9	AFA	AFB	AFC	AFD	AFE	AFF	B00	B01	B02	B03	B04	B05
0	꾀 AF80	꾐 AF90	꾠 AFA0	꾰 AFB0	꿀 AFC0	꿐 AFD0	꿠 AFE0	꿰 AFF0	뀀 B000	뀐 B010	뀠 B020	뀰 B030	끀 B040	끐 B050
1	꾁 AF81	꾑 AF91	꾡 AFA1	꾱 AFB1	꿁 AFC1	꿑 AFD1	꿡 AFE1	꿱 AFF1	뀁 B001	뀑 B011	뀡 B021	뀱 B031	끁 B041	끑 B051
2	꾂 AF82	꾒 AF92	꾢 AFA2	꾲 AFB2	꿂 AFC2	꿒 AFD2	꿢 AFE2	꿲 AFF2	뀂 B002	뀒 B012	뀢 B022	뀲 B032	끂 B042	끒 B052
3	꾃 AF83	꾓 AF93	꾣 AFA3	꾳 AFB3	꿃 AFC3	꿓 AFD3	꿣 AFE3	꿳 AFF3	뀃 B003	뀓 B013	뀣 B023	뀳 B033	끃 B043	끓 B053
4	꾄 AF84	꾔 AF94	꾤 AFA4	꾴 AFB4	꿄 AFC4	꿔 AFD4	꿤 AFE4	꿴 AFF4	뀄 B004	뀔 B014	뀤 B024	뀴 B034	끄 B044	끔 B054
5	꾅 AF85	꾕 AF95	꾥 AFA5	꾵 AFB5	꿅 AFC5	꿕 AFD5	꿥 AFE5	꿵 AFF5	뀅 B005	뀕 B015	뀥 B025	뀵 B035	끅 B045	끕 B055
6	꾆 AF86	꾖 AF96	꾦 AFA6	꾶 AFB6	꿆 AFC6	꿖 AFD6	꿦 AFE6	꿶 AFF6	뀆 B006	뀖 B016	뀦 B026	뀶 B036	끆 B046	끖 B056
7	꾇 AF87	꾗 AF97	꾧 AFA7	꾷 AFB7	꿇 AFC7	꿗 AFD7	꿧 AFE7	꿷 AFF7	뀇 B007	뀗 B017	뀧 B027	뀷 B037	끇 B047	끗 B057
8	꾈 AF88	꾘 AF98	꾨 AFA8	꾸 AFB8	꿈 AFC8	꿘 AFD8	꿨 AFE8	꿸 AFF8	뀈 B008	뀘 B018	뀨 B028	뀸 B038	끈 B048	끘 B058
9	꾉 AF89	꾙 AF99	꾩 AFA9	꾹 AFB9	꿉 AFC9	꿙 AFD9	꿩 AFE9	꿹 AFF9	뀉 B009	뀙 B019	뀩 B029	뀹 B039	끉 B049	끙 B059
A	꾊 AF8A	꾚 AF9A	꾪 AFAA	꾺 AFBA	꿊 AFCA	꿚 AFDA	꿪 AFEA	꿺 AFFA	뀊 B00A	뀚 B01A	뀪 B02A	뀺 B03A	끊 B04A	끚 B05A
B	꾋 AF8B	꾛 AF9B	꾫 AFAB	꾻 AFBB	꿋 AFCB	꿛 AFDB	꿫 AFEB	꿻 AFFB	뀋 B00B	뀛 B01B	뀫 B02B	뀻 B03B	끋 B04B	끛 B05B
C	꾌 AF8C	꾜 AF9C	꾬 AFAC	꾼 AFBC	꿌 AFCC	꿜 AFDC	꿬 AFEC	꿼 AFFC	뀌 B00C	뀜 B01C	뀬 B02C	뀼 B03C	끌 B04C	끜 B05C
D	꾍 AF8D	꾝 AF9D	꾭 AFAD	꾽 AFBD	꿍 AFCD	꿝 AFDD	꿭 AFED	꿽 AFFD	뀍 B00D	뀝 B01D	뀭 B02D	뀽 B03D	끍 B04D	끝 B05D
E	꾎 AF8E	꾞 AF9E	꾮 AFAE	꾾 AFBE	꿎 AFCE	꿞 AFDE	꿮 AFEE	꿾 AFFE	뀎 B00E	뀞 B01E	뀮 B02E	뀾 B03E	끎 B04E	끞 B05E
F	꾏 AF8F	꾟 AF9F	꾯 AFAF	꾿 AFBF	꿏 AFCF	꿟 AFDF	꿯 AFEF	꿿 AFFF	뀏 B00F	뀟 B01F	뀯 B02F	뀿 B03F	끏 B04F	끟 B05F

	B06	B07	B08	B09	B0A	B0B	B0C	B0D	B0E	B0F	B10	B11	B12	B13
0	끠 B060	끰 B070	낀 B080	낐 B090	날 B0A0	낰 B0B0	냀 B0C0	냐 B0D0	냠 B0E0	냰 B0F0	넀 B100	널 B110	넠 B120	넰 B130
1	끡 B061	끱 B071	낁 B081	낑 B091	낡 B0A1	낱 B0B1	냁 B0C1	냑 B0D1	냡 B0E1	냱 B0F1	넁 B101	넑 B111	넡 B121	넱 B131
2	끢 B062	끲 B072	낂 B082	낒 B092	낢 B0A2	낲 B0B2	냂 B0C2	냒 B0D2	냢 B0E2	냲 B0F2	넂 B102	넒 B112	넢 B122	넲 B132
3	끣 B063	끳 B073	낃 B083	낓 B093	낣 B0A3	낳 B0B3	냃 B0C3	냓 B0D3	냣 B0E3	냳 B0F3	넃 B103	넓 B113	넣 B123	넳 B133
4	끤 B064	끴 B074	낄 B084	낔 B094	낤 B0A4	내 B0B4	냄 B0C4	냔 B0D4	냤 B0E4	냴 B0F4	넄 B104	넔 B114	네 B124	넴 B134
5	끥 B065	끵 B075	낅 B085	낕 B095	낥 B0A5	낵 B0B5	냅 B0C5	냕 B0D5	냥 B0E5	냵 B0F5	넅 B105	넕 B115	넥 B125	넵 B135
6	끦 B066	끶 B076	낆 B086	낖 B096	낦 B0A6	낶 B0B6	냆 B0C6	냖 B0D6	냦 B0E6	냶 B0F6	넆 B106	넖 B116	넦 B126	넶 B136
7	끧 B067	끷 B077	낇 B087	낗 B097	낧 B0A7	낷 B0B7	냇 B0C7	냗 B0D7	냧 B0E7	냷 B0F7	넇 B107	넗 B117	넧 B127	넷 B137
8	끨 B068	끸 B078	낈 B088	나 B098	남 B0A8	낸 B0B8	냈 B0C8	냘 B0D8	냨 B0E8	냸 B0F8	너 B108	넘 B118	넨 B128	넸 B138
9	끩 B069	끹 B079	낉 B089	낙 B099	납 B0A9	낹 B0B9	냉 B0C9	냙 B0D9	냩 B0E9	냹 B0F9	넉 B109	넙 B119	넩 B129	넹 B139
A	끪 B06A	끺 B07A	낊 B08A	낚 B09A	낪 B0AA	낺 B0BA	냊 B0CA	냚 B0DA	냪 B0EA	냺 B0FA	넊 B10A	넚 B11A	넪 B12A	넺 B13A
B	끫 B06B	끻 B07B	낋 B08B	낛 B09B	낫 B0AB	낻 B0BB	냋 B0CB	냛 B0DB	냫 B0EB	냻 B0FB	넋 B10B	넛 B11B	넫 B12B	넻 B13B
C	끬 B06C	끼 B07C	낌 B08C	난 B09C	났 B0AC	낼 B0BC	냌 B0CC	냜 B0DC	냬 B0EC	냼 B0FC	넌 B10C	넜 B11C	넬 B12C	넼 B13C
D	끭 B06D	끽 B07D	낍 B08D	낝 B09D	낭 B0AD	낽 B0BD	냍 B0CD	냝 B0DD	냭 B0ED	냽 B0FD	넍 B10D	넝 B11D	넭 B12D	넽 B13D
E	끮 B06E	끾 B07E	낎 B08E	낞 B09E	낮 B0AE	낾 B0BE	냎 B0CE	냞 B0DE	냮 B0EE	냾 B0FE	넎 B10E	넞 B11E	넮 B12E	넾 B13E
F	끯 B06F	끿 B07F	낏 B08F	낟 B09F	낯 B0AF	낿 B0BF	냏 B0CF	냟 B0DF	냯 B0EF	냿 B0FF	넏 B10F	넟 B11F	넯 B12F	넿 B13F

	B14	B15	B16	B17	B18	B19	B1A	B1B	B1C	B1D	B1E	B1F	B20	B21
0	녀 B140	념 B150	녠 B160	녰 B170	놀 B180	놐 B190	놠 B1A0	놰 B1B0	뇀 B1C0	뇐 B1D0	뇠 B1E0	뇰 B1F0	눀 B200	눐 B210
1	녁 B141	녑 B151	녡 B161	녱 B171	놁 B181	놑 B191	놡 B1A1	놱 B1B1	뇁 B1C1	뇑 B1D1	뇡 B1E1	뇱 B1F1	눁 B201	눑 B211
2	녂 B142	녒 B152	녢 B162	녲 B172	놂 B182	높 B192	놢 B1A2	놲 B1B2	뇂 B1C2	뇒 B1D2	뇢 B1E2	뇲 B1F2	눂 B202	눒 B212
3	녃 B143	녓 B153	녣 B163	녳 B173	놃 B183	놓 B193	놣 B1A3	놳 B1B3	뇃 B1C3	뇓 B1D3	뇣 B1E3	뇳 B1F3	눃 B203	눓 B213
4	년 B144	녔 B154	녤 B164	녴 B174	놄 B184	놔 B194	놤 B1A4	놴 B1B4	뇄 B1C4	뇔 B1D4	뇤 B1E4	뇴 B1F4	누 B204	눔 B214
5	녅 B145	녕 B155	녥 B165	녵 B175	놅 B185	놕 B195	놥 B1A5	놵 B1B5	뇅 B1C5	뇕 B1D5	뇥 B1E5	뇵 B1F5	눅 B205	눕 B215
6	녆 B146	녖 B156	녦 B166	녶 B176	놆 B186	놖 B196	놦 B1A6	놶 B1B6	뇆 B1C6	뇖 B1D6	뇦 B1E6	뇶 B1F6	눆 B206	눖 B216
7	녇 B147	녗 B157	녧 B167	녷 B177	놇 B187	놗 B197	놧 B1A7	놷 B1B7	뇇 B1C7	뇗 B1D7	뇧 B1E7	뇷 B1F7	눇 B207	눗 B217
8	녈 B148	녘 B158	녨 B168	노 B178	놈 B188	놘 B198	놨 B1A8	놸 B1B8	뇈 B1C8	뇘 B1D8	뇨 B1E8	뇸 B1F8	눈 B208	눘 B218
9	녉 B149	녙 B159	녩 B169	녹 B179	놉 B189	놙 B199	놩 B1A9	놹 B1B9	뇉 B1C9	뇙 B1D9	뇩 B1E9	뇹 B1F9	눉 B209	눙 B219
A	녊 B14A	녚 B15A	녪 B16A	녺 B17A	놊 B18A	놚 B19A	놪 B1AA	놺 B1BA	뇊 B1CA	뇚 B1DA	뇪 B1EA	뇺 B1FA	눊 B20A	눚 B21A
B	녋 B14B	녛 B15B	녫 B16B	녻 B17B	놋 B18B	놛 B19B	놫 B1AB	놻 B1BB	뇋 B1CB	뇛 B1DB	뇫 B1EB	뇻 B1FB	눋 B20B	눛 B21B
C	녌 B14C	녜 B15C	녬 B16C	논 B17C	놌 B18C	놜 B19C	놬 B1AC	놼 B1BC	뇌 B1CC	뇜 B1DC	뇬 B1EC	뇼 B1FC	눌 B20C	눜 B21C
D	녍 B14D	녝 B15D	녭 B16D	녽 B17D	농 B18D	놝 B19D	놭 B1AD	놽 B1BD	뇍 B1CD	뇝 B1DD	뇭 B1ED	뇽 B1FD	눍 B20D	눝 B21D
E	녎 B14E	녞 B15E	녮 B16E	녾 B17E	놎 B18E	놞 B19E	놮 B1AE	놾 B1BE	뇎 B1CE	뇞 B1DE	뇮 B1EE	뇾 B1FE	눎 B20E	눞 B21E
F	녏 B14F	녟 B15F	녯 B16F	녿 B17F	놏 B18F	놟 B19F	놯 B1AF	놿 B1BF	뇏 B1CF	뇟 B1DF	뇯 B1EF	뇿 B1FF	눏 B20F	눟 B21F

	B22	B23	B24	B25	B26	B27	B28	B29	B2A	B2B	B2C	B2D	B2E	B2F
0	눠 B220	눰 B230	뉀 B240	뉐 B250	뉠 B260	뉰 B270	늀 B280	느 B290	늠 B2A0	늰 B2B0	닀 B2C0	닐 B2D0	닠 B2E0	닰 B2F0
1	눡 B221	눱 B231	뉁 B241	뉑 B251	뉡 B261	뉱 B271	늁 B281	늑 B291	늡 B2A1	늱 B2B1	닁 B2C1	닑 B2D1	닡 B2E1	닱 B2F1
2	눢 B222	눲 B232	뉂 B242	뉒 B252	뉢 B262	뉲 B272	늂 B282	늒 B292	늢 B2A2	늲 B2B2	닂 B2C2	닒 B2D2	닢 B2E2	닲 B2F2
3	눣 B223	눳 B233	뉃 B243	뉓 B253	뉣 B263	뉳 B273	늃 B283	늓 B293	늣 B2A3	늳 B2B3	닃 B2C3	닓 B2D3	닣 B2E3	닳 B2F3
4	눤 B224	눴 B234	뉄 B244	뉔 B254	뉤 B264	뉴 B274	늄 B284	는 B294	늤 B2A4	늴 B2B4	닄 B2C4	닔 B2D4	다 B2E4	담 B2F4
5	눥 B225	눵 B235	뉅 B245	뉕 B255	뉥 B265	뉵 B275	늅 B285	늕 B295	능 B2A5	늵 B2B5	닅 B2C5	닕 B2D5	닥 B2E5	답 B2F5
6	눦 B226	눶 B236	뉆 B246	뉖 B256	뉦 B266	뉶 B276	늆 B286	늖 B296	늦 B2A6	늶 B2B6	닆 B2C6	닖 B2D6	닦 B2E6	닶 B2F6
7	눧 B227	눷 B237	뉇 B247	뉗 B257	뉧 B267	뉷 B277	늇 B287	늗 B297	늧 B2A7	늷 B2B7	닇 B2C7	닗 B2D7	닧 B2E7	닷 B2F7
8	눨 B228	눸 B238	뉈 B248	뉘 B258	뉨 B268	뉸 B278	늈 B288	늘 B298	늨 B2A8	늸 B2B8	니 B2C8	님 B2D8	단 B2E8	닸 B2F8
9	눩 B229	눹 B239	뉉 B249	뉙 B259	뉩 B269	뉹 B279	늉 B289	늙 B299	늩 B2A9	늹 B2B9	닉 B2C9	닙 B2D9	닩 B2E9	당 B2F9
A	눪 B22A	눺 B23A	뉊 B24A	뉚 B25A	뉪 B26A	뉺 B27A	늊 B28A	늚 B29A	늪 B2AA	늺 B2BA	닊 B2CA	닚 B2DA	닪 B2EA	닺 B2FA
B	눫 B22B	눻 B23B	뉋 B24B	뉛 B25B	뉫 B26B	뉻 B27B	늋 B28B	늛 B29B	늫 B2AB	늻 B2BB	닋 B2CB	닛 B2DB	닫 B2EB	닻 B2FB
C	눬 B22C	눼 B23C	뉌 B24C	뉜 B25C	뉬 B26C	뉼 B27C	늌 B28C	늜 B29C	늬 B2AC	늼 B2BC	닌 B2CC	닜 B2DC	달 B2EC	닼 B2FC
D	눭 B22D	눽 B23D	뉍 B24D	뉝 B25D	뉭 B26D	뉽 B27D	늍 B28D	늝 B29D	늭 B2AD	늽 B2BD	닍 B2CD	닝 B2DD	닭 B2ED	닽 B2FD
E	눮 B22E	눾 B23E	뉎 B24E	뉞 B25E	뉮 B26E	뉾 B27E	늎 B28E	늞 B29E	늮 B2AE	늾 B2BE	닎 B2CE	닞 B2DE	닮 B2EE	닾 B2FE
F	눯 B22F	눿 B23F	뉏 B24F	뉟 B25F	뉯 B26F	뉿 B27F	늏 B28F	늟 B29F	늯 B2AF	늿 B2BF	닏 B2CF	닟 B2DF	닯 B2EF	닿 B2FF

	B30	B31	B32	B33	B34	B35	B36	B37	B38	B39	B3A	B3B	B3C	B3D
0	대 B300	댐 B310	댠 B320	댰 B330	덀 B340	덐 B350	덠 B360	데 B370	뎀 B380	뎐 B390	뎠 B3A0	뎰 B3B0	돀 B3C0	돐 B3D0
1	댁 B301	댑 B311	댡 B321	댱 B331	덁 B341	덑 B351	덡 B361	덱 B371	뎁 B381	뎑 B391	뎡 B3A1	뎱 B3B1	돁 B3C1	돑 B3D1
2	댂 B302	댒 B312	댢 B322	댲 B332	덂 B342	덒 B352	덢 B362	덲 B372	뎂 B382	뎒 B392	뎢 B3A2	뎲 B3B2	돂 B3C2	돒 B3D2
3	댃 B303	댓 B313	댣 B323	댳 B333	덃 B343	덓 B353	덣 B363	덳 B373	뎃 B383	뎓 B393	뎣 B3A3	뎳 B3B3	돃 B3C3	돓 B3D3
4	댄 B304	댔 B314	댤 B324	댴 B334	덄 B344	더 B354	덤 B364	덴 B374	뎄 B384	뎔 B394	뎤 B3A4	뎴 B3B4	도 B3C4	돔 B3D4
5	댅 B305	댕 B315	댥 B325	댵 B335	덅 B345	덕 B355	덥 B365	덵 B375	뎅 B385	뎕 B395	뎥 B3A5	뎵 B3B5	독 B3C5	돕 B3D5
6	댆 B306	댖 B316	댦 B326	댶 B336	덆 B346	덖 B356	덦 B366	덶 B376	뎆 B386	뎖 B396	뎦 B3A6	뎶 B3B6	돆 B3C6	돖 B3D6
7	댇 B307	댗 B317	댧 B327	댷 B337	덇 B347	덗 B357	덧 B367	덷 B377	뎇 B387	뎗 B397	뎧 B3A7	뎷 B3B7	돇 B3C7	돗 B3D7
8	댈 B308	댘 B318	댨 B328	댸 B338	덈 B348	던 B358	덨 B368	델 B378	뎈 B388	뎘 B398	뎨 B3A8	뎸 B3B8	돈 B3C8	돘 B3D8
9	댉 B309	댙 B319	댩 B329	댹 B339	덉 B349	덙 B359	덩 B369	덹 B379	뎉 B389	뎙 B399	뎩 B3A9	뎹 B3B9	돉 B3C9	동 B3D9
A	댊 B30A	댚 B31A	댪 B32A	댺 B33A	덊 B34A	덚 B35A	덪 B36A	덺 B37A	뎊 B38A	뎚 B39A	뎪 B3AA	뎺 B3BA	돊 B3CA	돚 B3DA
B	댋 B30B	댛 B31B	댫 B32B	댻 B33B	덋 B34B	덛 B35B	덫 B36B	덻 B37B	뎋 B38B	뎛 B39B	뎫 B3AB	뎻 B3BB	돋 B3CB	돛 B3DB
C	댌 B30C	댜 B31C	댬 B32C	댼 B33C	덌 B34C	덜 B35C	덬 B36C	덼 B37C	뎌 B38C	뎜 B39C	뎬 B3AC	뎼 B3BC	돌 B3CC	돜 B3DC
D	댍 B30D	댝 B31D	댭 B32D	댽 B33D	덍 B34D	덝 B35D	덭 B36D	덽 B37D	뎍 B38D	뎝 B39D	뎭 B3AD	뎽 B3BD	돍 B3CD	돝 B3DD
E	댎 B30E	댞 B31E	댮 B32E	댾 B33E	덎 B34E	덞 B35E	덮 B36E	덾 B37E	뎎 B38E	뎞 B39E	뎮 B3AE	뎾 B3BE	돎 B3CE	돞 B3DE
F	댏 B30F	댟 B31F	댯 B32F	댿 B33F	덏 B34F	덟 B35F	덯 B36F	덿 B37F	뎏 B38F	뎟 B39F	뎯 B3AF	뎿 B3BF	돏 B3CF	돟 B3DF

	B3E	B3F	B40	B41	B42	B43	B44	B45	B46	B47	B48	B49	B4A	B4B
0	돠 B3E0	돰 B3F0	됀 B400	됐 B410	될 B420	됰 B430	둀 B440	두 B450	둠 B460	둰 B470	뒀 B480	뒐 B490	뒠 B4A0	뒰 B4B0
1	돡 B3E1	돱 B3F1	됁 B401	됑 B411	됡 B421	됱 B431	둁 B441	둑 B451	둡 B461	둱 B471	뒁 B481	뒑 B491	뒡 B4A1	뒱 B4B1
2	돢 B3E2	돲 B3F2	됂 B402	됒 B412	됢 B422	됲 B432	둂 B442	둒 B452	둢 B462	둲 B472	뒂 B482	뒒 B492	뒢 B4A2	뒲 B4B2
3	돣 B3E3	돳 B3F3	됃 B403	됓 B413	됣 B423	됳 B433	둃 B443	둓 B453	둣 B463	둳 B473	뒃 B483	뒓 B493	뒣 B4A3	뒳 B4B3
4	돤 B3E4	돴 B3F4	됄 B404	됔 B414	됤 B424	됴 B434	둄 B444	둔 B454	둤 B464	둴 B474	뒄 B484	뒔 B494	뒤 B4A4	뒴 B4B4
5	돥 B3E5	돵 B3F5	됅 B405	됕 B415	됥 B425	됵 B435	둅 B445	둕 B455	둥 B465	둵 B475	뒅 B485	뒕 B495	뒥 B4A5	뒵 B4B5
6	돦 B3E6	돶 B3F6	됆 B406	됖 B416	됦 B426	됶 B436	둆 B446	둖 B456	둦 B466	둶 B476	뒆 B486	뒖 B496	뒦 B4A6	뒶 B4B6
7	돧 B3E7	돷 B3F7	됇 B407	됗 B417	됧 B427	됷 B437	둇 B447	둗 B457	둧 B467	둷 B477	뒇 B487	뒗 B497	뒧 B4A7	뒷 B4B7
8	돨 B3E8	돸 B3F8	됈 B408	되 B418	됨 B428	됸 B438	둈 B448	둘 B458	둨 B468	둸 B478	뒈 B488	뒘 B498	뒨 B4A8	뒸 B4B8
9	돩 B3E9	돹 B3F9	됉 B409	됙 B419	됩 B429	됹 B439	둉 B449	둙 B459	둩 B469	둹 B479	뒉 B489	뒙 B499	뒩 B4A9	뒹 B4B9
A	돪 B3EA	돺 B3FA	됊 B40A	됚 B41A	됪 B42A	됺 B43A	둊 B44A	둚 B45A	둪 B46A	둺 B47A	뒊 B48A	뒚 B49A	뒪 B4AA	뒺 B4BA
B	돫 B3EB	돻 B3FB	됋 B40B	됛 B41B	됫 B42B	됻 B43B	둋 B44B	둛 B45B	둫 B46B	둻 B47B	뒋 B48B	뒛 B49B	뒫 B4AB	뒻 B4BB
C	돬 B3EC	돼 B3FC	됌 B40C	된 B41C	됬 B42C	됼 B43C	둌 B44C	둜 B45C	둬 B46C	둼 B47C	뒌 B48C	뒜 B49C	뒬 B4AC	뒼 B4BC
D	돭 B3ED	돽 B3FD	됍 B40D	됝 B41D	됭 B42D	됽 B43D	둍 B44D	둝 B45D	둭 B46D	둽 B47D	뒍 B48D	뒝 B49D	뒭 B4AD	뒽 B4BD
E	돮 B3EE	돾 B3FE	됎 B40E	됞 B41E	됮 B42E	됾 B43E	둎 B44E	둞 B45E	둮 B46E	둾 B47E	뒎 B48E	뒞 B49E	뒮 B4AE	뒾 B4BE
F	돯 B3EF	돿 B3FF	됏 B40F	됟 B41F	됯 B42F	됿 B43F	둏 B44F	둟 B45F	둯 B46F	둿 B47F	뒏 B48F	뒟 B49F	뒯 B4AF	뒿 B4BF

	B4C	B4D	B4E	B4F	B50	B51	B52	B53	B54	B55	B56	B57	B58	B59
0	듀 B4C0	듐 B4D0	든 B4E0	듰 B4F0	딀 B500	딐 B510	딠 B520	따 B530	땀 B540	땐 B550	땠 B560	땰 B570	떀 B580	떐 B590
1	듁 B4C1	듑 B4D1	듡 B4E1	등 B4F1	딁 B501	딑 B511	딡 B521	딱 B531	땁 B541	땑 B551	땡 B561	땱 B571	떁 B581	떑 B591
2	듂 B4C2	듒 B4D2	듢 B4E2	듲 B4F2	딂 B502	딒 B512	딢 B522	딲 B532	땂 B542	땒 B552	땢 B562	땲 B572	떂 B582	떒 B592
3	듃 B4C3	듓 B4D3	듣 B4E3	듳 B4F3	딃 B503	딓 B513	딣 B523	딳 B533	땃 B543	땓 B553	땣 B563	땳 B573	떃 B583	떓 B593
4	듄 B4C4	듔 B4D4	들 B4E4	듴 B4F4	딄 B504	디 B514	딤 B524	딴 B534	땄 B544	땔 B554	땤 B564	땴 B574	떄 B584	떔 B594
5	듅 B4C5	듕 B4D5	듥 B4E5	듵 B4F5	딅 B505	딕 B515	딥 B525	딵 B535	땅 B545	땕 B555	땥 B565	땵 B575	떅 B585	떕 B595
6	듆 B4C6	듖 B4D6	듦 B4E6	듶 B4F6	딆 B506	딖 B516	딦 B526	딶 B536	땆 B546	땖 B556	땦 B566	땶 B576	떆 B586	떖 B596
7	듇 B4C7	듗 B4D7	듧 B4E7	듷 B4F7	딇 B507	딗 B517	딧 B527	딷 B537	땇 B547	땗 B557	땧 B567	땷 B577	떇 B587	떗 B597
8	듈 B4C8	듘 B4D8	듨 B4E8	듸 B4F8	딈 B508	딘 B518	딨 B528	딸 B538	땈 B548	땘 B558	땨 B568	땸 B578	떈 B588	떘 B598
9	듉 B4C9	듙 B4D9	듩 B4E9	듹 B4F9	딉 B509	딙 B519	딩 B529	딹 B539	땉 B549	땙 B559	땩 B569	땹 B579	떉 B589	떙 B599
A	듊 B4CA	듚 B4DA	듪 B4EA	듺 B4FA	딊 B50A	딚 B51A	딪 B52A	딺 B53A	땊 B54A	땚 B55A	땪 B56A	땺 B57A	떊 B58A	떚 B59A
B	듋 B4CB	듛 B4DB	듫 B4EB	듻 B4FB	딋 B50B	딛 B51B	딫 B52B	딻 B53B	땋 B54B	땛 B55B	땫 B56B	땻 B57B	떋 B58B	떛 B59B
C	듌 B4CC	드 B4DC	듬 B4EC	듼 B4FC	딌 B50C	딜 B51C	딬 B52C	딼 B53C	때 B54C	땜 B55C	땬 B56C	땼 B57C	떌 B58C	떜 B59C
D	듍 B4CD	득 B4DD	듭 B4ED	듽 B4FD	딍 B50D	딝 B51D	딭 B52D	딽 B53D	땍 B54D	땝 B55D	땭 B56D	땽 B57D	떍 B58D	떝 B59D
E	듎 B4CE	듞 B4DE	듮 B4EE	듾 B4FE	딎 B50E	딞 B51E	딮 B52E	딾 B53E	땎 B54E	땞 B55E	땮 B56E	땾 B57E	떎 B58E	떞 B59E
F	듏 B4CF	듟 B4DF	듯 B4EF	듿 B4FF	딏 B50F	딟 B51F	딯 B52F	딿 B53F	땏 B54F	땟 B55F	땯 B56F	땿 B57F	떏 B58F	떟 B59F

	B5A	B5B	B5C	B5D	B5E	B5F	B60	B61	B62	B63	B64	B65	B66	B67
0	떠 B5A0	떰 B5B0	뗀 B5C0	뗐 B5D0	뗠 B5E0	뗰 B5F0	똀 B600	또 B610	똠 B620	똰 B630	뙀 B640	뙐 B650	뙠 B660	뙰 B670
1	떡 B5A1	떱 B5B1	뗁 B5C1	뗑 B5D1	뗡 B5E1	뗱 B5F1	똁 B601	똑 B611	똡 B621	똱 B631	뙁 B641	뙑 B651	뙡 B661	뙱 B671
2	떢 B5A2	떲 B5B2	뗂 B5C2	뗒 B5D2	뗢 B5E2	뗲 B5F2	똂 B602	똒 B612	똢 B622	똲 B632	뙂 B642	뙒 B652	뙢 B662	뙲 B672
3	떣 B5A3	떳 B5B3	뗃 B5C3	뗓 B5D3	뗣 B5E3	뗳 B5F3	똃 B603	똓 B613	똣 B623	똳 B633	뙃 B643	뙓 B653	뙣 B663	뙳 B673
4	떤 B5A4	떴 B5B4	뗄 B5C4	뗔 B5D4	뗤 B5E4	뗴 B5F4	똄 B604	똔 B614	똤 B624	똴 B634	뙄 B644	뙔 B654	뙤 B664	뙴 B674
5	떥 B5A5	떵 B5B5	뗅 B5C5	뗕 B5D5	뗥 B5E5	뗵 B5F5	똅 B605	똕 B615	똥 B625	똵 B635	뙅 B645	뙕 B655	뙥 B665	뙵 B675
6	떦 B5A6	떶 B5B6	뗆 B5C6	뗖 B5D6	뗦 B5E6	뗶 B5F6	똆 B606	똖 B616	똦 B626	똶 B636	뙆 B646	뙖 B656	뙦 B666	뙶 B676
7	떧 B5A7	떷 B5B7	뗇 B5C7	뗗 B5D7	뗧 B5E7	뗷 B5F7	똇 B607	똗 B617	똧 B627	똷 B637	뙇 B647	뙗 B657	뙧 B667	뙷 B677
8	떨 B5A8	떸 B5B8	뗈 B5C8	뗘 B5D8	뗨 B5E8	뗸 B5F8	똈 B608	똘 B618	똨 B628	똸 B638	뙈 B648	뙘 B658	뙨 B668	뙸 B678
9	떩 B5A9	떹 B5B9	뗉 B5C9	뗙 B5D9	뗩 B5E9	뗹 B5F9	똉 B609	똙 B619	똩 B629	똹 B639	뙉 B649	뙙 B659	뙩 B669	뙹 B679
A	떪 B5AA	떺 B5BA	뗊 B5CA	뗚 B5DA	뗪 B5EA	뗺 B5FA	똊 B60A	똚 B61A	똪 B62A	똺 B63A	뙊 B64A	뙚 B65A	뙪 B66A	뙺 B67A
B	떫 B5AB	떻 B5BB	뗋 B5CB	뗛 B5DB	뗫 B5EB	뗻 B5FB	똋 B60B	똛 B61B	똫 B62B	똻 B63B	뙋 B64B	뙛 B65B	뙫 B66B	뙻 B67B
C	떬 B5AC	떼 B5BC	뗌 B5CC	뗜 B5DC	뗬 B5EC	뗼 B5FC	똌 B60C	똜 B61C	똬 B62C	똼 B63C	뙌 B64C	뙜 B65C	뙬 B66C	뙼 B67C
D	떭 B5AD	떽 B5BD	뗍 B5CD	뗝 B5DD	뗭 B5ED	뗽 B5FD	똍 B60D	똝 B61D	똭 B62D	똽 B63D	뙍 B64D	뙝 B65D	뙭 B66D	뙽 B67D
E	떮 B5AE	떾 B5BE	뗎 B5CE	뗞 B5DE	뗮 B5EE	뗾 B5FE	똎 B60E	똞 B61E	똮 B62E	똾 B63E	뙎 B64E	뙞 B65E	뙮 B66E	뙾 B67E
F	떯 B5AF	떿 B5BF	뗏 B5CF	뗟 B5DF	뗯 B5EF	뗿 B5FF	똏 B60F	똟 B61F	똯 B62F	똿 B63F	뙏 B64F	뙟 B65F	뙯 B66F	뙿 B67F

	B68	B69	B6A	B6B	B6C	B6D	B6E	B6F	B70	B71	B72	B73	B74	B75
0	뚀 B680	뚐 B690	뚠 B6A0	뚰 B6B0	뛀 B6C0	뛐 B6D0	뛠 B6E0	뛰 B6F0	뜀 B700	뜐 B710	뜠 B720	뜰 B730	띀 B740	띐 B750
1	뚁 B681	뚑 B691	뚡 B6A1	뚱 B6B1	뛁 B6C1	뛑 B6D1	뛡 B6E1	뛱 B6F1	뜁 B701	뜑 B711	뜡 B721	뜱 B731	띁 B741	띑 B751
2	뚂 B682	뚒 B692	뚢 B6A2	뚲 B6B2	뛂 B6C2	뛒 B6D2	뛢 B6E2	뛲 B6F2	뜂 B702	뜒 B712	뜢 B722	뜲 B732	띂 B742	띒 B752
3	뚃 B683	뚓 B693	뚣 B6A3	뚳 B6B3	뛃 B6C3	뛓 B6D3	뛣 B6E3	뛳 B6F3	뜃 B703	뜓 B713	뜣 B723	뜳 B733	띃 B743	띓 B753
4	뚄 B684	뚔 B694	뚤 B6A4	뚴 B6B4	뛄 B6C4	뛔 B6D4	뛤 B6E4	뛴 B6F4	뜄 B704	뜔 B714	뜤 B724	뜴 B734	띄 B744	띔 B754
5	뚅 B685	뚕 B695	뚥 B6A5	뚵 B6B5	뛅 B6C5	뛕 B6D5	뛥 B6E5	뛵 B6F5	뜅 B705	뜕 B715	뜥 B725	뜵 B735	띅 B745	띕 B755
6	뚆 B686	뚖 B696	뚦 B6A6	뚶 B6B6	뛆 B6C6	뛖 B6D6	뛦 B6E6	뛶 B6F6	뜆 B706	뜖 B716	뜦 B726	뜶 B736	띆 B746	띖 B756
7	뚇 B687	뚗 B697	뚧 B6A7	뚷 B6B7	뛇 B6C7	뛗 B6D7	뛧 B6E7	뛷 B6F7	뜇 B707	뜗 B717	뜧 B727	뜷 B737	띇 B747	띗 B757
8	뚈 B688	뚘 B698	뚨 B6A8	뚸 B6B8	뛈 B6C8	뛘 B6D8	뛨 B6E8	뛸 B6F8	뜈 B708	뜘 B718	뜨 B728	뜸 B738	띈 B748	띘 B758
9	뚉 B689	뚙 B699	뚩 B6A9	뚹 B6B9	뛉 B6C9	뛙 B6D9	뛩 B6E9	뛹 B6F9	뜉 B709	뜙 B719	뜩 B729	뜹 B739	띉 B749	띙 B759
A	뚊 B68A	뚚 B69A	뚪 B6AA	뚺 B6BA	뛊 B6CA	뛚 B6DA	뛪 B6EA	뛺 B6FA	뜊 B70A	뜚 B71A	뜪 B72A	뜺 B73A	띊 B74A	띚 B75A
B	뚋 B68B	뚛 B69B	뚫 B6AB	뚻 B6BB	뛋 B6CB	뛛 B6DB	뛫 B6EB	뛻 B6FB	뜋 B70B	뜛 B71B	뜫 B72B	뜻 B73B	띋 B74B	띛 B75B
C	뚌 B68C	뚜 B69C	뚬 B6AC	뚼 B6BC	뛌 B6CC	뛜 B6DC	뛬 B6EC	뛼 B6FC	뜌 B70C	뜜 B71C	뜬 B72C	뜼 B73C	띌 B74C	띜 B75C
D	뚍 B68D	뚝 B69D	뚭 B6AD	뚽 B6BD	뛍 B6CD	뛝 B6DD	뛭 B6ED	뛽 B6FD	뜍 B70D	뜝 B71D	뜭 B72D	뜽 B73D	띍 B74D	띝 B75D
E	뚎 B68E	뚞 B69E	뚮 B6AE	뚾 B6BE	뛎 B6CE	뛞 B6DE	뛮 B6EE	뛾 B6FE	뜎 B70E	뜞 B71E	뜮 B72E	뜾 B73E	띎 B74E	띞 B75E
F	뚏 B68F	뚟 B69F	뚯 B6AF	뚿 B6BF	뛏 B6CF	뛟 B6DF	뛯 B6EF	뛿 B6FF	뜏 B70F	뜟 B71F	뜯 B72F	뜿 B73F	띏 B74F	띟 B75F

	B76	B77	B78	B79	B7A	B7B	B7C	B7D	B7E	B7F	B80	B81	B82	B83
0	띠 B760	띰 B770	란 B780	랐 B790	랠 B7A0	랰 B7B0	럀 B7C0	럐 B7D0	럠 B7E0	런 B7F0	렀 B800	렐 B810	렠 B820	렰 B830
1	띡 B761	띱 B771	랁 B781	랑 B791	랡 B7A1	랱 B7B1	럁 B7C1	럑 B7D1	럡 B7E1	럱 B7F1	렁 B801	렑 B811	렡 B821	렱 B831
2	띢 B762	띲 B772	랂 B782	랒 B792	랢 B7A2	랲 B7B2	럂 B7C2	럒 B7D2	럢 B7E2	럲 B7F2	렂 B802	렒 B812	렢 B822	렲 B832
3	띣 B763	띳 B773	랃 B783	랓 B793	랣 B7A3	랳 B7B3	럃 B7C3	럓 B7D3	럣 B7E3	럳 B7F3	렃 B803	렓 B813	렣 B823	렳 B833
4	띤 B764	띴 B774	랄 B784	랔 B794	랤 B7A4	랴 B7B4	럄 B7C4	럔 B7D4	럤 B7E4	럴 B7F4	렄 B804	렔 B814	려 B824	렴 B834
5	띥 B765	띵 B775	랅 B785	랕 B795	랥 B7A5	략 B7B5	럅 B7C5	럕 B7D5	럥 B7E5	럵 B7F5	렅 B805	렕 B815	력 B825	렵 B835
6	띦 B766	띶 B776	랆 B786	랖 B796	랦 B7A6	랶 B7B6	럆 B7C6	럖 B7D6	럦 B7E6	럶 B7F6	렆 B806	렖 B816	렦 B826	렶 B836
7	띧 B767	띷 B777	랇 B787	랗 B797	랧 B7A7	랷 B7B7	럇 B7C7	럗 B7D7	럧 B7E7	럷 B7F7	렇 B807	렗 B817	렧 B827	렷 B837
8	띨 B768	띸 B778	랈 B788	래 B798	램 B7A8	랸 B7B8	럈 B7C8	럘 B7D8	럨 B7E8	럸 B7F8	레 B808	렘 B818	련 B828	렸 B838
9	띩 B769	띹 B779	랉 B789	랙 B799	랩 B7A9	랹 B7B9	량 B7C9	럙 B7D9	럩 B7E9	럹 B7F9	렉 B809	렙 B819	렩 B829	령 B839
A	띪 B76A	띺 B77A	랊 B78A	랚 B79A	랪 B7AA	랺 B7BA	럊 B7CA	럚 B7DA	럪 B7EA	럺 B7FA	렊 B80A	렚 B81A	렪 B82A	렺 B83A
B	띫 B76B	띻 B77B	랋 B78B	랛 B79B	랫 B7AB	랻 B7BB	럋 B7CB	럛 B7DB	럫 B7EB	럻 B7FB	렋 B80B	렛 B81B	렫 B82B	렻 B83B
C	띬 B76C	라 B77C	람 B78C	랜 B79C	랬 B7AC	랼 B7BC	럌 B7CC	럜 B7DC	러 B7EC	럼 B7FC	렌 B80C	렜 B81C	렬 B82C	렼 B83C
D	띭 B76D	락 B77D	랍 B78D	랝 B79D	랭 B7AD	랽 B7BD	럍 B7CD	럝 B7DD	럭 B7ED	럽 B7FD	렍 B80D	렝 B81D	렭 B82D	렽 B83D
E	띮 B76E	띾 B77E	랎 B78E	랞 B79E	랮 B7AE	랾 B7BE	럎 B7CE	럞 B7DE	럮 B7EE	럾 B7FE	렎 B80E	렞 B81E	렮 B82E	렾 B83E
F	띯 B76F	띿 B77F	랏 B78F	랟 B79F	랯 B7AF	랿 B7BF	럏 B7CF	럟 B7DF	럯 B7EF	럿 B7FF	렏 B80F	렟 B81F	렯 B82F	렿 B83F

	B84	B85	B86	B87	B88	B89	B8A	B8B	B8C	B8D	B8E	B8F	B90	B91
0	례 B840	롐 B850	론 B860	롰 B870	뢀 B880	뢐 B890	뢠 B8A0	뢰 B8B0	룀 B8C0	룐 B8D0	룠 B8E0	룰 B8F0	뤀 B900	뤐 B910
1	롁 B841	롑 B851	롡 B861	롱 B871	뢁 B881	뢑 B891	뢡 B8A1	뢱 B8B1	룁 B8C1	룑 B8D1	룡 B8E1	룱 B8F1	뤁 B901	뤑 B911
2	롂 B842	롒 B852	롢 B862	롲 B872	뢂 B882	뢒 B892	뢢 B8A2	뢲 B8B2	룂 B8C2	룒 B8D2	룢 B8E2	룲 B8F2	뤂 B902	뤒 B912
3	롃 B843	롓 B853	롣 B863	롳 B873	뢃 B883	뢓 B893	뢣 B8A3	뢳 B8B3	룃 B8C3	룓 B8D3	룣 B8E3	룳 B8F3	뤃 B903	뤓 B913
4	롄 B844	롔 B854	롤 B864	롴 B874	뢄 B884	뢔 B894	뢤 B8A4	뢴 B8B4	룄 B8C4	룔 B8D4	룤 B8E4	룴 B8F4	뤄 B904	뤔 B914
5	롅 B845	롕 B855	롥 B865	롵 B875	뢅 B885	뢕 B895	뢥 B8A5	뢵 B8B5	룅 B8C5	룕 B8D5	룥 B8E5	룵 B8F5	뤅 B905	뤕 B915
6	롆 B846	롖 B856	롦 B866	롶 B876	뢆 B886	뢖 B896	뢦 B8A6	뢶 B8B6	룆 B8C6	룖 B8D6	룦 B8E6	룶 B8F6	뤆 B906	뤖 B916
7	롇 B847	롗 B857	롧 B867	롷 B877	뢇 B887	뢗 B897	뢧 B8A7	뢷 B8B7	룇 B8C7	룗 B8D7	룧 B8E7	룷 B8F7	뤇 B907	뤗 B917
8	롈 B848	롘 B858	롨 B868	롸 B878	뢈 B888	뢘 B898	뢨 B8A8	뢸 B8B8	룈 B8C8	룘 B8D8	루 B8E8	룸 B8F8	뤈 B908	뤘 B918
9	롉 B849	롙 B859	롩 B869	롹 B879	뢉 B889	뢙 B899	뢩 B8A9	뢹 B8B9	룉 B8C9	룙 B8D9	룩 B8E9	룹 B8F9	뤉 B909	뤙 B919
A	롊 B84A	롚 B85A	롪 B86A	롺 B87A	뢊 B88A	뢚 B89A	뢪 B8AA	뢺 B8BA	룊 B8CA	룚 B8DA	룪 B8EA	룺 B8FA	뤊 B90A	뤚 B91A
B	롋 B84B	롛 B85B	롫 B86B	롻 B87B	뢋 B88B	뢛 B89B	뢫 B8AB	뢻 B8BB	룋 B8CB	룛 B8DB	룫 B8EB	룻 B8FB	뤋 B90B	뤛 B91B
C	롌 B84C	로 B85C	롬 B86C	롼 B87C	뢌 B88C	뢜 B89C	뢬 B8AC	뢼 B8BC	료 B8CC	룜 B8DC	룬 B8EC	룼 B8FC	뤌 B90C	뤜 B91C
D	롍 B84D	록 B85D	롭 B86D	롽 B87D	뢍 B88D	뢝 B89D	뢭 B8AD	뢽 B8BD	룍 B8CD	룝 B8DD	룭 B8ED	룽 B8FD	뤍 B90D	뤝 B91D
E	롎 B84E	롞 B85E	롮 B86E	롾 B87E	뢎 B88E	뢞 B89E	뢮 B8AE	뢾 B8BE	룎 B8CE	룞 B8DE	룮 B8EE	룾 B8FE	뤎 B90E	뤞 B91E
F	롏 B84F	롟 B85F	롯 B86F	롿 B87F	뢏 B88F	뢟 B89F	뢯 B8AF	뢿 B8BF	룏 B8CF	룟 B8DF	룯 B8EF	룿 B8FF	뤏 B90F	뤟 B91F

	B92	B93	B94	B95	B96	B97	B98	B99	B9A	B9B	B9C	B9D	B9E	B9F
0	뤠 B920	뤰 B930	륀 B940	륐 B950	률 B960	륰 B970	릀 B980	릐 B990	릠 B9A0	린 B9B0	맀 B9C0	말 B9D0	맠 B9E0	맰 B9F0
1	뤡 B921	뤱 B931	륁 B941	륑 B951	륡 B961	륱 B971	릁 B981	릑 B991	릡 B9A1	릱 B9B1	링 B9C1	맑 B9D1	맡 B9E1	맱 B9F1
2	뤢 B922	뤲 B932	륂 B942	륒 B952	륢 B962	륲 B972	릂 B982	릒 B992	릢 B9A2	릲 B9B2	맂 B9C2	맒 B9D2	맢 B9E2	맲 B9F2
3	뤣 B923	뤳 B933	륃 B943	륓 B953	륣 B963	륳 B973	릃 B983	릓 B993	릣 B9A3	릳 B9B3	맃 B9C3	맓 B9D3	맣 B9E3	맳 B9F3
4	뤤 B924	뤴 B934	륄 B944	륔 B954	륤 B964	르 B974	름 B984	릔 B994	릤 B9A4	릴 B9B4	맄 B9C4	맔 B9D4	매 B9E4	맴 B9F4
5	뤥 B925	뤵 B935	륅 B945	륕 B955	륥 B965	륵 B975	릅 B985	릕 B995	릥 B9A5	릵 B9B5	맅 B9C5	맕 B9D5	맥 B9E5	맵 B9F5
6	뤦 B926	뤶 B936	륆 B946	륖 B956	륦 B966	륶 B976	릆 B986	릖 B996	릦 B9A6	릶 B9B6	맆 B9C6	맖 B9D6	맦 B9E6	맶 B9F6
7	뤧 B927	뤷 B937	륇 B947	륗 B957	륧 B967	륷 B977	릇 B987	릗 B997	릧 B9A7	릷 B9B7	맇 B9C7	맗 B9D7	맧 B9E7	맷 B9F7
8	뤨 B928	뤸 B938	륈 B948	류 B958	륨 B968	른 B978	릈 B988	릘 B998	릨 B9A8	릸 B9B8	마 B9C8	맘 B9D8	맨 B9E8	맸 B9F8
9	뤩 B929	뤹 B939	륉 B949	륙 B959	륩 B969	륹 B979	릉 B989	릙 B999	릩 B9A9	릹 B9B9	막 B9C9	맙 B9D9	맩 B9E9	맹 B9F9
A	뤪 B92A	뤺 B93A	륊 B94A	륚 B95A	륪 B96A	륺 B97A	릊 B98A	릚 B99A	릪 B9AA	릺 B9BA	맊 B9CA	맚 B9DA	맪 B9EA	맺 B9FA
B	뤫 B92B	뤻 B93B	륋 B94B	륛 B95B	륫 B96B	륻 B97B	릋 B98B	릛 B99B	릫 B9AB	릻 B9BB	맋 B9CB	맛 B9DB	맫 B9EB	맻 B9FB
C	뤬 B92C	뤼 B93C	륌 B94C	륜 B95C	륬 B96C	를 B97C	릌 B98C	릜 B99C	리 B9AC	림 B9BC	만 B9CC	맜 B9DC	맬 B9EC	맼 B9FC
D	뤭 B92D	뤽 B93D	륍 B94D	륝 B95D	륭 B96D	륽 B97D	릍 B98D	릝 B99D	릭 B9AD	립 B9BD	맍 B9CD	망 B9DD	맭 B9ED	맽 B9FD
E	뤮 B92E	뤾 B93E	륎 B94E	륞 B95E	륮 B96E	륾 B97E	릎 B98E	릞 B99E	릮 B9AE	릾 B9BE	많 B9CE	맞 B9DE	맮 B9EE	맾 B9FE
F	뤯 B92F	뤿 B93F	륏 B94F	륟 B95F	륯 B96F	륿 B97F	릏 B98F	릟 B99F	릯 B9AF	릿 B9BF	맏 B9CF	맟 B9DF	맯 B9EF	맿 B9FF

	BA0	BA1	BA2	BA3	BA4	BA5	BA6	BA7	BA8	BA9	BAA	BAB	BAC	BAD
0	먀 BA00	먐 BA10	먠 BA20	먰 BA30	멀 BA40	멐 BA50	멠 BA60	며 BA70	몀 BA80	몐 BA90	몠 BAA0	몰 BAB0	뫀 BAC0	뫐 BAD0
1	먁 BA01	먑 BA11	먡 BA21	먱 BA31	멁 BA41	멑 BA51	멡 BA61	멱 BA71	몁 BA81	몑 BA91	몡 BAA1	몱 BAB1	뫁 BAC1	뫑 BAD1
2	먂 BA02	먒 BA12	먢 BA22	먲 BA32	멂 BA42	멒 BA52	멢 BA62	멲 BA72	몂 BA82	몒 BA92	몢 BAA2	몲 BAB2	뫂 BAC2	뫒 BAD2
3	먃 BA03	먓 BA13	먣 BA23	먳 BA33	멃 BA43	멓 BA53	멣 BA63	멳 BA73	몃 BA83	몓 BA93	몣 BAA3	몳 BAB3	뫃 BAC3	뫓 BAD3
4	먄 BA04	먔 BA14	먤 BA24	먴 BA34	멄 BA44	메 BA54	멤 BA64	면 BA74	몄 BA84	몔 BA94	몤 BAA4	몴 BAB4	뫄 BAC4	뫔 BAD4
5	먅 BA05	먕 BA15	먥 BA25	먵 BA35	멅 BA45	멕 BA55	멥 BA65	멵 BA75	명 BA85	몕 BA95	몥 BAA5	몵 BAB5	뫅 BAC5	뫕 BAD5
6	먆 BA06	먖 BA16	먦 BA26	먶 BA36	멆 BA46	멖 BA56	멦 BA66	멶 BA76	몆 BA86	몖 BA96	몦 BAA6	몶 BAB6	뫆 BAC6	뫖 BAD6
7	먇 BA07	먗 BA17	먧 BA27	먷 BA37	멇 BA47	멗 BA57	멧 BA67	멷 BA77	몇 BA87	몗 BA97	몧 BAA7	몷 BAB7	뫇 BAC7	뫗 BAD7
8	먈 BA08	먘 BA18	먨 BA28	머 BA38	멈 BA48	멘 BA58	멨 BA68	멸 BA78	몈 BA88	몘 BA98	모 BAA8	몸 BAB8	뫈 BAC8	뫘 BAD8
9	먉 BA09	먙 BA19	먩 BA29	먹 BA39	멉 BA49	멙 BA59	멩 BA69	멹 BA79	몉 BA89	몙 BA99	목 BAA9	몹 BAB9	뫉 BAC9	뫙 BAD9
A	먊 BA0A	먚 BA1A	먪 BA2A	먺 BA3A	멊 BA4A	멚 BA5A	멪 BA6A	멺 BA7A	몊 BA8A	몚 BA9A	몪 BAAA	몺 BABA	뫊 BACA	뫚 BADA
B	먋 BA0B	먛 BA1B	먫 BA2B	먻 BA3B	멋 BA4B	멛 BA5B	멫 BA6B	멻 BA7B	몋 BA8B	몛 BA9B	몫 BAAB	못 BABB	뫋 BACB	뫛 BADB
C	먌 BA0C	먜 BA1C	먬 BA2C	먼 BA3C	멌 BA4C	멜 BA5C	멬 BA6C	멼 BA7C	몌 BA8C	몜 BA9C	몬 BAAC	몼 BABC	뫌 BACC	뫜 BADC
D	먍 BA0D	먝 BA1D	먭 BA2D	먽 BA3D	멍 BA4D	멝 BA5D	멭 BA6D	멽 BA7D	몍 BA8D	몝 BA9D	몭 BAAD	몽 BABD	뫍 BACD	뫝 BADD
E	먎 BA0E	먞 BA1E	먮 BA2E	먾 BA3E	멎 BA4E	멞 BA5E	멮 BA6E	멾 BA7E	몎 BA8E	몞 BA9E	몮 BAAE	몾 BABE	뫎 BACE	뫞 BADE
F	먏 BA0F	먟 BA1F	먯 BA2F	먿 BA3F	멏 BA4F	멟 BA5F	멯 BA6F	멿 BA7F	몏 BA8F	몟 BA9F	몯 BAAF	몿 BABF	뫏 BACF	뫟 BADF

	BAE	BAF	BB0	BB1	BB2	BB3	BB4	BB5	BB6	BB7	BB8	BB9	BBA	BBB
0	뫠 BAE0	뫰 BAF0	묀 BB00	묐 BB10	묠 BB20	묰 BB30	뭀 BB40	뭐 BB50	뭠 BB60	뭰 BB70	뮀 BB80	뮐 BB90	뮠 BBA0	뮰 BBB0
1	뫡 BAE1	뫱 BAF1	묁 BB01	묑 BB11	묡 BB21	묱 BB31	뭁 BB41	뭑 BB51	뭡 BB61	뭱 BB71	뮁 BB81	뮑 BB91	뮡 BBA1	뮱 BBB1
2	뫢 BAE2	뫲 BAF2	묂 BB02	묒 BB12	묢 BB22	묲 BB32	뭂 BB42	뭒 BB52	뭢 BB62	뭲 BB72	뮂 BB82	뮒 BB92	뮢 BBA2	뮲 BBB2
3	뫣 BAE3	뫳 BAF3	묃 BB03	묓 BB13	묣 BB23	묳 BB33	뭃 BB43	뭓 BB53	뭣 BB63	뭳 BB73	뮃 BB83	뮓 BB93	뮣 BBA3	뮳 BBB3
4	뫤 BAE4	뫴 BAF4	묄 BB04	묔 BB14	묤 BB24	무 BB34	뭄 BB44	뭔 BB54	뭤 BB64	뭴 BB74	뮄 BB84	뮔 BB94	뮤 BBA4	뮴 BBB4
5	뫥 BAE5	뫵 BAF5	묅 BB05	묕 BB15	묥 BB25	묵 BB35	뭅 BB45	뭕 BB55	뭥 BB65	뭵 BB75	뮅 BB85	뮕 BB95	뮥 BBA5	뮵 BBB5
6	뫦 BAE6	뫶 BAF6	묆 BB06	묖 BB16	묦 BB26	묶 BB36	뭆 BB46	뭖 BB56	뭦 BB66	뭶 BB76	뮆 BB86	뮖 BB96	뮦 BBA6	뮶 BBB6
7	뫧 BAE7	뫷 BAF7	묇 BB07	묗 BB17	묧 BB27	묷 BB37	뭇 BB47	뭗 BB57	뭧 BB67	뭷 BB77	뮇 BB87	뮗 BB97	뮧 BBA7	뮷 BBB7
8	뫨 BAE8	뫸 BAF8	묈 BB08	묘 BB18	묨 BB28	문 BB38	뭈 BB48	뭘 BB58	뭨 BB68	뭸 BB78	뮈 BB88	뮘 BB98	뮨 BBA8	뮸 BBB8
9	뫩 BAE9	뫹 BAF9	묉 BB09	묙 BB19	묩 BB29	묹 BB39	뭉 BB49	뭙 BB59	뭩 BB69	뭹 BB79	뮉 BB89	뮙 BB99	뮩 BBA9	뮹 BBB9
A	뫪 BAEA	뫺 BAFA	묊 BB0A	묚 BB1A	묪 BB2A	묺 BB3A	뭊 BB4A	뭚 BB5A	뭪 BB6A	뭺 BB7A	뮊 BB8A	뮚 BB9A	뮪 BBAA	뮺 BBBA
B	뫫 BAEB	뫻 BAFB	묋 BB0B	묛 BB1B	묫 BB2B	묻 BB3B	뭋 BB4B	뭛 BB5B	뭫 BB6B	뭻 BB7B	뮋 BB8B	뮛 BB9B	뮫 BBAB	뮻 BBBB
C	뫬 BAEC	뫼 BAFC	묌 BB0C	묜 BB1C	묬 BB2C	물 BB3C	뭌 BB4C	뭜 BB5C	뭬 BB6C	뭼 BB7C	뮌 BB8C	뮜 BB9C	뮬 BBAC	뮼 BBBC
D	뫭 BAED	뫽 BAFD	묍 BB0D	묝 BB1D	묭 BB2D	묽 BB3D	뭍 BB4D	뭝 BB5D	뭭 BB6D	뭽 BB7D	뮍 BB8D	뮝 BB9D	뮭 BBAD	뮽 BBBD
E	뫮 BAEE	뫾 BAFE	묎 BB0E	묞 BB1E	묮 BB2E	묾 BB3E	뭎 BB4E	뭞 BB5E	뭮 BB6E	뭾 BB7E	뮎 BB8E	뮞 BB9E	뮮 BBAE	뮾 BBBE
F	뫯 BAEF	뫿 BAFF	묏 BB0F	묟 BB1F	묯 BB2F	묿 BB3F	뭏 BB4F	뭟 BB5F	뭯 BB6F	뭿 BB7F	뮏 BB8F	뮟 BB9F	뮯 BBAF	뮿 BBBF

	BBC	BBD	BBE	BBF	BC0	BC1	BC2	BC3	BC4	BC5	BC6	BC7	BC8	BC9
0	므 BBC0	믐 BBD0	믠 BBE0	믰 BBF0	밀 BC00	밐 BC10	밠 BC20	배 BC30	뱀 BC40	뱐 BC50	뱠 BC60	뱰 BC70	벀 BC80	벐 BC90
1	믁 BBC1	믑 BBD1	믡 BBE1	믱 BBF1	밁 BC01	밑 BC11	밡 BC21	백 BC31	뱁 BC41	뱑 BC51	뱡 BC61	뱱 BC71	벁 BC81	벑 BC91
2	믂 BBC2	믒 BBD2	믢 BBE2	믲 BBF2	밂 BC02	밒 BC12	밢 BC22	밲 BC32	뱂 BC42	뱒 BC52	뱢 BC62	뱲 BC72	벂 BC82	벒 BC92
3	믃 BBC3	믓 BBD3	믣 BBE3	믳 BBF3	밃 BC03	밓 BC13	밣 BC23	밳 BC33	뱃 BC43	뱓 BC53	뱣 BC63	뱳 BC73	벃 BC83	벓 BC93
4	믄 BBC4	믔 BBD4	믤 BBE4	믴 BBF4	밄 BC04	바 BC14	밤 BC24	밴 BC34	뱄 BC44	뱔 BC54	뱤 BC64	뱴 BC74	버 BC84	범 BC94
5	믅 BBC5	믕 BBD5	믥 BBE5	믵 BBF5	밅 BC05	박 BC15	밥 BC25	밵 BC35	뱅 BC45	뱕 BC55	뱥 BC65	뱵 BC75	벅 BC85	법 BC95
6	믆 BBC6	믖 BBD6	믦 BBE6	믶 BBF6	밆 BC06	밖 BC16	밦 BC26	밶 BC36	뱆 BC46	뱖 BC56	뱦 BC66	뱶 BC76	벆 BC86	벖 BC96
7	믇 BBC7	믗 BBD7	믧 BBE7	믷 BBF7	밇 BC07	밗 BC17	밧 BC27	밷 BC37	뱇 BC47	뱗 BC57	뱧 BC67	뱷 BC77	벇 BC87	벗 BC97
8	믈 BBC8	믘 BBD8	믨 BBE8	미 BBF8	밈 BC08	반 BC18	밨 BC28	밸 BC38	뱈 BC48	뱘 BC58	뱨 BC68	뱸 BC78	번 BC88	벘 BC98
9	믉 BBC9	믙 BBD9	믩 BBE9	믹 BBF9	밉 BC09	밙 BC19	방 BC29	밹 BC39	뱉 BC49	뱙 BC59	뱩 BC69	뱹 BC79	벉 BC89	벙 BC99
A	믊 BBCA	믚 BBDA	믪 BBEA	믺 BBFA	밊 BC0A	밚 BC1A	밪 BC2A	밺 BC3A	뱊 BC4A	뱚 BC5A	뱪 BC6A	뱺 BC7A	벊 BC8A	벚 BC9A
B	믋 BBCB	믛 BBDB	믫 BBEB	믻 BBFB	밋 BC0B	받 BC1B	밫 BC2B	밻 BC3B	뱋 BC4B	뱛 BC5B	뱫 BC6B	뱻 BC7B	벋 BC8B	벛 BC9B
C	믌 BBCC	믜 BBDC	믬 BBEC	민 BBFC	밌 BC0C	발 BC1C	밬 BC2C	밼 BC3C	뱌 BC4C	뱜 BC5C	뱬 BC6C	뱼 BC7C	벌 BC8C	벜 BC9C
D	믍 BBCD	믝 BBDD	믭 BBED	믽 BBFD	밍 BC0D	밝 BC1D	밭 BC2D	밽 BC3D	뱍 BC4D	뱝 BC5D	뱭 BC6D	뱽 BC7D	벍 BC8D	벝 BC9D
E	믎 BBCE	믞 BBDE	믮 BBEE	믾 BBFE	밎 BC0E	밞 BC1E	밮 BC2E	밾 BC3E	뱎 BC4E	뱞 BC5E	뱮 BC6E	뱾 BC7E	벎 BC8E	벞 BC9E
F	믏 BBCF	믟 BBDF	믯 BBEF	믿 BBFF	및 BC0F	밟 BC1F	밯 BC2F	밿 BC3F	뱏 BC4F	뱟 BC5F	뱯 BC6F	뱿 BC7F	벏 BC8F	벟 BC9F

	BCA	BCB	BCC	BCD	BCE	BCF	BD0	BD1	BD2	BD3	BD4	BD5	BD6	BD7
0	베 BCA0	벰 BCB0	변 BCC0	볐 BCD0	볠 BCE0	볰 BCF0	봀 BD00	봐 BD10	봠 BD20	봰 BD30	뵀 BD40	뵐 BD50	뵠 BD60	뵰 BD70
1	벡 BCA1	벱 BCB1	볁 BCC1	병 BCD1	볡 BCE1	볱 BCF1	봁 BD01	봑 BD11	봡 BD21	봱 BD31	뵁 BD41	뵑 BD51	뵡 BD61	뵱 BD71
2	벢 BCA2	벲 BCB2	볂 BCC2	볒 BCD2	볢 BCE2	볲 BCF2	봂 BD02	봒 BD12	봢 BD22	봲 BD32	뵂 BD42	뵒 BD52	뵢 BD62	뵲 BD72
3	벣 BCA3	벳 BCB3	볃 BCC3	볓 BCD3	볣 BCE3	볳 BCF3	봃 BD03	봓 BD13	봣 BD23	봳 BD33	뵃 BD43	뵓 BD53	뵣 BD63	뵳 BD73
4	벤 BCA4	벴 BCB4	별 BCC4	볔 BCD4	볤 BCE4	보 BCF4	봄 BD04	봔 BD14	봤 BD24	봴 BD34	뵄 BD44	뵔 BD54	뵤 BD64	뵴 BD74
5	벥 BCA5	벵 BCB5	볅 BCC5	볕 BCD5	볥 BCE5	복 BCF5	봅 BD05	봕 BD15	봥 BD25	봵 BD35	뵅 BD45	뵕 BD55	뵥 BD65	뵵 BD75
6	벦 BCA6	벶 BCB6	볆 BCC6	볖 BCD6	볦 BCE6	볶 BCF6	봆 BD06	봖 BD16	봦 BD26	봶 BD36	뵆 BD46	뵖 BD56	뵦 BD66	뵶 BD76
7	벧 BCA7	벷 BCB7	볇 BCC7	볗 BCD7	볧 BCE7	볷 BCF7	봇 BD07	봗 BD17	봧 BD27	봷 BD37	뵇 BD47	뵗 BD57	뵧 BD67	뵷 BD77
8	벨 BCA8	벸 BCB8	볈 BCC8	볘 BCD8	볨 BCE8	본 BCF8	봈 BD08	봘 BD18	봨 BD28	봸 BD38	뵈 BD48	뵘 BD58	뵨 BD68	뵸 BD78
9	벩 BCA9	벹 BCB9	볉 BCC9	볙 BCD9	볩 BCE9	볹 BCF9	봉 BD09	봙 BD19	봩 BD29	봹 BD39	뵉 BD49	뵙 BD59	뵩 BD69	뵹 BD79
A	벪 BCAA	벺 BCBA	볊 BCCA	볚 BCDA	볪 BCEA	볺 BCFA	봊 BD0A	봚 BD1A	봪 BD2A	봺 BD3A	뵊 BD4A	뵚 BD5A	뵪 BD6A	뵺 BD7A
B	벫 BCAB	벻 BCBB	볋 BCCB	볛 BCDB	볫 BCEB	볻 BCFB	봋 BD0B	봛 BD1B	봫 BD2B	봻 BD3B	뵋 BD4B	뵛 BD5B	뵫 BD6B	뵻 BD7B
C	벬 BCAC	벼 BCBC	볌 BCCC	볜 BCDC	볬 BCEC	볼 BCFC	봌 BD0C	봜 BD1C	봬 BD2C	봼 BD3C	뵌 BD4C	뵜 BD5C	뵬 BD6C	뵼 BD7C
D	벭 BCAD	벽 BCBD	볍 BCCD	볝 BCDD	볭 BCED	볽 BCFD	봍 BD0D	봝 BD1D	봭 BD2D	봽 BD3D	뵍 BD4D	뵝 BD5D	뵭 BD6D	뵽 BD7D
E	벮 BCAE	벾 BCBE	볎 BCCE	볞 BCDE	볮 BCEE	볾 BCFE	봎 BD0E	봞 BD1E	봮 BD2E	봾 BD3E	뵎 BD4E	뵞 BD5E	뵮 BD6E	뵾 BD7E
F	벯 BCAF	벿 BCBF	볏 BCCF	볟 BCDF	볯 BCEF	볿 BCFF	봏 BD0F	봟 BD1F	봯 BD2F	봿 BD3F	뵏 BD4F	뵟 BD5F	뵯 BD6F	뵿 BD7F

	BD8	BD9	BDA	BDB	BDC	BDD	BDE	BDF	BE0	BE1	BE2	BE3	BE4	BE5
0	부 BD80	붐 BD90	붠 BDA0	붰 BDB0	뷀 BDC0	뷐 BDD0	뷠 BDE0	뷰 BDF0	븀 BE00	븐 BE10	븠 BE20	븰 BE30	빀 BE40	빐 BE50
1	북 BD81	붑 BD91	붡 BDA1	붱 BDB1	뷁 BDC1	뷑 BDD1	뷡 BDE1	뷱 BDF1	븁 BE01	븑 BE11	븡 BE21	븱 BE31	빁 BE41	빑 BE51
2	붂 BD82	붒 BD92	붢 BDA2	붲 BDB2	뷂 BDC2	뷒 BDD2	뷢 BDE2	뷲 BDF2	븂 BE02	븒 BE12	븢 BE22	븲 BE32	빂 BE42	빒 BE52
3	붃 BD83	붓 BD93	붣 BDA3	붳 BDB3	뷃 BDC3	뷓 BDD3	뷣 BDE3	뷳 BDF3	븃 BE03	븓 BE13	븣 BE23	븳 BE33	빃 BE43	빓 BE53
4	분 BD84	붔 BD94	붤 BDA4	붴 BDB4	뷄 BDC4	뷔 BDD4	뷤 BDE4	뷴 BDF4	븄 BE04	블 BE14	븤 BE24	븴 BE34	비 BE44	빔 BE54
5	붅 BD85	붕 BD95	붥 BDA5	붵 BDB5	뷅 BDC5	뷕 BDD5	뷥 BDE5	뷵 BDF5	븅 BE05	븕 BE15	븥 BE25	븵 BE35	빅 BE45	빕 BE55
6	붆 BD86	붖 BD96	붦 BDA6	붶 BDB6	뷆 BDC6	뷖 BDD6	뷦 BDE6	뷶 BDF6	븆 BE06	븖 BE16	븦 BE26	븶 BE36	빆 BE46	빖 BE56
7	붇 BD87	붗 BD97	붧 BDA7	붷 BDB7	뷇 BDC7	뷗 BDD7	뷧 BDE7	뷷 BDF7	븇 BE07	븗 BE17	븧 BE27	븷 BE37	빇 BE47	빗 BE57
8	불 BD88	붘 BD98	붨 BDA8	붸 BDB8	뷈 BDC8	뷘 BDD8	뷨 BDE8	뷸 BDF8	븈 BE08	븘 BE18	븨 BE28	븸 BE38	빈 BE48	빘 BE58
9	붉 BD89	붙 BD99	붩 BDA9	붹 BDB9	뷉 BDC9	뷙 BDD9	뷩 BDE9	뷹 BDF9	븉 BE09	븙 BE19	븩 BE29	븹 BE39	빉 BE49	빙 BE59
A	붊 BD8A	붚 BD9A	붪 BDAA	붺 BDBA	뷊 BDCA	뷚 BDDA	뷪 BDEA	뷺 BDFA	븊 BE0A	븚 BE1A	븪 BE2A	븺 BE3A	빊 BE4A	빚 BE5A
B	붋 BD8B	붛 BD9B	붫 BDAB	붻 BDBB	뷋 BDCB	뷛 BDDB	뷫 BDEB	뷻 BDFB	븋 BE0B	븛 BE1B	븫 BE2B	븻 BE3B	빋 BE4B	빛 BE5B
C	붌 BD8C	붜 BD9C	붬 BDAC	붼 BDBC	뷌 BDCC	뷜 BDDC	뷬 BDEC	뷼 BDFC	브 BE0C	븜 BE1C	븬 BE2C	븼 BE3C	빌 BE4C	빜 BE5C
D	붍 BD8D	붝 BD9D	붭 BDAD	붽 BDBD	뷍 BDCD	뷝 BDDD	뷭 BDED	뷽 BDFD	븍 BE0D	븝 BE1D	븭 BE2D	븽 BE3D	빍 BE4D	빝 BE5D
E	붎 BD8E	붞 BD9E	붮 BDAE	붾 BDBE	뷎 BDCE	뷞 BDDE	뷮 BDEE	뷾 BDFE	븎 BE0E	븞 BE1E	븮 BE2E	븾 BE3E	빎 BE4E	빞 BE5E
F	붏 BD8F	붟 BD9F	붯 BDAF	붿 BDBF	뷏 BDCF	뷟 BDDF	뷯 BDEF	뷿 BDFF	븏 BE0F	븟 BE1F	븯 BE2F	븿 BE3F	빏 BE4F	빟 BE5F

	BE6	BE7	BE8	BE9	BEA	BEB	BEC	BED	BEE	BEF	BF0	BF1	BF2	BF3
0	빠 BE60	빰 BE70	뺀 BE80	뺐 BE90	뺠 BEA0	뺰 BEB0	뻀 BEC0	뻐 BED0	뻠 BEE0	뻰 BEF0	뼀 BF00	뼐 BF10	뼠 BF20	뼰 BF30
1	빡 BE61	빱 BE71	뺁 BE81	뺑 BE91	뺡 BEA1	뺱 BEB1	뻁 BEC1	뻑 BED1	뻡 BEE1	뻱 BEF1	뼁 BF01	뼑 BF11	뼡 BF21	뼱 BF31
2	빢 BE62	빲 BE72	뺂 BE82	뺒 BE92	뺢 BEA2	뺲 BEB2	뻂 BEC2	뻒 BED2	뻢 BEE2	뻲 BEF2	뼂 BF02	뼒 BF12	뼢 BF22	뼲 BF32
3	빣 BE63	빳 BE73	뺃 BE83	뺓 BE93	뺣 BEA3	뺳 BEB3	뻃 BEC3	뻓 BED3	뻣 BEE3	뻳 BEF3	뼃 BF03	뼓 BF13	뼣 BF23	뼳 BF33
4	빤 BE64	빴 BE74	뺄 BE84	뺔 BE94	뺤 BEA4	뺴 BEB4	뻄 BEC4	뻔 BED4	뻤 BEE4	뻴 BEF4	뼄 BF04	뼔 BF14	뼤 BF24	뼴 BF34
5	빥 BE65	빵 BE75	뺅 BE85	뺕 BE95	뺥 BEA5	뺵 BEB5	뻅 BEC5	뻕 BED5	뻥 BEE5	뻵 BEF5	뼅 BF05	뼕 BF15	뼥 BF25	뼵 BF35
6	빦 BE66	빶 BE76	뺆 BE86	뺖 BE96	뺦 BEA6	뺶 BEB6	뻆 BEC6	뻖 BED6	뻦 BEE6	뻶 BEF6	뼆 BF06	뼖 BF16	뼦 BF26	뼶 BF36
7	빧 BE67	빷 BE77	뺇 BE87	뺗 BE97	뺧 BEA7	뺷 BEB7	뻇 BEC7	뻗 BED7	뻧 BEE7	뻷 BEF7	뼇 BF07	뼗 BF17	뼧 BF27	뼷 BF37
8	빨 BE68	빸 BE78	뺈 BE88	뺘 BE98	뺨 BEA8	뺸 BEB8	뻈 BEC8	뻘 BED8	뻨 BEE8	뻸 BEF8	뼈 BF08	뼘 BF18	뼨 BF28	뼸 BF38
9	빩 BE69	빹 BE79	뺉 BE89	뺙 BE99	뺩 BEA9	뺹 BEB9	뻉 BEC9	뻙 BED9	뻩 BEE9	뻹 BEF9	뼉 BF09	뼙 BF19	뼩 BF29	뼹 BF39
A	빪 BE6A	빺 BE7A	뺊 BE8A	뺚 BE9A	뺪 BEAA	뺺 BEBA	뻊 BECA	뻚 BEDA	뻪 BEEA	뻺 BEFA	뼊 BF0A	뼚 BF1A	뼪 BF2A	뼺 BF3A
B	빫 BE6B	빻 BE7B	뺋 BE8B	뺛 BE9B	뺫 BEAB	뺻 BEBB	뻋 BECB	뻛 BEDB	뻫 BEEB	뻻 BEFB	뼋 BF0B	뼛 BF1B	뼫 BF2B	뼻 BF3B
C	빬 BE6C	빼 BE7C	뺌 BE8C	뺜 BE9C	뺬 BEAC	뺼 BEBC	뻌 BECC	뻜 BEDC	뻬 BEEC	뻼 BEFC	뼌 BF0C	뼜 BF1C	뼬 BF2C	뼼 BF3C
D	빭 BE6D	빽 BE7D	뺍 BE8D	뺝 BE9D	뺭 BEAD	뺽 BEBD	뻍 BECD	뻝 BEDD	뻭 BEED	뻽 BEFD	뼍 BF0D	뼝 BF1D	뼭 BF2D	뼽 BF3D
E	빮 BE6E	빾 BE7E	뺎 BE8E	뺞 BE9E	뺮 BEAE	뺾 BEBE	뻎 BECE	뻞 BEDE	뻮 BEEE	뻾 BEFE	뼎 BF0E	뼞 BF1E	뼮 BF2E	뼾 BF3E
F	빯 BE6F	빿 BE7F	뺏 BE8F	뺟 BE9F	뺯 BEAF	뺿 BEBF	뻏 BECF	뻟 BEDF	뻯 BEEF	뻿 BEFF	뼏 BF0F	뼟 BF1F	뼯 BF2F	뼿 BF3F

	BF4	BF5	BF6	BF7	BF8	BF9	BFA	BFB	BFC	BFD	BFE	BFF	C00	C01
0	뽀 BF40	뽐 BF50	뽠 BF60	뽰 BF70	뾀 BF80	뾐 BF90	뾠 BFA0	뾰 BFB0	뿀 BFC0	뿐 BFD0	뿠 BFE0	뿰 BFF0	쀀 C000	쀐 C010
1	뽁 BF41	뽑 BF51	뽡 BF61	뽱 BF71	뾁 BF81	뾑 BF91	뾡 BFA1	뾱 BFB1	뿁 BFC1	뿑 BFD1	뿡 BFE1	뿱 BFF1	쀁 C001	쀑 C011
2	뽂 BF42	뽒 BF52	뽢 BF62	뽲 BF72	뾂 BF82	뾒 BF92	뾢 BFA2	뾲 BFB2	뿂 BFC2	뿒 BFD2	뿢 BFE2	뿲 BFF2	쀂 C002	쀒 C012
3	뽃 BF43	뽓 BF53	뽣 BF63	뽳 BF73	뾃 BF83	뾓 BF93	뾣 BFA3	뾳 BFB3	뿃 BFC3	뿓 BFD3	뿣 BFE3	뿳 BFF3	쀃 C003	쀓 C013
4	뽄 BF44	뽔 BF54	뽤 BF64	뽴 BF74	뾄 BF84	뾔 BF94	뾤 BFA4	뾴 BFB4	뿄 BFC4	뿔 BFD4	뿤 BFE4	뿴 BFF4	쀄 C004	쀔 C014
5	뽅 BF45	뽕 BF55	뽥 BF65	뽵 BF75	뾅 BF85	뾕 BF95	뾥 BFA5	뾵 BFB5	뿅 BFC5	뿕 BFD5	뿥 BFE5	뿵 BFF5	쀅 C005	쀕 C015
6	뽆 BF46	뽖 BF56	뽦 BF66	뽶 BF76	뾆 BF86	뾖 BF96	뾦 BFA6	뾶 BFB6	뿆 BFC6	뿖 BFD6	뿦 BFE6	뿶 BFF6	쀆 C006	쀖 C016
7	뽇 BF47	뽗 BF57	뽧 BF67	뽷 BF77	뾇 BF87	뾗 BF97	뾧 BFA7	뾷 BFB7	뿇 BFC7	뿗 BFD7	뿧 BFE7	뿷 BFF7	쀇 C007	쀗 C017
8	뽈 BF48	뽘 BF58	뽨 BF68	뽸 BF78	뾈 BF88	뾘 BF98	뾨 BFA8	뾸 BFB8	뿈 BFC8	뿘 BFD8	뿨 BFE8	뿸 BFF8	쀈 C008	쀘 C018
9	뽉 BF49	뽙 BF59	뽩 BF69	뽹 BF79	뾉 BF89	뾙 BF99	뾩 BFA9	뾹 BFB9	뿉 BFC9	뿙 BFD9	뿩 BFE9	뿹 BFF9	쀉 C009	쀙 C019
A	뽊 BF4A	뽚 BF5A	뽪 BF6A	뽺 BF7A	뾊 BF8A	뾚 BF9A	뾪 BFAA	뾺 BFBA	뿊 BFCA	뿚 BFDA	뿪 BFEA	뿺 BFFA	쀊 C00A	쀚 C01A
B	뽋 BF4B	뽛 BF5B	뽫 BF6B	뽻 BF7B	뾋 BF8B	뾛 BF9B	뾫 BFAB	뾻 BFBB	뿋 BFCB	뿛 BFDB	뿫 BFEB	뿻 BFFB	쀋 C00B	쀛 C01B
C	뽌 BF4C	뽜 BF5C	뽬 BF6C	뽼 BF7C	뾌 BF8C	뾜 BF9C	뾬 BFAC	뾼 BFBC	뿌 BFCC	뿜 BFDC	뿬 BFEC	뿼 BFFC	쀌 C00C	쀜 C01C
D	뽍 BF4D	뽝 BF5D	뽭 BF6D	뽽 BF7D	뾍 BF8D	뾝 BF9D	뾭 BFAD	뾽 BFBD	뿍 BFCD	뿝 BFDD	뿭 BFED	뿽 BFFD	쀍 C00D	쀝 C01D
E	뽎 BF4E	뽞 BF5E	뽮 BF6E	뽾 BF7E	뾎 BF8E	뾞 BF9E	뾮 BFAE	뾾 BFBE	뿎 BFCE	뿞 BFDE	뿮 BFEE	뿾 BFFE	쀎 C00E	쀞 C01E
F	뽏 BF4F	뽟 BF5F	뽯 BF6F	뽿 BF7F	뾏 BF8F	뾟 BF9F	뾯 BFAF	뾿 BFBF	뿏 BFCF	뿟 BFDF	뿯 BFEF	뿿 BFFF	쀏 C00F	쀟 C01F

	C02	C03	C04	C05	C06	C07	C08	C09	C0A	C0B	C0C	C0D	C0E	C0F
0	쀠 C020	쀰 C030	쁀 C040	쁐 C050	쁠 C060	쁰 C070	삀 C080	삐 C090	삠 C0A0	산 C0B0	샀 C0C0	샐 C0D0	샠 C0E0	샰 C0F0
1	쀡 C021	쀱 C031	쁁 C041	쁑 C051	쁡 C061	쁱 C071	삁 C081	삑 C091	삡 C0A1	삱 C0B1	상 C0C1	샑 C0D1	샡 C0E1	샱 C0F1
2	쀢 C022	쀲 C032	쁂 C042	쁒 C052	쁢 C062	쁲 C072	삂 C082	삒 C092	삢 C0A2	삲 C0B2	샂 C0C2	샒 C0D2	샢 C0E2	샲 C0F2
3	쀣 C023	쀳 C033	쁃 C043	쁓 C053	쁣 C063	쁳 C073	삃 C083	삓 C093	삣 C0A3	삳 C0B3	샃 C0C3	샓 C0D3	샣 C0E3	샳 C0F3
4	쀤 C024	쀴 C034	쁄 C044	쁔 C054	쁤 C064	쁴 C074	삄 C084	삔 C094	삤 C0A4	살 C0B4	샄 C0C4	샔 C0D4	샤 C0E4	샴 C0F4
5	쀥 C025	쀵 C035	쁅 C045	쁕 C055	쁥 C065	쁵 C075	삅 C085	삕 C095	삥 C0A5	삵 C0B5	샅 C0C5	샕 C0D5	샥 C0E5	샵 C0F5
6	쀦 C026	쀶 C036	쁆 C046	쁖 C056	쁦 C066	쁶 C076	삆 C086	삖 C096	삦 C0A6	삶 C0B6	샆 C0C6	샖 C0D6	샦 C0E6	샶 C0F6
7	쀧 C027	쀷 C037	쁇 C047	쁗 C057	쁧 C067	쁷 C077	삇 C087	삗 C097	삧 C0A7	삷 C0B7	샇 C0C7	샗 C0D7	샧 C0E7	샷 C0F7
8	쀨 C028	쀸 C038	쁈 C048	쁘 C058	쁨 C068	쁸 C078	삈 C088	삘 C098	삨 C0A8	삸 C0B8	새 C0C8	샘 C0D8	샨 C0E8	샸 C0F8
9	쀩 C029	쀹 C039	쁉 C049	쁙 C059	쁩 C069	쁹 C079	삉 C089	삙 C099	삩 C0A9	삹 C0B9	색 C0C9	샙 C0D9	샩 C0E9	샹 C0F9
A	쀪 C02A	쀺 C03A	쁊 C04A	쁚 C05A	쁪 C06A	쁺 C07A	삊 C08A	삚 C09A	삪 C0AA	삺 C0BA	샊 C0CA	샚 C0DA	샪 C0EA	샺 C0FA
B	쀫 C02B	쀻 C03B	쁋 C04B	쁛 C05B	쁫 C06B	쁻 C07B	삋 C08B	삛 C09B	삫 C0AB	삻 C0BB	샋 C0CB	샛 C0DB	샫 C0EB	샻 C0FB
C	쀬 C02C	쀼 C03C	쁌 C04C	쁜 C05C	쁬 C06C	쁼 C07C	삌 C08C	삜 C09C	사 C0AC	삼 C0BC	샌 C0CC	샜 C0DC	샬 C0EC	샼 C0FC
D	쀭 C02D	쀽 C03D	쁍 C04D	쁝 C05D	쁭 C06D	쁽 C07D	삍 C08D	삝 C09D	삭 C0AD	삽 C0BD	샍 C0CD	생 C0DD	샭 C0ED	샽 C0FD
E	쀮 C02E	쀾 C03E	쁎 C04E	쁞 C05E	쁮 C06E	쁾 C07E	삎 C08E	삞 C09E	삮 C0AE	삾 C0BE	샎 C0CE	샞 C0DE	샮 C0EE	샾 C0FE
F	쀯 C02F	쀿 C03F	쁏 C04F	쁟 C05F	쁯 C06F	쁿 C07F	삏 C08F	삟 C09F	삯 C0AF	삿 C0BF	샏 C0CF	샟 C0DF	샯 C0EF	샿 C0FF

	C10	C11	C12	C13	C14	C15	C16	C17	C18	C19	C1A	C1B	C1C	C1D
0	섀 C100	섐 C110	선 C120	섰 C130	셀 C140	셐 C150	셠 C160	셰 C170	솀 C180	손 C190	솠 C1A0	솰 C1B0	쇀 C1C0	쇐 C1D0
1	섁 C101	섑 C111	섡 C121	성 C131	셁 C141	셑 C151	셡 C161	셱 C171	솁 C181	솑 C191	송 C1A1	솱 C1B1	쇁 C1C1	쇑 C1D1
2	섂 C102	섒 C112	섢 C122	섲 C132	셂 C142	셒 C152	셢 C162	셲 C172	솂 C182	솒 C192	솢 C1A2	솲 C1B2	쇂 C1C2	쇒 C1D2
3	섃 C103	섓 C113	섣 C123	섳 C133	셃 C143	셓 C153	셣 C163	셳 C173	솃 C183	솓 C193	솣 C1A3	솳 C1B3	쇃 C1C3	쇓 C1D3
4	섄 C104	섔 C114	설 C124	섴 C134	셄 C144	셔 C154	셤 C164	셴 C174	솄 C184	솔 C194	솤 C1A4	솴 C1B4	쇄 C1C4	쇔 C1D4
5	섅 C105	섕 C115	섥 C125	섵 C135	셅 C145	셕 C155	셥 C165	셵 C175	솅 C185	솕 C195	솥 C1A5	솵 C1B5	쇅 C1C5	쇕 C1D5
6	섆 C106	섖 C116	섦 C126	섶 C136	셆 C146	셖 C156	셦 C166	셶 C176	솆 C186	솖 C196	솦 C1A6	솶 C1B6	쇆 C1C6	쇖 C1D6
7	섇 C107	섗 C117	섧 C127	섷 C137	셇 C147	셗 C157	셧 C167	셷 C177	솇 C187	솗 C197	솧 C1A7	솷 C1B7	쇇 C1C7	쇗 C1D7
8	섈 C108	섘 C118	섨 C128	세 C138	셈 C148	션 C158	셨 C168	셸 C178	솈 C188	솘 C198	솨 C1A8	솸 C1B8	쇈 C1C8	쇘 C1D8
9	섉 C109	섙 C119	섩 C129	섹 C139	셉 C149	셙 C159	셩 C169	셹 C179	솉 C189	솙 C199	솩 C1A9	솹 C1B9	쇉 C1C9	쇙 C1D9
A	섊 C10A	섚 C11A	섪 C12A	섺 C13A	셊 C14A	셚 C15A	셪 C16A	셺 C17A	솊 C18A	솚 C19A	솪 C1AA	솺 C1BA	쇊 C1CA	쇚 C1DA
B	섋 C10B	섛 C11B	섫 C12B	섻 C13B	셋 C14B	셛 C15B	셫 C16B	셻 C17B	솋 C18B	솛 C19B	솫 C1AB	솻 C1BB	쇋 C1CB	쇛 C1DB
C	섌 C10C	서 C11C	섬 C12C	센 C13C	셌 C14C	셜 C15C	셬 C16C	셼 C17C	소 C18C	솜 C19C	솬 C1AC	솼 C1BC	쇌 C1CC	쇜 C1DC
D	섍 C10D	석 C11D	섭 C12D	섽 C13D	셍 C14D	셝 C15D	셭 C16D	셽 C17D	속 C18D	솝 C19D	솭 C1AD	솽 C1BD	쇍 C1CD	쇝 C1DD
E	섎 C10E	섞 C11E	섮 C12E	섾 C13E	셎 C14E	셞 C15E	셮 C16E	셾 C17E	솎 C18E	솞 C19E	솮 C1AE	솾 C1BE	쇎 C1CE	쇞 C1DE
F	섏 C10F	섟 C11F	섯 C12F	섿 C13F	셏 C14F	셟 C15F	셯 C16F	셿 C17F	솏 C18F	솟 C19F	솯 C1AF	솿 C1BF	쇏 C1CF	쇟 C1DF

	C1E	C1F	C20	C21	C22	C23	C24	C25	C26	C27	C28	C29	C2A	C2B
0	쇠 C1E0	쇰 C1F0	숀 C200	숐 C210	술 C220	숰 C230	쉀 C240	쉐 C250	쉠 C260	쉰 C270	슀 C280	슐 C290	슠 C2A0	슰 C2B0
1	쇡 C1E1	쇱 C1F1	숁 C201	숑 C211	숡 C221	숱 C231	쉁 C241	쉑 C251	쉡 C261	쉱 C271	슁 C281	슑 C291	슡 C2A1	슱 C2B1
2	쇢 C1E2	쇲 C1F2	숂 C202	숒 C212	숢 C222	숲 C232	쉂 C242	쉒 C252	쉢 C262	쉲 C272	슂 C282	슒 C292	슢 C2A2	슲 C2B2
3	쇣 C1E3	쇳 C1F3	숃 C203	숓 C213	숣 C223	숳 C233	쉃 C243	쉓 C253	쉣 C263	쉳 C273	슃 C283	슓 C293	슣 C2A3	슳 C2B3
4	쇤 C1E4	쇴 C1F4	숄 C204	숔 C214	숤 C224	숴 C234	쉄 C244	쉔 C254	쉤 C264	쉴 C274	슄 C284	슔 C294	스 C2A4	슴 C2B4
5	쇥 C1E5	쇵 C1F5	숅 C205	숕 C215	숥 C225	숵 C235	쉅 C245	쉕 C255	쉥 C265	쉵 C275	슅 C285	슕 C295	슥 C2A5	습 C2B5
6	쇦 C1E6	쇶 C1F6	숆 C206	숖 C216	숦 C226	숶 C236	쉆 C246	쉖 C256	쉦 C266	쉶 C276	슆 C286	슖 C296	슦 C2A6	슶 C2B6
7	쇧 C1E7	쇷 C1F7	숇 C207	숗 C217	숧 C227	숷 C237	쉇 C247	쉗 C257	쉧 C267	쉷 C277	슇 C287	슗 C297	슧 C2A7	슷 C2B7
8	쇨 C1E8	쇸 C1F8	숈 C208	수 C218	숨 C228	숸 C238	쉈 C248	쉘 C258	쉨 C268	쉸 C278	슈 C288	슘 C298	슨 C2A8	슸 C2B8
9	쇩 C1E9	쇹 C1F9	숉 C209	숙 C219	숩 C229	숹 C239	쉉 C249	쉙 C259	쉩 C269	쉹 C279	슉 C289	슙 C299	슩 C2A9	승 C2B9
A	쇪 C1EA	쇺 C1FA	숊 C20A	숚 C21A	숪 C22A	숺 C23A	쉊 C24A	쉚 C25A	쉪 C26A	쉺 C27A	슊 C28A	슚 C29A	슪 C2AA	슺 C2BA
B	쇫 C1EB	쇻 C1FB	숋 C20B	숛 C21B	숫 C22B	숻 C23B	쉋 C24B	쉛 C25B	쉫 C26B	쉻 C27B	슋 C28B	슛 C29B	슫 C2AB	슻 C2BB
C	쇬 C1EC	쇼 C1FC	숌 C20C	순 C21C	숬 C22C	숼 C23C	쉌 C24C	쉜 C25C	쉬 C26C	쉼 C27C	슌 C28C	슜 C29C	슬 C2AC	슼 C2BC
D	쇭 C1ED	쇽 C1FD	숍 C20D	숝 C21D	숭 C22D	숽 C23D	쉍 C24D	쉝 C25D	쉭 C26D	쉽 C27D	슍 C28D	슝 C29D	슭 C2AD	슽 C2BD
E	쇮 C1EE	쇾 C1FE	숎 C20E	숞 C21E	숮 C22E	숾 C23E	쉎 C24E	쉞 C25E	쉮 C26E	쉾 C27E	슎 C28E	슞 C29E	슮 C2AE	슾 C2BE
F	쇯 C1EF	쇿 C1FF	숏 C20F	숟 C21F	숯 C22F	숿 C23F	쉏 C24F	쉟 C25F	쉯 C26F	쉿 C27F	슏 C28F	슟 C29F	슯 C2AF	슿 C2BF

	C2C	C2D	C2E	C2F	C30	C31	C32	C33	C34	C35	C36	C37	C38	C39
0	싀 C2C0	싐 C2D0	신 C2E0	싰 C2F0	쌀 C300	쌐 C310	쌠 C320	쌰 C330	썀 C340	썐 C350	썠 C360	썰 C370	쎀 C380	쎐 C390
1	싁 C2C1	싑 C2D1	싡 C2E1	싱 C2F1	쌁 C301	쌑 C311	쌡 C321	쌱 C331	썁 C341	썑 C351	썡 C361	썱 C371	쎁 C381	쎑 C391
2	싂 C2C2	싒 C2D2	싢 C2E2	싲 C2F2	쌂 C302	쌒 C312	쌢 C322	쌲 C332	썂 C342	썒 C352	썢 C362	썲 C372	쎂 C382	쎒 C392
3	싃 C2C3	싓 C2D3	싣 C2E3	싳 C2F3	쌃 C303	쌓 C313	쌣 C323	쌳 C333	썃 C343	썓 C353	썣 C363	썳 C373	쎃 C383	쎓 C393
4	싄 C2C4	싔 C2D4	실 C2E4	싴 C2F4	쌄 C304	쌔 C314	쌤 C324	쌴 C334	썄 C344	썔 C354	썤 C364	썴 C374	쎄 C384	쎔 C394
5	싅 C2C5	싕 C2D5	싥 C2E5	싵 C2F5	쌅 C305	쌕 C315	쌥 C325	쌵 C335	썅 C345	썕 C355	썥 C365	썵 C375	쎅 C385	쎕 C395
6	싆 C2C6	싖 C2D6	싦 C2E6	싶 C2F6	쌆 C306	쌖 C316	쌦 C326	쌶 C336	썆 C346	썖 C356	썦 C366	썶 C376	쎆 C386	쎖 C396
7	싇 C2C7	싗 C2D7	싧 C2E7	싷 C2F7	쌇 C307	쌗 C317	쌧 C327	쌷 C337	썇 C347	썗 C357	썧 C367	썷 C377	쎇 C387	쎗 C397
8	싈 C2C8	싘 C2D8	싨 C2E8	싸 C2F8	쌈 C308	쌘 C318	쌨 C328	쌸 C338	썈 C348	썘 C358	써 C368	썸 C378	쎈 C388	쎘 C398
9	싉 C2C9	싙 C2D9	싩 C2E9	싹 C2F9	쌉 C309	쌙 C319	쌩 C329	쌹 C339	썉 C349	썙 C359	썩 C369	썹 C379	쎉 C389	쎙 C399
A	싊 C2CA	싚 C2DA	싪 C2EA	싺 C2FA	쌊 C30A	쌚 C31A	쌪 C32A	쌺 C33A	썊 C34A	썚 C35A	썪 C36A	썺 C37A	쎊 C38A	쎚 C39A
B	싋 C2CB	싛 C2DB	싫 C2EB	싻 C2FB	쌋 C30B	쌛 C31B	쌫 C32B	쌻 C33B	썋 C34B	썛 C35B	썫 C36B	썻 C37B	쎋 C38B	쎛 C39B
C	싌 C2CC	시 C2DC	심 C2EC	싼 C2FC	쌌 C30C	쌜 C31C	쌬 C32C	쌼 C33C	썌 C34C	썜 C35C	썬 C36C	썼 C37C	쎌 C38C	쎜 C39C
D	싍 C2CD	식 C2DD	십 C2ED	싽 C2FD	쌍 C30D	쌝 C31D	쌭 C32D	쌽 C33D	썍 C34D	썝 C35D	썭 C36D	썽 C37D	쎍 C38D	쎝 C39D
E	싎 C2CE	싞 C2DE	싮 C2EE	싾 C2FE	쌎 C30E	쌞 C31E	쌮 C32E	쌾 C33E	썎 C34E	썞 C35E	썮 C36E	썾 C37E	쎎 C38E	쎞 C39E
F	싏 C2CF	싟 C2DF	싯 C2EF	싿 C2FF	쌏 C30F	쌟 C31F	쌯 C32F	쌿 C33F	썏 C34F	썟 C35F	썯 C36F	썿 C37F	쎏 C38F	쎟 C39F

	C3A	C3B	C3C	C3D	C3E	C3F	C40	C41	C42	C43	C44	C45	C46	C47
0	쎠 C3A0	쎰 C3B0	쏀 C3C0	쏐 C3D0	쏠 C3E0	쏰 C3F0	쐀 C400	쐐 C410	쐠 C420	쐰 C430	쑀 C440	쑐 C450	쑠 C460	쑰 C470
1	쎡 C3A1	쎱 C3B1	쏁 C3C1	쏑 C3D1	쏡 C3E1	쏱 C3F1	쐁 C401	쐑 C411	쐡 C421	쐱 C431	쑁 C441	쑑 C451	쑡 C461	쑱 C471
2	쎢 C3A2	쎲 C3B2	쏂 C3C2	쏒 C3D2	쏢 C3E2	쏲 C3F2	쐂 C402	쐒 C412	쐢 C422	쐲 C432	쑂 C442	쑒 C452	쑢 C462	쑲 C472
3	쎣 C3A3	쎳 C3B3	쏃 C3C3	쏓 C3D3	쏣 C3E3	쏳 C3F3	쐃 C403	쐓 C413	쐣 C423	쐳 C433	쑃 C443	쑓 C453	쑣 C463	쑳 C473
4	쎤 C3A4	쎴 C3B4	쏄 C3C4	쏔 C3D4	쏤 C3E4	쏴 C3F4	쐄 C404	쐔 C414	쐤 C424	쐴 C434	쑄 C444	쑔 C454	쑤 C464	쑴 C474
5	쎥 C3A5	쎵 C3B5	쏅 C3C5	쏕 C3D5	쏥 C3E5	쏵 C3F5	쐅 C405	쐕 C415	쐥 C425	쐵 C435	쑅 C445	쑕 C455	쑥 C465	쑵 C475
6	쎦 C3A6	쎶 C3B6	쏆 C3C6	쏖 C3D6	쏦 C3E6	쏶 C3F6	쐆 C406	쐖 C416	쐦 C426	쐶 C436	쑆 C446	쑖 C456	쑦 C466	쑶 C476
7	쎧 C3A7	쎷 C3B7	쏇 C3C7	쏗 C3D7	쏧 C3E7	쏷 C3F7	쐇 C407	쐗 C417	쐧 C427	쐷 C437	쑇 C447	쑗 C457	쑧 C467	쑷 C477
8	쎨 C3A8	쎸 C3B8	쏈 C3C8	쏘 C3D8	쏨 C3E8	쏸 C3F8	쐈 C408	쐘 C418	쐨 C428	쐸 C438	쑈 C448	쑘 C458	쑨 C468	쑸 C478
9	쎩 C3A9	쎹 C3B9	쏉 C3C9	쏙 C3D9	쏩 C3E9	쏹 C3F9	쐉 C409	쐙 C419	쐩 C429	쐹 C439	쑉 C449	쑙 C459	쑩 C469	쑹 C479
A	쎪 C3AA	쎺 C3BA	쏊 C3CA	쏚 C3DA	쏪 C3EA	쏺 C3FA	쐊 C40A	쐚 C41A	쐪 C42A	쐺 C43A	쑊 C44A	쑚 C45A	쑪 C46A	쑺 C47A
B	쎫 C3AB	쎻 C3BB	쏋 C3CB	쏛 C3DB	쏫 C3EB	쏻 C3FB	쐋 C40B	쐛 C41B	쐫 C42B	쐻 C43B	쑋 C44B	쑛 C45B	쑫 C46B	쑻 C47B
C	쎬 C3AC	쎼 C3BC	쏌 C3CC	쏜 C3DC	쏬 C3EC	쏼 C3FC	쐌 C40C	쐜 C41C	쐬 C42C	쐼 C43C	쑌 C44C	쑜 C45C	쑬 C46C	쑼 C47C
D	쎭 C3AD	쎽 C3BD	쏍 C3CD	쏝 C3DD	쏭 C3ED	쏽 C3FD	쐍 C40D	쐝 C41D	쐭 C42D	쐽 C43D	쑍 C44D	쑝 C45D	쑭 C46D	쑽 C47D
E	쎮 C3AE	쎾 C3BE	쏎 C3CE	쏞 C3DE	쏮 C3EE	쏾 C3FE	쐎 C40E	쐞 C41E	쐮 C42E	쐾 C43E	쑎 C44E	쑞 C45E	쑮 C46E	쑾 C47E
F	쎯 C3AF	쎿 C3BF	쏏 C3CF	쏟 C3DF	쏯 C3EF	쏿 C3FF	쐏 C40F	쐟 C41F	쐯 C42F	쐿 C43F	쑏 C44F	쑟 C45F	쑯 C46F	쑿 C47F

	C48	C49	C4A	C4B	C4C	C4D	C4E	C4F	C50	C51	C52	C53	C54	C55
0	쒀 C480	쒐 C490	쒠 C4A0	쒰 C4B0	쓀 C4C0	쓐 C4D0	쓠 C4E0	쓰 C4F0	씀 C500	씐 C510	씠 C520	씰 C530	앀 C540	앐 C550
1	쒁 C481	쒑 C491	쒡 C4A1	쒱 C4B1	쓁 C4C1	쓑 C4D1	쓡 C4E1	쓱 C4F1	씁 C501	씑 C511	씡 C521	씱 C531	앁 C541	앑 C551
2	쒂 C482	쒒 C492	쒢 C4A2	쒲 C4B2	쓂 C4C2	쓒 C4D2	쓢 C4E2	쓲 C4F2	씂 C502	씒 C512	씢 C522	씲 C532	앂 C542	앒 C552
3	쒃 C483	쒓 C493	쒣 C4A3	쒳 C4B3	쓃 C4C3	쓓 C4D3	쓣 C4E3	쓳 C4F3	씃 C503	씓 C513	씣 C523	씳 C533	앃 C543	앓 C553
4	쒄 C484	쒔 C494	쒤 C4A4	쒴 C4B4	쓄 C4C4	쓔 C4D4	쓤 C4E4	쓴 C4F4	씄 C504	씔 C514	씤 C524	씴 C534	아 C544	암 C554
5	쒅 C485	쒕 C495	쒥 C4A5	쒵 C4B5	쓅 C4C5	쓕 C4D5	쓥 C4E5	쓵 C4F5	씅 C505	씕 C515	씥 C525	씵 C535	악 C545	압 C555
6	쒆 C486	쒖 C496	쒦 C4A6	쒶 C4B6	쓆 C4C6	쓖 C4D6	쓦 C4E6	쓶 C4F6	씆 C506	씖 C516	씦 C526	씶 C536	앆 C546	앖 C556
7	쒇 C487	쒗 C497	쒧 C4A7	쒷 C4B7	쓇 C4C7	쓗 C4D7	쓧 C4E7	쓷 C4F7	씇 C507	씗 C517	씧 C527	씷 C537	앇 C547	앗 C557
8	쒈 C488	쒘 C498	쒨 C4A8	쒸 C4B8	쓈 C4C8	쓘 C4D8	쓨 C4E8	쓸 C4F8	씈 C508	씘 C518	씨 C528	씸 C538	안 C548	았 C558
9	쒉 C489	쒙 C499	쒩 C4A9	쒹 C4B9	쓉 C4C9	쓙 C4D9	쓩 C4E9	쓹 C4F9	씉 C509	씙 C519	씩 C529	씹 C539	앉 C549	앙 C559
A	쒊 C48A	쒚 C49A	쒪 C4AA	쒺 C4BA	쓊 C4CA	쓚 C4DA	쓪 C4EA	쓺 C4FA	씊 C50A	씚 C51A	씪 C52A	씺 C53A	않 C54A	앚 C55A
B	쒋 C48B	쒛 C49B	쒫 C4AB	쒻 C4BB	쓋 C4CB	쓛 C4DB	쓫 C4EB	쓻 C4FB	씋 C50B	씛 C51B	씫 C52B	씻 C53B	앋 C54B	앛 C55B
C	쒌 C48C	쒜 C49C	쒬 C4AC	쒼 C4BC	쓌 C4CC	쓜 C4DC	쓬 C4EC	쓼 C4FC	씌 C50C	씜 C51C	씬 C52C	씼 C53C	알 C54C	앜 C55C
D	쒍 C48D	쒝 C49D	쒭 C4AD	쒽 C4BD	쓍 C4CD	쓝 C4DD	쓭 C4ED	쓽 C4FD	씍 C50D	씝 C51D	씭 C52D	씽 C53D	앍 C54D	앝 C55D
E	쒎 C48E	쒞 C49E	쒮 C4AE	쒾 C4BE	쓎 C4CE	쓞 C4DE	쓮 C4EE	쓾 C4FE	씎 C50E	씞 C51E	씮 C52E	씾 C53E	앎 C54E	앞 C55E
F	쒏 C48F	쒟 C49F	쒯 C4AF	쒿 C4BF	쓏 C4CF	쓟 C4DF	쓯 C4EF	쓿 C4FF	씏 C50F	씟 C51F	씯 C52F	씿 C53F	앏 C54F	앟 C55F

	C56	C57	C58	C59	C5A	C5B	C5C	C5D	C5E	C5F	C60	C61	C62	C63
0	애 C560	앰 C570	얀 C580	얐 C590	얠 C5A0	얰 C5B0	엀 C5C0	에 C5D0	엠 C5E0	연 C5F0	였 C600	옐 C610	옠 C620	옰 C630
1	액 C561	앱 C571	얁 C581	양 C591	얡 C5A1	얱 C5B1	엁 C5C1	엑 C5D1	엡 C5E1	엱 C5F1	영 C601	옑 C611	옡 C621	옱 C631
2	앢 C562	앲 C572	얂 C582	얒 C592	얢 C5A2	얲 C5B2	엂 C5C2	엒 C5D2	엢 C5E2	엲 C5F2	옂 C602	옒 C612	옢 C622	옲 C632
3	앣 C563	앳 C573	얃 C583	얓 C593	얣 C5A3	얳 C5B3	엃 C5C3	엓 C5D3	엣 C5E3	엳 C5F3	옃 C603	옓 C613	옣 C623	옳 C633
4	앤 C564	앴 C574	얄 C584	얔 C594	얤 C5A4	어 C5B4	엄 C5C4	엔 C5D4	엤 C5E4	열 C5F4	옄 C604	옔 C614	오 C624	옴 C634
5	앥 C565	앵 C575	얅 C585	얕 C595	얥 C5A5	억 C5B5	업 C5C5	엕 C5D5	엥 C5E5	엵 C5F5	옅 C605	옕 C615	옥 C625	옵 C635
6	앦 C566	앶 C576	얆 C586	얖 C596	얦 C5A6	얶 C5B6	없 C5C6	엖 C5D6	엦 C5E6	엶 C5F6	옆 C606	옖 C616	옦 C626	옶 C636
7	앧 C567	앷 C577	얇 C587	얗 C597	얧 C5A7	얷 C5B7	엇 C5C7	엗 C5D7	엧 C5E7	엷 C5F7	옇 C607	옗 C617	옧 C627	옷 C637
8	앨 C568	앸 C578	얈 C588	얘 C598	얨 C5A8	언 C5B8	었 C5C8	엘 C5D8	엨 C5E8	엸 C5F8	예 C608	옘 C618	온 C628	옸 C638
9	앩 C569	앹 C579	얉 C589	얙 C599	얩 C5A9	얹 C5B9	엉 C5C9	엙 C5D9	엩 C5E9	엹 C5F9	옉 C609	옙 C619	옩 C629	옹 C639
A	앪 C56A	앺 C57A	얊 C58A	얚 C59A	얪 C5AA	얺 C5BA	엊 C5CA	엚 C5DA	엪 C5EA	엺 C5FA	옊 C60A	옚 C61A	옪 C62A	옺 C63A
B	앫 C56B	앻 C57B	얋 C58B	얛 C59B	얫 C5AB	얻 C5BB	엋 C5CB	엛 C5DB	엫 C5EB	엻 C5FB	옋 C60B	옛 C61B	옫 C62B	옻 C63B
C	앬 C56C	야 C57C	얌 C58C	얜 C59C	얬 C5AC	얼 C5BC	엌 C5CC	엜 C5DC	여 C5EC	염 C5FC	옌 C60C	옜 C61C	올 C62C	옼 C63C
D	앭 C56D	약 C57D	얍 C58D	얝 C59D	얭 C5AD	얽 C5BD	엍 C5CD	엝 C5DD	역 C5ED	엽 C5FD	옍 C60D	옝 C61D	옭 C62D	옽 C63D
E	앮 C56E	앾 C57E	얎 C58E	얞 C59E	얮 C5AE	얾 C5BE	엎 C5CE	엞 C5DE	엮 C5EE	엾 C5FE	옎 C60E	옞 C61E	옮 C62E	옾 C63E
F	앯 C56F	앿 C57F	얏 C58F	얟 C59F	얯 C5AF	얿 C5BF	엏 C5CF	엟 C5DF	엯 C5EF	엿 C5FF	옏 C60F	옟 C61F	옯 C62F	옿 C63F

	C64	C65	C66	C67	C68	C69	C6A	C6B	C6C	C6D	C6E	C6F	C70	C71
0	와 C640	왐 C650	왠 C660	왰 C670	욀 C680	욐 C690	욠 C6A0	우 C6B0	움 C6C0	원 C6D0	웠 C6E0	웰 C6F0	윀 C700	윐 C710
1	왁 C641	왑 C651	왡 C661	왱 C671	욁 C681	욑 C691	욡 C6A1	욱 C6B1	웁 C6C1	웑 C6D1	웡 C6E1	웱 C6F1	윁 C701	윑 C711
2	왂 C642	왒 C652	왢 C662	왲 C672	욂 C682	욒 C692	욢 C6A2	욲 C6B2	웂 C6C2	웒 C6D2	웢 C6E2	웲 C6F2	윂 C702	윒 C712
3	왃 C643	왓 C653	왣 C663	왳 C673	욃 C683	욓 C693	욣 C6A3	욳 C6B3	웃 C6C3	웓 C6D3	웣 C6E3	웳 C6F3	윃 C703	윓 C713
4	완 C644	왔 C654	왤 C664	왴 C674	욄 C684	요 C694	욤 C6A4	운 C6B4	웄 C6C4	월 C6D4	웤 C6E4	웴 C6F4	위 C704	윔 C714
5	왅 C645	왕 C655	왥 C665	왵 C675	욅 C685	욕 C695	욥 C6A5	욵 C6B5	웅 C6C5	웕 C6D5	웥 C6E5	웵 C6F5	윅 C705	윕 C715
6	왆 C646	왖 C656	왦 C666	왶 C676	욆 C686	욖 C696	욦 C6A6	욶 C6B6	웆 C6C6	웖 C6D6	웦 C6E6	웶 C6F6	윆 C706	윖 C716
7	왇 C647	왗 C657	왧 C667	왷 C677	욇 C687	욗 C697	욧 C6A7	욷 C6B7	웇 C6C7	웗 C6D7	웧 C6E7	웷 C6F7	윇 C707	윗 C717
8	왈 C648	왘 C658	왨 C668	외 C678	욈 C688	욘 C698	욨 C6A8	울 C6B8	웈 C6C8	웘 C6D8	웨 C6E8	웸 C6F8	윈 C708	윘 C718
9	왉 C649	왙 C659	왩 C669	왹 C679	욉 C689	욙 C699	용 C6A9	욹 C6B9	웉 C6C9	웙 C6D9	웩 C6E9	웹 C6F9	윉 C709	윙 C719
A	왊 C64A	왚 C65A	왪 C66A	왺 C67A	욊 C68A	욚 C69A	욪 C6AA	욺 C6BA	웊 C6CA	웚 C6DA	웪 C6EA	웺 C6FA	윊 C70A	윚 C71A
B	왋 C64B	왛 C65B	왫 C66B	왻 C67B	욋 C68B	욛 C69B	욫 C6AB	욻 C6BB	웋 C6CB	웛 C6DB	웫 C6EB	웻 C6FB	윋 C70B	윛 C71B
C	왌 C64C	왜 C65C	왬 C66C	왼 C67C	욌 C68C	욜 C69C	욬 C6AC	욼 C6BC	워 C6CC	웜 C6DC	웬 C6EC	웼 C6FC	윌 C70C	윜 C71C
D	왍 C64D	왝 C65D	왭 C66D	왽 C67D	욍 C68D	욝 C69D	욭 C6AD	욽 C6BD	웍 C6CD	웝 C6DD	웭 C6ED	웽 C6FD	윍 C70D	윝 C71D
E	왎 C64E	왞 C65E	왮 C66E	왾 C67E	욎 C68E	욞 C69E	욮 C6AE	욾 C6BE	웎 C6CE	웞 C6DE	웮 C6EE	웾 C6FE	윎 C70E	윞 C71E
F	왏 C64F	왟 C65F	왯 C66F	왿 C67F	욏 C68F	욟 C69F	욯 C6AF	욿 C6BF	웏 C6CF	웟 C6DF	웯 C6EF	웿 C6FF	윏 C70F	윟 C71F

	C72	C73	C74	C75	C76	C77	C78	C79	C7A	C7B	C7C	C7D	C7E	C7F
0	유 C720	윰 C730	은 C740	읐 C750	읠 C760	읰 C770	잀 C780	자 C790	잠 C7A0	잰 C7B0	쟀 C7C0	쟐 C7D0	쟠 C7E0	쟰 C7F0
1	육 C721	윱 C731	읁 C741	응 C751	읡 C761	읱 C771	잁 C781	작 C791	잡 C7A1	잱 C7B1	쟁 C7C1	쟑 C7D1	쟡 C7E1	쟱 C7F1
2	윢 C722	윲 C732	읂 C742	읒 C752	읢 C762	읲 C772	잂 C782	잒 C792	잢 C7A2	잲 C7B2	쟂 C7C2	쟒 C7D2	쟢 C7E2	쟲 C7F2
3	윣 C723	윳 C733	읃 C743	읓 C753	읣 C763	읳 C773	잃 C783	잓 C793	잣 C7A3	잳 C7B3	쟃 C7C3	쟓 C7D3	쟣 C7E3	쟳 C7F3
4	윤 C724	윴 C734	을 C744	읔 C754	읤 C764	이 C774	임 C784	잔 C794	잤 C7A4	잴 C7B4	쟄 C7C4	쟔 C7D4	쟤 C7E4	쟴 C7F4
5	윥 C725	융 C735	읅 C745	읕 C755	읥 C765	익 C775	입 C785	잕 C795	장 C7A5	잵 C7B5	쟅 C7C5	쟕 C7D5	쟥 C7E5	쟵 C7F5
6	윦 C726	윶 C736	읆 C746	읖 C756	읦 C766	읶 C776	잆 C786	잖 C796	잦 C7A6	잶 C7B6	쟆 C7C6	쟖 C7D6	쟦 C7E6	쟶 C7F6
7	윧 C727	윷 C737	읇 C747	읗 C757	읧 C767	읷 C777	잇 C787	잗 C797	잧 C7A7	잷 C7B7	쟇 C7C7	쟗 C7D7	쟧 C7E7	쟷 C7F7
8	율 C728	윸 C738	읈 C748	의 C758	읨 C768	인 C778	있 C788	잘 C798	잨 C7A8	잸 C7B8	쟈 C7C8	쟘 C7D8	쟨 C7E8	쟸 C7F8
9	윩 C729	윹 C739	읉 C749	읙 C759	읩 C769	읹 C779	잉 C789	잙 C799	잩 C7A9	잹 C7B9	쟉 C7C9	쟙 C7D9	쟩 C7E9	쟹 C7F9
A	윪 C72A	윺 C73A	읊 C74A	읚 C75A	읪 C76A	읺 C77A	잊 C78A	잚 C79A	잪 C7AA	잺 C7BA	쟊 C7CA	쟚 C7DA	쟪 C7EA	쟺 C7FA
B	윫 C72B	윻 C73B	읋 C74B	읛 C75B	읫 C76B	읻 C77B	잋 C78B	잛 C79B	잫 C7AB	잻 C7BB	쟋 C7CB	쟛 C7DB	쟫 C7EB	쟻 C7FB
C	윬 C72C	으 C73C	음 C74C	읜 C75C	읬 C76C	일 C77C	잌 C78C	잜 C79C	재 C7AC	잼 C7BC	쟌 C7CC	쟜 C7DC	쟬 C7EC	쟼 C7FC
D	윭 C72D	윽 C73D	읍 C74D	읝 C75D	읭 C76D	읽 C77D	잍 C78D	잝 C79D	잭 C7AD	잽 C7BD	쟍 C7CD	쟝 C7DD	쟭 C7ED	쟽 C7FD
E	윮 C72E	윾 C73E	읎 C74E	읞 C75E	읮 C76E	읾 C77E	잎 C78E	잞 C79E	잮 C7AE	잾 C7BE	쟎 C7CE	쟞 C7DE	쟮 C7EE	쟾 C7FE
F	윯 C72F	윿 C73F	읏 C74F	읟 C75F	읯 C76F	읿 C77F	잏 C78F	잟 C79F	잯 C7AF	잿 C7BF	쟏 C7CF	쟟 C7DF	쟯 C7EF	쟿 C7FF

	C80	C81	C82	C83	C84	C85	C86	C87	C88	C89	C8A	C8B	C8C	C8D
0	저 C800	점 C810	젠 C820	젰 C830	졀 C840	졐 C850	졠 C860	조 C870	좀 C880	좐 C890	좠 C8A0	좰 C8B0	죀 C8C0	죐 C8D0
1	적 C801	접 C811	젡 C821	젱 C831	졁 C841	졑 C851	졡 C861	족 C871	좁 C881	좑 C891	좡 C8A1	좱 C8B1	죁 C8C1	죑 C8D1
2	젂 C802	젒 C812	젢 C822	젲 C832	졂 C842	졒 C852	졢 C862	졲 C872	좂 C882	좒 C892	좢 C8A2	좲 C8B2	죂 C8C2	죒 C8D2
3	젃 C803	젓 C813	젣 C823	젳 C833	졃 C843	졓 C853	졣 C863	졳 C873	좃 C883	좓 C893	좣 C8A3	좳 C8B3	죃 C8C3	죓 C8D3
4	전 C804	젔 C814	젤 C824	젴 C834	졄 C844	졔 C854	졤 C864	존 C874	좄 C884	좔 C894	좤 C8A4	좴 C8B4	죄 C8C4	죔 C8D4
5	젅 C805	정 C815	젥 C825	젵 C835	졅 C845	졕 C855	졥 C865	졵 C875	종 C885	좕 C895	좥 C8A5	좵 C8B5	죅 C8C5	죕 C8D5
6	젆 C806	젖 C816	젦 C826	젶 C836	졆 C846	졖 C856	졦 C866	졶 C876	좆 C886	좖 C896	좦 C8A6	좶 C8B6	죆 C8C6	죖 C8D6
7	젇 C807	젗 C817	젧 C827	젷 C837	졇 C847	졗 C857	졧 C867	졷 C877	좇 C887	좗 C897	좧 C8A7	좷 C8B7	죇 C8C7	죗 C8D7
8	절 C808	젘 C818	젨 C828	져 C838	졈 C848	졘 C858	졨 C868	졸 C878	좈 C888	좘 C898	좨 C8A8	좸 C8B8	죈 C8C8	죘 C8D8
9	젉 C809	젙 C819	젩 C829	젹 C839	졉 C849	졙 C859	졩 C869	졹 C879	좉 C889	좙 C899	좩 C8A9	좹 C8B9	죉 C8C9	죙 C8D9
A	젊 C80A	젚 C81A	젪 C82A	젺 C83A	졊 C84A	졚 C85A	졪 C86A	졺 C87A	좊 C88A	좚 C89A	좪 C8AA	좺 C8BA	죊 C8CA	죚 C8DA
B	젋 C80B	젛 C81B	젫 C82B	젻 C83B	졋 C84B	졛 C85B	졫 C86B	졻 C87B	좋 C88B	좛 C89B	좫 C8AB	좻 C8BB	죋 C8CB	죛 C8DB
C	젌 C80C	제 C81C	젬 C82C	젼 C83C	졌 C84C	졜 C85C	졬 C86C	졼 C87C	좌 C88C	좜 C89C	좬 C8AC	좼 C8BC	죌 C8CC	죜 C8DC
D	젍 C80D	젝 C81D	젭 C82D	젽 C83D	졍 C84D	졝 C85D	졭 C86D	졽 C87D	좍 C88D	좝 C89D	좭 C8AD	좽 C8BD	죍 C8CD	죝 C8DD
E	젎 C80E	젞 C81E	젮 C82E	젾 C83E	졎 C84E	졞 C85E	졮 C86E	졾 C87E	좎 C88E	좞 C89E	좮 C8AE	좾 C8BE	죎 C8CE	죞 C8DE
F	젏 C80F	젟 C81F	젯 C82F	젿 C83F	졏 C84F	졟 C85F	졯 C86F	졿 C87F	좏 C88F	좟 C89F	좯 C8AF	좿 C8BF	죏 C8CF	죟 C8DF

	C8E	C8F	C90	C91	C92	C93	C94	C95	C96	C97	C98	C99	C9A	C9B
0	죠 C8E0	죰 C8F0	준 C900	줐 C910	줠 C920	줰 C930	쥀 C940	쥐 C950	쥠 C960	쥰 C970	즀 C980	즐 C990	즠 C9A0	즰 C9B0
1	죡 C8E1	죱 C8F1	줁 C901	중 C911	줡 C921	줱 C931	쥁 C941	쥑 C951	쥡 C961	쥱 C971	즁 C981	즑 C991	즡 C9A1	즱 C9B1
2	죢 C8E2	죲 C8F2	줂 C902	줒 C912	줢 C922	줲 C932	쥂 C942	쥒 C952	쥢 C962	쥲 C972	즂 C982	즒 C992	즢 C9A2	즲 C9B2
3	죣 C8E3	죳 C8F3	줃 C903	줓 C913	줣 C923	줳 C933	쥃 C943	쥓 C953	쥣 C963	쥳 C973	즃 C983	즓 C993	즣 C9A3	즳 C9B3
4	죤 C8E4	죴 C8F4	줄 C904	줔 C914	줤 C924	줴 C934	쥄 C944	쥔 C954	쥤 C964	쥴 C974	즄 C984	즔 C994	즤 C9A4	즴 C9B4
5	죥 C8E5	죵 C8F5	줅 C905	줕 C915	줥 C925	줵 C935	쥅 C945	쥕 C955	쥥 C965	쥵 C975	즅 C985	즕 C995	즥 C9A5	즵 C9B5
6	죦 C8E6	죶 C8F6	줆 C906	줖 C916	줦 C926	줶 C936	쥆 C946	쥖 C956	쥦 C966	쥶 C976	즆 C986	즖 C996	즦 C9A6	즶 C9B6
7	죧 C8E7	죷 C8F7	줇 C907	줗 C917	줧 C927	줷 C937	쥇 C947	쥗 C957	쥧 C967	쥷 C977	즇 C987	즗 C997	즧 C9A7	즷 C9B7
8	죨 C8E8	죸 C8F8	줈 C908	줘 C918	줨 C928	줸 C938	쥈 C948	쥘 C958	쥨 C968	쥸 C978	즈 C988	즘 C998	즨 C9A8	즸 C9B8
9	죩 C8E9	죹 C8F9	줉 C909	줙 C919	줩 C929	줹 C939	쥉 C949	쥙 C959	쥩 C969	쥹 C979	즉 C989	즙 C999	즩 C9A9	즹 C9B9
A	죪 C8EA	죺 C8FA	줊 C90A	줚 C91A	줪 C92A	줺 C93A	쥊 C94A	쥚 C95A	쥪 C96A	쥺 C97A	즊 C98A	즚 C99A	즪 C9AA	즺 C9BA
B	죫 C8EB	죻 C8FB	줋 C90B	줛 C91B	줫 C92B	줻 C93B	쥋 C94B	쥛 C95B	쥫 C96B	쥻 C97B	즋 C98B	즛 C99B	즫 C9AB	즻 C9BB
C	죬 C8EC	주 C8FC	줌 C90C	줜 C91C	줬 C92C	줼 C93C	쥌 C94C	쥜 C95C	쥬 C96C	쥼 C97C	즌 C98C	즜 C99C	즬 C9AC	즼 C9BC
D	죭 C8ED	죽 C8FD	줍 C90D	줝 C91D	줭 C92D	줽 C93D	쥍 C94D	쥝 C95D	쥭 C96D	쥽 C97D	즍 C98D	증 C99D	즭 C9AD	즽 C9BD
E	죮 C8EE	죾 C8FE	줎 C90E	줞 C91E	줮 C92E	줾 C93E	쥎 C94E	쥞 C95E	쥮 C96E	쥾 C97E	즎 C98E	즞 C99E	즮 C9AE	즾 C9BE
F	죯 C8EF	죿 C8FF	줏 C90F	줟 C91F	줯 C92F	줿 C93F	쥏 C94F	쥟 C95F	쥯 C96F	쥿 C97F	즏 C98F	즟 C99F	즯 C9AF	즿 C9BF

	C9C	C9D	C9E	C9F	CA0	CA1	CA2	CA3	CA4	CA5	CA6	CA7	CA8	CA9
0	지 C9C0	짐 C9D0	짠 C9E0	짰 C9F0	쨀 CA00	쨐 CA10	쨠 CA20	쨰 CA30	쩀 CA40	쩐 CA50	쩠 CA60	쩰 CA70	쪀 CA80	쪐 CA90
1	직 C9C1	집 C9D1	짡 C9E1	짱 C9F1	쨁 CA01	쨑 CA11	쨡 CA21	쨱 CA31	쩁 CA41	쩑 CA51	쩡 CA61	쩱 CA71	쪁 CA81	쪑 CA91
2	짂 C9C2	짒 C9D2	짢 C9E2	짲 C9F2	쨂 CA02	쨒 CA12	쨢 CA22	쨲 CA32	쩂 CA42	쩒 CA52	쩢 CA62	쩲 CA72	쪂 CA82	쪒 CA92
3	짃 C9C3	짓 C9D3	짣 C9E3	짳 C9F3	쨃 CA03	쨓 CA13	쨣 CA23	쨳 CA33	쩃 CA43	쩓 CA53	쩣 CA63	쩳 CA73	쪃 CA83	쪓 CA93
4	진 C9C4	짔 C9D4	짤 C9E4	짴 C9F4	쨄 CA04	쨔 CA14	쨤 CA24	쨴 CA34	쩄 CA44	쩔 CA54	쩤 CA64	쩴 CA74	쪄 CA84	쪔 CA94
5	짅 C9C5	징 C9D5	짥 C9E5	짵 C9F5	쨅 CA05	쨕 CA15	쨥 CA25	쨵 CA35	쩅 CA45	쩕 CA55	쩥 CA65	쩵 CA75	쪅 CA85	쪕 CA95
6	짆 C9C6	짖 C9D6	짦 C9E6	짶 C9F6	쨆 CA06	쨖 CA16	쨦 CA26	쨶 CA36	쩆 CA46	쩖 CA56	쩦 CA66	쩶 CA76	쪆 CA86	쪖 CA96
7	짇 C9C7	짗 C9D7	짧 C9E7	짷 C9F7	쨇 CA07	쨗 CA17	쨧 CA27	쨷 CA37	쩇 CA47	쩗 CA57	쩧 CA67	쩷 CA77	쪇 CA87	쪗 CA97
8	질 C9C8	짘 C9D8	짨 C9E8	째 C9F8	쨈 CA08	쨘 CA18	쨨 CA28	쨸 CA38	쩈 CA48	쩘 CA58	쩨 CA68	쩸 CA78	쪈 CA88	쪘 CA98
9	짉 C9C9	짙 C9D9	짩 C9E9	짹 C9F9	쨉 CA09	쨙 CA19	쨩 CA29	쨹 CA39	쩉 CA49	쩙 CA59	쩩 CA69	쩹 CA79	쪉 CA89	쪙 CA99
A	짊 C9CA	짚 C9DA	짪 C9EA	짺 C9FA	쨊 CA0A	쨚 CA1A	쨪 CA2A	쨺 CA3A	쩊 CA4A	쩚 CA5A	쩪 CA6A	쩺 CA7A	쪊 CA8A	쪚 CA9A
B	짋 C9CB	짛 C9DB	짫 C9EB	짻 C9FB	쨋 CA0B	쨛 CA1B	쨫 CA2B	쨻 CA3B	쩋 CA4B	쩛 CA5B	쩫 CA6B	쩻 CA7B	쪋 CA8B	쪛 CA9B
C	짌 C9CC	짜 C9DC	짬 C9EC	짼 C9FC	쨌 CA0C	쨜 CA1C	쨬 CA2C	쨼 CA3C	쩌 CA4C	쩜 CA5C	쩬 CA6C	쩼 CA7C	쪌 CA8C	쪜 CA9C
D	짍 C9CD	짝 C9DD	짭 C9ED	짽 C9FD	쨍 CA0D	쨝 CA1D	쨭 CA2D	쨽 CA3D	쩍 CA4D	쩝 CA5D	쩭 CA6D	쩽 CA7D	쪍 CA8D	쪝 CA9D
E	짎 C9CE	짞 C9DE	짮 C9EE	짾 C9FE	쨎 CA0E	쨞 CA1E	쨮 CA2E	쨾 CA3E	쩎 CA4E	쩞 CA5E	쩮 CA6E	쩾 CA7E	쪎 CA8E	쪞 CA9E
F	짏 C9CF	짟 C9DF	짯 C9EF	짿 C9FF	쨏 CA0F	쨟 CA1F	쨯 CA2F	쨿 CA3F	쩏 CA4F	쩟 CA5F	쩯 CA6F	쩿 CA7F	쪏 CA8F	쪟 CA9F

	CAA	CAB	CAC	CAD	CAE	CAF	CB0	CB1	CB2	CB3	CB4	CB5	CB6	CB7
0	쪠 CAA0	쪰 CAB0	쫀 CAC0	쫐 CAD0	쫠 CAE0	쫰 CAF0	쬀 CB00	쬐 CB10	쬠 CB20	쬰 CB30	쭀 CB40	쭐 CB50	쭠 CB60	쭰 CB70
1	쪡 CAA1	쪱 CAB1	쫁 CAC1	쫑 CAD1	쫡 CAE1	쫱 CAF1	쬁 CB01	쬑 CB11	쬡 CB21	쬱 CB31	쭁 CB41	쭑 CB51	쭡 CB61	쭱 CB71
2	쪢 CAA2	쪲 CAB2	쫂 CAC2	쫒 CAD2	쫢 CAE2	쫲 CAF2	쬂 CB02	쬒 CB12	쬢 CB22	쬲 CB32	쭂 CB42	쭒 CB52	쭢 CB62	쭲 CB72
3	쪣 CAA3	쪳 CAB3	쫃 CAC3	쫓 CAD3	쫣 CAE3	쫳 CAF3	쬃 CB03	쬓 CB13	쬣 CB23	쬳 CB33	쭃 CB43	쭓 CB53	쭣 CB63	쭳 CB73
4	쪤 CAA4	쪴 CAB4	쫄 CAC4	쫔 CAD4	쫤 CAE4	쫴 CAF4	쬄 CB04	쬔 CB14	쬤 CB24	쬴 CB34	쭄 CB44	쭔 CB54	쭤 CB64	쭴 CB74
5	쪥 CAA5	쪵 CAB5	쫅 CAC5	쫕 CAD5	쫥 CAE5	쫵 CAF5	쬅 CB05	쬕 CB15	쬥 CB25	쬵 CB35	쭅 CB45	쭕 CB55	쭥 CB65	쭵 CB75
6	쪦 CAA6	쪶 CAB6	쫆 CAC6	쫖 CAD6	쫦 CAE6	쫶 CAF6	쬆 CB06	쬖 CB16	쬦 CB26	쬶 CB36	쭆 CB46	쭖 CB56	쭦 CB66	쭶 CB76
7	쪧 CAA7	쪷 CAB7	쫇 CAC7	쫗 CAD7	쫧 CAE7	쫷 CAF7	쬇 CB07	쬗 CB17	쬧 CB27	쬷 CB37	쭇 CB47	쭗 CB57	쭧 CB67	쭷 CB77
8	쪨 CAA8	쪸 CAB8	쫈 CAC8	쫘 CAD8	쫨 CAE8	쫸 CAF8	쬈 CB08	쬘 CB18	쬨 CB28	쬸 CB38	쭈 CB48	쭘 CB58	쭨 CB68	쭸 CB78
9	쪩 CAA9	쪹 CAB9	쫉 CAC9	쫙 CAD9	쫩 CAE9	쫹 CAF9	쬉 CB09	쬙 CB19	쬩 CB29	쬹 CB39	쭉 CB49	쭙 CB59	쭩 CB69	쭹 CB79
A	쪪 CAAA	쪺 CABA	쫊 CACA	쫚 CADA	쫪 CAEA	쫺 CAFA	쬊 CB0A	쬚 CB1A	쬪 CB2A	쬺 CB3A	쭊 CB4A	쭚 CB5A	쭪 CB6A	쭺 CB7A
B	쪫 CAAB	쪻 CABB	쫋 CACB	쫛 CADB	쫫 CAEB	쫻 CAFB	쬋 CB0B	쬛 CB1B	쬫 CB2B	쬻 CB3B	쭋 CB4B	쭛 CB5B	쭫 CB6B	쭻 CB7B
C	쪬 CAAC	쪼 CABC	쫌 CACC	쫜 CADC	쫬 CAEC	쫼 CAFC	쬌 CB0C	쬜 CB1C	쬬 CB2C	쬼 CB3C	쭌 CB4C	쭜 CB5C	쭬 CB6C	쭼 CB7C
D	쪭 CAAD	쪽 CABD	쫍 CACD	쫝 CADD	쫭 CAED	쫽 CAFD	쬍 CB0D	쬝 CB1D	쬭 CB2D	쬽 CB3D	쭍 CB4D	쭝 CB5D	쭭 CB6D	쭽 CB7D
E	쪮 CAAE	쪾 CABE	쫎 CACE	쫞 CADE	쫮 CAEE	쫾 CAFE	쬎 CB0E	쬞 CB1E	쬮 CB2E	쬾 CB3E	쭎 CB4E	쭞 CB5E	쭮 CB6E	쭾 CB7E
F	쪯 CAAF	쪿 CABF	쫏 CACF	쫟 CADF	쫯 CAEF	쫿 CAFF	쬏 CB0F	쬟 CB1F	쬯 CB2F	쬿 CB3F	쭏 CB4F	쭟 CB5F	쭯 CB6F	쭿 CB7F

	CB8	CB9	CBA	CBB	CBC	CBD	CBE	CBF	CC0	CC1	CC2	CC3	CC4	CC5
0	쮀 CB80	쮐 CB90	쮠 CBA0	쮰 CBB0	쯀 CBC0	쯐 CBD0	쯠 CBE0	쯰 CBF0	찀 CC00	찐 CC10	찠 CC20	찰 CC30	챀 CC40	챐 CC50
1	쮁 CB81	쮑 CB91	쮡 CBA1	쮱 CBB1	쯁 CBC1	쯑 CBD1	쯡 CBE1	쯱 CBF1	찁 CC01	찑 CC11	찡 CC21	찱 CC31	챁 CC41	챑 CC51
2	쮂 CB82	쮒 CB92	쮢 CBA2	쮲 CBB2	쯂 CBC2	쯒 CBD2	쯢 CBE2	쯲 CBF2	찂 CC02	찒 CC12	찢 CC22	찲 CC32	챂 CC42	챒 CC52
3	쮃 CB83	쮓 CB93	쮣 CBA3	쮳 CBB3	쯃 CBC3	쯓 CBD3	쯣 CBE3	쯳 CBF3	찃 CC03	찓 CC13	찣 CC23	찳 CC33	챃 CC43	챓 CC53
4	쮄 CB84	쮔 CB94	쮤 CBA4	쮴 CBB4	쯄 CBC4	쯔 CBD4	쯤 CBE4	쯴 CBF4	찄 CC04	찔 CC14	찤 CC24	찴 CC34	채 CC44	챔 CC54
5	쮅 CB85	쮕 CB95	쮥 CBA5	쮵 CBB5	쯅 CBC5	쯕 CBD5	쯥 CBE5	쯵 CBF5	찅 CC05	찕 CC15	찥 CC25	찵 CC35	책 CC45	챕 CC55
6	쮆 CB86	쮖 CB96	쮦 CBA6	쮶 CBB6	쯆 CBC6	쯖 CBD6	쯦 CBE6	쯶 CBF6	찆 CC06	찖 CC16	찦 CC26	찶 CC36	챆 CC46	챖 CC56
7	쮇 CB87	쮗 CB97	쮧 CBA7	쮷 CBB7	쯇 CBC7	쯗 CBD7	쯧 CBE7	쯷 CBF7	찇 CC07	찗 CC17	찧 CC27	찷 CC37	챇 CC47	챗 CC57
8	쮈 CB88	쮘 CB98	쮨 CBA8	쮸 CBB8	쯈 CBC8	쯘 CBD8	쯨 CBE8	쯸 CBF8	찈 CC08	찘 CC18	차 CC28	참 CC38	챈 CC48	챘 CC58
9	쮉 CB89	쮙 CB99	쮩 CBA9	쮹 CBB9	쯉 CBC9	쯙 CBD9	쯩 CBE9	쯹 CBF9	찉 CC09	찙 CC19	착 CC29	찹 CC39	챉 CC49	챙 CC59
A	쮊 CB8A	쮚 CB9A	쮪 CBAA	쮺 CBBA	쯊 CBCA	쯚 CBDA	쯪 CBEA	쯺 CBFA	찊 CC0A	찚 CC1A	찪 CC2A	찺 CC3A	챊 CC4A	챚 CC5A
B	쮋 CB8B	쮛 CB9B	쮫 CBAB	쮻 CBBB	쯋 CBCB	쯛 CBDB	쯫 CBEB	쯻 CBFB	찋 CC0B	찛 CC1B	찫 CC2B	찻 CC3B	챋 CC4B	챛 CC5B
C	쮌 CB8C	쮜 CB9C	쮬 CBAC	쮼 CBBC	쯌 CBCC	쯜 CBDC	쯬 CBEC	쯼 CBFC	찌 CC0C	찜 CC1C	찬 CC2C	찼 CC3C	챌 CC4C	챜 CC5C
D	쮍 CB8D	쮝 CB9D	쮭 CBAD	쮽 CBBD	쯍 CBCD	쯝 CBDD	쯭 CBED	쯽 CBFD	찍 CC0D	찝 CC1D	찭 CC2D	창 CC3D	챍 CC4D	챝 CC5D
E	쮎 CB8E	쮞 CB9E	쮮 CBAE	쮾 CBBE	쯎 CBCE	쯞 CBDE	쯮 CBEE	쯾 CBFE	찎 CC0E	찞 CC1E	찮 CC2E	찾 CC3E	챎 CC4E	챞 CC5E
F	쮏 CB8F	쮟 CB9F	쮯 CBAF	쮿 CBBF	쯏 CBCF	쯟 CBDF	쯯 CBEF	쯿 CBFF	찏 CC0F	찟 CC1F	찯 CC2F	찿 CC3F	챏 CC4F	챟 CC5F

	CC6	CC7	CC8	CC9	CCA	CCB	CCC	CCD	CCE	CCF	CD0	CD1	CD2	CD3
0	챠 CC60	챰 CC70	첀 CC80	첐 CC90	철 CCA0	첰 CCB0	쳀 CCC0	쳐 CCD0	쳠 CCE0	쳰 CCF0	촀 CD00	촐 CD10	촠 CD20	촰 CD30
1	챡 CC61	챱 CC71	첁 CC81	첑 CC91	첡 CCA1	첱 CCB1	쳁 CCC1	쳑 CCD1	쳡 CCE1	쳱 CCF1	촁 CD01	촑 CD11	촡 CD21	촱 CD31
2	챢 CC62	챲 CC72	첂 CC82	첒 CC92	첢 CCA2	첲 CCB2	쳂 CCC2	쳒 CCD2	쳢 CCE2	쳲 CCF2	촂 CD02	촒 CD12	촢 CD22	촲 CD32
3	챣 CC63	챳 CC73	첃 CC83	첓 CC93	첣 CCA3	첳 CCB3	쳃 CCC3	쳓 CCD3	쳣 CCE3	쳳 CCF3	촃 CD03	촓 CD13	촣 CD23	촳 CD33
4	챤 CC64	챴 CC74	첄 CC84	첔 CC94	첤 CCA4	체 CCB4	쳄 CCC4	쳔 CCD4	쳤 CCE4	쳴 CCF4	촄 CD04	촔 CD14	촤 CD24	촴 CD34
5	챥 CC65	챵 CC75	첅 CC85	첕 CC95	첥 CCA5	첵 CCB5	쳅 CCC5	쳕 CCD5	쳥 CCE5	쳵 CCF5	촅 CD05	촕 CD15	촥 CD25	촵 CD35
6	챦 CC66	챶 CC76	첆 CC86	첖 CC96	첦 CCA6	첶 CCB6	쳆 CCC6	쳖 CCD6	쳦 CCE6	쳶 CCF6	촆 CD06	촖 CD16	촦 CD26	촶 CD36
7	챧 CC67	챷 CC77	첇 CC87	첗 CC97	첧 CCA7	첷 CCB7	쳇 CCC7	쳗 CCD7	쳧 CCE7	쳷 CCF7	촇 CD07	촗 CD17	촧 CD27	촷 CD37
8	챨 CC68	챸 CC78	첈 CC88	처 CC98	첨 CCA8	첸 CCB8	쳈 CCC8	쳘 CCD8	쳨 CCE8	쳸 CCF8	초 CD08	촘 CD18	촨 CD28	촸 CD38
9	챩 CC69	챹 CC79	첉 CC89	척 CC99	첩 CCA9	첹 CCB9	쳉 CCC9	쳙 CCD9	쳩 CCE9	쳹 CCF9	촉 CD09	촙 CD19	촩 CD29	촹 CD39
A	챪 CC6A	챺 CC7A	첊 CC8A	첚 CC9A	첪 CCAA	첺 CCBA	쳊 CCCA	쳚 CCDA	쳪 CCEA	쳺 CCFA	촊 CD0A	촚 CD1A	촪 CD2A	촺 CD3A
B	챫 CC6B	챻 CC7B	첋 CC8B	첛 CC9B	첫 CCAB	첻 CCBB	쳋 CCCB	쳛 CCDB	쳫 CCEB	쳻 CCFB	촋 CD0B	촛 CD1B	촫 CD2B	촻 CD3B
C	챬 CC6C	챼 CC7C	첌 CC8C	천 CC9C	첬 CCAC	첼 CCBC	쳌 CCCC	쳜 CCDC	쳬 CCEC	쳼 CCFC	촌 CD0C	촜 CD1C	촬 CD2C	촼 CD3C
D	챭 CC6D	챽 CC7D	첍 CC8D	첝 CC9D	청 CCAD	첽 CCBD	쳍 CCCD	쳝 CCDD	쳭 CCED	쳽 CCFD	촍 CD0D	총 CD1D	촭 CD2D	촽 CD3D
E	챮 CC6E	챾 CC7E	첎 CC8E	첞 CC9E	첮 CCAE	첾 CCBE	쳎 CCCE	쳞 CCDE	쳮 CCEE	쳾 CCFE	촎 CD0E	촞 CD1E	촮 CD2E	촾 CD3E
F	챯 CC6F	챿 CC7F	첏 CC8F	첟 CC9F	첯 CCAF	첿 CCBF	쳏 CCCF	쳟 CCDF	쳯 CCEF	쳿 CCFF	촏 CD0F	촟 CD1F	촯 CD2F	촿 CD3F

	CD4	CD5	CD6	CD7	CD8	CD9	CDA	CDB	CDC	CDD	CDE	CDF	CE0	CE1
0	쵀 CD40	쵐 CD50	쵠 CD60	쵰 CD70	춀 CD80	춐 CD90	춠 CDA0	춰 CDB0	췀 CDC0	췐 CDD0	췠 CDE0	췰 CDF0	츀 CE00	츐 CE10
1	쵁 CD41	쵑 CD51	쵡 CD61	쵱 CD71	춁 CD81	춑 CD91	춡 CDA1	춱 CDB1	췁 CDC1	췑 CDD1	췡 CDE1	췱 CDF1	츁 CE01	츑 CE11
2	쵂 CD42	쵒 CD52	쵢 CD62	쵲 CD72	춂 CD82	춒 CD92	춢 CDA2	춲 CDB2	췂 CDC2	췒 CDD2	췢 CDE2	췲 CDF2	츂 CE02	츒 CE12
3	쵃 CD43	쵓 CD53	쵣 CD63	쵳 CD73	춃 CD83	춓 CD93	춣 CDA3	춳 CDB3	췃 CDC3	췓 CDD3	췣 CDE3	췳 CDF3	츃 CE03	츓 CE13
4	쵄 CD44	쵔 CD54	쵤 CD64	쵴 CD74	춄 CD84	추 CD94	춤 CDA4	춴 CDB4	췄 CDC4	췔 CDD4	췤 CDE4	췴 CDF4	츄 CE04	츔 CE14
5	쵅 CD45	쵕 CD55	쵥 CD65	쵵 CD75	춅 CD85	축 CD95	춥 CDA5	춵 CDB5	췅 CDC5	췕 CDD5	췥 CDE5	췵 CDF5	츅 CE05	츕 CE15
6	쵆 CD46	쵖 CD56	쵦 CD66	쵶 CD76	춆 CD86	춖 CD96	춦 CDA6	춶 CDB6	췆 CDC6	췖 CDD6	췦 CDE6	췶 CDF6	츆 CE06	츖 CE16
7	쵇 CD47	쵗 CD57	쵧 CD67	쵷 CD77	춇 CD87	춗 CD97	춧 CDA7	춷 CDB7	췇 CDC7	췗 CDD7	췧 CDE7	췷 CDF7	츇 CE07	츗 CE17
8	쵈 CD48	쵘 CD58	쵨 CD68	쵸 CD78	춈 CD88	춘 CD98	춨 CDA8	춸 CDB8	췈 CDC8	췘 CDD8	취 CDE8	췸 CDF8	츈 CE08	츘 CE18
9	쵉 CD49	쵙 CD59	쵩 CD69	쵹 CD79	춉 CD89	춙 CD99	충 CDA9	춹 CDB9	췉 CDC9	췙 CDD9	췩 CDE9	췹 CDF9	츉 CE09	츙 CE19
A	쵊 CD4A	쵚 CD5A	쵪 CD6A	쵺 CD7A	춊 CD8A	춚 CD9A	춪 CDAA	춺 CDBA	췊 CDCA	췚 CDDA	췪 CDEA	췺 CDFA	츊 CE0A	츚 CE1A
B	쵋 CD4B	쵛 CD5B	쵫 CD6B	쵻 CD7B	춋 CD8B	춛 CD9B	춫 CDAB	춻 CDBB	췋 CDCB	췛 CDDB	췫 CDEB	췻 CDFB	츋 CE0B	츛 CE1B
C	쵌 CD4C	최 CD5C	쵬 CD6C	쵼 CD7C	춌 CD8C	출 CD9C	춬 CDAC	춼 CDBC	췌 CDCC	췜 CDDC	췬 CDEC	췼 CDFC	츌 CE0C	츜 CE1C
D	쵍 CD4D	쵝 CD5D	쵭 CD6D	쵽 CD7D	춍 CD8D	춝 CD9D	춭 CDAD	춽 CDBD	췍 CDCD	췝 CDDD	췭 CDED	췽 CDFD	츍 CE0D	츝 CE1D
E	쵎 CD4E	쵞 CD5E	쵮 CD6E	쵾 CD7E	춎 CD8E	춞 CD9E	춮 CDAE	춾 CDBE	췎 CDCE	췞 CDDE	췮 CDEE	췾 CDFE	츎 CE0E	츞 CE1E
F	쵏 CD4F	쵟 CD5F	쵯 CD6F	쵿 CD7F	춏 CD8F	춟 CD9F	춯 CDAF	춿 CDBF	췏 CDCF	췟 CDDF	췯 CDEF	췿 CDFF	츏 CE0F	츟 CE1F

	CE2	CE3	CE4	CE5	CE6	CE7	CE8	CE9	CEA	CEB	CEC	CED	CEE	CEF
0	츠 CE20	츰 CE30	칀 CE40	칐 CE50	칠 CE60	칰 CE70	캀 CE80	캐 CE90	캠 CEA0	캰 CEB0	컀 CEC0	컐 CED0	컠 CEE0	컰 CEF0
1	측 CE21	츱 CE31	칁 CE41	칑 CE51	칡 CE61	칱 CE71	캁 CE81	캑 CE91	캡 CEA1	캱 CEB1	컁 CEC1	컑 CED1	컡 CEE1	컱 CEF1
2	츢 CE22	츲 CE32	칂 CE42	칒 CE52	칢 CE62	칲 CE72	캂 CE82	캒 CE92	캢 CEA2	캲 CEB2	컂 CEC2	컒 CED2	컢 CEE2	컲 CEF2
3	츣 CE23	츳 CE33	칃 CE43	칓 CE53	칣 CE63	칳 CE73	캃 CE83	캓 CE93	캣 CEA3	캳 CEB3	컃 CEC3	컓 CED3	컣 CEE3	컳 CEF3
4	츤 CE24	츴 CE34	칄 CE44	칔 CE54	칤 CE64	카 CE74	캄 CE84	캔 CE94	캤 CEA4	캴 CEB4	컄 CEC4	컔 CED4	커 CEE4	컴 CEF4
5	츥 CE25	층 CE35	칅 CE45	칕 CE55	칥 CE65	칵 CE75	캅 CE85	캕 CE95	캥 CEA5	캵 CEB5	컅 CEC5	컕 CED5	컥 CEE5	컵 CEF5
6	츦 CE26	츶 CE36	칆 CE46	칖 CE56	칦 CE66	칶 CE76	캆 CE86	캖 CE96	캦 CEA6	캶 CEB6	컆 CEC6	컖 CED6	컦 CEE6	컶 CEF6
7	츧 CE27	츷 CE37	칇 CE47	칗 CE57	칧 CE67	칷 CE77	캇 CE87	캗 CE97	캧 CEA7	캷 CEB7	컇 CEC7	컗 CED7	컧 CEE7	컷 CEF7
8	츨 CE28	츸 CE38	칈 CE48	치 CE58	침 CE68	칸 CE78	캈 CE88	캘 CE98	캨 CEA8	캸 CEB8	컈 CEC8	컘 CED8	컨 CEE8	컸 CEF8
9	츩 CE29	츹 CE39	칉 CE49	칙 CE59	칩 CE69	칹 CE79	캉 CE89	캙 CE99	캩 CEA9	캹 CEB9	컉 CEC9	컙 CED9	컩 CEE9	컹 CEF9
A	츪 CE2A	츺 CE3A	칊 CE4A	칚 CE5A	칪 CE6A	칺 CE7A	캊 CE8A	캚 CE9A	캪 CEAA	캺 CEBA	컊 CECA	컚 CEDA	컪 CEEA	컺 CEFA
B	츫 CE2B	츻 CE3B	칋 CE4B	칛 CE5B	칫 CE6B	칻 CE7B	캋 CE8B	캛 CE9B	캫 CEAB	캻 CEBB	컋 CECB	컛 CEDB	컫 CEEB	컻 CEFB
C	츬 CE2C	츼 CE3C	칌 CE4C	친 CE5C	칬 CE6C	칼 CE7C	캌 CE8C	캜 CE9C	캬 CEAC	캼 CEBC	컌 CECC	컜 CEDC	컬 CEEC	컼 CEFC
D	츭 CE2D	츽 CE3D	칍 CE4D	칝 CE5D	칭 CE6D	칽 CE7D	캍 CE8D	캝 CE9D	캭 CEAD	캽 CEBD	컍 CECD	컝 CEDD	컭 CEED	컽 CEFD
E	츮 CE2E	츾 CE3E	칎 CE4E	칞 CE5E	칮 CE6E	칾 CE7E	캎 CE8E	캞 CE9E	캮 CEAE	캾 CEBE	컎 CECE	컞 CEDE	컮 CEEE	컾 CEFE
F	츯 CE2F	츿 CE3F	칏 CE4F	칟 CE5F	칯 CE6F	칿 CE7F	캏 CE8F	캟 CE9F	캯 CEAF	캿 CEBF	컏 CECF	컟 CEDF	컯 CEEF	컿 CEFF

	CF0	CF1	CF2	CF3	CF4	CF5	CF6	CF7	CF8	CF9	CFA	CFB	CFC	CFD
0	케 CF00	켐 CF10	켠 CF20	켰 CF30	콀 CF40	콐 CF50	콠 CF60	콰 CF70	쾀 CF80	쾐 CF90	쾠 CFA0	쾰 CFB0	쿀 CFC0	쿐 CFD0
1	켁 CF01	켑 CF11	켡 CF21	켱 CF31	콁 CF41	콑 CF51	콡 CF61	콱 CF71	쾁 CF81	쾑 CF91	쾡 CFA1	쾱 CFB1	쿁 CFC1	쿑 CFD1
2	켂 CF02	켒 CF12	켢 CF22	켲 CF32	콂 CF42	콒 CF52	콢 CF62	콲 CF72	쾂 CF82	쾒 CF92	쾢 CFA2	쾲 CFB2	쿂 CFC2	쿒 CFD2
3	켃 CF03	켓 CF13	켣 CF23	켳 CF33	콃 CF43	콓 CF53	콣 CF63	콳 CF73	쾃 CF83	쾓 CF93	쾣 CFA3	쾳 CFB3	쿃 CFC3	쿓 CFD3
4	켄 CF04	켔 CF14	켤 CF24	켴 CF34	콄 CF44	코 CF54	콤 CF64	콴 CF74	쾄 CF84	쾔 CF94	쾤 CFA4	쾴 CFB4	쿄 CFC4	쿔 CFD4
5	켅 CF05	켕 CF15	켥 CF25	켵 CF35	콅 CF45	콕 CF55	콥 CF65	콵 CF75	쾅 CF85	쾕 CF95	쾥 CFA5	쾵 CFB5	쿅 CFC5	쿕 CFD5
6	켆 CF06	켖 CF16	켦 CF26	켶 CF36	콆 CF46	콖 CF56	콦 CF66	콶 CF76	쾆 CF86	쾖 CF96	쾦 CFA6	쾶 CFB6	쿆 CFC6	쿖 CFD6
7	켇 CF07	켗 CF17	켧 CF27	켷 CF37	콇 CF47	콗 CF57	콧 CF67	콷 CF77	쾇 CF87	쾗 CF97	쾧 CFA7	쾷 CFB7	쿇 CFC7	쿗 CFD7
8	켈 CF08	켘 CF18	켨 CF28	켸 CF38	콈 CF48	콘 CF58	콨 CF68	콸 CF78	쾈 CF88	쾘 CF98	쾨 CFA8	쾸 CFB8	쿈 CFC8	쿘 CFD8
9	켉 CF09	켙 CF19	켩 CF29	켹 CF39	콉 CF49	콙 CF59	콩 CF69	콹 CF79	쾉 CF89	쾙 CF99	쾩 CFA9	쾹 CFB9	쿉 CFC9	쿙 CFD9
A	켊 CF0A	켚 CF1A	켪 CF2A	켺 CF3A	콊 CF4A	콚 CF5A	콪 CF6A	콺 CF7A	쾊 CF8A	쾚 CF9A	쾪 CFAA	쾺 CFBA	쿊 CFCA	쿚 CFDA
B	켋 CF0B	켛 CF1B	켫 CF2B	켻 CF3B	콋 CF4B	콛 CF5B	콫 CF6B	콻 CF7B	쾋 CF8B	쾛 CF9B	쾫 CFAB	쾻 CFBB	쿋 CFCB	쿛 CFDB
C	켌 CF0C	켜 CF1C	켬 CF2C	켼 CF3C	콌 CF4C	콜 CF5C	콬 CF6C	콼 CF7C	쾌 CF8C	쾜 CF9C	쾬 CFAC	쾼 CFBC	쿌 CFCC	쿜 CFDC
D	켍 CF0D	켝 CF1D	켭 CF2D	켽 CF3D	콍 CF4D	콝 CF5D	콭 CF6D	콽 CF7D	쾍 CF8D	쾝 CF9D	쾭 CFAD	쾽 CFBD	쿍 CFCD	쿝 CFDD
E	켎 CF0E	켞 CF1E	켮 CF2E	켾 CF3E	콎 CF4E	콞 CF5E	콮 CF6E	콾 CF7E	쾎 CF8E	쾞 CF9E	쾮 CFAE	쾾 CFBE	쿎 CFCE	쿞 CFDE
F	켏 CF0F	켟 CF1F	켯 CF2F	켿 CF3F	콏 CF4F	콟 CF5F	콯 CF6F	콿 CF7F	쾏 CF8F	쾟 CF9F	쾯 CFAF	쾿 CFBF	쿏 CFCF	쿟 CFDF

	CFE	CFF	D00	D01	D02	D03	D04	D05	D06	D07	D08	D09	D0A	D0B
0	쿠 CFE0	쿰 CFF0	퀀 D000	퀐 D010	퀠 D020	퀰 D030	큀 D040	큐 D050	큠 D060	큰 D070	킀 D080	킐 D090	킠 D0A0	킰 D0B0
1	쿡 CFE1	쿱 CFF1	퀁 D001	퀑 D011	퀡 D021	퀱 D031	큁 D041	큑 D051	큡 D061	큱 D071	킁 D081	킑 D091	킡 D0A1	킱 D0B1
2	쿢 CFE2	쿲 CFF2	퀂 D002	퀒 D012	퀢 D022	퀲 D032	큂 D042	큒 D052	큢 D062	큲 D072	킂 D082	킒 D092	킢 D0A2	킲 D0B2
3	쿣 CFE3	쿳 CFF3	퀃 D003	퀓 D013	퀣 D023	퀳 D033	큃 D043	큓 D053	큣 D063	큳 D073	킃 D083	킓 D093	킣 D0A3	킳 D0B3
4	쿤 CFE4	쿴 CFF4	퀄 D004	퀔 D014	퀤 D024	퀴 D034	큄 D044	큔 D054	큤 D064	클 D074	킄 D084	킔 D094	키 D0A4	킴 D0B4
5	쿥 CFE5	쿵 CFF5	퀅 D005	퀕 D015	퀥 D025	퀵 D035	큅 D045	큕 D055	큥 D065	큵 D075	킅 D085	킕 D095	킥 D0A5	킵 D0B5
6	쿦 CFE6	쿶 CFF6	퀆 D006	퀖 D016	퀦 D026	퀶 D036	큆 D046	큖 D056	큦 D066	큶 D076	킆 D086	킖 D096	킦 D0A6	킶 D0B6
7	쿧 CFE7	쿷 CFF7	퀇 D007	퀗 D017	퀧 D027	퀷 D037	큇 D047	큗 D057	큧 D067	큷 D077	킇 D087	킗 D097	킧 D0A7	킷 D0B7
8	쿨 CFE8	쿸 CFF8	퀈 D008	퀘 D018	퀨 D028	퀸 D038	큈 D048	큘 D058	큨 D068	큸 D078	킈 D088	킘 D098	킨 D0A8	킸 D0B8
9	쿩 CFE9	쿹 CFF9	퀉 D009	퀙 D019	퀩 D029	퀹 D039	큉 D049	큙 D059	큩 D069	큹 D079	킉 D089	킙 D099	킩 D0A9	킹 D0B9
A	쿪 CFEA	쿺 CFFA	퀊 D00A	퀚 D01A	퀪 D02A	퀺 D03A	큊 D04A	큚 D05A	큪 D06A	큺 D07A	킊 D08A	킚 D09A	킪 D0AA	킺 D0BA
B	쿫 CFEB	쿻 CFFB	퀋 D00B	퀛 D01B	퀫 D02B	퀻 D03B	큋 D04B	큛 D05B	큫 D06B	큻 D07B	킋 D08B	킛 D09B	킫 D0AB	킻 D0BB
C	쿬 CFEC	쿼 CFFC	퀌 D00C	퀜 D01C	퀬 D02C	퀼 D03C	큌 D04C	큜 D05C	크 D06C	큼 D07C	킌 D08C	킜 D09C	킬 D0AC	킼 D0BC
D	쿭 CFED	쿽 CFFD	퀍 D00D	퀝 D01D	퀭 D02D	퀽 D03D	큍 D04D	큝 D05D	큭 D06D	큽 D07D	킍 D08D	킝 D09D	킭 D0AD	킽 D0BD
E	쿮 CFEE	쿾 CFFE	퀎 D00E	퀞 D01E	퀮 D02E	퀾 D03E	큎 D04E	큞 D05E	큮 D06E	큾 D07E	킎 D08E	킞 D09E	킮 D0AE	킾 D0BE
F	쿯 CFEF	쿿 CFFF	퀏 D00F	퀟 D01F	퀯 D02F	퀿 D03F	큏 D04F	큟 D05F	큯 D06F	큿 D07F	킏 D08F	킟 D09F	킯 D0AF	킿 D0BF

	D0C	D0D	D0E	D0F	D10	D11	D12	D13	D14	D15	D16	D17	D18	D19
0	타 D0C0	탐 D0D0	탠 D0E0	탰 D0F0	턀 D100	턐 D110	턠 D120	터 D130	텀 D140	텐 D150	텠 D160	텰 D170	톀 D180	톐 D190
1	탁 D0C1	탑 D0D1	탡 D0E1	탱 D0F1	턁 D101	턑 D111	턡 D121	턱 D131	텁 D141	텑 D151	텡 D161	텱 D171	톁 D181	톑 D191
2	탂 D0C2	탒 D0D2	탢 D0E2	탲 D0F2	턂 D102	턒 D112	턢 D122	턲 D132	텂 D142	텒 D152	텢 D162	텲 D172	톂 D182	톒 D192
3	탃 D0C3	탓 D0D3	탣 D0E3	탳 D0F3	턃 D103	턓 D113	턣 D123	턳 D133	텃 D143	텓 D153	텣 D163	텳 D173	톃 D183	톓 D193
4	탄 D0C4	탔 D0D4	탤 D0E4	탴 D0F4	턄 D104	턔 D114	턤 D124	턴 D134	텄 D144	텔 D154	텤 D164	텴 D174	톄 D184	톔 D194
5	탅 D0C5	탕 D0D5	탥 D0E5	탵 D0F5	턅 D105	턕 D115	턥 D125	턵 D135	텅 D145	텕 D155	텥 D165	텵 D175	톅 D185	톕 D195
6	탆 D0C6	탖 D0D6	탦 D0E6	탶 D0F6	턆 D106	턖 D116	턦 D126	턶 D136	텆 D146	텖 D156	텦 D166	텶 D176	톆 D186	톖 D196
7	탇 D0C7	탗 D0D7	탧 D0E7	탷 D0F7	턇 D107	턗 D117	턧 D127	턷 D137	텇 D147	텗 D157	텧 D167	텷 D177	톇 D187	톗 D197
8	탈 D0C8	탘 D0D8	탨 D0E8	탸 D0F8	턈 D108	턘 D118	턨 D128	털 D138	텈 D148	텘 D158	텨 D168	텸 D178	톈 D188	톘 D198
9	탉 D0C9	탙 D0D9	탩 D0E9	탹 D0F9	턉 D109	턙 D119	턩 D129	턹 D139	텉 D149	텙 D159	텩 D169	텹 D179	톉 D189	톙 D199
A	탊 D0CA	탚 D0DA	탪 D0EA	탺 D0FA	턊 D10A	턚 D11A	턪 D12A	턺 D13A	텊 D14A	텚 D15A	텪 D16A	텺 D17A	톊 D18A	톚 D19A
B	탋 D0CB	탛 D0DB	탫 D0EB	탻 D0FB	턋 D10B	턛 D11B	턫 D12B	턻 D13B	텋 D14B	텛 D15B	텫 D16B	텻 D17B	톋 D18B	톛 D19B
C	탌 D0CC	태 D0DC	탬 D0EC	탼 D0FC	턌 D10C	턜 D11C	턬 D12C	턼 D13C	테 D14C	템 D15C	텬 D16C	텼 D17C	톌 D18C	톜 D19C
D	탍 D0CD	택 D0DD	탭 D0ED	탽 D0FD	턍 D10D	턝 D11D	턭 D12D	턽 D13D	텍 D14D	텝 D15D	텭 D16D	텽 D17D	톍 D18D	톝 D19D
E	탎 D0CE	탞 D0DE	탮 D0EE	탾 D0FE	턎 D10E	턞 D11E	턮 D12E	턾 D13E	텎 D14E	텞 D15E	텮 D16E	텾 D17E	톎 D18E	톞 D19E
F	탏 D0CF	탟 D0DF	탯 D0EF	탿 D0FF	턏 D10F	턟 D11F	턯 D12F	턿 D13F	텏 D14F	텟 D15F	텯 D16F	텿 D17F	톏 D18F	톟 D19F

	D1A	D1B	D1C	D1D	D1E	D1F	D20	D21	D22	D23	D24	D25	D26	D27
0	토 D1A0	톰 D1B0	퇀 D1C0	퇐 D1D0	퇠 D1E0	퇰 D1F0	툀 D200	툐 D210	툠 D220	툰 D230	퉀 D240	퉐 D250	퉠 D260	퉰 D270
1	톡 D1A1	톱 D1B1	퇁 D1C1	퇑 D1D1	퇡 D1E1	퇱 D1F1	툁 D201	툑 D211	툡 D221	툱 D231	퉁 D241	퉑 D251	퉡 D261	퉱 D271
2	톢 D1A2	톲 D1B2	퇂 D1C2	퇒 D1D2	퇢 D1E2	퇲 D1F2	툂 D202	툒 D212	툢 D222	툲 D232	퉂 D242	퉒 D252	퉢 D262	퉲 D272
3	톣 D1A3	톳 D1B3	퇃 D1C3	퇓 D1D3	퇣 D1E3	퇳 D1F3	툃 D203	툓 D213	툣 D223	툳 D233	퉃 D243	퉓 D253	퉣 D263	퉳 D273
4	톤 D1A4	톴 D1B4	퇄 D1C4	퇔 D1D4	퇤 D1E4	퇴 D1F4	툄 D204	툔 D214	툤 D224	툴 D234	퉄 D244	퉔 D254	퉤 D264	퉴 D274
5	톥 D1A5	통 D1B5	퇅 D1C5	퇕 D1D5	퇥 D1E5	퇵 D1F5	툅 D205	툕 D215	툥 D225	툵 D235	퉅 D245	퉕 D255	퉥 D265	퉵 D275
6	톦 D1A6	톶 D1B6	퇆 D1C6	퇖 D1D6	퇦 D1E6	퇶 D1F6	툆 D206	툖 D216	툦 D226	툶 D236	퉆 D246	퉖 D256	퉦 D266	퉶 D276
7	톧 D1A7	톷 D1B7	퇇 D1C7	퇗 D1D7	퇧 D1E7	퇷 D1F7	툇 D207	툗 D217	툧 D227	툷 D237	퉇 D247	퉗 D257	퉧 D267	퉷 D277
8	톨 D1A8	톸 D1B8	퇈 D1C8	퇘 D1D8	퇨 D1E8	퇸 D1F8	툈 D208	툘 D218	툨 D228	툸 D238	퉈 D248	퉘 D258	퉨 D268	퉸 D278
9	톩 D1A9	톹 D1B9	퇉 D1C9	퇙 D1D9	퇩 D1E9	퇹 D1F9	툉 D209	툙 D219	툩 D229	툹 D239	퉉 D249	퉙 D259	퉩 D269	퉹 D279
A	톪 D1AA	톺 D1BA	퇊 D1CA	퇚 D1DA	퇪 D1EA	퇺 D1FA	툊 D20A	툚 D21A	툪 D22A	툺 D23A	퉊 D24A	퉚 D25A	퉪 D26A	퉺 D27A
B	톫 D1AB	톻 D1BB	퇋 D1CB	퇛 D1DB	퇫 D1EB	퇻 D1FB	툋 D20B	툛 D21B	툫 D22B	툻 D23B	퉋 D24B	퉛 D25B	퉫 D26B	퉻 D27B
C	톬 D1AC	톼 D1BC	퇌 D1CC	퇜 D1DC	퇬 D1EC	퇼 D1FC	툌 D20C	툜 D21C	투 D22C	툼 D23C	퉌 D24C	퉜 D25C	퉬 D26C	퉼 D27C
D	톭 D1AD	톽 D1BD	퇍 D1CD	퇝 D1DD	퇭 D1ED	퇽 D1FD	툍 D20D	툝 D21D	툭 D22D	툽 D23D	퉍 D24D	퉝 D25D	퉭 D26D	퉽 D27D
E	톮 D1AE	톾 D1BE	퇎 D1CE	퇞 D1DE	퇮 D1EE	퇾 D1FE	툎 D20E	툞 D21E	툮 D22E	툾 D23E	퉎 D24E	퉞 D25E	퉮 D26E	퉾 D27E
F	톯 D1AF	톿 D1BF	퇏 D1CF	퇟 D1DF	퇯 D1EF	퇿 D1FF	툏 D20F	툟 D21F	툯 D22F	툿 D23F	퉏 D24F	퉟 D25F	퉯 D26F	퉿 D27F

	D28	D29	D2A	D2B	D2C	D2D	D2E	D2F	D30	D31	D32	D33	D34	D35
0	튀 D280	튐 D290	튠 D2A0	튰 D2B0	틀 D2C0	틐 D2D0	틠 D2E0	티 D2F0	팀 D300	판 D310	팠 D320	팰 D330	퍀 D340	퍐 D350
1	튁 D281	튑 D291	튡 D2A1	튱 D2B1	틁 D2C1	틑 D2D1	틡 D2E1	틱 D2F1	팁 D301	팑 D311	팡 D321	팱 D331	퍁 D341	퍑 D351
2	튂 D282	튒 D292	튢 D2A2	튲 D2B2	틂 D2C2	틒 D2D2	틢 D2E2	틲 D2F2	팂 D302	팒 D312	팢 D322	팲 D332	퍂 D342	퍒 D352
3	튃 D283	튓 D293	튣 D2A3	튳 D2B3	틃 D2C3	틓 D2D3	틣 D2E3	틳 D2F3	팃 D303	팓 D313	팣 D323	팳 D333	퍃 D343	퍓 D353
4	튄 D284	튔 D294	튤 D2A4	튴 D2B4	틄 D2C4	틔 D2D4	틤 D2E4	틴 D2F4	팄 D304	팔 D314	팤 D324	팴 D334	퍄 D344	퍔 D354
5	튅 D285	튕 D295	튥 D2A5	튵 D2B5	틅 D2C5	틕 D2D5	틥 D2E5	틵 D2F5	팅 D305	팕 D315	팥 D325	팵 D335	퍅 D345	퍕 D355
6	튆 D286	튖 D296	튦 D2A6	튶 D2B6	틆 D2C6	틖 D2D6	틦 D2E6	틶 D2F6	팆 D306	팖 D316	팦 D326	팶 D336	퍆 D346	퍖 D356
7	튇 D287	튗 D297	튧 D2A7	튷 D2B7	틇 D2C7	틗 D2D7	틧 D2E7	틷 D2F7	팇 D307	팗 D317	팧 D327	팷 D337	퍇 D347	퍗 D357
8	튈 D288	튘 D298	튨 D2A8	트 D2B8	틈 D2C8	틘 D2D8	틨 D2E8	틸 D2F8	팈 D308	팘 D318	패 D328	팸 D338	퍈 D348	퍘 D358
9	튉 D289	튙 D299	튩 D2A9	특 D2B9	틉 D2C9	틙 D2D9	틩 D2E9	틹 D2F9	팉 D309	팙 D319	팩 D329	팹 D339	퍉 D349	퍙 D359
A	튊 D28A	튚 D29A	튪 D2AA	튺 D2BA	틊 D2CA	틚 D2DA	틪 D2EA	틺 D2FA	팊 D30A	팚 D31A	팪 D32A	팺 D33A	퍊 D34A	퍚 D35A
B	튋 D28B	튛 D29B	튫 D2AB	튻 D2BB	틋 D2CB	틛 D2DB	틫 D2EB	틻 D2FB	팋 D30B	팛 D31B	팫 D32B	팻 D33B	퍋 D34B	퍛 D35B
C	튌 D28C	튜 D29C	튬 D2AC	튼 D2BC	틌 D2CC	틜 D2DC	틬 D2EC	틼 D2FC	파 D30C	팜 D31C	팬 D32C	팼 D33C	퍌 D34C	퍜 D35C
D	튍 D28D	튝 D29D	튭 D2AD	튽 D2BD	틍 D2CD	틝 D2DD	틭 D2ED	틽 D2FD	팍 D30D	팝 D31D	팭 D32D	팽 D33D	퍍 D34D	퍝 D35D
E	튎 D28E	튞 D29E	튮 D2AE	튾 D2BE	틎 D2CE	틞 D2DE	틮 D2EE	틾 D2FE	팎 D30E	팞 D31E	팮 D32E	팾 D33E	퍎 D34E	퍞 D35E
F	튏 D28F	튟 D29F	튯 D2AF	튿 D2BF	틏 D2CF	틟 D2DF	틯 D2EF	틿 D2FF	팏 D30F	팟 D31F	팯 D32F	팿 D33F	퍏 D34F	퍟 D35F

	D36	D37	D38	D39	D3A	D3B	D3C	D3D	D3E	D3F	D40	D41	D42	D43
0	퍠 D360	퍰 D370	펀 D380	펐 D390	펠 D3A0	펰 D3B0	폀 D3C0	폐 D3D0	폠 D3E0	폰 D3F0	퐀 D400	퐐 D410	퐠 D420	퐰 D430
1	퍡 D361	퍱 D371	펁 D381	펑 D391	펡 D3A1	펱 D3B1	폁 D3C1	폑 D3D1	폡 D3E1	폱 D3F1	퐁 D401	퐑 D411	퐡 D421	퐱 D431
2	퍢 D362	퍲 D372	펂 D382	펒 D392	펢 D3A2	펲 D3B2	폂 D3C2	폒 D3D2	폢 D3E2	폲 D3F2	퐂 D402	퐒 D412	퐢 D422	퐲 D432
3	퍣 D363	퍳 D373	펃 D383	펓 D393	펣 D3A3	펳 D3B3	폃 D3C3	폓 D3D3	폣 D3E3	폳 D3F3	퐃 D403	퐓 D413	퐣 D423	퐳 D433
4	퍤 D364	퍴 D374	펄 D384	펔 D394	펤 D3A4	펴 D3B4	폄 D3C4	폔 D3D4	폤 D3E4	폴 D3F4	퐄 D404	퐔 D414	퐤 D424	퐴 D434
5	퍥 D365	퍵 D375	펅 D385	펕 D395	펥 D3A5	펵 D3B5	폅 D3C5	폕 D3D5	폥 D3E5	폵 D3F5	퐅 D405	퐕 D415	퐥 D425	퐵 D435
6	퍦 D366	퍶 D376	펆 D386	펖 D396	펦 D3A6	펶 D3B6	폆 D3C6	폖 D3D6	폦 D3E6	폶 D3F6	퐆 D406	퐖 D416	퐦 D426	퐶 D436
7	퍧 D367	퍷 D377	펇 D387	펗 D397	펧 D3A7	펷 D3B7	폇 D3C7	폗 D3D7	폧 D3E7	폷 D3F7	퐇 D407	퐗 D417	퐧 D427	퐷 D437
8	퍨 D368	퍸 D378	펈 D388	페 D398	펨 D3A8	편 D3B8	폈 D3C8	폘 D3D8	폨 D3E8	폸 D3F8	퐈 D408	퐘 D418	퐨 D428	퐸 D438
9	퍩 D369	퍹 D379	펉 D389	펙 D399	펩 D3A9	펹 D3B9	평 D3C9	폙 D3D9	폩 D3E9	폹 D3F9	퐉 D409	퐙 D419	퐩 D429	퐹 D439
A	퍪 D36A	퍺 D37A	펊 D38A	펚 D39A	펪 D3AA	펺 D3BA	폊 D3CA	폚 D3DA	폪 D3EA	폺 D3FA	퐊 D40A	퐚 D41A	퐪 D42A	퐺 D43A
B	퍫 D36B	퍻 D37B	펋 D38B	펛 D39B	펫 D3AB	펻 D3BB	폋 D3CB	폛 D3DB	폫 D3EB	폻 D3FB	퐋 D40B	퐛 D41B	퐫 D42B	퐻 D43B
C	퍬 D36C	퍼 D37C	펌 D38C	펜 D39C	펬 D3AC	펼 D3BC	폌 D3CC	폜 D3DC	포 D3EC	폼 D3FC	퐌 D40C	퐜 D41C	퐬 D42C	퐼 D43C
D	퍭 D36D	퍽 D37D	펍 D38D	펝 D39D	펭 D3AD	펽 D3BD	폍 D3CD	폝 D3DD	폭 D3ED	폽 D3FD	퐍 D40D	퐝 D41D	퐭 D42D	퐽 D43D
E	퍮 D36E	퍾 D37E	펎 D38E	펞 D39E	펮 D3AE	펾 D3BE	폎 D3CE	폞 D3DE	폮 D3EE	폾 D3FE	퐎 D40E	퐞 D41E	퐮 D42E	퐾 D43E
F	퍯 D36F	퍿 D37F	펏 D38F	펟 D39F	펯 D3AF	펿 D3BF	폏 D3CF	폟 D3DF	폯 D3EF	폿 D3FF	퐏 D40F	퐟 D41F	퐯 D42F	퐿 D43F

	D44	D45	D46	D47	D48	D49	D4A	D4B	D4C	D4D	D4E	D4F	D50	D51
0	푀 D440	푐 D450	푠 D460	푰 D470	풀 D480	풐 D490	풠 D4A0	풰 D4B0	퓀 D4C0	퓐 D4D0	퓠 D4E0	퓰 D4F0	픀 D500	픐 D510
1	푁 D441	푑 D451	푡 D461	푱 D471	풁 D481	풑 D491	풡 D4A1	풱 D4B1	퓁 D4C1	퓑 D4D1	퓡 D4E1	퓱 D4F1	픁 D501	픑 D511
2	푂 D442	푒 D452	푢 D462	푲 D472	풂 D482	풒 D492	풢 D4A2	풲 D4B2	퓂 D4C2	퓒 D4D2	퓢 D4E2	퓲 D4F2	픂 D502	픒 D512
3	푃 D443	푓 D453	푣 D463	푳 D473	풃 D483	풓 D493	풣 D4A3	풳 D4B3	퓃 D4C3	퓓 D4D3	퓣 D4E3	퓳 D4F3	픃 D503	픓 D513
4	푄 D444	푔 D454	푤 D464	푴 D474	풄 D484	풔 D494	풤 D4A4	풴 D4B4	퓄 D4C4	퓔 D4D4	퓤 D4E4	퓴 D4F4	프 D504	픔 D514
5	푅 D445	푕 D455	푥 D465	푵 D475	풅 D485	풕 D495	풥 D4A5	풵 D4B5	퓅 D4C5	퓕 D4D5	퓥 D4E5	퓵 D4F5	픅 D505	픕 D515
6	푆 D446	푖 D456	푦 D466	푶 D476	풆 D486	풖 D496	풦 D4A6	풶 D4B6	퓆 D4C6	퓖 D4D6	퓦 D4E6	퓶 D4F6	픆 D506	픖 D516
7	푇 D447	푗 D457	푧 D467	푷 D477	풇 D487	풗 D497	풧 D4A7	풷 D4B7	퓇 D4C7	퓗 D4D7	퓧 D4E7	퓷 D4F7	픇 D507	픗 D517
8	푈 D448	푘 D458	푨 D468	푸 D478	품 D488	풘 D498	풨 D4A8	풸 D4B8	퓈 D4C8	퓘 D4D8	퓨 D4E8	퓸 D4F8	픈 D508	픘 D518
9	푉 D449	푙 D459	푩 D469	푹 D479	풉 D489	풙 D499	풩 D4A9	풹 D4B9	퓉 D4C9	퓙 D4D9	퓩 D4E9	퓹 D4F9	픉 D509	픙 D519
A	푊 D44A	푚 D45A	푪 D46A	푺 D47A	풊 D48A	풚 D49A	풪 D4AA	풺 D4BA	퓊 D4CA	퓚 D4DA	퓪 D4EA	퓺 D4FA	픊 D50A	픚 D51A
B	푋 D44B	푛 D45B	푫 D46B	푻 D47B	풋 D48B	풛 D49B	풫 D4AB	풻 D4BB	퓋 D4CB	퓛 D4DB	퓫 D4EB	퓻 D4FB	픋 D50B	픛 D51B
C	푌 D44C	표 D45C	푬 D46C	푼 D47C	풌 D48C	풜 D49C	풬 D4AC	풼 D4BC	퓌 D4CC	퓜 D4DC	퓬 D4EC	퓼 D4FC	플 D50C	픜 D51C
D	푍 D44D	푝 D45D	푭 D46D	푽 D47D	풍 D48D	풝 D49D	풭 D4AD	풽 D4BD	퓍 D4CD	퓝 D4DD	퓭 D4ED	퓽 D4FD	픍 D50D	픝 D51D
E	푎 D44E	푞 D45E	푮 D46E	푾 D47E	풎 D48E	풞 D49E	풮 D4AE	풾 D4BE	퓎 D4CE	퓞 D4DE	퓮 D4EE	퓾 D4FE	픎 D50E	픞 D51E
F	푏 D44F	푟 D45F	푯 D46F	푿 D47F	풏 D48F	풟 D49F	풯 D4AF	풿 D4BF	퓏 D4CF	퓟 D4DF	퓯 D4EF	퓿 D4FF	픏 D50F	픟 D51F

	D52	D53	D54	D55	D56	D57	D58	D59	D5A	D5B	D5C	D5D	D5E	D5F
0	픠 D520	픰 D530	핀 D540	핐 D550	할 D560	핰 D570	햀 D580	햐 D590	햠 D5A0	햰 D5B0	헀 D5C0	헐 D5D0	헠 D5E0	헰 D5F0
1	픡 D521	픱 D531	핁 D541	핑 D551	핡 D561	핱 D571	햁 D581	햑 D591	햡 D5A1	햱 D5B1	헁 D5C1	헑 D5D1	헡 D5E1	헱 D5F1
2	픢 D522	픲 D532	핂 D542	핒 D552	핢 D562	핲 D572	햂 D582	햒 D592	햢 D5A2	햲 D5B2	헂 D5C2	헒 D5D2	헢 D5E2	헲 D5F2
3	픣 D523	픳 D533	핃 D543	핓 D553	핣 D563	핳 D573	햃 D583	햓 D593	햣 D5A3	햳 D5B3	헃 D5C3	헓 D5D3	헣 D5E3	헳 D5F3
4	픤 D524	픴 D534	필 D544	핔 D554	핤 D564	해 D574	햄 D584	햔 D594	햤 D5A4	햴 D5B4	헄 D5C4	헔 D5D4	헤 D5E4	헴 D5F4
5	픥 D525	픵 D535	핅 D545	핕 D555	핥 D565	핵 D575	햅 D585	햕 D595	향 D5A5	햵 D5B5	헅 D5C5	헕 D5D5	헥 D5E5	헵 D5F5
6	픦 D526	픶 D536	핆 D546	핖 D556	핦 D566	핶 D576	햆 D586	햖 D596	햦 D5A6	햶 D5B6	헆 D5C6	헖 D5D6	헦 D5E6	헶 D5F6
7	픧 D527	픷 D537	핇 D547	핗 D557	핧 D567	핷 D577	햇 D587	햗 D597	햧 D5A7	햷 D5B7	헇 D5C7	헗 D5D7	헧 D5E7	헷 D5F7
8	픨 D528	픸 D538	핈 D548	하 D558	함 D568	핸 D578	했 D588	햘 D598	햨 D5A8	햸 D5B8	허 D5C8	험 D5D8	헨 D5E8	헸 D5F8
9	픩 D529	픹 D539	핉 D549	학 D559	합 D569	핹 D579	행 D589	햙 D599	햩 D5A9	햹 D5B9	헉 D5C9	헙 D5D9	헩 D5E9	헹 D5F9
A	픪 D52A	픺 D53A	핊 D54A	핚 D55A	핪 D56A	핺 D57A	햊 D58A	햚 D59A	햪 D5AA	햺 D5BA	헊 D5CA	헚 D5DA	헪 D5EA	헺 D5FA
B	픫 D52B	픻 D53B	핋 D54B	핛 D55B	핫 D56B	핻 D57B	햋 D58B	햛 D59B	햫 D5AB	햻 D5BB	헋 D5CB	헛 D5DB	헫 D5EB	헻 D5FB
C	픬 D52C	피 D53C	핌 D54C	한 D55C	핬 D56C	핼 D57C	햌 D58C	햜 D59C	햬 D5AC	햼 D5BC	헌 D5CC	헜 D5DC	헬 D5EC	헼 D5FC
D	픭 D52D	픽 D53D	핍 D54D	핝 D55D	항 D56D	핽 D57D	햍 D58D	햝 D59D	햭 D5AD	햽 D5BD	헍 D5CD	헝 D5DD	헭 D5ED	헽 D5FD
E	픮 D52E	픾 D53E	핎 D54E	핞 D55E	핮 D56E	핾 D57E	햎 D58E	햞 D59E	햮 D5AE	햾 D5BE	헎 D5CE	헞 D5DE	헮 D5EE	헾 D5FE
F	픯 D52F	픿 D53F	핏 D54F	핟 D55F	핯 D56F	핿 D57F	햏 D58F	햟 D59F	햯 D5AF	햿 D5BF	헏 D5CF	헟 D5DF	헯 D5EF	헿 D5FF

	D60	D61	D62	D63	D64	D65	D66	D67	D68	D69	D6A	D6B	D6C
0	혀 D600	혐 D610	혠 D620	혰 D630	홀 D640	홐 D650	홠 D660	홰 D670	횀 D680	횐 D690	횠 D6A0	횰 D6B0	훀 D6C0
1	혁 D601	협 D611	혡 D621	혱 D631	홁 D641	홑 D651	홡 D661	홱 D671	횁 D681	횑 D691	횡 D6A1	횱 D6B1	훁 D6C1
2	혂 D602	혒 D612	혢 D622	혲 D632	홂 D642	홒 D652	홢 D662	홲 D672	횂 D682	횒 D692	횢 D6A2	횲 D6B2	훂 D6C2
3	혃 D603	혓 D613	혣 D623	혳 D633	홃 D643	홓 D653	홣 D663	홳 D673	횃 D683	횓 D693	횣 D6A3	횳 D6B3	훃 D6C3
4	현 D604	혔 D614	혤 D624	혴 D634	홄 D644	화 D654	홤 D664	홴 D674	횄 D684	횔 D694	횤 D6A4	횴 D6B4	후 D6C4
5	혅 D605	형 D615	혥 D625	혵 D635	홅 D645	확 D655	홥 D665	홵 D675	횅 D685	횕 D695	횥 D6A5	횵 D6B5	훅 D6C5
6	혆 D606	혖 D616	혦 D626	혶 D636	홆 D646	홖 D656	홦 D666	홶 D676	횆 D686	횖 D696	횦 D6A6	횶 D6B6	훆 D6C6
7	혇 D607	혗 D617	혧 D627	혷 D637	홇 D647	홗 D657	홧 D667	홷 D677	횇 D687	횗 D697	횧 D6A7	횷 D6B7	훇 D6C7
8	혈 D608	혘 D618	혨 D628	호 D638	홈 D648	환 D658	홨 D668	홸 D678	횈 D688	횘 D698	효 D6A8	횸 D6B8	훈 D6C8
9	혉 D609	혙 D619	혩 D629	혹 D639	홉 D649	홙 D659	황 D669	홹 D679	횉 D689	횙 D699	횩 D6A9	횹 D6B9	훉 D6C9
A	혊 D60A	혚 D61A	혪 D62A	혺 D63A	홊 D64A	홚 D65A	홪 D66A	홺 D67A	횊 D68A	횚 D69A	횪 D6AA	횺 D6BA	훊 D6CA
B	혋 D60B	혛 D61B	혫 D62B	혻 D63B	홋 D64B	홛 D65B	홫 D66B	홻 D67B	횋 D68B	횛 D69B	횫 D6AB	횻 D6BB	훋 D6CB
C	혌 D60C	혜 D61C	혬 D62C	혼 D63C	홌 D64C	활 D65C	홬 D66C	홼 D67C	회 D68C	횜 D69C	횬 D6AC	횼 D6BC	훌 D6CC
D	혍 D60D	혝 D61D	혭 D62D	혽 D63D	홍 D64D	홝 D65D	홭 D66D	홽 D67D	획 D68D	횝 D69D	횭 D6AD	횽 D6BD	훍 D6CD
E	혎 D60E	혞 D61E	혮 D62E	혾 D63E	홎 D64E	홞 D65E	홮 D66E	홾 D67E	횎 D68E	횞 D69E	횮 D6AE	횾 D6BE	훎 D6CE
F	혏 D60F	혟 D61F	혯 D62F	혿 D63F	홏 D64F	홟 D65F	홯 D66F	홿 D67F	횏 D68F	횟 D69F	횯 D6AF	횿 D6BF	훏 D6CF

	D6D	D6E	D6F	D70	D71	D72	D73	D74	D75	D76	D77	D78	D79	D7A
0	훐 D6D0	훠 D6E0	훰 D6F0	휀 D700	휐 D710	휠 D720	휰 D730	흀 D740	흐 D750	흠 D760	흰 D770	힀 D780	힐 D790	힠 D7A0
1	훑 D6D1	훡 D6E1	훱 D6F1	휁 D701	휑 D711	휡 D721	휱 D731	흁 D741	흑 D751	흡 D761	흱 D771	힁 D781	힑 D791	힡 D7A1
2	훒 D6D2	훢 D6E2	훲 D6F2	휂 D702	휒 D712	휢 D722	휲 D732	흂 D742	흒 D752	흢 D762	흲 D772	힂 D782	힒 D792	힢 D7A2
3	훓 D6D3	훣 D6E3	훳 D6F3	휃 D703	휓 D713	휣 D723	휳 D733	흃 D743	흓 D753	흣 D763	흳 D773	힃 D783	힓 D793	힣 D7A3
4	훔 D6D4	훤 D6E4	훴 D6F4	휄 D704	휔 D714	휤 D724	휴 D734	흄 D744	흔 D754	흤 D764	흴 D774	힄 D784	힔 D794	
5	훕 D6D5	훥 D6E5	훵 D6F5	휅 D705	휕 D715	휥 D725	휵 D735	흅 D745	흕 D755	흥 D765	흵 D775	힅 D785	힕 D795	
6	훖 D6D6	훦 D6E6	훶 D6F6	휆 D706	휖 D716	휦 D726	휶 D736	흆 D746	흖 D756	흦 D766	흶 D776	힆 D786	힖 D796	
7	훗 D6D7	훧 D6E7	훷 D6F7	휇 D707	휗 D717	휧 D727	휷 D737	흇 D747	흗 D757	흧 D767	흷 D777	힇 D787	힗 D797	
8	훘 D6D8	훨 D6E8	훸 D6F8	휈 D708	휘 D718	휨 D728	휸 D738	흈 D748	흘 D758	흨 D768	흸 D778	히 D788	힘 D798	
9	훙 D6D9	훩 D6E9	훹 D6F9	휉 D709	휙 D719	휩 D729	휹 D739	흉 D749	흙 D759	흩 D769	흹 D779	힉 D789	힙 D799	
A	훚 D6DA	훪 D6EA	훺 D6FA	휊 D70A	휚 D71A	휪 D72A	휺 D73A	흊 D74A	흚 D75A	흪 D76A	흺 D77A	힊 D78A	힚 D79A	
B	훛 D6DB	훫 D6EB	훻 D6FB	휋 D70B	휛 D71B	휫 D72B	휻 D73B	흋 D74B	흛 D75B	흫 D76B	흻 D77B	힋 D78B	힛 D79B	
C	훜 D6DC	훬 D6EC	훼 D6FC	휌 D70C	휜 D71C	휬 D72C	휼 D73C	흌 D74C	흜 D75C	희 D76C	흼 D77C	힌 D78C	힜 D79C	
D	훝 D6DD	훭 D6ED	훽 D6FD	휍 D70D	휝 D71D	휭 D72D	휽 D73D	흍 D74D	흝 D75D	흭 D76D	흽 D77D	힍 D78D	힝 D79D	
E	훞 D6DE	훮 D6EE	훾 D6FE	휎 D70E	휞 D71E	휮 D72E	휾 D73E	흎 D74E	흞 D75E	흮 D76E	흾 D77E	힎 D78E	힞 D79E	
F	훟 D6DF	훯 D6EF	훿 D6FF	휏 D70F	휟 D71F	휯 D72F	휿 D73F	흏 D74F	흟 D75F	흯 D76F	흿 D77F	힏 D78F	힟 D79F	

	F90	F91	F92	F93	F94	F95	F96	F97
0	豈 8C48 F900	蘿 863F F910	鸞 9E1E F920	擄 64C4 F930	鹿 9E7F F940	縷 7E37 F950	怒 6012 F960	殺 6BBA F970
1	更 66F4 F901	螺 87BA F911	嵐 5D50 F921	櫓 6AD3 F931	論 8AD6 F941	陋 964B F951	率 7387 F961	辰 8FB0 F971
2	車 8ECA F902	裸 88F8 F912	濫 6FEB F922	爐 7210 F932	壟 58DF F942	勒 52D2 F952	異 7570 F962	沈 6C88 F972
3	賈 8CC8 F903	邏 908F F913	藍 85CD F923	盧 76E7 F933	弄 5F04 F943	肋 808B F953	北 5317 F963	拾 62FE F973
4	滑 6ED1 F904	樂 6A02 F914	襤 8964 F924	老 8001 F934	籠 7C60 F944	凜 51DC F954	磻 78FB F964	若 82E5 F974
5	串 4E32 F905	洛 6D1B F915	拉 62C9 F925	蘆 8606 F935	聾 807E F945	凌 51CC F955	便 4FBF F965	掠 63A0 F975
6	句 53E5 F906	烙 70D9 F916	臘 81D8 F926	虜 865C F936	牢 7262 F946	稜 7A1C F956	復 5FA9 F966	略 7565 F976
7	龜 9F9C F907	珞 73DE F917	蠟 881F F927	路 8DEF F937	磊 78CA F947	綾 7DBE F957	不 4E0D F967	亮 4EAE F977
8	龜 9F9C F908	落 843D F918	廊 5ECA F928	露 9732 F938	賂 8CC2 F948	菱 83F1 F958	泌 6CCC F968	兩 5169 F978
9	契 5951 F909	酪 916A F919	朗 6717 F929	魯 9B6F F939	雷 96F7 F949	陵 9675 F959	數 6578 F969	凉 51C9 F979
A	金 91D1 F90A	駱 99F1 F91A	浪 6D6A F92A	鷺 9DFA F93A	壘 58D8 F94A	讀 8B80 F95A	索 7D22 F96A	梁 6881 F97A
B	喇 5587 F90B	亂 4E82 F91B	狼 72FC F92B	碌 788C F93B	屢 5C62 F94B	拏 62CF F95B	參 53C3 F96B	糧 7CE7 F97B
C	奈 5948 F90C	卵 5375 F91C	郎 90CE F92C	祿 797F F93C	樓 6A13 F94C	樂 6A02 F95C	塞 585E F96C	良 826F F97C
D	懶 61F6 F90D	欄 6B04 F91D	來 4F86 F92D	綠 7DA0 F93D	淚 6DDA F94D	諾 8AFE F95D	省 7701 F96D	諒 8AD2 F97D
E	癩 7669 F90E	爛 721B F91E	冷 51B7 F92E	菉 83C9 F93E	漏 6F0F F94E	丹 4E39 F95E	葉 8449 F96E	量 91CF F97E
F	羅 7F85 F90F	蘭 862D F91F	勞 52DE F92F	錄 9304 F93F	累 7D2F F94F	寧 5BE7 F95F	說 8AAA F96F	勵 52F5 F97F

	F98	F99	F9A	F9B	F9C	F9D	F9E	F9F
0	呂 5442 F980	戀 6200 F990	裂 88C2 F9A0	聆 8046 F9B0	燎 71CE F9C0	類 985E F9D0	易 6613 F9E0	藺 85FA F9F0
1	女 5973 F981	撚 649A F991	說 8AAA F9A1	鈴 9234 F9B1	療 7642 F9C1	六 516D F9D1	李 674E F9E1	隣 96A3 F9F1
2	廬 5EEC F982	漣 6F23 F992	廉 5EC9 F9A2	零 96F6 F9B2	蓼 84FC F9C2	戮 622E F9D2	梨 68A8 F9E2	鱗 9C57 F9F2
3	旅 65C5 F983	煉 7149 F993	念 5FF5 F9A3	靈 9748 F9B3	遼 907C F9C3	陸 9678 F9D3	泥 6CE5 F9E3	麟 9E9F F9F3
4	濾 6FFE F984	璉 7489 F994	捻 637B F9A4	領 9818 F9B4	龍 9F8D F9C4	倫 502B F9D4	理 7406 F9E4	林 6797 F9F4
5	礪 792A F985	秊 79CA F995	殮 6BAE F9A5	例 4F8B F9B5	暈 6688 F9C5	崙 5D19 F9D5	痢 75E2 F9E5	淋 6DCB F9F5
6	閭 95AD F986	練 7DF4 F996	簾 7C3E F9A6	禮 79AE F9B6	阮 962E F9C6	淪 6DEA F9D6	罹 7F79 F9E6	臨 81E8 F9F6
7	驪 9A6A F987	聯 806F F997	獵 7375 F9A7	醴 91B4 F9B7	劉 5289 F9C7	輪 8F2A F9D7	裏 88CF F9E7	立 7ACB F9F7
8	麗 9E97 F988	輦 8F26 F998	令 4EE4 F9A8	隸 96B8 F9B8	杻 677B F9C8	律 5F8B F9D8	裡 88E1 F9E8	笠 7B20 F9F8
9	黎 9ECE F989	蓮 84EE F999	囹 56F9 F9A9	惡 60E1 F9B9	柳 67F3 F9C9	慄 6144 F9D9	里 91CC F9E9	粒 7C92 F9F9
A	力 529B F98A	連 9023 F99A	寧 5BE7 F9AA	了 4E86 F9BA	流 6D41 F9CA	栗 6817 F9DA	離 96E2 F9EA	狀 72C0 F9FA
B	曆 66C6 F98B	鍊 934A F99B	嶺 5DBA F9AB	僚 50DA F9BB	溜 6E9C F9CB	率 7387 F9DB	匿 533F F9EB	炙 7099 F9FB
C	歷 6B77 F98C	列 5217 F99C	怜 601C F9AC	寮 5BEE F9BC	琉 7409 F9CC	隆 9686 F9DC	溺 6EBA F9EC	識 8B58 F9FC
D	轢 8F62 F98D	劣 52A3 F99D	玲 73B2 F9AD	尿 5C3F F9BD	留 7559 F9CD	利 5229 F9DD	吝 541D F9ED	什 4EC0 F9FD
E	年 5E74 F98E	咽 54BD F99E	瑩 7469 F9AE	料 6599 F9BE	硫 786B F9CE	吏 540F F9DE	燐 71D0 F9EE	茶 8336 F9FE
F	憐 6190 F98F	烈 70C8 F99F	羚 7F9A F9AF	樂 6A02 F9BF	紐 7D10 F9CF	履 5C65 F9DF	璘 7498 F9EF	刺 523A F9FF

	FA0	FA1	FA2
0	切 5207 FA00	塚 585A FA10	蘒 8612 FA20
1	度 5EA6 FA01	﨑 FA11	﨡 FA21
2	拓 62D3 FA02	晴 6674 FA12	諸 8AF8 FA22
3	糖 7CD6 FA03	﨓 FA13	﨣 FA23
4	宅 5B85 FA04	﨔 FA14	﨤 FA24
5	洞 6D1E FA05	凞 51DE FA15	逸 9038 FA25
6	暴 66B4 FA06	猪 732A FA16	都 90FD FA26
7	輻 8F3B FA07	益 76CA FA17	﨧 FA27
8	行 884C FA08	礼 793C FA18	﨨 FA28
9	降 964D FA09	神 795E FA19	﨩 FA29
A	見 898B FA0A	祥 7965 FA1A	飯 98EF FA2A
B	廓 5ED3 FA0B	福 798F FA1B	飼 98FC FA2B
C	兀 5140 FA0C	靖 9756 FA1C	館 9928 FA2C
D	嗀 55C0 FA0D	精 7CBE FA1D	鶴 9DB4 FA2D
E	﨎 FA0E	羽 7FBD FA1E	
F	﨏 FA0F	﨟 FA1F	

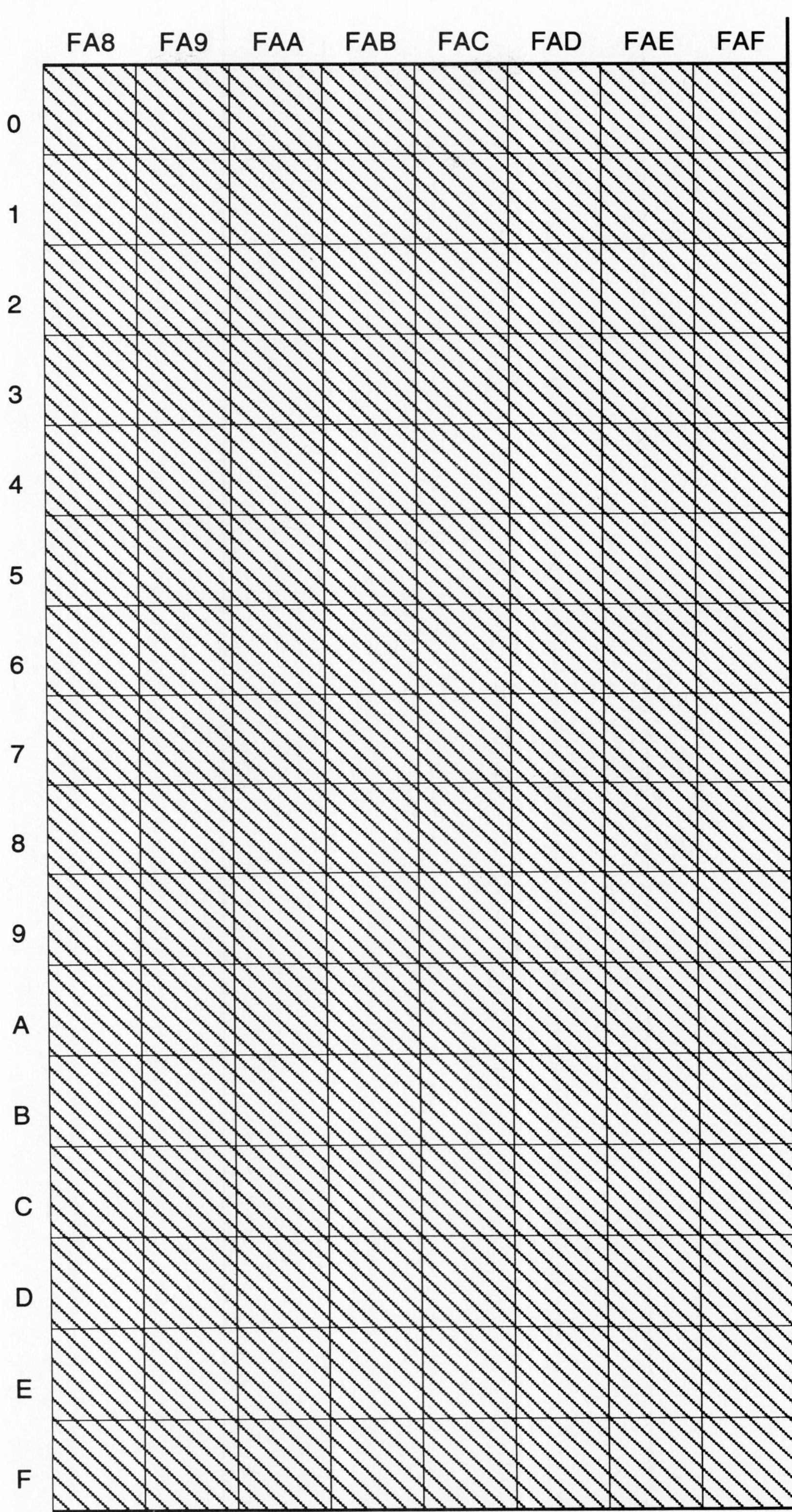
FA8
FA9
FAA
FAB
FAC
FAD
FAE
FAF
0
1
2
3
4
5
6
7
8
9
A
B
C
D
E
F

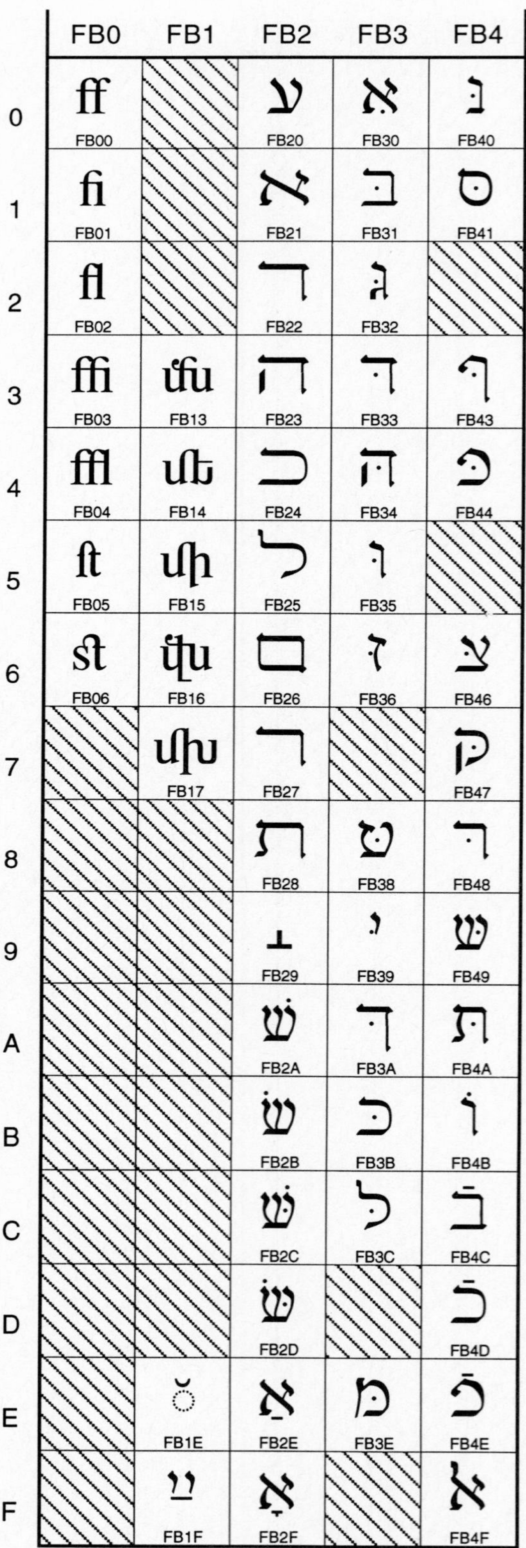

	FB0	FB1	FB2	FB3	FB4
0	ﬀ FB00		ﬠ FB20	אַ FB30	נּ FB40
1	ﬁ FB01		ﬡ FB21	בּ FB31	סּ FB41
2	ﬂ FB02		ﬢ FB22	גּ FB32	
3	ﬃ FB03	ﬓ FB13	ﬣ FB23	דּ FB33	ףּ FB43
4	ﬄ FB04	ﬔ FB14	ﬤ FB24	הּ FB34	פּ FB44
5	ﬅ FB05	ﬕ FB15	ﬥ FB25	וּ FB35	
6	ﬆ FB06	ﬖ FB16	ﬦ FB26	זּ FB36	צּ FB46
7		ﬗ FB17	ﬧ FB27		קּ FB47
8			ﬨ FB28	טּ FB38	רּ FB48
9			﬩ FB29	יּ FB39	שּ FB49
A			שׁ FB2A	ךּ FB3A	תּ FB4A
B			שׂ FB2B	כּ FB3B	וֹ FB4B
C			שּׁ FB2C	לּ FB3C	בֿ FB4C
D			שּׂ FB2D		כֿ FB4D
E		◌ﬞ FB1E	אַ FB2E	מּ FB3E	פֿ FB4E
F		ײַ FB1F	אָ FB2F		ﭏ FB4F

Alphabetic presentation forms

FB00 ﬀ LATIN SMALL LIGATURE FF
≈ 0066 f + 0066 f

FB01 ﬁ LATIN SMALL LIGATURE FI
≈ 0066 f + 0069 i

FB02 ﬂ LATIN SMALL LIGATURE FL
≈ 0066 f + 006C l

FB03 ﬃ LATIN SMALL LIGATURE FFI
≈ 0066 f + 0066 f + 0069 i

FB04 ﬄ LATIN SMALL LIGATURE FFL
≈ 0066 f + 0066 f + 006C l

FB05 ﬅ LATIN SMALL LIGATURE LONG S T
≈ 017F ſ + 0074 t

FB06 ﬆ LATIN SMALL LIGATURE ST
≈ 0073 s + 0074 t

FB13 ﬓ ARMENIAN SMALL LIGATURE MEN NOW
≈ 0574 մ + 0576 ն

FB14 ﬔ ARMENIAN SMALL LIGATURE MEN ECH
≈ 0574 մ + 0565 ե

FB15 ﬕ ARMENIAN SMALL LIGATURE MEN INI
≈ 0574 մ + 056B ի

FB16 ﬖ ARMENIAN SMALL LIGATURE VEW NOW
≈ 057E վ + 0576 ն

FB17 ﬗ ARMENIAN SMALL LIGATURE MEN XEH
≈ 0574 մ + 056D խ

FB1E ﬞ HEBREW POINT JUDEO-SPANISH VARIKA

FB1F ײַ HEBREW LIGATURE YIDDISH YOD YOD PATAH
≈ 05F2 ײ + 05B7 ַ

FB20 ﬠ HEBREW LETTER ALTERNATIVE AYIN
≈ <font> + 05E2 ע

FB21 ﬡ HEBREW LETTER WIDE ALEF
≈ <font> + 05D0 א

FB22 ﬢ HEBREW LETTER WIDE DALET
≈ <font> + 05D3 ד

FB23 ﬣ HEBREW LETTER WIDE HE
≈ <font> + 05D4 ה

FB24 ﬤ HEBREW LETTER WIDE KAF
≈ <font> + 05DB כ

FB25 ﬥ HEBREW LETTER WIDE LAMED
≈ <font> + 05DC ל

FB26 ﬦ HEBREW LETTER WIDE FINAL MEM
≈ <font> + 05DD ם

FB27 ﬧ HEBREW LETTER WIDE RESH
≈ <font> + 05E8 ר

FB28 ﬨ HEBREW LETTER WIDE TAV
≈ <font> + 05EA ת

FB29 ﬩ HEBREW LETTER ALTERNATIVE PLUS SIGN
≈ <font> + 002B +

FB2A שׁ HEBREW LETTER SHIN WITH SHIN DOT
≡ 05E9 ש + 05C1 ׁ

FB2B שׂ HEBREW LETTER SHIN WITH SIN DOT
≡ 05E9 ש + 05C2 ׂ

FB2C שּׁ HEBREW LETTER SHIN WITH DAGESH AND SHIN DOT
≡ 05E9 ש + 05BC ּ + 05C1 ׁ

FB2D שּׂ HEBREW LETTER SHIN WITH DAGESH AND SIN DOT
≡ 05E9 ש + 05BC ּ + 05C2 ׂ

FB2E אַ HEBREW LETTER ALEF WITH PATAH
≡ 05D0 א + 05B7 ַ

FB2F אָ HEBREW LETTER ALEF WITH QAMATS
≡ 05D0 א + 05B8 ָ

FB30 אּ HEBREW LETTER ALEF WITH MAPIQ
≡ 05D0 א + 05BC ּ

FB31 בּ HEBREW LETTER BET WITH DAGESH
≡ 05D1 ב + 05BC ּ

FB32 גּ HEBREW LETTER GIMEL WITH DAGESH
≡ 05D2 ג + 05BC ּ

FB33 דּ HEBREW LETTER DALET WITH DAGESH
≡ 05D3 ד + 05BC ּ

FB34 הּ HEBREW LETTER HE WITH MAPIQ
≡ 05D4 ה + 05BC ּ

FB35 וּ HEBREW LETTER VAV WITH DAGESH
≡ 05D5 ו + 05BC ּ

FB36 זּ HEBREW LETTER ZAYIN WITH DAGESH
≡ 05D6 ז + 05BC ּ

FB38 טּ HEBREW LETTER TET WITH DAGESH
≡ 05D8 ט + 05BC ּ

FB39 יּ HEBREW LETTER YOD WITH DAGESH
≡ 05D9 י + 05BC ּ

FB3A ךּ HEBREW LETTER FINAL KAF WITH DAGESH
≡ 05DA ך + 05BC ּ

FB3B כּ HEBREW LETTER KAF WITH DAGESH
≡ 05DB כ + 05BC ּ

FB3C לּ HEBREW LETTER LAMED WITH DAGESH
≡ 05DC ל + 05BC ◌ּ
FB3E מּ HEBREW LETTER MEM WITH DAGESH
≡ 05DE מ + 05BC ◌ּ
FB40 נּ HEBREW LETTER NUN WITH DAGESH
≡ 05E0 נ + 05BC ◌ּ
FB41 סּ HEBREW LETTER SAMEKH WITH DAGESH
≡ 05E1 ס + 05BC ◌ּ
FB43 ףּ HEBREW LETTER FINAL PE WITH DAGESH
≡ 05E3 ף + 05BC ◌ּ
FB44 פּ HEBREW LETTER PE WITH DAGESH
≡ 05E4 פ + 05BC ◌ּ
FB46 צּ HEBREW LETTER TSADI WITH DAGESH
≡ 05E6 צ + 05BC ◌ּ
FB47 קּ HEBREW LETTER QOF WITH DAGESH
≡ 05E7 ק + 05BC ◌ּ
FB48 רּ HEBREW LETTER RESH WITH DAGESH
≡ 05E8 ר + 05BC ◌ּ
FB49 שּ HEBREW LETTER SHIN WITH DAGESH
≡ 05E9 ש + 05BC ◌ּ
FB4A תּ HEBREW LETTER TAV WITH DAGESH
≡ 05EA ת + 05BC ◌ּ
FB4B וֹ HEBREW LETTER VAV WITH HOLAM
≡ 05D5 ו + 05B9 ◌ֹ
FB4C בֿ HEBREW LETTER BET WITH RAFE
≡ 05D1 ב + 05BF ◌ֿ
FB4D כֿ HEBREW LETTER KAF WITH RAFE
≡ 05DB כ + 05BF ◌ֿ
FB4E פֿ HEBREW LETTER PE WITH RAFE
≡ 05E4 פ + 05BF ◌ֿ
FB4F ﭏ HEBREW LIGATURE ALEF LAMED
≈ 05D0 א + 05DC ל

	FB5	FB6	FB7	FB8	FB9	FBA	FBB	FBC
0	ﭐ FB50	ﭠ FB60	ﭰ FB70	ﮀ FB80	ﮐ FB90	ﮠ FBA0	ﮰ FBB0	
1	ﭑ FB51	ﭡ FB61	ﭱ FB71	ﮁ FB81	ﮑ FB91	ﮡ FBA1	ﮱ FBB1	
2	ﭒ FB52	ﭢ FB62	ﭲ FB72	ﮂ FB82	ﮒ FB92	ﮢ FBA2		
3	ﭓ FB53	ﭣ FB63	ﭳ FB73	ﮃ FB83	ﮓ FB93	ﮣ FBA3		
4	ﭔ FB54	ﭤ FB64	ﭴ FB74	ﮄ FB84	ﮔ FB94	ﮤ FBA4		
5	ﭕ FB55	ﭥ FB65	ﭵ FB75	ﮅ FB85	ﮕ FB95	ﮥ FBA5		
6	ﭖ FB56	ﭦ FB66	ﭶ FB76	ﮆ FB86	ﮖ FB96	ﮦ FBA6		
7	ﭗ FB57	ﭧ FB67	ﭷ FB77	ﮇ FB87	ﮗ FB97	ﮧ FBA7		
8	ﭘ FB58	ﭨ FB68	ﭸ FB78	ﮈ FB88	ﮘ FB98	ﮨ FBA8		
9	ﭙ FB59	ﭩ FB69	ﭹ FB79	ﮉ FB89	ﮙ FB99	ﮩ FBA9		
A	ﭚ FB5A	ﭪ FB6A	ﭺ FB7A	ﮊ FB8A	ﮚ FB9A	ﮪ FBAA		
B	ﭛ FB5B	ﭫ FB6B	ﭻ FB7B	ﮋ FB8B	ﮛ FB9B	ﮫ FBAB		
C	ﭜ FB5C	ﭬ FB6C	ﭼ FB7C	ﮌ FB8C	ﮜ FB9C	ﮬ FBAC		
D	ﭝ FB5D	ﭭ FB6D	ﭽ FB7D	ﮍ FB8D	ﮝ FB9D	ﮭ FBAD		
E	ﭞ FB5E	ﭮ FB6E	ﭾ FB7E	ﮎ FB8E	ﮞ FB9E	ﮮ FBAE		
F	ﭟ FB5F	ﭯ FB6F	ﭿ FB7F	ﮏ FB8F	ﮟ FB9F	ﮯ FBAF		

	FBD	FBE	FBF	FC0	FC1	FC2	FC3	FC4
0		FBE0	FBF0	FC00	FC10	FC20	FC30	FC40
1		FBE1	FBF1	FC01	FC11	FC21	FC31	FC41
2		FBE2	FBF2	FC02	FC12	FC22	FC32	FC42
3	FBD3	FBE3	FBF3	FC03	FC13	FC23	FC33	FC43
4	FBD4	FBE4	FBF4	FC04	FC14	FC24	FC34	FC44
5	FBD5	FBE5	FBF5	FC05	FC15	FC25	FC35	FC45
6	FBD6	FBE6	FBF6	FC06	FC16	FC26	FC36	FC46
7	FBD7	FBE7	FBF7	FC07	FC17	FC27	FC37	FC47
8	FBD8	FBE8	FBF8	FC08	FC18	FC28	FC38	FC48
9	FBD9	FBE9	FBF9	FC09	FC19	FC29	FC39	FC49
A	FBDA	FBEA	FBFA	FC0A	FC1A	FC2A	FC3A	FC4A
B	FBDB	FBEB	FBFB	FC0B	FC1B	FC2B	FC3B	FC4B
C	FBDC	FBEC	FBFC	FC0C	FC1C	FC2C	FC3C	FC4C
D	FBDD	FBED	FBFD	FC0D	FC1D	FC2D	FC3D	FC4D
E	FBDE	FBEE	FBFE	FC0E	FC1E	FC2E	FC3E	FC4E
F	FBDF	FBEF	FBFF	FC0F	FC1F	FC2F	FC3F	FC4F

	FC5	FC6	FC7	FC8	FC9	FCA	FCB	FCC
0	FC50	FC60	FC70	FC80	FC90	FCA0	FCB0	FCC0
1	FC51	FC61	FC71	FC81	FC91	FCA1	FCB1	FCC1
2	FC52	FC62	FC72	FC82	FC92	FCA2	FCB2	FCC2
3	FC53	FC63	FC73	FC83	FC93	FCA3	FCB3	FCC3
4	FC54	FC64	FC74	FC84	FC94	FCA4	FCB4	FCC4
5	FC55	FC65	FC75	FC85	FC95	FCA5	FCB5	FCC5
6	FC56	FC66	FC76	FC86	FC96	FCA6	FCB6	FCC6
7	FC57	FC67	FC77	FC87	FC97	FCA7	FCB7	FCC7
8	FC58	FC68	FC78	FC88	FC98	FCA8	FCB8	FCC8
9	FC59	FC69	FC79	FC89	FC99	FCA9	FCB9	FCC9
A	FC5A	FC6A	FC7A	FC8A	FC9A	FCAA	FCBA	FCCA
B	FC5B	FC6B	FC7B	FC8B	FC9B	FCAB	FCBB	FCCB
C	FC5C	FC6C	FC7C	FC8C	FC9C	FCAC	FCBC	FCCC
D	FC5D	FC6D	FC7D	FC8D	FC9D	FCAD	FCBD	FCCD
E	FC5E	FC6E	FC7E	FC8E	FC9E	FCAE	FCBE	FCCE
F	FC5F	FC6F	FC7F	FC8F	FC9F	FCAF	FCBF	FCCF

	FCD	FCE	FCF	FD0	FD1	FD2	FD3	FD4
0	ﳐ FCD0	ﳠ FCE0	ﳰ FCF0	ﴀ FD00	ﴐ FD10	ﴠ FD20	ﴰ FD30	
1	ﳑ FCD1	ﳡ FCE1	ﳱ FCF1	ﴁ FD01	ﴑ FD11	ﴡ FD21	ﴱ FD31	
2	ﳒ FCD2	ﳢ FCE2	ﳲ FCF2	ﴂ FD02	ﴒ FD12	ﴢ FD22	ﴲ FD32	
3	ﳓ FCD3	ﳣ FCE3	ﳳ FCF3	ﴃ FD03	ﴓ FD13	ﴣ FD23	ﴳ FD33	
4	ﳔ FCD4	ﳤ FCE4	ﳴ FCF4	ﴄ FD04	ﴔ FD14	ﴤ FD24	ﴴ FD34	
5	ﳕ FCD5	ﳥ FCE5	ﳵ FCF5	ﴅ FD05	ﴕ FD15	ﴥ FD25	ﴵ FD35	
6	ﳖ FCD6	ﳦ FCE6	ﳶ FCF6	ﴆ FD06	ﴖ FD16	ﴦ FD26	ﴶ FD36	
7	ﳗ FCD7	ﳧ FCE7	ﳷ FCF7	ﴇ FD07	ﴗ FD17	ﴧ FD27	ﴷ FD37	
8	ﳘ FCD8	ﳨ FCE8	ﳸ FCF8	ﴈ FD08	ﴘ FD18	ﴨ FD28	ﴸ FD38	
9	ﳙ FCD9	ﳩ FCE9	ﳹ FCF9	ﴉ FD09	ﴙ FD19	ﴩ FD29	ﴹ FD39	
A	ﳚ FCDA	ﳪ FCEA	ﳺ FCFA	ﴊ FD0A	ﴚ FD1A	ﴪ FD2A	ﴺ FD3A	
B	ﳛ FCDB	ﳫ FCEB	ﳻ FCFB	ﴋ FD0B	ﴛ FD1B	ﴫ FD2B	ﴻ FD3B	
C	ﳜ FCDC	ﳬ FCEC	ﳼ FCFC	ﴌ FD0C	ﴜ FD1C	ﴬ FD2C	ﴼ FD3C	
D	ﳝ FCDD	ﳭ FCED	ﳽ FCFD	ﴍ FD0D	ﴝ FD1D	ﴭ FD2D	ﴽ FD3D	
E	ﳞ FCDE	ﳮ FCEE	ﳾ FCFE	ﴎ FD0E	ﴞ FD1E	ﴮ FD2E	﴾ FD3E	
F	ﳟ FCDF	ﳯ FCEF	ﳿ FCFF	ﴏ FD0F	ﴟ FD1F	ﴯ FD2F	﴿ FD3F	

	FD5	FD6	FD7	FD8	FD9	FDA	FDB	FDC
0	FD50	FD60	FD70	FD80		FDA0	FDB0	FDC0
1	FD51	FD61	FD71	FD81		FDA1	FDB1	FDC1
2	FD52	FD62	FD72	FD82	FD92	FDA2	FDB2	FDC2
3	FD53	FD63	FD73	FD83	FD93	FDA3	FDB3	FDC3
4	FD54	FD64	FD74	FD84	FD94	FDA4	FDB4	FDC4
5	FD55	FD65	FD75	FD85	FD95	FDA5	FDB5	FDC5
6	FD56	FD66	FD76	FD86	FD96	FDA6	FDB6	FDC6
7	FD57	FD67	FD77	FD87	FD97	FDA7	FDB7	FDC7
8	FD58	FD68	FD78	FD88	FD98	FDA8	FDB8	
9	FD59	FD69	FD79	FD89	FD99	FDA9	FDB9	
A	FD5A	FD6A	FD7A	FD8A	FD9A	FDAA	FDBA	
B	FD5B	FD6B	FD7B	FD8B	FD9B	FDAB	FDBB	
C	FD5C	FD6C	FD7C	FD8C	FD9C	FDAC	FDBC	
D	FD5D	FD6D	FD7D	FD8D	FD9D	FDAD	FDBD	
E	FD5E	FD6E	FD7E	FD8E	FD9E	FDAE	FDBE	
F	FD5F	FD6F	FD7F	FD8F	FD9F	FDAF	FDBF	

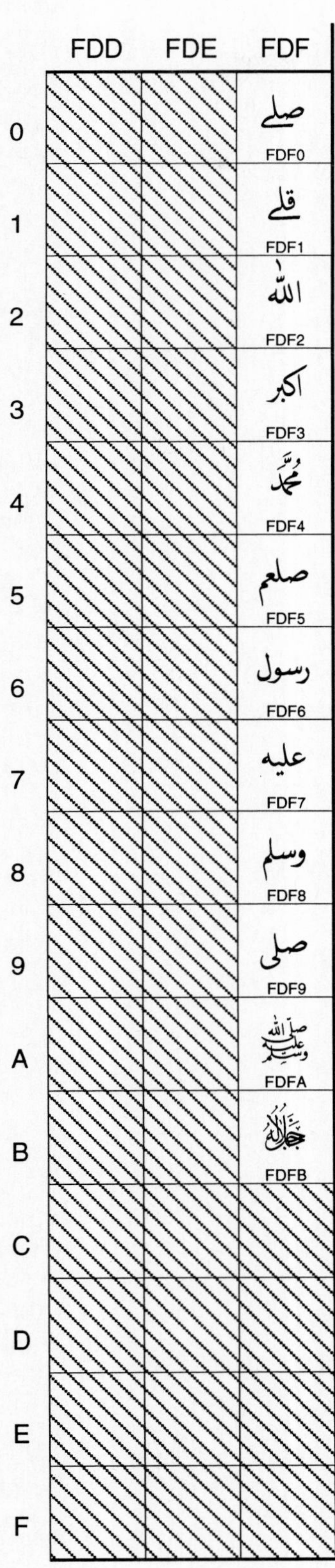

FDD
FDE
FDF
0
1
2
3
4
5
6
7
8
9
A
B
C
D
E
F
FDF0
FDF1
FDF2
FDF3
FDF4
FDF5
FDF6
FDF7
FDF8
FDF9
FDFA
FDFB

Arabic presentation forms-A

FB50 ﭐ ARABIC LETTER ALEF WASLA ISOLATED FORM
≈ <isolated> + 0671 ٱ

FB51 ﭑ ARABIC LETTER ALEF WASLA FINAL FORM
≈ <final> + 0671 ٱ

FB52 ﭒ ARABIC LETTER BEEH ISOLATED FORM
≈ <isolated> + 067B ٻ

FB53 ﭓ ARABIC LETTER BEEH FINAL FORM
≈ <final> + 067B ٻ

FB54 ﭔ ARABIC LETTER BEEH INITIAL FORM
≈ <initial> + 067B ٻ

FB55 ﭕ ARABIC LETTER BEEH MEDIAL FORM
≈ <medial> + 067B ٻ

FB56 ﭖ ARABIC LETTER PEH ISOLATED FORM
≈ <isolated> + 067E پ

FB57 ﭗ ARABIC LETTER PEH FINAL FORM
≈ <final> + 067E پ

FB58 ﭘ ARABIC LETTER PEH INITIAL FORM
≈ <initial> + 067E پ

FB59 ﭙ ARABIC LETTER PEH MEDIAL FORM
≈ <medial> + 067E پ

FB5A ﭚ ARABIC LETTER BEHEH ISOLATED FORM
≈ <isolated> + 0680 ڀ

FB5B ﭛ ARABIC LETTER BEHEH FINAL FORM
≈ <final> + 0680 ڀ

FB5C ﭜ ARABIC LETTER BEHEH INITIAL FORM
≈ <initial> + 0680 ڀ

FB5D ﭝ ARABIC LETTER BEHEH MEDIAL FORM
≈ <medial> + 0680 ڀ

FB5E ﭞ ARABIC LETTER TTEHEH ISOLATED FORM
≈ <isolated> + 067A ٺ

FB5F ﭟ ARABIC LETTER TTEHEH FINAL FORM
≈ <final> + 067A ٺ

FB60 ﭠ ARABIC LETTER TTEHEH INITIAL FORM
≈ <initial> + 067A ٺ

FB61 ﭡ ARABIC LETTER TTEHEH MEDIAL FORM
≈ <medial> + 067A ٺ

FB62 ﭢ ARABIC LETTER TEHEH ISOLATED FORM
≈ <isolated> + 067F ٿ

FB63 ﭣ ARABIC LETTER TEHEH FINAL FORM
≈ <final> + 067F ٿ

FB64 ﭤ ARABIC LETTER TEHEH INITIAL FORM
≈ <initial> + 067F ٿ

FB65 ﭥ ARABIC LETTER TEHEH MEDIAL FORM
≈ <medial> + 067F ٿ

FB66 ﭦ ARABIC LETTER TTEH ISOLATED FORM
≈ <isolated> + 0679 ٹ

FB67 ﭧ ARABIC LETTER TTEH FINAL FORM
≈ <final> + 0679 ٹ

FB68 ﭨ ARABIC LETTER TTEH INITIAL FORM
≈ <initial> + 0679 ٹ

FB69 ﭩ ARABIC LETTER TTEH MEDIAL FORM
≈ <medial> + 0679 ٹ

FB6A ﭪ ARABIC LETTER VEH ISOLATED FORM
≈ <isolated> + 06A4 ڤ

FB6B ﭫ ARABIC LETTER VEH FINAL FORM
≈ <final> + 06A4 ڤ

FB6C ﭬ ARABIC LETTER VEH INITIAL FORM
≈ <initial> + 06A4 ڤ

FB6D ﭭ ARABIC LETTER VEH MEDIAL FORM
≈ <medial> + 06A4 ڤ

FB6E ﭮ ARABIC LETTER PEHEH ISOLATED FORM
≈ <isolated> + 06A6 ڦ

FB6F ﭯ ARABIC LETTER PEHEH FINAL FORM
≈ <final> + 06A6 ڦ

FB70 ﭰ ARABIC LETTER PEHEH INITIAL FORM
≈ <initial> + 06A6 ڦ

FB71 ﭱ ARABIC LETTER PEHEH MEDIAL FORM
≈ <medial> + 06A6 ڦ

FB72 ﭲ ARABIC LETTER DYEH ISOLATED FORM
≈ <isolated> + 0684 ڄ

FB73 ﭳ ARABIC LETTER DYEH FINAL FORM
≈ <final> + 0684 ڄ

FB74 ﭴ ARABIC LETTER DYEH INITIAL FORM
≈ <initial> + 0684 ڄ

FB75 ﭵ ARABIC LETTER DYEH MEDIAL FORM
≈ <medial> + 0684 ڄ

FB76 ﭶ ARABIC LETTER NYEH ISOLATED FORM
≈ <isolated> + 0683 ڃ

FB77 ﭷ ARABIC LETTER NYEH FINAL FORM
≈ <final> + 0683 ڃ

FB78 ﭸ ARABIC LETTER NYEH INITIAL FORM
≈ <initial> + 0683 ڃ

FB79 ﭹ ARABIC LETTER NYEH MEDIAL FORM
≈ <medial> + 0683 ڃ

FB7A ﭺ ARABIC LETTER TCHEH ISOLATED FORM
≈ <isolated> + 0686 چ

FB7B ﭻ ARABIC LETTER TCHEH FINAL FORM
≈ <final> + 0686 چ

FB7C ﭼ ARABIC LETTER TCHEH INITIAL FORM
≈ <initial> + 0686 چ

FB7D ﭽ ARABIC LETTER TCHEH MEDIAL FORM
≈ <medial> + 0686 چ

FB7E ﭾ ARABIC LETTER TCHEHEH ISOLATED FORM
≈ <isolated> + 0687 ڇ

FB7F ﭿ ARABIC LETTER TCHEHEH FINAL FORM
≈ <final> + 0687 ڇ

FB80 ﮀ ARABIC LETTER TCHEHEH INITIAL FORM
≈ <initial> + 0687 ڇ

FB81 ﮁ ARABIC LETTER TCHEHEH MEDIAL FORM
≈ <medial> + 0687 ڇ

FB82 ﮂ ARABIC LETTER DDAHAL ISOLATED FORM
≈ <isolated> + 068D ڍ

FB83 ﮃ ARABIC LETTER DDAHAL FINAL FORM
≈ <final> + 068D ڍ

FB84 ﮄ ARABIC LETTER DAHAL ISOLATED FORM
≈ <isolated> + 068C ڌ

FB85 ﮅ ARABIC LETTER DAHAL FINAL FORM
≈ <final> + 068C ڌ

FB86 ﮆ ARABIC LETTER DUL ISOLATED FORM
≈ <isolated> + 068E ڎ

FB87 ﮇ ARABIC LETTER DUL FINAL FORM
≈ <final> + 068E ڎ

FB88 ﮈ ARABIC LETTER DDAL ISOLATED FORM
≈ <isolated> + 0688 ڈ

FB89 ﮉ ARABIC LETTER DDAL FINAL FORM
≈ <final> + 0688 ڈ

FB8A ﮊ ARABIC LETTER JEH ISOLATED FORM
≈ <isolated> + 0698 ژ

FB8B ﮋ ARABIC LETTER JEH FINAL FORM
≈ <final> + 0698 ژ

FB8C ﮌ ARABIC LETTER RREH ISOLATED FORM
≈ <isolated> + 0691 ڑ

FB8D ﮍ ARABIC LETTER RREH FINAL FORM
≈ <final> + 0691 ڑ

FB8E ﮎ ARABIC LETTER KEHEH ISOLATED FORM
≈ <isolated> + 06A9 ک

FB8F ﮏ ARABIC LETTER KEHEH FINAL FORM
≈ <final> + 06A9 ک

FB90 ﮐ ARABIC LETTER KEHEH INITIAL FORM
≈ <initial> + 06A9 ک

FB91 ﮑ ARABIC LETTER KEHEH MEDIAL FORM
≈ <medial> + 06A9 ک

FB92 ﮒ ARABIC LETTER GAF ISOLATED FORM
≈ <isolated> + 06AF گ

FB93 ﮓ ARABIC LETTER GAF FINAL FORM
≈ <final> + 06AF گ

FB94 ﮔ ARABIC LETTER GAF INITIAL FORM
≈ <initial> + 06AF گ

FB95 ﮕ ARABIC LETTER GAF MEDIAL FORM
≈ <medial> + 06AF گ

FB96 ﮖ ARABIC LETTER GUEH ISOLATED FORM
≈ <isolated> + 06B3 ڳ

FB97 ﮗ ARABIC LETTER GUEH FINAL FORM
≈ <final> + 06B3 ڳ

FB98 ﮘ ARABIC LETTER GUEH INITIAL FORM
≈ <initial> + 06B3 ڳ

FB99 ﮙ ARABIC LETTER GUEH MEDIAL FORM
≈ <medial> + 06B3 ڳ

FB9A ﮚ ARABIC LETTER NGOEH ISOLATED FORM
≈ <isolated> + 06B1 ڱ

FB9B ﮛ ARABIC LETTER NGOEH FINAL FORM
≈ <final> + 06B1 ڱ

FB9C ﮜ ARABIC LETTER NGOEH INITIAL FORM
≈ <initial> + 06B1 ڱ

FB9D ﮝ ARABIC LETTER NGOEH MEDIAL FORM
≈ <medial> + 06B1 ڱ

FB9E ﮞ ARABIC LETTER NOON GHUNNA ISOLATED FORM
≈ <isolated> + 06BA ں

FB9F ﮟ ARABIC LETTER NOON GHUNNA FINAL FORM
≈ <final> + 06BA ں

FBA0 ﮠ ARABIC LETTER RNOON ISOLATED FORM
≈ <isolated> + 06BB ڻ

FBA1 ﮡ ARABIC LETTER RNOON FINAL FORM
≈ <final> + 06BB ڻ

FBA2 ﮢ ARABIC LETTER RNOON INITIAL FORM
≈ <initial> + 06BB ڻ

FBA3 ﮣ ARABIC LETTER RNOON MEDIAL FORM
≈ <medial> + 06BB ڻ

FBA4 ﮤ ARABIC LETTER HEH WITH YEH ABOVE ISOLATED FORM
≈ <isolated> + 06C0 ۀ

FBA5 ﮥ ARABIC LETTER HEH WITH YEH ABOVE FINAL FORM
≈ <final> + 06C0 ۀ

FBA6 ﮦ ARABIC LETTER HEH GOAL ISOLATED FORM
≈ <isolated> + 06C1 ہ

FBA7 ﮧ ARABIC LETTER HEH GOAL FINAL FORM
≈ <final> + 06C1 ہ

FBA8 ﮨ ARABIC LETTER HEH GOAL INITIAL FORM
≈ <initial> + 06C1 ہ

FBA9 ﮩ ARABIC LETTER HEH GOAL MEDIAL FORM
≈ <medial> + 06C1 ہ

FBAA ﮪ ARABIC LETTER HEH DOACHASHMEE ISOLATED FORM
≈ <isolated> + 06BE ھ

FBAB ﮫ ARABIC LETTER HEH DOACHASHMEE FINAL FORM
≈ <final> + 06BE ھ

FBAC ﮬ ARABIC LETTER HEH DOACHASHMEE INITIAL FORM
≈ <initial> + 06BE ھ

FBAD ﮭ ARABIC LETTER HEH DOACHASHMEE MEDIAL FORM
≈ <medial> + 06BE ھ

FBAE ﮮ ARABIC LETTER YEH BARREE ISOLATED FORM
≈ <isolated> + 06D2 ے

FBAF ﮯ ARABIC LETTER YEH BARREE FINAL FORM
≈ <final> + 06D2 ے

FBB0 ﮰ ARABIC LETTER YEH BARREE WITH HAMZA ABOVE ISOLATED FORM
≈ <isolated> + 06D3 ۓ

FBB1 ﮱ ARABIC LETTER YEH BARREE WITH HAMZA ABOVE FINAL FORM
≈ <final> + 06D3 ۓ

FBB2 <reserved>
FBB3 <reserved>
FBB4 <reserved>
FBB5 <reserved>
FBB6 <reserved>
FBB7 <reserved>
FBB8 <reserved>
FBB9 <reserved>
FBBA <reserved>
FBBB <reserved>
FBBC <reserved>
FBBD <reserved>
FBBE <reserved>
FBBF <reserved>
FBC0 <reserved>
FBC1 <reserved>
FBC2 <reserved>
FBC3 <reserved>
FBC4 <reserved>
FBC5 <reserved>
FBC6 <reserved>
FBC7 <reserved>
FBC8 <reserved>
FBC9 <reserved>
FBCA <reserved>
FBCB <reserved>
FBCC <reserved>
FBCD <reserved>
FBCE <reserved>
FBCF <reserved>
FBD0 <reserved>
FBD1 <reserved>
FBD2 <reserved>

FBD3 ﯓ ARABIC LETTER NG ISOLATED FORM
≈ <isolated> + 06AD ڭ

FBD4 ﯔ ARABIC LETTER NG FINAL FORM
≈ <final> + 06AD ڭ

FBD5 ﯕ ARABIC LETTER NG INITIAL FORM
≈ <initial> + 06AD ڭ

FBD6 ﯖ ARABIC LETTER NG MEDIAL FORM
≈ <medial> + 06AD ڭ

FBD7 ﯗ ARABIC LETTER U ISOLATED FORM
≈ <isolated> + 06C7 ۇ

FBD8 ﯘ ARABIC LETTER U FINAL FORM
≈ <final> + 06C7 ۇ

FBD9 ﯙ ARABIC LETTER OE ISOLATED FORM
≈ <isolated> + 06C6 ۆ

FBDA ﯚ ARABIC LETTER OE FINAL FORM
≈ <final> + 06C6 ۆ

FBDB ﯛ ARABIC LETTER YU ISOLATED FORM
≈ <isolated> + 06C8 ۈ

FBDC ﯜ ARABIC LETTER YU FINAL FORM
≈ <final> + 06C8 ۈ

FBDD ﯝ ARABIC LETTER U WITH HAMZA ABOVE ISOLATED FORM
≈ <isolated> + 0677 ٷ

FBDE ﯞ ARABIC LETTER VE ISOLATED FORM
≈ <isolated> + 06CB ۋ

FBDF ﯟ ARABIC LETTER VE FINAL FORM
≈ <final> + 06CB ۋ

FBE0 ﯠ ARABIC LETTER KIRGHIZ OE ISOLATED FORM
≈ <isolated> + 06C5 ۅ

FBE1 ﯡ ARABIC LETTER KIRGHIZ OE FINAL FORM
≈ <final> + 06C5 ۅ

FBE2 ﯢ ARABIC LETTER KIRGHIZ YU ISOLATED FORM
≈ <isolated> + 06C9 ۉ

FBE3 ﯣ ARABIC LETTER KIRGHIZ YU FINAL FORM
≈ <final> + 06C9 ۉ

FBE4 ﯤ ARABIC LETTER E ISOLATED FORM
≈ <isolated> + 06D0 ې

FBE5 ﯥ ARABIC LETTER E FINAL FORM
≈ <final> + 06D0 ې

FBE6 ﯦ ARABIC LETTER E INITIAL FORM
≈ <initial> + 06D0 ې

FBE7 ﯧ ARABIC LETTER E MEDIAL FORM
≈ <medial> + 06D0 ې

FBE8 ﯨ ARABIC LETTER UIGHUR KAZAKH KIRGHIZ ALEF MAKSURA INITIAL FORM

FBE9 ﯩ ARABIC LETTER UIGHUR KAZAKH KIRGHIZ ALEF MAKSURA MEDIAL FORM

FBEA ﯪ ARABIC LIGATURE YEH WITH HAMZA ABOVE WITH ALEF ISOLATED FORM
≈ <isolated> + 0626 ئ + 0627 ا

FBEB ﯫ ARABIC LIGATURE YEH WITH HAMZA ABOVE WITH ALEF FINAL FORM
≈ <final> + 0626 ئ + 0627 ا

FBEC ﯬ ARABIC LIGATURE YEH WITH HAMZA ABOVE WITH AE ISOLATED FORM
≈ <isolated> + 0626 ئ + 06D5 ە

FBED ﯭ ARABIC LIGATURE YEH WITH HAMZA ABOVE WITH AE FINAL FORM
≈ <final> + 0626 ئ + 06D5 ە

FBEE ﯮ ARABIC LIGATURE YEH WITH HAMZA ABOVE WITH WAW ISOLATED FORM
≈ <isolated> + 0626 ئ + 0648 و

FBEF ﯯ ARABIC LIGATURE YEH WITH HAMZA ABOVE WITH WAW FINAL FORM
≈ <final> + 0626 ئ + 0648 و

FBF0 ﯰ ARABIC LIGATURE YEH WITH HAMZA ABOVE WITH U ISOLATED FORM
≈ <isolated> + 0626 ئ + 06C7 ۇ

FBF1 ﯱ ARABIC LIGATURE YEH WITH HAMZA ABOVE WITH U FINAL FORM
≈ <final> + 0626 ئ + 06C7 ۇ

FBF2 ﯲ ARABIC LIGATURE YEH WITH HAMZA ABOVE WITH OE ISOLATED FORM
≈ <isolated> + 0626 ئ + 06C6 ۆ

FBF3 ﯳ ARABIC LIGATURE YEH WITH HAMZA ABOVE WITH OE FINAL FORM
≈ <final> + 0626 ئ + 06C6 ۆ

FBF4 ﯴ ARABIC LIGATURE YEH WITH HAMZA ABOVE WITH YU ISOLATED FORM
≈ <isolated> + 0626 ئ + 06C8 ۈ

FBF5 ﯵ ARABIC LIGATURE YEH WITH HAMZA ABOVE WITH YU FINAL FORM
≈ <final> + 0626 ئ + 06C8 ۈ

FBF6 ﯶ ARABIC LIGATURE YEH WITH HAMZA ABOVE WITH E ISOLATED FORM
≈ <isolated> + 0626 ئ + 06D0 ې

FBF7 ﯷ ARABIC LIGATURE YEH WITH HAMZA ABOVE WITH E FINAL FORM
≈ <final> + 0626 ئ + 06D0 ې

FBF8 ﯸ ARABIC LIGATURE YEH WITH HAMZA ABOVE WITH E INITIAL FORM
≈ <initial> + 0626 ئ + 06D0 ې

FBF9 ﯹ ARABIC LIGATURE UIGHUR KIRGHIZ YEH WITH HAMZA ABOVE WITH ALEF MAKSURA ISOLATED FORM

FBFA ﯺ ARABIC LIGATURE UIGHUR KIRGHIZ YEH WITH HAMZA ABOVE WITH ALEF MAKSURA FINAL FORM

FBFB ﯻ ARABIC LIGATURE UIGHUR KIRGHIZ YEH WITH HAMZA ABOVE WITH ALEF MAKSURA INITIAL FORM

FBFC ﯼ ARABIC LETTER FARSI YEH ISOLATED FORM
≈ <isolated> + 06CC ی

FBFD ﯽ ARABIC LETTER FARSI YEH FINAL FORM
≈ <final> + 06CC ی

FBFE ﯾ ARABIC LETTER FARSI YEH INITIAL FORM
≈ <initial> + 06CC ی

FBFF ﯿ ARABIC LETTER FARSI YEH MEDIAL FORM
≈ <medial> + 06CC ی

FC00 ﰀ ARABIC LIGATURE YEH WITH HAMZA ABOVE WITH JEEM ISOLATED FORM
≈ <isolated> + 0626 ئ + 062C ج

FC01 ﰁ ARABIC LIGATURE YEH WITH HAMZA ABOVE WITH HAH ISOLATED FORM
≈ <isolated> + 0626 ئ + 062D ح

FC02 ﰂ ARABIC LIGATURE YEH WITH HAMZA ABOVE WITH MEEM ISOLATED FORM
≈ <isolated> + 0626 ئ + 0645 م

FC03 ﰃ ARABIC LIGATURE YEH WITH HAMZA ABOVE WITH ALEF MAKSURA ISOLATED FORM
≈ <isolated> + 0626 ئ + 0649 ى

FC04 ﰄ ARABIC LIGATURE YEH WITH HAMZA ABOVE WITH YEH ISOLATED FORM
≈ <isolated> + 0626 ئ + 064A ي

FC05 ﰅ ARABIC LIGATURE BEH WITH JEEM ISOLATED FORM
≈ <isolated> + 0628 ب + 062C ج

FC06 ﰆ ARABIC LIGATURE BEH WITH HAH ISOLATED FORM
≈ <isolated> + 0628 ب + 062D ح

FC07 ﰇ ARABIC LIGATURE BEH WITH KHAH ISOLATED FORM
≈ <isolated> + 0628 ب + 062E خ

FC08 ﰈ ARABIC LIGATURE BEH WITH MEEM ISOLATED FORM
≈ <isolated> + 0628 ب + 0645 م

FC09 ﰉ ARABIC LIGATURE BEH WITH ALEF MAKSURA ISOLATED FORM
≈ <isolated> + 0628 ب + 0649 ى

FC0A ﰊ ARABIC LIGATURE BEH WITH YEH ISOLATED FORM
≈ <isolated> + 0628 ب + 064A ي

FC0B ﰋ ARABIC LIGATURE TEH WITH JEEM ISOLATED FORM
≈ <isolated> + 062A ت + 062C ج

FC0C ﰌ ARABIC LIGATURE TEH WITH HAH ISOLATED FORM
≈ <isolated> + 062A ت + 062D ح

FC0D ﰍ ARABIC LIGATURE TEH WITH KHAH ISOLATED FORM
≈ <isolated> + 062A ت + 062E خ

FC0E ﰎ ARABIC LIGATURE TEH WITH MEEM ISOLATED FORM
≈ <isolated> + 062A ت + 0645 م

FC0F ﰏ ARABIC LIGATURE TEH WITH ALEF MAKSURA ISOLATED FORM
≈ <isolated> + 062A ت + 0649 ى

FC10 ﰐ ARABIC LIGATURE TEH WITH YEH ISOLATED FORM
≈ <isolated> + 062A ت + 064A ي

FC11 ﰑ ARABIC LIGATURE THEH WITH JEEM ISOLATED FORM
≈ <isolated> + 062B ث + 062C ج

FC12 ﰒ ARABIC LIGATURE THEH WITH MEEM ISOLATED FORM
≈ <isolated> + 062B ث + 0645 م

FC13 ﰓ ARABIC LIGATURE THEH WITH ALEF MAKSURA ISOLATED FORM
≈ <isolated> + 062B ث + 0649 ى

FC14 ﰔ ARABIC LIGATURE THEH WITH YEH ISOLATED FORM
≈ <isolated> + 062B ث + 064A ي

FC15 ﰕ ARABIC LIGATURE JEEM WITH HAH ISOLATED FORM
≈ <isolated> + 062C ج + 062D ح

FC16 ﰖ ARABIC LIGATURE JEEM WITH MEEM ISOLATED FORM
≈ <isolated> + 062C ج + 0645 م

FC17 ﰗ ARABIC LIGATURE HAH WITH JEEM ISOLATED FORM
≈ <isolated> + 062D ح + 062C ج

FC18 ﰘ ARABIC LIGATURE HAH WITH MEEM ISOLATED FORM
≈ <isolated> + 062D ح + 0645 م

FC19 ﰙ ARABIC LIGATURE KHAH WITH JEEM ISOLATED FORM
≈ <isolated> + 062E خ + 062C ج

FC1A ﰚ ARABIC LIGATURE KHAH WITH HAH ISOLATED FORM
≈ <isolated> + 062E خ + 062D ح

FC1B ﰛ ARABIC LIGATURE KHAH WITH MEEM ISOLATED FORM
≈ <isolated> + 062E خ + 0645 م

FC1C ﰜ ARABIC LIGATURE SEEN WITH JEEM ISOLATED FORM
≈ <isolated> + 0633 س + 062C ج

FC1D ﰝ ARABIC LIGATURE SEEN WITH HAH ISOLATED FORM
≈ <isolated> + 0633 س + 062D ح

FC1E ﰞ ARABIC LIGATURE SEEN WITH KHAH ISOLATED FORM
≈ <isolated> + 0633 س + 062E خ

FC1F ﰟ ARABIC LIGATURE SEEN WITH MEEM ISOLATED FORM
≈ <isolated> + 0633 س + 0645 م

FC20 ﰠ ARABIC LIGATURE SAD WITH HAH ISOLATED FORM
≈ <isolated> + 0635 ص + 062D ح

FC21 ﰡ ARABIC LIGATURE SAD WITH MEEM ISOLATED FORM
≈ <isolated> + 0635 ص + 0645 م

FC22 ﰢ ARABIC LIGATURE DAD WITH JEEM ISOLATED FORM
≈ <isolated> + 0636 ض + 062C ج

FC23 ﰣ ARABIC LIGATURE DAD WITH HAH ISOLATED FORM
≈ <isolated> + 0636 ض + 062D ح

FC24 ﰤ ARABIC LIGATURE DAD WITH KHAH ISOLATED FORM
≈ <isolated> + 0636 ض + 062E خ

FC25 ﰥ ARABIC LIGATURE DAD WITH MEEM ISOLATED FORM
≈ <isolated> + 0636 ض + 0645 م

FC26 ﰦ ARABIC LIGATURE TAH WITH HAH ISOLATED FORM
≈ <isolated> + 0637 ط + 062D ح

FC27 ﰧ ARABIC LIGATURE TAH WITH MEEM ISOLATED FORM
≈ <isolated> + 0637 ط + 0645 م

FC28 ﰨ ARABIC LIGATURE ZAH WITH MEEM ISOLATED FORM
≈ <isolated> + 0638 ظ + 0645 م

FC29 ﰩ ARABIC LIGATURE AIN WITH JEEM ISOLATED FORM
≈ <isolated> + 0639 ع + 062C ج

FC2A ﰪ ARABIC LIGATURE AIN WITH MEEM ISOLATED FORM
≈ <isolated> + 0639 ع + 0645 م

FC2B ﰫ ARABIC LIGATURE GHAIN WITH JEEM ISOLATED FORM
≈ <isolated> + 063A غ + 062C ج

FC2C ﰬ ARABIC LIGATURE GHAIN WITH MEEM ISOLATED FORM
≈ <isolated> + 063A غ + 0645 م

FC2D ﰭ ARABIC LIGATURE FEH WITH JEEM ISOLATED FORM
≈ <isolated> + 0641 ف + 062C ج

FC2E ﰮ ARABIC LIGATURE FEH WITH HAH ISOLATED FORM
≈ <isolated> + 0641 ف + 062D ح

FC2F ﰯ ARABIC LIGATURE FEH WITH KHAH ISOLATED FORM
≈ <isolated> + 0641 ف + 062E خ

FC30 ﰰ ARABIC LIGATURE FEH WITH MEEM ISOLATED FORM
≈ <isolated> + 0641 ف + 0645 م

FC31 ﰱ ARABIC LIGATURE FEH WITH ALEF MAKSURA ISOLATED FORM
≈ <isolated> + 0641 ف + 0649 ى

FC32 ﰲ ARABIC LIGATURE FEH WITH YEH ISOLATED FORM
≈ <isolated> + 0641 ف + 064A ي

FC33 ﰳ ARABIC LIGATURE QAF WITH HAH ISOLATED FORM
≈ <isolated> + 0642 ق + 062D ح

FC34 ﰴ ARABIC LIGATURE QAF WITH MEEM ISOLATED FORM
≈ <isolated> + 0642 ق + 0645 م

FC35 ﰵ ARABIC LIGATURE QAF WITH ALEF MAKSURA ISOLATED FORM
≈ <isolated> + 0642 ق + 0649 ى

FC36 ﰶ ARABIC LIGATURE QAF WITH YEH ISOLATED FORM
≈ <isolated> + 0642 ق + 064A ي

FC37 ﰷ ARABIC LIGATURE KAF WITH ALEF ISOLATED FORM
≈ <isolated> + 0643 ك + 0627 ا

FC38 ﰸ ARABIC LIGATURE KAF WITH JEEM ISOLATED FORM
≈ <isolated> + 0643 ك + 062C ج

FC39 ﰹ ARABIC LIGATURE KAF WITH HAH ISOLATED FORM
≈ <isolated> + 0643 ك + 062D ح

FC3A ﰺ ARABIC LIGATURE KAF WITH KHAH ISOLATED FORM
≈ <isolated> + 0643 ك + 062E خ

FC3B ﰻ ARABIC LIGATURE KAF WITH LAM ISOLATED FORM
≈ <isolated> + 0643 ك + 0644 ل

FC3C ﰼ ARABIC LIGATURE KAF WITH MEEM ISOLATED FORM
≈ <isolated> + 0643 ك + 0645 م

FC3D ﰽ ARABIC LIGATURE KAF WITH ALEF MAKSURA ISOLATED FORM
≈ <isolated> + 0643 ك + 0649 ى

FC3E ﰾ ARABIC LIGATURE KAF WITH YEH ISOLATED FORM
≈ <isolated> + 0643 ك + 064A ي

FC3F ﰿ ARABIC LIGATURE LAM WITH JEEM ISOLATED FORM
≈ <isolated> + 0644 ل + 062C ج

FC40 ﱀ ARABIC LIGATURE LAM WITH HAH ISOLATED FORM
≈ <isolated> + 0644 ل + 062D ح

FC41 ﱁ ARABIC LIGATURE LAM WITH KHAH ISOLATED FORM
≈ <isolated> + 0644 ل + 062E خ

FC42 ﱂ ARABIC LIGATURE LAM WITH MEEM ISOLATED FORM
≈ <isolated> + 0644 ل + 0645 م

FC43 ﱃ ARABIC LIGATURE LAM WITH ALEF MAKSURA ISOLATED FORM
≈ <isolated> + 0644 ل + 0649 ى

FC44 ﱄ ARABIC LIGATURE LAM WITH YEH ISOLATED FORM
≈ <isolated> + 0644 ل + 064A ي

FC45 ﱅ ARABIC LIGATURE MEEM WITH JEEM ISOLATED FORM
≈ <isolated> + 0645 م + 062C ج

FC46 ﱆ ARABIC LIGATURE MEEM WITH HAH ISOLATED FORM
≈ <isolated> + 0645 م + 062D ح

FC47 ﱇ ARABIC LIGATURE MEEM WITH KHAH ISOLATED FORM
≈ <isolated> + 0645 م + 062E خ

FC48 ﱈ ARABIC LIGATURE MEEM WITH MEEM ISOLATED FORM
≈ <isolated> + 0645 م + 0645 م

FC49 ﱉ ARABIC LIGATURE MEEM WITH ALEF MAKSURA ISOLATED FORM
≈ <isolated> + 0645 م + 0649 ى

FC4A ﱊ ARABIC LIGATURE MEEM WITH YEH ISOLATED FORM
≈ <isolated> + 0645 م + 064A ي

FC4B ﱋ ARABIC LIGATURE NOON WITH JEEM ISOLATED FORM
≈ <isolated> + 0646 ن + 062C ج

FC4C ﱌ ARABIC LIGATURE NOON WITH HAH ISOLATED FORM
≈ <isolated> + 0646 ن + 062D ح

FC4D ﱍ ARABIC LIGATURE NOON WITH KHAH ISOLATED FORM
≈ <isolated> + 0646 ن + 062E خ

FC4E ﱎ ARABIC LIGATURE NOON WITH MEEM ISOLATED FORM
≈ <isolated> + 0646 ن + 0645 م

FC4F ﱏ ARABIC LIGATURE NOON WITH ALEF MAKSURA ISOLATED FORM
≈ <isolated> + 0646 ن + 0649 ى

FC50 ﱐ ARABIC LIGATURE NOON WITH YEH ISOLATED FORM
≈ <isolated> + 0646 ن + 064A ي

FC51 ﱑ ARABIC LIGATURE HEH WITH JEEM ISOLATED FORM
≈ <isolated> + 0647 ه + 062C ج

FC52 ﱒ ARABIC LIGATURE HEH WITH MEEM ISOLATED FORM
≈ <isolated> + 0647 ه + 0645 م

FC53 ﱓ ARABIC LIGATURE HEH WITH ALEF MAKSURA ISOLATED FORM
≈ <isolated> + 0647 ه + 0649 ى

FC54 ﱔ ARABIC LIGATURE HEH WITH YEH ISOLATED FORM
≈ <isolated> + 0647 ه + 064A ي

FC55 ﱕ ARABIC LIGATURE YEH WITH JEEM ISOLATED FORM
≈ <isolated> + 064A ي + 062C ج

FC56 ﱖ ARABIC LIGATURE YEH WITH HAH ISOLATED FORM
≈ <isolated> + 064A ي + 062D ح

FC57 ﱗ ARABIC LIGATURE YEH WITH KHAH ISOLATED FORM
≈ <isolated> + 064A ي + 062E خ

FC58 ﱘ ARABIC LIGATURE YEH WITH MEEM ISOLATED FORM
≈ <isolated> + 064A ي + 0645 م

FC59 ﱙ ARABIC LIGATURE YEH WITH ALEF MAKSURA ISOLATED FORM
≈ <isolated> + 064A ي + 0649 ى

FC5A ﱚ ARABIC LIGATURE YEH WITH YEH ISOLATED FORM
≈ <isolated> + 064A ي + 064A ي

FC5B ﱛ ARABIC LIGATURE THAL WITH SUPERSCRIPT ALEF ISOLATED FORM
≈ <isolated> + 0630 ذ + 0670 ◌ٰ

FC5C ﱜ ARABIC LIGATURE REH WITH SUPERSCRIPT ALEF ISOLATED FORM
≈ <isolated> + 0631 ر + 0670 ◌ٰ

FC5D ﱝ ARABIC LIGATURE ALEF MAKSURA WITH SUPERSCRIPT ALEF ISOLATED FORM
≈ <isolated> + 0649 ى + 0670 ◌ٰ

FC5E ﱞ ARABIC LIGATURE SHADDA WITH DAMMATAN ISOLATED FORM
≈ <isolated> + 0020 SP + 0651 ◌ّ + 064C ◌ٌ

FC5F ﱟ ARABIC LIGATURE SHADDA WITH KASRATAN ISOLATED FORM
≈ <isolated> + 0020 SP + 0651 ◌ّ + 064D ◌ٍ

FC60 ﱠ ARABIC LIGATURE SHADDA WITH FATHA ISOLATED FORM
≈ <isolated> + 0020 SP + 0651 ◌ّ + 064E ◌َ

FC61 ﱡ ARABIC LIGATURE SHADDA WITH DAMMA ISOLATED FORM
≈ <isolated> + 0020 [SP] + 0651 ◌ّ + 064F ◌ُ

FC62 ﱢ ARABIC LIGATURE SHADDA WITH KASRA ISOLATED FORM
≈ <isolated> + 0020 [SP] + 0651 ◌ّ + 0650 ◌ِ

FC63 ﱣ ARABIC LIGATURE SHADDA WITH SUPERSCRIPT ALEF ISOLATED FORM
≈ <isolated> + 0020 [SP] + 0651 ◌ّ + 0670 ◌ٰ

FC64 ﱤ ARABIC LIGATURE YEH WITH HAMZA ABOVE WITH REH FINAL FORM
≈ <final> + 0626 ئ + 0631 ر

FC65 ﱥ ARABIC LIGATURE YEH WITH HAMZA ABOVE WITH ZAIN FINAL FORM
≈ <final> + 0626 ئ + 0632 ز

FC66 ﱦ ARABIC LIGATURE YEH WITH HAMZA ABOVE WITH MEEM FINAL FORM
≈ <final> + 0626 ئ + 0645 م

FC67 ﱧ ARABIC LIGATURE YEH WITH HAMZA ABOVE WITH NOON FINAL FORM
≈ <final> + 0626 ئ + 0646 ن

FC68 ﱨ ARABIC LIGATURE YEH WITH HAMZA ABOVE WITH ALEF MAKSURA FINAL FORM
≈ <final> + 0626 ئ + 0649 ى

FC69 ﱩ ARABIC LIGATURE YEH WITH HAMZA ABOVE WITH YEH FINAL FORM
≈ <final> + 0626 ئ + 064A ي

FC6A ﱪ ARABIC LIGATURE BEH WITH REH FINAL FORM
≈ <final> + 0628 ب + 0631 ر

FC6B ﱫ ARABIC LIGATURE BEH WITH ZAIN FINAL FORM
≈ <final> + 0628 ب + 0632 ز

FC6C ﱬ ARABIC LIGATURE BEH WITH MEEM FINAL FORM
≈ <final> + 0628 ب + 0645 م

FC6D ﱭ ARABIC LIGATURE BEH WITH NOON FINAL FORM
≈ <final> + 0628 ب + 0646 ن

FC6E ﱮ ARABIC LIGATURE BEH WITH ALEF MAKSURA FINAL FORM
≈ <final> + 0628 ب + 0649 ى

FC6F ﱯ ARABIC LIGATURE BEH WITH YEH FINAL FORM
≈ <final> + 0628 ب + 064A ي

FC70 ﱰ ARABIC LIGATURE TEH WITH REH FINAL FORM
≈ <final> + 062A ت + 0631 ر

FC71 ﱱ ARABIC LIGATURE TEH WITH ZAIN FINAL FORM
≈ <final> + 062A ت + 0632 ز

FC72 ﱲ ARABIC LIGATURE TEH WITH MEEM FINAL FORM
≈ <final> + 062A ت + 0645 م

FC73 ﱳ ARABIC LIGATURE TEH WITH NOON FINAL FORM
≈ <final> + 062A ت + 0646 ن

FC74 ﱴ ARABIC LIGATURE TEH WITH ALEF MAKSURA FINAL FORM
≈ <final> + 062A ت + 0649 ى

FC75 ﱵ ARABIC LIGATURE TEH WITH YEH FINAL FORM
≈ <final> + 062A ت + 064A ي

FC76 ﱶ ARABIC LIGATURE THEH WITH REH FINAL FORM
≈ <final> + 062B ث + 0631 ر

FC77 ﱷ ARABIC LIGATURE THEH WITH ZAIN FINAL FORM
≈ <final> + 062B ث + 0632 ز

FC78 ﱸ ARABIC LIGATURE THEH WITH MEEM FINAL FORM
≈ <final> + 062B ث + 0645 م

FC79 ﱹ ARABIC LIGATURE THEH WITH NOON FINAL FORM
≈ <final> + 062B ث + 0646 ن

FC7A ﱺ ARABIC LIGATURE THEH WITH ALEF MAKSURA FINAL FORM
≈ <final> + 062B ث + 0649 ى

FC7B ﱻ ARABIC LIGATURE THEH WITH YEH FINAL FORM
≈ <final> + 062B ث + 064A ي

FC7C ﱼ ARABIC LIGATURE FEH WITH ALEF MAKSURA FINAL FORM
≈ <final> + 0641 ف + 0649 ى

FC7D ﱽ ARABIC LIGATURE FEH WITH YEH FINAL FORM
≈ <final> + 0641 ف + 064A ي

FC7E ﱾ ARABIC LIGATURE QAF WITH ALEF MAKSURA FINAL FORM
≈ <final> + 0642 ق + 0649 ى

FC7F ﱿ ARABIC LIGATURE QAF WITH YEH FINAL FORM
≈ <final> + 0642 ق + 064A ي

FC80 ﲀ ARABIC LIGATURE KAF WITH ALEF FINAL FORM
≈ <final> + 0643 ك + 0627 ا

FC81 ﲁ ARABIC LIGATURE KAF WITH LAM FINAL FORM
≈ <final> + 0643 ك + 0644 ل

FC82 ﲂ ARABIC LIGATURE KAF WITH MEEM FINAL FORM
≈ <final> + 0643 ك + 0645 م

FC83 ﲃ ARABIC LIGATURE KAF WITH ALEF MAKSURA FINAL FORM
≈ <final> + 0643 ك + 0649 ى

FC84 ﲄ ARABIC LIGATURE KAF WITH YEH FINAL FORM
≈ <final> + 0643 ك + 064A ي

FC85 ﲅ ARABIC LIGATURE LAM WITH MEEM FINAL FORM
≈ <final> + 0644 ل + 0645 م

FC86 ﲆ ARABIC LIGATURE LAM WITH ALEF MAKSURA FINAL FORM
≈ <final> + 0644 ل + 0649 ى

FC87 ﲇ ARABIC LIGATURE LAM WITH YEH FINAL FORM
≈ <final> + 0644 ل + 064A ي

FC88 ﲈ ARABIC LIGATURE MEEM WITH ALEF FINAL FORM
≈ <final> + 0645 م + 0627 ا

FC89 ﲉ ARABIC LIGATURE MEEM WITH MEEM FINAL FORM
≈ <final> + 0645 م + 0645 م

FC8A ﲊ ARABIC LIGATURE NOON WITH REH FINAL FORM
≈ <final> + 0646 ن + 0631 ر

FC8B ﲋ ARABIC LIGATURE NOON WITH ZAIN FINAL FORM
≈ <final> + 0646 ن + 0632 ز

FC8C ﲌ ARABIC LIGATURE NOON WITH MEEM FINAL FORM
≈ <final> + 0646 ن + 0645 م

FC8D ﲍ ARABIC LIGATURE NOON WITH NOON FINAL FORM
≈ <final> + 0646 ن + 0646 ن

FC8E ﲎ ARABIC LIGATURE NOON WITH ALEF MAKSURA FINAL FORM
≈ <final> + 0646 ن + 0649 ى

FC8F ﲏ ARABIC LIGATURE NOON WITH YEH FINAL FORM
≈ <final> + 0646 ن + 064A ي

FC90 ﲐ ARABIC LIGATURE ALEF MAKSURA WITH SUPERSCRIPT ALEF FINAL FORM
≈ <final> + 0649 ى + 0670 ◌ٰ

FC91 ﲑ ARABIC LIGATURE YEH WITH REH FINAL FORM
≈ <final> + 064A ي + 0631 ر

FC92 ﲒ ARABIC LIGATURE YEH WITH ZAIN FINAL FORM
≈ <final> + 064A ي + 0632 ز

FC93 ﲓ ARABIC LIGATURE YEH WITH MEEM FINAL FORM
≈ <final> + 064A ي + 0645 م

FC94 ﲔ ARABIC LIGATURE YEH WITH NOON FINAL FORM
≈ <final> + 064A ي + 0646 ن

FC95 ﲕ ARABIC LIGATURE YEH WITH ALEF MAKSURA FINAL FORM
≈ <final> + 064A ي + 0649 ى

FC96 ﲖ ARABIC LIGATURE YEH WITH YEH FINAL FORM
≈ <final> + 064A ي + 064A ي

FC97 ﲗ ARABIC LIGATURE YEH WITH HAMZA ABOVE WITH JEEM INITIAL FORM
≈ <initial> + 0626 ئ + 062C ج

FC98 ﲘ ARABIC LIGATURE YEH WITH HAMZA ABOVE WITH HAH INITIAL FORM
≈ <initial> + 0626 ئ + 062D ح

FC99 ﲙ ARABIC LIGATURE YEH WITH HAMZA ABOVE WITH KHAH INITIAL FORM
≈ <initial> + 0626 ئ + 062E خ

FC9A ﲚ ARABIC LIGATURE YEH WITH HAMZA ABOVE WITH MEEM INITIAL FORM
≈ <initial> + 0626 ئ + 0645 م

FC9B ﲛ ARABIC LIGATURE YEH WITH HAMZA ABOVE WITH HEH INITIAL FORM
≈ <initial> + 0626 ئ + 0647 ه

FC9C ﲜ ARABIC LIGATURE BEH WITH JEEM INITIAL FORM
≈ <initial> + 0628 ب + 062C ج

FC9D ﲝ ARABIC LIGATURE BEH WITH HAH INITIAL FORM
≈ <initial> + 0628 ب + 062D ح

FC9E ﲞ ARABIC LIGATURE BEH WITH KHAH INITIAL FORM
≈ <initial> + 0628 ب + 062E خ

FC9F ﲟ ARABIC LIGATURE BEH WITH MEEM INITIAL FORM
≈ <initial> + 0628 ب + 0645 م

FCA0 ﲠ ARABIC LIGATURE BEH WITH HEH INITIAL FORM
≈ <initial> + 0628 ب + 0647 ه

FCA1 ﲡ ARABIC LIGATURE TEH WITH JEEM INITIAL FORM
≈ <initial> + 062A ت + 062C ج

FCA2 ﲢ ARABIC LIGATURE TEH WITH HAH INITIAL FORM
≈ <initial> + 062A ت + 062D ح

FCA3 ﲣ ARABIC LIGATURE TEH WITH KHAH INITIAL FORM
≈ <initial> + 062A ت + 062E خ

FCA4 ﲤ ARABIC LIGATURE TEH WITH MEEM INITIAL FORM
≈ <initial> + 062A ت + 0645 م

FCA5 ﲥ ARABIC LIGATURE TEH WITH HEH INITIAL FORM
≈ <initial> + 062A ت + 0647 ه

FCA6 ﲦ ARABIC LIGATURE THEH WITH MEEM INITIAL FORM
≈ <initial> + 062B ث + 0645 م

FCA7 ﲧ ARABIC LIGATURE JEEM WITH HAH INITIAL FORM
≈ <initial> + 062C ج + 062D ح

FCA8 ﲨ ARABIC LIGATURE JEEM WITH MEEM INITIAL FORM
≈ <initial> + 062C ج + 0645 م

FCA9 ﲩ ARABIC LIGATURE HAH WITH JEEM INITIAL FORM
≈ <initial> + 062D ح + 062C ج

FCAA ﲪ ARABIC LIGATURE HAH WITH MEEM INITIAL FORM
≈ <initial> + 062D ح + 0645 م

FCAB ﲫ ARABIC LIGATURE KHAH WITH JEEM INITIAL FORM
≈ <initial> + 062E خ + 062C ج

FCAC ﲬ ARABIC LIGATURE KHAH WITH MEEM INITIAL FORM
≈ <initial> + 062E خ + 0645 م

FCAD ﲭ ARABIC LIGATURE SEEN WITH JEEM INITIAL FORM
≈ <initial> + 0633 س + 062C ج

FCAE ﲮ ARABIC LIGATURE SEEN WITH HAH INITIAL FORM
≈ <initial> + 0633 س + 062D ح

FCAF ﲯ ARABIC LIGATURE SEEN WITH KHAH INITIAL FORM
≈ <initial> + 0633 س + 062E خ

FCB0 ﲰ ARABIC LIGATURE SEEN WITH MEEM INITIAL FORM
≈ <initial> + 0633 س + 0645 م

FCB1 ﲱ ARABIC LIGATURE SAD WITH HAH INITIAL FORM
≈ <initial> + 0635 ص + 062D ح

FCB2 ﲲ ARABIC LIGATURE SAD WITH KHAH INITIAL FORM
≈ <initial> + 0635 ص + 062E خ

FCB3 ﲳ ARABIC LIGATURE SAD WITH MEEM INITIAL FORM
≈ <initial> + 0635 ص + 0645 م

FCB4 ﲴ ARABIC LIGATURE DAD WITH JEEM INITIAL FORM
≈ <initial> + 0636 ض + 062C ج

FCB5 ﲵ ARABIC LIGATURE DAD WITH HAH INITIAL FORM
≈ <initial> + 0636 ض + 062D ح

FCB6 ﲶ ARABIC LIGATURE DAD WITH KHAH INITIAL FORM
≈ <initial> + 0636 ض + 062E خ

FCB7 ﲷ ARABIC LIGATURE DAD WITH MEEM INITIAL FORM
≈ <initial> + 0636 ض + 0645 م

FCB8 ﲸ ARABIC LIGATURE TAH WITH HAH INITIAL FORM
≈ <initial> + 0637 ط + 062D ح

FCB9 ﲹ ARABIC LIGATURE ZAH WITH MEEM INITIAL FORM
≈ <initial> + 0638 ظ + 0645 م

FCBA ﲺ ARABIC LIGATURE AIN WITH JEEM INITIAL FORM
≈ <initial> + 0639 ع + 062C ج

FCBB ﲻ ARABIC LIGATURE AIN WITH MEEM INITIAL FORM
≈ <initial> + 0639 ع + 0645 م

FCBC ﲼ ARABIC LIGATURE GHAIN WITH JEEM INITIAL FORM
≈ <initial> + 063A غ + 062C ج

FCBD ﲽ ARABIC LIGATURE GHAIN WITH MEEM INITIAL FORM
≈ <initial> + 063A غ + 0645 م

FCBE ﲾ ARABIC LIGATURE FEH WITH JEEM INITIAL FORM
≈ <initial> + 0641 ف + 062C ج

FCBF ﲿ ARABIC LIGATURE FEH WITH HAH INITIAL FORM
≈ <initial> + 0641 ف + 062D ح

FCC0 ﳀ ARABIC LIGATURE FEH WITH KHAH INITIAL FORM
≈ <initial> + 0641 ف + 062E خ

FCC1 ﳁ ARABIC LIGATURE FEH WITH MEEM INITIAL FORM
≈ <initial> + 0641 ف + 0645 م

FCC2 ﳂ ARABIC LIGATURE QAF WITH HAH INITIAL FORM
≈ <initial> + 0642 ق + 062D ح

FCC3 ﳃ ARABIC LIGATURE QAF WITH MEEM INITIAL FORM
≈ <initial> + 0642 ق + 0645 م

FCC4 ﳄ ARABIC LIGATURE KAF WITH JEEM INITIAL FORM
≈ <initial> + 0643 ك + 062C ج

FCC5 ﳅ ARABIC LIGATURE KAF WITH HAH INITIAL FORM
≈ <initial> + 0643 ك + 062D ح

FCC6 ﳆ ARABIC LIGATURE KAF WITH KHAH INITIAL FORM
≈ <initial> + 0643 ك + 062E خ

FCC7 ﳇ ARABIC LIGATURE KAF WITH LAM INITIAL FORM
≈ <initial> + 0643 ك + 0644 ل

FCC8 ﳈ ARABIC LIGATURE KAF WITH MEEM INITIAL FORM
≈ <initial> + 0643 ك + 0645 م

FCC9 ﳉ ARABIC LIGATURE LAM WITH JEEM INITIAL FORM
≈ <initial> + 0644 ل + 062C ج

FCCA ﳊ ARABIC LIGATURE LAM WITH HAH INITIAL FORM
≈ <initial> + 0644 ل + 062D ح

FCCB ﳋ ARABIC LIGATURE LAM WITH KHAH INITIAL FORM
≈ <initial> + 0644 ل + 062E خ

FCCC ﳌ ARABIC LIGATURE LAM WITH MEEM INITIAL FORM
≈ <initial> + 0644 ل + 0645 م

FCCD ﳍ ARABIC LIGATURE LAM WITH HEH INITIAL FORM
≈ <initial> + 0644 ل + 0647 ه

FCCE ﳎ ARABIC LIGATURE MEEM WITH JEEM INITIAL FORM
≈ <initial> + 0645 م + 062C ج

FCCF ﳏ ARABIC LIGATURE MEEM WITH HAH INITIAL FORM
≈ <initial> + 0645 م + 062D ح

FCD0 ﳐ ARABIC LIGATURE MEEM WITH KHAH INITIAL FORM
≈ <initial> + 0645 م + 062E خ

FCD1 ﳑ ARABIC LIGATURE MEEM WITH MEEM INITIAL FORM
≈ <initial> + 0645 م + 0645 م

FCD2 ﳒ ARABIC LIGATURE NOON WITH JEEM INITIAL FORM
≈ <initial> + 0646 ن + 062C ج

FCD3 ﳓ ARABIC LIGATURE NOON WITH HAH INITIAL FORM
≈ <initial> + 0646 ن + 062D ح

FCD4 ﳔ ARABIC LIGATURE NOON WITH KHAH INITIAL FORM
≈ <initial> + 0646 ن + 062E خ

FCD5 ﳕ ARABIC LIGATURE NOON WITH MEEM INITIAL FORM
≈ <initial> + 0646 ن + 0645 م

FCD6 ﳖ ARABIC LIGATURE NOON WITH HEH INITIAL FORM
≈ <initial> + 0646 ن + 0647 ه

FCD7 ﳗ ARABIC LIGATURE HEH WITH JEEM INITIAL FORM
≈ <initial> + 0647 ه + 062C ج

FCD8 ﳘ ARABIC LIGATURE HEH WITH MEEM INITIAL FORM
≈ <initial> + 0647 ه + 0645 م

FCD9 ﳙ ARABIC LIGATURE HEH WITH SUPERSCRIPT ALEF INITIAL FORM
≈ <initial> + 0647 ه + 0670 ٰ

FCDA ﳚ ARABIC LIGATURE YEH WITH JEEM INITIAL FORM
≈ <initial> + 064A ي + 062C ج

FCDB ﳛ ARABIC LIGATURE YEH WITH HAH INITIAL FORM
≈ <initial> + 064A ي + 062D ح

FCDC ﳜ ARABIC LIGATURE YEH WITH KHAH INITIAL FORM
≈ <initial> + 064A ي + 062E خ

FCDD ﳝ ARABIC LIGATURE YEH WITH MEEM INITIAL FORM
≈ <initial> + 064A ي + 0645 م

FCDE ﳞ ARABIC LIGATURE YEH WITH HEH INITIAL FORM
≈ <initial> + 064A ي + 0647 ه

FCDF ﳟ ARABIC LIGATURE YEH WITH HAMZA ABOVE WITH MEEM MEDIAL FORM
≈ <medial> + 0626 ئ + 0645 م

FCE0 ﳠ ARABIC LIGATURE YEH WITH HAMZA ABOVE WITH HEH MEDIAL FORM
≈ <medial> + 0626 ئ + 0647 ه

FCE1 ﳡ ARABIC LIGATURE BEH WITH MEEM MEDIAL FORM
≈ <medial> + 0628 ب + 0645 م

FCE2 ﳢ ARABIC LIGATURE BEH WITH HEH MEDIAL FORM
≈ <medial> + 0628 ب + 0647 ه

FCE3 ﳣ ARABIC LIGATURE TEH WITH MEEM MEDIAL FORM
≈ <medial> + 062A ت + 0645 م

FCE4 ﳤ ARABIC LIGATURE TEH WITH HEH MEDIAL FORM
≈ <medial> + 062A ت + 0647 ه

FCE5 ﳥ ARABIC LIGATURE THEH WITH MEEM MEDIAL FORM
≈ <medial> + 062B ث + 0645 م

FCE6 ﳦ ARABIC LIGATURE THEH WITH HEH MEDIAL FORM
≈ <medial> + 062B ث + 0647 ه

FCE7 ﳧ ARABIC LIGATURE SEEN WITH MEEM MEDIAL FORM
≈ <medial> + 0633 س + 0645 م

FCE8 ﳨ ARABIC LIGATURE SEEN WITH HEH MEDIAL FORM
≈ <medial> + 0633 س + 0647 ه

FCE9 ﳩ ARABIC LIGATURE SHEEN WITH MEEM MEDIAL FORM
≈ <medial> + 0634 ش + 0645 م

FCEA ﳪ ARABIC LIGATURE SHEEN WITH HEH MEDIAL FORM
≈ <medial> + 0634 ش + 0647 ه

FCEB ﳫ ARABIC LIGATURE KAF WITH LAM MEDIAL FORM
≈ <medial> + 0643 ك + 0644 ل

FCEC ﳬ ARABIC LIGATURE KAF WITH MEEM MEDIAL FORM
≈ <medial> + 0643 ك + 0645 م

FCED ﳭ ARABIC LIGATURE LAM WITH MEEM MEDIAL FORM
≈ <medial> + 0644 ل + 0645 م

FCEE ﳮ ARABIC LIGATURE NOON WITH MEEM MEDIAL FORM
≈ <medial> + 0646 ن + 0645 م

FCEF ﳯ ARABIC LIGATURE NOON WITH HEH MEDIAL FORM
≈ <medial> + 0646 ن + 0647 ه

FCF0 ﳰ ARABIC LIGATURE YEH WITH MEEM MEDIAL FORM
≈ <medial> + 064A ي + 0645 م

FCF1 ﳱ ARABIC LIGATURE YEH WITH HEH MEDIAL FORM
≈ <medial> + 064A ي + 0647 ه

FCF2 ﳲ ARABIC LIGATURE SHADDA WITH FATHA MEDIAL FORM
≈ <medial> + 0020 [SP] + 0651 ◌ّ + 064E ◌َ

FCF3 ﳳ ARABIC LIGATURE SHADDA WITH DAMMA MEDIAL FORM
≈ <medial> + 0020 [SP] + 0651 ◌ّ + 064F ◌ُ

FCF4 ﳴ ARABIC LIGATURE SHADDA WITH KASRA MEDIAL FORM
≈ <medial> + 0020 [SP] + 0651 ◌ّ + 0650 ◌ِ

FCF5 ﳵ ARABIC LIGATURE TAH WITH ALEF MAKSURA ISOLATED FORM
≈ <isolated> + 0637 ط + 0649 ى

FCF6 ﳶ ARABIC LIGATURE TAH WITH YEH ISOLATED FORM
≈ <isolated> + 0637 ط + 064A ي

FCF7 ﳷ ARABIC LIGATURE AIN WITH ALEF MAKSURA ISOLATED FORM
≈ <isolated> + 0639 ع + 0649 ى

FCF8 ﳸ ARABIC LIGATURE AIN WITH YEH ISOLATED FORM
≈ <isolated> + 0639 ع + 064A ي

FCF9 ﳹ ARABIC LIGATURE GHAIN WITH ALEF MAKSURA ISOLATED FORM
≈ <isolated> + 063A غ + 0649 ى

FCFA ﳺ ARABIC LIGATURE GHAIN WITH YEH ISOLATED FORM
≈ <isolated> + 063A غ + 064A ي

FCFB ﳻ ARABIC LIGATURE SEEN WITH ALEF MAKSURA ISOLATED FORM
≈ <isolated> + 0633 س + 0649 ى

FCFC ﳼ ARABIC LIGATURE SEEN WITH YEH ISOLATED FORM
≈ <isolated> + 0633 س + 064A ي

FCFD ﳽ ARABIC LIGATURE SHEEN WITH ALEF MAKSURA ISOLATED FORM
≈ <isolated> + 0634 ش + 0649 ى

FCFE ﳾ ARABIC LIGATURE SHEEN WITH YEH ISOLATED FORM
≈ <isolated> + 0634 ش + 064A ي

FCFF ﳿ ARABIC LIGATURE HAH WITH ALEF MAKSURA ISOLATED FORM
≈ <isolated> + 062D ح + 0649 ى

FD00 ﴀ ARABIC LIGATURE HAH WITH YEH ISOLATED FORM
≈ <isolated> + 062D ح + 064A ي

FD01 ﴁ ARABIC LIGATURE JEEM WITH ALEF MAKSURA ISOLATED FORM
≈ <isolated> + 062C ج + 0649 ى

FD02 ﴂ ARABIC LIGATURE JEEM WITH YEH ISOLATED FORM
≈ <isolated> + 062C ج + 064A ي

FD03 ﴃ ARABIC LIGATURE KHAH WITH ALEF MAKSURA ISOLATED FORM
≈ <isolated> + 062E خ + 0649 ى

FD04 ﴄ ARABIC LIGATURE KHAH WITH YEH ISOLATED FORM
≈ <isolated> + 062E خ + 064A ي

FD05 ﴅ ARABIC LIGATURE SAD WITH ALEF MAKSURA ISOLATED FORM
≈ <isolated> + 0635 ص + 0649 ى

FD06 ﴆ ARABIC LIGATURE SAD WITH YEH ISOLATED FORM
≈ <isolated> + 0635 ص + 064A ي

FD07 ﴇ ARABIC LIGATURE DAD WITH ALEF MAKSURA ISOLATED FORM
≈ <isolated> + 0636 ض + 0649 ى

FD08 ﴈ ARABIC LIGATURE DAD WITH YEH ISOLATED FORM
≈ <isolated> + 0636 ض + 064A ي

FD09 ﴉ ARABIC LIGATURE SHEEN WITH JEEM ISOLATED FORM
≈ <isolated> + 0634 ش + 062C ج

FD0A ﴊ ARABIC LIGATURE SHEEN WITH HAH ISOLATED FORM
≈ <isolated> + 0634 ش + 062D ح

FD0B ﴋ ARABIC LIGATURE SHEEN WITH KHAH ISOLATED FORM
≈ <isolated> + 0634 ش + 062E خ

FD0C ﴌ ARABIC LIGATURE SHEEN WITH MEEM ISOLATED FORM
≈ <isolated> + 0634 ش + 0645 م

FD0D ﴍ ARABIC LIGATURE SHEEN WITH REH ISOLATED FORM
≈ <isolated> + 0634 ش + 0631 ر

FD0E ﴎ ARABIC LIGATURE SEEN WITH REH ISOLATED FORM
≈ <isolated> + 0633 س + 0631 ر

FD0F ﴏ ARABIC LIGATURE SAD WITH REH ISOLATED FORM
≈ <isolated> + 0635 ص + 0631 ر

FD10 ﴐ ARABIC LIGATURE DAD WITH REH ISOLATED FORM
≈ <isolated> + 0636 ض + 0631 ر

FD11 ﴑ ARABIC LIGATURE TAH WITH ALEF MAKSURA FINAL FORM
≈ <final> + 0637 ط + 0649 ى

FD12 ﴒ ARABIC LIGATURE TAH WITH YEH FINAL FORM
≈ <final> + 0637 ط + 064A ي

FD13 ﴓ ARABIC LIGATURE AIN WITH ALEF MAKSURA FINAL FORM
≈ <final> + 0639 ع + 0649 ى

FD14 ﴔ ARABIC LIGATURE AIN WITH YEH FINAL FORM
≈ <final> + 0639 ع + 064A ي

FD15 ﴕ ARABIC LIGATURE GHAIN WITH ALEF MAKSURA FINAL FORM
≈ <final> + 063A غ + 0649 ى

FD16 ﴖ ARABIC LIGATURE GHAIN WITH YEH FINAL FORM
≈ <final> + 063A غ + 064A ي

FD17 ﴗ ARABIC LIGATURE SEEN WITH ALEF MAKSURA FINAL FORM
≈ <final> + 0633 س + 0649 ى

FD18 ﴘ ARABIC LIGATURE SEEN WITH YEH FINAL FORM
≈ <final> + 0633 س + 064A ي

FD19 ﴙ ARABIC LIGATURE SHEEN WITH ALEF MAKSURA FINAL FORM
≈ <final> + 0634 ش + 0649 ى

FD1A ﴚ ARABIC LIGATURE SHEEN WITH YEH FINAL FORM
≈ <final> + 0634 ش + 064A ي

FD1B ﴛ ARABIC LIGATURE HAH WITH ALEF MAKSURA FINAL FORM
≈ <final> + 062D ح + 0649 ى

FD1C ﴜ ARABIC LIGATURE HAH WITH YEH FINAL FORM
≈ <final> + 062D ح + 064A ي

FD1D ﴝ ARABIC LIGATURE JEEM WITH ALEF MAKSURA FINAL FORM
≈ <final> + 062C ج + 0649 ى

FD1E ﴞ ARABIC LIGATURE JEEM WITH YEH FINAL FORM
≈ <final> + 062C ج + 064A ي

FD1F ﴟ ARABIC LIGATURE KHAH WITH ALEF MAKSURA FINAL FORM
≈ <final> + 062E خ + 0649 ى

FD20 ﴠ ARABIC LIGATURE KHAH WITH YEH FINAL FORM
≈ <final> + 062E خ + 064A ي

FD21 ﴡ ARABIC LIGATURE SAD WITH ALEF MAKSURA FINAL FORM
≈ <final> + 0635 ص + 0649 ى

FD22 ﴢ ARABIC LIGATURE SAD WITH YEH FINAL FORM
≈ <final> + 0635 ص + 064A ي

FD23 ﴣ ARABIC LIGATURE DAD WITH ALEF MAKSURA FINAL FORM
≈ <final> + 0636 ض + 0649 ى

FD24 ﴤ ARABIC LIGATURE DAD WITH YEH FINAL FORM
≈ <final> + 0636 ض + 064A ي

FD25 ﴥ ARABIC LIGATURE SHEEN WITH JEEM FINAL FORM
≈ <final> + 0634 ش + 062C ج

FD26 ﴦ ARABIC LIGATURE SHEEN WITH HAH FINAL FORM
≈ <final> + 0634 ش + 062D ح

FD27 ﴧ ARABIC LIGATURE SHEEN WITH KHAH FINAL FORM
≈ <final> + 0634 ش + 062E خ

FD28 ﴨ ARABIC LIGATURE SHEEN WITH MEEM FINAL FORM
≈ <final> + 0634 ش + 0645 م

FD29 ﴩ ARABIC LIGATURE SHEEN WITH REH FINAL FORM
≈ <final> + 0634 ش + 0631 ر

FD2A ﴪ ARABIC LIGATURE SEEN WITH REH FINAL FORM
≈ <final> + 0633 س + 0631 ر

FD2B ﴫ ARABIC LIGATURE SAD WITH REH FINAL FORM
≈ <final> + 0635 ص + 0631 ر

FD2C ﴬ ARABIC LIGATURE DAD WITH REH FINAL FORM
≈ <final> + 0636 ض + 0631 ر

FD2D ﴭ ARABIC LIGATURE SHEEN WITH JEEM INITIAL FORM
≈ <initial> + 0634 ش + 062C ج

FD2E ﴮ ARABIC LIGATURE SHEEN WITH HAH INITIAL FORM
≈ <initial> + 0634 ش + 062D ح

FD2F ﴯ ARABIC LIGATURE SHEEN WITH KHAH INITIAL FORM
≈ <initial> + 0634 ش + 062E خ

FD30 ﴰ ARABIC LIGATURE SHEEN WITH MEEM INITIAL FORM
≈ <initial> + 0634 ش + 0645 م

FD31 ﴱ ARABIC LIGATURE SEEN WITH HEH INITIAL FORM
≈ <initial> + 0633 س + 0647 ه

FD32 ﴲ ARABIC LIGATURE SHEEN WITH HEH INITIAL FORM
≈ <initial> + 0634 ش + 0647 ه

FD33 ﴳ ARABIC LIGATURE TAH WITH MEEM INITIAL FORM
≈ <initial> + 0637 ط + 0645 م

FD34 ﴴ ARABIC LIGATURE SEEN WITH JEEM MEDIAL FORM
≈ <medial> + 0633 س + 062C ج

FD35 ﴵ ARABIC LIGATURE SEEN WITH HAH MEDIAL FORM
≈ <medial> + 0633 س + 062D ح

FD36 ﴶ ARABIC LIGATURE SEEN WITH KHAH MEDIAL FORM
≈ <medial> + 0633 س + 062E خ

FD37 ﴷ ARABIC LIGATURE SHEEN WITH JEEM MEDIAL FORM
≈ <medial> + 0634 ش + 062C ج

FD38 ﴸ ARABIC LIGATURE SHEEN WITH HAH MEDIAL FORM
≈ <medial> + 0634 ش + 062D ح

FD39 ﴹ ARABIC LIGATURE SHEEN WITH KHAH MEDIAL FORM
≈ <medial> + 0634 ش + 062E خ

FD3A ﴺ ARABIC LIGATURE TAH WITH MEEM MEDIAL FORM
≈ <medial> + 0637 ط + 0645 م

FD3B ﴻ ARABIC LIGATURE ZAH WITH MEEM MEDIAL FORM
≈ <medial> + 0638 ظ + 0645 م

FD3C ﴼ ARABIC LIGATURE ALEF WITH FATHATAN FINAL FORM
≈ <final> + 0627 ا + 064B ً

FD3D ﴽ ARABIC LIGATURE ALEF WITH FATHATAN ISOLATED FORM
≈ <isolated> + 0627 ا + 064B ً

FD3E ﴾ ORNATE LEFT PARENTHESIS

FD3F ﴿ ORNATE RIGHT PARENTHESIS

FD40 <reserved>

FD41 <reserved>

FD42 <reserved>

FD43 <reserved>

FD44 <reserved>

FD45 <reserved>

FD46 <reserved>

FD47 <reserved>

FD48 <reserved>

FD49 <reserved>

FD4A <reserved>

FD4B <reserved>

FD4C <reserved>

FD4D <reserved>

FD4E <reserved>

FD4F <reserved>

FD50 ﵐ ARABIC LIGATURE TEH WITH JEEM WITH MEEM INITIAL FORM
≈ <initial> + 062A ت + 062C ج + 0645 م

FD51 ﵑ ARABIC LIGATURE TEH WITH HAH WITH JEEM FINAL FORM
≈ <final> + 062A ت + 062D ح + 062C ج

FD52 ﵒ ARABIC LIGATURE TEH WITH HAH WITH JEEM INITIAL FORM
≈ <initial> + 062A ت + 062D ح + 062C ج

FD53 ﵓ ARABIC LIGATURE TEH WITH HAH WITH MEEM INITIAL FORM
≈ <initial> + 062A ت + 062D ح + 0645 م

FD54 ﵔ ARABIC LIGATURE TEH WITH KHAH WITH MEEM INITIAL FORM
≈ <initial> + 062A ت + 062E خ + 0645 م

FD55 ﵕ ARABIC LIGATURE TEH WITH MEEM WITH JEEM INITIAL FORM
≈ <initial> + 062A ت + 0645 م + 062C ج

FD56 ﵖ ARABIC LIGATURE TEH WITH MEEM WITH HAH INITIAL FORM
≈ <initial> + 062A ت + 0645 م + 062D ح

FD57 ﵗ ARABIC LIGATURE TEH WITH MEEM WITH KHAH INITIAL FORM
≈ <initial> + 062A ت + 0645 م + 062E خ

FD58 ﵘ ARABIC LIGATURE JEEM WITH MEEM WITH HAH FINAL FORM
≈ <final> + 062C ج + 0645 م + 062D ح

FD59 ﵙ ARABIC LIGATURE JEEM WITH MEEM WITH HAH INITIAL FORM
≈ <initial> + 062C ج + 0645 م + 062D ح

FD5A ﵚ ARABIC LIGATURE HAH WITH MEEM WITH YEH FINAL FORM
≈ <final> + 062D ح + 0645 م + 064A ي

FD5B ﵛ ARABIC LIGATURE HAH WITH MEEM WITH ALEF MAKSURA FINAL FORM
≈ <final> + 062D ح + 0645 م + 0649 ى

FD5C ﵜ ARABIC LIGATURE SEEN WITH HAH WITH JEEM INITIAL FORM
≈ <initial> + 0633 س + 062D ح + 062C ج

FD5D ﵝ ARABIC LIGATURE SEEN WITH JEEM WITH HAH INITIAL FORM
≈ <initial> + 0633 س + 062C ج + 062D ح

FD5E ﵞ ARABIC LIGATURE SEEN WITH JEEM WITH ALEF MAKSURA FINAL FORM
≈ <final> + 0633 س + 062C ج + 0649 ى

FD5F ﵟ ARABIC LIGATURE SEEN WITH MEEM WITH HAH FINAL FORM
≈ <final> + 0633 س + 0645 م + 062D ح

FD60 ﵠ ARABIC LIGATURE SEEN WITH MEEM WITH HAH INITIAL FORM
≈ <initial> + 0633 س + 0645 م + 062D ح

FD61 ﵡ ARABIC LIGATURE SEEN WITH MEEM WITH JEEM INITIAL FORM
≈ <initial> + 0633 س + 0645 م + 062C ج

FD62 ﵢ ARABIC LIGATURE SEEN WITH MEEM WITH MEEM FINAL FORM
≈ <final> + 0633 س + 0645 م + 0645 م

FD63 ﵣ ARABIC LIGATURE SEEN WITH MEEM WITH MEEM INITIAL FORM
≈ <initial> + 0633 س + 0645 م + 0645 م

FD64 ﵤ ARABIC LIGATURE SAD WITH HAH WITH HAH FINAL FORM
≈ <final> + 0635 ص + 062D ح + 062D ح

FD65 ﵥ ARABIC LIGATURE SAD WITH HAH WITH HAH INITIAL FORM
≈ <initial> + 0635 ص + 062D ح + 062D ح

FD66 ﵦ ARABIC LIGATURE SAD WITH MEEM WITH MEEM FINAL FORM
≈ <final> + 0635 ص + 0645 م + 0645 م

FD67 ﵧ ARABIC LIGATURE SHEEN WITH HAH WITH MEEM FINAL FORM
≈ <final> + 0634 ش + 062D ح + 0645 م

FD68 ﵨ ARABIC LIGATURE SHEEN WITH HAH WITH MEEM INITIAL FORM
≈ <initial> + 0634 ش + 062D ح + 0645 م

FD69 ﵩ ARABIC LIGATURE SHEEN WITH JEEM WITH YEH FINAL FORM
≈ <final> + 0634 ش + 062C ج + 064A ي

FD6A ﵪ ARABIC LIGATURE SHEEN WITH MEEM WITH KHAH FINAL FORM
≈ <final> + 0634 ش + 0645 م + 062E خ

FD6B ﵫ ARABIC LIGATURE SHEEN WITH MEEM WITH KHAH INITIAL FORM
≈ <initial> + 0634 ش + 0645 م + 062E خ

FD6C ﵬ ARABIC LIGATURE SHEEN WITH MEEM WITH MEEM FINAL FORM
≈ <final> + 0634 ش + 0645 م + 0645 م

FD6D ﵭ ARABIC LIGATURE SHEEN WITH MEEM WITH MEEM INITIAL FORM
≈ <initial> + 0634 ش + 0645 م + 0645 م

FD6E ﵮ ARABIC LIGATURE DAD WITH HAH WITH ALEF MAKSURA FINAL FORM
≈ <final> + 0636 ض + 062D ح + 0649 ى

FD6F ﵯ ARABIC LIGATURE DAD WITH KHAH WITH MEEM FINAL FORM
≈ <final> + 0636 ض + 062E خ + 0645 م

FD70 ﵰ ARABIC LIGATURE DAD WITH KHAH WITH MEEM INITIAL FORM
≈ <initial> + 0636 ض + 062E خ + 0645 م

FD71 ﵱ ARABIC LIGATURE TAH WITH MEEM WITH HAH FINAL FORM
≈ <final> + 0637 ط + 0645 م + 062D ح

FD72 ﵲ ARABIC LIGATURE TAH WITH MEEM WITH HAH INITIAL FORM
≈ <initial> + 0637 ط + 0645 م + 062D ح

FD73 ﵳ ARABIC LIGATURE TAH WITH MEEM WITH MEEM INITIAL FORM
≈ <initial> + 0637 ط + 0645 م + 0645 م

FD74 ﵴ ARABIC LIGATURE TAH WITH MEEM WITH YEH FINAL FORM
≈ <final> + 0637 ط + 0645 م + 064A ي

FD75 ﵵ ARABIC LIGATURE AIN WITH JEEM WITH MEEM FINAL FORM
≈ <final> + 0639 ع + 062C ج + 0645 م

FD76 ﵶ ARABIC LIGATURE AIN WITH MEEM WITH MEEM FINAL FORM
≈ <final> + 0639 ع + 0645 م + 0645 م

FD77 ﵷ ARABIC LIGATURE AIN WITH MEEM WITH MEEM INITIAL FORM
≈ <initial> + 0639 ع + 0645 م + 0645 م

FD78 ﵸ ARABIC LIGATURE AIN WITH MEEM WITH ALEF MAKSURA FINAL FORM
≈ <final> + 0639 ع + 0645 م + 0649 ى

FD79 ﵹ ARABIC LIGATURE GHAIN WITH MEEM WITH MEEM FINAL FORM
≈ <final> + 063A غ + 0645 م + 0645 م

FD7A ﵺ ARABIC LIGATURE GHAIN WITH MEEM WITH YEH FINAL FORM
≈ <final> + 063A غ + 0645 م + 064A ي

FD7B ﵻ ARABIC LIGATURE GHAIN WITH MEEM WITH ALEF MAKSURA FINAL FORM
≈ <final> + 063A غ + 0645 م + 0649 ى

FD7C ﵼ ARABIC LIGATURE FEH WITH KHAH WITH MEEM FINAL FORM
≈ <final> + 0641 ف + 062E خ + 0645 م

FD7D ﵽ ARABIC LIGATURE FEH WITH KHAH WITH MEEM INITIAL FORM
≈ <initial> + 0641 ف + 062E خ + 0645 م

FD7E ﵾ ARABIC LIGATURE QAF WITH MEEM WITH HAH FINAL FORM
≈ <final> + 0642 ق + 0645 م + 062D ح

FD7F ﵿ ARABIC LIGATURE QAF WITH MEEM WITH MEEM FINAL FORM
≈ <final> + 0642 ق + 0645 م + 0645 م

FD80 ﶀ ARABIC LIGATURE LAM WITH HAH WITH MEEM FINAL FORM
≈ <final> + 0644 ل + 062D ح + 0645 م

FD81 ﶁ ARABIC LIGATURE LAM WITH HAH WITH YEH FINAL FORM
≈ <final> + 0644 ل + 062D ح + 064A ي

FD82 ﶂ ARABIC LIGATURE LAM WITH HAH WITH ALEF MAKSURA FINAL FORM
≈ <final> + 0644 ل + 062D ح + 0649 ى

FD83 ﶃ ARABIC LIGATURE LAM WITH JEEM WITH JEEM INITIAL FORM
≈ <initial> + 0644 ل + 062C ج + 062C ج

FD84 ﶄ ARABIC LIGATURE LAM WITH JEEM WITH JEEM FINAL FORM
≈ <final> + 0644 ل + 062C ج + 062C ج

FD85 ﶅ ARABIC LIGATURE LAM WITH KHAH WITH MEEM FINAL FORM
≈ <final> + 0644 ل + 062E خ + 0645 م

FD86 ﶆ ARABIC LIGATURE LAM WITH KHAH WITH MEEM INITIAL FORM
≈ <initial> + 0644 ل + 062E خ + 0645 م

FD87 ﶇ ARABIC LIGATURE LAM WITH MEEM WITH HAH FINAL FORM
≈ <final> + 0644 ل + 0645 م + 062D ح

FD88 ﶈ ARABIC LIGATURE LAM WITH MEEM WITH HAH INITIAL FORM
≈ <initial> + 0644 ل + 0645 م + 062D ح

FD89 ﶉ ARABIC LIGATURE MEEM WITH HAH WITH JEEM INITIAL FORM
≈ <initial> + 0645 م + 062D ح + 062C ج

FD8A ﶊ ARABIC LIGATURE MEEM WITH HAH WITH MEEM INITIAL FORM
≈ <initial> + 0645 م + 062D ح + 0645 م

FD8B ﶋ ARABIC LIGATURE MEEM WITH HAH WITH YEH FINAL FORM
≈ <final> + 0645 م + 062D ح + 064A ي

FD8C ﶌ ARABIC LIGATURE MEEM WITH JEEM WITH HAH INITIAL FORM
≈ <initial> + 0645 م + 062C ج + 062D ح

FD8D ﶍ ARABIC LIGATURE MEEM WITH JEEM WITH MEEM INITIAL FORM
≈ <initial> + 0645 م + 062C ج + 0645 م

FD8E ﶎ ARABIC LIGATURE MEEM WITH KHAH WITH JEEM INITIAL FORM
≈ <initial> + 0645 م + 062E خ + 062C ج

FD8F ﶏ ARABIC LIGATURE MEEM WITH KHAH WITH MEEM INITIAL FORM
≈ <initial> + 0645 م + 062E خ + 0645 م

FD90 <reserved>

FD91 <reserved>

FD92 ﶒ ARABIC LIGATURE MEEM WITH JEEM WITH KHAH INITIAL FORM
≈ <initial> + 0645 م + 062C ج + 062E خ

FD93 ﶓ ARABIC LIGATURE HEH WITH MEEM WITH JEEM INITIAL FORM
≈ <initial> + 0647 ه + 0645 م + 062C ج

FD94 ﶔ ARABIC LIGATURE HEH WITH MEEM WITH MEEM INITIAL FORM
≈ <initial> + 0647 ه + 0645 م + 0645 م

FD95 ﶕ ARABIC LIGATURE NOON WITH HAH WITH MEEM INITIAL FORM
≈ <initial> + 0646 ن + 062D ح + 0645 م

FD96 ﶖ ARABIC LIGATURE NOON WITH HAH WITH ALEF MAKSURA FINAL FORM
≈ <final> + 0646 ن + 062D ح + 0649 ى

FD97 ﶗ ARABIC LIGATURE NOON WITH JEEM WITH MEEM FINAL FORM
≈ <final> + 0646 ن + 062C ج + 0645 م

FD98 ﶘ ARABIC LIGATURE NOON WITH JEEM WITH MEEM INITIAL FORM
≈ <initial> + 0646 ن + 062C ج + 0645 م

FD99 ﶙ ARABIC LIGATURE NOON WITH JEEM WITH ALEF MAKSURA FINAL FORM
≈ <final> + 0646 ن + 062C ج + 0649 ى

FD9A ﶚ ARABIC LIGATURE NOON WITH MEEM WITH YEH FINAL FORM
≈ <final> + 0646 ن + 0645 م + 064A ي

FD9B ﶛ ARABIC LIGATURE NOON WITH MEEM WITH ALEF MAKSURA FINAL FORM
≈ <final> + 0646 ن + 0645 م + 0649 ى

FD9C ﶜ ARABIC LIGATURE YEH WITH MEEM WITH MEEM FINAL FORM
≈ <final> + 064A ي + 0645 م + 0645 م

FD9D ﶝ ARABIC LIGATURE YEH WITH MEEM WITH MEEM INITIAL FORM
≈ <initial> + 064A ي + 0645 م + 0645 م

FD9E ﶞ ARABIC LIGATURE BEH WITH KHAH WITH YEH FINAL FORM
≈ <final> + 0628 ب + 062E خ + 064A ي

FD9F ﶟ ARABIC LIGATURE TEH WITH JEEM WITH YEH FINAL FORM
≈ <final> + 062A ت + 062C ج + 064A ي

FDA0 ﶠ ARABIC LIGATURE TEH WITH JEEM WITH ALEF MAKSURA FINAL FORM
≈ <final> + 062A ت + 062C ج + 0649 ى

FDA1 ﶡ ARABIC LIGATURE TEH WITH KHAH WITH YEH FINAL FORM
≈ <final> + 062A ت + 062E خ + 064A ي

FDA2 ﶢ ARABIC LIGATURE TEH WITH KHAH WITH ALEF MAKSURA FINAL FORM
≈ <final> + 062A ت + 062E خ + 0649 ى

FDA3 ﶣ ARABIC LIGATURE TEH WITH MEEM WITH YEH FINAL FORM
≈ <final> + 062A ت + 0645 م + 064A ي

FDA4 ﶤ ARABIC LIGATURE TEH WITH MEEM WITH ALEF MAKSURA FINAL FORM
≈ <final> + 062A ت + 0645 م + 0649 ى

FDA5 ﶥ ARABIC LIGATURE JEEM WITH MEEM WITH YEH FINAL FORM
≈ <final> + 062C ج + 0645 م + 064A ي

FDA6 ﶦ ARABIC LIGATURE JEEM WITH HAH WITH ALEF MAKSURA FINAL FORM
≈ <final> + 062C ج + 062D ح + 0649 ى

FDA7 جمى ARABIC LIGATURE JEEM WITH MEEM WITH ALEF MAKSURA FINAL FORM
≈ <final> + 062C ج + 0645 م + 0649 ى

FDA8 سخى ARABIC LIGATURE SEEN WITH KHAH WITH ALEF MAKSURA FINAL FORM
≈ <final> + 0633 س + 062E خ + 0649 ى

FDA9 صحي ARABIC LIGATURE SAD WITH HAH WITH YEH FINAL FORM
≈ <final> + 0635 ص + 062D ح + 064A ي

FDAA شحي ARABIC LIGATURE SHEEN WITH HAH WITH YEH FINAL FORM
≈ <final> + 0634 ش + 062D ح + 064A ي

FDAB ضحي ARABIC LIGATURE DAD WITH HAH WITH YEH FINAL FORM
≈ <final> + 0636 ض + 062D ح + 064A ي

FDAC لجي ARABIC LIGATURE LAM WITH JEEM WITH YEH FINAL FORM
≈ <final> + 0644 ل + 062C ج + 064A ي

FDAD لمي ARABIC LIGATURE LAM WITH MEEM WITH YEH FINAL FORM
≈ <final> + 0644 ل + 0645 م + 064A ي

FDAE يحي ARABIC LIGATURE YEH WITH HAH WITH YEH FINAL FORM
≈ <final> + 064A ي + 062D ح + 064A ي

FDAF يجي ARABIC LIGATURE YEH WITH JEEM WITH YEH FINAL FORM
≈ <final> + 064A ي + 062C ج + 064A ي

FDB0 يمي ARABIC LIGATURE YEH WITH MEEM WITH YEH FINAL FORM
≈ <final> + 064A ي + 0645 م + 064A ي

FDB1 ممي ARABIC LIGATURE MEEM WITH MEEM WITH YEH FINAL FORM
≈ <final> + 0645 م + 0645 م + 064A ي

FDB2 قمي ARABIC LIGATURE QAF WITH MEEM WITH YEH FINAL FORM
≈ <final> + 0642 ق + 0645 م + 064A ي

FDB3 نحي ARABIC LIGATURE NOON WITH HAH WITH YEH FINAL FORM
≈ <final> + 0646 ن + 062D ح + 064A ي

FDB4 قمح ARABIC LIGATURE QAF WITH MEEM WITH HAH INITIAL FORM
≈ <initial> + 0642 ق + 0645 م + 062D ح

FDB5 لحم ARABIC LIGATURE LAM WITH HAH WITH MEEM INITIAL FORM
≈ <initial> + 0644 ل + 062D ح + 0645 م

FDB6 عمي ARABIC LIGATURE AIN WITH MEEM WITH YEH FINAL FORM
≈ <final> + 0639 ع + 0645 م + 064A ي

FDB7 كمي ARABIC LIGATURE KAF WITH MEEM WITH YEH FINAL FORM
≈ <final> + 0643 ك + 0645 م + 064A ي

FDB8 نجح ARABIC LIGATURE NOON WITH JEEM WITH HAH INITIAL FORM
≈ <initial> + 0646 ن + 062C ج + 062D ح

FDB9 مخي ARABIC LIGATURE MEEM WITH KHAH WITH YEH FINAL FORM
≈ <final> + 0645 م + 062E خ + 064A ي

FDBA لجم ARABIC LIGATURE LAM WITH JEEM WITH MEEM INITIAL FORM
≈ <initial> + 0644 ل + 062C ج + 0645 م

FDBB كمم ARABIC LIGATURE KAF WITH MEEM WITH MEEM FINAL FORM
≈ <final> + 0643 ك + 0645 م + 0645 م

FDBC لجم ARABIC LIGATURE LAM WITH JEEM WITH MEEM FINAL FORM
≈ <final> + 0644 ل + 062C ج + 0645 م

FDBD نجح ARABIC LIGATURE NOON WITH JEEM WITH HAH FINAL FORM
≈ <final> + 0646 ن + 062C ج + 062D ح

FDBE جحي ARABIC LIGATURE JEEM WITH HAH WITH YEH FINAL FORM
≈ <final> + 062C ج + 062D ح + 064A ي

FDBF حجي ARABIC LIGATURE HAH WITH JEEM WITH YEH FINAL FORM
≈ <final> + 062D ح + 062C ج + 064A ي

FDC0 مجي ARABIC LIGATURE MEEM WITH JEEM WITH YEH FINAL FORM
≈ <final> + 0645 م + 062C ج + 064A ي

FDC1 فمي ARABIC LIGATURE FEH WITH MEEM WITH YEH FINAL FORM
≈ <final> + 0641 ف + 0645 م + 064A ي

FDC2 بحي ARABIC LIGATURE BEH WITH HAH WITH YEH FINAL FORM
≈ <final> + 0628 ب + 062D ح + 064A ي

FDC3 كمم ARABIC LIGATURE KAF WITH MEEM WITH MEEM INITIAL FORM
≈ <initial> + 0643 ك + 0645 م + 0645 م

FDC4 عجم ARABIC LIGATURE AIN WITH JEEM WITH MEEM INITIAL FORM
≈ <initial> + 0639 ع + 062C ج + 0645 م

FDC5 صمم ARABIC LIGATURE SAD WITH MEEM WITH MEEM INITIAL FORM
≈ <initial> + 0635 ص + 0645 م + 0645 م

FDC6 سخي ARABIC LIGATURE SEEN WITH KHAH WITH YEH FINAL FORM
≈ <final> + 0633 س + 062E خ + 064A ي

FDC7 نجي ARABIC LIGATURE NOON WITH JEEM WITH YEH FINAL FORM
≈ <final> + 0646 ن + 062C ج + 064A ي

FDC8 <reserved>
FDC9 <reserved>
FDCA <reserved>
FDCB <reserved>
FDCC <reserved>
FDCD <reserved>

FDCE <reserved>
FDCF <reserved>
FDD0 <reserved>
FDD1 <reserved>
FDD2 <reserved>
FDD3 <reserved>
FDD4 <reserved>
FDD5 <reserved>
FDD6 <reserved>
FDD7 <reserved>
FDD8 <reserved>
FDD9 <reserved>
FDDA <reserved>
FDDB <reserved>
FDDC <reserved>
FDDD <reserved>
FDDE <reserved>
FDDF <reserved>
FDE0 <reserved>
FDE1 <reserved>
FDE2 <reserved>
FDE3 <reserved>
FDE4 <reserved>
FDE5 <reserved>
FDE6 <reserved>
FDE7 <reserved>
FDE8 <reserved>
FDE9 <reserved>
FDEA <reserved>
FDEB <reserved>
FDEC <reserved>
FDED <reserved>
FDEE <reserved>
FDEF <reserved>

FDF0 ﷰ ARABIC LIGATURE SALLA USED AS KORANIC STOP SIGN ISOLATED FORM
≈ <isolated> + 0635 ص + 0644 ل + 06D2 ے

FDF1 ﷱ ARABIC LIGATURE QALA USED AS KORANIC STOP SIGN ISOLATED FORM
≈ <isolated> + 0642 ق + 0644 ل + 06D2 ے

FDF2 ﷲ ARABIC LIGATURE ALLAH ISOLATED FORM
≈ <isolated> + 0627 ا + 0644 ل + 0644 ل + 0647 ه

FDF3 ﷳ ARABIC LIGATURE AKBAR ISOLATED FORM
≈ <isolated> + 0627 ا + 0643 ك + 0628 ب + 0631 ر

FDF4 ﷴ ARABIC LIGATURE MOHAMMAD ISOLATED FORM
≈ <isolated> + 0645 م + 062D ح + 0645 م + 062F د

FDF5 ﷵ ARABIC LIGATURE SALAM ISOLATED FORM
≈ <isolated> + 0635 ص + 0644 ل + 0639 ع + 0645 م

FDF6 ﷶ ARABIC LIGATURE RASOUL ISOLATED FORM
≈ <isolated> + 0631 ر + 0633 س + 0648 و + 0644 ل

FDF7 ﷷ ARABIC LIGATURE ALAYHE ISOLATED FORM
≈ <isolated> + 0639 ع + 0644 ل + 064A ي + 0647 ه

FDF8 ﷸ ARABIC LIGATURE WASALLAM ISOLATED FORM
≈ <isolated> + 0648 و + 0633 س + 0644 ل + 0645 م

FDF9 ﷹ ARABIC LIGATURE SALLA ISOLATED FORM
≈ <isolated> + 0635 ص + 0644 ل + 0649 ى

FDFA ﷺ ARABIC LIGATURE SALLALLAHOU ALAYHE WASALLAM
≈ <isolated> + 0635 ص + 0644 ل + 0649 ى + 0020 SP + 0627 ا + 0644 ل + 0644 ل + 0647 ه + 0020 SP + 0639 ع + 0644 ل + 064A ي + 0647 ه + 0020 SP + 0648 و + 0633 س + 0644 ل + 0645 م

FDFB ﷻ ARABIC LIGATURE JALLAJALALOUHOU
≈ <isolated> + 062C ج + 0644 ل + 0020 SP + 062C ج + 0644 ل + 0627 ا + 0644 ل + 0647 ه

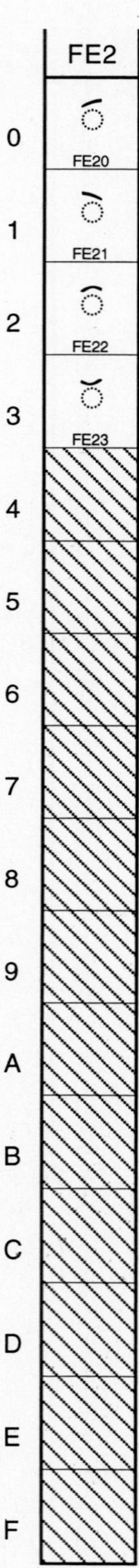
FE2
0
FE20
1
FE21
2
FE22
3
FE23
4
5
6
7
8
9
A
B
C
D
E
F

Combining half marks

FE20 ◌︠ COMBINING LIGATURE LEFT HALF
FE21 ◌︡ COMBINING LIGATURE RIGHT HALF
FE22 ◌︢ COMBINING DOUBLE TILDE LEFT HALF
FE23 ◌︣ COMBINING DOUBLE TILDE RIGHT HALF

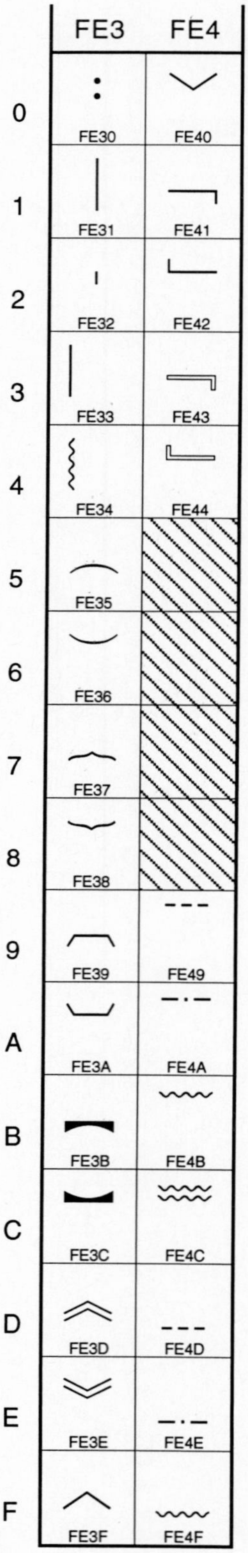

	FE3	FE4
0	FE30	FE40
1	FE31	FE41
2	FE32	FE42
3	FE33	FE43
4	FE34	FE44
5	FE35	
6	FE36	
7	FE37	
8	FE38	
9	FE39	FE49
A	FE3A	FE4A
B	FE3B	FE4B
C	FE3C	FE4C
D	FE3D	FE4D
E	FE3E	FE4E
F	FE3F	FE4F

Glyphs for vertical variants

FE30 ︰ PRESENTATION FORM FOR VERTICAL TWO DOT LEADER
≈ <vertical> + 2025 ‥

FE31 ︱ PRESENTATION FORM FOR VERTICAL EM DASH
≈ <vertical> + 2014 —

FE32 ︲ PRESENTATION FORM FOR VERTICAL EN DASH
≈ <vertical> + 2013 –

FE33 ︳ PRESENTATION FORM FOR VERTICAL LOW LINE
≈ <vertical> + 005F _

FE34 ︴ PRESENTATION FORM FOR VERTICAL WAVY LOW LINE
≈ <vertical> + 005F _

FE35 ︵ PRESENTATION FORM FOR VERTICAL LEFT PARENTHESIS
≈ <vertical> + 0028 (

FE36 ︶ PRESENTATION FORM FOR VERTICAL RIGHT PARENTHESIS
≈ <vertical> + 0029)

FE37 ︷ PRESENTATION FORM FOR VERTICAL LEFT CURLY BRACKET
≈ <vertical> + 007B {

FE38 ︸ PRESENTATION FORM FOR VERTICAL RIGHT CURLY BRACKET
≈ <vertical> + 007D }

FE39 ︹ PRESENTATION FORM FOR VERTICAL LEFT TORTOISE SHELL BRACKET
≈ <vertical> + 3014 〔

FE3A ︺ PRESENTATION FORM FOR VERTICAL RIGHT TORTOISE SHELL BRACKET
≈ <vertical> + 3015 〕

FE3B ︻ PRESENTATION FORM FOR VERTICAL LEFT BLACK LENTICULAR BRACKET
≈ <vertical> + 3010 【

FE3C ︼ PRESENTATION FORM FOR VERTICAL RIGHT BLACK LENTICULAR BRACKET
≈ <vertical> + 3011 】

FE3D ︽ PRESENTATION FORM FOR VERTICAL LEFT DOUBLE ANGLE BRACKET
≈ <vertical> + 300A 《

FE3E ︾ PRESENTATION FORM FOR VERTICAL RIGHT DOUBLE ANGLE BRACKET
≈ <vertical> + 300B 》

FE3F ︿ PRESENTATION FORM FOR VERTICAL LEFT ANGLE BRACKET
≈ <vertical> + 3008 〈

FE40 ﹀ PRESENTATION FORM FOR VERTICAL RIGHT ANGLE BRACKET
≈ <vertical> + 3009 〉

FE41 ﹁ PRESENTATION FORM FOR VERTICAL LEFT CORNER BRACKET
≈ <vertical> + 300C 「

FE42 ﹂ PRESENTATION FORM FOR VERTICAL RIGHT CORNER BRACKET
≈ <vertical> + 300D 」

FE43 ﹃ PRESENTATION FORM FOR VERTICAL LEFT WHITE CORNER BRACKET
≈ <vertical> + 300E 『

FE44 ﹄ PRESENTATION FORM FOR VERTICAL RIGHT WHITE CORNER BRACKET
≈ <vertical> + 300F 』

FE45 <reserved>

FE46 <reserved>

FE47 <reserved>

FE48 <reserved>

Overscores and underscores

FE49 ﹉ DASHED OVERLINE
≈ 203E ‾

FE4A ﹊ CENTRELINE OVERLINE
≈ 203E ‾

FE4B ﹋ WAVY OVERLINE
≈ 203E ‾

FE4C ﹌ DOUBLE WAVY OVERLINE
≈ 203E ‾

FE4D ﹍ DASHED LOW LINE
≈ 005F _

FE4E ﹎ CENTRELINE LOW LINE
≈ 005F _

FE4F ﹏ WAVY LOW LINE
≈ 005F _

	FE5	FE6
0	, FE50	& FE60
1	、 FE51	* FE61
2	. FE52	+ FE62
3		- FE63
4	; FE54	< FE64
5	: FE55	> FE65
6	? FE56	= FE66
7	! FE57	
8	- FE58	\ FE68
9	(FE59	$ FE69
A	) FE5A	% FE6A
B	{ FE5B	@ FE6B
C	} FE5C	
D	〔 FE5D	
E	〕 FE5E	
F	# FE5F	

Small form variants

FE50 , SMALL COMMA
≈ <small> + 002C ,

FE51 、 SMALL IDEOGRAPHIC COMMA
≈ <small> + 3001 、

FE52 . SMALL FULL STOP
≈ <small> + 002E .

FE53 <reserved>
→ 00B7 · middle dot

FE54 ; SMALL SEMICOLON
≈ <small> + 003B ;

FE55 : SMALL COLON
≈ <small> + 003A :

FE56 ? SMALL QUESTION MARK
≈ <small> + 003F ?

FE57 ! SMALL EXCLAMATION MARK
≈ <small> + 0021 !

FE58 — SMALL EM DASH
≈ <small> + 2014 —

FE59 (SMALL LEFT PARENTHESIS
≈ <small> + 0028 (

FE5A) SMALL RIGHT PARENTHESIS
≈ <small> + 0029)

FE5B { SMALL LEFT CURLY BRACKET
≈ <small> + 007B {

FE5C } SMALL RIGHT CURLY BRACKET
≈ <small> + 007D }

FE5D 〔 SMALL LEFT TORTOISE SHELL BRACKET
≈ <small> + 3014 〔

FE5E 〕 SMALL RIGHT TORTOISE SHELL BRACKET
≈ <small> + 3015 〕

FE5F # SMALL NUMBER SIGN
≈ <small> + 0023 #

FE60 & SMALL AMPERSAND
≈ <small> + 0026 &

FE61 * SMALL ASTERISK
≈ <small> + 002A *

FE62 + SMALL PLUS SIGN
≈ <small> + 002B +

FE63 - SMALL HYPHEN-MINUS
≈ <small> + 002D -

FE64 < SMALL LESS-THAN SIGN
≈ <small> + 003C <

FE65 > SMALL GREATER-THAN SIGN
≈ <small> + 003E >

FE66 = SMALL EQUALS SIGN
≈ <small> + 003D =

FE67 <reserved>
→ 2215 / division slash

FE68 \ SMALL REVERSE SOLIDUS
≈ <small> + 005C \

FE69 $ SMALL DOLLAR SIGN
≈ <small> + 0024 $

FE6A % SMALL PERCENT SIGN
≈ <small> + 0025 %

FE6B @ SMALL COMMERCIAL AT
≈ <small> + 0040 @

	FE7	FE8	FE9	FEA	FEB	FEC	FED	FEE	FEF
0	ﹰ FE70	ﺀ FE80	ﺐ FE90	ﺠ FEA0	ﺰ FEB0	ﻀ FEC0	ﻐ FED0	ﻠ FEE0	ﻰ FEF0
1	ﹱ FE71	ﺁ FE81	ﺑ FE91	ﺡ FEA1	ﺱ FEB1	ﻁ FEC1	ﻑ FED1	ﻡ FEE1	ﻱ FEF1
2	ﹲ FE72	ﺂ FE82	ﺒ FE92	ﺢ FEA2	ﺲ FEB2	ﻂ FEC2	ﻒ FED2	ﻢ FEE2	ﻲ FEF2
3		ﺃ FE83	ﺓ FE93	ﺣ FEA3	ﺳ FEB3	ﻃ FEC3	ﻓ FED3	ﻣ FEE3	ﻳ FEF3
4	FE74	ﺄ FE84	ﺔ FE94	ﺤ FEA4	ﺴ FEB4	ﻄ FEC4	ﻔ FED4	ﻤ FEE4	ﻴ FEF4
5		ﺅ FE85	ﺕ FE95	ﺥ FEA5	ﺵ FEB5	ﻅ FEC5	ﻕ FED5	ﻥ FEE5	ﻵ FEF5
6	ﹶ FE76	ﺆ FE86	ﺖ FE96	ﺦ FEA6	ﺶ FEB6	ﻆ FEC6	ﻖ FED6	ﻦ FEE6	ﻶ FEF6
7	ﹷ FE77	ﺇ FE87	ﺗ FE97	ﺧ FEA7	ﺷ FEB7	ﻇ FEC7	ﻗ FED7	ﻧ FEE7	ﻷ FEF7
8	ﹸ FE78	ﺈ FE88	ﺘ FE98	ﺨ FEA8	ﺸ FEB8	ﻈ FEC8	ﻘ FED8	ﻨ FEE8	ﻸ FEF8
9	ﹹ FE79	ﺉ FE89	ﺙ FE99	ﺩ FEA9	ﺹ FEB9	ﻉ FEC9	ﻙ FED9	ﻩ FEE9	ﻹ FEF9
A	FE7A	ﺊ FE8A	ﺚ FE9A	ﺪ FEAA	ﺺ FEBA	ﻊ FECA	ﻚ FEDA	ﻪ FEEA	ﻺ FEFA
B	ﹻ FE7B	ﺋ FE8B	ﺛ FE9B	ﺫ FEAB	ﺻ FEBB	ﻋ FECB	ﻛ FEDB	ﻫ FEEB	ﻻ FEFB
C	ﹼ FE7C	ﺌ FE8C	ﺜ FE9C	ﺬ FEAC	ﺼ FEBC	ﻌ FECC	ﻜ FEDC	ﻬ FEEC	ﻼ FEFC
D	ﹽ FE7D	ﺍ FE8D	ﺝ FE9D	ﺭ FEAD	ﺽ FEBD	ﻍ FECD	ﻝ FEDD	ﻭ FEED	
E	ﹾ FE7E	ﺎ FE8E	ﺞ FE9E	ﺮ FEAE	ﺾ FEBE	ﻎ FECE	ﻞ FEDE	ﻮ FEEE	
F	ﹿ FE7F	ﺏ FE8F	ﺟ FE9F	ﺯ FEAF	ﺿ FEBF	ﻏ FECF	ﻟ FEDF	ﻯ FEEF	ZWN BSP FEFF

Glyphs for spacing forms of Arabic points

FE70 ً ARABIC FATHATAN ISOLATED FORM
≈ <isolated> + 0020 [SP] + 064B ً

FE71 ـً ARABIC TATWEEL WITH FATHATAN ABOVE
≈ <medial> + 0640 ـ + 064B ً

FE72 ٌ ARABIC DAMMATAN ISOLATED FORM
≈ <isolated> + 0020 [SP] + 064C ٌ

FE73 <reserved>

FE74 ٍ ARABIC KASRATAN ISOLATED FORM
≈ <isolated> + 0020 [SP] + 064D ٍ

FE75 <reserved>

FE76 َ ARABIC FATHA ISOLATED FORM
≈ <isolated> + 0020 [SP] + 064E َ

FE77 ـَ ARABIC FATHA MEDIAL FORM
≈ <medial> + 0640 ـ + 064E َ

FE78 ُ ARABIC DAMMA ISOLATED FORM
≈ <isolated> + 0020 [SP] + 064F ُ

FE79 ـُ ARABIC DAMMA MEDIAL FORM
≈ <medial> + 0640 ـ + 064F ُ

FE7A ِ ARABIC KASRA ISOLATED FORM
≈ <isolated> + 0020 [SP] + 0650 ِ

FE7B ـِ ARABIC KASRA MEDIAL FORM
≈ <medial> + 0640 ـ + 0650 ِ

FE7C ّ ARABIC SHADDA ISOLATED FORM
≈ <isolated> + 0020 [SP] + 0651 ّ

FE7D ـّ ARABIC SHADDA MEDIAL FORM
≈ <medial> + 0640 ـ + 0651 ّ

FE7E ْ ARABIC SUKUN ISOLATED FORM
≈ <isolated> + 0020 [SP] + 0652 ْ

FE7F ـْ ARABIC SUKUN MEDIAL FORM
≈ <medial> + 0640 ـ + 0652 ْ

Basic glyphs for Arabic language contextual forms

FE80 ء ARABIC LETTER HAMZA ISOLATED FORM
≈ <isolated> + 0621 ء

FE81 آ ARABIC LETTER ALEF WITH MADDA ABOVE ISOLATED FORM
≈ <isolated> + 0622 آ

FE82 ـآ ARABIC LETTER ALEF WITH MADDA ABOVE FINAL FORM
≈ <final> + 0622 آ

FE83 أ ARABIC LETTER ALEF WITH HAMZA ABOVE ISOLATED FORM
≈ <isolated> + 0623 أ

FE84 ـأ ARABIC LETTER ALEF WITH HAMZA ABOVE FINAL FORM
≈ <final> + 0623 أ

FE85 ؤ ARABIC LETTER WAW WITH HAMZA ABOVE ISOLATED FORM
≈ <isolated> + 0624 ؤ

FE86 ـؤ ARABIC LETTER WAW WITH HAMZA ABOVE FINAL FORM
≈ <final> + 0624 ؤ

FE87 إ ARABIC LETTER ALEF WITH HAMZA BELOW ISOLATED FORM
≈ <isolated> + 0625 إ

FE88 ـإ ARABIC LETTER ALEF WITH HAMZA BELOW FINAL FORM
≈ <final> + 0625 إ

FE89 ئ ARABIC LETTER YEH WITH HAMZA ABOVE ISOLATED FORM
≈ <isolated> + 0626 ئ

FE8A ـئ ARABIC LETTER YEH WITH HAMZA ABOVE FINAL FORM
≈ <final> + 0626 ئ

FE8B ئـ ARABIC LETTER YEH WITH HAMZA ABOVE INITIAL FORM
≈ <initial> + 0626 ئ

FE8C ـئـ ARABIC LETTER YEH WITH HAMZA ABOVE MEDIAL FORM
≈ <medial> + 0626 ئ

FE8D ا ARABIC LETTER ALEF ISOLATED FORM
≈ <isolated> + 0627 ا

FE8E ـا ARABIC LETTER ALEF FINAL FORM
≈ <final> + 0627 ا

FE8F ب ARABIC LETTER BEH ISOLATED FORM
≈ <isolated> + 0628 ب

FE90 ـب ARABIC LETTER BEH FINAL FORM
≈ <final> + 0628 ب

FE91 بـ ARABIC LETTER BEH INITIAL FORM
≈ <initial> + 0628 ب

FE92 ـبـ ARABIC LETTER BEH MEDIAL FORM
≈ <medial> + 0628 ب

FE93 ة ARABIC LETTER TEH MARBUTA ISOLATED FORM
≈ <isolated> + 0629 ة

FE94 ـة ARABIC LETTER TEH MARBUTA FINAL FORM
≈ <final> + 0629 ة

FE95 ت ARABIC LETTER TEH ISOLATED FORM
≈ <isolated> + 062A ت

FE96 ـت ARABIC LETTER TEH FINAL FORM
≈ <final> + 062A ت

FE97 تـ ARABIC LETTER TEH INITIAL FORM
≈ <initial> + 062A ت

FE98 ﺘ ARABIC LETTER TEH MEDIAL FORM
≈ <medial> + 062A ت

FE99 ﺙ ARABIC LETTER THEH ISOLATED FORM
≈ <isolated> + 062B ث

FE9A ﺚ ARABIC LETTER THEH FINAL FORM
≈ <final> + 062B ث

FE9B ﺛ ARABIC LETTER THEH INITIAL FORM
≈ <initial> + 062B ث

FE9C ﺜ ARABIC LETTER THEH MEDIAL FORM
≈ <medial> + 062B ث

FE9D ﺝ ARABIC LETTER JEEM ISOLATED FORM
≈ <isolated> + 062C ج

FE9E ﺞ ARABIC LETTER JEEM FINAL FORM
≈ <final> + 062C ج

FE9F ﺟ ARABIC LETTER JEEM INITIAL FORM
≈ <initial> + 062C ج

FEA0 ﺠ ARABIC LETTER JEEM MEDIAL FORM
≈ <medial> + 062C ج

FEA1 ﺡ ARABIC LETTER HAH ISOLATED FORM
≈ <isolated> + 062D ح

FEA2 ﺢ ARABIC LETTER HAH FINAL FORM
≈ <final> + 062D ح

FEA3 ﺣ ARABIC LETTER HAH INITIAL FORM
≈ <initial> + 062D ح

FEA4 ﺤ ARABIC LETTER HAH MEDIAL FORM
≈ <medial> + 062D ح

FEA5 ﺥ ARABIC LETTER KHAH ISOLATED FORM
≈ <isolated> + 062E خ

FEA6 ﺦ ARABIC LETTER KHAH FINAL FORM
≈ <final> + 062E خ

FEA7 ﺧ ARABIC LETTER KHAH INITIAL FORM
≈ <initial> + 062E خ

FEA8 ﺨ ARABIC LETTER KHAH MEDIAL FORM
≈ <medial> + 062E خ

FEA9 ﺩ ARABIC LETTER DAL ISOLATED FORM
≈ <isolated> + 062F د

FEAA ﺪ ARABIC LETTER DAL FINAL FORM
≈ <final> + 062F د

FEAB ﺫ ARABIC LETTER THAL ISOLATED FORM
≈ <isolated> + 0630 ذ

FEAC ﺬ ARABIC LETTER THAL FINAL FORM
≈ <final> + 0630 ذ

FEAD ﺭ ARABIC LETTER REH ISOLATED FORM
≈ <isolated> + 0631 ر

FEAE ﺮ ARABIC LETTER REH FINAL FORM
≈ <final> + 0631 ر

FEAF ﺯ ARABIC LETTER ZAIN ISOLATED FORM
≈ <isolated> + 0632 ز

FEB0 ﺰ ARABIC LETTER ZAIN FINAL FORM
≈ <final> + 0632 ز

FEB1 ﺱ ARABIC LETTER SEEN ISOLATED FORM
≈ <isolated> + 0633 س

FEB2 ﺲ ARABIC LETTER SEEN FINAL FORM
≈ <final> + 0633 س

FEB3 ﺳ ARABIC LETTER SEEN INITIAL FORM
≈ <initial> + 0633 س

FEB4 ﺴ ARABIC LETTER SEEN MEDIAL FORM
≈ <medial> + 0633 س

FEB5 ﺵ ARABIC LETTER SHEEN ISOLATED FORM
≈ <isolated> + 0634 ش

FEB6 ﺶ ARABIC LETTER SHEEN FINAL FORM
≈ <final> + 0634 ش

FEB7 ﺷ ARABIC LETTER SHEEN INITIAL FORM
≈ <initial> + 0634 ش

FEB8 ﺸ ARABIC LETTER SHEEN MEDIAL FORM
≈ <medial> + 0634 ش

FEB9 ﺹ ARABIC LETTER SAD ISOLATED FORM
≈ <isolated> + 0635 ص

FEBA ﺺ ARABIC LETTER SAD FINAL FORM
≈ <final> + 0635 ص

FEBB ﺻ ARABIC LETTER SAD INITIAL FORM
≈ <initial> + 0635 ص

FEBC ﺼ ARABIC LETTER SAD MEDIAL FORM
≈ <medial> + 0635 ص

FEBD ﺽ ARABIC LETTER DAD ISOLATED FORM
≈ <isolated> + 0636 ض

FEBE ﺾ ARABIC LETTER DAD FINAL FORM
≈ <final> + 0636 ض

FEBF ﺿ ARABIC LETTER DAD INITIAL FORM
≈ <initial> + 0636 ض

FEC0 ﻀ ARABIC LETTER DAD MEDIAL FORM
≈ <medial> + 0636 ض

FEC1 ﻁ ARABIC LETTER TAH ISOLATED FORM
≈ <isolated> + 0637 ط

FEC2 ﻂ ARABIC LETTER TAH FINAL FORM
≈ <final> + 0637 ط

FEC3 ﻃ ARABIC LETTER TAH INITIAL FORM
≈ <initial> + 0637 ط

FEC4 ﻄ ARABIC LETTER TAH MEDIAL FORM
≈ <medial> + 0637 ط

FEC5 ﻅ ARABIC LETTER ZAH ISOLATED FORM
≈ <isolated> + 0638 ظ

FEC6 ﻆ ARABIC LETTER ZAH FINAL FORM
≈ <final> + 0638 ظ

FEC7 ﻇ ARABIC LETTER ZAH INITIAL FORM
≈ <initial> + 0638 ظ

FEC8 ﻈ ARABIC LETTER ZAH MEDIAL FORM
≈ <medial> + 0638 ظ

FEC9 ﻉ ARABIC LETTER AIN ISOLATED FORM
≈ <isolated> + 0639 ع

FECA ﻊ ARABIC LETTER AIN FINAL FORM
≈ <final> + 0639 ع

FECB ﻋ ARABIC LETTER AIN INITIAL FORM
≈ <initial> + 0639 ع

FECC ﻌ ARABIC LETTER AIN MEDIAL FORM
≈ <medial> + 0639 ع

FECD ﻍ ARABIC LETTER GHAIN ISOLATED FORM
≈ <isolated> + 063A غ

FECE ﻎ ARABIC LETTER GHAIN FINAL FORM
≈ <final> + 063A غ

FECF ﻏ ARABIC LETTER GHAIN INITIAL FORM
≈ <initial> + 063A غ

FED0 ﻐ ARABIC LETTER GHAIN MEDIAL FORM
≈ <medial> + 063A غ

FED1 ﻑ ARABIC LETTER FEH ISOLATED FORM
≈ <isolated> + 0641 ف

FED2 ﻒ ARABIC LETTER FEH FINAL FORM
≈ <final> + 0641 ف

FED3 ﻓ ARABIC LETTER FEH INITIAL FORM
≈ <initial> + 0641 ف

FED4 ﻔ ARABIC LETTER FEH MEDIAL FORM
≈ <medial> + 0641 ف

FED5 ﻕ ARABIC LETTER QAF ISOLATED FORM
≈ <isolated> + 0642 ق

FED6 ﻖ ARABIC LETTER QAF FINAL FORM
≈ <final> + 0642 ق

FED7 ﻗ ARABIC LETTER QAF INITIAL FORM
≈ <initial> + 0642 ق

FED8 ﻘ ARABIC LETTER QAF MEDIAL FORM
≈ <medial> + 0642 ق

FED9 ﻙ ARABIC LETTER KAF ISOLATED FORM
≈ <isolated> + 0643 ك

FEDA ﻚ ARABIC LETTER KAF FINAL FORM
≈ <final> + 0643 ك

FEDB ﻛ ARABIC LETTER KAF INITIAL FORM
≈ <initial> + 0643 ك

FEDC ﻜ ARABIC LETTER KAF MEDIAL FORM
≈ <medial> + 0643 ك

FEDD ﻝ ARABIC LETTER LAM ISOLATED FORM
≈ <isolated> + 0644 ل

FEDE ﻞ ARABIC LETTER LAM FINAL FORM
≈ <final> + 0644 ل

FEDF ﻟ ARABIC LETTER LAM INITIAL FORM
≈ <initial> + 0644 ل

FEE0 ﻠ ARABIC LETTER LAM MEDIAL FORM
≈ <medial> + 0644 ل

FEE1 ﻡ ARABIC LETTER MEEM ISOLATED FORM
≈ <isolated> + 0645 م

FEE2 ﻢ ARABIC LETTER MEEM FINAL FORM
≈ <final> + 0645 م

FEE3 ﻣ ARABIC LETTER MEEM INITIAL FORM
≈ <initial> + 0645 م

FEE4 ﻤ ARABIC LETTER MEEM MEDIAL FORM
≈ <medial> + 0645 م

FEE5 ﻥ ARABIC LETTER NOON ISOLATED FORM
≈ <isolated> + 0646 ن

FEE6 ﻦ ARABIC LETTER NOON FINAL FORM
≈ <final> + 0646 ن

FEE7 ﻧ ARABIC LETTER NOON INITIAL FORM
≈ <initial> + 0646 ن

FEE8 ﻨ ARABIC LETTER NOON MEDIAL FORM
≈ <medial> + 0646 ن

FEE9 ه ARABIC LETTER HEH ISOLATED FORM
≈ <isolated> + 0647 ه

FEEA ـه ARABIC LETTER HEH FINAL FORM
≈ <final> + 0647 ه

FEEB هـ ARABIC LETTER HEH INITIAL FORM
≈ <initial> + 0647 ه

FEEC ـهـ ARABIC LETTER HEH MEDIAL FORM
≈ <medial> + 0647 ه

FEED و ARABIC LETTER WAW ISOLATED FORM
≈ <isolated> + 0648 و

FEEE ـو ARABIC LETTER WAW FINAL FORM
≈ <final> + 0648 و

FEEF ى ARABIC LETTER ALEF MAKSURA ISOLATED FORM
≈ <isolated> + 0649 ى

FEF0 ـى ARABIC LETTER ALEF MAKSURA FINAL FORM
≈ <final> + 0649 ى

FEF1 ي ARABIC LETTER YEH ISOLATED FORM
≈ <isolated> + 064A ي

FEF2 ـي ARABIC LETTER YEH FINAL FORM
≈ <final> + 064A ي

FEF3 يـ ARABIC LETTER YEH INITIAL FORM
≈ <initial> + 064A ي

FEF4 ـيـ ARABIC LETTER YEH MEDIAL FORM
≈ <medial> + 064A ي

FEF5 ﻵ ARABIC LIGATURE LAM WITH ALEF WITH MADDA ABOVE ISOLATED FORM
≈ <isolated> + 0644 ل + 0622 آ

FEF6 ﻶ ARABIC LIGATURE LAM WITH ALEF WITH MADDA ABOVE FINAL FORM
≈ <final> + 0644 ل + 0622 آ

FEF7 ﻷ ARABIC LIGATURE LAM WITH ALEF WITH HAMZA ABOVE ISOLATED FORM
≈ <isolated> + 0644 ل + 0623 أ

FEF8 ﻸ ARABIC LIGATURE LAM WITH ALEF WITH HAMZA ABOVE FINAL FORM
≈ <final> + 0644 ل + 0623 أ

FEF9 ﻹ ARABIC LIGATURE LAM WITH ALEF WITH HAMZA BELOW ISOLATED FORM
≈ <isolated> + 0644 ل + 0625 إ

FEFA ﻺ ARABIC LIGATURE LAM WITH ALEF WITH HAMZA BELOW FINAL FORM
≈ <final> + 0644 ل + 0625 إ

FEFB ﻻ ARABIC LIGATURE LAM WITH ALEF ISOLATED FORM
≈ <isolated> + 0644 ل + 0627 ا

FEFC ﻼ ARABIC LIGATURE LAM WITH ALEF FINAL FORM
≈ <final> + 0644 ل + 0627 ا

FEFD <reserved>

FEFE <reserved>

Special

FEFF ZWNBSP ZERO WIDTH NO-BREAK SPACE
= BYTE ORDER MARK
= BOM
• may be used to detect byte order by contrast with FFFE which is not a character
• may also be used as zero width no-break space
→ FFFE <not a character>

	FF0	FF1	FF2	FF3	FF4	FF5	FF6	FF7
0		０ FF10	＠ FF20	Ｐ FF30	｀ FF40	ｐ FF50		ｰ FF70
1	！ FF01	１ FF11	Ａ FF21	Ｑ FF31	ａ FF41	ｑ FF51	｡ FF61	ｱ FF71
2	＂ FF02	２ FF12	Ｂ FF22	Ｒ FF32	ｂ FF42	ｒ FF52	｢ FF62	ｲ FF72
3	＃ FF03	３ FF13	Ｃ FF23	Ｓ FF33	ｃ FF43	ｓ FF53	｣ FF63	ｳ FF73
4	＄ FF04	４ FF14	Ｄ FF24	Ｔ FF34	ｄ FF44	ｔ FF54	､ FF64	ｴ FF74
5	％ FF05	５ FF15	Ｅ FF25	Ｕ FF35	ｅ FF45	ｕ FF55	･ FF65	ｵ FF75
6	＆ FF06	６ FF16	Ｆ FF26	Ｖ FF36	ｆ FF46	ｖ FF56	ｦ FF66	ｶ FF76
7	＇ FF07	７ FF17	Ｇ FF27	Ｗ FF37	ｇ FF47	ｗ FF57	ｧ FF67	ｷ FF77
8	（ FF08	８ FF18	Ｈ FF28	Ｘ FF38	ｈ FF48	ｘ FF58	ｨ FF68	ｸ FF78
9	） FF09	９ FF19	Ｉ FF29	Ｙ FF39	ｉ FF49	ｙ FF59	ｩ FF69	ｹ FF79
A	＊ FF0A	： FF1A	Ｊ FF2A	Ｚ FF3A	ｊ FF4A	ｚ FF5A	ｪ FF6A	ｺ FF7A
B	＋ FF0B	； FF1B	Ｋ FF2B	［ FF3B	ｋ FF4B	｛ FF5B	ｫ FF6B	ｻ FF7B
C	， FF0C	＜ FF1C	Ｌ FF2C	＼ FF3C	ｌ FF4C	｜ FF5C	ｬ FF6C	ｼ FF7C
D	－ FF0D	＝ FF1D	Ｍ FF2D	］ FF3D	ｍ FF4D	｝ FF5D	ｭ FF6D	ｽ FF7D
E	． FF0E	＞ FF1E	Ｎ FF2E	＾ FF3E	ｎ FF4E	～ FF5E	ｮ FF6E	ｾ FF7E
F	／ FF0F	？ FF1F	Ｏ FF2F	＿ FF3F	ｏ FF4F		ｯ FF6F	ｿ FF7F

	FF8	FF9	FFA	FFB	FFC	FFD	FFE
0	ﾀ FF80	ﾐ FF90	HW HF FFA0	ﾰ FFB0			￠ FFE0
1	ﾁ FF81	ﾑ FF91	ﾡ FFA1	ﾱ FFB1			￡ FFE1
2	ﾂ FF82	ﾒ FF92	ﾢ FFA2	ﾲ FFB2	ￂ FFC2	ￒ FFD2	￢ FFE2
3	ﾃ FF83	ﾓ FF93	ﾣ FFA3	ﾳ FFB3	ￃ FFC3	ￓ FFD3	￣ FFE3
4	ﾄ FF84	ﾔ FF94	ﾤ FFA4	ﾴ FFB4	ￄ FFC4	ￔ FFD4	￤ FFE4
5	ﾅ FF85	ﾕ FF95	ﾥ FFA5	ﾵ FFB5	ￅ FFC5	ￕ FFD5	￥ FFE5
6	ﾆ FF86	ﾖ FF96	ﾦ FFA6	ﾶ FFB6	ￆ FFC6	ￖ FFD6	￦ FFE6
7	ﾇ FF87	ﾗ FF97	ﾧ FFA7	ﾷ FFB7	ￇ FFC7	ￗ FFD7	
8	ﾈ FF88	ﾘ FF98	ﾨ FFA8	ﾸ FFB8			￨ FFE8
9	ﾉ FF89	ﾙ FF99	ﾩ FFA9	ﾹ FFB9			￩ FFE9
A	ﾊ FF8A	ﾚ FF9A	ﾪ FFAA	ﾺ FFBA	ￊ FFCA	ￚ FFDA	￪ FFEA
B	ﾋ FF8B	ﾛ FF9B	ﾫ FFAB	ﾻ FFBB	ￋ FFCB	ￛ FFDB	￫ FFEB
C	ﾌ FF8C	ﾜ FF9C	ﾬ FFAC	ﾼ FFBC	ￌ FFCC	ￜ FFDC	￬ FFEC
D	ﾍ FF8D	ﾝ FF9D	ﾭ FFAD	ﾽ FFBD	ￍ FFCD		￭ FFED
E	ﾎ FF8E	ﾞ FF9E	ﾮ FFAE	ﾾ FFBE	ￎ FFCE		￮ FFEE
F	ﾏ FF8F	ﾟ FF9F	ﾯ FFAF		ￏ FFCF		

Fullwidth ASCII variants

FF00 <reserved>

FF01 ！ FULLWIDTH EXCLAMATION MARK
≈ <wide> + 0021 !

FF02 ＂ FULLWIDTH QUOTATION MARK
≈ <wide> + 0022 "

FF03 ＃ FULLWIDTH NUMBER SIGN
≈ <wide> + 0023 #

FF04 ＄ FULLWIDTH DOLLAR SIGN
≈ <wide> + 0024 $

FF05 ％ FULLWIDTH PERCENT SIGN
≈ <wide> + 0025 %

FF06 ＆ FULLWIDTH AMPERSAND
≈ <wide> + 0026 &

FF07 ＇ FULLWIDTH APOSTROPHE
≈ <wide> + 0027 '

FF08 （ FULLWIDTH LEFT PARENTHESIS
≈ <wide> + 0028 (

FF09 ） FULLWIDTH RIGHT PARENTHESIS
≈ <wide> + 0029)

FF0A ＊ FULLWIDTH ASTERISK
≈ <wide> + 002A *

FF0B ＋ FULLWIDTH PLUS SIGN
≈ <wide> + 002B +

FF0C ， FULLWIDTH COMMA
≈ <wide> + 002C ,

FF0D － FULLWIDTH HYPHEN-MINUS
≈ <wide> + 002D -

FF0E ． FULLWIDTH FULL STOP
≈ <wide> + 002E .

FF0F ／ FULLWIDTH SOLIDUS
≈ <wide> + 002F /

FF10 ０ FULLWIDTH DIGIT ZERO
≈ <wide> + 0030 0

FF11 １ FULLWIDTH DIGIT ONE
≈ <wide> + 0031 1

FF12 ２ FULLWIDTH DIGIT TWO
≈ <wide> + 0032 2

FF13 ３ FULLWIDTH DIGIT THREE
≈ <wide> + 0033 3

FF14 ４ FULLWIDTH DIGIT FOUR
≈ <wide> + 0034 4

FF15 ５ FULLWIDTH DIGIT FIVE
≈ <wide> + 0035 5

FF16 ６ FULLWIDTH DIGIT SIX
≈ <wide> + 0036 6

FF17 ７ FULLWIDTH DIGIT SEVEN
≈ <wide> + 0037 7

FF18 ８ FULLWIDTH DIGIT EIGHT
≈ <wide> + 0038 8

FF19 ９ FULLWIDTH DIGIT NINE
≈ <wide> + 0039 9

FF1A ： FULLWIDTH COLON
≈ <wide> + 003A :

FF1B ； FULLWIDTH SEMICOLON
≈ <wide> + 003B ;

FF1C ＜ FULLWIDTH LESS-THAN SIGN
≈ <wide> + 003C <

FF1D ＝ FULLWIDTH EQUALS SIGN
≈ <wide> + 003D =

FF1E ＞ FULLWIDTH GREATER-THAN SIGN
≈ <wide> + 003E >

FF1F ？ FULLWIDTH QUESTION MARK
≈ <wide> + 003F ?

FF20 ＠ FULLWIDTH COMMERCIAL AT
≈ <wide> + 0040 @

FF21 Ａ FULLWIDTH LATIN CAPITAL LETTER A
≈ <wide> + 0041 A

FF22 Ｂ FULLWIDTH LATIN CAPITAL LETTER B
≈ <wide> + 0042 B

FF23 Ｃ FULLWIDTH LATIN CAPITAL LETTER C
≈ <wide> + 0043 C

FF24 Ｄ FULLWIDTH LATIN CAPITAL LETTER D
≈ <wide> + 0044 D

FF25 Ｅ FULLWIDTH LATIN CAPITAL LETTER E
≈ <wide> + 0045 E

FF26 Ｆ FULLWIDTH LATIN CAPITAL LETTER F
≈ <wide> + 0046 F

FF27 Ｇ FULLWIDTH LATIN CAPITAL LETTER G
≈ <wide> + 0047 G

FF28 Ｈ FULLWIDTH LATIN CAPITAL LETTER H
≈ <wide> + 0048 H

FF29 Ｉ FULLWIDTH LATIN CAPITAL LETTER I
≈ <wide> + 0049 I

FF2A Ｊ FULLWIDTH LATIN CAPITAL LETTER J
≈ <wide> + 004A J

FF2B Ｋ FULLWIDTH LATIN CAPITAL LETTER K
≈ <wide> + 004B K

FF2C Ｌ FULLWIDTH LATIN CAPITAL LETTER L
≈ <wide> + 004C L

FF2D Ｍ FULLWIDTH LATIN CAPITAL LETTER M
≈ <wide> + 004D M

FF2E N FULLWIDTH LATIN CAPITAL LETTER N
≈ <wide> + 004E N

FF2F O FULLWIDTH LATIN CAPITAL LETTER O
≈ <wide> + 004F O

FF30 P FULLWIDTH LATIN CAPITAL LETTER P
≈ <wide> + 0050 P

FF31 Q FULLWIDTH LATIN CAPITAL LETTER Q
≈ <wide> + 0051 Q

FF32 R FULLWIDTH LATIN CAPITAL LETTER R
≈ <wide> + 0052 R

FF33 S FULLWIDTH LATIN CAPITAL LETTER S
≈ <wide> + 0053 S

FF34 T FULLWIDTH LATIN CAPITAL LETTER T
≈ <wide> + 0054 T

FF35 U FULLWIDTH LATIN CAPITAL LETTER U
≈ <wide> + 0055 U

FF36 V FULLWIDTH LATIN CAPITAL LETTER V
≈ <wide> + 0056 V

FF37 W FULLWIDTH LATIN CAPITAL LETTER W
≈ <wide> + 0057 W

FF38 X FULLWIDTH LATIN CAPITAL LETTER X
≈ <wide> + 0058 X

FF39 Y FULLWIDTH LATIN CAPITAL LETTER Y
≈ <wide> + 0059 Y

FF3A Z FULLWIDTH LATIN CAPITAL LETTER Z
≈ <wide> + 005A Z

FF3B [FULLWIDTH LEFT SQUARE BRACKET
≈ <wide> + 005B [

FF3C \ FULLWIDTH REVERSE SOLIDUS
≈ <wide> + 005C \

FF3D] FULLWIDTH RIGHT SQUARE BRACKET
≈ <wide> + 005D]

FF3E ^ FULLWIDTH CIRCUMFLEX ACCENT
≈ <wide> + 005E ^

FF3F _ FULLWIDTH LOW LINE
≈ <wide> + 005F _

FF40 ` FULLWIDTH GRAVE ACCENT
≈ <wide> + 0060 `

FF41 a FULLWIDTH LATIN SMALL LETTER A
≈ <wide> + 0061 a

FF42 b FULLWIDTH LATIN SMALL LETTER B
≈ <wide> + 0062 b

FF43 c FULLWIDTH LATIN SMALL LETTER C
≈ <wide> + 0063 c

FF44 d FULLWIDTH LATIN SMALL LETTER D
≈ <wide> + 0064 d

FF45 e FULLWIDTH LATIN SMALL LETTER E
≈ <wide> + 0065 e

FF46 f FULLWIDTH LATIN SMALL LETTER F
≈ <wide> + 0066 f

FF47 g FULLWIDTH LATIN SMALL LETTER G
≈ <wide> + 0067 g

FF48 h FULLWIDTH LATIN SMALL LETTER H
≈ <wide> + 0068 h

FF49 i FULLWIDTH LATIN SMALL LETTER I
≈ <wide> + 0069 i

FF4A j FULLWIDTH LATIN SMALL LETTER J
≈ <wide> + 006A j

FF4B k FULLWIDTH LATIN SMALL LETTER K
≈ <wide> + 006B k

FF4C l FULLWIDTH LATIN SMALL LETTER L
≈ <wide> + 006C l

FF4D m FULLWIDTH LATIN SMALL LETTER M
≈ <wide> + 006D m

FF4E n FULLWIDTH LATIN SMALL LETTER N
≈ <wide> + 006E n

FF4F o FULLWIDTH LATIN SMALL LETTER O
≈ <wide> + 006F o

FF50 p FULLWIDTH LATIN SMALL LETTER P
≈ <wide> + 0070 p

FF51 q FULLWIDTH LATIN SMALL LETTER Q
≈ <wide> + 0071 q

FF52 r FULLWIDTH LATIN SMALL LETTER R
≈ <wide> + 0072 r

FF53 ｓ FULLWIDTH LATIN SMALL LETTER S
≈ <wide> + 0073 s

FF54 ｔ FULLWIDTH LATIN SMALL LETTER T
≈ <wide> + 0074 t

FF55 ｕ FULLWIDTH LATIN SMALL LETTER U
≈ <wide> + 0075 u

FF56 ｖ FULLWIDTH LATIN SMALL LETTER V
≈ <wide> + 0076 v

FF57 ｗ FULLWIDTH LATIN SMALL LETTER W
≈ <wide> + 0077 w

FF58 ｘ FULLWIDTH LATIN SMALL LETTER X
≈ <wide> + 0078 x

FF59 ｙ FULLWIDTH LATIN SMALL LETTER Y
≈ <wide> + 0079 y

FF5A ｚ FULLWIDTH LATIN SMALL LETTER Z
≈ <wide> + 007A z

FF5B ｛ FULLWIDTH LEFT CURLY BRACKET
≈ <wide> + 007B {

FF5C ｜ FULLWIDTH VERTICAL LINE
≈ <wide> + 007C |

FF5D ｝ FULLWIDTH RIGHT CURLY BRACKET
≈ <wide> + 007D }

FF5E ～ FULLWIDTH TILDE
≈ <wide> + 007E ~

FF5F <reserved>

Halfwidth Katakana variants

FF60 <reserved>

FF61 ｡ HALFWIDTH IDEOGRAPHIC FULL STOP
≈ <narrow> + 3002 。

FF62 ｢ HALFWIDTH LEFT CORNER BRACKET
≈ <narrow> + 300C 「

FF63 ｣ HALFWIDTH RIGHT CORNER BRACKET
≈ <narrow> + 300D 」

FF64 ､ HALFWIDTH IDEOGRAPHIC COMMA
≈ <narrow> + 3001 、

FF65 ･ HALFWIDTH KATAKANA MIDDLE DOT
≈ <narrow> + 30FB ・

FF66 ｦ HALFWIDTH KATAKANA LETTER WO
≈ <narrow> + 30F2 ヲ

FF67 ｧ HALFWIDTH KATAKANA LETTER SMALL A
≈ <narrow> + 30A1 ァ

FF68 ｨ HALFWIDTH KATAKANA LETTER SMALL I
≈ <narrow> + 30A3 ィ

FF69 ｩ HALFWIDTH KATAKANA LETTER SMALL U
≈ <narrow> + 30A5 ゥ

FF6A ｪ HALFWIDTH KATAKANA LETTER SMALL E
≈ <narrow> + 30A7 ェ

FF6B ｫ HALFWIDTH KATAKANA LETTER SMALL O
≈ <narrow> + 30A9 ォ

FF6C ｬ HALFWIDTH KATAKANA LETTER SMALL YA
≈ <narrow> + 30E3 ャ

FF6D ｭ HALFWIDTH KATAKANA LETTER SMALL YU
≈ <narrow> + 30E5 ュ

FF6E ｮ HALFWIDTH KATAKANA LETTER SMALL YO
≈ <narrow> + 30E7 ョ

FF6F ｯ HALFWIDTH KATAKANA LETTER SMALL TU
≈ <narrow> + 30C3 ッ

FF70 ｰ HALFWIDTH KATAKANA-HIRAGANA PROLONGED SOUND MARK
≈ <narrow> + 30FC ー

FF71 ｱ HALFWIDTH KATAKANA LETTER A
≈ <narrow> + 30A2 ア

FF72 ｲ HALFWIDTH KATAKANA LETTER I
≈ <narrow> + 30A4 イ

FF73 ｳ HALFWIDTH KATAKANA LETTER U
≈ <narrow> + 30A6 ウ

FF74 ｴ HALFWIDTH KATAKANA LETTER E
≈ <narrow> + 30A8 エ

FF75 ｵ HALFWIDTH KATAKANA LETTER O
≈ <narrow> + 30AA オ

FF76 ｶ HALFWIDTH KATAKANA LETTER KA
≈ <narrow> + 30AB カ

FF77 ｷ HALFWIDTH KATAKANA LETTER KI
≈ <narrow> + 30AD キ

FF78 ｸ HALFWIDTH KATAKANA LETTER KU
≈ <narrow> + 30AF ク

FF79 ｹ HALFWIDTH KATAKANA LETTER KE
≈ <narrow> + 30B1 ケ

FF7A ｺ HALFWIDTH KATAKANA LETTER KO
≈ <narrow> + 30B3 コ

FF7B ｻ HALFWIDTH KATAKANA LETTER SA
≈ <narrow> + 30B5 サ

FF7C ｼ HALFWIDTH KATAKANA LETTER SI
≈ <narrow> + 30B7 シ

FF7D ｽ HALFWIDTH KATAKANA LETTER SU
≈ <narrow> + 30B9 ス

FF7E ｾ HALFWIDTH KATAKANA LETTER SE
≈ <narrow> + 30BB セ

FF7F ｿ HALFWIDTH KATAKANA LETTER SO
≈ <narrow> + 30BD ソ

FF80 ﾀ HALFWIDTH KATAKANA LETTER TA
≈ <narrow> + 30BF タ

FF81 ﾁ HALFWIDTH KATAKANA LETTER TI
≈ <narrow> + 30C1 チ

FF82 ﾂ HALFWIDTH KATAKANA LETTER TU
≈ <narrow> + 30C4 ツ

FF83 ﾃ HALFWIDTH KATAKANA LETTER TE
≈ <narrow> + 30C6 テ

FF84 ﾄ HALFWIDTH KATAKANA LETTER TO
≈ <narrow> + 30C8 ト

FF85 ﾅ HALFWIDTH KATAKANA LETTER NA
≈ <narrow> + 30CA ナ

FF86 ﾆ HALFWIDTH KATAKANA LETTER NI
≈ <narrow> + 30CB ニ

FF87 ﾇ HALFWIDTH KATAKANA LETTER NU
≈ <narrow> + 30CC ヌ

FF88 ﾈ HALFWIDTH KATAKANA LETTER NE
≈ <narrow> + 30CD ネ

FF89 ﾉ HALFWIDTH KATAKANA LETTER NO
≈ <narrow> + 30CE ノ

FF8A ﾊ HALFWIDTH KATAKANA LETTER HA
≈ <narrow> + 30CF ハ

FF8B ﾋ HALFWIDTH KATAKANA LETTER HI
≈ <narrow> + 30D2 ヒ

FF8C ﾌ HALFWIDTH KATAKANA LETTER HU
≈ <narrow> + 30D5 フ

FF8D ﾍ HALFWIDTH KATAKANA LETTER HE
≈ <narrow> + 30D8 ヘ

FF8E ﾎ HALFWIDTH KATAKANA LETTER HO
≈ <narrow> + 30DB ホ

FF8F ﾏ HALFWIDTH KATAKANA LETTER MA
≈ <narrow> + 30DE マ

FF90 ﾐ HALFWIDTH KATAKANA LETTER MI
≈ <narrow> + 30DF ミ

FF91 ﾑ HALFWIDTH KATAKANA LETTER MU
≈ <narrow> + 30E0 ム

FF92 ﾒ HALFWIDTH KATAKANA LETTER ME
≈ <narrow> + 30E1 メ

FF93 ﾓ HALFWIDTH KATAKANA LETTER MO
≈ <narrow> + 30E2 モ

FF94 ﾔ HALFWIDTH KATAKANA LETTER YA
≈ <narrow> + 30E4 ヤ

FF95 ﾕ HALFWIDTH KATAKANA LETTER YU
≈ <narrow> + 30E6 ユ

FF96 ﾖ HALFWIDTH KATAKANA LETTER YO
≈ <narrow> + 30E8 ヨ

FF97 ﾗ HALFWIDTH KATAKANA LETTER RA
≈ <narrow> + 30E9 ラ

FF98 ﾘ HALFWIDTH KATAKANA LETTER RI
≈ <narrow> + 30EA リ

FF99 ﾙ HALFWIDTH KATAKANA LETTER RU
≈ <narrow> + 30EB ル

FF9A ﾚ HALFWIDTH KATAKANA LETTER RE
≈ <narrow> + 30EC レ

FF9B ﾛ HALFWIDTH KATAKANA LETTER RO
≈ <narrow> + 30ED ロ

FF9C ﾜ HALFWIDTH KATAKANA LETTER WA
≈ <narrow> + 30EF ワ

FF9D ﾝ HALFWIDTH KATAKANA LETTER N
≈ <narrow> + 30F3 ン

FF9E ﾞ HALFWIDTH KATAKANA VOICED SOUND MARK
≈ <narrow> + 309B ゛

FF9F ﾟ HALFWIDTH KATAKANA SEMI-VOICED SOUND MARK
≈ <narrow> + 309C ゜

Halfwidth Hangul variants

FFA0 HALFWIDTH HANGUL FILLER
≈ <narrow> + 3164

FFA1 ﾡ HALFWIDTH HANGUL LETTER KIYEOK
≈ <narrow> + 3131 ㄱ

FFA2 ﾢ HALFWIDTH HANGUL LETTER SSANGKIYEOK
≈ <narrow> + 3132 ㄲ

FFA3 ﾣ HALFWIDTH HANGUL LETTER KIYEOK-SIOS
≈ <narrow> + 3133 ㄳ

FFA4 ﾤ HALFWIDTH HANGUL LETTER NIEUN
≈ <narrow> + 3134 ㄴ

FFA5 ﾥ HALFWIDTH HANGUL LETTER NIEUN-CIEUC
≈ <narrow> + 3135 ㄵ

FFA6 ﾦ HALFWIDTH HANGUL LETTER NIEUN-HIEUH
≈ <narrow> + 3136 ㄶ

FFA7 ﾧ HALFWIDTH HANGUL LETTER TIKEUT
≈ <narrow> + 3137 ㄷ

FFA8 ﾨ HALFWIDTH HANGUL LETTER SSANGTIKEUT
≈ <narrow> + 3138 ㄸ

FFA9 ﾩ HALFWIDTH HANGUL LETTER RIEUL
≈ <narrow> + 3139 ㄹ

FFAA ﾪ HALFWIDTH HANGUL LETTER RIEUL-KIYEOK
≈ <narrow> + 313A ㄺ

FFAB ﾫ HALFWIDTH HANGUL LETTER RIEUL-MIEUM
≈ <narrow> + 313B ㄻ

FFAC ﾬ HALFWIDTH HANGUL LETTER RIEUL-PIEUP
≈ <narrow> + 313C ㄼ

FFAD ﾭ HALFWIDTH HANGUL LETTER RIEUL-SIOS
≈ <narrow> + 313D ㄽ

FFAE ﾮ HALFWIDTH HANGUL LETTER RIEUL-THIEUTH
≈ <narrow> + 313E ㄾ

FFAF ﾯ HALFWIDTH HANGUL LETTER RIEUL-PHIEUPH
≈ <narrow> + 313F ㄿ

FFB0 ﾰ HALFWIDTH HANGUL LETTER RIEUL-HIEUH
≈ <narrow> + 3140 ㅀ

FFB1 ﾱ HALFWIDTH HANGUL LETTER MIEUM
≈ <narrow> + 3141 ㅁ

FFB2 ﾲ HALFWIDTH HANGUL LETTER PIEUP
≈ <narrow> + 3142 ㅂ

FFB3 ﾳ HALFWIDTH HANGUL LETTER SSANGPIEUP
≈ <narrow> + 3143 ㅃ

FFB4 ﾴ HALFWIDTH HANGUL LETTER PIEUP-SIOS
≈ <narrow> + 3144 ㅄ

FFB5 ﾵ HALFWIDTH HANGUL LETTER SIOS
≈ <narrow> + 3145 ㅅ

FFB6 ﾶ HALFWIDTH HANGUL LETTER SSANGSIOS
≈ <narrow> + 3146 ㅆ

FFB7 ﾷ HALFWIDTH HANGUL LETTER IEUNG
≈ <narrow> + 3147 ㅇ

FFB8 ﾸ HALFWIDTH HANGUL LETTER CIEUC
≈ <narrow> + 3148 ㅈ

FFB9 ﾹ HALFWIDTH HANGUL LETTER SSANGCIEUC
≈ <narrow> + 3149 ㅉ

FFBA ﾺ HALFWIDTH HANGUL LETTER CHIEUCH
≈ <narrow> + 314A ㅊ

FFBB ﾻ HALFWIDTH HANGUL LETTER KHIEUKH
≈ <narrow> + 314B ㅋ

FFBC ﾼ HALFWIDTH HANGUL LETTER THIEUTH
≈ <narrow> + 314C ㅌ

FFBD ﾽ HALFWIDTH HANGUL LETTER PHIEUPH
≈ <narrow> + 314D ㅍ

FFBE ﾾ HALFWIDTH HANGUL LETTER HIEUH
≈ <narrow> + 314E ㅎ

FFBF <reserved>

FFC0 <reserved>

FFC1 <reserved>

FFC2 ￂ HALFWIDTH HANGUL LETTER A
≈ <narrow> + 314F ㅏ

FFC3 ￃ HALFWIDTH HANGUL LETTER AE
≈ <narrow> + 3150 ㅐ

FFC4 ￄ HALFWIDTH HANGUL LETTER YA
≈ <narrow> + 3151 ㅑ

FFC5 ￅ HALFWIDTH HANGUL LETTER YAE
≈ <narrow> + 3152 ㅒ

FFC6 ￆ HALFWIDTH HANGUL LETTER EO
≈ <narrow> + 3153 ㅓ

FFC7 ￇ HALFWIDTH HANGUL LETTER E
≈ <narrow> + 3154 ㅔ

FFC8 <reserved>

FFC9 <reserved>
FFCA ￊ HALFWIDTH HANGUL LETTER YEO
≈ <narrow> + 3155 ㅕ
FFCB ￋ HALFWIDTH HANGUL LETTER YE
≈ <narrow> + 3156 ㅖ
FFCC ￌ HALFWIDTH HANGUL LETTER O
≈ <narrow> + 3157 ㅗ
FFCD ￍ HALFWIDTH HANGUL LETTER WA
≈ <narrow> + 3158 ㅘ
FFCE ￎ HALFWIDTH HANGUL LETTER WAE
≈ <narrow> + 3159 ㅙ
FFCF ￏ HALFWIDTH HANGUL LETTER OE
≈ <narrow> + 315A ㅚ
FFD0 <reserved>
FFD1 <reserved>
FFD2 ￒ HALFWIDTH HANGUL LETTER YO
≈ <narrow> + 315B ㅛ
FFD3 ￓ HALFWIDTH HANGUL LETTER U
≈ <narrow> + 315C ㅜ
FFD4 ￔ HALFWIDTH HANGUL LETTER WEO
≈ <narrow> + 315D ㅝ
FFD5 ￕ HALFWIDTH HANGUL LETTER WE
≈ <narrow> + 315E ㅞ
FFD6 ￖ HALFWIDTH HANGUL LETTER WI
≈ <narrow> + 315F ㅟ
FFD7 ￗ HALFWIDTH HANGUL LETTER YU
≈ <narrow> + 3160 ㅠ
FFD8 <reserved>
FFD9 <reserved>
FFDA ￚ HALFWIDTH HANGUL LETTER EU
≈ <narrow> + 3161 ㅡ
FFDB ￛ HALFWIDTH HANGUL LETTER YI
≈ <narrow> + 3162 ㅢ
FFDC ￜ HALFWIDTH HANGUL LETTER I
≈ <narrow> + 3163 ㅣ
FFDD <reserved>
FFDE <reserved>
FFDF <reserved>

Fullwidth symbol variants

FFE0 ￠ FULLWIDTH CENT SIGN
≈ <wide> + 00A2 ¢
FFE1 ￡ FULLWIDTH POUND SIGN
≈ <wide> + 00A3 £
FFE2 ￢ FULLWIDTH NOT SIGN
≈ <wide> + 00AC ¬
FFE3 ￣ FULLWIDTH MACRON
≈ <wide> + 00AF ¯
FFE4 ￤ FULLWIDTH BROKEN BAR
≈ <wide> + 00A6 ¦
FFE5 ￥ FULLWIDTH YEN SIGN
≈ <wide> + 00A5 ¥
FFE6 ￦ FULLWIDTH WON SIGN
≈ <wide> + 20A9 ₩
FFE7 <reserved>
FFE8 ￨ HALFWIDTH FORMS LIGHT VERTICAL
≈ <narrow> + 2502 │
FFE9 ￩ HALFWIDTH LEFTWARDS ARROW
≈ <narrow> + 2190 ←
FFEA ￪ HALFWIDTH UPWARDS ARROW
≈ <narrow> + 2191 ↑
FFEB ￫ HALFWIDTH RIGHTWARDS ARROW
≈ <narrow> + 2192 →
FFEC ￬ HALFWIDTH DOWNWARDS ARROW
≈ <narrow> + 2193 ↓
FFED ￭ HALFWIDTH BLACK SQUARE
≈ <narrow> + 25A0 ■
FFEE ￮ HALFWIDTH WHITE CIRCLE
≈ <narrow> + 25CB ○

FFF
0
1
2
3
4
5
6
7
8
9
A
B
C
D
FFFD
E
F

Specials

FFF0 ▧ <reserved>
FFF1 ▧ <reserved>
FFF2 ▧ <reserved>
FFF3 ▧ <reserved>
FFF4 ▧ <reserved>
FFF5 ▧ <reserved>
FFF6 ▧ <reserved>
FFF7 ▧ <reserved>
FFF8 ▧ <reserved>
FFF9 ▧ <reserved>
FFFA ▧ <reserved>
FFFB ▧ <reserved>
FFFC ▧ <reserved>
FFFD � REPLACEMENT CHARACTER
• used to replace incoming characters whose values are unknown or unrepresentable in Unicode
→ 001A SUB substitute

Not character codes

FFFE ■ <not a character>
• the value FFFE ■ is guaranteed not to be a Unicode character at all
• may be used to detect byte order by contrast with FEFF ZWNBSP which is a character
→ FEFF ZWNBSP zero width no-break space

FFFF ■ <not a character>
• the value FFFF ■ is guaranteed not to be a Unicode character at all

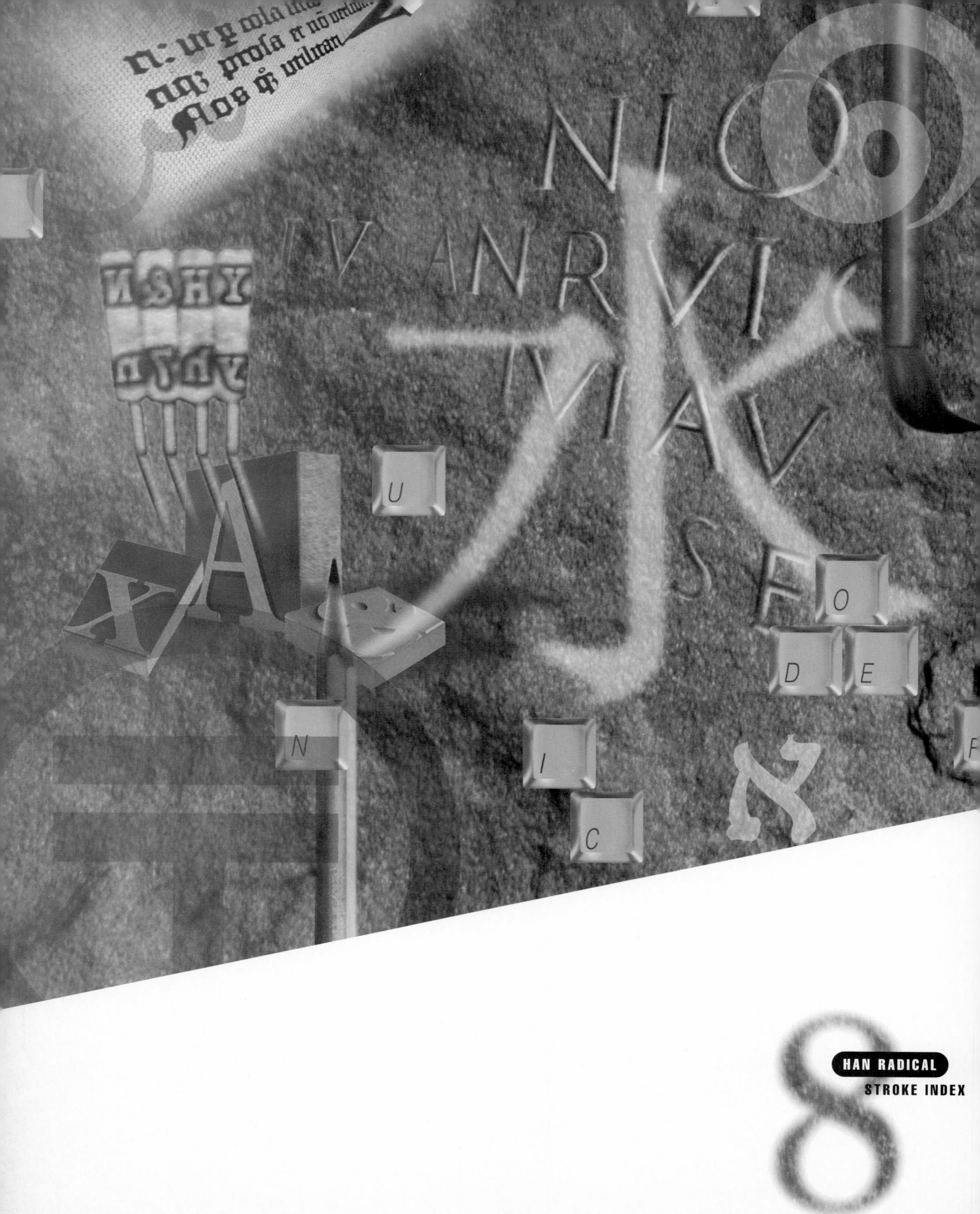

8

HAN RADICAL STROKE INDEX

Chapter 8

Han Radical-Stroke Index

To expedite locating specific Han ideographic characters within the Unicode Han ideographic set, this chapter contains a set of radical-stroke charts. Under the traditional radical-stroke system, each Han ideograph is considered to be written with one of a number of different character elements or radicals and a number of additional strokes. For example, the character 說 has the radical 言 and seven additional strokes. To find the character 說 within a dictionary, one would first locate the section for its radical, 言, and then find the subsection for characters with seven additional strokes.

This method is complicated by the fact that there are occasional ambiguities in the counting of strokes. Even worse, some characters are considered by different authorities to be written with different radicals; there is not in fact universal agreement about which set of radicals to use for certain characters, particularly with the increased use of simplified characters.

The most influential authority for radical-stroke information is the eighteenth century *KangXi* dictionary, which contains 214 radicals. The main problem in using *KangXi* radicals today is that many simplified characters are difficult to classify under any of the 214 *KangXi* radicals. As a result, various modern radical sets have been introduced. None, however, is in general use, and the 214 *KangXi* radicals remain the best known.

The Unicode radical-stroke charts are based on the *KangXi* radicals. The Unicode Standard follows a number of different sources for radical-stroke classification. Where two sources are at odds as to radical or stroke count for a given character, the character is shown in *both* positions in the radical-stroke charts.

Simplified characters are, as a rule, considered to have the same radical as their traditional forms and are found under the appropriate radical. For example, the character 伣 is found under the same radical, 人, as its traditional form (俔). The only exceptions are those characters for which the radical itself is simplified. Characters with a simplified radical are placed in a block separate from their traditional forms; this block follows immediately after the block for characters with the traditional radical. Thus, immediately following the block of characters with the radical 言 is a block of characters with its simplified form, 讠. The simplified character 说 is found in the latter block; its traditional counterpart, 說, in the former.

Characters within the compatibility range (U+F900 → U+FAFF) are not included in the radical-stroke charts.

一 (1) 一 4E00 **1** 丁 4E01 丂 4E02 七 4E03 丄 4E04 丅 4E05 丆 4E06 **2** 万 4E07 丈 4E08 三 4E09 上 4E0A 下 4E0B 丌 4E0C **3** 不 4E0D 与 4E0E 丏 4E0F 丐 4E10 丑 4E11 丒 4E12 专 4E13
丗 4E17 **4** 且 4E14 丕 4E15 世 4E16 丘 4E18 丙 4E19 业 4E1A 丛 4E1B 东 4E1C 丝 4E1D **5** 丞 4E1E 丟 4E1F 丠 4E20 両 4E21 丢 4E22 **6** 丣 4E23 两 4E24 严 4E25 **7** 並 4E26

丨 (2) 丨 4E28 **1** 丩 4E29 **2** 个 4E2A 丫 4E2B **3** 中 4E2D 丮 4E2E 丯 4E2F 丰 4E30 **4** 丱 4E31 **6** 串 4E32 **7** 丳 4E33 **8** 临 4E34 **9** 丵 4E35

丶 (3) 丶 4E36 **1** 丷 4E37 **2** 丸 4E38 凡 51E1 **3** 丹 4E39 为 4E3A **4** 主 4E3B 丼 4E3C **7** 丽 4E3D **8** 举 4E3E

丿 (4) 丿 4E3F 乀 4E40 乁 4E41 **1** 乂 4E42 乃 4E43 乄 4E44 **2** 久 4E45 乆 4E46 乇 4E47 么 4E48 义 4E49 乊 4E4A 凢 51E2 **3** 之 4E4B 乌 4E4C **4** 乍 4E4D 乎 4E4E 乏 4E4F 乐 4E50
5 乑 4E51 乒 4E52 乓 4E53 乔 4E54 **6** 乕 4E55 **7** 乖 4E56 **8** 乗 4E57 **9** 乘 4E58

乙 (5) 乙 4E59 乚 4E5A 乛 4E5B **1** 乜 4E5C 九 4E5D **2** 乞 4E5E 也 4E5F 习 4E60 卫 536B **3** 乢 4E62 乣 4E63 乤 4E64 乥 4E65 书 4E66 **4** 乧 4E67 **5** 乨 4E68 乩 4E69 乪 4E6A
乫 4E6B 乬 4E6C 乭 4E6D 乮 4E6E 乯 4E6F 买 4E70 厾 53BE **6** 乱 4E71 乲 4E72 **7** 乳 4E73 乴 4E74 乵 4E75 乶 4E76 乷 4E77 **8** 乹 4E79 乺 4E7A 乻 4E7B 乼 4E7C **9** 乽 4E7D
10 乾 4E7E 乿 4E7F 亀 4E80 **11** 亁 4E81 **12** 亂 4E82 亃 4E83 亄 4E84

亅 (6) 亅 4E85 **1** 了 4E86 **2** 亇 4E87 **3** 予 4E88 **5** 争 4E89 **6** 亊 4E8A **7** 事 4E8B

二 (7) 二 4E8C **1** 亍 4E8D 于 4E8E 亏 4E8F 亐 4E90 **2** 云 4E91 互 4E92 亓 4E93 五 4E94 井 4E95 亖 4E96 **3** 亗 4E97 **4** 亘 4E98 亙 4E99 亚 4E9A **5** 些 4E9B 亜 4E9C
6 亝 4E9D 亞 4E9E 亟 4E9F

亠 (8) 亠 4EA0 **1** 亡 4EA1 **2** 亢 4EA2 亣 4EA3 **4** 交 4EA4 亥 4EA5 亦 4EA6 产 4EA7 **5** 亨 4EA8 亩 4EA9 亪 4EAA **6** 享 4EAB 京 4EAC **7** 亭 4EAD 亮 4EAE 亯 4EAF 亰 4EB0
亱 4EB1 亲 4EB2 **8** 亳 4EB3 **10** 亴 4EB4 亵 4EB5 **11** 亶 4EB6 亷 4EB7 **14** 亸 4EB8 **15** 赢 8D62 **19** 亹 4EB9

人 (9) 人 4EBA 亻 4EBB **1** 亼 4EBC 亽 4EBD 亾 4EBE 亿 4EBF **2** 什 4EC0 仁 4EC1 仂 4EC2 仃 4EC3 仄 4EC4 仅 4EC5 仆 4EC6 仇 4EC7 仈 4EC8 仉 4EC9 今 4ECA 介 4ECB 仌 4ECC 仍 4ECD 从 4ECE

人 9 仏 4ECF 仐 4ED0 仑 4ED1 仒 4ED2 仓 4ED3 **3** 仔 4ED4 仕 4ED5 他 4ED6 仗 4ED7 付 4ED8 仙 4ED9 仚 4EDA 仛 4EDB 仜 4EDC 仝 4EDD 仞 4EDE 仟 4EDF 仠 4EE0 仡 4EE1 仢 4EE2 代 4EE3 令 4EE4

以 4EE5 仦 4EE6 仧 4EE7 仨 4EE8 仩 4EE9 仪 4EEA 仫 4EEB 们 4EEC 仭 4EED **4** 仮 4EEE 仯 4EEF 仰 4EF0 仱 4EF1 仲 4EF2 仳 4EF3 仴 4EF4 仵 4EF5 件 4EF6 价 4EF7 仸 4EF8 仹 4EF9 仺 4EFA

任 4EFB 仼 4EFC 份 4EFD 仾 4EFE 仿 4EFF 伀 4F00 企 4F01 伂 4F02 伃 4F03 伄 4F04 伅 4F05 伆 4F06 伇 4F07 伈 4F08 伉 4F09 伊 4F0A 伋 4F0B 伌 4F0C 伍 4F0D 伎 4F0E 伏 4F0F 伐 4F10 休 4F11

伒 4F12 伓 4F13 伔 4F14 伕 4F15 伖 4F16 众 4F17 优 4F18 伙 4F19 会 4F1A 伛 4F1B 伜 4F1C 伝 4F1D 伞 4F1E 伟 4F1F 传 4F20 伡 4F21 伢 4F22 伣 4F23 伤 4F24 伦 4F26 伧 4F27 伨 4F28 伩 4F29

伪 4F2A 伫 4F2B 伬 4F2C 全 5168 氽 6C3D **5** 伥 4F25 伭 4F2D 伮 4F2E 伯 4F2F 估 4F30 伱 4F31 伲 4F32 伳 4F33 伴 4F34 伵 4F35 伶 4F36 伷 4F37 伸 4F38 伹 4F39 伺 4F3A 伻 4F3B 似 4F3C

伽 4F3D 伾 4F3E 伿 4F3F 佀 4F40 佁 4F41 佂 4F42 佃 4F43 佄 4F44 佅 4F45 但 4F46 佇 4F47 佈 4F48 佉 4F49 佊 4F4A 佋 4F4B 佌 4F4C 位 4F4D 低 4F4E 住 4F4F 佐 4F50 佑 4F51 佒 4F52 体 4F53

佔 4F54 何 4F55 佖 4F56 佗 4F57 佘 4F58 余 4F59 佚 4F5A 佛 4F5B 作 4F5C 佝 4F5D 佞 4F5E 佟 4F5F 你 4F60 佡 4F61 佢 4F62 佣 4F63 佤 4F64 佥 4F65 佦 4F66 佧 4F67 佨 4F68 **6** 佩 4F69

佪 4F6A 佫 4F6B 佬 4F6C 佭 4F6D 佮 4F6E 佯 4F6F 佰 4F70 佱 4F71 佲 4F72 佳 4F73 佴 4F74 佶 4F76 佷 4F77 佸 4F78 佹 4F79 佺 4F7A 佻 4F7B 佼 4F7C 佽 4F7D 佾 4F7E 使 4F7F 侀 4F80 侁 4F81

侂 4F82 侃 4F83 侄 4F84 侅 4F85 來 4F86 侇 4F87 侈 4F88 侉 4F89 侊 4F8A 例 4F8B 侌 4F8C 侍 4F8D 侎 4F8E 侏 4F8F 侐 4F90 侑 4F91 侒 4F92 侓 4F93 侔 4F94 侕 4F95 侖 4F96 侗 4F97 侘 4F98

侙 4F99 侚 4F9A 供 4F9B 侜 4F9C 依 4F9D 侞 4F9E 侟 4F9F 侠 4FA0 価 4FA1 侢 4FA2 侣 4FA3 侤 4FA4 侥 4FA5 侦 4FA6 侧 4FA7 侨 4FA8 侩 4FA9 侪 4FAA 侫 4FAB 侬 4FAC 侭 4FAD **7** 侮 4FAE

侯 4FAF 侰 4FB0 侱 4FB1 侲 4FB2 侳 4FB3 侴 4FB4 侵 4FB5 侶 4FB6 侷 4FB7 侸 4FB8 侹 4FB9 侺 4FBA 侻 4FBB 侼 4FBC 侽 4FBD 侾 4FBE 便 4FBF 俀 4FC0 俁 4FC1 係 4FC2 促 4FC3 俄 4FC4 俅 4FC5

俆 4FC6 俇 4FC7 俈 4FC8 俉 4FC9 俊 4FCA 俋 4FCB 俌 4FCC 俍 4FCD 俎 4FCE 俏 4FCF 俐 4FD0 俑 4FD1 俒 4FD2 俓 4FD3 俔 4FD4 俕 4FD5 俖 4FD6 俗 4FD7 俘 4FD8 俙 4FD9 俚 4FDA 俛 4FDB 俜 4FDC

保 4FDD 俞 4FDE 俟 4FDF 俠 4FE0 信 4FE1 俢 4FE2 俣 4FE3 俤 4FE4 俥 4FE5 俦 4FE6 俧 4FE7 俨 4FE8 俩 4FE9 俪 4FEA 俫 4FEB 俬 4FEC 俭 4FED **8** 併 4F75 修 4FEE 俯 4FEF 俰 4FF0 俱 4FF1

俲 4FF2 俳 4FF3 俴 4FF4 俵 4FF5 俶 4FF6 俷 4FF7 俸 4FF8 俹 4FF9 俺 4FFA 俻 4FFB 俼 4FFC 俽 4FFD 俾 4FFE 俿 4FFF 倀 5000 倁 5001 倂 5002 倃 5003 倄 5004 倅 5005 倆 5006 倇 5007 倈 5008

倉 5009 倊 500A 個 500B 倌 500C 倍 500D 倎 500E 倏 500F 倐 5010 們 5011 倒 5012 倓 5013 倔 5014 倕 5015 倖 5016 倗 5017 倘 5018 候 5019 倚 501A 倛 501B 倜 501C 倝 501D 倞 501E 借 501F

倠 5020 倡 5021 倢 5022 倣 5023 値 5024 倥 5025 倦 5026 倧 5027 倨 5028 倩 5029 倪 502A 倫 502B 倬 502C 倭 502D 倮 502E 倯 502F 倰 5030 倱 5031 倲 5032 倳 5033 倴 5034 倵 5035 倶 5036

倷 5037 倸 5038 倹 5039 债 503A 值 503C 倽 503D 倾 503E 倿 503F **9** 倻 503B 偀 5040 偁 5041 偂 5042 偃 5043 偄 5044 偅 5045 偆 5046 假 5047 偈 5048 偉 5049 偊 504A 偋 504B 偌 504C

偍 504D 偎 504E 偏 504F 偐 5050 偑 5051 偒 5052 偓 5053 偔 5054 偕 5055 偖 5056 偗 5057 偘 5058 偙 5059 做 505A 偛 505B 停 505C 偝 505D 偞 505E 偟 505F 偠 5060 偡 5061 偢 5062 偣 5063

偤 5064 健 5065 偦 5066 偧 5067 偨 5068 偩 5069 偪 506A 偫 506B 偬 506C 偭 506D 偮 506E 偯 506F 偰 5070 偱 5071 偲 5072 偳 5073 側 5074 偵 5075 偶 5076 偷 5077 偸 5078 偹 5079 偺 507A

偻 507B 偼 507C 偽 507D 偾 507E 偿 507F **10** 傀 5080 傁 5081 傂 5082 傃 5083 傄 5084 傅 5085 傆 5086 傇 5087 傈 5088 傉 5089 傊 508A 傋 508B 傌 508C 傍 508D 傎 508E 傏 508F 傐 5090

傑 5091 傒 5092 傓 5093 傔 5094 傕 5095 傖 5096 傗 5097 傘 5098 備 5099 傚 509A 傛 509B 傜 509C 傝 509D 傞 509E 傟 509F 傠 50A0 傡 50A1 傢 50A2 傣 50A3 傥 50A5 傦 50A6 傧 50A7 储 50A8

傩 50A9 **11** 傪 50AA 傫 50AB 催 50AC 傭 50AD 傮 50AE 傯 50AF 傰 50B0 傱 50B1 傲 50B2 傳 50B3 傴 50B4 債 50B5 傶 50B6 傷 50B7 傸 50B8 傹 50B9 傺 50BA 傻 50BB 傼 50BC 傽 50BD 傾 50BE

傿 50BF 僀 50C0 僁 50C1 僂 50C2 僃 50C3 僄 50C4 僅 50C5 僆 50C6 僇 50C7 僈 50C8 僉 50C9 僊 50CA 僋 50CB 僌 50CC 働 50CD **12** 僎 50CE 像 50CF 僐 50D0 僑 50D1 僒 50D2 僓 50D3 僔 50D4

人 9 **12** 僎 50CE 像 50CF 僐 50D0 僑 50D1 僒 50D2 僓 50D3 僔 50D4 僕 50D5 僖 50D6 僗 50D7 僘 50D8 僙 50D9 僚 50DA 僛 50DB 僜 50DC 僝 50DD 僞 50DE 僟 50DF 僠 50E0 僡 50E1 僢 50E2 僣 50E3
僤 50E4 僥 50E5 僦 50E6 僧 50E7 僨 50E8 僩 50E9 僪 50EA 僫 50EB 僬 50EC 僭 50ED 僮 50EE 僯 50EF 僰 50F0 僱 50F1 僳 50F3 僴 50F4 儰 5130 **13** 傤 50A4 僲 50F2 僵 50F5 僶 50F6 僷 50F7
僸 50F8 價 50F9 僺 50FA 僻 50FB 僼 50FC 僽 50FD 僾 50FE 僿 50FF 儀 5100 儁 5101 儂 5102 儃 5103 億 5104 儅 5105 儆 5106 儇 5107 儈 5108 儉 5109 儊 510A 儋 510B 儌 510C 儍 510D 儎 510E
儏 510F **14** 儐 5110 儑 5111 儒 5112 儓 5113 儔 5114 儕 5115 儖 5116 儗 5117 儘 5118 儙 5119 儚 511A 儛 511B 儜 511C 儝 511D 儞 511E **15** 償 511F 儠 5120 儡 5121 儢 5122 儣 5123
儤 5124 儥 5125 儦 5126 儧 5127 儨 5128 儩 5129 優 512A 儫 512B 儬 512C **16** 儭 512D 儮 512E 儯 512F 儱 5131 儲 5132 **17** 儳 5133 儴 5134 儵 5135 **18** 儶 5136 **19** 儷 5137
儸 5138 儹 5139 儺 513A **20** 儻 513B 儼 513C **21** 儽 513D **22** 儾 513E

儿 10 儿 513F **1** 兀 5140 **2** 允 5141 兂 5142 元 5143 **3** 兄 5144 充 5145 **4** 兆 5146 兇 5147 先 5148 光 5149 兊 514A **5** 克 514B 兌 514C 兎 514E 兏 514F 児 5150 兑 5151
6 免 514D 兒 5152 兓 5153 兔 5154 兕 5155 兖 5156 **7** 兗 5157 兘 5158 兙 5159 **8** 党 515A 兛 515B **9** 兜 515C 兝 515D 兞 515E **10** 兟 515F **11** 兡 5161
12 兢 5162 **14** 兣 5163 **19** 兤 5164

入 11 入 5165 **1** 兦 5166 **2** 內 5167 **6** 兩 5169 **7** 兪 516A

八 12 八 516B **2** 公 516C 六 516D 兮 516E **3** 兰 5170 **4** 共 5171 兲 5172 关 5173 兴 5174 **5** 兵 5175 **6** 其 5176 具 5177 典 5178 **7** 养 517B **8** 兺 517A 兼 517C
9 兽 517D **11** 兾 517E **14** 冀 5180 **16** 冁 5181

冂 13 冂 5182 **2** 冃 5183 冄 5184 内 5185 円 5186 冇 5187 冈 5188 **3** 冉 5189 冊 518A 冋 518B 册 518C **4** 再 518D 冎 518E **5** 冏 518F **6** 冐 5190 **7** 冑 5191 冒 5192
8 冓 5193 冔 5194 **9** 冕 5195

冖 14 冖 5196 **2** 冗 5197 冘 5198 **3** 写 5199 冚 519A **4** 农 519C **5** 冝 519D **6** 冞 519E **7** 冟 519F 冠 51A0 **8** 冡 51A1 冢 51A2 冣 51A3 冤 51A4 冥 51A5 冦 51A6
冧 51A7 **9** 冨 51A8 **12** 冩 51A9 **14** 冪 51AA

冫 15 冫 51AB **3** 冬 51AC 冭 51AD 冮 51AE **4** 冰 51B0 冱 51B1 冲 51B2 决 51B3 冴 51B4 **5** 况 51B5 冶 51B6 冷 51B7 冸 51B8 冹 51B9 冺 51BA 冻 51BB **6** 冼 51BC 冽 51BD 冾 51BE

冫 15 冿 51BF 净 51C0 **7** 凁 51C1 凂 51C2 凃 51C3 **8** 凄 51C4 凅 51C5 准 51C6 凇 51C7 凈 51C8 凉 51C9 凊 51CA 凋 51CB 凌 51CC 凍 51CD 凎 51CE **9** 减 51CF 凐 51D0 凑 51D1
10 凒 51D2 凓 51D3 凔 51D4 凕 51D5 凖 51D6 **11** 凗 51D7 **12** 凘 51D8 **13** 凙 51D9 凚 51DA 凛 51DB 凜 51DC **14** 凝 51DD 凞 51DE **15** 凟 51DF

几 16 几 51E0 **1** 凣 51E3 **2** 凤 51E4 **3** 凥 51E5 凧 51E7 **4** 凨 51E8 凩 51E9 凪 51EA 凫 51EB **6** 凭 51ED 凮 51EE 凯 51EF **9** 凰 51F0 **10** 兠 5160 凱 51F1 凲 51F2
12 凳 51F3 凴 51F4

凵 17 凵 51F5 **2** 凶 51F6 **3** 凷 51F7 凸 51F8 凹 51F9 出 51FA 击 51FB **6** 函 51FD **7** 凾 51FE **10** 凿 51FF

刀 18 刀 5200 刁 5201 刂 5202 **1** 刃 5203 刄 5204 **2** 刅 5205 分 5206 切 5207 刈 5208 **3** 刉 5209 刊 520A 刋 520B 刌 520C **4** 刎 520E 刏 520F 刐 5210 刑 5211 划 5212 刓 5213
刔 5214 刕 5215 刖 5216 列 5217 刘 5218 则 5219 刚 521A 创 521B **5** 刜 521C 初 521D 刞 521E 刟 521F 删 5220 刡 5221 刢 5222 刣 5223 判 5224 別 5225 刦 5226 刧 5227 刨 5228 利 5229
刪 522A 别 522B 刬 522C 刭 522D **6** 刮 522E 刯 522F 到 5230 刱 5231 刲 5232 刳 5233 刴 5234 刵 5235 制 5236 刷 5237 券 5238 刹 5239 刺 523A 刻 523B 刼 523C 刽 523D 刾 523E 刿 523F
剀 5240 剁 5241 剂 5242 **7** 剃 5243 剄 5244 剅 5245 剆 5246 則 5247 剈 5248 剉 5249 削 524A 剋 524B 剌 524C 前 524D 剎 524E 剏 524F 剐 5250 剑 5251 **8** 剒 5252 剓 5253 剔 5254
剕 5255 剖 5256 剗 5257 剘 5258 剙 5259 剚 525A 剛 525B 剜 525C 剝 525D 剞 525E 剟 525F 剠 5260 剡 5261 剢 5262 剣 5263 剤 5264 剥 5265 剦 5266 剧 5267 荆 8346 **9** 剨 5268 剪 526A
剫 526B 剬 526C 剭 526D 剮 526E 副 526F 剰 5270 剱 5271 剶 5276 **10** 剩 5269 割 5272 剳 5273 剴 5274 創 5275 **11** 剷 5277 剸 5278 剹 5279 剺 527A 剻 527B 剼 527C 剽 527D 剾 527E
12 劀 5280 劁 5281 劂 5282 劃 5283 劄 5284 **13** 劅 5285 劆 5286 劇 5287 劈 5288 劉 5289 劊 528A 劋 528B 劌 528C 劍 528D 劎 528E 劏 528F **14** 剿 527F 劐 5290 劑 5291 劒 5292
劓 5293 劔 5294 辧 8FA7 **15** 劕 5295 **17** 劖 5296 **19** 劗 5297 劘 5298 **21** 劙 5299 劚 529A

力 19 力 529B **1** 劜 529C **2** 劝 529D 办 529E **3** 功 529F 加 52A0 劢 52A2 **4** 劣 52A3 劤 52A4 劥 52A5 劦 52A6 劧 52A7 动 52A8 **5** 助 52A9 努 52AA 劫 52AB 劬 52AC 劭 52AD
劮 52AE 劯 52AF 劰 52B0 励 52B1 劲 52B2 劳 52B3 労 52B4 **6** 劵 52B5 劶 52B6 劷 52B7 劸 52B8 効 52B9 劺 52BA 劻 52BB 劼 52BC 劽 52BD 劾 52BE 势 52BF **7** 勀 52C0 勁 52C1 勂 52C2
勃 52C3 勄 52C4 勅 52C5 勆 52C6 勇 52C7 勈 52C8 勉 52C9 勊 52CA 勋 52CB **8** 勌 52CC 勍 52CD 勎 52CE 勏 52CF 勐 52D0 勑 52D1 **9** 勒 52D2 勓 52D3 勔 52D4 動 52D5 勖 52D6 勗 52D7
勘 52D8 務 52D9 勚 52DA **10** 勛 52DB 勜 52DC 勝 52DD 勞 52DE **11** 募 52DF 勠 52E0 勡 52E1 勢 52E2 勣 52E3 勤 52E4 勥 52E5 勦 52E6 勧 52E7 **12** 勨 52E8 勩 52E9 勪 52EA 勫 52EB
勬 52EC 勭 52ED **13** 勮 52EE 勯 52EF 勰 52F0 勱 52F1 **14** 勳 52F3 **15** 勴 52F4 勵 52F5 勶 52F6 **17** 勷 52F7 **18** 勸 52F8

勹 20 | 勹 52F9 | **1** 勺 52FA | **2** 勻 52FB 勼 52FC 勽 52FD 勾 52FE 勿 52FF 匀 5300 匁 5301 匂 5302 | **3** 匃 5303 匄 5304 包 5305 匆 5306 匇 5307 | **4** 匈 5308 | **5** 匉 5309
6 匊 530A 匋 530B 匌 530C | **7** 匍 530D 甮 752E | **8** 匎 530E | **9** 匏 530F 匐 5310 | **10** 匑 5311 匒 5312 | **11** 匓 5313 | **13** 匔 5314

匕 21 | 匕 5315 | **2** 化 5316 | **3** 北 5317 | **9** 匘 5318 匙 5319 莻 83BB | **11** 蒊 848A

匚 22 | 匚 531A | **3** 匛 531B 匜 531C 匝 531D 匞 531E | **4** 匟 531F 匠 5320 匡 5321 匢 5322 | **5** 匣 5323 匤 5324 匥 5325 | **6** 匦 5326 | **7** 匧 5327 匨 5328 匩 5329 | **8** 匪 532A
匫 532B | **9** 匬 532C 匭 532D 匮 532E | **11** 匯 532F | **12** 匰 5330 匱 5331 匲 5332 | **13** 匳 5333 赜 8D5C | **14** 匴 5334 | **15** 匵 5335 | **18** 匶 5336 匷 5337

匸 23 | 匸 5338 | **2** 匹 5339 区 533A | **5** 医 533B | **6** 匼 533C | **7** 匽 533D | **9** 匾 533E 匿 533F 區 5340

十 24 | 十 5341 | **1** 卂 5342 千 5343 卄 5344 | **2** 卅 5345 卆 5346 升 5347 午 5348 | **3** 卉 5349 半 534A | **4** 卋 534B 卌 534C 卍 534D 华 534E 协 534F 卐 5350 | **6** 丧 4E27 卑 5351
卒 5352 卓 5353 協 5354 单 5355 卖 5356 | **7** 南 5357 | **9** 卙 5359 | **10** 博 535A | **19** 卛 535B 颦 98A6

卜 25 | 卜 535C | **2** 卝 535D 卞 535E | **3** 占 5360 卡 5361 卢 5362 | **4** 贞 8D1E | **5** 卣 5363 卤 5364 | **6** 卥 5365 卦 5366 卧 5367 | **9** 卨 5368

卩 26 | 卩 5369 | **1** 卪 536A | **2** 兯 516F 卬 536C | **3** 卭 536D 卮 536E 卯 536F | **4** 印 5370 危 5371 | **5** 卲 5372 即 5373 却 5374 卵 5375 | **6** 卶 5376 卷 5377 卹 5379 卺 537A
7 卸 5378 卻 537B 卼 537C 卽 537D | **9** 卾 537E 卿 537F | **11** 厀 5380 厁 5381

厂 27 | 厂 5382 | **2** 厃 5383 厄 5384 厅 5385 历 5386 | **3** 厇 5387 厈 5388 厉 5389 | **4** 厊 538A 压 538B 厌 538C 厍 538D 质 8D28 | **5** 厎 538E 厏 538F 厐 5390 厑 5391 | **6** 厒 5392
厓 5393 厔 5394 厕 5395 | **7** 厖 5396 厗 5397 厘 5398 厙 5399 厚 539A 厛 539B | **8** 厜 539C 厝 539D 厞 539E 原 539F | **9** 厠 53A0 厡 53A1 厢 53A2 厣 53A3 厩 53A9 | **10** 厤 53A4
厥 53A5 厦 53A6 厧 53A7 厨 53A8 | **11** 厪 53AA 厫 53AB | **12** 厬 53AC 厭 53AD 厮 53AE 厰 53B0 | **13** 厱 53B1 厲 53B2 靥 9765 | **14** 赝 8D5D | **15** 厳 53B3 | **17** 厴 53B4
28 厵 53B5

厶 28 厶 53B6 **2** 厷 53B7 厸 53B8 厹 53B9 **3** 厺 53BA 去 53BB **4** 厽 53BD **5** 县 53BF **6** 叀 53C0 叁 53C1 参 53C2 **9** 參 53C3 叄 53C4 **10** 叅 53C5 **11** 兿 517F
12 叆 53C6 **13** 叇 53C7

又 29 又 53C8 **1** 叉 53C9 **2** 及 53CA 友 53CB 双 53CC 反 53CD 収 53CE **3** 叏 53CF 叐 53D0 发 53D1 **4** 叒 53D2 **5** 叓 53D3 **6** 叔 53D4 叕 53D5 取 53D6 受 53D7 变 53D8
艰 8270 **7** 叙 53D9 叚 53DA 叛 53DB 叜 53DC 叝 53DD **8** 叞 53DE 叟 53DF 难 96BE **11** 叠 53E0 **14** 叡 53E1 **16** 叢 53E2

口 30 口 53E3 **2** 卟 535F 古 53E4 句 53E5 另 53E6 叧 53E7 叨 53E8 叩 53E9 只 53EA 叫 53EB 召 53EC 叭 53ED 叮 53EE 可 53EF 台 53F0 叱 53F1 史 53F2 右 53F3 叴 53F4 叵 53F5 叶 53F6 号 53F7
司 53F8 叹 53F9 叺 53FA 叻 53FB 叼 53FC 叽 53FD 叾 53FE **3** 叿 53FF 吀 5400 吁 5401 吂 5402 吃 5403 各 5404 吅 5405 吆 5406 吇 5407 合 5408 吉 5409 吊 540A 吋 540B 同 540C 名 540D
后 540E 吏 540F 吐 5410 向 5411 吒 5412 吓 5413 吔 5414 吕 5415 吖 5416 吗 5417 **4** 吘 5418 吙 5419 吚 541A 君 541B 吜 541C 吝 541D 吞 541E 吟 541F 吠 5420 吡 5421 吢 5422 吣 5423
吤 5424 吥 5425 否 5426 吧 5427 吨 5428 吩 5429 吪 542A 含 542B 听 542C 吭 542D 吮 542E 启 542F 吰 5430 吱 5431 吲 5432 吳 5433 吴 5434 吵 5435 吶 5436 吷 5437 吸 5438 吹 5439 吺 543A
吻 543B 吼 543C 吽 543D 吾 543E 吿 543F 呀 5440 呁 5441 呂 5442 呃 5443 呄 5444 呅 5445 呆 5446 呇 5447 呈 5448 呉 5449 告 544A 呋 544B 呌 544C 呍 544D 呎 544E 呏 544F 呐 5450 呑 5451
呒 5452 呓 5453 呔 5454 呕 5455 呖 5456 呗 5457 员 5458 呙 5459 呚 545A 呛 545B 呜 545C **5** 呝 545D 呞 545E 呟 545F 呠 5460 呡 5461 呢 5462 呣 5463 呤 5464 呥 5465 呦 5466 呧 5467
周 5468 呩 5469 呪 546A 呫 546B 呬 546C 呭 546D 呮 546E 呯 546F 呰 5470 呱 5471 呲 5472 味 5473 呴 5474 呵 5475 呶 5476 呷 5477 呸 5478 呹 5479 呺 547A 呻 547B 呼 547C 命 547D 呾 547E
呿 547F 咀 5480 咁 5481 咂 5482 咃 5483 咄 5484 咅 5485 咆 5486 咇 5487 咈 5488 咉 5489 咊 548A 咋 548B 和 548C 咍 548D 咎 548E 咏 548F 咐 5490 咑 5491 咒 5492 咓 5493 咔 5494 咕 5495
咖 5496 咗 5497 咘 5498 咙 5499 咚 549A 咛 549B 咜 549C 咝 549D 鸣 9E23 **6** 咞 549E 咟 549F 咠 54A0 咡 54A1 咢 54A2 咣 54A3 咤 54A4 咥 54A5 咦 54A6 咧 54A7 咨 54A8 咩 54A9 咪 54AA
咫 54AB 咬 54AC 咭 54AD 咮 54AE 咯 54AF 咰 54B0 咱 54B1 咲 54B2 咳 54B3 咴 54B4 咵 54B5 咶 54B6 咷 54B7 咸 54B8 咹 54B9 咺 54BA 咻 54BB 咼 54BC 咽 54BD 咾 54BE 咿 54BF 哀 54C0 品 54C1
哂 54C2 哃 54C3 哄 54C4 哅 54C5 哆 54C6 哇 54C7 哈 54C8 哉 54C9 哊 54CA 哋 54CB 哌 54CC 响 54CD 哎 54CE 哏 54CF 哐 54D0 哑 54D1 哒 54D2 哓 54D3 哔 54D4 哕 54D5 哖 54D6 哗 54D7 哘 54D8
哙 54D9 哚 54DA 哛 54DB 哜 54DC 哝 54DD 哞 54DE 哟 54DF 器 5668 骂 9A82 **7** 哠 54E0 員 54E1 哢 54E2 哣 54E3 哤 54E4 哥 54E5 哦 54E6 哧 54E7 哨 54E8 哩 54E9 哪 54EA 哫 54EB 哬 54EC
哭 54ED 哮 54EE 哯 54EF 哰 54F0 哱 54F1 哲 54F2 哳 54F3 哴 54F4 哵 54F5 哶 54F6 哷 54F7 哸 54F8 哹 54F9 哺 54FA 哻 54FB 哼 54FC 哽 54FD 哾 54FE 哿 54FF 唀 5500 唁 5501 唂 5502 唃 5503
唄 5504 唅 5505 唆 5506 唇 5507 唈 5508 唉 5509 唊 550A 唋 550B 唌 550C 唍 550D 唎 550E 唏 550F 唐 5510 唑 5511 唒 5512 唓 5513 唔 5514 唕 5515 唖 5516 唗 5517 唘 5518 唙 5519 唚 551A
唛 551B 唝 551D 唞 551E 唟 551F 唠 5520 唡 5521 唢 5522 唣 5523 唤 5524 唥 5525 唦 5526 唧 5527 **8** 唨 5528 唩 5529 唪 552A 唫 552B 唬 552C 唭 552D 售 552E 唯 552F 唰 5530 唱 5531
唲 5532 唳 5533 唴 5534 唵 5535 唶 5536 唷 5537 唸 5538 唹 5539 唺 553A 唻 553B 唼 553C 唽 553D 唾 553E 唿 553F 啀 5540 啁 5541 啂 5542 啃 5543 啄 5544 啅 5545 商 5546 啇 5547 啈 5548
啉 5549 啊 554A 啋 554B 啌 554C 啍 554D 啎 554E 問 554F 啐 5550 啑 5551 啒 5552 啓 5553 啔 5554 啕 5555 啖 5556 啗 5557 啘 5558 啚 555A 啛 555B 啜 555C 啝 555D 啞 555E 啠 5560 啡 5561

口 30 啜 555C 啝 555D 啞 555E 啠 5560 啡 5561 啢 5562 啣 5563 啤 5564 啥 5565 啦 5566 啧 5567 啨 5568 啩 5569 啪 556A 啬 556C 啭 556D 啮 556E 啯 556F 啰 5570 啱 5571 啲 5572 啳 5573 啴 5574

啵 5575 啶 5576 啷 5577 啸 5578 啹 5579 **9** 啙 5559 啫 556B 啺 557A 啻 557B 啼 557C 啽 557D 啾 557E 啿 557F 喀 5580 喁 5581 喂 5582 喃 5583 善 5584 喅 5585 喆 5586 喇 5587 喈 5588

喉 5589 喊 558A 喋 558B 喌 558C 喍 558D 喎 558E 喏 558F 喐 5590 喑 5591 喒 5592 喓 5593 喔 5594 喕 5595 喖 5596 喗 5597 喘 5598 喙 5599 喚 559A 喛 559B 喜 559C 喞 559E 喟 559F 喠 55A0

喡 55A1 喢 55A2 喣 55A3 喤 55A4 喥 55A5 喦 55A6 喧 55A7 喨 55A8 喩 55A9 喪 55AA 喫 55AB 喬 55AC 喭 55AD 單 55AE 喯 55AF 喰 55B0 喱 55B1 喲 55B2 喳 55B3 喴 55B4 喵 55B5 喷 55B7 喸 55B8

喹 55B9 喺 55BA 喻 55BB 喼 55BC 喽 55BD 喾 55BE 噅 5645 **10** 喿 55BF 嗀 55C0 嗁 55C1 嗂 55C2 嗃 55C3 嗄 55C4 嗅 55C5 嗆 55C6 嗇 55C7 嗈 55C8 嗉 55C9 嗊 55CA 嗋 55CB 嗌 55CC 嗍 55CD

嗎 55CE 嗏 55CF 嗐 55D0 嗑 55D1 嗒 55D2 嗓 55D3 嗔 55D4 嗕 55D5 嗖 55D6 嗗 55D7 嗘 55D8 嗙 55D9 嗚 55DA 嗛 55DB 嗜 55DC 嗝 55DD 嗞 55DE 嗟 55DF 嗠 55E0 嗡 55E1 嗢 55E2 嗣 55E3 嗤 55E4

嗥 55E5 嗦 55E6 嗧 55E7 嗨 55E8 嗩 55E9 嗪 55EA 嗫 55EB 嗬 55EC 嗭 55ED 嗮 55EE 嗯 55EF 嗰 55F0 嗱 55F1 嗲 55F2 嗳 55F3 嗴 55F4 嗵 55F5 辔 8F94 **11** 嗶 55F6 嗷 55F7 嗸 55F8 嗹 55F9

嗺 55FA 嗻 55FB 嗼 55FC 嗽 55FD 嗾 55FE 嗿 55FF 嘀 5600 嘁 5601 嘂 5602 嘃 5603 嘄 5604 嘅 5605 嘆 5606 嘇 5607 嘈 5608 嘉 5609 嘊 560A 嘋 560B 嘌 560C 嘍 560D 嘎 560E 嘏 560F 嘐 5610

嘑 5611 嘒 5612 嘓 5613 嘔 5614 嘕 5615 嘖 5616 嘗 5617 嘘 5618 嘙 5619 嘚 561A 嘛 561B 嘜 561C 嘝 561D 嘞 561E 嘡 5621 嘢 5622 嘣 5623 嘤 5624 嘥 5625 嘧 5627 噑 5651 噓 5653

12 嘟 561F 嘠 5620 嘨 5628 嘩 5629 嘪 562A 嘫 562B 嘬 562C 嘭 562D 嘮 562E 嘯 562F 嘰 5630 嘱 5631 嘲 5632 嘳 5633 嘴 5634 嘵 5635 嘶 5636 嘷 5637 嘸 5638 嘹 5639 嘺 563A 嘻 563B

嘼 563C 嘽 563D 嘾 563E 嘿 563F 噀 5640 噁 5641 噂 5642 噃 5643 噄 5644 噆 5646 噇 5647 噈 5648 噉 5649 噊 564A 噋 564B 噌 564C 噍 564D 噎 564E 噏 564F 噐 5650 噒 5652 噔 5654 噖 5656

噗 5657 噘 5658 噙 5659 噚 565A 噛 565B 噜 565C 噝 565D 噴 5674 **13** 噞 565E 噟 565F 噠 5660 噡 5661 噢 5662 噣 5663 噤 5664 噥 5665 噦 5666 噧 5667 噩 5669 噪 566A 噫 566B 噬 566C

噭 566D 噮 566E 噯 566F 噰 5670 噱 5671 噲 5672 噳 5673 噵 5675 噶 5676 噷 5677 噸 5678 噹 5679 噺 567A 噻 567B 噼 567C 駡 99E1 **14** 噽 567D 噾 567E 噿 567F 嚀 5680 嚁 5681 嚂 5682

嚃 5683 嚄 5684 嚅 5685 嚆 5686 嚇 5687 嚈 5688 嚉 5689 嚊 568A 嚋 568B 嚌 568C 嚍 568D 嚎 568E 嚏 568F 嚐 5690 嚑 5691 嚒 5692 嚓 5693 嚺 56BA **15** 嚔 5694 嚕 5695 嚖 5696 嚗 5697

嚘 5698 嚙 5699 嚚 569A 嚛 569B 嚜 569C 嚝 569D 嚞 569E 嚟 569F 嚠 56A0 嚡 56A1 嚢 56A2 嚣 56A3 嚤 56A4 **16** 嚥 56A5 嚦 56A6 嚧 56A7 嚨 56A8 嚩 56A9 嚪 56AA 嚫 56AB 嚬 56AC 嚭 56AD

嚮 56AE 嚯 56AF 嚰 56B0 **17** 嚱 56B1 嚲 56B2 嚳 56B3 嚴 56B4 嚵 56B5 嚶 56B6 嚷 56B7 嚸 56B8 嚹 56B9 **18** 嚻 56BB 嚼 56BC 嚽 56BD 嚾 56BE 嚿 56BF 囀 56C0 囁 56C1 囂 56C2 囃 56C3

囄 56C4 囍 56CD **19** 囅 56C5 囆 56C6 囇 56C7 囈 56C8 囉 56C9 囊 56CA 囋 56CB 囎 56CE **20** 囌 56CC 囏 56CF 囐 56D0 **21** 囑 56D1 囒 56D2 囓 56D3 **22** 囔 56D4 囕 56D5

25 囖 56D6

囗 31 囗 56D7 **2** 囘 56D8 囙 56D9 囚 56DA 四 56DB 囜 56DC **3** 囝 56DD 回 56DE 囟 56DF 因 56E0 囡 56E1 团 56E2 団 56E3 **4** 囤 56E4 囥 56E5 囦 56E6 囧 56E7 囨 56E8 囩 56E9 囪 56EA

囫 56EB 囬 56EC 园 56ED 囮 56EE 囯 56EF 困 56F0 囱 56F1 囲 56F2 図 56F3 围 56F4 囵 56F5 **5** 囶 56F6 囷 56F7 囸 56F8 囹 56F9 固 56FA 囻 56FB 囼 56FC 国 56FD 图 56FE **6** 囿 56FF

圀 5700 **7** 圁 5701 圂 5702 圃 5703 圄 5704 圅 5705 圆 5706 **8** 圇 5707 圈 5708 圉 5709 圊 570A 國 570B 圏 570F **9** 圌 570C 圍 570D 圎 570E 圐 5710 **10** 圑 5711 園 5712

圓 5713 圔 5714 圕 5715 **11** 圖 5716 圗 5717 團 5718 圙 5719 **12** 圚 571A **13** 圛 571B 圜 571C **19** 圝 571D **23** 圞 571E

土 32 土 571F **1** 圠 5720 圡 5721 **2** 圢 5722 圣 5723 圤 5724 圥 5725 圦 5726 圧 5727 **3** 在 5728 圩 5729 圪 572A 圫 572B 圬 572C 圭 572D 圮 572E 圯 572F 地 5730 圱 5731 圲 5732
圳 5733 圴 5734 圵 5735 圶 5736 圷 5737 圸 5738 圹 5739 场 573A **4** 圻 573B 圼 573C 圽 573D 圾 573E 圿 573F 址 5740 坁 5741 坂 5742 坃 5743 坄 5744 坅 5745 坆 5746 均 5747 坈 5748
坉 5749 坊 574A 坋 574B 坌 574C 坍 574D 坎 574E 坏 574F 坐 5750 坑 5751 坒 5752 坓 5753 坔 5754 坕 5755 坖 5756 块 5757 坘 5758 坙 5759 坚 575A 坛 575B 坜 575C 坝 575D 坞 575E 坟 575F
坠 5760 **5** 坡 5761 坢 5762 坣 5763 坤 5764 坥 5765 坦 5766 坧 5767 坨 5768 坩 5769 坪 576A 坫 576B 坬 576C 坭 576D 坮 576E 坯 576F 坰 5770 坱 5771 坲 5772 坳 5773 坴 5774 坵 5775
坶 5776 坷 5777 坸 5778 坹 5779 坺 577A 坻 577B 坼 577C 坽 577D 坾 577E 坿 577F 垀 5780 垁 5781 垂 5782 垃 5783 垄 5784 垅 5785 垆 5786 垇 5787 垈 5788 垉 5789 垊 578A **6** 型 578B
垌 578C 垍 578D 垎 578E 垏 578F 垐 5790 垑 5791 垒 5792 垓 5793 垔 5794 垕 5795 垖 5796 垗 5797 垘 5798 垙 5799 垚 579A 垛 579B 垜 579C 垝 579D 垞 579E 垟 579F 垠 57A0 垡 57A1 垢 57A2
垣 57A3 垤 57A4 垥 57A5 垦 57A6 垧 57A7 垨 57A8 垩 57A9 垪 57AA 垫 57AB 垬 57AC 垭 57AD 垮 57AE 垯 57AF 垰 57B0 垱 57B1 垲 57B2 垳 57B3 垴 57B4 垵 57B5 **7** 垶 57B6 垷 57B7 垸 57B8
垹 57B9 垺 57BA 垻 57BB 垼 57BC 垽 57BD 垾 57BE 垿 57BF 埀 57C0 埁 57C1 埂 57C2 埃 57C3 埄 57C4 埅 57C5 埆 57C6 埇 57C7 埈 57C8 埉 57C9 埋 57CB 埌 57CC 埍 57CD 城 57CE 埏 57CF 埐 57D0
埑 57D1 埒 57D2 埓 57D3 埔 57D4 埕 57D5 埖 57D6 埗 57D7 埘 57D8 埙 57D9 埚 57DA 埛 57DB **8** 埜 57DC 埝 57DD 埞 57DE 域 57DF 埠 57E0 埡 57E1 埢 57E2 埣 57E3 埤 57E4 埥 57E5 埦 57E6
埧 57E7 埨 57E8 埩 57E9 埫 57EB 埬 57EC 埭 57ED 埮 57EE 埯 57EF 埰 57F0 埱 57F1 埲 57F2 埳 57F3 埴 57F4 埵 57F5 埶 57F6 執 57F7 埸 57F8 培 57F9 基 57FA 埻 57FB 埼 57FC 埽 57FD 埾 57FE
埿 57FF 堀 5800 堁 5801 堂 5802 堃 5803 堄 5804 堅 5805 堆 5806 堇 5807 堈 5808 堉 5809 堊 580A 堋 580B 堌 580C 堍 580D 堎 580E 堏 580F 堐 5810 堑 5811 堒 5812 堓 5813 堔 5814
9 埪 57EA 堕 5815 堖 5816 堗 5817 堘 5818 堙 5819 堚 581A 堛 581B 堜 581C 堝 581D 堞 581E 堟 581F 堠 5820 堡 5821 堢 5822 堣 5823 堤 5824 堥 5825 堦 5826 堧 5827 堨 5828 堩 5829
堪 582A 堫 582B 堬 582C 堭 582D 堮 582E 堯 582F 堰 5830 報 5831 堲 5832 堳 5833 場 5834 堵 5835 堶 5836 堷 5837 堸 5838 堹 5839 堺 583A 堻 583B 堼 583C 堽 583D 堾 583E 堿 583F 塀 5840
塁 5841 塂 5842 塄 5844 塅 5845 塆 5846 塇 5847 塈 5848 塚 585A **10** 塃 5843 塉 5849 塊 584A 塋 584B 塌 584C 塍 584D 塎 584E 塏 584F 塐 5850 塑 5851 塒 5852 塓 5853 塔 5854 塕 5855
塖 5856 塗 5857 塘 5858 塙 5859 塛 585B 塜 585C 塝 585D 塞 585E 塟 585F 塠 5860 塡 5861 塢 5862 塣 5863 塤 5864 塥 5865 塦 5866 塧 5867 塨 5868 塩 5869 塪 586A 填 586B 塬 586C 塭 586D
塮 586E 塯 586F 塰 5870 塱 5871 **11** 塲 5872 塳 5873 塴 5874 塵 5875 塶 5876 塷 5877 塸 5878 塹 5879 塺 587A 塻 587B 塼 587C 塽 587D 塾 587E 塿 587F 墀 5880 墁 5881 墂 5882 境 5883
墄 5884 墅 5885 墆 5886 墇 5887 墈 5888 墉 5889 墊 588A 墋 588B 墌 588C 墍 588D 墎 588E 墏 588F 墐 5890 墑 5891 墒 5892 墓 5893 墔 5894 墕 5895 墖 5896 増 5897 墘 5898 墙 5899 墚 589A
墛 589B **12** 墜 589C 墝 589D 增 589E 墟 589F 墠 58A0 墡 58A1 墢 58A2 墣 58A3 墤 58A4 墥 58A5 墦 58A6 墧 58A7 墨 58A8 墩 58A9 墪 58AA 墫 58AB 墬 58AC 墭 58AD 墮 58AE 墯 58AF 墰 58B0
墱 58B1 墲 58B2 墳 58B3 墴 58B4 墵 58B5 墶 58B6 墷 58B7 墸 58B8 墹 58B9 **13** 墺 58BA 墻 58BB 墼 58BC 墽 58BD 墾 58BE 墿 58BF 壀 58C0 壁 58C1 壂 58C2 壃 58C3 壄 58C4 壅 58C5 壆 58C6
壇 58C7 壈 58C8 壉 58C9 壊 58CA 壋 58CB 壌 58CC **14** 壍 58CD 壎 58CE 壏 58CF 壐 58D0 壑 58D1 壒 58D2 壓 58D3 壔 58D4 壕 58D5 壖 58D6 壗 58D7 **15** 壘 58D8 壙 58D9 **16** 壚 58DA
壛 58DB 壜 58DC 壝 58DD 壞 58DE 壟 58DF 壠 58E0 壡 58E1 壢 58E2 **17** 壣 58E3 壤 58E4 壥 58E5 **18** 壦 58E6 **20** 壧 58E7 壨 58E8 **21** 壩 58E9 **22** 壪 58EA

士 33 士 58EB **1** 壬 58EC **2** 壭 58ED **3** 壮 58EE **4** 壯 58EF 声 58F0 壱 58F1 売 58F2 **5** 壳 58F3 **6** 壴 58F4 壵 58F5 **7** 壶 58F6 **8** 壷 58F7 壸 58F8

士 33 **9** 壹 58F9 壺 58FA 壻 58FB **10** 壼 58FC **11** 壽 58FD 壾 58FE **12** 壿 58FF 夀 5900 **13** 夁 5901

夂 34 夂 5902 **1** 夃 5903 **2** 処 51E6 务 52A1 处 5904 **3** 夅 5905 **4** 夆 5906 **5** 备 5907 **6** 夈 5908

夊 35 夊 590A **4** 夋 590B **5** 夌 590C **6** 変 5909 复 590D **7** 夎 590E 夏 590F **11** 夐 5910 **15** 夓 5913 **16** 夒 5912 **19** 夔 5914

夕 36 夕 5915 **2** 外 5916 夗 5917 夘 5918 **3** 夙 5919 多 591A 夛 591B **5** 夜 591C 夝 591D **7** 夞 591E **8** 够 591F 夠 5920 **9** 夡 5921 **11** 夢 5922 夣 5923 夤 5924 夥 5925 **12** 夦 5926

大 37 大 5927 夨 5928 **1** 天 5929 太 592A 夫 592B 夬 592C 夭 592D **2** 央 592E 夯 592F 夰 5930 失 5931 夲 5932 夳 5933 头 5934 **3** 夵 5935 夶 5936 夷 5937 夸 5938 夹 5939 夺 593A 夻 593B 夼 593C **4** 夽 593D 夾 593E 夿 593F 奀 5940 奁 5941 奂 5942 **5** 奃 5943 奄 5944 奅 5945 奆 5946 奇 5947 奈 5948 奉 5949 奋 594B 奌 594C 奍 594D **6** 奎 594E 奏 594F 奐 5950 契 5951 奒 5952 奓 5953 奔 5954 奕 5955 奖 5956 类 7C7B **7** 奊 594A 套 5957 奘 5958 奙 5959 奚 595A **8** 奛 595B 奜 595C 奝 595D 奞 595E **9** 奟 595F 奠 5960 奡 5961 奢 5962 奣 5963 奤 5964 奥 5965 **10** 奦 5966 奧 5967 奨 5968 **11** 奩 5969 奪 596A 奫 596B 奬 596C **12** 奭 596D **13** 奮 596E 奯 596F **15** 奰 5970 **19** 奱 5971 **21** 奲 5972

女 38 女 5973 **2** 奴 5974 奵 5975 奶 5976 **3** 奷 5977 奸 5978 她 5979 奺 597A 奻 597B 奼 597C 好 597D 奾 597E 奿 597F 妀 5980 妁 5981 如 5982 妃 5983 妄 5984 妅 5985 妆 5986 妇 5987 妈 5988 **4** 妉 5989 妊 598A 妋 598B 妌 598C 妎 598E 妏 598F 妐 5990 妑 5991 妒 5992 妓 5993 妔 5994 妕 5995 妖 5996 妗 5997 妘 5998 妙 5999 妚 599A 妜 599C 妝 599D 妞 599E 妟 599F 妠 59A0 妡 59A1 妢 59A2 妣 59A3 妤 59A4 妥 59A5 妦 59A6 妧 59A7 妨 59A8 妩 59A9 妪 59AA 妫 59AB **5** 妬 59AC 妭 59AD 妮 59AE 妯 59AF 妰 59B0 妱 59B1 妲 59B2 妳 59B3 妴 59B4 妵 59B5 妶 59B6 妷 59B7 妸 59B8 妹 59B9 妺 59BA 妻 59BB 妼 59BC 妽 59BD 妾 59BE 妿 59BF 姀 59C0 姁 59C1 姂 59C2 姃 59C3 姄 59C4 姅 59C5 姆 59C6 姇 59C7 姈 59C8 姉 59C9 姊 59CA 始 59CB 姌 59CC 姍 59CD 姎 59CE 姏 59CF 姐 59D0 姑 59D1 姒 59D2 姓 59D3 委 59D4 姕 59D5 姖 59D6 姗 59D7 **6** 妍 598D 姘 59D8 姙 59D9 姚 59DA 姛 59DB 姜 59DC 姝 59DD 姞 59DE 姟 59DF 姠 59E0 姡 59E1 姢 59E2 姣 59E3 姤 59E4 姥 59E5 姦 59E6 姧 59E7 姨 59E8 姩 59E9 姪 59EA 姫 59EB 姭 59ED 姮 59EE 姯 59EF 姰 59F0 姱 59F1 姲 59F2 姳 59F3 姴 59F4 姵 59F5 姶 59F6 姷 59F7 姸 59F8 姹 59F9 姺 59FA 姻 59FB 姼 59FC 姽 59FD 姾 59FE 姿 59FF 娀 5A00 威 5A01 娂 5A02 娃 5A03 娄 5A04 娅 5A05 娆 5A06 娇 5A07 娈 5A08 **7** 姬 59EC 娉 5A09 娊 5A0A 娋 5A0B 娌 5A0C 娍 5A0D 娎 5A0E 娏 5A0F 娐 5A10 娑 5A11 娒 5A12 娓 5A13 娔 5A14 娕 5A15 娖 5A16 娗 5A17 娘 5A18 娙 5A19 娚 5A1A 娛 5A1B 娜 5A1C 娝 5A1D 娞 5A1E 娟 5A1F 娠 5A20 娡 5A21 娢 5A22 娣 5A23 娤 5A24 娥 5A25

女 38 娥 5A25 娦 5A26 娧 5A27 娨 5A28 娩 5A29 娪 5A2A 娫 5A2B 娭 5A2D 娮 5A2E 娯 5A2F 娰 5A30 娱 5A31 娲 5A32 娳 5A33 娴 5A34 娽 5A3D **8** 娬 5A2C 娵 5A35 娶 5A36 娷 5A37 娸 5A38 娹 5A39
娺 5A3A 娻 5A3B 娼 5A3C 娾 5A3E 娿 5A3F 婀 5A40 婁 5A41 婂 5A42 婃 5A43 婄 5A44 婅 5A45 婆 5A46 婇 5A47 婈 5A48 婉 5A49 婊 5A4A 婋 5A4B 婌 5A4C 婍 5A4D 婎 5A4E 婏 5A4F 婐 5A50 婑 5A51
婒 5A52 婓 5A53 婔 5A54 婕 5A55 婖 5A56 婗 5A57 婘 5A58 婙 5A59 婚 5A5A 婛 5A5B 婜 5A5C 婝 5A5D 婞 5A5E 婟 5A5F 婠 5A60 婡 5A61 婢 5A62 婣 5A63 婤 5A64 婥 5A65 婦 5A66 婧 5A67 婨 5A68
婩 5A69 婪 5A6A 婫 5A6B 婬 5A6C 婭 5A6D 婮 5A6E 婯 5A6F 婰 5A70 婱 5A71 婲 5A72 婳 5A73 婴 5A74 婵 5A75 婶 5A76 **9** 婷 5A77 婸 5A78 婹 5A79 婺 5A7A 婻 5A7B 婼 5A7C 婽 5A7D 婾 5A7E
婿 5A7F 媀 5A80 媁 5A81 媂 5A82 媃 5A83 媄 5A84 媅 5A85 媆 5A86 媇 5A87 媈 5A88 媉 5A89 媊 5A8A 媋 5A8B 媌 5A8C 媍 5A8D 媎 5A8E 媏 5A8F 媑 5A91 媒 5A92 媓 5A93 媔 5A94 媕 5A95 媖 5A96
媗 5A97 媘 5A98 媙 5A99 媚 5A9A 媛 5A9B 媜 5A9C 媝 5A9D 媞 5A9E 媟 5A9F 媠 5AA0 媡 5AA1 媢 5AA2 媣 5AA3 媤 5AA4 媥 5AA5 媦 5AA6 媧 5AA7 媨 5AA8 媩 5AA9 媪 5AAA 媫 5AAB 媬 5AAC 媭 5AAD
媮 5AAE 媯 5AAF 媼 5ABC 嫏 5ACF **10** 嘦 5626 媐 5A90 媰 5AB0 媱 5AB1 媲 5AB2 媳 5AB3 媴 5AB4 媵 5AB5 媶 5AB6 媷 5AB7 媸 5AB8 媹 5AB9 媺 5ABA 媻 5ABB 媽 5ABD 媾 5ABE 媿 5ABF 嫀 5AC0
嫁 5AC1 嫂 5AC2 嫃 5AC3 嫄 5AC4 嫅 5AC5 嫆 5AC6 嫇 5AC7 嫈 5AC8 嫉 5AC9 嫊 5ACA 嫋 5ACB 嫌 5ACC 嫍 5ACD 嫎 5ACE 嫐 5AD0 嫑 5AD1 嫒 5AD2 嫓 5AD3 嫔 5AD4 **11** 嫕 5AD5 嫖 5AD6 嫗 5AD7
嫘 5AD8 嫙 5AD9 嫚 5ADA 嫛 5ADB 嫜 5ADC 嫝 5ADD 嫞 5ADE 嫟 5ADF 嫠 5AE0 嫡 5AE1 嫢 5AE2 嫣 5AE3 嫤 5AE4 嫥 5AE5 嫦 5AE6 嫧 5AE7 嫨 5AE8 嫩 5AE9 嫪 5AEA 嫫 5AEB 嫬 5AEC 嫭 5AED 嫮 5AEE
嫯 5AEF 嫰 5AF0 嫱 5AF1 嫲 5AF2 **12** 嫳 5AF3 嫴 5AF4 嫵 5AF5 嫶 5AF6 嫷 5AF7 嫸 5AF8 嫹 5AF9 嫺 5AFA 嫻 5AFB 嫼 5AFC 嫽 5AFD 嫾 5AFE 嫿 5AFF 嬀 5B00 嬁 5B01 嬂 5B02 嬃 5B03 嬄 5B04
嬅 5B05 嬆 5B06 嬇 5B07 嬈 5B08 嬉 5B09 嬊 5B0A 嬋 5B0B 嬌 5B0C 嬍 5B0D 嬎 5B0E 嬏 5B0F **13** 嬐 5B10 嬑 5B11 嬒 5B12 嬓 5B13 嬔 5B14 嬕 5B15 嬖 5B16 嬗 5B17 嬘 5B18 嬙 5B19 嬚 5B1A
嬛 5B1B 嬜 5B1C 嬝 5B1D 嬞 5B1E 嬟 5B1F 嬠 5B20 嬡 5B21 嬢 5B22 **14** 嬣 5B23 嬤 5B24 嬥 5B25 嬦 5B26 嬧 5B27 嬨 5B28 嬩 5B29 嬪 5B2A 嬫 5B2B 嬬 5B2C 嬭 5B2D 嬮 5B2E 嬯 5B2F 嬰 5B30
嬱 5B31 嬲 5B32 嬳 5B33 嬴 5B34 嬵 5B35 嬶 5B36 嬷 5B37 **15** 嬸 5B38 嬺 5B3A 嬻 5B3B 嬼 5B3C 嬽 5B3D **16** 嬹 5B39 嬾 5B3E 嬿 5B3F **17** 孀 5B40 孁 5B41 孂 5B42 孃 5B43 孄 5B44
孅 5B45 孆 5B46 **18** 孇 5B47 孈 5B48 孉 5B49 **19** 孊 5B4A 孋 5B4B 孌 5B4C **20** 孍 5B4D **21** 孎 5B4E 孏 5B4F

子 39 子 5B50 孑 5B51 孒 5B52 孓 5B53 **1** 孔 5B54 **2** 孕 5B55 **3** 孖 5B56 字 5B57 存 5B58 孙 5B59 **4** 孚 5B5A 孛 5B5B 孜 5B5C 孝 5B5D 孞 5B5E **5** 孟 5B5F 孠 5B60 孡 5B61
孢 5B62 季 5B63 孤 5B64 孥 5B65 学 5B66 孧 5B67 **6** 孨 5B68 孩 5B69 孪 5B6A **7** 孫 5B6B 孬 5B6C 孭 5B6D **8** 孮 5B6E 孯 5B6F 孰 5B70 **9** 孱 5B71 孲 5B72 **10** 孳 5B73
孴 5B74 **11** 孵 5B75 孶 5B76 孷 5B77 **13** 學 5B78 孹 5B79 **14** 孺 5B7A 孻 5B7B **16** 孼 5B7C **17** 孽 5B7D 孾 5B7E **19** 孿 5B7F

宀 40 宀 5B80 **2** 宁 5B81 宂 5B82 它 5B83 宄 5B84 **3** 宅 5B85 宆 5B86 宇 5B87 守 5B88 安 5B89 **4** 宊 5B8A 宋 5B8B 完 5B8C 宍 5B8D 宎 5B8E 宏 5B8F 宐 5B90 宑 5B91 宒 5B92
5 宓 5B93 宔 5B94 宕 5B95 宖 5B96 宗 5B97 官 5B98 宙 5B99 定 5B9A 宛 5B9B 宜 5B9C 宝 5B9D 实 5B9E 実 5B9F 宠 5BA0 审 5BA1 **6** 客 5BA2 宣 5BA3 室 5BA4 宥 5BA5 宦 5BA6 宨 5BA8
宩 5BA9 宪 5BAA 宫 5BAB **7** 宧 5BA7 宬 5BAC 宭 5BAD 宮 5BAE 宯 5BAF 宰 5BB0 宱 5BB1 宲 5BB2 害 5BB3 宴 5BB4 宵 5BB5 家 5BB6 宷 5BB7 宸 5BB8 容 5BB9 宺 5BBA 宻 5BBB 宼 5BBC 宽 5BBD
宾 5BBE **8** 宿 5BBF 寀 5BC0 寁 5BC1 寂 5BC2 寃 5BC3 寄 5BC4 寅 5BC5 密 5BC6 寇 5BC7 寈 5BC8 寉 5BC9 **9** 寊 5BCA 寋 5BCB 富 5BCC 寍 5BCD 寎 5BCE 寏 5BCF 寐 5BD0 寑 5BD1 寒 5BD2

宀 40 寓 5BD3 寔 5BD4 寕 5BD5 寪 5BEA **10** 寖 5BD6 寗 5BD7 寘 5BD8 寙 5BD9 寚 5BDA 寛 5BDB 寜 5BDC 寝 5BDD **11** 寞 5BDE 察 5BDF 寠 5BE0 寡 5BE1 寢 5BE2 寣 5BE3 寤 5BE4 寥 5BE5 實 5BE6
寧 5BE7 寨 5BE8 赛 8D5B **12** 審 5BE9 寫 5BEB 寬 5BEC 寭 5BED 寮 5BEE **13** 寯 5BEF 寰 5BF0 **14** 寱 5BF1 寲 5BF2 **16** 寳 5BF3 寴 5BF4 寵 5BF5 **17** 寶 5BF6 **18** 寷 5BF7

寸 41 寸 5BF8 **2** 对 5BF9 **3** 寺 5BFA 导 5BFC **4** 寽 5BFD 对 5BFE 寿 5BFF **5** 尀 5C00 **6** 封 5C01 専 5C02 **7** 尃 5C03 射 5C04 尅 5C05 **8** 將 5C07 專 5C08 尉 5C09
9 尊 5C0A 尋 5C0B 尌 5C0C **11** 對 5C0D **12** 導 5C0E

小 42 小 5C0F **1** 尐 5C10 少 5C11 **2** 厼 53BC 尒 5C12 尓 5C13 尔 5C14 尕 5C15 **3** 尖 5C16 尗 5C17 尘 5C18 **5** 尙 5C19 尚 5C1A 鼡 9F21 **6** 単 5358 尛 5C1B 尜 5C1C 尝 5C1D
8 蛍 86CD **9** 営 55B6 尞 5C1E 辉 8F89 **10** 尟 5C1F 尠 5C20

尢 43 尢 5C22 尣 5C23 **1** 尤 5C24 **3** 尥 5C25 尦 5C26 尧 5C27 **4** 尨 5C28 尩 5C29 尪 5C2A 尫 5C2B 尬 5C2C **5** 尭 5C2D **6** 尮 5C2E 尯 5C2F **9** 尰 5C30 就 5C31
10 尲 5C32 尳 5C33 尴 5C34 **12** 尵 5C35 **14** 尶 5C36 尷 5C37

尸 44 尸 5C38 **1** 尹 5C39 尺 5C3A **2** 尻 5C3B 尼 5C3C **3** 尽 5C3D **4** 尾 5C3E 尿 5C3F 局 5C40 屁 5C41 层 5C42 屃 5C43 **5** 屄 5C44 居 5C45 屆 5C46 屇 5C47 屈 5C48 屉 5C49
届 5C4A **6** 屋 5C4B 屌 5C4C 屍 5C4D 屎 5C4E 屏 5C4F **7** 屐 5C50 屑 5C51 屒 5C52 屓 5C53 屔 5C54 展 5C55 屖 5C56 屗 5C57 屘 5C58 **8** 屙 5C59 屚 5C5A 屛 5C5B 屜 5C5C 屝 5C5D
9 属 5C5E 屟 5C5F 屠 5C60 屡 5C61 **11** 屢 5C62 屣 5C63 **12** 層 5C64 履 5C65 屦 5C66 屧 5C67 **14** 屨 5C68 **15** 屩 5C69 屪 5C6A **16** 屫 5C6B **18** 屬 5C6C
21 屭 5C6D

屮 45 屮 5C6E **1** 屯 5C6F **3** 屰 5C70

山 46 山 5C71 **1** 屲 5C72 **2** 屳 5C73 屴 5C74 屵 5C75 屶 5C76 屷 5C77 **3** 屸 5C78 屹 5C79 屺 5C7A 屻 5C7B 屼 5C7C 屽 5C7D 屾 5C7E 屿 5C7F 岀 5C80 岁 5C81 岂 5C82 岃 5C83
4 妛 599B 岄 5C84 岅 5C85 岆 5C86 岇 5C87 岈 5C88 岉 5C89 岊 5C8A 岋 5C8B 岌 5C8C 岎 5C8E 岏 5C8F 岐 5C90 岑 5C91 岒 5C92 岓 5C93 岔 5C94 岕 5C95 岖 5C96 岗 5C97 岘 5C98 岙 5C99
岚 5C9A 岛 5C9B 岜 5C9C **5** 岝 5C9D 岞 5C9E 岟 5C9F 岠 5CA0 岡 5CA1 岢 5CA2 岣 5CA3 岤 5CA4 岥 5CA5 岦 5CA6 岧 5CA7 岨 5CA8 岩 5CA9 岪 5CAA 岫 5CAB 岬 5CAC 岭 5CAD 岮 5CAE 岯 5CAF
岰 5CB0 岱 5CB1 岲 5CB2 岳 5CB3 岴 5CB4 岵 5CB5 岶 5CB6 岷 5CB7 岸 5CB8 岹 5CB9 岺 5CBA 岻 5CBB 岼 5CBC 岽 5CBD 岾 5CBE 岿 5CBF 峀 5CC0 峁 5CC1 峂 5CC2 峃 5CC3 峄 5CC4 峅 5CC5

山 46 **6** 岍 5C8D 峆 5CC6 峇 5CC7 峈 5CC8 峉 5CC9 峊 5CCA 峋 5CCB 峌 5CCC 峍 5CCD 峎 5CCE 峏 5CCF 峐 5CD0 峑 5CD1 峒 5CD2 峓 5CD3 峔 5CD4 峕 5CD5 峖 5CD6 峗 5CD7 峘 5CD8 峙 5CD9 峚 5CDA

峛 5CDB 峜 5CDC 峝 5CDD 峞 5CDE 峟 5CDF 峠 5CE0 峡 5CE1 峢 5CE2 峣 5CE3 峤 5CE4 峥 5CE5 峦 5CE6 峧 5CE7 **7** 埊 57CA 峨 5CE8 峩 5CE9 峪 5CEA 峫 5CEB 峬 5CEC 峭 5CED 峮 5CEE 峯 5CEF

峰 5CF0 峱 5CF1 峲 5CF2 峳 5CF3 峴 5CF4 峵 5CF5 島 5CF6 峷 5CF7 峸 5CF8 峹 5CF9 峺 5CFA 峻 5CFB 峼 5CFC 峽 5CFD 峾 5CFE 峿 5CFF 崀 5D00 崁 5D01 崂 5D02 崃 5D03 崄 5D04 崅 5D05

8 崆 5D06 崇 5D07 崈 5D08 崉 5D09 崊 5D0A 崋 5D0B 崌 5D0C 崍 5D0D 崎 5D0E 崏 5D0F 崐 5D10 崑 5D11 崒 5D12 崓 5D13 崔 5D14 崕 5D15 崖 5D16 崗 5D17 崘 5D18 崙 5D19 崚 5D1A 崛 5D1B

崜 5D1C 崝 5D1D 崞 5D1E 崟 5D1F 崠 5D20 崡 5D21 崢 5D22 崣 5D23 崤 5D24 崥 5D25 崦 5D26 崧 5D27 崨 5D28 崩 5D29 崪 5D2A 崫 5D2B 崬 5D2C 崭 5D2D 崮 5D2E 崯 5D2F 崰 5D30 **9** 崱 5D31

崲 5D32 崳 5D33 崴 5D34 崵 5D35 崶 5D36 崷 5D37 崸 5D38 崹 5D39 崺 5D3A 崻 5D3B 崼 5D3C 崽 5D3D 崾 5D3E 崿 5D3F 嵀 5D40 嵁 5D41 嵂 5D42 嵃 5D43 嵄 5D44 嵅 5D45 嵆 5D46 嵇 5D47 嵈 5D48

嵉 5D49 嵋 5D4B 嵌 5D4C 嵍 5D4D 嵎 5D4E 嵏 5D4F 嵐 5D50 嵑 5D51 嵒 5D52 嵓 5D53 嵔 5D54 嵕 5D55 嵖 5D56 嵗 5D57 嵘 5D58 嵙 5D59 嵚 5D5A 嵛 5D5B 嵜 5D5C 嵝 5D5D **10** 嵊 5D4A 嵞 5D5E

嵟 5D5F 嵠 5D60 嵡 5D61 嵢 5D62 嵣 5D63 嵤 5D64 嵥 5D65 嵦 5D66 嵧 5D67 嵨 5D68 嵩 5D69 嵪 5D6A 嵫 5D6B 嵬 5D6C 嵭 5D6D 嵮 5D6E 嵯 5D6F 嵰 5D70 嵱 5D71 嵲 5D72 嵳 5D73 嵴 5D74 嵵 5D75

嵶 5D76 **11** 嵷 5D77 嵸 5D78 嵹 5D79 嵺 5D7A 嵻 5D7B 嵼 5D7C 嵽 5D7D 嵾 5D7E 嵿 5D7F 嶀 5D80 嶁 5D81 嶂 5D82 嶃 5D83 嶄 5D84 嶅 5D85 嶆 5D86 嶇 5D87 嶈 5D88 嶉 5D89 嶊 5D8A 嶋 5D8B

嶌 5D8C 嶍 5D8D 嶎 5D8E **12** 嶏 5D8F 嶐 5D90 嶑 5D91 嶒 5D92 嶓 5D93 嶔 5D94 嶕 5D95 嶖 5D96 嶗 5D97 嶘 5D98 嶙 5D99 嶚 5D9A 嶛 5D9B 嶜 5D9C 嶝 5D9D 嶞 5D9E 嶟 5D9F 嶠 5DA0 嶡 5DA1

嶢 5DA2 嶣 5DA3 嶤 5DA4 嶥 5DA5 **13** 嶦 5DA6 嶧 5DA7 嶨 5DA8 嶩 5DA9 嶪 5DAA 嶫 5DAB 嶬 5DAC 嶭 5DAD 嶮 5DAE 嶯 5DAF 嶰 5DB0 嶱 5DB1 嶲 5DB2 嶳 5DB3 嶴 5DB4 嶵 5DB5 嶶 5DB6

14 嶷 5DB7 嶸 5DB8 嶹 5DB9 嶺 5DBA 嶼 5DBC 嶽 5DBD 嶾 5DBE 嶿 5DBF **15** 巀 5DC0 巁 5DC1 巂 5DC2 **16** 嶻 5DBB 巃 5DC3 巄 5DC4 巅 5DC5 **17** 巆 5DC6 巇 5DC7 巈 5DC8 巉 5DC9

巊 5DCA 巋 5DCB 巌 5DCC **18** 巍 5DCD 巏 5DCF 巐 5DD0 **19** 巎 5DCE 巑 5DD1 巒 5DD2 巓 5DD3 巔 5DD4 巕 5DD5 **20** 巖 5DD6 巗 5DD7 巘 5DD8 巙 5DD9 巚 5DDA

巛 47 巛 5DDB 巜 5DDC 川 5DDD **3** 州 5DDE 巟 5DDF **4** 巠 5DE0 巡 5DE1 **8** 巢 5DE2 巣 5DE3 **12** 巤 5DE4

工 48 工 5DE5 **2** 左 5DE6 巧 5DE7 巨 5DE8 **3** 巩 5DE9 巪 5DEA **4** 巫 5DEB **6** 巬 5DEC 巭 5DED **7** 差 5DEE **9** 巯 5DEF **10** 巰 5DF0

己 49 己 5DF1 已 5DF2 巳 5DF3 **1** 巴 5DF4 **4** 巵 5DF5 **5** 巶 5DF6 **6** 巷 5DF7 巸 5DF8 巹 5DF9 巺 5DFA 巻 5DFB **7** 巼 5DFC **9** 巽 5DFD

巾 50 巾 5DFE **1** 巿 5DFF 帀 5E00 币 5E01 **2** 市 5E02 布 5E03 帄 5E04 帅 5E05 **3** 帆 5E06 帇 5E07 师 5E08 **4** 帉 5E09 帊 5E0A 帋 5E0B 希 5E0C 帍 5E0D 帎 5E0E 帏 5E0F 帐 5E10

5 帑 5E11 帒 5E12 帓 5E13 帔 5E14 帕 5E15 帖 5E16 帗 5E17 帘 5E18 帙 5E19 帚 5E1A 帛 5E1B 帜 5E1C **6** 帝 5E1D 帞 5E1E 帟 5E1F 帠 5E20 帡 5E21 帢 5E22 帣 5E23 帤 5E24 帥 5E25

带 5E26 帧 5E27 **7** 帨 5E28 帩 5E29 帪 5E2A 師 5E2B 帬 5E2C 席 5E2D 帮 5E2E 帯 5E2F 帱 5E31 **8** 帲 5E32 帳 5E33 帴 5E34 帵 5E35 帶 5E36 帷 5E37 常 5E38 帹 5E39 帺 5E3A 帻 5E3B

巾 50 帼 5E3C **9** 帽 5E3D 帾 5E3E 帿 5E3F 幀 5E40 幁 5E41 幂 5E42 幃 5E43 幄 5E44 幅 5E45 幆 5E46 幇 5E47 幈 5E48 幉 5E49 **10** 幊 5E4A 幋 5E4B 幌 5E4C 幍 5E4D 幎 5E4E 幏 5E4F 幐 5E50
11 幑 5E51 幒 5E52 幓 5E53 幔 5E54 幕 5E55 幖 5E56 幗 5E57 幘 5E58 幙 5E59 幛 5E5B **12** 幚 5E5A 幜 5E5C 幝 5E5D 幞 5E5E 帜 5E5F 幠 5E60 幡 5E61 幢 5E62 幣 5E63 幤 5E64 幥 5E65
13 幦 5E66 幧 5E67 幨 5E68 幩 5E69 **14** 幪 5E6A 幫 5E6B 幬 5E6C **15** 幭 5E6D 幮 5E6E 幯 5E6F **16** 幰 5E70 **17** 幱 5E71

干 51 干 5E72 **2** 平 5E73 **3** 年 5E74 幵 5E75 **5** 并 5E76 幷 5E77 幸 5E78 **6** 顸 9878 **10** 幹 5E79

乡 52 乡 4E61 幺 5E7A **1** 幻 5E7B **2** 幼 5E7C **6** 幽 5E7D **8** 喝 559D **9** 幾 5E7E

广 53 广 5E7F **2** 庀 5E80 庁 5E81 庂 5E82 広 5E83 **3** 庄 5E84 庅 5E85 庆 5E86 **4** 庇 5E87 庈 5E88 庉 5E89 床 5E8A 庋 5E8B 庌 5E8C 庍 5E8D 庎 5E8E 序 5E8F 庐 5E90 庑 5E91 庒 5E92
库 5E93 应 5E94 庘 5E98 **5** 底 5E95 庖 5E96 店 5E97 庙 5E99 庚 5E9A 庛 5E9B 府 5E9C 庝 5E9D 庞 5E9E 废 5E9F **6** 庠 5EA0 庡 5EA1 庢 5EA2 庣 5EA3 庤 5EA4 庥 5EA5 度 5EA6
7 座 5EA7 庨 5EA8 庩 5EA9 庪 5EAA 庫 5EAB 庬 5EAC 庭 5EAD 庮 5EAE 庯 5EAF **8** 庰 5EB0 庱 5EB1 庲 5EB2 庳 5EB3 庴 5EB4 庵 5EB5 庶 5EB6 康 5EB7 庸 5EB8 庹 5EB9 庺 5EBA 庻 5EBB
庼 5EBC **9** 庽 5EBD 庾 5EBE 庿 5EBF 廀 5EC0 廁 5EC1 廂 5EC2 廃 5EC3 廊 5ECA 赓 8D53 **10** 廅 5EC5 廆 5EC6 廇 5EC7 廈 5EC8 廉 5EC9 廋 5ECB 廌 5ECC **11** 廄 5EC4 廍 5ECD 廎 5ECE
廏 5ECF 廐 5ED0 廑 5ED1 廒 5ED2 廓 5ED3 廔 5ED4 廕 5ED5 廖 5ED6 廗 5ED7 廘 5ED8 **12** 廙 5ED9 廚 5EDA 廛 5EDB 廜 5EDC 廝 5EDD 廞 5EDE 廟 5EDF 廠 5EE0 廡 5EE1 廢 5EE2 廣 5EE3 廤 5EE4
13 廥 5EE5 廦 5EE6 廧 5EE7 廨 5EE8 廩 5EE9 廪 5EEA **15** 廫 5EEB **16** 廬 5EEC 廭 5EED **17** 廮 5EEE 廯 5EEF 廰 5EF0 **18** 廱 5EF1 **19** 廲 5EF2 **22** 廳 5EF3

廴 54 廴 5EF4 **3** 廵 5EF5 **4** 延 5EF6 廷 5EF7 **5** 廸 5EF8 廹 5EF9 **6** 建 5EFA 廻 5EFB 廼 5EFC **7** 廽 5EFD

廾 55 廾 5EFE **1** 廿 5EFF 开 5F00 **2** 弁 5F01 **3** 异 5F02 **4** 弃 5F03 弄 5F04 弅 5F05 **5** 弆 5F06 **6** 弇 5F07 弈 5F08 **7** 弉 5F09 **12** 弊 5F0A

弋 56 弋 5F0B **1** 弌 5F0C **2** 弍 5F0D **3** 弎 5F0E 式 5F0F 弐 5F10 **6** 贰 8D30 **9** 弑 5F11 **10** 弒 5F12

弓 57 弓 5F13 **1** 弔 5F14 引 5F15 弖 5F16 **2** 弗 5F17 弘 5F18 **3** 弙 5F19 弚 5F1A 弛 5F1B 弜 5F1C **4** 弝 5F1D 弞 5F1E 弟 5F1F 张 5F20 **5** 弡 5F21 弢 5F22 弣 5F23 弤 5F24
弥 5F25 弦 5F26 弧 5F27 弨 5F28 弩 5F29 弪 5F2A **6** 弫 5F2B 弬 5F2C 弭 5F2D 弮 5F2E 弯 5F2F **7** 弰 5F30 弱 5F31 弲 5F32 弳 5F33 **8** 弴 5F34 張 5F35 弶 5F36 強 5F37 弸 5F38

弓 57 · 弹 5F39 · **9** 强 5F3A · 弻 5F3B · 弼 5F3C · 弽 5F3D · 弾 5F3E · **10** 弿 5F3F · 彀 5F40 · 彁 5F41 · 彂 5F42 · **11** 彃 5F43 · 彄 5F44 · 彅 5F45 · **12** 彆 5F46 · 彇 5F47 · 彈 5F48 · 彉 5F49 · **13** 彊 5F4A ·
彋 5F4B · **14** 彌 5F4C · **15** 彍 5F4D · **19** 彎 5F4E · **20** 彏 5F4F

彐 58 · 彐 5F50 · 彑 5F51 · **2** 刍 520D · 归 5F52 · **3** 寻 5BFB · 当 5F53 · **5** 彔 5F54 · 录 5F55 · **6** 彖 5F56 · **7** 帰 5E30 · **8** 彗 5F57 · **9** 彘 5F58 · **10** 彙 5F59 · 彚 5F5A
13 彛 5F5B · 彜 5F5C · **15** 彝 5F5D · 彞 5F5E · **23** 彟 5F5F · 彠 5F60

彡 59 · 彡 5F61 · **4** 形 5F62 · 彣 5F63 · 彤 5F64 · **6** 彥 5F65 · 彦 5F66 · 须 987B · **7** 彧 5F67 · 彨 5F68 · **8** 彩 5F69 · 彪 5F6A · 彫 5F6B · 彬 5F6C · **9** 彭 5F6D · **10** 彮 5F6E · **11** 彯 5F6F ·
彰 5F70 · **12** 影 5F71 · **19** 彲 5F72

彳 60 · 彳 5F73 · **3** 彴 5F74 · 彵 5F75 · **4** 彶 5F76 · 彷 5F77 · 彸 5F78 · 役 5F79 · 彺 5F7A · 彻 5F7B · **5** 彼 5F7C · 彽 5F7D · 彾 5F7E · 彿 5F7F · 往 5F80 · 征 5F81 · 徂 5F82 · 徃 5F83 · 径 5F84 · **6** 待 5F85 ·
徆 5F86 · 徇 5F87 · 很 5F88 · 徉 5F89 · 徊 5F8A · 律 5F8B · 後 5F8C · 徍 5F8D · 徔 5F94 · **7** 徎 5F8E · 徏 5F8F · 徐 5F90 · 徑 5F91 · 徒 5F92 · 従 5F93 · 徕 5F95 · **8** 徖 5F96 · 得 5F97 · 徘 5F98 · 徙 5F99 · 徛 5F9B ·
徜 5F9C · 徝 5F9D · 從 5F9E · 徟 5F9F · 徠 5FA0 · 御 5FA1 · 徢 5FA2 · 徣 5FA3 · 衔 8854 · **9** 徚 5F9A · 徤 5FA4 · 徥 5FA5 · 徦 5FA6 · 徧 5FA7 · 徨 5FA8 · 復 5FA9 · 循 5FAA · 徫 5FAB · **10** 徬 5FAC · 徭 5FAD · 微 5FAE ·
徯 5FAF · 徰 5FB0 · **11** 徱 5FB1 · 徳 5FB3 · 徴 5FB4 · **12** 徲 5FB2 · 徵 5FB5 · 徶 5FB6 · 德 5FB7 · 徸 5FB8 · 徹 5FB9 · 徺 5FBA · **13** 徻 5FBB · 徼 5FBC · **14** 徽 5FBD · 徾 5FBE · **16** 徿 5FBF
17 忀 5FC0 · 忁 5FC1 · **18** 忂 5FC2

心 61 · 心 5FC3 · 忄 5FC4 · **1** 必 5FC5 · 忆 5FC6 · **2** 忇 5FC7 · 忈 5FC8 · 忉 5FC9 · 忊 5FCA · **3** 忋 5FCB · 忌 5FCC · 忍 5FCD · 忎 5FCE · 忏 5FCF · 忐 5FD0 · 忑 5FD1 · 忒 5FD2 · 忓 5FD3 · 忔 5FD4 · 忕 5FD5 · 忖 5FD6 ·
志 5FD7 · 忘 5FD8 · 忙 5FD9 · 忚 5FDA · 忛 5FDB · 応 5FDC · **4** 忝 5FDD · 忞 5FDE · 忟 5FDF · 忠 5FE0 · 忡 5FE1 · 忢 5FE2 · 忣 5FE3 · 忤 5FE4 · 忥 5FE5 · 忦 5FE6 · 忧 5FE7 · 忨 5FE8 · 忩 5FE9 · 忪 5FEA · 快 5FEB · 忬 5FEC ·
忭 5FED · 忮 5FEE · 忯 5FEF · 忰 5FF0 · 忱 5FF1 · 忲 5FF2 · 忳 5FF3 · 忴 5FF4 · 念 5FF5 · 忶 5FF6 · 忷 5FF7 · 忸 5FF8 · 忹 5FF9 · 忺 5FFA · 忻 5FFB · 忼 5FFC · 忽 5FFD · 忾 5FFE · 忿 5FFF · 怀 6000 · 态 6001 · 怂 6002 · 怄 6004 ·
怅 6005 · 怆 6006 · **5** 怃 6003 · 怇 6007 · 怈 6008 · 怉 6009 · 怊 600A · 怋 600B · 怌 600C · 怍 600D · 怎 600E · 怏 600F · 怐 6010 · 怑 6011 · 怒 6012 · 怓 6013 · 怔 6014 · 怕 6015 · 怖 6016 · 怗 6017 · 怘 6018 · 怙 6019 ·
怚 601A · 怛 601B · 怜 601C · 思 601D · 怞 601E · 怟 601F · 怠 6020 · 怡 6021 · 怢 6022 · 怣 6023 · 怤 6024 · 急 6025 · 怦 6026 · 性 6027 · 怨 6028 · 怩 6029 · 怪 602A · 怫 602B · 怬 602C · 怭 602D · 怮 602E · 怯 602F · 怰 6030 ·
怱 6031 · 怲 6032 · 怳 6033 · 怴 6034 · 怵 6035 · 怶 6036 · 怷 6037 · 怸 6038 · 怹 6039 · 怺 603A · 总 603B · 怼 603C · 怽 603D · 怾 603E · 怿 603F · **6** 恀 6040 · 恁 6041 · 恂 6042 · 恃 6043 · 恄 6044 · 恅 6045 · 恆 6046 ·
恇 6047 · 恈 6048 · 恉 6049 · 恊 604A · 恋 604B · 恌 604C · 恍 604D · 恎 604E · 恏 604F · 恐 6050 · 恑 6051 · 恒 6052 · 恓 6053 · 恔 6054 · 恕 6055 · 恖 6056 · 恗 6057 · 恘 6058 · 恙 6059 · 恚 605A · 恛 605B · 恜 605C · 恝 605D ·
恞 605E · 恟 605F · 恠 6060 · 恡 6061 · 恢 6062 · 恣 6063 · 恤 6064 · 恥 6065 · 恦 6066 · 恧 6067 · 恨 6068 · 恩 6069 · 恪 606A · 恫 606B · 恬 606C · 恭 606D · 恮 606E · 息 606F · 恰 6070 · 恱 6071 · 恲 6072 · 恳 6073 · 恴 6074

心 61 · 恲 6072 · 恳 6073 · 恴 6074 · 恵 6075 · 恶 6076 · 恷 6077 · 恸 6078 · 恹 6079 · 恺 607A · 恻 607B · 恼 607C · 恽 607D · 虑 8651 · **7** · 恾 607E · 恿 607F · 悀 6080 · 悁 6081 · 悂 6082 · 悃 6083 · 悄 6084 · 悅 6085 · 悆 6086

悇 6087 · 悈 6088 · 悉 6089 · 悊 608A · 悋 608B · 悌 608C · 悍 608D · 悎 608E · 悏 608F · 悐 6090 · 悑 6091 · 悒 6092 · 悓 6093 · 悔 6094 · 悕 6095 · 悖 6096 · 悗 6097 · 悘 6098 · 悙 6099 · 悚 609A · 悛 609B · 悜 609C · 悝 609D

悞 609E · 悟 609F · 悠 60A0 · 悡 60A1 · 悢 60A2 · 患 60A3 · 悤 60A4 · 悥 60A5 · 悦 60A6 · 悧 60A7 · 您 60A8 · 悩 60A9 · 悪 60AA · 悫 60AB · 悬 60AC · 悭 60AD · 悮 60AE · 悯 60AF · **8** · 悰 60B0 · 悱 60B1 · 悲 60B2 · 悳 60B3

悴 60B4 · 悵 60B5 · 悶 60B6 · 悷 60B7 · 悸 60B8 · 悹 60B9 · 悺 60BA · 悻 60BB · 悼 60BC · 悽 60BD · 悾 60BE · 悿 60BF · 惀 60C0 · 惁 60C1 · 惂 60C2 · 惃 60C3 · 惄 60C4 · 情 60C5 · 惆 60C6 · 惇 60C7 · 惈 60C8 · 惉 60C9 · 惊 60CA

惋 60CB · 惌 60CC · 惍 60CD · 惎 60CE · 惏 60CF · 惐 60D0 · 惑 60D1 · 惒 60D2 · 惓 60D3 · 惔 60D4 · 惕 60D5 · 惖 60D6 · 惗 60D7 · 惘 60D8 · 惙 60D9 · 惚 60DA · 惛 60DB · 惜 60DC · 惝 60DD · 惞 60DE · 惟 60DF · 惠 60E0 · 惡 60E1

惢 60E2 · 惣 60E3 · 惤 60E4 · 惥 60E5 · 惦 60E6 · 惧 60E7 · 惨 60E8 · 惩 60E9 · 惪 60EA · 惫 60EB · 惬 60EC · 惭 60ED · 惮 60EE · 惯 60EF · **9** · 惰 60F0 · 惱 60F1 · 惲 60F2 · 想 60F3 · 惴 60F4 · 惵 60F5 · 惶 60F6 · 惷 60F7

惸 60F8 · 惹 60F9 · 惺 60FA · 惻 60FB · 惼 60FC · 惽 60FD · 惾 60FE · 惿 60FF · 愀 6100 · 愁 6101 · 愂 6102 · 愃 6103 · 愄 6104 · 愅 6105 · 愆 6106 · 愇 6107 · 愈 6108 · 愉 6109 · 愊 610A · 愋 610B · 愌 610C · 愍 610D · 愎 610E

意 610F · 愐 6110 · 愑 6111 · 愒 6112 · 愓 6113 · 愔 6114 · 愕 6115 · 愖 6116 · 愗 6117 · 愘 6118 · 愙 6119 · 愚 611A · 愛 611B · 愜 611C · 愝 611D · 愞 611E · 感 611F · 愠 6120 · 愡 6121 · 愢 6122 · 愣 6123 · 愤 6124 · 愥 6125

愦 6126 · 慈 6148 · 慨 6168 · **10** · 厯 53AF · 愧 6127 · 愨 6128 · 愩 6129 · 愪 612A · 愫 612B · 愬 612C · 愭 612D · 愮 612E · 愯 612F · 愰 6130 · 愱 6131 · 愲 6132 · 愳 6133 · 愴 6134 · 愵 6135 · 愶 6136 · 愷 6137 · 愸 6138

愺 613A · 愻 613B · 愼 613C · 愽 613D · 愾 613E · 愿 613F · 慀 6140 · 慁 6141 · 慂 6142 · 慃 6143 · 慄 6144 · 慅 6145 · 慆 6146 · 慇 6147 · 慉 6149 · 慊 614A · 態 614B · 慌 614C · 慍 614D · 慎 614E · 慏 614F · 慐 6150 · 慑 6151

11 · 慒 6152 · 慓 6153 · 慔 6154 · 慕 6155 · 慖 6156 · 慗 6157 · 慘 6158 · 慙 6159 · 慚 615A · 慛 615B · 慜 615C · 慝 615D · 慞 615E · 慟 615F · 慠 6160 · 慡 6161 · 慢 6162 · 慣 6163 · 慤 6164 · 慥 6165 · 慦 6166 · 慧 6167

慩 6169 · 慪 616A · 慫 616B · 慬 616C · 慮 616E · 慯 616F · 慰 6170 · 慱 6171 · 慲 6172 · 慳 6173 · 慴 6174 · 慵 6175 · 慶 6176 · 慷 6177 · 慸 6178 · 慹 6179 · 慺 617A · 慻 617B · 慼 617C · 慽 617D · 慾 617E · 慿 617F · 憀 6180

憁 6181 · 憂 6182 · 憃 6183 · 憄 6184 · 憅 6185 · 憆 6186 · 憇 6187 · 憈 6188 · **12** · 慭 616D · 憉 6189 · 憊 618A · 憋 618B · 憌 618C · 憍 618D · 憎 618E · 憏 618F · 憐 6190 · 憑 6191 · 憒 6192 · 憓 6193 · 憔 6194 · 憕 6195

憖 6196 · 憗 6197 · 憘 6198 · 憙 6199 · 憚 619A · 憛 619B · 憜 619C · 憝 619D · 憞 619E · 憟 619F · 憠 61A0 · 憡 61A1 · 憢 61A2 · 憣 61A3 · 憤 61A4 · 憥 61A5 · 憦 61A6 · 憧 61A7 · 憨 61A8 · 憩 61A9 · 憪 61AA · 憫 61AB · 憬 61AC

憭 61AD · 憮 61AE · 憯 61AF · 憰 61B0 · 憱 61B1 · 憲 61B2 · 憳 61B3 · **13** · 憴 61B4 · 憵 61B5 · 憶 61B6 · 憷 61B7 · 憸 61B8 · 憹 61B9 · 憺 61BA · 憼 61BC · 憽 61BD · 憾 61BE · 憿 61BF · 懀 61C0 · 懁 61C1 · 懂 61C2 · 懃 61C3

懄 61C4 · 懅 61C5 · 懆 61C6 · 懇 61C7 · 懈 61C8 · 應 61C9 · 懊 61CA · 懋 61CB · 懌 61CC · 懍 61CD · 懎 61CE · 懏 61CF · 懐 61D0 · 懑 61D1 · 懒 61D2 · 懓 61D3 · 懔 61D4 · **14** · 憻 61BB · 懕 61D5 · 懖 61D6 · 懗 61D7 · 懘 61D8

懙 61D9 · 懚 61DA · 懛 61DB · 懜 61DC · 懝 61DD · 懞 61DE · 懟 61DF · 懠 61E0 · 懡 61E1 · 懢 61E2 · 懣 61E3 · 懤 61E4 · 懥 61E5 · 懦 61E6 · 懧 61E7 · 懨 61E8 · **15** · 懩 61E9 · 懪 61EA · 懫 61EB · 懬 61EC · 懭 61ED · 懮 61EE

懯 61EF · 懰 61F0 · 懱 61F1 · 懲 61F2 · 懳 61F3 · 懴 61F4 · **16** · 懵 61F5 · 懶 61F6 · 懷 61F7 · 懸 61F8 · **17** · 懹 61F9 · 懺 61FA · 懻 61FB · **18** · 懼 61FC · 懽 61FD · 懾 61FE · 懿 61FF · **19** · 愹 6139 · 戀 6200

戁 6201 · 戂 6202 · **20** · 戃 6203 · 戄 6204 · **21** · 戅 6205 · 戆 6206 · **24** · 戇 6207

戈 62 · 戈 6208 · **1** · 戉 6209 · 戊 620A · 戋 620B · **2** · 戌 620C · 戍 620D · 戎 620E · 戏 620F · **3** · 成 6210 · 我 6211 · 戒 6212 · 戓 6213 · **4** · 戔 6214 · 戕 6215 · 或 6216 · 戗 6217 · **5** · 战 6218

6 · 戙 6219 · 载 8F7D · **7** · 戚 621A · 戛 621B · 戜 621C · 戝 621D · **8** · 戞 621E · 戟 621F · **9** · 戠 6220 · 戡 6221 · 戢 6222 · 戣 6223 · 戤 6224 · 戥 6225 · 戦 6226 · **10** · 戧 6227 · 戨 6228 · 戩 6229

截 622A · 戫 622B · 戬 622C · **11** · 戭 622D · 戮 622E · 戯 622F · 戱 6231 · **12** · 戰 6230 · **13** · 戲 6232 · **14** · 戳 6233 · 戴 6234 · **18** · 戵 6235

戶 63 | 戶 6236 | 户 6237 | 戸 6238 | **1** | 戹 6239 | **3** | 戺 623A | 戻 623B | 戼 623C | **4** | 戽 623D | 戾 623E | 房 623F | 所 6240 | **5** | 扁 6241 | 扂 6242 | 扃 6243 | **6** | 扄 6244 | 扅 6245 | 扆 6246 | 扇 6247
7 | 扈 6248 | **8** | 扉 6249 | 扊 624A

手 64 | 手 624B | 扌 624C | 才 624D | **1** | 扎 624E | **2** | 扐 6250 | 扑 6251 | 扒 6252 | 打 6253 | 扔 6254 | 払 6255 | 扖 6256 | **3** | 扏 624F | 扗 6257 | 托 6258 | 扙 6259 | 扚 625A | 扛 625B | 扜 625C | 扝 625D | 扞 625E
扠 6260 | 扡 6261 | 扢 6262 | 扣 6263 | 扤 6264 | 扥 6265 | 扦 6266 | 执 6267 | 扨 6268 | 扩 6269 | 扪 626A | 扫 626B | 扬 626C | **4** | 扟 625F | 扭 626D | 扮 626E | 扯 626F | 扰 6270 | 扱 6271 | 扲 6272 | 扳 6273 | 扴 6274
扵 6275 | 扶 6276 | 扷 6277 | 批 6279 | 扺 627A | 扻 627B | 扼 627C | 扽 627D | 找 627E | 承 627F | 技 6280 | 抁 6281 | 抂 6282 | 抃 6283 | 抄 6284 | 抅 6285 | 抆 6286 | 抇 6287 | 抈 6288 | 抉 6289 | 把 628A | 抌 628C | 抍 628D
抎 628E | 抏 628F | 抐 6290 | 抑 6291 | 抒 6292 | 抓 6293 | 抔 6294 | 投 6295 | 抖 6296 | 抗 6297 | 折 6298 | 抙 6299 | 抚 629A | 抛 629B | 抜 629C | 抝 629D | 択 629E | 抟 629F | 抠 62A0 | 抡 62A1 | 抢 62A2 | 抣 62A3 | 护 62A4
报 62A5 | **5** | 扸 6278 | 抋 628B | 抦 62A6 | 抧 62A7 | 抨 62A8 | 抩 62A9 | 抪 62AA | 披 62AB | 抬 62AC | 抭 62AD | 抮 62AE | 抯 62AF | 抰 62B0 | 抱 62B1 | 抳 62B3 | 抴 62B4 | 抵 62B5 | 抶 62B6 | 抷 62B7 | 抸 62B8 | 抹 62B9
抺 62BA | 抻 62BB | 押 62BC | 抽 62BD | 抾 62BE | 抿 62BF | 拀 62C0 | 拁 62C1 | 拂 62C2 | 拃 62C3 | 拄 62C4 | 担 62C5 | 拆 62C6 | 拇 62C7 | 拈 62C8 | 拉 62C9 | 拊 62CA | 拋 62CB | 拌 62CC | 拍 62CD | 拎 62CE | 拏 62CF | 拐 62D0
拑 62D1 | 拒 62D2 | 拓 62D3 | 拔 62D4 | 拕 62D5 | 拖 62D6 | 拗 62D7 | 拘 62D8 | 拙 62D9 | 拚 62DA | 招 62DB | 拜 62DC | 拝 62DD | 拞 62DE | 拟 62DF | 拠 62E0 | 拡 62E1 | 拢 62E2 | 拣 62E3 | 拤 62E4 | 拥 62E5 | 拦 62E6 | 拧 62E7
拨 62E8 | 择 62E9 | **6** | 拪 62EA | 拫 62EB | 括 62EC | 拭 62ED | 拮 62EE | 拯 62EF | 拰 62F0 | 拱 62F1 | 拲 62F2 | 拳 62F3 | 拴 62F4 | 拵 62F5 | 拶 62F6 | 拷 62F7 | 拸 62F8 | 拹 62F9 | 拺 62FA | 拻 62FB | 拼 62FC | 拽 62FD
拾 62FE | 拿 62FF | 挀 6300 | 持 6301 | 挂 6302 | 挃 6303 | 挄 6304 | 挅 6305 | 挆 6306 | 指 6307 | 挈 6308 | 按 6309 | 挊 630A | 挌 630C | 挍 630D | 挎 630E | 挏 630F | 挐 6310 | 挑 6311 | 挒 6312 | 挓 6313 | 挔 6314 | 挕 6315
挖 6316 | 挗 6317 | 挘 6318 | 挙 6319 | 挚 631A | 挛 631B | 挝 631D | 挞 631E | 挟 631F | 挠 6320 | 挡 6321 | 挢 6322 | 挣 6323 | 挤 6324 | 挥 6325 | 挦 6326 | 挧 6327 | **7** | 挋 630B | 挨 6328 | 挩 6329 | 挪 632A | 挫 632B
挬 632C | 挭 632D | 挮 632E | 振 632F | 挰 6330 | 挱 6331 | 挲 6332 | 挳 6333 | 挴 6334 | 挵 6335 | 挶 6336 | 挷 6337 | 挸 6338 | 挹 6339 | 挺 633A | 挻 633B | 挼 633C | 挽 633D | 挾 633E | 挿 633F | 捀 6340 | 捁 6341 | 捂 6342
捃 6343 | 捄 6344 | 捅 6345 | 捆 6346 | 捇 6347 | 捈 6348 | 捉 6349 | 捊 634A | 捋 634B | 捌 634C | 捍 634D | 捎 634E | 捏 634F | 捐 6350 | 捑 6351 | 捒 6352 | 捔 6354 | 捕 6355 | 捖 6356 | 捗 6357 | 捘 6358 | 捙 6359 | 捚 635A
捛 635B | 捜 635C | 捝 635D | 捞 635E | 损 635F | 捠 6360 | 捡 6361 | 换 6362 | 捣 6363 | 捤 6364 | **8** | 挜 631C | 捓 6353 | 捥 6365 | 捦 6366 | 捧 6367 | 捨 6368 | 捩 6369 | 捪 636A | 捫 636B | 捬 636C | 捭 636D | 据 636E
捯 636F | 捰 6370 | 捱 6371 | 捲 6372 | 捳 6373 | 捴 6374 | 捵 6375 | 捶 6376 | 捷 6377 | 捸 6378 | 捹 6379 | 捺 637A | 捻 637B | 捼 637C | 捽 637D | 捾 637E | 捿 637F | 掀 6380 | 掁 6381 | 掂 6382 | 掃 6383 | 掄 6384 | 掅 6385
掆 6386 | 掇 6387 | 授 6388 | 掉 6389 | 掊 638A | 掋 638B | 掌 638C | 掍 638D | 掎 638E | 掏 638F | 掐 6390 | 掑 6391 | 排 6392 | 掓 6393 | 掕 6395 | 掖 6396 | 掗 6397 | 掘 6398 | 掙 6399 | 掚 639A | 掛 639B | 掜 639C | 掝 639D
掞 639E | 掟 639F | 掠 63A0 | 採 63A1 | 探 63A2 | 掣 63A3 | 掤 63A4 | 接 63A5 | 掦 63A6 | 控 63A7 | 推 63A8 | 掩 63A9 | 措 63AA | 掫 63AB | 掬 63AC | 掭 63AD | 掮 63AE | 掯 63AF | 掰 63B0 | 掱 63B1 | 掳 63B3 | 掴 63B4 | 掵 63B5
掶 63B6 | 掷 63B7 | 掸 63B8 | 掹 63B9 | 掺 63BA | 掻 63BB | 掼 63BC | **9** | 掔 6394 | 掲 63B2 | 掽 63BD | 掾 63BE | 掿 63BF | 揀 63C0 | 揁 63C1 | 揂 63C2 | 揃 63C3 | 揄 63C4 | 揅 63C5 | 揆 63C6 | 揇 63C7 | 揈 63C8 | 揉 63C9
揊 63CA | 揋 63CB | 揌 63CC | 揍 63CD | 揎 63CE | 描 63CF | 提 63D0 | 揑 63D1 | 插 63D2 | 揓 63D3 | 揔 63D4 | 揕 63D5 | 揖 63D6 | 揗 63D7 | 揘 63D8 | 揙 63D9 | 揚 63DA | 換 63DB | 揜 63DC | 揝 63DD | 揞 63DE | 揟 63DF | 揠 63E0
握 63E1 | 揢 63E2 | 揣 63E3 | 揤 63E4 | 揥 63E5 | 揦 63E6 | 揧 63E7 | 揨 63E8 | 揩 63E9 | 揪 63EA | 揫 63EB | 揬 63EC | 揭 63ED | 揮 63EE | 揯 63EF | 揰 63F0 | 揱 63F1 | 揲 63F2 | 揳 63F3 | 援 63F4 | 揵 63F5 | 揶 63F6 | 揷 63F7
揸 63F8 | 揹 63F9 | 揺 63FA | 揻 63FB | 揼 63FC | 揽 63FD | 揾 63FE | 揿 63FF | 搀 6400 | 搁 6401 | 搂 6402 | 搃 6403 | 搄 6404 | 搅 6405 | 搽 643D | 撝 649D | **10** | 搆 6406 | 搇 6407 | 搈 6408 | 搉 6409 | 搊 640A | 搋 640B

手 64

10 搆 6406 搇 6407 搈 6408 搉 6409 搊 640A 搋 640B 搌 640C 損 640D 搎 640E 搏 640F 搐 6410 搑 6411 搒 6412 搓 6413 搔 6414 搕 6415 搖 6416 搗 6417 搘 6418 搙 6419 搚 641A 搛 641B 搜 641C 搝 641D 搞 641E 搟 641F 搠 6420 搡 6421 搢 6422 搣 6423 搤 6424 搥 6425 搦 6426 搧 6427 搨 6428 搩 6429 搪 642A 搫 642B 搬 642C 搭 642D 搮 642E 搯 642F 搰 6430 搲 6432 搳 6433 搴 6434 搵 6435 搶 6436 搷 6437 搸 6438 搹 6439 携 643A 搻 643B 搼 643C 搾 643E 搿 643F 摀 6440 摁 6441 摂 6442 摃 6443 摄 6444 摅 6445 摆 6446 摇 6447 摈 6448 摉 6449 摊 644A

11 抲 62B2 摋 644B 摌 644C 摍 644D 摎 644E 摏 644F 摐 6450 摑 6451 摒 6452 摓 6453 摔 6454 摕 6455 摗 6457 摘 6458 摙 6459 摚 645A 摛 645B 摜 645C 摝 645D 摞 645E 摟 645F 摠 6460 摢 6462 摣 6463 摤 6464 摥 6465 摦 6466 摧 6467 摩 6469 摪 646A 摫 646B 摬 646C 摭 646D 摮 646E 摯 646F 摰 6470 摱 6471 摲 6472 摳 6473 摴 6474 摵 6475 摶 6476 摷 6477 摸 6478 摹 6479 摺 647A 摻 647B 摼 647C 摽 647D 摾 647E 摿 647F 撀 6480 撁 6481 撂 6482 撃 6483 撄 6484

12 搱 6431 摖 6456 摡 6461 摨 6468 撅 6485 撆 6486 撇 6487 撈 6488 撉 6489 撊 648A 撋 648B 撌 648C 撍 648D 撎 648E 撏 648F 撐 6490 撑 6491 撒 6492 撓 6493 撔 6494 撕 6495 撖 6496 撗 6497 撘 6498 撙 6499 撚 649A 撜 649C 撞 649E 撟 649F 撠 64A0 撡 64A1 撢 64A2 撣 64A3 撤 64A4 撥 64A5 撦 64A6 撧 64A7 撨 64A8 撩 64A9 撪 64AA 撫 64AB 撬 64AC 播 64AD 撮 64AE 撯 64AF 撰 64B0 撱 64B1 撲 64B2 撳 64B3 撴 64B4 撵 64B5 撶 64B6 撷 64B7 撸 64B8 撹 64B9 撺 64BA 擆 64C6

13 撛 649B 撻 64BB 撼 64BC 撽 64BD 撾 64BE 撿 64BF 擀 64C0 擁 64C1 擂 64C2 擃 64C3 擄 64C4 擅 64C5 擇 64C7 擈 64C8 擉 64C9 擊 64CA 擋 64CB 擌 64CC 操 64CD 擎 64CE 擏 64CF 擐 64D0 擑 64D1 擒 64D2 擓 64D3 擔 64D4 擕 64D5 擖 64D6 擗 64D7 擘 64D8 擙 64D9 據 64DA 擛 64DB 擜 64DC 擝 64DD 擞 64DE

14 擟 64DF 擠 64E0 擡 64E1 擢 64E2 擣 64E3 擤 64E4 擦 64E6 擧 64E7 擨 64E8 擩 64E9 擪 64EA 擫 64EB 擬 64EC 擭 64ED 擮 64EE 擯 64EF 擰 64F0 擱 64F1

15 擥 64E5 擲 64F2 擳 64F3 擴 64F4 擵 64F5 擶 64F6 擷 64F7 擸 64F8 擹 64F9 擺 64FA 擻 64FB 擼 64FC 擽 64FD 擾 64FE 擿 64FF 攀 6500 攁 6501 攂 6502 攃 6503 攄 6504 攅 6505 攆 6506

16 攇 6507 攈 6508 攉 6509 攊 650A 攋 650B 攌 650C 攍 650D 攎 650E 攏 650F 攐 6510 攒 6512

17 攑 6511 攓 6513 攔 6514 攕 6515 攖 6516 攗 6517 攘 6518 攙 6519 攚 651A

18 攛 651B 攜 651C 攝 651D

19 攞 651E 攟 651F 攠 6520 攡 6521 攢 6522 攣 6523 攤 6524 攦 6526 攧 6527

20 攥 6525 攨 6528 攩 6529 攪 652A 攫 652B

21 攬 652C 攭 652D

22 攮 652E

支 65

支 652F **2** 攰 6530 **5** 攱 6531 **8** 攲 6532 **12** 攳 6533

攴 66

攴 6534 攵 6535

2 收 6536 攷 6537

3 攸 6538 改 6539 攺 653A 攻 653B 攼 653C

4 攽 653D 放 653E 政 653F

5 敀 6540 敁 6541 敂 6542 敃 6543 敄 6544 故 6545

6 敆 6546 敇 6547 效 6548 敉 6549 敊 654A 敋 654B 敌 654C

7 啟 555F 敍 654D 敎 654E 敏 654F 敐 6550 救 6551 敒 6552 敓 6553 敔 6554 敕 6555 敖 6556 敗 6557 敘 6558 教 6559 敚 655A 敛 655B

8 敜 655C 敝 655D 敞 655E 敟 655F 敠 6560 敡 6561 敢 6562 散 6563 敤 6564 敥 6565 敦 6566 敧 6567 敨 6568 敩 6569 敪 656A 敭 656D

9 敫 656B 敬 656C 敮 656E 敯 656F 数 6570

10 敱 6571 敲 6572 敳 6573

11 整 6574 敵 6575 敶 6576 敷 6577 數 6578 敹 6579 敺 657A 敻 657B

12 敼 657C 敽 657D 敾 657E 敿 657F

13 斀 6580 斁 6581 斂 6582

14 斃 6583 贁 8D01

15 斄 6584

16 斅 6585 斆 6586

文 67 文 6587 **3** 斈 6588 **4** 斉 6589 **6** 斊 658A 斋 658B **7** 斌 658C 斍 658D 斎 658E 斏 658F **8** 斐 6590 斑 6591 **9** 斒 6592 **12** 斓 6593 **15** 斔 6594
17 斕 6595 **19** 斖 6596

斗 68 斗 6597 **3** 斘 6598 **6** 料 6599 斚 659A **7** 斛 659B 斜 659C **8** 斝 659D **9** 斞 659E 斟 659F **10** 斠 65A0 斡 65A1 **12** 斢 65A2 **13** 斣 65A3

斤 69 斤 65A4 **1** 斥 65A5 **4** 斦 65A6 斧 65A7 斨 65A8 斩 65A9 **5** 斪 65AA 斫 65AB **6** 颀 9880 **7** 斬 65AC 断 65AD **8** 斮 65AE 斯 65AF **9** 新 65B0 斱 65B1
11 斲 65B2 斳 65B3 **12** 斴 65B4 **13** 斵 65B5 斶 65B6 **14** 斷 65B7 **21** 斸 65B8

方 70 方 65B9 **4** 斺 65BA 斻 65BB 於 65BC **5** 施 65BD 斾 65BE 斿 65BF 旀 65C0 **6** 旁 65C1 旂 65C2 旃 65C3 旄 65C4 旅 65C5 旆 65C6 旊 65CA **7** 旇 65C7 旈 65C8 旉 65C9 旋 65CB
旌 65CC 旍 65CD 旎 65CE 族 65CF **8** 旐 65D0 旑 65D1 **9** 旒 65D2 旓 65D3 旔 65D4 旕 65D5 **10** 旖 65D6 旗 65D7 **12** 旘 65D8 旙 65D9 **13** 旚 65DA **14** 旛 65DB
15 旜 65DC 旝 65DD 旞 65DE **16** 旟 65DF

无 71 无 65E0 **1** 旡 65E1 **5** 既 65E2 **7** 旣 65E3 **9** 旤 65E4

日 72 日 65E5 **1** 旦 65E6 旧 65E7 **2** 旨 65E8 早 65E9 旪 65EA 旫 65EB 旬 65EC 旭 65ED 旮 65EE 旯 65EF **3** 旰 65F0 旱 65F1 旲 65F2 旳 65F3 旴 65F4 旵 65F5 时 65F6 旷 65F7 旸 65F8
4 旹 65F9 旺 65FA 旻 65FB 旼 65FC 旽 65FD 旾 65FE 旿 65FF 昀 6600 昁 6601 昂 6602 昃 6603 昄 6604 昅 6605 昆 6606 昇 6607 昈 6608 昉 6609 昊 660A 昋 660B 昌 660C 昍 660D 明 660E
昏 660F 昐 6610 昑 6611 昒 6612 易 6613 昔 6614 昕 6615 昖 6616 昗 6617 昘 6618 昙 6619 畅 7545 **5** 昚 661A 昛 661B 昜 661C 昝 661D 昞 661E 星 661F 映 6620 昡 6621 昢 6622 昣 6623
昤 6624 春 6625 昦 6626 昧 6627 昨 6628 昩 6629 昪 662A 昫 662B 昬 662C 昭 662D 昮 662E 是 662F 昰 6630 昱 6631 昲 6632 昳 6633 昴 6634 昵 6635 昶 6636 昷 6637 昸 6638 昹 6639 昺 663A
昻 663B 昼 663C 昽 663D 显 663E 昿 663F **6** 晀 6640 晁 6641 時 6642 晃 6643 晄 6644 晅 6645 晆 6646 晇 6647 晈 6648 晉 6649 晊 664A 晋 664B 晌 664C 晍 664D 晎 664E 晏 664F 晐 6650
晑 6651 晒 6652 晓 6653 晔 6654 晕 6655 晖 6656 **7** 晗 6657 晘 6658 晙 6659 晚 665A 晛 665B 晜 665C 晝 665D 晞 665E 晟 665F 晠 6660 晡 6661 晢 6662 晣 6663 晤 6664 晥 6665 晦 6666
晧 6667 晨 6668 晩 6669 曽 66FD **8** 晪 666A 晫 666B 晬 666C 晭 666D 普 666E 景 666F 晰 6670 晱 6671 晲 6672 晳 6673 晴 6674 晵 6675 晶 6676 晷 6677 晸 6678 晹 6679 智 667A 晻 667B
晼 667C 晽 667D 晾 667E 晿 667F 暀 6680 暁 6681 暂 6682 暃 6683 **9** 暄 6684 暅 6685 暆 6686 暇 6687 暈 6688 暉 6689 暊 668A 暋 668B 暌 668C 暍 668D 暎 668E 暏 668F 暐 6690 暑 6691
暒 6692 暓 6693 暔 6694 暕 6695 暖 6696 暗 6697 暘 6698 暙 6699 稥 7A25 **10** 尡 5C21 暚 669A 暛 669B 暜 669C 暝 669D 暞 669E 暟 669F 暠 66A0 暡 66A1 暢 66A2 暣 66A3 暤 66A4 暥 66A5

日 72 暤 66A4 暥 66A5 暦 66A6 暧 66A7 暨 66A8 **11** 暩 66A9 暪 66AA 暫 66AB 暬 66AC 暭 66AD 暮 66AE 暯 66AF 暰 66B0 暱 66B1 暲 66B2 暳 66B3 暴 66B4 暵 66B5 暶 66B6 暷 66B7 **12** 暸 66B8
暹 66B9 暺 66BA 暻 66BB 暼 66BC 暽 66BD 暾 66BE 暿 66BF 曀 66C0 曁 66C1 曂 66C2 曃 66C3 曄 66C4 曅 66C5 曆 66C6 曇 66C7 曈 66C8 曉 66C9 曊 66CA 曋 66CB 曌 66CC 曍 66CD **13** 曎 66CE
曏 66CF 曐 66D0 曑 66D1 曒 66D2 曓 66D3 曔 66D4 曕 66D5 曖 66D6 曗 66D7 **14** 曘 66D8 曙 66D9 曚 66DA 曛 66DB 曜 66DC **15** 曝 66DD 曞 66DE 曟 66DF 曠 66E0 曡 66E1 曢 66E2
16 曣 66E3 曤 66E4 曥 66E5 曦 66E6 曧 66E7 曨 66E8 **17** 曩 66E9 **19** 曪 66EA 曫 66EB 曬 66EC **20** 曭 66ED 曮 66EE **21** 曯 66EF

曰 73 曰 66F0 **1** 曱 66F1 电 7535 **2** 曲 66F2 曳 66F3 **3** 更 66F4 曵 66F5 **4** 曶 66F6 **5** 曷 66F7 **6** 書 66F8 曺 66FA **7** 曹 66F9 曻 66FB 曼 66FC **8** 曾 66FE
替 66FF 最 6700 朁 6701 朂 6702 **9** 會 6703 **10** 朄 6704 朅 6705 **12** 朆 6706 **17** 朇 6707

月 74 月 6708 **2** 有 6709 **4** 朊 670A 朋 670B 朌 670C 服 670D **5** 朎 670E 朏 670F 朐 6710 朑 6711 **6** 朒 6712 朓 6713 朔 6714 朕 6715 **7** 朖 6716 朗 6717 朘 6718 朙 6719
朚 671A 望 671B **8** 朜 671C 朝 671D 朞 671E 期 671F **9** 朠 6720 朡 6721 **10** 朢 6722 **11** 膤 81A4 **12** 朣 6723 朤 6724 朥 6725 膶 81B6 **14** 朦 6726 **16** 朧 6727

木 75 木 6728 朩 6729 **1** 未 672A 末 672B 本 672C 札 672D 朮 672E 术 672F 朰 6730 **2** 朱 6731 朲 6732 朳 6733 朴 6734 朵 6735 朶 6736 朷 6737 朸 6738 朹 6739 机 673A 朻 673B 朼 673C
朽 673D 朾 673E 朿 673F 杀 6740 杁 6741 杂 6742 权 6743 **3** 杄 6744 杅 6745 杆 6746 杇 6747 杈 6748 杉 6749 杊 674A 杋 674B 杌 674C 杍 674D 李 674E 杏 674F 材 6750 村 6751 杒 6752
杓 6753 杔 6754 杕 6755 杖 6756 杗 6757 杘 6758 杙 6759 杚 675A 杛 675B 杜 675C 杝 675D 杞 675E 束 675F 杠 6760 条 6761 杢 6762 杣 6763 杤 6764 来 6765 杦 6766 杧 6767 杨 6768 杩 6769
极 6781 **4** 杪 676A 杫 676B 杬 676C 杭 676D 杮 676E 杯 676F 杰 6770 東 6771 杲 6772 杳 6773 杴 6774 杵 6775 杶 6776 杷 6777 杸 6778 杹 6779 杺 677A 杻 677B 杼 677C 杽 677D 松 677E
板 677F 枀 6780 枂 6782 枃 6783 构 6784 枅 6785 枆 6786 枇 6787 枈 6788 枉 6789 枊 678A 枋 678B 枌 678C 枍 678D 枎 678E 枏 678F 析 6790 枑 6791 枒 6792 枓 6793 枔 6794 枕 6795 枖 6796
林 6797 枘 6798 枙 6799 枚 679A 枛 679B 果 679C 枝 679D 枞 679E 枟 679F 枠 67A0 枡 67A1 枢 67A2 枣 67A3 枤 67A4 枥 67A5 枦 67A6 枧 67A7 枨 67A8 枩 67A9 枪 67AA 枫 67AB 枬 67AC 枭 67AD
5 枮 67AE 枯 67AF 枰 67B0 枱 67B1 枲 67B2 枳 67B3 枴 67B4 枵 67B5 架 67B6 枷 67B7 枸 67B8 枹 67B9 枺 67BA 枻 67BB 枼 67BC 枽 67BD 枾 67BE 枿 67BF 柀 67C0 柁 67C1 柂 67C2 柃 67C3
柄 67C4 柅 67C5 柆 67C6 柇 67C7 柈 67C8 柉 67C9 柊 67CA 柋 67CB 柌 67CC 柍 67CD 柎 67CE 柏 67CF 某 67D0 柑 67D1 柒 67D2 染 67D3 柔 67D4 柕 67D5 柖 67D6 柗 67D7 柘 67D8 柙 67D9 柚 67DA
柛 67DB 柜 67DC 柝 67DD 柞 67DE 柟 67DF 柠 67E0 柡 67E1 柢 67E2 柣 67E3 柤 67E4 查 67E5 柦 67E6 柧 67E7 柨 67E8 柩 67E9 柪 67EA 柫 67EB 柬 67EC 柭 67ED 柮 67EE 柯 67EF 柰 67F0 柱 67F1
柲 67F2 柳 67F3 柴 67F4 柵 67F5 柶 67F6 柷 67F7 柸 67F8 柹 67F9 柺 67FA 査 67FB 柼 67FC 柽 67FD 柾 67FE 柿 67FF 栀 6800 栁 6801 栂 6802 栃 6803 栄 6804 栅 6805 栆 6806 标 6807 栈 6808
栉 6809 栊 680A 栋 680B 栌 680C 栍 680D 栎 680E 栏 680F 栐 6810 树 6811 **6** 唜 551C 栒 6812 栓 6813 栔 6814 栕 6815 栖 6816 栗 6817 栘 6818 栙 6819 栚 681A 栛 681B 栜 681C 栝 681D
栞 681E 栟 681F 栠 6820 校 6821 栢 6822 栣 6823 栤 6824 栥 6825 栦 6826 栧 6827 栨 6828 栩 6829 株 682A 栫 682B 栬 682C 栭 682D 栮 682E 栯 682F 栰 6830 栱 6831 栲 6832 栳 6833 栴 6834

木 75 | 栱 6831 | 栲 6832 | 栳 6833 | 栴 6834 | 栵 6835 | 栶 6836 | 样 6837 | 核 6838 | 根 6839 | 栺 683A | 栻 683B | 格 683C | 栽 683D | 栾 683E | 栿 683F | 桀 6840 | 桁 6841 | 桂 6842 | 桃 6843 | 桄 6844 | 桅 6845 | 框 6846 | 桇 6847

案 6848 | 桉 6849 | 桊 684A | 桋 684B | 桌 684C | 桍 684D | 桎 684E | 桏 684F | 桐 6850 | 桑 6851 | 桒 6852 | 桓 6853 | 桔 6854 | 桕 6855 | 桖 6856 | 桗 6857 | 桘 6858 | 桙 6859 | 桚 685A | 桛 685B | 桜 685C | 桝 685D | 桞 685E

桟 685F | 桠 6860 | 桡 6861 | 桢 6862 | 档 6863 | 桤 6864 | 桥 6865 | 桦 6866 | 桧 6867 | 桨 6868 | 桩 6869 | 桪 686A | **7** | 桫 686B | 桬 686C | 桭 686D | 桮 686E | 桯 686F | 桰 6870 | 桱 6871 | 桲 6872 | 桳 6873 | 桴 6874

桵 6875 | 桶 6876 | 桷 6877 | 桸 6878 | 桹 6879 | 桺 687A | 桻 687B | 桼 687C | 桽 687D | 桾 687E | 桿 687F | 梀 6880 | 梁 6881 | 梂 6882 | 梃 6883 | 梄 6884 | 梅 6885 | 梆 6886 | 梇 6887 | 梈 6888 | 梉 6889 | 梊 688A | 梋 688B

梌 688C | 梍 688D | 梎 688E | 梏 688F | 梐 6890 | 梑 6891 | 梒 6892 | 梓 6893 | 梔 6894 | 梕 6895 | 梖 6896 | 梗 6897 | 梘 6898 | 梙 6899 | 梚 689A | 梛 689B | 梜 689C | 條 689D | 梞 689E | 梟 689F | 梠 68A0 | 梡 68A1 | 梢 68A2

梣 68A3 | 梤 68A4 | 梥 68A5 | 梦 68A6 | 梧 68A7 | 梨 68A8 | 梩 68A9 | 梪 68AA | 梫 68AB | 梬 68AC | 梭 68AD | 梮 68AE | 梯 68AF | 械 68B0 | 梱 68B1 | 梲 68B2 | 梳 68B3 | 梴 68B4 | 梵 68B5 | 梶 68B6 | 梷 68B7 | 梸 68B8 | 梹 68B9

梺 68BA | 梻 68BB | 梼 68BC | 梽 68BD | 梾 68BE | 梿 68BF | 检 68C0 | 棁 68C1 | 棂 68C2 | **8** | 棃 68C3 | 棄 68C4 | 棅 68C5 | 棆 68C6 | 棇 68C7 | 棈 68C8 | 棉 68C9 | 棊 68CA | 棋 68CB | 棌 68CC | 棍 68CD | 棎 68CE | 棏 68CF

棐 68D0 | 棑 68D1 | 棒 68D2 | 棓 68D3 | 棔 68D4 | 棕 68D5 | 棖 68D6 | 棗 68D7 | 棘 68D8 | 棙 68D9 | 棚 68DA | 棛 68DB | 棜 68DC | 棝 68DD | 棞 68DE | 棟 68DF | 棠 68E0 | 棡 68E1 | 棢 68E2 | 棣 68E3 | 棤 68E4 | 棥 68E5 | 棦 68E6

棧 68E7 | 棨 68E8 | 棩 68E9 | 棪 68EA | 棫 68EB | 棬 68EC | 棭 68ED | 森 68EE | 棯 68EF | 棰 68F0 | 棱 68F1 | 棲 68F2 | 棳 68F3 | 棴 68F4 | 棵 68F5 | 棶 68F6 | 棷 68F7 | 棸 68F8 | 棹 68F9 | 棺 68FA | 棻 68FB | 棼 68FC | 棽 68FD

棾 68FE | 棿 68FF | 椀 6900 | 椁 6901 | 椂 6902 | 椃 6903 | 椄 6904 | 椅 6905 | 椆 6906 | 椇 6907 | 椈 6908 | 椉 6909 | 椊 690A | 椋 690B | 椌 690C | 植 690D | 椎 690E | 椏 690F | 椐 6910 | 椑 6911 | 椒 6912 | 椓 6913 | 椔 6914

椕 6915 | 椖 6916 | 椗 6917 | 椘 6918 | 椙 6919 | 椚 691A | 椛 691B | 検 691C | 椝 691D | 椞 691E | 椟 691F | 椠 6920 | 椡 6921 | 椢 6922 | 椣 6923 | 椤 6924 | 椥 6925 | 椦 6926 | 椧 6927 | 椨 6928 | 椩 6929 | 椪 692A | 椫 692B

椬 692C | 椭 692D | 椮 692E | **9** | 椯 692F | 椰 6930 | 椱 6931 | 椲 6932 | 椳 6933 | 椴 6934 | 椵 6935 | 椶 6936 | 椷 6937 | 椸 6938 | 椹 6939 | 椺 693A | 椻 693B | 椼 693C | 椽 693D | 椾 693E | 椿 693F | 楀 6940 | 楁 6941

楂 6942 | 楃 6943 | 楄 6944 | 楅 6945 | 楆 6946 | 楇 6947 | 楈 6948 | 楉 6949 | 楊 694A | 楋 694B | 楌 694C | 楍 694D | 楎 694E | 楏 694F | 楐 6950 | 楑 6951 | 楒 6952 | 楓 6953 | 楔 6954 | 楕 6955 | 楖 6956 | 楗 6957 | 楘 6958

楙 6959 | 楚 695A | 楛 695B | 楜 695C | 楝 695D | 楞 695E | 楟 695F | 楠 6960 | 楡 6961 | 楢 6962 | 楣 6963 | 楤 6964 | 楥 6965 | 楦 6966 | 楧 6967 | 楨 6968 | 楩 6969 | 楪 696A | 楫 696B | 楬 696C | 業 696D | 楮 696E | 楯 696F

楰 6970 | 楱 6971 | 楲 6972 | 楳 6973 | 楴 6974 | 極 6975 | 楶 6976 | 楷 6977 | 楸 6978 | 楹 6979 | 楺 697A | 楻 697B | 楼 697C | 楽 697D | 楾 697E | 楿 697F | 榀 6980 | 榁 6981 | 概 6982 | 榃 6983 | 榄 6984 | 榅 6985 | 榆 6986

榇 6987 | 榈 6988 | 榉 6989 | 榊 698A | 榋 698B | 榌 698C | 榔 6994 | 榘 6998 | **10** | 榍 698D | 榎 698E | 榏 698F | 榐 6990 | 榑 6991 | 榒 6992 | 榓 6993 | 榕 6995 | 榖 6996 | 榗 6997 | 榙 6999 | 榚 699A | 榛 699B | 榜 699C

榝 699D | 榞 699E | 榟 699F | 榠 69A0 | 榡 69A1 | 榢 69A2 | 榣 69A3 | 榤 69A4 | 榥 69A5 | 榦 69A6 | 榧 69A7 | 榨 69A8 | 榩 69A9 | 榪 69AA | 榫 69AB | 榬 69AC | 榭 69AD | 榮 69AE | 榯 69AF | 榰 69B0 | 榱 69B1 | 榲 69B2 | 榳 69B3

榴 69B4 | 榵 69B5 | 榶 69B6 | 榷 69B7 | 榸 69B8 | 榹 69B9 | 榺 69BA | 榻 69BB | 榼 69BC | 榽 69BD | 榾 69BE | 榿 69BF | 槀 69C0 | 槁 69C1 | 槂 69C2 | 槃 69C3 | 槄 69C4 | 槅 69C5 | 槆 69C6 | 槇 69C7 | 槈 69C8 | 槉 69C9 | 槊 69CA

構 69CB | 槌 69CC | 槍 69CD | 槎 69CE | 槏 69CF | 槐 69D0 | 槑 69D1 | 槒 69D2 | 槓 69D3 | 槔 69D4 | 槕 69D5 | 槖 69D6 | 槗 69D7 | 様 69D8 | 槙 69D9 | 槛 69DB | 槜 69DC | 槝 69DD | 槞 69DE | 槟 69DF | 槠 69E0 | 槡 69E1 | 槩 69E9

樮 6A2E | 欅 6B05 | **11** | 槢 69E2 | 槣 69E3 | 槤 69E4 | 槥 69E5 | 槦 69E6 | 槧 69E7 | 槨 69E8 | 槪 69EA | 槫 69EB | 槬 69EC | 槭 69ED | 槮 69EE | 槯 69EF | 槰 69F0 | 槱 69F1 | 槲 69F2 | 槳 69F3 | 槴 69F4 | 槵 69F5 | 槶 69F6

槷 69F7 | 槸 69F8 | 槹 69F9 | 槺 69FA | 槻 69FB | 槼 69FC | 槽 69FD | 槾 69FE | 槿 69FF | 樀 6A00 | 樁 6A01 | 樂 6A02 | 樃 6A03 | 樄 6A04 | 樅 6A05 | 樆 6A06 | 樇 6A07 | 樈 6A08 | 樉 6A09 | 樊 6A0A | 樋 6A0B | 樌 6A0C | 樍 6A0D

樎 6A0E | 樏 6A0F | 樐 6A10 | 樑 6A11 | 樒 6A12 | 樓 6A13 | 樔 6A14 | 樕 6A15 | 樖 6A16 | 樗 6A17 | 樘 6A18 | 標 6A19 | 樚 6A1A | 樛 6A1B | 樜 6A1C | 樝 6A1D | 樞 6A1E | 樟 6A1F | 樠 6A20 | 模 6A21 | 樢 6A22 | 樣 6A23 | 樤 6A24

樥 6A25 | 樦 6A26 | 樧 6A27 | 樨 6A28 | 権 6A29 | 横 6A2A | 樫 6A2B | 樬 6A2C | 樭 6A2D | 樯 6A2F | 樰 6A30 | 樱 6A31 | 橴 6A74 | **12** | 樲 6A32 | 樳 6A33 | 樴 6A34 | 樵 6A35 | 樶 6A36 | 樷 6A37 | 樸 6A38 | 樹 6A39 | 樺 6A3A

木 75 樶 6A36 樷 6A37 樸 6A38 樹 6A39 樺 6A3A 樻 6A3B 樼 6A3C 樽 6A3D 樾 6A3E 樿 6A3F 橀 6A40 橁 6A41 橂 6A42 橃 6A43 橄 6A44 橅 6A45 橆 6A46 橇 6A47 橈 6A48 橉 6A49 橊 6A4A 橋 6A4B 橌 6A4C
橍 6A4D 橎 6A4E 橏 6A4F 橐 6A50 橑 6A51 橒 6A52 橓 6A53 橔 6A54 橕 6A55 橖 6A56 橗 6A57 橘 6A58 橙 6A59 橚 6A5A 橛 6A5B 橜 6A5C 橝 6A5D 橞 6A5E 機 6A5F 橠 6A60 橡 6A61 橢 6A62 橣 6A63
橤 6A64 橥 6A65 橦 6A66 橧 6A67 橨 6A68 橩 6A69 橪 6A6A 橫 6A6B 橬 6A6C 橭 6A6D 橮 6A6E 橯 6A6F 橰 6A70 橱 6A71 橲 6A72 橳 6A73 橵 6A75 橶 6A76 橷 6A77 橸 6A78 橹 6A79 橺 6A7A 橻 6A7B
橼 6A7C **13** 槚 69DA 橽 6A7D 橾 6A7E 橿 6A7F 檀 6A80 檁 6A81 檂 6A82 檃 6A83 檄 6A84 檅 6A85 檆 6A86 檇 6A87 檈 6A88 檉 6A89 檊 6A8A 檋 6A8B 檌 6A8C 檍 6A8D 檎 6A8E 檏 6A8F 檐 6A90
檑 6A91 檒 6A92 檓 6A93 檔 6A94 檕 6A95 檖 6A96 檗 6A97 檘 6A98 檙 6A99 檚 6A9A 檛 6A9B 檜 6A9C 檝 6A9D 檞 6A9E 檟 6A9F 檠 6AA0 檡 6AA1 檢 6AA2 檣 6AA3 檤 6AA4 檥 6AA5 檦 6AA6 檧 6AA7
檨 6AA8 檩 6AA9 檪 6AAA **14** 檫 6AAB 檬 6AAC 檭 6AAD 檮 6AAE 檯 6AAF 檰 6AB0 檱 6AB1 檲 6AB2 檳 6AB3 檴 6AB4 檵 6AB5 檶 6AB6 檷 6AB7 檸 6AB8 檹 6AB9 檺 6ABA 檻 6ABB 檼 6ABC 檽 6ABD
檾 6ABE 檿 6ABF 櫀 6AC0 櫁 6AC1 櫂 6AC2 櫃 6AC3 櫄 6AC4 櫅 6AC5 櫆 6AC6 櫇 6AC7 櫈 6AC8 櫉 6AC9 櫊 6ACA **15** 櫋 6ACB 櫌 6ACC 櫍 6ACD 櫎 6ACE 櫏 6ACF 櫐 6AD0 櫑 6AD1 櫒 6AD2 櫓 6AD3
櫔 6AD4 櫕 6AD5 櫖 6AD6 櫗 6AD7 櫘 6AD8 櫙 6AD9 櫚 6ADA 櫛 6ADB 櫜 6ADC 櫝 6ADD 櫞 6ADE 櫟 6ADF 櫠 6AE0 櫡 6AE1 櫢 6AE2 櫣 6AE3 櫤 6AE4 櫥 6AE5 櫦 6AE6 櫭 6AED **16** 櫧 6AE7 櫨 6AE8
櫩 6AE9 櫪 6AEA 櫫 6AEB 櫬 6AEC 櫮 6AEE 櫯 6AEF 櫰 6AF0 櫱 6AF1 櫲 6AF2 櫳 6AF3 櫴 6AF4 櫵 6AF5 櫶 6AF6 **17** 櫸 6AF8 櫹 6AF9 櫺 6AFA 櫻 6AFB 櫼 6AFC 櫽 6AFD 櫾 6AFE 櫿 6AFF 欀 6B00
欁 6B01 欂 6B02 欃 6B03 欄 6B04 欌 6B0C **18** 櫷 6AF7 欆 6B06 欇 6B07 欈 6B08 欉 6B09 權 6B0A 欋 6B0B 欍 6B0D 欎 6B0E **19** 欏 6B0F 欐 6B10 欑 6B11 欒 6B12 **20** 欓 6B13 欔 6B14
欕 6B15 **21** 欖 6B16 欗 6B17 欘 6B18 欙 6B19 欚 6B1A 欛 6B1B **22** 欜 6B1C 欝 6B1D **24** 欞 6B1E 欟 6B1F

欠 76 欠 6B20 **2** 次 6B21 欢 6B22 **3** 欤 6B24 **4** 欣 6B23 欥 6B25 欦 6B26 欧 6B27 **5** 欨 6B28 欪 6B2A **6** 欫 6B2B 欬 6B2C 欭 6B2D 欮 6B2E 欯 6B2F 欰 6B30 欱 6B31
7 欲 6B32 欳 6B33 欴 6B34 欵 6B35 欶 6B36 欷 6B37 欸 6B38 **8** 欹 6B39 欺 6B3A 欻 6B3B 欼 6B3C 欽 6B3D 款 6B3E 欿 6B3F **9** 欩 6B29 歀 6B40 歁 6B41 歂 6B42 歃 6B43 歄 6B44
歅 6B45 歆 6B46 歇 6B47 歈 6B48 **10** 歉 6B49 歊 6B4A 歋 6B4B 歌 6B4C 歍 6B4D **11** 歎 6B4E 歏 6B4F 歐 6B50 歑 6B51 歒 6B52 歓 6B53 **12** 歔 6B54 歖 6B56 歗 6B57 歘 6B58 歙 6B59
歚 6B5A **13** 歕 6B55 歛 6B5B 歜 6B5C 歝 6B5D **14** 歞 6B5E 歟 6B5F **15** 歠 6B60 **18** 歡 6B61

止 77 止 6B62 **1** 正 6B63 **2** 此 6B64 **3** 步 6B65 **4** 武 6B66 歧 6B67 歨 6B68 歩 6B69 **5** 歪 6B6A 歫 6B6B **6** 歬 6B6C 歭 6B6D **8** 歮 6B6E 歯 6B6F **9** 歰 6B70
歱 6B71 歲 6B72 歳 6B73 **10** 歴 6B74 **11** 歵 6B75 歶 6B76 **12** 歷 6B77 **14** 歸 6B78

歹 78 歹 6B79 **1** 歺 6B7A **2** 死 6B7B **3** 歼 6B7C **4** 歽 6B7D 歾 6B7E 歿 6B7F 殀 6B80 殁 6B81 **5** 殂 6B82 殃 6B83 殄 6B84 殅 6B85 殆 6B86 殇 6B87 **6** 殈 6B88 殉 6B89
殊 6B8A 残 6B8B **7** 殌 6B8C 殍 6B8D 殎 6B8E 殏 6B8F 殐 6B90 殑 6B91 殒 6B92 殓 6B93 **8** 殔 6B94 殕 6B95 殖 6B96 殗 6B97 殘 6B98 殙 6B99 殚 6B9A **9** 殛 6B9B 殜 6B9C 飱 98F1
10 殝 6B9D 殞 6B9E 殟 6B9F 殠 6BA0 殡 6BA1 **11** 殢 6BA2 殣 6BA3 殤 6BA4 殥 6BA5 殦 6BA6 **12** 殧 6BA7 殨 6BA8 殩 6BA9 殪 6BAA 殫 6BAB **13** 殬 6BAC 殭 6BAD 殮 6BAE

歹 78 **14** 殯 6BAF **15** 殰 6BB0 殱 6BB1 **17** 殲 6BB2

殳 79 殳 6BB3 **4** 殴 6BB4 **5** 段 6BB5 殶 6BB6 **6** 殷 6BB7 **7** 殸 6BB8 殹 6BB9 殺 6BBA 殻 6BBB **8** 殼 6BBC 殽 6BBD **9** 殾 6BBE 殿 6BBF 毀 6BC0 毁 6BC1 毂 6BC2
10 毃 6BC3 毄 6BC4 **11** 毅 6BC5 毆 6BC6 **12** 毇 6BC7 毈 6BC8 **15** 毉 6BC9 **19** 毊 6BCA

毋 80 毋 6BCB 毌 6BCC **1** 母 6BCD **2** 毎 6BCE **3** 乸 4E78 每 6BCF 毐 6BD0 **4** 毑 6BD1 毒 6BD2 **9** 毓 6BD3

比 81 比 6BD4 **2** 毕 6BD5 **5** 毖 6BD6 毗 6BD7 毘 6BD8 **6** 毙 6BD9 **13** 毚 6BDA

毛 82 毛 6BDB **3** 毜 6BDC 毝 6BDD **4** 毞 6BDE 毟 6BDF **5** 毠 6BE0 毡 6BE1 **6** 毢 6BE2 毣 6BE3 毤 6BE4 毥 6BE5 毦 6BE6 毧 6BE7 毨 6BE8 毩 6BE9 毪 6BEA **7** 毫 6BEB 毬 6BEC
毭 6BED 毮 6BEE **8** 毯 6BEF 毰 6BF0 毱 6BF1 毲 6BF2 毳 6BF3 毴 6BF4 毵 6BF5 毶 6BF6 **9** 毷 6BF7 毸 6BF8 毹 6BF9 毺 6BFA 毻 6BFB 毼 6BFC 毽 6BFD **10** 毾 6BFE **11** 毿 6BFF
氀 6C00 氁 6C01 氂 6C02 **12** 氃 6C03 氄 6C04 氅 6C05 氆 6C06 氇 6C07 **13** 氈 6C08 氉 6C09 氊 6C0A **14** 氋 6C0B **15** 氌 6C0C **18** 氍 6C0D **22** 氎 6C0E

氏 83 氏 6C0F **1** 氐 6C10 民 6C11 **2** 氒 6C12 **4** 氓 6C13

气 84 气 6C14 **1** 氕 6C15 **2** 氖 6C16 気 6C17 氘 6C18 **3** 氙 6C19 氚 6C1A **4** 氛 6C1B 氜 6C1C 氝 6C1D **5** 氞 6C1E 氟 6C1F 氠 6C20 氡 6C21 氢 6C22 **6** 氣 6C23 氤 6C24
氥 6C25 氦 6C26 氧 6C27 氨 6C28 氩 6C29 **7** 氪 6C2A 氫 6C2B **8** 氬 6C2C 氭 6C2D 氮 6C2E 氯 6C2F 氰 6C30 **9** 氱 6C31 **10** 氲 6C32 氳 6C33

水 85 水 6C34 氵 6C35 **1** 氶 6C36 氷 6C37 永 6C38 氹 6C39 氺 6C3A **2** 凼 51FC 氻 6C3B 氼 6C3C 氾 6C3E 氿 6C3F 汀 6C40 汁 6C41 求 6C42 汃 6C43 汄 6C44 汅 6C45 汆 6C46 汇 6C47 汈 6C48
汉 6C49 **3** 汊 6C4A 汋 6C4B 汌 6C4C 汍 6C4D 汎 6C4E 汏 6C4F 汐 6C50 汑 6C51 汒 6C52 汓 6C53 汔 6C54 汕 6C55 汖 6C56 汗 6C57 汘 6C58 汙 6C59 汚 6C5A 汛 6C5B 汜 6C5C 汝 6C5D 汞 6C5E
江 6C5F 池 6C60 污 6C61 汢 6C62 汣 6C63 汤 6C64 **4** 汥 6C65 汦 6C66 汧 6C67 汨 6C68 汩 6C69 汪 6C6A 汫 6C6B 汬 6C6C 汭 6C6D 汮 6C6E 汯 6C6F 汰 6C70 汱 6C71 汲 6C72 汳 6C73 汴 6C74
汵 6C75 汶 6C76 汷 6C77 汸 6C78 汹 6C79 決 6C7A 汻 6C7B 汼 6C7C 汽 6C7D 汾 6C7E 汿 6C7F 沀 6C80 沁 6C81 沂 6C82 沃 6C83 沄 6C84 沅 6C85 沆 6C86 沇 6C87 沈 6C88 沉 6C89 沊 6C8A 沋 6C8B
沌 6C8C 沍 6C8D 沎 6C8E 沏 6C8F 沐 6C90 沑 6C91 沒 6C92 沓 6C93 沔 6C94 沕 6C95 沖 6C96 沗 6C97 沘 6C98 沙 6C99 沚 6C9A 沛 6C9B 沜 6C9C 沝 6C9D 沞 6C9E 沟 6C9F 沠 6CA0 没 6CA1 沢 6CA2

水 85 沣 6CA3 沤 6CA4 沥 6CA5 沦 6CA6 沧 6CA7 沨 6CA8 沩 6CA9 沪 6CAA **5** 沫 6CAB 沬 6CAC 沭 6CAD 沮 6CAE 沯 6CAF 沰 6CB0 沱 6CB1 沲 6CB2 河 6CB3 沴 6CB4 沵 6CB5 沶 6CB6 沷 6CB7 沸 6CB8

油 6CB9 沺 6CBA 治 6CBB 沼 6CBC 沽 6CBD 沾 6CBE 沿 6CBF 泀 6CC0 況 6CC1 泂 6CC2 泃 6CC3 泄 6CC4 泅 6CC5 泆 6CC6 泇 6CC7 泈 6CC8 泉 6CC9 泊 6CCA 泋 6CCB 泌 6CCC 泍 6CCD 泎 6CCE 泏 6CCF

泐 6CD0 泑 6CD1 泓 6CD3 泔 6CD4 法 6CD5 泖 6CD6 泗 6CD7 泘 6CD8 泙 6CD9 泛 6CDB 泜 6CDC 泝 6CDD 泞 6CDE 泟 6CDF 泠 6CE0 泡 6CE1 波 6CE2 泣 6CE3 泤 6CE4 泥 6CE5 泦 6CE6 泧 6CE7 注 6CE8

泩 6CE9 泪 6CEA 泫 6CEB 泬 6CEC 泭 6CED 泮 6CEE 泯 6CEF 泰 6CF0 泱 6CF1 泲 6CF2 泳 6CF3 泴 6CF4 泵 6CF5 泶 6CF6 泷 6CF7 泸 6CF8 泹 6CF9 泺 6CFA 泻 6CFB 泼 6CFC 泽 6CFD 泾 6CFE 畓 7553

6 泒 6CD2 泚 6CDA 泿 6CFF 洀 6D00 洁 6D01 洂 6D02 洃 6D03 洄 6D04 洅 6D05 洆 6D06 洇 6D07 洈 6D08 洉 6D09 洊 6D0A 洋 6D0B 洌 6D0C 洎 6D0E 洏 6D0F 洐 6D10 洑 6D11 洒 6D12 洓 6D13

洔 6D14 洕 6D15 洗 6D17 洘 6D18 洙 6D19 洚 6D1A 洛 6D1B 洜 6D1C 洝 6D1D 洞 6D1E 洟 6D1F 洠 6D20 洡 6D21 洢 6D22 洣 6D23 洤 6D24 津 6D25 洦 6D26 洧 6D27 洨 6D28 洩 6D29 洪 6D2A 洫 6D2B

洬 6D2C 洭 6D2D 洮 6D2E 洯 6D2F 洰 6D30 洱 6D31 洲 6D32 洳 6D33 洴 6D34 洵 6D35 洶 6D36 洷 6D37 洸 6D38 洹 6D39 洺 6D3A 活 6D3B 洼 6D3C 洽 6D3D 派 6D3E 洿 6D3F 浀 6D40 流 6D41 浂 6D42

浃 6D43 浄 6D44 浅 6D45 浆 6D46 浇 6D47 浈 6D48 浉 6D49 浊 6D4A 测 6D4B 浌 6D4C 浍 6D4D 济 6D4E 浏 6D4F 浐 6D50 浑 6D51 浒 6D52 浓 6D53 浔 6D54 浕 6D55 **7** 洍 6D0D 洖 6D16 浖 6D56

浗 6D57 浘 6D58 浙 6D59 浚 6D5A 浛 6D5B 浜 6D5C 浝 6D5D 浞 6D5E 浟 6D5F 浠 6D60 浡 6D61 浢 6D62 浣 6D63 浤 6D64 浥 6D65 浦 6D66 浧 6D67 浨 6D68 浩 6D69 浪 6D6A 浫 6D6B 浬 6D6C 浭 6D6D

浮 6D6E 浯 6D6F 浰 6D70 浱 6D71 浲 6D72 浳 6D73 浴 6D74 浵 6D75 浶 6D76 海 6D77 浸 6D78 浹 6D79 浺 6D7A 浻 6D7B 浼 6D7C 浽 6D7D 浾 6D7E 浿 6D7F 涀 6D80 涁 6D81 涂 6D82 涃 6D83 涄 6D84

涅 6D85 涆 6D86 涇 6D87 消 6D88 涉 6D89 涊 6D8A 涋 6D8B 涌 6D8C 涍 6D8D 涎 6D8E 涏 6D8F 涐 6D90 涑 6D91 涒 6D92 涓 6D93 涔 6D94 涕 6D95 涖 6D96 涗 6D97 涘 6D98 涚 6D9A 涛 6D9B 涜 6D9C

涝 6D9D 涞 6D9E 涟 6D9F 涠 6DA0 涡 6DA1 涢 6DA2 涣 6DA3 涤 6DA4 涥 6DA5 润 6DA6 涧 6DA7 涨 6DA8 涩 6DA9 **8** 涙 6D99 涪 6DAA 涫 6DAB 涬 6DAC 涭 6DAD 涮 6DAE 涯 6DAF 涰 6DB0 涱 6DB1

液 6DB2 涳 6DB3 涴 6DB4 涵 6DB5 涶 6DB6 涷 6DB7 涸 6DB8 涹 6DB9 涺 6DBA 涻 6DBB 涼 6DBC 涽 6DBD 涾 6DBE 涿 6DBF 淀 6DC0 淁 6DC1 淂 6DC2 淃 6DC3 淄 6DC4 淅 6DC5 淆 6DC6 淇 6DC7 淈 6DC8

淉 6DC9 淊 6DCA 淋 6DCB 淌 6DCC 淍 6DCD 淎 6DCE 淏 6DCF 淐 6DD0 淑 6DD1 淒 6DD2 淓 6DD3 淔 6DD4 淕 6DD5 淖 6DD6 淗 6DD7 淘 6DD8 淙 6DD9 淚 6DDA 淛 6DDB 淜 6DDC 淝 6DDD 淞 6DDE 淟 6DDF

淠 6DE0 淡 6DE1 淢 6DE2 淣 6DE3 淤 6DE4 淥 6DE5 淦 6DE6 淧 6DE7 淨 6DE8 淩 6DE9 淪 6DEA 淫 6DEB 淬 6DEC 淭 6DED 淮 6DEE 淯 6DEF 淰 6DF0 深 6DF1 淲 6DF2 淳 6DF3 淴 6DF4 淵 6DF5 淶 6DF6

混 6DF7 淸 6DF8 淹 6DF9 淺 6DFA 添 6DFB 淼 6DFC 淽 6DFD 淾 6DFE 淿 6DFF 渀 6E00 渁 6E01 渂 6E02 渄 6E04 清 6E05 渆 6E06 渇 6E07 済 6E08 渉 6E09 渊 6E0A 渋 6E0B 渌 6E0C 渍 6E0D 渎 6E0E

渏 6E0F 渐 6E10 渑 6E11 渒 6E12 渓 6E13 渔 6E14 渕 6E15 渖 6E16 渗 6E17 湴 6E74 颍 988D **9** 渃 6E03 渘 6E18 渙 6E19 渚 6E1A 減 6E1B 渜 6E1C 渝 6E1D 渞 6E1E 渟 6E1F 渠 6E20 渡 6E21

渢 6E22 渣 6E23 渤 6E24 渥 6E25 渦 6E26 渧 6E27 渨 6E28 温 6E29 渪 6E2A 渫 6E2B 測 6E2C 渭 6E2D 渮 6E2E 港 6E2F 渰 6E30 渱 6E31 渲 6E32 渳 6E33 渴 6E34 渵 6E35 渶 6E36 渷 6E37 游 6E38

渹 6E39 渺 6E3A 渻 6E3B 渼 6E3C 渽 6E3D 渾 6E3E 渿 6E3F 湀 6E40 湁 6E41 湂 6E42 湃 6E43 湄 6E44 湅 6E45 湆 6E46 湇 6E47 湈 6E48 湉 6E49 湊 6E4A 湋 6E4B 湌 6E4C 湍 6E4D 湎 6E4E 湏 6E4F

湐 6E50 湑 6E51 湒 6E52 湓 6E53 湔 6E54 湕 6E55 湖 6E56 湗 6E57 湘 6E58 湙 6E59 湚 6E5A 湛 6E5B 湜 6E5C 湝 6E5D 湞 6E5E 湟 6E5F 湠 6E60 湡 6E61 湢 6E62 湣 6E63 湤 6E64 湥 6E65 湦 6E66

湧 6E67 湨 6E68 湩 6E69 湪 6E6A 湫 6E6B 湬 6E6C 湭 6E6D 湮 6E6E 湯 6E6F 湰 6E70 湱 6E71 湲 6E72 湳 6E73 湵 6E75 湶 6E76 湷 6E77 湸 6E78 湹 6E79 湺 6E7A 湻 6E7B 湼 6E7C 湽 6E7D 湾 6E7E

湿 6E7F 満 6E80 溁 6E81 溂 6E82 溃 6E83 溄 6E84 溅 6E85 溆 6E86 溇 6E87 溈 6E88 溉 6E89 溊 6E8A 溋 6E8B 溌 6E8C 溫 6EAB 滋 6ECB 滞 6EDE **10** 溍 6E8D 溎 6E8E 溏 6E8F 源 6E90 溑 6E91

溒 6E92 溓 6E93 溔 6E94 溕 6E95 準 6E96 溗 6E97 溘 6E98 溙 6E99 溚 6E9A 溛 6E9B 溜 6E9C 溝 6E9D 溞 6E9E 溟 6E9F 溠 6EA0 溡 6EA1 溢 6EA2 溣 6EA3 溤 6EA4 溥 6EA5 溦 6EA6 溧 6EA7 溨 6EA8

水 85 溟 6E9F 溠 6EA0 溡 6EA1 溢 6EA2 溣 6EA3 溤 6EA4 溥 6EA5 溦 6EA6 溧 6EA7 溨 6EA8 溩 6EA9 溪 6EAA 溬 6EAC 溭 6EAD 溮 6EAE 溯 6EAF 溰 6EB0 溱 6EB1 溲 6EB2 溳 6EB3 溴 6EB4 溵 6EB5 溶 6EB6

溷 6EB7 溸 6EB8 溹 6EB9 溺 6EBA 溻 6EBB 溼 6EBC 溽 6EBD 溾 6EBE 溿 6EBF 滀 6EC0 滁 6EC1 滂 6EC2 滃 6EC3 滄 6EC4 滅 6EC5 滆 6EC6 滇 6EC7 滈 6EC8 滉 6EC9 滊 6ECA 滍 6ECD 滎 6ECE 滏 6ECF

滐 6ED0 滑 6ED1 滒 6ED2 滓 6ED3 滔 6ED4 滕 6ED5 滖 6ED6 滗 6ED7 滘 6ED8 滙 6ED9 滛 6EDB 滜 6EDC 滝 6EDD 滟 6EDF 滠 6EE0 满 6EE1 滢 6EE2 滣 6EE3 滤 6EE4 滥 6EE5 滦 6EE6 滧 6EE7 滨 6EE8

滩 6EE9 **11** 滌 6ECC 滚 6EDA 滫 6EEB 滬 6EEC 滭 6EED 滮 6EEE 滯 6EEF 滰 6EF0 滱 6EF1 滲 6EF2 滳 6EF3 滴 6EF4 滵 6EF5 滶 6EF6 滷 6EF7 滸 6EF8 滹 6EF9 滺 6EFA 滻 6EFB 滼 6EFC 滽 6EFD

滾 6EFE 滿 6EFF 漀 6F00 漁 6F01 漂 6F02 漃 6F03 漄 6F04 漅 6F05 漆 6F06 漇 6F07 漈 6F08 漉 6F09 漊 6F0A 漌 6F0C 漍 6F0D 漎 6F0E 漏 6F0F 漐 6F10 漑 6F11 漒 6F12 漓 6F13 演 6F14 漕 6F15

漖 6F16 漗 6F17 漘 6F18 漙 6F19 漚 6F1A 漛 6F1B 漜 6F1C 漝 6F1D 漞 6F1E 漟 6F1F 漠 6F20 漡 6F21 漢 6F22 漣 6F23 漤 6F24 漥 6F25 漦 6F26 漧 6F27 漨 6F28 漩 6F29 漪 6F2A 漫 6F2B 漬 6F2C

漭 6F2D 漮 6F2E 漯 6F2F 漰 6F30 漱 6F31 漲 6F32 漳 6F33 漴 6F34 漵 6F35 漶 6F36 漷 6F37 漸 6F38 漹 6F39 漺 6F3A 漻 6F3B 漼 6F3C 漾 6F3E 漿 6F3F 潀 6F40 潁 6F41 潂 6F42 潃 6F43 潄 6F44

潅 6F45 潆 6F46 潇 6F47 潈 6F48 潉 6F49 潊 6F4A 潋 6F4B 潌 6F4C 潍 6F4D **12** 漋 6F0B 漽 6F3D 潎 6F4E 潏 6F4F 潐 6F50 潑 6F51 潒 6F52 潓 6F53 潔 6F54 潕 6F55 潖 6F56 潗 6F57 潘 6F58

潙 6F59 潛 6F5B 潜 6F5C 潝 6F5D 潟 6F5F 潠 6F60 潡 6F61 潢 6F62 潣 6F63 潤 6F64 潥 6F65 潦 6F66 潧 6F67 潨 6F68 潩 6F69 潪 6F6A 潫 6F6B 潬 6F6C 潭 6F6D 潮 6F6E 潯 6F6F 潰 6F70 潱 6F71

潲 6F72 潳 6F73 潴 6F74 潵 6F75 潶 6F76 潷 6F77 潸 6F78 潹 6F79 潺 6F7A 潻 6F7B 潼 6F7C 潽 6F7D 潿 6F7F 澁 6F81 澂 6F82 澃 6F83 澄 6F84 澅 6F85 澆 6F86 澇 6F87 澈 6F88 澉 6F89 澊 6F8A

澋 6F8B 澌 6F8C 澍 6F8D 澎 6F8E 澏 6F8F 澐 6F90 澑 6F91 澒 6F92 澓 6F93 澔 6F94 澕 6F95 澖 6F96 澗 6F97 澘 6F98 澚 6F9A 澜 6F9C 澝 6F9D 濐 6FD0 **13** 滪 6EEA 潚 6F5A 潞 6F5E 潾 6F7E

澙 6F99 澞 6F9E 澟 6F9F 澠 6FA0 澡 6FA1 澢 6FA2 澣 6FA3 澤 6FA4 澥 6FA5 澦 6FA6 澧 6FA7 澨 6FA8 澩 6FA9 澪 6FAA 澫 6FAB 澬 6FAC 澭 6FAD 澮 6FAE 澯 6FAF 澰 6FB0 澱 6FB1 澲 6FB2 澳 6FB3

澴 6FB4 澵 6FB5 澶 6FB6 澷 6FB7 澸 6FB8 澹 6FB9 澺 6FBA 澻 6FBB 澼 6FBC 澽 6FBD 澾 6FBE 澿 6FBF 激 6FC0 濁 6FC1 濂 6FC2 濃 6FC3 濄 6FC4 濅 6FC5 濆 6FC6 濇 6FC7 濈 6FC8 濉 6FC9 濊 6FCA

濋 6FCB 濌 6FCC 濍 6FCD 濎 6FCE 濏 6FCF 濑 6FD1 濒 6FD2 濓 6FD3 濖 6FD6 **14** 澀 6F80 濔 6FD4 濕 6FD5 濗 6FD7 濘 6FD8 濙 6FD9 濚 6FDA 濛 6FDB 濜 6FDC 濝 6FDD 濞 6FDE 济 6FDF 濠 6FE0

濡 6FE1 濢 6FE2 濣 6FE3 濤 6FE4 濥 6FE5 濦 6FE6 濧 6FE7 濨 6FE8 濩 6FE9 濪 6FEA 濫 6FEB 濬 6FEC 濭 6FED 濮 6FEE 濯 6FEF 濰 6FF0 濱 6FF1 濲 6FF2 濴 6FF4 濵 6FF5 濶 6FF6 濸 6FF8

15 澛 6F9B 濷 6FF7 濹 6FF9 濺 6FFA 濻 6FFB 濼 6FFC 濽 6FFD 濾 6FFE 濿 6FFF 瀀 7000 瀁 7001 瀂 7002 瀃 7003 瀄 7004 瀅 7005 瀆 7006 瀇 7007 瀈 7008 瀉 7009 瀊 700A 瀋 700B 瀌 700C

瀍 700D 瀎 700E 瀏 700F 瀐 7010 瀑 7011 瀒 7012 瀓 7013 瀔 7014 **16** 濳 6FF3 瀕 7015 瀖 7016 瀗 7017 瀘 7018 瀙 7019 瀚 701A 瀛 701B 瀜 701C 瀝 701D 瀞 701E 瀟 701F 瀠 7020 瀡 7021

瀢 7022 瀣 7023 瀤 7024 瀥 7025 瀦 7026 瀧 7027 瀨 7028 瀩 7029 瀪 702A 瀫 702B 瀬 702C 瀭 702D 瀮 702E **17** 瀯 702F 瀰 7030 瀱 7031 瀲 7032 瀳 7033 瀴 7034 瀵 7035 瀶 7036 瀷 7037

瀸 7038 瀹 7039 瀺 703A 瀻 703B 瀼 703C 瀽 703D 瀾 703E 瀿 703F 灀 7040 灁 7041 **18** 灂 7042 灃 7043 灄 7044 灅 7045 灆 7046 灇 7047 灈 7048 灉 7049 灊 704A 灋 704B 灌 704C 灍 704D

灏 704F 灐 7050 **19** 灑 7051 灒 7052 灓 7053 灔 7054 灕 7055 灖 7056 灗 7057 灘 7058 **20** 灙 7059 灚 705A 灛 705B 灜 705C **21** 灝 705D 灞 705E 灟 705F 灠 7060 灡 7061

22 灢 7062 灣 7063 **23** 灎 704E 灤 7064 灥 7065 灦 7066 **24** 灧 7067 灨 7068 **28** 灩 7069 **29** 灪 706A

火 86 火 706B 灬 706C **1** 灭 706D **2** 灮 706E 灯 706F 灰 7070 灱 7071 灲 7072 灳 7073 炇 7087 **3** 灴 7074 灵 7075 灶 7076 灷 7077 灸 7078 灹 7079 灺 707A 灻 707B 灼 707C 災 707D

火 86 · 灾 707E · 灿 707F · 炀 7080 · **4** · 炂 7082 · 炃 7083 · 炄 7084 · 炅 7085 · 炆 7086 · 炈 7088 · 炉 7089 · 炊 708A · 炋 708B · 炌 708C · 炍 708D · 炎 708E · 炏 708F · 炐 7090 · 炑 7091 · 炒 7092 · 炓 7093 · 炔 7094 · 炕 7095

炖 7096 · 炗 7097 · 炘 7098 · 炙 7099 · 炚 709A · 炛 709B · 炜 709C · 炝 709D · 炞 709E · **5** · 炁 7081 · 炟 709F · 炠 70A0 · 炡 70A1 · 炢 70A2 · 炣 70A3 · 炤 70A4 · 炥 70A5 · 炦 70A6 · 炧 70A7 · 炨 70A8 · 炩 70A9 · 炪 70AA

炫 70AB · 炬 70AC · 炭 70AD · 炮 70AE · 炯 70AF · 炰 70B0 · 炱 70B1 · 炲 70B2 · 炳 70B3 · 炴 70B4 · 炵 70B5 · 炶 70B6 · 炷 70B7 · 炸 70B8 · 点 70B9 · 為 70BA · 炻 70BB · 炼 70BC · 炽 70BD · 炾 70BE · 炿 70BF · 烀 70C0 · 烁 70C1

烂 70C2 · 烃 70C3 · 畑 7551 · 秌 79CC · **6** · 烄 70C4 · 烅 70C5 · 烆 70C6 · 烇 70C7 · 烈 70C8 · 烉 70C9 · 烊 70CA · 烋 70CB · 烌 70CC · 烍 70CD · 烎 70CE · 烏 70CF · 烐 70D0 · 烑 70D1 · 烒 70D2 · 烓 70D3 · 烔 70D4 · 烕 70D5

烖 70D6 · 烗 70D7 · 烘 70D8 · 烙 70D9 · 烚 70DA · 烛 70DB · 烜 70DC · 烝 70DD · 烞 70DE · 烟 70DF · 烠 70E0 · 烡 70E1 · 烢 70E2 · 烣 70E3 · 烤 70E4 · 烥 70E5 · 烦 70E6 · 烧 70E7 · 烨 70E8 · 烩 70E9 · 烪 70EA · 烫 70EB · 烬 70EC

热 70ED · 烮 70EE · 缹 7F39 · **7** · 烯 70EF · 烰 70F0 · 烱 70F1 · 烲 70F2 · 烳 70F3 · 烴 70F4 · 烵 70F5 · 烶 70F6 · 烷 70F7 · 烸 70F8 · 烹 70F9 · 烺 70FA · 烻 70FB · 烼 70FC · 烽 70FD · 烾 70FE · 烿 70FF · 焀 7100 · 焁 7101

焂 7102 · 焃 7103 · 焄 7104 · 焅 7105 · 焆 7106 · 焇 7107 · 焈 7108 · 焉 7109 · 焊 710A · 焋 710B · 焌 710C · 焍 710D · 焎 710E · 焏 710F · 焐 7110 · 焑 7111 · 焒 7112 · 焓 7113 · 焕 7115 · 焖 7116 · 焗 7117 · 焘 7118

8 · 焔 7114 · 焙 7119 · 焚 711A · 焛 711B · 焜 711C · 焝 711D · 焞 711E · 焟 711F · 焠 7120 · 無 7121 · 焢 7122 · 焣 7123 · 焤 7124 · 焥 7125 · 焦 7126 · 焧 7127 · 焨 7128 · 焩 7129 · 焪 712A · 焫 712B · 焬 712C · 焭 712D

焮 712E · 焯 712F · 焰 7130 · 焱 7131 · 焲 7132 · 焳 7133 · 焴 7134 · 焵 7135 · 然 7136 · 焷 7137 · 焸 7138 · 焹 7139 · 焺 713A · 焻 713B · 焼 713C · 焽 713D · 焾 713E · 焿 713F · 煀 7140 · 颎 988E · **9** · 煁 7141 · 煂 7142

煃 7143 · 煄 7144 · 煅 7145 · 煆 7146 · 煇 7147 · 煈 7148 · 煉 7149 · 煊 714A · 煋 714B · 煌 714C · 煍 714D · 煎 714E · 煏 714F · 煐 7150 · 煑 7151 · 煒 7152 · 煓 7153 · 煔 7154 · 煕 7155 · 煖 7156 · 煗 7157 · 煘 7158 · 煙 7159

煚 715A · 煛 715B · 煜 715C · 煝 715D · 煞 715E · 煟 715F · 煠 7160 · 煡 7161 · 煢 7162 · 煣 7163 · 煤 7164 · 煥 7165 · 煦 7166 · 照 7167 · 煨 7168 · 煩 7169 · 煪 716A · 煫 716B · 煬 716C · 煭 716D · 煮 716E · 煯 716F · 煰 7170

煱 7171 · 煲 7172 · 煳 7173 · 煴 7174 · 煵 7175 · 煶 7176 · 煷 7177 · 煸 7178 · 煺 717A · 熙 7199 · **10** · 煹 7179 · 煻 717B · 煼 717C · 煽 717D · 煾 717E · 煿 717F · 熀 7180 · 熁 7181 · 熂 7182 · 熃 7183 · 熄 7184 · 熅 7185

熆 7186 · 熇 7187 · 熈 7188 · 熉 7189 · 熊 718A · 熋 718B · 熌 718C · 熍 718D · 熎 718E · 熏 718F · 熐 7190 · 熑 7191 · 熒 7192 · 熓 7193 · 熔 7194 · 熕 7195 · 熖 7196 · 熗 7197 · 熘 7198 · 熦 71A6 · **11** · 勲 52F2 · 熚 719A

熛 719B · 熜 719C · 熝 719D · 熞 719E · 熟 719F · 熠 71A0 · 熡 71A1 · 熢 71A2 · 熣 71A3 · 熤 71A4 · 熥 71A5 · 熧 71A7 · 熨 71A8 · 熩 71A9 · 熪 71AA · 熫 71AB · 熬 71AC · 熭 71AD · 熮 71AE · 熯 71AF · 熰 71B0 · 熱 71B1 · 熲 71B2

熳 71B3 · 熴 71B4 · 熵 71B5 · **12** · 熶 71B6 · 熷 71B7 · 熸 71B8 · 熹 71B9 · 熺 71BA · 熻 71BB · 熼 71BC · 熽 71BD · 熾 71BE · 熿 71BF · 燀 71C0 · 燁 71C1 · 燂 71C2 · 燃 71C3 · 燄 71C4 · 燅 71C5 · 燆 71C6 · 燇 71C7 · 燈 71C8

燉 71C9 · 燊 71CA · 燋 71CB · 燌 71CC · 燍 71CD · 燎 71CE · 燏 71CF · 燐 71D0 · 燑 71D1 · 燒 71D2 · 燓 71D3 · 燔 71D4 · 燕 71D5 · 燖 71D6 · 燗 71D7 · 燘 71D8 · 燙 71D9 · 燚 71DA · 燛 71DB · 燜 71DC · 燝 71DD · 燞 71DE

13 · 營 71DF · 燠 71E0 · 燡 71E1 · 燢 71E2 · 燣 71E3 · 燤 71E4 · 燥 71E5 · 燦 71E6 · 燧 71E7 · 燨 71E8 · 燩 71E9 · 燪 71EA · 燫 71EB · 燬 71EC · 燭 71ED · 燮 71EE · 燯 71EF · 燰 71F0 · 燱 71F1 · 燲 71F2 · 燳 71F3 · 燴 71F4

燵 71F5 · 燶 71F6 · 燷 71F7 · **14** · 燸 71F8 · 燹 71F9 · 燺 71FA · 燻 71FB · 燼 71FC · 燽 71FD · 燾 71FE · 燿 71FF · 爀 7200 · 爁 7201 · 爂 7202 · 爃 7203 · **15** · 夑 5911 · 爄 7204 · 爅 7205 · 爆 7206 · 爇 7207 · 爈 7208

爉 7209 · 爊 720A · 爌 720C · 爍 720D · 爎 720E · 爕 7215 · **16** · 爋 720B · 爏 720F · 爐 7210 · 爑 7211 · 爒 7212 · 爓 7213 · 爔 7214 · 爖 7216 · 爗 7217 · 爘 7218 · **17** · 爙 7219 · 爚 721A · 爛 721B · **18** · 爜 721C

爝 721D · 爞 721E · 爟 721F · 爠 7220 · **19** · 爡 7221 · 爢 7222 · **20** · 爣 7223 · **21** · 爤 7224 · 爥 7225 · 爦 7226 · **24** · 爧 7227 · **25** · 爨 7228 · **29** · 爩 7229

爪 87 · 爪 722A · 爫 722B · **4** · 爬 722C · 爭 722D · 觅 89C5 · **5** · 爮 722E · 爯 722F · 爰 7230 · **6** · 爱 7231 · **8** · 爲 7232 · **10** · 爳 7233 · **11** · 噕 5655 · 爴 7234 · **14** · 爵 7235

父 88 — 父 7236 · **2** 爷 7237 · **4** 爸 7238 · **6** 爹 7239 · **9** 爺 723A

爻 89 — 爻 723B · **5** 爼 723C · **7** 爽 723D · **10** 爾 723E

丬 90 — 丬 4E2C · 爿 723F · **4** 牀 7240 · **5** 牁 7241 · **6** 将 5C06 · 牂 7242 · **9** 牃 7243 · **10** 牄 7244 · **11** 牅 7245 · **13** 牆 7246

片 91 — 片 7247 · **4** 版 7248 · **5** 牉 7249 · 牊 724A · **8** 牋 724B · 牌 724C · 牍 724D · **9** 牎 724E · 牏 724F · 牐 7250 · 牑 7251 · 牒 7252 · **10** 牓 7253 · 牔 7254 · **11** 牕 7255 · 牖 7256 · 牗 7257 · **15** 牘 7258

牙 92 — 牙 7259 · **8** 牚 725A

牛 93 — 牛 725B · 牜 725C · **2** 牝 725D · 牞 725E · 牟 725F · **3** 牠 7260 · 牡 7261 · 牢 7262 · 牣 7263 · 牤 7264 · **4** 牥 7265 · 牦 7266 · 牧 7267 · 牨 7268 · 物 7269 · 牪 726A · 牫 726B · 牬 726C · **5** 牭 726D · 牮 726E · 牯 726F · 牰 7270 · 牱 7271 · 牲 7272 · 牳 7273 · 牴 7274 · 牵 7275 · **6** 牶 7276 · 牷 7277 · 牸 7278 · 特 7279 · 牺 727A · **7** 牻 727B · 牼 727C · 牽 727D · 牾 727E · 牿 727F · 犁 7281 · **8** 犀 7280 · 犂 7282 · 犃 7283 · 犄 7284 · 犅 7285 · 犆 7286 · 犇 7287 · 犈 7288 · 犉 7289 · 犊 728A · 犋 728B · **9** 犌 728C · 犍 728D · 犎 728E · 犏 728F · 犐 7290 · 犑 7291 · **10** 犒 7292 · 犓 7293 · 犔 7294 · 犕 7295 · 犖 7296 · 犗 7297 · **11** 犘 7298 · 犙 7299 · 犚 729A · 犛 729B · **12** 犜 729C · 犝 729D · 犞 729E · 犟 729F · **13** 犠 72A0 · **15** 犡 72A1 · 犢 72A2 · 犣 72A3 · 犤 72A4 · 犥 72A5 · 犦 72A6 · **16** 犧 72A7 · 犨 72A8 · **18** 犩 72A9 · **20** 犪 72AA · **23** 犫 72AB

犬 94 — 犬 72AC · 犭 72AD · **1** 犮 72AE · **2** 犯 72AF · 犰 72B0 · **3** 犱 72B1 · 犲 72B2 · 犳 72B3 · 犴 72B4 · 犵 72B5 · 状 72B6 · 犷 72B7 · 犸 72B8 · **4** 犹 72B9 · 犺 72BA · 犻 72BB · 犼 72BC · 犽 72BD · 犾 72BE · 犿 72BF · 狀 72C0 · 狁 72C1 · 狂 72C2 · 狃 72C3 · 狄 72C4 · 狅 72C5 · 狆 72C6 · 狇 72C7 · 狈 72C8 · **5** 狉 72C9 · 狊 72CA · 狋 72CB · 狌 72CC · 狍 72CD · 狎 72CE · 狏 72CF · 狐 72D0 · 狑 72D1 · 狒 72D2 · 狓 72D3 · 狔 72D4 · 狕 72D5 · 狖 72D6 · 狗 72D7 · 狘 72D8 · 狙 72D9 · 狚 72DA · 狛 72DB · 狜 72DC · 狝 72DD · 狞 72DE · **6** 狟 72DF · 狠 72E0 · 狡 72E1 · 狢 72E2 · 狣 72E3 · 狤 72E4 · 狥 72E5 · 狦 72E6 · 狧 72E7 · 狨 72E8 · 狩 72E9 · 狪 72EA · 狫 72EB · 独 72EC · 狭 72ED · 狮 72EE · 狯 72EF · 狰 72F0 · 狱 72F1 · 狲 72F2 · **7** 狳 72F3 · 狴 72F4 · 狵 72F5 · 狶 72F6 · 狷 72F7 · 狸 72F8 · 狹 72F9 · 狺 72FA · 狻 72FB · 狼 72FC · 狽 72FD · 狾 72FE · 狿 72FF · 猀 7300 · 猁 7301 · 猂 7302 · 猃 7303 · **8** 猄 7304 · 猅 7305 · 猆 7306 · 猇 7307 · 猈 7308 · 猉 7309 · 猊 730A · 猋 730B · 猌 730C · 猍 730D · 猎 730E · 猏 730F · 猐 7310 · 猑 7311 · 猒 7312 · 猓 7313 · 猔 7314 · 猕 7315 · 猖 7316 · 猗 7317 · 猘 7318 · 猙 7319 · 猚 731A · 猛 731B · 猜 731C · 猝 731D · 猞 731E · 猟 731F · 猠 7320 · 猡 7321 · 猪 732A · **9** 猢 7322 · 猣 7323 · 猤 7324 · 猥 7325 · 猦 7326 · 猧 7327 · 猨 7328 · 猩 7329 · 猫 732B · 猬 732C

犬 94 — 猫 732B 猬 732C 猭 732D 献 732E 猯 732F 猰 7330 猱 7331 猲 7332 猳 7333 猴 7334 猵 7335 猶 7336 猷 7337 猸 7338 猹 7339 獁 7341 獓 7353 **10** 猺 733A 猻 733B 猼 733C 猽 733D 猾 733E
猿 733F 獀 7340 獂 7342 獃 7343 獄 7344 獅 7345 獆 7346 獇 7347 獈 7348 獉 7349 獊 734A **11** 獌 734C 獍 734D 獎 734E 獏 734F 獐 7350 獑 7351 獒 7352 獔 7354 獕 7355 **12** 獋 734B
獖 7356 獗 7357 獘 7358 獙 7359 獚 735A 獛 735B 獜 735C 獝 735D 獞 735E 獟 735F 獠 7360 獡 7361 獢 7362 獣 7363 獤 7364 **13** 獥 7365 獦 7366 獧 7367 獨 7368 獩 7369 獪 736A 獫 736B
獬 736C 獭 736D **14** 獮 736E 獯 736F 獰 7370 獱 7371 獲 7372 獳 7373 獴 7374 **15** 獵 7375 獶 7376 獷 7377 獸 7378 **16** 獹 7379 獺 737A 獻 737B **17** 獼 737C 獽 737D
18 獾 737E 獿 737F **19** 玀 7380 **20** 玁 7381 玂 7382 玃 7383

玄 95 — 玄 7384 **4** 玅 7385 **5** 玆 7386 **6** 率 7387 玈 7388

玉 96 — 玉 7389 玊 738A 王 738B **1** 玌 738C 玍 738D **2** 玎 738E 玏 738F 玐 7390 玑 7391 **3** 玒 7392 玓 7393 玔 7394 玕 7395 玖 7396 玗 7397 玘 7398 玙 7399 玚 739A 玛 739B
4 玜 739C 玝 739D 玞 739E 玟 739F 玠 73A0 玡 73A1 玢 73A2 玣 73A3 玤 73A4 玥 73A5 玦 73A6 玧 73A7 玨 73A8 玩 73A9 玪 73AA 玫 73AB 玬 73AC 玭 73AD 玮 73AE 环 73AF 现 73B0 玱 73B1
5 玲 73B2 玳 73B3 玴 73B4 玵 73B5 玶 73B6 玷 73B7 玸 73B8 玹 73B9 玺 73BA 玻 73BB 玼 73BC 玽 73BD 玾 73BE 玿 73BF 珀 73C0 珁 73C1 珂 73C2 珃 73C3 珄 73C4 珅 73C5 珆 73C6 珇 73C7
珈 73C8 珉 73C9 珊 73CA 珋 73CB 珌 73CC 珍 73CD 珎 73CE 珏 73CF 珐 73D0 珑 73D1 **6** 珒 73D2 珓 73D3 珔 73D4 珕 73D5 珖 73D6 珗 73D7 珘 73D8 珙 73D9 珚 73DA 珛 73DB 珜 73DC 珝 73DD
珞 73DE 珟 73DF 珠 73E0 珡 73E1 珢 73E2 珣 73E3 珤 73E4 珥 73E5 珦 73E6 珧 73E7 珨 73E8 珩 73E9 珪 73EA 珫 73EB 珬 73EC 班 73ED 珮 73EE 珯 73EF 珰 73F0 珱 73F1 珲 73F2 顼 987C
7 珳 73F3 珴 73F4 珵 73F5 珶 73F6 珸 73F8 珹 73F9 珺 73FA 珻 73FB 珼 73FC 珽 73FD 現 73FE 珿 73FF 琀 7400 琁 7401 琂 7402 球 7403 琄 7404 琅 7405 理 7406 琇 7407 琈 7408 琉 7409
琋 740B 琌 740C 琍 740D 琎 740E 琏 740F 琐 7410 琑 7411 琒 7412 琓 7413 **8** 珷 73F7 琊 740A 琔 7414 琕 7415 琖 7416 琗 7417 琘 7418 琙 7419 琚 741A 琛 741B 琜 741C 琝 741D 琟 741F
琠 7420 琡 7421 琢 7422 琣 7423 琤 7424 琥 7425 琦 7426 琧 7427 琨 7428 琩 7429 琪 742A 琫 742B 琬 742C 琭 742D 琮 742E 琯 742F 琰 7430 琱 7431 琲 7432 琳 7433 琴 7434 琵 7435 琶 7436
琷 7437 琸 7438 琹 7439 琺 743A 琻 743B 琼 743C **9** 琞 741E 琽 743D 琾 743E 琿 743F 瑀 7440 瑁 7441 瑂 7442 瑃 7443 瑄 7444 瑅 7445 瑆 7446 瑇 7447 瑈 7448 瑉 7449 瑊 744A 瑋 744B
瑌 744C 瑍 744D 瑎 744E 瑏 744F 瑐 7450 瑑 7451 瑒 7452 瑓 7453 瑔 7454 瑕 7455 瑖 7456 瑗 7457 瑘 7458 瑙 7459 瑚 745A 瑛 745B 瑜 745C 瑝 745D 瑞 745E 瑟 745F 瑶 7476 **10** 瑠 7460
瑡 7461 瑢 7462 瑣 7463 瑤 7464 瑥 7465 瑦 7466 瑧 7467 瑨 7468 瑩 7469 瑪 746A 瑫 746B 瑬 746C 瑭 746D 瑮 746E 瑯 746F 瑰 7470 瑱 7471 瑲 7472 瑳 7473 瑴 7474 瑵 7475 瑷 7477 瑸 7478
11 瑹 7479 瑺 747A 瑻 747B 瑼 747C 瑽 747D 瑾 747E 瑿 747F 璀 7480 璁 7481 璂 7482 璃 7483 璄 7484 璅 7485 璆 7486 璇 7487 璈 7488 璉 7489 璊 748A 璋 748B 璌 748C 璎 748E
12 璍 748D 璏 748F 璑 7491 璒 7492 璓 7493 璔 7494 璕 7495 璖 7496 璗 7497 璙 7499 璚 749A 璛 749B 璜 749C 璝 749D 璞 749E 璟 749F 璠 74A0 璡 74A1 璣 74A3 璤 74A4 **13** 璐 7490
璘 7498 璢 74A2 璥 74A5 璦 74A6 璧 74A7 璨 74A8 璩 74A9 璪 74AA 璫 74AB 璬 74AC 璭 74AD 璮 74AE 璯 74AF 環 74B0 璱 74B1 璲 74B2 璳 74B3 璴 74B4 **14** 璵 74B5 璶 74B6 璸 74B8 璹 74B9
璺 74BA 璻 74BB 璼 74BC 璽 74BD 璾 74BE 璿 74BF 瓀 74C0 瓁 74C1 瓂 74C2 **15** 璷 74B7 瓃 74C3 瓄 74C4 瓅 74C5 瓆 74C6 瓇 74C7 瓈 74C8 瓉 74C9 瓊 74CA 瓋 74CB **16** 瓌 74CC 瓍 74CD

玉 96 瓊 74CA 瓋 74CB **16** 瓌 74CC 瓍 74CD 瓎 74CE 瓏 74CF 瓐 74D0 瓑 74D1 瓒 74D2 **17** 瓓 74D3 瓔 74D4 瓕 74D5 瓖 74D6 **18** 瓗 74D7 瓘 74D8 瓙 74D9 **19** 瓚 74DA **20** 瓛 74DB

瓜 97 瓜 74DC **3** 瓝 74DD **5** 瓞 74DE 瓟 74DF **6** 瓠 74E0 **8** 瓡 74E1 **11** 瓢 74E2 **14** 瓣 74E3 **17** 瓤 74E4 **19** 瓥 74E5

瓦 98 瓦 74E6 **2** 瓧 74E7 **3** 瓨 74E8 瓩 74E9 **4** 瓪 74EA 瓫 74EB 瓬 74EC 瓭 74ED 瓮 74EE 瓯 74EF 瓰 74F0 瓱 74F1 瓲 74F2 **5** 瓳 74F3 瓴 74F4 瓵 74F5 **6** 瓶 74F6 瓷 74F7 瓸 74F8 **7** 瓹 74F9 瓺 74FA 瓻 74FB 瓼 74FC **8** 瓽 74FD 瓾 74FE 瓿 74FF 甀 7500 甁 7501 **9** 甂 7502 甃 7503 甄 7504 甅 7505 甆 7506 **10** 甇 7507 甈 7508 甉 7509 **11** 甊 750A 甋 750B 甌 750C 甍 750D 甎 750E **12** 甏 750F 甐 7510 甑 7511 甒 7512 **13** 甓 7513 甔 7514 甕 7515 **14** 甖 7516 **16** 甗 7517

甘 99 甘 7518 **3** 甙 7519 **4** 甚 751A **6** 甛 751B 甜 751C **8** 甝 751D 甞 751E

生 100 生 751F **4** 甠 7520 **5** 甡 7521 **6** 產 7522 産 7523 **7** 甤 7524 甥 7525 甦 7526 **9** 甧 7527

用 101 用 7528 甩 7529 **1** 甪 752A **2** 甫 752B 甬 752C **4** 甭 752D **7** 甯 752F

田 102 田 7530 由 7531 甲 7532 申 7533 甴 7534 **1** 甶 7536 **2** 男 7537 甸 7538 甹 7539 町 753A 甼 753C **3** 画 753B 甽 753D 甾 753E 甿 753F 畀 7540 畁 7541 畂 7542 畃 7543 畄 7544 **4** 畆 7546 畇 7547 畈 7548 畉 7549 畊 754A 畋 754B 界 754C 畍 754D 畎 754E 畏 754F 畐 7550 畒 7552 **5** 畔 7554 畕 7555 畖 7556 畗 7557 畘 7558 留 7559 畚 755A 畛 755B 畜 755C 畝 755D 畞 755E 畟 755F **6** 畡 7561 畢 7562 畣 7563 畤 7564 略 7565 畦 7566 畧 7567 畩 7569 **7** 番 756A 畫 756B 畬 756C 畭 756D 畮 756E 畯 756F 異 7570 畲 7572 畳 7573 畴 7574 **8** 畵 7575 當 7576 畷 7577 畸 7578 畹 7579 畺 757A **9** 畱 7571 畻 757B 畼 757C 畽 757D **10** 畾 757E 畿 757F **11** 疀 7580 疁 7581 疂 7582 **12** 疃 7583 疄 7584 **13** 疅 7585 **14** 疆 7586 疇 7587 **15** 疈 7588 **17** 疉 7589 疊 758A

疋 103 疋 758B **3** 疌 758C **5** 疍 758D **7** 疎 758E 疏 758F **9** 疐 7590 疑 7591

疒 104 疒 7592 **2** 疓 7593 疔 7594 疕 7595 疖 7596 疗 7597 **3** 疘 7598 疙 7599 疚 759A 疛 759B 疜 759C 疝 759D 疞 759E 疟 759F 疠 75A0 **4** 疡 75A1 疢 75A2 疣 75A3 疤 75A4 疥 75A5

疒 104 疦 75A6 疧 75A7 疨 75A8 疩 75A9 疪 75AA 疫 75AB 疬 75AC 疭 75AD 疮 75AE 疯 75AF 疺 75BA **5** 疰 75B0 疱 75B1 疲 75B2 疳 75B3 疴 75B4 疵 75B5 疶 75B6 疷 75B7 疸 75B8 疹 75B9 疻 75BB

疼 75BC 疽 75BD 疾 75BE 疿 75BF 痀 75C0 痁 75C1 痂 75C2 痃 75C3 痄 75C4 病 75C5 痆 75C6 症 75C7 痈 75C8 痉 75C9 **6** 痊 75CA 痋 75CB 痌 75CC 痍 75CD 痎 75CE 痏 75CF 痐 75D0 痑 75D1

痒 75D2 痓 75D3 痔 75D4 痕 75D5 痖 75D6 **7** 痗 75D7 痘 75D8 痙 75D9 痚 75DA 痛 75DB 痜 75DC 痝 75DD 痞 75DE 痟 75DF 痠 75E0 痡 75E1 痢 75E2 痣 75E3 痤 75E4 痥 75E5 痦 75E6 痧 75E7

痨 75E8 痩 75E9 痪 75EA 痫 75EB **8** 痬 75EC 痭 75ED 痮 75EE 痯 75EF 痰 75F0 痱 75F1 痲 75F2 痳 75F3 痴 75F4 痵 75F5 痶 75F6 痷 75F7 痸 75F8 痹 75F9 痺 75FA 痻 75FB 痼 75FC 痽 75FD

痾 75FE 痿 75FF 瘀 7600 瘁 7601 瘂 7602 瘃 7603 瘄 7604 瘅 7605 瘆 7606 **9** 瘇 7607 瘈 7608 瘉 7609 瘊 760A 瘋 760B 瘌 760C 瘍 760D 瘎 760E 瘏 760F 瘐 7610 瘑 7611 瘒 7612 瘓 7613

瘔 7614 瘕 7615 瘖 7616 瘗 7617 瘘 7618 瘟 761F 瘩 7629 癈 7648 **10** 瘙 7619 瘚 761A 瘛 761B 瘜 761C 瘝 761D 瘞 761E 瘠 7620 瘡 7621 瘢 7622 瘣 7623 瘤 7624 瘥 7625 瘦 7626 瘧 7627

瘨 7628 瘪 762A 瘫 762B **11** 瘬 762C 瘭 762D 瘮 762E 瘯 762F 瘰 7630 瘱 7631 瘲 7632 瘳 7633 瘴 7634 瘵 7635 瘶 7636 瘷 7637 瘸 7638 瘹 7639 瘺 763A 瘻 763B 瘼 763C 瘽 763D 瘾 763E

瘿 763F 癊 764A **12** 癀 7640 癁 7641 療 7642 癃 7643 癄 7644 癅 7645 癆 7646 癇 7647 癉 7649 癋 764B 癌 764C 癍 764D 癎 764E **13** 癏 764F 癐 7650 癑 7651 癒 7652 癓 7653 癔 7654

癕 7655 癖 7656 癗 7657 癘 7658 癙 7659 癚 765A 癛 765B 癜 765C 癝 765D 癞 765E **14** 癟 765F 癠 7660 癡 7661 癣 7663 **15** 癢 7662 癤 7664 癥 7665 癦 7666 **16** 癧 7667 癨 7668

癩 7669 癪 766A 癫 766B **17** 癬 766C 癭 766D 癮 766E **18** 癯 766F 癰 7670 **19** 癱 7671 癲 7672 **21** 癳 7673 **23** 癴 7674 **25** 癵 7675

癶 105 癶 7676 **3** 癷 7677 **4** 癸 7678 癹 7679 発 767A **7** 登 767B 發 767C

白 106 白 767D **1** 百 767E 癿 767F **2** 皀 7680 皁 7681 皂 7682 皃 7683 **3** 的 7684 **4** 皅 7685 皆 7686 皇 7687 皈 7688 **5** 畠 7560 皉 7689 皊 768A 皋 768B 皌 768C 皍 768D

6 皎 768E 皏 768F 皐 7690 皑 7691 **7** 皒 7692 皓 7693 皔 7694 皕 7695 皖 7696 **8** 皗 7697 皘 7698 皙 7699 **10** 皚 769A 皛 769B 皜 769C 皝 769D 皞 769E **11** 皟 769F

皠 76A0 皡 76A1 **12** 皢 76A2 皣 76A3 皤 76A4 皥 76A5 **13** 皦 76A6 皧 76A7 皨 76A8 **14** 皩 76A9 **15** 皪 76AA 皫 76AB **16** 皬 76AC **18** 皭 76AD

皮 107 皮 76AE **3** 皯 76AF **5** 皰 76B0 皱 76B1 **6** 皲 76B2 **7** 皳 76B3 皴 76B4 **8** 皵 76B5 **9** 皶 76B6 皷 76B7 皸 76B8 皹 76B9 **10** 皺 76BA **11** 皻 76BB

12 皼 76BC **13** 皽 76BD **15** 皾 76BE

皿 108 皿 76BF **2** 盀 76C0 盁 76C1 **3** 盂 76C2 **4** 盃 76C3 盄 76C4 盅 76C5 盆 76C6 盇 76C7 盈 76C8 **5** 盉 76C9 益 76CA 盋 76CB 盌 76CC 盍 76CD 盎 76CE 盏 76CF 盐 76D0 监 76D1

6 盒 76D2 盓 76D3 盔 76D4 盕 76D5 盖 76D6 盗 76D7 盘 76D8 **7** 盙 76D9 盚 76DA 盛 76DB 盜 76DC **8** 盝 76DD 盞 76DE 盟 76DF **9** 盠 76E0 盡 76E1 盢 76E2 監 76E3

10 盤 76E4 **11** 盥 76E5 盦 76E6 盧 76E7 **12** 盨 76E8 盩 76E9 盪 76EA **13** 盫 76EB 盬 76EC **15** 盭 76ED

目 109
目 76EE **2** 盯 76EF **3** 盰 76F0 盱 76F1 盲 76F2 盳 76F3 直 76F4 盵 76F5 **4** 盶 76F6 盷 76F7 相 76F8 盹 76F9 盺 76FA 盻 76FB 盼 76FC 盽 76FD 盾 76FE 盿 76FF 眀 7700 省 7701
眂 7702 眃 7703 眄 7704 眅 7705 眆 7706 眇 7707 眈 7708 眉 7709 眊 770A 看 770B 県 770C 眍 770D **5** 眎 770E 眏 770F 眐 7710 眑 7711 眒 7712 眓 7713 眔 7714 眕 7715 眖 7716 眗 7717
眘 7718 眙 7719 眚 771A 眛 771B 眜 771C 眝 771D 眞 771E 真 771F 眠 7720 眡 7721 眢 7722 眣 7723 眤 7724 眥 7725 眦 7726 眧 7727 眨 7728 眩 7729 眪 772A 眫 772B 眬 772C 眿 773F
6 眭 772D 眮 772E 眯 772F 眰 7730 眱 7731 眲 7732 眳 7733 眴 7734 眵 7735 眶 7736 眷 7737 眸 7738 眹 7739 眺 773A 眻 773B 眼 773C 眽 773D 眾 773E 睁 7741 **7** 睂 7742 睃 7743
睄 7744 睅 7745 睆 7746 睇 7747 睈 7748 睉 7749 睊 774A 睋 774B 睌 774C 睍 774D 睎 774E 睏 774F 睐 7750 睑 7751 **8** 睒 7752 睓 7753 睔 7754 睕 7755 睖 7756 睗 7757 睘 7758 睙 7759
睚 775A 睛 775B 睜 775C 睝 775D 睞 775E 睟 775F 睠 7760 睡 7761 睢 7762 督 7763 睤 7764 睥 7765 睦 7766 睧 7767 睨 7768 睩 7769 睪 776A 睫 776B 睬 776C 睭 776D **9** 睮 776E 睯 776F
睰 7770 睱 7771 睲 7772 睳 7773 睴 7774 睵 7775 睶 7776 睸 7778 睹 7779 睺 777A 睻 777B 睼 777C 睽 777D 睾 777E 睿 777F 瞀 7780 瞁 7781 瞂 7782 瞃 7783 瞄 7784 瞅 7785 瞆 7786
10 瞇 7787 瞈 7788 瞉 7789 瞊 778A 瞋 778B 瞌 778C 瞍 778D 瞎 778E 瞏 778F 瞐 7790 瞑 7791 瞒 7792 瞓 7793 **11** 瞔 7794 瞕 7795 瞖 7796 瞗 7797 瞘 7798 瞙 7799 瞚 779A 瞛 779B
瞜 779C 瞝 779D 瞞 779E 瞟 779F 瞠 77A0 瞡 77A1 瞢 77A2 瞣 77A3 **12** 瞤 77A4 瞥 77A5 瞦 77A6 瞧 77A7 瞨 77A8 瞩 77A9 瞪 77AA 瞫 77AB 瞬 77AC 瞭 77AD 瞮 77AE 瞯 77AF 瞰 77B0 瞱 77B1
瞲 77B2 瞳 77B3 瞴 77B4 瞵 77B5 瞶 77B6 瞷 77B7 **13** 瞸 77B8 瞹 77B9 瞺 77BA 瞻 77BB 瞼 77BC 瞽 77BD 瞾 77BE 瞿 77BF 矀 77C0 矁 77C1 矂 77C2 **14** 矃 77C3 矄 77C4 矅 77C5 矆 77C6
矇 77C7 矈 77C8 矉 77C9 矊 77CA **15** 矋 77CB 矌 77CC 矍 77CD 矎 77CE 矏 77CF **16** 矐 77D0 矑 77D1 矒 77D2 矓 77D3 **18** 矔 77D4 **19** 睷 7777 矕 77D5 矗 77D7 **20** 矘 77D8
矙 77D9 **21** 矖 77D6 矚 77DA

矛 110
矛 77DB **4** 矜 77DC **5** 矝 77DD **7** 矞 77DE 矟 77DF **8** 矠 77E0 **20** 矡 77E1

矢 111
矢 77E2 **2** 矣 77E3 **3** 矤 77E4 知 77E5 **4** 矦 77E6 矧 77E7 矨 77E8 **5** 矩 77E9 **6** 矪 77EA 矫 77EB **7** 矬 77EC 短 77ED **8** 矮 77EE **12** 矯 77EF 矰 77F0
14 矱 77F1 **15** 矲 77F2

石 112
石 77F3 **2** 矴 77F4 矵 77F5 矶 77F6 **3** 矷 77F7 矸 77F8 矹 77F9 矺 77FA 矻 77FB 矼 77FC 矽 77FD 矾 77FE 矿 77FF 码 7801 **4** 砀 7800 砂 7802 砃 7803 砄 7804 砅 7805 砆 7806
砇 7807 砈 7808 砉 7809 砊 780A 砋 780B 砌 780C 砍 780D 砎 780E 砏 780F 砐 7810 砒 7812 砓 7813 砕 7815 砖 7816 砗 7817 砘 7818 砙 7819 砚 781A 砛 781B 砜 781C **5** 砑 7811 砝 781D
砞 781E 砟 781F 砠 7820 砡 7821 砢 7822 砣 7823 砤 7824 砥 7825 砦 7826 砧 7827 砨 7828 砩 7829 砪 782A 砫 782B 砬 782C 砭 782D 砮 782E 砯 782F 砰 7830 砱 7831 砲 7832 砳 7833 破 7834
砵 7835 砶 7836 砷 7837 砸 7838 砹 7839 砺 783A 砼 783C 砽 783D 砾 783E 砿 783F 础 7840 硁 7841 **6** 研 7814 硂 7842 硃 7843 硄 7844 硅 7845 硆 7846 硇 7847 硈 7848 硉 7849 硊 784A
硋 784B 硌 784C 硍 784D 硎 784E 硏 784F 硐 7850 硑 7851 硒 7852 硓 7853 硔 7854 硕 7855 硖 7856 硗 7857 硘 7858 硙 7859 硚 785A 硛 785B **7** 硜 785C 硝 785D 硞 785E 硟 785F 硠 7860

石 112 硡 7861 硢 7862 硣 7863 硤 7864 硥 7865 硦 7866 硧 7867 硨 7868 硩 7869 硪 786A 硫 786B 硬 786C 硭 786D 确 786E 硯 786F 硰 7870 硱 7871 硲 7872 硳 7873 硴 7874 硵 7875 硶 7876 硷 7877
8 硸 7878 硹 7879 硺 787A 硻 787B 硼 787C 硽 787D 硿 787F 碀 7880 碁 7881 碂 7882 碃 7883 碄 7884 碅 7885 碆 7886 碇 7887 碈 7888 碉 7889 碊 788A 碋 788B 碌 788C 碍 788D 碎 788E
碏 788F 碐 7890 碑 7891 碒 7892 碓 7893 碔 7894 碕 7895 碖 7896 碗 7897 碘 7898 碙 7899 碚 789A 碛 789B 碜 789C **9** 硾 787E 碝 789D 碞 789E 碟 789F 碠 78A0 碡 78A1 碢 78A2 碣 78A3
碤 78A4 碥 78A5 碦 78A6 碧 78A7 碨 78A8 碩 78A9 碪 78AA 碫 78AB 碬 78AC 碭 78AD 碮 78AE 碯 78AF 碰 78B0 碱 78B1 碲 78B2 碳 78B3 碴 78B4 碵 78B5 碶 78B6 碷 78B7 碸 78B8 碹 78B9 磁 78C1
10 確 78BA 碻 78BB 碼 78BC 碽 78BD 碾 78BE 碿 78BF 磀 78C0 磂 78C2 磃 78C3 磄 78C4 磅 78C5 磆 78C6 磇 78C7 磈 78C8 磉 78C9 磊 78CA 磋 78CB 磌 78CC 磍 78CD 磎 78CE 磏 78CF 磐 78D0
磑 78D1 磒 78D2 磓 78D3 磔 78D4 磕 78D5 磖 78D6 磗 78D7 磘 78D8 磙 78D9 磜 78DC **11** 磚 78DA 磛 78DB 磝 78DD 磞 78DE 磟 78DF 磠 78E0 磡 78E1 磢 78E2 磣 78E3 磤 78E4 磥 78E5 磦 78E6
磧 78E7 磨 78E8 磩 78E9 磪 78EA 磫 78EB 磬 78EC 磭 78ED 磮 78EE **12** 磯 78EF 磰 78F0 磱 78F1 磲 78F2 磳 78F3 磴 78F4 磵 78F5 磶 78F6 磸 78F8 磹 78F9 磺 78FA 磻 78FB 磼 78FC 磽 78FD
磾 78FE 磿 78FF 礀 7900 礁 7901 礂 7902 礃 7903 礄 7904 礅 7905 **13** 磷 78F7 礆 7906 礇 7907 礈 7908 礉 7909 礊 790A 礋 790B 礌 790C 礍 790D 礎 790E 礏 790F 礐 7910 礑 7911 礒 7912
礓 7913 礔 7914 礕 7915 礖 7916 **14** 礗 7917 礘 7918 礙 7919 礚 791A 礛 791B 礜 791C 礝 791D 礞 791E 礟 791F 礠 7920 礡 7921 **15** 礢 7922 礣 7923 礤 7924 礦 7926 礧 7927 礨 7928
礩 7929 礪 792A 礫 792B 礬 792C **16** 礥 7925 礭 792D 礮 792E 礯 792F 礰 7930 礱 7931 礲 7932 礳 7933 礴 7934 **17** 礵 7935 **18** 礶 7936 礷 7937 **19** 礸 7938 **20** 礹 7939

示 113 示 793A 礻 793B **1** 礼 793C **2** 礽 793D **3** 社 793E 礿 793F 祀 7940 祁 7941 祂 7942 祃 7943 **4** 祄 7944 祅 7945 祆 7946 祇 7947 祈 7948 祉 7949 祊 794A 祋 794B 祌 794C
祍 794D 祎 794E **5** 祏 794F 祐 7950 祑 7951 祒 7952 祓 7953 祔 7954 祕 7955 祖 7956 祗 7957 祘 7958 祙 7959 祚 795A 祛 795B 祜 795C 祝 795D 神 795E 祟 795F 祠 7960 祡 7961 祢 7962
6 祣 7963 祤 7964 祥 7965 祧 7967 票 7968 祩 7969 祪 796A 祫 796B 祬 796C 祭 796D 祮 796E 祯 796F **7** 祦 7966 祰 7970 祱 7971 祲 7972 祳 7973 祴 7974 祵 7975 祶 7976 祷 7977
祸 7978 禄 7984 **8** 祹 7979 祺 797A 祻 797B 祼 797C 祽 797D 祾 797E 祿 797F 禀 7980 禁 7981 禂 7982 禃 7983 禆 7986 **9** 禅 7985 禇 7987 禈 7988 禉 7989 禊 798A 禋 798B 禌 798C
禍 798D 禎 798E 福 798F 禐 7990 禑 7991 禒 7992 禓 7993 禔 7994 禕 7995 禖 7996 禗 7997 禘 7998 禙 7999 **10** 禚 799A 禛 799B 禜 799C 禝 799D 禞 799E 禟 799F 禠 79A0 禡 79A1 禢 79A2
禣 79A3 **11** 禤 79A4 禥 79A5 禦 79A6 **12** 禧 79A7 禨 79A8 禩 79A9 禪 79AA 禫 79AB **13** 禬 79AC 禭 79AD 禮 79AE 禯 79AF **14** 禰 79B0 禱 79B1 **15** 禲 79B2 **17** 禳 79B3
禴 79B4 **18** 禵 79B5 **19** 禶 79B6 禷 79B7

禸 114 禸 79B8 **4** 禹 79B9 禺 79BA **6** 离 79BB **7** 禼 79BC **8** 禽 79BD

禾 115 禾 79BE **2** 禿 79BF 秀 79C0 私 79C1 秂 79C2 秃 79C3 **3** 秄 79C4 秅 79C5 秆 79C6 秇 79C7 秈 79C8 秉 79C9 秊 79CA **4** 秋 79CB 种 79CD 秎 79CE 秏 79CF 秐 79D0 科 79D1 秒 79D2
秓 79D3 秔 79D4 秕 79D5 秖 79D6 秗 79D7 **5** 秘 79D8 秙 79D9 秚 79DA 秛 79DB 秜 79DC 秝 79DD 秞 79DE 租 79DF 秠 79E0 秡 79E1 秢 79E2 秣 79E3 秤 79E4 秥 79E5 秦 79E6 秧 79E7 秨 79E8

禾 115 秨 79E8 秩 79E9 秪 79EA 秫 79EB 秬 79EC 秭 79ED 秮 79EE 积 79EF 称 79F0 **6** 秱 79F1 秲 79F2 秳 79F3 秴 79F4 秵 79F5 秶 79F6 秷 79F7 秸 79F8 秹 79F9 秺 79FA 移 79FB 秼 79FC 秽 79FD
秾 79FE 稆 7A06 **7** 秿 79FF 稀 7A00 稁 7A01 稂 7A02 稃 7A03 稄 7A04 稅 7A05 稇 7A07 稈 7A08 稉 7A09 稊 7A0A 程 7A0B 稌 7A0C 稍 7A0D 税 7A0E **8** 稏 7A0F 稐 7A10 稑 7A11 稒 7A12
稓 7A13 稔 7A14 稕 7A15 稖 7A16 稗 7A17 稘 7A18 稙 7A19 稚 7A1A 稛 7A1B 稜 7A1C 稝 7A1D 稞 7A1E 稟 7A1F 稠 7A20 稡 7A21 稢 7A22 稤 7A24 **9** 稦 7A26 稧 7A27 稨 7A28 稩 7A29 稪 7A2A
稫 7A2B 稬 7A2C 稭 7A2D 種 7A2E 稯 7A2F 稰 7A30 稱 7A31 稲 7A32 稳 7A33 穀 7A40 **10** 稴 7A34 稵 7A35 稶 7A36 稷 7A37 稸 7A38 稹 7A39 稺 7A3A 稻 7A3B 稼 7A3C 稽 7A3D 稾 7A3E 稿 7A3F
穁 7A41 穂 7A42 穃 7A43 **11** 穄 7A44 穅 7A45 穆 7A46 穇 7A47 穈 7A48 穊 7A4A 穋 7A4B 穌 7A4C 積 7A4D 穎 7A4E 穏 7A4F 穐 7A50 穑 7A51 穒 7A52 **12** 穉 7A49 穓 7A53 穔 7A54 穕 7A55
穖 7A56 穗 7A57 穘 7A58 穙 7A59 穚 7A5A 穛 7A5B 穜 7A5C 穝 7A5D 穞 7A5E **13** 穟 7A5F 穠 7A60 穡 7A61 穢 7A62 穣 7A63 **14** 穤 7A64 穥 7A65 穦 7A66 穧 7A67 穨 7A68 穩 7A69 穪 7A6A
穫 7A6B **15** 穬 7A6C 穭 7A6D 穮 7A6E 穯 7A6F **17** 穰 7A70 穳 7A73 **18** 穱 7A71 **19** 穲 7A72

穴 116 穴 7A74 **1** 穵 7A75 **2** 究 7A76 穷 7A77 **3** 穸 7A78 穹 7A79 空 7A7A 穻 7A7B **4** 穼 7A7C 穽 7A7D 穾 7A7E 穿 7A7F 窀 7A80 窂 7A82 窃 7A83 **5** 窄 7A84 窅 7A85 窆 7A86
窇 7A87 窈 7A88 窉 7A89 窊 7A8A 窋 7A8B 窌 7A8C 窍 7A8D 窎 7A8E **6** 窏 7A8F 窐 7A90 窑 7A91 窒 7A92 窓 7A93 窔 7A94 窕 7A95 **7** 窖 7A96 窗 7A97 窘 7A98 窙 7A99 窚 7A9A 窛 7A9B
窜 7A9C 窝 7A9D **8** 窞 7A9E 窟 7A9F 窠 7AA0 窡 7AA1 窢 7AA2 窣 7AA3 窤 7AA4 窥 7AA5 窦 7AA6 窧 7AA7 **9** 窨 7AA8 窩 7AA9 窪 7AAA 窫 7AAB 窬 7AAC 窭 7AAD **10** 窮 7AAE 窯 7AAF
窰 7AB0 窱 7AB1 窲 7AB2 窳 7AB3 窴 7AB4 **11** 窵 7AB5 窶 7AB6 窷 7AB7 窸 7AB8 窹 7AB9 窺 7ABA 窻 7ABB 窼 7ABC 窽 7ABD **12** 窾 7ABE 窿 7ABF 竀 7AC0 竁 7AC1 竂 7AC2 **13** 竄 7AC4
竅 7AC5 **14** 竆 7AC6 **15** 竇 7AC7 **16** 竃 7AC3 竈 7AC8 竉 7AC9 **17** 竊 7ACA

立 117 立 7ACB **2** 竌 7ACC 竍 7ACD **3** 竎 7ACE 竏 7ACF **4** 竐 7AD0 竑 7AD1 竒 7AD2 竓 7AD3 竔 7AD4 竕 7AD5 竖 7AD6 竗 7AD7 **5** 竘 7AD8 站 7AD9 竚 7ADA 竛 7ADB 竜 7ADC 竝 7ADD
竞 7ADE **6** 竟 7ADF 章 7AE0 竡 7AE1 **7** 竢 7AE2 竣 7AE3 竤 7AE4 童 7AE5 竦 7AE6 竧 7AE7 **8** 竨 7AE8 竩 7AE9 竪 7AEA 竫 7AEB **9** 竬 7AEC 竭 7AED 端 7AEF 竰 7AF0
11 竮 7AEE 竱 7AF1 **12** 竲 7AF2 竳 7AF3 竴 7AF4 **13** 竵 7AF5 **15** 競 7AF6 竷 7AF7 **17** 竸 7AF8

竹 118 竹 7AF9 **2** 竺 7AFA 竻 7AFB **3** 竼 7AFC 竽 7AFD 竾 7AFE 竿 7AFF 笀 7B00 笁 7B01 笂 7B02 笃 7B03 **4** 笅 7B05 笆 7B06 笇 7B07 笈 7B08 笉 7B09 笊 7B0A 笋 7B0B 笌 7B0C 笍 7B0D
笎 7B0E 笏 7B0F 笐 7B10 笑 7B11 笒 7B12 笓 7B13 笔 7B14 笕 7B15 **5** 笖 7B16 笗 7B17 笘 7B18 笙 7B19 笚 7B1A 笛 7B1B 笜 7B1C 笝 7B1D 笞 7B1E 笠 7B20 笡 7B21 笢 7B22 笣 7B23 笤 7B24
笥 7B25 符 7B26 笧 7B27 笨 7B28 笩 7B29 笪 7B2A 笫 7B2B 第 7B2C 笭 7B2D 笮 7B2E 笯 7B2F 笰 7B30 笱 7B31 笲 7B32 笳 7B33 笴 7B34 笵 7B35 笶 7B36 笷 7B37 笸 7B38 笹 7B39 笺 7B3A 笻 7B3B
笼 7B3C 笽 7B3D **6** 笄 7B04 笟 7B1F 笾 7B3E 笿 7B3F 筀 7B40 筁 7B41 筂 7B42 筃 7B43 筄 7B44 筅 7B45 筆 7B46 筇 7B47 筈 7B48 等 7B49 筊 7B4A 筋 7B4B 筌 7B4C 筍 7B4D 筎 7B4E 筏 7B4F
筐 7B50 筑 7B51 筒 7B52 筓 7B53 答 7B54 筕 7B55 策 7B56 筗 7B57 筘 7B58 筙 7B59 筚 7B5A 筛 7B5B 筜 7B5C 筝 7B5D **7** 筞 7B5E 筟 7B5F 筠 7B60 筡 7B61 筢 7B62 筣 7B63 筤 7B64 筥 7B65

竹 118 — 筥 7B65 · 筦 7B66 · 筧 7B67 · 筨 7B68 · 筩 7B69 · 筪 7B6A · 筫 7B6B · 筬 7B6C · 筭 7B6D · 筮 7B6E · 筯 7B6F · 筰 7B70 · 筱 7B71 · 筲 7B72 · 筳 7B73 · 筴 7B74 · 筵 7B75 · 筶 7B76 · 筷 7B77 · 筸 7B78 · 筹 7B79 · 筺 7B7A · 筻 7B7B

筼 7B7C · 筽 7B7D · 签 7B7E · 筿 7B7F · 简 7B80 · **8** · 箁 7B81 · 箂 7B82 · 箃 7B83 · 箄 7B84 · 箅 7B85 · 箆 7B86 · 箇 7B87 · 箈 7B88 · 箉 7B89 · 箊 7B8A · 箋 7B8B · 箌 7B8C · 箍 7B8D · 箎 7B8E · 箏 7B8F · 箐 7B90 · 箑 7B91

箒 7B92 · 箓 7B93 · 箔 7B94 · 箕 7B95 · 箖 7B96 · 算 7B97 · 箘 7B98 · 箙 7B99 · 箚 7B9A · 箜 7B9C · 箝 7B9D · 箞 7B9E · 箟 7B9F · 箠 7BA0 · 管 7BA1 · 箢 7BA2 · 箣 7BA3 · 箤 7BA4 · 箥 7BA5 · 箦 7BA6 · 箧 7BA7 · 箨 7BA8 · 箩 7BA9

箫 7BAB · 節 7BC0 · **9** · 箛 7B9B · 箪 7BAA · 箬 7BAC · 箭 7BAD · 箮 7BAE · 箯 7BAF · 箰 7BB0 · 箱 7BB1 · 箲 7BB2 · 箳 7BB3 · 箴 7BB4 · 箵 7BB5 · 箶 7BB6 · 箷 7BB7 · 箸 7BB8 · 箹 7BB9 · 箺 7BBA · 箻 7BBB · 箼 7BBC · 箽 7BBD

箾 7BBE · 箿 7BBF · 篁 7BC1 · 篂 7BC2 · 篃 7BC3 · 範 7BC4 · 篅 7BC5 · 篆 7BC6 · 篇 7BC7 · 篈 7BC8 · 篊 7BCA · 篋 7BCB · 篌 7BCC · 篍 7BCD · 篎 7BCE · 篏 7BCF · 篐 7BD0 · 篑 7BD1 · 篒 7BD2 · 篓 7BD3 · **10** · 築 7BC9 · 篔 7BD4

篕 7BD5 · 篖 7BD6 · 篗 7BD7 · 篘 7BD8 · 篙 7BD9 · 篚 7BDA · 篛 7BDB · 篜 7BDC · 篝 7BDD · 篞 7BDE · 篟 7BDF · 篠 7BE0 · 篡 7BE1 · 篢 7BE2 · 篣 7BE3 · 篤 7BE4 · 篥 7BE5 · 篦 7BE6 · 篧 7BE7 · 篨 7BE8 · 篩 7BE9 · 篪 7BEA · 篫 7BEB

篬 7BEC · 篭 7BED · 篮 7BEE · 篯 7BEF · 簑 7C11 · 簕 7C15 · **11** · 篰 7BF0 · 篱 7BF1 · 篲 7BF2 · 篳 7BF3 · 篴 7BF4 · 篵 7BF5 · 篶 7BF6 · 篷 7BF7 · 篸 7BF8 · 篹 7BF9 · 篺 7BFA · 篻 7BFB · 篼 7BFC · 篽 7BFD · 篾 7BFE · 篿 7BFF

簀 7C00 · 簁 7C01 · 簂 7C02 · 簃 7C03 · 簄 7C04 · 簅 7C05 · 簆 7C06 · 簇 7C07 · 簈 7C08 · 簉 7C09 · 簊 7C0A · 簋 7C0B · 簌 7C0C · 簍 7C0D · 簎 7C0E · 簏 7C0F · 簐 7C10 · 簒 7C12 · 簓 7C13 · 簔 7C14 · 簖 7C16 · 簗 7C17

12 · 簘 7C18 · 簙 7C19 · 簚 7C1A · 簛 7C1B · 簜 7C1C · 簝 7C1D · 簞 7C1E · 簟 7C1F · 簠 7C20 · 簡 7C21 · 簢 7C22 · 簣 7C23 · 簤 7C24 · 簥 7C25 · 簦 7C26 · 簧 7C27 · 簨 7C28 · 簩 7C29 · 簪 7C2A · 簫 7C2B · 簬 7C2C · 簭 7C2D

簮 7C2E · 簯 7C2F · 簰 7C30 · 簱 7C31 · 簲 7C32 · **13** · 簳 7C33 · 簴 7C34 · 簵 7C35 · 簶 7C36 · 簷 7C37 · 簸 7C38 · 簹 7C39 · 簺 7C3A · 簻 7C3B · 簼 7C3C · 簽 7C3D · 簾 7C3E · 簿 7C3F · 籀 7C40 · 籁 7C41 · 籂 7C42

14 · 籃 7C43 · 籄 7C44 · 籅 7C45 · 籆 7C46 · 籇 7C47 · 籈 7C48 · 籉 7C49 · 籊 7C4A · 籋 7C4B · 籌 7C4C · 籍 7C4D · 籎 7C4E · 籏 7C4F · 籕 7C55 · 籖 7C56 · **15** · 籐 7C50 · 籑 7C51 · 籒 7C52 · 籓 7C53 · 籔 7C54

16 · 籗 7C57 · 籘 7C58 · 籙 7C59 · 籚 7C5A · 籛 7C5B · 籜 7C5C · 籝 7C5D · 籞 7C5E · 籟 7C5F · 籠 7C60 · 籡 7C61 · **17** · 籢 7C62 · 籣 7C63 · 籤 7C64 · 籥 7C65 · 籦 7C66 · 籧 7C67 · 籨 7C68 · **18** · 籪 7C6A

19 · 籩 7C69 · 籫 7C6B · 籬 7C6C · 籭 7C6D · 籮 7C6E · **20** · 籯 7C6F · 籰 7C70 · **24** · 籱 7C71 · **26** · 籲 7C72

米 119 — 米 7C73 · **2** · 籴 7C74 · 籵 7C75 · 籶 7C76 · **3** · 籷 7C77 · 籸 7C78 · 籹 7C79 · 籺 7C7A · 籼 7C7C · 籽 7C7D · 籾 7C7E · 籿 7C7F · 粀 7C80 · 粁 7C81 · 粂 7C82 · **4** · 粃 7C83 · 粄 7C84 · 粅 7C85 · 粆 7C86 · 粇 7C87

粈 7C88 · 粉 7C89 · 粊 7C8A · 粋 7C8B · 粌 7C8C · 粍 7C8D · 粎 7C8E · 粏 7C8F · 粐 7C90 · 粑 7C91 · **5** · 畨 7568 · 粒 7C92 · 粓 7C93 · 粔 7C94 · 粕 7C95 · 粖 7C96 · 粗 7C97 · 粘 7C98 · 粙 7C99 · 粚 7C9A · 粜 7C9C · 粝 7C9D

粣 7CA3 · **6** · 粞 7C9E · 粟 7C9F · 粠 7CA0 · 粡 7CA1 · 粢 7CA2 · 粤 7CA4 · 粥 7CA5 · 粧 7CA7 · 粨 7CA8 · 粩 7CA9 · 粪 7CAA · 粫 7CAB · 粬 7CAC · 粭 7CAD · **7** · 粦 7CA6 · 粮 7CAE · 粯 7CAF · 粰 7CB0 · 粱 7CB1 · 粲 7CB2

粳 7CB3 · 粴 7CB4 · 粵 7CB5 · **8** · 粶 7CB6 · 粷 7CB7 · 粸 7CB8 · 粹 7CB9 · 粺 7CBA · 粻 7CBB · 粼 7CBC · 粽 7CBD · 精 7CBE · 粿 7CBF · 糀 7CC0 · 糁 7CC1 · **9** · 糂 7CC2 · 糃 7CC3 · 糄 7CC4 · 糅 7CC5 · 糆 7CC6 · 糇 7CC7

糈 7CC8 · 糉 7CC9 · 糊 7CCA · 糋 7CCB · 糌 7CCC · 糍 7CCD · 糎 7CCE · **10** · 糏 7CCF · 糐 7CD0 · 糑 7CD1 · 糒 7CD2 · 糓 7CD3 · 糔 7CD4 · 糕 7CD5 · 糖 7CD6 · 糗 7CD7 · 糘 7CD8 · **11** · 糙 7CD9 · 糚 7CDA · 糛 7CDB · 糜 7CDC

糝 7CDD · 糞 7CDE · 糟 7CDF · 糠 7CE0 · 糡 7CE1 · 糢 7CE2 · 糨 7CE8 · **12** · 糣 7CE3 · 糤 7CE4 · 糥 7CE5 · 糦 7CE6 · 糧 7CE7 · **13** · 糩 7CE9 · 糪 7CEA · 糫 7CEB · 糬 7CEC · 糭 7CED · **14** · 糮 7CEE · 糯 7CEF · 糰 7CF0

15 · 糲 7CF2 · **16** · 糱 7CF1 · 糳 7CF3 · 糴 7CF4 · **17** · 糵 7CF5 · **19** · 糶 7CF6 · **21** · 糷 7CF7

糸 120 — 糸 7CF8 · 糹 7CF9 · **1** · 糺 7CFA · 系 7CFB · **2** · 糼 7CFC · 糽 7CFD · 糾 7CFE · 糿 7CFF · 纠 7EA0 · **3** · 紀 7D00 · 紁 7D01 · 紂 7D02 · 紃 7D03 · 約 7D04 · 紅 7D05 · 紆 7D06 · 紇 7D07 · 紈 7D08 · 紉 7D09 · 纡 7EA1

糸 120 红 7EA2 纣 7EA3 纤 7EA4 纥 7EA5 约 7EA6 级 7EA7 纨 7EA8 纩 7EA9 纪 7EAA 纫 7EAB
4
紊 7D0A 紋 7D0B 紌 7D0C 納 7D0D 紎 7D0E 紏 7D0F 紐 7D10 紑 7D11 紒 7D12 紓 7D13 純 7D14 紕 7D15

紖 7D16 紗 7D17 紘 7D18 紙 7D19 級 7D1A 紛 7D1B 紜 7D1C 紝 7D1D 紞 7D1E 紟 7D1F 素 7D20 紡 7D21 索 7D22 紣 7D23 紤 7D24 紥 7D25 紦 7D26 紧 7D27 纬 7EAC 纭 7EAD 纮 7EAE 纯 7EAF 纰 7EB0

纱 7EB1 纲 7EB2 纳 7EB3 纴 7EB4 纵 7EB5 纶 7EB6 纷 7EB7 纸 7EB8 纹 7EB9 纺 7EBA 纻 7EBB 纼 7EBC 纽 7EBD 纾 7EBE
5
紨 7D28 紩 7D29 紪 7D2A 紫 7D2B 紬 7D2C 紭 7D2D 紮 7D2E 累 7D2F

細 7D30 紱 7D31 紲 7D32 紳 7D33 紴 7D34 紵 7D35 紶 7D36 紷 7D37 紸 7D38 紹 7D39 紺 7D3A 紻 7D3B 紼 7D3C 紽 7D3D 紾 7D3E 紿 7D3F 絀 7D40 絁 7D41 終 7D42 絃 7D43 組 7D44 絅 7D45 絆 7D46

絇 7D47 絈 7D48 絉 7D49 絊 7D4A 絋 7D4B 経 7D4C 线 7EBF 绀 7EC0 绁 7EC1 绂 7EC2 练 7EC3 组 7EC4 绅 7EC5 细 7EC6 织 7EC7 终 7EC8 绉 7EC9 绊 7ECA 绋 7ECB 绌 7ECC 绍 7ECD 绎 7ECE 经 7ECF

绐 7ED0
6
絍 7D4D 絎 7D4E 絏 7D4F 結 7D50 絑 7D51 絒 7D52 絓 7D53 絔 7D54 絕 7D55 絖 7D56 絗 7D57 絘 7D58 絙 7D59 絚 7D5A 絜 7D5C 絝 7D5D 絞 7D5E 絟 7D5F 絠 7D60 絡 7D61 絢 7D62

絣 7D63 絤 7D64 絥 7D65 給 7D66 絧 7D67 絨 7D68 絩 7D69 絪 7D6A 絫 7D6B 絬 7D6C 絭 7D6D 絮 7D6E 絯 7D6F 絰 7D70 統 7D71 絲 7D72 絳 7D73 絴 7D74 絵 7D75 絶 7D76 絷 7D77 绑 7ED1 绒 7ED2

结 7ED3 绔 7ED4 绕 7ED5 绖 7ED6 绗 7ED7 绘 7ED8 给 7ED9 绚 7EDA 绛 7EDB 络 7EDC 绝 7EDD 绞 7EDE 统 7EDF
7
絛 7D5B 絸 7D78 絹 7D79 絺 7D7A 絻 7D7B 絼 7D7C 絽 7D7D 絾 7D7E 絿 7D7F

綀 7D80 綁 7D81 綂 7D82 綃 7D83 綄 7D84 綅 7D85 綆 7D86 綇 7D87 綈 7D88 綉 7D89 綊 7D8A 綋 7D8B 綌 7D8C 綍 7D8D 綎 7D8E 綏 7D8F 綐 7D90 綑 7D91 綒 7D92 經 7D93 綔 7D94 綕 7D95 綖 7D96

綗 7D97 綘 7D98 継 7D99 続 7D9A 綛 7D9B 绠 7EE0 绡 7EE1 绢 7EE2 绣 7EE3 绤 7EE4 绥 7EE5 绦 7EE6 继 7EE7 绨 7EE8
8
綜 7D9C 綝 7D9D 綞 7D9E 綟 7D9F 綠 7DA0 綡 7DA1 綢 7DA2 綣 7DA3

綤 7DA4 綥 7DA5 綦 7DA6 綧 7DA7 綨 7DA8 綩 7DA9 綪 7DAA 綫 7DAB 綬 7DAC 維 7DAD 綮 7DAE 綯 7DAF 綰 7DB0 綱 7DB1 網 7DB2 綳 7DB3 綴 7DB4 綵 7DB5 綶 7DB6 綷 7DB7 綸 7DB8 綹 7DB9 綺 7DBA

綻 7DBB 綼 7DBC 綽 7DBD 綾 7DBE 綿 7DBF 緀 7DC0 緁 7DC1 緂 7DC2 緃 7DC3 緄 7DC4 緅 7DC5 緆 7DC6 緇 7DC7 緈 7DC8 緉 7DC9 緊 7DCA 緋 7DCB 緌 7DCC 緍 7DCD 緎 7DCE 総 7DCF 緐 7DD0 緑 7DD1

緒 7DD2 緔 7DD4 緕 7DD5 绩 7EE9 绪 7EEA 绫 7EEB 续 7EED 绮 7EEE 绯 7EEF 绰 7EF0 绱 7EF1 绲 7EF2 绳 7EF3 维 7EF4 绵 7EF5 绶 7EF6 绷 7EF7 绸 7EF8 绹 7EF9 绺 7EFA 绻 7EFB 综 7EFC 绽 7EFD

绾 7EFE 绿 7EFF 缀 7F00 缁 7F01 缍 7F0D
9
緓 7DD3 緖 7DD6 緗 7DD7 緘 7DD8 緙 7DD9 線 7DDA 緛 7DDB 緜 7DDC 緝 7DDD 緞 7DDE 緟 7DDF 締 7DE0 緡 7DE1 緢 7DE2 緣 7DE3 緤 7DE4 緥 7DE5

緦 7DE6 緧 7DE7 編 7DE8 緩 7DE9 緪 7DEA 緫 7DEB 緬 7DEC 緭 7DED 緮 7DEE 緯 7DEF 緰 7DF0 緱 7DF1 緲 7DF2 緳 7DF3 練 7DF4 緵 7DF5 緶 7DF6 緷 7DF7 緸 7DF8 緹 7DF9 緺 7DFA 緻 7DFB 緼 7DFC

緽 7DFD 緾 7DFE 緿 7DFF 縀 7E00 縁 7E01 縂 7E02 縃 7E03 縄 7E04 縅 7E05 縆 7E06 縇 7E07 缂 7F02 缃 7F03 缄 7F04 缅 7F05 缆 7F06 缇 7F07 缈 7F08 缉 7F09 缋 7F0B 缌 7F0C 缎 7F0E 缏 7F0F

缐 7F10 缑 7F11 缒 7F12 缓 7F13 缔 7F14 缕 7F15 编 7F16 缗 7F17 缘 7F18
10
縈 7E08 縉 7E09 縊 7E0A 縋 7E0B 縌 7E0C 縍 7E0D 縎 7E0E 縏 7E0F 縐 7E10 縑 7E11 縒 7E12 縓 7E13 縔 7E14

縕 7E15 縖 7E16 縗 7E17 縘 7E18 縙 7E19 縚 7E1A 縛 7E1B 縜 7E1C 縝 7E1D 縞 7E1E 縟 7E1F 縠 7E20 縡 7E21 縢 7E22 縣 7E23 縤 7E24 縥 7E25 縦 7E26 縨 7E28 缊 7F0A 缙 7F19 缚 7F1A 缛 7F1B

缜 7F1C 缝 7F1D 缞 7F1E 缟 7F1F 缠 7F20 缡 7F21 缢 7F22 缣 7F23 缤 7F24
11
縧 7E27 縩 7E29 縪 7E2A 縫 7E2B 縬 7E2C 縭 7E2D 縮 7E2E 縯 7E2F 縰 7E30 縱 7E31 縲 7E32 縳 7E33 縴 7E34

縵 7E35 縶 7E36 縷 7E37 縸 7E38 縹 7E39 縺 7E3A 縻 7E3B 縼 7E3C 總 7E3D 績 7E3E 縿 7E3F 繀 7E40 繁 7E41 繂 7E42 繃 7E43 繄 7E44 繅 7E45 繆 7E46 繇 7E47 繉 7E49 繊 7E4A 繌 7E4C 繍 7E4D

缥 7F25 缦 7F26 缧 7F27 缨 7F28 缩 7F29 缪 7F2A 缫 7F2B
12
繈 7E48 繎 7E4E 繏 7E4F 繐 7E50 繑 7E51 繒 7E52 繓 7E53 織 7E54 繕 7E55 繖 7E56 繗 7E57 繘 7E58 繙 7E59 繚 7E5A 繛 7E5B

繜 7E5C 繝 7E5D 繞 7E5E 繟 7E5F 繠 7E60 繢 7E62 繣 7E63 繤 7E64 繥 7E65 繧 7E67 繱 7E71 缬 7F2C 缭 7F2D 缮 7F2E 缯 7F2F
13
繋 7E4B 繡 7E61 繦 7E66 繨 7E68 繩 7E69 繪 7E6A 繫 7E6B

繬 7E6C 繭 7E6D 繮 7E6E 繯 7E6F 繰 7E70 繲 7E72 繳 7E73 繴 7E74 繵 7E75 繶 7E76 繷 7E77 繸 7E78 繹 7E79 繺 7E7A 缰 7F30 缱 7F31 缲 7F32 缳 7F33 缴 7F34
14
繻 7E7B 繼 7E7C 繽 7E7D

糸 120 缱 7F31 缲 7F32 缳 7F33 缴 7F34 **14** 繻 7E7B 繼 7E7C 繽 7E7D 繾 7E7E 繿 7E7F 纀 7E80 纁 7E81 纂 7E82 纃 7E83 **15** 纄 7E84 纅 7E85 纆 7E86 纇 7E87 纈 7E88 纉 7E89 纊 7E8A 纋 7E8B
續 7E8C 纍 7E8D 纎 7E8E 纏 7E8F 纐 7E90 **16** 纑 7E91 纒 7E92 缵 7F35 **17** 纓 7E93 纔 7E94 纕 7E95 纖 7E96 **18** 纗 7E97 **19** 纘 7E98 纙 7E99 纚 7E9A 纛 7E9B **21** 纜 7E9C
纝 7E9D **23** 纞 7E9E

纟 120 纟 7E9F **8** 绬 7EEC

缶 121 缶 7F36 **2** 缷 7F37 **3** 缸 7F38 **4** 缺 7F3A 缼 7F3C **5** 缻 7F3B 缽 7F3D **6** 缾 7F3E 缿 7F3F 罀 7F40 **8** 罁 7F41 罂 7F42 **10** 罃 7F43 **11** 罄 7F44 罅 7F45
罆 7F46 **12** 罇 7F47 罈 7F48 罉 7F49 **13** 罊 7F4A 罋 7F4B **14** 罌 7F4C **15** 罍 7F4D **16** 罎 7F4E 罏 7F4F **18** 罐 7F50

网 122 网 7F51 罒 7F52 罓 7F53 **3** 罔 7F54 罕 7F55 罖 7F56 罗 7F57 **4** 罘 7F58 罙 7F59 罚 7F5A **5** 罜 7F5C 罝 7F5D 罞 7F5E 罟 7F5F 罠 7F60 罡 7F61 罢 7F62 **6** 罛 7F5B 罣 7F63
7 罤 7F64 罥 7F65 罦 7F66 **8** 罧 7F67 罨 7F68 罩 7F69 罪 7F6A 罫 7F6B 罬 7F6C 罭 7F6D 置 7F6E **9** 罯 7F6F 罰 7F70 罱 7F71 署 7F72 罳 7F73 罴 7F74 **10** 罵 7F75 罶 7F76
罷 7F77 罸 7F78 **11** 罹 7F79 罺 7F7A 罻 7F7B 罼 7F7C **12** 罽 7F7D 罾 7F7E 罿 7F7F 羀 7F80 羁 7F81 **13** 羂 7F82 **14** 羃 7F83 羄 7F84 羅 7F85 羆 7F86 **17** 羇 7F87
19 羈 7F88 羉 7F89

羊 123 羊 7F8A **1** 羋 7F8B **2** 羌 7F8C **3** 羍 7F8D 美 7F8E 羏 7F8F 羐 7F90 羑 7F91 **4** 羒 7F92 羓 7F93 羔 7F94 羖 7F96 羗 7F97 羘 7F98 羙 7F99 **5** 着 7740 羕 7F95 羚 7F9A
羛 7F9B 羜 7F9C 羝 7F9D 羞 7F9E 羟 7F9F **6** 羠 7FA0 羡 7FA1 羢 7FA2 **7** 羣 7FA3 群 7FA4 羥 7FA5 羦 7FA6 羧 7FA7 羨 7FA8 義 7FA9 羪 7FAA **8** 羫 7FAB **9** 羬 7FAC 羭 7FAD
羮 7FAE 羯 7FAF 羰 7FB0 **10** 羱 7FB1 羲 7FB2 **12** 羳 7FB3 羴 7FB4 羵 7FB5 **13** 羶 7FB6 羷 7FB7 羸 7FB8 羹 7FB9 **14** 羺 7FBA **15** 羻 7FBB 羼 7FBC

羽 124 羽 7FBD **3** 羾 7FBE 羿 7FBF **4** 翀 7FC0 翁 7FC1 翂 7FC2 翃 7FC3 翄 7FC4 翅 7FC5 翆 7FC6 **5** 翇 7FC7 翈 7FC8 翉 7FC9 翊 7FCA 翋 7FCB 翌 7FCC 翍 7FCD 翎 7FCE 翏 7FCF 翐 7FD0
翑 7FD1 習 7FD2 **6** 翓 7FD3 翔 7FD4 翕 7FD5 翖 7FD6 翗 7FD7 翘 7FD8 翙 7FD9 翚 7FDA **7** 翛 7FDB 翜 7FDC 翝 7FDD **8** 翞 7FDE 翟 7FDF 翠 7FE0 翡 7FE1 翢 7FE2 翣 7FE3 翤 7FE4
9 翥 7FE5 翦 7FE6 翧 7FE7 翨 7FE8 翩 7FE9 翪 7FEA 翫 7FEB 翬 7FEC 翭 7FED **10** 翮 7FEE 翯 7FEF 翰 7FF0 翱 7FF1 **11** 翲 7FF2 翳 7FF3 翴 7FF4 翶 7FF6 **12** 翷 7FF7 翸 7FF8
翹 7FF9 翺 7FFA 翻 7FFB 翼 7FFC **13** 翽 7FFD 翾 7FFE **14** 翿 7FFF 耀 8000

老 125 | 老 8001 | 耂 8002 | 考 8003 | **4** | 耄 8004 | 耆 8006 | **5** | 者 8005 | 耇 8007 | 耈 8008 | 耉 8009 | **6** | 耊 800A | 耋 800B

而 126 | 而 800C | **3** | 耍 800D | 耎 800E | 耏 800F | 耐 8010 | 耑 8011

耒 127 | 耒 8012 | **2** | 耓 8013 | **3** | 耔 8014 | **4** | 耕 8015 | 耖 8016 | 耗 8017 | 耘 8018 | 耙 8019 | **5** | 耚 801A | 耛 801B | 耜 801C | 耝 801D | 耞 801E | 耟 801F | **6** | 耠 8020 | **7** | 耡 8021 | 耢 8022
8 | 耣 8023 | 耤 8024 | 耥 8025 | **9** | 耦 8026 | 耧 8027 | **10** | 耨 8028 | 耩 8029 | 耪 802A | **11** | 耫 802B | 耬 802C | **12** | 耭 802D | 耮 802E | **14** | 耯 802F | **15** | 耰 8030 | **16** | 耱 8031
耲 8032

耳 128 | 耳 8033 | **1** | 耴 8034 | **2** | 耵 8035 | **3** | 耶 8036 | 耷 8037 | **4** | 耸 8038 | 耹 8039 | 耺 803A | 耻 803B | 耼 803C | 耽 803D | 耾 803E | 耿 803F | 聀 8040 | 聁 8041 | 聂 8042 | **5** | 聃 8043 | 聄 8044
聅 8045 | 聆 8046 | 聇 8047 | 聈 8048 | 聉 8049 | 聊 804A | 聋 804B | 职 804C | 聍 804D | **6** | 聎 804E | 聏 804F | 聐 8050 | 聑 8051 | 聒 8052 | 聓 8053 | 联 8054 | 聠 8060 | **7** | 聕 8055 | 聖 8056 | 聗 8057 | 聘 8058
8 | 聙 8059 | 聚 805A | 聛 805B | 聜 805C | 聝 805D | 聞 805E | 聟 805F | 聡 8061 | 聢 8062 | 聣 8063 | **9** | 聤 8064 | 聥 8065 | 聦 8066 | 聧 8067 | 聨 8068 | 聩 8069 | 聪 806A | 聫 806B | **10** | 聬 806C | 聭 806D
11 | 聯 806F | 聰 8070 | 聱 8071 | 聲 8072 | 聳 8073 | **12** | 聮 806E | 聴 8074 | 聵 8075 | 聶 8076 | 職 8077 | **13** | 聸 8078 | **14** | 聹 8079 | 聺 807A | 聻 807B | 聼 807C | **16** | 聽 807D | 聾 807E

聿 129 | 聿 807F | 肀 8080 | **4** | 肁 8081 | 肂 8082 | 肃 8083 | **6** | 粛 7C9B | **7** | 肄 8084 | 肅 8085 | 肆 8086 | **8** | 肇 8087 | 肈 8088

肉 130 | 肉 8089 | **1** | 肊 808A | **2** | 肋 808B | 肌 808C | 肍 808D | 肎 808E | 肏 808F | **3** | 肐 8090 | 肑 8091 | 肒 8092 | 肓 8093 | 肔 8094 | 肕 8095 | 肖 8096 | 肗 8097 | 肘 8098 | 肙 8099 | 肚 809A | 肛 809B | 肜 809C
肝 809D | 肞 809E | 肟 809F | 肠 80A0 | **4** | 股 80A1 | 肢 80A2 | 肣 80A3 | 肤 80A4 | 肥 80A5 | 肦 80A6 | 肧 80A7 | 肨 80A8 | 肩 80A9 | 肪 80AA | 肫 80AB | 肬 80AC | 肭 80AD | 肮 80AE | 肯 80AF | 肰 80B0 | 肱 80B1 | 育 80B2
肳 80B3 | 肴 80B4 | 肵 80B5 | 肶 80B6 | 肷 80B7 | 肸 80B8 | 肹 80B9 | 肺 80BA | 肻 80BB | 肼 80BC | 肽 80BD | 肾 80BE | 肿 80BF | 胀 80C0 | 胁 80C1 | **5** | 胂 80C2 | 胃 80C3 | 胄 80C4 | 胅 80C5 | 胆 80C6 | 胇 80C7 | 胈 80C8
胉 80C9 | 胊 80CA | 胋 80CB | 背 80CC | 胍 80CD | 胎 80CE | 胏 80CF | 胐 80D0 | 胑 80D1 | 胒 80D2 | 胓 80D3 | 胔 80D4 | 胕 80D5 | 胖 80D6 | 胗 80D7 | 胘 80D8 | 胙 80D9 | 胚 80DA | 胛 80DB | 胜 80DC | 胝 80DD | 胞 80DE | 胟 80DF
胠 80E0 | 胡 80E1 | 胢 80E2 | 胣 80E3 | 胤 80E4 | 胥 80E5 | 胦 80E6 | 胧 80E7 | 胨 80E8 | 胩 80E9 | 胪 80EA | 胫 80EB | 胬 80EC | **6** | 胭 80ED | 胯 80EF | 胰 80F0 | 胱 80F1 | 胲 80F2 | 胳 80F3 | 胴 80F4 | 胵 80F5 | 胶 80F6
胷 80F7 | 胸 80F8 | 胹 80F9 | 胺 80FA | 胻 80FB | 胼 80FC | 能 80FD | 胾 80FE | 胿 80FF | 脀 8100 | 脁 8101 | 脂 8102 | 脃 8103 | 脄 8104 | 脅 8105 | 脆 8106 | 脇 8107 | 脈 8108 | 脉 8109 | 脊 810A | 脋 810B | 脌 810C | 脍 810D
脎 810E | 脏 810F | 脐 8110 | 脑 8111 | 脒 8112 | 脓 8113 | 脔 8114 | **7** | 胮 80EE | 脕 8115 | 脖 8116 | 脗 8117 | 脘 8118 | 脙 8119 | 脚 811A | 脛 811B | 脜 811C | 脝 811D | 脞 811E | 脟 811F | 脠 8120 | 脡 8121 | 脢 8122
脣 8123 | 脤 8124 | 脥 8125 | 脦 8126 | 脧 8127 | 脨 8128 | 脩 8129 | 脪 812A | 脫 812B | 脬 812C | 脭 812D | 脮 812E | 脯 812F | 脰 8130 | 脱 8131 | 脲 8132 | 脳 8133 | 脴 8134 | 脵 8135 | 脶 8136 | 脷 8137 | 脸 8138

肉 130

8 脹 8139 脺 813A 脻 813B 脼 813C 脽 813D 脾 813E 脿 813F 腀 8140 腁 8141 腂 8142 腃 8143 腄 8144 腅 8145 腆 8146 腇 8147 腈 8148 腉 8149 腊 814A 腋 814B 腌 814C 腍 814D 腎 814E 腏 814F 腐 8150 腑 8151 腒 8152 腓 8153 腔 8154 腕 8155 腖 8156 腗 8157 腘 8158 腙 8159 腚 815A

9 腛 815B 腜 815C 腝 815D 腞 815E 腟 815F 腠 8160 腡 8161 腢 8162 腣 8163 腤 8164 腥 8165 腦 8166 腧 8167 腨 8168 腩 8169 腪 816A 腫 816B 腬 816C 腭 816D 腮 816E 腯 816F 腰 8170 腱 8171 腲 8172 腳 8173 腴 8174 腵 8175 腶 8176 腷 8177 腸 8178 腹 8179 腺 817A 腻 817B 腼 817C 腽 817D 腾 817E

10 腿 817F 膀 8180 膁 8181 膂 8182 膃 8183 膄 8184 膅 8185 膆 8186 膇 8187 膈 8188 膉 8189 膊 818A 膋 818B 膌 818C 膍 818D 膎 818E 膏 818F 膐 8190 膑 8191

11 膒 8192 膓 8193 膔 8194 膕 8195 膖 8196 膗 8197 膘 8198 膙 8199 膚 819A 膛 819B 膜 819C 膝 819D 膞 819E 膟 819F 膠 81A0 膡 81A1 膢 81A2 膣 81A3

12 膥 81A5 膦 81A6 膧 81A7 膨 81A8 膩 81A9 膪 81AA 膫 81AB 膬 81AC 膭 81AD 膮 81AE 膯 81AF 膰 81B0 膱 81B1 膲 81B2 膳 81B3 膴 81B4 膵 81B5

13 膷 81B7 膸 81B8 膹 81B9 膺 81BA 膻 81BB 膼 81BC 膽 81BD 膾 81BE 膿 81BF 臀 81C0 臁 81C1 臂 81C2 臃 81C3 臄 81C4 臅 81C5 臆 81C6 臇 81C7 臈 81C8 臉 81C9 臊 81CA 臋 81CB 臌 81CC

14 臍 81CD 臎 81CE 臏 81CF 臐 81D0 臑 81D1 臒 81D2 臓 81D3

15 臔 81D4 臕 81D5 臗 81D7 臘 81D8

16 臖 81D6 臙 81D9 臚 81DA 臛 81DB 臜 81DC

17 臝 81DD

18 臞 81DE 臟 81DF

19 臠 81E0 臡 81E1 臢 81E2

臣 131 臣 81E3

2 臤 81E4 臥 81E5

6 臦 81E6

8 臧 81E7

11 臨 81E8 臩 81E9

自 132 自 81EA

1 臫 81EB

4 臬 81EC 臭 81ED

6 臮 81EE 臯 81EF 臰 81F0

9 臱 81F1

10 臲 81F2

至 133 至 81F3

3 致 81F4

6 臵 81F5 臶 81F6 臷 81F7 臸 81F8

7 臹 81F9

8 臺 81FA

10 臻 81FB

臼 134 臼 81FC

2 臽 81FD 臾 81FE

3 臿 81FF

4 舀 8200 舁 8201

5 舂 8202

6 舃 8203 舄 8204

7 舅 8205

8 與 8207

9 興 8208

10 舆 8206 舉 8209

12 舊 820A

13 舋 820B

舌 135 舌 820C

2 舍 820D 舎 820E 舏 820F

4 舐 8210

5 舑 8211

6 舒 8212

8 舓 8213 舔 8214 舕 8215

9 舖 8216 舗 8217

10 舘 8218

12 舙 8219

13 舚 821A

舛 136 舛 821B

6 舜 821C

7 舝 821D

8 舞 821E

舟 137 舟 821F **2** 舠 8220 **3** 舡 8221 舢 8222 舣 8223 舤 8224 **4** 舥 8225 舦 8226 舧 8227 舨 8228 舩 8229 航 822A 舫 822B 般 822C 舭 822D 舮 822E 舯 822F 舰 8230 舱 8231
5 舲 8232 舳 8233 舴 8234 舵 8235 舶 8236 舷 8237 舸 8238 船 8239 舺 823A 舻 823B **6** 舼 823C 舽 823D 舾 823E 舿 823F **7** 艀 8240 艁 8241 艂 8242 艃 8243 艄 8244 艅 8245
艆 8246 艇 8247 艈 8248 艉 8249 **8** 艊 824A 艋 824B 艌 824C 艍 824D **9** 艎 824E 艏 824F 艐 8250 艑 8251 艒 8252 艓 8253 艔 8254 **10** 艕 8255 艖 8256 艗 8257 艘 8258 艙 8259
11 艚 825A 艛 825B 艜 825C 艝 825D **12** 艞 825E 艟 825F 艠 8260 **13** 艡 8261 艢 8262 艣 8263 艤 8264 艥 8265 **14** 艦 8266 艧 8267 艨 8268 艩 8269 **15** 艪 826A
16 艫 826B **17** 艬 826C **18** 艭 826D

艮 138 艮 826E **1** 良 826F **11** 艱 8271

色 139 色 8272 **4** 艳 8273 **5** 艴 8274 **8** 艵 8275 **13** 艶 8276 **18** 艷 8277

艸 140 艸 8278 艹 8279 **1** 艺 827A **2** 艻 827B 艼 827C 艽 827D 艾 827E 艿 827F 芀 8280 芁 8281 节 8282 **3** 芃 8283 芄 8284 芅 8285 芆 8286 芇 8287 芈 8288 芉 8289 芊 828A 芋 828B
芌 828C 芍 828D 芎 828E 芏 828F 芐 8290 芑 8291 芒 8292 芓 8293 芔 8294 芕 8295 芖 8296 芗 8297 **4** 芘 8298 芙 8299 芚 829A 芛 829B 芜 829C 芝 829D 芞 829E 芟 829F 芠 82A0 芡 82A1
芢 82A2 芣 82A3 芤 82A4 芥 82A5 芦 82A6 芧 82A7 芨 82A8 芩 82A9 芪 82AA 芫 82AB 芬 82AC 芭 82AD 芮 82AE 芯 82AF 芰 82B0 花 82B1 芲 82B2 芳 82B3 芴 82B4 芵 82B5 芶 82B6 芷 82B7 芸 82B8
芹 82B9 芺 82BA 芻 82BB 芼 82BC 芽 82BD 芾 82BE 苀 82C0 苁 82C1 苂 82C2 苃 82C3 苄 82C4 苅 82C5 苆 82C6 苇 82C7 苈 82C8 苉 82C9 苊 82CA 苋 82CB 苌 82CC 苍 82CD 苎 82CE 苏 82CF 茾 833E
5 芿 82BF 苐 82D0 苑 82D1 苒 82D2 苓 82D3 苔 82D4 苕 82D5 苖 82D6 苗 82D7 苘 82D8 苙 82D9 苚 82DA 苛 82DB 苜 82DC 苝 82DD 苞 82DE 苟 82DF 苠 82E0 苡 82E1 苢 82E2 苣 82E3 苤 82E4
若 82E5 苦 82E6 苧 82E7 苨 82E8 苩 82E9 苪 82EA 苫 82EB 苬 82EC 苭 82ED 苮 82EE 苯 82EF 苰 82F0 英 82F1 苲 82F2 苳 82F3 苴 82F4 苵 82F5 苶 82F6 苷 82F7 苸 82F8 苹 82F9 苺 82FA 苻 82FB
苼 82FC 苾 82FE 苿 82FF 茀 8300 茁 8301 茂 8302 范 8303 茄 8304 茅 8305 茆 8306 茇 8307 茈 8308 茉 8309 茊 830A 茋 830B 茌 830C 茍 830D 茎 830E 茏 830F 茐 8310 茓 8313 茔 8314 茕 8315
6 兹 5179 苽 82FD 茑 8311 茒 8312 茖 8316 茗 8317 茘 8318 茙 8319 茚 831A 茛 831B 茜 831C 茟 831F 茠 8320 茡 8321 茢 8322 茤 8324 茥 8325 茦 8326 茧 8327 茨 8328 茩 8329 茪 832A
茫 832B 茬 832C 茭 832D 茮 832E 茯 832F 茰 8330 茱 8331 茲 8332 茳 8333 茴 8334 茵 8335 茶 8336 茷 8337 茸 8338 茹 8339 茺 833A 茻 833B 茼 833C 茽 833D 茿 833F 荀 8340 荁 8341 荂 8342
荃 8343 荄 8344 荅 8345 荇 8347 荈 8348 草 8349 荊 834A 荋 834B 荌 834C 荍 834D 荎 834E 荏 834F 荐 8350 荑 8351 荒 8352 荔 8354 荕 8355 荖 8356 荗 8357 荘 8358 荙 8359 荚 835A 荛 835B
荜 835C 荞 835E 荟 835F 荠 8360 荢 8362 荣 8363 荤 8364 荥 8365 荦 8366 荧 8367 荨 8368 荩 8369 荪 836A 荬 836C 荭 836D 荮 836E 药 836F **7** 茝 831D 茞 831E 茣 8323 荡 8361 荫 836B
荰 8370 荱 8371 荲 8372 荳 8373 荴 8374 荵 8375 荶 8376 荷 8377 荸 8378 荹 8379 荺 837A 荻 837B 荼 837C 荽 837D 荾 837E 荿 837F 莀 8380 莁 8381 莂 8382 莃 8383 莄 8384 莅 8385 莆 8386
莇 8387 莈 8388 莉 8389 莊 838A 莋 838B 莌 838C 莍 838D 莎 838E 莏 838F 莐 8390 莑 8391 莒 8392 莓 8393 莔 8394 莕 8395 莖 8396 莗 8397 莘 8398 莙 8399 莚 839A 莛 839B 莜 839C 莝 839D

艸 140 莜 839C 莝 839D 莞 839E 莟 839F 莠 83A0 莡 83A1 莢 83A2 莣 83A3 莤 83A4 莥 83A5 莦 83A6 莧 83A7 莨 83A8 莩 83A9 莪 83AA 莫 83AB 莬 83AC 莮 83AE 莯 83AF 莰 83B0 莱 83B1 莳 83B3 莴 83B4

莵 83B5 莶 83B6 获 83B7 莸 83B8 莹 83B9 莺 83BA 莼 83BC **8** 荓 8353 莲 83B2 莽 83BD 莾 83BE 莿 83BF 菀 83C0 菁 83C1 菂 83C2 菃 83C3 菄 83C4 菅 83C5 菆 83C6 菇 83C7 菈 83C8 菉 83C9

菊 83CA 菋 83CB 菌 83CC 菍 83CD 菎 83CE 菏 83CF 菐 83D0 菑 83D1 菒 83D2 菓 83D3 菔 83D4 菕 83D5 菖 83D6 菗 83D7 菘 83D8 菙 83D9 菚 83DA 菛 83DB 菜 83DC 菝 83DD 菞 83DE 菟 83DF 菠 83E0

菡 83E1 菢 83E2 菣 83E3 菤 83E4 菥 83E5 菦 83E6 菧 83E7 菨 83E8 菩 83E9 菪 83EA 菫 83EB 菬 83EC 菭 83ED 菮 83EE 華 83EF 菰 83F0 菱 83F1 菲 83F2 菳 83F3 菴 83F4 菵 83F5 菶 83F6 菷 83F7

菸 83F8 菹 83F9 菺 83FA 菻 83FB 菼 83FC 菽 83FD 菾 83FE 菿 83FF 萀 8400 萁 8401 萂 8402 萃 8403 萄 8404 萅 8405 萆 8406 萇 8407 萈 8408 萉 8409 萊 840A 萋 840B 萌 840C 萍 840D 萎 840E

萏 840F 萐 8410 萑 8411 萒 8412 萓 8413 萔 8414 萕 8415 萖 8416 萗 8417 萘 8418 萙 8419 萚 841A 萛 841B 萜 841C 萝 841D 萞 841E 萟 841F 萠 8420 萡 8421 萢 8422 萣 8423 萤 8424 营 8425

萦 8426 萧 8427 **9** 荝 835D 莭 83AD 萨 8428 萩 8429 萪 842A 萫 842B 萬 842C 萭 842D 萮 842E 萯 842F 萰 8430 萱 8431 萲 8432 萳 8433 萴 8434 萵 8435 萶 8436 萷 8437 萸 8438 萹 8439

萺 843A 萻 843B 萼 843C 落 843D 萾 843E 萿 843F 葀 8440 葁 8441 葂 8442 葃 8443 葄 8444 葅 8445 葆 8446 葇 8447 葈 8448 葉 8449 葊 844A 葋 844B 葌 844C 葍 844D 葎 844E 葏 844F 葐 8450

葑 8451 葒 8452 葓 8453 葔 8454 葕 8455 葖 8456 著 8457 葘 8458 葙 8459 葚 845A 葛 845B 葜 845C 葝 845D 葞 845E 葟 845F 葠 8460 葡 8461 葢 8462 董 8463 葤 8464 葥 8465 葦 8466 葧 8467

葨 8468 葩 8469 葪 846A 葫 846B 葬 846C 葭 846D 葮 846E 葯 846F 葰 8470 葱 8471 葲 8472 葳 8473 葴 8474 葵 8475 葶 8476 葷 8477 葸 8478 葹 8479 葺 847A 葻 847B 葼 847C 葽 847D 葾 847E

葿 847F 蒀 8480 蒁 8481 蒂 8482 蒃 8483 蒄 8484 蒅 8485 蒆 8486 蒇 8487 蒈 8488 蒉 8489 蒋 848B 蒌 848C 蒍 848D 蒎 848E 蒏 848F **10** 蒐 8490 蒑 8491 蒒 8492 蒓 8493 蒔 8494 蒕 8495

蒖 8496 蒗 8497 蒘 8498 蒙 8499 蒚 849A 蒛 849B 蒜 849C 蒝 849D 蒞 849E 蒟 849F 蒠 84A0 蒡 84A1 蒢 84A2 蒣 84A3 蒤 84A4 蒥 84A5 蒦 84A6 蒧 84A7 蒨 84A8 蒩 84A9 蒪 84AA 蒫 84AB 蒬 84AC

蒭 84AD 蒮 84AE 蒯 84AF 蒰 84B0 蒱 84B1 蒲 84B2 蒳 84B3 蒴 84B4 蒵 84B5 蒶 84B6 蒷 84B7 蒸 84B8 蒹 84B9 蒺 84BA 蒻 84BB 蒼 84BC 蒽 84BD 蒾 84BE 蒿 84BF 蓀 84C0 蓁 84C1 蓂 84C2 蓃 84C3

蓄 84C4 蓅 84C5 蓆 84C6 蓇 84C7 蓈 84C8 蓉 84C9 蓊 84CA 蓋 84CB 蓌 84CC 蓍 84CD 蓎 84CE 蓐 84D0 蓑 84D1 蓒 84D2 蓓 84D3 蓔 84D4 蓕 84D5 蓖 84D6 蓗 84D7 蓘 84D8 蓙 84D9 蓚 84DA 蓛 84DB

蓜 84DC 蓝 84DD 蓞 84DE 蓟 84DF 蓠 84E0 蓡 84E1 蓢 84E2 蓣 84E3 蓤 84E4 **11** 蓥 84E5 蓧 84E7 蓨 84E8 蓩 84E9 蓪 84EA 蓫 84EB 蓬 84EC 蓭 84ED 蓮 84EE 蓯 84EF 蓰 84F0 蓱 84F1 蓲 84F2

蓳 84F3 蓴 84F4 蓵 84F5 蓶 84F6 蓷 84F7 蓸 84F8 蓹 84F9 蓺 84FA 蓻 84FB 蓼 84FC 蓽 84FD 蓾 84FE 蓿 84FF 蔀 8500 蔁 8501 蔂 8502 蔃 8503 蔄 8504 蔅 8505 蔆 8506 蔈 8508 蔉 8509 蔊 850A

蔋 850B 蔌 850C 蔍 850D 蔎 850E 蔏 850F 蔐 8510 蔑 8511 蔒 8512 蔓 8513 蔔 8514 蔕 8515 蔖 8516 蔗 8517 蔘 8518 蔙 8519 蔚 851A 蔛 851B 蔜 851C 蔝 851D 蔞 851E 蔟 851F 蔠 8520 蔡 8521

蔢 8522 蔣 8523 蔤 8524 蔥 8525 蔦 8526 蔧 8527 蔨 8528 蔩 8529 蔪 852A 蔫 852B 蔬 852C 蔭 852D 蔮 852E 蔯 852F 蔰 8530 蔱 8531 蔲 8532 蔳 8533 蔴 8534 蔵 8535 蔶 8536 蔷 8537 蔸 8538

蔹 8539 蔺 853A 蔻 853B 蔼 853C **12** 蓏 84CF 蔇 8507 蔽 853D 蔾 853E 蔿 853F 蕀 8540 蕁 8541 蕂 8542 蕃 8543 蕄 8544 蕅 8545 蕆 8546 蕇 8547 蕈 8548 蕉 8549 蕊 854A 蕋 854B 蕌 854C

蕍 854D 蕎 854E 蕏 854F 蕐 8550 蕑 8551 蕒 8552 蕓 8553 蕔 8554 蕕 8555 蕖 8556 蕗 8557 蕘 8558 蕙 8559 蕚 855A 蕛 855B 蕜 855C 蕝 855D 蕞 855E 蕟 855F 蕠 8560 蕡 8561 蕢 8562 蕣 8563

蕤 8564 蕥 8565 蕦 8566 蕧 8567 蕨 8568 蕩 8569 蕪 856A 蕫 856B 蕬 856C 蕭 856D 蕮 856E 蕯 856F 蕰 8570 蕱 8571 蕲 8572 蕳 8573 蕵 8575 **13** 蕶 8576 蕷 8577 蕸 8578 蕹 8579 蕺 857A

蕻 857B 蕼 857C 蕽 857D 蕾 857E 蕿 857F 薀 8580 薁 8581 薂 8582 薃 8583 薄 8584 薅 8585 薆 8586 薇 8587 薈 8588 薉 8589 薊 858A 薋 858B 薌 858C 薍 858D 薎 858E 薏 858F 薐 8590 薑 8591

薒 8592 薓 8593 薔 8594 薕 8595 薖 8596 薗 8597 薘 8598 薙 8599 薚 859A 薛 859B 薜 859C 薝 859D 薞 859E 薟 859F 薠 85A0 薡 85A1 薢 85A2 薣 85A3 薤 85A4 薥 85A5 薦 85A6 薧 85A7 薨 85A8

艸 140
薣 85A3 薤 85A4 薥 85A5 薦 85A6 薧 85A7 薨 85A8 薪 85AA 薫 85AB 薬 85AC 薮 85AE **14** 蕴 8574 薩 85A9 薭 85AD 薯 85AF 薰 85B0 薱 85B1 薲 85B2 薳 85B3 薴 85B4 薵 85B5 薶 85B6 薷 85B7
薸 85B8 薹 85B9 薺 85BA 薻 85BB 薼 85BC 薽 85BD 薾 85BE 薿 85BF 藀 85C0 藁 85C1 藂 85C2 藃 85C3 藄 85C4 藅 85C5 藆 85C6 藇 85C7 藈 85C8 藉 85C9 藊 85CA 藋 85CB 藌 85CC 藍 85CD 藎 85CE
藏 85CF 藐 85D0 藑 85D1 藒 85D2 藓 85D3 **15** 藔 85D4 藕 85D5 藖 85D6 藗 85D7 藘 85D8 藙 85D9 藚 85DA 藛 85DB 藜 85DC 藝 85DD 藞 85DE 藟 85DF 藠 85E0 藡 85E1 藢 85E2 藣 85E3 藤 85E4
藥 85E5 藦 85E6 藧 85E7 藨 85E8 藩 85E9 藪 85EA 藫 85EB 藬 85EC 藭 85ED 藯 85EF 藰 85F0 藱 85F1 藲 85F2 藳 85F3 藴 85F4 藵 85F5 **16** 藮 85EE 藶 85F6 藷 85F7 藸 85F8 藹 85F9 藺 85FA
藻 85FB 藼 85FC 藽 85FD 藾 85FE 藿 85FF 蘀 8600 蘁 8601 蘂 8602 蘃 8603 蘄 8604 蘅 8605 蘆 8606 蘇 8607 蘈 8608 蘉 8609 蘊 860A 蘋 860B 蘌 860C 蘍 860D 蘎 860E 蘏 860F 蘐 8610 蘑 8611
蘓 8613 蘔 8614 蘢 8622 **17** 蘒 8612 蘕 8615 蘖 8616 蘗 8617 蘘 8618 蘙 8619 蘚 861A 蘛 861B 蘜 861C 蘝 861D 蘞 861E 蘟 861F 蘠 8620 蘡 8621 蘣 8623 蘤 8624 蘥 8625 蘦 8626 蘧 8627
蘨 8628 蘩 8629 蘪 862A 蘫 862B 蘬 862C 蘭 862D 蘮 862E 蘯 862F 蘰 8630 **18** 蘲 8632 蘳 8633 蘴 8634 蘵 8635 蘶 8636 蘷 8637 **19** 蘱 8631 蘸 8638 蘹 8639 蘺 863A 蘻 863B 蘼 863C
蘽 863D 蘾 863E 蘿 863F 虀 8640 虁 8641 **20** 虂 8642 虃 8643 虄 8644 虅 8645 **21** 虆 8646 虇 8647 虈 8648 虉 8649 **23** 虊 864A **25** 虋 864B 虌 864C

虍 141
虍 864D **2** 虎 864E 虏 864F **3** 虐 8650 **4** 虒 8652 虓 8653 虔 8654 **5** 處 8655 虖 8656 虗 8657 虘 8658 虙 8659 虚 865A **6** 虛 865B 虝 865D **7** 虜 865C 虞 865E
號 865F **8** 虠 8660 虡 8661 **9** 虢 8662 虣 8663 **10** 虤 8664 虥 8665 虦 8666 **11** 虧 8667 虨 8668 **12** 虩 8669 **20** 虪 866A

虫 142
虫 866B **1** 虬 866C **2** 虭 866D 虮 866E 虯 866F 虰 8670 虱 8671 虲 8672 **3** 虳 8673 虴 8674 虵 8675 虶 8676 虷 8677 虸 8678 虹 8679 虺 867A 虻 867B 虼 867C 虽 867D 虾 867E
虿 867F 蚁 8681 蚂 8682 蚃 8683 **4** 蚄 8684 蚅 8685 蚆 8686 蚇 8687 蚉 8689 蚊 868A 蚋 868B 蚌 868C 蚍 868D 蚎 868E 蚏 868F 蚐 8690 蚑 8691 蚒 8692 蚓 8693 蚔 8694 蚕 8695 蚖 8696
蚗 8697 蚘 8698 蚙 8699 蚚 869A 蚛 869B 蚝 869D 蚞 869E 蚟 869F 蚠 86A0 蚡 86A1 蚢 86A2 蚣 86A3 蚤 86A4 蚥 86A5 蚦 86A6 蚧 86A7 蚨 86A8 蚩 86A9 蚪 86AA 蚬 86AC **5** 蚜 869C 蚫 86AB
蚭 86AD 蚮 86AE 蚯 86AF 蚰 86B0 蚱 86B1 蚲 86B2 蚳 86B3 蚴 86B4 蚵 86B5 蚶 86B6 蚷 86B7 蚸 86B8 蚹 86B9 蚺 86BA 蚻 86BB 蚼 86BC 蚽 86BD 蚾 86BE 蚿 86BF 蛀 86C0 蛁 86C1 蛂 86C2 蛃 86C3
蛄 86C4 蛅 86C5 蛆 86C6 蛇 86C7 蛈 86C8 蛉 86C9 蛊 86CA 蛋 86CB 蛌 86CC 蛎 86CE 蛏 86CF **6** 蚈 8688 蛐 86D0 蛑 86D1 蛒 86D2 蛓 86D3 蛔 86D4 蛕 86D5 蛗 86D7 蛘 86D8 蛙 86D9 蛚 86DA
蛛 86DB 蛜 86DC 蛝 86DD 蛞 86DE 蛟 86DF 蛠 86E0 蛡 86E1 蛢 86E2 蛣 86E3 蛤 86E4 蛥 86E5 蛦 86E6 蛧 86E7 蛨 86E8 蛩 86E9 蛪 86EA 蛫 86EB 蛬 86EC 蛭 86ED 蛮 86EE 蛯 86EF 蛰 86F0 蛱 86F1
蛲 86F2 蛳 86F3 蛴 86F4 **7** 蛖 86D6 蛵 86F5 蛶 86F6 蛷 86F7 蛸 86F8 蛹 86F9 蛺 86FA 蛻 86FB 蛼 86FC 蛽 86FD 蛾 86FE 蛿 86FF 蜀 8700 蜁 8701 蜂 8702 蜃 8703 蜄 8704 蜅 8705 蜆 8706
蜇 8707 蜈 8708 蜉 8709 蜊 870A 蜋 870B 蜌 870C 蜍 870D 蜎 870E 蜏 870F 蜐 8710 蜑 8711 蜒 8712 蜓 8713 蜔 8714 蜕 8715 蜖 8716 蜗 8717 蜫 872B 蝆 8746 **8** 蜘 8718 蜙 8719 蜚 871A
蜛 871B 蜜 871C 蜝 871D 蜞 871E 蜟 871F 蜠 8720 蜡 8721 蜢 8722 蜣 8723 蜤 8724 蜥 8725 蜦 8726 蜧 8727 蜨 8728 蜩 8729 蜪 872A 蜬 872C 蜭 872D 蜮 872E 蜯 872F 蜰 8730 蜱 8731 蜲 8732
蜳 8733 蜴 8734 蜵 8735 蜶 8736 蜷 8737 蜸 8738 蜹 8739 蜺 873A 蜻 873B 蜼 873C 蜽 873D 蜾 873E 蜿 873F 蝀 8740 蝁 8741 蝂 8742 蝃 8743 蝄 8744 蝅 8745 蝇 8747 蝈 8748 蝊 874A 蝋 874B
9 蝉 8749 蝌 874C 蝍 874D 蝎 874E 蝏 874F 蝐 8750 蝑 8751 蝒 8752 蝓 8753 蝔 8754 蝕 8755 蝖 8756 蝗 8757 蝘 8758 蝙 8759 蝚 875A 蝛 875B 蝜 875C 蝝 875D 蝞 875E 蝟 875F 蝠 8760

虫 142 蝠 8760 蝡 8761 蝢 8762 蝣 8763 蝤 8764 蝥 8765 蝦 8766 蝧 8767 蝨 8768 蝩 8769 蝪 876A 蝫 876B 蝬 876C 蝭 876D 蝮 876E 蝯 876F 蝰 8770 蝱 8771 蝲 8772 蝳 8773 蝴 8774 蝵 8775 蝶 8776
蝷 8777 蝸 8778 蝺 877A 蝻 877B 蝼 877C 蝽 877D 蝾 877E 蝿 877F 螀 8780 蟡 87E1 **10** 蝹 8779 螁 8781 螂 8782 螃 8783 螄 8784 螅 8785 螆 8786 螇 8787 螈 8788 螉 8789 螊 878A 螋 878B
螌 878C 融 878D 螎 878E 螏 878F 螐 8790 螑 8791 螒 8792 螓 8793 螔 8794 螕 8795 螖 8796 螗 8797 螘 8798 螙 8799 螚 879A 螛 879B 螜 879C 螝 879D 螞 879E 螟 879F 螠 87A0 螡 87A1 螢 87A2
螣 87A3 螤 87A4 螥 87A5 螦 87A6 螧 87A7 螨 87A8 螩 87A9 **11** 螪 87AA 螫 87AB 螬 87AC 螭 87AD 螮 87AE 螯 87AF 螰 87B0 螱 87B1 螲 87B2 螳 87B3 螴 87B4 螵 87B5 螶 87B6 螷 87B7 螸 87B8
螹 87B9 螺 87BA 螻 87BB 螼 87BC 螽 87BD 螾 87BE 螿 87BF 蟀 87C0 蟁 87C1 蟂 87C2 蟃 87C3 蟄 87C4 蟅 87C5 蟆 87C6 蟇 87C7 蟈 87C8 蟉 87C9 蟊 87CA 蟋 87CB 蟌 87CC 蟍 87CD 蟎 87CE 蟏 87CF
蟐 87D0 蟑 87D1 **12** 蟓 87D3 蟔 87D4 蟕 87D5 蟖 87D6 蟗 87D7 蟘 87D8 蟙 87D9 蟚 87DA 蟛 87DB 蟜 87DC 蟝 87DD 蟞 87DE 蟟 87DF 蟠 87E0 蟢 87E2 蟣 87E3 蟤 87E4 蟥 87E5 蟦 87E6 蟧 87E7
蟨 87E8 蟩 87E9 蟪 87EA 蟫 87EB 蟬 87EC 蟭 87ED 蟮 87EE 蟯 87EF 蟰 87F0 蟱 87F1 蟲 87F2 蟳 87F3 蟴 87F4 蟵 87F5 蠎 880E **13** 蟒 87D2 蟶 87F6 蟷 87F7 蟸 87F8 蟹 87F9 蟺 87FA 蟻 87FB
蟼 87FC 蟽 87FD 蟾 87FE 蟿 87FF 蠀 8800 蠁 8801 蠂 8802 蠃 8803 蠄 8804 蠅 8805 蠆 8806 蠇 8807 蠈 8808 蠉 8809 蠊 880A 蠋 880B 蠌 880C 蠍 880D 蠏 880F **14** 蠐 8810 蠑 8811 蠒 8812
蠓 8813 蠔 8814 蠕 8815 蠖 8816 蠗 8817 蠘 8818 蠙 8819 **15** 蠚 881A 蠛 881B 蠜 881C 蠝 881D 蠞 881E 蠟 881F 蠠 8820 蠡 8821 蠢 8822 蠣 8823 蠤 8824 蠴 8834 **16** 蠥 8825 蠦 8826
蠧 8827 蠨 8828 蠩 8829 蠪 882A 蠫 882B 蠬 882C **17** 蠭 882D 蠮 882E 蠯 882F 蠰 8830 蠱 8831 蠲 8832 蠳 8833 **18** 蠵 8835 蠶 8836 蠷 8837 蠸 8838 蠹 8839 蠺 883A **19** 蠻 883B
20 蠼 883C **21** 蠽 883D 蠾 883E **22** 蠿 883F

血 143 血 8840 **3** 衁 8841 衂 8842 **4** 衃 8843 衄 8844 **5** 衅 8845 **6** 衆 8846 衇 8847 衈 8848 衉 8849 **15** 衊 884A **18** 衋 884B

行 144 行 884C **3** 衍 884D 衎 884E **4** 衏 884F **5** 衐 8850 衑 8851 衒 8852 術 8853 **6** 衕 8855 衖 8856 街 8857 衘 8858 **7** 衙 8859 **9** 衚 885A 衛 885B 衜 885C 衝 885D
10 衞 885E 衟 885F 衠 8860 衡 8861 **18** 衢 8862

衣 145 衣 8863 衤 8864 **2** 补 8865 **3** 衦 8866 衧 8867 表 8868 衩 8869 衪 886A 衫 886B 衬 886C **4** 衭 886D 衮 886E 衯 886F 衰 8870 衱 8871 衲 8872 衳 8873 衴 8874 衵 8875 衶 8876
衷 8877 衸 8878 衹 8879 衺 887A 衻 887B 衼 887C 衽 887D 衾 887E 衿 887F 袀 8880 袁 8881 袂 8882 袃 8883 袄 8884 袅 8885 袆 8886 袇 8887 **5** 袈 8888 袉 8889 袊 888A 袋 888B 袌 888C
袍 888D 袎 888E 袏 888F 袐 8890 袑 8891 袒 8892 袓 8893 袔 8894 袕 8895 袖 8896 袗 8897 袘 8898 袙 8899 袚 889A 袛 889B 袜 889C 袝 889D 袞 889E 袟 889F 袠 88A0 袡 88A1 袢 88A2 袣 88A3
袤 88A4 袥 88A5 袦 88A6 袧 88A7 袨 88A8 袩 88A9 袪 88AA 被 88AB 袬 88AC 袮 88AE 袰 88B0 **6** 袯 88AF 袱 88B1 袲 88B2 袳 88B3 袴 88B4 袵 88B5 袶 88B6 袷 88B7 袸 88B8 袹 88B9 袺 88BA
袻 88BB 袼 88BC 袽 88BD 袾 88BE 袿 88BF 裀 88C0 裁 88C1 裂 88C2 裃 88C3 裄 88C4 装 88C5 裆 88C6 裇 88C7 裈 88C8 裉 88C9 **7** 裊 88CA 裋 88CB 裌 88CC 裍 88CD 裎 88CE 裏 88CF 裐 88D0
裑 88D1 裒 88D2 裓 88D3 裔 88D4 裕 88D5 裖 88D6 裗 88D7 裘 88D8 裙 88D9 裚 88DA 裛 88DB 補 88DC 裝 88DD 裞 88DE 裟 88DF 裠 88E0 裡 88E1 裢 88E2 裣 88E3 裤 88E4 裥 88E5 **8** 裧 88E7

衣 145 **8** 裧 88E7 裨 88E8 裩 88E9 裪 88EA 裫 88EB 裬 88EC 裭 88ED 裮 88EE 裯 88EF 裰 88F0 裱 88F1 裲 88F2 裳 88F3 裴 88F4 裵 88F5 裶 88F6 裷 88F7 裸 88F8 裹 88F9 裺 88FA 裻 88FB 裼 88FC
製 88FD 裾 88FE 裿 88FF 褀 8900 褁 8901 褂 8902 褃 8903 褄 8904 **9** 裦 88E6 褅 8905 褆 8906 複 8907 褈 8908 褉 8909 褊 890A 褋 890B 褌 890C 褍 890D 褎 890E 褏 890F 褐 8910 褑 8911
褒 8912 褓 8913 褔 8914 褕 8915 褖 8916 褗 8917 褘 8918 褙 8919 褚 891A 褛 891B 褜 891C 褝 891D **10** 褞 891E 褟 891F 褠 8920 褡 8921 褢 8922 褣 8923 褤 8924 褥 8925 褦 8926 褧 8927
褨 8928 褩 8929 褪 892A 褫 892B 褬 892C 褭 892D 褮 892E 褯 892F 褰 8930 褱 8931 褲 8932 褴 8934 **11** 褳 8933 褵 8935 褶 8936 褷 8937 褸 8938 褹 8939 褺 893A 褻 893B 褼 893C 褽 893D
褾 893E 褿 893F 襀 8940 襁 8941 襂 8942 襃 8943 襄 8944 襅 8945 襔 8954 **12** 襆 8946 襇 8947 襈 8948 襉 8949 襊 894A 襋 894B 襌 894C 襍 894D 襎 894E 襏 894F 襐 8950 襑 8951 襒 8952
襓 8953 襕 8955 襰 8970 **13** 襖 8956 襗 8957 襘 8958 襙 8959 襚 895A 襛 895B 襜 895C 襝 895D 襞 895E 襟 895F 襠 8960 襡 8961 襢 8962 **14** 襣 8963 襤 8964 襥 8965 襦 8966 襧 8967
襨 8968 **15** 襩 8969 襪 896A 襫 896B 襬 896C 襭 896D 襮 896E **16** 襯 896F 襱 8971 襲 8972 **17** 襳 8973 襴 8974 襽 897D **18** 襵 8975 襶 8976 襷 8977 **19** 襸 8978 襹 8979
襺 897A 襻 897B 襼 897C

襾 146 襾 897E 西 897F 覀 8980 **3** 要 8981 **5** 覂 8982 **6** 覃 8983 覄 8984 **7** 覅 8985 **12** 覆 8986 **13** 覇 8987 覈 8988 **17** 覉 8989 **19** 覊 898A

見 147 見 898B **2** 覌 898C 覙 8999 观 89C2 **3** 覍 898D 覎 898E **4** 規 898F 覐 8990 覑 8991 覒 8992 覓 8993 覔 8994 规 89C4 视 89C6 **5** 覕 8995 視 8996 覗 8997 覘 8998 覚 899A
觇 89C7 览 89C8 觉 89C9 **6** 覛 899B 覜 899C 觊 89CA **7** 覝 899D 覞 899E 覟 899F 覠 89A0 覡 89A1 觋 89CB **8** 覢 89A2 覣 89A3 覤 89A4 覥 89A5 觌 89CC 觍 89CD **9** 覦 89A6
覧 89A7 覨 89A8 覩 89A9 親 89AA 觎 89CE **10** 覫 89AB 覬 89AC 覭 89AD 覮 89AE 覯 89AF 觏 89CF **11** 覰 89B0 覱 89B1 覲 89B2 観 89B3 觐 89D0 觑 89D1 **12** 覴 89B4 覵 89B5 覶 89B6
覷 89B7 覸 89B8 **13** 覹 89B9 覺 89BA 覻 89BB **14** 覼 89BC 覽 89BD **15** 覾 89BE 覿 89BF **18** 觀 89C0

见 147 见 89C1 **3** 觃 89C3

角 148 角 89D2 **2** 觓 89D3 觔 89D4 **4** 觕 89D5 觖 89D6 觗 89D7 觘 89D8 觙 89D9 **5** 觚 89DA 觛 89DB 觝 89DD 觞 89DE **6** 觜 89DC 觟 89DF 觠 89E0 觡 89E1 觢 89E2 解 89E3 觤 89E4
觥 89E5 触 89E6 觧 89E7 **7** 觨 89E8 觩 89E9 觪 89EA 觫 89EB **8** 觬 89EC 觭 89ED 觮 89EE 觯 89EF **9** 觰 89F0 觱 89F1 **10** 觲 89F2 觳 89F3 **11** 觴 89F4 **12** 觵 89F5
觶 89F6 **13** 觷 89F7 觸 89F8 觹 89F9 **14** 觺 89FA **15** 觻 89FB 觼 89FC **16** 觽 89FD 觾 89FE **18** 觿 89FF

言 149 言 8A00 訁 8A01 **2** 訂 8A02 訃 8A03 訄 8A04 訅 8A05 訆 8A06 訇 8A07 計 8A08 计 8BA1 订 8BA2 讣 8BA3 认 8BA4 讥 8BA5 **3** 訉 8A09 訊 8A0A 訋 8A0B 訌 8A0C 訍 8A0D 討 8A0E 訏 8A0F

言 149 訐 8A10 訑 8A11 訒 8A12 訓 8A13 訔 8A14 訕 8A15 訖 8A16 託 8A17 記 8A18 訙 8A19 訚 8A1A 讦 8BA6 讧 8BA7 讨 8BA8 让 8BA9 讪 8BAA 讫 8BAB 讬 8BAC 训 8BAD 议 8BAE 讯 8BAF 记 8BB0 讱 8BB1

4 訛 8A1B 訜 8A1C 訝 8A1D 訞 8A1E 訟 8A1F 訠 8A20 訡 8A21 訢 8A22 訣 8A23 訤 8A24 訥 8A25 訦 8A26 訧 8A27 訨 8A28 訩 8A29 訪 8A2A 訫 8A2B 訬 8A2C 設 8A2D 訮 8A2E 訯 8A2F 訰 8A30
許 8A31 訲 8A32 訳 8A33 讲 8BB2 讳 8BB3 讴 8BB4 讶 8BB6 讷 8BB7 许 8BB8 讹 8BB9 论 8BBA 讻 8BBB 讼 8BBC 讽 8BBD 设 8BBE 访 8BBF 诀 8BC0

5 訴 8A34 訵 8A35 訶 8A36 訷 8A37 訸 8A38
訹 8A39 診 8A3A 註 8A3B 証 8A3C 訽 8A3D 訾 8A3E 訿 8A3F 詀 8A40 詁 8A41 詂 8A42 詃 8A43 詄 8A44 詅 8A45 詆 8A46 詇 8A47 詈 8A48 詉 8A49 詊 8A4A 詋 8A4B 詌 8A4C 詍 8A4D 詎 8A4E 詏 8A4F
詐 8A50 詑 8A51 詒 8A52 詓 8A53 詔 8A54 評 8A55 詖 8A56 詗 8A57 詘 8A58 詙 8A59 詚 8A5A 詛 8A5B 詜 8A5C 詝 8A5D 詞 8A5E 詟 8A5F 詠 8A60 讵 8BB5 证 8BC1 诂 8BC2 诃 8BC3 评 8BC4 诅 8BC5
识 8BC6 诇 8BC7 诈 8BC8 诉 8BC9 诊 8BCA 诋 8BCB 诌 8BCC 词 8BCD 诎 8BCE 诏 8BCF 诐 8BD0 译 8BD1 诒 8BD2

6 詡 8A61 詢 8A62 詣 8A63 詤 8A64 詥 8A65 試 8A66 詧 8A67 詨 8A68 詩 8A69
詪 8A6A 詫 8A6B 詬 8A6C 詭 8A6D 詮 8A6E 詯 8A6F 詰 8A70 話 8A71 該 8A72 詳 8A73 詴 8A74 詵 8A75 詶 8A76 詷 8A77 詸 8A78 詹 8A79 詺 8A7A 詻 8A7B 詼 8A7C 詽 8A7D 詾 8A7E 詿 8A7F 誀 8A80
誁 8A81 誂 8A82 誃 8A83 誄 8A84 誅 8A85 誆 8A86 誇 8A87 誈 8A88 誉 8A89 誊 8A8A 诓 8BD3 诔 8BD4 试 8BD5 诖 8BD6 诗 8BD7 诘 8BD8 诙 8BD9 诚 8BDA 诛 8BDB 诜 8BDC 话 8BDD 诟 8BDF 诠 8BE0
诡 8BE1 询 8BE2 诣 8BE3 诤 8BE4 该 8BE5 详 8BE6 诧 8BE7 诨 8BE8 诩 8BE9

7 誋 8A8B 誌 8A8C 認 8A8D 誎 8A8E 誏 8A8F 誐 8A90 誑 8A91 誒 8A92 誓 8A93 誔 8A94 誕 8A95 誖 8A96 誗 8A97
誘 8A98 誙 8A99 誚 8A9A 誛 8A9B 誜 8A9C 誝 8A9D 語 8A9E 誟 8A9F 誠 8AA0 誡 8AA1 誢 8AA2 誣 8AA3 誤 8AA4 誥 8AA5 誦 8AA6 誧 8AA7 誨 8AA8 誩 8AA9 說 8AAA 誫 8AAB 説 8AAC 読 8AAD 誮 8AAE
诫 8BEB 诬 8BEC 语 8BED 诮 8BEE 误 8BEF 诰 8BF0 诱 8BF1 诲 8BF2 诳 8BF3 说 8BF4 诵 8BF5 诶 8BF6

8 誯 8AAF 誰 8AB0 誱 8AB1 課 8AB2 誳 8AB3 誴 8AB4 誵 8AB5 誶 8AB6 誷 8AB7 誸 8AB8
誹 8AB9 誺 8ABA 誻 8ABB 誼 8ABC 誽 8ABD 誾 8ABE 調 8ABF 諀 8AC0 諁 8AC1 諂 8AC2 諃 8AC3 諄 8AC4 諅 8AC5 諆 8AC6 談 8AC7 諈 8AC8 諉 8AC9 諊 8ACA 請 8ACB 諌 8ACC 諍 8ACD 諎 8ACE 諏 8ACF
諐 8AD0 諑 8AD1 諒 8AD2 諓 8AD3 諔 8AD4 諕 8AD5 論 8AD6 諗 8AD7 諘 8AD8 諙 8AD9 諚 8ADA 諩 8AE9 诞 8BDE 请 8BF7 诸 8BF8 诹 8BF9 诺 8BFA 读 8BFB 诼 8BFC 诽 8BFD 课 8BFE 诿 8BFF 谀 8C00
谁 8C01 谂 8C02 调 8C03 谄 8C04 谅 8C05 谆 8C06 谇 8C07 谈 8C08 谉 8C09 谊 8C0A

9 諛 8ADB 諜 8ADC 諝 8ADD 諞 8ADE 諟 8ADF 諠 8AE0 諡 8AE1 諢 8AE2 諣 8AE3 諤 8AE4 諥 8AE5 諦 8AE6
諧 8AE7 諨 8AE8 諪 8AEA 諫 8AEB 諬 8AEC 諭 8AED 諮 8AEE 諯 8AEF 諰 8AF0 諱 8AF1 諲 8AF2 諳 8AF3 諴 8AF4 諵 8AF5 諶 8AF6 諷 8AF7 諸 8AF8 諹 8AF9 諺 8AFA 諻 8AFB 諼 8AFC 諽 8AFD 諾 8AFE
諿 8AFF 謀 8B00 謁 8B01 謂 8B02 謃 8B03 謊 8B0A 謡 8B21 谋 8C0B 谌 8C0C 谍 8C0D 谎 8C0E 谏 8C0F 谐 8C10 谑 8C11 谒 8C12 谓 8C13 谔 8C14 谕 8C15 谖 8C16 谗 8C17 谘 8C18 谙 8C19 谚 8C1A
谛 8C1B 谜 8C1C 谝 8C1D 谞 8C1E

10 謄 8B04 謅 8B05 謆 8B06 謇 8B07 謈 8B08 謉 8B09 謌 8B0C 謍 8B0D 謎 8B0E 謏 8B0F 謐 8B10 謑 8B11 謒 8B12 謓 8B13 謔 8B14 謕 8B15 謖 8B16 謗 8B17
謘 8B18 謙 8B19 謚 8B1A 講 8B1B 謜 8B1C 謝 8B1D 謞 8B1E 謟 8B1F 謠 8B20 謢 8B22 谟 8C1F 谠 8C20 谡 8C21 谢 8C22 谣 8C23 谤 8C24 谥 8C25 谦 8C26 谧 8C27

11 謋 8B0B 謣 8B23 謤 8B24
謥 8B25 謦 8B26 謧 8B27 謨 8B28 謩 8B29 謪 8B2A 謫 8B2B 謬 8B2C 謭 8B2D 謮 8B2E 謯 8B2F 謰 8B30 謱 8B31 謲 8B32 謳 8B33 謴 8B34 謵 8B35 謶 8B36 謷 8B37 謸 8B38 謹 8B39 謺 8B3A 謻 8B3B
謼 8B3C 謽 8B3D 謾 8B3E 谨 8C28 谩 8C29 谪 8C2A 谫 8C2B 谬 8C2C

12 謿 8B3F 譀 8B40 譁 8B41 譂 8B42 譃 8B43 譄 8B44 譆 8B46 譇 8B47 譈 8B48 證 8B49 譊 8B4A 譋 8B4B 譌 8B4C 譎 8B4E
譏 8B4F 譐 8B50 譑 8B51 譒 8B52 譓 8B53 譔 8B54 譕 8B55 譖 8B56 譗 8B57 識 8B58 譙 8B59 譚 8B5A 譛 8B5B 譜 8B5C 谭 8C2D 谮 8C2E 谯 8C2F 谰 8C30 谱 8C31 谲 8C32

13 譍 8B4D 譝 8B5D
譞 8B5E 譟 8B5F 譠 8B60 譡 8B61 譢 8B62 譣 8B63 譤 8B64 譥 8B65 警 8B66 譧 8B67 譨 8B68 譩 8B69 譪 8B6A 譫 8B6B 譬 8B6C 譭 8B6D 譮 8B6E 譯 8B6F 議 8B70 譱 8B71 譲 8B72 谳 8C33 谴 8C34
谵 8C35

14 譅 8B45 譳 8B73 譴 8B74 譵 8B75 譶 8B76 護 8B77 譸 8B78 譹 8B79 譺 8B7A 譻 8B7B 譽 8B7D 诪 8BEA

15 譼 8B7C 譾 8B7E 譿 8B7F 讀 8B80 讁 8B81 讂 8B82 讃 8B83 讄 8B84

言 149 譾 8B7E 譿 8B7F 讀 8B80 讁 8B81 讂 8B82 讃 8B83 讄 8B84 讅 8B85 **16** 讆 8B86 讇 8B87 讈 8B88 讉 8B89 變 8B8A 讋 8B8B 讌 8B8C 讍 8B8D 讎 8B8E 讏 8B8F 讐 8B90 **17** 讑 8B91 讒 8B92
讓 8B93 讔 8B94 讕 8B95 讖 8B96 谶 8C36 **18** 讗 8B97 讘 8B98 讙 8B99 **19** 讚 8B9A 讛 8B9B **20** 讜 8B9C 讝 8B9D 讞 8B9E **22** 讟 8B9F

讠 149 讠 8BA0

谷 150 谷 8C37 **3** 谸 8C38 **4** 谹 8C39 谺 8C3A 谻 8C3B **6** 谼 8C3C **7** 谽 8C3D **8** 谾 8C3E **10** 谿 8C3F 豀 8C40 豁 8C41 **11** 豂 8C42 **12** 豃 8C43 **15** 豄 8C44
16 豅 8C45

豆 151 豆 8C46 **3** 豇 8C47 豈 8C48 **4** 豉 8C49 **6** 豊 8C4A 豋 8C4B **8** 豌 8C4C 豍 8C4D 豎 8C4E **10** 豏 8C4F **11** 豐 8C50 **13** 豑 8C51 **18** 豒 8C52 **20** 豓 8C53
21 豔 8C54

豕 152 豕 8C55 **1** 豖 8C56 **3** 豗 8C57 **4** 豘 8C58 豙 8C59 豚 8C5A 豛 8C5B 豜 8C5C 豝 8C5D **5** 豞 8C5E 豟 8C5F 豠 8C60 象 8C61 **6** 豢 8C62 豣 8C63 豤 8C64 豥 8C65 豦 8C66
7 豧 8C67 豨 8C68 豩 8C69 豪 8C6A **9** 豫 8C6B 豬 8C6C 豭 8C6D 豮 8C6E **10** 豯 8C6F 豰 8C70 豱 8C71 豲 8C72 豳 8C73 **11** 豴 8C74 豵 8C75 **12** 豷 8C77 **13** 豶 8C76

豸 153 豸 8C78 **3** 豹 8C79 豺 8C7A 豻 8C7B **4** 豼 8C7C 豽 8C7D **5** 豾 8C7E 豿 8C7F 貀 8C80 貁 8C81 貂 8C82 貃 8C83 **6** 貄 8C84 貅 8C85 貆 8C86 貇 8C87 貈 8C88 貉 8C89 貊 8C8A
7 貋 8C8B 貌 8C8C 貍 8C8D **8** 貎 8C8E 貏 8C8F **9** 貐 8C90 貑 8C91 貒 8C92 貓 8C93 **10** 貔 8C94 貕 8C95 貖 8C96 **11** 貗 8C97 貘 8C98 貙 8C99 **12** 貚 8C9A
18 貛 8C9B **20** 貜 8C9C

貝 154 貝 8C9D **2** 貞 8C9E 貟 8C9F 負 8CA0 负 8D1F 贠 8D20 **3** 財 8CA1 貢 8CA2 貣 8CA3 貤 8CA4 贡 8D21 财 8D22 **4** 貥 8CA5 貦 8CA6 貧 8CA7 貨 8CA8 販 8CA9 貪 8CAA 貫 8CAB 責 8CAC
貭 8CAD 貮 8CAE 责 8D23 贤 8D24 败 8D25 账 8D26 货 8D27 贩 8D29 贪 8D2A 贫 8D2B 购 8D2D 贮 8D2E 贯 8D2F **5** 貯 8CAF 貰 8CB0 貱 8CB1 貲 8CB2 貳 8CB3 貴 8CB4 貵 8CB5 貶 8CB6 買 8CB7
貸 8CB8 貹 8CB9 貺 8CBA 費 8CBB 貼 8CBC 貽 8CBD 貾 8CBE 貿 8CBF 賀 8CC0 賁 8CC1 贬 8D2C 贱 8D31 贲 8D32 贳 8D33 贴 8D34 贵 8D35 贶 8D36 贷 8D37 贸 8D38 费 8D39 贺 8D3A 贻 8D3B
6 賂 8CC2 賃 8CC3 賄 8CC4 賅 8CC5 賆 8CC6 資 8CC7 賈 8CC8 賉 8CC9 賊 8CCA 賋 8CCB 賌 8CCC 賍 8CCD 賎 8CCE 贼 8D3C 贽 8D3D 贾 8D3E 贿 8D3F 赀 8D40 赁 8D41 赂 8D42 赃 8D43 资 8D44
赅 8D45 赆 8D46 **7** 賏 8CCF 賐 8CD0 賑 8CD1 賒 8CD2 賔 8CD4 賕 8CD5 賖 8CD6 賗 8CD7 賘 8CD8 赇 8D47 赈 8D48 赉 8D49 赊 8D4A **8** 賓 8CD3 賙 8CD9 賚 8CDA 賛 8CDB 賜 8CDC 賝 8CDD

貝 154 賞 8CDE 賟 8CDF 賠 8CE0 賡 8CE1 賢 8CE2 賣 8CE3 賤 8CE4 賥 8CE5 賦 8CE6 賧 8CE7 賨 8CE8 賩 8CE9 質 8CEA 賫 8CEB 賬 8CEC 赋 8D4B 赌 8D4C 赍 8D4D 赎 8D4E 赏 8D4F 赐 8D50 赒 8D52 赔 8D54
赕 8D55 **9** 賭 8CED 賮 8CEE 賯 8CEF 賰 8CF0 賱 8CF1 賲 8CF2 賳 8CF3 賴 8CF4 賵 8CF5 赖 8D56 赗 8D57 **10** 賶 8CF6 賷 8CF7 賸 8CF8 賹 8CF9 賺 8CFA 賻 8CFB 購 8CFC 賽 8CFD 赘 8D58
赙 8D59 赚 8D5A **11** 賾 8CFE 賿 8CFF 贀 8D00 贂 8D02 贃 8D03 贄 8D04 贅 8D05 **12** 贆 8D06 贇 8D07 贈 8D08 贉 8D09 贊 8D0A 贋 8D0B 贌 8D0C 赞 8D5E 赟 8D5F 赠 8D60 **13** 贍 8D0D
贎 8D0E 贏 8D0F 赡 8D61 **14** 贐 8D10 贑 8D11 贒 8D12 贓 8D13 贔 8D14 赑 8D51 **15** 贕 8D15 贖 8D16 贗 8D17 贘 8D18 **16** 贙 8D19 贚 8D1A **17** 贛 8D1B 赣 8D63 **18** 贜 8D1C

贝 154 贝 8D1D

赤 155 赤 8D64 **4** 赥 8D65 赦 8D66 **5** 赧 8D67 **6** 赨 8D68 赩 8D69 赪 8D6A **7** 赫 8D6B **9** 赬 8D6C 赭 8D6D 赮 8D6E **10** 赯 8D6F

走 156 走 8D70 赱 8D71 **2** 赲 8D72 赳 8D73 赴 8D74 赵 8D75 **3** 赶 8D76 起 8D77 赸 8D78 **4** 赹 8D79 赺 8D7A 赻 8D7B 赼 8D7C 赽 8D7D 赾 8D7E 赿 8D7F **5** 趀 8D80 趁 8D81 趂 8D82
趃 8D83 趄 8D84 超 8D85 趆 8D86 趇 8D87 趈 8D88 趉 8D89 越 8D8A 趋 8D8B **6** 趌 8D8C 趍 8D8D 趎 8D8E 趏 8D8F 趐 8D90 趑 8D91 趒 8D92 趓 8D93 趔 8D94 **7** 趕 8D95 趖 8D96 趗 8D97
趘 8D98 趙 8D99 趚 8D9A **8** 趛 8D9B 趜 8D9C 趝 8D9D 趞 8D9E 趟 8D9F 趠 8DA0 趡 8DA1 趢 8DA2 趣 8DA3 趤 8DA4 **9** 趥 8DA5 趦 8DA6 趧 8DA7 **10** 趨 8DA8 **12** 趩 8DA9 趪 8DAA
趫 8DAB 趬 8DAC 趭 8DAD **13** 趮 8DAE **14** 趯 8DAF 趰 8DB0 **16** 趱 8DB1 **19** 趲 8DB2

足 157 足 8DB3 **2** 趴 8DB4 **3** 趵 8DB5 趶 8DB6 趷 8DB7 趸 8DB8 **4** 趹 8DB9 趺 8DBA 趻 8DBB 趽 8DBD 趾 8DBE 趿 8DBF 跀 8DC0 跁 8DC1 跂 8DC2 跃 8DC3 跄 8DC4 **5** 跅 8DC5 跆 8DC6
跇 8DC7 跈 8DC8 跉 8DC9 跊 8DCA 跋 8DCB 跌 8DCC 跍 8DCD 跎 8DCE 跏 8DCF 跐 8DD0 跑 8DD1 跒 8DD2 跓 8DD3 跔 8DD4 跕 8DD5 跖 8DD6 跗 8DD7 跘 8DD8 跙 8DD9 跚 8DDA 跛 8DDB 跜 8DDC 距 8DDD
跞 8DDE **6** 趼 8DBC 跟 8DDF 跠 8DE0 跡 8DE1 跢 8DE2 跣 8DE3 跤 8DE4 跥 8DE5 跦 8DE6 跧 8DE7 跨 8DE8 跩 8DE9 跪 8DEA 跫 8DEB 跬 8DEC 跭 8DED 跮 8DEE 路 8DEF 跰 8DF0 跱 8DF1 跲 8DF2
跳 8DF3 跴 8DF4 践 8DF5 跶 8DF6 跷 8DF7 跸 8DF8 跹 8DF9 跺 8DFA 跻 8DFB **7** 跼 8DFC 跽 8DFD 跾 8DFE 跿 8DFF 踀 8E00 踁 8E01 踂 8E02 踃 8E03 踄 8E04 踅 8E05 踆 8E06 踇 8E07 踈 8E08
踉 8E09 踊 8E0A 踋 8E0B 踌 8E0C 踍 8E0D 踎 8E0E **8** 踏 8E0F 踐 8E10 踑 8E11 踒 8E12 踓 8E13 踔 8E14 踕 8E15 踖 8E16 踗 8E17 踘 8E18 踙 8E19 踚 8E1A 踛 8E1B 踜 8E1C 踝 8E1D 踞 8E1E
踟 8E1F 踠 8E20 踡 8E21 踢 8E22 踣 8E23 踤 8E24 踥 8E25 踦 8E26 踧 8E27 踨 8E28 踩 8E29 踪 8E2A 踬 8E2C 踭 8E2D 踮 8E2E 踯 8E2F 踺 8E3A **9** 踫 8E2B 踰 8E30 踱 8E31 踲 8E32 踳 8E33
踴 8E34 踵 8E35 踶 8E36 踷 8E37 踸 8E38 踹 8E39 踻 8E3B 踼 8E3C 踽 8E3D 踾 8E3E 踿 8E3F 蹀 8E40 蹁 8E41 蹂 8E42 蹃 8E43 蹄 8E44 蹅 8E45 **10** 蹆 8E46 蹇 8E47 蹈 8E48 蹉 8E49 蹊 8E4A
蹋 8E4B 蹌 8E4C 蹍 8E4D 蹎 8E4E 蹏 8E4F 蹐 8E50 蹑 8E51 蹒 8E52 蹓 8E53 **11** 蹔 8E54 蹕 8E55 蹖 8E56 蹗 8E57 蹘 8E58 蹙 8E59 蹚 8E5A 蹛 8E5B 蹜 8E5C 蹝 8E5D 蹞 8E5E 蹟 8E5F 蹠 8E60
蹡 8E61 蹢 8E62 蹣 8E63 蹤 8E64 蹥 8E65 蹦 8E66 蹧 8E67 躀 8E80 **12** 蹨 8E68 蹩 8E69 蹪 8E6A 蹫 8E6B 蹬 8E6C 蹭 8E6D 蹮 8E6E 蹯 8E6F 蹰 8E70 蹱 8E71 蹲 8E72 蹳 8E73 蹴 8E74 蹵 8E75

足 157 蹵 8E75 蹶 8E76 蹷 8E77 蹸 8E78 蹹 8E79 蹺 8E7A 蹻 8E7B 蹼 8E7C 蹽 8E7D 蹾 8E7E 蹿 8E7F **13** 躁 8E81 躂 8E82 躃 8E83 躄 8E84 躅 8E85 躆 8E86 躇 8E87 躈 8E88 躉 8E89 **14** 躊 8E8A 躋 8E8B 躌 8E8C 躍 8E8D 躎 8E8E 躏 8E8F **15** 躐 8E90 躑 8E91 躒 8E92 躓 8E93 躔 8E94 躕 8E95 躖 8E96 **16** 躗 8E97 躘 8E98 躙 8E99 躚 8E9A 躛 8E9B 躜 8E9C **17** 躝 8E9D 躞 8E9E 躟 8E9F 躠 8EA0 **18** 躡 8EA1 躢 8EA2 躣 8EA3 躤 8EA4 躥 8EA5 **19** 躦 8EA6 躧 8EA7 **20** 躩 8EA9 躪 8EAA **22** 躨 8EA8

身 158 身 8EAB **3** 躬 8EAC **4** 躭 8EAD 躮 8EAE 躯 8EAF **5** 躰 8EB0 **6** 躱 8EB1 躲 8EB2 **7** 躳 8EB3 躴 8EB4 躵 8EB5 **8** 躶 8EB6 躷 8EB7 躸 8EB8 躹 8EB9 躺 8EBA 躻 8EBB 躼 8EBC **9** 躽 8EBD 躾 8EBE **10** 躿 8EBF **11** 軀 8EC0 軁 8EC1 **12** 軂 8EC2 軃 8EC3 軄 8EC4 軅 8EC5 **13** 軆 8EC6 **14** 軇 8EC7 **17** 軈 8EC8 **20** 軉 8EC9

車 159 車 8ECA **1** 軋 8ECB 轧 8F67 **2** 军 519B 軌 8ECC 軍 8ECD 轨 8F68 **3** 軎 8ECE 軏 8ECF 軐 8ED0 軑 8ED1 軒 8ED2 軓 8ED3 軔 8ED4 軕 8ED5 轩 8F69 轪 8F6A 轫 8F6B **4** 軖 8ED6 軗 8ED7 軘 8ED8 軙 8ED9 軚 8EDA 軛 8EDB 軜 8EDC 軝 8EDD 軞 8EDE 軟 8EDF 軠 8EE0 軡 8EE1 転 8EE2 軣 8EE3 转 8F6C 轭 8F6D 轮 8F6E 软 8F6F 轰 8F70 **5** 軤 8EE4 軥 8EE5 軦 8EE6 軧 8EE7 軨 8EE8 軩 8EE9 軪 8EEA 軫 8EEB 軬 8EEC 軮 8EEE 軯 8EEF 軰 8EF0 軲 8EF2 軳 8EF3 軴 8EF4 軵 8EF5 軶 8EF6 軷 8EF7 軸 8EF8 軹 8EF9 軺 8EFA 軻 8EFB 軼 8EFC 軽 8EFD 轱 8F71 轲 8F72 轳 8F73 轴 8F74 轵 8F75 轶 8F76 轷 8F77 轸 8F78 轹 8F79 轺 8F7A 轻 8F7B **6** 軭 8EED 軱 8EF1 軾 8EFE 軿 8EFF 輀 8F00 輁 8F01 輂 8F02 較 8F03 輄 8F04 輅 8F05 輆 8F06 輇 8F07 輈 8F08 載 8F09 輊 8F0A 輋 8F0B 輌 8F0C 轼 8F7C 轾 8F7E 轿 8F7F 辀 8F80 辁 8F81 辂 8F82 较 8F83 **7** 輍 8F0D 輎 8F0E 輏 8F0F 輐 8F10 輑 8F11 輒 8F12 輓 8F13 輔 8F14 輕 8F15 辄 8F84 辅 8F85 辆 8F86 **8** 輖 8F16 輗 8F17 輘 8F18 輙 8F19 輚 8F1A 輛 8F1B 輜 8F1C 輝 8F1D 輞 8F1E 輟 8F1F 輠 8F20 輡 8F21 輢 8F22 輣 8F23 輤 8F24 輥 8F25 輦 8F26 輧 8F27 輨 8F28 輩 8F29 輪 8F2A 輫 8F2B 輬 8F2C 辇 8F87 辊 8F8A 辋 8F8B 辌 8F8C 辍 8F8D 辎 8F8E **9** 輭 8F2D 輮 8F2E 輯 8F2F 輰 8F30 輱 8F31 輲 8F32 輳 8F33 輴 8F34 輵 8F35 輶 8F36 輷 8F37 輸 8F38 輹 8F39 輺 8F3A 輻 8F3B 輼 8F3C 辏 8F8F 辐 8F90 辑 8F91 辒 8F92 输 8F93 **10** 輽 8F3D 輾 8F3E 輿 8F3F 轀 8F40 轁 8F41 轂 8F42 轃 8F43 轄 8F44 轅 8F45 辕 8F95 辖 8F96 辗 8F97 **11** 轆 8F46 轇 8F47 轈 8F48 轉 8F49 轊 8F4A 轋 8F4B 轌 8F4C 辘 8F98 **12** 轍 8F4D 轎 8F4E 轏 8F4F 轐 8F50 轑 8F51 轒 8F52 轓 8F53 辙 8F99 辚 8F9A **13** 轔 8F54 轕 8F55 轖 8F56 轗 8F57 轘 8F58 轙 8F59 轚 8F5A **14** 轛 8F5B 轜 8F5C 轝 8F5D 轞 8F5E 轟 8F5F **15** 轠 8F60 轡 8F61 轢 8F62 **16** 轣 8F63 轤 8F64 **20** 轥 8F65

车 159 车 8F66

辛 160 辛 8F9B **5** 辜 8F9C 辝 8F9D **6** 辞 8F9E 辟 8F9F 辠 8FA0 **7** 辡 8FA1 辢 8FA2 辣 8FA3 **8** 辤 8FA4 **9** 辥 8FA5 辦 8FA6 辨 8FA8 辩 8FA9 辪 8FAA **10** 辫 8FAB **11** 辬 8FAC **12** 辭 8FAD **13** 辮 8FAE **14** 辯 8FAF

辰 161 辰 8FB0 **3** 辱 8FB1 **6** 農 8FB2 **8** 辳 8FB3 **12** 辴 8FB4

辵 162 辵 8FB5 辶 8FB6 **1** 辷 8FB7 **2** 辸 8FB8 边 8FB9 辺 8FBA 辻 8FBB 込 8FBC 辽 8FBD **3** 达 8FBE 辿 8FBF 迀 8FC0 迁 8FC1 迂 8FC2 迃 8FC3 迄 8FC4 迅 8FC5 迆 8FC6 过 8FC7 迈 8FC8

迉 8FC9 **4** 迊 8FCA 迋 8FCB 迌 8FCC 迍 8FCD 迎 8FCE 迏 8FCF 运 8FD0 近 8FD1 迒 8FD2 返 8FD4 迕 8FD5 迖 8FD6 迗 8FD7 还 8FD8 这 8FD9 迚 8FDA 进 8FDB 远 8FDC 违 8FDD 连 8FDE 迟 8FDF

迬 8FEC **5** 迓 8FD3 迠 8FE0 迡 8FE1 迢 8FE2 迣 8FE3 迤 8FE4 迥 8FE5 迦 8FE6 迧 8FE7 迨 8FE8 迩 8FE9 迪 8FEA 迫 8FEB 迭 8FED 迮 8FEE 迯 8FEF 述 8FF0 迱 8FF1 迲 8FF2 迳 8FF3

6 迴 8FF4 迵 8FF5 迶 8FF6 迷 8FF7 迹 8FF9 迺 8FFA 迻 8FFB 迼 8FFC 追 8FFD 迾 8FFE 迿 8FFF 退 9000 送 9001 适 9002 逃 9003 逅 9005 逆 9006 逇 9007 逈 9008 选 9009 逊 900A

7 逄 9004 逋 900B 逌 900C 逍 900D 逎 900E 透 900F 逐 9010 逑 9011 递 9012 逓 9013 途 9014 逕 9015 逖 9016 逗 9017 逘 9018 這 9019 通 901A 逛 901B 逜 901C 逝 901D 逞 901E 速 901F

造 9020 逡 9021 逢 9022 連 9023 逤 9024 逥 9025 逦 9026 逧 9027 **8** 迸 8FF8 逨 9028 逩 9029 逪 902A 逫 902B 逬 902C 逭 902D 逮 902E 逯 902F 逰 9030 週 9031 進 9032 逳 9033 逴 9034

逵 9035 逶 9036 逷 9037 逸 9038 逹 9039 逺 903A 逻 903B **9** 逼 903C 逽 903D 逾 903E 逿 903F 遀 9040 遁 9041 遂 9042 遃 9043 遄 9044 遅 9045 遆 9046 遇 9047 遈 9048 遉 9049 遊 904A

運 904B 遌 904C 遍 904D 過 904E 遏 904F 遐 9050 遑 9051 遒 9052 道 9053 達 9054 違 9055 遖 9056 遗 9057 遥 9065 **10** 遘 9058 遙 9059 遚 905A 遛 905B 遜 905C 遝 905D 遞 905E 遟 905F

遠 9060 遡 9061 遢 9062 遣 9063 遤 9064 **11** 遦 9066 遧 9067 遨 9068 適 9069 遪 906A 遫 906B 遬 906C 遭 906D 遮 906E 遯 906F 遰 9070 遱 9071 遳 9073 **12** 遲 9072 遵 9075 遶 9076

遷 9077 選 9078 遹 9079 遺 907A 遻 907B 遼 907C 邆 9086 **13** 遴 9074 遽 907D 遾 907E 避 907F 邀 9080 邁 9081 邂 9082 還 9084 邅 9085 **14** 邃 9083 邇 9087 邈 9088 邉 9089

15 邊 908A 邋 908B 邌 908C **16** 邍 908D **17** 邎 908E **19** 邏 908F 邐 9090

邑 163 邑 9091 **2** 邒 9092 邓 9093 **3** 邔 9094 邕 9095 邖 9096 邗 9097 邘 9098 邙 9099 邚 909A 邛 909B 邜 909C 邝 909D **4** 邞 909E 邟 909F 邠 90A0 邡 90A1 邢 90A2 那 90A3 邤 90A4

邥 90A5 邦 90A6 邧 90A7 邨 90A8 邩 90A9 邪 90AA 邫 90AB 邬 90AC **5** 邭 90AD 邮 90AE 邯 90AF 邰 90B0 邱 90B1 邲 90B2 邳 90B3 邴 90B4 邵 90B5 邶 90B6 邷 90B7 邸 90B8 邹 90B9 邺 90BA

邻 90BB **6** 邼 90BC 邽 90BD 邾 90BE 邿 90BF 郀 90C0 郁 90C1 郂 90C2 郃 90C3 郄 90C4 郅 90C5 郆 90C6 郇 90C7 郈 90C8 郉 90C9 郊 90CA 郋 90CB 郌 90CC 郍 90CD 郎 90CE 郏 90CF 郐 90D0

郑 90D1 郓 90D3 **7** 郒 90D2 郔 90D4 郕 90D5 郖 90D6 郗 90D7 郘 90D8 郙 90D9 郚 90DA 郛 90DB 郜 90DC 郝 90DD 郞 90DE 郟 90DF 郠 90E0 郡 90E1 郢 90E2 郣 90E3 郤 90E4 郥 90E5 郦 90E6

郧 90E7 **8** 部 90E8 郩 90E9 郪 90EA 郫 90EB 郬 90EC 郭 90ED 郮 90EE 郯 90EF 郰 90F0 郱 90F1 郲 90F2 郳 90F3 郴 90F4 郵 90F5 郶 90F6 郷 90F7 郸 90F8 **9** 郹 90F9 郺 90FA 郻 90FB

郼 90FC 都 90FD 郾 90FE 郿 90FF 鄀 9100 鄁 9101 鄂 9102 鄃 9103 鄄 9104 鄅 9105 鄆 9106 鄇 9107 鄈 9108 鄉 9109 鄊 910A **10** 鄋 910B 鄌 910C 鄍 910D 鄎 910E 鄏 910F 鄐 9110 鄑 9111

鄒 9112 鄓 9113 鄔 9114 鄕 9115 鄖 9116 鄗 9117 **11** 鄘 9118 鄙 9119 鄚 911A 鄛 911B 鄜 911C 鄝 911D 鄞 911E 鄟 911F 鄠 9120 鄡 9121 鄢 9122 鄣 9123 鄤 9124 鄥 9125 **12** 鄦 9126

鄧 9127 鄨 9128 鄩 9129 鄪 912A 鄫 912B 鄬 912C 鄭 912D 鄮 912E 鄯 912F 鄰 9130 鄱 9131 鄲 9132 **13** 鄳 9133 鄴 9134 鄵 9135 鄶 9136 鄷 9137 **14** 鄸 9138 鄹 9139 **15** 鄺 913A

鄻 913B 鄼 913C 鄽 913D 鄾 913E **16** 鄿 913F 酀 9140 酂 9142 **17** 酁 9141 酃 9143 **18** 酄 9144 酅 9145 酆 9146 **19** 酇 9147 酈 9148

酉 164 酉 9149 **2** 酊 914A 酋 914B **3** 酌 914C 配 914D 酎 914E 酏 914F 酐 9150 酑 9151 酒 9152 **4** 酓 9153 酔 9154 酕 9155 酖 9156 酗 9157 酘 9158 酙 9159 酚 915A 酛 915B 酜 915C
酝 915D 酞 915E **5** 酟 915F 酠 9160 酡 9161 酢 9162 酣 9163 酤 9164 酥 9165 **6** 酦 9166 酧 9167 酨 9168 酩 9169 酪 916A 酫 916B 酬 916C 酭 916D 酮 916E 酯 916F 酰 9170 酱 9171
7 酲 9172 酳 9173 酴 9174 酵 9175 酶 9176 酷 9177 酸 9178 酹 9179 酺 917A 酻 917B 酼 917C 酽 917D 酾 917E 酿 917F **8** 醀 9180 醁 9181 醂 9182 醃 9183 醄 9184 醅 9185 醆 9186
醇 9187 醈 9188 醉 9189 醊 918A 醋 918B 醌 918C **9** 醍 918D 醎 918E 醏 918F 醐 9190 醑 9191 醒 9192 醓 9193 醔 9194 醕 9195 醖 9196 醗 9197 **10** 醘 9198 醙 9199 醚 919A 醛 919B
醜 919C 醝 919D 醞 919E 醟 919F 醠 91A0 醡 91A1 醢 91A2 醣 91A3 醤 91A4 **11** 醥 91A5 醦 91A6 醧 91A7 醨 91A8 醩 91A9 醪 91AA 醫 91AB 醬 91AC **12** 醭 91AD 醮 91AE 醯 91AF 醰 91B0
醱 91B1 **13** 醲 91B2 醳 91B3 醴 91B4 醵 91B5 醶 91B6 醷 91B7 醸 91B8 **14** 醹 91B9 醺 91BA 醻 91BB **16** 醼 91BC **17** 醽 91BD 醾 91BE 醿 91BF 釀 91C0 **18** 釁 91C1 釂 91C2
19 釃 91C3 釄 91C4 **20** 釅 91C5

釆 165 釆 91C6 **1** 采 91C7 **4** 釈 91C8 **5** 釉 91C9 释 91CA **13** 釋 91CB

里 166 里 91CC **2** 重 91CD **4** 野 91CE **5** 量 91CF **11** 釐 91D0

金 167 金 91D1 釒 91D2 **1** 釓 91D3 釔 91D4 钆 9486 钇 9487 **2** 釕 91D5 釖 91D6 釗 91D7 釘 91D8 釙 91D9 釚 91DA 釛 91DB 釜 91DC 針 91DD 釞 91DE 釟 91DF 釠 91E0 釡 91E1 釢 91E2 针 9488
钉 9489 钊 948A 钋 948B 钌 948C **3** 突 7A81 釣 91E3 釤 91E4 釥 91E5 釦 91E6 釧 91E7 釨 91E8 釩 91E9 釪 91EA 釫 91EB 釬 91EC 釭 91ED 釮 91EE 釯 91EF 釰 91F0 釱 91F1 釲 91F2 釳 91F3
釴 91F4 釵 91F5 釶 91F6 釷 91F7 釸 91F8 釹 91F9 釺 91FA 釻 91FB 釼 91FC 钍 948D 钎 948E 钏 948F 钐 9490 钑 9491 钒 9492 钓 9493 钔 9494 钕 9495 钖 9496 钗 9497 **4** 釽 91FD 釾 91FE
釿 91FF 鈀 9200 鈁 9201 鈂 9202 鈃 9203 鈄 9204 鈅 9205 鈆 9206 鈇 9207 鈈 9208 鈉 9209 鈊 920A 鈋 920B 鈌 920C 鈍 920D 鈎 920E 鈏 920F 鈐 9210 鈑 9211 鈒 9212 鈓 9213 鈔 9214 鈕 9215
鈖 9216 鈗 9217 鈘 9218 鈙 9219 鈚 921A 鈛 921B 鈜 921C 鈝 921D 鈞 921E 鈟 921F 鈠 9220 鈡 9221 鈢 9222 鈣 9223 鈤 9224 鈥 9225 鈦 9226 鈧 9227 鈨 9228 鈩 9229 鈪 922A 鈫 922B 鈬 922C
钘 9498 钙 9499 钚 949A 钛 949B 钜 949C 钝 949D 钞 949E 钟 949F 钠 94A0 钡 94A1 钢 94A2 钣 94A3 钤 94A4 钥 94A5 钦 94A6 钧 94A7 钪 94AA 钫 94AB 钬 94AC 钭 94AD 钮 94AE 钯 94AF
5 鈭 922D 鈮 922E 鈯 922F 鈰 9230 鈱 9231 鈲 9232 鈳 9233 鈴 9234 鈵 9235 鈶 9236 鈷 9237 鈸 9238 鈹 9239 鈺 923A 鈻 923B 鈼 923C 鈽 923D 鈾 923E 鈿 923F 鉀 9240 鉁 9241 鉂 9242
鉃 9243 鉄 9244 鉅 9245 鉆 9246 鉇 9247 鉈 9248 鉉 9249 鉊 924A 鉋 924B 鉌 924C 鉍 924D 鉎 924E 鉏 924F 鉐 9250 鉑 9251 鉒 9252 鉓 9253 鉔 9254 鉕 9255 鉖 9256 鉗 9257 鉘 9258 鉙 9259
鉚 925A 鉛 925B 鉜 925C 鉝 925D 鉞 925E 鉟 925F 鉠 9260 鉡 9261 鉢 9262 鉣 9263 鉤 9264 鉥 9265 鉦 9266 鉧 9267 鉨 9268 鉩 9269 鉪 926A 鉫 926B 鉬 926C 鉭 926D 鉮 926E 鉯 926F 鉰 9270
鉱 9271 鉲 9272 鉳 9273 鉴 9274 銏 928F 钨 94A8 钩 94A9 钰 94B0 钱 94B1 钲 94B2 钳 94B3 钴 94B4 钵 94B5 钶 94B6 钷 94B7 钸 94B8 钹 94B9 钺 94BA 钻 94BB 钼 94BC 钽 94BD 钾 94BE 钿 94BF
铀 94C0 铁 94C1 铂 94C2 铃 94C3 铄 94C4 铅 94C5 铆 94C6 铇 94C7 铈 94C8 铉 94C9 铊 94CA 铋 94CB 铌 94CC 铍 94CD 铎 94CE 铳 94F3 **6** 鉵 9275 鉶 9276 鉷 9277 鉸 9278 鉹 9279 鉺 927A

金 167 鉻 927B 鉽 927D 鉾 927E 鉿 927F 銀 9280 銁 9281 銂 9282 銃 9283 銄 9284 銅 9285 銆 9286 銇 9287 銈 9288 銉 9289 銊 928A 銋 928B 銌 928C 銍 928D 銎 928E 銐 9290 銑 9291 銒 9292 銓 9293

銔 9294 銕 9295 銖 9296 銗 9297 銘 9298 銙 9299 銚 929A 銛 929B 銜 929C 銝 929D 銞 929E 銟 929F 銠 92A0 銡 92A1 銢 92A2 銣 92A3 銤 92A4 銥 92A5 銦 92A6 銧 92A7 銨 92A8 銩 92A9 銪 92AA

銫 92AB 銬 92AC 銭 92AD 銮 92AE 銯 92AF 銰 92B0 銱 92B1 铏 94CF 铐 94D0 铑 94D1 铒 94D2 铕 94D5 铖 94D6 铗 94D7 铙 94D9 铚 94DA 铛 94DB 铜 94DC 铝 94DD 铞 94DE 铟 94DF 铠 94E0 铡 94E1

铢 94E2 铣 94E3 铥 94E5 铦 94E6 铧 94E7 铨 94E8 铩 94E9 铪 94EA 铫 94EB 铬 94EC 铭 94ED 铯 94EF 铰 94F0 铱 94F1 铲 94F2 铵 94F5 银 94F6 铷 94F7

7

銲 92B2 銳 92B3 銴 92B4 銵 92B5

銶 92B6 銷 92B7 銸 92B8 銹 92B9 銺 92BA 銻 92BB 銼 92BC 銽 92BD 銾 92BE 銿 92BF 鋀 92C0 鋁 92C1 鋂 92C2 鋃 92C3 鋄 92C4 鋅 92C5 鋆 92C6 鋇 92C7 鋈 92C8 鋉 92C9 鋊 92CA 鋋 92CB 鋌 92CC

鋍 92CD 鋎 92CE 鋏 92CF 鋐 92D0 鋑 92D1 鋒 92D2 鋓 92D3 鋔 92D4 鋕 92D5 鋖 92D6 鋗 92D7 鋘 92D8 鋙 92D9 鋚 92DA 鋛 92DB 鋜 92DC 鋝 92DD 鋞 92DE 鋟 92DF 鋠 92E0 鋡 92E1 鋢 92E2 鋤 92E4

鋥 92E5 鋦 92E6 鋧 92E7 鋨 92E8 鋩 92E9 鋪 92EA 鋫 92EB 鋬 92EC 鋭 92ED 鋮 92EE 鋯 92EF 鋰 92F0 鋱 92F1 鋲 92F2 鋳 92F3 鋴 92F4 鋵 92F5 鋶 92F6 铓 94D3 铘 94D8 铤 94E4 铴 94F4 铸 94F8

铹 94F9 铺 94FA 铻 94FB 铼 94FC 铽 94FD 链 94FE 铿 94FF 销 9500 锁 9501 锂 9502 锃 9503 锄 9504 锅 9505 锆 9506 锇 9507 锈 9508 锉 9509 锊 950A 锋 950B 锌 950C 锍 950D 锎 950E 锏 950F

锐 9510 锑 9511 锒 9512 锓 9513 锔 9514

8

鉼 927C 鋣 92E3 鋷 92F7 鋸 92F8 鋹 92F9 鋺 92FA 鋼 92FC 鋽 92FD 鋾 92FE 鋿 92FF 錀 9300 錁 9301 錂 9302 錃 9303 錄 9304 錅 9305 錆 9306

錇 9307 錈 9308 錉 9309 錊 930A 錋 930B 錌 930C 錍 930D 錎 930E 錏 930F 錐 9310 錑 9311 錒 9312 錓 9313 錔 9314 錕 9315 錖 9316 錗 9317 錘 9318 錙 9319 錚 931A 錛 931B 錜 931C 錝 931D

錞 931E 錟 931F 錠 9320 錡 9321 錢 9322 錣 9323 錤 9324 錥 9325 錦 9326 錧 9327 錩 9329 錪 932A 錫 932B 錬 932C 錭 932D 錮 932E 錯 932F 錰 9330 錱 9331 録 9332 錳 9333 錴 9334 錵 9335

錶 9336 錷 9337 錸 9338 錹 9339 錺 933A 錻 933B 錼 933C 錽 933D 錾 933E 錿 933F 鍀 9340 鍁 9341 鍂 9342 鍃 9343 鍄 9344 鍅 9345 鍆 9346 鍈 9348 铔 94D4 铮 94EE 锕 9515 锖 9516 锗 9517

锘 9518 错 9519 锚 951A 锛 951B 锜 951C 锝 951D 锞 951E 锟 951F 锠 9520 锡 9521 锢 9522 锣 9523 锤 9524 锥 9525 锦 9526 锨 9528 锩 9529 锪 952A 锫 952B 锬 952C 锭 952D 键 952E 锯 952F

锰 9530 锱 9531 锳 9533

9

鋻 92FB 錨 9328 鍇 9347 鍉 9349 鍊 934A 鍋 934B 鍌 934C 鍍 934D 鍎 934E 鍏 934F 鍐 9350 鍑 9351 鍒 9352 鍓 9353 鍔 9354 鍕 9355 鍖 9356 鍗 9357 鍘 9358

鍙 9359 鍚 935A 鍛 935B 鍜 935C 鍝 935D 鍞 935E 鍟 935F 鍠 9360 鍡 9361 鍢 9362 鍣 9363 鍤 9364 鍥 9365 鍦 9366 鍧 9367 鍨 9368 鍩 9369 鍪 936A 鍫 936B 鍬 936C 鍭 936D 鍮 936E 鍯 936F

鍰 9370 鍱 9371 鍲 9372 鍳 9373 鍴 9374 鍵 9375 鍶 9376 鍷 9377 鍸 9378 鍹 9379 鍺 937A 鍻 937B 鍼 937C 鍽 937D 鍾 937E 鍿 937F 鎀 9380 鎁 9381 鎂 9382 鎃 9383 鎄 9384 鎅 9385 鎆 9386

鎇 9387 鎡 93A1 锲 9532 锴 9534 锵 9535 锶 9536 锷 9537 锸 9538 锹 9539 锺 953A 锻 953B 锼 953C 锽 953D 锾 953E 锿 953F 镀 9540 镁 9541 镂 9542 镃 9543 镄 9544 镅 9545

10

鎈 9388

鎉 9389 鎊 938A 鎋 938B 鎌 938C 鎍 938D 鎎 938E 鎏 938F 鎐 9390 鎑 9391 鎒 9392 鎓 9393 鎔 9394 鎕 9395 鎖 9396 鎗 9397 鎘 9398 鎙 9399 鎚 939A 鎛 939B 鎜 939C 鎝 939D 鎞 939E 鎟 939F

鎠 93A0 鎢 93A2 鎣 93A3 鎤 93A4 鎥 93A5 鎦 93A6 鎧 93A7 鎨 93A8 鎪 93AA 鎫 93AB 鎬 93AC 鎭 93AD 鎮 93AE 鎯 93AF 鎰 93B0 鎱 93B1 鎲 93B2 鎳 93B3 鎴 93B4 鎵 93B5 鎶 93B6 鎷 93B7 鎸 93B8

鎹 93B9 鎺 93BA 鎻 93BB 鎼 93BC 鎽 93BD 鎾 93BE 鎿 93BF 镆 9546 镇 9547 镈 9548 镉 9549 镊 954A 镌 954C 镍 954D 镎 954E 镏 954F 镐 9550 镑 9551 镒 9552 镓 9553 镔 9554 镕 9555

11

鎩 93A9 鏀 93C0 鏁 93C1 鏂 93C2 鏃 93C3 鏄 93C4 鏅 93C5 鏆 93C6 鏇 93C7 鏈 93C8 鏉 93C9 鏊 93CA 鏋 93CB 鏌 93CC 鏍 93CD 鏎 93CE 鏏 93CF 鏐 93D0 鏑 93D1 鏒 93D2 鏓 93D3 鏔 93D4

鏕 93D5 鏖 93D6 鏗 93D7 鏘 93D8 鏙 93D9 鏚 93DA 鏛 93DB 鏜 93DC 鏝 93DD 鏞 93DE 鏟 93DF 鏠 93E0 鏡 93E1 鏢 93E2 鏣 93E3 鏤 93E4 鏥 93E5 鏦 93E6 鏧 93E7 鏨 93E8 鏩 93E9 鏪 93EA 鏫 93EB

鏬 93EC 鏭 93ED 鏮 93EE 鏯 93EF 鏰 93F0 鏱 93F1 鏲 93F2 鏹 93F9 镖 9556 镗 9557 镘 9558 镙 9559 镚 955A 镛 955B 镜 955C 镝 955D 镞 955E 镟 955F 镠 9560

12

鏳 93F3 鏵 93F5 鏶 93F6

金 167 **12** 鏳 93F3 鏵 93F5 鏶 93F6 鏷 93F7 鏸 93F8 鏺 93FA 鏼 93FC 鏾 93FE 鏿 93FF 鐀 9400 鐁 9401 鐂 9402 鐃 9403 鐄 9404 鐅 9405 鐆 9406 鐇 9407 鐈 9408 鐉 9409 鐊 940A 鐋 940B 鐌 940C
鐍 940D 鐎 940E 鐏 940F 鐐 9410 鐑 9411 鐒 9412 鐓 9413 鐔 9414 鐖 9416 鐗 9417 鐘 9418 鐙 9419 鐚 941A 鐛 941B 鐜 941C 鐝 941D 鐞 941E 鐟 941F 鐠 9420 鐡 9421 鐢 9422 鐣 9423 鐥 9425
鐦 9426 鐧 9427 鐨 9428 镡 9561 镢 9562 镣 9563 镤 9564 镥 9565 镦 9566 镧 9567 镨 9568 镩 9569 镪 956A 镫 956B **13** 鏴 93F4 鏻 93FB 鏽 93FD 鐤 9424 鐩 9429 鐪 942A 鐫 942B 鐬 942C
鐭 942D 鐮 942E 鐯 942F 鐰 9430 鐱 9431 鐲 9432 鐳 9433 鐴 9434 鐵 9435 鐶 9436 鐷 9437 鐸 9438 鐹 9439 鐺 943A 鐻 943B 鐼 943C 鐽 943D 鐾 943E 鐿 943F 鑀 9440 鑁 9441 镬 956C 镭 956D
镮 956E 镯 956F 镰 9570 镱 9571 镲 9572 **14** 鐕 9415 鑂 9442 鑃 9443 鑄 9444 鑅 9445 鑆 9446 鑇 9447 鑈 9448 鑉 9449 鑊 944A 鑋 944B 鑌 944C 鑍 944D 鑎 944E 鑏 944F 鑐 9450 鑑 9451
鑒 9452 鑓 9453 鑔 9454 鑧 9467 **15** 鑕 9455 鑖 9456 鑗 9457 鑘 9458 鑙 9459 鑚 945A 鑛 945B 鑜 945C 鑝 945D 鑞 945E 鑟 945F 鑠 9460 鑡 9461 鑢 9462 鑣 9463 鑤 9464 鑥 9465 鑦 9466
锧 9527 镳 9573 镴 9574 **16** 鑨 9468 鑩 9469 鑪 946A 鑫 946B 鑬 946C **17** 鑭 946D 鑮 946E 鑯 946F 鑰 9470 鑱 9471 鑲 9472 鑳 9473 钄 9484 镵 9575 镶 9576 **18** 鑴 9474 鑵 9475
鑶 9476 鑷 9477 鑸 9478 鑹 9479 鑺 947A **19** 鑻 947B 鑼 947C 鑽 947D 鑾 947E **20** 鑿 947F 钀 9480 钁 9481 钂 9482 镋 954B **21** 钃 9483

钅 167 钅 9485

長 168 長 9577 镸 9578 **3** 镹 9579 **4** 镺 957A **5** 镻 957B **8** 镼 957C **12** 镽 957D **14** 镾 957E

长 168 长 957F

門 169 門 9580 **1** 閁 9581 閂 9582 闩 95E9 **2** 閃 9583 閄 9584 閅 9585 闪 95EA **3** 閆 9586 閇 9587 閈 9588 閉 9589 閊 958A 闫 95EB 闬 95EC 闭 95ED 问 95EE 闯 95EF **4** 開 958B
閌 958C 閍 958D 閎 958E 閏 958F 閐 9590 閑 9591 閒 9592 間 9593 閔 9594 閕 9595 閖 9596 閗 9597 闰 95F0 闱 95F1 闲 95F2 闳 95F3 间 95F4 闵 95F5 闶 95F6 闷 95F7 **5** 閘 9598 閙 9599
閚 959A 閛 959B 閜 959C 閝 959D 閞 959E 閟 959F 閠 95A0 闸 95F8 闹 95F9 **6** 閡 95A1 関 95A2 閣 95A3 閤 95A4 閥 95A5 閦 95A6 閧 95A7 閨 95A8 閩 95A9 閪 95AA 闺 95FA 闻 95FB 闼 95FC
闽 95FD 闾 95FE 阀 9600 阁 9601 阂 9602 **7** 閫 95AB 閬 95AC 閭 95AD 閮 95AE 閯 95AF 閰 95B0 閱 95B1 閲 95B2 閳 95B3 閴 95B4 阃 9603 阄 9604 阅 9605 阆 9606 **8** 閵 95B5 閶 95B6
閸 95B8 閹 95B9 閺 95BA 閻 95BB 閼 95BC 閽 95BD 閾 95BE 閿 95BF 闀 95C0 闁 95C1 闂 95C2 阈 9608 阉 9609 阊 960A 阋 960B 阌 960C 阍 960D 阎 960E 阏 960F 阐 9610 **9** 閷 95B7 闃 95C3
闄 95C4 闅 95C5 闆 95C6 闇 95C7 闈 95C8 闉 95C9 闊 95CA 闋 95CB 闌 95CC 闍 95CD 闎 95CE 闏 95CF 阇 9607 阑 9611 阒 9612 阓 9613 阔 9614 阕 9615 **10** 闐 95D0 闑 95D1 闒 95D2 闓 95D3
闔 95D4 闕 95D5 闖 95D6 闗 95D7 闘 95D8 闿 95FF 阖 9616 阗 9617 阘 9618 阙 9619 **11** 闙 95D9 闚 95DA 闛 95DB 關 95DC 闝 95DD 阚 961A **12** 闞 95DE 闟 95DF 闠 95E0 闡 95E1
13 闢 95E2 闣 95E3 闤 95E4 闥 95E5 闦 95E6 阛 961B **14** 闧 95E7

门 169 门 95E8

阜 170 阜 961C 阝 961D **2** 阞 961E 队 961F **3** 阠 9620 阡 9621 阢 9622 阣 9623 阤 9624 **4** 阥 9625 阦 9626 阧 9627 阨 9628 阩 9629 阪 962A 阫 962B 阬 962C 阭 962D 阮 962E 阯 962F
阰 9630 阱 9631 防 9632 阳 9633 阴 9634 阵 9635 阶 9636 **5** 阷 9637 阸 9638 阹 9639 阺 963A 阻 963B 阼 963C 阽 963D 阾 963E 阿 963F 陀 9640 陁 9641 陂 9642 陃 9643 附 9644 际 9645
陆 9646 陇 9647 陈 9648 陉 9649 **6** 陊 964A 陋 964B 陌 964C 降 964D 陎 964E 陏 964F 限 9650 陑 9651 陒 9652 陓 9653 陔 9654 陕 9655 **7** 陖 9656 陗 9657 陘 9658 陙 9659 陛 965B
陜 965C 陝 965D 陞 965E 陟 965F 陠 9660 陡 9661 院 9662 陣 9663 除 9664 陥 9665 陦 9666 陧 9667 陨 9668 险 9669 **8** 陚 965A 陪 966A 陫 966B 陬 966C 陭 966D 陮 966E 陯 966F 陰 9670
陱 9671 陲 9672 陳 9673 陴 9674 陵 9675 陶 9676 陷 9677 陸 9678 陹 9679 険 967A **9** 陻 967B 陼 967C 陽 967D 陾 967E 陿 967F 隀 9680 隁 9681 隂 9682 隃 9683 隄 9684 隅 9685 隆 9686
隇 9687 隈 9688 隉 9689 隊 968A 隋 968B 隌 968C 隍 968D 階 968E 随 968F 隐 9690 **10** 隑 9691 隒 9692 隓 9693 隔 9694 隕 9695 隖 9696 隗 9697 隘 9698 隙 9699 **11** 隚 969A 際 969B
障 969C 隝 969D 隞 969E 隟 969F 隠 96A0 隡 96A1 **12** 隢 96A2 隣 96A3 隤 96A4 隥 96A5 **13** 隦 96A6 隧 96A7 隨 96A8 隩 96A9 險 96AA 隫 96AB **14** 隬 96AC 隭 96AD 隮 96AE 隯 96AF
隰 96B0 隱 96B1 隲 96B2 **15** 隳 96B3 **16** 隴 96B4 **17** 隵 96B5

隶 171 隶 96B6 **8** 隷 96B7 **9** 隸 96B8

隹 172 隹 96B9 **2** 隺 96BA 隻 96BB 隼 96BC 隽 96BD **3** 隿 96BF 雀 96C0 **4** 雁 96C1 雂 96C2 雃 96C3 雄 96C4 雅 96C5 集 96C6 雇 96C7 雈 96C8 **5** 雉 96C9 雊 96CA 雋 96CB 雌 96CC
雍 96CD 雎 96CE 雏 96CF **6** 雐 96D0 雑 96D1 雒 96D2 **7** 雓 96D3 **8** 雔 96D4 雕 96D5 **9** 雖 96D6 **10** 雗 96D7 雘 96D8 雙 96D9 雚 96DA 雛 96DB 雜 96DC 雝 96DD 雞 96DE
雟 96DF 雠 96E0 **11** 雡 96E1 離 96E2 難 96E3 **13** 雤 96E4 **16** 雥 96E5 雦 96E6 **20** 雧 96E7

雨 173 雨 96E8 **3** 雩 96E9 雪 96EA 雫 96EB **4** 雬 96EC 雭 96ED 雮 96EE 雯 96EF 雰 96F0 雱 96F1 雲 96F2 雳 96F3 **5** 雴 96F4 雵 96F5 零 96F6 雷 96F7 雸 96F8 雹 96F9 雺 96FA 電 96FB
雼 96FC 雽 96FD 雾 96FE **6** 雿 96FF 需 9700 霁 9701 **7** 霂 9702 霃 9703 霄 9704 霅 9705 霆 9706 震 9707 霈 9708 霉 9709 霊 970A **8** 霋 970B 霌 970C 霍 970D 霎 970E 霏 970F
霐 9710 霑 9711 霒 9712 霓 9713 霔 9714 霕 9715 霖 9716 霗 9717 **9** 霘 9718 霙 9719 霚 971A 霛 971B 霜 971C 霝 971D 霞 971E 霟 971F 霠 9720 **10** 霡 9721 霢 9722 霣 9723 霤 9724
霥 9725 **11** 霦 9726 霧 9727 霨 9728 霩 9729 霪 972A 霫 972B 霬 972C 霭 972D **12** 霮 972E 霯 972F 霰 9730 霱 9731 露 9732 霳 9733 霴 9734 **13** 霵 9735 霶 9736 霷 9737 霸 9738
霹 9739 霺 973A 霻 973B **14** 霼 973C 霽 973D 霾 973E 霿 973F 靀 9740 **15** 靁 9741 **16** 靂 9742 靃 9743 靄 9744 靅 9745 靆 9746 靇 9747 靈 9748 **17** 靉 9749 **18** 靊 974A
19 靋 974B 靌 974C 靍 974D 靎 974E **21** 靏 974F **31** 靐 9750

青 174 · 青 9751 · 靑 9752 · **4** 靓 9753 · 靔 9754 · **5** 靕 9755 · 靖 9756 · **6** 靗 9757 · 靘 9758 · 静 9759 · **7** 靚 975A · **8** 靛 975B · 靜 975C · **10** 靝 975D

非 175 · 非 975E · **4** 辈 8F88 · 靟 975F · **7** 靠 9760 · **11** 靡 9761

面 176 · 面 9762 · 靣 9763 · **5** 靤 9764 · **7** 靦 9766 · **12** 靧 9767 · **14** 靨 9768

革 177 · 革 9769 · **2** 靪 976A · **3** 靫 976B · 靬 976C · 靭 976D · 靮 976E · 靯 976F · 靰 9770 · 靱 9771 · **4** 靲 9772 · 靳 9773 · 靴 9774 · 靵 9775 · 靶 9776 · 靷 9777 · 靸 9778 · 靹 9779 · **5** 靺 977A · 靻 977B · 靼 977C · 靽 977D · 靾 977E · 靿 977F · 鞀 9780 · 鞁 9781 · 鞂 9782 · 鞃 9783 · 鞄 9784 · 鞅 9785 · 鞆 9786 · **6** 鞇 9787 · 鞈 9788 · 鞉 9789 · 鞊 978A · 鞋 978B · 鞌 978C · 鞍 978D · 鞎 978E · 鞏 978F · 鞐 9790 · 鞑 9791 · 鞒 9792 · **7** 鞓 9793 · 鞔 9794 · 鞕 9795 · 鞖 9796 · 鞗 9797 · 鞘 9798 · 鞙 9799 · **8** 鞚 979A · 鞛 979B · 鞜 979C · 鞝 979D · 鞞 979E · 鞟 979F · 鞠 97A0 · 鞡 97A1 · **9** 鞢 97A2 · 鞣 97A3 · 鞤 97A4 · 鞥 97A5 · 鞦 97A6 · 鞧 97A7 · 鞨 97A8 · 鞩 97A9 · 鞪 97AA · 鞫 97AB · 鞬 97AC · 鞭 97AD · 鞮 97AE · 鞯 97AF · 鞰 97B0 · **10** 鞱 97B1 · 鞲 97B2 · 鞳 97B3 · 鞴 97B4 · 鞵 97B5 · 鞶 97B6 · 鞷 97B7 · **11** 鞸 97B8 · 鞹 97B9 · 鞺 97BA · 鞻 97BB · **12** 鞼 97BC · 鞽 97BD · 鞾 97BE · 鞿 97BF · **13** 韀 97C0 · 韁 97C1 · 韂 97C2 · 韃 97C3 · **14** 韄 97C4 · 韅 97C5 · **15** 韆 97C6 · 韇 97C7 · 韈 97C8 · **17** 韉 97C9 · **21** 韊 97CA

韋 178 · 韋 97CB · **3** 韌 97CC · 韧 97E7 · **5** 韍 97CD · 韎 97CE · 韨 97E8 · **6** 韏 97CF · 韐 97D0 · 韑 97D1 · **7** 韒 97D2 · **8** 韓 97D3 · 韔 97D4 · 韕 97D5 · 韩 97E9 · **9** 韖 97D6 · 韗 97D7 · 韘 97D8 · 韙 97D9 · 韚 97DA · 韪 97EA · 韫 97EB · **10** 韜 97DC · 韝 97DD · 韞 97DE · 韟 97DF · 韬 97EC · **11** 韛 97DB · 韠 97E0 · **12** 韡 97E1 · 韢 97E2 · **13** 韣 97E3 · **15** 韤 97E4 · 韥 97E5

韦 178 · 韦 97E6

韭 179 · 韭 97ED · **4** 韮 97EE · **6** 韯 97EF · **7** 韰 97F0 · **8** 韱 97F1 · **10** 韲 97F2

音 180 · 音 97F3 · **4** 韴 97F4 · 韵 97F5 · **5** 韶 97F6 · 韷 97F7 · **7** 韸 97F8 · **9** 韹 97F9 · 韺 97FA · **10** 韻 97FB · 韼 97FC · **11** 韽 97FD · 韾 97FE · **13** 響 97FF · **14** 頀 9800

頁 181 · 頁 9801 · **2** 頂 9802 · 頃 9803 · 頄 9804 · 顶 9876 · 顷 9877 · **3** 項 9805 · 順 9806 · 頇 9807 · 須 9808 · 頉 9809 · 项 9879 · 顺 987A · **4** 頊 980A · 頋 980B · 頌 980C · 頍 980D · 頎 980E · 頏 980F · 預 9810 · 頑 9811 · 頒 9812 · 頓 9813 · 顽 987D · 顾 987E · 顿 987F · 颁 9881 · 颂 9882 · 颃 9883 · 预 9884 · **5** 頔 9814 · 頕 9815 · 頖 9816 · 頗 9817 · 領 9818 · 頙 9819 · 頚 981A · 颅 9885 · 领 9886 · 颇 9887 · 颈 9888

頁 181 **6** 頛 981B 頜 981C 頝 981D 頞 981E 頟 981F 頠 9820 頡 9821 頢 9822 頦 9826 頧 9827 頨 9828 頩 9829 頪 982A 頫 982B 頬 982C 颉 9889 颊 988A 颋 988B 颌 988C 颏 988F **7** 頣 9823
頤 9824 頭 982D 頮 982E 頯 982F 頰 9830 頱 9831 頲 9832 頳 9833 頴 9834 頵 9835 頶 9836 頷 9837 頸 9838 頹 9839 頺 983A 頼 983C 頽 983D 颐 9890 频 9891 颒 9892 颓 9893 颔 9894 颕 9895
颖 9896 **8** 頥 9825 頻 983B 頿 983F 顀 9840 顁 9841 顂 9842 顃 9843 顄 9844 顅 9845 顆 9846 顇 9847 顈 9848 顉 9849 顊 984A 颗 9897 **9** 頾 983E 顋 984B 題 984C 額 984D 顎 984E
顏 984F 顐 9850 顑 9851 顒 9852 顓 9853 顔 9854 顕 9855 類 985E 题 9898 颙 9899 颚 989A 颛 989B 颜 989C 额 989D 颞 989E **10** 顖 9856 顗 9857 願 9858 顙 9859 顚 985A 顛 985B 顜 985C
顝 985D 颟 989F 颠 98A0 颡 98A1 **11** 顟 985F 顠 9860 顡 9861 顢 9862 顣 9863 **12** 顤 9864 顥 9865 顦 9866 顧 9867 顨 9868 颢 98A2 **13** 顩 9869 顪 986A 顫 986B 颤 98A4
14 顬 986C 顭 986D 顮 986E 顯 986F 颥 98A5 **15** 顰 9870 **16** 顱 9871 顲 9872 **17** 颧 98A7 **18** 顳 9873 顴 9874

页 181 页 9875 **12** 颣 98A3

凬 182 凬 51EC 風 98A8 **3** 颩 98A9 颪 98AA **4** 颫 98AB 颬 98AC **5** 颭 98AD 颮 98AE 颯 98AF 颰 98B0 颱 98B1 飐 98D0 飑 98D1 飒 98D2 **6** 颲 98B2 颳 98B3 **7** 颴 98B4 颵 98B5
8 颶 98B6 颷 98B7 飓 98D3 **9** 颸 98B8 颹 98B9 颺 98BA 飏 98CF 飔 98D4 **10** 颻 98BB 颼 98BC 颽 98BD 颾 98BE 颿 98BF 飀 98C0 飕 98D5 飖 98D6 飗 98D7 **11** 飁 98C1 飂 98C2
飃 98C3 飄 98C4 飘 98D8 **12** 飅 98C5 飆 98C6 飇 98C7 飈 98C8 飉 98C9 飊 98CA 飙 98D9 飚 98DA **13** 飋 98CB **18** 飌 98CC 飍 98CD

风 182 风 98CE

飛 183 飛 98DB **12** 飜 98DC **18** 飝 98DD

飞 183 飞 98DE

食 184 食 98DF 飠 98E0 **2** 飡 98E1 飢 98E2 飣 98E3 飤 98E4 饤 9964 饥 9965 **3** 飥 98E5 飦 98E6 飧 98E7 飨 98E8 饦 9966 饧 9967 **4** 飩 98E9 飪 98EA 飫 98EB 飬 98EC 飭 98ED 飮 98EE
飯 98EF 飰 98F0 飲 98F2 饨 9968 饩 9969 饪 996A 饫 996B 饬 996C 饭 996D 饮 996E **5** 飳 98F3 飴 98F4 飵 98F5 飶 98F6 飷 98F7 飸 98F8 飹 98F9 飻 98FB 飼 98FC 飽 98FD 飾 98FE 飿 98FF
饯 996F 饰 9970 饱 9971 饲 9972 饳 9973 饴 9974 **6** 蚀 8680 飺 98FA 餀 9900 餁 9901 餂 9902 餃 9903 餄 9904 餆 9906 餇 9907 餈 9908 餉 9909 養 990A 餋 990B 餌 990C 餍 990D 餎 990E
餏 990F 饵 9975 饶 9976 饷 9977 饸 9978 饹 9979 饺 997A 饻 997B 饼 997C **7** 餐 9910 餑 9911 餒 9912 餓 9913 餔 9914 餕 9915 餖 9916 餗 9917 餘 9918 餙 9919 饽 997D 饾 997E 饿 997F

食 184 饾 997E 饿 997F 馀 9980 馁 9981 馂 9982 **8** 餅 9905 餚 991A 餛 991B 餜 991C 餝 991D 餞 991E 餟 991F 餠 9920 餡 9921 餢 9922 餣 9923 餤 9924 餥 9925 餦 9926 餧 9927 館 9928 餩 9929

馃 9983 馄 9984 馅 9985 馆 9986 **9** 餪 992A 餫 992B 餬 992C 餭 992D 餮 992E 餯 992F 餰 9930 餱 9931 餲 9932 餳 9933 餴 9934 餵 9935 餷 9937 馇 9987 馈 9988 馊 998A 馋 998B

10 餶 9936 餸 9938 餹 9939 餺 993A 餻 993B 餼 993C 餽 993D 餾 993E 餿 993F 饀 9940 饁 9941 饂 9942 馉 9989 馌 998C 馍 998D 馎 998E 馏 998F **11** 饃 9943 饄 9944 饅 9945 饆 9946

饇 9947 饈 9948 饉 9949 馐 9990 馑 9991 馒 9992 **12** 饊 994A 饋 994B 饌 994C 饍 994D 饎 994E 饏 994F 饐 9950 饑 9951 饒 9952 饓 9953 馓 9993 馔 9994 **13** 饔 9954 饕 9955 饖 9956

饗 9957 饘 9958 饙 9959 **14** 饚 995A 饛 995B 饜 995C **16** 饝 995D **17** 饞 995E 饟 995F **19** 饠 9960 饡 9961 **22** 饢 9962 馕 9995

饣 184 饣 9963

首 185 首 9996 **2** 馗 9997 **8** 馘 9998

香 186 香 9999 **4** 馚 999A **5** 馛 999B 馜 999C 馝 999D **7** 馞 999E 馟 999F 馠 99A0 **8** 馡 99A1 馢 99A2 馣 99A3 **9** 馤 99A4 馥 99A5 **10** 馦 99A6 馧 99A7 **11** 馨 99A8

12 馩 99A9 **14** 馪 99AA **18** 馫 99AB

馬 187 馬 99AC **2** 冯 51AF 馭 99AD 馮 99AE 馱 99B1 驭 9A6D **3** 馯 99AF 馰 99B0 馲 99B2 馳 99B3 馴 99B4 馵 99B5 驮 9A6E 驯 9A6F 驰 9A70 **4** 馶 99B6 馷 99B7 馸 99B8 馹 99B9 馺 99BA

馻 99BB 馼 99BC 馽 99BD 馾 99BE 馿 99BF 駀 99C0 駁 99C1 駂 99C2 駃 99C3 駄 99C4 駅 99C5 駆 99C6 駇 99C7 驱 9A71 驲 9A72 驳 9A73 驴 9A74 **5** 駈 99C8 駉 99C9 駊 99CA 駋 99CB 駌 99CC

駍 99CD 駎 99CE 駏 99CF 駐 99D0 駑 99D1 駒 99D2 駓 99D3 駔 99D4 駕 99D5 駖 99D6 駗 99D7 駘 99D8 駙 99D9 駚 99DA 駛 99DB 駜 99DC 駝 99DD 駞 99DE 駟 99DF 駠 99E0 驵 9A75 驶 9A76 驷 9A77

驸 9A78 驹 9A79 驺 9A7A 驻 9A7B 驼 9A7C 驽 9A7D 驾 9A7E 驿 9A7F 骀 9A80 **6** 駢 99E2 駣 99E3 駤 99E4 駥 99E5 駦 99E6 駧 99E7 駨 99E8 駩 99E9 駪 99EA 駫 99EB 駬 99EC 駭 99ED 駮 99EE

駯 99EF 駰 99F0 駱 99F1 駲 99F2 骁 9A81 骃 9A83 骄 9A84 骅 9A85 骆 9A86 骇 9A87 骈 9A88 骉 9A89 **7** 駴 99F4 駵 99F5 駶 99F6 駷 99F7 駸 99F8 駹 99F9 駺 99FA 駻 99FB 駼 99FC 駽 99FD

駾 99FE 駿 99FF 騀 9A00 騁 9A01 騂 9A02 騃 9A03 骊 9A8A 骋 9A8B 验 9A8C 骍 9A8D 骎 9A8E 骏 9A8F **8** 駳 99F3 騄 9A04 騅 9A05 騆 9A06 騇 9A07 騈 9A08 騉 9A09 騊 9A0A 騋 9A0B 騌 9A0C

騍 9A0D 騎 9A0E 騏 9A0F 騐 9A10 騑 9A11 騒 9A12 験 9A13 骐 9A90 骑 9A91 骒 9A92 骓 9A93 骔 9A94 骖 9A96 **9** 騔 9A14 騕 9A15 騖 9A16 騗 9A17 騘 9A18 騙 9A19 騚 9A1A 騛 9A1B 騜 9A1C

騝 9A1D 騞 9A1E 騟 9A1F 騠 9A20 騡 9A21 騢 9A22 騣 9A23 騤 9A24 騥 9A25 騦 9A26 騧 9A27 騨 9A28 骗 9A97 骘 9A98 骙 9A99 骚 9A9A 骛 9A9B **10** 蓦 84E6 騩 9A29 騪 9A2A 騫 9A2B 騬 9A2C

騭 9A2D 騮 9A2E 騯 9A2F 騰 9A30 騱 9A31 騲 9A32 騳 9A33 騴 9A34 騵 9A35 騶 9A36 騷 9A37 騸 9A38 骜 9A9C 骝 9A9D 骞 9A9E 骟 9A9F **11** 騹 9A39 騺 9A3A 騻 9A3B 騼 9A3C 騽 9A3D 騾 9A3E

騿 9A3F 驀 9A40 驁 9A41 驂 9A42 驃 9A43 驄 9A44 驅 9A45 驆 9A46 驇 9A47 骠 9AA0 骡 9AA1 骢 9AA2 **12** 驈 9A48 驉 9A49 驊 9A4A 驋 9A4B 驍 9A4D 驎 9A4E 驏 9A4F 驐 9A50 驑 9A51 驒 9A52

馬 187 驒 9A52 驓 9A53 驔 9A54 驕 9A55 骕 9A95 骣 9AA3 **13** 驌 9A4C 驖 9A56 驗 9A57 驘 9A58 驙 9A59 驚 9A5A 驛 9A5B 驜 9A5C **14** 驝 9A5D 驞 9A5E 驟 9A5F 骤 9AA4 **16** 驠 9A60 驡 9A61 驢 9A62 驣 9A63 骥 9AA5 **17** 驤 9A64 驥 9A65 驦 9A66 驧 9A67 骦 9AA6 骧 9AA7 **18** 驨 9A68 驩 9A69 **19** 驪 9A6A **20** 驫 9A6B

马 187 马 9A6C

骨 188 骨 9AA8 **2** 骩 9AA9 **3** 骪 9AAA 骫 9AAB 骬 9AAC 骭 9AAD 骮 9AAE **4** 骯 9AAF 骰 9AB0 骱 9AB1 **5** 骲 9AB2 骳 9AB3 骴 9AB4 骵 9AB5 骶 9AB6 骷 9AB7 **6** 骸 9AB8 骹 9AB9 骺 9ABA 骻 9ABB 骼 9ABC **7** 骽 9ABD 骾 9ABE **8** 骿 9ABF 髀 9AC0 髁 9AC1 **9** 髂 9AC2 髃 9AC3 髄 9AC4 髅 9AC5 **10** 髆 9AC6 髇 9AC7 髈 9AC8 髉 9AC9 髊 9ACA 髋 9ACB 髌 9ACC **11** 髍 9ACD 髎 9ACE 髏 9ACF **12** 髐 9AD0 **13** 髑 9AD1 髒 9AD2 髓 9AD3 體 9AD4 **14** 髕 9AD5 **15** 髖 9AD6 **16** 髗 9AD7

高 189 高 9AD8 髙 9AD9 **4** 髚 9ADA **5** 髛 9ADB **8** 髜 9ADC **12** 髝 9ADD **13** 髞 9ADE

髟 190 髟 9ADF **2** 髠 9AE0 **3** 髡 9AE1 髢 9AE2 **4** 髣 9AE3 髤 9AE4 髥 9AE5 髦 9AE6 髧 9AE7 髨 9AE8 髩 9AE9 髪 9AEA **5** 髫 9AEB 髬 9AEC 髭 9AED 髮 9AEE 髯 9AEF 髰 9AF0 髱 9AF1 髲 9AF2 髳 9AF3 髴 9AF4 **6** 髵 9AF5 髶 9AF6 髷 9AF7 髸 9AF8 髹 9AF9 髺 9AFA 髻 9AFB 鬇 9B07 **7** 髼 9AFC 髽 9AFD 髾 9AFE 髿 9AFF 鬀 9B00 鬁 9B01 鬂 9B02 **8** 鬃 9B03 鬄 9B04 鬅 9B05 鬆 9B06 鬈 9B08 **9** 鬉 9B09 鬊 9B0A 鬋 9B0B 鬌 9B0C 鬍 9B0D 鬎 9B0E 鬏 9B0F **10** 鬐 9B10 鬑 9B11 鬒 9B12 鬓 9B13 **11** 鬔 9B14 鬕 9B15 鬖 9B16 鬗 9B17 鬘 9B18 鬝 9B1D **12** 鬙 9B19 鬚 9B1A 鬛 9B1B 鬜 9B1C **13** 鬞 9B1E 鬟 9B1F 鬠 9B20 **14** 鬡 9B21 鬢 9B22 **15** 鬣 9B23 **17** 鬤 9B24

鬥 191 鬥 9B25 **4** 鬦 9B26 **5** 鬧 9B27 **6** 鬨 9B28 **8** 鬩 9B29 **10** 鬪 9B2A **12** 鬫 9B2B **14** 鬬 9B2C 鬭 9B2D **17** 鬮 9B2E

鬯 192 鬯 9B2F **17** 鬰 9B30 **19** 鬱 9B31

鬲 193 鬲 9B32 **6** 鬳 9B33 **7** 鬴 9B34 **8** 鬵 9B35 鬶 9B36 **9** 鬷 9B37 **10** 鬸 9B38 **11** 鬹 9B39 鬺 9B3A **12** 鬻 9B3B

鬼 194 鬼 9B3C **3** 鬽 9B3D **4** 鬾 9B3E 鬿 9B3F 魀 9B40 魁 9B41 魂 9B42 **5** 魃 9B43 魄 9B44 魅 9B45 魆 9B46 **6** 魇 9B47 **7** 魈 9B48 魉 9B49 **8** 魊 9B4A 魋 9B4B 魌 9B4C

鬼 194 魍 9B4D 魎 9B4E 魏 9B4F **10** 魐 9B50 **11** 魑 9B51 魒 9B52 魓 9B53 魔 9B54 **12** 魕 9B55 魖 9B56 **14** 魗 9B57 魘 9B58 魙 9B59

魚 195 魚 9B5A **2** 魛 9B5B 魜 9B5C 魝 9B5D 魞 9B5E 鱽 9C7D **3** 魟 9B5F 魠 9B60 魡 9B61 魢 9B62 鱾 9C7E **4** 魣 9B63 魤 9B64 魥 9B65 魦 9B66 魧 9B67 魨 9B68 魩 9B69 魪 9B6A 魫 9B6B
魬 9B6C 魭 9B6D 魮 9B6E 魯 9B6F 魰 9B70 魱 9B71 魲 9B72 魳 9B73 魴 9B74 魵 9B75 魶 9B76 魷 9B77 魸 9B78 魹 9B79 鱿 9C7F 鲀 9C80 鲁 9C81 鲂 9C82 鲃 9C83 **5** 稣 7A23 魺 9B7A 魻 9B7B
魼 9B7C 魽 9B7D 魾 9B7E 魿 9B7F 鮀 9B80 鮁 9B81 鮂 9B82 鮃 9B83 鮄 9B84 鮅 9B85 鮆 9B86 鮇 9B87 鮈 9B88 鮉 9B89 鮊 9B8A 鮋 9B8B 鮌 9B8C 鮍 9B8D 鮎 9B8E 鮏 9B8F 鮐 9B90 鮑 9B91 鮒 9B92
鮓 9B93 鮔 9B94 鮕 9B95 鮖 9B96 鮗 9B97 鮘 9B98 鮣 9BA3 鲄 9C84 鲅 9C85 鲆 9C86 鲇 9C87 鲈 9C88 鲉 9C89 鲊 9C8A 鲋 9C8B 鲌 9C8C 鲍 9C8D 鲎 9C8E 鲏 9C8F 鲐 9C90 **6** 鮙 9B99 鮚 9B9A
鮛 9B9B 鮜 9B9C 鮝 9B9D 鮞 9B9E 鮟 9B9F 鮠 9BA0 鮡 9BA1 鮢 9BA2 鮤 9BA4 鮥 9BA5 鮦 9BA6 鮧 9BA7 鮨 9BA8 鮩 9BA9 鮪 9BAA 鮫 9BAB 鮬 9BAC 鮭 9BAD 鮮 9BAE 鮯 9BAF 鮰 9BB0 鮱 9BB1 鮲 9BB2
鮳 9BB3 鮴 9BB4 鲑 9C91 鲒 9C92 鲓 9C93 鲔 9C94 鲕 9C95 鲖 9C96 鲗 9C97 鲙 9C99 鲚 9C9A 鲛 9C9B 鲜 9C9C 鲝 9C9D 鲞 9C9E 鲟 9C9F **7** 鮵 9BB5 鮶 9BB6 鮷 9BB7 鮸 9BB8 鮹 9BB9 鮺 9BBA
鮻 9BBB 鮼 9BBC 鮽 9BBD 鮾 9BBE 鮿 9BBF 鯀 9BC0 鯁 9BC1 鯂 9BC2 鯃 9BC3 鯄 9BC4 鯅 9BC5 鯆 9BC6 鯇 9BC7 鯈 9BC8 鯉 9BC9 鯊 9BCA 鯋 9BCB 鯌 9BCC 鯍 9BCD 鯎 9BCE 鯏 9BCF 鯐 9BD0 鯑 9BD1
鯒 9BD2 鯓 9BD3 鲠 9CA0 鲡 9CA1 鲣 9CA3 鲤 9CA4 鲥 9CA5 鲦 9CA6 鲧 9CA7 鲨 9CA8 鲩 9CA9 鲪 9CAA 鲫 9CAB 鲬 9CAC **8** 鯔 9BD4 鯕 9BD5 鯖 9BD6 鯗 9BD7 鯘 9BD8 鯙 9BD9 鯚 9BDA 鯛 9BDB
鯜 9BDC 鯝 9BDD 鯞 9BDE 鯟 9BDF 鯠 9BE0 鯡 9BE1 鯢 9BE2 鯣 9BE3 鯤 9BE4 鯥 9BE5 鯦 9BE6 鯧 9BE7 鯨 9BE8 鯩 9BE9 鯪 9BEA 鯫 9BEB 鯬 9BEC 鯭 9BED 鯮 9BEE 鯯 9BEF 鯰 9BF0 鯱 9BF1 鯲 9BF2
鯳 9BF3 鯴 9BF4 鯵 9BF5 鯻 9BFB 鲢 9CA2 鲭 9CAD 鲮 9CAE 鲯 9CAF 鲰 9CB0 鲱 9CB1 鲲 9CB2 鲳 9CB3 鲴 9CB4 鲵 9CB5 鲶 9CB6 鲷 9CB7 鲸 9CB8 鲹 9CB9 鲺 9CBA 鲻 9CBB **9** 鯶 9BF6 鯷 9BF7
鯸 9BF8 鯹 9BF9 鯺 9BFA 鯼 9BFC 鯽 9BFD 鯾 9BFE 鯿 9BFF 鰀 9C00 鰁 9C01 鰂 9C02 鰃 9C03 鰄 9C04 鰅 9C05 鰆 9C06 鰇 9C07 鰈 9C08 鰉 9C09 鰊 9C0A 鰋 9C0B 鰌 9C0C 鰍 9C0D 鰎 9C0E 鰏 9C0F
鰐 9C10 鰑 9C11 鰒 9C12 鰓 9C13 鰔 9C14 鰕 9C15 鰖 9C16 鰗 9C17 鰘 9C18 鰙 9C19 鰚 9C1A 鰛 9C1B 鰠 9C20 鰦 9C26 鲼 9CBC 鲽 9CBD 鲿 9CBF 鳀 9CC0 鳁 9CC1 鳂 9CC2 鳃 9CC3 鳄 9CC4 鳅 9CC5
鳆 9CC6 鳇 9CC7 鳈 9CC8 鳉 9CC9 鳊 9CCA 鳋 9CCB **10** 鰜 9C1C 鰝 9C1D 鰞 9C1E 鰟 9C1F 鰡 9C21 鰢 9C22 鰣 9C23 鰤 9C24 鰥 9C25 鰧 9C27 鰨 9C28 鰩 9C29 鰪 9C2A 鰫 9C2B 鰬 9C2C 鰭 9C2D
鰮 9C2E 鰯 9C2F 鰰 9C30 鲾 9CBE 鳌 9CCC 鳍 9CCD 鳎 9CCE 鳏 9CCF 鳐 9CD0 鳑 9CD1 鳒 9CD2 **11** 鰱 9C31 鰲 9C32 鰳 9C33 鰴 9C34 鰵 9C35 鰶 9C36 鰷 9C37 鰸 9C38 鰹 9C39 鰺 9C3A 鰻 9C3B
鰼 9C3C 鰽 9C3D 鰾 9C3E 鰿 9C3F 鱀 9C40 鱁 9C41 鱂 9C42 鱃 9C43 鱄 9C44 鱅 9C45 鱆 9C46 鱇 9C47 鱈 9C48 鳓 9CD3 鳔 9CD4 鳕 9CD5 鳖 9CD6 鳗 9CD7 鳘 9CD8 鳙 9CD9 鳚 9CDA 鳛 9CDB
12 鱉 9C49 鱊 9C4A 鱋 9C4B 鱌 9C4C 鱍 9C4D 鱎 9C4E 鱏 9C4F 鱐 9C50 鱑 9C51 鱒 9C52 鱓 9C53 鱔 9C54 鱕 9C55 鱖 9C56 鱗 9C57 鱘 9C58 鱙 9C59 鱚 9C5A 鱛 9C5B 鳜 9CDC 鳝 9CDD 鳞 9CDE
鳟 9CDF **13** 鱜 9C5C 鱝 9C5D 鱞 9C5E 鱟 9C5F 鱠 9C60 鱡 9C61 鱢 9C62 鱣 9C63 鱤 9C64 鱥 9C65 鱦 9C66 鱧 9C67 鱩 9C69 鱪 9C6A 鱫 9C6B 鳠 9CE0 鳡 9CE1 鳢 9CE2 鳣 9CE3 **14** 鱨 9C68
鱬 9C6C 鱭 9C6D 鱮 9C6E 鱯 9C6F 鱰 9C70 鳤 9CE4 **15** 鱱 9C71 鱲 9C72 鱳 9C73 鱴 9C74 鱵 9C75 鱶 9C76 **16** 鱷 9C77 鱸 9C78 **18** 鱹 9C79 **19** 鱺 9C7A **22** 鱻 9C7B

鱼 195 鱼 9C7C **6** 鲘 9C98

鳥 196 | 鳥 9CE5 | **1** | 鳦 9CE6 | **2** | 鳧 9CE7 | 鳨 9CE8 | 鳩 9CE9 | 鳪 9CEA | 鳫 9CEB | 鳬 9CEC | 鳮 9CEE | 鳯 9CEF | 鳰 9CF0 | 鸠 9E20 | 鸡 9E21 | **3** | 鳭 9CED | 鳱 9CF1 | 鳲 9CF2 | 鳳 9CF3 | 鳴 9CF4 | 鳵 9CF5 | 鳶 9CF6

鸢 9E22 | 鸤 9E24 | **4** | 鳷 9CF7 | 鳸 9CF8 | 鳹 9CF9 | 鳺 9CFA | 鳻 9CFB | 鳼 9CFC | 鳽 9CFD | 鳾 9CFE | 鳿 9CFF | 鴀 9D00 | 鴁 9D01 | 鴂 9D02 | 鴃 9D03 | 鴄 9D04 | 鴅 9D05 | 鴆 9D06 | 鴇 9D07 | 鴈 9D08 | 鴉 9D09 | 鴋 9D0B

鴌 9D0C | 鴍 9D0D | 鴎 9D0E | 鸥 9E25 | 鸦 9E26 | 鸧 9E27 | 鸨 9E28 | 鸩 9E29 | **5** | 鴊 9D0A | 鴏 9D0F | 鴐 9D10 | 鴑 9D11 | 鴒 9D12 | 鴓 9D13 | 鴔 9D14 | 鴕 9D15 | 鴖 9D16 | 鴗 9D17 | 鴘 9D18 | 鴙 9D19 | 鴚 9D1A | 鴛 9D1B

鴜 9D1C | 鴝 9D1D | 鴞 9D1E | 鴟 9D1F | 鴠 9D20 | 鴡 9D21 | 鴢 9D22 | 鴣 9D23 | 鴤 9D24 | 鴥 9D25 | 鴦 9D26 | 鴧 9D27 | 鴨 9D28 | 鴩 9D29 | 鴪 9D2A | 鴫 9D2B | 鴬 9D2C | 鸪 9E2A | 鸫 9E2B | 鸬 9E2C | 鸭 9E2D | 鸮 9E2E | 鸯 9E2F

鸰 9E30 | 鸱 9E31 | 鸲 9E32 | 鸳 9E33 | 鸵 9E35 | 鸶 9E36 | **6** | 翵 7FF5 | 鴭 9D2D | 鴮 9D2E | 鴯 9D2F | 鴰 9D30 | 鴱 9D31 | 鴲 9D32 | 鴳 9D33 | 鴴 9D34 | 鴵 9D35 | 鴶 9D36 | 鴷 9D37 | 鴸 9D38 | 鴹 9D39 | 鴺 9D3A | 鴻 9D3B

鴼 9D3C | 鴽 9D3D | 鴾 9D3E | 鴿 9D3F | 鵀 9D40 | 鵁 9D41 | 鵂 9D42 | 鵃 9D43 | 鵄 9D44 | 鵅 9D45 | 鵆 9D46 | 鵇 9D47 | 鵈 9D48 | 鵉 9D49 | 鸷 9E37 | 鸸 9E38 | 鸹 9E39 | 鸺 9E3A | 鸻 9E3B | 鸼 9E3C | 鸽 9E3D | 鸾 9E3E | 鸿 9E3F

7 | 鵊 9D4A | 鵋 9D4B | 鵌 9D4C | 鵍 9D4D | 鵎 9D4E | 鵏 9D4F | 鵐 9D50 | 鵑 9D51 | 鵒 9D52 | 鵓 9D53 | 鵔 9D54 | 鵕 9D55 | 鵖 9D56 | 鵗 9D57 | 鵘 9D58 | 鵙 9D59 | 鵚 9D5A | 鵛 9D5B | 鵜 9D5C | 鵝 9D5D | 鵞 9D5E | 鵟 9D5F

鵠 9D60 | 鵡 9D61 | 鵢 9D62 | 鵣 9D63 | 鵤 9D64 | 鵥 9D65 | 鹀 9E40 | 鹁 9E41 | 鹂 9E42 | 鹃 9E43 | 鹄 9E44 | 鹅 9E45 | 鹆 9E46 | 鹇 9E47 | 鹈 9E48 | **8** | 鵦 9D66 | 鵧 9D67 | 鵨 9D68 | 鵩 9D69 | 鵪 9D6A | 鵫 9D6B | 鵬 9D6C

鵭 9D6D | 鵮 9D6E | 鵯 9D6F | 鵰 9D70 | 鵱 9D71 | 鵲 9D72 | 鵳 9D73 | 鵴 9D74 | 鵵 9D75 | 鵶 9D76 | 鵷 9D77 | 鵸 9D78 | 鵹 9D79 | 鵺 9D7A | 鵻 9D7B | 鵼 9D7C | 鵽 9D7D | 鵾 9D7E | 鵿 9D7F | 鶀 9D80 | 鶁 9D81 | 鶂 9D82 | 鶃 9D83

鶄 9D84 | 鶅 9D85 | 鶆 9D86 | 鶇 9D87 | 鶈 9D88 | 鶉 9D89 | 鶊 9D8A | 鶋 9D8B | 鶌 9D8C | 鶍 9D8D | 鶎 9D8E | 鶏 9D8F | 鶑 9D91 | 鹉 9E49 | 鹊 9E4A | 鹌 9E4C | 鹍 9E4D | 鹎 9E4E | 鹏 9E4F | 鹑 9E51 | 鹒 9E52 | 鹓 9E53

9 | 鶐 9D90 | 鶒 9D92 | 鶓 9D93 | 鶔 9D94 | 鶕 9D95 | 鶖 9D96 | 鶗 9D97 | 鶘 9D98 | 鶙 9D99 | 鶚 9D9A | 鶛 9D9B | 鶜 9D9C | 鶝 9D9D | 鶞 9D9E | 鶟 9D9F | 鶠 9DA0 | 鶡 9DA1 | 鶢 9DA2 | 鶣 9DA3 | 鶤 9DA4 | 鶥 9DA5 | 鶦 9DA6

鶧 9DA7 | 鶨 9DA8 | 鶩 9DA9 | 鶪 9DAA | 鶫 9DAB | 鶿 9DBF | 鹋 9E4B | 鹕 9E55 | 鹖 9E56 | 鹗 9E57 | 鹙 9E59 | 鹚 9E5A | 鹛 9E5B | 鹜 9E5C | **10** | 鶬 9DAC | 鶭 9DAD | 鶮 9DAE | 鶯 9DAF | 鶰 9DB0 | 鶱 9DB1 | 鶲 9DB2 | 鶳 9DB3

鶴 9DB4 | 鶵 9DB5 | 鶶 9DB6 | 鶷 9DB7 | 鶸 9DB8 | 鶹 9DB9 | 鶺 9DBA | 鶻 9DBB | 鶼 9DBC | 鶽 9DBD | 鶾 9DBE | 鷀 9DC0 | 鷁 9DC1 | 鷂 9DC2 | 鷃 9DC3 | 鷄 9DC4 | 鷅 9DC5 | 鷆 9DC6 | 鷇 9DC7 | 鷈 9DC8 | 鷉 9DC9 | 鷊 9DCA | 鷌 9DCC

鷍 9DCD | 鷎 9DCE | 鷏 9DCF | 鹘 9E58 | 鹝 9E5D | 鹞 9E5E | 鹟 9E5F | 鹠 9E60 | 鹡 9E61 | 鹢 9E62 | 鹣 9E63 | 鹤 9E64 | **11** | 鷋 9DCB | 鷐 9DD0 | 鷑 9DD1 | 鷒 9DD2 | 鷓 9DD3 | 鷔 9DD4 | 鷕 9DD5 | 鷖 9DD6 | 鷗 9DD7 | 鷘 9DD8

鷙 9DD9 | 鷚 9DDA | 鷛 9DDB | 鷜 9DDC | 鷝 9DDD | 鷞 9DDE | 鷟 9DDF | 鷠 9DE0 | 鹥 9E65 | 鹦 9E66 | 鹧 9E67 | 鹨 9E68 | **12** | 鷡 9DE1 | 鷢 9DE2 | 鷣 9DE3 | 鷤 9DE4 | 鷥 9DE5 | 鷦 9DE6 | 鷧 9DE7 | 鷨 9DE8 | 鷩 9DE9 | 鷪 9DEA

鷬 9DEC | 鷭 9DED | 鷮 9DEE | 鷯 9DEF | 鷰 9DF0 | 鷱 9DF1 | 鷲 9DF2 | 鷳 9DF3 | 鷴 9DF4 | 鷵 9DF5 | 鷶 9DF6 | 鷷 9DF7 | 鷸 9DF8 | 鷺 9DFA | 鷻 9DFB | 鷼 9DFC | 鹔 9E54 | 鹩 9E69 | 鹪 9E6A | 鹫 9E6B | 鹬 9E6C | **13** | 鷫 9DEB

鷹 9DF9 | 鷽 9DFD | 鷾 9DFE | 鷿 9DFF | 鸀 9E00 | 鸁 9E01 | 鸂 9E02 | 鸃 9E03 | 鸄 9E04 | 鸅 9E05 | 鸆 9E06 | 鸇 9E07 | 鸈 9E08 | 鸉 9E09 | 鸊 9E0A | 鸴 9E34 | 鹭 9E6D | 鹮 9E6E | 鹯 9E6F | 鹰 9E70 | **14** | 鸋 9E0B | 鸌 9E0C

鸍 9E0D | 鸎 9E0E | 鸏 9E0F | 鸐 9E10 | 鸑 9E11 | 鸒 9E12 | 鹱 9E71 | 鹲 9E72 | **15** | 鸓 9E13 | 鸔 9E14 | **16** | 鸕 9E15 | 鸖 9E16 | 鸗 9E17 | **17** | 鸘 9E18 | 鸙 9E19 | 鸚 9E1A | 鹳 9E73 | 鹴 9E74 | **18** | 鸛 9E1B

鸜 9E1C | **19** | 鸝 9E1D | 鸞 9E1E

鸟 196 | 鸟 9E1F | **8** | 鹐 9E50

鹵 197 | 鹵 9E75 | **4** | 鹶 9E76 | **5** | 鹷 9E77 | **8** | 鹸 9E78 | **9** | 鹹 9E79 | 鹾 9E7E | **10** | 鹺 9E7A | 鹻 9E7B | **13** | 鹼 9E7C | 鹽 9E7D

鹿 198 鹿 9E7F **2** 麀 9E80 麁 9E81 麂 9E82 **4** 麃 9E83 麄 9E84 **5** 麅 9E85 麆 9E86 麇 9E87 麈 9E88 **6** 麉 9E89 麊 9E8A 麋 9E8B **7** 麌 9E8C 麍 9E8D 麎 9E8E 麏 9E8F 麐 9E90
8 麑 9E91 麒 9E92 麓 9E93 麔 9E94 麕 9E95 麖 9E96 麗 9E97 **9** 麘 9E98 麙 9E99 麚 9E9A 麛 9E9B **10** 麜 9E9C 麝 9E9D **11** 麞 9E9E **12** 麟 9E9F **13** 麠 9EA0
14 麡 9EA1 **17** 麢 9EA2 **20** 麣 9EA3 **22** 麤 9EA4

麥 199 麥 9EA5 **3** 麧 9EA7 **4** 麨 9EA8 麩 9EA9 麪 9EAA 麫 9EAB 麸 9EB8 **5** 麬 9EAC 麭 9EAD 麮 9EAE **6** 麯 9EAF 麰 9EB0 **7** 麱 9EB1 麲 9EB2 **8** 麳 9EB3 麴 9EB4 麹 9EB9
9 麵 9EB5 麺 9EBA **11** 麶 9EB6 **18** 麷 9EB7

麦 199 麦 9EA6

麻 200 麻 9EBB **3** 麼 9EBC 麽 9EBD **4** 麾 9EBE **7** 麿 9EBF **8** 黀 9EC0 **9** 黁 9EC1 **13** 黂 9EC2

黃 201 黃 9EC3 黄 9EC4 **4** 黅 9EC5 黆 9EC6 **5** 黇 9EC7 黈 9EC8 黉 9EC9 **6** 黊 9ECA 黋 9ECB **13** 黌 9ECC

黍 202 黍 9ECD **3** 黎 9ECE **5** 黏 9ECF **11** 黐 9ED0

黑 203 黑 9ED1 黒 9ED2 **3** 黓 9ED3 **4** 黔 9ED4 黕 9ED5 黖 9ED6 黗 9ED7 默 9ED8 **5** 黚 9EDA 黛 9EDB 黜 9EDC 黝 9EDD 點 9EDE **6** 黟 9EDF 黠 9EE0 黡 9EE1 **7** 黢 9EE2 黣 9EE3
8 黤 9EE4 黥 9EE5 黦 9EE6 黧 9EE7 黨 9EE8 黩 9EE9 黪 9EEA **9** 黫 9EEB 黬 9EEC 黭 9EED 黮 9EEE 黯 9EEF **10** 黰 9EF0 黱 9EF1 **11** 黙 9ED9 黲 9EF2 黳 9EF3 黴 9EF4
13 黵 9EF5 **14** 黶 9EF6 **15** 黷 9EF7 **16** 黸 9EF8

黹 204 黹 9EF9 **4** 黺 9EFA **5** 黻 9EFB **7** 黼 9EFC

黽 205 黽 9EFD 黾 9EFE **4** 黿 9EFF **5** 鼀 9F00 鼁 9F01 鼂 9F02 鼌 9F0C **6** 鼃 9F03 鼄 9F04 **8** 鼅 9F05 **10** 鼆 9F06 **11** 鼇 9F07 **12** 鼈 9F08 鼉 9F09 鼍 9F0D
13 鼊 9F0A

鼎 206 鼎 9F0E **2** 鼏 9F0F 鼐 9F10 鼑 9F11 **3** 鼒 9F12

鼓 207 鼓 9F13 鼔 9F14 **5** 鼕 9F15 鼖 9F16 **6** 鼗 9F17 **8** 鼘 9F18 鼙 9F19 鼚 9F1A 鼛 9F1B **10** 鼜 9F1C **11** 鼝 9F1D 鼞 9F1E **12** 鼟 9F1F

鼠 208 鼠 9F20 **4** 鼢 9F22 鼣 9F23 鼤 9F24 **5** 鼥 9F25 鼦 9F26 鼧 9F27 鼨 9F28 鼩 9F29 鼪 9F2A 鼫 9F2B 鼬 9F2C **6** 鼭 9F2D **7** 鼮 9F2E 鼯 9F2F 鼰 9F30 **8** 鼱 9F31 **9** 鼲 9F32 鼳 9F33 鼴 9F34 鼵 9F35 **10** 鼶 9F36 鼷 9F37 鼸 9F38 鼹 9F39 **15** 鼺 9F3A

鼻 209 鼻 9F3B **2** 鼼 9F3C 鼽 9F3D **3** 鼾 9F3E 鼿 9F3F **5** 齀 9F40 齁 9F41 **8** 齂 9F42 **9** 齃 9F43 齄 9F44 **10** 齅 9F45 齆 9F46 **11** 齇 9F47 **13** 齈 9F48 **22** 齉 9F49

齊 210 齊 9F4A **3** 齋 9F4B **4** 齌 9F4C **5** 齍 9F4D **7** 齎 9F4E **9** 齏 9F4F 齑 9F51

齐 210 齐 9F50

齒 211 齒 9F52 **1** 齓 9F53 **2** 齔 9F54 龀 9F80 **3** 齕 9F55 龁 9F81 **4** 齗 9F57 齘 9F58 龂 9F82 **5** 齖 9F56 齙 9F59 齚 9F5A 齛 9F5B 齜 9F5C 齝 9F5D 齞 9F5E 齟 9F5F 齠 9F60 齡 9F61 齢 9F62 齣 9F63 龃 9F83 龄 9F84 龅 9F85 龆 9F86 **6** 齤 9F64 齥 9F65 齦 9F66 齧 9F67 齨 9F68 齩 9F69 龇 9F87 龈 9F88 **7** 齪 9F6A 齫 9F6B 齬 9F6C 龉 9F89 龊 9F8A **8** 齭 9F6D 齮 9F6E 齯 9F6F 齰 9F70 齱 9F71 **9** 齲 9F72 齳 9F73 齴 9F74 齵 9F75 齶 9F76 齷 9F77 龋 9F8B 龌 9F8C **10** 齸 9F78 齹 9F79 齺 9F7A 齻 9F7B **13** 齼 9F7C 齽 9F7D **20** 齾 9F7E

齿 211 齿 9F7F

龍 212 龍 9F8D **2** 龎 9F8E **3** 龏 9F8F 龐 9F90 **4** 龑 9F91 **5** 砻 783B 龒 9F92 **6** 袭 88AD 龓 9F93 龔 9F94 龕 9F95 龚 9F9A 龛 9F9B **16** 龖 9F96 **17** 龗 9F97 **32** 龘 9F98

龙 龙
212 9F99

龜 龜 **4** 鼋 **5** 龝 **12** 龞
213 9F9C 9F0B 9F9D 9F9E

龟 龟
213 9F9F

龠 龠 **4** 龡 **5** 龢 **8** 龣 **9** 龤 龥
214 9FA0 9FA1 9FA2 9FA3 9FA4 9FA5

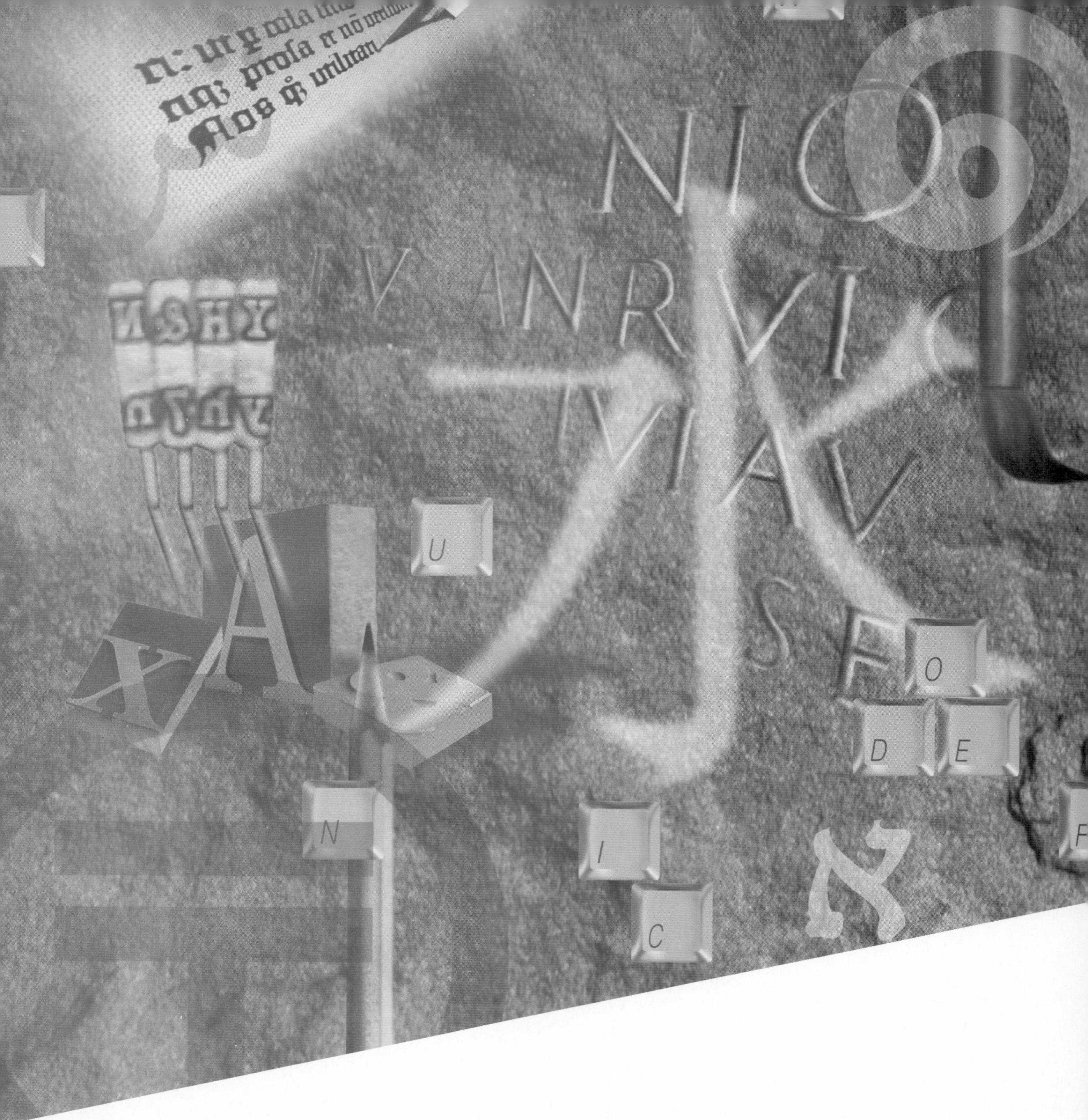

APPENDIX A

Transformation Formats

Appendix A

Transformation Formats

Existing software and practices in information technology frequently depend on character data being represented as a sequence of bytes. Older, but still prevalent practices often assume that only 7 bits of each byte are significant for the purpose of interchanging character data. To make use of Unicode character data in such systems, it is necessary to transform individual Unicode character values and pairs of surrogates into a sequence of one or more bytes that represent the same information, but which are restricted in their numerical range, so they can be interchanged with or transmitted through such systems. Typically, a transformation format allows a certain number of code values in the ASCII range to be transmitted as-is (except for truncation of the leading zero byte), a property known as *transparency*—while other code values are represented through an escape mechanism. This approach typically makes use of a variable-length encoding to achieve greater efficiency when invoking the escape mechanism.

Two transformation formats have been developed to meet the needs just described. There are two transformation formats instead of just one due to differences in the transparency requirements of the expected transmission channels. These are known as *UTFs* (Universal Character Set Transformation Formats); specifically UTF-7 and UTF-8. Both UTF-7 and UTF-8 can be used with MIME; UTF-8 is often used as a file code in X/Open environments. UTF-8 is included as Amendment Number 2 of ISO/IEC 10646. UTF-7 is not part of ISO/IEC 10646 as of this writing.

A.1 UTF-7

The term UTF-7 stands for UCS Transformation Format, 7-bit form.

Many existing character transmission media support only 7 bits of significant data within individual bytes; furthermore, in the majority of these cases, only a subset of the integral values 0...127 may be interchanged transparently. Typically, C0 (0...31) and DEL (127) and certain other values are not transparent in these media. Examples of such media include the most common mail transport agents employed in the Internet, particularly those based on the Simple Mail Transport Protocol (SMTP).

To address the needs of such transmission media and, in particular, to address the needs of the developing Multimedia Internet Mail Extensions (MIME) standard, a transformation format was devised which supports the necessary transparency to facilitate effective interchange of Unicode (UCS-2) character data in such environments. This format is known as UTF-7. UTF-7 is described in Internet Network Working Group RFC-1642 and is available in electronic form via the `unicode.org` World Wide Web Page and from the `unicode.org` FTP archive (see *Section 1.6, Resources,* for addresses).

The following discussion is a summary of the RFC. Character set UTF-7 is safe for Internet mail transmission and therefore may be used with any content transfer encoding in MIME (except where line length and line break restrictions are violated). Specifically, the 7-bit encoding for bodies and the Q encoding for headers are both acceptable. The MIME character set identifier is UNICODE-1-1-UTF-7.

Specification of UTF-7 depends on some definitions of US-ASCII character subsets.

Set D (directly encoded characters, derived from RFC 1521, Appendix B) consists of the upper and lower case letters A through Z and a through z, the 10 digits 0-9, and nine special characters listed in Table A-1 (note that "+" and "=" are omitted).

Table A-1. UTF-7 Set D Special Characters

Character	ASCII & Unicode Value (decimal)
'	39
(	40
)	41
,	44
-	45
.	46
/	47
:	58
?	63

Set O (optional direct characters) consists of the characters listed in Table A-2 (note that "\" and "~" are omitted because they are often redefined in variants of ASCII).

Table A-2. UTF-7 Set O

Character	ASCII & Unicode Value (decimal)
!	33
"	34
#	35
$	36
%	37
&	38
*	42
;	59
<	60
=	61
>	62
@	64
[	91
]	93
^	94
_	95
`	96
{	123
|	124
}	125

Set B (Modified Base 64) is the set of characters in the Base64 alphabet defined in Internet RFC 1521, excluding the pad character "=" (decimal value 61). The pad character "=" is excluded because UTF-7 is designed for use within header fields as set forth in RFC 1522. Since the only readable encoding in RFC 1522 is "Q" (based on RFC 1521's Quoted-Printable), the "=" character is not available for use (without a lot of escape sequences).

A UTF-7 stream represents 16-bit Unicode characters in 7-bit US-ASCII as follows.

Rule 1: Direct Encoding

Unicode characters in Set D may be encoded directly as their ASCII equivalents. Unicode characters in Set O may optionally be encoded directly as their ASCII equivalents; bear in mind that many of these characters are illegal in header fields, or may not pass correctly through some mail gateways.

Rule 2: Unicode Shifted Encoding

Any Unicode character sequence may be encoded using a sequence of characters in set B, when preceded by the shift character "+" (US-ASCII character value decimal 43). The "+" signals that subsequent bytes are to be interpreted as elements of the Modified Base64 alphabet until a character not in that alphabet is encountered. Such characters include control characters such as carriage returns and line feeds; thus, a Unicode shifted sequence always terminates at the end of a line. As a special case, if the sequence terminates with the character "-" (US-ASCII decimal 45) then that character is absorbed; other terminating characters are not absorbed and are processed normally. A terminating character is necessary when the next character after the Modified Base64 sequence is part of character set B. The sequence "+-" may be used to encode the character "+". A "+" character followed immediately by any character other than members of set B or "-" is an ill-formed sequence.

Unicode data is encoded using Modified Base64 by first converting Unicode 16-bit quantities to a byte stream (with the most significant byte first). Text with an odd number of bytes is ill-formed.

The byte stream is then encoded by applying the Base64 content transfer encoding algorithm as defined in RFC 1521, modified to omit the "=" pad character. Instead, when encoding, zero bits are added to pad to a Base64 character boundary. When decoding, any bits at the end of the Modified Base64 sequence that do not constitute a complete 16-bit Unicode character are discarded. If such discarded bits are non-zero the sequence is ill-formed. The pad character "=" is not used when encoding Modified Base64 because that conflicts with its use as an escape character for the Q content transfer encoding in RFC 1522 header fields.

Rule 3: ASCII Equivalents

The space (decimal 32), tab (decimal 9), carriage return (decimal 13), and line feed (decimal 10) characters may be directly represented by their ASCII equivalents. However, note that MIME content transfer encodings have rules concerning the use of such characters. Usage that does not conform to the restrictions of RFC 822, for example, would have to be encoded using MIME content transfer encodings other than 7-bit or 8-bit, such as quoted-printable, binary, or base64.

Given this set of rules, Unicode characters that may be encoded via rules 1 or 3 take one byte per character, and other Unicode characters are encoded on average with 2 2/3 bytes per character plus one byte to switch into Modified Base64 and an optional byte to switch out.

Sample Implementation of the UTF-7 Conversions

```
/* ================================================================ */
/*      The following definitions are compiler-specific.
   I would use wchar_t for UniChar, except that the C standard
   does not guarantee that it has at least 16 bits, so wchar_t is
   no more portable than unsigned short!
*/

typedef unsigned short  UniChar;
```

```
/* ================================================================ */
/*      Each of these routines converts the text between *sourceStart and
sourceEnd, putting the result into the buffer between *targetStart and
targetEnd. Note: the end pointers are *after* the last item: e.g.
*(sourceEnd - 1) is the last item.

    The return result indicates whether the conversion was successful,
and if not, whether the problem was in the source or target buffers.

    After the conversion, *sourceStart and *targetStart are both
updated to point to the end of last text successfully converted in
the respective buffers.

        In ConvertUniChartoUTF7, optional indicates whether UTF-7 optional
characters should be directly encoded, and verbose controls whether the
shift-out character, "-", is always emitted at the end of a shifted
sequence.
*/

typedef enum {
    ok,                             /* conversion successful */
    sourceCorrupt,          /* source contains invalid UTF-7 */
    targetExhausted         /* insuff. room in target for conversion */
} ConversionResult;

extern ConversionResult         ConvertUniChartoUTF7 (
        UniChar** sourceStart, UniChar* sourceEnd,
        char** targetStart, char* targetEnd,
        int optional, int verbose);

extern ConversionResult         ConvertUTF7toUniChar (
        char** sourceStart, char* sourceEnd,
        UniChar** targetStart, UniChar* targetEnd);

/* ================================================================ */


#include "ConvertUTF7.h"

static char base64[]
    = "ABCDEFGHIJKLMNOPQRSTUVWXYZabcdefghijklmnopqrstuvwxyz0123456789+/";
static short invbase64[128];

static char direct[] =
    "ABCDEFGHIJKLMNOPQRSTUVWXYZabcdefghijklmnopqrstuvwxyz0123456789'(),-./:?";
static char optional[] = "!\"#$%&*;<=>@[]^_`{|}";
static char spaces[] = " \011\015\012";/* space, tab, return, line feed */
static char mustshiftsafe[128];
static char mustshiftopt[128];

static int needtables = 1;

#define SHIFT_IN '+'
#define SHIFT_OUT '-'

static void
tabinit()
{
    int i, limit;

    for (i = 0; i < 128; ++i)
    {
        mustshiftopt[i] = mustshiftsafe[i] = 1;
        invbase64[i] = -1;
    }
    limit = strlen(direct);
    for (i = 0; i < limit; ++i)
        mustshiftopt[direct[i]] = mustshiftsafe[direct[i]] = 0;
    limit = strlen(spaces);
    for (i = 0; i < limit; ++i)
        mustshiftopt[spaces[i]] = mustshiftsafe[spaces[i]] = 0;
    limit = strlen(optional);
    for (i = 0; i < limit; ++i)
        mustshiftopt[optional[i]] = 0;
    limit = strlen(base64);
    for (i = 0; i < limit; ++i)
        invbase64[base64[i]] = i;

    needtables = 0;
}

#define DECLARE_BIT_BUFFER \
    register unsigned long BITbuffer = 0, buffertemp = 0; int bufferbits = 0
#define BITS_IN_BUFFER bufferbits
#define WRITE_N_BITS(x, n) \
    ((BITbuffer |= ( ((x) & ~(-1L<<(n))) << (32-(n)-bufferbits) ) ), \
    bufferbits += (n) )
#define READ_N_BITS(n) \
    ((buffertemp = (BITbuffer >> (32-(n)))), \
        (BITbuffer <<= (n)), (bufferbits -= (n)), buffertemp)
#define TARGETCHECK  {if (target >= targetEnd) {result = targetExhausted; break;}}
```

```
ConversionResult ConvertUniChartoUTF7(
        UniChar** sourceStart, UniChar* sourceEnd,
        char** targetStart, char* targetEnd,
        int optional, int verbose)
{
    ConversionResult result = ok;
    DECLARE_BIT_BUFFER;
    int shifted = 0, needshift = 0, done = 0;
    register UniChar *source = *sourceStart;
    register char *target = *targetStart;
    char *mustshift;

    if (needtables)
        tabinit();

    if (optional)
        mustshift = mustshiftopt;
    else
        mustshift = mustshiftsafe;

    do
    {
        register UniChar r;

        if (!(done = (source >= sourceEnd)))
            r = *source++;
        needshift = (!done && ((r > 0x7f) || mustshift[r]));

        if (needshift && !shifted)
        {
            TARGETCHECK;
            *target++ = SHIFT_IN;
            /* Special case handling of the SHIFT_IN character */
            if (r == (UniChar)SHIFT_IN) {
                TARGETCHECK;
                *target++ = SHIFT_OUT;
            }
            else
                shifted = 1;
        }

        if (shifted)
        {
            /* Either write the character to the bit buffer, or pad
               the bit buffer out to a full base64 character.
               */
            if (needshift)
                WRITE_N_BITS(r, 16);
            else
                WRITE_N_BITS(0, (6 - (BITS_IN_BUFFER % 6))%6);

            /* Flush out as many full base64 characters as possible
               from the bit buffer.
               */
            while ((target < targetEnd) && BITS_IN_BUFFER >= 6)
            {
                *target++ = base64[READ_N_BITS(6)];
            }

            if (BITS_IN_BUFFER >= 6)
                TARGETCHECK;

            if (!needshift)
            {
                /* Write the explicit shift out character if
                    1) The caller has requested we always do it, or
                    2) The directly encoded character is in the
                    base64 set.
                    */
                if (verbose || ((!done) && invbase64[r] >= 0))
                {
                    TARGETCHECK;
                    *target++ = SHIFT_OUT;
                }
                shifted = 0;
            }
        }

        /* The character can be directly encoded as ASCII. */
        if (!needshift && !done)
        {
            TARGETCHECK;
            *target++ = (char) r;
        }

    }
    while (!done);

    *sourceStart = source;
    *targetStart = target;
    return result;
}
```

```
ConversionResult ConvertUTF7toUniChar(
        char** sourceStart, char* sourceEnd,
        UniChar** targetStart, UniChar* targetEnd)
{
    ConversionResult result = ok;
    DECLARE_BIT_BUFFER;
    int shifted = 0, first = 0, wroteone = 0, base64EOF, base64value, done;
    unsigned int c, prevc;
    unsigned long junk;
    register char *source = *sourceStart;
    register UniChar *target = *targetStart;

    if (needtables)
        tabinit();

    do
    {
        /* read an ASCII character c */
        if (!(done = (source >= sourceEnd)))
            c = *source++;
        if (shifted)
        {
            /* We're done with a base64 string if we hit EOF, it's not a valid
               ASCII character, or it's not in the base64 set.
               */
            base64EOF = done || (c > 0x7f) || (base64value = invbase64[c]) < 0;
            if (base64EOF)
            {
                shifted = 0;
                /* If the character causing us to drop out was SHIFT_IN or
                   SHIFT_OUT, it may be a special escape for SHIFT_IN. The
                   test for SHIFT_IN is not necessary, but allows an alternate
                   form of UTF-7 where SHIFT_IN is escaped by SHIFT_IN. This
                   only works for some values of SHIFT_IN.
                   */
                if (!done && (c == SHIFT_IN || c == SHIFT_OUT))
                {
                    /* get another character c */
                    prevc = c;
                    if (!(done = (source >= sourceEnd)))
                        c = *source++;
                    /* If no base64 characters were encountered, and the
                       character terminating the shift sequence was
                       SHIFT_OUT, then it's a special escape for SHIFT_IN.
                       */
                    if (first && prevc == SHIFT_OUT)
                    {
                        /* write SHIFT_IN unicode */
                        TARGETCHECK;
                        *target++ = (UniChar)SHIFT_IN;
                    }
                    else if (!wroteone)
                    {
                        result = sourceCorrupt;
                    }
                }
                else if (!wroteone)
                {
                    result = sourceCorrupt;
                }
            }
            else
            {
                /* Add another 6 bits of base64 to the bit buffer. */
                WRITE_N_BITS(base64value, 6);
                first = 0;
            }

            /* Extract as many full 16 bit characters as possible from the
               bit buffer.
               */
            while (BITS_IN_BUFFER >= 16 && (target < targetEnd))
            {
                /* write a unicode */
                *target++ = READ_N_BITS(16);
                wroteone = 1;
            }

            if (BITS_IN_BUFFER >= 16)
                TARGETCHECK;

            if (base64EOF)
            {
                junk = READ_N_BITS(BITS_IN_BUFFER);
                if (junk)
                {
                    result = sourceCorrupt;
                }
            }
        }
```

```
        if (!shifted && !done)
        {
            if (c == SHIFT_IN)
            {
                shifted = 1;
                first = 1;
                wroteone = 0;
            }
            else
            {
                /* It must be a directly encoded character. */
                if (c > 0x7f)
                {
                    result = sourceCorrupt;
                }
                /* write a unicode */
                TARGETCHECK;
                *target++ = c;
            }
        }
    }
    while (!done);

    *sourceStart = source;
    *targetStart = target;
    return result;
}
```

A.2 UTF-8

The term UTF-8 stands for UCS Transformation Format, 8-bit form.

To address the use of Unicode character data in 8-bit UNIX environments, X/Open developed and promulgated a transformation format known as File System Safe UTF (FSS-UTF, also known as UTF-2). Since that time, this UTF has been accepted as a normative addendum to ISO/IEC 10646 and has been renamed UTF-8, for UCS Transformation Format, 8-bit form.UTF-8 is described in ISO/IEC 10646 AM1. It is available in electronic form via the `unicode.org` World Wide Web Page and the `unicode.org` FTP archive (see *Section 1.6, Resources,* for addresses).

The UTF-8 transformation form maintains transparency for *all* of the ASCII code values (0...127). Furthermore, the values 0...127 do not appear in any byte of a transformed result except as the direct representation of these ASCII values. Each code value (non-surrogates) is represented in UTF-8 by 1, 2, or 3 bytes, depending on the code value. Pairs of surrogates take 4 bytes.

UTF-8 is a variable length encoding of the Unicode Standard using 8-bit sequences, where the high bits indicate which part of the sequence a byte belongs to. Table A-3 shows how the bits in a Unicode value (or surrogate pair) are distributed among the bytes in the UTF-8 encoding.

Table A-3. UTF-8 Bit Distribution

Unicode value	1st Byte	2nd Byte	3rd Byte	4th Byte
000000000xxxxxxx	0xxxxxxx			
00000yyyyyxxxxxx	110yyyyy	10xxxxxx		
zzzzyyyyyyxxxxxx	1110zzzz	10yyyyyy	10xxxxxx	
110110wwwwzzzzyy+ 110111yyyyxxxxxx	11110uuu [a]	10uuzzzz	10yyyyyy	10xxxxxx

a. where uuuuu = wwww + 1
(to account for addition of 10000_{16} as in *Section 3.7, Surrogates*)

Thus the ASCII range (U+0000 ⟶ U+007F) can be expressed as single bytes; most non-ideographics (U+0080 ⟶ U+07FF) can be expressed as 2 bytes; the remaining Unicode values can be expressed as 3 bytes, and surrogate pairs can be expressed as 4 bytes.

When converting Unicode values to UTF-8, always use the shortest form that can represent those values. This preserves uniqueness of encoding. For example, the Unicode value <0000000000000001> is encoded as <00000001>, not as <11000000 10000001>. The latter is an example of an unused UTF-8 byte sequence. *Do not make use of these unused byte sequences for encoding any other information.*

When converting from UTF-8 to Unicode values, however, implementations do not need to check that the shortest encoding is being used, which simplifies the conversion algorithm.

Some of the important characteristics of UTF-8 are

- Unicode characters from U+0000 to U+007E (ASCII repertoire) map to UTF-8 bytes 00 to 7E (ASCII values).
- ASCII values do *not* otherwise occur in a UTF-8 transformation. This provides compatibility with historical file systems and other systems which parse for ASCII bytes.
- It is very simple and efficient to convert to and from Unicode text.
- The first byte indicates the number of bytes to follow in a multi-byte sequence. This allows for efficient forward parsing.
- It is efficient to find the start of a character starting from an arbitrary location in an byte stream. You need to search at most four bytes backwards, and it is simple to recognize an initial byte. For example, in C
  `isInitialByte = ((byte & 0xC0) != 0x80);`
- UTF-8 is reasonably compact in terms of number of bytes used for encoding.

Sample Implementation of the UTF-8 Conversions

The following is provided as a sample implementation. For brevity, it does not deal with all possible error conditions.

```
/* ================================================================ */

#include <stdio.h>
#include <stdlib.h>
#include <string.h>

/* ================================================================ */
/*  The following 4 definitions are compiler-specific.
*/

typedef unsigned longUCS4;
typedef unsigned shortSimpleUniChar;
typedef unsigned shortUniChar;
typedef unsigned charUTF8;

typedef enum {false, true} Boolean;


const UCS4 kReplacementCharacter =0x0000FFFDUL;
const UCS4 kMaximumSimpleUniChar =0x0000FFFFUL;
const UCS4 kMaximumUniChar =0x0010FFFFUL;
const UCS4 kMaximumUCS4 =0x7FFFFFFFUL;

/* ================================================================ */
/*  Each of these routines converts the text between *sourceStart and
sourceEnd, putting the result into the buffer between *targetStart and
targetEnd. Note: the end pointers are *after* the last item: e.g.
*(sourceEnd - 1) is the last item.

    The return result indicates whether the conversion was successful,
and if not, whether the problem was in the source or target buffers.
```

```
    After the conversion, *sourceStart and *targetStart are both
updated to point to the end of last text successfully converted in
the respective buffers.
*/

typedef enum {
    ok,              /* conversion successful */
    sourceExhausted,/* partial character in source, but hit end */
    targetExhausted/* insuff. room in target for conversion */
} ConversionResult;

ConversionResultConvertUCS4toUniChar (
        UCS4** sourceStart, const UCS4* sourceEnd,
        UniChar** targetStart, const UniChar* targetEnd);

ConversionResultConvertUniChartoUCS4 (
        UniChar** sourceStart, UniChar* sourceEnd,
        UCS4** targetStart, const UCS4* targetEnd);

ConversionResultConvertUniChartoUTF8 (
        UniChar** sourceStart, const UniChar* sourceEnd,
        UTF8** targetStart, const UTF8* targetEnd);

ConversionResultConvertUTF8toUniChar (
        UTF8** sourceStart, UTF8* sourceEnd,
        UniChar** targetStart, const UniChar* targetEnd);

/* ================================================================ */

#include "ConvertUTF.h"

const int halfShift= 10;
const UCS4 halfBase= 0x0010000UL;
const UCS4 halfMask= 0x3FFUL;
const UCS4 kSurrogateHighStart= 0xD800UL;
const UCS4 kSurrogateHighEnd= 0xDBFFUL;
const UCS4 kSurrogateLowStart= 0xDC00UL;
const UCS4 kSurrogateLowEnd= 0xDFFFUL;

/* ================================================================ */

ConversionResultConvertUCS4toUniChar (
        UCS4** sourceStart, const UCS4* sourceEnd,
        UniChar** targetStart, const UniChar* targetEnd) {
    ConversionResult result = ok;
    register UCS4* source = *sourceStart;
    register UniChar* target = *targetStart;
    while (source < sourceEnd) {
        register UCS4 ch;
        if (target >= targetEnd) {
            result = targetExhausted; break;
        };
        ch = *source++;
        if (ch <= kMaximumSimpleUniChar) {
            *target++ = ch;
        } else if (ch > kMaximumUniChar) {
            *target++ = kReplacementCharacter;
        } else {
            if (target + 1 >= targetEnd) {
                result = targetExhausted; break;
            };
            ch -= halfBase;
            *target++ = (ch >> halfShift) + kSurrogateHighStart;
            *target++ = (ch & halfMask) + kSurrogateLowStart;
        };
    };
    *sourceStart = source;
    *targetStart = target;
    return result;
};

/* ================================================================ */

ConversionResultConvertUniChartoUCS4 (
        UniChar** sourceStart, UniChar* sourceEnd,
        UCS4** targetStart, const UCS4* targetEnd) {
    ConversionResult result = ok;
    register UniChar* source = *sourceStart;
    register UCS4* target = *targetStart;
    while (source < sourceEnd) {
        register UCS4 ch;
        ch = *source++;
        if (ch >= kSurrogateHighStart && ch <= kSurrogateHighEnd
                && source < sourceEnd) {
            register UCS4 ch2 = *source;
            if (ch2 >= kSurrogateLowStart && ch2 <= kSurrogateLowEnd) {
                ch = ((ch - kSurrogateHighStart) << halfShift)
                    + (ch2 - kSurrogateLowStart) + halfBase;
                ++source;
            };
        };
        if (target >= targetEnd) {
```

```
                result = targetExhausted; break;
            };
            *target++ = ch;
        };
        *sourceStart = source;
        *targetStart = target;
        return result;
};

/* ================================================================ */

UCS4 offsetsFromUTF8[6] ={0x00000000UL, 0x00003080UL, 0x000E2080UL,
                          0x03C82080UL, 0xFA082080UL, 0x82082080UL};
char bytesFromUTF8[256] = {
    0,0,0,0,0,0,0,0,0,0,0,0,0,0,0,0, 0,0,0,0,0,0,0,0,0,0,0,0,0,0,0,0,
    0,0,0,0,0,0,0,0,0,0,0,0,0,0,0,0, 0,0,0,0,0,0,0,0,0,0,0,0,0,0,0,0,
    0,0,0,0,0,0,0,0,0,0,0,0,0,0,0,0, 0,0,0,0,0,0,0,0,0,0,0,0,0,0,0,0,
    0,0,0,0,0,0,0,0,0,0,0,0,0,0,0,0, 0,0,0,0,0,0,0,0,0,0,0,0,0,0,0,0,
    0,0,0,0,0,0,0,0,0,0,0,0,0,0,0,0, 0,0,0,0,0,0,0,0,0,0,0,0,0,0,0,0,
    0,0,0,0,0,0,0,0,0,0,0,0,0,0,0,0, 0,0,0,0,0,0,0,0,0,0,0,0,0,0,0,0,
    1,1,1,1,1,1,1,1,1,1,1,1,1,1,1,1, 1,1,1,1,1,1,1,1,1,1,1,1,1,1,1,1,
    2,2,2,2,2,2,2,2,2,2,2,2,2,2,2,2, 3,3,3,3,3,3,3,3,4,4,4,4,5,5,5,5};

UTF8 firstByteMark[7] = {0x00, 0x00, 0xC0, 0xE0, 0xF0, 0xF8, 0xFC};

/* ================================================================ */
/*  This code is similar in effect to making successive calls on the
mbtowc and wctomb routines in FSS-UTF. However, it is considerably
different in code:
* it is adapted to be consistent with Unicode characters with surrogates,
* the interface converts a whole buffer to avoid function-call overhead
* constants have been gathered.
* loops & conditionals have been removed as much as possible for
efficiency, in favor of drop-through switch statements.
*/

/* ================================================================ */
ConversionResultConvertUniChartoUTF8 (
        UniChar** sourceStart, const UniChar* sourceEnd,
        UTF8** targetStart, const UTF8* targetEnd)
{
    ConversionResult result = ok;
    register UniChar* source = *sourceStart;
    register UTF8* target = *targetStart;
    while (source < sourceEnd) {
        register UCS4 ch;
        register unsigned short bytesToWrite = 0;
        register const UCS4 byteMask = 0xBF;
        register const UCS4 byteMark = 0x80;
        ch = *source++;
        if (ch >= kSurrogateHighStart && ch <= kSurrogateHighEnd
                && source < sourceEnd) {
            register UCS4 ch2 = *source;
            if (ch2 >= kSurrogateLowStart && ch2 <= kSurrogateLowEnd) {
                ch = ((ch - kSurrogateHighStart) << halfShift)
                    + (ch2 - kSurrogateLowStart) + halfBase;
                ++source;
            };
        };
        if (ch < 0x80) { bytesToWrite = 1;
        } else if (ch < 0x800) {bytesToWrite = 2;
        } else if (ch < 0x10000) {bytesToWrite = 3;
        } else if (ch < 0x200000) {bytesToWrite = 4;
        } else if (ch < 0x4000000) {bytesToWrite = 5;
        } else if (ch <= kMaximumUCS4){bytesToWrite = 6;
        } else {                    bytesToWrite = 2;
                                            ch = kReplacementCharacter;
        }; /* I wish there were a smart way to avoid this conditional */

        target += bytesToWrite;
        if (target > targetEnd) {
            target -= bytesToWrite; result = targetExhausted; break;
        };
        switch (bytesToWrite) {/* note: code falls through cases! */
            case 6:*--target = (ch | byteMark) & byteMask; ch >>= 6;
            case 5:*--target = (ch | byteMark) & byteMask; ch >>= 6;
            case 4:*--target = (ch | byteMark) & byteMask; ch >>= 6;
            case 3:*--target = (ch | byteMark) & byteMask; ch >>= 6;
            case 2:*--target = (ch | byteMark) & byteMask; ch >>= 6;
            case 1:*--target =  ch | firstByteMark[bytesToWrite];
        };
        target += bytesToWrite;
    };
    *sourceStart = source;
    *targetStart = target;
    return result;
};

/* ================================================================ */

ConversionResultConvertUTF8toUniChar (
        UTF8** sourceStart, UTF8* sourceEnd,
```

```
        UniChar** targetStart, const UniChar* targetEnd)
{
    ConversionResult result = ok;
    register UTF8* source = *sourceStart;
    register UniChar* target = *targetStart;
    while (source < sourceEnd) {
        register UCS4 ch = 0;
        register unsigned short extraBytesToWrite = bytesFromUTF8[*source];
        if (source + extraBytesToWrite > sourceEnd) {
            result = sourceExhausted; break;
        };
        switch(extraBytesToWrite) {/* note: code falls through cases! */
            case 5:ch += *source++; ch <<= 6;
            case 4:ch += *source++; ch <<= 6;
            case 3:ch += *source++; ch <<= 6;
            case 2:ch += *source++; ch <<= 6;
            case 1:ch += *source++; ch <<= 6;
            case 0:ch += *source++;
        };
        ch -= offsetsFromUTF8[extraBytesToWrite];

        if (target >= targetEnd) {
            result = targetExhausted; break;
        };
        if (ch <= kMaximumSimpleUniChar) {
            *target++ = ch;
        } else if (ch > kMaximumUniChar) {
            *target++ = kReplacementCharacter;
        } else {
            if (target + 1 >= targetEnd) {
                result = targetExhausted; break;
            };
            ch -= halfBase;
            *target++ = (ch >> halfShift) + kSurrogateHighStart;
            *target++ = (ch & halfMask) + kSurrogateLowStart;
        };
    };
    *sourceStart = source;
    *targetStart = target;
    return result;
};
```

APPENDIX

B

Submitting New Character

Appendix B

Submitting New Characters

The Unicode Consortium accepts proposals for inclusion of new characters or scripts in the Unicode Standard. All proposals must be in writing, must include at least one picture of each proposed character (normally from a printed source), and must include documentation justifying the proposal. The identification of the sponsor(s) must be included, along with a postal or electronic mail address, and/or a phone number. General guidelines for the preparation of a proposal appear next, and more detailed information is available electronically through the consortium's World Wide Web server.

The Unicode Standard definition of character is stated in the Glossary. Before preparing a proposal, sponsors should note in particular the distinction between the terms *character* and *glyph* as therein defined. Because of this distinction, graphics such as ligatures, conjunct consonants, minor variant written forms, or abbreviations of longer forms are generally not acceptable as Unicode characters. The Unicode Consortium is interested in obtaining information on known glyphs, minor variants, precomposed characters (including ligatures, conjunct consonants, and accented characters) and other such "non-characters," mainly for cataloging and research purposes; however, they are generally not acceptable for character proposals.

B.1 Proposals

Each proposal received will be evaluated by members of the Unicode Technical Committee, and the result of this evaluation will be communicated to the sponsor(s) of the proposal. All proposals (whether successful or not) will be retained by the Unicode Consortium..

Send proposals to:

The Unicode Consortium
P.O. Box 700519
San Jose, CA 95170-0519
USA

Internet: unicode-inc@unicode.org

The sponsor proposing the addition of a new character to the Unicode Standard should follow these guidelines:

1. Determine that each proposed addition is a character according to the definition given in the Unicode Standard and that the proposed addition does not already exist in the Standard. Ensure that documentation supporting the proposal states whether any Unicode characters were examined as possible equiva-

lents for the proposed character and, if so, why each was rejected.

2. If the character is a Han (ideographic) character, strong evidence for its uniqueness, indispensability, and value to users must be submitted, including printed contexts where it is used. If it could be considered a variant of a character already included in the Unicode Standard, the proposed character should be shown in a context that demonstrates why it must be distinguished as a separate character and not considered a variant of the character already included.

3. If the character is part of a dead language or obsolete/rare script, cite the most important modern sources of information on the script. Names (including academic affiliation) of researchers in the relevant field are welcomed.

4. Proposals to include entire scripts (Egyptian hieroglyphics, for example) should also cite modern, definitive sources of information regarding such scripts. Sponsorship by the relevant academic bodies (such as The International Association of Egyptologists) may be helpful in determining the proper scope for encoding of characters in such cases.

5. The Unicode Consortium works closely with ISO JTC1/SC2/WG2 in proposing additions as well as monitoring the status of proposals by various national bodies. Therefore, proposals may eventually be formulated as ISO/IEC documents and significant detailed information will be required. The form N-1116-F, *Proposal Summary Form to Accompany Submissions for Additional Repertoire of ISO/IEC 10646*, has been designed for this purpose, and its use is encouraged for all proposals. The form is available via anonymous FTP (at the time of writing, it is available as ftp://dkuug.dk/JTC1/SC2/WG2/n1252.doc), and requires the following further information (paraphrased):

- the repertoire, including proposed character names
- the name and contact information for a company or individual who would agree to provide a computerized font (True Type, PostScript, or 96x96 bit-map) for publication of the standard
- references to dictionaries and descriptive texts establishing authoritative information
- names and addresses of appropriate contacts within national body or user organizations
- the context within which the proposed characters are used (for example, current, historical, and so on)
- especially for sporadic additions, what similarities or relationships the proposed characters bear to existing characters already encoded in the standard

In the meantime, there are ways for programmers and scholarly organizations to make use of Unicode character encoding, even if the script they want to use or transmit is not yet (or may never be) part of the Unicode Standard. Individual groups that make use of rare scripts or special characters can reach a private agreement about interchange and set aside part of the Private Use Area to encode their private set of characters.

A few living scripts are very likely to be included in the near future, including Ethiopian, Mongolian, Sinhala, Burmese, Khmer, and Cree/Inuktitut. The Unicode Consortium has also published three technical reports that contain proposals or draft proposals for encoding a number of additional scripts. These reports and the scripts they cover are as follows:

Unicode Technical Report #1, Draft Proposals, October 1992.
  Burmese, Khmer, and Ethiopian

Unicode Technical Report #2, Preliminary Draft Proposals, October 1992.
Mongolian, Sinhala, and Tibetan (superseded by the Tibetan block in the Unicode Standard, Version 2.0).

Unicode Technical Report #3, Exploratory Proposals, October 1992.
Early Aramaic, Balti, Batak, Buginese, Cherokee, Etruscan, Glagolitic, Kirat (Limbu), Linear B, Maldivian (Dihevi), Manipuri (Meithei), Meroïtic, Ogham, Pahlavi/Avestan, Old Persian Cuneiform, Phœnician, Róng (Lepcha), Northern Runes, Epigraphic South Arabian, Syriac, Tagalog and Mangyan (Buhid), Tai Lu, Tai Mau (Tai Nua), Tifinagh (Numidian), and Ugaritic Cuneiform.

Additional characters that have been proposed to ISO JTC1/SC2/WG2 include the following:

> Aboriginal Canadian Scripts (Syllabics), Additional CJK Typesetting symbols, Arabic Script Extensions for Uighur, Kazakh, and Kirghiz, Braille, Cham, Chữ Nôm, Irish Gaelic Precomposed Latin Letters, Egyptian Hieroglyphics, Unified CJK Ideograph extensions, Xishuang Banna Dai, and Yi.

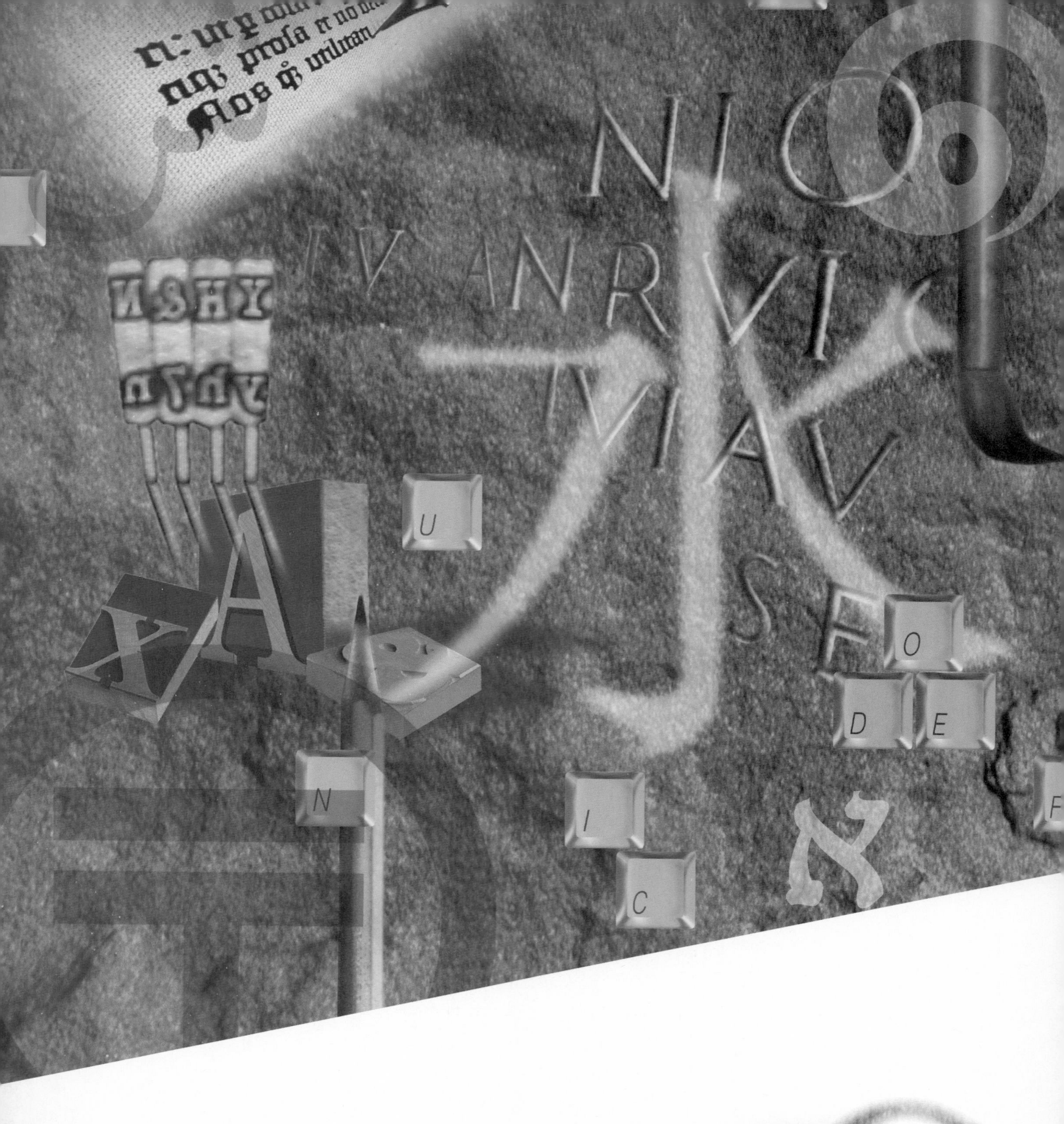

APPENDIX

C

Relationship to ISO/IEC 10646

Appendix C

Relationship to ISO/ IEC 10646

Having recognized the benefits of developing a single universal character code standard, members of the Unicode Consortium worked with representatives from the International Organization for Standardization (ISO) during October of 1991 to pursue this goal. Meetings between the two bodies resulted in mutually acceptable changes to both Unicode Version 1.0 and the first ISO/IEC Draft International Standard DIS 10646.1, which merged their combined repertoire into a single numerical character encoding. This work culminated in the Unicode Standard, Version 1.1.

A second draft, DIS 10646.2, which reflected the result of this merger effort, was distributed for international ballot in January 1992 with a passing vote taken in late June 1992. After final editorial changes were made to accommodate the comments of voting members, the final standard was published in May 1993 as ISO/IEC 10646-1:1993, *Information technology—Universal Multiple-Octet*[1] *Coded Character Set (UCS)—Part 1: Architecture and Basic Multilingual Plane*. The Unicode Standard, Version 1.1 reflected the additional characters introduced from the DIS 10646.1 repetoire and incorporated minor editorial changes.

C.1 Timeline

Year	Version	Summary
1989	DP 10646	Draft proposal, independent of Unicode
1990	Unicode Pre-pub...	Pre-publication review draft
1990	Unicode 1.0	Edition published by Addison-Wesley
1990	DIS-1 10646	First draft, independent of Unicode
1992	Unicode 1.0.1	Modified for merger compatibility
1992	DIS-2 10646	Second draft, merged with Unicode
1993	IS 10646-1:1993	Merged standard
1993	Unicode 1.1	Revised to match IS 10646-1:1993
1995	10646 amendments	Korean realigned, plus 201 additions
1996	Unicode 2.0	Revised to cover 10646 amendments

The combined repertoire presented in ISO/IEC 10646 is a superset of the Unicode Standard, Version 1.0 repertoire as amended by the Unicode Standard, Version 1.0.1. The Unicode Standard, Version 1.0 was amended by the *Unicode 1.0.1 Addendum* in order to make the Unicode Standard a proper subset of ISO/IEC 10646. This entailed both moving and eliminating certain characters. The Unicode Standard, Version 2.0 covers the repertoire of

1. *Octet* is ISO/IEC terminology for *byte*, that is, an ordered sequence of 8 bits considered as a unit.

the Unicode Standard, Version 1.1 (and IS 10646), plus the first seven amendments to IS 10646, as follows:

1: UTF-16

2: UTF-8

3: Coding of C1 Controls

4: Removal of Annex G: UTF-1

5: Korean Hangul Character Collection

6: Tibetan Character Collection

7: 33 Additional Characters (Hebrew, Long S, Dong)

In addition, the Unicode Standard, Version 2.0 also covers Technical Corrigendum No. 1 (on renaming of Æ LIGATURE to LETTER), and such Editorial Corrigenda to ISO/IEC 10646 as were applicable to the Unicode Standard.

C.2 Structure of ISO/IEC 10646

ISO/IEC 10646 defines two alternative forms of encoding:

- A four-octet (31-bit) encoding containing 2^{31} code positions. These code positions are conceptually divided into 128 *groups* of 256 *planes*, each plane containing 256 *rows* of 256 *cells*.
- A two-octet encoding consisting of plane zero, the *Basic Multilingual Plane* (or BMP).

The 31-bit form is referred to as UCS-4 (Universal Character Set coded in 4 bytes) and the 16-bit form is referred to as UCS-2 (Universal Character Set coded in 2 bytes).

The code numbers from 0 through 65,535 decimal (0 - FFFF hexadecimal) can be represented by character code values of 16 bits. The most useful characters (that is, the characters found in major existing standards worldwide) are assigned in this range (that is, in the BMP). ISO/IEC 10646 does not currently define any characters in other planes.

Merging the Unicode Standard, Version 1.0 and DIS 10646.1 consisted of aligning the numerical values of identical characters and then filling in some groups of characters that were present in DIS 10646.1 but not in the Unicode Standard. As a result, the character code values of ISO/IEC 10646 UCS-2 and the Unicode Standard, Version1.1 are precisely the same. The Unicode Standard, Version 2.0 has added more characters, matching recent additions to ISO/IEC 10646-1:1993. The specific adjustments made to the Unicode Standard, Version 1.0 in order to achieve these goals are listed in *Appendix D, Cumulative Changes.*

Since ISO/IEC 10646 does not currently encode any characters outside of the BMP, the character repertoires and encoding assignments of the Unicode Standard and ISO/IEC 10646 are identical. For instance, the character "A", U+0041 LATIN CAPITAL LETTER A, has the unchanging numerical value 41 hexadecimal. This value may be extended by any quantity of leading zeros to serve in the context of the following fixed-length encoding standards (see Table C-1).

This design eliminates the problem of disparate code values in all systems that use any of the standards just mentioned.

Table C-1. Zero Extending

Bits	Standard	Binary	Hex	Dec	Char
7	ASCII	1000001	41	65	A
8	8859-1	01000001	41	65	A
16	Unicode, UCS-2	00000000 01000001	41	65	A
31	UCS-4	0000000 00000000 00000000 01000001	41	65	A

C.3 UTF-16

The term UTF-16 stands for UCS Transformation Format for Planes of Group 00.

UTF-16 is the ISO/IEC encoding that is equivalent to the Unicode Standard with the use of surrogates as described in *Chapter 3, Conformance*. In UTF-16, each UCS-2 code value represents itself. Non-BMP code values of ISO/IEC 10646 in planes $1...16_{10}$ are represented using pairs of special codes. UTF-16 defines the transformation between the UCS-4 code positions in planes 1 to 16 of Group 00 and the pairs of special codes, and is precisely identical to the transformation defined in the Unicode Standard under D.28 in *Section 3.7, Surrogates*. Sample code for transforming UCS-4 into the Unicode Standard with surrogates is located in *Section A.2, UTF-8*.

As in the Unicode Standard, the first element of each surrogate code pair must be a UCS-2 code value in the range $D800\text{-}DBFF_{16}$; the second element must be a UCS-2 code value in the range $DC00...DFFF_{16}$. These two ranges are known as the *high-half zone* and *low-half zone*, respectively. Together, they constitute the newly defined S (Special) Zone of the BMP. Because each of these two ranges provide 1024_{10} values, a total of 1024^2 (= 1,048,576) code values may be represented through this mechanism. These code values are drawn from planes $1...16_{10}$ of group 0 of UCS-4, that is, the range of UCS-4 code values $00010000...0010FFFF_{16}$.

UTF-16 does not support the representation of all the UCS-4 code space but is limited to the BMP and the next 16 planes. This should not be an undue limitation since ISO JTC1/SC2/WG2 has stipulated that planes 1..14 will be filled first with future character assignments. Furthermore, of these additional planes, plane 15 ($000F0000...000FFFFF_{16}$) and plane 16 ($00100000...0010FFFF_{16}$) will be reserved for private use. There are other UCS-4 private use code values (in groups 60 to 7F and in planes E0 to FF in group 00) that are not accessible using UTF-16. Use of these private use code values is *strongly* discouraged because data encoded with these code values will not be interchangeable with Unicode implementations. Planes 15 and 16 should be used instead.

Applications interchanging ISO/IEC 10646 data containing non-BMP code values in planes 1..16 of ISO/IEC 10646 should use UTF-16 as the default encoding form in the absence of information to the contrary. Data exchanged with Unicode applications must be in UCS-2 form: if the data contains non-BMP encoded characters, they must be first transformed into UTF-16.

C.4 The Unicode Standard and ISO/IEC 10646

The goal of merging the Unicode Standard and DIS 10646.1 has been realized; making character code assignments *identical* in the Unicode Standard and ISO/IEC 10646 UCS-2 (that is, the ISO/IEC 10646 BMP). Programmers and system users should treat the character code values from the Unicode Standard, UCS-2, and BMP as identities, especially in the transmission of raw character data across system boundaries.

However, the Unicode Standard and ISO/IEC 10646 differ in the precise terms of their conformance specifications. Any Unicode implementation will conform to ISO/IEC 10646, Level 3, but because Unicode Standard imposes additional constraints on character semantics and transmittability, not all implementations that are compliant with ISO/IEC 10646 will be compliant with the Unicode Standard.

C.5 The Unicode Standard as a Profile of 10646

ISO/IEC 10646 provides mechanisms for specifying a number of implementation parameters, generating what may be termed various instantiations of the standard. ISO/IEC 10646 contains no means of explicitly declaring a profile matching the Unicode Standard as such. As a whole, however, the Unicode Standard may be considered as encompassing the entire repertoire of ISO/IEC 10646 and having the following profile values (as well as additional semantics):

- Numbered subset 300 (BMP)
- UTF-16 (if surrogates are used; UCS-2 otherwise)
- Implementation level 3 (allowing both combining marks and precomposed characters)
- Device type 1 (receiving device with full retransmission capability)

Few applications are expected to make use of all of the 38,000-plus characters defined in the ISO/IEC 10646 Basic Multilingual Plane. The conformance clauses of the two standards address this situation in very different ways. ISO/IEC 10646 provides a mechanism for specifying included subsets of the character repertoire, permitting implementations to ignore characters that are not included (see Informative Annex A of ISO/IEC 10646). A Unicode implementation requires a minimal level of handling all character codes, namely the ability to store and retransmit them undamaged. Thus the Unicode Standard encompasses the entire ISO/IEC 10646 Basic Multilingual Plane without requiring that any particular subset be implemented.

The Unicode Standard does not provide mechanisms for identifying a stream of bytes as Unicode characters, although to some extent this function is served by use of the *byte order mark* (U+FEFF) to indicate byte ordering. ISO/IEC 10646 also allows the use of U+FEFF as a "signature" as described in Informative Annex F to ISO/IEC 10646. Since UCS-2 is equivalent in repertoire and encoding to the Unicode Standard, Version 1.1, this optional "signature" convention for discerning between forms UCS-2 and UCS-4 is brought to the attention of Unicode implementers. The method is summarized in the Specials subsection of *Section 6.8, Compatibility Area and Specials.*

C.6 Character Names

Unicode character names follow the ISO/IEC character naming guidelines (summarized in Informative Annex K of ISO/IEC 10646). In the prior version of the Unicode Standard, the naming convention followed the ISO/IEC naming convention,[1] but with some differences which were largely editorial. For example:

1. The names adopted by the Unicode Standard are from the English-language version of ISO/IEC 10646, even if other language versions are published by ISO.

ISO/IEC 10646 name	029A	LATIN SMALL LETTER CLOSED OPEN E
Unicode 1.0 name	029A	LATIN SMALL LETTER CLOSED EPSILON

In the ISO/IEC framework, the unique character name is viewed as the major resource for both character semantics and cross-mapping among standards. In the framework of the Unicode Standard, character semantics are indicated via alias names, usage annotations, character properties, and functional specifications as mentioned in *Chapter 3, Conformance*, while cross-mappings among standards are provided in the form of explicit tables. The disparities between the Unicode Standard, Version 1.0 names and ISO/IEC 10646 names have been remedied by adoption of ISO/IEC 10646 names in the Unicode Standard. If the Unicode Standard, Version 1.0 name differed from the ISO/IEC 10646 name, then the previous name is provided as a cross reference in the *Unicode Character Database*.

C.7 Character Functional Specifications

The core of a character code standard is a mapping of code values to characters, but in some cases the semantics or even identity of the character may be unclear. Certainly a character is not simply the representative glyph used to depict it in the standard. For this reason, the Unicode Standard undertakes to supply as much information as possible to clarify the semantics of the characters it encodes.

Thus the Unicode Standard consists of far more than a chart of code values. It contains many peripheral ingredients that give it coherence and make it implementable. Also necessary to a complete standard is a set of extensive character functional specifications and substantial background material designed to help implementers better understand how the characters interact and, in general, how best to implement the standard. The Unicode Standard specifies properties and algorithms. Compliant implementations of the Unicode Standard will also be compliant with ISO/IEC 10646, Level 3; *however, not necessarily vice-versa.*

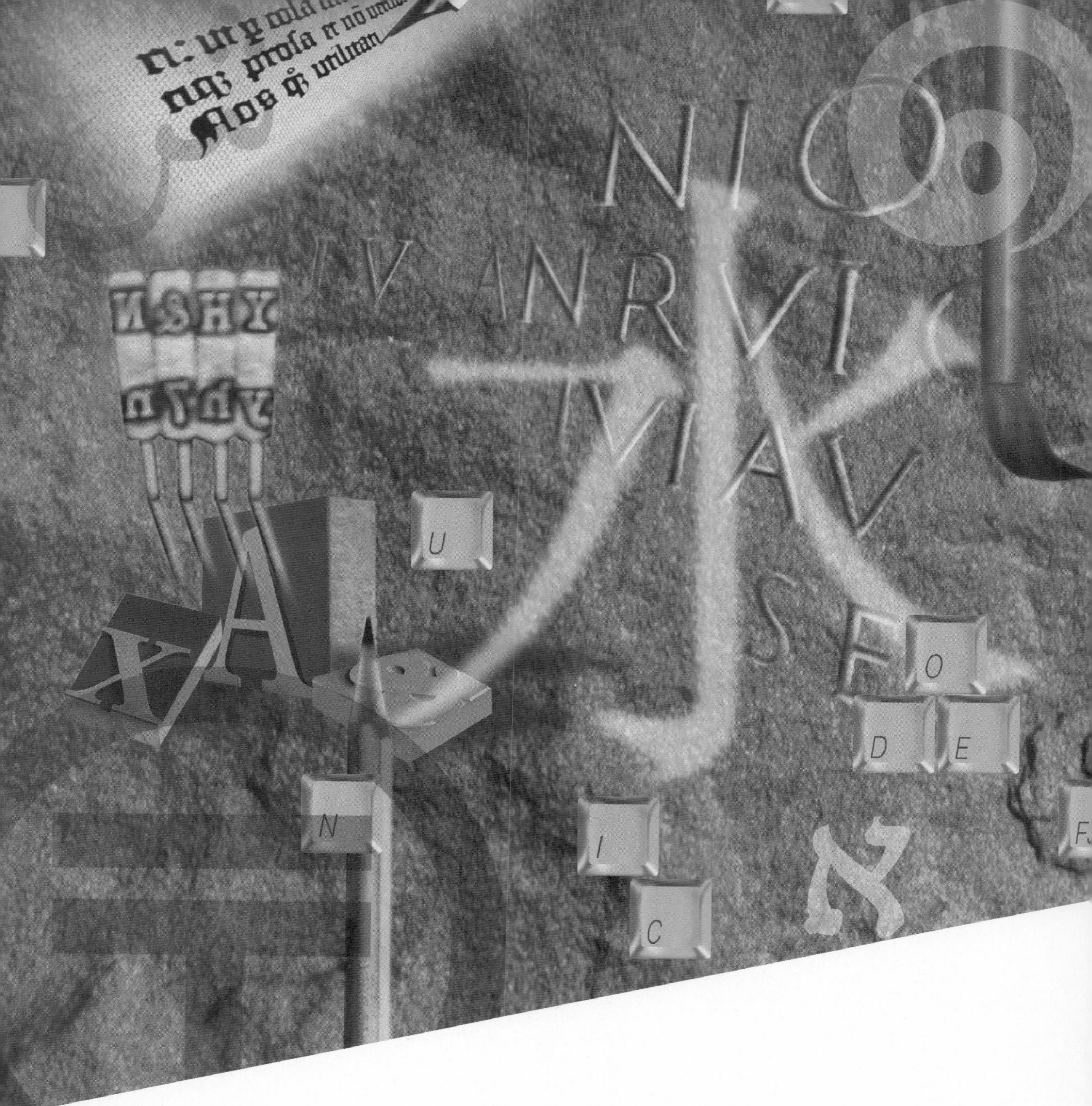

APPENDIX

D

Cumulative Changes

Appendix D

Cumulative Changes

D.1 Versions of the Unicode Standard

The Unicode Technical Committee has accepted changes to the Unicode Standard in order to maintain a single numerical encoding provided by the Unicode Standard and the standard ISO/IEC 10646-1:1993. There have been three formally numbered versions of the Unicode Standard, relating to versions of ISO 10646 as shown in Table D-1.

Table D-1. Versions of the Unicode Standard

Year	Version	Published	Content Relation to ISO 10646
1991	Unicode 1.0	Addison-Wesley	Basis of Draft-2 ISO 10646
1993	Unicode 1.1	Unicode Tech Report #4	Matches ISO 10646
1996	Unicode 2.0	Addison-Wesley	Matches ISO 10646 plus amendments

The Unicode Standard since version 1.1 has been kept in synch with ISO 10646 so that the two standards match precisely in character content and naming; the history of this relationship is given in *Appendix C, Relationship to ISO/IEC 10646*. This appendix enumerates the specific character content, name, and semantic changes made from Unicode Standard, Version 1.0 to Version 1.1 and from Version 1.1 to Version 2.0 to maintain alignment with ISO 10646.

D.2 Changes from Unicode 1.0 to 1.1

Areas Redefined

Private Use Area. In the Unicode Standard, Version 1.0, the Private Use Area ranged from U+E800 → U+FDFF (5,632 code positions). In the Unicode Standard, Version 1.1, this area was enlarged and shifted to the range U+E000 → U+F8FF (6,400 code positions).

Characters Removed

Four Greek letters were removed as part of a realignment of the Greek block; these case forms were judged inappropriate:

```
U+03DB  GREEK SMALL LETTER STIGMA
U+03DD  GREEK SMALL LETTER DIGAMMA
U+03DF  GREEK SMALL LETTER KOPPA
U+03E1  GREEK SMALL LETTER SAMPI
```

One Gurmukhi sign was removed:

```
U+0A3D  GURMUKHI SIGN AVAGRAHA
```

Five Thai phonetic order vowel signs were removed at the request of the Thai National Body as part of the ISO/IEC 10646 merger process in order to conduct further study on their utilization. Consequently, the alternate ordering described in the Unicode Standard, Version 1.0 no longer applies:

```
U+0E70  THAI PHONETIC ORDER VOWEL SIGN SARA E
U+0E71  THAI PHONETIC ORDER VOWEL SIGN SARA AE
U+0E72  THAI PHONETIC ORDER VOWEL SIGN SARA O
U+0E73  THAI PHONETIC ORDER VOWEL SIGN SARA MAI
           MUAN
U+0E74  THAI PHONETIC ORDER VOWEL SIGN SARA MAI
           MALAI
```

Five Lao phonetic order vowel signs were removed analogously with those in Thai:

```
U+0EF0  LAO PHONETIC ORDER VOWEL SIGN E
U+0EF1  LAO PHONETIC ORDER VOWEL SIGN EI
U+0EF2  LAO PHONETIC ORDER VOWEL SIGN O
U+0EF3  LAO PHONETIC ORDER VOWEL SIGN AY
U+0EF4  LAO PHONETIC ORDER VOWEL SIGN AI
```

The entire Tibetan block of the Unicode Standard, Version 1.0, comprising 71 assigned characters (U+1000 → U+105F), was removed for further study. (Tibetan has returned in the Unicode Standard, Version 2.0, occupying a reorganized block in the range U+0F00 → U+0FBF, see additions below.):

Two APL symbols were removed as part of a realignment of the APL group:

```
U+2300  APL COMPOSE OPERATOR[1]
U+2301  APL OUT
```

And note removal of a glyph shown by error in the Unicode Standard, Version 1.0 chart:

```
U+27B0  (never was a character)
```

Characters Unified

Three Greek letters were unified (that is, moved to merge with another existing character) as part of a realignment of the Greek block. Four Cyrillic letters were unified as being variants. One CJK punctuation symbol was unified as being an ideographic character. See Table D-2.

Table D-2. Characters Unified

From	To/With	1.0 Name
U+0371	U+0314	GREEK NON-SPACING DASIA PNEUMATA
U+0372	U+0313	GREEK NON-SPACING PSILI PNEUMATA
U+0384	U+030D	GREEK NON-SPACING TONOS[a]
U+04C5	U+049A	CYRILLIC CAPITAL LETTER KA OGONEK
U+04C6	U+049B	CYRILLIC SMALL LETTER KA OGONEK
U+04C9	U+04B2	CYRILLIC CAPITAL LETTER KHA OGONEK
U+04CA	U+04B3	CYRILLIC SMALL LETTER KHA OGONEK
U+3004	U+4EDD	IDEOGRAPHIC DITTO MARK[b]

a. This code has been assigned to a moved character, GREEK TONOS (renamed from GREEK SPACING TONOS).

b. This code has been assigned to a moved character, JAPANESE INDUSTRIAL STANDARD SYMBOL.

1. This code has been assigned to a new character, DIAMETER SIGN.

Characters Moved

Eight Greek characters were moved as part of a realignment of the Greek block. One Hebrew mark was moved to the Alphabetic Presentation Forms block. One Japanese symbol was moved. See Table D-3.

Table D-3. Characters Moved

From	To	1.0 Name
U+0370	U+0345	GREEK NON-SPACING IOTA BELOW
U+0385	U+0344	GREEK NON-SPACING DIAERESIS TONOS
U+03D7	U+037E	GREEK QUESTION MARK
U+03D8	U+0374	GREEK UPPER NUMERAL SIGN
U+03D9	U+0375	GREEK LOWER NUMERAL SIGN
U+03F3	U+0384	GREEK SPACING TONOS[a]
U+03F4	U+0385	GREEK SPACING DIAERESIS TONOS[b]
U+03F5	U+037A	GREEK SPACING IOTA BELOW
U+05F5	U+FB1E	HEBREW POINT VARIKA
U+32FF	U+3004	JAPANESE INDUSTRIAL STANDARD SYMBOL[c]

a. This replaces U+0384 GREEK NON-SPACING TONOS; the code U+03F3 has been assigned to a new character, GREEK LETTER YOT.

b. This replaces U+0385 GREEK NON-SPACING DIAERESIS TONOS; the code U+03F4 has been assigned to a moved character, GREEK DIALYTIKA TONOS (renamed from GREEK SPACING DIAERESIS TONOS).

c. This replaces U+3004 IDEOGRAPHIC DITTO MARK.

All 47 circled Katakana characters (U+32D0 → U+32FE) were reordered from I-RO-HA order to A-I-U-E-O order.

All 69 Arabic contextual-variant glyphs in the Arabic Presentation Forms-B block (U+FE8A → U+FEF4) were reordered from INITIAL-MEDIAL-FINAL order to FINAL-INITIAL-MEDIAL order.

Code Values Whose Assignment Has Changed

The information in Tables D-4 and D-5 is not additional to the previous categories; it can be derived from the foregoing. However, because of its importance it is presented here in summary form. These are all the code values for which the Unicode Standard, Version 1.0 and the Unicode Standard, Version 1.1 have *different characters* at the same codepoint.

Table D-4. Changed Assignments

Code	Unicode 1.0 Character	Unicode 1.1 Character
U+0384	GREEK NON-SPACING TONOS	GREEK TONOS
U+0385	GREEK NON-SPACING DIAERESIS TONOS	GREEK DIALYTIKA TONOS
U+03F3	GREEK SPACING TONOS	GREEK LETTER YOT
U+2300	APL COMPOSE OPERATOR	DIAMETER SIGN
U+3004	IDEOGRAPHIC DITTO MARK	JAPANESE INDUSTRIAL STANDARD SYMBOL

Table D-5. Reordered Character Groups

Code Range	Character Group
U+32D0 → U+32FE	Circled Katakana
U+FE8A → U+FEF4	Arabic contextual-variant glyphs

Apart from the 5 individual codepoints just enumerated plus two groups totaling 116 others, the following conclusion can be drawn: If the Unicode Standard, Version 1.0 and the

Unicode Standard, Version 1.1 both contain a given codepoint but the names attached to that codepoint differ, then this difference represents merely a *name change* for the same character assignment, not a differing character assignment.

New Characters Added

In the Unicode Standard, Version 1.1, a total of 4,306 Korean Hangul "Supplementary Syllables" plus 1,964 other items from drafts of ISO 10646 were annexed into code positions that had been unassigned in the Unicode Standard, Version 1.0. The Hangul supplementary syllables have since been removed in the Unicode Standard, Version 2.0; most of the remaining additions from the Unicode Standard, Version 1.0 to the Unicode Standard, Version 1.1 are presentation forms whose use as characters is discouraged in the Unicode Standard. These additions are listed below by the Unicode Standard, Version 2.0 block; in this listing, the relatively few additions that constitute substantive characters are enumerated explicitly.

In block Latin Extended-A, 1 additional precomposed diacritic combination.

In block Latin Extended-B, 35 additional precomposed diacritic combinations.

In block Combining Diacritical Marks, 6 additions:

```
U+0342  COMBINING GREEK PERISPOMENI
U+0343  COMBINING GREEK KORONIS
U+0344  COMBINING GREEK DIALYTIKA TONOS
U+0345  COMBINING GREEK YPOGEGRAMMENI
U+0360  COMBINING DOUBLE TILDE
U+0361  COMBINING DOUBLE INVERTED BREVE
```

In block Greek, 5 additions:

```
U+0374  GREEK NUMERAL SIGN
U+0375  GREEK LOWER NUMERAL SIGN
U+037A  GREEK YPOGEGRAMMENI
U+037E  GREEK QUESTION MARK
U+0387  GREEK ANO TELEIA
```

In block Cyrillic, 38 additional precomposed diacritic combinations.

In block Armenian, 1 additional ligature.

In block Arabic, 25 additions, largely Koranic reading symbols:

```
U+066D  ARABIC FIVE POINTED STAR
U+06D6  ARABIC SMALL HIGH LIGATURE SAD WITH LAM
            WITH ALEF MAKSURA
U+06D7  ARABIC SMALL HIGH LIGATURE QAF WITH LAM
            WITH ALEF MAKSURA
U+06D8  ARABIC SMALL HIGH MEEM INITIAL FORM
U+06D9  ARABIC SMALL HIGH LAM ALEF
U+06DA  ARABIC SMALL HIGH JEEM
U+06DB  ARABIC SMALL HIGH THREE DOTS
U+06DC  ARABIC SMALL HIGH SEEN
U+06DD  ARABIC END OF AYAH
U+06DE  ARABIC START OF RUB EL HIZB
U+06DF  ARABIC SMALL HIGH ROUNDED ZERO
U+06E0  ARABIC SMALL HIGH UPRIGHT RECTANGULAR
            ZERO
U+06E1  ARABIC SMALL HIGH DOTLESS HEAD OF KHAH
U+06E2  ARABIC SMALL HIGH MEEM ISOLATED FORM
U+06E3  ARABIC SMALL LOW SEEN
U+06E4  ARABIC SMALL HIGH MADDA
U+06E5  ARABIC SMALL WAW
```

```
U+06E6  ARABIC SMALL YEH
U+06E7  ARABIC SMALL HIGH YEH
U+06E8  ARABIC SMALL HIGH NOON
U+06E9  ARABIC PLACE OF SAJDAH
U+06EA  ARABIC EMPTY CENTRE LOW STOP
U+06EB  ARABIC EMPTY CENTRE HIGH STOP
U+06EC  ARABIC ROUNDED HIGH STOP WITH FILLED
           CENTRE
U+06ED  ARABIC SMALL LOW MEEM
```

In block Gurmukhi, 1 addition:

```
U+0A4D  GURMUKHI SIGN VIRAMA
```

In block Gujarati, 3 additions:

```
U+0A8D  GUJARATI VOWEL CANDRA E
U+0A91  GUJARATI VOWEL CANDRA O
U+0AC9  GUJARATI VOWEL SIGN CANDRA O
```

In block Oriya, 1 addition:

```
U+0B56  ORIYA AI LENGTH MARK
```

The whole block Hangul Jamo, comprising 240 additions.

The whole block Latin Extended Additional, comprising 245 additional precomposed diacritic combinations.

The whole block Greek Extended, comprising 233 additional precomposed diacritic combinations.

In block General Punctuation, 3 additions:

```
U+203F  UNDERTIE
U+2045  LEFT SQUARE BRACKET WITH QUILL
U+2046  RIGHT SQUARE BRACKET WITH QUILL
```

Also in block General Punctuation, 6 additional form-shaping controls.

In block Miscellaneous Technical, 9 additions:

```
U+232D  CYLINDRICITY
U+232E  ALL AROUND-PROFILE
U+232F  SYMMETRY
U+2330  TOTAL RUNOUT
U+2331  DIMENSION ORIGIN
U+2332  CONICAL TAPER
U+2333  SLOPE
U+2334  COUNTERBORE
U+2335  COUNTERSINK
```

Also in block Miscellaneous Technical, 69 additional precomposed APL functional symbols.

In block Geometric Shapes, 1 addition:

```
U+25EF  LARGE CIRCLE
```

In block CJK Symbols and Punctuation, 1 addition:

```
U+3037  IDEOGRAPHIC TELEGRAPH LINE FEED SEPARA-
           TOR SYMBOL
```

In block Katakana, 4 additions:

```
U+30F7  KATAKANA LETTER VA
U+30F8  KATAKANA LETTER VI
U+30F9  KATAKANA LETTER VE
U+30FA  KATAKANA LETTER VO
```

In block Enclosed CJK Letters and Months, 12 additional telegraph symbols for the months.

In block CJK Compatibility, 62 additions, mostly telegraph symbols.

The whole block Hangul Supplementary Syllables A, comprising 1,930 modern Korean Hangul syllables from the standard KS C 5659-1990—*removed in the Unicode Standard, Version 2.0.*

The whole block Hangul Supplementary Syllables B, comprising 2,376 old Korean Hangul syllables from the standard KS C 5657-1991—*removed in the Unicode Standard, Version 2.0.*

The whole block CJK Compatibility Ideographs, comprising 302 additional compatibility variants

The whole block Alphabetic Presentation Forms, comprising 57 additional presentation forms.

The whole block Arabic Presentation Forms-A, comprising 593 additional presentation forms.

The whole block Combining Half Marks, comprising 4 additional presentation forms

In block Halfwidth and Fullwidth Forms, 7 additional halfwidth forms.

Character Name Changes

Characters in the Unicode Standard and ISO 10646, except for CJK Ideographs and Hangul Syllables, are each given a unique name written in all uppercase, with at most a hyphen for punctuation. ISO 10646 names may also have appended a parenthesized comment, which are only informational. In the Unicode Standard, Version 1.1, the character names were adjusted to match the ISO 10646 names precisely. This involved changing the names of 1,890 characters, though in most cases the changes were only minor editorial variations.

The full list of editorial changes will not be enumerated here, as the full set of the Unicode Standard, Version 1.0 character names may be found on the Unicode CD-ROM as part of the *Unicode Character Database*. As was stated in the subsection "Code Values Whose Assignment Has Changed", only 5 individual codepoints, plus two groups totaling 116 others, actually changed in character assignment from the Unicode Standard, Version 1.0 to the Unicode Standard, Version 1.1. In all other cases where the names attached to a codepoint differ, this difference represents an editorial change in the character name.

A few comments may be added concerning the nature of the editorial name changes. Some changes apply mainly or solely to a single block while others are applied throughout the names list. For example, the Unicode Standard, Version 1.0 has "PERIOD" where the Unicode Standard, Version 1.1 has "FULL STOP", this change is made consistently in the whole names list, for example:

Code	1.0 Name	1.1 Name
002E	PERIOD	FULL STOP
0589	ARMENIAN PERIOD	ARMENIAN FULL STOP
06D4	ARABIC PERIOD	ARABIC FULL STOP
2488	DIGIT ONE PERIOD	DIGIT ONE FULL STOP

There are other cases of terminology change which apply to many characters but which do not map 100% systematically between the two versions. There are also some changes which are individual to particular single characters.

For reference, *Table D-6 1.1 Name Changes*, on page D-7 shows *all* the name differences, regardless of consistency, occurring within the first 256 codepoints:

Table D-6. 1.1 Name Changes

Code	Unicode 1.0	Unicode 1.1
0027	APOSTROPHE-QUOTE	APOSTROPHE
0028	OPENING PARENTHESIS	LEFT PARENTHESIS
0029	CLOSING PARENTHESIS	RIGHT PARENTHESIS
002E	PERIOD	FULL STOP
002F	SLASH	SOLIDUS
005B	OPENING SQUARE BRACKET	LEFT SQUARE BRACKET
005C	BACKSLASH	REVERSE SOLIDUS
005D	CLOSING SQUARE BRACKET	RIGHT SQUARE BRACKET
005E	SPACING CIRCUMFLEX	CIRCUMFLEX ACCENT
005F	SPACING UNDERSCORE	LOW LINE
0060	SPACING GRAVE	GRAVE ACCENT
007B	OPENING CURLY BRACKET	LEFT CURLY BRACKET
007C	VERTICAL BAR	VERTICAL LINE
007D	CLOSING CURLY BRACKET	RIGHT CURLY BRACKET
00A0	NON-BREAKING SPACE	NO-BREAK SPACE
00A6	BROKEN VERTICAL BAR	BROKEN BAR
00A8	SPACING DIAERESIS	DIAERESIS
00AB	LEFT POINTING GUILLEMET	LEFT-POINTING DOUBLE ANGLE QUOTATION MARK
00AE	REGISTERED TRADE MARK SIGN	REGISTERED SIGN
00AF	SPACING MACRON	MACRON
00B1	PLUS-OR-MINUS SIGN	PLUS-MINUS SIGN
00B2	SUPERSCRIPT DIGIT TWO	SUPERSCRIPT TWO
00B3	SUPERSCRIPT DIGIT THREE	SUPERSCRIPT THREE
00B4	SPACING ACUTE	ACUTE ACCENT
00B6	PARAGRAPH SIGN	PILCROW SIGN
00B8	SPACING CEDILLA	CEDILLA
00B9	SUPERSCRIPT DIGIT ONE	SUPERSCRIPT ONE
00BB	RIGHT POINTING GUILLEMET	RIGHT-POINTING DOUBLE ANGLE QUOTATION MARK
00BC	FRACTION ONE QUARTER	VULGAR FRACTION ONE QUARTER
00BD	FRACTION ONE HALF	VULGAR FRACTION ONE HALF
00BE	FRACTION THREE QUARTERS	VULGAR FRACTION THREE QUARTERS
Also note in particular:		
FEFF	BYTE ORDER MARK	ZERO WIDTH NO-BREAK SPACE

The character U+FEFF retains the semantics of *byte order mark*, but it has been renamed to ZERO WIDTH NON-BREAK SPACE and given additional semantics as described *Section 2.4, Special Character and Non-Character Values.*

Character Semantics Changes

Joiners no longer can be used to request use of ligatures, nor to request that they not be used. The *byte order mark* gained additional semantics, as noted earlier.

D.3 Changes from Unicode 1.1 to Unicode 2.0

No characters have been removed or unified from the Unicode Standard, Version 1.1 to the Unicode Standard, Version 2.0.

Areas Redefined

Surrogates Area. In the Unicode Standard, Version 2.0, the range U+D800 → U+DFFF is newly defined as the Surrogates Area (see *Chapter 6, Character Block Descriptions*).

Hangul Syllables Area. The the Unicode Standard, Version 1.0 Hangul Area (U+3400 → U+3D2D) and the the Unicode Standard, Version 1.1 Hangul Supplementary Syllables A and B areas (U+3D2E → U+4DFF) containing 4,306 Korean Hangul syllables have been removed. In their stead in the Unicode Standard, Version 2.0, the Hangul Syllables Area (U+AC00 → U+D7A3) containing 11,172 Korean Hangul syllables has been added.

Characters Moved

The redefinition of the Hangul Syllables Area resulted in the movement of previously-encoded Hangul Syllables to the new area. No other characters have been moved in the transition from the Unicode Standard, Version 1.1 to the Unicode Standard, Version 2.0.

New Characters Added

The redefinition of the Hangul Syllables Area resulted in the addition of Hangul Syllables to the new area to complete the modern 11,172 Korean Hangul Syllable set.

In the Unicode Standard, Version 2.0, an additional 201 items also included in amendments to ISO 10646 were annexed into code positions that had been unassigned in the Unicode Standard, Version 1.1. These additions are listed below by block.

In the Hebrew block, 31 additional cantillation marks:

U+0591 → U+05AF
U+05C4 HEBREW MARK UPPER DOT

The whole Tibetan block, comprising 168 additions:

U+0F00 → U+0FBF

In the Latin Extended Additional block, 1 additional precomposed character:

U+1E9B LATIN SMALL LETTER LONG S WITH DOT ABOVE

In block Currency Symbols, 1 addition from Vietnam:

U+20AB DONG SIGN

Character Name Changes

LIGATURE was changed to LETTER in these 6 names:

Table D-7. 2.0 Name Changes

Code	Unicode 1.1	Unicode 2.0
00C6	LATIN CAPITAL LIGATURE AE	LATIN CAPITAL LETTER AE
00E6	LATIN SMALL LIGATURE AE	LATIN SMALL LETTER AE
01E2	LATIN CAPITAL LIGATURE AE WITH MACRON	LATIN CAPITAL LETTER AE WITH MACRON
01E3	LATIN SMALL LIGATURE AE WITH MACRON	LATIN SMALL LETTER AE WITH MACRON
01FC	LATIN CAPITAL LIGATURE AE WITH ACUTE	LATIN CAPITAL LETTER AE WITH ACUTE
01FD	LATIN SMALL LIGATURE AE WITH ACUTE	LATIN SMALL LETTER AE WITH ACUTE

ISO/IEC JTC1/SC2/WG2 and the Unicode Technical Committee have resolved that there shall be no further character name changes in the future.

Character Semantics Changes

The order of joiner characters used for Indic half-forms changed.

The Unicode Standard, Version 1.1 *Appendix G, Symmetric Swapping* became the normative property *mirrored.* See *Section 4.7, Mirrored.* See also ISO/IEC 10646, Annex C (Informative).

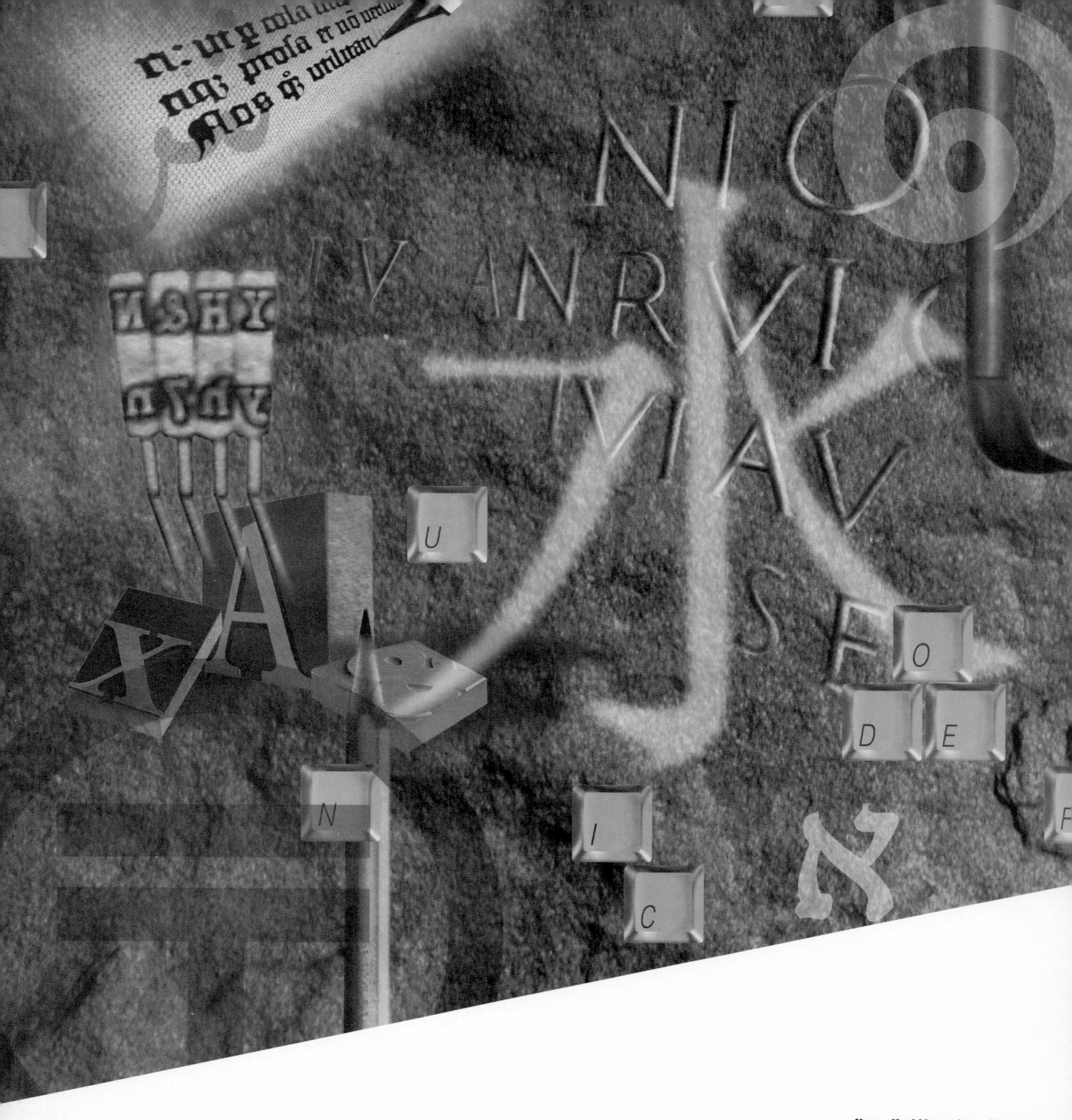

Han Unification History

APPENDIX E

Appendix E

Han Unification History

Efforts to create a unified Han character encoding are at least as venerable as the existing national standards. The Chinese Character Code for Information Interchange (CCCII) developed in Taiwan has been in use since 1980. It contains characters for use in China, Taiwan, and Japan. In somewhat modified form, it has been adopted for use in the United states as ANSI Z39.64-1989, also known as the East Asian Character Code (EACC) for bibliographic use. In 1981, Takahashi Tokutaro of Japan's National Diet Library proposed standardization of a character set for common use among East Asian countries.

The Unicode Han character set began with a project to create a Han character cross-reference database at Xerox in 1986. In 1988, a parallel effort began at Apple based on the Research Libraries Information Network's CJK Thesaurus, which is used to maintain EACC. The merger of the Apple and Xerox databases in 1989 led to the first draft of the Unicode Han character set. At the September, 1989 meeting of X3L2 (an accredited standards committee for codes and character sets operating under the procedures of the American National Standards Institute), the Unicode Working Group proposed this set for inclusion in ISO 10646.

The primary difference between the Unicode Han character repertoire and earlier efforts was that the Unicode Han character set extended the bibliographic sets to guarantee complete coverage of industry and newer national standards. The unification criteria employed in this original Unicode Han character repertoire were based on rules used by JIS and on a set of Han character identity principles (*rentong yuanze*) being developed in China by experts working with the Association for a Common Chinese Code (ACCC). An important principle was to preserve all character distinctions within existing and proposed national and industry standards.

The Unicode Han proposal stimulated interest in a unified Han set for inclusion in ISO 10646, which led to the first ISO *ad hoc* meeting to discuss the issue of unification, held in Beijing in October 1989. The October 1989 meeting was the beginning of informal cooperation between the Unicode Working Group and the ACCC to exchange information on each group's proposals for Han unification.

A second ISO *ad hoc* meeting on Han Unification was held in Seoul in February 1990. At this meeting, the Korean delegation proposed the establishment of a group composed of the East Asian countries and other interested organizations to study a unified Han encoding. From this informal meeting emerged the Chinese/Japanese/Korean Joint Research Group (hereafter referred to as the CJK-JRG).

A second draft of the Unicode Han character repertoire was sent out for widespread review in December 1990 to coincide with the announcement of the formation of the Unicode Consortium. The December 1990 draft of the Unicode Han character set differed from the first in that it used the principle of *KangXi* radical/stroke ordering of the characters. In order to verify independently the soundness and accuracy of the unification, the Consortium arranged to have this draft reviewed in detail by East Asian scholars at the University of Toronto.

In the meantime, China announced that it was about to complete its own proposal for a Han Character Set, GB 13000. Concluding that the two drafts were similar in content and philosophy, the Unicode Consortium and the Center for Computer and Information Development Research, Ministry of Machinery and Electronic Industry (CCID, China's computer standards body) agreed to merge the two efforts into a single proposal. Each added missing characters from the other set and agreed upon a method for ordering the characters using the four-dictionary ordering scheme described in *Section 6.4, CJK Ideographs Area*. Both proposals benefited greatly from programmatic comparisons of the two databases.

As a result of the agreement to merge the Unicode Standard and ISO 10646, the Unicode Consortium agreed to adopt the unified Han character repertoire that was to be developed by the CJK-JRG.

The first CJK-JRG meeting was held in Tokyo, in July 1991. The group recognized that there was a compelling requirement for unification of the existing CJK ideographic characters into one coherent coding standard. Two basic decisions were made: to use GB 13000 (previously merged with the Unicode Han repertoire) as the basis for what would be termed "The Unified Repertoire and Ordering," and to verify the unification results based on rules that had been developed by professor Miyazawa Akira and other members of the Japanese delegation.

The formal review of GB 13000 began immediately. Subsequent meetings were held in Beijing and Hong Kong. On March 27, 1992 the CJK-JRG completed the *Unified Repertoire and Ordering* (URO), *Version 2.0*. This repertoire was subsequently published both by the Unicode Consortium in The Unicode Standard, Version 1.0, Volume 2 and by ISO in ISO/IEC 10646-1:1993.

In October 1993, the CJK-JRG became a formal subgroup of ISO/IEC JTC1/SC2/WG2 and was renamed to the Ideographic Rapporteur Group (IRG). The IRG now has the formal responsibility of developing extensions to the URO 2.0 in order to expand the encoded repertoire of unified CJK ideographs. The Unicode Consortium particpates in this group as a liaison member of ISO.

In its second meeting in Hanoi in February 1994, the IRG agreed to include Vietnamese Chữ Nôm ideographs in a future version of the URO and to add a fifth reference dictionary to the ordering scheme.

At the present time (November, 1995), the IRG is considering a total of 21,252 additional CJKV ideographs submitted by China, Japan, Korea, Taiwan, and Vietnam as extensions to the URO 2.0. The actual number of new ideographs to be added to the URO is expected to be smaller than this number once the unification process has been performed on these additions. The actual encoded positions of any extensions will be determined by ISO SC2/WG2, and not by the IRG.

GLOSSARY

Glossary

Abstract Character. A unit of information used for the organization, control, or representation of textual data. (See also *character* (1, 2) and *surrogate pair.*)

Accent mark. A mark placed above, below, or to the side of a character to alter its phonetic value. (See also *diacritic.*)

Alphabet. A collection of symbols which, in the context of a particular written language, represent the sounds of that language. The correspondence between symbols and sounds may be either more or less exact; most alphabets do not exhibit a one-to-one correspondence between distinct sounds (phonemes) and distinct symbols (graphemes).

ANSI. (1) The American National Standards Institute. (2) The Microsoft collective name for all the Windows code pages. Sometimes used specifically for code page 1252, which is a superset of ISO/IEC 8859-1.

Arabic Digits. Forms of decimal digits used in most parts of the Arabic world (for instance, U+0660 ٠ , U+0661 ١ , U+0662 ٢ , U+0663 ٣). Although European digits derive historically from these forms, they are visually distinct and are coded separately. (Arabic digits are sometimes called Indic numerals; however, this leads to confusion with the digits currently used with the scripts of India.) Arabic digits are referred to as *Arabic-Indic digits* in the Unicode Standard.

Area. An organizational unit of the Unicode Standard larger than the *block.* The areas are enumerated in *Chapter 2, General Structure,* and are further described in *Chapter 6, Character Block Descriptions.*

ASCII. Acronym for American Standard Code for Information Interchange, a 7-bit code that is the US national variant of ISO/IEC 646. Formally, the U.S. standard ANSI X3.4.

Base Character. A character that does not graphically combine with preceding characters.

BIDI. Abbreviation of bidirectional, in reference to mixed left-to-right and right-to-left text.

Bidirectional Display. The process or result of mixing left-to-right oriented text and right-to-left oriented text in a single line.

Big-endian. A computer architecture that stores multiple-byte numerical values with the most significant byte (MSB) values first.

Binary Files. Files containing non-textual information.

Block. A grouping of related characters within the Unicode encoding space. A block may contain unassigned positions, which are reserved.

BOM. Acronym for *byte order mark.* The Unicode character U+FEFF ZERO WIDTH NO-BREAK SPACE is used to indicate the byte order of a text. The BOM allows a receiver of Unicode text to distinguish between text arriving in big-endian order from text arriving in little-endian order *in the absence of a higher level protocol.* (See *Chapter 5, Implementation Guidelines* and the Specials subsection in *Section 6.8, Compatibility Area and Specials.*)

Bopomofo. An alphabetic script used primarily in the Republic of China (Taiwan) to write the sounds of Mandarin Chinese. Each symbol corresponds to either the syllable initial or syllable final sounds; it is therefore a sub-syllabic script in its primary usage. The name is derived from the names of its first four elements. More properly known as *zhuyin zimu* or *zhuyin fuhao* (in Mandarin Chinese).

Canonical. (1) Conforming to the general rules for encoding, that is, not compressed, compacted, or in any other form specified by a higher protocol. (2) Characteristic of a normative mapping and form of equivalence specified in the Conformance chapter of this standard.

Canonical Decomposition. The decomposition of a character which results from applying canonical mappings and then reordering non-spacing marks according to the Canonical Ordering Algorithm. (See *Chapter 3, Conformance.*)

Canonical Equivalent. Two character sequences are said to be canonical equivalents if their canonical decompositions are identical. (See *Chapter 3, Conformance.*)

Cantillation Mark. A mark that is used to indicate how a text is to be chanted or sung.

Character. (1) The smallest component of written language that has semantic value; refers to the abstract meaning and/or shape, rather than a specific shape (see also *glyph*), though in code tables some form of visual representation is essential for the reader's understanding. (2) Synonym for *abstract character.* (3) Loosely, the basic unit of encoding for the Unicode character encoding, a 16-bit unit of textual information. (4) Synonym for *code value.* (5) The English name for the ideographic written elements of Chinese origin. (See *ideograph (2).*)

Character Properties. An unordered list of property names and property values associated with individual character code elements. (See *Chapter 4, Character Properties.*)

Character Repertoire. (See *repertoire.*)

CJK. Abbreviation for Chinese, Japanese, and Korean.

Character Set. A collection of elements used to represent textual information.

Chữ Hán. The name for Han characters used in Vietnam; derived from Hanzi.

Chữ Nôm. A demotic script of Vietnam developed from components of Han characters. Its creators used methods similar to those used by the Chinese in creating Han characters.

Code Element. (See *code point.*)

Code Page. A coded character set, often referring to a coded character set used by a personal computer; for example, PC code page 437, the default coded character set used by the U.S. English version of the DOS operating system.

Code Point. (1) A numerical index (or position) in an encoding table used for encoding characters. (2) Synonym for *code value.*

Code Space. A range of numerical values available for encoding characters.

Code Value. A minimal bit combination that can represent a unit of encoded text for processing or interchange. Also known as *code point.*

Coded Character Representation. An ordered sequence of one or more code values associated with an abstract character in a given character repertoire. (See *Chapter 3, Conformance.*)

Coded Character Set. A character set in which each character is assigned a numeric code value. Frequently abbreviated as *character set, charset* or *code set.*

Collation. The process of ordering units of textual information. Collation is usually specific to a particular language. Also known as *alphabetizing* or *alphabetic sorting.*

Combining Character. A character that graphically combines with a preceding base character. (See also *non-spacing mark.*)

Combining Character Sequence. A character sequence consisting of a base character followed by one or more combining characters. Also called *composed character sequence.*

Compatibility. (1) Consistency with existing practice or pre-existing character encoding standards. (2) Characteristic of a normative mapping and form of equivalence specified in the Conformance chapter of this standard.

Compatibility Area. An area of the Unicode Standard, which contains characters included only for compatibility with pre-existing character encoding standards.

Compatibility Character. (1) A character encoded only for compatibility. (2) A character which has a compatibility decomposition.

Compatibility Decomposition. The decomposition of a character which results from applying the compatibility mappings and then reordering non-spacing marks according to the Canonical Ordering Algorithm. (See *Chapter 3, Conformance.*)

Compatibility Equivalent. Two character sequences are said to be compatibility equivalents if their compatibility decompositions are identical.

Composite Character. (See *decomposable character.*)

Conjunct Form. A type of ligature that appears in most scripts based on the Brahmi family of Indic scripts. (See the Devanagari character block description.)

Contextual Variant. A text element can have a presentation form that depends upon textual context in which it is rendered. This presentation form is known as a *contextual variant.*

DBCS. Abbreviation for double-byte character set.

Dead Consonant. An Indic consonant character followed by a *virama* character. This sequence indicates that the consonant has lost its inherent vowel. (See the Devanagari character block description.)

Decomposable Character. A character that is equivalent to a sequence of one or more other characters. Also known as a *precomposed character* or a *composite character.*

Decomposition. (1) The process of separating or analyzing a text element into component units. These component units may not have any functional status, but may be simply formal units, that is, abstract shapes. (2) A sequence of one or more characters that is equivalent to a decomposable character. (See *decomposable character* and *Chapter 3, Conformance.*)

Demotic Script. (1) A script or a form of a script used to write the vernacular or common speech of some language community. (2) A simplified form of the ancient Egyptian hieratic writing. (See cover.)

Dependent Vowel. A symbol or sign that represents a vowel and which is attached or combined with another symbol, usually one that represents a consonant. For example, in writing systems based on Arabic, Hebrew, and Indic scripts, vowels are normally represented as dependent vowel signs.

Diacritic. (1) A mark applied or attached to a symbol in order to create a new symbol that represents an modified or new value. (2) A mark applied to a symbol irrespective of whether it changes the value of that symbol. In the latter case, the diacritic usually represents an independent value (for example, an accent, tone, or some other linguistic information). Also called *diacritical mark* or *diacritical.* (See also *combining character* and *non-spacing mark.*)

Diaeresis. Two horizontal dots over a letter, as in *naïve.* The same Unicode character is used to represent the *umlaut.* (See *umlaut.*)

Digits. (See *Arabic digits, European digits,* and *Indic digits.*)

Digraph. A pair of signs or symbols (two graphs), which together represent a single sound or a single linguistic unit. The English writing system employs many digraphs (for example, *th, ch, sh, qu,* and so on). The same two symbols may not always be interpreted as a digraph (for example, *cathode* versus *cathouse*). When three signs are so combined, they are called a *trigraph.* More than three are usually called an *n-graph.*

Diphthong. A pair of vowels that are considered a single vowel for the purpose of phonemic distinction. One of the two vowels is more prominent than the other. In writing systems, diphthongs are sometimes written with one symbol, and sometimes with more than one symbol (for example, with a *digraph*).

Directionality. A property of every graphic character that determines its horizontal ordering as specified in the Unicode Bidirectional Algorithm. (See *Chapter 3, Conformance.*)

Display Cell. A rectangular region on a display device within which one or more glyphs are imaged.

Double-Byte Character Set. One of a number of character sets defined for representing Chinese, Japanese, or Korean text (for example, JIS X 0208-1990). These character sets are often encoded in such a way as to allow double-byte character encodings to be mixed with single-byte character encodings. Abbreviated DBCS. (See also multi-byte character set.)

Ductility. The ability of a cursive font to stretch or compress the connective baseline to effect text justification.

Encapsulated Text. (1) Plain text surrounded by formatting information. (2) Text recoded to pass through narrow transmission channels or to match communication protocols.

Equivalence. In the context of text processing, the process or result of establishing whether two text elements are identical in some respect.

European Digits. Forms of decimal digits first used in Europe and now used worldwide. Historically, these derive from the Arabic digits; they are sometimes called Arabic numerals, but this leads to confusion with the real Arabic digits.

Fancy Text. Also known as *rich text.* The result of adding additional information to plain text. Examples of information that can be added include font data, color, formatting information, phonetic annotations, interlinear text, and so on. The Unicode Standard does not address the representation of fancy text. It is expected that systems and applications will implement proprietary forms of fancy text. Some public forms of fancy text are available (for example, ODA, HTML, and SGML). When everything but primary content is removed from fancy text, only plain text should remain.

Floating (diacritic, accent, mark). (See *non-spacing mark.*)

Font. A collection of glyphs used for the visual depiction of character data. A font is often associated with a set of parameters(for example, size, posture, weight, and serifness), which, when set to particular values, generate a collection of imagable glyphs.

Formatted Text. (See *fancy text.*)

Formatting Codes. Characters that are inherently invisible but which have an effect on the surrounding characters. An example is U+206E NATIONAL DIGIT SHAPES.

GCGID. Acronym for Graphic Character Global Identifier. These are listed in the IBM document *Character Data Representation Architecture, Level 1, Registry SC09-1391.*

Glyph. (1) An abstract form that represents one or more glyph images. (2) A synonym for *glyph image.* In displaying Unicode character data, one or more glyphs may be selected to depict a particular character. These glyphs are selected by a rendering engine during composition and layout processing. (See also *character.*)

Glyph Code. A code value that refers to a glyph. Usually, the glyphs contained in a font are referenced by their glyph code. Glyph codes may be local to a particular font; that is, a different font containing the same glyphs may use different codes.

Glyph Identifier. Similar to a glyph code, a glyph identifier is a label used to refer to a glyph within a font. A font may employ both local and global glyph identifiers. A collection of global or universal glyph identifiers is defined by the Association for Font Information and Interchange (AFII).

Glyph Image. The actual, concrete image of a glyph representation having been rasterized or otherwise imaged onto some display surface.

Glyph Metrics. A collection of properties that specify the relative size and positioning along with other features of a glyph.

Grapheme. A minimally distinctive unit of writing in the context of a particular writing system. For example, ‹b› and ‹d› are distinct graphemes in English writing systems since there exist distinct words like big and dig. Conversely, ‹*a*› and ‹a› are not distinct graphemes since no word is distinguished on the basis of these two different forms. A grapheme is for a writing system what a phoneme is for a phonology.

Graphic Character. (1) A character typically associated with a visible display representation. (See also *glyph.*) (2) Any character that is not primarily associated with a control or formatting function.

Halant. A synonym for the *virama* character. It literally means *killer,* referring to its function of *killing* the inherent vowel of a consonant letter. (See *virama.*)

Half-form Consonant. In the Devanagari script, and certain other scripts of the Brahmi family of Indic scripts, a dead consonant may be depicted in the so-called half-form. This form is composed of the distinctive part of a consonant letter symbol without its vertical stem. It may be used to create conjunct forms that follow a horizontal layout pattern.

Han Character. Ideographic characters of Chinese origin.

Han Unification. The process of identifying Han characters that are in common among the writing systems of Chinese, Japanese, Korean, and Vietnamese.

Hangul. The name of the script used to write the Korean language.

Hanja. The name for Han characters used in Korean; derived from the Chinese word hanzi.

Hankaku. Japanese for *halfwidth*; refers to glyph images designed to fit half the display space of a Han character.

Hanzi. The Chinese name for Han characters. The Han script was first codified during the Han dynasty (in the 3rd century BC). The name hanzi is derived from two Han characters, signifying Han (that is, "Chinese") and character respectively.

Hiragana. One of two standard syllabaries associated with the Japanese writing system. Hiragana syllables are typically used in representation of native Japanese words and grammatical particles.

Ideograph. (1) Any symbol that primarily denotes an idea (or meaning) in contrast to a sound (or pronunciation); for example, ☎ and ♥. (2) A common term used to refer to Han characters.

Independent Vowel. In Indic scripts, certain vowels are depicted using independent letter symbols that stand on their own. This is often true when a word starts with a vowel or a word consists only of a vowel.

Indic Digits. Forms of decimal digits used in various Indic scripts (for example, Devanagari: U+0966 ०, U+0967 १, U+0968 २, U+0969 ३). Arabic digits (and, eventually, European digits) derive historically from these forms.

Informative. Information in this standard that is not normative but which contributes to the correct use and implementation of the standard.

Inherent Vowel. In writing systems based on a script in the Brahmi family of Indic scripts, a consonant letter symbol normally has an inherent vowel, unless otherwise indicated. The phonetic value of this vowel differs among the various languages written with these writing systems. An inherent vowel is overridden either by indicating another vowel with an explicit vowel sign or by using *virama* to create a dead consonant.

ISCII. (1) Indian Standard Code for Information Interchange. (2) Iranian Standard Code for Information Interchange

Jamo. The Korean name for a single letter of the Hangul script. Jamo are used to form Hangul syllables.

Joiner. An invisible character that affects the joining behavior of surrounding characters. (See the General Punctuation character block description.)

Kana. The name of a primarily syllabic script used by the Japanese writing system. It comes in two forms, *hiragana* and *katakana.* The former is used to write particles, grammatical affixes, and words which have no *kanji* form; the latter is used primarily to write foreign words.

Kanji. The name for Han characters used in Japanese; derived from the Chinese word hanzi. Also romanized as *kanzi.*

Katakana. One of two standard syllabaries associated with the Japanese writing system. Katakana syllables are typically used in representation of borrowed vocabulary (other than that of Chinese origin), sound-symbolic interjections, or phonetic representation of "difficult" kanji characters in Japanese.

Letter. An element of an alphabet. In a broad sense, includes elements of syllabaries and ideographs.

Ligature. A glyph representing a combination of two or more characters. In the Latin script, there are only a few in modern use, such as the ligatures between "f" and "i" (= ﬁ) or "f" and "l" (= ﬂ). Other scripts make use of many ligatures, depending on the font and style.

Little-endian. A computer architecture that stores multiple-byte numerical values with the least significant byte (LSB) values first.

Logical Order. The order in which text is typed on a keyboard. For the most part, logical order corresponds to phonetic order. (For more information, see *Chapter 2, General Structure.*)

LSB. Abbreviation for *least significant byte.*

LZW. Abbreviation for *Lempel-Ziv-Welch,* a standard algorithm widely used for compression of data.

Mirrored. A property of characters whose images are mirrored horizontally in text that is laid out from right to left (versus left to right). (See *Chapter 3, Conformance.*)

MSB. Abbreviation for *most significant byte.*

Multi-Byte Character Set. A character set encoded with a variable number of bytes per character. Many large character sets have been defined as MBCS in order to keep strict compatibility with the ASCII subset and/or ISO/IEC 2022. Abbreviated as MBCS.

Neutral character. A character that can be written either right-to-left or left-to-right, depending on context.

Non-Joiner. An invisible character that affects the joining behavior of surrounding characters. (See the General Punctuation character block description.)

Non-spacing Diacritic. A diacritic that is a non-spacing mark.

Non-spacing Mark. A combining character whose positioning in presentation is dependent on its base character. A non-spacing mark generally does not consume space along the visual baseline in and of itself. (See also *combining character.*)

Normative. Required for conformance with the Unicode Standard.

NSM. Abbreviation for *non-spacing mark.*

Phoneme. A minimally distinct sound in the context of a particular spoken language. For example, in American English, /p/ and /b/ are distinct phonemes because pat and bat are distinct; however, the two different sounds of /t/ in tick and stick are not distinct in English, even though they are distinct in other languages such as in Thai.

Plain Text. Computer encoded text that consists *only* of a sequence of code elements from a given standard, with no other formatting or structural information. Plain text interchange is commonly used between computer systems that do not share higher level protocols. (See also *fancy text.*)

Points. (1)The non-spacing vowels and other signs of written Hebrew. (2) A unit of measurement in typography.

Precomposed Character. (See *decomposable character.*)

Presentation Form. A ligature or variant glyph which has been encoded as a character for compatibility. (See also *compatibility character.*)

Private Use. Refers to code values and areas of the standard whose interpretation is not specified by the standard and whose use may be determined by private agreement among cooperating users.

Property. (See *character properties.*)

Radical. A structural component of a Han character conventionally used for indexing. The traditional number of such radicals is 214.

Rendering. (1) The process of selecting and laying out glyphs for the purpose of depicting characters. (2) The process of making glyphs visible on a display device.

Repertoire. The collection of characters included in a character set.

Replacement Character. Character used as a substitute for an uninterpretable character from another encoding. The Unicode Standard uses U+FFFD REPLACEMENT CHARACTER for this function.

Replacement Glyph. A glyph used to render a character that cannot be rendered with the correct appearance in a particular font. It often is shown as an open ❑ or black ▮ rectangle. Also known as a *missing glyph.* (See *Section 5.4, Unknown and Missing Characters.*)

Rich Text. (See *fancy text.*)

SBCS. Acronym for *single byte character set.* Any 1-byte character encoding. This term is generally used in contrast with DBCS and/or MBCS.

Script. A collection of symbols used to represent textual information in one or more writing systems.

Spacing Mark. A combining character that is not a non-spacing mark. (See *non-spacing mark.*)

Surrogate, High. A Unicode code value in the range U+D800 through U+DBFF.

Surrogate, Low. A Unicode code value in the range U+DC00 through U+DFFF.

Surrogate Pair. A coded character representation for a single abstract character that consists of a sequence of two Unicode values, where the first value of the pair is a high-surrogate and the second is a low-surrogate.

Syllabary. An alphabet whose symbols typically represent multiple phonemes of a language. These multiple phonemes are generally combinations of consonants and vowels.

Syllable. (1) An element of a syllabary. (2) A basic unit of articulation that corresponds to a pulmonary pulse.

Symmetric Swapping. (See *mirrored.*)

Text Element. A minimum unit of text in relation to a particular text process, in the context of a particular writing system. In general, the mapping between text elements and code elements is many-to-many. (See *Chapter 2, General Structure.*)

Titlecase. Uppercased initial letters followed by lowercase letters in words. A casing convention often used in titles, headers, and entries, as exemplified in this glossary.

Tone Mark. A diacritic or non-spacing mark that represents a phonemic tone. Tone languages are common in Southeast Asia and Africa. Since tones always accompany vowels (the syllabic nucleus), they are most frequently written using functionally independent marks attached to a vowel symbol. However, some writing systems such as Thai place tone marks on consonant symbols; Chinese does not use tone marks (except when it is written phonemically).

UCS-2. ISO/IEC 10646 encoding form: Universal Character Set coded in 2 octets. (See *Appendix C, Relationship to ISO/IEC 10646.)*

UCS-4. ISO/IEC 10646 encoding form: Universal Character Set coded in 4 octets. (See *Appendix C, Relationship to ISO/IEC 10646.)*

Umlaut. Two horizontal dots over a letter, as in German *Köpfe.* The same Unicode character is used to represent the *diaeresis.* (See *diaeresis.*)

Unification. The process of identifying characters that are in common among writing systems.

UTF-7. Unicode (or UCS) Transformation Format, 7-bit form. (See *Appendix A, Transformation Formats.*)

UTF-8. Unicode (or UCS) Transformation Format, 8-bit form. (See *Appendix A, Transformation Formats.*)

UTF-16. The ISO/IEC 10646 encoding that is equivalent to the Unicode Standard with the use of surrogates as described in *Section 3.7, Surrogates.* (See also *Appendix C, Relationship to ISO/IEC 10646.)*

Virama. The name of a symbol used with Indic scripts to indicate a dead consonant. (See the Devanagari and Tamil character block descriptions.)

Vowel Sign. In many scripts, a mark used to indicate a vowel or vowel quality.

wchar_t. The ANSI C defined *wide character* type, usually implemented as either 16 or 32 bits. ANSI specifies that `wchar_t` be an integral type and that the C language source character set be mappable by simple extension (zero- or sign-extension).

Writing Direction. The direction or orientation of writing characters within lines of text in a writing system. Three directions are common in modern writing systems: left to right, right to left, and top to bottom.

Writing System. A set of rules for using one or more scripts to write a particular language. Examples include the American English writing system, the British English writing system, the French writing system, and the Japanese writing system.

Written Language. A non-oral form of language. A writing system is the means by which a language is written.

Zenkaku. Japanese for *fullwidth*; refers to glyph images designed to fit the same display space as a Han character.

Zero Width. Characteristic of some spaces or format control characters that do not advance text along the horizontal baseline. (See *non-spacing mark.*)

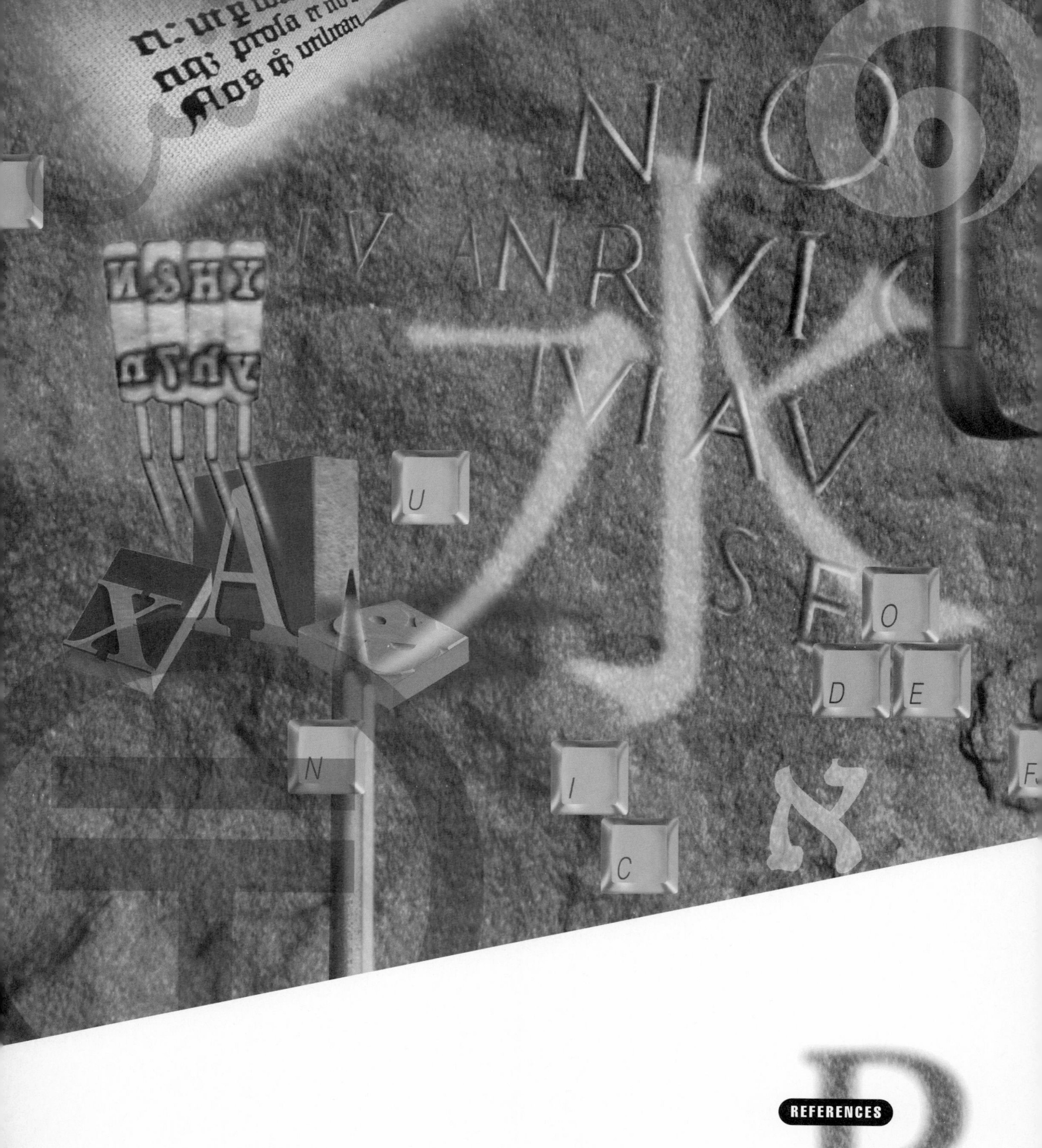

REFERENCES

References

Citations are given for the standards and dictionaries that were used as resources for *The Unicode Standard*, primarily for Version 1.0. A revised or reaffirmed version, with a different date, may have been published subsequently. Where a Draft International Standard is known to have progressed to International Standard status, the entry for the DIS has been revised.

In *Selected Resources,* the latest known edition is cited.

In general, American library practice has been followed for the romanization of titles and names written in non-Roman script. Exceptions are the use of *Pinyin* for Chinese, and when the rendering supplied by an author had to be used because the name or title in the original script was unavailable.

Due to the pending publication of many ISO standards, references to these standards as "ISO" or "ISO/IEC" standards is in flux. Citations below and in the rest of this standard represent the best information readily available at the time of publication.

R.1 Source Standards

ANSI X3.4: American National Standards Institute. *Coded character set—7-bit American national standard code for information interchange.* New York, 1986. (ANSI X3.4 - 1986).

ANSI X3.32: American National Standards Institute. *American national standard graphic representation of the control characters of American national standard code for information interchange.* New York, 1973. (ANSI X3.32-1973).

ANSI Y10.20: American National Standards Institute. *Mathematic signs and symbols for use in physical sciences and technology.* New York, 1988. (ANSI Y10.20 - 1975 (R1988)).

ANSI Z39.47: American National Standards Institute. *Extended Latin alphabet coded character set for bibliographic use.* New York, 1985. (ANSI Z39.47 - 1985).

ANSI Z39.64: American National Standards Institute. *East Asian character code for bibliographic use.* New Brunswick, Transaction, 1991. (ANSI Z39.64 - 1989).

ASMO 449: Arab Organization for Standardization and Metrology. *Data processing 7-bit coded character set for information interchange.* [s.l.], 1983. (Arab standard specifications; 449-1982). Authorized English translation.

CCCII: *Zhongwen Zixun Jiaohuanma (Chinese Character Code for Information Interchange).* Revised edition. Taipei, Xingzhengyuan Wenhua Jianshe Xiaozu (Executive Yuan Committee for Cultural Construction), 1985.

Alternative romanization of title: *Chung wen tzu hsün chiao huan ma.*

CNS 11643: *Tongyong hanzi biaozhun jiaohuanma (Han Character Standard Interchange Code for General Use).* Taipei, Xingzhengyuan (Executive Yuan), 1986.

ECMA Registry: (*See* ISO Register.)

GB 2312: *Code of Chinese Graphic Character Set for Information Interchange, Primary Set.* Beijing, Jishu Biaozhun Chubanshe (Technical Standards Press), 1981. (GB 2312 - 1980).

GB 13000: Information Technology—Universal Multiple-Octet Coded Character Set (UCS)—Part 1: Architecture and Basic Multilingual Plane. Beijing, 1993. (GB 13000.1-93) (ISO/IEC 10646.1-1993).

ISCII: India Department of Electronics. *Indian standard code for information interchange.* New Delhi, 1988.

ISO Register: International Organization for Standardization. *ISO international register of character sets to be used with escape sequences.* [Geneva], 1990.

ISO/IEC 646: International Organization for Standardization. *Information processing—ISO 7-bit coded character set for information interchange.* [Geneva], 1991. (ISO 646:1991).

ISO 2047: International Organization for Standardization. *Information processing—Graphical representations for the control characters of the 7-bit coded character set.* [Geneva], 1975. (ISO 2047:1975).

ISO/IEC 2022: International Organization for Standardization. *Information processing—ISO 7-bit and 8-bit coded character sets—Code extension techniques.* 3d ed. [Geneva], 1986. (ISO 2022:1994).

ISO 2033: International Organization for Standardization. *Information processing—Coding of machine-readable characters (OCR and MICR).* 2d ed. [Geneva], 1983. (ISO 2033:1983).

ISO/IEC 4873: International Organization for Standardization. *Information technology—ISO 8 bit code for Information Interchange—Structure and Rules for Implementation.* [Geneva], 1991. (ISO 4873:1991).

ISO 5426: International Organization for Standardization. *Extension of the Latin alphabet coded character set for bibliographic information interchange.* 2d ed. [Geneva], 1983. (ISO 5426:1983).

ISO 5427: International Organization for Standardization. *Extension of the Cyrillic alphabet coded character set for bibliographic information interchange.* [Geneva], 1984. (ISO 5427:1984).

ISO 5428: International Organization for Standardization. *Greek alphabet coded character set for bibliographic information interchange.* [Geneva], 1984. (ISO 5428-1984).

ISO/IEC 6429: International Organization for Standardization. *Information technology—Control functions for coded character sets.* [Geneva], 1992. (ISO 6429:1992).

ISO 6438: International Organization for Standardization. *Documentation—African coded character set for bibliographic information interchange.* [Geneva], 1983. (ISO 6438:1983).

ISO 6861.2: International Organization for Standardization. *Information and documentation—Glagolitic alphabet coded character set for bibliographic information interchange.* [Geneva], in press.

ISO DIS 6862: International Organization for Standardization. *Information and documentation—Mathematics character set for bibliographic information interchange.* [Geneva], in press.

ISO/IEC 6937: International Organization for Standardization. *Information processing—Coded character sets for text communication.* [Geneva], 1984.

ISO/IEC 8859: International Organization for Standardization. *Information processing—8-bit single-byte coded graphic character sets.* [Geneva], 1987.

ISO 8879: International Organization for Standardization. *Information processing—Text and office systems—Standard generalized markup language (SGML).* [Geneva], 1986. (ISO 8879:1986).

ISO DIS 8957: International Organization for Standardization. *Information and documentation—Hebrew alphabet coded character sets for bibliographic information interchange.* [Geneva], in press.

ISO 9036: International Organization for Standardization. *Information processing—Arabic 7-bit coded character set for information interchange.* [Geneva], 1987. (ISO 9036:1987).

ISO/IEC 10367: International Organization for Standardization. Joint Technical Committee 1. Subcommittee 2. Working Group 3. *Information processing—Repertoire of standardized coded graphic character sets for use in 8-bit codes.* Geneva, 1991. (ISO/IEC 10367-1:1991).

ISO DIS 10585: International Organization for Standardization. *Information and documentation—Armenian alphabet coded character set for bibliographic information interchange.* [Geneva], in press.

ISO DIS 10586: International Organization for Standardization. *Information and documentation—Georgian alphabet coded character set for bibliographic information interchange.* [Geneva], in press.

ISO/IEC 10646: International Organization for Standardization. *Information Technology—Universal Multiple-Octet Coded Character Set (UCS)—Part 1: Architecture and Basic Multilingual Plane.* [Geneva], 1993. (ISO/IEC 10646-1:1993).

ISO 10754: International Organization for Standardization. *Information and documentation—Extension of the Cyrillic alphabet coded character set for non-Slavic languages for bibliographic information interchange.* [Geneva], in press.

ISO DIS 10822: International Organization for Standardization. *Information and documentation—Extended Arabic coded character set for bibliographic information interchange.* [Geneva], in press.

JIS X 0208: Japanese Standards Association. *Jouhou koukan you kanji fugoukei (Code of the Japanese Graphic Character Set for Information Interchange).* Tokyo, 1990. (JIS X 0208-1990) Revision of the 1983 edition.

JIS X 0212: Japanese Standards Association. *Jouhou koukan you kanji fugou-hojo kanji (Code of the supplementary Japanese graphic character set for information interchange).* Tokyo, 1990. (JIS X 0212-1990) 1990 extensions to JIS.

JIS X 0221: Information Technology—Universal Multiple-Octet Coded Character Set (UCS)—Part 1: Architecture and Basic Multilingual Plane. Tokyo, 1995. (JIS X0221-1995).

KS C 5601-1987: Korea Industrial Standards Association. *Chongbo kyohwanyong puho (Han'gul mit Hancha).* Seoul, 1989. (KS C 5601-1987).

KS C 5601-1992: Korea Industrial Standards Association. *Chongbo kyohwanyong puho (Han'gul mit Hancha).* Seoul, 1992. (KS C 5601-1992).

KS C 5657: Korea Industrial Standards Association. *Chongbo kyohwanyong puho hwakchang set'u.* Seoul, 1991. (KS C 5657-1991).

RFC 1642: *UTF-7: A Mail-Safe Transformation Format of Unicode*, by D. Goldsmith and M. Davis (Taligent, Inc.). Category: Experimental. July 1994.

Available by anonymous ftp from: `ftp://ds.internic.net/rfc/rfc1642.txt`

TIS 620-2529: Thai Industrial Standards Institute, Ministry of Industry. *Thai Industrial Standard for Thai Character Code for Computer.* Bangkok, 1986. (TIS 620-2529 - 1986).

R.2 Source Dictionaries for Han Unification

Dae Jaweon. Seoul, Samseong Publishing Co. Ltd, 1988.

Dai Kan-Wa Jiten / Morohashi Tetsuji cho. Shu teiban. Tokyo, Taishukan Shoten, Showa 59-61 [1984-86].

Hanyu Da Zidian. 1st edition. Chendu, Sichuan Cishu Publishing, 1986.

KangXi Zidian. 7th edition. Beijing: Zhonghua Bookstore, 1989.

R.3 Selected Resources

Allworth, Edward. *Nationalities of the Soviet East: Publications and Writing Systems.* New York, London, Columbia University Press, 1971.

The Alphabet Makers: a Presentation from the Museum of the Alphabet. Waxhaw, North Carolina. 2nd ed. Huntington Beach, CA, Summer Institute of Linguistics, 1991. ISBN 0938978136.

Alphabete und Schriftzeichen des Morgen- und Abendlandes. 2. übearb, u. erw. Aufl. Berlin, Bundesdruckerei, 1969.

Bergsträsser, Gotthelf. *Introduction to the Semitic Languages: Text Speciments and Grammatical Sketches.* Translated ... with an appendix on the scripts by Peter T. Daniels. Winona Lake, Eisenbrauns, 1983. ISBN 093146417X; 0931464102 (pbk.).

Translation of *Einführung in die semitschen Sprachen*, 1928.

The Book of a Thousand Tongues, by Eugene A. Nida. Rev. ed. London, United Bible Society, 1972.

First ed. by Eric M. North, 1928.

The Gospel in Many Tongues: Specimens of 875 Languages ... London, British and Foreign Bible Society, 1965.

Campbell, George L. *Compendium of the World's Languages.* London, New York, Routledge, 1990. ISBN 0415069376 (set); 0415069785 (v.1); 0415069793 (v.2).

Clews, John. *Language Automation Worldwide: The Development of Character Set Standards.* Harrogate (North Yorkshire), SESAME Computer Projects, 1988. ISBN 1870095014.

Comrie, Bernard, ed. *The World's Major Languages.* New York, Oxford, Oxford University Press, 1987. ISBN 0195205219; 0195065115 (pbk.).

Comrie, Bernard, ed. *The Languages of the Soviet Union.* Cambridge, New York, Cambridge University Press, 1981. ISBN 0521232309; 051298776 (pbk.).

Cotter, Sean. *Inside Taligent Technology* / Sean Cotter with Mike Potel. Reading, MA, Addison-Wesley, 1995. ISBN 0201409704.

Coulmas, Florian. *The Blackwell Encyclopedia of Writing Systems.* Cambridge, MA, Blackwell, 1996. ISBN 0631194460.

Coulmas, Florian. *The Writing Systems of the World.* Oxford, New York, Blackwell, 1989. ISBN 0631165134.

DeFrancis, John. *Visible Speech: The Diverse Oneness of Writing Systems.* Honolulu, University of Hawaii Press, 1989. ISBN 0824812077.

Diringer, David. *The Alphabet: A Key To The History of Mankind.* 3d ed., completely rev. with the assistance of Reinhold Regensburger. New York, Funk and Wagnalls, 1968.

Also published: London, Hutchinson. ISBN 090676408.

Diringer, David. *Writing.* London, Thames and Hudson, 1962.

Also published: New York, Praeger.

Dixon, Robert M. W. *The Languages of Australia.* Cambridge, New York, Cambridge University Press, 1980. ISBN 0521223296.

Esling, John. *Computer coding of the IPA: supplementary report.* Journal of the International Phonetic Association, 20:1 (1990), p. 22-26.

Endo, Shotoku. *Hayawakari Chugoku Kantai-ji.* Tokyo, Kokusho Kankokai, Showa 61 [1986].

Faulmann, Carl. *Schriftzeichen und Alphabete aller Zeiten und Völker.* Reprint of *Das Buch Der Schrift* ...,1880. Augsburg, Augustus Verlag, 1990. ISBN 3804301428.

Flanagan, David. *Java in a Nutshell.* Sebastopol, CA, O'Reilly, 1996. ISBN 1565921836.

Friedrich, Johannes. *Geschichte der Schrift.* Heidelberg, C. Winter, 1966.

Gaur, Albertine. *A History of Writing.* Rev. ed. New York, Cross River Press, 1992. ISBN 1558593586.

Also published: London, British Library. ISBN 0712302700.

Gelb, Ignace J. *A Study of Writing.* Rev. ed. Chicago, University of Chicago Press, 1963. ISBN 0226286053; 0226286061 (pbk.).

Gilyarevsky, Rudzhero S. *Languages Identification Guide*, by Rudzhero S. Gilyarevsky and Vladimir S. Grivnin. Moscow, Nauka, 1970.

Haarmann, Harald. *Universalgeschichte der Schrift.* Frankfurt, New York, Campus Verlag, 1990. ISBN 3593343460.

Habein, Yaeko Sato. *The History of the Japanese Written Language.* Tokyo, University of Tokyo Press, 1984. ISBN 0860083470; 4130870475.

Heller, Martin. *Advanced Win32 Programming.* New York, Wiley, 1993. ISBN 0471592455.

Hipson, Peter D. *What Every Visual C++ 2 Programmer Should Know.* Indianapolis, Sams, 1994. ISBN 0672304937.

Huang, K'o-tung. *An Introduction to Chinese, Japanese and Korean Computing,* by Jack K. T. Huang and Timothy D. Huang. Singapore, Teaneck, NJ, World Scientific, 1989. ISBN 9971506645.

IBM. *National Language Support Reference Manual.* 4th ed. North York, ON, IBM Canada Ltd., National Language Technical Center, 1994. (National Language Design Guide, 2) (SE09-8002-03).

Ifrah, Georges. *From One to Zero, A Universal History of Numbers.* New York, Penguin, 1987 ©1985. ISBN 0140099190.

Also published: New York, Viking, 1985. ISBN 0670373958.

Translation of *Histoire universelle des chiffres.*

Insider's Guide to Windows95 Programming. Forrest Houlette [et al]. Indianapolis, Que 1995. ISBN 1565296796.

Isaev, Magomet Izmailovich. *Sto Tridtsat' Ravnopravnykh; O Iazykakh Narodov SSSR.* Moskva, Nauka, 1970.

Jensen, Hans. *Sign, Symbol and Script: An Account of Man's Efforts to Write.* New York, Putnam, 1969.

Also published: London, Allen & Unwin. ISBN 0044000219.

Translation of *Die Schrift in Vergangenheit und Gegenwart* (Berlin, Deuthscher Verlag, 1969).

Kano, Nadine. *Developing International Software For Windows 95 And Windows NT.* Redmond, WA, Microsoft Press, 1995. ISBN 1556158408.

Katzner, Kenneth. *The Languages of the World.* New ed. London: Routledge, 1995. ISBN 0415118093.

Knuth, Donald E. *The* $\mathrm{T_EX}$*book.* 21st. printing, rev. Reading, MA, Addison-Wesley, 1992. ISBN 0201134489.

Lunde, Ken. *Understanding Japanese Information Processing.* Sebastopol, CA, O'Reilly, 1993. ISBN 1565920430.

Malherbe, Michel. *Les Langages de l'Humanité: une Encyclopédie des 3000 Langues Parlées dans le Monde.* Paris, Laffont, 1995. ISBN 2221059476.

Microsoft Win32 Programmer's Reference. Redmond, WA, Microsoft Press, 1995.

Muller, Siegfried H. *The World's Living Languages: Basic Facts of their Structure, Kinship, Location, and Number of Speakers.* New York, Ungar, 1964.

Murray, William H. *Application Programming for Windows NT* / William H. Murray III & Chris H. Pappas. Berkeley, Osborne McGraw-Hill, 1993. ISBN 0078819334.

Musaev, Kenesbai Musaevich. *Alfavity Iazykov Narodov SSSR.* Moskva, Nauka, 1965.

Myers, Brian. *Mastering Windows NT Programming* / Brian Myers & Eric Hamer. San Francisco, Sybex 1993. ISBN 0782112641.

Naik, Bapurao S. *Typography of Devanagari.* 1st ed., rev. Bombay. Directorate of Languages, Govt. of Maharashtra, 1971.

Nakanishi, Akira. *Writing Systems of the World: Alphabets, Syllabaries, Pictograms.* Rutland, VT, Tokyo, Tuttle, 1980. ISBN 0804812934; 0804816549 (pbk.).

Revised translation of *Sekai no monji.*

Nida, Eugene A. *The Book of a Thousand Tongues.* (See *The Book of a Thousand Tongues.*)

Nonroman Scripts in the Bibliographic Environment. In Encyclopedia of Library and Information Science, 56 (supplement 19), 260-83. New York, Dekker, 1995.

O'Donnell, Sandra Martin. *Programming for the World, A Guide to Internationalization.* Englewood Cliffs, NJ, PRT Prentice-Hall, 1994. ISBN 0137221908.

Pavlenko, Nikolai Andreevich. *Istoria Pis'ma.* 2. izd. Minsk, Vysshaia shkola, 1987.

Pullum, Geoffrey K. *Phonetic Symbol Guide* / Geoffrey K. Pullum and William A. Ladusaw. 2nd ed. Chicago, University of Chicago Press, 1996. ISBN 0226685357; 0226685365 (pbk.).

Pullum, Geoffrey K. *Remarks on the 1989 revision of the International Phonetic Alphabet.* Journal of the International Phonetic Association, 20:1 (1990), p. 33-40.

Ramsey, S. Robert. *The Languages of China.* 2d printing with revisions. Princeton, Princeton University Press, 1989 ©1987. ISBN 069101468X.

Richter, Jeffrey. *Advanced Windows: The Developer's Guide to the Win32 API for Windows 3.5 and Windows 95.* Redmond, WA, Microsoft Press, 1995. ISBN 1556156774.

Robinson, Andrew. *The Story of Writing.* London, New York, Thames and Hudson, 1995. ISBN 0500016658.

Ruhlen, Merritt. *A Guide to the World's Languages, Volume 1: Classification, with a Postscript on Recent Developments.* Stanford, CA, Stanford University Press, 1991. ISBN 0804718946 (v. 1).

Also published: London, Arnold. ISBN 0340561866 (v. 1).

Sampson, Geoffrey. *Writing Systems: A Linguistic Introduction.* Stanford, CA, Stanford University Press, 1985. ISBN 0804712549.

Also published: London, Hutchinson. ISBN 009156980X.

Senner, Wayne M. *The Origins of Writing.* Lincoln, University of Nebraska Press, 1989. ISBN 0803242026; 0803291671 (pbk.).

Shepherd, Walter. *Shepherd's Glossary Of Graphic Signs And Symbols.* Compiled and classified for ready reference by Walter Shepherd. New York, Dover, 1971. ISBN 0486207005.

Also published: London, Dent. ISBN 0460038184.

Shinmura, Izuru. *Kojien* / Shinmura Izuru hen. Dai 4-han. Tokyo, Iwanami Shoten, 1991.

Suarez, Jorge A. *The Mesoamerican Indian Languages.* Cambridge, New York, Cambridge University Press, 1983. ISBN 0521228344; 0521296692 (pbk.).

Taligent's Guide to Designing Programs: Well-Mannered Object-Oriented Design in C++. Cupertino, CA, Taligent Press; Reading, MA, Addison-Wesley, 1994. ISBN 0201408880.

von Ostermann, Georg F. *Manual of Foreign Languages.* 4th ed., revised and enlarged New York, Central Book Company, 1952.

Universal Multiple-Octet Coded Character Set Coexistence and Migration. High Wycombe, X/Open Company, 1994. (X/Open Technical Study, E401.) ISBN 1859120318.

Wemyss, Stanley. *The Languages of the World, Ancient and Modern: the Alphabets, Ideographs, and Other Written Characters of the World in Sound and Symbol.* Philadelphia, 1950.

The World's Writing Systems. Edited by Peter T. Daniels and William Bright. New York, Oxford University Press, 1995. ISBN 0195079930.

INDICES

Indices

I.1 Unicode Names Index

The Unicode Names index contains three types of entries.

- Formal character names—all uppercase
- Alternative character names (aliases)—all lowercase
- Character group names—mixed case (titlecase)

Formal character names are unmodified from the character names lists, although the name strings may be indexed by different words in the names. Alternative character names and character group names are occasionally modified slightly to make them understandable out of context (for example, from "boot" to "armenian boot").

Not every character is indexed. Large groups of similar characters, including CJK ideographs, Korean Hangul syllables, and compatibility characters, are indexed by their character group names, such as block names, subblocks, alphabet names, relevant standards, or group summaries (for example, "Roman Numerals").

Neighboring paired characters (such as capital/small case pairs, mathematical symbols and their negations, and left/right brackets) are generally indexed under only one member of the pair.

I.2 General Index

The general index is a guide to the written text only. To find the range for a particular script, see the Contents. To find the code for a specific character, see the preceding Unicode Names Index. For the definition of specific terms, see the Glossary.